PRESENTED TO

_____

_____

BY

_____

_____

ON THE OCCASION OF

_____

_____

DATE

_____

_____

Your word is a lamp to guide my feet
and a light for my path.

PSALM 119:105

HOLY BIBLE

CATHOLIC

HOLY
BIBLE

NLT
CATHOLIC
EDITION

Tyndale House Publishers, Inc.
Carol Stream, Illinois

Concerning the New Living Translation:

NIHIL OBSTAT

Gali Bali
Bishop of Guntur

IMPRIMATUR

Oswald Cardinal Gracias
Archbishop of Bombay
President, Conference of Catholic Bishops of India
April 29, 2015
[Not for Liturgical Use]

Concerning the book introductions in this Bible:

NIHIL OBSTAT

Reverend John Balluff, S.T.D.
Censor Deputatus
June 29, 2016

PERMISSION TO PUBLISH

Most Reverend Joseph M. Siegel, D.D., S.T.L.
Vicar General
Diocese of Joliet
June 30, 2016

The *Nihil Obstat* and *Permission to Publish* are official declarations that a text is free of doctrinal and moral error. No implication is contained therein that those who have granted the *Nihil Obstat* and *Permission to Publish* agree with the content, opinions, or statements expressed. Nor do they assume any legal responsibility associated with publication. The *Permission to Publish* granted herein refers only to the introductory paragraphs to each book contained in this Bible.

Tyndale House Publishers and Wycliffe Bible Translators share the vision for an understandable, accurate translation of the Bible for every person in the world. Each sale of the *Holy Bible,* New Living Translation, benefits Wycliffe Bible Translators. Wycliffe is working with partners around the world to accomplish Vision 2025—an initiative to start a Bible translation program in every language group that needs it by the year 2025.

CONTENTS

The Old Testament

The New Testament

ALPHABETICAL LISTING
OF BIBLE BOOKS

Introduction to

THE NEW LIVING TRANSLATION
CATHOLIC EDITION

Translation Philosophy and Methodology

English Bible translations tend to be governed by one of two general translation theories. The first theory has been called "formal-equivalence," "literal," or "word-for-word" translation. According to this theory, the translator attempts to render each word of the original language into English and seeks to preserve the original syntax and sentence structure as much as possible in translation. The second theory has been called "dynamic-equivalence," "functional-equivalence," or "thought-for-thought" translation. The goal of this translation theory is to produce in English the closest natural equivalent of the message expressed by the original-language text, both in meaning and in style.

Both of these translation theories have their strengths. A formal-equivalence translation preserves aspects of the original text—including ancient idioms, term consistency, and original-language syntax—that are valuable for scholars and professional study. It allows a reader to trace formal elements of the original-language text through the English translation. A dynamic-equivalence translation, on the other hand, focuses on translating the message of the original-language text. It ensures that the meaning of the text is readily apparent to the contemporary reader. This allows the message to come through with immediacy, without requiring the reader to struggle with foreign idioms and awkward syntax.

The translators of the New Living Translation set out to render the message of the original texts of Scripture into clear, contemporary English. As they did so, they kept the concerns of both formal-equivalence and dynamic-equivalence in mind. On the one hand, they translated as simply and literally as possible when that approach yielded an accurate, clear, and natural English text. Many words and phrases were rendered literally and consistently into English, preserving essential literary and rhetorical devices, ancient metaphors, and word choices that give structure to the text and provide echoes of meaning from one passage to the next.

On the other hand, the translators rendered the message more dynamically when the literal rendering was hard to understand, was misleading, or yielded archaic or foreign wording. They clarified difficult metaphors and terms to aid in the reader's understanding. The translators first struggled with the meaning of the words and phrases in the ancient context; then they rendered the message into clear, natural English. Their goal was to be faithful to the ancient texts while creating an eminently readable translation.

Translation Process and Team

To produce an accurate translation of the Bible into contemporary English, the translation team needed the skills necessary to enter into the thought patterns of the ancient authors and then to render their ideas, connotations, and effects into clear, contemporary English. To begin this process, qualified biblical scholars were needed to interpret the meaning of the original text. In order to guard against personal and theological biases, the translators needed to represent a diverse group of scholars who would employ the best exegetical tools. Then to work alongside the scholars, skilled English stylists were needed to shape the translated text into clear, contemporary English.

With these concerns in mind, the Bible Translation Committee recruited teams of scholars that represented a broad spectrum of denominations, theological perspectives, and backgrounds. Each book of the Bible was assigned to three different scholars with proven expertise in the book or group of books to be reviewed. Each of these scholars made a thorough review of a base translation and submitted suggested revisions to the appropriate Senior Translator. The Senior Translator then reviewed and summarized these suggestions and proposed a draft that served as the basis for several additional phases of exegetical and stylistic committee review. Finally, the Bible Translation Committee jointly reviewed and approved every verse of the final translation.

The New Living Translation was first published in 1996. Shortly after its initial publication, the Bible Translation Committee began a process of further committee review and translation refinement. The purpose of this continued revision was to increase the level of precision without sacrificing the text's easy-to-understand quality. This second-edition text was completed in 2004, with minor changes subsequently introduced in 2007, 2013, and 2015.

The text of the NLT was reviewed by a group of eminent Catholic scholars, and the imprimatur was granted by Oswald Cardinal Gracias, Archbishop of Bombay, April 29, 2015. This Catholic Edition, including the deuterocanonical books, was first published in 2015.

Written to Be Read Aloud
It is evident in Scripture that the biblical documents were written to be read aloud, often in public worship (see Nehemiah 8; Luke 4:16-20; 1 Timothy 4:13; Revelation 1:3). It is still the case today that more people will hear the Bible read aloud than are likely to read it for themselves. Therefore, a new translation must communicate with clarity and power when it is read publicly. Clarity was a primary goal for the NLT translators, not only to facilitate private reading and understanding, but also to ensure that it would be excellent for public reading and make an immediate and powerful impact on any listener.

The Texts behind the New Living Translation
The Old Testament translators used the Masoretic Text of the Hebrew Bible as represented in *Biblia Hebraica Stuttgartensia* (1977), with its extensive system of textual notes. The translators also took into account the Dead Sea Scrolls, the Septuagint and other Greek manuscripts, the Samaritan Pentateuch, the Syriac Peshitta, the Latin Vulgate, and any other versions or manuscripts that shed light on difficult passages.

The New Testament translators used the two standard editions of the Greek New Testament: the *Greek New Testament*, published by the United Bible Societies (UBS, fourth revised edition, 1993), and *Novum Testamentum Graece*, edited by Nestle and Aland (NA, twenty-seventh edition, 1993). These two editions, which have the same text but differ in punctuation and textual notes, represent, for the most part, the best in modern textual scholarship. However, in cases where strong textual or other scholarly evidence supported the decision, the translators sometimes chose to differ from the UBS and NA Greek texts and followed variant readings found in other ancient witnesses. Significant textual variants of this sort are always noted in the textual notes of the New Living Translation.

The translators of the deuterocanonical books used as their standard text the Greek version known as *Septuaginta*, compiled by Alfred Rahlfs (Stuttgart, 1979 edition). For the book of Tobit, the text of Codex Sinaiticus was used as the primary Greek text. For the additions to Daniel, the Greek text of Theodotion was the primary Greek text.

Translation Issues
The translators have made a conscious effort to provide a text that can be easily understood by the typical reader of modern English. To this end, we sought to use only vocabulary and language structures in common use today. We avoided using language likely to become quickly dated or that reflects only a narrow subdialect of English, with the goal of making the New Living Translation as broadly useful and timeless as possible.

But our concern for readability goes beyond the concerns of vocabulary and sentence structure. We are also concerned about historical and cultural barriers to understanding the Bible, and we have sought to translate terms shrouded in history and culture in ways that can be immediately understood. To this end:

- We have converted ancient weights and measures (for example, "ephah" [a unit of dry volume] or "cubit" [a unit of length]) to modern English (American) equivalents, since the ancient measures are not generally meaningful to today's readers. Then in the textual footnotes we offer the literal Hebrew, Aramaic, or Greek measures, along with modern metric equivalents.
- Instead of translating ancient monetary values literally, we have expressed them in common terms that communicate the message. For example, in the Old Testament, "ten shekels of silver" becomes "ten pieces of silver" to convey the intended message.
- Since the names of Hebrew months are unknown to most contemporary readers, and since the Hebrew lunar calendar fluctuates from year to year in relation to the solar calendar used today, we have looked for clear ways to communicate the time of year the Hebrew months (such as Abib) refer to. Where it is possible to define a specific ancient date in terms of our modern calendar, we use modern dates in the text. A textual footnote then gives the literal Hebrew date and states the rationale for our rendering. (See, for example, the text and note at Ezra 6:15.)
- Since ancient references to the time of day differ from our modern methods of denoting time, we have used renderings that are instantly understandable to the modern reader. Accordingly, we have rendered specific times of day by using approximate equivalents in terms of our common "o'clock" system.
- When the meaning of a proper name (or a wordplay inherent in a proper name) is relevant to the message of the text, its meaning is often illuminated with a textual footnote. For example, in Exodus 2:10 the text reads: "The princess named him Moses, for she explained, 'I lifted him out of the water.' " The accompanying footnote reads: *"Moses* sounds like a Hebrew term that means 'to lift out.' "

   Sometimes, when the actual meaning of a name is clear, that meaning is included in parentheses within the text itself. For example, the text at Genesis 16:11 reads: "You are to name him Ishmael (*which means 'God hears'*), for the LORD has heard your cry of distress." Since the original hearers and readers would have instantly understood the meaning of the name "Ishmael," we have provided modern readers with the same information so they can experience the text in a similar way.
- Many words and phrases carry a great deal of cultural meaning that was obvious to the original readers but needs explanation in our own culture. For example, the phrase "they beat their breasts" (Luke 23:48) in ancient times meant that people were very upset, often in mourning. In our translation we chose to translate this phrase dynamically for clarity: "They went home in *deep sorrow*."
- Metaphorical language is sometimes difficult for contemporary readers to understand, so at times we have chosen to translate or illuminate the meaning of a metaphor. For example, the ancient poet writes, "Your neck is *like* the tower of David" (Song of Songs 4:4). We have rendered it "Your neck is *as beautiful as* the tower of David" to clarify the intended positive meaning of the metaphor.
- When the content of the original language text is poetic in character, we have rendered it in English poetic form. Hebrew poetry often uses parallelism, a literary form where a second phrase echoes the initial phrase in some way. Whenever possible, we sought to represent these parallel phrases in natural poetic English.
- The Greek term *hoi Ioudaioi* is literally translated "the Jews" in many English translations. In the Gospel of John, however, this term doesn't always refer to the Jewish people generally. In some contexts, it refers more particularly to the Jewish religious leaders. We have attempted to capture the meaning in these different contexts by using terms such as "the people" (with a footnote: Greek *the Jewish people*) or "the Jewish leaders," where appropriate.
- One challenge we faced was how to translate accurately the ancient biblical text that was originally written in a context where male-oriented terms were used to refer to humanity generally. We needed to respect the nature of the ancient context while also trying to make the translation clear to a modern audience that tends to read male-oriented language as applying only to males. Often the original text, though using masculine terms, clearly intends that the message be applied to both men and women. A typical example is found in the New Testament letters, where the believers are called "brothers" (*adelphoi*). Yet it is

clear from the content of these letters that they were addressed to all the believers—male and female. Thus, we have usually translated this Greek word as "brothers and sisters" in order to represent the historical situation more accurately.

We have also been sensitive to passages where the text applies generally to human beings or to the human condition. In some instances we have used plural pronouns (they, them) in place of the masculine singular (he, him). For example, a traditional rendering of Proverbs 22:6 is: "Train up a child in the way he should go, and when he is old he will not turn from it." We have rendered it: "Direct your children onto the right path, and when they are older, they will not leave it." At times, we have also replaced third person pronouns with the second person to ensure clarity. A traditional rendering of Proverbs 26:27 is: "He who digs a pit will fall into it, and he who rolls a stone, it will come back on him." We have rendered it: "If you set a trap for others, you will get caught in it yourself. If you roll a boulder down on others, it will crush you instead."

We should emphasize that all masculine nouns and pronouns used to represent God (for example, "Father") have been maintained without exception. All decisions of this kind have been driven by the concern to reflect accurately the intended meaning of the original texts of Scripture.

Lexical Consistency in Terminology

For the sake of clarity, we have translated certain original-language terms consistently, especially within synoptic passages and for commonly repeated rhetorical phrases, and within certain word categories such as divine names and non-theological technical terminology (e.g., liturgical, legal, cultural, zoological, and botanical terms). For theological terms, we have allowed a greater semantic range of acceptable English words or phrases for a single Hebrew or Greek word. We have avoided some theological terms that are not readily understood by many modern readers. For example, we avoided using words such as "justification" and "sanctification," which are often unfamiliar to modern readers. In place of these words, we have provided renderings such as "made right with God" and "made holy."

Many individuals in the Bible, especially the Old Testament, are known by more than one name (e.g., Uzziah/Azariah). For the sake of clarity, we have tried to use a single spelling for any one individual, footnoting the literal spelling whenever we vary from it. This is especially helpful in delineating the kings of Israel and Judah. King Joash/Jehoash of Israel has been consistently called Jehoash, while King Joash/Jehoash of Judah is called Joash. A similar distinction has been used to distinguish between Joram/Jehoram of Israel and Joram/Jehoram of Judah. All such decisions were made with the goal of clarifying the text for the reader. When the ancient biblical writers clearly had a theological purpose in their choice of a variant name (e.g., Esh-baal/Ishbosheth), the different names have been maintained with an explanatory footnote.

For the names Jacob and Israel, which are used interchangeably for both the individual patriarch and the nation, we generally render it "Israel" when it refers to the nation and "Jacob" when it refers to the individual. When our rendering of the name differs from the underlying Hebrew text, we provide a textual footnote, which includes this explanation: "The names 'Jacob' and 'Israel' are often interchanged throughout the Old Testament, referring sometimes to the individual patriarch and sometimes to the nation."

The Rendering of Divine Names

In the Old Testament, all appearances of 'el, 'elohim, or 'eloah have been translated "God," except where the context demands the translation "god(s)." We have generally rendered the tetragrammaton (YHWH) consistently as "the LORD," utilizing a form with small capitals that is common among English translations. This will distinguish it from the name 'adonai, which we render "Lord." When 'adonai and YHWH appear together, we have rendered it "Sovereign LORD." When 'elohim and YHWH appear together, we have rendered it "LORD God." When YH (the short form of YHWH) and YHWH appear together, we have rendered it "LORD GOD." When YHWH appears with the term tseba'oth, we have rendered it "LORD of Heaven's Armies" to translate the meaning of the name. In a few cases, we have utilized the transliteration, Yahweh, when the personal character of the name is being invoked in contrast to another divine name or the name of some other god (for example, see Exodus 3:15; 6:2-3).

Gary Smith, *Union University*
John Walton, *Wheaton College*

Jeremiah, Lamentations

G. Herbert Livingston, *Asbury Theological Seminary*
Elmer A. Martens, *Mennonite Brethren Biblical Seminary*

Ezekiel

Daniel I. Block, *Wheaton College*
David H. Engelhard, *Calvin Theological Seminary*
David Thompson, *Asbury Theological Seminary*

Daniel, Haggai—Malachi

Joyce Baldwin Caine, *Trinity College, Bristol*
Douglas Gropp, *Catholic University of America*
Roy Hayden, *Oral Roberts School of Theology*
Andrew Hill, *Wheaton College*
Tremper Longman III, *Westmont College*

Hosea—Zephaniah

Joseph Coleson, *Nazarene Theological Seminary*
Roy Hayden, *Oral Roberts School of Theology*
Andrew Hill, *Wheaton College*
Richard Patterson, *Liberty University*

GOSPELS AND ACTS

Grant R. Osborne, Senior Translator
  Trinity Evangelical Divinity School

Matthew

Craig Blomberg, *Denver Seminary*
Donald A. Hagner, *Fuller Theological Seminary*
David Turner, *Grand Rapids Baptist Seminary*

Mark

Robert Guelich, *Fuller Theological Seminary*
George Guthrie, *Union University*
Grant R. Osborne, *Trinity Evangelical Divinity School*

Luke

Darrell Bock, *Dallas Theological Seminary*
Scot McKnight, *North Park University*
Robert Stein, *The Southern Baptist Theological Seminary*

John

Gary M. Burge, *Wheaton College*
Philip W. Comfort, *Coastal Carolina University*
Marianne Meye Thompson, *Fuller Theological Seminary*

Acts

D. A. Carson, *Trinity Evangelical Divinity School*
William J. Larkin, *Columbia International University*
Roger Mohrlang, *Whitworth University*

LETTERS AND REVELATION

Norman R. Ericson, Senior Translator
  Wheaton College

Romans, Galatians

Gerald Borchert, *Northern Baptist Theological Seminary*
Douglas J. Moo, *Wheaton College*
Thomas R. Schreiner, *The Southern Baptist Theological Seminary*

1 & 2 Corinthians

Joseph Alexanian, *Trinity International University*
Linda Belleville, *Bethel College, Mishawaka, Indiana*
Douglas A. Oss, *Central Bible College*
Robert Sloan, *Houston Baptist University*

Ephesians—Philemon

Harold W. Hoehner, *Dallas Theological Seminary*
Moises Silva, *Gordon-Conwell Theological Seminary*
Klyne Snodgrass, *North Park Theological Seminary*

Hebrews, James, 1 & 2 Peter, Jude

Peter Davids, *St. Stephen's University*
Norman R. Ericson, *Wheaton College*
William Lane, *Seattle Pacific University*
J. Ramsey Michaels, *S. W. Missouri State University*

1—3 John, Revelation

Greg Beale, *Westminster Theological Seminary*
Robert Mounce, *Whitworth University*
M. Robert Mulholland Jr., *Asbury Theological Seminary*

DEUTEROCANONICAL BOOKS

Philip W. Comfort, *Coastal Carolina University*
J. Julius Scott, *Wheaton College*
David P. Barrett, *Coordinating Editor*
James A. Swanson, *Academic Editor*

SPECIAL REVIEWERS

F. F. Bruce, *University of Manchester*
Kenneth N. Taylor, *Translator,* The Living Bible

COORDINATING TEAM

Mark D. Taylor, *Director and Chief Stylist*
Ronald A. Beers, *Executive Director and Stylist*
Mark R. Norton, *Managing Editor and O.T. Coordinating Editor*
Philip W. Comfort, *N.T. Coordinating Editor*
Daniel W. Taylor, *Bethel University, Senior Stylist*
Sean A. Harrison, *Editor and Stylist*
James A. Swanson, *Lexical Reviewer*

BIBLE TRANSLATION TEAM

Holy Bible, New Living Translation

PENTATEUCH

Daniel I. Block, Senior Translator
Wheaton College

Genesis
Allen Ross, *Beeson Divinity School, Samford University*
Gordon Wenham, *Trinity College, Bristol*

Exodus
Robert Bergen, *Hannibal-LaGrange College*
Daniel I. Block, *Wheaton College*
Eugene Carpenter, *Bethel College, Mishawaka, Indiana*

Leviticus
David Baker, *Ashland Theological Seminary*
Victor Hamilton, *Asbury University*
Kenneth Mathews, *Beeson Divinity School, Samford University*

Numbers
Dale A. Brueggemann, *Assemblies of God Division of Foreign Missions*
R. K. Harrison, *Wycliffe College*
Paul R. House, *Beeson Divinity School, Samford University*
Gerald L. Mattingly, *Johnson Bible College*

Deuteronomy
J. Gordon McConville, *University of Gloucester*
Eugene H. Merrill, *Dallas Theological Seminary*
John A. Thompson, *University of Melbourne*

HISTORICAL BOOKS

Barry J. Beitzel, Senior Translator
Trinity Evangelical Divinity School

Joshua, Judges
Carl E. Armerding, *Schloss Mittersill Study Centre*
Barry J. Beitzel, *Trinity Evangelical Divinity School*
Lawson Stone, *Asbury Theological Seminary*

1 & 2 Samuel
Robert Gordon, *Cambridge University*
V. Philips Long, *Regent College*
J. Robert Vannoy, *Biblical Theological Seminary*

1 & 2 Kings
Bill T. Arnold, *Asbury Theological Seminary*

William H. Barnes, *North Central University*
Frederic W. Bush, *Fuller Theological Seminary*

1 & 2 Chronicles
Raymond B. Dillard, *Westminster Theological Seminary*
David A. Dorsey, *Evangelical School of Theology*
Terry Eves, *Erskine College*

Ruth, Ezra—Esther
William C. Williams, *Vanguard University*
H. G. M. Williamson, *Oxford University*

WISDOM BOOKS

Tremper Longman III, Senior Translator
Westmont College

Job
August Konkel, *Providence Theological Seminary*
Tremper Longman III, *Westmont College*
Al Wolters, *Redeemer College*

Psalms 1–75
Mark D. Futato, *Reformed Theological Seminary*
Douglas Green, *Westminster Theological Seminary*
Richard Pratt, *Reformed Theological Seminary*

Psalms 76–150
David M. Howard Jr., *Bethel Theological Seminary*
Raymond C. Ortlund Jr., *Immanuel Church, Nashville, Tennessee*
Willem VanGemeren, *Trinity Evangelical Divinity School*

Proverbs
Ted Hildebrandt, *Gordon College*
Richard Schultz, *Wheaton College*
Raymond C. Van Leeuwen, *Eastern College*

Ecclesiastes, Song of Songs
Daniel C. Fredericks, *Belhaven College*
David Hubbard, *Fuller Theological Seminary*
Tremper Longman III, *Westmont College*

PROPHETS

John N. Oswalt, Senior Translator
Asbury Theological Seminary

Isaiah
John N. Oswalt, *Asbury Theological Seminary*

Until the discovery of the Dead Sea Scrolls, these additional texts could be found only in the Greek version of the Scriptures called the Septuagint. The texts were written later than the rest of the Old Testament, so although they were created within the Jewish community, they have never been accepted as part of the Jewish canon of Scripture. The Roman Catholic Church refers to these additional books as deuterocanonical (literally, "second canon"). Protestants often refer to them as apocryphal (literally, "hidden").

While there are varying lists of deuterocanonical books, this edition of the New Living Translation includes the following books that were decreed as part of the Old Testament canon by the Council of Trent in 1546: Tobit, Judith, the Greek additions to Esther, Wisdom (also called Wisdom of Solomon), Sirach (also called Ecclesiasticus), Baruch (including the Letter of Jeremiah), the Greek additions to Daniel (i.e., The Prayer of Azariah, The Song of the Three Young Men, Susanna and the Elders, and Bel and the Dragon), and 1 and 2 Maccabees. This translation does not include other books (e.g., Prayer of Manasseh, 1 and 2 Esdras) that were included in some manuscripts of the Latin Vulgate but were denied canonical status by the Council of Trent.

The Greek additions to Esther are traditionally designated by the letters A, B, C, D, E, and F, and this translation follows that tradition. Accordingly, the reader can readily distinguish between the content of the Hebrew text of Esther and the expansions found in Greek versions.

There are three Greek additions to the book of Daniel. The first addition expands the account of the fiery furnace in chapter 3 with The Prayer of Azariah and The Song of the Three Young Men. These are included in this edition as verses 3:23-90. The second addition, often called Susanna and the Elders, is presented as chapter 13. The third addition, often called Bel and the Dragon, is presented as chapter 14.

As WE SUBMIT this translation for publication, we recognize that any translation of the Scriptures is subject to limitations and imperfections. Anyone who has attempted to communicate the richness of God's word into another language will realize it is impossible to make a perfect translation. Recognizing these limitations, we sought God's guidance and wisdom throughout this project. Now we pray that he will accept our efforts and use this translation for the benefit of the church and of all people.

We pray that the New Living Translation will overcome some of the barriers of history, culture, and language that have kept people from reading and understanding God's word. We hope that readers unfamiliar with the Bible will find the words clear and easy to understand and that readers well versed in the Scriptures will gain a fresh perspective. We pray that readers will gain insight and wisdom for living, but most of all that they will meet the God of the Bible and be forever changed by knowing him.

The Bible Translation Committee

In the Gospels and Acts, the Greek word *christos* has normally been translated as "Messiah" when the context assumes a Jewish audience. When a Gentile audience can be assumed (which is consistently the case in the Epistles and Revelation), *christos* has been translated as "Christ." The Greek word *kurios* is consistently translated "Lord," except that it is translated "Lᴏʀᴅ" wherever the New Testament text explicitly quotes from the Old Testament, and the text there has it in small capitals.

Since the texts used to translate the deuterocanonical books were written in Greek, our renderings of the divine names in these books more closely resemble our New Testament practice. (This is true even though the deuterocanonical books are considered an extension of the Old Testament.) In the Greek text of these books (as in the Septuagint, the Greek translation of the Old Testament), the term *kurios* is used to represent a number of possible Hebrew terms, including both *'adonai* and *YHWH*. Since it is difficult to determine which underlying term was intended in many cases, we simply rendered *kurios* consistently as "Lord" throughout the text of these books.

Textual Footnotes

The New Living Translation provides several kinds of textual footnotes, all designated in the text with an asterisk:

- When for the sake of clarity the NLT renders a difficult or potentially confusing phrase dynamically, we generally give the literal rendering in a textual footnote. This allows the reader to see the literal source of our dynamic rendering and how our translation relates to other more literal translations. These notes are prefaced with "Hebrew," "Aramaic," or "Greek," identifying the language of the underlying source text. For example, in Acts 2:42 we translated the literal "breaking of bread" (from the Greek) as "the Lord's Supper" to clarify that this verse refers to the ceremonial practice of the church rather than just an ordinary meal. Then we attached a footnote to "the Lord's Supper," which reads: "Greek *the breaking of bread.*"

- Textual footnotes are also used to show alternative renderings, prefaced with the word "Or." These normally occur for passages where an aspect of the meaning is debated. On occasion, we also provide notes on words or phrases that represent a departure from long-standing tradition. These notes are prefaced with "Traditionally rendered." For example, the footnote to the translation "serious skin disease" at Leviticus 13:2 says: "Traditionally rendered *leprosy.* The Hebrew word used throughout this passage is used to describe various skin diseases."

- When our translators follow a textual variant that differs significantly from our standard Hebrew or Greek texts (listed earlier), we document that difference with a footnote. We also footnote cases where the NLT does not translate a passage that is included in the Greek text known as the *Textus Receptus* (and familiar to readers through its translation in the King James Version). In such cases, we offer a translation of the excluded text in a footnote, even though it is generally recognized as a later addition to the Greek text and not part of the original Greek New Testament.

- All Old Testament passages that are quoted in the New Testament are identified by a textual footnote at the New Testament location. When the New Testament clearly quotes from the Greek translation of the Old Testament, and when it differs significantly in wording from the Hebrew text, we also provide a textual footnote at the Old Testament location. This note includes a rendering of the Greek version, along with a cross-reference to the New Testament passage(s) where it is cited (for example, see notes on Psalms 8:2; 53:3; Proverbs 3:12).

- Some textual footnotes provide cultural and historical information on places, things, and people in the Bible that are probably obscure to modern readers. Such notes should aid the reader in understanding the message of the text. For example, in Acts 12:1, "King Herod" is named in this translation as "King Herod Agrippa" and is identified in a footnote as being "the nephew of Herod Antipas and a grandson of Herod the Great."

Deuterocanonical Books

The thirty-nine books of the original Old Testament canon were written in Hebrew. During the third to first centuries ʙᴄ, additional texts were written, some in Greek and some in Hebrew.

Old Testament

Genesis

AS ITS NAME IMPLIES, Genesis is the book of beginnings. It starts with the creation of the world and every creature in it. It records the first marriage, the first sin, the first consequences of sin, and the first reference to God's plan to redeem humanity. After recounting the stories of the Flood and the Tower of Babel, Genesis also tells the story of the birth of the nation of Israel. The story begins as God calls Abraham, the forefather of the Israelites, to leave his home, Ur (located in modern-day Iraq), and move to Canaan—the land God would promise his descendants. Eventually, the Redeemer of the world would come from the descendants of Abraham. The story then shifts to events concerning Isaac, Abraham's son, and then to Jacob, Abraham's grandson. Genesis concludes with the remarkable experiences of Joseph, one of Jacob's twelve sons.

■ **Author:** Moses, according to Jewish tradition

■ **Date Written:** Uncertain, perhaps between 1450 and 1410 BC

■ **Purpose:** To show how the world and everything in it came about and to show God's desire to have a people set apart to worship him

■ **Themes:** Origin of the world, humanity, sin, and the nation of Israel; the sovereignty and trustworthiness of God; obedience and blessing

■ **Outline**

The Account of Creation

1 In the beginning God created the heavens and the earth.* ²The earth was formless and empty, and darkness covered the deep waters. And the Spirit of God was hovering over the surface of the waters.

³Then God said, "Let there be light," and there was light. ⁴And God saw that the light was good. Then he separated the light from the darkness. ⁵God called the light "day" and the darkness "night."

And evening passed and morning came, marking the first day.

⁶Then God said, "Let there be a space between the waters, to separate the waters of the heavens from the waters of the earth." ⁷And that is what happened. God made this space to separate the waters of the earth from the waters of the heavens. ⁸God called the space "sky."

And evening passed and morning came, marking the second day.

⁹Then God said, "Let the waters beneath the sky flow together into one place, so dry ground may appear." And that is what happened. ¹⁰God called the dry ground "land" and the waters "seas." And God saw that it was good. ¹¹Then God said, "Let the land sprout with vegetation—every sort of seed-bearing plant, and trees that grow seed-bearing fruit. These seeds will then produce the kinds of plants and trees from which they came." And that is what happened. ¹²The land produced vegetation—all sorts of seed-bearing plants, and trees with seed-bearing fruit. Their seeds produced plants and trees of

1:1 Or *In the beginning when God created the heavens and the earth,* . . . Or *When God began to create the heavens and the earth,* . . .

the same kind. And God saw that it was good. ¹³And evening passed and morning came, marking the third day.

¹⁴Then God said, "Let lights appear in the sky to separate the day from the night. Let them be signs to mark the seasons, days, and years. ¹⁵Let these lights in the sky shine down on the earth." And that is what happened. ¹⁶God made two great lights—the larger one to govern the day, and the smaller one to govern the night. He also made the stars. ¹⁷God set these lights in the sky to light the earth, ¹⁸to govern the day and night, and to separate the light from the darkness. And God saw that it was good. ¹⁹And evening passed and morning came, marking the fourth day.

²⁰Then God said, "Let the waters swarm with fish and other life. Let the skies be filled with birds of every kind." ²¹So God created great sea creatures and every living thing that scurries and swarms in the water, and every sort of bird—each producing offspring of the same kind. And God saw that it was good. ²²Then God blessed them, saying, "Be fruitful and multiply. Let the fish fill the seas, and let the birds multiply on the earth."

²³And evening passed and morning came, marking the fifth day.

²⁴Then God said, "Let the earth produce every sort of animal, each producing offspring of the same kind—livestock, small animals that scurry along the ground, and wild animals." And that is what happened. ²⁵God made all sorts of wild animals, livestock, and small animals, each able to produce offspring of the same kind. And God saw that it was good.

²⁶Then God said, "Let us make human beings* in our image, to be like us. They will reign over the fish in the sea, the birds in the sky, the livestock, all the wild animals on the earth,* and the small animals that scurry along the ground."

²⁷ So God created human beings* in his own image.

In the image of God he created them; male and female he created them.

²⁸Then God blessed them and said, "Be fruitful and multiply. Fill the earth and govern it. Reign over the fish in the sea, the birds in the sky, and all the animals that scurry along the ground."

²⁹Then God said, "Look! I have given you every seed-bearing plant throughout the earth and all the fruit trees for your food. ³⁰And I have given every green plant as food for all the wild animals, the birds in the sky, and the small animals that scurry along the ground—everything that has life." And that is what happened.

³¹Then God looked over all he had made, and he saw that it was very good!

And evening passed and morning came, marking the sixth day.

2 So the creation of the heavens and the earth and everything in them was completed. ²On the seventh day God had finished his work of creation, so he rested* from all his work. ³And God blessed the seventh day and declared it holy, because it was the day when he rested from all his work of creation.

⁴This is the account of the creation of the heavens and the earth.

The Man and Woman in Eden

When the LORD God made the earth and the heavens, ⁵neither wild plants nor grains were growing on the earth. For the LORD God had not yet sent rain to water the earth, and there were no people to cultivate the soil. ⁶Instead, springs* came up from the ground and watered all the land. ⁷Then the LORD God formed the man from the dust of the ground. He breathed the breath of life into the man's nostrils, and the man became a living person.

⁸Then the LORD God planted a garden in Eden in the east, and there he placed the man he had made. ⁹The LORD God made all sorts of trees grow up from the ground—trees that were beautiful and that produced delicious fruit. In the middle of the garden he placed the tree of life and the tree of the knowledge of good and evil.

¹⁰A river flowed from the land of Eden, watering the garden and then dividing into

---

1:26a Or *man;* Hebrew reads *adam.*　　1:26b As in Syriac version; Hebrew reads *all the earth.*　　1:27 Or *the man;* Hebrew reads *ha-adam.*　　2:2 Or *ceased;* also in 2:3.　　2:6 Or *mist.*

four branches. [11]The first branch, called the Pishon, flowed around the entire land of Havilah, where gold is found. [12]The gold of that land is exceptionally pure; aromatic resin and onyx stone are also found there. [13]The second branch, called the Gihon, flowed around the entire land of Cush. [14]The third branch, called the Tigris, flowed east of the land of Asshur. The fourth branch is called the Euphrates.

[15]The LORD God placed the man in the Garden of Eden to tend and watch over it. [16]But the LORD God warned him, "You may freely eat the fruit of every tree in the garden—[17]except the tree of the knowledge of good and evil. If you eat its fruit, you are sure to die."

[18]Then the LORD God said, "It is not good for the man to be alone. I will make a helper who is just right for him." [19]So the LORD God formed from the ground all the wild animals and all the birds of the sky. He brought them to the man* to see what he would call them, and the man chose a name for each one. [20]He gave names to all the livestock, all the birds of the sky, and all the wild animals. But still there was no helper just right for him.

[21]So the LORD God caused the man to fall into a deep sleep. While the man slept, the LORD God took out one of the man's ribs* and closed up the opening. [22]Then the LORD God made a woman from the rib, and he brought her to the man.

[23]"At last!" the man exclaimed.

"This one is bone from my bone,
    and flesh from my flesh!
She will be called 'woman,'
    because she was taken from 'man.'"

[24]This explains why a man leaves his father and mother and is joined to his wife, and the two are united into one.

[25]Now the man and his wife were both naked, but they felt no shame.

The Man and Woman Sin

3 The serpent was the shrewdest of all the wild animals the LORD God had made. One day he asked the woman, "Did God really say you must not eat the fruit from any of the trees in the garden?"

[2]"Of course we may eat fruit from the trees in the garden," the woman replied. [3]"It's only the fruit from the tree in the middle of the garden that we are not allowed to eat. God said, 'You must not eat it or even touch it; if you do, you will die.'"

[4]"You won't die!" the serpent replied to the woman. [5]"God knows that your eyes will be opened as soon as you eat it, and you will be like God, knowing both good and evil."

[6]The woman was convinced. She saw that the tree was beautiful and its fruit looked delicious, and she wanted the wisdom it would give her. So she took some of the fruit and ate it. Then she gave some to her husband, who was with her, and he ate it, too. [7]At that moment their eyes were opened, and they suddenly felt shame at their nakedness. So they sewed fig leaves together to cover themselves.

[8]When the cool evening breezes were blowing, the man* and his wife heard the LORD God walking about in the garden. So they hid from the LORD God among the trees. [9]Then the LORD God called to the man, "Where are you?"

[10]He replied, "I heard you walking in the garden, so I hid. I was afraid because I was naked."

[11]"Who told you that you were naked?" the LORD God asked. "Have you eaten from the tree whose fruit I commanded you not to eat?"

[12]The man replied, "It was the woman you gave me who gave me the fruit, and I ate it."

[13]Then the LORD God asked the woman, "What have you done?"

"The serpent deceived me," she replied. "That's why I ate it."

[14]Then the LORD God said to the serpent,

"Because you have done this, you are cursed
    more than all animals, domestic and
    wild.
You will crawl on your belly,
    groveling in the dust as long as you live.
[15] And I will cause hostility between you and
        the woman,
    and between your offspring and her
        offspring.
He will strike* your head,
    and you will strike his heel."

[16]Then he said to the woman,

"I will sharpen the pain of your pregnancy,
    and in pain you will give birth.
And you will desire to control your
        husband,
    but he will rule over you.*"

2:19 Or *Adam,* and so throughout the chapter.   **2:21** Or *took a part of the man's side.*   **3:8** Or *Adam,* and so throughout the chapter.   **3:15** Or *bruise;* also in 3:15b.   **3:16** Or *And though you will have desire for your husband, / he will rule over you.*

17And to the man he said,

"Since you listened to your wife and ate
     from the tree
     whose fruit I commanded you not to eat,
the ground is cursed because of you.
     All your life you will struggle to scratch
     a living from it.
18 It will grow thorns and thistles for you,
     though you will eat of its grains.
19 By the sweat of your brow
     will you have food to eat
until you return to the ground
     from which you were made.
For you were made from dust,
     and to dust you will return."

Paradise Lost: God's Judgment

20Then the man—Adam—named his wife Eve,
because she would be the mother of all who
live.* 21And the LORD God made clothing from
animal skins for Adam and his wife.

22Then the LORD God said, "Look, the
human beings* have become like us, knowing
both good and evil. What if they reach out, take
fruit from the tree of life, and eat it? Then they
will live forever!" 23So the LORD God banished
them from the Garden of Eden, and he sent
Adam out to cultivate the ground from which
he had been made. 24After sending them out,
the LORD God stationed mighty cherubim to
the east of the Garden of Eden. And he placed
a flaming sword that flashed back and forth to
guard the way to the tree of life.

Cain and Abel

4 Now Adam* had sexual relations with his
wife, Eve, and she became pregnant. When
she gave birth to Cain, she said, "With the
LORD's help, I have produced* a man!" 2Later
she gave birth to his brother and named him
Abel.

When they grew up, Abel became a shepherd, while Cain cultivated the ground. 3When
it was time for the harvest, Cain presented
some of his crops as a gift to the LORD. 4Abel
also brought a gift—the best portions of the
firstborn lambs from his flock. The LORD accepted Abel and his gift, 5but he did not accept
Cain and his gift. This made Cain very angry,
and he looked dejected.

6"Why are you so angry?" the LORD asked

Cain. "Why do you look so dejected? 7You will
be accepted if you do what is right. But if you
refuse to do what is right, then watch out! Sin
is crouching at the door, eager to control you.
But you must subdue it and be its master."

8One day Cain suggested to his brother,
"Let's go out into the fields."* And while they
were in the field, Cain attacked his brother,
Abel, and killed him.

9Afterward the LORD asked Cain, "Where is
your brother? Where is Abel?"

"I don't know," Cain responded. "Am I my
brother's guardian?"

10But the LORD said, "What have you done?
Listen! Your brother's blood cries out to me
from the ground! 11Now you are cursed and
banished from the ground, which has swallowed your brother's blood. 12No longer will
the ground yield good crops for you, no matter
how hard you work! From now on you will be
a homeless wanderer on the earth."

13Cain replied to the LORD, "My punishment* is too great for me to bear! 14You have
banished me from the land and from your presence; you have made me a homeless wanderer.
Anyone who finds me will kill me!"

15The LORD replied, "No, for I will give a
sevenfold punishment to anyone who kills
you." Then the LORD put a mark on Cain to
warn anyone who might try to kill him. 16So
Cain left the LORD's presence and settled in
the land of Nod,* east of Eden.

The Descendants of Cain

17Cain had sexual relations with his wife, and
she became pregnant and gave birth to Enoch.
Then Cain founded a city, which he named
Enoch, after his son. 18Enoch had a son named
Irad. Irad became the father of* Mehujael.
Mehujael became the father of Methushael.
Methushael became the father of Lamech.

19Lamech married two women. The first
was named Adah, and the second was Zillah.
20Adah gave birth to Jabal, who was the first
of those who raise livestock and live in tents.
21His brother's name was Jubal, the first of
all who play the harp and flute. 22Lamech's
other wife, Zillah, gave birth to a son named
Tubal-cain. He became an expert in forging
tools of bronze and iron. Tubal-cain had a sister named Naamah. 23One day Lamech said to
his wives,

3:20 Eve sounds like a Hebrew term that means "to give life."   3:22 Or the man; Hebrew reads ha-adam.   4:1a Or the man;
also in 4:25.   4:1b Or I have acquired. Cain sounds like a Hebrew term that can mean "produce" or "acquire."   4:8 As
in Samaritan Pentateuch, Greek and Syriac versions, and Latin Vulgate; Masoretic Text lacks "Let's go out into the fields."
4:13 Or My sin.   4:16 Nod means "wandering."   4:18 Or the ancestor of, and so throughout the verse.

"Adah and Zillah, hear my voice;
    listen to me, you wives of Lamech.
I have killed a man who attacked me,
    a young man who wounded me.
²⁴ If someone who kills Cain is punished
        seven times,
    then the one who kills me will be
        punished seventy-seven times!"

The Birth of Seth

²⁵Adam had sexual relations with his wife again, and she gave birth to another son. She named him Seth,* for she said, "God has granted me another son in place of Abel, whom Cain killed." ²⁶When Seth grew up, he had a son and named him Enosh. At that time people first began to worship the LORD by name.

The Descendants of Adam

5 This is the written account of the descendants of Adam. When God created human beings,* he made them to be like himself. ²He created them male and female, and he blessed them and called them "human."

³When Adam was 130 years old, he became the father of a son who was just like him—in his very image. He named his son Seth. ⁴After the birth of Seth, Adam lived another 800 years, and he had other sons and daughters. ⁵Adam lived 930 years, and then he died.

⁶When Seth was 105 years old, he became the father of* Enosh. ⁷After the birth of* Enosh, Seth lived another 807 years, and he had other sons and daughters. ⁸Seth lived 912 years, and then he died.

⁹When Enosh was 90 years old, he became the father of Kenan. ¹⁰After the birth of Kenan, Enosh lived another 815 years, and he had other sons and daughters. ¹¹Enosh lived 905 years, and then he died.

¹²When Kenan was 70 years old, he became the father of Mahalalel. ¹³After the birth of Mahalalel, Kenan lived another 840 years, and he had other sons and daughters. ¹⁴Kenan lived 910 years, and then he died.

¹⁵When Mahalalel was 65 years old, he became the father of Jared. ¹⁶After the birth of Jared, Mahalalel lived another 830 years, and he had other sons and

daughters. ¹⁷Mahalalel lived 895 years, and then he died.

¹⁸When Jared was 162 years old, he became the father of Enoch. ¹⁹After the birth of Enoch, Jared lived another 800 years, and he had other sons and daughters. ²⁰Jared lived 962 years, and then he died.

²¹When Enoch was 65 years old, he became the father of Methuselah. ²²After the birth of Methuselah, Enoch lived in close fellowship with God for another 300 years, and he had other sons and daughters. ²³Enoch lived 365 years, ²⁴walking in close fellowship with God. Then one day he disappeared, because God took him.

²⁵When Methuselah was 187 years old, he became the father of Lamech. ²⁶After the birth of Lamech, Methuselah lived another 782 years, and he had other sons and daughters. ²⁷Methuselah lived 969 years, and then he died.

²⁸When Lamech was 182 years old, he became the father of a son. ²⁹Lamech named his son Noah, for he said, "May he bring us relief* from our work and the painful labor of farming this ground that the LORD has cursed." ³⁰After the birth of Noah, Lamech lived another 595 years, and he had other sons and daughters. ³¹Lamech lived 777 years, and then he died.

³²After Noah was 500 years old, he became the father of Shem, Ham, and Japheth.

A World Gone Wrong

6 Then the people began to multiply on the earth, and daughters were born to them. ²The sons of God saw the beautiful women* and took any they wanted as their wives. ³Then the LORD said, "My Spirit will not put up with* humans for such a long time, for they are only mortal flesh. In the future, their normal lifespan will be no more than 120 years."

⁴In those days, and for some time after, giant Nephilites lived on the earth, for whenever the sons of God had intercourse with women, they gave birth to children who became the heroes and famous warriors of ancient times.

⁵The LORD observed the extent of human wickedness on the earth, and he saw that everything they thought or imagined was consistently and totally evil. ⁶So the LORD was sorry he had ever made them and put them on the

---

4:25 *Seth* probably means "granted"; the name may also mean "appointed."   5:1 Or *man*; Hebrew reads *adam*; similarly in 5:2.   5:6 Or *the ancestor of*; also in 5:9, 12, 15, 18, 21, 25.   5:7 Or *the birth of this ancestor of*; also in 5:10, 13, 16, 19, 22, 26.   5:29 *Noah* sounds like a Hebrew term that can mean "relief" or "comfort."   6:2 Hebrew *daughters of men*; also in 6:4.   6:3 Greek version reads *will not remain in.*

earth. It broke his heart. ⁷And the Lord said, "I will wipe this human race I have created from the face of the earth. Yes, and I will destroy every living thing—all the people, the large animals, the small animals that scurry along the ground, and even the birds of the sky. I am sorry I ever made them." ⁸But Noah found favor with the Lord.

The Story of Noah

⁹This is the account of Noah and his family. Noah was a righteous man, the only blameless person living on earth at the time, and he walked in close fellowship with God. ¹⁰Noah was the father of three sons: Shem, Ham, and Japheth.

¹¹Now God saw that the earth had become corrupt and was filled with violence. ¹²God observed all this corruption in the world, for everyone on earth was corrupt. ¹³So God said to Noah, "I have decided to destroy all living creatures, for they have filled the earth with violence. Yes, I will wipe them all out along with the earth!

¹⁴"Build a large boat* from cypress wood* and waterproof it with tar, inside and out. Then construct decks and stalls throughout its interior. ¹⁵Make the boat 450 feet long, 75 feet wide, and 45 feet high.* ¹⁶Leave an 18-inch opening* below the roof all the way around the boat. Put the door on the side, and build three decks inside the boat—lower, middle, and upper.

¹⁷"Look! I am about to cover the earth with a flood that will destroy every living thing that breathes. Everything on earth will die. ¹⁸But I will confirm my covenant with you. So enter the boat—you and your wife and your sons and their wives. ¹⁹Bring a pair of every kind of animal—a male and a female—into the boat with you to keep them alive during the flood. ²⁰Pairs of every kind of bird, and every kind of animal, and every kind of small animal that scurries along the ground, will come to you to be kept alive. ²¹And be sure to take on board enough food for your family and for all the animals."

²²So Noah did everything exactly as God had commanded him.

The Flood Covers the Earth

7 When everything was ready, the Lord said to Noah, "Go into the boat with all your family, for among all the people of the earth, I can see that you alone are righteous. ²Take with you seven pairs—male and female—of each animal I have approved for eating and for sacrifice,* and take one pair of each of the others. ³Also take seven pairs of every kind of bird. There must be a male and a female in each pair to ensure that all life will survive on the earth after the flood. ⁴Seven days from now I will make the rains pour down on the earth. And it will rain for forty days and forty nights, until I have wiped from the earth all the living things I have created."

⁵So Noah did everything as the Lord commanded him.

⁶Noah was 600 years old when the flood covered the earth. ⁷He went on board the boat to escape the flood—he and his wife and his sons and their wives. ⁸With them were all the various kinds of animals—those approved for eating and for sacrifice and those that were not—along with all the birds and the small animals that scurry along the ground. ⁹They entered the boat in pairs, male and female, just as God had commanded Noah. ¹⁰After seven days, the waters of the flood came and covered the earth.

¹¹When Noah was 600 years old, on the seventeenth day of the second month, all the underground waters erupted from the earth, and the rain fell in mighty torrents from the sky. ¹²The rain continued to fall for forty days and forty nights.

¹³That very day Noah had gone into the boat with his wife and his sons—Shem, Ham, and Japheth—and their wives. ¹⁴With them in the boat were pairs of every kind of animal—domestic and wild, large and small—along with birds of every kind. ¹⁵Two by two they came into the boat, representing every living thing that breathes. ¹⁶A male and a female of each kind entered, just as God had commanded Noah. Then the Lord closed the door behind them.

¹⁷For forty days the floodwaters grew deeper, covering the ground and lifting the boat high above the earth. ¹⁸As the waters rose higher and higher above the ground, the boat floated safely on the surface. ¹⁹Finally, the water covered even the highest mountains on the earth, ²⁰rising more than twenty-two feet* above the highest peaks. ²¹All the living things on earth died—birds, domestic animals, wild animals, small animals that scurry along the ground, and all the people. ²²Everything that

6:14a Traditionally rendered an ark.   6:14b Or gopher wood.   6:15 Hebrew 300 cubits [138 meters] long, 50 cubits [23 meters] wide, and 30 cubits [13.8 meters] high.   6:16 Hebrew an opening of 1 cubit [46 centimeters].   7:2 Hebrew of each clean animal; similarly in 7:8.   7:20 Hebrew 15 cubits [6.9 meters].

breathed and lived on dry land died. ²³God wiped out every living thing on the earth—people, livestock, small animals that scurry along the ground, and the birds of the sky. All were destroyed. The only people who survived were Noah and those with him in the boat. ²⁴And the floodwaters covered the earth for 150 days.

The Flood Recedes

8 But God remembered Noah and all the wild animals and livestock with him in the boat. He sent a wind to blow across the earth, and the floodwaters began to recede. ²The underground waters stopped flowing, and the torrential rains from the sky were stopped. ³So the floodwaters gradually receded from the earth. After 150 days, ⁴exactly five months from the time the flood began,* the boat came to rest on the mountains of Ararat. ⁵Two and a half months later,* as the waters continued to go down, other mountain peaks became visible.

⁶After another forty days, Noah opened the window he had made in the boat ⁷and released a raven. The bird flew back and forth until the floodwaters on the earth had dried up. ⁸He also released a dove to see if the water had receded and it could find dry ground. ⁹But the dove could find no place to land because the water still covered the ground. So it returned to the boat, and Noah held out his hand and drew the dove back inside. ¹⁰After waiting another seven days, Noah released the dove again. ¹¹This time the dove returned to him in the evening with a fresh olive leaf in its beak. Then Noah knew that the floodwaters were almost gone. ¹²He waited another seven days and then released the dove again. This time it did not come back.

¹³Noah was now 601 years old. On the first day of the new year, ten and a half months after the flood began,* the floodwaters had almost dried up from the earth. Noah lifted back the covering of the boat and saw that the surface of the ground was drying. ¹⁴Two more months went by,* and at last the earth was dry!

¹⁵Then God said to Noah, ¹⁶"Leave the boat, all of you—you and your wife, and your sons and their wives. ¹⁷Release all the animals—the birds, the livestock, and the small animals that scurry along the ground—so they can be fruitful and multiply throughout the earth."

¹⁸So Noah, his wife, and his sons and their wives left the boat. ¹⁹And all of the large and small animals and birds came out of the boat, pair by pair.

²⁰Then Noah built an altar to the LORD, and there he sacrificed as burnt offerings the animals and birds that had been approved for that purpose.* ²¹And the LORD was pleased with the aroma of the sacrifice and said to himself, "I will never again curse the ground because of the human race, even though everything they think or imagine is bent toward evil from childhood. I will never again destroy all living things. ²²As long as the earth remains, there will be planting and harvest, cold and heat, summer and winter, day and night."

God Confirms His Covenant

9 Then God blessed Noah and his sons and told them, "Be fruitful and multiply. Fill the earth. ²All the animals of the earth, all the birds of the sky, all the small animals that scurry along the ground, and all the fish in the sea will look on you with fear and terror. I have placed them in your power. ³I have given them to you for food, just as I have given you grain and vegetables. ⁴But you must never eat any meat that still has the lifeblood in it.

⁵"And I will require the blood of anyone who takes another person's life. If a wild animal kills a person, it must die. And anyone who murders a fellow human must die. ⁶If anyone takes a human life, that person's life will also be taken by human hands. For God made human beings* in his own image. ⁷Now be fruitful and multiply, and repopulate the earth."

⁸Then God told Noah and his sons, ⁹"I hereby confirm my covenant with you and your descendants, ¹⁰and with all the animals that were on the boat with you—the birds, the livestock, and all the wild animals—every living creature on earth. ¹¹Yes, I am confirming my covenant with you. Never again will floodwaters kill all living creatures; never again will a flood destroy the earth."

¹²Then God said, "I am giving you a sign of my covenant with you and with all living creatures, for all generations to come. ¹³I have placed my rainbow in the clouds. It is the sign of my covenant with you and with all the earth. ¹⁴When I send clouds over the earth, the rainbow will appear in the clouds, ¹⁵and I will remember my covenant with you

8:4 Hebrew *on the seventeenth day of the seventh month;* see 7:11. on 8:4.   8:13 Hebrew *On the first day of the first month;* see 7:11.   8:14 Hebrew *The twenty-seventh day of the second month arrived;* see note on 8:13.   8:20 Hebrew *every clean animal and every clean bird.*   9:6 Or *man;* Hebrew reads *ha-adam.*

and with all living creatures. Never again will the floodwaters destroy all life. [16]When I see the rainbow in the clouds, I will remember the eternal covenant between God and every living creature on earth." [17]Then God said to Noah, "Yes, this rainbow is the sign of the covenant I am confirming with all the creatures on earth."

Noah's Sons

[18]The sons of Noah who came out of the boat with their father were Shem, Ham, and Japheth. (Ham is the father of Canaan.) [19]From these three sons of Noah came all the people who now populate the earth.

[20]After the flood, Noah began to cultivate the ground, and he planted a vineyard. [21]One day he drank some wine he had made, and he became drunk and lay naked inside his tent. [22]Ham, the father of Canaan, saw that his father was naked and went outside and told his brothers. [23]Then Shem and Japheth took a robe, held it over their shoulders, and backed into the tent to cover their father. As they did this, they looked the other way so they would not see him naked.

[24]When Noah woke up from his stupor, he learned what Ham, his youngest son, had done. [25]Then he cursed Canaan, the son of Ham:

"May Canaan be cursed!
　　May he be the lowest of servants to his
　　　relatives."

[26]Then Noah said,

"May the LORD, the God of Shem, be
　　blessed,
　　and may Canaan be his servant!
[27]　May God expand the territory of Japheth!
　　May Japheth share the prosperity of
　　　Shem,*
　　and may Canaan be his servant."

[28]Noah lived another 350 years after the great flood. [29]He lived 950 years, and then he died.

10 This is the account of the families of Shem, Ham, and Japheth, the three sons of Noah. Many children were born to them after the great flood.

Descendants of Japheth

[2]The descendants of Japheth were Gomer, Magog, Madai, Javan, Tubal, Meshech, and Tiras.
[3]The descendants of Gomer were Ashkenaz, Riphath, and Togarmah.
[4]The descendants of Javan were Elishah, Tarshish, Kittim, and Rodanim.* [5]Their descendants became the seafaring peoples that spread out to various lands, each identified by its own language, clan, and national identity.

Descendants of Ham

[6]The descendants of Ham were Cush, Mizraim, Put, and Canaan.
[7]The descendants of Cush were Seba, Havilah, Sabtah, Raamah, and Sabteca. The descendants of Raamah were Sheba and Dedan.
　　[8]Cush was also the ancestor of Nimrod, who was the first heroic warrior on earth. [9]Since he was the greatest hunter in the world,* his name became proverbial. People would say, "This man is like Nimrod, the greatest hunter in the world." [10]He built his kingdom in the land of Babylonia,* with the cities of Babylon, Erech, Akkad, and Calneh. [11]From there he expanded his territory to Assyria,* building the cities of Nineveh, Rehoboth-ir, Calah, [12]and Resen (the great city located between Nineveh and Calah).
[13]Mizraim was the ancestor of the Ludites, Anamites, Lehabites, Naphtuhites, [14]Pathrusites, Casluhites, and the Caphtorites, from whom the Philistines came.*
[15]Canaan's oldest son was Sidon, the ancestor of the Sidonians. Canaan was also the ancestor of the Hittites,* [16]Jebusites, Amorites, Girgashites, [17]Hivites, Arkites, Sinites, [18]Arvadites, Zemarites, and Hamathites. The Canaanite clans eventually spread out, [19]and the territory of Canaan extended from Sidon in the north to Gerar and Gaza in the south, and east as far as Sodom, Gomorrah, Admah, and Zeboiim, near Lasha.
[20]These were the descendants of Ham, identified by clan, language, territory, and national identity.

9:27 Hebrew *May he live in the tents of Shem*.　　10:4 As in some Hebrew manuscripts and Greek version (see also 1 Chr 1:7); most Hebrew manuscripts read *Dodanim*.　　10:9 Hebrew *a great hunter before the LORD*; also in 10:9b.　　10:10 Hebrew *Shinar*. 10:11 Or *From that land Assyria went out*.　　10:14 Hebrew *Casluhites, from whom the Philistines came, and Caphtorites*. Compare Jer 47:4; Amos 9:7.　　10:15 Hebrew *ancestor of Heth*.

Descendants of Shem

²¹Sons were also born to Shem, the older brother of Japheth.* Shem was the ancestor of all the descendants of Eber. ²²The descendants of Shem were Elam, Asshur, Arphaxad, Lud, and Aram. ²³The descendants of Aram were Uz, Hul, Gether, and Mash. ²⁴Arphaxad was the father of Shelah,* and Shelah was the father of Eber. ²⁵Eber had two sons. The first was named Peleg (which means "division"), for during his lifetime the people of the world were divided into different language groups. His brother's name was Joktan. ²⁶Joktan was the ancestor of Almodad, Sheleph, Hazarmaveth, Jerah, ²⁷Hadoram, Uzal, Diklah, ²⁸Obal, Abimael, Sheba, ²⁹Ophir, Havilah, and Jobab. All these were descendants of Joktan. ³⁰The territory they occupied extended from Mesha all the way to Sephar in the eastern mountains. ³¹These were the descendants of Shem, identified by clan, language, territory, and national identity.

Conclusion

³²These are the clans that descended from Noah's sons, arranged by nation according to their lines of descent. All the nations of the earth descended from these clans after the great flood.

The Tower of Babel

11 At one time all the people of the world spoke the same language and used the same words. ²As the people migrated to the east, they found a plain in the land of Babylonia* and settled there.

³They began saying to each other, "Let's make bricks and harden them with fire." (In this region bricks were used instead of stone, and tar was used for mortar.) ⁴Then they said, "Come, let's build a great city for ourselves with a tower that reaches into the sky. This will make us famous and keep us from being scattered all over the world."

⁵But the LORD came down to look at the city and the tower the people were building. ⁶"Look!" he said. "The people are united, and they all speak the same language. After this, nothing they set out to do will be impossible for them! ⁷Come, let's go down and confuse the people with different languages. Then they won't be able to understand each other."

⁸In that way, the LORD scattered them all over the world, and they stopped building the city. ⁹That is why the city was called Babel,* because that is where the LORD confused the people with different languages. In this way he scattered them all over the world.

The Line of Descent from Shem to Abram

¹⁰This is the account of Shem's family.

Two years after the great flood, when Shem was 100 years old, he became the father of* Arphaxad. ¹¹After the birth of* Arphaxad, Shem lived another 500 years and had other sons and daughters.

¹²When Arphaxad was 35 years old, he became the father of Shelah. ¹³After the birth of Shelah, Arphaxad lived another 403 years and had other sons and daughters.*

¹⁴When Shelah was 30 years old, he became the father of Eber. ¹⁵After the birth of Eber, Shelah lived another 403 years and had other sons and daughters.

¹⁶When Eber was 34 years old, he became the father of Peleg. ¹⁷After the birth of Peleg, Eber lived another 430 years and had other sons and daughters.

¹⁸When Peleg was 30 years old, he became the father of Reu. ¹⁹After the birth of Reu, Peleg lived another 209 years and had other sons and daughters.

²⁰When Reu was 32 years old, he became the father of Serug. ²¹After the birth of Serug, Reu lived another 207 years and had other sons and daughters.

²²When Serug was 30 years old, he became the father of Nahor. ²³After the birth of Nahor, Serug lived another 200 years and had other sons and daughters.

²⁴When Nahor was 29 years old, he became the father of Terah. ²⁵After the birth of Terah, Nahor lived another 119 years and had other sons and daughters.

²⁶After Terah was 70 years old, he became the father of Abram, Nahor, and Haran.

10:21 Or *Shem, whose older brother was Japheth.*   **10:24** Greek version reads *Arphaxad was the father of Cainan, Cainan was the father of Shelah.* Compare Luke 3:36.   **11:2** Hebrew *Shinar.*   **11:9** Or *Babylon. Babel* sounds like a Hebrew term that means "confusion."   **11:10** Or *the ancestor of;* also in 11:12, 14, 16, 18, 20, 22, 24.   **11:11** Or *the birth of this ancestor of;* also in 11:13, 15, 17, 19, 21, 23, 25.   **11:12-13** Greek version reads ¹²*When Arphaxad was 135 years old, he became the father of Cainan.* ¹³*After the birth of Cainan, Arphaxad lived another 430 years and had other sons and daughters, and then he died. When Cainan was 130 years old, he became the father of Shelah. After the birth of Shelah, Cainan lived another 330 years and had other sons and daughters, and then he died.* Compare Luke 3:35-36.

The Family of Terah

27This is the account of Terah's family. Terah was the father of Abram, Nahor, and Haran; and Haran was the father of Lot. 28But Haran died in Ur of the Chaldeans, the land of his birth, while his father, Terah, was still living. 29Meanwhile, Abram and Nahor both married. The name of Abram's wife was Sarai, and the name of Nahor's wife was Milcah. (Milcah and her sister Iscah were daughters of Nahor's brother Haran.) 30But Sarai was unable to become pregnant and had no children.

31One day Terah took his son Abram, his daughter-in-law Sarai (his son Abram's wife), and his grandson Lot (his son Haran's child) and moved away from Ur of the Chaldeans. He was headed for the land of Canaan, but they stopped at Haran and settled there. 32Terah lived for 205 years* and died while still in Haran.

The Call of Abram

12 The LORD had said to Abram, "Leave your native country, your relatives, and your father's family, and go to the land that I will show you. 2I will make you into a great nation. I will bless you and make you famous, and you will be a blessing to others. 3I will bless those who bless you and curse those who treat you with contempt. All the families on earth will be blessed through you."

4So Abram departed as the LORD had instructed, and Lot went with him. Abram was seventy-five years old when he left Haran. 5He took his wife, Sarai, his nephew Lot, and all his wealth—his livestock and all the people he had taken into his household at Haran—and headed for the land of Canaan. When they arrived in Canaan, 6Abram traveled through the land as far as Shechem. There he set up camp beside the oak of Moreh. At that time, the area was inhabited by Canaanites.

7Then the LORD appeared to Abram and said, "I will give this land to your descendants.*" And Abram built an altar there and dedicated it to the LORD, who had appeared to him. 8After that, Abram traveled south and set up camp in the hill country, with Bethel to the west and Ai to the east. There he built another altar and dedicated it to the LORD, and he worshiped the LORD. 9Then Abram continued traveling south by stages toward the Negev.

Abram and Sarai in Egypt

10At that time a severe famine struck the land of Canaan, forcing Abram to go down to Egypt, where he lived as a foreigner. 11As he was approaching the border of Egypt, Abram said to his wife, Sarai, "Look, you are a very beautiful woman. 12When the Egyptians see you, they will say, 'This is his wife. Let's kill him; then we can have her!' 13So please tell them you are my sister. Then they will spare my life and treat me well because of their interest in you."

14And sure enough, when Abram arrived in Egypt, everyone noticed Sarai's beauty. 15When the palace officials saw her, they sang her praises to Pharaoh, their king, and Sarai was taken into his palace. 16Then Pharaoh gave Abram many gifts because of her—sheep, goats, cattle, male and female donkeys, male and female servants, and camels.

17But the LORD sent terrible plagues upon Pharaoh and his household because of Sarai, Abram's wife. 18So Pharaoh summoned Abram and accused him sharply. "What have you done to me?" he demanded. "Why didn't you tell me she was your wife? 19Why did you say, 'She is my sister,' and allow me to take her as my wife? Now then, here is your wife. Take her and get out of here!" 20Pharaoh ordered some of his men to escort them, and he sent Abram out of the country, along with his wife and all his possessions.

Abram and Lot Separate

13 So Abram left Egypt and traveled north into the Negev, along with his wife and Lot and all that they owned. 2(Abram was very rich in livestock, silver, and gold.) 3From the Negev, they continued traveling by stages toward Bethel, and they pitched their tents between Bethel and Ai, where they had camped before. 4This was the same place where Abram had built the altar, and there he worshiped the LORD again.

5Lot, who was traveling with Abram, had also become very wealthy with flocks of sheep and goats, herds of cattle, and many tents. 6But the land could not support both Abram and Lot with all their flocks and herds living so close together. 7So disputes broke out between the herdsmen of Abram and Lot. (At that time Canaanites and Perizzites were also living in the land.)

8Finally Abram said to Lot, "Let's not allow this conflict to come between us or our herdsmen. After all, we are close relatives! 9The whole countryside is open to you. Take your choice of any section of the land you want, and we will separate. If you want the land to

11:32 Some ancient versions read 145 years; compare 11:26 and 12:4.   12:7 Hebrew seed.

the left, then I'll take the land on the right. If you prefer the land on the right, then I'll go to the left."

¹⁰Lot took a long look at the fertile plains of the Jordan Valley in the direction of Zoar. The whole area was well watered everywhere, like the garden of the LORD or the beautiful land of Egypt. (This was before the LORD destroyed Sodom and Gomorrah.) ¹¹Lot chose for himself the whole Jordan Valley to the east of them. He went there with his flocks and servants and parted company with his uncle Abram. ¹²So Abram settled in the land of Canaan, and Lot moved his tents to a place near Sodom and settled among the cities of the plain. ¹³But the people of this area were extremely wicked and constantly sinned against the LORD.

¹⁴After Lot had gone, the LORD said to Abram, "Look as far as you can see in every direction—north and south, east and west. ¹⁵I am giving all this land, as far as you can see, to you and your descendants* as a permanent possession. ¹⁶And I will give you so many descendants that, like the dust of the earth, they cannot be counted! ¹⁷Go and walk through the land in every direction, for I am giving it to you."

¹⁸So Abram moved his camp to Hebron and settled near the oak grove belonging to Mamre. There he built another altar to the LORD.

Abram Rescues Lot

14 About this time war broke out in the region. King Amraphel of Babylonia,* King Arioch of Ellasar, King Kedorlaomer of Elam, and King Tidal of Goiim ²fought against King Bera of Sodom, King Birsha of Gomorrah, King Shinab of Admah, King Shemeber of Zeboiim, and the king of Bela (also called Zoar). ³This second group of kings joined forces in Siddim Valley (that is, the valley of the Dead Sea*). ⁴For twelve years they had been subject to King Kedorlaomer, but in the thirteenth year they rebelled against him.

⁵One year later Kedorlaomer and his allies arrived and defeated the Rephaites at Ashteroth-karnaim, the Zuzites at Ham, the Emites at Shaveh-kiriathaim, ⁶and the Horites at Mount Seir, as far as El-paran at the edge of the wilderness. ⁷Then they turned back and came to En-mishpat (now called Kadesh) and conquered all the territory of the Amalekites, and also the Amorites living in Hazazon-tamar. ⁸Then the rebel kings of Sodom, Gomorrah, Admah, Zeboiim, and Bela (also called Zoar)

prepared for battle in the valley of the Dead Sea.* ⁹They fought against King Kedorlaomer of Elam, King Tidal of Goiim, King Amraphel of Babylonia, and King Arioch of Ellasar—four kings against five. ¹⁰As it happened, the valley of the Dead Sea was filled with tar pits. And as the army of the kings of Sodom and Gomorrah fled, some fell into the tar pits, while the rest escaped into the mountains. ¹¹The victorious invaders then plundered Sodom and Gomorrah and headed for home, taking with them all the spoils of war and the food supplies. ¹²They also captured Lot—Abram's nephew who lived in Sodom—and carried off everything he owned.

¹³But one of Lot's men escaped and reported everything to Abram the Hebrew, who was living near the oak grove belonging to Mamre the Amorite. Mamre and his relatives, Eshcol and Aner, were Abram's allies.

¹⁴When Abram heard that his nephew Lot had been captured, he mobilized the 318 trained men who had been born into his household. Then he pursued Kedorlaomer's army until he caught up with them at Dan. ¹⁵There he divided his men and attacked during the night. Kedorlaomer's army fled, but Abram chased them as far as Hobah, north of Damascus. ¹⁶Abram recovered all the goods that had been taken, and he brought back his nephew Lot with his possessions and all the women and other captives.

Melchizedek Blesses Abram

¹⁷After Abram returned from his victory over Kedorlaomer and all his allies, the king of Sodom went out to meet him in the valley of Shaveh (that is, the King's Valley).

¹⁸And Melchizedek, the king of Salem and a priest of God Most High,* brought Abram some bread and wine. ¹⁹Melchizedek blessed Abram with this blessing:

"Blessed be Abram by God Most High,
    Creator of heaven and earth.
²⁰ And blessed be God Most High,
    who has defeated your enemies for you."

Then Abram gave Melchizedek a tenth of all the goods he had recovered.

²¹The king of Sodom said to Abram, "Give back my people who were captured. But you may keep for yourself all the goods you have recovered."

²²Abram replied to the king of Sodom, "I

13:15 Hebrew *seed*; also in 13:16.   14:1 Hebrew *Shinar*; also in 14:9.   14:3 Hebrew *Salt Sea*.   14:8 Hebrew *Siddim Valley* (see 14:3); also in 14:10.   14:18 Hebrew *El-Elyon*; also in 14:19, 20, 22.

solemnly swear to the LORD, God Most High, Creator of heaven and earth, 23that I will not take so much as a single thread or sandal thong from what belongs to you. Otherwise you might say, 'I am the one who made Abram rich.' 24I will accept only what my young warriors have already eaten, and I request that you give a fair share of the goods to my allies—Aner, Eshcol, and Mamre."

The LORD's Covenant Promise to Abram

15 Some time later, the LORD spoke to Abram in a vision and said to him, "Do not be afraid, Abram, for I will protect you, and your reward will be great."

2But Abram replied, "O Sovereign LORD, what good are all your blessings when I don't even have a son? Since you've given me no children, Eliezer of Damascus, a servant in my household, will inherit all my wealth. 3You have given me no descendants of my own, so one of my servants will be my heir."

4Then the LORD said to him, "No, your servant will not be your heir, for you will have a son of your own who will be your heir." 5Then the LORD took Abram outside and said to him, "Look up into the sky and count the stars if you can. That's how many descendants you will have!"

6And Abram believed the LORD, and the LORD counted him as righteous because of his faith.

7Then the LORD told him, "I am the LORD who brought you out of Ur of the Chaldeans to give you this land as your possession."

8But Abram replied, "O Sovereign LORD, how can I be sure that I will actually possess it?"

9The LORD told him, "Bring me a three-year-old heifer, a three-year-old female goat, a three-year-old ram, a turtledove, and a young pigeon." 10So Abram presented all these to him and killed them. Then he cut each animal down the middle and laid the halves side by side; he did not, however, cut the birds in half. 11Some vultures swooped down to eat the carcasses, but Abram chased them away.

12As the sun was going down, Abram fell into a deep sleep, and a terrifying darkness came down over him. 13Then the LORD said to Abram, "You can be sure that your descendants will be strangers in a foreign land, where they will be oppressed as slaves for 400 years. 14But I will punish the nation that enslaves them, and in the end they will come away with great wealth. 15(As for you, you will die in peace and be buried at a ripe old age.) 16After four generations your descendants will return here to this land, for the sins of the Amorites do not yet warrant their destruction."

17After the sun went down and darkness fell, Abram saw a smoking firepot and a flaming torch pass between the halves of the carcasses. 18So the LORD made a covenant with Abram that day and said, "I have given this land to your descendants, all the way from the border of Egypt* to the great Euphrates River—19the land now occupied by the Kenites, Kenizzites, Kadmonites, 20Hittites, Perizzites, Rephaites, 21Amorites, Canaanites, Girgashites, and Jebusites."

The Birth of Ishmael

16 Now Sarai, Abram's wife, had not been able to bear children for him. But she had an Egyptian servant named Hagar. 2So Sarai said to Abram, "The LORD has prevented me from having children. Go and sleep with my servant. Perhaps I can have children through her." And Abram agreed with Sarai's proposal. 3So Sarai, Abram's wife, took Hagar the Egyptian servant and gave her to Abram as a wife. (This happened ten years after Abram had settled in the land of Canaan.)

4So Abram had sexual relations with Hagar, and she became pregnant. But when Hagar knew she was pregnant, she began to treat her mistress, Sarai, with contempt. 5Then Sarai said to Abram, "This is all your fault! I put my servant into your arms, but now that she's pregnant she treats me with contempt. The LORD will show who's wrong—you or me!"

6Abram replied, "Look, she is your servant, so deal with her as you see fit." Then Sarai treated Hagar so harshly that she finally ran away.

7The angel of the LORD found Hagar beside a spring of water in the wilderness, along the road to Shur. 8The angel said to her, "Hagar, Sarai's servant, where have you come from, and where are you going?"

"I'm running away from my mistress, Sarai," she replied.

9The angel of the LORD said to her, "Return to your mistress, and submit to her authority." 10Then he added, "I will give you more descendants than you can count."

11And the angel also said, "You are now pregnant and will give birth to a son. You are to name him Ishmael (which means 'God hears'), for the LORD has heard your cry of distress.

15:18 Hebrew *the river of Egypt,* referring either to an eastern branch of the Nile River or to the Brook of Egypt in the Sinai (see Num 34:5).

¹²This son of yours will be a wild man, as untamed as a wild donkey! He will raise his fist against everyone, and everyone will be against him. Yes, he will live in open hostility against all his relatives."

¹³Thereafter, Hagar used another name to refer to the LORD, who had spoken to her. She said, "You are the God who sees me."* She also said, "Have I truly seen the One who sees me?" ¹⁴So that well was named Beer-lahai-roi (which means "well of the Living One who sees me"). It can still be found between Kadesh and Bered.

¹⁵So Hagar gave Abram a son, and Abram named him Ishmael. ¹⁶Abram was eighty-six years old when Ishmael was born.

Abram Is Named Abraham

17 When Abram was ninety-nine years old, the LORD appeared to him and said, "I am El-Shaddai—'God Almighty.' Serve me faithfully and live a blameless life. ²I will make a covenant with you, by which I will guarantee to give you countless descendants."

³At this, Abram fell face down on the ground. Then God said to him, ⁴"This is my covenant with you: I will make you the father of a multitude of nations! ⁵What's more, I am changing your name. It will no longer be Abram. Instead, you will be called Abraham,* for you will be the father of many nations. ⁶I will make you extremely fruitful. Your descendants will become many nations, and kings will be among them!

⁷"I will confirm my covenant with you and your descendants* after you, from generation to generation. This is the everlasting covenant: I will always be your God and the God of your descendants after you. ⁸And I will give the entire land of Canaan, where you now live as a foreigner, to you and your descendants. It will be their possession forever, and I will be their God."

The Mark of the Covenant

⁹Then God said to Abraham, "Your responsibility is to obey the terms of the covenant. You and all your descendants have this continual responsibility. ¹⁰This is the covenant that you and your descendants must keep: Each male among you must be circumcised. ¹¹You must cut off the flesh of your foreskin as a sign of the covenant between me and you. ¹²From generation to generation, every male child must be circumcised on the eighth day after his birth. This applies not only to members of your family but also to the servants born in your household and the foreign-born servants whom you have purchased. ¹³All must be circumcised. Your bodies will bear the mark of my everlasting covenant. ¹⁴Any male who fails to be circumcised will be cut off from the covenant family for breaking the covenant."

Sarai Is Named Sarah

¹⁵Then God said to Abraham, "Regarding Sarai, your wife—her name will no longer be Sarai. From now on her name will be Sarah.* ¹⁶And I will bless her and give you a son from her! Yes, I will bless her richly, and she will become the mother of many nations. Kings of nations will be among her descendants."

¹⁷Then Abraham bowed down to the ground, but he laughed to himself in disbelief. "How could I become a father at the age of 100?" he thought. "And how can Sarah have a baby when she is ninety years old?" ¹⁸So Abraham said to God, "May Ishmael live under your special blessing!"

¹⁹But God replied, "No—Sarah, your wife, will give birth to a son for you. You will name him Isaac,* and I will confirm my covenant with him and his descendants as an everlasting covenant. ²⁰As for Ishmael, I will bless him also, just as you have asked. I will make him extremely fruitful and multiply his descendants. He will become the father of twelve princes, and I will make him a great nation. ²¹But my covenant will be confirmed with Isaac, who will be born to you and Sarah about this time next year." ²²When God had finished speaking, he left Abraham.

²³On that very day Abraham took his son, Ishmael, and every male in his household, including those born there and those he had bought. Then he circumcised them, cutting off their foreskins, just as God had told him. ²⁴Abraham was ninety-nine years old when he was circumcised, ²⁵and Ishmael, his son, was thirteen. ²⁶Both Abraham and his son, Ishmael, were circumcised on that same day, ²⁷along with all the other men and boys of the household, whether they were born there or bought as servants. All were circumcised with him.

A Son Is Promised to Sarah

18 The LORD appeared again to Abraham near the oak grove belonging to Mamre. One day Abraham was sitting at the entrance

---

16:13 Hebrew *El-roi.*   17:5 *Abram* means "exalted father"; *Abraham* sounds like a Hebrew term that means "father of many."
17:7 Hebrew *seed*; also in 17:7b, 8, 9, 10, 19.   17:15 *Sarai* and *Sarah* both mean "princess"; the change in spelling may reflect
the difference in dialect between Ur and Canaan.   17:19 *Isaac* means "he laughs."

to his tent during the hottest part of the day. ²He looked up and noticed three men standing nearby. When he saw them, he ran to meet them and welcomed them, bowing low to the ground.

³"My lord," he said, "if it pleases you, stop here for a while. ⁴Rest in the shade of this tree while water is brought to wash your feet. ⁵And since you've honored your servant with this visit, let me prepare some food to refresh you before you continue on your journey."

"All right," they said. "Do as you have said."

⁶So Abraham ran back to the tent and said to Sarah, "Hurry! Get three large measures* of your best flour, knead it into dough, and bake some bread." ⁷Then Abraham ran out to the herd and chose a tender calf and gave it to his servant, who quickly prepared it. ⁸When the food was ready, Abraham took some yogurt and milk and the roasted meat, and he served it to the men. As they ate, Abraham waited on them in the shade of the trees.

⁹"Where is Sarah, your wife?" the visitors asked.

"She's inside the tent," Abraham replied.

¹⁰Then one of them said, "I will return to you about this time next year, and your wife, Sarah, will have a son!"

Sarah was listening to this conversation from the tent. ¹¹Abraham and Sarah were both very old by this time, and Sarah was long past the age of having children. ¹²So she laughed silently to herself and said, "How could a worn-out woman like me enjoy such pleasure, especially when my master—my husband—is also so old?"

¹³Then the LORD said to Abraham, "Why did Sarah laugh? Why did she say, 'Can an old woman like me have a baby?' ¹⁴Is anything too hard for the LORD? I will return about this time next year, and Sarah will have a son."

¹⁵Sarah was afraid, so she denied it, saying, "I didn't laugh."

But the LORD said, "No, you did laugh."

Abraham Intercedes for Sodom

¹⁶Then the men got up from their meal and looked out toward Sodom. As they left, Abraham went with them to send them on their way.

¹⁷"Should I hide my plan from Abraham?" the LORD asked. ¹⁸"For Abraham will certainly become a great and mighty nation, and all the nations of the earth will be blessed through him. ¹⁹I have singled him out so that he will direct his sons and their families to keep the way of the LORD by doing what is right and just. Then I will do for Abraham all that I have promised."

²⁰So the LORD told Abraham, "I have heard a great outcry from Sodom and Gomorrah, because their sin is so flagrant. ²¹I am going down to see if their actions are as wicked as I have heard. If not, I want to know."

²²The other men turned and headed toward Sodom, but the LORD remained with Abraham. ²³Abraham approached him and said, "Will you sweep away both the righteous and the wicked? ²⁴Suppose you find fifty righteous people living there in the city—will you still sweep it away and not spare it for their sakes? ²⁵Surely you wouldn't do such a thing, destroying the righteous along with the wicked. Why, you would be treating the righteous and the wicked exactly the same! Surely you wouldn't do that! Should not the Judge of all the earth do what is right?"

²⁶And the LORD replied, "If I find fifty righteous people in Sodom, I will spare the entire city for their sake."

²⁷Then Abraham spoke again. "Since I have begun, let me speak further to my Lord, even though I am but dust and ashes. ²⁸Suppose there are only forty-five righteous people rather than fifty? Will you destroy the whole city for lack of five?"

And the LORD said, "I will not destroy it if I find forty-five righteous people there."

²⁹Then Abraham pressed his request further. "Suppose there are only forty?"

And the LORD replied, "I will not destroy it for the sake of the forty."

³⁰"Please don't be angry, my Lord," Abraham pleaded. "Let me speak—suppose only thirty righteous people are found?"

And the LORD replied, "I will not destroy it if I find thirty."

³¹Then Abraham said, "Since I have dared to speak to the Lord, let me continue—suppose there are only twenty?"

And the LORD replied, "Then I will not destroy it for the sake of the twenty."

³²Finally, Abraham said, "Lord, please don't be angry with me if I speak one more time. Suppose only ten are found there?"

And the LORD replied, "Then I will not destroy it for the sake of the ten."

³³When the LORD had finished his conversation with Abraham, he went on his way, and Abraham returned to his tent.

18:6 Hebrew *3 seahs,* about half a bushel or 22 liters.

Sodom and Gomorrah Destroyed

19 That evening the two angels came to the entrance of the city of Sodom. Lot was sitting there, and when he saw them, he stood up to meet them. Then he welcomed them and bowed with his face to the ground. ²"My lords," he said, "come to my home to wash your feet, and be my guests for the night. You may then get up early in the morning and be on your way again."

"Oh no," they replied. "We'll just spend the night out here in the city square."

³But Lot insisted, so at last they went home with him. Lot prepared a feast for them, complete with fresh bread made without yeast, and they ate. ⁴But before they retired for the night, all the men of Sodom, young and old, came from all over the city and surrounded the house. ⁵They shouted to Lot, "Where are the men who came to spend the night with you? Bring them out to us so we can have sex with them!"

⁶So Lot stepped outside to talk to them, shutting the door behind him. ⁷"Please, my brothers," he begged, "don't do such a wicked thing. ⁸Look, I have two virgin daughters. Let me bring them out to you, and you can do with them as you wish. But please, leave these men alone, for they are my guests and are under my protection."

⁹"Stand back!" they shouted. "This fellow came to town as an outsider, and now he's acting like our judge! We'll treat you far worse than those other men!" And they lunged toward Lot to break down the door.

¹⁰But the two angels* reached out, pulled Lot into the house, and bolted the door. ¹¹Then they blinded all the men, young and old, who were at the door of the house, so they gave up trying to get inside.

¹²Meanwhile, the angels questioned Lot. "Do you have any other relatives here in the city?" they asked. "Get them out of this place—your sons-in-law, sons, daughters, or anyone else. ¹³For we are about to destroy this city completely. The outcry against this place is so great it has reached the LORD, and he has sent us to destroy it."

¹⁴So Lot rushed out to tell his daughters' fiancés, "Quick, get out of the city! The LORD is about to destroy it." But the young men thought he was only joking.

¹⁵At dawn the next morning the angels became insistent. "Hurry," they said to Lot. "Take your wife and your two daughters who are

19:10 Hebrew *men*; also in 19:12, 16.

here. Get out right now, or you will be swept away in the destruction of the city!"

¹⁶When Lot still hesitated, the angels seized his hand and the hands of his wife and two daughters and rushed them to safety outside the city, for the LORD was merciful. ¹⁷When they were safely out of the city, one of the angels ordered, "Run for your lives! And don't look back or stop anywhere in the valley! Escape to the mountains, or you will be swept away!"

¹⁸"Oh no, my lord!" Lot begged. ¹⁹"You have been so gracious to me and saved my life, and you have shown such great kindness. But I cannot go to the mountains. Disaster would catch up to me there, and I would soon die. ²⁰See, there is a small village nearby. Please let me go there instead; don't you see how small it is? Then my life will be saved."

²¹"All right," the angel said, "I will grant your request. I will not destroy the little village. ²²But hurry! Escape to it, for I can do nothing until you arrive there." (This explains why that village was known as Zoar, which means "little place.")

²³Lot reached the village just as the sun was rising over the horizon. ²⁴Then the LORD rained down fire and burning sulfur from the sky on Sodom and Gomorrah. ²⁵He utterly destroyed them, along with the other cities and villages of the plain, wiping out all the people and every bit of vegetation. ²⁶But Lot's wife looked back as she was following behind him, and she turned into a pillar of salt.

²⁷Abraham got up early that morning and hurried out to the place where he had stood in the LORD's presence. ²⁸He looked out across the plain toward Sodom and Gomorrah and watched as columns of smoke rose from the cities like smoke from a furnace.

²⁹But God had listened to Abraham's request and kept Lot safe, removing him from the disaster that engulfed the cities on the plain.

Lot and His Daughters

³⁰Afterward Lot left Zoar because he was afraid of the people there, and he went to live in a cave in the mountains with his two daughters. ³¹One day the older daughter said to her sister, "There are no men left anywhere in this entire area, so we can't get married like everyone else. And our father will soon be too old to have children. ³²Come, let's get him drunk with wine, and then we will have sex with him. That way we will preserve our family line through our father."

33So that night they got him drunk with wine, and the older daughter went in and had intercourse with her father. He was unaware of her lying down or getting up again.

34The next morning the older daughter said to her younger sister, "I had sex with our father last night. Let's get him drunk with wine again tonight, and you go in and have sex with him. That way we will preserve our family line through our father." 35So that night they got him drunk with wine again, and the younger daughter went in and had intercourse with him. As before, he was unaware of her lying down or getting up again.

36As a result, both of Lot's daughters became pregnant by their own father. 37When the older daughter gave birth to a son, she named him Moab.* He became the ancestor of the nation now known as the Moabites. 38When the younger daughter gave birth to a son, she named him Ben-ammi.* He became the ancestor of the nation now known as the Ammonites.

Abraham Deceives Abimelech

20 Abraham moved south to the Negev and lived for a while between Kadesh and Shur, and then he moved on to Gerar. While living there as a foreigner, 2Abraham introduced his wife, Sarah, by saying, "She is my sister." So King Abimelech of Gerar sent for Sarah and had her brought to him at his palace.

3But that night God came to Abimelech in a dream and told him, "You are a dead man, for that woman you have taken is already married!"

4But Abimelech had not slept with her yet, so he said, "Lord, will you destroy an innocent nation? 5Didn't Abraham tell me, 'She is my sister'? And she herself said, 'Yes, he is my brother.' I acted in complete innocence! My hands are clean."

6In the dream God responded, "Yes, I know you are innocent. That's why I kept you from sinning against me, and why I did not let you touch her. 7Now return the woman to her husband, and he will pray for you, for he is a prophet. Then you will live. But if you don't return her to him, you can be sure that you and all your people will die."

8Abimelech got up early the next morning and quickly called all his servants together. When he told them what had happened, his men were terrified. 9Then Abimelech called

for Abraham. "What have you done to us?" he demanded. "What crime have I committed that deserves treatment like this, making me and my kingdom guilty of this great sin? No one should ever do what you have done! 10Whatever possessed you to do such a thing?"

11Abraham replied, "I thought, 'This is a godless place. They will want my wife and will kill me to get her.' 12And she really is my sister, for we both have the same father, but different mothers. And I married her. 13When God called me to leave my father's home and to travel from place to place, I told her, 'Do me a favor. Wherever we go, tell the people that I am your brother.'"

14Then Abimelech took some of his sheep and goats, cattle, and male and female servants, and he presented them to Abraham. He also returned his wife, Sarah, to him. 15Then Abimelech said, "Look over my land and choose any place where you would like to live." 16And he said to Sarah, "Look, I am giving your 'brother' 1,000 pieces of silver* in the presence of all these witnesses. This is to compensate you for any wrong I may have done to you. This will settle any claim against me, and your reputation is cleared."

17Then Abraham prayed to God, and God healed Abimelech, his wife, and his female servants, so they could have children. 18For the LORD had caused all the women to be infertile because of what happened with Abraham's wife, Sarah.

The Birth of Isaac

21 The LORD kept his word and did for Sarah exactly what he had promised. 2She became pregnant, and she gave birth to a son for Abraham in his old age. This happened at just the time God had said it would. 3And Abraham named their son Isaac. 4Eight days after Isaac was born, Abraham circumcised him as God had commanded. 5Abraham was 100 years old when Isaac was born.

6And Sarah declared, "God has brought me laughter.* All who hear about this will laugh with me. 7Who would have said to Abraham that Sarah would nurse a baby? Yet I have given Abraham a son in his old age!"

Hagar and Ishmael Are Sent Away

8When Isaac grew up and was about to be weaned, Abraham prepared a huge feast to celebrate the occasion. 9But Sarah saw

19:37 Moab sounds like a Hebrew term that means "from father."   19:38 Ben-ammi means "son of my kinsman."
20:16 Hebrew 1,000 [shekels] of silver, about 25 pounds or 11.4 kilograms in weight.   21:6 The name Isaac means "he laughs."

Ishmael—the son of Abraham and her Egyptian servant Hagar—making fun of her son, Isaac.* ¹⁰So she turned to Abraham and demanded, "Get rid of that slave woman and her son. He is not going to share the inheritance with my son, Isaac. I won't have it!"

¹¹This upset Abraham very much because Ishmael was his son. ¹²But God told Abraham, "Do not be upset over the boy and your servant. Do whatever Sarah tells you, for Isaac is the son through whom your descendants will be counted. ¹³But I will also make a nation of the descendants of Hagar's son because he is your son, too."

¹⁴So Abraham got up early the next morning, prepared food and a container of water, and strapped them on Hagar's shoulders. Then he sent her away with their son, and she wandered aimlessly in the wilderness of Beersheba.

¹⁵When the water was gone, she put the boy in the shade of a bush. ¹⁶Then she went and sat down by herself about a hundred yards* away. "I don't want to watch the boy die," she said, as she burst into tears.

¹⁷But God heard the boy crying, and the angel of God called to Hagar from heaven, "Hagar, what's wrong? Do not be afraid! God has heard the boy crying as he lies there. ¹⁸Go to him and comfort him, for I will make a great nation from his descendants."

¹⁹Then God opened Hagar's eyes, and she saw a well full of water. She quickly filled her water container and gave the boy a drink.

²⁰And God was with the boy as he grew up in the wilderness. He became a skillful archer, ²¹and he settled in the wilderness of Paran. His mother arranged for him to marry a woman from the land of Egypt.

Abraham's Covenant with Abimelech

²²About this time, Abimelech came with Phicol, his army commander, to visit Abraham. "God is obviously with you, helping you in everything you do," Abimelech said. ²³"Swear to me in God's name that you will never deceive me, my children, or any of my descendants. I have been loyal to you, so now swear that you will be loyal to me and to this country where you are living as a foreigner."

²⁴Abraham replied, "Yes, I swear to it!" ²⁵Then Abraham complained to Abimelech about a well that Abimelech's servants had taken by force from Abraham's servants.

²⁶"This is the first I've heard of it," Abimelech answered. "I have no idea who is responsible. You have never complained about this before."

²⁷Abraham then gave some of his sheep, goats, and cattle to Abimelech, and they made a treaty. ²⁸But Abraham also took seven additional female lambs and set them off by themselves. ²⁹Abimelech asked, "Why have you set these seven apart from the others?"

³⁰Abraham replied, "Please accept these seven lambs to show your agreement that I dug this well." ³¹Then he named the place Beersheba (which means "well of the oath"), because that was where they had sworn the oath.

³²After making their covenant at Beersheba, Abimelech left with Phicol, the commander of his army, and they returned home to the land of the Philistines. ³³Then Abraham planted a tamarisk tree at Beersheba, and there he worshiped the LORD, the Eternal God.* ³⁴And Abraham lived as a foreigner in Philistine country for a long time.

Abraham's Faith Tested

22 Some time later, God tested Abraham's faith. "Abraham!" God called.

"Yes," he replied. "Here I am."

²"Take your son, your only son—yes, Isaac, whom you love so much—and go to the land of Moriah. Go and sacrifice him as a burnt offering on one of the mountains, which I will show you."

³The next morning Abraham got up early. He saddled his donkey and took two of his servants with him, along with his son, Isaac. Then he chopped wood for a fire for a burnt offering and set out for the place God had told him about. ⁴On the third day of their journey, Abraham looked up and saw the place in the distance. ⁵"Stay here with the donkey," Abraham told the servants. "The boy and I will travel a little farther. We will worship there, and then we will come right back."

⁶So Abraham placed the wood for the burnt offering on Isaac's shoulders, while he himself carried the fire and the knife. As the two of them walked on together, ⁷Isaac turned to Abraham and said, "Father?"

"Yes, my son?" Abraham replied.

"We have the fire and the wood," the boy said, "but where is the sheep for the burnt offering?"

⁸"God will provide a sheep for the burnt offering, my son," Abraham answered. And they both walked on together.

⁹When they arrived at the place where God

had told him to go, Abraham built an altar and arranged the wood on it. Then he tied his son, Isaac, and laid him on the altar on top of the wood. ¹⁰And Abraham picked up the knife to kill his son as a sacrifice. ¹¹At that moment the angel of the LORD called to him from heaven, "Abraham! Abraham!"

"Yes," Abraham replied. "Here I am!"

¹²"Don't lay a hand on the boy!" the angel said. "Do not hurt him in any way, for now I know that you truly fear God. You have not withheld from me even your son, your only son."

¹³Then Abraham looked up and saw a ram caught by its horns in a thicket. So he took the ram and sacrificed it as a burnt offering in place of his son. ¹⁴Abraham named the place Yahweh-Yireh (which means "the LORD will provide"). To this day, people still use that name as a proverb: "On the mountain of the LORD it will be provided."

¹⁵Then the angel of the LORD called again to Abraham from heaven. ¹⁶"This is what the LORD says: Because you have obeyed me and have not withheld even your son, your only son, I swear by my own name that ¹⁷I will certainly bless you. I will multiply your descendants* beyond number, like the stars in the sky and the sand on the seashore. Your descendants will conquer the cities of their enemies. ¹⁸And through your descendants all the nations of the earth will be blessed—all because you have obeyed me."

¹⁹Then they returned to the servants and traveled back to Beersheba, where Abraham continued to live.

²⁰Soon after this, Abraham heard that Milcah, his brother Nahor's wife, had borne Nahor eight sons. ²¹The oldest was named Uz, the next oldest was Buz, followed by Kemuel (the ancestor of the Arameans), ²²Kesed, Hazo, Pildash, Jidlaph, and Bethuel. ²³(Bethuel became the father of Rebekah.) In addition to these eight sons from Milcah, ²⁴Nahor had four other children from his concubine Reumah. Their names were Tebah, Gaham, Tahash, and Maacah.

The Burial of Sarah

23 When Sarah was 127 years old, ²she died at Kiriath-arba (now called Hebron) in the land of Canaan. There Abraham mourned and wept for her.

³Then, leaving her body, he said to the Hittite elders, ⁴"Here I am, a stranger and a foreigner among you. Please sell me a piece of land so I can give my wife a proper burial."

⁵The Hittites replied to Abraham, ⁶"Listen, my lord, you are an honored prince among us. Choose the finest of our tombs and bury her there. No one here will refuse to help you in this way."

⁷Then Abraham bowed low before the Hittites ⁸and said, "Since you are willing to help me in this way, be so kind as to ask Ephron son of Zohar ⁹to let me buy his cave at Machpelah, down at the end of his field. I will pay the full price in the presence of witnesses, so I will have a permanent burial place for my family."

¹⁰Ephron was sitting there among the others, and he answered Abraham as the others listened, speaking publicly before all the Hittite elders of the town. ¹¹"No, my lord," he said to Abraham, "please listen to me. I will give you the field and the cave. Here in the presence of my people, I give it to you. Go and bury your dead."

¹²Abraham again bowed low before the citizens of the land, ¹³and he replied to Ephron as everyone listened. "No, listen to me. I will buy it from you. Let me pay the full price for the field so I can bury my dead there."

¹⁴Ephron answered Abraham, ¹⁵"My lord, please listen to me. The land is worth 400 pieces* of silver, but what is that between friends? Go ahead and bury your dead."

¹⁶So Abraham agreed to Ephron's price and paid the amount he had suggested—400 pieces of silver, weighed according to the market standard. The Hittite elders witnessed the transaction.

¹⁷So Abraham bought the plot of land belonging to Ephron at Machpelah, near Mamre. This included the field itself, the cave that was in it, and all the surrounding trees. ¹⁸It was transferred to Abraham as his permanent possession in the presence of the Hittite elders at the city gate. ¹⁹Then Abraham buried his wife, Sarah, there in Canaan, in the cave of Machpelah, near Mamre (also called Hebron). ²⁰So the field and the cave were transferred from the Hittites to Abraham for use as a permanent burial place.

A Wife for Isaac

24 Abraham was now a very old man, and the LORD had blessed him in every way. ²One day Abraham said to his oldest servant, the man in charge of his household, "Take an oath by putting your hand under my thigh. ³Swear by the LORD, the God of heaven and

22:17 Hebrew *seed*; also in 22:17b, 18.   23:15 Hebrew *400 shekels*, about 10 pounds or 4.6 kilograms in weight; also in 23:16.

earth, that you will not allow my son to marry one of these local Canaanite women. ⁴Go instead to my homeland, to my relatives, and find a wife there for my son Isaac."

⁵The servant asked, "But what if I can't find a young woman who is willing to travel so far from home? Should I then take Isaac there to live among your relatives in the land you came from?"

⁶"No!" Abraham responded. "Be careful never to take my son there. ⁷For the Lord, the God of heaven, who took me from my father's house and my native land, solemnly promised to give this land to my descendants.* He will send his angel ahead of you, and he will see to it that you find a wife there for my son. ⁸If she is unwilling to come back with you, then you are free from this oath of mine. But under no circumstances are you to take my son there."

⁹So the servant took an oath by putting his hand under the thigh of his master, Abraham. He swore to follow Abraham's instructions. ¹⁰Then he loaded ten of Abraham's camels with all kinds of expensive gifts from his master, and he traveled to distant Aram-naharaim. There he went to the town where Abraham's brother Nahor had settled. ¹¹He made the camels kneel beside a well just outside the town. It was evening, and the women were coming out to draw water.

¹²"O Lord, God of my master, Abraham," he prayed. "Please give me success today, and show unfailing love to my master, Abraham. ¹³See, I am standing here beside this spring, and the young women of the town are coming out to draw water. ¹⁴This is my request. I will ask one of them, 'Please give me a drink from your jug.' If she says, 'Yes, have a drink, and I will water your camels, too!'—let her be the one you have selected as Isaac's wife. This is how I will know that you have shown unfailing love to my master."

¹⁵Before he had finished praying, he saw a young woman named Rebekah coming out with her water jug on her shoulder. She was the daughter of Bethuel, who was the son of Abraham's brother Nahor and his wife, Milcah. ¹⁶Rebekah was very beautiful and old enough to be married, but she was still a virgin. She went down to the spring, filled her jug, and came up again. ¹⁷Running over to her, the servant said, "Please give me a little drink of water from your jug."

¹⁸"Yes, my lord," she answered, "have a drink." And she quickly lowered her jug from her shoulder and gave him a drink. ¹⁹When she had given him a drink, she said, "I'll draw water for your camels, too, until they have had enough to drink." ²⁰So she quickly emptied her jug into the watering trough and ran back to the well to draw water for all his camels.

²¹The servant watched her in silence, wondering whether or not the Lord had given him success in his mission. ²²Then at last, when the camels had finished drinking, he took out a gold ring for her nose and two large gold bracelets* for her wrists.

²³"Whose daughter are you?" he asked. "And please tell me, would your father have any room to put us up for the night?"

²⁴"I am the daughter of Bethuel," she replied. "My grandparents are Nahor and Milcah. ²⁵Yes, we have plenty of straw and feed for the camels, and we have room for guests."

²⁶The man bowed low and worshiped the Lord. ²⁷"Praise the Lord, the God of my master, Abraham," he said. "The Lord has shown unfailing love and faithfulness to my master, for he has led me straight to my master's relatives."

²⁸The young woman ran home to tell her family everything that had happened. ²⁹Now Rebekah had a brother named Laban, who ran out to meet the man at the spring. ³⁰He had seen the nose-ring and the bracelets on his sister's wrists, and had heard Rebekah tell what the man had said. So he rushed out to the spring, where the man was still standing beside his camels. ³¹Laban said to him, "Come and stay with us, you who are blessed by the Lord! Why are you standing here outside the town when I have a room all ready for you and a place prepared for the camels?"

³²So the man went home with Laban, and Laban unloaded the camels, gave him straw for their bedding, fed them, and provided water for the man and the camel drivers to wash their feet. ³³Then food was served. But Abraham's servant said, "I don't want to eat until I have told you why I have come."

"All right," Laban said, "tell us."

³⁴"I am Abraham's servant," he explained. ³⁵"And the Lord has greatly blessed my master; he has become a wealthy man. The Lord has given him flocks of sheep and goats, herds of cattle, a fortune in silver and gold, and many male and female servants and camels and donkeys.

24:7 Hebrew *seed*; also in 24:60. 24:22 Hebrew *a gold nose-ring weighing a beka* [0.2 ounces or 6 grams] *and two gold bracelets weighing 10* [shekels] [4 ounces or 114 grams].

³⁶"When Sarah, my master's wife, was very old, she gave birth to my master's son, and my master has given him everything he owns. ³⁷And my master made me take an oath. He said, 'Do not allow my son to marry one of these local Canaanite women. ³⁸Go instead to my father's house, to my relatives, and find a wife there for my son.'

³⁹"But I said to my master, 'What if I can't find a young woman who is willing to go back with me?' ⁴⁰He responded, 'The LORD, in whose presence I have lived, will send his angel with you and will make your mission successful. Yes, you must find a wife for my son from among my relatives, from my father's family. ⁴¹Then you will have fulfilled your obligation. But if you go to my relatives and they refuse to let her go with you, you will be free from my oath.'

⁴²"So today when I came to the spring, I prayed this prayer: 'O LORD, God of my master, Abraham, please give me success on this mission. ⁴³See, I am standing here beside this spring. This is my request. When a young woman comes to draw water, I will say to her, "Please give me a little drink of water from your jug." ⁴⁴If she says, "Yes, have a drink, and I will draw water for your camels, too," let her be the one you have selected to be the wife of my master's son.'

⁴⁵"Before I had finished praying in my heart, I saw Rebekah coming out with her water jug on her shoulder. She went down to the spring and drew water. So I said to her, 'Please give me a drink.' ⁴⁶She quickly lowered her jug from her shoulder and said, 'Yes, have a drink, and I will water your camels, too!' So I drank, and then she watered the camels.

⁴⁷"Then I asked, 'Whose daughter are you?' She replied, 'I am the daughter of Bethuel, and my grandparents are Nahor and Milcah.' So I put the ring on her nose, and the bracelets on her wrists.

⁴⁸"Then I bowed low and worshiped the LORD. I praised the LORD, the God of my master, Abraham, because he had led me straight to my master's niece to be his son's wife. ⁴⁹So tell me—will you or won't you show unfailing love and faithfulness to my master? Please tell me yes or no, and then I'll know what to do next."

⁵⁰Then Laban and Bethuel replied, "The LORD has obviously brought you here, so there is nothing we can say. ⁵¹Here is Rebekah; take her and go. Yes, let her be the wife of your master's son, as the LORD has directed."

⁵²When Abraham's servant heard their answer, he bowed down to the ground and worshiped the LORD. ⁵³Then he brought out silver and gold jewelry and clothing and presented them to Rebekah. He also gave expensive presents to her brother and mother. ⁵⁴Then they ate their meal, and the servant and the men with him stayed there overnight.

But early the next morning, Abraham's servant said, "Send me back to my master."

⁵⁵"But we want Rebekah to stay with us at least ten days," her brother and mother said. "Then she can go."

⁵⁶But he said, "Don't delay me. The LORD has made my mission successful; now send me back so I can return to my master."

⁵⁷"Well," they said, "we'll call Rebekah and ask her what she thinks." ⁵⁸So they called Rebekah. "Are you willing to go with this man?" they asked her.

And she replied, "Yes, I will go."

⁵⁹So they said good-bye to Rebekah and sent her away with Abraham's servant and his men. The woman who had been Rebekah's childhood nurse went along with her. ⁶⁰They gave her this blessing as she parted:

"Our sister, may you become
    the mother of many millions!
May your descendants be strong
    and conquer the cities of their enemies."

⁶¹Then Rebekah and her servant girls mounted the camels and followed the man. So Abraham's servant took Rebekah and went on his way.

⁶²Meanwhile, Isaac, whose home was in the Negev, had returned from Beer-lahai-roi. ⁶³One evening as he was walking and meditating in the fields, he looked up and saw the camels coming. ⁶⁴When Rebekah looked up and saw Isaac, she quickly dismounted from her camel. ⁶⁵"Who is that man walking through the fields to meet us?" she asked the servant.

And he replied, "It is my master." So Rebekah covered her face with her veil. ⁶⁶Then the servant told Isaac everything he had done.

⁶⁷And Isaac brought Rebekah into his mother Sarah's tent, and she became his wife. He loved her deeply, and she was a special comfort to him after the death of his mother.

The Death of Abraham

25 Abraham married another wife, whose name was Keturah. ²She gave birth to Zimran, Jokshan, Medan, Midian, Ishbak, and Shuah. ³Jokshan was the father of Sheba and Dedan. Dedan's descendants were the As-shurites, Letushites, and Leummites. 4Midian's sons were Ephah, Epher, Hanoch, Abida, and Eldaah. These were all descendants of Abraham through Keturah.

5Abraham gave everything he owned to his son Isaac. 6But before he died, he gave gifts to the sons of his concubines and sent them off to a land in the east, away from Isaac.

7Abraham lived for 175 years, 8and he died at a ripe old age, having lived a long and satisfying life. He breathed his last and joined his ancestors in death. 9His sons Isaac and Ishmael buried him in the cave of Machpelah, near Mamre, in the field of Ephron son of Zohar the Hittite. 10This was the field Abraham had purchased from the Hittites and where he had buried his wife Sarah. 11After Abraham's death, God blessed his son Isaac, who settled near Beer-lahai-roi in the Negev.

Ishmael's Descendants

12This is the account of the family of Ishmael, the son of Abraham through Hagar, Sarah's Egyptian servant. 13Here is a list, by their names and clans, of Ishmael's descendants: The oldest was Nebaioth, followed by Kedar, Adbeel, Mibsam, 14Mishma, Dumah, Massa, 15Hadad, Tema, Jetur, Naphish, and Kedemah. 16These twelve sons of Ishmael became the founders of twelve tribes named after them, listed according to the places they settled and camped. 17Ishmael lived for 137 years. Then he breathed his last and joined his ancestors in death. 18Ishmael's descendants occupied the region from Havilah to Shur, which is east of Egypt in the direction of Asshur. There they lived in open hostility toward all their relatives.*

The Births of Esau and Jacob

19This is the account of the family of Isaac, the son of Abraham. 20When Isaac was forty years old, he married Rebekah, the daughter of Bethuel the Aramean from Paddan-aram and the sister of Laban the Aramean.

21Isaac pleaded with the LORD on behalf of his wife, because she was unable to have children. The LORD answered Isaac's prayer, and Rebekah became pregnant with twins. 22But the two children struggled with each other in her womb. So she went to ask the LORD about it. "Why is this happening to me?" she asked. 23And the LORD told her, "The sons in your womb will become two nations. From the very

beginning, the two nations will be rivals. One nation will be stronger than the other; and your older son will serve your younger son."

24And when the time came to give birth, Rebekah discovered that she did indeed have twins! 25The first one was very red at birth and covered with thick hair like a fur coat. So they named him Esau.* 26Then the other twin was born with his hand grasping Esau's heel. So they named him Jacob.* Isaac was sixty years old when the twins were born.

Esau Sells His Birthright

27As the boys grew up, Esau became a skillful hunter. He was an outdoorsman, but Jacob had a quiet temperament, preferring to stay at home. 28Isaac loved Esau because he enjoyed eating the wild game Esau brought home, but Rebekah loved Jacob.

29One day when Jacob was cooking some stew, Esau arrived home from the wilderness exhausted and hungry. 30Esau said to Jacob, "I'm starved! Give me some of that red stew!" (This is how Esau got his other name, Edom, which means "red.")

31"All right," Jacob replied, "but trade me your rights as the firstborn son."

32"Look, I'm dying of starvation!" said Esau. "What good is my birthright to me now?"

33But Jacob said, "First you must swear that your birthright is mine." So Esau swore an oath, thereby selling all his rights as the firstborn to his brother, Jacob.

34Then Jacob gave Esau some bread and lentil stew. Esau ate the meal, then got up and left. He showed contempt for his rights as the firstborn.

Isaac Deceives Abimelech

26 A severe famine now struck the land, as had happened before in Abraham's time. So Isaac moved to Gerar, where Abimelech, king of the Philistines, lived.

2The LORD appeared to Isaac and said, "Do not go down to Egypt, but do as I tell you. 3Live here as a foreigner in this land, and I will be with you and bless you. I hereby confirm that I will give all these lands to you and your descendants,* just as I solemnly promised Abraham, your father. 4I will cause your descendants to become as numerous as the stars of the sky, and I will give them all these lands. And through your descendants all the nations of the earth will be blessed. 5I will do this because Abraham

25:18 The meaning of the Hebrew is uncertain.   25:25 Esau sounds like a Hebrew term that means "hair."   25:26 Jacob sounds like the Hebrew words for "heel" and "deceiver."   26:3 Hebrew seed; also in 26:4, 24.

listened to me and obeyed all my requirements, commands, decrees, and instructions." ⁶So Isaac stayed in Gerar.

⁷When the men who lived there asked Isaac about his wife, Rebekah, he said, "She is my sister." He was afraid to say, "She is my wife." He thought, "They will kill me to get her, because she is so beautiful." ⁸But some time later, Abimelech, king of the Philistines, looked out his window and saw Isaac caressing Rebekah.

⁹Immediately, Abimelech called for Isaac and exclaimed, "She is obviously your wife! Why did you say, 'She is my sister'?"

"Because I was afraid someone would kill me to get her from me," Isaac replied.

¹⁰"How could you do this to us?" Abimelech exclaimed. "One of my people might easily have taken your wife and slept with her, and you would have made us guilty of great sin."

¹¹Then Abimelech issued a public proclamation: "Anyone who touches this man or his wife will be put to death!"

Conflict over Water Rights

¹²When Isaac planted his crops that year, he harvested a hundred times more grain than he planted, for the LORD blessed him. ¹³He became a very rich man, and his wealth continued to grow. ¹⁴He acquired so many flocks of sheep and goats, herds of cattle, and servants that the Philistines became jealous of him. ¹⁵So the Philistines filled up all of Isaac's wells with dirt. These were the wells that had been dug by the servants of his father, Abraham.

¹⁶Finally, Abimelech ordered Isaac to leave the country. "Go somewhere else," he said, "for you have become too powerful for us."

¹⁷So Isaac moved away to the Gerar Valley, where he set up their tents and settled down. ¹⁸He reopened the wells his father had dug, which the Philistines had filled in after Abraham's death. Isaac also restored the names Abraham had given them.

¹⁹Isaac's servants also dug in the Gerar Valley and discovered a well of fresh water. ²⁰But then the shepherds from Gerar came and claimed the spring. "This is our water," they said, and they argued over it with Isaac's herdsmen. So Isaac named the well Esek (which means "argument"). ²¹Isaac's men then dug another well, but again there was a dispute over it. So Isaac named it Sitnah (which means "hostility"). ²²Abandoning that one, Isaac moved on and dug another well. This time there was no dispute over it, so Isaac named the place Rehoboth (which means "open space"), for he said, "At last the LORD has created enough space for us to prosper in this land."

²³From there Isaac moved to Beersheba, ²⁴where the LORD appeared to him on the night of his arrival. "I am the God of your father, Abraham," he said. "Do not be afraid, for I am with you and will bless you. I will multiply your descendants, and they will become a great nation. I will do this because of my promise to Abraham, my servant." ²⁵Then Isaac built an altar there and worshiped the LORD. He set up his camp at that place, and his servants dug another well.

Isaac's Covenant with Abimelech

²⁶One day King Abimelech came from Gerar with his adviser, Ahuzzath, and also Phicol, his army commander. ²⁷"Why have you come here?" Isaac asked. "You obviously hate me, since you kicked me off your land."

²⁸They replied, "We can plainly see that the LORD is with you. So we want to enter into a sworn treaty with you. Let's make a covenant. ²⁹Swear that you will not harm us, just as we have never troubled you. We have always treated you well, and we sent you away from us in peace. And now look how the LORD has blessed you!"

³⁰So Isaac prepared a covenant feast to celebrate the treaty, and they ate and drank together. ³¹Early the next morning, they each took a solemn oath not to interfere with each other. Then Isaac sent them home again, and they left him in peace.

³²That very day Isaac's servants came and told him about a new well they had dug. "We've found water!" they exclaimed. ³³So Isaac named the well Shibah (which means "oath"). And to this day the town that grew up there is called Beersheba (which means "well of the oath").

³⁴At the age of forty, Esau married two Hittite wives: Judith, the daughter of Beeri, and Basemath, the daughter of Elon. ³⁵But Esau's wives made life miserable for Isaac and Rebekah.

Jacob Steals Esau's Blessing

27 One day when Isaac was old and turning blind, he called for Esau, his older son, and said, "My son."

"Yes, Father?" Esau replied.

²"I am an old man now," Isaac said, "and I don't know when I may die. ³Take your bow and a quiver full of arrows, and go out into the open country to hunt some wild game for me.

⁴Prepare my favorite dish, and bring it here for me to eat. Then I will pronounce the blessing that belongs to you, my firstborn son, before I die."

⁵But Rebekah overheard what Isaac had said to his son Esau. So when Esau left to hunt for the wild game, ⁶she said to her son Jacob, "Listen. I overheard your father say to Esau, ⁷'Bring me some wild game and prepare me a delicious meal. Then I will bless you in the LORD's presence before I die.' ⁸Now, my son, listen to me. Do exactly as I tell you. ⁹Go out to the flocks, and bring me two fine young goats. I'll use them to prepare your father's favorite dish. ¹⁰Then take the food to your father so he can eat it and bless you before he dies."

¹¹"But look," Jacob replied to Rebekah, "my brother, Esau, is a hairy man, and my skin is smooth. ¹²What if my father touches me? He'll see that I'm trying to trick him, and then he'll curse me instead of blessing me."

¹³But his mother replied, "Then let the curse fall on me, my son! Just do what I tell you. Go out and get the goats for me!"

¹⁴So Jacob went out and got the young goats for his mother. Rebekah took them and prepared a delicious meal, just the way Isaac liked it. ¹⁵Then she took Esau's favorite clothes, which were there in the house, and gave them to her younger son, Jacob. ¹⁶She covered his arms and the smooth part of his neck with the skin of the young goats. ¹⁷Then she gave Jacob the delicious meal, including freshly baked bread.

¹⁸So Jacob took the food to his father. "My father?" he said.

"Yes, my son," Isaac answered. "Who are you—Esau or Jacob?"

¹⁹Jacob replied, "It's Esau, your firstborn son. I've done as you told me. Here is the wild game. Now sit up and eat it so you can give me your blessing."

²⁰Isaac asked, "How did you find it so quickly, my son?"

"The LORD your God put it in my path!" Jacob replied.

²¹Then Isaac said to Jacob, "Come closer so I can touch you and make sure that you really are Esau." ²²So Jacob went closer to his father, and Isaac touched him. "The voice is Jacob's, but the hands are Esau's," Isaac said. ²³But he did not recognize Jacob, because Jacob's hands felt hairy just like Esau's. So Isaac prepared to bless Jacob. ²⁴"But are you really my son Esau?" he asked.

"Yes, I am," Jacob replied.

²⁵Then Isaac said, "Now, my son, bring me the wild game. Let me eat it, and then I will give you my blessing." So Jacob took the food to his father, and Isaac ate it. He also drank the wine that Jacob served him. ²⁶Then Isaac said to Jacob, "Please come a little closer and kiss me, my son."

²⁷So Jacob went over and kissed him. And when Isaac caught the smell of his clothes, he was finally convinced, and he blessed his son. He said, "Ah! The smell of my son is like the smell of the outdoors, which the LORD has blessed!

²⁸ "From the dew of heaven
       and the richness of the earth,
    may God always give you abundant
       harvests of grain
    and bountiful new wine.
²⁹ May many nations become your servants,
       and may they bow down to you.
    May you be the master over your brothers,
       and may your mother's sons bow down
       to you.
    All who curse you will be cursed,
       and all who bless you will be blessed."

³⁰As soon as Isaac had finished blessing Jacob, and almost before Jacob had left his father, Esau returned from his hunt. ³¹Esau prepared a delicious meal and brought it to his father. Then he said, "Sit up, my father, and eat my wild game so you can give me your blessing."

³²But Isaac asked him, "Who are you?"

Esau replied, "It's your son, your firstborn son, Esau."

³³Isaac began to tremble uncontrollably and said, "Then who just served me wild game? I have already eaten it, and I blessed him just before you came. And yes, that blessing must stand!"

³⁴When Esau heard his father's words, he let out a loud and bitter cry. "Oh my father, what about me? Bless me, too!" he begged.

³⁵But Isaac said, "Your brother was here, and he tricked me. He has taken away your blessing."

³⁶Esau exclaimed, "No wonder his name is Jacob, for now he has cheated me twice.* First he took my rights as the firstborn, and now he has stolen my blessing. Oh, haven't you saved even one blessing for me?"

³⁷Isaac said to Esau, "I have made Jacob your

27:36 *Jacob* sounds like the Hebrew words for "heel" and "deceiver."

master and have declared that all his brothers will be his servants. I have guaranteed him an abundance of grain and wine—what is left for me to give you, my son?"

38Esau pleaded, "But do you have only one blessing? Oh my father, bless me, too!" Then Esau broke down and wept.

39Finally, his father, Isaac, said to him,

"You will live away from the richness of
    the earth,
    and away from the dew of the heaven
    above.
40 You will live by your sword,
    and you will serve your brother.
But when you decide to break free,
    you will shake his yoke from your neck."

Jacob Flees to Paddan-Aram

41From that time on, Esau hated Jacob because their father had given Jacob the blessing. And Esau began to scheme: "I will soon be mourning my father's death. Then I will kill my brother, Jacob."

42But Rebekah heard about Esau's plans. So she sent for Jacob and told him, "Listen, Esau is consoling himself by plotting to kill you. 43So listen carefully, my son. Get ready and flee to my brother, Laban, in Haran. 44Stay there with him until your brother cools off. 45When he calms down and forgets what you have done to him, I will send for you to come back. Why should I lose both of you in one day?"

46Then Rebekah said to Isaac, "I'm sick and tired of these local Hittite women! I would rather die than see Jacob marry one of them."

28 So Isaac called for Jacob, blessed him, and said, "You must not marry any of these Canaanite women. 2Instead, go at once to Paddan-aram, to the house of your grandfather Bethuel, and marry one of your uncle Laban's daughters. 3May God Almighty* bless you and give you many children. And may your descendants multiply and become many nations! 4May God pass on to you and your descendants* the blessings he promised to Abraham. May you own this land where you are now living as a foreigner, for God gave this land to Abraham."

5So Isaac sent Jacob away, and he went to Paddan-aram to stay with his uncle Laban, his mother's brother, the son of Bethuel the Aramean.

6Esau knew that his father, Isaac, had blessed Jacob and sent him to Paddan-aram to find a wife, and that he had warned Jacob, "You must not marry a Canaanite woman." 7He also knew that Jacob had obeyed his parents and gone to Paddan-aram. 8It was now very clear to Esau that his father did not like the local Canaanite women. 9So Esau visited his uncle Ishmael's family and married one of Ishmael's daughters, in addition to the wives he already had. His new wife's name was Mahalath. She was the sister of Nebaioth and the daughter of Ishmael, Abraham's son.

Jacob's Dream at Bethel

10Meanwhile, Jacob left Beersheba and traveled toward Haran. 11At sundown he arrived at a good place to set up camp and stopped there for the night. Jacob found a stone to rest his head against and lay down to sleep. 12As he slept, he dreamed of a stairway that reached from the earth up to heaven. And he saw the angels of God going up and down the stairway.

13At the top of the stairway stood the LORD, and he said, "I am the LORD, the God of your grandfather Abraham, and the God of your father, Isaac. The ground you are lying on belongs to you. I am giving it to you and your descendants. 14Your descendants will be as numerous as the dust of the earth! They will spread out in all directions—to the west and the east, to the north and the south. And all the families of the earth will be blessed through you and your descendants. 15What's more, I am with you, and I will protect you wherever you go. One day I will bring you back to this land. I will not leave you until I have finished giving you everything I have promised you."

16Then Jacob awoke from his sleep and said, "Surely the LORD is in this place, and I wasn't even aware of it!" 17But he was also afraid and said, "What an awesome place this is! It is none other than the house of God, the very gateway to heaven!"

18The next morning Jacob got up very early. He took the stone he had rested his head against, and he set it upright as a memorial pillar. Then he poured olive oil over it. 19He named that place Bethel (which means "house of God"), although it was previously called Luz.

20Then Jacob made this vow: "If God will indeed be with me and protect me on this journey, and if he will provide me with food and clothing, 21and if I return safely to my father's home, then the LORD will certainly be my God. 22And this memorial pillar I have set

28:3 Hebrew *El-Shaddai*.   28:4 Hebrew *seed*; also in 28:13, 14.

up will become a place for worshiping God, and I will present to God a tenth of everything he gives me."

Jacob Arrives at Paddan-Aram

29 Then Jacob hurried on, finally arriving in the land of the east. ²He saw a well in the distance. Three flocks of sheep and goats lay in an open field beside it, waiting to be watered. But a heavy stone covered the mouth of the well.

³It was the custom there to wait for all the flocks to arrive before removing the stone and watering the animals. Afterward the stone would be placed back over the mouth of the well. ⁴Jacob went over to the shepherds and asked, "Where are you from, my friends?"

"We are from Haran," they answered.

⁵"Do you know a man there named Laban, the grandson of Nahor?" he asked.

"Yes, we do," they replied.

⁶"Is he doing well?" Jacob asked.

"Yes, he's well," they answered. "Look, here comes his daughter Rachel with the flock now."

⁷Jacob said, "Look, it's still broad daylight—too early to round up the animals. Why don't you water the sheep and goats so they can get back out to pasture?"

⁸"We can't water the animals until all the flocks have arrived," they replied. "Then the shepherds move the stone from the mouth of the well, and we water all the sheep and goats."

⁹Jacob was still talking with them when Rachel arrived with her father's flock, for she was a shepherd. ¹⁰And because Rachel was his cousin—the daughter of Laban, his mother's brother—and because the sheep and goats belonged to his uncle Laban, Jacob went over to the well and moved the stone from its mouth and watered his uncle's flock. ¹¹Then Jacob kissed Rachel, and he wept aloud. ¹²He explained to Rachel that he was her cousin on her father's side—the son of her aunt Rebekah. So Rachel quickly ran and told her father, Laban.

¹³As soon as Laban heard that his nephew Jacob had arrived, he ran out to meet him. He embraced and kissed him and brought him home. When Jacob had told him his story, ¹⁴Laban exclaimed, "You really are my own flesh and blood!"

Jacob Marries Leah and Rachel

After Jacob had stayed with Laban for about a month, ¹⁵Laban said to him, "You shouldn't work for me without pay just because we are relatives. Tell me how much your wages should be."

¹⁶Now Laban had two daughters. The older daughter was named Leah, and the younger one was Rachel. ¹⁷There was no sparkle in Leah's eyes,* but Rachel had a beautiful figure and a lovely face. ¹⁸Since Jacob was in love with Rachel, he told her father, "I'll work for you for seven years if you'll give me Rachel, your younger daughter, as my wife."

¹⁹"Agreed!" Laban replied. "I'd rather give her to you than to anyone else. Stay and work with me." ²⁰So Jacob worked seven years to pay for Rachel. But his love for her was so strong that it seemed to him but a few days.

²¹Finally, the time came for him to marry her. "I have fulfilled my agreement," Jacob said to Laban. "Now give me my wife so I can sleep with her."

²²So Laban invited everyone in the neighborhood and prepared a wedding feast. ²³But that night, when it was dark, Laban took Leah to Jacob, and he slept with her. ²⁴(Laban had given Leah a servant, Zilpah, to be her maid.)

²⁵But when Jacob woke up in the morning—it was Leah! "What have you done to me?" Jacob raged at Laban. "I worked seven years for Rachel! Why have you tricked me?"

²⁶"It's not our custom here to marry off a younger daughter ahead of the firstborn," Laban replied. ²⁷"But wait until the bridal week is over; then we'll give you Rachel, too—provided you promise to work another seven years for me."

²⁸So Jacob agreed to work seven more years. A week after Jacob had married Leah, Laban gave him Rachel, too. ²⁹(Laban gave Rachel a servant, Bilhah, to be her maid.) ³⁰So Jacob slept with Rachel, too, and he loved her much more than Leah. He then stayed and worked for Laban the additional seven years.

Jacob's Many Children

³¹When the LORD saw that Leah was unloved, he enabled her to have children, but Rachel could not conceive. ³²So Leah became pregnant and gave birth to a son. She named him Reuben,* for she said, "The LORD has noticed my misery, and now my husband will love me."

³³She soon became pregnant again and gave birth to another son. She named him Simeon,* for she said, "The LORD heard that I was unloved and has given me another son."

29:17 Or *Leah had dull eyes,* or *Leah had soft eyes.* The meaning of the Hebrew is uncertain.   **29:32** *Reuben* means "Look, a son!" It also sounds like the Hebrew for "He has seen my misery."   **29:33** *Simeon* probably means "one who hears."

[34]Then she became pregnant a third time and gave birth to another son. He was named Levi,* for she said, "Surely this time my husband will feel affection for me, since I have given him three sons!"

[35]Once again Leah became pregnant and gave birth to another son. She named him Judah,* for she said, "Now I will praise the LORD!" And then she stopped having children.

30 When Rachel saw that she wasn't having any children for Jacob, she became jealous of her sister. She pleaded with Jacob, "Give me children, or I'll die!"

[2]Then Jacob became furious with Rachel. "Am I God?" he asked. "He's the one who has kept you from having children!"

[3]Then Rachel told him, "Take my maid, Bilhah, and sleep with her. She will bear children for me,* and through her I can have a family, too." [4]So Rachel gave her servant, Bilhah, to Jacob as a wife, and he slept with her. [5]Bilhah became pregnant and presented him with a son. [6]Rachel named him Dan,* for she said, "God has vindicated me! He has heard my request and given me a son." [7]Then Bilhah became pregnant again and gave Jacob a second son. [8]Rachel named him Naphtali,* for she said, "I have struggled hard with my sister, and I'm winning!"

[9]Meanwhile, Leah realized that she wasn't getting pregnant anymore, so she took her servant, Zilpah, and gave her to Jacob as a wife. [10]Soon Zilpah presented him with a son. [11]Leah named him Gad,* for she said, "How fortunate I am!" [12]Then Zilpah gave Jacob a second son. [13]And Leah named him Asher,* for she said, "What joy is mine! Now the other women will celebrate with me."

[14]One day during the wheat harvest, Reuben found some mandrakes growing in a field and brought them to his mother, Leah. Rachel begged Leah, "Please give me some of your son's mandrakes."

[15]But Leah angrily replied, "Wasn't it enough that you stole my husband? Now will you steal my son's mandrakes, too?"

Rachel answered, "I will let Jacob sleep with you tonight if you give me some of the mandrakes."

[16]So that evening, as Jacob was coming home from the fields, Leah went out to meet him.

"You must come and sleep with me tonight!" she said. "I have paid for you with some mandrakes that my son found." So that night he slept with Leah. [17]And God answered Leah's prayers. She became pregnant again and gave birth to a fifth son for Jacob. [18]She named him Issachar,* for she said, "God has rewarded me for giving my servant to my husband as a wife." [19]Then Leah became pregnant again and gave birth to a sixth son for Jacob. [20]She named him Zebulun,* for she said, "God has given me a good reward. Now my husband will treat me with respect, for I have given him six sons." [21]Later she gave birth to a daughter and named her Dinah.

[22]Then God remembered Rachel's plight and answered her prayers by enabling her to have children. [23]She became pregnant and gave birth to a son. "God has removed my disgrace," she said. [24]And she named him Joseph,* for she said, "May the LORD add yet another son to my family."

Jacob's Wealth Increases

[25]Soon after Rachel had given birth to Joseph, Jacob said to Laban, "Please release me so I can go home to my own country. [26]Let me take my wives and children, for I have earned them by serving you, and let me be on my way. You certainly know how hard I have worked for you."

[27]"Please listen to me," Laban replied. "I have become wealthy, for* the LORD has blessed me because of you. [28]Tell me how much I owe you. Whatever it is, I'll pay it."

[29]Jacob replied, "You know how hard I've worked for you, and how your flocks and herds have grown under my care. [30]You had little indeed before I came, but your wealth has increased enormously. The LORD has blessed you through everything I've done. But now, what about me? When can I start providing for my own family?"

[31]"What wages do you want?" Laban asked again.

Jacob replied, "Don't give me anything. Just do this one thing, and I'll continue to tend and watch over your flocks. [32]Let me inspect your flocks today and remove all the sheep and goats that are speckled or spotted, along with all the black sheep. Give these to me as my wages. [33]In the future, when you check on the animals you have given me as my wages, you'll see that I

29:34 *Levi* sounds like a Hebrew term that means "being attached" or "feeling affection for." 29:35 *Judah* is related to the Hebrew term for "praise." 30:3 Hebrew *bear children on my knees.* 30:6 *Dan* means "he judged" or "he vindicated." 30:8 *Naphtali* means "my struggle." 30:11 *Gad* means "good fortune." 30:13 *Asher* means "happy." 30:18 *Issachar* sounds like a Hebrew term that means "reward." 30:20 *Zebulun* probably means "honor." 30:24 *Joseph* means "may he add." 30:27 Or *I have learned by divination that.*

have been honest. If you find in my flock any goats without speckles or spots, or any sheep that are not black, you will know that I have stolen them from you."

³⁴"All right," Laban replied. "It will be as you say." ³⁵But that very day Laban went out and removed the male goats that were streaked and spotted, all the female goats that were speckled and spotted or had white patches, and all the black sheep. He placed them in the care of his own sons, ³⁶who took them a three-days' journey from where Jacob was. Meanwhile, Jacob stayed and cared for the rest of Laban's flock.

³⁷Then Jacob took some fresh branches from poplar, almond, and plane trees and peeled off strips of bark, making white streaks on them. ³⁸Then he placed these peeled branches in the watering troughs where the flocks came to drink, for that was where they mated. ³⁹And when they mated in front of the white-streaked branches, they gave birth to young that were streaked, speckled, and spotted. ⁴⁰Jacob separated those lambs from Laban's flock. And at mating time he turned the flock to face Laban's animals that were streaked or black. This is how he built his own flock instead of increasing Laban's.

⁴¹Whenever the stronger females were ready to mate, Jacob would place the peeled branches in the watering troughs in front of them. Then they would mate in front of the branches. ⁴²But he didn't do this with the weaker ones, so the weaker lambs belonged to Laban, and the stronger ones were Jacob's. ⁴³As a result, Jacob became very wealthy, with large flocks of sheep and goats, female and male servants, and many camels and donkeys.

Jacob Flees from Laban

31 But Jacob soon learned that Laban's sons were grumbling about him. "Jacob has robbed our father of everything!" they said. "He has gained all his wealth at our father's expense." ²And Jacob began to notice a change in Laban's attitude toward him.

³Then the LORD said to Jacob, "Return to the land of your father and grandfather and to your relatives there, and I will be with you."

⁴So Jacob called Rachel and Leah out to the field where he was watching his flock. ⁵He said to them, "I have noticed that your father's attitude toward me has changed. But the God of my father has been with me. ⁶You know how hard I have worked for your father, ⁷but he has cheated me, changing my wages ten times. But

God has not allowed him to do me any harm. ⁸For if he said, 'The speckled animals will be your wages,' the whole flock began to produce speckled young. And when he changed his mind and said, 'The striped animals will be your wages,' then the whole flock produced striped young. ⁹In this way, God has taken your father's animals and given them to me.

¹⁰"One time during the mating season, I had a dream and saw that the male goats mating with the females were streaked, speckled, and spotted. ¹¹Then in my dream, the angel of God said to me, 'Jacob!' And I replied, 'Yes, here I am.'

¹²"The angel said, 'Look up, and you will see that only the streaked, speckled, and spotted males are mating with the females of your flock. For I have seen how Laban has treated you. ¹³I am the God who appeared to you at Bethel,* the place where you anointed the pillar of stone and made your vow to me. Now get ready and leave this country and return to the land of your birth.'"

¹⁴Rachel and Leah responded, "That's fine with us! We won't inherit any of our father's wealth anyway. ¹⁵He has reduced our rights to those of foreign women. And after he sold us, he wasted the money you paid him for us. ¹⁶All the wealth God has given you from our father legally belongs to us and our children. So go ahead and do whatever God has told you."

¹⁷So Jacob put his wives and children on camels, ¹⁸and he drove all his livestock in front of him. He packed all the belongings he had acquired in Paddan-aram and set out for the land of Canaan, where his father, Isaac, lived. ¹⁹At the time they left, Laban was some distance away, shearing his sheep. Rachel stole her father's household idols and took them with her. ²⁰Jacob outwitted Laban the Aramean, for they set out secretly and never told Laban they were leaving. ²¹So Jacob took all his possessions with him and crossed the Euphrates River,* heading for the hill country of Gilead.

Laban Pursues Jacob

²²Three days later, Laban was told that Jacob had fled. ²³So he gathered a group of his relatives and set out in hot pursuit. He caught up with Jacob seven days later in the hill country of Gilead. ²⁴But the previous night God had appeared to Laban the Aramean in a dream and told him, "I'm warning you—leave Jacob alone!"

²⁵Laban caught up with Jacob as he was

31:13 As in Greek version and an Aramaic Targum; Hebrew reads *the God of Bethel.* 31:21 Hebrew *the river.*

camped in the hill country of Gilead, and he set up his camp not far from Jacob's. ²⁶"What do you mean by deceiving me like this?" Laban demanded. "How dare you drag my daughters away like prisoners of war? ²⁷Why did you slip away secretly? Why did you deceive me? And why didn't you say you wanted to leave? I would have given you a farewell feast, with singing and music, accompanied by tambourines and harps. ²⁸Why didn't you let me kiss my daughters and grandchildren and tell them good-bye? You have acted very foolishly! ²⁹I could destroy you, but the God of your father appeared to me last night and warned me, 'Leave Jacob alone!' ³⁰I can understand your feeling that you must go, and your intense longing for your father's home. But why have you stolen my gods?"

³¹"I rushed away because I was afraid," Jacob answered. "I thought you would take your daughters from me by force. ³²But as for your gods, see if you can find them, and let the person who has taken them die! And if you find anything else that belongs to you, identify it before all these relatives of ours, and I will give it back!" But Jacob did not know that Rachel had stolen the household idols.

³³Laban went first into Jacob's tent to search there, then into Leah's, and then the tents of the two servant wives—but he found nothing. Finally, he went into Rachel's tent. ³⁴But Rachel had taken the household idols and hidden them in her camel saddle, and now she was sitting on them. When Laban had thoroughly searched her tent without finding them, ³⁵she said to her father, "Please, sir, forgive me if I don't get up for you. I'm having my monthly period." So Laban continued his search, but he could not find the household idols.

³⁶Then Jacob became very angry, and he challenged Laban. "What's my crime?" he demanded. "What have I done wrong to make you chase after me as though I were a criminal? ³⁷You have rummaged through everything I own. Now show me what you found that belongs to you! Set it out here in front of us, before our relatives, for all to see. Let them judge between us!

³⁸"For twenty years I have been with you, caring for your flocks. In all that time your sheep and goats never miscarried. In all those years I never used a single ram of yours for food. ³⁹If any were attacked and killed by wild animals, I never showed you the carcass and asked you to reduce the count of your flock. No, I took the loss myself! You made me pay

for every stolen animal, whether it was taken in broad daylight or in the dark of night. ⁴⁰"I worked for you through the scorching heat of the day and through cold and sleepless nights. ⁴¹Yes, for twenty years I slaved in your house! I worked for fourteen years earning your two daughters, and then six more years for your flock. And you changed my wages ten times! ⁴²In fact, if the God of my father had not been on my side—the God of Abraham and the fearsome God of Isaac*—you would have sent me away empty-handed. But God has seen your abuse and my hard work. That is why he appeared to you last night and rebuked you!"

Jacob's Treaty with Laban

⁴³Then Laban replied to Jacob, "These women are my daughters, these children are my grandchildren, and these flocks are my flocks—in fact, everything you see is mine. But what can I do now about my daughters and their children? ⁴⁴So come, let's make a covenant, you and I, and it will be a witness to our commitment."

⁴⁵So Jacob took a stone and set it up as a monument. ⁴⁶Then he told his family members, "Gather some stones." So they gathered stones and piled them in a heap. Then Jacob and Laban sat down beside the pile of stones to eat a covenant meal. ⁴⁷To commemorate the event, Laban called the place Jegar-sahadutha (which means "witness pile" in Aramaic), and Jacob called it Galeed (which means "witness pile" in Hebrew).

⁴⁸Then Laban declared, "This pile of stones will stand as a witness to remind us of the covenant we have made today." This explains why it was called Galeed—"Witness Pile." ⁴⁹But it was also called Mizpah (which means "watchtower"), for Laban said, "May the LORD keep watch between us to make sure that we keep this covenant when we are out of each other's sight. ⁵⁰If you mistreat my daughters or if you marry other wives, God will see it even if no one else does. He is a witness to this covenant between us.

⁵¹"See this pile of stones," Laban continued, "and see this monument I have set between us. ⁵²They stand between us as witnesses of our vows. I will never pass this pile of stones to harm you, and you must never pass these stones or this monument to harm me. ⁵³I call on the God of our ancestors—the God of your grandfather Abraham and the God of my grandfather Nahor—to serve as a judge between us."

So Jacob took an oath before the fearsome

31:42 Or *and the Fear of Isaac.*

God of his father, Isaac,* to respect the boundary line. 54Then Jacob offered a sacrifice to God there on the mountain and invited everyone to a covenant feast. After they had eaten, they spent the night on the mountain.

55*Laban got up early the next morning, and he kissed his grandchildren and his daughters and blessed them. Then he left and returned home.

32 1*As Jacob started on his way again, angels of God came to meet him. 2When Jacob saw them, he exclaimed, "This is God's camp!" So he named the place Mahanaim.*

Jacob Sends Gifts to Esau

3Then Jacob sent messengers ahead to his brother, Esau, who was living in the region of Seir in the land of Edom. 4He told them, "Give this message to my master Esau: 'Humble greetings from your servant Jacob. Until now I have been living with Uncle Laban, 5and now I own cattle, donkeys, flocks of sheep and goats, and many servants, both men and women. I have sent these messengers to inform my lord of my coming, hoping that you will be friendly to me.'"

6After delivering the message, the messengers returned to Jacob and reported, "We met your brother, Esau, and he is already on his way to meet you—with an army of 400 men!" 7Jacob was terrified at the news. He divided his household, along with the flocks and herds and camels, into two groups. 8He thought, "If Esau meets one group and attacks it, perhaps the other group can escape."

9Then Jacob prayed, "O God of my grandfather Abraham, and God of my father, Isaac—O LORD, you told me, 'Return to your own land and to your relatives.' And you promised me, 'I will treat you kindly.' 10I am not worthy of all the unfailing love and faithfulness you have shown to me, your servant. When I left home and crossed the Jordan River, I owned nothing except a walking stick. Now my household fills two large camps! 11O LORD, please rescue me from the hand of my brother, Esau. I am afraid that he is coming to attack me, along with my wives and children. 12But you promised me, 'I will surely treat you kindly, and I will multiply your descendants until they become as numerous as the sands along the seashore—too many to count.'"

13Jacob stayed where he was for the night. Then he selected these gifts from his possessions to present to his brother, Esau: 14200 female goats, 20 male goats, 200 ewes, 20 rams, 1530 female camels with their young, 40 cows, 10 bulls, 20 female donkeys, and 10 male donkeys. 16He divided these animals into herds and assigned each to different servants. Then he told his servants, "Go ahead of me with the animals, but keep some distance between the herds."

17He gave these instructions to the men leading the first group: "When my brother, Esau, meets you, he will ask, 'Whose servants are you? Where are you going? Who owns these animals?' 18You must reply, 'They belong to your servant Jacob, but they are a gift for his master Esau. Look, he is coming right behind us.'"

19Jacob gave the same instructions to the second and third herdsmen and to all who followed behind the herds: "You must say the same thing to Esau when you meet him. 20And be sure to say, 'Look, your servant Jacob is right behind us.'"

Jacob thought, "I will try to appease him by sending gifts ahead of me. When I see him in person, perhaps he will be friendly to me." 21So the gifts were sent on ahead, while Jacob himself spent that night in the camp.

Jacob Wrestles with God

22During the night Jacob got up and took his two wives, his two servant wives, and his eleven sons and crossed the Jabbok River with them. 23After taking them to the other side, he sent over all his possessions.

24This left Jacob all alone in the camp, and a man came and wrestled with him until the dawn began to break. 25When the man saw that he would not win the match, he touched Jacob's hip and wrenched it out of its socket. 26Then the man said, "Let me go, for the dawn is breaking!"

But Jacob said, "I will not let you go unless you bless me."

27"What is your name?" the man asked.

He replied, "Jacob."

28"Your name will no longer be Jacob," the man told him. "From now on you will be called Israel,* because you have fought with God and with men and have won."

29"Please tell me your name," Jacob said.

"Why do you want to know my name?" the man replied. Then he blessed Jacob there.

31:53 Or *the Fear of his father, Isaac.*   31:55 Verse 31:55 is numbered 32:1 in Hebrew text.   32:1 Verses 32:1-32 are numbered 32:2-33 in Hebrew text.   32:2 *Mahanaim* means "two camps."   32:28 *Jacob* sounds like the Hebrew words for "heel" and "deceiver." *Israel* means "God fights."

³⁰Jacob named the place Peniel (which means "face of God"), for he said, "I have seen God face to face, yet my life has been spared." ³¹The sun was rising as Jacob left Peniel,* and he was limping because of the injury to his hip. ³²(Even today the people of Israel don't eat the tendon near the hip socket because of what happened that night when the man strained the tendon of Jacob's hip.)

Jacob and Esau Make Peace

33 Then Jacob looked up and saw Esau coming with his 400 men. So he divided the children among Leah, Rachel, and his two servant wives. ²He put the servant wives and their children at the front, Leah and her children next, and Rachel and Joseph last. ³Then Jacob went on ahead. As he approached his brother, he bowed to the ground seven times before him. ⁴Then Esau ran to meet him and embraced him, threw his arms around his neck, and kissed him. And they both wept.

⁵Then Esau looked at the women and children and asked, "Who are these people with you?"

"These are the children God has graciously given to me, your servant," Jacob replied. ⁶Then the servant wives came forward with their children and bowed before him. ⁷Next came Leah with her children, and they bowed before him. Finally, Joseph and Rachel came forward and bowed before him.

⁸"And what were all the flocks and herds I met as I came?" Esau asked.

Jacob replied, "They are a gift, my lord, to ensure your friendship."

⁹"My brother, I have plenty," Esau answered. "Keep what you have for yourself."

¹⁰But Jacob insisted, "No, if I have found favor with you, please accept this gift from me. And what a relief to see your friendly smile. It is like seeing the face of God! ¹¹Please take this gift I have brought you, for God has been very gracious to me. I have more than enough." And because Jacob insisted, Esau finally accepted the gift.

¹²"Well," Esau said, "let's be going. I will lead the way."

¹³But Jacob replied, "You can see, my lord, that some of the children are very young, and the flocks and herds have their young, too. If they are driven too hard, even for one day, all the animals could die. ¹⁴Please, my lord, go ahead of your servant. We will follow slowly, at a pace that is comfortable for the livestock and the children. I will meet you at Seir."

¹⁵"All right," Esau said, "but at least let me assign some of my men to guide and protect you."

Jacob responded, "That's not necessary. It's enough that you've received me warmly, my lord!"

¹⁶So Esau turned around and started back to Seir that same day. ¹⁷Jacob, on the other hand, traveled on to Succoth. There he built himself a house and made shelters for his livestock. That is why the place was named Succoth (which means "shelters").

¹⁸Later, having traveled all the way from Paddan-aram, Jacob arrived safely at the town of Shechem, in the land of Canaan. There he set up camp outside the town. ¹⁹Jacob bought the plot of land where he camped from the family of Hamor, the father of Shechem, for 100 pieces of silver.* ²⁰And there he built an altar and named it El-Elohe-Israel.*

Revenge against Shechem

34 One day Dinah, the daughter of Jacob and Leah, went to visit some of the young women who lived in the area. ²But when the local prince, Shechem son of Hamor the Hivite, saw Dinah, he seized her and raped her. ³But then he fell in love with her, and he tried to win her affection with tender words. ⁴He said to his father, Hamor, "Get me this young girl. I want to marry her."

⁵Soon Jacob heard that Shechem had defiled his daughter, Dinah. But since his sons were out in the fields herding his livestock, he said nothing until they returned. ⁶Hamor, Shechem's father, came to discuss the matter with Jacob. ⁷Meanwhile, Jacob's sons had come in from the field as soon as they heard what had happened. They were shocked and furious that their sister had been raped. Shechem had done a disgraceful thing against Jacob's family,* something that should never be done.

⁸Hamor tried to speak with Jacob and his sons. "My son Shechem is truly in love with your daughter," he said. "Please let him marry her. ⁹In fact, let's arrange other marriages, too. You give us your daughters for our sons, and we will give you our daughters for your sons. ¹⁰And you may live among us; the land is open to you! Settle here and trade with us. And feel free to buy property in the area."

¹¹Then Shechem himself spoke to Dinah's

32:31 Hebrew *Penuel*, a variant spelling of Peniel.   **33:19** Hebrew *100 kesitahs*; the value or weight of the kesitah is no longer known.   **33:20** *El-Elohe-Israel* means "God, the God of Israel."   **34:7** Hebrew *a disgraceful thing in Israel.*

father and brothers. "Please be kind to me, and let me marry her," he begged. "I will give you whatever you ask. [12]No matter what dowry or gift you demand, I will gladly pay it—just give me the girl as my wife."

[13]But since Shechem had defiled their sister, Dinah, Jacob's sons responded deceitfully to Shechem and his father, Hamor. [14]They said to them, "We couldn't possibly allow this, because you're not circumcised. It would be a disgrace for our sister to marry a man like you! [15]But here is a solution. If every man among you will be circumcised like we are, [16]then we will give you our daughters, and we'll take your daughters for ourselves. We will live among you and become one people. [17]But if you don't agree to be circumcised, we will take her and be on our way."

[18]Hamor and his son Shechem agreed to their proposal. [19]Shechem wasted no time in acting on this request, for he wanted Jacob's daughter desperately. Shechem was a highly respected member of his family, [20]and he went with his father, Hamor, to present this proposal to the leaders at the town gate.

[21]"These men are our friends," they said. "Let's invite them to live here among us and trade freely. Look, the land is large enough to hold them. We can take their daughters as wives and let them marry ours. [22]But they will consider staying here and becoming one people with us only if all of our men are circumcised, just as they are. [23]But if we do this, all their livestock and possessions will eventually be ours. Come, let's agree to their terms and let them settle here among us."

[24]So all the men in the town council agreed with Hamor and Shechem, and every male in the town was circumcised. [25]But three days later, when their wounds were still sore, two of Jacob's sons, Simeon and Levi, who were Dinah's full brothers, took their swords and entered the town without opposition. Then they slaughtered every male there, [26]including Hamor and his son Shechem. They killed them with their swords, then took Dinah from Shechem's house and returned to their camp.

[27]Meanwhile, the rest of Jacob's sons arrived. Finding the men slaughtered, they plundered the town because their sister had been defiled there. [28]They seized all the flocks and herds and donkeys—everything they could lay their hands on, both inside the town and outside in the fields. [29]They looted all their wealth and plundered their houses. They also took all their little children and wives and led them away as captives.

[30]Afterward Jacob said to Simeon and Levi, "You have ruined me! You've made me stink among all the people of this land—among all the Canaanites and Perizzites. We are so few that they will join forces and crush us. I will be ruined, and my entire household will be wiped out!"

[31]"But why should we let him treat our sister like a prostitute?" they retorted angrily.

Jacob's Return to Bethel

35 Then God said to Jacob, "Get ready and move to Bethel and settle there. Build an altar there to the God who appeared to you when you fled from your brother, Esau."

[2]So Jacob told everyone in his household, "Get rid of all your pagan idols, purify yourselves, and put on clean clothing. [3]We are now going to Bethel, where I will build an altar to the God who answered my prayers when I was in distress. He has been with me wherever I have gone."

[4]So they gave Jacob all their pagan idols and earrings, and he buried them under the great tree near Shechem. [5]As they set out, a terror from God spread over the people in all the towns of that area, so no one attacked Jacob's family.

[6]Eventually, Jacob and his household arrived at Luz (also called Bethel) in Canaan. [7]Jacob built an altar there and named the place El-bethel (which means "God of Bethel"), because God had appeared to him there when he was fleeing from his brother, Esau.

[8]Soon after this, Rebekah's old nurse, Deborah, died. She was buried beneath the oak tree in the valley below Bethel. Ever since, the tree has been called Allon-bacuth (which means "oak of weeping").

[9]Now that Jacob had returned from Paddan-aram, God appeared to him again at Bethel. God blessed him, [10]saying, "Your name is Jacob, but you will not be called Jacob any longer. From now on your name will be Israel."* So God renamed him Israel.

[11]Then God said, "I am El-Shaddai—'God Almighty.' Be fruitful and multiply. You will become a great nation, even many nations. Kings will be among your descendants! [12]And I will give you the land I once gave to Abraham and Isaac. Yes, I will give it to you and to your descendants after you." [13]Then God went up from the place where he had spoken to Jacob.

35:10 *Jacob* sounds like the Hebrew words for "heel" and "deceiver." *Israel* means "God fights."

[14]Jacob set up a stone pillar to mark the place where God had spoken to him. Then he poured wine over it as an offering to God and anointed the pillar with olive oil. [15]And Jacob named the place Bethel (which means "house of God"), because God had spoken to him there.

The Deaths of Rachel and Isaac

[16]Leaving Bethel, Jacob and his clan moved on toward Ephrath. But Rachel went into labor while they were still some distance away. Her labor pains were intense. [17]After a very hard delivery, the midwife finally exclaimed, "Don't be afraid—you have another son!" [18]Rachel was about to die, but with her last breath she named the baby Ben-oni (which means "son of my sorrow"). The baby's father, however, called him Benjamin (which means "son of my right hand"). [19]So Rachel died and was buried on the way to Ephrath (that is, Bethlehem). [20]Jacob set up a stone monument over Rachel's grave, and it can be seen there to this day.

[21]Then Jacob* traveled on and camped beyond Migdal-eder. [22]While he was living there, Reuben had intercourse with Bilhah, his father's concubine, and Jacob soon heard about it.

These are the names of the twelve sons of Jacob:

[23]The sons of Leah were Reuben (Jacob's oldest son), Simeon, Levi, Judah, Issachar, and Zebulun.

[24]The sons of Rachel were Joseph and Benjamin.

[25]The sons of Bilhah, Rachel's servant, were Dan and Naphtali.

[26]The sons of Zilpah, Leah's servant, were Gad and Asher.

These are the names of the sons who were born to Jacob at Paddan-aram.

[27]So Jacob returned to his father, Isaac, in Mamre, which is near Kiriath-arba (now called Hebron), where Abraham and Isaac had both lived as foreigners. [28]Isaac lived for 180 years. [29]Then he breathed his last and died at a ripe old age, joining his ancestors in death. And his sons, Esau and Jacob, buried him.

Descendants of Esau

36 This is the account of the descendants of Esau (also known as Edom). [2]Esau married two young women from Canaan: Adah, the daughter of Elon the Hittite; and Oholibamah, the daughter of Anah and granddaughter of Zibeon the Hivite. [3]He also married his cousin Basemath, who was the daughter of Ishmael and the sister of Nebaioth. [4]Adah gave birth to a son named Eliphaz for Esau. Basemath gave birth to a son named Reuel. [5]Oholibamah gave birth to sons named Jeush, Jalam, and Korah. All these sons were born to Esau in the land of Canaan.

[6]Esau took his wives, his children, and his entire household, along with his livestock and cattle—all the wealth he had acquired in the land of Canaan—and moved away from his brother, Jacob. [7]There was not enough land to support them both because of all the livestock and possessions they had acquired. [8]So Esau (also known as Edom) settled in the hill country of Seir.

[9]This is the account of Esau's descendants, the Edomites, who lived in the hill country of Seir.

[10]These are the names of Esau's sons:
Eliphaz, the son of Esau's wife Adah; and Reuel, the son of Esau's wife Basemath.

[11]The descendants of Eliphaz were Teman, Omar, Zepho, Gatam, and Kenaz. [12]Timna, the concubine of Esau's son Eliphaz, gave birth to a son named Amalek. These are the descendants of Esau's wife Adah.

[13]The descendants of Reuel were Nahath, Zerah, Shammah, and Mizzah. These are the descendants of Esau's wife Basemath.

[14]Esau also had sons through Oholibamah, the daughter of Anah and granddaughter of Zibeon. Their names were Jeush, Jalam, and Korah.

[15]These are the descendants of Esau who became the leaders of various clans:

The descendants of Esau's oldest son, Eliphaz, became the leaders of the clans of Teman, Omar, Zepho, Kenaz, [16]Korah, Gatam, and Amalek. These are the clan leaders in the land of Edom who descended from Eliphaz. All these were descendants of Esau's wife Adah.

[17]The descendants of Esau's son Reuel became the leaders of the clans of Nahath, Zerah, Shammah, and Mizzah. These are the clan leaders in the land of Edom who descended from Reuel. All these were descendants of Esau's wife Basemath.

18The descendants of Esau and his wife Oholibamah became the leaders of the clans of Jeush, Jalam, and Korah. These are the clan leaders who descended from Esau's wife Oholibamah, the daughter of Anah.

19These are the clans descended from Esau (also known as Edom), identified by their clan leaders.

Original Peoples of Edom

20These are the names of the tribes that descended from Seir the Horite. They lived in the land of Edom: Lotan, Shobal, Zibeon, Anah, 21Dishon, Ezer, and Dishan. These were the Horite clan leaders, the descendants of Seir, who lived in the land of Edom.

22The descendants of Lotan were Hori and Hemam. Lotan's sister was named Timna.

23The descendants of Shobal were Alvan, Manahath, Ebal, Shepho, and Onam.

24The descendants of Zibeon were Aiah and Anah. (This is the Anah who discovered the hot springs in the wilderness while he was grazing his father's donkeys.)

25The descendants of Anah were his son, Dishon, and his daughter, Oholibamah.

26The descendants of Dishon* were Hemdan, Eshban, Ithran, and Keran.

27The descendants of Ezer were Bilhan, Zaavan, and Akan.

28The descendants of Dishan were Uz and Aran.

29So these were the leaders of the Horite clans: Lotan, Shobal, Zibeon, Anah, 30Dishon, Ezer, and Dishan. The Horite clans are named after their clan leaders, who lived in the land of Seir.

Rulers of Edom

31These are the kings who ruled in the land of Edom before any king ruled over the Israelites*:

32Bela son of Beor, who ruled in Edom from his city of Dinhabah.

33When Bela died, Jobab son of Zerah from Bozrah became king in his place.

34When Jobab died, Husham from the land of the Temanites became king in his place.

35When Husham died, Hadad son of Bedad became king in his place and ruled from the city of Avith. He was the one who defeated the Midianites in the land of Moab.

36When Hadad died, Samlah from the city of Masrekah became king in his place.

37When Samlah died, Shaul from the city of Rehoboth-on-the-River became king in his place.

38When Shaul died, Baal-hanan son of Acbor became king in his place.

39When Baal-hanan son of Acbor died, Hadad* became king in his place and ruled from the city of Pau. His wife was Mehetabel, the daughter of Matred and granddaughter of Me-zahab.

40These are the names of the leaders of the clans descended from Esau, who lived in the places named for them: Timna, Alvah, Jetheth, 41Oholibamah, Elah, Pinon, 42Kenaz, Teman, Mibzar, 43Magdiel, and Iram. These are the leaders of the clans of Edom, listed according to their settlements in the land they occupied. They all descended from Esau, the ancestor of the Edomites.

Joseph's Dreams

37 So Jacob settled again in the land of Canaan, where his father had lived as a foreigner.

2This is the account of Jacob and his family. When Joseph was seventeen years old, he often tended his father's flocks. He worked for his half brothers, the sons of his father's wives Bilhah and Zilpah. But Joseph reported to his father some of the bad things his brothers were doing.

3Jacob* loved Joseph more than any of his other children because Joseph had been born to him in his old age. So one day Jacob had a special gift made for Joseph—a beautiful robe.* 4But his brothers hated Joseph because their father loved him more than the rest of them. They couldn't say a kind word to him.

5One night Joseph had a dream, and when he told his brothers about it, they hated him more than ever. 6"Listen to this dream," he said. 7"We were out in the field, tying up bundles of grain. Suddenly my bundle stood up, and your bundles all gathered around and bowed low before mine!"

8His brothers responded, "So you think you will be our king, do you? Do you actually think

---

36:26 Hebrew *Dishan*, a variant spelling of Dishon; compare 36:21, 28.   36:31 Or *before an Israelite king ruled over them.*
36:39 As in some Hebrew manuscripts, Samaritan Pentateuch, and Syriac version (see also 1 Chr 1:50); most Hebrew manuscripts read *Hadar.*   37:3a Hebrew *Israel;* also in 37:13. See note on 35:21.   37:3b Traditionally rendered *a coat of many colors.* The exact meaning of the Hebrew is uncertain.

you will reign over us?" And they hated him all the more because of his dreams and the way he talked about them.

⁹Soon Joseph had another dream, and again he told his brothers about it. "Listen, I have had another dream," he said. "The sun, moon, and eleven stars bowed low before me!"

¹⁰This time he told the dream to his father as well as to his brothers, but his father scolded him. "What kind of dream is that?" he asked. "Will your mother and I and your brothers actually come and bow to the ground before you?" ¹¹But while his brothers were jealous of Joseph, his father wondered what the dreams meant.

¹²Soon after this, Joseph's brothers went to pasture their father's flocks at Shechem. ¹³When they had been gone for some time, Jacob said to Joseph, "Your brothers are pasturing the sheep at Shechem. Get ready, and I will send you to them."

"I'm ready to go," Joseph replied.

¹⁴"Go and see how your brothers and the flocks are getting along," Jacob said. "Then come back and bring me a report." So Jacob sent him on his way, and Joseph traveled to Shechem from their home in the valley of Hebron.

¹⁵When he arrived there, a man from the area noticed him wandering around the countryside. "What are you looking for?" he asked.

¹⁶"I'm looking for my brothers," Joseph replied. "Do you know where they are pasturing their sheep?"

¹⁷"Yes," the man told him. "They have moved on from here, but I heard them say, 'Let's go on to Dothan.'" So Joseph followed his brothers to Dothan and found them there.

Joseph Sold into Slavery

¹⁸When Joseph's brothers saw him coming, they recognized him in the distance. As he approached, they made plans to kill him. ¹⁹"Here comes the dreamer!" they said. ²⁰"Come on, let's kill him and throw him into one of these cisterns. We can tell our father, 'A wild animal has eaten him.' Then we'll see what becomes of his dreams!"

²¹But when Reuben heard of their scheme, he came to Joseph's rescue. "Let's not kill him," he said. ²²"Why should we shed any blood? Let's just throw him into this empty cistern here in the wilderness. Then he'll die without

our laying a hand on him." Reuben was secretly planning to rescue Joseph and return him to his father.

²³So when Joseph arrived, his brothers ripped off the beautiful robe he was wearing. ²⁴Then they grabbed him and threw him into the cistern. Now the cistern was empty; there was no water in it. ²⁵Then, just as they were sitting down to eat, they looked up and saw a caravan of camels in the distance coming toward them. It was a group of Ishmaelite traders taking a load of gum, balm, and aromatic resin from Gilead down to Egypt.

²⁶Judah said to his brothers, "What will we gain by killing our brother? We'd have to cover up the crime.* ²⁷Instead of hurting him, let's sell him to those Ishmaelite traders. After all, he is our brother—our own flesh and blood!" And his brothers agreed. ²⁸So when the Ishmaelites, who were Midianite traders, came by, Joseph's brothers pulled him out of the cistern and sold him to them for twenty pieces* of silver. And the traders took him to Egypt.

²⁹Some time later, Reuben returned to get Joseph out of the cistern. When he discovered that Joseph was missing, he tore his clothes in grief. ³⁰Then he went back to his brothers and lamented, "The boy is gone! What will I do now?"

³¹Then the brothers killed a young goat and dipped Joseph's robe in its blood. ³²They sent the beautiful robe to their father with this message: "Look at what we found. Doesn't this robe belong to your son?"

³³Their father recognized it immediately. "Yes," he said, "it is my son's robe. A wild animal must have eaten him. Joseph has clearly been torn to pieces!" ³⁴Then Jacob tore his clothes and dressed himself in burlap. He mourned deeply for his son for a long time. ³⁵His family all tried to comfort him, but he refused to be comforted. "I will go to my grave* mourning for my son," he would say, and then he would weep.

³⁶Meanwhile, the Midianite traders* arrived in Egypt, where they sold Joseph to Potiphar, an officer of Pharaoh, the king of Egypt. Potiphar was captain of the palace guard.

Judah and Tamar

38 About this time, Judah left home and moved to Adullam, where he stayed with a man named Hirah. ²There he saw a

---

37:26 Hebrew *cover his blood.*   37:28 Hebrew *20 [shekels],* about 8 ounces or 228 grams in weight.   37:35 Hebrew *go down to Sheol.*   37:36 Hebrew *the Medanites.* The relationship between the Midianites and Medanites is unclear; compare 37:28. See also 25:2.

Canaanite woman, the daughter of Shua, and he married her. When he slept with her, ³she became pregnant and gave birth to a son, and he named the boy Er. ⁴Then she became pregnant again and gave birth to another son, and she named him Onan. ⁵And when she gave birth to a third son, she named him Shelah. At the time of Shelah's birth, they were living at Kezib.

⁶In the course of time, Judah arranged for his firstborn son, Er, to marry a young woman named Tamar. ⁷But Er was a wicked man in the LORD's sight, so the LORD took his life. ⁸Then Judah said to Er's brother Onan, "Go and marry Tamar, as our law requires of the brother of a man who has died. You must produce an heir for your brother."

⁹But Onan was not willing to have a child who would not be his own heir. So whenever he had intercourse with his brother's wife, he spilled the semen on the ground. This prevented her from having a child who would belong to his brother. ¹⁰But the LORD considered it evil for Onan to deny a child to his dead brother. So the LORD took Onan's life, too.

¹¹Then Judah said to Tamar, his daughter-in-law, "Go back to your parents' home and remain a widow until my son Shelah is old enough to marry you." (But Judah didn't really intend to do this because he was afraid Shelah would also die, like his two brothers.) So Tamar went back to live in her father's home.

¹²Some years later Judah's wife died. After the time of mourning was over, Judah and his friend Hirah the Adullamite went up to Timnah to supervise the shearing of his sheep. ¹³Someone told Tamar, "Look, your father-in-law is going up to Timnah to shear his sheep."

¹⁴Tamar was aware that Shelah had grown up, but no arrangements had been made for her to come and marry him. So she changed out of her widow's clothing and covered herself with a veil to disguise herself. Then she sat beside the road at the entrance to the village of Enaim, which is on the road to Timnah. ¹⁵Judah noticed her and thought she was a prostitute, since she had covered her face. ¹⁶So he stopped and propositioned her. "Let me have sex with you," he said, not realizing that she was his own daughter-in-law.

"How much will you pay to have sex with me?" Tamar asked.

¹⁷"I'll send you a young goat from my flock," Judah promised.

"But what will you give me to guarantee that you will send the goat?" she asked.

¹⁸"What kind of guarantee do you want?" he replied.

She answered, "Leave me your identification seal and its cord and the walking stick you are carrying." So Judah gave them to her. Then he had intercourse with her, and she became pregnant. ¹⁹Afterward she went back home, took off her veil, and put on her widow's clothing as usual.

²⁰Later Judah asked his friend Hirah the Adullamite to take the young goat to the woman and to pick up the things he had given her as his guarantee. But Hirah couldn't find her. ²¹So he asked the men who lived there, "Where can I find the shrine prostitute who was sitting beside the road at the entrance to Enaim?"

"We've never had a shrine prostitute here," they replied.

²²So Hirah returned to Judah and told him, "I couldn't find her anywhere, and the men of the village claim they've never had a shrine prostitute there."

²³"Then let her keep the things I gave her," Judah said. "I sent the young goat as we agreed, but you couldn't find her. We'd be the laughingstock of the village if we went back again to look for her."

²⁴About three months later, Judah was told, "Tamar, your daughter-in-law, has acted like a prostitute. And now, because of this, she's pregnant."

"Bring her out, and let her be burned!" Judah demanded.

²⁵But as they were taking her out to kill her, she sent this message to her father-in-law: "The man who owns these things made me pregnant. Look closely. Whose seal and cord and walking stick are these?"

²⁶Judah recognized them immediately and said, "She is more righteous than I am, because I didn't arrange for her to marry my son Shelah." And Judah never slept with Tamar again.

²⁷When the time came for Tamar to give birth, it was discovered that she was carrying twins. ²⁸While she was in labor, one of the babies reached out his hand. The midwife grabbed it and tied a scarlet string around the child's wrist, announcing, "This one came out first." ²⁹But then he pulled back his hand, and out came his brother! "What!" the midwife exclaimed. "How did you break out first?" So he was named Perez.* ³⁰Then the baby with the scarlet string on his wrist was born, and he was named Zerah.*

38:29 *Perez* means "breaking out."   **38:30** *Zerah* means "scarlet" or "brightness."

Joseph in Potiphar's House

39 When Joseph was taken to Egypt by the Ishmaelite traders, he was purchased by Potiphar, an Egyptian officer. Potiphar was captain of the guard for Pharaoh, the king of Egypt.

²The LORD was with Joseph, so he succeeded in everything he did as he served in the home of his Egyptian master. ³Potiphar noticed this and realized that the LORD was with Joseph, giving him success in everything he did. ⁴This pleased Potiphar, so he soon made Joseph his personal attendant. He put him in charge of his entire household and everything he owned. ⁵From the day Joseph was put in charge of his master's household and property, the LORD began to bless Potiphar's household for Joseph's sake. All his household affairs ran smoothly, and his crops and livestock flourished. ⁶So Potiphar gave Joseph complete administrative responsibility over everything he owned. With Joseph there, he didn't worry about a thing—except what kind of food to eat!

Joseph was a very handsome and well-built young man, ⁷and Potiphar's wife soon began to look at him lustfully. "Come and sleep with me," she demanded.

⁸But Joseph refused. "Look," he told her, "my master trusts me with everything in his entire household. ⁹No one here has more authority than I do. He has held back nothing from me except you, because you are his wife. How could I do such a wicked thing? It would be a great sin against God."

¹⁰She kept putting pressure on Joseph day after day, but he refused to sleep with her, and he kept out of her way as much as possible. ¹¹One day, however, no one else was around when he went in to do his work. ¹²She came and grabbed him by his cloak, demanding, "Come on, sleep with me!" Joseph tore himself away, but he left his cloak in her hand as he ran from the house.

¹³When she saw that she was holding his cloak and he had fled, ¹⁴she called out to her servants. Soon all the men came running. "Look!" she said. "My husband has brought this Hebrew slave here to make fools of us! He came into my room to rape me, but I screamed. ¹⁵When he heard me scream, he ran outside and got away, but he left his cloak behind with me."

¹⁶She kept the cloak with her until her husband came home. ¹⁷Then she told him her story. "That Hebrew slave you've brought into our house tried to come in and fool around with me," she said. ¹⁸"But when I screamed, he ran outside, leaving his cloak with me!"

Joseph Put in Prison

¹⁹Potiphar was furious when he heard his wife's story about how Joseph had treated her. ²⁰So he took Joseph and threw him into the prison where the king's prisoners were held, and there he remained. ²¹But the LORD was with Joseph in the prison and showed him his faithful love. And the LORD made Joseph a favorite with the prison warden. ²²Before long, the warden put Joseph in charge of all the other prisoners and over everything that happened in the prison. ²³The warden had no more worries, because Joseph took care of everything. The LORD was with him and caused everything he did to succeed.

Joseph Interprets Two Dreams

40 Some time later, Pharaoh's chief cupbearer and chief baker offended their royal master. ²Pharaoh became angry with these two officials, ³and he put them in the prison where Joseph was, in the palace of the captain of the guard. ⁴They remained in prison for quite some time, and the captain of the guard assigned them to Joseph, who looked after them.

⁵While they were in prison, Pharaoh's cupbearer and baker each had a dream one night, and each dream had its own meaning. ⁶When Joseph saw them the next morning, he noticed that they both looked upset. ⁷"Why do you look so worried today?" he asked them.

⁸And they replied, "We both had dreams last night, but no one can tell us what they mean."

"Interpreting dreams is God's business," Joseph replied. "Go ahead and tell me your dreams."

⁹So the chief cup-bearer told Joseph his dream first. "In my dream," he said, "I saw a grapevine in front of me. ¹⁰The vine had three branches that began to bud and blossom, and soon it produced clusters of ripe grapes. ¹¹I was holding Pharaoh's wine cup in my hand, so I took a cluster of grapes and squeezed the juice into the cup. Then I placed the cup in Pharaoh's hand."

¹²"This is what the dream means," Joseph said. "The three branches represent three days. ¹³Within three days Pharaoh will lift you up and restore you to your position as his chief cupbearer. ¹⁴And please remember me and do me a favor when things go well for you. Mention me to Pharaoh, so he might let me out of this place. ¹⁵For I was kidnapped from my homeland, the land of the Hebrews, and now I'm here in prison, but I did nothing to deserve it."

16When the chief baker saw that Joseph had given the first dream such a positive interpretation, he said to Joseph, "I had a dream, too. In my dream there were three baskets of white pastries stacked on my head. 17The top basket contained all kinds of pastries for Pharaoh, but the birds came and ate them from the basket on my head."

18"This is what the dream means," Joseph told him. "The three baskets also represent three days. 19Three days from now Pharaoh will lift you up and impale your body on a pole. Then birds will come and peck away at your flesh."

20Pharaoh's birthday came three days later, and he prepared a banquet for all his officials and staff. He summoned* his chief cup-bearer and chief baker to join the other officials. 21He then restored the chief cup-bearer to his former position, so he could again hand Pharaoh his cup. 22But Pharaoh impaled the chief baker, just as Joseph had predicted when he interpreted his dream. 23Pharaoh's chief cup-bearer, however, forgot all about Joseph, never giving him another thought.

Pharaoh's Dreams

41 Two full years later, Pharaoh dreamed that he was standing on the bank of the Nile River. 2In his dream he saw seven fat, healthy cows come up out of the river and begin grazing in the marsh grass. 3Then he saw seven more cows come up behind them from the Nile, but these were scrawny and thin. These cows stood beside the fat cows on the riverbank. 4Then the scrawny, thin cows ate the seven healthy, fat cows! At this point in the dream, Pharaoh woke up.

5But he fell asleep again and had a second dream. This time he saw seven heads of grain, plump and beautiful, growing on a single stalk. 6Then seven more heads of grain appeared, but these were shriveled and withered by the east wind. 7And these thin heads swallowed up the seven plump, well-formed heads! Then Pharaoh woke up again and realized it was a dream.

8The next morning Pharaoh was very disturbed by the dreams. So he called for all the magicians and wise men of Egypt. When Pharaoh told them his dreams, not one of them could tell him what they meant.

9Finally, the king's chief cup-bearer spoke up. "Today I have been reminded of my failure," he told Pharaoh. 10"Some time ago, you

were angry with the chief baker and me, and you imprisoned us in the palace of the captain of the guard. 11One night the chief baker and I each had a dream, and each dream had its own meaning. 12There was a young Hebrew man with us in the prison who was a slave of the captain of the guard. We told him our dreams, and he told us what each of our dreams meant. 13And everything happened just as he had predicted. I was restored to my position as cupbearer, and the chief baker was executed and impaled on a pole."

14Pharaoh sent for Joseph at once, and he was quickly brought from the prison. After he shaved and changed his clothes, he went in and stood before Pharaoh. 15Then Pharaoh said to Joseph, "I had a dream last night, and no one here can tell me what it means. But I have heard that when you hear about a dream you can interpret it."

16"It is beyond my power to do this," Joseph replied. "But God can tell you what it means and set you at ease."

17So Pharaoh told Joseph his dream. "In my dream," he said, "I was standing on the bank of the Nile River, 18and I saw seven fat, healthy cows come up out of the river and begin grazing in the marsh grass. 19But then I saw seven sick-looking cows, scrawny and thin, come up after them. I've never seen such sorry-looking animals in all the land of Egypt. 20These thin, scrawny cows ate the seven fat cows. 21But afterward you wouldn't have known it, for they were still as thin and scrawny as before! Then I woke up.

22"In my dream I also saw seven heads of grain, full and beautiful, growing on a single stalk. 23Then seven more heads of grain appeared, but these were blighted, shriveled, and withered by the east wind. 24And the shriveled heads swallowed the seven healthy heads. I told these dreams to the magicians, but no one could tell me what they mean."

25Joseph responded, "Both of Pharaoh's dreams mean the same thing. God is telling Pharaoh in advance what he is about to do. 26The seven healthy cows and the seven healthy heads of grain both represent seven years of prosperity. 27The seven thin, scrawny cows that came up later and the seven thin heads of grain, withered by the east wind, represent seven years of famine.

28"This will happen just as I have described it, for God has revealed to Pharaoh in advance what he is about to do. 29The next seven years

40:20 Hebrew *He lifted up the head of.*

will be a period of great prosperity throughout the land of Egypt. ³⁰But afterward there will be seven years of famine so great that all the prosperity will be forgotten in Egypt. Famine will destroy the land. ³¹This famine will be so severe that even the memory of the good years will be erased. ³²As for having two similar dreams, it means that these events have been decreed by God, and he will soon make them happen.

³³"Therefore, Pharaoh should find an intelligent and wise man and put him in charge of the entire land of Egypt. ³⁴Then Pharaoh should appoint supervisors over the land and let them collect one-fifth of all the crops during the seven good years. ³⁵Have them gather all the food produced in the good years that are just ahead and bring it to Pharaoh's storehouses. Store it away, and guard it so there will be food in the cities. ³⁶That way there will be enough to eat when the seven years of famine come to the land of Egypt. Otherwise this famine will destroy the land."

Joseph Made Ruler of Egypt

³⁷Joseph's suggestions were well received by Pharaoh and his officials. ³⁸So Pharaoh asked his officials, "Can we find anyone else like this man so obviously filled with the spirit of God?" ³⁹Then Pharaoh said to Joseph, "Since God has revealed the meaning of the dreams to you, clearly no one else is as intelligent or wise as you are. ⁴⁰You will be in charge of my court, and all my people will take orders from you. Only I, sitting on my throne, will have a rank higher than yours."

⁴¹Pharaoh said to Joseph, "I hereby put you in charge of the entire land of Egypt." ⁴²Then Pharaoh removed his signet ring from his hand and placed it on Joseph's finger. He dressed him in fine linen clothing and hung a gold chain around his neck. ⁴³Then he had Joseph ride in the chariot reserved for his second-in-command. And wherever Joseph went, the command was shouted, "Kneel down!" So Pharaoh put Joseph in charge of all Egypt. ⁴⁴And Pharaoh said to him, "I am Pharaoh, but no one will lift a hand or foot in the entire land of Egypt without your approval."

⁴⁵Then Pharaoh gave Joseph a new Egyptian name, Zaphenath-paneah.* He also gave him a wife, whose name was Asenath. She was the daughter of Potiphera, the priest of On.* So Joseph took charge of the entire land of Egypt.

⁴⁶He was thirty years old when he began serving in the court of Pharaoh, the king of Egypt. And when Joseph left Pharaoh's presence, he inspected the entire land of Egypt.

⁴⁷As predicted, for seven years the land produced bumper crops. ⁴⁸During those years, Joseph gathered all the crops grown in Egypt and stored the grain from the surrounding fields in the cities. ⁴⁹He piled up huge amounts of grain like sand on the seashore. Finally, he stopped keeping records because there was too much to measure.

⁵⁰During this time, before the first of the famine years, two sons were born to Joseph and his wife, Asenath, the daughter of Potiphera, the priest of On. ⁵¹Joseph named his older son Manasseh,* for he said, "God has made me forget all my troubles and everyone in my father's family." ⁵²Joseph named his second son Ephraim,* for he said, "God has made me fruitful in this land of my grief."

⁵³At last the seven years of bumper crops throughout the land of Egypt came to an end. ⁵⁴Then the seven years of famine began, just as Joseph had predicted. The famine also struck all the surrounding countries, but throughout Egypt there was plenty of food. ⁵⁵Eventually, however, the famine spread throughout the land of Egypt as well. And when the people cried out to Pharaoh for food, he told them, "Go to Joseph, and do whatever he tells you." ⁵⁶So with severe famine everywhere, Joseph opened up the storehouses and distributed grain to the Egyptians, for the famine was severe throughout the land of Egypt. ⁵⁷And people from all around came to Egypt to buy grain from Joseph because the famine was severe throughout the world.

Joseph's Brothers Go to Egypt

42 When Jacob heard that grain was available in Egypt, he said to his sons, "Why are you standing around looking at one another? ²I have heard there is grain in Egypt. Go down there, and buy enough grain to keep us alive. Otherwise we'll die."

³So Joseph's ten older brothers went down to Egypt to buy grain. ⁴But Jacob wouldn't let Joseph's younger brother, Benjamin, go with them, for fear some harm might come to him. ⁵So Jacob's* sons arrived in Egypt along with others to buy food, for the famine was in Canaan as well.

41:45a Zaphenath-paneah probably means "God speaks and lives."   41:45b Greek version reads of Heliopolis; also in 41:50.
41:51 Manasseh sounds like a Hebrew term that means "causing to forget."   41:52 Ephraim sounds like a Hebrew term that means "fruitful."   42:5 Hebrew Israel's. See note on 35:21.

6Since Joseph was governor of all Egypt and in charge of selling grain to all the people, it was to him that his brothers came. When they arrived, they bowed before him with their faces to the ground. 7Joseph recognized his brothers instantly, but he pretended to be a stranger and spoke harshly to them. "Where are you from?" he demanded.

"From the land of Canaan," they replied. "We have come to buy food."

8Although Joseph recognized his brothers, they didn't recognize him. 9And he remembered the dreams he'd had about them many years before. He said to them, "You are spies! You have come to see how vulnerable our land has become."

10"No, my lord!" they exclaimed. "Your servants have simply come to buy food. 11We are all brothers—members of the same family. We are honest men, sir! We are not spies!"

12"Yes, you are!" Joseph insisted. "You have come to see how vulnerable our land has become."

13"Sir," they said, "there are actually twelve of us. We, your servants, are all brothers, sons of a man living in the land of Canaan. Our youngest brother is back there with our father right now, and one of our brothers is no longer with us."

14But Joseph insisted, "As I said, you are spies! 15This is how I will test your story. I swear by the life of Pharaoh that you will never leave Egypt unless your youngest brother comes here! 16One of you must go and get your brother. I'll keep the rest of you here in prison. Then we'll find out whether or not your story is true. By the life of Pharaoh, if it turns out that you don't have a younger brother, then I'll know you are spies."

17So Joseph put them all in prison for three days. 18On the third day Joseph said to them, "I am a God-fearing man. If you do as I say, you will live. 19If you really are honest men, choose one of your brothers to remain in prison. The rest of you may go home with grain for your starving families. 20But you must bring your youngest brother back to me. This will prove that you are telling the truth, and you will not die." To this they agreed.

21Speaking among themselves, they said, "Clearly we are being punished because of what we did to Joseph long ago. We saw his anguish when he pleaded for his life, but we wouldn't listen. That's why we're in this trouble."

22"Didn't I tell you not to sin against the boy?" Reuben asked. "But you wouldn't listen. And now we have to answer for his blood!"

23Of course, they didn't know that Joseph understood them, for he had been speaking to them through an interpreter. 24Now he turned away from them and began to weep. When he regained his composure, he spoke to them again. Then he chose Simeon from among them and had him tied up right before their eyes.

25Joseph then ordered his servants to fill the men's sacks with grain, but he also gave secret instructions to return each brother's payment at the top of his sack. He also gave them supplies for their journey home. 26So the brothers loaded their donkeys with the grain and headed for home.

27But when they stopped for the night and one of them opened his sack to get grain for his donkey, he found his money in the top of his sack. 28"Look!" he exclaimed to his brothers. "My money has been returned; it's here in my sack!" Then their hearts sank. Trembling, they said to each other, "What has God done to us?"

29When the brothers came to their father, Jacob, in the land of Canaan, they told him everything that had happened to them. 30"The man who is governor of the land spoke very harshly to us," they told him. "He accused us of being spies scouting the land. 31But we said, 'We are honest men, not spies. 32We are twelve brothers, sons of one father. One brother is no longer with us, and the youngest is at home with our father in the land of Canaan.'

33"Then the man who is governor of the land told us, 'This is how I will find out if you are honest men. Leave one of your brothers here with me, and take grain for your starving families and go on home. 34But you must bring your youngest brother back to me. Then I will know you are honest men and not spies. Then I will give you back your brother, and you may trade freely in the land.' "

35As they emptied out their sacks, there in each man's sack was the bag of money he had paid for the grain! The brothers and their father were terrified when they saw the bags of money. 36Jacob exclaimed, "You are robbing me of my children! Joseph is gone! Simeon is gone! And now you want to take Benjamin, too. Everything is going against me!"

37Then Reuben said to his father, "You may kill my two sons if I don't bring Benjamin back to you. I'll be responsible for him, and I promise to bring him back."

38But Jacob replied, "My son will not go down with you. His brother Joseph is dead, and he is all I have left. If anything should happen to him on your journey, you would send this grieving, white-haired man to his grave.*"

The Brothers Return to Egypt

43 But the famine continued to ravage the land of Canaan. [2]When the grain they had brought from Egypt was almost gone, Jacob said to his sons, "Go back and buy us a little more food."

[3]But Judah said, "The man was serious when he warned us, 'You won't see my face again unless your brother is with you.' [4]If you send Benjamin with us, we will go down and buy more food. [5]But if you don't let Benjamin go, we won't go either. Remember, the man said, 'You won't see my face again unless your brother is with you.'"

[6]"Why were you so cruel to me?" Jacob* moaned. "Why did you tell him you had another brother?"

[7]"The man kept asking us questions about our family," they replied. "He asked, 'Is your father still alive? Do you have another brother?' So we answered his questions. How could we know he would say, 'Bring your brother down here'?"

[8]Judah said to his father, "Send the boy with me, and we will be on our way. Otherwise we will all die of starvation—and not only we, but you and our little ones. [9]I personally guarantee his safety. You may hold me responsible if I don't bring him back to you. Then let me bear the blame forever. [10]If we hadn't wasted all this time, we could have gone and returned twice by now."

[11]So their father, Jacob, finally said to them, "If it can't be avoided, then at least do this. Pack your bags with the best products of this land. Take them down to the man as gifts—balm, honey, gum, aromatic resin, pistachio nuts, and almonds. [12]Also take double the money that was put back in your sacks, as it was probably someone's mistake. [13]Then take your brother, and go back to the man. [14]May God Almighty* give you mercy as you go before the man, so that he will release Simeon and let Benjamin return. But if I must lose my children, so be it."

[15]So the men packed Jacob's gifts and double the money and headed off with Benjamin. They finally arrived in Egypt and presented themselves to Joseph. [16]When Joseph saw Benjamin with them, he said to the manager of his household, "These men will eat with me this noon. Take them inside the palace. Then go slaughter an animal, and prepare a big feast."

[17]So the man did as Joseph told him and took them into Joseph's palace.

[18]The brothers were terrified when they saw that they were being taken into Joseph's house. "It's because of the money someone put in our sacks last time we were here," they said. "He plans to pretend that we stole it. Then he will seize us, make us slaves, and take our donkeys."

A Feast at Joseph's Palace

[19]The brothers approached the manager of Joseph's household and spoke to him at the entrance to the palace. [20]"Sir," they said, "we came to Egypt once before to buy food. [21]But as we were returning home, we stopped for the night and opened our sacks. Then we discovered that each man's money—the exact amount paid—was in the top of his sack! Here it is; we have brought it back with us. [22]We also have additional money to buy more food. We have no idea who put our money in our sacks."

[23]"Relax. Don't be afraid," the household manager told them. "Your God, the God of your father, must have put this treasure into your sacks. I know I received your payment." Then he released Simeon and brought him out to them.

[24]The manager then led the men into Joseph's palace. He gave them water to wash their feet and provided food for their donkeys. [25]They were told they would be eating there, so they prepared their gifts for Joseph's arrival at noon.

[26]When Joseph came home, they gave him the gifts they had brought him, then bowed low to the ground before him. [27]After greeting them, he asked, "How is your father, the old man you spoke about? Is he still alive?"

[28]"Yes," they replied. "Our father, your servant, is alive and well." And they bowed low again.

[29]Then Joseph looked at his brother Benjamin, the son of his own mother. "Is this your youngest brother, the one you told me about?" Joseph asked. "May God be gracious to you, my son." [30]Then Joseph hurried from the room because he was overcome with emotion for his brother. He went into his private room, where he broke down and wept. [31]After washing his face, he came back out, keeping himself under control. Then he ordered, "Bring out the food!"

[32]The waiters served Joseph at his own table, and his brothers were served at a separate table. The Egyptians who ate with Joseph sat at their own table, because Egyptians despise Hebrews

42:38 Hebrew *to Sheol.*   43:6 Hebrew *Israel;* also in 43:11. See note on 35:21.   43:14 Hebrew *El-Shaddai.*

and refuse to eat with them. ³³Joseph told each of his brothers where to sit, and to their amazement, he seated them according to age, from oldest to youngest. ³⁴And Joseph filled their plates with food from his own table, giving Benjamin five times as much as he gave the others. So they feasted and drank freely with him.

Joseph's Silver Cup

44 When his brothers were ready to leave, Joseph gave these instructions to his palace manager: "Fill each of their sacks with as much grain as they can carry, and put each man's money back into his sack. ²Then put my personal silver cup at the top of the youngest brother's sack, along with the money for his grain." So the manager did as Joseph instructed him.

³The brothers were up at dawn and were sent on their journey with their loaded donkeys. ⁴But when they had gone only a short distance and were barely out of the city, Joseph said to his palace manager, "Chase after them and stop them. When you catch up with them, ask them, 'Why have you repaid my kindness with such evil? ⁵Why have you stolen my master's silver cup,* which he uses to predict the future? What a wicked thing you have done!'"

⁶When the palace manager caught up with the men, he spoke to them as he had been instructed.

⁷"What are you talking about?" the brothers responded. "We are your servants and would never do such a thing! ⁸Didn't we return the money we found in our sacks? We brought it back all the way from the land of Canaan. Why would we steal silver or gold from your master's house? ⁹If you find his cup with any one of us, let that man die. And all the rest of us, my lord, will be your slaves."

¹⁰"That's fair," the man replied. "But only the one who stole the cup will be my slave. The rest of you may go free."

¹¹They all quickly took their sacks from the backs of their donkeys and opened them. ¹²The palace manager searched the brothers' sacks, from the oldest to the youngest. And the cup was found in Benjamin's sack! ¹³When the brothers saw this, they tore their clothing in despair. Then they loaded their donkeys again and returned to the city.

¹⁴Joseph was still in his palace when Judah and his brothers arrived, and they fell to the ground before him. ¹⁵"What have you done?"

Joseph demanded. "Don't you know that a man like me can predict the future?"

¹⁶Judah answered, "Oh, my lord, what can we say to you? How can we explain this? How can we prove our innocence? God is punishing us for our sins. My lord, we have all returned to be your slaves—all of us, not just our brother who had your cup in his sack."

¹⁷"No," Joseph said. "I would never do such a thing! Only the man who stole the cup will be my slave. The rest of you may go back to your father in peace."

Judah Speaks for His Brothers

¹⁸Then Judah stepped forward and said, "Please, my lord, let your servant say just one word to you. Please, do not be angry with me, even though you are as powerful as Pharaoh himself.

¹⁹"My lord, previously you asked us, your servants, 'Do you have a father or a brother?' ²⁰And we responded, 'Yes, my lord, we have a father who is an old man, and his youngest son is a child of his old age. His full brother is dead, and he alone is left of his mother's children, and his father loves him very much.'

²¹"And you said to us, 'Bring him here so I can see him with my own eyes.' ²²But we said to you, 'My lord, the boy cannot leave his father, for his father would die.' ²³But you told us, 'Unless your youngest brother comes with you, you will never see my face again.'

²⁴"So we returned to your servant, our father, and told him what you had said. ²⁵Later, when he said, 'Go back again and buy us more food,' ²⁶we replied, 'We can't go unless you let our youngest brother go with us. We'll never get to see the man's face unless our youngest brother is with us.'

²⁷"Then my father said to us, 'As you know, my wife had two sons, ²⁸and one of them went away and never returned. Doubtless he was torn to pieces by some wild animal. I have never seen him since. ²⁹Now if you take his brother away from me, and any harm comes to him, you will send this grieving, white-haired man to his grave.*'

³⁰"And now, my lord, I cannot go back to my father without the boy. Our father's life is bound up in the boy's life. ³¹If he sees that the boy is not with us, our father will die. We, your servants, will indeed be responsible for sending that grieving, white-haired man to his grave. ³²My lord, I guaranteed to my father that I would take care of the boy. I told him, 'If

44:5 As in Greek version; Hebrew lacks this phrase.   44:29 Hebrew *to Sheol*; also in 44:31.

I don't bring him back to you, I will bear the blame forever.'

33"So please, my lord, let me stay here as a slave instead of the boy, and let the boy return with his brothers. 34For how can I return to my father if the boy is not with me? I couldn't bear to see the anguish this would cause my father!"

Joseph Reveals His Identity

45 Joseph could stand it no longer. There were many people in the room, and he said to his attendants, "Out, all of you!" So he was alone with his brothers when he told them who he was. 2Then he broke down and wept. He wept so loudly the Egyptians could hear him, and word of it quickly carried to Pharaoh's palace.

3"I am Joseph!" he said to his brothers. "Is my father still alive?" But his brothers were speechless! They were stunned to realize that Joseph was standing there in front of them. 4"Please, come closer," he said to them. So they came closer. And he said again, "I am Joseph, your brother, whom you sold into slavery in Egypt. 5But don't be upset, and don't be angry with yourselves for selling me to this place. It was God who sent me here ahead of you to preserve your lives. 6This famine that has ravaged the land for two years will last five more years, and there will be neither plowing nor harvesting. 7God has sent me ahead of you to keep you and your families alive and to preserve many survivors.* 8So it was God who sent me here, not you! And he is the one who made me an adviser* to Pharaoh—the manager of his entire palace and the governor of all Egypt.

9"Now hurry back to my father and tell him, 'This is what your son Joseph says: God has made me master over all the land of Egypt. So come down to me immediately! 10You can live in the region of Goshen, where you can be near me with all your children and grandchildren, your flocks and herds, and everything you own. 11I will take care of you there, for there are still five years of famine ahead of us. Otherwise you, your household, and all your animals will starve.'"

12Then Joseph added, "Look! You can see for yourselves, and so can my brother Benjamin, that I really am Joseph! 13Go tell my father of my honored position here in Egypt. Describe for him everything you have seen, and then bring my father here quickly." 14Weeping with joy, he embraced Benjamin, and Benjamin did the same. 15Then Joseph kissed each of his brothers and wept over them, and after that they began talking freely with him.

Pharaoh Invites Jacob to Egypt

16The news soon reached Pharaoh's palace: "Joseph's brothers have arrived!" Pharaoh and his officials were all delighted to hear this.

17Pharaoh said to Joseph, "Tell your brothers, 'This is what you must do: Load your pack animals, and hurry back to the land of Canaan. 18Then get your father and all of your families, and return here to me. I will give you the very best land in Egypt, and you will eat from the best that the land produces.'"

19Then Pharaoh said to Joseph, "Tell your brothers, 'Take wagons from the land of Egypt to carry your little children and your wives, and bring your father here. 20Don't worry about your personal belongings, for the best of all the land of Egypt is yours.'"

21So the sons of Jacob* did as they were told. Joseph provided them with wagons, as Pharaoh had commanded, and he gave them supplies for the journey. 22And he gave each of them new clothes—but to Benjamin he gave five changes of clothes and 300 pieces* of silver. 23He also sent his father ten male donkeys loaded with the finest products of Egypt, and ten female donkeys loaded with grain and bread and other supplies he would need on his journey.

24So Joseph sent his brothers off, and as they left, he called after them, "Don't quarrel about all this along the way!" 25And they left Egypt and returned to their father, Jacob, in the land of Canaan.

26"Joseph is still alive!" they told him. "And he is governor of all the land of Egypt!" Jacob was stunned at the news—he couldn't believe it. 27But when they repeated to Jacob everything Joseph had told them, and when he saw the wagons Joseph had sent to carry him, their father's spirits revived.

28Then Jacob exclaimed, "It must be true! My son Joseph is alive! I must go and see him before I die."

Jacob's Journey to Egypt

46 So Jacob* set out for Egypt with all his possessions. And when he came to Beersheba, he offered sacrifices to the God of

---

45:7 Or *and to save you with an extraordinary rescue.* The meaning of the Hebrew is uncertain.   45:8 Hebrew *a father.*
45:21 Hebrew *Israel;* also in 45:28. See note on 35:21.   45:22 Hebrew *300 [shekels],* about 7.5 pounds or 3.4 kilograms
in weight.   46:1 Hebrew *Israel;* also in 46:29, 30. See note on 35:21.

his father, Isaac. [2]During the night God spoke to him in a vision. "Jacob! Jacob!" he called.

"Here I am," Jacob replied.

[3]"I am God,* the God of your father," the voice said. "Do not be afraid to go down to Egypt, for there I will make your family into a great nation. [4]I will go with you down to Egypt, and I will bring you back again. You will die in Egypt, but Joseph will be with you to close your eyes."

[5]So Jacob left Beersheba, and his sons took him to Egypt. They carried him and their little ones and their wives in the wagons Pharaoh had provided for them. [6]They also took all their livestock and all the personal belongings they had acquired in the land of Canaan. So Jacob and his entire family went to Egypt—[7]sons and grandsons, daughters and granddaughters— all his descendants.

[8]These are the names of the descendants of Israel—the sons of Jacob—who went to Egypt:

Reuben was Jacob's oldest son. [9]The sons of Reuben were Hanoch, Pallu, Hezron, and Carmi.

[10]The sons of Simeon were Jemuel, Jamin, Ohad, Jakin, Zohar, and Shaul. (Shaul's mother was a Canaanite woman.)

[11]The sons of Levi were Gershon, Kohath, and Merari.

[12]The sons of Judah were Er, Onan, Shelah, Perez, and Zerah (though Er and Onan had died in the land of Canaan). The sons of Perez were Hezron and Hamul.

[13]The sons of Issachar were Tola, Puah,* Jashub,* and Shimron.

[14]The sons of Zebulun were Sered, Elon, and Jahleel.

[15]These were the sons of Leah and Jacob who were born in Paddan-aram, in addition to their daughter, Dinah. The number of Jacob's de- scendants (male and female) through Leah was thirty-three.

[16]The sons of Gad were Zephon,* Haggi, Shuni, Ezbon, Eri, Arodi, and Areli.

[17]The sons of Asher were Imnah, Ishvah, Ishvi, and Beriah. Their sister was Serah. Beriah's sons were Heber and Malkiel.

[18]These were the sons of Zilpah, the servant given to Leah by her father, Laban. The number of Jacob's descendants through Zilpah was sixteen.

[19]The sons of Jacob's wife Rachel were Joseph and Benjamin.

[20]Joseph's sons, born in the land of Egypt, were Manasseh and Ephraim. Their mother was Asenath, daughter of Potiphera, the priest of On.*

[21]Benjamin's sons were Bela, Beker, Ashbel, Gera, Naaman, Ehi, Rosh, Muppim, Huppim, and Ard.

[22]These were the sons of Rachel and Jacob. The number of Jacob's descendants through Rachel was fourteen.

[23]The son of Dan was Hushim.

[24]The sons of Naphtali were Jahzeel, Guni, Jezer, and Shillem.

[25]These were the sons of Bilhah, the servant given to Rachel by her father, Laban. The num- ber of Jacob's descendants through Bilhah was seven.

[26]The total number of Jacob's direct descen- dants who went with him to Egypt, not count- ing his sons' wives, was sixty-six. [27]In addition, Joseph had two sons* who were born in Egypt. So altogether, there were seventy* members of Jacob's family in the land of Egypt.

Jacob's Family Arrives in Goshen

[28]As they neared their destination, Jacob sent Judah ahead to meet Joseph and get directions to the region of Goshen. And when they finally arrived there, [29]Joseph prepared his chariot and traveled to Goshen to meet his father, Jacob. When Joseph arrived, he embraced his father and wept, holding him for a long time. [30]Fi- nally, Jacob said to Joseph, "Now I am ready to die, since I have seen your face again and know you are still alive."

[31]And Joseph said to his brothers and to his father's entire family, "I will go to Pharaoh and tell him, 'My brothers and my father's entire family have come to me from the land of Canaan. [32]These men are shepherds, and they raise livestock. They have brought with them their flocks and herds and everything they own.'"

[33]Then he said, "When Pharaoh calls for you and asks you about your occupation, [34]you

---

46:3 Hebrew *I am El.*   46:13a As in Syriac version and Samaritan Pentateuch (see also 1 Chr 7:1); Hebrew reads *Puvah*.
46:13b As in some Greek manuscripts and Samaritan Pentateuch (see also Num 26:24; 1 Chr 7:1); Hebrew reads *Iob*.
46:16 As in Greek version and Samaritan Pentateuch (see also Num 26:15); Hebrew reads *Ziphion*.   46:20 Greek version reads *of Heliopolis.*   46:27a Greek version reads *nine sons,* probably including Joseph's grandsons through Ephraim and Manasseh (see 1 Chr 7:14-20).   46:27b Greek version reads *seventy-five;* see note on Exod 1:5.

must tell him, 'We, your servants, have raised livestock all our lives, as our ancestors have always done.' When you tell him this, he will let you live here in the region of Goshen, for the Egyptians despise shepherds."

Jacob Blesses Pharaoh

47 Then Joseph went to see Pharaoh and told him, "My father and my brothers have arrived from the land of Canaan. They have come with all their flocks and herds and possessions, and they are now in the region of Goshen." 2Joseph took five of his brothers with him and presented them to Pharaoh. 3And Pharaoh asked the brothers, "What is your occupation?"

They replied, "We, your servants, are shepherds, just like our ancestors. 4We have come to live here in Egypt for a while, for there is no pasture for our flocks in Canaan. The famine is very severe there. So please, we request permission to live in the region of Goshen."

5Then Pharaoh said to Joseph, "Now that your father and brothers have joined you here, 6choose any place in the entire land of Egypt for them to live. Give them the best land of Egypt. Let them live in the region of Goshen. And if any of them have special skills, put them in charge of my livestock, too."

7Then Joseph brought in his father, Jacob, and presented him to Pharaoh. And Jacob blessed Pharaoh.

8"How old are you?" Pharaoh asked him.

9Jacob replied, "I have traveled this earth for 130 hard years. But my life has been short compared to the lives of my ancestors." 10Then Jacob blessed Pharaoh again before leaving his court.

11So Joseph assigned the best land of Egypt—the region of Rameses—to his father and his brothers, and he settled them there, just as Pharaoh had commanded. 12And Joseph provided food for his father and his brothers in amounts appropriate to the number of their dependents, including the smallest children.

Joseph's Leadership in the Famine

13Meanwhile, the famine became so severe that all the food was used up, and people were starving throughout the lands of Egypt and Canaan. 14By selling grain to the people, Joseph eventually collected all the money in Egypt and Canaan, and he put the money in Pharaoh's treasury. 15When the people of Egypt and Canaan ran out of money, all the Egyptians came to Joseph. "Our money is gone!" they cried. "But please give us food, or we will die before your very eyes!"

16Joseph replied, "Since your money is gone, bring me your livestock. I will give you food in exchange for your livestock." 17So they brought their livestock to Joseph in exchange for food. In exchange for their horses, flocks of sheep and goats, herds of cattle, and donkeys, Joseph provided them with food for another year.

18But that year ended, and the next year they came again and said, "We cannot hide the truth from you, my lord. Our money is gone, and all our livestock and cattle are yours. We have nothing left to give but our bodies and our land. 19Why should we die before your very eyes? Buy us and our land in exchange for food; we offer our land and ourselves as slaves for Pharaoh. Just give us grain so we may live and not die, and so the land does not become empty and desolate."

20So Joseph bought all the land of Egypt for Pharaoh. All the Egyptians sold him their fields because the famine was so severe, and soon all the land belonged to Pharaoh. 21As for the people, he made them all slaves,* from one end of Egypt to the other. 22The only land he did not buy was the land belonging to the priests. They received an allotment of food directly from Pharaoh, so they didn't need to sell their land.

23Then Joseph said to the people, "Look, today I have bought you and your land for Pharaoh. I will provide you with seed so you can plant the fields. 24Then when you harvest it, one-fifth of your crop will belong to Pharaoh. You may keep the remaining four-fifths as seed for your fields and as food for you, your households, and your little ones."

25"You have saved our lives!" they exclaimed. "May it please you, my lord, to let us be Pharaoh's servants." 26Joseph then issued a decree still in effect in the land of Egypt, that Pharaoh should receive one-fifth of all the crops grown on his land. Only the land belonging to the priests was not given to Pharaoh.

27Meanwhile, the people of Israel settled in the region of Goshen in Egypt. There they acquired property, and they were fruitful, and their population grew rapidly. 28Jacob lived for seventeen years after his arrival in Egypt, so he lived 147 years in all.

29As the time of his death drew near, Jacob*

47:21 As in Greek version and Samaritan Pentateuch; Hebrew reads *he moved them all into the towns.*   47:29 Hebrew *Israel*; also in 47:31b. See note on 35:21.

called for his son Joseph and said to him, "Please do me this favor. Put your hand under my thigh and swear that you will treat me with unfailing love by honoring this last request: Do not bury me in Egypt. 30When I die, please take my body out of Egypt and bury me with my ancestors."

So Joseph promised, "I will do as you ask."

31"Swear that you will do it," Jacob insisted. So Joseph gave his oath, and Jacob bowed humbly at the head of his bed.*

Jacob Blesses Manasseh and Ephraim

48 One day not long after this, word came to Joseph, "Your father is failing rapidly." So Joseph went to visit his father, and he took with him his two sons, Manasseh and Ephraim.

2When Joseph arrived, Jacob was told, "Your son Joseph has come to see you." So Jacob* gathered his strength and sat up in his bed.

3Jacob said to Joseph, "God Almighty* appeared to me at Luz in the land of Canaan and blessed me. 4He said to me, 'I will make you fruitful, and I will multiply your descendants. I will make you a multitude of nations. And I will give this land of Canaan to your descendants* after you as an everlasting possession.'

5"Now I am claiming as my own sons these two boys of yours, Ephraim and Manasseh, who were born here in the land of Egypt before I arrived. They will be my sons, just as Reuben and Simeon are. 6But any children born to you in the future will be your own, and they will inherit land within the territories of their brothers Ephraim and Manasseh.

7"Long ago, as I was returning from Paddanaram,* Rachel died in the land of Canaan. We were still on the way, some distance from Ephrath (that is, Bethlehem). So with great sorrow I buried her there beside the road to Ephrath."

8Then Jacob looked over at the two boys. "Are these your sons?" he asked.

9"Yes," Joseph told him, "these are the sons God has given me here in Egypt."

And Jacob said, "Bring them closer to me, so I can bless them."

10Jacob was half blind because of his age and could hardly see. So Joseph brought the boys close to him, and Jacob kissed and embraced them. 11Then Jacob said to Joseph, "I never thought I would see your face again, but now God has let me see your children, too!"

12Joseph moved the boys, who were at their grandfather's knees, and he bowed with his face to the ground. 13Then he positioned the boys in front of Jacob. With his right hand he directed Ephraim toward Jacob's left hand, and with his left hand he put Manasseh at Jacob's right hand. 14But Jacob crossed his arms as he reached out to lay his hands on the boys' heads. He put his right hand on the head of Ephraim, though he was the younger boy, and his left hand on the head of Manasseh, though he was the firstborn. 15Then he blessed Joseph and said,

"May the God before whom my
       grandfather Abraham
   and my father, Isaac, walked—
the God who has been my shepherd
   all my life, to this very day,
16 the Angel who has redeemed me from
       all harm—
   may he bless these boys.
May they preserve my name
   and the names of Abraham and
   Isaac.
And may their descendants multiply
       greatly
   throughout the earth."

17But Joseph was upset when he saw that his father placed his right hand on Ephraim's head. So Joseph lifted it to move it from Ephraim's head to Manasseh's head. 18"No, my father," he said. "This one is the firstborn. Put your right hand on his head."

19But his father refused. "I know, my son; I know," he replied. "Manasseh will also become a great people, but his younger brother will become even greater. And his descendants will become a multitude of nations."

20So Jacob blessed the boys that day with this blessing: "The people of Israel will use your names when they give a blessing. They will say, 'May God make you as prosperous as Ephraim and Manasseh.'" In this way, Jacob put Ephraim ahead of Manasseh.

21Then Jacob said to Joseph, "Look, I am about to die, but God will be with you and will take you back to Canaan, the land of your ancestors. 22And beyond what I have given your brothers, I am giving you an extra portion of the land* that I took from the Amorites with my sword and bow."

47:31 Greek version reads and Israel bowed in worship as he leaned on his staff. Compare Heb 11:21. 48:2 Hebrew Israel; also in 48:8, 10, 11, 13, 14, 21. See note on 35:21. 48:3 Hebrew El-Shaddai. 48:4 Hebrew seed; also in 48:19. 48:7 Hebrew Paddan, referring to Paddan-aram; compare Gen 35:9. 48:22 Or an extra ridge of land. The meaning of the Hebrew is uncertain.

Jacob's Last Words to His Sons

49 Then Jacob called together all his sons and said, "Gather around me, and I will tell you what will happen to each of you in the days to come.

2 "Come and listen, you sons of Jacob;
  listen to Israel, your father.

3 "Reuben, you are my firstborn, my strength,
  the child of my vigorous youth.
  You are first in rank and first in power.
4 But you are as unruly as a flood,
  and you will be first no longer.
  For you went to bed with my wife;
  you defiled my marriage couch.

5 "Simeon and Levi are two of a kind;
  their weapons are instruments of violence.
6 May I never join in their meetings;
  may I never be a party to their plans.
  For in their anger they murdered men,
  and they crippled oxen just for sport.
7 A curse on their anger, for it is fierce;
  a curse on their wrath, for it is cruel.
I will scatter them among the descendants of Jacob;
  I will disperse them throughout Israel.

8 "Judah, your brothers will praise you.
  You will grasp your enemies by the neck.
  All your relatives will bow before you.
9 Judah, my son, is a young lion
  that has finished eating its prey.
  Like a lion he crouches and lies down;
  like a lioness—who dares to rouse him?
10 The scepter will not depart from Judah,
  nor the ruler's staff from his descendants,*
  until the coming of the one to whom it belongs,*
  the one whom all nations will honor.
11 He ties his foal to a grapevine,
  the colt of his donkey to a choice vine.
  He washes his clothes in wine,
  his robes in the blood of grapes.
12 His eyes are darker than wine,
  and his teeth are whiter than milk.

13 "Zebulun will settle by the seashore
  and will be a harbor for ships;
  his borders will extend to Sidon.

14 "Issachar is a sturdy donkey,
  resting between two saddlepacks.*
15 When he sees how good the countryside is
  and how pleasant the land,
he will bend his shoulder to the load
  and submit himself to hard labor.

16 "Dan will govern his people,
  like any other tribe in Israel.
17 Dan will be a snake beside the road,
  a poisonous viper along the path
that bites the horse's hooves
  so its rider is thrown off.
18 I trust in you for salvation, O LORD!

19 "Gad will be attacked by marauding bands,
  but he will attack them when they retreat.

20 "Asher will dine on rich foods
  and produce food fit for kings.

21 "Naphtali is a doe set free
  that bears beautiful fawns.

22 "Joseph is the foal of a wild donkey,
  the foal of a wild donkey at a spring—
  one of the wild donkeys on the ridge.*
23 Archers attacked him savagely;
  they shot at him and harassed him.
24 But his bow remained taut,
  and his arms were strengthened
by the hands of the Mighty One of Jacob,
  by the Shepherd, the Rock of Israel.
25 May the God of your father help you;
  may the Almighty bless you
with the blessings of the heavens above,
  and blessings of the watery depths below,
  and blessings of the breasts and womb.
26 May my fatherly blessings on you
  surpass the blessings of my ancestors,*
  reaching to the heights of the eternal hills.
May these blessings rest on the head of Joseph,
  who is a prince among his brothers.

49:10a Hebrew *from between his feet.*   49:10b Or *until tribute is brought to him and the peoples obey*; traditionally rendered *until Shiloh comes.*   49:14 Or *sheepfolds*, or *hearths.*   49:22 Or *Joseph is a fruitful tree, / a fruitful tree beside a spring, / His branches reach over the wall. The meaning of the Hebrew is uncertain.*   49:26 Or *of the ancient mountains.*

27 "Benjamin is a ravenous wolf,
    devouring his enemies in the
       morning
    and dividing his plunder in the
       evening."

28These are the twelve tribes of Israel, and this is what their father said as he told his sons good-bye. He blessed each one with an appropriate message.

Jacob's Death and Burial

29Then Jacob instructed them, "Soon I will die and join my ancestors. Bury me with my father and grandfather in the cave in the field of Ephron the Hittite. 30This is the cave in the field of Machpelah, near Mamre in Canaan, that Abraham bought from Ephron the Hittite as a permanent burial site. 31There Abraham and his wife Sarah are buried. There Isaac and his wife, Rebekah, are buried. And there I buried Leah. 32It is the plot of land and the cave that my grandfather Abraham bought from the Hittites."

33When Jacob had finished this charge to his sons, he drew his feet into the bed, breathed his last, and joined his ancestors in death.

50 Joseph threw himself on his father and wept over him and kissed him. 2Then Joseph told the physicians who served him to embalm his father's body; so Jacob* was embalmed. 3The embalming process took the usual forty days. And the Egyptians mourned his death for seventy days.

4When the period of mourning was over, Joseph approached Pharaoh's advisers and said, "Please do me this favor and speak to Pharaoh on my behalf. 5Tell him that my father made me swear an oath. He said to me, 'Listen, I am about to die. Take my body back to the land of Canaan, and bury me in the tomb I prepared for myself.' So please allow me to go and bury my father. After his burial, I will return without delay."

6Pharaoh agreed to Joseph's request. "Go and bury your father, as he made you promise," he said. 7So Joseph went up to bury his father. He was accompanied by all of Pharaoh's officials, all the senior members of Pharaoh's household, and all the senior officers of Egypt. 8Joseph also took his entire household and his brothers and their households. But they left their little children and flocks and herds in the land of Goshen. 9A great number of chariots and charioteers accompanied Joseph.

10When they arrived at the threshing floor of Atad, near the Jordan River, they held a very great and solemn memorial service, with a seven-day period of mourning for Joseph's father. 11The local residents, the Canaanites, watched them mourning at the threshing floor of Atad. Then they renamed that place (which is near the Jordan) Abel-mizraim,* for they said, "This is a place of deep mourning for these Egyptians."

12So Jacob's sons did as he had commanded them. 13They carried his body to the land of Canaan and buried him in the cave in the field of Machpelah, near Mamre. This is the cave that Abraham had bought as a permanent burial site from Ephron the Hittite.

Joseph Reassures His Brothers

14After burying Jacob, Joseph returned to Egypt with his brothers and all who had accompanied him to his father's burial. 15But now that their father was dead, Joseph's brothers became fearful. "Now Joseph will show his anger and pay us back for all the wrong we did to him," they said.

16So they sent this message to Joseph: "Before your father died, he instructed us 17to say to you: 'Please forgive your brothers for the great wrong they did to you—for their sin in treating you so cruelly.' So we, the servants of the God of your father, beg you to forgive our sin." When Joseph received the message, he broke down and wept. 18Then his brothers came and threw themselves down before Joseph. "Look, we are your slaves!" they said.

19But Joseph replied, "Don't be afraid of me. Am I God, that I can punish you? 20You intended to harm me, but God intended it all for good. He brought me to this position so I could save the lives of many people. 21No, don't be afraid. I will continue to take care of you and your children." So he reassured them by speaking kindly to them.

The Death of Joseph

22So Joseph and his brothers and their families continued to live in Egypt. Joseph lived to the age of 110. 23He lived to see three generations of descendants of his son Ephraim, and he lived to see the birth of the children of Manasseh's son Makir, whom he claimed as his own.*

24"Soon I will die," Joseph told his brothers,

50:2 Hebrew *Israel*. See note on 35:21.   50:11 *Abel-mizraim* means "mourning of the Egyptians."   50:23 Hebrew *who were born on Joseph's knees.*

"but God will surely come to help you and lead you out of this land of Egypt. He will bring you back to the land he solemnly promised to give to Abraham, to Isaac, and to Jacob."

²⁵Then Joseph made the sons of Israel swear an oath, and he said, "When God comes to help you and lead you back, you must take my bones with you." ²⁶So Joseph died at the age of 110. The Egyptians embalmed him, and his body was placed in a coffin in Egypt.

Exodus

EVERY COUNTRY HAS ITS own national history—a record of the events leading to its independence. The book of Exodus records Israel's history, recounting its earliest years and God's covenant with its people. Exodus takes its name from the main event of the book: the Israelites' deliverance from slavery in Egypt. The book begins with a short account of how the Israelites became slaves in Egypt. The focus then shifts to the birth and life of Moses, God's chosen leader for Israel. From a burning bush in the Sinai Desert, God called Moses to return to his homeland of Egypt and lead the Israelites to freedom. But Pharaoh refused to free the Israelites, and as a result he brought God's ten plagues upon Egypt. The final plague not only changed Pharaoh's mind; it became a memorial of God's deliverance, celebrated in the observance of Passover. Once set free, the Israelites traveled to the wilderness of Sinai to worship God. But Pharaoh chased them to the Red Sea, where God displayed his power by parting it for the Israelites to cross but closing it over the pursuing Egyptians. The Israelites were then free to travel to Mount Sinai. There God established his covenant with them, giving them the Ten Commandments and plans for the Tabernacle. After the Israelites constructed the Tabernacle, God filled it with his glory, signifying his presence with them.

- **Author:** Moses, according to Jewish tradition
- **Date Written:** Uncertain, perhaps between 1450 and 1410 BC
- **Purpose:** To record the events of Israel's deliverance from Egypt and development as a nation
- **Themes:** God's sovereignty, guidance, redemption, and covenant with Israel; obedience
- **Outline**
  1:1-22 Israel's bondage in Egypt
  2:1–7:7 The birth and calling of Moses
  7:8–15:21 The plagues, the Passover, and the Exodus
  15:22–24:18 The trip to Sinai and the giving of the Law
  25:1–31:18 Instructions for the Tabernacle
  32:1–35:3 Israel's sin and repentance
  35:4–40:38 The building of the Tabernacle

The Israelites in Egypt

1 These are the names of the sons of Israel (that is, Jacob) who moved to Egypt with their father, each with his family: ²Reuben, Simeon, Levi, Judah, ³Issachar, Zebulun, Benjamin, ⁴Dan, Naphtali, Gad, and Asher. ⁵In all, Jacob had seventy* descendants in Egypt, including Joseph, who was already there.

⁶In time, Joseph and all of his brothers died, ending that entire generation. ⁷But their descendants, the Israelites, had many children and grandchildren. In fact, they multiplied so greatly that they became extremely powerful and filled the land.

⁸Eventually, a new king came to power in Egypt who knew nothing about Joseph or what he had done. ⁹He said to his people, "Look, the people of Israel now outnumber us and are stronger than we are. ¹⁰We must make a plan to keep them from growing even more. If we don't, and if war breaks out, they will join our enemies and fight against us. Then they will escape from the country.*"

¹¹So the Egyptians made the Israelites their slaves. They appointed brutal slave drivers over them, hoping to wear them down with crushing labor. They forced them to build the cities of Pithom and Rameses as supply centers for the

1:5 Dead Sea Scrolls and Greek version read *seventy-five*; see notes on Gen 46:27.   1:10 Or *will take the country.*

king. [12] But the more the Egyptians oppressed them, the more the Israelites multiplied and spread, and the more alarmed the Egyptians became. [13] So the Egyptians worked the people of Israel without mercy. [14] They made their lives bitter, forcing them to mix mortar and make bricks and do all the work in the fields. They were ruthless in all their demands.

[15] Then Pharaoh, the king of Egypt, gave this order to the Hebrew midwives, Shiphrah and Puah: [16] "When you help the Hebrew women as they give birth, watch as they deliver.* If the baby is a boy, kill him; if it is a girl, let her live." [17] But because the midwives feared God, they refused to obey the king's orders. They allowed the boys to live, too.

[18] So the king of Egypt called for the midwives. "Why have you done this?" he demanded. "Why have you allowed the boys to live?"

[19] "The Hebrew women are not like the Egyptian women," the midwives replied. "They are more vigorous and have their babies so quickly that we cannot get there in time."

[20] So God was good to the midwives, and the Israelites continued to multiply, growing more and more powerful. [21] And because the midwives feared God, he gave them families of their own.

[22] Then Pharaoh gave this order to all his people: "Throw every newborn Hebrew boy into the Nile River. But you may let the girls live."

The Birth of Moses

2 About this time, a man and woman from the tribe of Levi got married. [2] The woman became pregnant and gave birth to a son. She saw that he was a special baby and kept him hidden for three months. [3] But when she could no longer hide him, she got a basket made of papyrus reeds and waterproofed it with tar and pitch. She put the baby in the basket and laid it among the reeds along the bank of the Nile River. [4] The baby's sister then stood at a distance, watching to see what would happen to him.

[5] Soon Pharaoh's daughter came down to bathe in the river, and her attendants walked along the riverbank. When the princess saw the basket among the reeds, she sent her maid to get it for her. [6] When the princess opened it, she saw the baby. The little boy was crying, and she felt sorry for him. "This must be one of the Hebrew children," she said.

[7] Then the baby's sister approached the princess. "Should I go and find one of the Hebrew women to nurse the baby for you?" she asked.

[8] "Yes, do!" the princess replied. So the girl went and called the baby's mother.

[9] "Take this baby and nurse him for me," the princess told the baby's mother. "I will pay you for your help." So the woman took her baby home and nursed him.

[10] Later, when the boy was older, his mother brought him back to Pharaoh's daughter, who adopted him as her own son. The princess named him Moses,* for she explained, "I lifted him out of the water."

Moses Escapes to Midian

[11] Many years later, when Moses had grown up, he went out to visit his own people, the Hebrews, and he saw how hard they were forced to work. During his visit, he saw an Egyptian beating one of his fellow Hebrews. [12] After looking in all directions to make sure no one was watching, Moses killed the Egyptian and hid the body in the sand.

[13] The next day, when Moses went out to visit his people again, he saw two Hebrew men fighting. "Why are you beating up your friend?" Moses said to the one who had started the fight.

[14] The man replied, "Who appointed you to be our prince and judge? Are you going to kill me as you killed that Egyptian yesterday?"

Then Moses was afraid, thinking, "Everyone knows what I did." [15] And sure enough, Pharaoh heard what had happened, and he tried to kill Moses. But Moses fled from Pharaoh and went to live in the land of Midian.

When Moses arrived in Midian, he sat down beside a well. [16] Now the priest of Midian had seven daughters who came as usual to draw water and fill the water troughs for their father's flocks. [17] But some other shepherds came and chased them away. So Moses jumped up and rescued the girls from the shepherds. Then he drew water for their flocks.

[18] When the girls returned to Reuel, their father, he asked, "Why are you back so soon today?"

[19] "An Egyptian rescued us from the shepherds," they answered. "And then he drew water for us and watered our flocks."

[20] "Then where is he?" their father asked. "Why did you leave him there? Invite him to come and eat with us."

1:16 Hebrew *look upon the two stones;* perhaps the reference is to a birthstool.   2:10 *Moses* sounds like a Hebrew term that means "to lift out."

²¹Moses accepted the invitation, and he settled there with him. In time, Reuel gave Moses his daughter Zipporah to be his wife. ²²Later she gave birth to a son, and Moses named him Gershom,* for he explained, "I have been a foreigner in a foreign land."

²³Years passed, and the king of Egypt died. But the Israelites continued to groan under their burden of slavery. They cried out for help, and their cry rose up to God. ²⁴God heard their groaning, and he remembered his covenant promise to Abraham, Isaac, and Jacob. ²⁵He looked down on the people of Israel and knew it was time to act.*

Moses and the Burning Bush

3 One day Moses was tending the flock of his father-in-law, Jethro,* the priest of Midian. He led the flock far into the wilderness and came to Sinai,* the mountain of God. ²There the angel of the LORD appeared to him in a blazing fire from the middle of a bush. Moses stared in amazement. Though the bush was engulfed in flames, it didn't burn up. ³"This is amazing," Moses said to himself. "Why isn't that bush burning up? I must go see it."

⁴When the LORD saw Moses coming to take a closer look, God called to him from the middle of the bush, "Moses! Moses!"

"Here I am!" Moses replied.

⁵"Do not come any closer," the LORD warned. "Take off your sandals, for you are standing on holy ground. ⁶I am the God of your father*— the God of Abraham, the God of Isaac, and the God of Jacob." When Moses heard this, he covered his face because he was afraid to look at God.

⁷Then the LORD told him, "I have certainly seen the oppression of my people in Egypt. I have heard their cries of distress because of their harsh slave drivers. Yes, I am aware of their suffering. ⁸So I have come down to rescue them from the power of the Egyptians and lead them out of Egypt into their own fertile and spacious land. It is a land flowing with milk and honey—the land where the Canaanites, Hittites, Amorites, Perizzites, Hivites, and Jebusites now live. ⁹Look! The cry of the people of Israel has reached me, and I have seen how harshly the Egyptians abuse them. ¹⁰Now go, for I am sending you to Pharaoh. You must lead my people Israel out of Egypt."

¹¹But Moses protested to God, "Who am I to appear before Pharaoh? Who am I to lead the people of Israel out of Egypt?"

¹²God answered, "I will be with you. And this is your sign that I am the one who has sent you: When you have brought the people out of Egypt, you will worship God at this very mountain."

¹³But Moses protested, "If I go to the people of Israel and tell them, 'The God of your ancestors has sent me to you,' they will ask me, 'What is his name?' Then what should I tell them?"

¹⁴God replied to Moses, "I AM WHO I AM.* Say this to the people of Israel: I AM has sent me to you." ¹⁵God also said to Moses, "Say this to the people of Israel: Yahweh,* the God of your ancestors—the God of Abraham, the God of Isaac, and the God of Jacob—has sent me to you.

This is my eternal name,
    my name to remember for all
        generations.

¹⁶"Now go and call together all the elders of Israel. Tell them, 'Yahweh, the God of your ancestors—the God of Abraham, Isaac, and Jacob—has appeared to me. He told me, "I have been watching closely, and I see how the Egyptians are treating you. ¹⁷I have promised to rescue you from your oppression in Egypt. I will lead you to a land flowing with milk and honey—the land where the Canaanites, Hittites, Amorites, Perizzites, Hivites, and Jebusites now live."'

¹⁸"The elders of Israel will accept your message. Then you and the elders must go to the king of Egypt and tell him, 'The LORD, the God of the Hebrews, has met with us. So please let us take a three-day journey into the wilderness to offer sacrifices to the LORD, our God.'

¹⁹"But I know that the king of Egypt will not let you go unless a mighty hand forces him.* ²⁰So I will raise my hand and strike the Egyptians, performing all kinds of miracles among them. Then at last he will let you go. ²¹And I will cause the Egyptians to look favorably on you. They will give you gifts when you go so you will not leave empty-handed. ²²Every Israelite woman will ask for articles of silver and gold and fine clothing from her Egyptian neighbors and from the foreign women

2:22 Gershom sounds like a Hebrew term that means "a foreigner there." 2:25 Or and acknowledged his obligation to help them. 3:1a Moses' father-in-law went by two names, Jethro and Reuel. 3:1b Hebrew Horeb, another name for Sinai. 3:6 Greek version reads your fathers. 3:14 Or I WILL BE WHAT I WILL BE. 3:15 Yahweh (also in 3:16) is a transliteration of the proper name YHWH that is sometimes rendered "Jehovah"; in this translation it is usually rendered "the LORD" (note the use of small capitals). 3:19 As in Greek and Latin versions; Hebrew reads will not let you go, not by a mighty hand.

in their houses. You will dress your sons and daughters with these, stripping the Egyptians of their wealth."

Signs of the LORD's Power

4 But Moses protested again, "What if they won't believe me or listen to me? What if they say, 'The LORD never appeared to you'?"

²Then the LORD asked him, "What is that in your hand?"

"A shepherd's staff," Moses replied.

³"Throw it down on the ground," the LORD told him. So Moses threw down the staff, and it turned into a snake! Moses jumped back. ⁴Then the LORD told him, "Reach out and grab its tail." So Moses reached out and grabbed it, and it turned back into a shepherd's staff in his hand.

⁵"Perform this sign," the LORD told him. "Then they will believe that the LORD, the God of their ancestors—the God of Abraham, the God of Isaac, and the God of Jacob—really has appeared to you."

⁶Then the LORD said to Moses, "Now put your hand inside your cloak." So Moses put his hand inside his cloak, and when he took it out again, his hand was white as snow with a severe skin disease.* ⁷"Now put your hand back into your cloak," the LORD said. So Moses put his hand back in, and when he took it out again, it was as healthy as the rest of his body.

⁸The LORD said to Moses, "If they do not believe you and are not convinced by the first miraculous sign, they will be convinced by the second sign. ⁹And if they don't believe you or listen to you even after these two signs, then take some water from the Nile River and pour it out on the dry ground. When you do, the water from the Nile will turn to blood on the ground."

¹⁰But Moses pleaded with the LORD, "O Lord, I'm not very good with words. I never have been, and I'm not now, even though you have spoken to me. I get tongue-tied, and my words get tangled."

¹¹Then the LORD asked Moses, "Who makes a person's mouth? Who decides whether people speak or do not speak, hear or do not hear, see or do not see? Is it not I, the LORD? ¹²Now go! I will be with you as you speak, and I will instruct you in what to say."

¹³But Moses again pleaded, "Lord, please! Send anyone else."

¹⁴Then the LORD became angry with Moses.

"All right," he said. "What about your brother, Aaron the Levite? I know he speaks well. And look! He is on his way to meet you now. He will be delighted to see you. ¹⁵Talk to him, and put the words in his mouth. I will be with both of you as you speak, and I will instruct you both in what to do. ¹⁶Aaron will be your spokesman to the people. He will be your mouthpiece, and you will stand in the place of God for him, telling him what to say. ¹⁷And take your shepherd's staff with you, and use it to perform the miraculous signs I have shown you."

Moses Returns to Egypt

¹⁸So Moses went back home to Jethro, his father-in-law. "Please let me return to my relatives in Egypt," Moses said. "I don't even know if they are still alive."

"Go in peace," Jethro replied.

¹⁹Before Moses left Midian, the LORD said to him, "Return to Egypt, for all those who wanted to kill you have died."

²⁰So Moses took his wife and sons, put them on a donkey, and headed back to the land of Egypt. In his hand he carried the staff of God.

²¹And the LORD told Moses, "When you arrive back in Egypt, go to Pharaoh and perform all the miracles I have empowered you to do. But I will harden his heart so he will refuse to let the people go. ²²Then you will tell him, 'This is what the LORD says: Israel is my firstborn son. ²³I commanded you, "Let my son go, so he can worship me." But since you have refused, I will now kill your firstborn son!'"

²⁴On the way to Egypt, at a place where Moses and his family had stopped for the night, the LORD confronted him and was about to kill him. ²⁵But Moses' wife, Zipporah, took a flint knife and circumcised her son. She touched his feet* with the foreskin and said, "Now you are a bridegroom of blood to me." ²⁶(When she said "a bridegroom of blood," she was referring to the circumcision.) After that, the LORD left him alone.

²⁷Now the LORD had said to Aaron, "Go out into the wilderness to meet Moses." So Aaron went and met Moses at the mountain of God, and he embraced him. ²⁸Moses then told Aaron everything the LORD had commanded him to say. And he told him about the miraculous signs the LORD had commanded him to perform.

²⁹Then Moses and Aaron returned to Egypt and called all the elders of Israel together.

4:6 Or *with leprosy.* The Hebrew word used here can describe various skin diseases.   4:25 The Hebrew word for "feet" may refer here to the male sex organ.

30Aaron told them everything the LORD had told Moses, and Moses performed the miraculous signs as they watched. 31Then the people of Israel were convinced that the LORD had sent Moses and Aaron. When they heard that the LORD was concerned about them and had seen their misery, they bowed down and worshiped.

Moses and Aaron Speak to Pharaoh

5 After this presentation to Israel's leaders, Moses and Aaron went and spoke to Pharaoh. They told him, "This is what the LORD, the God of Israel, says: Let my people go so they may hold a festival in my honor in the wilderness."

2"Is that so?" retorted Pharaoh. "And who is the LORD? Why should I listen to him and let Israel go? I don't know the LORD, and I will not let Israel go."

3But Aaron and Moses persisted. "The God of the Hebrews has met with us," they declared. "So let us take a three-day journey into the wilderness so we can offer sacrifices to the LORD our God. If we don't, he will kill us with a plague or with the sword."

4Pharaoh replied, "Moses and Aaron, why are you distracting the people from their tasks? Get back to work! 5Look, there are many of your people in the land, and you are stopping them from their work."

Making Bricks without Straw

6That same day Pharaoh sent this order to the Egyptian slave drivers and the Israelite foremen: 7"Do not supply any more straw for making bricks. Make the people get it themselves! 8But still require them to make the same number of bricks as before. Don't reduce the quota. They are lazy. That's why they are crying out, 'Let us go and offer sacrifices to our God.' 9Load them down with more work. Make them sweat! That will teach them to listen to lies!"

10So the slave drivers and foremen went out and told the people: "This is what Pharaoh says: I will not provide any more straw for you. 11Go and get it yourselves. Find it wherever you can. But you must produce just as many bricks as before!" 12So the people scattered throughout the land of Egypt in search of stubble to use as straw.

13Meanwhile, the Egyptian slave drivers continued to push hard. "Meet your daily quota of bricks, just as you did when we provided you with straw!" they demanded. 14Then they whipped the Israelite foremen they had put in charge of the work crews. "Why haven't you met your quotas either yesterday or today?" they demanded.

15So the Israelite foremen went to Pharaoh and pleaded with him. "Please don't treat your servants like this," they begged. 16"We are given no straw, but the slave drivers still demand, 'Make bricks!' We are being beaten, but it isn't our fault! Your own people are to blame!"

17But Pharaoh shouted, "You're just lazy! Lazy! That's why you're saying, 'Let us go and offer sacrifices to the LORD.' 18Now get back to work! No straw will be given to you, but you must still produce the full quota of bricks."

19The Israelite foremen could see that they were in serious trouble when they were told, "You must not reduce the number of bricks you make each day." 20As they left Pharaoh's court, they confronted Moses and Aaron, who were waiting outside for them. 21The foremen said to them, "May the LORD judge and punish you for making us stink before Pharaoh and his officials. You have put a sword into their hands, an excuse to kill us!"

22Then Moses went back to the LORD and protested, "Why have you brought all this trouble on your own people, Lord? Why did you send me? 23Ever since I came to Pharaoh as your spokesman, he has been even more brutal to your people. And you have done nothing to rescue them!"

Promises of Deliverance

6 Then the LORD told Moses, "Now you will see what I will do to Pharaoh. When he feels the force of my strong hand, he will let the people go. In fact, he will force them to leave his land!"

2And God said to Moses, "I am Yahweh—'the LORD.'* 3I appeared to Abraham, to Isaac, and to Jacob as El-Shaddai—'God Almighty'*—but I did not reveal my name, Yahweh, to them. 4And I reaffirmed my covenant with them. Under its terms, I promised to give them the land of Canaan, where they were living as foreigners. 5You can be sure that I have heard the groans of the people of Israel, who are now slaves to the Egyptians. And I am well aware of my covenant with them.

6"Therefore, say to the people of Israel: 'I am the LORD. I will free you from your oppression

---

6:2 Yahweh is a transliteration of the proper name YHWH that is sometimes rendered "Jehovah"; in this translation it is usually rendered "the LORD" (note the use of small capitals).   6:3 El-Shaddai, which means "God Almighty," is the name for God used in Gen 17:1; 28:3; 35:11; 43:14; 48:3.

and will rescue you from your slavery in Egypt. I will redeem you with a powerful arm and great acts of judgment. [7]I will claim you as my own people, and I will be your God. Then you will know that I am the LORD your God who has freed you from your oppression in Egypt. [8]I will bring you into the land I swore to give to Abraham, Isaac, and Jacob. I will give it to you as your very own possession. I am the LORD!'"

[9]So Moses told the people of Israel what the LORD had said, but they refused to listen anymore. They had become too discouraged by the brutality of their slavery.

[10]Then the LORD said to Moses, [11]"Go back to Pharaoh, the king of Egypt, and tell him to let the people of Israel leave his country."

[12]"But LORD!" Moses objected. "My own people won't listen to me anymore. How can I expect Pharaoh to listen? I'm such a clumsy speaker!*"

[13]But the LORD spoke to Moses and Aaron and gave them orders for the Israelites and for Pharaoh, the king of Egypt. The LORD commanded Moses and Aaron to lead the people of Israel out of Egypt.

The Ancestors of Moses and Aaron

[14]These are the ancestors of some of the clans of Israel:

The sons of Reuben, Israel's oldest son, were Hanoch, Pallu, Hezron, and Carmi. Their descendants became the clans of Reuben. [15]The sons of Simeon were Jemuel, Jamin, Ohad, Jakin, Zohar, and Shaul. (Shaul's mother was a Canaanite woman.) Their descendants became the clans of Simeon. [16]These are the descendants of Levi, as listed in their family records: The sons of Levi were Gershon, Kohath, and Merari. (Levi lived to be 137 years old.)

[17]The descendants of Gershon included Libni and Shimei, each of whom became the ancestor of a clan.

[18]The descendants of Kohath included Amram, Izhar, Hebron, and Uzziel. (Kohath lived to be 133 years old.)

[19]The descendants of Merari included Mahli and Mushi.

These are the clans of the Levites, as listed in their family records.

[20]Amram married his father's sister Jochebed, and she gave birth to his sons, Aaron and Moses. (Amram lived to be 137 years old.)

[21]The sons of Izhar were Korah, Nepheg, and Zicri.

[22]The sons of Uzziel were Mishael, Elzaphan, and Sithri.

[23]Aaron married Elisheba, the daughter of Amminadab and sister of Nahshon, and she gave birth to his sons, Nadab, Abihu, Eleazar, and Ithamar.

[24]The sons of Korah were Assir, Elkanah, and Abiasaph. Their descendants became the clans of Korah.

[25]Eleazar son of Aaron married one of the daughters of Putiel, and she gave birth to his son, Phinehas.

These are the ancestors of the Levite families, listed according to their clans.

[26]The Aaron and Moses named in this list are the same ones to whom the LORD said, "Lead the people of Israel out of the land of Egypt like an army." [27]It was Moses and Aaron who spoke to Pharaoh, the king of Egypt, about leading the people of Israel out of Egypt.

[28]When the LORD spoke to Moses in the land of Egypt, [29]he said to him, "I am the LORD! Tell Pharaoh, the king of Egypt, everything I am telling you." [30]But Moses argued with the LORD, saying, "I can't do it! I'm such a clumsy speaker! Why should Pharaoh listen to me?"

Aaron's Staff Becomes a Serpent

7 Then the LORD said to Moses, "Pay close attention to this. I will make you seem like God to Pharaoh, and your brother, Aaron, will be your prophet. [2]Tell Aaron everything I command you, and Aaron must command Pharaoh to let the people of Israel leave his country. [3]But I will make Pharaoh's heart stubborn so I can multiply my miraculous signs and wonders in the land of Egypt. [4]Even then Pharaoh will refuse to listen to you. So I will bring down my fist on Egypt. Then I will rescue my forces—my people, the Israelites—from the land of Egypt with great acts of judgment. [5]When I raise my powerful hand and bring out the Israelites, the Egyptians will know that I am the LORD."

[6]So Moses and Aaron did just as the LORD had commanded them. [7]Moses was eighty years old, and Aaron was eighty-three when they made their demands to Pharaoh.

[8]Then the LORD said to Moses and Aaron, [9]"Pharaoh will demand, 'Show me a miracle.'

6:12 Hebrew *I have uncircumcised lips;* also in 6:30.

When he does this, say to Aaron, 'Take your staff and throw it down in front of Pharaoh, and it will become a serpent.*' "

¹⁰So Moses and Aaron went to Pharaoh and did what the LORD had commanded them. Aaron threw down his staff before Pharaoh and his officials, and it became a serpent! ¹¹Then Pharaoh called in his own wise men and sorcerers, and these Egyptian magicians did the same thing with their magic. ¹²They threw down their staffs, which also became serpents! But then Aaron's staff swallowed up their staffs. ¹³Pharaoh's heart, however, remained hard. He still refused to listen, just as the LORD had predicted.

A Plague of Blood

¹⁴Then the LORD said to Moses, "Pharaoh's heart is stubborn,* and he still refuses to let the people go. ¹⁵So go to Pharaoh in the morning as he goes down to the river. Stand on the bank of the Nile and meet him there. Be sure to take along the staff that turned into a snake. ¹⁶Then announce to him, 'The LORD, the God of the Hebrews, has sent me to tell you, "Let my people go, so they can worship me in the wilderness." Until now, you have refused to listen to him. ¹⁷So this is what the LORD says: "I will show you that I am the LORD." Look! I will strike the water of the Nile with this staff in my hand, and the river will turn to blood. ¹⁸The fish in it will die, and the river will stink. The Egyptians will not be able to drink any water from the Nile.' "

¹⁹Then the LORD said to Moses: "Tell Aaron, 'Take your staff and raise your hand over the waters of Egypt—all its rivers, canals, ponds, and all the reservoirs. Turn all the water to blood. Everywhere in Egypt the water will turn to blood, even the water stored in wooden bowls and stone pots.' "

²⁰So Moses and Aaron did just as the LORD commanded them. As Pharaoh and all of his officials watched, Aaron raised his staff and struck the water of the Nile. Suddenly, the whole river turned to blood! ²¹The fish in the river died, and the water became so foul that the Egyptians couldn't drink it. There was blood everywhere throughout the land of Egypt. ²²But again the magicians of Egypt used their magic, and they, too, turned water into blood. So Pharaoh's heart remained hard. He refused to listen to Moses and Aaron, just as the LORD had predicted. ²³Pharaoh returned to his palace and put the whole thing out of his mind. ²⁴Then all the Egyptians dug along the riverbank to find drinking water, for they couldn't drink the water from the Nile.

²⁵Seven days passed from the time the LORD struck the Nile.

A Plague of Frogs

8 ¹*Then the LORD said to Moses, "Go back to Pharaoh and announce to him, 'This is what the LORD says: Let my people go, so they can worship me. ²If you refuse to let them go, I will send a plague of frogs across your entire land. ³The Nile River will swarm with frogs. They will come up out of the river and into your palace, even into your bedroom and onto your bed! They will enter the houses of your officials and your people. They will even jump into your ovens and your kneading bowls. ⁴Frogs will jump on you, your people, and all your officials.' "

⁵*Then the LORD said to Moses, "Tell Aaron, 'Raise the staff in your hand over all the rivers, canals, and ponds of Egypt, and bring up frogs over all the land.' " ⁶So Aaron raised his hand over the waters of Egypt, and frogs came up and covered the whole land! ⁷But the magicians were able to do the same thing with their magic. They, too, caused frogs to come up on the land of Egypt.

⁸Then Pharaoh summoned Moses and Aaron and begged, "Plead with the LORD to take the frogs away from me and my people. I will let your people go, so they can offer sacrifices to the LORD."

⁹"You set the time!" Moses replied. "Tell me when you want me to pray for you, your officials, and your people. Then you and your houses will be rid of the frogs. They will remain only in the Nile River."

¹⁰"Do it tomorrow," Pharaoh said.

"All right," Moses replied, "it will be as you have said. Then you will know that there is no one like the LORD our God. ¹¹The frogs will leave you and your houses, your officials, and your people. They will remain only in the Nile River."

¹²So Moses and Aaron left Pharaoh's palace, and Moses cried out to the LORD about the frogs he had inflicted on Pharaoh. ¹³And the LORD did just what Moses had predicted. The frogs in the houses, the courtyards, and the fields all died. ¹⁴The Egyptians piled them into great heaps, and a terrible stench filled

---

7:9 Hebrew *tannin*, which elsewhere refers to a sea monster. Greek version translates it "dragon."   7:14 Hebrew *heavy*.
8:1 Verses 8:1-4 are numbered 7:26-29 in Hebrew text.   8:5 Verses 8:5-32 are numbered 8:1-28 in Hebrew text.

the land. ¹⁵But when Pharaoh saw that relief had come, he became stubborn.* He refused to listen to Moses and Aaron, just as the LORD had predicted.

A Plague of Gnats

¹⁶So the LORD said to Moses, "Tell Aaron, 'Raise your staff and strike the ground. The dust will turn into swarms of gnats throughout the land of Egypt.'" ¹⁷So Moses and Aaron did just as the LORD had commanded them. When Aaron raised his hand and struck the ground with his staff, gnats infested the entire land, covering the Egyptians and their animals. All the dust in the land of Egypt turned into gnats. ¹⁸Pharaoh's magicians tried to do the same thing with their secret arts, but this time they failed. And the gnats covered everyone, people and animals alike.

¹⁹"This is the finger of God!" the magicians exclaimed to Pharaoh. But Pharaoh's heart remained hard. He wouldn't listen to them, just as the LORD had predicted.

A Plague of Flies

²⁰Then the LORD told Moses, "Get up early in the morning and stand in Pharaoh's way as he goes down to the river. Say to him, 'This is what the LORD says: Let my people go, so they can worship me. ²¹If you refuse, then I will send swarms of flies on you, your officials, your people, and all the houses. The Egyptian homes will be filled with flies, and the ground will be covered with them. ²²But this time I will spare the region of Goshen, where my people live. No flies will be found there. Then you will know that I am the LORD and that I am present even in the heart of your land. ²³I will make a clear distinction between* my people and your people. This miraculous sign will happen tomorrow.'"

²⁴And the LORD did just as he had said. A thick swarm of flies filled Pharaoh's palace and the houses of his officials. The whole land of Egypt was thrown into chaos by the flies.

²⁵Pharaoh called for Moses and Aaron. "All right! Go ahead and offer sacrifices to your God," he said. "But do it here in this land."

²⁶But Moses replied, "That wouldn't be right. The Egyptians detest the sacrifices that we offer to the LORD our God. Look, if we offer our sacrifices here where the Egyptians can see us, they will stone us. ²⁷We must take a three-day trip into the wilderness to offer sacrifices to the LORD our God, just as he has commanded us."

²⁸"All right, go ahead," Pharaoh replied. "I will let you go into the wilderness to offer sacrifices to the LORD your God. But don't go too far away. Now hurry and pray for me."

²⁹Moses answered, "As soon as I leave you, I will pray to the LORD, and tomorrow the swarms of flies will disappear from you and your officials and all your people. But I am warning you, Pharaoh, don't lie to us again and refuse to let the people go to sacrifice to the LORD."

³⁰So Moses left Pharaoh's palace and pleaded with the LORD to remove all the flies. ³¹And the LORD did as Moses asked and caused the swarms of flies to disappear from Pharaoh, his officials, and his people. Not a single fly remained. ³²But Pharaoh again became stubborn and refused to let the people go.

A Plague against Livestock

9 "Go back to Pharaoh," the LORD commanded Moses. "Tell him, 'This is what the LORD, the God of the Hebrews, says: Let my people go, so they can worship me. ²If you continue to hold them and refuse to let them go, ³the hand of the LORD will strike all your livestock—your horses, donkeys, camels, cattle, sheep, and goats—with a deadly plague. ⁴But the LORD will again make a distinction between the livestock of the Israelites and that of the Egyptians. Not a single one of Israel's animals will die! ⁵The LORD has already set the time for the plague to begin. He has declared that he will strike the land tomorrow.'"

⁶And the LORD did just as he had said. The next morning all the livestock of the Egyptians died, but the Israelites didn't lose a single animal. ⁷Pharaoh sent his officials to investigate, and they discovered that the Israelites had not lost a single animal! But even so, Pharaoh's heart remained stubborn,* and he still refused to let the people go.

A Plague of Festering Boils

⁸Then the LORD said to Moses and Aaron, "Take handfuls of soot from a brick kiln, and have Moses toss it into the air while Pharaoh watches. ⁹The ashes will spread like fine dust over the whole land of Egypt, causing festering boils to break out on people and animals throughout the land."

¹⁰So they took soot from a brick kiln and

8:15 Hebrew *made his heart heavy;* also in 8:32. 8:23 As in Greek and Latin versions; Hebrew reads *I will set redemption between.* 9:7 Hebrew *heavy.*

went and stood before Pharaoh. As Pharaoh watched, Moses threw the soot into the air, and boils broke out on people and animals alike. ¹¹Even the magicians were unable to stand before Moses, because the boils had broken out on them and all the Egyptians. ¹²But the LORD hardened Pharaoh's heart, and just as the LORD had predicted to Moses, Pharaoh refused to listen.

A Plague of Hail

¹³Then the LORD said to Moses, "Get up early in the morning and stand before Pharaoh. Tell him, 'This is what the LORD, the God of the Hebrews, says: Let my people go, so they can worship me. ¹⁴If you don't, I will send more plagues on you* and your officials and your people. Then you will know that there is no one like me in all the earth. ¹⁵By now I could have lifted my hand and struck you and your people with a plague to wipe you off the face of the earth. ¹⁶But I have spared you for a purpose—to show you my power* and to spread my fame throughout the earth. ¹⁷But you still lord it over my people and refuse to let them go. ¹⁸So tomorrow at this time I will send a hailstorm more devastating than any in all the history of Egypt. ¹⁹Quick! Order your livestock and servants to come in from the fields to find shelter. Any person or animal left outside will die when the hail falls.'"

²⁰Some of Pharaoh's officials were afraid because of what the LORD had said. They quickly brought their servants and livestock in from the fields. ²¹But those who paid no attention to the word of the LORD left theirs out in the open.

²²Then the LORD said to Moses, "Lift your hand toward the sky so hail may fall on the people, the livestock, and all the plants throughout the land of Egypt." ²³So Moses lifted his staff toward the sky, and the LORD sent thunder and hail, and lightning flashed toward the earth. The LORD sent a tremendous hailstorm against all the land of Egypt. ²⁴Never in all the history of Egypt had there been a storm like that, with such devastating hail and continuous lightning. ²⁵It left all of Egypt in ruins. The hail struck down everything in the open field—people, animals, and plants alike. Even the trees were destroyed. ²⁶The only place without hail was the region of Goshen, where the people of Israel lived.

²⁷Then Pharaoh quickly summoned Moses and Aaron. "This time I have sinned," he confessed. "The LORD is the righteous one, and my people and I are wrong. ²⁸Please beg the LORD to end this terrifying thunder and hail. We've had enough. I will let you go; you don't need to stay any longer."

²⁹"All right," Moses replied. "As soon as I leave the city, I will lift my hands and pray to the LORD. Then the thunder and hail will stop, and you will know that the earth belongs to the LORD. ³⁰But I know that you and your officials still do not fear the LORD God."

³¹(All the flax and barley were ruined by the hail, because the barley had formed heads and the flax was budding. ³²But the wheat and the emmer wheat were spared, because they had not yet sprouted from the ground.)

³³So Moses left Pharaoh's court and went out of the city. When he lifted his hands to the LORD, the thunder and hail stopped, and the downpour ceased. ³⁴But when Pharaoh saw that the rain, hail, and thunder had stopped, he and his officials sinned again, and Pharaoh again became stubborn.* ³⁵Because his heart was hard, Pharaoh refused to let the people leave, just as the LORD had predicted through Moses.

A Plague of Locusts

10 Then the LORD said to Moses, "Return to Pharaoh and make your demands again. I have made him and his officials stubborn* so I can display my miraculous signs among them. ²I've also done it so you can tell your children and grandchildren about how I made a mockery of the Egyptians and about the signs I displayed among them—and so you will know that I am the LORD."

³So Moses and Aaron went to Pharaoh and said, "This is what the LORD, the God of the Hebrews, says: How long will you refuse to submit to me? Let my people go, so they can worship me. ⁴If you refuse, watch out! For tomorrow I will bring a swarm of locusts on your country. ⁵They will cover the land so that you won't be able to see the ground. They will devour what little is left of your crops after the hailstorm, including all the trees growing in the fields. ⁶They will overrun your palaces and the homes of your officials and all the houses in Egypt. Never in the history of Egypt have your ancestors seen a plague like this one!" And with that, Moses turned and left Pharaoh.

9:14 Hebrew on your heart.   9:16 Greek version reads to display my power in you; compare Rom 9:17.   9:34 Hebrew made his heart heavy.   10:1 Hebrew have made his heart and his officials' hearts heavy.

7Pharaoh's officials now came to Pharaoh and appealed to him. "How long will you let this man hold us hostage? Let the men go to worship the LORD their God! Don't you realize that Egypt lies in ruins?"

8So Moses and Aaron were brought back to Pharaoh. "All right," he told them, "go and worship the LORD your God. But who exactly will be going with you?"

9Moses replied, "We will all go—young and old, our sons and daughters, and our flocks and herds. We must all join together in celebrating a festival to the LORD."

10Pharaoh retorted, "The LORD will certainly need to be with you if I let you take your little ones! I can see through your evil plan. 11Never! Only the men may go and worship the LORD, since that is what you requested." And Pharaoh threw them out of the palace.

12Then the LORD said to Moses, "Raise your hand over the land of Egypt to bring on the locusts. Let them cover the land and devour every plant that survived the hailstorm."

13So Moses raised his staff over Egypt, and the LORD caused an east wind to blow over the land all that day and through the night. When morning arrived, the east wind had brought the locusts. 14And the locusts swarmed over the whole land of Egypt, settling in dense swarms from one end of the country to the other. It was the worst locust plague in Egyptian history, and there has never been another one like it. 15For the locusts covered the whole country and darkened the land. They devoured every plant in the fields and all the fruit on the trees that had survived the hailstorm. Not a single leaf was left on the trees and plants throughout the land of Egypt.

16Pharaoh quickly summoned Moses and Aaron. "I have sinned against the LORD your God and against you," he confessed. 17"Forgive my sin, just this once, and plead with the LORD your God to take away this death from me."

18So Moses left Pharaoh's court and pleaded with the LORD. 19The LORD responded by shifting the wind, and the strong west wind blew the locusts into the Red Sea.* Not a single locust remained in all the land of Egypt. 20But the LORD hardened Pharaoh's heart again, so he refused to let the people go.

A Plague of Darkness

21Then the LORD said to Moses, "Lift your hand toward heaven, and the land of Egypt will be covered with a darkness so thick you can feel

10:19 Hebrew *sea of reeds.*

it." 22So Moses lifted his hand to the sky, and a deep darkness covered the entire land of Egypt for three days. 23During all that time the people could not see each other, and no one moved. But there was light as usual where the people of Israel lived.

24Finally, Pharaoh called for Moses. "Go and worship the LORD," he said. "But leave your flocks and herds here. You may even take your little ones with you."

25"No," Moses said, "you must provide us with animals for sacrifices and burnt offerings to the LORD our God. 26All our livestock must go with us, too; not a hoof can be left behind. We must choose our sacrifices for the LORD our God from among these animals. And we won't know how we are to worship the LORD until we get there."

27But the LORD hardened Pharaoh's heart once more, and he would not let them go. 28"Get out of here!" Pharaoh shouted at Moses. "I'm warning you. Never come back to see me again! The day you see my face, you will die!"

29"Very well," Moses replied. "I will never see your face again."

Death for Egypt's Firstborn

11 Then the LORD said to Moses, "I will strike Pharaoh and the land of Egypt with one more blow. After that, Pharaoh will let you leave this country. In fact, he will be so eager to get rid of you that he will force you all to leave. 2Tell all the Israelite men and women to ask their Egyptian neighbors for articles of silver and gold." 3(Now the LORD had caused the Egyptians to look favorably on the people of Israel. And Moses was considered a very great man in the land of Egypt, respected by Pharaoh's officials and the Egyptian people alike.)

4Moses had announced to Pharaoh, "This is what the LORD says: At midnight tonight I will pass through the heart of Egypt. 5All the firstborn sons will die in every family in Egypt, from the oldest son of Pharaoh, who sits on his throne, to the oldest son of his lowliest servant girl who grinds the flour. Even the firstborn of all the livestock will die. 6Then a loud wail will rise throughout the land of Egypt, a wail like no one has heard before or will ever hear again. 7But among the Israelites it will be so peaceful that not even a dog will bark. Then you will know that the LORD makes a distinction between the Egyptians and the Israelites. 8All the officials of Egypt will run to me and fall to the ground before me. 'Please leave!' they will beg. 'Hurry! And take all your followers with you.' Only then will I go!" Then, burning with anger, Moses left Pharaoh.

⁹Now the LORD had told Moses earlier, "Pharaoh will not listen to you, but then I will do even more mighty miracles in the land of Egypt." ¹⁰Moses and Aaron performed these miracles in Pharaoh's presence, but the LORD hardened Pharaoh's heart, and he wouldn't let the Israelites leave the country.

The First Passover

12 While the Israelites were still in the land of Egypt, the LORD gave the following instructions to Moses and Aaron: ²"From now on, this month will be the first month of the year for you. ³Announce to the whole community of Israel that on the tenth day of this month each family must choose a lamb or a young goat for a sacrifice, one animal for each household. ⁴If a family is too small to eat a whole animal, let them share with another family in the neighborhood. Divide the animal according to the size of each family and how much they can eat. ⁵The animal you select must be a one-year-old male, either a sheep or a goat, with no defects.

⁶"Take special care of this chosen animal until the evening of the fourteenth day of this first month. Then the whole assembly of the community of Israel must slaughter their lamb or young goat at twilight. ⁷They are to take some of the blood and smear it on the sides and top of the doorframes of the houses where they eat the animal. ⁸That same night they must roast the meat over a fire and eat it along with bitter salad greens and bread made without yeast. ⁹Do not eat any of the meat raw or boiled in water. The whole animal—including the head, legs, and internal organs—must be roasted over a fire. ¹⁰Do not leave any of it until the next morning. Burn whatever is not eaten before morning.

¹¹"These are your instructions for eating this meal: Be fully dressed,* wear your sandals, and carry your walking stick in your hand. Eat the meal with urgency, for this is the LORD's Passover. ¹²On that night I will pass through the land of Egypt and strike down every firstborn son and firstborn male animal in the land of Egypt. I will execute judgment against all the gods of Egypt, for I am the LORD! ¹³But the blood on your doorposts will serve as a sign, marking the houses where you are staying.

12:11 Hebrew *Bind up your loins.*

When I see the blood, I will pass over you. This plague of death will not touch you when I strike the land of Egypt.

¹⁴"This is a day to remember. Each year, from generation to generation, you must celebrate it as a special festival to the LORD. This is a law for all time. ¹⁵For seven days the bread you eat must be made without yeast. On the first day of the festival, remove every trace of yeast from your homes. Anyone who eats bread made with yeast during the seven days of the festival will be cut off from the community of Israel. ¹⁶On the first day of the festival and again on the seventh day, all the people must observe an official day for holy assembly. No work of any kind may be done on these days except in the preparation of food.

¹⁷"Celebrate this Festival of Unleavened Bread, for it will remind you that I brought your forces out of the land of Egypt on this very day. This festival will be a permanent law for you; celebrate this day from generation to generation. ¹⁸The bread you eat must be made without yeast from the evening of the fourteenth day of the first month until the evening of the twenty-first day of that month. ¹⁹During those seven days, there must be no trace of yeast in your homes. Anyone who eats anything made with yeast during this week will be cut off from the community of Israel. These regulations apply both to the foreigners living among you and to the native-born Israelites. ²⁰During those days you must not eat anything made with yeast. Wherever you live, eat only bread made without yeast."

²¹Then Moses called all the elders of Israel together and said to them, "Go, pick out a lamb or young goat for each of your families, and slaughter the Passover animal. ²²Drain the blood into a basin. Then take a bundle of hyssop branches and dip it into the blood. Brush the hyssop across the top and sides of the doorframes of your houses. And no one may go out through the door until morning. ²³For the LORD will pass through the land to strike down the Egyptians. But when he sees the blood on the top and sides of the doorframe, the LORD will pass over your home. He will not permit his death angel to enter your house and strike you down.

²⁴"Remember, these instructions are a permanent law that you and your descendants must observe forever. ²⁵When you enter the land the LORD has promised to give you, you will continue to observe this ceremony. ²⁶Then

your children will ask, 'What does this ceremony mean?' 27 And you will reply, 'It is the Passover sacrifice to the LORD, for he passed over the houses of the Israelites in Egypt. And though he struck the Egyptians, he spared our families.'" When Moses had finished speaking, all the people bowed down to the ground and worshiped.

28 So the people of Israel did just as the LORD had commanded through Moses and Aaron. 29 And that night at midnight, the LORD struck down all the firstborn sons in the land of Egypt, from the firstborn son of Pharaoh, who sat on his throne, to the firstborn son of the prisoner in the dungeon. Even the firstborn of their livestock were killed. 30 Pharaoh and all his officials and all the people of Egypt woke up during the night, and loud wailing was heard throughout the land of Egypt. There was not a single house where someone had not died.

Israel's Exodus from Egypt

31 Pharaoh sent for Moses and Aaron during the night. "Get out!" he ordered. "Leave my people—and take the rest of the Israelites with you! Go and worship the LORD as you have requested. 32 Take your flocks and herds, as you said, and be gone. Go, but bless me as you leave." 33 All the Egyptians urged the people of Israel to get out of the land as quickly as possible, for they thought, "We will all die!"

34 The Israelites took their bread dough before yeast was added. They wrapped their kneading boards in their cloaks and carried them on their shoulders. 35 And the people of Israel did as Moses had instructed; they asked the Egyptians for clothing and articles of silver and gold. 36 The LORD caused the Egyptians to look favorably on the Israelites, and they gave the Israelites whatever they asked for. So they stripped the Egyptians of their wealth!

37 That night the people of Israel left Rameses and started for Succoth. There were about 600,000 men,* plus all the women and children. 38 A rabble of non-Israelites went with them, along with great flocks and herds of livestock. 39 For bread they baked flat cakes from the dough without yeast they had brought from Egypt. It was made without yeast because the people were driven out of Egypt in such a hurry that they had no time to prepare the bread or other food.

40 The people of Israel had lived in Egypt* for 430 years. 41 In fact, it was on the last day of the 430th year that all the LORD's forces left the land. 42 On this night the LORD kept his promise to bring his people out of the land of Egypt. So this night belongs to him, and it must be commemorated every year by all the Israelites, from generation to generation.

Instructions for the Passover

43 Then the LORD said to Moses and Aaron, "These are the instructions for the festival of Passover. No outsiders are allowed to eat the Passover meal. 44 But any slave who has been purchased may eat it if he has been circumcised. 45 Temporary residents and hired servants may not eat it. 46 Each Passover lamb must be eaten in one house. Do not carry any of its meat outside, and do not break any of its bones. 47 The whole community of Israel must celebrate this Passover festival.

48 "If there are foreigners living among you who want to celebrate the LORD's Passover, let all their males be circumcised. Only then may they celebrate the Passover with you like any native-born Israelite. But no uncircumcised male may ever eat the Passover meal. 49 This instruction applies to everyone, whether a native-born Israelite or a foreigner living among you."

50 So all the people of Israel followed all the LORD's commands to Moses and Aaron. 51 On that very day the LORD brought the people of Israel out of the land of Egypt like an army.

Dedication of the Firstborn

13 Then the LORD said to Moses, 2 "Dedicate to me every firstborn among the Israelites. The first offspring to be born, of both humans and animals, belongs to me."

3 So Moses said to the people, "This is a day to remember forever—the day you left Egypt, the place of your slavery. Today the LORD has brought you out by the power of his mighty hand. (Remember, eat no food containing yeast.) 4 On this day in early spring, in the month of Abib,* you have been set free. 5 You must celebrate this event in this month each year after the LORD brings you into the land of the Canaanites, Hittites, Amorites, Hivites, and Jebusites. (He swore to your ancestors that he would give you this land—a land flowing with milk and honey.) 6 For seven days the bread you eat must be made without yeast. Then on

---

12:37 Or *fighting men*; Hebrew reads *men on foot*.   12:40 Samaritan Pentateuch reads *in Canaan and Egypt*; Greek version reads *in Egypt and Canaan*.   13:4 Hebrew *On this day in the month of Abib*. This first month of the ancient Hebrew lunar calendar usually occurs within the months of March and April.

the seventh day, celebrate a feast to the LORD. 7Eat bread without yeast during those seven days. In fact, there must be no yeast bread or any yeast at all found within the borders of your land during this time.

8"On the seventh day you must explain to your children, 'I am celebrating what the LORD did for me when I left Egypt.' 9This annual festival will be a visible sign to you, like a mark branded on your hand or your forehead. Let it remind you always to recite this teaching of the LORD: 'With a strong hand, the LORD rescued you from Egypt.'* 10So observe the decree of this festival at the appointed time each year.

11"This is what you must do when the LORD fulfills the promise he swore to you and to your ancestors. When he gives you the land where the Canaanites now live, 12you must present all firstborn sons and firstborn male animals to the LORD, for they belong to him. 13A firstborn donkey may be bought back from the LORD by presenting a lamb or young goat in its place. But if you do not buy it back, you must break its neck. However, you must buy back every firstborn son.

14"And in the future, your children will ask you, 'What does all this mean?' Then you will tell them, 'With the power of his mighty hand, the LORD brought us out of Egypt, the place of our slavery. 15Pharaoh stubbornly refused to let us go, so the LORD killed all the firstborn males throughout the land of Egypt, both people and animals. That is why I now sacrifice all the firstborn males to the LORD—except that the firstborn sons are always bought back.' 16This ceremony will be like a mark branded on your hand or your forehead. It is a reminder that the power of the LORD's mighty hand brought us out of Egypt."

Israel's Wilderness Detour

17When Pharaoh finally let the people go, God did not lead them along the main road that runs through Philistine territory, even though that was the shortest route to the Promised Land. God said, "If the people are faced with a battle, they might change their minds and return to Egypt." 18So God led them in a roundabout way through the wilderness toward the Red Sea.* Thus the Israelites left Egypt like an army ready for battle.*

19Moses took the bones of Joseph with him, for Joseph had made the sons of Israel swear to do this. He said, "God will certainly come to help you. When he does, you must take my bones with you from this place."

20The Israelites left Succoth and camped at Etham on the edge of the wilderness. 21The LORD went ahead of them. He guided them during the day with a pillar of cloud, and he provided light at night with a pillar of fire. This allowed them to travel by day or by night. 22And the LORD did not remove the pillar of cloud or pillar of fire from its place in front of the people.

14 Then the LORD gave these instructions to Moses: 2"Order the Israelites to turn back and camp by Pi-hahiroth between Migdol and the sea. Camp there along the shore, across from Baal-zephon. 3Then Pharaoh will think, 'The Israelites are confused. They are trapped in the wilderness!' 4And once again I will harden Pharaoh's heart, and he will chase after you.* I have planned this in order to display my glory through Pharaoh and his whole army. After this the Egyptians will know that I am the LORD!" So the Israelites camped there as they were told.

The Egyptians Pursue Israel

5When word reached the king of Egypt that the Israelites had fled, Pharaoh and his officials changed their minds. "What have we done, letting all those Israelite slaves get away?" they asked. 6So Pharaoh harnessed his chariot and called up his troops. 7He took with him 600 of Egypt's best chariots, along with the rest of the chariots of Egypt, each with its commander. 8The LORD hardened the heart of Pharaoh, the king of Egypt, so he chased after the people of Israel, who had left with fists raised in defiance. 9The Egyptians chased after them with all the forces in Pharaoh's army—all his horses and chariots, his charioteers, and his troops. The Egyptians caught up with the people of Israel as they were camped beside the shore near Pi-hahiroth, across from Baal-zephon.

10As Pharaoh approached, the people of Israel looked up and panicked when they saw the Egyptians overtaking them. They cried out to the LORD, 11and they said to Moses, "Why did you bring us out here to die in the wilderness? Weren't there enough graves for us in Egypt? What have you done to us? Why did you make us leave Egypt? 12Didn't we tell you this would happen while we were still in Egypt? We said, 'Leave us alone! Let us be slaves to the Egyptians. It's better to be a slave in Egypt than a corpse in the wilderness!'"

[13] But Moses told the people, "Don't be afraid. Just stand still and watch the LORD rescue you today. The Egyptians you see today will never be seen again. [14] The LORD himself will fight for you. Just stay calm."

Escape through the Red Sea

[15] Then the LORD said to Moses, "Why are you crying out to me? Tell the people to get moving! [16] Pick up your staff and raise your hand over the sea. Divide the water so the Israelites can walk through the middle of the sea on dry ground. [17] And I will harden the hearts of the Egyptians, and they will charge in after the Israelites. My great glory will be displayed through Pharaoh and his troops, his chariots, and his charioteers. [18] When my glory is displayed through them, all Egypt will see my glory and know that I am the LORD!"

[19] Then the angel of God, who had been leading the people of Israel, moved to the rear of the camp. The pillar of cloud also moved from the front and stood behind them. [20] The cloud settled between the Egyptian and Israelite camps. As darkness fell, the cloud turned to fire, lighting up the night. But the Egyptians and Israelites did not approach each other all night.

[21] Then Moses raised his hand over the sea, and the LORD opened up a path through the water with a strong east wind. The wind blew all that night, turning the seabed into dry land. [22] So the people of Israel walked through the middle of the sea on dry ground, with walls of water on each side!

[23] Then the Egyptians—all of Pharaoh's horses, chariots, and charioteers—chased them into the middle of the sea. [24] But just before dawn the LORD looked down on the Egyptian army from the pillar of fire and cloud, and he threw their forces into total confusion. [25] He twisted* their chariot wheels, making their chariots difficult to drive. "Let's get out of here—away from these Israelites!" the Egyptians shouted. "The LORD is fighting for them against Egypt!"

[26] When all the Israelites had reached the other side, the LORD said to Moses, "Raise your hand over the sea again. Then the waters will rush back and cover the Egyptians and their chariots and charioteers." [27] So as the sun began to rise, Moses raised his hand over the sea, and the water rushed back into its usual place. The Egyptians tried to escape, but the LORD swept them into the sea. [28] Then the waters returned and covered all the chariots and charioteers—the entire army of Pharaoh. Of all the Egyptians who had chased the Israelites into the sea, not a single one survived.

[29] But the people of Israel had walked through the middle of the sea on dry ground, as the water stood up like a wall on both sides. [30] That is how the LORD rescued Israel from the hand of the Egyptians that day. And the Israelites saw the bodies of the Egyptians washed up on the seashore. [31] When the people of Israel saw the mighty power that the LORD had unleashed against the Egyptians, they were filled with awe before him. They put their faith in the LORD and in his servant Moses.

A Song of Deliverance

15 Then Moses and the people of Israel sang this song to the LORD:

"I will sing to the LORD,
  for he has triumphed gloriously;
he has hurled both horse and rider
  into the sea.
[2] The LORD is my strength and my song;
  he has given me victory.
This is my God, and I will praise him—
  my father's God, and I will exalt him!
[3] The LORD is a warrior;
  Yahweh* is his name!
[4] Pharaoh's chariots and army
  he has hurled into the sea.
The finest of Pharaoh's officers
  are drowned in the Red Sea.*
[5] The deep waters gushed over them;
  they sank to the bottom like a stone.

[6] "Your right hand, O LORD,
  is glorious in power.
Your right hand, O LORD,
  smashes the enemy.
[7] In the greatness of your majesty,
  you overthrow those who rise against
    you.
You unleash your blazing fury;
  it consumes them like straw.
[8] At the blast of your breath,
  the waters piled up!

14:25 As in Greek version, Samaritan Pentateuch, and Syriac version; Hebrew reads *He removed.*   15:3 *Yahweh* is a transliteration of the proper name *YHWH* that is sometimes rendered "Jehovah"; in this translation it is usually rendered "the LORD" (note the use of small capitals).   15:4 Hebrew *sea of reeds;* also in 15:22.

The surging waters stood straight like a
    wall;
in the heart of the sea the deep waters
    became hard.

9 "The enemy boasted, 'I will chase them
    and catch up with them.
I will plunder them
    and consume them.
I will flash my sword;
    my powerful hand will destroy them.'
10 But you blew with your breath,
    and the sea covered them.
They sank like lead
    in the mighty waters.

11 "Who is like you among the gods,
    O LORD—
glorious in holiness,
awesome in splendor,
    performing great wonders?
12 You raised your right hand,
    and the earth swallowed our enemies.

13 "With your unfailing love you lead
    the people you have redeemed.
In your might, you guide them
    to your sacred home.
14 The peoples hear and tremble;
    anguish grips those who live in
    Philistia.
15 The leaders of Edom are terrified;
    the nobles of Moab tremble.
All who live in Canaan melt away;
16   terror and dread fall upon them.
The power of your arm
    makes them lifeless as stone
until your people pass by, O LORD,
    until the people you purchased pass by.
17 You will bring them in and plant them on
    your own mountain—
the place, O LORD, reserved for your
    own dwelling,
the sanctuary, O Lord, that your hands
    have established.
18 The LORD will reign forever and ever!"

19 When Pharaoh's horses, chariots, and
charioteers rushed into the sea, the LORD
brought the water crashing down on them.
But the people of Israel had walked through
the middle of the sea on dry ground!
20 Then Miriam the prophet, Aaron's sister,
took a tambourine and led all the women as
they played their tambourines and danced.
21 And Miriam sang this song:

"Sing to the LORD,
    for he has triumphed gloriously;
he has hurled both horse and rider
    into the sea."

Bitter Water at Marah

22 Then Moses led the people of Israel away
from the Red Sea, and they moved out into the
desert of Shur. They traveled in this desert for
three days without finding any water. 23 When
they came to the oasis of Marah, the water was
too bitter to drink. So they called the place Ma-
rah (which means "bitter"). 24 Then the people complained and turned
against Moses. "What are we going to drink?"
they demanded. 25 So Moses cried out to the
LORD for help, and the LORD showed him a
piece of wood. Moses threw it into the water,
and this made the water good to drink.

It was there at Marah that the LORD set before them the following decree as a standard to
test their faithfulness to him. 26 He said, "If you
will listen carefully to the voice of the LORD
your God and do what is right in his sight,
obeying his commands and keeping all his
decrees, then I will not make you suffer any of
the diseases I sent on the Egyptians; for I am
the LORD who heals you."

27 After leaving Marah, the Israelites traveled on to the oasis of Elim, where they found
twelve springs and seventy palm trees. They
camped there beside the water.

Manna and Quail from Heaven

16 Then the whole community of Israel set
out from Elim and journeyed into the
wilderness of Sin,* between Elim and Mount
Sinai. They arrived there on the fifteenth day
of the second month, one month after leaving the land of Egypt.* 2 There, too, the whole
community of Israel complained about Moses
and Aaron.

3 "If only the LORD had killed us back in
Egypt," they moaned. "There we sat around
pots filled with meat and ate all the bread we
wanted. But now you have brought us into this
wilderness to starve us all to death."

4 Then the LORD said to Moses, "Look, I'm
going to rain down food from heaven for you.
Each day the people can go out and pick up
as much food as they need for that day. I will

16:1a The geographical name *Sin* is related to *Sinai* and should not be confused with the English word *sin*.   16:1b The
Exodus had occurred on the fifteenth day of the first month (see Num 33:3).

test them in this to see whether or not they will follow my instructions. ⁵On the sixth day they will gather food, and when they prepare it, there will be twice as much as usual."

⁶So Moses and Aaron said to all the people of Israel, "By evening you will realize it was the LORD who brought you out of the land of Egypt. ⁷In the morning you will see the glory of the LORD, because he has heard your complaints, which are against him, not against us. What have we done that you should complain about us?" ⁸Then Moses added, "The LORD will give you meat to eat in the evening and bread to satisfy you in the morning, for he has heard all your complaints against him. What have we done? Yes, your complaints are against the LORD, not against us."

⁹Then Moses said to Aaron, "Announce this to the entire community of Israel: 'Present yourselves before the LORD, for he has heard your complaining.'" ¹⁰And as Aaron spoke to the whole community of Israel, they looked out toward the wilderness. There they could see the awesome glory of the LORD in the cloud.

¹¹Then the LORD said to Moses, ¹²"I have heard the Israelites' complaints. Now tell them, 'In the evening you will have meat to eat, and in the morning you will have all the bread you want. Then you will know that I am the LORD your God.'"

¹³That evening vast numbers of quail flew in and covered the camp. And the next morning the area around the camp was wet with dew. ¹⁴When the dew evaporated, a flaky substance as fine as frost blanketed the ground. ¹⁵The Israelites were puzzled when they saw it. "What is it?" they asked each other. They had no idea what it was.

And Moses told them, "It is the food the LORD has given you to eat. ¹⁶These are the LORD's instructions: Each household should gather as much as it needs. Pick up two quarts* for each person in your tent."

¹⁷So the people of Israel did as they were told. Some gathered a lot, some only a little. ¹⁸But when they measured it out,* everyone had just enough. Those who gathered a lot had nothing left over, and those who gathered only a little had enough. Each family had just what it needed.

¹⁹Then Moses told them, "Do not keep any of it until morning." ²⁰But some of them didn't listen and kept some of it until morning. But

by then it was full of maggots and had a terrible smell. Moses was very angry with them.

²¹After this the people gathered the food morning by morning, each family according to its need. And as the sun became hot, the flakes they had not picked up melted and disappeared. ²²On the sixth day, they gathered twice as much as usual—four quarts* for each person instead of two. Then all the leaders of the community came and asked Moses for an explanation. ²³He told them, "This is what the LORD commanded: Tomorrow will be a day of complete rest, a holy Sabbath day set apart for the LORD. So bake or boil as much as you want today, and set aside what is left for tomorrow."

²⁴So they put some aside until morning, just as Moses had commanded. And in the morning the leftover food was wholesome and good, without maggots or odor. ²⁵Moses said, "Eat this food today, for today is a Sabbath day dedicated to the LORD. There will be no food on the ground today. ²⁶You may gather the food for six days, but the seventh day is the Sabbath. There will be no food on the ground that day."

²⁷Some of the people went out anyway on the seventh day, but they found no food. ²⁸The LORD asked Moses, "How long will these people refuse to obey my commands and instructions? ²⁹They must realize that the Sabbath is the LORD's gift to you. That is why he gives you a two-day supply on the sixth day, so there will be enough for two days. On the Sabbath day you must each stay in your place. Do not go out to pick up food on the seventh day." ³⁰So the people did not gather any food on the seventh day.

³¹The Israelites called the food manna.* It was white like coriander seed, and it tasted like honey wafers.

³²Then Moses said, "This is what the LORD has commanded: Fill a two-quart container with manna to preserve it for your descendants. Then later generations will be able to see the food I gave you in the wilderness when I set you free from Egypt."

³³Moses said to Aaron, "Get a jar and fill it with two quarts of manna. Then put it in a sacred place before the LORD to preserve it for all future generations." ³⁴Aaron did just as the LORD had commanded Moses. He eventually placed it in the Ark of the Covenant—in front of the stone tablets inscribed with the terms of the covenant.* ³⁵So the people of Israel ate

16:16 Hebrew *1 omer* [2.2 liters]; also in 16:32, 33.   16:18 Hebrew *measured it with an omer.*   16:22 Hebrew *2 omers* [4.4 liters].
16:31 *Manna* means "What is it?" See 16:15.   16:34 Hebrew *He placed it in front of the Testimony;* see note on 25:16.

manna for forty years until they arrived at the land where they would settle. They ate manna until they came to the border of the land of Canaan. [36]The container used to measure the manna was an omer, which was one-tenth of an ephah; it held about two quarts.*

Water from the Rock

17 At the LORD's command, the whole community of Israel left the wilderness of Sin* and moved from place to place. Eventually they camped at Rephidim, but there was no water there for the people to drink. [2]So once more the people complained against Moses. "Give us water to drink!" they demanded.

"Quiet!" Moses replied. "Why are you complaining against me? And why are you testing the LORD?"

[3]But tormented by thirst, they continued to argue with Moses. "Why did you bring us out of Egypt? Are you trying to kill us, our children, and our livestock with thirst?"

[4]Then Moses cried out to the LORD, "What should I do with these people? They are ready to stone me!"

[5]The LORD said to Moses, "Walk out in front of the people. Take your staff, the one you used when you struck the water of the Nile, and call some of the elders of Israel to join you. [6]I will stand before you on the rock at Mount Sinai.* Strike the rock, and water will come gushing out. Then the people will be able to drink." So Moses struck the rock as he was told, and water gushed out as the elders looked on.

[7]Moses named the place Massah (which means "test") and Meribah (which means "arguing") because the people of Israel argued with Moses and tested the LORD by saying, "Is the LORD here with us or not?"

Israel Defeats the Amalekites

[8]While the people of Israel were still at Rephidim, the warriors of Amalek attacked them. [9]Moses commanded Joshua, "Choose some men to go out and fight the army of Amalek for us. Tomorrow, I will stand at the top of the hill, holding the staff of God in my hand." [10]So Joshua did what Moses had commanded and fought the army of Amalek. Meanwhile, Moses, Aaron, and Hur climbed to the top of a nearby hill. [11]As long as Moses held up the staff in his hand, the Israelites had the advantage. But whenever he dropped his hand, the Amalekites gained the advantage. [12]Moses' arms soon became so tired he could no longer hold them up. So Aaron and Hur found a stone for him to sit on. Then they stood on each side of Moses, holding up his hands. So his hands held steady until sunset. [13]As a result, Joshua overwhelmed the army of Amalek in battle.

[14]After the victory, the LORD instructed Moses, "Write this down on a scroll as a permanent reminder, and read it aloud to Joshua: I will erase the memory of Amalek from under heaven." [15]Moses built an altar there and named it Yahweh-Nissi (which means "the LORD is my banner"). [16]He said, "They have raised their fist against the LORD's throne, so now* the LORD will be at war with Amalek generation after generation."

Jethro's Visit to Moses

18 Moses' father-in-law, Jethro, the priest of Midian, heard about everything God had done for Moses and his people, the Israelites. He heard especially about how the LORD had rescued them from Egypt.

[2]Earlier, Moses had sent his wife, Zipporah, and his two sons back to Jethro, who had taken them in. [3](Moses' first son was named Gershom,* for Moses had said when the boy was born, "I have been a foreigner in a foreign land." [4]His second son was named Eliezer,* for Moses had said, "The God of my ancestors was my helper; he rescued me from the sword of Pharaoh.") [5]Jethro, Moses' father-in-law, now came to visit Moses in the wilderness. He brought Moses' wife and two sons with him, and they arrived while Moses and the people were camped near the mountain of God. [6]Jethro had sent a message to Moses, saying, "I, Jethro, your father-in-law, am coming to see you with your wife and your two sons."

[7]So Moses went out to meet his father-in-law. He bowed low and kissed him. They asked about each other's welfare and then went into Moses' tent. [8]Moses told his father-in-law everything the LORD had done to Pharaoh and Egypt on behalf of Israel. He also told about all the hardships they had experienced along the way and how the LORD had rescued his people from all their troubles. [9]Jethro was delighted when he heard about all the good things the

---

16:36 Hebrew *An omer is one-tenth of an ephah.*   17:1 The geographical name *Sin* is related to *Sinai* and should not be confused with the English word *sin.*   17:6 Hebrew *Horeb,* another name for Sinai.   17:16 Or *Hands have been lifted up to the LORD's throne, and now.*   18:3 *Gershom* sounds like a Hebrew term that means "a foreigner there."   18:4 *Eliezer* means "God is my helper."

LORD had done for Israel as he rescued them from the hand of the Egyptians.

¹⁰"Praise the LORD," Jethro said, "for he has rescued you from the Egyptians and from Pharaoh. Yes, he has rescued Israel from the powerful hand of Egypt! ¹¹I know now that the LORD is greater than all other gods, because he rescued his people from the oppression of the proud Egyptians."

¹²Then Jethro, Moses' father-in-law, brought a burnt offering and sacrifices to God. Aaron and all the elders of Israel came out and joined him in a sacrificial meal in God's presence.

Jethro's Wise Advice

¹³The next day, Moses took his seat to hear the people's disputes against each other. They waited before him from morning till evening.

¹⁴When Moses' father-in-law saw all that Moses was doing for the people, he asked, "What are you really accomplishing here? Why are you trying to do all this alone while everyone stands around you from morning till evening?"

¹⁵Moses replied, "Because the people come to me to get a ruling from God. ¹⁶When a dispute arises, they come to me, and I am the one who settles the case between the quarreling parties. I inform the people of God's decrees and give them his instructions."

¹⁷"This is not good!" Moses' father-in-law exclaimed. ¹⁸"You're going to wear yourself out—and the people, too. This job is too heavy a burden for you to handle all by yourself. ¹⁹Now listen to me, and let me give you a word of advice, and may God be with you. You should continue to be the people's representative before God, bringing their disputes to him. ²⁰Teach them God's decrees, and give them his instructions. Show them how to conduct their lives. ²¹But select from all the people some capable, honest men who fear God and hate bribes. Appoint them as leaders over groups of one thousand, one hundred, fifty, and ten. ²²They should always be available to solve the people's common disputes, but have them bring the major cases to you. Let the leaders decide the smaller matters themselves. They will help you carry the load, making the task easier for you. ²³If you follow this advice, and if God commands you to do so, then you will be able to endure the pressures, and all these people will go home in peace."

²⁴Moses listened to his father-in-law's advice and followed his suggestions. ²⁵He chose capable men from all over Israel and appointed them as leaders over the people. He put them in charge of groups of one thousand, one hundred, fifty, and ten. ²⁶These men were always available to solve the people's common disputes. They brought the major cases to Moses, but they took care of the smaller matters themselves.

²⁷Soon after this, Moses said good-bye to his father-in-law, who returned to his own land.

The LORD Reveals Himself at Sinai

19 Exactly two months after the Israelites left Egypt,* they arrived in the wilderness of Sinai. ²After breaking camp at Rephidim, they came to the wilderness of Sinai and set up camp there at the base of Mount Sinai.

³Then Moses climbed the mountain to appear before God. The LORD called to him from the mountain and said, "Give these instructions to the family of Jacob; announce it to the descendants of Israel: ⁴'You have seen what I did to the Egyptians. You know how I carried you on eagles' wings and brought you to myself. ⁵Now if you will obey me and keep my covenant, you will be my own special treasure from among all the peoples on earth; for all the earth belongs to me. ⁶And you will be my kingdom of priests, my holy nation.' This is the message you must give to the people of Israel."

⁷So Moses returned from the mountain and called together the elders of the people and told them everything the LORD had commanded him. ⁸And all the people responded together, "We will do everything the LORD has commanded." So Moses brought the people's answer back to the LORD.

⁹Then the LORD said to Moses, "I will come to you in a thick cloud, Moses, so the people themselves can hear me when I speak with you. Then they will always trust you."

Moses told the LORD what the people had said. ¹⁰Then the LORD told Moses, "Go down and prepare the people for my arrival. Consecrate them today and tomorrow, and have them wash their clothing. ¹¹Be sure they are ready on the third day, for on that day the LORD will come down on Mount Sinai as all the people watch. ¹²Mark off a boundary all around the mountain. Warn the people, 'Be careful! Do not go up on the mountain or even touch its boundaries. Anyone who touches the

---

19:1 Hebrew *In the third month after the Israelites left Egypt, on the very day,* i.e., two lunar months to the day after leaving Egypt. Compare Num 33:3.

mountain will certainly be put to death. ¹³No hand may touch the person or animal that crosses the boundary; instead, stone them or shoot them with arrows. They must be put to death.' However, when the ram's horn sounds a long blast, then the people may go up on the mountain.*"

¹⁴So Moses went down to the people. He consecrated them for worship, and they washed their clothes. ¹⁵He told them, "Get ready for the third day, and until then abstain from having sexual intercourse."

¹⁶On the morning of the third day, thunder roared and lightning flashed, and a dense cloud came down on the mountain. There was a long, loud blast from a ram's horn, and all the people trembled. ¹⁷Moses led them out from the camp to meet with God, and they stood at the foot of the mountain. ¹⁸All of Mount Sinai was covered with smoke because the LORD had descended on it in the form of fire. The smoke billowed into the sky like smoke from a brick kiln, and the whole mountain shook violently. ¹⁹As the blast of the ram's horn grew louder and louder, Moses spoke, and God thundered his reply. ²⁰The LORD came down on the top of Mount Sinai and called Moses to the top of the mountain. So Moses climbed the mountain.

²¹Then the LORD told Moses, "Go back down and warn the people not to break through the boundaries to see the LORD, or they will die. ²²Even the priests who regularly come near to the LORD must purify themselves so that the LORD does not break out and destroy them."

²³"But LORD," Moses protested, "the people cannot come up to Mount Sinai. You already warned us. You told me, 'Mark off a boundary all around the mountain to set it apart as holy.'"

²⁴But the LORD said, "Go down and bring Aaron back up with you. In the meantime, do not let the priests or the people break through to approach the LORD, or he will break out and destroy them."

²⁵So Moses went down to the people and told them what the LORD had said.

Ten Commandments for the Covenant Community

20 Then God gave the people all these instructions*:

²"I am the LORD your God, who rescued you from the land of Egypt, the place of your slavery.

³"You must not have any other god but me.

⁴"You must not make for yourself an idol of any kind or an image of anything in the heavens or on the earth or in the sea. ⁵You must not bow down to them or worship them, for I, the LORD your God, am a jealous God who will not tolerate your affection for any other gods. I lay the sins of the parents upon their children; the entire family is affected—even children in the third and fourth generations of those who reject me. ⁶But I lavish unfailing love for a thousand generations on those* who love me and obey my commands.

⁷"You must not misuse the name of the LORD your God. The LORD will not let you go unpunished if you misuse his name.

⁸"Remember to observe the Sabbath day by keeping it holy. ⁹You have six days each week for your ordinary work, ¹⁰but the seventh day is a Sabbath day of rest dedicated to the LORD your God. On that day no one in your household may do any work. This includes you, your sons and daughters, your male and female servants, your livestock, and any foreigners living among you. ¹¹For in six days the LORD made the heavens, the earth, the sea, and everything in them; but on the seventh day he rested. That is why the LORD blessed the Sabbath day and set it apart as holy.

¹²"Honor your father and mother. Then you will live a long, full life in the land the LORD your God is giving you.

¹³"You must not murder.

¹⁴"You must not commit adultery.

¹⁵"You must not steal.

¹⁶"You must not testify falsely against your neighbor.

¹⁷"You must not covet your neighbor's house. You must not covet your neighbor's wife, male or female servant, ox or donkey, or anything else that belongs to your neighbor."

¹⁸When the people heard the thunder and the loud blast of the ram's horn, and when they saw the flashes of lightning and the smoke billowing from the mountain, they stood at a distance, trembling with fear.

¹⁹And they said to Moses, "You speak to us, and we will listen. But don't let God speak directly to us, or we will die!"

²⁰"Don't be afraid," Moses answered them, "for God has come in this way to test you, and

19:13 Or *up to the mountain.*   20:1 Hebrew *all these words.*   20:6 Hebrew *for thousands of those.*

so that your fear of him will keep you from sinning!"

²¹As the people stood in the distance, Moses approached the dark cloud where God was.

Proper Use of Altars

²²And the Lord said to Moses, "Say this to the people of Israel: You saw for yourselves that I spoke to you from heaven. ²³Remember, you must not make any idols of silver or gold to rival me.

²⁴"Build for me an altar made of earth, and offer your sacrifices to me—your burnt offerings and peace offerings, your sheep and goats, and your cattle. Build my altar wherever I cause my name to be remembered, and I will come to you and bless you. ²⁵If you use stones to build my altar, use only natural, uncut stones. Do not shape the stones with a tool, for that would make the altar unfit for holy use. ²⁶And do not approach my altar by going up steps. If you do, someone might look up under your clothing and see your nakedness.

Fair Treatment of Slaves

21 "These are the regulations you must present to Israel.

²"If you buy a Hebrew slave, he may serve for no more than six years. Set him free in the seventh year, and he will owe you nothing for his freedom. ³If he was single when he became your slave, he shall leave single. But if he was married before he became a slave, then his wife must be freed with him.

⁴"If his master gave him a wife while he was a slave and they had sons or daughters, then only the man will be free in the seventh year, but his wife and children will still belong to his master. ⁵But the slave may declare, 'I love my master, my wife, and my children. I don't want to go free.' ⁶If he does this, his master must present him before God.* Then his master must take him to the door or doorpost and publicly pierce his ear with an awl. After that, the slave will serve his master for life.

⁷"When a man sells his daughter as a slave, she will not be freed at the end of six years as the men are. ⁸If she does not satisfy her owner, he must allow her to be bought back again. But he is not allowed to sell her to foreigners, since he is the one who broke the contract with her. ⁹But if the slave's owner arranges for her to marry his son, he may no longer treat her as a slave but as a daughter.

¹⁰"If a man who has married a slave wife takes another wife for himself, he must not neglect the rights of the first wife to food, clothing, and sexual intimacy. ¹¹If he fails in any of these three obligations, she may leave as a free woman without making any payment.

Cases of Personal Injury

¹²"Anyone who assaults and kills another person must be put to death. ¹³But if it was simply an accident permitted by God, I will appoint a place of refuge where the slayer can run for safety. ¹⁴However, if someone deliberately kills another person, then the slayer must be dragged even from my altar and be put to death.

¹⁵"Anyone who strikes father or mother must be put to death.

¹⁶"Kidnappers must be put to death, whether they are caught in possession of their victims or have already sold them as slaves.

¹⁷"Anyone who dishonors* father or mother must be put to death.

¹⁸"Now suppose two men quarrel, and one hits the other with a stone or fist, and the injured person does not die but is confined to bed. ¹⁹If he is later able to walk outside again, even with a crutch, the assailant will not be punished but must compensate his victim for lost wages and provide for his full recovery.

²⁰"If a man beats his male or female slave with a club and the slave dies as a result, the owner must be punished. ²¹But if the slave recovers within a day or two, then the owner shall not be punished, since the slave is his property.

²²"Now suppose two men are fighting, and in the process they accidentally strike a pregnant woman so she gives birth prematurely.* If no further injury results, the man who struck the woman must pay the amount of compensation the woman's husband demands and the judges approve. ²³But if there is further injury, the punishment must match the injury: a life for a life, ²⁴an eye for an eye, a tooth for a tooth, a hand for a hand, a foot for a foot, ²⁵a burn for a burn, a wound for a wound, a bruise for a bruise.

²⁶"If a man hits his male or female slave in the eye and the eye is blinded, he must let the slave go free to compensate for the eye. ²⁷And if a man knocks out the tooth of his male or female slave, he must let the slave go free to compensate for the tooth.

²⁸"If an ox* gores a man or woman to death,

21:6 Or *before the judges.*   21:17 Greek version reads *Anyone who speaks disrespectfully of.* Compare Matt 15:4; Mark 7:10.
21:22 Or *so she has a miscarriage;* Hebrew reads *so her children come out.*   21:28 Or *bull,* or *cow;* also in 21:29-36.

the ox must be stoned, and its flesh may not be eaten. In such a case, however, the owner will not be held liable. ²⁹But suppose the ox had a reputation for goring, and the owner had been informed but failed to keep it under control. If the ox then kills someone, it must be stoned, and the owner must also be put to death. ³⁰However, the dead person's relatives may accept payment to compensate for the loss of life. The owner of the ox may redeem his life by paying whatever is demanded.

³¹"The same regulation applies if the ox gores a boy or a girl. ³²But if the ox gores a slave, either male or female, the animal's owner must pay the slave's owner thirty silver coins,* and the ox must be stoned.

³³"Suppose someone digs or uncovers a pit and fails to cover it, and then an ox or a donkey falls into it. ³⁴The owner of the pit must pay full compensation to the owner of the animal, but then he gets to keep the dead animal.

³⁵"If someone's ox injures a neighbor's ox and the injured ox dies, then the two owners must sell the live ox and divide the price equally between them. They must also divide the dead animal. ³⁶But if the ox had a reputation for goring, yet its owner failed to keep it under control, he must pay full compensation—a live ox for the dead one—but he may keep the dead ox.

Protection of Property

22 ¹*"If someone steals an ox* or sheep and then kills or sells it, the thief must pay back five oxen for each ox stolen, and four sheep for each sheep stolen.

²*"If a thief is caught in the act of breaking into a house and is struck and killed in the process, the person who killed the thief is not guilty of murder. ³But if it happens in daylight, the one who killed the thief is guilty of murder.

"A thief who is caught must pay in full for everything he stole. If he cannot pay, he must be sold as a slave to pay for his theft. ⁴If someone steals an ox or a donkey or a sheep and it is found in the thief's possession, then the thief must pay double the value of the stolen animal.

⁵"If an animal is grazing in a field or vineyard and the owner lets it stray into someone else's field to graze, then the animal's owner must pay compensation from the best of his own grain or grapes.

⁶"If you are burning thornbushes and the fire gets out of control and spreads into another person's field, destroying the sheaves or the uncut grain or the whole crop, the one who started the fire must pay for the lost crop.

⁷"Suppose someone leaves money or goods with a neighbor for safekeeping, and they are stolen from the neighbor's house. If the thief is caught, the compensation is double the value of what was stolen. ⁸But if the thief is not caught, the neighbor must appear before God,* who will determine if he stole the property.

⁹"Suppose there is a dispute between two people who both claim to own a particular ox, donkey, sheep, article of clothing, or any lost property. Both parties must come before God, and the person whom God declares* guilty must pay double compensation to the other.

¹⁰"Now suppose someone leaves a donkey, ox, sheep, or any other animal with a neighbor for safekeeping, but it dies or is injured or is taken away, and no one sees what happened. ¹¹The neighbor must then take an oath in the presence of the LORD. If the LORD confirms that the neighbor did not steal the property, the owner must accept the verdict, and no payment will be required. ¹²But if the animal was indeed stolen, the guilty person must pay compensation to the owner. ¹³If it was torn to pieces by a wild animal, the remains of the carcass must be shown as evidence, and no compensation will be required.

¹⁴"If someone borrows an animal from a neighbor and it is injured or dies when the owner is absent, the person who borrowed it must pay full compensation. ¹⁵But if the owner was present, no compensation is required. And no compensation is required if the animal was rented, for this loss is covered by the rental fee.

Social Responsibility

¹⁶"If a man seduces a virgin who is not engaged to anyone and has sex with her, he must pay the customary bride price and marry her. ¹⁷But if her father refuses to let him marry her, the man must still pay him an amount equal to the bride price of a virgin.

¹⁸"You must not allow a sorceress to live.

¹⁹"Anyone who has sexual relations with an animal must certainly be put to death.

²⁰"Anyone who sacrifices to any god other than the LORD must be destroyed.*

21:32 Hebrew 30 shekels of silver, about 12 ounces or 342 grams in weight.   22:1a Verse 22:1 is numbered 21:37 in Hebrew text.   22:1b Or bull, or cow; also in 22:4, 9, 10.   22:2 Verses 22:2-31 are numbered 22:1-30 in Hebrew text.   22:8 Or before the judges.   22:9 Or before the judges, and the person whom the judges declare.   22:20 The Hebrew term used here refers to the complete consecration of things or people to the LORD, either by destroying them or by giving them as an offering.

²¹"You must not mistreat or oppress foreigners in any way. Remember, you yourselves were once foreigners in the land of Egypt.

²²"You must not exploit a widow or an orphan. ²³If you exploit them in any way and they cry out to me, then I will certainly hear their cry. ²⁴My anger will blaze against you, and I will kill you with the sword. Then your wives will be widows and your children fatherless.

²⁵"If you lend money to any of my people who are in need, do not charge interest as a money lender would. ²⁶If you take your neighbor's cloak as security for a loan, you must return it before sunset. ²⁷This coat may be the only blanket your neighbor has. How can a person sleep without it? If you do not return it and your neighbor cries out to me for help, then I will hear, for I am merciful.

²⁸"You must not dishonor God or curse any of your rulers.

²⁹"You must not hold anything back when you give me offerings from your crops and your wine.

"You must give me your firstborn sons.

³⁰"You must also give me the firstborn of your cattle, sheep, and goats. But leave the newborn animal with its mother for seven days; then give it to me on the eighth day.

³¹"You must be my holy people. Therefore, do not eat any animal that has been torn up and killed by wild animals. Throw it to the dogs.

A Call for Justice

23 "You must not pass along false rumors. You must not cooperate with evil people by lying on the witness stand.

²"You must not follow the crowd in doing wrong. When you are called to testify in a dispute, do not be swayed by the crowd to twist justice. ³And do not slant your testimony in favor of a person just because that person is poor.

⁴"If you come upon your enemy's ox or donkey that has strayed away, take it back to its owner. ⁵If you see that the donkey of someone who hates you has collapsed under its load, do not walk by. Instead, stop and help.

⁶"In a lawsuit, you must not deny justice to the poor.

⁷"Be sure never to charge anyone falsely with evil. Never sentence an innocent or blameless person to death, for I never declare a guilty person to be innocent.

⁸"Take no bribes, for a bribe makes you ignore something that you clearly see. A bribe makes even a righteous person twist the truth.

⁹"You must not oppress foreigners. You know what it's like to be a foreigner, for you yourselves were once foreigners in the land of Egypt.

¹⁰"Plant and harvest your crops for six years, ¹¹but let the land be renewed and lie uncultivated during the seventh year. Then let the poor among you harvest whatever grows on its own. Leave the rest for wild animals to eat. The same applies to your vineyards and olive groves.

¹²"You have six days each week for your ordinary work, but on the seventh day you must stop working. This gives your ox and your donkey a chance to rest. It also allows your slaves and the foreigners living among you to be refreshed.

¹³"Pay close attention to all my instructions. You must not call on the name of any other gods. Do not even speak their names.

Three Annual Festivals

¹⁴"Each year you must celebrate three festivals in my honor. ¹⁵First, celebrate the Festival of Unleavened Bread. For seven days the bread you eat must be made without yeast, just as I commanded you. Celebrate this festival annually at the appointed time in early spring, in the month of Abib,* for that is the anniversary of your departure from Egypt. No one may appear before me without an offering.

¹⁶"Second, celebrate the Festival of Harvest,* when you bring me the first crops of your harvest.

"Finally, celebrate the Festival of the Final Harvest* at the end of the harvest season, when you have harvested all the crops from your fields. ¹⁷At these three times each year, every man in Israel must appear before the Sovereign, the Lord.

¹⁸"You must not offer the blood of my sacrificial offerings together with any baked goods containing yeast. And do not leave the fat from the festival offerings until the next morning.

¹⁹"As you harvest your crops, bring the very best of the first harvest to the house of the Lord your God.

23:15 Hebrew *appointed time in the month of Abib.* This first month of the ancient Hebrew lunar calendar usually occurs within the months of March and April.   **23:16a** Or *Festival of Weeks.* This was later called the Festival of Pentecost (see Acts 2:1). It is celebrated today as Shavuot (or Shabuoth).   **23:16b** Or *Festival of Ingathering.* This was later called the Festival of Shelters or Festival of Tabernacles (see Lev 23:33-36). It is celebrated today as Sukkot (or Succoth).

"You must not cook a young goat in its mother's milk.

A Promise of the LORD's Presence

20"See, I am sending an angel before you to protect you on your journey and lead you safely to the place I have prepared for you. 21Pay close attention to him, and obey his instructions. Do not rebel against him, for he is my representative, and he will not forgive your rebellion. 22But if you are careful to obey him, following all my instructions, then I will be an enemy to your enemies, and I will oppose those who oppose you. 23For my angel will go before you and bring you into the land of the Amorites, Hittites, Perizzites, Canaanites, Hivites, and Jebusites, so you may live there. And I will destroy them completely. 24You must not worship the gods of these nations or serve them in any way or imitate their evil practices. Instead, you must utterly destroy them and smash their sacred pillars.

25"You must serve only the LORD your God. If you do, I* will bless you with food and water, and I will protect you from illness. 26There will be no miscarriages or infertility in your land, and I will give you long, full lives.

27"I will send my terror ahead of you and create panic among all the people whose lands you invade. I will make all your enemies turn and run. 28I will send terror* ahead of you to drive out the Hivites, Canaanites, and Hittites. 29But I will not drive them out in a single year, because the land would become desolate and the wild animals would multiply and threaten you. 30I will drive them out a little at a time until your population has increased enough to take possession of the land. 31And I will fix your boundaries from the Red Sea to the Mediterranean Sea,* and from the eastern wilderness to the Euphrates River.* I will hand over to you the people now living in the land, and you will drive them out ahead of you.

32"Make no treaties with them or their gods. 33They must not live in your land, or they will cause you to sin against me. If you serve their gods, you will be caught in the trap of idolatry."

Israel Accepts the LORD's Covenant

24 Then the LORD instructed Moses: "Come up here to me, and bring along Aaron, Nadab, Abihu, and seventy of Israel's elders. All of you must worship from a distance. 2Only Moses is allowed to come near to the LORD. The others must not come near, and none of the other people are allowed to climb up the mountain with him."

3Then Moses went down to the people and repeated all the instructions and regulations the LORD had given him. All the people answered with one voice, "We will do everything the LORD has commanded."

4Then Moses carefully wrote down all the LORD's instructions. Early the next morning Moses got up and built an altar at the foot of the mountain. He also set up twelve pillars, one for each of the twelve tribes of Israel. 5Then he sent some of the young Israelite men to present burnt offerings and to sacrifice bulls as peace offerings to the LORD. 6Moses drained half the blood from these animals into basins. The other half he splattered against the altar. 7Then he took the Book of the Covenant and read it aloud to the people. Again they all responded, "We will do everything the LORD has commanded. We will obey."

8Then Moses took the blood from the basins and splattered it over the people, declaring, "Look, this blood confirms the covenant the LORD has made with you in giving you these instructions."

9Then Moses, Aaron, Nadab, Abihu, and the seventy elders of Israel climbed up the mountain. 10There they saw the God of Israel. Under his feet there seemed to be a surface of brilliant blue lapis lazuli, as clear as the sky itself. 11And though these nobles of Israel gazed upon God, he did not destroy them. In fact, they ate a covenant meal, eating and drinking in his presence!

12Then the LORD said to Moses, "Come up to me on the mountain. Stay there, and I will give you the tablets of stone on which I have inscribed the instructions and commands so you can teach the people." 13So Moses and his assistant Joshua set out, and Moses climbed up the mountain of God.

14Moses told the elders, "Stay here and wait for us until we come back. Aaron and Hur are here with you. If anyone has a dispute while I am gone, consult with them."

15Then Moses climbed up the mountain, and the cloud covered it. 16And the glory of the LORD settled down on Mount Sinai, and the cloud covered it for six days. On the seventh day the LORD called to Moses from inside the cloud. 17To the Israelites at the foot of the mountain, the glory of the LORD appeared at the summit like a consuming fire.

23:25 As in Greek and Latin versions; Hebrew reads *he.*   23:28 Often rendered *the hornet.* The meaning of the Hebrew is uncertain.   23:31a Hebrew *from the sea of reeds to the sea of the Philistines.*   23:31b Hebrew *from the wilderness to the river.*

18Then Moses disappeared into the cloud as he climbed higher up the mountain. He remained on the mountain forty days and forty nights.

Offerings for the Tabernacle

25 The LORD said to Moses, 2"Tell the people of Israel to bring me their sacred offerings. Accept the contributions from all whose hearts are moved to offer them. 3Here is a list of sacred offerings you may accept from them:

gold, silver, and bronze;
4 blue, purple, and scarlet thread;
fine linen and goat hair for cloth;
5 tanned ram skins and fine goatskin leather;
acacia wood;
6 olive oil for the lamps;
spices for the anointing oil and the
fragrant incense;
7 onyx stones, and other gemstones to be set
in the ephod and the priest's chestpiece.

8"Have the people of Israel build me a holy sanctuary so I can live among them. 9You must build this Tabernacle and its furnishings exactly according to the pattern I will show you.

Plans for the Ark of the Covenant

10"Have the people make an Ark of acacia wood—a sacred chest 45 inches long, 27 inches wide, and 27 inches high.* 11Overlay it inside and outside with pure gold, and run a molding of gold all around it. 12Cast four gold rings and attach them to its four feet, two rings on each side. 13Make poles from acacia wood, and overlay them with gold. 14Insert the poles into the rings at the sides of the Ark to carry it. 15These carrying poles must stay inside the rings; never remove them. 16When the Ark is finished, place inside it the stone tablets inscribed with the terms of the covenant,* which I will give to you. 17"Then make the Ark's cover—the place of atonement—from pure gold. It must be 45 inches long and 27 inches wide.* 18Then make two cherubim from hammered gold, and place them on the two ends of the atonement cover. 19Mold the cherubim on each end of the atonement cover, making it all of one piece of gold. 20The cherubim will face each other and look down on the atonement cover. With

their wings spread above it, they will protect it. 21Place inside the Ark the stone tablets inscribed with the terms of the covenant, which I will give to you. Then put the atonement cover on top of the Ark. 22I will meet with you there and talk to you from above the atonement cover between the gold cherubim that hover over the Ark of the Covenant.* From there I will give you my commands for the people of Israel.

Plans for the Table

23"Then make a table of acacia wood, 36 inches long, 18 inches wide, and 27 inches high.* 24Overlay it with pure gold and run a gold molding around the edge. 25Decorate it with a 3-inch border* all around, and run a gold molding along the border. 26Make four gold rings for the table and attach them at the four corners next to the four legs. 27Attach the rings near the border to hold the poles that are used to carry the table. 28Make these poles from acacia wood, and overlay them with gold. 29Make special containers of pure gold for the table—bowls, ladles, pitchers, and jars—to be used in pouring out liquid offerings. 30Place the Bread of the Presence on the table to remain before me at all times.

Plans for the Lampstand

31"Make a lampstand of pure, hammered gold. Make the entire lampstand and its decorations of one piece—the base, center stem, lamp cups, buds, and petals. 32Make it with six branches going out from the center stem, three on each side. 33Each of the six branches will have three lamp cups shaped like almond blossoms, complete with buds and petals. 34Craft the center stem of the lampstand with four lamp cups shaped like almond blossoms, complete with buds and petals. 35There will also be an almond bud beneath each pair of branches where the six branches extend from the center stem. 36The almond buds and branches must all be of one piece with the center stem, and they must be hammered from pure gold. 37Then make the seven lamps for the lampstand, and set them so they reflect their light forward. 38The lamp snuffers and trays must also be made of pure gold. 39You will need 75 pounds* of pure gold for the lampstand and its accessories. 40"Be sure that you make everything accord-

---

25:10 Hebrew *2.5 cubits* [115 centimeters] *long, 1.5 cubits* [69 centimeters] *wide, and 1.5 cubits high.*   25:16 Hebrew *Place inside the Ark the Testimony;* similarly in 25:21. The Hebrew word for "testimony" refers to the terms of the LORD's covenant with Israel as written on stone tablets, and also to the covenant itself.   25:17 Hebrew *2.5 cubits* [115 centimeters] *long and 1.5 cubits* [69 centimeters] *wide.*   25:22 Or *Ark of the Testimony.*   25:23 Hebrew *2 cubits* [92 centimeters] *long, 1 cubit* [46 centimeters] *wide, and 1.5 cubits* [69 centimeters] *high.*   25:25 Hebrew *a border of a handbreadth* [8 centimeters].   25:39 Hebrew *1 talent* [34 kilograms].

ing to the pattern I have shown you here on the mountain.

Plans for the Tabernacle

26 "Make the Tabernacle from ten curtains of finely woven linen. Decorate the curtains with blue, purple, and scarlet thread and with skillfully embroidered cherubim. 2These ten curtains must all be exactly the same size—42 feet long and 6 feet wide.* 3Join five of these curtains together to make one long curtain, then join the other five into a second long curtain. 4Put loops of blue yarn along the edge of the last curtain in each set. 5The fifty loops along the edge of one curtain are to match the fifty loops along the edge of the other curtain. 6Then make fifty gold clasps and fasten the long curtains together with the clasps. In this way, the Tabernacle will be made of one continuous piece.

7"Make eleven curtains of goat-hair cloth to serve as a tent covering for the Tabernacle. 8These eleven curtains must all be exactly the same size—45 feet long and 6 feet wide.* 9Join five of these curtains together to make one long curtain, and join the other six into a second long curtain. Allow 3 feet of material from the second set of curtains to hang over the front* of the sacred tent. 10Make fifty loops for one edge of each large curtain. 11Then make fifty bronze clasps, and fasten the loops of the long curtains with the clasps. In this way, the tent covering will be made of one continuous piece. 12The remaining 3 feet* of this tent covering will be left to hang over the back of the Tabernacle. 13Allow 18 inches* of remaining material to hang down over each side, so the Tabernacle is completely covered. 14Complete the tent covering with a protective layer of tanned ram skins and a layer of fine goatskin leather.

15"For the framework of the Tabernacle, construct frames of acacia wood. 16Each frame must be 15 feet high and 27 inches wide,* 17with two pegs under each frame. Make all the frames identical. 18Make twenty of these frames to support the curtains on the south side of the Tabernacle. 19Also make forty silver bases—two bases under each frame, with the pegs fitting securely into the bases. 20For the north side of the Tabernacle, make another twenty frames, 21with their forty silver bases, two bases under each frame. 22Make six frames for the rear—the

west side of the Tabernacle—23along with two additional frames to reinforce the rear corners of the Tabernacle. 24These corner frames will be matched at the bottom and firmly attached at the top with a single ring, forming a single corner unit. Make both of these corner units the same way. 25So there will be eight frames at the rear of the Tabernacle, set in sixteen silver bases—two bases under each frame.

26"Make crossbars of acacia wood to link the frames, five crossbars for the north side of the Tabernacle 27and five for the south side. Also make five crossbars for the rear of the Tabernacle, which will face west. 28The middle crossbar, attached halfway up the frames, will run all the way from one end of the Tabernacle to the other. 29Overlay the frames with gold, and make gold rings to hold the crossbars. Overlay the crossbars with gold as well.

30"Set up this Tabernacle according to the pattern you were shown on the mountain.

31"For the inside of the Tabernacle, make a special curtain of finely woven linen. Decorate it with blue, purple, and scarlet thread and with skillfully embroidered cherubim. 32Hang this curtain on gold hooks attached to four posts of acacia wood. Overlay the posts with gold, and set them in four silver bases. 33Hang the inner curtain from clasps, and put the Ark of the Covenant* in the room behind it. This curtain will separate the Holy Place from the Most Holy Place.

34"Then put the Ark's cover—the place of atonement—on top of the Ark of the Covenant inside the Most Holy Place. 35Place the table outside the inner curtain on the north side of the Tabernacle, and place the lampstand across the room on the south side.

36"Make another curtain for the entrance to the sacred tent. Make it of finely woven linen and embroider it with exquisite designs, using blue, purple, and scarlet thread. 37Craft five posts from acacia wood. Overlay them with gold, and hang the curtain from them with gold hooks. Cast five bronze bases for the posts.

Plans for the Altar of Burnt Offering

27 "Using acacia wood, construct a square altar 7½ feet wide, 7½ feet long, and 4½ feet high.* 2Make horns for each of its four corners so that the horns and altar are all one piece. Overlay the altar with bronze. 3Make ash

---

26:2 Hebrew 28 cubits [12.9 meters] long and 4 cubits [1.8 meters] wide.   26:8 Hebrew 30 cubits [13.8 meters] long and 4 cubits [1.8 meters] wide.   26:9 Hebrew Double over the sixth sheet at the front.   26:12 Hebrew The half sheet that is left over. 26:13 Hebrew 1 cubit [46 centimeters].   26:16 Hebrew 10 cubits [4.6 meters] high and 1.5 meters [69 centimeters] wide.   26:33 Or Ark of the Testimony; also in 26:34.   27:1 Hebrew 5 cubits [2.3 meters] wide, 5 cubits long, a square, and 3 cubits [1.4 meters] high.

buckets, shovels, basins, meat forks, and fire-pans, all of bronze. ⁴Make a bronze grating for it, and attach four bronze rings at its four corners. ⁵Install the grating halfway down the side of the altar, under the ledge. ⁶For carrying the altar, make poles from acacia wood, and overlay them with bronze. ⁷Insert the poles through the rings on the two sides of the altar. ⁸The altar must be hollow, made from planks. Build it just as you were shown on the mountain.

Plans for the Courtyard

⁹"Then make the courtyard for the Tabernacle, enclosed with curtains made of finely woven linen. On the south side, make the curtains 150 feet long.* ¹⁰They will be held up by twenty posts set securely in twenty bronze bases. Hang the curtains with silver hooks and rings. ¹¹Make the curtains the same on the north side—150 feet of curtains held up by twenty posts set securely in bronze bases. Hang the curtains with silver hooks and rings. ¹²The curtains on the west end of the courtyard will be 75 feet long,* supported by ten posts set into ten bases. ¹³The east end of the courtyard, the front, will also be 75 feet long. ¹⁴The courtyard entrance will be on the east end, flanked by two curtains. The curtain on the right side will be 22½ feet long,* supported by three posts set into three bases. ¹⁵The curtain on the left side will also be 22½ feet long, supported by three posts set into three bases.

¹⁶"For the entrance to the courtyard, make a curtain that is 30 feet long.* Make it from finely woven linen, and decorate it with beautiful embroidery in blue, purple, and scarlet thread. Support it with four posts, each securely set in its own base. ¹⁷All the posts around the courtyard must have silver rings and hooks and bronze bases. ¹⁸So the entire courtyard will be 150 feet long and 75 feet wide, with curtain walls 7½ feet high,* made from finely woven linen. The bases for the posts will be made of bronze. ¹⁹All the articles used in the rituals of the Tabernacle, including all the tent pegs used to support the Tabernacle and the courtyard curtains, must be made of bronze.

Light for the Tabernacle

²⁰"Command the people of Israel to bring you pure oil of pressed olives for the light, to keep the lamps burning continually. ²¹The lampstand will stand in the Tabernacle, in front of the inner curtain that shields the Ark of the Covenant.* Aaron and his sons must keep the lamps burning in the LORD's presence all night. This is a permanent law for the people of Israel, and it must be observed from generation to generation.

Clothing for the Priests

28 "Call for your brother, Aaron, and his sons, Nadab, Abihu, Eleazar, and Ithamar. Set them apart from the rest of the people of Israel so they may minister to me and be my priests. ²Make sacred garments for Aaron that are glorious and beautiful. ³Instruct all the skilled craftsmen whom I have filled with the spirit of wisdom. Have them make garments for Aaron that will distinguish him as a priest set apart for my service. ⁴These are the garments they are to make: a chestpiece, an ephod, a robe, a patterned tunic, a turban, and a sash. They are to make these sacred garments for your brother, Aaron, and his sons to wear when they serve me as priests. ⁵So give them fine linen cloth, gold thread, and blue, purple, and scarlet thread.

Design of the Ephod

⁶"The craftsmen must make the ephod of finely woven linen and skillfully embroider it with gold and with blue, purple, and scarlet thread. ⁷It will consist of two pieces, front and back, joined at the shoulders with two shoulder-pieces. ⁸The decorative sash will be made of the same materials: finely woven linen embroidered with gold and with blue, purple, and scarlet thread.

⁹"Take two onyx stones, and engrave on them the names of the tribes of Israel. ¹⁰Six names will be on each stone, arranged in the order of the births of the original sons of Israel. ¹¹Engrave these names on the two stones in the same way a jeweler engraves a seal. Then mount the stones in settings of gold filigree. ¹²Fasten the two stones on the shoulder-pieces of the ephod as a reminder that Aaron represents the people of Israel. Aaron will carry these names on his shoulders as a constant reminder whenever he goes before the LORD. ¹³Make settings of gold filigree, ¹⁴then braid two cords of pure gold and attach them to the filigree settings on the shoulders of the ephod.

27:9 Hebrew *100 cubits* [46 meters]; also in 27:11.   27:12 Hebrew *50 cubits* [23 meters]; also in 27:13.   27:14 Hebrew *15 cubits* [6.9 meters]; also in 27:15.   27:16 Hebrew *20 cubits* [9.2 meters].   27:18 Hebrew *100 cubits* [46 meters] *long and 50 by 50* [23 meters] *wide and 5 cubits* [2.3 meters] *high.*   27:21 Hebrew *in the Tent of Meeting, outside the inner curtain that is in front of the Testimony.* See note on 25:16.

Design of the Chestpiece

15 "Then, with great skill and care, make a chestpiece to be worn for seeking a decision from God.* Make it to match the ephod, using finely woven linen embroidered with gold and with blue, purple, and scarlet thread. 16 Make the chestpiece of a single piece of cloth folded to form a pouch nine inches* square. 17 Mount four rows of gemstones* on it. The first row will contain a red carnelian, a pale-green peridot, and an emerald. 18 The second row will contain a turquoise, a blue lapis lazuli, and a white moonstone. 19 The third row will contain an orange jacinth, an agate, and a purple amethyst. 20 The fourth row will contain a blue-green beryl, an onyx, and a green jasper. All these stones will be set in gold filigree. 21 Each stone will represent one of the twelve sons of Israel, and the name of that tribe will be engraved on it like a seal.

22 "To attach the chestpiece to the ephod, make braided cords of pure gold thread. 23 Then make two gold rings and attach them to the top corners of the chestpiece. 24 Tie the two gold cords to the two rings on the chestpiece. 25 Tie the other ends of the cords to the gold settings on the shoulder-pieces of the ephod. 26 Then make two more gold rings and attach them to the inside edges of the chestpiece next to the ephod. 27 And make two more gold rings and attach them to the front of the ephod, below the shoulder-pieces, just above the knot where the decorative sash is fastened to the ephod. 28 Then attach the bottom rings of the chestpiece to the rings on the ephod with blue cords. This will hold the chestpiece securely to the ephod above the decorative sash.

29 "In this way, Aaron will carry the names of the tribes of Israel on the sacred chestpiece* over his heart when he goes into the Holy Place. This will be a continual reminder that he represents the people when he comes before the LORD. 30 Insert the Urim and Thummim into the sacred chestpiece so they will be carried over Aaron's heart when he goes into the LORD's presence. In this way, Aaron will always carry over his heart the objects used to determine the LORD's will for his people whenever he goes in before the LORD.

Additional Clothing for the Priests

31 "Make the robe that is worn with the ephod from a single piece of blue cloth, 32 with an opening for Aaron's head in the middle of it. Reinforce the opening with a woven collar* so it will not tear. 33 Make pomegranates out of blue, purple, and scarlet yarn, and attach them to the hem of the robe, with gold bells between them. 34 The gold bells and pomegranates are to alternate all around the hem. 35 Aaron will wear this robe whenever he ministers before the LORD, and the bells will tinkle as he goes in and out of the LORD's presence in the Holy Place. If he wears it, he will not die.

36 "Next make a medallion of pure gold, and engrave it like a seal with these words: HOLY TO THE LORD. 37 Attach the medallion with a blue cord to the front of Aaron's turban, where it must remain. 38 Aaron must wear it on his forehead so he may take on himself any guilt of the people of Israel when they consecrate their sacred offerings. He must always wear it on his forehead so the LORD will accept the people.

39 "Weave Aaron's patterned tunic from fine linen cloth. Fashion the turban from this linen as well. Also make a sash, and decorate it with colorful embroidery.

40 "For Aaron's sons, make tunics, sashes, and special head coverings that are glorious and beautiful. 41 Clothe your brother, Aaron, and his sons with these garments, and then anoint and ordain them. Consecrate them so they can serve as my priests. 42 Also make linen undergarments for them, to be worn next to their bodies, reaching from their hips to their thighs. 43 These must be worn whenever Aaron and his sons enter the Tabernacle* or approach the altar in the Holy Place to perform their priestly duties. Then they will not incur guilt and die. This is a permanent law for Aaron and all his descendants after him.

Dedication of the Priests

29 "This is the ceremony you must follow when you consecrate Aaron and his sons to serve me as priests: Take a young bull and two rams with no defects. 2 Then, using choice wheat flour and no yeast, make loaves of bread, thin cakes mixed with olive oil, and wafers spread with oil. 3 Place them all in a single basket, and present them at the entrance of the Tabernacle, along with the young bull and the two rams.

4 "Present Aaron and his sons at the entrance of the Tabernacle,* and wash them with water. 5 Dress Aaron in his priestly garments—the

---

28:15 Hebrew a chestpiece for decision.   28:16 Hebrew 1 span [23 centimeters].   28:17 The identification of some of these gemstones is uncertain.   28:29 Hebrew the chestpiece for decision; also in 28:30. See 28:15.   28:32 The meaning of the Hebrew is uncertain.   28:43 Hebrew Tent of Meeting.   29:4 Hebrew Tent of Meeting; also in 29:10, 11, 30, 32, 42, 44.

tunic, the robe worn with the ephod, the ephod itself, and the chestpiece. Then wrap the decorative sash of the ephod around him. ⁶Place the turban on his head, and fasten the sacred medallion to the turban. ⁷Then anoint him by pouring the anointing oil over his head. ⁸Next present his sons, and dress them in their tunics. ⁹Wrap the sashes around the waists of Aaron and his sons, and put their special head coverings on them. Then the right to the priesthood will be theirs by law forever. In this way, you will ordain Aaron and his sons.

¹⁰"Bring the young bull to the entrance of the Tabernacle, where Aaron and his sons will lay their hands on its head. ¹¹Then slaughter the bull in the LORD's presence at the entrance of the Tabernacle. ¹²Put some of its blood on the horns of the altar with your finger, and pour out the rest at the base of the altar. ¹³Take all the fat around the internal organs, the long lobe of the liver, and the two kidneys and the fat around them, and burn it all on the altar. ¹⁴Then take the rest of the bull, including its hide, meat, and dung, and burn it outside the camp as a sin offering.

¹⁵"Next Aaron and his sons must lay their hands on the head of one of the rams. ¹⁶Then slaughter the ram, and splatter its blood against all sides of the altar. ¹⁷Cut the ram into pieces, and wash off the internal organs and the legs. Set them alongside the head and the other pieces of the body, ¹⁸then burn the entire animal on the altar. This is a burnt offering to the LORD; it is a pleasing aroma, a special gift presented to the LORD.

¹⁹"Now take the other ram, and have Aaron and his sons lay their hands on its head. ²⁰Then slaughter it, and apply some of its blood to the right earlobes of Aaron and his sons. Also put it on the thumbs of their right hands and the big toes of their right feet. Splatter the rest of the blood against all sides of the altar. ²¹Then take some of the blood from the altar and some of the anointing oil, and sprinkle it on Aaron and his sons and on their garments. In this way, they and their garments will be set apart as holy.

²²"Since this is the ram for the ordination of Aaron and his sons, take the fat of the ram, including the fat of the broad tail, the fat around the internal organs, the long lobe of the liver, and the two kidneys and the fat around them, along with the right thigh. ²³Then take one round loaf of bread, one thin cake mixed with olive oil, and one wafer from the basket of bread without yeast that was placed in the LORD's presence. ²⁴Put all these in the hands of Aaron and his sons to be lifted up as a special offering to the LORD. ²⁵Afterward take the various breads from their hands, and burn them on the altar along with the burnt offering. It is a pleasing aroma to the LORD, a special gift for him. ²⁶Then take the breast of Aaron's ordination ram, and lift it up in the LORD's presence as a special offering to him. Then keep it as your own portion.

²⁷"Set aside the portions of the ordination ram that belong to Aaron and his sons. This includes the breast and the thigh that were lifted up before the LORD as a special offering. ²⁸In the future, whenever the people of Israel lift up a peace offering, a portion of it must be set aside for Aaron and his descendants. This is their permanent right, and it is a sacred offering from the Israelites to the LORD.

²⁹"Aaron's sacred garments must be preserved for his descendants who succeed him, and they will wear them when they are anointed and ordained. ³⁰The descendant who succeeds him as high priest will wear these clothes for seven days as he ministers in the Tabernacle and the Holy Place.

³¹"Take the ram used in the ordination ceremony, and boil its meat in a sacred place. ³²Then Aaron and his sons will eat this meat, along with the bread in the basket, at the Tabernacle entrance. ³³They alone may eat the meat and bread used for their purification* in the ordination ceremony. No one else may eat them, for these things are set apart and holy. ³⁴If any of the ordination meat or bread remains until the morning, it must be burned. It may not be eaten, for it is holy.

³⁵"This is how you will ordain Aaron and his sons to their offices, just as I have commanded you. The ordination ceremony will go on for seven days. ³⁶Each day you must sacrifice a young bull as a sin offering to purify them, making them right with the LORD.* Afterward, cleanse the altar by purifying it*; make it holy by anointing it with oil. ³⁷Purify the altar, and consecrate it every day for seven days. After that, the altar will be absolutely holy, and whatever touches it will become holy.

³⁸"These are the sacrifices you are to offer regularly on the altar. Each day, offer two lambs that are a year old, ³⁹one in the morning and the other in the evening. ⁴⁰With one of them, offer two quarts of choice flour mixed with one quart of pure oil of pressed olives; also,

29:33 Or *their atonement.*   29:36a Or *to make atonement.*   29:36b Or *by making atonement for it;* similarly in 29:37.

offer one quart of wine* as a liquid offering. 41Offer the other lamb in the evening, along with the same offerings of flour and wine as in the morning. It will be a pleasing aroma, a special gift presented to the LORD.

42"These burnt offerings are to be made each day from generation to generation. Offer them in the LORD's presence at the Tabernacle entrance; there I will meet with you and speak with you. 43I will meet the people of Israel there, in the place made holy by my glorious presence. 44Yes, I will consecrate the Tabernacle and the altar, and I will consecrate Aaron and his sons to serve me as priests. 45Then I will live among the people of Israel and be their God, 46and they will know that I am the LORD their God. I am the one who brought them out of the land of Egypt so that I could live among them. I am the LORD their God.

Plans for the Incense Altar

30 "Then make another altar of acacia wood for burning incense. 2Make it 18 inches square and 36 inches high,* with horns at the corners carved from the same piece of wood as the altar itself. 3Overlay the top, sides, and horns of the altar with pure gold, and run a gold molding around the entire altar. 4Make two gold rings, and attach them on opposite sides of the altar below the gold molding to hold the carrying poles. 5Make the poles of acacia wood and overlay them with gold. 6Place the incense altar just outside the inner curtain that shields the Ark of the Covenant,* in front of the Ark's cover—the place of atonement— that covers the tablets inscribed with the terms of the covenant.* I will meet with you there.

7"Every morning when Aaron maintains the lamps, he must burn fragrant incense on the altar. 8And each evening when he lights the lamps, he must again burn incense in the LORD's presence. This must be done from generation to generation. 9Do not offer any unholy incense on this altar, or any burnt offerings, grain offerings, or liquid offerings.

10"Once a year Aaron must purify* the altar by smearing its horns with blood from the offering made to purify the people from their sin. This will be a regular, annual event from generation to generation, for this is the LORD's most holy altar."

Money for the Tabernacle

11Then the LORD said to Moses, 12"Whenever you take a census of the people of Israel, each man who is counted must pay a ransom for himself to the LORD. Then no plague will strike the people as you count them. 13Each person who is counted must give a small piece of silver as a sacred offering to the LORD. (This payment is half a shekel,* based on the sanctuary shekel, which equals twenty gerahs.) 14All who have reached their twentieth birthday must give this sacred offering to the LORD. 15When this offering is given to the LORD to purify your lives, making you right with him,* the rich must not give more than the specified amount, and the poor must not give less. 16Receive this ransom money from the Israelites, and use it for the care of the Tabernacle.* It will bring the Israelites to the LORD's attention, and it will purify your lives."

Plans for the Washbasin

17Then the LORD said to Moses, 18"Make a bronze washbasin with a bronze stand. Place it between the Tabernacle and the altar, and fill it with water. 19Aaron and his sons will wash their hands and feet there. 20They must wash with water whenever they go into the Tabernacle to appear before the LORD and when they approach the altar to burn up their special gifts to the LORD—or they will die! 21They must always wash their hands and feet, or they will die. This is a permanent law for Aaron and his descendants, to be observed from generation to generation."

The Anointing Oil

22Then the LORD said to Moses, 23"Collect choice spices—12½ pounds of pure myrrh, 6¼ pounds of fragrant cinnamon, 6¼ pounds of fragrant calamus,* 24and 12½ pounds of cassia*—as measured by the weight of the sanctuary shekel. Also get one gallon of olive oil.* 25Like a skilled incense maker, blend these ingredients to make a holy anointing oil. 26Use this sacred oil to anoint the Tabernacle, the Ark of the Covenant, 27the table and all its utensils, the lampstand and all its accessories, the incense altar, 28the altar of burnt offering and all its utensils, and the washbasin with its stand. 29Consecrate them to make them absolutely

29:40 Hebrew ⅒ [of an ephah] [2.2 liters] of choice flour ... ¼ of a hin [1 liter] of pure oil ... ¼ of a hin of wine.   30:2 Hebrew 1 cubit [46 centimeters] long and 1 cubit wide, a square, and 2 cubits [92 centimeters] high.   30:6a Or Ark of the Testimony; also in 30:26. 30:6b Hebrew that covers the Testimony; see note on 25:16.   30:10 Or make atonement for; also in 30:10b.   30:13 Or 0.2 ounces [6 grams].   30:15 Or to make atonement for your lives; similarly in 30:16.   30:16 Hebrew Tent of Meeting; also in 30:18, 20, 26, 36. 30:23 Hebrew 500 [shekels] [5.7 kilograms] of pure myrrh, 250 [shekels] [2.9 kilograms] of fragrant cinnamon, 250 [shekels] of fragrant calamus.   30:24a Hebrew 500 [shekels] [5.7 kilograms] of cassia.   30:24b Hebrew 1 hin [3.8 liters] of olive oil.

holy. After this, whatever touches them will also become holy.

³⁰"Anoint Aaron and his sons also, consecrating them to serve me as priests. ³¹And say to the people of Israel, 'This holy anointing oil is reserved for me from generation to generation. ³²It must never be used to anoint anyone else, and you must never make any blend like it for yourselves. It is holy, and you must treat it as holy. ³³Anyone who makes a blend like it or anoints someone other than a priest will be cut off from the community.'"

The Incense

³⁴Then the LORD said to Moses, "Gather fragrant spices—resin droplets, mollusk shell, and galbanum—and mix these fragrant spices with pure frankincense, weighed out in equal amounts. ³⁵Using the usual techniques of the incense maker, blend the spices together and sprinkle them with salt to produce a pure and holy incense. ³⁶Grind some of the mixture into a very fine powder and put it in front of the Ark of the Covenant,* where I will meet with you in the Tabernacle. You must treat this incense as most holy. ³⁷Never use this formula to make this incense for yourselves. It is reserved for the LORD, and you must treat it as holy. ³⁸Anyone who makes incense like this for personal use will be cut off from the community."

Craftsmen: Bezalel and Oholiab

31 Then the LORD said to Moses, ²"Look, I have specifically chosen Bezalel son of Uri, grandson of Hur, of the tribe of Judah. ³I have filled him with the Spirit of God, giving him great wisdom, ability, and expertise in all kinds of crafts. ⁴He is a master craftsman, expert in working with gold, silver, and bronze. ⁵He is skilled in engraving and mounting gemstones and in carving wood. He is a master at every craft!

⁶"And I have personally appointed Oholiab son of Ahisamach, of the tribe of Dan, to be his assistant. Moreover, I have given special skill to all the gifted craftsmen so they can make all the things I have commanded you to make:

⁷ the Tabernacle;*
the Ark of the Covenant;*
the Ark's cover—the place of atonement;
all the furnishings of the Tabernacle;
⁸ the table and its utensils;

the pure gold lampstand with all its accessories;
the incense altar;
⁹ the altar of burnt offering with all its utensils;
the washbasin with its stand;
¹⁰ the beautifully stitched garments—the sacred garments for Aaron the priest, and the garments for his sons to wear as they minister as priests;
¹¹ the anointing oil;
the fragrant incense for the Holy Place.

The craftsmen must make everything as I have commanded you."

Instructions for the Sabbath

¹²The LORD then gave these instructions to Moses: ¹³"Tell the people of Israel: 'Be careful to keep my Sabbath day, for the Sabbath is a sign of the covenant between me and you from generation to generation. It is given so you may know that I am the LORD, who makes you holy. ¹⁴You must keep the Sabbath day, for it is a holy day for you. Anyone who desecrates it must be put to death; anyone who works on that day will be cut off from the community. ¹⁵You have six days each week for your ordinary work, but the seventh day must be a Sabbath day of complete rest, a holy day dedicated to the LORD. Anyone who works on the Sabbath must be put to death. ¹⁶The people of Israel must keep the Sabbath day by observing it from generation to generation. This is a covenant obligation for all time. ¹⁷It is a permanent sign of my covenant with the people of Israel. For in six days the LORD made heaven and earth, but on the seventh day he stopped working and was refreshed.'"

¹⁸When the LORD finished speaking with Moses on Mount Sinai, he gave him the two stone tablets inscribed with the terms of the covenant,* written by the finger of God.

The Gold Calf

32 When the people saw how long it was taking Moses to come back down the mountain, they gathered around Aaron. "Come on," they said, "make us some gods who can lead us. We don't know what happened to this fellow Moses, who brought us here from the land of Egypt."

²So Aaron said, "Take the gold rings from the

30:36 Hebrew *in front of the Testimony;* see note on 25:16.   31:7a Hebrew *the Tent of Meeting.*   31:7b Hebrew *the Ark of the Testimony.*   31:18 Hebrew *the two tablets of the Testimony;* see note on 25:16.

ears of your wives and sons and daughters, and bring them to me."

3All the people took the gold rings from their ears and brought them to Aaron. 4Then Aaron took the gold, melted it down, and molded it into the shape of a calf. When the people saw it, they exclaimed, "O Israel, these are the gods who brought you out of the land of Egypt!"

5Aaron saw how excited the people were, so he built an altar in front of the calf. Then he announced, "Tomorrow will be a festival to the LORD!"

6The people got up early the next morning to sacrifice burnt offerings and peace offerings. After this, they celebrated with feasting and drinking, and they indulged in pagan revelry.

7The LORD told Moses, "Quick! Go down the mountain! Your people whom you brought from the land of Egypt have corrupted themselves. 8How quickly they have turned away from the way I commanded them to live! They have melted down gold and made a calf, and they have bowed down and sacrificed to it. They are saying, 'These are your gods, O Israel, who brought you out of the land of Egypt.'"

9Then the LORD said, "I have seen how stubborn and rebellious these people are. 10Now leave me alone so my fierce anger can blaze against them, and I will destroy them. Then I will make you, Moses, into a great nation."

11But Moses tried to pacify the LORD his God. "O LORD!" he said. "Why are you so angry with your own people whom you brought from the land of Egypt with such great power and such a strong hand? 12Why let the Egyptians say, 'Their God rescued them with the evil intention of slaughtering them in the mountains and wiping them from the face of the earth'? Turn away from your fierce anger. Change your mind about this terrible disaster you have threatened against your people! 13Remember your servants Abraham, Isaac, and Jacob.* You bound yourself with an oath to them, saying, 'I will make your descendants as numerous as the stars of heaven. And I will give them all of this land that I have promised to your descendants, and they will possess it forever.'"

14So the LORD changed his mind about the terrible disaster he had threatened to bring on his people.

15Then Moses turned and went down the mountain. He held in his hands the two stone tablets inscribed with the terms of the covenant.* They were inscribed on both sides, front and back. 16These tablets were God's work; the words on them were written by God himself.

17When Joshua heard the boisterous noise of the people shouting below them, he exclaimed to Moses, "It sounds like war in the camp!"

18But Moses replied, "No, it's not a shout of victory nor the wailing of defeat. I hear the sound of a celebration."

19When they came near the camp, Moses saw the calf and the dancing, and he burned with anger. He threw the stone tablets to the ground, smashing them at the foot of the mountain. 20He took the calf they had made and burned it. Then he ground it into powder, threw it into the water, and forced the people to drink it.

21Finally, he turned to Aaron and demanded, "What did these people do to you to make you bring such terrible sin upon them?"

22"Don't get so upset, my lord," Aaron replied. "You yourself know how evil these people are. 23They said to me, 'Make us gods who will lead us. We don't know what happened to this fellow Moses, who brought us here from the land of Egypt.' 24So I told them, 'Whoever has gold jewelry, take it off.' When they brought it to me, I simply threw it into the fire—and out came this calf!"

25Moses saw that Aaron had let the people get completely out of control, much to the amusement of their enemies.* 26So he stood at the entrance to the camp and shouted, "All of you who are on the LORD's side, come here and join me." And all the Levites gathered around him.

27Moses told them, "This is what the LORD, the God of Israel, says: Each of you, take your swords and go back and forth from one end of the camp to the other. Kill everyone—even your brothers, friends, and neighbors." 28The Levites obeyed Moses' command, and about 3,000 people died that day.

29Then Moses told the Levites, "Today you have ordained yourselves* for the service of the LORD, for you obeyed him even though it meant killing your own sons and brothers. Today you have earned a blessing."

Moses Intercedes for Israel

30The next day Moses said to the people, "You have committed a terrible sin, but I will go back

---

32:13 Hebrew *Israel.* The names "Jacob" and "Israel" are often interchanged throughout the Old Testament, referring sometimes to the individual patriarch and sometimes to the nation.   32:15 Hebrew *the two tablets of the Testimony;* see note on 25:16.   32:25 Or *out of control, and they mocked anyone who opposed them.* The meaning of the Hebrew is uncertain. 32:29 As in Greek and Latin versions; Hebrew reads *Today ordain yourselves.*

up to the Lord on the mountain. Perhaps I will be able to obtain forgiveness* for your sin."

³¹So Moses returned to the Lord and said, "Oh, what a terrible sin these people have committed. They have made gods of gold for themselves. ³²But now, if you will only forgive their sin—but if not, erase my name from the record you have written!"

³³But the Lord replied to Moses, "No, I will erase the name of everyone who has sinned against me. ³⁴Now go, lead the people to the place I told you about. Look! My angel will lead the way before you. And when I come to call the people to account, I will certainly hold them responsible for their sins."

³⁵Then the Lord sent a great plague upon the people because they had worshiped the calf Aaron had made.

33 The Lord said to Moses, "Get going, you and the people you brought up from the land of Egypt. Go up to the land I swore to give to Abraham, Isaac, and Jacob. I told them, 'I will give this land to your descendants.' ²And I will send an angel before you to drive out the Canaanites, Amorites, Hittites, Perizzites, Hivites, and Jebusites. ³Go up to this land that flows with milk and honey. But I will not travel among you, for you are a stubborn and rebellious people. If I did, I would surely destroy you along the way."

⁴When the people heard these stern words, they went into mourning and stopped wearing their jewelry and fine clothes. ⁵For the Lord had told Moses to tell them, "You are a stubborn and rebellious people. If I were to travel with you for even a moment, I would destroy you. Remove your jewelry and fine clothes while I decide what to do with you." ⁶So from the time they left Mount Sinai,* the Israelites wore no more jewelry or fine clothes.

⁷It was Moses' practice to take the Tent of Meeting* and set it up some distance from the camp. Everyone who wanted to make a request of the Lord would go to the Tent of Meeting outside the camp.

⁸Whenever Moses went out to the Tent of Meeting, all the people would get up and stand in the entrances of their own tents. They would all watch Moses until he disappeared inside. ⁹As he went into the tent, the pillar of cloud would come down and hover at its entrance while the Lord spoke with Moses. ¹⁰When the

people saw the cloud standing at the entrance of the tent, they would stand and bow down in front of their own tents. ¹¹Inside the Tent of Meeting, the Lord would speak to Moses face to face, as one speaks to a friend. Afterward Moses would return to the camp, but the young man who assisted him, Joshua son of Nun, would remain behind in the Tent of Meeting.

Moses Sees the Lord's Glory

¹²One day Moses said to the Lord, "You have been telling me, 'Take these people up to the Promised Land.' But you haven't told me whom you will send with me. You have told me, 'I know you by name, and I look favorably on you.' ¹³If it is true that you look favorably on me, let me know your ways so I may understand you more fully and continue to enjoy your favor. And remember that this nation is your very own people."

¹⁴The Lord replied, "I will personally go with you, Moses, and I will give you rest—everything will be fine for you."

¹⁵Then Moses said, "If you don't personally go with us, don't make us leave this place. ¹⁶How will anyone know that you look favorably on me—on me and on your people—if you don't go with us? For your presence among us sets your people and me apart from all other people on the earth."

¹⁷The Lord replied to Moses, "I will indeed do what you have asked, for I look favorably on you, and I know you by name."

¹⁸Moses responded, "Then show me your glorious presence."

¹⁹The Lord replied, "I will make all my goodness pass before you, and I will call out my name, Yahweh,* before you. For I will show mercy to anyone I choose, and I will show compassion to anyone I choose. ²⁰But you may not look directly at my face, for no one may see me and live." ²¹The Lord continued, "Look, stand near me on this rock. ²²As my glorious presence passes by, I will hide you in the crevice of the rock and cover you with my hand until I have passed by. ²³Then I will remove my hand and let you see me from behind. But my face will not be seen."

A New Copy of the Covenant

34 Then the Lord told Moses, "Chisel out two stone tablets like the first ones. I will write on them the same words that were

---

32:30 Or *to make atonement.* 33:6 Hebrew *Horeb,* another name for Sinai. 33:7 This "Tent of Meeting" is different from the Tabernacle described in chapters 26 and 36. 33:19 *Yahweh* is a transliteration of the proper name *YHWH* that is sometimes rendered "Jehovah"; in this translation it is usually rendered "the Lord" (note the use of small capitals).

on the tablets you smashed. ²Be ready in the morning to climb up Mount Sinai and present yourself to me on the top of the mountain. ³No one else may come with you. In fact, no one is to appear anywhere on the mountain. Do not even let the flocks or herds graze near the mountain."

⁴So Moses chiseled out two tablets of stone like the first ones. Early in the morning he climbed Mount Sinai as the LORD had commanded him, and he carried the two stone tablets in his hands.

⁵Then the LORD came down in a cloud and stood there with him; and he called out his own name, Yahweh.* ⁶The LORD passed in front of Moses, calling out,

"Yahweh!* The LORD!
    The God of compassion and mercy!
I am slow to anger
    and filled with unfailing love and
        faithfulness.
⁷ I lavish unfailing love to a thousand
        generations.*
    I forgive iniquity, rebellion, and sin.
But I do not excuse the guilty.
    I lay the sins of the parents upon their
        children and grandchildren;
the entire family is affected—
    even children in the third and fourth
        generations."

⁸Moses immediately threw himself to the ground and worshiped. ⁹And he said, "O Lord, if it is true that I have found favor with you, then please travel with us. Yes, this is a stubborn and rebellious people, but please forgive our iniquity and our sins. Claim us as your own special possession."

¹⁰The LORD replied, "Listen, I am making a covenant with you in the presence of all your people. I will perform miracles that have never been performed anywhere in all the earth or in any nation. And all the people around you will see the power of the LORD—the awesome power I will display for you. ¹¹But listen carefully to everything I command you today. Then I will go ahead of you and drive out the Amorites, Canaanites, Hittites, Perizzites, Hivites, and Jebusites.

¹²"Be very careful never to make a treaty with the people who live in the land where you are going. If you do, you will follow their evil ways and be trapped. ¹³Instead, you must break down their pagan altars, smash their sacred pillars, and cut down their Asherah poles. ¹⁴You must worship no other gods, for the LORD, whose very name is Jealous, is a God who is jealous about his relationship with you.

¹⁵"You must not make a treaty of any kind with the people living in the land. They lust after their gods, offering sacrifices to them. They will invite you to join them in their sacrificial meals, and you will go with them. ¹⁶Then you will accept their daughters, who sacrifice to other gods, as wives for your sons. And they will seduce your sons to commit adultery against me by worshiping other gods. ¹⁷You must not make any gods of molten metal for yourselves.

¹⁸"You must celebrate the Festival of Unleavened Bread. For seven days the bread you eat must be made without yeast, just as I commanded you. Celebrate this festival annually at the appointed time in early spring, in the month of Abib,* for that is the anniversary of your departure from Egypt.

¹⁹"The firstborn of every animal belongs to me, including the firstborn males* from your herds of cattle and your flocks of sheep and goats. ²⁰A firstborn donkey may be bought back from the LORD by presenting a lamb or young goat in its place. But if you do not buy it back, you must break its neck. However, you must buy back every firstborn son.

"No one may appear before me without an offering.

²¹"You have six days each week for your ordinary work, but on the seventh day you must stop working, even during the seasons of plowing and harvest.

²²"You must celebrate the Festival of Harvest* with the first crop of the wheat harvest, and celebrate the Festival of the Final Harvest* at the end of the harvest season. ²³Three times each year every man in Israel must appear before the Sovereign, the LORD, the God of Israel. ²⁴I will drive out the other nations ahead of you and expand your territory, so no

---

34:5 *Yahweh* is a transliteration of the proper name *YHWH* that is sometimes rendered "Jehovah"; in this translation it is usually rendered "the LORD" (note the use of small capitals). **34:6** See note on 34:5. **34:7** Hebrew *for thousands.* **34:18** Hebrew *appointed time in the month of Abib.* This first month of the ancient Hebrew lunar calendar usually occurs within the months of March and April. **34:19** As in Greek version; the meaning of the Hebrew word is uncertain. **34:22a** Hebrew *Festival of Weeks;* compare 23:16. This was later called the Festival of Pentecost. It is celebrated today as Shavuot (or Shabuoth). **34:22b** Or *Festival of Ingathering.* This was later called the Festival of Shelters or Festival of Tabernacles (see Lev 23:33-36). It is celebrated today as Sukkot (or Succoth).

one will covet and conquer your land while you appear before the LORD your God three times each year.

25"You must not offer the blood of my sacrificial offerings together with any baked goods containing yeast. And none of the meat of the Passover sacrifice may be kept over until the next morning.

26"As you harvest your crops, bring the very best of the first harvest to the house of the LORD your God.

"You must not cook a young goat in its mother's milk."

27Then the LORD said to Moses, "Write down all these instructions, for they represent the terms of the covenant I am making with you and with Israel."

28Moses remained there on the mountain with the LORD forty days and forty nights. In all that time he ate no bread and drank no water. And the LORD* wrote the terms of the covenant—the Ten Commandments*—on the stone tablets.

29When Moses came down Mount Sinai carrying the two stone tablets inscribed with the terms of the covenant,* he wasn't aware that his face had become radiant because he had spoken to the LORD. 30So when Aaron and the people of Israel saw the radiance of Moses' face, they were afraid to come near him.

31But Moses called out to them and asked Aaron and all the leaders of the community to come over, and he talked with them. 32Then all the people of Israel approached him, and Moses gave them all the instructions the LORD had given him on Mount Sinai. 33When Moses finished speaking with them, he covered his face with a veil. 34But whenever he went into the Tent of Meeting to speak with the LORD, he would remove the veil until he came out again. Then he would give the people whatever instructions the LORD had given him, 35and the people of Israel would see the radiant glow of his face. So he would put the veil over his face until he returned to speak with the LORD.

Instructions for the Sabbath

35 Then Moses called together the whole community of Israel and told them, "These are the instructions the LORD has commanded you to follow. 2You have six days each week for your ordinary work, but the seventh day must be a Sabbath day of complete rest, a holy day dedicated to the LORD. Anyone who works on that day must be put to death. 3You

must not even light a fire in any of your homes on the Sabbath."

Offerings for the Tabernacle

4Then Moses said to the whole community of Israel, "This is what the LORD has commanded: 5Take a sacred offering for the LORD. Let those with generous hearts present the following gifts to the LORD:

gold, silver, and bronze;
6 blue, purple, and scarlet thread;
fine linen and goat hair for cloth;
7 tanned ram skins and fine goatskin
leather;
acacia wood;
8 olive oil for the lamps;
spices for the anointing oil and the
fragrant incense;
9 onyx stones, and other gemstones to be set
in the ephod and the priest's chestpiece.

10"Come, all of you who are gifted craftsmen. Construct everything that the LORD has commanded:

11 the Tabernacle and its sacred tent, its
covering, clasps, frames, crossbars,
posts, and bases;
12 the Ark and its carrying poles;
the Ark's cover—the place of atonement;
the inner curtain to shield the Ark;
13 the table, its carrying poles, and all its
utensils;
the Bread of the Presence;
14 for light, the lampstand, its accessories,
the lamp cups, and the olive oil for
lighting;
15 the incense altar and its carrying poles;
the anointing oil and fragrant incense;
the curtain for the entrance of the
Tabernacle;
16 the altar of burnt offering;
the bronze grating of the altar and its
carrying poles and utensils;
the washbasin with its stand;
17 the curtains for the walls of the courtyard;
the posts and their bases;
the curtain for the entrance to the
courtyard;
18 the tent pegs of the Tabernacle and
courtyard and their ropes;
19 the beautifully stitched garments for the
priests to wear while ministering in
the Holy Place—the sacred garments

34:28a Hebrew he.   34:28b Hebrew the ten words.   34:29 Hebrew the two tablets of the Testimony; see note on 25:16.

for Aaron the priest, and the garments for his sons to wear as they minister as priests."

²⁰So the whole community of Israel left Moses and returned to their tents. ²¹All whose hearts were stirred and whose spirits were moved came and brought their sacred offerings to the LORD. They brought all the materials needed for the Tabernacle,* for the performance of its rituals, and for the sacred garments. ²²Both men and women came, all whose hearts were willing. They brought to the LORD their offerings of gold—brooches, earrings, rings from their fingers, and necklaces. They presented gold objects of every kind as a special offering to the LORD. ²³All those who owned the following items willingly brought them: blue, purple, and scarlet thread; fine linen and goat hair for cloth; and tanned ram skins and fine goatskin leather. ²⁴And all who had silver and bronze objects gave them as a sacred offering to the LORD. And those who had acacia wood brought it for use in the project.

²⁵All the women who were skilled in sewing and spinning prepared blue, purple, and scarlet thread, and fine linen cloth. ²⁶All the women who were willing used their skills to spin the goat hair into yarn. ²⁷The leaders brought onyx stones and the special gemstones to be set in the ephod and the priest's chestpiece. ²⁸They also brought spices and olive oil for the light, the anointing oil, and the fragrant incense. ²⁹So the people of Israel—every man and woman who was eager to help in the work the LORD had given them through Moses—brought their gifts and gave them freely to the LORD.

³⁰Then Moses told the people of Israel, "The LORD has specifically chosen Bezalel son of Uri, grandson of Hur, of the tribe of Judah. ³¹The LORD has filled Bezalel with the Spirit of God, giving him great wisdom, ability, and expertise in all kinds of crafts. ³²He is a master craftsman, expert in working with gold, silver, and bronze. ³³He is skilled in engraving and mounting gemstones and in carving wood. He is a master at every craft. ³⁴And the LORD has given both him and Oholiab son of Ahisamach, of the tribe of Dan, the ability to teach their skills to others. ³⁵The LORD has given them special skills as engravers, designers, embroiderers in blue, purple, and scarlet thread on fine linen cloth, and weavers. They excel as craftsmen and as designers.

36 "The LORD has gifted Bezalel, Oholiab, and the other skilled craftsmen with wisdom and ability to perform any task involved in building the sanctuary. Let them construct and furnish the Tabernacle, just as the LORD has commanded."

²So Moses summoned Bezalel and Oholiab and all the others who were specially gifted by the LORD and were eager to get to work. ³Moses gave them the materials donated by the people of Israel as sacred offerings for the completion of the sanctuary. But the people continued to bring additional gifts each morning. ⁴Finally the craftsmen who were working on the sanctuary left their work. ⁵They went to Moses and reported, "The people have given more than enough materials to complete the job the LORD has commanded us to do!"

⁶So Moses gave the command, and this message was sent throughout the camp: "Men and women, don't prepare any more gifts for the sanctuary. We have enough!" So the people stopped bringing their sacred offerings. ⁷Their contributions were more than enough to complete the whole project.

Building the Tabernacle

⁸The skilled craftsmen made ten curtains of finely woven linen for the Tabernacle. Then Bezalel* decorated the curtains with blue, purple, and scarlet thread and with skillfully embroidered cherubim. ⁹All ten curtains were exactly the same size—42 feet long and 6 feet wide.* ¹⁰Five of these curtains were joined together to make one long curtain, and the other five were joined to make a second long curtain. ¹¹He made fifty loops of blue yarn and put them along the edge of the last curtain in each set. ¹²The fifty loops along the edge of one curtain matched the fifty loops along the edge of the other curtain. ¹³Then he made fifty gold clasps and fastened the long curtains together with the clasps. In this way, the Tabernacle was made of one continuous piece.

¹⁴He made eleven curtains of goat-hair cloth to serve as a tent covering for the Tabernacle. ¹⁵These eleven curtains were all exactly the same size—45 feet long and 6 feet wide.* ¹⁶Bezalel joined five of these curtains together to make one long curtain, and the other six were joined to make a second long curtain. ¹⁷He made fifty loops for the edge of each large curtain. ¹⁸He also made fifty bronze clasps to fasten the long curtains together. In this way,

35:21 Hebrew *Tent of Meeting.*   36:8 Hebrew *he;* also in 36:16, 20, 35. See 37:1.   36:9 Hebrew *28 cubits* [12.9 meters] *long and 4 cubits* [1.8 meters] *wide.*   36:15 Hebrew *30 cubits* [13.8 meters] *long and 4 cubits* [1.8 meters] *wide.*

the tent covering was made of one continuous piece. ¹⁹He completed the tent covering with a layer of tanned ram skins and a layer of fine goatskin leather.

²⁰For the framework of the Tabernacle, Bezalel constructed frames of acacia wood. ²¹Each frame was 15 feet high and 27 inches wide,* ²²with two pegs under each frame. All the frames were identical. ²³He made twenty of these frames to support the curtains on the south side of the Tabernacle. ²⁴He also made forty silver bases—two bases under each frame, with the pegs fitting securely into the bases. ²⁵For the north side of the Tabernacle, he made another twenty frames, ²⁶with their forty silver bases, two bases under each frame. ²⁷He made six frames for the rear—the west side of the Tabernacle—²⁸along with two additional frames to reinforce the rear corners of the Tabernacle. ²⁹These corner frames were matched at the bottom and firmly attached at the top with a single ring, forming a single corner unit. Both of these corner units were made the same way. ³⁰So there were eight frames at the rear of the Tabernacle, set in sixteen silver bases—two bases under each frame.

³¹Then he made crossbars of acacia wood to link the frames, five crossbars for the north side of the Tabernacle ³²and five for the south side. He also made five crossbars for the rear of the Tabernacle, which faced west. ³³He made the middle crossbar to attach halfway up the frames; it ran all the way from one end of the Tabernacle to the other. ³⁴He overlaid the frames with gold and made gold rings to hold the crossbars. Then he overlaid the crossbars with gold as well.

³⁵For the inside of the Tabernacle, Bezalel made a special curtain of finely woven linen. He decorated it with blue, purple, and scarlet thread and with skillfully embroidered cherubim. ³⁶For the curtain, he made four posts of acacia wood and four gold hooks. He overlaid the posts with gold and set them in four silver bases.

³⁷Then he made another curtain for the entrance to the sacred tent. He made it of finely woven linen and embroidered it with exquisite designs using blue, purple, and scarlet thread. ³⁸This curtain was hung on gold hooks attached to five posts. The posts with their decorated tops and hooks were overlaid

with gold, and the five bases were cast from bronze.

Building the Ark of the Covenant

37 Next Bezalel made the Ark of acacia wood—a sacred chest 45 inches long, 27 inches wide, and 27 inches high.* ²He overlaid it inside and outside with pure gold, and he ran a molding of gold all around it. ³He cast four gold rings and attached them to its four feet, two rings on each side. ⁴Then he made poles from acacia wood and overlaid them with gold. ⁵He inserted the poles into the rings at the sides of the Ark to carry it.

⁶Then he made the Ark's cover—the place of atonement—from pure gold. It was 45 inches long and 27 inches wide.* ⁷He made two cherubim from hammered gold and placed them on the two ends of the atonement cover. ⁸He molded the cherubim on each end of the atonement cover, making it all of one piece of gold. ⁹The cherubim faced each other and looked down on the atonement cover. With their wings spread above it, they protected it.

Building the Table

¹⁰Then Bezalel* made the table of acacia wood, 36 inches long, 18 inches wide, and 27 inches high.* ¹¹He overlaid it with pure gold and ran a gold molding around the edge. ¹²He decorated it with a 3-inch border* all around, and he ran a gold molding along the border. ¹³Then he cast four gold rings for the table and attached them at the four corners next to the four legs. ¹⁴The rings were attached near the border to hold the poles that were used to carry the table. ¹⁵He made these poles from acacia wood and overlaid them with gold. ¹⁶Then he made special containers of pure gold for the table—bowls, ladles, jars, and pitchers—to be used in pouring out liquid offerings.

Building the Lampstand

¹⁷Then Bezalel made the lampstand of pure, hammered gold. He made the entire lampstand and its decorations of one piece—the base, center stem, lamp cups, buds, and petals. ¹⁸The lampstand had six branches going out from the center stem, three on each side. ¹⁹Each of the six branches had three lamp cups shaped like almond blossoms, complete with buds and petals. ²⁰The center stem of

36:21 Hebrew 10 cubits [4.6 meters] high and 1.5 cubits [69 centimeters] wide.   37:1 Hebrew 2.5 cubits [115 centimeters] long, 1.5 cubits [69 centimeters] wide, and 1.5 cubits high.   37:6 Hebrew 2.5 cubits [115 centimeters] long and 1.5 cubits [69 centimeters] wide.   37:10a Hebrew he; also in 37:17, 25.   37:10b Hebrew 2 cubits [92 centimeters] long, 1 cubit [46 centimeters] wide, and 1.5 cubits [69 centimeters] high.   37:12 Hebrew a border of a handbreadth [8 centimeters].

the lampstand was crafted with four lamp cups shaped like almond blossoms, complete with buds and petals. 21There was an almond bud beneath each pair of branches where the six branches extended from the center stem, all made of one piece. 22The almond buds and branches were all of one piece with the center stem, and they were hammered from pure gold.

23He also made seven lamps for the lampstand, lamp snuffers, and trays, all of pure gold. 24The entire lampstand, along with its accessories, was made from 75 pounds* of pure gold.

Building the Incense Altar

25Then Bezalel made the incense altar of acacia wood. It was 18 inches square and 36 inches high,* with horns at the corners carved from the same piece of wood as the altar itself. 26He overlaid the top, sides, and horns of the altar with pure gold, and he ran a gold molding around the entire altar. 27He made two gold rings and attached them on opposite sides of the altar below the gold molding to hold the carrying poles. 28He made the poles of acacia wood and overlaid them with gold.

29Then he made the sacred anointing oil and the fragrant incense, using the techniques of a skilled incense maker.

Building the Altar of Burnt Offering

38 Next Bezalel* used acacia wood to construct the square altar of burnt offering. It was 7½ feet wide, 7½ feet long, and 4½ feet high.* 2He made horns for each of its four corners so that the horns and altar were all one piece. He overlaid the altar with bronze. 3Then he made all the altar utensils of bronze—the ash buckets, shovels, basins, meat forks, and firepans. 4Next he made a bronze grating and installed it halfway down the side of the altar, under the ledge. 5He cast four rings and attached them to the corners of the bronze grating to hold the carrying poles. 6He made the poles from acacia wood and overlaid them with bronze. 7He inserted the poles through the rings on the sides of the altar. The altar was hollow and was made from planks.

Building the Washbasin

8Bezalel made the bronze washbasin and its bronze stand from bronze mirrors donated by the women who served at the entrance of the Tabernacle.*

Building the Courtyard

9Then Bezalel made the courtyard, which was enclosed with curtains made of finely woven linen. On the south side the curtains were 150 feet long.* 10They were held up by twenty posts set securely in twenty bronze bases. He hung the curtains with silver hooks and rings. 11He made a similar set of curtains for the north side—150 feet of curtains held up by twenty posts set securely in bronze bases. He hung the curtains with silver hooks and rings. 12The curtains on the west end of the courtyard were 75 feet long,* hung with silver hooks and rings and supported by ten posts set into ten bases. 13The east end, the front, was also 75 feet long.

14The courtyard entrance was on the east end, flanked by two curtains. The curtain on the right side was 22½ feet long* and was supported by three posts set into three bases. 15The curtain on the left side was also 22½ feet long and was supported by three posts set into three bases. 16All the curtains used in the courtyard were made of finely woven linen. 17Each post had a bronze base, and all the hooks and rings were silver. The tops of the posts of the courtyard were overlaid with silver, and the rings to hold up the curtains were made of silver.

18He made the curtain for the entrance to the courtyard of finely woven linen, and he decorated it with beautiful embroidery in blue, purple, and scarlet thread. It was 30 feet long, and its height was 7½ feet,* just like the curtains of the courtyard walls. 19It was supported by four posts, each set securely in its own bronze base. The tops of the posts were overlaid with silver, and the hooks and rings were also made of silver.

20All the tent pegs used in the Tabernacle and courtyard were made of bronze.

Inventory of Materials

21This is an inventory of the materials used in building the Tabernacle of the Covenant.* The Levites compiled the figures, as Moses directed, and Ithamar son of Aaron the priest served as recorder. 22Bezalel son of Uri, grandson of Hur, of the tribe of Judah, made everything just as

37:24 Hebrew 1 talent [34 kilograms]. 37:25 Hebrew 1 cubit [46 centimeters] long and 1 cubit wide, a square, and 2 cubits [92 centimeters] high. 38:1a Hebrew he; also in 38:8, 9. 38:1b Hebrew 5 cubits [2.3 meters] wide, 5 cubits long, a square, and 3 cubits [1.4 meters] high. 38:8 Hebrew Tent of Meeting; also in 38:30. 38:9 Hebrew 100 cubits [46 meters]; also in 38:11. 38:12 Hebrew 50 cubits [23 meters]; also in 38:13. 38:14 Hebrew 15 cubits [6.9 meters]; also in 38:15. 38:18 Hebrew 20 cubits [9.2 meters] long and 5 cubits [2.3 meters] high. 38:21 Hebrew the Tabernacle, the Tabernacle of the Testimony.

the LORD had commanded Moses. ²³He was assisted by Oholiab son of Ahisamach, of the tribe of Dan, a craftsman expert at engraving, designing, and embroidering with blue, purple, and scarlet thread on fine linen cloth.

²⁴The people brought special offerings of gold totaling 2,193 pounds,* as measured by the weight of the sanctuary shekel. This gold was used throughout the Tabernacle.

²⁵The whole community of Israel gave 7,545 pounds* of silver, as measured by the weight of the sanctuary shekel. ²⁶This silver came from the tax collected from each man registered in the census. (The tax is one beka, which is half a shekel,* based on the sanctuary shekel.) The tax was collected from 603,550 men who had reached their twentieth birthday. ²⁷The hundred bases for the frames of the sanctuary walls and for the posts supporting the inner curtain required 7,500 pounds of silver, about 75 pounds for each base.* ²⁸The remaining 45 pounds* of silver was used to make the hooks and rings and to overlay the tops of the posts.

²⁹The people also brought as special offerings 5,310 pounds* of bronze, ³⁰which was used for casting the bases for the posts at the entrance to the Tabernacle, and for the bronze altar with its bronze grating and all the altar utensils. ³¹Bronze was also used to make the bases for the posts that supported the curtains around the courtyard, the bases for the curtain at the entrance of the courtyard, and all the tent pegs for the Tabernacle and the courtyard.

Clothing for the Priests

39 The craftsmen made beautiful sacred garments of blue, purple, and scarlet cloth—clothing for Aaron to wear while ministering in the Holy Place, just as the LORD had commanded Moses.

Making the Ephod

²Bezalel* made the ephod of finely woven linen and embroidered it with gold and with blue, purple, and scarlet thread. ³He made gold thread by hammering out thin sheets of gold and cutting it into fine strands. With great skill and care, he worked it into the fine linen with the blue, purple, and scarlet thread.

⁴The ephod consisted of two pieces, front and back, joined at the shoulders with two shoulder-pieces. ⁵The decorative sash was made of the same materials: finely woven linen embroidered with gold and with blue, purple, and scarlet thread, just as the LORD had commanded Moses. ⁶They mounted the two onyx stones in settings of gold filigree. The stones were engraved with the names of the tribes of Israel, just as a seal is engraved. ⁷He fastened these stones on the shoulder-pieces of the ephod as a reminder that the priest represents the people of Israel. All this was done just as the LORD had commanded Moses.

Making the Chestpiece

⁸Bezalel made the chestpiece with great skill and care. He made it to match the ephod, using finely woven linen embroidered with gold and with blue, purple, and scarlet thread. ⁹He made the chestpiece of a single piece of cloth folded to form a pouch nine inches* square. ¹⁰They mounted four rows of gemstones* on it. The first row contained a red carnelian, a pale-green peridot, and an emerald. ¹¹The second row contained a turquoise, a blue lapis lazuli, and a white moonstone. ¹²The third row contained an orange jacinth, an agate, and a purple amethyst. ¹³The fourth row contained a blue-green beryl, an onyx, and a green jasper. All these stones were set in gold filigree. ¹⁴Each stone represented one of the twelve sons of Israel, and the name of that tribe was engraved on it like a seal.

¹⁵To attach the chestpiece to the ephod, they made braided cords of pure gold thread. ¹⁶They also made two settings of gold filigree and two gold rings and attached them to the top corners of the chestpiece. ¹⁷They tied the two gold cords to the rings on the chestpiece. ¹⁸They tied the other ends of the cords to the gold settings on the shoulder-pieces of the ephod. ¹⁹Then they made two more gold rings and attached them to the inside edges of the chestpiece next to the ephod. ²⁰Then they made two more gold rings and attached them to the front of the ephod, below the shoulder-pieces, just above the knot where the decorative sash was fastened to the ephod. ²¹They attached the bottom rings of the chestpiece to the rings on the ephod with blue cords. In this way, the chestpiece was held securely to the ephod above the decorative sash. All this was done just as the LORD had commanded Moses.

38:24 Hebrew *29 talents and 730 shekels* [994 kilograms]. Each shekel weighed about 0.4 ounces or 11 grams.   38:25 Hebrew *100 talents and 1,775 shekels* [3,420 kilograms].   38:26 Or *0.2 ounces* [6 grams].   38:27 Hebrew *100 talents* [3,400 kilograms] *of silver, 1 talent* [34 kilograms] *for each base.*   38:28 Hebrew *1,775* [*shekels*] [20.2 kilograms].   38:29 Hebrew *70 talents and 2,400 shekels* [2,407 kilograms].   39:2 Hebrew *He*; also in 39:8, 22.   39:9 Hebrew *1 span* [23 centimeters].   39:10 The identification of some of these gemstones is uncertain.

Additional Clothing for the Priests

22Bezalel made the robe that is worn with the ephod from a single piece of blue woven cloth, 23with an opening for Aaron's head in the middle of it. The opening was reinforced with a woven collar* so it would not tear. 24They made pomegranates of blue, purple, and scarlet yarn, and attached them to the hem of the robe. 25They also made bells of pure gold and placed them between the pomegranates along the hem of the robe, 26with bells and pomegranates alternating all around the hem. This robe was to be worn whenever the priest ministered before the LORD, just as the LORD had commanded Moses.

27They made tunics for Aaron and his sons from fine linen cloth. 28The turban and the special head coverings were made of fine linen, and the undergarments were also made of finely woven linen. 29The sashes were made of finely woven linen and embroidered with blue, purple, and scarlet thread, just as the LORD had commanded Moses.

30Finally, they made the sacred medallion—the badge of holiness—of pure gold. They engraved it like a seal with these words: HOLY TO THE LORD. 31They attached the medallion with a blue cord to Aaron's turban, just as the LORD had commanded Moses.

Moses Inspects the Work

32And so at last the Tabernacle* was finished. The Israelites had done everything just as the LORD had commanded Moses. 33And they brought the entire Tabernacle to Moses:

the sacred tent with all its furnishings, clasps, frames, crossbars, posts, and bases;
34 the tent coverings of tanned ram skins and fine goatskin leather; the inner curtain to shield the Ark;
35 the Ark of the Covenant* and its carrying poles; the Ark's cover—the place of atonement;
36 the table and all its utensils; the Bread of the Presence;
37 the pure gold lampstand with its symmetrical lamp cups, all its accessories, and the olive oil for lighting;
38 the gold altar;

the anointing oil and fragrant incense; the curtain for the entrance of the sacred tent;
39 the bronze altar; the bronze grating and its carrying poles and utensils; the washbasin with its stand;
40 the curtains for the walls of the courtyard; the posts and their bases; the curtain for the entrance to the courtyard; the ropes and tent pegs; all the furnishings to be used in worship at the Tabernacle;
41 the beautifully stitched garments for the priests to wear while ministering in the Holy Place—the sacred garments for Aaron the priest, and the garments for his sons to wear as they minister as priests.

42So the people of Israel followed all of the LORD's instructions to Moses. 43Then Moses inspected all their work. When he found it had been done just as the LORD had commanded him, he blessed them.

The Tabernacle Completed

40 Then the LORD said to Moses, 2"Set up the Tabernacle* on the first day of the new year.* 3Place the Ark of the Covenant* inside, and install the inner curtain to enclose the Ark within the Most Holy Place. 4Then bring in the table, and arrange the utensils on it. And bring in the lampstand, and set up the lamps.

5"Place the gold incense altar in front of the Ark of the Covenant. Then hang the curtain at the entrance of the Tabernacle. 6Place the altar of burnt offering in front of the Tabernacle entrance. 7Set the washbasin between the Tabernacle* and the altar, and fill it with water. 8Then set up the courtyard around the outside of the tent, and hang the curtain for the courtyard entrance.

9"Take the anointing oil and anoint the Tabernacle and all its furnishings to consecrate them and make them holy. 10Anoint the altar of burnt offering and its utensils to consecrate them. Then the altar will become absolutely holy. 11Next anoint the washbasin and its stand to consecrate them.

12"Present Aaron and his sons at the entrance

39:23 The meaning of the Hebrew is uncertain.   39:32 Hebrew *the Tabernacle, the Tent of Meeting;* also in 39:40.   39:35 Or *Ark of the Testimony.*   40:2a Hebrew *the Tabernacle, the Tent of Meeting;* also in 40:6, 29.   40:2b Hebrew *the first day of the first month.* This day of the ancient Hebrew lunar calendar occurred in March or April.   40:3 Or *Ark of the Testimony;* also in 40:5, 21.   40:7 Hebrew *Tent of Meeting;* also in 40:12, 22, 24, 26, 30, 32, 34, 35.

of the Tabernacle, and wash them with water. 13Dress Aaron with the sacred garments and anoint him, consecrating him to serve me as a priest. 14Then present his sons and dress them in their tunics. 15Anoint them as you did their father, so they may also serve me as priests. With their anointing, Aaron's descendants are set apart for the priesthood forever, from generation to generation."

16Moses proceeded to do everything just as the LORD had commanded him. 17So the Tabernacle was set up on the first day of the first month of the second year. 18Moses erected the Tabernacle by setting down its bases, inserting the frames, attaching the crossbars, and setting up the posts. 19Then he spread the coverings over the Tabernacle framework and put on the protective layers, just as the LORD had commanded him.

20He took the stone tablets inscribed with the terms of the covenant and placed them* inside the Ark. Then he attached the carrying poles to the Ark, and he set the Ark's cover—the place of atonement—on top of it. 21Then he brought the Ark of the Covenant into the Tabernacle and hung the inner curtain to shield it from view, just as the LORD had commanded him.

22Next Moses placed the table in the Tabernacle, along the north side of the Holy Place, just outside the inner curtain. 23And he arranged the Bread of the Presence on the table before the LORD, just as the LORD had commanded him.

24He set the lampstand in the Tabernacle across from the table on the south side of the Holy Place. 25Then he lit the lamps in the LORD's presence, just as the LORD had

40:20 Hebrew *He placed the Testimony;* see note on 25:16.

commanded him. 26He also placed the gold incense altar in the Tabernacle, in the Holy Place in front of the inner curtain. 27On it he burned the fragrant incense, just as the LORD had commanded him.

28He hung the curtain at the entrance of the Tabernacle, 29and he placed the altar of burnt offering near the Tabernacle entrance. On it he offered a burnt offering and a grain offering, just as the LORD had commanded him.

30Next Moses placed the washbasin between the Tabernacle and the altar. He filled it with water so the priests could wash themselves. 31Moses and Aaron and Aaron's sons used water from it to wash their hands and feet. 32Whenever they approached the altar and entered the Tabernacle, they washed themselves, just as the LORD had commanded Moses.

33Then he hung the curtains forming the courtyard around the Tabernacle and the altar. And he set up the curtain at the entrance of the courtyard. So at last Moses finished the work.

The LORD's Glory Fills the Tabernacle

34Then the cloud covered the Tabernacle, and the glory of the LORD filled the Tabernacle. 35Moses could no longer enter the Tabernacle because the cloud had settled down over it, and the glory of the LORD filled the Tabernacle.

36Now whenever the cloud lifted from the Tabernacle, the people of Israel would set out on their journey, following it. 37But if the cloud did not rise, they remained where they were until it lifted. 38The cloud of the LORD hovered over the Tabernacle during the day, and at night fire glowed inside the cloud so the whole family of Israel could see it. This continued throughout all their journeys.

Leviticus

OUR ENTIRE LIVES should glorify God— from our religious worship to our daily tasks. With this in mind, the book of Leviticus was written as a handbook for the religious servants (the priests and Levites) of Israel. Leviticus gives detailed rules concerning the daily lives of the Israelites and special procedures for the worship of the Lord. It provides instructions for offering sacrifices. Leviticus also describes the proper methods for the Israelites to observe major festivals and holidays and for the priests to carry out the duties of their office.

- **Author:** Moses, according to Jewish tradition
- **Date Written:** Uncertain, perhaps between 1445 and 1444 BC
- **Purpose:** To outline the Levites' duties in worship and to teach the Israelites how to live holy lives
- **Themes:** Sacrifice and offering, proper worship, healthy living, the importance of holiness
- **Outline**
1:1–15:33 The sacrificial system
16:1-34 The great Day of Atonement
17:1–20:27 Various regulations
21:1–22:33 Rules for the priests
23:1–25:55 Rules concerning the festivals
26:1–27:34 Obedience, vows, and tithes

Procedures for the Burnt Offering

1 The Lord called to Moses from the Tabernacle* and said to him, ²"Give the following instructions to the people of Israel. When you present an animal as an offering to the Lord, you may take it from your herd of cattle or your flock of sheep and goats.

³"If the animal you present as a burnt offering is from the herd, it must be a male with no defects. Bring it to the entrance of the Tabernacle so you* may be accepted by the Lord. ⁴Lay your hand on the animal's head, and the Lord will accept its death in your place to purify you, making you right with him.* ⁵Then slaughter the young bull in the Lord's presence, and Aaron's sons, the priests, will present the animal's blood by splattering it against all sides of the altar that stands at the entrance to the Tabernacle. ⁶Then skin the animal and cut it into pieces. ⁷The sons of Aaron the priest will build a wood fire on the altar. ⁸They will arrange the pieces of the offering, including the head and fat, on the wood burning on the altar. ⁹But the internal organs and the legs must first be washed with water. Then the priest will burn the entire sacrifice on the altar

as a burnt offering. It is a special gift, a pleasing aroma to the Lord.

¹⁰"If the animal you present as a burnt offering is from the flock, it may be either a sheep or a goat, but it must be a male with no defects. ¹¹Slaughter the animal on the north side of the altar in the Lord's presence, and Aaron's sons, the priests, will splatter its blood against all sides of the altar. ¹²Then cut the animal in pieces, and the priests will arrange the pieces of the offering, including the head and fat, on the wood burning on the altar. ¹³But the internal organs and the legs must first be washed with water. Then the priest will burn the entire sacrifice on the altar as a burnt offering. It is a special gift, a pleasing aroma to the Lord.

¹⁴"If you present a bird as a burnt offering to the Lord, choose either a turtledove or a young pigeon. ¹⁵The priest will take the bird to the altar, wring off its head, and burn it on the altar. But first he must drain its blood against the side of the altar. ¹⁶The priest must also remove the crop and the feathers* and throw them in the ashes on the east side of the altar. ¹⁷Then, grasping the bird by its wings, the priest will tear the bird open, but without

1:1 Hebrew *Tent of Meeting;* also in 1:3, 5.   1:3 Or *it.*   1:4 Or *to make atonement for you.*   1:16 Or *the crop and its contents.* The meaning of the Hebrew is uncertain.

tearing it apart. Then he will burn it as a burnt offering on the wood burning on the altar. It is a special gift, a pleasing aroma to the LORD.

Procedures for the Grain Offering

2 "When you present grain as an offering to the LORD, the offering must consist of choice flour. You are to pour olive oil on it, sprinkle it with frankincense, [2]and bring it to Aaron's sons, the priests. The priest will scoop out a handful of the flour moistened with oil, together with all the frankincense, and burn this representative portion on the altar. It is a special gift, a pleasing aroma to the LORD. [3]The rest of the grain offering will then be given to Aaron and his sons. This offering will be considered a most holy part of the special gifts presented to the LORD.

[4]"If your offering is a grain offering baked in an oven, it must be made of choice flour, but without any yeast. It may be presented in the form of thin cakes mixed with olive oil or wafers spread with olive oil. [5]If your grain offering is cooked on a griddle, it must be made of choice flour mixed with olive oil but without any yeast. [6]Break it in pieces and pour olive oil on it; it is a grain offering. [7]If your grain offering is prepared in a pan, it must be made of choice flour and olive oil.

[8]"No matter how a grain offering for the LORD has been prepared, bring it to the priest, who will present it at the altar. [9]The priest will take a representative portion of the grain offering and burn it on the altar. It is a special gift, a pleasing aroma to the LORD. [10]The rest of the grain offering will then be given to Aaron and his sons as their food. This offering will be considered a most holy part of the special gifts presented to the LORD.

[11]"Do not use yeast in preparing any of the grain offerings you present to the LORD, because no yeast or honey may be burned as a special gift presented to the LORD. [12]You may add yeast and honey to an offering of the first crops of your harvest, but these must never be offered on the altar as a pleasing aroma to the LORD. [13]Season all your grain offerings with salt to remind you of God's eternal covenant. Never forget to add salt to your grain offerings.

[14]"If you present a grain offering to the LORD from the first portion of your harvest, bring fresh grain that is coarsely ground and roasted on a fire. [15]Put olive oil on this grain offering, and sprinkle it with frankincense. [16]The priest will take a representative portion of the grain moistened with oil, together with all the frankincense, and burn it as a special gift presented to the LORD.

Procedures for the Peace Offering

3 "If you present an animal from the herd as a peace offering to the LORD, it may be a male or a female, but it must have no defects. [2]Lay your hand on the animal's head, and slaughter it at the entrance of the Tabernacle.* Then Aaron's sons, the priests, will splatter its blood against all sides of the altar. [3]The priest must present part of this peace offering as a special gift to the LORD. This includes all the fat around the internal organs, [4]the two kidneys and the fat around them near the loins, and the long lobe of the liver. These must be removed with the kidneys, [5]and Aaron's sons will burn them on top of the burnt offering on the wood burning on the altar. It is a special gift, a pleasing aroma to the LORD.

[6]"If you present an animal from the flock as a peace offering to the LORD, it may be a male or a female, but it must have no defects. [7]If you present a sheep as your offering, bring it to the LORD, [8]lay your hand on its head, and slaughter it in front of the Tabernacle. Aaron's sons will then splatter the sheep's blood against all sides of the altar. [9]The priest must present the fat of this peace offering as a special gift to the LORD. This includes the fat of the broad tail cut off near the backbone, all the fat around the internal organs, [10]the two kidneys and the fat around them near the loins, and the long lobe of the liver. These must be removed with the kidneys, [11]and the priest will burn them on the altar. It is a special gift of food presented to the LORD.

[12]"If you present a goat as your offering, bring it to the LORD, [13]lay your hand on its head, and slaughter it in front of the Tabernacle. Aaron's sons will then splatter the goat's blood against all sides of the altar. [14]The priest must present part of this offering as a special gift to the LORD. This includes all the fat around the internal organs, [15]the two kidneys and the fat around them near the loins, and the long lobe of the liver. These must be removed with the kidneys, [16]and the priest will burn them on the altar. It is a special gift of food, a pleasing aroma to the LORD. All the fat belongs to the LORD.

[17]"You must never eat any fat or blood. This is a permanent law for you, and it must

3:2 Hebrew *Tent of Meeting;* also in 3:8, 13.

be observed from generation to generation, wherever you live."

Procedures for the Sin Offering

4 Then the LORD said to Moses, [2]"Give the following instructions to the people of Israel. This is how you are to deal with those who sin unintentionally by doing anything that violates one of the LORD's commands.

[3]"If the high priest* sins, bringing guilt upon the entire community, he must give a sin offering for the sin he has committed. He must present to the LORD a young bull with no defects. [4]He must bring the bull to the LORD at the entrance of the Tabernacle,* lay his hand on the bull's head, and slaughter it before the LORD. [5]The high priest will then take some of the bull's blood into the Tabernacle, [6]dip his finger in the blood, and sprinkle it seven times before the LORD in front of the inner curtain of the sanctuary. [7]The priest will then put some of the blood on the horns of the altar for fragrant incense that stands in the LORD's presence inside the Tabernacle. He will pour out the rest of the bull's blood at the base of the altar for burnt offerings at the entrance of the Tabernacle. [8]Then the priest must remove all the fat of the bull to be offered as a sin offering. This includes all the fat around the internal organs, [9]the two kidneys and the fat around them near the loins, and the long lobe of the liver. He must remove these along with the kidneys, [10]just as he does with cattle offered as a peace offering, and burn them on the altar of burnt offerings. [11]But he must take whatever is left of the bull—its hide, meat, head, legs, internal organs, and dung—[12]and carry it away to a place outside the camp that is ceremonially clean, the place where the ashes are dumped. There, on the ash heap, he will burn it on a wood fire.

[13]"If the entire Israelite community sins by violating one of the LORD's commands, but the people don't realize it, they are still guilty. [14]When they become aware of their sin, the people must bring a young bull as an offering for their sin and present it before the Tabernacle. [15]The elders of the community must then lay their hands on the bull's head and slaughter it before the LORD. [16]The high priest will then take some of the bull's blood into the Tabernacle, [17]dip his finger in the blood, and sprinkle it seven times before the LORD in front of the inner curtain. [18]He will then put some of the blood on the horns of the altar for fragrant incense that stands in the LORD's presence inside the Tabernacle. He will pour out the rest of the blood at the base of the altar for burnt offerings at the entrance of the Tabernacle. [19]Then the priest must remove all the animal's fat and burn it on the altar, [20]just as he does with the bull offered as a sin offering for the high priest. Through this process, the priest will purify the people, making them right with the LORD,* and they will be forgiven. [21]Then the priest must take what is left of the bull and carry it outside the camp and burn it there, just as is done with the sin offering for the high priest. This offering is for the sin of the entire congregation of Israel.

[22]"If one of Israel's leaders sins by violating one of the commands of the LORD his God but doesn't realize it, he is still guilty. [23]When he becomes aware of his sin, he must bring as his offering a male goat with no defects. [24]He must lay his hand on the goat's head and slaughter it at the place where burnt offerings are slaughtered before the LORD. This is an offering for his sin. [25]Then the priest will dip his finger in the blood of the sin offering and put it on the horns of the altar for burnt offerings. He will pour out the rest of the blood at the base of the altar. [26]Then he must burn all the goat's fat on the altar, just as he does with the peace offering. Through this process, the priest will purify the leader from his sin, making him right with the LORD, and he will be forgiven.

[27]"If any of the common people sin by violating one of the LORD's commands, but they don't realize it, they are still guilty. [28]When they become aware of their sin, they must bring as an offering for their sin a female goat with no defects. [29]They must lay a hand on the head of the sin offering and slaughter it at the place where burnt offerings are slaughtered. [30]Then the priest will dip his finger in the blood and put it on the horns of the altar for burnt offerings. He will pour out the rest of the blood at the base of the altar. [31]Then he must remove all the goat's fat, just as he does with the fat of the peace offering. He will burn the fat on the altar, and it will be a pleasing aroma to the LORD. Through this process, the priest will purify the people, making them right with the LORD, and they will be forgiven.

[32]"If the people bring a sheep as their sin offering, it must be a female with no defects. [33]They must lay a hand on the head of the sin offering and slaughter it at the place where

---

4:3 Hebrew *the anointed priest;* also in 4:5, 16.   4:4 Hebrew *Tent of Meeting;* also in 4:5, 7, 14, 16, 18.   4:20 Or *will make atonement for the people;* similarly in 4:26, 31, 35.

burnt offerings are slaughtered. ³⁴Then the priest will dip his finger in the blood of the sin offering and put it on the horns of the altar for burnt offerings. He will pour out the rest of the blood at the base of the altar. ³⁵Then he must remove all the sheep's fat, just as he does with the fat of a sheep presented as a peace offering. He will burn the fat on the altar on top of the special gifts presented to the LORD. Through this process, the priest will purify the people from their sin, making them right with the LORD, and they will be forgiven.

Sins Requiring a Sin Offering

5 "If you are called to testify about something you have seen or that you know about, it is sinful to refuse to testify, and you will be punished for your sin.

²"Or suppose you unknowingly touch something that is ceremonially unclean, such as the carcass of an unclean animal. When you realize what you have done, you must admit your defilement and your guilt. This is true whether it is a wild animal, a domestic animal, or an animal that scurries along the ground.

³"Or suppose you unknowingly touch something that makes a person unclean. When you realize what you have done, you must admit your guilt.

⁴"Or suppose you make a foolish vow of any kind, whether its purpose is for good or for bad. When you realize its foolishness, you must admit your guilt.

⁵"When you become aware of your guilt in any of these ways, you must confess your sin. ⁶Then you must bring to the LORD as the penalty for your sin a female from the flock, either a sheep or a goat. This is a sin offering with which the priest will purify you from your sin, making you right with the LORD.*

⁷"But if you cannot afford to bring a sheep, you may bring to the LORD two turtledoves or two young pigeons as the penalty for your sin. One of the birds will be for a sin offering, and the other for a burnt offering. ⁸You must bring them to the priest, who will present the first bird as the sin offering. He will wring its neck but without severing its head from the body. ⁹Then he will sprinkle some of the blood of the sin offering against the sides of the altar, and the rest of the blood will be drained out at the base of the altar. This is an offering for sin. ¹⁰The priest will then prepare the second bird as a burnt offering, following

all the procedures that have been prescribed. Through this process the priest will purify you from your sin, making you right with the LORD, and you will be forgiven.

¹¹"If you cannot afford to bring two turtledoves or two young pigeons, you may bring two quarts* of choice flour for your sin offering. Since it is an offering for sin, you must not moisten it with olive oil or put any frankincense on it. ¹²Take the flour to the priest, who will scoop out a handful as a representative portion. He will burn it on the altar on top of the special gifts presented to the LORD. It is an offering for sin. ¹³Through this process, the priest will purify those who are guilty of any of these sins, making them right with the LORD, and they will be forgiven. The rest of the flour will belong to the priest, just as with the grain offering."

Procedures for the Guilt Offering

¹⁴Then the LORD said to Moses, ¹⁵"If one of you commits a sin by unintentionally defiling the LORD's sacred property, you must bring a guilt offering to the LORD. The offering must be your own ram with no defects, or you may buy one of equal value with silver, as measured by the weight of the sanctuary shekel.* ¹⁶You must make restitution for the sacred property you have harmed by paying for the loss, plus an additional 20 percent. When you give the payment to the priest, he will purify you with the ram sacrificed as a guilt offering, making you right with the LORD, and you will be forgiven.

¹⁷"Suppose you sin by violating one of the LORD's commands. Even if you are unaware of what you have done, you are guilty and will be punished for your sin. ¹⁸For a guilt offering, you must bring to the priest your own ram with no defects, or you may buy one of equal value. Through this process the priest will purify you from your unintentional sin, making you right with the LORD, and you will be forgiven. ¹⁹This is a guilt offering, for you have been guilty of an offense against the LORD."

Sins Requiring a Guilt Offering

6 ¹*Then the LORD said to Moses, ²"Suppose one of you sins against your associate and is unfaithful to the LORD. Suppose you cheat in a deal involving a security deposit, or you steal or commit fraud, ³or you find lost property and lie about it, or you lie while swearing to tell the truth, or you commit any other such sin. ⁴If

---

5:6 Or *will make atonement for you for your sin;* similarly in 5:10, 13, 16, 18.   5:11 Hebrew ⅒ *of an ephah* [2.2 liters].   5:15 Each shekel was about 0.4 ounces or 11 grams in weight.   6:1 Verses 6:1-7 are numbered 5:20-26 in Hebrew text.

you have sinned in any of these ways, you are guilty. You must give back whatever you stole, or the money you took by extortion, or the security deposit, or the lost property you found, [5]or anything obtained by swearing falsely. You must make restitution by paying the full price plus an additional 20 percent to the person you have harmed. On the same day you must present a guilt offering. [6]As a guilt offering to the LORD, you must bring to the priest your own ram with no defects, or you may buy one of equal value. [7]Through this process, the priest will purify you before the LORD, making you right with him,* and you will be forgiven for any of these sins you have committed."

Further Instructions for the Burnt Offering

[8]*Then the LORD said to Moses, [9]"Give Aaron and his sons the following instructions regarding the burnt offering. The burnt offering must be left on top of the altar until the next morning, and the fire on the altar must be kept burning all night. [10]In the morning, after the priest on duty has put on his official linen clothing and linen undergarments, he must clean out the ashes of the burnt offering and put them beside the altar. [11]Then he must take off these garments, change back into his regular clothes, and carry the ashes outside the camp to a place that is ceremonially clean. [12]Meanwhile, the fire on the altar must be kept burning; it must never go out. Each morning the priest will add fresh wood to the fire and arrange the burnt offering on it. He will then burn the fat of the peace offerings on it. [13]Remember, the fire must be kept burning on the altar at all times. It must never go out.

Further Instructions for the Grain Offering

[14]"These are the instructions regarding the grain offering. Aaron's sons must present this offering to the LORD in front of the altar. [15]The priest on duty will take from the grain offering a handful of the choice flour moistened with olive oil, together with all the frankincense. He will burn this representative portion on the altar as a pleasing aroma to the LORD. [16]Aaron and his sons may eat the rest of the flour, but it must be baked without yeast and eaten in a sacred place within the courtyard of the Tabernacle.* [17]Remember, it must never be prepared with yeast. I have given it to the priests as their share of the special gifts presented to me.

Like the sin offering and the guilt offering, it is most holy. [18]Any of Aaron's male descendants may eat from the special gifts presented to the LORD. This is their permanent right from generation to generation. Anyone or anything that touches these offerings will become holy."

Procedures for the Ordination Offering

[19]Then the LORD said to Moses, [20]"On the day Aaron and his sons are anointed, they must present to the LORD the standard grain offering of two quarts* of choice flour, half to be offered in the morning and half to be offered in the evening. [21]It must be carefully mixed with olive oil and cooked on a griddle. Then slice* this grain offering and present it as a pleasing aroma to the LORD. [22]In each generation, the high priest* who succeeds Aaron must prepare this same offering. It belongs to the LORD and must be burned up completely. This is a permanent law. [23]All such grain offerings of a priest must be burned up entirely. None of it may be eaten."

Further Instructions for the Sin Offering

[24]Then the LORD said to Moses, [25]"Give Aaron and his sons the following instructions regarding the sin offering. The animal given as an offering for sin is a most holy offering, and it must be slaughtered in the LORD's presence at the place where the burnt offerings are slaughtered. [26]The priest who offers the sacrifice as a sin offering must eat his portion in a sacred place within the courtyard of the Tabernacle. [27]Anyone or anything that touches the sacrificial meat will become holy. If any of the sacrificial blood spatters on a person's clothing, the soiled garment must be washed in a sacred place. [28]If a clay pot is used to boil the sacrificial meat, it must then be broken. If a bronze pot is used, it must be scoured and thoroughly rinsed with water. [29]Any male from a priest's family may eat from this offering; it is most holy. [30]But the offering for sin may not be eaten if its blood was brought into the Tabernacle as an offering for purification* in the Holy Place. It must be completely burned with fire.

Further Instructions for the Guilt Offering

7 "These are the instructions for the guilt offering. It is most holy. [2]The animal sacrificed as a guilt offering must be slaughtered at the place where the burnt offerings are

---

6:7 Or *will make atonement for you before the LORD.*   6:8 Verses 6:8-30 are numbered 6:1-23 in Hebrew text.   6:16 Hebrew *Tent of Meeting;* also in 6:26, 30.   6:20 Hebrew *⅒ of an ephah* [2.2 liters].   6:21 The meaning of this Hebrew term is uncertain.   6:22 Hebrew *the anointed priest.*   6:30 Or *an offering to make atonement.*

slaughtered, and its blood must be splattered against all sides of the altar. ³The priest will then offer all its fat on the altar, including the fat of the broad tail, the fat around the internal organs, ⁴the two kidneys and the fat around them near the loins, and the long lobe of the liver. These are to be removed with the kidneys, ⁵and the priests will burn them on the altar as a special gift presented to the LORD. This is the guilt offering. ⁶Any male from a priest's family may eat the meat. It must be eaten in a sacred place, for it is most holy.

⁷"The same instructions apply to both the guilt offering and the sin offering. Both belong to the priest who uses them to purify someone, making that person right with the LORD.* ⁸In the case of the burnt offering, the priest may keep the hide of the sacrificed animal. ⁹Any grain offering that has been baked in an oven, prepared in a pan, or cooked on a griddle belongs to the priest who presents it. ¹⁰All other grain offerings, whether made of dry flour or flour moistened with olive oil, are to be shared equally among all the priests, the descendants of Aaron.

Further Instructions for the Peace Offering

¹¹"These are the instructions regarding the different kinds of peace offerings that may be presented to the LORD. ¹²If you present your peace offering as an expression of thanksgiving, the usual animal sacrifice must be accompanied by various kinds of bread made without yeast—thin cakes mixed with olive oil, wafers spread with oil, and cakes made of choice flour mixed with olive oil. ¹³This peace offering of thanksgiving must also be accompanied by loaves of bread made with yeast. ¹⁴One of each kind of bread must be presented as a gift to the LORD. It will then belong to the priest who splatters the blood of the peace offering against the altar. ¹⁵The meat of the peace offering of thanksgiving must be eaten on the same day it is offered. None of it may be saved for the next morning.

¹⁶"If you bring an offering to fulfill a vow or as a voluntary offering, the meat must be eaten on the same day the sacrifice is offered, but whatever is left over may be eaten on the second day. ¹⁷Any meat left over until the third day must be completely burned up. ¹⁸If any of the meat from the peace offering is eaten on the third day, the person who presented it will not be accepted by the LORD. You will receive no credit for offering it. By then the meat will

be contaminated; if you eat it, you will be punished for your sin.

¹⁹"Meat that touches anything ceremonially unclean may not be eaten; it must be completely burned up. The rest of the meat may be eaten, but only by people who are ceremonially clean. ²⁰If you are ceremonially unclean and you eat meat from a peace offering that was presented to the LORD, you will be cut off from the community. ²¹If you touch anything that is unclean (whether it is human defilement or an unclean animal or any other unclean, detestable thing) and then eat meat from a peace offering presented to the LORD, you will be cut off from the community."

The Forbidden Blood and Fat

²²Then the LORD said to Moses, ²³"Give the following instructions to the people of Israel. You must never eat fat, whether from cattle, sheep, or goats. ²⁴The fat of an animal found dead or torn to pieces by wild animals must never be eaten, though it may be used for any other purpose. ²⁵Anyone who eats fat from an animal presented as a special gift to the LORD will be cut off from the community. ²⁶No matter where you live, you must never consume the blood of any bird or animal. ²⁷Anyone who consumes blood will be cut off from the community."

A Portion for the Priests

²⁸Then the LORD said to Moses, ²⁹"Give the following instructions to the people of Israel. When you present a peace offering to the LORD, bring part of it as a gift to the LORD. ³⁰Present it to the LORD with your own hands as a special gift to the LORD. Bring the fat of the animal, together with the breast, and lift up the breast as a special offering to the LORD. ³¹Then the priest will burn the fat on the altar, but the breast will belong to Aaron and his descendants. ³²Give the right thigh of your peace offering to the priest as a gift. ³³The right thigh must always be given to the priest who offers the blood and the fat of the peace offering. ³⁴For I have reserved the breast of the special offering and the right thigh of the sacred offering for the priests. It is the permanent right of Aaron and his descendants to share in the peace offerings brought by the people of Israel. ³⁵This is their rightful share. The special gifts presented to the LORD have been reserved for Aaron and his descendants from the time they were set apart to serve the LORD as priests. ³⁶On the day they were anointed, the LORD commanded the

7:7 Or to make atonement.

Israelites to give these portions to the priests as their permanent share from generation to generation."

37These are the instructions for the burnt offering, the grain offering, the sin offering, and the guilt offering, as well as the ordination offering and the peace offering. 38The LORD gave these instructions to Moses on Mount Sinai when he commanded the Israelites to present their offerings to the LORD in the wilderness of Sinai.

Ordination of the Priests

8 Then the LORD said to Moses, 2"Bring Aaron and his sons, along with their sacred garments, the anointing oil, the bull for the sin offering, the two rams, and the basket of bread made without yeast, 3and call the entire community of Israel together at the entrance of the Tabernacle.*"

4So Moses followed the LORD's instructions, and the whole community assembled at the Tabernacle entrance. 5Moses announced to them, "This is what the LORD has commanded us to do!" 6Then he presented Aaron and his sons and washed them with water. 7He put the official tunic on Aaron and tied the sash around his waist. He dressed him in the robe, placed the ephod on him, and attached the ephod securely with its decorative sash. 8Then Moses placed the chestpiece on Aaron and put the Urim and the Thummim inside it. 9He placed the turban on Aaron's head and attached the gold medallion—the badge of holiness—to the front of the turban, just as the LORD had commanded him.

10Then Moses took the anointing oil and anointed the Tabernacle and everything in it, making them holy. 11He sprinkled the oil on the altar seven times, anointing it and all its utensils, as well as the washbasin and its stand, making them holy. 12Then he poured some of the anointing oil on Aaron's head, anointing him and making him holy for his work. 13Next Moses presented Aaron's sons. He clothed them in their tunics, tied their sashes around them, and put their special head coverings on them, just as the LORD had commanded him.

14Then Moses presented the bull for the sin offering. Aaron and his sons laid their hands on the bull's head, 15and Moses slaughtered it. Moses took some of the blood, and with his finger he put it on the four horns of the altar

to purify it. He poured out the rest of the blood at the base of the altar. Through this process, he made the altar holy by purifying it.* 16Then Moses took all the fat around the internal organs, the long lobe of the liver, and the two kidneys and the fat around them, and he burned it all on the altar. 17He took the rest of the bull, including its hide, meat, and dung, and burned it on a fire outside the camp, just as the LORD had commanded him.

18Then Moses presented the ram for the burnt offering. Aaron and his sons laid their hands on the ram's head, 19and Moses slaughtered it. Then Moses took the ram's blood and splattered it against all sides of the altar. 20Then he cut the ram into pieces, and he burned the head, some of its pieces, and the fat on the altar. 21After washing the internal organs and the legs with water, Moses burned the entire ram on the altar as a burnt offering. It was a pleasing aroma, a special gift presented to the LORD, just as the LORD had commanded him.

22Then Moses presented the other ram, which was the ram of ordination. Aaron and his sons laid their hands on the ram's head, 23and Moses slaughtered it. Then Moses took some of its blood and applied it to the lobe of Aaron's right ear, the thumb of his right hand, and the big toe of his right foot. 24Next Moses presented Aaron's sons and applied some of the blood to the lobes of their right ears, the thumbs of their right hands, and the big toes of their right feet. He then splattered the rest of the blood against all sides of the altar.

25Next Moses took the fat, including the fat of the broad tail, the fat around the internal organs, the long lobe of the liver, and the two kidneys and the fat around them, along with the right thigh. 26On top of these he placed a thin cake of bread made without yeast, a cake of bread mixed with olive oil, and a wafer spread with olive oil. All these were taken from the basket of bread made without yeast that was placed in the LORD's presence. 27He put all these in the hands of Aaron and his sons, and he lifted these gifts as a special offering to the LORD. 28Moses then took all the offerings back from them and burned them on the altar on top of the burnt offering. This was the ordination offering. It was a pleasing aroma, a special gift presented to the LORD. 29Then Moses took the breast and lifted it up as a special offering to the LORD. This was Moses' portion of the ram of ordination, just as the LORD had commanded him.

8:3 Hebrew *Tent of Meeting;* also in 8:4, 31, 33, 35.   8:15 Or *by making atonement for it;* or *that offerings for purification might be made on it.*

³⁰Next Moses took some of the anointing oil and some of the blood that was on the altar, and he sprinkled them on Aaron and his garments and on his sons and their garments. In this way, he made Aaron and his sons and their garments holy.

³¹Then Moses said to Aaron and his sons, "Boil the remaining meat of the offerings at the Tabernacle entrance, and eat it there, along with the bread that is in the basket of offerings for the ordination, just as I commanded when I said, 'Aaron and his sons will eat it.' ³²Any meat or bread that is left over must then be burned up. ³³You must not leave the Tabernacle entrance for seven days, for that is when the ordination ceremony will be completed. ³⁴Everything we have done today was commanded by the LORD in order to purify you, making you right with him.* ³⁵Now stay at the entrance of the Tabernacle day and night for seven days, and do everything the LORD requires. If you fail to do this, you will die, for this is what the LORD has commanded." ³⁶So Aaron and his sons did everything the LORD had commanded through Moses.

The Priests Begin Their Work

9 After the ordination ceremony, on the eighth day, Moses called together Aaron and his sons and the elders of Israel. ²He said to Aaron, "Take a young bull for a sin offering and a ram for a burnt offering, both without defects, and present them to the LORD. ³Then tell the Israelites, 'Take a male goat for a sin offering, and take a calf and a lamb, both a year old and without defects, for a burnt offering. ⁴Also take a bull* and a ram for a peace offering and flour moistened with olive oil for a grain offering. Present all these offerings to the LORD because the LORD will appear to you today.'"

⁵So the people presented all these things at the entrance of the Tabernacle,* just as Moses had commanded. Then the whole community came forward and stood before the LORD. ⁶And Moses said, "This is what the LORD has commanded you to do so that the glory of the LORD may appear to you."

⁷Then Moses said to Aaron, "Come to the altar and sacrifice your sin offering and your burnt offering to purify yourself and the people. Then present the offerings of the people to purify them, making them right with the LORD,* just as he has commanded."

⁸So Aaron went to the altar and slaughtered the calf as a sin offering for himself. ⁹His sons brought him the blood, and he dipped his finger in it and put it on the horns of the altar. He poured out the rest of the blood at the base of the altar. ¹⁰Then he burned on the altar the fat, the kidneys, and the long lobe of the liver from the sin offering, just as the LORD had commanded Moses. ¹¹The meat and the hide, however, he burned outside the camp.

¹²Next Aaron slaughtered the animal for the burnt offering. His sons brought him the blood, and he splattered it against all sides of the altar. ¹³Then they handed him each piece of the burnt offering, including the head, and he burned them on the altar. ¹⁴Then he washed the internal organs and the legs and burned them on the altar along with the rest of the burnt offering.

¹⁵Next Aaron presented the offerings of the people. He slaughtered the people's goat and presented it as an offering for their sin, just as he had first done with the offering for his own sin. ¹⁶Then he presented the burnt offering and sacrificed it in the prescribed way. ¹⁷He also presented the grain offering, burning a handful of the flour mixture on the altar, in addition to the regular burnt offering for the morning.

¹⁸Then Aaron slaughtered the bull and the ram for the people's peace offering. His sons brought him the blood, and he splattered it against all sides of the altar. ¹⁹Then he took the fat of the bull and the ram—the fat of the broad tail and from around the internal organs—along with the kidneys and the long lobes of the livers. ²⁰He placed these fat portions on top of the breasts of these animals and burned them on the altar. ²¹Aaron then lifted up the breasts and right thighs as a special offering to the LORD, just as Moses had commanded.

²²After that, Aaron raised his hands toward the people and blessed them. Then, after presenting the sin offering, the burnt offering, and the peace offering, he stepped down from the altar. ²³Then Moses and Aaron went into the Tabernacle, and when they came back out, they blessed the people again, and the glory of the LORD appeared to the whole community. ²⁴Fire blazed forth from the LORD's presence and consumed the burnt offering and the fat on the altar. When the people saw this, they shouted with joy and fell face down on the ground.

8:34 Or *to make atonement for you.*   9:4 Or *cow;* also in 9:18, 19. 9:5 Hebrew *Tent of Meeting;* also in 9:23.   9:7 Or *to make atonement for them.*

The Sin of Nadab and Abihu

10 Aaron's sons Nadab and Abihu put coals of fire in their incense burners and sprinkled incense over them. In this way, they disobeyed the Lord by burning before him the wrong kind of fire, different than he had commanded. ²So fire blazed forth from the Lord's presence and burned them up, and they died there before the Lord.

³Then Moses said to Aaron, "This is what the Lord meant when he said,

'I will display my holiness
    through those who come near me.
I will display my glory
    before all the people.'"

And Aaron was silent.

⁴Then Moses called for Mishael and Elzaphan, Aaron's cousins, the sons of Aaron's uncle Uzziel. He said to them, "Come forward and carry away the bodies of your relatives from in front of the sanctuary to a place outside the camp." ⁵So they came forward and picked them up by their garments and carried them out of the camp, just as Moses had commanded.

⁶Then Moses said to Aaron and his sons Eleazar and Ithamar, "Do not show grief by leaving your hair uncombed* or by tearing your clothes. If you do, you will die, and the Lord's anger will strike the whole community of Israel. However, the rest of the Israelites, your relatives, may mourn because of the Lord's fiery destruction of Nadab and Abihu. ⁷But you must not leave the entrance of the Tabernacle* or you will die, for you have been anointed with the Lord's anointing oil." So they did as Moses commanded.

Instructions for Priestly Conduct

⁸Then the Lord said to Aaron, ⁹"You and your descendants must never drink wine or any other alcoholic drink before going into the Tabernacle. If you do, you will die. This is a permanent law for you, and it must be observed from generation to generation. ¹⁰You must distinguish between what is sacred and what is common, between what is ceremonially unclean and what is clean. ¹¹And you must teach the Israelites all the decrees that the Lord has given them through Moses."

¹²Then Moses said to Aaron and his remaining sons, Eleazar and Ithamar, "Take what is left of the grain offering after a portion has been presented as a special gift to the Lord, and eat it beside the altar. Make sure it contains no yeast, for it is most holy. ¹³You must eat it in a sacred place, for it has been given to you and your descendants as your portion of the special gifts presented to the Lord. These are the commands I have been given. ¹⁴But the breast and thigh that were lifted up as a special offering may be eaten in any place that is ceremonially clean. These parts have been given to you and your descendants as your portion of the peace offerings presented by the people of Israel. ¹⁵You must lift up the thigh and breast as a special offering to the Lord, along with the fat of the special gifts. These parts will belong to you and your descendants as your permanent right, just as the Lord has commanded."

¹⁶Moses then asked them what had happened to the goat of the sin offering. When he discovered it had been burned up, he became very angry with Eleazar and Ithamar, Aaron's remaining sons. ¹⁷"Why didn't you eat the sin offering in the sacred area?" he demanded. "It is a holy offering! The Lord has given it to you to remove the guilt of the community and to purify the people, making them right with the Lord.* ¹⁸Since the animal's blood was not brought into the Holy Place, you should have eaten the meat in the sacred area as I ordered you."

¹⁹Then Aaron answered Moses, "Today my sons presented both their sin offering and their burnt offering to the Lord. And yet this tragedy has happened to me. If I had eaten the people's sin offering on such a tragic day as this, would the Lord have been pleased?" ²⁰And when Moses heard this, he was satisfied.

Ceremonially Clean and Unclean Animals

11 Then the Lord said to Moses and Aaron, ²"Give the following instructions to the people of Israel.

"Of all the land animals, these are the ones you may use for food. ³You may eat any animal that has completely split hooves and chews the cud. ⁴You may not, however, eat the following animals* that have split hooves or that chew the cud, but not both. The camel chews the cud but does not have split hooves, so it is ceremonially unclean for you. ⁵The hyrax* chews the cud but does not have split hooves, so it is unclean. ⁶The hare chews the cud but does not have split hooves, so it is unclean. ⁷The pig

---

10:6 Or *by uncovering your heads.*   10:7 Hebrew *Tent of Meeting;* also in 10:9.   10:17 Or *to make atonement for the people before the Lord.*   11:4 The identification of some of the animals, birds, and insects in this chapter is uncertain.   11:5 Or *coney,* or *rock badger.*

has evenly split hooves but does not chew the cud, so it is unclean. 8You may not eat the meat of these animals or even touch their carcasses. They are ceremonially unclean for you.

9"Of all the marine animals, these are ones you may use for food. You may eat anything from the water if it has both fins and scales, whether taken from salt water or from streams. 10But you must never eat animals from the sea or from rivers that do not have both fins and scales. They are detestable to you. This applies both to little creatures that live in shallow water and to all creatures that live in deep water. 11They will always be detestable to you. You must never eat their meat or even touch their dead bodies. 12Any marine animal that does not have both fins and scales is detestable to you.

13"These are the birds that are detestable to you. You must never eat them: the griffon vulture, the bearded vulture, the black vulture, 14the kite, falcons of all kinds, 15ravens of all kinds, 16the eagle owl, the short-eared owl, the seagull, hawks of all kinds, 17the little owl, the cormorant, the great owl, 18the barn owl, the desert owl, the Egyptian vulture, 19the stork, herons of all kinds, the hoopoe, and the bat.

20"You must not eat winged insects that walk along the ground; they are detestable to you. 21You may, however, eat winged insects that walk along the ground and have jointed legs so they can jump. 22The insects you are permitted to eat include all kinds of locusts, bald locusts, crickets, and grasshoppers. 23All other winged insects that walk along the ground are detestable to you.

24"The following creatures will make you ceremonially unclean. If any of you touch their carcasses, you will be defiled until evening. 25If you pick up their carcasses, you must wash your clothes, and you will remain defiled until evening.

26"Any animal that has split hooves that are not evenly divided or that does not chew the cud is unclean for you. If you touch the carcass of such an animal, you will be defiled. 27Of the animals that walk on all fours, those that have paws are unclean. If you touch the carcass of such an animal, you will be defiled until evening. 28If you pick up its carcass, you must wash your clothes, and you will remain defiled until evening. These animals are unclean for you.

29"Of the small animals that scurry along the ground, these are unclean for you: the mole rat, the rat, large lizards of all kinds, 30the gecko, the monitor lizard, the common lizard, the sand lizard, and the chameleon. 31All these small animals are unclean for you. If any of you touch the dead body of such an animal, you will be defiled until evening. 32If such an animal dies and falls on something, that object will be unclean. This is true whether the object is made of wood, cloth, leather, or burlap. Whatever its use, you must dip it in water, and it will remain defiled until evening. After that, it will be ceremonially clean and may be used again.

33"If such an animal falls into a clay pot, everything in the pot will be defiled, and the pot must be smashed. 34If the water from such a container spills on any food, the food will be defiled. And any beverage in such a container will be defiled. 35Any object on which the carcass of such an animal falls will be defiled. If it is an oven or hearth, it must be destroyed, for it is defiled, and you must treat it accordingly.

36"However, if the carcass of such an animal falls into a spring or a cistern, the water will still be clean. But anyone who touches the carcass will be defiled. 37If the carcass falls on seed grain to be planted in the field, the seed will still be considered clean. 38But if the seed is wet when the carcass falls on it, the seed will be defiled.

39"If an animal you are permitted to eat dies and you touch its carcass, you will be defiled until evening. 40If you eat any of its meat or carry away its carcass, you must wash your clothes, and you will remain defiled until evening.

41"All small animals that scurry along the ground are detestable, and you must never eat them. 42This includes all animals that slither along on their bellies, as well as those with four legs and those with many feet. All such animals that scurry along the ground are detestable, and you must never eat them. 43Do not defile yourselves by touching them. You must not make yourselves ceremonially unclean because of them. 44For I am the LORD your God. You must consecrate yourselves and be holy, because I am holy. So do not defile yourselves with any of these small animals that scurry along the ground. 45For I, the LORD, am the one who brought you up from the land of Egypt, that I might be your God. Therefore, you must be holy because I am holy.

46"These are the instructions regarding land animals, birds, marine creatures, and animals that scurry along the ground. 47By these instructions you will know what is unclean and clean, and which animals may be eaten and which may not be eaten."

Purification after Childbirth

12 The LORD said to Moses, [2]"Give the following instructions to the people of Israel. If a woman becomes pregnant and gives birth to a son, she will be ceremonially unclean for seven days, just as she is unclean during her menstrual period. [3]On the eighth day the boy's foreskin must be circumcised. [4]After waiting thirty-three days, she will be purified from the bleeding of childbirth. During this time of purification, she must not touch anything that is set apart as holy. And she must not enter the sanctuary until her time of purification is over. [5]If a woman gives birth to a daughter, she will be ceremonially unclean for two weeks, just as she is unclean during her menstrual period. After waiting sixty-six days, she will be purified from the bleeding of childbirth.

[6]"When the time of purification is completed for either a son or a daughter, the woman must bring a one-year-old lamb for a burnt offering and a young pigeon or turtledove for a purification offering. She must bring her offerings to the priest at the entrance of the Tabernacle.* [7]The priest will then present them to the LORD to purify her.* Then she will be ceremonially clean again after her bleeding at childbirth. These are the instructions for a woman after the birth of a son or a daughter.

[8]"If a woman cannot afford to bring a lamb, she must bring two turtledoves or two young pigeons. One will be for the burnt offering and the other for the purification offering. The priest will sacrifice them to purify her, and she will be ceremonially clean.'"

Serious Skin Diseases

13 The LORD said to Moses and Aaron, [2]"If anyone has a swelling or a rash or discolored skin that might develop into a serious skin disease,* that person must be brought to Aaron the priest or to one of his sons.* [3]The priest will examine the affected area of the skin. If the hair in the affected area has turned white and the problem appears to be more than skin-deep, it is a serious skin disease, and the priest who examines it must pronounce the person ceremonially unclean.

[4]"But if the affected area of the skin is only a white discoloration and does not appear to be more than skin-deep, and if the hair on the spot has not turned white, the priest will quarantine the person for seven days. [5]On the seventh day the priest will make another examination.

If he finds the affected area has not changed and the problem has not spread on the skin, the priest will quarantine the person for seven more days. [6]On the seventh day the priest will make another examination. If he finds the affected area has faded and has not spread, the priest will pronounce the person ceremonially clean. It was only a rash. The person's clothing must be washed, and the person will be ceremonially clean. [7]But if the rash continues to spread after the person has been examined by the priest and has been pronounced clean, the infected person must return to be examined again. [8]If the priest finds that the rash has spread, he must pronounce the person ceremonially unclean, for it is indeed a skin disease.

[9]"Anyone who develops a serious skin disease must go to the priest for an examination. [10]If the priest finds a white swelling on the skin, and some hair on the spot has turned white, and there is an open sore in the affected area, [11]it is a chronic skin disease, and the priest must pronounce the person ceremonially unclean. In such cases the person need not be quarantined, for it is obvious that the skin is defiled by the disease.

[12]"Now suppose the disease has spread all over the person's skin, covering the body from head to foot. [13]When the priest examines the infected person and finds that the disease covers the entire body, he will pronounce the person ceremonially clean. Since the skin has turned completely white, the person is clean. [14]But if any open sores appear, the infected person will be pronounced ceremonially unclean. [15]The priest must make this pronouncement as soon as he sees an open sore, since open sores indicate the presence of a skin disease. [16]However, if the open sores heal and turn white like the rest of the skin, the person must return to the priest [17]for another examination. If the affected areas have indeed turned white, the priest will then pronounce the person ceremonially clean by declaring, 'You are clean!'

[18]"If anyone has a boil on the skin that has started to heal, [19]but a white swelling or a reddish white spot develops in its place, that person must go to the priest to be examined. [20]If the priest examines it and finds it to be more than skin-deep, and if the hair in the affected area has turned white, the priest must pronounce the person ceremonially unclean. The boil has become a serious skin disease. [21]But if the priest finds no white hair on the affected

---

12:6 Hebrew *Tent of Meeting.*   12:7 Or *to make atonement for her;* also in 12:8.   13:2a Traditionally rendered *leprosy.* The Hebrew word used throughout this passage is used to describe various skin diseases.   13:2b Or *one of his descendants.*

area and the problem appears to be no more than skin-deep and has faded, the priest must quarantine the person for seven days. ²²If during that time the affected area spreads on the skin, the priest must pronounce the person ceremonially unclean, because it is a serious disease. ²³But if the area grows no larger and does not spread, it is merely the scar from the boil, and the priest will pronounce the person ceremonially clean.

²⁴"If anyone has suffered a burn on the skin and the burned area changes color, becoming either reddish white or shiny white, ²⁵the priest must examine it. If he finds that the hair in the affected area has turned white and the problem appears to be more than skin-deep, a skin disease has broken out in the burn. The priest must then pronounce the person ceremonially unclean, for it is clearly a serious skin disease. ²⁶But if the priest finds no white hair on the affected area and the problem appears to be no more than skin-deep and has faded, the priest must quarantine the infected person for seven days. ²⁷On the seventh day the priest must examine the person again. If the affected area has spread on the skin, the priest must pronounce that person ceremonially unclean, for it is clearly a serious skin disease. ²⁸But if the affected area has not changed or spread on the skin and has faded, it is simply a swelling from the burn. The priest will then pronounce the person ceremonially clean, for it is only the scar from the burn.

²⁹"If anyone, either a man or woman, has a sore on the head or chin, ³⁰the priest must examine it. If he finds it is more than skin-deep and has fine yellow hair on it, the priest must pronounce the person ceremonially unclean. It is a scabby sore of the head or chin. ³¹If the priest examines the scabby sore and finds that it is only skin-deep but there is no black hair on it, he must quarantine the person for seven days. ³²On the seventh day the priest must examine the sore again. If he finds that the scabby sore has not spread, and there is no yellow hair on it, and it appears to be only skin-deep, ³³the person must shave off all hair except the hair on the affected area. Then the priest must quarantine the person for another seven days. ³⁴On the seventh day he will examine the sore again. If it has not spread and appears to be no more than skin-deep, the priest will pronounce the person ceremonially clean. The person's clothing must be washed, and the person will be ceremonially clean. ³⁵But if the scabby sore begins to spread after the person is pronounced clean, ³⁶the priest must do another examination. If he finds that the sore has spread, the priest does not need to look for yellow hair. The infected person is ceremonially unclean. ³⁷But if the color of the scabby sore does not change and black hair has grown on it, it has healed. The priest will then pronounce the person ceremonially clean.

³⁸"If anyone, either a man or woman, has shiny white patches on the skin, ³⁹the priest must examine the affected area. If he finds that the shiny patches are only pale white, this is a harmless skin rash, and the person is ceremonially clean.

⁴⁰"If a man loses his hair and his head becomes bald, he is still ceremonially clean. ⁴¹And if he loses hair on his forehead, he simply has a bald forehead; he is still clean. ⁴²However, if a reddish white sore appears on the bald area on top of his head or on his forehead, this is a skin disease. ⁴³The priest must examine him, and if he finds swelling around the reddish white sore anywhere on the man's head and it looks like a skin disease, ⁴⁴the man is indeed infected with a skin disease and is unclean. The priest must pronounce him ceremonially unclean because of the sore on his head.

⁴⁵"Those who suffer from a serious skin disease must tear their clothing and leave their hair uncombed.* They must cover their mouth and call out, 'Unclean! Unclean!' ⁴⁶As long as the serious disease lasts, they will be ceremonially unclean. They must live in isolation in their place outside the camp.

Treatment of Contaminated Clothing

⁴⁷"Now suppose mildew* contaminates some woolen or linen clothing, ⁴⁸woolen or linen fabric, the hide of an animal, or anything made of leather. ⁴⁹If the contaminated area in the clothing, the animal hide, the fabric, or the leather article has turned greenish or reddish, it is contaminated with mildew and must be shown to the priest. ⁵⁰After examining the affected spot, the priest will put the article in quarantine for seven days. ⁵¹On the seventh day the priest must inspect it again. If the contaminated area has spread, the clothing or fabric or leather is clearly contaminated by a serious mildew and is ceremonially unclean. ⁵²The priest must burn the item—the clothing, the woolen or linen fabric, or piece of leather—for

13:45 Or *and uncover their heads.*   13:47 Traditionally rendered *leprosy.* The Hebrew term used throughout this passage is the same term used for the various skin diseases described in 13:1-46.

it has been contaminated by a serious mildew. It must be completely destroyed by fire.

53"But if the priest examines it and finds that the contaminated area has not spread in the clothing, the fabric, or the leather, 54the priest will order the object to be washed and then quarantined for seven more days. 55Then the priest must examine the object again. If he finds that the contaminated area has not changed color after being washed, even if it did not spread, the object is defiled. It must be completely burned up, whether the contaminated spot* is on the inside or outside. 56But if the priest examines it and finds that the contaminated area has faded after being washed, he must cut the spot from the clothing, the fabric, or the leather. 57If the spot later reappears on the clothing, the fabric, or the leather article, the mildew is clearly spreading, and the contaminated object must be burned up. 58But if the spot disappears from the clothing, the fabric, or the leather article after it has been washed, it must be washed again; then it will be ceremonially clean.

59"These are the instructions for dealing with mildew that contaminates woolen or linen clothing or fabric or anything made of leather. This is how the priest will determine whether these items are ceremonially clean or unclean."

Cleansing from Skin Diseases

14 And the LORD said to Moses, 2"The following instructions are for those seeking ceremonial purification from a skin disease.* Those who have been healed must be brought to the priest, 3who will examine them at a place outside the camp. If the priest finds that someone has been healed of a serious skin disease, 4he will perform a purification ceremony, using two live birds that are ceremonially clean, a stick of cedar,* some scarlet yarn, and a hyssop branch. 5The priest will order that one bird be slaughtered over a clay pot filled with fresh water. 6He will take the live bird, the cedar stick, the scarlet yarn, and the hyssop branch, and dip them into the blood of the bird that was slaughtered over the fresh water. 7The priest will then sprinkle the blood of the dead bird seven times on the person being purified of the skin disease. When the priest has purified the person, he will release the live bird in the open field to fly away.

8"The persons being purified must then wash their clothes, shave off all their hair, and bathe themselves in water. Then they will be ceremonially clean and may return to the camp. However, they must remain outside their tents for seven days. 9On the seventh day they must again shave all the hair from their heads, including the hair of the beard and eyebrows. They must also wash their clothes and bathe themselves in water. Then they will be ceremonially clean.

10"On the eighth day each person being purified must bring two male lambs and a one-year-old female lamb, all with no defects, along with a grain offering of six quarts* of choice flour moistened with olive oil, and a cup* of olive oil. 11Then the officiating priest will present that person for purification, along with the offerings, before the LORD at the entrance of the Tabernacle.* 12The priest will take one of the male lambs and the olive oil and present them as a guilt offering, lifting them up as a special offering before the LORD. 13He will then slaughter the male lamb in the sacred area where sin offerings and burnt offerings are slaughtered. As with the sin offering, the guilt offering belongs to the priest. It is a most holy offering. 14The priest will then take some of the blood of the guilt offering and apply it to the lobe of the right ear, the thumb of the right hand, and the big toe of the right foot of the person being purified.

15"Then the priest will pour some of the olive oil into the palm of his own left hand. 16He will dip his right finger into the oil in his palm and sprinkle some of it with his finger seven times before the LORD. 17The priest will then apply some of the oil in his palm over the blood from the guilt offering that is on the lobe of the right ear, the thumb of the right hand, and the big toe of the right foot of the person being purified. 18The priest will apply the oil remaining in his hand to the head of the person being purified. Through this process, the priest will purify* the person before the LORD.

19"Then the priest must present the sin offering to purify the person who was cured of the skin disease. After that, the priest will slaughter the burnt offering 20and offer it on the altar along with the grain offering. Through this process, the priest will purify the person who was healed, and the person will be ceremonially clean.

13:55 The meaning of the Hebrew is uncertain.   14:2 Traditionally rendered leprosy; see note on 13:2a.   14:4 Or juniper; also in 14:6, 49, 51.   14:10a Hebrew ³⁄₁₀ of an ephah [6.6 liters].   14:10b Hebrew 1 log [0.3 liters]; also in 14:21.   14:11 Hebrew Tent of Meeting; also in 14:23.   14:18 Or will make atonement for; similarly in 14:19, 20, 21, 29, 31, 53.

²¹"But anyone who is too poor and cannot afford these offerings may bring one male lamb for a guilt offering, to be lifted up as a special offering for purification. The person must also bring two quarts* of choice flour moistened with olive oil for the grain offering and a cup of olive oil. ²²The offering must also include two turtledoves or two young pigeons, whichever the person can afford. One of the pair must be used for the sin offering and the other for a burnt offering. ²³On the eighth day of the purification ceremony, the person being purified must bring the offerings to the priest in the LORD's presence at the entrance of the Tabernacle. ²⁴The priest will take the lamb for the guilt offering, along with the olive oil, and lift them up as a special offering to the LORD. ²⁵Then the priest will slaughter the lamb for the guilt offering. He will take some of its blood and apply it to the lobe of the right ear, the thumb of the right hand, and the big toe of the right foot of the person being purified.

²⁶"The priest will also pour some of the olive oil into the palm of his own left hand. ²⁷He will dip his right finger into the oil in his palm and sprinkle some of it seven times before the LORD. ²⁸The priest will then apply some of the oil in his palm over the blood from the guilt offering that is on the lobe of the right ear, the thumb of the right hand, and the big toe of the right foot of the person being purified. ²⁹The priest will apply the oil remaining in his hand to the head of the person being purified. Through this process, the priest will purify the person before the LORD.

³⁰"Then the priest will offer the two turtledoves or the two young pigeons, whichever the person can afford. ³¹One of them is for a sin offering and the other for a burnt offering, to be presented along with the grain offering. Through this process, the priest will purify the person before the LORD. ³²These are the instructions for purification for those who have recovered from a serious skin disease but who cannot afford to bring the offerings normally required for the ceremony of purification."

Treatment of Contaminated Houses

³³Then the LORD said to Moses and Aaron, ³⁴"When you arrive in Canaan, the land I am giving you as your own possession, I may contaminate some of the houses in your land with mildew.* ³⁵The owner of such a house must then go to the priest and say, 'It appears that my house has some kind of mildew.' ³⁶Before the priest goes in to inspect the house, he must have the house emptied so nothing inside will be pronounced ceremonially unclean. ³⁷Then the priest will go in and examine the mildew on the walls. If he finds greenish or reddish streaks and the contamination appears to go deeper than the wall's surface, ³⁸the priest will step outside the door and put the house in quarantine for seven days. ³⁹On the seventh day the priest must return for another inspection. If he finds that the mildew on the walls of the house has spread, ⁴⁰the priest must order that the stones from those areas be removed. The contaminated material will then be taken outside the town to an area designated as ceremonially unclean. ⁴¹Next the inside walls of the entire house must be scraped thoroughly and the scrapings dumped in the unclean place outside the town. ⁴²Other stones will be brought in to replace the ones that were removed, and the walls will be replastered.

⁴³"But if the mildew reappears after all the stones have been replaced and the house has been scraped and replastered, ⁴⁴the priest must return and inspect the house again. If he finds that the mildew has spread, the walls are clearly contaminated with a serious mildew, and the house is defiled. ⁴⁵It must be torn down, and all its stones, timbers, and plaster must be carried out of town to the place designated as ceremonially unclean. ⁴⁶Those who enter the house during the period of quarantine will be ceremonially unclean until evening, ⁴⁷and all who sleep or eat in the house must wash their clothing.

⁴⁸"But if the priest returns for his inspection and finds that the mildew has not reappeared in the house after the fresh plastering, he will pronounce it clean because the mildew is clearly gone. ⁴⁹To purify the house the priest must take two birds, a stick of cedar, some scarlet yarn, and a hyssop branch. ⁵⁰He will slaughter one of the birds over a clay pot filled with fresh water. ⁵¹He will take the cedar stick, the hyssop branch, the scarlet yarn, and the live bird, and dip them into the blood of the slaughtered bird and into the fresh water. Then he will sprinkle the house seven times. ⁵²When the priest has purified the house in exactly this way, ⁵³he will release the live bird in the open fields outside the town. Through this process, the priest will purify the house, and it will be ceremonially clean.

⁵⁴"These are the instructions for dealing

14:21 Hebrew ¹/₁₀ of an ephah [2.2 liters].   14:34 Traditionally rendered leprosy; see note on 13:47.

with serious skin diseases,* including scabby sores; 55and mildew,* whether on clothing or in a house; 56and a swelling on the skin, a rash, or discolored skin. 57This procedure will determine whether a person or object is ceremonially clean or unclean.

"These are the instructions regarding skin diseases and mildew."

Bodily Discharges

15 The LORD said to Moses and Aaron, 2"Give the following instructions to the people of Israel.

"Any man who has a bodily discharge is ceremonially unclean. 3This defilement is caused by his discharge, whether the discharge continues or stops. In either case the man is unclean. 4Any bed on which the man with the discharge lies and anything on which he sits will be ceremonially unclean. 5So if you touch the man's bed, you must wash your clothes and bathe yourself in water, and you will remain unclean until evening. 6If you sit where the man with the discharge has sat, you must wash your clothes and bathe yourself in water, and you will remain unclean until evening. 7If you touch the man with the discharge, you must wash your clothes and bathe yourself in water, and you will remain unclean until evening. 8If the man spits on you, you must wash your clothes and bathe yourself in water, and you will remain unclean until evening. 9Any saddle blanket on which the man rides will be ceremonially unclean. 10If you touch anything that was under the man, you will be unclean until evening. You must wash your clothes and bathe yourself in water, and you will remain unclean until evening. 11If the man touches you without first rinsing his hands, you must wash your clothes and bathe yourself in water, and you will remain unclean until evening. 12Any clay pot the man touches must be broken, and any wooden utensil he touches must be rinsed with water.

13"When the man with the discharge is healed, he must count off seven days for the period of purification. Then he must wash his clothes and bathe himself in fresh water, and he will be ceremonially clean. 14On the eighth day he must get two turtledoves or two young pigeons and come before the LORD at the entrance of the Tabernacle* and give his offerings to the priest. 15The priest will offer one bird for a sin offering and the other for a burnt offering.

Through this process, the priest will purify* the man before the LORD for his discharge.

16"Whenever a man has an emission of semen, he must bathe his entire body in water, and he will remain ceremonially unclean until the next evening.* 17Any clothing or leather with semen on it must be washed in water, and it will remain unclean until evening. 18After a man and a woman have sexual intercourse, they must each bathe in water, and they will remain unclean until the next evening.

19"Whenever a woman has her menstrual period, she will be ceremonially unclean for seven days. Anyone who touches her during that time will be unclean until evening. 20Anything on which the woman lies or sits during the time of her period will be unclean. 21If any of you touch her bed, you must wash your clothes and bathe yourself in water, and you will remain unclean until evening. 22If you touch any object she has sat on, you must wash your clothes and bathe yourself in water, and you will remain unclean until evening. 23This includes her bed or any other object she has sat on; you will be unclean until evening if you touch it. 24If a man has sexual intercourse with her and her blood touches him, her menstrual impurity will be transmitted to him. He will remain unclean for seven days, and any bed on which he lies will be unclean.

25"If a woman has a flow of blood for many days that is unrelated to her menstrual period, or if the blood continues beyond the normal period, she is ceremonially unclean. As during her menstrual period, the woman will be unclean as long as the discharge continues. 26Any bed she lies on and any object she sits on during that time will be unclean, just as during her normal menstrual period. 27If any of you touch these things, you will be ceremonially unclean. You must wash your clothes and bathe yourself in water, and you will remain unclean until evening.

28"When the woman's bleeding stops, she must count off seven days. Then she will be ceremonially clean. 29On the eighth day she must bring two turtledoves or two young pigeons and present them to the priest at the entrance of the Tabernacle. 30The priest will offer one for a sin offering and the other for a burnt offering. Through this process, the priest will purify her before the LORD for the ceremonial impurity caused by her bleeding.

14:54 Traditionally rendered *leprosy;* see note on 13:2a.   14:55 Traditionally rendered *leprosy;* see note on 13:47.
15:14 Hebrew *Tent of Meeting;* also in 15:29.   15:15 Or *will make atonement for;* also in 15:30.   15:16 Hebrew *until evening;* also in 15:18.

³¹"This is how you will guard the people of Israel from ceremonial uncleanness. Otherwise they would die, for their impurity would defile my Tabernacle that stands among them. ³²These are the instructions for dealing with anyone who has a bodily discharge—a man who is unclean because of an emission of semen ³³or a woman during her menstrual period. It applies to any man or woman who has a bodily discharge, and to a man who has sexual intercourse with a woman who is ceremonially unclean."

The Day of Atonement

16 The LORD spoke to Moses after the death of Aaron's two sons, who died after they entered the LORD's presence and burned the wrong kind of fire before him. ²The LORD said to Moses, "Warn your brother, Aaron, not to enter the Most Holy Place behind the inner curtain whenever he chooses; if he does, he will die. For the Ark's cover—the place of atonement—is there, and I myself am present in the cloud above the atonement cover.

³"When Aaron enters the sanctuary area, he must follow these instructions fully. He must bring a young bull for a sin offering and a ram for a burnt offering. ⁴He must put on his linen tunic and the linen undergarments worn next to his body. He must tie the linen sash around his waist and put the linen turban on his head. These are sacred garments, so he must bathe himself in water before he puts them on. ⁵Aaron must take from the community of Israel two male goats for a sin offering and a ram for a burnt offering.

⁶"Aaron will present his own bull as a sin offering to purify himself and his family, making them right with the LORD.* ⁷Then he must take the two male goats and present them to the LORD at the entrance of the Tabernacle.* ⁸He is to cast sacred lots to determine which goat will be reserved as an offering to the LORD and which will carry the sins of the people to the wilderness of Azazel. ⁹Aaron will then present as a sin offering the goat chosen by lot for the LORD. ¹⁰The other goat, the scapegoat chosen by lot to be sent away, will be kept alive, standing before the LORD. When it is sent away to Azazel in the wilderness, the people will be purified and made right with the LORD.*

¹¹"Aaron will present his own bull as a sin offering to purify himself and his family, making them right with the LORD. After he has slaughtered the bull as a sin offering, ¹²he will fill an incense burner with burning coals from the altar that stands before the LORD. Then he will take two handfuls of fragrant powdered incense and will carry the burner and the incense behind the inner curtain. ¹³There in the LORD's presence he will put the incense on the burning coals so that a cloud of incense will rise over the Ark's cover—the place of atonement—that rests on the Ark of the Covenant.* If he follows these instructions, he will not die. ¹⁴Then he must take some of the blood of the bull, dip his finger in it, and sprinkle it on the east side of the atonement cover. He must sprinkle blood seven times with his finger in front of the atonement cover.

¹⁵"Then Aaron must slaughter the first goat as a sin offering for the people and carry its blood behind the inner curtain. There he will sprinkle the goat's blood over the atonement cover and in front of it, just as he did with the bull's blood. ¹⁶Through this process, he will purify* the Most Holy Place, and he will do the same for the entire Tabernacle, because of the defiling sin and rebellion of the Israelites. ¹⁷No one else is allowed inside the Tabernacle when Aaron enters it for the purification ceremony in the Most Holy Place. No one may enter until he comes out again after purifying himself, his family, and all the congregation of Israel, making them right with the LORD.

¹⁸"Then Aaron will come out to purify the altar that stands before the LORD. He will do this by taking some of the blood from the bull and the goat and putting it on each of the horns of the altar. ¹⁹Then he must sprinkle the blood with his finger seven times over the altar. In this way, he will cleanse it from Israel's defilement and make it holy.

²⁰"When Aaron has finished purifying the Most Holy Place and the Tabernacle and the altar, he must present the live goat. ²¹He will lay both of his hands on the goat's head and confess over it all the wickedness, rebellion, and sins of the people of Israel. In this way, he will transfer the people's sins to the head of the goat. Then a man specially chosen for the task will drive the goat into the wilderness. ²²As the goat goes into the wilderness, it will

---

16:6 Or *to make atonement for himself and his family;* similarly in 16:11, 17b, 24, 34.   16:7 Hebrew *Tent of Meeting;* also in 16:16, 17, 20, 23, 33.   16:10 Or *wilderness, it will make atonement for the people.*   16:13 Hebrew *that is above the Testimony.* The Hebrew word for "testimony" refers to the terms of the LORD's covenant with Israel as written on stone tablets, which were kept in the Ark, and also to the covenant itself.   16:16 Or *make atonement for;* similarly in 16:17a, 18, 20, 27, 33.

carry all the people's sins upon itself into a desolate land.

²³"When Aaron goes back into the Tabernacle, he must take off the linen garments he was wearing when he entered the Most Holy Place, and he must leave the garments there. ²⁴Then he must bathe himself with water in a sacred place, put on his regular garments, and go out to sacrifice a burnt offering for himself and a burnt offering for the people. Through this process, he will purify himself and the people, making them right with the LORD. ²⁵He must then burn all the fat of the sin offering on the altar.

²⁶"The man chosen to drive the scapegoat into the wilderness of Azazel must wash his clothes and bathe himself in water. Then he may return to the camp.

²⁷"The bull and the goat presented as sin offerings, whose blood Aaron takes into the Most Holy Place for the purification ceremony, will be carried outside the camp. The animals' hides, internal organs, and dung are all to be burned. ²⁸The man who burns them must wash his clothes and bathe himself in water before returning to the camp.

²⁹"On the tenth day of the appointed month in early autumn,* you must deny yourselves.* Neither native-born Israelites nor foreigners living among you may do any kind of work. This is a permanent law for you. ³⁰On that day offerings of purification will be made for you,* and you will be purified in the LORD's presence from all your sins. ³¹It will be a Sabbath day of complete rest for you, and you must deny yourselves. This is a permanent law for you. ³²In future generations, the purification* ceremony will be performed by the priest who has been anointed and ordained to serve as high priest in place of his ancestor Aaron. He will put on the holy linen garments ³³and purify the Most Holy Place, the Tabernacle, the altar, the priests, and the entire congregation. ³⁴This is a permanent law for you, to purify the people of Israel from their sins, making them right with the LORD once each year."

Moses followed all these instructions exactly as the LORD had commanded him.

Prohibitions against Eating Blood

17 Then the LORD said to Moses, ²"Give the following instructions to Aaron and his sons and all the people of Israel. This is what the LORD has commanded.

³"If any native Israelite sacrifices a bull* or a lamb or a goat anywhere inside or outside the camp ⁴instead of bringing it to the entrance of the Tabernacle* to present it as an offering to the LORD, that person will be as guilty as a murderer.* Such a person has shed blood and will be cut off from the community. ⁵The purpose of this rule is to stop the Israelites from sacrificing animals in the open fields. It will ensure that they bring their sacrifices to the priest at the entrance of the Tabernacle, so he can present them to the LORD as peace offerings. ⁶Then the priest will be able to splatter the blood against the LORD's altar at the entrance of the Tabernacle, and he will burn the fat as a pleasing aroma to the LORD. ⁷The people must no longer be unfaithful to the LORD by offering sacrifices to the goat idols.* This is a permanent law for them, to be observed from generation to generation.

⁸"Give them this command as well. If any native Israelite or foreigner living among you offers a burnt offering or a sacrifice ⁹but does not bring it to the entrance of the Tabernacle to offer it to the LORD, that person will be cut off from the community.

¹⁰"And if any native Israelite or foreigner living among you eats or drinks blood in any form, I will turn against that person and cut him off from the community of your people, ¹¹for the life of the body is in its blood. I have given you the blood on the altar to purify you, making you right with the LORD.* It is the blood, given in exchange for a life, that makes purification possible. ¹²That is why I have said to the people of Israel, 'You must never eat or drink blood—neither you nor the foreigners living among you.'

¹³"And if any native Israelite or foreigner living among you goes hunting and kills an animal or bird that is approved for eating, he must drain its blood and cover it with earth. ¹⁴The life of every creature is in its blood. That is why I have said to the people of Israel, 'You must never eat or drink blood, for the life of any creature is in its blood.' So whoever consumes blood will be cut off from the community.

¹⁵"And if any native-born Israelites or foreigners eat the meat of an animal that died naturally or was torn up by wild animals,

---

16:29a Hebrew *On the tenth day of the seventh month.* This day in the ancient Hebrew lunar calendar occurred in September or October.   16:29b Or *must fast;* also in 16:31.   16:30 Or *atonement will be made for you, to purify you.*   16:32 Or *atonement.* 17:3 Or *cow.*   17:4a Hebrew *Tent of Meeting;* also in 17:5, 6, 9.   17:4b Hebrew *will be guilty of blood.*   17:7 Or *goat demons.* 17:11 Or *to make atonement for you.*

they must wash their clothes and bathe themselves in water. They will remain ceremonially unclean until evening, but then they will be clean. ¹⁶But if they do not wash their clothes and bathe themselves, they will be punished for their sin."

Forbidden Sexual Practices

18 Then the LORD said to Moses, ²"Give the following instructions to the people of Israel. I am the LORD your God. ³So do not act like the people in Egypt, where you used to live, or like the people of Canaan, where I am taking you. You must not imitate their way of life. ⁴You must obey all my regulations and be careful to obey my decrees, for I am the LORD your God. ⁵If you obey my decrees and my regulations, you will find life through them. I am the LORD.

⁶"You must never have sexual relations with a close relative, for I am the LORD.

⁷"Do not violate your father by having sexual relations with your mother. She is your mother; you must not have sexual relations with her.

⁸"Do not have sexual relations with any of your father's wives, for this would violate your father.

⁹"Do not have sexual relations with your sister or half sister, whether she is your father's daughter or your mother's daughter, whether she was born into your household or someone else's.

¹⁰"Do not have sexual relations with your granddaughter, whether she is your son's daughter or your daughter's daughter, for this would violate yourself.

¹¹"Do not have sexual relations with your stepsister, the daughter of any of your father's wives, for she is your sister.

¹²"Do not have sexual relations with your father's sister, for she is your father's close relative.

¹³"Do not have sexual relations with your mother's sister, for she is your mother's close relative.

¹⁴"Do not violate your uncle, your father's brother, by having sexual relations with his wife, for she is your aunt.

¹⁵"Do not have sexual relations with your daughter-in-law; she is your son's wife, so you must not have sexual relations with her.

¹⁶"Do not have sexual relations with your brother's wife, for this would violate your brother.

¹⁷"Do not have sexual relations with both a woman and her daughter. And do not take* her granddaughter, whether her son's daughter or her daughter's daughter, and have sexual relations with her. They are close relatives, and this would be a wicked act.

¹⁸"While your wife is living, do not marry her sister and have sexual relations with her, for they would be rivals.

¹⁹"Do not have sexual relations with a woman during her period of menstrual impurity.

²⁰"Do not defile yourself by having sexual intercourse with your neighbor's wife.

²¹"Do not permit any of your children to be offered as a sacrifice to Molech, for you must not bring shame on the name of your God. I am the LORD.

²²"Do not practice homosexuality, having sex with another man as with a woman. It is a detestable sin.

²³"A man must not defile himself by having sex with an animal. And a woman must not offer herself to a male animal to have intercourse with it. This is a perverse act.

²⁴"Do not defile yourselves in any of these ways, for the people I am driving out before you have defiled themselves in all these ways. ²⁵Because the entire land has become defiled, I am punishing the people who live there. I will cause the land to vomit them out. ²⁶You must obey all my decrees and regulations. You must not commit any of these detestable sins. This applies both to native-born Israelites and to the foreigners living among you.

²⁷"All these detestable activities are practiced by the people of the land where I am taking you, and this is how the land has become defiled. ²⁸So do not defile the land and give it a reason to vomit you out, as it will vomit out the people who live there now. ²⁹Whoever commits any of these detestable sins will be cut off from the community of Israel. ³⁰So obey my instructions, and do not defile yourselves by committing any of these detestable practices that were committed by the people who lived in the land before you. I am the LORD your God."

Holiness in Personal Conduct

19 The LORD also said to Moses, ²"Give the following instructions to the entire community of Israel. You must be holy because I, the LORD your God, am holy.

³"Each of you must show great respect for your mother and father, and you must always

18:17 Or *do not marry.*

observe my Sabbath days of rest. I am the LORD your God.

4"Do not put your trust in idols or make metal images of gods for yourselves. I am the LORD your God.

5"When you sacrifice a peace offering to the LORD, offer it properly so you* will be accepted by God. 6The sacrifice must be eaten on the same day you offer it or on the next day. Whatever is left over until the third day must be completely burned up. 7If any of the sacrifice is eaten on the third day, it will be contaminated, and I will not accept it. 8Anyone who eats it on the third day will be punished for defiling what is holy to the LORD and will be cut off from the community.

9"When you harvest the crops of your land, do not harvest the grain along the edges of your fields, and do not pick up what the harvesters drop. 10It is the same with your grape crop—do not strip every last bunch of grapes from the vines, and do not pick up the grapes that fall to the ground. Leave them for the poor and the foreigners living among you. I am the LORD your God.

11"Do not steal.

"Do not deceive or cheat one another.

12"Do not bring shame on the name of your God by using it to swear falsely. I am the LORD.

13"Do not defraud or rob your neighbor.

"Do not make your hired workers wait until the next day to receive their pay.

14"Do not insult the deaf or cause the blind to stumble. You must fear your God; I am the LORD.

15"Do not twist justice in legal matters by favoring the poor or being partial to the rich and powerful. Always judge people fairly.

16"Do not spread slanderous gossip among your people.*

"Do not stand idly by when your neighbor's life is threatened. I am the LORD.

17"Do not nurse hatred in your heart for any of your relatives.* Confront people directly so you will not be held guilty for their sin.

18"Do not seek revenge or bear a grudge against a fellow Israelite, but love your neighbor as yourself. I am the LORD.

19"You must obey all my decrees.

"Do not mate two different kinds of animals. Do not plant your field with two different kinds of seed. Do not wear clothing woven from two different kinds of thread.

20"If a man has sex with a slave girl whose freedom has never been purchased but who is committed to become another man's wife, he must pay full compensation to her master. But since she is not a free woman, neither the man nor the woman will be put to death. 21The man, however, must bring a ram as a guilt offering and present it to the LORD at the entrance of the Tabernacle.* 22The priest will then purify him* before the LORD with the ram of the guilt offering, and the man's sin will be forgiven.

23"When you enter the land and plant fruit trees, leave the fruit unharvested for the first three years and consider it forbidden.* Do not eat it. 24In the fourth year the entire crop must be consecrated to the LORD as a celebration of praise. 25Finally, in the fifth year you may eat the fruit. If you follow this pattern, your harvest will increase. I am the LORD your God.

26"Do not eat meat that has not been drained of its blood.

"Do not practice fortune-telling or witchcraft.

27"Do not trim off the hair on your temples or trim your beards.

28"Do not cut your bodies for the dead, and do not mark your skin with tattoos. I am the LORD.

29"Do not defile your daughter by making her a prostitute, or the land will be filled with prostitution and wickedness.

30"Keep my Sabbath days of rest, and show reverence toward my sanctuary. I am the LORD.

31"Do not defile yourselves by turning to mediums or to those who consult the spirits of the dead. I am the LORD your God.

32"Stand up in the presence of the elderly, and show respect for the aged. Fear your God. I am the LORD.

33"Do not take advantage of foreigners who live among you in your land. 34Treat them like native-born Israelites, and love them as you love yourself. Remember that you were once foreigners living in the land of Egypt. I am the LORD your God.

35"Do not use dishonest standards when measuring length, weight, or volume. 36Your scales and weights must be accurate. Your containers for measuring dry materials or liquids must be accurate.* I am the LORD your God who brought you out of the land of Egypt.

37"You must be careful to keep all of my decrees and regulations by putting them into practice. I am the LORD."

19:5 Or it.   19:16 Hebrew *Do not act as a merchant toward your own people.*   19:17 Hebrew *for your brother.*   19:21 Hebrew *Tent of Meeting.*   19:22 Or *make atonement for him.*   19:23 Hebrew *consider it uncircumcised.*   19:36 Hebrew *Use an honest ephah* [a dry measure] *and an honest hin* [a liquid measure].

Punishments for Disobedience

20 The LORD said to Moses, 2"Give the people of Israel these instructions, which apply both to native Israelites and to the foreigners living in Israel.

"If any of them offer their children as a sacrifice to Molech, they must be put to death. The people of the community must stone them to death. 3I myself will turn against them and cut them off from the community, because they have defiled my sanctuary and brought shame on my holy name by offering their children to Molech. 4And if the people of the community ignore those who offer their children to Molech and refuse to execute them, 5I myself will turn against them and their families and will cut them off from the community. This will happen to all who commit spiritual prostitution by worshiping Molech.

6"I will also turn against those who commit spiritual prostitution by putting their trust in mediums or in those who consult the spirits of the dead. I will cut them off from the community. 7So set yourselves apart to be holy, for I am the LORD your God. 8Keep all my decrees by putting them into practice, for I am the LORD who makes you holy.

9"Anyone who dishonors* father or mother must be put to death. Such a person is guilty of a capital offense.

10"If a man commits adultery with his neighbor's wife, both the man and the woman who have committed adultery must be put to death.

11"If a man violates his father by having sex with one of his father's wives, both the man and the woman must be put to death, for they are guilty of a capital offense.

12"If a man has sex with his daughter-in-law, both must be put to death. They have committed a perverse act and are guilty of a capital offense.

13"If a man practices homosexuality, having sex with another man as with a woman, both men have committed a detestable act. They must both be put to death, for they are guilty of a capital offense.

14"If a man marries both a woman and her mother, he has committed a wicked act. The man and both women must be burned to death to wipe out such wickedness from among you.

15"If a man has sex with an animal, he must be put to death, and the animal must be killed.

16"If a woman presents herself to a male animal to have intercourse with it, she and the animal must both be put to death. You must kill both, for they are guilty of a capital offense.

17"If a man marries his sister, the daughter of either his father or his mother, and they have sexual relations, it is a shameful disgrace. They must be publicly cut off from the community. Since the man has violated his sister, he will be punished for his sin.

18"If a man has sexual relations with a woman during her menstrual period, both of them must be cut off from the community, for together they have exposed the source of her blood flow.

19"Do not have sexual relations with your aunt, whether your mother's sister or your father's sister. This would dishonor a close relative. Both parties are guilty and will be punished for their sin.

20"If a man has sex with his uncle's wife, he has violated his uncle. Both the man and woman will be punished for their sin, and they will die childless.

21"If a man marries his brother's wife, it is an act of impurity. He has violated his brother, and the guilty couple will remain childless.

22"You must keep all my decrees and regulations by putting them into practice; otherwise the land to which I am bringing you as your new home will vomit you out. 23Do not live according to the customs of the people I am driving out before you. It is because they do these shameful things that I detest them. 24But I have promised you, 'You will possess their land because I will give it to you as your possession—a land flowing with milk and honey.' I am the LORD your God, who has set you apart from all other people.

25"You must therefore make a distinction between ceremonially clean and unclean animals, and between clean and unclean birds. You must not defile yourselves by eating any unclean animal or bird or creature that scurries along the ground. I have identified them as being unclean for you. 26You must be holy because I, the LORD, am holy. I have set you apart from all other people to be my very own.

27"Men and women among you who act as mediums or who consult the spirits of the dead must be put to death by stoning. They are guilty of a capital offense."

Instructions for the Priests

21 The LORD said to Moses, "Give the following instructions to the priests, the descendants of Aaron.

20:9 Greek version reads *Anyone who speaks disrespectfully of.* Compare Matt 15:4; Mark 7:10.

"A priest must not make himself ceremonially unclean by touching the dead body of a relative. ²The only exceptions are his closest relatives—his mother or father, son or daughter, brother, ³or his virgin sister who depends on him because she has no husband. ⁴But a priest must not defile himself and make himself unclean for someone who is related to him only by marriage.

⁵"The priests must not shave their heads or trim their beards or cut their bodies. ⁶They must be set apart as holy to their God and must never bring shame on the name of God. They must be holy, for they are the ones who present the special gifts to the LORD, gifts of food for their God.

⁷"Priests may not marry a woman defiled by prostitution, and they may not marry a woman who is divorced from her husband, for the priests are set apart as holy to their God. ⁸You must treat them as holy because they offer up food to your God. You must consider them holy because I, the LORD, am holy, and I make you holy.

⁹"If a priest's daughter defiles herself by becoming a prostitute, she also defiles her father's holiness, and she must be burned to death.

¹⁰"The high priest has the highest rank of all the priests. The anointing oil has been poured on his head, and he has been ordained to wear the priestly garments. He must never leave his hair uncombed* or tear his clothing. ¹¹He must not defile himself by going near a dead body. He may not make himself ceremonially unclean even for his father or mother. ¹²He must not defile the sanctuary of his God by leaving it to attend to a dead person, for he has been made holy by the anointing oil of his God. I am the LORD.

¹³"The high priest may marry only a virgin. ¹⁴He may not marry a widow, a woman who is divorced, or a woman who has defiled herself by prostitution. She must be a virgin from his own clan, ¹⁵so that he will not dishonor his descendants among his clan, for I am the LORD who makes him holy."

¹⁶Then the LORD said to Moses, ¹⁷"Give the following instructions to Aaron: In all future generations, none of your descendants who has any defect will qualify to offer food to his God. ¹⁸No one who has a defect qualifies, whether he is blind, lame, disfigured, deformed, ¹⁹or has a broken foot or arm, ²⁰or is hunchbacked or dwarfed, or has a defective eye, or skin sores or scabs, or damaged testicles. ²¹No descendant

of Aaron who has a defect may approach the altar to present special gifts to the LORD. Since he has a defect, he may not approach the altar to offer food to his God. ²²However, he may eat from the food offered to God, including the holy offerings and the most holy offerings. ²³Yet because of his physical defect, he may not enter the room behind the inner curtain or approach the altar, for this would defile my holy places. I am the LORD who makes them holy."

²⁴So Moses gave these instructions to Aaron and his sons and to all the Israelites.

22 The LORD said to Moses, ²"Tell Aaron and his sons to be very careful with the sacred gifts that the Israelites set apart for me, so they do not bring shame on my holy name. I am the LORD. ³Give them the following instructions.

"In all future generations, if any of your descendants is ceremonially unclean when he approaches the sacred offerings that the people of Israel consecrate to the LORD, he must be cut off from my presence. I am the LORD.

⁴"If any of Aaron's descendants has a skin disease* or any kind of discharge that makes him ceremonially unclean, he may not eat from the sacred offerings until he has been pronounced clean. He also becomes unclean by touching a corpse, or by having an emission of semen, ⁵or by touching a small animal that is unclean, or by touching someone who is ceremonially unclean for any reason. ⁶The man who is defiled in any of these ways will remain unclean until evening. He may not eat from the sacred offerings until he has bathed himself in water. ⁷When the sun goes down, he will be ceremonially clean again and may eat from the sacred offerings, for this is his food. ⁸He may not eat an animal that has died a natural death or has been torn apart by wild animals, for this would defile him. I am the LORD.

⁹"The priests must follow my instructions carefully. Otherwise they will be punished for their sin and will die for violating my instructions. I am the LORD who makes them holy.

¹⁰"No one outside a priest's family may eat the sacred offerings. Even guests and hired workers in a priest's home are not allowed to eat them. ¹¹However, if the priest buys a slave for himself, the slave may eat from the sacred offerings. And if his slaves have children, they also may share his food. ¹²If a priest's daughter marries someone outside the priestly family, she may no longer eat the sacred offerings.

21:10 Or *never uncover his head.*   22:4 Traditionally rendered *leprosy;* see note on 13:2a.

¹³But if she becomes a widow or is divorced and has no children to support her, and she returns to live in her father's home as in her youth, she may eat her father's food again. Otherwise, no one outside a priest's family may eat the sacred offerings.

¹⁴"Any such person who eats the sacred offerings without realizing it must pay the priest for the amount eaten, plus an additional 20 percent. ¹⁵The priests must not let the Israelites defile the sacred offerings brought to the LORD ¹⁶by allowing unauthorized people to eat them. This would bring guilt upon them and require them to pay compensation. I am the LORD who makes them holy."

Worthy and Unworthy Offerings

¹⁷And the LORD said to Moses, ¹⁸"Give Aaron and his sons and all the Israelites these instructions, which apply both to native Israelites and to the foreigners living among you.

"If you present a gift as a burnt offering to the LORD, whether it is to fulfill a vow or is a voluntary offering, ¹⁹you* will be accepted only if your offering is a male animal with no defects. It may be a bull, a ram, or a male goat. ²⁰Do not present an animal with defects, because the LORD will not accept it on your behalf.

²¹"If you present a peace offering to the LORD from the herd or the flock, whether it is to fulfill a vow or is a voluntary offering, you must offer a perfect animal. It may have no defect of any kind. ²²You must not offer an animal that is blind, crippled, or injured, or that has a wart, a skin sore, or scabs. Such animals must never be offered on the altar as special gifts to the LORD. ²³If a bull* or lamb has a leg that is too long or too short, it may be offered as a voluntary offering, but it may not be offered to fulfill a vow. ²⁴If an animal has damaged testicles or is castrated, you may not offer it to the LORD. You must never do this in your own land, ²⁵and you must not accept such an animal from foreigners and then offer it as a sacrifice to your God. Such animals will not be accepted on your behalf, for they are mutilated or defective."

²⁶And the LORD said to Moses, ²⁷"When a calf or lamb or goat is born, it must be left with its mother for seven days. From the eighth day on, it will be acceptable as a special gift to the LORD. ²⁸But you must not slaughter a mother animal and her offspring on the same day, whether from the herd or the flock. ²⁹When you bring a thanksgiving offering to the LORD, sacrifice it properly so you will be accepted. ³⁰Eat the entire sacrificial animal on the day it is presented. Do not leave any of it until the next morning. I am the LORD.

³¹"You must faithfully keep all my commands by putting them into practice, for I am the LORD. ³²Do not bring shame on my holy name, for I will display my holiness among the people of Israel. I am the LORD who makes you holy. ³³It was I who rescued you from the land of Egypt, that I might be your God. I am the LORD."

The Appointed Festivals

23 The LORD said to Moses, ²"Give the following instructions to the people of Israel. These are the LORD's appointed festivals, which you are to proclaim as official days for holy assembly.

³"You have six days each week for your ordinary work, but the seventh day is a Sabbath day of complete rest, an official day for holy assembly. It is the LORD's Sabbath day, and it must be observed wherever you live.

⁴"In addition to the Sabbath, these are the LORD's appointed festivals, the official days for holy assembly that are to be celebrated at their proper times each year.

Passover and the Festival of Unleavened Bread

⁵"The LORD's Passover begins at sundown on the fourteenth day of the first month.* ⁶On the next day, the fifteenth day of the month, you must begin celebrating the Festival of Unleavened Bread. This festival to the LORD continues for seven days, and during that time the bread you eat must be made without yeast. ⁷On the first day of the festival, all the people must stop their ordinary work and observe an official day for holy assembly. ⁸For seven days you must present special gifts to the LORD. On the seventh day the people must again stop all their ordinary work to observe an official day for holy assembly."

Celebration of First Harvest

⁹Then the LORD said to Moses, ¹⁰"Give the following instructions to the people of Israel. When you enter the land I am giving you and you harvest its first crops, bring the priest a bundle of grain from the first cutting of your grain harvest. ¹¹On the day after the Sabbath, the priest will lift it up before the LORD so it may be accepted on your behalf. ¹²On that same

22:19 Or *it.*   22:23 Or *cow.*   23:5 This day in the ancient Hebrew lunar calendar occurred in late March, April, or early May.

day you must sacrifice a one-year-old male lamb with no defects as a burnt offering to the Lord. 13With it you must present a grain offering consisting of four quarts* of choice flour moistened with olive oil. It will be a special gift, a pleasing aroma to the Lord. You must also offer one quart* of wine as a liquid offering. 14Do not eat any bread or roasted grain or fresh kernels on that day until you bring this offering to your God. This is a permanent law for you, and it must be observed from generation to generation wherever you live.

The Festival of Harvest

15"From the day after the Sabbath—the day you bring the bundle of grain to be lifted up as a special offering—count off seven full weeks. 16Keep counting until the day after the seventh Sabbath, fifty days later. Then present an offering of new grain to the Lord. 17From wherever you live, bring two loaves of bread to be lifted up before the Lord as a special offering. Make these loaves from four quarts of choice flour, and bake them with yeast. They will be an offering to the Lord from the first of your crops. 18Along with the bread, present seven one-year-old male lambs with no defects, one young bull, and two rams as burnt offerings to the Lord. These burnt offerings, together with the grain offerings and liquid offerings, will be a special gift, a pleasing aroma to the Lord. 19Then you must offer one male goat as a sin offering and two one-year-old male lambs as a peace offering.

20"The priest will lift up the two lambs as a special offering to the Lord, together with the loaves representing the first of your crops. These offerings, which are holy to the Lord, belong to the priests. 21That same day will be proclaimed an official day for holy assembly, a day on which you do no ordinary work. This is a permanent law for you, and it must be observed from generation to generation wherever you live.*

22"When you harvest the crops of your land, do not harvest the grain along the edges of your fields, and do not pick up what the harvesters drop. Leave it for the poor and the foreigners living among you. I am the Lord your God."

The Festival of Trumpets

23The Lord said to Moses, 24"Give the following instructions to the people of Israel. On the first day of the appointed month in early autumn,* you are to observe a day of complete rest. It will be an official day for holy assembly, a day commemorated with loud blasts of a trumpet. 25You must do no ordinary work on that day. Instead, you are to present special gifts to the Lord."

The Day of Atonement

26Then the Lord said to Moses, 27"Be careful to celebrate the Day of Atonement on the tenth day of that same month—nine days after the Festival of Trumpets.* You must observe it as an official day for holy assembly, a day to deny yourselves* and present special gifts to the Lord. 28Do no work during that entire day because it is the Day of Atonement, when offerings of purification are made for you, making you right with* the Lord your God. 29All who do not deny themselves that day will be cut off from God's people. 30And I will destroy anyone among you who does any work on that day. 31You must not do any work at all! This is a permanent law for you, and it must be observed from generation to generation wherever you live. 32This will be a Sabbath day of complete rest for you, and on that day you must deny yourselves. This day of rest will begin at sundown on the ninth day of the month and extend until sundown on the tenth day."

The Festival of Shelters

33And the Lord said to Moses, 34"Give the following instructions to the people of Israel. Begin celebrating the Festival of Shelters* on the fifteenth day of the appointed month—five days after the Day of Atonement.* This festival to the Lord will last for seven days. 35On the first day of the festival you must proclaim an official day for holy assembly, when you do no ordinary work. 36For seven days you must present special gifts to the Lord. The eighth day is another holy day on which you present your special gifts to the Lord. This will be a solemn occasion, and no ordinary work may be done that day.

23:13a Hebrew 2⁄10 of an ephah [4.4 liters]; also in 23:17.   23:13b Hebrew 1⁄4 of a hin [1 liter].   23:21 This celebration, called the Festival of Harvest or the Festival of Weeks, was later called the Festival of Pentecost (see Acts 2:1). It is celebrated today as Shavuot (or Shabuoth).   23:24 Hebrew On the first day of the seventh month. This day in the ancient Hebrew lunar calendar occurred in September or October. This festival is celebrated today as Rosh Hashanah, the Jewish new year.   23:27a Hebrew on the tenth day of the seventh month; see 23:24 and the note there. This day in the ancient Hebrew lunar calendar occurred in September or October. It is celebrated today as Yom Kippur.   23:27b Or to fast; similarly in 23:29, 32.   23:28 Or when atonement is made for you before.   23:34a Or Festival of Booths, or Festival of Tabernacles. This was earlier called the Festival of the Final Harvest or Festival of Ingathering (see Exod 23:16b). It is celebrated today as Sukkot (or Succoth).   23:34b Hebrew on the fifteenth day of the seventh month; see 23:27a and the note there.

37("These are the LORD's appointed festivals. Celebrate them each year as official days for holy assembly by presenting special gifts to the LORD—burnt offerings, grain offerings, sacrifices, and liquid offerings—each on its proper day. 38These festivals must be observed in addition to the LORD's regular Sabbath days, and the offerings are in addition to your personal gifts, the offerings you give to fulfill your vows, and the voluntary offerings you present to the LORD.)

39"Remember that this seven-day festival to the LORD—the Festival of Shelters—begins on the fifteenth day of the appointed month,* after you have harvested all the produce of the land. The first day and the eighth day of the festival will be days of complete rest. 40On the first day gather branches from magnificent trees*—palm fronds, boughs from leafy trees, and willows that grow by the streams. Then celebrate with joy before the LORD your God for seven days. 41You must observe this festival to the LORD for seven days every year. This is a permanent law for you, and it must be observed in the appointed month* from generation to generation. 42For seven days you must live outside in little shelters. All native-born Israelites must live in shelters. 43This will remind each new generation of Israelites that I made their ancestors live in shelters when I rescued them from the land of Egypt. I am the LORD your God."

44So Moses gave the Israelites these instructions regarding the annual festivals of the LORD.

Pure Oil and Holy Bread

24 The LORD said to Moses, 2"Command the people of Israel to bring you pure oil of pressed olives for the light, to keep the lamps burning continually. 3This is the lampstand that stands in the Tabernacle, in front of the inner curtain that shields the Ark of the Covenant.* Aaron must keep the lamps burning in the LORD's presence all night. This is a permanent law for you, and it must be observed from generation to generation. 4Aaron and the priests must tend the lamps on the pure gold lampstand continually in the LORD's presence.

5"You must bake twelve flat loaves of bread from choice flour, using four quarts* of flour for each loaf. 6Place the bread before the LORD on the pure gold table, and arrange the loaves in two stacks, with six loaves in each stack. 7Put some pure frankincense near each stack to serve as a representative offering, a special gift presented to the LORD. 8Every Sabbath day this bread must be laid out before the LORD as a gift from the Israelites; it is an ongoing expression of the eternal covenant. 9The loaves of bread will belong to Aaron and his descendants, who must eat them in a sacred place, for they are most holy. It is the permanent right of the priests to claim this portion of the special gifts presented to the LORD."

An Example of Just Punishment

10One day a man who had an Israelite mother and an Egyptian father came out of his tent and got into a fight with one of the Israelite men. 11During the fight, this son of an Israelite woman blasphemed the Name of the LORD* with a curse. So the man was brought to Moses for judgment. His mother was Shelomith, the daughter of Dibri of the tribe of Dan. 12They kept the man in custody until the LORD's will in the matter should become clear to them.

13Then the LORD said to Moses, 14"Take the blasphemer outside the camp, and tell all those who heard the curse to lay their hands on his head. Then let the entire community stone him to death. 15Say to the people of Israel: Those who curse their God will be punished for their sin. 16Anyone who blasphemes the Name of the LORD must be stoned to death by the whole community of Israel. Any native-born Israelite or foreigner among you who blasphemes the Name of the LORD must be put to death.

17"Anyone who takes another person's life must be put to death.

18"Anyone who kills another person's animal must pay for it in full—a live animal for the animal that was killed.

19"Anyone who injures another person must be dealt with according to the injury inflicted—20a fracture for a fracture, an eye for an eye, a tooth for a tooth. Whatever anyone does to injure another person must be paid back in kind.

21"Whoever kills an animal must pay for it in full, but whoever kills another person must be put to death.

22"This same standard applies both to native-born Israelites and to the foreigners living among you. I am the LORD your God."

23After Moses gave all these instructions to

23:39 Hebrew *on the fifteenth day of the seventh month.*   23:40 Or *gather fruit from majestic trees.*   23:41 Hebrew *the seventh month.*
24:3 Hebrew *in the Tent of Meeting, outside the inner curtain of the Testimony;* see note on 16:13.   24:5 Hebrew ²⁄₁₀ *of an ephah* [4.4 liters].   24:11 Hebrew *the Name;* also in 24:16b.

the Israelites, they took the blasphemer outside the camp and stoned him to death. The Israelites did just as the LORD had commanded Moses.

The Sabbath Year

25 While Moses was on Mount Sinai, the LORD said to him, 2"Give the following instructions to the people of Israel. When you have entered the land I am giving you, the land itself must observe a Sabbath rest before the LORD every seventh year. 3For six years you may plant your fields and prune your vineyards and harvest your crops, 4but during the seventh year the land must have a Sabbath year of complete rest. It is the LORD's Sabbath. Do not plant your fields or prune your vineyards during that year. 5And don't store away the crops that grow on their own or gather the grapes from your unpruned vines. The land must have a year of complete rest. 6But you may eat whatever the land produces on its own during its Sabbath. This applies to you, your male and female servants, your hired workers, and the temporary residents who live with you. 7Your livestock and the wild animals in your land will also be allowed to eat what the land produces.

The Year of Jubilee

8"In addition, you must count off seven Sabbath years, seven sets of seven years, adding up to forty-nine years in all. 9Then on the Day of Atonement in the fiftieth year,* blow the ram's horn loud and long throughout the land. 10Set this year apart as holy, a time to proclaim freedom throughout the land for all who live there. It will be a jubilee year for you, when each of you may return to the land that belonged to your ancestors and return to your own clan. 11This fiftieth year will be a jubilee for you. During that year you must not plant your fields or store away any of the crops that grow on their own, and don't gather the grapes from your unpruned vines. 12It will be a jubilee year for you, and you must keep it holy. But you may eat whatever the land produces on its own. 13In the Year of Jubilee each of you may return to the land that belonged to your ancestors.

14"When you make an agreement with your neighbor to buy or sell property, you must not take advantage of each other. 15When you buy land from your neighbor, the price you pay must be based on the number of years since the last jubilee. The seller must set the price by taking into account the number of years

remaining until the next Year of Jubilee. 16The more years until the next jubilee, the higher the price; the fewer years, the lower the price. After all, the person selling the land is actually selling you a certain number of harvests. 17Show your fear of God by not taking advantage of each other. I am the LORD your God.

18"If you want to live securely in the land, follow my decrees and obey my regulations. 19Then the land will yield large crops, and you will eat your fill and live securely in it. 20But you might ask, 'What will we eat during the seventh year, since we are not allowed to plant or harvest crops that year?' 21Be assured that I will send my blessing for you in the sixth year, so the land will produce a crop large enough for three years. 22When you plant your fields in the eighth year, you will still be eating from the large crop of the sixth year. In fact, you will still be eating from that large crop when the new crop is harvested in the ninth year.

Redemption of Property

23"The land must never be sold on a permanent basis, for the land belongs to me. You are only foreigners and tenant farmers working for me. 24"With every purchase of land you must grant the seller the right to buy it back. 25If one of your fellow Israelites falls into poverty and is forced to sell some family land, then a close relative should buy it back for him. 26If there is no close relative to buy the land, but the person who sold it gets enough money to buy it back, 27he then has the right to redeem it from the one who bought it. The price of the land will be discounted according to the number of years until the next Year of Jubilee. In this way the original owner can then return to the land. 28But if the original owner cannot afford to buy back the land, it will remain with the new owner until the next Year of Jubilee. In the jubilee year, the land must be returned to the original owners so they can return to their family land.

29"Anyone who sells a house inside a walled town has the right to buy it back for a full year after its sale. During that year, the seller retains the right to buy it back. 30But if it is not bought back within a year, the sale of the house within the walled town cannot be reversed. It will become the permanent property of the buyer. It will not be returned to the original owner in the Year of Jubilee. 31But a house in a village— a settlement without fortified walls—will be treated like property in the countryside. Such

25:9 Hebrew *on the tenth day of the seventh month, on the Day of Atonement;* see 23:27a and the note there.

a house may be bought back at any time, and it must be returned to the original owner in the Year of Jubilee.

³²"The Levites always have the right to buy back a house they have sold within the towns allotted to them. ³³And any property that is sold by the Levites—all houses within the Levitical towns—must be returned in the Year of Jubilee. After all, the houses in the towns reserved for the Levites are the only property they own in all Israel. ³⁴The open pastureland around the Levitical towns may never be sold. It is their permanent possession.

Redemption of the Poor and Enslaved

³⁵"If one of your fellow Israelites falls into poverty and cannot support himself, support him as you would a foreigner or a temporary resident and allow him to live with you. ³⁶Do not charge interest or make a profit at his expense. Instead, show your fear of God by letting him live with you as your relative. ³⁷Remember, do not charge interest on money you lend him or make a profit on food you sell him. ³⁸I am the LORD your God, who brought you out of the land of Egypt to give you the land of Canaan and to be your God.

³⁹"If one of your fellow Israelites falls into poverty and is forced to sell himself to you, do not treat him as a slave. ⁴⁰Treat him instead as a hired worker or as a temporary resident who lives with you, and he will serve you only until the Year of Jubilee. ⁴¹At that time he and his children will no longer be obligated to you, and they will return to their clans and go back to the land originally allotted to their ancestors. ⁴²The people of Israel are my servants, whom I brought out of the land of Egypt, so they must never be sold as slaves. ⁴³Show your fear of God by not treating them harshly.

⁴⁴"However, you may purchase male and female slaves from among the nations around you. ⁴⁵You may also purchase the children of temporary residents who live among you, including those who have been born in your land. You may treat them as your property, ⁴⁶passing them on to your children as a permanent inheritance. You may treat them as slaves, but you must never treat your fellow Israelites this way.

⁴⁷"Suppose a foreigner or temporary resident becomes rich while living among you. If any of your fellow Israelites fall into poverty and are forced to sell themselves to such a foreigner or to a member of his family, ⁴⁸they still retain the right to be bought back, even after they have been purchased. They may be bought back by a brother, ⁴⁹an uncle, or a cousin. In fact, anyone from the extended family may buy them back. They may also redeem themselves if they have prospered. ⁵⁰They will negotiate the price of their freedom with the person who bought them. The price will be based on the number of years from the time they were sold until the next Year of Jubilee—whatever it would cost to hire a worker for that period of time. ⁵¹If many years still remain until the jubilee, they will repay the proper proportion of what they received when they sold themselves. ⁵²If only a few years remain until the Year of Jubilee, they will repay a small amount for their redemption. ⁵³The foreigner must treat them as workers hired on a yearly basis. You must not allow a foreigner to treat any of your fellow Israelites harshly. ⁵⁴If any Israelites have not been bought back by the time the Year of Jubilee arrives, they and their children must be set free at that time. ⁵⁵For the people of Israel belong to me. They are my servants, whom I brought out of the land of Egypt. I am the LORD your God.

Blessings for Obedience

26 "Do not make idols or set up carved images, or sacred pillars, or sculptured stones in your land so you may worship them. I am the LORD your God. ²You must keep my Sabbath days of rest and show reverence for my sanctuary. I am the LORD.

³"If you follow my decrees and are careful to obey my commands, ⁴I will send you the seasonal rains. The land will then yield its crops, and the trees of the field will produce their fruit. ⁵Your threshing season will overlap with the grape harvest, and your grape harvest will overlap with the season of planting grain. You will eat your fill and live securely in your own land.

⁶"I will give you peace in the land, and you will be able to sleep with no cause for fear. I will rid the land of wild animals and keep your enemies out of your land. ⁷In fact, you will chase down your enemies and slaughter them with your swords. ⁸Five of you will chase a hundred, and a hundred of you will chase ten thousand! All your enemies will fall beneath your sword.

⁹"I will look favorably upon you, making you fertile and multiplying your people. And I will fulfill my covenant with you. ¹⁰You will have such a surplus of crops that you will need to clear out the old grain to make room for the

new harvest! [11]I will live among you, and I will not despise you. [12]I will walk among you; I will be your God, and you will be my people. [13]I am the LORD your God, who brought you out of the land of Egypt so you would no longer be their slaves. I broke the yoke of slavery from your neck so you can walk with your heads held high.

Punishments for Disobedience

[14]"However, if you do not listen to me or obey all these commands, [15]and if you break my covenant by rejecting my decrees, treating my regulations with contempt, and refusing to obey my commands, [16]I will punish you. I will bring sudden terrors upon you—wasting diseases and burning fevers that will cause your eyes to fail and your life to ebb away. You will plant your crops in vain because your enemies will eat them. [17]I will turn against you, and you will be defeated by your enemies. Those who hate you will rule over you, and you will run even when no one is chasing you!

[18]"And if, in spite of all this, you still disobey me, I will punish you seven times over for your sins. [19]I will break your proud spirit by making the skies as unyielding as iron and the earth as hard as bronze. [20]All your work will be for nothing, for your land will yield no crops, and your trees will bear no fruit.

[21]"If even then you remain hostile toward me and refuse to obey me, I will inflict disaster on you seven times over for your sins. [22]I will send wild animals that will rob you of your children and destroy your livestock. Your numbers will dwindle, and your roads will be deserted.

[23]"And if you fail to learn the lesson and continue your hostility toward me, [24]then I myself will be hostile toward you. I will personally strike you with calamity seven times over for your sins. [25]I will send armies against you to carry out the curse of the covenant you have broken. When you run to your towns for safety, I will send a plague to destroy you there, and you will be handed over to your enemies. [26]I will destroy your food supply, so that ten women will need only one oven to bake bread for their families. They will ration your food by weight, and though you have food to eat, you will not be satisfied.

[27]"If in spite of all this you still refuse to listen and still remain hostile toward me, [28]then I will give full vent to my hostility. I myself will punish you seven times over for your sins. [29]Then you will eat the flesh of your own sons and daughters. [30]I will destroy your pagan shrines and knock down your places of worship. I will leave your lifeless corpses piled on top of your lifeless idols,* and I will despise you. [31]I will make your cities desolate and destroy your places of pagan worship. I will take no pleasure in your offerings that should be a pleasing aroma to me. [32]Yes, I myself will devastate your land, and your enemies who come to occupy it will be appalled at what they see. [33]I will scatter you among the nations and bring out my sword against you. Your land will become desolate, and your cities will lie in ruins. [34]Then at last the land will enjoy its neglected Sabbath years as it lies desolate while you are in exile in the land of your enemies. Then the land will finally rest and enjoy the Sabbaths it missed. [35]As long as the land lies in ruins, it will enjoy the rest you never allowed it to take every seventh year while you lived in it.

[36]"And for those of you who survive, I will demoralize you in the land of your enemies. You will live in such fear that the sound of a leaf driven by the wind will send you fleeing. You will run as though fleeing from a sword, and you will fall even when no one pursues you. [37]Though no one is chasing you, you will stumble over each other as though fleeing from a sword. You will have no power to stand up against your enemies. [38]You will die among the foreign nations and be devoured in the land of your enemies. [39]Those of you who survive will waste away in your enemies' lands because of their sins and the sins of their ancestors.

[40]"But at last my people will confess their sins and the sins of their ancestors for betraying me and being hostile toward me. [41]When I have turned their hostility back on them and brought them to the land of their enemies, then at last their stubborn hearts will be humbled, and they will pay for their sins. [42]Then I will remember my covenant with Jacob and my covenant with Isaac and my covenant with Abraham, and I will remember the land. [43]For the land must be abandoned to enjoy its years of Sabbath rest as it lies deserted. At last the people will pay for their sins, for they have continually rejected my regulations and despised my decrees.

[44]"But despite all this, I will not utterly reject or despise them while they are in exile in the land of their enemies. I will not cancel my covenant with them by wiping them out, for I am

26:30 The Hebrew term (literally *round things*) probably alludes to dung.

the Lord their God. [45]For their sakes I will remember my ancient covenant with their ancestors, whom I brought out of the land of Egypt in the sight of all the nations, that I might be their God. I am the Lord."

[46]These are the decrees, regulations, and instructions that the Lord gave through Moses on Mount Sinai as evidence of the relationship between himself and the Israelites.

Redemption of Gifts Offered to the Lord

27 The Lord said to Moses, [2]"Give the following instructions to the people of Israel. If anyone makes a special vow to dedicate someone to the Lord by paying the value of that person, [3]here is the scale of values to be used. A man between the ages of twenty and sixty is valued at fifty shekels* of silver, as measured by the sanctuary shekel. [4]A woman of that age is valued at thirty shekels* of silver. [5]A boy between the ages of five and twenty is valued at twenty shekels of silver; a girl of that age is valued at ten shekels* of silver. [6]A boy between the ages of one month and five years is valued at five shekels of silver; a girl of that age is valued at three shekels* of silver. [7]A man older than sixty is valued at fifteen shekels of silver; a woman of that age is valued at ten shekels* of silver. [8]If you desire to make such a vow but cannot afford to pay the required amount, take the person to the priest. He will determine the amount for you to pay based on what you can afford.

[9]"If your vow involves giving an animal that is acceptable as an offering to the Lord, any gift to the Lord will be considered holy. [10]You may not exchange or substitute it for another animal—neither a good animal for a bad one nor a bad animal for a good one. But if you do exchange one animal for another, then both the original animal and its substitute will be considered holy. [11]If your vow involves an unclean animal—one that is not acceptable as an offering to the Lord—then you must bring the animal to the priest. [12]He will assess its value, and his assessment will be final, whether high or low. [13]If you want to buy back the animal, you must pay the value set by the priest, plus 20 percent.

[14]"If someone dedicates a house to the Lord, the priest will come to assess its value. The priest's assessment will be final, whether high or low. [15]If the person who dedicated the house wants to buy it back, he must pay the value set by the priest, plus 20 percent. Then the house will again be his.

[16]"If someone dedicates to the Lord a piece of his family property, its value will be assessed according to the amount of seed required to plant it—fifty shekels of silver for a field planted with five bushels of barley seed.* [17]If the field is dedicated to the Lord in the Year of Jubilee, then the entire assessment will apply. [18]But if the field is dedicated after the Year of Jubilee, the priest will assess the land's value in proportion to the number of years left until the next Year of Jubilee. Its assessed value is reduced each year. [19]If the person who dedicated the field wants to buy it back, he must pay the value set by the priest, plus 20 percent. Then the field will again be legally his. [20]But if he does not want to buy it back, and it is sold to someone else, the field can no longer be bought back. [21]When the field is released in the Year of Jubilee, it will be holy, a field specially set apart* for the Lord. It will become the property of the priests.

[22]"If someone dedicates to the Lord a field he has purchased but which is not part of his family property, [23]the priest will assess its value based on the number of years left until the next Year of Jubilee. On that day he must give the assessed value of the land as a sacred donation to the Lord. [24]In the Year of Jubilee the field must be returned to the person from whom he purchased it, the one who inherited it as family property. [25](All the payments must be measured by the weight of the sanctuary shekel,* which equals twenty gerahs.)

[26]"You may not dedicate a firstborn animal to the Lord, for the firstborn of your cattle, sheep, and goats already belong to him. [27]However, you may buy back the firstborn of a ceremonially unclean animal by paying the priest's assessment of its worth, plus 20 percent. If you do not buy it back, the priest will sell it at its assessed value.

[28]"However, anything specially set apart for the Lord—whether a person, an animal, or family property—must never be sold or bought back. Anything devoted in this way has been set apart as holy, and it belongs to

---

27:3 Or 20 ounces [570 grams].   27:4 Or 12 ounces [342 grams].   27:5 Or A boy . . . 8 ounces [228 grams] of silver; a girl . . . 4 ounces [114 grams].   27:6 Or A boy . . . 2 ounces [57 grams] of silver; a girl . . . 1.2 ounces [34 grams].   27:7 Or A man . . . 6 ounces [171 grams] of silver; a woman . . . 4 ounces [114 grams].   27:16 Hebrew 50 shekels [20 ounces or 570 grams] of silver for a homer [220 liters] of barley seed.   27:21 The Hebrew term used here refers to the complete consecration of things or people to the Lord, either by destroying them or by giving them as an offering; also in 27:28, 29.   27:25 Each shekel was about 0.4 ounces [11 grams] in weight.

the Lord. ²⁹No person specially set apart for destruction may be bought back. Such a person must be put to death.

³⁰"One-tenth of the produce of the land, whether grain from the fields or fruit from the trees, belongs to the Lord and must be set apart to him as holy. ³¹If you want to buy back the Lord's tenth of the grain or fruit, you must pay its value, plus 20 percent. ³²Count off every tenth animal from your herds and flocks and set them apart for the Lord as holy. ³³You may not pick and choose between good and bad animals, and you may not substitute one for another. But if you do exchange one animal for another, then both the original animal and its substitute will be considered holy and cannot be bought back."

³⁴These are the commands that the Lord gave through Moses on Mount Sinai for the Israelites.

Numbers

THE DISCONTENTED WHINING of a young child can be difficult to ignore. Likewise, the childish whining of the Israelites in the wilderness characterizes the book of Numbers. This book picks up where Exodus leaves off, with the Israelites camped at the base of Mount Sinai. From there the Israelites journeyed to the wilderness of Paran, south of the Promised Land. Scouts were sent to explore the Promised Land and give a report on its inhabitants. When they returned to the camp, their report was unfavorable. The people doubted God's ability to give them their inheritance, and they complained against him. Because of their unfaithfulness, God condemned them to wander in the wilderness until the generation of complainers died and a new generation took their place. Forty years later they slowly made their way back to Canaan—this time ready to obey God's commands. After winning some important battles east of the Jordan River, the Israelites prepared to enter the heart of the Promised Land they had waited so long to see.

■ **Author:** Moses, according to Jewish tradition

■ **Date Written:** Uncertain, perhaps between 1450 and 1410 BC

■ **Purpose:** To tell the story of how Israel prepared to enter the Promised Land, how they sinned and were punished, and how they returned again to enter the land

■ **Themes:** Rebellion, faith, God's justice and faithfulness

■ **Outline**
1:1–2:34 The census of the men for battle
3:1–10:10 Special regulations for the Israelites
10:11–14:45 The journey to Canaan and the great rebellion
15:1–19:22 Wandering in the wilderness
20:1–25:18 The journey to the plains of Moab and Balaam's oracles
26:1–36:13 Preparations in Moab for entry into Canaan

Registration of Israel's Troops

1 A year after Israel's departure from Egypt, the LORD spoke to Moses in the Tabernacle* in the wilderness of Sinai. On the first day of the second month* of that year he said, 2"From the whole community of Israel, record the names of all the warriors by their clans and families. List all the men 3twenty years old or older who are able to go to war. You and Aaron must register the troops, 4and you will be assisted by one family leader from each tribe.

5"These are the tribes and the names of the leaders who will assist you:

Tribe	Leader
Reuben	Elizur son of Shedeur
6 Simeon	Shelumiel son of Zurishaddai
7 Judah	Nahshon son of Amminadab
8 Issachar	Nethanel son of Zuar
9 Zebulun	Eliab son of Helon
10 Ephraim son of Joseph	Elishama son of Ammihud
Manasseh son of Joseph	Gamaliel son of Pedahzur
11 Benjamin	Abidan son of Gideoni
12 Dan	Ahiezer son of Ammishaddai
13 Asher	Pagiel son of Ocran
14 Gad	Eliasaph son of Deuel
15 Naphtali	Ahira son of Enan

16These are the chosen leaders of the community, the leaders of their ancestral tribes, the heads of the clans of Israel."

17So Moses and Aaron called together these

1:1a Hebrew *the Tent of Meeting.*   1:1b This day in the ancient Hebrew lunar calendar occurred in April or May.

chosen leaders, [18]and they assembled the whole community of Israel on that very day.* All the people were registered according to their ancestry by their clans and families. The men of Israel who were twenty years old or older were listed one by one, [19]just as the LORD had commanded Moses. So Moses recorded their names in the wilderness of Sinai.

[20-21]This is the number of men twenty years old or older who were able to go to war, as their names were listed in the records of their clans and families*:

Tribe	Number
Reuben (Jacob's* oldest son)	46,500
[22-23] Simeon	59,300
[24-25] Gad	45,650
[26-27] Judah	74,600
[28-29] Issachar	54,400
[30-31] Zebulun	57,400
[32-33] Ephraim son of Joseph	40,500
[34-35] Manasseh son of Joseph	32,200
[36-37] Benjamin	35,400
[38-39] Dan	62,700
[40-41] Asher	41,500
[42-43] Naphtali	53,400

[44]These were the men registered by Moses and Aaron and the twelve leaders of Israel, all listed according to their ancestral descent. [45]They were registered by families—all the men of Israel who were twenty years old or older and able to go to war. [46]The total number was 603,550.

[47]But this total did not include the Levites. [48]For the LORD had said to Moses, [49]"Do not include the tribe of Levi in the registration; do not count them with the rest of the Israelites. [50]Put the Levites in charge of the Tabernacle of the Covenant,* along with all its furnishings and equipment. They must carry the Tabernacle and all its furnishings as you travel, and they must take care of it and camp around it. [51]Whenever it is time for the Tabernacle to move, the Levites will take it down. And when it is time to stop, they will set it up again. But any unauthorized person who goes too near the Tabernacle must be put to death. [52]Each tribe of Israel will camp in a designated area with its own family banner. [53]But the Levites will camp around the Tabernacle of the Covenant to protect the community of Israel from the LORD's anger. The Levites are responsible to stand guard around the Tabernacle."

[54]So the Israelites did everything just as the LORD had commanded Moses.

Organization for Israel's Camp

2 Then the LORD gave these instructions to Moses and Aaron: [2]"When the Israelites set up camp, each tribe will be assigned its own area. The tribal divisions will camp beneath their family banners on all four sides of the Tabernacle,* but at some distance from it.

[3-4]"The divisions of Judah, Issachar, and Zebulun are to camp toward the sunrise on the east side of the Tabernacle, beneath their family banners. These are the names of the tribes, their leaders, and the numbers of their registered troops:

Tribe	Leader	Number
Judah	Nahshon son of Amminadab	74,600
[5-6] Issachar	Nethanel son of Zuar	54,400
[7-8] Zebulun	Eliab son of Helon	57,400

[9]So the total of all the troops on Judah's side of the camp is 186,400. These three tribes are to lead the way whenever the Israelites travel to a new campsite.

[10-11]"The divisions of Reuben, Simeon, and Gad are to camp on the south side of the Tabernacle, beneath their family banners. These are the names of the tribes, their leaders, and the numbers of their registered troops:

Tribe	Leader	Number
Reuben	Elizur son of Shedeur	46,500
[12-13] Simeon	Shelumiel son of Zurishaddai	59,300
[14-15] Gad	Eliasaph son of Deuel*	45,650

[16]So the total of all the troops on Reuben's side of the camp is 151,450. These three tribes will be second in line whenever the Israelites travel.

[17]"Then the Tabernacle, carried by the Levites, will set out from the middle of the camp. All the tribes are to travel in the same order

1:18 Hebrew *on the first day of the second month*; see 1:1. 1:20-21a In the Hebrew text, this sentence (*This is the number of men twenty years old or older who were able to go to war, as their names were listed in the records of their clans and families*) is repeated in 1:22, 24, 26, 28, 30, 32, 34, 36, 38, 40, 42. 1:20-21b Hebrew *Israel's*. The names "Jacob" and "Israel" are often interchanged throughout the Old Testament, referring sometimes to the individual patriarch and sometimes to the nation. 1:50 Or *Tabernacle of the Testimony*; also in 1:53. 2:2 Hebrew *the Tent of Meeting*; also in 2:17. 2:14-15 As in many Hebrew manuscripts, Samaritan Pentateuch, and Latin Vulgate (see also 1:14); most Hebrew manuscripts read *son of Reuel*.

that they camp, each in position under the appropriate family banner.

18-19"The divisions of Ephraim, Manasseh, and Benjamin are to camp on the west side of the Tabernacle, beneath their family banners. These are the names of the tribes, their leaders, and the numbers of their registered troops:

Tribe	Leader	Number
Ephraim	Elishama son of Ammihud	40,500
20-21 Manasseh	Gamaliel son of Pedahzur	32,200
22-23 Benjamin	Abidan son of Gideoni	35,400

24So the total of all the troops on Ephraim's side of the camp is 108,100. These three tribes will be third in line whenever the Israelites travel.

25-26"The divisions of Dan, Asher, and Naphtali are to camp on the north side of the Tabernacle, beneath their family banners. These are the names of the tribes, their leaders, and the numbers of their registered troops:

Tribe	Leader	Number
Dan	Ahiezer son of Ammishaddai	62,700
27-28 Asher	Pagiel son of Ocran	41,500
29-30 Naphtali	Ahira son of Enan	53,400

31So the total of all the troops on Dan's side of the camp is 157,600. These three tribes will be last, marching under their banners whenever the Israelites travel."

32In summary, the troops of Israel listed by their families totaled 603,550. 33But as the LORD had commanded, the Levites were not included in this registration. 34So the people of Israel did everything as the LORD had commanded Moses. Each clan and family set up camp and marched under their banners exactly as the LORD had instructed them.

Levites Appointed for Service

3 This is the family line of Aaron and Moses as it was recorded when the LORD spoke to Moses on Mount Sinai: 2The names of Aaron's sons were Nadab (the oldest), Abihu, Eleazar, and Ithamar. 3These sons of Aaron were anointed and ordained to minister as priests. 4But Nadab and Abihu died in the LORD's presence in the wilderness of Sinai when they burned before the LORD the wrong kind of fire, different than he had commanded. Since they

had no sons, this left only Eleazar and Ithamar to serve as priests with their father, Aaron.

5Then the LORD said to Moses, 6"Call forward the tribe of Levi, and present them to Aaron the priest to serve as his assistants. 7They will serve Aaron and the whole community, performing their sacred duties in and around the Tabernacle.* 8They will also maintain all the furnishings of the sacred tent,* serving in the Tabernacle on behalf of all the Israelites. 9Assign the Levites to Aaron and his sons. They have been given from among all the people of Israel to serve as their assistants. 10Appoint Aaron and his sons to carry out the duties of the priesthood. But any unauthorized person who goes too near the sanctuary must be put to death."

11And the LORD said to Moses, 12"Look, I have chosen the Levites from among the Israelites to serve as substitutes for all the firstborn sons of the people of Israel. The Levites belong to me, 13for all the firstborn males are mine. On the day I struck down all the firstborn sons of the Egyptians, I set apart for myself all the firstborn in Israel, both of people and of animals. They are mine; I am the LORD."

Registration of the Levites

14The LORD spoke again to Moses in the wilderness of Sinai. He said, 15"Record the names of the members of the tribe of Levi by their families and clans. List every male who is one month old or older." 16So Moses listed them, just as the LORD had commanded.

17Levi had three sons, whose names were Gershon, Kohath, and Merari.
18The clans descended from Gershon were named after two of his descendants, Libni and Shimei.
19The clans descended from Kohath were named after four of his descendants, Amram, Izhar, Hebron, and Uzziel.
20The clans descended from Merari were named after two of his descendants, Mahli and Mushi.
These were the Levite clans, listed according to their family groups.

21The descendants of Gershon were composed of the clans descended from Libni and Shimei. 22There were 7,500 males one month old or older among these Gershonite clans. 23They were assigned the area to the west of the Tabernacle for their camp. 24The leader

3:7 Hebrew *around the Tent of Meeting, doing service at the Tabernacle.*   3:8 Hebrew *the Tent of Meeting;* also in 3:25.

of the Gershonite clans was Eliasaph son of Lael. 25These two clans were responsible to care for the Tabernacle, including the sacred tent with its layers of coverings, the curtain at its entrance, 26the curtains of the courtyard that surrounded the Tabernacle and altar, the curtain at the courtyard entrance, the ropes, and all the equipment related to their use.

27The descendants of Kohath were composed of the clans descended from Amram, Izhar, Hebron, and Uzziel. 28There were 8,600* males one month old or older among these Kohathite clans. They were responsible for the care of the sanctuary, 29and they were assigned the area south of the Tabernacle for their camp. 30The leader of the Kohathite clans was Elizaphan son of Uzziel. 31These four clans were responsible for the care of the Ark, the table, the lampstand, the altars, the various articles used in the sanctuary, the inner curtain, and all the equipment related to their use. 32Eleazar, son of Aaron the priest, was the chief administrator over all the Levites, with special responsibility for the oversight of the sanctuary.

33The descendants of Merari were composed of the clans descended from Mahli and Mushi. 34There were 6,200 males one month old or older among these Merarite clans. 35They were assigned the area north of the Tabernacle for their camp. The leader of the Merarite clans was Zuriel son of Abihail. 36These two clans were responsible for the care of the frames supporting the Tabernacle, the crossbars, the pillars, the bases, and all the equipment related to their use. 37They were also responsible for the posts of the courtyard and all their bases, pegs, and ropes.

38The area in front of the Tabernacle, in the east toward the sunrise,* was reserved for the tents of Moses and of Aaron and his sons, who had the final responsibility for the sanctuary on behalf of the people of Israel. Anyone other than a priest or Levite who went too near the sanctuary was to be put to death.

39When Moses and Aaron counted the Levite clans at the LORD's command, the total number was 22,000 males one month old or older.

Redeeming the Firstborn Sons

40Then the LORD said to Moses, "Now count all the firstborn sons in Israel who are one month old or older, and make a list of their names. 41The Levites must be reserved for me

as substitutes for the firstborn sons of Israel; I am the LORD. And the Levites' livestock must be reserved for me as substitutes for the firstborn livestock of the whole nation of Israel."

42So Moses counted the firstborn sons of the people of Israel, just as the LORD had commanded. 43The number of firstborn sons who were one month old or older was 22,273.

44Then the LORD said to Moses, 45"Take the Levites as substitutes for the firstborn sons of the people of Israel. And take the livestock of the Levites as substitutes for the firstborn livestock of the people of Israel. The Levites belong to me; I am the LORD. 46There are 273 more firstborn sons of Israel than there are Levites. To redeem these extra firstborn sons, 47collect five pieces of silver* for each of them (each piece weighing the same as the sanctuary shekel, which equals twenty gerahs). 48Give the silver to Aaron and his sons as the redemption price for the extra firstborn sons."

49So Moses collected the silver for redeeming the firstborn sons of Israel who exceeded the number of Levites. 50He collected 1,365 pieces of silver* on behalf of these firstborn sons of Israel (each piece weighing the same as the sanctuary shekel). 51And Moses gave the silver for the redemption to Aaron and his sons, just as the LORD had commanded.

Duties of the Kohathite Clan

4 Then the LORD said to Moses and Aaron, 2"Record the names of the members of the clans and families of the Kohathite division of the tribe of Levi. 3List all the men between the ages of thirty and fifty who are eligible to serve in the Tabernacle.*

4"The duties of the Kohathites at the Tabernacle will relate to the most sacred objects. 5When the camp moves, Aaron and his sons must enter the Tabernacle first to take down the inner curtain and cover the Ark of the Covenant* with it. 6Then they must cover the inner curtain with fine goatskin leather and spread over that a single piece of blue cloth. Finally, they must put the carrying poles of the Ark in place.

7"Next they must spread a blue cloth over the table where the Bread of the Presence is displayed, and on the cloth they will place the bowls, ladles, jars, pitchers, and the special bread. 8They must spread a scarlet cloth over all of this, and finally a covering of fine goatskin

---

3:28 Some Greek manuscripts read 8,300; see total in 3:39.   3:38 Hebrew toward the sunrise, in front of the Tent of Meeting.
3:47 Hebrew 5 shekels [2 ounces or 57 grams].   3:50 Hebrew 1,365 [shekels] of silver [34 pounds or 15.5 kilograms].   4:3 Hebrew
the Tent of Meeting; also in 4:4, 15, 23, 25, 28, 30, 31, 33, 35, 37, 39, 41, 43, 47.   4:5 Or Ark of the Testimony.

leather on top of the scarlet cloth. Then they must insert the carrying poles into the table.

9"Next they must cover the lampstand with a blue cloth, along with its lamps, lamp snuffers, trays, and special jars of olive oil. 10Then they must cover the lampstand and its accessories with fine goatskin leather and place the bundle on a carrying frame.

11"Next they must spread a blue cloth over the gold incense altar and cover this cloth with fine goatskin leather. Then they must attach the carrying poles to the altar. 12They must take all the remaining furnishings of the sanctuary and wrap them in a blue cloth, cover them with fine goatskin leather, and place them on the carrying frame.

13"They must remove the ashes from the altar for sacrifices and cover the altar with a purple cloth. 14All the altar utensils—the firepans, meat forks, shovels, basins, and all the containers—must be placed on the cloth, and a covering of fine goatskin leather must be spread over them. Finally, they must put the carrying poles in place. 15The camp will be ready to move when Aaron and his sons have finished covering the sanctuary and all the sacred articles. The Kohathites will come and carry these things to the next destination. But they must not touch the sacred objects, or they will die. So these are the things from the Tabernacle that the Kohathites must carry.

16"Eleazar son of Aaron the priest will be responsible for the oil of the lampstand, the fragrant incense, the daily grain offering, and the anointing oil. In fact, Eleazar will be responsible for the entire Tabernacle and everything in it, including the sanctuary and its furnishings."

17Then the LORD said to Moses and Aaron, 18"Do not let the Kohathite clans be destroyed from among the Levites! 19This is what you must do so they will live and not die when they approach the most sacred objects. Aaron and his sons must always go in with them and assign a specific duty or load to each person. 20The Kohathites must never enter the sanctuary to look at the sacred objects for even a moment, or they will die."

Duties of the Gershonite Clan

21And the LORD said to Moses, 22"Record the names of the members of the clans and families of the Gershonite division of the tribe of Levi. 23List all the men between the ages of thirty and fifty who are eligible to serve in the Tabernacle. 24"These Gershonite clans will be responsible for general service and carrying loads. 25They must carry the curtains of the Tabernacle, the Tabernacle itself with its coverings, the outer covering of fine goatskin leather, and the curtain for the Tabernacle entrance. 26They are also to carry the curtains for the courtyard walls that surround the Tabernacle and altar, the curtain across the courtyard entrance, the ropes, and all the equipment related to their use. The Gershonites are responsible for all these items. 27Aaron and his sons will direct the Gershonites regarding all their duties, whether it involves moving the equipment or doing other work. They must assign the Gershonites responsibility for the loads they are to carry. 28So these are the duties assigned to the Gershonite clans at the Tabernacle. They will be directly responsible to Ithamar son of Aaron the priest.

Duties of the Merarite Clan

29"Now record the names of the members of the clans and families of the Merarite division of the tribe of Levi. 30List all the men between the ages of thirty and fifty who are eligible to serve in the Tabernacle. 31"Their only duty at the Tabernacle will be to carry loads. They will carry the frames of the Tabernacle, the crossbars, the posts, and the bases; 32also the posts for the courtyard walls with their bases, pegs, and ropes; and all the accessories and everything else related to their use. Assign the various loads to each man by name. 33So these are the duties of the Merarite clans at the Tabernacle. They are directly responsible to Ithamar son of Aaron the priest."

Summary of the Registration

34So Moses, Aaron, and the other leaders of the community listed the members of the Kohathite division by their clans and families. 35The list included all the men between thirty and fifty years of age who were eligible for service in the Tabernacle, 36and the total number came to 2,750. 37So this was the total of all those from the Kohathite clans who were eligible to serve at the Tabernacle. Moses and Aaron listed them, just as the LORD had commanded through Moses.

38The Gershonite division was also listed by its clans and families. 39The list included all the men between thirty and fifty years of age who were eligible for service in the Tabernacle, 40and the total number came to 2,630. 41So this was the total of all those from the Gershonite clans who were eligible to serve at the Tabernacle. Moses and Aaron listed them, just as the LORD had commanded.

42The Merarite division was also listed by its clans and families. 43The list included all the men between thirty and fifty years of age who were eligible for service in the Tabernacle, 44and the total number came to 3,200. 45So this was the total of all those from the Merarite clans who were eligible for service. Moses and Aaron listed them, just as the LORD had commanded through Moses.

46So Moses, Aaron, and the leaders of Israel listed all the Levites by their clans and families. 47All the men between thirty and fifty years of age who were eligible for service in the Tabernacle and for its transportation 48numbered 8,580. 49When their names were recorded, as the LORD had commanded through Moses, each man was assigned his task and told what to carry.

And so the registration was completed, just as the LORD had commanded Moses.

Purity in Israel's Camp

5 The LORD gave these instructions to Moses: 2"Command the people of Israel to remove from the camp anyone who has a skin disease* or a discharge, or who has become ceremonially unclean by touching a dead person. 3This command applies to men and women alike. Remove them so they will not defile the camp in which I live among them." 4So the Israelites did as the LORD had commanded Moses and removed such people from the camp.

5Then the LORD said to Moses, 6"Give the following instructions to the people of Israel: If any of the people—men or women—betray the LORD by doing wrong to another person, they are guilty. 7They must confess their sin and make full restitution for what they have done, adding an additional 20 percent and returning it to the person who was wronged. 8But if the person who was wronged is dead, and there are no near relatives to whom restitution can be made, the payment belongs to the LORD and must be given to the priest. Those who are guilty must also bring a ram as a sacrifice, and they will be purified and made right with the LORD.* 9All the sacred offerings that the Israelites bring to a priest will belong to him. 10Each priest may keep all the sacred donations that he receives."

Protecting Marital Faithfulness

11And the LORD said to Moses, 12"Give the following instructions to the people of Israel.

"Suppose a man's wife goes astray, and she is unfaithful to her husband 13and has sex with another man, but neither her husband nor anyone else knows about it. She has defiled herself, even though there was no witness and she was not caught in the act. 14If her husband becomes jealous and is suspicious of his wife and needs to know whether or not she has defiled herself, 15the husband must bring his wife to the priest. He must also bring an offering of two quarts* of barley flour to be presented on her behalf. Do not mix it with olive oil or frankincense, for it is a jealousy offering—an offering to prove whether or not she is guilty.

16"The priest will then present her to stand trial before the LORD. 17He must take some holy water in a clay jar and pour into it dust he has taken from the Tabernacle floor. 18When the priest has presented the woman before the LORD, he must unbind her hair and place in her hands the offering of proof—the jealousy offering to determine whether her husband's suspicions are justified. The priest will stand before her, holding the jar of bitter water that brings a curse to those who are guilty. 19The priest will then put the woman under oath and say to her, 'If no other man has had sex with you, and you have not gone astray and defiled yourself while under your husband's authority, may you be immune from the effects of this bitter water that brings on the curse. 20But if you have gone astray by being unfaithful to your husband, and have defiled yourself by having sex with another man—'

21"At this point the priest must put the woman under oath by saying, 'May the people know that the LORD's curse is upon you when he makes you infertile, causing your womb to shrivel* and your abdomen to swell. 22Now may this water that brings the curse enter your body and cause your abdomen to swell and your womb to shrivel.*' And the woman will be required to say, 'Yes, let it be so.' 23And the priest will write these curses on a piece of leather and wash them off into the bitter water. 24He will make the woman drink the bitter water that brings on the curse. When the water enters her body, it will cause bitter suffering if she is guilty.

25"The priest will take the jealousy offering

5:2 Traditionally rendered *leprosy*. The Hebrew word used here describes various skin diseases.   5:8 Or *bring a ram for atonement, which will make atonement for them.*   5:15 Hebrew 1/10 of an ephah [2.2 liters].   5:21 Hebrew *when he causes your thigh to waste away.*   5:22 Hebrew *and your thigh to waste away.*

from the woman's hand, lift it up before the LORD, and carry it to the altar. 26He will take a handful of the flour as a token portion and burn it on the altar, and he will require the woman to drink the water. 27If she has defiled herself by being unfaithful to her husband, the water that brings on the curse will cause bitter suffering. Her abdomen will swell and her womb will shrink,* and her name will become a curse among her people. 28But if she has not defiled herself and is pure, then she will be unharmed and will still be able to have children.

29"This is the ritual law for dealing with suspicion. If a woman goes astray and defiles herself while under her husband's authority, 30or if a man becomes jealous and is suspicious that his wife has been unfaithful, the husband must present his wife before the LORD, and the priest will apply this entire ritual law to her. 31The husband will be innocent of any guilt in this matter, but his wife will be held accountable for her sin."

Nazirite Laws

6 Then the LORD said to Moses, 2"Give the following instructions to the people of Israel.

"If any of the people, either men or women, take the special vow of a Nazirite, setting themselves apart to the LORD in a special way, 3they must give up wine and other alcoholic drinks. They must not use vinegar made from wine or from other alcoholic drinks, they must not drink fresh grape juice, and they must not eat grapes or raisins. 4As long as they are bound by their Nazirite vow, they are not allowed to eat or drink anything that comes from a grapevine—not even the grape seeds or skins.

5"They must never cut their hair throughout the time of their vow, for they are holy and set apart to the LORD. Until the time of their vow has been fulfilled, they must let their hair grow long. 6And they must not go near a dead body during the entire period of their vow to the LORD. 7Even if the dead person is their own father, mother, brother, or sister, they must not defile themselves, for the hair on their head is the symbol of their separation to God. 8This requirement applies as long as they are set apart to the LORD.

9"If someone falls dead beside them, the hair they have dedicated will be defiled. They must wait for seven days and then shave their heads. Then they will be cleansed from their defilement. 10On the eighth day they must bring two turtledoves or two young pigeons to the priest at the entrance of the Tabernacle.* 11The priest will offer one of the birds for a sin offering and the other for a burnt offering. In this way, he will purify them* from the guilt they incurred through contact with the dead body. Then they must reaffirm their commitment and let their hair begin to grow again. 12The days of their vow that were completed before their defilement no longer count. They must rededicate themselves to the LORD as a Nazirite for the full term of their vow, and each must bring a one-year-old male lamb for a guilt offering.

13"This is the ritual law for Nazirites. At the conclusion of their time of separation as Nazirites, they must each go to the entrance of the Tabernacle 14and offer their sacrifices to the LORD: a one-year-old male lamb without defect for a burnt offering, a one-year-old female lamb without defect for a sin offering, a ram without defect for a peace offering, 15a basket of bread made without yeast—cakes of choice flour mixed with olive oil and wafers spread with olive oil—along with their prescribed grain offerings and liquid offerings. 16The priest will present these offerings before the LORD: first the sin offering and the burnt offering; 17then the ram for a peace offering, along with the basket of bread made without yeast. The priest must also present the prescribed grain offering and liquid offering to the LORD.

18"Then the Nazirites will shave their heads at the entrance of the Tabernacle. They will take the hair that had been dedicated and place it on the fire beneath the peace-offering sacrifice. 19After the Nazirite's head has been shaved, the priest will take for each of them the boiled shoulder of the ram, and he will take from the basket a cake and a wafer made without yeast. He will put them all into the Nazirite's hands. 20Then the priest will lift them up as a special offering before the LORD. These are holy portions for the priest, along with the breast of the special offering and the thigh of the sacred offering that are lifted up before the LORD. After this ceremony the Nazirites may again drink wine.

21"This is the ritual law of the Nazirites, who vow to bring these offerings to the LORD. They may also bring additional offerings if they can afford it. And they must be careful to do whatever they vowed when they set themselves apart as Nazirites."

5:27 Hebrew *and her thigh will waste away.*   6:10 Hebrew *the Tent of Meeting;* also in 6:13, 18.   6:11 Or *make atonement for them.*

The Priestly Blessing

22Then the LORD said to Moses, 23"Tell Aaron and his sons to bless the people of Israel with this special blessing:

24 'May the LORD bless you
and protect you.
25 May the LORD smile on you
and be gracious to you.
26 May the LORD show you his favor
and give you his peace.'

27Whenever Aaron and his sons bless the people of Israel in my name, I myself will bless them."

Offerings of Dedication

7 On the day Moses set up the Tabernacle, he anointed it and set it apart as holy. He also anointed and set apart all its furnishings and the altar with its utensils. 2Then the leaders of Israel—the tribal leaders who had registered the troops—came and brought their offerings. 3Together they brought six large wagons and twelve oxen. There was a wagon for every two leaders and an ox for each leader. They presented these to the LORD in front of the Tabernacle.

4Then the LORD said to Moses, 5"Receive their gifts, and use these oxen and wagons for transporting the Tabernacle.* Distribute them among the Levites according to the work they have to do." 6So Moses took the wagons and oxen and presented them to the Levites. 7He gave two wagons and four oxen to the Gershonite division for their work, 8and he gave four wagons and eight oxen to the Merarite division for their work. All their work was done under the leadership of Ithamar son of Aaron the priest. 9But he gave none of the wagons or oxen to the Kohathite division, since they were required to carry the sacred objects of the Tabernacle on their shoulders.

10The leaders also presented dedication gifts for the altar at the time it was anointed. They each placed their gifts before the altar. 11The LORD said to Moses, "Let one leader bring his gift each day for the dedication of the altar."

12On the first day Nahshon son of Amminadab, leader of the tribe of Judah, presented his offering.

13His offering consisted of a silver platter weighing 3¼ pounds and a silver basin weighing 1¾ pounds* (as measured by the weight of the sanctuary shekel). These were both filled with grain offerings of choice flour moistened with olive oil. 14He also brought a gold container weighing four ounces,* which was filled with incense. 15He brought a young bull, a ram, and a one-year-old male lamb for a burnt offering, 16and a male goat for a sin offering. 17For a peace offering he brought two bulls, five rams, five male goats, and five one-year-old male lambs. This was the offering brought by Nahshon son of Amminadab.

18On the second day Nethanel son of Zuar, leader of the tribe of Issachar, presented his offering.

19His offering consisted of a silver platter weighing 3¼ pounds and a silver basin weighing 1¾ pounds (as measured by the weight of the sanctuary shekel). These were both filled with grain offerings of choice flour moistened with olive oil. 20He also brought a gold container weighing four ounces, which was filled with incense. 21He brought a young bull, a ram, and a one-year-old male lamb for a burnt offering, 22and a male goat for a sin offering. 23For a peace offering he brought two bulls, five rams, five male goats, and five one-year-old male lambs. This was the offering brought by Nethanel son of Zuar.

24On the third day Eliab son of Helon, leader of the tribe of Zebulun, presented his offering.

25His offering consisted of a silver platter weighing 3¼ pounds and a silver basin weighing 1¾ pounds (as measured by the weight of the sanctuary shekel). These were both filled with grain offerings of choice flour moistened with olive oil. 26He also brought a gold container weighing four ounces, which was filled with incense. 27He brought a young bull, a ram, and a one-year-old male lamb for a burnt offering, 28and a male goat for a sin offering. 29For a peace offering he brought two bulls, five rams, five male goats, and five one-year-old male lambs. This was the offering brought by Eliab son of Helon.

7:5 Hebrew *the Tent of Meeting;* also in 7:89.   7:13 Hebrew *silver platter weighing 130 [shekels]* [1.5 kilograms] *and a silver basin weighing 70 shekels* [800 grams]; also in 7:19, 25, 31, 37, 43, 49, 55, 61, 67, 73, 79, 85.   7:14 Hebrew *10 [shekels]* [114 grams]; also in 7:20, 26, 32, 38, 44, 50, 56, 62, 68, 74, 80, 86.

³⁰On the fourth day Elizur son of Shedeur, leader of the tribe of Reuben, presented his offering.

³¹His offering consisted of a silver platter weighing 3¼ pounds and a silver basin weighing 1¾ pounds (as measured by the weight of the sanctuary shekel). These were both filled with grain offerings of choice flour moistened with olive oil. ³²He also brought a gold container weighing four ounces, which was filled with incense. ³³He brought a young bull, a ram, and a one-year-old male lamb for a burnt offering, ³⁴and a male goat for a sin offering. ³⁵For a peace offering he brought two bulls, five rams, five male goats, and five one-year-old male lambs. This was the offering brought by Elizur son of Shedeur.

³⁶On the fifth day Shelumiel son of Zurishaddai, leader of the tribe of Simeon, presented his offering.

³⁷His offering consisted of a silver platter weighing 3¼ pounds and a silver basin weighing 1¾ pounds (as measured by the weight of the sanctuary shekel). These were both filled with grain offerings of choice flour moistened with olive oil. ³⁸He also brought a gold container weighing four ounces, which was filled with incense. ³⁹He brought a young bull, a ram, and a one-year-old male lamb for a burnt offering, ⁴⁰and a male goat for a sin offering. ⁴¹For a peace offering he brought two bulls, five rams, five male goats, and five one-year-old male lambs. This was the offering brought by Shelumiel son of Zurishaddai.

⁴²On the sixth day Eliasaph son of Deuel, leader of the tribe of Gad, presented his offering.

⁴³His offering consisted of a silver platter weighing 3¼ pounds and a silver basin weighing 1¾ pounds (as measured by the weight of the sanctuary shekel). These were both filled with grain offerings of choice flour moistened with olive oil. ⁴⁴He also brought a gold container weighing four ounces, which was filled with incense. ⁴⁵He brought a young bull, a ram, and a one-year-old male lamb for a burnt offering, ⁴⁶and a male goat for a sin offering. ⁴⁷For a peace offering he brought two bulls, five rams, five male goats, and five one-year-old male lambs. This was the offering brought by Eliasaph son of Deuel.

⁴⁸On the seventh day Elishama son of Ammihud, leader of the tribe of Ephraim, presented his offering.

⁴⁹His offering consisted of a silver platter weighing 3¼ pounds and a silver basin weighing 1¾ pounds (as measured by the weight of the sanctuary shekel). These were both filled with grain offerings of choice flour moistened with olive oil. ⁵⁰He also brought a gold container weighing four ounces, which was filled with incense. ⁵¹He brought a young bull, a ram, and a one-year-old male lamb for a burnt offering, ⁵²and a male goat for a sin offering. ⁵³For a peace offering he brought two bulls, five rams, five male goats, and five one-year-old male lambs. This was the offering brought by Elishama son of Ammihud.

⁵⁴On the eighth day Gamaliel son of Pedahzur, leader of the tribe of Manasseh, presented his offering.

⁵⁵His offering consisted of a silver platter weighing 3¼ pounds and a silver basin weighing 1¾ pounds (as measured by the weight of the sanctuary shekel). These were both filled with grain offerings of choice flour moistened with olive oil. ⁵⁶He also brought a gold container weighing four ounces, which was filled with incense. ⁵⁷He brought a young bull, a ram, and a one-year-old male lamb for a burnt offering, ⁵⁸and a male goat for a sin offering. ⁵⁹For a peace offering he brought two bulls, five rams, five male goats, and five one-year-old male lambs. This was the offering brought by Gamaliel son of Pedahzur.

⁶⁰On the ninth day Abidan son of Gideoni, leader of the tribe of Benjamin, presented his offering.

⁶¹His offering consisted of a silver platter weighing 3¼ pounds and a silver basin weighing 1¾ pounds (as measured by the weight of the sanctuary shekel). These were both filled with grain offerings of choice flour moistened with olive oil. ⁶²He also brought a gold container weighing four ounces, which was filled with incense. ⁶³He brought a young bull, a ram, and a one-year-old male lamb for a burnt offering, ⁶⁴and a male goat for a sin offering. ⁶⁵For a peace offering he brought two bulls, five rams, five male goats, and

five one-year-old male lambs. This was the offering brought by Abidan son of Gideoni.

⁶⁶On the tenth day Ahiezer son of Ammishaddai, leader of the tribe of Dan, presented his offering.

⁶⁷His offering consisted of a silver platter weighing 3¼ pounds and a silver basin weighing 1¾ pounds (as measured by the weight of the sanctuary shekel). These were both filled with grain offerings of choice flour moistened with olive oil. ⁶⁸He also brought a gold container weighing four ounces, which was filled with incense. ⁶⁹He brought a young bull, a ram, and a one-year-old male lamb for a burnt offering, ⁷⁰and a male goat for a sin offering. ⁷¹For a peace offering he brought two bulls, five rams, five male goats, and five one-year-old male lambs. This was the offering brought by Ahiezer son of Ammishaddai.

⁷²On the eleventh day Pagiel son of Ocran, leader of the tribe of Asher, presented his offering.

⁷³His offering consisted of a silver platter weighing 3¼ pounds and a silver basin weighing 1¾ pounds (as measured by the weight of the sanctuary shekel). These were both filled with grain offerings of choice flour moistened with olive oil. ⁷⁴He also brought a gold container weighing four ounces, which was filled with incense. ⁷⁵He brought a young bull, a ram, and a one-year-old male lamb for a burnt offering, ⁷⁶and a male goat for a sin offering. ⁷⁷For a peace offering he brought two bulls, five rams, five male goats, and five one-year-old male lambs. This was the offering brought by Pagiel son of Ocran.

⁷⁸On the twelfth day Ahira son of Enan, leader of the tribe of Naphtali, presented his offering.

⁷⁹His offering consisted of a silver platter weighing 3¼ pounds and a silver basin weighing 1¾ pounds (as measured by the weight of the sanctuary shekel). These were both filled with grain offerings of choice flour moistened with olive oil. ⁸⁰He also brought a gold container weighing four ounces, which was filled with incense. ⁸¹He brought a young bull, a ram, and a one-year-old male lamb for a

burnt offering, ⁸²and a male goat for a sin offering. ⁸³For a peace offering he brought two bulls, five rams, five male goats, and five one-year-old male lambs. This was the offering brought by Ahira son of Enan.

⁸⁴So this was the dedication offering brought by the leaders of Israel at the time the altar was anointed: twelve silver platters, twelve silver basins, and twelve gold incense containers. ⁸⁵Each silver platter weighed 3¼ pounds, and each silver basin weighed 1¾ pounds. The total weight of the silver was 60 pounds* (as measured by the weight of the sanctuary shekel). ⁸⁶Each of the twelve gold containers that was filled with incense weighed four ounces (as measured by the weight of the sanctuary shekel). The total weight of the gold was three pounds.* ⁸⁷Twelve young bulls, twelve rams, and twelve one-year-old male lambs were donated for the burnt offerings, along with their prescribed grain offerings. Twelve male goats were brought for the sin offerings. ⁸⁸Twenty-four bulls, sixty rams, sixty male goats, and sixty one-year-old male lambs were donated for the peace offerings. This was the dedication offering for the altar after it was anointed.

⁸⁹Whenever Moses went into the Tabernacle to speak with the LORD, he heard the voice speaking to him from between the two cherubim above the Ark's cover—the place of atonement—that rests on the Ark of the Covenant.* The LORD spoke to him from there.

Preparing the Lamps

8 The LORD said to Moses, ²"Give Aaron the following instructions: When you set up the seven lamps in the lampstand, place them so their light shines forward in front of the lampstand." ³So Aaron did this. He set up the seven lamps so they reflected their light forward, just as the LORD had commanded Moses. ⁴The entire lampstand, from its base to its decorative blossoms, was made of beaten gold. It was built according to the exact design the LORD had shown Moses.

The Levites Dedicated

⁵Then the LORD said to Moses, ⁶"Now set the Levites apart from the rest of the people of Israel and make them ceremonially clean. ⁷Do this by sprinkling them with the water of purification, and have them shave their entire body and wash their clothing. Then they

7:85 Hebrew 2,400 [shekels] [27.6 kilograms].   7:86 Hebrew 120 [shekels] [1.4 kilograms].   7:89 Or Ark of the Testimony.

will be ceremonially clean. [8]Have them bring a young bull and a grain offering of choice flour moistened with olive oil, along with a second young bull for a sin offering. [9]Then assemble the whole community of Israel, and present the Levites at the entrance of the Tabernacle.* [10]When you present the Levites before the LORD, the people of Israel must lay their hands on them. [11]Raising his hands, Aaron must then present the Levites to the LORD as a special offering from the people of Israel, thus dedicating them to the LORD's service.

[12]"Next the Levites will lay their hands on the heads of the young bulls. Present one as a sin offering and the other as a burnt offering to the LORD, to purify the Levites and make them right with the LORD.* [13]Then have the Levites stand in front of Aaron and his sons, and raise your hands and present them as a special offering to the LORD. [14]In this way, you will set the Levites apart from the rest of the people of Israel, and the Levites will belong to me. [15]After this, they may go into the Tabernacle to do their work, because you have purified them and presented them as a special offering.

[16]"Of all the people of Israel, the Levites are reserved for me. I have claimed them for myself in place of all the firstborn sons of the Israelites; I have taken the Levites as their substitutes. [17]For all the firstborn males among the people of Israel are mine, both of people and of animals. I set them apart for myself on the day I struck down all the firstborn sons of the Egyptians. [18]Yes, I have claimed the Levites in place of all the firstborn sons of Israel. [19]And of all the Israelites, I have assigned the Levites to Aaron and his sons. They will serve in the Tabernacle on behalf of the Israelites and make sacrifices to purify* the people so no plague will strike them when they approach the sanctuary."

[20]So Moses, Aaron, and the whole community of Israel dedicated the Levites, carefully following all the LORD's instructions to Moses. [21]The Levites purified themselves from sin and washed their clothes, and Aaron lifted them up and presented them to the LORD as a special offering. He then offered a sacrifice to purify them and make them right with the LORD.* [22]After that the Levites went into the Tabernacle to perform their duties, assisting Aaron and his sons. So they carried out all the commands that the LORD gave Moses concerning the Levites.

[23]The LORD also instructed Moses, [24]"This is the rule the Levites must follow: They must begin serving in the Tabernacle at the age of twenty-five, [25]and they must retire at the age of fifty. [26]After retirement they may assist their fellow Levites by serving as guards at the Tabernacle, but they may not officiate in the service. This is how you must assign duties to the Levites."

The Second Passover

9 A year after Israel's departure from Egypt, the LORD spoke to Moses in the wilderness of Sinai. In the first month* of that year he said, [2]"Tell the Israelites to celebrate the Passover at the prescribed time, [3]at twilight on the fourteenth day of the first month.* Be sure to follow all my decrees and regulations concerning this celebration."

[4]So Moses told the people to celebrate the Passover [5]in the wilderness of Sinai as twilight fell on the fourteenth day of the month. And they celebrated the festival there, just as the LORD had commanded Moses. [6]But some of the men had been ceremonially defiled by touching a dead body, so they could not celebrate the Passover that day. They came to Moses and Aaron that day [7]and said, "We have become ceremonially unclean by touching a dead body. But why should we be prevented from presenting the LORD's offering at the proper time with the rest of the Israelites?"

[8]Moses answered, "Wait here until I have received instructions for you from the LORD."

[9]This was the LORD's reply to Moses. [10]"Give the following instructions to the people of Israel: If any of the people now or in future generations are ceremonially unclean at Passover time because of touching a dead body, or if they are on a journey and cannot be present at the ceremony, they may still celebrate the LORD's Passover. [11]They must offer the Passover sacrifice one month later, at twilight on the fourteenth day of the second month.* They must eat the Passover lamb at that time with bitter salad greens and bread made without yeast. [12]They must not leave any of the lamb until the next morning, and they must not break any of its bones. They must follow all the normal regulations concerning the Passover.

8:9 Hebrew *the Tent of Meeting;* also in 8:15, 19, 22, 24, 26.   8:12 Or *to make atonement for the Levites.*   8:19 Or *make atonement for.* 8:21 Or *then made atonement for them to purify them.*   9:1 The first month of the ancient Hebrew lunar calendar usually occurs within the months of March and April.   9:3 This day in the ancient Hebrew lunar calendar occurred in late March, April, or early May.   9:11 This day in the ancient Hebrew lunar calendar occurred in late April, May, or early June.

¹³"But those who neglect to celebrate the Passover at the regular time, even though they are ceremonially clean and not away on a trip, will be cut off from the community of Israel. If they fail to present the LORD's offering at the proper time, they will suffer the consequences of their guilt. ¹⁴And if foreigners living among you want to celebrate the Passover to the LORD, they must follow these same decrees and regulations. The same laws apply both to native-born Israelites and to the foreigners living among you."

The Fiery Cloud

¹⁵On the day the Tabernacle was set up, the cloud covered it.* But from evening until morning the cloud over the Tabernacle looked like a pillar of fire. ¹⁶This was the regular pattern—at night the cloud that covered the Tabernacle had the appearance of fire. ¹⁷Whenever the cloud lifted from over the sacred tent, the people of Israel would break camp and follow it. And wherever the cloud settled, the people of Israel would set up camp. ¹⁸In this way, they traveled and camped at the LORD's command wherever he told them to go. Then they remained in their camp as long as the cloud stayed over the Tabernacle. ¹⁹If the cloud remained over the Tabernacle for a long time, the Israelites stayed and performed their duty to the LORD. ²⁰Sometimes the cloud would stay over the Tabernacle for only a few days, so the people would stay for only a few days, as the LORD commanded. Then at the LORD's command they would break camp and move on. ²¹Sometimes the cloud stayed only overnight and lifted the next morning. But day or night, when the cloud lifted, the people broke camp and moved on. ²²Whether the cloud stayed above the Tabernacle for two days, a month, or a year, the people of Israel stayed in camp and did not move on. But as soon as it lifted, they broke camp and moved on. ²³So they camped or traveled at the LORD's command, and they did whatever the LORD told them through Moses.

The Silver Trumpets

10 Now the LORD said to Moses, ²"Make two trumpets of hammered silver for calling the community to assemble and for signaling the breaking of camp. ³When both trumpets are blown, everyone must gather before you at the entrance of the Tabernacle.*

⁴But if only one trumpet is blown, then only the leaders—the heads of the clans of Israel—must present themselves to you.

⁵"When you sound the signal to move on, the tribes camped on the east side of the Tabernacle must break camp and move forward. ⁶When you sound the signal a second time, the tribes camped on the south will follow. You must sound short blasts as the signal for moving on. ⁷But when you call the people to an assembly, blow the trumpets with a different signal. ⁸Only the priests, Aaron's descendants, are allowed to blow the trumpets. This is a permanent law for you, to be observed from generation to generation.

⁹"When you arrive in your own land and go to war against your enemies who attack you, sound the alarm with the trumpets. Then the LORD your God will remember you and rescue you from your enemies. ¹⁰Blow the trumpets in times of gladness, too, sounding them at your annual festivals and at the beginning of each month. And blow the trumpets over your burnt offerings and peace offerings. The trumpets will remind your God of his covenant with you. I am the LORD your God."

The Israelites Leave Sinai

¹¹In the second year after Israel's departure from Egypt—on the twentieth day of the second month*—the cloud lifted from the Tabernacle of the Covenant.* ¹²So the Israelites set out from the wilderness of Sinai and traveled on from place to place until the cloud stopped in the wilderness of Paran.

¹³When the people set out for the first time, following the instructions the LORD had given through Moses, ¹⁴Judah's troops led the way. They marched behind their banner, and their leader was Nahshon son of Amminadab. ¹⁵They were joined by the troops of the tribe of Issachar, led by Nethanel son of Zuar, ¹⁶and the troops of the tribe of Zebulun, led by Eliab son of Helon.

¹⁷Then the Tabernacle was taken down, and the Gershonite and Merarite divisions of the Levites were next in the line of march, carrying the Tabernacle with them. ¹⁸Reuben's troops went next, marching behind their banner. Their leader was Elizur son of Shedeur. ¹⁹They were joined by the troops of the tribe of Simeon, led by Shelumiel son of Zurishaddai, ²⁰and the troops of the tribe of Gad, led by Eliasaph son of Deuel.

9:15 Hebrew *covered the Tabernacle, the Tent of the Testimony.* 10:3 Hebrew *Tent of Meeting.* 10:11a This day in the ancient Hebrew lunar calendar occurred in late April, May, or early June. 10:11b Or *Tabernacle of the Testimony.*

²¹Next came the Kohathite division of the Levites, carrying the sacred objects from the Tabernacle. Before they arrived at the next camp, the Tabernacle would already be set up at its new location. ²²Ephraim's troops went next, marching behind their banner. Their leader was Elishama son of Ammihud. ²³They were joined by the troops of the tribe of Manasseh, led by Gamaliel son of Pedahzur, ²⁴and the troops of the tribe of Benjamin, led by Abidan son of Gideoni.

²⁵Dan's troops went last, marching behind their banner and serving as the rear guard for all the tribal camps. Their leader was Ahiezer son of Ammishaddai. ²⁶They were joined by the troops of the tribe of Asher, led by Pagiel son of Ocran, ²⁷and the troops of the tribe of Naphtali, led by Ahira son of Enan.

²⁸This was the order in which the Israelites marched, division by division.

²⁹One day Moses said to his brother-in-law, Hobab son of Reuel the Midianite, "We are on our way to the place the Lord promised us, for he said, 'I will give it to you.' Come with us and we will treat you well, for the Lord has promised wonderful blessings for Israel!"

³⁰But Hobab replied, "No, I will not go. I must return to my own land and family."

³¹"Please don't leave us," Moses pleaded. "You know the places in the wilderness where we should camp. Come, be our guide. ³²If you do, we'll share with you all the blessings the Lord gives us."

³³They marched for three days after leaving the mountain of the Lord, with the Ark of the Lord's Covenant moving ahead of them to show them where to stop and rest. ³⁴As they moved on each day, the cloud of the Lord hovered over them. ³⁵And whenever the Ark set out, Moses would shout, "Arise, O Lord, and let your enemies be scattered! Let them flee before you!" ³⁶And when the Ark was set down, he would say, "Return, O Lord, to the countless thousands of Israel!"

The People Complain to Moses

11 Soon the people began to complain about their hardship, and the Lord heard everything they said. Then the Lord's anger blazed against them, and he sent a fire to rage among them, and he destroyed some of the people in the outskirts of the camp. ²Then the people screamed to Moses for help, and when he prayed to the Lord, the fire stopped. ³After that, the area was known as Taberah (which means "the place of burning"), because fire from the Lord had burned among them there.

⁴Then the foreign rabble who were traveling with the Israelites began to crave the good things of Egypt. And the people of Israel also began to complain. "Oh, for some meat!" they exclaimed. ⁵"We remember the fish we used to eat for free in Egypt. And we had all the cucumbers, melons, leeks, onions, and garlic we wanted. ⁶But now our appetites are gone. All we ever see is this manna!"

⁷The manna looked like small coriander seeds, and it was pale yellow like gum resin. ⁸The people would go out and gather it from the ground. They made flour by grinding it with hand mills or pounding it in mortars. Then they boiled it in a pot and made it into flat cakes. These cakes tasted like pastries baked with olive oil. ⁹The manna came down on the camp with the dew during the night.

¹⁰Moses heard all the families standing in the doorways of their tents whining, and the Lord became extremely angry. Moses was also very aggravated. ¹¹And Moses said to the Lord, "Why are you treating me, your servant, so harshly? Have mercy on me! What did I do to deserve the burden of all these people? ¹²Did I give birth to them? Did I bring them into the world? Why did you tell me to carry them in my arms like a mother carries a nursing baby? How can I carry them to the land you swore to give their ancestors? ¹³Where am I supposed to get meat for all these people? They keep whining to me, saying, 'Give us meat to eat!' ¹⁴I can't carry all these people by myself! The load is far too heavy! ¹⁵If this is how you intend to treat me, just go ahead and kill me. Do me a favor and spare me this misery!"

Moses Chooses Seventy Leaders

¹⁶Then the Lord said to Moses, "Gather before me seventy men who are recognized as elders and leaders of Israel. Bring them to the Tabernacle* to stand there with you. ¹⁷I will come down and talk to you there. I will take some of the Spirit that is upon you, and I will put the Spirit upon them also. They will bear the burden of the people along with you, so you will not have to carry it alone.

¹⁸"And say to the people, 'Purify yourselves, for tomorrow you will have meat to eat. You were whining, and the Lord heard you when you cried, "Oh, for some meat! We were better off in Egypt!" Now the Lord will give you

11:16 Hebrew *the Tent of Meeting.*

meat, and you will have to eat it. ¹⁹And it won't be for just a day or two, or for five or ten or even twenty. ²⁰You will eat it for a whole month until you gag and are sick of it. For you have rejected the Lord, who is here among you, and you have whined to him, saying, "Why did we ever leave Egypt?"'"

²¹But Moses responded to the Lord, "There are 600,000 foot soldiers here with me, and yet you say, 'I will give them meat for a whole month!' ²²Even if we butchered all our flocks and herds, would that satisfy them? Even if we caught all the fish in the sea, would that be enough?"

²³Then the Lord said to Moses, "Has my arm lost its power? Now you will see whether or not my word comes true!"

²⁴So Moses went out and reported the Lord's words to the people. He gathered the seventy elders and stationed them around the Tabernacle.* ²⁵And the Lord came down in the cloud and spoke to Moses. Then he gave the seventy elders the same Spirit that was upon Moses. And when the Spirit rested upon them, they prophesied. But this never happened again.

²⁶Two men, Eldad and Medad, had stayed behind in the camp. They were listed among the elders, but they had not gone out to the Tabernacle. Yet the Spirit rested upon them as well, so they prophesied there in the camp. ²⁷A young man ran and reported to Moses, "Eldad and Medad are prophesying in the camp!"

²⁸Joshua son of Nun, who had been Moses' assistant since his youth, protested, "Moses, my master, make them stop!"

²⁹But Moses replied, "Are you jealous for my sake? I wish that all the Lord's people were prophets and that the Lord would put his Spirit upon them all!" ³⁰Then Moses returned to the camp with the elders of Israel.

The Lord Sends Quail

³¹Now the Lord sent a wind that brought quail from the sea and let them fall all around the camp. For miles in every direction there were quail flying about three feet above the ground.* ³²So the people went out and caught quail all that day and throughout the night and all the next day, too. No one gathered less than fifty bushels*! They spread the quail all around the camp to dry. ³³But while they were gorging themselves on the meat—while it was still in their mouths—the anger of

the Lord blazed against the people, and he struck them with a severe plague. ³⁴So that place was called Kibroth-hattaavah (which means "graves of gluttony") because there they buried the people who had craved meat from Egypt. ³⁵From Kibroth-hattaavah the Israelites traveled to Hazeroth, where they stayed for some time.

The Complaints of Miriam and Aaron

12 While they were at Hazeroth, Miriam and Aaron criticized Moses because he had married a Cushite woman. ²They said, "Has the Lord spoken only through Moses? Hasn't he spoken through us, too?" But the Lord heard them. ³(Now Moses was very humble—more humble than any other person on earth.)

⁴So immediately the Lord called to Moses, Aaron, and Miriam and said, "Go out to the Tabernacle,* all three of you!" So the three of them went to the Tabernacle. ⁵Then the Lord descended in the pillar of cloud and stood at the entrance of the Tabernacle.* "Aaron and Miriam!" he called, and they stepped forward. ⁶And the Lord said to them, "Now listen to what I say:

"If there were prophets among you,
    I, the Lord, would reveal myself in
        visions.
    I would speak to them in dreams.
⁷ But not with my servant Moses.
    Of all my house, he is the one I trust.
⁸ I speak to him face to face,
    clearly, and not in riddles!
    He sees the Lord as he is.
So why were you not afraid
    to criticize my servant Moses?"

⁹The Lord was very angry with them, and he departed. ¹⁰As the cloud moved from above the Tabernacle, there stood Miriam, her skin as white as snow from leprosy.* When Aaron saw what had happened to her, ¹¹he cried out to Moses, "Oh, my master! Please don't punish us for this sin we have so foolishly committed. ¹²Don't let her be like a stillborn baby, already decayed at birth."

¹³So Moses cried out to the Lord, "O God, I beg you, please heal her!"

¹⁴But the Lord said to Moses, "If her father had done nothing more than spit in her face,

11:24 Hebrew *the tent;* also in 11:26.   11:31 Or *there were quail about 3 feet* [2 cubits or 92 centimeters] *deep on the ground.*
11:32 Hebrew *10 homers* [2.2 kiloliters].   12:4 Hebrew *the Tent of Meeting.*   12:5 Hebrew *the tent;* also in 12:10.   12:10 Or *with a skin disease.* The Hebrew word used here can describe various skin diseases.

wouldn't she be defiled for seven days? So keep her outside the camp for seven days, and after that she may be accepted back."

¹⁵So Miriam was kept outside the camp for seven days, and the people waited until she was brought back before they traveled again. ¹⁶Then they left Hazeroth and camped in the wilderness of Paran.

Twelve Scouts Explore Canaan

13 The LORD now said to Moses, ²"Send out men to explore the land of Canaan, the land I am giving to the Israelites. Send one leader from each of the twelve ancestral tribes." ³So Moses did as the LORD commanded him. He sent out twelve men, all tribal leaders of Israel, from their camp in the wilderness of Paran. ⁴These were the tribes and the names of their leaders:

Tribe	Leader
Reuben	Shammua son of Zaccur
⁵ Simeon	Shaphat son of Hori
⁶ Judah............	Caleb son of Jephunneh
⁷ Issachar...............	Igal son of Joseph
⁸ Ephraim	Hoshea son of Nun
⁹ Benjamin	Palti son of Raphu
¹⁰ Zebulun	Gaddiel son of Sodi
¹¹ Manasseh son of Joseph	Gaddi son of Susi
¹² Dan	Ammiel son of Gemalli
¹³ Asher...............	Sethur son of Michael
¹⁴ Naphtali	Nahbi son of Vophsi
¹⁵ Gad	Geuel son of Maki

¹⁶These are the names of the men Moses sent out to explore the land. (Moses called Hoshea son of Nun by the name Joshua.)

¹⁷Moses gave the men these instructions as he sent them out to explore the land: "Go north through the Negev into the hill country. ¹⁸See what the land is like, and find out whether the people living there are strong or weak, few or many. ¹⁹See what kind of land they live in. Is it good or bad? Do their towns have walls, or are they unprotected like open camps? ²⁰Is the soil fertile or poor? Are there many trees? Do your best to bring back samples of the crops you see." (It happened to be the season for harvesting the first ripe grapes.)

²¹So they went up and explored the land from the wilderness of Zin as far as Rehob, near Lebo-hamath. ²²Going north, they passed through the Negev and arrived at Hebron, where Ahiman, Sheshai, and Talmai—all

descendants of Anak—lived. (The ancient town of Hebron was founded seven years before the Egyptian city of Zoan.) ²³When they came to the valley of Eshcol, they cut down a branch with a single cluster of grapes so large that it took two of them to carry it on a pole between them! They also brought back samples of the pomegranates and figs. ²⁴That place was called the valley of Eshcol (which means "cluster"), because of the cluster of grapes the Israelite men cut there.

The Scouting Report

²⁵After exploring the land for forty days, the men returned ²⁶to Moses, Aaron, and the whole community of Israel at Kadesh in the wilderness of Paran. They reported to the whole community what they had seen and showed them the fruit they had taken from the land. ²⁷This was their report to Moses: "We entered the land you sent us to explore, and it is indeed a bountiful country—a land flowing with milk and honey. Here is the kind of fruit it produces. ²⁸But the people living there are powerful, and their towns are large and fortified. We even saw giants there, the descendants of Anak! ²⁹The Amalekites live in the Negev, and the Hittites, Jebusites, and Amorites live in the hill country. The Canaanites live along the coast of the Mediterranean Sea* and along the Jordan Valley."

³⁰But Caleb tried to quiet the people as they stood before Moses. "Let's go at once to take the land," he said. "We can certainly conquer it!"

³¹But the other men who had explored the land with him disagreed. "We can't go up against them! They are stronger than we are!" ³²So they spread this bad report about the land among the Israelites: "The land we traveled through and explored will devour anyone who goes to live there. All the people we saw were huge. ³³We even saw giants* there, the descendants of Anak. Next to them we felt like grasshoppers, and that's what they thought, too!"

The People Rebel

14 Then the whole community began weeping aloud, and they cried all night. ²Their voices rose in a great chorus of protest against Moses and Aaron. "If only we had died in Egypt, or even here in the wilderness!" they complained. ³"Why is the LORD taking us to this country only to have us die in battle? Our wives and our little ones will be carried off as plunder! Wouldn't it be better for us to return

13:29 Hebrew *the sea.*   13:33 Hebrew *nephilim.*

to Egypt?" ⁴Then they plotted among themselves, "Let's choose a new leader and go back to Egypt!"

⁵Then Moses and Aaron fell face down on the ground before the whole community of Israel. ⁶Two of the men who had explored the land, Joshua son of Nun and Caleb son of Jephunneh, tore their clothing. ⁷They said to all the people of Israel, "The land we traveled through and explored is a wonderful land! ⁸And if the LORD is pleased with us, he will bring us safely into that land and give it to us. It is a rich land flowing with milk and honey. ⁹Do not rebel against the LORD, and don't be afraid of the people of the land. They are only helpless prey to us! They have no protection, but the LORD is with us! Don't be afraid of them!"

¹⁰But the whole community began to talk about stoning Joshua and Caleb. Then the glorious presence of the LORD appeared to all the Israelites at the Tabernacle.* ¹¹And the LORD said to Moses, "How long will these people treat me with contempt? Will they never believe me, even after all the miraculous signs I have done among them? ¹²I will disown them and destroy them with a plague. Then I will make you into a nation greater and mightier than they are!"

Moses Intercedes for the People

¹³But Moses objected. "What will the Egyptians think when they hear about it?" he asked the LORD. "They know full well the power you displayed in rescuing your people from Egypt. ¹⁴Now if you destroy them, the Egyptians will send a report to the inhabitants of this land, who have already heard that you live among your people. They know, LORD, that you have appeared to your people face to face and that your pillar of cloud hovers over them. They know that you go before them in the pillar of cloud by day and the pillar of fire by night. ¹⁵Now if you slaughter all these people with a single blow, the nations that have heard of your fame will say, ¹⁶'The LORD was not able to bring them into the land he swore to give them, so he killed them in the wilderness.'

¹⁷"Please, Lord, prove that your power is as great as you have claimed. For you said, ¹⁸'The LORD is slow to anger and filled with unfailing love, forgiving every kind of sin and rebellion. But he does not excuse the guilty. He lays the sins of the parents upon their children; the entire family is affected—even children in the third and fourth generations.' ¹⁹In keeping

with your magnificent, unfailing love, please pardon the sins of this people, just as you have forgiven them ever since they left Egypt."

²⁰Then the LORD said, "I will pardon them as you have requested. ²¹But as surely as I live, and as surely as the earth is filled with the LORD's glory, ²²not one of these people will ever enter that land. They have all seen my glorious presence and the miraculous signs I performed both in Egypt and in the wilderness, but again and again they have tested me by refusing to listen to my voice. ²³They will never even see the land I swore to give their ancestors. None of those who have treated me with contempt will ever see it. ²⁴But my servant Caleb has a different attitude than the others have. He has remained loyal to me, so I will bring him into the land he explored. His descendants will possess their full share of that land. ²⁵Now turn around, and don't go on toward the land where the Amalekites and Canaanites live. Tomorrow you must set out for the wilderness in the direction of the Red Sea.*"

The LORD Punishes the Israelites

²⁶Then the LORD said to Moses and Aaron, ²⁷"How long must I put up with this wicked community and its complaints about me? Yes, I have heard the complaints the Israelites are making against me. ²⁸Now tell them this: 'As surely as I live, declares the LORD, I will do to you the very things I heard you say. ²⁹You will all drop dead in this wilderness! Because you complained against me, every one of you who is twenty years old or older and was included in the registration will die. ³⁰You will not enter and occupy the land I swore to give you. The only exceptions will be Caleb son of Jephunneh and Joshua son of Nun.

³¹"'You said your children would be carried off as plunder. Well, I will bring them safely into the land, and they will enjoy what you have despised. ³²But as for you, you will drop dead in this wilderness. ³³And your children will be like shepherds, wandering in the wilderness for forty years. In this way, they will pay for your faithlessness, until the last of you lies dead in the wilderness.

³⁴"'Because your men explored the land for forty days, you must wander in the wilderness for forty years—a year for each day, suffering the consequences of your sins. Then you will discover what it is like to have me for an enemy.' ³⁵I, the LORD, have spoken! I will certainly do these things to every member of

14:10 Hebrew *the Tent of Meeting.*   14:25 Hebrew *sea of reeds.*

the community who has conspired against me. They will be destroyed here in this wilderness, and here they will die!”

36The ten men Moses had sent to explore the land—the ones who incited rebellion against the Lord with their bad report—37were struck dead with a plague before the Lord. 38Of the twelve who had explored the land, only Joshua and Caleb remained alive.

39When Moses reported the Lord's words to all the Israelites, the people were filled with grief. 40Then they got up early the next morning and went to the top of the range of hills. “Let's go,” they said. “We realize that we have sinned, but now we are ready to enter the land the Lord has promised us.”

41But Moses said, “Why are you now disobeying the Lord's orders to return to the wilderness? It won't work. 42Do not go up into the land now. You will only be crushed by your enemies because the Lord is not with you. 43When you face the Amalekites and Canaanites in battle, you will be slaughtered. The Lord will abandon you because you have abandoned the Lord.”

44But the people defiantly pushed ahead toward the hill country, even though neither Moses nor the Ark of the Lord's Covenant left the camp. 45Then the Amalekites and the Canaanites who lived in those hills came down and attacked them and chased them back as far as Hormah.

Laws concerning Offerings

15 Then the Lord told Moses, 2“Give the following instructions to the people of Israel.

“When you finally settle in the land I am giving you, 3you will offer special gifts as a pleasing aroma to the Lord. These gifts may take the form of a burnt offering, a sacrifice to fulfill a vow, a voluntary offering, or an offering at any of your annual festivals, and they may be taken from your herds of cattle or your flocks of sheep and goats. 4When you present these offerings, you must also give the Lord a grain offering of two quarts* of choice flour mixed with one quart* of olive oil. 5For each lamb offered as a burnt offering or a special sacrifice, you must also present one quart of wine as a liquid offering.

6“If the sacrifice is a ram, give a grain offering of four quarts* of choice flour mixed with

a third of a gallon* of olive oil, 7and give a third of a gallon of wine as a liquid offering. This will be a pleasing aroma to the Lord.

8“When you present a young bull as a burnt offering or as a sacrifice to fulfill a vow or as a peace offering to the Lord, 9you must also give a grain offering of six quarts* of choice flour mixed with two quarts* of olive oil, 10and give two quarts of wine as a liquid offering. This will be a special gift, a pleasing aroma to the Lord.

11“Each sacrifice of a bull, ram, lamb, or young goat should be prepared in this way. 12Follow these instructions with each offering you present. 13All of you native-born Israelites must follow these instructions when you offer a special gift as a pleasing aroma to the Lord. 14And if any foreigners visit you or live among you and want to present a special gift as a pleasing aroma to the Lord, they must follow these same procedures. 15Native-born Israelites and foreigners are equal before the Lord and are subject to the same decrees. This is a permanent law for you, to be observed from generation to generation. 16The same instructions and regulations will apply both to you and to the foreigners living among you.”

17Then the Lord said to Moses, 18“Give the following instructions to the people of Israel.

“When you arrive in the land where I am taking you, 19and you eat the crops that grow there, you must set some aside as a sacred offering to the Lord. 20Present a cake from the first of the flour you grind, and set it aside as a sacred offering, as you do with the first grain from the threshing floor. 21Throughout the generations to come, you are to present a sacred offering to the Lord each year from the first of your ground flour.

22“But suppose you unintentionally fail to carry out all these commands that the Lord has given you through Moses. 23And suppose your descendants in the future fail to do everything the Lord has commanded through Moses. 24If the mistake was made unintentionally, and the community was unaware of it, the whole community must present a young bull for a burnt offering as a pleasing aroma to the Lord. It must be offered along with its prescribed grain offering and liquid offering and with one male goat for a sin offering. 25With it the priest will purify the whole community of Israel, making them right with the Lord,*

15:4a Hebrew 1/10 of an ephah [2.2 liters].   15:4b Hebrew 1/4 of a hin [1 liter]; also in 15:5.   15:6a Hebrew 2/10 of an ephah [4.4 liters].
15:6b Hebrew 1/3 of a hin [1.3 liters]; also in 15:7.   15:9a Hebrew 3/10 of an ephah [6.6 liters].   15:9b Hebrew 1/2 of a hin [2 liters]; also in 15:10.   15:25 Or will make atonement for the whole community of Israel.

and they will be forgiven. For it was an unintentional sin, and they have corrected it with their offerings to the LORD—the special gift and the sin offering. 26The whole community of Israel will be forgiven, including the foreigners living among you, for all the people were involved in the sin.

27 "If one individual commits an unintentional sin, the guilty person must bring a one-year-old female goat for a sin offering. 28The priest will sacrifice it to purify* the guilty person before the LORD, and that person will be forgiven. 29These same instructions apply both to native-born Israelites and to the foreigners living among you.

30"But those who brazenly violate the LORD's will, whether native-born Israelites or foreigners, have blasphemed the LORD, and they must be cut off from the community. 31Since they have treated the LORD's word with contempt and deliberately disobeyed his command, they must be completely cut off and suffer the punishment for their guilt."

Penalty for Breaking the Sabbath

32One day while the people of Israel were in the wilderness, they discovered a man gathering wood on the Sabbath day. 33The people who found him doing this took him before Moses, Aaron, and the rest of the community. 34They held him in custody because they did not know what to do with him. 35Then the LORD said to Moses, "The man must be put to death! The whole community must stone him outside the camp." 36So the whole community took the man outside the camp and stoned him to death, just as the LORD had commanded Moses.

Tassels on Clothing

37Then the LORD said to Moses, 38"Give the following instructions to the people of Israel: Throughout the generations to come you must make tassels for the hems of your clothing and attach them with a blue cord. 39When you see the tassels, you will remember and obey all the commands of the LORD instead of following your own desires and defiling yourselves, as you are prone to do. 40The tassels will help you remember that you must obey all my commands and be holy to your God. 41I am the LORD your God who brought you out of the land of Egypt that I might be your God. I am the LORD your God!"

Korah's Rebellion

16 One day Korah son of Izhar, a descendant of Kohath son of Levi, conspired with Dathan and Abiram, the sons of Eliab, and On son of Peleth, from the tribe of Reuben. 2They incited a rebellion against Moses, along with 250 other leaders of the community, all prominent members of the assembly. 3They united against Moses and Aaron and said, "You have gone too far! The whole community of Israel has been set apart by the LORD, and he is with all of us. What right do you have to act as though you are greater than the rest of the LORD's people?"

4When Moses heard what they were saying, he fell face down on the ground. 5Then he said to Korah and his followers, "Tomorrow morning the LORD will show us who belongs to him* and who is holy. The LORD will allow only those whom he selects to enter his own presence. 6Korah, you and all your followers must prepare your incense burners. 7Light fires in them tomorrow, and burn incense before the LORD. Then we will see whom the LORD chooses as his holy one. You Levites are the ones who have gone too far!"

8Then Moses spoke again to Korah: "Now listen, you Levites! 9Does it seem insignificant to you that the God of Israel has chosen you from among all the community of Israel to be near him so you can serve in the LORD's Tabernacle and stand before the people to minister to them? 10Korah, he has already given this special ministry to you and your fellow Levites. Are you now demanding the priesthood as well? 11The LORD is the one you and your followers are really revolting against! For who is Aaron that you are complaining about him?"

12Then Moses summoned Dathan and Abiram, the sons of Eliab, but they replied, "We refuse to come before you! 13Isn't it enough that you brought us out of Egypt, a land flowing with milk and honey, to kill us here in this wilderness, and that you now treat us like your subjects? 14What's more, you haven't brought us into another land flowing with milk and honey. You haven't given us a new homeland with fields and vineyards. Are you trying to fool these men?* We will not come."

15Then Moses became very angry and said to the LORD, "Do not accept their grain offerings! I have not taken so much as a donkey from them, and I have never hurt a single one of them." 16And Moses said to Korah, "You

15:28 Or to make atonement for.   16:5 Greek version reads God has visited and knows those who are his. Compare 2 Tim 2:19.
16:14 Hebrew Are you trying to put out the eyes of these men?

and all your followers must come here tomorrow and present yourselves before the LORD. Aaron will also be here. [17] You and each of your 250 followers must prepare an incense burner and put incense on it, so you can all present them before the LORD. Aaron will also bring his incense burner."

[18] So each of these men prepared an incense burner, lit the fire, and placed incense on it. Then they all stood at the entrance of the Tabernacle* with Moses and Aaron. [19] Meanwhile, Korah had stirred up the entire community against Moses and Aaron, and they all gathered at the Tabernacle entrance. Then the glorious presence of the LORD appeared to the whole community, [20] and the LORD said to Moses and Aaron, [21] "Get away from all these people so that I may instantly destroy them!"

[22] But Moses and Aaron fell face down on the ground. "O God," they pleaded, "you are the God who gives breath to all creatures. Must you be angry with all the people when only one man sins?"

[23] And the LORD said to Moses, [24] "Then tell all the people to get away from the tents of Korah, Dathan, and Abiram."

[25] So Moses got up and rushed over to the tents of Dathan and Abiram, followed by the elders of Israel. [26] "Quick!" he told the people. "Get away from the tents of these wicked men, and don't touch anything that belongs to them. If you do, you will be destroyed for their sins." [27] So all the people stood back from the tents of Korah, Dathan, and Abiram. Then Dathan and Abiram came out and stood at the entrances of their tents, together with their wives and children and little ones.

[28] And Moses said, "This is how you will know that the LORD has sent me to do all these things that I have done—for I have not done them on my own. [29] If these men die a natural death, or if nothing unusual happens, then the LORD has not sent me. [30] But if the LORD does something entirely new and the ground opens its mouth and swallows them and all their belongings, and they go down alive into the grave,* then you will know that these men have shown contempt for the LORD."

[31] He had hardly finished speaking the words when the ground suddenly split open beneath them. [32] The earth opened its mouth and swallowed the men, along with their households and all their followers who were standing with them, and everything they owned. [33] So they

went down alive into the grave, along with all their belongings. The earth closed over them, and they all vanished from among the people of Israel. [34] All the people around them fled when they heard their screams. "The earth will swallow us, too!" they cried. [35] Then fire blazed forth from the LORD and burned up the 250 men who were offering incense.

[36]* And the LORD said to Moses, [37] "Tell Eleazar son of Aaron the priest to pull all the incense burners from the fire, for they are holy. Also tell him to scatter the burning coals. [38] Take the incense burners of these men who have sinned at the cost of their lives, and hammer the metal into a thin sheet to overlay the altar. Since these burners were used in the LORD's presence, they have become holy. Let them serve as a warning to the people of Israel."

[39] So Eleazar the priest collected the 250 bronze incense burners that had been used by the men who died in the fire, and the bronze was hammered into a thin sheet to overlay the altar. [40] This would warn the Israelites that no unauthorized person—no one who was not a descendant of Aaron—should ever enter the LORD's presence to burn incense. If anyone did, the same thing would happen to him as happened to Korah and his followers. So the LORD's instructions to Moses were carried out.

[41] But the very next morning the whole community of Israel began muttering again against Moses and Aaron, saying, "You have killed the LORD's people!" [42] As the community gathered to protest against Moses and Aaron, they turned toward the Tabernacle and saw that the cloud had covered it, and the glorious presence of the LORD appeared.

[43] Moses and Aaron came and stood in front of the Tabernacle, [44] and the LORD said to Moses, [45] "Get away from all these people so that I can instantly destroy them!" But Moses and Aaron fell face down on the ground.

[46] And Moses said to Aaron, "Quick, take an incense burner and place burning coals on it from the altar. Lay incense on it, and carry it out among the people to purify them and make them right with the LORD.* The LORD's anger is blazing against them—the plague has already begun."

[47] Aaron did as Moses told him and ran out among the people. The plague had already begun to strike down the people, but Aaron burned the incense and purified* the people. [48] He stood between the dead and the

---

16:18 Hebrew *the Tent of Meeting;* also in 16:19, 42, 43, 50.   16:30 Hebrew *into Sheol;* also in 16:33.   16:36 Verses 16:36-50 are numbered 17:1-15 in Hebrew text.   16:46 Or *to make atonement for them.*   16:47 Or *and made atonement for.*

living, and the plague stopped. ⁴⁹But 14,700 people died in that plague, in addition to those who had died in the affair involving Korah. ⁵⁰Then because the plague had stopped, Aaron returned to Moses at the entrance of the Tabernacle.

The Budding of Aaron's Staff

17 ¹*Then the Lord said to Moses, ²"Tell the people of Israel to bring you twelve wooden staffs, one from each leader of Israel's ancestral tribes, and inscribe each leader's name on his staff. ³Inscribe Aaron's name on the staff of the tribe of Levi, for there must be one staff for the leader of each ancestral tribe. ⁴Place these staffs in the Tabernacle in front of the Ark containing the tablets of the Covenant,* where I meet with you. ⁵Buds will sprout on the staff belonging to the man I choose. Then I will finally put an end to the people's murmuring and complaining against you."

⁶So Moses gave the instructions to the people of Israel, and each of the twelve tribal leaders, including Aaron, brought Moses a staff. ⁷Moses placed the staffs in the Lord's presence in the Tabernacle of the Covenant.* ⁸When he went into the Tabernacle of the Covenant the next day, he found that Aaron's staff, representing the tribe of Levi, had sprouted, budded, blossomed, and produced ripe almonds!

⁹When Moses brought all the staffs out from the Lord's presence, he showed them to the people. Each man claimed his own staff. ¹⁰And the Lord said to Moses: "Place Aaron's staff permanently before the Ark of the Covenant* to serve as a warning to rebels. This should put an end to their complaints against me and prevent any further deaths." ¹¹So Moses did as the Lord commanded him.

¹²Then the people of Israel said to Moses, "Look, we are doomed! We are dead! We are ruined! ¹³Everyone who even comes close to the Tabernacle of the Lord dies. Are we all doomed to die?"

Duties of Priests and Levites

18 Then the Lord said to Aaron: "You, your sons, and your relatives from the tribe of Levi will be held responsible for any offenses related to the sanctuary. But you and your sons alone will be held responsible for violations connected with the priesthood.

²"Bring your relatives of the tribe of Levi— your ancestral tribe—to assist you and your sons as you perform the sacred duties in front of the Tabernacle of the Covenant.* ³But as the Levites go about all their assigned duties at the Tabernacle, they must be careful not to go near any of the sacred objects or the altar. If they do, both you and they will die. ⁴The Levites must join you in fulfilling their responsibilities for the care and maintenance of the Tabernacle,* but no unauthorized person may assist you.

⁵"You yourselves must perform the sacred duties inside the sanctuary and at the altar. If you follow these instructions, the Lord's anger will never again blaze against the people of Israel. ⁶I myself have chosen your fellow Levites from among the Israelites to be your special assistants. They are a gift to you, dedicated to the Lord for service in the Tabernacle. ⁷But you and your sons, the priests, must personally handle all the priestly rituals associated with the altar and with everything behind the inner curtain. I am giving you the priesthood as your special privilege of service. Any unauthorized person who comes too near the sanctuary will be put to death."

Support for the Priests and Levites

⁸The Lord gave these further instructions to Aaron: "I myself have put you in charge of all the holy offerings that are brought to me by the people of Israel. I have given all these consecrated offerings to you and your sons as your permanent share. ⁹You are allotted the portion of the most holy offerings that is not burned on the fire. This portion of all the most holy offerings—including the grain offerings, sin offerings, and guilt offerings—will be most holy, and it belongs to you and your sons. ¹⁰You must eat it as a most holy offering. All the males may eat of it, and you must treat it as most holy.

¹¹"All the sacred offerings and special offerings presented to me when the Israelites lift them up before the altar also belong to you. I have given them to you and to your sons and daughters as your permanent share. Any member of your family who is ceremonially clean may eat of these offerings.

¹²"I also give you the harvest gifts brought by the people as offerings to the Lord—the best of the olive oil, new wine, and grain. ¹³All the first crops of their land that the people

---

17:1 Verses 17:1-13 are numbered 17:16-28 in Hebrew text.   17:4 Hebrew *in the Tent of Meeting before the Testimony.* The Hebrew word for "testimony" refers to the terms of the Lord's covenant with Israel as written on stone tablets, which were kept in the Ark, and also to the covenant itself.   17:7 Or *Tabernacle of the Testimony;* also in 17:8.   17:10 Hebrew *before the Testimony;* see note on 17:4.   18:2 Or *Tabernacle of the Testimony.*   18:4 Hebrew *the Tent of Meeting;* also in 18:6, 21, 22, 23, 31.

present to the LORD belong to you. Any member of your family who is ceremonially clean may eat this food.

¹⁴"Everything in Israel that is specially set apart for the LORD* also belongs to you.

¹⁵"The firstborn of every mother, whether human or animal, that is offered to the LORD will be yours. But you must always redeem your firstborn sons and the firstborn of ceremonially unclean animals. ¹⁶Redeem them when they are one month old. The redemption price is five pieces of silver* (as measured by the weight of the sanctuary shekel, which equals twenty gerahs).

¹⁷"However, you may not redeem the firstborn of cattle, sheep, or goats. They are holy and have been set apart for the LORD. Sprinkle their blood on the altar, and burn their fat as a special gift, a pleasing aroma to the LORD. ¹⁸The meat of these animals will be yours, just like the breast and right thigh that are presented by lifting them up as a special offering before the altar. ¹⁹Yes, I am giving you all these holy offerings that the people of Israel bring to the LORD. They are for you and your sons and daughters, to be eaten as your permanent share. This is an eternal and unbreakable covenant* between the LORD and you, and it also applies to your descendants."

²⁰And the LORD said to Aaron, "You priests will receive no allotment of land or share of property among the people of Israel. I am your share and your allotment. ²¹As for the tribe of Levi, your relatives, I will compensate them for their service in the Tabernacle. Instead of an allotment of land, I will give them the tithes from the entire land of Israel.

²²"From now on, no Israelites except priests or Levites may approach the Tabernacle. If they come too near, they will be judged guilty and will die. ²³Only the Levites may serve at the Tabernacle, and they will be held responsible for any offenses against it. This is a permanent law for you, to be observed from generation to generation. The Levites will receive no allotment of land among the Israelites, ²⁴because I have given them the Israelites' tithes, which have been presented as sacred offerings to the LORD. This will be the Levites' share. That is why I said they would receive no allotment of land among the Israelites."

²⁵The LORD also told Moses, ²⁶"Give these instructions to the Levites: When you receive from the people of Israel the tithes I have assigned as your allotment, give a tenth of the tithes you receive—a tithe of the tithe—to the LORD as a sacred offering. ²⁷The LORD will consider this offering to be your harvest offering, as though it were the first grain from your own threshing floor or wine from your own winepress. ²⁸You must present one-tenth of the tithe received from the Israelites as a sacred offering to the LORD. This is the LORD's sacred portion, and you must present it to Aaron the priest. ²⁹Be sure to give to the LORD the best portions of the gifts given to you.

³⁰"Also, give these instructions to the Levites: When you present the best part as your offering, it will be considered as though it came from your own threshing floor or winepress. ³¹You Levites and your families may eat this food anywhere you wish, for it is your compensation for serving in the Tabernacle. ³²You will not be considered guilty for accepting the LORD's tithes if you give the best portion to the priests. But be careful not to treat the holy gifts of the people of Israel as though they were common. If you do, you will die."

The Water of Purification

19 The LORD said to Moses and Aaron, ²"Here is another legal requirement commanded by the LORD: Tell the people of Israel to bring you a red heifer, a perfect animal that has no defects and has never been yoked to a plow. ³Give it to Eleazar the priest, and it will be taken outside the camp and slaughtered in his presence. ⁴Eleazar will take some of its blood on his finger and sprinkle it seven times toward the front of the Tabernacle.* ⁵As Eleazar watches, the heifer must be burned—its hide, meat, blood, and dung. ⁶Eleazar the priest must then take a stick of cedar,* a hyssop branch, and some scarlet yarn and throw them into the fire where the heifer is burning.

⁷"Then the priest must wash his clothes and bathe himself in water. Afterward he may return to the camp, though he will remain ceremonially unclean until evening. ⁸The man who burns the animal must also wash his clothes and bathe himself in water, and he, too, will remain unclean until evening. ⁹Then someone who is ceremonially clean will gather up the ashes of the heifer and deposit them in a purified place outside the camp. They will be kept there for the community of Israel to

---

18:14 The Hebrew term used here refers to the complete consecration of things or people to the LORD, either by destroying them or by giving them as an offering.   18:16 Hebrew *5 shekels* [2 ounces or 57 grams] *of silver.*   18:19 Hebrew *a covenant of salt.*   19:4 Hebrew *the Tent of Meeting.*   19:6 Or *juniper.*

use in the water for the purification ceremony. This ceremony is performed for the removal of sin. [10]The man who gathers up the ashes of the heifer must also wash his clothes, and he will remain ceremonially unclean until evening. This is a permanent law for the people of Israel and any foreigners who live among them.

[11]"All those who touch a dead human body will be ceremonially unclean for seven days. [12]They must purify themselves on the third and seventh days with the water of purification; then they will be purified. But if they do not do this on the third and seventh days, they will continue to be unclean even after the seventh day. [13]All those who touch a dead body and do not purify themselves in the proper way defile the LORD's Tabernacle, and they will be cut off from the community of Israel. Since the water of purification was not sprinkled on them, their defilement continues.

[14]"This is the ritual law that applies when someone dies inside a tent: All those who enter that tent and those who were inside when the death occurred will be ceremonially unclean for seven days. [15]Any open container in the tent that was not covered with a lid is also defiled. [16]And if someone in an open field touches the corpse of someone who was killed with a sword or who died a natural death, or if someone touches a human bone or a grave, that person will be defiled for seven days.

[17]"To remove the defilement, put some of the ashes from the burnt purification offering in a jar, and pour fresh water over them. [18]Then someone who is ceremonially clean must take a hyssop branch and dip it into the water. That person must sprinkle the water on the tent, on all the furnishings in the tent, and on the people who were in the tent; also on the person who touched a human bone, or touched someone who was killed or who died naturally, or touched a grave. [19]On the third and seventh days the person who is ceremonially clean must sprinkle the water on those who are defiled. Then on the seventh day the people being cleansed must wash their clothes and bathe themselves, and that evening they will be cleansed of their defilement. [20]"But those who become defiled and do not purify themselves will be cut off from the community, for they have defiled the sanctuary of the LORD. Since the water of purification has not been sprinkled on them, they remain defiled. [21]This is a permanent

law for the people. Those who sprinkle the water of purification must afterward wash their clothes, and anyone who then touches the water used for purification will remain defiled until evening. [22]Anything and anyone that a defiled person touches will be ceremonially unclean until evening."

Moses Strikes the Rock

20 In the first month of the year,* the whole community of Israel arrived in the wilderness of Zin and camped at Kadesh. While they were there, Miriam died and was buried.

[2]There was no water for the people to drink at that place, so they rebelled against Moses and Aaron. [3]The people blamed Moses and said, "If only we had died in the LORD's presence with our brothers! [4]Why have you brought the congregation of the LORD's people into this wilderness to die, along with all our livestock? [5]Why did you make us leave Egypt and bring us here to this terrible place? This land has no grain, no figs, no grapes, no pomegranates, and no water to drink!"

[6]Moses and Aaron turned away from the people and went to the entrance of the Tabernacle,* where they fell face down on the ground. Then the glorious presence of the LORD appeared to them, [7]and the LORD said to Moses, [8]"You and Aaron must take the staff and assemble the entire community. As the people watch, speak to the rock over there, and it will pour out its water. You will provide enough water from the rock to satisfy the whole community and their livestock."

[9]So Moses did as he was told. He took the staff from the place where it was kept before the LORD. [10]Then he and Aaron summoned the people to come and gather at the rock. "Listen, you rebels!" he shouted. "Must we bring you water from this rock?" [11]Then Moses raised his hand and struck the rock twice with the staff, and water gushed out. So the entire community and their livestock drank their fill.

[12]But the LORD said to Moses and Aaron, "Because you did not trust me enough to demonstrate my holiness to the people of Israel, you will not lead them into the land I am giving them!" [13]This place was known as the waters of Meribah (which means "arguing") because there the people of Israel argued with the LORD, and there he demonstrated his holiness among them.

20:1 The first month of the ancient Hebrew lunar calendar usually occurs within the months of March and April. The number of years since leaving Egypt is not specified.   20:6 Hebrew *the Tent of Meeting.*

Edom Refuses Israel Passage

¹⁴While Moses was at Kadesh, he sent ambassadors to the king of Edom with this message:

"This is what your relatives, the people of Israel, say: You know all the hardships we have been through. ¹⁵Our ancestors went down to Egypt, and we lived there a long time, and we and our ancestors were brutally mistreated by the Egyptians. ¹⁶But when we cried out to the LORD, he heard us and sent an angel who brought us out of Egypt. Now we are camped at Kadesh, a town on the border of your land. ¹⁷Please let us travel through your land. We will be careful not to go through your fields and vineyards. We won't even drink water from your wells. We will stay on the king's road and never leave it until we have passed through your territory."

¹⁸But the king of Edom said, "Stay out of my land, or I will meet you with an army!"

¹⁹The Israelites answered, "We will stay on the main road. If our livestock drink your water, we will pay for it. Just let us pass through your country. That's all we ask."

²⁰But the king of Edom replied, "Stay out! You may not pass through our land." With that he mobilized his army and marched out against them with an imposing force. ²¹Because Edom refused to allow Israel to pass through their country, Israel was forced to turn around.

The Death of Aaron

²²The whole community of Israel left Kadesh and arrived at Mount Hor. ²³There, on the border of the land of Edom, the LORD said to Moses and Aaron, ²⁴"The time has come for Aaron to join his ancestors in death. He will not enter the land I am giving the people of Israel, because the two of you rebelled against my instructions concerning the water at Meribah. ²⁵Now take Aaron and his son Eleazar up Mount Hor. ²⁶There you will remove Aaron's priestly garments and put them on Eleazar, his son. Aaron will die there and join his ancestors."

²⁷So Moses did as the LORD commanded. The three of them went up Mount Hor together as the whole community watched. ²⁸At the summit, Moses removed the priestly garments from Aaron and put them on Eleazar, Aaron's son. Then Aaron died there on top of the mountain, and Moses and Eleazar went back down. ²⁹When the people realized that Aaron had died, all Israel mourned for him thirty days.

Victory over the Canaanites

21 The Canaanite king of Arad, who lived in the Negev, heard that the Israelites were approaching on the road through Atharim. So he attacked the Israelites and took some of them as prisoners. ²Then the people of Israel made this vow to the LORD: "If you will hand these people over to us, we will completely destroy* all their towns." ³The LORD heard the Israelites' request and gave them victory over the Canaanites. The Israelites completely destroyed them and their towns, and the place has been called Hormah* ever since.

The Bronze Snake

⁴Then the people of Israel set out from Mount Hor, taking the road to the Red Sea* to go around the land of Edom. But the people grew impatient with the long journey, ⁵and they began to speak against God and Moses. "Why have you brought us out of Egypt to die here in the wilderness?" they complained. "There is nothing to eat here and nothing to drink. And we hate this horrible manna!"

⁶So the LORD sent poisonous snakes among the people, and many were bitten and died. ⁷Then the people came to Moses and cried out, "We have sinned by speaking against the LORD and against you. Pray that the LORD will take away the snakes." So Moses prayed for the people.

⁸Then the LORD told him, "Make a replica of a poisonous snake and attach it to a pole. All who are bitten will live if they simply look at it!" ⁹So Moses made a snake out of bronze and attached it to a pole. Then anyone who was bitten by a snake could look at the bronze snake and be healed!

Israel's Journey to Moab

¹⁰The Israelites traveled next to Oboth and camped there. ¹¹Then they went on to Iyeabarim, in the wilderness on the eastern border of Moab. ¹²From there they traveled to the valley of Zered Brook and set up camp. ¹³Then they moved out and camped on the far side of the Arnon River, in the wilderness adjacent to the territory of the Amorites. The Arnon is the boundary line between the Moabites and

---

21:2 The Hebrew term used here refers to the complete consecration of things or people to the LORD, either by destroying them or by giving them as an offering; also in 21:3.   21:3 *Hormah* means "destruction."   21:4 Hebrew *sea of reeds.*

the Amorites. ¹⁴For this reason *The Book of the Wars of the* Lord speaks of "the town of Waheb in the area of Suphah, and the ravines of the Arnon River, ¹⁵and the ravines that extend as far as the settlement of Ar on the border of Moab."

¹⁶From there the Israelites traveled to Beer,* which is the well where the Lord said to Moses, "Assemble the people, and I will give them water." ¹⁷There the Israelites sang this song:

"Spring up, O well!
  Yes, sing its praises!
¹⁸ Sing of this well,
  which princes dug,
  which great leaders hollowed out
  with their scepters and staffs."

Then the Israelites left the wilderness and proceeded on through Mattanah, ¹⁹Nahaliel, and Bamoth. ²⁰After that they went to the valley in Moab where Pisgah Peak overlooks the wasteland.*

Victory over Sihon and Og

²¹The Israelites sent ambassadors to King Sihon of the Amorites with this message:

²²"Let us travel through your land. We will be careful not to go through your fields and vineyards. We won't even drink water from your wells. We will stay on the king's road until we have passed through your territory."

²³But King Sihon refused to let them cross his territory. Instead, he mobilized his entire army and attacked Israel in the wilderness, engaging them in battle at Jahaz. ²⁴But the Israelites slaughtered them with their swords and occupied their land from the Arnon River to the Jabbok River. They went only as far as the Ammonite border because the boundary of the Ammonites was fortified.*

²⁵So Israel captured all the towns of the Amorites and settled in them, including the city of Heshbon and its surrounding villages. ²⁶Heshbon had been the capital of King Sihon of the Amorites. He had defeated a former Moabite king and seized all his land as far as the Arnon River. ²⁷Therefore, the ancient poets wrote this about him:

"Come to Heshbon and let it be rebuilt!
  Let the city of Sihon be restored.
²⁸ A fire flamed forth from Heshbon,
  a blaze from the city of Sihon.
It burned the city of Ar in Moab;
  it destroyed the rulers of the Arnon
  heights.
²⁹ What sorrow awaits you, O people of
  Moab!
You are finished, O worshipers of
  Chemosh!
Chemosh has left his sons as refugees,
  his daughters as captives of Sihon,
  the Amorite king.
³⁰ We have utterly destroyed them,
  from Heshbon to Dibon.
We have completely wiped them out
  as far away as Nophah and Medeba.*"

³¹So the people of Israel occupied the territory of the Amorites. ³²After Moses sent men to explore the Jazer area, they captured all the towns in the region and drove out the Amorites who lived there. ³³Then they turned and marched up the road to Bashan, but King Og of Bashan and all his people attacked them at Edrei. ³⁴The Lord said to Moses, "Do not be afraid of him, for I have handed him over to you, along with all his people and his land. Do the same to him as you did to King Sihon of the Amorites, who ruled in Heshbon." ³⁵And Israel killed King Og, his sons, and all his subjects; not a single survivor remained. Then Israel occupied their land.

Balak Sends for Balaam

22 Then the people of Israel traveled to the plains of Moab and camped east of the Jordan River, across from Jericho. ²Balak son of Zippor, the Moabite king, had seen everything the Israelites did to the Amorites. ³And when the people of Moab saw how many Israelites there were, they were terrified. ⁴The king of Moab said to the elders of Midian, "This mob will devour everything in sight, like an ox devours grass in the field!"

So Balak, king of Moab, ⁵sent messengers to call Balaam son of Beor, who was living in his native land of Pethor* near the Euphrates River.* His message said:

"Look, a vast horde of people has arrived from Egypt. They cover the face of the

---

21:16 *Beer* means "well." 21:20 Or *overlooks Jeshimon.* 21:24 Or *because the terrain of the Ammonite frontier was rugged;* Hebrew reads *because the boundary of the Ammonites was strong.* 21:30 Or *until fire spread to Medeba.* The meaning of the Hebrew is uncertain. 22:5a Or *who was at Pethor in the land of the Amavites.* 22:5b Hebrew *the river.*

earth and are threatening me. 6Please come and curse these people for me because they are too powerful for me. Then perhaps I will be able to conquer them and drive them from the land. I know that blessings fall on any people you bless, and curses fall on people you curse."

7Balak's messengers, who were elders of Moab and Midian, set out with money to pay Balaam to place a curse upon Israel.* They went to Balaam and delivered Balak's message to him. 8"Stay here overnight," Balaam said. "In the morning I will tell you whatever the Lord directs me to say." So the officials from Moab stayed there with Balaam.

9That night God came to Balaam and asked him, "Who are these men visiting you?"

10Balaam said to God, "Balak son of Zippor, king of Moab, has sent me this message: 11'Look, a vast horde of people has arrived from Egypt, and they cover the face of the earth. Come and curse these people for me. Then perhaps I will be able to stand up to them and drive them from the land.'"

12But God told Balaam, "Do not go with them. You are not to curse these people, for they have been blessed!"

13The next morning Balaam got up and told Balak's officials, "Go on home! The Lord will not let me go with you."

14So the Moabite officials returned to King Balak and reported, "Balaam refused to come with us." 15Then Balak tried again. This time he sent a larger number of even more distinguished officials than those he had sent the first time. 16They went to Balaam and delivered this message to him:

"This is what Balak son of Zippor says: Please don't let anything stop you from coming to help me. 17I will pay you very well and do whatever you tell me. Just come and curse these people for me!"

18But Balaam responded to Balak's messengers, "Even if Balak were to give me his palace filled with silver and gold, I would be powerless to do anything against the will of the Lord my God. 19But stay here one more night, and I will see if the Lord has anything else to say to me."

20That night God came to Balaam and told him, "Since these men have come for you, get up and go with them. But do only what I tell you to do."

22:7 Hebrew *set out with the money of divination in their hand.*

Balaam and His Donkey

21So the next morning Balaam got up, saddled his donkey, and started off with the Moabite officials. 22But God was angry that Balaam was going, so he sent the angel of the Lord to stand in the road to block his way. As Balaam and two servants were riding along, 23Balaam's donkey saw the angel of the Lord standing in the road with a drawn sword in his hand. The donkey bolted off the road into a field, but Balaam beat it and turned it back onto the road. 24Then the angel of the Lord stood at a place where the road narrowed between two vineyard walls. 25When the donkey saw the angel of the Lord, it tried to squeeze by and crushed Balaam's foot against the wall. So Balaam beat the donkey again. 26Then the angel of the Lord moved farther down the road and stood in a place too narrow for the donkey to get by at all. 27This time when the donkey saw the angel, it lay down under Balaam. In a fit of rage Balaam beat the animal again with his staff.

28Then the Lord gave the donkey the ability to speak. "What have I done to you that deserves your beating me three times?" it asked Balaam.

29"You have made me look like a fool!" Balaam shouted. "If I had a sword with me, I would kill you!"

30"But I am the same donkey you have ridden all your life," the donkey answered. "Have I ever done anything like this before?"

"No," Balaam admitted.

31Then the Lord opened Balaam's eyes, and he saw the angel of the Lord standing in the roadway with a drawn sword in his hand. Balaam bowed his head and fell face down on the ground before him.

32"Why did you beat your donkey those three times?" the angel of the Lord demanded. "Look, I have come to block your way because you are stubbornly resisting me. 33Three times the donkey saw me and shied away; otherwise, I would certainly have killed you by now and spared the donkey."

34Then Balaam confessed to the angel of the Lord, "I have sinned. I didn't realize you were standing in the road to block my way. I will return home if you are against my going."

35But the angel of the Lord told Balaam, "Go with these men, but say only what I tell you to say." So Balaam went on with Balak's officials. 36When King Balak heard that Balaam was on the way, he went out to meet him at a Moabite town on the Arnon River at the farthest border of his land. ³⁷"Didn't I send you an urgent invitation? Why didn't you come right away?" Balak asked Balaam. "Didn't you believe me when I said I would reward you richly?"

³⁸Balaam replied, "Look, now I have come, but I have no power to say whatever I want. I will speak only the message that God puts in my mouth." ³⁹Then Balaam accompanied Balak to Kiriath-huzoth, ⁴⁰where the king sacrificed cattle and sheep. He sent portions of the meat to Balaam and the officials who were with him. ⁴¹The next morning Balak took Balaam up to Bamoth-baal. From there he could see some of the people of Israel spread out below him.

Balaam Blesses Israel

23 Then Balaam said to King Balak, "Build me seven altars here, and prepare seven young bulls and seven rams for me to sacrifice." ²Balak followed his instructions, and the two of them sacrificed a young bull and a ram on each altar.

³Then Balaam said to Balak, "Stand here by your burnt offerings, and I will go to see if the LORD will respond to me. Then I will tell you whatever he reveals to me." So Balaam went alone to the top of a bare hill, ⁴and God met him there. Balaam said to him, "I have prepared seven altars and have sacrificed a young bull and a ram on each altar." ⁵The LORD gave Balaam a message for King Balak. Then he said, "Go back to Balak and give him my message."

⁶So Balaam returned and found the king standing beside his burnt offerings with all the officials of Moab. ⁷This was the message Balaam delivered:

"Balak summoned me to come from Aram;
    the king of Moab brought me from the
        eastern hills.
'Come,' he said, 'curse Jacob for me!
    Come and announce Israel's doom.'
⁸ But how can I curse those
    whom God has not cursed?
How can I condemn those
    whom the LORD has not condemned?
⁹ I see them from the cliff tops;
    I watch them from the hills.
I see a people who live by themselves,
    set apart from other nations.
¹⁰ Who can count Jacob's descendants, as
    numerous as dust?

Who can count even a fourth of Israel's
    people?
Let me die like the righteous;
    let my life end like theirs."

¹¹Then King Balak demanded of Balaam, "What have you done to me? I brought you to curse my enemies. Instead, you have blessed them!"

¹²But Balaam replied, "I will speak only the message that the LORD puts in my mouth."

Balaam's Second Message

¹³Then King Balak told him, "Come with me to another place. There you will see another part of the nation of Israel, but not all of them. Curse at least that many!" ¹⁴So Balak took Balaam to the plateau of Zophim on Pisgah Peak. He built seven altars there and offered a young bull and a ram on each altar.

¹⁵Then Balaam said to the king, "Stand here by your burnt offerings while I go over there to meet the LORD."

¹⁶And the LORD met Balaam and gave him a message. Then he said, "Go back to Balak and give him my message."

¹⁷So Balaam returned and found the king standing beside his burnt offerings with all the officials of Moab. "What did the LORD say?" Balak asked eagerly.

¹⁸This was the message Balaam delivered:

"Rise up, Balak, and listen!
    Hear me, son of Zippor.
¹⁹ God is not a man, so he does not lie.
    He is not human, so he does not change
        his mind.
Has he ever spoken and failed to act?
    Has he ever promised and not carried it
        through?
²⁰ Listen, I received a command to bless;
    God has blessed, and I cannot reverse it!
²¹ No misfortune is in his plan for Jacob;
    no trouble is in store for Israel.
For the LORD their God is with them;
    he has been proclaimed their king.
²² God brought them out of Egypt;
    for them he is as strong as a wild ox.
²³ No curse can touch Jacob;
    no magic has any power against Israel.
For now it will be said of Jacob,
    'What wonders God has done for
        Israel!'
²⁴ These people rise up like a lioness,
    like a majestic lion rousing itself.
They refuse to rest

until they have feasted on prey,
   drinking the blood of the
      slaughtered!"

²⁵Then Balak said to Balaam, "Fine, but if you won't curse them, at least don't bless them!"

²⁶But Balaam replied to Balak, "Didn't I tell you that I can do only what the LORD tells me?"

Balaam's Third Message

²⁷Then King Balak said to Balaam, "Come, I will take you to one more place. Perhaps it will please God to let you curse them from there."

²⁸So Balak took Balaam to the top of Mount Peor, overlooking the wasteland.* ²⁹Balaam again told Balak, "Build me seven altars, and prepare seven young bulls and seven rams for me to sacrifice." ³⁰So Balak did as Balaam ordered and offered a young bull and a ram on each altar.

24 By now Balaam realized that the LORD was determined to bless Israel, so he did not resort to divination as before. Instead, he turned and looked out toward the wilderness, ²where he saw the people of Israel camped, tribe by tribe. Then the Spirit of God came upon him, ³and this is the message he delivered:

"This is the message of Balaam son of
      Beor,
   the message of the man whose eyes see
      clearly,
⁴ the message of one who hears the words
      of God,
   who sees a vision from the Almighty,
   who bows down with eyes wide open:
⁵ How beautiful are your tents, O Jacob;
   how lovely are your homes, O Israel!
⁶ They spread before me like palm groves,*
   like gardens by the riverside.
They are like tall trees planted by the
      LORD,
   like cedars beside the waters.
⁷ Water will flow from their buckets;
   their offspring have all they need.
Their king will be greater than Agag;
   their kingdom will be exalted.
⁸ God brought them out of Egypt;
   for them he is as strong as a wild ox.
He devours all the nations that oppose
      him,

breaking their bones in pieces,
   shooting them with arrows.
⁹ Like a lion, Israel crouches and lies
      down;
   like a lioness, who dares to arouse her?
Blessed is everyone who blesses you,
      O Israel,
   and cursed is everyone who curses
      you."

¹⁰King Balak flew into a rage against Balaam. He angrily clapped his hands and shouted, "I called you to curse my enemies! Instead, you have blessed them three times. ¹¹Now get out of here! Go back home! I promised to reward you richly, but the LORD has kept you from your reward."

¹²Balaam told Balak, "Don't you remember what I told your messengers? I said, ¹³'Even if Balak were to give me his palace filled with silver and gold, I would be powerless to do anything against the will of the LORD.' I told you that I could say only what the LORD says! ¹⁴Now I am returning to my own people. But first let me tell you what the Israelites will do to your people in the future."

Balaam's Final Messages

¹⁵This is the message Balaam delivered:

"This is the message of Balaam son of
      Beor,
   the message of the man whose eyes see
      clearly,
¹⁶ the message of one who hears the words
      of God,
   who has knowledge from the Most
      High,
   who sees a vision from the Almighty,
   who bows down with eyes wide open:
¹⁷ I see him, but not here and now.
   I perceive him, but far in the distant
      future.
A star will rise from Jacob;
   a scepter will emerge from Israel.
It will crush the heads of Moab's people,
   cracking the skulls* of the people of
      Sheth.
¹⁸ Edom will be taken over,
   and Seir, its enemy, will be conquered,
   while Israel marches on in triumph.
¹⁹ A ruler will rise in Jacob
   who will destroy the survivors
      of Ir."

23:28 Or *overlooking Jeshimon.* 24:6 Or *like a majestic valley.* 24:17 As in Samaritan Pentateuch; the meaning of the Hebrew word is uncertain.

²⁰Then Balaam looked over toward the people of Amalek and delivered this message:

"Amalek was the greatest of nations,
    but its destiny is destruction!"

²¹Then he looked over toward the Kenites and delivered this message:

"Your home is secure;
    your nest is set in the rocks.
²² But the Kenites will be destroyed
    when Assyria* takes you captive."

²³Balaam concluded his messages by saying:

"Alas, who can survive
    unless God has willed it?
²⁴ Ships will come from the coasts of
    Cyprus*;
    they will oppress Assyria and afflict
    Eber,
    but they, too, will be utterly
    destroyed."

²⁵Then Balaam left and returned home, and Balak also went on his way.

Moab Seduces Israel

25 While the Israelites were camped at Acacia Grove,* some of the men defiled themselves by having* sexual relations with local Moabite women. ²These women invited them to attend sacrifices to their gods, so the Israelites feasted with them and worshiped the gods of Moab. ³In this way, Israel joined in the worship of Baal of Peor, causing the LORD's anger to blaze against his people.

⁴The LORD issued the following command to Moses: "Seize all the ringleaders and execute them before the LORD in broad daylight, so his fierce anger will turn away from the people of Israel."

⁵So Moses ordered Israel's judges, "Each of you must put to death the men under your authority who have joined in worshiping Baal of Peor."

⁶Just then one of the Israelite men brought a Midianite woman into his tent, right before the eyes of Moses and all the people, as everyone was weeping at the entrance of the Tabernacle.* ⁷When Phinehas son of Eleazar and grandson of Aaron the priest saw this, he jumped up and left the assembly. He took a spear ⁸and rushed after the man into his tent. Phinehas thrust the spear all the way through the man's body and into the woman's stomach. So the plague against the Israelites was stopped, ⁹but not before 24,000 people had died.

¹⁰Then the LORD said to Moses, ¹¹"Phinehas son of Eleazar and grandson of Aaron the priest has turned my anger away from the Israelites by being as zealous among them as I was. So I stopped destroying all Israel as I had intended to do in my zealous anger. ¹²Now tell him that I am making my special covenant of peace with him. ¹³In this covenant, I give him and his descendants a permanent right to the priesthood, for in his zeal for me, his God, he purified the people of Israel, making them right with me.*'"

¹⁴The Israelite man killed with the Midianite woman was named Zimri son of Salu, the leader of a family from the tribe of Simeon. ¹⁵The woman's name was Cozbi; she was the daughter of Zur, the leader of a Midianite clan.

¹⁶Then the LORD said to Moses, ¹⁷"Attack the Midianites and destroy them, ¹⁸because they assaulted you with deceit and tricked you into worshiping Baal of Peor, and because of Cozbi, the daughter of a Midianite leader, who was killed at the time of the plague because of what happened at Peor."

The Second Registration of Israel's Troops

26 After the plague had ended,* the LORD said to Moses and to Eleazar son of Aaron the priest, ²"From the whole community of Israel, record the names of all the warriors by their families. List all the men twenty years old or older who are able to go to war."

³So there on the plains of Moab beside the Jordan River, across from Jericho, Moses and Eleazar the priest issued these instructions to the leaders of Israel: ⁴"List all the men of Israel twenty years old and older, just as the LORD commanded Moses."

This is the record of all the descendants of Israel who came out of Egypt.

The Tribe of Reuben

⁵These were the clans descended from the sons of Reuben, Jacob's* oldest son:
    The Hanochite clan, named after their
      ancestor Hanoch.

24:22 Hebrew *Asshur*; also in 24:24.　　24:24 Hebrew *Kittim*.　　25:1a Hebrew *Shittim*.　　25:1b As in Greek version; Hebrew reads *some of the men began having*.　　25:6 Hebrew *the Tent of Meeting*.　　25:13 Or *he made atonement for the people of Israel*.
26:1 The initial phrase in verse 26:1 is numbered 25:19 in Hebrew text.　　26:5 Hebrew *Israel's*; see note on 1:20-21b.

The Palluite clan, named after their ancestor Pallu.

6 The Hezronite clan, named after their ancestor Hezron.

The Carmite clan, named after their ancestor Carmi.

7These were the clans of Reuben. Their registered troops numbered 43,730.

8Pallu was the ancestor of Eliab, 9and Eliab was the father of Nemuel, Dathan, and Abiram. This Dathan and Abiram are the same community leaders who conspired with Korah against Moses and Aaron, rebelling against the LORD. 10But the earth opened up its mouth and swallowed them with Korah, and fire devoured 250 of their followers. This served as a warning to the entire nation of Israel. 11However, the sons of Korah did not die that day.

The Tribe of Simeon

12These were the clans descended from the sons of Simeon:

The Jemuelite clan, named after their ancestor Jemuel.*

The Jaminite clan, named after their ancestor Jamin.

The Jakinite clan, named after their ancestor Jakin.

13 The Zoharite clan, named after their ancestor Zohar.*

The Shaulite clan, named after their ancestor Shaul.

14These were the clans of Simeon. Their registered troops numbered 22,200.

The Tribe of Gad

15These were the clans descended from the sons of Gad:

The Zephonite clan, named after their ancestor Zephon.

The Haggite clan, named after their ancestor Haggi.

The Shunite clan, named after their ancestor Shuni.

16 The Oznite clan, named after their ancestor Ozni.

The Erite clan, named after their ancestor Eri.

17 The Arodite clan, named after their ancestor Arodi.*

The Arelite clan, named after their ancestor Areli.

18These were the clans of Gad. Their registered troops numbered 40,500.

The Tribe of Judah

19Judah had two sons, Er and Onan, who had died in the land of Canaan. 20These were the clans descended from Judah's surviving sons:

The Shelanite clan, named after their ancestor Shelah.

The Perezite clan, named after their ancestor Perez.

The Zerahite clan, named after their ancestor Zerah.

21These were the subclans descended from the Perezites:

The Hezronites, named after their ancestor Hezron.

The Hamulites, named after their ancestor Hamul.

22These were the clans of Judah. Their registered troops numbered 76,500.

The Tribe of Issachar

23These were the clans descended from the sons of Issachar:

The Tolaite clan, named after their ancestor Tola.

The Puite clan, named after their ancestor Puah.*

24 The Jashubite clan, named after their ancestor Jashub.

The Shimronite clan, named after their ancestor Shimron.

25These were the clans of Issachar. Their registered troops numbered 64,300.

The Tribe of Zebulun

26These were the clans descended from the sons of Zebulun:

The Seredite clan, named after their ancestor Sered.

The Elonite clan, named after their ancestor Elon.

The Jahleelite clan, named after their ancestor Jahleel.

26:12 As in Syriac version (see also Gen 46:10; Exod 6:15); Hebrew reads *Nemuelite . . . Nemuel.*   26:13 As in parallel texts at Gen 46:10 and Exod 6:15; Hebrew reads *Zerahite . . . Zerah.*   26:17 As in Samaritan Pentateuch and Greek and Syriac versions (see also Gen 46:16); Hebrew reads *Arod.*   26:23 As in Samaritan Pentateuch, Greek and Syriac versions, and Latin Vulgate (see also 1 Chr 7:1); Hebrew reads *The Punite clan, named after its ancestor Puvah.*

27These were the clans of Zebulun. Their registered troops numbered 60,500.

The Tribe of Manasseh
28Two clans were descended from Joseph through Manasseh and Ephraim.

29These were the clans descended from Manasseh:

The Makirite clan, named after their ancestor Makir.

The Gileadite clan, named after their ancestor Gilead, Makir's son.

30These were the subclans descended from the Gileadites:

The Iezerites, named after their ancestor Iezer.

The Helekites, named after their ancestor Helek.

31 The Asrielites, named after their ancestor Asriel.

The Shechemites, named after their ancestor Shechem.

32 The Shemidaites, named after their ancestor Shemida.

The Hepherites, named after their ancestor Hepher.

33 (One of Hepher's descendants, Zelophehad, had no sons, but his daughters' names were Mahlah, Noah, Hoglah, Milcah, and Tirzah.)

34These were the clans of Manasseh. Their registered troops numbered 52,700.

The Tribe of Ephraim
35These were the clans descended from the sons of Ephraim:

The Shuthelahite clan, named after their ancestor Shuthelah.

The Bekerite clan, named after their ancestor Beker.

The Tahanite clan, named after their ancestor Tahan.

36This was the subclan descended from the Shuthelahites:

The Eranites, named after their ancestor Eran.

37These were the clans of Ephraim. Their registered troops numbered 32,500.

These clans of Manasseh and Ephraim were all descendants of Joseph.

The Tribe of Benjamin
38These were the clans descended from the sons of Benjamin:

The Belaite clan, named after their ancestor Bela.

The Ashbelite clan, named after their ancestor Ashbel.

The Ahiramite clan, named after their ancestor Ahiram.

39 The Shuphamite clan, named after their ancestor Shupham.*

The Huphamite clan, named after their ancestor Hupham.

40These were the subclans descended from the Belaites:

The Ardites, named after their ancestor Ard.*

The Naamites, named after their ancestor Naaman.

41These were the clans of Benjamin. Their registered troops numbered 45,600.

The Tribe of Dan
42These were the clans descended from the sons of Dan:

The Shuhamite clan, named after their ancestor Shuham.

43These were the Shuhamite clans of Dan. Their registered troops numbered 64,400.

The Tribe of Asher
44These were the clans descended from the sons of Asher:

The Imnite clan, named after their ancestor Imnah.

The Ishvite clan, named after their ancestor Ishvi.

The Beriite clan, named after their ancestor Beriah.

45These were the subclans descended from the Beriites:

The Heberites, named after their ancestor Heber.

The Malkielites, named after their ancestor Malkiel.

26:39 As in some Hebrew manuscripts, Samaritan Pentateuch, Greek and Syriac versions, and Latin Vulgate; most Hebrew manuscripts read *Shephupham*. 26:40 As in Samaritan Pentateuch, some Greek manuscripts, and Latin Vulgate; Hebrew lacks *named after their ancestor Ard*.

⁴⁶Asher also had a daughter named Serah.

⁴⁷These were the clans of Asher. Their registered troops numbered 53,400.

The Tribe of Naphtali
⁴⁸These were the clans descended from the sons of Naphtali:
The Jahzeelite clan, named after their ancestor Jahzeel.
The Gunite clan, named after their ancestor Guni.
⁴⁹ The Jezerite clan, named after their ancestor Jezer.
The Shillemite clan, named after their ancestor Shillem.

⁵⁰These were the clans of Naphtali. Their registered troops numbered 45,400.

Results of the Registration
⁵¹In summary, the registered troops of all Israel numbered 601,730.

⁵²Then the LORD said to Moses, ⁵³"Divide the land among the tribes, and distribute the grants of land in proportion to the tribes' populations, as indicated by the number of names on the list. ⁵⁴Give the larger tribes more land and the smaller tribes less land, each group receiving a grant in proportion to the size of its population. ⁵⁵But you must assign the land by lot, and give land to each ancestral tribe according to the number of names on the list. ⁵⁶Each grant of land must be assigned by lot among the larger and smaller tribal groups."

The Tribe of Levi
⁵⁷This is the record of the Levites who were counted according to their clans:
The Gershonite clan, named after their ancestor Gershon.
The Kohathite clan, named after their ancestor Kohath.
The Merarite clan, named after their ancestor Merari.

⁵⁸The Libnites, the Hebronites, the Mahlites, the Mushites, and the Korahites were all subclans of the Levites.
Now Kohath was the ancestor of Amram, ⁵⁹and Amram's wife was named Jochebed. She also was a descendant of Levi, born among the Levites in the land of Egypt. Amram and Jochebed became the parents of Aaron, Moses, and their sister, Miriam. ⁶⁰To Aaron were born

Nadab, Abihu, Eleazar, and Ithamar. ⁶¹But Nadab and Abihu died when they burned before the LORD the wrong kind of fire, different than he had commanded.

⁶²The men from the Levite clans who were one month old or older numbered 23,000. But the Levites were not included in the registration of the rest of the people of Israel because they were not given an allotment of land when it was divided among the Israelites.

⁶³So these are the results of the registration of the people of Israel as conducted by Moses and Eleazar the priest on the plains of Moab beside the Jordan River, across from Jericho. ⁶⁴Not one person on this list had been among those listed in the previous registration taken by Moses and Aaron in the wilderness of Sinai. ⁶⁵For the LORD had said of them, "They will all die in the wilderness." Not one of them survived except Caleb son of Jephunneh and Joshua son of Nun.

The Daughters of Zelophehad
27 One day a petition was presented by the daughters of Zelophehad—Mahlah, Noah, Hoglah, Milcah, and Tirzah. Their father, Zelophehad, was a descendant of Hepher son of Gilead, son of Makir, son of Manasseh, son of Joseph. ²These women stood before Moses, Eleazar the priest, the tribal leaders, and the entire community at the entrance of the Tabernacle.* ³"Our father died in the wilderness," they said. "He was not among Korah's followers, who rebelled against the LORD; he died because of his own sin. But he had no sons. ⁴Why should the name of our father disappear from his clan just because he had no sons? Give us property along with the rest of our relatives."

⁵So Moses brought their case before the LORD. ⁶And the LORD replied to Moses, ⁷"The claim of the daughters of Zelophehad is legitimate. You must give them a grant of land along with their father's relatives. Assign them the property that would have been given to their father.

⁸"And give the following instructions to the people of Israel: If a man dies and has no son, then give his inheritance to his daughters. ⁹And if he has no daughter either, transfer his inheritance to his brothers. ¹⁰If he has no brothers, give his inheritance to his father's brothers. ¹¹But if his father has no brothers, give his inheritance to the nearest relative in his clan. This is a legal requirement for the people of Israel, just as the LORD commanded Moses."

27:2 Hebrew *the Tent of Meeting.*

Joshua Chosen to Lead Israel

¹²One day the LORD said to Moses, "Climb one of the mountains east of the river,* and look out over the land I have given the people of Israel. ¹³After you have seen it, you will die like your brother, Aaron, ¹⁴for you both rebelled against my instructions in the wilderness of Zin. When the people of Israel rebelled, you failed to demonstrate my holiness to them at the waters." (These are the waters of Meribah at Kadesh* in the wilderness of Zin.)

¹⁵Then Moses said to the LORD, ¹⁶"O LORD, you are the God who gives breath to all creatures. Please appoint a new man as leader for the community. ¹⁷Give them someone who will guide them wherever they go and will lead them into battle, so the community of the LORD will not be like sheep without a shepherd."

¹⁸The LORD replied, "Take Joshua son of Nun, who has the Spirit in him, and lay your hands on him. ¹⁹Present him to Eleazar the priest before the whole community, and publicly commission him to lead the people. ²⁰Transfer some of your authority to him so the whole community of Israel will obey him. ²¹When direction from the LORD is needed, Joshua will stand before Eleazar the priest, who will use the Urim—one of the sacred lots cast before the LORD—to determine his will. This is how Joshua and the rest of the community of Israel will determine everything they should do."

²²So Moses did as the LORD commanded. He presented Joshua to Eleazar the priest and the whole community. ²³Moses laid his hands on him and commissioned him to lead the people, just as the LORD had commanded through Moses.

The Daily Offerings

28 The LORD said to Moses, ²"Give these instructions to the people of Israel: The offerings you present as special gifts are a pleasing aroma to me; they are my food. See to it that they are brought at the appointed times and offered according to my instructions.

³"Say to the people: This is the special gift you must present to the LORD as your daily burnt offering. You must offer two one-year-old male lambs with no defects. ⁴Sacrifice one lamb in the morning and the other in the evening. ⁵With each lamb you must offer a grain offering of two quarts* of choice flour mixed with one quart* of pure oil of pressed olives. ⁶This is the regular burnt offering instituted at Mount Sinai as a special gift, a pleasing aroma to the LORD. ⁷Along with it you must present the proper liquid offering of one quart of alcoholic drink with each lamb, poured out in the Holy Place as an offering to the LORD. ⁸Offer the second lamb in the evening with the same grain offering and liquid offering. It, too, is a special gift, a pleasing aroma to the LORD.

The Sabbath Offerings

⁹"On the Sabbath day, sacrifice two one-year-old male lambs with no defects. They must be accompanied by a grain offering of four quarts* of choice flour moistened with olive oil, and a liquid offering. ¹⁰This is the burnt offering to be presented each Sabbath day, in addition to the regular burnt offering and its accompanying liquid offering.

The Monthly Offerings

¹¹"On the first day of each month, present an extra burnt offering to the LORD of two young bulls, one ram, and seven one-year-old male lambs, all with no defects. ¹²These must be accompanied by grain offerings of choice flour moistened with olive oil—six quarts* with each bull, four quarts with the ram, ¹³and two quarts with each lamb. This burnt offering will be a special gift, a pleasing aroma to the LORD. ¹⁴You must also present a liquid offering with each sacrifice: two quarts* of wine for each bull, a third of a gallon* for the ram, and one quart* for each lamb. Present this monthly burnt offering on the first day of each month throughout the year.

¹⁵"On the first day of each month, you must also offer one male goat for a sin offering to the LORD. This is in addition to the regular burnt offering and its accompanying liquid offering.

Offerings for the Passover

¹⁶"On the fourteenth day of the first month,* you must celebrate the LORD's Passover. ¹⁷On the following day—the fifteenth day of the month—a joyous, seven-day festival will begin, but no bread made with yeast may be eaten. ¹⁸The first day of the festival will be an official day for holy assembly, and no ordinary

27:12 Or *the mountains of Abarim.*   27:14 Hebrew *waters of Meribath-kadesh.*   28:5a Hebrew *¹⁄₁₀ of an ephah* [2.2 liters]; also in 28:13, 21, 29.   28:5b Hebrew *¹⁄₄ of a hin* [1 liter]; also in 28:7.   28:9 Hebrew *²⁄₁₀ of an ephah* [4.4 liters]; also in 28:12, 20, 28. 28:12 Hebrew *³⁄₁₀ of an ephah* [6.6 liters]; also in 28:20, 28.   28:14a Hebrew *½ of a hin* [2 liters].   28:14b Hebrew *⅓ of a hin* [1.3 liters].   28:14c Hebrew *¼ of a hin* [1 liter].   28:16 This day in the ancient Hebrew lunar calendar occurred in late March, April, or early May.

work may be done on that day. ¹⁹As a special gift you must present a burnt offering to the LORD—two young bulls, one ram, and seven one-year-old male lambs, all with no defects. ²⁰These will be accompanied by grain offerings of choice flour moistened with olive oil—six quarts with each bull, four quarts with the ram, ²¹and two quarts with each of the seven lambs. ²²You must also offer a male goat as a sin offering to purify yourselves and make yourselves right with the LORD.* ²³Present these offerings in addition to your regular morning burnt offering. ²⁴On each of the seven days of the festival, this is how you must prepare the food offering that is presented as a special gift, a pleasing aroma to the LORD. These will be offered in addition to the regular burnt offerings and liquid offerings. ²⁵The seventh day of the festival will be another official day for holy assembly, and no ordinary work may be done on that day.

Offerings for the Festival of Harvest

²⁶"At the Festival of Harvest,* when you present the first of your new grain to the LORD, you must call an official day for holy assembly, and you may do no ordinary work on that day. ²⁷Present a special burnt offering on that day as a pleasing aroma to the LORD. It will consist of two young bulls, one ram, and seven one-year-old male lambs. ²⁸These will be accompanied by grain offerings of choice flour moistened with olive oil—six quarts with each bull, four quarts with the ram, ²⁹and two quarts with each of the seven lambs. ³⁰Also, offer one male goat to purify yourselves and make yourselves right with the LORD. ³¹Prepare these special burnt offerings, along with their liquid offerings, in addition to the regular burnt offering and its accompanying grain offering. Be sure that all the animals you sacrifice have no defects.

Offerings for the Festival of Trumpets

29 "Celebrate the Festival of Trumpets each year on the first day of the appointed month in early autumn.* You must call an official day for holy assembly, and you may do no ordinary work. ²On that day you must

present a burnt offering as a pleasing aroma to the LORD. It will consist of one young bull, one ram, and seven one-year-old male lambs, all with no defects. ³These must be accompanied by grain offerings of choice flour moistened with olive oil—six quarts* with the bull, four quarts* with the ram, ⁴and two quarts* with each of the seven lambs. ⁵In addition, you must sacrifice a male goat as a sin offering to purify yourselves and make yourselves right with the LORD.* ⁶These special sacrifices are in addition to your regular monthly and daily burnt offerings, and they must be given with their prescribed grain offerings and liquid offerings. These offerings are given as a special gift to the LORD, a pleasing aroma to him.

Offerings for the Day of Atonement

⁷"Ten days later, on the tenth day of the same month,* you must call another holy assembly. On that day, the Day of Atonement, the people must go without food and must do no ordinary work. ⁸You must present a burnt offering as a pleasing aroma to the LORD. It will consist of one young bull, one ram, and seven one-year-old male lambs, all with no defects. ⁹These offerings must be accompanied by the prescribed grain offerings of choice flour moistened with olive oil—six quarts of choice flour with the bull, four quarts of choice flour with the ram, ¹⁰and two quarts of choice flour with each of the seven lambs. ¹¹You must also sacrifice one male goat for a sin offering. This is in addition to the sin offering of atonement and the regular daily burnt offering with its grain offering, and their accompanying liquid offerings.

Offerings for the Festival of Shelters

¹²"Five days later, on the fifteenth day of the same month,* you must call another holy assembly of all the people, and you may do no ordinary work on that day. It is the beginning of the Festival of Shelters,* a seven-day festival to the LORD. ¹³On the first day of the festival, you must present a burnt offering as a special gift, a pleasing aroma to the LORD. It will consist of thirteen young bulls, two rams, and fourteen one-year-old male lambs, all with no

---

28:22 Or *to make atonement for yourselves;* also in 28:30.   28:26 Hebrew *Festival of Weeks.* This was later called the Festival of Pentecost (see Acts 2:1). It is celebrated today as Shavuot (or Shabuoth).   29:1 Hebrew *the first day of the seventh month.* This day in the ancient Hebrew lunar calendar occurred in September or October. This festival is celebrated today as Rosh Hashanah, the Jewish new year.   29:3a Hebrew *³⁄₁₀ of an ephah* [6.6 liters]; also in 29:9, 14.   29:3b Hebrew *²⁄₁₀ of an ephah* [4.4 liters]; also in 29:9, 14.   29:4 Hebrew *¹⁄₁₀ of an ephah* [2.2 liters]; also in 29:10, 15.   29:5 Or *to make atonement for yourselves.* 29:7 Hebrew *On the tenth day of the seventh month;* see 29:1 and the note there. This day in the ancient Hebrew lunar calendar occurred in September or October. It is celebrated today as Yom Kippur.   29:12a Hebrew *On the fifteenth day of the seventh month;* see 29:1, 7 and the notes there. This day in the ancient Hebrew lunar calendar occurred in late September, October, or early November.   29:12b Or *Festival of Booths,* or *Festival of Tabernacles.* This was earlier called the Festival of the Final Harvest or Festival of Ingathering (see Exod 23:16b). It is celebrated today as Sukkot (or Succoth).

defects. ¹⁴Each of these offerings must be accompanied by a grain offering of choice flour moistened with olive oil—six quarts for each of the thirteen bulls, four quarts for each of the two rams, ¹⁵and two quarts for each of the fourteen lambs. ¹⁶You must also sacrifice a male goat as a sin offering, in addition to the regular burnt offering with its accompanying grain offering and liquid offering.

¹⁷"On the second day of this seven-day festival, sacrifice twelve young bulls, two rams, and fourteen one-year-old male lambs, all with no defects. ¹⁸Each of these offerings of bulls, rams, and lambs must be accompanied by its prescribed grain offering and liquid offering. ¹⁹You must also sacrifice a male goat as a sin offering, in addition to the regular burnt offering with its accompanying grain offering and liquid offering.

²⁰"On the third day of the festival, sacrifice eleven young bulls, two rams, and fourteen one-year-old male lambs, all with no defects. ²¹Each of these offerings of bulls, rams, and lambs must be accompanied by its prescribed grain offering and liquid offering. ²²You must also sacrifice a male goat as a sin offering, in addition to the regular burnt offering with its accompanying grain offering and liquid offering.

²³"On the fourth day of the festival, sacrifice ten young bulls, two rams, and fourteen one-year-old male lambs, all with no defects. ²⁴Each of these offerings of bulls, rams, and lambs must be accompanied by its prescribed grain offering and liquid offering. ²⁵You must also sacrifice a male goat as a sin offering, in addition to the regular burnt offering with its accompanying grain offering and liquid offering.

²⁶"On the fifth day of the festival, sacrifice nine young bulls, two rams, and fourteen one-year-old male lambs, all with no defects. ²⁷Each of these offerings of bulls, rams, and lambs must be accompanied by its prescribed grain offering and liquid offering. ²⁸You must also sacrifice a male goat as a sin offering, in addition to the regular burnt offering with its accompanying grain offering and liquid offering.

²⁹"On the sixth day of the festival, sacrifice eight young bulls, two rams, and fourteen one-year-old male lambs, all with no defects. ³⁰Each of these offerings of bulls, rams, and lambs must be accompanied by its prescribed grain offering and liquid offering. ³¹You must also sacrifice a male goat as a sin offering, in addition to the regular burnt offering with its accompanying grain offering and liquid offering.

³²"On the seventh day of the festival, sacrifice seven young bulls, two rams, and fourteen one-year-old male lambs, all with no defects. ³³Each of these offerings of bulls, rams, and lambs must be accompanied by its prescribed grain offering and liquid offering. ³⁴You must also sacrifice one male goat as a sin offering, in addition to the regular burnt offering with its accompanying grain offering and liquid offering.

³⁵"On the eighth day of the festival, proclaim another holy day. You must do no ordinary work on that day. ³⁶You must present a burnt offering as a special gift, a pleasing aroma to the LORD. It will consist of one young bull, one ram, and seven one-year-old male lambs, all with no defects. ³⁷Each of these offerings must be accompanied by its prescribed grain offering and liquid offering. ³⁸You must also sacrifice one male goat as a sin offering, in addition to the regular burnt offering with its accompanying grain offering and liquid offering.

³⁹"You must present these offerings to the LORD at your annual festivals. These are in addition to the sacrifices and offerings you present in connection with vows, or as voluntary offerings, burnt offerings, grain offerings, liquid offerings, or peace offerings."

⁴⁰*So Moses gave all of these instructions to the people of Israel as the LORD had commanded him.

Laws concerning Vows

30 ¹*Then Moses summoned the leaders of the tribes of Israel and told them, "This is what the LORD has commanded: ²A man who makes a vow to the LORD or makes a pledge under oath must never break it. He must do exactly what he said he would do.

³"If a young woman makes a vow to the LORD or a pledge under oath while she is still living at her father's home, ⁴and her father hears of the vow or pledge and does not object to it, then all her vows and pledges will stand. ⁵But if her father refuses to let her fulfill the vow or pledge on the day he hears of it, then all her vows and pledges will become invalid. The LORD will forgive her because her father would not let her fulfill them.

⁶"Now suppose a young woman makes a vow or binds herself with an impulsive pledge and later marries. ⁷If her husband learns of her vow or pledge and does not object on the day he

29:40 Verse 29:40 is numbered 30:1 in Hebrew text. 30:1 Verses 30:1-16 are numbered 30:2-17 in Hebrew text.

hears of it, her vows and pledges will stand. [8]But if her husband refuses to accept her vow or impulsive pledge on the day he hears of it, he nullifies her commitments, and the LORD will forgive her. [9]If, however, a woman is a widow or is divorced, she must fulfill all her vows and pledges.

[10]"But suppose a woman is married and living in her husband's home when she makes a vow or binds herself with a pledge. [11]If her husband hears of it and does not object to it, her vow or pledge will stand. [12]But if her husband refuses to accept it on the day he hears of it, her vow or pledge will be nullified, and the LORD will forgive her. [13]So her husband may either confirm or nullify any vows or pledges she makes to deny herself. [14]But if he does not object on the day he hears of it, then he is agreeing to all her vows and pledges. [15]If he waits more than a day and then tries to nullify a vow or pledge, he will be punished for her guilt."

[16]These are the regulations the LORD gave Moses concerning relationships between a man and his wife, and between a father and a young daughter who still lives at home.

Conquest of the Midianites

31 Then the LORD said to Moses, [2]"On behalf of the people of Israel, take revenge on the Midianites for leading them into idolatry. After that, you will die and join your ancestors."

[3]So Moses said to the people, "Choose some men, and arm them to fight the LORD's war of revenge against Midian. [4]From each tribe of Israel, send 1,000 men into battle." [5]So they chose 1,000 men from each tribe of Israel, a total of 12,000 men armed for battle. [6]Then Moses sent them out, 1,000 men from each tribe, and Phinehas son of Eleazar the priest led them into battle. They carried along the holy objects of the sanctuary and the trumpets for sounding the charge. [7]They attacked Midian as the LORD had commanded Moses, and they killed all the men. [8]All five of the Midianite kings—Evi, Rekem, Zur, Hur, and Reba—died in the battle. They also killed Balaam son of Beor with the sword.

[9]Then the Israelite army captured the Midianite women and children and seized their cattle and flocks and all their wealth as plunder. [10]They burned all the towns and villages where the Midianites had lived. [11]After they had gathered the plunder and captives, both people and animals, [12]they brought them all to

Moses and Eleazar the priest, and to the whole community of Israel, which was camped on the plains of Moab beside the Jordan River, across from Jericho. [13]Moses, Eleazar the priest, and all the leaders of the community went to meet them outside the camp. [14]But Moses was furious with all the generals and captains* who had returned from the battle.

[15]"Why have you let all the women live?" he demanded. [16]"These are the very ones who followed Balaam's advice and caused the people of Israel to rebel against the LORD at Mount Peor. They are the ones who caused the plague to strike the LORD's people. [17]So kill all the boys and all the women who have had intercourse with a man. [18]Only the young girls who are virgins may live; you may keep them for yourselves. [19]And all of you who have killed anyone or touched a dead body must stay outside the camp for seven days. You must purify yourselves and your captives on the third and seventh days. [20]Purify all your clothing, too, and everything made of leather, goat hair, or wood."

[21]Then Eleazar the priest said to the men who were in the battle, "The LORD has given Moses this legal requirement: [22]Anything made of gold, silver, bronze, iron, tin, or lead—[23]that is, all metals that do not burn—must be passed through fire in order to be made ceremonially pure. These metal objects must then be further purified with the water of purification. But everything that burns must be purified by the water alone. [24]On the seventh day you must wash your clothes and be purified. Then you may return to the camp."

Division of the Plunder

[25]And the LORD said to Moses, [26]"You and Eleazar the priest and the family leaders of each tribe are to make a list of all the plunder taken in the battle, including the people and animals. [27]Then divide the plunder into two parts, and give half to the men who fought the battle and half to the rest of the people. [28]From the army's portion, first give the LORD his share of the plunder—one of every 500 of the prisoners and of the cattle, donkeys, sheep, and goats. [29]Give this share of the army's half to Eleazar the priest as an offering to the LORD. [30]From the half that belongs to the people of Israel, take one of every fifty of the prisoners and of the cattle, donkeys, sheep, goats, and other animals. Give this share to the Levites, who are in charge of maintaining the LORD's Tabernacle."

31:14 Hebrew *the commanders of thousands, and the commanders of hundreds;* also in 31:48, 52, 54.

³¹So Moses and Eleazar the priest did as the LORD commanded Moses.

³²The plunder remaining from everything the fighting men had taken totaled 675,000 sheep and goats, ³³72,000 cattle, ³⁴61,000 donkeys, ³⁵and 32,000 virgin girls.

³⁶Half of the plunder was given to the fighting men. It totaled 337,500 sheep and goats, ³⁷of which 675 were the LORD's share; ³⁸36,000 cattle, of which 72 were the LORD's share; ³⁹30,500 donkeys, of which 61 were the LORD's share; ⁴⁰and 16,000 virgin girls, of whom 32 were the LORD's share. ⁴¹Moses gave all the LORD's share to Eleazar the priest, just as the LORD had directed him.

⁴²Half of the plunder belonged to the people of Israel, and Moses separated it from the half belonging to the fighting men. ⁴³It totaled 337,500 sheep and goats, ⁴⁴36,000 cattle, ⁴⁵30,500 donkeys, ⁴⁶and 16,000 virgin girls. ⁴⁷From the half-share given to the people, Moses took one of every fifty prisoners and animals and gave them to the Levites, who maintained the LORD's Tabernacle. All this was done as the LORD had commanded Moses.

⁴⁸Then all the generals and captains came to Moses ⁴⁹and said, "We, your servants, have accounted for all the men who went out to battle under our command; not one of us is missing! ⁵⁰So we are presenting the items of gold we captured as an offering to the LORD from our share of the plunder—armbands, bracelets, rings, earrings, and necklaces. This will purify our lives before the LORD and make us right with him.*"

⁵¹So Moses and Eleazar the priest received the gold from all the military commanders—all kinds of jewelry and crafted objects. ⁵²In all, the gold that the generals and captains presented as a gift to the LORD weighed about 420 pounds.* ⁵³All the fighting men had taken some of the plunder for themselves. ⁵⁴So Moses and Eleazar the priest accepted the gifts from the generals and captains and brought the gold to the Tabernacle* as a reminder to the LORD that the people of Israel belong to him.

The Tribes East of the Jordan

32 The tribes of Reuben and Gad owned vast numbers of livestock. So when they saw that the lands of Jazer and Gilead were ideally suited for their flocks and herds, ²they came to Moses, Eleazar the priest, and the other leaders of the community. They said, ³"Notice the towns of Ataroth, Dibon, Jazer, Nimrah, Heshbon, Elealeh, Sibmah,* Nebo, and Beon. ⁴The LORD has conquered this whole area for the community of Israel, and it is ideally suited for all our livestock. ⁵If we have found favor with you, please let us have this land as our property instead of giving us land across the Jordan River."

⁶"Do you intend to stay here while your brothers go across and do all the fighting?" Moses asked the men of Gad and Reuben. ⁷"Why do you want to discourage the rest of the people of Israel from going across to the land the LORD has given them? ⁸Your ancestors did the same thing when I sent them from Kadesh-barnea to explore the land. ⁹After they went up to the valley of Eshcol and explored the land, they discouraged the people of Israel from entering the land the LORD was giving them. ¹⁰Then the LORD was very angry with them, and he vowed, ¹¹'Of all those I rescued from Egypt, no one who is twenty years old or older will ever see the land I swore to give to Abraham, Isaac, and Jacob, for they have not obeyed me wholeheartedly. ¹²The only exceptions are Caleb son of Jephunneh the Kenizzite and Joshua son of Nun, for they have wholeheartedly followed the LORD.'

¹³"The LORD was angry with Israel and made them wander in the wilderness for forty years until the entire generation that sinned in the LORD's sight had died. ¹⁴But here you are, a brood of sinners, doing exactly the same thing! You are making the LORD even angrier with Israel. ¹⁵If you turn away from him like this and he abandons them again in the wilderness, you will be responsible for destroying this entire nation!"

¹⁶But they approached Moses and said, "We simply want to build pens for our livestock and fortified towns for our wives and children. ¹⁷Then we will arm ourselves and lead our fellow Israelites into battle until we have brought them safely to their land. Meanwhile, our families will stay in the fortified towns we build here, so they will be safe from any attacks by the local people. ¹⁸We will not return to our homes until all the people of Israel have received their portions of land. ¹⁹But we do not claim any of the land on the other side of the Jordan. We would rather live here on the east side and accept this as our grant of land."

²⁰Then Moses said, "If you keep your word and arm yourselves for the LORD's battles,

31:50 Or *will make atonement for our lives before the LORD.* 31:52 Hebrew *16,750 shekels* [191 kilograms]. 31:54 Hebrew *the Tent of Meeting.* 32:3 As in Samaritan Pentateuch and Greek version (see also 32:38); Hebrew reads *Sebam.*

²¹and if your troops cross the Jordan and keep fighting until the LORD has driven out his enemies, ²²then you may return when the LORD has conquered the land. You will have fulfilled your duty to the LORD and to the rest of the people of Israel. And the land on the east side of the Jordan will be your property from the LORD. ²³But if you fail to keep your word, then you will have sinned against the LORD, and you may be sure that your sin will find you out. ²⁴Go ahead and build towns for your families and pens for your flocks, but do everything you have promised."

²⁵Then the men of Gad and Reuben replied, "We, your servants, will follow your instructions exactly. ²⁶Our children, wives, flocks, and cattle will stay here in the towns of Gilead. ²⁷But all who are able to bear arms will cross over to fight for the LORD, just as you have said."

²⁸So Moses gave orders to Eleazar the priest, Joshua son of Nun, and the leaders of the clans of Israel. ²⁹He said, "The men of Gad and Reuben who are armed for battle must cross the Jordan with you to fight for the LORD. If they do, give them the land of Gilead as their property when the land is conquered. ³⁰But if they refuse to arm themselves and cross over with you, then they must accept land with the rest of you in the land of Canaan."

³¹The tribes of Gad and Reuben said again, "We are your servants, and we will do as the LORD has commanded! ³²We will cross the Jordan into Canaan fully armed to fight for the LORD, but our property will be here on this side of the Jordan."

³³So Moses assigned land to the tribes of Gad, Reuben, and half the tribe of Manasseh son of Joseph. He gave them the territory of King Sihon of the Amorites and the land of King Og of Bashan—the whole land with its cities and surrounding lands. ³⁴The descendants of Gad built the towns of Dibon, Ataroth, Aroer, ³⁵Atroth-shophan, Jazer, Jogbehah, ³⁶Beth-nimrah, and Beth-haran. These were all fortified towns with pens for their flocks.

³⁷The descendants of Reuben built the towns of Heshbon, Elealeh, Kiriathaim, ³⁸Nebo, Baalmeon, and Sibmah. They changed the names of some of the towns they conquered and rebuilt.

³⁹Then the descendants of Makir of the tribe of Manasseh went to Gilead and conquered it, and they drove out the Amorites living there. ⁴⁰So Moses gave Gilead to the Makirites, descendants of Manasseh, and they settled there. ⁴¹The people of Jair, another clan of the tribe of Manasseh, captured many of the towns in Gilead and changed the name of that region to the Towns of Jair.* ⁴²Meanwhile, a man named Nobah captured the town of Kenath and its surrounding villages, and he renamed that area Nobah after himself.

Remembering Israel's Journey

33 This is the route the Israelites followed as they marched out of Egypt under the leadership of Moses and Aaron. ²At the LORD's direction, Moses kept a written record of their progress. These are the stages of their march, identified by the different places where they stopped along the way.

³They set out from the city of Rameses in early spring—on the fifteenth day of the first month*—on the morning after the first Passover celebration. The people of Israel left defiantly, in full view of all the Egyptians. ⁴Meanwhile, the Egyptians were burying all their firstborn sons, whom the LORD had killed the night before. The LORD had defeated the gods of Egypt that night with great acts of judgment!

⁵After leaving Rameses, the Israelites set up camp at Succoth.
⁶Then they left Succoth and camped at Etham on the edge of the wilderness.
⁷They left Etham and turned back toward Pi-hahiroth, opposite Baal-zephon, and camped near Migdol.
⁸They left Pi-hahiroth* and crossed the Red Sea* into the wilderness beyond. Then they traveled for three days into the Etham wilderness and camped at Marah.
⁹They left Marah and camped at Elim, where there were twelve springs of water and seventy palm trees.
¹⁰They left Elim and camped beside the Red Sea.*
¹¹They left the Red Sea and camped in the wilderness of Sin.*
¹²They left the wilderness of Sin and camped at Dophkah.
¹³They left Dophkah and camped at Alush.

32:41 Hebrew *Havvoth-jair*.   33:3 This day in the ancient Hebrew lunar calendar occurred in late March, April, or early May. 33:8a As in many Hebrew manuscripts, Samaritan Pentateuch, and Latin Vulgate (see also 33:7); most Hebrew manuscripts read *left from in front of Hahiroth*.   33:8b Hebrew *the sea*.   33:10 Hebrew *sea of reeds*; also in 33:11.   33:11 The geographical name *Sin* is related to *Sinai* and should not be confused with the English word *sin*.

¹⁴They left Alush and camped at Rephidim, where there was no water for the people to drink.
¹⁵They left Rephidim and camped in the wilderness of Sinai.
¹⁶They left the wilderness of Sinai and camped at Kibroth-hattaavah.
¹⁷They left Kibroth-hattaavah and camped at Hazeroth.
¹⁸They left Hazeroth and camped at Rithmah.
¹⁹They left Rithmah and camped at Rimmon-perez.
²⁰They left Rimmon-perez and camped at Libnah.
²¹They left Libnah and camped at Rissah.
²²They left Rissah and camped at Kehelathah.
²³They left Kehelathah and camped at Mount Shepher.
²⁴They left Mount Shepher and camped at Haradah.
²⁵They left Haradah and camped at Makheloth.
²⁶They left Makheloth and camped at Tahath.
²⁷They left Tahath and camped at Terah.
²⁸They left Terah and camped at Mithcah.
²⁹They left Mithcah and camped at Hashmonah.
³⁰They left Hashmonah and camped at Moseroth.
³¹They left Moseroth and camped at Bene-jaakan.
³²They left Bene-jaakan and camped at Hor-haggidgad.
³³They left Hor-haggidgad and camped at Jotbathah.
³⁴They left Jotbathah and camped at Abronah.
³⁵They left Abronah and camped at Ezion-geber.
³⁶They left Ezion-geber and camped at Kadesh in the wilderness of Zin.
³⁷They left Kadesh and camped at Mount Hor, at the border of Edom. ³⁸While they were at the foot of Mount Hor, Aaron the priest was directed by the LORD to go up the mountain, and there he died. This happened in midsummer, on the first day of the fifth month* of the fortieth year after Israel's departure from Egypt. ³⁹Aaron was 123 years old when he died there on Mount Hor.
⁴⁰At that time the Canaanite king of Arad, who lived in the Negev in the land of Canaan, heard that the people of Israel were approaching his land.
⁴¹Meanwhile, the Israelites left Mount Hor and camped at Zalmonah.
⁴²Then they left Zalmonah and camped at Punon.
⁴³They left Punon and camped at Oboth.
⁴⁴They left Oboth and camped at Iye-abarim on the border of Moab.
⁴⁵They left Iye-abarim* and camped at Dibon-gad.
⁴⁶They left Dibon-gad and camped at Almon-diblathaim.
⁴⁷They left Almon-diblathaim and camped in the mountains east of the river,* near Mount Nebo.
⁴⁸They left the mountains east of the river and camped on the plains of Moab beside the Jordan River, across from Jericho. ⁴⁹Along the Jordan River they camped from Beth-jeshimoth as far as the meadows of Acacia* on the plains of Moab.

⁵⁰While they were camped near the Jordan River on the plains of Moab opposite Jericho, the LORD said to Moses, ⁵¹"Give the following instructions to the people of Israel: When you cross the Jordan River into the land of Canaan, ⁵²you must drive out all the people living there. You must destroy all their carved and molten images and demolish all their pagan shrines. ⁵³Take possession of the land and settle in it, because I have given it to you to occupy. ⁵⁴You must distribute the land among the clans by sacred lot and in proportion to their size. A larger portion of land will be allotted to each of the larger clans, and a smaller portion will be allotted to each of the smaller clans. The decision of the sacred lot is final. In this way, the portions of land will be divided among your ancestral tribes. ⁵⁵But if you fail to drive out the people who live in the land, those who remain will be like splinters in your eyes and thorns in your sides. They will harass you in the land where you live. ⁵⁶And I will do to you what I had planned to do to them."

Boundaries of the Land

34 Then the LORD said to Moses, ²"Give these instructions to the Israelites: When you come into the land of Canaan, which I am giving you as your special possession, these will be the boundaries. ³The southern portion of your country will extend

33:38 This day in the ancient Hebrew lunar calendar occurred in July or August.   33:45 As in 33:44; Hebrew reads *Iyim*, another name for Iye-abarim.   33:47 Or *the mountains of Abarim*; also in 33:48.   33:49 Hebrew *as far as Abel-shittim*.

from the wilderness of Zin, along the edge of Edom. The southern boundary will begin on the east at the Dead Sea.* 4It will then run south past Scorpion Pass* in the direction of Zin. Its southernmost point will be Kadesh-barnea, from which it will go to Hazar-addar, and on to Azmon. 5From Azmon the boundary will turn toward the Brook of Egypt and end at the Mediterranean Sea.*

6"Your western boundary will be the coastline of the Mediterranean Sea.

7"Your northern boundary will begin at the Mediterranean Sea and run east to Mount Hor, 8then to Lebo-hamath, and on through Zedad 9and Ziphron to Hazar-enan. This will be your northern boundary.

10"The eastern boundary will start at Hazar-enan and run south to Shepham, 11then down to Riblah on the east side of Ain. From there the boundary will run down along the eastern edge of the Sea of Galilee,* 12and then along the Jordan River to the Dead Sea. These are the boundaries of your land."

13Then Moses told the Israelites, "This territory is the homeland you are to divide among yourselves by sacred lot. The LORD has commanded that the land be divided among the nine and a half remaining tribes. 14The families of the tribes of Reuben, Gad, and half the tribe of Manasseh have already received their grants of land 15on the east side of the Jordan River, across from Jericho toward the sunrise."

Leaders to Divide the Land

16And the LORD said to Moses, 17"Eleazar the priest and Joshua son of Nun are the men designated to divide the grants of land among the people. 18Enlist one leader from each tribe to help them with the task. 19These are the tribes and the names of the leaders:

Tribe	Leader
Judah	Caleb son of Jephunneh
20 Simeon	Shemuel son of Ammihud
21 Benjamin	Elidad son of Kislon
22 Dan	Bukki son of Jogli
23 Manasseh son of Joseph	Hanniel son of Ephod
24 Ephraim son of Joseph	Kemuel son of Shiphtan
25 Zebulun	Elizaphan son of Parnach
26 Issachar	Paltiel son of Azzan
27 Asher	Ahihud son of Shelomi
28 Naphtali	Pedahel son of Ammihud

29These are the men the LORD has appointed to divide the grants of land in Canaan among the Israelites."

Towns for the Levites

35 While Israel was camped beside the Jordan on the plains of Moab across from Jericho, the LORD said to Moses, 2"Command the people of Israel to give to the Levites from their property certain towns to live in, along with the surrounding pasturelands. 3These towns will be for the Levites to live in, and the surrounding lands will provide pasture for their cattle, flocks, and other livestock. 4The pastureland assigned to the Levites around these towns will extend 1,500 feet* from the town walls in every direction. 5Measure off 3,000 feet* outside the town walls in every direction—east, south, west, north—with the town at the center. This area will serve as the larger pastureland for the towns.

6"Six of the towns you give the Levites will be cities of refuge, where a person who has accidentally killed someone can flee for safety. In addition, give them forty-two other towns. 7In all, forty-eight towns with the surrounding pastureland will be given to the Levites. 8These towns will come from the property of the people of Israel. The larger tribes will give more towns to the Levites, while the smaller tribes will give fewer. Each tribe will give property in proportion to the size of its land."

Cities of Refuge

9The LORD said to Moses, 10"Give the following instructions to the people of Israel.

"When you cross the Jordan into the land of Canaan, 11designate cities of refuge to which people can flee if they have killed someone accidentally. 12These cities will be places of protection from a dead person's relatives who want to avenge the death. The slayer must not be put to death before being tried by the community. 13Designate six cities of refuge for yourselves, 14three on the east side of the Jordan River and three on the west in the land of Canaan. 15These cities are for the protection of Israelites, foreigners living among you, and traveling merchants. Anyone who accidentally kills someone may flee there for safety.

16"But if someone strikes and kills another person with a piece of iron, it is murder, and the murderer must be executed. 17Or if someone with a stone in his hand strikes and kills

---

34:3 Hebrew *Salt Sea;* also in 34:12.   34:4 Or *the ascent of Akrabbim.*   34:5 Hebrew *the sea;* also in 34:6, 7.   34:11 Hebrew *Sea of Kinnereth.*   35:4 Hebrew *1,000 cubits* [460 meters].   35:5 Hebrew *2,000 cubits* [920 meters].

another person, it is murder, and the murderer must be put to death. [18]Or if someone strikes and kills another person with a wooden object, it is murder, and the murderer must be put to death. [19]The victim's nearest relative is responsible for putting the murderer to death. When they meet, the avenger must put the murderer to death. [20]So if someone hates another person and waits in ambush, then pushes him or throws something at him and he dies, it is murder. [21]Or if someone hates another person and hits him with a fist and he dies, it is murder. In such cases, the avenger must put the murderer to death when they meet.

[22]"But suppose someone pushes another person without having shown previous hostility, or throws something that unintentionally hits another person, [23]or accidentally drops a huge stone on someone, though they were not enemies, and the person dies. [24]If this should happen, the community must follow these regulations in making a judgment between the slayer and the avenger, the victim's nearest relative: [25]The community must protect the slayer from the avenger and must escort the slayer back to live in the city of refuge to which he fled. There he must remain until the death of the high priest, who was anointed with the sacred oil.

[26]"But if the slayer ever leaves the limits of the city of refuge, [27]and the avenger finds him outside the city and kills him, it will not be considered murder. [28]The slayer should have stayed inside the city of refuge until the death of the high priest. But after the death of the high priest, the slayer may return to his own property. [29]These are legal requirements for you to observe from generation to generation, wherever you may live.

[30]"All murderers must be put to death, but only if evidence is presented by more than one witness. No one may be put to death on the testimony of only one witness. [31]Also, you must never accept a ransom payment for the life of someone judged guilty of murder and subject to execution; murderers must always be put to death. [32]And never accept a ransom payment from someone who has fled to a city of refuge, allowing a slayer to return to his property before the death of the high priest. [33]This will ensure that the land where you live will not be polluted, for murder pollutes the land. And no sacrifice except the execution of the murderer can purify the land from murder.* [34]You must not defile the land where you live, for I live there myself. I am the LORD, who lives among the people of Israel."

Women Who Inherit Property

36 Then the heads of the clans of Gilead— descendants of Makir, son of Manasseh, son of Joseph—came to Moses and the family leaders of Israel with a petition. [2]They said, "Sir, the LORD instructed you to divide the land by sacred lot among the people of Israel. You were told by the LORD to give the grant of land owned by our brother Zelophehad to his daughters. [3]But if they marry men from another tribe, their grants of land will go with them to the tribe into which they marry. In this way, the total area of our tribal land will be reduced. [4]Then when the Year of Jubilee comes, their portion of land will be added to that of the new tribe, causing it to be lost forever to our ancestral tribe."

[5]So Moses gave the Israelites this command from the LORD: "The claim of the men of the tribe of Joseph is legitimate. [6]This is what the LORD commands concerning the daughters of Zelophehad: Let them marry anyone they like, as long as it is within their own ancestral tribe. [7]None of the territorial land may pass from tribe to tribe, for all the land given to each tribe must remain within the tribe to which it was first allotted. [8]The daughters throughout the tribes of Israel who are in line to inherit property must marry within their tribe, so that all the Israelites will keep their ancestral property. [9]No grant of land may pass from one tribe to another; each tribe of Israel must keep its allotted portion of land."

[10]The daughters of Zelophehad did as the LORD commanded Moses. [11]Mahlah, Tirzah, Hoglah, Milcah, and Noah all married cousins on their father's side. [12]They married into the clans of Manasseh son of Joseph. Thus, their inheritance of land remained within their ancestral tribe.

[13]These are the commands and regulations that the LORD gave to the people of Israel through Moses while they were camped on the plains of Moab beside the Jordan River, across from Jericho.

35:33 Or *can make atonement for murder.*

Deuteronomy

THE BOOK OF DEUTERONOMY records the covenant between God and Israel. It calls each new generation of Israelites to remember who God is and what he has done for them. Through a series of speeches, this fifth and final book of Moses summarizes the events that led up to that moment in Israel's history: the eve of Israel's entry into the Promised Land. Moses exhorted the Israelites to remain faithful and obedient and called them to rededicate their lives to the task God had given them. Then Moses led the people in worship. Finally, Moses appointed his successor, Joshua, and went off to a mountain by himself to view the Promised Land from a distance before he died.

- **Author:** Moses, according to Jewish tradition (except for the final summary, possibly written by Joshua)

- **Date Written:** Uncertain, perhaps between 1407 and 1406 BC

- **Purpose:** To remind the people of what God had done for them and to encourage them to rededicate their lives to him

- **Themes:** God's faithfulness, God's laws for his people, the consequences of sin, the importance of obedience, God's love for his people

- **Outline**
  1:1–4:49 Moses' first address
  5:1–26:19 Moses' second address
  27:1–28:68 Summary of various laws
  29:1–32:43 Moses' third address and the appointment of Joshua
  32:44–34:12 Moses' final words and death

Introduction to Moses' First Address

1 These are the words that Moses spoke to all the people of Israel while they were in the wilderness east of the Jordan River. They were camped in the Jordan Valley* near Suph, between Paran on one side and Tophel, Laban, Hazeroth, and Di-zahab on the other. ²Normally it takes only eleven days to travel from Mount Sinai* to Kadesh-barnea, going by way of Mount Seir. ³But forty years after the Israelites left Egypt, on the first day of the eleventh month,* Moses addressed the people of Israel, telling them everything the LORD had commanded him to say. ⁴This took place after he had defeated King Sihon of the Amorites, who ruled in Heshbon, and at Edrei had defeated King Og of Bashan, who ruled in Ashtaroth.

⁵While the Israelites were in the land of Moab east of the Jordan River, Moses carefully explained the LORD's instructions as follows.

The Command to Leave Sinai

⁶"When we were at Mount Sinai, the LORD our God said to us, 'You have stayed at this mountain long enough. ⁷It is time to break camp and move on. Go to the hill country of the Amorites and to all the neighboring regions—the Jordan Valley, the hill country, the western foothills,* the Negev, and the coastal plain. Go to the land of the Canaanites and to Lebanon, and all the way to the great Euphrates River. ⁸Look, I am giving all this land to you! Go in and occupy it, for it is the land the LORD swore to give to your ancestors Abraham, Isaac, and Jacob, and to all their descendants.'"

Moses Appoints Leaders from Each Tribe

⁹Moses continued, "At that time I told you, 'You are too great a burden for me to carry all by myself. ¹⁰The LORD your God has increased your population, making you as numerous as the stars! ¹¹And may the LORD, the God

---

1:1 Hebrew *the Arabah;* also in 1:7.   **1:2** Hebrew *Horeb,* another name for Sinai; also in 1:6, 19.   **1:3** Hebrew *In the fortieth year, on the first day of the eleventh month.* This day in the ancient Hebrew lunar calendar occurred in January or February. **1:7** Hebrew *the Shephelah.*

of your ancestors, multiply you a thousand times more and bless you as he promised! ¹²But you are such a heavy load to carry! How can I deal with all your problems and bickering? ¹³Choose some well-respected men from each tribe who are known for their wisdom and understanding, and I will appoint them as your leaders.'

¹⁴"Then you responded, 'Your plan is a good one.' ¹⁵So I took the wise and respected men you had selected from your tribes and appointed them to serve as judges and officials over you. Some were responsible for a thousand people, some for a hundred, some for fifty, and some for ten.

¹⁶"At that time I instructed the judges, 'You must hear the cases of your fellow Israelites and the foreigners living among you. Be perfectly fair in your decisions ¹⁷and impartial in your judgments. Hear the cases of those who are poor as well as those who are rich. Don't be afraid of anyone's anger, for the decision you make is God's decision. Bring me any cases that are too difficult for you, and I will handle them.'

¹⁸"At that time I gave you instructions about everything you were to do.

Scouts Explore the Land

¹⁹"Then, just as the LORD our God commanded us, we left Mount Sinai and traveled through the great and terrifying wilderness, as you yourselves remember, and headed toward the hill country of the Amorites. When we arrived at Kadesh-barnea, ²⁰I said to you, 'You have now reached the hill country of the Amorites that the LORD our God is giving us. ²¹Look! He has placed the land in front of you. Go and occupy it as the LORD, the God of your ancestors, has promised you. Don't be afraid! Don't be discouraged!'

²²"But you all came to me and said, 'First, let's send out scouts to explore the land for us. They will advise us on the best route to take and which towns we should enter.'

²³"This seemed like a good idea to me, so I chose twelve scouts, one from each of your tribes. ²⁴They headed for the hill country and came to the valley of Eshcol and explored it. ²⁵They picked some of its fruit and brought it back to us. And they reported, 'The land the LORD our God has given us is indeed a good land.'

Israel's Rebellion against the LORD

²⁶"But you rebelled against the command of the LORD your God and refused to go in. ²⁷You

1:40 Hebrew *sea of reeds.*

complained in your tents and said, 'The LORD must hate us. That's why he has brought us here from Egypt—to hand us over to the Amorites to be slaughtered. ²⁸Where can we go? Our brothers have demoralized us with their report. They tell us, "The people of the land are taller and more powerful than we are, and their towns are large, with walls rising high into the sky! We even saw giants there—the descendants of Anak!"'

²⁹"But I said to you, 'Don't be shocked or afraid of them! ³⁰The LORD your God is going ahead of you. He will fight for you, just as you saw him do in Egypt. ³¹And you saw how the LORD your God cared for you all along the way as you traveled through the wilderness, just as a father cares for his child. Now he has brought you to this place.'

³²"But even after all he did, you refused to trust the LORD your God, ³³who goes before you looking for the best places to camp, guiding you with a pillar of fire by night and a pillar of cloud by day.

³⁴"When the LORD heard your complaining, he became very angry. So he solemnly swore, ³⁵'Not one of you from this wicked generation will live to see the good land I swore to give your ancestors, ³⁶except Caleb son of Jephunneh. He will see this land because he has followed the LORD completely. I will give to him and his descendants some of the very land he explored during his scouting mission.'

³⁷"And the LORD was also angry with me because of you. He said to me, 'Moses, not even you will enter the Promised Land! ³⁸Instead, your assistant, Joshua son of Nun, will lead the people into the land. Encourage him, for he will lead Israel as they take possession of it. ³⁹I will give the land to your little ones—your innocent children. You were afraid they would be captured, but they will be the ones who occupy it. ⁴⁰As for you, turn around now and go on back through the wilderness toward the Red Sea.'

⁴¹"Then you confessed, 'We have sinned against the LORD! We will go into the land and fight for it, as the LORD our God has commanded us.' So your men strapped on their weapons, thinking it would be easy to attack the hill country.

⁴²"But the LORD told me to tell you, 'Do not attack, for I am not with you. If you go ahead on your own, you will be crushed by your enemies.'

⁴³"This is what I told you, but you would not listen. Instead, you again rebelled against

the LORD's command and arrogantly went into the hill country to fight. 44But the Amorites who lived there came out against you like a swarm of bees. They chased and battered you all the way from Seir to Hormah. 45Then you returned and wept before the LORD, but he refused to listen. 46So you stayed there at Kadesh for a long time.

Remembering Israel's Wanderings

2 "Then we turned around and headed back across the wilderness toward the Red Sea,* just as the LORD had instructed me, and we wandered around in the region of Mount Seir for a long time.

2"Then at last the LORD said to me, 3'You have been wandering around in this hill country long enough; turn to the north. 4Give these orders to the people: "You will pass through the country belonging to your relatives the Edomites, the descendants of Esau, who live in Seir. The Edomites will feel threatened, so be careful. 5Do not bother them, for I have given them all the hill country around Mount Seir as their property, and I will not give you even one square foot of their land. 6If you need food to eat or water to drink, pay them for it. 7For the LORD your God has blessed you in everything you have done. He has watched your every step through this great wilderness. During these forty years, the LORD your God has been with you, and you have lacked nothing."'

8"So we bypassed the territory of our relatives, the descendants of Esau, who live in Seir. We avoided the road through the Arabah Valley that comes up from Elath and Ezion-geber.

"Then as we turned north along the desert route through Moab, 9the LORD warned us, 'Do not bother the Moabites, the descendants of Lot, or start a war with them. I have given them Ar as their property, and I will not give you any of their land.'"

10(A race of giants called the Emites had once lived in the area of Ar. They were as strong and numerous and tall as the Anakites, another race of giants. 11Both the Emites and the Anakites are also known as the Rephaites, though the Moabites call them Emites. 12In earlier times the Horites had lived in Seir, but they were driven out and displaced by the descendants of Esau, just as Israel drove out the people of Canaan when the LORD gave Israel their land.)

13Moses continued, "Then the LORD said to us, 'Get moving. Cross the Zered Brook.' So we crossed the brook.

14"Thirty-eight years passed from the time we first left Kadesh-barnea until we finally crossed the Zered Brook! By then, all the men old enough to fight in battle had died in the wilderness, as the LORD had vowed would happen. 15The LORD struck them down until they had all been eliminated from the community.

16"When all the men of fighting age had died, 17the LORD said to me, 18'Today you will cross the border of Moab at Ar 19and enter the land of the Ammonites, the descendants of Lot. But do not bother them or start a war with them. I have given the land of Ammon to them as their property, and I will not give you any of their land.'"

20(That area was once considered the land of the Rephaites, who had lived there, though the Ammonites call them Zamzummites. 21They were also as strong and numerous and tall as the Anakites. But the LORD destroyed them so the Ammonites could occupy their land. 22He had done the same for the descendants of Esau who lived in Seir, for he destroyed the Horites so they could settle there in their place. The descendants of Esau live there to this day. 23A similar thing happened when the Caphtorites from Crete* invaded and destroyed the Avvites, who had lived in villages in the area of Gaza.)

24Moses continued, "Then the LORD said, 'Now get moving! Cross the Arnon Gorge. Look, I will hand over to you Sihon the Amorite, king of Heshbon, and I will give you his land. Attack him and begin to occupy the land. 25Beginning today I will make people throughout the earth terrified because of you. When they hear reports about you, they will tremble with dread and fear.'"

Victory over Sihon of Heshbon

26Moses continued, "From the wilderness of Kedemoth I sent ambassadors to King Sihon of Heshbon with this proposal of peace:

27'Let us travel through your land. We will stay on the main road and won't turn off into the fields on either side. 28Sell us food to eat and water to drink, and we will pay for it. All we want is permission to pass through your land. 29The descendants of Esau who live in Seir allowed us to go through their country, and so did the Moabites, who live in Ar. Let us pass through until we cross the Jordan into the land the LORD our God is giving us.'

2:1 Hebrew *sea of reeds.* 2:23 Hebrew *from Caphtor.*

³⁰"But King Sihon of Heshbon refused to allow us to pass through, because the LORD your God made Sihon stubborn and defiant so he could help you defeat him, as he has now done.

³¹"Then the LORD said to me, 'Look, I have begun to hand King Sihon and his land over to you. Begin now to conquer and occupy his land.'

³²"Then King Sihon declared war on us and mobilized his forces at Jahaz. ³³But the LORD our God handed him over to us, and we crushed him, his sons, and all his people. ³⁴We conquered all his towns and completely destroyed* everyone—men, women, and children. Not a single person was spared. ³⁵We took all the livestock as plunder for ourselves, along with anything of value from the towns we ransacked.

³⁶"The LORD our God also helped us conquer Aroer on the edge of the Arnon Gorge, and the town in the gorge, and the whole area as far as Gilead. No town had walls too strong for us. ³⁷However, we avoided the land of the Ammonites all along the Jabbok River and the towns in the hill country—all the places the LORD our God had commanded us to leave alone.

Victory over Og of Bashan

3 "Next we turned and headed for the land of Bashan, where King Og and his entire army attacked us at Edrei. ²But the LORD told me, 'Do not be afraid of him, for I have given you victory over Og and his entire army, and I will give you all his land. Treat him just as you treated King Sihon of the Amorites, who ruled in Heshbon.'

³"So the LORD our God handed King Og and all his people over to us, and we killed them all. Not a single person survived. ⁴We conquered all sixty of his towns—the entire Argob region in his kingdom of Bashan. Not a single town escaped our conquest. ⁵These towns were all fortified with high walls and barred gates. We also took many unwalled villages at the same time. ⁶We completely destroyed* the kingdom of Bashan, just as we had destroyed King Sihon of Heshbon. We destroyed all the people in every town we conquered—men, women, and children alike. ⁷But we kept all the livestock for ourselves and took plunder from all the towns.

⁸"So we took the land of the two Amorite kings east of the Jordan River—all the way from the Arnon Gorge to Mount Hermon. ⁹(Mount Hermon is called Sirion by the Sidonians, and the Amorites call it Senir.) ¹⁰We had now conquered all the cities on the plateau and all Gilead and Bashan, as far as the towns of Salecah and Edrei, which were part of Og's kingdom in Bashan. ¹¹(King Og of Bashan was the last survivor of the giant Rephaites. His bed was made of iron and was more than thirteen feet long and six feet wide.* It can still be seen in the Ammonite city of Rabbah.)

Land Division East of the Jordan

¹²"When we took possession of this land, I gave to the tribes of Reuben and Gad the territory beyond Aroer along the Arnon Gorge, plus half of the hill country of Gilead with its towns. ¹³Then I gave the rest of Gilead and all of Bashan—Og's former kingdom—to the half-tribe of Manasseh. (This entire Argob region of Bashan used to be known as the land of the Rephaites. ¹⁴Jair, a leader from the tribe of Manasseh, conquered the whole Argob region in Bashan, all the way to the border of the Geshurites and Maacathites. Jair renamed this region after himself, calling it the Towns of Jair,* as it is still known today.) ¹⁵I gave Gilead to the clan of Makir. ¹⁶But I also gave part of Gilead to the tribes of Reuben and Gad. The area I gave them extended from the middle of the Arnon Gorge in the south to the Jabbok River on the Ammonite frontier. ¹⁷They also received the Jordan Valley, all the way from the Sea of Galilee down to the Dead Sea,* with the Jordan River serving as the western boundary. To the east were the slopes of Pisgah.

¹⁸"At that time I gave this command to the tribes that would live east of the Jordan: 'Although the LORD your God has given you this land as your property, all your fighting men must cross the Jordan ahead of your Israelite relatives, armed and ready to assist them. ¹⁹Your wives, children, and numerous livestock, however, may stay behind in the towns I have given you. ²⁰When the LORD has given security to the rest of the Israelites, as he has to you, and when they occupy the land the LORD your God is giving them across the Jordan River, then you may all return here to the land I have given you.'

2:34 The Hebrew term used here refers to the complete consecration of things or people to the LORD, either by destroying them or by giving them as an offering.   **3:6** The Hebrew term used here refers to the complete consecration of things or people to the LORD, either by destroying them or by giving them as an offering; also in 3:6b.   **3:11** Hebrew *9 cubits* [4.1 meters] *long and 4 cubits* [1.8 meters] *wide.*   **3:14** Hebrew *Havvoth-jair.*   **3:17** Hebrew *from Kinnereth to the Sea of the Arabah, the Salt Sea.*

Moses Forbidden to Enter the Land

21"At that time I gave Joshua this charge: 'You have seen for yourself everything the LORD your God has done to these two kings. He will do the same to all the kingdoms on the west side of the Jordan. 22Do not be afraid of the nations there, for the LORD your God will fight for you.'

23"At that time I pleaded with the LORD and said, 24'O Sovereign LORD, you have only begun to show your greatness and the strength of your hand to me, your servant. Is there any god in heaven or on earth who can perform such great and mighty deeds as you do? 25Please let me cross the Jordan to see the wonderful land on the other side, the beautiful hill country and the Lebanon mountains.'

26"But the LORD was angry with me because of you, and he would not listen to me. 'That's enough!' he declared. 'Speak of it no more. 27But go up to Pisgah Peak, and look over the land in every direction. Take a good look, but you may not cross the Jordan River. 28Instead, commission Joshua and encourage and strengthen him, for he will lead the people across the Jordan. He will give them all the land you now see before you as their possession.' 29So we stayed in the valley near Beth-peor.

Moses Urges Israel to Obey

4 "And now, Israel, listen carefully to these decrees and regulations that I am about to teach you. Obey them so that you may live, so you may enter and occupy the land that the LORD, the God of your ancestors, is giving you. 2Do not add to or subtract from these commands I am giving you. Just obey the commands of the LORD your God that I am giving you.

3"You saw for yourself what the LORD did to you at Baal-peor. There the LORD your God destroyed everyone who had worshiped Baal, the god of Peor. 4But all of you who were faithful to the LORD your God are still alive today—every one of you.

5"Look, I now teach you these decrees and regulations just as the LORD my God commanded me, so that you may obey them in the land you are about to enter and occupy. 6Obey them completely, and you will display your wisdom and intelligence among the surrounding nations. When they hear all these decrees, they will exclaim, 'How wise and prudent are the people of this great nation!' 7For what great nation has a god as near to them as the LORD

our God is near to us whenever we call on him? 8And what great nation has decrees and regulations as righteous and fair as this body of instructions that I am giving you today?

9"But watch out! Be careful never to forget what you yourself have seen. Do not let these memories escape from your mind as long as you live! And be sure to pass them on to your children and grandchildren. 10Never forget the day when you stood before the LORD your God at Mount Sinai,* where he told me, 'Summon the people before me, and I will personally instruct them. Then they will learn to fear me as long as they live, and they will teach their children to fear me also.'

11"You came near and stood at the foot of the mountain, while flames from the mountain shot into the sky. The mountain was shrouded in black clouds and deep darkness. 12And the LORD spoke to you from the heart of the fire. You heard the sound of his words but didn't see his form; there was only a voice. 13He proclaimed his covenant—the Ten Commandments*—which he commanded you to keep, and which he wrote on two stone tablets. 14It was at that time that the LORD commanded me to teach you his decrees and regulations so you would obey them in the land you are about to enter and occupy.

A Warning against Idolatry

15"But be very careful! You did not see the LORD's form on the day he spoke to you from the heart of the fire at Mount Sinai. 16So do not corrupt yourselves by making an idol in any form—whether of a man or a woman, 17an animal on the ground, a bird in the sky, 18a small animal that scurries along the ground, or a fish in the deepest sea. 19And when you look up into the sky and see the sun, moon, and stars—all the forces of heaven—don't be seduced into worshiping them. The LORD your God gave them to all the peoples of the earth. 20Remember that the LORD rescued you from the iron-smelting furnace of Egypt in order to make you his very own people and his special possession, which is what you are today.

21"But the LORD was angry with me because of you. He vowed that I would not cross the Jordan River into the good land the LORD your God is giving you as your special possession. 22You will cross the Jordan to occupy the land, but I will not. Instead, I will die here on the east side of the river. 23So be careful not to break the covenant the LORD your God has made

4:10 Hebrew *Horeb*, another name for Sinai; also in 4:15.   4:13 Hebrew *the ten words*.

with you. Do not make idols of any shape or form, for the LORD your God has forbidden this. ²⁴The LORD your God is a devouring fire; he is a jealous God.

²⁵"In the future, when you have children and grandchildren and have lived in the land a long time, do not corrupt yourselves by making idols of any kind. This is evil in the sight of the LORD your God and will arouse his anger. ²⁶"Today I call on heaven and earth as witnesses against you. If you break my covenant, you will quickly disappear from the land you are crossing the Jordan to occupy. You will live there only a short time; then you will be utterly destroyed. ²⁷For the LORD will scatter you among the nations, where only a few of you will survive. ²⁸There, in a foreign land, you will worship idols made from wood and stone—gods that neither see nor hear nor eat nor smell. ²⁹But from there you will search again for the LORD your God. And if you search for him with all your heart and soul, you will find him.

³⁰"In the distant future, when you are suffering all these things, you will finally return to the LORD your God and listen to what he tells you. ³¹For the LORD your God is a merciful God; he will not abandon you or destroy you or forget the solemn covenant he made with your ancestors.

There Is Only One God

³²"Now search all of history, from the time God created people on the earth until now, and search from one end of the heavens to the other. Has anything as great as this ever been seen or heard before? ³³Has any nation ever heard the voice of God* speaking from fire—as you did—and survived? ³⁴Has any other god dared to take a nation for himself out of another nation by means of trials, miraculous signs, wonders, war, a strong hand, a powerful arm, and terrifying acts? Yet that is what the LORD your God did for you in Egypt, right before your eyes.

³⁵"He showed you these things so you would know that the LORD is God and there is no other. ³⁶He let you hear his voice from heaven so he could instruct you. He let you see his great fire here on earth so he could speak to you from it. ³⁷Because he loved your ancestors, he chose to bless their descendants, and he personally brought you out of Egypt with a great display of power. ³⁸He drove out nations far greater than you, so he could bring you in

and give you their land as your special possession, as it is today.

³⁹"So remember this and keep it firmly in mind: The LORD is God both in heaven and on earth, and there is no other. ⁴⁰If you obey all the decrees and commands I am giving you today, all will be well with you and your children. I am giving you these instructions so you will enjoy a long life in the land the LORD your God is giving you for all time."

Eastern Cities of Refuge

⁴¹Then Moses set apart three cities of refuge east of the Jordan River. ⁴²Anyone who killed another person unintentionally, without previous hostility, could flee there to live in safety. ⁴³These were the cities: Bezer on the wilderness plateau for the tribe of Reuben; Ramoth in Gilead for the tribe of Gad; Golan in Bashan for the tribe of Manasseh.

Introduction to Moses' Second Address

⁴⁴This is the body of instruction that Moses presented to the Israelites. ⁴⁵These are the laws, decrees, and regulations that Moses gave to the people of Israel when they left Egypt, ⁴⁶and as they camped in the valley near Beth-peor east of the Jordan River. (This land was formerly occupied by the Amorites under King Sihon, who ruled from Heshbon. But Moses and the Israelites destroyed him and his people when they came up from Egypt. ⁴⁷Israel took possession of his land and that of King Og of Bashan—the two Amorite kings east of the Jordan. ⁴⁸So Israel conquered the entire area from Aroer at the edge of the Arnon Gorge all the way to Mount Sirion,* also called Mount Hermon. ⁴⁹And they conquered the eastern bank of the Jordan River as far south as the Dead Sea,* below the slopes of Pisgah.)

Ten Commandments for the Covenant Community

5 Moses called all the people of Israel together and said, "Listen carefully, Israel. Hear the decrees and regulations I am giving you today, so you may learn them and obey them!

²"The LORD our God made a covenant with us at Mount Sinai.* ³The LORD did not make this covenant with our ancestors, but with all of us who are alive today. ⁴At the mountain the LORD spoke to you face to face from the heart of the fire. ⁵I stood as an intermediary between

---

4:33 Or *voice of a god.* 4:48 As in Syriac version (see also 3:9); Hebrew reads *Mount Sion.* 4:49 Hebrew *took the Arabah on the east side of the Jordan as far as the sea of the Arabah.* 5:2 Hebrew *Horeb,* another name for Sinai.

you and the LORD, for you were afraid of the fire and did not want to approach the mountain. He spoke to me, and I passed his words on to you. This is what he said:

⁶"I am the LORD your God, who rescued you from the land of Egypt, the place of your slavery.

⁷"You must not have any other god but me.

⁸"You must not make for yourself an idol of any kind, or an image of anything in the heavens or on the earth or in the sea. ⁹You must not bow down to them or worship them, for I, the LORD your God, am a jealous God who will not tolerate your affection for any other gods. I lay the sins of the parents upon their children; the entire family is affected—even children in the third and fourth generations of those who reject me. ¹⁰But I lavish unfailing love for a thousand generations on those* who love me and obey my commands.

¹¹"You must not misuse the name of the LORD your God. The LORD will not let you go unpunished if you misuse his name.

¹²"Observe the Sabbath day by keeping it holy, as the LORD your God has commanded you. ¹³You have six days each week for your ordinary work, ¹⁴but the seventh day is a Sabbath day of rest dedicated to the LORD your God. On that day no one in your household may do any work. This includes you, your sons and daughters, your male and female servants, your oxen and donkeys and other livestock, and any foreigners living among you. All your male and female servants must rest as you do. ¹⁵Remember that you were once slaves in Egypt, but the LORD your God brought you out with his strong hand and powerful arm. That is why the LORD your God has commanded you to rest on the Sabbath day.

¹⁶"Honor your father and mother, as the LORD your God commanded you. Then you will live a long, full life in the land the LORD your God is giving you.

¹⁷"You must not murder.

¹⁸"You must not commit adultery.

¹⁹"You must not steal.

²⁰"You must not testify falsely against your neighbor.

²¹"You must not covet your neighbor's wife. You must not covet your neighbor's house or land, male or female servant, ox or donkey, or anything else that belongs to your neighbor.

²²"The LORD spoke these words to all of you assembled there at the foot of the mountain. He spoke with a loud voice from the heart of the fire, surrounded by clouds and deep darkness. This was all he said at that time, and he wrote his words on two stone tablets and gave them to me.

²³"But when you heard the voice from the heart of the darkness, while the mountain was blazing with fire, all your tribal leaders and elders came to me. ²⁴They said, 'Look, the LORD our God has shown us his glory and greatness, and we have heard his voice from the heart of the fire. Today we have seen that God can speak to us humans, and yet we live! ²⁵But now, why should we risk death again? If the LORD our God speaks to us again, we will certainly die and be consumed by this awesome fire. ²⁶Can any living thing hear the voice of the living God from the heart of the fire as we did and yet survive? ²⁷Go yourself and listen to what the LORD our God says. Then come and tell us everything he tells you, and we will listen and obey.'

²⁸"The LORD heard the request you made to me. And he said, 'I have heard what the people said to you, and they are right. ²⁹Oh, that they would always have hearts like this, that they might fear me and obey all my commands! If they did, they and their descendants would prosper forever. ³⁰Go and tell them, "Return to your tents." ³¹But you stand here with me so I can give you all my commands, decrees, and regulations. You must teach them to the people so they can obey them in the land I am giving them as their possession.'"

³²So Moses told the people, "You must be careful to obey all the commands of the LORD your God, following his instructions in every detail. ³³Stay on the path that the LORD your God has commanded you to follow. Then you will live long and prosperous lives in the land you are about to enter and occupy.

A Call for Wholehearted Commitment

6 "These are the commands, decrees, and regulations that the LORD your God commanded me to teach you. You must obey them in the land you are about to enter and occupy, ²and you and your children and grandchildren must fear the LORD your God as long as you live. If you obey all his decrees and commands,

5:10 Hebrew *for thousands of those.*

you will enjoy a long life. ³Listen closely, Israel, and be careful to obey. Then all will go well with you, and you will have many children in the land flowing with milk and honey, just as the LORD, the God of your ancestors, promised you.

⁴"Listen, O Israel! The LORD is our God, the LORD alone.* ⁵And you must love the LORD your God with all your heart, all your soul, and all your strength. ⁶And you must commit yourselves wholeheartedly to these commands that I am giving you today. ⁷Repeat them again and again to your children. Talk about them when you are at home and when you are on the road, when you are going to bed and when you are getting up. ⁸Tie them to your hands and wear them on your forehead as reminders. ⁹Write them on the doorposts of your house and on your gates.

¹⁰"The LORD your God will soon bring you into the land he swore to give you when he made a vow to your ancestors Abraham, Isaac, and Jacob. It is a land with large, prosperous cities that you did not build. ¹¹The houses will be richly stocked with goods you did not produce. You will draw water from cisterns you did not dig, and you will eat from vineyards and olive trees you did not plant. When you have eaten your fill in this land, ¹²be careful not to forget the LORD, who rescued you from slavery in the land of Egypt. ¹³You must fear the LORD your God and serve him. When you take an oath, you must use only his name.

¹⁴"You must not worship any of the gods of neighboring nations, ¹⁵for the LORD your God, who lives among you, is a jealous God. His anger will flare up against you, and he will wipe you from the face of the earth. ¹⁶You must not test the LORD your God as you did when you complained at Massah. ¹⁷You must diligently obey the commands of the LORD your God—all the laws and decrees he has given you. ¹⁸Do what is right and good in the LORD's sight, so all will go well with you. Then you will enter and occupy the good land that the LORD swore to give your ancestors. ¹⁹You will drive out all the enemies living in the land, just as the LORD said you would.

²⁰"In the future your children will ask you, 'What is the meaning of these laws, decrees, and regulations that the LORD our God has commanded us to obey?'

²¹"Then you must tell them, 'We were Pharaoh's slaves in Egypt, but the LORD brought us out of Egypt with his strong hand. ²²The LORD did miraculous signs and wonders before our eyes, dealing terrifying blows against Egypt and Pharaoh and all his people. ²³He brought us out of Egypt so he could give us this land he had sworn to give our ancestors. ²⁴And the LORD our God commanded us to obey all these decrees and to fear him so he can continue to bless us and preserve our lives, as he has done to this day. ²⁵For we will be counted as righteous when we obey all the commands the LORD our God has given us.'

The Privilege of Holiness

7 "When the LORD your God brings you into the land you are about to enter and occupy, he will clear away many nations ahead of you: the Hittites, Girgashites, Amorites, Canaanites, Perizzites, Hivites, and Jebusites. These seven nations are greater and more numerous than you. ²When the LORD your God hands these nations over to you and you conquer them, you must completely destroy* them. Make no treaties with them and show them no mercy. ³You must not intermarry with them. Do not let your daughters and sons marry their sons and daughters, ⁴for they will lead your children away from me to worship other gods. Then the anger of the LORD will burn against you, and he will quickly destroy you. ⁵This is what you must do. You must break down their pagan altars and shatter their sacred pillars. Cut down their Asherah poles and burn their idols. ⁶For you are a holy people, who belong to the LORD your God. Of all the people on earth, the LORD your God has chosen you to be his own special treasure.

⁷"The LORD did not set his heart on you and choose you because you were more numerous than other nations, for you were the smallest of all nations! ⁸Rather, it was simply that the LORD loves you, and he was keeping the oath he had sworn to your ancestors. That is why the LORD rescued you with such a strong hand from your slavery and from the oppressive hand of Pharaoh, king of Egypt. ⁹Understand, therefore, that the LORD your God is indeed God. He is the faithful God who keeps his covenant for a thousand generations and lavishes his unfailing love on those who love him and obey his commands. ¹⁰But he does not hesitate to punish and destroy those who reject

6:4 Or The LORD our God is one LORD; or The LORD our God, the LORD is one; or The LORD is our God, the LORD is one.   7:2 The Hebrew term used here refers to the complete consecration of things or people to the LORD, either by destroying them or by giving them as an offering; also in 7:26.

him. ¹¹Therefore, you must obey all these commands, decrees, and regulations I am giving you today.

¹²"If you listen to these regulations and faithfully obey them, the LORD your God will keep his covenant of unfailing love with you, as he promised with an oath to your ancestors. ¹³He will love you and bless you, and he will give you many children. He will give fertility to your land and your animals. When you arrive in the land he swore to give your ancestors, you will have large harvests of grain, new wine, and olive oil, and great herds of cattle, sheep, and goats. ¹⁴You will be blessed above all the nations of the earth. None of your men or women will be childless, and all your livestock will bear young. ¹⁵And the LORD will protect you from all sickness. He will not let you suffer from the terrible diseases you knew in Egypt, but he will inflict them on all your enemies!

¹⁶"You must destroy all the nations the LORD your God hands over to you. Show them no mercy, and do not worship their gods, or they will trap you. ¹⁷Perhaps you will think to yourselves, 'How can we ever conquer these nations that are so much more powerful than we are?' ¹⁸But don't be afraid of them! Just remember what the LORD your God did to Pharaoh and to all the land of Egypt. ¹⁹Remember the great terrors the LORD your God sent against them. You saw it all with your own eyes! And remember the miraculous signs and wonders, and the strong hand and powerful arm with which he brought you out of Egypt. The LORD your God will use this same power against all the people you fear. ²⁰And then the LORD your God will send terror* to drive out the few survivors still hiding from you!

²¹"No, do not be afraid of those nations, for the LORD your God is among you, and he is a great and awesome God. ²²The LORD your God will drive those nations out ahead of you little by little. You will not clear them away all at once, otherwise the wild animals would multiply too quickly for you. ²³But the LORD your God will hand them over to you. He will throw them into complete confusion until they are destroyed. ²⁴He will put their kings in your power, and you will erase their names from the face of the earth. No one will be able to stand against you, and you will destroy them all.

²⁵"You must burn their idols in fire, and you must not covet the silver or gold that covers them. You must not take it or it will become a trap to you, for it is detestable to the LORD your God. ²⁶Do not bring any detestable objects into your home, for then you will be destroyed, just like them. You must utterly detest such things, for they are set apart for destruction.

A Call to Remember and Obey

8 "Be careful to obey all the commands I am giving you today. Then you will live and multiply, and you will enter and occupy the land the LORD swore to give your ancestors. ²Remember how the LORD your God led you through the wilderness for these forty years, humbling you and testing you to prove your character, and to find out whether or not you would obey his commands. ³Yes, he humbled you by letting you go hungry and then feeding you with manna, a food previously unknown to you and your ancestors. He did it to teach you that people do not live by bread alone; rather, we live by every word that comes from the mouth of the LORD. ⁴For all these forty years your clothes didn't wear out, and your feet didn't blister or swell. ⁵Think about it: Just as a parent disciplines a child, the LORD your God disciplines you for your own good.

⁶"So obey the commands of the LORD your God by walking in his ways and fearing him. ⁷For the LORD your God is bringing you into a good land of flowing streams and pools of water, with fountains and springs that gush out in the valleys and hills. ⁸It is a land of wheat and barley; of grapevines, fig trees, and pomegranates; of olive oil and honey. ⁹It is a land where food is plentiful and nothing is lacking. It is a land where iron is as common as stone, and copper is abundant in the hills. ¹⁰When you have eaten your fill, be sure to praise the LORD your God for the good land he has given you.

¹¹"But that is the time to be careful! Beware that in your plenty you do not forget the LORD your God and disobey his commands, regulations, and decrees that I am giving you today. ¹²For when you have become full and prosperous and have built fine homes to live in, ¹³and when your flocks and herds have become very large and your silver and gold have multiplied along with everything else, be careful! ¹⁴Do not become proud at that time and forget the LORD your God, who rescued you from slavery in the land of Egypt. ¹⁵Do not forget that he led you through the great and terrifying wilderness with its poisonous snakes and scorpions, where it was so hot and dry. He gave you water from the rock! ¹⁶He fed you with manna in the wilderness, a food unknown to your ancestors.

7:20 Often rendered *the hornet*. The meaning of the Hebrew is uncertain.

He did this to humble you and test you for your own good. [17]He did all this so you would never say to yourself, 'I have achieved this wealth with my own strength and energy.' [18]Remember the LORD your God. He is the one who gives you power to be successful, in order to fulfill the covenant he confirmed to your ancestors with an oath.

[19]"But I assure you of this: If you ever forget the LORD your God and follow other gods, worshiping and bowing down to them, you will certainly be destroyed. [20]Just as the LORD has destroyed other nations in your path, you also will be destroyed if you refuse to obey the LORD your God.

Victory by God's Grace

9 "Listen, O Israel! Today you are about to cross the Jordan River to take over the land belonging to nations much greater and more powerful than you. They live in cities with walls that reach to the sky! [2]The people are strong and tall—descendants of the famous Anakite giants. You've heard the saying, 'Who can stand up to the Anakites?' [3]But recognize today that the LORD your God is the one who will cross over ahead of you like a devouring fire to destroy them. He will subdue them so that you will quickly conquer them and drive them out, just as the LORD has promised.

[4]"After the LORD your God has done this for you, don't say in your hearts, 'The LORD has given us this land because we are such good people!' No, it is because of the wickedness of the other nations that he is pushing them out of your way. [5]It is not because you are so good or have such integrity that you are about to occupy their land. The LORD your God will drive these nations out ahead of you only because of their wickedness, and to fulfill the oath he swore to your ancestors Abraham, Isaac, and Jacob. [6]You must recognize that the LORD your God is not giving you this good land because you are good, for you are not—you are a stubborn people.

Remembering the Gold Calf

[7]"Remember and never forget how angry you made the LORD your God out in the wilderness. From the day you left Egypt until now, you have been constantly rebelling against him. [8]Even at Mount Sinai* you made the LORD so angry he was ready to destroy you. [9]This happened when I was on the mountain receiving the tablets of stone inscribed with the words of the covenant that the LORD had made with you. I was there for forty days and forty nights, and all that time I ate no food and drank no water. [10]The LORD gave me the two tablets on which God had written with his own finger all the words he had spoken to you from the heart of the fire when you were assembled at the mountain.

[11]"At the end of the forty days and nights, the LORD handed me the two stone tablets inscribed with the words of the covenant. [12]Then the LORD said to me, 'Get up! Go down immediately, for the people you brought out of Egypt have corrupted themselves. How quickly they have turned away from the way I commanded them to live! They have melted gold and made an idol for themselves!'

[13]"The LORD also said to me, 'I have seen how stubborn and rebellious these people are. [14]Leave me alone so I may destroy them and erase their name from under heaven. Then I will make a mighty nation of your descendants, a nation larger and more powerful than they are.'

[15]"So while the mountain was blazing with fire I turned and came down, holding in my hands the two stone tablets inscribed with the terms of the covenant. [16]There below me I could see that you had sinned against the LORD your God. You had melted gold and made a calf idol for yourselves. How quickly you had turned away from the path the LORD had commanded you to follow! [17]So I took the stone tablets and threw them to the ground, smashing them before your eyes.

[18]"Then, as before, I threw myself down before the LORD for forty days and nights. I ate no bread and drank no water because of the great sin you had committed by doing what the LORD hated, provoking him to anger. [19]I feared that the furious anger of the LORD, which turned him against you, would drive him to destroy you. But again he listened to me. [20]The LORD was so angry with Aaron that he wanted to destroy him, too. But I prayed for Aaron, and the LORD spared him. [21]I took your sin—the calf you had made—and I melted it down in the fire and ground it into fine dust. Then I threw the dust into the stream that flows down the mountain.

[22]"You also made the LORD angry at Taberah,* Massah,* and Kibroth-hattaavah.* [23]And at Kadesh-barnea the LORD sent you out with

9:8 Hebrew *Horeb,* another name for Sinai.   9:22a *Taberah* means "place of burning." See Num 11:1-3.   9:22b *Massah* means "place of testing." See Exod 17:1-7.   9:22c *Kibroth-hattaavah* means "graves of gluttony." See Num 11:31-34.

this command: 'Go up and take over the land I have given you.' But you rebelled against the command of the LORD your God and refused to put your trust in him or obey him. 24Yes, you have been rebelling against the LORD as long as I have known you.

25"That is why I threw myself down before the LORD for forty days and nights—for the LORD said he would destroy you. 26I prayed to the LORD and said, 'O Sovereign LORD, do not destroy them. They are your own people. They are your special possession, whom you redeemed from Egypt by your mighty power and your strong hand. 27Please overlook the stubbornness and the awful sin of these people, and remember instead your servants Abraham, Isaac, and Jacob. 28If you destroy these people, the Egyptians will say, "The Israelites died because the LORD wasn't able to bring them to the land he had promised to give them." Or they might say, "He destroyed them because he hated them; he deliberately took them into the wilderness to slaughter them." 29But they are your people and your special possession, whom you brought out of Egypt by your great strength and powerful arm.'

A New Copy of the Covenant

10 "At that time the LORD said to me, 'Chisel out two stone tablets like the first ones. Also make a wooden Ark—a sacred chest to store them in. Come up to me on the mountain, 2and I will write on the tablets the same words that were on the ones you smashed. Then place the tablets in the Ark.'

3"So I made an Ark of acacia wood and cut two stone tablets like the first two. Then I went up the mountain with the tablets in my hand. 4Once again the LORD wrote the Ten Commandments* on the tablets and gave them to me. They were the same words the LORD had spoken to you from the heart of the fire on the day you were assembled at the foot of the mountain. 5Then I turned and came down the mountain and placed the tablets in the Ark of the Covenant, which I had made, just as the LORD commanded me. And the tablets are still there in the Ark."

6(The people of Israel set out from the wells of the people of Jaakan* and traveled to Moserah, where Aaron died and was buried. His son Eleazar ministered as high priest in his place. 7Then they journeyed to Gudgodah, and from there to Jotbathah, a land with many brooks and streams. 8At that time the LORD set apart the tribe of Levi to carry the Ark of the LORD's Covenant, and to stand before the LORD as his ministers, and to pronounce blessings in his name. These are their duties to this day. 9That is why the Levites have no share of property or possession of land among the other Israelite tribes. The LORD himself is their special possession, as the LORD your God told them.)

10"As for me, I stayed on the mountain in the LORD's presence for forty days and nights, as I had done the first time. And once again the LORD listened to my pleas and agreed not to destroy you. 11Then the LORD said to me, 'Get up and resume the journey, and lead the people to the land I swore to give to their ancestors, so they may take possession of it.'

A Call to Love and Obedience

12"And now, Israel, what does the LORD your God require of you? He requires only that you fear the LORD your God, and live in a way that pleases him, and love him and serve him with all your heart and soul. 13And you must always obey the LORD's commands and decrees that I am giving you today for your own good.

14"Look, the highest heavens and the earth and everything in it all belong to the LORD your God. 15Yet the LORD chose your ancestors as the objects of his love. And he chose you, their descendants, above all other nations, as is evident today. 16Therefore, change your hearts* and stop being stubborn.

17"For the LORD your God is the God of gods and Lord of lords. He is the great God, the mighty and awesome God, who shows no partiality and cannot be bribed. 18He ensures that orphans and widows receive justice. He shows love to the foreigners living among you and gives them food and clothing. 19So you, too, must show love to foreigners, for you yourselves were once foreigners in the land of Egypt. 20You must fear the LORD your God and worship him and cling to him. Your oaths must be in his name alone. 21He alone is your God, the only one who is worthy of your praise, the one who has done these mighty miracles that you have seen with your own eyes. 22When your ancestors went down into Egypt, there were only seventy of them. But now the LORD your God has made you as numerous as the stars in the sky!

11 "You must love the LORD your God and always obey his requirements, decrees, regulations, and commands. 2Keep in mind

10:4 Hebrew *the ten words.*   10:6 Or *set out from Beeroth of Bene-jaakan.*   10:16 Hebrew *circumcise the foreskin of your hearts.*

that I am not talking now to your children, who have never experienced the discipline of the LORD your God or seen his greatness and his strong hand and powerful arm. ³They didn't see the miraculous signs and wonders he performed in Egypt against Pharaoh and all his land. ⁴They didn't see what the LORD did to the armies of Egypt and to their horses and chariots—how he drowned them in the Red Sea* as they were chasing you. He destroyed them, and they have not recovered to this very day!

⁵"Your children didn't see how the LORD cared for you in the wilderness until you arrived here. ⁶They didn't see what he did to Dathan and Abiram (the sons of Eliab, a descendant of Reuben) when the earth opened its mouth in the Israelite camp and swallowed them, along with their households and tents and every living thing that belonged to them. ⁷But you have seen the LORD perform all these mighty deeds with your own eyes!

The Blessings of Obedience

⁸"Therefore, be careful to obey every command I am giving you today, so you may have strength to go in and take over the land you are about to enter. ⁹If you obey, you will enjoy a long life in the land the LORD swore to give to your ancestors and to you, their descendants—a land flowing with milk and honey! ¹⁰For the land you are about to enter and take over is not like the land of Egypt from which you came, where you planted your seed and made irrigation ditches with your foot as in a vegetable garden. ¹¹Rather, the land you will soon take over is a land of hills and valleys with plenty of rain—¹²a land that the LORD your God cares for. He watches over it through each season of the year!

¹³"If you carefully obey the commands I am giving you today, and if you love the LORD your God and serve him with all your heart and soul, ¹⁴then he will send the rains in their proper seasons—the early and late rains—so you can bring in your harvests of grain, new wine, and olive oil. ¹⁵He will give you lush pastureland for your livestock, and you yourselves will have all you want to eat.

¹⁶"But be careful. Don't let your heart be deceived so that you turn away from the LORD and serve and worship other gods. ¹⁷If you do, the LORD's anger will burn against you. He will shut up the sky and hold back the rain, and the ground will fail to produce its harvests. Then

you will quickly die in that good land the LORD is giving you.

¹⁸"So commit yourselves wholeheartedly to these words of mine. Tie them to your hands and wear them on your forehead as reminders. ¹⁹Teach them to your children. Talk about them when you are at home and when you are on the road, when you are going to bed and when you are getting up. ²⁰Write them on the doorposts of your house and on your gates, ²¹so that as long as the sky remains above the earth, you and your children may flourish in the land the LORD swore to give your ancestors.

²²"Be careful to obey all these commands I am giving you. Show love to the LORD your God by walking in his ways and holding tightly to him. ²³Then the LORD will drive out all the nations ahead of you, though they are much greater and stronger than you, and you will take over their land. ²⁴Wherever you set foot, that land will be yours. Your frontiers will stretch from the wilderness in the south to Lebanon in the north, and from the Euphrates River in the east to the Mediterranean Sea in the west.* ²⁵No one will be able to stand against you, for the LORD your God will cause the people to fear and dread you, as he promised, wherever you go in the whole land.

²⁶"Look, today I am giving you the choice between a blessing and a curse! ²⁷You will be blessed if you obey the commands of the LORD your God that I am giving you today. ²⁸But you will be cursed if you reject the commands of the LORD your God and turn away from him and worship gods you have not known before.

²⁹"When the LORD your God brings you into the land and helps you take possession of it, you must pronounce the blessing at Mount Gerizim and the curse at Mount Ebal. ³⁰(These two mountains are west of the Jordan River in the land of the Canaanites who live in the Jordan Valley,* near the town of Gilgal, not far from the oaks of Moreh.) ³¹For you are about to cross the Jordan River to take over the land the LORD your God is giving you. When you take that land and are living in it, ³²you must be careful to obey all the decrees and regulations I am giving you today.

The LORD's Chosen Place for Worship

12 "These are the decrees and regulations you must be careful to obey when you live in the land that the LORD, the God of your ancestors, is giving you. You must obey them as long as you live.

11:4 Hebrew *sea of reeds.*   11:24 Hebrew *to the western sea.*   11:30 Hebrew *the Arabah.*

²"When you drive out the nations that live there, you must destroy all the places where they worship their gods—high on the mountains, up on the hills, and under every green tree. ³Break down their altars and smash their sacred pillars. Burn their Asherah poles and cut down their carved idols. Completely erase the names of their gods!

⁴"Do not worship the LORD your God in the way these pagan peoples worship their gods. ⁵Rather, you must seek the LORD your God at the place of worship he himself will choose from among all the tribes—the place where his name will be honored. ⁶There you will bring your burnt offerings, your sacrifices, your tithes, your sacred offerings, your offerings to fulfill a vow, your voluntary offerings, and your offerings of the firstborn animals of your herds and flocks. ⁷There you and your families will feast in the presence of the LORD your God, and you will rejoice in all you have accomplished because the LORD your God has blessed you.

⁸"Your pattern of worship will change. Today all of you are doing as you please, ⁹because you have not yet arrived at the place of rest, the land the LORD your God is giving you as your special possession. ¹⁰But you will soon cross the Jordan River and live in the land the LORD your God is giving you. When he gives you rest from all your enemies and you're living safely in the land, ¹¹you must bring everything I command you—your burnt offerings, your sacrifices, your tithes, your sacred offerings, and your offerings to fulfill a vow—to the designated place of worship, the place the LORD your God chooses for his name to be honored.

¹²"You must celebrate there in the presence of the LORD your God with your sons and daughters and all your servants. And remember to include the Levites who live in your towns, for they will receive no allotment of land among you. ¹³Be careful not to sacrifice your burnt offerings just anywhere you like. ¹⁴You may do so only at the place the LORD will choose within one of your tribal territories. There you must offer your burnt offerings and do everything I command you.

¹⁵"But you may butcher your animals and eat their meat in any town whenever you want. You may freely eat the animals with which the LORD your God blesses you. All of you, whether ceremonially clean or unclean, may eat that meat, just as you now eat gazelle and deer. ¹⁶But you must not consume the blood. You must pour it out on the ground like water.

¹⁷"But you may not eat your offerings in your hometown—neither the tithe of your grain and new wine and olive oil, nor the firstborn of your flocks and herds, nor any offering to fulfill a vow, nor your voluntary offerings, nor your sacred offerings. ¹⁸You must eat these in the presence of the LORD your God at the place he will choose. Eat them there with your children, your servants, and the Levites who live in your towns, celebrating in the presence of the LORD your God in all you do. ¹⁹And be very careful never to neglect the Levites as long as you live in your land.

²⁰"When the LORD your God expands your territory as he has promised, and you have the urge to eat meat, you may freely eat meat whenever you want. ²¹It might happen that the designated place of worship—the place the LORD your God chooses for his name to be honored—is a long way from your home. If so, you may butcher any of the cattle, sheep, or goats the LORD has given you, and you may freely eat the meat in your hometown, as I have commanded you. ²²Anyone, whether ceremonially clean or unclean, may eat that meat, just as you do now with gazelle and deer. ²³But never consume the blood, for the blood is the life, and you must not consume the lifeblood with the meat. ²⁴Instead, pour out the blood on the ground like water. ²⁵Do not consume the blood, so that all may go well with you and your children after you, because you will be doing what pleases the LORD.

²⁶"Take your sacred gifts and your offerings given to fulfill a vow to the place the LORD chooses. ²⁷You must offer the meat and blood of your burnt offerings on the altar of the LORD your God. The blood of your other sacrifices must be poured out on the altar of the LORD your God, but you may eat the meat. ²⁸Be careful to obey all my commands, so that all will go well with you and your children after you, because you will be doing what is good and pleasing to the LORD your God.

²⁹"When the LORD your God goes ahead of you and destroys the nations and you drive them out and live in their land, ³⁰do not fall into the trap of following their customs and worshiping their gods. Do not inquire about their gods, saying, 'How do these nations worship their gods? I want to follow their example.' ³¹You must not worship the LORD your God the way the other nations worship their gods, for they perform for their gods every detestable act that the LORD hates. They even burn their sons and daughters as sacrifices to their gods.

32*"So be careful to obey all the commands I give you. You must not add anything to them or subtract anything from them.

A Warning against Idolatry

13 1*"Suppose there are prophets among you or those who dream dreams about the future, and they promise you signs or miracles, 2and the predicted signs or miracles occur. If they then say, 'Come, let us worship other gods'—gods you have not known before—3do not listen to them. The LORD your God is testing you to see if you truly love him with all your heart and soul. 4Serve only the LORD your God and fear him alone. Obey his commands, listen to his voice, and cling to him. 5The false prophets or visionaries who try to lead you astray must be put to death, for they encourage rebellion against the LORD your God, who redeemed you from slavery and brought you out of the land of Egypt. Since they try to lead you astray from the way the LORD your God commanded you to live, you must put them to death. In this way you will purge the evil from among you.

6"Suppose someone secretly entices you—even your brother, your son or daughter, your beloved wife, or your closest friend—and says, 'Let us go worship other gods'—gods that neither you nor your ancestors have known. 7They might suggest that you worship the gods of peoples who live nearby or who come from the ends of the earth. 8But do not give in or listen. Have no pity, and do not spare or protect them. 9You must put them to death! Strike the first blow yourself, and then all the people must join in. 10Stone the guilty ones to death because they have tried to draw you away from the LORD your God, who rescued you from the land of Egypt, the place of slavery. 11Then all Israel will hear about it and be afraid, and no one will act so wickedly again.

12"When you begin living in the towns the LORD your God is giving you, you may hear 13that scoundrels among you are leading their fellow citizens astray by saying, 'Let us go worship other gods'—gods you have not known before. 14In such cases, you must examine the facts carefully. If you find that the report is true and such a detestable act has been committed among you, 15you must attack that town and completely destroy* all its inhabitants, as well as all the livestock. 16Then you must pile all the plunder in the middle of the open square and burn it. Burn the entire town as a burnt offering to the LORD your God. That town must remain a ruin forever; it may never be rebuilt. 17Keep none of the plunder that has been set apart for destruction. Then the LORD will turn from his fierce anger and be merciful to you. He will have compassion on you and make you a large nation, just as he swore to your ancestors. 18"The LORD your God will be merciful only if you listen to his voice and keep all his commands that I am giving you today, doing what pleases him.

Ceremonially Clean and Unclean Animals

14 "Since you are the people of the LORD your God, never cut yourselves or shave the hair above your foreheads in mourning for the dead. 2You have been set apart as holy to the LORD your God, and he has chosen you from all the nations of the earth to be his own special treasure.

3"You must not eat any detestable animals that are ceremonially unclean. 4These are the animals* you may eat: the ox, the sheep, the goat, 5the deer, the gazelle, the roe deer, the wild goat, the addax, the antelope, and the mountain sheep.

6"You may eat any animal that has completely split hooves and chews the cud, 7but if the animal doesn't have both, it may not be eaten. So you may not eat the camel, the hare, or the hyrax.* They chew the cud but do not have split hooves, so they are ceremonially unclean for you. 8And you may not eat the pig. It has split hooves but does not chew the cud, so it is ceremonially unclean for you. You may not eat the meat of these animals or even touch their carcasses.

9"Of all the marine animals, you may eat whatever has both fins and scales. 10You may not, however, eat marine animals that do not have both fins and scales. They are ceremonially unclean for you.

11"You may eat any bird that is ceremonially clean. 12These are the birds you may not eat: the griffon vulture, the bearded vulture, the black vulture, 13the kite, the falcon, buzzards of all kinds, 14ravens of all kinds, 15the eagle owl, the short-eared owl, the seagull, hawks of all kinds, 16the little owl, the great owl, the barn

---

12:32 Verse 12:32 is numbered 13:1 in Hebrew text. 13:1 Verses 13:1-18 are numbered 13:2-19 in Hebrew text. 13:15 The Hebrew term used here refers to the complete consecration of things or people to the LORD, either by destroying them or by giving them as an offering; similarly in 13:17. 14:4 The identification of some of the animals and birds listed in this chapter is uncertain. 14:7 Or *coney*, or *rock badger*.

owl, [17]the desert owl, the Egyptian vulture, the cormorant, [18]the stork, herons of all kinds, the hoopoe, and the bat.

[19]"All winged insects that walk along the ground are ceremonially unclean for you and may not be eaten. [20]But you may eat any winged bird or insect that is ceremonially clean.

[21]"You must not eat anything that has died a natural death. You may give it to a foreigner living in your town, or you may sell it to a stranger. But do not eat it yourselves, for you are set apart as holy to the LORD your God.

"You must not cook a young goat in its mother's milk.

The Giving of Tithes

[22]"You must set aside a tithe of your crops—one-tenth of all the crops you harvest each year. [23]Bring this tithe to the designated place of worship—the place the LORD your God chooses for his name to be honored—and eat it there in his presence. This applies to your tithes of grain, new wine, olive oil, and the firstborn males of your flocks and herds. Doing this will teach you always to fear the LORD your God.

[24]"Now when the LORD your God blesses you with a good harvest, the place of worship he chooses for his name to be honored might be too far for you to bring the tithe. [25]If so, you may sell the tithe portion of your crops and herds, put the money in a pouch, and go to the place the LORD your God has chosen. [26]When you arrive, you may use the money to buy any kind of food you want—cattle, sheep, goats, wine, or other alcoholic drink. Then feast there in the presence of the LORD your God and celebrate with your household. [27]And do not neglect the Levites in your town, for they will receive no allotment of land among you.

[28]"At the end of every third year, bring the entire tithe of that year's harvest and store it in the nearest town. [29]Give it to the Levites, who will receive no allotment of land among you, as well as to the foreigners living among you, the orphans, and the widows in your towns, so they can eat and be satisfied. Then the LORD your God will bless you in all your work.

Release for Debtors

15 "At the end of every seventh year you must cancel the debts of everyone who owes you money. [2]This is how it must be done. Everyone must cancel the loans they have made to their fellow Israelites. They must not

15:12 Or *If a Hebrew man or woman is sold to you.*

demand payment from their neighbors or relatives, for the LORD's time of release has arrived. [3]This release from debt, however, applies only to your fellow Israelites—not to the foreigners living among you.

[4]"There should be no poor among you, for the LORD your God will greatly bless you in the land he is giving you as a special possession. [5]You will receive this blessing if you are careful to obey all the commands of the LORD your God that I am giving you today. [6]The LORD your God will bless you as he has promised. You will lend money to many nations but will never need to borrow. You will rule many nations, but they will not rule over you.

[7]"But if there are any poor Israelites in your towns when you arrive in the land the LORD your God is giving you, do not be hard-hearted or tightfisted toward them. [8]Instead, be generous and lend them whatever they need. [9]Do not be mean-spirited and refuse someone a loan because the year for canceling debts is close at hand. If you refuse to make the loan and the needy person cries out to the LORD, you will be considered guilty of sin. [10]Give generously to the poor, not grudgingly, for the LORD your God will bless you in everything you do. [11]There will always be some in the land who are poor. That is why I am commanding you to share freely with the poor and with other Israelites in need.

Release for Hebrew Slaves

[12]"If a fellow Hebrew sells himself or herself to be your servant* and serves you for six years, in the seventh year you must set that servant free.

[13]"When you release a male servant, do not send him away empty-handed. [14]Give him a generous farewell gift from your flock, your threshing floor, and your winepress. Share with him some of the bounty with which the LORD your God has blessed you. [15]Remember that you were once slaves in the land of Egypt and the LORD your God redeemed you! That is why I am giving you this command.

[16]"But suppose your servant says, 'I will not leave you,' because he loves you and your family, and he has done well with you. [17]In that case, take an awl and push it through his earlobe into the door. After that, he will be your servant for life. And do the same for your female servants.

[18]"You must not consider it a hardship when you release your servants. Remember that for six years they have given you services worth

double the wages of hired workers, and the LORD your God will bless you in all you do.

Sacrificing Firstborn Male Animals

19"You must set aside for the LORD your God all the firstborn males from your flocks and herds. Do not use the firstborn of your herds to work your fields, and do not shear the firstborn of your flocks. 20Instead, you and your family must eat these animals in the presence of the LORD your God each year at the place he chooses. 21But if this firstborn animal has any defect, such as lameness or blindness, or if anything else is wrong with it, you must not sacrifice it to the LORD your God. 22Instead, use it for food for your family in your hometown. Anyone, whether ceremonially clean or unclean, may eat it, just as anyone may eat a gazelle or deer. 23But you must not consume the blood. You must pour it out on the ground like water.

Passover and the Festival of Unleavened Bread

16 "In honor of the LORD your God, celebrate the Passover each year in the early spring, in the month of Abib,* for that was the month in which the LORD your God brought you out of Egypt by night. 2Your Passover sacrifice may be from either the flock or the herd, and it must be sacrificed to the LORD your God at the designated place of worship—the place he chooses for his name to be honored. 3Eat it with bread made without yeast. For seven days the bread you eat must be made without yeast, as when you escaped from Egypt in such a hurry. Eat this bread—the bread of suffering—so that as long as you live you will remember the day you departed from Egypt. 4Let no yeast be found in any house throughout your land for those seven days. And when you sacrifice the Passover lamb on the evening of the first day, do not let any of the meat remain until the next morning.

5"You may not sacrifice the Passover in just any of the towns that the LORD your God is giving you. 6You must offer it only at the designated place of worship—the place the LORD your God chooses for his name to be honored. Sacrifice it there in the evening as the sun goes down on the anniversary of your exodus from Egypt. 7Roast the lamb and eat it in the place the LORD your God chooses. Then you may go

back to your tents the next morning. 8For the next six days you may not eat any bread made with yeast. On the seventh day proclaim another holy day in honor of the LORD your God, and no work may be done on that day.

The Festival of Harvest

9"Count off seven weeks from when you first begin to cut the grain at the time of harvest. 10Then celebrate the Festival of Harvest* to honor the LORD your God. Bring him a voluntary offering in proportion to the blessings you have received from him. 11This is a time to celebrate before the LORD your God at the designated place of worship he will choose for his name to be honored. Celebrate with your sons and daughters, your male and female servants, the Levites from your towns, and the foreigners, orphans, and widows who live among you. 12Remember that you were once slaves in Egypt, so be careful to obey all these decrees.

The Festival of Shelters

13"You must observe the Festival of Shelters* for seven days at the end of the harvest season, after the grain has been threshed and the grapes have been pressed. 14This festival will be a happy time of celebrating with your sons and daughters, your male and female servants, and the Levites, foreigners, orphans, and widows from your towns. 15For seven days you must celebrate this festival to honor the LORD your God at the place he chooses, for it is he who blesses you with bountiful harvests and gives you success in all your work. This festival will be a time of great joy for all.

16"Each year every man in Israel must celebrate these three festivals: the Festival of Unleavened Bread, the Festival of Harvest, and the Festival of Shelters. On each of these occasions, all men must appear before the LORD your God at the place he chooses, but they must not appear before the LORD without a gift for him. 17All must give as they are able, according to the blessings given to them by the LORD your God.

Justice for the People

18"Appoint judges and officials for yourselves from each of your tribes in all the towns the LORD your God is giving you. They must judge the people fairly. 19You must never twist justice

16:1 Hebrew *Observe the month of Abib, and keep the Passover unto the LORD your God.* Abib, the first month of the ancient Hebrew lunar calendar, usually occurs within the months of March and April.   16:10 Hebrew *Festival of Weeks;* also in 16:16. This was later called the Festival of Pentecost (see Acts 2:1). It is celebrated today as Shavuot (or Shabuoth).   16:13 Or *Festival of Booths,* or *Festival of Tabernacles;* also in 16:16. This was earlier called the Festival of the Final Harvest or Festival of Ingathering (see Exod 23:16b). It is celebrated today as Sukkot (or Succoth).

or show partiality. Never accept a bribe, for bribes blind the eyes of the wise and corrupt the decisions of the godly. ²⁰Let true justice prevail, so you may live and occupy the land that the Lord your God is giving you.

²¹"You must never set up a wooden Asherah pole beside the altar you build for the Lord your God. ²²And never set up sacred pillars for worship, for the Lord your God hates them.

17 "Never sacrifice sick or defective cattle, sheep, or goats to the Lord your God, for he detests such gifts.

²"When you begin living in the towns the Lord your God is giving you, a man or woman among you might do evil in the sight of the Lord your God and violate the covenant. ³For instance, they might serve other gods or worship the sun, the moon, or any of the stars—the forces of heaven—which I have strictly forbidden. ⁴When you hear about it, investigate the matter thoroughly. If it is true that this detestable thing has been done in Israel, ⁵then the man or woman who has committed such an evil act must be taken to the gates of the town and stoned to death. ⁶But never put a person to death on the testimony of only one witness. There must always be two or three witnesses. ⁷The witnesses must throw the first stones, and then all the people may join in. In this way, you will purge the evil from among you.

⁸"Suppose a case arises in a local court that is too hard for you to decide—for instance, whether someone is guilty of murder or only of manslaughter, or a difficult lawsuit, or a case involving different kinds of assault. Take such legal cases to the place the Lord your God will choose, ⁹and present them to the Levitical priests or the judge on duty at that time. They will hear the case and declare the verdict. ¹⁰You must carry out the verdict they announce and the sentence they prescribe at the place the Lord chooses. You must do exactly what they say. ¹¹After they have interpreted the law and declared their verdict, the sentence they impose must be fully executed; do not modify it in any way. ¹²Anyone arrogant enough to reject the verdict of the judge or of the priest who represents the Lord your God must die. In this way you will purge the evil from Israel. ¹³Then everyone else will hear about it and be afraid to act so arrogantly.

Guidelines for a King

¹⁴"You are about to enter the land the Lord your God is giving you. When you take it over

and settle there, you may think, 'We should select a king to rule over us like the other nations around us.' ¹⁵If this happens, be sure to select as king the man the Lord your God chooses. You must appoint a fellow Israelite; he may not be a foreigner.

¹⁶"The king must not build up a large stable of horses for himself or send his people to Egypt to buy horses, for the Lord has told you, 'You must never return to Egypt.' ¹⁷The king must not take many wives for himself, because they will turn his heart away from the Lord. And he must not accumulate large amounts of wealth in silver and gold for himself.

¹⁸"When he sits on the throne as king, he must copy for himself this body of instruction on a scroll in the presence of the Levitical priests. ¹⁹He must always keep that copy with him and read it daily as long as he lives. That way he will learn to fear the Lord his God by obeying all the terms of these instructions and decrees. ²⁰This regular reading will prevent him from becoming proud and acting as if he is above his fellow citizens. It will also prevent him from turning away from these commands in the smallest way. And it will ensure that he and his descendants will reign for many generations in Israel.

Gifts for the Priests and Levites

18 "Remember that the Levitical priests— that is, the whole of the tribe of Levi— will receive no allotment of land among the other tribes in Israel. Instead, the priests and Levites will eat from the special gifts given to the Lord, for that is their share. ²They will have no land of their own among the Israelites. The Lord himself is their special possession, just as he promised them.

³"These are the parts the priests may claim as their share from the cattle, sheep, and goats that the people bring as offerings: the shoulder, the cheeks, and the stomach. ⁴You must also give to the priests the first share of the grain, the new wine, the olive oil, and the wool at shearing time. ⁵For the Lord your God chose the tribe of Levi out of all your tribes to minister in the Lord's name forever.

⁶"Suppose a Levite chooses to move from his town in Israel, wherever he is living, to the place the Lord chooses for worship. ⁷He may minister there in the name of the Lord his God, just like all his fellow Levites who are serving the Lord there. ⁸He may eat his share of the sacrifices and offerings, even if he also receives support from his family.

A Call to Holy Living

9"When you enter the land the LORD your God is giving you, be very careful not to imitate the detestable customs of the nations living there. 10For example, never sacrifice your son or daughter as a burnt offering.* And do not let your people practice fortune-telling, or use sorcery, or interpret omens, or engage in witchcraft, 11or cast spells, or function as mediums or psychics, or call forth the spirits of the dead. 12Anyone who does these things is detestable to the LORD. It is because the other nations have done these detestable things that the LORD your God will drive them out ahead of you. 13But you must be blameless before the LORD your God. 14The nations you are about to displace consult sorcerers and fortune-tellers, but the LORD your God forbids you to do such things."

True and False Prophets

15Moses continued, "The LORD your God will raise up for you a prophet like me from among your fellow Israelites. You must listen to him. 16For this is what you yourselves requested of the LORD your God when you were assembled at Mount Sinai.* You said, 'Don't let us hear the voice of the LORD our God anymore or see this blazing fire, for we will die.'

17"Then the LORD said to me, 'What they have said is right. 18I will raise up a prophet like you from among their fellow Israelites. I will put my words in his mouth, and he will tell the people everything I command him. 19I will personally deal with anyone who will not listen to the messages the prophet proclaims on my behalf. 20But any prophet who falsely claims to speak in my name or who speaks in the name of another god must die.'

21"But you may wonder, 'How will we know whether or not a prophecy is from the LORD?' 22If the prophet speaks in the LORD's name but his prediction does not happen or come true, you will know that the LORD did not give that message. That prophet has spoken without my authority and need not be feared.

Cities of Refuge

19 "When the LORD your God destroys the nations whose land he is giving you, you will take over their land and settle in their towns and homes. 2Then you must set apart three cities of refuge in the land the LORD your God is giving you. 3Survey the territory,*

and divide the land the LORD your God is giving you into three districts, with one of these cities in each district. Then anyone who has killed someone can flee to one of the cities of refuge for safety.

4"If someone kills another person unintentionally, without previous hostility, the slayer may flee to any of these cities to live in safety. 5For example, suppose someone goes into the forest with a neighbor to cut wood. And suppose one of them swings an ax to chop down a tree, and the ax head flies off the handle, killing the other person. In such cases, the slayer may flee to one of the cities of refuge to live in safety.

6"If the distance to the nearest city of refuge is too far, an enraged avenger might be able to chase down and kill the person who caused the death. Then the slayer would die unfairly, since he had never shown hostility toward the person who died. 7That is why I am commanding you to set aside three cities of refuge.

8"And if the LORD your God enlarges your territory, as he swore to your ancestors, and gives you all the land he promised them, 9you must designate three additional cities of refuge. (He will give you this land if you are careful to obey all the commands I have given you—if you always love the LORD your God and walk in his ways.) 10That way you will prevent the death of innocent people in the land the LORD your God is giving you as your special possession. You will not be held responsible for the death of innocent people.

11"But suppose someone is hostile toward a neighbor and deliberately ambushes and murders him and then flees to one of the cities of refuge. 12In that case, the elders of the murderer's hometown must send agents to the city of refuge to bring him back and hand him over to the dead person's avenger to be put to death. 13Do not feel sorry for that murderer! Purge from Israel the guilt of murdering innocent people; then all will go well with you.

Concern for Justice

14"When you arrive in the land the LORD your God is giving you as your special possession, you must never steal anyone's land by moving the boundary markers your ancestors set up to mark their property.

15"You must not convict anyone of a crime on the testimony of only one witness. The facts

---

18:10 Or *never make your son or daughter pass through the fire.*   18:16 Hebrew *Horeb,* another name for Sinai.   19:3 Or *Keep the roads in good repair.*

of the case must be established by the testimony of two or three witnesses.

¹⁶"If a malicious witness comes forward and accuses someone of a crime, ¹⁷then both the accuser and accused must appear before the LORD by coming to the priests and judges in office at that time. ¹⁸The judges must investigate the case thoroughly. If the accuser has brought false charges against his fellow Israelite, ¹⁹you must impose on the accuser the sentence he intended for the other person. In this way, you will purge such evil from among you. ²⁰Then the rest of the people will hear about it and be afraid to do such an evil thing. ²¹You must show no pity for the guilty! Your rule should be life for life, eye for eye, tooth for tooth, hand for hand, foot for foot.

Regulations concerning War

20 "When you go out to fight your enemies and you face horses and chariots and an army greater than your own, do not be afraid. The LORD your God, who brought you out of the land of Egypt, is with you! ²When you prepare for battle, the priest must come forward to speak to the troops. ³He will say to them, 'Listen to me, all you men of Israel! Do not be afraid as you go out to fight your enemies today! Do not lose heart or panic or tremble before them. ⁴For the LORD your God is going with you! He will fight for you against your enemies, and he will give you victory!'

⁵"Then the officers of the army must address the troops and say, 'Has anyone here just built a new house but not yet dedicated it? If so, you may go home! You might be killed in the battle, and someone else would dedicate your house. ⁶Has anyone here just planted a vineyard but not yet eaten any of its fruit? If so, you may go home! You might die in battle, and someone else would eat the first fruit. ⁷Has anyone here just become engaged to a woman but not yet married her? Well, you may go home and get married! You might die in the battle, and someone else would marry her.'

⁸"Then the officers will also say, 'Is anyone here afraid or worried? If you are, you may go home before you frighten anyone else.' ⁹When the officers have finished speaking to their troops, they will appoint the unit commanders.

¹⁰"As you approach a town to attack it, you must first offer its people terms for peace. ¹¹If they accept your terms and open the gates to you, then all the people inside will serve you in forced labor. ¹²But if they refuse to make peace and prepare to fight, you must attack the town. ¹³When the LORD your God hands the town over to you, use your swords to kill every man in the town. ¹⁴But you may keep for yourselves all the women, children, livestock, and other plunder. You may enjoy the plunder from your enemies that the LORD your God has given you.

¹⁵"But these instructions apply only to distant towns, not to the towns of the nations in the land you will enter. ¹⁶In those towns that the LORD your God is giving you as a special possession, destroy every living thing. ¹⁷You must completely destroy* the Hittites, Amorites, Canaanites, Perizzites, Hivites, and Jebusites, just as the LORD your God has commanded you. ¹⁸This will prevent the people of the land from teaching you to imitate their detestable customs in the worship of their gods, which would cause you to sin deeply against the LORD your God.

¹⁹"When you are attacking a town and the war drags on, you must not cut down the trees with your axes. You may eat the fruit, but do not cut down the trees. Are the trees your enemies, that you should attack them? ²⁰You may only cut down trees that you know are not valuable for food. Use them to make the equipment you need to attack the enemy town until it falls.

Cleansing for Unsolved Murder

21 "When you are in the land the LORD your God is giving you, someone may be found murdered in a field, and you don't know who committed the murder. ²In such a case, your elders and judges must measure the distance from the site of the crime to the nearby towns. ³When the nearest town has been determined, that town's elders must select from the herd a heifer that has never been trained or yoked to a plow. ⁴They must lead it down to a valley that has not been plowed or planted and that has a stream running through it. There in the valley they must break the heifer's neck. ⁵Then the Levitical priests must step forward, for the LORD your God has chosen them to minister before him and to pronounce blessings in the LORD's name. They are to decide all legal and criminal cases.

⁶"The elders of the town must wash their hands over the heifer whose neck was broken. ⁷Then they must say, 'Our hands did not shed this person's blood, nor did we see it happen. ⁸O LORD, forgive your people Israel whom you

---

20:17 The Hebrew term used here refers to the complete consecration of things or people to the LORD, either by destroying them or by giving them as an offering.

have redeemed. Do not charge your people with the guilt of murdering an innocent person.' Then they will be absolved of the guilt of this person's blood. ⁹By following these instructions, you will do what is right in the LORD's sight and will cleanse the guilt of murder from your community.

Marriage to a Captive Woman

¹⁰"Suppose you go out to war against your enemies and the LORD your God hands them over to you, and you take some of them as captives. ¹¹And suppose you see among the captives a beautiful woman, and you are attracted to her and want to marry her. ¹²If this happens, you may take her to your home, where she must shave her head, cut her nails, ¹³and change the clothes she was wearing when she was captured. She will stay in your home, but let her mourn for her father and mother for a full month. Then you may marry her, and you will be her husband and she will be your wife. ¹⁴But if you marry her and she does not please you, you must let her go free. You may not sell her or treat her as a slave, for you have humiliated her.

Rights of the Firstborn

¹⁵"Suppose a man has two wives, but he loves one and not the other, and both have given him sons. And suppose the firstborn son is the son of the wife he does not love. ¹⁶When the man divides his inheritance, he may not give the larger inheritance to his younger son, the son of the wife he loves, as if he were the firstborn son. ¹⁷He must recognize the rights of his oldest son, the son of the wife he does not love, by giving him a double portion. He is the first son of his father's virility, and the rights of the firstborn belong to him.

Dealing with a Rebellious Son

¹⁸"Suppose a man has a stubborn and rebellious son who will not obey his father or mother, even though they discipline him. ¹⁹In such a case, the father and mother must take the son to the elders as they hold court at the town gate. ²⁰The parents must say to the elders, 'This son of ours is stubborn and rebellious and refuses to obey. He is a glutton and a drunkard.' ²¹Then all the men of his town must stone him to death. In this way, you will purge this evil from among you, and all Israel will hear about it and be afraid.

Various Regulations

²²"If someone has committed a crime worthy of death and is executed and hung on a tree,* ²³the body must not remain hanging from the tree overnight. You must bury the body that same day, for anyone who is hung* is cursed in the sight of God. In this way, you will prevent the defilement of the land the LORD your God is giving you as your special possession.

22 "If you see your neighbor's ox or sheep or goat wandering away, don't ignore your responsibility.* Take it back to its owner. ²If its owner does not live nearby or you don't know who the owner is, take it to your place and keep it until the owner comes looking for it. Then you must return it. ³Do the same if you find your neighbor's donkey, clothing, or anything else your neighbor loses. Don't ignore your responsibility.

⁴"If you see that your neighbor's donkey or ox has collapsed on the road, do not look the other way. Go and help your neighbor get it back on its feet!

⁵"A woman must not put on men's clothing, and a man must not wear women's clothing. Anyone who does this is detestable in the sight of the LORD your God.

⁶"If you happen to find a bird's nest in a tree or on the ground, and there are young ones or eggs in it with the mother sitting in the nest, do not take the mother with the young. ⁷You may take the young, but let the mother go, so you may prosper and enjoy a long life.

⁸"When you build a new house, you must build a railing around the edge of its flat roof. That way you will not be considered guilty of murder if someone falls from the roof.

⁹"You must not plant any other crop between the rows of your vineyard. If you do, you are forbidden to use either the grapes from the vineyard or the other crop.

¹⁰"You must not plow with an ox and a donkey harnessed together.

¹¹"You must not wear clothing made of wool and linen woven together.

¹²"You must put four tassels on the hem of the cloak with which you cover yourself—on the front, back, and sides.

Regulations for Sexual Purity

¹³"Suppose a man marries a woman, but after sleeping with her, he turns against her ¹⁴and publicly accuses her of shameful conduct,

---

21:22 Or *impaled on a pole;* similarly in 21:23.   21:23 Greek version reads *for everyone who is hung on a tree.* Compare Gal 3:13.
22:1 Hebrew *don't hide yourself;* similarly in 22:3.

saying, 'When I married this woman, I discovered she was not a virgin.' [15]Then the woman's father and mother must bring the proof of her virginity to the elders as they hold court at the town gate. [16]Her father must say to them, 'I gave my daughter to this man to be his wife, and now he has turned against her. [17]He has accused her of shameful conduct, saying, "I discovered that your daughter was not a virgin." But here is the proof of my daughter's virginity.' Then they must spread her bed sheet before the elders. [18]The elders must then take the man and punish him. [19]They must also fine him 100 pieces of silver,* which he must pay to the woman's father because he publicly accused a virgin of Israel of shameful conduct. The woman will then remain the man's wife, and he may never divorce her.

[20]"But suppose the man's accusations are true, and he can show that she was not a virgin. [21]The woman must be taken to the door of her father's home, and there the men of the town must stone her to death, for she has committed a disgraceful crime in Israel by being promiscuous while living in her parents' home. In this way, you will purge this evil from among you.

[22]"If a man is discovered committing adultery, both he and the woman must die. In this way, you will purge Israel of such evil.

[23]"Suppose a man meets a young woman, a virgin who is engaged to be married, and he has sexual intercourse with her. If this happens within a town, [24]you must take both of them to the gates of that town and stone them to death. The woman is guilty because she did not scream for help. The man must die because he violated another man's wife. In this way, you will purge this evil from among you.

[25]"But if the man meets the engaged woman out in the country, and he rapes her, then only the man must die. [26]Do nothing to the young woman; she has committed no crime worthy of death. She is as innocent as a murder victim. [27]Since the man raped her out in the country, it must be assumed that she screamed, but there was no one to rescue her.

[28]"Suppose a man has intercourse with a young woman who is a virgin but is not engaged to be married. If they are discovered, [29]he must pay her father fifty pieces of silver.* Then he must marry the young woman because he violated her, and he may never divorce her as long as he lives.

[30]*"A man must not marry his father's former wife, for this would violate his father.

Regulations concerning Worship

23 [1]*"If a man's testicles are crushed or his penis is cut off, he may not be admitted to the assembly of the LORD.

[2]"If a person is illegitimate by birth, neither he nor his descendants for ten generations may be admitted to the assembly of the LORD.

[3]"No Ammonite or Moabite or any of their descendants for ten generations may be admitted to the assembly of the LORD. [4]These nations did not welcome you with food and water when you came out of Egypt. Instead, they hired Balaam son of Beor from Pethor in distant Aram-naharaim to curse you. [5]But the LORD your God refused to listen to Balaam. He turned the intended curse into a blessing because the LORD your God loves you. [6]As long as you live, you must never promote the welfare and prosperity of the Ammonites or Moabites.

[7]"Do not detest the Edomites or the Egyptians, because the Edomites are your relatives and you lived as foreigners among the Egyptians. [8]The third generation of Edomites and Egyptians may enter the assembly of the LORD.

Miscellaneous Regulations

[9]"When you go to war against your enemies, be sure to stay away from anything that is impure. [10]"Any man who becomes ceremonially defiled because of a nocturnal emission must leave the camp and stay away all day. [11]Toward evening he must bathe himself, and at sunset he may return to the camp.

[12]"You must have a designated area outside the camp where you can go to relieve yourself. [13]Each of you must have a spade as part of your equipment. Whenever you relieve yourself, dig a hole with the spade and cover the excrement. [14]The camp must be holy, for the LORD your God moves around in your camp to protect you and to defeat your enemies. He must not see any shameful thing among you, or he will turn away from you.

[15]"If slaves should escape from their masters and take refuge with you, you must not hand them over to their masters. [16]Let them live among you in any town they choose, and do not oppress them.

[17]"No Israelite, whether man or woman, may become a temple prostitute. [18]When you are

22:19 Hebrew 100 [shekels] of silver, about 2.5 pounds or 1.1 kilograms in weight.   22:29 Hebrew 50 [shekels] of silver, about 1.25 pounds or 570 grams in weight.   22:30 Verse 22:30 is numbered 23:1 in Hebrew text.   23:1 Verses 23:1-25 are numbered 23:2-26 in Hebrew text.

bringing an offering to fulfill a vow, you must not bring to the house of the LORD your God any offering from the earnings of a prostitute, whether a man* or a woman, for both are detestable to the LORD your God.

¹⁹"Do not charge interest on the loans you make to a fellow Israelite, whether you loan money, or food, or anything else. ²⁰You may charge interest to foreigners, but you may not charge interest to Israelites, so that the LORD your God may bless you in everything you do in the land you are about to enter and occupy.

²¹"When you make a vow to the LORD your God, be prompt in fulfilling whatever you promised him. For the LORD your God demands that you promptly fulfill all your vows, or you will be guilty of sin. ²²However, it is not a sin to refrain from making a vow. ²³But once you have voluntarily made a vow, be careful to fulfill your promise to the LORD your God.

²⁴"When you enter your neighbor's vineyard, you may eat your fill of grapes, but you must not carry any away in a basket. ²⁵And when you enter your neighbor's field of grain, you may pluck the heads of grain with your hand, but you must not harvest it with a sickle.

24 "Suppose a man marries a woman but she does not please him. Having discovered something wrong with her, he writes a document of divorce, hands it to her, and sends her away from his house. ²When she leaves his house, she is free to marry another man. ³But if the second husband also turns against her, writes a document of divorce, hands it to her, and sends her away, or if he dies, ⁴the first husband may not marry her again, for she has been defiled. That would be detestable to the LORD. You must not bring guilt upon the land the LORD your God is giving you as a special possession.

⁵"A newly married man must not be drafted into the army or be given any other official responsibilities. He must be free to spend one year at home, bringing happiness to the wife he has married.

⁶"It is wrong to take a set of millstones, or even just the upper millstone, as security for a loan, for the owner uses it to make a living.

⁷"If anyone kidnaps a fellow Israelite and treats him as a slave or sells him, the kidnapper must die. In this way, you will purge the evil from among you.

⁸"In all cases involving serious skin diseases,* be careful to follow the instructions of the Levitical priests; obey all the commands I have given them. ⁹Remember what the LORD your God did to Miriam as you were coming from Egypt.

¹⁰"If you lend anything to your neighbor, do not enter his house to pick up the item he is giving as security. ¹¹You must wait outside while he goes in and brings it out to you. ¹²If your neighbor is poor and gives you his cloak as security for a loan, do not keep the cloak overnight. ¹³Return the cloak to its owner by sunset so he can stay warm through the night and bless you, and the LORD your God will count you as righteous.

¹⁴"Never take advantage of poor and destitute laborers, whether they are fellow Israelites or foreigners living in your towns. ¹⁵You must pay them their wages each day before sunset because they are poor and are counting on it. If you don't, they might cry out to the LORD against you, and it would be counted against you as sin.

¹⁶"Parents must not be put to death for the sins of their children, nor children for the sins of their parents. Those deserving to die must be put to death for their own crimes.

¹⁷"True justice must be given to foreigners living among you and to orphans, and you must never accept a widow's garment as security for her debt. ¹⁸Always remember that you were slaves in Egypt and that the LORD your God redeemed you from your slavery. That is why I have given you this command.

¹⁹"When you are harvesting your crops and forget to bring in a bundle of grain from your field, don't go back to get it. Leave it for the foreigners, orphans, and widows. Then the LORD your God will bless you in all you do. ²⁰When you beat the olives from your olive trees, don't go over the boughs twice. Leave the remaining olives for the foreigners, orphans, and widows. ²¹When you gather the grapes in your vineyard, don't glean the vines after they are picked. Leave the remaining grapes for the foreigners, orphans, and widows. ²²Remember that you were slaves in the land of Egypt. That is why I am giving you this command.

25 "Suppose two people take a dispute to court, and the judges declare that one is right and the other is wrong. ²If the person in the wrong is sentenced to be flogged, the judge must command him to lie down and be beaten in his presence with the number of lashes appropriate to the crime. ³But never give more

23:18 Hebrew *a dog.*   24:8 Traditionally rendered *leprosy.* The Hebrew word used here can describe various skin diseases.

than forty lashes; more than forty lashes would publicly humiliate your neighbor.

⁴"You must not muzzle an ox to keep it from eating as it treads out the grain.

⁵"If two brothers are living together on the same property and one of them dies without a son, his widow may not be married to anyone from outside the family. Instead, her husband's brother should marry her and have intercourse with her to fulfill the duties of a brother-in-law. ⁶The first son she bears to him will be considered the son of the dead brother, so that his name will not be forgotten in Israel.

⁷"But if the man refuses to marry his brother's widow, she must go to the town gate and say to the elders assembled there, 'My husband's brother refuses to preserve his brother's name in Israel—he refuses to fulfill the duties of a brother-in-law by marrying me.' ⁸The elders of the town will then summon him and talk with him. If he still refuses and says, 'I don't want to marry her,' ⁹the widow must walk over to him in the presence of the elders, pull his sandal from his foot, and spit in his face. Then she must declare, 'This is what happens to a man who refuses to provide his brother with children.' ¹⁰Ever afterward in Israel his family will be referred to as 'the family of the man whose sandal was pulled off'!

¹¹"If two Israelite men get into a fight and the wife of one tries to rescue her husband by grabbing the testicles of the other man, ¹²you must cut off her hand. Show her no pity.

¹³"You must use accurate scales when you weigh out merchandise, ¹⁴and you must use full and honest measures. ¹⁵Yes, always use honest weights and measures, so that you may enjoy a long life in the land the LORD your God is giving you. ¹⁶All who cheat with dishonest weights and measures are detestable to the LORD your God.

¹⁷"Never forget what the Amalekites did to you as you came from Egypt. ¹⁸They attacked you when you were exhausted and weary, and they struck down those who were straggling behind. They had no fear of God. ¹⁹Therefore, when the LORD your God has given you rest from all your enemies in the land he is giving you as a special possession, you must destroy the Amalekites and erase their memory from under heaven. Never forget this!

Harvest Offerings and Tithes

26 "When you enter the land the LORD your God is giving you as a special possession and you have conquered it and settled there, ²put some of the first produce from each crop you harvest into a basket and bring it to the designated place of worship—the place the LORD your God chooses for his name to be honored. ³Go to the priest in charge at that time and say to him, 'With this gift I acknowledge to the LORD your God that I have entered the land he swore to our ancestors he would give us.' ⁴The priest will then take the basket from your hand and set it before the altar of the LORD your God.

⁵"You must then say in the presence of the LORD your God, 'My ancestor Jacob was a wandering Aramean who went to live as a foreigner in Egypt. His family arrived few in number, but in Egypt they became a large and mighty nation. ⁶When the Egyptians oppressed and humiliated us by making us their slaves, ⁷we cried out to the LORD, the God of our ancestors. He heard our cries and saw our hardship, toil, and oppression. ⁸So the LORD brought us out of Egypt with a strong hand and powerful arm, with overwhelming terror, and with miraculous signs and wonders. ⁹He brought us to this place and gave us this land flowing with milk and honey! ¹⁰And now, O LORD, I have brought you the first portion of the harvest you have given me from the ground.' Then place the produce before the LORD your God, and bow to the ground in worship before him. ¹¹Afterward you may go and celebrate because of all the good things the LORD your God has given to you and your household. Remember to include the Levites and the foreigners living among you in the celebration.

¹²"Every third year you must offer a special tithe of your crops. In this year of the special tithe you must give your tithes to the Levites, foreigners, orphans, and widows, so that they will have enough to eat in your towns. ¹³Then you must declare in the presence of the LORD your God, 'I have taken the sacred gift from my house and have given it to the Levites, foreigners, orphans, and widows, just as you commanded me. I have not violated or forgotten any of your commands. ¹⁴I have not eaten any of it while in mourning; I have not handled it while I was ceremonially unclean; and I have not offered any of it to the dead. I have obeyed the LORD my God and have done everything you commanded me. ¹⁵Now look down from your holy dwelling place in heaven and bless your people Israel and the land you swore to our ancestors to give us—a land flowing with milk and honey.'

A Call to Obey the LORD's Commands

16 "Today the LORD your God has commanded you to obey all these decrees and regulations. So be careful to obey them wholeheartedly. 17 You have declared today that the LORD is your God. And you have promised to walk in his ways, and to obey his decrees, commands, and regulations, and to do everything he tells you. 18 The LORD has declared today that you are his people, his own special treasure, just as he promised, and that you must obey all his commands. 19 And if you do, he will set you high above all the other nations he has made. Then you will receive praise, honor, and renown. You will be a nation that is holy to the LORD your God, just as he promised."

The Altar on Mount Ebal

27 Then Moses and the leaders of Israel gave this charge to the people: "Obey all these commands that I am giving you today. 2 When you cross the Jordan River and enter the land the LORD your God is giving you, set up some large stones and coat them with plaster. 3 Write this whole body of instruction on them when you cross the river to enter the land the LORD your God is giving you—a land flowing with milk and honey, just as the LORD, the God of your ancestors, promised you. 4 When you cross the Jordan, set up these stones at Mount Ebal and coat them with plaster, as I am commanding you today.

5 "Then build an altar there to the LORD your God, using natural, uncut stones. You must not shape the stones with an iron tool. 6 Build the altar of uncut stones, and use it to offer burnt offerings to the LORD your God. 7 Also sacrifice peace offerings on it, and celebrate by feasting there before the LORD your God. 8 You must clearly write all these instructions on the stones coated with plaster."

9 Then Moses and the Levitical priests addressed all Israel as follows: "O Israel, be quiet and listen! Today you have become the people of the LORD your God. 10 So you must obey the LORD your God by keeping all these commands and decrees that I am giving you today."

Curses from Mount Ebal

11 That same day Moses also gave this charge to the people: 12 "When you cross the Jordan River, the tribes of Simeon, Levi, Judah, Issachar, Joseph, and Benjamin must stand on Mount Gerizim to proclaim a blessing over the people. 13 And the tribes of Reuben, Gad, Asher, Zebulun, Dan, and Naphtali must stand on Mount Ebal to proclaim a curse.

14 "Then the Levites will shout to all the people of Israel:

15 'Cursed is anyone who carves or casts an idol and secretly sets it up. These idols, the work of craftsmen, are detestable to the LORD.'

And all the people will reply, 'Amen.'

16 'Cursed is anyone who dishonors father or mother.'

And all the people will reply, 'Amen.'

17 'Cursed is anyone who steals property from a neighbor by moving a boundary marker.'

And all the people will reply, 'Amen.'

18 'Cursed is anyone who leads a blind person astray on the road.'

And all the people will reply, 'Amen.'

19 'Cursed is anyone who denies justice to foreigners, orphans, or widows.'

And all the people will reply, 'Amen.'

20 'Cursed is anyone who has sexual intercourse with one of his father's wives, for he has violated his father.'

And all the people will reply, 'Amen.'

21 'Cursed is anyone who has sexual intercourse with an animal.'

And all the people will reply, 'Amen.'

22 'Cursed is anyone who has sexual intercourse with his sister, whether she is the daughter of his father or his mother.'

And all the people will reply, 'Amen.'

23 'Cursed is anyone who has sexual intercourse with his mother-in-law.'

And all the people will reply, 'Amen.'

24 'Cursed is anyone who attacks a neighbor in secret.'

And all the people will reply, 'Amen.'

25 'Cursed is anyone who accepts payment to kill an innocent person.'

And all the people will reply, 'Amen.'

26 'Cursed is anyone who does not affirm and obey the terms of these instructions.'

And all the people will reply, 'Amen.'

Blessings for Obedience

28 "If you fully obey the LORD your God and carefully keep all his commands that I am giving you today, the LORD your God will set you high above all the nations of the world. ²You will experience all these blessings if you obey the LORD your God:

³ Your towns and your fields
   will be blessed.
⁴ Your children and your crops
   will be blessed.
 The offspring of your herds and flocks
   will be blessed.
⁵ Your fruit baskets and breadboards
   will be blessed.
⁶ Wherever you go and whatever you do,
   you will be blessed.

⁷"The LORD will conquer your enemies when they attack you. They will attack you from one direction, but they will scatter from you in seven!

⁸"The LORD will guarantee a blessing on everything you do and will fill your storehouses with grain. The LORD your God will bless you in the land he is giving you.

⁹"If you obey the commands of the LORD your God and walk in his ways, the LORD will establish you as his holy people as he swore he would do. ¹⁰Then all the nations of the world will see that you are a people claimed by the LORD, and they will stand in awe of you.

¹¹"The LORD will give you prosperity in the land he swore to your ancestors to give you, blessing you with many children, numerous livestock, and abundant crops. ¹²The LORD will send rain at the proper time from his rich treasury in the heavens and will bless all the work you do. You will lend to many nations, but you will never need to borrow from them. ¹³If you listen to these commands of the LORD your God that I am giving you today, and if you carefully obey them, the LORD will make you the head and not the tail, and you will always be on top and never at the bottom. ¹⁴You must not turn away from any of the commands I am giving you today, nor follow after other gods and worship them.

Curses for Disobedience

¹⁵"But if you refuse to listen to the LORD your God and do not obey all the commands and decrees I am giving you today, all these curses will come and overwhelm you:

¹⁶ Your towns and your fields
   will be cursed.
¹⁷ Your fruit baskets and breadboards
   will be cursed.
¹⁸ Your children and your crops
   will be cursed.
 The offspring of your herds and flocks
   will be cursed.
¹⁹ Wherever you go and whatever you do,
   you will be cursed.

²⁰"The LORD himself will send on you curses, confusion, and frustration in everything you do, until at last you are completely destroyed for doing evil and abandoning me. ²¹The LORD will afflict you with diseases until none of you are left in the land you are about to enter and occupy. ²²The LORD will strike you with wasting diseases, fever, and inflammation, with scorching heat and drought, and with blight and mildew. These disasters will pursue you until you die. ²³The skies above will be as unyielding as bronze, and the earth beneath will be as hard as iron. ²⁴The LORD will change the rain that falls on your land into powder, and dust will pour down from the sky until you are destroyed.

²⁵"The LORD will cause you to be defeated by your enemies. You will attack your enemies from one direction, but you will scatter from them in seven! You will be an object of horror to all the kingdoms of the earth. ²⁶Your corpses will be food for all the scavenging birds and wild animals, and no one will be there to chase them away.

²⁷"The LORD will afflict you with the boils of Egypt and with tumors, scurvy, and the itch, from which you cannot be cured. ²⁸The LORD will strike you with madness, blindness, and panic. ²⁹You will grope around in broad daylight like a blind person groping in the darkness, but you will not find your way. You will be oppressed and robbed continually, and no one will come to save you.

³⁰"You will be engaged to a woman, but another man will sleep with her. You will build a house, but someone else will live in it. You will plant a vineyard, but you will never enjoy its fruit. ³¹Your ox will be butchered before your eyes, but you will not eat a single bite of the meat. Your donkey will be taken from you, never to be returned. Your sheep and goats will be given to your enemies, and no one will be there to help you. ³²You will watch as your sons and daughters are taken away as slaves. Your heart will break for them, but you won't be able

to help them. ³³A foreign nation you have never heard about will eat the crops you worked so hard to grow. You will suffer under constant oppression and harsh treatment. ³⁴You will go mad because of all the tragedy you see around you. ³⁵The LORD will cover your knees and legs with incurable boils. In fact, you will be covered from head to foot.

³⁶"The LORD will exile you and your king to a nation unknown to you and your ancestors. There in exile you will worship gods of wood and stone! ³⁷You will become an object of horror, ridicule, and mockery among all the nations to which the LORD sends you.

³⁸"You will plant much but harvest little, for locusts will eat your crops. ³⁹You will plant vineyards and care for them, but you will not drink the wine or eat the grapes, for worms will destroy the vines. ⁴⁰You will grow olive trees throughout your land, but you will never use the olive oil, for the fruit will drop before it ripens. ⁴¹You will have sons and daughters, but you will lose them, for they will be led away into captivity. ⁴²Swarms of insects will destroy your trees and crops.

⁴³"The foreigners living among you will become stronger and stronger, while you become weaker and weaker. ⁴⁴They will lend money to you, but you will not lend to them. They will be the head, and you will be the tail!

⁴⁵"If you refuse to listen to the LORD your God and to obey the commands and decrees he has given you, all these curses will pursue and overtake you until you are destroyed. ⁴⁶These horrors will serve as a sign and warning among you and your descendants forever. ⁴⁷If you do not serve the LORD your God with joy and enthusiasm for the abundant benefits you have received, ⁴⁸you will serve your enemies whom the LORD will send against you. You will be left hungry, thirsty, naked, and lacking in everything. The LORD will put an iron yoke on your neck, oppressing you harshly until he has destroyed you.

⁴⁹"The LORD will bring a distant nation against you from the end of the earth, and it will swoop down on you like a vulture. It is a nation whose language you do not understand, ⁵⁰a fierce and heartless nation that shows no respect for the old and no pity for the young. ⁵¹Its armies will devour your livestock and crops, and you will be destroyed. They will leave you no grain, new wine, olive oil, calves, or lambs, and you will starve to death. ⁵²They will attack your cities until all the fortified walls in your land—the walls you trusted to protect you—are knocked down. They will attack all the towns in the land the LORD your God has given you.

⁵³"The siege and terrible distress of the enemy's attack will be so severe that you will eat the flesh of your own sons and daughters, whom the LORD your God has given you. ⁵⁴The most tenderhearted man among you will have no compassion for his own brother, his beloved wife, and his surviving children. ⁵⁵He will refuse to share with them the flesh he is devouring—the flesh of one of his own children—because he has nothing else to eat during the siege and terrible distress that your enemy will inflict on all your towns. ⁵⁶The most tender and delicate woman among you—so delicate she would not so much as touch the ground with her foot—will be selfish toward the husband she loves and toward her own son or daughter. ⁵⁷She will hide from them the afterbirth and the new baby she has borne, so that she herself can secretly eat them. She will have nothing else to eat during the siege and terrible distress that your enemy will inflict on all your towns.

⁵⁸"If you refuse to obey all the words of instruction that are written in this book, and if you do not fear the glorious and awesome name of the LORD your God, ⁵⁹then the LORD will overwhelm you and your children with indescribable plagues. These plagues will be intense and without relief, making you miserable and unbearably sick. ⁶⁰He will afflict you with all the diseases of Egypt that you feared so much, and you will have no relief. ⁶¹The LORD will afflict you with every sickness and plague there is, even those not mentioned in this Book of Instruction, until you are destroyed. ⁶²Though you become as numerous as the stars in the sky, few of you will be left because you would not listen to the LORD your God.

⁶³"Just as the LORD has found great pleasure in causing you to prosper and multiply, the LORD will find pleasure in destroying you. You will be torn from the land you are about to enter and occupy. ⁶⁴For the LORD will scatter you among all the nations from one end of the earth to the other. There you will worship foreign gods that neither you nor your ancestors have known, gods made of wood and stone! ⁶⁵There among those nations you will find no peace or place to rest. And the LORD will cause your heart to tremble, your eyesight to fail, and your soul to despair. ⁶⁶Your life will constantly hang in the balance. You will live night and day in fear, unsure if you will survive. ⁶⁷In the

morning you will say, 'If only it were night!' And in the evening you will say, 'If only it were morning!' For you will be terrified by the awful horrors you see around you. [68]Then the LORD will send you back to Egypt in ships, to a destination I promised you would never see again. There you will offer to sell yourselves to your enemies as slaves, but no one will buy you."

29

[1]*These are the terms of the covenant the LORD commanded Moses to make with the Israelites while they were in the land of Moab, in addition to the covenant he had made with them at Mount Sinai.*

Moses Reviews the Covenant

[2]*Moses summoned all the Israelites and said to them, "You have seen with your own eyes everything the LORD did in the land of Egypt to Pharaoh and to all his servants and to his whole country—[3]all the great tests of strength, the miraculous signs, and the amazing wonders. [4]But to this day the LORD has not given you minds that understand, nor eyes that see, nor ears that hear! [5]For forty years I led you through the wilderness, yet your clothes and sandals did not wear out. [6]You ate no bread and drank no wine or other alcoholic drink, but he provided for you so you would know that he is the LORD your God.

[7]"When we came here, King Sihon of Heshbon and King Og of Bashan came out to fight against us, but we defeated them. [8]We took their land and gave it to the tribes of Reuben and Gad and to the half-tribe of Manasseh as their grant of land.

[9]"Therefore, obey the terms of this covenant so that you will prosper in everything you do. [10]All of you—tribal leaders, elders, officers, all the men of Israel—are standing today in the presence of the LORD your God. [11]Your little ones and your wives are with you, as well as the foreigners living among you who chop your wood and carry your water. [12]You are standing here today to enter into the covenant of the LORD your God. The LORD is making this covenant, including the curses. [13]By entering into the covenant today, he will establish you as his people and confirm that he is your God, just as he promised you and as he swore to your ancestors Abraham, Isaac, and Jacob.

[14]"But you are not the only ones with whom I am making this covenant with its curses. [15]I am making this covenant both with you who stand here today in the presence of the LORD our God, and also with the future generations who are not standing here today.

[16]"You remember how we lived in the land of Egypt and how we traveled through the lands of enemy nations as we left. [17]You have seen their detestable practices and their idols* made of wood, stone, silver, and gold. [18]I am making this covenant with you so that no one among you—no man, woman, clan, or tribe—will turn away from the LORD our God to worship these gods of other nations, and so that no root among you bears bitter and poisonous fruit.

[19]"Those who hear the warnings of this curse should not congratulate themselves, thinking, 'I am safe, even though I am following the desires of my own stubborn heart.' This would lead to utter ruin! [20]The LORD will never pardon such people. Instead his anger and jealousy will burn against them. All the curses written in this book will come down on them, and the LORD will erase their names from under heaven. [21]The LORD will separate them from all the tribes of Israel, to pour out on them all the curses of the covenant recorded in this Book of Instruction.

[22]"Then the generations to come, both your own descendants and the foreigners who come from distant lands, will see the devastation of the land and the diseases the LORD inflicts on it. [23]They will exclaim, 'The whole land is devastated by sulfur and salt. It is a wasteland with nothing planted and nothing growing, not even a blade of grass. It is like the cities of Sodom and Gomorrah, Admah and Zeboiim, which the LORD destroyed in his intense anger.' [24]"And all the surrounding nations will ask, 'Why has the LORD done this to this land? Why was he so angry?'

[25]"And the answer will be, 'This happened because the people of the land abandoned the covenant that the LORD, the God of their ancestors, made with them when he brought them out of the land of Egypt. [26]Instead, they turned away to serve and worship gods they had not known before, gods that were not from the LORD. [27]That is why the LORD's anger has burned against this land, bringing down on it every curse recorded in this book. [28]In great anger and fury the LORD uprooted his people from their land and banished them to another land, where they still live today!'

[29]"The LORD our God has secrets known to

29:1a Verse 29:1 is numbered 28:69 in Hebrew text.   29:1b Hebrew *Horeb,* another name for Sinai.   29:2 Verses 29:2-29 are numbered 29:1-28 in Hebrew text.   29:17 The Hebrew term (literally *round things*) probably alludes to dung.

no one. We are not accountable for them, but we and our children are accountable forever for all that he has revealed to us, so that we may obey all the terms of these instructions.

A Call to Return to the LORD

30 "In the future, when you experience all these blessings and curses I have listed for you, and when you are living among the nations to which the LORD your God has exiled you, take to heart all these instructions. ²If at that time you and your children return to the LORD your God, and if you obey with all your heart and all your soul all the commands I have given you today, ³then the LORD your God will restore your fortunes. He will have mercy on you and gather you back from all the nations where he has scattered you. ⁴Even though you are banished to the ends of the earth,* the LORD your God will gather you from there and bring you back again. ⁵The LORD your God will return you to the land that belonged to your ancestors, and you will possess that land again. Then he will make you even more prosperous and numerous than your ancestors!

⁶"The LORD your God will change your heart* and the hearts of all your descendants, so that you will love him with all your heart and soul and so you may live! ⁷The LORD your God will inflict all these curses on your enemies and on those who hate and persecute you. ⁸Then you will again obey the LORD and keep all his commands that I am giving you today.

⁹"The LORD your God will then make you successful in everything you do. He will give you many children and numerous livestock, and he will cause your fields to produce abundant harvests, for the LORD will again delight in being good to you as he was to your ancestors. ¹⁰The LORD your God will delight in you if you obey his voice and keep the commands and decrees written in this Book of Instruction, and if you turn to the LORD your God with all your heart and soul.

The Choice of Life or Death

¹¹"This command I am giving you today is not too difficult for you, and it is not beyond your reach. ¹²It is not kept in heaven, so distant that you must ask, 'Who will go up to heaven and bring it down so we can hear it and obey?' ¹³It is not kept beyond the sea, so far away that you must ask, 'Who will cross the sea to bring it to us so we can hear it and obey?' ¹⁴No, the message is very close at hand; it is on your lips and in your heart so that you can obey it.

¹⁵"Now listen! Today I am giving you a choice between life and death, between prosperity and disaster. ¹⁶For I command you this day to love the LORD your God and to keep his commands, decrees, and regulations by walking in his ways. If you do this, you will live and multiply, and the LORD your God will bless you and the land you are about to enter and occupy.

¹⁷"But if your heart turns away and you refuse to listen, and if you are drawn away to serve and worship other gods, ¹⁸then I warn you now that you will certainly be destroyed. You will not live a long, good life in the land you are crossing the Jordan to occupy.

¹⁹"Today I have given you the choice between life and death, between blessings and curses. Now I call on heaven and earth to witness the choice you make. Oh, that you would choose life, so that you and your descendants might live! ²⁰You can make this choice by loving the LORD your God, obeying him, and committing yourself firmly to him. This* is the key to your life. And if you love and obey the LORD, you will live long in the land the LORD swore to give your ancestors Abraham, Isaac, and Jacob."

Joshua Becomes Israel's Leader

31 When Moses had finished giving these instructions* to all the people of Israel, ²he said, "I am now 120 years old, and I am no longer able to lead you. The LORD has told me, 'You will not cross the Jordan River.' ³But the LORD your God himself will cross over ahead of you. He will destroy the nations living there, and you will take possession of their land. Joshua will lead you across the river, just as the LORD promised.

⁴"The LORD will destroy the nations living in the land, just as he destroyed Sihon and Og, the kings of the Amorites. ⁵The LORD will hand over to you the people who live there, and you must deal with them as I have commanded you. ⁶So be strong and courageous! Do not be afraid and do not panic before them. For the LORD your God will personally go ahead of you. He will neither fail you nor abandon you."

⁷Then Moses called for Joshua, and as all Israel watched, he said to him, "Be strong and courageous! For you will lead these people into the land that the LORD swore to their ancestors he would give them. You are the one who will divide it among them as their grants of land.

30:4 Hebrew *of the heavens.*   30:6 Hebrew *circumcise your heart.*   30:20 Or He.   31:1 As in Dead Sea Scrolls and Greek version; Masoretic Text reads *Moses went and spoke.*

8Do not be afraid or discouraged, for the LORD will personally go ahead of you. He will be with you; he will neither fail you nor abandon you."

Public Reading of the Book of Instruction

9So Moses wrote this entire body of instruction in a book and gave it to the priests, who carried the Ark of the LORD's Covenant, and to the elders of Israel. 10Then Moses gave them this command: "At the end of every seventh year, the Year of Release, during the Festival of Shelters, 11you must read this Book of Instruction to all the people of Israel when they assemble before the LORD your God at the place he chooses. 12Call them all together—men, women, children, and the foreigners living in your towns—so they may hear this Book of Instruction and learn to fear the LORD your God and carefully obey all the terms of these instructions. 13Do this so that your children who have not known these instructions will hear them and will learn to fear the LORD your God. Do this as long as you live in the land you are crossing the Jordan to occupy."

Israel's Disobedience Predicted

14Then the LORD said to Moses, "The time has come for you to die. Call Joshua and present yourselves at the Tabernacle,* so that I may commission him there." So Moses and Joshua went and presented themselves at the Tabernacle. 15And the LORD appeared to them in a pillar of cloud that stood at the entrance to the sacred tent.

16The LORD said to Moses, "You are about to die and join your ancestors. After you are gone, these people will begin to worship foreign gods, the gods of the land where they are going. They will abandon me and break my covenant that I have made with them. 17Then my anger will blaze forth against them. I will abandon them, hiding my face from them, and they will be devoured. Terrible trouble will come down on them, and on that day they will say, 'These disasters have come down on us because God is no longer among us!' 18At that time I will hide my face from them on account of all the evil they commit by worshiping other gods.

19"So write down the words of this song, and teach it to the people of Israel. Help them learn it, so it may serve as a witness for me against them. 20For I will bring them into the land I swore to give their ancestors—a land flowing with milk and honey. There they will become prosperous, eat all the food they want, and

become fat. But they will begin to worship other gods; they will despise me and break my covenant. 21And when great disasters come down on them, this song will stand as evidence against them, for it will never be forgotten by their descendants. I know the intentions of these people, even now before they have entered the land I swore to give them."

22So that very day Moses wrote down the words of the song and taught it to the Israelites.

23Then the LORD commissioned Joshua son of Nun with these words: "Be strong and courageous, for you must bring the people of Israel into the land I swore to give them. I will be with you."

24When Moses had finished writing this entire body of instruction in a book, 25he gave this command to the Levites who carried the Ark of the LORD's Covenant: 26"Take this Book of Instruction and place it beside the Ark of the Covenant of the LORD your God, so it may remain there as a witness against the people of Israel. 27For I know how rebellious and stubborn you are. Even now, while I am still alive and am here with you, you have rebelled against the LORD. How much more rebellious will you be after my death!

28"Now summon all the elders and officials of your tribes, so that I can speak to them directly and call heaven and earth to witness against them. 29I know that after my death you will become utterly corrupt and will turn from the way I have commanded you to follow. In the days to come, disaster will come down on you, for you will do what is evil in the LORD's sight, making him very angry with your actions."

The Song of Moses

30So Moses recited this entire song publicly to the assembly of Israel:

32

1 "Listen, O heavens, and I will speak!
    Hear, O earth, the words that I say!
2 Let my teaching fall on you like rain;
    let my speech settle like dew.
Let my words fall like rain on tender grass,
    like gentle showers on young plants.
3 I will proclaim the name of the LORD;
    how glorious is our God!
4 He is the Rock; his deeds are perfect.
    Everything he does is just and fair.
He is a faithful God who does no wrong;
    how just and upright he is!

31:14 Hebrew *Tent of Meeting;* also in 31:14b.

5 "But they have acted corruptly toward
       him;
  when they act so perversely,
  are they really his children?*
       They are a deceitful and twisted
           generation.
6 Is this the way you repay the LORD,
       you foolish and senseless people?
  Isn't he your Father who created you?
       Has he not made you and established
           you?
7 Remember the days of long ago;
       think about the generations past.
  Ask your father, and he will inform you.
       Inquire of your elders, and they will tell
           you.
8 When the Most High assigned lands to the
       nations,
       when he divided up the human race,
  he established the boundaries of the
       peoples
       according to the number in his heavenly
           court.*

9 "For the people of Israel belong to the
       LORD;
       Jacob is his special possession.
10 He found them in a desert land,
       in an empty, howling wasteland.
  He surrounded them and watched over
       them;
       he guarded them as he would guard his
           own eyes.*
11 Like an eagle that rouses her chicks
       and hovers over her young,
  so he spread his wings to take them up
       and carried them safely on his
           pinions.
12 The LORD alone guided them;
       they followed no foreign gods.
13 He let them ride over the highlands
       and feast on the crops of the fields.
  He nourished them with honey from
       the rock
       and olive oil from the stony ground.
14 He fed them yogurt from the herd
       and milk from the flock,
       together with the fat of lambs.
  He gave them choice rams from Bashan,
       and goats,
       together with the choicest wheat.
  You drank the finest wine,
       made from the juice of grapes.

15 "But Israel* soon became fat and unruly;
       the people grew heavy, plump, and
           stuffed!
  Then they abandoned the God who had
       made them;
       they made light of the Rock of their
           salvation.
16 They stirred up his jealousy by worshiping
       foreign gods;
       they provoked his fury with detestable
           deeds.
17 They offered sacrifices to demons, which
       are not God,
       to gods they had not known before,
  to new gods only recently arrived,
       to gods their ancestors had never
           feared.
18 You neglected the Rock who had fathered
       you;
       you forgot the God who had given you
           birth.

19 "The LORD saw this and drew back,
       provoked to anger by his own sons and
           daughters.
20 He said, 'I will abandon them;
       then see what becomes of them.
  For they are a twisted generation,
       children without integrity.
21 They have roused my jealousy by
       worshiping things that are not God;
       they have provoked my anger with their
           useless idols.
  Now I will rouse their jealousy through
       people who are not even a people;
  I will provoke their anger through the
       foolish Gentiles.
22 For my anger blazes forth like fire
       and burns to the depths of the grave.*
  It devours the earth and all its crops
       and ignites the foundations of the
           mountains.
23 I will heap disasters upon them
       and shoot them down with my arrows.
24 I will weaken them with famine,
       burning fever, and deadly disease.
  I will send the fangs of wild beasts
       and poisonous snakes that glide in the
           dust.
25 Outside, the sword will bring death,
       and inside, terror will strike
  both young men and young women,
       both infants and the aged.

32:5 The meaning of the Hebrew is uncertain.   32:8 As in Dead Sea Scrolls, which read *the number of the sons of God,* and
Greek version, which reads *the number of the angels of God;* Masoretic Text reads *the number of the sons of Israel.*   32:10 Hebrew
as the pupil of his eye.   32:15 Hebrew *Jeshurun,* a term of endearment for Israel.   32:22 Hebrew *of Sheol.*

26 I would have annihilated them,
   wiping out even the memory of them.
27 But I feared the taunt of Israel's enemy,
   who might misunderstand and say,
   "Our own power has triumphed!
   The LORD had nothing to do with this!" '

28 "But Israel is a senseless nation;
   the people are foolish, without
   understanding.
29 Oh, that they were wise and could
   understand this!
   Oh, that they might know their fate!
30 How could one person chase a thousand
   of them,
   and two people put ten thousand to
   flight,
   unless their Rock had sold them,
   unless the LORD had given them up?
31 But the rock of our enemies is not like our
   Rock,
   as even they recognize.*
32 Their vine grows from the vine of Sodom,
   from the vineyards of Gomorrah.
   Their grapes are poison,
   and their clusters are bitter.
33 Their wine is the venom of serpents,
   the deadly poison of cobras.

34 "The LORD says, 'Am I not storing up these
   things,
   sealing them away in my treasury?
35 I will take revenge; I will pay them back.
   In due time their feet will slip.
   Their day of disaster will arrive,
   and their destiny will overtake them.'

36 "Indeed, the LORD will give justice to his
   people,
   and he will change his mind about* his
   servants,
   when he sees their strength is gone
   and no one is left, slave or free.
37 Then he will ask, 'Where are their gods,
   the rocks they fled to for refuge?
38 Where now are those gods,
   who ate the fat of their sacrifices
   and drank the wine of their offerings?
   Let those gods arise and help you!
   Let them provide you with shelter!
39 Look now; I myself am he!
   There is no other god but me!

I am the one who kills and gives life;
   I am the one who wounds and heals;
   no one can be rescued from my powerful
   hand!
40 Now I raise my hand to heaven
   and declare, "As surely as I live,
41 when I sharpen my flashing sword
   and begin to carry out justice,
   I will take revenge on my enemies
   and repay those who reject me.
42 I will make my arrows drunk with blood,
   and my sword will devour flesh—
   the blood of the slaughtered and the
   captives,
   and the heads of the enemy leaders." '

43 "Rejoice with him, you heavens,
   and let all of God's angels worship him.*
   Rejoice with his people, you Gentiles,
   and let all the angels be strengthened
   in him.*
   For he will avenge the blood of his
   children*;
   he will take revenge against his
   enemies.
   He will repay those who hate him*
   and cleanse his people's land."

44So Moses came with Joshua* son of Nun and recited all the words of this song to the people.

45When Moses had finished reciting all these words to the people of Israel, 46he added: "Take to heart all the words of warning I have given you today. Pass them on as a command to your children so they will obey every word of these instructions. 47These instructions are not empty words—they are your life! By obeying them you will enjoy a long life in the land you will occupy when you cross the Jordan River."

Moses' Death Foretold

48That same day the LORD said to Moses, 49"Go to Moab, to the mountains east of the river,* and climb Mount Nebo, which is across from Jericho. Look out across the land of Canaan, the land I am giving to the people of Israel as their own special possession. 50Then you will die there on the mountain. You will join your ancestors, just as Aaron, your brother, died on Mount Hor and joined his ancestors. 51For both of you betrayed me with the Israelites at the waters of Meribah at Kadesh* in the wilderness of Zin. You failed to demonstrate my holiness to the people of Israel there. 52So you will see the land from a distance, but you may not enter the land I am giving to the people of Israel."

Moses Blesses the People

33 This is the blessing that Moses, the man of God, gave to the people of Israel before his death:

2 "The LORD came from Mount Sinai
  and dawned upon us* from Mount Seir;
he shone forth from Mount Paran
  and came from Meribah-kadesh
  with flaming fire at his right hand.*
3 Indeed, he loves his people;*
  all his holy ones are in his hands.
They follow in his steps
  and accept his teaching.
4 Moses gave us the LORD's instruction,
  the special possession of the people of
    Israel.*
5 The LORD became king in Israel*—
  when the leaders of the people
    assembled,
  when the tribes of Israel gathered as one."

6Moses said this about the tribe of Reuben:*

"Let the tribe of Reuben live and not die
    out,
  though they are few in number."

7Moses said this about the tribe of Judah:

"O LORD, hear the cry of Judah
  and bring them together as a people.
Give them strength to defend their cause;
  help them against their enemies!"

8Moses said this about the tribe of Levi:

"O LORD, you have given your Thummim
    and Urim—the sacred lots—
  to your faithful servants the Levites.*
You put them to the test at Massah
  and struggled with them at the waters
    of Meribah.
9 The Levites obeyed your word
  and guarded your covenant.

They were more loyal to you
  than to their own parents.
They ignored their relatives
  and did not acknowledge their own
    children.
10 They teach your regulations to Jacob;
  they give your instructions to Israel.
They present incense before you
  and offer whole burnt offerings on the
    altar.
11 Bless the ministry of the Levites, O LORD,
  and accept all the work of their hands.
Hit their enemies where it hurts the most;
  strike down their foes so they never rise
    again."

12Moses said this about the tribe of Benjamin:

"The people of Benjamin are loved by the
    LORD
  and live in safety beside him.
He surrounds them continuously
  and preserves them from every harm."

13Moses said this about the tribes of Joseph:

"May their land be blessed by the LORD
  with the precious gift of dew from the
    heavens
  and water from beneath the earth;
14 with the rich fruit that grows in the sun,
  and the rich harvest produced each
    month;
15 with the finest crops of the ancient
    mountains,
  and the abundance from the everlasting
    hills;
16 with the best gifts of the earth and its
    bounty,
  and the favor of the one who appeared
    in the burning bush.
May these blessings rest on Joseph's head,
  crowning the brow of the prince among
    his brothers.
17 Joseph has the majesty of a young bull;
  he has the horns of a wild ox.
He will gore distant nations,
  even to the ends of the earth.
This is my blessing for the multitudes
    of Ephraim
  and the thousands of Manasseh."

32:51 Hebrew *waters of Meribath-kadesh.* 33:2a As in Greek and Syriac versions; Hebrew reads *upon them.* 33:2b Or *came from myriads of holy ones, from the south, from his mountain slopes.* The meaning of the Hebrew is uncertain. 33:3 As in Greek version; Hebrew reads *Indeed, lover of the peoples.* 33:4 Hebrew *of Jacob.* The names "Jacob" and "Israel" are often interchanged throughout the Old Testament, referring sometimes to the individual patriarch and sometimes to the nation. 33:5 Hebrew *in Jeshurun,* a term of endearment for Israel. 33:6 Hebrew lacks *Moses said this about the tribe of Reuben.* 33:8 As in Greek version; Hebrew lacks *the Levites.*

18Moses said this about the tribes of Zebulun and Issachar*:

> "May the people of Zebulun prosper in
>   their travels.
> May the people of Issachar prosper at
>   home in their tents.
> 19 They summon the people to the mountain
>   to offer proper sacrifices there.
> They benefit from the riches of the sea
>   and the hidden treasures in the sand."

20Moses said this about the tribe of Gad:

> "Blessed is the one who enlarges Gad's
>   territory!
> Gad is poised there like a lion
>   to tear off an arm or a head.
> 21 The people of Gad took the best land for
>   themselves;
>   a leader's share was assigned to them.
> When the leaders of the people were
>   assembled,
>   they carried out the LORD's justice
>   and obeyed his regulations for Israel."

22Moses said this about the tribe of Dan:

> "Dan is a lion's cub,
>   leaping out from Bashan."

23Moses said this about the tribe of Naphtali:

> "O Naphtali, you are rich in favor
>   and full of the LORD's blessings;
>   may you possess the west and the
>   south."

24Moses said this about the tribe of Asher:

> "May Asher be blessed above other sons;
>   may he be esteemed by his brothers;
>   may he bathe his feet in olive oil.
> 25 May the bolts of your gates be of iron and
>   bronze;
>   may you be secure all your days."

> 26 "There is no one like the God of Israel.*
>   He rides across the heavens to help you,
>   across the skies in majestic splendor.
> 27 The eternal God is your refuge,
>   and his everlasting arms are under you.

> He drives out the enemy before you;
>   he cries out, 'Destroy them!'
> 28 So Israel will live in safety,
>   prosperous Jacob in security,
> in a land of grain and new wine,
>   while the heavens drop down dew.
> 29 How blessed you are, O Israel!
>   Who else is like you, a people saved by
>   the LORD?
> He is your protecting shield
>   and your triumphant sword!
> Your enemies will cringe before you,
>   and you will stomp on their backs!"

The Death of Moses

34 Then Moses went up to Mount Nebo from the plains of Moab and climbed Pisgah Peak, which is across from Jericho. And the LORD showed him the whole land, from Gilead as far as Dan; 2all the land of Naphtali; the land of Ephraim and Manasseh; all the land of Judah, extending to the Mediterranean Sea*; 3the Negev; the Jordan Valley with Jericho—the city of palms—as far as Zoar. 4Then the LORD said to Moses, "This is the land I promised on oath to Abraham, Isaac, and Jacob when I said, 'I will give it to your descendants.' I have now allowed you to see it with your own eyes, but you will not enter the land."

5So Moses, the servant of the LORD, died there in the land of Moab, just as the LORD had said. 6The LORD buried him* in a valley near Beth-peor in Moab, but to this day no one knows the exact place. 7Moses was 120 years old when he died, yet his eyesight was clear, and he was as strong as ever. 8The people of Israel mourned for Moses on the plains of Moab for thirty days, until the customary period of mourning was over.

9Now Joshua son of Nun was full of the spirit of wisdom, for Moses had laid his hands on him. So the people of Israel obeyed him, doing just as the LORD had commanded Moses.

10There has never been another prophet in Israel like Moses, whom the LORD knew face to face. 11The LORD sent him to perform all the miraculous signs and wonders in the land of Egypt against Pharaoh, and all his servants, and his entire land. 12With mighty power, Moses performed terrifying acts in the sight of all Israel.

33:18 Hebrew lacks and Issachar.   33:26 Hebrew of Jeshurun, a term of endearment for Israel.   34:2 Hebrew the western sea.
34:6 Hebrew He buried him; Samaritan Pentateuch and some Greek manuscripts read They buried him.

Joshua

THE BOOK OF JOSHUA is about leadership—more specifically, about Joshua's leadership of the Israelites. At the opening of the book, Moses had already died, and Joshua had been appointed his successor. While the Israelites waited on the plains of Moab, Joshua prepared them for battle. Once they were ready, Joshua led them across the Jordan River to begin their conquest of the land God promised them. The Israelites then fought three campaigns: (1) one in the central region, (2) one in the south, and (3) one in the north. After the initial victories, Joshua and his people divided the land among the tribes of Israel. At the book's end, Joshua was old and close to death, and he urged the Israelites to follow the Lord their God.

■ **Author:** Joshua, according to Jewish tradition (except for the ending, possibly written by Phinehas the high priest)

■ **Date Written:** Uncertain, perhaps around 1380 BC

■ **Purpose:** To give the history of Israel's conquest of the Promised Land

■ **Themes:** Obedience, faith, guidance, godly leadership

■ **Outline**
1:1–5:15 Mobilizing Israel and entering the Promised Land
6:1–8:35 The central campaign
9:1–10:43 The southern campaign
11:1-15 The northern campaign
11:16–22:34 Summary and division of the land
23:1–24:33 Joshua's final words and death

The LORD's Charge to Joshua

1 After the death of Moses the LORD's servant, the LORD spoke to Joshua son of Nun, Moses' assistant. He said, ²"Moses my servant is dead. Therefore, the time has come for you to lead these people, the Israelites, across the Jordan River into the land I am giving them. ³I promise you what I promised Moses: 'Wherever you set foot, you will be on land I have given you—⁴from the Negev wilderness in the south to the Lebanon mountains in the north, from the Euphrates River in the east to the Mediterranean Sea* in the west, including all the land of the Hittites.' ⁵No one will be able to stand against you as long as you live. For I will be with you as I was with Moses. I will not fail you or abandon you.

⁶"Be strong and courageous, for you are the one who will lead these people to possess all the land I swore to their ancestors I would give them. ⁷Be strong and very courageous. Be careful to obey all the instructions Moses gave you. Do not deviate from them, turning either to the right or to the left. Then you will

1:4 Hebrew *the Great Sea.*

be successful in everything you do. ⁸Study this Book of Instruction continually. Meditate on it day and night so you will be sure to obey everything written in it. Only then will you prosper and succeed in all you do. ⁹This is my command—be strong and courageous! Do not be afraid or discouraged. For the LORD your God is with you wherever you go."

Joshua's Charge to the Israelites

¹⁰Joshua then commanded the officers of Israel, ¹¹"Go through the camp and tell the people to get their provisions ready. In three days you will cross the Jordan River and take possession of the land the LORD your God is giving you."

¹²Then Joshua called together the tribes of Reuben, Gad, and the half-tribe of Manasseh. He told them, ¹³"Remember what Moses, the servant of the LORD, commanded you: 'The LORD your God is giving you a place of rest. He has given you this land.' ¹⁴Your wives, children, and livestock may remain here in the land Moses assigned to you on the east side of the Jordan River. But your strong warriors,

fully armed, must lead the other tribes across the Jordan to help them conquer their territory. Stay with them ¹⁵until the LORD gives them rest, as he has given you rest, and until they, too, possess the land the LORD your God is giving them. Only then may you return and settle here on the east side of the Jordan River in the land that Moses, the servant of the LORD, assigned to you."

¹⁶They answered Joshua, "We will do whatever you command us, and we will go wherever you send us. ¹⁷We will obey you just as we obeyed Moses. And may the LORD your God be with you as he was with Moses. ¹⁸Anyone who rebels against your orders and does not obey your words and everything you command will be put to death. So be strong and courageous!"

Rahab Protects the Spies

2 Then Joshua secretly sent out two spies from the Israelite camp at Acacia Grove.* He instructed them, "Scout out the land on the other side of the Jordan River, especially around Jericho." So the two men set out and came to the house of a prostitute named Rahab and stayed there that night.

²But someone told the king of Jericho, "Some Israelites have come here tonight to spy out the land." ³So the king of Jericho sent orders to Rahab: "Bring out the men who have come into your house, for they have come here to spy out the whole land."

⁴Rahab had hidden the two men, but she replied, "Yes, the men were here earlier, but I didn't know where they were from. ⁵They left the town at dusk, as the gates were about to close. I don't know where they went. If you hurry, you can probably catch up with them." ⁶(Actually, she had taken them up to the roof and hidden them beneath bundles of flax she had laid out.) ⁷So the king's men went looking for the spies along the road leading to the shallow crossings of the Jordan River. And as soon as the king's men had left, the gate of Jericho was shut.

⁸Before the spies went to sleep that night, Rahab went up on the roof to talk with them. ⁹"I know the LORD has given you this land," she told them. "We are all afraid of you. Everyone in the land is living in terror. ¹⁰For we have heard how the LORD made a dry path for you through the Red Sea* when you left Egypt. And we know what you did to Sihon and Og, the two Amorite kings east of the Jordan River,

whose people you completely destroyed.* ¹¹No wonder our hearts have melted in fear! No one has the courage to fight after hearing such things. For the LORD your God is the supreme God of the heavens above and the earth below.

¹²"Now swear to me by the LORD that you will be kind to me and my family since I have helped you. Give me some guarantee that ¹³when Jericho is conquered, you will let me live, along with my father and mother, my brothers and sisters, and all their families."

¹⁴"We offer our own lives as a guarantee for your safety," the men agreed. "If you don't betray us, we will keep our promise and be kind to you when the LORD gives us the land."

¹⁵Then, since Rahab's house was built into the town wall, she let them down by a rope through the window. ¹⁶"Escape to the hill country," she told them. "Hide there for three days from the men searching for you. Then, when they have returned, you can go on your way."

¹⁷Before they left, the men told her, "We will be bound by the oath we have taken only if you follow these instructions. ¹⁸When we come into the land, you must leave this scarlet rope hanging from the window through which you let us down. And all your family members—your father, mother, brothers, and all your relatives—must be here inside the house. ¹⁹If they go out into the street and are killed, it will not be our fault. But if anyone lays a hand on people inside this house, we will accept the responsibility for their death. ²⁰If you betray us, however, we are not bound by this oath in any way."

²¹"I accept your terms," she replied. And she sent them on their way, leaving the scarlet rope hanging from the window.

²²The spies went up into the hill country and stayed there three days. The men who were chasing them searched everywhere along the road, but they finally returned without success. ²³Then the two spies came down from the hill country, crossed the Jordan River, and reported to Joshua all that had happened to them. ²⁴"The LORD has given us the whole land," they said, "for all the people in the land are terrified of us."

The Israelites Cross the Jordan

3 Early the next morning Joshua and all the Israelites left Acacia Grove* and arrived at the banks of the Jordan River, where they camped before crossing. ²Three days later the

2:1 Hebrew *Shittim.*   2:10a Hebrew *sea of reeds.*   2:10b The Hebrew term used here refers to the complete consecration of things or people to the LORD, either by destroying them or by giving them as an offering.   3:1 Hebrew *Shittim.*

Israelite officers went through the camp, [3]giving these instructions to the people: "When you see the Levitical priests carrying the Ark of the Covenant of the LORD your God, move out from your positions and follow them. [4]Since you have never traveled this way before, they will guide you. Stay about half a mile* behind them, keeping a clear distance between you and the Ark. Make sure you don't come any closer."

[5]Then Joshua told the people, "Purify yourselves, for tomorrow the LORD will do great wonders among you."

[6]In the morning Joshua said to the priests, "Lift up the Ark of the Covenant and lead the people across the river." And so they started out and went ahead of the people.

[7]The LORD told Joshua, "Today I will begin to make you a great leader in the eyes of all the Israelites. They will know that I am with you, just as I was with Moses. [8]Give this command to the priests who carry the Ark of the Covenant: 'When you reach the banks of the Jordan River, take a few steps into the river and stop there.'"

[9]So Joshua told the Israelites, "Come and listen to what the LORD your God says. [10]Today you will know that the living God is among you. He will surely drive out the Canaanites, Hittites, Hivites, Perizzites, Girgashites, Amorites, and Jebusites ahead of you. [11]Look, the Ark of the Covenant, which belongs to the Lord of the whole earth, will lead you across the Jordan River! [12]Now choose twelve men from the tribes of Israel, one from each tribe. [13]The priests will carry the Ark of the LORD, the Lord of all the earth. As soon as their feet touch the water, the flow of water will be cut off upstream, and the river will stand up like a wall."

[14]So the people left their camp to cross the Jordan, and the priests who were carrying the Ark of the Covenant went ahead of them. [15]It was the harvest season, and the Jordan was overflowing its banks. But as soon as the feet of the priests who were carrying the Ark touched the water at the river's edge, [16]the water above that point began backing up a great distance away at a town called Adam, which is near Zarethan. And the water below that point flowed on to the Dead Sea* until the riverbed was dry. Then all the people crossed over near the town of Jericho.

[17]Meanwhile, the priests who were carrying the Ark of the LORD's Covenant stood on dry ground in the middle of the riverbed as the people passed by. They waited there until the whole nation of Israel had crossed the Jordan on dry ground.

Memorials to the Jordan Crossing

4 When all the people had crossed the Jordan, the LORD said to Joshua, [2]"Now choose twelve men, one from each tribe. [3]Tell them, 'Take twelve stones from the very place where the priests are standing in the middle of the Jordan. Carry them out and pile them up at the place where you will camp tonight.'"

[4]So Joshua called together the twelve men he had chosen—one from each of the tribes of Israel. [5]He told them, "Go into the middle of the Jordan, in front of the Ark of the LORD your God. Each of you must pick up one stone and carry it out on your shoulder—twelve stones in all, one for each of the twelve tribes of Israel. [6]We will use these stones to build a memorial. In the future your children will ask you, 'What do these stones mean?' [7]Then you can tell them, 'They remind us that the Jordan River stopped flowing when the Ark of the LORD's Covenant went across.' These stones will stand as a memorial among the people of Israel forever."

[8]So the men did as Joshua had commanded them. They took twelve stones from the middle of the Jordan River, one for each tribe, just as the LORD had told Joshua. They carried them to the place where they camped for the night and constructed the memorial there.

[9]Joshua also set up another pile of twelve stones in the middle of the Jordan, at the place where the priests who carried the Ark of the Covenant were standing. And they are there to this day.

[10]The priests who were carrying the Ark stood in the middle of the river until all of the LORD's commands that Moses had given to Joshua were carried out. Meanwhile, the people hurried across the riverbed. [11]And when everyone was safely on the other side, the priests crossed over with the Ark of the LORD as the people watched.

[12]The armed warriors from the tribes of Reuben, Gad, and the half-tribe of Manasseh led the Israelites across the Jordan, just as Moses had directed. [13]These armed men—about 40,000 strong—were ready for battle, and the LORD was with them as they crossed over to the plains of Jericho.

[14]That day the LORD made Joshua a great

3:4 Hebrew *about 2,000 cubits* [920 meters].   3:16 Hebrew *the sea of the Arabah, the Salt Sea.*

leader in the eyes of all the Israelites, and for the rest of his life they revered him as much as they had revered Moses.

¹⁵The LORD had said to Joshua, ¹⁶"Command the priests carrying the Ark of the Covenant* to come up out of the riverbed." ¹⁷So Joshua gave the command. ¹⁸As soon as the priests carrying the Ark of the LORD's Covenant came up out of the riverbed and their feet were on high ground, the water of the Jordan returned and overflowed its banks as before.

¹⁹The people crossed the Jordan on the tenth day of the first month.* Then they camped at Gilgal, just east of Jericho. ²⁰It was there at Gilgal that Joshua piled up the twelve stones taken from the Jordan River.

²¹Then Joshua said to the Israelites, "In the future your children will ask, 'What do these stones mean?' ²²Then you can tell them, 'This is where the Israelites crossed the Jordan on dry ground.' ²³For the LORD your God dried up the river right before your eyes, and he kept it dry until you were all across, just as he did at the Red Sea* when he dried it up until we had all crossed over. ²⁴He did this so all the nations of the earth might know that the LORD's hand is powerful, and so you might fear the LORD your God forever."

5 When all the Amorite kings west of the Jordan and all the Canaanite kings who lived along the Mediterranean coast* heard how the LORD had dried up the Jordan River so the people of Israel could cross, they lost heart and were paralyzed with fear because of them.

Israel Reestablishes Covenant Ceremonies

²At that time the LORD told Joshua, "Make flint knives and circumcise this second generation of Israelites.*" ³So Joshua made flint knives and circumcised the entire male population of Israel at Gibeath-haaraloth.*

⁴Joshua had to circumcise them because all the men who were old enough to fight in battle when they left Egypt had died in the wilderness. ⁵Those who left Egypt had all been circumcised, but none of those born after the Exodus, during the years in the wilderness, had been circumcised. ⁶The Israelites had traveled in the wilderness for forty years until all the men who were old enough to fight in battle when they left Egypt had died. For they

had disobeyed the LORD, and the LORD vowed he would not let them enter the land he had sworn to give us—a land flowing with milk and honey. ⁷So Joshua circumcised their sons—those who had grown up to take their fathers' places—for they had not been circumcised on the way to the Promised Land. ⁸After all the males had been circumcised, they rested in the camp until they were healed.

⁹Then the LORD said to Joshua, "Today I have rolled away the shame of your slavery in Egypt." So that place has been called Gilgal* to this day.

¹⁰While the Israelites were camped at Gilgal on the plains of Jericho, they celebrated Passover on the evening of the fourteenth day of the first month.* ¹¹The very next day they began to eat unleavened bread and roasted grain harvested from the land. ¹²No manna appeared on the day they first ate from the crops of the land, and it was never seen again. So from that time on the Israelites ate from the crops of Canaan.

The LORD's Commander Confronts Joshua

¹³When Joshua was near the town of Jericho, he looked up and saw a man standing in front of him with sword in hand. Joshua went up to him and demanded, "Are you friend or foe?"

¹⁴"Neither one," he replied. "I am the commander of the LORD's army."

At this, Joshua fell with his face to the ground in reverence. "I am at your command," Joshua said. "What do you want your servant to do?"

¹⁵The commander of the LORD's army replied, "Take off your sandals, for the place where you are standing is holy." And Joshua did as he was told.

The Fall of Jericho

6 Now the gates of Jericho were tightly shut because the people were afraid of the Israelites. No one was allowed to go out or in. ²But the LORD said to Joshua, "I have given you Jericho, its king, and all its strong warriors. ³You and your fighting men should march around the town once a day for six days. ⁴Seven priests will walk ahead of the Ark, each carrying a ram's horn. On the seventh day you are to march around the town seven times, with the priests blowing the horns. ⁵When you hear the

---

4:16 Hebrew *Ark of the Testimony.*   4:19 This day in the ancient Hebrew lunar calendar occurred in late March, April, or early May.   4:23 Hebrew *sea of reeds.*   5:1 Hebrew *along the sea.*   5:2 Or *circumcise the Israelites a second time.*   5:3 Gibeath-haaraloth means "hill of foreskins."   5:9 *Gilgal* sounds like the Hebrew word *galal,* meaning "to roll."   5:10 This day in the ancient Hebrew lunar calendar occurred in late March, April, or early May.

priests give one long blast on the rams' horns, have all the people shout as loud as they can. Then the walls of the town will collapse, and the people can charge straight into the town."

⁶So Joshua called together the priests and said, "Take up the Ark of the LORD's Covenant, and assign seven priests to walk in front of it, each carrying a ram's horn." ⁷Then he gave orders to the people: "March around the town, and the armed men will lead the way in front of the Ark of the LORD."

⁸After Joshua spoke to the people, the seven priests with the rams' horns started marching in the presence of the LORD, blowing the horns as they marched. And the Ark of the LORD's Covenant followed behind them. ⁹Some of the armed men marched in front of the priests with the horns and some behind the Ark, with the priests continually blowing the horns. ¹⁰"Do not shout; do not even talk," Joshua commanded. "Not a single word from any of you until I tell you to shout. Then shout!" ¹¹So the Ark of the LORD was carried around the town once that day, and then everyone returned to spend the night in the camp.

¹²Joshua got up early the next morning, and the priests again carried the Ark of the LORD. ¹³The seven priests with the rams' horns marched in front of the Ark of the LORD, blowing their horns. Again the armed men marched both in front of the priests with the horns and behind the Ark of the LORD. All this time the priests were blowing their horns. ¹⁴On the second day they again marched around the town once and returned to the camp. They followed this pattern for six days.

¹⁵On the seventh day the Israelites got up at dawn and marched around the town as they had done before. But this time they went around the town seven times. ¹⁶The seventh time around, as the priests sounded the long blast on their horns, Joshua commanded the people, "Shout! For the LORD has given you the town! ¹⁷Jericho and everything in it must be completely destroyed* as an offering to the LORD. Only Rahab the prostitute and the others in her house will be spared, for she protected our spies.

¹⁸"Do not take any of the things set apart for destruction, or you yourselves will be completely destroyed, and you will bring trouble on the camp of Israel. ¹⁹Everything made from

silver, gold, bronze, or iron is sacred to the LORD and must be brought into his treasury."

²⁰When the people heard the sound of the rams' horns, they shouted as loud as they could. Suddenly, the walls of Jericho collapsed, and the Israelites charged straight into the town and captured it. ²¹They completely destroyed everything in it with their swords—men and women, young and old, cattle, sheep, goats, and donkeys.

²²Meanwhile, Joshua said to the two spies, "Keep your promise. Go to the prostitute's house and bring her out, along with all her family."

²³The men who had been spies went in and brought out Rahab, her father, mother, brothers, and all the other relatives who were with her. They moved her whole family to a safe place near the camp of Israel.

²⁴Then the Israelites burned the town and everything in it. Only the things made from silver, gold, bronze, or iron were kept for the treasury of the LORD's house. ²⁵So Joshua spared Rahab the prostitute and her relatives who were with her in the house, because she had hidden the spies Joshua sent to Jericho. And she lives among the Israelites to this day.

²⁶At that time Joshua invoked this curse:

"May the curse of the LORD fall on anyone
    who tries to rebuild the town of Jericho.
At the cost of his firstborn son,
    he will lay its foundation.
At the cost of his youngest son,
    he will set up its gates."

²⁷So the LORD was with Joshua, and his reputation spread throughout the land.

Ai Defeats the Israelites

7 But Israel violated the instructions about the things set apart for the LORD.* A man named Achan had stolen some of these dedicated things, so the LORD was very angry with the Israelites. Achan was the son of Carmi, a descendant of Zimri* son of Zerah, of the tribe of Judah.

²Joshua sent some of his men from Jericho to spy out the town of Ai, east of Bethel, near Beth-aven. ³When they returned, they told Joshua, "There's no need for all of us to go up there; it won't take more than two or three

---

6:17 The Hebrew term used here refers to the complete consecration of things or people to the LORD, either by destroying them or by giving them as an offering; similarly in 6:18, 21.   7:1a The Hebrew term used here refers to the complete consecration of things or people to the LORD, either by destroying them or by giving them as an offering; similarly in 7:11, 12, 13, 15.   7:1b As in parallel text at 1 Chr 2:6; Hebrew reads Zabdi. Also in 7:17, 18.

thousand men to attack Ai. Since there are so few of them, don't make all our people struggle to go up there."

4So approximately 3,000 warriors were sent, but they were soundly defeated. The men of Ai 5chased the Israelites from the town gate as far as the quarries,* and they killed about thirty-six who were retreating down the slope. The Israelites were paralyzed with fear at this turn of events, and their courage melted away.

6Joshua and the elders of Israel tore their clothing in dismay, threw dust on their heads, and bowed face down to the ground before the Ark of the LORD until evening. 7Then Joshua cried out, "Oh, Sovereign LORD, why did you bring us across the Jordan River if you are going to let the Amorites kill us? If only we had been content to stay on the other side! 8Lord, what can I say now that Israel has fled from its enemies? 9For when the Canaanites and all the other people living in the land hear about it, they will surround us and wipe our name off the face of the earth. And then what will happen to the honor of your great name?"

10But the LORD said to Joshua, "Get up! Why are you lying on your face like this? 11Israel has sinned and broken my covenant! They have stolen some of the things that I commanded must be set apart for me. And they have not only stolen them but have lied about it and hidden the things among their own belongings. 12That is why the Israelites are running from their enemies in defeat. For now Israel itself has been set apart for destruction. I will not remain with you any longer unless you destroy the things among you that were set apart for destruction.

13"Get up! Command the people to purify themselves in preparation for tomorrow. For this is what the LORD, the God of Israel, says: Hidden among you, O Israel, are things set apart for the LORD. You will never defeat your enemies until you remove these things from among you.

14"In the morning you must present yourselves by tribes, and the LORD will point out the tribe to which the guilty man belongs. That tribe must come forward with its clans, and the LORD will point out the guilty clan. That clan will then come forward, and the LORD will point out the guilty family. Finally, each member of the guilty family must come forward one by one. 15The one who has stolen what was set apart for destruction will himself be burned

with fire, along with everything he has, for he has broken the covenant of the LORD and has done a horrible thing in Israel."

Achan's Sin

16Early the next morning Joshua brought the tribes of Israel before the LORD, and the tribe of Judah was singled out. 17Then the clans of Judah came forward, and the clan of Zerah was singled out. Then the families of Zerah came forward, and the family of Zimri was singled out. 18Every member of Zimri's family was brought forward person by person, and Achan was singled out.

19Then Joshua said to Achan, "My son, give glory to the LORD, the God of Israel, by telling the truth. Make your confession and tell me what you have done. Don't hide it from me."

20Achan replied, "It is true! I have sinned against the LORD, the God of Israel. 21Among the plunder I saw a beautiful robe from Babylon,* 200 silver coins,* and a bar of gold weighing more than a pound.* I wanted them so much that I took them. They are hidden in the ground beneath my tent, with the silver buried deeper than the rest."

22So Joshua sent some men to make a search. They ran to the tent and found the stolen goods hidden there, just as Achan had said, with the silver buried beneath the rest. 23They took the things from the tent and brought them to Joshua and all the Israelites. Then they laid them on the ground in the presence of the LORD.

24Then Joshua and all the Israelites took Achan, the silver, the robe, the bar of gold, his sons, daughters, cattle, donkeys, sheep, goats, tent, and everything he had, and they brought them to the valley of Achor. 25Then Joshua said to Achan, "Why have you brought trouble on us? The LORD will now bring trouble on you." And all the Israelites stoned Achan and his family and burned their bodies. 26They piled a great heap of stones over Achan, which remains to this day. That is why the place has been called the Valley of Trouble* ever since. So the LORD was no longer angry.

The Israelites Defeat Ai

8 Then the LORD said to Joshua, "Do not be afraid or discouraged. Take all your fighting men and attack Ai, for I have given you the king of Ai, his people, his town, and his land. 2You will destroy them as you destroyed Jericho and its king. But this time you may keep

---

7:5 Or as far as Shebarim.   7:21a Hebrew Shinar.   7:21b Hebrew 200 shekels of silver, about 5 pounds or 2.3 kilograms in weight.   7:21c Hebrew 50 shekels, about 20 ounces or 570 grams in weight.   7:26 Hebrew valley of Achor.

the plunder and the livestock for yourselves. Set an ambush behind the town."

³So Joshua and all the fighting men set out to attack Ai. Joshua chose 30,000 of his best warriors and sent them out at night ⁴with these orders: "Hide in ambush close behind the town and be ready for action. ⁵When our main army attacks, the men of Ai will come out to fight as they did before, and we will run away from them. ⁶We will let them chase us until we have drawn them away from the town. For they will say, 'The Israelites are running away from us as they did before.' Then, while we are running from them, ⁷you will jump up from your ambush and take possession of the town, for the Lord your God will give it to you. ⁸Set the town on fire, as the Lord has commanded. You have your orders."

⁹So they left and went to the place of ambush between Bethel and the west side of Ai. But Joshua remained among the people in the camp that night. ¹⁰Early the next morning Joshua roused his men and started toward Ai, accompanied by the elders of Israel. ¹¹All the fighting men who were with Joshua marched in front of the town and camped on the north side of Ai, with a valley between them and the town. ¹²That night Joshua sent about 5,000 men to lie in ambush between Bethel and Ai, on the west side of the town. ¹³So they stationed the main army north of the town and the ambush west of the town. Joshua himself spent that night in the valley.

¹⁴When the king of Ai saw the Israelites across the valley, he and all his army hurried out early in the morning and attacked the Israelites at a place overlooking the Jordan Valley.* But he didn't realize there was an ambush behind the town. ¹⁵Joshua and the Israelite army fled toward the wilderness as though they were badly beaten. ¹⁶Then all the men in the town were called out to chase after them. In this way, they were lured away from the town. ¹⁷There was not a man left in Ai or Bethel* who did not chase after the Israelites, and the town was left wide open.

¹⁸Then the Lord said to Joshua, "Point the spear in your hand toward Ai, for I will hand the town over to you." Joshua did as he was commanded. ¹⁹As soon as Joshua gave this signal, all the men in ambush jumped up from their position and poured into the town. They quickly captured it and set it on fire.

²⁰When the men of Ai looked behind them, smoke from the town was filling the sky, and they had nowhere to go. For the Israelites who had fled in the direction of the wilderness now turned on their pursuers. ²¹When Joshua and all the other Israelites saw that the ambush had succeeded and that smoke was rising from the town, they turned and attacked the men of Ai. ²²Meanwhile, the Israelites who were inside the town came out and attacked the enemy from the rear. So the men of Ai were caught in the middle, with Israelite fighters on both sides. Israel attacked them, and not a single person survived or escaped. ²³Only the king of Ai was taken alive and brought to Joshua.

²⁴When the Israelite army finished chasing and killing all the men of Ai in the open fields, they went back and finished off everyone inside. ²⁵So the entire population of Ai, including men and women, was wiped out that day—12,000 in all. ²⁶For Joshua kept holding out his spear until everyone who had lived in Ai was completely destroyed.* ²⁷Only the livestock and the treasures of the town were not destroyed, for the Israelites kept these as plunder for themselves, as the Lord had commanded Joshua. ²⁸So Joshua burned the town of Ai,* and it became a permanent mound of ruins, desolate to this very day.

²⁹Joshua impaled the king of Ai on a sharpened pole and left him there until evening. At sunset the Israelites took down the body, as Joshua commanded, and threw it in front of the town gate. They piled a great heap of stones over him that can still be seen today.

The Lord's Covenant Renewed

³⁰Then Joshua built an altar to the Lord, the God of Israel, on Mount Ebal. ³¹He followed the commands that Moses the Lord's servant had written in the Book of Instruction: "Make me an altar from stones that are uncut and have not been shaped with iron tools."* Then on the altar they presented burnt offerings and peace offerings to the Lord. ³²And as the Israelites watched, Joshua copied onto the stones of the altar* the instructions Moses had given them.

³³Then all the Israelites—foreigners and native-born alike—along with the elders, officers, and judges, were divided into two groups. One group stood in front of Mount Gerizim, the other in front of Mount Ebal. Each group faced the other, and between them

---

8:14 Hebrew *the Arabah.*   8:17 Some manuscripts lack *or Bethel.*   8:26 The Hebrew term used here refers to the complete consecration of things or people to the Lord, either by destroying them or by giving them as an offering.   8:28 *Ai* means "ruin."   8:31 Exod 20:25; Deut 27:5-6.   8:32 Hebrew *onto the stones.*

stood the Levitical priests carrying the Ark of the LORD's Covenant. This was all done according to the commands that Moses, the servant of the LORD, had previously given for blessing the people of Israel.

34Joshua then read to them all the blessings and curses Moses had written in the Book of Instruction. 35Every word of every command that Moses had ever given was read to the entire assembly of Israel, including the women and children and the foreigners who lived among them.

The Gibeonites Deceive Israel

9 Now all the kings west of the Jordan River heard about what had happened. These were the kings of the Hittites, Amorites, Canaanites, Perizzites, Hivites, and Jebusites, who lived in the hill country, in the western foothills,* and along the coast of the Mediterranean Sea* as far north as the Lebanon mountains. 2These kings combined their armies to fight as one against Joshua and the Israelites.

3But when the people of Gibeon heard what Joshua had done to Jericho and Ai, 4they resorted to deception to save themselves. They sent ambassadors to Joshua, loading their donkeys with weathered saddlebags and old, patched wineskins. 5They put on worn-out, patched sandals and ragged clothes. And the bread they took with them was dry and moldy. 6When they arrived at the camp of Israel at Gilgal, they told Joshua and the men of Israel, "We have come from a distant land to ask you to make a peace treaty with us."

7The Israelites replied to these Hivites, "How do we know you don't live nearby? For if you do, we cannot make a treaty with you."

8They replied, "We are your servants."

"But who are you?" Joshua demanded. "Where do you come from?"

9They answered, "Your servants have come from a very distant country. We have heard of the might of the LORD your God and of all he did in Egypt. 10We have also heard what he did to the two Amorite kings east of the Jordan River—King Sihon of Heshbon and King Og of Bashan (who lived in Ashtaroth). 11So our elders and all our people instructed us, 'Take supplies for a long journey. Go meet with the people of Israel and tell them, "We are your servants; please make a treaty with us."'

12"This bread was hot from the ovens when we left our homes. But now, as you can see, it is dry and moldy. 13These wineskins were new when we filled them, but now they are old and split open. And our clothing and sandals are worn out from our very long journey."

14So the Israelites examined their food, but they did not consult the LORD. 15Then Joshua made a peace treaty with them and guaranteed their safety, and the leaders of the community ratified their agreement with a binding oath.

16Three days after making the treaty, they learned that these people actually lived nearby! 17The Israelites set out at once to investigate and reached their towns in three days. The names of these towns were Gibeon, Kephirah, Beeroth, and Kiriath-jearim. 18But the Israelites did not attack the towns, for the Israelite leaders had made a vow to them in the name of the LORD, the God of Israel.

The people of Israel grumbled against their leaders because of the treaty. 19But the leaders replied, "Since we have sworn an oath in the presence of the LORD, the God of Israel, we cannot touch them. 20This is what we must do. We must let them live, for divine anger would come upon us if we broke our oath. 21Let them live." So they made them woodcutters and water carriers for the entire community, as the Israelite leaders directed.

22Joshua called together the Gibeonites and said, "Why did you lie to us? Why did you say that you live in a distant land when you live right here among us? 23May you be cursed! From now on you will always be servants who cut wood and carry water for the house of my God."

24They replied, "We did it because we—your servants—were clearly told that the LORD your God commanded his servant Moses to give you this entire land and to destroy all the people living in it. So we feared greatly for our lives because of you. That is why we have done this. 25Now we are at your mercy—do to us whatever you think is right."

26So Joshua did not allow the people of Israel to kill them. 27But that day he made the Gibeonites the woodcutters and water carriers for the community of Israel and for the altar of the LORD—wherever the LORD would choose to build it. And that is what they do to this day.

Israel Defeats the Southern Armies

10 Adoni-zedek, king of Jerusalem, heard that Joshua had captured and completely destroyed* Ai and killed its king, just

---

9:1a Hebrew *the Shephelah*.   9:1b Hebrew *the Great Sea*.   10:1 The Hebrew term used here refers to the complete consecration of things or people to the LORD, either by destroying them or by giving them as an offering; also in 10:28, 35, 37, 39, 40.

as he had destroyed the town of Jericho and killed its king. He also learned that the Gibeonites had made peace with Israel and were now their allies. 2He and his people became very afraid when they heard all this because Gibeon was a large town—as large as the royal cities and larger than Ai. And the Gibeonite men were strong warriors.

3So King Adoni-zedek of Jerusalem sent messengers to several other kings: Hoham of Hebron, Piram of Jarmuth, Japhia of Lachish, and Debir of Eglon. 4"Come and help me destroy Gibeon," he urged them, "for they have made peace with Joshua and the people of Israel." 5So these five Amorite kings combined their armies for a united attack. They moved all their troops into place and attacked Gibeon.

6The men of Gibeon quickly sent messengers to Joshua at his camp in Gilgal. "Don't abandon your servants now!" they pleaded. "Come at once! Save us! Help us! For all the Amorite kings who live in the hill country have joined forces to attack us."

7So Joshua and his entire army, including his best warriors, left Gilgal and set out for Gibeon. 8"Do not be afraid of them," the LORD said to Joshua, "for I have given you victory over them. Not a single one of them will be able to stand up to you."

9Joshua traveled all night from Gilgal and took the Amorite armies by surprise. 10The LORD threw them into a panic, and the Israelites slaughtered great numbers of them at Gibeon. Then the Israelites chased the enemy along the road to Beth-horon, killing them all along the way to Azekah and Makkedah. 11As the Amorites retreated down the road from Beth-horon, the LORD destroyed them with a terrible hailstorm from heaven that continued until they reached Azekah. The hail killed more of the enemy than the Israelites killed with the sword.

12On the day the LORD gave the Israelites victory over the Amorites, Joshua prayed to the LORD in front of all the people of Israel. He said,

"Let the sun stand still over Gibeon,
   and the moon over the valley of Aijalon."

13So the sun stood still and the moon stayed in place until the nation of Israel had defeated its enemies.

Is this event not recorded in *The Book of Jashar**? The sun stayed in the middle of the sky,

and it did not set as on a normal day.* 14There has never been a day like this one before or since, when the LORD answered such a prayer. Surely the LORD fought for Israel that day!

15Then Joshua and the Israelite army returned to their camp at Gilgal.

Joshua Kills the Five Southern Kings

16During the battle the five kings escaped and hid in a cave at Makkedah. 17When Joshua heard that they had been found, 18he issued this command: "Cover the opening of the cave with large rocks, and place guards at the entrance to keep the kings inside. 19The rest of you continue chasing the enemy and cut them down from the rear. Don't give them a chance to get back to their towns, for the LORD your God has given you victory over them."

20So Joshua and the Israelite army continued the slaughter and completely crushed the enemy. They totally wiped out the five armies except for a tiny remnant that managed to reach their fortified towns. 21Then the Israelites returned safely to Joshua in the camp at Makkedah. After that, no one dared to speak even a word against Israel.

22Then Joshua said, "Remove the rocks covering the opening of the cave, and bring the five kings to me." 23So they brought the five kings out of the cave—the kings of Jerusalem, Hebron, Jarmuth, Lachish, and Eglon. 24When they brought them out, Joshua told the commanders of his army, "Come and put your feet on the kings' necks." And they did as they were told.

25"Don't ever be afraid or discouraged," Joshua told his men. "Be strong and courageous, for the LORD is going to do this to all of your enemies." 26Then Joshua killed each of the five kings and impaled them on five sharpened poles, where they hung until evening.

27As the sun was going down, Joshua gave instructions for the bodies of the kings to be taken down from the poles and thrown into the cave where they had been hiding. Then they covered the opening of the cave with a pile of large rocks, which remains to this very day.

Israel Destroys the Southern Towns

28That same day Joshua captured and destroyed the town of Makkedah. He killed everyone in it, including the king, leaving no survivors. He destroyed them all, and he killed the king of Makkedah as he had killed the king of Jericho. 29Then Joshua and the Israelites went to

10:13a Or *The Book of the Upright.*   10:13b Or *did not set for about a whole day.*

Libnah and attacked it. ³⁰There, too, the LORD gave them the town and its king. He killed everyone in it, leaving no survivors. Then Joshua killed the king of Libnah as he had killed the king of Jericho.

³¹From Libnah, Joshua and the Israelites went to Lachish and attacked it. ³²Here again, the LORD gave them Lachish. Joshua took it on the second day and killed everyone in it, just as he had done at Libnah. ³³During the attack on Lachish, King Horam of Gezer arrived with his army to help defend the town. But Joshua's men killed him and his army, leaving no survivors.

³⁴Then Joshua and the Israelite army went on to Eglon and attacked it. ³⁵They captured it that day and killed everyone in it. He completely destroyed everyone, just as he had done at Lachish. ³⁶From Eglon, Joshua and the Israelite army went up to Hebron and attacked it. ³⁷They captured the town and killed everyone in it, including its king, leaving no survivors. They did the same thing to all of its surrounding villages. And just as he had done at Eglon, he completely destroyed the entire population.

³⁸Then Joshua and the Israelites turned back and attacked Debir. ³⁹He captured the town, its king, and all of its surrounding villages. He completely destroyed everyone in it, leaving no survivors. He did to Debir and its king just what he had done to Hebron and to Libnah and its king.

⁴⁰So Joshua conquered the whole region— the kings and people of the hill country, the Negev, the western foothills,* and the mountain slopes. He completely destroyed everyone in the land, leaving no survivors, just as the LORD, the God of Israel, had commanded. ⁴¹Joshua slaughtered them from Kadesh-barnea to Gaza and from the region around the town of Goshen up to Gibeon. ⁴²Joshua conquered all these kings and their land in a single campaign, for the LORD, the God of Israel, was fighting for his people.

⁴³Then Joshua and the Israelite army returned to their camp at Gilgal.

Israel Defeats the Northern Armies

11 When King Jabin of Hazor heard what had happened, he sent messages to the following kings: King Jobab of Madon; the king of Shimron; the king of Acshaph; ²all the kings of the northern hill country; the kings in the Jordan Valley south of Galilee*; the kings in the

Galilean foothills*; the kings of Naphoth-dor on the west; ³the kings of Canaan, both east and west; the kings of the Amorites, the Hittites, the Perizzites, the Jebusites in the hill country, and the Hivites in the towns on the slopes of Mount Hermon in the land of Mizpah.

⁴All these kings came out to fight. Their combined armies formed a vast horde. And with all their horses and chariots, they covered the landscape like the sand on the seashore. ⁵The kings joined forces and established their camp around the water near Merom to fight against Israel.

⁶Then the LORD said to Joshua, "Do not be afraid of them. By this time tomorrow I will hand all of them over to Israel as dead men. Then you must cripple their horses and burn their chariots."

⁷So Joshua and all his fighting men traveled to the water near Merom and attacked suddenly. ⁸And the LORD gave them victory over their enemies. The Israelites chased them as far as Greater Sidon and Misrephoth-maim, and eastward into the valley of Mizpah, until not one enemy warrior was left alive. ⁹Then Joshua crippled the horses and burned all the chariots, as the LORD had instructed.

¹⁰Joshua then turned back and captured Hazor and killed its king. (Hazor had at one time been the capital of all these kingdoms.) ¹¹The Israelites completely destroyed* every living thing in the city, leaving no survivors. Not a single person was spared. And then Joshua burned the city.

¹²Joshua slaughtered all the other kings and their people, completely destroying them, just as Moses, the servant of the LORD, had commanded. ¹³But the Israelites did not burn any of the towns built on mounds except Hazor, which Joshua burned. ¹⁴And the Israelites took all the plunder and livestock of the ravaged towns for themselves. But they killed all the people, leaving no survivors. ¹⁵As the LORD had commanded his servant Moses, so Moses commanded Joshua. And Joshua did as he was told, carefully obeying all the commands that the LORD had given to Moses.

¹⁶So Joshua conquered the entire region— the hill country, the entire Negev, the whole area around the town of Goshen, the western foothills, the Jordan Valley,* the mountains of Israel, and the Galilean foothills. ¹⁷The Israelite territory now extended all the way from Mount

---

10:40 Hebrew *the Shephelah.*　11:2a Hebrew *in the Arabah south of Kinnereth.*　11:2b Hebrew *the Shephelah;* also in 11:16.
11:11 The Hebrew term used here refers to the complete consecration of things or people to the LORD, either by destroying them or by giving them as an offering; also in 11:12, 20, 21.　11:16 Hebrew *the Shephelah, the Arabah.*

Halak, which leads up to Seir in the south, as far north as Baal-gad at the foot of Mount Hermon in the valley of Lebanon. Joshua killed all the kings of those territories, [18]waging war for a long time to accomplish this. [19]No one in this region made peace with the Israelites except the Hivites of Gibeon. All the others were defeated. [20]For the LORD hardened their hearts and caused them to fight the Israelites. So they were completely destroyed without mercy, as the LORD had commanded Moses.

[21]During this period Joshua destroyed all the descendants of Anak, who lived in the hill country of Hebron, Debir, Anab, and the entire hill country of Judah and Israel. He killed them all and completely destroyed their towns. [22]None of the descendants of Anak were left in all the land of Israel, though some still remained in Gaza, Gath, and Ashdod.

[23]So Joshua took control of the entire land, just as the LORD had instructed Moses. He gave it to the people of Israel as their special possession, dividing the land among the tribes. So the land finally had rest from war.

Kings Defeated East of the Jordan

12 These are the kings east of the Jordan River who had been killed by the Israelites and whose land was taken. Their territory extended from the Arnon Gorge to Mount Hermon and included all the land east of the Jordan Valley.*

[2]King Sihon of the Amorites, who lived in Heshbon, was defeated. His kingdom included Aroer, on the edge of the Arnon Gorge, and extended from the middle of the Arnon Gorge to the Jabbok River, which serves as a border for the Ammonites. This territory included the southern half of the territory of Gilead. [3]Sihon also controlled the Jordan Valley and regions to the east—from as far north as the Sea of Galilee to as far south as the Dead Sea,* including the road to Beth-jeshimoth and southward to the slopes of Pisgah.

[4]King Og of Bashan, the last of the Rephaites, lived at Ashtaroth and Edrei. [5]He ruled a territory stretching from Mount Hermon to Salecah in the north and to all of Bashan in the east, and westward to the borders of the kingdoms of Geshur and Maacah. This territory included the northern half of Gilead, as far as the boundary of King Sihon of Heshbon.

[6]Moses, the servant of the LORD, and the Israelites had destroyed the people of King Sihon and King Og. And Moses gave their land as a possession to the tribes of Reuben, Gad, and the half-tribe of Manasseh.

Kings Defeated West of the Jordan

[7]The following is a list of the kings that Joshua and the Israelite armies defeated on the west side of the Jordan, from Baal-gad in the valley of Lebanon to Mount Halak, which leads up to Seir. (Joshua gave this land to the tribes of Israel as their possession, [8]including the hill country, the western foothills,* the Jordan Valley, the mountain slopes, the Judean wilderness, and the Negev. The people who lived in this region were the Hittites, the Amorites, the Canaanites, the Perizzites, the Hivites, and the Jebusites.) These are the kings Israel defeated:

[9] The king of Jericho
    The king of Ai, near Bethel
[10] The king of Jerusalem
    The king of Hebron
[11] The king of Jarmuth
    The king of Lachish
[12] The king of Eglon
    The king of Gezer
[13] The king of Debir
    The king of Geder
[14] The king of Hormah
    The king of Arad
[15] The king of Libnah
    The king of Adullam
[16] The king of Makkedah
    The king of Bethel
[17] The king of Tappuah
    The king of Hepher
[18] The king of Aphek
    The king of Lasharon
[19] The king of Madon
    The king of Hazor
[20] The king of Shimron-meron
    The king of Acshaph
[21] The king of Taanach
    The king of Megiddo
[22] The king of Kedesh
    The king of Jokneam in Carmel
[23] The king of Dor in the town of
       Naphoth-dor*
    The king of Goyim in Gilgal*
[24] The king of Tirzah.

In all, thirty-one kings were defeated.

12:1 Hebrew *the Arabah;* also in 12:3, 8.   12:3 Hebrew *from the Sea of Kinnereth to the Sea of the Arabah, which is the Salt Sea.*
12:8 Hebrew *the Shephelah.*   12:23a Hebrew *Naphath-dor,* a variant spelling of Naphoth-dor.   12:23b Greek version reads *Goyim in Galilee.*

The Land Yet to Be Conquered

13 When Joshua was an old man, the LORD said to him, "You are growing old, and much land remains to be conquered. ²This is the territory that remains: all the regions of the Philistines and the Geshurites, ³and the larger territory of the Canaanites, extending from the stream of Shihor on the border of Egypt, northward to the boundary of Ekron. It includes the territory of the five Philistine rulers of Gaza, Ashdod, Ashkelon, Gath, and Ekron. The land of the Avvites ⁴in the south also remains to be conquered. In the north, the following area has not yet been conquered: all the land of the Canaanites, including Mearah (which belongs to the Sidonians), stretching northward to Aphek on the border of the Amorites; ⁵the land of the Gebalites and all of the Lebanon mountain area to the east, from Baal-gad below Mount Hermon to Lebo-hamath; ⁶and all the hill country from Lebanon to Misrephoth-maim, including all the land of the Sidonians.

"I myself will drive these people out of the land ahead of the Israelites. So be sure to give this land to Israel as a special possession, just as I have commanded you. ⁷Include all this territory as Israel's possession when you divide this land among the nine tribes and the half-tribe of Manasseh."

The Land Divided East of the Jordan

⁸Half the tribe of Manasseh and the tribes of Reuben and Gad had already received their grants of land on the east side of the Jordan, for Moses, the servant of the LORD, had previously assigned this land to them.

⁹Their territory extended from Aroer on the edge of the Arnon Gorge (including the town in the middle of the gorge) to the plain beyond Medeba, as far as Dibon. ¹⁰It also included all the towns of King Sihon of the Amorites, who had reigned in Heshbon, and extended as far as the borders of Ammon. ¹¹It included Gilead, the territory of the kingdoms of Geshur and Maacah, all of Mount Hermon, all of Bashan as far as Salecah, ¹²and all the territory of King Og of Bashan, who had reigned in Ashtaroth and Edrei. King Og was the last of the Rephaites, for Moses had attacked them and driven them out. ¹³But the Israelites failed to drive out the people of Geshur

and Maacah, so they continue to live among the Israelites to this day.

An Allotment for the Tribe of Levi

¹⁴Moses did not assign any allotment of land to the tribe of Levi. Instead, as the LORD had promised them, their allotment came from the offerings burned on the altar to the LORD, the God of Israel.

The Land Given to the Tribe of Reuben

¹⁵Moses had assigned the following area to the clans of the tribe of Reuben.

¹⁶Their territory extended from Aroer on the edge of the Arnon Gorge (including the town in the middle of the gorge) to the plain beyond Medeba. ¹⁷It included Heshbon and the other towns on the plain—Dibon, Bamoth-baal, Beth-baal-meon, ¹⁸Jahaz, Kedemoth, Mephaath, ¹⁹Kiriathaim, Sibmah, Zereth-shahar on the hill above the valley, ²⁰Beth-peor, the slopes of Pisgah, and Beth-jeshimoth.

²¹The land of Reuben also included all the towns of the plain and the entire kingdom of Sihon. Sihon was the Amorite king who had reigned in Heshbon and was killed by Moses along with the leaders of Midian—Evi, Rekem, Zur, Hur, and Reba—princes living in the region who were allied with Sihon. ²²The Israelites had also killed Balaam son of Beor, who used magic to tell the future. ²³The Jordan River marked the western boundary for the tribe of Reuben. The towns and their surrounding villages in this area were given as a homeland to the clans of the tribe of Reuben.

The Land Given to the Tribe of Gad

²⁴Moses had assigned the following area to the clans of the tribe of Gad.

²⁵Their territory included Jazer, all the towns of Gilead, and half of the land of Ammon, as far as the town of Aroer just west of* Rabbah. ²⁶It extended from Heshbon to Ramath-mizpeh and Betonim, and from Mahanaim to the territory of Lo-debar.* ²⁷In the valley were Beth-haram, Beth-nimrah, Succoth, Zaphon, and the rest of the kingdom of King Sihon of Heshbon. The western boundary ran

---

13:25 Hebrew *in front of.*   13:26 Hebrew *Li-debir,* apparently a variant spelling of Lo-debar (compare 2 Sam 9:4; 17:27; Amos 6:13).

along the Jordan River, extended as far north as the tip of the Sea of Galilee,* and then turned eastward. 28The towns and their surrounding villages in this area were given as a homeland to the clans of the tribe of Gad.

The Land Given to the Half-Tribe of Manasseh

29Moses had assigned the following area to the clans of the half-tribe of Manasseh.

30Their territory extended from Mahanaim, including all of Bashan, all the former kingdom of King Og, and the sixty towns of Jair in Bashan. 31It also included half of Gilead and King Og's royal cities of Ashtaroth and Edrei. All this was given to the clans of the descendants of Makir, who was Manasseh's son.

32These are the allotments Moses had made while he was on the plains of Moab, across the Jordan River, east of Jericho. 33But Moses gave no allotment of land to the tribe of Levi, for the LORD, the God of Israel, had promised that he himself would be their allotment.

The Land Divided West of the Jordan

14 The remaining tribes of Israel received land in Canaan as allotted by Eleazar the priest, Joshua son of Nun, and the tribal leaders. 2These nine and a half tribes received their grants of land by means of sacred lots, in accordance with the LORD's command through Moses. 3Moses had already given a grant of land to the two and a half tribes on the east side of the Jordan River, but he had given the Levites no such allotment. 4The descendants of Joseph had become two separate tribes—Manasseh and Ephraim. And the Levites were given no land at all, only towns to live in with surrounding pasturelands for their livestock and all their possessions. 5So the land was distributed in strict accordance with the LORD's commands to Moses.

Caleb Requests His Land

6A delegation from the tribe of Judah, led by Caleb son of Jephunneh the Kenizzite, came to Joshua at Gilgal. Caleb said to Joshua, "Remember what the LORD said to Moses, the man of God, about you and me when we were at Kadesh-barnea. 7I was forty years old when Moses, the servant of the LORD, sent me from Kadesh-barnea to explore the land of Canaan. I returned and gave an honest report, 8but my brothers who went with me frightened the people from entering the Promised Land. For my part, I wholeheartedly followed the LORD my God. 9So that day Moses solemnly promised me, 'The land of Canaan on which you were just walking will be your grant of land and that of your descendants forever, because you wholeheartedly followed the LORD my God.'

10"Now, as you can see, the LORD has kept me alive and well as he promised for all these forty-five years since Moses made this promise—even while Israel wandered in the wilderness. Today I am eighty-five years old. 11I am as strong now as I was when Moses sent me on that journey, and I can still travel and fight as well as I could then. 12So give me the hill country that the LORD promised me. You will remember that as scouts we found the descendants of Anak living there in great, walled towns. But if the LORD is with me, I will drive them out of the land, just as the LORD said."

13So Joshua blessed Caleb son of Jephunneh and gave Hebron to him as his portion of land. 14Hebron still belongs to the descendants of Caleb son of Jephunneh the Kenizzite because he wholeheartedly followed the LORD, the God of Israel. 15(Previously Hebron had been called Kiriath-arba. It had been named after Arba, a great hero of the descendants of Anak.)

And the land had rest from war.

The Land Given to the Tribe of Judah

15 The allotment for the clans of the tribe of Judah reached southward to the border of Edom, as far south as the wilderness of Zin.

2The southern boundary began at the south bay of the Dead Sea,* 3ran south of Scorpion Pass* into the wilderness of Zin, and then went south of Kadesh-barnea to Hezron. Then it went up to Addar, where it turned toward Karka. 4From there it passed to Azmon until it finally reached the Brook of Egypt, which it followed to the Mediterranean Sea.* This was their* southern boundary.

5The eastern boundary extended along the Dead Sea to the mouth of the Jordan River.

The northern boundary began at the

13:27 Hebrew *Sea of Kinnereth*.   15:2 Hebrew *the Salt Sea*; also in 15:5.   15:3 Hebrew *Akrabbim*.   15:4a Hebrew *the sea*; also in 15:11.   15:4b Hebrew *your*.

bay where the Jordan River empties into the Dead Sea, ⁶went up from there to Beth-hoglah, then proceeded north of Beth-arabah to the Stone of Bohan. (Bohan was Reuben's son.) ⁷From that point it went through the valley of Achor to Debir, turning north toward Gilgal, which is across from the slopes of Adummim on the south side of the valley. From there the boundary extended to the springs at En-shemesh and on to En-rogel. ⁸The boundary then passed through the valley of Ben-Hinnom, along the southern slopes of the Jebusites, where the city of Jerusalem is located. Then it went west to the top of the mountain above the valley of Hinnom, and on up to the northern end of the valley of Rephaim. ⁹From there the boundary extended from the top of the mountain to the spring at the waters of Nephtoah,* and from there to the towns on Mount Ephron. Then it turned toward Baalah (that is, Kiriath-jearim). ¹⁰The boundary circled west of Baalah to Mount Seir, passed along to the town of Kesalon on the northern slope of Mount Jearim, and went down to Beth-shemesh and on to Timnah. ¹¹The boundary then proceeded to the slope of the hill north of Ekron, where it turned toward Shikkeron and Mount Baalah. It passed Jabneel and ended at the Mediterranean Sea.

¹²The western boundary was the shoreline of the Mediterranean Sea.*

These are the boundaries for the clans of the tribe of Judah.

The Land Given to Caleb

¹³The LORD commanded Joshua to assign some of Judah's territory to Caleb son of Jephunneh. So Caleb was given the town of Kiriath-arba (that is, Hebron), which had been named after Anak's ancestor. ¹⁴Caleb drove out the three groups of Anakites—the descendants of Sheshai, Ahiman, and Talmai, the sons of Anak. ¹⁵From there he went to fight against the people living in the town of Debir (formerly called Kiriath-sepher). ¹⁶Caleb said, "I will give my daughter Acsah in marriage to the one who attacks and captures Kiriath-sepher." ¹⁷Othniel, the son of Caleb's brother Kenaz, was the one who conquered it, so Acsah became Othniel's wife.

¹⁸When Acsah married Othniel, she urged him* to ask her father for a field. As she got down off her donkey, Caleb asked her, "What's the matter?"

¹⁹She said, "Give me another gift. You have already given me land in the Negev; now please give me springs of water, too." So Caleb gave her the upper and lower springs.

The Towns Allotted to Judah

²⁰This was the homeland allocated to the clans of the tribe of Judah.

²¹The towns of Judah situated along the borders of Edom in the extreme south were Kabzeel, Eder, Jagur, ²²Kinah, Dimonah, Adadah, ²³Kedesh, Hazor, Ithnan, ²⁴Ziph, Telem, Bealoth, ²⁵Hazor-hadattah, Kerioth-hezron (that is, Hazor), ²⁶Amam, Shema, Moladah, ²⁷Hazar-gaddah, Heshmon, Beth-pelet, ²⁸Hazar-shual, Beersheba, Biziothiah, ²⁹Baalah, Iim, Ezem, ³⁰Eltolad, Kesil, Hormah, ³¹Ziklag, Madmannah, Sansannah, ³²Lebaoth, Shilhim, Ain, and Rimmon—twenty-nine towns with their surrounding villages.

³³The following towns situated in the western foothills* were also given to Judah: Eshtaol, Zorah, Ashnah, ³⁴Zanoah, En-gannim, Tappuah, Enam, ³⁵Jarmuth, Adullam, Socoh, Azekah, ³⁶Shaaraim, Adithaim, Gederah, and Gederothaim—fourteen towns with their surrounding villages.

³⁷Also included were Zenan, Hadashah, Migdal-gad, ³⁸Dilean, Mizpeh, Joktheel, ³⁹Lachish, Bozkath, Eglon, ⁴⁰Cabbon, Lahmam, Kitlish, ⁴¹Gederoth, Beth-dagon, Naamah, and Makkedah—sixteen towns with their surrounding villages.

⁴²Besides these, there were Libnah, Ether, Ashan, ⁴³Iphtah, Ashnah, Nezib, ⁴⁴Keilah, Aczib, and Mareshah—nine towns with their surrounding villages.

⁴⁵The territory of the tribe of Judah also included Ekron and its surrounding settlements and villages. ⁴⁶From Ekron the boundary extended west and included the towns near Ashdod with their surrounding villages. ⁴⁷It also included Ashdod with its surrounding settlements and villages and Gaza with its settlements and villages, as far as the Brook of Egypt

15:9 Or *the spring at Me-nephtoah.*   15:12 Hebrew *the Great Sea;* also in 15:47.   15:18 Some Greek manuscripts read *he urged her.*
15:33 Hebrew *the Shephelah.*

and along the coast of the Mediterranean Sea.

48Judah also received the following towns in the hill country: Shamir, Jattir, Socoh, 49Dannah, Kiriath-sannah (that is, Debir), 50Anab, Eshtemoh, Anim, 51Goshen, Holon, and Giloh—eleven towns with their surrounding villages.

52Also included were the towns of Arab, Dumah, Eshan, 53Janim, Beth-tappuah, Aphekah, 54Humtah, Kiriath-arba (that is, Hebron), and Zior—nine towns with their surrounding villages.

55Besides these, there were Maon, Carmel, Ziph, Juttah, 56Jezreel, Jokdeam, Zanoah, 57Kain, Gibeah, and Timnah—ten towns with their surrounding villages.

58In addition, there were Halhul, Beth-zur, Gedor, 59Maarath, Beth-anoth, and Eltekon—six towns with their surrounding villages.

60There were also Kiriath-baal (that is, Kiriath-jearim) and Rabbah—two towns with their surrounding villages.

61In the wilderness there were the towns of Beth-arabah, Middin, Secacah, 62Nibshan, the City of Salt, and En-gedi—six towns with their surrounding villages.

63But the tribe of Judah could not drive out the Jebusites, who lived in the city of Jerusalem, so the Jebusites live there among the people of Judah to this day.

The Land Given to Ephraim and West Manasseh

16 The allotment for the descendants of Joseph extended from the Jordan River near Jericho, east of the springs of Jericho, through the wilderness and into the hill country of Bethel. 2From Bethel (that is, Luz)* it ran over to Ataroth in the territory of the Arkites. 3Then it descended westward to the territory of the Japhletites as far as Lower Beth-horon, then to Gezer and over to the Mediterranean Sea.*

4This was the homeland allocated to the families of Joseph's sons, Manasseh and Ephraim.

The Land Given to Ephraim

5The following territory was given to the clans of the tribe of Ephraim.

The boundary of their homeland began at Ataroth-addar in the east. From there it ran to Upper Beth-horon, 6then on to the Mediterranean Sea. From Micmethath on the north, the boundary curved eastward past Taanath-shiloh to the east of Janoah. 7From Janoah it turned southward to Ataroth and Naarah, touched Jericho, and ended at the Jordan River. 8From Tappuah the boundary extended westward, following the Kanah Ravine to the Mediterranean Sea. This is the homeland allocated to the clans of the tribe of Ephraim.

9In addition, some towns with their surrounding villages in the territory allocated to the half-tribe of Manasseh were set aside for the tribe of Ephraim. 10They did not drive the Canaanites out of Gezer, however, so the people of Gezer live as slaves among the people of Ephraim to this day.

The Land Given to West Manasseh

17 The next allotment of land was given to the half-tribe of Manasseh, the descendants of Joseph's older son. Makir, the firstborn son of Manasseh, was the father of Gilead. Because his descendants were experienced soldiers, the regions of Gilead and Bashan on the east side of the Jordan had already been given to them. 2So the allotment on the west side of the Jordan was for the remaining families within the clans of the tribe of Manasseh: Abiezer, Helek, Asriel, Shechem, Hepher, and Shemida. These clans represent the male descendants of Manasseh son of Joseph.

3However, Zelophehad, a descendant of Hepher son of Gilead, son of Makir, son of Manasseh, had no sons. He had only daughters, whose names were Mahlah, Noah, Hoglah, Milcah, and Tirzah. 4These women came to Eleazar the priest, Joshua son of Nun, and the Israelite leaders and said, "The LORD commanded Moses to give us a grant of land along with the men of our tribe."

So Joshua gave them a grant of land along with their uncles, as the LORD had commanded. 5As a result, Manasseh's total allocation came to ten parcels of land, in addition to the land of Gilead and Bashan across the Jordan River, 6because the female descendants of Manasseh received a grant of land along with the male descendants. (The land of Gilead was given to the rest of the male descendants of Manasseh.)

16:2 As in Greek version (also see 18:13); Hebrew reads *From Bethel to Luz.*   16:3 Hebrew *the sea;* also in 16:6, 8.

7The boundary of the tribe of Manasseh extended from the border of Asher to Micmethath, near Shechem. Then the boundary went south from Micmethath to the settlement near the spring of Tappuah. 8The land surrounding Tappuah belonged to Manasseh, but the town of Tappuah itself, on the border of Manasseh's territory, belonged to the tribe of Ephraim. 9From the spring of Tappuah, the boundary of Manasseh followed the Kanah Ravine to the Mediterranean Sea.* Several towns south of the ravine were inside Manasseh's territory, but they actually belonged to the tribe of Ephraim. 10In general, however, the land south of the ravine belonged to Ephraim, and the land north of the ravine belonged to Manasseh. Manasseh's boundary ran along the northern side of the ravine and ended at the Mediterranean Sea. North of Manasseh was the territory of Asher, and to the east was the territory of Issachar.

11The following towns within the territory of Issachar and Asher, however, were given to Manasseh: Beth-shan,* Ibleam, Dor (that is, Naphoth-dor),* Endor, Taanach, and Megiddo, each with their surrounding settlements.

12But the descendants of Manasseh were unable to occupy these towns because the Canaanites were determined to stay in that region. 13Later, however, when the Israelites became strong enough, they forced the Canaanites to work as slaves. But they did not drive them out of the land.

14The descendants of Joseph came to Joshua and asked, "Why have you given us only one portion of land as our homeland when the LORD has blessed us with so many people?"

15Joshua replied, "If there are so many of you, and if the hill country of Ephraim is not large enough for you, clear out land for yourselves in the forest where the Perizzites and Rephaites live."

16The descendants of Joseph responded, "It's true that the hill country is not large enough for us. But all the Canaanites in the lowlands have iron chariots, both those in Beth-shan and its surrounding settlements and those in the valley of Jezreel. They are too strong for us."

17Then Joshua said to the tribes of Ephraim and Manasseh, the descendants of Joseph,

"Since you are so large and strong, you will be given more than one portion. 18The forests of the hill country will be yours as well. Clear as much of the land as you wish, and take possession of its farthest corners. And you will drive out the Canaanites from the valleys, too, even though they are strong and have iron chariots."

The Allotments of the Remaining Land

18 Now that the land was under Israelite control, the entire community of Israel gathered at Shiloh and set up the Tabernacle.* 2But there remained seven tribes who had not yet been allotted their grants of land.

3Then Joshua asked them, "How long are you going to wait before taking possession of the remaining land the LORD, the God of your ancestors, has given to you? 4Select three men from each tribe, and I will send them out to explore the land and map it out. They will then return to me with a written report of their proposed divisions of their new homeland. 5Let them divide the land into seven sections, excluding Judah's territory in the south and Joseph's territory in the north. 6And when you record the seven divisions of the land and bring them to me, I will cast sacred lots in the presence of the LORD our God to assign land to each tribe.

7"The Levites, however, will not receive any allotment of land. Their role as priests of the LORD is their allotment. And the tribes of Gad, Reuben, and the half-tribe of Manasseh won't receive any more land, for they have already received their grant of land, which Moses, the servant of the LORD, gave them on the east side of the Jordan River."

8As the men started on their way to map out the land, Joshua commanded them, "Go and explore the land and write a description of it. Then return to me, and I will assign the land to the tribes by casting sacred lots here in the presence of the LORD at Shiloh." 9The men did as they were told and mapped the entire territory into seven sections, listing the towns in each section. They made a written record and then returned to Joshua in the camp at Shiloh. 10And there at Shiloh, Joshua cast sacred lots in the presence of the LORD to determine which tribe should have each section.

The Land Given to Benjamin

11The first allotment of land went to the clans of the tribe of Benjamin. It lay between the

17:9 Hebrew the sea; also in 17:10.   17:11a Hebrew Beth-shean, a variant spelling of Beth-shan; also in 17:16.   17:11b The meaning of the Hebrew here is uncertain.   18:1 Hebrew Tent of Meeting.

territory assigned to the tribes of Judah and Joseph.

¹²The northern boundary of Benjamin's land began at the Jordan River, went north of the slope of Jericho, then west through the hill country and the wilderness of Beth-aven. ¹³From there the boundary went south to Luz (that is, Bethel) and proceeded down to Ataroth-addar on the hill that lies south of Lower Beth-horon. ¹⁴The boundary then made a turn and swung south along the western edge of the hill facing Beth-horon, ending at the village of Kiriath-baal (that is, Kiriath-jearim), a town belonging to the tribe of Judah. This was the western boundary. ¹⁵The southern boundary began at the outskirts of Kiriath-jearim. From that western point it ran* to the spring at the waters of Nephtoah,* ¹⁶and down to the base of the mountain beside the valley of Ben-Hinnom, at the northern end of the valley of Rephaim. From there it went down the valley of Hinnom, crossing south of the slope where the Jebusites lived, and continued down to En-rogel. ¹⁷From En-rogel the boundary proceeded in a northerly direction and came to En-shemesh and on to Geliloth (which is across from the slopes of Adummim). Then it went down to the Stone of Bohan. (Bohan was Reuben's son.) ¹⁸From there it passed along the north side of the slope overlooking the Jordan Valley.* The border then went down into the valley, ¹⁹ran past the north slope of Beth-hoglah, and ended at the north bay of the Dead Sea,* which is the southern end of the Jordan River. This was the southern boundary. ²⁰The eastern boundary was the Jordan River.

These were the boundaries of the homeland allocated to the clans of the tribe of Benjamin.

The Towns Given to Benjamin
²¹These were the towns given to the clans of the tribe of Benjamin.

Jericho, Beth-hoglah, Emek-keziz, ²²Beth-arabah, Zemaraim, Bethel, ²³Avvim, Parah, Ophrah, ²⁴Kephar-ammoni, Ophni, and Geba—twelve towns with their surrounding villages. ²⁵Also Gibeon, Ramah, Beeroth, ²⁶Mizpah, Kephirah, Mozah, ²⁷Rekem, Irpeel, Taralah, ²⁸Zela, Haeleph, the Jebusite town (that is, Jerusalem), Gibeah, and Kiriath-jearim*—fourteen towns with their surrounding villages.

This was the homeland allocated to the clans of the tribe of Benjamin.

The Land Given to Simeon
19 The second allotment of land went to the clans of the tribe of Simeon. Their homeland was surrounded by Judah's territory.

²Simeon's homeland included Beersheba, Sheba, Moladah, ³Hazar-shual, Balah, Ezem, ⁴Eltolad, Bethul, Hormah, ⁵Ziklag, Beth-marcaboth, Hazar-susah, ⁶Beth-lebaoth, and Sharuhen—thirteen towns with their surrounding villages. ⁷It also included Ain, Rimmon, Ether, and Ashan—four towns with their villages, ⁸including all the surrounding villages as far south as Baalath-beer (also known as Ramah of the Negev).

This was the homeland allocated to the clans of the tribe of Simeon. ⁹Their allocation of land came from part of what had been given to Judah because Judah's territory was too large for them. So the tribe of Simeon received an allocation within the territory of Judah.

The Land Given to Zebulun
¹⁰The third allotment of land went to the clans of the tribe of Zebulun.

The boundary of Zebulun's homeland started at Sarid. ¹¹From there it went west, going past Maralah, touching Dabbesheth, and proceeding to the brook east of Jokneam. ¹²In the other direction, the boundary went east from Sarid to the border of Kisloth-tabor, and from there to Daberath and up to Japhia. ¹³Then it continued east to Gath-hepher, Eth-kazin, and Rimmon and turned toward Neah. ¹⁴The northern boundary of Zebulun passed Hannathon and ended at the valley

---

18:15a Or *From there it went to Mozah*. The meaning of the Hebrew is uncertain.   18:15b Or *the spring at Me-nephtoah*.
18:18 Hebrew *overlooking the Arabah*, or *overlooking Beth-arabah*.   18:19 Hebrew *Salt Sea*.   18:28 As in Greek version; Hebrew reads *Kiriath*.

of Iphtah-el. [15]The towns in these areas included Kattath, Nahalal, Shimron, Idalah, and Bethlehem—twelve towns with their surrounding villages.

[16]The homeland allocated to the clans of the tribe of Zebulun included these towns and their surrounding villages.

The Land Given to Issachar
[17]The fourth allotment of land went to the clans of the tribe of Issachar.

[18]Its boundaries included the following towns: Jezreel, Kesulloth, Shunem, [19]Hapharaim, Shion, Anaharath, [20]Rabbith, Kishion, Ebez, [21]Remeth, En-gannim, En-haddah, and Beth-pazzez. [22]The boundary also touched Tabor, Shahazumah, and Beth-shemesh, ending at the Jordan River—sixteen towns with their surrounding villages.

[23]The homeland allocated to the clans of the tribe of Issachar included these towns and their surrounding villages.

The Land Given to Asher
[24]The fifth allotment of land went to the clans of the tribe of Asher.

[25]Its boundaries included these towns: Helkath, Hali, Beten, Acshaph, [26]Allammelech, Amad, and Mishal. The boundary on the west touched Carmel and Shihor-libnath, [27]then it turned east toward Beth-dagon, and ran as far as Zebulun in the valley of Iphtah-el, going north to Beth-emek and Neiel. It then continued north to Cabul, [28]Abdon,* Rehob, Hammon, Kanah, and as far as Greater Sidon. [29]Then the boundary turned toward Ramah and the fortress of Tyre, where it turned toward Hosah and came to the Mediterranean Sea.* The territory also included Mehebel, Aczib, [30]Ummah, Aphek, and Rehob—twenty-two towns with their surrounding villages.

[31]The homeland allocated to the clans of the tribe of Asher included these towns and their surrounding villages.

The Land Given to Naphtali
[32]The sixth allotment of land went to the clans of the tribe of Naphtali.

[33]Its boundary ran from Heleph, from the oak at Zaanannim, and extended across to Adami-nekeb, Jabneel, and as far as Lakkum, ending at the Jordan River. [34]The western boundary ran past Aznoth-tabor, then to Hukkok, and touched the border of Zebulun in the south, the border of Asher on the west, and the Jordan River* on the east. [35]The fortified towns included in this territory were Ziddim, Zer, Hammath, Rakkath, Kinnereth, [36]Adamah, Ramah, Hazor, [37]Kedesh, Edrei, En-hazor, [38]Yiron, Migdal-el, Horem, Beth-anath, and Beth-shemesh—nineteen towns with their surrounding villages.

[39]The homeland allocated to the clans of the tribe of Naphtali included these towns and their surrounding villages.

The Land Given to Dan
[40]The seventh allotment of land went to the clans of the tribe of Dan.

[41]The land allocated as their homeland included the following towns: Zorah, Eshtaol, Ir-shemesh, [42]Shaalabbin, Aijalon, Ithlah, [43]Elon, Timnah, Ekron, [44]Eltekeh, Gibbethon, Baalath, [45]Jehud, Bene-berak, Gath-rimmon, [46]Me-jarkon, Rakkon, and the territory across from Joppa.

[47]But the tribe of Dan had trouble taking possession of their land,* so they attacked the town of Laish.* They captured it, slaughtered its people, and settled there. They renamed the town Dan after their ancestor.

[48]The homeland allocated to the clans of the tribe of Dan included these towns and their surrounding villages.

The Land Given to Joshua
[49]After all the land was divided among the tribes, the Israelites gave a piece of land to Joshua as his allocation. [50]For the LORD had said he could have any town he wanted. He chose Timnath-serah in the hill country of Ephraim. He rebuilt the town and lived there.

19:28 As in some Hebrew manuscripts (see also 21:30); most Hebrew manuscripts read *Ebron.*   19:29 Hebrew *the sea.*
19:34 Hebrew *and Judah at the Jordan River.*   19:47a Or *had trouble holding on to their land.*   19:47b Hebrew *Leshem,* a variant spelling of Laish.

⁵¹These are the territories that Eleazar the priest, Joshua son of Nun, and the tribal leaders allocated as grants of land to the tribes of Israel by casting sacred lots in the presence of the LORD at the entrance of the Tabernacle* at Shiloh. So the division of the land was completed.

The Cities of Refuge

20 The LORD said to Joshua, ²"Now tell the Israelites to designate the cities of refuge, as I instructed Moses. ³Anyone who kills another person accidentally and unintentionally can run to one of these cities; they will be places of refuge from relatives seeking revenge for the person who was killed.

⁴"Upon reaching one of these cities, the one who caused the death will appear before the elders at the city gate and present his case. They must allow him to enter the city and give him a place to live among them. ⁵If the relatives of the victim come to avenge the killing, the leaders must not release the slayer to them, for he killed the other person unintentionally and without previous hostility. ⁶But the slayer must stay in that city and be tried by the local assembly, which will render a judgment. And he must continue to live in that city until the death of the high priest who was in office at the time of the accident. After that, he is free to return to his own home in the town from which he fled."

⁷The following cities were designated as cities of refuge: Kedesh of Galilee, in the hill country of Naphtali; Shechem, in the hill country of Ephraim; and Kiriath-arba (that is, Hebron), in the hill country of Judah. ⁸On the east side of the Jordan River, across from Jericho, the following cities were designated: Bezer, in the wilderness plain of the tribe of Reuben; Ramoth in Gilead, in the territory of the tribe of Gad; and Golan in Bashan, in the land of the tribe of Manasseh. ⁹These cities were set apart for all the Israelites as well as the foreigners living among them. Anyone who accidentally killed another person could take refuge in one of these cities. In this way, they could escape being killed in revenge prior to standing trial before the local assembly.

The Towns Given to the Levites

21 Then the leaders of the tribe of Levi came to consult with Eleazar the priest, Joshua son of Nun, and the leaders of the other tribes of Israel. ²They came to them at Shiloh in the land of Canaan and said, "The LORD

19:51 Hebrew *Tent of Meeting.*

commanded Moses to give us towns to live in and pasturelands for our livestock." ³So by the command of the LORD the people of Israel gave the Levites the following towns and pasturelands out of their own grants of land.

⁴The descendants of Aaron, who were members of the Kohathite clan within the tribe of Levi, were allotted thirteen towns that were originally assigned to the tribes of Judah, Simeon, and Benjamin. ⁵The other families of the Kohathite clan were allotted ten towns from the tribes of Ephraim, Dan, and the half-tribe of Manasseh.

⁶The clan of Gershon was allotted thirteen towns from the tribes of Issachar, Asher, Naphtali, and the half-tribe of Manasseh in Bashan.

⁷The clan of Merari was allotted twelve towns from the tribes of Reuben, Gad, and Zebulun.

⁸So the Israelites obeyed the LORD's command to Moses and assigned these towns and pasturelands to the Levites by casting sacred lots.

⁹The Israelites gave the following towns from the tribes of Judah and Simeon ¹⁰to the descendants of Aaron, who were members of the Kohathite clan within the tribe of Levi, since the sacred lot fell to them first: ¹¹Kiriath-arba (that is, Hebron), in the hill country of Judah, along with its surrounding pasturelands. (Arba was an ancestor of Anak.) ¹²But the open fields beyond the town and the surrounding villages were given to Caleb son of Jephunneh as his possession.

¹³The following towns with their pasturelands were given to the descendants of Aaron the priest: Hebron (a city of refuge for those who accidentally killed someone), Libnah, ¹⁴Jattir, Eshtemoa, ¹⁵Holon, Debir, ¹⁶Ain, Juttah, and Beth-shemesh—nine towns from these two tribes.

¹⁷From the tribe of Benjamin the priests were given the following towns with their pasturelands: Gibeon, Geba, ¹⁸Anathoth, and Almon—four towns. ¹⁹So in all, thirteen towns with their pasturelands were given to the priests, the descendants of Aaron.

²⁰The rest of the Kohathite clan from the tribe of Levi was allotted the following towns and pasturelands from the tribe of Ephraim: ²¹Shechem in the hill country of Ephraim (a city of refuge for those who accidentally killed someone), Gezer, ²²Kibzaim, and Beth-horon—four towns.

²³The following towns and pasturelands

were allotted to the priests from the tribe of Dan: Eltekeh, Gibbethon, 24Aijalon, and Gath-rimmon—four towns.

25The half-tribe of Manasseh allotted the following towns with their pasturelands to the priests: Taanach and Gath-rimmon—two towns. 26So in all, ten towns with their pasturelands were given to the rest of the Kohathite clan.

27The descendants of Gershon, another clan within the tribe of Levi, received the following towns with their pasturelands from the half-tribe of Manasseh: Golan in Bashan (a city of refuge for those who accidentally killed someone) and Be-eshterah—two towns.

28From the tribe of Issachar they received the following towns with their pasturelands: Kishion, Daberath, 29Jarmuth, and En-gannim—four towns.

30From the tribe of Asher they received the following towns with their pasturelands: Mishal, Abdon, 31Helkath, and Rehob—four towns.

32From the tribe of Naphtali they received the following towns with their pasturelands: Kedesh in Galilee (a city of refuge for those who accidentally killed someone), Hammoth-dor, and Kartan—three towns. 33So in all, thirteen towns with their pasturelands were allotted to the clan of Gershon.

34The rest of the Levites—the Merari clan—were given the following towns with their pasturelands from the tribe of Zebulun: Jokneam, Kartah, 35Dimnah, and Nahalal—four towns.

36From the tribe of Reuben they received the following towns with their pasturelands: Bezer, Jahaz,* 37Kedemoth, and Mephaath—four towns.

38From the tribe of Gad they received the following towns with their pasturelands: Ramoth in Gilead (a city of refuge for those who accidentally killed someone), Mahanaim, 39Heshbon, and Jazer—four towns. 40So in all, twelve towns were allotted to the clan of Merari.

41The total number of towns and pasturelands within Israelite territory given to the Levites came to forty-eight. 42Every one of these towns had pasturelands surrounding it.

43So the LORD gave to Israel all the land he had sworn to give their ancestors, and they took possession of it and settled there. 44And the LORD gave them rest on every side, just as he had solemnly promised their ancestors. None of their enemies could stand against

them, for the LORD helped them conquer all their enemies. 45Not a single one of all the good promises the LORD had given to the family of Israel was left unfulfilled; everything he had spoken came true.

The Eastern Tribes Return Home

22 Then Joshua called together the tribes of Reuben, Gad, and the half-tribe of Manasseh. 2He told them, "You have done as Moses, the servant of the LORD, commanded you, and you have obeyed every order I have given you. 3During all this time you have not deserted the other tribes. You have been careful to obey the commands of the LORD your God right up to the present day. 4And now the LORD your God has given the other tribes rest, as he promised them. So go back home to the land that Moses, the servant of the LORD, gave you as your possession on the east side of the Jordan River. 5But be very careful to obey all the commands and the instructions that Moses gave to you. Love the LORD your God, walk in all his ways, obey his commands, hold firmly to him, and serve him with all your heart and all your soul." 6So Joshua blessed them and sent them away, and they went home.

7Moses had given the land of Bashan, east of the Jordan River, to the half-tribe of Manasseh. (The other half of the tribe was given land west of the Jordan.) As Joshua sent them away and blessed them, 8he said to them, "Go back to your homes with the great wealth you have taken from your enemies—the vast herds of livestock, the silver, gold, bronze, and iron, and the large supply of clothing. Share the plunder with your relatives."

9So the men of Reuben, Gad, and the half-tribe of Manasseh left the rest of Israel at Shiloh in the land of Canaan. They started the journey back to their own land of Gilead, the territory that belonged to them according to the LORD's command through Moses.

The Eastern Tribes Build an Altar

10But while they were still in Canaan, and when they came to a place called Geliloth* near the Jordan River, the men of Reuben, Gad, and the half-tribe of Manasseh stopped to build a large and imposing altar.

11The rest of Israel heard that the people of Reuben, Gad, and the half-tribe of Manasseh had built an altar at Geliloth at the edge of the land of Canaan, on the west side of the Jordan River. 12So the whole community of

21:36 Hebrew *Jahzah*, a variant spelling of Jahaz.   22:10 Or *to the circle of stones;* similarly in 22:11.

Israel gathered at Shiloh and prepared to go to war against them. [13]First, however, they sent a delegation led by Phinehas son of Eleazar, the priest, to talk with the tribes of Reuben, Gad, and the half-tribe of Manasseh. [14]In this delegation were ten leaders of Israel, one from each of the ten tribes, and each the head of his family within the clans of Israel.

[15]When they arrived in the land of Gilead, they said to the tribes of Reuben, Gad, and the half-tribe of Manasseh, [16]"The whole community of the LORD demands to know why you are betraying the God of Israel. How could you turn away from the LORD and build an altar for yourselves in rebellion against him? [17]Was our sin at Peor not enough? To this day we are not fully cleansed of it, even after the plague that struck the entire community of the LORD. [18]And yet today you are turning away from following the LORD. If you rebel against the LORD today, he will be angry with all of us tomorrow.

[19]"If you need the altar because the land you possess is defiled, then join us in the LORD's land, where the Tabernacle of the LORD is situated, and share our land with us. But do not rebel against the LORD or against us by building an altar other than the one true altar of the LORD our God. [20]Didn't divine anger fall on the entire community of Israel when Achan, a member of the clan of Zerah, sinned by stealing the things set apart for the LORD*? He was not the only one who died because of his sin."

[21]Then the people of Reuben, Gad, and the half-tribe of Manasseh answered the heads of the clans of Israel: [22]"The LORD, the Mighty One, is God! The LORD, the Mighty One, is God! He knows the truth, and may Israel know it, too! We have not built the altar in treacherous rebellion against the LORD. If we have done so, do not spare our lives this day. [23]If we have built an altar for ourselves to turn away from the LORD or to offer burnt offerings or grain offerings or peace offerings, may the LORD himself punish us.

[24]"The truth is, we have built this altar because we fear that in the future your descendants will say to ours, 'What right do you have to worship the LORD, the God of Israel? [25]The LORD has placed the Jordan River as a barrier between our people and you people of Reuben and Gad. You have no claim to the LORD.' So your descendants may prevent our descendants from worshiping the LORD.

[26]"So we decided to build the altar, not for burnt offerings or sacrifices, [27]but as a memorial. It will remind our descendants and your descendants that we, too, have the right to worship the LORD at his sanctuary with our burnt offerings, sacrifices, and peace offerings. Then your descendants will not be able to say to ours, 'You have no claim to the LORD.'

[28]"If they say this, our descendants can reply, 'Look at this copy of the LORD's altar that our ancestors made. It is not for burnt offerings or sacrifices; it is a reminder of the relationship both of us have with the LORD.' [29]Far be it from us to rebel against the LORD or turn away from him by building our own altar for burnt offerings, grain offerings, or sacrifices. Only the altar of the LORD our God that stands in front of the Tabernacle may be used for that purpose."

[30]When Phinehas the priest and the leaders of the community—the heads of the clans of Israel—heard this from the tribes of Reuben, Gad, and the half-tribe of Manasseh, they were satisfied. [31]Phinehas son of Eleazar, the priest, replied to them, "Today we know the LORD is among us because you have not committed this treachery against the LORD as we thought. Instead, you have rescued Israel from being destroyed by the hand of the LORD."

[32]Then Phinehas son of Eleazar, the priest, and the other leaders left the tribes of Reuben and Gad in Gilead and returned to the land of Canaan to tell the Israelites what had happened. [33]And all the Israelites were satisfied and praised God and spoke no more of war against Reuben and Gad.

[34]The people of Reuben and Gad named the altar "Witness,"* for they said, "It is a witness between us and them that the LORD is our God, too."

Joshua's Final Words to Israel

23 The years passed, and the LORD had given the people of Israel rest from all their enemies. Joshua, who was now very old, [2]called together all the elders, leaders, judges, and officers of Israel. He said to them, "I am now a very old man. [3]You have seen everything the LORD your God has done for you during my lifetime. The LORD your God has fought for you against your enemies. [4]I have allotted to you as your homeland all the land of the nations yet unconquered, as well as the land of those we have already conquered—from the Jordan River to the Mediterranean Sea*

22:20 The Hebrew term used here refers to the complete consecration of things or people to the LORD, either by destroying them or by giving them as an offering. 22:34 Some manuscripts lack this word. 23:4 Hebrew *the Great Sea.*

in the west. ⁵This land will be yours, for the LORD your God will himself drive out all the people living there now. You will take possession of their land, just as the LORD your God promised you.

⁶"So be very careful to follow everything Moses wrote in the Book of Instruction. Do not deviate from it, turning either to the right or to the left. ⁷Make sure you do not associate with the other people still remaining in the land. Do not even mention the names of their gods, much less swear by them or serve them or worship them. ⁸Rather, cling tightly to the LORD your God as you have done until now.

⁹"For the LORD has driven out great and powerful nations for you, and no one has yet been able to defeat you. ¹⁰Each one of you will put to flight a thousand of the enemy, for the LORD your God fights for you, just as he has promised. ¹¹So be very careful to love the LORD your God.

¹²"But if you turn away from him and cling to the customs of the survivors of these nations remaining among you, and if you intermarry with them, ¹³then know for certain that the LORD your God will no longer drive them out of your land. Instead, they will be a snare and a trap to you, a whip for your backs and thorny brambles in your eyes, and you will vanish from this good land the LORD your God has given you.

¹⁴"Soon I will die, going the way of everything on earth. Deep in your hearts you know that every promise of the LORD your God has come true. Not a single one has failed! ¹⁵But as surely as the LORD your God has given you the good things he promised, he will also bring disaster on you if you disobey him. He will completely destroy you from this good land he has given you. ¹⁶If you break the covenant of the LORD your God by worshiping and serving other gods, his anger will burn against you, and you will quickly vanish from the good land he has given you."

The LORD's Covenant Renewed

24 Then Joshua summoned all the tribes of Israel to Shechem, including their elders, leaders, judges, and officers. So they came and presented themselves to God.

²Joshua said to the people, "This is what the LORD, the God of Israel, says: Long ago your ancestors, including Terah, the father of Abraham and Nahor, lived beyond the Euphrates River,* and they worshiped other gods. ³But I took your ancestor Abraham from the land beyond the Euphrates and led him into the land of Canaan. I gave him many descendants through his son Isaac. ⁴To Isaac I gave Jacob and Esau. To Esau I gave the mountains of Seir, while Jacob and his children went down into Egypt.

⁵"Then I sent Moses and Aaron, and I brought terrible plagues on Egypt; and afterward I brought you out as a free people. ⁶But when your ancestors arrived at the Red Sea,* the Egyptians chased after you with chariots and charioteers. ⁷When your ancestors cried out to the LORD, I put darkness between you and the Egyptians. I brought the sea crashing down on the Egyptians, drowning them. With your very own eyes you saw what I did. Then you lived in the wilderness for many years.

⁸"Finally, I brought you into the land of the Amorites on the east side of the Jordan. They fought against you, but I destroyed them before you. I gave you victory over them, and you took possession of their land. ⁹Then Balak son of Zippor, king of Moab, started a war against Israel. He summoned Balaam son of Beor to curse you, ¹⁰but I would not listen to him. Instead, I made Balaam bless you, and so I rescued you from Balak.

¹¹"When you crossed the Jordan River and came to Jericho, the men of Jericho fought against you, as did the Amorites, the Perizzites, the Canaanites, the Hittites, the Girgashites, the Hivites, and the Jebusites. But I gave you victory over them. ¹²And I sent terror* ahead of you to drive out the two kings of the Amorites. It was not your swords or bows that brought you victory. ¹³I gave you land you had not worked on, and I gave you towns you did not build—the towns where you are now living. I gave you vineyards and olive groves for food, though you did not plant them.

¹⁴"So fear the LORD and serve him wholeheartedly. Put away forever the idols your ancestors worshiped when they lived beyond the Euphrates River and in Egypt. Serve the LORD alone. ¹⁵But if you refuse to serve the LORD, then choose today whom you will serve. Would you prefer the gods your ancestors served beyond the Euphrates? Or will it be the gods of the Amorites in whose land you now live? But as for me and my family, we will serve the LORD."

¹⁶The people replied, "We would never

24:2 Hebrew *the river;* also in 24:3, 14, 15.   24:6 Hebrew *sea of reeds.*   24:12 Often rendered *the hornet.* The meaning of the Hebrew is uncertain.

abandon the LORD and serve other gods. [17]For the LORD our God is the one who rescued us and our ancestors from slavery in the land of Egypt. He performed mighty miracles before our very eyes. As we traveled through the wilderness among our enemies, he preserved us. [18]It was the LORD who drove out the Amorites and the other nations living here in the land. So we, too, will serve the LORD, for he alone is our God."

[19]Then Joshua warned the people, "You are not able to serve the LORD, for he is a holy and jealous God. He will not forgive your rebellion and your sins. [20]If you abandon the LORD and serve other gods, he will turn against you and destroy you, even though he has been so good to you."

[21]But the people answered Joshua, "No, we will serve the LORD!"

[22]"You are a witness to your own decision," Joshua said. "You have chosen to serve the LORD."

"Yes," they replied, "we are witnesses to what we have said."

[23]"All right then," Joshua said, "destroy the idols among you, and turn your hearts to the LORD, the God of Israel."

[24]The people said to Joshua, "We will serve the LORD our God. We will obey him alone."

[25]So Joshua made a covenant with the people that day at Shechem, committing them to follow the decrees and regulations of the LORD. [26]Joshua recorded these things in the Book of God's Instructions. As a reminder of their agreement, he took a huge stone and rolled it beneath the terebinth tree beside the Tabernacle of the LORD.

[27]Joshua said to all the people, "This stone has heard everything the LORD said to us. It will be a witness to testify against you if you go back on your word to God."

[28]Then Joshua sent all the people away to their own homelands.

Leaders Buried in the Promised Land

[29]After this, Joshua son of Nun, the servant of the LORD, died at the age of 110. [30]They buried him in the land he had been allocated, at Timnath-serah in the hill country of Ephraim, north of Mount Gaash.

[31]The people of Israel served the LORD throughout the lifetime of Joshua and of the elders who outlived him—those who had personally experienced all that the LORD had done for Israel.

[32]The bones of Joseph, which the Israelites had brought along with them when they left Egypt, were buried at Shechem, in the plot of land Jacob had bought from the sons of Hamor for 100 pieces of silver.* This land was located in the territory allotted to the descendants of Joseph.

[33]Eleazar son of Aaron also died. He was buried in the hill country of Ephraim, in the town of Gibeah, which had been given to his son Phinehas.

24:32 Hebrew *100 kesitahs*; the value or weight of the kesitah is no longer known.

Judges

OFTEN THE GREATEST HEROES appear in the midst of the worst chaos and confusion. This is true in the book of Judges, where true heroes and heroines are called upon repeatedly to save the day after the people had fallen into sin. After Joshua's armies conquered Canaan, the twelve tribes of Israel settled their allotted portions of land. They had no earthly king, because God was to serve as their king. But this required that the people follow and obey God—a situation that rarely existed during this period. The people soon became unfaithful to God and practiced their pagan neighbors' ways. To punish their disobedience, God allowed the Israelites' neighbors to oppress them. The Israelites repented and asked God to rescue them, and he raised up various leaders among them to drive out the enemy. These leaders were known as judges. They not only defeated their enemies and drove them from the land, but they turned the Israelites' hearts back to God. But time after time, soon after the people were delivered from their oppressive neighbors, they lost their zeal for God, and the cycle began again.

■ **Author:** Samuel, according to Jewish tradition

■ **Date Written:** Uncertain, perhaps around 1000 BC

■ **Purpose:** To show the pitfalls of Israel's lack of central authority, the consequences of sin, and God's willingness to rescue those who repent

■ **Themes:** Compromise, unfaithfulness, punishment for sin, repentance, deliverance

■ **Outline**
1:1–3:4 Summary of current events
3:5-31 The first judges—Othniel, Ehud, and Shamgar
4:1–5:31 Deborah and Barak's victory
6:1–8:35 The story of Gideon
9:1-57 The story of Abimelech
10:1–12:15 The stories of Tola, Jair, Jephthah, Ibzan, Elon, and Abdon
13:1–16:31 The story of Samson
17:1–21:25 Anarchy in the land

Judah and Simeon Conquer the Land

1 After the death of Joshua, the Israelites asked the LORD, "Which tribe should go first to attack the Canaanites?"

²The LORD answered, "Judah, for I have given them victory over the land."

³The men of Judah said to their relatives from the tribe of Simeon, "Join with us to fight against the Canaanites living in the territory allotted to us. Then we will help you conquer your territory." So the men of Simeon went with Judah.

⁴When the men of Judah attacked, the LORD gave them victory over the Canaanites and Perizzites, and they killed 10,000 enemy warriors at the town of Bezek. ⁵While at Bezek they

1:9 Hebrew *the Shephelah.*

encountered King Adoni-bezek and fought against him, and the Canaanites and Perizzites were defeated. ⁶Adoni-bezek escaped, but the Israelites soon captured him and cut off his thumbs and big toes.

⁷Adoni-bezek said, "I once had seventy kings with their thumbs and big toes cut off, eating scraps from under my table. Now God has paid me back for what I did to them." They took him to Jerusalem, and he died there.

⁸The men of Judah attacked Jerusalem and captured it, killing all its people and setting the city on fire. ⁹Then they went down to fight the Canaanites living in the hill country, the Negev, and the western foothills.* ¹⁰Judah marched against the Canaanites in Hebron (formerly

called Kiriath-arba), defeating the forces of Sheshai, Ahiman, and Talmai.

[11]From there they went to fight against the people living in the town of Debir (formerly called Kiriath-sepher). [12]Caleb said, "I will give my daughter Acsah in marriage to the one who attacks and captures Kiriath-sepher." [13]Othniel, the son of Caleb's younger brother, Kenaz, was the one who conquered it, so Acsah became Othniel's wife.

[14]When Acsah married Othniel, she urged him* to ask her father for a field. As she got down off her donkey, Caleb asked her, "What's the matter?"

[15]She said, "Let me have another gift. You have already given me land in the Negev; now please give me springs of water, too." So Caleb gave her the upper and lower springs.

[16]When the tribe of Judah left Jericho—the city of palms—the Kenites, who were descendants of Moses' father-in-law, traveled with them into the wilderness of Judah. They settled among the people there, near the town of Arad in the Negev.

[17]Then Judah joined with Simeon to fight against the Canaanites living in Zephath, and they completely destroyed* the town. So the town was named Hormah.* [18]In addition, Judah captured the towns of Gaza, Ashkelon, and Ekron, along with their surrounding territories.

Israel Fails to Conquer the Land

[19]The LORD was with the people of Judah, and they took possession of the hill country. But they failed to drive out the people living in the plains, who had iron chariots. [20]The town of Hebron was given to Caleb as Moses had promised. And Caleb drove out the people living there, who were descendants of the three sons of Anak.

[21]The tribe of Benjamin, however, failed to drive out the Jebusites, who were living in Jerusalem. So to this day the Jebusites live in Jerusalem among the people of Benjamin.

[22]The descendants of Joseph attacked the town of Bethel, and the LORD was with them. [23]They sent men to scout out Bethel (formerly known as Luz). [24]They confronted a man coming out of the town and said to him, "Show us a way into the town, and we will have mercy on you." [25]So he showed them a way in, and they killed everyone in the town except that man and his family. [26]Later the man moved to

the land of the Hittites, where he built a town. He named it Luz, which is its name to this day.

[27]The tribe of Manasseh failed to drive out the people living in Beth-shan,* Taanach, Dor, Ibleam, Megiddo, and all their surrounding settlements, because the Canaanites were determined to stay in that region. [28]When the Israelites grew stronger, they forced the Canaanites to work as slaves, but they never did drive them completely out of the land.

[29]The tribe of Ephraim failed to drive out the Canaanites living in Gezer, so the Canaanites continued to live there among them.

[30]The tribe of Zebulun failed to drive out the residents of Kitron and Nahalol, so the Canaanites continued to live among them. But the Canaanites were forced to work as slaves for the people of Zebulun.

[31]The tribe of Asher failed to drive out the residents of Acco, Sidon, Ahlab, Aczib, Helbah, Aphik, and Rehob. [32]Instead, the people of Asher moved in among the Canaanites, who controlled the land, for they failed to drive them out.

[33]Likewise, the tribe of Naphtali failed to drive out the residents of Beth-shemesh and Beth-anath. Instead, they moved in among the Canaanites, who controlled the land. Nevertheless, the people of Beth-shemesh and Beth-anath were forced to work as slaves for the people of Naphtali.

[34]As for the tribe of Dan, the Amorites forced them back into the hill country and would not let them come down into the plains. [35]The Amorites were determined to stay in Mount Heres, Aijalon, and Shaalbim, but when the descendants of Joseph became stronger, they forced the Amorites to work as slaves. [36]The boundary of the Amorites ran from Scorpion Pass* to Sela and continued upward from there.

The LORD's Messenger Comes to Bokim

2 The angel of the LORD went up from Gilgal to Bokim and said to the Israelites, "I brought you out of Egypt into this land that I swore to give your ancestors, and I said I would never break my covenant with you. [2]For your part, you were not to make any covenants with the people living in this land; instead, you were to destroy their altars. But you disobeyed my command. Why did you do this? [3]So now I declare that I will no longer drive out the people living in your land. They will

---

1:14 Greek version and Latin Vulgate read *he urged her.*   1:17a The Hebrew term used here refers to the complete consecration of things or people to the LORD, either by destroying them or by giving them as an offering.   1:17b *Hormah* means "destruction."   1:27 Hebrew *Beth-shean,* a variant spelling of Beth-shan.   1:36 Hebrew *Akrabbim.*

be thorns in your sides,* and their gods will be a constant temptation to you."

⁴When the angel of the LORD finished speaking to all the Israelites, the people wept loudly. ⁵So they called the place Bokim (which means "weeping"), and they offered sacrifices there to the LORD.

The Death of Joshua

⁶After Joshua sent the people away, each of the tribes left to take possession of the land allotted to them. ⁷And the Israelites served the LORD throughout the lifetime of Joshua and the leaders who outlived him—those who had seen all the great things the LORD had done for Israel.

⁸Joshua son of Nun, the servant of the LORD, died at the age of 110. ⁹They buried him in the land he had been allocated, at Timnath-serah* in the hill country of Ephraim, north of Mount Gaash.

Israel Disobeys the LORD

¹⁰After that generation died, another generation grew up who did not acknowledge the LORD or remember the mighty things he had done for Israel.

¹¹The Israelites did evil in the LORD's sight and served the images of Baal. ¹²They abandoned the LORD, the God of their ancestors, who had brought them out of Egypt. They went after other gods, worshiping the gods of the people around them. And they angered the LORD. ¹³They abandoned the LORD to serve Baal and the images of Ashtoreth. ¹⁴This made the LORD burn with anger against Israel, so he handed them over to raiders who stole their possessions. He turned them over to their enemies all around, and they were no longer able to resist them. ¹⁵Every time Israel went out to battle, the LORD fought against them, causing them to be defeated, just as he had warned. And the people were in great distress.

The LORD Rescues His People

¹⁶Then the LORD raised up judges to rescue the Israelites from their attackers. ¹⁷Yet Israel did not listen to the judges but prostituted themselves by worshiping other gods. How quickly they turned away from the path of their ancestors, who had walked in obedience to the LORD's commands. ¹⁸Whenever the LORD raised up a judge over

Israel, he was with that judge and rescued the people from their enemies throughout the judge's lifetime. For the LORD took pity on his people, who were burdened by oppression and suffering. ¹⁹But when the judge died, the people returned to their corrupt ways, behaving worse than those who had lived before them. They went after other gods, serving and worshiping them. And they refused to give up their evil practices and stubborn ways.

²⁰So the LORD burned with anger against Israel. He said, "Because these people have violated my covenant, which I made with their ancestors, and have ignored my commands, ²¹I will no longer drive out the nations that Joshua left unconquered when he died. ²²I did this to test Israel—to see whether or not they would follow the ways of the LORD as their ancestors did." ²³That is why the LORD left those nations in place. He did not quickly drive them out or allow Joshua to conquer them all.

The Nations Left in Canaan

3 These are the nations that the LORD left in the land to test those Israelites who had not experienced the wars of Canaan. ²He did this to teach warfare to generations of Israelites who had no experience in battle. ³These are the nations: the Philistines (those living under the five Philistine rulers), all the Canaanites, the Sidonians, and the Hivites living in the mountains of Lebanon from Mount Baal-hermon to Lebo-hamath. ⁴These people were left to test the Israelites—to see whether they would obey the commands the LORD had given to their ancestors through Moses.

⁵So the people of Israel lived among the Canaanites, Hittites, Amorites, Perizzites, Hivites, and Jebusites, ⁶and they intermarried with them. Israelite sons married their daughters, and Israelite daughters were given in marriage to their sons. And the Israelites served their gods.

Othniel Becomes Israel's Judge

⁷The Israelites did evil in the LORD's sight. They forgot about the LORD their God, and they served the images of Baal and the Asherah poles. ⁸Then the LORD burned with anger against Israel, and he turned them over to King Cushan-rishathaim of Aram-naharaim.* And the Israelites served Cushan-rishathaim for eight years.

2:3 Hebrew *They will be in your sides;* compare Num 33:55.   2:9 As in parallel text at Josh 24:30; Hebrew reads *Timnath-heres,* a variant spelling of Timnath-serah.   3:8 *Aram-naharaim* means "Aram of the two rivers," thought to have been located between the Euphrates and Balih Rivers in northwestern Mesopotamia.

9But when the people of Israel cried out to the LORD for help, the LORD raised up a rescuer to save them. His name was Othniel, the son of Caleb's younger brother, Kenaz. 10The Spirit of the LORD came upon him, and he became Israel's judge. He went to war against King Cushan-rishathaim of Aram, and the LORD gave Othniel victory over him. 11So there was peace in the land for forty years. Then Othniel son of Kenaz died.

Ehud Becomes Israel's Judge

12Once again the Israelites did evil in the LORD's sight, and the LORD gave King Eglon of Moab control over Israel because of their evil. 13Eglon enlisted the Ammonites and Amalekites as allies, and then he went out and defeated Israel, taking possession of Jericho, the city of palms. 14And the Israelites served Eglon of Moab for eighteen years.

15But when the people of Israel cried out to the LORD for help, the LORD again raised up a rescuer to save them. His name was Ehud son of Gera, a left-handed man of the tribe of Benjamin. The Israelites sent Ehud to deliver their tribute money to King Eglon of Moab. 16So Ehud made a double-edged dagger that was about a foot* long, and he strapped it to his right thigh, keeping it hidden under his clothing. 17He brought the tribute money to Eglon, who was very fat.

18After delivering the payment, Ehud started home with those who had helped carry the tribute. 19But when Ehud reached the stone idols near Gilgal, he turned back. He came to Eglon and said, "I have a secret message for you."

So the king commanded his servants, "Be quiet!" and he sent them all out of the room.

20Ehud walked over to Eglon, who was sitting alone in a cool upstairs room. And Ehud said, "I have a message from God for you!" As King Eglon rose from his seat, 21Ehud reached with his left hand, pulled out the dagger strapped to his right thigh, and plunged it into the king's belly. 22The dagger went so deep that the handle disappeared beneath the king's fat. So Ehud did not pull out the dagger, and the king's bowels emptied.* 23Then Ehud closed and locked the doors of the room and escaped down the latrine.*

24After Ehud was gone, the king's servants returned and found the doors to the upstairs room locked. They thought he might be using the latrine in the room, 25so they waited. But when the king didn't come out after a long delay, they became concerned and got a key. And when they opened the doors, they found their master dead on the floor.

26While the servants were waiting, Ehud escaped, passing the stone idols on his way to Seirah. 27When he arrived in the hill country of Ephraim, Ehud sounded a call to arms. Then he led a band of Israelites down from the hills.

28"Follow me," he said, "for the LORD has given you victory over Moab your enemy." So they followed him. And the Israelites took control of the shallow crossings of the Jordan River across from Moab, preventing anyone from crossing.

29They attacked the Moabites and killed about 10,000 of their strongest and most able-bodied warriors. Not one of them escaped. 30So Moab was conquered by Israel that day, and there was peace in the land for eighty years.

Shamgar Becomes Israel's Judge

31After Ehud, Shamgar son of Anath rescued Israel. He once killed 600 Philistines with an ox goad.

Deborah Becomes Israel's Judge

4 After Ehud's death, the Israelites again did evil in the LORD's sight. 2So the LORD turned them over to King Jabin of Hazor, a Canaanite king. The commander of his army was Sisera, who lived in Harosheth-haggoyim. 3Sisera, who had 900 iron chariots, ruthlessly oppressed the Israelites for twenty years. Then the people of Israel cried out to the LORD for help.

4Deborah, the wife of Lappidoth, was a prophet who was judging Israel at that time. 5She would sit under the Palm of Deborah, between Ramah and Bethel in the hill country of Ephraim, and the Israelites would go to her for judgment. 6One day she sent for Barak son of Abinoam, who lived in Kedesh in the land of Naphtali. She said to him, "This is what the LORD, the God of Israel, commands you: Call out 10,000 warriors from the tribes of Naphtali and Zebulun at Mount Tabor. 7And I will call out Sisera, commander of Jabin's army, along with his chariots and warriors, to the Kishon River. There I will give you victory over him."

8Barak told her, "I will go, but only if you go with me."

9"Very well," she replied, "I will go with you. But you will receive no honor in this venture, for the LORD's victory over Sisera will be

---

3:16 Hebrew *gomed*, the length of which is uncertain.   3:22 Or *and it came out behind.*   3:23 Or *and went out through the porch;* the meaning of the Hebrew is uncertain.

at the hands of a woman." So Deborah went with Barak to Kedesh. [10]At Kedesh, Barak called together the tribes of Zebulun and Naphtali, and 10,000 warriors went up with him. Deborah also went with him.

[11]Now Heber the Kenite, a descendant of Moses' brother-in-law* Hobab, had moved away from the other members of his tribe and pitched his tent by the oak of Zaanannim near Kedesh.

[12]When Sisera was told that Barak son of Abinoam had gone up to Mount Tabor, [13]he called for all 900 of his iron chariots and all of his warriors, and they marched from Harosheth-haggoyim to the Kishon River.

[14]Then Deborah said to Barak, "Get ready! This is the day the LORD will give you victory over Sisera, for the LORD is marching ahead of you." So Barak led his 10,000 warriors down the slopes of Mount Tabor into battle. [15]When Barak attacked, the LORD threw Sisera and all his chariots and warriors into a panic. Sisera leaped down from his chariot and escaped on foot. [16]Then Barak chased the chariots and the enemy army all the way to Harosheth-haggoyim, killing all of Sisera's warriors. Not a single one was left alive.

[17]Meanwhile, Sisera ran to the tent of Jael, the wife of Heber the Kenite, because Heber's family was on friendly terms with King Jabin of Hazor. [18]Jael went out to meet Sisera and said to him, "Come into my tent, sir. Come in. Don't be afraid." So he went into her tent, and she covered him with a blanket.

[19]"Please give me some water," he said. "I'm thirsty." So she gave him some milk from a leather bag and covered him again.

[20]"Stand at the door of the tent," he told her. "If anybody comes and asks you if there is anyone here, say no."

[21]But when Sisera fell asleep from exhaustion, Jael quietly crept up to him with a hammer and tent peg in her hand. Then she drove the tent peg through his temple and into the ground, and so he died.

[22]When Barak came looking for Sisera, Jael went out to meet him. She said, "Come, and I will show you the man you are looking for." So he followed her into the tent and found Sisera lying there dead, with the tent peg through his temple.

[23]So on that day Israel saw God defeat Jabin, the Canaanite king. [24]And from that time on Israel became stronger and stronger against King Jabin until they finally destroyed him.

The Song of Deborah

5 On that day Deborah and Barak son of Abinoam sang this song:

[2] "Israel's leaders took charge,
   and the people gladly followed.
Praise the LORD!

[3] "Listen, you kings!
   Pay attention, you mighty rulers!
For I will sing to the LORD.
   I will make music to the LORD, the God of Israel.

[4] "LORD, when you set out from Seir
   and marched across the fields of Edom,
the earth trembled,
   and the cloudy skies poured down rain.

[5] The mountains quaked in the presence of the LORD,
   the God of Mount Sinai—
in the presence of the LORD,
   the God of Israel.

[6] "In the days of Shamgar son of Anath,
   and in the days of Jael,
people avoided the main roads,
   and travelers stayed on winding pathways.

[7] There were few people left in the villages of Israel*—
   until Deborah arose as a mother for Israel.

[8] When Israel chose new gods,
   war erupted at the city gates.
Yet not a shield or spear could be seen
   among forty thousand warriors in Israel!

[9] My heart is with the commanders of Israel,
   with those who volunteered for war.
Praise the LORD!

[10] "Consider this, you who ride on fine donkeys,
   you who sit on fancy saddle blankets,
   and you who walk along the road.

[11] Listen to the village musicians*
   gathered at the watering holes.
They recount the righteous victories of the LORD
   and the victories of his villagers in Israel.

4:11 Or *father-in-law.*   5:7 The meaning of the Hebrew is uncertain.   5:11 The meaning of the Hebrew is uncertain.

Then the people of the LORD
marched down to the city gates.

12 "Wake up, Deborah, wake up!
Wake up, wake up, and sing a song!
Arise, Barak!
Lead your captives away, son of
Abinoam!

13 "Down from Tabor marched the few
against the nobles.
The people of the LORD marched down
against mighty warriors.

14 They came down from Ephraim—
a land that once belonged to the
Amalekites;
they followed you, Benjamin, with your
troops.
From Makir the commanders marched
down;
from Zebulun came those who carry a
commander's staff.

15 The princes of Issachar were with Deborah
and Barak.
They followed Barak, rushing into the
valley.
But in the tribe of Reuben
there was great indecision.*

16 Why did you sit at home among the
sheepfolds—
to hear the shepherds whistle for their
flocks?
Yes, in the tribe of Reuben
there was great indecision.

17 Gilead remained east of the Jordan.
And why did Dan stay home?
Asher sat unmoved at the seashore,
remaining in his harbors.

18 But Zebulun risked his life,
as did Naphtali, on the heights of the
battlefield.

19 "The kings of Canaan came and fought,
at Taanach near Megiddo's springs,
but they carried off no silver treasures.

20 The stars fought from heaven.
The stars in their orbits fought against
Sisera.

21 The Kishon River swept them away—
that ancient torrent, the Kishon.
March on with courage, my soul!

22 Then the horses' hooves hammered the
ground,
the galloping, galloping of Sisera's
mighty steeds.

23 'Let the people of Meroz be cursed,' said
the angel of the LORD.
'Let them be utterly cursed,
because they did not come to help the
LORD—
to help the LORD against the mighty
warriors.'

24 "Most blessed among women is Jael,
the wife of Heber the Kenite.
May she be blessed above all women
who live in tents.

25 Sisera asked for water,
and she gave him milk.
In a bowl fit for nobles,
she brought him yogurt.

26 Then with her left hand she reached for
a tent peg,
and with her right hand for the
workman's hammer.
She struck Sisera with the hammer,
crushing his head.
With a shattering blow, she pierced his
temples.

27 He sank, he fell,
he lay still at her feet.
And where he sank,
there he died.

28 "From the window Sisera's mother looked
out.
Through the window she watched for
his return, saying,
'Why is his chariot so long in coming?
Why don't we hear the sound of chariot
wheels?'

29 "Her wise women answer,
and she repeats these words to herself:

30 'They must be dividing the captured
plunder—
with a woman or two for every man.
There will be colorful robes for Sisera,
and colorful, embroidered robes
for me.
Yes, the plunder will include
colorful robes embroidered on both
sides.'

31 "LORD, may all your enemies die like
Sisera!
But may those who love you rise like the
sun in all its power!"

Then there was peace in the land for forty years.

5:15 As in some Hebrew manuscripts and Syriac version, which read *searchings of heart*; Masoretic Text reads *resolve of heart*.

Gideon Becomes Israel's Judge

6 The Israelites did evil in the LORD's sight. So the LORD handed them over to the Midianites for seven years. ²The Midianites were so cruel that the Israelites made hiding places for themselves in the mountains, caves, and strongholds. ³Whenever the Israelites planted their crops, marauders from Midian, Amalek, and the people of the east would attack Israel, ⁴camping in the land and destroying crops as far away as Gaza. They left the Israelites with nothing to eat, taking all the sheep, goats, cattle, and donkeys. ⁵These enemy hordes, coming with their livestock and tents, were as thick as locusts; they arrived on droves of camels too numerous to count. And they stayed until the land was stripped bare. ⁶So Israel was reduced to starvation by the Midianites. Then the Israelites cried out to the LORD for help.

⁷When they cried out to the LORD because of Midian, ⁸the LORD sent a prophet to the Israelites. He said, "This is what the LORD, the God of Israel, says: I brought you up out of slavery in Egypt. ⁹I rescued you from the Egyptians and from all who oppressed you. I drove out your enemies and gave you their land. ¹⁰I told you, 'I am the LORD your God. You must not worship the gods of the Amorites, in whose land you now live.' But you have not listened to me."

¹¹Then the angel of the LORD came and sat beneath the great tree at Ophrah, which belonged to Joash of the clan of Abiezer. Gideon son of Joash was threshing wheat at the bottom of a winepress to hide the grain from the Midianites. ¹²The angel of the LORD appeared to him and said, "Mighty hero, the LORD is with you!"

¹³"Sir," Gideon replied, "if the LORD is with us, why has all this happened to us? And where are all the miracles our ancestors told us about? Didn't they say, 'The LORD brought us up out of Egypt'? But now the LORD has abandoned us and handed us over to the Midianites."

¹⁴Then the LORD turned to him and said, "Go with the strength you have, and rescue Israel from the Midianites. I am sending you!"

¹⁵"But Lord," Gideon replied, "how can I rescue Israel? My clan is the weakest in the whole tribe of Manasseh, and I am the least in my entire family!"

¹⁶The LORD said to him, "I will be with you. And you will destroy the Midianites as if you were fighting against one man."

¹⁷Gideon replied, "If you are truly going to help me, show me a sign to prove that it is really the LORD speaking to me. ¹⁸Don't go away until I come back and bring my offering to you."

He answered, "I will stay here until you return."

¹⁹Gideon hurried home. He cooked a young goat, and with a basket* of flour he baked some bread without yeast. Then, carrying the meat in a basket and the broth in a pot, he brought them out and presented them to the angel, who was under the great tree.

²⁰The angel of God said to him, "Place the meat and the unleavened bread on this rock, and pour the broth over it." And Gideon did as he was told. ²¹Then the angel of the LORD touched the meat and bread with the tip of the staff in his hand, and fire flamed up from the rock and consumed all he had brought. And the angel of the LORD disappeared.

²²When Gideon realized that it was the angel of the LORD, he cried out, "Oh, Sovereign LORD, I'm doomed! I have seen the angel of the LORD face to face!"

²³"It is all right," the LORD replied. "Do not be afraid. You will not die." ²⁴And Gideon built an altar to the LORD there and named it Yahweh-Shalom (which means "the LORD is peace"). The altar remains in Ophrah in the land of the clan of Abiezer to this day.

²⁵That night the LORD said to Gideon, "Take the second bull from your father's herd, the one that is seven years old. Pull down your father's altar to Baal, and cut down the Asherah pole standing beside it. ²⁶Then build an altar to the LORD your God here on this hilltop sanctuary, laying the stones carefully. Sacrifice the bull as a burnt offering on the altar, using as fuel the wood of the Asherah pole you cut down."

²⁷So Gideon took ten of his servants and did as the LORD had commanded. But he did it at night because he was afraid of the other members of his father's household and the people of the town.

²⁸Early the next morning, as the people of the town began to stir, someone discovered that the altar of Baal had been broken down and that the Asherah pole beside it had been cut down. In their place a new altar had been built, and on it were the remains of the bull that had been sacrificed. ²⁹The people said to each other, "Who did this?" And after asking around and making a careful search, they learned that it was Gideon, the son of Joash.

³⁰"Bring out your son," the men of the town

6:19 Hebrew *an ephah* [20 quarts or 22 liters].

demanded of Joash. "He must die for destroying the altar of Baal and for cutting down the Asherah pole."

31 But Joash shouted to the mob that confronted him, "Why are you defending Baal? Will you argue his case? Whoever pleads his case will be put to death by morning! If Baal truly is a god, let him defend himself and destroy the one who broke down his altar!" 32 From then on Gideon was called Jerub-baal, which means "Let Baal defend himself," because he broke down Baal's altar.

Gideon Asks for a Sign

33 Soon afterward the armies of Midian, Amalek, and the people of the east formed an alliance against Israel and crossed the Jordan, camping in the valley of Jezreel. 34 Then the Spirit of the LORD clothed Gideon with power. He blew a ram's horn as a call to arms, and the men of the clan of Abiezer came to him. 35 He also sent messengers throughout Manasseh, Asher, Zebulun, and Naphtali, summoning their warriors, and all of them responded.

36 Then Gideon said to God, "If you are truly going to use me to rescue Israel as you promised, 37 prove it to me in this way. I will put a wool fleece on the threshing floor tonight. If the fleece is wet with dew in the morning but the ground is dry, then I will know that you are going to help me rescue Israel as you promised." 38 And that is just what happened. When Gideon got up early the next morning, he squeezed the fleece and wrung out a whole bowlful of water.

39 Then Gideon said to God, "Please don't be angry with me, but let me make one more request. Let me use the fleece for one more test. This time let the fleece remain dry while the ground around it is wet with dew." 40 So that night God did as Gideon asked. The fleece was dry in the morning, but the ground was covered with dew.

Gideon Defeats the Midianites

7 So Jerub-baal (that is, Gideon) and his army got up early and went as far as the spring of Harod. The armies of Midian were camped north of them in the valley near the hill of Moreh. 2 The LORD said to Gideon, "You have too many warriors with you. If I let all of you fight the Midianites, the Israelites will boast to me that they saved themselves by their own strength. 3 Therefore, tell the people, 'Whoever is timid or afraid may leave this mountain* and go home.'" So 22,000 of them went home, leaving only 10,000 who were willing to fight.

4 But the LORD told Gideon, "There are still too many! Bring them down to the spring, and I will test them to determine who will go with you and who will not." 5 When Gideon took his warriors down to the water, the LORD told him, "Divide the men into two groups. In one group put all those who cup water in their hands and lap it up with their tongues like dogs. In the other group put all those who kneel down and drink with their mouths in the stream." 6 Only 300 of the men drank from their hands. All the others got down on their knees and drank with their mouths in the stream.

7 The LORD told Gideon, "With these 300 men I will rescue you and give you victory over the Midianites. Send all the others home." 8 So Gideon collected the provisions and rams' horns of the other warriors and sent them home. But he kept the 300 men with him.

The Midianite camp was in the valley just below Gideon. 9 That night the LORD said, "Get up! Go down into the Midianite camp, for I have given you victory over them! 10 But if you are afraid to attack, go down to the camp with your servant Purah. 11 Listen to what the Midianites are saying, and you will be greatly encouraged. Then you will be eager to attack."

So Gideon took Purah and went down to the edge of the enemy camp. 12 The armies of Midian, Amalek, and the people of the east had settled in the valley like a swarm of locusts. Their camels were like grains of sand on the seashore—too many to count! 13 Gideon crept up just as a man was telling his companion about a dream. The man said, "I had this dream, and in my dream a loaf of barley bread came tumbling down into the Midianite camp. It hit a tent, turned it over, and knocked it flat!"

14 His companion answered, "Your dream can mean only one thing—God has given Gideon son of Joash, the Israelite, victory over Midian and all its allies!"

15 When Gideon heard the dream and its interpretation, he bowed in worship before the LORD.* Then he returned to the Israelite camp and shouted, "Get up! For the LORD has given you victory over the Midianite hordes!" 16 He divided the 300 men into three groups and gave each man a ram's horn and a clay jar with a torch in it.

17 Then he said to them, "Keep your eyes on

7:3 Hebrew *may leave Mount Gilead.* The identity of Mount Gilead is uncertain in this context. It is perhaps used here as another name for Mount Gilboa.   7:15 As in Greek version; Hebrew reads *he bowed.*

me. When I come to the edge of the camp, do just as I do. [18]As soon as I and those with me blow the rams' horns, blow your horns, too, all around the entire camp, and shout, 'For the LORD and for Gideon!'"

[19]It was just after midnight,* after the changing of the guard, when Gideon and the 100 men with him reached the edge of the Midianite camp. Suddenly, they blew the rams' horns and broke their clay jars. [20]Then all three groups blew their horns and broke their jars. They held the blazing torches in their left hands and the horns in their right hands, and they all shouted, "A sword for the LORD and for Gideon!"

[21]Each man stood at his position around the camp and watched as all the Midianites rushed around in a panic, shouting as they ran to escape. [22]When the 300 Israelites blew their rams' horns, the LORD caused the warriors in the camp to fight against each other with their swords. Those who were not killed fled to places as far away as Beth-shittah near Zererah and to the border of Abel-meholah near Tabbath.

[23]Then Gideon sent for the warriors of Naphtali, Asher, and Manasseh, who joined in chasing the army of Midian. [24]Gideon also sent messengers throughout the hill country of Ephraim, saying, "Come down to attack the Midianites. Cut them off at the shallow crossings of the Jordan River at Beth-barah."

So all the men of Ephraim did as they were told. [25]They captured Oreb and Zeeb, the two Midianite commanders, killing Oreb at the rock of Oreb, and Zeeb at the winepress of Zeeb. And they continued to chase the Midianites. Afterward the Israelites brought the heads of Oreb and Zeeb to Gideon, who was by the Jordan River.

Gideon Kills Zebah and Zalmunna

8 Then the people of Ephraim asked Gideon, "Why have you treated us this way? Why didn't you send for us when you first went out to fight the Midianites?" And they argued heatedly with Gideon.

[2]But Gideon replied, "What have I accomplished compared to you? Aren't even the leftover grapes of Ephraim's harvest better than the entire crop of my little clan of Abiezer? [3]God gave you victory over Oreb and Zeeb, the commanders of the Midianite army. What have I accomplished compared to that?" When the men of Ephraim heard Gideon's answer, their anger subsided.

[4]Gideon then crossed the Jordan River with his 300 men, and though exhausted, they continued to chase the enemy. [5]When they reached Succoth, Gideon asked the leaders of the town, "Please give my warriors some food. They are very tired. I am chasing Zebah and Zalmunna, the kings of Midian."

[6]But the officials of Succoth replied, "Catch Zebah and Zalmunna first, and then we will feed your army."

[7]So Gideon said, "After the LORD gives me victory over Zebah and Zalmunna, I will return and tear your flesh with the thorns and briers from the wilderness."

[8]From there Gideon went up to Peniel* and again asked for food, but he got the same answer. [9]So he said to the people of Peniel, "After I return in victory, I will tear down this tower."

[10]By this time Zebah and Zalmunna were in Karkor with about 15,000 warriors—all that remained of the allied armies of the east, for 120,000 had already been killed. [11]Gideon circled around by the caravan route east of Nobah and Jogbehah, taking the Midianite army by surprise. [12]Zebah and Zalmunna, the two Midianite kings, fled, but Gideon chased them down and captured all their warriors.

[13]After this, Gideon returned from the battle by way of Heres Pass. [14]There he captured a young man from Succoth and demanded that he write down the names of all the seventy-seven officials and elders in the town. [15]Gideon then returned to Succoth and said to the leaders, "Here are Zebah and Zalmunna. When we were here before, you taunted me, saying, 'Catch Zebah and Zalmunna first, and then we will feed your exhausted army.'" [16]Then Gideon took the elders of the town and taught them a lesson, punishing them with thorns and briers from the wilderness. [17]He also tore down the tower of Peniel and killed all the men in the town.

[18]Then Gideon asked Zebah and Zalmunna, "The men you killed at Tabor—what were they like?"

"Like you," they replied. "They all had the look of a king's son."

[19]"They were my brothers, the sons of my own mother!" Gideon exclaimed. "As surely as the LORD lives, I wouldn't kill you if you hadn't killed them."

[20]Turning to Jether, his oldest son, he said, "Kill them!" But Jether did not draw his sword, for he was only a boy and was afraid.

[21]Then Zebah and Zalmunna said to Gideon,

7:19 Hebrew *at the beginning of the second watch.*   8:8 Hebrew *Penuel,* a variant spelling of Peniel; also in 8:9, 17.

"Be a man! Kill us yourself!" So Gideon killed them both and took the royal ornaments from the necks of their camels.

Gideon's Sacred Ephod

22Then the Israelites said to Gideon, "Be our ruler! You and your son and your grandson will be our rulers, for you have rescued us from Midian."

23But Gideon replied, "I will not rule over you, nor will my son. The LORD will rule over you! 24However, I do have one request—that each of you give me an earring from the plunder you collected from your fallen enemies." (The enemies, being Ishmaelites, all wore gold earrings.)

25"Gladly!" they replied. They spread out a cloak, and each one threw in a gold earring he had gathered from the plunder. 26The weight of the gold earrings was forty-three pounds,* not including the royal ornaments and pendants, the purple clothing worn by the kings of Midian, or the chains around the necks of their camels.

27Gideon made a sacred ephod from the gold and put it in Ophrah, his hometown. But soon all the Israelites prostituted themselves by worshiping it, and it became a trap for Gideon and his family.

28That is the story of how the people of Israel defeated Midian, which never recovered. Throughout the rest of Gideon's lifetime—about forty years—there was peace in the land. 29Then Gideon* son of Joash returned home. 30He had seventy sons born to him, for he had many wives. 31He also had a concubine in Shechem, who gave birth to a son, whom he named Abimelech. 32Gideon died when he was very old, and he was buried in the grave of his father, Joash, at Ophrah in the land of the clan of Abiezer.

33As soon as Gideon died, the Israelites prostituted themselves by worshiping the images of Baal, making Baal-berith their god. 34They forgot the LORD their God, who had rescued them from all their enemies surrounding them. 35Nor did they show any loyalty to the family of Jerub-baal (that is, Gideon), despite all the good he had done for Israel.

Abimelech Rules over Shechem

9 One day Gideon's* son Abimelech went to Shechem to visit his uncles—his mother's brothers. He said to them and to the rest of his mother's family, 2"Ask the leading citizens of Shechem whether they want to be ruled by all seventy of Gideon's sons or by one man. And remember that I am your own flesh and blood!"

3So Abimelech's uncles gave his message to all the citizens of Shechem on his behalf. And after listening to this proposal, the people of Shechem decided in favor of Abimelech because he was their relative. 4They gave him seventy silver coins from the temple of Baal-berith, which he used to hire some reckless troublemakers who agreed to follow him. 5He went to his father's home at Ophrah, and there, on one stone, they killed all seventy of his half brothers, the sons of Gideon.* But the youngest brother, Jotham, escaped and hid.

6Then all the leading citizens of Shechem and Beth-millo called a meeting under the oak beside the pillar* at Shechem and made Abimelech their king.

Jotham's Parable

7When Jotham heard about this, he climbed to the top of Mount Gerizim and shouted,

"Listen to me, citizens of Shechem!
    Listen to me if you want God to listen
        to you!
8 Once upon a time the trees decided to
        choose a king.
    First they said to the olive tree,
        'Be our king!'
9 But the olive tree refused, saying,
    'Should I quit producing the olive oil
        that blesses both God and people,
        just to wave back and forth over the
            trees?'

10 "Then they said to the fig tree,
        'You be our king!'
11 But the fig tree also refused, saying,
    'Should I quit producing my sweet
            fruit
        just to wave back and forth over the
            trees?'

12 "Then they said to the grapevine,
        'You be our king!'
13 But the grapevine also refused, saying,
    'Should I quit producing the wine
        that cheers both God and people,
        just to wave back and forth over the
            trees?'

8:26 Hebrew 1,700 [shekels] [19.4 kilograms].   8:29 Hebrew Jerub-baal; see 6:32.   9:1 Hebrew Jerub-baal's (see 6:32); also in 9:2, 24.   9:5 Hebrew Jerub-baal (see 6:32); also in 9:16, 19, 28, 57.   9:6 The meaning of the Hebrew is uncertain.

¹⁴ "Then all the trees finally turned to the
  thornbush and said,
  'Come, you be our king!'
¹⁵ And the thornbush replied to the trees,
  'If you truly want to make me your king,
  come and take shelter in my shade.
  If not, let fire come out from me
  and devour the cedars of Lebanon.'"

¹⁶Jotham continued, "Now make sure you have acted honorably and in good faith by making Abimelech your king, and that you have done right by Gideon and all of his descendants. Have you treated him with the honor he deserves for all he accomplished? ¹⁷For he fought for you and risked his life when he rescued you from the Midianites. ¹⁸But today you have revolted against my father and his descendants, killing his seventy sons on one stone. And you have chosen his slave woman's son, Abimelech, to be your king just because he is your relative.

¹⁹"If you have acted honorably and in good faith toward Gideon and his descendants today, then may you find joy in Abimelech, and may he find joy in you. ²⁰But if you have not acted in good faith, then may fire come out from Abimelech and devour the leading citizens of Shechem and Beth-millo; and may fire come out from the citizens of Shechem and Beth-millo and devour Abimelech!"

²¹Then Jotham escaped and lived in Beer because he was afraid of his brother Abimelech.

Shechem Rebels against Abimelech

²²After Abimelech had ruled over Israel for three years, ²³God sent a spirit that stirred up trouble between Abimelech and the leading citizens of Shechem, and they revolted. ²⁴God was punishing Abimelech for murdering Gideon's seventy sons, and the citizens of Shechem for supporting him in this treachery of murdering his brothers. ²⁵The citizens of Shechem set an ambush for Abimelech on the hilltops and robbed everyone who passed that way. But someone warned Abimelech about their plot.

²⁶One day Gaal son of Ebed moved to Shechem with his brothers and gained the confidence of the leading citizens of Shechem. ²⁷During the annual harvest festival at Shechem, held in the temple of the local god, the wine flowed freely, and everyone began cursing Abimelech. ²⁸"Who is Abimelech?"* Gaal shouted. "He's not a true son of Shechem,* so

why should we be his servants? He's merely the son of Gideon, and this Zebul is merely his deputy. Serve the true sons of Hamor, the founder of Shechem. Why should we serve Abimelech? ²⁹If I were in charge here, I would get rid of Abimelech. I would say* to him, 'Get some soldiers, and come out and fight!'"

³⁰But when Zebul, the leader of the city, heard what Gaal was saying, he was furious. ³¹He sent messengers to Abimelech in Arumah,* telling him, "Gaal son of Ebed and his brothers have come to live in Shechem, and now they are inciting the city to rebel against you. ³²Come by night with an army and hide out in the fields. ³³In the morning, as soon as it is daylight, attack the city. When Gaal and those who are with him come out against you, you can do with them as you wish."

³⁴So Abimelech and all his men went by night and split into four groups, stationing themselves around Shechem. ³⁵Gaal was standing at the city gates when Abimelech and his army came out of hiding. ³⁶When Gaal saw them, he said to Zebul, "Look, there are people coming down from the hilltops!"

Zebul replied, "It's just the shadows on the hills that look like men."

³⁷But again Gaal said, "No, people are coming down from the hills.* And another group is coming down the road past the Diviners' Oak.*"

³⁸Then Zebul turned on him and asked, "Now where is that big mouth of yours? Wasn't it you that said, 'Who is Abimelech, and why should we be his servants?' The men you mocked are right outside the city! Go out and fight them!"

³⁹So Gaal led the leading citizens of Shechem into battle against Abimelech. ⁴⁰But Abimelech chased him, and many of Shechem's men were wounded and fell along the road as they retreated to the city gate. ⁴¹Abimelech returned to Arumah, and Zebul drove Gaal and his brothers out of Shechem.

⁴²The next day the people of Shechem went out into the fields to battle. When Abimelech heard about it, ⁴³he divided his men into three groups and set an ambush in the fields. When Abimelech saw the people coming out of the city, he and his men jumped up from their hiding places and attacked them. ⁴⁴Abimelech and his group stormed the city gate to keep the men of Shechem from getting back in, while Abimelech's other two groups cut them down in the

9:28 Hebrew *Who is Shechem?*   9:29 As in Greek version; Hebrew reads *And he said.*   9:31 Or *in secret;* Hebrew reads *in Tormah;* compare 9:41.   9:37a Or *the center of the land.*   9:37b Hebrew *Elon-meonenim.*

fields. 45The battle went on all day before Abimelech finally captured the city. He killed the people, leveled the city, and scattered salt all over the ground.

46When the leading citizens who lived in the tower of Shechem heard what had happened, they ran and hid in the temple of Baal-berith.* 47Someone reported to Abimelech that the citizens had gathered in the temple, 48so he led his forces to Mount Zalmon. He took an ax and chopped some branches from a tree, then put them on his shoulder. "Quick, do as I have done!" he told his men. 49So each of them cut down some branches, following Abimelech's example. They piled the branches against the walls of the temple and set them on fire. So all the people who had lived in the tower of Shechem died—about 1,000 men and women.

50Then Abimelech attacked the town of Thebez and captured it. 51But there was a strong tower inside the town, and all the men and women—the entire population—fled to it. They barricaded themselves in and climbed up to the roof of the tower. 52Abimelech followed them to attack the tower. But as he prepared to set fire to the entrance, 53a woman on the roof dropped a millstone that landed on Abimelech's head and crushed his skull.

54He quickly said to his young armor bearer, "Draw your sword and kill me! Don't let it be said that a woman killed Abimelech!" So the young man ran him through with his sword, and he died. 55When Abimelech's men saw that he was dead, they disbanded and returned to their homes.

56In this way, God punished Abimelech for the evil he had done against his father by murdering his seventy brothers. 57God also punished the men of Shechem for all their evil. So the curse of Jotham son of Gideon was fulfilled.

Tola Becomes Israel's Judge

10 After Abimelech died, Tola son of Puah, son of Dodo, was the next person to rescue Israel. He was from the tribe of Issachar but lived in the town of Shamir in the hill country of Ephraim. 2He judged Israel for twenty-three years. When he died, he was buried in Shamir.

Jair Becomes Israel's Judge

3After Tola died, Jair from Gilead judged Israel for twenty-two years. 4His thirty sons rode around on thirty donkeys, and they owned thirty towns in the land of Gilead, which are still called the Towns of Jair.* 5When Jair died, he was buried in Kamon.

The Ammonites Oppress Israel

6Again the Israelites did evil in the LORD's sight. They served the images of Baal and Ashtoreth, and the gods of Aram, Sidon, Moab, Ammon, and Philistia. They abandoned the LORD and no longer served him at all. 7So the LORD burned with anger against Israel, and he turned them over to the Philistines and the Ammonites, 8who began to oppress them that year. For eighteen years they oppressed all the Israelites east of the Jordan River in the land of the Amorites (that is, in Gilead). 9The Ammonites also crossed to the west side of the Jordan and attacked Judah, Benjamin, and Ephraim.

The Israelites were in great distress. 10Finally, they cried out to the LORD for help, saying, "We have sinned against you because we have abandoned you as our God and have served the images of Baal."

11The LORD replied, "Did I not rescue you from the Egyptians, the Amorites, the Ammonites, the Philistines, 12the Sidonians, the Amalekites, and the Maonites? When they oppressed you, you cried out to me for help, and I rescued you. 13Yet you have abandoned me and served other gods. So I will not rescue you anymore. 14Go and cry out to the gods you have chosen! Let them rescue you in your hour of distress!"

15But the Israelites pleaded with the LORD and said, "We have sinned. Punish us as you see fit, only rescue us today from our enemies." 16Then the Israelites put aside their foreign gods and served the LORD. And he was grieved by their misery.

17At that time the armies of Ammon had gathered for war and were camped in Gilead, and the people of Israel assembled and camped at Mizpah. 18The leaders of Gilead said to each other, "Whoever attacks the Ammonites first will become ruler over all the people of Gilead."

Jephthah Becomes Israel's Judge

11 Now Jephthah of Gilead was a great warrior. He was the son of Gilead, but his mother was a prostitute. 2Gilead's wife also had several sons, and when these half brothers grew up, they chased Jephthah off the land. "You will not get any of our father's inheritance," they said, "for you are the son of a prostitute." 3So Jephthah fled from his brothers and

---

9:46 Hebrew *El-berith,* another name for Baal-berith; compare 9:4.   10:4 Hebrew *Havvoth-jair.*

lived in the land of Tob. Soon he had a band of worthless rebels following him.

⁴At about this time, the Ammonites began their war against Israel. ⁵When the Ammonites attacked, the elders of Gilead sent for Jephthah in the land of Tob. ⁶The elders said, "Come and be our commander! Help us fight the Ammonites!"

⁷But Jephthah said to them, "Aren't you the ones who hated me and drove me from my father's house? Why do you come to me now when you're in trouble?"

⁸"Because we need you," the elders replied. "If you lead us in battle against the Ammonites, we will make you ruler over all the people of Gilead."

⁹Jephthah said to the elders, "Let me get this straight. If I come with you and if the LORD gives me victory over the Ammonites, will you really make me ruler over all the people?"

¹⁰"The LORD is our witness," the elders replied. "We promise to do whatever you say."

¹¹So Jephthah went with the elders of Gilead, and the people made him their ruler and commander of the army. At Mizpah, in the presence of the LORD, Jephthah repeated what he had said to the elders.

¹²Then Jephthah sent messengers to the king of Ammon, asking, "Why have you come out to fight against my land?"

¹³The king of Ammon answered Jephthah's messengers, "When the Israelites came out of Egypt, they stole my land from the Arnon River to the Jabbok River and all the way to the Jordan. Now then, give back the land peaceably."

¹⁴Jephthah sent this message back to the Ammonite king:

¹⁵"This is what Jephthah says: Israel did not steal any land from Moab or Ammon. ¹⁶When the people of Israel arrived at Kadesh on their journey from Egypt after crossing the Red Sea,* ¹⁷they sent messengers to the king of Edom asking for permission to pass through his land. But their request was denied. Then they asked the king of Moab for similar permission, but he wouldn't let them pass through either. So the people of Israel stayed in Kadesh.

¹⁸"Finally, they went around Edom and Moab through the wilderness. They traveled along Moab's eastern border and camped on the other side of the Arnon River. But they never once crossed the Arnon River into Moab, for the Arnon was the border of Moab.

¹⁹"Then Israel sent messengers to King Sihon of the Amorites, who ruled from Heshbon, asking for permission to cross through his land to get to their destination. ²⁰But King Sihon didn't trust Israel to pass through his land. Instead, he mobilized his army at Jahaz and attacked them. ²¹But the LORD, the God of Israel, gave his people victory over King Sihon. So Israel took control of all the land of the Amorites, who lived in that region, ²²from the Arnon River to the Jabbok River, and from the eastern wilderness to the Jordan.

²³"So you see, it was the LORD, the God of Israel, who took away the land from the Amorites and gave it to Israel. Why, then, should we give it back to you? ²⁴You keep whatever your god Chemosh gives you, and we will keep whatever the LORD our God gives us. ²⁵Are you any better than Balak son of Zippor, king of Moab? Did he try to make a case against Israel for disputed land? Did he go to war against them?

²⁶"Israel has been living here for 300 years, inhabiting Heshbon and its surrounding settlements, all the way to Aroer and its settlements, and in all the towns along the Arnon River. Why have you made no effort to recover it before now? ²⁷Therefore, I have not sinned against you. Rather, you have wronged me by attacking me. Let the LORD, who is judge, decide today which of us is right—Israel or Ammon."

²⁸But the king of Ammon paid no attention to Jephthah's message.

Jephthah's Vow

²⁹At that time the Spirit of the LORD came upon Jephthah, and he went throughout the land of Gilead and Manasseh, including Mizpah in Gilead, and from there he led an army against the Ammonites. ³⁰And Jephthah made a vow to the LORD. He said, "If you give me victory over the Ammonites, ³¹I will give to the LORD whatever comes out of my house to meet me when I return in triumph. I will sacrifice it as a burnt offering."

³²So Jephthah led his army against the Ammonites, and the LORD gave him victory. ³³He crushed the Ammonites, devastating about

11:16 Hebrew *sea of reeds.*

twenty towns from Aroer to an area near Minnith and as far away as Abel-keramim. In this way Israel defeated the Ammonites.

34When Jephthah returned home to Mizpah, his daughter came out to meet him, playing on a tambourine and dancing for joy. She was his one and only child; he had no other sons or daughters. 35When he saw her, he tore his clothes in anguish. "Oh, my daughter!" he cried out. "You have completely destroyed me! You've brought disaster on me! For I have made a vow to the LORD, and I cannot take it back."

36And she said, "Father, if you have made a vow to the LORD, you must do to me what you have vowed, for the LORD has given you a great victory over your enemies, the Ammonites. 37But first let me do this one thing: Let me go up and roam in the hills and weep with my friends for two months, because I will die a virgin."

38"You may go," Jephthah said. And he sent her away for two months. She and her friends went into the hills and wept because she would never have children. 39When she returned home, her father kept the vow he had made, and she died a virgin.

So it has become a custom in Israel 40for young Israelite women to go away for four days each year to lament the fate of Jephthah's daughter.

Ephraim Fights with Jephthah

12 Then the people of Ephraim mobilized an army and crossed over the Jordan River to Zaphon. They sent this message to Jephthah: "Why didn't you call for us to help you fight against the Ammonites? We are going to burn down your house with you in it!"

2Jephthah replied, "I summoned you at the beginning of the dispute, but you refused to come! You failed to help us in our struggle against Ammon. 3So when I realized you weren't coming, I risked my life and went to battle without you, and the LORD gave me victory over the Ammonites. So why have you now come to fight me?"

4The people of Ephraim responded, "You men of Gilead are nothing more than fugitives from Ephraim and Manasseh." So Jephthah gathered all the men of Gilead and attacked the men of Ephraim and defeated them.

5Jephthah captured the shallow crossings of the Jordan River, and whenever a fugitive from Ephraim tried to go back across, the men of Gilead would challenge him. "Are you a member

13:4 Hebrew *any unclean thing;* also in 13:7, 14.

of the tribe of Ephraim?" they would ask. If the man said, "No, I'm not," 6they would tell him to say "Shibboleth." If he was from Ephraim, he would say "Sibboleth," because people from Ephraim cannot pronounce the word correctly. Then they would take him and kill him at the shallow crossings of the Jordan. In all, 42,000 Ephraimites were killed at that time.

7Jephthah judged Israel for six years. When he died, he was buried in one of the towns of Gilead.

Ibzan Becomes Israel's Judge

8After Jephthah died, Ibzan from Bethlehem judged Israel. 9He had thirty sons and thirty daughters. He sent his daughters to marry men outside his clan, and he brought in thirty young women from outside his clan to marry his sons. Ibzan judged Israel for seven years. 10When he died, he was buried at Bethlehem.

Elon Becomes Israel's Judge

11After Ibzan died, Elon from the tribe of Zebulun judged Israel for ten years. 12When he died, he was buried at Aijalon in Zebulun.

Abdon Becomes Israel's Judge

13After Elon died, Abdon son of Hillel, from Pirathon, judged Israel. 14He had forty sons and thirty grandsons, who rode on seventy donkeys. He judged Israel for eight years. 15When he died, he was buried at Pirathon in Ephraim, in the hill country of the Amalekites.

The Birth of Samson

13 Again the Israelites did evil in the LORD's sight, so the LORD handed them over to the Philistines, who oppressed them for forty years.

2In those days a man named Manoah from the tribe of Dan lived in the town of Zorah. His wife was unable to become pregnant, and they had no children. 3The angel of the LORD appeared to Manoah's wife and said, "Even though you have been unable to have children, you will soon become pregnant and give birth to a son. 4So be careful; you must not drink wine or any other alcoholic drink nor eat any forbidden food.* 5You will become pregnant and give birth to a son, and his hair must never be cut. For he will be dedicated to God as a Nazirite from birth. He will begin to rescue Israel from the Philistines."

6The woman ran and told her husband, "A man of God appeared to me! He looked like one of God's angels, terrifying to see. I didn't ask where he was from, and he didn't tell me his name. 7But he told me, 'You will become pregnant and give birth to a son. You must not drink wine or any other alcoholic drink nor eat any forbidden food. For your son will be dedicated to God as a Nazirite from the moment of his birth until the day of his death.'"

8Then Manoah prayed to the LORD, saying, "Lord, please let the man of God come back to us again and give us more instructions about this son who is to be born."

9God answered Manoah's prayer, and the angel of God appeared once again to his wife as she was sitting in the field. But her husband, Manoah, was not with her. 10So she quickly ran and told her husband, "The man who appeared to me the other day is here again!"

11Manoah ran back with his wife and asked, "Are you the man who spoke to my wife the other day?"

"Yes," he replied, "I am."

12So Manoah asked him, "When your words come true, what kind of rules should govern the boy's life and work?"

13The angel of the LORD replied, "Be sure your wife follows the instructions I gave her. 14She must not eat grapes or raisins, drink wine or any other alcoholic drink, or eat any forbidden food."

15Then Manoah said to the angel of the LORD, "Please stay here until we can prepare a young goat for you to eat."

16"I will stay," the angel of the LORD replied, "but I will not eat anything. However, you may prepare a burnt offering as a sacrifice to the LORD." (Manoah didn't realize it was the angel of the LORD.)

17Then Manoah asked the angel of the LORD, "What is your name? For when all this comes true, we want to honor you."

18"Why do you ask my name?" the angel of the LORD replied. "It is too wonderful for you to understand."

19Then Manoah took a young goat and a grain offering and offered it on a rock as a sacrifice to the LORD. And as Manoah and his wife watched, the LORD did an amazing thing. 20As the flames from the altar shot up toward the sky, the angel of the LORD ascended in the fire. When Manoah and his wife saw this, they fell with their faces to the ground.

21The angel did not appear again to Manoah and his wife. Manoah finally realized

14:11 Hebrew *they.*

it was the angel of the LORD, 22and he said to his wife, "We will certainly die, for we have seen God!"

23But his wife said, "If the LORD were going to kill us, he wouldn't have accepted our burnt offering and grain offering. He wouldn't have appeared to us and told us this wonderful thing and done these miracles."

24When her son was born, she named him Samson. And the LORD blessed him as he grew up. 25And the Spirit of the LORD began to stir him while he lived in Mahaneh-dan, which is located between the towns of Zorah and Eshtaol.

Samson's Riddle

14 One day when Samson was in Timnah, one of the Philistine women caught his eye. 2When he returned home, he told his father and mother, "A young Philistine woman in Timnah caught my eye. I want to marry her. Get her for me."

3His father and mother objected. "Isn't there even one woman in our tribe or among all the Israelites you could marry?" they asked. "Why must you go to the pagan Philistines to find a wife?"

But Samson told his father, "Get her for me! She looks good to me." 4His father and mother didn't realize the LORD was at work in this, creating an opportunity to work against the Philistines, who ruled over Israel at that time.

5As Samson and his parents were going down to Timnah, a young lion suddenly attacked Samson near the vineyards of Timnah. 6At that moment the Spirit of the LORD came powerfully upon him, and he ripped the lion's jaws apart with his bare hands. He did it as easily as if it were a young goat. But he didn't tell his father or mother about it. 7When Samson arrived in Timnah, he talked with the woman and was very pleased with her.

8Later, when he returned to Timnah for the wedding, he turned off the path to look at the carcass of the lion. And he found that a swarm of bees had made some honey in the carcass. 9He scooped some of the honey into his hands and ate it along the way. He also gave some to his father and mother, and they ate it. But he didn't tell them he had taken the honey from the carcass of the lion.

10As his father was making final arrangements for the marriage, Samson threw a party at Timnah, as was the custom for elite young men. 11When the bride's parents* saw him, they selected thirty young men from the town to be his companions.

¹²Samson said to them, "Let me tell you a riddle. If you solve my riddle during these seven days of the celebration, I will give you thirty fine linen robes and thirty sets of festive clothing. ¹³But if you can't solve it, then you must give me thirty fine linen robes and thirty sets of festive clothing."

"All right," they agreed, "let's hear your riddle."

¹⁴So he said:

"Out of the one who eats came something
    to eat;
    out of the strong came something
    sweet."

Three days later they were still trying to figure it out. ¹⁵On the fourth* day they said to Samson's wife, "Entice your husband to explain the riddle for us, or we will burn down your father's house with you in it. Did you invite us to this party just to make us poor?"

¹⁶So Samson's wife came to him in tears and said, "You don't love me; you hate me! You have given my people a riddle, but you haven't told me the answer."

"I haven't even given the answer to my father or mother," he replied. "Why should I tell you?" ¹⁷So she cried whenever she was with him and kept it up for the rest of the celebration. At last, on the seventh day he told her the answer because she was tormenting him with her nagging. Then she explained the riddle to the young men.

¹⁸So before sunset of the seventh day, the men of the town came to Samson with their answer:

"What is sweeter than honey?
    What is stronger than a lion?"

Samson replied, "If you hadn't plowed with my heifer, you wouldn't have solved my riddle!"

¹⁹Then the Spirit of the LORD came powerfully upon him. He went down to the town of Ashkelon, killed thirty men, took their belongings, and gave their clothing to the men who had solved his riddle. But Samson was furious about what had happened, and he went back home to live with his father and mother. ²⁰So his wife was given in marriage to the man who had been Samson's best man at the wedding.

14:15 As in Greek version; Hebrew reads *seventh.*

Samson's Vengeance on the Philistines

15 Later on, during the wheat harvest, Samson took a young goat as a present to his wife. He said, "I'm going into my wife's room to sleep with her," but her father wouldn't let him in.

²"I truly thought you must hate her," her father explained, "so I gave her in marriage to your best man. But look, her younger sister is even more beautiful than she is. Marry her instead."

³Samson said, "This time I cannot be blamed for everything I am going to do to you Philistines." ⁴Then he went out and caught 300 foxes. He tied their tails together in pairs, and he fastened a torch to each pair of tails. ⁵Then he lit the torches and let the foxes run through the grain fields of the Philistines. He burned all their grain to the ground, including the sheaves and the uncut grain. He also destroyed their vineyards and olive groves.

⁶"Who did this?" the Philistines demanded.

"Samson," was the reply, "because his father-in-law from Timnah gave Samson's wife to be married to his best man." So the Philistines went and got the woman and her father and burned them to death.

⁷"Because you did this," Samson vowed, "I won't rest until I take my revenge on you!" ⁸So he attacked the Philistines with great fury and killed many of them. Then he went to live in a cave in the rock of Etam.

⁹The Philistines retaliated by setting up camp in Judah and spreading out near the town of Lehi. ¹⁰The men of Judah asked the Philistines, "Why are you attacking us?"

The Philistines replied, "We've come to capture Samson. We've come to pay him back for what he did to us."

¹¹So 3,000 men of Judah went down to get Samson at the cave in the rock of Etam. They said to Samson, "Don't you realize the Philistines rule over us? What are you doing to us?"

But Samson replied, "I only did to them what they did to me."

¹²But the men of Judah told him, "We have come to tie you up and hand you over to the Philistines."

"All right," Samson said. "But promise that you won't kill me yourselves."

¹³"We will only tie you up and hand you over to the Philistines," they replied. "We won't kill you." So they tied him up with two new ropes and brought him up from the rock.

¹⁴As Samson arrived at Lehi, the Philistines

came shouting in triumph. But the Spirit of the LORD came powerfully upon Samson, and he snapped the ropes on his arms as if they were burnt strands of flax, and they fell from his wrists. ¹⁵Then he found the jawbone of a recently killed donkey. He picked it up and killed 1,000 Philistines with it. ¹⁶Then Samson said,

> "With the jawbone of a donkey,
>   I've piled them in heaps!
> With the jawbone of a donkey,
>   I've killed a thousand men!"

¹⁷When he finished his boasting, he threw away the jawbone; and the place was named Jawbone Hill.*

¹⁸Samson was now very thirsty, and he cried out to the LORD, "You have accomplished this great victory by the strength of your servant. Must I now die of thirst and fall into the hands of these pagans?" ¹⁹So God caused water to gush out of a hollow in the ground at Lehi, and Samson was revived as he drank. Then he named that place "The Spring of the One Who Cried Out,"* and it is still in Lehi to this day.

²⁰Samson judged Israel for twenty years during the period when the Philistines dominated the land.

Samson Carries Away Gaza's Gates

16 One day Samson went to the Philistine town of Gaza and spent the night with a prostitute. ²Word soon spread* that Samson was there, so the men of Gaza gathered together and waited all night at the town gates. They kept quiet during the night, saying to themselves, "When the light of morning comes, we will kill him."

³But Samson stayed in bed only until midnight. Then he got up, took hold of the doors of the town gate, including the two posts, and lifted them up, bar and all. He put them on his shoulders and carried them all the way to the top of the hill across from Hebron.

Samson and Delilah

⁴Some time later Samson fell in love with a woman named Delilah, who lived in the valley of Sorek. ⁵The rulers of the Philistines went to her and said, "Entice Samson to tell you what makes him so strong and how he can be

overpowered and tied up securely. Then each of us will give you 1,100 pieces* of silver."

⁶So Delilah said to Samson, "Please tell me what makes you so strong and what it would take to tie you up securely."

⁷Samson replied, "If I were tied up with seven new bowstrings that have not yet been dried, I would become as weak as anyone else."

⁸So the Philistine rulers brought Delilah seven new bowstrings, and she tied Samson up with them. ⁹She had hidden some men in one of the inner rooms of her house, and she cried out, "Samson! The Philistines have come to capture you!" But Samson snapped the bowstrings as a piece of string snaps when it is burned by a fire. So the secret of his strength was not discovered.

¹⁰Afterward Delilah said to him, "You've been making fun of me and telling me lies! Now please tell me how you can be tied up securely."

¹¹Samson replied, "If I were tied up with brand-new ropes that had never been used, I would become as weak as anyone else."

¹²So Delilah took new ropes and tied him up with them. The men were hiding in the inner room as before, and again Delilah cried out, "Samson! The Philistines have come to capture you!" But again Samson snapped the ropes from his arms as if they were thread.

¹³Then Delilah said, "You've been making fun of me and telling me lies! Now tell me how you can be tied up securely."

Samson replied, "If you were to weave the seven braids of my hair into the fabric on your loom and tighten it with the loom shuttle, I would become as weak as anyone else."

So while he slept, Delilah wove the seven braids of his hair into the fabric. ¹⁴Then she tightened it with the loom shuttle.* Again she cried out, "Samson! The Philistines have come to capture you!" But Samson woke up, pulled back the loom shuttle, and yanked his hair away from the loom and the fabric.

¹⁵Then Delilah pouted, "How can you tell me, 'I love you,' when you don't share your secrets with me? You've made fun of me three times now, and you still haven't told me what makes you so strong!" ¹⁶She tormented him with her nagging day after day until he was sick to death of it.

¹⁷Finally, Samson shared his secret with her.

15:17 Hebrew *Ramath-lehi.*   15:19 Hebrew *En-hakkore.*   16:2 As in Greek and Syriac versions and Latin Vulgate; Hebrew lacks *Word soon spread.*   16:5 Hebrew *1,100 [shekels],* about 28 pounds or 12.5 kilograms in weight.   16:13-14 As in Greek version and Latin Vulgate; Hebrew lacks *I would become as weak as anyone else. / So while he slept, Delilah wove the seven braids of his hair into the fabric.* ¹⁴*Then she tightened it with the loom shuttle.*

"My hair has never been cut," he confessed, "for I was dedicated to God as a Nazirite from birth. If my head were shaved, my strength would leave me, and I would become as weak as anyone else."

18Delilah realized he had finally told her the truth, so she sent for the Philistine rulers. "Come back one more time," she said, "for he has finally told me his secret." So the Philistine rulers returned with the money in their hands. 19Delilah lulled Samson to sleep with his head in her lap, and then she called in a man to shave off the seven locks of his hair. In this way she began to bring him down,* and his strength left him.

20Then she cried out, "Samson! The Philistines have come to capture you!"

When he woke up, he thought, "I will do as before and shake myself free." But he didn't realize the LORD had left him.

21So the Philistines captured him and gouged out his eyes. They took him to Gaza, where he was bound with bronze chains and forced to grind grain in the prison.

22But before long, his hair began to grow back.

Samson's Final Victory

23The Philistine rulers held a great festival, offering sacrifices and praising their god, Dagon. They said, "Our god has given us victory over our enemy Samson!"

24When the people saw him, they praised their god, saying, "Our god has delivered our enemy to us! The one who killed so many of us is now in our power!"

25Half drunk by now, the people demanded, "Bring out Samson so he can amuse us!" So he was brought from the prison to amuse them, and they had him stand between the pillars supporting the roof. 26Samson said to the young servant who was leading him by the hand, "Place my hands against the pillars that hold up the temple. I want to rest against them." 27Now the temple was completely filled with people. All the Philistine rulers were there, and there were about 3,000 men and women on the roof who were watching as Samson amused them.

28Then Samson prayed to the LORD, "Sovereign LORD, remember me again. O God, please strengthen me just one more time. With one blow let me pay back the Philistines for the loss of my two eyes." 29Then Samson put his hands on the two center pillars that held up the temple. Pushing against them with both hands, 30he prayed, "Let me die with the Philistines." And the temple crashed down on the Philistine rulers and all the people. So he killed more people when he died than he had during his entire lifetime.

31Later his brothers and other relatives went down to get his body. They took him back home and buried him between Zorah and Eshtaol, where his father, Manoah, was buried. Samson had judged Israel for twenty years.

Micah's Idols

17 There was a man named Micah, who lived in the hill country of Ephraim. 2One day he said to his mother, "I heard you place a curse on the person who stole 1,100 pieces* of silver from you. Well, I have the money. I was the one who took it."

"The LORD bless you for admitting it," his mother replied. 3He returned the money to her, and she said, "I now dedicate these silver coins to the LORD. In honor of my son, I will have an image carved and an idol cast."

4So when he returned the money to his mother, she took 200 silver coins and gave them to a silversmith, who made them into an image and an idol. And these were placed in Micah's house. 5Micah set up a shrine for the idol, and he made a sacred ephod and some household idols. Then he installed one of his sons as his personal priest.

6In those days Israel had no king; all the people did whatever seemed right in their own eyes.

7One day a young Levite, who had been living in Bethlehem in Judah, arrived in that area. 8He had left Bethlehem in search of another place to live, and as he traveled, he came to the hill country of Ephraim. He happened to stop at Micah's house as he was traveling through. 9"Where are you from?" Micah asked him.

He replied, "I am a Levite from Bethlehem in Judah, and I am looking for a place to live."

10"Stay here with me," Micah said, "and you can be a father and priest to me. I will give you ten pieces of silver* a year, plus a change of clothes and your food." 11The Levite agreed to this, and the young man became like one of Micah's sons.

12So Micah installed the Levite as his personal priest, and he lived in Micah's house. 13"I know the LORD will bless me now," Micah

16:19 Or she began to torment him. Greek version reads He began to grow weak.   17:2 Hebrew 1,100 [shekels], about 28 pounds or 12.5 kilograms in weight.   17:10 Hebrew 10 [shekels] of silver, about 4 ounces or 114 grams in weight.

said, "because I have a Levite serving as my priest."

Idolatry in the Tribe of Dan

18 Now in those days Israel had no king. And the tribe of Dan was trying to find a place where they could settle, for they had not yet moved into the land assigned to them when the land was divided among the tribes of Israel. ²So the men of Dan chose from their clans five capable warriors from the towns of Zorah and Eshtaol to scout out a land for them to settle in.

When these warriors arrived in the hill country of Ephraim, they came to Micah's house and spent the night there. ³While at Micah's house, they recognized the young Levite's accent, so they went over and asked him, "Who brought you here, and what are you doing in this place? Why are you here?" ⁴He told them about his agreement with Micah and that he had been hired as Micah's personal priest.

⁵Then they said, "Ask God whether or not our journey will be successful."

⁶"Go in peace," the priest replied. "For the LORD is watching over your journey."

⁷So the five men went on to the town of Laish, where they noticed the people living carefree lives, like the Sidonians; they were peaceful and secure.* The people were also wealthy because their land was very fertile. And they lived a great distance from Sidon and had no allies nearby.

⁸When the men returned to Zorah and Eshtaol, their relatives asked them, "What did you find?"

⁹The men replied, "Come on, let's attack them! We have seen the land, and it is very good. What are you waiting for? Don't hesitate to go and take possession of it. ¹⁰When you get there, you will find the people living carefree lives. God has given us a spacious and fertile land, lacking in nothing!"

¹¹So 600 men from the tribe of Dan, armed with weapons of war, set out from Zorah and Eshtaol. ¹²They camped at a place west of Kiriath-jearim in Judah, which is called Mahaneh-dan* to this day. ¹³Then they went on from there into the hill country of Ephraim and came to the house of Micah.

¹⁴The five men who had scouted out the land around Laish explained to the others, "These buildings contain a sacred ephod, as well as some household idols, a carved image, and a cast idol. What do you think you should do?" ¹⁵Then the five men turned off the road

and went over to Micah's house, where the young Levite lived, and greeted him kindly. ¹⁶As the 600 armed warriors from the tribe of Dan stood at the entrance of the gate, ¹⁷the five scouts entered the shrine and removed the carved image, the sacred ephod, the household idols, and the cast idol. Meanwhile, the priest was standing at the gate with the 600 armed warriors.

¹⁸When the priest saw the men carrying all the sacred objects out of Micah's shrine, he said, "What are you doing?"

¹⁹"Be quiet and come with us," they said. "Be a father and priest to all of us. Isn't it better to be a priest for an entire tribe and clan of Israel than for the household of just one man?"

²⁰The young priest was quite happy to go with them, so he took along the sacred ephod, the household idols, and the carved image. ²¹They turned and started on their way again, placing their children, livestock, and possessions in front of them.

²²When the people from the tribe of Dan were quite a distance from Micah's house, the people who lived near Micah came chasing after them. ²³They were shouting as they caught up with them. The men of Dan turned around and said to Micah, "What's the matter? Why have you called these men together and chased after us like this?"

²⁴"What do you mean, 'What's the matter?' " Micah replied. "You've taken away all the gods I have made, and my priest, and I have nothing left!"

²⁵The men of Dan said, "Watch what you say! There are some short-tempered men around here who might get angry and kill you and your family." ²⁶So the men of Dan continued on their way. When Micah saw that there were too many of them for him to attack, he turned around and went home.

²⁷Then, with Micah's idols and his priest, the men of Dan came to the town of Laish, whose people were peaceful and secure. They attacked with swords and burned the town to the ground. ²⁸There was no one to rescue the people, for they lived a great distance from Sidon and had no allies nearby. This happened in the valley near Beth-rehob.

Then the people of the tribe of Dan rebuilt the town and lived there. ²⁹They renamed the town Dan after their ancestor, Israel's son, but it had originally been called Laish.

³⁰Then they set up the carved image, and they appointed Jonathan son of Gershom, son

18:7 The meaning of the Hebrew is uncertain.　18:12 *Mahaneh-dan* means "the camp of Dan."

of Moses,* as their priest. This family continued as priests for the tribe of Dan until the Exile. ³¹So Micah's carved image was worshiped by the tribe of Dan as long as the Tabernacle of God remained at Shiloh.

The Levite and His Concubine

19 Now in those days Israel had no king. There was a man from the tribe of Levi living in a remote area of the hill country of Ephraim. One day he brought home a woman from Bethlehem in Judah to be his concubine. ²But she became angry with him* and returned to her father's home in Bethlehem.

After about four months, ³her husband set out for Bethlehem to speak personally to her and persuade her to come back. He took with him a servant and a pair of donkeys. When he arrived at* her father's house, her father saw him and welcomed him. ⁴Her father urged him to stay awhile, so he stayed three days, eating, drinking, and sleeping there.

⁵On the fourth day the man was up early, ready to leave, but the woman's father said to his son-in-law, "Have something to eat before you go." ⁶So the two men sat down together and had something to eat and drink. Then the woman's father said, "Please stay another night and enjoy yourself." ⁷The man got up to leave, but his father-in-law kept urging him to stay, so he finally gave in and stayed the night.

⁸On the morning of the fifth day he was up early again, ready to leave, and again the woman's father said, "Have something to eat; then you can leave later this afternoon." So they had another day of feasting. ⁹Later, as the man and his concubine and servant were preparing to leave, his father-in-law said, "Look, it's almost evening. Stay the night and enjoy yourself. Tomorrow you can get up early and be on your way."

¹⁰But this time the man was determined to leave. So he took his two saddled donkeys and his concubine and headed in the direction of Jebus (that is, Jerusalem). ¹¹It was late in the day when they neared Jebus, and the man's servant said to him, "Let's stop at this Jebusite town and spend the night there."

¹²"No," his master said, "we can't stay in this foreign town where there are no Israelites. Instead, we will go on to Gibeah. ¹³Come on, let's try to get as far as Gibeah or Ramah, and we'll spend the night in one of those towns." ¹⁴So

they went on. The sun was setting as they came to Gibeah, a town in the land of Benjamin, ¹⁵so they stopped there to spend the night. They rested in the town square, but no one took them in for the night.

¹⁶That evening an old man came home from his work in the fields. He was from the hill country of Ephraim, but he was living in Gibeah, where the people were from the tribe of Benjamin. ¹⁷When he saw the travelers sitting in the town square, he asked them where they were from and where they were going.

¹⁸"We have been in Bethlehem in Judah," the man replied. "We are on our way to a remote area in the hill country of Ephraim, which is my home. I traveled to Bethlehem, and now I'm returning home.* But no one has taken us in for the night, ¹⁹even though we have everything we need. We have straw and feed for our donkeys and plenty of bread and wine for ourselves."

²⁰"You are welcome to stay with me," the old man said. "I will give you anything you might need. But whatever you do, don't spend the night in the square." ²¹So he took them home with him and fed the donkeys. After they washed their feet, they ate and drank together.

²²While they were enjoying themselves, a crowd of troublemakers from the town surrounded the house. They began beating at the door and shouting to the old man, "Bring out the man who is staying with you so we can have sex with him."

²³The old man stepped outside to talk to them. "No, my brothers, don't do such an evil thing. For this man is a guest in my house, and such a thing would be shameful. ²⁴Here, take my virgin daughter and this man's concubine. I will bring them out to you, and you can abuse them and do whatever you like. But don't do such a shameful thing to this man."

²⁵But they wouldn't listen to him. So the Levite took hold of his concubine and pushed her out the door. The men of the town abused her all night, taking turns raping her until morning. Finally, at dawn they let her go. ²⁶At daybreak the woman returned to the house where her husband was staying. She collapsed at the door of the house and lay there until it was light.

²⁷When her husband opened the door to leave, there lay his concubine with her hands on the threshold. ²⁸He said, "Get up! Let's go!"

18:30 As in an ancient Hebrew tradition, some Greek manuscripts, and Latin Vulgate; Masoretic Text reads *son of Manasseh*. 19:2 Or *she was unfaithful to him*.   19:3 As in Greek version; Hebrew reads *When she brought him to*.   19:18 As in Greek version (see also 19:29); Hebrew reads *now I'm going to the Tabernacle of the LORD*.

But there was no answer.* So he put her body on his donkey and took her home.

²⁹When he got home, he took a knife and cut his concubine's body into twelve pieces. Then he sent one piece to each tribe throughout all the territory of Israel.

³⁰Everyone who saw it said, "Such a horrible crime has not been committed in all the time since Israel left Egypt. Think about it! What are we going to do? Who's going to speak up?"

Israel's War with Benjamin

20 Then all the Israelites were united as one man, from Dan in the north to Beersheba in the south, including those from across the Jordan in the land of Gilead. The entire community assembled in the presence of the Lord at Mizpah. ²The leaders of all the people and all the tribes of Israel—400,000 warriors armed with swords—took their positions in the assembly of the people of God. ³(Word soon reached the land of Benjamin that the other tribes had gone up to Mizpah.) The Israelites then asked how this terrible crime had happened.

⁴The Levite, the husband of the woman who had been murdered, said, "My concubine and I came to spend the night in Gibeah, a town that belongs to the people of Benjamin. ⁵That night some of the leading citizens of Gibeah surrounded the house, planning to kill me, and they raped my concubine until she was dead. ⁶So I cut her body into twelve pieces and sent the pieces throughout the territory assigned to Israel, for these men have committed a terrible and shameful crime. ⁷Now then, all of you—the entire community of Israel—must decide here and now what should be done about this!"

⁸And all the people rose to their feet in unison and declared, "None of us will return home! No, not even one of us! ⁹Instead, this is what we will do to Gibeah; we will draw lots to decide who will attack it. ¹⁰One-tenth of the men* from each tribe will be chosen to supply the warriors with food, and the rest of us will take revenge on Gibeah* of Benjamin for this shameful thing they have done in Israel." ¹¹So all the Israelites were completely united, and they gathered together to attack the town.

¹²The Israelites sent messengers to the tribe of Benjamin, saying, "What a terrible thing has been done among you! ¹³Give up those evil men, those troublemakers from Gibeah, so we can execute them and purge Israel of this evil."

But the people of Benjamin would not listen. ¹⁴Instead, they came from their towns and gathered at Gibeah to fight the Israelites. ¹⁵In all, 26,000 of their warriors armed with swords arrived in Gibeah to join the 700 elite troops who lived there. ¹⁶Among Benjamin's elite troops, 700 were left-handed, and each of them could sling a rock and hit a target within a hairsbreadth without missing. ¹⁷Israel had 400,000 experienced soldiers armed with swords, not counting Benjamin's warriors.

¹⁸Before the battle the Israelites went to Bethel and asked God, "Which tribe should go first to attack the people of Benjamin?"

The Lord answered, "Judah is to go first."

¹⁹So the Israelites left early the next morning and camped near Gibeah. ²⁰Then they advanced toward Gibeah to attack the men of Benjamin. ²¹But Benjamin's warriors, who were defending the town, came out and killed 22,000 Israelites on the battlefield that day.

²²But the Israelites encouraged each other and took their positions again at the same place they had fought the previous day. ²³For they had gone up to Bethel and wept in the presence of the Lord until evening. They had asked the Lord, "Should we fight against our relatives from Benjamin again?"

And the Lord had said, "Go out and fight against them."

²⁴So the next day they went out again to fight against the men of Benjamin, ²⁵but the men of Benjamin killed another 18,000 Israelites, all of whom were experienced with the sword.

²⁶Then all the Israelites went up to Bethel and wept in the presence of the Lord and fasted until evening. They also brought burnt offerings and peace offerings to the Lord. ²⁷The Israelites went up seeking direction from the Lord. (In those days the Ark of the Covenant of God was in Bethel, ²⁸and Phinehas son of Eleazar and grandson of Aaron was the priest.) The Israelites asked the Lord, "Should we fight against our relatives from Benjamin again, or should we stop?"

The Lord said, "Go! Tomorrow I will hand them over to you."

²⁹So the Israelites set an ambush all around Gibeah. ³⁰They went out on the third day and took their positions at the same place as before. ³¹When the men of Benjamin came out to attack, they were drawn away from the town. And as they had done before, they began to kill the Israelites. About thirty Israelites died in the

---

19:28 Greek version adds *for she was dead*.   20:10a Hebrew *10 men from every hundred, 100 men from every thousand, and 1,000 men from every 10,000*.   20:10b Hebrew *Geba*, in this case a variant spelling of Gibeah; also in 20:33.

open fields and along the roads, one leading to Bethel and the other leading back to Gibeah. ³²Then the warriors of Benjamin shouted, "We're defeating them as we did before!" But the Israelites had planned in advance to run away so that the men of Benjamin would chase them along the roads and be drawn away from the town.

³³When the main group of Israelite warriors reached Baal-tamar, they turned and took up their positions. Meanwhile, the Israelites hiding in ambush to the west* of Gibeah jumped up to fight. ³⁴There were 10,000 elite Israelite troops who advanced against Gibeah. The fighting was so heavy that Benjamin didn't realize the impending disaster. ³⁵So the Lord helped Israel defeat Benjamin, and that day the Israelites killed 25,100 of Benjamin's warriors, all of whom were experienced swordsmen. ³⁶Then the men of Benjamin saw that they were beaten.

The Israelites had retreated from Benjamin's warriors in order to give those hiding in ambush more room to maneuver against Gibeah. ³⁷Then those who were hiding rushed in from all sides and killed everyone in the town. ³⁸They had arranged to send up a large cloud of smoke from the town as a signal. ³⁹When the Israelites saw the smoke, they turned and attacked Benjamin's warriors.

By that time Benjamin's warriors had killed about thirty Israelites, and they shouted, "We're defeating them as we did in the first battle!" ⁴⁰But when the warriors of Benjamin looked behind them and saw the smoke rising into the sky from every part of the town, ⁴¹the men of Israel turned and attacked. At this point the men of Benjamin became terrified, because they realized disaster was close at hand. ⁴²So they turned around and fled before the Israelites toward the wilderness. But they couldn't escape the battle, and the people who came out of the nearby towns were also killed.* ⁴³The Israelites surrounded the men of Benjamin and chased them relentlessly, finally overtaking them east of Gibeah.* ⁴⁴That day 18,000 of Benjamin's strongest warriors died in battle. ⁴⁵The survivors fled into the wilderness toward the rock of Rimmon, but Israel killed 5,000 of them along the road. They continued the chase until they had killed another 2,000 near Gidom.

⁴⁶So that day the tribe of Benjamin lost 25,000 strong warriors armed with swords, ⁴⁷leaving only 600 men who escaped to the rock of Rimmon, where they lived for four months. ⁴⁸And the Israelites returned and slaughtered every living thing in all the towns—the people, the livestock, and everything they found. They also burned down all the towns they came to.

Israel Provides Wives for Benjamin

21 The Israelites had vowed at Mizpah, "We will never give our daughters in marriage to a man from the tribe of Benjamin." ²Now the people went to Bethel and sat in the presence of God until evening, weeping loudly and bitterly. ³"O Lord, God of Israel," they cried out, "why has this happened in Israel? Now one of our tribes is missing from Israel!"

⁴Early the next morning the people built an altar and presented their burnt offerings and peace offerings on it. ⁵Then they said, "Who among the tribes of Israel did not join us at Mizpah when we held our assembly in the presence of the Lord?" At that time they had taken a solemn oath in the Lord's presence, vowing that anyone who refused to come would be put to death.

⁶The Israelites felt sorry for their brother Benjamin and said, "Today one of the tribes of Israel has been cut off. ⁷How can we find wives for the few who remain, since we have sworn by the Lord not to give them our daughters in marriage?"

⁸So they asked, "Who among the tribes of Israel did not join us at Mizpah when we assembled in the presence of the Lord?" And they discovered that no one from Jabesh-gilead had attended the assembly. ⁹For after they counted all the people, no one from Jabesh-gilead was present.

¹⁰So the assembly sent 12,000 of their best warriors to Jabesh-gilead with orders to kill everyone there, including women and children. ¹¹"This is what you are to do," they said. "Completely destroy* all the males and every woman who is not a virgin." ¹²Among the residents of Jabesh-gilead they found 400 young virgins who had never slept with a man, and they brought them to the camp at Shiloh in the land of Canaan.

¹³The Israelite assembly sent a peace delegation to the remaining people of Benjamin who

---

20:33 As in Greek and Syriac versions and Latin Vulgate; Hebrew reads *hiding in the open space.*   20:42 Or *battle, for the people from the nearby towns also came out and killed them.*   20:43 The meaning of the Hebrew is uncertain.   21:11 The Hebrew term used here refers to the complete consecration of things or people to the Lord, either by destroying them or by giving them as an offering.

were living at the rock of Rimmon. ¹⁴Then the men of Benjamin returned to their homes, and the 400 women of Jabesh-gilead who had been spared were given to them as wives. But there were not enough women for all of them.

¹⁵The people felt sorry for Benjamin because the LORD had made this gap among the tribes of Israel. ¹⁶So the elders of the assembly asked, "How can we find wives for the few who remain, since the women of the tribe of Benjamin are dead? ¹⁷There must be heirs for the survivors so that an entire tribe of Israel is not wiped out. ¹⁸But we cannot give them our own daughters in marriage because we have sworn with a solemn oath that anyone who does this will fall under God's curse."

¹⁹Then they thought of the annual festival of the LORD held in Shiloh, south of Lebonah and north of Bethel, along the east side of the road that goes from Bethel to Shechem. ²⁰They told the men of Benjamin who still needed wives, "Go and hide in the vineyards. ²¹When you see the young women of Shiloh come out for their dances, rush out from the vineyards, and each of you can take one of them home to the land of Benjamin to be your wife! ²²And when their fathers and brothers come to us in protest, we will tell them, 'Please be sympathetic. Let them have your daughters, for we didn't find wives for all of them when we destroyed Jabesh-gilead. And you are not guilty of breaking the vow since you did not actually give your daughters to them in marriage.'"

²³So the men of Benjamin did as they were told. Each man caught one of the women as she danced in the celebration and carried her off to be his wife. They returned to their own land, and they rebuilt their towns and lived in them.

²⁴Then the people of Israel departed by tribes and families, and they returned to their own homes.

²⁵In those days Israel had no king; all the people did whatever seemed right in their own eyes.

Ruth

GOD OFTEN USES the most unlikely people to accomplish his plans and purposes. In this book, Ruth, a Moabite widow, willingly left her homeland to care for her mother-in-law, Naomi, who was also a widow. Being a Moabite, Ruth was not a part of God's chosen people, Israel, but she chose to follow God, anyway. God rewarded her for her faithfulness and her kindness to her mother-in-law. First, he provided for Ruth's physical needs. As Ruth went out to get food, she came to a field, the

- **Author:** Samuel, according to Jewish tradition (although the closing genealogy suggests it was written after his death)
- **Date Written:** Uncertain, perhaps between 1375 and 1050 BC
- **Purpose:** To show that God rewards those who trust in him
- **Themes:** Faithfulness, kindness, integrity, God's protection and blessing
- **Outline**
  1:1-10 Naomi's tragedy
  1:11-22 Ruth's loyalty to Naomi
  2:1–3:18 The friendship of Naomi's relative Boaz
  4:1-17 The marriage of Boaz and Ruth
  4:18-22 The genealogy of King David

owner of which allowed her to gather as much leftover grain as she needed. But God's provision did not stop at Ruth's immediate physical needs. The owner of the field, Boaz, was also a relative of Naomi. Boaz took a sincere interest in Ruth, and eventually they were married. God continued to show his faithful love to Ruth and Boaz by honoring them through their descendants—King David and, hundreds of years later, Jesus Christ.

Elimelech Moves His Family to Moab

1 In the days when the judges ruled in Israel, a severe famine came upon the land. So a man from Bethlehem in Judah left his home and went to live in the country of Moab, taking his wife and two sons with him. ²The man's name was Elimelech, and his wife was Naomi. Their two sons were Mahlon and Kilion. They were Ephrathites from Bethlehem in the land of Judah. And when they reached Moab, they settled there.

³Then Elimelech died, and Naomi was left with her two sons. ⁴The two sons married Moabite women. One married a woman named Orpah, and the other a woman named Ruth. But about ten years later, ⁵both Mahlon and Kilion died. This left Naomi alone, without her two sons or her husband.

Naomi and Ruth Return

⁶Then Naomi heard in Moab that the LORD had blessed his people in Judah by giving them good crops again. So Naomi and her daughters-in-law got ready to leave Moab to return to her homeland. ⁷With her two daughters-in-law she set out from the place where she had been living, and they took the road that would lead them back to Judah.

⁸But on the way, Naomi said to her two daughters-in-law, "Go back to your mothers' homes. And may the LORD reward you for your kindness to your husbands and to me. ⁹May the LORD bless you with the security of another marriage." Then she kissed them good-bye, and they all broke down and wept.

¹⁰"No," they said. "We want to go with you to your people."

¹¹But Naomi replied, "Why should you go on with me? Can I still give birth to other sons who could grow up to be your husbands? ¹²No, my daughters, return to your parents' homes, for I am too old to marry again. And even if it were possible, and I were to get married tonight and bear sons, then what? ¹³Would you

wait for them to grow up and refuse to marry someone else? No, of course not, my daughters! Things are far more bitter for me than for you, because the LORD himself has raised his fist against me."

¹⁴And again they wept together, and Orpah kissed her mother-in-law good-bye. But Ruth clung tightly to Naomi. ¹⁵"Look," Naomi said to her, "your sister-in-law has gone back to her people and to her gods. You should do the same."

¹⁶But Ruth replied, "Don't ask me to leave you and turn back. Wherever you go, I will go; wherever you live, I will live. Your people will be my people, and your God will be my God. ¹⁷Wherever you die, I will die, and there I will be buried. May the LORD punish me severely if I allow anything but death to separate us!" ¹⁸When Naomi saw that Ruth was determined to go with her, she said nothing more.

¹⁹So the two of them continued on their journey. When they came to Bethlehem, the entire town was excited by their arrival. "Is it really Naomi?" the women asked.

²⁰"Don't call me Naomi," she responded. "Instead, call me Mara,* for the Almighty has made life very bitter for me. ²¹I went away full, but the LORD has brought me home empty. Why call me Naomi when the LORD has caused me to suffer* and the Almighty has sent such tragedy upon me?"

²²So Naomi returned from Moab, accompanied by her daughter-in-law Ruth, the young Moabite woman. They arrived in Bethlehem in late spring, at the beginning of the barley harvest.

Ruth Works in Boaz's Field

2 Now there was a wealthy and influential man in Bethlehem named Boaz, who was a relative of Naomi's husband, Elimelech.

²One day Ruth the Moabite said to Naomi, "Let me go out into the harvest fields to pick up the stalks of grain left behind by anyone who is kind enough to let me do it."

Naomi replied, "All right, my daughter, go ahead." ³So Ruth went out to gather grain behind the harvesters. And as it happened, she found herself working in a field that belonged to Boaz, the relative of her father-in-law, Elimelech.

⁴While she was there, Boaz arrived from Bethlehem and greeted the harvesters. "The LORD be with you!" he said.

"The LORD bless you!" the harvesters replied.

⁵Then Boaz asked his foreman, "Who is that young woman over there? Who does she belong to?"

⁶And the foreman replied, "She is the young woman from Moab who came back with Naomi. ⁷She asked me this morning if she could gather grain behind the harvesters. She has been hard at work ever since, except for a few minutes' rest in the shelter."

⁸Boaz went over and said to Ruth, "Listen, my daughter. Stay right here with us when you gather grain; don't go to any other fields. Stay right behind the young women working in my field. ⁹See which part of the field they are harvesting, and then follow them. I have warned the young men not to treat you roughly. And when you are thirsty, help yourself to the water they have drawn from the well."

¹⁰Ruth fell at his feet and thanked him warmly. "What have I done to deserve such kindness?" she asked. "I am only a foreigner."

¹¹"Yes, I know," Boaz replied. "But I also know about everything you have done for your mother-in-law since the death of your husband. I have heard how you left your father and mother and your own land to live here among complete strangers. ¹²May the LORD, the God of Israel, under whose wings you have come to take refuge, reward you fully for what you have done."

¹³"I hope I continue to please you, sir," she replied. "You have comforted me by speaking so kindly to me, even though I am not one of your workers."

¹⁴At mealtime Boaz called to her, "Come over here, and help yourself to some food. You can dip your bread in the sour wine." So she sat with his harvesters, and Boaz gave her some roasted grain to eat. She ate all she wanted and still had some left over.

¹⁵When Ruth went back to work again, Boaz ordered his young men, "Let her gather grain right among the sheaves without stopping her. ¹⁶And pull out some heads of barley from the bundles and drop them on purpose for her. Let her pick them up, and don't give her a hard time!"

¹⁷So Ruth gathered barley there all day, and when she beat out the grain that evening, it filled an entire basket.* ¹⁸She carried it back into town and showed it to her mother-in-law.

1:20 *Naomi* means "pleasant"; *Mara* means "bitter." 1:21 Or *has testified against me.* 2:17 Hebrew *it was about an ephah* [20 quarts or 22 liters].

Ruth also gave her the roasted grain that was left over from her meal.

¹⁹"Where did you gather all this grain today?" Naomi asked. "Where did you work? May the LORD bless the one who helped you!"

So Ruth told her mother-in-law about the man in whose field she had worked. She said, "The man I worked with today is named Boaz."

²⁰"May the LORD bless him!" Naomi told her daughter-in-law. "He is showing his kindness to us as well as to your dead husband.* That man is one of our closest relatives, one of our family redeemers."

²¹Then Ruth* said, "What's more, Boaz even told me to come back and stay with his harvesters until the entire harvest is completed."

²²"Good!" Naomi exclaimed. "Do as he said, my daughter. Stay with his young women right through the whole harvest. You might be harassed in other fields, but you'll be safe with him."

²³So Ruth worked alongside the women in Boaz's fields and gathered grain with them until the end of the barley harvest. Then she continued working with them through the wheat harvest in early summer. And all the while she lived with her mother-in-law.

Ruth at the Threshing Floor

3 One day Naomi said to Ruth, "My daughter, it's time that I found a permanent home for you, so that you will be provided for. ²Boaz is a close relative of ours, and he's been very kind by letting you gather grain with his young women. Tonight he will be winnowing barley at the threshing floor. ³Now do as I tell you—take a bath and put on perfume and dress in your nicest clothes. Then go to the threshing floor, but don't let Boaz see you until he has finished eating and drinking. ⁴Be sure to notice where he lies down; then go and uncover his feet and lie down there. He will tell you what to do."

⁵"I will do everything you say," Ruth replied. ⁶So she went down to the threshing floor that night and followed the instructions of her mother-in-law.

⁷After Boaz had finished eating and drinking and was in good spirits, he lay down at the far end of the pile of grain and went to sleep. Then Ruth came quietly, uncovered his feet, and lay down. ⁸Around midnight Boaz suddenly woke up and turned over. He was surprised to find a woman lying at his feet! ⁹"Who are you?" he asked.

"I am your servant Ruth," she replied. "Spread the corner of your covering over me, for you are my family redeemer."

¹⁰"The LORD bless you, my daughter!" Boaz exclaimed. "You are showing even more family loyalty now than you did before, for you have not gone after a younger man, whether rich or poor. ¹¹Now don't worry about a thing, my daughter. I will do what is necessary, for everyone in town knows you are a virtuous woman. ¹²But while it's true that I am one of your family redeemers, there is another man who is more closely related to you than I am. ¹³Stay here tonight, and in the morning I will talk to him. If he is willing to redeem you, very well. Let him marry you. But if he is not willing, then as surely as the LORD lives, I will redeem you myself! Now lie down here until morning."

¹⁴So Ruth lay at Boaz's feet until the morning, but she got up before it was light enough for people to recognize each other. For Boaz had said, "No one must know that a woman was here at the threshing floor." ¹⁵Then Boaz said to her, "Bring your cloak and spread it out." He measured six scoops* of barley into the cloak and placed it on her back. Then he* returned to the town.

¹⁶When Ruth went back to her mother-in-law, Naomi asked, "What happened, my daughter?"

Ruth told Naomi everything Boaz had done for her, ¹⁷and she added, "He gave me these six scoops of barley and said, 'Don't go back to your mother-in-law empty-handed.'"

¹⁸Then Naomi said to her, "Just be patient, my daughter, until we hear what happens. The man won't rest until he has settled things today."

Boaz Marries Ruth

4 Boaz went to the town gate and took a seat there. Just then the family redeemer he had mentioned came by, so Boaz called out to him, "Come over here and sit down, friend. I want to talk to you." So they sat down together. ²Then Boaz called ten leaders from the town and asked them to sit as witnesses. ³And Boaz said to the family redeemer, "You know Naomi, who came back from Moab. She is selling the land that belonged to our relative Elimelech. ⁴I thought I should speak to you about it so that you can redeem it if you wish.

2:20 Hebrew *to the living and to the dead.*   2:21 Hebrew *Ruth the Moabite.*   3:15a Hebrew *six measures,* an unknown quantity. 3:15b Most Hebrew manuscripts read *he;* many Hebrew manuscripts, Syriac version, and Latin Vulgate read *she.*

If you want the land, then buy it here in the presence of these witnesses. But if you don't want it, let me know right away, because I am next in line to redeem it after you."

The man replied, "All right, I'll redeem it."

⁵Then Boaz told him, "Of course, your purchase of the land from Naomi also requires that you marry Ruth, the Moabite widow. That way she can have children who will carry on her husband's name and keep the land in the family."

⁶"Then I can't redeem it," the family redeemer replied, "because this might endanger my own estate. You redeem the land; I cannot do it."

⁷Now in those days it was the custom in Israel for anyone transferring a right of purchase to remove his sandal and hand it to the other party. This publicly validated the transaction. ⁸So the other family redeemer drew off his sandal as he said to Boaz, "You buy the land."

⁹Then Boaz said to the elders and to the crowd standing around, "You are witnesses that today I have bought from Naomi all the property of Elimelech, Kilion, and Mahlon. ¹⁰And with the land I have acquired Ruth, the Moabite widow of Mahlon, to be my wife. This way she can have a son to carry on the family name of her dead husband and to inherit the family property here in his hometown. You are all witnesses today."

¹¹Then the elders and all the people standing in the gate replied, "We are witnesses! May the LORD make this woman who is coming into your home like Rachel and Leah, from whom all the nation of Israel descended! May you

4:20 As in some Greek manuscripts (see also 4:21); Hebrew reads *Salma*.

prosper in Ephrathah and be famous in Bethlehem. ¹²And may the LORD give you descendants by this young woman who will be like those of our ancestor Perez, the son of Tamar and Judah."

The Descendants of Boaz

¹³So Boaz took Ruth into his home, and she became his wife. When he slept with her, the LORD enabled her to become pregnant, and she gave birth to a son. ¹⁴Then the women of the town said to Naomi, "Praise the LORD, who has now provided a redeemer for your family! May this child be famous in Israel. ¹⁵May he restore your youth and care for you in your old age. For he is the son of your daughter-in-law who loves you and has been better to you than seven sons!"

¹⁶Naomi took the baby and cuddled him to her breast. And she cared for him as if he were her own. ¹⁷The neighbor women said, "Now at last Naomi has a son again!" And they named him Obed. He became the father of Jesse and the grandfather of David.

¹⁸This is the genealogical record of their ancestor Perez:

Perez was the father of Hezron.
¹⁹ Hezron was the father of Ram.
Ram was the father of Amminadab.
²⁰ Amminadab was the father of Nahshon.
Nahshon was the father of Salmon.*
²¹ Salmon was the father of Boaz.
Boaz was the father of Obed.
²² Obed was the father of Jesse.
Jesse was the father of David.

1 Samuel

THE CHOICES PEOPLE MAKE say a lot about their character. The book of 1 Samuel is full of choices—some good and some bad. The first significant choice in 1 Samuel is made by Hannah, a woman who was unable to have children. She cried out to God for a child, and God heard her prayer and granted her request. Grateful to God for his goodness, Hannah dedicated her child, Samuel, to the Lord from the time he was born. So Samuel grew up among the priests at the Tabernacle, and eventually he became the leading priest.

■ **Author:** Uncertain; some have suggested Samuel and the prophets Nathan and Gad

■ **Date Written:** Uncertain, perhaps around 1000 BC

■ **Purpose:** To record the life of Israel's last judge, Samuel, the reign and decline of Israel's first king, Saul, and the selection and preparation of Israel's greatest king, David

■ **Themes:** Israel's rejection of God as king, leadership, obedience, God's faithfulness

■ **Outline**
1:1–7:17 Samuel's early ministry and the Philistine war
8:1–15:35 King Saul's early successes
16:1–20:42 Saul's decline and the rise of David
21:1–24:22 Saul's persecution of David
25:1–31:13 David's growing strength and the death of Saul

Toward the end of Samuel's life, the Israelites rejected Samuel's sons as judges over Israel and asked him to appoint a king over them. Samuel warned the Israelites that a king would oppress them, but they chose to have one, anyway. Thus began the history of Israel's kings. Samuel anointed a tall, handsome man named Saul to be Israel's first king. At first Saul appeared to make some good decisions. But soon he made some very bad choices, and God brought an end to his reign. David, a shepherd from Bethlehem, was chosen to take Saul's place. Saul tried several times to kill David, but by the end of the book, Saul is dead, and David is soon to become the next king.

Elkanah and His Family

1 There was a man named Elkanah who lived in Ramah in the region of Zuph* in the hill country of Ephraim. He was the son of Jeroham, son of Elihu, son of Tohu, son of Zuph, of Ephraim. ²Elkanah had two wives, Hannah and Peninnah. Peninnah had children, but Hannah did not.

³Each year Elkanah would travel to Shiloh to worship and sacrifice to the LORD of Heaven's Armies at the Tabernacle. The priests of the LORD at that time were the two sons of Eli—Hophni and Phinehas. ⁴On the days Elkanah presented his sacrifice, he would give portions of the meat to Peninnah and each of her children. ⁵And though he loved Hannah, he would give her only one choice portion* because the LORD had given her no children. ⁶So Peninnah would taunt Hannah and make fun of her because the LORD had kept her from having children. ⁷Year after year it was the same—Peninnah would taunt Hannah as they went to the Tabernacle.* Each time, Hannah would be reduced to tears and would not even eat.

⁸"Why are you crying, Hannah?" Elkanah would ask. "Why aren't you eating? Why be downhearted just because you have no children? You have me—isn't that better than having ten sons?"

1:1 As in Greek version; Hebrew reads in Ramathaim-zophim; compare 1:19. 1:5 Or And because he loved Hannah, he would give her a choice portion. The meaning of the Hebrew is uncertain. 1:7 Hebrew the house of the LORD; also in 1:24.

Hannah's Prayer for a Son

⁹Once after a sacrificial meal at Shiloh, Hannah got up and went to pray. Eli the priest was sitting at his customary place beside the entrance of the Tabernacle.* ¹⁰Hannah was in deep anguish, crying bitterly as she prayed to the LORD. ¹¹And she made this vow: "O LORD of Heaven's Armies, if you will look upon my sorrow and answer my prayer and give me a son, then I will give him back to you. He will be yours for his entire lifetime, and as a sign that he has been dedicated to the LORD, his hair will never be cut.*"

¹²As she was praying to the LORD, Eli watched her. ¹³Seeing her lips moving but hearing no sound, he thought she had been drinking. ¹⁴"Must you come here drunk?" he demanded. "Throw away your wine!"

¹⁵"Oh no, sir!" she replied. "I haven't been drinking wine or anything stronger. But I am very discouraged, and I was pouring out my heart to the LORD. ¹⁶Don't think I am a wicked woman! For I have been praying out of great anguish and sorrow."

¹⁷"In that case," Eli said, "go in peace! May the God of Israel grant the request you have asked of him."

¹⁸"Oh, thank you, sir!" she exclaimed. Then she went back and began to eat again, and she was no longer sad.

Samuel's Birth and Dedication

¹⁹The entire family got up early the next morning and went to worship the LORD once more. Then they returned home to Ramah. When Elkanah slept with Hannah, the LORD remembered her plea, ²⁰and in due time she gave birth to a son. She named him Samuel,* for she said, "I asked the LORD for him."

²¹The next year Elkanah and his family went on their annual trip to offer a sacrifice to the LORD and to keep his vow. ²²But Hannah did not go. She told her husband, "Wait until the boy is weaned. Then I will take him to the Tabernacle and leave him there with the LORD permanently.*"

²³"Whatever you think is best," Elkanah agreed. "Stay here for now, and may the LORD help you keep your promise.*" So she stayed home and nursed the boy until he was weaned.

²⁴When the child was weaned, Hannah took him to the Tabernacle in Shiloh. They brought along a three-year-old bull* for the sacrifice and a basket* of flour and some wine. ²⁵After sacrificing the bull, they brought the boy to Eli. ²⁶"Sir, do you remember me?" Hannah asked. "I am the very woman who stood here several years ago praying to the LORD. ²⁷I asked the LORD to give me this boy, and he has granted my request. ²⁸Now I am giving him to the LORD, and he will belong to the LORD his whole life." And they* worshiped the LORD there.

Hannah's Prayer of Praise

2 Then Hannah prayed:

"My heart rejoices in the LORD!
  The LORD has made me strong.*
Now I have an answer for my enemies;
  I rejoice because you rescued me.
² No one is holy like the LORD!
  There is no one besides you;
  there is no Rock like our God.

³ "Stop acting so proud and haughty!
  Don't speak with such arrogance!
For the LORD is a God who knows what
    you have done;
  he will judge your actions.
⁴ The bow of the mighty is now broken,
  and those who stumbled are now
    strong.
⁵ Those who were well fed are now starving,
  and those who were starving are now
    full.
The childless woman now has seven
    children,
  and the woman with many children
    wastes away.
⁶ The LORD gives both death and life;
  he brings some down to the grave* but
    raises others up.
⁷ The LORD makes some poor and others
    rich;
  he brings some down and lifts
    others up.
⁸ He lifts the poor from the dust
  and the needy from the garbage
    dump.
He sets them among princes,
  placing them in seats of honor.
For all the earth is the LORD's,
  and he has set the world in order.

1:9 Hebrew *the Temple of the LORD.*   1:11 Some manuscripts add *He will drink neither wine nor intoxicants.*   1:20 *Samuel* sounds like the Hebrew term for "asked of God" or "heard by God."   1:22 Some manuscripts add *I will offer him as a Nazirite for all time.*   1:23 As in Dead Sea Scrolls and Greek version; Masoretic Text reads *may the LORD keep his promise.*   1:24a As in Dead Sea Scrolls, Greek and Syriac versions; Masoretic Text reads *three bulls.*   1:24b Hebrew *and an ephah* [20 quarts or 22 liters].   1:28 Hebrew *he.*   2:1 Hebrew *has exalted my horn.*   2:6 Hebrew *to Sheol.*

9 "He will protect his faithful ones,
　　but the wicked will disappear in
　　　darkness.
　No one will succeed by strength alone.
10 　Those who fight against the LORD will
　　　be shattered.
　He thunders against them from heaven;
　　the LORD judges throughout the earth.
　He gives power to his king;
　　he increases the strength* of his
　　　anointed one."

11 Then Elkanah returned home to Ramah without Samuel. And the boy served the LORD by assisting Eli the priest.

Eli's Wicked Sons

12 Now the sons of Eli were scoundrels who had no respect for the LORD 13 or for their duties as priests. Whenever anyone offered a sacrifice, Eli's sons would send over a servant with a three-pronged fork. While the meat of the sacrificed animal was still boiling, 14 the servant would stick the fork into the pot and demand that whatever it brought up be given to Eli's sons. All the Israelites who came to worship at Shiloh were treated this way. 15 Sometimes the servant would come even before the animal's fat had been burned on the altar. He would demand raw meat before it had been boiled so that it could be used for roasting.

16 The man offering the sacrifice might reply, "Take as much as you want, but the fat must be burned first." Then the servant would demand, "No, give it to me now, or I'll take it by force." 17 So the sin of these young men was very serious in the LORD's sight, for they treated the LORD's offerings with contempt.

18 But Samuel, though he was only a boy, served the LORD. He wore a linen garment like that of a priest.* 19 Each year his mother made a small coat for him and brought it to him when she came with her husband for the sacrifice. 20 Before they returned home, Eli would bless Elkanah and his wife and say, "May the LORD give you other children to take the place of this one she gave to the LORD.*" 21 And the LORD blessed Hannah, and she conceived and gave birth to three sons and two daughters. Meanwhile, Samuel grew up in the presence of the LORD.

22 Now Eli was very old, but he was aware of what his sons were doing to the people of Israel. He knew, for instance, that his sons were seducing the young women who assisted at the entrance of the Tabernacle.* 23 Eli said to them, "I have been hearing reports from all the people about the wicked things you are doing. Why do you keep sinning? 24 You must stop, my sons! The reports I hear among the LORD's people are not good. 25 If someone sins against another person, God* can mediate for the guilty party. But if someone sins against the LORD, who can intercede?" But Eli's sons wouldn't listen to their father, for the LORD was already planning to put them to death.

26 Meanwhile, the boy Samuel grew taller and grew in favor with the LORD and with the people.

A Warning for Eli's Family

27 One day a man of God came to Eli and gave him this message from the LORD: "I revealed myself* to your ancestors when they were Pharaoh's slaves in Egypt. 28 I chose your ancestor Aaron* from among all the tribes of Israel to be my priest, to offer sacrifices on my altar, to burn incense, and to wear the priestly vest* as he served me. And I assigned the sacrificial offerings to you priests. 29 So why do you scorn my sacrifices and offerings? Why do you give your sons more honor than you give me—for you and they have become fat from the best offerings of my people Israel!

30 "Therefore, the LORD, the God of Israel, says: I promised that your branch of the tribe of Levi* would always be my priests. But I will honor those who honor me, and I will despise those who think lightly of me. 31 The time is coming when I will put an end to your family, so it will no longer serve as my priests. All the members of your family will die before their time. None will reach old age. 32 You will watch with envy as I pour out prosperity on the people of Israel. But no members of your family will ever live out their days. 33 The few not cut off from serving at my altar will survive, but only so their eyes can go blind and their hearts break, and their children will die a violent death.* 34 And to prove that what I have said will come true, I will cause your two sons, Hophni and Phinehas, to die on the same day!

35 "Then I will raise up a faithful priest who

2:10 Hebrew *he exalts the horn.*　　2:18 Hebrew *He wore a linen ephod.*　　2:20 As in Dead Sea Scrolls and Greek version; Masoretic Text reads *this one he requested of the LORD.*　　2:22 Hebrew *Tent of Meeting.* Some manuscripts lack this entire sentence.　　2:25 Or *the judges.*　　2:27 As in Greek and Syriac versions; Hebrew reads *Did I reveal myself.*　　2:28a Hebrew *your father.*　　2:28b Hebrew *an ephod.*　　2:30 Hebrew *that your house and your father's house.*　　2:33 As in Dead Sea Scrolls and Greek version, which read *die by the sword;* Masoretic Text reads *die like mortals.*

will serve me and do what I desire. I will establish his family, and they will be priests to my anointed kings forever. [36]Then all of your surviving family will bow before him, begging for money and food. 'Please,' they will say, 'give us jobs among the priests so we will have enough to eat.'"

The Lord Speaks to Samuel

3 Meanwhile, the boy Samuel served the Lord by assisting Eli. Now in those days messages from the Lord were very rare, and visions were quite uncommon.

[2]One night Eli, who was almost blind by now, had gone to bed. [3]The lamp of God had not yet gone out, and Samuel was sleeping in the Tabernacle* near the Ark of God. [4]Suddenly the Lord called out, "Samuel!"

"Yes?" Samuel replied. "What is it?" [5]He got up and ran to Eli. "Here I am. Did you call me?"

"I didn't call you," Eli replied. "Go back to bed." So he did.

[6]Then the Lord called out again, "Samuel!"

Again Samuel got up and went to Eli. "Here I am. Did you call me?"

"I didn't call you, my son," Eli said. "Go back to bed."

[7]Samuel did not yet know the Lord because he had never had a message from the Lord before. [8]So the Lord called a third time, and once more Samuel got up and went to Eli. "Here I am. Did you call me?"

Then Eli realized it was the Lord who was calling the boy. [9]So he said to Samuel, "Go and lie down again, and if someone calls again, say, 'Speak, Lord, your servant is listening.'" So Samuel went back to bed.

[10]And the Lord came and called as before, "Samuel! Samuel!"

And Samuel replied, "Speak, your servant is listening."

[11]Then the Lord said to Samuel, "I am about to do a shocking thing in Israel. [12]I am going to carry out all my threats against Eli and his family, from beginning to end. [13]I have warned him that judgment is coming upon his family forever, because his sons are blaspheming God* and he hasn't disciplined them. [14]So I have vowed that the sins of Eli and his sons will never be forgiven by sacrifices or offerings."

Samuel Speaks for the Lord

[15]Samuel stayed in bed until morning, then got up and opened the doors of the Tabernacle* as usual. He was afraid to tell Eli what the Lord had said to him. [16]But Eli called out to him, "Samuel, my son."

"Here I am," Samuel replied.

[17]"What did the Lord say to you? Tell me everything. And may God strike you and even kill you if you hide anything from me!" [18]So Samuel told Eli everything; he didn't hold anything back. "It is the Lord's will," Eli replied. "Let him do what he thinks best."

[19]As Samuel grew up, the Lord was with him, and everything Samuel said proved to be reliable. [20]And all Israel, from Dan in the north to Beersheba in the south, knew that Samuel was confirmed as a prophet of the Lord. [21]The Lord continued to appear at Shiloh and gave messages to Samuel there at the Tabernacle. [4:1]And Samuel's words went out to all the people of Israel.

The Philistines Capture the Ark

4 At that time Israel was at war with the Philistines. The Israelite army was camped near Ebenezer, and the Philistines were at Aphek. [2]The Philistines attacked and defeated the army of Israel, killing 4,000 men. [3]After the battle was over, the troops retreated to their camp, and the elders of Israel asked, "Why did the Lord allow us to be defeated by the Philistines?" Then they said, "Let's bring the Ark of the Covenant of the Lord from Shiloh. If we carry it into battle with us, it* will save us from our enemies."

[4]So they sent men to Shiloh to bring the Ark of the Covenant of the Lord of Heaven's Armies, who is enthroned between the cherubim. Hophni and Phinehas, the sons of Eli, were also there with the Ark of the Covenant of God. [5]When all the Israelites saw the Ark of the Covenant of the Lord coming into the camp, their shout of joy was so loud it made the ground shake!

[6]"What's going on?" the Philistines asked. "What's all the shouting about in the Hebrew camp?" When they were told it was because the Ark of the Lord had arrived, [7]they panicked. "The gods have* come into their camp!" they cried. "This is a disaster! We have never had to face anything like this before! [8]Help! Who can save us from these mighty gods of Israel? They are the same gods who destroyed the Egyptians with plagues when Israel was in the wilderness. [9]Fight as never before, Philistines! If you don't, we will become the

---

3:3 Hebrew *the Temple of the Lord.*   3:13 As in Greek version; Hebrew reads *his sons have made themselves contemptible.*
3:15 Hebrew *the house of the Lord.*   4:3 Or *he.*   4:7 Or *A god has.*

Hebrews' slaves just as they have been ours! Stand up like men and fight!"

¹⁰So the Philistines fought desperately, and Israel was defeated again. The slaughter was great; 30,000 Israelite soldiers died that day. The survivors turned and fled to their tents. ¹¹The Ark of God was captured, and Hophni and Phinehas, the two sons of Eli, were killed.

The Death of Eli

¹²A man from the tribe of Benjamin ran from the battlefield and arrived at Shiloh later that same day. He had torn his clothes and put dust on his head to show his grief. ¹³Eli was waiting beside the road to hear the news of the battle, for his heart trembled for the safety of the Ark of God. When the messenger arrived and told what had happened, an outcry resounded throughout the town.

¹⁴"What is all the noise about?" Eli asked.

The messenger rushed over to Eli, ¹⁵who was ninety-eight years old and blind. ¹⁶He said to Eli, "I have just come from the battlefield—I was there this very day."

"What happened, my son?" Eli demanded.

¹⁷"Israel has been defeated by the Philistines," the messenger replied. "The people have been slaughtered, and your two sons, Hophni and Phinehas, were also killed. And the Ark of God has been captured."

¹⁸When the messenger mentioned what had happened to the Ark of God, Eli fell backward from his seat beside the gate. He broke his neck and died, for he was old and overweight. He had been Israel's judge for forty years.

¹⁹Eli's daughter-in-law, the wife of Phinehas, was pregnant and near her time of delivery. When she heard that the Ark of God had been captured and that her father-in-law and husband were dead, she went into labor and gave birth. ²⁰She died in childbirth, but before she passed away the midwives tried to encourage her. "Don't be afraid," they said. "You have a baby boy!" But she did not answer or pay attention to them.

²¹She named the child Ichabod (which means "Where is the glory?"), for she said, "Israel's glory is gone." She named him this because the Ark of God had been captured and because her father-in-law and husband were dead. ²²Then she said, "The glory has departed from Israel, for the Ark of God has been captured."

The Ark in Philistia

5 After the Philistines captured the Ark of God, they took it from the battleground at Ebenezer to the town of Ashdod. ²They carried the Ark of God into the temple of Dagon and placed it beside an idol of Dagon. ³But when the citizens of Ashdod went to see it the next morning, Dagon had fallen with his face to the ground in front of the Ark of the LORD! So they took Dagon and put him in his place again. ⁴But the next morning the same thing happened—Dagon had fallen face down before the Ark of the LORD again. This time his head and hands had broken off and were lying in the doorway. Only the trunk of his body was left intact. ⁵That is why to this day neither the priests of Dagon nor anyone who enters the temple of Dagon in Ashdod will step on its threshold.

⁶Then the LORD's heavy hand struck the people of Ashdod and the nearby villages with a plague of tumors.* ⁷When the people realized what was happening, they cried out, "We can't keep the Ark of the God of Israel here any longer! He is against us! We will all be destroyed along with Dagon, our god." ⁸So they called together the rulers of the Philistine towns and asked, "What should we do with the Ark of the God of Israel?"

The rulers discussed it and replied, "Move it to the town of Gath." So they moved the Ark of the God of Israel to Gath. ⁹But when the Ark arrived at Gath, the LORD's heavy hand fell on its men, young and old; he struck them with a plague of tumors, and there was a great panic.

¹⁰So they sent the Ark of God to the town of Ekron, but when the people of Ekron saw it coming they cried out, "They are bringing the Ark of the God of Israel here to kill us, too!" ¹¹The people summoned the Philistine rulers again and begged them, "Please send the Ark of the God of Israel back to its own country, or it* will kill us all." For the deadly plague from God had already begun, and great fear was sweeping across the town. ¹²Those who didn't die were afflicted with tumors; and the cry from the town rose to heaven.

The Philistines Return the Ark

6 The Ark of the LORD remained in Philistine territory seven months in all. ²Then the Philistines called in their priests and diviners and asked them, "What should we do about the Ark of the LORD? Tell us how to return it to its own country."

5:6 Greek version and Latin Vulgate read *tumors; and rats appeared in their land, and death and destruction were throughout the city.*
5:11 Or *he.*

³"Send the Ark of the God of Israel back with a gift," they were told. "Send a guilt offering so the plague will stop. Then, if you are healed, you will know it was his hand that caused the plague."

⁴"What sort of guilt offering should we send?" they asked.

And they were told, "Since the plague has struck both you and your five rulers, make five gold tumors and five gold rats, just like those that have ravaged your land. ⁵Make these things to show honor to the God of Israel. Perhaps then he will stop afflicting you, your gods, and your land. ⁶Don't be stubborn and rebellious as Pharaoh and the Egyptians were. By the time God was finished with them, they were eager to let Israel go.

⁷"Now build a new cart, and find two cows that have just given birth to calves. Make sure the cows have never been yoked to a cart. Hitch the cows to the cart, but shut their calves away from them in a pen. ⁸Put the Ark of the LORD on the cart, and beside it place a chest containing the gold rats and gold tumors you are sending as a guilt offering. Then let the cows go wherever they want. ⁹If they cross the border of our land and go to Beth-shemesh, we will know it was the LORD who brought this great disaster upon us. If they don't, we will know it was not his hand that caused the plague. It came simply by chance."

¹⁰So these instructions were carried out. Two cows were hitched to the cart, and their newborn calves were shut up in a pen. ¹¹Then the Ark of the LORD and the chest containing the gold rats and gold tumors were placed on the cart. ¹²And sure enough, without veering off in other directions, the cows went straight along the road toward Beth-shemesh, lowing as they went. The Philistine rulers followed them as far as the border of Beth-shemesh.

¹³The people of Beth-shemesh were harvesting wheat in the valley, and when they saw the Ark, they were overjoyed! ¹⁴The cart came into the field of a man named Joshua and stopped beside a large rock. So the people broke up the wood of the cart for a fire and killed the cows and sacrificed them to the LORD as a burnt offering. ¹⁵Several men of the tribe of Levi lifted the Ark of the LORD and the chest containing the gold rats and gold tumors from the cart and placed them on the large rock. Many sacrifices and burnt offerings were offered to the LORD

that day by the people of Beth-shemesh. ¹⁶The five Philistine rulers watched all this and then returned to Ekron that same day.

¹⁷The five gold tumors sent by the Philistines as a guilt offering to the LORD were gifts from the rulers of Ashdod, Gaza, Ashkelon, Gath, and Ekron. ¹⁸The five gold rats represented the five Philistine towns and their surrounding villages, which were controlled by the five rulers. The large rock* at Beth-shemesh, where they set the Ark of the LORD, still stands in the field of Joshua as a witness to what happened there.

The Ark Moved to Kiriath-Jearim

¹⁹But the LORD killed seventy men* from Beth-shemesh because they looked into the Ark of the LORD. And the people mourned greatly because of what the LORD had done. ²⁰"Who is able to stand in the presence of the LORD, this holy God?" they cried out. "Where can we send the Ark from here?"

²¹So they sent messengers to the people at Kiriath-jearim and told them, "The Philistines have returned the Ark of the LORD. Come here and get it!"

7 So the men of Kiriath-jearim came to get the Ark of the LORD. They took it to the hillside home of Abinadab and ordained Eleazar, his son, to be in charge of it. ²The Ark remained in Kiriath-jearim for a long time— twenty years in all. During that time all Israel mourned because it seemed the LORD had abandoned them.

Samuel Leads Israel to Victory

³Then Samuel said to all the people of Israel, "If you want to return to the LORD with all your hearts, get rid of your foreign gods and your images of Ashtoreth. Turn your hearts to the LORD and obey him alone; then he will rescue you from the Philistines." ⁴So the Israelites got rid of their images of Baal and Ashtoreth and worshiped only the LORD.

⁵Then Samuel told them, "Gather all of Israel to Mizpah, and I will pray to the LORD for you." ⁶So they gathered at Mizpah and, in a great ceremony, drew water from a well and poured it out before the LORD. They also went without food all day and confessed that they had sinned against the LORD. (It was at Mizpah that Samuel became Israel's judge.)

⁷When the Philistine rulers heard that Israel

6:18 As in some Hebrew manuscripts and Greek version; most Hebrew manuscripts read *great meadow* or *Abel-haggedolah*.
6:19 As in a few Hebrew manuscripts; most Hebrew manuscripts read *70 men, 50,000 men*. Perhaps the text should be understood to read *the LORD killed 70 men and 50 oxen*.

had gathered at Mizpah, they mobilized their army and advanced. The Israelites were badly frightened when they learned that the Philistines were approaching. 8"Don't stop pleading with the LORD our God to save us from the Philistines!" they begged Samuel. 9So Samuel took a young lamb and offered it to the LORD as a whole burnt offering. He pleaded with the LORD to help Israel, and the LORD answered him.

10Just as Samuel was sacrificing the burnt offering, the Philistines arrived to attack Israel. But the LORD spoke with a mighty voice of thunder from heaven that day, and the Philistines were thrown into such confusion that the Israelites defeated them. 11The men of Israel chased them from Mizpah to a place below Beth-car, slaughtering them all along the way. 12Samuel then took a large stone and placed it between the towns of Mizpah and Jeshanah.* He named it Ebenezer (which means "the stone of help"), for he said, "Up to this point the LORD has helped us!"

13So the Philistines were subdued and didn't invade Israel again for some time. And throughout Samuel's lifetime, the LORD's powerful hand was raised against the Philistines. 14The Israelite villages near Ekron and Gath that the Philistines had captured were restored to Israel, along with the rest of the territory that the Philistines had taken. And there was peace between Israel and the Amorites in those days.

15Samuel continued as Israel's judge for the rest of his life. 16Each year he traveled around, setting up his court first at Bethel, then at Gilgal, and then at Mizpah. He judged the people of Israel at each of these places. 17Then he would return to his home at Ramah, and he would hear cases there, too. And Samuel built an altar to the LORD at Ramah.

Israel Requests a King

8 As Samuel grew old, he appointed his sons to be judges over Israel. 2Joel and Abijah, his oldest sons, held court in Beersheba. 3But they were not like their father, for they were greedy for money. They accepted bribes and perverted justice.

4Finally, all the elders of Israel met at Ramah to discuss the matter with Samuel. 5"Look," they told him, "you are now old, and your sons are not like you. Give us a king to judge us like all the other nations have."

6Samuel was displeased with their request and went to the LORD for guidance. 7"Do everything they say to you," the LORD replied, "for they are rejecting me, not you. They don't want me to be their king any longer. 8Ever since I brought them from Egypt they have continually abandoned me and followed other gods. And now they are giving you the same treatment. 9Do as they ask, but solemnly warn them about the way a king will reign over them."

Samuel Warns against a Kingdom

10So Samuel passed on the LORD's warning to the people who were asking him for a king. 11"This is how a king will reign over you," Samuel said. "The king will draft your sons and assign them to his chariots and his charioteers, making them run before his chariots. 12Some will be generals and captains in his army,* some will be forced to plow in his fields and harvest his crops, and some will make his weapons and chariot equipment. 13The king will take your daughters from you and force them to cook and bake and make perfumes for him. 14He will take away the best of your fields and vineyards and olive groves and give them to his own officials. 15He will take a tenth of your grain and your grape harvest and distribute it among his officers and attendants. 16He will take your male and female slaves and demand the finest of your cattle* and donkeys for his own use. 17He will demand a tenth of your flocks, and you will be his slaves. 18When that day comes, you will beg for relief from this king you are demanding, but then the LORD will not help you."

19But the people refused to listen to Samuel's warning. "Even so, we still want a king," they said. 20"We want to be like the nations around us. Our king will judge us and lead us into battle."

21So Samuel repeated to the LORD what the people had said, 22and the LORD replied, "Do as they say, and give them a king." Then Samuel agreed and sent the people home.

Saul Meets Samuel

9 There was a wealthy, influential man named Kish from the tribe of Benjamin. He was the son of Abiel, son of Zeror, son of Becorath, son of Aphiah, of the tribe of Benjamin. 2His son Saul was the most handsome man in Israel—head and shoulders taller than anyone else in the land.

3One day Kish's donkeys strayed away, and

7:12 As in Greek and Syriac versions; Hebrew reads *Shen*.   8:12 Hebrew *commanders of thousands and commanders of fifties.*
8:16 As in Greek version; Hebrew reads *young men.*

he told Saul, "Take a servant with you, and go look for the donkeys." 4So Saul took one of the servants and traveled through the hill country of Ephraim, the land of Shalishah, the Shaalim area, and the entire land of Benjamin, but they couldn't find the donkeys anywhere.

5Finally, they entered the region of Zuph, and Saul said to his servant, "Let's go home. By now my father will be more worried about us than about the donkeys!"

6But the servant said, "I've just thought of something! There is a man of God who lives here in this town. He is held in high honor by all the people because everything he says comes true. Let's go find him. Perhaps he can tell us which way to go."

7"But we don't have anything to offer him," Saul replied. "Even our food is gone, and we don't have a thing to give him."

8"Well," the servant said, "I have one small silver piece.* We can at least offer it to the man of God and see what happens!" 9(In those days if people wanted a message from God, they would say, "Let's go and ask the seer," for prophets used to be called seers.)

10"All right," Saul agreed, "let's try it!" So they started into the town where the man of God lived.

11As they were climbing the hill to the town, they met some young women coming out to draw water. So Saul and his servant asked, "Is the seer here today?"

12"Yes," they replied. "Stay right on this road. He is at the town gates. He has just arrived to take part in a public sacrifice up at the place of worship. 13Hurry and catch him before he goes up there to eat. The guests won't begin eating until he arrives to bless the food."

14So they entered the town, and as they passed through the gates, Samuel was coming out toward them to go up to the place of worship.

15Now the LORD had told Samuel the previous day, 16"About this time tomorrow I will send you a man from the land of Benjamin. Anoint him to be the leader of my people, Israel. He will rescue them from the Philistines, for I have looked down on my people in mercy and have heard their cry."

17When Samuel saw Saul, the LORD said, "That's the man I told you about! He will rule my people."

18Just then Saul approached Samuel at the gateway and asked, "Can you please tell me where the seer's house is?"

19"I am the seer!" Samuel replied. "Go up to the place of worship ahead of me. We will eat there together, and in the morning I'll tell you what you want to know and send you on your way. 20And don't worry about those donkeys that were lost three days ago, for they have been found. And I am here to tell you that you and your family are the focus of all Israel's hopes."

21Saul replied, "But I'm only from the tribe of Benjamin, the smallest tribe in Israel, and my family is the least important of all the families of that tribe! Why are you talking like this to me?"

22Then Samuel brought Saul and his servant into the hall and placed them at the head of the table, honoring them above the thirty special guests. 23Samuel then instructed the cook to bring Saul the finest cut of meat, the piece that had been set aside for the guest of honor. 24So the cook brought in the meat and placed it before Saul. "Go ahead and eat it," Samuel said. "I was saving it for you even before I invited these others!" So Saul ate with Samuel that day.

25When they came down from the place of worship and returned to town, Samuel took Saul up to the roof of the house and prepared a bed for him there.* 26At daybreak the next morning, Samuel called to Saul, "Get up! It's time you were on your way." So Saul got ready, and he and Samuel left the house together. 27When they reached the edge of town, Samuel told Saul to send his servant on ahead. After the servant was gone, Samuel said, "Stay here, for I have received a special message for you from God."

Samuel Anoints Saul as King

10 Then Samuel took a flask of olive oil and poured it over Saul's head. He kissed Saul and said, "I am doing this because the LORD has appointed you to be the ruler over Israel, his special possession.* 2When you leave me today, you will see two men beside Rachel's tomb at Zelzah, on the border of Benjamin. They will tell you that the donkeys have been found and that your father has stopped worrying about them and is now worried about you. He is asking, 'Have you seen my son?'

3"When you get to the oak of Tabor, you will see three men coming toward you who are on their way to worship God at Bethel. One will be

---

9:8 Hebrew ¼ shekel of silver, about 0.1 ounces or 3 grams in weight.   9:25 As in Greek version; Hebrew reads and talked with him there.   10:1 Greek version reads over Israel. And you will rule over the LORD's people and save them from their enemies around them. This will be the sign to you that the LORD has appointed you to be leader over his special possession.

bringing three young goats, another will have three loaves of bread, and the third will be carrying a wineskin full of wine. ⁴They will greet you and offer you two of the loaves, which you are to accept.

⁵"When you arrive at Gibeah of God,* where the garrison of the Philistines is located, you will meet a band of prophets coming down from the place of worship. They will be playing a harp, a tambourine, a flute, and a lyre, and they will be prophesying. ⁶At that time the Spirit of the LORD will come powerfully upon you, and you will prophesy with them. You will be changed into a different person. ⁷After these signs take place, do what must be done, for God is with you. ⁸Then go down to Gilgal ahead of me. I will join you there to sacrifice burnt offerings and peace offerings. You must wait for seven days until I arrive and give you further instructions."

Samuel's Signs Are Fulfilled

⁹As Saul turned and started to leave, God gave him a new heart, and all Samuel's signs were fulfilled that day. ¹⁰When Saul and his servant arrived at Gibeah, they saw a group of prophets coming toward them. Then the Spirit of God came powerfully upon Saul, and he, too, began to prophesy. ¹¹When those who knew Saul heard about it, they exclaimed, "What? Is even Saul a prophet? How did the son of Kish become a prophet?"

¹²And one of those standing there said, "Can anyone become a prophet, no matter who his father is?"* So that is the origin of the saying "Is even Saul a prophet?"

¹³When Saul had finished prophesying, he went up to the place of worship. ¹⁴"Where have you been?" Saul's uncle asked him and his servant.

"We were looking for the donkeys," Saul replied, "but we couldn't find them. So we went to Samuel to ask him where they were."

¹⁵"Oh? And what did he say?" his uncle asked.

¹⁶"He told us that the donkeys had already been found," Saul replied. But Saul didn't tell his uncle what Samuel said about the kingdom.

Saul Is Acclaimed King

¹⁷Later Samuel called all the people of Israel to meet before the LORD at Mizpah. ¹⁸And he said, "This is what the LORD, the God of Israel,

has declared: I brought you from Egypt and rescued you from the Egyptians and from all of the nations that were oppressing you. ¹⁹But though I have rescued you from your misery and distress, you have rejected your God today and have said, 'No, we want a king instead!' Now, therefore, present yourselves before the LORD by tribes and clans."

²⁰So Samuel brought all the tribes of Israel before the LORD, and the tribe of Benjamin was chosen by lot. ²¹Then he brought each family of the tribe of Benjamin before the LORD, and the family of the Matrites was chosen. And finally Saul son of Kish was chosen from among them. But when they looked for him, he had disappeared! ²²So they asked the LORD, "Where is he?"

And the LORD replied, "He is hiding among the baggage." ²³So they found him and brought him out, and he stood head and shoulders above anyone else.

²⁴Then Samuel said to all the people, "This is the man the LORD has chosen as your king. No one in all Israel is like him!"

And all the people shouted, "Long live the king!"

²⁵Then Samuel told the people what the rights and duties of a king were. He wrote them down on a scroll and placed it before the LORD. Then Samuel sent the people home again.

²⁶When Saul returned to his home at Gibeah, a group of men whose hearts God had touched went with him. ²⁷But there were some scoundrels who complained, "How can this man save us?" And they scorned him and refused to bring him gifts. But Saul ignored them.

[Nahash, king of the Ammonites, had been grievously oppressing the people of Gad and Reuben who lived east of the Jordan River. He gouged out the right eye of each of the Israelites living there, and he didn't allow anyone to come and rescue them. In fact, of all the Israelites east of the Jordan, there wasn't a single one whose right eye Nahash had not gouged out. But there were 7,000 men who had escaped from the Ammonites, and they had settled in Jabesh-gilead.]*

Saul Defeats the Ammonites

11 About a month later,* King Nahash of Ammon led his army against the Israelite town of Jabesh-gilead. But all the citizens

---

10:5 Hebrew *Gibeath-haelohim.*   10:12 Hebrew *said, "Who is their father?"*   10:27 This paragraph, which is not included in the Masoretic Text, is found in Dead Sea Scroll 4QSam². 11:1 As in Dead Sea Scroll 4QSam² and Greek version; Masoretic Text lacks *About a month later.*

of Jabesh asked for peace. "Make a treaty with us, and we will be your servants," they pleaded. ²"All right," Nahash said, "but only on one condition. I will gouge out the right eye of every one of you as a disgrace to all Israel!"

³"Give us seven days to send messengers throughout Israel!" replied the elders of Jabesh. "If no one comes to save us, we will agree to your terms."

⁴When the messengers came to Gibeah of Saul and told the people about their plight, everyone broke into tears. ⁵Saul had been plowing a field with his oxen, and when he returned to town, he asked, "What's the matter? Why is everyone crying?" So they told him about the message from Jabesh.

⁶Then the Spirit of God came powerfully upon Saul, and he became very angry. ⁷He took two oxen and cut them into pieces and sent the messengers to carry them throughout Israel with this message: "This is what will happen to the oxen of anyone who refuses to follow Saul and Samuel into battle!" And the LORD made the people afraid of Saul's anger, and all of them came out together as one. ⁸When Saul mobilized them at Bezek, he found that there were 300,000 men from Israel and 30,000* men from Judah.

⁹So Saul sent the messengers back to Jabesh-gilead to say, "We will rescue you by noontime tomorrow!" There was great joy throughout the town when that message arrived!

¹⁰The men of Jabesh then told their enemies, "Tomorrow we will come out to you, and you can do to us whatever you wish." ¹¹But before dawn the next morning, Saul arrived, having divided his army into three detachments. He launched a surprise attack against the Ammonites and slaughtered them the whole morning. The remnant of their army was so badly scattered that no two of them were left together.

¹²Then the people exclaimed to Samuel, "Now where are those men who said, 'Why should Saul rule over us?' Bring them here, and we will kill them!"

¹³But Saul replied, "No one will be executed today, for today the LORD has rescued Israel!"

¹⁴Then Samuel said to the people, "Come, let us all go to Gilgal to renew the kingdom." ¹⁵So they all went to Gilgal, and in a solemn ceremony before the LORD they made Saul

king. Then they offered peace offerings to the LORD, and Saul and all the Israelites were filled with joy.

Samuel's Farewell Address

12 Then Samuel addressed all Israel: "I have done as you asked and given you a king. ²Your king is now your leader. I stand here before you—an old, gray-haired man—and my sons serve you. I have served as your leader from the time I was a boy to this very day. ³Now testify against me in the presence of the LORD and before his anointed one. Whose ox or donkey have I stolen? Have I ever cheated any of you? Have I ever oppressed you? Have I ever taken a bribe and perverted justice? Tell me and I will make right whatever I have done wrong."

⁴"No," they replied, "you have never cheated or oppressed us, and you have never taken even a single bribe."

⁵"The LORD and his anointed one are my witnesses today," Samuel declared, "that my hands are clean."

"Yes, he is a witness," they replied.

⁶"It was the LORD who appointed Moses and Aaron," Samuel continued. "He brought your ancestors out of the land of Egypt. ⁷Now stand here quietly before the LORD as I remind you of all the great things the LORD has done for you and your ancestors.

⁸"When the Israelites were* in Egypt and cried out to the LORD, he sent Moses and Aaron to rescue them from Egypt and to bring them into this land. ⁹But the people soon forgot about the LORD their God, so he handed them over to Sisera, the commander of Hazor's army, and also to the Philistines and to the king of Moab, who fought against them.

¹⁰"Then they cried to the LORD again and confessed, 'We have sinned by turning away from the LORD and worshiping the images of Baal and Ashtoreth. But we will worship you and you alone if you will rescue us from our enemies.' ¹¹Then the LORD sent Gideon,* Bedan,* Jephthah, and Samuel* to save you, and you lived in safety.

¹²"But when you were afraid of Nahash, the king of Ammon, you came to me and said that you wanted a king to reign over you, even though the LORD your God was already your king. ¹³All right, here is the king you have

---

11:8 Dead Sea Scrolls and Greek version read 70,000. 12:8 Hebrew *When Jacob was.* The names "Jacob" and "Israel" are often interchanged throughout the Old Testament, referring sometimes to the individual patriarch and sometimes to the nation. 12:11a Hebrew *Jerub-baal,* another name for Gideon; see Judg 6:32. 12:11b Greek and Syriac versions read *Barak.* 12:11c Greek and Syriac versions read *Samson.*

chosen. You asked for him, and the LORD has granted your request.

14"Now if you fear and worship the LORD and listen to his voice, and if you do not rebel against the LORD's commands, then both you and your king will show that you recognize the LORD as your God. 15But if you rebel against the LORD's commands and refuse to listen to him, then his hand will be as heavy upon you as it was upon your ancestors.

16"Now stand here and see the great thing the LORD is about to do. 17You know that it does not rain at this time of the year during the wheat harvest. I will ask the LORD to send thunder and rain today. Then you will realize how wicked you have been in asking the LORD for a king!"

18So Samuel called to the LORD, and the LORD sent thunder and rain that day. And all the people were terrified of the LORD and of Samuel. 19"Pray to the LORD your God for us, or we will die!" they all said to Samuel. "For now we have added to our sins by asking for a king."

20"Don't be afraid," Samuel reassured them. "You have certainly done wrong, but make sure now that you worship the LORD with all your heart, and don't turn your back on him. 21Don't go back to worshiping worthless idols that cannot help or rescue you—they are totally useless! 22The LORD will not abandon his people, because that would dishonor his great name. For it has pleased the LORD to make you his very own people.

23"As for me, I will certainly not sin against the LORD by ending my prayers for you. And I will continue to teach you what is good and right. 24But be sure to fear the LORD and faithfully serve him. Think of all the wonderful things he has done for you. 25But if you continue to sin, you and your king will be swept away."

Continued War with Philistia

13 Saul was thirty* years old when he became king, and he reigned for forty-two years.* 2Saul selected 3,000 special troops from the army of Israel and sent the rest of the men home. He took 2,000 of the chosen men with him to Micmash and the hill country of Bethel. The other 1,000 went with Saul's son Jonathan to Gibeah in the land of Benjamin.

3Soon after this, Jonathan attacked and defeated the garrison of Philistines at Geba. The news spread quickly among the Philistines. So Saul blew the ram's horn throughout the land, saying, "Hebrews, hear this! Rise up in revolt!" 4All Israel heard the news that Saul had destroyed the Philistine garrison at Geba and that the Philistines now hated the Israelites more than ever. So the entire Israelite army was summoned to join Saul at Gilgal.

5The Philistines mustered a mighty army of 3,000* chariots, 6,000 charioteers, and as many warriors as the grains of sand on the seashore! They camped at Micmash east of Beth-aven. 6The men of Israel saw what a tight spot they were in; and because they were hard pressed by the enemy, they tried to hide in caves, thickets, rocks, holes, and cisterns. 7Some of them crossed the Jordan River and escaped into the land of Gad and Gilead.

Saul's Disobedience and Samuel's Rebuke

Meanwhile, Saul stayed at Gilgal, and his men were trembling with fear. 8Saul waited there seven days for Samuel, as Samuel had instructed him earlier, but Samuel still didn't come. Saul realized that his troops were rapidly slipping away. 9So he demanded, "Bring me the burnt offering and the peace offerings!" And Saul sacrificed the burnt offering himself.

10Just as Saul was finishing with the burnt offering, Samuel arrived. Saul went out to meet and welcome him, 11but Samuel said, "What is this you have done?"

Saul replied, "I saw my men scattering from me, and you didn't arrive when you said you would, and the Philistines are at Micmash ready for battle. 12So I said, 'The Philistines are ready to march against us at Gilgal, and I haven't even asked for the LORD's help!' So I felt compelled to offer the burnt offering myself before you came."

13"How foolish!" Samuel exclaimed. "You have not kept the command the LORD your God gave you. Had you kept it, the LORD would have established your kingdom over Israel forever. 14But now your kingdom must end, for the LORD has sought out a man after his own heart. The LORD has already appointed him to be the leader of his people, because you have not kept the LORD's command."

Israel's Military Disadvantage

15Samuel then left Gilgal and went on his way, but the rest of the troops went with Saul to meet the army. They went up from Gilgal to

---

13:1a As in a few Greek manuscripts; the number is missing in the Hebrew.   13:1b Hebrew *reigned . . . and two;* the number is incomplete in the Hebrew. Compare Acts 13:21.   13:5 As in Greek and Syriac versions; Hebrew reads *30,000.*

Gibeah in the land of Benjamin.* When Saul counted the men who were still with him, he found only 600 were left! ¹⁶Saul and Jonathan and the troops with them were staying at Geba in the land of Benjamin. The Philistines set up their camp at Micmash. ¹⁷Three raiding parties soon left the camp of the Philistines. One went north toward Ophrah in the land of Shual, ¹⁸another went west to Beth-horon, and the third moved toward the border above the valley of Zeboim near the wilderness.

¹⁹There were no blacksmiths in the land of Israel in those days. The Philistines wouldn't allow them for fear they would make swords and spears for the Hebrews. ²⁰So whenever the Israelites needed to sharpen their plowshares, picks, axes, or sickles,* they had to take them to a Philistine blacksmith. ²¹The charges were as follows: a quarter of an ounce* of silver for sharpening a plowshare or a pick, and an eighth of an ounce* for sharpening an ax or making the point of an ox goad. ²²So on the day of the battle none of the people of Israel had a sword or spear, except for Saul and Jonathan.

²³The pass at Micmash had meanwhile been secured by a contingent of the Philistine army.

Jonathan's Daring Plan

14 One day Jonathan said to his armor bearer, "Come on, let's go over to where the Philistines have their outpost." But Jonathan did not tell his father what he was doing.

²Meanwhile, Saul and his 600 men were camped on the outskirts of Gibeah, around the pomegranate tree* at Migron. ³Among Saul's men was Ahijah the priest, who was wearing the ephod, the priestly vest. Ahijah was the son of Ichabod's brother Ahitub, son of Phinehas, son of Eli, the priest of the LORD who had served at Shiloh.

No one realized that Jonathan had left the Israelite camp. ⁴To reach the Philistine outpost, Jonathan had to go down between two rocky cliffs that were called Bozez and Seneh. ⁵The cliff on the north was in front of Micmash, and the one on the south was in front of Geba. ⁶"Let's go across to the outpost of those pagans," Jonathan said to his armor bearer. "Perhaps the LORD will help us, for nothing can hinder the LORD. He can win a battle whether he has many warriors or only a few!"

⁷"Do what you think is best," the armor bearer replied. "I'm with you completely, whatever you decide."

⁸"All right, then," Jonathan told him. "We will cross over and let them see us. ⁹If they say to us, 'Stay where you are or we'll kill you,' then we will stop and not go up to them. ¹⁰But if they say, 'Come on up and fight,' then we will go up. That will be the LORD's sign that he will help us defeat them."

¹¹When the Philistines saw them coming, they shouted, "Look! The Hebrews are crawling out of their holes!" ¹²Then the men from the outpost shouted to Jonathan, "Come on up here, and we'll teach you a lesson!"

"Come on, climb right behind me," Jonathan said to his armor bearer, "for the LORD will help us defeat them!"

¹³So they climbed up using both hands and feet, and the Philistines fell before Jonathan, and his armor bearer killed those who came behind them. ¹⁴They killed some twenty men in all, and their bodies were scattered over about half an acre.*

¹⁵Suddenly, panic broke out in the Philistine army, both in the camp and in the field, including even the outposts and raiding parties. And just then an earthquake struck, and everyone was terrified.

Israel Defeats the Philistines

¹⁶Saul's lookouts in Gibeah of Benjamin saw a strange sight—the vast army of Philistines began to melt away in every direction.* ¹⁷"Call the roll and find out who's missing," Saul ordered. And when they checked, they found that Jonathan and his armor bearer were gone.

¹⁸Then Saul shouted to Ahijah, "Bring the ephod here!" For at that time Ahijah was wearing the ephod in front of the Israelites.* ¹⁹But while Saul was talking to the priest, the confusion in the Philistine camp grew louder and louder. So Saul said to the priest, "Never mind; let's get going!"*

²⁰Then Saul and all his men rushed out to the battle and found the Philistines killing each other. There was terrible confusion everywhere. ²¹Even the Hebrews who had previously gone over to the Philistine army revolted and joined in with Saul, Jonathan, and the rest of the Israelites. ²²Likewise, the men of Israel who

13:15 As in Greek version; Hebrew reads *Samuel then left Gilgal and went to Gibeah in the land of Benjamin.* 13:20 As in Greek version; Hebrew reads *or plowshares.* 13:21a Hebrew *1 pim* [8 grams]. 13:21b Hebrew ⅓ *[of a shekel]* [4 grams]. 14:2 Or *around the rock of Rimmon;* compare Judg 20:45, 47; 21:13. 14:14 Hebrew *half a yoke;* a "yoke" was the amount of land plowed by a pair of yoked oxen in one day. 14:16 As in Greek version; Hebrew reads *they went and there.* 14:18 As in some Greek manuscripts; Hebrew reads *"Bring the Ark of God."* For at that time the Ark of God was with the Israelites. 14:19 Hebrew *Withdraw your hand.*

were hiding in the hill country of Ephraim joined the chase when they saw the Philistines running away. 23So the LORD saved Israel that day, and the battle continued to rage even beyond Beth-aven.

Saul's Foolish Oath

24Now the men of Israel were pressed to exhaustion that day, because Saul had placed them under an oath, saying, "Let a curse fall on anyone who eats before evening—before I have full revenge on my enemies." So no one ate anything all day, 25even though they had all found honeycomb on the ground in the forest. 26They didn't dare touch the honey because they all feared the oath they had taken.

27But Jonathan had not heard his father's command, and he dipped the end of his stick into a piece of honeycomb and ate the honey. After he had eaten it, he felt refreshed.* 28But one of the men saw him and said, "Your father made the army take a strict oath that anyone who eats food today will be cursed. That is why everyone is weary and faint."

29"My father has made trouble for us all!" Jonathan exclaimed. "A command like that only hurts us. See how refreshed I am now that I have eaten this little bit of honey. 30If the men had been allowed to eat freely from the food they found among our enemies, think how many more Philistines we could have killed!"

31They chased and killed the Philistines all day from Micmash to Aijalon, growing more and more faint. 32That evening they rushed for the battle plunder and butchered the sheep, goats, cattle, and calves, but they ate them without draining the blood. 33Someone reported to Saul, "Look, the men are sinning against the LORD by eating meat that still has blood in it."

"That is very wrong," Saul said. "Find a large stone and roll it over here. 34Then go out among the troops and tell them, 'Bring the cattle, sheep, and goats here to me. Kill them here, and drain the blood before you eat them. Do not sin against the LORD by eating meat with the blood still in it.'"

So that night all the troops brought their animals and slaughtered them there. 35Then Saul built an altar to the LORD; it was the first of the altars he built to the LORD.

36Then Saul said, "Let's chase the Philistines all night and plunder them until sunrise. Let's destroy every last one of them."

His men replied, "We'll do whatever you think is best."

But the priest said, "Let's ask God first."

37So Saul asked God, "Should we go after the Philistines? Will you help us defeat them?" But God made no reply that day.

38Then Saul said to the leaders, "Something's wrong! I want all my army commanders to come here. We must find out what sin was committed today. 39I vow by the name of the LORD who rescued Israel that the sinner will surely die, even if it is my own son Jonathan!" But no one would tell him what the trouble was.

40Then Saul said, "Jonathan and I will stand over here, and all of you stand over there."

And the people responded to Saul, "Whatever you think is best."

41Then Saul prayed, "O LORD, God of Israel, please show us who is guilty and who is innocent.*" Then they cast sacred lots, and Jonathan and Saul were chosen as the guilty ones, and the people were declared innocent.

42Then Saul said, "Now cast lots again and choose between me and Jonathan." And Jonathan was shown to be the guilty one.

43"Tell me what you have done," Saul demanded of Jonathan.

"I tasted a little honey," Jonathan admitted. "It was only a little bit on the end of my stick. Does that deserve death?"

44"Yes, Jonathan," Saul said, "you must die! May God strike me and even kill me if you do not die for this."

45But the people broke in and said to Saul, "Jonathan has won this great victory for Israel. Should he die? Far from it! As surely as the LORD lives, not one hair on his head will be touched, for God helped him do a great deed today." So the people rescued Jonathan, and he was not put to death.

46Then Saul called back the army from chasing the Philistines, and the Philistines returned home.

Saul's Military Successes

47Now when Saul had secured his grasp on Israel's throne, he fought against his enemies in every direction—against Moab, Ammon, Edom, the kings of Zobah, and the Philistines. And wherever he turned, he was victorious.* 48He performed great deeds and conquered the Amalekites, saving Israel from all those who had plundered them.

14:27 Or his eyes brightened; similarly in 14:29.   14:41 Greek version adds If the fault is with me or my son Jonathan, respond with Urim; but if the men of Israel are at fault, respond with Thummim.   14:47 As in Greek version; Hebrew reads he acted wickedly.

⁴⁹Saul's sons included Jonathan, Ishbosheth,* and Malkishua. He also had two daughters: Merab, who was older, and Michal. ⁵⁰Saul's wife was Ahinoam, the daughter of Ahimaaz. The commander of Saul's army was Abner, the son of Saul's uncle Ner. ⁵¹Saul's father, Kish, and Abner's father, Ner, were both sons of Abiel.

⁵²The Israelites fought constantly with the Philistines throughout Saul's lifetime. So whenever Saul observed a young man who was brave and strong, he drafted him into his army.

Saul Defeats the Amalekites

15 One day Samuel said to Saul, "It was the LORD who told me to anoint you as king of his people, Israel. Now listen to this message from the LORD! ²This is what the LORD of Heaven's Armies has declared: I have decided to settle accounts with the nation of Amalek for opposing Israel when they came from Egypt. ³Now go and completely destroy* the entire Amalekite nation—men, women, children, babies, cattle, sheep, goats, camels, and donkeys."

⁴So Saul mobilized his army at Telaim. There were 200,000 soldiers from Israel and 10,000 men from Judah. ⁵Then Saul and his army went to a town of the Amalekites and lay in wait in the valley. ⁶Saul sent this warning to the Kenites: "Move away from where the Amalekites live, or you will die with them. For you showed kindness to all the people of Israel when they came up from Egypt." So the Kenites packed up and left.

⁷Then Saul slaughtered the Amalekites from Havilah all the way to Shur, east of Egypt. ⁸He captured Agag, the Amalekite king, but completely destroyed everyone else. ⁹Saul and his men spared Agag's life and kept the best of the sheep and goats, the cattle, the fat calves, and the lambs—everything, in fact, that appealed to them. They destroyed only what was worthless or of poor quality.

The LORD Rejects Saul

¹⁰Then the LORD said to Samuel, ¹¹"I am sorry that I ever made Saul king, for he has not been loyal to me and has refused to obey my command." Samuel was so deeply moved when he heard this that he cried out to the LORD all night.

¹²Early the next morning Samuel went to find Saul. Someone told him, "Saul went to the town of Carmel to set up a monument to himself; then he went on to Gilgal."

¹³When Samuel finally found him, Saul greeted him cheerfully. "May the LORD bless you," he said. "I have carried out the LORD's command!"

¹⁴"Then what is all the bleating of sheep and goats and the lowing of cattle I hear?" Samuel demanded.

¹⁵"It's true that the army spared the best of the sheep, goats, and cattle," Saul admitted. "But they are going to sacrifice them to the LORD your God. We have destroyed everything else."

¹⁶Then Samuel said to Saul, "Stop! Listen to what the LORD told me last night!"

"What did he tell you?" Saul asked.

¹⁷And Samuel told him, "Although you may think little of yourself, are you not the leader of the tribes of Israel? The LORD has anointed you king of Israel. ¹⁸And the LORD sent you on a mission and told you, 'Go and completely destroy the sinners, the Amalekites, until they are all dead.' ¹⁹Why haven't you obeyed the LORD? Why did you rush for the plunder and do what was evil in the LORD's sight?"

²⁰"But I did obey the LORD," Saul insisted. "I carried out the mission he gave me. I brought back King Agag, but I destroyed everyone else. ²¹Then my troops brought in the best of the sheep, goats, cattle, and plunder to sacrifice to the LORD your God in Gilgal."

²²But Samuel replied,

"What is more pleasing to the LORD:
　your burnt offerings and sacrifices
　or your obedience to his voice?
Listen! Obedience is better than sacrifice,
　and submission is better than offering
　　the fat of rams.
²³ Rebellion is as sinful as witchcraft,
　and stubbornness as bad as worshiping
　　idols.
So because you have rejected the command
　of the LORD,
　he has rejected you as king."

Saul Pleads for Forgiveness

²⁴Then Saul admitted to Samuel, "Yes, I have sinned. I have disobeyed your instructions and the LORD's command, for I was afraid of the people and did what they demanded. ²⁵But now, please forgive my sin and come back with me so that I may worship the LORD."

²⁶But Samuel replied, "I will not go back

14:49 Hebrew *Ishvi,* a variant name for Ishbosheth; also known as Esh-baal.　15:3 The Hebrew term used here refers to the complete consecration of things or people to the LORD, either by destroying them or by giving them as an offering; also in 15:8, 9, 15, 18, 20, 21.

with you! Since you have rejected the LORD's command, he has rejected you as king of Israel."

27As Samuel turned to go, Saul tried to hold him back and tore the hem of his robe. 28And Samuel said to him, "The LORD has torn the kingdom of Israel from you today and has given it to someone else—one who is better than you. 29And he who is the Glory of Israel will not lie, nor will he change his mind, for he is not human that he should change his mind!"

30Then Saul pleaded again, "I know I have sinned. But please, at least honor me before the elders of my people and before Israel by coming back with me so that I may worship the LORD your God." 31So Samuel finally agreed and went back with him, and Saul worshiped the LORD.

Samuel Executes King Agag

32Then Samuel said, "Bring King Agag to me." Agag arrived full of hope, for he thought, "Surely the worst is over, and I have been spared!"* 33But Samuel said, "As your sword has killed the sons of many mothers, now your mother will be childless." And Samuel cut Agag to pieces before the LORD at Gilgal.

34Then Samuel went home to Ramah, and Saul returned to his house at Gibeah of Saul. 35Samuel never went to meet with Saul again, but he mourned constantly for him. And the LORD was sorry he had ever made Saul king of Israel.

Samuel Anoints David as King

16 Now the LORD said to Samuel, "You have mourned long enough for Saul. I have rejected him as king of Israel, so fill your flask with olive oil and go to Bethlehem. Find a man named Jesse who lives there, for I have selected one of his sons to be my king."

2But Samuel asked, "How can I do that? If Saul hears about it, he will kill me."

"Take a heifer with you," the LORD replied, "and say that you have come to make a sacrifice to the LORD. 3Invite Jesse to the sacrifice, and I will show you which of his sons to anoint for me."

4So Samuel did as the LORD instructed. When he arrived at Bethlehem, the elders of the town came trembling to meet him. "What's wrong?" they asked. "Do you come in peace?"

5"Yes," Samuel replied. "I have come to sacrifice to the LORD. Purify yourselves and come with me to the sacrifice." Then Samuel performed the purification rite for Jesse and his sons and invited them to the sacrifice, too.

6When they arrived, Samuel took one look at Eliab and thought, "Surely this is the LORD's anointed!"

7But the LORD said to Samuel, "Don't judge by his appearance or height, for I have rejected him. The LORD doesn't see things the way you see them. People judge by outward appearance, but the LORD looks at the heart."

8Then Jesse told his son Abinadab to step forward and walk in front of Samuel. But Samuel said, "This is not the one the LORD has chosen." 9Next Jesse summoned Shimea,* but Samuel said, "Neither is this the one the LORD has chosen." 10In the same way all seven of Jesse's sons were presented to Samuel. But Samuel said to Jesse, "The LORD has not chosen any of these." 11Then Samuel asked, "Are these all the sons you have?"

"There is still the youngest," Jesse replied. "But he's out in the fields watching the sheep and goats."

"Send for him at once," Samuel said. "We will not sit down to eat until he arrives."

12So Jesse sent for him. He was dark and handsome, with beautiful eyes.

And the LORD said, "This is the one; anoint him."

13So as David stood there among his brothers, Samuel took the flask of olive oil he had brought and anointed David with the oil. And the Spirit of the LORD came powerfully upon David from that day on. Then Samuel returned to Ramah.

David Serves in Saul's Court

14Now the Spirit of the LORD had left Saul, and the LORD sent a tormenting spirit* that filled him with depression and fear.

15Some of Saul's servants said to him, "A tormenting spirit from God is troubling you. 16Let us find a good musician to play the harp whenever the tormenting spirit troubles you. He will play soothing music, and you will soon be well again."

17"All right," Saul said. "Find me someone who plays well, and bring him here."

18One of the servants said to Saul, "One of Jesse's sons from Bethlehem is a talented harp player. Not only that—he is a brave warrior, a man of war, and has good judgment. He is

---

15:32 Dead Sea Scrolls and Greek version read *Agag arrived hesitantly, for he thought, "Surely this is the bitterness of death."*
16:9 Hebrew *Shammah*, a variant spelling of Shimea; compare 1 Chr 2:13; 20:7.   16:14 Or *an evil spirit*; also in 16:15, 16, 23.

also a fine-looking young man, and the LORD is with him."

¹⁹So Saul sent messengers to Jesse to say, "Send me your son David, the shepherd." ²⁰Jesse responded by sending David to Saul, along with a young goat, a donkey loaded with bread, and a wineskin full of wine.

²¹So David went to Saul and began serving him. Saul loved David very much, and David became his armor bearer.

²²Then Saul sent word to Jesse asking, "Please let David remain in my service, for I am very pleased with him."

²³And whenever the tormenting spirit from God troubled Saul, David would play the harp. Then Saul would feel better, and the tormenting spirit would go away.

Goliath Challenges the Israelites

17 The Philistines now mustered their army for battle and camped between Socoh in Judah and Azekah at Ephes-dammim. ²Saul countered by gathering his Israelite troops near the valley of Elah. ³So the Philistines and Israelites faced each other on opposite hills, with the valley between them.

⁴Then Goliath, a Philistine champion from Gath, came out of the Philistine ranks to face the forces of Israel. He was over nine feet* tall! ⁵He wore a bronze helmet, and his bronze coat of mail weighed 125 pounds.* ⁶He also wore bronze leg armor, and he carried a bronze javelin on his shoulder. ⁷The shaft of his spear was as heavy and thick as a weaver's beam, tipped with an iron spearhead that weighed 15 pounds.* His armor bearer walked ahead of him carrying a shield.

⁸Goliath stood and shouted a taunt across to the Israelites. "Why are you all coming out to fight?" he called. "I am the Philistine champion, but you are only the servants of Saul. Choose one man to come down here and fight me! ⁹If he kills me, then we will be your slaves. But if I kill him, you will be our slaves! ¹⁰I defy the armies of Israel today! Send me a man who will fight me!" ¹¹When Saul and the Israelites heard this, they were terrified and deeply shaken.

Jesse Sends David to Saul's Camp

¹²Now David was the son of a man named Jesse, an Ephrathite from Bethlehem in the land of Judah. Jesse was an old man at that time, and he had eight sons. ¹³Jesse's three oldest sons—Eliab, Abinadab, and Shimea*—had already joined Saul's army to fight the Philistines. ¹⁴David was the youngest son. David's three oldest brothers stayed with Saul's army, ¹⁵but David went back and forth so he could help his father with the sheep in Bethlehem.

¹⁶For forty days, every morning and evening, the Philistine champion strutted in front of the Israelite army.

¹⁷One day Jesse said to David, "Take this basket* of roasted grain and these ten loaves of bread, and carry them quickly to your brothers. ¹⁸And give these ten cuts of cheese to their captain. See how your brothers are getting along, and bring back a report on how they are doing.*" ¹⁹David's brothers were with Saul and the Israelite army at the valley of Elah, fighting against the Philistines.

²⁰So David left the sheep with another shepherd and set out early the next morning with the gifts, as Jesse had directed him. He arrived at the camp just as the Israelite army was leaving for the battlefield with shouts and battle cries. ²¹Soon the Israelite and Philistine forces stood facing each other, army against army. ²²David left his things with the keeper of supplies and hurried out to the ranks to greet his brothers. ²³As he was talking with them, Goliath, the Philistine champion from Gath, came out from the Philistine ranks. Then David heard him shout his usual taunt to the army of Israel.

²⁴As soon as the Israelite army saw him, they began to run away in fright. ²⁵"Have you seen the giant?" the men asked. "He comes out each day to defy Israel. The king has offered a huge reward to anyone who kills him. He will give that man one of his daughters for a wife, and the man's entire family will be exempted from paying taxes!"

²⁶David asked the soldiers standing nearby, "What will a man get for killing this Philistine and ending his defiance of Israel? Who is this pagan Philistine anyway, that he is allowed to defy the armies of the living God?"

²⁷And these men gave David the same reply. They said, "Yes, that is the reward for killing him."

²⁸But when David's oldest brother, Eliab, heard David talking to the men, he was angry.

17:4 Hebrew *6 cubits and 1 span* [which totals about 9.75 feet or 3 meters]; Dead Sea Scrolls and Greek version read *4 cubits and 1 span* [which totals about 6.75 feet or 2 meters].   17:5 Hebrew *5,000 shekels* [57 kilograms].   17:7 Hebrew *600 shekels* [6.8 kilograms].   17:13 Hebrew *Shammah,* a variant spelling of Shimea; compare 1 Chr 2:13; 20:7.   17:17 Hebrew *ephah* [20 quarts or 22 liters].   17:18 Hebrew *and take their pledge.*

"What are you doing around here anyway?" he demanded. "What about those few sheep you're supposed to be taking care of? I know about your pride and deceit. You just want to see the battle!"

29"What have I done now?" David replied. "I was only asking a question!" 30He walked over to some others and asked them the same thing and received the same answer. 31Then David's question was reported to King Saul, and the king sent for him.

David Kills Goliath

32"Don't worry about this Philistine," David told Saul. "I'll go fight him!"

33"Don't be ridiculous!" Saul replied. "There's no way you can fight this Philistine and possibly win! You're only a boy, and he's been a man of war since his youth."

34But David persisted. "I have been taking care of my father's sheep and goats," he said. "When a lion or a bear comes to steal a lamb from the flock, 35I go after it with a club and rescue the lamb from its mouth. If the animal turns on me, I catch it by the jaw and club it to death. 36I have done this to both lions and bears, and I'll do it to this pagan Philistine, too, for he has defied the armies of the living God! 37The LORD who rescued me from the claws of the lion and the bear will rescue me from this Philistine!"

Saul finally consented. "All right, go ahead," he said. "And may the LORD be with you!"

38Then Saul gave David his own armor—a bronze helmet and a coat of mail. 39David put it on, strapped the sword over it, and took a step or two to see what it was like, for he had never worn such things before.

"I can't go in these," he protested to Saul. "I'm not used to them." So David took them off again. 40He picked up five smooth stones from a stream and put them into his shepherd's bag. Then, armed only with his shepherd's staff and sling, he started across the valley to fight the Philistine.

41Goliath walked out toward David with his shield bearer ahead of him, 42sneering in contempt at this ruddy-faced boy. 43"Am I a dog," he roared at David, "that you come at me with a stick?" And he cursed David by the names of his gods. 44"Come over here, and I'll give your flesh to the birds and wild animals!" Goliath yelled.

45David replied to the Philistine, "You come to me with sword, spear, and javelin, but I come

to you in the name of the LORD of Heaven's Armies—the God of the armies of Israel, whom you have defied. 46Today the LORD will conquer you, and I will kill you and cut off your head. And then I will give the dead bodies of your men to the birds and wild animals, and the whole world will know that there is a God in Israel! 47And everyone assembled here will know that the LORD rescues his people, but not with sword and spear. This is the LORD's battle, and he will give you to us!"

48As Goliath moved closer to attack, David quickly ran out to meet him. 49Reaching into his shepherd's bag and taking out a stone, he hurled it with his sling and hit the Philistine in the forehead. The stone sank in, and Goliath stumbled and fell face down on the ground.

50So David triumphed over the Philistine with only a sling and a stone, for he had no sword. 51Then David ran over and pulled Goliath's sword from its sheath. David used it to kill him and cut off his head.

Israel Routs the Philistines

When the Philistines saw that their champion was dead, they turned and ran. 52Then the men of Israel and Judah gave a great shout of triumph and rushed after the Philistines, chasing them as far as Gath* and the gates of Ekron. The bodies of the dead and wounded Philistines were strewn all along the road from Shaaraim, as far as Gath and Ekron. 53Then the Israelite army returned and plundered the deserted Philistine camp. 54(David took the Philistine's head to Jerusalem, but he stored the man's armor in his own tent.)

55As Saul watched David go out to fight the Philistine, he asked Abner, the commander of his army, "Abner, whose son is this young man?"

"I really don't know," Abner declared.

56"Well, find out who he is!" the king told him.

57As soon as David returned from killing Goliath, Abner brought him to Saul with the Philistine's head still in his hand. 58"Tell me about your father, young man," Saul said.

And David replied, "His name is Jesse, and we live in Bethlehem."

Saul Becomes Jealous of David

18 After David had finished talking with Saul, he met Jonathan, the king's son. There was an immediate bond between them, for Jonathan loved David. 2From that day on

17:52 As in some Greek manuscripts; Hebrew reads *a valley.*

Saul kept David with him and wouldn't let him return home. ³And Jonathan made a solemn pact with David, because he loved him as he loved himself. ⁴Jonathan sealed the pact by taking off his robe and giving it to David, together with his tunic, sword, bow, and belt.

⁵Whatever Saul asked David to do, David did it successfully. So Saul made him a commander over the men of war, an appointment that was welcomed by the people and Saul's officers alike.

⁶When the victorious Israelite army was returning home after David had killed the Philistine, women from all the towns of Israel came out to meet King Saul. They sang and danced for joy with tambourines and cymbals.* ⁷This was their song:

"Saul has killed his thousands,
    and David his ten thousands!"

⁸This made Saul very angry. "What's this?" he said. "They credit David with ten thousands and me with only thousands. Next they'll be making him their king!" ⁹So from that time on Saul kept a jealous eye on David.

¹⁰The very next day a tormenting spirit* from God overwhelmed Saul, and he began to rave in his house like a madman. David was playing the harp, as he did each day. But Saul had a spear in his hand, ¹¹and he suddenly hurled it at David, intending to pin him to the wall. But David escaped him twice.

¹²Saul was then afraid of David, for the LORD was with David and had turned away from Saul. ¹³Finally, Saul sent him away and appointed him commander over 1,000 men, and David faithfully led his troops into battle.

¹⁴David continued to succeed in everything he did, for the LORD was with him. ¹⁵When Saul recognized this, he became even more afraid of him. ¹⁶But all Israel and Judah loved David because he was so successful at leading his troops into battle.

David Marries Saul's Daughter

¹⁷One day Saul said to David, "I am ready to give you my older daughter, Merab, as your wife. But first you must prove yourself to be a real warrior by fighting the LORD's battles." For Saul thought, "I'll send him out against the Philistines and let them kill him rather than doing it myself."

¹⁸"Who am I, and what is my family in Israel that I should be the king's son-in-law?" David

exclaimed. "My father's family is nothing!" ¹⁹So* when the time came for Saul to give his daughter Merab in marriage to David, he gave her instead to Adriel, a man from Meholah.

²⁰In the meantime, Saul's daughter Michal had fallen in love with David, and Saul was delighted when he heard about it. ²¹"Here's another chance to see him killed by the Philistines!" Saul said to himself. But to David he said, "Today you have a second chance to become my son-in-law!"

²²Then Saul told his men to say to David, "The king really likes you, and so do we. Why don't you accept the king's offer and become his son-in-law?"

²³When Saul's men said these things to David, he replied, "How can a poor man from a humble family afford the bride price for the daughter of a king?"

²⁴When Saul's men reported this back to the king, ²⁵he told them, "Tell David that all I want for the bride price is 100 Philistine foreskins! Vengeance on my enemies is all I really want." But what Saul had in mind was that David would be killed in the fight.

²⁶David was delighted to accept the offer. Before the time limit expired, ²⁷he and his men went out and killed 200 Philistines. Then David fulfilled the king's requirement by presenting all their foreskins to him. So Saul gave his daughter Michal to David to be his wife.

²⁸When Saul realized that the LORD was with David and how much his daughter Michal loved him, ²⁹Saul became even more afraid of him, and he remained David's enemy for the rest of his life.

³⁰Every time the commanders of the Philistines attacked, David was more successful against them than all the rest of Saul's officers. So David's name became very famous.

Saul Tries to Kill David

19 Saul now urged his servants and his son Jonathan to assassinate David. But Jonathan, because of his strong affection for David, ²told him what his father was planning. "Tomorrow morning," he warned him, "you must find a hiding place out in the fields. ³I'll ask my father to go out there with me, and I'll talk to him about you. Then I'll tell you everything I can find out."

⁴The next morning Jonathan spoke with his father about David, saying many good things about him. "The king must not sin against his servant David," Jonathan said. "He's never

18:6 The type of instrument represented by the word *cymbals* is uncertain.   18:10 Or *an evil spirit*.   18:19 Or *But*.

done anything to harm you. He has always helped you in any way he could. ⁵Have you forgotten about the time he risked his life to kill the Philistine giant and how the Lord brought a great victory to all Israel as a result? You were certainly happy about it then. Why should you murder an innocent man like David? There is no reason for it at all!"

⁶So Saul listened to Jonathan and vowed, "As surely as the Lord lives, David will not be killed."

⁷Afterward Jonathan called David and told him what had happened. Then he brought David to Saul, and David served in the court as before.

⁸War broke out again after that, and David led his troops against the Philistines. He attacked them with such fury that they all ran away.

⁹But one day when Saul was sitting at home, with spear in hand, the tormenting spirit* from the Lord suddenly came upon him again. As David played his harp, ¹⁰Saul hurled his spear at David. But David dodged out of the way, and leaving the spear stuck in the wall, he fled and escaped into the night.

Michal Saves David's Life
¹¹Then Saul sent troops to watch David's house. They were told to kill David when he came out the next morning. But Michal, David's wife, warned him, "If you don't escape tonight, you will be dead by morning." ¹²So she helped him climb out through a window, and he fled and escaped. ¹³Then she took an idol* and put it in his bed, covered it with blankets, and put a cushion of goat's hair at its head.

¹⁴When the troops came to arrest David, she told them he was sick and couldn't get out of bed.

¹⁵But Saul sent the troops back to get David. He ordered, "Bring him to me in his bed so I can kill him!" ¹⁶But when they came to carry David out, they discovered that it was only an idol in the bed with a cushion of goat's hair at its head.

¹⁷"Why have you betrayed me like this and let my enemy escape?" Saul demanded of Michal.

"I had to," Michal replied. "He threatened to kill me if I didn't help him."

¹⁸So David escaped and went to Ramah to see Samuel, and he told him all that Saul had done to him. Then Samuel took David with him to live at Naioth. ¹⁹When the report reached Saul

19:9 Or *evil spirit.* 19:13 Hebrew *teraphim;* also in 19:16.

that David was at Naioth in Ramah, ²⁰he sent troops to capture him. But when they arrived and saw Samuel leading a group of prophets who were prophesying, the Spirit of God came upon Saul's men, and they also began to prophesy. ²¹When Saul heard what had happened, he sent other troops, but they, too, prophesied! The same thing happened a third time. ²²Finally, Saul himself went to Ramah and arrived at the great well in Secu. "Where are Samuel and David?" he demanded.

"They are at Naioth in Ramah," someone told him.

²³But on the way to Naioth in Ramah the Spirit of God came even upon Saul, and he, too, began to prophesy all the way to Naioth! ²⁴He tore off his clothes and lay naked on the ground all day and all night, prophesying in the presence of Samuel. The people who were watching exclaimed, "What? Is even Saul a prophet?"

Jonathan Helps David
20 David now fled from Naioth in Ramah and found Jonathan. "What have I done?" he exclaimed. "What is my crime? How have I offended your father that he is so determined to kill me?"

²"That's not true!" Jonathan protested. "You're not going to die. He always tells me everything he's going to do, even the little things. I know my father wouldn't hide something like this from me. It just isn't so!"

³Then David took an oath before Jonathan and said, "Your father knows perfectly well about our friendship, so he has said to himself, 'I won't tell Jonathan—why should I hurt him?' But I swear to you that I am only a step away from death! I swear it by the Lord and by your own soul!"

⁴"Tell me what I can do to help you," Jonathan exclaimed.

⁵David replied, "Tomorrow we celebrate the new moon festival. I've always eaten with the king on this occasion, but tomorrow I'll hide in the field and stay there until the evening of the third day. ⁶If your father asks where I am, tell him I asked permission to go home to Bethlehem for an annual family sacrifice. ⁷If he says, 'Fine!' you will know all is well. But if he is angry and loses his temper, you will know he is determined to kill me. ⁸Show me this loyalty as my sworn friend—for we made a solemn pact before the Lord—or kill me yourself if I have sinned against your father. But please don't betray me to him!"

⁹"Never!" Jonathan exclaimed. "You know that if I had the slightest notion my father was planning to kill you, I would tell you at once."

¹⁰Then David asked, "How will I know whether or not your father is angry?"

¹¹"Come out to the field with me," Jonathan replied. And they went out there together. ¹²Then Jonathan told David, "I promise by the LORD, the God of Israel, that by this time tomorrow, or the next day at the latest, I will talk to my father and let you know at once how he feels about you. If he speaks favorably about you, I will let you know. ¹³But if he is angry and wants you killed, may the LORD strike me and even kill me if I don't warn you so you can escape and live. May the LORD be with you as he used to be with my father. ¹⁴And may you treat me with the faithful love of the LORD as long as I live. But if I die, ¹⁵treat my family with this faithful love, even when the LORD destroys all your enemies from the face of the earth."

¹⁶So Jonathan made a solemn pact with David,* saying, "May the LORD destroy all your enemies!" ¹⁷And Jonathan made David reaffirm his vow of friendship again, for Jonathan loved David as he loved himself.

¹⁸Then Jonathan said, "Tomorrow we celebrate the new moon festival. You will be missed when your place at the table is empty. ¹⁹The day after tomorrow, toward evening, go to the place where you hid before, and wait there by the stone pile.* ²⁰I will come out and shoot three arrows to the side of the stone pile as though I were shooting at a target. ²¹Then I will send a boy to bring the arrows back. If you hear me tell him, 'They're on this side,' then you will know, as surely as the LORD lives, that all is well, and there is no trouble. ²²But if I tell him, 'Go farther—the arrows are still ahead of you,' then it will mean that you must leave immediately, for the LORD is sending you away. ²³And may the LORD make us keep our promises to each other, for he has witnessed them."

²⁴So David hid himself in the field, and when the new moon festival began, the king sat down to eat. ²⁵He sat at his usual place against the wall, with Jonathan sitting opposite him* and Abner beside him. But David's place was empty. ²⁶Saul didn't say anything about it that day, for he said to himself, "Something must have made David ceremonially unclean." ²⁷But when David's place was empty again the next day, Saul asked Jonathan, "Why hasn't the son of Jesse been here for the meal either yesterday or today?"

²⁸Jonathan replied, "David earnestly asked me if he could go to Bethlehem. ²⁹He said, 'Please let me go, for we are having a family sacrifice. My brother demanded that I be there. So please let me get away to see my brothers.' That's why he isn't here at the king's table."

³⁰Saul boiled with rage at Jonathan. "You stupid son of a whore!"* he swore at him. "Do you think I don't know that you want him to be king in your place, shaming yourself and your mother? ³¹As long as that son of Jesse is alive, you'll never be king. Now go and get him so I can kill him!"

³²"But why should he be put to death?" Jonathan asked his father. "What has he done?" ³³Then Saul hurled his spear at Jonathan, intending to kill him. So at last Jonathan realized that his father was really determined to kill David.

³⁴Jonathan left the table in fierce anger and refused to eat on that second day of the festival, for he was crushed by his father's shameful behavior toward David.

³⁵The next morning, as agreed, Jonathan went out into the field and took a young boy with him to gather his arrows. ³⁶"Start running," he told the boy, "so you can find the arrows as I shoot them." So the boy ran, and Jonathan shot an arrow beyond him. ³⁷When the boy had almost reached the arrow, Jonathan shouted, "The arrow is still ahead of you. ³⁸Hurry, hurry, don't wait." So the boy quickly gathered up the arrows and ran back to his master. ³⁹He, of course, suspected nothing; only Jonathan and David understood the signal. ⁴⁰Then Jonathan gave his bow and arrows to the boy and told him to take them back to town.

⁴¹As soon as the boy was gone, David came out from where he had been hiding near the stone pile.* Then David bowed three times to Jonathan with his face to the ground. Both of them were in tears as they embraced each other and said good-bye, especially David.

⁴²At last Jonathan said to David, "Go in peace, for we have sworn loyalty to each other in the LORD's name. The LORD is the witness of a bond between us and our children forever." Then David left, and Jonathan returned to the town.*

20:16 Hebrew *with the house of David.* 20:19 Hebrew *the stone Ezel.* The meaning of the Hebrew is uncertain. 20:25 As in Greek version; Hebrew reads *with Jonathan standing.* 20:30 Hebrew *You son of a perverse and rebellious woman.* 20:41 As in Greek version; Hebrew reads *near the south edge.* 20:42 This sentence is numbered 21:1 in Hebrew text.

David Runs from Saul

21 1*David went to the town of Nob to see Ahimelech the priest. Ahimelech trembled when he saw him. "Why are you alone?" he asked. "Why is no one with you?"

2"The king has sent me on a private matter," David said. "He told me not to tell anyone why I am here. I have told my men where to meet me later. 3Now, what is there to eat? Give me five loaves of bread or anything else you have."

4"We don't have any regular bread," the priest replied. "But there is the holy bread, which you can have if your young men have not slept with any women recently."

5"Don't worry," David replied. "I never allow my men to be with women when we are on a campaign. And since they stay clean even on ordinary trips, how much more on this one!"

6Since there was no other food available, the priest gave him the holy bread—the Bread of the Presence that was placed before the LORD in the Tabernacle. It had just been replaced that day with fresh bread.

7Now Doeg the Edomite, Saul's chief herdsman, was there that day, having been detained before the LORD.*

8David asked Ahimelech, "Do you have a spear or sword? The king's business was so urgent that I didn't even have time to grab a weapon!"

9"I only have the sword of Goliath the Philistine, whom you killed in the valley of Elah," the priest replied. "It is wrapped in a cloth behind the ephod. Take that if you want it, for there is nothing else here."

"There is nothing like it!" David replied. "Give it to me!"

10So David escaped from Saul and went to King Achish of Gath. 11But the officers of Achish were unhappy about his being there. "Isn't this David, the king of the land?" they asked. "Isn't he the one the people honor with dances, singing,

'Saul has killed his thousands,
    and David his ten thousands'?"

12David heard these comments and was very afraid of what King Achish of Gath might do to him. 13So he pretended to be insane, scratching on doors and drooling down his beard.

14Finally, King Achish said to his men, "Must you bring me a madman? 15We already have enough of them around here! Why should I let someone like this be my guest?"

David at the Cave of Adullam

22 So David left Gath and escaped to the cave of Adullam. Soon his brothers and all his other relatives joined him there. 2Then others began coming—men who were in trouble or in debt or who were just discontented—until David was the captain of about 400 men.

3Later David went to Mizpeh in Moab, where he asked the king, "Please allow my father and mother to live here with you until I know what God is going to do for me." 4So David's parents stayed in Moab with the king during the entire time David was living in his stronghold.

5One day the prophet Gad told David, "Leave the stronghold and return to the land of Judah." So David went to the forest of Hereth.

6The news of his arrival in Judah soon reached Saul. At the time, the king was sitting beneath the tamarisk tree on the hill at Gibeah, holding his spear and surrounded by his officers.

7"Listen here, you men of Benjamin!" Saul shouted to his officers when he heard the news. "Has that son of Jesse promised every one of you fields and vineyards? Has he promised to make you all generals and captains in his army?* 8Is that why you have conspired against me? For not one of you told me when my own son made a solemn pact with the son of Jesse. You're not even sorry for me. Think of it! My own son—encouraging him to kill me, as he is trying to do this very day!"

9Then Doeg the Edomite, who was standing there with Saul's men, spoke up. "When I was at Nob," he said, "I saw the son of Jesse talking to the priest, Ahimelech son of Ahitub. 10Ahimelech consulted the LORD for him. Then he gave him food and the sword of Goliath the Philistine."

The Slaughter of the Priests

11King Saul immediately sent for Ahimelech and all his family, who served as priests at Nob. 12When they arrived, Saul shouted at him, "Listen to me, you son of Ahitub!"

"What is it, my king?" Ahimelech asked.

13"Why have you and the son of Jesse conspired against me?" Saul demanded. "Why did you give him food and a sword? Why have you

---

consulted God for him? Why have you encouraged him to kill me, as he is trying to do this very day?"

¹⁴"But sir," Ahimelech replied, "is anyone among all your servants as faithful as David, your son-in-law? Why, he is the captain of your bodyguard and a highly honored member of your household! ¹⁵This was certainly not the first time I had consulted God for him! May the king not accuse me and my family in this matter, for I knew nothing at all of any plot against you."

¹⁶"You will surely die, Ahimelech, along with your entire family!" the king shouted. ¹⁷And he ordered his bodyguards, "Kill these priests of the LORD, for they are allies and conspirators with David! They knew he was running away from me, but they didn't tell me!" But Saul's men refused to kill the LORD's priests.

¹⁸Then the king said to Doeg, "You do it." So Doeg the Edomite turned on them and killed them that day, eighty-five priests in all, still wearing their priestly garments. ¹⁹Then he went to Nob, the town of the priests, and killed the priests' families—men and women, children and babies—and all the cattle, donkeys, sheep, and goats.

²⁰Only Abiathar, one of the sons of Ahimelech, escaped and fled to David. ²¹When he told David that Saul had killed the priests of the LORD, ²²David exclaimed, "I knew it! When I saw Doeg the Edomite there that day, I knew he was sure to tell Saul. Now I have caused the death of all your father's family. ²³Stay here with me, and don't be afraid. I will protect you with my own life, for the same person wants to kill us both."

David Protects the Town of Keilah

23 One day news came to David that the Philistines were at Keilah stealing grain from the threshing floors. ²David asked the LORD, "Should I go and attack them?"

"Yes, go and save Keilah," the LORD told him.

³But David's men said, "We're afraid even here in Judah. We certainly don't want to go to Keilah to fight the whole Philistine army!"

⁴So David asked the LORD again, and again the LORD replied, "Go down to Keilah, for I will help you conquer the Philistines."

⁵So David and his men went to Keilah. They slaughtered the Philistines and took all their livestock and rescued the people of Keilah. ⁶Now when Abiathar son of Ahimelech fled to

23:11 Some manuscripts lack the first sentence of 23:11.

David at Keilah, he brought the ephod with him.

⁷Saul soon learned that David was at Keilah. "Good!" he exclaimed. "We've got him now! God has handed him over to me, for he has trapped himself in a walled town!" ⁸So Saul mobilized his entire army to march to Keilah and besiege David and his men.

⁹But David learned of Saul's plan and told Abiathar the priest to bring the ephod and ask the LORD what he should do. ¹⁰Then David prayed, "O LORD, God of Israel, I have heard that Saul is planning to come and destroy Keilah because I am here. ¹¹Will the leaders of Keilah betray me to him?* And will Saul actually come as I have heard? O LORD, God of Israel, please tell me."

And the LORD said, "He will come."

¹²Again David asked, "Will the leaders of Keilah betray me and my men to Saul?"

And the LORD replied, "Yes, they will betray you."

David Hides in the Wilderness

¹³So David and his men—about 600 of them now—left Keilah and began roaming the countryside. Word soon reached Saul that David had escaped, so he didn't go to Keilah after all. ¹⁴David now stayed in the strongholds of the wilderness and in the hill country of Ziph. Saul hunted him day after day, but God didn't let Saul find him.

¹⁵One day near Horesh, David received the news that Saul was on the way to Ziph to search for him and kill him. ¹⁶Jonathan went to find David and encouraged him to stay strong in his faith in God. ¹⁷"Don't be afraid," Jonathan reassured him. "My father will never find you! You are going to be the king of Israel, and I will be next to you, as my father, Saul, is well aware." ¹⁸So the two of them renewed their solemn pact before the LORD. Then Jonathan returned home, while David stayed at Horesh.

¹⁹But now the men of Ziph went to Saul in Gibeah and betrayed David to him. "We know where David is hiding," they said. "He is in the strongholds of Horesh on the hill of Hakilah, which is in the southern part of Jeshimon. ²⁰Come down whenever you're ready, O king, and we will catch him and hand him over to you!"

²¹"The LORD bless you," Saul said. "At last someone is concerned about me! ²²Go and check again to be sure of where he is staying and who has seen him there, for I know that

he is very crafty. ²³Discover his hiding places, and come back when you are sure. Then I'll go with you. And if he is in the area at all, I'll track him down, even if I have to search every hiding place in Judah!" ²⁴So the men of Ziph returned home ahead of Saul.

Meanwhile, David and his men had moved into the wilderness of Maon in the Arabah Valley south of Jeshimon. ²⁵When David heard that Saul and his men were searching for him, he went even farther into the wilderness to the great rock, and he remained there in the wilderness of Maon. But Saul kept after him in the wilderness.

²⁶Saul and David were now on opposite sides of a mountain. Just as Saul and his men began to close in on David and his men, ²⁷an urgent message reached Saul that the Philistines were raiding Israel again. ²⁸So Saul quit chasing David and returned to fight the Philistines. Ever since that time, the place where David was camped has been called the Rock of Escape.* ²⁹*David then went to live in the strongholds of En-gedi.

David Spares Saul's Life

24 ¹*After Saul returned from fighting the Philistines, he was told that David had gone into the wilderness of En-gedi. ²So Saul chose 3,000 elite troops from all Israel and went to search for David and his men near the rocks of the wild goats.

³At the place where the road passes some sheepfolds, Saul went into a cave to relieve himself. But as it happened, David and his men were hiding farther back in that very cave!

⁴"Now's your opportunity!" David's men whispered to him. "Today the LORD is telling you, 'I will certainly put your enemy into your power, to do with as you wish.'" So David crept forward and cut off a piece of the hem of Saul's robe.

⁵But then David's conscience began bothering him because he had cut Saul's robe. ⁶He said to his men, "The LORD forbid that I should do this to my lord the king. I shouldn't attack the LORD's anointed one, for the LORD himself has chosen him." ⁷So David restrained his men and did not let them kill Saul.

After Saul had left the cave and gone on his way, ⁸David came out and shouted after him, "My lord the king!" And when Saul looked around, David bowed low before him.

⁹Then he shouted to Saul, "Why do you listen to the people who say I am trying to harm you? ¹⁰This very day you can see with your own eyes it isn't true. For the LORD placed you at my mercy back there in the cave. Some of my men told me to kill you, but I spared you. For I said, 'I will never harm the king—he is the LORD's anointed one.' ¹¹Look, my father, at what I have in my hand. It is a piece of the hem of your robe! I cut it off, but I didn't kill you. This proves that I am not trying to harm you and that I have not sinned against you, even though you have been hunting for me to kill me.

¹²"May the LORD judge between us. Perhaps the LORD will punish you for what you are trying to do to me, but I will never harm you. ¹³As that old proverb says, 'From evil people come evil deeds.' So you can be sure I will never harm you. ¹⁴Who is the king of Israel trying to catch anyway? Should he spend his time chasing one who is as worthless as a dead dog or a single flea? ¹⁵May the LORD therefore judge which of us is right and punish the guilty one. He is my advocate, and he will rescue me from your power!"

¹⁶When David had finished speaking, Saul called back, "Is that really you, my son David?" Then he began to cry. ¹⁷And he said to David, "You are a better man than I am, for you have repaid me good for evil. ¹⁸Yes, you have been amazingly kind to me today, for when the LORD put me in a place where you could have killed me, you didn't do it. ¹⁹Who else would let his enemy get away when he had him in his power? May the LORD reward you well for the kindness you have shown me today. ²⁰And now I realize that you are surely going to be king, and that the kingdom of Israel will flourish under your rule. ²¹Now swear to me by the LORD that when that happens you will not kill my family and destroy my line of descendants!"

²²So David promised this to Saul with an oath. Then Saul went home, but David and his men went back to their stronghold.

The Death of Samuel

25 Now Samuel died, and all Israel gathered for his funeral. They buried him at his house in Ramah.

Nabal Angers David

Then David moved down to the wilderness of Maon.* ²There was a wealthy man from

23:28 Hebrew *Sela-hammahlekoth.*   23:29 Verse 23:29 is numbered 24:1 in Hebrew text.   24:1 Verses 24:1-22 are numbered 24:2-23 in Hebrew text.   25:1 As in Greek version (see also 25:2); Hebrew reads *Paran.*

Maon who owned property near the town of Carmel. He had 3,000 sheep and 1,000 goats, and it was sheep-shearing time. ³This man's name was Nabal, and his wife, Abigail, was a sensible and beautiful woman. But Nabal, a descendant of Caleb, was crude and mean in all his dealings.

⁴When David heard that Nabal was shearing his sheep, ⁵he sent ten of his young men to Carmel with this message for Nabal: ⁶"Peace and prosperity to you, your family, and everything you own! ⁷I am told that it is sheep-shearing time. While your shepherds stayed among us near Carmel, we never harmed them, and nothing was ever stolen from them. ⁸Ask your own men, and they will tell you this is true. So would you be kind to us, since we have come at a time of celebration? Please share any provisions you might have on hand with us and with your friend David." ⁹David's young men gave this message to Nabal in David's name, and they waited for a reply.

¹⁰"Who is this fellow David?" Nabal sneered to the young men. "Who does this son of Jesse think he is? There are lots of servants these days who run away from their masters. ¹¹Should I take my bread and my water and my meat that I've slaughtered for my shearers and give it to a band of outlaws who come from who knows where?"

¹²So David's young men returned and told him what Nabal had said. ¹³"Get your swords!" was David's reply as he strapped on his own. Then 400 men started off with David, and 200 remained behind to guard their equipment.

¹⁴Meanwhile, one of Nabal's servants went to Abigail and told her, "David sent messengers from the wilderness to greet our master, but he screamed insults at them. ¹⁵These men have been very good to us, and we never suffered any harm from them. Nothing was stolen from us the whole time they were with us. ¹⁶In fact, day and night they were like a wall of protection to us and the sheep. ¹⁷You need to know this and figure out what to do, for there is going to be trouble for our master and his whole family. He's so ill-tempered that no one can even talk to him!"

¹⁸Abigail wasted no time. She quickly gathered 200 loaves of bread, two wineskins full of wine, five sheep that had been slaughtered, nearly a bushel* of roasted grain, 100 clusters of raisins, and 200 fig cakes. She packed them on donkeys ¹⁹and said to her servants, "Go on ahead. I will follow you shortly." But she didn't tell her husband Nabal what she was doing.

²⁰As she was riding her donkey into a mountain ravine, she saw David and his men coming toward her. ²¹David had just been saying, "A lot of good it did to help this fellow. We protected his flocks in the wilderness, and nothing he owned was lost or stolen. But he has repaid me evil for good. ²²May God strike me and kill me* if even one man of his household is still alive tomorrow morning!"

Abigail Intercedes for Nabal

²³When Abigail saw David, she quickly got off her donkey and bowed low before him. ²⁴She fell at his feet and said, "I accept all blame in this matter, my lord. Please listen to what I have to say. ²⁵I know Nabal is a wicked and ill-tempered man; please don't pay any attention to him. He is a fool, just as his name suggests.* But I never even saw the young men you sent.

²⁶"Now, my lord, as surely as the LORD lives and you yourself live, since the LORD has kept you from murdering and taking vengeance into your own hands, let all your enemies and those who try to harm you be as cursed as Nabal is. ²⁷And here is a present that I, your servant, have brought to you and your young men. ²⁸Please forgive me if I have offended you in any way. The LORD will surely reward you with a lasting dynasty, for you are fighting the LORD's battles. And you have not done wrong throughout your entire life.

²⁹"Even when you are chased by those who seek to kill you, your life is safe in the care of the LORD your God, secure in his treasure pouch! But the lives of your enemies will disappear like stones shot from a sling! ³⁰When the LORD has done all he promised and has made you leader of Israel, ³¹don't let this be a blemish on your record. Then your conscience won't have to bear the staggering burden of needless bloodshed and vengeance. And when the LORD has done these great things for you, please remember me, your servant!"

³²David replied to Abigail, "Praise the LORD, the God of Israel, who has sent you to meet me today! ³³Thank God for your good sense! Bless you for keeping me from murder and from carrying out vengeance with my own hands. ³⁴For I swear by the LORD, the God

25:18 Hebrew *5 seahs* [36.5 liters]. 25:22 As in Greek version; Hebrew reads *May God strike and kill the enemies of David.* 25:25 The name *Nabal* means "fool."

of Israel, who has kept me from hurting you, that if you had not hurried out to meet me, not one of Nabal's men would still be alive tomorrow morning." [35] Then David accepted her present and told her, "Return home in peace. I have heard what you said. We will not kill your husband."

[36] When Abigail arrived home, she found that Nabal was throwing a big party and was celebrating like a king. He was very drunk, so she didn't tell him anything about her meeting with David until dawn the next day. [37] In the morning when Nabal was sober, his wife told him what had happened. As a result he had a stroke,* and he lay paralyzed on his bed like a stone. [38] About ten days later, the LORD struck him, and he died.

David Marries Abigail

[39] When David heard that Nabal was dead, he said, "Praise the LORD, who has avenged the insult I received from Nabal and has kept me from doing it myself. Nabal has received the punishment for his sin." Then David sent messengers to Abigail to ask her to become his wife.

[40] When the messengers arrived at Carmel, they told Abigail, "David has sent us to take you back to marry him."

[41] She bowed low to the ground and responded, "I, your servant, would be happy to marry David. I would even be willing to become a slave, washing the feet of his servants!" [42] Quickly getting ready, she took along five of her servant girls as attendants, mounted her donkey, and went with David's messengers. And so she became his wife. [43] David also married Ahinoam from Jezreel, making both of them his wives. [44] Saul, meanwhile, had given his daughter Michal, David's wife, to a man from Gallim named Palti son of Laish.

David Spares Saul Again

26 Now some men from Ziph came to Saul at Gibeah to tell him, "David is hiding on the hill of Hakilah, which overlooks Jeshimon."

[2] So Saul took 3,000 of Israel's elite troops and went to hunt him down in the wilderness of Ziph. [3] Saul camped along the road beside the hill of Hakilah, near Jeshimon, where David was hiding. When David learned that Saul had come after him into the wilderness, [4] he sent out spies to verify the report of Saul's arrival.

[5] David slipped over to Saul's camp one night to look around. Saul and Abner son of Ner, the commander of his army, were sleeping inside a ring formed by the slumbering warriors. [6] "Who will volunteer to go in there with me?" David asked Ahimelech the Hittite and Abishai son of Zeruiah, Joab's brother.

"I'll go with you," Abishai replied. [7] So David and Abishai went right into Saul's camp and found him asleep, with his spear stuck in the ground beside his head. Abner and the soldiers were lying asleep around him.

[8] "God has surely handed your enemy over to you this time!" Abishai whispered to David. "Let me pin him to the ground with one thrust of the spear; I won't need to strike twice!"

[9] "No!" David said. "Don't kill him. For who can remain innocent after attacking the LORD's anointed one? [10] Surely the LORD will strike Saul down someday, or he will die of old age or in battle. [11] The LORD forbid that I should kill the one he has anointed! But take his spear and that jug of water beside his head, and then let's get out of here!"

[12] So David took the spear and jug of water that were near Saul's head. Then he and Abishai got away without anyone seeing them or even waking up, because the LORD had put Saul's men into a deep sleep.

[13] David climbed the hill opposite the camp until he was at a safe distance. [14] Then he shouted down to the soldiers and to Abner son of Ner, "Wake up, Abner!"

"Who is it?" Abner demanded.

[15] "Well, Abner, you're a great man, aren't you?" David taunted. "Where in all Israel is there anyone as mighty? So why haven't you guarded your master the king when someone came to kill him? [16] This isn't good at all! I swear by the LORD that you and your men deserve to die, because you failed to protect your master, the LORD's anointed! Look around! Where are the king's spear and the jug of water that were beside his head?"

[17] Saul recognized David's voice and called out, "Is that you, my son David?"

And David replied, "Yes, my lord the king. [18] Why are you chasing me? What have I done? What is my crime? [19] But now let my lord the king listen to his servant. If the LORD has stirred you up against me, then let him accept my offering. But if this is simply a human scheme, then may those involved be cursed by the LORD. For they have driven me from my home, so I can no longer live among the

LORD's people, and they have said, 'Go, worship pagan gods.' ²⁰Must I die on foreign soil, far from the presence of the LORD? Why has the king of Israel come out to search for a single flea? Why does he hunt me down like a partridge on the mountains?"

²¹Then Saul confessed, "I have sinned. Come back home, my son, and I will no longer try to harm you, for you valued my life today. I have been a fool and very, very wrong."

²²"Here is your spear, O king," David replied. "Let one of your young men come over and get it. ²³The LORD gives his own reward for doing good and for being loyal, and I refused to kill you even when the LORD placed you in my power, for you are the LORD's anointed one. ²⁴Now may the LORD value my life, even as I have valued yours today. May he rescue me from all my troubles."

²⁵And Saul said to David, "Blessings on you, my son David. You will do many heroic deeds, and you will surely succeed." Then David went away, and Saul returned home.

David among the Philistines

27 But David kept thinking to himself, "Someday Saul is going to get me. The best thing I can do is escape to the Philistines. Then Saul will stop hunting for me in Israelite territory, and I will finally be safe."

²So David took his 600 men and went over and joined Achish son of Maoch, the king of Gath. ³David and his men and their families settled there with Achish at Gath. David brought his two wives along with him— Ahinoam from Jezreel and Abigail, Nabal's widow from Carmel. ⁴Word soon reached Saul that David had fled to Gath, so he stopped hunting for him.

⁵One day David said to Achish, "If it is all right with you, we would rather live in one of the country towns instead of here in the royal city."

⁶So Achish gave him the town of Ziklag (which still belongs to the kings of Judah to this day), ⁷and they lived there among the Philistines for a year and four months.

⁸David and his men spent their time raiding the Geshurites, the Girzites, and the Amalekites—people who had lived near Shur, toward the land of Egypt, since ancient times. ⁹David did not leave one person alive in the villages he attacked. He took the sheep, goats, cattle, donkeys, camels, and clothing before returning home to see King Achish.

28:6 Hebrew *by Urim.*

¹⁰"Where did you make your raid today?" Achish would ask.

And David would reply, "Against the south of Judah, the Jerahmeelites, and the Kenites."

¹¹No one was left alive to come to Gath and tell where he had really been. This happened again and again while he was living among the Philistines. ¹²Achish believed David and thought to himself, "By now the people of Israel must hate him bitterly. Now he will have to stay here and serve me forever!"

Saul Consults a Medium

28 About that time the Philistines mustered their armies for another war with Israel. King Achish told David, "You and your men will be expected to join me in battle."

²"Very well!" David agreed. "Now you will see for yourself what we can do."

Then Achish told David, "I will make you my personal bodyguard for life."

³Meanwhile, Samuel had died, and all Israel had mourned for him. He was buried in Ramah, his hometown. And Saul had banned from the land of Israel all mediums and those who consult the spirits of the dead.

⁴The Philistines set up their camp at Shunem, and Saul gathered all the army of Israel and camped at Gilboa. ⁵When Saul saw the vast Philistine army, he became frantic with fear. ⁶He asked the LORD what he should do, but the LORD refused to answer him, either by dreams or by sacred lots* or by the prophets. ⁷Saul then said to his advisers, "Find a woman who is a medium, so I can go and ask her what to do."

His advisers replied, "There is a medium at Endor."

⁸So Saul disguised himself by wearing ordinary clothing instead of his royal robes. Then he went to the woman's home at night, accompanied by two of his men.

"I have to talk to a man who has died," he said. "Will you call up his spirit for me?"

⁹"Are you trying to get me killed?" the woman demanded. "You know that Saul has outlawed all the mediums and all who consult the spirits of the dead. Why are you setting a trap for me?"

¹⁰But Saul took an oath in the name of the LORD and promised, "As surely as the LORD lives, nothing bad will happen to you for doing this."

¹¹Finally, the woman said, "Well, whose spirit do you want me to call up?"

"Call up Samuel," Saul replied.

¹²When the woman saw Samuel, she screamed, "You've deceived me! You are Saul!"

¹³"Don't be afraid!" the king told her. "What do you see?"

"I see a god* coming up out of the earth," she said.

¹⁴"What does he look like?" Saul asked.

"He is an old man wrapped in a robe," she replied. Saul realized it was Samuel, and he fell to the ground before him.

¹⁵"Why have you disturbed me by calling me back?" Samuel asked Saul.

"Because I am in deep trouble," Saul replied. "The Philistines are at war with me, and God has left me and won't reply by prophets or dreams. So I have called for you to tell me what to do."

¹⁶But Samuel replied, "Why ask me, since the LORD has left you and has become your enemy? ¹⁷The LORD has done just as he said he would. He has torn the kingdom from you and given it to your rival, David. ¹⁸The LORD has done this to you today because you refused to carry out his fierce anger against the Amalekites. ¹⁹What's more, the LORD will hand you and the army of Israel over to the Philistines tomorrow, and you and your sons will be here with me. The LORD will bring down the entire army of Israel in defeat."

²⁰Saul fell full length on the ground, paralyzed with fright because of Samuel's words. He was also faint with hunger, for he had eaten nothing all day and all night.

²¹When the woman saw how distraught he was, she said, "Sir, I obeyed your command at the risk of my life. ²²Now do what I say, and let me give you a little something to eat so you can regain your strength for the trip back."

²³But Saul refused to eat anything. Then his advisers joined the woman in urging him to eat, so he finally yielded and got up from the ground and sat on the couch.

²⁴The woman had been fattening a calf, so she hurried out and killed it. She took some flour, kneaded it into dough and baked unleavened bread. ²⁵She brought the meal to Saul and his advisers, and they ate it. Then they went out into the night.

The Philistines Reject David

29 The entire Philistine army now mobilized at Aphek, and the Israelites camped at the spring in Jezreel. ²As the Philistine rulers were leading out their troops in

28:13 Or *gods*.

groups of hundreds and thousands, David and his men marched at the rear with King Achish. ³But the Philistine commanders demanded, "What are these Hebrews doing here?"

And Achish told them, "This is David, the servant of King Saul of Israel. He's been with me for years, and I've never found a single fault in him from the day he arrived until today."

⁴But the Philistine commanders were angry. "Send him back to the town you've given him!" they demanded. "He can't go into the battle with us. What if he turns against us in battle and becomes our adversary? Is there any better way for him to reconcile himself with his master than by handing our heads over to him? ⁵Isn't this the same David about whom the women of Israel sing in their dances,

'Saul has killed his thousands,
and David his ten thousands'?"

⁶So Achish finally summoned David and said to him, "I swear by the LORD that you have been a trustworthy ally. I think you should go with me into battle, for I've never found a single flaw in you from the day you arrived until today. But the other Philistine rulers won't hear of it. ⁷Please don't upset them, but go back quietly."

⁸"What have I done to deserve this treatment?" David demanded. "What have you ever found in your servant, that I can't go and fight the enemies of my lord the king?"

⁹But Achish insisted, "As far as I'm concerned, you're as perfect as an angel of God. But the Philistine commanders are afraid to have you with them in the battle. ¹⁰Now get up early in the morning, and leave with your men as soon as it gets light."

¹¹So David and his men headed back into the land of the Philistines, while the Philistine army went on to Jezreel.

David Destroys the Amalekites

30 Three days later, when David and his men arrived home at their town of Ziklag, they found that the Amalekites had made a raid into the Negev and Ziklag; they had crushed Ziklag and burned it to the ground. ²They had carried off the women and children and everyone else but without killing anyone.

³When David and his men saw the ruins and realized what had happened to their families, ⁴they wept until they could weep no more. ⁵David's two wives, Ahinoam from

Jezreel and Abigail, the widow of Nabal from Carmel, were among those captured. 6David was now in great danger because all his men were very bitter about losing their sons and daughters, and they began to talk of stoning him. But David found strength in the LORD his God.

7Then he said to Abiathar the priest, "Bring me the ephod!" So Abiathar brought it. 8Then David asked the LORD, "Should I chase after this band of raiders? Will I catch them?"

And the LORD told him, "Yes, go after them. You will surely recover everything that was taken from you!"

9So David and his 600 men set out, and they came to the brook Besor. 10But 200 of the men were too exhausted to cross the brook, so David continued the pursuit with 400 men.

11Along the way they found an Egyptian man in a field and brought him to David. They gave him some bread to eat and water to drink. 12They also gave him part of a fig cake and two clusters of raisins, for he hadn't had anything to eat or drink for three days and nights. Before long his strength returned.

13"To whom do you belong, and where do you come from?" David asked him.

"I am an Egyptian—the slave of an Amalekite," he replied. "My master abandoned me three days ago because I was sick. 14We were on our way back from raiding the Kerethites in the Negev, the territory of Judah, and the land of Caleb, and we had just burned Ziklag."

15"Will you lead me to this band of raiders?" David asked.

The young man replied, "If you take an oath in God's name that you will not kill me or give me back to my master, then I will guide you to them."

16So he led David to them, and they found the Amalekites spread out across the fields, eating and drinking and dancing with joy because of the vast amount of plunder they had taken from the Philistines and the land of Judah. 17David and his men rushed in among them and slaughtered them throughout that night and the entire next day until evening. None of the Amalekites escaped except 400 young men who fled on camels. 18David got back everything the Amalekites had taken, and he rescued his two wives. 19Nothing was missing: small or great, son or daughter, nor anything else that had been taken. David brought everything back. 20He also recovered all the flocks and herds, and his men drove

30:29 Greek version reads *Carmel*.

them ahead of the other livestock. "This plunder belongs to David!" they said.

21Then David returned to the brook Besor and met up with the 200 men who had been left behind because they were too exhausted to go with him. They went out to meet David and his men, and David greeted them joyfully. 22But some evil troublemakers among David's men said, "They didn't go with us, so they can't have any of the plunder we recovered. Give them their wives and children, and tell them to be gone."

23But David said, "No, my brothers! Don't be selfish with what the LORD has given us. He has kept us safe and helped us defeat the band of raiders that attacked us. 24Who will listen when you talk like this? We share and share alike—those who go to battle and those who guard the equipment." 25From then on David made this a decree and regulation for Israel, and it is still followed today.

26When he arrived at Ziklag, David sent part of the plunder to the elders of Judah, who were his friends. "Here is a present for you, taken from the LORD's enemies," he said.

27The gifts were sent to the people of the following towns David had visited: Bethel, Ramoth-negev, Jattir, 28Aroer, Siphmoth, Eshtemoa, 29Racal,* the towns of the Jerahmeelites, the towns of the Kenites, 30Hormah, Bor-ashan, Athach, 31Hebron, and all the other places David and his men had visited.

The Death of Saul

31 Now the Philistines attacked Israel, and the men of Israel fled before them. Many were slaughtered on the slopes of Mount Gilboa. 2The Philistines closed in on Saul and his sons, and they killed three of his sons— Jonathan, Abinadab, and Malkishua. 3The fighting grew very fierce around Saul, and the Philistine archers caught up with him and wounded him severely.

4Saul groaned to his armor bearer, "Take your sword and kill me before these pagan Philistines come to run me through and taunt and torture me."

But his armor bearer was afraid and would not do it. So Saul took his own sword and fell on it. 5When his armor bearer realized that Saul was dead, he fell on his own sword and died beside the king. 6So Saul, his three sons, his armor bearer, and his troops all died together that same day.

7When the Israelites on the other side of

the Jezreel Valley and beyond the Jordan saw that the Israelite army had fled and that Saul and his sons were dead, they abandoned their towns and fled. So the Philistines moved in and occupied their towns.

⁸The next day, when the Philistines went out to strip the dead, they found the bodies of Saul and his three sons on Mount Gilboa. ⁹So they cut off Saul's head and stripped off his armor. Then they proclaimed the good news of Saul's death in their pagan temple and to the people throughout the land of Philistia. ¹⁰They placed his armor in the temple of the Ashtoreths, and they fastened his body to the wall of the city of Beth-shan.

¹¹But when the people of Jabesh-gilead heard what the Philistines had done to Saul, ¹²all their mighty warriors traveled through the night to Beth-shan and took the bodies of Saul and his sons down from the wall. They brought them to Jabesh, where they burned the bodies. ¹³Then they took their bones and buried them beneath the tamarisk tree at Jabesh, and they fasted for seven days.

2 Samuel

AMONG THE GODLY MEN AND WOMEN mentioned in the Bible, King David stands as one of the most prominent. The prophet Samuel had said that God wanted "a man after his own heart," and David was that man. The book of 2 Samuel tells King David's story, covering a period of approximately forty years, the bulk of David's reign as king. It begins with David's being proclaimed king of Israel. Soon after his inauguration, David solidified his position against rivals to the throne. After conquering Jerusalem, David made it his capital and brought the sacred Ark of the Covenant there. Then he defeated the Philistines— neighbors who had harassed the Israelites for hundreds of years. But 2 Samuel also describes the darker side of David's career, including his affair with Bathsheba and the rebellion led by his son Absalom. The book comes to a close near the end of David's long reign.

■ **Author:** Uncertain; some have suggested Nathan's son Zabud and the prophets Nathan and Gad

■ **Date Written:** Uncertain, perhaps around 930 BC, not long after David's reign (1050–970 BC)

■ **Purpose:** To record the history of David's reign, to validate the Davidic dynasty, and to depict David as the ideal example of good leadership

■ **Themes:** Prosperity under David, ideal leadership, justice, consequences of sin

■ **Outline**
1:1–6:23 David's first acts as king
7:1-29 God's covenant with David
8:1–10:19 David's victories over his enemies
11:1–12:25 David's sin with Bathsheba and Nathan's rebuke
12:26–21:22 David's troubled reign
22:1–23:7 David's final praise
23:8–24:25 Further problems in David's reign

David Learns of Saul's Death

1 After the death of Saul, David returned from his victory over the Amalekites and spent two days in Ziklag. ²On the third day a man arrived from Saul's army camp. He had torn his clothes and put dirt on his head to show that he was in mourning. He fell to the ground before David in deep respect.

³"Where have you come from?" David asked.

"I escaped from the Israelite camp," the man replied.

⁴"What happened?" David demanded. "Tell me how the battle went."

The man replied, "Our entire army fled from the battle. Many of the men are dead, and Saul and his son Jonathan are also dead."

⁵"How do you know Saul and Jonathan are dead?" David demanded of the young man.

⁶The man answered, "I happened to be on Mount Gilboa, and there was Saul leaning on his spear with the enemy chariots and charioteers closing in on him. ⁷When he turned and saw me, he cried out for me to come to him. 'How can I help?' I asked him.

⁸"He responded, 'Who are you?'

"'I am an Amalekite,' I told him.

⁹"Then he begged me, 'Come over here and put me out of my misery, for I am in terrible pain and want to die.'

¹⁰"So I killed him," the Amalekite told David, "for I knew he couldn't live. Then I took his crown and his armband, and I have brought them here to you, my lord."

¹¹David and his men tore their clothes in sorrow when they heard the news. ¹²They mourned and wept and fasted all day for Saul and his son Jonathan, and for the LORD's army and the nation of Israel, because they had died by the sword that day.

¹³Then David said to the young man who had brought the news, "Where are you from?"

And he replied, "I am a foreigner, an Amalekite, who lives in your land."

¹⁴"Why were you not afraid to kill the LORD's anointed one?" David asked.

¹⁵Then David said to one of his men, "Kill him!" So the man thrust his sword into the Amalekite and killed him. ¹⁶"You have condemned yourself," David said, "for you yourself confessed that you killed the LORD's anointed one."

David's Song for Saul and Jonathan

¹⁷Then David composed a funeral song for Saul and Jonathan, ¹⁸and he commanded that it be taught to the people of Judah. It is known as the Song of the Bow, and it is recorded in *The Book of Jashar.**

¹⁹ Your pride and joy, O Israel, lies dead on
the hills!
Oh, how the mighty heroes have fallen!
²⁰ Don't announce the news in Gath,
don't proclaim it in the streets of
Ashkelon,
or the daughters of the Philistines will
rejoice
and the pagans will laugh in triumph.

²¹ O mountains of Gilboa,
let there be no dew or rain upon you,
nor fruitful fields producing offerings
of grain.*
For there the shield of the mighty heroes
was defiled;
the shield of Saul will no longer be
anointed with oil.
²² The bow of Jonathan was powerful,
and the sword of Saul did its mighty
work.
They shed the blood of their enemies
and pierced the bodies of mighty heroes.

²³ How beloved and gracious were Saul and
Jonathan!
They were together in life and in death.
They were swifter than eagles,
stronger than lions.
²⁴ O women of Israel, weep for Saul,
for he dressed you in luxurious scarlet
clothing,
in garments decorated with gold.

²⁵ Oh, how the mighty heroes have fallen in
battle!
Jonathan lies dead on the hills.

²⁶ How I weep for you, my brother Jonathan!
Oh, how much I loved you!
And your love for me was deep,
deeper than the love of women!

²⁷ Oh, how the mighty heroes have fallen!
Stripped of their weapons, they lie dead.

David Anointed King of Judah

2 After this, David asked the LORD, "Should I move back to one of the towns of Judah?"

"Yes," the LORD replied.

Then David asked, "Which town should I go to?"

"To Hebron," the LORD answered.

²David's two wives were Ahinoam from Jezreel and Abigail, the widow of Nabal from Carmel. So David and his wives ³and his men and their families all moved to Judah, and they settled in the villages near Hebron. ⁴Then the men of Judah came to David and anointed him king over the people of Judah.

When David heard that the men of Jabesh-gilead had buried Saul, ⁵he sent them this message: "May the LORD bless you for being so loyal to your master Saul and giving him a decent burial. ⁶May the LORD be loyal to you in return and reward you with his unfailing love! And I, too, will reward you for what you have done. ⁷Now that Saul is dead, I ask you to be my strong and loyal subjects like the people of Judah, who have anointed me as their new king."

Ishbosheth Proclaimed King of Israel

⁸But Abner son of Ner, the commander of Saul's army, had already gone to Mahanaim with Saul's son Ishbosheth.* ⁹There he proclaimed Ishbosheth king over Gilead, Jezreel, Ephraim, Benjamin, the land of the Ashurites, and all the rest of Israel.

¹⁰Ishbosheth, Saul's son, was forty years old when he became king, and he ruled from Mahanaim for two years. Meanwhile, the people of Judah remained loyal to David. ¹¹David made Hebron his capital, and he ruled as king of Judah for seven and a half years.

War between Israel and Judah

¹²One day Abner led Ishbosheth's troops from Mahanaim to Gibeon. ¹³About the same time, Joab son of Zeruiah led David's troops out and met them at the pool of Gibeon. The two groups sat down there, facing each other from opposite sides of the pool.

1:18 Or *The Book of the Upright.*   1:21 The meaning of the Hebrew is uncertain.   2:8 *Ishbosheth* is another name for Esh-baal.

¹⁴Then Abner suggested to Joab, "Let's have a few of our warriors fight hand to hand here in front of us."

"All right," Joab agreed. ¹⁵So twelve men were chosen to fight from each side—twelve men of Benjamin representing Ishbosheth son of Saul, and twelve representing David. ¹⁶Each one grabbed his opponent by the hair and thrust his sword into the other's side so that all of them died. So this place at Gibeon has been known ever since as the Field of Swords.*

¹⁷A fierce battle followed that day, and Abner and the men of Israel were defeated by the forces of David.

The Death of Asahel

¹⁸Joab, Abishai, and Asahel—the three sons of Zeruiah—were among David's forces that day. Asahel could run like a gazelle, ¹⁹and he began chasing Abner. He pursued him relentlessly, not stopping for anything. ²⁰When Abner looked back and saw him coming, he called out, "Is that you, Asahel?"

"Yes, it is," he replied.

²¹"Go fight someone else!" Abner warned. "Take on one of the younger men, and strip him of his weapons." But Asahel kept right on chasing Abner.

²²Again Abner shouted to him, "Get away from here! I don't want to kill you. How could I ever face your brother Joab again?"

²³But Asahel refused to turn back, so Abner thrust the butt end of his spear through Asahel's stomach, and the spear came out through his back. He stumbled to the ground and died there. And everyone who came by that spot stopped and stood still when they saw Asahel lying there.

²⁴When Joab and Abishai found out what had happened, they set out after Abner. The sun was just going down as they arrived at the hill of Ammah near Giah, along the road to the wilderness of Gibeon. ²⁵Abner's troops from the tribe of Benjamin regrouped there at the top of the hill to take a stand.

²⁶Abner shouted down to Joab, "Must we always be killing each other? Don't you realize that bitterness is the only result? When will you call off your men from chasing their Israelite brothers?"

²⁷Then Joab said, "God only knows what would have happened if you hadn't spoken, for we would have chased you all night if necessary." ²⁸So Joab blew the ram's horn, and his men stopped chasing the troops of Israel.

²⁹All that night Abner and his men retreated through the Jordan Valley.* They crossed the Jordan River, traveling all through the morning,* and didn't stop until they arrived at Mahanaim.

³⁰Meanwhile, Joab and his men also returned home. When Joab counted his casualties, he discovered that only 19 men were missing in addition to Asahel. ³¹But 360 of Abner's men had been killed, all from the tribe of Benjamin. ³²Joab and his men took Asahel's body to Bethlehem and buried him there in his father's tomb. Then they traveled all night and reached Hebron at daybreak.

3 That was the beginning of a long war between those who were loyal to Saul and those loyal to David. As time passed David became stronger and stronger, while Saul's dynasty became weaker and weaker.

David's Sons Born in Hebron

²These are the sons who were born to David in Hebron:

The oldest was Amnon, whose mother was Ahinoam from Jezreel.
³ The second was Daniel,* whose mother was Abigail, the widow of Nabal from Carmel.
The third was Absalom, whose mother was Maacah, the daughter of Talmai, king of Geshur.
⁴ The fourth was Adonijah, whose mother was Haggith.
The fifth was Shephatiah, whose mother was Abital.
⁵ The sixth was Ithream, whose mother was Eglah, David's wife.

These sons were all born to David in Hebron.

Abner Joins Forces with David

⁶As the war between the house of Saul and the house of David went on, Abner became a powerful leader among those loyal to Saul. ⁷One day Ishbosheth,* Saul's son, accused Abner of sleeping with one of his father's concubines, a woman named Rizpah, daughter of Aiah.

⁸Abner was furious. "Am I some Judean dog

2:16 Hebrew *Helkath-hazzurim.* 2:29a Hebrew *the Arabah.* 2:29b Or *continued on through the Bithron.* The meaning of the Hebrew is uncertain. 3:3 As in parallel text at 1 Chr 3:1 (see also Greek version, which reads *Daluia,* and possible support by Dead Sea Scrolls); Hebrew reads *Kileab.* 3:7 *Ishbosheth* is another name for Esh-baal.

to be kicked around like this?" he shouted. "After all I have done for your father, Saul, and his family and friends by not handing you over to David, is this my reward—that you find fault with me about this woman? ⁹May God strike me and even kill me if I don't do everything I can to help David get what the LORD has promised him! ¹⁰I'm going to take Saul's kingdom and give it to David. I will establish the throne of David over Israel as well as Judah, all the way from Dan in the north to Beersheba in the south." ¹¹Ishbosheth didn't dare say another word because he was afraid of what Abner might do.

¹²Then Abner sent messengers to David, saying, "Doesn't the entire land belong to you? Make a solemn pact with me, and I will help turn over all of Israel to you."

¹³"All right," David replied, "but I will not negotiate with you unless you bring back my wife Michal, Saul's daughter, when you come."

¹⁴David then sent this message to Ishbosheth, Saul's son: "Give me back my wife Michal, for I bought her with the lives* of 100 Philistines."

¹⁵So Ishbosheth took Michal away from her husband, Palti* son of Laish. ¹⁶Palti followed along behind her as far as Bahurim, weeping as he went. Then Abner told him, "Go back home!" So Palti returned.

¹⁷Meanwhile, Abner had consulted with the elders of Israel. "For some time now," he told them, "you have wanted to make David your king. ¹⁸Now is the time! For the LORD has said, 'I have chosen David to save my people Israel from the hands of the Philistines and from all their other enemies.'" ¹⁹Abner also spoke with the men of Benjamin. Then he went to Hebron to tell David that all the people of Israel and Benjamin had agreed to support him.

²⁰When Abner and twenty of his men came to Hebron, David entertained them with a great feast. ²¹Then Abner said to David, "Let me go and call an assembly of all Israel to support my lord the king. They will make a covenant with you to make you their king, and you will rule over everything your heart desires." So David sent Abner safely on his way.

Joab Murders Abner

²²But just after David had sent Abner away in safety, Joab and some of David's troops returned from a raid, bringing much plunder with them. ²³When Joab arrived, he was told that Abner had just been there visiting the king and had been sent away in safety.

²⁴Joab rushed to the king and demanded, "What have you done? What do you mean by letting Abner get away? ²⁵You know perfectly well that he came to spy on you and find out everything you're doing!"

²⁶Joab then left David and sent messengers to catch up with Abner, asking him to return. They found him at the well of Sirah and brought him back, though David knew nothing about it. ²⁷When Abner arrived back at Hebron, Joab took him aside at the gateway as if to speak with him privately. But then he stabbed Abner in the stomach and killed him in revenge for killing his brother Asahel.

²⁸When David heard about it, he declared, "I vow by the LORD that I and my kingdom are forever innocent of this crime against Abner son of Ner. ²⁹Joab and his family are the guilty ones. May the family of Joab be cursed in every generation with a man who has open sores or leprosy* or who walks on crutches* or dies by the sword or begs for food!"

³⁰So Joab and his brother Abishai killed Abner because Abner had killed their brother Asahel at the battle of Gibeon.

David Mourns Abner's Death

³¹Then David said to Joab and all those who were with him, "Tear your clothes and put on burlap. Mourn for Abner." And King David himself walked behind the procession to the grave. ³²They buried Abner in Hebron, and the king and all the people wept at his graveside. ³³Then the king sang this funeral song for Abner:

"Should Abner have died as fools die?
³⁴ Your hands were not bound;
    your feet were not chained.
No, you were murdered—
    the victim of a wicked plot."

All the people wept again for Abner. ³⁵David had refused to eat anything on the day of the funeral, and now everyone begged him to eat. But David had made a vow, saying, "May God strike me and even kill me if I eat anything before sundown."

³⁶This pleased the people very much. In fact, everything the king did pleased them! ³⁷So

---

3:14 Hebrew *the foreskins.*   3:15 As in 1 Sam 25:44; Hebrew reads *Paltiel,* a variant spelling of Palti.   3:29a Or *or a contagious skin disease.* The Hebrew word used here can describe various skin diseases.   3:29b Or *who is effeminate;* Hebrew reads *who handles a spindle.*

everyone in Judah and all Israel understood that David was not responsible for Abner's murder.

38Then King David said to his officials, "Don't you realize that a great commander has fallen today in Israel? 39And even though I am the anointed king, these two sons of Zeruiah—Joab and Abishai—are too strong for me to control. So may the LORD repay these evil men for their evil deeds."

The Murder of Ishbosheth

4 When Ishbosheth,* Saul's son, heard about Abner's death at Hebron, he lost all courage, and all Israel became paralyzed with fear. 2Now there were two brothers, Baanah and Recab, who were captains of Ishbosheth's raiding parties. They were sons of Rimmon, a member of the tribe of Benjamin who lived in Beeroth. The town of Beeroth is now part of Benjamin's territory 3because the original people of Beeroth fled to Gittaim, where they still live as foreigners.

4(Saul's son Jonathan had a son named Mephibosheth,* who was crippled as a child. He was five years old when the report came from Jezreel that Saul and Jonathan had been killed in battle. When the child's nurse heard the news, she picked him up and fled. But as she hurried away, she dropped him, and he became crippled.)

5One day Recab and Baanah, the sons of Rimmon from Beeroth, went to Ishbosheth's house around noon as he was taking his midday rest. 6The doorkeeper, who had been sifting wheat, became drowsy and fell asleep. So Recab and Baanah slipped past her.* 7They went into the house and found Ishbosheth sleeping on his bed. They struck and killed him and cut off his head. Then, taking his head with them, they fled across the Jordan Valley* through the night. 8When they arrived at Hebron, they presented Ishbosheth's head to David. "Look!" they exclaimed to the king. "Here is the head of Ishbosheth, the son of your enemy Saul who tried to kill you. Today the LORD has given my lord the king revenge on Saul and his entire family!"

9But David said to Recab and Baanah, "The LORD, who saves me from all my enemies, is my witness. 10Someone once told me, 'Saul is dead,' thinking he was bringing me good news. But I

seized him and killed him at Ziklag. That's the reward I gave him for his news! 11How much more should I reward evil men who have killed an innocent man in his own house and on his own bed? Shouldn't I hold you responsible for his blood and rid the earth of you?"

12So David ordered his young men to kill them, and they did. They cut off their hands and feet and hung their bodies beside the pool in Hebron. Then they took Ishbosheth's head and buried it in Abner's tomb in Hebron.

David Becomes King of All Israel

5 Then all the tribes of Israel went to David at Hebron and told him, "We are your own flesh and blood. 2In the past,* when Saul was our king, you were the one who really led the forces of Israel. And the LORD told you, 'You will be the shepherd of my people Israel. You will be Israel's leader.'"

3So there at Hebron, King David made a covenant before the LORD with all the elders of Israel. And they anointed him king of Israel.

4David was thirty years old when he began to reign, and he reigned forty years in all. 5He had reigned over Judah from Hebron for seven years and six months, and from Jerusalem he reigned over all Israel and Judah for thirty-three years.

David Captures Jerusalem

6David then led his men to Jerusalem to fight against the Jebusites, the original inhabitants of the land who were living there. The Jebusites taunted David, saying, "You'll never get in here! Even the blind and lame could keep you out!" For the Jebusites thought they were safe. 7But David captured the fortress of Zion, which is now called the City of David.

8On the day of the attack, David said to his troops, "I hate those 'lame' and 'blind' Jebusites.* Whoever attacks them should strike by going into the city through the water tunnel.*" That is the origin of the saying, "The blind and the lame may not enter the house."*

9So David made the fortress his home, and he called it the City of David. He extended the city, starting at the supporting terraces* and working inward. 10And David became more and more powerful, because the LORD God of Heaven's Armies was with him.

11Then King Hiram of Tyre sent messengers

4:1 Ishbosheth is another name for Esh-baal.   4:4 Mephibosheth is another name for Merib-baal.   4:6 As in Greek version; Hebrew reads So they went into the house pretending to fetch wheat, but they stabbed him in the stomach. Then Recab and Baanah escaped.   4:7 Hebrew the Arabah.   5:2 Or For some time.   5:8a Or Those 'lame' and 'blind' Jebusites hate me.   5:8b Or with scaling hooks. The meaning of the Hebrew is uncertain.   5:8c The meaning of this saying is uncertain.   5:9 Hebrew the millo. The meaning of the Hebrew is uncertain.

to David, along with cedar timber and carpenters and stonemasons, and they built David a palace. [12]And David realized that the LORD had confirmed him as king over Israel and had blessed his kingdom for the sake of his people Israel.

[13]After moving from Hebron to Jerusalem, David married more concubines and wives, and they had more sons and daughters. [14]These are the names of David's sons who were born in Jerusalem: Shammua, Shobab, Nathan, Solomon, [15]Ibhar, Elishua, Nepheg, Japhia, [16]Elishama, Eliada, and Eliphelet.

David Conquers the Philistines

[17]When the Philistines heard that David had been anointed king of Israel, they mobilized all their forces to capture him. But David was told they were coming, so he went into the stronghold. [18]The Philistines arrived and spread out across the valley of Rephaim. [19]So David asked the LORD, "Should I go out to fight the Philistines? Will you hand them over to me?"

The LORD replied to David, "Yes, go ahead. I will certainly hand them over to you."

[20]So David went to Baal-perazim and defeated the Philistines there. "The LORD did it!" David exclaimed. "He burst through my enemies like a raging flood!" So he named that place Baal-perazim (which means "the Lord who bursts through"). [21]The Philistines had abandoned their idols there, so David and his men confiscated them.

[22]But after a while the Philistines returned and again spread out across the valley of Rephaim. [23]And again David asked the LORD what to do. "Do not attack them straight on," the LORD replied. "Instead, circle around behind and attack them near the poplar* trees. [24]When you hear a sound like marching feet in the tops of the poplar trees, be on the alert! That will be the signal that the LORD is moving ahead of you to strike down the Philistine army." [25]So David did what the LORD commanded, and he struck down the Philistines all the way from Gibeon* to Gezer.

Moving the Ark to Jerusalem

6 Then David again gathered all the elite troops in Israel, 30,000 in all. [2]He led them to Baalah of Judah* to bring back the Ark of God,

which bears the name of the LORD of Heaven's Armies,* who is enthroned between the cherubim. [3]They placed the Ark of God on a new cart and brought it from Abinadab's house, which was on a hill. Uzzah and Ahio, Abinadab's sons, were guiding the cart [4]that carried the Ark of God.* Ahio walked in front of the Ark. [5]David and all the people of Israel were celebrating before the LORD, singing songs* and playing all kinds of musical instruments—lyres, harps, tambourines, castanets, and cymbals.

[6]But when they arrived at the threshing floor of Nacon, the oxen stumbled, and Uzzah reached out his hand and steadied the Ark of God. [7]Then the LORD's anger was aroused against Uzzah, and God struck him dead because of this.* So Uzzah died right there beside the Ark of God.

[8]David was angry because the LORD's anger had burst out against Uzzah. He named that place Perez-uzzah (which means "to burst out against Uzzah"), as it is still called today.

[9]David was now afraid of the LORD, and he asked, "How can I ever bring the Ark of the LORD back into my care?" [10]So David decided not to move the Ark of the LORD into the City of David. Instead, he took it to the house of Obed-edom of Gath. [11]The Ark of the LORD remained there in Obed-edom's house for three months, and the LORD blessed Obed-edom and his entire household.

[12]Then King David was told, "The LORD has blessed Obed-edom's household and everything he has because of the Ark of God." So David went there and brought the Ark of God from the house of Obed-edom to the City of David with a great celebration. [13]After the men who were carrying the Ark of the LORD had gone six steps, David sacrificed a bull and a fattened calf. [14]And David danced before the LORD with all his might, wearing a priestly garment.* [15]So David and all the people of Israel brought up the Ark of the LORD with shouts of joy and the blowing of rams' horns.

Michal's Contempt for David

[16]But as the Ark of the LORD entered the City of David, Michal, the daughter of Saul, looked down from her window. When she saw King David leaping and dancing before the LORD, she was filled with contempt for him.

5:23 Or aspen, or balsam; also in 5:24. The exact identification of this tree is uncertain.   5:25 As in Greek version (see also 1 Chr 14:16); Hebrew reads Geba.   6:2a Hebrew Baale of Judah, another name for Kiriath-jearim; compare 1 Chr 13:6. 6:2b Or the Ark of God where the Name is proclaimed—the name of the LORD of Heaven's Armies.   6:4 As in Dead Sea Scrolls and some Greek manuscripts; Masoretic Text reads [4]and they brought it from Abinadab's house, which was on a hill, with the Ark of God.   6:5 As in Dead Sea Scrolls and Greek version (see also 1 Chr 13:8); Masoretic Text reads before the LORD with all manner of cypress wood.   6:7 As in Dead Sea Scrolls; Masoretic Text reads because of his irreverence.   6:14 Hebrew a linen ephod.

¹⁷They brought the Ark of the LORD and set it in its place inside the special tent David had prepared for it. And David sacrificed burnt offerings and peace offerings to the LORD. ¹⁸When he had finished his sacrifices, David blessed the people in the name of the LORD of Heaven's Armies. ¹⁹Then he gave to every Israelite man and woman in the crowd a loaf of bread, a cake of dates,* and a cake of raisins. Then all the people returned to their homes.

²⁰When David returned home to bless his own family, Michal, the daughter of Saul, came out to meet him. She said in disgust, "How distinguished the king of Israel looked today, shamelessly exposing himself to the servant girls like any vulgar person might do!"

²¹David retorted to Michal, "I was dancing before the LORD, who chose me above your father and all his family! He appointed me as the leader of Israel, the people of the LORD, so I celebrate before the LORD. ²²Yes, and I am willing to look even more foolish than this, even to be humiliated in my own eyes! But those servant girls you mentioned will indeed think I am distinguished!" ²³So Michal, the daughter of Saul, remained childless throughout her entire life.

The LORD's Covenant Promise to David

7 When King David was settled in his palace and the LORD had given him rest from all the surrounding enemies, ²the king summoned Nathan the prophet. "Look," David said, "I am living in a beautiful cedar palace,* but the Ark of God is out there in a tent!"

³Nathan replied to the king, "Go ahead and do whatever you have in mind, for the LORD is with you."

⁴But that same night the LORD said to Nathan,

⁵"Go and tell my servant David, 'This is what the LORD has declared: Are you the one to build a house for me to live in? ⁶I have never lived in a house, from the day I brought the Israelites out of Egypt until this very day. I have always moved from one place to another with a tent and a Tabernacle as my dwelling. ⁷Yet no matter where I have gone with the Israelites, I have never once complained to Israel's tribal leaders, the shepherds of my people Israel. I have never asked them, "Why haven't you built me a beautiful cedar house?"'

⁸"Now go and say to my servant David,

'This is what the LORD of Heaven's Armies has declared: I took you from tending sheep in the pasture and selected you to be the leader of my people Israel. ⁹I have been with you wherever you have gone, and I have destroyed all your enemies before your eyes. Now I will make your name as famous as anyone who has ever lived on the earth! ¹⁰And I will provide a homeland for my people Israel, planting them in a secure place where they will never be disturbed. Evil nations won't oppress them as they've done in the past, ¹¹starting from the time I appointed judges to rule my people Israel. And I will give you rest from all your enemies.

"'Furthermore, the LORD declares that he will make a house for you—a dynasty of kings! ¹²For when you die and are buried with your ancestors, I will raise up one of your descendants, your own offspring, and I will make his kingdom strong. ¹³He is the one who will build a house—a temple—for my name. And I will secure his royal throne forever. ¹⁴I will be his father, and he will be my son. If he sins, I will correct and discipline him with the rod, like any father would do. ¹⁵But my favor will not be taken from him as I took it from Saul, whom I removed from your sight. ¹⁶Your house and your kingdom will continue before me* for all time, and your throne will be secure forever.'"

¹⁷So Nathan went back to David and told him everything the LORD had said in this vision.

David's Prayer of Thanks

¹⁸Then King David went in and sat before the LORD and prayed,

"Who am I, O Sovereign LORD, and what is my family, that you have brought me this far? ¹⁹And now, Sovereign LORD, in addition to everything else, you speak of giving your servant a lasting dynasty! Do you deal with everyone this way, O Sovereign LORD?*

²⁰"What more can I say to you? You know what your servant is really like, Sovereign LORD. ²¹Because of your promise and according to your will, you have done all these great things and have made them known to your servant.

[22]"How great you are, O Sovereign LORD! There is no one like you. We have never even heard of another God like you! [23]What other nation on earth is like your people Israel? What other nation, O God, have you redeemed from slavery to be your own people? You made a great name for yourself when you redeemed your people from Egypt. You performed awesome miracles and drove out the nations and gods that stood in their way.* [24]You made Israel your very own people forever, and you, O LORD, became their God.

[25]"And now, O LORD God, I am your servant; do as you have promised concerning me and my family. Confirm it as a promise that will last forever. [26]And may your name be honored forever so that everyone will say, 'The LORD of Heaven's Armies is God over Israel!' And may the house of your servant David continue before you forever.

[27]"O LORD of Heaven's Armies, God of Israel, I have been bold enough to pray this prayer to you because you have revealed all this to your servant, saying, 'I will build a house for you—a dynasty of kings!' [28]For you are God, O Sovereign LORD. Your words are truth, and you have promised these good things to your servant. [29]And now, may it please you to bless the house of your servant, so that it may continue forever before you. For you have spoken, and when you grant a blessing to your servant, O Sovereign LORD, it is an eternal blessing!"

David's Military Victories

8 After this, David defeated and subdued the Philistines by conquering Gath, their largest town.* [2]David also conquered the land of Moab. He made the people lie down on the ground in a row, and he measured them off in groups with a length of rope. He measured off two groups to be executed for every one group to be spared. The Moabites who were spared became David's subjects and paid him tribute money.

[3]David also destroyed the forces of Hadadezer son of Rehob, king of Zobah, when Hadadezer marched out to strengthen his control along the Euphrates River. [4]David captured 1,000 chariots, 7,000 charioteers,* and 20,000 foot soldiers. He crippled all the chariot horses except enough for 100 chariots.

[5]When Arameans from Damascus arrived to help King Hadadezer, David killed 22,000 of them. [6]Then he placed several army garrisons in Damascus, the Aramean capital, and the Arameans became David's subjects and paid him tribute money. So the LORD made David victorious wherever he went.

[7]David brought the gold shields of Hadadezer's officers to Jerusalem, [8]along with a large amount of bronze from Hadadezer's towns of Tebah* and Berothai.

[9]When King Toi of Hamath heard that David had destroyed the entire army of Hadadezer, [10]he sent his son Joram to congratulate King David for his successful campaign. Hadadezer and Toi had been enemies and were often at war. Joram presented David with many gifts of silver, gold, and bronze.

[11]King David dedicated all these gifts to the LORD, as he did with the silver and gold from the other nations he had defeated—[12]from Edom,* Moab, Ammon, Philistia, and Amalek—and from Hadadezer son of Rehob, king of Zobah.

[13]So David became even more famous when he returned from destroying 18,000 Edomites* in the Valley of Salt. [14]He placed army garrisons throughout Edom, and all the Edomites became David's subjects. In fact, the LORD made David victorious wherever he went.

[15]So David reigned over all Israel and did what was just and right for all his people. [16]Joab son of Zeruiah was commander of the army. Jehoshaphat son of Ahilud was the royal historian. [17]Zadok son of Ahitub and Ahimelech son of Abiathar were the priests. Seraiah was the court secretary. [18]Benaiah son of Jehoiada was captain of the king's bodyguard.* And David's sons served as priestly leaders.*

David's Kindness to Mephibosheth

9 One day David asked, "Is anyone in Saul's family still alive—anyone to whom I can show kindness for Jonathan's sake?" [2]He summoned a man named Ziba, who had been one

---

7:23 As in Greek version (see also 1 Chr 17:21); Hebrew reads *You made a name for yourself and awesome miracles for your land in the sight of your people, whom you redeemed from Egypt, the nations and their gods.* 8:1 Hebrew *by conquering Metheg-ammah,* a name that means "the bridle," possibly referring to the size of the town or the tribute money taken from it. Compare 1 Chr 18:1. 8:4 As in Dead Sea Scrolls and Greek version (see also 1 Chr 18:4); Masoretic Text reads *captured 1,700 charioteers.* 8:8 As in some Greek manuscripts (see also 1 Chr 18:8); Hebrew reads *Betah.* 8:12 As in a few Hebrew manuscripts and Greek and Syriac versions (see also 8:14; 1 Chr 18:11); most Hebrew manuscripts read *Aram.* 8:13 As in a few Hebrew manuscripts and Greek and Syriac versions (see also 8:14; 1 Chr 18:12); most Hebrew manuscripts read *Arameans.* 8:18a Hebrew *of the Kerethites and Pelethites.* 8:18b Hebrew *David's sons were priests;* compare parallel text at 1 Chr 18:17.

of Saul's servants. "Are you Ziba?" the king asked.

"Yes sir, I am," Ziba replied.

³The king then asked him, "Is anyone still alive from Saul's family? If so, I want to show God's kindness to them."

Ziba replied, "Yes, one of Jonathan's sons is still alive. He is crippled in both feet."

⁴"Where is he?" the king asked.

"In Lo-debar," Ziba told him, "at the home of Makir son of Ammiel."

⁵So David sent for him and brought him from Makir's home. ⁶His name was Mephibosheth*; he was Jonathan's son and Saul's grandson. When he came to David, he bowed low to the ground in deep respect. David said, "Greetings, Mephibosheth."

Mephibosheth replied, "I am your servant."

⁷"Don't be afraid!" David said. "I intend to show kindness to you because of my promise to your father, Jonathan. I will give you all the property that once belonged to your grandfather Saul, and you will eat here with me at the king's table!"

⁸Mephibosheth bowed respectfully and exclaimed, "Who is your servant, that you should show such kindness to a dead dog like me?"

⁹Then the king summoned Saul's servant Ziba and said, "I have given your master's grandson everything that belonged to Saul and his family. ¹⁰You and your sons and servants are to farm the land for him to produce food for your master's household.* But Mephibosheth, your master's grandson, will eat here at my table." (Ziba had fifteen sons and twenty servants.)

¹¹Ziba replied, "Yes, my lord the king; I am your servant, and I will do all that you have commanded." And from that time on, Mephibosheth ate regularly at David's table,* like one of the king's own sons.

¹²Mephibosheth had a young son named Mica. From then on, all the members of Ziba's household were Mephibosheth's servants. ¹³And Mephibosheth, who was crippled in both feet, lived in Jerusalem and ate regularly at the king's table.

David Defeats the Ammonites

10 Some time after this, King Nahash* of the Ammonites died, and his son Hanun became king. ²David said, "I am going to show loyalty to Hanun just as his father, Nahash, was always loyal to me." So David sent ambassadors to express sympathy to Hanun about his father's death.

But when David's ambassadors arrived in the land of Ammon, ³the Ammonite commanders said to Hanun, their master, "Do you really think these men are coming here to honor your father? No! David has sent them to spy out the city so they can come in and conquer it!" ⁴So Hanun seized David's ambassadors and shaved off half of each man's beard, cut off their robes at the buttocks, and sent them back to David in shame.

⁵When David heard what had happened, he sent messengers to tell the men, "Stay at Jericho until your beards grow out, and then come back." For they felt deep shame because of their appearance.

⁶When the people of Ammon realized how seriously they had angered David, they sent and hired 20,000 Aramean foot soldiers from the lands of Beth-rehob and Zobah, 1,000 from the king of Maacah, and 12,000 from the land of Tob. ⁷When David heard about this, he sent Joab and all his warriors to fight them. ⁸The Ammonite troops came out and drew up their battle lines at the entrance of the city gate, while the Arameans from Zobah and Rehob and the men from Tob and Maacah positioned themselves to fight in the open fields.

⁹When Joab saw that he would have to fight on both the front and the rear, he chose some of Israel's elite troops and placed them under his personal command to fight the Arameans in the fields. ¹⁰He left the rest of the army under the command of his brother Abishai, who was to attack the Ammonites. ¹¹"If the Arameans are too strong for me, then come over and help me," Joab told his brother. "And if the Ammonites are too strong for you, I will come and help you. ¹²Be courageous! Let us fight bravely for our people and the cities of our God. May the LORD's will be done."

¹³When Joab and his troops attacked, the Arameans began to run away. ¹⁴And when the Ammonites saw the Arameans running, they ran from Abishai and retreated into the city. After the battle was over, Joab returned to Jerusalem.

¹⁵The Arameans now realized that they were no match for Israel. So when they regrouped, ¹⁶they were joined by additional Aramean troops summoned by Hadadezer from the other side of the Euphrates River.* These troops arrived at Helam under the command

---

9:6 *Mephibosheth* is another name for Merib-baal.   9:10 As in Greek version; Hebrew reads *your master's grandson.*   9:11 As in Greek version; Hebrew reads *my table.*   10:1 As in parallel text at 1 Chr 19:1; Hebrew reads *the king.*   10:16 Hebrew *the river.*

of Shobach, the commander of Hadadezer's forces.

[17]When David heard what was happening, he mobilized all Israel, crossed the Jordan River, and led the army to Helam. The Arameans positioned themselves in battle formation and fought against David. [18]But again the Arameans fled from the Israelites. This time David's forces killed 700 charioteers and 40,000 foot soldiers,* including Shobach, the commander of their army. [19]When all the kings allied with Hadadezer saw that they had been defeated by Israel, they surrendered to Israel and became their subjects. After that, the Arameans were afraid to help the Ammonites.

David and Bathsheba

11 In the spring of the year,* when kings normally go out to war, David sent Joab and the Israelite army to fight the Ammonites. They destroyed the Ammonite army and laid siege to the city of Rabbah. However, David stayed behind in Jerusalem.

[2]Late one afternoon, after his midday rest, David got out of bed and was walking on the roof of the palace. As he looked out over the city, he noticed a woman of unusual beauty taking a bath. [3]He sent someone to find out who she was, and he was told, "She is Bathsheba, the daughter of Eliam and the wife of Uriah the Hittite." [4]Then David sent messengers to get her; and when she came to the palace, he slept with her. She had just completed the purification rites after having her menstrual period. Then she returned home. [5]Later, when Bathsheba discovered that she was pregnant, she sent David a message, saying, "I'm pregnant."

[6]Then David sent word to Joab: "Send me Uriah the Hittite." So Joab sent him to David. [7]When Uriah arrived, David asked him how Joab and the army were getting along and how the war was progressing. [8]Then he told Uriah, "Go on home and relax.*" David even sent a gift to Uriah after he had left the palace. [9]But Uriah didn't go home. He slept that night at the palace entrance with the king's palace guard.

[10]When David heard that Uriah had not gone home, he summoned him and asked, "What's the matter? Why didn't you go home last night after being away for so long?"

[11]Uriah replied, "The Ark and the armies of Israel and Judah are living in tents,* and Joab and my master's men are camping in the open fields. How could I go home to wine and dine and sleep with my wife? I swear that I would never do such a thing."

[12]"Well, stay here today," David told him, "and tomorrow you may return to the army." So Uriah stayed in Jerusalem that day and the next. [13]Then David invited him to dinner and got him drunk. But even then he couldn't get Uriah to go home to his wife. Again he slept at the palace entrance with the king's palace guard.

David Arranges for Uriah's Death

[14]So the next morning David wrote a letter to Joab and gave it to Uriah to deliver. [15]The letter instructed Joab, "Station Uriah on the front lines where the battle is fiercest. Then pull back so that he will be killed." [16]So Joab assigned Uriah to a spot close to the city wall where he knew the enemy's strongest men were fighting. [17]And when the enemy soldiers came out of the city to fight, Uriah the Hittite was killed along with several other Israelite soldiers.

[18]Then Joab sent a battle report to David. [19]He told his messenger, "Report all the news of the battle to the king. [20]But he might get angry and ask, 'Why did the troops go so close to the city? Didn't they know there would be shooting from the walls? [21]Wasn't Abimelech son of Gideon* killed at Thebez by a woman who threw a millstone down on him from the wall? Why would you get so close to the wall?' Then tell him, 'Uriah the Hittite was killed, too.'"

[22]So the messenger went to Jerusalem and gave a complete report to David. [23]"The enemy came out against us in the open fields," he said. "And as we chased them back to the city gate, [24]the archers on the wall shot arrows at us. Some of the king's men were killed, including Uriah the Hittite."

[25]"Well, tell Joab not to be discouraged," David said. "The sword devours this one today and that one tomorrow! Fight harder next time, and conquer the city!"

[26]When Uriah's wife heard that her husband was dead, she mourned for him. [27]When the period of mourning was over, David sent for her and brought her to the palace, and she became one of his wives. Then she gave birth to a son. But the LORD was displeased with what David had done.

10:18 As in some Greek manuscripts (see also 1 Chr 19:18); Hebrew reads *charioteers*. 11:1 Hebrew *At the turn of the year*. The first day of the year in the ancient Hebrew lunar calendar occurred in March or April. 11:8 Hebrew *and wash your feet*, an expression that may also have a connotation of ritualistic washing. 11:11 Or *at Succoth*. 11:21 Hebrew *son of Jerub-besheth*. Jerub-besheth is a variation on the name Jerub-baal, which is another name for Gideon; see Judg 6:32.

Nathan Rebukes David

12 So the LORD sent Nathan the prophet to tell David this story: "There were two men in a certain town. One was rich, and one was poor. ²The rich man owned a great many sheep and cattle. ³The poor man owned nothing but one little lamb he had bought. He raised that little lamb, and it grew up with his children. It ate from the man's own plate and drank from his cup. He cuddled it in his arms like a baby daughter. ⁴One day a guest arrived at the home of the rich man. But instead of killing an animal from his own flock or herd, he took the poor man's lamb and killed it and prepared it for his guest."

⁵David was furious. "As surely as the LORD lives," he vowed, "any man who would do such a thing deserves to die! ⁶He must repay four lambs to the poor man for the one he stole and for having no pity."

⁷Then Nathan said to David, "You are that man! The LORD, the God of Israel, says: I anointed you king of Israel and saved you from the power of Saul. ⁸I gave you your master's house and his wives and the kingdoms of Israel and Judah. And if that had not been enough, I would have given you much, much more. ⁹Why, then, have you despised the word of the LORD and done this horrible deed? For you have murdered Uriah the Hittite with the sword of the Ammonites and stolen his wife. ¹⁰From this time on, your family will live by the sword because you have despised me by taking Uriah's wife to be your own.

¹¹"This is what the LORD says: Because of what you have done, I will cause your own household to rebel against you. I will give your wives to another man before your very eyes, and he will go to bed with them in public view. ¹²You did it secretly, but I will make this happen to you openly in the sight of all Israel."

David Confesses His Guilt

¹³Then David confessed to Nathan, "I have sinned against the LORD."

Nathan replied, "Yes, but the LORD has forgiven you, and you won't die for this sin. ¹⁴Nevertheless, because you have shown utter contempt for the word of the LORD* by doing this, your child will die."

¹⁵After Nathan returned to his home, the LORD sent a deadly illness to the child of David

and Uriah's wife. ¹⁶David begged God to spare the child. He went without food and lay all night on the bare ground. ¹⁷The elders of his household pleaded with him to get up and eat with them, but he refused.

¹⁸Then on the seventh day the child died. David's advisers were afraid to tell him. "He wouldn't listen to reason while the child was ill," they said. "What drastic thing will he do when we tell him the child is dead?"

¹⁹When David saw them whispering, he realized what had happened. "Is the child dead?" he asked.

"Yes," they replied, "he is dead."

²⁰Then David got up from the ground, washed himself, put on lotions,* and changed his clothes. He went to the Tabernacle and worshiped the LORD. After that, he returned to the palace and was served food and ate.

²¹His advisers were amazed. "We don't understand you," they told him. "While the child was still living, you wept and refused to eat. But now that the child is dead, you have stopped your mourning and are eating again."

²²David replied, "I fasted and wept while the child was alive, for I said, 'Perhaps the LORD will be gracious to me and let the child live.' ²³But why should I fast when he is dead? Can I bring him back again? I will go to him one day, but he cannot return to me."

²⁴Then David comforted Bathsheba, his wife, and slept with her. She became pregnant and gave birth to a son, and David* named him Solomon. The LORD loved the child ²⁵and sent word through Nathan the prophet that they should name him Jedidiah (which means "beloved of the LORD"), as the LORD had commanded.*

David Captures Rabbah

²⁶Meanwhile, Joab was fighting against Rabbah, the capital of Ammon, and he captured the royal fortifications.* ²⁷Joab sent messengers to tell David, "I have fought against Rabbah and captured its water supply.* ²⁸Now bring the rest of the army and capture the city. Otherwise, I will capture it and get credit for the victory."

²⁹So David gathered the rest of the army and went to Rabbah, and he fought against it and captured it. ³⁰David removed the crown from the king's head,* and it was placed on his own head. The crown was made of gold and set with

---

12:14 As in Dead Sea Scrolls; Masoretic Text reads *the enemies of the LORD.*   12:20 Hebrew *anointed himself.*   12:24 Hebrew *he;* an alternate Hebrew reading and some Hebrew manuscripts read *she.*   12:25 As in Greek version; Hebrew reads *because of the LORD.*   12:26 Or *the royal city.*   12:27 Or *captured the city of water.*   12:30a Or *from the head of Milcom* (as in Greek version). Milcom, also called Molech, was the god of the Ammonites.

gems, and it weighed seventy-five pounds.* David took a vast amount of plunder from the city. 31He also made slaves of the people of Rabbah and forced them to labor with* saws, iron picks, and iron axes, and to work in the brick kilns.* That is how he dealt with the people of all the Ammonite towns. Then David and all the army returned to Jerusalem.

The Rape of Tamar

13 Now David's son Absalom had a beautiful sister named Tamar. And Amnon, her half brother, fell desperately in love with her. 2Amnon became so obsessed with Tamar that he became ill. She was a virgin, and Amnon thought he could never have her.

3But Amnon had a very crafty friend—his cousin Jonadab. He was the son of David's brother Shimea.* 4One day Jonadab said to Amnon, "What's the trouble? Why should the son of a king look so dejected morning after morning?"

So Amnon told him, "I am in love with Tamar, my brother Absalom's sister."

5"Well," Jonadab said, "I'll tell you what to do. Go back to bed and pretend you are ill. When your father comes to see you, ask him to let Tamar come and prepare some food for you. Tell him you'll feel better if she prepares it as you watch and feeds you with her own hands."

6So Amnon lay down and pretended to be sick. And when the king came to see him, Amnon asked him, "Please let my sister Tamar come and cook my favorite dish* as I watch. Then I can eat it from her own hands." 7So David agreed and sent Tamar to Amnon's house to prepare some food for him.

8When Tamar arrived at Amnon's house, she went to the place where he was lying down so he could watch her mix some dough. Then she baked his favorite dish for him. 9But when she set the serving tray before him, he refused to eat. "Everyone get out of here," Amnon told his servants. So they all left.

10Then he said to Tamar, "Now bring the food into my bedroom and feed it to me here." So Tamar took his favorite dish to him. 11But as she was feeding him, he grabbed her and demanded, "Come to bed with me, my darling sister."

12"No, my brother!" she cried. "Don't be foolish! Don't do this to me! Such wicked things aren't done in Israel. 13Where could I go in my shame? And you would be called one of the greatest fools in Israel. Please, just speak to the king about it, and he will let you marry me."

14But Amnon wouldn't listen to her, and since he was stronger than she was, he raped her. 15Then suddenly Amnon's love turned to hate, and he hated her even more than he had loved her. "Get out of here!" he snarled at her.

16"No, no!" Tamar cried. "Sending me away now is worse than what you've already done to me."

But Amnon wouldn't listen to her. 17He shouted for his servant and demanded, "Throw this woman out, and lock the door behind her!"

18So the servant put her out and locked the door behind her. She was wearing a long, beautiful robe,* as was the custom in those days for the king's virgin daughters. 19But now Tamar tore her robe and put ashes on her head. And then, with her face in her hands, she went away crying.

20Her brother Absalom saw her and asked, "Is it true that Amnon has been with you? Well, my sister, keep quiet for now, since he's your brother. Don't you worry about it." So Tamar lived as a desolate woman in her brother Absalom's house.

21When King David heard what had happened, he was very angry.* 22And though Absalom never spoke to Amnon about this, he hated Amnon deeply because of what he had done to his sister.

Absalom's Revenge on Amnon

23Two years later, when Absalom's sheep were being sheared at Baal-hazor near Ephraim, Absalom invited all the king's sons to come to a feast. 24He went to the king and said, "My sheep-shearers are now at work. Would the king and his servants please come to celebrate the occasion with me?"

25The king replied, "No, my son. If we all came, we would be too much of a burden on you." Absalom pressed him, but the king would not come, though he gave Absalom his blessing.

26"Well, then," Absalom said, "if you can't come, how about sending my brother Amnon with us?"

"Why Amnon?" the king asked. 27But Absalom kept on pressing the king until he finally

12:30b Hebrew 1 talent [34 kilograms].   12:31a Hebrew He also brought out the people [of Rabbah] and put them under.
12:31b Hebrew and he made them pass through the brick kilns.   13:3 Hebrew Shimeah (also in 13:32), a variant spelling of Shimea;
compare 1 Chr 2:13.   13:6 Or a couple of cakes; also in 13:8, 10.   13:18 Or a robe with sleeves, or an ornamented robe. The meaning
of the Hebrew is uncertain.   13:21 Dead Sea Scrolls and Greek version add But he did not punish his son Amnon, because he loved
him, for he was his firstborn.

agreed to let all his sons attend, including Amnon. So Absalom prepared a feast fit for a king.* ²⁸Absalom told his men, "Wait until Amnon gets drunk; then at my signal, kill him! Don't be afraid. I'm the one who has given the command. Take courage and do it!" ²⁹So at Absalom's signal they murdered Amnon. Then the other sons of the king jumped on their mules and fled.

³⁰As they were on the way back to Jerusalem, this report reached David: "Absalom has killed all the king's sons; not one is left alive!" ³¹The king got up, tore his robe, and threw himself on the ground. His advisers also tore their clothes in horror and sorrow.

³²But just then Jonadab, the son of David's brother Shimea, arrived and said, "No, don't believe that all the king's sons have been killed! It was only Amnon! Absalom has been plotting this ever since Amnon raped his sister Tamar. ³³No, my lord the king, your sons aren't all dead! It was only Amnon." ³⁴Meanwhile Absalom escaped.

Then the watchman on the Jerusalem wall saw a great crowd coming down the hill on the road from the west. He ran to tell the king, "I see a crowd of people coming from the Horonaim road along the side of the hill."*

³⁵"Look!" Jonadab told the king. "There they are now! The king's sons are coming, just as I said."

³⁶They soon arrived, weeping and sobbing, and the king and all his servants wept bitterly with them. ³⁷And David mourned many days for his son Amnon.

Absalom fled to his grandfather, Talmai son of Ammihud, the king of Geshur. ³⁸He stayed there in Geshur for three years. ³⁹And King David,* now reconciled to Amnon's death, longed to be reunited with his son Absalom.*

Joab Arranges for Absalom's Return

14 Joab realized how much the king longed to see Absalom. ²So he sent for a woman from Tekoa who had a reputation for great wisdom. He said to her, "Pretend you are in mourning; wear mourning clothes and don't put on lotions.* Act like a woman who has been mourning for the dead for a long time. ³Then go to the king and tell him the story I am about to tell you." Then Joab told her what to say.

⁴When the woman from Tekoa approached*

the king, she bowed with her face to the ground in deep respect and cried out, "O king! Help me!"

⁵"What's the trouble?" the king asked.

"Alas, I am a widow!" she replied. "My husband is dead. ⁶My two sons had a fight out in the field. And since no one was there to stop it, one of them was killed. ⁷Now the rest of the family is demanding, 'Let us have your son. We will execute him for murdering his brother. He doesn't deserve to inherit his family's property.' They want to extinguish the only coal I have left, and my husband's name and family will disappear from the face of the earth."

⁸"Leave it to me," the king told her. "Go home, and I'll see to it that no one touches him."

⁹"Oh, thank you, my lord the king," the woman from Tekoa replied. "If you are criticized for helping me, let the blame fall on me and on my father's house, and let the king and his throne be innocent."

¹⁰"If anyone objects," the king said, "bring him to me. I can assure you he will never harm you again!"

¹¹Then she said, "Please swear to me by the LORD your God that you won't let anyone take vengeance against my son. I want no more bloodshed."

"As surely as the LORD lives," he replied, "not a hair on your son's head will be disturbed!"

¹²"Please allow me to ask one more thing of my lord the king," she said.

"Go ahead and speak," he responded.

¹³She replied, "Why don't you do as much for the people of God as you have promised to do for me? You have convicted yourself in making this decision, because you have refused to bring home your own banished son. ¹⁴All of us must die eventually. Our lives are like water spilled out on the ground, which cannot be gathered up again. But God does not just sweep life away; instead, he devises ways to bring us back when we have been separated from him.

¹⁵"I have come to plead with my lord the king because people have threatened me. I said to myself, 'Perhaps the king will listen to me ¹⁶and rescue us from those who would cut us off from the inheritance* God has given us. ¹⁷Yes, my lord the king will give us peace of mind again.' I know that you are like an angel

---

13:27 As in Greek and Latin versions (compare also Dead Sea Scrolls); the Hebrew text lacks this sentence.　13:34 As in Greek version; Hebrew lacks this sentence.　13:39a Dead Sea Scrolls and Greek version read *And the spirit of the king.* 13:39b Or *no longer felt a need to go out after Absalom.*　14:2 Hebrew *don't anoint yourself with oil.*　14:4 As in many Hebrew manuscripts and Greek and Syriac versions; Masoretic Text reads *spoke to.*　14:16 Or *the property;* or *the people.*

of God in discerning good from evil. May the LORD your God be with you."

18"I must know one thing," the king replied, "and tell me the truth."

"Yes, my lord the king," she responded.

19"Did Joab put you up to this?"

And the woman replied, "My lord the king, how can I deny it? Nobody can hide anything from you. Yes, Joab sent me and told me what to say. 20He did it to place the matter before you in a different light. But you are as wise as an angel of God, and you understand everything that happens among us!"

21So the king sent for Joab and told him, "All right, go and bring back the young man Absalom."

22Joab bowed with his face to the ground in deep respect and said, "At last I know that I have gained your approval, my lord the king, for you have granted me this request!"

23Then Joab went to Geshur and brought Absalom back to Jerusalem. 24But the king gave this order: "Absalom may go to his own house, but he must never come into my presence." So Absalom did not see the king.

Absalom Reconciled to David

25Now Absalom was praised as the most handsome man in all Israel. He was flawless from head to foot. 26He cut his hair only once a year, and then only because it was so heavy. When he weighed it out, it came to five pounds!* 27He had three sons and one daughter. His daughter's name was Tamar, and she was very beautiful.

28Absalom lived in Jerusalem for two years, but he never got to see the king. 29Then Absalom sent for Joab to ask him to intercede for him, but Joab refused to come. Absalom sent for him a second time, but again Joab refused to come. 30So Absalom said to his servants, "Go and set fire to Joab's barley field, the field next to mine." So they set his field on fire, as Absalom had commanded.

31Then Joab came to Absalom at his house and demanded, "Why did your servants set my field on fire?"

32And Absalom replied, "Because I wanted you to ask the king why he brought me back from Geshur if he didn't intend to see me. I might as well have stayed there. Let me see the king; if he finds me guilty of anything, then let him kill me."

33So Joab told the king what Absalom had said. Then at last David summoned Absalom, who came and bowed low before the king, and the king kissed him.

Absalom's Rebellion

15 After this, Absalom bought a chariot and horses, and he hired fifty bodyguards to run ahead of him. 2He got up early every morning and went out to the gate of the city. When people brought a case to the king for judgment, Absalom would ask where in Israel they were from, and they would tell him their tribe. 3Then Absalom would say, "You've really got a strong case here! It's too bad the king doesn't have anyone to hear it. 4I wish I were the judge. Then everyone could bring their cases to me for judgment, and I would give them justice!"

5When people tried to bow before him, Absalom wouldn't let them. Instead, he took them by the hand and kissed them. 6Absalom did this with everyone who came to the king for judgment, and so he stole the hearts of all the people of Israel.

7After four years,* Absalom said to the king, "Let me go to Hebron to offer a sacrifice to the LORD and fulfill a vow I made to him. 8For while your servant was at Geshur in Aram, I promised to sacrifice to the LORD in Hebron* if he would bring me back to Jerusalem."

9"All right," the king told him. "Go and fulfill your vow."

So Absalom went to Hebron. 10But while he was there, he sent secret messengers to all the tribes of Israel to stir up a rebellion against the king. "As soon as you hear the ram's horn," his message read, "you are to say, 'Absalom has been crowned king in Hebron.'" 11He took 200 men from Jerusalem with him as guests, but they knew nothing of his intentions. 12While Absalom was offering the sacrifices, he sent for Ahithophel, one of David's counselors who lived in Giloh. Soon many others also joined Absalom, and the conspiracy gained momentum.

David Escapes from Jerusalem

13A messenger soon arrived in Jerusalem to tell David, "All Israel has joined Absalom in a conspiracy against you!"

14"Then we must flee at once, or it will be too late!" David urged his men. "Hurry! If we get out of the city before Absalom arrives, both we and the city of Jerusalem will be spared from disaster."

14:26 Hebrew *200 shekels* [2.3 kilograms] *by the royal standard.* 15:7 As in Greek and Syriac versions; Hebrew reads *forty years.*
15:8 As in some Greek manuscripts; Hebrew lacks *in Hebron.*

¹⁵"We are with you," his advisers replied. "Do what you think is best."

¹⁶So the king and all his household set out at once. He left no one behind except ten of his concubines to look after the palace. ¹⁷The king and all his people set out on foot, pausing at the last house ¹⁸to let all the king's men move past to lead the way. There were 600 men from Gath who had come with David, along with the king's bodyguard.*

¹⁹Then the king turned and said to Ittai, a leader of the men from Gath, "Why are you coming with us? Go on back to King Absalom, for you are a guest in Israel, a foreigner in exile. ²⁰You arrived only recently, and should I force you today to wander with us? I don't even know where we will go. Go on back and take your kinsmen with you, and may the LORD show you his unfailing love and faithfulness.*"

²¹But Ittai said to the king, "I vow by the LORD and by your own life that I will go wherever my lord the king goes, no matter what happens—whether it means life or death."

²²David replied, "All right, come with us." So Ittai and all his men and their families went along.

²³Everyone cried loudly as the king and his followers passed by. They crossed the Kidron Valley and then went out toward the wilderness.

²⁴Zadok and all the Levites also came along, carrying the Ark of the Covenant of God. They set down the Ark of God, and Abiathar offered sacrifices* until everyone had passed out of the city.

²⁵Then the king instructed Zadok to take the Ark of God back into the city. "If the LORD sees fit," David said, "he will bring me back to see the Ark and the Tabernacle* again. ²⁶But if he is through with me, then let him do what seems best to him."

²⁷The king also told Zadok the priest, "Look,* here is my plan. You and Abiathar* should return quietly to the city with your son Ahimaaz and Abiathar's son Jonathan. ²⁸I will stop at the shallows of the Jordan River* and wait there for a report from you." ²⁹So Zadok and Abiathar took the Ark of God back to the city and stayed there.

³⁰David walked up the road to the Mount of Olives, weeping as he went. His head was covered and his feet were bare as a sign of mourning. And the people who were with him covered their heads and wept as they climbed the hill. ³¹When someone told David that his adviser Ahithophel was now backing Absalom, David prayed, "O LORD, let Ahithophel give Absalom foolish advice!"

³²When David reached the summit of the Mount of Olives where people worshiped God, Hushai the Arkite was waiting there for him. Hushai had torn his clothing and put dirt on his head as a sign of mourning. ³³But David told him, "If you go with me, you will only be a burden. ³⁴Return to Jerusalem and tell Absalom, 'I will now be your adviser, O king, just as I was your father's adviser in the past.' Then you can frustrate and counter Ahithophel's advice. ³⁵Zadok and Abiathar, the priests, will be there. Tell them about the plans being made in the king's palace, ³⁶and they will send their sons Ahimaaz and Jonathan to tell me what is going on."

³⁷So David's friend Hushai returned to Jerusalem, getting there just as Absalom arrived.

David and Ziba

16 When David had gone a little beyond the summit of the Mount of Olives, Ziba, the servant of Mephibosheth,* was waiting there for him. He had two donkeys loaded with 200 loaves of bread, 100 clusters of raisins, 100 bunches of summer fruit, and a wineskin full of wine.

²"What are these for?" the king asked Ziba.

Ziba replied, "The donkeys are for the king's people to ride on, and the bread and summer fruit are for the young men to eat. The wine is for those who become exhausted in the wilderness."

³"And where is Mephibosheth, Saul's grandson?" the king asked him.

"He stayed in Jerusalem," Ziba replied. "He said, 'Today I will get back the kingdom of my grandfather Saul.'"

⁴"In that case," the king told Ziba, "I give you everything Mephibosheth owns."

"I bow before you," Ziba replied. "May I always be pleasing to you, my lord the king."

Shimei Curses David

⁵As King David came to Bahurim, a man came out of the village cursing them. It was Shimei son of Gera, from the same clan as Saul's family.

15:18 Hebrew *the Kerethites and Pelethites.*   15:20 As in Greek version; Hebrew reads *and may unfailing love and faithfulness go with you.*   15:24 Or *Abiathar went up.*   15:25 Hebrew *and his dwelling place.*   15:27a As in Greek version; Hebrew reads *Are you a seer?* or *Do you see?*   15:27b Hebrew lacks *and Abiathar;* compare 15:29.   15:28 Hebrew *at the crossing points of the wilderness.*
16:1 *Mephibosheth* is another name for Merib-baal.

⁶He threw stones at the king and the king's officers and all the mighty warriors who surrounded him. ⁷"Get out of here, you murderer, you scoundrel!" he shouted at David. ⁸"The LORD is paying you back for all the bloodshed in Saul's clan. You stole his throne, and now the LORD has given it to your son Absalom. At last you will taste some of your own medicine, for you are a murderer!"

⁹"Why should this dead dog curse my lord the king?" Abishai son of Zeruiah demanded. "Let me go over and cut off his head!"

¹⁰"No!" the king said. "Who asked your opinion, you sons of Zeruiah! If the LORD has told him to curse me, who are you to stop him?"

¹¹Then David said to Abishai and to all his servants, "My own son is trying to kill me. Doesn't this relative of Saul* have even more reason to do so? Leave him alone and let him curse, for the LORD has told him to do it. ¹²And perhaps the LORD will see that I am being wronged* and will bless me because of these curses today." ¹³So David and his men continued down the road, and Shimei kept pace with them on a nearby hillside, cursing and throwing stones and dirt at David.

¹⁴The king and all who were with him grew weary along the way, so they rested when they reached the Jordan River.*

Ahithophel Advises Absalom

¹⁵Meanwhile, Absalom and all the army of Israel arrived at Jerusalem, accompanied by Ahithophel. ¹⁶When David's friend Hushai the Arkite arrived, he went immediately to see Absalom. "Long live the king!" he exclaimed. "Long live the king!"

¹⁷"Is this the way you treat your friend David?" Absalom asked him. "Why aren't you with him?"

¹⁸"I'm here because I belong to the man who is chosen by the LORD and by all the men of Israel," Hushai replied. ¹⁹"And anyway, why shouldn't I serve you? Just as I was your father's adviser, now I will be your adviser!"

²⁰Then Absalom turned to Ahithophel and asked him, "What should I do next?"

²¹Ahithophel told him, "Go and sleep with your father's concubines, for he has left them here to look after the palace. Then all Israel will know that you have insulted your father beyond hope of reconciliation, and they will throw their support to you." ²²So they set up a tent on the palace roof where everyone could see it, and Absalom went in and had sex with his father's concubines.

²³Absalom followed Ahithophel's advice, just as David had done. For every word Ahithophel spoke seemed as wise as though it had come directly from the mouth of God.

17

Now Ahithophel urged Absalom, "Let me choose 12,000 men to start out after David tonight. ²I will catch up with him while he is weary and discouraged. He and his troops will panic, and everyone will run away. Then I will kill only the king, ³and I will bring all the people back to you as a bride returns to her husband. After all, it is only one man's life that you seek.* Then you will be at peace with all the people." ⁴This plan seemed good to Absalom and to all the elders of Israel.

Hushai Counters Ahithophel's Advice

⁵But then Absalom said, "Bring in Hushai the Arkite. Let's see what he thinks about this." ⁶When Hushai arrived, Absalom told him what Ahithophel had said. Then he asked, "What is your opinion? Should we follow Ahithophel's advice? If not, what do you suggest?"

⁷"Well," Hushai replied to Absalom, "this time Ahithophel has made a mistake. ⁸You know your father and his men; they are mighty warriors. Right now they are as enraged as a mother bear who has been robbed of her cubs. And remember that your father is an experienced man of war. He won't be spending the night among the troops. ⁹He has probably already hidden in some pit or cave. And when he comes out and attacks and a few of your men fall, there will be panic among your troops, and the word will spread that Absalom's men are being slaughtered. ¹⁰Then even the bravest soldiers, though they have the heart of a lion, will be paralyzed with fear. For all Israel knows what a mighty warrior your father is and how courageous his men are.

¹¹"I recommend that you mobilize the entire army of Israel, bringing them from as far away as Dan in the north and Beersheba in the south. That way you will have an army as numerous as the sand on the seashore. And I advise that you personally lead the troops. ¹²When we find David, we'll fall on him like dew that falls on the ground. Then neither he nor any of his men will be left alive. ¹³And if David were to escape

---

16:11 Hebrew *this Benjaminite.*   16:12 As in Greek and Syriac versions; Hebrew reads *see my iniquity.*   16:14 As in Greek version (see also 17:16); Hebrew reads *when they reached their destination.*   17:3 As in Greek version; Hebrew reads *like the return of all is the man whom you seek.*

into some town, you will have all Israel there at your command. Then we can take ropes and drag the walls of the town into the nearest valley until every stone is torn down."

¹⁴Then Absalom and all the men of Israel said, "Hushai's advice is better than Ahithophel's." For the LORD had determined to defeat the counsel of Ahithophel, which really was the better plan, so that he could bring disaster on Absalom!

Hushai Warns David to Escape

¹⁵Hushai told Zadok and Abiathar, the priests, what Ahithophel had said to Absalom and the elders of Israel and what he himself had advised instead. ¹⁶"Quick!" he told them. "Find David and urge him not to stay at the shallows of the Jordan River* tonight. He must go across at once into the wilderness beyond. Otherwise he will die and his entire army with him."

¹⁷Jonathan and Ahimaaz had been staying at En-rogel so as not to be seen entering and leaving the city. Arrangements had been made for a servant girl to bring them the message they were to take to King David. ¹⁸But a boy spotted them at En-rogel, and he told Absalom about it. So they quickly escaped to Bahurim, where a man hid them down inside a well in his courtyard. ¹⁹The man's wife put a cloth over the top of the well and scattered grain on it to dry in the sun; so no one suspected they were there.

²⁰When Absalom's men arrived, they asked her, "Have you seen Ahimaaz and Jonathan?"

The woman replied, "They were here, but they crossed over the brook." Absalom's men looked for them without success and returned to Jerusalem.

²¹Then the two men crawled out of the well and hurried on to King David. "Quick!" they told him, "cross the Jordan tonight!" And they told him how Ahithophel had advised that he be captured and killed. ²²So David and all the people with him went across the Jordan River during the night, and they were all on the other bank before dawn.

²³When Ahithophel realized that his advice had not been followed, he saddled his donkey, went to his hometown, set his affairs in order, and hanged himself. He died there and was buried in the family tomb.

²⁴David soon arrived at Mahanaim. By now,

Absalom had mobilized the entire army of Israel and was leading his troops across the Jordan River. ²⁵Absalom had appointed Amasa as commander of his army, replacing Joab, who had been commander under David. (Amasa was Joab's cousin. His father was Jether,* an Ishmaelite.* His mother, Abigail daughter of Nahash, was the sister of Joab's mother, Zeruiah.) ²⁶Absalom and the Israelite army set up camp in the land of Gilead.

²⁷When David arrived at Mahanaim, he was warmly greeted by Shobi son of Nahash, who came from Rabbah of the Ammonites, and by Makir son of Ammiel from Lo-debar, and by Barzillai of Gilead from Rogelim. ²⁸They brought sleeping mats, cooking pots, serving bowls, wheat and barley, flour and roasted grain, beans, lentils, ²⁹honey, butter, sheep, goats, and cheese for David and those who were with him. For they said, "You must all be very hungry and tired and thirsty after your long march through the wilderness."

Absalom's Defeat and Death

18 David now mustered the men who were with him and appointed generals and captains* to lead them. ²He sent the troops out in three groups, placing one group under Joab, one under Joab's brother Abishai son of Zeruiah, and one under Ittai, the man from Gath. The king told his troops, "I am going out with you."

³But his men objected strongly. "You must not go," they urged. "If we have to turn and run—and even if half of us die—it will make no difference to Absalom's troops; they will be looking only for you. You are worth 10,000 of us,* and it is better that you stay here in the town and send help if we need it."

⁴"If you think that's the best plan, I'll do it," the king answered. So he stood alongside the gate of the town as all the troops marched out in groups of hundreds and of thousands.

⁵And the king gave this command to Joab, Abishai, and Ittai: "For my sake, deal gently with young Absalom." And all the troops heard the king give this order to his commanders.

⁶So the battle began in the forest of Ephraim, ⁷and the Israelite troops were beaten back by David's men. There was a great slaughter that day, and 20,000 men laid down their lives. ⁸The battle raged all across the countryside,

---

17:16 Hebrew *at the crossing points of the wilderness.*   17:25a Hebrew *Ithra,* a variant spelling of Jether.   17:25b As in some Greek manuscripts (see also 1 Chr 2:17); Hebrew reads *an Israelite.*   18:1 Hebrew *appointed commanders of thousands and commanders of hundreds.*   18:3 As in two Hebrew manuscripts and some Greek and Latin manuscripts; most Hebrew manuscripts read *Now there are 10,000 like us.*

and more men died because of the forest than were killed by the sword.

⁹During the battle, Absalom happened to come upon some of David's men. He tried to escape on his mule, but as he rode beneath the thick branches of a great tree, his hair* got caught in the tree. His mule kept going and left him dangling in the air. ¹⁰One of David's men saw what had happened and told Joab, "I saw Absalom dangling from a great tree."

¹¹"What?" Joab demanded. "You saw him there and didn't kill him? I would have rewarded you with ten pieces of silver* and a hero's belt!"

¹²"I would not kill the king's son for even a thousand pieces of silver,*" the man replied to Joab. "We all heard the king say to you and Abishai and Ittai, 'For my sake, please spare young Absalom.' ¹³And if I had betrayed the king by killing his son—and the king would certainly find out who did it—you yourself would be the first to abandon me."

¹⁴"Enough of this nonsense," Joab said. Then he took three daggers and plunged them into Absalom's heart as he dangled, still alive, in the great tree. ¹⁵Ten of Joab's young armor bearers then surrounded Absalom and killed him.

¹⁶Then Joab blew the ram's horn, and his men returned from chasing the army of Israel. ¹⁷They threw Absalom's body into a deep pit in the forest and piled a great heap of stones over it. And all Israel fled to their homes.

¹⁸During his lifetime, Absalom had built a monument to himself in the King's Valley, for he said, "I have no son to carry on my name." He named the monument after himself, and it is known as Absalom's Monument to this day.

David Mourns Absalom's Death

¹⁹Then Zadok's son Ahimaaz said, "Let me run to the king with the good news that the LORD has rescued him from his enemies."

²⁰"No," Joab told him, "it wouldn't be good news to the king that his son is dead. You can be my messenger another time, but not today." ²¹Then Joab said to a man from Ethiopia,* "Go tell the king what you have seen." The man bowed and ran off.

²²But Ahimaaz continued to plead with Joab, "Whatever happens, please let me go, too."

"Why should you go, my son?" Joab replied. "There will be no reward for your news."

²³"Yes, but let me go anyway," he begged.

Joab finally said, "All right, go ahead." So Ahimaaz took the less demanding route by way of the plain and ran to Mahanaim ahead of the Ethiopian.

²⁴While David was sitting between the inner and outer gates of the town, the watchman climbed to the roof of the gateway by the wall. As he looked, he saw a lone man running toward them. ²⁵He shouted the news down to David, and the king replied, "If he is alone, he has news."

As the messenger came closer, ²⁶the watchman saw another man running toward them. He shouted down, "Here comes another one!"

The king replied, "He also will have news."

²⁷"The first man runs like Ahimaaz son of Zadok," the watchman said.

"He is a good man and comes with good news," the king replied.

²⁸Then Ahimaaz cried out to the king, "Everything is all right!" He bowed before the king with his face to the ground and said, "Praise to the LORD your God, who has handed over the rebels who dared to stand against my lord the king."

²⁹"What about young Absalom?" the king demanded. "Is he all right?"

Ahimaaz replied, "When Joab told me to come, there was a lot of commotion. But I didn't know what was happening."

³⁰"Wait here," the king told him. So Ahimaaz stepped aside.

³¹Then the man from Ethiopia arrived and said, "I have good news for my lord the king. Today the LORD has rescued you from all those who rebelled against you."

³²"What about young Absalom?" the king demanded. "Is he all right?"

And the Ethiopian replied, "May all of your enemies, my lord the king, both now and in the future, share the fate of that young man!"

³³*The king was overcome with emotion. He went up to the room over the gateway and burst into tears. And as he went, he cried, "O my son Absalom! My son, my son Absalom! If only I had died instead of you! O Absalom, my son, my son."

Joab Rebukes the King

19 ¹*Word soon reached Joab that the king was weeping and mourning for Absalom. ²As all the people heard of the king's deep grief for his son, the joy of that day's victory

---

18:9 Hebrew *his head.*   **18:11** Hebrew *10 [shekels] of silver,* about 4 ounces or 114 grams in weight.   **18:12** Hebrew *1,000 [shekels] of silver,* about 25 pounds or 11.4 kilograms in weight.   **18:21** Hebrew *from Cush;* similarly in 18:23, 31, 32.   **18:33** Verse 18:33 is numbered 19:1 in Hebrew text.   **19:1** Verses 19:1-43 are numbered 19:2-44 in Hebrew text.

was turned into deep sadness. ³They crept back into the town that day as though they were ashamed and had deserted in battle. ⁴The king covered his face with his hands and kept on crying, "O my son Absalom! O Absalom, my son, my son!"

⁵Then Joab went to the king's room and said to him, "We saved your life today and the lives of your sons, your daughters, and your wives and concubines. Yet you act like this, making us feel ashamed of ourselves. ⁶You seem to love those who hate you and hate those who love you. You have made it clear today that your commanders and troops mean nothing to you. It seems that if Absalom had lived and all of us had died, you would be pleased. ⁷Now go out there and congratulate your troops, for I swear by the LORD that if you don't go out, not a single one of them will remain here tonight. Then you will be worse off than ever before."

⁸So the king went out and took his seat at the town gate, and as the news spread throughout the town that he was there, everyone went to him.

Meanwhile, the Israelites who had supported Absalom fled to their homes. ⁹And throughout all the tribes of Israel there was much discussion and argument going on. The people were saying, "The king rescued us from our enemies and saved us from the Philistines, but Absalom chased him out of the country. ¹⁰Now Absalom, whom we anointed to rule over us, is dead. Why not ask David to come back and be our king again?"

¹¹Then King David sent Zadok and Abiathar, the priests, to say to the elders of Judah, "Why are you the last ones to welcome back the king into his palace? For I have heard that all Israel is ready. ¹²You are my relatives, my own tribe, my own flesh and blood! So why are you the last ones to welcome back the king?" ¹³And David told them to tell Amasa, "Since you are my own flesh and blood, like Joab, may God strike me and even kill me if I do not appoint you as commander of my army in his place."

¹⁴Then Amasa* convinced all the men of Judah, and they responded unanimously. They sent word to the king, "Return to us, and bring back all who are with you."

David's Return to Jerusalem

¹⁵So the king started back to Jerusalem. And when he arrived at the Jordan River, the people of Judah came to Gilgal to meet him and escort him across the river. ¹⁶Shimei son of Gera, the man from Bahurim in Benjamin, hurried across with the men of Judah to welcome King David. ¹⁷A thousand other men from the tribe of Benjamin were with him, including Ziba, the chief servant of the house of Saul, and Ziba's fifteen sons and twenty servants. They rushed down to the Jordan to meet the king. ¹⁸They crossed the shallows of the Jordan to bring the king's household across the river, helping him in every way they could.

David's Mercy to Shimei

As the king was about to cross the river, Shimei fell down before him. ¹⁹"My lord the king, please forgive me," he pleaded. "Forget the terrible thing your servant did when you left Jerusalem. May the king put it out of his mind. ²⁰I know how much I sinned. That is why I have come here today, the very first person in all Israel* to greet my lord the king."

²¹Then Abishai son of Zeruiah said, "Shimei should die, for he cursed the LORD's anointed king!"

²²"Who asked your opinion, you sons of Zeruiah!" David exclaimed. "Why have you become my adversary* today? This is not a day for execution, for today I am once again the king of Israel!" ²³Then, turning to Shimei, David vowed, "Your life will be spared."

David's Kindness to Mephibosheth

²⁴Now Mephibosheth,* Saul's grandson, came down from Jerusalem to meet the king. He had not cared for his feet, trimmed his beard, or washed his clothes since the day the king left Jerusalem. ²⁵"Why didn't you come with me, Mephibosheth?" the king asked him.

²⁶Mephibosheth replied, "My lord the king, my servant Ziba deceived me. I told him, 'Saddle my donkey* so I can go with the king.' For as you know I am crippled. ²⁷Ziba has slandered me by saying that I refused to come. But I know that my lord the king is like an angel of God, so do what you think is best. ²⁸All my relatives and I could expect only death from you, my lord, but instead you have honored me by allowing me to eat at your own table! What more can I ask?"

²⁹"You've said enough," David replied. "I've decided that you and Ziba will divide your land equally between you."

³⁰"Give him all of it," Mephibosheth said.

19:14 Or David; Hebrew reads he.   19:20 Hebrew in the house of Joseph.   19:22 Or my prosecutor.   19:24 Mephibosheth is another name for Merib-baal.   19:26 As in Greek, Syriac, and Latin versions; Hebrew reads I will saddle a donkey for myself.

"I am content just to have you safely back again, my lord the king!"

David's Kindness to Barzillai
31Barzillai of Gilead had come down from Rogelim to escort the king across the Jordan. 32He was very old—eighty years of age—and very wealthy. He was the one who had provided food for the king during his stay in Mahanaim. 33"Come across with me and live in Jerusalem," the king said to Barzillai. "I will take care of you there."

34"No," he replied, "I am far too old to go with the king to Jerusalem. 35I am eighty years old today, and I can no longer enjoy anything. Food and wine are no longer tasty, and I cannot hear the singers as they sing. I would only be a burden to my lord the king. 36Just to go across the Jordan River with the king is all the honor I need! 37Then let me return again to die in my own town, where my father and mother are buried. But here is your servant, my son Kimham. Let him go with my lord the king and receive whatever you want to give him."

38"Good," the king agreed. "Kimham will go with me, and I will help him in any way you would like. And I will do for you anything you want." 39So all the people crossed the Jordan with the king. After David had blessed Barzillai and kissed him, Barzillai returned to his own home.

40The king then crossed over to Gilgal, taking Kimham with him. All the troops of Judah and half the troops of Israel escorted the king on his way.

An Argument over the King
41But all the men of Israel complained to the king, "The men of Judah stole the king and didn't give us the honor of helping take you, your household, and all your men across the Jordan."

42The men of Judah replied, "The king is one of our own kinsmen. Why should this make you angry? We haven't eaten any of the king's food or received any special favors!"

43"But there are ten tribes in Israel," the others replied. "So we have ten times as much right to the king as you do. What right do you have to treat us with such contempt? Weren't we the first to speak of bringing him back to be our king again?" The argument continued back and forth, and the men of Judah spoke even more harshly than the men of Israel.

The Revolt of Sheba
20 There happened to be a troublemaker there named Sheba son of Bicri, a man from the tribe of Benjamin. Sheba blew a ram's horn and began to chant:

"Down with the dynasty of David!
  We have no interest in the son of Jesse.
Come on, you men of Israel,
  back to your homes!"

2So all the men of Israel deserted David and followed Sheba son of Bicri. But the men of Judah stayed with their king and escorted him from the Jordan River to Jerusalem.

3When David came to his palace in Jerusalem, he took the ten concubines he had left to look after the palace and placed them in seclusion. Their needs were provided for, but he no longer slept with them. So each of them lived like a widow until she died.

4Then the king told Amasa, "Mobilize the army of Judah within three days, and report back at that time." 5So Amasa went out to notify Judah, but it took him longer than the time he had been given.

6Then David said to Abishai, "Sheba son of Bicri is going to hurt us more than Absalom did. Quick, take my troops and chase after him before he gets into a fortified town where we can't reach him."

7So Abishai and Joab,* together with the king's bodyguard* and all the mighty warriors, set out from Jerusalem to go after Sheba. 8As they arrived at the great stone in Gibeon, Amasa met them. Joab was wearing his military tunic with a dagger strapped to his belt. As he stepped forward to greet Amasa, he slipped the dagger from its sheath.*

9"How are you, my cousin?" Joab said and took him by the beard with his right hand as though to kiss him. 10Amasa didn't notice the dagger in his left hand, and Joab stabbed him in the stomach with it so that his insides gushed out onto the ground. Joab did not need to strike again, and Amasa soon died. Joab and his brother Abishai left him lying there and continued after Sheba.

11One of Joab's young men shouted to Amasa's troops, "If you are for Joab and David, come and follow Joab." 12But Amasa lay in his blood in the middle of the road, and Joab's man saw that everyone was stopping to stare at him. So he pulled him off the road into a field and

20:7a Hebrew So Joab's men.   20:7b Hebrew the Kerethites and Pelethites; also in 20:23.   20:8 Hebrew As he stepped forward, it fell out.

threw a cloak over him. 13With Amasa's body out of the way, everyone went on with Joab to capture Sheba son of Bicri.

14Meanwhile, Sheba traveled through all the tribes of Israel and eventually came to the town of Abel-beth-maacah. All the members of his own clan, the Bicrites,* assembled for battle and followed him into the town. 15When Joab's forces arrived, they attacked Abel-beth-maacah. They built a siege ramp against the town's fortifications and began battering down the wall. 16But a wise woman in the town called out to Joab, "Listen to me, Joab. Come over here so I can talk to you." 17As he approached, the woman asked, "Are you Joab?"

"I am," he replied.

So she said, "Listen carefully to your servant."

"I'm listening," he said.

18Then she continued, "There used to be a saying, 'If you want to settle an argument, ask advice at the town of Abel.' 19I am one who is peace loving and faithful in Israel. But you are destroying an important town in Israel.* Why do you want to devour what belongs to the LORD?"

20And Joab replied, "Believe me, I don't want to devour or destroy your town! 21That's not my purpose. All I want is a man named Sheba son of Bicri from the hill country of Ephraim, who has revolted against King David. If you hand over this one man to me, I will leave the town in peace."

"All right," the woman replied, "we will throw his head over the wall to you." 22Then the woman went to all the people with her wise advice, and they cut off Sheba's head and threw it out to Joab. So he blew the ram's horn and called his troops back from the attack. They all returned to their homes, and Joab returned to the king at Jerusalem.

23Now Joab was the commander of the army of Israel. Benaiah son of Jehoiada was captain of the king's bodyguard. 24Adoniram* was in charge of forced labor. Jehoshaphat son of Ahilud was the royal historian. 25Sheva was the court secretary. Zadok and Abiathar were the priests. 26And Ira, a descendant of Jair, was David's personal priest.

David Avenges the Gibeonites

21 There was a famine during David's reign that lasted for three years, so David asked the LORD about it. And the LORD said,

"The famine has come because Saul and his family are guilty of murdering the Gibeonites."

2So the king summoned the Gibeonites. They were not part of Israel but were all that was left of the nation of the Amorites. The people of Israel had sworn not to kill them, but Saul, in his zeal for Israel and Judah, had tried to wipe them out. 3David asked them, "What can I do for you? How can I make amends so that you will bless the LORD's people again?"

4"Well, money can't settle this matter between us and the family of Saul," the Gibeonites replied. "Neither can we demand the life of anyone in Israel."

"What can I do then?" David asked. "Just tell me and I will do it for you."

5Then they replied, "It was Saul who planned to destroy us, to keep us from having any place at all in the territory of Israel. 6So let seven of Saul's sons be handed over to us, and we will execute them before the LORD at Gibeon, on the mountain of the LORD.*"

"All right," the king said, "I will do it." 7The king spared Jonathan's son Mephibosheth,* who was Saul's grandson, because of the oath David and Jonathan had sworn before the LORD. 8But he gave them Saul's two sons Armoni and Mephibosheth, whose mother was Rizpah daughter of Aiah. He also gave them the five sons of Saul's daughter Merab,* the wife of Adriel son of Barzillai from Meholah. 9The men of Gibeon executed them on the mountain before the LORD. So all seven of them died together at the beginning of the barley harvest.

10Then Rizpah daughter of Aiah, the mother of two of the men, spread burlap on a rock and stayed there the entire harvest season. She prevented the scavenger birds from tearing at their bodies during the day and stopped wild animals from eating them at night. 11When David learned what Rizpah, Saul's concubine, had done, 12he went to the people of Jabesh-gilead and retrieved the bones of Saul and his son Jonathan. (When the Philistines had killed Saul and Jonathan on Mount Gilboa, the people of Jabesh-gilead stole their bodies from the public square of Beth-shan, where the Philistines had hung them.) 13So David obtained the bones of Saul and Jonathan, as well as the bones of the men the Gibeonites had executed.

14Then the king ordered that they bury the

20:14 As in Greek and Latin versions; Hebrew reads *All the Berites.*   20:19 Hebrew *a town that is a mother in Israel.*   20:24 As in Greek version (see also 1 Kgs 4:6; 5:14); Hebrew reads *Adoram.*   21:6 As in Greek version (see also 21:9); Hebrew reads *at Gibeah of Saul, the chosen of the LORD.*   21:7 *Mephibosheth* is another name for Merib-baal.   21:8 As in a few Hebrew and Greek manuscripts and Syriac version (see also 1 Sam 18:19); most Hebrew manuscripts read *Michal.*

bones in the tomb of Kish, Saul's father, at the town of Zela in the land of Benjamin. After that, God ended the famine in the land.

Battles against Philistine Giants

15Once again the Philistines were at war with Israel. And when David and his men were in the thick of battle, David became weak and exhausted. 16Ishbi-benob was a descendant of the giants*; his bronze spearhead weighed more than seven pounds,* and he was armed with a new sword. He had cornered David and was about to kill him. 17But Abishai son of Zeruiah came to David's rescue and killed the Philistine. Then David's men declared, "You are not going out to battle with us again! Why risk snuffing out the light of Israel?"

18After this, there was another battle against the Philistines at Gob. As they fought, Sibbecai from Hushah killed Saph, another descendant of the giants.

19During another battle at Gob, Elhanan son of Jair* from Bethlehem killed the brother of Goliath of Gath.* The handle of his spear was as thick as a weaver's beam!

20In another battle with the Philistines at Gath, they encountered a huge man* with six fingers on each hand and six toes on each foot, twenty-four in all, who was also a descendant of the giants. 21But when he defied and taunted Israel, he was killed by Jonathan, the son of David's brother Shimea.*

22These four Philistines were descendants of the giants of Gath, but David and his warriors killed them.

David's Song of Praise

22 David sang this song to the LORD on the day the LORD rescued him from all his enemies and from Saul. 2He sang:

"The LORD is my rock, my fortress, and my savior;
3   my God is my rock, in whom I find protection.
He is my shield, the power that saves me, and my place of safety.
He is my refuge, my savior, the one who saves me from violence.
4 I called on the LORD, who is worthy of praise, and he saved me from my enemies.

5 "The waves of death overwhelmed me; floods of destruction swept over me.
6 The grave* wrapped its ropes around me; death laid a trap in my path.
7 But in my distress I cried out to the LORD; yes, I cried to my God for help.
He heard me from his sanctuary; my cry reached his ears.

8 "Then the earth quaked and trembled. The foundations of the heavens shook; they quaked because of his anger.
9 Smoke poured from his nostrils; fierce flames leaped from his mouth. Glowing coals blazed forth from him.
10 He opened the heavens and came down; dark storm clouds were beneath his feet.
11 Mounted on a mighty angelic being,* he flew, soaring* on the wings of the wind.
12 He shrouded himself in darkness, veiling his approach with dense rain clouds.
13 A great brightness shone around him, and burning coals* blazed forth.
14 The LORD thundered from heaven; the voice of the Most High resounded.
15 He shot arrows and scattered his enemies; his lightning flashed, and they were confused.
16 Then at the command of the LORD, at the blast of his breath,
the bottom of the sea could be seen, and the foundations of the earth were laid bare.

17 "He reached down from heaven and rescued me; he drew me out of deep waters.
18 He rescued me from my powerful enemies, from those who hated me and were too strong for me.
19 They attacked me at a moment when I was in distress, but the LORD supported me.
20 He led me to a place of safety; he rescued me because he delights in me.
21 The LORD rewarded me for doing right; he restored me because of my innocence.
22 For I have kept the ways of the LORD;

21:16a Or *a descendant of the Rapha;* also in 21:18, 20, 22.   21:16b Hebrew *300 [shekels]* [3.4 kilograms].   21:19a As in parallel text at 1 Chr 20:5; Hebrew reads *son of Jaare-oregim.*   21:19b As in parallel text at 1 Chr 20:5; Hebrew reads *killed Goliath of Gath.*   21:20 As in parallel text at 1 Chr 20:6; Hebrew reads *a Midianite.*   21:21 As in parallel text at 1 Chr 20:7; Hebrew reads *Shimei,* a variant spelling of Shimea.   22:6 Hebrew *Sheol.*   22:11a Hebrew *a cherub.*   22:11b As in some Hebrew manuscripts (see also Ps 18:10); other Hebrew manuscripts read *appearing.*   22:13 Or *and lightning bolts.*

I have not turned from my God to
  follow evil.
23 I have followed all his regulations;
  I have never abandoned his decrees.
24 I am blameless before God;
  I have kept myself from sin.
25 The LORD rewarded me for doing right.
  He has seen my innocence.

26 "To the faithful you show yourself
    faithful;
  to those with integrity you show
    integrity.
27 To the pure you show yourself pure,
  but to the crooked you show yourself
    shrewd.
28 You rescue the humble,
  but your eyes watch the proud and
    humiliate them.
29 O LORD, you are my lamp.
  The LORD lights up my darkness.
30 In your strength I can crush an army;
  with my God I can scale any wall.

31 "God's way is perfect.
  All the LORD's promises prove true.
  He is a shield for all who look to him
    for protection.
32 For who is God except the LORD?
  Who but our God is a solid rock?
33 God is my strong fortress,
  and he makes my way perfect.
34 He makes me as surefooted as a deer,
  enabling me to stand on mountain
    heights.
35 He trains my hands for battle;
  he strengthens my arm to draw a
    bronze bow.
36 You have given me your shield of victory;
  your help* has made me great.
37 You have made a wide path for my feet
  to keep them from slipping.

38 "I chased my enemies and destroyed
    them;
  I did not stop until they were
    conquered.
39 I consumed them;
  I struck them down so they did not
    get up;
  they fell beneath my feet.
40 You have armed me with strength for the
    battle;

you have subdued my enemies under
  my feet.
41 You placed my foot on their necks.
  I have destroyed all who hated me.
42 They looked for help, but no one came to
    their rescue.
  They even cried to the LORD, but he
    refused to answer.
43 I ground them as fine as the dust of the
    earth;
  I trampled them* in the gutter like dirt.

44 "You gave me victory over my accusers.
  You preserved me as the ruler over
    nations;
  people I don't even know now serve me.
45 Foreign nations cringe before me;
  as soon as they hear of me, they submit.
46 They all lose their courage
  and come trembling* from their
    strongholds.

47 "The LORD lives! Praise to my Rock!
  May God, the Rock of my salvation,
    be exalted!
48 He is the God who pays back those who
    harm me;
  he brings down the nations under me
49   and delivers me from my enemies.
  You hold me safe beyond the reach of my
    enemies;
  you save me from violent opponents.
50 For this, O LORD, I will praise you among
    the nations;
  I will sing praises to your name.
51 You give great victories to your king;
  you show unfailing love to your
    anointed,
    to David and all his descendants
    forever."

David's Last Words

23 These are the last words of David:

  "David, the son of Jesse, speaks—
  David, the man who was raised up so
    high,
  David, the man anointed by the God of
    Jacob,
  David, the sweet psalmist of Israel.*

2 "The Spirit of the LORD speaks through me;
  his words are upon my tongue.

22:36 As in Dead Sea Scrolls; Masoretic Text reads *your answering.*   22:43 As in Dead Sea Scrolls (see also Ps 18:42); Masoretic Text reads *I crushed and trampled them.*   22:46 As in parallel text at Ps 18:45; Hebrew reads *come girding themselves.*   23:1 Or the *favorite subject of the songs of Israel;* or *the favorite of the Strong One of Israel.*

³ The God of Israel spoke.
  The Rock of Israel said to me:
  'The one who rules righteously,
    who rules in the fear of God,
⁴ is like the light of morning at sunrise,
    like a morning without clouds,
  like the gleaming of the sun
    on new grass after rain.'

⁵ "Is it not my family God has chosen?
    Yes, he has made an everlasting
      covenant with me.
  His agreement is arranged and guaranteed
    in every detail.
  He will ensure my safety and success.
⁶ But the godless are like thorns to be
    thrown away,
  for they tear the hand that touches
    them.
⁷ One must use iron tools to chop them
    down;
  they will be totally consumed by fire."

David's Mightiest Warriors

⁸These are the names of David's mightiest warriors. The first was Jashobeam the Hacmonite,* who was leader of the Three*—the three mightiest warriors among David's men. He once used his spear to kill 800 enemy warriors in a single battle.*

⁹Next in rank among the Three was Eleazar son of Dodai, a descendant of Ahoah. Once Eleazar and David stood together against the Philistines when the entire Israelite army had fled. ¹⁰He killed Philistines until his hand was too tired to lift his sword, and the LORD gave him a great victory that day. The rest of the army did not return until it was time to collect the plunder!

¹¹Next in rank was Shammah son of Agee from Harar. One time the Philistines gathered at Lehi and attacked the Israelites in a field full of lentils. The Israelite army fled, ¹²but Shammah* held his ground in the middle of the field and beat back the Philistines. So the LORD brought about a great victory.

¹³Once during the harvest, when David was at the cave of Adullam, the Philistine army was camped in the valley of Rephaim. The Three (who were among the Thirty—an elite group among David's fighting men) went down to meet him there. ¹⁴David was staying in the stronghold at the time, and a Philistine detachment had occupied the town of Bethlehem.

¹⁵David remarked longingly to his men, "Oh, how I would love some of that good water from the well by the gate in Bethlehem." ¹⁶So the Three broke through the Philistine lines, drew some water from the well by the gate in Bethlehem, and brought it back to David. But he refused to drink it. Instead, he poured it out as an offering to the LORD. ¹⁷"The LORD forbid that I should drink this!" he exclaimed. "This water is as precious as the blood of these men* who risked their lives to bring it to me." So David did not drink it. These are examples of the exploits of the Three.

David's Thirty Mighty Men

¹⁸Abishai son of Zeruiah, the brother of Joab, was the leader of the Thirty.* He once used his spear to kill 300 enemy warriors in a single battle. It was by such feats that he became as famous as the Three. ¹⁹Abishai was the most famous of the Thirty* and was their commander, though he was not one of the Three.

²⁰There was also Benaiah son of Jehoiada, a valiant warrior* from Kabzeel. He did many heroic deeds, which included killing two champions* of Moab. Another time, on a snowy day, he chased a lion down into a pit and killed it. ²¹Once, armed only with a club, he killed an imposing Egyptian warrior who was armed with a spear. Benaiah wrenched the spear from the Egyptian's hand and killed him with it. ²²Deeds like these made Benaiah as famous as the Three mightiest warriors. ²³He was more honored than the other members of the Thirty, though he was not one of the Three. And David made him captain of his bodyguard.

²⁴Other members of the Thirty included:

Asahel, Joab's brother;
Elhanan son of Dodo from Bethlehem;
²⁵ Shammah from Harod;
Elika from Harod;
²⁶ Helez from Pelon*;
Ira son of Ikkesh from Tekoa;

23:8a As in parallel text at 1 Chr 11:11; Hebrew reads *Josheb-basshebeth the Tahkemonite*.   23:8b As in Greek and Latin versions (see also 1 Chr 11:11); the meaning of the Hebrew is uncertain.   23:8c As in some Greek manuscripts (see also 1 Chr 11:11); the meaning of the Hebrew is uncertain, though it might be rendered *the Three*. *It was Adino the Eznite who killed 800 men at one time.*   23:12 Hebrew *he*.   23:17 Hebrew *Shall I drink the blood of these men?*   23:18 As in a few Hebrew manuscripts and Syriac version; most Hebrew manuscripts read *the Three*.   23:19 As in Syriac version; Hebrew reads *the Three*.   23:20a Or *son of Jehoiada, son of Ish-hai*.   23:20b Hebrew *two of Ariel*.   23:26 As in parallel text at 1 Chr 11:27 (see also 1 Chr 27:10); Hebrew reads *from Palti*.

²⁷ Abiezer from Anathoth;
Sibbecai* from Hushah;
²⁸ Zalmon from Ahoah;
Maharai from Netophah;
²⁹ Heled* son of Baanah from Netophah;
Ithai* son of Ribai from Gibeah (in the
land of Benjamin);
³⁰ Benaiah from Pirathon;
Hurai* from Nahale-gaash*;
³¹ Abi-albon from Arabah;
Azmaveth from Bahurim;
³² Eliahba from Shaalbon;
the sons of Jashen;
Jonathan ³³son of Shagee* from Harar;
Ahiam son of Sharar from Harar;
³⁴ Eliphelet son of Ahasbai from Maacah;
Eliam son of Ahithophel from Giloh;
³⁵ Hezro from Carmel;
Paarai from Arba;
³⁶ Igal son of Nathan from Zobah;
Bani from Gad;
³⁷ Zelek from Ammon;
Naharai from Beeroth, the armor bearer
of Joab son of Zeruiah;
³⁸ Ira from Jattir;
Gareb from Jattir;
³⁹ Uriah the Hittite.

There were thirty-seven in all.

David Takes a Census

24 Once again the anger of the LORD burned against Israel, and he caused David to harm them by taking a census. "Go and count the people of Israel and Judah," the LORD told him.

²So the king said to Joab and the commanders* of the army, "Take a census of all the tribes of Israel—from Dan in the north to Beersheba in the south—so I may know how many people there are."

³But Joab replied to the king, "May the LORD your God let you live to see a hundred times as many people as there are now! But why, my lord the king, do you want to do this?"

⁴But the king insisted that they take the census, so Joab and the commanders of the army went out to count the people of Israel. ⁵First they crossed the Jordan and camped at Aroer, south of the town in the valley, in the direction of Gad. Then they went on to Jazer, ⁶then to Gilead in the land of Tahtim-hodshi* and to Dan-jaan and around to Sidon. ⁷Then they came to the fortress of Tyre, and all the towns of the Hivites and Canaanites. Finally, they went south to Judah* as far as Beersheba.

⁸Having gone through the entire land for nine months and twenty days, they returned to Jerusalem. ⁹Joab reported the number of people to the king. There were 800,000 capable warriors in Israel who could handle a sword, and 500,000 in Judah.

Judgment for David's Sin

¹⁰But after he had taken the census, David's conscience began to bother him. And he said to the LORD, "I have sinned greatly by taking this census. Please forgive my guilt, LORD, for doing this foolish thing."

¹¹The next morning the word of the LORD came to the prophet Gad, who was David's seer. This was the message: ¹²"Go and say to David, 'This is what the LORD says: I will give you three choices. Choose one of these punishments, and I will inflict it on you.'"

¹³So Gad came to David and asked him, "Will you choose three* years of famine throughout your land, three months of fleeing from your enemies, or three days of severe plague throughout your land? Think this over and decide what answer I should give the LORD who sent me."

¹⁴"I'm in a desperate situation!" David replied to Gad. "But let us fall into the hands of the LORD, for his mercy is great. Do not let me fall into human hands."

¹⁵So the LORD sent a plague upon Israel that morning, and it lasted for three days.* A total of 70,000 people died throughout the nation, from Dan in the north to Beersheba in the south. ¹⁶But as the angel was preparing to destroy Jerusalem, the LORD relented and said to the death angel, "Stop! That is enough!" At that moment the angel of the LORD was by the threshing floor of Araunah the Jebusite.

¹⁷When David saw the angel, he said to the LORD, "I am the one who has sinned and done wrong! But these people are as innocent as sheep—what have they done? Let your anger fall against me and my family."

23:27 As in some Greek manuscripts (see also 1 Chr 11:29); Hebrew reads *Mebunnai*.   23:29a As in some Hebrew manuscripts (see also 1 Chr 11:30); most Hebrew manuscripts read *Heleb*.   23:29b As in parallel text at 1 Chr 11:31; Hebrew reads *Ittai*.   23:30a As in some Greek manuscripts (see also 1 Chr 11:32); Hebrew reads *Hiddai*.   23:30b Or *from the ravines of Gaash*.   23:33 As in parallel text at 1 Chr 11:34; Hebrew reads *Jonathan, Shammah;* some Greek manuscripts read *Jonathan son of Shammah*.   24:2 As in Greek version (see also 24:4 and 1 Chr 21:2); Hebrew reads *Joab the commander*.   24:6 Greek version reads *to Gilead and to Kadesh in the land of the Hittites*.   24:7 Or *they went to the Negev of Judah*.   24:13 As in Greek version (see also 1 Chr 21:12); Hebrew reads *seven*.   24:15 Hebrew *for the designated time*.

David Builds an Altar

¹⁸That day Gad came to David and said to him, "Go up and build an altar to the LORD on the threshing floor of Araunah the Jebusite."

¹⁹So David went up to do what the LORD had commanded him. ²⁰When Araunah saw the king and his men coming toward him, he came and bowed before the king with his face to the ground. ²¹"Why have you come, my lord the king?" Araunah asked.

David replied, "I have come to buy your threshing floor and to build an altar to the LORD there, so that he will stop the plague."

²²"Take it, my lord the king, and use it as you wish," Araunah said to David. "Here are

oxen for the burnt offering, and you can use the threshing boards and ox yokes for wood to build a fire on the altar. ²³I will give it all to you, Your Majesty, and may the LORD your God accept your sacrifice."

²⁴But the king replied to Araunah, "No, I insist on buying it, for I will not present burnt offerings to the LORD my God that have cost me nothing." So David paid him fifty pieces of silver* for the threshing floor and the oxen.

²⁵David built an altar there to the LORD and sacrificed burnt offerings and peace offerings. And the LORD answered his prayer for the land, and the plague on Israel was stopped.

24:24 Hebrew *50 shekels of silver,* about 20 ounces or 570 grams in weight.

1 Kings

EFFECTIVE LEADERSHIP often has more to do with character than accomplishments. At least that seems to be the case in the book of 1 Kings. The books of 1 and 2 Kings form one book in the Hebrew Bible, covering the period when kings ruled Israel after David's reign. First Kings opens with the death of David, followed by the reign of Solomon and the building of the Temple in Jerusalem. The book then records Solomon's death and the division of the kingdom into northern and southern halves (Israel and Judah, respectively). This division resulted from a foolish decision by Solomon's heir, Rehoboam. Despite wise advice from his older advisers, Rehoboam chose to follow a policy of harsh rule, and the northern tribes rebelled. First Kings then begins a chronicle of each king who ruled Israel or Judah, giving him a rating of either good or bad, depending on his faithfulness to God and the covenant. The book closes with a great conflict between Elijah the prophet and Ahab, king of Israel.

■ **Author:** Uncertain; some have suggested Jeremiah or a group of prophets

■ **Date Written:** Uncertain, possibly around 562 BC, shortly after King Jehoiachin's release

■ **Purpose:** To contrast the lives of the godly and ungodly kings throughout the history of Israel and Judah and to demonstrate the consequences of idolatry and wickedness

■ **Themes:** Idolatry, the Temple, good and bad kings, the rise of the prophet movement, sin and its consequences

■ **Outline**
1:1–2:11 The death of David
2:12–11:43 The reign of Solomon
12:1-24 The division of the kingdom
12:25–16:28 The rivalry between Israel and Judah up to Ahab
16:29–22:40 Elijah and Ahab
22:41-53 The reigns of Jehoshaphat and Ahaziah

David in His Old Age

1 King David was now very old, and no matter how many blankets covered him, he could not keep warm. ²So his advisers told him, "Let us find a young virgin to wait on you and look after you, my lord. She will lie in your arms and keep you warm."

³So they searched throughout the land of Israel for a beautiful girl, and they found Abishag from Shunem and brought her to the king. ⁴The girl was very beautiful, and she looked after the king and took care of him. But the king had no sexual relations with her.

Adonijah Claims the Throne

⁵About that time David's son Adonijah, whose mother was Haggith, began boasting, "I will make myself king." So he provided himself with chariots and charioteers and recruited fifty men to run in front of him. ⁶Now his father, King David, had never disciplined him at any time, even by asking, "Why are you doing that?" Adonijah had been born next after Absalom, and he was very handsome.

⁷Adonijah took Joab son of Zeruiah and Abiathar the priest into his confidence, and they agreed to help him become king. ⁸But Zadok the priest, Benaiah son of Jehoiada, Nathan the prophet, Shimei, Rei, and David's personal bodyguard refused to support Adonijah.

⁹Adonijah went to the Stone of Zoheleth* near the spring of En-rogel, where he sacrificed sheep, cattle, and fattened calves. He invited all his brothers—the other sons of King David—and all the royal officials of Judah. ¹⁰But he did not invite Nathan the prophet or Benaiah or the king's bodyguard or his brother Solomon.

1:9 Or *to the Serpent's Stone*; Greek version supports reading *Zoheleth* as a proper name.

¹¹Then Nathan went to Bathsheba, Solomon's mother, and asked her, "Haven't you heard that Haggith's son, Adonijah, has made himself king, and our lord David doesn't even know about it? ¹²If you want to save your own life and the life of your son Solomon, follow my advice. ¹³Go at once to King David and say to him, 'My lord the king, didn't you make a vow and say to me, "Your son Solomon will surely be the next king and will sit on my throne"? Why then has Adonijah become king?' ¹⁴And while you are still talking with him, I will come and confirm everything you have said."

¹⁵So Bathsheba went into the king's bedroom. (He was very old now, and Abishag was taking care of him.) ¹⁶Bathsheba bowed down before the king.

"What can I do for you?" he asked her.

¹⁷She replied, "My lord, you made a vow before the LORD your God when you said to me, 'Your son Solomon will surely be the next king and will sit on my throne.' ¹⁸But instead, Adonijah has made himself king, and my lord the king does not even know about it. ¹⁹He has sacrificed many cattle, fattened calves, and sheep, and he has invited all the king's sons to attend the celebration. He also invited Abiathar the priest and Joab, the commander of the army. But he did not invite your servant Solomon. ²⁰And now, my lord the king, all Israel is waiting for you to announce who will become king after you. ²¹If you do not act, my son Solomon and I will be treated as criminals as soon as my lord the king has died."

²²While she was still speaking with the king, Nathan the prophet arrived. ²³The king's officials told him, "Nathan the prophet is here to see you."

Nathan went in and bowed before the king with his face to the ground. ²⁴Nathan asked, "My lord the king, have you decided that Adonijah will be the next king and that he will sit on your throne? ²⁵Today he has sacrificed many cattle, fattened calves, and sheep, and he has invited all the king's sons to attend the celebration. He also invited the commanders of the army and Abiathar the priest. They are feasting and drinking with him and shouting, 'Long live King Adonijah!' ²⁶But he did not invite me or Zadok the priest or Benaiah or your servant Solomon. ²⁷Has my lord the king really done this without letting any of his officials know who should be the next king?"

David Makes Solomon King

²⁸King David responded, "Call Bathsheba!" So she came back in and stood before the king. ²⁹And the king repeated his vow: "As surely as the LORD lives, who has rescued me from every danger, ³⁰your son Solomon will be the next king and will sit on my throne this very day, just as I vowed to you before the LORD, the God of Israel."

³¹Then Bathsheba bowed down with her face to the ground before the king and exclaimed, "May my lord King David live forever!"

³²Then King David ordered, "Call Zadok the priest, Nathan the prophet, and Benaiah son of Jehoiada." When they came into the king's presence, ³³the king said to them, "Take Solomon and my officials down to Gihon Spring. Solomon is to ride on my own mule. ³⁴There Zadok the priest and Nathan the prophet are to anoint him king over Israel. Blow the ram's horn and shout, 'Long live King Solomon!' ³⁵Then escort him back here, and he will sit on my throne. He will succeed me as king, for I have appointed him to be ruler over Israel and Judah."

³⁶"Amen!" Benaiah son of Jehoiada replied. "May the LORD, the God of my lord the king, decree that it happen. ³⁷And may the LORD be with Solomon as he has been with you, my lord the king, and may he make Solomon's reign even greater than yours!"

³⁸So Zadok the priest, Nathan the prophet, Benaiah son of Jehoiada, and the king's bodyguard* took Solomon down to Gihon Spring, with Solomon riding on King David's own mule. ³⁹There Zadok the priest took the flask of olive oil from the sacred tent and anointed Solomon with the oil. Then they sounded the ram's horn and all the people shouted, "Long live King Solomon!" ⁴⁰And all the people followed Solomon into Jerusalem, playing flutes and shouting for joy. The celebration was so joyous and noisy that the earth shook with the sound.

⁴¹Adonijah and his guests heard the celebrating and shouting just as they were finishing their banquet. When Joab heard the sound of the ram's horn, he asked, "What's going on? Why is the city in such an uproar?"

⁴²And while he was still speaking, Jonathan son of Abiathar the priest arrived. "Come in," Adonijah said to him, "for you are a good man. You must have good news."

⁴³"Not at all!" Jonathan replied. "Our lord King David has just declared Solomon king!

1:38 Hebrew *the Kerethites and Pelethites;* also in 1:44.

44The king sent him down to Gihon Spring with Zadok the priest, Nathan the prophet, and Benaiah son of Jehoiada, protected by the king's bodyguard. They had him ride on the king's own mule, 45and Zadok and Nathan have anointed him at Gihon Spring as the new king. They have just returned, and the whole city is celebrating and rejoicing. That's what all the noise is about. 46What's more, Solomon is now sitting on the royal throne as king. 47And all the royal officials have gone to King David and congratulated him, saying, 'May your God make Solomon's fame even greater than your own, and may Solomon's reign be even greater than yours!' Then the king bowed his head in worship as he lay in his bed, 48and he said, 'Praise the LORD, the God of Israel, who today has chosen a successor to sit on my throne while I am still alive to see it.'"

49Then all of Adonijah's guests jumped up in panic from the banquet table and quickly scattered. 50Adonijah was afraid of Solomon, so he rushed to the sacred tent and grabbed on to the horns of the altar. 51Word soon reached Solomon that Adonijah had seized the horns of the altar in fear, and that he was pleading, "Let King Solomon swear today that he will not kill me!"

52Solomon replied, "If he proves himself to be loyal, not a hair on his head will be touched. But if he makes trouble, he will die." 53So King Solomon summoned Adonijah, and they brought him down from the altar. He came and bowed respectfully before King Solomon, who dismissed him, saying, "Go on home."

David's Final Instructions to Solomon

2 As the time of King David's death approached, he gave this charge to his son Solomon:

2"I am going where everyone on earth must someday go. Take courage and be a man. 3Observe the requirements of the LORD your God, and follow all his ways. Keep the decrees, commands, regulations, and laws written in the Law of Moses so that you will be successful in all you do and wherever you go. 4If you do this, then the LORD will keep the promise he made to me. He told me, 'If your descendants live as they should and follow me faithfully with all their heart and soul, one of them will always sit on the throne of Israel.'

5"And there is something else. You know what Joab son of Zeruiah did to me when he murdered my two army commanders, Abner son of Ner and Amasa son of Jether. He pretended that it was an act of war, but it was done in a time of peace,* staining his belt and sandals with innocent blood.* 6Do with him what you think best, but don't let him grow old and go to his grave in peace.*

7"Be kind to the sons of Barzillai of Gilead. Make them permanent guests at your table, for they took care of me when I fled from your brother Absalom.

8"And remember Shimei son of Gera, the man from Bahurim in Benjamin. He cursed me with a terrible curse as I was fleeing to Mahanaim. When he came down to meet me at the Jordan River, I swore by the LORD that I would not kill him. 9But that oath does not make him innocent. You are a wise man, and you will know how to arrange a bloody death for him.*"

10Then David died and was buried with his ancestors in the City of David. 11David had reigned over Israel for forty years, seven of them in Hebron and thirty-three in Jerusalem. 12Solomon became king and sat on the throne of David his father, and his kingdom was firmly established.

Solomon Establishes His Rule

13One day Adonijah, whose mother was Haggith, came to see Bathsheba, Solomon's mother. "Have you come with peaceful intentions?" she asked him.

"Yes," he said, "I come in peace. 14In fact, I have a favor to ask of you."

"What is it?" she asked.

15He replied, "As you know, the kingdom was rightfully mine; all Israel wanted me to be the next king. But the tables were turned, and the kingdom went to my brother instead; for that is the way the LORD wanted it. 16So now I have just one favor to ask of you. Please don't turn me down."

"What is it?" she asked.

17He replied, "Speak to King Solomon on my behalf, for I know he will do anything you request. Ask him to let me marry Abishag, the girl from Shunem."

18"All right," Bathsheba replied. "I will speak to the king for you."

19So Bathsheba went to King Solomon to speak on Adonijah's behalf. The king rose from

---

2:5a Or He murdered them during a time of peace as revenge for deaths they had caused in time of war. 2:5b As in some Greek and Old Latin manuscripts; Hebrew reads with the blood of war. 2:6 Hebrew don't let his white head go down to Sheol in peace. 2:9 Hebrew how to bring his white head down to Sheol in blood.

his throne to meet her, and he bowed down before her. When he sat down on his throne again, the king ordered that a throne be brought for his mother, and she sat at his right hand.

20"I have one small request to make of you," she said. "I hope you won't turn me down."

"What is it, my mother?" he asked. "You know I won't refuse you."

21"Then let your brother Adonijah marry Abishag, the girl from Shunem," she replied.

22"How can you possibly ask me to give Abishag to Adonijah?" King Solomon demanded. "You might as well ask me to give him the kingdom! You know that he is my older brother, and that he has Abiathar the priest and Joab son of Zeruiah on his side."

23Then King Solomon made a vow before the LORD: "May God strike me and even kill me if Adonijah has not sealed his fate with this request. 24The LORD has confirmed me and placed me on the throne of my father, David; he has established my dynasty as he promised. So as surely as the LORD lives, Adonijah will die this very day!" 25So King Solomon ordered Benaiah son of Jehoiada to execute him, and Adonijah was put to death.

26Then the king said to Abiathar the priest, "Go back to your home in Anathoth. You deserve to die, but I will not kill you now, because you carried the Ark of the Sovereign LORD for David my father and you shared all his hardships." 27So Solomon deposed Abiathar from his position as priest of the LORD, thereby fulfilling the prophecy the LORD had given at Shiloh concerning the descendants of Eli.

28Joab had not joined Absalom's earlier rebellion, but he had joined Adonijah's rebellion. So when Joab heard about Adonijah's death, he ran to the sacred tent of the LORD and grabbed on to the horns of the altar. 29When this was reported to King Solomon, he sent Benaiah son of Jehoiada to execute him.

30Benaiah went to the sacred tent of the LORD and said to Joab, "The king orders you to come out!"

But Joab answered, "No, I will die here."

So Benaiah returned to the king and told him what Joab had said.

31"Do as he said," the king replied. "Kill him there beside the altar and bury him. This will remove the guilt of Joab's senseless murders from me and from my father's family. 32The LORD will repay him* for the murders of two men who were more righteous and better than he. For my father knew nothing about the

2:32 Hebrew *will return his blood on his own head.*

deaths of Abner son of Ner, commander of the army of Israel, and of Amasa son of Jether, commander of the army of Judah. 33May their blood be on Joab and his descendants forever, and may the LORD grant peace forever to David, his descendants, his dynasty, and his throne."

34So Benaiah son of Jehoiada returned to the sacred tent and killed Joab, and he was buried at his home in the wilderness. 35Then the king appointed Benaiah to command the army in place of Joab, and he installed Zadok the priest to take the place of Abiathar.

36The king then sent for Shimei and told him, "Build a house here in Jerusalem and live there. But don't step outside the city to go anywhere else. 37On the day you so much as cross the Kidron Valley, you will surely die; and your blood will be on your own head."

38Shimei replied, "Your sentence is fair; I will do whatever my lord the king commands." So Shimei lived in Jerusalem for a long time.

39But three years later two of Shimei's slaves ran away to King Achish son of Maacah of Gath. When Shimei learned where they were, 40he saddled his donkey and went to Gath to search for them. When he found them, he brought them back to Jerusalem.

41Solomon heard that Shimei had left Jerusalem and had gone to Gath and returned. 42So the king sent for Shimei and demanded, "Didn't I make you swear by the LORD and warn you not to go anywhere else or you would surely die? And you replied, 'The sentence is fair; I will do as you say.' 43Then why haven't you kept your oath to the LORD and obeyed my command?"

44The king also said to Shimei, "You certainly remember all the wicked things you did to my father, David. May the LORD now bring that evil on your own head. 45But may I, King Solomon, receive the LORD's blessings, and may one of David's descendants always sit on this throne in the presence of the LORD." 46Then, at the king's command, Benaiah son of Jehoiada took Shimei outside and killed him.

So the kingdom was now firmly in Solomon's grip.

Solomon Asks for Wisdom

3 Solomon made an alliance with Pharaoh, the king of Egypt, and married one of his daughters. He brought her to live in the City of David until he could finish building his palace and the Temple of the LORD and the wall around the city. 2At that time the people

of Israel sacrificed their offerings at local places of worship, for a temple honoring the name of the LORD had not yet been built.

³Solomon loved the LORD and followed all the decrees of his father, David, except that Solomon, too, offered sacrifices and burned incense at the local places of worship. ⁴The most important of these places of worship was at Gibeon, so the king went there and sacrificed 1,000 burnt offerings. ⁵That night the LORD appeared to Solomon in a dream, and God said, "What do you want? Ask, and I will give it to you!"

⁶Solomon replied, "You showed great and faithful love to your servant my father, David, because he was honest and true and faithful to you. And you have continued to show this great and faithful love to him today by giving him a son to sit on his throne.

⁷"Now, O LORD my God, you have made me king instead of my father, David, but I am like a little child who doesn't know his way around. ⁸And here I am in the midst of your own chosen people, a nation so great and numerous they cannot be counted! ⁹Give me an understanding heart so that I can govern your people well and know the difference between right and wrong. For who by himself is able to govern this great people of yours?"

¹⁰The Lord was pleased that Solomon had asked for wisdom. ¹¹So God replied, "Because you have asked for wisdom in governing my people with justice and have not asked for a long life or wealth or the death of your enemies—¹²I will give you what you asked for! I will give you a wise and understanding heart such as no one else has had or ever will have! ¹³And I will also give you what you did not ask for—riches and fame! No other king in all the world will be compared to you for the rest of your life! ¹⁴And if you follow me and obey my decrees and my commands as your father, David, did, I will give you a long life."

¹⁵Then Solomon woke up and realized it had been a dream. He returned to Jerusalem and stood before the Ark of the Lord's Covenant, where he sacrificed burnt offerings and peace offerings. Then he invited all his officials to a great banquet.

Solomon Judges Wisely

¹⁶Some time later two prostitutes came to the king to have an argument settled. ¹⁷"Please, my lord," one of them began, "this woman and I live in the same house. I gave birth to a baby while she was with me in the house. ¹⁸Three days later this woman also had a baby. We were alone; there were only two of us in the house. ¹⁹"But her baby died during the night when she rolled over on it. ²⁰Then she got up in the night and took my son from beside me while I was asleep. She laid her dead child in my arms and took mine to sleep beside her. ²¹And in the morning when I tried to nurse my son, he was dead! But when I looked more closely in the morning light, I saw that it wasn't my son at all."

²²Then the other woman interrupted, "It certainly was your son, and the living child is mine."

"No," the first woman said, "the living child is mine, and the dead one is yours." And so they argued back and forth before the king.

²³Then the king said, "Let's get the facts straight. Both of you claim the living child is yours, and each says that the dead one belongs to the other. ²⁴All right, bring me a sword." So a sword was brought to the king.

²⁵Then he said, "Cut the living child in two, and give half to one woman and half to the other!"

²⁶Then the woman who was the real mother of the living child, and who loved him very much, cried out, "Oh no, my lord! Give her the child—please do not kill him!"

But the other woman said, "All right, he will be neither yours nor mine; divide him between us!"

²⁷Then the king said, "Do not kill the child, but give him to the woman who wants him to live, for she is his mother!"

²⁸When all Israel heard the king's decision, the people were in awe of the king, for they saw the wisdom God had given him for rendering justice.

Solomon's Officials and Governors

4 King Solomon now ruled over all Israel, ²and these were his high officials:

Azariah son of Zadok was the priest.
³ Elihoreph and Ahijah, the sons of Shisha, were court secretaries.
Jehoshaphat son of Ahilud was the royal historian.
⁴ Benaiah son of Jehoiada was commander of the army.
Zadok and Abiathar were priests.
⁵ Azariah son of Nathan was in charge of the district governors.
Zabud son of Nathan, a priest, was a trusted adviser to the king.

6 Ahishar was manager of the palace property.
Adoniram son of Abda was in charge of forced labor.

7 Solomon also had twelve district governors who were over all Israel. They were responsible for providing food for the king's household. Each of them arranged provisions for one month of the year. 8 These are the names of the twelve governors:

Ben-hur, in the hill country of Ephraim.
9 Ben-deker, in Makaz, Shaalbim, Beth-shemesh, and Elon-bethhanan.
10 Ben-hesed, in Arubboth, including Socoh and all the land of Hepher.
11 Ben-abinadab, in all of Naphoth-dor.* (He was married to Taphath, one of Solomon's daughters.)
12 Baana son of Ahilud, in Taanach and Megiddo, all of Beth-shan* near Zarethan below Jezreel, and all the territory from Beth-shan to Abel-meholah and over to Jokmeam.
13 Ben-geber, in Ramoth-gilead, including the Towns of Jair (named for Jair of the tribe of Manasseh*) in Gilead, and in the Argob region of Bashan, including sixty large fortified towns with bronze bars on their gates.
14 Ahinadab son of Iddo, in Mahanaim.
15 Ahimaaz, in Naphtali. (He was married to Basemath, another of Solomon's daughters.)
16 Baana son of Hushai, in Asher and in Aloth.
17 Jehoshaphat son of Paruah, in Issachar.
18 Shimei son of Ela, in Benjamin.
19 Geber son of Uri, in the land of Gilead,* including the territories of King Sihon of the Amorites and King Og of Bashan. There was also one governor over the land of Judah.*

Solomon's Prosperity and Wisdom

20 The people of Judah and Israel were as numerous as the sand on the seashore. They were very contented, with plenty to eat and drink. 21*Solomon ruled over all the kingdoms from the Euphrates River* in the north to the land of the Philistines and the border of Egypt in the south. The conquered peoples of those lands sent tribute money to Solomon and continued to serve him throughout his lifetime.

22 The daily food requirements for Solomon's palace were 150 bushels of choice flour and 300 bushels of meal*; 23 also 10 oxen from the fattening pens, 20 pasture-fed cattle, 100 sheep or goats, as well as deer, gazelles, roe deer, and choice poultry.*

24 Solomon's dominion extended over all the kingdoms west of the Euphrates River, from Tiphsah to Gaza. And there was peace on all his borders. 25 During the lifetime of Solomon, all of Judah and Israel lived in peace and safety. And from Dan in the north to Beersheba in the south, each family had its own home and garden.*

26 Solomon had 4,000* stalls for his chariot horses, and he had 12,000 horses.*

27 The district governors faithfully provided food for King Solomon and his court; each made sure nothing was lacking during the month assigned to him. 28 They also brought the necessary barley and straw for the royal horses in the stables.

29 God gave Solomon very great wisdom and understanding, and knowledge as vast as the sands of the seashore. 30 In fact, his wisdom exceeded that of all the wise men of the East and the wise men of Egypt. 31 He was wiser than anyone else, including Ethan the Ezrahite and the sons of Mahol—Heman, Calcol, and Darda. His fame spread throughout all the surrounding nations. 32 He composed some 3,000 proverbs and wrote 1,005 songs. 33 He could speak with authority about all kinds of plants, from the great cedar of Lebanon to the tiny hyssop that grows from cracks in a wall. He could also speak about animals, birds, small creatures, and fish. 34 And kings from every nation sent their ambassadors to listen to the wisdom of Solomon.

Preparations for Building the Temple

5 1*King Hiram of Tyre had always been a loyal friend of David. When Hiram learned that David's son Solomon was the new king of Israel, he sent ambassadors to congratulate him.

4:11 Hebrew *Naphath-dor*, a variant spelling of Naphoth-dor.   4:12 Hebrew *Beth-shean*, a variant spelling of Beth-shan; also in 4:12b.   4:13 Hebrew *Jair son of Manasseh*; compare 1 Chr 2:22.   4:19a Greek version reads *of Gad*; compare 4:13.   4:19b As in some Greek manuscripts; Hebrew lacks *of Judah*. The meaning of the Hebrew is uncertain.   4:21a Verses 4:21-34 are numbered 5:1-14 in Hebrew text.   4:21b Hebrew *the river*; also in 4:24.   4:22 Hebrew *30 cors* [6.6 kiloliters] *of choice flour and 60 cors* [13.2 kiloliters] *of meal*.   4:23 Or *and fattened geese*.   4:25 Hebrew *each family lived under its own grapevine and under its own fig tree*.   4:26a As in some Greek manuscripts (see also 2 Chr 9:25); Hebrew reads *40,000*.   4:26b Or *12,000 charioteers*.   5:1 Verses 5:1-18 are numbered 5:15-32 in Hebrew text.

²Then Solomon sent this message back to Hiram:

³"You know that my father, David, was not able to build a Temple to honor the name of the LORD his God because of the many wars waged against him by surrounding nations. He could not build until the LORD gave him victory over all his enemies. ⁴But now the LORD my God has given me peace on every side; I have no enemies, and all is well. ⁵So I am planning to build a Temple to honor the name of the LORD my God, just as he had instructed my father, David. For the LORD told him, 'Your son, whom I will place on your throne, will build the Temple to honor my name.'

⁶"Therefore, please command that cedars from Lebanon be cut for me. Let my men work alongside yours, and I will pay your men whatever wages you ask. As you know, there is no one among us who can cut timber like you Sidonians!"

⁷When Hiram received Solomon's message, he was very pleased and said, "Praise the LORD today for giving David a wise son to be king of the great nation of Israel." ⁸Then he sent this reply to Solomon:

"I have received your message, and I will supply all the cedar and cypress timber you need. ⁹My servants will bring the logs from the Lebanon mountains to the Mediterranean Sea* and make them into rafts and float them along the coast to whatever place you choose. Then we will break the rafts apart so you can carry the logs away. You can pay me by supplying me with food for my household."

¹⁰So Hiram supplied as much cedar and cypress timber as Solomon desired. ¹¹In return, Solomon sent him an annual payment of 100,000 bushels* of wheat for his household and 110,000 gallons* of pure olive oil. ¹²So the LORD gave wisdom to Solomon, just as he had promised. And Hiram and Solomon made a formal alliance of peace.

¹³Then King Solomon conscripted a labor force of 30,000 men from all Israel. ¹⁴He sent them to Lebanon in shifts, 10,000 every month, so that each man would be one month in Lebanon and two months at home. Adoniram was in charge of this labor force. ¹⁵Solomon also had 70,000 common laborers, 80,000 quarry workers in the hill country, ¹⁶and 3,600* foremen to supervise the work. ¹⁷At the king's command, they quarried large blocks of high-quality stone and shaped them to make the foundation of the Temple. ¹⁸Men from the city of Gebal helped Solomon's and Hiram's builders prepare the timber and stone for the Temple.

Solomon Builds the Temple

6 It was in midspring, in the month of Ziv,* during the fourth year of Solomon's reign, that he began to construct the Temple of the LORD. This was 480 years after the people of Israel were rescued from their slavery in the land of Egypt.

²The Temple that King Solomon built for the LORD was 90 feet long, 30 feet wide, and 45 feet high.* ³The entry room at the front of the Temple was 30 feet* wide, running across the entire width of the Temple. It projected outward 15 feet* from the front of the Temple. ⁴Solomon also made narrow recessed windows throughout the Temple.

⁵He built a complex of rooms against the outer walls of the Temple, all the way around the sides and rear of the building. ⁶The complex was three stories high, the bottom floor being 7½ feet wide, the second floor 9 feet wide, and the top floor 10½ feet wide.* The rooms were connected to the walls of the Temple by beams resting on ledges built out from the wall. So the beams were not inserted into the walls themselves.

⁷The stones used in the construction of the Temple were finished at the quarry, so there was no sound of hammer, ax, or any other iron tool at the building site.

⁸The entrance to the bottom floor* was on the south side of the Temple. There were winding stairs going up to the second floor, and another flight of stairs between the second and third floors. ⁹After completing the Temple structure, Solomon put in a ceiling made of cedar beams and planks. ¹⁰As already stated,

---

5:9 Hebrew *the sea.*   5:11a Hebrew *20,000 cors* [4,400 kiloliters].   5:11b As in Greek version, which reads *20,000 baths* [420 kiloliters] (see also 2 Chr 2:10); Hebrew reads *20 cors,* about 1,000 gallons or 4.4 kiloliters in volume.   5:16 As in some Greek manuscripts (see also 2 Chr 2:2, 18); Hebrew reads *3,300.*   6:1 Hebrew *It was in the month of Ziv, which is the second month.* This month of the ancient Hebrew lunar calendar usually occurs within the months of April and May.   6:2 Hebrew *60 cubits* [27.6 meters] *long, 20 cubits* [9.2 meters] *wide, and 30 cubits* [13.8 meters] *high.*   6:3a Hebrew *20 cubits* [9.2 meters]; also in 6:16, 20.   6:3b Hebrew *10 cubits* [4.6 meters].   6:6 Hebrew *the bottom floor being 5 cubits* [2.3 meters] *wide, the second floor 6 cubits* [2.8 meters] *wide, and the top floor 7 cubits* [3.2 meters] *wide.*   6:8 As in Greek version; Hebrew reads *middle floor.*

he built a complex of rooms along the sides of the building, attached to the Temple walls by cedar timbers. Each story of the complex was 7½ feet* high.

¹¹Then the LORD gave this message to Solomon: ¹²"Concerning this Temple you are building, if you keep all my decrees and regulations and obey all my commands, I will fulfill through you the promise I made to your father, David. ¹³I will live among the Israelites and will never abandon my people Israel."

The Temple's Interior

¹⁴So Solomon finished building the Temple. ¹⁵The entire inside, from floor to ceiling, was paneled with wood. He paneled the walls and ceilings with cedar, and he used planks of cypress for the floors. ¹⁶He partitioned off an inner sanctuary—the Most Holy Place—at the far end of the Temple. It was 30 feet deep and was paneled with cedar from floor to ceiling. ¹⁷The main room of the Temple, outside the Most Holy Place, was 60 feet* long. ¹⁸Cedar paneling completely covered the stone walls throughout the Temple, and the paneling was decorated with carvings of gourds and open flowers.

¹⁹He prepared the inner sanctuary at the far end of the Temple, where the Ark of the LORD's Covenant would be placed. ²⁰This inner sanctuary was 30 feet long, 30 feet wide, and 30 feet high. He overlaid the inside with solid gold. He also overlaid the altar made of cedar.* ²¹Then Solomon overlaid the rest of the Temple's interior with solid gold, and he made gold chains to protect the entrance* to the Most Holy Place. ²²So he finished overlaying the entire Temple with gold, including the altar that belonged to the Most Holy Place.

²³He made two cherubim of wild olive* wood, each 15 feet* tall, and placed them in the inner sanctuary. ²⁴The wingspan of each of the cherubim was 15 feet, each wing being 7½ feet* long. ²⁵The two cherubim were identical in shape and size; ²⁶each was 15 feet tall. ²⁷He placed them side by side in the inner sanctuary of the Temple. Their outspread wings reached from wall to wall, while their inner wings touched at the center of the room. ²⁸He overlaid the two cherubim with gold.

²⁹He decorated all the walls of the inner sanctuary and the main room with carvings of cherubim, palm trees, and open flowers. ³⁰He overlaid the floor in both rooms with gold.

³¹For the entrance to the inner sanctuary, he made double doors of wild olive wood with five-sided doorposts.* ³²These double doors were decorated with carvings of cherubim, palm trees, and open flowers. The doors, including the decorations of cherubim and palm trees, were overlaid with gold.

³³Then he made four-sided doorposts of wild olive wood for the entrance to the Temple. ³⁴There were two folding doors of cypress wood, and each door was hinged to fold back upon itself. ³⁵These doors were decorated with carvings of cherubim, palm trees, and open flowers—all overlaid evenly with gold.

³⁶The walls of the inner courtyard were built so that there was one layer of cedar beams between every three layers of finished stone.

³⁷The foundation of the LORD's Temple was laid in midspring, in the month of Ziv,* during the fourth year of Solomon's reign. ³⁸The entire building was completed in every detail by midautumn, in the month of Bul,* during the eleventh year of his reign. So it took seven years to build the Temple.

Solomon Builds His Palace

7 Solomon also built a palace for himself, and it took him thirteen years to complete the construction.

²One of Solomon's buildings was called the Palace of the Forest of Lebanon. It was 150 feet long, 75 feet wide, and 45 feet high.* There were four rows of cedar pillars, and great cedar beams rested on the pillars. ³The hall had a cedar roof. Above the beams on the pillars were forty-five side rooms,* arranged in three tiers of fifteen each. ⁴On each end of the long hall were three rows of windows facing each other. ⁵All the doorways and doorposts* had rectangular frames and were arranged in sets of three, facing each other.

⁶Solomon also built the Hall of Pillars, which was 75 feet long and 45 feet wide.* There was a porch in front, along with a canopy supported by pillars.

6:10 Hebrew 5 cubits [2.3 meters]. 6:17 Hebrew 40 cubits [18.4 meters]. 6:20 Or overlaid the altar with cedar. The meaning of the Hebrew is uncertain. 6:21 Or to draw curtains across. The meaning of the Hebrew is uncertain. 6:23a Or pine; Hebrew reads oil tree; also in 6:31, 33. 6:23b Hebrew 10 cubits [4.6 meters]; also in 6:24, 26. 6:24 Hebrew 5 cubits [2.3 meters]. 6:31 The meaning of the Hebrew is uncertain. 6:37 Hebrew was laid in the month of Ziv. This month of the ancient Hebrew lunar calendar usually occurs within the months of April and May. 6:38 Hebrew by the month of Bul, which is the eighth month. This month of the ancient Hebrew lunar calendar usually occurs within the months of October and November. 7:2 Hebrew 100 cubits [46 meters] long, 50 cubits [23 meters] wide, and 30 cubits [13.8 meters] high. 7:3 Or 45 rafters, or 45 beams, or 45 pillars. The architectural details in 7:2-6 can be interpreted in many different ways. 7:5 Greek version reads windows. 7:6 Hebrew 50 cubits [23 meters] long and 30 cubits [13.8 meters] wide.

7Solomon also built the throne room, known as the Hall of Justice, where he sat to hear legal matters. It was paneled with cedar from floor to ceiling.* 8Solomon's living quarters surrounded a courtyard behind this hall, and they were constructed the same way. He also built similar living quarters for Pharaoh's daughter, whom he had married.

9From foundation to eaves, all these buildings were built from huge blocks of high-quality stone, cut with saws and trimmed to exact measure on all sides. 10Some of the huge foundation stones were 15 feet long, and some were 12 feet* long. 11The blocks of high-quality stone used in the walls were also cut to measure, and cedar beams were also used. 12The walls of the great courtyard were built so that there was one layer of cedar beams between every three layers of finished stone, just like the walls of the inner courtyard of the LORD's Temple with its entry room.

Furnishings for the Temple

13King Solomon then asked for a man named Huram* to come from Tyre. 14He was half Israelite, since his mother was a widow from the tribe of Naphtali, and his father had been a craftsman in bronze from Tyre. Huram was extremely skillful and talented in any work in bronze, and he came to do all the metal work for King Solomon.

15Huram cast two bronze pillars, each 27 feet tall and 18 feet in circumference.* 16For the tops of the pillars he cast bronze capitals, each 7½ feet* tall. 17Each capital was decorated with seven sets of latticework and interwoven chains. 18He also encircled the latticework with two rows of pomegranates to decorate the capitals over the pillars. 19The capitals on the columns inside the entry room were shaped like water lilies, and they were six feet* tall. 20The capitals on the two pillars had 200 pomegranates in two rows around them, beside the rounded surface next to the latticework. 21Huram set the pillars at the entrance of the Temple, one toward the south and one toward the north. He named the one on the south Jakin, and the one on the north Boaz.* 22The capitals on the pillars were shaped like water lilies. And so the work on the pillars was finished.

23Then Huram cast a great round basin, 15 feet across from rim to rim, called the Sea. It was 7½ feet deep and about 45 feet in circumference.* 24It was encircled just below its rim by two rows of decorative gourds. There were about six gourds per foot* all the way around, and they were cast as part of the basin.

25The Sea was placed on a base of twelve bronze oxen,* all facing outward. Three faced north, three faced west, three faced south, and three faced east, and the Sea rested on them. 26The walls of the Sea were about three inches* thick, and its rim flared out like a cup and resembled a water lily blossom. It could hold about 11,000 gallons* of water.

27Huram also made ten bronze water carts, each 6 feet long, 6 feet wide, and 4½ feet tall.* 28They were constructed with side panels braced with crossbars. 29Both the panels and the crossbars were decorated with carved lions, oxen, and cherubim. Above and below the lions and oxen were wreath decorations. 30Each of these carts had four bronze wheels and bronze axles. There were supporting posts for the bronze basins at the corners of the carts; these supports were decorated on each side with carvings of wreaths. 31The top of each cart had a rounded frame for the basin. It projected 1½ feet* above the cart's top like a round pedestal, and its opening was 2¼ feet* across; it was decorated on the outside with carvings of wreaths. The panels of the carts were square, not round. 32Under the panels were four wheels that were connected to axles that had been cast as one unit with the cart. The wheels were 2¼ feet in diameter 33and were similar to chariot wheels. The axles, spokes, rims, and hubs were all cast from molten bronze.

34There were handles at each of the four corners of the carts, and these, too, were cast as one unit with the cart. 35Around the top of each cart was a rim nine inches wide.* The corner supports and side panels were cast as one unit with the cart. 36Carvings of cherubim, lions, and palm trees decorated the panels and corner supports wherever there was room, and there

---

7:7 As in Syriac version and Latin Vulgate; Hebrew reads *from floor to floor.*   7:10 Hebrew *10 cubits* [4.6 meters] . . . *8 cubits* [3.7 meters].   7:13 Hebrew *Hiram* (also in 7:40, 45); compare 2 Chr 2:13. This is not the same person mentioned in 5:1.   7:15 Hebrew *18 cubits* [8.3 meters] *tall and 12 cubits* [5.5 meters] *in circumference.*   7:16 Hebrew *5 cubits* [2.3 meters].   7:19 Hebrew *4 cubits* [1.8 meters]; also in 7:38.   7:21 *Jakin* probably means "he establishes"; *Boaz* probably means "in him is strength."   7:23 Hebrew *10 cubits* [4.6 meters] *across. . . . 5 cubits* [2.3 meters] *deep and 30 cubits* [13.8 meters] *in circumference.*   7:24 Or *20 gourds per meter*; Hebrew reads *10 per cubit.*   7:25 Hebrew *12 oxen*; compare 2 Kgs 16:17, which specifies *bronze oxen.*   7:26a Hebrew *a handbreadth* [8 centimeters].   7:26b Hebrew *2,000 baths* [42 kiloliters].   7:27 Hebrew *4 cubits* [1.8 meters] *long, 4 cubits wide, and 3 cubits* [1.4 meters] *high.*   7:31a Hebrew *a cubit* [46 centimeters].   7:31b Hebrew *1½ cubits* [69 centimeters]; also in 7:32.   7:35 Hebrew *half a cubit wide* [23 centimeters].

were wreaths all around. 37All ten water carts were the same size and were made alike, for each was cast from the same mold.

38Huram also made ten smaller bronze basins, one for each cart. Each basin was six feet across and could hold 220 gallons* of water. 39He set five water carts on the south side of the Temple and five on the north side. The great bronze basin called the Sea was placed near the southeast corner of the Temple. 40He also made the necessary washbasins, shovels, and bowls.

So at last Huram completed everything King Solomon had assigned him to make for the Temple of the LORD:

41 the two pillars;
   the two bowl-shaped capitals on top of the pillars;
   the two networks of interwoven chains that decorated the capitals;
42 the 400 pomegranates that hung from the chains on the capitals (two rows of pomegranates for each of the chain networks that decorated the capitals on top of the pillars);
43 the ten water carts holding the ten basins;
44 the Sea and the twelve oxen under it;
45 the ash buckets, the shovels, and the bowls.

Huram made all these things of burnished bronze for the Temple of the LORD, just as King Solomon had directed. 46The king had them cast in clay molds in the Jordan Valley between Succoth and Zarethan. 47Solomon did not weigh all these things because there were so many; the weight of the bronze could not be measured.

48Solomon also made all the furnishings of the Temple of the LORD:

   the gold altar;
   the gold table for the Bread of the Presence;
49 the lampstands of solid gold, five on the south and five on the north, in front of the Most Holy Place;
   the flower decorations, lamps, and tongs—all of gold;
50 the small bowls, lamp snuffers, bowls, ladles, and incense burners—all of solid gold;

the doors for the entrances to the Most Holy Place and the main room of the Temple, with their fronts overlaid with gold.

51So King Solomon finished all his work on the Temple of the LORD. Then he brought all the gifts his father, David, had dedicated—the silver, the gold, and the various articles—and he stored them in the treasuries of the LORD's Temple.

The Ark Brought to the Temple

8 Solomon then summoned to Jerusalem the elders of Israel and all the heads of the tribes—the leaders of the ancestral families of the Israelites. They were to bring the Ark of the LORD's Covenant to the Temple from its location in the City of David, also known as Zion. 2So all the men of Israel assembled before King Solomon at the annual Festival of Shelters, which is held in early autumn in the month of Ethanim.*

3When all the elders of Israel arrived, the priests picked up the Ark. 4The priests and Levites brought up the Ark of the LORD along with the special tent* and all the sacred items that had been in it. 5There, before the Ark, King Solomon and the entire community of Israel sacrificed so many sheep, goats, and cattle that no one could keep count!

6Then the priests carried the Ark of the LORD's Covenant into the inner sanctuary of the Temple—the Most Holy Place—and placed it beneath the wings of the cherubim. 7The cherubim spread their wings over the Ark, forming a canopy over the Ark and its carrying poles. 8These poles were so long that their ends could be seen from the Holy Place, which is in front of the Most Holy Place, but not from the outside. They are still there to this day. 9Nothing was in the Ark except the two stone tablets that Moses had placed in it at Mount Sinai,* where the LORD made a covenant with the people of Israel when they left the land of Egypt.

10When the priests came out of the Holy Place, a thick cloud filled the Temple of the LORD. 11The priests could not continue their service because of the cloud, for the glorious presence of the LORD filled the Temple of the LORD.

7:38 Hebrew 40 baths [840 liters].   8:2 Hebrew at the festival in the month Ethanim, which is the seventh month. The Festival of Shelters began on the fifteenth day of the seventh month of the ancient Hebrew lunar calendar. This day occurred in late September, October, or early November.   8:4 Hebrew the Tent of Meeting; i.e., the tent mentioned in 2 Sam 6:17 and 1 Chr 16:1.   8:9 Hebrew at Horeb, another name for Sinai.

Solomon Praises the LORD

12Then Solomon prayed, "O LORD, you have said that you would live in a thick cloud of darkness. 13Now I have built a glorious Temple for you, a place where you can live forever!*"

14Then the king turned around to the entire community of Israel standing before him and gave this blessing: 15"Praise the LORD, the God of Israel, who has kept the promise he made to my father, David. For he told my father, 16'From the day I brought my people Israel out of Egypt, I have never chosen a city among any of the tribes of Israel as the place where a Temple should be built to honor my name. But I have chosen David to be king over my people Israel.'"

17Then Solomon said, "My father, David, wanted to build this Temple to honor the name of the LORD, the God of Israel. 18But the LORD told him, 'You wanted to build the Temple to honor my name. Your intention is good, 19but you are not the one to do it. One of your own sons will build the Temple to honor me.'

20"And now the LORD has fulfilled the promise he made, for I have become king in my father's place, and now I sit on the throne of Israel, just as the LORD promised. I have built this Temple to honor the name of the LORD, the God of Israel. 21And I have prepared a place there for the Ark, which contains the covenant that the LORD made with our ancestors when he brought them out of Egypt."

Solomon's Prayer of Dedication

22Then Solomon stood before the altar of the LORD in front of the entire community of Israel. He lifted his hands toward heaven, 23and he prayed,

"O LORD, God of Israel, there is no God like you in all of heaven above or on the earth below. You keep your covenant and show unfailing love to all who walk before you in wholehearted devotion. 24You have kept your promise to your servant David, my father. You made that promise with your own mouth, and with your own hands you have fulfilled it today.

25"And now, O LORD, God of Israel, carry out the additional promise you made to your servant David, my father. For you said to him, 'If your descendants guard their behavior and faithfully follow me as you have done, one of them will always sit on the throne of Israel.' 26Now, O God of

Israel, fulfill this promise to your servant David, my father.

27"But will God really live on earth? Why, even the highest heavens cannot contain you. How much less this Temple I have built! 28Nevertheless, listen to my prayer and my plea, O LORD my God. Hear the cry and the prayer that your servant is making to you today. 29May you watch over this Temple night and day, this place where you have said, 'My name will be there.' May you always hear the prayers I make toward this place. 30May you hear the humble and earnest requests from me and your people Israel when we pray toward this place. Yes, hear us from heaven where you live, and when you hear, forgive.

31"If someone wrongs another person and is required to take an oath of innocence in front of your altar in this Temple, 32then hear from heaven and judge between your servants—the accuser and the accused. Punish the guilty as they deserve. Acquit the innocent because of their innocence.

33"If your people Israel are defeated by their enemies because they have sinned against you, and if they turn to you and acknowledge your name and pray to you here in this Temple, 34then hear from heaven and forgive the sin of your people Israel and return them to this land you gave their ancestors.

35"If the skies are shut up and there is no rain because your people have sinned against you, and if they pray toward this Temple and acknowledge your name and turn from their sins because you have punished them, 36then hear from heaven and forgive the sins of your servants, your people Israel. Teach them to follow the right path, and send rain on your land that you have given to your people as their special possession.

37"If there is a famine in the land or a plague or crop disease or attacks of locusts or caterpillars, or if your people's enemies are in the land besieging their towns—whatever disaster or disease there is—38and if your people Israel pray about their troubles, raising their hands toward this Temple, 39then hear from heaven where you live, and forgive. Give your people what their actions deserve, for you alone know each human heart. 40Then

8:13 Some Greek texts add the line *Is this not written in the Book of Jashar?*

they will fear you as long as they live in the land you gave to our ancestors.

⁴¹"In the future, foreigners who do not belong to your people Israel will hear of you. They will come from distant lands because of your name, ⁴²for they will hear of your great name and your strong hand and your powerful arm. And when they pray toward this Temple, ⁴³then hear from heaven where you live, and grant what they ask of you. In this way, all the people of the earth will come to know and fear you, just as your own people Israel do. They, too, will know that this Temple I have built honors your name.

⁴⁴"If your people go out where you send them to fight their enemies, and if they pray to the LORD by turning toward this city you have chosen and toward this Temple I have built to honor your name, ⁴⁵then hear their prayers from heaven and uphold their cause.

⁴⁶"If they sin against you—and who has never sinned?—you might become angry with them and let their enemies conquer them and take them captive to their land far away or near. ⁴⁷But in that land of exile, they might turn to you in repentance and pray, 'We have sinned, done evil, and acted wickedly.' ⁴⁸If they turn to you with their whole heart and soul in the land of their enemies and pray toward the land you gave to their ancestors—toward this city you have chosen, and toward this Temple I have built to honor your name—⁴⁹then hear their prayers and their petition from heaven where you live, and uphold their cause. ⁵⁰Forgive your people who have sinned against you. Forgive all the offenses they have committed against you. Make their captors merciful to them, ⁵¹for they are your people—your special possession—whom you brought out of the iron-smelting furnace of Egypt.

⁵²"May your eyes be open to my requests and to the requests of your people Israel. May you hear and answer them whenever they cry out to you. ⁵³For when you brought our ancestors out of Egypt, O Sovereign LORD, you told your servant Moses that you had set Israel apart from all the nations of the earth to be your own special possession."

The Dedication of the Temple

⁵⁴When Solomon finished making these prayers and petitions to the LORD, he stood up in front of the altar of the LORD, where he had been kneeling with his hands raised toward heaven. ⁵⁵He stood and in a loud voice blessed the entire congregation of Israel:

⁵⁶"Praise the LORD who has given rest to his people Israel, just as he promised. Not one word has failed of all the wonderful promises he gave through his servant Moses. ⁵⁷May the LORD our God be with us as he was with our ancestors; may he never leave us or abandon us. ⁵⁸May he give us the desire to do his will in everything and to obey all the commands, decrees, and regulations that he gave our ancestors. ⁵⁹And may these words that I have prayed in the presence of the LORD be before him constantly, day and night, so that the LORD our God may give justice to me and to his people Israel, according to each day's needs. ⁶⁰Then people all over the earth will know that the LORD alone is God and there is no other. ⁶¹And may you be completely faithful to the LORD our God. May you always obey his decrees and commands, just as you are doing today."

⁶²Then the king and all Israel with him offered sacrifices to the LORD. ⁶³Solomon offered to the LORD a peace offering of 22,000 cattle and 120,000 sheep and goats. And so the king and all the people of Israel dedicated the Temple of the LORD.

⁶⁴That same day the king consecrated the central area of the courtyard in front of the LORD's Temple. He offered burnt offerings, grain offerings, and the fat of peace offerings there, because the bronze altar in the LORD's presence was too small to hold all the burnt offerings, grain offerings, and the fat of the peace offerings.

⁶⁵Then Solomon and all Israel celebrated the Festival of Shelters* in the presence of the LORD our God. A large congregation had gathered from as far away as Lebo-hamath in the north and the Brook of Egypt in the south. The celebration went on for fourteen days in all—seven days for the dedication of the altar and seven days for the Festival of Shelters.* ⁶⁶After the festival was over,* Solomon sent the people home. They blessed the king and went to their homes joyful and glad because the LORD had been good to his servant David and to his people Israel.

8:65a Hebrew *the festival;* see note on 8:2.   8:65b Hebrew *seven days and seven days, fourteen days;* compare parallel text at 2 Chr 7:8-10.   8:66 Hebrew *On the eighth day,* probably referring to the day following the seven-day Festival of Shelters; compare parallel text at 2 Chr 7:9-10.

The LORD's Response to Solomon

9 So Solomon finished building the Temple of the LORD, as well as the royal palace. He completed everything he had planned to do. ²Then the LORD appeared to Solomon a second time, as he had done before at Gibeon. ³The LORD said to him,

"I have heard your prayer and your petition. I have set this Temple apart to be holy—this place you have built where my name will be honored forever. I will always watch over it, for it is dear to my heart.

⁴"As for you, if you will follow me with integrity and godliness, as David your father did, obeying all my commands, decrees, and regulations, ⁵then I will establish the throne of your dynasty over Israel forever. For I made this promise to your father, David: 'One of your descendants will always sit on the throne of Israel.'

⁶"But if you or your descendants abandon me and disobey the commands and decrees I have given you, and if you serve and worship other gods, ⁷then I will uproot Israel from this land that I have given them. I will reject this Temple that I have made holy to honor my name. I will make Israel an object of mockery and ridicule among the nations. ⁸And though this Temple is impressive now, all who pass by will be appalled and will gasp in horror. They will ask, 'Why did the LORD do such terrible things to this land and to this Temple?'

⁹"And the answer will be, 'Because his people abandoned the LORD their God, who brought their ancestors out of Egypt, and they worshiped other gods instead and bowed down to them. That is why the LORD has brought all these disasters on them.'"

Solomon's Agreement with Hiram

¹⁰It took Solomon twenty years to build the LORD's Temple and his own royal palace. At the end of that time, ¹¹he gave twenty towns in the land of Galilee to King Hiram of Tyre. (Hiram had previously provided all the cedar and cypress timber and gold that Solomon had requested.) ¹²But when Hiram came from Tyre to see the towns Solomon had given him, he was not at all pleased with them. ¹³"What kind of towns are these, my brother?" he asked. So Hiram called that area Cabul (which means "worthless"), as it is still known today. ¹⁴Nevertheless, Hiram paid* Solomon 9,000 pounds* of gold.

Solomon's Many Achievements

¹⁵This is the account of the forced labor that King Solomon conscripted to build the LORD's Temple, the royal palace, the supporting terraces,* the wall of Jerusalem, and the cities of Hazor, Megiddo, and Gezer. ¹⁶(Pharaoh, the king of Egypt, had attacked and captured Gezer, killing the Canaanite population and burning it down. He gave the city to his daughter as a wedding gift when she married Solomon. ¹⁷So Solomon rebuilt the city of Gezer.) He also built up the towns of Lower Bethhoron, ¹⁸Baalath, and Tamar* in the wilderness within his land. ¹⁹He built towns as supply centers and constructed towns where his chariots and horses* could be stationed. He built everything he desired in Jerusalem and Lebanon and throughout his entire realm.

²⁰There were still some people living in the land who were not Israelites, including Amorites, Hittites, Perizzites, Hivites, and Jebusites. ²¹These were descendants of the nations whom the people of Israel had not completely destroyed.* So Solomon conscripted them as slaves, and they serve as forced laborers to this day. ²²But Solomon did not conscript any of the Israelites for forced labor. Instead, he assigned them to serve as fighting men, government officials, officers and captains in his army, commanders of his chariots, and charioteers. ²³Solomon appointed 550 of them to supervise the people working on his various projects.

²⁴Solomon moved his wife, Pharaoh's daughter, from the City of David to the new palace he had built for her. Then he constructed the supporting terraces.

²⁵Three times each year Solomon presented burnt offerings and peace offerings on the altar he had built for the LORD. He also burned incense to the LORD. And so he finished the work of building the Temple.

²⁶King Solomon also built a fleet of ships at Ezion-geber, a port near Elath* in the land of Edom, along the shore of the Red Sea.* ²⁷Hiram sent experienced crews of sailors to sail the

---

9:14a Or *For Hiram had paid.*   9:14b Hebrew *120 talents* [4,000 kilograms].   9:15 Hebrew *the millo;* also in 9:24. The meaning of the Hebrew is uncertain.   9:18 An alternate reading in the Masoretic Text reads *Tadmor.*   9:19 Or *and charioteers.* 9:21 The Hebrew term used here refers to the complete consecration of things or people to the LORD, either by destroying them or by giving them as an offering.   9:26a As in Greek version (see also 2 Kgs 14:22; 16:6); Hebrew reads *Eloth,* a variant spelling of Elath.   9:26b Hebrew *sea of reeds.*

ships with Solomon's men. ²⁸They sailed to Ophir and brought back to Solomon some sixteen tons* of gold.

Visit of the Queen of Sheba

10 When the queen of Sheba heard of Solomon's fame, which brought honor to the name of the LORD,* she came to test him with hard questions. ²She arrived in Jerusalem with a large group of attendants and a great caravan of camels loaded with spices, large quantities of gold, and precious jewels. When she met with Solomon, she talked with him about everything she had on her mind. ³Solomon had answers for all her questions; nothing was too hard for the king to explain to her. ⁴When the queen of Sheba realized how very wise Solomon was, and when she saw the palace he had built, ⁵she was overwhelmed. She was also amazed at the food on his tables, the organization of his officials and their splendid clothing, the cup-bearers, and the burnt offerings Solomon made at the Temple of the LORD.

⁶She exclaimed to the king, "Everything I heard in my country about your achievements* and wisdom is true! ⁷I didn't believe what was said until I arrived here and saw it with my own eyes. In fact, I had not heard the half of it! Your wisdom and prosperity are far beyond what I was told. ⁸How happy your people* must be! What a privilege for your officials to stand here day after day, listening to your wisdom! ⁹Praise the LORD your God, who delights in you and has placed you on the throne of Israel. Because of the LORD's eternal love for Israel, he has made you king so you can rule with justice and righteousness."

¹⁰Then she gave the king a gift of 9,000 pounds* of gold, great quantities of spices, and precious jewels. Never again were so many spices brought in as those the queen of Sheba gave to King Solomon.

¹¹(In addition, Hiram's ships brought gold from Ophir, and they also brought rich cargoes of red sandalwood* and precious jewels. ¹²The king used the sandalwood to make railings for the Temple of the LORD and the royal palace, and to construct lyres and harps for the musicians. Never before or since has there been such a supply of sandalwood.)

¹³King Solomon gave the queen of Sheba whatever she asked for, besides all the customary gifts he had so generously given. Then she and all her attendants returned to their own land.

Solomon's Wealth and Splendor

¹⁴Each year Solomon received about 25 tons* of gold. ¹⁵This did not include the additional revenue he received from merchants and traders, all the kings of Arabia, and the governors of the land.

¹⁶King Solomon made 200 large shields of hammered gold, each weighing more than fifteen pounds.* ¹⁷He also made 300 smaller shields of hammered gold, each weighing nearly four pounds.* The king placed these shields in the Palace of the Forest of Lebanon.

¹⁸Then the king made a huge throne, decorated with ivory and overlaid with fine gold. ¹⁹The throne had six steps and a rounded back. There were armrests on both sides of the seat, and the figure of a lion stood on each side of the throne. ²⁰There were also twelve other lions, one standing on each end of the six steps. No other throne in all the world could be compared with it!

²¹All of King Solomon's drinking cups were solid gold, as were all the utensils in the Palace of the Forest of Lebanon. They were not made of silver, for silver was considered worthless in Solomon's day!

²²The king had a fleet of trading ships of Tarshish that sailed with Hiram's fleet. Once every three years the ships returned, loaded with gold, silver, ivory, apes, and peacocks.*

²³So King Solomon became richer and wiser than any other king on earth. ²⁴People from every nation came to consult him and to hear the wisdom God had given him. ²⁵Year after year everyone who visited brought him gifts of silver and gold, clothing, weapons, spices, horses, and mules.

²⁶Solomon built up a huge force of chariots and horses.* He had 1,400 chariots and 12,000 horses. He stationed some of them in the chariot cities and some near him in Jerusalem. ²⁷The king made silver as plentiful in Jerusalem as stone. And valuable cedar timber was as common as the sycamore-fig trees that grow in the foothills of Judah.* ²⁸Solomon's horses were imported from Egypt* and from Cilicia*;

9:28 Hebrew *420 talents* [14 metric tons].   10:1 Or *which was due to the name of the* LORD. The meaning of the Hebrew is uncertain.
10:6 Hebrew *your words.*   10:8 Greek and Syriac versions and Latin Vulgate read *your wives.*   10:10 Hebrew *120 talents* [4,000 kilograms].   10:11 Hebrew *almug wood;* also in 10:12.   10:14 Hebrew *666 talents* [23 metric tons].   10:16 Hebrew *600* [shekels] *of gold* [6.8 kilograms].   10:17 Hebrew *3 minas* [1.8 kilograms].   10:22 Or *and baboons.*   10:26 Or *charioteers;* also in 10:26b.
10:27 Hebrew *the Shephelah.*   10:28a Possibly *Muzur,* a district near Cilicia; also in 10:29.   10:28b Hebrew *Kue,* probably another name for Cilicia.

the king's traders acquired them from Cilicia at the standard price. ²⁹At that time chariots from Egypt could be purchased for 600 pieces of silver,* and horses for 150 pieces of silver.* They were then exported to the kings of the Hittites and the kings of Aram.

Solomon's Many Wives

11 Now King Solomon loved many foreign women. Besides Pharaoh's daughter, he married women from Moab, Ammon, Edom, Sidon, and from among the Hittites. ²The LORD had clearly instructed the people of Israel, "You must not marry them, because they will turn your hearts to their gods." Yet Solomon insisted on loving them anyway. ³He had 700 wives of royal birth and 300 concubines. And in fact, they did turn his heart away from the LORD.

⁴In Solomon's old age, they turned his heart to worship other gods instead of being completely faithful to the LORD his God, as his father, David, had been. ⁵Solomon worshiped Ashtoreth, the goddess of the Sidonians, and Molech,* the detestable god of the Ammonites. ⁶In this way, Solomon did what was evil in the LORD's sight; he refused to follow the LORD completely, as his father, David, had done.

⁷On the Mount of Olives, east of Jerusalem,* he even built a pagan shrine for Chemosh, the detestable god of Moab, and another for Molech, the detestable god of the Ammonites. ⁸Solomon built such shrines for all his foreign wives to use for burning incense and sacrificing to their gods.

⁹The LORD was very angry with Solomon, for his heart had turned away from the LORD, the God of Israel, who had appeared to him twice. ¹⁰He had warned Solomon specifically about worshiping other gods, but Solomon did not listen to the LORD's command. ¹¹So now the LORD said to him, "Since you have not kept my covenant and have disobeyed my decrees, I will surely tear the kingdom away from you and give it to one of your servants. ¹²But for the sake of your father, David, I will not do this while you are still alive. I will take the kingdom away from your son. ¹³And even so, I will not take away the entire kingdom; I will let him be king of one tribe, for the sake of my servant David and for the sake of Jerusalem, my chosen city."

Solomon's Adversaries

¹⁴Then the LORD raised up Hadad the Edomite, a member of Edom's royal family, to be Solomon's adversary. ¹⁵Years before, David had defeated Edom. Joab, his army commander, had stayed to bury some of the Israelite soldiers who had died in battle. While there, they killed every male in Edom. ¹⁶Joab and the army of Israel had stayed there for six months, killing them.

¹⁷But Hadad and a few of his father's royal officials escaped and headed for Egypt. (Hadad was just a boy at the time.) ¹⁸They set out from Midian and went to Paran, where others joined them. Then they traveled to Egypt and went to Pharaoh, who gave them a home, food, and some land. ¹⁹Pharaoh grew very fond of Hadad, and he gave him his wife's sister in marriage—the sister of Queen Tahpenes. ²⁰She bore him a son named Genubath. Tahpenes raised him* in Pharaoh's palace among Pharaoh's own sons.

²¹When the news reached Hadad in Egypt that David and his commander Joab were both dead, he said to Pharaoh, "Let me return to my own country."

²²"Why?" Pharaoh asked him. "What do you lack here that makes you want to go home?"

"Nothing," he replied. "But even so, please let me return home."

²³God also raised up Rezon son of Eliada as Solomon's adversary. Rezon had fled from his master, King Hadadezer of Zobah, ²⁴and had become the leader of a gang of rebels. After David conquered Hadadezer, Rezon and his men fled to Damascus, where he became king. ²⁵Rezon was Israel's bitter adversary for the rest of Solomon's reign, and he made trouble, just as Hadad did. Rezon hated Israel intensely and continued to reign in Aram.

Jeroboam Rebels against Solomon

²⁶Another rebel leader was Jeroboam son of Nebat, one of Solomon's own officials. He came from the town of Zeredah in Ephraim, and his mother was Zeruah, a widow.

²⁷This is the story behind his rebellion. Solomon was rebuilding the supporting terraces* and repairing the walls of the city of his father, David. ²⁸Jeroboam was a very capable young man, and when Solomon saw how industrious he was, he put him in charge of the

---

10:29a Hebrew *600 [shekels] of silver*, about 15 pounds or 6.8 kilograms in weight.   **10:29b** Hebrew *150 [shekels]*, about 3.8 pounds or 1.7 kilograms in weight.   **11:5** Hebrew *Milcom*, a variant spelling of Molech; also in 11:33.   **11:7** Hebrew *On the mountain east of Jerusalem*.   **11:20** As in Greek version; Hebrew reads *weaned him*.   **11:27** Hebrew *the millo*. The meaning of the Hebrew is uncertain.

labor force from the tribes of Ephraim and Manasseh, the descendants of Joseph.

²⁹One day as Jeroboam was leaving Jerusalem, the prophet Ahijah from Shiloh met him along the way. Ahijah was wearing a new cloak. The two of them were alone in a field, ³⁰and Ahijah took hold of the new cloak he was wearing and tore it into twelve pieces. ³¹Then he said to Jeroboam, "Take ten of these pieces, for this is what the LORD, the God of Israel, says: 'I am about to tear the kingdom from the hand of Solomon, and I will give ten of the tribes to you! ³²But I will leave him one tribe for the sake of my servant David and for the sake of Jerusalem, which I have chosen out of all the tribes of Israel. ³³For Solomon has* abandoned me and worshiped Ashtoreth, the goddess of the Sidonians; Chemosh, the god of Moab; and Molech, the god of the Ammonites. He has not followed my ways and done what is pleasing in my sight. He has not obeyed my decrees and regulations as David his father did.

³⁴"'But I will not take the entire kingdom from Solomon at this time. For the sake of my servant David, the one whom I chose and who obeyed my commands and decrees, I will keep Solomon as leader for the rest of his life. ³⁵But I will take the kingdom away from his son and give ten of the tribes to you. ³⁶His son will have one tribe so that the descendants of David my servant will continue to reign, shining like a lamp in Jerusalem, the city I have chosen to be the place for my name. ³⁷And I will place you on the throne of Israel, and you will rule over all that your heart desires. ³⁸If you listen to what I tell you and follow my ways and do whatever I consider to be right, and if you obey my decrees and commands, as my servant David did, then I will always be with you. I will establish an enduring dynasty for you as I did for David, and I will give Israel to you. ³⁹Because of Solomon's sin I will punish the descendants of David—though not forever.'"

⁴⁰Solomon tried to kill Jeroboam, but he fled to King Shishak of Egypt and stayed there until Solomon died.

Summary of Solomon's Reign

⁴¹The rest of the events in Solomon's reign, including all his deeds and his wisdom, are recorded in *The Book of the Acts of Solomon.* ⁴²Solomon ruled in Jerusalem over all Israel for forty years. ⁴³When he died, he was buried in the City of David, named for his father. Then his son Rehoboam became the next king.

The Northern Tribes Revolt

12 Rehoboam went to Shechem, where all Israel had gathered to make him king. ²When Jeroboam son of Nebat heard of this, he returned from Egypt,* for he had fled to Egypt to escape from King Solomon. ³The leaders of Israel summoned him, and Jeroboam and the whole assembly of Israel went to speak with Rehoboam. ⁴"Your father was a hard master," they said. "Lighten the harsh labor demands and heavy taxes that your father imposed on us. Then we will be your loyal subjects."

⁵Rehoboam replied, "Give me three days to think this over. Then come back for my answer." So the people went away.

⁶Then King Rehoboam discussed the matter with the older men who had counseled his father, Solomon. "What is your advice?" he asked. "How should I answer these people?"

⁷The older counselors replied, "If you are willing to be a servant to these people today and give them a favorable answer, they will always be your loyal subjects."

⁸But Rehoboam rejected the advice of the older men and instead asked the opinion of the young men who had grown up with him and were now his advisers. ⁹"What is your advice?" he asked them. "How should I answer these people who want me to lighten the burdens imposed by my father?"

¹⁰The young men replied, "This is what you should tell those complainers who want a lighter burden: 'My little finger is thicker than my father's waist! ¹¹Yes, my father laid heavy burdens on you, but I'm going to make them even heavier! My father beat you with whips, but I will beat you with scorpions!'"

¹²Three days later Jeroboam and all the people returned to hear Rehoboam's decision, just as the king had ordered. ¹³But Rehoboam spoke harshly to the people, for he rejected the advice of the older counselors ¹⁴and followed the counsel of his younger advisers. He told the people, "My father laid heavy burdens on you, but I'm going to make them even heavier! My father beat you with whips, but I will beat you with scorpions!"

¹⁵So the king paid no attention to the people. This turn of events was the will of the LORD, for it fulfilled the LORD's message to Jeroboam

---

11:33 As in Greek, Syriac, and Latin Vulgate; Hebrew reads *For they have.*   12:2 As in Greek version and Latin Vulgate (see also 2 Chr 10:2); Hebrew reads *he lived in Egypt.*

son of Nebat through the prophet Ahijah from Shiloh.

16When all Israel realized that the king had refused to listen to them, they responded,

"Down with the dynasty of David!
We have no interest in the son of Jesse.
Back to your homes, O Israel!
Look out for your own house, O David!"

So the people of Israel returned home. 17But Rehoboam continued to rule over the Israelites who lived in the towns of Judah.

18King Rehoboam sent Adoniram,* who was in charge of forced labor, to restore order, but the people of Israel stoned him to death. When this news reached King Rehoboam, he quickly jumped into his chariot and fled to Jerusalem. 19And to this day the northern tribes of Israel have refused to be ruled by a descendant of David.

20When the people of Israel learned of Jeroboam's return from Egypt, they called an assembly and made him king over all Israel. So only the tribe of Judah remained loyal to the family of David.

Shemaiah's Prophecy

21When Rehoboam arrived at Jerusalem, he mobilized the men of Judah and the tribe of Benjamin—180,000 select troops—to fight against the men of Israel and to restore the kingdom to himself.

22But God said to Shemaiah, the man of God, 23"Say to Rehoboam son of Solomon, king of Judah, and to all the people of Judah and Benjamin, and to the rest of the people, 24'This is what the LORD says: Do not fight against your relatives, the Israelites. Go back home, for what has happened is my doing!'" So they obeyed the message of the LORD and went home, as the LORD had commanded.

Jeroboam Makes Gold Calves

25Jeroboam then built up the city of Shechem in the hill country of Ephraim, and it became his capital. Later he went and built up the town of Peniel.*

26Jeroboam thought to himself, "Unless I am careful, the kingdom will return to the dynasty of David. 27When these people go to Jerusalem to offer sacrifices at the Temple of the LORD, they will again give their allegiance to King Rehoboam of Judah. They will kill me and make him their king instead."

28So on the advice of his counselors, the king made two gold calves. He said to the people,* "It is too much trouble for you to worship in Jerusalem. Look, Israel, these are the gods who brought you out of Egypt!"

29He placed these calf idols in Bethel and in Dan—at either end of his kingdom. 30But this became a great sin, for the people worshiped the idols, traveling as far north as Dan to worship the one there.

31Jeroboam also erected buildings at the pagan shrines and ordained priests from the common people—those who were not from the priestly tribe of Levi. 32And Jeroboam instituted a religious festival in Bethel, held on the fifteenth day of the eighth month,* in imitation of the annual Festival of Shelters in Judah. There at Bethel he himself offered sacrifices to the calves he had made, and he appointed priests for the pagan shrines he had made. 33So on the fifteenth day of the eighth month, a day that he himself had designated, Jeroboam offered sacrifices on the altar at Bethel. He instituted a religious festival for Israel, and he went up to the altar to burn incense.

A Prophet Denounces Jeroboam

13 At the LORD's command, a man of God from Judah went to Bethel, arriving there just as Jeroboam was approaching the altar to burn incense. 2Then at the LORD's command, he shouted, "O altar, altar! This is what the LORD says: A child named Josiah will be born into the dynasty of David. On you he will sacrifice the priests from the pagan shrines who come here to burn incense, and human bones will be burned on you." 3That same day the man of God gave a sign to prove his message. He said, "The LORD has promised to give this sign: This altar will split apart, and its ashes will be poured out on the ground."

4When King Jeroboam heard the man of God speaking against the altar at Bethel, he pointed at him and shouted, "Seize that man!" But instantly the king's hand became paralyzed in that position, and he couldn't pull it back. 5At the same time a wide crack appeared in the altar, and the ashes poured out, just as the man of God had predicted in his message from the LORD.

6The king cried out to the man of God,

12:18 As in some Greek manuscripts and Syriac version (see also 4:6; 5:14); Hebrew reads *Adoram*.   12:25 Hebrew *Penuel,* a variant spelling of Peniel.   12:28 Hebrew *to them.*   12:32 This day of the ancient Hebrew lunar calendar occurred in late October or early November, exactly one month after the annual Festival of Shelters in Judah (see Lev 23:34).

"Please ask the LORD your God to restore my hand again!" So the man of God prayed to the LORD, and the king's hand was restored and he could move it again.

⁷Then the king said to the man of God, "Come to the palace with me and have something to eat, and I will give you a gift."

⁸But the man of God said to the king, "Even if you gave me half of everything you own, I would not go with you. I would not eat or drink anything in this place. ⁹For the LORD gave me this command: 'You must not eat or drink anything while you are there, and do not return to Judah by the same way you came.'" ¹⁰So he left Bethel and went home another way.

¹¹As it happened, there was an old prophet living in Bethel, and his sons* came home and told him what the man of God had done in Bethel that day. They also told their father what the man had said to the king. ¹²The old prophet asked them, "Which way did he go?" So they showed their father* which road the man of God had taken. ¹³"Quick, saddle the donkey," the old man said. So they saddled the donkey for him, and he mounted it.

¹⁴Then he rode after the man of God and found him sitting under a great tree. The old prophet asked him, "Are you the man of God who came from Judah?"

"Yes, I am," he replied.

¹⁵Then he said to the man of God, "Come home with me and eat some food."

¹⁶"No, I cannot," he replied. "I am not allowed to eat or drink anything here in this place. ¹⁷For the LORD gave me this command: 'You must not eat or drink anything while you are there, and do not return to Judah by the same way you came.'"

¹⁸But the old prophet answered, "I am a prophet, too, just as you are. And an angel gave me this command from the LORD: 'Bring him home with you so he can have something to eat and drink.'" But the old man was lying to him. ¹⁹So they went back together, and the man of God ate and drank at the prophet's home.

²⁰Then while they were sitting at the table, a command from the LORD came to the old prophet. ²¹He cried out to the man of God from Judah, "This is what the LORD says: You have defied the word of the LORD and have disobeyed the command the LORD your God gave you. ²²You came back to this place and ate and drank where he told you not to eat or drink. Because of this, your body will not be buried in the grave of your ancestors."

²³After the man of God had finished eating and drinking, the old prophet saddled his own donkey for him, ²⁴and the man of God started off again. But as he was traveling along, a lion came out and killed him. His body lay there on the road, with the donkey and the lion standing beside it. ²⁵People who passed by saw the body lying in the road and the lion standing beside it, and they went and reported it in Bethel, where the old prophet lived.

²⁶When the prophet heard the report, he said, "It is the man of God who disobeyed the LORD's command. The LORD has fulfilled his word by causing the lion to attack and kill him."

²⁷Then the prophet said to his sons, "Saddle a donkey for me." So they saddled a donkey, ²⁸and he went out and found the body lying in the road. The donkey and lion were still standing there beside it, for the lion had not eaten the body nor attacked the donkey. ²⁹So the prophet laid the body of the man of God on the donkey and took it back to the town to mourn over him and bury him. ³⁰He laid the body in his own grave, crying out in grief, "Oh, my brother!"

³¹Afterward the prophet said to his sons, "When I die, bury me in the grave where the man of God is buried. Lay my bones beside his bones. ³²For the message the LORD told him to proclaim against the altar in Bethel and against the pagan shrines in the towns of Samaria will certainly come true."

³³But even after this, Jeroboam did not turn from his evil ways. He continued to choose priests from the common people. He appointed anyone who wanted to become a priest for the pagan shrines. ³⁴This became a great sin and resulted in the utter destruction of Jeroboam's dynasty from the face of the earth.

Ahijah's Prophecy against Jeroboam

14 At that time Jeroboam's son Abijah became very sick. ²So Jeroboam told his wife, "Disguise yourself so that no one will recognize you as my wife. Then go to the prophet Ahijah at Shiloh—the man who told me I would become king. ³Take him a gift of ten loaves of bread, some cakes, and a jar of honey, and ask him what will happen to the boy."

⁴So Jeroboam's wife went to Ahijah's home at Shiloh. He was an old man now and could no longer see. ⁵But the LORD had told Ahijah, "Jeroboam's wife will come here, pretending to be someone else. She will ask you about her

13:11 As in Greek version; Hebrew reads *son.*   13:12 As in Greek version; Hebrew reads *They had seen.*

son, for he is very sick. Give her the answer I give you."

⁶So when Ahijah heard her footsteps at the door, he called out, "Come in, wife of Jeroboam! Why are you pretending to be someone else?" Then he told her, "I have bad news for you. ⁷Give your husband, Jeroboam, this message from the LORD, the God of Israel: 'I promoted you from the ranks of the common people and made you ruler over my people Israel. ⁸I ripped the kingdom away from the family of David and gave it to you. But you have not been like my servant David, who obeyed my commands and followed me with all his heart and always did whatever I wanted. ⁹You have done more evil than all who lived before you. You have made other gods for yourself and have made me furious with your gold calves. And since you have turned your back on me, ¹⁰I will bring disaster on your dynasty and will destroy every one of your male descendants, slave and free alike, anywhere in Israel. I will burn up your royal dynasty as one burns up trash until it is all gone. ¹¹The members of Jeroboam's family who die in the city will be eaten by dogs, and those who die in the field will be eaten by vultures. I, the LORD, have spoken.'"

¹²Then Ahijah said to Jeroboam's wife, "Go on home, and when you enter the city, the child will die. ¹³All Israel will mourn for him and bury him. He is the only member of your family who will have a proper burial, for this child is the only good thing that the LORD, the God of Israel, sees in the entire family of Jeroboam.

¹⁴"In addition, the LORD will raise up a king over Israel who will destroy the family of Jeroboam. This will happen today, even now! ¹⁵Then the LORD will shake Israel like a reed whipped about in a stream. He will uproot the people of Israel from this good land that he gave their ancestors and will scatter them beyond the Euphrates River,* for they have angered the LORD with the Asherah poles they have set up for worship. ¹⁶He will abandon Israel because Jeroboam sinned and made Israel sin along with him."

¹⁷So Jeroboam's wife returned to Tirzah, and the child died just as she walked through the door of her home. ¹⁸And all Israel buried him and mourned for him, as the LORD had promised through the prophet Ahijah.

¹⁹The rest of the events in Jeroboam's reign, including all his wars and how he ruled, are recorded in *The Book of the History of the Kings of Israel.* ²⁰Jeroboam reigned in Israel twenty-two years. When Jeroboam died, his son Nadab became the next king.

Rehoboam Rules in Judah

²¹Meanwhile, Rehoboam son of Solomon was king in Judah. He was forty-one years old when he became king, and he reigned seventeen years in Jerusalem, the city the LORD had chosen from among all the tribes of Israel as the place to honor his name. Rehoboam's mother was Naamah, an Ammonite woman.

²²During Rehoboam's reign, the people of Judah did what was evil in the LORD's sight, provoking his anger with their sin, for it was even worse than that of their ancestors. ²³For they also built for themselves pagan shrines and set up sacred pillars and Asherah poles on every high hill and under every green tree. ²⁴There were even male and female shrine prostitutes throughout the land. The people imitated the detestable practices of the pagan nations the LORD had driven from the land ahead of the Israelites.

²⁵In the fifth year of King Rehoboam's reign, King Shishak of Egypt came up and attacked Jerusalem. ²⁶He ransacked the treasuries of the LORD's Temple and the royal palace; he stole everything, including all the gold shields Solomon had made. ²⁷King Rehoboam later replaced them with bronze shields as substitutes, and he entrusted them to the care of the commanders of the guard who protected the entrance to the royal palace. ²⁸Whenever the king went to the Temple of the LORD, the guards would also take the shields and then return them to the guardroom.

²⁹The rest of the events in Rehoboam's reign and everything he did are recorded in *The Book of the History of the Kings of Judah.* ³⁰There was constant war between Rehoboam and Jeroboam. ³¹When Rehoboam died, he was buried among his ancestors in the City of David. His mother was Naamah, an Ammonite woman. Then his son Abijam* became the next king.

Abijam Rules in Judah

15 Abijam* began to rule over Judah in the eighteenth year of Jeroboam's reign in Israel. ²He reigned in Jerusalem three years. His mother was Maacah, the granddaughter of Absalom.*

³He committed the same sins as his father before him, and he was not faithful to the LORD

14:15 Hebrew *the river.*   14:31 Also known as *Abijah.*   15:1 Also known as *Abijah.*   15:2 Hebrew *Abishalom* (also in 15:10), a variant spelling of Absalom; compare 2 Chr 11:20.

his God, as his ancestor David had been. ⁴But for David's sake, the LORD his God allowed his descendants to continue ruling, shining like a lamp, and he gave Abijam a son to rule after him in Jerusalem. ⁵For David had done what was pleasing in the LORD's sight and had obeyed the LORD's commands throughout his life, except in the affair concerning Uriah the Hittite.

⁶There was war between Abijam and Jeroboam* throughout Abijam's reign. ⁷The rest of the events in Abijam's reign and everything he did are recorded in *The Book of the History of the Kings of Judah*. There was constant war between Abijam and Jeroboam. ⁸When Abijam died, he was buried in the City of David. Then his son Asa became the next king.

Asa Rules in Judah

⁹Asa began to rule over Judah in the twentieth year of Jeroboam's reign in Israel. ¹⁰He reigned in Jerusalem forty-one years. His grandmother* was Maacah, the granddaughter of Absalom.

¹¹Asa did what was pleasing in the LORD's sight, as his ancestor David had done. ¹²He banished the male and female shrine prostitutes from the land and got rid of all the idols* his ancestors had made. ¹³He even deposed his grandmother Maacah from her position as queen mother because she had made an obscene Asherah pole. He cut down her obscene pole and burned it in the Kidron Valley. ¹⁴Although the pagan shrines were not removed, Asa's heart remained completely faithful to the LORD throughout his life. ¹⁵He brought into the Temple of the LORD the silver and gold and the various items that he and his father had dedicated.

¹⁶There was constant war between King Asa of Judah and King Baasha of Israel. ¹⁷King Baasha of Israel invaded Judah and fortified Ramah in order to prevent anyone from entering or leaving King Asa's territory in Judah.

¹⁸Asa responded by removing all the silver and gold that was left in the treasuries of the Temple of the LORD and the royal palace. He sent it with some of his officials to Ben-hadad son of Tabrimmon, son of Hezion, the king of Aram, who was ruling in Damascus, along with this message:

¹⁹"Let there be a treaty* between you and me like the one between your father and my father. See, I am sending you a gift of silver and gold. Break your treaty with King Baasha of Israel so that he will leave me alone."

²⁰Ben-hadad agreed to King Asa's request and sent the commanders of his army to attack the towns of Israel. They conquered the towns of Ijon, Dan, Abel-beth-maacah, and all Kinnereth, and all the land of Naphtali. ²¹As soon as Baasha of Israel heard what was happening, he abandoned his project of fortifying Ramah and withdrew to Tirzah. ²²Then King Asa sent an order throughout Judah, requiring that everyone, without exception, help to carry away the building stones and timbers that Baasha had been using to fortify Ramah. Asa used these materials to fortify the town of Geba in Benjamin and the town of Mizpah.

²³The rest of the events in Asa's reign—the extent of his power, everything he did, and the names of the cities he built—are recorded in *The Book of the History of the Kings of Judah*. In his old age his feet became diseased. ²⁴When Asa died, he was buried with his ancestors in the City of David.

Then Jehoshaphat, Asa's son, became the next king.

Nadab Rules in Israel

²⁵Nadab son of Jeroboam began to rule over Israel in the second year of King Asa's reign in Judah. He reigned in Israel two years. ²⁶But he did what was evil in the LORD's sight and followed the example of his father, continuing the sins that Jeroboam had led Israel to commit.

²⁷Then Baasha son of Ahijah, from the tribe of Issachar, plotted against Nadab and assassinated him while he and the Israelite army were laying siege to the Philistine town of Gibbethon. ²⁸Baasha killed Nadab in the third year of King Asa's reign in Judah, and he became the next king of Israel.

²⁹He immediately slaughtered all the descendants of King Jeroboam, so that not one of the royal family was left, just as the LORD had promised concerning Jeroboam by the prophet Ahijah from Shiloh. ³⁰This was done because Jeroboam had provoked the anger of the LORD, the God of Israel, by the sins he had committed and the sins he had led Israel to commit.

³¹The rest of the events in Nadab's reign and everything he did are recorded in *The Book of the History of the Kings of Israel*.

15:6 As in a few Hebrew and Greek manuscripts; most Hebrew manuscripts read *between Rehoboam and Jeroboam*.   15:10 Or *The queen mother;* Hebrew reads *His mother* (also in 15:13); compare 15:2.   15:12 The Hebrew term (literally *round things*) probably alludes to dung.   15:19 As in Greek version; Hebrew reads *There is a treaty*.

Baasha Rules in Israel

³²There was constant war between King Asa of Judah and King Baasha of Israel. ³³Baasha son of Ahijah began to rule over all Israel in the third year of King Asa's reign in Judah. Baasha reigned in Tirzah twenty-four years. ³⁴But he did what was evil in the LORD's sight and followed the example of Jeroboam, continuing the sins that Jeroboam had led Israel to commit.

16 This message from the LORD was delivered to King Baasha by the prophet Jehu son of Hanani: ²"I lifted you out of the dust to make you ruler of my people Israel, but you have followed the evil example of Jeroboam. You have provoked my anger by causing my people Israel to sin. ³So now I will destroy you and your family, just as I destroyed the descendants of Jeroboam son of Nebat. ⁴The members of Baasha's family who die in the city will be eaten by dogs, and those who die in the field will be eaten by vultures."

⁵The rest of the events in Baasha's reign and the extent of his power are recorded in *The Book of the History of the Kings of Israel.* ⁶When Baasha died, he was buried in Tirzah. Then his son Elah became the next king.

⁷The message from the LORD against Baasha and his family came through the prophet Jehu son of Hanani. It was delivered because Baasha had done what was evil in the LORD's sight (just as the family of Jeroboam had done), and also because Baasha had destroyed the family of Jeroboam. The LORD's anger was provoked by Baasha's sins.

Elah Rules in Israel

⁸Elah son of Baasha began to rule over Israel in the twenty-sixth year of King Asa's reign in Judah. He reigned in the city of Tirzah for two years.

⁹Then Zimri, who commanded half of the royal chariots, made plans to kill him. One day in Tirzah, Elah was getting drunk at the home of Arza, the supervisor of the palace. ¹⁰Zimri walked in and struck him down and killed him. This happened in the twenty-seventh year of King Asa's reign in Judah. Then Zimri became the next king.

¹¹Zimri immediately killed the entire royal family of Baasha, leaving him not even a single male child. He even destroyed distant relatives and friends. ¹²So Zimri destroyed the dynasty of Baasha as the LORD had promised through

the prophet Jehu. ¹³This happened because of all the sins Baasha and his son Elah had committed, and because of the sins they led Israel to commit. They provoked the anger of the LORD, the God of Israel, with their worthless idols.

¹⁴The rest of the events in Elah's reign and everything he did are recorded in *The Book of the History of the Kings of Israel.*

Zimri Rules in Israel

¹⁵Zimri began to rule over Israel in the twenty-seventh year of King Asa's reign in Judah, but his reign in Tirzah lasted only seven days. The army of Israel was then attacking the Philistine town of Gibbethon. ¹⁶When they heard that Zimri had committed treason and had assassinated the king, that very day they chose Omri, commander of the army, as the new king of Israel. ¹⁷So Omri led the entire army of Israel up from Gibbethon to attack Tirzah, Israel's capital. ¹⁸When Zimri saw that the city had been taken, he went into the citadel of the palace and burned it down over himself and died in the flames. ¹⁹For he, too, had done what was evil in the LORD's sight. He followed the example of Jeroboam in all the sins he had committed and led Israel to commit.

²⁰The rest of the events in Zimri's reign and his conspiracy are recorded in *The Book of the History of the Kings of Israel.*

Omri Rules in Israel

²¹But now the people of Israel were split into two factions. Half the people tried to make Tibni son of Ginath their king, while the other half supported Omri. ²²But Omri's supporters defeated the supporters of Tibni. So Tibni was killed, and Omri became the next king.

²³Omri began to rule over Israel in the thirty-first year of King Asa's reign in Judah. He reigned twelve years in all, six of them in Tirzah. ²⁴Then Omri bought the hill now known as Samaria from its owner, Shemer, for 150 pounds of silver.* He built a city on it and called the city Samaria in honor of Shemer.

²⁵But Omri did what was evil in the LORD's sight, even more than any of the kings before him. ²⁶He followed the example of Jeroboam son of Nebat in all the sins he had committed and led Israel to commit. The people provoked the anger of the LORD, the God of Israel, with their worthless idols.

²⁷The rest of the events in Omri's reign, the extent of his power, and everything he did are

16:24 Hebrew *for 2 talents* [68 kilograms] *of silver.*

recorded in *The Book of the History of the Kings of Israel.* 28When Omri died, he was buried in Samaria. Then his son Ahab became the next king.

Ahab Rules in Israel

29Ahab son of Omri began to rule over Israel in the thirty-eighth year of King Asa's reign in Judah. He reigned in Samaria twenty-two years. 30But Ahab son of Omri did what was evil in the LORD's sight, even more than any of the kings before him. 31And as though it were not enough to follow the sinful example of Jeroboam, he married Jezebel, the daughter of King Ethbaal of the Sidonians, and he began to bow down in worship of Baal. 32First Ahab built a temple and an altar for Baal in Samaria. 33Then he set up an Asherah pole. He did more to provoke the anger of the LORD, the God of Israel, than any of the other kings of Israel before him.

34It was during his reign that Hiel, a man from Bethel, rebuilt Jericho. When he laid its foundations, it cost him the life of his oldest son, Abiram. And when he completed it and set up its gates, it cost him the life of his youngest son, Segub.* This all happened according to the message from the LORD concerning Jericho spoken by Joshua son of Nun.

Elijah Fed by Ravens

17 Now Elijah, who was from Tishbe in Gilead, told King Ahab, "As surely as the LORD, the God of Israel, lives—the God I serve—there will be no dew or rain during the next few years until I give the word!"

2Then the LORD said to Elijah, 3"Go to the east and hide by Kerith Brook, near where it enters the Jordan River. 4Drink from the brook and eat what the ravens bring you, for I have commanded them to bring you food."

5So Elijah did as the LORD told him and camped beside Kerith Brook, east of the Jordan. 6The ravens brought him bread and meat each morning and evening, and he drank from the brook. 7But after a while the brook dried up, for there was no rainfall anywhere in the land.

The Widow at Zarephath

8Then the LORD said to Elijah, 9"Go and live in the village of Zarephath, near the city of Sidon. I have instructed a widow there to feed you."

10So he went to Zarephath. As he arrived at the gates of the village, he saw a widow gathering sticks, and he asked her, "Would you please bring me a little water in a cup?" 11As she was going to get it, he called to her, "Bring me a bite of bread, too."

12But she said, "I swear by the LORD your God that I don't have a single piece of bread in the house. And I have only a handful of flour left in the jar and a little cooking oil in the bottom of the jug. I was just gathering a few sticks to cook this last meal, and then my son and I will die."

13But Elijah said to her, "Don't be afraid! Go ahead and do just what you've said, but make a little bread for me first. Then use what's left to prepare a meal for yourself and your son. 14For this is what the LORD, the God of Israel, says: There will always be flour and olive oil left in your containers until the time when the LORD sends rain and the crops grow again!"

15So she did as Elijah said, and she and Elijah and her family continued to eat for many days. 16There was always enough flour and olive oil left in the containers, just as the LORD had promised through Elijah.

17Some time later the woman's son became sick. He grew worse and worse, and finally he died. 18Then she said to Elijah, "O man of God, what have you done to me? Have you come here to point out my sins and kill my son?"

19But Elijah replied, "Give me your son." And he took the child's body from her arms, carried him up the stairs to the room where he was staying, and laid the body on his bed. 20Then Elijah cried out to the LORD, "O LORD my God, why have you brought tragedy to this widow who has opened her home to me, causing her son to die?"

21And he stretched himself out over the child three times and cried out to the LORD, "O LORD my God, please let this child's life return to him." 22The LORD heard Elijah's prayer, and the life of the child returned, and he revived! 23Then Elijah brought him down from the upper room and gave him to his mother. "Look!" he said. "Your son is alive!"

24Then the woman told Elijah, "Now I know for sure that you are a man of God, and that the LORD truly speaks through you."

The Contest on Mount Carmel

18 Later on, in the third year of the drought, the LORD said to Elijah, "Go and present yourself to King Ahab. Tell him

16:34 An ancient Hebrew scribal tradition reads *He killed his oldest son when he laid its foundations, and he killed his youngest son when he set up its gates.*

that I will soon send rain!" ²So Elijah went to appear before Ahab.

Meanwhile, the famine had become very severe in Samaria. ³So Ahab summoned Obadiah, who was in charge of the palace. (Obadiah was a devoted follower of the LORD. ⁴Once when Jezebel had tried to kill all the LORD's prophets, Obadiah had hidden 100 of them in two caves. He put fifty prophets in each cave and supplied them with food and water.) ⁵Ahab said to Obadiah, "We must check every spring and valley in the land to see if we can find enough grass to save at least some of my horses and mules." ⁶So they divided the land between them. Ahab went one way by himself, and Obadiah went another way by himself.

⁷As Obadiah was walking along, he suddenly saw Elijah coming toward him. Obadiah recognized him at once and bowed low to the ground before him. "Is it really you, my lord Elijah?" he asked.

⁸"Yes, it is," Elijah replied. "Now go and tell your master, 'Elijah is here.'"

⁹"Oh, sir," Obadiah protested, "what harm have I done to you that you are sending me to my death at the hands of Ahab? ¹⁰For I swear by the LORD your God that the king has searched every nation and kingdom on earth from end to end to find you. And each time he was told, 'Elijah isn't here,' King Ahab forced the king of that nation to swear to the truth of his claim. ¹¹And now you say, 'Go and tell your master, "Elijah is here."' ¹²But as soon as I leave you, the Spirit of the LORD will carry you away to who knows where. When Ahab comes and cannot find you, he will kill me. Yet I have been a true servant of the LORD all my life. ¹³Has no one told you, my lord, about the time when Jezebel was trying to kill the LORD's prophets? I hid 100 of them in two caves and supplied them with food and water. ¹⁴And now you say, 'Go and tell your master, "Elijah is here."' Sir, if I do that, Ahab will certainly kill me."

¹⁵But Elijah said, "I swear by the LORD Almighty, in whose presence I stand, that I will present myself to Ahab this very day."

¹⁶So Obadiah went to tell Ahab that Elijah had come, and Ahab went out to meet Elijah. ¹⁷When Ahab saw him, he exclaimed, "So, is it really you, you troublemaker of Israel?"

¹⁸"I have made no trouble for Israel," Elijah replied. "You and your family are the troublemakers, for you have refused to obey the commands of the LORD and have worshiped the images of Baal instead. ¹⁹Now summon all Israel to join me at Mount Carmel, along with the 450 prophets of Baal and the 400 prophets of Asherah who are supported by Jezebel.*"

²⁰So Ahab summoned all the people of Israel and the prophets to Mount Carmel. ²¹Then Elijah stood in front of them and said, "How much longer will you waver, hobbling between two opinions? If the LORD is God, follow him! But if Baal is God, then follow him!" But the people were completely silent.

²²Then Elijah said to them, "I am the only prophet of the LORD who is left, but Baal has 450 prophets. ²³Now bring two bulls. The prophets of Baal may choose whichever one they wish and cut it into pieces and lay it on the wood of their altar, but without setting fire to it. I will prepare the other bull and lay it on the wood on the altar, but not set fire to it. ²⁴Then call on the name of your god, and I will call on the name of the LORD. The god who answers by setting fire to the wood is the true God!" And all the people agreed.

²⁵Then Elijah said to the prophets of Baal, "You go first, for there are many of you. Choose one of the bulls, and prepare it and call on the name of your god. But do not set fire to the wood."

²⁶So they prepared one of the bulls and placed it on the altar. Then they called on the name of Baal from morning until noontime, shouting, "O Baal, answer us!" But there was no reply of any kind. Then they danced, hobbling around the altar they had made.

²⁷About noontime Elijah began mocking them. "You'll have to shout louder," he scoffed, "for surely he is a god! Perhaps he is daydreaming, or is relieving himself.* Or maybe he is away on a trip, or is asleep and needs to be wakened!"

²⁸So they shouted louder, and following their normal custom, they cut themselves with knives and swords until the blood gushed out. ²⁹They raved all afternoon until the time of the evening sacrifice, but still there was no sound, no reply, no response.

³⁰Then Elijah called to the people, "Come over here!" They all crowded around him as he repaired the altar of the LORD that had been torn down. ³¹He took twelve stones, one to represent each of the tribes of Israel,* ³²and he used the stones to rebuild the altar in the name of the LORD. Then he dug a trench around the altar large enough to hold about three gallons.*

18:19 Hebrew who eat at Jezebel's table.   18:27 Or is busy somewhere else, or is engaged in business.   18:31 Hebrew each of the tribes of the sons of Jacob to whom the LORD had said, "Your name will be Israel."   18:32 Hebrew 2 seahs [14.6 liters] of seed.

³³He piled wood on the altar, cut the bull into pieces, and laid the pieces on the wood.*

Then he said, "Fill four large jars with water, and pour the water over the offering and the wood."

³⁴After they had done this, he said, "Do the same thing again!" And when they were finished, he said, "Now do it a third time!" So they did as he said, ³⁵and the water ran around the altar and even filled the trench.

³⁶At the usual time for offering the evening sacrifice, Elijah the prophet walked up to the altar and prayed, "O LORD, God of Abraham, Isaac, and Jacob,* prove today that you are God in Israel and that I am your servant. Prove that I have done all this at your command. ³⁷O LORD, answer me! Answer me so these people will know that you, O LORD, are God and that you have brought them back to yourself."

³⁸Immediately the fire of the LORD flashed down from heaven and burned up the young bull, the wood, the stones, and the dust. It even licked up all the water in the trench! ³⁹And when all the people saw it, they fell face down on the ground and cried out, "The LORD—he is God! Yes, the LORD is God!"

⁴⁰Then Elijah commanded, "Seize all the prophets of Baal. Don't let a single one escape!" So the people seized them all, and Elijah took them down to the Kishon Valley and killed them there.

Elijah Prays for Rain

⁴¹Then Elijah said to Ahab, "Go get something to eat and drink, for I hear a mighty rainstorm coming!"

⁴²So Ahab went to eat and drink. But Elijah climbed to the top of Mount Carmel and bowed low to the ground and prayed with his face between his knees.

⁴³Then he said to his servant, "Go and look out toward the sea."

The servant went and looked, then returned to Elijah and said, "I didn't see anything."

Seven times Elijah told him to go and look. ⁴⁴Finally the seventh time, his servant told him, "I saw a little cloud about the size of a man's hand rising from the sea."

Then Elijah shouted, "Hurry to Ahab and tell him, 'Climb into your chariot and go back home. If you don't hurry, the rain will stop you!'"

⁴⁵And soon the sky was black with clouds.

A heavy wind brought a terrific rainstorm, and Ahab left quickly for Jezreel. ⁴⁶Then the LORD gave special strength to Elijah. He tucked his cloak into his belt* and ran ahead of Ahab's chariot all the way to the entrance of Jezreel.

Elijah Flees to Sinai

19 When Ahab got home, he told Jezebel everything Elijah had done, including the way he had killed all the prophets of Baal. ²So Jezebel sent this message to Elijah: "May the gods strike me and even kill me if by this time tomorrow I have not killed you just as you killed them."

³Elijah was afraid and fled for his life. He went to Beersheba, a town in Judah, and he left his servant there. ⁴Then he went on alone into the wilderness, traveling all day. He sat down under a solitary broom tree and prayed that he might die. "I have had enough, LORD," he said. "Take my life, for I am no better than my ancestors who have already died."

⁵Then he lay down and slept under the broom tree. But as he was sleeping, an angel touched him and told him, "Get up and eat!" ⁶He looked around and there beside his head was some bread baked on hot stones and a jar of water! So he ate and drank and lay down again.

⁷Then the angel of the LORD came again and touched him and said, "Get up and eat some more, or the journey ahead will be too much for you."

⁸So he got up and ate and drank, and the food gave him enough strength to travel forty days and forty nights to Mount Sinai,* the mountain of God. ⁹There he came to a cave, where he spent the night.

The LORD Speaks to Elijah

But the LORD said to him, "What are you doing here, Elijah?"

¹⁰Elijah replied, "I have zealously served the LORD God Almighty. But the people of Israel have broken their covenant with you, torn down your altars, and killed every one of your prophets. I am the only one left, and now they are trying to kill me, too."

¹¹"Go out and stand before me on the mountain," the LORD told him. And as Elijah stood there, the LORD passed by, and a mighty windstorm hit the mountain. It was such a terrible blast that the rocks were torn loose, but the LORD was not in the wind. After the wind there

---

18:33 Verse 18:34 in the Hebrew text begins here. 18:36 Hebrew *and Israel.* The names "Jacob" and "Israel" are often interchanged throughout the Old Testament, referring sometimes to the individual patriarch and sometimes to the nation. 18:46 Hebrew *He bound up his loins.* 19:8 Hebrew *to Horeb,* another name for Sinai.

was an earthquake, but the LORD was not in the earthquake. [12]And after the earthquake there was a fire, but the LORD was not in the fire. And after the fire there was the sound of a gentle whisper. [13]When Elijah heard it, he wrapped his face in his cloak and went out and stood at the entrance of the cave.

And a voice said, "What are you doing here, Elijah?"

[14]He replied again, "I have zealously served the LORD God Almighty. But the people of Israel have broken their covenant with you, torn down your altars, and killed every one of your prophets. I am the only one left, and now they are trying to kill me, too."

[15]Then the LORD told him, "Go back the same way you came, and travel to the wilderness of Damascus. When you arrive there, anoint Hazael to be king of Aram. [16]Then anoint Jehu grandson of Nimshi* to be king of Israel, and anoint Elisha son of Shaphat from the town of Abel-meholah to replace you as my prophet. [17]Anyone who escapes from Hazael will be killed by Jehu, and those who escape Jehu will be killed by Elisha! [18]Yet I will preserve 7,000 others in Israel who have never bowed down to Baal or kissed him!"

The Call of Elisha

[19]So Elijah went and found Elisha son of Shaphat plowing a field. There were twelve teams of oxen in the field, and Elisha was plowing with the twelfth team. Elijah went over to him and threw his cloak across his shoulders and then walked away. [20]Elisha left the oxen standing there, ran after Elijah, and said to him, "First let me go and kiss my father and mother good-bye, and then I will go with you!"

Elijah replied, "Go on back, but think about what I have done to you."

[21]So Elisha returned to his oxen and slaughtered them. He used the wood from the plow to build a fire to roast their flesh. He passed around the meat to the townspeople, and they all ate. Then he went with Elijah as his assistant.

Ben-Hadad Attacks Samaria

20 About that time King Ben-hadad of Aram mobilized his army, supported by the chariots and horses of thirty-two allied kings. They went to besiege Samaria, the capital of Israel, and launched attacks against it. [2]Ben-hadad sent messengers into the city to relay this message to King Ahab of Israel: "This

is what Ben-hadad says: [3]'Your silver and gold are mine, and so are your wives and the best of your children!'"

[4]"All right, my lord the king," Israel's king replied. "All that I have is yours!"

[5]Soon Ben-hadad's messengers returned again and said, "This is what Ben-hadad says: 'I have already demanded that you give me your silver, gold, wives, and children. [6]But about this time tomorrow I will send my officials to search your palace and the homes of your officials. They will take away everything you consider valuable!'"

[7]Then Ahab summoned all the elders of the land and said to them, "Look how this man is stirring up trouble! I already agreed with his demand that I give him my wives and children and silver and gold."

[8]"Don't give in to any more demands," all the elders and the people advised.

[9]So Ahab told the messengers from Ben-hadad, "Say this to my lord the king: 'I will give you everything you asked for the first time, but I cannot accept this last demand of yours.'" So the messengers returned to Ben-hadad with that response.

[10]Then Ben-hadad sent this message to Ahab: "May the gods strike me and even kill me if there remains enough dust from Samaria to provide even a handful for each of my soldiers."

[11]The king of Israel sent back this answer: "A warrior putting on his sword for battle should not boast like a warrior who has already won."

[12]Ahab's reply reached Ben-hadad and the other kings as they were drinking in their tents.* "Prepare to attack!" Ben-hadad commanded his officers. So they prepared to attack the city.

Ahab's Victory over Ben-Hadad

[13]Then a certain prophet came to see King Ahab of Israel and told him, "This is what the LORD says: Do you see all these enemy forces? Today I will hand them all over to you. Then you will know that I am the LORD."

[14]Ahab asked, "How will he do it?"

And the prophet replied, "This is what the LORD says: The troops of the provincial commanders will do it."

"Should we attack first?" Ahab asked.

"Yes," the prophet answered.

[15]So Ahab mustered the troops of the 232 provincial commanders. Then he called out the rest of the army of Israel, some 7,000 men. [16]About noontime, as Ben-hadad and the thirty-two allied kings were still in their tents

19:16 Hebrew *descendant of Nimshi*; compare 2 Kgs 9:2, 14.   20:12 Or *in Succoth*; also in 20:16.

drinking themselves into a stupor, 17 the troops of the provincial commanders marched out of the city as the first contingent.

As they approached, Ben-hadad's scouts reported to him, "Some troops are coming from Samaria."

18 "Take them alive," Ben-hadad commanded, "whether they have come for peace or for war."

19 But Ahab's provincial commanders and the entire army had now come out to fight. 20 Each Israelite soldier killed his Aramean opponent, and suddenly the entire Aramean army panicked and fled. The Israelites chased them, but King Ben-hadad and a few of his charioteers escaped on horses. 21 However, the king of Israel destroyed the other horses and chariots and slaughtered the Arameans.

22 Afterward the prophet said to King Ahab, "Get ready for another attack. Begin making plans now, for the king of Aram will come back next spring.*"

Ben-Hadad's Second Attack

23 After their defeat, Ben-hadad's officers said to him, "The Israelite gods are gods of the hills; that is why they won. But we can beat them easily on the plains. 24 Only this time replace the kings with field commanders! 25 Recruit another army like the one you lost. Give us the same number of horses, chariots, and men, and we will fight against them on the plains. There's no doubt that we will beat them." So King Ben-hadad did as they suggested.

26 The following spring he called up the Aramean army and marched out against Israel, this time at Aphek. 27 Israel then mustered its army, set up supply lines, and marched out for battle. But the Israelite army looked like two little flocks of goats in comparison to the vast Aramean forces that filled the countryside!

28 Then the man of God went to the king of Israel and said, "This is what the LORD says: The Arameans have said, 'The LORD is a god of the hills and not of the plains.' So I will defeat this vast army for you. Then you will know that I am the LORD."

29 The two armies camped opposite each other for seven days, and on the seventh day the battle began. The Israelites killed 100,000 Aramean foot soldiers in one day. 30 The rest fled into the town of Aphek, but the wall fell on them and killed another 27,000. Ben-hadad fled into the town and hid in a secret room.

31 Ben-hadad's officers said to him, "Sir, we have heard that the kings of Israel are merciful. So let's humble ourselves by wearing burlap around our waists and putting ropes on our heads, and surrender to the king of Israel. Then perhaps he will let you live."

32 So they put on burlap and ropes, and they went to the king of Israel and begged, "Your servant Ben-hadad says, 'Please let me live!'"

The king of Israel responded, "Is he still alive? He is my brother!"

33 The men took this as a good sign and quickly picked up on his words. "Yes," they said, "your brother Ben-hadad!"

"Go and get him," the king of Israel told them. And when Ben-hadad arrived, Ahab invited him up into his chariot.

34 Ben-hadad told him, "I will give back the towns my father took from your father, and you may establish places of trade in Damascus, as my father did in Samaria."

Then Ahab said, "I will release you under these conditions." So they made a new treaty, and Ben-hadad was set free.

A Prophet Condemns Ahab

35 Meanwhile, the LORD instructed one of the group of prophets to say to another man, "Hit me!" But the man refused to hit the prophet.

36 Then the prophet told him, "Because you have not obeyed the voice of the LORD, a lion will kill you as soon as you leave me." And when he had gone, a lion did attack and kill him.

37 Then the prophet turned to another man and said, "Hit me!" So he struck the prophet and wounded him.

38 The prophet placed a bandage over his eyes to disguise himself and then waited beside the road for the king. 39 As the king passed by, the prophet called out to him, "Sir, I was in the thick of battle, and suddenly a man brought me a prisoner. He said, 'Guard this man; if for any reason he gets away, you will either die or pay a fine of seventy-five pounds* of silver!' 40 But while I was busy doing something else, the prisoner disappeared!"

"Well, it's your own fault," the king replied. "You have brought the judgment on yourself."

41 Then the prophet quickly pulled the bandage from his eyes, and the king of Israel recognized him as one of the prophets. 42 The prophet said to him, "This is what the LORD says: Because you have spared the man I said

20:22 Hebrew *at the turn of the year;* similarly in 20:26. The first day of the year in the ancient Hebrew lunar calendar occurred in March or April.   20:39 Hebrew *1 talent* [34 kilograms].

must be destroyed,* now you must die in his place, and your people will die instead of his people." ⁴³So the king of Israel went home to Samaria angry and sullen.

Naboth's Vineyard

21 Now there was a man named Naboth, from Jezreel, who owned a vineyard in Jezreel beside the palace of King Ahab of Samaria. ²One day Ahab said to Naboth, "Since your vineyard is so convenient to my palace, I would like to buy it to use as a vegetable garden. I will give you a better vineyard in exchange, or if you prefer, I will pay you for it."

³But Naboth replied, "The LORD forbid that I should give you the inheritance that was passed down by my ancestors."

⁴So Ahab went home angry and sullen because of Naboth's answer. The king went to bed with his face to the wall and refused to eat!

⁵"What's the matter?" his wife Jezebel asked him. "What's made you so upset that you're not eating?"

⁶"I asked Naboth to sell me his vineyard or trade it, but he refused!" Ahab told her.

⁷"Are you the king of Israel or not?" Jezebel demanded. "Get up and eat something, and don't worry about it. I'll get you Naboth's vineyard!"

⁸So she wrote letters in Ahab's name, sealed them with his seal, and sent them to the elders and other leaders of the town where Naboth lived. ⁹In her letters she commanded: "Call the citizens together for a time of fasting, and give Naboth a place of honor. ¹⁰And then seat two scoundrels across from him who will accuse him of cursing God and the king. Then take him out and stone him to death."

¹¹So the elders and other town leaders followed the instructions Jezebel had written in the letters. ¹²They called for a fast and put Naboth at a prominent place before the people. ¹³Then the two scoundrels came and sat down across from him. And they accused Naboth before all the people, saying, "He cursed God and the king." So he was dragged outside the town and stoned to death. ¹⁴The town leaders then sent word to Jezebel, "Naboth has been stoned to death."

¹⁵When Jezebel heard the news, she said to Ahab, "You know the vineyard Naboth wouldn't sell you? Well, you can have it now!

He's dead!" ¹⁶So Ahab immediately went down to the vineyard of Naboth to claim it.

¹⁷But the LORD said to Elijah,* ¹⁸"Go down to meet King Ahab of Israel, who rules in Samaria. He will be at Naboth's vineyard in Jezreel, claiming it for himself. ¹⁹Give him this message: 'This is what the LORD says: Wasn't it enough that you killed Naboth? Must you rob him, too? Because you have done this, dogs will lick your blood at the very place where they licked the blood of Naboth!'"

²⁰"So, my enemy, you have found me!" Ahab exclaimed to Elijah.

"Yes," Elijah answered, "I have come because you have sold yourself to what is evil in the LORD's sight. ²¹So now the LORD says,* 'I will bring disaster on you and consume you. I will destroy every one of your male descendants, slave and free alike, anywhere in Israel! ²²I am going to destroy your family as I did the family of Jeroboam son of Nebat and the family of Baasha son of Ahijah, for you have made me very angry and have led Israel into sin.'

²³"And regarding Jezebel, the LORD says, 'Dogs will eat Jezebel's body at the plot of land in Jezreel.*'

²⁴"The members of Ahab's family who die in the city will be eaten by dogs, and those who die in the field will be eaten by vultures."

²⁵(No one else so completely sold himself to what was evil in the LORD's sight as Ahab did under the influence of his wife Jezebel. ²⁶His worst outrage was worshiping idols* just as the Amorites had done—the people whom the LORD had driven out from the land ahead of the Israelites.)

²⁷But when Ahab heard this message, he tore his clothing, dressed in burlap, and fasted. He even slept in burlap and went about in deep mourning.

²⁸Then another message from the LORD came to Elijah: ²⁹"Do you see how Ahab has humbled himself before me? Because he has done this, I will not do what I promised during his lifetime. It will happen to his sons; I will destroy his dynasty."

Jehoshaphat and Ahab

22 For three years there was no war between Aram and Israel. ²Then during the third year, King Jehoshaphat of Judah went to visit King Ahab of Israel. ³During the visit,

---

20:42 The Hebrew term used here refers to the complete consecration of things or people to the LORD, either by destroying them or by giving them as an offering.   21:17 Hebrew *Elijah the Tishbite*; also in 21:28.   21:21 As in Greek version; Hebrew lacks *So now the LORD says*.   21:23 As in several Hebrew manuscripts, Syriac, and Latin Vulgate (see also 2 Kgs 9:26, 36); most Hebrew manuscripts read *at the city wall*.   21:26 The Hebrew term (literally *round things*) probably alludes to dung.

the king of Israel said to his officials, "Do you realize that the town of Ramoth-gilead belongs to us? And yet we've done nothing to recapture it from the king of Aram!"

⁴Then he turned to Jehoshaphat and asked, "Will you join me in battle to recover Ramoth-gilead?"

Jehoshaphat replied to the king of Israel, "Why, of course! You and I are as one. My troops are your troops, and my horses are your horses." ⁵Then Jehoshaphat added, "But first let's find out what the LORD says."

⁶So the king of Israel summoned the prophets, about 400 of them, and asked them, "Should I go to war against Ramoth-gilead, or should I hold back?"

They all replied, "Yes, go right ahead! The Lord will give the king victory."

⁷But Jehoshaphat asked, "Is there not also a prophet of the LORD here? We should ask him the same question."

⁸The king of Israel replied to Jehoshaphat, "There is one more man who could consult the LORD for us, but I hate him. He never prophesies anything but trouble for me! His name is Micaiah son of Imlah."

Jehoshaphat replied, "That's not the way a king should talk! Let's hear what he has to say."

⁹So the king of Israel called one of his officials and said, "Quick! Bring Micaiah son of Imlah."

Micaiah Prophesies against Ahab

¹⁰King Ahab of Israel and King Jehoshaphat of Judah, dressed in their royal robes, were sitting on thrones at the threshing floor near the gate of Samaria. All of Ahab's prophets were prophesying there in front of them. ¹¹One of them, Zedekiah son of Kenaanah, made some iron horns and proclaimed, "This is what the LORD says: With these horns you will gore the Arameans to death!"

¹²All the other prophets agreed. "Yes," they said, "go up to Ramoth-gilead and be victorious, for the LORD will give the king victory!"

¹³Meanwhile, the messenger who went to get Micaiah said to him, "Look, all the prophets are promising victory for the king. Be sure that you agree with them and promise success."

¹⁴But Micaiah replied, "As surely as the LORD lives, I will say only what the LORD tells me to say."

¹⁵When Micaiah arrived before the king, Ahab asked him, "Micaiah, should we go to war against Ramoth-gilead, or should we hold back?"

Micaiah replied sarcastically, "Yes, go up and be victorious, for the LORD will give the king victory!"

¹⁶But the king replied sharply, "How many times must I demand that you speak only the truth to me when you speak for the LORD?"

¹⁷Then Micaiah told him, "In a vision I saw all Israel scattered on the mountains, like sheep without a shepherd. And the LORD said, 'Their master has been killed.* Send them home in peace.'"

¹⁸"Didn't I tell you?" the king of Israel exclaimed to Jehoshaphat. "He never prophesies anything but trouble for me."

¹⁹Then Micaiah continued, "Listen to what the LORD says! I saw the LORD sitting on his throne with all the armies of heaven around him, on his right and on his left. ²⁰And the LORD said, 'Who can entice Ahab to go into battle against Ramoth-gilead so he can be killed?'

"There were many suggestions, ²¹and finally a spirit approached the LORD and said, 'I can do it!'

²²"'How will you do this?' the LORD asked.

"And the spirit replied, 'I will go out and inspire all of Ahab's prophets to speak lies.'

"'You will succeed,' said the LORD. 'Go ahead and do it.'

²³"So you see, the LORD has put a lying spirit in the mouths of all your prophets. For the LORD has pronounced your doom."

²⁴Then Zedekiah son of Kenaanah walked up to Micaiah and slapped him across the face. "Since when did the Spirit of the LORD leave me to speak to you?" he demanded.

²⁵And Micaiah replied, "You will find out soon enough when you are trying to hide in some secret room!"

²⁶"Arrest him!" the king of Israel ordered. "Take him back to Amon, the governor of the city, and to my son Joash. ²⁷Give them this order from the king: 'Put this man in prison, and feed him nothing but bread and water until I return safely from the battle!'"

²⁸But Micaiah replied, "If you return safely, it will mean that the LORD has not spoken through me!" Then he added to those standing around, "Everyone mark my words!"

The Death of Ahab

²⁹So King Ahab of Israel and King Jehoshaphat of Judah led their armies against Ramoth-gilead. ³⁰The king of Israel said to Jehoshaphat,

22:17 Hebrew *These people have no master.*

"As we go into battle, I will disguise myself so no one will recognize me, but you wear your royal robes." So the king of Israel disguised himself, and they went into battle.

³¹Meanwhile, the king of Aram had issued these orders to his thirty-two chariot commanders: "Attack only the king of Israel. Don't bother with anyone else!" ³²So when the Aramean chariot commanders saw Jehoshaphat in his royal robes, they went after him. "There is the king of Israel!" they shouted. But when Jehoshaphat called out, ³³the chariot commanders realized he was not the king of Israel, and they stopped chasing him.

³⁴An Aramean soldier, however, randomly shot an arrow at the Israelite troops and hit the king of Israel between the joints of his armor. "Turn the horses* and get me out of here!" Ahab groaned to the driver of his chariot. "I'm badly wounded!"

³⁵The battle raged all that day, and the king remained propped up in his chariot facing the Arameans. The blood from his wound ran down to the floor of his chariot, and as evening arrived he died. ³⁶Just as the sun was setting, the cry ran through his troops: "We're done for! Run for your lives!"

³⁷So the king died, and his body was taken to Samaria and buried there. ³⁸Then his chariot was washed beside the pool of Samaria, and dogs came and licked his blood at the place where the prostitutes bathed,* just as the LORD had promised.

³⁹The rest of the events in Ahab's reign and everything he did, including the story of the ivory palace and the towns he built, are recorded in *The Book of the History of the Kings of Israel.* ⁴⁰So Ahab died, and his son Ahaziah became the next king.

Jehoshaphat Rules in Judah

⁴¹Jehoshaphat son of Asa began to rule over Judah in the fourth year of King Ahab's reign in Israel. ⁴²Jehoshaphat was thirty-five years old when he became king, and he reigned in Jerusalem twenty-five years. His mother was Azubah, the daughter of Shilhi.

⁴³Jehoshaphat was a good king, following the example of his father, Asa. He did what was pleasing in the LORD's sight. *During his reign, however, he failed to remove all the pagan shrines, and the people still offered sacrifices and burned incense there. ⁴⁴Jehoshaphat also made peace with the king of Israel.

⁴⁵The rest of the events in Jehoshaphat's reign, the extent of his power, and the wars he waged are recorded in *The Book of the History of the Kings of Judah.* ⁴⁶He banished from the land the rest of the male and female shrine prostitutes, who still continued their practices from the days of his father, Asa.

⁴⁷(There was no king in Edom at that time, only a deputy.)

⁴⁸Jehoshaphat also built a fleet of trading ships* to sail to Ophir for gold. But the ships never set sail, for they met with disaster in their home port of Ezion-geber. ⁴⁹At one time Ahaziah son of Ahab had proposed to Jehoshaphat, "Let my men sail with your men in the ships." But Jehoshaphat refused the request.

⁵⁰When Jehoshaphat died, he was buried with his ancestors in the City of David. Then his son Jehoram became the next king.

Ahaziah Rules in Israel

⁵¹Ahaziah son of Ahab began to rule over Israel in the seventeenth year of King Jehoshaphat's reign in Judah. He reigned in Samaria two years. ⁵²But he did what was evil in the LORD's sight, following the example of his father and mother and the example of Jeroboam son of Nebat, who had led Israel to sin. ⁵³He served Baal and worshiped him, provoking the anger of the LORD, the God of Israel, just as his father had done.

22:34 Hebrew *Turn your hand.*   22:38 Or *his blood, and the prostitutes bathed [in it];* or *his blood, and they washed his armor.*
22:43 Verses 22:43b-53 are numbered 22:44-54 in Hebrew text.   22:48 Hebrew *fleet of ships of Tarshish.*

2 Kings

IF YOU HAVE EVER SEEN a fish struggling to swim upstream, you have an idea of what it was like to be a good king in Israel or Judah. In 2 Kings, most of the kings simply go along with the current of evil. Only a handful struggled to follow the God of Israel, rejecting the idolatry, immorality, and complacency that surrounded them. In order to counter this widespread wickedness, the prophets often took center stage, warning kings and others about the consequences of sin. Ultimately, however, wickedness prevailed, and 2 Kings describes two tragedies that changed the

■ **Author:** Uncertain; some have suggested Jeremiah or a group of prophets

■ **Date Written:** Uncertain, possibly around 562 BC, shortly after King Jehoiachin's release

■ **Purpose:** To contrast the lives of the godly and ungodly kings throughout the history of Israel and Judah and to demonstrate the consequences of idolatry and wickedness

■ **Themes:** Idolatry, the Temple, good and bad kings, the rise of the prophet movement, sin and its consequences

■ **Outline**

1:1–2:11 The end of Elijah's ministry
2:12–8:15 The ministry of Elisha the prophet
8:16–17:41 The kings of Israel and Judah until the fall of Israel
18:1–25:30 The kingdom of Judah until the fall of Jerusalem

face of Israel's history. In 722 BC, the northern kingdom of Israel was destroyed by the Assyrians, and in 586 BC, the southern kingdom of Judah was dismantled by the Babylonians. As in the book of 1 Kings, all these events are interpreted as the direct result of the idolatry and wickedness that pervaded the nations of Israel and Judah.

Elijah Confronts King Ahaziah

1 After King Ahab's death, the land of Moab rebelled against Israel.

²One day Israel's new king, Ahaziah, fell through the latticework of an upper room at his palace in Samaria and was seriously injured. So he sent messengers to the temple of Baal-zebub, the god of Ekron, to ask whether he would recover.

³But the angel of the LORD told Elijah, who was from Tishbe, "Go and confront the messengers of the king of Samaria and ask them, 'Is there no God in Israel? Why are you going to Baal-zebub, the god of Ekron, to ask whether the king will recover? ⁴Now, therefore, this is what the LORD says: You will never leave the bed you are lying on; you will surely die.'" So Elijah went to deliver the message.

⁵When the messengers returned to the king, he asked them, "Why have you returned so soon?"

⁶They replied, "A man came up to us and

told us to go back to the king and give him this message. 'This is what the LORD says: Is there no God in Israel? Why are you sending men to Baal-zebub, the god of Ekron, to ask whether you will recover? Therefore, because you have done this, you will never leave the bed you are lying on; you will surely die.'"

⁷"What sort of man was he?" the king demanded. "What did he look like?"

⁸They replied, "He was a hairy man,* and he wore a leather belt around his waist."

"Elijah from Tishbe!" the king exclaimed.

⁹Then he sent an army captain with fifty soldiers to arrest him. They found him sitting on top of a hill. The captain said to him, "Man of God, the king has commanded you to come down with us."

¹⁰But Elijah replied to the captain, "If I am a man of God, let fire come down from heaven and destroy you and your fifty men!" Then fire fell from heaven and killed them all.

¹¹So the king sent another captain with fifty

1:8 Or *He was wearing clothing made of hair.*

men. The captain said to him, "Man of God, the king demands that you come down at once."

¹²Elijah replied, "If I am a man of God, let fire come down from heaven and destroy you and your fifty men!" And again the fire of God fell from heaven and killed them all.

¹³Once more the king sent a third captain with fifty men. But this time the captain went up the hill and fell to his knees before Elijah. He pleaded with him, "O man of God, please spare my life and the lives of these, your fifty servants. ¹⁴See how the fire from heaven came down and destroyed the first two groups. But now please spare my life!"

¹⁵Then the angel of the LORD said to Elijah, "Go down with him, and don't be afraid of him." So Elijah got up and went with him to the king.

¹⁶And Elijah said to the king, "This is what the LORD says: Why did you send messengers to Baal-zebub, the god of Ekron, to ask whether you will recover? Is there no God in Israel to answer your question? Therefore, because you have done this, you will never leave the bed you are lying on; you will surely die."

¹⁷So Ahaziah died, just as the LORD had promised through Elijah. Since Ahaziah did not have a son to succeed him, his brother Joram* became the next king. This took place in the second year of the reign of Jehoram son of Jehoshaphat, king of Judah.

¹⁸The rest of the events in Ahaziah's reign and everything he did are recorded in *The Book of the History of the Kings of Israel.*

Elijah Taken into Heaven

2 When the LORD was about to take Elijah up to heaven in a whirlwind, Elijah and Elisha were traveling from Gilgal. ²And Elijah said to Elisha, "Stay here, for the LORD has told me to go to Bethel."

But Elisha replied, "As surely as the LORD lives and you yourself live, I will never leave you!" So they went down together to Bethel.

³The group of prophets from Bethel came to Elisha and asked him, "Did you know that the LORD is going to take your master away from you today?"

"Of course I know," Elisha answered. "But be quiet about it."

⁴Then Elijah said to Elisha, "Stay here, for the LORD has told me to go to Jericho."

But Elisha replied again, "As surely as the LORD lives and you yourself live, I will never leave you." So they went on together to Jericho.

⁵Then the group of prophets from Jericho came to Elisha and asked him, "Did you know that the LORD is going to take your master away from you today?"

"Of course I know," Elisha answered. "But be quiet about it."

⁶Then Elijah said to Elisha, "Stay here, for the LORD has told me to go to the Jordan River."

But again Elisha replied, "As surely as the LORD lives and you yourself live, I will never leave you." So they went on together.

⁷Fifty men from the group of prophets also went and watched from a distance as Elijah and Elisha stopped beside the Jordan River. ⁸Then Elijah folded his cloak together and struck the water with it. The river divided, and the two of them went across on dry ground!

⁹When they came to the other side, Elijah said to Elisha, "Tell me what I can do for you before I am taken away."

And Elisha replied, "Please let me inherit a double share of your spirit and become your successor."

¹⁰"You have asked a difficult thing," Elijah replied. "If you see me when I am taken from you, then you will get your request. But if not, then you won't."

¹¹As they were walking along and talking, suddenly a chariot of fire appeared, drawn by horses of fire. It drove between the two men, separating them, and Elijah was carried by a whirlwind into heaven. ¹²Elisha saw it and cried out, "My father! My father! I see the chariots and charioteers of Israel!" And as they disappeared from sight, Elisha tore his clothes in distress.

¹³Elisha picked up Elijah's cloak, which had fallen when he was taken up. Then Elisha returned to the bank of the Jordan River. ¹⁴He struck the water with Elijah's cloak and cried out, "Where is the LORD, the God of Elijah?" Then the river divided, and Elisha went across.

¹⁵When the group of prophets from Jericho saw from a distance what happened, they exclaimed, "Elijah's spirit rests upon Elisha!" And they went to meet him and bowed to the ground before him. ¹⁶"Sir," they said, "just say the word and fifty of our strongest men will search the wilderness for your master. Perhaps the Spirit of the LORD has left him on some mountain or in some valley."

"No," Elisha said, "don't send them." ¹⁷But they kept urging him until they shamed him into agreeing, and he finally said, "All right, send them." So fifty men searched for three

1:17 Hebrew *Jehoram,* a variant spelling of Joram.

days but did not find Elijah. [18]Elisha was still at Jericho when they returned. "Didn't I tell you not to go?" he asked.

Elisha's First Miracles
[19]One day the leaders of the town of Jericho visited Elisha. "We have a problem, my lord," they told him. "This town is located in pleasant surroundings, as you can see. But the water is bad, and the land is unproductive."

[20]Elisha said, "Bring me a new bowl with salt in it." So they brought it to him. [21]Then he went out to the spring that supplied the town with water and threw the salt into it. And he said, "This is what the LORD says: I have purified this water. It will no longer cause death or infertility.*" [22]And the water has remained pure ever since, just as Elisha said.

[23]Elisha left Jericho and went up to Bethel. As he was walking along the road, a group of boys from the town began mocking and making fun of him. "Go away, baldy!" they chanted. "Go away, baldy!" [24]Elisha turned around and looked at them, and he cursed them in the name of the LORD. Then two bears came out of the woods and mauled forty-two of them. [25]From there Elisha went to Mount Carmel and finally returned to Samaria.

War between Israel and Moab
3 Ahab's son Joram* began to rule over Israel in the eighteenth year of King Jehoshaphat's reign in Judah. He reigned in Samaria twelve years. [2]He did what was evil in the LORD's sight, but not to the same extent as his father and mother. He at least tore down the sacred pillar of Baal that his father had set up. [3]Nevertheless, he continued in the sins that Jeroboam son of Nebat had committed and led the people of Israel to commit.

[4]King Mesha of Moab was a sheep breeder. He used to pay the king of Israel an annual tribute of 100,000 lambs and the wool of 100,000 rams. [5]But after Ahab's death, the king of Moab rebelled against the king of Israel. [6]So King Joram promptly mustered the army of Israel and marched from Samaria. [7]On the way, he sent this message to King Jehoshaphat of Judah: "The king of Moab has rebelled against me. Will you join me in battle against him?"

And Jehoshaphat replied, "Why, of course! You and I are as one. My troops are your troops, and my horses are your horses." [8]Then Jehoshaphat asked, "What route will we take?"

"We will attack from the wilderness of Edom," Joram replied.

[9]The king of Edom and his troops joined them, and all three armies traveled along a roundabout route through the wilderness for seven days. But there was no water for the men or their animals.

[10]"What should we do?" the king of Israel cried out. "The LORD has brought the three of us here to let the king of Moab defeat us."

[11]But King Jehoshaphat of Judah asked, "Is there no prophet of the LORD with us? If there is, we can ask the LORD what to do through him."

One of King Joram's officers replied, "Elisha son of Shaphat is here. He used to be Elijah's personal assistant.*"

[12]Jehoshaphat said, "Yes, the LORD speaks through him." So the king of Israel, King Jehoshaphat of Judah, and the king of Edom went to consult with Elisha.

[13]"Why are you coming to me?"* Elisha asked the king of Israel. "Go to the pagan prophets of your father and mother!"

But King Joram of Israel said, "No! For it was the LORD who called us three kings here—only to be defeated by the king of Moab!"

[14]Elisha replied, "As surely as the LORD Almighty lives, whom I serve, I wouldn't even bother with you except for my respect for King Jehoshaphat of Judah. [15]Now bring me someone who can play the harp."

While the harp was being played, the power* of the LORD came upon Elisha, [16]and he said, "This is what the LORD says: This dry valley will be filled with pools of water! [17]You will see neither wind nor rain, says the LORD, but this valley will be filled with water. You will have plenty for yourselves and your cattle and other animals. [18]But this is only a simple thing for the LORD, for he will make you victorious over the army of Moab! [19]You will conquer the best of their towns, even the fortified ones. You will cut down all their good trees, stop up all their springs, and ruin all their good land with stones."

[20]The next day at about the time when the morning sacrifice was offered, water suddenly appeared! It was flowing from the direction of Edom, and soon there was water everywhere.

[21]Meanwhile, when the people of Moab

2:21 Or *or make the land unproductive*; Hebrew reads *or barrenness.*   3:1 Hebrew *Jehoram,* a variant spelling of Joram; also in 3:6.   3:11 Hebrew *He used to pour water on the hands of Elijah.*   3:13 Hebrew *What is there in common between you and me?*   3:15 Hebrew *the hand.*

heard about the three armies marching against them, they mobilized every man who was old enough to strap on a sword, and they stationed themselves along their border. 22But when they got up the next morning, the sun was shining across the water, making it appear red to the Moabites—like blood. 23"It's blood!" the Moabites exclaimed. "The three armies must have attacked and killed each other! Let's go, men of Moab, and collect the plunder!"

24But when the Moabites arrived at the Israelite camp, the army of Israel rushed out and attacked them until they turned and ran. The army of Israel chased them into the land of Moab, destroying everything as they went.* 25They destroyed the towns, covered their good land with stones, stopped up all the springs, and cut down all the good trees. Finally, only Kir-hareseth and its stone walls were left, but men with slings surrounded and attacked it.

26When the king of Moab saw that he was losing the battle, he led 700 of his swordsmen in a desperate attempt to break through the enemy lines near the king of Edom, but they failed. 27Then the king of Moab took his oldest son, who would have been the next king, and sacrificed him as a burnt offering on the wall. So there was great anger against Israel,* and the Israelites withdrew and returned to their own land.

Elisha Helps a Poor Widow

4 One day the widow of a member of the group of prophets came to Elisha and cried out, "My husband who served you is dead, and you know how he feared the LORD. But now a creditor has come, threatening to take my two sons as slaves."

2"What can I do to help you?" Elisha asked. "Tell me, what do you have in the house?"

"Nothing at all, except a flask of olive oil," she replied.

3And Elisha said, "Borrow as many empty jars as you can from your friends and neighbors. 4Then go into your house with your sons and shut the door behind you. Pour olive oil from your flask into the jars, setting each one aside when it is filled."

5So she did as she was told. Her sons kept bringing jars to her, and she filled one after another. 6Soon every container was full to the brim!

"Bring me another jar," she said to one of her sons.

"There aren't any more!" he told her. And then the olive oil stopped flowing.

7When she told the man of God what had happened, he said to her, "Now sell the olive oil and pay your debts, and you and your sons can live on what is left over."

Elisha and the Woman from Shunem

8One day Elisha went to the town of Shunem. A wealthy woman lived there, and she urged him to come to her home for a meal. After that, whenever he passed that way, he would stop there for something to eat.

9She said to her husband, "I am sure this man who stops in from time to time is a holy man of God. 10Let's build a small room for him on the roof and furnish it with a bed, a table, a chair, and a lamp. Then he will have a place to stay whenever he comes by."

11One day Elisha returned to Shunem, and he went up to this upper room to rest. 12He said to his servant Gehazi, "Tell the woman from Shunem I want to speak to her." When she appeared, 13Elisha said to Gehazi, "Tell her, 'We appreciate the kind concern you have shown us. What can we do for you? Can we put in a good word for you to the king or to the commander of the army?'"

"No," she replied, "my family takes good care of me."

14Later Elisha asked Gehazi, "What can we do for her?"

Gehazi replied, "She doesn't have a son, and her husband is an old man."

15"Call her back again," Elisha told him. When the woman returned, Elisha said to her as she stood in the doorway, 16"Next year at this time you will be holding a son in your arms!"

"No, my lord!" she cried. "O man of God, don't deceive me and get my hopes up like that."

17But sure enough, the woman soon became pregnant. And at that time the following year she had a son, just as Elisha had said.

18One day when her child was older, he went out to help his father, who was working with the harvesters. 19Suddenly he cried out, "My head hurts! My head hurts!"

His father said to one of the servants, "Carry him home to his mother."

20So the servant took him home, and his mother held him on her lap. But around noontime he died. 21She carried him up and laid him on the bed of the man of God, then shut the door and left him there. 22She sent a message

3:24 The meaning of the Hebrew is uncertain.   3:27 Or *So Israel's anger was great.* The meaning of the Hebrew is uncertain.

to her husband: "Send one of the servants and a donkey so that I can hurry to the man of God and come right back."

²³"Why go today?" he asked. "It is neither a new moon festival nor a Sabbath."

But she said, "It will be all right."

²⁴So she saddled the donkey and said to the servant, "Hurry! Don't slow down unless I tell you to."

²⁵As she approached the man of God at Mount Carmel, Elisha saw her in the distance. He said to Gehazi, "Look, the woman from Shunem is coming. ²⁶Run out to meet her and ask her, 'Is everything all right with you, your husband, and your child?'"

"Yes," the woman told Gehazi, "everything is fine."

²⁷But when she came to the man of God at the mountain, she fell to the ground before him and caught hold of his feet. Gehazi began to push her away, but the man of God said, "Leave her alone. She is deeply troubled, but the LORD has not told me what it is."

²⁸Then she said, "Did I ask you for a son, my lord? And didn't I say, 'Don't deceive me and get my hopes up'?"

²⁹Then Elisha said to Gehazi, "Get ready to travel*; take my staff and go! Don't talk to anyone along the way. Go quickly and lay the staff on the child's face."

³⁰But the boy's mother said, "As surely as the LORD lives and you yourself live, I won't go home unless you go with me." So Elisha returned with her.

³¹Gehazi hurried on ahead and laid the staff on the child's face, but nothing happened. There was no sign of life. He returned to meet Elisha and told him, "The child is still dead."

³²When Elisha arrived, the child was indeed dead, lying there on the prophet's bed. ³³He went in alone and shut the door behind him and prayed to the LORD. ³⁴Then he lay down on the child's body, placing his mouth on the child's mouth, his eyes on the child's eyes, and his hands on the child's hands. And as he stretched out on him, the child's body began to grow warm again! ³⁵Elisha got up, walked back and forth across the room once, and then stretched himself out again on the child. This time the boy sneezed seven times and opened his eyes!

³⁶Then Elisha summoned Gehazi. "Call the child's mother!" he said. And when she came in, Elisha said, "Here, take your son!" ³⁷She fell at his feet and bowed before him, overwhelmed with gratitude. Then she took her son in her arms and carried him downstairs.

Miracles during a Famine

³⁸Elisha now returned to Gilgal, and there was a famine in the land. One day as the group of prophets was seated before him, he said to his servant, "Put a large pot on the fire, and make some stew for the rest of the group."

³⁹One of the young men went out into the field to gather herbs and came back with a pocketful of wild gourds. He shredded them and put them into the pot without realizing they were poisonous. ⁴⁰Some of the stew was served to the men. But after they had eaten a bite or two they cried out, "Man of God, there's poison in this stew!" So they would not eat it.

⁴¹Elisha said, "Bring me some flour." Then he threw it into the pot and said, "Now it's all right; go ahead and eat." And then it did not harm them.

⁴²One day a man from Baal-shalishah brought the man of God a sack of fresh grain and twenty loaves of barley bread made from the first grain of his harvest. Elisha said, "Give it to the people so they can eat."

⁴³"What?" his servant exclaimed. "Feed a hundred people with only this?"

But Elisha repeated, "Give it to the people so they can eat, for this is what the LORD says: Everyone will eat, and there will even be some left over!" ⁴⁴And when they gave it to the people, there was plenty for all and some left over, just as the LORD had promised.

The Healing of Naaman

5 The king of Aram had great admiration for Naaman, the commander of his army, because through him the LORD had given Aram great victories. But though Naaman was a mighty warrior, he suffered from leprosy.*

²At this time Aramean raiders had invaded the land of Israel, and among their captives was a young girl who had been given to Naaman's wife as a maid. ³One day the girl said to her mistress, "I wish my master would go to see the prophet in Samaria. He would heal him of his leprosy."

⁴So Naaman told the king what the young girl from Israel had said. ⁵"Go and visit the prophet," the king of Aram told him. "I will send a letter of introduction for you to take to the king of Israel." So Naaman started

4:29 Hebrew *Bind up your loins.* **5:1** Or *from a contagious skin disease.* The Hebrew word used here and throughout this passage can describe various skin diseases.

out, carrying as gifts 750 pounds of silver, 150 pounds of gold,* and ten sets of clothing. 6The letter to the king of Israel said: "With this letter I present my servant Naaman. I want you to heal him of his leprosy."

7When the king of Israel read the letter, he tore his clothes in dismay and said, "Am I God, that I can give life and take it away? Why is this man asking me to heal someone with leprosy? I can see that he's just trying to pick a fight with me."

8But when Elisha, the man of God, heard that the king of Israel had torn his clothes in dismay, he sent this message to him: "Why are you so upset? Send Naaman to me, and he will learn that there is a true prophet here in Israel."

9So Naaman went with his horses and chariots and waited at the door of Elisha's house. 10But Elisha sent a messenger out to him with this message: "Go and wash yourself seven times in the Jordan River. Then your skin will be restored, and you will be healed of your leprosy."

11But Naaman became angry and stalked away. "I thought he would certainly come out to meet me!" he said. "I expected him to wave his hand over the leprosy and call on the name of the LORD his God and heal me! 12Aren't the rivers of Damascus, the Abana and the Pharpar, better than any of the rivers of Israel? Why shouldn't I wash in them and be healed?" So Naaman turned and went away in a rage.

13But his officers tried to reason with him and said, "Sir,* if the prophet had told you to do something very difficult, wouldn't you have done it? So you should certainly obey him when he says simply, 'Go and wash and be cured!'" 14So Naaman went down to the Jordan River and dipped himself seven times, as the man of God had instructed him. And his skin became as healthy as the skin of a young child, and he was healed!

15Then Naaman and his entire party went back to find the man of God. They stood before him, and Naaman said, "Now I know that there is no God in all the world except in Israel. So please accept a gift from your servant."

16But Elisha replied, "As surely as the LORD lives, whom I serve, I will not accept any gifts." And though Naaman urged him to take the gift, Elisha refused.

17Then Naaman said, "All right, but please allow me to load two of my mules with earth from this place, and I will take it back home with me. From now on I will never again offer burnt offerings or sacrifices to any other god except the LORD. 18However, may the LORD pardon me in this one thing: When my master the king goes into the temple of the god Rimmon to worship there and leans on my arm, may the LORD pardon me when I bow, too."

19"Go in peace," Elisha said. So Naaman started home again.

The Greed of Gehazi

20But Gehazi, the servant of Elisha, the man of God, said to himself, "My master should not have let this Aramean get away without accepting any of his gifts. As surely as the LORD lives, I will chase after him and get something from him." 21So Gehazi set off after Naaman.

When Naaman saw Gehazi running after him, he climbed down from his chariot and went to meet him. "Is everything all right?" Naaman asked.

22"Yes," Gehazi said, "but my master has sent me to tell you that two young prophets from the hill country of Ephraim have just arrived. He would like 75 pounds* of silver and two sets of clothing to give to them."

23"By all means, take twice as much* silver," Naaman insisted. He gave him two sets of clothing, tied up the money in two bags, and sent two of his servants to carry the gifts for Gehazi. 24But when they arrived at the citadel,* Gehazi took the gifts from the servants and sent the men back. Then he went and hid the gifts inside the house.

25When he went in to his master, Elisha asked him, "Where have you been, Gehazi?"

"I haven't been anywhere," he replied.

26But Elisha asked him, "Don't you realize that I was there in spirit when Naaman stepped down from his chariot to meet you? Is this the time to receive money and clothing, olive groves and vineyards, sheep and cattle, and male and female servants? 27Because you have done this, you and your descendants will suffer from Naaman's leprosy forever." When Gehazi left the room, he was covered with leprosy; his skin was white as snow.

The Floating Ax Head

6 One day the group of prophets came to Elisha and told him, "As you can see, this place where we meet with you is too small. 2Let's go down to the Jordan River, where there are

---

5:5 Hebrew 10 talents [340 kilograms] of silver, 6,000 [shekels] [68 kilograms] of gold.   5:13 Hebrew My father.   5:22 Hebrew 1 talent [34 kilograms].   5:23 Hebrew take 2 talents [150 pounds or 68 kilograms].   5:24 Hebrew the Ophel.

plenty of logs. There we can build a new place for us to meet."

"All right," he told them, "go ahead."

3"Please come with us," someone suggested.

"I will," he said. 4So he went with them.

When they arrived at the Jordan, they began cutting down trees. 5But as one of them was cutting a tree, his ax head fell into the river. "Oh, sir!" he cried. "It was a borrowed ax!"

6"Where did it fall?" the man of God asked. When he showed him the place, Elisha cut a stick and threw it into the water at that spot. Then the ax head floated to the surface. 7"Grab it," Elisha said. And the man reached out and grabbed it.

Elisha Traps the Arameans

8When the king of Aram was at war with Israel, he would confer with his officers and say, "We will mobilize our forces at such and such a place."

9But immediately Elisha, the man of God, would warn the king of Israel, "Do not go near that place, for the Arameans are planning to mobilize their troops there." 10So the king of Israel would send word to the place indicated by the man of God. Time and again Elisha warned the king, so that he would be on the alert there.

11The king of Aram became very upset over this. He called his officers together and demanded, "Which of you is the traitor? Who has been informing the king of Israel of my plans?"

12"It's not us, my lord the king," one of the officers replied. "Elisha, the prophet in Israel, tells the king of Israel even the words you speak in the privacy of your bedroom!"

13"Go and find out where he is," the king commanded, "so I can send troops to seize him." And the report came back: "Elisha is at Dothan." 14So one night the king of Aram sent a great army with many chariots and horses to surround the city.

15When the servant of the man of God got up early the next morning and went outside, there were troops, horses, and chariots everywhere. "Oh, sir, what will we do now?" the young man cried to Elisha.

16"Don't be afraid!" Elisha told him. "For there are more on our side than on theirs!"

17Then Elisha prayed, "O Lord, open his eyes and let him see!" The Lord opened the young man's eyes, and when he looked up, he saw that the hillside around Elisha was filled with horses and chariots of fire.

18As the Aramean army advanced toward him, Elisha prayed, "O Lord, please make them blind." So the Lord struck them with blindness as Elisha had asked.

19Then Elisha went out and told them, "You have come the wrong way! This isn't the right city! Follow me, and I will take you to the man you are looking for." And he led them to the city of Samaria.

20As soon as they had entered Samaria, Elisha prayed, "O Lord, now open their eyes and let them see." So the Lord opened their eyes, and they discovered that they were in the middle of Samaria.

21When the king of Israel saw them, he shouted to Elisha, "My father, should I kill them? Should I kill them?"

22"Of course not!" Elisha replied. "Do we kill prisoners of war? Give them food and drink and send them home again to their master."

23So the king made a great feast for them and then sent them home to their master. After that, the Aramean raiders stayed away from the land of Israel.

Ben-Hadad Besieges Samaria

24Some time later, however, King Ben-hadad of Aram mustered his entire army and besieged Samaria. 25As a result, there was a great famine in the city. The siege lasted so long that a donkey's head sold for eighty pieces of silver, and a cup of dove's dung sold for five pieces* of silver.

26One day as the king of Israel was walking along the wall of the city, a woman called to him, "Please help me, my lord the king!"

27He answered, "If the Lord doesn't help you, what can I do? I have neither food from the threshing floor nor wine from the press to give you." 28But then the king asked, "What is the matter?"

She replied, "This woman said to me: 'Come on, let's eat your son today, then we will eat my son tomorrow.' 29So we cooked my son and ate him. Then the next day I said to her, 'Kill your son so we can eat him,' but she has hidden her son."

30When the king heard this, he tore his clothes in despair. And as the king walked along the wall, the people could see that he was wearing burlap under his robe next to his skin. 31"May God strike me and even kill me if I don't separate Elisha's head from his shoulders this very day," the king vowed.

32Elisha was sitting in his house with the

6:25 Hebrew *sold for 80 [shekels]* [2 pounds or 0.9 kilograms] *of silver, and ¼ of a cab* [0.3 liters] *of dove's dung sold for 5 [shekels]* [2 ounces or 57 grams]. *Dove's dung* may be a variety of wild vegetable.

elders of Israel when the king sent a messenger to summon him. But before the messenger arrived, Elisha said to the elders, "A murderer has sent a man to cut off my head. When he arrives, shut the door and keep him out. We will soon hear his master's steps following him."

33While Elisha was still saying this, the messenger arrived. And the king* said, "All this misery is from the LORD! Why should I wait for the LORD any longer?"

7 Elisha replied, "Listen to this message from the LORD! This is what the LORD says: By this time tomorrow in the markets of Samaria, six quarts of choice flour will cost only one piece of silver,* and twelve quarts of barley grain will cost only one piece of silver.*"

2The officer assisting the king said to the man of God, "That couldn't happen even if the LORD opened the windows of heaven!"

But Elisha replied, "You will see it happen with your own eyes, but you won't be able to eat any of it!"

Outcasts Visit the Enemy Camp

3Now there were four men with leprosy* sitting at the entrance of the city gates. "Why should we sit here waiting to die?" they asked each other. 4"We will starve if we stay here, but with the famine in the city, we will starve if we go back there. So we might as well go out and surrender to the Aramean army. If they let us live, so much the better. But if they kill us, we would have died anyway."

5So at twilight they set out for the camp of the Arameans. But when they came to the edge of the camp, no one was there! 6For the Lord had caused the Aramean army to hear the clatter of speeding chariots and the galloping of horses and the sounds of a great army approaching. "The king of Israel has hired the Hittites and Egyptians* to attack us!" they cried to one another. 7So they panicked and ran into the night, abandoning their tents, horses, donkeys, and everything else, as they fled for their lives.

8When the men with leprosy arrived at the edge of the camp, they went into one tent after another, eating and drinking wine; and they carried off silver and gold and clothing and hid it. 9Finally, they said to each other, "This is not right. This is a day of good news, and we aren't sharing it with anyone! If we wait until morning, some calamity will certainly fall upon us. Come on, let's go back and tell the people at the palace."

10So they went back to the city and told the gatekeepers what had happened. "We went out to the Aramean camp," they said, "and no one was there! The horses and donkeys were tethered and the tents were all in order, but there wasn't a single person around!" 11Then the gatekeepers shouted the news to the people in the palace.

Israel Plunders the Camp

12The king got out of bed in the middle of the night and told his officers, "I know what has happened. The Arameans know we are starving, so they have left their camp and have hidden in the fields. They are expecting us to leave the city, and then they will take us alive and capture the city."

13One of his officers replied, "We had better send out scouts to check into this. Let them take five of the remaining horses. If something happens to them, it will be no worse than if they stay here and die with the rest of us."

14So two chariots with horses were prepared, and the king sent scouts to see what had happened to the Aramean army. 15They went all the way to the Jordan River, following a trail of clothing and equipment that the Arameans had thrown away in their mad rush to escape. The scouts returned and told the king about it. 16Then the people of Samaria rushed out and plundered the Aramean camp. So it was true that six quarts of choice flour were sold that day for one piece of silver, and twelve quarts of barley grain were sold for one piece of silver, just as the LORD had promised. 17The king appointed his officer to control the traffic at the gate, but he was knocked down and trampled to death as the people rushed out.

So everything happened exactly as the man of God had predicted when the king came to his house. 18The man of God had said to the king, "By this time tomorrow in the markets of Samaria, six quarts of choice flour will cost one piece of silver, and twelve quarts of barley grain will cost one piece of silver."

19The king's officer had replied, "That couldn't happen even if the LORD opened the windows of heaven!" And the man of God had said, "You will see it happen with your own

---

6:33 Hebrew *he.*   7:1a Hebrew *1 seah* [7.3 liters] *of choice flour will cost 1 shekel* [0.4 ounces or 11 grams]; also in 7:16, 18.
7:1b Hebrew *2 seahs* [14.6 liters] *of barley grain will cost 1 shekel* [0.4 ounces or 11 grams]; also in 7:16, 18.   7:3 Or *with a contagious skin disease.* The Hebrew word used here and throughout this passage can describe various skin diseases.   7:6 Possibly *and the people of Muzur,* a district near Cilicia.

eyes, but you won't be able to eat any of it!" [20]And so it was, for the people trampled him to death at the gate!

The Woman from Shunem Returns Home

8 Elisha had told the woman whose son he had brought back to life, "Take your family and move to some other place, for the LORD has called for a famine on Israel that will last for seven years." [2]So the woman did as the man of God instructed. She took her family and settled in the land of the Philistines for seven years.

[3]After the famine ended she returned from the land of the Philistines, and she went to see the king about getting back her house and land. [4]As she came in, the king was talking with Gehazi, the servant of the man of God. The king had just said, "Tell me some stories about the great things Elisha has done." [5]And Gehazi was telling the king about the time Elisha had brought a boy back to life. At that very moment, the mother of the boy walked in to make her appeal to the king about her house and land.

"Look, my lord the king!" Gehazi exclaimed. "Here is the woman now, and this is her son— the very one Elisha brought back to life!"

[6]"Is this true?" the king asked her. And she told him the story. So he directed one of his officials to see that everything she had lost was restored to her, including the value of any crops that had been harvested during her absence.

Hazael Murders Ben-Hadad

[7]Elisha went to Damascus, the capital of Aram, where King Ben-hadad lay sick. When someone told the king that the man of God had come, [8]the king said to Hazael, "Take a gift to the man of God. Then tell him to ask the LORD, 'Will I recover from this illness?'"

[9]So Hazael loaded down forty camels with the finest products of Damascus as a gift for Elisha. He went to him and said, "Your servant Ben-hadad, the king of Aram, has sent me to ask, 'Will I recover from this illness?'"

[10]And Elisha replied, "Go and tell him, 'You will surely recover.' But actually the LORD has shown me that he will surely die!" [11]Elisha stared at Hazael* with a fixed gaze until Hazael became uneasy.* Then the man of God started weeping.

[12]"What's the matter, my lord?" Hazael asked him.

Elisha replied, "I know the terrible things you will do to the people of Israel. You will burn their fortified cities, kill their young men with the sword, dash their little children to the ground, and rip open their pregnant women!"

[13]Hazael responded, "How could a nobody like me* ever accomplish such great things?"

Elisha answered, "The LORD has shown me that you are going to be the king of Aram."

[14]When Hazael left Elisha and went back, the king asked him, "What did Elisha tell you?"

And Hazael replied, "He told me that you will surely recover."

[15]But the next day Hazael took a blanket, soaked it in water, and held it over the king's face until he died. Then Hazael became the next king of Aram.

Jehoram Rules in Judah

[16]Jehoram son of King Jehoshaphat of Judah began to rule over Judah in the fifth year of the reign of Joram son of Ahab, king of Israel. [17]Jehoram was thirty-two years old when he became king, and he reigned in Jerusalem eight years. [18]But Jehoram followed the example of the kings of Israel and was as wicked as King Ahab, for he had married one of Ahab's daughters. So Jehoram did what was evil in the LORD's sight. [19]But the LORD did not want to destroy Judah, for he had promised his servant David that his descendants would continue to rule, shining like a lamp forever.

[20]During Jehoram's reign, the Edomites revolted against Judah and crowned their own king. [21]So Jehoram* went with all his chariots to attack the town of Zair.* The Edomites surrounded him and his chariot commanders, but he went out at night and attacked them* under cover of darkness. But Jehoram's army deserted him and fled to their homes. [22]So Edom has been independent from Judah to this day. The town of Libnah also revolted about that same time.

[23]The rest of the events in Jehoram's reign and everything he did are recorded in *The Book of the History of the Kings of Judah.* [24]When Jehoram died, he was buried with his ancestors in the City of David. Then his son Ahaziah became the next king.

Ahaziah Rules in Judah

[25]Ahaziah son of Jehoram began to rule over Judah in the twelfth year of the reign of Joram son of Ahab, king of Israel.

8:11a Hebrew *He stared at him.*   8:11b The meaning of the Hebrew is uncertain.   8:13 Hebrew *a dog.*   8:21a Hebrew *Joram,* a variant spelling of Jehoram; also in 8:23, 24.   8:21b Greek version reads *Seir.*   8:21c Or *he went out and escaped.* The meaning of the Hebrew is uncertain.

²⁶Ahaziah was twenty-two years old when he became king, and he reigned in Jerusalem one year. His mother was Athaliah, a granddaughter of King Omri of Israel. ²⁷Ahaziah followed the evil example of King Ahab's family. He did what was evil in the LORD's sight, just as Ahab's family had done, for he was related by marriage to the family of Ahab.

²⁸Ahaziah joined Joram son of Ahab in his war against King Hazael of Aram at Ramoth-gilead. When the Arameans wounded King Joram in the battle, ²⁹he returned to Jezreel to recover from the wounds he had received at Ramoth.* Because Joram was wounded, King Ahaziah of Judah went to Jezreel to visit him.

Jehu Anointed King of Israel

9 Meanwhile, Elisha the prophet had summoned a member of the group of prophets. "Get ready to travel,"* he told him, "and take this flask of olive oil with you. Go to Ramoth-gilead, ²and find Jehu son of Jehoshaphat, son of Nimshi. Call him into a private room away from his friends, ³and pour the oil over his head. Say to him, 'This is what the LORD says: I anoint you to be the king over Israel.' Then open the door and run for your life!"

⁴So the young prophet did as he was told and went to Ramoth-gilead. ⁵When he arrived there, he found Jehu sitting around with the other army officers. "I have a message for you, Commander," he said.

"For which one of us?" Jehu asked.

"For you, Commander," he replied.

⁶So Jehu left the others and went into the house. Then the young prophet poured the oil over Jehu's head and said, "This is what the LORD, the God of Israel, says: I anoint you king over the LORD's people, Israel. ⁷You are to destroy the family of Ahab, your master. In this way, I will avenge the murder of my prophets and all the LORD's servants who were killed by Jezebel. ⁸The entire family of Ahab must be wiped out. I will destroy every one of his male descendants, slave and free alike, anywhere in Israel. ⁹I will destroy the family of Ahab as I destroyed the families of Jeroboam son of Nebat and of Baasha son of Ahijah. ¹⁰Dogs will eat Ahab's wife Jezebel at the plot of land in Jezreel, and no one will bury her." Then the young prophet opened the door and ran.

¹¹Jehu went back to his fellow officers, and one of them asked him, "What did that madman want? Is everything all right?"

"You know how a man like that babbles on," Jehu replied.

¹²"You're hiding something," they said. "Tell us."

So Jehu told them, "He said to me, 'This is what the LORD says: I have anointed you to be king over Israel.'"

¹³Then they quickly spread out their cloaks on the bare steps and blew the ram's horn, shouting, "Jehu is king!"

Jehu Kills Joram and Ahaziah

¹⁴So Jehu son of Jehoshaphat, son of Nimshi, led a conspiracy against King Joram. (Now Joram had been with the army at Ramoth-gilead, defending Israel against the forces of King Hazael of Aram. ¹⁵But King Joram* was wounded in the fighting and returned to Jezreel to recover from his wounds.) So Jehu told the men with him, "If you want me to be king, don't let anyone leave town and go to Jezreel to report what we have done."

¹⁶Then Jehu got into a chariot and rode to Jezreel to find King Joram, who was lying there wounded. King Ahaziah of Judah was there, too, for he had gone to visit him. ¹⁷The watchman on the tower of Jezreel saw Jehu and his company approaching, so he shouted to Joram, "I see a company of troops coming!"

"Send out a rider to ask if they are coming in peace," King Joram ordered.

¹⁸So a horseman went out to meet Jehu and said, "The king wants to know if you are coming in peace."

Jehu replied, "What do you know about peace? Fall in behind me!"

The watchman called out to the king, "The messenger has met them, but he's not returning."

¹⁹So the king sent out a second horseman. He rode up to them and said, "The king wants to know if you come in peace."

Again Jehu answered, "What do you know about peace? Fall in behind me!"

²⁰The watchman exclaimed, "The messenger has met them, but he isn't returning either! It must be Jehu son of Nimshi, for he's driving like a madman."

²¹"Quick! Get my chariot ready!" King Joram commanded.

Then King Joram of Israel and King Ahaziah of Judah rode out in their chariots to

8:29 Hebrew *Ramah*, a variant spelling of Ramoth.   9:1 Hebrew *Bind up your loins.*   9:15 Hebrew *Jehoram*, a variant spelling of Joram; also in 9:17, 21, 22, 23, 24.

meet Jehu. They met him at the plot of land that had belonged to Naboth of Jezreel. ²²King Joram demanded, "Do you come in peace, Jehu?"

Jehu replied, "How can there be peace as long as the idolatry and witchcraft of your mother, Jezebel, are all around us?"

²³Then King Joram turned the horses around* and fled, shouting to King Ahaziah, "Treason, Ahaziah!" ²⁴But Jehu drew his bow and shot Joram between the shoulders. The arrow pierced his heart, and he sank down dead in his chariot.

²⁵Jehu said to Bidkar, his officer, "Throw him into the plot of land that belonged to Naboth of Jezreel. Do you remember when you and I were riding along behind his father, Ahab? The LORD pronounced this message against him: ²⁶'I solemnly swear that I will repay him here on this plot of land, says the LORD, for the murder of Naboth and his sons that I saw yesterday.' So throw him out on Naboth's property, just as the LORD said."

²⁷When King Ahaziah of Judah saw what was happening, he fled along the road to Beth-haggan. Jehu rode after him, shouting, "Shoot him, too!" So they shot Ahaziah* in his chariot at the Ascent of Gur, near Ibleam. He was able to go on as far as Megiddo, but he died there. ²⁸His servants took him by chariot to Jerusalem, where they buried him with his ancestors in the City of David. ²⁹Ahaziah had become king over Judah in the eleventh year of the reign of Joram son of Ahab.

The Death of Jezebel

³⁰When Jezebel, the queen mother, heard that Jehu had come to Jezreel, she painted her eyelids and fixed her hair and sat at a window. ³¹When Jehu entered the gate of the palace, she shouted at him, "Have you come in peace, you murderer? You're just like Zimri, who murdered his master!"*

³²Jehu looked up and saw her at the window and shouted, "Who is on my side?" And two or three eunuchs looked out at him. ³³"Throw her down!" Jehu yelled. So they threw her out of the window, and her blood spattered against the wall and on the horses. And Jehu trampled her body under his horses' hooves.

³⁴Then Jehu went into the palace and ate and drank. Afterward he said, "Someone go and bury this cursed woman, for she is the daughter of a king." ³⁵But when they went out to bury her, they found only her skull, her feet, and her hands.

³⁶When they returned and told Jehu, he stated, "This fulfills the message from the LORD, which he spoke through his servant Elijah from Tishbe: 'At the plot of land in Jezreel, dogs will eat Jezebel's body. ³⁷Her remains will be scattered like dung on the plot of land in Jezreel, so that no one will be able to recognize her.'"

Jehu Kills Ahab's Family

10 Ahab had seventy sons living in the city of Samaria. So Jehu wrote letters and sent them to Samaria, to the elders and officials of the city,* and to the guardians of King Ahab's sons. He said, ²"The king's sons are with you, and you have at your disposal chariots, horses, a fortified city, and weapons. As soon as you receive this letter, ³select the best qualified of your master's sons to be your king, and prepare to fight for Ahab's dynasty."

⁴But they were paralyzed with fear and said, "We've seen that two kings couldn't stand against this man! What can we do?"

⁵So the palace and city administrators, together with the elders and the guardians of the king's sons, sent this message to Jehu: "We are your servants and will do anything you tell us. We will not make anyone king; do whatever you think is best."

⁶Jehu responded with a second letter: "If you are on my side and are going to obey me, bring the heads of your master's sons to me at Jezreel by this time tomorrow." Now the seventy sons of the king were being cared for by the leaders of Samaria, where they had been raised since childhood. ⁷When the letter arrived, the leaders killed all seventy of the king's sons. They placed their heads in baskets and presented them to Jehu at Jezreel.

⁸A messenger went to Jehu and said, "They have brought the heads of the king's sons."

So Jehu ordered, "Pile them in two heaps at the entrance of the city gate, and leave them there until morning."

⁹In the morning he went out and spoke to the crowd that had gathered around them. "You are not to blame," he told them. "I am the one who conspired against my master and killed him. But who killed all these? ¹⁰You can be sure that the message of the LORD that was

---

9:23 Hebrew *turned his hands.* 9:27 As in Greek and Syriac versions; Hebrew lacks *So they shot Ahaziah.* 9:31 See 1 Kgs 16:9-10, where Zimri killed his master, King Elah. 10:1 As in some Greek manuscripts and Latin Vulgate (see also 10:6); Hebrew reads *of Jezreel.*

spoken concerning Ahab's family will not fail. The LORD declared through his servant Elijah that this would happen." [11] Then Jehu killed all who were left of Ahab's relatives living in Jezreel and all his important officials, his personal friends, and his priests. So Ahab was left without a single survivor.

[12] Then Jehu set out for Samaria. Along the way, while he was at Beth-eked of the Shepherds, [13] he met some relatives of King Ahaziah of Judah. "Who are you?" he asked them.

And they replied, "We are relatives of King Ahaziah. We are going to visit the sons of King Ahab and the sons of the queen mother."

[14] "Take them alive!" Jehu shouted to his men. And they captured all forty-two of them and killed them at the well of Beth-eked. None of them escaped.

[15] When Jehu left there, he met Jehonadab son of Recab, who was coming to meet him. After they had greeted each other, Jehu said to him, "Are you as loyal to me as I am to you?"

"Yes, I am," Jehonadab replied.

"If you are," Jehu said, "then give me your hand." So Jehonadab put out his hand, and Jehu helped him into the chariot. [16] Then Jehu said, "Now come with me, and see how devoted I am to the LORD." So Jehonadab rode along with him.

[17] When Jehu arrived in Samaria, he killed everyone who was left there from Ahab's family, just as the LORD had promised through Elijah.

Jehu Kills the Priests of Baal

[18] Then Jehu called a meeting of all the people of the city and said to them, "Ahab's worship of Baal was nothing compared to the way I will worship him! [19] Therefore, summon all the prophets and worshipers of Baal, and call together all his priests. See to it that every one of them comes, for I am going to offer a great sacrifice to Baal. Anyone who fails to come will be put to death." But Jehu's cunning plan was to destroy all the worshipers of Baal.

[20] Then Jehu ordered, "Prepare a solemn assembly to worship Baal!" So they did. [21] He sent messengers throughout all Israel summoning those who worshiped Baal. They all came—not a single one remained behind—and they filled the temple of Baal from one end to the other. [22] And Jehu instructed the keeper of the wardrobe, "Be sure that every worshiper of Baal wears one of these robes." So robes were given to them.

[23] Then Jehu went into the temple of Baal with Jehonadab son of Recab. Jehu said to the worshipers of Baal, "Make sure no one who worships the LORD is here—only those who worship Baal." [24] So they were all inside the temple to offer sacrifices and burnt offerings. Now Jehu had stationed eighty of his men outside the building and had warned them, "If you let anyone escape, you will pay for it with your own life."

[25] As soon as Jehu had finished sacrificing the burnt offering, he commanded his guards and officers, "Go in and kill all of them. Don't let a single one escape!" So they killed them all with their swords, and the guards and officers dragged their bodies outside.* Then Jehu's men went into the innermost fortress* of the temple of Baal. [26] They dragged out the sacred pillar* used in the worship of Baal and burned it. [27] They smashed the sacred pillar and wrecked the temple of Baal, converting it into a public toilet, as it remains to this day.

[28] In this way, Jehu destroyed every trace of Baal worship from Israel. [29] He did not, however, destroy the gold calves at Bethel and Dan, with which Jeroboam son of Nebat had caused Israel to sin.

[30] Nonetheless the LORD said to Jehu, "You have done well in following my instructions to destroy the family of Ahab. Therefore, your descendants will be kings of Israel down to the fourth generation." [31] But Jehu did not obey the Law of the LORD, the God of Israel, with all his heart. He refused to turn from the sins that Jeroboam had led Israel to commit.

The Death of Jehu

[32] At about that time the LORD began to cut down the size of Israel's territory. King Hazael conquered several sections of the country [33] east of the Jordan River, including all of Gilead, Gad, Reuben, and Manasseh. He conquered the area from the town of Aroer by the Arnon Gorge to as far north as Gilead and Bashan.

[34] The rest of the events in Jehu's reign—everything he did and all his achievements—are recorded in The Book of the History of the Kings of Israel.

[35] When Jehu died, he was buried in Samaria. Then his son Jehoahaz became the next king. [36] In all, Jehu reigned over Israel from Samaria for twenty-eight years.

10:25a Or and they left their bodies lying there; or and they threw them out into the outermost court.   10:25b Hebrew city.   10:26 As in Greek and Syriac versions and Latin Vulgate; Hebrew reads sacred pillars.

Queen Athaliah Rules in Judah

11 When Athaliah, the mother of King Ahaziah of Judah, learned that her son was dead, she began to destroy the rest of the royal family. ²But Ahaziah's sister Jehosheba, the daughter of King Jehoram,* took Ahaziah's infant son, Joash, and stole him away from among the rest of the king's children, who were about to be killed. She put Joash and his nurse in a bedroom, and they hid him from Athaliah, so the child was not murdered. ³Joash remained hidden in the Temple of the LORD for six years while Athaliah ruled over the land.

Revolt against Athaliah

⁴In the seventh year of Athaliah's reign, Jehoiada the priest summoned the commanders, the Carite mercenaries, and the palace guards to come to the Temple of the LORD. He made a solemn pact with them and made them swear an oath of loyalty there in the LORD's Temple; then he showed them the king's son.

⁵Jehoiada told them, "This is what you must do. A third of you who are on duty on the Sabbath are to guard the royal palace itself. ⁶Another third of you are to stand guard at the Sur Gate. And the final third must stand guard behind the palace guard. These three groups will all guard the palace. ⁷The other two units who are off duty on the Sabbath must stand guard for the king at the LORD's Temple. ⁸Form a bodyguard around the king and keep your weapons in hand. Kill anyone who tries to break through. Stay with the king wherever he goes."

⁹So the commanders did everything as Jehoiada the priest ordered. The commanders took charge of the men reporting for duty that Sabbath, as well as those who were going off duty. They brought them all to Jehoiada the priest, ¹⁰and he supplied them with the spears and small shields that had once belonged to King David and were stored in the Temple of the LORD. ¹¹The palace guards stationed themselves around the king, with their weapons ready. They formed a line from the south side of the Temple around to the north side and all around the altar.

¹²Then Jehoiada brought out Joash, the king's son, placed the crown on his head, and presented him with a copy of God's laws.* They anointed him and proclaimed him king, and everyone clapped their hands and shouted, "Long live the king!"

The Death of Athaliah

¹³When Athaliah heard the noise made by the palace guards and the people, she hurried to the LORD's Temple to see what was happening. ¹⁴When she arrived, she saw the newly crowned king standing in his place of authority by the pillar, as was the custom at times of coronation. The commanders and trumpeters were surrounding him, and people from all over the land were rejoicing and blowing trumpets. When Athaliah saw all this, she tore her clothes in despair and shouted, "Treason! Treason!"

¹⁵Then Jehoiada the priest ordered the commanders who were in charge of the troops, "Take her to the soldiers in front of the Temple,* and kill anyone who tries to rescue her." For the priest had said, "She must not be killed in the Temple of the LORD." ¹⁶So they seized her and led her out to the gate where horses enter the palace grounds, and she was killed there.

Jehoiada's Religious Reforms

¹⁷Then Jehoiada made a covenant between the LORD and the king and the people that they would be the LORD's people. He also made a covenant between the king and the people. ¹⁸And all the people of the land went over to the temple of Baal and tore it down. They demolished the altars and smashed the idols to pieces, and they killed Mattan the priest of Baal in front of the altars.

Jehoiada the priest stationed guards at the Temple of the LORD. ¹⁹Then the commanders, the Carite mercenaries, the palace guards, and all the people of the land escorted the king from the Temple of the LORD. They went through the gate of the guards and into the palace, and the king took his seat on the royal throne. ²⁰So all the people of the land rejoiced, and the city was peaceful because Athaliah had been killed at the king's palace.

²¹*Joash* was seven years old when he became king.

Joash Repairs the Temple

12 ¹*Joash* began to rule over Judah in the seventh year of King Jehu's reign in Israel. He reigned in Jerusalem forty years. His

---

11:2 Hebrew *Joram*, a variant spelling of Jehoram.　11:12 Or *a copy of the covenant.*　11:15 Or *Bring her out from between the ranks;* or *Take her out of the Temple precincts.* The meaning of the Hebrew is uncertain.　11:21a Verse 11:21 is numbered 12:1 in Hebrew text.　11:21b Hebrew *Jehoash*, a variant spelling of Joash.　12:1a Verses 12:1-21 are numbered 12:2-22 in Hebrew text. 12:1b Hebrew *Jehoash*, a variant spelling of Joash; also in 12:2, 4, 6, 7, 18.

mother was Zibiah from Beersheba. ²All his life Joash did what was pleasing in the LORD's sight because Jehoiada the priest instructed him. ³Yet even so, he did not destroy the pagan shrines, and the people still offered sacrifices and burned incense there.

⁴One day King Joash said to the priests, "Collect all the money brought as a sacred offering to the LORD's Temple, whether it is a regular assessment, a payment of vows, or a voluntary gift. ⁵Let the priests take some of that money to pay for whatever repairs are needed at the Temple."

⁶But by the twenty-third year of Joash's reign, the priests still had not repaired the Temple. ⁷So King Joash called for Jehoiada and the other priests and asked them, "Why haven't you repaired the Temple? Don't use any more money for your own needs. From now on, it must all be spent on Temple repairs." ⁸So the priests agreed not to accept any more money from the people, and they also agreed to let others take responsibility for repairing the Temple.

⁹Then Jehoiada the priest bored a hole in the lid of a large chest and set it on the right-hand side of the altar at the entrance of the Temple of the LORD. The priests guarding the entrance put all of the people's contributions into the chest. ¹⁰Whenever the chest became full, the court secretary and the high priest counted the money that had been brought to the LORD's Temple and put it into bags. ¹¹Then they gave the money to the construction supervisors, who used it to pay the people working on the LORD's Temple—the carpenters, the builders, ¹²the masons, and the stonecutters. They also used the money to buy the timber and the finished stone needed for repairing the LORD's Temple, and they paid any other expenses related to the Temple's restoration.

¹³The money brought to the Temple was not used for making silver bowls, lamp snuffers, basins, trumpets, or other articles of gold or silver for the Temple of the LORD. ¹⁴It was paid to the workmen, who used it for the Temple repairs. ¹⁵No accounting of this money was required from the construction supervisors, because they were honest and trustworthy men. ¹⁶However, the money that was contributed for guilt offerings and sin offerings was not brought into the LORD's Temple. It was given to the priests for their own use.

The End of Joash's Reign

¹⁷About this time King Hazael of Aram went to war against Gath and captured it. Then he turned to attack Jerusalem. ¹⁸King Joash collected all the sacred objects that Jehoshaphat, Jehoram, and Ahaziah, the previous kings of Judah, had dedicated, along with what he himself had dedicated. He sent them all to Hazael, along with all the gold in the treasuries of the LORD's Temple and the royal palace. So Hazael called off his attack on Jerusalem.

¹⁹The rest of the events in Joash's reign and everything he did are recorded in *The Book of the History of the Kings of Judah.*

²⁰Joash's officers plotted against him and assassinated him at Beth-millo on the road to Silla. ²¹The assassins were Jozacar* son of Shimeath and Jehozabad son of Shomer—both trusted advisers. Joash was buried with his ancestors in the City of David. Then his son Amaziah became the next king.

Jehoahaz Rules in Israel

13 Jehoahaz son of Jehu began to rule over Israel in the twenty-third year of King Joash's reign in Judah. He reigned in Samaria seventeen years. ²But he did what was evil in the LORD's sight. He followed the example of Jeroboam son of Nebat, continuing the sins that Jeroboam had led Israel to commit. ³So the LORD was very angry with Israel, and he allowed King Hazael of Aram and his son Ben-hadad to defeat them repeatedly.

⁴Then Jehoahaz prayed for the LORD's help, and the LORD heard his prayer, for he could see how severely the king of Aram was oppressing Israel. ⁵So the LORD provided someone to rescue the Israelites from the tyranny of the Arameans. Then Israel lived in safety again as they had in former days.

⁶But they continued to sin, following the evil example of Jeroboam. They also allowed the Asherah pole in Samaria to remain standing. ⁷Finally, Jehoahaz's army was reduced to 50 charioteers, 10 chariots, and 10,000 foot soldiers. The king of Aram had killed the others, trampling them like dust under his feet.

⁸The rest of the events in Jehoahaz's reign—everything he did and the extent of his power—are recorded in *The Book of the History of the Kings of Israel.* ⁹When Jehoahaz died, he was buried in Samaria. Then his son Jehoash* became the next king.

12:21 As in Greek and Syriac versions; Hebrew reads *Jozabad.* 12, 13, 14, 25.   13:9 Hebrew *Joash,* a variant spelling of Jehoash; also in 13:10,

Jehoash Rules in Israel

¹⁰Jehoash son of Jehoahaz began to rule over Israel in the thirty-seventh year of King Joash's reign in Judah. He reigned in Samaria sixteen years. ¹¹But he did what was evil in the LORD's sight. He refused to turn from the sins that Jeroboam son of Nebat had led Israel to commit.

¹²The rest of the events in Jehoash's reign and everything he did, including the extent of his power and his war with King Amaziah of Judah, are recorded in *The Book of the History of the Kings of Israel.* ¹³When Jehoash died, he was buried in Samaria with the kings of Israel. Then his son Jeroboam II became the next king.

Elisha's Final Prophecy

¹⁴When Elisha was in his last illness, King Jehoash of Israel visited him and wept over him. "My father! My father! I see the chariots and charioteers of Israel!" he cried.

¹⁵Elisha told him, "Get a bow and some arrows." And the king did as he was told. ¹⁶Elisha told him, "Put your hand on the bow," and Elisha laid his own hands on the king's hands. ¹⁷Then he commanded, "Open that eastern window," and he opened it. Then he said, "Shoot!" So he shot an arrow. Elisha proclaimed, "This is the LORD's arrow, an arrow of victory over Aram, for you will completely conquer the Arameans at Aphek."

¹⁸Then he said, "Now pick up the other arrows and strike them against the ground." So the king picked them up and struck the ground three times. ¹⁹But the man of God was angry with him. "You should have struck the ground five or six times!" he exclaimed. "Then you would have beaten Aram until it was entirely destroyed. Now you will be victorious only three times."

²⁰Then Elisha died and was buried.

Groups of Moabite raiders used to invade the land each spring. ²¹Once when some Israelites were burying a man, they spied a band of these raiders. So they hastily threw the corpse into the tomb of Elisha and fled. But as soon as the body touched Elisha's bones, the dead man revived and jumped to his feet!

²²King Hazael of Aram had oppressed Israel during the entire reign of King Jehoahaz. ²³But the LORD was gracious and merciful to the people of Israel, and they were not totally destroyed. He pitied them because of his covenant with Abraham, Isaac, and Jacob. And to this day he still has not completely destroyed them or banished them from his presence.

²⁴King Hazael of Aram died, and his son Ben-hadad became the next king. ²⁵Then Jehoash son of Jehoahaz recaptured from Ben-hadad son of Hazael the towns that had been taken from Jehoash's father, Jehoahaz. Jehoash defeated Ben-hadad on three occasions, and he recovered the Israelite towns.

Amaziah Rules in Judah

14 Amaziah son of Joash began to rule over Judah in the second year of the reign of King Jehoash* of Israel. ²Amaziah was twenty-five years old when he became king, and he reigned in Jerusalem twenty-nine years. His mother was Jehoaddin from Jerusalem. ³Amaziah did what was pleasing in the LORD's sight, but not like his ancestor David. Instead, he followed the example of his father, Joash. ⁴Amaziah did not destroy the pagan shrines, and the people still offered sacrifices and burned incense there.

⁵When Amaziah was well established as king, he executed the officials who had assassinated his father. ⁶However, he did not kill the children of the assassins, for he obeyed the command of the LORD as written by Moses in the Book of the Law: "Parents must not be put to death for the sins of their children, nor children for the sins of their parents. Those deserving to die must be put to death for their own crimes."*

⁷Amaziah also killed 10,000 Edomites in the Valley of Salt. He also conquered Sela and changed its name to Joktheel, as it is called to this day.

⁸One day Amaziah sent messengers with this challenge to Israel's king Jehoash, the son of Jehoahaz and grandson of Jehu: "Come and meet me in battle!"*

⁹But King Jehoash of Israel replied to King Amaziah of Judah with this story: "Out in the Lebanon mountains, a thistle sent a message to a mighty cedar tree: 'Give your daughter in marriage to my son.' But just then a wild animal of Lebanon came by and stepped on the thistle, crushing it!

¹⁰"You have indeed defeated Edom, and you are proud of it. But be content with your victory and stay at home! Why stir up trouble that will only bring disaster on you and the people of Judah?"

¹¹But Amaziah refused to listen, so King

14:1 Hebrew *Joash,* a variant spelling of Jehoash; also in 14:13, 23, 27.   14:6 Deut 24:16.   14:8 Hebrew *Come, let us look one another in the face.*

Jehoash of Israel mobilized his army against King Amaziah of Judah. The two armies drew up their battle lines at Beth-shemesh in Judah. [12]Judah was routed by the army of Israel, and its army scattered and fled for home. [13]King Jehoash of Israel captured Judah's king, Amaziah son of Joash and grandson of Ahaziah, at Beth-shemesh. Then he marched to Jerusalem, where he demolished 600 feet* of Jerusalem's wall, from the Ephraim Gate to the Corner Gate. [14]He carried off all the gold and silver and all the articles from the Temple of the LORD. He also seized the treasures from the royal palace, along with hostages, and then returned to Samaria.

[15]The rest of the events in Jehoash's reign and everything he did, including the extent of his power and his war with King Amaziah of Judah, are recorded in *The Book of the History of the Kings of Israel.* [16]When Jehoash died, he was buried in Samaria with the kings of Israel. And his son Jeroboam II became the next king.

[17]King Amaziah of Judah lived for fifteen years after the death of King Jehoash of Israel. [18]The rest of the events in Amaziah's reign are recorded in *The Book of the History of the Kings of Judah.*

[19]There was a conspiracy against Amaziah's life in Jerusalem, and he fled to Lachish. But his enemies sent assassins after him, and they killed him there. [20]They brought his body back to Jerusalem on a horse, and he was buried with his ancestors in the City of David.

[21]All the people of Judah had crowned Amaziah's sixteen-year-old son, Uzziah,* as king in place of his father, Amaziah. [22]After his father's death, Uzziah rebuilt the town of Elath and restored it to Judah.

Jeroboam II Rules in Israel

[23]Jeroboam II, the son of Jehoash, began to rule over Israel in the fifteenth year of King Amaziah's reign in Judah. He reigned in Samaria forty-one years. [24]He did what was evil in the LORD's sight. He refused to turn from the sins that Jeroboam son of Nebat had led Israel to commit. [25]Jeroboam II recovered the territories of Israel between Lebo-hamath and the Dead Sea,* just as the LORD, the God of Israel, had promised through Jonah son of Amittai, the prophet from Gath-hepher.

[26]For the LORD saw the bitter suffering of everyone in Israel, and that there was no one in Israel, slave or free, to help them. [27]And because the LORD had not said he would blot out the name of Israel completely, he used Jeroboam II, the son of Jehoash, to save them.

[28]The rest of the events in the reign of Jeroboam II and everything he did—including the extent of his power, his wars, and how he recovered for Israel both Damascus and Hamath, which had belonged to Judah*—are recorded in *The Book of the History of the Kings of Israel.* [29]When Jeroboam II died, he was buried in Samaria* with the kings of Israel. Then his son Zechariah became the next king.

Uzziah Rules in Judah

15 Uzziah* son of Amaziah began to rule over Judah in the twenty-seventh year of the reign of King Jeroboam II of Israel. [2]He was sixteen years old when he became king, and he reigned in Jerusalem fifty-two years. His mother was Jecoliah from Jerusalem.

[3]He did what was pleasing in the LORD's sight, just as his father, Amaziah, had done. [4]But he did not destroy the pagan shrines, and the people still offered sacrifices and burned incense there. [5]The LORD struck the king with leprosy,* which lasted until the day he died. He lived in isolation in a separate house. The king's son Jotham was put in charge of the royal palace, and he governed the people of the land.

[6]The rest of the events in Uzziah's reign and everything he did are recorded in *The Book of the History of the Kings of Judah.* [7]When Uzziah died, he was buried with his ancestors in the City of David. And his son Jotham became the next king.

Zechariah Rules in Israel

[8]Zechariah son of Jeroboam II began to rule over Israel in the thirty-eighth year of King Uzziah's reign in Judah. He reigned in Samaria six months. [9]Zechariah did what was evil in the LORD's sight, as his ancestors had done. He refused to turn from the sins that Jeroboam son of Nebat had led Israel to commit. [10]Then Shallum son of Jabesh conspired against Zechariah, assassinated him in public,* and became the next king.

[11]The rest of the events in Zechariah's reign are recorded in *The Book of the History of the Kings*

14:13 Hebrew *400 cubits* [180 meters].   14:21 Hebrew *Azariah,* a variant spelling of Uzziah.   14:25 Hebrew *the sea of the Arabah.*
14:28 Or *to Yaudi.* The meaning of the Hebrew is uncertain.   14:29 As in some Greek manuscripts; Hebrew lacks *he was buried in Samaria.*   15:1 Hebrew *Azariah,* a variant spelling of Uzziah; also in 15:6, 7, 8, 17, 23, 27.   15:5 Or *with a contagious skin disease.* The Hebrew word used here and throughout this passage can describe various skin diseases.   15:10 Or *at Ibleam.*

of Israel. ¹²So the LORD's message to Jehu came true: "Your descendants will be kings of Israel down to the fourth generation."

Shallum Rules in Israel

¹³Shallum son of Jabesh began to rule over Israel in the thirty-ninth year of King Uzziah's reign in Judah. Shallum reigned in Samaria only one month. ¹⁴Then Menahem son of Gadi went to Samaria from Tirzah and assassinated him, and he became the next king.

¹⁵The rest of the events in Shallum's reign, including his conspiracy, are recorded in *The Book of the History of the Kings of Israel.*

Menahem Rules in Israel

¹⁶At that time Menahem destroyed the town of Tappuah* and all the surrounding countryside as far as Tirzah, because its citizens refused to surrender the town. He killed the entire population and ripped open the pregnant women.

¹⁷Menahem son of Gadi began to rule over Israel in the thirty-ninth year of King Uzziah's reign in Judah. He reigned in Samaria ten years. ¹⁸But Menahem did what was evil in the LORD's sight. During his entire reign, he refused to turn from the sins that Jeroboam son of Nebat had led Israel to commit.

¹⁹Then King Tiglath-pileser* of Assyria invaded the land. But Menahem paid him thirty-seven tons* of silver to gain his support in tightening his grip on royal power. ²⁰Menahem extorted the money from the rich of Israel, demanding that each of them pay fifty pieces* of silver to the king of Assyria. So the king of Assyria turned from attacking Israel and did not stay in the land.

²¹The rest of the events in Menahem's reign and everything he did are recorded in *The Book of the History of the Kings of Israel.* ²²When Menahem died, his son Pekahiah became the next king.

Pekahiah Rules in Israel

²³Pekahiah son of Menahem began to rule over Israel in the fiftieth year of King Uzziah's reign in Judah. He reigned in Samaria two years. ²⁴But Pekahiah did what was evil in the LORD's sight. He refused to turn from the sins that Jeroboam son of Nebat had led Israel to commit.

²⁵Then Pekah son of Remaliah, the commander of Pekahiah's army, conspired against him. With fifty men from Gilead, Pekah assassinated the king, along with Argob and Arieh, in the citadel of the palace at Samaria. And Pekah reigned in his place.

²⁶The rest of the events in Pekahiah's reign and everything he did are recorded in *The Book of the History of the Kings of Israel.*

Pekah Rules in Israel

²⁷Pekah son of Remaliah began to rule over Israel in the fifty-second year of King Uzziah's reign in Judah. He reigned in Samaria twenty years. ²⁸But Pekah did what was evil in the LORD's sight. He refused to turn from the sins that Jeroboam son of Nebat had led Israel to commit.

²⁹During Pekah's reign, King Tiglath-pileser of Assyria attacked Israel again, and he captured the towns of Ijon, Abel-beth-maacah, Janoah, Kedesh, and Hazor. He also conquered the regions of Gilead, Galilee, and all of Naphtali, and he took the people to Assyria as captives. ³⁰Then Hoshea son of Elah conspired against Pekah and assassinated him. He began to rule over Israel in the twentieth year of Jotham son of Uzziah.

³¹The rest of the events in Pekah's reign and everything he did are recorded in *The Book of the History of the Kings of Israel.*

Jotham Rules in Judah

³²Jotham son of Uzziah began to rule over Judah in the second year of King Pekah's reign in Israel. ³³He was twenty-five years old when he became king, and he reigned in Jerusalem sixteen years. His mother was Jerusha, the daughter of Zadok.

³⁴Jotham did what was pleasing in the LORD's sight. He did everything his father, Uzziah, had done. ³⁵But he did not destroy the pagan shrines, and the people still offered sacrifices and burned incense there. He rebuilt the upper gate of the Temple of the LORD.

³⁶The rest of the events in Jotham's reign and everything he did are recorded in *The Book of the History of the Kings of Judah.* ³⁷In those days the LORD began to send King Rezin of Aram and King Pekah of Israel to attack Judah. ³⁸When Jotham died, he was buried with his ancestors in the City of David. And his son Ahaz became the next king.

Ahaz Rules in Judah

16 Ahaz son of Jotham began to rule over Judah in the seventeenth year of King Pekah's reign in Israel. ²Ahaz was twenty years

---

15:16 As in some Greek manuscripts; Hebrew reads *Tiphsah.* **15:19a** Hebrew *Pul,* another name for Tiglath-pileser. **15:19b** Hebrew *1,000 talents* [34 metric tons]. **15:20** Hebrew *50 shekels* [20 ounces or 570 grams].

old when he became king, and he reigned in Jerusalem sixteen years. He did not do what was pleasing in the sight of the LORD his God, as his ancestor David had done. ³Instead, he followed the example of the kings of Israel, even sacrificing his own son in the fire.* In this way, he followed the detestable practices of the pagan nations the LORD had driven from the land ahead of the Israelites. ⁴He offered sacrifices and burned incense at the pagan shrines and on the hills and under every green tree.

⁵Then King Rezin of Aram and King Pekah of Israel came up to attack Jerusalem. They besieged Ahaz but could not conquer him. ⁶At that time the king of Edom* recovered the town of Elath for Edom.* He drove out the people of Judah and sent Edomites* to live there, as they do to this day.

⁷King Ahaz sent messengers to King Tiglathpileser of Assyria with this message: "I am your servant and your vassal.* Come up and rescue me from the attacking armies of Aram and Israel." ⁸Then Ahaz took the silver and gold from the Temple of the LORD and the palace treasury and sent it as a payment to the Assyrian king. ⁹So the king of Assyria attacked the Aramean capital of Damascus and led its population away as captives, resettling them in Kir. He also killed King Rezin.

¹⁰King Ahaz then went to Damascus to meet with King Tiglath-pileser of Assyria. While he was there, he took special note of the altar. Then he sent a model of the altar to Uriah the priest, along with its design in full detail. ¹¹Uriah followed the king's instructions and built an altar just like it, and it was ready before the king returned from Damascus. ¹²When the king returned, he inspected the altar and made offerings on it. ¹³He presented a burnt offering and a grain offering, he poured out a liquid offering, and he sprinkled the blood of peace offerings on the altar.

¹⁴Then King Ahaz removed the old bronze altar from its place in front of the LORD's Temple, between the entrance and the new altar, and placed it on the north side of the new altar. ¹⁵He told Uriah the priest, "Use the new altar* for the morning sacrifices of burnt offering, the evening grain offering, the king's burnt offering and grain offering, and the burnt offerings of all the people, as well as their grain offerings and liquid offerings.

Sprinkle the blood from all the burnt offerings and sacrifices on the new altar. The bronze altar will be for my personal use only." ¹⁶Uriah the priest did just as King Ahaz commanded him.

¹⁷Then the king removed the side panels and basins from the portable water carts. He also removed the great bronze basin called the Sea from the backs of the bronze oxen and placed it on the stone pavement. ¹⁸In deference to the king of Assyria, he also removed the canopy that had been constructed inside the palace for use on the Sabbath day,* as well as the king's outer entrance to the Temple of the LORD.

¹⁹The rest of the events in Ahaz's reign and everything he did are recorded in *The Book of the History of the Kings of Judah.* ²⁰When Ahaz died, he was buried with his ancestors in the City of David. Then his son Hezekiah became the next king.

Hoshea Rules in Israel

17 Hoshea son of Elah began to rule over Israel in the twelfth year of King Ahaz's reign in Judah. He reigned in Samaria nine years. ²He did what was evil in the LORD's sight, but not to the same extent as the kings of Israel who ruled before him.

³King Shalmaneser of Assyria attacked King Hoshea, so Hoshea was forced to pay heavy tribute to Assyria. ⁴But Hoshea stopped paying the annual tribute and conspired against the king of Assyria by asking King So of Egypt* to help him shake free of Assyria's power. When the king of Assyria discovered this treachery, he seized Hoshea and put him in prison.

Samaria Falls to Assyria

⁵Then the king of Assyria invaded the entire land, and for three years he besieged the city of Samaria. ⁶Finally, in the ninth year of King Hoshea's reign, Samaria fell, and the people of Israel were exiled to Assyria. They were settled in colonies in Halah, along the banks of the Habor River in Gozan, and in the cities of the Medes.

⁷This disaster came upon the people of Israel because they worshiped other gods. They sinned against the LORD their God, who had brought them safely out of Egypt and had rescued them from the power of Pharaoh, the king of Egypt. ⁸They had followed the practices of the pagan nations the LORD had driven from

16:3 Or *even making his son pass through the fire.*   16:6a As in Latin Vulgate; Hebrew reads *Rezin king of Aram.*   16:6b As in Latin Vulgate; Hebrew reads *Aram.*   16:6c As in Greek version, Latin Vulgate, and an alternate reading of the Masoretic Text; the other alternate reads *Arameans.*   16:7 Hebrew *your son.*   16:15 Hebrew *the great altar.*   16:18 The meaning of the Hebrew is uncertain.   17:4 Or *by asking the king of Egypt at Sais.*

the land ahead of them, as well as the practices the kings of Israel had introduced. 9The people of Israel had also secretly done many things that were not pleasing to the LORD their God. They built pagan shrines for themselves in all their towns, from the smallest outpost to the largest walled city. 10They set up sacred pillars and Asherah poles at the top of every hill and under every green tree. 11They offered sacrifices on all the hilltops, just like the nations the LORD had driven from the land ahead of them. So the people of Israel had done many evil things, arousing the LORD's anger. 12Yes, they worshiped idols,* despite the LORD's specific and repeated warnings.

13Again and again the LORD had sent his prophets and seers to warn both Israel and Judah: "Turn from all your evil ways. Obey my commands and decrees—the entire law that I commanded your ancestors to obey, and that I gave you through my servants the prophets."

14But the Israelites would not listen. They were as stubborn as their ancestors who had refused to believe in the LORD their God. 15They rejected his decrees and the covenant he had made with their ancestors, and they despised all his warnings. They worshiped worthless idols, so they became worthless themselves. They followed the example of the nations around them, disobeying the LORD's command not to imitate them.

16They rejected all the commands of the LORD their God and made two calves from metal. They set up an Asherah pole and worshiped Baal and all the forces of heaven. 17They even sacrificed their own sons and daughters in the fire.* They consulted fortune-tellers and practiced sorcery and sold themselves to evil, arousing the LORD's anger.

18Because the LORD was very angry with Israel, he swept them away from his presence. Only the tribe of Judah remained in the land. 19But even the people of Judah refused to obey the commands of the LORD their God, for they followed the evil practices that Israel had introduced. 20The LORD rejected all the descendants of Israel. He punished them by handing them over to their attackers until he had banished Israel from his presence.

21For when the LORD* tore Israel away from the kingdom of David, they chose Jeroboam son of Nebat as their king. But Jeroboam drew Israel away from following the LORD and made them commit a great sin. 22And the people of Israel persisted in all the evil ways of Jeroboam. They did not turn from these sins 23until the LORD finally swept them away from his presence, just as all his prophets had warned. So Israel was exiled from their land to Assyria, where they remain to this day.

Foreigners Settle in Israel

24The king of Assyria transported groups of people from Babylon, Cuthah, Avva, Hamath, and Sepharvaim and resettled them in the towns of Samaria, replacing the people of Israel. They took possession of Samaria and lived in its towns. 25But since these foreign settlers did not worship the LORD when they first arrived, the LORD sent lions among them, which killed some of them.

26So a message was sent to the king of Assyria: "The people you have sent to live in the towns of Samaria do not know the religious customs of the God of the land. He has sent lions among them to destroy them because they have not worshiped him correctly."

27The king of Assyria then commanded, "Send one of the exiled priests back to Samaria. Let him live there and teach the new residents the religious customs of the God of the land." 28So one of the priests who had been exiled from Samaria returned to Bethel and taught the new residents how to worship the LORD.

29But these various groups of foreigners also continued to worship their own gods. In town after town where they lived, they placed their idols at the pagan shrines that the people of Samaria had built. 30Those from Babylon worshiped idols of their god Succoth-benoth. Those from Cuthah worshiped their god Nergal. And those from Hamath worshiped Ashima. 31The Avvites worshiped their gods Nibhaz and Tartak. And the people from Sepharvaim even burned their own children as sacrifices to their gods Adrammelech and Anammelech.

32These new residents worshiped the LORD, but they also appointed from among themselves all sorts of people as priests to offer sacrifices at their places of worship. 33And though they worshiped the LORD, they continued to follow their own gods according to the religious customs of the nations from which they came. 34And this is still going on today. They continue to follow their former practices instead of truly worshiping the LORD and obeying the decrees, regulations, instructions, and

---

17:12 The Hebrew term (literally *round things*) probably alludes to dung.   17:17 Or *They even made their sons and daughters pass through the fire.*   17:21 Hebrew *he*; compare 1 Kgs 11:31-32.

commands he gave the descendants of Jacob, whose name he changed to Israel.

35For the LORD had made a covenant with the descendants of Jacob and commanded them: "Do not worship any other gods or bow before them or serve them or offer sacrifices to them. 36But worship only the LORD, who brought you out of Egypt with great strength and a powerful arm. Bow down to him alone, and offer sacrifices only to him. 37Be careful at all times to obey the decrees, regulations, instructions, and commands that he wrote for you. You must not worship other gods. 38Do not forget the covenant I made with you, and do not worship other gods. 39You must worship only the LORD your God. He is the one who will rescue you from all your enemies."

40But the people would not listen and continued to follow their former practices. 41So while these new residents worshiped the LORD, they also worshiped their idols. And to this day their descendants do the same.

Hezekiah Rules in Judah

18 Hezekiah son of Ahaz began to rule over Judah in the third year of King Hoshea's reign in Israel. 2He was twenty-five years old when he became king, and he reigned in Jerusalem twenty-nine years. His mother was Abijah,* the daughter of Zechariah. 3He did what was pleasing in the LORD's sight, just as his ancestor David had done. 4He removed the pagan shrines, smashed the sacred pillars, and cut down the Asherah poles. He broke up the bronze serpent that Moses had made, because the people of Israel had been offering sacrifices to it. The bronze serpent was called Nehushtan.*

5Hezekiah trusted in the LORD, the God of Israel. There was no one like him among all the kings of Judah, either before or after his time. 6He remained faithful to the LORD in everything, and he carefully obeyed all the commands the LORD had given Moses. 7So the LORD was with him, and Hezekiah was successful in everything he did. He revolted against the king of Assyria and refused to pay him tribute. 8He also conquered the Philistines as far distant as Gaza and its territory, from their smallest outpost to their largest walled city.

9During the fourth year of Hezekiah's reign, which was the seventh year of King Hoshea's reign in Israel, King Shalmaneser of Assyria attacked the city of Samaria and began a siege against it. 10Three years later, during the sixth year of King Hezekiah's reign and the ninth year of King Hoshea's reign in Israel, Samaria fell. 11At that time the king of Assyria exiled the Israelites to Assyria and placed them in colonies in Halah, along the banks of the Habor River in Gozan, and in the cities of the Medes. 12For they refused to listen to the LORD their God and obey him. Instead, they violated his covenant—all the laws that Moses the LORD's servant had commanded them to obey.

Assyria Invades Judah

13In the fourteenth year of King Hezekiah's reign,* King Sennacherib of Assyria came to attack the fortified towns of Judah and conquered them. 14King Hezekiah sent this message to the king of Assyria at Lachish: "I have done wrong. I will pay whatever tribute money you demand if you will only withdraw." The king of Assyria then demanded a settlement of more than eleven tons of silver and one ton of gold.* 15To gather this amount, King Hezekiah used all the silver stored in the Temple of the LORD and in the palace treasury. 16Hezekiah even stripped the gold from the doors of the LORD's Temple and from the doorposts he had overlaid with gold, and he gave it all to the Assyrian king.

17Nevertheless, the king of Assyria sent his commander in chief, his field commander, and his chief of staff* from Lachish with a huge army to confront King Hezekiah in Jerusalem. The Assyrians took up a position beside the aqueduct that feeds water into the upper pool, near the road leading to the field where cloth is washed.* 18They summoned King Hezekiah, but the king sent these officials to meet with them: Eliakim son of Hilkiah, the palace administrator; Shebna the court secretary; and Joah son of Asaph, the royal historian.

Sennacherib Threatens Jerusalem

19Then the Assyrian king's chief of staff told them to give this message to Hezekiah:

"This is what the great king of Assyria says: What are you trusting in that makes you so confident? 20Do you think that mere words can substitute for military skill and

---

18:2 As in parallel text at 2 Chr 29:1; Hebrew reads *Abi,* a variant spelling of Abijah.   18:4 *Nehushtan* sounds like the Hebrew terms that mean "snake," "bronze," and "unclean thing."   18:13 The fourteenth year of Hezekiah's reign was 701 B.C.
18:14 Hebrew *300 talents* [10 metric tons] *of silver and 30 talents* [1 metric ton] *of gold.*   18:17a Or *the rabshakeh;* also in 18:19, 26, 27, 28, 37.   18:17b Or *bleached.*

strength? Who are you counting on, that you have rebelled against me? ²¹On Egypt? If you lean on Egypt, it will be like a reed that splinters beneath your weight and pierces your hand. Pharaoh, the king of Egypt, is completely unreliable!

²²"But perhaps you will say to me, 'We are trusting in the LORD our God!' But isn't he the one who was insulted by Hezekiah? Didn't Hezekiah tear down his shrines and altars and make everyone in Judah and Jerusalem worship only at the altar here in Jerusalem?

²³"I'll tell you what! Strike a bargain with my master, the king of Assyria. I will give you 2,000 horses if you can find that many men to ride on them! ²⁴With your tiny army, how can you think of challenging even the weakest contingent of my master's troops, even with the help of Egypt's chariots and charioteers? ²⁵What's more, do you think we have invaded your land without the LORD's direction? The LORD himself told us, 'Attack this land and destroy it!'"

²⁶Then Eliakim son of Hilkiah, Shebna, and Joah said to the Assyrian chief of staff, "Please speak to us in Aramaic, for we understand it well. Don't speak in Hebrew,* for the people on the wall will hear."

²⁷But Sennacherib's chief of staff replied, "Do you think my master sent this message only to you and your master? He wants all the people to hear it, for when we put this city under siege, they will suffer along with you. They will be so hungry and thirsty that they will eat their own dung and drink their own urine."

²⁸Then the chief of staff stood and shouted in Hebrew to the people on the wall, "Listen to this message from the great king of Assyria! ²⁹This is what the king says: Don't let Hezekiah deceive you. He will never be able to rescue you from my power. ³⁰Don't let him fool you into trusting in the LORD by saying, 'The LORD will surely rescue us. This city will never fall into the hands of the Assyrian king!'

³¹"Don't listen to Hezekiah! These are the terms the king of Assyria is offering: Make peace with me—open the gates and come out. Then each of you can continue eating from your own grapevine and fig tree and drinking from your own well. ³²Then I will arrange to take you to another land like this one—a land

of grain and new wine, bread and vineyards, olive groves and honey. Choose life instead of death!

"Don't listen to Hezekiah when he tries to mislead you by saying, 'The LORD will rescue us!' ³³Have the gods of any other nations ever saved their people from the king of Assyria? ³⁴What happened to the gods of Hamath and Arpad? And what about the gods of Sepharvaim, Hena, and Ivvah? Did any god rescue Samaria from my power? ³⁵What god of any nation has ever been able to save its people from my power? So what makes you think that the LORD can rescue Jerusalem from me?"

³⁶But the people were silent and did not utter a word because Hezekiah had commanded them, "Do not answer him."

³⁷Then Eliakim son of Hilkiah, the palace administrator; Shebna the court secretary; and Joah son of Asaph, the royal historian, went back to Hezekiah. They tore their clothes in despair, and they went in to see the king and told him what the Assyrian chief of staff had said.

Hezekiah Seeks the LORD's Help

19 When King Hezekiah heard their report, he tore his clothes and put on burlap and went into the Temple of the LORD. ²And he sent Eliakim the palace administrator, Shebna the court secretary, and the leading priests, all dressed in burlap, to the prophet Isaiah son of Amoz. ³They told him, "This is what King Hezekiah says: Today is a day of trouble, insults, and disgrace. It is like when a child is ready to be born, but the mother has no strength to deliver the baby. ⁴But perhaps the LORD your God has heard the Assyrian chief of staff,* sent by the king to defy the living God, and will punish him for his words. Oh, pray for those of us who are left!"

⁵After King Hezekiah's officials delivered the king's message to Isaiah, ⁶the prophet replied, "Say to your master, 'This is what the LORD says: Do not be disturbed by this blasphemous speech against me from the Assyrian king's messengers. ⁷Listen! I myself will move against him,* and the king will receive a message that he is needed at home. So he will return to his land, where I will have him killed with a sword.'"

⁸Meanwhile, the Assyrian chief of staff left Jerusalem and went to consult the king of Assyria, who had left Lachish and was attacking Libnah.

⁹Soon afterward King Sennacherib received

18:26 Hebrew *in the dialect of Judah;* also in 18:28.   19:4 Or *the rabshakeh;* also in 19:8.   19:7 Hebrew *I will put a spirit in him.*

word that King Tirhakah of Ethiopia* was leading an army to fight against him. Before leaving to meet the attack, he sent messengers back to Hezekiah in Jerusalem with this message:

10 "This message is for King Hezekiah of Judah. Don't let your God, in whom you trust, deceive you with promises that Jerusalem will not be captured by the king of Assyria. 11 You know perfectly well what the kings of Assyria have done wherever they have gone. They have completely destroyed everyone who stood in their way! Why should you be any different? 12 Have the gods of other nations rescued them—such nations as Gozan, Haran, Rezeph, and the people of Eden who were in Tel-assar? My predecessors destroyed them all! 13 What happened to the king of Hamath and the king of Arpad? What happened to the kings of Sepharvaim, Hena, and Ivvah?"

14 After Hezekiah received the letter from the messengers and read it, he went up to the LORD's Temple and spread it out before the LORD. 15 And Hezekiah prayed this prayer before the LORD: "O LORD, God of Israel, you are enthroned between the mighty cherubim! You alone are God of all the kingdoms of the earth. You alone created the heavens and the earth. 16 Bend down, O LORD, and listen! Open your eyes, O LORD, and see! Listen to Sennacherib's words of defiance against the living God.

17 "It is true, LORD, that the kings of Assyria have destroyed all these nations. 18 And they have thrown the gods of these nations into the fire and burned them. But of course the Assyrians could destroy them! They were not gods at all—only idols of wood and stone shaped by human hands. 19 Now, O LORD our God, rescue us from his power; then all the kingdoms of the earth will know that you alone, O LORD, are God."

Isaiah Predicts Judah's Deliverance

20 Then Isaiah son of Amoz sent this message to Hezekiah: "This is what the LORD, the God of Israel, says: I have heard your prayer about King Sennacherib of Assyria. 21 And the LORD has spoken this word against him:

"The virgin daughter of Zion
    despises you and laughs at you.

19:9 Hebrew *of Cush.*

The daughter of Jerusalem
    shakes her head in derision as you flee.

22 "Whom have you been defying and
        ridiculing?
    Against whom did you raise your voice?
    At whom did you look with such haughty
        eyes?
    It was the Holy One of Israel!
23 By your messengers you have defied the
        Lord.
    You have said, 'With my many chariots
    I have conquered the highest mountains—
        yes, the remotest peaks of Lebanon.
    I have cut down its tallest cedars
        and its finest cypress trees.
    I have reached its farthest corners
        and explored its deepest forests.
24 I have dug wells in many foreign lands
        and refreshed myself with their water.
    With the sole of my foot
        I stopped up all the rivers of Egypt!'

25 "But have you not heard?
        I decided this long ago.
    Long ago I planned it,
        and now I am making it happen.
    I planned for you to crush fortified cities
        into heaps of rubble.
26 That is why their people have so little
        power
        and are so frightened and confused.
    They are as weak as grass,
        as easily trampled as tender green
            shoots.
    They are like grass sprouting on a
            housetop,
        scorched before it can grow lush and
            tall.

27 "But I know you well—
        where you stay
    and when you come and go.
        I know the way you have raged
            against me.
28 And because of your raging against me
        and your arrogance, which I have heard
            for myself,
    I will put my hook in your nose
        and my bit in your mouth.
    I will make you return
        by the same road on which you came."

29 Then Isaiah said to Hezekiah, "Here is the proof that what I say is true:

"This year you will eat only what grows up
　　by itself,
　　and next year you will eat what springs
　　　up from that.
But in the third year you will plant crops
　　and harvest them;
　　you will tend vineyards and eat their
　　　fruit.
30 And you who are left in Judah,
　　who have escaped the ravages of the
　　　siege,
　　will put roots down in your own soil
　　and will grow up and flourish.
31 For a remnant of my people will spread
　　out from Jerusalem,
　　a group of survivors from Mount Zion.
The passionate commitment of the LORD
　　of Heaven's Armies*
　　will make this happen!

32 "And this is what the LORD says about the
king of Assyria:

"His armies will not enter Jerusalem.
　　They will not even shoot an arrow at it.
They will not march outside its gates with
　　their shields
　　nor build banks of earth against its
　　　walls.
33 The king will return to his own country
　　by the same road on which he came.
He will not enter this city,
　　says the LORD.
34 For my own honor and for the sake of my
　　servant David,
　　I will defend this city and protect it."

35 That night the angel of the LORD went
out to the Assyrian camp and killed 185,000
Assyrian soldiers. When the surviving Assyrians* woke up the next morning, they found
corpses everywhere. 36 Then King Sennacherib
of Assyria broke camp and returned to his own
land. He went home to his capital of Nineveh
and stayed there.
37 One day while he was worshiping in the
temple of his god Nisroch, his sons* Adrammelech and Sharezer killed him with their swords.
They then escaped to the land of Ararat, and
another son, Esarhaddon, became the next
king of Assyria.

Hezekiah's Sickness and Recovery

20 About that time Hezekiah became
deathly ill, and the prophet Isaiah son
of Amoz went to visit him. He gave the king
this message: "This is what the LORD says: Set
your affairs in order, for you are going to die.
You will not recover from this illness."

2 When Hezekiah heard this, he turned
his face to the wall and prayed to the LORD,
3 "Remember, O LORD, how I have always been
faithful to you and have served you singlemindedly, always doing what pleases you."
Then he broke down and wept bitterly.

4 But before Isaiah had left the middle courtyard,* this message came to him from the
LORD: 5 "Go back to Hezekiah, the leader of my
people. Tell him, 'This is what the LORD, the
God of your ancestor David, says: I have heard
your prayer and seen your tears. I will heal you,
and three days from now you will get out of
bed and go to the Temple of the LORD. 6 I will
add fifteen years to your life, and I will rescue
you and this city from the king of Assyria. I will
defend this city for my own honor and for the
sake of my servant David.'"

7 Then Isaiah said, "Make an ointment from
figs." So Hezekiah's servants spread the ointment over the boil, and Hezekiah recovered!

8 Meanwhile, Hezekiah had said to Isaiah,
"What sign will the LORD give to prove that he
will heal me and that I will go to the Temple of
the LORD three days from now?"

9 Isaiah replied, "This is the sign from the
LORD to prove that he will do as he promised.
Would you like the shadow on the sundial to
go forward ten steps or backward ten steps?*"

10 "The shadow always moves forward," Hezekiah replied, "so that would be easy. Make it
go ten steps backward instead." 11 So Isaiah
the prophet asked the LORD to do this, and he
caused the shadow to move ten steps backward
on the sundial* of Ahaz!

Envoys from Babylon

12 Soon after this, Merodach-baladan* son of
Baladan, king of Babylon, sent Hezekiah his
best wishes and a gift, for he had heard that
Hezekiah had been very sick. 13 Hezekiah received the Babylonian envoys and showed
them everything in his treasure-houses—the
silver, the gold, the spices, and the aromatic

19:31 As in Greek and Syriac versions, Latin Vulgate, and an alternate reading of the Masoretic Text (see also Isa 37:32);
the other alternate reads *the LORD*.　　19:35 Hebrew *When they*.　　19:37 As in Greek version and an alternate reading of the
Masoretic Text (see also Isa 37:38); the other alternate reading lacks *his sons*.　　20:4 As in Greek version and an alternate
reading in the Masoretic Text; the other alternate reads *the middle of the city*.　　20:9 Or *The shadow on the sundial has gone
forward ten steps; do you want it to go backward ten steps?*　　20:11 Hebrew *the steps*.　　20:12 As in some Hebrew manuscripts
and Greek and Syriac versions (see also Isa 39:1); Masoretic Text reads *Berodach-baladan*.

oils. He also took them to see his armory and showed them everything in his royal treasuries! There was nothing in his palace or kingdom that Hezekiah did not show them.

¹⁴Then Isaiah the prophet went to King Hezekiah and asked him, "What did those men want? Where were they from?"

Hezekiah replied, "They came from the distant land of Babylon."

¹⁵"What did they see in your palace?" Isaiah asked.

"They saw everything," Hezekiah replied. "I showed them everything I own—all my royal treasuries."

¹⁶Then Isaiah said to Hezekiah, "Listen to this message from the LORD: ¹⁷The time is coming when everything in your palace—all the treasures stored up by your ancestors until now—will be carried off to Babylon. Nothing will be left, says the LORD. ¹⁸Some of your very own sons will be taken away into exile. They will become eunuchs who will serve in the palace of Babylon's king."

¹⁹Then Hezekiah said to Isaiah, "This message you have given me from the LORD is good." For the king was thinking, "At least there will be peace and security during my lifetime."

²⁰The rest of the events in Hezekiah's reign, including the extent of his power and how he built a pool and dug a tunnel* to bring water into the city, are recorded in *The Book of the History of the Kings of Judah.* ²¹Hezekiah died, and his son Manasseh became the next king.

Manasseh Rules in Judah

21 Manasseh was twelve years old when he became king, and he reigned in Jerusalem fifty-five years. His mother was Hephzibah. ²He did what was evil in the LORD's sight, following the detestable practices of the pagan nations that the LORD had driven from the land ahead of the Israelites. ³He rebuilt the pagan shrines his father, Hezekiah, had destroyed. He constructed altars for Baal and set up an Asherah pole, just as King Ahab of Israel had done. He also bowed before all the powers of the heavens and worshiped them.

⁴He built pagan altars in the Temple of the LORD, the place where the LORD had said, "My name will remain in Jerusalem forever." ⁵He built these altars for all the powers of the heavens in both courtyards of the LORD's Temple. ⁶Manasseh also sacrificed his own son in the fire.* He practiced sorcery and divination, and

he consulted with mediums and psychics. He did much that was evil in the LORD's sight, arousing his anger.

⁷Manasseh even made a carved image of Asherah and set it up in the Temple, the very place where the LORD had told David and his son Solomon: "My name will be honored forever in this Temple and in Jerusalem—the city I have chosen from among all the tribes of Israel. ⁸If the Israelites will be careful to obey my commands—all the laws my servant Moses gave them—I will not send them into exile from this land that I gave their ancestors." ⁹But the people refused to listen, and Manasseh led them to do even more evil than the pagan nations that the LORD had destroyed when the people of Israel entered the land.

¹⁰Then the LORD said through his servants the prophets: ¹¹"King Manasseh of Judah has done many detestable things. He is even more wicked than the Amorites, who lived in this land before Israel. He has caused the people of Judah to sin with his idols.* ¹²So this is what the LORD, the God of Israel, says: I will bring such disaster on Jerusalem and Judah that the ears of those who hear about it will tingle with horror. ¹³I will judge Jerusalem by the same standard I used for Samaria and the same measure* I used for the family of Ahab. I will wipe away the people of Jerusalem as one wipes a dish and turns it upside down. ¹⁴Then I will reject even the remnant of my own people who are left, and I will hand them over as plunder for their enemies. ¹⁵For they have done great evil in my sight and have angered me ever since their ancestors came out of Egypt."

¹⁶Manasseh also murdered many innocent people until Jerusalem was filled from one end to the other with innocent blood. This was in addition to the sin that he caused the people of Judah to commit, leading them to do evil in the LORD's sight.

¹⁷The rest of the events in Manasseh's reign and everything he did, including the sins he committed, are recorded in *The Book of the History of the Kings of Judah.* ¹⁸When Manasseh died, he was buried in the palace garden, the garden of Uzza. Then his son Amon became the next king.

Amon Rules in Judah

¹⁹Amon was twenty-two years old when he became king, and he reigned in Jerusalem

20:20 Hebrew *watercourse.* 21:6 Or *also made his son pass through the fire.* 21:11 The Hebrew term (literally *round things*) probably alludes to dung; also in 21:21. 21:13 Hebrew *the same plumb line I used for Samaria and the same plumb bob.*

two years. His mother was Meshullemeth, the daughter of Haruz from Jotbah. ²⁰He did what was evil in the LORD's sight, just as his father, Manasseh, had done. ²¹He followed the example of his father, worshiping the same idols his father had worshiped. ²²He abandoned the LORD, the God of his ancestors, and he refused to follow the LORD's ways.

²³Then Amon's own officials conspired against him and assassinated him in his palace. ²⁴But the people of the land killed all those who had conspired against King Amon, and they made his son Josiah the next king.

²⁵The rest of the events in Amon's reign and what he did are recorded in *The Book of the History of the Kings of Judah.* ²⁶He was buried in his tomb in the garden of Uzza. Then his son Josiah became the next king.

Josiah Rules in Judah

22 Josiah was eight years old when he became king, and he reigned in Jerusalem thirty-one years. His mother was Jedidah, the daughter of Adaiah from Bozkath. ²He did what was pleasing in the LORD's sight and followed the example of his ancestor David. He did not turn away from doing what was right.

³In the eighteenth year of his reign, King Josiah sent Shaphan son of Azaliah and grandson of Meshullam, the court secretary, to the Temple of the LORD. He told him, ⁴"Go to Hilkiah the high priest and have him count the money the gatekeepers have collected from the people at the LORD's Temple. ⁵Entrust this money to the men assigned to supervise the restoration of the LORD's Temple. Then they can use it to pay workers to repair the Temple. ⁶They will need to hire carpenters, builders, and masons. Also have them buy the timber and the finished stone needed to repair the Temple. ⁷But don't require the construction supervisors to keep account of the money they receive, for they are honest and trustworthy men."

Hilkiah Discovers God's Law

⁸Hilkiah the high priest said to Shaphan the court secretary, "I have found the Book of the Law in the LORD's Temple!" Then Hilkiah gave the scroll to Shaphan, and he read it.

⁹Shaphan went to the king and reported, "Your officials have turned over the money collected at the Temple of the LORD to the workers and supervisors at the Temple." ¹⁰Shaphan also told the king, "Hilkiah the priest has given me a scroll." So Shaphan read it to the king.

¹¹When the king heard what was written in the Book of the Law, he tore his clothes in despair. ¹²Then he gave these orders to Hilkiah the priest, Ahikam son of Shaphan, Acbor son of Micaiah, Shaphan the court secretary, and Asaiah the king's personal adviser: ¹³"Go to the Temple and speak to the LORD for me and for the people and for all Judah. Inquire about the words written in this scroll that has been found. For the LORD's great anger is burning against us because our ancestors have not obeyed the words in this scroll. We have not been doing everything it says we must do."

¹⁴So Hilkiah the priest, Ahikam, Acbor, Shaphan, and Asaiah went to the New Quarter* of Jerusalem to consult with the prophet Huldah. She was the wife of Shallum son of Tikvah, son of Harhas, the keeper of the Temple wardrobe.

¹⁵She said to them, "The LORD, the God of Israel, has spoken! Go back and tell the man who sent you, ¹⁶'This is what the LORD says: I am going to bring disaster on this city* and its people. All the words written in the scroll that the king of Judah has read will come true. ¹⁷For my people have abandoned me and offered sacrifices to pagan gods, and I am very angry with them for everything they have done. My anger will burn against this place, and it will not be quenched.'

¹⁸"But go to the king of Judah who sent you to seek the LORD and tell him: 'This is what the LORD, the God of Israel, says concerning the message you have just heard: ¹⁹You were sorry and humbled yourself before the LORD when you heard what I said against this city and its people—that this land would be cursed and become desolate. You tore your clothing in despair and wept before me in repentance. And I have indeed heard you, says the LORD. ²⁰So I will not send the promised disaster until after you have died and been buried in peace. You will not see the disaster I am going to bring on this city.'"

So they took her message back to the king.

Josiah's Religious Reforms

23 Then the king summoned all the elders of Judah and Jerusalem. ²And the king went up to the Temple of the LORD with all the people of Judah and Jerusalem, along with the priests and the prophets—all the people from the least to the greatest. There the king read to them the entire Book of the Covenant that had been found in the LORD's Temple. ³The king took his place of authority beside the pillar and renewed the covenant in the LORD's presence. He pledged to obey the LORD by keeping all his commands, laws, and decrees with all his heart and soul. In this way, he confirmed all the terms of the covenant that were written in the scroll, and all the people pledged themselves to the covenant.

⁴Then the king instructed Hilkiah the high priest and the priests of the second rank and the Temple gatekeepers to remove from the LORD's Temple all the articles that were used to worship Baal, Asherah, and all the powers of the heavens. The king had all these things burned outside Jerusalem on the terraces of the Kidron Valley, and he carried the ashes away to Bethel. ⁵He did away with the idolatrous priests, who had been appointed by the previous kings of Judah, for they had offered sacrifices at the pagan shrines throughout Judah and even in the vicinity of Jerusalem. They had also offered sacrifices to Baal, and to the sun, the moon, the constellations, and to all the powers of the heavens. ⁶The king removed the Asherah pole from the LORD's Temple and took it outside Jerusalem to the Kidron Valley, where he burned it. Then he ground the ashes of the pole to dust and threw the dust over the graves of the people. ⁷He also tore down the living quarters of the male and female shrine prostitutes that were inside the Temple of the LORD, where the women wove coverings for the Asherah pole.

⁸Josiah brought to Jerusalem all the priests who were living in other towns of Judah. He also defiled the pagan shrines, where they had offered sacrifices—all the way from Geba to Beersheba. He destroyed the shrines at the entrance to the gate of Joshua, the governor of Jerusalem. This gate was located to the left of the city gate as one enters the city. ⁹The priests who had served at the pagan shrines were not allowed to serve at* the LORD's altar in Jerusalem, but they were allowed to eat unleavened bread with the other priests.

¹⁰Then the king defiled the altar of Topheth in the valley of Ben-Hinnom, so no one could ever again use it to sacrifice a son or daughter in the fire* as an offering to Molech. ¹¹He removed from the entrance of the LORD's Temple the horse statues that the former kings of Judah had dedicated to the sun. They were near the quarters of Nathan-melech the eunuch, an officer of the court.* The king also burned the chariots dedicated to the sun.

¹²Josiah tore down the altars that the kings of Judah had built on the palace roof above the upper room of Ahaz. The king destroyed the altars that Manasseh had built in the two courtyards of the LORD's Temple. He smashed them to bits* and scattered the pieces in the Kidron Valley. ¹³The king also desecrated the pagan shrines east of Jerusalem, to the south of the Mount of Corruption, where King Solomon of Israel had built shrines for Ashtoreth, the detestable goddess of the Sidonians; and for Chemosh, the detestable god of the Moabites; and for Molech,* the vile god of the Ammonites. ¹⁴He smashed the sacred pillars and cut down the Asherah poles. Then he desecrated these places by scattering human bones over them.

¹⁵The king also tore down the altar at Bethel—the pagan shrine that Jeroboam son of Nebat had made when he caused Israel to sin. He burned down the shrine and ground it to dust, and he burned the Asherah pole. ¹⁶Then Josiah turned around and noticed several tombs in the side of the hill. He ordered that the bones be brought out, and he burned them on the altar at Bethel to desecrate it. (This happened just as the LORD had promised through the man of God when Jeroboam stood beside the altar at the festival.)

Then Josiah turned and looked up at the tomb of the man of God* who had predicted these things. ¹⁷"What is that monument over there?" Josiah asked.

And the people of the town told him, "It is the tomb of the man of God who came from Judah and predicted the very things that you have just done to the altar at Bethel!"

¹⁸Josiah replied, "Leave it alone. Don't disturb his bones." So they did not burn his bones or those of the old prophet from Samaria.

¹⁹Then Josiah demolished all the buildings at the pagan shrines in the towns of Samaria, just as he had done at Bethel. They had been built by the various kings of Israel and had made the LORD* very angry. ²⁰He executed the priests of the pagan shrines on their own altars, and he burned human bones on the

23:9 Hebrew *did not come up to.*   23:10 Or *to make a son or daughter pass through the fire.*   23:11 The meaning of the Hebrew is uncertain.   23:12 Or *He quickly removed them.*   23:13 Hebrew *Milcom,* a variant spelling of Molech.   23:16 As in Greek version; Hebrew lacks *when Jeroboam stood beside the altar at the festival. Then Josiah turned and looked up at the tomb of the man of God.*   23:19 As in Greek and Syriac versions and Latin Vulgate; Hebrew lacks *the LORD.*

altars to desecrate them. Finally, he returned to Jerusalem.

Josiah Celebrates Passover

²¹King Josiah then issued this order to all the people: "You must celebrate the Passover to the LORD your God, as required in this Book of the Covenant." ²²There had not been a Passover celebration like that since the time when the judges ruled in Israel, nor throughout all the years of the kings of Israel and Judah. ²³But in the eighteenth year of King Josiah's reign, this Passover was celebrated to the LORD in Jerusalem.

²⁴Josiah also got rid of the mediums and psychics, the household gods, the idols,* and every other kind of detestable practice, both in Jerusalem and throughout the land of Judah. He did this in obedience to the laws written in the scroll that Hilkiah the priest had found in the LORD's Temple. ²⁵Never before had there been a king like Josiah, who turned to the LORD with all his heart and soul and strength, obeying all the laws of Moses. And there has never been a king like him since.

²⁶Even so, the LORD was very angry with Judah because of all the wicked things Manasseh had done to provoke him. ²⁷For the LORD said, "I will also banish Judah from my presence just as I have banished Israel. And I will reject my chosen city of Jerusalem and the Temple where my name was to be honored."

²⁸The rest of the events in Josiah's reign and all his deeds are recorded in *The Book of the History of the Kings of Judah*.

²⁹While Josiah was king, Pharaoh Neco, king of Egypt, went to the Euphrates River to help the king of Assyria. King Josiah and his army marched out to fight him,* but King Neco* killed him when they met at Megiddo. ³⁰Josiah's officers took his body back in a chariot from Megiddo to Jerusalem and buried him in his own tomb. Then the people of the land anointed Josiah's son Jehoahaz and made him the next king.

Jehoahaz Rules in Judah

³¹Jehoahaz was twenty-three years old when he became king, and he reigned in Jerusalem three months. His mother was Hamutal, the daughter of Jeremiah from Libnah. ³²He did what was evil in the LORD's sight, just as his ancestors had done.

³³Pharaoh Neco put Jehoahaz in prison at Riblah in the land of Hamath to prevent him from ruling* in Jerusalem. He also demanded that Judah pay 7,500 pounds of silver and 75 pounds of gold* as tribute.

Jehoiakim Rules in Judah

³⁴Pharaoh Neco then installed Eliakim, another of Josiah's sons, to reign in place of his father, and he changed Eliakim's name to Jehoiakim. Jehoahaz was taken to Egypt as a prisoner, where he died.

³⁵In order to get the silver and gold demanded as tribute by Pharaoh Neco, Jehoiakim collected a tax from the people of Judah, requiring them to pay in proportion to their wealth.

³⁶Jehoiakim was twenty-five years old when he became king, and he reigned in Jerusalem eleven years. His mother was Zebidah, the daughter of Pedaiah from Rumah. ³⁷He did what was evil in the LORD's sight, just as his ancestors had done.

24 During Jehoiakim's reign, King Nebuchadnezzar of Babylon invaded the land of Judah. Jehoiakim surrendered and paid him tribute for three years but then rebelled. ²Then the LORD sent bands of Babylonian,* Aramean, Moabite, and Ammonite raiders against Judah to destroy it, just as the LORD had promised through his prophets. ³These disasters happened to Judah because of the LORD's command. He had decided to banish Judah from his presence because of the many sins of Manasseh, ⁴who had filled Jerusalem with innocent blood. The LORD would not forgive this.

⁵The rest of the events in Jehoiakim's reign and all his deeds are recorded in *The Book of the History of the Kings of Judah*. ⁶When Jehoiakim died, his son Jehoiachin became the next king.

⁷The king of Egypt did not venture out of his country after that, for the king of Babylon captured the entire area formerly claimed by Egypt—from the Brook of Egypt to the Euphrates River.

Jehoiachin Rules in Judah

⁸Jehoiachin was eighteen years old when he became king, and he reigned in Jerusalem three months. His mother was Nehushta, the daughter of Elnathan from Jerusalem. ⁹Jehoiachin

---

23:24 The Hebrew term (literally *round things*) probably alludes to dung.   23:29a Or *Josiah went out to meet him.*
23:29b Hebrew *he.*   23:33a The meaning of the Hebrew is uncertain.   23:33b Hebrew *100 talents* [3,400 kilograms] *of silver and 1 talent* [34 kilograms] *of gold.*   24:2 Or *Chaldean.*

did what was evil in the LORD's sight, just as his father had done.

¹⁰During Jehoiachin's reign, the officers of King Nebuchadnezzar of Babylon came up against Jerusalem and besieged it. ¹¹Nebuchadnezzar himself arrived at the city during the siege. ¹²Then King Jehoiachin, along with the queen mother, his advisers, his commanders, and his officials, surrendered to the Babylonians.

In the eighth year of Nebuchadnezzar's reign, he took Jehoiachin prisoner. ¹³As the LORD had said beforehand, Nebuchadnezzar carried away all the treasures from the LORD's Temple and the royal palace. He stripped away* all the gold objects that King Solomon of Israel had placed in the Temple. ¹⁴King Nebuchadnezzar took all of Jerusalem captive, including all the commanders and the best of the soldiers, craftsmen, and artisans—10,000 in all. Only the poorest people were left in the land.

¹⁵Nebuchadnezzar led King Jehoiachin away as a captive to Babylon, along with the queen mother, his wives and officials, and all Jerusalem's elite. ¹⁶He also exiled 7,000 of the best troops and 1,000 craftsmen and artisans, all of whom were strong and fit for war. ¹⁷Then the king of Babylon installed Mattaniah, Jehoiachin's* uncle, as the next king, and he changed Mattaniah's name to Zedekiah.

Zedekiah Rules in Judah

¹⁸Zedekiah was twenty-one years old when he became king, and he reigned in Jerusalem eleven years. His mother was Hamutal, the daughter of Jeremiah from Libnah. ¹⁹But Zedekiah did what was evil in the LORD's sight, just as Jehoiakim had done. ²⁰These things happened because of the LORD's anger against the people of Jerusalem and Judah, until he finally banished them from his presence and sent them into exile.

The Fall of Jerusalem

Zedekiah rebelled against the king of Babylon.

25 So on January 15,* during the ninth year of Zedekiah's reign, King Nebuchadnezzar of Babylon led his entire army against Jerusalem. They surrounded the city and built siege ramps against its walls. ²Jerusalem was kept under siege until the eleventh year of King Zedekiah's reign.

³By July 18 in the eleventh year of Zedekiah's reign,* the famine in the city had become very severe, and the last of the food was entirely gone. ⁴Then a section of the city wall was broken down. Since the city was surrounded by the Babylonians,* the soldiers waited for nightfall and escaped* through the gate between the two walls behind the king's garden. Then they headed toward the Jordan Valley.*

⁵But the Babylonian* troops chased the king and overtook him on the plains of Jericho, for his men had all deserted him and scattered. ⁶They captured the king and took him to the king of Babylon at Riblah, where they pronounced judgment upon Zedekiah. ⁷They made Zedekiah watch as they slaughtered his sons. Then they gouged out Zedekiah's eyes, bound him in bronze chains, and led him away to Babylon.

The Temple Destroyed

⁸On August 14 of that year,* which was the nineteenth year of King Nebuchadnezzar's reign, Nebuzaradan, the captain of the guard and an official of the Babylonian king, arrived in Jerusalem. ⁹He burned down the Temple of the LORD, the royal palace, and all the houses of Jerusalem. He destroyed all the important buildings* in the city. ¹⁰Then he supervised the entire Babylonian army as they tore down the walls of Jerusalem on every side. ¹¹Then Nebuzaradan, the captain of the guard, took as exiles the rest of the people who remained in the city, the defectors who had declared their allegiance to the king of Babylon, and the rest of the population. ¹²But the captain of the guard allowed some of the poorest people to stay behind to care for the vineyards and fields.

¹³The Babylonians broke up the bronze pillars in front of the LORD's Temple, the bronze water carts, and the great bronze basin called the Sea, and they carried all the bronze away to Babylon. ¹⁴They also took all the ash buckets, shovels, lamp snuffers, ladles, and all the other bronze articles used for making sacrifices at the Temple. ¹⁵The captain of the guard also took the incense burners and basins, and all the other articles made of pure gold or silver.

24:13 Or *He cut apart.* 24:17 Hebrew *his.* 25:1 Hebrew *on the tenth day of the tenth month,* of the ancient Hebrew lunar calendar. A number of events in 2 Kings can be cross-checked with dates in surviving Babylonian records and related accurately to our modern calendar. This day was January 15, 588 B.C. 25:3 Hebrew *By the ninth day of the [fourth] month* [in the eleventh year of Zedekiah's reign] (compare Jer 39:2; 52:6 and the notes below). This day was July 18, 586 B.C.; also see note on 25:1. 25:4a Or *the Chaldeans;* also in 25:13, 25, 26. 25:4b As in Greek version (see also Jer 39:4; 52:7); Hebrew lacks *escaped.* 25:4c Hebrew *the Arabah.* 25:5 Or *Chaldean;* also in 25:10, 24. 25:8 Hebrew *On the seventh day of the fifth month,* of the ancient Hebrew lunar calendar. This day was August 14, 586 B.C.; also see note on 25:1. 25:9 Or *destroyed the houses of all the important people.*

¹⁶The weight of the bronze from the two pillars, the Sea, and the water carts was too great to be measured. These things had been made for the LORD's Temple in the days of Solomon. ¹⁷Each of the pillars was 27 feet* tall. The bronze capital on top of each pillar was 7½ feet* high and was decorated with a network of bronze pomegranates all the way around.

¹⁸Nebuzaradan, the captain of the guard, took with him as prisoners Seraiah the high priest, Zephaniah the priest of the second rank, and the three chief gatekeepers. ¹⁹And from among the people still hiding in the city, he took an officer who had been in charge of the Judean army; five of the king's personal advisers; the army commander's chief secretary, who was in charge of recruitment; and sixty other citizens. ²⁰Nebuzaradan, the captain of the guard, took them all to the king of Babylon at Riblah. ²¹And there at Riblah, in the land of Hamath, the king of Babylon had them all put to death. So the people of Judah were sent into exile from their land.

Gedaliah Governs in Judah

²²Then King Nebuchadnezzar appointed Gedaliah son of Ahikam and grandson of Shaphan as governor over the people he had left in Judah. ²³When all the army commanders and their men learned that the king of Babylon had appointed Gedaliah as governor, they went to see him at Mizpah. These included Ishmael son of Nethaniah, Johanan son of Kareah, Seraiah son of Tanhumeth the Netophathite, Jezaniah* son of the Maacathite, and all their men.

²⁴Gedaliah vowed to them that the Babylonian officials meant them no harm. "Don't be afraid of them. Live in the land and serve the king of Babylon, and all will go well for you," he promised.

²⁵But in midautumn of that year,* Ishmael son of Nethaniah and grandson of Elishama, who was a member of the royal family, went to Mizpah with ten men and killed Gedaliah. He also killed all the Judeans and Babylonians who were with him at Mizpah.

²⁶Then all the people of Judah, from the least to the greatest, as well as the army commanders, fled in panic to Egypt, for they were afraid of what the Babylonians would do to them.

Hope for Israel's Royal Line

²⁷In the thirty-seventh year of the exile of King Jehoiachin of Judah, Evil-merodach ascended to the Babylonian throne. He was kind to* Jehoiachin and released him* from prison on April 2 of that year.* ²⁸He spoke kindly to Jehoiachin and gave him a higher place than all the other exiled kings in Babylon. ²⁹He supplied Jehoiachin with new clothes to replace his prison garb and allowed him to dine in the king's presence for the rest of his life. ³⁰So the king gave him a regular food allowance as long as he lived.

25:17a Hebrew 18 cubits [8.3 meters]. 25:17b As in parallel texts at 1 Kgs 7:16, 2 Chr 3:15, and Jer 52:22, all of which read 5 cubits [2.3 meters]; Hebrew reads 3 cubits, which is 4.5 feet or 1.4 meters. 25:23 As in parallel text at Jer 40:8; Hebrew reads Jaazaniah, a variant spelling of Jezaniah. 25:25 Hebrew in the seventh month, of the ancient Hebrew lunar calendar. This month occurred within the months of October and November 586 B.C.; also see note on 25:1. 25:27a Hebrew He raised the head of. 25:27b As in some Hebrew manuscripts and Greek and Syriac versions (see also Jer 52:31); Masoretic Text lacks released him. 25:27c Hebrew on the twenty-seventh day of the twelfth month, of the ancient Hebrew lunar calendar. This day was April 2, 561 B.C.; also see note on 25:1.

1 Chronicles

UNDERSTANDING your family's history is important. Knowing where your ancestors came from and what they accomplished provides a sense of identity, heritage, and destiny. These are some of the reasons the writer of Chronicles penned this extensive account of Israel's family history. The book of 1 Chronicles begins with a series of genealogies that trace the roots of both King David and the Levites. This list represents more than just names; it represents the chosen people of God—the ancestors of God's covenant people. After the genealogies comes the account of Israel's first two kings, Saul and David. Their successes and failures are shown to stem largely from their spiritual choices. Special emphasis is given to the admirable accomplishments of David's reign. The book closes with David's vision for the Temple that is to be built.

- **Author:** Ezra, according to Jewish tradition
- **Date Written:** Around 430 BC, recording events between 1000 and 960 BC
- **Purpose:** To unify God's people, to trace the roots of King David and of the twelve tribes, and to teach that genuine worship ought to be the center of individual and national life
- **Themes:** Israel's history as God's chosen people, the accomplishments of King David, true worship, the Temple, the priests
- **Outline**
  1:1–9:44 The genealogies
  10:1-14 The death of Saul
  11:1–23:1 The reign of David
  23:2–27:34 The Temple, the Levites, and the tribal leaders
  28:1–29:30 David's final years

From Adam to Noah's Sons

1 The descendants of Adam were Seth, Enosh, ²Kenan, Mahalalel, Jared, ³Enoch, Methuselah, Lamech, ⁴and Noah.
The sons of Noah were* Shem, Ham, and Japheth.

Descendants of Japheth

⁵The descendants of Japheth were Gomer, Magog, Madai, Javan, Tubal, Meshech, and Tiras.
⁶The descendants of Gomer were Ashkenaz, Riphath,* and Togarmah.
⁷The descendants of Javan were Elishah, Tarshish, Kittim, and Rodanim.

Descendants of Ham

⁸The descendants of Ham were Cush, Mizraim,* Put, and Canaan.
⁹The descendants of Cush were Seba,
Havilah, Sabtah, Raamah, and Sabteca.
The descendants of Raamah were Sheba and Dedan. ¹⁰Cush was also the ancestor of Nimrod, who was the first heroic warrior on earth.
¹¹Mizraim was the ancestor of the Ludites, Anamites, Lehabites, Naphtuhites, ¹²Pathrusites, Casluhites, and the Caphtorites, from whom the Philistines came.*
¹³Canaan's oldest son was Sidon, the ancestor of the Sidonians. Canaan was also the ancestor of the Hittites,* ¹⁴Jebusites, Amorites, Girgashites, ¹⁵Hivites, Arkites, Sinites, ¹⁶Arvadites, Zemarites, and Hamathites.

Descendants of Shem

¹⁷The descendants of Shem were Elam, Asshur, Arphaxad, Lud, and Aram.

1:4 As in Greek version (see also Gen 5:3-32); Hebrew lacks *The sons of Noah were.* **1:6** As in some Hebrew manuscripts and Greek version (see also Gen 10:3); most Hebrew manuscripts read *Diphath.* **1:8** Or *Egypt;* also in 1:11. **1:12** Hebrew *Casluhites, from whom the Philistines came, Caphtorites.* See Jer 47:4; Amos 9:7. **1:13** Hebrew *ancestor of Heth.*

The descendants of Aram were* Uz, Hul, Gether, and Mash.*

¹⁸Arphaxad was the father of Shelah. Shelah was the father of Eber.

¹⁹Eber had two sons. The first was named Peleg (which means "division"), for during his lifetime the people of the world were divided into different language groups. His brother's name was Joktan.

²⁰Joktan was the ancestor of Almodad, Sheleph, Hazarmaveth, Jerah, ²¹Hadoram, Uzal, Diklah, ²²Obal,* Abimael, Sheba, ²³Ophir, Havilah, and Jobab. All these were descendants of Joktan.

²⁴So this is the family line descended from Shem: Arphaxad, Shelah,* ²⁵Eber, Peleg, Reu, ²⁶Serug, Nahor, Terah, ²⁷and Abram, later known as Abraham.

Descendants of Abraham

²⁸The sons of Abraham were Isaac and Ishmael. ²⁹These are their genealogical records:

The sons of Ishmael were Nebaioth (the oldest), Kedar, Adbeel, Mibsam, ³⁰Mishma, Dumah, Massa, Hadad, Tema, ³¹Jetur, Naphish, and Kedemah. These were the sons of Ishmael.

³²The sons of Keturah, Abraham's concubine, were Zimran, Jokshan, Medan, Midian, Ishbak, and Shuah.

The sons of Jokshan were Sheba and Dedan.

³³The sons of Midian were Ephah, Epher, Hanoch, Abida, and Eldaah.

All these were descendants of Abraham through his concubine Keturah.

Descendants of Isaac

³⁴Abraham was the father of Isaac. The sons of Isaac were Esau and Israel.*

Descendants of Esau

³⁵The sons of Esau were Eliphaz, Reuel, Jeush, Jalam, and Korah.

³⁶The descendants of Eliphaz were Teman, Omar, Zepho,* Gatam, Kenaz, and Amalek, who was born to Timna.*

³⁷The descendants of Reuel were Nahath, Zerah, Shammah, and Mizzah.

Original Peoples of Edom

³⁸The descendants of Seir were Lotan, Shobal, Zibeon, Anah, Dishon, Ezer, and Dishan.

³⁹The descendants of Lotan were Hori and Hemam.* Lotan's sister was named Timna.

⁴⁰The descendants of Shobal were Alvan,* Manahath, Ebal, Shepho,* and Onam.

The descendants of Zibeon were Aiah and Anah.

⁴¹The son of Anah was Dishon.

The descendants of Dishon were Hemdan,* Eshban, Ithran, and Keran.

⁴²The descendants of Ezer were Bilhan, Zaavan, and Akan.*

The descendants of Dishan* were Uz and Aran.

Rulers of Edom

⁴³These are the kings who ruled in the land of Edom before any king ruled over the Israelites*:

Bela son of Beor, who ruled from his city of Dinhabah.

⁴⁴When Bela died, Jobab son of Zerah from Bozrah became king in his place.

⁴⁵When Jobab died, Husham from the land of the Temanites became king in his place.

⁴⁶When Husham died, Hadad son of Bedad became king in his place and ruled from the city of Avith. He was the one who destroyed the Midianite army in the land of Moab.

⁴⁷When Hadad died, Samlah from the city of Masrekah became king in his place.

⁴⁸When Samlah died, Shaul from the city of Rehoboth-on-the-River became king in his place.

⁴⁹When Shaul died, Baal-hanan son of Acbor became king in his place.

⁵⁰When Baal-hanan died, Hadad became king in his place and ruled from the city of Pau.* His wife was Mehetabel, the

---

1:17a As in one Hebrew manuscript and some Greek manuscripts (see also Gen 10:23); most Hebrew manuscripts lack *The descendants of Aram were.* 1:17b As in parallel text at Gen 10:23; Hebrew reads *and Meshech.* 1:22 As in some Hebrew manuscripts and Syriac version (see also Gen 10:28); most Hebrew manuscripts read *Ebal.* 1:24 Some Greek manuscripts read *Arphaxad, Cainan, Shelah.* See notes on Gen 10:24; 11:12-13. 1:34 *Israel* is the name that God gave to Jacob. 1:36a As in many Hebrew manuscripts and a few Greek manuscripts (see also Gen 36:11); most Hebrew manuscripts read *Zephi.* 1:36b As in some Greek manuscripts (see also Gen 36:12); Hebrew reads *Kenaz, Timna, and Amalek.* 1:39 As in parallel text at Gen 36:22; Hebrew reads *and Homam.* 1:40a As in many Hebrew manuscripts and a few Greek manuscripts (see also Gen 36:23); most Hebrew manuscripts read *Alian.* 1:40b As in some Hebrew manuscripts (see also Gen 36:23); most Hebrew manuscripts read *Shephi.* 1:41 As in many Hebrew manuscripts and some Greek manuscripts (see also Gen 36:26); most Hebrew manuscripts read *Hamran.* 1:42a As in many Hebrew and Greek manuscripts (see also Gen 36:27); most Hebrew manuscripts read *Jaakan.* 1:42b Hebrew *Dishon;* compare 1:38 and parallel text at Gen 36:28. 1:43 Or *before an Israelite king ruled over them.* 1:50 As in many Hebrew manuscripts, some Greek manuscripts, Syriac version, and Latin Vulgate (see also Gen 36:39); most Hebrew manuscripts read *Pai.*

daughter of Matred and granddaughter of Me-zahab. ⁵¹Then Hadad died.

The clan leaders of Edom were Timna, Alvah,* Jetheth, ⁵²Oholibamah, Elah, Pinon, ⁵³Kenaz, Teman, Mibzar, ⁵⁴Magdiel, and Iram. These are the clan leaders of Edom.

Descendants of Israel

2 The sons of Israel* were Reuben, Simeon, Levi, Judah, Issachar, Zebulun, ²Dan, Joseph, Benjamin, Naphtali, Gad, and Asher.

Descendants of Judah

³Judah had three sons from Bathshua, a Canaanite woman. Their names were Er, Onan, and Shelah. But the LORD saw that the oldest son, Er, was a wicked man, so he killed him. ⁴Later Judah had twin sons from Tamar, his widowed daughter-in-law. Their names were Perez and Zerah. So Judah had five sons in all.

⁵The sons of Perez were Hezron and Hamul.

⁶The sons of Zerah were Zimri, Ethan, Heman, Calcol, and Darda*—five in all.

⁷The son of Carmi (a descendant of Zimri) was Achan,* who brought disaster on Israel by taking plunder that had been set apart for the LORD.*

⁸The son of Ethan was Azariah.

From Judah's Grandson Hezron to David

⁹The sons of Hezron were Jerahmeel, Ram, and Caleb.*

10 Ram was the father of Amminadab. Amminadab was the father of Nahshon, a leader of Judah.

11 Nahshon was the father of Salmon.* Salmon was the father of Boaz.

12 Boaz was the father of Obed. Obed was the father of Jesse.

¹³Jesse's first son was Eliab, his second was Abinadab, his third was Shimea, ¹⁴his fourth was Nethanel, his fifth was Raddai, ¹⁵his sixth was Ozem, and his seventh was David.

¹⁶Their sisters were named Zeruiah and Abigail. Zeruiah had three sons

named Abishai, Joab, and Asahel. ¹⁷Abigail married a man named Jether, an Ishmaelite, and they had a son named Amasa.

Other Descendants of Hezron

¹⁸Hezron's son Caleb had sons from his wife Azubah and from Jerioth.* Her sons were named Jesher, Shobab, and Ardon. ¹⁹After Azubah died, Caleb married Ephrathah,* and they had a son named Hur. ²⁰Hur was the father of Uri. Uri was the father of Bezalel.

²¹When Hezron was sixty years old, he married Gilead's sister, the daughter of Makir. They had a son named Segub. ²²Segub was the father of Jair, who ruled twenty-three towns in the land of Gilead. ²³(But Geshur and Aram captured the Towns of Jair* and also took Kenath and its sixty surrounding villages.) All these were descendants of Makir, the father of Gilead. ²⁴Soon after Hezron died in the town of Caleb-ephrathah, his wife Abijah gave birth to a son named Ashhur (the father of* Tekoa).

Descendants of Hezron's Son Jerahmeel

²⁵The sons of Jerahmeel, the oldest son of Hezron, were Ram (the firstborn), Bunah, Oren, Ozem, and Ahijah. ²⁶Jerahmeel had a second wife named Atarah. She was the mother of Onam.

²⁷The sons of Ram, the oldest son of Jerahmeel, were Maaz, Jamin, and Eker.

²⁸The sons of Onam were Shammai and Jada. The sons of Shammai were Nadab and Abishur.

²⁹The sons of Abishur and his wife Abihail were Ahban and Molid.

³⁰The sons of Nadab were Seled and Appaim. Seled died without children, ³¹but Appaim had a son named Ishi. The son of Ishi was Sheshan. Sheshan had a descendant named Ahlai.

³²The sons of Jada, Shammai's brother, were Jether and Jonathan. Jether died without children, ³³but Jonathan had two sons named Peleth and Zaza.

These were all descendants of Jerahmeel.

1:51 As in an alternate reading of the Masoretic Text (see also Gen 36:40); the other alternate reads *Aliah.*   2:1 *Israel* is the name that God gave to Jacob.   2:6 As in many Hebrew manuscripts, some Greek manuscripts, and Syriac version (see also 1 Kgs 4:31); Hebrew reads *Dara.*   2:7a Hebrew *Achar;* compare Josh 7:1. *Achar* means "disaster."   2:7b The Hebrew term used here refers to the complete consecration of things or people to the LORD, either by destroying them or by giving them as an offering.   2:9 Hebrew *Kelubai,* a variant spelling of Caleb; compare 2:18.   2:11 As in Greek version (see also Ruth 4:20); Hebrew reads *Salma.*   2:18 Or *Caleb had a daughter named Jerioth from his wife, Azubah.* The meaning of the Hebrew is uncertain.   2:19 Hebrew *Ephrath,* a variant spelling of Ephrathah; compare 2:50 and 4:4.   2:23 Or *captured Havvoth-jair.* 2:24 Or *the founder of;* also in 2:42, 45, 49.

³⁴Sheshan had no sons, though he did have daughters. He also had an Egyptian servant named Jarha. ³⁵Sheshan gave one of his daughters to be the wife of Jarha, and they had a son named Attai.

³⁶ Attai was the father of Nathan. Nathan was the father of Zabad.
³⁷ Zabad was the father of Ephlal. Ephlal was the father of Obed.
³⁸ Obed was the father of Jehu. Jehu was the father of Azariah.
³⁹ Azariah was the father of Helez. Helez was the father of Eleasah.
⁴⁰ Eleasah was the father of Sismai. Sismai was the father of Shallum.
⁴¹ Shallum was the father of Jekamiah. Jekamiah was the father of Elishama.

Descendants of Hezron's Son Caleb

⁴²The descendants of Caleb, the brother of Jerahmeel, included Mesha (the firstborn), who became the father of Ziph. Caleb's descendants also included the sons of Mareshah, the father of Hebron.* ⁴³The sons of Hebron were Korah, Tappuah, Rekem, and Shema. ⁴⁴Shema was the father of Raham. Raham was the father of Jorkeam. Rekem was the father of Shammai. ⁴⁵The son of Shammai was Maon. Maon was the father of Beth-zur. ⁴⁶Caleb's concubine Ephah gave birth to Haran, Moza, and Gazez. Haran was the father of Gazez.

⁴⁷The sons of Jahdai were Regem, Jotham, Geshan, Pelet, Ephah, and Shaaph. ⁴⁸Another of Caleb's concubines, Maacah, gave birth to Sheber and Tirhanah. ⁴⁹She also gave birth to Shaaph (the father of Madmannah) and Sheva (the father of Macbenah and Gibea). Caleb also had a daughter named Acsah. ⁵⁰These were all descendants of Caleb.

Descendants of Caleb's Son Hur

The sons of Hur, the oldest son of Caleb's wife Ephrathah, were Shobal (the founder of Kiriath-jearim), ⁵¹Salma (the founder of Bethlehem), and Hareph (the founder of Beth-gader). ⁵²The descendants of Shobal (the founder of Kiriath-jearim) were Haroeh, half the Manahathites, ⁵³and the families of

Kiriath-jearim—the Ithrites, Puthites, Shumathites, and Mishraites, from whom came the people of Zorah and Eshtaol. ⁵⁴The descendants of Salma were the people of Bethlehem, the Netophathites, Atroth-beth-joab, the other half of the Manahathites, the Zorites, ⁵⁵and the families of scribes living at Jabez—the Tirathites, Shimeathites, and Sucathites. All these were Kenites who descended from Hammath, the father of the family of Recab.*

Descendants of David

3 These are the sons of David who were born in Hebron:

The oldest was Amnon, whose mother was Ahinoam from Jezreel.
The second was Daniel, whose mother was Abigail from Carmel.
² The third was Absalom, whose mother was Maacah, the daughter of Talmai, king of Geshur.
The fourth was Adonijah, whose mother was Haggith.
³ The fifth was Shephatiah, whose mother was Abital.
The sixth was Ithream, whose mother was Eglah, David's wife.

⁴These six sons were born to David in Hebron, where he reigned seven and a half years.

Then David reigned another thirty-three years in Jerusalem. ⁵The sons born to David in Jerusalem included Shammua,* Shobab, Nathan, and Solomon. Their mother was Bathsheba,* the daughter of Ammiel. ⁶David also had nine other sons: Ibhar, Elishua,* Elpelet,* ⁷Nogah, Nepheg, Japhia, ⁸Elishama, Eliada, and Eliphelet.

⁹These were the sons of David, not including his sons born to his concubines. Their sister was named Tamar.

Descendants of Solomon

¹⁰The descendants of Solomon were Rehoboam, Abijah, Asa, Jehoshaphat, ¹¹Jehoram,* Ahaziah, Joash, ¹²Amaziah, Uzziah,* Jotham, ¹³Ahaz, Hezekiah, Manasseh, ¹⁴Amon, and Josiah. ¹⁵The sons of Josiah were Johanan (the

---

2:42 Or *who founded Hebron*. The meaning of the Hebrew is uncertain.   **2:55** Or *the founder of Beth-recab*.   **3:5a** As in Syriac version (see also 14:4; 2 Sam 5:14); Hebrew reads *Shimea*.   **3:5b** Hebrew *Bathshua*, a variant spelling of Bathsheba.   **3:6a** As in some Hebrew and Greek manuscripts (see also 14:5-7 and 2 Sam 5:15); most Hebrew manuscripts read *Elishama*.   **3:6b** Hebrew *Eliphelet;* compare parallel text at 14:5-7.   **3:11** Hebrew *Joram*, a variant spelling of Jehoram.   **3:12** Hebrew *Azariah*, a variant spelling of Uzziah.

oldest), Jehoiakim (the second), Zedekiah (the third), and Jehoahaz* (the fourth). ¹⁶The successors of Jehoiakim were his son Jehoiachin and his brother Zedekiah.*

Descendants of Jehoiachin

¹⁷The sons of Jehoiachin,* who was taken prisoner by the Babylonians, were Shealtiel, ¹⁸Malkiram, Pedaiah, Shenazzar, Jekamiah, Hoshama, and Nedabiah. ¹⁹The sons of Pedaiah were Zerubbabel and Shimei.

The sons of Zerubbabel were Meshullam and Hananiah. (Their sister was Shelomith.) ²⁰His five other sons were Hashubah, Ohel, Berekiah, Hasadiah, and Jushab-hesed. ²¹The sons of Hananiah were Pelatiah and Jeshaiah. Jeshaiah's son was Rephaiah. Rephaiah's son was Arnan. Arnan's son was Obadiah. Obadiah's son was Shecaniah. ²²The descendants of Shecaniah were Shemaiah and his sons, Hattush, Igal, Bariah, Neariah, and Shaphat—six in all. ²³The sons of Neariah were Elioenai, Hizkiah, and Azrikam—three in all. ²⁴The sons of Elioenai were Hodaviah, Eliashib, Pelaiah, Akkub, Johanan, Delaiah, and Anani—seven in all.

Other Descendants of Judah

4 The descendants of Judah were Perez, Hezron, Carmi, Hur, and Shobal. ²Shobal's son Reaiah was the father of Jahath. Jahath was the father of Ahumai and Lahad. These were the families of the Zorathites. ³The descendants of* Etam were Jezreel, Ishma, Idbash, their sister Hazzelelponi, ⁴Penuel (the father of* Gedor), and Ezer (the father of Hushah). These were the descendants of Hur (the firstborn of Ephrathah), the ancestor of Bethlehem. ⁵Ashhur (the father of Tekoa) had two wives, named Helah and Naarah. ⁶Naarah gave birth to Ahuzzam, Hepher, Temeni, and Haahashtari. ⁷Helah gave birth to Zereth, Izhar,* Ethnan, ⁸and Koz, who became the ancestor of Anub, Zobebah, and all the families of Aharhel son of Harum. ⁹There was a man named Jabez who was more honorable than any of his brothers.

His mother named him Jabez* because his birth had been so painful. ¹⁰He was the one who prayed to the God of Israel, "Oh, that you would bless me and expand my territory! Please be with me in all that I do, and keep me from all trouble and pain!" And God granted him his request.

¹¹Kelub (the brother of Shuhah) was the father of Mehir. Mehir was the father of Eshton. ¹²Eshton was the father of Beth-rapha, Paseah, and Tehinnah. Tehinnah was the father of Ir-nahash. These were the descendants of Recah.

¹³The sons of Kenaz were Othniel and Seraiah. Othniel's sons were Hathath and Meonothai.* ¹⁴Meonothai was the father of Ophrah. Seraiah was the father of Joab, the founder of the Valley of Craftsmen,* so called because they were craftsmen.

¹⁵The sons of Caleb son of Jephunneh were Iru, Elah, and Naam. The son of Elah was Kenaz.

¹⁶The sons of Jehallelel were Ziph, Ziphah, Tiria, and Asarel.

¹⁷The sons of Ezrah were Jether, Mered, Epher, and Jalon. One of Mered's wives became* the mother of Miriam, Shammai, and Ishbah (the father of Eshtemoa). ¹⁸He married a woman from Judah, who became the mother of Jered (the father of Gedor), Heber (the father of Soco), and Jekuthiel (the father of Zanoah). Mered also married Bithia, a daughter of Pharaoh, and she bore him children. ¹⁹Hodiah's wife was the sister of Naham. One of her sons was the father of Keilah the Garmite, and another was the father of Eshtemoa the Maacathite. ²⁰The sons of Shimon were Amnon, Rinnah, Ben-hanan, and Tilon.

The descendants of Ishi were Zoheth and Ben-zoheth.

Descendants of Judah's Son Shelah

²¹Shelah was one of Judah's sons. The descendants of Shelah were Er (the father of Lecah); Laadah (the father of Mareshah); the families of linen workers at Beth-ashbea; ²²Jokim; the men of Cozeba; and Joash and Saraph, who ruled over Moab

---

3:15 Hebrew *Shallum*, another name for Jehoahaz.   3:16 Hebrew *The sons of Jehoiakim were his son Jeconiah* [a variant spelling of Jehoiachin] *and his son Zedekiah*.   3:17 Hebrew *Jeconiah*, a variant spelling of Jehoiachin.   4:3 As in Greek version; Hebrew reads *father of*. The meaning of the Hebrew is uncertain.   4:4 Or *the founder of*; also in 4:5, 12, 14, 17, 18, and perhaps other instances where the text reads *the father of*.   4:7 As in an alternate reading in the Masoretic Text (see also Latin Vulgate); the other alternate and the Greek version read *Zohar*.   4:9 *Jabez* sounds like a Hebrew word meaning "distress" or "pain."   4:13 As in some Greek manuscripts and Latin Vulgate; Hebrew lacks *and Meonothai*.   4:14 Or *Joab, the father of Ge-harashim*.   4:17 Or *Jether's wife became*; Hebrew reads *She became*.

and Jashubi-lehem. These names all come from ancient records. 23They were the pottery makers who lived in Netaim and Gederah. They lived there and worked for the king.

Descendants of Simeon

24The sons of Simeon were Jemuel,* Jamin, Jarib, Zohar,* and Shaul. 25The descendants of Shaul were Shallum, Mibsam, and Mishma. 26The descendants of Mishma were Hammuel, Zaccur, and Shimei. 27Shimei had sixteen sons and six daughters, but none of his brothers had large families. So Simeon's tribe never grew as large as the tribe of Judah.

28They lived in Beersheba, Moladah, Hazarshual, 29Bilhah, Ezem, Tolad, 30Bethuel, Hormah, Ziklag, 31Beth-marcaboth, Hazar-susim, Beth-biri, and Shaaraim. These towns were under their control until the time of King David. 32Their descendants also lived in Etam, Ain, Rimmon, Token, and Ashan—five towns 33and their surrounding villages as far away as Baalath.* This was their territory, and these names are listed in their genealogical records.

34Other descendants of Simeon included Meshobab, Jamlech, Joshah son of Amaziah, 35Joel, Jehu son of Joshibiah, son of Seraiah, son of Asiel, 36Elioenai, Jaakobah, Jeshohaiah, Asaiah, Adiel, Jesimiel, Benaiah, 37and Ziza son of Shiphi, son of Allon, son of Jedaiah, son of Shimri, son of Shemaiah.

38These were the names of some of the leaders of Simeon's wealthy clans. Their families grew, 39and they traveled to the region of Gerar,* in the east part of the valley, seeking pastureland for their flocks. 40They found lush pastures there, and the land was spacious, quiet, and peaceful. Some of Ham's descendants had been living in that region. 41But during the reign of King Hezekiah of Judah, these leaders of Simeon invaded the region and completely destroyed* the homes of the descendants of Ham and of the Meunites. No trace of them remains today.

They killed everyone who lived there and took the land for themselves, because they wanted its good pastureland for their flocks. 42Five hundred of these invaders from the tribe of Simeon went to Mount Seir, led by Pelatiah, Neariah, Rephaiah, and Uzziel—all sons of Ishi. 43They destroyed the few Amalekites who had survived, and they have lived there ever since.

Descendants of Reuben

5 The oldest son of Israel* was Reuben. But since he dishonored his father by sleeping with one of his father's concubines, his birthright was given to the sons of his brother Joseph. For this reason, Reuben is not listed in the genealogical records as the firstborn son. 2The descendants of Judah became the most powerful tribe and provided a ruler for the nation,* but the birthright belonged to Joseph.

3The sons of Reuben, the oldest son of Israel, were Hanoch, Pallu, Hezron, and Carmi. 4The descendants of Joel were Shemaiah, Gog, Shimei, 5Micah, Reaiah, Baal, 6and Beerah. Beerah was the leader of the Reubenites when they were taken into captivity by King Tiglath-pileser* of Assyria. 7Beerah's* relatives are listed in their genealogical records by their clans: Jeiel (the leader), Zechariah, 8and Bela son of Azaz, son of Shema, son of Joel. The Reubenites lived in the area that stretches from Aroer to Nebo and Baalmeon. 9And since they had so many livestock in the land of Gilead, they spread east toward the edge of the desert that stretches to the Euphrates River. 10During the reign of Saul, the Reubenites defeated the Hagrites in battle. Then they moved into the Hagrite settlements all along the eastern edge of Gilead.

Descendants of Gad

11Next to the Reubenites, the descendants of Gad lived in the land of Bashan as far east as Salecah. 12Joel was the leader in the land of Bashan, and Shapham was second-in-command, followed by Janai and Shaphat. 13Their relatives, the leaders of seven other clans, were Michael, Meshullam, Sheba, Jorai, Jacan, Zia, and Eber. 14These were all

4:24a As in Syriac version (see also Gen 46:10; Exod 6:15); Hebrew reads Nemuel.   4:24b As in parallel texts at Gen 46:10 and Exod 6:15; Hebrew reads Zerah.   4:33 As in some Greek manuscripts (see also Josh 19:8); Hebrew reads Baal.   4:39 As in Greek version; Hebrew reads Gedor.   4:41 The Hebrew term used here refers to the complete consecration of things or people to the LORD, either by destroying them or by giving them as an offering.   5:1 Israel is the name that God gave to Jacob.   5:2 Or and from Judah came a prince.   5:6 Hebrew Tilgath-pilneser, a variant spelling of Tiglath-pileser; also in 5:26.   5:7 Hebrew His.

descendants of Abihail son of Huri, son of Jaroah, son of Gilead, son of Michael, son of Jeshishai, son of Jahdo, son of Buz. 15Ahi son of Abdiel, son of Guni, was the leader of their clans.

16The Gadites lived in the land of Gilead, in Bashan and its villages, and throughout all the pasturelands of Sharon. 17All of these were listed in the genealogical records during the days of King Jotham of Judah and King Jeroboam of Israel.

The Tribes East of the Jordan

18There were 44,760 capable warriors in the armies of Reuben, Gad, and the half-tribe of Manasseh. They were all skilled in combat and armed with shields, swords, and bows. 19They waged war against the Hagrites, the Jeturites, the Naphishites, and the Nodabites. 20They cried out to God during the battle, and he answered their prayer because they trusted in him. So the Hagrites and all their allies were defeated. 21The plunder taken from the Hagrites included 50,000 camels, 250,000 sheep and goats, 2,000 donkeys, and 100,000 captives. 22Many of the Hagrites were killed in the battle because God was fighting against them. The people of Reuben, Gad, and Manasseh lived in their land until they were taken into exile.

23The half-tribe of Manasseh was very large and spread through the land from Bashan to Baal-hermon, Senir, and Mount Hermon. 24These were the leaders of their clans: Epher,* Ishi, Eliel, Azriel, Jeremiah, Hodaviah, and Jahdiel. These men had a great reputation as mighty warriors and leaders of their clans.

25But these tribes were unfaithful to the God of their ancestors. They worshiped the gods of the nations that God had destroyed. 26So the God of Israel caused King Pul of Assyria (also known as Tiglath-pileser) to invade the land and take away the people of Reuben, Gad, and the half-tribe of Manasseh as captives. The Assyrians exiled them to Halah, Habor, Hara, and the Gozan River, where they remain to this day.

The Priestly Line

6 1*The sons of Levi were Gershon, Kohath, and Merari. 2The descendants of Kohath included Amram, Izhar, Hebron, and Uzziel.

3The children of Amram were Aaron, Moses, and Miriam.
The sons of Aaron were Nadab, Abihu, Eleazar, and Ithamar.
4 Eleazar was the father of Phinehas. Phinehas was the father of Abishua.
5 Abishua was the father of Bukki. Bukki was the father of Uzzi.
6 Uzzi was the father of Zerahiah. Zerahiah was the father of Meraioth.
7 Meraioth was the father of Amariah. Amariah was the father of Ahitub.
8 Ahitub was the father of Zadok. Zadok was the father of Ahimaaz.
9 Ahimaaz was the father of Azariah. Azariah was the father of Johanan.
10 Johanan was the father of Azariah, the high priest at the Temple* built by Solomon in Jerusalem.
11 Azariah was the father of Amariah. Amariah was the father of Ahitub.
12 Ahitub was the father of Zadok. Zadok was the father of Shallum.
13 Shallum was the father of Hilkiah. Hilkiah was the father of Azariah.
14 Azariah was the father of Seraiah. Seraiah was the father of Jehozadak, 15who went into exile when the LORD sent the people of Judah and Jerusalem into captivity under Nebuchadnezzar.

The Levite Clans

16*The sons of Levi were Gershon,* Kohath, and Merari.
17The descendants of Gershon included Libni and Shimei.
18The descendants of Kohath included Amram, Izhar, Hebron, and Uzziel.
19The descendants of Merari included Mahli and Mushi.

The following were the Levite clans, listed according to their ancestral descent:

20The descendants of Gershon included Libni, Jahath, Zimmah, 21Joah, Iddo, Zerah, and Jeatherai.
22The descendants of Kohath included Amminadab, Korah, Assir, 23Elkanah, Abiasaph,* Assir, 24Tahath, Uriel, Uzziah, and Shaul.

5:24 As in Greek version and Latin Vulgate; Hebrew reads *and Epher.*   6:1 Verses 6:1-15 are numbered 5:27-41 in Hebrew text.   6:10 Hebrew *the house.*   6:16a Verses 6:16-81 are numbered 6:1-66 in Hebrew text.   6:16b Hebrew *Gershom,* a variant spelling of Gershon (see 6:1); also in 6:17, 20, 43, 62, 71.   6:23 Hebrew *Ebiasaph,* a variant spelling of Abiasaph (also in 6:37); compare parallel text at Exod 6:24.

25The descendants of Elkanah included Amasai, Ahimoth, 26Elkanah, Zophai, Nahath, 27Eliab, Jeroham, Elkanah, and Samuel.*

28The sons of Samuel were Joel* (the older) and Abijah (the second).

29The descendants of Merari included Mahli, Libni, Shimei, Uzzah, 30Shimea, Haggiah, and Asaiah.

The Temple Musicians

31David assigned the following men to lead the music at the house of the LORD after the Ark was placed there. 32They ministered with music at the Tabernacle* until Solomon built the Temple of the LORD in Jerusalem. They carried out their work, following all the regulations handed down to them. 33These are the men who served, along with their sons:

Heman the musician was from the clan of Kohath. His genealogy was traced back through Joel, Samuel, 34Elkanah, Jeroham, Eliel, Toah, 35Zuph, Elkanah, Mahath, Amasai, 36Elkanah, Joel, Azariah, Zephaniah, 37Tahath, Assir, Abiasaph, Korah, 38Izhar, Kohath, Levi, and Israel.*

39Heman's first assistant was Asaph from the clan of Gershon.* Asaph's genealogy was traced back through Berekiah, Shimea, 40Michael, Baaseiah, Malkijah, 41Ethni, Zerah, Adaiah, 42Ethan, Zimmah, Shimei, 43Jahath, Gershon, and Levi.

44Heman's second assistant was Ethan from the clan of Merari. Ethan's genealogy was traced back through Kishi, Abdi, Malluch, 45Hashabiah, Amaziah, Hilkiah, 46Amzi, Bani, Shemer, 47Mahli, Mushi, Merari, and Levi.

48Their fellow Levites were appointed to various other tasks in the Tabernacle, the house of God.

Aaron's Descendants

49Only Aaron and his descendants served as priests. They presented the offerings on the altar of burnt offering and the altar of incense, and they performed all the other duties related to the Most Holy Place. They made atonement for Israel by doing everything that Moses, the servant of God, had commanded them.

50The descendants of Aaron were Eleazar, Phinehas, Abishua, 51Bukki, Uzzi, Zerahiah, 52Meraioth, Amariah, Ahitub, 53Zadok, and Ahimaaz.

Territory for the Levites

54This is a record of the towns and territory assigned by means of sacred lots to the descendants of Aaron, who were from the clan of Kohath. 55This territory included Hebron and its surrounding pasturelands in Judah, 56but the fields and outlying areas belonging to the city were given to Caleb son of Jephunneh. 57So the descendants of Aaron were given the following towns, each with its pasturelands: Hebron (a city of refuge),* Libnah, Jattir, Eshtemoa, 58Holon,* Debir, 59Ain,* Juttah,* and Beth-shemesh. 60And from the territory of Benjamin they were given Gibeon,* Geba, Alemeth, and Anathoth, each with its pasturelands. So thirteen towns were given to the descendants of Aaron. 61The remaining descendants of Kohath received ten towns from the territory of the half-tribe of Manasseh by means of sacred lots.

62The descendants of Gershon received by sacred lots thirteen towns from the territories of Issachar, Asher, Naphtali, and from the Bashan area of Manasseh, east of the Jordan.

63The descendants of Merari received by sacred lots twelve towns from the territories of Reuben, Gad, and Zebulun.

64So the people of Israel assigned all these towns and pasturelands to the Levites. 65The towns in the territories of Judah, Simeon, and Benjamin, mentioned above, were assigned to them by means of sacred lots.

66The descendants of Kohath were given the following towns from the territory of Ephraim, each with its pasturelands: 67Shechem (a city of refuge in the hill country of Ephraim),* Gezer, 68Jokmeam, Beth-horon, 69Aijalon, and Gathrimmon. 70The remaining descendants of Kohath were assigned the towns of Aner and Bileam from the territory of the half-tribe of Manasseh, each with its pasturelands.

6:27 As in some Greek manuscripts (see also 6:33-34); Hebrew lacks *and Samuel.* 6:28 As in some Greek manuscripts and the Syriac version (see also 6:33 and 1 Sam 8:2); Hebrew lacks *Joel.* 6:32 Hebrew *the Tabernacle, the Tent of Meeting.* 6:38 *Israel* is the name that God gave to Jacob. 6:39 Hebrew lacks *from the clan of Gershon;* see 6:43. 6:57 As in parallel text at Josh 21:13; Hebrew reads *were given the cities of refuge: Hebron, and the following towns, each with its pasturelands.* 6:58 As in parallel text at Josh 21:15; Masoretic Text reads *Hilez;* other manuscripts read *Hilen.* 6:59a As in parallel text at Josh 21:16; Hebrew reads *Ashan.* 6:59b As in Syriac version (see also Josh 21:16); Hebrew lacks *Juttah.* 6:60 As in parallel text at Josh 21:17; Hebrew lacks *Gibeon.* 6:66-67 As in parallel text at Josh 21:21; Hebrew text reads *were given the cities of refuge: Shechem in the hill country of Ephraim, and the following towns, each with its pasturelands.*

71The descendants of Gershon received the towns of Golan (in Bashan) and Ashtaroth from the territory of the half-tribe of Manasseh, each with its pasturelands. 72From the territory of Issachar, they were given Kedesh, Daberath, 73Ramoth, and Anem, each with its pasturelands. 74From the territory of Asher, they received Mashal, Abdon, 75Hukok, and Rehob, each with its pasturelands. 76From the territory of Naphtali, they were given Kedesh in Galilee, Hammon, and Kiriathaim, each with its pasturelands.

77The remaining descendants of Merari received the towns of Jokneam, Kartah,* Rimmon,* and Tabor from the territory of Zebulun, each with its pasturelands. 78From the territory of Reuben, east of the Jordan River opposite Jericho, they received Bezer (a desert town), Jahaz,* 79Kedemoth, and Mephaath, each with its pasturelands. 80And from the territory of Gad, they received Ramoth in Gilead, Mahanaim, 81Heshbon, and Jazer, each with its pasturelands.

Descendants of Issachar

7 The four sons of Issachar were Tola, Puah, Jashub, and Shimron. 2The sons of Tola were Uzzi, Rephaiah, Jeriel, Jahmai, Ibsam, and Shemuel. Each of them was the leader of an ancestral clan. At the time of King David, the total number of mighty warriors listed in the records of these clans was 22,600.

3The son of Uzzi was Izrahiah. The sons of Izrahiah were Michael, Obadiah, Joel, and Isshiah. These five became the leaders of clans. 4All of them had many wives and many sons, so the total number of men available for military service among their descendants was 36,000.

5The total number of mighty warriors from all the clans of the tribe of Issachar was 87,000. All of them were listed in their genealogical records.

Descendants of Benjamin

6Three of Benjamin's sons were Bela, Beker, and Jediael. 7The five sons of Bela were Ezbon, Uzzi, Uzziel, Jerimoth, and Iri. Each of them was the leader of an ancestral clan. The total number of mighty warriors from

these clans was 22,034, as listed in their genealogical records. 8The sons of Beker were Zemirah, Joash, Eliezer, Elioenai, Omri, Jeremoth, Abijah, Anathoth, and Alemeth. 9Each of them was the leader of an ancestral clan. The total number of mighty warriors and leaders from these clans was 20,200, as listed in their genealogical records. 10The son of Jediael was Bilhan. The sons of Bilhan were Jeush, Benjamin, Ehud, Kenaanah, Zethan, Tarshish, and Ahishahar. 11Each of them was the leader of an ancestral clan. From these clans the total number of mighty warriors ready for war was 17,200. 12The sons of Ir were Shuppim and Huppim. Hushim was the son of Aher.

Descendants of Naphtali

13The sons of Naphtali were Jahzeel,* Guni, Jezer, and Shillem.* They were all descendants of Jacob's concubine Bilhah.

Descendants of Manasseh

14The descendants of Manasseh through his Aramean concubine included Asriel. She also bore Makir, the father of Gilead. 15Makir found wives for* Huppim and Shuppim. Makir had a sister named Maacah. One of his descendants was Zelophehad, who had only daughters. 16Makir's wife, Maacah, gave birth to a son whom she named Peresh. His brother's name was Sheresh. The sons of Peresh were Ulam and Rakem. 17The son of Ulam was Bedan. All these were considered Gileadites, descendants of Makir son of Manasseh. 18Makir's sister Hammoleketh gave birth to Ishhod, Abiezer, and Mahlah. 19The sons of Shemida were Ahian, Shechem, Likhi, and Aniam.

Descendants of Ephraim

20The descendants of Ephraim were Shuthelah, Bered, Tahath, Eleadah, Tahath, 21Zabad, Shuthelah, Ezer, and Elead. These two were killed trying to steal livestock from the local farmers near Gath. 22Their father, Ephraim, mourned for them a long time, and his relatives came to comfort him. 23Afterward Ephraim slept with his wife, and she became pregnant and gave birth to a son. Ephraim named him Beriah* because of the tragedy his family had suffered. 24He had a daughter named Sheerah. She built the towns of Lower and Upper Beth-horon and Uzzen-sheerah.

25The descendants of Ephraim included Rephah, Resheph, Telah, Tahan, 26Ladan, Ammihud, Elishama, 27Nun, and Joshua.

28The descendants of Ephraim lived in the territory that included Bethel and its surrounding towns to the south, Naaran to the east, Gezer and its villages to the west, and Shechem and its surrounding villages to the north as far as Ayyah and its towns. 29Along the border of Manasseh were the towns of Beth-shan,* Taanach, Megiddo, Dor, and their surrounding villages. The descendants of Joseph son of Israel* lived in these towns.

Descendants of Asher

30The sons of Asher were Imnah, Ishvah, Ishvi, and Beriah. They had a sister named Serah.

31The sons of Beriah were Heber and Malkiel (the father of Birzaith).

32The sons of Heber were Japhlet, Shomer, and Hotham. They had a sister named Shua.

33The sons of Japhlet were Pasach, Bimhal, and Ashvath.

34The sons of Shomer were Ahi,* Rohgah, Hubbah, and Aram.

35The sons of his brother Helem* were Zophah, Imna, Shelesh, and Amal.

36The sons of Zophah were Suah, Harnepher, Shual, Beri, Imrah, 37Bezer, Hod, Shamma, Shilshah, Ithran,* and Beera.

38The sons of Jether were Jephunneh, Pispah, and Ara.

39The sons of Ulla were Arah, Hanniel, and Rizia.

40Each of these descendants of Asher was the head of an ancestral clan. They were all select men—mighty warriors and outstanding leaders. The total number of men available for military service was 26,000, as listed in their genealogical records.

Descendants of Benjamin

8 Benjamin's first son was Bela, the second was Ashbel, the third was Aharah, 2the fourth was Nohah, and the fifth was Rapha.

3The sons of Bela were Addar, Gera, Abihud,* 4Abishua, Naaman, Ahoah, 5Gera, Shephuphan, and Huram.

6The sons of Ehud, leaders of the clans living at Geba, were exiled to Manahath. 7Ehud's sons were Naaman, Ahijah, and Gera. Gera, who led them into exile, was the father of Uzza and Ahihud.*

8After Shaharaim divorced his wives Hushim and Baara, he had children in the land of Moab. 9His wife Hodesh gave birth to Jobab, Zibia, Mesha, Malcam, 10Jeuz, Sakia, and Mirmah. These sons all became the leaders of clans.

11Shaharaim's wife Hushim had already given birth to Abitub and Elpaal. 12The sons of Elpaal were Eber, Misham, Shemed (who built the towns of Ono and Lod and their nearby villages), 13Beriah, and Shema. They were the leaders of the clans living in Aijalon, and they drove out the inhabitants of Gath.

14Ahio, Shashak, Jeremoth, 15Zebadiah, Arad, Eder, 16Michael, Ishpah, and Joha were the sons of Beriah.

17Zebadiah, Meshullam, Hizki, Heber, 18Ishmerai, Izliah, and Jobab were the sons of Elpaal.

19Jakim, Zicri, Zabdi, 20Elienai, Zillethai, Eliel, 21Adaiah, Beraiah, and Shimrath were the sons of Shimei.

22Ishpan, Eber, Eliel, 23Abdon, Zicri, Hanan, 24Hananiah, Elam, Anthothijah, 25Iphdeiah, and Penuel were the sons of Shashak.

26Shamsherai, Shehariah, Athaliah, 27Jaareshiah, Elijah, and Zicri were the sons of Jeroham.

28These were the leaders of the ancestral clans; they were listed in their genealogical records, and they all lived in Jerusalem.

The Family of Saul

29Jeiel* (the father of* Gibeon) lived in the town of Gibeon. His wife's name was Maacah, 30and his oldest son was named Abdon. Jeiel's other sons were

---

7:23 Beriah sounds like a Hebrew term meaning "tragedy" or "misfortune." 7:29a Hebrew Beth-shean, a variant spelling of Beth-shan. 7:29b Israel is the name that God gave to Jacob. 7:34 Or The sons of Shomer, his brother, were. 7:35 Possibly another name for Hotham; compare 7:32. 7:37 Possibly another name for Jether; compare 7:38. 8:3 Possibly Gera the father of Ehud; compare 8:6. 8:7 Or Gera, that is Heglam, was the father of Uzza and Ahihud. 8:29a As in some Greek manuscripts (see also 9:35); Hebrew lacks Jeiel. 8:29b Or the founder of.

Zur, Kish, Baal, Ner,* Nadab, 31Gedor,
Ahio, Zechariah,* 32and Mikloth,
who was the father of Shimeam.* All
these families lived near each other
in Jerusalem.

33 Ner was the father of Kish.
Kish was the father of Saul.
Saul was the father of Jonathan,
Malkishua, Abinadab, and Esh-baal.
34 Jonathan was the father of Merib-baal.
Merib-baal was the father of Micah.
35 Micah was the father of Pithon, Melech,
Tahrea,* and Ahaz.
36 Ahaz was the father of Jadah.*
Jadah was the father of Alemeth,
Azmaveth, and Zimri.
Zimri was the father of Moza.
37 Moza was the father of Binea.
Binea was the father of Rephaiah.*
Rephaiah was the father of Eleasah.
Eleasah was the father of Azel.
38Azel had six sons: Azrikam, Bokeru,
Ishmael, Sheariah, Obadiah, and Hanan.
These were the sons of Azel.
39Azel's brother Eshek had three sons: the
first was Ulam, the second was Jeush,
and the third was Eliphelet. 40Ulam's
sons were all mighty warriors and
expert archers. They had many sons and
grandsons—150 in all.

All these were descendants of Benjamin.

9 So all Israel was listed in the genealogical
records in *The Book of the Kings of Israel.*

The Returning Exiles
The people of Judah were exiled to Babylon
because they were unfaithful to the LORD. 2The
first of the exiles to return to their property
in their former towns were priests, Levites,
Temple servants, and other Israelites. 3Some
of the people from the tribes of Judah, Benjamin, Ephraim, and Manasseh came and settled
in Jerusalem.

4One family that returned was that of Uthai
son of Ammihud, son of Omri, son of Imri,
son of Bani, a descendant of Perez son of
Judah.
5Others returned from the Shilonite clan,
including Asaiah (the oldest) and his sons.

6From the Zerahite clan, Jeuel returned with
his relatives.
In all, 690 families from the tribe of Judah
returned.

7From the tribe of Benjamin came Sallu son
of Meshullam, son of Hodaviah, son of
Hassenuah; 8Ibneiah son of Jeroham; Elah
son of Uzzi, son of Micri; and Meshullam
son of Shephatiah, son of Reuel, son of
Ibnijah.
9These men were all leaders of clans, and they
were listed in their genealogical records. In
all, 956 families from the tribe of Benjamin
returned.

The Returning Priests
10Among the priests who returned were
Jedaiah, Jehoiarib, Jakin, 11Azariah son of
Hilkiah, son of Meshullam, son of Zadok,
son of Meraioth, son of Ahitub. Azariah
was the chief officer of the house of God.
12Other returning priests were Adaiah son of
Jeroham, son of Pashhur, son of Malkijah,
and Maasai son of Adiel, son of Jahzerah,
son of Meshullam, son of Meshillemith,
son of Immer.
13In all, 1,760 priests returned. They were heads
of clans and very able men. They were responsible for ministering at the house of God.

The Returning Levites
14The Levites who returned were Shemaiah
son of Hasshub, son of Azrikam, son
of Hashabiah, a descendant of Merari;
15Bakbakkar; Heresh; Galal; Mattaniah
son of Mica, son of Zicri, son of Asaph;
16Obadiah son of Shemaiah, son of Galal,
son of Jeduthun; and Berekiah son of Asa,
son of Elkanah, who lived in the area of
Netophah.
17The gatekeepers who returned were
Shallum, Akkub, Talmon, Ahiman, and
their relatives. Shallum was the chief
gatekeeper. 18Prior to this time, they were
responsible for the King's Gate on the east
side. These men served as gatekeepers for
the camps of the Levites. 19Shallum was
the son of Kore, a descendant of Abiasaph,*
from the clan of Korah. He and his
relatives, the Korahites, were responsible
for guarding the entrance to the sanctuary,

8:30 As in some Greek manuscripts (see also 9:36); Hebrew lacks *Ner.* 8:31 As in parallel text at 9:37; Hebrew reads *Zeker,*
a variant spelling of Zechariah. 8:32 As in parallel text at 9:38; Hebrew reads *Shimeah,* a variant spelling of Shimeam.
8:35 As in parallel text at 9:41; Hebrew reads *Tarea,* a variant spelling of Tahrea. 8:36 As in parallel text at 9:42; Hebrew
reads *Jehoaddah,* a variant spelling of Jadah. 8:37 As in parallel text at 9:43; Hebrew reads *Raphah,* a variant spelling of
Rephaiah. 9:19 Hebrew *Ebiasaph,* a variant spelling of Abiasaph; compare Exod 6:24.

just as their ancestors had guarded the Tabernacle in the camp of the LORD.

²⁰Phinehas son of Eleazar had been in charge of the gatekeepers in earlier times, and the LORD had been with him. ²¹And later Zechariah son of Meshelemiah was responsible for guarding the entrance to the Tabernacle.*

²²In all, there were 212 gatekeepers in those days, and they were listed according to the genealogies in their villages. David and Samuel the seer had appointed their ancestors because they were reliable men. ²³These gatekeepers and their descendants, by their divisions, were responsible for guarding the entrance to the house of the LORD when that house was a tent. ²⁴The gatekeepers were stationed on all four sides—east, west, north, and south. ²⁵Their relatives in the villages came regularly to share their duties for seven-day periods.

²⁶The four chief gatekeepers, all Levites, were trusted officials, for they were responsible for the rooms and treasuries at the house of God. ²⁷They would spend the night around the house of God, since it was their duty to guard it and to open the gates every morning. ²⁸Some of the gatekeepers were assigned to care for the various articles used in worship. They checked them in and out to avoid any loss. ²⁹Others were responsible for the furnishings, the items in the sanctuary, and the supplies, such as choice flour, wine, olive oil, frankincense, and spices. ³⁰But it was the priests who blended the spices. ³¹Mattithiah, a Levite and the oldest son of Shallum the Korahite, was entrusted with baking the bread used in the offerings. ³²And some members of the clan of Kohath were in charge of preparing the bread to be set on the table each Sabbath day.

³³The musicians, all prominent Levites, lived at the Temple. They were exempt from other responsibilities since they were on duty at all hours. ³⁴All these men lived in Jerusalem. They were the heads of Levite families and were listed as prominent leaders in their genealogical records.

King Saul's Family Tree

³⁵Jeiel (the father of* Gibeon) lived in the town of Gibeon. His wife's name was Maacah, ³⁶and his oldest son was named Abdon. Jeiel's other sons were Zur, Kish, Baal, Ner, Nadab, ³⁷Gedor, Ahio, Zechariah,

and Mikloth. ³⁸Mikloth was the father of Shimeam. All these families lived near each other in Jerusalem.

³⁹ Ner was the father of Kish.
Kish was the father of Saul.
Saul was the father of Jonathan,
    Malkishua, Abinadab, and Esh-baal.
⁴⁰ Jonathan was the father of Merib-baal.
Merib-baal was the father of Micah.
⁴¹ The sons of Micah were Pithon, Melech,
    Tahrea, and Ahaz.*
⁴² Ahaz was the father of Jadah.*
Jadah was the father of Alemeth,
    Azmaveth, and Zimri.
Zimri was the father of Moza.
⁴³ Moza was the father of Binea.
Binea's son was Rephaiah.
Rephaiah's son was Eleasah.
Eleasah's son was Azel.
⁴⁴Azel had six sons, whose names were
    Azrikam, Bokeru, Ishmael, Sheariah,
    Obadiah, and Hanan. These were the sons
    of Azel.

The Death of King Saul

10 Now the Philistines attacked Israel, and the men of Israel fled before them. Many were slaughtered on the slopes of Mount Gilboa. ²The Philistines closed in on Saul and his sons, and they killed three of his sons—Jonathan, Abinadab, and Malkishua. ³The fighting grew very fierce around Saul, and the Philistine archers caught up with him and wounded him.

⁴Saul groaned to his armor bearer, "Take your sword and kill me before these pagan Philistines come to taunt and torture me."

But his armor bearer was afraid and would not do it. So Saul took his own sword and fell on it. ⁵When his armor bearer realized that Saul was dead, he fell on his own sword and died. ⁶So Saul and his three sons died there together, bringing his dynasty to an end.

⁷When all the Israelites in the Jezreel Valley saw that their army had fled and that Saul and his sons were dead, they abandoned their towns and fled. So the Philistines moved in and occupied their towns.

⁸The next day, when the Philistines went out to strip the dead, they found the bodies of Saul and his sons on Mount Gilboa. ⁹So they stripped off Saul's armor and cut off his head. Then they proclaimed the good news of Saul's death before their idols and to the people throughout the land of Philistia. ¹⁰They placed

9:21 Hebrew *Tent of Meeting.*   9:35 Or *the founder of.*   9:41 As in Syriac version and Latin Vulgate (see also 8:35); Hebrew lacks *and Ahaz.*   9:42 As in some Hebrew manuscripts and Greek version (see also 8:36); Hebrew reads *Jarah.*

his armor in the temple of their gods, and they fastened his head to the temple of Dagon.

¹¹But when everyone in Jabesh-gilead heard about everything the Philistines had done to Saul, ¹²all their mighty warriors brought the bodies of Saul and his sons back to Jabesh. Then they buried their bones beneath the great tree at Jabesh, and they fasted for seven days.

¹³So Saul died because he was unfaithful to the Lord. He failed to obey the Lord's command, and he even consulted a medium ¹⁴instead of asking the Lord for guidance. So the Lord killed him and turned the kingdom over to David son of Jesse.

David Becomes King of All Israel

11 Then all Israel gathered before David at Hebron and told him, "We are your own flesh and blood. ²In the past,* even when Saul was king, you were the one who really led the forces of Israel. And the Lord your God told you, 'You will be the shepherd of my people Israel. You will be the leader of my people Israel.'"

³So there at Hebron, David made a covenant before the Lord with all the elders of Israel. And they anointed him king of Israel, just as the Lord had promised through Samuel.

David Captures Jerusalem

⁴Then David and all Israel went to Jerusalem (or Jebus, as it used to be called), where the Jebusites, the original inhabitants of the land, were living. ⁵The people of Jebus taunted David, saying, "You'll never get in here!" But David captured the fortress of Zion, which is now called the City of David.

⁶David had said to his troops, "Whoever is first to attack the Jebusites will become the commander of my armies!" And Joab, the son of David's sister Zeruiah, was first to attack, so he became the commander of David's armies.

⁷David made the fortress his home, and that is why it is called the City of David. ⁸He extended the city from the supporting terraces* to the surrounding area, while Joab rebuilt the rest of Jerusalem. ⁹And David became more and more powerful, because the Lord of Heaven's Armies was with him.

David's Mightiest Warriors

¹⁰These are the leaders of David's mighty warriors. Together with all Israel, they decided to make David their king, just as the Lord had promised concerning Israel.

¹¹Here is the record of David's mightiest warriors: The first was Jashobeam the Hacmonite, who was leader of the Three—the mightiest warriors among David's men.* He once used his spear to kill 300 enemy warriors in a single battle.

¹²Next in rank among the Three was Eleazar son of Dodai,* a descendant of Ahoah. ¹³He was with David when the Philistines gathered for battle at Pas-dammim and attacked the Israelites in a field full of barley. The Israelite army fled, ¹⁴but Eleazar and David* held their ground in the middle of the field and beat back the Philistines. So the Lord saved them by giving them a great victory.

¹⁵Once when David was at the rock near the cave of Adullam, the Philistine army was camped in the valley of Rephaim. The Three (who were among the Thirty—an elite group among David's fighting men) went down to meet him there. ¹⁶David was staying in the stronghold at the time, and a Philistine detachment had occupied the town of Bethlehem.

¹⁷David remarked longingly to his men, "Oh, how I would love some of that good water from the well by the gate in Bethlehem." ¹⁸So the Three broke through the Philistine lines, drew some water from the well by the gate in Bethlehem, and brought it back to David. But David refused to drink it. Instead, he poured it out as an offering to the Lord. ¹⁹"God forbid that I should drink this!" he exclaimed. "This water is as precious as the blood of these men* who risked their lives to bring it to me." So David did not drink it. These are examples of the exploits of the Three.

David's Thirty Mighty Men

²⁰Abishai, the brother of Joab, was the leader of the Thirty.* He once used his spear to kill 300 enemy warriors in a single battle. It was by such feats that he became as famous as the Three. ²¹Abishai was the most famous of the Thirty and was their commander, though he was not one of the Three.

²²There was also Benaiah son of Jehoiada, a valiant warrior from Kabzeel. He did many heroic deeds, which included killing two champions* of Moab. Another time, on

---

11:2 Or *For some time.*   11:8 Hebrew *the millo.* The meaning of the Hebrew is uncertain.   11:11 As in some Greek manuscripts (see also 2 Sam 23:8); Hebrew reads *leader of the Thirty,* or *leader of the captains.*   11:12 As in parallel text at 2 Sam 23:9 (see also 1 Chr 27:4); Hebrew reads *Dodo,* a variant spelling of Dodai.   11:14 Hebrew *they.*   11:19 Hebrew *Shall I drink the lifeblood of these men?*   11:20 As in Syriac version; Hebrew reads *the Three;* also in 11:21.   11:22 Or *two sons of Ariel.*

a snowy day, he chased a lion down into a pit and killed it. ²³Once, armed only with a club, he killed an Egyptian warrior who was 7½ feet* tall and who was armed with a spear as thick as a weaver's beam. Benaiah wrenched the spear from the Egyptian's hand and killed him with it. ²⁴Deeds like these made Benaiah as famous as the three mightiest warriors. ²⁵He was more honored than the other members of the Thirty, though he was not one of the Three. And David made him captain of his bodyguard.

²⁶David's mighty warriors also included:

Asahel, Joab's brother;
Elhanan son of Dodo from Bethlehem;
²⁷ Shammah from Harod;*
Helez from Pelon;
²⁸ Ira son of Ikkesh from Tekoa;
Abiezer from Anathoth;
²⁹ Sibbecai from Hushah;
Zalmon* from Ahoah;
³⁰ Maharai from Netophah;
Heled son of Baanah from Netophah;
³¹ Ithai son of Ribai from Gibeah (in the land of Benjamin);
Benaiah from Pirathon;
³² Hurai from near Nahale-gaash*;
Abi-albon* from Arabah;
³³ Azmaveth from Bahurim*;
Eliahba from Shaalbon;
³⁴ the sons of Jashen* from Gizon;
Jonathan son of Shagee from Harar;
³⁵ Ahiam son of Sharar* from Harar;
Eliphal son of Ur;
³⁶ Hepher from Mekerah;
Ahijah from Pelon;
³⁷ Hezro from Carmel;
Paarai* son of Ezbai;
³⁸ Joel, the brother of Nathan;
Mibhar son of Hagri;
³⁹ Zelek from Ammon;
Naharai from Beeroth, the armor bearer of Joab son of Zeruiah;
⁴⁰ Ira from Jattir;
Gareb from Jattir;
⁴¹ Uriah the Hittite;
Zabad son of Ahlai;
⁴² Adina son of Shiza, the Reubenite leader who had thirty men with him;
⁴³ Hanan son of Maacah;
Joshaphat from Mithna;

⁴⁴ Uzzia from Ashtaroth;
Shama and Jeiel, the sons of Hotham, from Aroer;
⁴⁵ Jediael son of Shimri;
Joha, his brother, from Tiz;
⁴⁶ Eliel from Mahavah;
Jeribai and Joshaviah, the sons of Elnaam;
Ithmah from Moab;
⁴⁷ Eliel and Obed;
Jaasiel from Zobah.*

Warriors Join David's Army

12 The following men joined David at Ziklag while he was hiding from Saul son of Kish. They were among the warriors who fought beside David in battle. ²All of them were expert archers, and they could shoot arrows or sling stones with their left hand as well as their right. They were all relatives of Saul from the tribe of Benjamin. ³Their leader was Ahiezer son of Shemaah from Gibeah; his brother Joash was second-in-command. These were the other warriors:

Jeziel and Pelet, sons of Azmaveth;
Beracah;
Jehu from Anathoth;
⁴ Ishmaiah from Gibeon, a famous warrior and leader among the Thirty;
*Jeremiah, Jahaziel, Johanan, and Jozabad from Gederah;
⁵ Eluzai, Jerimoth, Bealiah, Shemariah, and Shephatiah from Haruph;
⁶ Elkanah, Isshiah, Azarel, Joezer, and Jashobeam, who were Korahites;
⁷ Joelah and Zebadiah, sons of Jeroham from Gedor.

⁸Some brave and experienced warriors from the tribe of Gad also defected to David while he was at the stronghold in the wilderness. They were expert with both shield and spear, as fierce as lions and as swift as deer on the mountains.

⁹ Ezer was their leader.
Obadiah was second.
Eliab was third.
¹⁰ Mishmannah was fourth.
Jeremiah was fifth.
¹¹ Attai was sixth.
Eliel was seventh.

11:23 Hebrew 5 cubits [2.3 meters]. 11:27 As in parallel text at 2 Sam 23:25; Hebrew reads Shammoth from Haror. 11:29 As in parallel text at 2 Sam 23:28; Hebrew reads Ilai. 11:32a Or from the ravines of Gaash. 11:32b As in parallel text at 2 Sam 23:31; Hebrew reads Abiel. 11:33 As in parallel text at 2 Sam 23:31; Hebrew reads Baharum. 11:34 As in parallel text at 2 Sam 23:32; Hebrew reads sons of Hashem. 11:35 As in parallel text at 2 Sam 23:33; Hebrew reads son of Sacar. 11:37 As in parallel text at 2 Sam 23:35; Hebrew reads Naarai. 11:47 Or the Mezobaite. 12:4 Verses 12:4b-40 are numbered 12:5-41 in Hebrew text.

¹² Johanan was eighth.
Elzabad was ninth.
¹³ Jeremiah was tenth.
Macbannai was eleventh.

¹⁴These warriors from Gad were army commanders. The weakest among them could take on a hundred regular troops, and the strongest could take on a thousand! ¹⁵These were the men who crossed the Jordan River during its seasonal flooding at the beginning of the year and drove out all the people living in the lowlands on both the east and west banks.

¹⁶Others from Benjamin and Judah came to David at the stronghold. ¹⁷David went out to meet them and said, "If you have come in peace to help me, we are friends. But if you have come to betray me to my enemies when I am innocent, then may the God of our ancestors see it and punish you."

¹⁸Then the Spirit came upon Amasai, the leader of the Thirty, and he said,

"We are yours, David!
We are on your side, son of Jesse.
Peace and prosperity be with you,
and success to all who help you,
for your God is the one who helps
you."

So David let them join him, and he made them officers over his troops.

¹⁹Some men from Manasseh defected from the Israelite army and joined David when he set out with the Philistines to fight against Saul. But as it turned out, the Philistine rulers refused to let David and his men go with them. After much discussion, they sent them back, for they said, "It will cost us our heads if David switches loyalties to Saul and turns against us."

²⁰Here is a list of the men from Manasseh who defected to David as he was returning to Ziklag: Adnah, Jozabad, Jediael, Michael, Jozabad, Elihu, and Zillethai. Each commanded 1,000 troops from the tribe of Manasseh. ²¹They helped David chase down bands of raiders, for they were all brave and able warriors who became commanders in his army. ²²Day after day more men joined David until he had a great army, like the army of God.

²³These are the numbers of armed warriors who joined David at Hebron. They were all eager to see David become king instead of Saul, just as the LORD had promised.

²⁴From the tribe of Judah, there were 6,800 warriors armed with shields and spears. ²⁵From the tribe of Simeon, there were 7,100 brave warriors. ²⁶From the tribe of Levi, there were 4,600 warriors. ²⁷This included Jehoiada, leader of the family of Aaron, who had 3,700 under his command. ²⁸This also included Zadok, a brave young warrior, with 22 members of his family who were all officers.

²⁹From the tribe of Benjamin, Saul's relatives, there were 3,000 warriors. Most of the men from Benjamin had remained loyal to Saul until this time. ³⁰From the tribe of Ephraim, there were 20,800 brave warriors, each highly respected in his own clan. ³¹From the half-tribe of Manasseh west of the Jordan, 18,000 men were designated by name to help David become king. ³²From the tribe of Issachar, there were 200 leaders of the tribe with their relatives. All these men understood the signs of the times and knew the best course for Israel to take. ³³From the tribe of Zebulun, there were 50,000 skilled warriors. They were fully armed and prepared for battle and completely loyal to David. ³⁴From the tribe of Naphtali, there were 1,000 officers and 37,000 warriors armed with shields and spears. ³⁵From the tribe of Dan, there were 28,600 warriors, all prepared for battle. ³⁶From the tribe of Asher, there were 40,000 trained warriors, all prepared for battle. ³⁷From the east side of the Jordan River— where the tribes of Reuben and Gad and the half-tribe of Manasseh lived—there were 120,000 troops armed with every kind of weapon.

³⁸All these men came in battle array to Hebron with the single purpose of making David the king over all Israel. In fact, everyone in Israel agreed that David should be their king. ³⁹They feasted and drank with David for three days, for preparations had been made by their relatives for their arrival. ⁴⁰And people from as far away as Issachar, Zebulun, and Naphtali brought food on donkeys, camels, mules, and oxen. Vast supplies of flour, fig cakes, clusters of raisins, wine, olive oil, cattle, sheep, and goats were brought to the celebration. There was great joy throughout the land of Israel.

David Attempts to Move the Ark

13 David consulted with all his officials, including the generals and captains of his army.* ²Then he addressed the entire assembly of Israel as follows: "If you approve and if it is the will of the LORD our God, let us send messages to all the Israelites throughout the land, including the priests and Levites in their towns and pasturelands. Let us invite them to come and join us. ³It is time to bring back the Ark of our God, for we neglected it during the reign of Saul."

⁴The whole assembly agreed to this, for the people could see it was the right thing to do. ⁵So David summoned all Israel, from the Shihor Brook of Egypt in the south all the way to the town of Lebo-hamath in the north, to join in bringing the Ark of God from Kiriath-jearim. ⁶Then David and all Israel went to Baalah of Judah (also called Kiriath-jearim) to bring back the Ark of God, which bears the name* of the LORD who is enthroned between the cherubim. ⁷They placed the Ark of God on a new cart and brought it from Abinadab's house. Uzzah and Ahio were guiding the cart. ⁸David and all Israel were celebrating before God with all their might, singing songs and playing all kinds of musical instruments—lyres, harps, tambourines, cymbals, and trumpets.

⁹But when they arrived at the threshing floor of Nacon,* the oxen stumbled, and Uzzah reached out his hand to steady the Ark. ¹⁰Then the LORD's anger was aroused against Uzzah, and he struck him dead because he had laid his hand on the Ark. So Uzzah died there in the presence of God.

¹¹David was angry because the LORD's anger had burst out against Uzzah. He named that place Perez-uzzah (which means "to burst out against Uzzah"), as it is still called today. ¹²David was now afraid of God, and he asked, "How can I ever bring the Ark of God back into my care?" ¹³So David did not move the Ark into the City of David. Instead, he took it to the house of Obed-edom of Gath. ¹⁴The Ark of God remained there in Obed-edom's house for three months, and the LORD blessed the household of Obed-edom and everything he owned.

David's Palace and Family

14 Then King Hiram of Tyre sent messengers to David, along with cedar timber, and stonemasons and carpenters to build him a palace. ²And David realized that the LORD had confirmed him as king over Israel and had greatly blessed his kingdom for the sake of his people Israel.

³Then David married more wives in Jerusalem, and they had more sons and daughters. ⁴These are the names of David's sons who were born in Jerusalem: Shammua, Shobab, Nathan, Solomon, ⁵Ibhar, Elishua, Elpelet, ⁶Nogah, Nepheg, Japhia, ⁷Elishama, Eliada,* and Eliphelet.

David Conquers the Philistines

⁸When the Philistines heard that David had been anointed king over all Israel, they mobilized all their forces to capture him. But David was told they were coming, so he marched out to meet them. ⁹The Philistines arrived and made a raid in the valley of Rephaim. ¹⁰So David asked God, "Should I go out to fight the Philistines? Will you hand them over to me?"

The LORD replied, "Yes, go ahead. I will hand them over to you."

¹¹So David and his troops went up to Baal-perazim and defeated the Philistines there. "God did it!" David exclaimed. "He used me to burst through my enemies like a raging flood!" So they named that place Baal-perazim (which means "the Lord who bursts through"). ¹²The Philistines had abandoned their gods there, so David gave orders to burn them.

¹³But after a while the Philistines returned and raided the valley again. ¹⁴And once again David asked God what to do. "Do not attack them straight on," God replied. "Instead, circle around behind and attack them near the poplar* trees. ¹⁵When you hear a sound like marching feet in the tops of the poplar trees, go out and attack! That will be the signal that God is moving ahead of you to strike down the Philistine army." ¹⁶So David did what God commanded, and they struck down the Philistine army all the way from Gibeon to Gezer.

¹⁷So David's fame spread everywhere, and the LORD caused all the nations to fear David.

Preparing to Move the Ark

15 David now built several buildings for himself in the City of David. He also prepared a place for the Ark of God and set up a special tent for it. ²Then he commanded, "No one except the Levites may carry the Ark of God. The LORD has chosen them to carry the Ark of the LORD and to serve him forever."

13:1 Hebrew *the commanders of thousands and of hundreds.*   13:6 Or *the Ark of God, where the Name is proclaimed—the name.*
13:9 As in parallel text at 2 Sam 6:6; Hebrew reads *Kidon.*   14:7 Hebrew *Beeliada,* a variant spelling of Eliada; compare 3:8 and parallel text at 2 Sam 5:16.   14:14 Or *aspen,* or *balsam;* also in 14:15. The exact identification of this tree is uncertain.

³Then David summoned all Israel to Jerusalem to bring the Ark of the LORD to the place he had prepared for it. ⁴This is the number of the descendants of Aaron (the priests) and the Levites who were called together:

⁵From the clan of Kohath, 120, with Uriel as their leader.
⁶From the clan of Merari, 220, with Asaiah as their leader.
⁷From the clan of Gershon,* 130, with Joel as their leader.
⁸From the descendants of Elizaphan, 200, with Shemaiah as their leader.
⁹From the descendants of Hebron, 80, with Eliel as their leader.
¹⁰From the descendants of Uzziel, 112, with Amminadab as their leader.

¹¹Then David summoned the priests, Zadok and Abiathar, and these Levite leaders: Uriel, Asaiah, Joel, Shemaiah, Eliel, and Amminadab. ¹²He said to them, "You are the leaders of the Levite families. You must purify yourselves and all your fellow Levites, so you can bring the Ark of the LORD, the God of Israel, to the place I have prepared for it. ¹³Because you Levites did not carry the Ark the first time, the anger of the LORD our God burst out against us. We failed to ask God how to move it properly." ¹⁴So the priests and the Levites purified themselves in order to bring the Ark of the LORD, the God of Israel, to Jerusalem. ¹⁵Then the Levites carried the Ark of God on their shoulders with its carrying poles, just as the LORD had instructed Moses.

¹⁶David also ordered the Levite leaders to appoint a choir of Levites who were singers and musicians to sing joyful songs to the accompaniment of harps, lyres, and cymbals. ¹⁷So the Levites appointed Heman son of Joel along with his fellow Levites: Asaph son of Berekiah, and Ethan son of Kushaiah from the clan of Merari. ¹⁸The following men were chosen as their assistants: Zechariah, Jaaziel,* Shemiramoth, Jehiel, Unni, Eliab, Benaiah, Maaseiah, Mattithiah, Eliphelehu, Mikneiah, and the gatekeepers—Obed-edom and Jeiel. ¹⁹The musicians Heman, Asaph, and Ethan were chosen to sound the bronze cymbals. ²⁰Zechariah, Aziel, Shemiramoth, Jehiel, Unni, Eliab, Maaseiah, and Benaiah were chosen to play the harps.* ²¹Mattithiah, Eliphelehu, Mikneiah, Obed-edom, Jeiel, and Azaziah were chosen to play the lyres.* ²²Kenaniah, the head Levite, was chosen as the choir leader because of his skill.

²³Berekiah and Elkanah were chosen to guard* the Ark. ²⁴Shebaniah, Joshaphat, Nethanel, Amasai, Zechariah, Benaiah, and Eliezer—all of whom were priests—were chosen to blow the trumpets as they marched in front of the Ark of God. Obed-edom and Jehiah were chosen to guard the Ark.

Moving the Ark to Jerusalem

²⁵Then David and the elders of Israel and the generals of the army* went to the house of Obed-edom to bring the Ark of the LORD's Covenant up to Jerusalem with a great celebration. ²⁶And because God was clearly helping the Levites as they carried the Ark of the LORD's Covenant, they sacrificed seven bulls and seven rams.

²⁷David was dressed in a robe of fine linen, as were all the Levites who carried the Ark, and also the singers, and Kenaniah the choir leader. David was also wearing a priestly garment.* ²⁸So all Israel brought up the Ark of the LORD's Covenant with shouts of joy, the blowing of rams' horns and trumpets, the crashing of cymbals, and loud playing on harps and lyres.

²⁹But as the Ark of the LORD's Covenant entered the City of David, Michal, the daughter of Saul, looked down from her window. When she saw King David skipping about and laughing with joy, she was filled with contempt for him.

16 They brought the Ark of God and placed it inside the special tent David had prepared for it. And they presented burnt offerings and peace offerings to God. ²When he had finished his sacrifices, David blessed the people in the name of the LORD. ³Then he gave to every man and woman in all Israel a loaf of bread, a cake of dates,* and a cake of raisins.

⁴David appointed the following Levites to lead the people in worship before the Ark of the LORD—to invoke his blessings, to give thanks, and to praise the LORD, the God of Israel. ⁵Asaph, the leader of this group, sounded the cymbals. Second to him was Zechariah, followed by Jeiel, Shemiramoth, Jehiel,

15:7 Hebrew *Gershom,* a variant spelling of Gershon.   15:18 As in several Hebrew manuscripts and Greek version (see also parallel lists in 15:20; 16:5); Masoretic Text reads *Zechariah ben Jaaziel.*   15:20 Hebrew adds *according to Alamoth,* which is probably a musical term. The meaning of the Hebrew is uncertain.   15:21 Hebrew adds *according to the Sheminith,* which is probably a musical term. The meaning of the Hebrew is uncertain.   15:23 Hebrew *chosen as gatekeepers for;* also in 15:24.   15:25 Hebrew *the commanders of thousands.*   15:27 Hebrew *a linen ephod.*   16:3 Or *a portion of meat.* The meaning of the Hebrew is uncertain.

Mattithiah, Eliab, Benaiah, Obed-edom, and Jeiel. They played the harps and lyres. ⁶The priests, Benaiah and Jahaziel, played the trumpets regularly before the Ark of God's Covenant.

David's Song of Praise

⁷On that day David gave to Asaph and his fellow Levites this song of thanksgiving to the LORD:

⁸ Give thanks to the LORD and proclaim his greatness.
   Let the whole world know what he has done.
⁹ Sing to him; yes, sing his praises.
   Tell everyone about his wonderful deeds.
¹⁰ Exult in his holy name;
   rejoice, you who worship the LORD.
¹¹ Search for the LORD and for his strength;
   continually seek him.
¹² Remember the wonders he has performed,
   his miracles, and the rulings he has given,
¹³ you children of his servant Israel,
   you descendants of Jacob, his chosen ones.

¹⁴ He is the LORD our God.
   His justice is seen throughout the land.
¹⁵ Remember his covenant forever—
   the commitment he made to a thousand generations.
¹⁶ This is the covenant he made with Abraham
   and the oath he swore to Isaac.
¹⁷ He confirmed it to Jacob as a decree,
   and to the people of Israel as a never-ending covenant:
¹⁸ "I will give you the land of Canaan
   as your special possession."

¹⁹ He said this when you were few in number,
   a tiny group of strangers in Canaan.
²⁰ They wandered from nation to nation,
   from one kingdom to another.
²¹ Yet he did not let anyone oppress them.
   He warned kings on their behalf:
²² "Do not touch my chosen people,
   and do not hurt my prophets."

²³ Let the whole earth sing to the LORD!
   Each day proclaim the good news that he saves.
²⁴ Publish his glorious deeds among the nations.
   Tell everyone about the amazing things he does.
²⁵ Great is the LORD! He is most worthy of praise!
   He is to be feared above all gods.
²⁶ The gods of other nations are mere idols,
   but the LORD made the heavens!
²⁷ Honor and majesty surround him;
   strength and joy fill his dwelling.

²⁸ O nations of the world, recognize the LORD,
   recognize that the LORD is glorious and strong.
²⁹ Give to the LORD the glory he deserves!
   Bring your offering and come into his presence.
   Worship the LORD in all his holy splendor.
³⁰ Let all the earth tremble before him.
   The world stands firm and cannot be shaken.

³¹ Let the heavens be glad, and the earth rejoice!
   Tell all the nations, "The LORD reigns!"
³² Let the sea and everything in it shout his praise!
   Let the fields and their crops burst out with joy!
³³ Let the trees of the forest sing for joy before the LORD,
   for he is coming to judge the earth.

³⁴ Give thanks to the LORD, for he is good!
   His faithful love endures forever.
³⁵ Cry out, "Save us, O God of our salvation!
   Gather and rescue us from among the nations,
   so we can thank your holy name
   and rejoice and praise you."

³⁶ Praise the LORD, the God of Israel,
   who lives from everlasting to everlasting!

And all the people shouted "Amen!" and praised the LORD.

Worship at Jerusalem and Gibeon

³⁷David arranged for Asaph and his fellow Levites to serve regularly before the Ark of the LORD's Covenant, doing whatever needed to be done each day. ³⁸This group included Obed-edom (son of Jeduthun), Hosah, and sixty-eight other Levites as gatekeepers.

³⁹Meanwhile, David stationed Zadok the priest and his fellow priests at the Tabernacle

of the LORD at the place of worship in Gibeon, where they continued to minister before the LORD. ⁴⁰They sacrificed the regular burnt offerings to the LORD each morning and evening on the altar set aside for that purpose, obeying everything written in the Law of the LORD, as he had commanded Israel. ⁴¹David also appointed Heman, Jeduthun, and the others chosen by name to give thanks to the LORD, for "his faithful love endures forever." ⁴²They used their trumpets, cymbals, and other instruments to accompany their songs of praise to God.* And the sons of Jeduthun were appointed as gatekeepers.

⁴³Then all the people returned to their homes, and David turned and went home to bless his own family.

The LORD's Covenant Promise to David

17 When David was settled in his palace, he summoned Nathan the prophet. "Look," David said, "I am living in a beautiful cedar palace,* but the Ark of the LORD's Covenant is out there under a tent!"

²Nathan replied to David, "Do whatever you have in mind, for God is with you."

³But that same night God said to Nathan,

⁴"Go and tell my servant David, 'This is what the LORD has declared: You are not the one to build a house for me to live in. ⁵I have never lived in a house, from the day I brought the Israelites out of Egypt until this very day. My home has always been a tent, moving from one place to another in a Tabernacle. ⁶Yet no matter where I have gone with the Israelites, I have never once complained to Israel's leaders, the shepherds of my people. I have never asked them, "Why haven't you built me a beautiful cedar house?"'

⁷"Now go and say to my servant David, 'This is what the LORD of Heaven's Armies has declared: I took you from tending sheep in the pasture and selected you to be the leader of my people Israel. ⁸I have been with you wherever you have gone, and I have destroyed all your enemies before your eyes. Now I will make your name as famous as anyone who has ever lived on the earth! ⁹And I will provide a homeland for my people Israel, planting them in a secure place where they will never be disturbed. Evil nations won't oppress them as they've done in the past, ¹⁰starting from the time I appointed judges to rule my people Israel. And I will defeat all your enemies.

"'Furthermore, I declare that the LORD will build a house for you—a dynasty of kings! ¹¹For when you die and join your ancestors, I will raise up one of your descendants, one of your sons, and I will make his kingdom strong. ¹²He is the one who will build a house—a temple—for me. And I will secure his throne forever. ¹³I will be his father, and he will be my son. I will never take my favor from him as I took it from the one who ruled before you. ¹⁴I will confirm him as king over my house and my kingdom for all time, and his throne will be secure forever.'"

¹⁵So Nathan went back to David and told him everything the LORD had said in this vision.

David's Prayer of Thanks

¹⁶Then King David went in and sat before the LORD and prayed,

"Who am I, O LORD God, and what is my family, that you have brought me this far? ¹⁷And now, O God, in addition to everything else, you speak of giving your servant a lasting dynasty! You speak as though I were someone very great,* O LORD God!

¹⁸"What more can I say to you about the way you have honored me? You know what your servant is really like. ¹⁹For the sake of your servant, O LORD, and according to your will, you have done all these great things and have made them known.

²⁰"O LORD, there is no one like you. We have never even heard of another God like you! ²¹What other nation on earth is like your people Israel? What other nation, O God, have you redeemed from slavery to be your own people? You made a great name for yourself when you redeemed your people from Egypt. You performed awesome miracles and drove out the nations that stood in their way. ²²You chose Israel to be your very own people forever, and you, O LORD, became their God.

²³"And now, O LORD, I am your servant; do as you have promised concerning me and my family. May it be a promise that

---

16:42 Or *to accompany the sacred music;* or *to accompany singing to God.* 17:1 Hebrew *a house of cedar.* 17:17 The meaning of the Hebrew is uncertain.

will last forever. ²⁴And may your name be established and honored forever so that everyone will say, 'The LORD of Heaven's Armies, the God of Israel, is Israel's God!' And may the house of your servant David continue before you forever.

²⁵"O my God, I have been bold enough to pray to you because you have revealed to your servant that you will build a house for him—a dynasty of kings! ²⁶For you are God, O LORD. And you have promised these good things to your servant. ²⁷And now, it has pleased you to bless the house of your servant, so that it will continue forever before you. For when you grant a blessing, O LORD, it is an eternal blessing!"

David's Military Victories

18 After this, David defeated and subdued the Philistines by conquering Gath and its surrounding towns. ²David also conquered the land of Moab, and the Moabites who were spared became David's subjects and paid him tribute money.

³David also destroyed the forces of Hadadezer, king of Zobah, as far as Hamath,* when Hadadezer marched out to strengthen his control along the Euphrates River. ⁴David captured 1,000 chariots, 7,000 charioteers, and 20,000 foot soldiers. He crippled all the chariot horses except enough for 100 chariots.

⁵When Arameans from Damascus arrived to help King Hadadezer, David killed 22,000 of them. ⁶Then he placed several army garrisons* in Damascus, the Aramean capital, and the Arameans became David's subjects and paid him tribute money. So the LORD made David victorious wherever he went.

⁷David brought the gold shields of Hadadezer's officers to Jerusalem, ⁸along with a large amount of bronze from Hadadezer's towns of Tebah* and Cun. Later Solomon melted the bronze and molded it into the great bronze basin called the Sea, the pillars, and the various bronze articles used at the Temple.

⁹When King Toi* of Hamath heard that David had destroyed the entire army of King Hadadezer of Zobah, ¹⁰he sent his son Joram* to congratulate King David for his successful campaign. Hadadezer and Toi had been enemies and were often at war. Joram presented David with many gifts of gold, silver, and bronze.

¹¹King David dedicated all these gifts to the LORD, along with the silver and gold he had taken from the other nations—from Edom, Moab, Ammon, Philistia, and Amalek.

¹²Abishai son of Zeruiah destroyed 18,000 Edomites in the Valley of Salt. ¹³He placed army garrisons in Edom, and all the Edomites became David's subjects. In fact, the LORD made David victorious wherever he went.

¹⁴So David reigned over all Israel and did what was just and right for all his people. ¹⁵Joab son of Zeruiah was commander of the army. Jehoshaphat son of Ahilud was the royal historian. ¹⁶Zadok son of Ahitub and Ahimelech* son of Abiathar were the priests. Seraiah* was the court secretary. ¹⁷Benaiah son of Jehoiada was captain of the king's bodyguard.* And David's sons served as the king's chief assistants.

David Defeats the Ammonites

19 Some time after this, King Nahash of the Ammonites died, and his son Hanun* became king. ²David said, "I am going to show loyalty to Hanun because his father, Nahash, was always loyal to me." So David sent messengers to express sympathy to Hanun about his father's death.

But when David's ambassadors arrived in the land of Ammon, ³the Ammonite commanders said to Hanun, "Do you really think these men are coming here to honor your father? No! David has sent them to spy out the land so they can come in and conquer it!" ⁴So Hanun seized David's ambassadors and shaved them, cut off their robes at the buttocks, and sent them back to David in shame.

⁵When David heard what had happened to the men, he sent messengers to tell them, "Stay at Jericho until your beards grow out, and then come back." For they felt deep shame because of their appearance.

⁶When the people of Ammon realized how seriously they had angered David, Hanun and the Ammonites sent 75,000 pounds* of silver to hire chariots and charioteers from Aramnaharaim, Aram-maacah, and Zobah. ⁷They also hired 32,000 chariots and secured the support of the king of Maacah and his army.

18:3 The meaning of the Hebrew is uncertain.   18:6 As in Greek version and Latin Vulgate (see also 2 Sam 8:6); Hebrew lacks *several army garrisons*.   18:8 Hebrew reads *Tibhath*, a variant spelling of Tebah; compare parallel text at 2 Sam 8:8. 18:9 As in parallel text at 2 Sam 8:9; Hebrew reads *Tou;* also in 18:10.   18:10 As in parallel text at 2 Sam 8:10; Hebrew reads *Hadoram*, a variant spelling of Joram.   18:16a As in some Hebrew manuscripts, Syriac version, and Latin Vulgate (see also 2 Sam 8:17); most Hebrew manuscripts read *Abimelech*.   18:16b As in parallel text at 2 Sam 8:17; Hebrew reads *Shavsha*. 18:17 Hebrew *of the Kerethites and Pelethites*.   19:1 As in parallel text at 2 Sam 10:1; Hebrew lacks *Hanun*.   19:6 Hebrew *1,000 talents* [34,000 kilograms].

These forces camped at Medeba, where they were joined by the Ammonite troops that Hanun had recruited from his own towns. [8]When David heard about this, he sent Joab and all his warriors to fight them. [9]The Ammonite troops came out and drew up their battle lines at the entrance of the city, while the other kings positioned themselves to fight in the open fields.

[10]When Joab saw that he would have to fight on both the front and the rear, he chose some of Israel's elite troops and placed them under his personal command to fight the Arameans in the fields. [11]He left the rest of the army under the command of his brother Abishai, who was to attack the Ammonites. [12]"If the Arameans are too strong for me, then come over and help me," Joab told his brother. "And if the Ammonites are too strong for you, I will help you. [13]Be courageous! Let us fight bravely for our people and the cities of our God. May the LORD's will be done."

[14]When Joab and his troops attacked, the Arameans began to run away. [15]And when the Ammonites saw the Arameans running, they also ran from Abishai and retreated into the city. Then Joab returned to Jerusalem.

[16]The Arameans now realized that they were no match for Israel, so they sent messengers and summoned additional Aramean troops from the other side of the Euphrates River.* These troops were under the command of Shobach,* the commander of Hadadezer's forces.

[17]When David heard what was happening, he mobilized all Israel, crossed the Jordan River, and positioned his troops in battle formation. Then David engaged the Arameans in battle, and they fought against him. [18]But again the Arameans fled from the Israelites. This time David's forces killed 7,000 charioteers and 40,000 foot soldiers, including Shobach, the commander of their army. [19]When Hadadezer's allies saw that they had been defeated by Israel, they surrendered to David and became his subjects. After that, the Arameans were no longer willing to help the Ammonites.

David Captures Rabbah

20 In the spring of the year,* when kings normally go out to war, Joab led the Israelite army in successful attacks against the land of the Ammonites. In the process he laid siege to the city of Rabbah, attacking and destroying it. However, David stayed behind in Jerusalem.

[2]Then David went to Rabbah and removed the crown from the king's head,* and it was placed on his own head. The crown was made of gold and set with gems, and he found that it weighed seventy-five pounds.* David took a vast amount of plunder from the city. [3]He also made slaves of the people of Rabbah and forced them to labor with saws, iron picks, and iron axes.* That is how David dealt with the people of all the Ammonite towns. Then David and all the army returned to Jerusalem.

Battles against Philistine Giants

[4]After this, war broke out with the Philistines at Gezer. As they fought, Sibbecai from Hushah killed Saph,* a descendant of the giants,* and so the Philistines were subdued.

[5]During another battle with the Philistines, Elhanan son of Jair killed Lahmi, the brother of Goliath of Gath. The handle of Lahmi's spear was as thick as a weaver's beam!

[6]In another battle with the Philistines at Gath, they encountered a huge man with six fingers on each hand and six toes on each foot, twenty-four in all, who was also a descendant of the giants. [7]But when he defied and taunted Israel, he was killed by Jonathan, the son of David's brother Shimea.

[8]These Philistines were descendants of the giants of Gath, but David and his warriors killed them.

David Takes a Census

21 Satan rose up against Israel and caused David to take a census of the people of Israel. [2]So David said to Joab and the commanders of the army, "Take a census of all the people of Israel—from Beersheba in the south to Dan in the north—and bring me a report so I may know how many there are."

[3]But Joab replied, "May the LORD increase the number of his people a hundred times over! But why, my lord the king, do you want to do this? Are they not all your servants? Why must you cause Israel to sin?"

[4]But the king insisted that they take the census, so Joab traveled throughout all Israel to count the people. Then he returned to

---

19:16a Hebrew *the river*.   19:16b As in parallel text at 2 Sam 10:16; Hebrew reads *Shophach*; also in 19:18.   20:1 Hebrew *At the turn of the year*. The first day of the year in the ancient Hebrew lunar calendar occurred in March or April.   20:2a Or *from the head of Milcom* (as in Greek version and Latin Vulgate). Milcom, also called Molech, was the god of the Ammonites. 20:2b Hebrew *1 talent* [34 kilograms].   20:3 As in parallel text at 2 Sam 12:31; Hebrew reads *and cut them with saws, iron picks, and saws*.   20:4a As in parallel text at 2 Sam 21:18; Hebrew reads *Sippai*.   20:4b Hebrew *descendant of the Rephaites*; also in 20:6, 8.

Jerusalem ⁵and reported the number of people to David. There were 1,100,000 warriors in all Israel who could handle a sword, and 470,000 in Judah. ⁶But Joab did not include the tribes of Levi and Benjamin in the census because he was so distressed at what the king had made him do.

Judgment for David's Sin

⁷God was very displeased with the census, and he punished Israel for it. ⁸Then David said to God, "I have sinned greatly by taking this census. Please forgive my guilt for doing this foolish thing."

⁹Then the LORD spoke to Gad, David's seer. This was the message: ¹⁰"Go and say to David, 'This is what the LORD says: I will give you three choices. Choose one of these punishments, and I will inflict it on you.'"

¹¹So Gad came to David and said, "These are the choices the LORD has given you. ¹²You may choose three years of famine, three months of destruction by the sword of your enemies, or three days of severe plague as the angel of the LORD brings devastation throughout the land of Israel. Decide what answer I should give the LORD who sent me."

¹³"I'm in a desperate situation!" David replied to Gad. "But let me fall into the hands of the LORD, for his mercy is very great. Do not let me fall into human hands."

¹⁴So the LORD sent a plague upon Israel, and 70,000 people died as a result. ¹⁵And God sent an angel to destroy Jerusalem. But just as the angel was preparing to destroy it, the LORD relented and said to the death angel, "Stop! That is enough!" At that moment the angel of the LORD was standing by the threshing floor of Araunah* the Jebusite.

¹⁶David looked up and saw the angel of the LORD standing between heaven and earth with his sword drawn, reaching out over Jerusalem. So David and the leaders of Israel put on burlap to show their deep distress and fell face down on the ground. ¹⁷And David said to God, "I am the one who called for the census! I am the one who has sinned and done wrong! But these people are as innocent as sheep—what have they done? O LORD my God, let your anger fall against me and my family, but do not destroy your people."

David Builds an Altar

¹⁸Then the angel of the LORD told Gad to instruct David to go up and build an altar to the LORD on the threshing floor of Araunah the Jebusite. ¹⁹So David went up to do what the LORD had commanded him through Gad. ²⁰Araunah, who was busy threshing wheat at the time, turned and saw the angel there. His four sons, who were with him, ran away and hid. ²¹When Araunah saw David approaching, he left his threshing floor and bowed before David with his face to the ground.

²²David said to Araunah, "Let me buy this threshing floor from you at its full price. Then I will build an altar to the LORD there, so that he will stop the plague."

²³"Take it, my lord the king, and use it as you wish," Araunah said to David. "I will give the oxen for the burnt offerings, and the threshing boards for wood to build a fire on the altar, and the wheat for the grain offering. I will give it all to you."

²⁴But King David replied to Araunah, "No, I insist on buying it for the full price. I will not take what is yours and give it to the LORD. I will not present burnt offerings that have cost me nothing!" ²⁵So David gave Araunah 600 pieces of gold* in payment for the threshing floor.

²⁶David built an altar there to the LORD and sacrificed burnt offerings and peace offerings. And when David prayed, the LORD answered him by sending fire from heaven to burn up the offering on the altar. ²⁷Then the LORD spoke to the angel, who put the sword back into its sheath.

²⁸When David saw that the LORD had answered his prayer, he offered sacrifices there at Araunah's threshing floor. ²⁹At that time the Tabernacle of the LORD and the altar of burnt offering that Moses had made in the wilderness were located at the place of worship in Gibeon. ³⁰But David was not able to go there to inquire of God, because he was terrified by the drawn sword of the angel of the LORD.

22 Then David said, "This will be the location for the Temple of the LORD God and the place of the altar for Israel's burnt offerings!"

Preparations for the Temple

²So David gave orders to call together the foreigners living in Israel, and he assigned them the task of preparing finished stone for building the Temple of God. ³David provided large amounts of iron for the nails that would be needed for the doors in the gates and for the

---

21:15 As in parallel text at 2 Sam 24:16; Hebrew reads *Ornan*, another name for Araunah; also in 21:18-28.   21:25 Hebrew *600 shekels of gold*, about 15 pounds or 6.8 kilograms in weight.

clamps, and he gave more bronze than could be weighed. [4]He also provided innumerable cedar logs, for the men of Tyre and Sidon had brought vast amounts of cedar to David.

[5]David said, "My son Solomon is still young and inexperienced. And since the Temple to be built for the LORD must be a magnificent structure, famous and glorious throughout the world, I will begin making preparations for it now." So David collected vast amounts of building materials before his death.

[6]Then David sent for his son Solomon and instructed him to build a Temple for the LORD, the God of Israel. [7]"My son, I wanted to build a Temple to honor the name of the LORD my God," David told him. [8]"But the LORD said to me, 'You have killed many men in the battles you have fought. And since you have shed so much blood in my sight, you will not be the one to build a Temple to honor my name. [9]But you will have a son who will be a man of peace. I will give him peace with his enemies in all the surrounding lands. His name will be Solomon,* and I will give peace and quiet to Israel during his reign. [10]He is the one who will build a Temple to honor my name. He will be my son, and I will be his father. And I will secure the throne of his kingdom over Israel forever.'

[11]"Now, my son, may the LORD be with you and give you success as you follow his directions in building the Temple of the LORD your God. [12]And may the LORD give you wisdom and understanding, that you may obey the Law of the LORD your God as you rule over Israel. [13]For you will be successful if you carefully obey the decrees and regulations that the LORD gave to Israel through Moses. Be strong and courageous; do not be afraid or lose heart!

[14]"I have worked hard to provide materials for building the Temple of the LORD—nearly 4,000 tons of gold, 40,000 tons of silver,* and so much iron and bronze that it cannot be weighed. I have also gathered timber and stone for the walls, though you may need to add more. [15]You have a large number of skilled stonemasons and carpenters and craftsmen of every kind. [16]You have expert goldsmiths and silversmiths and workers of bronze and iron. Now begin the work, and may the LORD be with you!"

[17]Then David ordered all the leaders of Israel to assist Solomon in this project. [18]"The LORD your God is with you," he declared. "He has given you peace with the surrounding nations. He has handed them over to me, and they are now subject to the LORD and his people. [19]Now seek the LORD your God with all your heart and soul. Build the sanctuary of the LORD God so that you can bring the Ark of the LORD's Covenant and the holy vessels of God into the Temple built to honor the LORD's name."

Duties of the Levites

23 When David was an old man, he appointed his son Solomon to be king over Israel. [2]David summoned all the leaders of Israel, together with the priests and Levites. [3]All the Levites who were thirty years old or older were counted, and the total came to 38,000. [4]Then David said, "From all the Levites, 24,000 will supervise the work at the Temple of the LORD. Another 6,000 will serve as officials and judges. [5]Another 4,000 will work as gatekeepers, and 4,000 will praise the LORD with the musical instruments I have made." [6]Then David divided the Levites into divisions named after the clans descended from the three sons of Levi—Gershon, Kohath, and Merari.

The Gershonites

[7]The Gershonite family units were defined by their lines of descent from Libni* and Shimei, the sons of Gershon. [8]Three of the descendants of Libni were Jehiel (the family leader), Zetham, and Joel. [9]These were the leaders of the family of Libni. Three of the descendants of Shimei were Shelomoth, Haziel, and Haran. [10]Four other descendants of Shimei were Jahath, Ziza,* Jeush, and Beriah. [11]Jahath was the family leader, and Ziza was next. Jeush and Beriah were counted as a single family because neither had many sons.

The Kohathites

[12]Four of the descendants of Kohath were Amram, Izhar, Hebron, and Uzziel. [13]The sons of Amram were Aaron and Moses. Aaron and his descendants were set apart to dedicate the most holy things, to offer sacrifices in the LORD's presence, to serve the LORD, and to pronounce blessings in his name forever.

[14]As for Moses, the man of God, his sons were included with the tribe of Levi. [15]The sons of Moses were Gershom and Eliezer.

22:9 Solomon sounds like and is probably derived from the Hebrew word for "peace." 22:14 Hebrew 100,000 talents [3,400 metric tons] of gold, 1,000,000 talents [34,000 metric tons] of silver. 23:7 Hebrew Ladan (also in 23:8, 9), a variant spelling of Libni; compare 6:17. 23:10 As in Greek version and Latin Vulgate (see also 23:11); Hebrew reads Zina.

[16] The descendants of Gershom included Shebuel, the family leader. [17] Eliezer had only one son, Rehabiah, the family leader. Rehabiah had numerous descendants. [18] The descendants of Izhar included Shelomith, the family leader. [19] The descendants of Hebron included Jeriah (the family leader), Amariah (the second), Jahaziel (the third), and Jekameam (the fourth). [20] The descendants of Uzziel included Micah (the family leader) and Isshiah (the second).

The Merarites

[21] The descendants of Merari included Mahli and Mushi.

The sons of Mahli were Eleazar and Kish. [22] Eleazar died with no sons, only daughters. His daughters married their cousins, the sons of Kish. [23] Three of the descendants of Mushi were Mahli, Eder, and Jerimoth.

[24] These were the descendants of Levi by clans, the leaders of their family groups, registered carefully by name. Each had to be twenty years old or older to qualify for service in the house of the LORD. [25] For David said, "The LORD, the God of Israel, has given us peace, and he will always live in Jerusalem. [26] Now the Levites will no longer need to carry the Tabernacle and its furnishings from place to place." [27] In accordance with David's final instructions, all the Levites twenty years old or older were registered for service.

[28] The work of the Levites was to assist the priests, the descendants of Aaron, as they served at the house of the LORD. They also took care of the courtyards and side rooms, helped perform the ceremonies of purification, and served in many other ways in the house of God. [29] They were in charge of the sacred bread that was set out on the table, the choice flour for the grain offerings, the wafers made without yeast, the cakes cooked in olive oil, and the other mixed breads. They were also responsible to check all the weights and measures. [30] And each morning and evening they stood before the LORD to sing songs of thanks and praise to him. [31] They assisted with the burnt offerings that were presented to the LORD on Sabbath days, at new moon celebrations, and at all the appointed festivals. The required number of Levites served in the LORD's presence at all times, following all the procedures they had been given.

23:32 Hebrew *the Tent of Meeting and the sanctuary.*

[32] And so, under the supervision of the priests, the Levites watched over the Tabernacle and the Temple* and faithfully carried out their duties of service at the house of the LORD.

Duties of the Priests

24 This is how Aaron's descendants, the priests, were divided into groups for service. The sons of Aaron were Nadab, Abihu, Eleazar, and Ithamar. [2] But Nadab and Abihu died before their father, and they had no sons. So only Eleazar and Ithamar were left to carry on as priests.

[3] With the help of Zadok, who was a descendant of Eleazar, and of Ahimelech, who was a descendant of Ithamar, David divided Aaron's descendants into groups according to their various duties. [4] Eleazar's descendants were divided into sixteen groups and Ithamar's into eight, for there were more family leaders among the descendants of Eleazar.

[5] All tasks were assigned to the various groups by means of sacred lots so that no preference would be shown, for there were many qualified officials serving God in the sanctuary from among the descendants of both Eleazar and Ithamar. [6] Shemaiah son of Nethanel, a Levite, acted as secretary and wrote down the names and assignments in the presence of the king, the officials, Zadok the priest, Ahimelech son of Abiathar, and the family leaders of the priests and Levites. The descendants of Eleazar and Ithamar took turns casting lots.

[7] The first lot fell to Jehoiarib.
The second lot fell to Jedaiah.
[8] The third lot fell to Harim.
The fourth lot fell to Seorim.
[9] The fifth lot fell to Malkijah.
The sixth lot fell to Mijamin.
[10] The seventh lot fell to Hakkoz.
The eighth lot fell to Abijah.
[11] The ninth lot fell to Jeshua.
The tenth lot fell to Shecaniah.
[12] The eleventh lot fell to Eliashib.
The twelfth lot fell to Jakim.
[13] The thirteenth lot fell to Huppah.
The fourteenth lot fell to Jeshebeab.
[14] The fifteenth lot fell to Bilgah.
The sixteenth lot fell to Immer.
[15] The seventeenth lot fell to Hezir.
The eighteenth lot fell to Happizzez.
[16] The nineteenth lot fell to Pethahiah.
The twentieth lot fell to Jehezkel.

17 The twenty-first lot fell to Jakin.
The twenty-second lot fell to Gamul.
18 The twenty-third lot fell to Delaiah.
The twenty-fourth lot fell to Maaziah.

19Each group carried out its appointed duties in the house of the LORD according to the procedures established by their ancestor Aaron in obedience to the commands of the LORD, the God of Israel.

Family Leaders among the Levites

20These were the other family leaders descended from Levi:

From the descendants of Amram, the leader was Shebuel.*
From the descendants of Shebuel, the leader was Jehdeiah.
21 From the descendants of Rehabiah, the leader was Isshiah.
22 From the descendants of Izhar, the leader was Shelomith.*
From the descendants of Shelomith, the leader was Jahath.
23 From the descendants of Hebron, Jeriah was the leader,* Amariah was second, Jahaziel was third, and Jekameam was fourth.
24 From the descendants of Uzziel, the leader was Micah.
From the descendants of Micah, the leader was Shamir, 25along with Isshiah, the brother of Micah.
From the descendants of Isshiah, the leader was Zechariah.
26 From the descendants of Merari, the leaders were Mahli and Mushi.
From the descendants of Jaaziah, the leader was Beno.
27 From the descendants of Merari through Jaaziah, the leaders were Beno, Shoham, Zaccur, and Ibri.
28 From the descendants of Mahli, the leader was Eleazar, though he had no sons.
29 From the descendants of Kish, the leader was Jerahmeel.
30 From the descendants of Mushi, the leaders were Mahli, Eder, and Jerimoth.

These were the descendants of Levi in their various families. 31Like the descendants of Aaron, they were assigned to their duties by means of sacred lots, without regard to age or rank. Lots were drawn in the presence of King David, Zadok, Ahimelech, and the family leaders of the priests and the Levites.

Duties of the Musicians

25 David and the army commanders then appointed men from the families of Asaph, Heman, and Jeduthun to proclaim God's messages to the accompaniment of lyres, harps, and cymbals. Here is a list of their names and their work:

2From the sons of Asaph, there were Zaccur, Joseph, Nethaniah, and Asarelah. They worked under the direction of their father, Asaph, who proclaimed God's messages by the king's orders.
3From the sons of Jeduthun, there were Gedaliah, Zeri, Jeshaiah, Shimei,* Hashabiah, and Mattithiah, six in all. They worked under the direction of their father, Jeduthun, who proclaimed God's messages to the accompaniment of the lyre, offering thanks and praise to the LORD.
4From the sons of Heman, there were Bukkiah, Mattaniah, Uzziel, Shubael,* Jerimoth, Hananiah, Hanani, Eliathah, Giddalti, Romamti-ezer, Joshbekashah, Mallothi, Hothir, and Mahazioth. 5All these were the sons of Heman, the king's seer, for God had honored him with fourteen sons and three daughters.

6All these men were under the direction of their fathers as they made music at the house of the LORD. Their responsibilities included the playing of cymbals, harps, and lyres at the house of God. Asaph, Jeduthun, and Heman reported directly to the king. 7They and their families were all trained in making music before the LORD, and each of them—288 in all—was an accomplished musician. 8The musicians were appointed to their term of service by means of sacred lots, without regard to whether they were young or old, teacher or student.

9 The first lot fell to Joseph of the Asaph clan and twelve of his sons and relatives.*
The second lot fell to Gedaliah and twelve of his sons and relatives.

24:20 Hebrew *Shubael* (also in 24:20b), a variant spelling of Shebuel; compare 23:16 and 26:24.   24:22 Hebrew *Shelomoth* (also in 24:22b), a variant spelling of Shelomith; compare 23:18.   24:23 Hebrew *From the descendants of Jeriah*; compare 23:19. 25:3 As in one Hebrew manuscript and some Greek manuscripts (see also 25:17); most Hebrew manuscripts lack *Shimei*. 25:4 Hebrew *Shebuel*, a variant spelling of Shubael; compare 25:20.   25:9 As in Greek version; Hebrew lacks *and twelve of his sons and relatives.*

¹⁰ The third lot fell to Zaccur and twelve of his sons and relatives.

¹¹ The fourth lot fell to Zeri* and twelve of his sons and relatives.

¹² The fifth lot fell to Nethaniah and twelve of his sons and relatives.

¹³ The sixth lot fell to Bukkiah and twelve of his sons and relatives.

¹⁴ The seventh lot fell to Asarelah* and twelve of his sons and relatives.

¹⁵ The eighth lot fell to Jeshaiah and twelve of his sons and relatives.

¹⁶ The ninth lot fell to Mattaniah and twelve of his sons and relatives.

¹⁷ The tenth lot fell to Shimei and twelve of his sons and relatives.

¹⁸ The eleventh lot fell to Uzziel* and twelve of his sons and relatives.

¹⁹ The twelfth lot fell to Hashabiah and twelve of his sons and relatives.

²⁰ The thirteenth lot fell to Shubael and twelve of his sons and relatives.

²¹ The fourteenth lot fell to Mattithiah and twelve of his sons and relatives.

²² The fifteenth lot fell to Jerimoth* and twelve of his sons and relatives.

²³ The sixteenth lot fell to Hananiah and twelve of his sons and relatives.

²⁴ The seventeenth lot fell to Joshbekashah* and twelve of his sons and relatives.

²⁵ The eighteenth lot fell to Hanani and twelve of his sons and relatives.

²⁶ The nineteenth lot fell to Mallothi and twelve of his sons and relatives.

²⁷ The twentieth lot fell to Eliathah and twelve of his sons and relatives.

²⁸ The twenty-first lot fell to Hothir and twelve of his sons and relatives.

²⁹ The twenty-second lot fell to Giddalti and twelve of his sons and relatives.

³⁰ The twenty-third lot fell to Mahazioth and twelve of his sons and relatives.

³¹ The twenty-fourth lot fell to Romamti-ezer and twelve of his sons and relatives.

Duties of the Gatekeepers

26 These are the divisions of the gatekeepers:

From the Korahites, there was Meshelemiah son of Kore, of the family of Abiasaph.*

²The sons of Meshelemiah were Zechariah (the oldest), Jediael (the second), Zebadiah (the third), Jathniel (the fourth), ³Elam (the fifth), Jehohanan (the sixth), and Eliehoenai (the seventh).

⁴The sons of Obed-edom, also gatekeepers, were Shemaiah (the oldest), Jehozabad (the second), Joah (the third), Sacar (the fourth), Nethanel (the fifth), ⁵Ammiel (the sixth), Issachar (the seventh), and Peullethai (the eighth). God had richly blessed Obed-edom.

⁶Obed-edom's son Shemaiah had sons with great ability who earned positions of great authority in the clan. ⁷Their names were Othni, Rephael, Obed, and Elzabad. Their relatives, Elihu and Semakiah, were also very capable men.

⁸All of these descendants of Obed-edom, including their sons and grandsons—sixty-two of them in all—were very capable men, well qualified for their work.

⁹Meshelemiah's eighteen sons and relatives were also very capable men.

¹⁰Hosah, of the Merari clan, appointed Shimri as the leader among his sons, though he was not the oldest. ¹¹His other sons included Hilkiah (the second), Tebaliah (the third), and Zechariah (the fourth). Hosah's sons and relatives, who served as gatekeepers, numbered thirteen in all.

¹²These divisions of the gatekeepers were named for their family leaders, and like the other Levites, they served at the house of the LORD. ¹³They were assigned by families for guard duty at the various gates, without regard to age or training, for it was all decided by means of sacred lots.

¹⁴The responsibility for the east gate went to Meshelemiah* and his group. The north gate was assigned to his son Zechariah, a man of unusual wisdom. ¹⁵The south gate went to Obed-edom, and his sons were put in charge of the storehouse. ¹⁶Shuppim and Hosah were assigned the west gate and the gateway leading up to the Temple.* Guard duties were divided evenly. ¹⁷Six Levites were assigned each day to the east gate, four to the north gate, four to the

25:11 Hebrew *Izri*, a variant spelling of Zeri; compare 25:3.   25:14 Hebrew *Jesarelah*, a variant spelling of Asarelah; compare 25:2.   25:18 Hebrew *Azarel*, a variant spelling of Uzziel; compare 25:4.   25:22 Hebrew *Jeremoth*, a variant spelling of Jerimoth; compare 25:4.   25:24 Hebrew *Joshbekasha*, a variant spelling of Joshbekashah; compare 25:4.   26:1 As in Greek version (see also Exod 6:24); Hebrew reads *Asaph*.   26:14 Hebrew *Shelemiah*, a variant spelling of Meshelemiah; compare 26:2.   26:16 Or *the gate of Shalleketh on the upper road* (also in 26:18). The meaning of the Hebrew is uncertain.

south gate, and two pairs at the storehouse. ¹⁸Six were assigned each day to the west gate, four to the gateway leading up to the Temple, and two to the courtyard.*

¹⁹These were the divisions of the gatekeepers from the clans of Korah and Merari.

Treasurers and Other Officials

²⁰Other Levites, led by Ahijah, were in charge of the treasuries of the house of God and the treasuries of the gifts dedicated to the LORD. ²¹From the family of Libni* in the clan of Gershon, Jehiel* was the leader. ²²The sons of Jehiel, Zetham and his brother Joel, were in charge of the treasuries of the house of the LORD.

²³These are the leaders that descended from Amram, Izhar, Hebron, and Uzziel:

²⁴From the clan of Amram, Shebuel was a descendant of Gershom son of Moses. He was the chief officer of the treasuries. ²⁵His relatives through Eliezer were Rehabiah, Jeshaiah, Joram, Zicri, and Shelomoth.

²⁶Shelomoth and his relatives were in charge of the treasuries containing the gifts that King David, the family leaders, and the generals and captains* and other officers of the army had dedicated to the LORD. ²⁷These men dedicated some of the plunder they had gained in battle to maintain the house of the LORD. ²⁸Shelomoth* and his relatives also cared for the gifts dedicated to the LORD by Samuel the seer, Saul son of Kish, Abner son of Ner, and Joab son of Zeruiah. All the other dedicated gifts were in their care, too.

²⁹From the clan of Izhar came Kenaniah. He and his sons were given administrative responsibilities* over Israel as officials and judges.

³⁰From the clan of Hebron came Hashabiah. He and his relatives—1,700 capable men—were put in charge of the Israelite lands west of the Jordan River. They were responsible for all matters related to the things of the LORD and the service of the king in that area.

³¹Also from the clan of Hebron came Jeriah,* who was the leader of the Hebronites according to the genealogical records. (In the fortieth year of David's reign, a search was made in the records, and capable men from the clan of Hebron were found at Jazer in the land of Gilead.) ³²There were 2,700 capable men among the relatives of Jeriah. King David sent them to the east side of the Jordan River and put them in charge of the tribes of Reuben and Gad and the half-tribe of Manasseh. They were responsible for all matters related to God and to the king.

Military Commanders and Divisions

27 This is the list of Israelite generals and captains,* and their officers, who served the king by supervising the army divisions that were on duty each month of the year. Each division served for one month and had 24,000 troops.

²Jashobeam son of Zabdiel was commander of the first division of 24,000 troops, which was on duty during the first month. ³He was a descendant of Perez and was in charge of all the army officers for the first month.

⁴Dodai, a descendant of Ahoah, was commander of the second division of 24,000 troops, which was on duty during the second month. Mikloth was his chief officer.

⁵Benaiah son of Jehoiada the priest was commander of the third division of 24,000 troops, which was on duty during the third month. ⁶This was the Benaiah who commanded David's elite military group known as the Thirty. His son Ammizabad was his chief officer.

⁷Asahel, the brother of Joab, was commander of the fourth division of 24,000 troops, which was on duty during the fourth month. Asahel was succeeded by his son Zebadiah.

⁸Shammah* the Izrahite was commander of the fifth division of 24,000 troops, which was on duty during the fifth month.

⁹Ira son of Ikkesh from Tekoa was commander of the sixth division of 24,000 troops, which was on duty during the sixth month.

26:18 Or *the colonnade.* The meaning of the Hebrew is uncertain.   26:21a Hebrew *Ladan,* a variant spelling of Libni; compare 6:17.   26:21b Hebrew *Jehieli* (also in 26:22), a variant spelling of Jehiel; compare 23:8.   26:26 Hebrew *the commanders of thousands and of hundreds.*   26:28 Hebrew *Shelomith,* a variant spelling of Shelomoth.   26:29 Or *were given outside work;* or *were given work away from the Temple area.*   26:31 Hebrew *Jerijah,* a variant spelling of Jeriah; compare 23:19.   27:1 Hebrew *commanders of thousands and of hundreds.*   27:8 Hebrew *Shamhuth,* a variant spelling of Shammah; compare 11:27 and 2 Sam 23:25.

¹⁰Helez, a descendant of Ephraim from Pelon, was commander of the seventh division of 24,000 troops, which was on duty during the seventh month. ¹¹Sibbecai, a descendant of Zerah from Hushah, was commander of the eighth division of 24,000 troops, which was on duty during the eighth month. ¹²Abiezer from Anathoth in the territory of Benjamin was commander of the ninth division of 24,000 troops, which was on duty during the ninth month. ¹³Maharai, a descendant of Zerah from Netophah, was commander of the tenth division of 24,000 troops, which was on duty during the tenth month. ¹⁴Benaiah from Pirathon in Ephraim was commander of the eleventh division of 24,000 troops, which was on duty during the eleventh month. ¹⁵Heled,* a descendant of Othniel from Netophah, was commander of the twelfth division of 24,000 troops, which was on duty during the twelfth month.

Leaders of the Tribes

¹⁶The following were the tribes of Israel and their leaders:

Tribe	Leader
Reuben	Eliezer son of Zicri
Simeon	Shephatiah son of Maacah
¹⁷ Levi	Hashabiah son of Kemuel
Aaron (the priests)	Zadok
¹⁸ Judah	Elihu (a brother of David)
Issachar	Omri son of Michael
¹⁹ Zebulun	Ishmaiah son of Obadiah
Naphtali	Jeremoth son of Azriel
²⁰ Ephraim	Hoshea son of Azaziah
Manasseh (west)	Joel son of Pedaiah
²¹ Manasseh in Gilead (east)	Iddo son of Zechariah
Benjamin	Jaasiel son of Abner
²² Dan	Azarel son of Jeroham

These were the leaders of the tribes of Israel.

²³When David took his census, he did not count those who were younger than twenty years of age, because the LORD had promised to make the Israelites as numerous as the stars in heaven. ²⁴Joab son of Zeruiah began the census but never finished it because* the anger of God fell on Israel. The total number was never recorded in King David's official records.

Officials of David's Kingdom

²⁵Azmaveth son of Adiel was in charge of the palace treasuries.

Jonathan son of Uzziah was in charge of the regional treasuries throughout the towns, villages, and fortresses of Israel. ²⁶Ezri son of Kelub was in charge of the field workers who farmed the king's lands. ²⁷Shimei from Ramah was in charge of the king's vineyards.

Zabdi from Shepham was responsible for the grapes and the supplies of wine. ²⁸Baal-hanan from Geder was in charge of the king's olive groves and sycamore-fig trees in the foothills of Judah.*

Joash was responsible for the supplies of olive oil. ²⁹Shitrai from Sharon was in charge of the cattle on the Sharon Plain.

Shaphat son of Adlai was responsible for the cattle in the valleys. ³⁰Obil the Ishmaelite was in charge of the camels.

Jehdeiah from Meronoth was in charge of the donkeys. ³¹Jaziz the Hagrite was in charge of the king's flocks of sheep and goats.

All these officials were overseers of King David's property.

³²Jonathan, David's uncle, was a wise counselor to the king, a man of great insight, and a scribe. Jehiel the Hacmonite was responsible for teaching the king's sons. ³³Ahithophel was the royal adviser. Hushai the Arkite was the king's friend. ³⁴Ahithophel was succeeded by Jehoiada son of Benaiah and by Abiathar. Joab was commander of the king's army.

David's Instructions to Solomon

28 David summoned all the officials of Israel to Jerusalem—the leaders of the tribes, the commanders of the army divisions, the other generals and captains,* the overseers of the royal property and livestock, the palace officials, the mighty men, and all the other brave warriors in the kingdom. ²David rose to his feet and said: "My brothers and my people! It was my desire to build a Temple where the Ark of the LORD's Covenant, God's footstool, could rest permanently. I made the necessary preparations for building it, ³but God said to me, 'You must not build a Temple to honor my name, for you are a warrior and have shed much blood.'

27:15 Hebrew *Heldai*, a variant spelling of Heled; compare 11:30 and 2 Sam 23:29.   27:24 Or *never finished it, and yet*.
27:28 Hebrew *the Shephelah*.   28:1 Hebrew *the commanders of thousands and commanders of hundreds*.

⁴"Yet the LORD, the God of Israel, has chosen me from among all my father's family to be king over Israel forever. For he has chosen the tribe of Judah to rule, and from among the families of Judah he chose my father's family. And from among my father's sons the LORD was pleased to make me king over all Israel. ⁵And from among my sons—for the LORD has given me many—he chose Solomon to succeed me on the throne of Israel and to rule over the LORD's kingdom. ⁶He said to me, 'Your son Solomon will build my Temple and its courtyards, for I have chosen him as my son, and I will be his father. ⁷And if he continues to obey my commands and regulations as he does now, I will make his kingdom last forever.'

⁸"So now, with God as our witness, and in the sight of all Israel—the LORD's assembly—I give you this charge. Be careful to obey all the commands of the LORD your God, so that you may continue to possess this good land and leave it to your children as a permanent inheritance.

⁹"And Solomon, my son, learn to know the God of your ancestors intimately. Worship and serve him with your whole heart and a willing mind. For the LORD sees every heart and knows every plan and thought. If you seek him, you will find him. But if you forsake him, he will reject you forever. ¹⁰So take this seriously. The LORD has chosen you to build a Temple as his sanctuary. Be strong, and do the work."

¹¹Then David gave Solomon the plans for the Temple and its surroundings, including the entry room, the storerooms, the upstairs rooms, the inner rooms, and the inner sanctuary—which was the place of atonement. ¹²David also gave Solomon all the plans he had in mind* for the courtyards of the LORD's Temple, the outside rooms, the treasuries, and the rooms for the gifts dedicated to the LORD. ¹³The king also gave Solomon the instructions concerning the work of the various divisions of priests and Levites in the Temple of the LORD. And he gave specifications for the items in the Temple that were to be used for worship.

¹⁴David gave instructions regarding how much gold and silver should be used to make the items needed for service. ¹⁵He told Solomon the amount of gold needed for the gold lampstands and lamps, and the amount of silver for the silver lampstands and lamps, depending on how each would be used. ¹⁶He designated the amount of gold for the table on which the Bread of the Presence would be placed and the amount of silver for other tables.

¹⁷David also designated the amount of gold for the solid gold meat hooks used to handle the sacrificial meat and for the basins, pitchers, and dishes, as well as the amount of silver for every dish. ¹⁸He designated the amount of refined gold for the altar of incense. Finally, he gave him a plan for the LORD's "chariot"—the gold cherubim* whose wings were stretched out over the Ark of the LORD's Covenant. ¹⁹"Every part of this plan," David told Solomon, "was given to me in writing from the hand of the LORD.*"

²⁰Then David continued, "Be strong and courageous, and do the work. Don't be afraid or discouraged, for the LORD God, my God, is with you. He will not fail you or forsake you. He will see to it that all the work related to the Temple of the LORD is finished correctly. ²¹The various divisions of priests and Levites will serve in the Temple of God. Others with skills of every kind will volunteer, and the officials and the entire nation are at your command."

Gifts for Building the Temple

29 Then King David turned to the entire assembly and said, "My son Solomon, whom God has clearly chosen as the next king of Israel, is still young and inexperienced. The work ahead of him is enormous, for the Temple he will build is not for mere mortals—it is for the LORD God himself! ²Using every resource at my command, I have gathered as much as I could for building the Temple of my God. Now there is enough gold, silver, bronze, iron, and wood, as well as great quantities of onyx, other precious stones, costly jewels, and all kinds of fine stone and marble.

³"And now, because of my devotion to the Temple of my God, I am giving all of my own private treasures of gold and silver to help in the construction. This is in addition to the building materials I have already collected for his holy Temple. ⁴I am donating more than 112 tons of gold* from Ophir and 262 tons of refined silver* to be used for overlaying the walls of the buildings ⁵and for the other gold and silver work to be done by the craftsmen. Now then, who will follow my example and give offerings to the LORD today?"

⁶Then the family leaders, the leaders of the tribes of Israel, the generals and captains of the

---

28:12 Or *the plans of the spirit that was with him.*   28:18 Hebrew *for the gold cherub chariot.*   28:19 Or *was written under the direction of the LORD.*   29:4a Hebrew *3,000 talents* [102 metric tons] *of gold.*   29:4b Hebrew *7,000 talents* [238 metric tons] *of silver.*

army,* and the king's administrative officers all gave willingly. 7For the construction of the Temple of God, they gave about 188 tons of gold,* 10,000 gold coins,* 375 tons of silver,* 675 tons of bronze,* and 3,750 tons of iron.* 8They also contributed numerous precious stones, which were deposited in the treasury of the house of the LORD under the care of Jehiel, a descendant of Gershon. 9The people rejoiced over the offerings, for they had given freely and wholeheartedly to the LORD, and King David was filled with joy.

David's Prayer of Praise

10Then David praised the LORD in the presence of the whole assembly:

"O LORD, the God of our ancestor Israel,* may you be praised forever and ever! 11Yours, O LORD, is the greatness, the power, the glory, the victory, and the majesty. Everything in the heavens and on earth is yours, O LORD, and this is your kingdom. We adore you as the one who is over all things. 12Wealth and honor come from you alone, for you rule over everything. Power and might are in your hand, and at your discretion people are made great and given strength.

13"O our God, we thank you and praise your glorious name! 14But who am I, and who are my people, that we could give anything to you? Everything we have has come from you, and we give you only what you first gave us! 15We are here for only a moment, visitors and strangers in the land as our ancestors were before us. Our days on earth are like a passing shadow, gone so soon without a trace.

16"O LORD our God, even this material we have gathered to build a Temple to honor your holy name comes from you! It all belongs to you! 17I know, my God, that you examine our hearts and rejoice when you find integrity there. You know I have done all this with good motives, and I have watched your people offer their gifts willingly and joyously.

18"O LORD, the God of our ancestors Abraham, Isaac, and Israel, make your people always want to obey you. See to it that their love for you never changes. 19Give my son Solomon the wholehearted desire to obey all your commands, laws, and decrees, and to do everything necessary to build this Temple, for which I have made these preparations."

20Then David said to the whole assembly, "Give praise to the LORD your God!" And the entire assembly praised the LORD, the God of their ancestors, and they bowed low and knelt before the LORD and the king.

Solomon Named as King

21The next day they brought 1,000 bulls, 1,000 rams, and 1,000 male lambs as burnt offerings to the LORD. They also brought liquid offerings and many other sacrifices on behalf of all Israel. 22They feasted and drank in the LORD's presence with great joy that day.

And again they crowned David's son Solomon as their new king. They anointed him before the LORD as their leader, and they anointed Zadok as priest. 23So Solomon took the throne of the LORD in place of his father, David, and he succeeded in everything, and all Israel obeyed him. 24All the officials, the warriors, and the sons of King David pledged their loyalty to King Solomon. 25And the LORD exalted Solomon in the sight of all Israel, and he gave Solomon greater royal splendor than any king in Israel before him.

Summary of David's Reign

26So David son of Jesse reigned over all Israel. 27He reigned over Israel for forty years, seven of them in Hebron and thirty-three in Jerusalem. 28He died at a ripe old age, having enjoyed long life, wealth, and honor. Then his son Solomon ruled in his place.

29All the events of King David's reign, from beginning to end, are written in *The Record of Samuel the Seer*, *The Record of Nathan the Prophet*, and *The Record of Gad the Seer*. 30These accounts include the mighty deeds of his reign and everything that happened to him and to Israel and to all the surrounding kingdoms.

29:6 Hebrew *the commanders of thousands and commanders of hundreds.*   29:7a Hebrew *5,000 talents* [170 metric tons] *of gold.* 29:7b Hebrew *10,000 darics* [a Persian coin] *of gold,* about 185 pounds or 84 kilograms in weight.   29:7c Hebrew *10,000 talents* [340 metric tons] *of silver.*   29:7d Hebrew *18,000 talents* [612 metric tons] *of bronze.*   29:7e Hebrew *100,000 talents* [3,400 metric tons] *of iron.*   29:10 *Israel* is the name that God gave to Jacob.

2 Chronicles

IT IS EASY AS CHRISTIANS to look down upon people from cultures known to worship idols. But meanwhile, many of us devotedly serve idols of wealth, prestige, and self-fulfillment. Second Chronicles, however, calls us back to wholehearted, single-minded devotion to God. Continuing the history of Israel and Judah that was begun in 1 Chronicles, this book recounts the glory of Solomon's reign, highlighting the construction and dedication of the Temple. It also records the actions of the kings of Judah who came after Solomon, taking

- **Author:** Ezra, according to Jewish tradition
- **Date Written:** Around 430 BC, recording events from the beginning of Solomon's reign (970 BC) to the beginning of the Babylonian captivity (586 BC)
- **Purpose:** To unify the nation around true worship of God by showing the rewards of faithfulness and the consequences of sin
- **Themes:** Rewards of faithfulness, consequences of sin, the Temple, reform, national collapse, restoration
- **Outline**
  1:1–17 The beginning of Solomon's reign
  2:1–7:22 The building and dedication of the Temple
  8:1–9:31 The glory of Solomon's reign
  10:1–36:23 The remaining kings of Judah

special note of each one's attention to the religious affairs of their nation. Second Chronicles highlights the deeds of Hezekiah, under whose reign an extended revival took place. The writer also describes the destruction of Jerusalem and the exile to Babylon. The book ends on a positive note, however, as King Cyrus of Persia decrees that the people of Judah are free to return home. As the writer of 2 Chronicles provides his readers with a history of Israel's past, he indirectly urges his readers to rededicate their lives to the one true God.

Solomon Asks for Wisdom

1 Solomon son of David took firm control of his kingdom, for the LORD his God was with him and made him very powerful.

2 Solomon called together all the leaders of Israel—the generals and captains of the army,* the judges, and all the political and clan leaders. 3 Then he led the entire assembly to the place of worship in Gibeon, for God's Tabernacle* was located there. (This was the Tabernacle that Moses, the LORD's servant, had made in the wilderness.)

4 David had already moved the Ark of God from Kiriath-jearim to the tent he had prepared for it in Jerusalem. 5 But the bronze altar made by Bezalel son of Uri and grandson of Hur was there* at Gibeon in front of the Tabernacle of

the LORD. So Solomon and the people gathered in front of it to consult the LORD.* 6 There in front of the Tabernacle, Solomon went up to the bronze altar in the LORD's presence and sacrificed 1,000 burnt offerings on it.

7 That night God appeared to Solomon and said, "What do you want? Ask, and I will give it to you!"

8 Solomon replied to God, "You showed great and faithful love to David, my father, and now you have made me king in his place. 9 O LORD God, please continue to keep your promise to David my father, for you have made me king over a people as numerous as the dust of the earth! 10 Give me the wisdom and knowledge to lead them properly,* for who could possibly govern this great people of yours?"

1:2 Hebrew *the commanders of thousands and of hundreds.* 1:3 Hebrew *Tent of Meeting;* also in 1:6, 13. 1:5a As in Greek version and Latin Vulgate, and some Hebrew manuscripts; Masoretic Text reads *he placed.* 1:5b Hebrew *to consult him.* 1:10 Hebrew *to go out and come in before this people.*

¹¹God said to Solomon, "Because your greatest desire is to help your people, and you did not ask for wealth, riches, fame, or even the death of your enemies or a long life, but rather you asked for wisdom and knowledge to properly govern my people—¹²I will certainly give you the wisdom and knowledge you requested. But I will also give you wealth, riches, and fame such as no other king has had before you or will ever have in the future!"

¹³Then Solomon returned to Jerusalem from the Tabernacle at the place of worship in Gibeon, and he reigned over Israel.

¹⁴Solomon built up a huge force of chariots and horses.* He had 1,400 chariots and 12,000 horses. He stationed some of them in the chariot cities and some near him in Jerusalem. ¹⁵The king made silver and gold as plentiful in Jerusalem as stone. And valuable cedar timber was as common as the sycamore-fig trees that grow in the foothills of Judah.* ¹⁶Solomon's horses were imported from Egypt* and from Cilicia*; the king's traders acquired them from Cilicia at the standard price. ¹⁷At that time chariots from Egypt could be purchased for 600 pieces of silver,* and horses for 150 pieces of silver.* They were then exported to the kings of the Hittites and the kings of Aram.

Preparations for Building the Temple

2 ¹*Solomon decided to build a Temple to honor the name of the LORD, and also a royal palace for himself. ²*He enlisted a force of 70,000 laborers, 80,000 men to quarry stone in the hill country, and 3,600 foremen.

³Solomon also sent this message to King Hiram* at Tyre:

"Send me cedar logs as you did for my father, David, when he was building his palace. ⁴I am about to build a Temple to honor the name of the LORD my God. It will be a place set apart to burn fragrant incense before him, to display the special sacrificial bread, and to sacrifice burnt offerings each morning and evening, on the Sabbaths, at new moon celebrations, and at the other appointed festivals of the LORD our God. He has commanded Israel to do these things forever.

⁵"This must be a magnificent Temple because our God is greater than all other gods. ⁶But who can really build him a worthy home? Not even the highest heavens can contain him! So who am I to consider building a Temple for him, except as a place to burn sacrifices to him?

⁷"So send me a master craftsman who can work with gold, silver, bronze, and iron, as well as with purple, scarlet, and blue cloth. He must be a skilled engraver who can work with the craftsmen of Judah and Jerusalem who were selected by my father, David.

⁸"Also send me cedar, cypress, and red sandalwood* logs from Lebanon, for I know that your men are without equal at cutting timber in Lebanon. I will send my men to help them. ⁹An immense amount of timber will be needed, for the Temple I am going to build will be very large and magnificent. ¹⁰In payment for your woodcutters, I will send 100,000 bushels of crushed wheat, 100,000 bushels of barley,* 110,000 gallons of wine, and 110,000 gallons of olive oil.*"

¹¹King Hiram sent this letter of reply to Solomon:

"It is because the LORD loves his people that he has made you their king! ¹²Praise the LORD, the God of Israel, who made the heavens and the earth! He has given King David a wise son, gifted with skill and understanding, who will build a Temple for the LORD and a royal palace for himself.

¹³"I am sending you a master craftsman named Huram-abi, who is extremely talented. ¹⁴His mother is from the tribe of Dan in Israel, and his father is from Tyre. He is skillful at making things from gold, silver, bronze, and iron, and he also works with stone and wood. He can work with purple, blue, and scarlet cloth and fine linen. He is also an engraver and can follow any design given to him. He will work with your craftsmen and those appointed by my lord David, your father. ¹⁵"Send along the wheat, barley, olive

---

1:14 Or *charioteers*; also in 1:14b. 1:15 Hebrew *the Shephelah*. 1:16a Possibly *Muzur*, a district near Cilicia; also in 1:17. 1:16b Hebrew *Kue*, probably another name for Cilicia. 1:17a Hebrew *600 [shekels] of silver*, about 15 pounds or 6.8 kilograms in weight. 1:17b Hebrew *150 [shekels]*, about 3.8 pounds or 1.7 kilograms in weight. 2:1 Verse 2:1 is numbered 1:18 in Hebrew text. 2:2 Verses 2:2-18 are numbered 2:1-17 in Hebrew text. 2:3 Hebrew *Huram*, a variant spelling of Hiram; also in 2:11. 2:8 Or *juniper*; Hebrew reads *algum*, perhaps a variant spelling of *almug*; compare 9:10-11 and parallel text at 1 Kgs 10:11-12. 2:10a Hebrew *20,000 cors [4,400 kiloliters] of crushed wheat, 20,000 cors of barley*. 2:10b Hebrew *20,000 baths* [420 kiloliters] *of wine, and 20,000 baths of olive oil*.

oil, and wine that my lord has mentioned. ¹⁶We will cut whatever timber you need from the Lebanon mountains and will float the logs in rafts down the coast of the Mediterranean Sea* to Joppa. From there you can transport the logs up to Jerusalem."

¹⁷Solomon took a census of all foreigners in the land of Israel, like the census his father had taken, and he counted 153,600. ¹⁸He assigned 70,000 of them as common laborers, 80,000 as quarry workers in the hill country, and 3,600 as foremen.

Solomon Builds the Temple

3 So Solomon began to build the Temple of the LORD in Jerusalem on Mount Moriah, where the LORD had appeared to David, his father. The Temple was built on the threshing floor of Araunah* the Jebusite, the site that David had selected. ²The construction began in midspring,* during the fourth year of Solomon's reign.

³These are the dimensions Solomon used for the foundation of the Temple of God (using the old standard of measurement).* It was 90 feet long and 30 feet wide.* ⁴The entry room at the front of the Temple was 30 feet* wide, running across the entire width of the Temple, and 30 feet* high. He overlaid the inside with pure gold.

⁵He paneled the main room of the Temple with cypress wood, overlaid it with fine gold, and decorated it with carvings of palm trees and chains. ⁶He decorated the walls of the Temple with beautiful jewels and with gold from the land of Parvaim. ⁷He overlaid the beams, thresholds, walls, and doors throughout the Temple with gold, and he carved figures of cherubim on the walls.

⁸He made the Most Holy Place 30 feet wide, corresponding to the width of the Temple, and 30 feet deep. He overlaid its interior with 23 tons* of fine gold. ⁹The gold nails that were used weighed 20 ounces* each. He also overlaid the walls of the upper rooms with gold.

¹⁰He made two figures shaped like cherubim, overlaid them with gold, and placed them in the Most Holy Place. ¹¹The total wingspan of the two cherubim standing side by side was 30 feet. One wing of the first figure was 7½ feet* long, and it touched the Temple wall. The other wing, also 7½ feet long, touched one of the wings of the second figure. ¹²In the same way, the second figure had one wing 7½ feet long that touched the opposite wall. The other wing, also 7½ feet long, touched the wing of the first figure. ¹³So the wingspan of the two cherubim side by side was 30 feet. They stood on their feet and faced out toward the main room of the Temple.

¹⁴Across the entrance of the Most Holy Place he hung a curtain made of fine linen, decorated with blue, purple, and scarlet thread and embroidered with figures of cherubim.

¹⁵For the front of the Temple, he made two pillars that were 27 feet* tall, each topped by a capital extending upward another 7½ feet. ¹⁶He made a network of interwoven chains* and used them to decorate the tops of the pillars. He also made 100 decorative pomegranates and attached them to the chains. ¹⁷Then he set up the two pillars at the entrance of the Temple, one to the south of the entrance and the other to the north. He named the one on the south Jakin, and the one on the north Boaz.*

Furnishings for the Temple

4 Solomon* also made a bronze altar 30 feet long, 30 feet wide, and 15 feet high.* ²Then he cast a great round basin, 15 feet across from rim to rim, called the Sea. It was 7½ feet deep and about 45 feet in circumference.* ³It was encircled just below its rim by two rows of figures that resembled oxen. There were about six oxen per foot* all the way around, and they were cast as part of the basin.

⁴The Sea was placed on a base of twelve bronze oxen, all facing outward. Three faced north, three faced west, three faced south, and three faced east, and the Sea rested on them. ⁵The walls of the Sea were about three inches*

thick, and its rim flared out like a cup and resembled a water lily blossom. It could hold about 16,500 gallons* of water.

[6] He also made ten smaller basins for washing the utensils for the burnt offerings. He set five on the south side and five on the north. But the priests washed themselves in the Sea.

[7] He then cast ten gold lampstands according to the specifications that had been given, and he put them in the Temple. Five were placed against the south wall, and five were placed against the north wall.

[8] He also built ten tables and placed them in the Temple, five along the south wall and five along the north wall. Then he molded 100 gold basins.

[9] He then built a courtyard for the priests, and also the large outer courtyard. He made doors for the courtyard entrances and overlaid them with bronze. [10] The great bronze basin called the Sea was placed near the southeast corner of the Temple.

[11] Huram-abi also made the necessary washbasins, shovels, and bowls.

So at last Huram-abi completed everything King Solomon had assigned him to make for the Temple of God:

[12] the two pillars;
the two bowl-shaped capitals on top of the pillars;
the two networks of interwoven chains that decorated the capitals;
[13] the 400 pomegranates that hung from the chains on the capitals (two rows of pomegranates for each of the chain networks that decorated the capitals on top of the pillars);
[14] the water carts holding the basins;
[15] the Sea and the twelve oxen under it;
[16] the ash buckets, the shovels, the meat hooks, and all the related articles.

Huram-abi made all these things of burnished bronze for the Temple of the LORD, just as King Solomon had directed. [17] The king had them cast in clay molds in the Jordan Valley between Succoth and Zarethan.* [18] Solomon used such great quantities of bronze that its weight could not be determined.

[19] Solomon also made all the furnishings for the Temple of God:

the gold altar;
the tables for the Bread of the Presence;
[20] the lampstands and their lamps of solid gold, to burn in front of the Most Holy Place as prescribed;
[21] the flower decorations, lamps, and tongs—all of the purest gold;
[22] the lamp snuffers, bowls, ladles, and incense burners—all of solid gold;
the doors for the entrances to the Most Holy Place and the main room of the Temple, overlaid with gold.

5 So Solomon finished all his work on the Temple of the LORD. Then he brought all the gifts his father, David, had dedicated—the silver, the gold, and the various articles—and he stored them in the treasuries of the Temple of God.

The Ark Brought to the Temple

[2] Solomon then summoned to Jerusalem the elders of Israel and all the heads of tribes—the leaders of the ancestral families of Israel. They were to bring the Ark of the LORD's Covenant to the Temple from its location in the City of David, also known as Zion. [3] So all the men of Israel assembled before the king at the annual Festival of Shelters, which is held in early autumn.*

[4] When all the elders of Israel arrived, the Levites picked up the Ark. [5] The priests and Levites brought up the Ark along with the special tent* and all the sacred items that had been in it. [6] There, before the Ark, King Solomon and the entire community of Israel sacrificed so many sheep, goats, and cattle that no one could keep count!

[7] Then the priests carried the Ark of the LORD's Covenant into the inner sanctuary of the Temple—the Most Holy Place—and placed it beneath the wings of the cherubim. [8] The cherubim spread their wings over the Ark, forming a canopy over the Ark and its carrying poles. [9] These poles were so long that their ends could be seen from the Holy Place,* which is in front of the Most Holy Place, but not from the outside. They are still there to this day. [10] Nothing was in the Ark except the two stone tablets that Moses had placed in it at Mount Sinai,* where the LORD made a covenant with the people of Israel when they left Egypt.

4:5b Hebrew *3,000 baths* [63 kiloliters]. 4:17 As in parallel text at 1 Kgs 7:46; Hebrew reads *Zeredah.* 5:3 Hebrew *at the festival that is in the seventh month.* The Festival of Shelters began on the fifteenth day of the seventh month of the ancient Hebrew lunar calendar. This day occurred in late September, October, or early November. 5:5 Hebrew *the Tent of Meeting;* i.e., the tent mentioned in 2 Sam 6:17 and 1 Chr 16:1. 5:9 As in some Hebrew manuscripts and Greek version (see also 1 Kgs 8:8); Masoretic Text reads *from the Ark.* 5:10 Hebrew *Horeb,* another name for Sinai.

¹¹Then the priests left the Holy Place. All the priests who were present had purified themselves, whether or not they were on duty that day. ¹²And the Levites who were musicians—Asaph, Heman, Jeduthun, and all their sons and brothers—were dressed in fine linen robes and stood at the east side of the altar playing cymbals, lyres, and harps. They were joined by 120 priests who were playing trumpets. ¹³The trumpeters and singers performed together in unison to praise and give thanks to the LORD. Accompanied by trumpets, cymbals, and other instruments, they raised their voices and praised the LORD with these words:

"He is good!
His faithful love endures forever!"

At that moment a thick cloud filled the Temple of the LORD. ¹⁴The priests could not continue their service because of the cloud, for the glorious presence of the LORD filled the Temple of God.

Solomon Praises the LORD

6 Then Solomon prayed, "O LORD, you have said that you would live in a thick cloud of darkness. ²Now I have built a glorious Temple for you, a place where you can live forever!"

³Then the king turned around to the entire community of Israel standing before him and gave this blessing: ⁴"Praise the LORD, the God of Israel, who has kept the promise he made to my father, David. For he told my father, ⁵'From the day I brought my people out of the land of Egypt, I have never chosen a city among any of the tribes of Israel as the place where a Temple should be built to honor my name. Nor have I chosen a king to lead my people Israel. ⁶But now I have chosen Jerusalem as the place for my name to be honored, and I have chosen David to be king over my people Israel.'"

⁷Then Solomon said, "My father, David, wanted to build this Temple to honor the name of the LORD, the God of Israel. ⁸But the LORD told him, 'You wanted to build the Temple to honor my name. Your intention is good, ⁹but you are not the one to do it. One of your own sons will build the Temple to honor me.'

¹⁰"And now the LORD has fulfilled the promise he made, for I have become king in my father's place, and now I sit on the throne of Israel, just as the LORD promised. I have built this Temple to honor the name of the LORD, the God of Israel. ¹¹There I have placed the Ark, which contains the covenant that the LORD made with the people of Israel."

Solomon's Prayer of Dedication

¹²Then Solomon stood before the altar of the LORD in front of the entire community of Israel, and he lifted his hands in prayer. ¹³Now Solomon had made a bronze platform 7½ feet long, 7½ feet wide, and 4½ feet high* and had placed it at the center of the Temple's outer courtyard. He stood on the platform, and then he knelt in front of the entire community of Israel and lifted his hands toward heaven. ¹⁴He prayed,

"O LORD, God of Israel, there is no God like you in all of heaven and earth. You keep your covenant and show unfailing love to all who walk before you in wholehearted devotion. ¹⁵You have kept your promise to your servant David, my father. You made that promise with your own mouth, and with your own hands you have fulfilled it today.

¹⁶"And now, O LORD, God of Israel, carry out the additional promise you made to your servant David, my father. For you said to him, 'If your descendants guard their behavior and faithfully follow my Law as you have done, one of them will always sit on the throne of Israel.' ¹⁷Now, O LORD, God of Israel, fulfill this promise to your servant David.

¹⁸"But will God really live on earth among people? Why, even the highest heavens cannot contain you. How much less this Temple I have built! ¹⁹Nevertheless, listen to my prayer and my plea, O LORD my God. Hear the cry and the prayer that your servant is making to you. ²⁰May you watch over this Temple day and night, this place where you have said you would put your name. May you always hear the prayers I make toward this place. ²¹May you hear the humble and earnest requests from me and your people Israel when we pray toward this place. Yes, hear us from heaven where you live, and when you hear, forgive.

²²"If someone wrongs another person and is required to take an oath of innocence in front of your altar at this Temple, ²³then hear from heaven and judge between your servants—the accuser and the accused. Pay back the guilty as

6:13 Hebrew *5 cubits* [2.3 meters] *long, 5 cubits wide, and 3 cubits* [1.4 meters] *high.*

they deserve. Acquit the innocent because of their innocence.

24"If your people Israel are defeated by their enemies because they have sinned against you, and if they turn back and acknowledge your name and pray to you here in this Temple, 25then hear from heaven and forgive the sin of your people Israel and return them to this land you gave to them and to their ancestors.

26"If the skies are shut up and there is no rain because your people have sinned against you, and if they pray toward this Temple and acknowledge your name and turn from their sins because you have punished them, 27then hear from heaven and forgive the sins of your servants, your people Israel. Teach them to follow the right path, and send rain on your land that you have given to your people as their special possession.

28"If there is a famine in the land or a plague or crop disease or attacks of locusts or caterpillars, or if your people's enemies are in the land besieging their towns—whatever disaster or disease there is—29and if your people Israel pray about their troubles or sorrow, raising their hands toward this Temple, 30then hear from heaven where you live, and forgive. Give your people what their actions deserve, for you alone know each human heart. 31Then they will fear you and walk in your ways as long as they live in the land you gave to our ancestors.

32"In the future, foreigners who do not belong to your people Israel will hear of you. They will come from distant lands when they hear of your great name and your strong hand and your powerful arm. And when they pray toward this Temple, 33then hear from heaven where you live, and grant what they ask of you. In this way, all the people of the earth will come to know and fear you, just as your own people Israel do. They, too, will know that this Temple I have built honors your name.

34"If your people go out where you send them to fight their enemies, and if they pray to you by turning toward this city you have chosen and toward this Temple I have built to honor your name, 35then hear their prayers from heaven and uphold their cause.

36"If they sin against you—and who has

never sinned?—you might become angry with them and let their enemies conquer them and take them captive to a foreign land far away or near. 37But in that land of exile, they might turn to you in repentance and pray, 'We have sinned, done evil, and acted wickedly.' 38If they turn to you with their whole heart and soul in the land of their captivity and pray toward the land you gave to their ancestors—toward this city you have chosen, and toward this Temple I have built to honor your name—39then hear their prayers and their petitions from heaven where you live, and uphold their cause. Forgive your people who have sinned against you.

40"O my God, may your eyes be open and your ears attentive to all the prayers made to you in this place.

41 "And now arise, O LORD God, and enter
        your resting place,
     along with the Ark, the symbol of
        your power.
May your priests, O LORD God, be
        clothed with salvation;
     may your loyal servants rejoice in
        your goodness.
42 O LORD God, do not reject the king you
        have anointed.
     Remember your unfailing love for
        your servant David."

The Dedication of the Temple

7 When Solomon finished praying, fire flashed down from heaven and burned up the burnt offerings and sacrifices, and the glorious presence of the LORD filled the Temple. 2The priests could not enter the Temple of the LORD because the glorious presence of the LORD filled it. 3When all the people of Israel saw the fire coming down and the glorious presence of the LORD filling the Temple, they fell face down on the ground and worshiped and praised the LORD, saying,

"He is good!
     His faithful love endures forever!"

4Then the king and all the people offered sacrifices to the LORD. 5King Solomon offered a sacrifice of 22,000 cattle and 120,000 sheep and goats. And so the king and all the people dedicated the Temple of God. 6The priests took their assigned positions, and so did the Levites who were singing, "His faithful love endures forever!" They accompanied the singing with music from the instruments King David had made for praising the LORD. Across from the Levites, the priests blew the trumpets, while all Israel stood.

⁷Solomon then consecrated the central area of the courtyard in front of the LORD's Temple. He offered burnt offerings and the fat of peace offerings there, because the bronze altar he had built could not hold all the burnt offerings, grain offerings, and sacrificial fat.

⁸For the next seven days Solomon and all Israel celebrated the Festival of Shelters.* A large congregation had gathered from as far away as Lebo-hamath in the north and the Brook of Egypt in the south. ⁹On the eighth day they had a closing ceremony, for they had celebrated the dedication of the altar for seven days and the Festival of Shelters for seven days. ¹⁰Then at the end of the celebration,* Solomon sent the people home. They were all joyful and glad because the LORD had been so good to David and to Solomon and to his people Israel.

The LORD's Response to Solomon

¹¹So Solomon finished the Temple of the LORD, as well as the royal palace. He completed everything he had planned to do in the construction of the Temple and the palace. ¹²Then one night the LORD appeared to Solomon and said,

"I have heard your prayer and have chosen this Temple as the place for making sacrifices. ¹³At times I might shut up the heavens so that no rain falls, or command grasshoppers to devour your crops, or send plagues among you. ¹⁴Then if my people who are called by my name will humble themselves and pray and seek my face and turn from their wicked ways, I will hear from heaven and will forgive their sins and restore their land. ¹⁵My eyes will be open and my ears attentive to every prayer made in this place. ¹⁶For I have chosen this Temple and set it apart to be holy—a place where my name will be honored forever. I will always watch over it, for it is dear to my heart.

¹⁷"As for you, if you faithfully follow me as David your father did, obeying all my commands, decrees, and regulations, ¹⁸then I will establish the throne of your dynasty. For I made this covenant with your father, David, when I said, 'One of your descendants will always rule over Israel.'

¹⁹"But if you or your descendants abandon me and disobey the decrees and commands I have given you, and if you serve and worship other gods, ²⁰then I will uproot the people from this land that I have given them. I will reject this Temple that I have made holy to honor my name. I will make it an object of mockery and ridicule among the nations. ²¹And though this Temple is impressive now, all who pass by will be appalled. They will ask, 'Why did the LORD do such terrible things to this land and to this Temple?'

²²"And the answer will be, 'Because his people abandoned the LORD, the God of their ancestors, who brought them out of Egypt, and they worshiped other gods instead and bowed down to them. That is why he has brought all these disasters on them.'"

Solomon's Many Achievements

8 It took Solomon twenty years to build the LORD's Temple and his own royal palace. At the end of that time, ²Solomon turned his attention to rebuilding the towns that King Hiram* had given him, and he settled Israelites in them.

³Solomon also fought against the town of Hamath-zobah and conquered it. ⁴He rebuilt Tadmor in the wilderness and built towns in the region of Hamath as supply centers. ⁵He fortified the towns of Upper Beth-horon and Lower Beth-horon, rebuilding their walls and installing barred gates. ⁶He also rebuilt Baalath and other supply centers and constructed towns where his chariots and horses* could be stationed. He built everything he desired in Jerusalem and Lebanon and throughout his entire realm.

⁷There were still some people living in the land who were not Israelites, including the Hittites, Amorites, Perizzites, Hivites, and Jebusites. ⁸These were descendants of the nations whom the people of Israel had not destroyed. So Solomon conscripted them for his labor force, and they serve as forced laborers to this day. ⁹But Solomon did not conscript any of the Israelites for his labor force. Instead, he assigned them to serve as fighting men, officers in his army, commanders of his chariots, and

---

7:8 Hebrew *the festival* (also in 7:9); see note on 5:3.   7:10 Hebrew *Then on the twenty-third day of the seventh month.* This day of the ancient Hebrew lunar calendar occurred in October or early November.   8:2 Hebrew *Huram,* a variant spelling of Hiram; also in 8:18.   8:6 Or *and charioteers.*

charioteers. ¹⁰King Solomon appointed 250 of them to supervise the people.

¹¹Solomon moved his wife, Pharaoh's daughter, from the City of David to the new palace he had built for her. He said, "My wife must not live in King David's palace, for the Ark of the LORD has been there, and it is holy ground."

¹²Then Solomon presented burnt offerings to the LORD on the altar he had built for him in front of the entry room of the Temple. ¹³He offered the sacrifices for the Sabbaths, the new moon festivals, and the three annual festivals—the Passover celebration, the Festival of Harvest,* and the Festival of Shelters—as Moses had commanded.

¹⁴In assigning the priests to their duties, Solomon followed the regulations of his father, David. He also assigned the Levites to lead the people in praise and to assist the priests in their daily duties. And he assigned the gatekeepers to their gates by their divisions, following the commands of David, the man of God. ¹⁵Solomon did not deviate in any way from David's commands concerning the priests and Levites and the treasuries.

¹⁶So Solomon made sure that all the work related to building the Temple of the LORD was carried out, from the day its foundation was laid to the day of its completion.

¹⁷Later Solomon went to Ezion-geber and Elath,* ports along the shore of the Red Sea* in the land of Edom. ¹⁸Hiram sent him ships commanded by his own officers and manned by experienced crews of sailors. These ships sailed to Ophir with Solomon's men and brought back to Solomon almost seventeen tons* of gold.

Visit of the Queen of Sheba

9 When the queen of Sheba heard of Solomon's fame, she came to Jerusalem to test him with hard questions. She arrived with a large group of attendants and a great caravan of camels loaded with spices, large quantities of gold, and precious jewels. When she met with Solomon, she talked with him about everything she had on her mind. ²Solomon had answers for all her questions; nothing was too hard for him to explain to her. ³When the queen of Sheba realized how wise Solomon was, and when she saw the palace he had built, ⁴she was overwhelmed. She was also amazed at the food on his tables, the organization of his officials and their splendid clothing, the cup-bearers and their robes, and the burnt offerings* Solomon made at the Temple of the LORD.

⁵She exclaimed to the king, "Everything I heard in my country about your achievements* and wisdom is true! ⁶I didn't believe what was said until I arrived here and saw it with my own eyes. In fact, I had not heard the half of your great wisdom! It is far beyond what I was told. ⁷How happy your people must be! What a privilege for your officials to stand here day after day, listening to your wisdom! ⁸Praise the LORD your God, who delights in you and has placed you on the throne as king to rule for him. Because God loves Israel and desires this kingdom to last forever, he has made you king over them so you can rule with justice and righteousness."

⁹Then she gave the king a gift of 9,000 pounds* of gold, great quantities of spices, and precious jewels. Never before had there been spices as fine as those the queen of Sheba gave to King Solomon.

¹⁰(In addition, the crews of Hiram and Solomon brought gold from Ophir, and they also brought red sandalwood* and precious jewels. ¹¹The king used the sandalwood to make steps* for the Temple of the LORD and the royal palace, and to construct lyres and harps for the musicians. Never before had such beautiful things been seen in Judah.)

¹²King Solomon gave the queen of Sheba whatever she asked for—gifts of greater value than the gifts she had given him. Then she and all her attendants returned to their own land.

Solomon's Wealth and Splendor

¹³Each year Solomon received about 25 tons* of gold. ¹⁴This did not include the additional revenue he received from merchants and traders. All the kings of Arabia and the governors of the provinces also brought gold and silver to Solomon.

¹⁵King Solomon made 200 large shields of hammered gold, each weighing more than 15 pounds.* ¹⁶He also made 300 smaller shields of hammered gold, each weighing more than 7½ pounds.* The king placed these shields in the Palace of the Forest of Lebanon.

¹⁷Then the king made a huge throne, decorated with ivory and overlaid with pure gold.

8:13 Or Festival of Weeks. 8:17a As in Greek version (see also 2 Kgs 14:22; 16:6); Hebrew reads Eloth, a variant spelling of Elath. 8:17b As in parallel text at 1 Kgs 9:26; Hebrew reads the sea. 8:18 Hebrew 450 talents [15.3 metric tons]. 9:4 As in Greek and Syriac versions (see also 1 Kgs 10:5); Hebrew reads and the ascent. 9:5 Hebrew your words. 9:9 Hebrew 120 talents [4,000 kilograms]. 9:10 Hebrew algum wood (also in 9:11); perhaps a variant spelling of almug. Compare parallel text at 1 Kgs 10:11-12. 9:11 Or gateways. The meaning of the Hebrew is uncertain. 9:13 Hebrew 666 talents [23 metric tons]. 9:15 Hebrew 600 [shekels] of hammered gold [6.8 kilograms]. 9:16 Hebrew 300 [shekels] of gold [3.4 kilograms].

18The throne had six steps, with a footstool of gold. There were armrests on both sides of the seat, and the figure of a lion stood on each side of the throne. 19There were also twelve other lions, one standing on each end of the six steps. No other throne in all the world could be compared with it!

20All of King Solomon's drinking cups were solid gold, as were all the utensils in the Palace of the Forest of Lebanon. They were not made of silver, for silver was considered worthless in Solomon's day!

21The king had a fleet of trading ships of Tarshish manned by the sailors sent by Hiram.* Once every three years the ships returned, loaded with gold, silver, ivory, apes, and peacocks.*

22So King Solomon became richer and wiser than any other king on earth. 23Kings from every nation came to consult him and to hear the wisdom God had given him. 24Year after year everyone who visited brought him gifts of silver and gold, clothing, weapons, spices, horses, and mules.

25Solomon had 4,000 stalls for his horses and chariots, and he had 12,000 horses.* He stationed some of them in the chariot cities, and some near him in Jerusalem. 26He ruled over all the kings from the Euphrates River* in the north to the land of the Philistines and the border of Egypt in the south. 27The king made silver as plentiful in Jerusalem as stone. And valuable cedar timber was as common as the sycamore-fig trees that grow in the foothills of Judah.* 28Solomon's horses were imported from Egypt* and many other countries.

Summary of Solomon's Reign

29The rest of the events of Solomon's reign, from beginning to end, are recorded in *The Record of Nathan the Prophet,* and *The Prophecy of Ahijah from Shiloh,* and also in *The Visions of Iddo the Seer,* concerning Jeroboam son of Nebat. 30Solomon ruled in Jerusalem over all Israel for forty years. 31When he died, he was buried in the City of David, named for his father. Then his son Rehoboam became the next king.

The Northern Tribes Revolt

10 Rehoboam went to Shechem, where all Israel had gathered to make him king. 2When Jeroboam son of Nebat heard of this, he returned from Egypt, for he had fled to Egypt to escape from King Solomon. 3The leaders of Israel summoned him, and Jeroboam and all Israel went to speak with Rehoboam. 4"Your father was a hard master," they said. "Lighten the harsh labor demands and heavy taxes that your father imposed on us. Then we will be your loyal subjects."

5Rehoboam replied, "Come back in three days for my answer." So the people went away.

6Then King Rehoboam discussed the matter with the older men who had counseled his father, Solomon. "What is your advice?" he asked. "How should I answer these people?"

7The older counselors replied, "If you are good to these people and do your best to please them and give them a favorable answer, they will always be your loyal subjects."

8But Rehoboam rejected the advice of the older men and instead asked the opinion of the young men who had grown up with him and were now his advisers. 9"What is your advice?" he asked them. "How should I answer these people who want me to lighten the burdens imposed by my father?"

10The young men replied, "This is what you should tell those complainers who want a lighter burden: 'My little finger is thicker than my father's waist! 11Yes, my father laid heavy burdens on you, but I'm going to make them even heavier! My father beat you with whips, but I will beat you with scorpions!'"

12Three days later Jeroboam and all the people returned to hear Rehoboam's decision, just as the king had ordered. 13But Rehoboam spoke harshly to them, for he rejected the advice of the older counselors 14and followed the counsel of his younger advisers. He told the people, "My father laid* heavy burdens on you, but I'm going to make them even heavier! My father beat you with whips, but I will beat you with scorpions!"

15So the king paid no attention to the people. This turn of events was the will of God, for it fulfilled the LORD's message to Jeroboam son of Nebat through the prophet Ahijah from Shiloh.

16When all Israel realized* that the king had refused to listen to them, they responded,

"Down with the dynasty of David!
We have no interest in the son of Jesse.

9:21a Hebrew *Huram,* a variant spelling of Hiram.   9:21b Or *and baboons.*   9:25 Or *12,000 charioteers.*   9:26 Hebrew *the river.*   9:27 Hebrew *the Shephelah.*   9:28 Possibly *Muzur,* a district near Cilicia.   10:14 As in Greek version and many Hebrew manuscripts (see also 1 Kgs 12:14); Masoretic Text reads *I will lay.*   10:16 As in Syriac version, Latin Vulgate, and many Hebrew manuscripts (see also 1 Kgs 12:16); Masoretic Text lacks *realized.*

Back to your homes, O Israel!
Look out for your own house, O David!"

So all the people of Israel returned home. [17]But Rehoboam continued to rule over the Israelites who lived in the towns of Judah.

[18]King Rehoboam sent Adoniram,* who was in charge of forced labor, to restore order, but the people of Israel stoned him to death. When this news reached King Rehoboam, he quickly jumped into his chariot and fled to Jerusalem. [19]And to this day the northern tribes of Israel have refused to be ruled by a descendant of David.

Shemaiah's Prophecy

11 When Rehoboam arrived at Jerusalem, he mobilized the men of Judah and Benjamin—180,000 select troops—to fight against Israel and to restore the kingdom to himself. [2]But the LORD said to Shemaiah, the man of God, [3]"Say to Rehoboam son of Solomon, king of Judah, and to all the Israelites in Judah and Benjamin: [4]'This is what the LORD says: Do not fight against your relatives. Go back home, for what has happened is my doing!'" So they obeyed the message of the LORD and did not fight against Jeroboam.

Rehoboam Fortifies Judah

[5]Rehoboam remained in Jerusalem and fortified various towns for the defense of Judah. [6]He built up Bethlehem, Etam, Tekoa, [7]Beth-zur, Soco, Adullam, [8]Gath, Mareshah, Ziph, [9]Adoraim, Lachish, Azekah, [10]Zorah, Aijalon, and Hebron. These became the fortified towns of Judah and Benjamin. [11]Rehoboam strengthened their defenses and stationed commanders in them, and he stored supplies of food, olive oil, and wine. [12]He also put shields and spears in these towns as a further safety measure. So only Judah and Benjamin remained under his control.

[13]But all the priests and Levites living among the northern tribes of Israel sided with Rehoboam. [14]The Levites even abandoned their pasturelands and property and moved to Judah and Jerusalem, because Jeroboam and his sons would not allow them to serve the LORD as priests. [15]Jeroboam appointed his own priests to serve at the pagan shrines, where they worshiped the goat and calf idols he had made. [16]From all the tribes of Israel, those who sincerely wanted to worship the LORD, the God

of Israel, followed the Levites to Jerusalem, where they could offer sacrifices to the LORD, the God of their ancestors. [17]This strengthened the kingdom of Judah, and for three years they supported Rehoboam son of Solomon, for during those years they faithfully followed in the footsteps of David and Solomon.

Rehoboam's Family

[18]Rehoboam married his cousin Mahalath, the daughter of David's son Jerimoth and of Abihail, the daughter of Eliab son of Jesse. [19]Mahalath had three sons—Jeush, Shemariah, and Zaham.

[20]Later Rehoboam married another cousin, Maacah, the granddaughter of Absalom. Maacah gave birth to Abijah, Attai, Ziza, and Shelomith. [21]Rehoboam loved Maacah more than any of his other wives and concubines. In all, he had eighteen wives and sixty concubines, and they gave birth to twenty-eight sons and sixty daughters.

[22]Rehoboam appointed Maacah's son Abijah as leader among the princes, making it clear that he would be the next king. [23]Rehoboam also wisely gave responsibilities to his other sons and stationed some of them in the fortified towns throughout the land of Judah and Benjamin. He provided them with generous provisions, and he found many wives for them.

Egypt Invades Judah

12 But when Rehoboam was firmly established and strong, he abandoned the Law of the LORD, and all Israel followed him in this sin. [2]Because they were unfaithful to the LORD, King Shishak of Egypt came up and attacked Jerusalem in the fifth year of King Rehoboam's reign. [3]He came with 1,200 chariots, 60,000 horses,* and a countless army of foot soldiers, including Libyans, Sukkites, and Ethiopians.* [4]Shishak conquered Judah's fortified towns and then advanced to attack Jerusalem.

[5]The prophet Shemaiah then met with Rehoboam and Judah's leaders, who had all fled to Jerusalem because of Shishak. Shemaiah told them, "This is what the LORD says: You have abandoned me, so I am abandoning you to Shishak."

[6]Then the leaders of Israel and the king humbled themselves and said, "The LORD is right in doing this to us!"

[7]When the LORD saw their change of heart, he gave this message to Shemaiah: "Since the

10:18 Hebrew *Hadoram,* a variant spelling of Adoniram; compare 1 Kgs 4:6; 5:14; 12:18.   12:3a Or *charioteers,* or *horsemen.*
12:3b Hebrew *and Cushites.*

people have humbled themselves, I will not completely destroy them and will soon give them some relief. I will not use Shishak to pour out my anger on Jerusalem. ⁸But they will become his subjects, so they will know the difference between serving me and serving earthly rulers."

⁹So King Shishak of Egypt came up and attacked Jerusalem. He ransacked the treasuries of the LORD's Temple and the royal palace; he stole everything, including all the gold shields Solomon had made. ¹⁰King Rehoboam later replaced them with bronze shields as substitutes, and he entrusted them to the care of the commanders of the guard who protected the entrance to the royal palace. ¹¹Whenever the king went to the Temple of the LORD, the guards would also take the shields and then return them to the guardroom. ¹²Because Rehoboam humbled himself, the LORD's anger was turned away, and he did not destroy him completely. There were still some good things in the land of Judah.

Summary of Rehoboam's Reign

¹³King Rehoboam firmly established himself in Jerusalem and continued to rule. He was forty-one years old when he became king, and he reigned seventeen years in Jerusalem, the city the LORD had chosen from among all the tribes of Israel as the place to honor his name. Rehoboam's mother was Naamah, a woman from Ammon. ¹⁴But he was an evil king, for he did not seek the LORD with all his heart.

¹⁵The rest of the events of Rehoboam's reign, from beginning to end, are recorded in *The Record of Shemaiah the Prophet* and *The Record of Iddo the Seer,* which are part of the genealogical record. Rehoboam and Jeroboam were continually at war with each other. ¹⁶When Rehoboam died, he was buried in the City of David. Then his son Abijah became the next king.

Abijah's War with Jeroboam

13 Abijah began to rule over Judah in the eighteenth year of Jeroboam's reign in Israel. ²He reigned in Jerusalem three years. His mother was Maacah,* the daughter of Uriel from Gibeah.

Then war broke out between Abijah and Jeroboam. ³Judah, led by King Abijah, fielded 400,000 select warriors, while Jeroboam mustered 800,000 select troops from Israel.

⁴When the army of Judah arrived in the hill country of Ephraim, Abijah stood on Mount Zemaraim and shouted to Jeroboam and all Israel: "Listen to me! ⁵Don't you realize that the LORD, the God of Israel, made a lasting covenant* with David, giving him and his descendants the throne of Israel forever? ⁶Yet Jeroboam son of Nebat, a mere servant of David's son Solomon, rebelled against his master. ⁷Then a whole gang of scoundrels joined him, defying Solomon's son Rehoboam when he was young and inexperienced and could not stand up to them.

⁸"Do you really think you can stand against the kingdom of the LORD that is led by the descendants of David? You may have a vast army, and you have those gold calves that Jeroboam made as your gods. ⁹But you have chased away the priests of the LORD (the descendants of Aaron) and the Levites, and you have appointed your own priests, just like the pagan nations. You let anyone become a priest these days! Whoever comes to be dedicated with a young bull and seven rams can become a priest of these so-called gods of yours!

¹⁰"But as for us, the LORD is our God, and we have not abandoned him. Only the descendants of Aaron serve the LORD as priests, and the Levites alone may help them in their work. ¹¹They present burnt offerings and fragrant incense to the LORD every morning and evening. They place the Bread of the Presence on the holy table, and they light the gold lampstand every evening. We are following the instructions of the LORD our God, but you have abandoned him. ¹²So you see, God is with us. He is our leader. His priests blow their trumpets and lead us into battle against you. O people of Israel, do not fight against the LORD, the God of your ancestors, for you will not succeed!"

¹³Meanwhile, Jeroboam had secretly sent part of his army around behind the men of Judah to ambush them. ¹⁴When Judah realized that they were being attacked from the front and the rear, they cried out to the LORD for help. Then the priests blew the trumpets, ¹⁵and the men of Judah began to shout. At the sound of their battle cry, God defeated Jeroboam and all Israel and routed them before Abijah and the army of Judah.

¹⁶The Israelite army fled from Judah, and God handed them over to Judah in defeat. ¹⁷Abijah and his army inflicted heavy losses on them; 500,000 of Israel's select troops were killed that day. ¹⁸So Judah defeated Israel on

13:2 As in most Greek manuscripts and Syriac version (see also 2 Chr 11:20-21; 1 Kgs 15:2); Hebrew reads *Micaiah,* a variant spelling of Maacah.   13:5 Hebrew *a covenant of salt.*

that occasion because they trusted in the LORD, the God of their ancestors. ¹⁹Abijah and his army pursued Jeroboam's troops and captured some of his towns, including Bethel, Jeshanah, and Ephron, along with their surrounding villages.

²⁰So Jeroboam of Israel never regained his power during Abijah's lifetime, and finally the LORD struck him down and he died. ²¹Meanwhile, Abijah of Judah grew more and more powerful. He married fourteen wives and had twenty-two sons and sixteen daughters.

²²The rest of the events of Abijah's reign, including his words and deeds, are recorded in *The Commentary of Iddo the Prophet.*

Early Years of Asa's Reign

14 ¹*When Abijah died, he was buried in the City of David. Then his son Asa became the next king. There was peace in the land for ten years. ²*Asa did what was pleasing and good in the sight of the LORD his God. ³He removed the foreign altars and the pagan shrines. He smashed the sacred pillars and cut down the Asherah poles. ⁴He commanded the people of Judah to seek the LORD, the God of their ancestors, and to obey his law and his commands. ⁵Asa also removed the pagan shrines, as well as the incense altars from every one of Judah's towns. So Asa's kingdom enjoyed a period of peace. ⁶During those peaceful years, he was able to build up the fortified towns throughout Judah. No one tried to make war against him at this time, for the LORD was giving him rest from his enemies.

⁷Asa told the people of Judah, "Let us build towns and fortify them with walls, towers, gates, and bars. The land is still ours because we sought the LORD our God, and he has given us peace on every side." So they went ahead with these projects and brought them to completion.

⁸King Asa had an army of 300,000 warriors from the tribe of Judah, armed with large shields and spears. He also had an army of 280,000 warriors from the tribe of Benjamin, armed with small shields and bows. Both armies were composed of well-trained fighting men.

⁹Once an Ethiopian* named Zerah attacked Judah with an army of 1,000,000 men* and 300 chariots. They advanced to the town of Mareshah, ¹⁰so Asa deployed his armies for battle in the valley north of Mareshah.* ¹¹Then Asa cried out to the LORD his God, "O LORD, no one but you can help the powerless against the mighty! Help us, O LORD our God, for we trust in you alone. It is in your name that we have come against this vast horde. O LORD, you are our God; do not let mere men prevail against you!"

¹²So the LORD defeated the Ethiopians* in the presence of Asa and the army of Judah, and the enemy fled. ¹³Asa and his army pursued them as far as Gerar, and so many Ethiopians fell that they were unable to rally. They were destroyed by the LORD and his army, and the army of Judah carried off a vast amount of plunder.

¹⁴While they were at Gerar, they attacked all the towns in that area, and terror from the LORD came upon the people there. As a result, a vast amount of plunder was taken from these towns, too. ¹⁵They also attacked the camps of herdsmen and captured many sheep, goats, and camels before finally returning to Jerusalem.

Asa's Religious Reforms

15 Then the Spirit of God came upon Azariah son of Oded, ²and he went out to meet King Asa as he was returning from the battle. "Listen to me, Asa!" he shouted. "Listen, all you people of Judah and Benjamin! The LORD will stay with you as long as you stay with him! Whenever you seek him, you will find him. But if you abandon him, he will abandon you. ³For a long time Israel was without the true God, without a priest to teach them, and without the Law to instruct them. ⁴But whenever they were in trouble and turned to the LORD, the God of Israel, and sought him out, they found him.

⁵"During those dark times, it was not safe to travel. Problems troubled the people of every land. ⁶Nation fought against nation, and city against city, for God was troubling them with every kind of problem. ⁷But as for you, be strong and courageous, for your work will be rewarded."

⁸When Asa heard this message from Azariah the prophet,* he took courage and removed all the detestable idols from the land of Judah and Benjamin and in the towns he had captured in the hill country of Ephraim. And he repaired the altar of the LORD, which stood in front of the entry room of the LORD's Temple.

14:1 Verse 14:1 is numbered 13:23 in Hebrew text.   14:2 Verses 14:2-15 are numbered 14:1-14 in Hebrew text.   14:9a Hebrew *a Cushite.*   14:9b Or *an army of thousands and thousands;* Hebrew reads *an army of a thousand thousands.*   14:10 As in Greek version; Hebrew reads *valley of Zephathah near Mareshah.*   14:12 Hebrew *Cushites;* also in 14:13.   15:8 As in Syriac version and Latin Vulgate (see also 15:1); Hebrew reads *from Oded the prophet.*

⁹Then Asa called together all the people of Judah and Benjamin, along with the people of Ephraim, Manasseh, and Simeon who had settled among them. For many from Israel had moved to Judah during Asa's reign when they saw that the LORD his God was with him. ¹⁰The people gathered at Jerusalem in late spring,* during the fifteenth year of Asa's reign.

¹¹On that day they sacrificed to the LORD 700 cattle and 7,000 sheep and goats from the plunder they had taken in the battle. ¹²Then they entered into a covenant to seek the LORD, the God of their ancestors, with all their heart and soul. ¹³They agreed that anyone who refused to seek the LORD, the God of Israel, would be put to death—whether young or old, man or woman. ¹⁴They shouted out their oath of loyalty to the LORD with trumpets blaring and rams' horns sounding. ¹⁵All in Judah were happy about this covenant, for they had entered into it with all their heart. They earnestly sought after God, and they found him. And the LORD gave them rest from their enemies on every side.

¹⁶King Asa even deposed his grandmother* Maacah from her position as queen mother because she had made an obscene Asherah pole. He cut down her obscene pole, broke it up, and burned it in the Kidron Valley. ¹⁷Although the pagan shrines were not removed from Israel, Asa's heart remained completely faithful throughout his life. ¹⁸He brought into the Temple of God the silver and gold and the various items that he and his father had dedicated.

¹⁹So there was no more war until the thirty-fifth year of Asa's reign.

Final Years of Asa's Reign

16 In the thirty-sixth year of Asa's reign, King Baasha of Israel invaded Judah and fortified Ramah in order to prevent anyone from entering or leaving King Asa's territory in Judah.

²Asa responded by removing the silver and gold from the treasuries of the Temple of the LORD and the royal palace. He sent it to King Ben-hadad of Aram, who was ruling in Damascus, along with this message:

³"Let there be a treaty* between you and me like the one between your father and my father. See, I am sending you silver and gold. Break your treaty with King Baasha of Israel so that he will leave me alone."

⁴Ben-hadad agreed to King Asa's request and sent the commanders of his army to attack the towns of Israel. They conquered the towns of Ijon, Dan, Abel-beth-maacah,* and all the store cities in Naphtali. ⁵As soon as Baasha of Israel heard what was happening, he abandoned his project of fortifying Ramah and stopped all work on it. ⁶Then King Asa called out all the men of Judah to carry away the building stones and timbers that Baasha had been using to fortify Ramah. Asa used these materials to fortify the towns of Geba and Mizpah.

⁷At that time Hanani the seer came to King Asa and told him, "Because you have put your trust in the king of Aram instead of in the LORD your God, you missed your chance to destroy the army of the king of Aram. ⁸Don't you remember what happened to the Ethiopians* and Libyans and their vast army, with all of their chariots and charioteers?* At that time you relied on the LORD, and he handed them over to you. ⁹The eyes of the LORD search the whole earth in order to strengthen those whose hearts are fully committed to him. What a fool you have been! From now on you will be at war."

¹⁰Asa became so angry with Hanani for saying this that he threw him into prison and put him in stocks. At that time Asa also began to oppress some of his people.

Summary of Asa's Reign

¹¹The rest of the events of Asa's reign, from beginning to end, are recorded in *The Book of the Kings of Judah and Israel.* ¹²In the thirty-ninth year of his reign, Asa developed a serious foot disease. Yet even with the severity of his disease, he did not seek the LORD's help but turned only to his physicians. ¹³So he died in the forty-first year of his reign. ¹⁴He was buried in the tomb he had carved out for himself in the City of David. He was laid on a bed perfumed with sweet spices and fragrant ointments, and the people built a huge funeral fire in his honor.

Jehoshaphat Rules in Judah

17 Then Jehoshaphat, Asa's son, became the next king. He strengthened Judah to stand against any attack from Israel. ²He

---

15:10 Hebrew *in the third month.* This month of the ancient Hebrew lunar calendar usually occurs within the months of May and June.   15:16 Hebrew *his mother.*   16:3 As in Greek version; Hebrew reads *There is a treaty.*   16:4 As in parallel text at 1 Kgs 15:20; Hebrew reads *Abel-maim,* another name for Abel-beth-maacah.   16:8a Hebrew *Cushites.*   16:8b Or *and horsemen?*

stationed troops in all the fortified towns of Judah, and he assigned additional garrisons to the land of Judah and to the towns of Ephraim that his father, Asa, had captured.

³The LORD was with Jehoshaphat because he followed the example of his father's early years* and did not worship the images of Baal. ⁴He sought his father's God and obeyed his commands instead of following the evil practices of the kingdom of Israel. ⁵So the LORD established Jehoshaphat's control over the kingdom of Judah. All the people of Judah brought gifts to Jehoshaphat, so he became very wealthy and highly esteemed. ⁶He was deeply committed to* the ways of the LORD. He removed the pagan shrines and Asherah poles from Judah.

⁷In the third year of his reign Jehoshaphat sent his officials to teach in all the towns of Judah. These officials included Ben-hail, Obadiah, Zechariah, Nethanel, and Micaiah. ⁸He sent Levites along with them, including Shemaiah, Nethaniah, Zebadiah, Asahel, Shemiramoth, Jehonathan, Adonijah, Tobijah, and Tob-adonijah. He also sent out the priests Elishama and Jehoram. ⁹They took copies of the Book of the Law of the LORD and traveled around through all the towns of Judah, teaching the people.

¹⁰Then the fear of the LORD fell over all the surrounding kingdoms so that none of them wanted to declare war on Jehoshaphat. ¹¹Some of the Philistines brought him gifts and silver as tribute, and the Arabs brought 7,700 rams and 7,700 male goats.

¹²So Jehoshaphat became more and more powerful and built fortresses and storage cities throughout Judah. ¹³He stored numerous supplies in Judah's towns and stationed an army of seasoned troops at Jerusalem. ¹⁴His army was enrolled according to ancestral clans.

From Judah there were 300,000 troops organized in units of 1,000, under the command of Adnah. ¹⁵Next in command was Jehohanan, who commanded 280,000 troops. ¹⁶Next was Amasiah son of Zicri, who volunteered for the LORD's service, with 200,000 troops under his command. ¹⁷From Benjamin there were 200,000 troops equipped with bows and shields. They were under the command of Eliada, a veteran soldier. ¹⁸Next in command was Jehozabad, who commanded 180,000 armed men.

¹⁹These were the troops stationed in Jerusalem to serve the king, besides those Jehoshaphat stationed in the fortified towns throughout Judah.

Jehoshaphat and Ahab

18 Jehoshaphat enjoyed great riches and high esteem, and he made an alliance with Ahab of Israel by having his son marry Ahab's daughter. ²A few years later he went to Samaria to visit Ahab, who prepared a great banquet for him and his officials. They butchered great numbers of sheep, goats, and cattle for the feast. Then Ahab enticed Jehoshaphat to join forces with him to recover Ramoth-gilead.

³"Will you go with me to Ramoth-gilead?" King Ahab of Israel asked King Jehoshaphat of Judah.

Jehoshaphat replied, "Why, of course! You and I are as one, and my troops are your troops. We will certainly join you in battle." ⁴Then Jehoshaphat added, "But first let's find out what the LORD says."

⁵So the king of Israel summoned the prophets, 400 of them, and asked them, "Should we go to war against Ramoth-gilead, or should I hold back?"

They all replied, "Yes, go right ahead! God will give the king victory."

⁶But Jehoshaphat asked, "Is there not also a prophet of the LORD here? We should ask him the same question."

⁷The king of Israel replied to Jehoshaphat, "There is one more man who could consult the LORD for us, but I hate him. He never prophesies anything but trouble for me! His name is Micaiah son of Imlah."

Jehoshaphat replied, "That's not the way a king should talk! Let's hear what he has to say."

⁸So the king of Israel called one of his officials and said, "Quick! Bring Micaiah son of Imlah."

Micaiah Prophesies against Ahab

⁹King Ahab of Israel and King Jehoshaphat of Judah, dressed in their royal robes, were sitting on thrones at the threshing floor near the gate of Samaria. All of Ahab's prophets were prophesying there in front of them. ¹⁰One of them, Zedekiah son of Kenaanah, made some iron horns and proclaimed, "This is what the LORD says: With these horns you will gore the Arameans to death!"

¹¹All the other prophets agreed. "Yes,"

17:3 Some Hebrew manuscripts read *the example of his father, David.*   17:6 Hebrew *His heart was courageous in.*

they said, "go up to Ramoth-gilead and be victorious, for the LORD will give the king victory!"

¹²Meanwhile, the messenger who went to get Micaiah said to him, "Look, all the prophets are promising victory for the king. Be sure that you agree with them and promise success."

¹³But Micaiah replied, "As surely as the LORD lives, I will say only what my God says."

¹⁴When Micaiah arrived before the king, Ahab asked him, "Micaiah, should we go to war against Ramoth-gilead, or should I hold back?"

Micaiah replied sarcastically, "Yes, go up and be victorious, for you will have victory over them!"

¹⁵But the king replied sharply, "How many times must I demand that you speak only the truth to me when you speak for the LORD?"

¹⁶Then Micaiah told him, "In a vision I saw all Israel scattered on the mountains, like sheep without a shepherd. And the LORD said, 'Their master has been killed.* Send them home in peace.'"

¹⁷"Didn't I tell you?" the king of Israel exclaimed to Jehoshaphat. "He never prophesies anything but trouble for me."

¹⁸Then Micaiah continued, "Listen to what the LORD says! I saw the LORD sitting on his throne with all the armies of heaven around him, on his right and on his left. ¹⁹And the LORD said, 'Who can entice King Ahab of Israel to go into battle against Ramoth-gilead so he can be killed?'

"There were many suggestions, ²⁰and finally a spirit approached the LORD and said, 'I can do it!'

"'How will you do this?' the LORD asked.

²¹"And the spirit replied, 'I will go out and inspire all of Ahab's prophets to speak lies.'

"'You will succeed,' said the LORD. 'Go ahead and do it.'

²²"So you see, the LORD has put a lying spirit in the mouths of your prophets. For the LORD has pronounced your doom."

²³Then Zedekiah son of Kenaanah walked up to Micaiah and slapped him across the face. "Since when did the Spirit of the LORD leave me to speak to you?" he demanded.

²⁴And Micaiah replied, "You will find out soon enough when you are trying to hide in some secret room!"

²⁵"Arrest him!" the king of Israel ordered. "Take him back to Amon, the governor of the city, and to my son Joash. ²⁶Give them this order from the king: 'Put this man in prison,

and feed him nothing but bread and water until I return safely from the battle!'"

²⁷But Micaiah replied, "If you return safely, it will mean that the LORD has not spoken through me!" Then he added to those standing around, "Everyone mark my words!"

The Death of Ahab

²⁸So King Ahab of Israel and King Jehoshaphat of Judah led their armies against Ramoth-gilead. ²⁹The king of Israel said to Jehoshaphat, "As we go into battle, I will disguise myself so no one will recognize me, but you wear your royal robes." So the king of Israel disguised himself, and they went into battle.

³⁰Meanwhile, the king of Aram had issued these orders to his chariot commanders: "Attack only the king of Israel! Don't bother with anyone else." ³¹So when the Aramean chariot commanders saw Jehoshaphat in his royal robes, they went after him. "There is the king of Israel!" they shouted. But Jehoshaphat called out, and the LORD saved him. God helped him by turning the attackers away from him. ³²As soon as the chariot commanders realized he was not the king of Israel, they stopped chasing him.

³³An Aramean soldier, however, randomly shot an arrow at the Israelite troops and hit the king of Israel between the joints of his armor. "Turn the horses* and get me out of here!" Ahab groaned to the driver of the chariot. "I'm badly wounded!"

³⁴The battle raged all that day, and the king of Israel propped himself up in his chariot facing the Arameans. In the evening, just as the sun was setting, he died.

Jehoshaphat Appoints Judges

19 When King Jehoshaphat of Judah arrived safely home in Jerusalem, ²Jehu son of Hanani the seer went out to meet him. "Why should you help the wicked and love those who hate the LORD?" he asked the king. "Because of what you have done, the LORD is very angry with you. ³Even so, there is some good in you, for you have removed the Asherah poles throughout the land, and you have committed yourself to seeking God."

⁴Jehoshaphat lived in Jerusalem, but he went out among the people, traveling from Beersheba to the hill country of Ephraim, encouraging the people to return to the LORD, the God of their ancestors. ⁵He appointed judges throughout the nation in

18:16 Hebrew *These people have no master.*   18:33 Hebrew *Turn your hand.*

all the fortified towns, [6]and he said to them, "Always think carefully before pronouncing judgment. Remember that you do not judge to please people but to please the LORD. He will be with you when you render the verdict in each case. [7]Fear the LORD and judge with integrity, for the LORD our God does not tolerate perverted justice, partiality, or the taking of bribes."

[8]In Jerusalem, Jehoshaphat appointed some of the Levites and priests and clan leaders in Israel to serve as judges* for cases involving the LORD's regulations and for civil disputes. [9]These were his instructions to them: "You must always act in the fear of the LORD, with faithfulness and an undivided heart. [10]Whenever a case comes to you from fellow citizens in an outlying town, whether a murder case or some other violation of God's laws, commands, decrees, or regulations, you must warn them not to sin against the LORD, so that he will not be angry with you and them. Do this and you will not be guilty.

[11]"Amariah the high priest will have final say in all cases involving the LORD. Zebadiah son of Ishmael, a leader from the tribe of Judah, will have final say in all civil cases. The Levites will assist you in making sure that justice is served. Take courage as you fulfill your duties, and may the LORD be with those who do what is right."

War with Surrounding Nations

20 After this, the armies of the Moabites, Ammonites, and some of the Meunites* declared war on Jehoshaphat. [2]Messengers came and told Jehoshaphat, "A vast army from Edom* is marching against you from beyond the Dead Sea.* They are already at Hazazon-tamar." (This was another name for En-gedi.) [3]Jehoshaphat was terrified by this news and begged the LORD for guidance. He also ordered everyone in Judah to begin fasting. [4]So people from all the towns of Judah came to Jerusalem to seek the LORD's help.

[5]Jehoshaphat stood before the community of Judah and Jerusalem in front of the new courtyard at the Temple of the LORD. [6]He prayed, "O LORD, God of our ancestors, you alone are the God who is in heaven. You are ruler of all the kingdoms of the earth. You are powerful and mighty; no one can stand against you! [7]O our God, did you not drive out those

who lived in this land when your people Israel arrived? And did you not give this land forever to the descendants of your friend Abraham? [8]Your people settled here and built this Temple to honor your name. [9]They said, 'Whenever we are faced with any calamity such as war,* plague, or famine, we can come to stand in your presence before this Temple where your name is honored. We can cry out to you to save us, and you will hear us and rescue us.'

[10]"And now see what the armies of Ammon, Moab, and Mount Seir are doing. You would not let our ancestors invade those nations when Israel left Egypt, so they went around them and did not destroy them. [11]Now see how they reward us! For they have come to throw us out of your land, which you gave us as an inheritance. [12]O our God, won't you stop them? We are powerless against this mighty army that is about to attack us. We do not know what to do, but we are looking to you for help."

[13]As all the men of Judah stood before the LORD with their little ones, wives, and children, [14]the Spirit of the LORD came upon one of the men standing there. His name was Jahaziel son of Zechariah, son of Benaiah, son of Jeiel, son of Mattaniah, a Levite who was a descendant of Asaph.

[15]He said, "Listen, all you people of Judah and Jerusalem! Listen, King Jehoshaphat! This is what the LORD says: Do not be afraid! Don't be discouraged by this mighty army, for the battle is not yours, but God's. [16]Tomorrow, march out against them. You will find them coming up through the ascent of Ziz at the end of the valley that opens into the wilderness of Jeruel. [17]But you will not even need to fight. Take your positions; then stand still and watch the LORD's victory. He is with you, O people of Judah and Jerusalem. Do not be afraid or discouraged. Go out against them tomorrow, for the LORD is with you!"

[18]Then King Jehoshaphat bowed low with his face to the ground. And all the people of Judah and Jerusalem did the same, worshiping the LORD. [19]Then the Levites from the clans of Kohath and Korah stood to praise the LORD, the God of Israel, with a very loud shout.

[20]Early the next morning the army of Judah went out into the wilderness of Tekoa. On the way Jehoshaphat stopped and said, "Listen to me, all you people of Judah and Jerusalem! Believe in the LORD your God, and you will be

19:8 As in Greek version; the meaning of the Hebrew is uncertain.   20:1 As in some Greek manuscripts (see also 26:7); Hebrew repeats *Ammonites.*   20:2a As in one Hebrew manuscript; most Hebrew manuscripts and ancient versions read *Aram.*   20:2b Hebrew *the sea.*   20:9 Or *sword of judgment; or sword, judgment.*

able to stand firm. Believe in his prophets, and you will succeed."

²¹After consulting the people, the king appointed singers to walk ahead of the army, singing to the LORD and praising him for his holy splendor. This is what they sang:

"Give thanks to the LORD;
    his faithful love endures forever!"

²²At the very moment they began to sing and give praise, the LORD caused the armies of Ammon, Moab, and Mount Seir to start fighting among themselves. ²³The armies of Moab and Ammon turned against their allies from Mount Seir and killed every one of them. After they had destroyed the army of Seir, they began attacking each other. ²⁴So when the army of Judah arrived at the lookout point in the wilderness, all they saw were dead bodies lying on the ground as far as they could see. Not a single one of the enemy had escaped.

²⁵King Jehoshaphat and his men went out to gather the plunder. They found vast amounts of equipment, clothing,* and other valuables—more than they could carry. There was so much plunder that it took them three days just to collect it all! ²⁶On the fourth day they gathered in the Valley of Blessing,* which got its name that day because the people praised and thanked the LORD there. It is still called the Valley of Blessing today.

²⁷Then all the men returned to Jerusalem, with Jehoshaphat leading them, overjoyed that the LORD had given them victory over their enemies. ²⁸They marched into Jerusalem to the music of harps, lyres, and trumpets, and they proceeded to the Temple of the LORD.

²⁹When all the surrounding kingdoms heard that the LORD himself had fought against the enemies of Israel, the fear of God came over them. ³⁰So Jehoshaphat's kingdom was at peace, for his God had given him rest on every side.

Summary of Jehoshaphat's Reign

³¹So Jehoshaphat ruled over the land of Judah. He was thirty-five years old when he became king, and he reigned in Jerusalem twenty-five years. His mother was Azubah, the daughter of Shilhi.

³²Jehoshaphat was a good king, following the ways of his father, Asa. He did what was pleasing in the LORD's sight. ³³During his reign, however, he failed to remove all the pagan shrines, and the people never fully committed themselves to follow the God of their ancestors.

³⁴The rest of the events of Jehoshaphat's reign, from beginning to end, are recorded in *The Record of Jehu Son of Hanani,* which is included in *The Book of the Kings of Israel.*

³⁵Some time later King Jehoshaphat of Judah made an alliance with King Ahaziah of Israel, who was very wicked.* ³⁶Together they built a fleet of trading ships* at the port of Ezion-geber. ³⁷Then Eliezer son of Dodavahu from Mareshah prophesied against Jehoshaphat. He said, "Because you have allied yourself with King Ahaziah, the LORD will destroy your work." So the ships met with disaster and never put out to sea.*

Jehoram Rules in Judah

21 When Jehoshaphat died, he was buried with his ancestors in the City of David. Then his son Jehoram became the next king.

²Jehoram's brothers—the other sons of Jehoshaphat—were Azariah, Jehiel, Zechariah, Azariahu, Michael, and Shephatiah; all these were the sons of Jehoshaphat king of Judah.* ³Their father had given each of them valuable gifts of silver, gold, and costly items, and also some of Judah's fortified towns. However, he designated Jehoram as the next king because he was the oldest. ⁴But when Jehoram had become solidly established as king, he killed all his brothers and some of the other leaders of Judah.

⁵Jehoram was thirty-two years old when he became king, and he reigned in Jerusalem eight years. ⁶But Jehoram followed the example of the kings of Israel and was as wicked as King Ahab, for he had married one of Ahab's daughters. So Jehoram did what was evil in the LORD's sight. ⁷But the LORD did not want to destroy David's dynasty, for he had made a covenant with David and promised that his descendants would continue to rule, shining like a lamp forever.

⁸During Jehoram's reign, the Edomites revolted against Judah and crowned their own king. ⁹So Jehoram went out with his full army and all his chariots. The Edomites surrounded

---

20:25 As in some Hebrew manuscripts and Latin Vulgate; most Hebrew manuscripts read *corpses.*   20:26 Hebrew *valley of Beracah.*   20:35 Or *who made him do what was wicked.*   20:36 Hebrew *fleet of ships that could go to Tarshish.*   20:37 Hebrew *never set sail for Tarshish.*   21:2 Masoretic Text reads *of Israel;* also in 21:4. The author of Chronicles sees Judah as representative of the true Israel. (Some Hebrew manuscripts, Greek and Syriac versions, and Latin Vulgate read *of Judah.*)

him and his chariot commanders, but he went out at night and attacked them* under cover of darkness. ¹⁰Even so, Edom has been independent from Judah to this day. The town of Libnah also revolted about that same time. All this happened because Jehoram had abandoned the LORD, the God of his ancestors. ¹¹He had built pagan shrines in the hill country of Judah and had led the people of Jerusalem and Judah to give themselves to pagan gods and to go astray.

¹²Then Elijah the prophet wrote Jehoram this letter:

"This is what the LORD, the God of your ancestor David, says: You have not followed the good example of your father, Jehoshaphat, or your grandfather King Asa of Judah. ¹³Instead, you have been as evil as the kings of Israel. You have led the people of Jerusalem and Judah to worship idols, just as King Ahab did in Israel. And you have even killed your own brothers, men who were better than you. ¹⁴So now the LORD is about to strike you, your people, your children, your wives, and all that is yours with a heavy blow. ¹⁵You yourself will suffer with a severe intestinal disease that will get worse each day until your bowels come out."

¹⁶Then the LORD stirred up the Philistines and the Arabs, who lived near the Ethiopians,* to attack Jehoram. ¹⁷They marched against Judah, broke down its defenses, and carried away everything of value in the royal palace, including the king's sons and his wives. Only his youngest son, Ahaziah,* was spared.

¹⁸After all this, the LORD struck Jehoram with an incurable intestinal disease. ¹⁹The disease grew worse and worse, and at the end of two years it caused his bowels to come out, and he died in agony. His people did not build a great funeral fire to honor him as they had done for his ancestors.

²⁰Jehoram was thirty-two years old when he became king, and he reigned in Jerusalem eight years. No one was sorry when he died. They buried him in the City of David, but not in the royal cemetery.

Ahaziah Rules in Judah

22 Then the people of Jerusalem made Ahaziah, Jehoram's youngest son, their next king, since the marauding bands who came with the Arabs* had killed all the older sons. So Ahaziah son of Jehoram reigned as king of Judah.

²Ahaziah was twenty-two* years old when he became king, and he reigned in Jerusalem one year. His mother was Athaliah, a granddaughter of King Omri. ³Ahaziah also followed the evil example of King Ahab's family, for his mother encouraged him in doing wrong. ⁴He did what was evil in the LORD's sight, just as Ahab's family had done. They even became his advisers after the death of his father, and they led him to ruin.

⁵Following their evil advice, Ahaziah joined Joram,* the son of King Ahab of Israel, in his war against King Hazael of Aram at Ramoth-gilead. When the Arameans* wounded Joram in the battle, ⁶he returned to Jezreel to recover from the wounds he had received at Ramoth.* Because Joram was wounded, King Ahaziah* of Judah went to Jezreel to visit him.

⁷But God had decided that this visit would be Ahaziah's downfall. While he was there, Ahaziah went out with Joram to meet Jehu grandson of Nimshi,* whom the LORD had appointed to destroy the dynasty of Ahab.

⁸While Jehu was executing judgment against the family of Ahab, he happened to meet some of Judah's officials and Ahaziah's relatives* who were traveling with Ahaziah. So Jehu killed them all. ⁹Then Jehu's men searched for Ahaziah, and they found him hiding in the city of Samaria. They brought him to Jehu, who killed him. Ahaziah was given a decent burial because the people said, "He was the grandson of Jehoshaphat—a man who sought the LORD with all his heart." But none of the surviving members of Ahaziah's family was capable of ruling the kingdom.

Queen Athaliah Rules in Judah

¹⁰When Athaliah, the mother of King Ahaziah of Judah, learned that her son was dead, she began to destroy the rest of Judah's royal family. ¹¹But Ahaziah's sister Jehosheba,* the daughter of King Jehoram, took Ahaziah's

21:9 Or *he went out and escaped*. The meaning of the Hebrew is uncertain.   21:16 Hebrew *the Cushites*.   21:17 Hebrew *Jehoahaz*, a variant spelling of Ahaziah; compare 22:1.   22:1 Or *marauding bands of Arabs*.   22:2 As in some Greek manuscripts and Syriac version (see also 2 Kgs 8:26); Hebrew reads *forty-two*.   22:5a Hebrew *Jehoram*, a variant spelling of Joram; also in 22:6, 7.   22:5b As in two Hebrew manuscripts and Latin Vulgate (see also 2 Kgs 8:28); Masoretic Text reads *the archers*. 22:6a Hebrew *Ramah*, a variant spelling of Ramoth.   22:6b As in some Hebrew manuscripts, Greek and Syriac versions, and Latin Vulgate (see also 2 Kgs 8:29); most Hebrew manuscripts read *Azariah*.   22:7 Hebrew *descendant of Nimshi*; compare 2 Kgs 9:2, 14.   22:8 As in Greek version (see also 2 Kgs 10:13); Hebrew reads *and sons of the brothers of Ahaziah*.   22:11 As in parallel text at 2 Kgs 11:2; Hebrew lacks *Ahaziah's sister* and reads *Jehoshabeath* [a variant spelling of Jehosheba].

infant son, Joash, and stole him away from among the rest of the king's children, who were about to be killed. She put Joash and his nurse in a bedroom. In this way, Jehosheba, wife of Jehoiada the priest and sister of Ahaziah, hid the child so that Athaliah could not murder him. ¹²Joash remained hidden in the Temple of God for six years while Athaliah ruled over the land.

Revolt against Athaliah

23 In the seventh year of Athaliah's reign, Jehoiada the priest decided to act. He summoned his courage and made a pact with five army commanders: Azariah son of Jeroham, Ishmael son of Jehohanan, Azariah son of Obed, Maaseiah son of Adaiah, and Elishaphat son of Zicri. ²These men traveled secretly throughout Judah and summoned the Levites and clan leaders in all the towns to come to Jerusalem. ³They all gathered at the Temple of God, where they made a solemn pact with Joash, the young king.

Jehoiada said to them, "Here is the king's son! The time has come for him to reign! The LORD has promised that a descendant of David will be our king. ⁴This is what you must do. When you priests and Levites come on duty on the Sabbath, a third of you will serve as gatekeepers. ⁵Another third will go over to the royal palace, and the final third will be at the Foundation Gate. Everyone else should stay in the courtyards of the LORD's Temple. ⁶Remember, only the priests and Levites on duty may enter the Temple of the LORD, for they are set apart as holy. The rest of the people must obey the LORD's instructions and stay outside. ⁷You Levites, form a bodyguard around the king and keep your weapons in hand. Kill anyone who tries to enter the Temple. Stay with the king wherever he goes."

⁸So the Levites and all the people of Judah did everything as Jehoiada the priest ordered. The commanders took charge of the men reporting for duty that Sabbath, as well as those who were going off duty. Jehoiada the priest did not let anyone go home after their shift ended. ⁹Then Jehoiada supplied the commanders with the spears and the large and small shields that had once belonged to King David and were stored in the Temple of God. ¹⁰He stationed all the people around the king, with their weapons ready. They formed a line from the south side of the Temple around to the north side and all around the altar.

¹¹Then Jehoiada and his sons brought out Joash, the king's son, placed the crown on his head, and presented him with a copy of God's laws.* They anointed him and proclaimed him king, and everyone shouted, "Long live the king!"

The Death of Athaliah

¹²When Athaliah heard the noise of the people running and the shouts of praise to the king, she hurried to the LORD's Temple to see what was happening. ¹³When she arrived, she saw the newly crowned king standing in his place of authority by the pillar at the Temple entrance. The commanders and trumpeters were surrounding him, and people from all over the land were rejoicing and blowing trumpets. Singers with musical instruments were leading the people in a great celebration. When Athaliah saw all this, she tore her clothes in despair and shouted, "Treason! Treason!"

¹⁴Then Jehoiada the priest ordered the commanders who were in charge of the troops, "Take her to the soldiers in front of the Temple,* and kill anyone who tries to rescue her." For the priest had said, "She must not be killed in the Temple of the LORD." ¹⁵So they seized her and led her out to the entrance of the Horse Gate on the palace grounds, and they killed her there.

Jehoiada's Religious Reforms

¹⁶Then Jehoiada made a covenant between himself and the king and the people that they would be the LORD's people. ¹⁷And all the people went over to the temple of Baal and tore it down. They demolished the altars and smashed the idols, and they killed Mattan the priest of Baal in front of the altars.

¹⁸Jehoiada now put the priests and Levites in charge of the Temple of the LORD, following all the directions given by David. He also commanded them to present burnt offerings to the LORD, as prescribed by the Law of Moses, and to sing and rejoice as David had instructed. ¹⁹He also stationed gatekeepers at the gates of the LORD's Temple to keep out those who for any reason were ceremonially unclean.

²⁰Then the commanders, nobles, rulers, and all the people of the land escorted the king from the Temple of the LORD. They went through the upper gate and into the palace, and they seated the king on the royal throne. ²¹So all the people of the land rejoiced, and

---

23:11 Or *a copy of the covenant.* 23:14 Or *Bring her out from between the ranks;* or *Take her out of the Temple precincts.* The meaning of the Hebrew is uncertain.

the city was peaceful because Athaliah had been killed.

Joash Repairs the Temple

24 Joash was seven years old when he became king, and he reigned in Jerusalem forty years. His mother was Zibiah from Beersheba. ²Joash did what was pleasing in the LORD's sight throughout the lifetime of Jehoiada the priest. ³Jehoiada chose two wives for Joash, and he had sons and daughters.

⁴At one point Joash decided to repair and restore the Temple of the LORD. ⁵He summoned the priests and Levites and gave them these instructions: "Go to all the towns of Judah and collect the required annual offerings, so that we can repair the Temple of your God. Do not delay!" But the Levites did not act immediately.

⁶So the king called for Jehoiada the high priest and asked him, "Why haven't you demanded that the Levites go out and collect the Temple taxes from the towns of Judah and from Jerusalem? Moses, the servant of the LORD, levied this tax on the community of Israel in order to maintain the Tabernacle of the Covenant.*"

⁷Over the years the followers of wicked Athaliah had broken into the Temple of God, and they had used all the dedicated things from the Temple of the LORD to worship the images of Baal.

⁸So now the king ordered a chest to be made and set outside the gate leading to the Temple of the LORD. ⁹Then a proclamation was sent throughout Judah and Jerusalem, telling the people to bring to the LORD the tax that Moses, the servant of God, had required of the Israelites in the wilderness. ¹⁰This pleased all the leaders and the people, and they gladly brought their money and filled the chest with it.

¹¹Whenever the chest became full, the Levites would carry it to the king's officials. Then the court secretary and an officer of the high priest would come and empty the chest and take it back to the Temple again. This went on day after day, and a large amount of money was collected. ¹²The king and Jehoiada gave the money to the construction supervisors, who hired masons and carpenters to restore the Temple of the LORD. They also hired metalworkers, who made articles of iron and bronze for the LORD's Temple.

¹³The men in charge of the renovation worked hard and made steady progress. They restored the Temple of God according to its original design and strengthened it. ¹⁴When all the repairs were finished, they brought the remaining money to the king and Jehoiada. It was used to make various articles for the Temple of the LORD—articles for worship services and for burnt offerings, including ladles and other articles made of gold and silver. And the burnt offerings were sacrificed continually in the Temple of the LORD during the lifetime of Jehoiada the priest.

¹⁵Jehoiada lived to a very old age, finally dying at 130. ¹⁶He was buried among the kings in the City of David, because he had done so much good in Israel for God and his Temple.

Jehoiada's Reforms Reversed

¹⁷But after Jehoiada's death, the leaders of Judah came and bowed before King Joash and persuaded him to listen to their advice. ¹⁸They decided to abandon the Temple of the LORD, the God of their ancestors, and they worshiped Asherah poles and idols instead! Because of this sin, divine anger fell on Judah and Jerusalem. ¹⁹Yet the LORD sent prophets to bring them back to him. The prophets warned them, but still the people would not listen.

²⁰Then the Spirit of God came upon Zechariah son of Jehoiada the priest. He stood before the people and said, "This is what God says: Why do you disobey the LORD's commands and keep yourselves from prospering? You have abandoned the LORD, and now he has abandoned you!"

²¹Then the leaders plotted to kill Zechariah, and King Joash ordered that they stone him to death in the courtyard of the LORD's Temple. ²²That was how King Joash repaid Jehoiada for his loyalty—by killing his son. Zechariah's last words as he died were, "May the LORD see what they are doing and avenge my death!"

The End of Joash's Reign

²³In the spring of the year* the Aramean army marched against Joash. They invaded Judah and Jerusalem and killed all the leaders of the nation. Then they sent all the plunder back to their king in Damascus. ²⁴Although the Arameans attacked with only a small army, the LORD helped them conquer the much larger army of Judah. The people of Judah had abandoned the LORD, the God of their ancestors, so judgment was carried out against Joash.

²⁵The Arameans withdrew, leaving Joash

24:6 Hebrew *Tent of the Testimony.*   24:23 Hebrew *At the turn of the year.* The first day of the year in the ancient Hebrew lunar calendar occurred in March or April.

severely wounded. But his own officials plotted to kill him for murdering the son* of Jehoiada the priest. They assassinated him as he lay in bed. Then he was buried in the City of David, but not in the royal cemetery. 26 The assassins were Jozacar,* the son of an Ammonite woman named Shimeath, and Jehozabad, the son of a Moabite woman named Shomer.*

27 The account of the sons of Joash, the prophecies about him, and the record of his restoration of the Temple of God are written in *The Commentary on the Book of the Kings.* His son Amaziah became the next king.

Amaziah Rules in Judah

25 Amaziah was twenty-five years old when he became king, and he reigned in Jerusalem twenty-nine years. His mother was Jehoaddin* from Jerusalem. 2 Amaziah did what was pleasing in the LORD's sight, but not wholeheartedly.

3 When Amaziah was well established as king, he executed the officials who had assassinated his father. 4 However, he did not kill the children of the assassins, for he obeyed the command of the LORD as written by Moses in the Book of the Law: "Parents must not be put to death for the sins of their children, nor children for the sins of their parents. Those deserving to die must be put to death for their own crimes."*

5 Then Amaziah organized the army, assigning generals and captains* for all Judah and Benjamin. He took a census and found that he had an army of 300,000 select troops, twenty years old and older, all trained in the use of spear and shield. 6 He also paid about 7,500 pounds* of silver to hire 100,000 experienced fighting men from Israel.

7 But a man of God came to him and said, "Your Majesty, do not hire troops from Israel, for the LORD is not with Israel. He will not help those people of Ephraim! 8 If you let them go with your troops into battle, you will be defeated by the enemy no matter how well you fight. God will overthrow you, for he has the power to help you or to trip you up."

9 Amaziah asked the man of God, "But what about all that silver I paid to hire the army of Israel?"

The man of God replied, "The LORD is able to give you much more than this!" 10 So Am-

aziah discharged the hired troops and sent them back to Ephraim. This made them very angry with Judah, and they returned home in a great rage.

11 Then Amaziah summoned his courage and led his army to the Valley of Salt, where they killed 10,000 Edomite troops from Seir. 12 They captured another 10,000 and took them to the top of a cliff and threw them off, dashing them to pieces on the rocks below.

13 Meanwhile, the hired troops that Amaziah had sent home raided several of the towns of Judah between Samaria and Beth-horon. They killed 3,000 people and carried off great quantities of plunder.

14 When King Amaziah returned from slaughtering the Edomites, he brought with him idols taken from the people of Seir. He set them up as his own gods, bowed down in front of them, and offered sacrifices to them! 15 This made the LORD very angry, and he sent a prophet to ask, "Why do you turn to gods who could not even save their own people from you?"

16 But the king interrupted him and said, "Since when have I made you the king's counselor? Be quiet now before I have you killed!"

So the prophet stopped with this warning: "I know that God has determined to destroy you because you have done this and have refused to accept my counsel."

17 After consulting with his advisers, King Amaziah of Judah sent this challenge to Israel's king Jehoash,* the son of Jehoahaz and grandson of Jehu: "Come and meet me in battle!"*

18 But King Jehoash of Israel replied to King Amaziah of Judah with this story: "Out in the Lebanon mountains, a thistle sent a message to a mighty cedar tree: 'Give your daughter in marriage to my son.' But just then a wild animal of Lebanon came by and stepped on the thistle, crushing it!

19 "You are saying, 'I have defeated Edom,' and you are very proud of it. But my advice is to stay at home. Why stir up trouble that will only bring disaster on you and the people of Judah?"

20 But Amaziah refused to listen, for God was determined to destroy him for turning to the gods of Edom. 21 So King Jehoash of Israel mobilized his army against King Amaziah of Judah. The two armies drew up their battle lines at Beth-shemesh in Judah. 22 Judah was routed

---

24:25 As in Greek version and Latin Vulgate; Hebrew reads *sons.* 24:26a As in parallel text at 2 Kgs 12:21; Hebrew reads *Zabad.* 24:26b As in parallel text at 2 Kgs 12:21; Hebrew reads *Shimrith,* a variant spelling of Shomer. 25:1 As in parallel text at 2 Kgs 14:2; Hebrew reads *Jehoaddan,* a variant spelling of Jehoaddin. 25:4 Deut 24:16. 25:5 Hebrew *commanders of thousands and commanders of hundreds.* 25:6 Hebrew *100 talents* [3,400 kilograms]. 25:17a Hebrew *Joash,* a variant spelling of Jehoash; also in 25:18, 21, 23, 25. 25:17b Hebrew *Come, let us look one another in the face.*

by the army of Israel, and its army scattered and fled for home. 23King Jehoash of Israel captured Judah's king, Amaziah son of Joash and grandson of Ahaziah, at Beth-shemesh. Then he brought him to Jerusalem, where he demolished 600 feet* of Jerusalem's wall, from the Ephraim Gate to the Corner Gate. 24He carried off all the gold and silver and all the articles from the Temple of God that had been in the care of Obed-edom. He also seized the treasures of the royal palace, along with hostages, and then returned to Samaria.

25King Amaziah of Judah lived for fifteen years after the death of King Jehoash of Israel. 26The rest of the events in Amaziah's reign, from beginning to end, are recorded in *The Book of the Kings of Judah and Israel.*

27After Amaziah turned away from the LORD, there was a conspiracy against his life in Jerusalem, and he fled to Lachish. But his enemies sent assassins after him, and they killed him there. 28They brought his body back on a horse, and he was buried with his ancestors in the City of David.*

Uzziah Rules in Judah

26 All the people of Judah had crowned Amaziah's sixteen-year-old son, Uzziah, as king in place of his father. 2After his father's death, Uzziah rebuilt the town of Elath* and restored it to Judah.

3Uzziah was sixteen years old when he became king, and he reigned in Jerusalem fifty-two years. His mother was Jecoliah from Jerusalem. 4He did what was pleasing in the LORD's sight, just as his father, Amaziah, had done. 5Uzziah sought God during the days of Zechariah, who taught him to fear God.* And as long as the king sought guidance from the LORD, God gave him success.

6Uzziah declared war on the Philistines and broke down the walls of Gath, Jabneh, and Ashdod. Then he built new towns in the Ashdod area and in other parts of Philistia. 7God helped him in his wars against the Philistines, his battles with the Arabs of Gur,* and his wars with the Meunites. 8The Meunites* paid annual tribute to him, and his fame spread even to Egypt, for he had become very powerful.

9Uzziah built fortified towers in Jerusalem at the Corner Gate, at the Valley Gate, and at the angle in the wall. 10He also constructed forts in the wilderness and dug many water cisterns, because he kept great herds of livestock in the foothills of Judah* and on the plains. He was also a man who loved the soil. He had many workers who cared for his farms and vineyards, both on the hillsides and in the fertile valleys.

11Uzziah had an army of well-trained warriors, ready to march into battle, unit by unit. This army had been mustered and organized by Jeiel, the secretary of the army, and his assistant, Maaseiah. They were under the direction of Hananiah, one of the king's officials. 12These regiments of mighty warriors were commanded by 2,600 clan leaders. 13The army consisted of 307,500 men, all elite troops. They were prepared to assist the king against any enemy.

14Uzziah provided the entire army with shields, spears, helmets, coats of mail, bows, and sling stones. 15And he built structures on the walls of Jerusalem, designed by experts to protect those who shot arrows and hurled large stones* from the towers and the corners of the wall. His fame spread far and wide, for the LORD gave him marvelous help, and he became very powerful.

Uzziah's Sin and Punishment

16But when he had become powerful, he also became proud, which led to his downfall. He sinned against the LORD his God by entering the sanctuary of the LORD's Temple and personally burning incense on the incense altar. 17Azariah the high priest went in after him with eighty other priests of the LORD, all brave men. 18They confronted King Uzziah and said, "It is not for you, Uzziah, to burn incense to the LORD. That is the work of the priests alone, the descendants of Aaron who are set apart for this work. Get out of the sanctuary, for you have sinned. The LORD God will not honor you for this!"

19Uzziah, who was holding an incense burner, became furious. But as he was standing there raging at the priests before the incense altar in the LORD's Temple, leprosy* suddenly broke out on his forehead. 20When Azariah the high priest and all the other priests saw the leprosy, they rushed him out. And the king himself was eager to get out because the LORD had struck him. 21So King Uzziah had leprosy

25:23 Hebrew *400 cubits* [180 meters].   25:28 As in some Hebrew manuscripts and other ancient versions (see also 2 Kgs 14:20); most Hebrew manuscripts read *the city of Judah.*   26:2 As in Greek version (see also 2 Kgs 14:22; 16:6); Hebrew reads *Eloth,* a variant spelling of Elath.   26:5 As in Syriac and Greek versions; Hebrew reads *who instructed him in divine visions.*   26:7 As in Greek version; Hebrew reads *Gur-baal.*   26:8 As in Greek version; Hebrew reads *Ammonites.* Compare 26:7.   26:10 Hebrew *the Shephelah.*   26:15 Or *to shoot arrows and hurl large stones.*   26:19 Or *a contagious skin disease.* The Hebrew word used here and throughout this passage can describe various skin diseases.

until the day he died. He lived in isolation in a separate house, for he was excluded from the Temple of the Lord. His son Jotham was put in charge of the royal palace, and he governed the people of the land.

²²The rest of the events of Uzziah's reign, from beginning to end, are recorded by the prophet Isaiah son of Amoz. ²³When Uzziah died, he was buried with his ancestors; his grave was in a nearby burial field belonging to the kings, for the people said, "He had leprosy." And his son Jotham became the next king.

Jotham Rules in Judah

27 Jotham was twenty-five years old when he became king, and he reigned in Jerusalem sixteen years. His mother was Jerusha, the daughter of Zadok.

²Jotham did what was pleasing in the Lord's sight. He did everything his father, Uzziah, had done, except that Jotham did not sin by entering the Temple of the Lord. But the people continued in their corrupt ways.

³Jotham rebuilt the upper gate of the Temple of the Lord. He also did extensive rebuilding on the wall at the hill of Ophel. ⁴He built towns in the hill country of Judah and constructed fortresses and towers in the wooded areas. ⁵Jotham went to war against the Ammonites and conquered them. Over the next three years he received from them an annual tribute of 7,500 pounds* of silver, 50,000 bushels of wheat, and 50,000 bushels of barley.*

⁶King Jotham became powerful because he was careful to live in obedience to the Lord his God.

⁷The rest of the events of Jotham's reign, including all his wars and other activities, are recorded in *The Book of the Kings of Israel and Judah*. ⁸He was twenty-five years old when he became king, and he reigned in Jerusalem sixteen years. ⁹When Jotham died, he was buried in the City of David. And his son Ahaz became the next king.

Ahaz Rules in Judah

28 Ahaz was twenty years old when he became king, and he reigned in Jerusalem sixteen years. He did not do what was pleasing in the sight of the Lord, as his ancestor David had done. ²Instead, he followed the example of the kings of Israel. He cast metal images for the worship of Baal. ³He offered sacrifices in the valley of Ben-Hinnom, even sacrificing his own sons in the fire.* In this way, he followed the detestable practices of the pagan nations the Lord had driven from the land ahead of the Israelites. ⁴He offered sacrifices and burned incense at the pagan shrines and on the hills and under every green tree.

⁵Because of all this, the Lord his God allowed the king of Aram to defeat Ahaz and to exile large numbers of his people to Damascus. The armies of the king of Israel also defeated Ahaz and inflicted many casualties on his army. ⁶In a single day Pekah son of Remaliah, Israel's king, killed 120,000 of Judah's troops, all of them experienced warriors, because they had abandoned the Lord, the God of their ancestors. ⁷Then Zicri, a warrior from Ephraim, killed Maaseiah, the king's son; Azrikam, the king's palace commander; and Elkanah, the king's second-in-command. ⁸The armies of Israel captured 200,000 women and children from Judah and seized tremendous amounts of plunder, which they took back to Samaria.

⁹But a prophet of the Lord named Oded was there in Samaria when the army of Israel returned home. He went out to meet them and said, "The Lord, the God of your ancestors, was angry with Judah and let you defeat them. But you have gone too far, killing them without mercy, and all heaven is disturbed. ¹⁰And now you are planning to make slaves of these people from Judah and Jerusalem. What about your own sins against the Lord your God? ¹¹Listen to me and return these prisoners you have taken, for they are your own relatives. Watch out, because now the Lord's fierce anger has been turned against you!"

¹²Then some of the leaders of Israel*— Azariah son of Jehohanan, Berekiah son of Meshillemoth, Jehizkiah son of Shallum, and Amasa son of Hadlai—agreed with this and confronted the men returning from battle. ¹³"You must not bring the prisoners here!" they declared. "We cannot afford to add to our sins and guilt. Our guilt is already great, and the Lord's fierce anger is already turned against Israel."

¹⁴So the warriors released the prisoners and handed over the plunder in the sight of the leaders and all the people. ¹⁵Then the four men just mentioned by name came forward and distributed clothes from the plunder to the prisoners who were naked. They provided clothing and sandals to wear, gave them enough food and drink, and dressed their

27:5a Hebrew *100 talents* [3,400 kilograms]. 27:5b Hebrew *10,000 cors* [2,200 kiloliters] *of wheat, and 10,000 cors of barley.* 28:3 Or *even making his sons pass through the fire.* 28:12 Hebrew *Ephraim,* referring to the northern kingdom of Israel.

wounds with olive oil. They put those who were weak on donkeys and took all the prisoners back to their own people in Jericho, the city of palms. Then they returned to Samaria.

Ahaz Closes the Temple

¹⁶At that time King Ahaz of Judah asked the king of Assyria for help. ¹⁷The armies of Edom had again invaded Judah and taken captives. ¹⁸And the Philistines had raided towns located in the foothills of Judah* and in the Negev of Judah. They had already captured and occupied Beth-shemesh, Aijalon, Gederoth, Soco with its villages, Timnah with its villages, and Gimzo with its villages. ¹⁹The LORD was humbling Judah because of King Ahaz of Judah,* for he had encouraged his people to sin and had been utterly unfaithful to the LORD.

²⁰So when King Tiglath-pileser* of Assyria arrived, he attacked Ahaz instead of helping him. ²¹Ahaz took valuable items from the LORD's Temple, the royal palace, and from the homes of his officials and gave them to the king of Assyria as tribute. But this did not help him. ²²Even during this time of trouble, King Ahaz continued to reject the LORD. ²³He offered sacrifices to the gods of Damascus who had defeated him, for he said, "Since these gods helped the kings of Aram, they will help me, too, if I sacrifice to them." But instead, they led to his ruin and the ruin of all Judah.

²⁴The king took the various articles from the Temple of God and broke them into pieces. He shut the doors of the LORD's Temple so that no one could worship there, and he set up altars to pagan gods in every corner of Jerusalem. ²⁵He made pagan shrines in all the towns of Judah for offering sacrifices to other gods. In this way, he aroused the anger of the LORD, the God of his ancestors.

²⁶The rest of the events of Ahaz's reign and everything he did, from beginning to end, are recorded in *The Book of the Kings of Judah and Israel.* ²⁷When Ahaz died, he was buried in Jerusalem but not in the royal cemetery of the kings of Judah. Then his son Hezekiah became the next king.

Hezekiah Rules in Judah

29 Hezekiah was twenty-five years old when he became the king of Judah, and he reigned in Jerusalem twenty-nine years. His mother was Abijah, the daughter of Zechariah.

²He did what was pleasing in the LORD's sight, just as his ancestor David had done.

Hezekiah Reopens the Temple

³In the very first month of the first year of his reign, Hezekiah reopened the doors of the Temple of the LORD and repaired them. ⁴He summoned the priests and Levites to meet him at the courtyard east of the Temple. ⁵He said to them, "Listen to me, you Levites! Purify yourselves, and purify the Temple of the LORD, the God of your ancestors. Remove all the defiled things from the sanctuary. ⁶Our ancestors were unfaithful and did what was evil in the sight of the LORD our God. They abandoned the LORD and his dwelling place; they turned their backs on him. ⁷They also shut the doors to the Temple's entry room, and they snuffed out the lamps. They stopped burning incense and presenting burnt offerings at the sanctuary of the God of Israel.

⁸"That is why the LORD's anger has fallen upon Judah and Jerusalem. He has made them an object of dread, horror, and ridicule, as you can see with your own eyes. ⁹Because of this, our fathers have been killed in battle, and our sons and daughters and wives have been captured. ¹⁰But now I will make a covenant with the LORD, the God of Israel, so that his fierce anger will turn away from us. ¹¹My sons, do not neglect your duties any longer! The LORD has chosen you to stand in his presence, to minister to him, and to lead the people in worship and present offerings to him."

¹²Then these Levites got right to work:

From the clan of Kohath: Mahath son of Amasai and Joel son of Azariah.
From the clan of Merari: Kish son of Abdi and Azariah son of Jehallelel.
From the clan of Gershon: Joah son of Zimmah and Eden son of Joah.
¹³ From the family of Elizaphan: Shimri and Jeiel.
From the family of Asaph: Zechariah and Mattaniah.
¹⁴ From the family of Heman: Jehiel and Shimei.
From the family of Jeduthun: Shemaiah and Uzziel.

¹⁵These men called together their fellow Levites, and they all purified themselves. Then

they began to cleanse the Temple of the Lord, just as the king had commanded. They were careful to follow all the Lord's instructions in their work. ¹⁶The priests went into the sanctuary of the Temple of the Lord to cleanse it, and they took out to the Temple courtyard all the defiled things they found. From there the Levites carted it all out to the Kidron Valley.

¹⁷They began the work in early spring, on the first day of the new year,* and in eight days they had reached the entry room of the Lord's Temple. Then they purified the Temple of the Lord itself, which took another eight days. So the entire task was completed in sixteen days.

The Temple Rededication

¹⁸Then the Levites went to King Hezekiah and gave him this report: "We have cleansed the entire Temple of the Lord, the altar of burnt offering with all its utensils, and the table of the Bread of the Presence with all its utensils. ¹⁹We have also recovered all the items discarded by King Ahaz when he was unfaithful and closed the Temple. They are now in front of the altar of the Lord, purified and ready for use."

²⁰Early the next morning King Hezekiah gathered the city officials and went to the Temple of the Lord. ²¹They brought seven bulls, seven rams, and seven male lambs as a burnt offering, together with seven male goats as a sin offering for the kingdom, for the Temple, and for Judah. The king commanded the priests, who were descendants of Aaron, to sacrifice the animals on the altar of the Lord. ²²So they killed the bulls, and the priests took the blood and sprinkled it on the altar. Next they killed the rams and sprinkled their blood on the altar. And finally, they did the same with the male lambs. ²³The male goats for the sin offering were then brought before the king and the assembly of people, who laid their hands on them. ²⁴The priests then killed the goats as a sin offering and sprinkled their blood on the altar to make atonement for the sins of all Israel. The king had specifically commanded that this burnt offering and sin offering should be made for all Israel.

²⁵King Hezekiah then stationed the Levites at the Temple of the Lord with cymbals, lyres, and harps. He obeyed all the commands that the Lord had given to King David through Gad, the king's seer, and the prophet Nathan. ²⁶The Levites then took their positions around the Temple with the instruments of David, and the priests took their positions with the trumpets.

²⁷Then Hezekiah ordered that the burnt offering be placed on the altar. As the burnt offering was presented, songs of praise to the Lord were begun, accompanied by the trumpets and other instruments of David, the former king of Israel. ²⁸The entire assembly worshiped the Lord as the singers sang and the trumpets blew, until all the burnt offerings were finished. ²⁹Then the king and everyone with him bowed down in worship. ³⁰King Hezekiah and the officials ordered the Levites to praise the Lord with the psalms written by David and by Asaph the seer. So they offered joyous praise and bowed down in worship.

³¹Then Hezekiah declared, "Now that you have consecrated yourselves to the Lord, bring your sacrifices and thanksgiving offerings to the Temple of the Lord." So the people brought their sacrifices and thanksgiving offerings, and all whose hearts were willing brought burnt offerings, too. ³²The people brought to the Lord 70 bulls, 100 rams, and 200 male lambs for burnt offerings. ³³They also brought 600 cattle and 3,000 sheep and goats as sacred offerings.

³⁴But there were too few priests to prepare all the burnt offerings. So their relatives the Levites helped them until the work was finished and more priests had been purified, for the Levites had been more conscientious about purifying themselves than the priests had been. ³⁵There was an abundance of burnt offerings, along with the usual liquid offerings, and a great deal of fat from the many peace offerings.

So the Temple of the Lord was restored to service. ³⁶And Hezekiah and all the people rejoiced because of what God had done for the people, for everything had been accomplished so quickly.

Preparations for Passover

30 King Hezekiah now sent word to all Israel and Judah, and he wrote letters of invitation to the people of Ephraim and Manasseh. He asked everyone to come to the Temple of the Lord at Jerusalem to celebrate the Passover of the Lord, the God of Israel. ²The king, his officials, and all the community of Jerusalem decided to celebrate Passover a month later than usual.* ³They were unable to

---

29:17 Hebrew *on the first day of the first month.* This day in the ancient Hebrew lunar calendar occurred in March or early April, 715 B.C.   30:2 Hebrew *in the second month.* Passover was normally observed in the first month (of the ancient Hebrew lunar calendar).

celebrate it at the prescribed time because not enough priests could be purified by then, and the people had not yet assembled at Jerusalem.

⁴This plan for keeping the Passover seemed right to the king and all the people. ⁵So they sent a proclamation throughout all Israel, from Beersheba in the south to Dan in the north, inviting everyone to come to Jerusalem to celebrate the Passover of the LORD, the God of Israel. The people had not been celebrating it in great numbers as required in the Law.

⁶At the king's command, runners were sent throughout Israel and Judah. They carried letters that said:

"O people of Israel, return to the LORD, the God of Abraham, Isaac, and Israel,* so that he will return to the few of us who have survived the conquest of the Assyrian kings. ⁷Do not be like your ancestors and relatives who abandoned the LORD, the God of their ancestors, and became an object of derision, as you yourselves can see. ⁸Do not be stubborn, as they were, but submit yourselves to the LORD. Come to his Temple, which he has set apart as holy forever. Worship the LORD your God so that his fierce anger will turn away from you.

⁹"For if you return to the LORD, your relatives and your children will be treated mercifully by their captors, and they will be able to return to this land. For the LORD your God is gracious and merciful. If you return to him, he will not continue to turn his face from you."

Celebration of Passover

¹⁰The runners went from town to town throughout Ephraim and Manasseh and as far as the territory of Zebulun. But most of the people just laughed at the runners and made fun of them. ¹¹However, some people from Asher, Manasseh, and Zebulun humbled themselves and went to Jerusalem.

¹²At the same time, God's hand was on the people in the land of Judah, giving them all one heart to obey the orders of the king and his officials, who were following the word of the LORD. ¹³So a huge crowd assembled at Jerusalem in midspring* to celebrate the Festival of Unleavened Bread. ¹⁴They set to work and removed the pagan altars from Jerusalem. They

took away all the incense altars and threw them into the Kidron Valley.

¹⁵On the fourteenth day of the second month, one month later than usual,* the people slaughtered the Passover lamb. This shamed the priests and Levites, so they purified themselves and brought burnt offerings to the Temple of the LORD. ¹⁶Then they took their places at the Temple as prescribed in the Law of Moses, the man of God. The Levites brought the sacrificial blood to the priests, who then sprinkled it on the altar.

¹⁷Since many of the people had not purified themselves, the Levites had to slaughter their Passover lamb for them, to set them apart for the LORD. ¹⁸Most of those who came from Ephraim, Manasseh, Issachar, and Zebulun had not purified themselves. But King Hezekiah prayed for them, and they were allowed to eat the Passover meal anyway, even though this was contrary to the requirements of the Law. For Hezekiah said, "May the LORD, who is good, pardon those ¹⁹who decide to follow the LORD, the God of their ancestors, even though they are not properly cleansed for the ceremony." ²⁰And the LORD listened to Hezekiah's prayer and healed the people.

²¹So the people of Israel who were present in Jerusalem joyously celebrated the Festival of Unleavened Bread for seven days. Each day the Levites and priests sang to the LORD, accompanied by loud instruments.* ²²Hezekiah encouraged all the Levites regarding the skill they displayed as they served the LORD. The celebration continued for seven days. Peace offerings were sacrificed, and the people gave thanks to the LORD, the God of their ancestors.

²³The entire assembly then decided to continue the festival another seven days, so they celebrated joyfully for another week. ²⁴King Hezekiah gave the people 1,000 bulls and 7,000 sheep and goats for offerings, and the officials donated 1,000 bulls and 10,000 sheep and goats. Meanwhile, many more priests purified themselves.

²⁵The entire assembly of Judah rejoiced, including the priests, the Levites, all who came from the land of Israel, the foreigners who came to the festival, and all those who lived in Judah. ²⁶There was great joy in the city, for Jerusalem had not seen a celebration like this one since the days of Solomon, King David's son. ²⁷Then the priests and Levites stood and

---

30:6 *Israel* is the name that God gave to Jacob.   30:13 Hebrew *in the second month.* The second month of the ancient Hebrew lunar calendar usually occurs within the months of April and May.   30:15 Hebrew *On the fourteenth day of the second month.* Passover normally began on the fourteenth day of the first month (see Lev 23:5).   30:21 Or *sang to the LORD with all their strength.*

blessed the people, and God heard their prayer from his holy dwelling in heaven.

Hezekiah's Religious Reforms

31 When the festival ended, the Israelites who attended went to all the towns of Judah, Benjamin, Ephraim, and Manasseh, and they smashed all the sacred pillars, cut down the Asherah poles, and removed the pagan shrines and altars. After this, the Israelites returned to their own towns and homes.

²Hezekiah then organized the priests and Levites into divisions to offer the burnt offerings and peace offerings, and to worship and give thanks and praise to the LORD at the gates of the Temple. ³The king also made a personal contribution of animals for the daily morning and evening burnt offerings, the weekly Sabbath festivals, the monthly new moon festivals, and the annual festivals as prescribed in the Law of the LORD. ⁴In addition, he required the people in Jerusalem to bring a portion of their goods to the priests and Levites, so they could devote themselves fully to the Law of the LORD.

⁵When the people of Israel heard these requirements, they responded generously by bringing the first share of their grain, new wine, olive oil, honey, and all the produce of their fields. They brought a large quantity—a tithe of all they produced. ⁶The people who had moved to Judah from Israel, and the people of Judah themselves, brought in the tithes of their cattle, sheep, and goats and a tithe of the things that had been dedicated to the LORD their God, and they piled them up in great heaps. ⁷They began piling them up in late spring, and the heaps continued to grow until early autumn.* ⁸When Hezekiah and his officials came and saw these huge piles, they thanked the LORD and his people Israel!

⁹"Where did all this come from?" Hezekiah asked the priests and Levites.

¹⁰And Azariah the high priest, from the family of Zadok, replied, "Since the people began bringing their gifts to the LORD's Temple, we have had enough to eat and plenty to spare. The LORD has blessed his people, and all this is left over."

¹¹Hezekiah ordered that storerooms be prepared in the Temple of the LORD. When this was done, ¹²the people faithfully brought all the gifts, tithes, and other items dedicated for use in the Temple. Conaniah the Levite was put in charge, assisted by his brother Shimei.

¹³The supervisors under them were Jehiel, Azaziah, Nahath, Asahel, Jerimoth, Jozabad, Eliel, Ismakiah, Mahath, and Benaiah. These appointments were made by King Hezekiah and Azariah, the chief official in the Temple of God.

¹⁴Kore son of Imnah the Levite, who was the gatekeeper at the East Gate, was put in charge of distributing the voluntary offerings given to God, the gifts, and the things that had been dedicated to the LORD. ¹⁵His faithful assistants were Eden, Miniamin, Jeshua, Shemaiah, Amariah, and Shecaniah. They distributed the gifts among the families of priests in their towns by their divisions, dividing the gifts fairly among old and young alike. ¹⁶They distributed the gifts to all males three years old or older, regardless of their place in the genealogical records. The distribution went to all who would come to the LORD's Temple to perform their daily duties according to their divisions. ¹⁷They distributed gifts to the priests who were listed by their families in the genealogical records, and to the Levites twenty years old or older who were listed according to their jobs and their divisions. ¹⁸Food allotments were also given to the families of all those listed in the genealogical records, including their little babies, wives, sons, and daughters. For they had all been faithful in purifying themselves.

¹⁹As for the priests, the descendants of Aaron, who were living in the open villages around the towns, men were appointed by name to distribute portions to every male among the priests and to all the Levites listed in the genealogical records.

²⁰In this way, King Hezekiah handled the distribution throughout all Judah, doing what was pleasing and good in the sight of the LORD his God. ²¹In all that he did in the service of the Temple of God and in his efforts to follow God's laws and commands, Hezekiah sought his God wholeheartedly. As a result, he was very successful.

Assyria Invades Judah

32 After Hezekiah had faithfully carried out this work, King Sennacherib of Assyria invaded Judah. He laid siege to the fortified towns, giving orders for his army to break through their walls. ²When Hezekiah realized that Sennacherib also intended to attack Jerusalem, ³he consulted with his officials and military advisers, and they decided to stop the

---

31:7 Hebrew *in the third month . . . until the seventh month.* The third month of the ancient Hebrew lunar calendar usually occurs within the months of May and June; the seventh month usually occurs within September and October.

flow of the springs outside the city. ⁴They organized a huge work crew to stop the flow of the springs, cutting off the brook that ran through the fields. For they said, "Why should the kings of Assyria come here and find plenty of water?" ⁵Then Hezekiah worked hard at repairing all the broken sections of the wall, erecting towers, and constructing a second wall outside the first. He also reinforced the supporting terraces* in the City of David and manufactured large numbers of weapons and shields. ⁶He appointed military officers over the people and assembled them before him in the square at the city gate. Then Hezekiah encouraged them by saying: ⁷"Be strong and courageous! Don't be afraid or discouraged because of the king of Assyria or his mighty army, for there is a power far greater on our side! ⁸He may have a great army, but they are merely men. We have the LORD our God to help us and to fight our battles for us!" Hezekiah's words greatly encouraged the people.

Sennacherib Threatens Jerusalem

⁹While King Sennacherib of Assyria was still besieging the town of Lachish, he sent his officers to Jerusalem with this message for Hezekiah and all the people in the city:

¹⁰"This is what King Sennacherib of Assyria says: What are you trusting in that makes you think you can survive my siege of Jerusalem? ¹¹Hezekiah has said, 'The LORD our God will rescue us from the king of Assyria.' Surely Hezekiah is misleading you, sentencing you to death by famine and thirst! ¹²Don't you realize that Hezekiah is the very person who destroyed all the LORD's shrines and altars? He commanded Judah and Jerusalem to worship only at the altar at the Temple and to offer sacrifices on it alone.

¹³"Surely you must realize what I and the other kings of Assyria before me have done to all the people of the earth! Were any of the gods of those nations able to rescue their people from my power? ¹⁴Which of their gods was able to rescue its people from the destructive power of my predecessors? What makes you think your God can rescue you from me? ¹⁵Don't let Hezekiah deceive you! Don't let him fool you like this! I say it again—no god of any nation or kingdom has ever yet been able to rescue his people from me or my ancestors. How much less will your God rescue you from my power!"

¹⁶And Sennacherib's officers further mocked the LORD God and his servant Hezekiah, heaping insult upon insult. ¹⁷The king also sent letters scorning the LORD, the God of Israel. He wrote, "Just as the gods of all the other nations failed to rescue their people from my power, so the God of Hezekiah will also fail." ¹⁸The Assyrian officials who brought the letters shouted this in Hebrew* to the people gathered on the walls of the city, trying to terrify them so it would be easier to capture the city. ¹⁹These officers talked about the God of Jerusalem as though he were one of the pagan gods, made by human hands.

²⁰Then King Hezekiah and the prophet Isaiah son of Amoz cried out in prayer to God in heaven. ²¹And the LORD sent an angel who destroyed the Assyrian army with all its commanders and officers. So Sennacherib was forced to return home in disgrace to his own land. And when he entered the temple of his god, some of his own sons killed him there with a sword.

²²That is how the LORD rescued Hezekiah and the people of Jerusalem from King Sennacherib of Assyria and from all the others who threatened them. So there was peace throughout the land. ²³From then on King Hezekiah became highly respected among all the surrounding nations, and many gifts for the LORD arrived at Jerusalem, with valuable presents for King Hezekiah, too.

Hezekiah's Sickness and Recovery

²⁴About that time Hezekiah became deathly ill. He prayed to the LORD, who healed him and gave him a miraculous sign. ²⁵But Hezekiah did not respond appropriately to the kindness shown him, and he became proud. So the LORD's anger came against him and against Judah and Jerusalem. ²⁶Then Hezekiah humbled himself and repented of his pride, as did the people of Jerusalem. So the LORD's anger did not fall on them during Hezekiah's lifetime. ²⁷Hezekiah was very wealthy and highly honored. He built special treasury buildings for his silver, gold, precious stones, and spices, and for his shields and other valuable items. ²⁸He also constructed many storehouses for his grain, new wine, and olive oil; and he made many stalls for his cattle and pens for his flocks of sheep and goats. ²⁹He built many towns and

32:5 Hebrew *the millo.* The meaning of the Hebrew is uncertain.   32:18 Hebrew *in the dialect of Judah.*

acquired vast flocks and herds, for God had given him great wealth. [30]He blocked up the upper spring of Gihon and brought the water down through a tunnel to the west side of the City of David. And so he succeeded in everything he did.

[31]However, when ambassadors arrived from Babylon to ask about the remarkable events that had taken place in the land, God withdrew from Hezekiah in order to test him and to see what was really in his heart.

Summary of Hezekiah's Reign

[32]The rest of the events in Hezekiah's reign and his acts of devotion are recorded in *The Vision of the Prophet Isaiah Son of Amoz,* which is included in *The Book of the Kings of Judah and Israel.* [33]When Hezekiah died, he was buried in the upper area of the royal cemetery, and all Judah and Jerusalem honored him at his death. And his son Manasseh became the next king.

Manasseh Rules in Judah

33 Manasseh was twelve years old when he became king, and he reigned in Jerusalem fifty-five years. [2]He did what was evil in the LORD's sight, following the detestable practices of the pagan nations that the LORD had driven from the land ahead of the Israelites. [3]He rebuilt the pagan shrines his father, Hezekiah, had broken down. He constructed altars for the images of Baal and set up Asherah poles. He also bowed before all the powers of the heavens and worshiped them.

[4]He built pagan altars in the Temple of the LORD, the place where the LORD had said, "My name will remain in Jerusalem forever." [5]He built these altars for all the powers of the heavens in both courtyards of the LORD's Temple. [6]Manasseh also sacrificed his own sons in the fire* in the valley of Ben-Hinnom. He practiced sorcery, divination, and witchcraft, and he consulted with mediums and psychics. He did much that was evil in the LORD's sight, arousing his anger.

[7]Manasseh even took a carved idol he had made and set it up in God's Temple, the very place where God had told David and his son Solomon: "My name will be honored forever in this Temple and in Jerusalem—the city I have chosen from among all the tribes of Israel. [8]If the Israelites will be careful to obey my commands—all the laws, decrees, and regulations given through Moses—I will not send them into exile from this land that I set

aside for your ancestors." [9]But Manasseh led the people of Judah and Jerusalem to do even more evil than the pagan nations that the LORD had destroyed when the people of Israel entered the land.

[10]The LORD spoke to Manasseh and his people, but they ignored all his warnings. [11]So the LORD sent the commanders of the Assyrian armies, and they took Manasseh prisoner. They put a ring through his nose, bound him in bronze chains, and led him away to Babylon. [12]But while in deep distress, Manasseh sought the LORD his God and sincerely humbled himself before the God of his ancestors. [13]And when he prayed, the LORD listened to him and was moved by his request. So the LORD brought Manasseh back to Jerusalem and to his kingdom. Then Manasseh finally realized that the LORD alone is God!

[14]After this Manasseh rebuilt the outer wall of the City of David, from west of the Gihon Spring in the Kidron Valley to the Fish Gate, and continuing around the hill of Ophel. He built the wall very high. And he stationed his military officers in all of the fortified towns of Judah. [15]Manasseh also removed the foreign gods and the idol from the LORD's Temple. He tore down all the altars he had built on the hill where the Temple stood and all the altars that were in Jerusalem, and he dumped them outside the city. [16]Then he restored the altar of the LORD and sacrificed peace offerings and thanksgiving offerings on it. He also encouraged the people of Judah to worship the LORD, the God of Israel. [17]However, the people still sacrificed at the pagan shrines, though only to the LORD their God.

[18]The rest of the events of Manasseh's reign, his prayer to God, and the words the seers spoke to him in the name of the LORD, the God of Israel, are recorded in *The Book of the Kings of Israel.* [19]Manasseh's prayer, the account of the way God answered him, and an account of all his sins and unfaithfulness are recorded in *The Record of the Seers.** It includes a list of the locations where he built pagan shrines and set up Asherah poles and idols before he humbled himself and repented. [20]When Manasseh died, he was buried in his palace. Then his son Amon became the next king.

Amon Rules in Judah

[21]Amon was twenty-two years old when he became king, and he reigned in Jerusalem two years. [22]He did what was evil in the LORD's

33:6 Or *also made his sons pass through the fire.*   33:19 Or *The Record of Hozai.*

sight, just as his father, Manasseh, had done. He worshiped and sacrificed to all the idols his father had made. ²³But unlike his father, he did not humble himself before the LORD. Instead, Amon sinned even more.

²⁴Then Amon's own officials conspired against him and assassinated him in his palace. ²⁵But the people of the land killed all those who had conspired against King Amon, and they made his son Josiah the next king.

Josiah Rules in Judah

34 Josiah was eight years old when he became king, and he reigned in Jerusalem thirty-one years. ²He did what was pleasing in the LORD's sight and followed the example of his ancestor David. He did not turn away from doing what was right.

³During the eighth year of his reign, while he was still young, Josiah began to seek the God of his ancestor David. Then in the twelfth year he began to purify Judah and Jerusalem, destroying all the pagan shrines, the Asherah poles, and the carved idols and cast images. ⁴He ordered that the altars of Baal be demolished and that the incense altars which stood above them be broken down. He also made sure that the Asherah poles, the carved idols, and the cast images were smashed and scattered over the graves of those who had sacrificed to them. ⁵He burned the bones of the pagan priests on their own altars, and so he purified Judah and Jerusalem.

⁶He did the same thing in the towns of Manasseh, Ephraim, and Simeon, even as far as Naphtali, and in the regions* all around them. ⁷He destroyed the pagan altars and the Asherah poles, and he crushed the idols into dust. He cut down all the incense altars throughout the land of Israel. Finally, he returned to Jerusalem.

⁸In the eighteenth year of his reign, after he had purified the land and the Temple, Josiah appointed Shaphan son of Azaliah, Maaseiah the governor of Jerusalem, and Joah son of Joahaz, the royal historian, to repair the Temple of the LORD his God. ⁹They gave Hilkiah the high priest the money that had been collected by the Levites who served as gatekeepers at the Temple of God. The gifts were brought by people from Manasseh, Ephraim, and from all the remnant of Israel, as well as from all Judah, Benjamin, and the people of Jerusalem. ¹⁰He entrusted the money to the men

assigned to supervise the restoration of the LORD's Temple. Then they paid the workers who did the repairs and renovation of the Temple. ¹¹They hired carpenters and builders, who purchased finished stone for the walls and timber for the rafters and beams. They restored what earlier kings of Judah had allowed to fall into ruin.

¹²The workers served faithfully under the leadership of Jahath and Obadiah, Levites of the Merarite clan, and Zechariah and Meshullam, Levites of the Kohathite clan. Other Levites, all of whom were skilled musicians, ¹³were put in charge of the laborers of the various trades. Still others assisted as secretaries, officials, and gatekeepers.

Hilkiah Discovers God's Law

¹⁴While they were bringing out the money collected at the LORD's Temple, Hilkiah the priest found the Book of the Law of the LORD that was written by Moses. ¹⁵Hilkiah said to Shaphan the court secretary, "I have found the Book of the Law in the LORD's Temple!" Then Hilkiah gave the scroll to Shaphan.

¹⁶Shaphan took the scroll to the king and reported, "Your officials are doing everything they were assigned to do. ¹⁷The money that was collected at the Temple of the LORD has been turned over to the supervisors and workmen." ¹⁸Shaphan also told the king, "Hilkiah the priest has given me a scroll." So Shaphan read it to the king.

¹⁹When the king heard what was written in the Law, he tore his clothes in despair. ²⁰Then he gave these orders to Hilkiah, Ahikam son of Shaphan, Acbor son of Micaiah,* Shaphan the court secretary, and Asaiah the king's personal adviser: ²¹"Go to the Temple and speak to the LORD for me and for all the remnant of Israel and Judah. Inquire about the words written in the scroll that has been found. For the LORD's great anger has been poured out on us because our ancestors have not obeyed the word of the LORD. We have not been doing everything this scroll says we must do."

²²So Hilkiah and the other men went to the New Quarter* of Jerusalem to consult with the prophet Huldah. She was the wife of Shallum son of Tikvah, son of Harhas,* the keeper of the Temple wardrobe.

²³She said to them, "The LORD, the God of Israel, has spoken! Go back and tell the man

---

34:6 As in Syriac version; Hebrew reads *in their temples,* or *in their ruins.* The meaning of the Hebrew is uncertain. 34:20 As in parallel text at 2 Kgs 22:12; Hebrew reads *Abdon son of Micah.* 34:22a Or *the Second Quarter,* a newer section of Jerusalem. Hebrew reads *the Mishneh.* 34:22b As in parallel text at 2 Kgs 22:14; Hebrew reads *son of Tokhath, son of Hasrah.*

who sent you, ²⁴"This is what the LORD says: I am going to bring disaster on this city* and its people. All the curses written in the scroll that was read to the king of Judah will come true. ²⁵For my people have abandoned me and offered sacrifices to pagan gods, and I am very angry with them for everything they have done. My anger will be poured out on this place, and it will not be quenched.'

²⁶"But go to the king of Judah who sent you to seek the LORD and tell him: 'This is what the LORD, the God of Israel, says concerning the message you have just heard: ²⁷You were sorry and humbled yourself before God when you heard his words against this city and its people. You humbled yourself and tore your clothing in despair and wept before me in repentance. And I have indeed heard you, says the LORD. ²⁸So I will not send the promised disaster until after you have died and been buried in peace. You yourself will not see the disaster I am going to bring on this city and its people.'"

So they took her message back to the king.

Josiah's Religious Reforms

²⁹Then the king summoned all the elders of Judah and Jerusalem. ³⁰And the king went up to the Temple of the LORD with all the people of Judah and Jerusalem, along with the priests and the Levites—all the people from the greatest to the least. There the king read to them the entire Book of the Covenant that had been found in the LORD's Temple. ³¹The king took his place of authority beside the pillar and renewed the covenant in the LORD's presence. He pledged to obey the LORD by keeping all his commands, laws, and decrees with all his heart and soul. He promised to obey all the terms of the covenant that were written in the scroll. ³²And he required everyone in Jerusalem and the people of Benjamin to make a similar pledge. The people of Jerusalem did so, renewing their covenant with God, the God of their ancestors.

³³So Josiah removed all detestable idols from the entire land of Israel and required everyone to worship the LORD their God. And throughout the rest of his lifetime, they did not turn away from the LORD, the God of their ancestors.

Josiah Celebrates Passover

35 Then Josiah announced that the Passover of the LORD would be celebrated in Jerusalem, and so the Passover lamb was slaughtered on the fourteenth day of the first month.* ²Josiah also assigned the priests to their duties and encouraged them in their work at the Temple of the LORD. ³He issued this order to the Levites, who were to teach all Israel and who had been set apart to serve the LORD: "Put the holy Ark in the Temple that was built by Solomon son of David, the king of Israel. You no longer need to carry it back and forth on your shoulders. Now spend your time serving the LORD your God and his people Israel. ⁴Report for duty according to the family divisions of your ancestors, following the directions of King David of Israel and the directions of his son Solomon.

⁵"Then stand in the sanctuary at the place appointed for your family division and help the families assigned to you as they bring their offerings to the Temple. ⁶Slaughter the Passover lambs, purify yourselves, and prepare to help those who come. Follow all the directions that the LORD gave through Moses."

⁷Then Josiah provided 30,000 lambs and young goats for the people's Passover offerings, along with 3,000 cattle, all from the king's own flocks and herds. ⁸The king's officials also made willing contributions to the people, priests, and Levites. Hilkiah, Zechariah, and Jehiel, the administrators of God's Temple, gave the priests 2,600 lambs and young goats and 300 cattle as Passover offerings. ⁹The Levite leaders—Conaniah and his brothers Shemaiah and Nethanel, as well as Hashabiah, Jeiel, and Jozabad—gave 5,000 lambs and young goats and 500 cattle to the Levites for their Passover offerings.

¹⁰When everything was ready for the Passover celebration, the priests and the Levites took their places, organized by their divisions, as the king had commanded. ¹¹The Levites then slaughtered the Passover lambs and presented the blood to the priests, who sprinkled the blood on the altar while the Levites prepared the animals. ¹²They divided the burnt offerings among the people by their family groups, so they could offer them to the LORD as prescribed in the Book of Moses. They did the same with the cattle. ¹³Then they roasted the Passover lambs as prescribed; and they boiled the holy offerings in pots, kettles, and pans, and brought them out quickly so the people could eat them.

¹⁴Afterward the Levites prepared Passover offerings for themselves and for the priests—the descendants of Aaron—because the priests

34:24 Hebrew *this place;* also in 34:27, 28.   35:1 This day in the ancient Hebrew lunar calendar was April 5, 622 B.C.

had been busy from morning till night offering the burnt offerings and the fat portions. The Levites took responsibility for all these preparations.

¹⁵The musicians, descendants of Asaph, were in their assigned places, following the commands that had been given by David, Asaph, Heman, and Jeduthun, the king's seer. The gatekeepers guarded the gates and did not need to leave their posts of duty, for their Passover offerings were prepared for them by their fellow Levites.

¹⁶The entire ceremony for the LORD's Passover was completed that day. All the burnt offerings were sacrificed on the altar of the LORD, as King Josiah had commanded. ¹⁷All the Israelites present in Jerusalem celebrated Passover and the Festival of Unleavened Bread for seven days. ¹⁸Never since the time of the prophet Samuel had there been such a Passover. None of the kings of Israel had ever kept a Passover as Josiah did, involving all the priests and Levites, all the people of Jerusalem, and people from all over Judah and Israel. ¹⁹This Passover was celebrated in the eighteenth year of Josiah's reign.

Josiah Dies in Battle

²⁰After Josiah had finished restoring the Temple, King Neco of Egypt led his army up from Egypt to do battle at Carchemish on the Euphrates River, and Josiah and his army marched out to fight him.* ²¹But King Neco sent messengers to Josiah with this message:

"What do you want with me, king of Judah? I have no quarrel with you today! I am on my way to fight another nation, and God has told me to hurry! Do not interfere with God, who is with me, or he will destroy you."

²²But Josiah refused to listen to Neco, to whom God had indeed spoken, and he would not turn back. Instead, he disguised himself and led his army into battle on the plain of Megiddo. ²³But the enemy archers hit King Josiah with their arrows and wounded him. He cried out to his men, "Take me from the battle, for I am badly wounded!"

²⁴So they lifted Josiah out of his chariot and placed him in another chariot. Then they brought him back to Jerusalem, where he died. He was buried there in the royal cemetery. And all Judah and Jerusalem mourned for him. ²⁵The prophet Jeremiah composed funeral songs for Josiah, and to this day choirs still sing these sad songs about his death. These songs of sorrow have become a tradition and are recorded in *The Book of Laments*.

²⁶The rest of the events of Josiah's reign and his acts of devotion (carried out according to what was written in the Law of the LORD), ²⁷from beginning to end—all are recorded in *The Book of the Kings of Israel and Judah*.

Jehoahaz Rules in Judah

36 Then the people of the land took Josiah's son Jehoahaz and made him the next king in Jerusalem.

²Jehoahaz* was twenty-three years old when he became king, and he reigned in Jerusalem three months.

³Then he was deposed by the king of Egypt, who demanded that Judah pay 7,500 pounds of silver and 75 pounds of gold* as tribute.

Jehoiakim Rules in Judah

⁴The king of Egypt then installed Eliakim, the brother of Jehoahaz, as the next king of Judah and Jerusalem, and he changed Eliakim's name to Jehoiakim. Then Neco took Jehoahaz to Egypt as a prisoner.

⁵Jehoiakim was twenty-five years old when he became king, and he reigned in Jerusalem eleven years. He did what was evil in the sight of the LORD his God.

⁶Then King Nebuchadnezzar of Babylon came to Jerusalem and captured it, and he bound Jehoiakim in bronze chains and led him away to Babylon. ⁷Nebuchadnezzar also took some of the treasures from the Temple of the LORD, and he placed them in his palace* in Babylon.

⁸The rest of the events in Jehoiakim's reign, including all the evil things he did and everything found against him, are recorded in *The Book of the Kings of Israel and Judah*. Then his son Jehoiachin became the next king.

Jehoiachin Rules in Judah

⁹Jehoiachin was eighteen* years old when he became king, and he reigned in Jerusalem three months and ten days. Jehoiachin did what was evil in the LORD's sight.

35:20 Or *Josiah went out to meet him.*   36:2 Hebrew *Joahaz*, a variant spelling of Jehoahaz; also in 36:4.   36:3 Hebrew *100 talents* [3,400 kilograms] *of silver and 1 talent* [34 kilograms] *of gold.*   36:7 Or *temple.*   36:9 As in one Hebrew manuscript, some Greek manuscripts, and Syriac version (see also 2 Kgs 24:8); most Hebrew manuscripts read *eight.*

¹⁰In the spring of the year* King Nebuchadnezzar took Jehoiachin to Babylon. Many treasures from the Temple of the LORD were also taken to Babylon at that time. And Nebuchadnezzar installed Jehoiachin's uncle,* Zedekiah, as the next king in Judah and Jerusalem.

Zedekiah Rules in Judah

¹¹Zedekiah was twenty-one years old when he became king, and he reigned in Jerusalem eleven years. ¹²But Zedekiah did what was evil in the sight of the LORD his God, and he refused to humble himself when the prophet Jeremiah spoke to him directly from the LORD. ¹³He also rebelled against King Nebuchadnezzar, even though he had taken an oath of loyalty in God's name. Zedekiah was a hard and stubborn man, refusing to turn to the LORD, the God of Israel.

¹⁴Likewise, all the leaders of the priests and the people became more and more unfaithful. They followed all the pagan practices of the surrounding nations, desecrating the Temple of the LORD that had been consecrated in Jerusalem.

¹⁵The LORD, the God of their ancestors, repeatedly sent his prophets to warn them, for he had compassion on his people and his Temple. ¹⁶But the people mocked these messengers of God and despised their words. They scoffed at the prophets until the LORD's anger could no longer be restrained and nothing could be done.

The Fall of Jerusalem

¹⁷So the LORD brought the king of Babylon against them. The Babylonians* killed Judah's young men, even chasing after them into the Temple. They had no pity on the people, killing both young men and young women, the old and the infirm. God handed all of them over to Nebuchadnezzar. ¹⁸The king took home to Babylon all the articles, large and small, used in the Temple of God, and the treasures from both the LORD's Temple and from the palace of the king and his officials. ¹⁹Then his army burned the Temple of God, tore down the walls of Jerusalem, burned all the palaces, and completely destroyed everything of value.* ²⁰The few who survived were taken as exiles to Babylon, and they became servants to the king and his sons until the kingdom of Persia came to power.

²¹So the message of the LORD spoken through Jeremiah was fulfilled. The land finally enjoyed its Sabbath rest, lying desolate until the seventy years were fulfilled, just as the prophet had said.

Cyrus Allows the Exiles to Return

²²In the first year of King Cyrus of Persia,* the LORD fulfilled the prophecy he had given through Jeremiah.* He stirred the heart of Cyrus to put this proclamation in writing and to send it throughout his kingdom:

²³"This is what King Cyrus of Persia says:
"The LORD, the God of heaven, has given me all the kingdoms of the earth. He has appointed me to build him a Temple at Jerusalem, which is in Judah. Any of you who are his people may go there for this task. And may the LORD your God be with you!"

36:10a Hebrew *At the turn of the year*. The first day of this year in the ancient Hebrew lunar calendar was April 13, 597 B.C.   36:10b As in parallel text at 2 Kgs 24:17; Hebrew reads *brother*, or *relative*.   36:17 Or *Chaldeans*.   36:19 Or *destroyed all the valuable articles from the Temple*.   36:22a The first year of Cyrus's reign over Babylon was 538 B.C.   36:22b See Jer 25:11-12; 29:10.

Ezra

MANY GREAT MEN AND WOMEN
never gain celebrity status. They do their
deeds in relative obscurity, yet their contributions profoundly impact the lives of
those who come after them. Ezra was
such a person. The book of Ezra details
the Israelites' return to the land of Palestine after their captivity in Babylon. The
book opens with the return of a large
group of exiles and the rebuilding of
the Temple under Zerubbabel. Halfway
through the book, we are introduced
to Ezra, a scribe schooled in the laws

- **Author:** Ezra, according to Jewish tradition
- **Date Written:** Around 430 BC, recording
events between 538 and 430 BC
- **Purpose:** To show God's faithfulness in
restoring his people to their land
- **Themes:** The return of the exiles, rebuilding
the Temple, faithfulness to the law of Moses
- **Outline**
1:1–2:70 The return of the first group of exiles
to Jerusalem
3:1-13 The rebuilding of the Temple begun
4:1-24 The work on the Temple halted
5:1–6:22 The completion and rededication
of the Temple
7:1–10:44 The ministry of Ezra

of Moses. The book records how Ezra dealt with the problems that arose, such
as marriages between Israelites and non-Israelites. After a great deal of struggle
regarding the rebuilding of the Temple, the project was finally completed and dedicated to the glory of God.

Cyrus Allows the Exiles to Return

1 In the first year of King Cyrus of Persia,* the
LORD fulfilled the prophecy he had given
through Jeremiah.* He stirred the heart of Cyrus to put this proclamation in writing and to
send it throughout his kingdom:

2"This is what King Cyrus of Persia says:
   "The LORD, the God of heaven, has
given me all the kingdoms of the earth.
He has appointed me to build him a
Temple at Jerusalem, which is in Judah.
3Any of you who are his people may go to
Jerusalem in Judah to rebuild this Temple
of the LORD, the God of Israel, who lives in
Jerusalem. And may your God be with you!
4Wherever this Jewish remnant is found,
let their neighbors contribute toward their
expenses by giving them silver and gold,
supplies for the journey, and livestock, as
well as a voluntary offering for the Temple
of God in Jerusalem."

5Then God stirred the hearts of the priests
and Levites and the leaders of the tribes of
Judah and Benjamin to go to Jerusalem to
rebuild the Temple of the LORD. 6And all their
neighbors assisted by giving them articles
of silver and gold, supplies for the journey,
and livestock. They gave them many valuable gifts in addition to all the voluntary offerings.

7King Cyrus himself brought out the
articles that King Nebuchadnezzar had taken
from the LORD's Temple in Jerusalem and had
placed in the temple of his own gods. 8Cyrus
directed Mithredath, the treasurer of Persia,
to count these items and present them to
Sheshbazzar, the leader of the exiles returning to Judah.* 9This is a list of the items that
were returned:

gold basins............................30
silver basins 1,000
silver incense burners* 29

1:1a The first year of Cyrus's reign over Babylon was 538 B.C.   1:1b See Jer 25:11-12; 29:10.   1:8 Hebrew *Sheshbazzar, the prince*
of Judah.   1:9 The meaning of this Hebrew word is uncertain.

¹⁰ gold bowls 30
   silver bowls 410
   other items. 1,000

¹¹In all, there were 5,400 articles of gold and silver. Sheshbazzar brought all of these along when the exiles went from Babylon to Jerusalem.

Exiles Who Returned with Zerubbabel

2 Here is the list of the Jewish exiles of the provinces who returned from their captivity. King Nebuchadnezzar had deported them to Babylon, but now they returned to Jerusalem and the other towns in Judah where they originally lived. ²Their leaders were Zerubbabel, Jeshua, Nehemiah, Seraiah, Reelaiah, Mordecai, Bilshan, Mispar, Bigvai, Rehum, and Baanah.

This is the number of the men of Israel who returned from exile:
³ The family of Parosh 2,172
⁴ The family of Shephatiah 372
⁵ The family of Arah 775
⁶ The family of Pahath-moab
   (descendants of Jeshua and Joab) . . 2,812
⁷ The family of Elam. 1,254
⁸ The family of Zattu 945
⁹ The family of Zaccai. 760
¹⁰ The family of Bani 642
¹¹ The family of Bebai 623
¹² The family of Azgad. 1,222
¹³ The family of Adonikam. 666
¹⁴ The family of Bigvai. 2,056
¹⁵ The family of Adin 454
¹⁶ The family of Ater (descendants of
   Hezekiah). 98
¹⁷ The family of Bezai 323
¹⁸ The family of Jorah 112
¹⁹ The family of Hashum 223
²⁰ The family of Gibbar 95
²¹ The people of Bethlehem 123
²² The people of Netophah. 56
²³ The people of Anathoth 128
²⁴ The people of Beth-azmaveth* 42
²⁵ The people of Kiriath-jearim,*
   Kephirah, and Beeroth 743
²⁶ The people of Ramah and Geba 621
²⁷ The people of Micmash. 122
²⁸ The people of Bethel and Ai 223
²⁹ The citizens of Nebo 52
³⁰ The citizens of Magbish 156

³¹ The citizens of West Elam*. 1,254
³² The citizens of Harim 320
³³ The citizens of Lod, Hadid, and Ono. . . 725
³⁴ The citizens of Jericho. 345
³⁵ The citizens of Senaah. 3,630

³⁶These are the priests who returned from exile:
   The family of Jedaiah (through the line of
      Jeshua) 973
³⁷ The family of Immer 1,052
³⁸ The family of Pashhur. 1,247
³⁹ The family of Harim 1,017

⁴⁰These are the Levites who returned from exile:
   The families of Jeshua and Kadmiel
      (descendants of Hodaviah). 74
⁴¹ The singers of the family of Asaph 128
⁴² The gatekeepers of the families of
      Shallum, Ater, Talmon, Akkub, Hatita,
      and Shobai 139

⁴³The descendants of the following Temple servants returned from exile:
   Ziha, Hasupha, Tabbaoth,
⁴⁴ Keros, Siaha, Padon,
⁴⁵ Lebanah, Hagabah, Akkub,
⁴⁶ Hagab, Shalmai,* Hanan,
⁴⁷ Giddel, Gahar, Reaiah,
⁴⁸ Rezin, Nekoda, Gazzam,
⁴⁹ Uzza, Paseah, Besai,
⁵⁰ Asnah, Meunim, Nephusim,
⁵¹ Bakbuk, Hakupha, Harhur,
⁵² Bazluth, Mehida, Harsha,
⁵³ Barkos, Sisera, Temah,
⁵⁴ Neziah, and Hatipha.

⁵⁵The descendants of these servants of King Solomon returned from exile:
   Sotai, Hassophereth, Peruda,
⁵⁶ Jaalah, Darkon, Giddel,
⁵⁷ Shephatiah, Hattil, Pokereth-hazzebaim,
   and Ami.

⁵⁸In all, the Temple servants and the descendants of Solomon's servants numbered 392.

⁵⁹Another group returned at this time from the towns of Tel-melah, Tel-harsha, Kerub, Addan, and Immer. However, they could not prove that they or their families were descendants of Israel. ⁶⁰This group included the

2:24 As in parallel text at Neh 7:28; Hebrew reads *Azmaveth.* 2:25 As in some Hebrew manuscripts and Greek version (see also Neh 7:29); Hebrew reads *Kiriath-arim.* 2:31 Or *of the other Elam.* 2:46 As in an alternate reading of the Masoretic Text (see also Neh 7:48); the other alternate reads *Shamlai.*

families of Delaiah, Tobiah, and Nekoda—a total of 652 people.

[61]Three families of priests—Hobaiah, Hakkoz, and Barzillai—also returned. (This Barzillai had married a woman who was a descendant of Barzillai of Gilead, and he had taken her family name.) [62]They searched for their names in the genealogical records, but they were not found, so they were disqualified from serving as priests. [63]The governor told them not to eat the priests' share of food from the sacrifices until a priest could consult the LORD about the matter by using the Urim and Thummim—the sacred lots.

[64]So a total of 42,360 people returned to Judah, [65]in addition to 7,337 servants and 200 singers, both men and women. [66]They took with them 736 horses, 245 mules, [67]435 camels, and 6,720 donkeys.

[68]When they arrived at the Temple of the LORD in Jerusalem, some of the family leaders made voluntary offerings toward the rebuilding of God's Temple on its original site, [69]and each leader gave as much as he could. The total of their gifts came to 61,000 gold coins,* 6,250 pounds* of silver, and 100 robes for the priests.

[70]So the priests, the Levites, the singers, the gatekeepers, the Temple servants, and some of the common people settled in villages near Jerusalem. The rest of the people returned to their own towns throughout Israel.

The Altar Is Rebuilt

3 In early autumn,* when the Israelites had settled in their towns, all the people assembled in Jerusalem with a unified purpose. [2]Then Jeshua son of Jehozadak* joined his fellow priests and Zerubbabel son of Shealtiel with his family in rebuilding the altar of the God of Israel. They wanted to sacrifice burnt offerings on it, as instructed in the Law of Moses, the man of God. [3]Even though the people were afraid of the local residents, they rebuilt the altar at its old site. Then they began to sacrifice burnt offerings on the altar to the LORD each morning and evening.

[4]They celebrated the Festival of Shelters as prescribed in the Law, sacrificing the number of burnt offerings specified for each day of the festival. [5]They also offered the regular burnt offerings and the offerings required for the new moon celebrations and the annual festivals as prescribed by the LORD. The people also gave voluntary offerings to the LORD. [6]Fifteen days before the Festival of Shelters began,* the priests had begun to sacrifice burnt offerings to the LORD. This was even before they had started to lay the foundation of the LORD's Temple.

The People Begin to Rebuild the Temple

[7]Then the people hired masons and carpenters and bought cedar logs from the people of Tyre and Sidon, paying them with food, wine, and olive oil. The logs were brought down from the Lebanon mountains and floated along the coast of the Mediterranean Sea* to Joppa, for King Cyrus had given permission for this.

[8]The construction of the Temple of God began in midspring,* during the second year after they arrived in Jerusalem. The work force was made up of everyone who had returned from exile, including Zerubbabel son of Shealtiel, Jeshua son of Jehozadak and his fellow priests, and all the Levites. The Levites who were twenty years old or older were put in charge of rebuilding the LORD's Temple. [9]The workers at the Temple of God were supervised by Jeshua with his sons and relatives, and Kadmiel and his sons, all descendants of Hodaviah.* They were helped in this task by the Levites of the family of Henadad.

[10]When the builders completed the foundation of the LORD's Temple, the priests put on their robes and took their places to blow their trumpets. And the Levites, descendants of Asaph, clashed their cymbals to praise the LORD, just as King David had prescribed. [11]With praise and thanks, they sang this song to the LORD:

"He is so good!
His faithful love for Israel endures forever!"

Then all the people gave a great shout, praising the LORD because the foundation of the LORD's Temple had been laid.

2:69a Hebrew 61,000 darics of gold, about 1,100 pounds or 500 kilograms in weight.   2:69b Hebrew 5,000 minas [3,000 kilograms].   3:1 Hebrew In the seventh month. The year is not specified, so it may have been during Cyrus's first year (538 B.C.) or second year (537 B.C.). The seventh month of the ancient Hebrew lunar calendar occurred within the months of September/October 538 B.C. and October/November 537 B.C.   3:2 Hebrew Jozadak, a variant spelling of Jehozadak; also in 3:8.   3:6 Hebrew On the first day of the seventh month. This day in the ancient Hebrew lunar calendar occurred in September or October. The Festival of Shelters began on the fifteenth day of the seventh month.   3:7 Hebrew the sea. 3:8 Hebrew in the second month. This month in the ancient Hebrew lunar calendar occurred within the months of April and May 536 B.C.   3:9 Hebrew sons of Judah (i.e., bene Yehudah). Bene might also be read here as the proper name Binnui; Yehudah is probably another name for Hodaviah. Compare 2:40; Neh 7:43; 1 Esdras 5:58.

¹²But many of the older priests, Levites, and other leaders who had seen the first Temple wept aloud when they saw the new Temple's foundation. The others, however, were shouting for joy. ¹³The joyful shouting and weeping mingled together in a loud noise that could be heard far in the distance.

Enemies Oppose the Rebuilding

4 The enemies of Judah and Benjamin heard that the exiles were rebuilding a Temple to the LORD, the God of Israel. ²So they approached Zerubbabel and the other leaders and said, "Let us build with you, for we worship your God just as you do. We have sacrificed to him ever since King Esarhaddon of Assyria brought us here."

³But Zerubbabel, Jeshua, and the other leaders of Israel replied, "You may have no part in this work. We alone will build the Temple for the LORD, the God of Israel, just as King Cyrus of Persia commanded us."

⁴Then the local residents tried to discourage and frighten the people of Judah to keep them from their work. ⁵They bribed agents to work against them and to frustrate their plans. This went on during the entire reign of King Cyrus of Persia and lasted until King Darius of Persia took the throne.*

Later Opposition under Xerxes and Artaxerxes

⁶Years later when Xerxes* began his reign, the enemies of Judah wrote a letter of accusation against the people of Judah and Jerusalem.

⁷Even later, during the reign of King Artaxerxes of Persia,* the enemies of Judah, led by Bishlam, Mithredath, and Tabeel, sent a letter to Artaxerxes in the Aramaic language, and it was translated for the king.

⁸*Rehum the governor and Shimshai the court secretary wrote the letter, telling King Artaxerxes about the situation in Jerusalem. ⁹They greeted the king for all their colleagues—the judges and local leaders, the people of Tarpel, the Persians, the Babylonians, and the people of Erech and Susa (that is, Elam). ¹⁰They also sent greetings from the rest of the people whom the great and noble Ashurbanipal* had deported and relocated in Samaria and throughout the neighboring lands of the province west of the Euphrates River.* ¹¹This is a copy of their letter:

"To King Artaxerxes, from your loyal subjects in the province west of the Euphrates River.

¹²"The king should know that the Jews who came here to Jerusalem from Babylon are rebuilding this rebellious and evil city. They have already laid the foundation and will soon finish its walls. ¹³And the king should know that if this city is rebuilt and its walls are completed, it will be much to your disadvantage, for the Jews will then refuse to pay their tribute, customs, and tolls to you.

¹⁴"Since we are your loyal subjects* and do not want to see the king dishonored in this way, we have sent the king this information. ¹⁵We suggest that a search be made in your ancestors' records, where you will discover what a rebellious city this has been in the past. In fact, it was destroyed because of its long and troublesome history of revolt against the kings and countries who controlled it. ¹⁶We declare to the king that if this city is rebuilt and its walls are completed, the province west of the Euphrates River will be lost to you."

¹⁷Then King Artaxerxes sent this reply:

"To Rehum the governor, Shimshai the court secretary, and their colleagues living in Samaria and throughout the province west of the Euphrates River. Greetings.

¹⁸"The letter you sent has been translated and read to me. ¹⁹I ordered a search of the records and have found that Jerusalem has indeed been a hotbed of insurrection against many kings. In fact, rebellion and revolt are normal there! ²⁰Powerful kings have ruled over Jerusalem and the entire province west of the Euphrates River, receiving tribute, customs, and tolls. ²¹Therefore, issue orders to have these men stop their work. That city must not be rebuilt except at my express command. ²²Be diligent, and don't neglect this matter, for we must not permit the situation to harm the king's interests."

²³When this letter from King Artaxerxes was read to Rehum, Shimshai, and their colleagues, they hurried to Jerusalem. Then,

---

4:5 Darius reigned 521–486 B.C.   4:6 Hebrew *Ahasuerus,* another name for Xerxes. He reigned 486–465 B.C.   4:7 Artaxerxes reigned 465–424 B.C.   4:8 The original text of 4:8–6:18 is in Aramaic.   4:10a Aramaic *Osnappar,* another name for Ashurbanipal.   4:10b Aramaic *the province beyond the river;* also in 4:11, 16, 17, 20.   4:14 Aramaic *Since we eat the salt of the palace.*

with a show of strength, they forced the Jews to stop building.

The Rebuilding Resumes

24So the work on the Temple of God in Jerusalem had stopped, and it remained at a standstill until the second year of the reign of King Darius of Persia.*

5 At that time the prophets Haggai and Zechariah son of Iddo prophesied to the Jews in Judah and Jerusalem. They prophesied in the name of the God of Israel who was over them. 2Zerubbabel son of Shealtiel and Jeshua son of Jehozadak* responded by starting again to rebuild the Temple of God in Jerusalem. And the prophets of God were with them and helped them.

3But Tattenai, governor of the province west of the Euphrates River,* and Shethar-bozenai and their colleagues soon arrived in Jerusalem and asked, "Who gave you permission to rebuild this Temple and restore this structure?" 4They also asked for* the names of all the men working on the Temple. 5But because their God was watching over them, the leaders of the Jews were not prevented from building until a report was sent to Darius and he returned his decision.

Tattenai's Letter to King Darius

6This is a copy of the letter that Tattenai the governor, Shethar-bozenai, and the other officials of the province west of the Euphrates River sent to King Darius:

7"To King Darius. Greetings.

8"The king should know that we went to the construction site of the Temple of the great God in the province of Judah. It is being rebuilt with specially prepared stones, and timber is being laid in its walls. The work is going forward with great energy and success.

9"We asked the leaders, 'Who gave you permission to rebuild this Temple and restore this structure?' 10And we demanded their names so that we could tell you who the leaders were.

11"This was their answer: 'We are the servants of the God of heaven and earth, and we are rebuilding the Temple that was built here many years ago by a great king of Israel. 12But because our ancestors angered the God of heaven, he abandoned them to King Nebuchadnezzar of Babylon,* who destroyed this Temple and exiled the people to Babylonia. 13However, King Cyrus of Babylon,* during the first year of his reign, issued a decree that the Temple of God should be rebuilt. 14King Cyrus returned the gold and silver cups that Nebuchadnezzar had taken from the Temple of God in Jerusalem and had placed in the temple of Babylon. These cups were taken from that temple and presented to a man named Sheshbazzar, whom King Cyrus appointed as governor of Judah. 15The king instructed him to return the cups to their place in Jerusalem and to rebuild the Temple of God there on its original site. 16So this Sheshbazzar came and laid the foundations of the Temple of God in Jerusalem. The people have been working on it ever since, though it is not yet completed.'

17"Therefore, if it pleases the king, we request that a search be made in the royal archives of Babylon to discover whether King Cyrus ever issued a decree to rebuild God's Temple in Jerusalem. And then let the king send us his decision in this matter."

Darius Approves the Rebuilding

6 So King Darius issued orders that a search be made in the Babylonian archives, which were stored in the treasury. 2But it was at the fortress at Ecbatana in the province of Media that a scroll was found. This is what it said:

"Memorandum:

3"In the first year of King Cyrus's reign, a decree was sent out concerning the Temple of God at Jerusalem.

"Let the Temple be rebuilt on the site where Jews used to offer their sacrifices, using the original foundations. Its height will be ninety feet, and its width will be ninety feet.* 4Every three layers of specially prepared stones will be topped by a layer of timber. All expenses will be paid by the

4:24 The second year of Darius's reign was 520 B.C. The narrative started in 4:1-5 is resumed at verse 24. 5:2 Aramaic *Jozadak,* a variant spelling of Jehozadak. 5:3 Aramaic *the province beyond the river;* also in 5:6. 5:4 As in one Hebrew manuscript and Greek and Syriac versions; Masoretic Text reads *Then we told them.* 5:12 Aramaic *Nebuchadnezzar the Chaldean.* 5:13 King Cyrus of Persia is here identified as the king of Babylon because Persia had conquered the Babylonian Empire. 6:3 Aramaic *Its height will be 60 cubits* [27.6 meters], *and its width will be 60 cubits.* It is commonly held that this verse should be emended to read: "Its height will be 30 cubits [45 feet or 13.8 meters], its length will be 60 cubits [90 feet or 27.6 meters], and its width will be 20 cubits [30 feet or 9.2 meters]"; compare 1 Kgs 6:2. The emendation regarding the width is supported by the Syriac version.

royal treasury. ⁵Furthermore, the gold and silver cups, which were taken to Babylon by Nebuchadnezzar from the Temple of God in Jerusalem, must be returned to Jerusalem and put back where they belong. Let them be taken back to the Temple of God."

⁶So King Darius sent this message:

"Now therefore, Tattenai, governor of the province west of the Euphrates River,* and Shethar-bozenai, and your colleagues and other officials west of the Euphrates River—stay away from there! ⁷Do not disturb the construction of the Temple of God. Let it be rebuilt on its original site, and do not hinder the governor of Judah and the elders of the Jews in their work.

⁸"Moreover, I hereby decree that you are to help these elders of the Jews as they rebuild this Temple of God. You must pay the full construction costs, without delay, from my taxes collected in the province west of the Euphrates River so that the work will not be interrupted. ⁹"Give the priests in Jerusalem whatever is needed in the way of young bulls, rams, and male lambs for the burnt offerings presented to the God of heaven. And without fail, provide them with as much wheat, salt, wine, and olive oil as they need each day. ¹⁰Then they will be able to offer acceptable sacrifices to the God of heaven and pray for the welfare of the king and his sons.

¹¹"Those who violate this decree in any way will have a beam pulled from their house. Then they will be lifted up and impaled on it, and their house will be reduced to a pile of rubble.* ¹²May the God who has chosen the city of Jerusalem as the place to honor his name destroy any king or nation that violates this command and destroys this Temple.

"I, Darius, have issued this decree. Let it be obeyed with all diligence."

The Temple's Dedication

¹³Tattenai, governor of the province west of the Euphrates River, and Shethar-bozenai and their colleagues complied at once with the command of King Darius. ¹⁴So the Jewish elders continued their work, and they were greatly encouraged by the preaching of the prophets Haggai and Zechariah son of Iddo. The Temple was finally finished, as had been commanded by the God of Israel and decreed by Cyrus, Darius, and Artaxerxes, the kings of Persia. ¹⁵The Temple was completed on March 12,* during the sixth year of King Darius's reign.

¹⁶The Temple of God was then dedicated with great joy by the people of Israel, the priests, the Levites, and the rest of the people who had returned from exile. ¹⁷During the dedication ceremony for the Temple of God, 100 young bulls, 200 rams, and 400 male lambs were sacrificed. And 12 male goats were presented as a sin offering for the twelve tribes of Israel. ¹⁸Then the priests and Levites were divided into their various divisions to serve at the Temple of God in Jerusalem, as prescribed in the Book of Moses.

Celebration of Passover

¹⁹On April 21* the returned exiles celebrated Passover. ²⁰The priests and Levites had purified themselves and were ceremonially clean. So they slaughtered the Passover lamb for all the returned exiles, for their fellow priests, and for themselves. ²¹The Passover meal was eaten by the people of Israel who had returned from exile and by the others in the land who had turned from their corrupt practices to worship the LORD, the God of Israel. ²²Then they celebrated the Festival of Unleavened Bread for seven days. There was great joy throughout the land because the LORD had caused the king of Assyria* to be favorable to them, so that he helped them to rebuild the Temple of God, the God of Israel.

Ezra Arrives in Jerusalem

7 Many years later, during the reign of King Artaxerxes of Persia,* there was a man named Ezra. He was the son* of Seraiah, son of Azariah, son of Hilkiah, ²son of Shallum, son of Zadok, son of Ahitub, ³son of Amariah, son of Azariah, son* of Meraioth, ⁴son of Zerahiah, son of Uzzi, son of Bukki, ⁵son of Abishua, son of Phinehas, son of Eleazar,

6:6 Aramaic *the province beyond the river;* also in 6:6b, 8, 13.   6:11 Aramaic *a dunghill.*   6:15 Aramaic *on the third day of the month Adar,* of the ancient Hebrew lunar calendar. A number of events in Ezra can be cross-checked with dates in surviving Persian records and related accurately to our modern calendar. This day was March 12, 515 B.C.   6:19 Hebrew *On the fourteenth day of the first month,* of the ancient Hebrew lunar calendar. This day was April 21, 515 B.C.; also see note on 6:15.   6:22 King Darius of Persia is here identified as the king of Assyria because Persia had conquered the Babylonian Empire, which included the earlier Assyrian Empire.   7:1a Artaxerxes reigned 465–424 B.C.   7:1b Or *descendant;* see 1 Chr 6:14.   7:3 Or *descendant;* see 1 Chr 6:6-10.

son of Aaron the high priest.* ⁶This Ezra was a scribe who was well versed in the Law of Moses, which the LORD, the God of Israel, had given to the people of Israel. He came up to Jerusalem from Babylon, and the king gave him everything he asked for, because the gracious hand of the LORD his God was on him. ⁷Some of the people of Israel, as well as some of the priests, Levites, singers, gatekeepers, and Temple servants, traveled up to Jerusalem with him in the seventh year of King Artaxerxes' reign.

⁸Ezra arrived in Jerusalem in August* of that year. ⁹He had arranged to leave Babylon on April 8, the first day of the new year,* and he arrived at Jerusalem on August 4,* for the gracious hand of his God was on him. ¹⁰This was because Ezra had determined to study and obey the Law of the LORD and to teach those decrees and regulations to the people of Israel.

Artaxerxes' Letter to Ezra

¹¹King Artaxerxes had given a copy of the following letter to Ezra, the priest and scribe who studied and taught the commands and decrees of the LORD to Israel:

¹²*"From Artaxerxes, the king of kings, to Ezra the priest, the teacher of the law of the God of heaven. Greetings.

¹³"I decree that any of the people of Israel in my kingdom, including the priests and Levites, may volunteer to return to Jerusalem with you. ¹⁴I and my council of seven hereby instruct you to conduct an inquiry into the situation in Judah and Jerusalem, based on your God's law, which is in your hand. ¹⁵We also commission you to take with you silver and gold, which we are freely presenting as an offering to the God of Israel who lives in Jerusalem.

¹⁶"Furthermore, you are to take any silver and gold that you may obtain from the province of Babylon, as well as the voluntary offerings of the people and the priests that are presented for the Temple of their God in Jerusalem. ¹⁷These donations are to be used specifically for the purchase of bulls, rams, male lambs, and the appropriate grain offerings and liquid offerings, all of which will be offered on the altar of the Temple of your God in Jerusalem. ¹⁸Any silver and gold that is left over may be used in whatever way you and your colleagues feel is the will of your God.

¹⁹"But as for the cups we are entrusting to you for the service of the Temple of your God, deliver them all to the God of Jerusalem. ²⁰If you need anything else for your God's Temple or for any similar needs, you may take it from the royal treasury.

²¹"I, Artaxerxes the king, hereby send this decree to all the treasurers in the province west of the Euphrates River*: 'You are to give Ezra, the priest and teacher of the law of the God of heaven, whatever he requests of you. ²²You are to give him up to 7,500 pounds* of silver, 500 bushels* of wheat, 550 gallons of wine, 550 gallons of olive oil,* and an unlimited supply of salt. ²³Be careful to provide whatever the God of heaven demands for his Temple, for why should we risk bringing God's anger against the realm of the king and his sons? ²⁴I also decree that no priest, Levite, singer, gatekeeper, Temple servant, or other worker in this Temple of God will be required to pay tribute, customs, or tolls of any kind.'

²⁵"And you, Ezra, are to use the wisdom your God has given you to appoint magistrates and judges who know your God's laws to govern all the people in the province west of the Euphrates River. Teach the law to anyone who does not know it. ²⁶Anyone who refuses to obey the law of your God and the law of the king will be punished immediately, either by death, banishment, confiscation of goods, or imprisonment."

Ezra Praises the LORD

²⁷Praise the LORD, the God of our ancestors, who made the king want to beautify the Temple of the LORD in Jerusalem! ²⁸And praise him for demonstrating such unfailing love to me by honoring me before the king, his council, and all his mighty nobles! I felt encouraged because the gracious hand of the LORD my God was on me. And I gathered some of the leaders of Israel to return with me to Jerusalem.

7:5 Or *the first priest.*   7:8 Hebrew *in the fifth month.* This month in the ancient Hebrew lunar calendar occurred within the months of August and September 458 B.C.   7:9a Hebrew *on the first day of the first month,* of the ancient Hebrew lunar calendar. This day was April 8, 458 B.C.; also see note on 6:15.   7:9b Hebrew *on the first day of the fifth month,* of the ancient Hebrew lunar calendar. This day was August 4, 458 B.C.; also see note on 6:15.   7:12 The original text of 7:12-26 is in Aramaic.   7:21 Aramaic *the province beyond the river;* also in 7:25.   7:22a Aramaic *100 talents* [3,400 kilograms].   7:22b Aramaic *100 cors* [22 kiloliters].   7:22c Aramaic *100 baths* [2.1 kiloliters] *of wine, 100 baths of olive oil.*

Exiles Who Returned with Ezra

8 Here is a list of the family leaders and the genealogies of those who came with me from Babylon during the reign of King Artaxerxes:

2 From the family of Phinehas: Gershom.
From the family of Ithamar: Daniel.
From the family of David: Hattush, 3a descendant of Shecaniah.
From the family of Parosh: Zechariah and 150 other men were registered.
4 From the family of Pahath-moab: Eliehoenai son of Zerahiah and 200 other men.
5 From the family of Zattu*: Shecaniah son of Jahaziel and 300 other men.
6 From the family of Adin: Ebed son of Jonathan and 50 other men.
7 From the family of Elam: Jeshaiah son of Athaliah and 70 other men.
8 From the family of Shephatiah: Zebadiah son of Michael and 80 other men.
9 From the family of Joab: Obadiah son of Jehiel and 218 other men.
10 From the family of Bani*: Shelomith son of Josiphiah and 160 other men.
11 From the family of Bebai: Zechariah son of Bebai and 28 other men.
12 From the family of Azgad: Johanan son of Hakkatan and 110 other men.
13 From the family of Adonikam, who came later*: Eliphelet, Jeuel, Shemaiah, and 60 other men.
14 From the family of Bigvai: Uthai, Zaccur,* and 70 other men.

Ezra's Journey to Jerusalem

15 I assembled the exiles at the Ahava Canal, and we camped there for three days while I went over the lists of the people and the priests who had arrived. I found that not one Levite had volunteered to come along. 16So I sent for Eliezer, Ariel, Shemaiah, Elnathan, Jarib, Elnathan, Nathan, Zechariah, and Meshullam, who were leaders of the people. I also sent for Joiarib and Elnathan, who were men of discernment. 17I sent them to Iddo, the leader of the Levites at Casiphia, to ask him and his relatives and the Temple servants to send us ministers for the Temple of God at Jerusalem. 18Since the gracious hand of our God was on us, they sent us a man named Sherebiah, along with eighteen of his sons and brothers. He was a very astute man and a descendant of Mahli, who was a descendant of Levi son of Israel.* 19They also sent Hashabiah, together with Jeshaiah from the descendants of Merari, and twenty of his sons and brothers, 20and 220 Temple servants. The Temple servants were assistants to the Levites—a group of Temple workers first instituted by King David and his officials. They were all listed by name.

21And there by the Ahava Canal, I gave orders for all of us to fast and humble ourselves before our God. We prayed that he would give us a safe journey and protect us, our children, and our goods as we traveled. 22For I was ashamed to ask the king for soldiers and horsemen* to accompany us and protect us from enemies along the way. After all, we had told the king, "Our God's hand of protection is on all who worship him, but his fierce anger rages against those who abandon him." 23So we fasted and earnestly prayed that our God would take care of us, and he heard our prayer.

24I appointed twelve leaders of the priests—Sherebiah, Hashabiah, and ten other priests—25to be in charge of transporting the silver, the gold, the gold bowls, and the other items that the king, his council, his officials, and all the people of Israel had presented for the Temple of God. 26I weighed the treasure as I gave it to them and found the totals to be as follows:

24 tons* of silver,
7,500 pounds* of silver articles,
7,500 pounds of gold,
27 20 gold bowls, equal in value to 1,000 gold coins,*
2 fine articles of polished bronze, as precious as gold.

28And I said to these priests, "You and these treasures have been set apart as holy to the LORD. This silver and gold is a voluntary offering to the LORD, the God of our ancestors. 29Guard these treasures well until you present them to the leading priests, the Levites, and the leaders of Israel, who will weigh them at the storerooms of the LORD's Temple in Jerusalem." 30So the priests and the Levites accepted the task of transporting these treasures

8:5 As in some Greek manuscripts (see also 1 Esdras 8:32); Hebrew lacks *Zattu*. 8:10 As in some Greek manuscripts (see also 1 Esdras 8:36); Hebrew lacks *Bani*. 8:13 Or *who were the last of his family*. 8:14 As in Greek and Syriac versions and an alternate reading of the Masoretic Text; the other alternate reads *Zabbud*. 8:18 *Israel* is the name that God gave to Jacob. 8:22 Or *charioteers*. 8:26a Hebrew *650 talents* [22 metric tons]. 8:26b Hebrew *100 talents* [3,400 kilograms]; also in 8:26c. 8:27 Hebrew *1,000 darics*, about 19 pounds or 8.6 kilograms in weight.

of silver and gold to the Temple of our God in Jerusalem.

³¹We broke camp at the Ahava Canal on April 19* and started off to Jerusalem. And the gracious hand of our God protected us and saved us from enemies and bandits along the way. ³²So we arrived safely in Jerusalem, where we rested for three days.

³³On the fourth day after our arrival, the silver, gold, and other valuables were weighed at the Temple of our God and entrusted to Meremoth son of Uriah the priest and to Eleazar son of Phinehas, along with Jozabad son of Jeshua and Noadiah son of Binnui—both of whom were Levites. ³⁴Everything was accounted for by number and weight, and the total weight was officially recorded.

³⁵Then the exiles who had come out of captivity sacrificed burnt offerings to the God of Israel. They presented twelve bulls for all the people of Israel, as well as ninety-six rams and seventy-seven male lambs. They also offered twelve male goats as a sin offering. All this was given as a burnt offering to the LORD. ³⁶The king's decrees were delivered to his highest officers and the governors of the province west of the Euphrates River,* who then cooperated by supporting the people and the Temple of God.

Ezra's Prayer concerning Intermarriage

9 When these things had been done, the Jewish leaders came to me and said, "Many of the people of Israel, and even some of the priests and Levites, have not kept themselves separate from the other peoples living in the land. They have taken up the detestable practices of the Canaanites, Hittites, Perizzites, Jebusites, Ammonites, Moabites, Egyptians, and Amorites. ²For the men of Israel have married women from these people and have taken them as wives for their sons. So the holy race has become polluted by these mixed marriages. Worse yet, the leaders and officials have led the way in this outrage."

³When I heard this, I tore my cloak and my shirt, pulled hair from my head and beard, and sat down utterly shocked. ⁴Then all who trembled at the words of the God of Israel came and sat with me because of this outrage committed by the returned exiles. And I sat there utterly appalled until the time of the evening sacrifice.

⁵At the time of the sacrifice, I stood up from where I had sat in mourning with my clothes torn. I fell to my knees and lifted my hands to the LORD my God. ⁶I prayed,

"O my God, I am utterly ashamed; I blush to lift up my face to you. For our sins are piled higher than our heads, and our guilt has reached to the heavens. ⁷From the days of our ancestors until now, we have been steeped in sin. That is why we and our kings and our priests have been at the mercy of the pagan kings of the land. We have been killed, captured, robbed, and disgraced, just as we are today.

⁸"But now we have been given a brief moment of grace, for the LORD our God has allowed a few of us to survive as a remnant. He has given us security in this holy place. Our God has brightened our eyes and granted us some relief from our slavery. ⁹For we were slaves, but in his unfailing love our God did not abandon us in our slavery. Instead, he caused the kings of Persia to treat us favorably. He revived us so we could rebuild the Temple of our God and repair its ruins. He has given us a protective wall in Judah and Jerusalem.

¹⁰"And now, O our God, what can we say after all of this? For once again we have abandoned your commands! ¹¹Your servants the prophets warned us when they said, 'The land you are entering to possess is totally defiled by the detestable practices of the people living there. From one end to the other, the land is filled with corruption. ¹²Don't let your daughters marry their sons! Don't take their daughters as wives for your sons. Don't ever promote the peace and prosperity of those nations. If you follow these instructions, you will be strong and will enjoy the good things the land produces, and you will leave this prosperity to your children forever.'

¹³"Now we are being punished because of our wickedness and our great guilt. But we have actually been punished far less than we deserve, for you, our God, have allowed some of us to survive as a remnant. ¹⁴But even so, we are again breaking your commands and intermarrying with people who do these detestable things. Won't your anger be enough to destroy us, so that even this little remnant no longer survives?

8:31 Hebrew *on the twelfth day of the first month,* of the ancient Hebrew lunar calendar. This day was April 19, 458 B.C.; also see note on 6:15. 8:36 Hebrew *the province beyond the river.*

¹⁵O Lord, God of Israel, you are just. We come before you in our guilt as nothing but an escaped remnant, though in such a condition none of us can stand in your presence."

The People Confess Their Sin

10 While Ezra prayed and made this confession, weeping and lying face down on the ground in front of the Temple of God, a very large crowd of people from Israel—men, women, and children—gathered and wept bitterly with him. ²Then Shecaniah son of Jehiel, a descendant of Elam, said to Ezra, "We have been unfaithful to our God, for we have married these pagan women of the land. But in spite of this there is hope for Israel. ³Let us now make a covenant with our God to divorce our pagan wives and to send them away with their children. We will follow the advice given by you and by the others who respect the commands of our God. Let it be done according to the Law of God. ⁴Get up, for it is your duty to tell us how to proceed in setting things straight. We are behind you, so be strong and take action."

⁵So Ezra stood up and demanded that the leaders of the priests and the Levites and all the people of Israel swear that they would do as Shecaniah had said. And they all swore a solemn oath. ⁶Then Ezra left the front of the Temple of God and went to the room of Jehohanan son of Eliashib. He spent the night* there without eating or drinking anything. He was still in mourning because of the unfaithfulness of the returned exiles.

⁷Then a proclamation was made throughout Judah and Jerusalem that all the exiles should come to Jerusalem. ⁸Those who failed to come within three days would, if the leaders and elders so decided, forfeit all their property and be expelled from the assembly of the exiles.

⁹Within three days, all the people of Judah and Benjamin had gathered in Jerusalem. This took place on December 19,* and all the people were sitting in the square before the Temple of God. They were trembling both because of the seriousness of the matter and because it was raining. ¹⁰Then Ezra the priest stood and said to them: "You have committed a terrible sin. By marrying pagan women, you have increased Israel's guilt. ¹¹So now confess your sin to the Lord, the God of your ancestors, and do what he

demands. Separate yourselves from the people of the land and from these pagan women."

¹²Then the whole assembly raised their voices and answered, "Yes, you are right; we must do as you say!" ¹³Then they added, "This isn't something that can be done in a day or two, for many of us are involved in this extremely sinful affair. And this is the rainy season, so we cannot stay out here much longer. ¹⁴Let our leaders act on behalf of us all. Let everyone who has a pagan wife come at a scheduled time, accompanied by the leaders and judges of his city, so that the fierce anger of our God concerning this affair may be turned away from us."

¹⁵Only Jonathan son of Asahel and Jahzeiah son of Tikvah opposed this course of action, and they were supported by Meshullam and Shabbethai the Levite.

¹⁶So this was the plan they followed. Ezra selected leaders to represent their families, designating each of the representatives by name. On December 29,* the leaders sat down to investigate the matter. ¹⁷By March 27, the first day of the new year,* they had finished dealing with all the men who had married pagan wives.

Those Guilty of Intermarriage

¹⁸These are the priests who had married pagan wives:

From the family of Jeshua son of Jehozadak* and his brothers: Maaseiah, Eliezer, Jarib, and Gedaliah. ¹⁹They vowed to divorce their wives, and they each acknowledged their guilt by offering a ram as a guilt offering.

²⁰From the family of Immer: Hanani and Zebadiah.

²¹From the family of Harim: Maaseiah, Elijah, Shemaiah, Jehiel, and Uzziah.

²²From the family of Pashhur: Elioenai, Maaseiah, Ishmael, Nethanel, Jozabad, and Elasah.

²³These are the Levites who were guilty: Jozabad, Shimei, Kelaiah (also called Kelita), Pethahiah, Judah, and Eliezer.

²⁴This is the singer who was guilty: Eliashib.

These are the gatekeepers who were guilty: Shallum, Telem, and Uri.

10:6 As in parallel text at 1 Esdras 9:2; Hebrew reads *He went.* 10:9 Hebrew *on the twentieth day of the ninth month,* of the ancient Hebrew lunar calendar. This day was December 19, 458 b.c.; also see note on 6:15. 10:16 Hebrew *On the first day of the tenth month,* of the ancient Hebrew lunar calendar. This day was December 29, 458 b.c.; also see note on 6:15. 10:17 Hebrew *By the first day of the first month,* of the ancient Hebrew lunar calendar. This day was March 27, 457 b.c.; also see note on 6:15. 10:18 Hebrew *Jozadak,* a variant spelling of Jehozadak.

25These are the other people of Israel who were guilty:

From the family of Parosh: Ramiah, Izziah, Malkijah, Mijamin, Eleazar, Hashabiah,* and Benaiah.

26From the family of Elam: Mattaniah, Zechariah, Jehiel, Abdi, Jeremoth, and Elijah.

27From the family of Zattu: Elioenai, Eliashib, Mattaniah, Jeremoth, Zabad, and Aziza.

28From the family of Bebai: Jehohanan, Hananiah, Zabbai, and Athlai.

29From the family of Bani: Meshullam, Malluch, Adaiah, Jashub, Sheal, and Jeremoth.

30From the family of Pahath-moab: Adna, Kelal, Benaiah, Maaseiah, Mattaniah, Bezalel, Binnui, and Manasseh.

31From the family of Harim: Eliezer, Ishijah, Malkijah, Shemaiah, Shimeon, 32Benjamin, Malluch, and Shemariah.

33From the family of Hashum: Mattenai, Mattattah, Zabad, Eliphelet, Jeremai, Manasseh, and Shimei.

34From the family of Bani: Maadai, Amram, Uel, 35Benaiah, Bedeiah, Keluhi, 36Vaniah, Meremoth, Eliashib, 37Mattaniah, Mattenai, and Jaasu.

38From the family of Binnui*: Shimei, 39Shelemiah, Nathan, Adaiah, 40Macnadebai, Shashai, Sharai, 41Azarel, Shelemiah, Shemariah, 42Shallum, Amariah, and Joseph.

43From the family of Nebo: Jeiel, Mattithiah, Zabad, Zebina, Jaddai, Joel, and Benaiah.

44Each of these men had a pagan wife, and some even had children by these wives.*

10:25 As in parallel text at 1 Esdras 9:26; Hebrew reads *Malkijah.*   10:37-38 As in Greek version; Hebrew reads *Jaasu, 38Bani, Binnui.*   10:44 Or *and they sent them away with their children.* The meaning of the Hebrew is uncertain.

Nehemiah

IT IS EASY TO ANALYZE, scrutinize, and talk about all the problems in the world, but we need people who will do something about them. The book of Nehemiah shows what happens when such a person steps forward. Nehemiah learned of a situation that greatly distressed him: The city walls of Jerusalem were broken down, and the city was defenseless. The small number of Jews who had returned to their homeland after decades of Babylonian captivity desperately needed the walls to be rebuilt. Nehemiah knew that the task could not wait, so he obtained permission from the king of Persia and traveled to Jerusalem. There he surveyed the situation and led the reconstruction of the walls. Despite several setbacks from enemies of Jerusalem, the task was completed within a very short time, and the walls were dedicated to the glory of God. Ezra also led the people to recommit their lives to following God's laws.

■ **Author:** Possibly Ezra, although Nehemiah's words are written in first person, suggesting that he contributed to the book

■ **Date Written:** Around 430 BC

■ **Purpose:** To chronicle the return of the exiles to Jerusalem and the rebuilding of Jerusalem's walls and to encourage the people to remain faithful to God's laws

■ **Themes:** Vision/leadership, prayer, repentance/revival

■ **Outline**

1:1–2:20 Nehemiah's arrival in Jerusalem
3:1–7:73 The work on the walls begun
8:1–10:39 The reading of the law and national repentance
11:1–13:31 The dedication of the walls and Nehemiah's reforms

---

1 These are the memoirs of Nehemiah son of Hacaliah.

Nehemiah's Concern for Jerusalem
In late autumn, in the month of Kislev, in the twentieth year of King Artaxerxes' reign,* I was at the fortress of Susa. ²Hanani, one of my brothers, came to visit me with some other men who had just arrived from Judah. I asked them about the Jews who had returned there from captivity and about how things were going in Jerusalem.

³They said to me, "Things are not going well for those who returned to the province of Judah. They are in great trouble and disgrace. The wall of Jerusalem has been torn down, and the gates have been destroyed by fire."

⁴When I heard this, I sat down and wept. In fact, for days I mourned, fasted, and prayed to the God of heaven. ⁵Then I said,

"O LORD, God of heaven, the great and awesome God who keeps his covenant of unfailing love with those who love him and obey his commands, ⁶listen to my prayer! Look down and see me praying night and day for your people Israel. I confess that we have sinned against you. Yes, even my own family and I have sinned! ⁷We have sinned terribly by not obeying the commands, decrees, and regulations that you gave us through your servant Moses.

⁸"Please remember what you told your servant Moses: 'If you are unfaithful to me, I will scatter you among the nations.

1:1 Hebrew *In the month of Kislev of the twentieth year.* A number of dates in the book of Nehemiah can be cross-checked with dates in surviving Persian records and related accurately to our modern calendar. This month of the ancient Hebrew lunar calendar occurred within the months of November and December 446 B.C. The *twentieth year* probably refers to the reign of King Artaxerxes I; compare 2:1; 5:14.

⁹But if you return to me and obey my commands and live by them, then even if you are exiled to the ends of the earth,* I will bring you back to the place I have chosen for my name to be honored.'

¹⁰"The people you rescued by your great power and strong hand are your servants. ¹¹O Lord, please hear my prayer! Listen to the prayers of those of us who delight in honoring you. Please grant me success today by making the king favorable to me.* Put it into his heart to be kind to me."

In those days I was the king's cup-bearer.

Nehemiah Goes to Jerusalem

2 Early the following spring, in the month of Nisan,* during the twentieth year of King Artaxerxes' reign, I was serving the king his wine. I had never before appeared sad in his presence. ²So the king asked me, "Why are you looking so sad? You don't look sick to me. You must be deeply troubled."

Then I was terrified, ³but I replied, "Long live the king! How can I not be sad? For the city where my ancestors are buried is in ruins, and the gates have been destroyed by fire."

⁴The king asked, "Well, how can I help you?"

With a prayer to the God of heaven, ⁵I replied, "If it please the king, and if you are pleased with me, your servant, send me to Judah to rebuild the city where my ancestors are buried."

⁶The king, with the queen sitting beside him, asked, "How long will you be gone? When will you return?" After I told him how long I would be gone, the king agreed to my request.

⁷I also said to the king, "If it please the king, let me have letters addressed to the governors of the province west of the Euphrates River,* instructing them to let me travel safely through their territories on my way to Judah. ⁸And please give me a letter addressed to Asaph, the manager of the king's forest, instructing him to give me timber. I will need it to make beams for the gates of the Temple fortress, for the city walls, and for a house for myself." And the king granted these requests, because the gracious hand of God was on me.

⁹When I came to the governors of the province west of the Euphrates River, I delivered the king's letters to them. The king, I should add, had sent along army officers and horsemen* to protect me. ¹⁰But when Sanballat the Horonite and Tobiah the Ammonite official heard of my arrival, they were very displeased that someone had come to help the people of Israel.

Nehemiah Inspects Jerusalem's Wall

¹¹So I arrived in Jerusalem. Three days later, ¹²I slipped out during the night, taking only a few others with me. I had not told anyone about the plans God had put in my heart for Jerusalem. We took no pack animals with us except the donkey I was riding. ¹³After dark I went out through the Valley Gate, past the Jackal's Well,* and over to the Dung Gate to inspect the broken walls and burned gates. ¹⁴Then I went to the Fountain Gate and to the King's Pool, but my donkey couldn't get through the rubble. ¹⁵So, though it was still dark, I went up the Kidron Valley* instead, inspecting the wall before I turned back and entered again at the Valley Gate.

¹⁶The city officials did not know I had been out there or what I was doing, for I had not yet said anything to anyone about my plans. I had not yet spoken to the Jewish leaders—the priests, the nobles, the officials, or anyone else in the administration. ¹⁷But now I said to them, "You know very well what trouble we are in. Jerusalem lies in ruins, and its gates have been destroyed by fire. Let us rebuild the wall of Jerusalem and end this disgrace!" ¹⁸Then I told them about how the gracious hand of God had been on me, and about my conversation with the king.

They replied at once, "Yes, let's rebuild the wall!" So they began the good work.

¹⁹But when Sanballat, Tobiah, and Geshem the Arab heard of our plan, they scoffed contemptuously. "What are you doing? Are you rebelling against the king?" they asked.

²⁰I replied, "The God of heaven will help us succeed. We, his servants, will start rebuilding this wall. But you have no share, legal right, or historic claim in Jerusalem."

Rebuilding the Wall of Jerusalem

3 Then Eliashib the high priest and the other priests started to rebuild at the Sheep Gate. They dedicated it and set up its doors, building the wall as far as the Tower of the Hundred, which they dedicated, and the Tower of Hananel. ²People from the town of Jericho worked

---

1:9 Hebrew *of the heavens.*   1:11 Hebrew *today in the sight of this man.*   2:1 Hebrew *In the month of Nisan.* This month of the ancient Hebrew lunar calendar occurred within the months of April and May 445 B.C.   2:7 Hebrew *the province beyond the river;* also in 2:9.   2:9 Or *charioteers.*   2:13 Or *Serpent's Well.*   2:15 Hebrew *the valley.*

next to them, and beyond them was Zaccur son of Imri.

³The Fish Gate was built by the sons of Hassenaah. They laid the beams, set up its doors, and installed its bolts and bars. ⁴Meremoth son of Uriah and grandson of Hakkoz repaired the next section of wall. Beside him were Meshullam son of Berekiah and grandson of Meshezabel, and then Zadok son of Baana. ⁵Next were the people from Tekoa, though their leaders refused to work with the construction supervisors.

⁶The Old City Gate* was repaired by Joiada son of Paseah and Meshullam son of Besodeiah. They laid the beams, set up its doors, and installed its bolts and bars. ⁷Next to them were Melatiah from Gibeon, Jadon from Meronoth, people from Gibeon, and people from Mizpah, the headquarters of the governor of the province west of the Euphrates River.* ⁸Next was Uzziel son of Harhaiah, a goldsmith by trade, who also worked on the wall. Beyond him was Hananiah, a manufacturer of perfumes. They left out a section of Jerusalem as they built the Broad Wall.*

⁹Rephaiah son of Hur, the leader of half the district of Jerusalem, was next to them on the wall. ¹⁰Next Jedaiah son of Harumaph repaired the wall across from his own house, and next to him was Hattush son of Hashabneiah. ¹¹Then came Malkijah son of Harim and Hasshub son of Pahath-moab, who repaired another section of the wall and the Tower of the Ovens. ¹²Shallum son of Hallohesh and his daughters repaired the next section. He was the leader of the other half of the district of Jerusalem.

¹³The Valley Gate was repaired by the people from Zanoah, led by Hanun. They set up its doors and installed its bolts and bars. They also repaired the 1,500 feet* of wall to the Dung Gate.

¹⁴The Dung Gate was repaired by Malkijah son of Recab, the leader of the Beth-hakkerem district. He rebuilt it, set up its doors, and installed its bolts and bars.

¹⁵The Fountain Gate was repaired by Shallum* son of Col-hozeh, the leader of the Mizpah district. He rebuilt it, roofed it, set up its doors, and installed its bolts and bars. Then he repaired the wall of the pool of Siloam* near the king's garden, and he rebuilt the wall as far as the stairs that descend from the City of David. ¹⁶Next to him was Nehemiah son of Azbuk, the leader of half the district of Beth-zur. He rebuilt the wall from a place across from the tombs of David's family as far as the water reservoir and the House of the Warriors.

¹⁷Next to him, repairs were made by a group of Levites working under the supervision of Rehum son of Bani. Then came Hashabiah, the leader of half the district of Keilah, who supervised the building of the wall on behalf of his own district. ¹⁸Next down the line were his countrymen led by Binnui* son of Henadad, the leader of the other half of the district of Keilah.

¹⁹Next to them, Ezer son of Jeshua, the leader of Mizpah, repaired another section of wall across from the ascent to the armory near the angle in the wall. ²⁰Next to him was Baruch son of Zabbai, who zealously repaired an additional section from the angle to the door of the house of Eliashib the high priest. ²¹Meremoth son of Uriah and grandson of Hakkoz rebuilt another section of the wall extending from the door of Eliashib's house to the end of the house.

²²The next repairs were made by the priests from the surrounding region. ²³After them, Benjamin and Hasshub repaired the section across from their house, and Azariah son of Maaseiah and grandson of Ananiah repaired the section across from his house. ²⁴Next was Binnui son of Henadad, who rebuilt another section of the wall from Azariah's house to the angle and the corner. ²⁵Palal son of Uzai carried on the work from a point opposite the angle and the tower that projects up from the king's upper house beside the court of the guard. Next to him were Pedaiah son of Parosh, ²⁶with the Temple servants living on the hill of Ophel, who repaired the wall as far as a point across from the Water Gate to the east and the projecting tower. ²⁷Then came the people of Tekoa, who repaired another section across from the great projecting tower and over to the wall of Ophel.

²⁸Above the Horse Gate, the priests repaired the wall. Each one repaired the section immediately across from his own house. ²⁹Next Zadok son of Immer also rebuilt the wall across from his own house, and beyond him was Shemaiah son of Shecaniah, the gatekeeper of the East Gate. ³⁰Next Hananiah son of Shelemiah

3:6 Or The Mishneh Gate, or The Jeshanah Gate.   3:7 Hebrew the province beyond the river.   3:8 Or They fortified Jerusalem up to the Broad Wall.   3:13 Hebrew 1,000 cubits [460 meters].   3:15a As in Syriac version; Hebrew reads Shallun.   3:15b Hebrew pool of Shelah, another name for the pool of Siloam.   3:18 As in a few Hebrew manuscripts, some Greek manuscripts, and Syriac version (see also 3:24; 10:9); most Hebrew manuscripts read Bavvai.

and Hanun, the sixth son of Zalaph, repaired another section, while Meshullam son of Berekiah rebuilt the wall across from where he lived. [31]Malkijah, one of the goldsmiths, repaired the wall as far as the housing for the Temple servants and merchants, across from the Inspection Gate. Then he continued as far as the upper room at the corner. [32]The other goldsmiths and merchants repaired the wall from that corner to the Sheep Gate.

Enemies Oppose the Rebuilding

4 [1]*Sanballat was very angry when he learned that we were rebuilding the wall. He flew into a rage and mocked the Jews, [2]saying in front of his friends and the Samarian army officers, "What does this bunch of poor, feeble Jews think they're doing? Do they think they can build the wall in a single day by just offering a few sacrifices?* Do they actually think they can make something of stones from a rubbish heap—and charred ones at that?"

[3]Tobiah the Ammonite, who was standing beside him, remarked, "That stone wall would collapse if even a fox walked along the top of it!"

[4]Then I prayed, "Hear us, our God, for we are being mocked. May their scoffing fall back on their own heads, and may they themselves become captives in a foreign land! [5]Do not ignore their guilt. Do not blot out their sins, for they have provoked you to anger here in front of* the builders."

[6]At last the wall was completed to half its height around the entire city, for the people had worked with enthusiasm.

[7]*But when Sanballat and Tobiah and the Arabs, Ammonites, and Ashdodites heard that the work was going ahead and that the gaps in the wall of Jerusalem were being repaired, they were furious. [8]They all made plans to come and fight against Jerusalem and throw us into confusion. [9]But we prayed to our God and guarded the city day and night to protect ourselves.

[10]Then the people of Judah began to complain, "The workers are getting tired, and there is so much rubble to be moved. We will never be able to build the wall by ourselves."

[11]Meanwhile, our enemies were saying, "Before they know what's happening, we will swoop down on them and kill them and end their work."

[12]The Jews who lived near the enemy came and told us again and again, "They will come from all directions and attack us!"* [13]So I placed armed guards behind the lowest parts of the wall in the exposed areas. I stationed the people to stand guard by families, armed with swords, spears, and bows.

[14]Then as I looked over the situation, I called together the nobles and the rest of the people and said to them, "Don't be afraid of the enemy! Remember the Lord, who is great and glorious, and fight for your brothers, your sons, your daughters, your wives, and your homes!"

[15]When our enemies heard that we knew of their plans and that God had frustrated them, we all returned to our work on the wall. [16]But from then on, only half my men worked while the other half stood guard with spears, shields, bows, and coats of mail. The leaders stationed themselves behind the people of Judah [17]who were building the wall. The laborers carried on their work with one hand supporting their load and one hand holding a weapon. [18]All the builders had a sword belted to their side. The trumpeter stayed with me to sound the alarm.

[19]Then I explained to the nobles and officials and all the people, "The work is very spread out, and we are widely separated from each other along the wall. [20]When you hear the blast of the trumpet, rush to wherever it is sounding. Then our God will fight for us!"

[21]We worked early and late, from sunrise to sunset. And half the men were always on guard. [22]I also told everyone living outside the walls to stay in Jerusalem. That way they and their servants could help with guard duty at night and work during the day. [23]During this time, none of us—not I, nor my relatives, nor my servants, nor the guards who were with me—ever took off our clothes. We carried our weapons with us at all times, even when we went for water.*

Nehemiah Defends the Oppressed

5 About this time some of the men and their wives raised a cry of protest against their fellow Jews. [2]They were saying, "We have such large families. We need more food to survive."

[3]Others said, "We have mortgaged our fields, vineyards, and homes to get food during the famine."

4:1 Verses 4:1-6 are numbered 3:33-38 in Hebrew text.   4:2 The meaning of the Hebrew is uncertain.   4:5 Or for they have thrown insults in the face of.   4:7 Verses 4:7-23 are numbered 4:1-17 in Hebrew text.   4:12 The meaning of the Hebrew is uncertain.   4:23 Or Each carried his weapon in his right hand. Hebrew reads Each his weapon the water. The meaning of the Hebrew is uncertain.

⁴And others said, "We have had to borrow money on our fields and vineyards to pay our taxes. ⁵We belong to the same family as those who are wealthy, and our children are just like theirs. Yet we must sell our children into slavery just to get enough money to live. We have already sold some of our daughters, and we are helpless to do anything about it, for our fields and vineyards are already mortgaged to others."

⁶When I heard their complaints, I was very angry. ⁷After thinking it over, I spoke out against these nobles and officials. I told them, "You are hurting your own relatives by charging interest when they borrow money!" Then I called a public meeting to deal with the problem.

⁸At the meeting I said to them, "We are doing all we can to redeem our Jewish relatives who have had to sell themselves to pagan foreigners, but you are selling them back into slavery again. How often must we redeem them?" And they had nothing to say in their defense.

⁹Then I pressed further, "What you are doing is not right! Should you not walk in the fear of our God in order to avoid being mocked by enemy nations? ¹⁰I myself, as well as my brothers and my workers, have been lending the people money and grain, but now let us stop this business of charging interest. ¹¹You must restore their fields, vineyards, olive groves, and homes to them this very day. And repay the interest you charged when you lent them money, grain, new wine, and olive oil."

¹²They replied, "We will give back everything and demand nothing more from the people. We will do as you say." Then I called the priests and made the nobles and officials swear to do what they had promised.

¹³I shook out the folds of my robe and said, "If you fail to keep your promise, may God shake you like this from your homes and from your property!"

The whole assembly responded, "Amen," and they praised the LORD. And the people did as they had promised.

¹⁴For the entire twelve years that I was governor of Judah—from the twentieth year to the thirty-second year of the reign of King Artaxerxes*—neither I nor my officials drew on our official food allowance. ¹⁵The former governors, in contrast, had laid heavy burdens on the people, demanding a daily ration of food and wine, besides forty pieces* of silver. Even their assistants took advantage of the people. But because I feared God, I did not act that way.

¹⁶I also devoted myself to working on the wall and refused to acquire any land. And I required all my servants to spend time working on the wall. ¹⁷I asked for nothing, even though I regularly fed 150 Jewish officials at my table, besides all the visitors from other lands! ¹⁸The provisions I paid for each day included one ox, six choice sheep or goats, and a large number of poultry. And every ten days we needed a large supply of all kinds of wine. Yet I refused to claim the governor's food allowance because the people already carried a heavy burden.

¹⁹Remember, O my God, all that I have done for these people, and bless me for it.

Continued Opposition to Rebuilding

6 Sanballat, Tobiah, Geshem the Arab, and the rest of our enemies found out that I had finished rebuilding the wall and that no gaps remained—though we had not yet set up the doors in the gates. ²So Sanballat and Geshem sent a message asking me to meet them at one of the villages* in the plain of Ono.

But I realized they were plotting to harm me, ³so I replied by sending this message to them: "I am engaged in a great work, so I can't come. Why should I stop working to come and meet with you?"

⁴Four times they sent the same message, and each time I gave the same reply. ⁵The fifth time, Sanballat's servant came with an open letter in his hand, ⁶and this is what it said:

"There is a rumor among the surrounding nations, and Geshem* tells me it is true, that you and the Jews are planning to rebel and that is why you are building the wall. According to his reports, you plan to be their king. ⁷He also reports that you have appointed prophets in Jerusalem to proclaim about you, 'Look! There is a king in Judah!'

"You can be very sure that this report will get back to the king, so I suggest that you come and talk it over with me."

⁸I replied, "There is no truth in any part of your story. You are making up the whole thing."

5:14 That is, 445–433 B.C.   5:15 Hebrew *40 shekels* [1 pound or 456 grams].   6:2 As in Greek version; Hebrew reads *at Kephirim.*
6:6 Hebrew *Gashmu,* a variant spelling of Geshem.

[9]They were just trying to intimidate us, imagining that they could discourage us and stop the work. So I continued the work with even greater determination.*

[10]Later I went to visit Shemaiah son of Delaiah and grandson of Mehetabel, who was confined to his home. He said, "Let us meet together inside the Temple of God and bolt the doors shut. Your enemies are coming to kill you tonight."

[11]But I replied, "Should someone in my position run from danger? Should someone in my position enter the Temple to save his life? No, I won't do it!" [12]I realized that God had not spoken to him, but that he had uttered this prophecy against me because Tobiah and Sanballat had hired him. [13]They were hoping to intimidate me and make me sin. Then they would be able to accuse and discredit me.

[14]Remember, O my God, all the evil things that Tobiah and Sanballat have done. And remember Noadiah the prophet and all the prophets like her who have tried to intimidate me.

The Builders Complete the Wall

[15]So on October 2* the wall was finished—just fifty-two days after we had begun. [16]When our enemies and the surrounding nations heard about it, they were frightened and humiliated. They realized this work had been done with the help of our God.

[17]During those fifty-two days, many letters went back and forth between Tobiah and the nobles of Judah. [18]For many in Judah had sworn allegiance to him because his father-in-law was Shecaniah son of Arah, and his son Jehohanan was married to the daughter of Meshullam son of Berekiah. [19]They kept telling me about Tobiah's good deeds, and then they told him everything I said. And Tobiah kept sending threatening letters to intimidate me.

7 After the wall was finished and I had set up the doors in the gates, the gatekeepers, singers, and Levites were appointed. [2]I gave the responsibility of governing Jerusalem to my brother Hanani, along with Hananiah, the commander of the fortress, for he was a faithful man who feared God more than most. [3]I said to them, "Do not leave the gates open during the hottest part of the day.* And even while the gatekeepers are on duty, have them shut and bar the doors. Appoint the residents of Jerusalem to act as guards, everyone on a regular watch. Some will serve at sentry posts and some in front of their own homes."

Nehemiah Registers the People

[4]At that time the city was large and spacious, but the population was small, and none of the houses had been rebuilt. [5]So my God gave me the idea to call together all the nobles and leaders of the city, along with the ordinary citizens, for registration. I had found the genealogical record of those who had first returned to Judah. This is what was written there:

[6]Here is the list of the Jewish exiles of the provinces who returned from their captivity. King Nebuchadnezzar had deported them to Babylon, but now they returned to Jerusalem and the other towns in Judah where they originally lived. [7]Their leaders were Zerubbabel, Jeshua, Nehemiah, Seraiah,* Reelaiah,* Nahamani, Mordecai, Bilshan, Mispar,* Bigvai, Rehum,* and Baanah.

This is the number of the men of Israel who returned from exile:

[8]	The family of Parosh	2,172
[9]	The family of Shephatiah	372
[10]	The family of Arah	652
[11]	The family of Pahath-moab (descendants of Jeshua and Joab)	2,818
[12]	The family of Elam	1,254
[13]	The family of Zattu	845
[14]	The family of Zaccai	760
[15]	The family of Bani*	648
[16]	The family of Bebai	628
[17]	The family of Azgad	2,322
[18]	The family of Adonikam	667
[19]	The family of Bigvai	2,067
[20]	The family of Adin	655
[21]	The family of Ater (descendants of Hezekiah)	98
[22]	The family of Hashum	328
[23]	The family of Bezai	324

6:9 As in Greek version; Hebrew reads *But now to strengthen my hands.*   6:15 Hebrew *on the twenty-fifth day of the month Elul,* of the ancient Hebrew lunar calendar. This day was October 2, 445 B.C.; also see note on 1:1.   7:3 Or *Keep the gates of Jerusalem closed until the sun is hot.*   7:7a As in parallel text at Ezra 2:2; Hebrew reads *Azariah.*   7:7b As in parallel text at Ezra 2:2; Hebrew reads *Raamiah.*   7:7c As in parallel text at Ezra 2:2; Hebrew reads *Mispereth.*   7:7d As in parallel text at Ezra 2:2; Hebrew reads *Nehum.*   7:15 As in parallel text at Ezra 2:10; Hebrew reads *Binnui.*

²⁴ The family of Jorah*...............112

²⁵ The family of Gibbar*............. 95

²⁶ The people of Bethlehem and
Netophah.....................188

²⁷ The people of Anathoth........... 128

²⁸ The people of Beth-azmaveth....... 42

²⁹ The people of Kiriath-jearim,
Kephirah, and Beeroth.......... 743

³⁰ The people of Ramah and Geba 621

³¹ The people of Micmash...........122

³² The people of Bethel and Ai.......123

³³ The people of West Nebo*.......... 52

³⁴ The citizens of West Elam*........1,254

³⁵ The citizens of Harim............. 320

³⁶ The citizens of Jericho............. 345

³⁷ The citizens of Lod, Hadid,
and Ono......................721

³⁸ The citizens of Senaah...........3,930

³⁹These are the priests who returned from exile:

The family of Jedaiah (through the
line of Jeshua).................. 973

⁴⁰ The family of Immer.............1,052

⁴¹ The family of Pashhur...........1,247

⁴² The family of Harim 1,017

⁴³These are the Levites who returned from exile:

The families of Jeshua and Kadmiel
(descendants of Hodaviah*)....... 74

⁴⁴ The singers of the family of Asaph .. 148

⁴⁵ The gatekeepers of the families of
Shallum, Ater, Talmon, Akkub,
Hatita, and Shobai..............138

⁴⁶The descendants of the following Temple servants returned from exile:
Ziha, Hasupha, Tabbaoth,

⁴⁷ Keros, Siaha,* Padon,

⁴⁸ Lebanah, Hagabah, Shalmai,

⁴⁹ Hanan, Giddel, Gahar,

⁵⁰ Reaiah, Rezin, Nekoda,

⁵¹ Gazzam, Uzza, Paseah,

⁵² Besai, Meunim, Nephusim,*

⁵³ Bakbuk, Hakupha, Harhur,

⁵⁴ Bazluth,* Mehida, Harsha,

⁵⁵ Barkos, Sisera, Temah,

⁵⁶ Neziah, and Hatipha.

⁵⁷The descendants of these servants of King Solomon returned from exile:
Sotai, Hassophereth, Peruda,*

⁵⁸ Jaalah,* Darkon, Giddel,

⁵⁹ Shephatiah, Hattil, Pokereth-hazzebaim, and Ami.*

⁶⁰In all, the Temple servants and the descendants of Solomon's servants numbered 392.

⁶¹Another group returned at this time from the towns of Tel-melah, Tel-harsha, Kerub, Addan,* and Immer. However, they could not prove that they or their families were descendants of Israel. ⁶²This group included the families of Delaiah, Tobiah, and Nekoda—a total of 642 people.

⁶³Three families of priests—Hobaiah, Hakkoz, and Barzillai—also returned. (This Barzillai had married a woman who was a descendant of Barzillai of Gilead, and he had taken her family name.) ⁶⁴They searched for their names in the genealogical records, but they were not found, so they were disqualified from serving as priests. ⁶⁵The governor told them not to eat the priests' share of food from the sacrifices until a priest could consult the LORD about the matter by using the Urim and Thummim—the sacred lots.

⁶⁶So a total of 42,360 people returned to Judah, ⁶⁷in addition to 7,337 servants and 245 singers, both men and women. ⁶⁸They took with them 736 horses, 245 mules,* ⁶⁹435 camels, and 6,720 donkeys.

⁷⁰Some of the family leaders gave gifts for the work. The governor gave to the treasury 1,000 gold coins,* 50 gold basins, and 530 robes for the priests. ⁷¹The other leaders gave to the treasury a total of 20,000 gold coins* and some 2,750 pounds* of silver for the work. ⁷²The rest of the people gave 20,000 gold coins, about 2,500 pounds* of silver, and 67 robes for the priests.

⁷³So the priests, the Levites, the gatekeepers, the singers, the Temple

---

7:24 As in parallel text at Ezra 2:18; Hebrew reads *Hariph.* **7:25** As in parallel text at Ezra 2:20; Hebrew reads *Gibeon.* **7:33** Or *of the other Nebo.* **7:34** Or *of the other Elam.* **7:43** As in parallel text at Ezra 2:40; Hebrew reads *Hodevah.* **7:47** As in parallel text at Ezra 2:44; Hebrew reads *Sia.* **7:52** As in parallel text at Ezra 2:50; Hebrew reads *Nephushesim.* **7:54** As in parallel text at Ezra 2:52; Hebrew reads *Bazlith.* **7:57** As in parallel text at Ezra 2:55; Hebrew reads *Sotai, Sophereth, Perida.* **7:58** As in parallel text at Ezra 2:56; Hebrew reads *Jaala.* **7:59** As in parallel text at Ezra 2:57; Hebrew reads *Amon.* **7:61** As in parallel text at Ezra 2:59; Hebrew reads *Addon.* **7:68** As in some Hebrew manuscripts (see also Ezra 2:66); most Hebrew manuscripts lack this verse. Verses 7:69-73 are numbered 7:68-72 in Hebrew text. **7:70** Hebrew *1,000 darics of gold,* about 19 pounds or 8.6 kilograms in weight. **7:71a** Hebrew *20,000 darics of gold,* about 375 pounds or 170 kilograms in weight; also in 7:72. **7:71b** Hebrew *2,200 minas* [1,300 kilograms]. **7:72** Hebrew *2,000 minas* [1,200 kilograms].

servants, and some of the common people settled near Jerusalem. The rest of the people returned to their own towns throughout Israel.

Ezra Reads the Law

8 In October,* when the Israelites had settled in their towns, 8:1all the people assembled with a unified purpose at the square just inside the Water Gate. They asked Ezra the scribe to bring out the Book of the Law of Moses, which the LORD had given for Israel to obey.

²So on October 8* Ezra the priest brought the Book of the Law before the assembly, which included the men and women and all the children old enough to understand. ³He faced the square just inside the Water Gate from early morning until noon and read aloud to everyone who could understand. All the people listened closely to the Book of the Law.

⁴Ezra the scribe stood on a high wooden platform that had been made for the occasion. To his right stood Mattithiah, Shema, Anaiah, Uriah, Hilkiah, and Maaseiah. To his left stood Pedaiah, Mishael, Malkijah, Hashum, Hashbaddanah, Zechariah, and Meshullam. ⁵Ezra stood on the platform in full view of all the people. When they saw him open the book, they all rose to their feet.

⁶Then Ezra praised the LORD, the great God, and all the people chanted, "Amen! Amen!" as they lifted their hands. Then they bowed down and worshiped the LORD with their faces to the ground.

⁷The Levites—Jeshua, Bani, Sherebiah, Jamin, Akkub, Shabbethai, Hodiah, Maaseiah, Kelita, Azariah, Jozabad, Hanan, and Pelaiah—then instructed the people in the Law while everyone remained in their places. ⁸They read from the Book of the Law of God and clearly explained the meaning of what was being read, helping the people understand each passage.

⁹Then Nehemiah the governor, Ezra the priest and scribe, and the Levites who were interpreting for the people said to them, "Don't mourn or weep on such a day as this! For today is a sacred day before the LORD your God." For the people had all been weeping as they listened to the words of the Law.

¹⁰And Nehemiah* continued, "Go and celebrate with a feast of rich foods and sweet drinks, and share gifts of food with people who have nothing prepared. This is a sacred day before our Lord. Don't be dejected and sad, for the joy of the LORD is your strength!"

¹¹And the Levites, too, quieted the people, telling them, "Hush! Don't weep! For this is a sacred day." ¹²So the people went away to eat and drink at a festive meal, to share gifts of food, and to celebrate with great joy because they had heard God's words and understood them.

The Festival of Shelters

¹³On October 9* the family leaders of all the people, together with the priests and Levites, met with Ezra the scribe to go over the Law in greater detail. ¹⁴As they studied the Law, they discovered that the LORD had commanded through Moses that the Israelites should live in shelters during the festival to be held that month.* ¹⁵He had said that a proclamation should be made throughout their towns and in Jerusalem, telling the people to go to the hills to get branches from olive, wild olive,* myrtle, palm, and other leafy trees. They were to use these branches to make shelters in which they would live during the festival, as prescribed in the Law.

¹⁶So the people went out and cut branches and used them to build shelters on the roofs of their houses, in their courtyards, in the courtyards of God's Temple, or in the squares just inside the Water Gate and the Ephraim Gate. ¹⁷So everyone who had returned from captivity lived in these shelters during the festival, and they were all filled with great joy! The Israelites had not celebrated like this since the days of Joshua* son of Nun.

¹⁸Ezra read from the Book of the Law of God on each of the seven days of the festival. Then on the eighth day they held a solemn assembly, as was required by law.

The People Confess Their Sins

9 On October 31* the people assembled again, and this time they fasted and dressed in burlap and sprinkled dust on their heads. ²Those of Israelite descent separated themselves from

---

7:73 Hebrew *In the seventh month.* This month of the ancient Hebrew lunar calendar occurred within the months of October and November 445 B.C.   8:2 Hebrew *on the first day of the seventh month,* of the ancient Hebrew lunar calendar. This day was October 8, 445 B.C.; also see note on 1:1.   8:10 Hebrew *he.*   8:13 Hebrew *On the second day,* of the seventh month of the ancient Hebrew lunar calendar. This day was October 9, 445 B.C.; also see notes on 1:1 and 8:2.   8:14 Hebrew *in the seventh month.* This month of the ancient Hebrew lunar calendar usually occurs within the months of September and October. See Lev 23:39-43.   8:15 Or *pine;* Hebrew reads *oil tree.*   8:17 Hebrew *Jeshua,* a variant spelling of Joshua.   9:1 Hebrew *On the twenty-fourth day of that same month,* the seventh month of the ancient Hebrew lunar calendar. This day was October 31, 445 B.C.; also see notes on 1:1 and 8:2.

all foreigners as they confessed their own sins and the sins of their ancestors. ³They remained standing in place for three hours* while the Book of the Law of the LORD their God was read aloud to them. Then for three more hours they confessed their sins and worshiped the LORD their God. ⁴The Levites—Jeshua, Bani, Kadmiel, Shebaniah, Bunni, Sherebiah, Bani, and Kenani—stood on the stairway of the Levites and cried out to the LORD their God with loud voices.

⁵Then the leaders of the Levites—Jeshua, Kadmiel, Bani, Hashabneiah, Sherebiah, Hodiah, Shebaniah, and Pethahiah—called out to the people: "Stand up and praise the LORD your God, for he lives from everlasting to everlasting!" Then they prayed:

"May your glorious name be praised! May it be exalted above all blessing and praise!

⁶"You alone are the LORD. You made the skies and the heavens and all the stars. You made the earth and the seas and everything in them. You preserve them all, and the angels of heaven worship you.

⁷"You are the LORD God, who chose Abram and brought him from Ur of the Chaldeans and renamed him Abraham. ⁸When he had proved himself faithful, you made a covenant with him to give him and his descendants the land of the Canaanites, Hittites, Amorites, Perizzites, Jebusites, and Girgashites. And you have done what you promised, for you are always true to your word.

⁹"You saw the misery of our ancestors in Egypt, and you heard their cries from beside the Red Sea.* ¹⁰You displayed miraculous signs and wonders against Pharaoh, his officials, and all his people, for you knew how arrogantly they were treating our ancestors. You have a glorious reputation that has never been forgotten. ¹¹You divided the sea for your people so they could walk through on dry land! And then you hurled their enemies into the depths of the sea. They sank like stones beneath the mighty waters. ¹²You led our ancestors by a pillar of cloud during the day and a pillar of fire at night so that they could find their way.

¹³"You came down at Mount Sinai and spoke to them from heaven. You gave them regulations and instructions that

were just, and decrees and commands that were good. ¹⁴You instructed them concerning your holy Sabbath. And you commanded them, through Moses your servant, to obey all your commands, decrees, and instructions.

¹⁵"You gave them bread from heaven when they were hungry and water from the rock when they were thirsty. You commanded them to go and take possession of the land you had sworn to give them.

¹⁶"But our ancestors were proud and stubborn, and they paid no attention to your commands. ¹⁷They refused to obey and did not remember the miracles you had done for them. Instead, they became stubborn and appointed a leader to take them back to their slavery in Egypt.* But you are a God of forgiveness, gracious and merciful, slow to become angry, and rich in unfailing love. You did not abandon them, ¹⁸even when they made an idol shaped like a calf and said, 'This is your god who brought you out of Egypt!' They committed terrible blasphemies.

¹⁹"But in your great mercy you did not abandon them to die in the wilderness. The pillar of cloud still led them forward by day, and the pillar of fire showed them the way through the night. ²⁰You sent your good Spirit to instruct them, and you did not stop giving them manna from heaven or water for their thirst. ²¹For forty years you sustained them in the wilderness, and they lacked nothing. Their clothes did not wear out, and their feet did not swell!

²²"Then you helped our ancestors conquer kingdoms and nations, and you placed your people in every corner of the land.* They took over the land of King Sihon of Heshbon and the land of King Og of Bashan. ²³You made their descendants as numerous as the stars in the sky and brought them into the land you had promised to their ancestors.

²⁴"They went in and took possession of the land. You subdued whole nations before them. Even the Canaanites, who inhabited the land, were powerless! Your people could deal with these nations and their kings as they pleased. ²⁵Our ancestors captured fortified cities and fertile land. They took over houses full of good things,

9:3 Hebrew *for a quarter of a day.*   9:9 Hebrew *sea of reeds.*   9:17 As in Greek version; Hebrew reads *in their rebellion.*   9:22 The meaning of the Hebrew is uncertain.

with cisterns already dug and vineyards and olive groves and fruit trees in abundance. So they ate until they were full and grew fat and enjoyed themselves in all your blessings.

26"But despite all this, they were disobedient and rebelled against you. They turned their backs on your Law, they killed your prophets who warned them to return to you, and they committed terrible blasphemies. 27So you handed them over to their enemies, who made them suffer. But in their time of trouble they cried to you, and you heard them from heaven. In your great mercy, you sent them liberators who rescued them from their enemies.

28"But as soon as they were at peace, your people again committed evil in your sight, and once more you let their enemies conquer them. Yet whenever your people turned and cried to you again for help, you listened once more from heaven. In your wonderful mercy, you rescued them many times!

29"You warned them to return to your Law, but they became proud and obstinate and disobeyed your commands. They did not follow your regulations, by which people will find life if only they obey. They stubbornly turned their backs on you and refused to listen. 30In your love, you were patient with them for many years. You sent your Spirit, who warned them through the prophets. But still they wouldn't listen! So once again you allowed the peoples of the land to conquer them. 31But in your great mercy, you did not destroy them completely or abandon them forever. What a gracious and merciful God you are!

32"And now, our God, the great and mighty and awesome God, who keeps his covenant of unfailing love, do not let all the hardships we have suffered seem insignificant to you. Great trouble has come upon us and upon our kings and leaders and priests and prophets and ancestors—all of your people—from the days when the kings of Assyria first triumphed over us until now. 33Every time you punished us you were being just. We have sinned greatly, and you gave us only what we deserved. 34Our kings, leaders, priests, and ancestors did not obey your Law or listen to the warnings in your commands and laws. 35Even while they had their own kingdom, they did not serve you, though you showered your goodness on them. You gave them a large, fertile land, but they refused to turn from their wickedness.

36"So now today we are slaves in the land of plenty that you gave our ancestors for their enjoyment! We are slaves here in this good land. 37The lush produce of this land piles up in the hands of the kings whom you have set over us because of our sins. They have power over us and our livestock. We serve them at their pleasure, and we are in great misery."

The People Agree to Obey

38*The people responded, "In view of all this,* we are making a solemn promise and putting it in writing. On this sealed document are the names of our leaders and Levites and priests."

10 1*The document was ratified and sealed with the following names:

The governor:
Nehemiah son of Hacaliah, and also Zedekiah.

2The following priests:
Seraiah, Azariah, Jeremiah, 3Pashhur, Amariah, Malkijah, 4Hattush, Shebaniah, Malluch, 5Harim, Meremoth, Obadiah, 6Daniel, Ginnethon, Baruch, 7Meshullam, Abijah, Mijamin, 8Maaziah, Bilgai, and Shemaiah. These were the priests.

9The following Levites:
Jeshua son of Azaniah, Binnui from the family of Henadad, Kadmiel, 10and their fellow Levites: Shebaniah, Hodiah, Kelita, Pelaiah, Hanan, 11Mica, Rehob, Hashabiah, 12Zaccur, Sherebiah, Shebaniah, 13Hodiah, Bani, and Beninu.

14The following leaders:
Parosh, Pahath-moab, Elam, Zattu, Bani, 15Bunni, Azgad, Bebai, 16Adonijah, Bigvai, Adin, 17Ater, Hezekiah, Azzur, 18Hodiah, Hashum, Bezai, 19Hariph, Anathoth, Nebai, 20Magpiash, Meshullam, Hezir, 21Meshezabel, Zadok, Jaddua, 22Pelatiah, Hanan, Anaiah, 23Hoshea, Hananiah, Hasshub, 24Hallohesh, Pilha, Shobek, 25Rehum, Hashabnah, Maaseiah, 26Ahiah, Hanan, Anan, 27Malluch, Harim, and Baanah.

9:38a Verse 9:38 is numbered 10:1 in Hebrew text.   9:38b Or In spite of all this.   10:1 Verses 10:1-39 are numbered 10:2-40 in Hebrew text.

The Vow of the People

28Then the rest of the people—the priests, Levites, gatekeepers, singers, Temple servants, and all who had separated themselves from the pagan people of the land in order to obey the Law of God, together with their wives, sons, daughters, and all who were old enough to understand—29joined their leaders and bound themselves with an oath. They swore a curse on themselves if they failed to obey the Law of God as issued by his servant Moses. They solemnly promised to carefully follow all the commands, regulations, and decrees of the Lord our Lord:

30"We promise not to let our daughters marry the pagan people of the land, and not to let our sons marry their daughters.

31"We also promise that if the people of the land should bring any merchandise or grain to be sold on the Sabbath or on any other holy day, we will refuse to buy it. Every seventh year we will let our land rest, and we will cancel all debts owed to us.

32"In addition, we promise to obey the command to pay the annual Temple tax of one-eighth of an ounce of silver* for the care of the Temple of our God. 33This will provide for the Bread of the Presence; for the regular grain offerings and burnt offerings; for the offerings on the Sabbaths, the new moon celebrations, and the annual festivals; for the holy offerings; and for the sin offerings to make atonement for Israel. It will provide for everything necessary for the work of the Temple of our God.

34"We have cast sacred lots to determine when—at regular times each year—the families of the priests, Levites, and the common people should bring wood to God's Temple to be burned on the altar of the Lord our God, as is written in the Law.

35"We promise to bring the first part of every harvest to the Lord's Temple year after year—whether it be a crop from the soil or from our fruit trees. 36We agree to give God our oldest sons and the firstborn of all our herds and flocks, as prescribed in the Law. We will present them to the priests who minister in the Temple of our God. 37We will store the produce in the storerooms of the Temple of our God. We will bring the best of our flour and other grain offerings, the best of our fruit, and the best of our new wine and olive oil. And we promise to bring to the Levites a tenth of everything our land produces, for it is the Levites who collect the tithes in all our rural towns.

38"A priest—a descendant of Aaron—will be with the Levites as they receive these tithes. And a tenth of all that is collected as tithes will be delivered by the Levites to the Temple of our God and placed in the storerooms. 39The people and the Levites must bring these offerings of grain, new wine, and olive oil to the storerooms and place them in the sacred containers near the ministering priests, the gatekeepers, and the singers.

"We promise together not to neglect the Temple of our God."

The People Occupy Jerusalem

11 The leaders of the people were living in Jerusalem, the holy city. A tenth of the people from the other towns of Judah and Benjamin were chosen by sacred lots to live there, too, while the rest stayed where they were. 2And the people commended everyone who volunteered to resettle in Jerusalem.

3Here is a list of the names of the provincial officials who came to live in Jerusalem. (Most of the people, priests, Levites, Temple servants, and descendants of Solomon's servants continued to live in their own homes in the various towns of Judah, 4but some of the people from Judah and Benjamin resettled in Jerusalem.)

From the tribe of Judah:
Athaiah son of Uzziah, son of Zechariah, son of Amariah, son of Shephatiah, son of Mahalalel, of the family of Perez. 5Also Maaseiah son of Baruch, son of Col-hozeh, son of Hazaiah, son of Adaiah, son of Joiarib, son of Zechariah, of the family of Shelah.* 6There were 468 descendants of Perez who lived in Jerusalem—all outstanding men.

7From the tribe of Benjamin:
Sallu son of Meshullam, son of Joed, son of Pedaiah, son of Kolaiah, son of Maaseiah, son of Ithiel, son of Jeshaiah. 8After him were Gabbai and Sallai and a total of 928 relatives. 9Their chief officer was Joel son of Zicri, who was assisted by Judah son of Hassenuah, second-in-command over the city.

10:32 Hebrew *tax of ⅓ of a shekel* [4 grams].   11:5 Hebrew *son of the Shilonite.*

[10]From the priests:

Jedaiah son of Joiarib; Jakin; [11]and Seraiah son of Hilkiah, son of Meshullam, son of Zadok, son of Meraioth, son of Ahitub, the supervisor of the Temple of God. [12]Also 822 of their associates, who worked at the Temple. Also Adaiah son of Jeroham, son of Pelaliah, son of Amzi, son of Zechariah, son of Pashhur, son of Malkijah, [13]along with 242 of his associates, who were heads of their families. Also Amashsai son of Azarel, son of Ahzai, son of Meshillemoth, son of Immer, [14]and 128 of his* outstanding associates. Their chief officer was Zabdiel son of Haggedolim.

[15]From the Levites:

Shemaiah son of Hasshub, son of Azrikam, son of Hashabiah, son of Bunni. [16]Also Shabbethai and Jozabad, who were in charge of the work outside the Temple of God. [17]Also Mattaniah son of Mica, son of Zabdi, a descendant of Asaph, who led in thanksgiving and prayer. Also Bakbukiah, who was Mattaniah's assistant, and Abda son of Shammua, son of Galal, son of Jeduthun. [18]In all, there were 284 Levites in the holy city.

[19]From the gatekeepers:

Akkub, Talmon, and 172 of their associates, who guarded the gates.

[20]The other priests, Levites, and the rest of the Israelites lived wherever their family inheritance was located in any of the towns of Judah. [21]The Temple servants, however, whose leaders were Ziha and Gishpa, all lived on the hill of Ophel.

[22]The chief officer of the Levites in Jerusalem was Uzzi son of Bani, son of Hashabiah, son of Mattaniah, son of Mica, a descendant of Asaph, whose family served as singers at God's Temple. [23]Their daily responsibilities were carried out according to the terms of a royal command.

[24]Pethahiah son of Meshezabel, a descendant of Zerah son of Judah, was the royal adviser in all matters of public administration.

[25]As for the surrounding villages with their open fields, some of the people of Judah lived in Kiriath-arba with its settlements, Dibon with its settlements, and Jekabzeel with its villages. [26]They also lived in Jeshua, Moladah, Beth-pelet, [27]Hazar-shual, Beersheba with its settlements, [28]Ziklag, and Meconah with its settlements. [29]They also lived in En-rimmon, Zorah, Jarmuth, [30]Zanoah, and Adullam with their surrounding villages. They also lived in Lachish with its nearby fields and Azekah with its surrounding villages. So the people of Judah were living all the way from Beersheba in the south to the valley of Hinnom.

[31]Some of the people of Benjamin lived at Geba, Micmash, Aija, and Bethel with its settlements. [32]They also lived in Anathoth, Nob, Ananiah, [33]Hazor, Ramah, Gittaim, [34]Hadid, Zeboim, Neballat, [35]Lod, Ono, and the Valley of Craftsmen.* [36]Some of the Levites who lived in Judah were sent to live with the tribe of Benjamin.

A History of the Priests and Levites

12 Here is the list of the priests and Levites who returned with Zerubbabel son of Shealtiel and Jeshua the high priest:

Seraiah, Jeremiah, Ezra,
[2] Amariah, Malluch, Hattush,
[3] Shecaniah, Harim,* Meremoth,
[4] Iddo, Ginnethon,* Abijah,
[5] Miniamin, Moadiah,* Bilgah,
[6] Shemaiah, Joiarib, Jedaiah,
[7] Sallu, Amok, Hilkiah, and Jedaiah.

These were the leaders of the priests and their associates in the days of Jeshua.

[8]The Levites who returned with them were Jeshua, Binnui, Kadmiel, Sherebiah, Judah, and Mattaniah, who with his associates was in charge of the songs of thanksgiving. [9]Their associates, Bakbukiah and Unni, stood opposite them during the service.

[10] Jeshua the high priest was the father of Joiakim.
Joiakim was the father of Eliashib.
Eliashib was the father of Joiada.
[11] Joiada was the father of Johanan.*
Johanan was the father of Jaddua.

[12]Now when Joiakim was high priest, the family leaders of the priests were as follows:

Meraiah was leader of the family of Seraiah.
Hananiah was leader of the family of Jeremiah.

11:14 As in Greek version; Hebrew reads *their.*   11:35 Or *and Ge-harashim.*   12:3 Hebrew *Rehum;* compare 7:42; 12:15; Ezra 2:39.   12:4 As in some Hebrew manuscripts and Latin Vulgate (see also 12:16); most Hebrew manuscripts read *Ginnethoi.*   12:5 Hebrew *Mijamin, Maadiah;* compare 12:17.   12:11 Hebrew *Jonathan;* compare 12:22.

13 Meshullam was leader of the family of
Ezra.
Jehohanan was leader of the family of
Amariah.
14 Jonathan was leader of the family of
Malluch.*
Joseph was leader of the family of
Shecaniah.*
15 Adna was leader of the family of Harim.
Helkai was leader of the family of
Meremoth.*
16 Zechariah was leader of the family of Iddo.
Meshullam was leader of the family of
Ginnethon.
17 Zicri was leader of the family of Abijah.
There was also a* leader of the family of
Miniamin.
Piltai was leader of the family of Moadiah.
18 Shammua was leader of the family of
Bilgah.
Jehonathan was leader of the family of
Shemaiah.
19 Mattenai was leader of the family of
Joiarib.
Uzzi was leader of the family of Jedaiah.
20 Kallai was leader of the family of Sallu.*
Eber was leader of the family of Amok.
21 Hashabiah was leader of the family of
Hilkiah.
Nethanel was leader of the family of
Jedaiah.

22A record of the Levite families was kept during the years when Eliashib, Joiada, Johanan, and Jaddua served as high priest. Another record of the priests was kept during the reign of Darius the Persian.* 23A record of the heads of the Levite families was kept in *The Book of History* down to the days of Johanan, the grandson* of Eliashib.

24These were the family leaders of the Levites: Hashabiah, Sherebiah, Jeshua, Binnui,* Kadmiel, and other associates, who stood opposite them during the ceremonies of praise and thanksgiving, one section responding to the other, as commanded by David, the man of God. 25This included Mattaniah, Bakbukiah, and Obadiah.

Meshullam, Talmon, and Akkub were the gatekeepers in charge of the storerooms at the gates. 26These all served in the days of Joiakim son of Jeshua, son of Jehozadak,* and in the days of Nehemiah the governor and of Ezra the priest and scribe.

Dedication of Jerusalem's Wall

27For the dedication of the new wall of Jerusalem, the Levites throughout the land were asked to come to Jerusalem to assist in the ceremonies. They were to take part in the joyous occasion with their songs of thanksgiving and with the music of cymbals, harps, and lyres. 28The singers were brought together from the region around Jerusalem and from the villages of the Netophathites. 29They also came from Beth-gilgal and the rural areas near Geba and Azmaveth, for the singers had built their own settlements around Jerusalem. 30The priests and Levites first purified themselves; then they purified the people, the gates, and the wall.

31I led the leaders of Judah to the top of the wall and organized two large choirs to give thanks. One of the choirs proceeded southward* along the top of the wall to the Dung Gate. 32Hoshaiah and half the leaders of Judah followed them, 33along with Azariah, Ezra, Meshullam, 34Judah, Benjamin, Shemaiah, and Jeremiah. 35Then came some priests who played trumpets, including Zechariah son of Jonathan, son of Shemaiah, son of Mattaniah, son of Micaiah, son of Zaccur, a descendant of Asaph. 36And Zechariah's colleagues were Shemaiah, Azarel, Milalai, Gilalai, Maai, Nethanel, Judah, and Hanani. They used the musical instruments prescribed by David, the man of God. Ezra the scribe led this procession. 37At the Fountain Gate they went straight up the steps on the ascent of the city wall toward the City of David. They passed the house of David and then proceeded to the Water Gate on the east.

38The second choir giving thanks went northward* around the other way to meet them. I followed them, together with the other half of the people, along the top of the wall past the Tower of the Ovens to the Broad Wall, 39then past the Ephraim Gate to the Old City Gate,* past the Fish Gate and the Tower of Hananel, and on to the Tower of the Hundred. Then we continued on to the Sheep Gate and stopped at the Guard Gate.

12:14a As in Greek version (see also 10:4; 12:2); Hebrew reads *Malluchi*.   12:14b As in many Hebrew manuscripts, some Greek manuscripts, and Syriac version (see also 12:3); most Hebrew manuscripts read *Shebaniah*.   12:15 As in some Greek manuscripts (see also 12:3); Hebrew reads *Meraioth*.   12:17 Hebrew lacks the name of this family leader.   12:20 Hebrew *Sallai*; compare 12:7.   12:22 *Darius the Persian* is probably Darius II, who reigned 423–404 B.C., or possibly Darius III, who reigned 336–331 B.C.   12:23 Hebrew *descendant*; compare 12:10-11.   12:24 Hebrew *son of* (i.e., *ben*), which should probably be read here as the proper name Binnui; compare Ezra 3:9 and the note there.   12:26 Hebrew *Jozadak*, a variant spelling of Jehozadak.   12:31 Hebrew *to the right*.   12:38 Hebrew *to the left*.   12:39 Or *the Mishneh Gate*, or *the Jeshanah Gate*.

⁴⁰The two choirs that were giving thanks then proceeded to the Temple of God, where they took their places. So did I, together with the group of leaders who were with me. ⁴¹We went together with the trumpet-playing priests—Eliakim, Maaseiah, Miniamin, Micaiah, Elioenai, Zechariah, and Hananiah—⁴²and the singers—Maaseiah, Shemaiah, Eleazar, Uzzi, Jehohanan, Malkijah, Elam, and Ezer. They played and sang loudly under the direction of Jezrahiah the choir director.

⁴³Many sacrifices were offered on that joyous day, for God had given the people cause for great joy. The women and children also participated in the celebration, and the joy of the people of Jerusalem could be heard far away.

Provisions for Temple Worship

⁴⁴On that day men were appointed to be in charge of the storerooms for the offerings, the first part of the harvest, and the tithes. They were responsible to collect from the fields outside the towns the portions required by the Law for the priests and Levites. For all the people of Judah took joy in the priests and Levites and their work. ⁴⁵They performed the service of their God and the service of purification, as commanded by David and his son Solomon, and so did the singers and the gatekeepers. ⁴⁶The custom of having choir directors to lead the choirs in hymns of praise and thanksgiving to God began long ago in the days of David and Asaph. ⁴⁷So now, in the days of Zerubbabel and of Nehemiah, all Israel brought a daily supply of food for the singers, the gatekeepers, and the Levites. The Levites, in turn, gave a portion of what they received to the priests, the descendants of Aaron.

Nehemiah's Various Reforms

13 On that same day, as the Book of Moses was being read to the people, the passage was found that said no Ammonite or Moabite should ever be permitted to enter the assembly of God.* ²For they had not provided the Israelites with food and water in the wilderness. Instead, they hired Balaam to curse them, though our God turned the curse into a blessing. ³When this passage of the Law was read, all those of foreign descent were immediately excluded from the assembly.

⁴Before this had happened, Eliashib the priest, who had been appointed as supervisor of the storerooms of the Temple of our God and who was also a relative of Tobiah, ⁵had converted a large storage room and placed it at Tobiah's disposal. The room had previously been used for storing the grain offerings, the frankincense, various articles for the Temple, and the tithes of grain, new wine, and olive oil (which were prescribed for the Levites, the singers, and the gatekeepers), as well as the offerings for the priests.

⁶I was not in Jerusalem at that time, for I had returned to King Artaxerxes of Babylon in the thirty-second year of his reign,* though I later asked his permission to return. ⁷When I arrived back in Jerusalem, I learned about Eliashib's evil deed in providing Tobiah with a room in the courtyards of the Temple of God. ⁸I became very upset and threw all of Tobiah's belongings out of the room. ⁹Then I demanded that the rooms be purified, and I brought back the articles for God's Temple, the grain offerings, and the frankincense.

¹⁰I also discovered that the Levites had not been given their prescribed portions of food, so they and the singers who were to conduct the worship services had all returned to work their fields. ¹¹I immediately confronted the leaders and demanded, "Why has the Temple of God been neglected?" Then I called all the Levites back again and restored them to their proper duties. ¹²And once more all the people of Judah began bringing their tithes of grain, new wine, and olive oil to the Temple storerooms.

¹³I assigned supervisors for the storerooms: Shelemiah the priest, Zadok the scribe, and Pedaiah, one of the Levites. And I appointed Hanan son of Zaccur and grandson of Mattaniah as their assistant. These men had an excellent reputation, and it was their job to make honest distributions to their fellow Levites.

¹⁴Remember this good deed, O my God, and do not forget all that I have faithfully done for the Temple of my God and its services.

¹⁵In those days I saw men of Judah treading out their winepresses on the Sabbath. They were also bringing in grain, loading it on donkeys, and bringing their wine, grapes, figs, and all sorts of produce to Jerusalem to sell on the Sabbath. So I rebuked them for selling their produce on that day. ¹⁶Some men from Tyre, who lived in Jerusalem, were bringing in fish and all kinds of merchandise. They

13:1 See Deut 23:3-6.   13:6 King Artaxerxes of Persia is here identified as the king of Babylon because Persia had conquered the Babylonian Empire. The thirty-second year of Artaxerxes was 433 B.C.

were selling it on the Sabbath to the people of Judah—and in Jerusalem at that!

¹⁷So I confronted the nobles of Judah. "Why are you profaning the Sabbath in this evil way?" I asked. ¹⁸"Wasn't it just this sort of thing that your ancestors did that caused our God to bring all this trouble upon us and our city? Now you are bringing even more wrath upon Israel by permitting the Sabbath to be desecrated in this way!"

¹⁹Then I commanded that the gates of Jerusalem should be shut as darkness fell every Friday evening,* not to be opened until the Sabbath ended. I sent some of my own servants to guard the gates so that no merchandise could be brought in on the Sabbath day. ²⁰The merchants and tradesmen with a variety of wares camped outside Jerusalem once or twice. ²¹But I spoke sharply to them and said, "What are you doing out here, camping around the wall? If you do this again, I will arrest you!" And that was the last time they came on the Sabbath. ²²Then I commanded the Levites to purify themselves and to guard the gates in order to preserve the holiness of the Sabbath.

Remember this good deed also, O my God! Have compassion on me according to your great and unfailing love.

²³About the same time I realized that some of the men of Judah had married women from Ashdod, Ammon, and Moab. ²⁴Furthermore,

13:19 Hebrew *on the day before the Sabbath.*

half their children spoke the language of Ashdod or of some other people and could not speak the language of Judah at all. ²⁵So I confronted them and called down curses on them. I beat some of them and pulled out their hair. I made them swear in the name of God that they would not let their children intermarry with the pagan people of the land.

²⁶"Wasn't this exactly what led King Solomon of Israel into sin?" I demanded. "There was no king from any nation who could compare to him, and God loved him and made him king over all Israel. But even he was led into sin by his foreign wives. ²⁷How could you even think of committing this sinful deed and acting unfaithfully toward God by marrying foreign women?"

²⁸One of the sons of Joiada son of Eliashib the high priest had married a daughter of Sanballat the Horonite, so I banished him from my presence.

²⁹Remember them, O my God, for they have defiled the priesthood and the solemn vows of the priests and Levites.

³⁰So I purged out everything foreign and assigned tasks to the priests and Levites, making certain that each knew his work. ³¹I also made sure that the supply of wood for the altar and the first portions of the harvest were brought at the proper times.

Remember this in my favor, O my God.

Tobit

THE ACCOUNT RECORDED IN the book of Tobit contains a wonderful blend of Jewish scripture and piety. The writer emphasizes that men and women must live a righteous life because of the righteous character of God. He tells the story through four characters: Tobit, a Jew living in Nineveh who continued to perform acts of charity even after he suffered great misfortunes; Tobiah, Tobit's handsome young son; Sarah, who saw seven prospective husbands die; and Raphael, an angel sent by God to solve their problems. This book gives us a good indication of the piety that characterized Jews after the exile and is a beautiful portrayal of Jewish family life during those times.

- **Author:** Unknown
- **Date Written:** Around 200 BC
- **Purpose:** To demonstrate the sovereignty, providence, and mercy of God, and to highlight the ultimate triumph of good over evil
- **Themes:** Commitment to God's laws; respect toward parents; purity in marriage; generosity to the poor; the reality of spiritual warfare
- **Outline**
  1:1–3:6 Tobit's trials
  3:7-17 The plight of Sarah
  4:1–10:13 The journey of Tobiah and his marriage to Sarah
  11:1–12:22 Tobiah's return and Raphael's revelation
  13:1-23 Tobit's song of praise
  14:1-17 Tobit's deathbed instructions

---

1 This is the story of Tobit son of Tobiel, son of Hananiel, son of Aduel, son of Gabael.* He belonged to the family of Asiel of the tribe of Naphtali. ²During the reign of Shalmaneser, king of Assyria, Tobit was taken into captivity from Thisbe, which is south of Kedesh Naphtali in Upper Galilee, above Asher* toward the west, and north of Phogor.

Tobit's Youth
³I, Tobit, have tried to live a life of truth and justice. I performed many goods deeds not only for my relatives but also for other captives who were with me in the city of Nineveh in Assyria. ⁴When I was a young man in my own country of Israel, the entire tribe of my ancestor Naphtali deserted the king who sat on the throne of David. They also deserted Jerusalem, the city where the Temple, God's dwelling place, was built and dedicated as a holy place for all generations forever. All the tribes of Israel had been instructed to offer their sacrifices in Jerusalem. ⁵Instead, my relatives and the entire tribe of Naphtali offered sacrifices on all the mountains of Galilee to the calf that King Jeroboam of Israel had made in Dan.

⁶So I alone went to Jerusalem for the frequent festivals, as all Israel was commanded to do. I would bring with me the first crops of the harvest, the firstborn of my flocks, the first wool from the sheep, and a tenth of my income.* ⁷I would give these to the priests, Aaron's descendants, as a sacrifice. In addition, I would give tithes of grain, wine, olive oil, pomegranates, figs, and other fruits to the Levites who were on duty in Jerusalem. Also, I would save a second tithe for six years and would distribute it in Jerusalem. ⁸Then every third year I would give a third tithe to orphans, widows, and those who had converted to Judaism, and we would eat a feast as required by the law of Moses. We also followed the instructions given by my father's mother, Deborah, who raised me after my father, Tobiel,* died and left me an orphan.

⁹When I came of age, I married Anna, a relative of mine, and we had a son, whom I named Tobiah.

1:1 Some manuscripts add *son of Raphael, son of Raguel.*   1:2 Or *Hazor.*   1:6 Greek *the tithes of the cattle.*   1:8 As in Latin Vulgate; Greek reads *Hananiel.*

Captivity in Nineveh

[10]After I was taken captive to Nineveh in Assyria, all my relatives and people ate Gentile food, [11]but I refused to eat any such food. [12]And because I obeyed God with all my heart, [13]the Most High brought me to the attention of King Shalmaneser, who made me his purchasing agent. [14]As long as the king lived, I went frequently to Media* to buy supplies. One time I left 750 pounds* of silver in the care of my relative Gabael, the brother of Gabri. [15]When Shalmaneser died and his son Sennacherib became king, the roads to Media were difficult to travel.

[16]During the reign of Shalmaneser, I was able to do many good deeds for my relatives and my people. [17]I shared my food with the hungry and clothed the naked. Whenever I saw the dead body of one of my people thrown outside the walls of Nineveh, I would bury it. [18]One time Sennacherib had to retreat from Judea because the King of heaven was punishing him for speaking blasphemous things. In his anger Sennacherib put to death many of the captives from Judea, but I stole the bodies and buried them secretly. When Sennacherib looked for the bodies, he could not find them. [19]One day someone from Nineveh told the king what I was doing. When I realized that the king knew all about me and wanted to put me to death, I became afraid and fled for my life. [20]All my property was taken from me and put in the royal treasury. All that was left to me was my wife, Anna, and my son, Tobiah.

[21]But less than forty days later the king was murdered by two of his sons, who escaped into the mountains of Ararat. He was succeeded by his son Esarhaddon, who appointed my nephew Ahikar* (my brother Hanael's son) to be his chief accountant and administrator. [22]Ahikar put in a good word for me, and I was able to return to Nineveh. (Ahikar had been Sennacherib's chief cup-bearer, guardian of the king's seal, administrator, and treasurer. When Esarhaddon became king, he reappointed Ahikar to office. As I said, Ahikar was my nephew, and so he was a close relative.)

2 So when Esarhaddon became king, I returned home to live with my wife, Anna, and my son, Tobiah. It was Pentecost, the Festival of Harvest,* and a fine dinner was prepared

for me. [2]When I saw all the food laid out on the table, I said to Tobiah, "My dear son, go and find a poor, sincere worshiper from among the Israelite captives here in Nineveh. Bring him home to share this dinner, and we will wait until you come back."

[3]Tobiah had hardly left when he returned. "Father!" he exclaimed.

"What is it, my son?" I replied.

Tobiah said, "One of our people has been strangled, and his body was dumped in the marketplace!"

[4]I hurried from the table without touching my food and found the body. I carried it back from the public square and put it in an outbuilding until I could bury it after sunset. [5]Then I returned to my own house, washed myself,* and ate my meal in sorrow. [6]As I ate, I thought of the prophecy of Amos against Bethel:

> "I will turn your celebrations into times
>   of mourning,
>   and your songs of joy will be turned
>   to weeping."*

Then I wept.

Tobit Becomes Blind

[7]At sunset I dug a grave and buried the dead man. [8]But my neighbors ridiculed me: "Will he never learn? He had to run away the last time he did such a thing, and here he is burying the dead again!"

[9]That same night I washed myself and went to bed along the inside wall of the courtyard. Because it was a hot night, I left my face uncovered. [10]I did not know there were sparrows on the wall until their droppings fell into my eyes, causing cataracts.* I went to the doctors to be healed, but the more they treated me with ointments, the worse my vision became. Finally, I was totally blind. I remained blind for four years. During this time my relatives grieved for me, and my nephew Ahikar took care of me for two years until he went to Elymais in Persia.

[11]My wife, Anna, supported us by making cloth.* [12]Each time she delivered to her employers what she had made, they paid her. On a certain day in late winter,* she finished a piece of work and took it to her employers. When they

2:14a Media was the northwestern part of present-day Iran.   2:14b Greek *10 talents* [340 kilograms].   2:21 Ahikar is a Jewish wise man in other ancient literature.   2:1 Or *Festival of Weeks,* a festival held 50 days after Passover.   2:5 According to the law of Moses, an Israelite was made unclean by touching a corpse.   2:6 Amos 8:10.   2:10 Greek *white films.*   2:11 Greek *by doing women's work.*   2:12 Greek *On the seventh of Dystrus.* This month of the Macedonian calendar corresponds to the 12th month of the Hebrew lunar calendar. This day occurs in March.

paid her in full for the cloth, they also gave her a young goat from their herd. ¹³As soon as she returned home, the goat began to bleat. I called out to her, "Where did you get that goat? You didn't steal it, did you? Give it back to its owners, for we cannot eat stolen food."

¹⁴She replied, "It was given to me as a bonus over and above what I earned." But I did not believe her. I became angry and told her to take the goat back. She answered, "And you're supposed to be a man of charity and righteous deeds! Now your true character is coming out!"

Tobit Prays for Death

3 I was struck with grief over my actions. I groaned and wept, and in my sadness I began to pray.

2 "You are just, O Lord,
and all your deeds are right.
Your ways are merciful and true.
You judge the world.
3 Remember me, Lord,
and look upon me with kindness.
Do not punish me for my sins,
both known and unknown,
or for the sins of my ancestors.
They sinned against you
4 and disobeyed your commandments.
So you gave us up to be plundered,
captured, and killed.
We became a laughingstock and an
object of scorn and derision
when you scattered us among the
nations.
5 I admit the justice of your many
judgments;
you are completely right to punish
my sins
and the sins of my ancestors.
For we have not kept your
commandments,
and we have not walked in your way
of truth.
6 Now deal with me as you please.
Command that my spirit be taken
from me
so that I may die and become dust.
It is better that I should die than live,
because I have had to endure
undeserved insults and lies,
and I am overwhelmed with grief.
O Lord, command that I be freed of this
misery
so that I can go to my everlasting home.

O Lord, do not turn your face
from me.
It is better for me to die
than to experience so much anguish
in my life
and to hear insults."

Sarah Falsely Accused

⁷On the very same day, at Ecbatana in Media, Sarah, the daughter of Raguel, was insulted by one of her father's servant girls. ⁸Sarah had been married to seven husbands, each of whom had been killed by the evil demon Asmodeus* before any of the marriages had been consummated. The servant said to her, "You are the one who kills your husbands. You have already had seven husbands and no children from any of them. ⁹Why do you punish us? Because your husbands died? Go with them! We never want to see a son or daughter of yours!"

Sarah Asks for Death

¹⁰Sarah was in deep anguish because of these insults. She went upstairs in tears, intending to hang herself. But she thought about it again and said, "People would reproach my father and say, 'Your only beloved daughter killed herself because of her troubles.' And I would bring my father in his old age down to his grave* in sorrow. It is better for me not to hang myself but to pray to the Lord to let me die. Then I won't have to hear these insults anymore." ¹¹So she spread out her hands at the window and prayed:

"I praise you, God of mercy.
I praise your name forever.
May all your creation praise you
forever.
12 To you, O Lord, I turn my face
and lift my eyes.
13 Command that I be allowed to die,
never more to hear insults.
14 You know, O Master, that I am innocent
of any impurity with a man.
15 I have disgraced neither my name
nor the name of my father in this land
of captivity.
I am my father's only child;
there is no one else to be his heir.
My father has no relatives
I can marry.
Seven husbands of mine have already
died—
so why should I live?

3:8 *Asmodeus* means "the Destroyer." **3:10** Greek *to Hades.*

But if you do not want to take my life,
O Lord,
   at least hear me concerning these insults."

Answers to Prayer

16At that very moment, the prayers of both Sarah and Tobit were heard in the glorious presence of God. 17Raphael was sent to answer their prayers for healing. He was going to heal Tobit's eyes so that he might once again see God's light. He also would arrange the marriage of Sarah, the daughter of Raguel, to Tobiah son of Tobit and would free Sarah from the demon Asmodeus. For Tobiah, more than anyone else who wanted her, was entitled to marry her. Tobit returned from the courtyard into his house at the same moment that Sarah came down from the upper room.

Tobit Instructs Tobiah his Son

4 That same day Tobit remembered the money he had entrusted to Gabael's care at Rages* in Media. 2He said to himself, "Since I have prayed for death, why shouldn't I tell my son, Tobiah, about this money before I die?"

3So Tobit called for Tobiah and said to him, "My son, give me a proper burial when I die. Honor your mother and care for her as long as she lives. Do what will please her and do nothing to make her sad. 4Remember, my dear son, that she went through many dangers for you while you were still in her womb. When she dies, bury her beside me in the same plot.

5"Remember the Lord every day of your life. Never sin deliberately or break his commandments. As long as you live, do what is right and never take part in wrongdoing. 6For those who live in the truth will succeed in all they do. To those who live righteous lives,* 7give generously from your possessions. But don't give a gift grudgingly. If you do not ignore the poor, God will not ignore you. 8Let your giving be in proportion to your possessions. If you have great wealth, give a generous amount. If you have few possessions, give from that little. 9In this way you will store up a great treasure for a time of need. 10For giving to people in need frees people from death and keeps them from going down into darkness. 11Giving to charity is a pleasing sacrifice to the Most High.

12"My dear son, be on your guard against all sexual immorality. It is important that you take a wife from your own tribe. Do not marry a foreign woman, for we are descendants of the prophets. My son, remember the example of Noah, Abraham, Isaac, and Jacob, our ancestors who took wives from among their relatives. They were blessed by the lives of their children, whose descendants will inherit their land. 13Be like them, my son; love your relatives. Do not proudly think you are better than your relatives, and do not hesitate to take a wife from your own tribe. Pride is the source of ruin and confusion. Idleness will result in famine.

14"Pay your workers each day; don't make them wait until the next day to receive their wages. If you serve God, you will be rewarded. Watch yourself, my son, in everything you do, and be disciplined in all your conduct. 15Don't do to others what you would hate to have them do to you. Don't drink too much wine or let drunkenness become a way of life. 16Give food to the hungry and clothing to the poor. Don't hesitate to give away your surplus to people in need. 17Place bread on the tombs of the just,* but give nothing to sinners.

18"Seek the counsel of every wise person, and do not reject useful advice. 19Bless the Lord God at every opportunity. Ask him to keep you on a straight path so that you will be successful in everything you do. The nations don't understand these things. It is the Lord who gives them good counsel, but if the Lord decides otherwise, he can bring them down to the grave.* So now remember these commands, my son, and never let them be erased from your heart.

20"Now, my son, I want to tell you that I have left 750 pounds* of silver in the care of Gabael son of Gabri at Rages in Media. 21Do not be anxious, my son, that we have become poor. You will have great wealth if you fear God, run from every sin, and do what is right in the sight of the Lord your God."

Raphael the Angel

5 Then Tobiah said to his father, "I will do everything you have told me. 2But how will I get your money from him, since I do not know him and he does not know me? What proof should I give him of my identity to convince him to give me the money? I do not even know the roads to Media."

3Tobit told him, "He and I made two copies of a written agreement. We tore one of them in half, and each of us kept one of the halves. I put the other copy with the money. Twenty years have passed since I deposited that money.

4:1 Rages was an important city near present-day Teheran.   4:6 Some manuscripts do not include 4:7-19a.   4:17 Or *Be generous with your food at the burial of the just.*   4:19 Greek *into deepest Hades.*   4:20 Greek *10 talents* [340 kilograms].

So find a reliable man to accompany you, my son. We will pay him for his time when you get back. Now go and reclaim this money from Gabael."

⁴Tobiah went out to find someone who knew the roads to Media and would accompany him there. He found Raphael standing outside, but Tobiah did not know that he was an angel of God. ⁵Tobiah asked him, "Who are you, young man?"

He replied, "I am an Israelite, one of your relatives, and I am looking for work."

Tobiah asked him, "Do you know the way to Media?"

⁶"Yes," Raphael answered. "I have gone there often and know all the roads. I used to stay with our relative Gabael in Rages. We will first have to travel to Ecbatana, which is on the plain east of here. Then it is two more long days to get to Rages, which is in the mountains."

⁷Tobiah said to him, "Wait for me, young man, while I go in and tell my father. I need someone to accompany me to Rages, and I will pay you to guide me."

⁸Raphael replied, "I am at your service, but don't be too long."

⁹Tobiah went in and told his father, "I have found a fellow Israelite who will go with me."

Tobit said, "Bring him to me, my son, so that I can find out about his family and tribe and decide if he should be trusted to go with you."

Tobiah went out and said to Raphael, "My father would like to meet you."

¹⁰When Raphael came in, Tobit immediately greeted him. Raphael replied, "And may all be well with you."

Tobit responded, "What! How can anything be well with me? I am blind and can no longer enjoy the sunlight. I might as well be dead, for everything is dark. Even though I'm still alive, I'm no better than a corpse. I hear voices, but I cannot even see who is speaking."

"Be brave," Raphael encouraged him. "God will heal you soon. Be confident."

Then Tobit said, "My son, Tobiah, wants to go to Media. Can you accompany him and guide him there? I will pay you, my brother."

"Yes, I can go with him," Raphael responded. "I know all the roads. I have often been to Media, crossing the plains and the mountains, so that I know every road."

¹¹Tobit inquired, "Tell me, brother, to what tribe and family do you belong?"

¹²"Why do you need to know my tribe?" replied Raphael.

Tobit said, "I really want to know who your family is and what your name is."

¹³Raphael answered, "I am Azariah, son of the great Hananiah,* one of your relatives."

¹⁴Tobit said, "Welcome, my brother. Do not be insulted because I wanted to know your tribe and family. You are a relative of mine, of good and noble stock. I knew Hananiah and Nathan,* the two sons of the great Shemeliah.* They used to make the pilgrimage to Jerusalem with me, and we would worship together. They did not turn away from keeping the law of Moses. Your relatives are good people, and you come from a good family. Again, welcome!" ¹⁵He added, "I will pay you a silver coin* for each day of your trip as well as all your expenses. ¹⁶I will also pay you a bonus if you both return safely."

Raphael replied, "I will go with him. Don't worry. We will return as healthy as we are now because the route is safe."

¹⁷Tobit said, "May God bless you, brother." Then he called Tobiah and said to him, "My son, prepare whatever is necessary for the trip. May God in heaven protect both of you as you travel and bring you back to me safely. May his angel guard your way."

Before setting out on the journey, Tobiah kissed his father and mother. Then Tobit said, "Have a safe journey."

¹⁸Tobiah's mother* began to weep. She said to Tobit, "Why have you sent my son away? Isn't he the one we depend on? ¹⁹Why do you want more money if it costs us the life of our son? ²⁰Can't we be satisfied with the life the Lord has given us?"

²¹Tobit said to her, "Don't worry. Our child is leaving in good health, and he will return the same way. You will see for yourself that he will be safe. Say no more. Do not fear for them, dear wife.* ²²A good angel will go with him. His mission will be successful, and he will return in good health."

⁶:¹So she stopped weeping.

The Journey to Rages

6 The young man and the angel left together, ²and Tobiah's dog followed them. They traveled until dusk and then spent the night beside the Tigris River.

³When Tobiah went down to wash his feet

5:13 Azariah means "The Lᴏʀᴅ helps," and Hananiah means "The Lᴏʀᴅ shows mercy."   5:14a Some manuscripts read *Jathan*.   5:14b Some manuscripts read *Shemaiah*.   5:15 Greek *a drachma*, which was the equivalent of a full day's wage.   5:18 Some manuscripts add *Anna*.   5:21 Greek *sister*.

in the river, a large fish jumped from the water and tried to swallow his foot. As Tobiah cried out, ⁴the angel shouted, "Catch the fish and hang on to it!" Tobiah grabbed the fish and pulled it up on the bank. ⁵Then the angel told him, "Cut open the fish, and save its heart, liver, and gall. Throw away the intestines. The heart, liver, and gall make good medicines." ⁶Tobiah did as the angel told him. Then he roasted the fish, ate some of it, and preserved the rest of it with salt.

The two traveled on together until they were near Media. ⁷Then the young man asked the angel, "Brother Azariah, what medicine can be made from the fish's heart, liver, and even the gall?"

⁸He replied, "If you burn the heart and liver and blow the smoke on a man or woman who is tormented by a demon or an evil spirit, the spirit will leave and never return. ⁹As for the gall, you can use it to anoint the eyes of a person who has cataracts.* Then, if you blow on the eyes, they will be healed."

¹⁰When they had entered Media and were getting close to Ecbatana, ¹¹Raphael spoke to the young man and said, "Brother Tobiah."

"Yes, what is it?" he replied.

Raphael said, "Tonight we must stay with your relative, Raguel. He has a daughter named Sarah. ¹²He has no male heir, and Sarah is his only daughter. Since you are the only eligible relative, you have the right to marry her and gain her inheritance. The young woman is sensible, courageous, and very beautiful, and her father is a good man." ¹³He continued: "You have the legal right to marry her. So, listen to me, brother. I will speak to the young woman's father tonight so that you can take her as your bride. When we return from Rages, we will celebrate the marriage. Raguel cannot keep her from you or promise her to another man, for that would be punishable by death according to the law of Moses. Raguel knows that you—above all others—are entitled to marry his daughter. So listen to me, brother. This very night we will arrange for you to marry her. And when we return from Rages, we will take her back with us to your house."

¹⁴But Tobiah said to Raphael, "Brother Azariah, I have heard that this woman has already been married seven times and that each husband died on his wedding night in the bridal chamber when he approached her. I have heard that it was a demon that killed them. ¹⁵The demon doesn't harm her, but it kills anyone

who wants to come near her. So I am afraid. I am my father's only son, and my death would bring my mother and father to their graves. Then there would be no son to bury them."

¹⁶Raphael said to him, "Remember your father's command to take a wife from your own tribe. Now listen to me, brother, and say no more about this demon. Take her as your wife. I know that she will marry you tonight. ¹⁷When you enter the bridal chamber, take the fish's liver and heart and lay them on the burning incense. The demon will smell the smoke and flee, never to return. ¹⁸Then, when you are about to go to bed with her, both of you must first stand up and pray. Ask the Lord of heaven to give you mercy and deliverance. Don't be afraid. Sarah was set apart for you from all eternity. You will rescue her and she will go with you. I have no doubt that you will have children by her, and they will be very dear to you. So don't worry!"

When Tobiah heard Raphael's words and realized that Sarah was his relative* on his father's side of the family, he fell deeply in love with her and his heart was set on her.

Meeting Raguel

7 When they reached Ecbatana, Tobiah said to Raphael, "Brother Azariah, take me straight to our brother Raguel." So they arrived at Raguel's house, where they found him seated by the courtyard door. They greeted Raguel, and he replied, "Greetings to you also, brothers. Welcome, and good health to you." Then Raguel brought them into the house ²and said to his wife, Edna, "This young man looks a lot like my relative Tobit!" ³Then Edna asked them, "Where are you from, brothers?"

They answered, "We belong to the descendants of Naphtali who are exiled in Nineveh."

⁴She asked them, "Do you know our relative Tobit?"

"We certainly do!"

Then she asked them, "Is he in good health?" ⁵They answered, "He is alive and well." Then Tobiah added, "He is my father!"

⁶Raguel jumped up, kissed him, and wept. ⁷Then he said, "Bless you, child. You are the son of a good and noble man. What an unfortunate calamity that such a righteous and charitable man became blind!" He embraced Tobiah and wept. ⁸His wife, Edna, also wept for Tobit, and even their daughter, Sarah, began to weep. ⁹They showed the visitors a warm welcome by preparing a young ram from the flock for a meal.

6:9 Greek *white films.*   6:18 Greek *sister.*

Marriage Arrangements

When they had washed and sat down* to eat, Tobiah said to Raphael, "Brother Azariah, how about asking Raguel if I can marry my relative* Sarah?"

¹⁰Raguel overheard the question, so he said to the young man, "Eat, drink, and be happy. No man is more entitled to my daughter than you. Indeed, I have no right to give her to anyone else since you are my closest relative. But, my son, let me explain the true situation to you. ¹¹I have given her to seven husbands from our family, and each of them died on his wedding night when he approached her. But don't be discouraged, my son. Eat and drink, for the Lord will make it work out for both of you."

But Tobiah said, "I will not eat or drink until we make a binding agreement."

So Raguel said, "I will do this. She is yours according to the law of Moses, and it has been decreed from heaven that she be given to you. Take her, for you belong to each other.* She is yours forever. May the Lord of heaven guide you, my son, and bless you both this night. May he grant you mercy and peace."

¹²Then Raguel called for his daughter, Sarah. When she came, he took her by the hand and gave away the bride to Tobiah, saying, "Here she is. Take her to be your wife according to the law of Moses. Take her to your father safely. And may the God of heaven prosper your journey with peace."

¹³Then Raguel called the young woman's mother and told her to bring him a scroll. On it he wrote out the marriage contract, stating that he was giving Sarah to Tobiah as his wife according to the law of Moses. ¹⁴Then they began to eat and drink.

¹⁵Then Raguel said to Edna, "Dear wife,* prepare the bedroom, and take our daughter there." ¹⁶So Edna went and made the bed as she was told. She took Sarah there and began to weep for her. Then she wiped away her tears and said, ¹⁷"Be brave, daughter. May the Lord of heaven grant you joy in the place of your sorrow. Be brave, my child." Then she left.

Tobiah Repels the Demon

8 After they had feasted, Tobiah wanted to go to bed with his bride. So the young woman's parents took him to the bedroom. ²Remembering Raphael's words, Tobiah took the fish's liver and heart out of his bag, and he put them on burning incense. ³The odor of the fish repelled the demon, and it fled through the air to Upper Egypt. (But Raphael followed him there and completely subdued him.)

⁴When the parents had left and shut the bedroom door, Tobiah got up from the bed and said to Sarah, "Stand up, dear wife.* We must pray to our Lord and ask him to grant us mercy and deliverance. ⁵So she got up, and they began to pray, asking God for deliverance. Tobiah said,

"We praise you, God of our ancestors.
    May your name be praised in all
        generations forever.
    Let the heavens and all creation praise
        you forever.
⁶ You made Adam, and then you made his
        wife, Eve,
    as his helper and support.
    And the entire human race has come
        from them.
    You said, 'It is not good for the man to
        be alone.
    I will make a companion who will help
        him.'*
⁷ I do not take this woman* as my wife
        for any lustful reason,
    but to show my fidelity.
    Grant us your mercy,
        and may she and I grow old together."

⁸They both said, "Amen, Amen." ⁹Then they went to bed and slept together.

But during the night Raguel arose and called his servants to help him dig a grave. ¹⁰He said, "Perhaps the man will die, so we will bury him before we are criticized and ridiculed." ¹¹When they had dug the grave, Raguel went back to his wife at the house and said to her, ¹²"Send one of your servant girls to see if Tobiah is still alive. If he is dead, we can bury him before it is daylight so that no one will know."

¹³So they sent one of the servants, who took a lighted lamp into the bedroom. She found them safe and sound, sleeping together. ¹⁴So the servant came out and told the parents, "He is alive. Nothing is wrong."

¹⁵Then they blessed the God of heaven. Raguel said,

"We praise you, O God, with pure
        blessings.
    May you be praised forever!
¹⁶ May you be praised because you have given
        me joy.

7:9a Greek *reclined.*   7:9b Greek *sister.*   7:11 Greek *you are her brother and she is your sister.*   7:15 Greek *Sister.*   8:4 Greek *sister.*
8:6 Gen 2:18.   8:7 Greek *my sister.*

It has not turned out as I had expected,
but you have shown us your great mercy.
[17] We praise you for having mercy
on these two children.
O Master, give them mercy and safety.
May their lives be filled with joy and
mercy."

[18]Then Raguel commanded his servants to fill
up the grave before dawn.

The Wedding Feast

[19]Raguel asked his wife to prepare many loaves
of bread. He also slaughtered two cows and
four young rams in preparation for a feast.
[20]And he said to Tobiah, "You must stay here
with me for fourteen days, eating and drinking and cheering up my daughter, for she has
been depressed. [21]Take half of what I own, and
return safely to your father. The other half will
be yours when my wife and I die. Be encouraged, my son. I am your father and Edna is your
mother, and all of us—including your wife*—
belong to you forever. Be encouraged, my son."

Raphael Gets the Money from Gabael

9 Then Tobiah said to Raphael, [2]"Brother
Azariah, take four household servants
and two camels with you, and go to Rages. Go
to Gabael, give him this portion of the written agreement, and get the money from him.
Invite him to return with you to my wedding
feast. [3]You know that my father is counting the
days until we return, and if I stay one day more
than necessary, he will be very worried. [4]You
know that Raguel made an oath, obligating
me to stay; I cannot violate his oath.*"

[5]So Raphael took the four servants and two
camels and went to Rages in Media, where he
stayed overnight with Gabael. Raphael gave
him Tobit's portion of the written agreement.
Then Raphael told Gabael that Tobit's son, Tobiah, had married, and he invited Gabael to the
wedding feast. So Gabael got up and counted
out the money bags, each properly sealed, and
loaded them on to camels.

[6]In the morning they both got up early and
went to the wedding celebration. When they
came to Raguel's house, they found Tobiah
sitting* at the table. He stood up and greeted
Gabael. Then Gabael began to weep, and he
blessed Tobiah with these words: "You are the
good and honorable son of a good and honorable man, who also is just and charitable. May
the Lord grant the blessings of heaven to you

and your wife and to your wife's father and
mother. Praise God, for I see that Tobiah looks
a lot like my relative Tobit."

Tobit and Anna Worry about Tobiah

10 Tobit had calculated the number of days
it would take Tobiah to reach Rages and
return again. He counted the days, and when
his son did not return, [2]he said, "What can be
detaining him? Do you think Gabael has died
and there is no one to give Tobiah the money?"
[3]Tobit began to worry. [4]His wife, Anna, said,
"My child has died and is no longer alive." She
began to weep and mourn for her son: [5]"How
terrible! Oh, my son, you are the light of my
eyes. Why did I let you take that journey?"
[6]But Tobit said to her, "Be quiet and stop
worrying, my dear wife.* Our son is safe. Probably something unexpected has happened. The
man we sent with him is a trustworthy relative.
Don't grieve for Tobiah. He will be here soon."
[7]She answered him, "You be quiet! Stop trying to deceive me. My child has died." Every
day she would rush out and look down the road
Tobiah had taken. No one could persuade her
to do otherwise. When the sun set, she would
go inside to mourn and weep all night long,
never getting any sleep.

Tobiah and Sarah Head Home

When the fourteen days of wedding festivities
(which Raguel had sworn to give his daughter)
had ended, Tobiah said to Raguel, "Send me
back. I know my father and mother think they
will never see me again. I beg you, father, let me
return to my own father, for you know that he
is old and blind."
[8]But Raguel said, "Don't go; stay with me,
my son. I will send messengers to your father
to tell him about you."
[9]But Tobiah responded, "No! I beg you to
send me back to my father!"
[10]So Raguel let Tobiah leave with his wife,
Sarah. He also gave Tobiah half of all his property: his male and female servants, cattle and
sheep, donkeys and camels, clothing, money,
and utensils. [11]As he sent them off, he embraced Tobiah and said to him, "Farewell, my
son. Travel safely. May the Lord of heaven give
you and your wife many good things. May my
eyes see my grandchildren before I die." [12]Then
he kissed his daughter, Sarah, and said to her,
"My daughter, honor your father-in-law and
mother-in-law because now they are your parents, just as we are. Go in peace, Daughter. As

8:21 Greek *sister.*   9:4 Some manuscripts place verse 4 before verse 3.   9:6 Greek *reclining.*   10:6 Greek *sister;* also in 10:13.

long as I live, may I hear that you are doing well." And then he let them go.

[13]Then Edna said to Tobiah, "My child and my beloved brother, may the Lord of heaven bring you home safely. And may I live long enough to see my grandchildren. In the sight of the Lord, I entrust my daughter, Sarah, to you. Don't ever do anything to make her sad. Go in peace, my son. From now on I am your mother and Sarah is your beloved wife. May we all have prosperous lives." Then she tenderly kissed them both and sent them on their way.

[14]And Tobiah left Raguel with great joy, praising the Lord of heaven and earth, the King of all, because he had given him a successful journey. Before leaving, he told Raguel and Edna, "May I fulfill the Lord's command to honor you all the days of my life."

The Journey Home

11 When they came to Kaserin, which is near Nineveh, Raphael said to Tobiah, [2]"You know that your father is old and blind. [3]Therefore, let us go ahead of your wife to get the house ready before the others arrive." [4]So they went on ahead, and Tobiah's dog followed them. As they traveled together, Raphael reminded Tobiah, "Make sure you're ready to use the gall of the fish."

[5]Anna sat looking down the road for her son, as she had been doing every day. [6]When she saw them coming, she said to her husband, "Look, your son is coming, along with the man who went with him!"

[7](Raphael had said to Tobiah, "I know that your father's eyes will be healed. [8]Anoint his eyes with the fish gall you carry. This will cause the cataracts* to fall off, and your father will regain his sight and see the light.")

[9]Anna ran to her son, embraced him, and said, "Now that I have seen you, my child, I can die in peace." And she wept.

[10]Despite his blindness, Tobit stood up and, hurrying to meet his son, stumbled through the courtyard door. Tobiah approached him [11]with the fish gall in his hand. He took hold of his father, blew into his eyes, and said, "Don't be afraid, Father." [12]Then Tobiah took the medicine and put it on his father's eyes, [13]causing him some pain. Using both of his hands, Tobiah pulled the cataracts from Tobit's eyes. Embracing Tobiah, [14]Tobit wept and said, "I can see you, my son; you are the light of my eyes!" Then he said,

"Praise God.
    Bless his great name.
    Bless all his holy angels.
May his great name be over us,
    and blessed be all his angels*
    for all eternity.
[15] Though he afflicted me,
    now I see Tobiah, my son."

So Tobit went inside, rejoicing and praising God as loudly as he could.

Tobiah told his father about the success of his journey—how he had gotten the money and married Sarah, the daughter of Raguel. Then he said that Sarah was at that very moment approaching the gate of Nineveh.

[16]Then Tobit, rejoicing and praising God, went out to meet his daughter-in-law at the gate of Nineveh. The people of Nineveh were amazed to see him walking along, fully restored and with no one leading him by the hand. [17]Tobiah told them all that God had been merciful to his father and restored his sight. When Tobit met Sarah, the wife of his son, Tobiah, he blessed her by saying, "Come in, my daughter. Praise God, who has brought you to us, my daughter. Blessed be your father's household, and blessed be my son, Tobiah, and you, my daughter. Come into your home now. May you have health, blessings, and joy."

On that day there was rejoicing among all the Jews in Nineveh. [18]Ahikar and his nephew Nadab came to join in the celebration with Tobit.*

Raphael's Wages

12 When the wedding festivities ended, Tobit said to Tobiah, "My son, take care of paying the wages of the man who traveled with you, and give him a bonus as well."

[2]Tobiah replied, "How much should I pay him, Father? How about half of the possessions I brought back with me? [3]He brought me back safely to you, he healed my wife, he brought the money back with me, and he healed you. How much extra shall I give him as a bonus?"

[4]Tobit said, "My son, he deserves to receive half of all he has brought back."

[5]So Tobiah said to Raphael, "For your wages, accept half of everything you brought back. Now go in peace."

[6]Then Raphael took the two men aside privately and said, "Praise God, and tell everyone about the good things he has done for you.

11:8 Greek *white films;* also in 11:13.   11:14 Some manuscripts read *May his holy name be blessed.*   11:18 Some manuscripts add *They celebrated Tobiah's wedding for seven days, and many gifts were given to him.*

Sing praises to his name. Honor God by telling everyone his words. Don't hold back from telling about him. [7]While it is good to hide the secret of a king, it is also good to reveal and praise the works of God.

"Do good so that evil will not overtake you. [8]Prayer made with true sincerity* is good, and charitable acts done with justice are better than wealth gotten by unjust means. It is better to give to the poor than to store up treasures of gold. [9]For charitable giving saves us from death and cleanses us from sin. Those who give charitably will be satisfied. [10]Those who do evil and commit sin are their own worst enemies.

Raphael Reveals His Identity

[11]"Now I will tell you the truth, hiding nothing from you. I already hinted at it when I said, 'While it is good to hide the secret of a king, it is also good to reveal and praise the works of God.' [12]When you prayed, Tobit, and when Sarah prayed, it was I who brought your prayer into the presence of the glorious Lord. And I was there whenever you buried the dead. [13]When you left your dinner to bury a dead man, I was sent to test you. [14]At the same time, God sent me to heal you and your daughter-in-law. [15]I am Raphael, one of the seven angels who stand ready and enter the glorious presence of the Lord."

[16]Tobit and Tobiah were greatly shaken. They fell with their faces to the ground. [17]But Raphael said to them, "Do not be afraid; peace be with you. Praise God forever. [18]When I was with you, I was there by the will of God. Praise him each and every day. Sing his praises. [19](By the way, if you thought I ate and drank with you, it was only imaginary—a vision.) [20]Praise the Lord of the earth,* and publicly acknowledge God. See, I am ascending to the one who sent me. Write down all the things that have happened to you." Then he ascended to heaven.

[21]They stood up and saw him no more. [22]Then they kept blessing God and singing his praises, and they openly acknowledged God for the wonderful things that happened when God's angel appeared to them.

Tobit's Praise

13

Then Tobit said:

"Praise God, who lives forever,
for his kingdom lasts for all ages.

[2]He both punishes and shows mercy.
He takes people to the place of the dead*
beneath the earth
and raises them up from great
destruction.
There is nothing that can escape his
hand.
[3]Praise him before the Gentiles, children
of Israel.
He has scattered you among them,
[4]yet he has shown you his greatness even
there.
Exalt him in the presence of every living
being,
because he is our Lord and our God.
He is our Father and our God forever.
[5]Although he punished you for your sins,
he will also show you his mercy—
you who have been scattered among the
nations.
[6]If you turn to him with all your heart and
all your soul
to practice truth in his presence,
then he will turn to you
and will no longer hide his face from
you.
[7]Now see what he has done for you,
and confess him with a loud voice.
Praise the King of justice,
and exalt his kingdom forever.*
In the land of my exile I confess him
and show his power and majesty to a
nation of sinners.
Turn around, sinners, and practice justice
before him.
Perhaps he will show you his mercy.
As for me, I will exalt my God,
and my soul rejoices in the King of
heaven.
[8]Let everyone speak of his majesty
and acknowledge him in Jerusalem.
[9]O Jerusalem, the holy city,
the Lord punished you for your
children's actions.*
But he will again have mercy on the
children of righteousness.
[10]Acknowledge the Lord, for he is good.
Bless the eternal King
so that his dwelling place* may be
rebuilt in you with joy.
May he cheer all the exiles among you
and love all who are in misery
throughout all generations forever.

12:8 Some manuscripts read *with fasting.*   12:20 Some manuscripts read *So now get up off the ground.*   13:2 Greek *Hades.*
13:7 Some manuscripts do not include 13:7b-10.   13:9 Some manuscripts read *for the deeds of your hands.*   13:10 Greek *his
tabernacle.*

11 A bright light will shine to the ends of the
    earth.
  Many nations will come to you from far
    away.
  People from the most remote places on
    earth will come to you, the holy city,*
    bringing gifts in their hands for the
    King of heaven.
  Generation after generation will be glad in
    your midst,
    and the name of the chosen city will live
    forever.
12 All who speak harshly against you will be
    cursed,
    as will all who overtake you and pull
    down your walls.
  Those who overthrow your towers and
    set your houses on fire will also be
    cursed.
  But all who respect you will be blessed
    forever.
13 Go and rejoice for the children of the
    righteous,
    for they will be gathered together
    and will praise the eternal Lord.
14 Blessed are all who love you
    and who rejoice to see you prosper.
  Blessed are all who grieve with you in your
    afflictions,
    for they will rejoice with you when they
    see your eternal glory.
15 O my soul, praise the Lord, the great
    King,*
16   for Jerusalem will be built as his eternal
    house.*
  I will be happy if some of my descendants
    live to see your glory, O Jerusalem,
    and acknowledge the King of heaven.
  The gates of Jerusalem will be built with
    sapphire and emerald,
    and all the surrounding walls with
    precious stones.
  The towers of Jerusalem will be built with
    gold,
    and their fortifications with pure gold.
17 The main streets of Jerusalem will be
    paved
    with rubies and precious stones of
    Ophir.
18 The gates of Jerusalem will sing hymns
    of joy,
    and all the houses will shout,
    'Hallelujah! Praise the God of
    Israel!'

In you, O Jerusalem, his holy name will
    be praised forever and ever."

14:1 So ended Tobit's praise.

Tobit's Final Words

14 2Tobit died in peace at the age of 112
    years and was buried with honor in
Nineveh. He was 62 years* old when he went
blind. After he was healed, he lived in prosperity, giving money to the poor, continually
praising God and acknowledging his majesty.

3When Tobit was on his deathbed, he sent
for his son, Tobiah, and gave him this command: "My son, take your children, 4and go
to Media. For I believe the message that God
has spoken by Nahum concerning Nineveh's
destruction. All the things Nahum said will
come upon Assyria and Nineveh. Everything
that was spoken by the prophets God sent to Israel will happen. None of their words will fail;
all will come true at the right time. So it will be
safer in Media than in Assyria and Babylon, for
I know and believe that whatever God has said
will happen. Not a single word of the prophets'
messages will fail. All of our fellow Israelites*
will be scattered from the good land, Israel,
and taken into captivity. The whole land of Israel will become desolate, including Samaria
and Jerusalem. And the Temple of God will be
burned to the ground for a while.

5"But God will again have mercy on them
and will bring his people back to the land of
Israel. They will rebuild the Temple of God,
though it won't be like the first one. This will
be the situation until the time comes for God's
promise to be fulfilled. Then the people of Israel will return from captivity to Jerusalem and
rebuild it with splendor. And the Temple of
God will be built in it, even as the prophets of
Israel said. 6Then all the nations of the earth
will turn from their ways and will truly worship God. All of them will abandon their idols,
which led them into error, 7and they will praise
the eternal God in righteousness. All the Israelites who are rescued in those days and who
truly acknowledge God will go to Jerusalem.
They will live safely forever in the land of Abraham, which will be handed over to them. Those
who truly love God will rejoice, and those who
practice sin and injustice will disappear from
the earth.

8-9"And now, my children, I give you these
commands: Serve God sincerely, and do what is

13:11 Greek will come to your holy name.   13:15 Or My soul praises the Lord, the great King.   13:16 Or for in that city his eternal Temple
will be built.   14:2 Some manuscripts read 58 years.   14:4 Greek brothers.

pleasing to him. Command your children to do what is right and to give charitably. They must remember God, blessing his name at all times in truth and with all their strength. Now, my son, leave Nineveh; do not stay here. [10]As soon as your mother dies and you have buried her beside me in the tomb, leave this city without delay. For I see that there is great injustice here; this city is full of treacherous and shameless people.

"My son, look at what Nadab did to Ahikar, who had raised him. Wasn't Ahikar forced to hide underground? But God personally repaid Nadab for his shameful treatment of Ahikar. Ahikar eventually returned to the light of day, but Nadab has gone into eternal darkness for trying to kill Ahikar. Because of his charitable acts, Ahikar escaped the deathly trap Nadab set for him. But Nadab fell into it himself—to his own destruction. [11]So now, my children, see what happens to those who are charitable. And see what happens to those who are unjust— they die!

"But now it is getting hard for me to breathe.*"

So they laid Tobit on his bed, and he died. Then they gave him a funeral with great honor.

[12]When Tobiah's mother died, Tobiah buried her beside his father. Then he and his wife* returned to Media and lived in Ecbatana with Raguel, his father-in-law. [13]Respecting the old age of his parents-in-law, he took care of them until they died. He buried them in Ecbatana of Media, and he inherited the property and possessions of Raguel, along with that of his father, Tobit.

[14]Then Tobiah died and was buried with honor at the age of 117. [15]But before he died, he not only heard about the destruction of Nineveh but witnessed it as well. He saw its captives being taken to Media by King Cyaxares.* Tobiah praised God for all that he had done to the people of Nineveh and Assyria. Before he died, he rejoiced over the destruction of Nineveh, and he praised the Lord God who lives forever and ever.

14:11 Or *now my spirit is about to leave me.*   14:12 Some manuscripts add *and children.*   14:15 Some manuscripts read *Nebuchadnezzar;* others read *Ahasuerus.*

Judith

THIS EXCITING STORY recounts a time when the "Assyrians" (a probable reference to the Babylonians) besieged the Israelites for refusing to pay tribute to King Nebuchadnezzar. The Assyrians, led by Holofernes, had already destroyed many other cities for refusing to pay tribute, but the people of Israel continued to resist. They mobilized their forces at strategic passes in the hills north of Jerusalem, while at the same time seeking God's favor. Ignoring warnings from an Ammonite that God was with the Israelites, Holofernes laid siege to the stronghold of Bethulia, cutting off the water supply and waiting for them to surrender. But Judith, a beautiful widow, asked God for assistance and devised a plan to single-handedly overcome Holofernes. She succeeded in her plan and killed the Assyrian commander while he lay in a drunken stupor. The next day the Assyrians discovered the disaster and fled, giving victory to the Israelites.

■ **Author:** Unknown

■ **Date Written:** Around 150 BC

■ **Purpose:** To encourage Jews to resist their enemies and to continue to faithfully observe the laws of God

■ **Themes:** Many virtues are highlighted and praised, including humility, justice, purity, courage, and faith; through faith in God, strength can be found in weakness.

■ **Outline**
1:1–3:14 The gathering storm
4:1–7:25 The siege against Bethulia
8:1–13:31 The deliverance by Judith
14:1–16:30 The victory

Arphaxad Builds Up Ecbatana

1 It was the twelfth year of the reign of Nebuchadnezzar,* who ruled over the Assyrians in the great city of Nineveh. At the same time, Arphaxad ruled over the Medes in Ecbatana. ²Arphaxad built walls around Ecbatana with huge stones 4½ feet thick and 9 feet long.* These walls were 105 feet high and 75 feet thick.* ³He also made towers that were 150 feet high and 90 feet wide* at the foundation. ⁴He built the gateways of the city 105 feet high and 60 feet wide* to allow his armies to march out in force, division by division. ⁵In those days King Nebuchadnezzar fought against King Arphaxad on the great plain near the borders of Ragau.* ⁶Nebuchadnezzar was joined by people from the hill country, from along the Euphrates, the Tigris, and the Hydaspes, and

from the plain where Arioch ruled over the Elymeans. In this way, many nations joined forces with the Babylonians.*

Nebuchadnezzar Calls for Allies

⁷Then Nebuchadnezzar, king of the Assyrians, sent a message to everyone in Persia and to all who lived in the west. The message went to those in Cilicia, Damascus, and the region of Lebanon and the Anti-Lebanon Mountains, and to all the people on the seacoast. ⁸The message also went to the people of Carmel, Gilead, Upper Galilee, the great plain of Esdraelon, ⁹the towns of Samaria, and to everyone who lived west of the Jordan River. This included Jerusalem, Bethany, Chelous, and Kadesh. The message went as far as the border of Egypt* to Tahpanhes, Rameses, and the whole land

---

1:1 The 12th year of Nebuchadnezzar's reign was 593 B.C.   1:2a Greek *3 cubits* [1.4 meters] *thick and 6 cubits* [2.8 meters] *long*. In this chapter, the distance measures are calculated from the Greek cubit at a ratio of 18 inches [46 centimeters] per cubit.   1:2b Greek *70 cubits* [32.2 meters] *high and 50 cubits* [23 meters] *thick.*   1:3 Greek *100 cubits* [46 meters] *high and 60 cubits* [27.6 meters] *wide.*   1:4 Greek *70 cubits* [32.2 meters] *high and 40 cubits* [18 meters] *wide.*   1:5 Ragau was a city located near present-day Teheran.   1:6 Greek *Chaldeans.*   1:9 Greek *the river of Egypt,* referring either to an eastern branch of the Nile River or to the brook of Egypt in the Sinai (see Num 34:5).

of Goshen. [10]It even went beyond Tanis and Memphis to the entire land of Egypt as far as the border of Ethiopia.

[11]But everyone throughout the region chose to disregard the summons from Nebuchadnezzar, king of the Assyrians, refusing to join him in war. They were not afraid of him; after all, he was just one man.* So they dishonored him by sending back his messengers with a negative response. [12]Then King Nebuchadnezzar became angry. He swore by his throne and kingdom that he would seek revenge on the whole territory of Cilicia and Damascus and Syria. He vowed to kill all the people of Moab, Ammon, Judea, and Egypt as far as the Mediterranean Sea and the Red Sea.*

Nebuchadnezzar Defeats Arphaxad

[13]In the seventeenth year of his reign,* Nebuchadnezzar led his forces against King Arphaxad and defeated him in battle, overpowering Arphaxad's entire army, including all his horsemen and chariots. [14]He took possession of all the towns and then conquered Ecbatana, capturing its towers, plundering its marketplaces, and reducing its glory to ruins. [15]He captured Arphaxad in the mountains of Ragau and killed him with spears, thus destroying him once and for all. [16]Then Nebuchadnezzar returned to Nineveh with his entire army, a vast number of troops. There he and his army rested and feasted for 120 days.

The Military Plan against the West

2 In the eighteenth year of Nebuchadnezzar's reign, on a certain day in midspring,* word went out from the palace of Nebuchadnezzar, king of the Assyrians, that he would seek revenge on the whole region, just as he had said. [2]He called all his advisers and governors and told them about his secret plan. And when he told them that the people throughout the region had refused to help him, [3]they decided that everyone who had disobeyed his command should be destroyed.

[4]After the council had finished making its plan, Nebuchadnezzar, king of the Assyrians, gave these orders to Holofernes, his commander who was second in power only to himself:

[5]"This is what the great king, the lord of the whole earth, says: Prepare for battle, and take with you 120,000 brave foot soldiers and 12,000 horsemen. [6]March out against all the lands to the west, for they disregarded my orders. [7]Tell them to prepare to submit to my authority,* for in my rage I am marching against them. I will cover the whole earth with my armies, and my troops will plunder it. [8]Their wounded will fill their valleys and ravines. Their dead will be thrown into the rivers, causing them to overflow. [9]I will lead them captive to the ends of the earth. [10]Go! Seize all their territory for me. All must surrender to you, and you are to hold them for me until I can punish them. [11]Show no mercy to those who resist. Slaughter and plunder them throughout the region. [12]For as I live, and by the power of my kingdom, I have spoken. I will accomplish all this by my own power. [13]Be careful, Holofernes, not to neglect any of your master's commands. Carry them out exactly as I have ordered you, and do so immediately."

Holofernes Prepares for War

[14]So Holofernes left the king and called together all the commanders, generals, and officers of the Assyrian army. [15]He arranged the 120,000 select troops by divisions, as the king had ordered him to do, together with 12,000 archers on horseback. [16]He organized them in battle formation. [17]He secured a vast number of camels, donkeys, and mules for carrying baggage, and innumerable sheep, oxen, and goats for food. [18]Everyone received plenty of rations and a large amount of gold and silver from the royal palace.

[19]Then Holofernes personally led his army ahead of King Nebuchadnezzar and overran the entire region to the west with chariots and horsemen and select troops. [20]After them followed a huge force of all sorts of people—like a swarm of locusts and the dust of the earth, too many to count.

Holofernes Advances

[21]They marched for three days from Nineveh to the plain of Bectileth, and they camped near Bectileth by the mountain to the north of Upper Cilicia. [22]From there Holofernes took his whole army—the foot soldiers, horsemen, and chariots—and went up to the hill country. [23]He devastated the region of Lydia* and carried away all the Rassisites and the Ishmaelites

1:11 Or just a human being.   1:12 Greek as far as the coast of the two seas.   1:13 The 17th year of Nebuchadnezzar's reign was 588 B.C.   2:1 Greek In the eighteenth year, on the twenty-second day of the first month, of the ancient Hebrew lunar calendar.   2:7 Greek to prepare earth and water.   2:23 Greek Put and Lud.

on the border of the desert south of the country of the Chelleans. ²⁴Then he marched along the Euphrates, crossed Mesopotamia, and destroyed all the fortified towns along Abron Brook as far as the sea. ²⁵He seized control of the territory of Cilicia and killed everyone who resisted him. Then he went to the southern borders of Japheth, across from Arabia. ²⁶He surrounded all the Midianites, burned their tents, and plundered their sheepfolds. ²⁷Then he went to the plain of Damascus during the wheat harvest. He burned their fields, destroyed their flocks and herds, plundered their towns, ravaged their lands, and slaughtered all their young men with the sword. ²⁸All the people who lived along the seacoast were terrified—those who lived in Sidon and Tyre and those in Sur, Ocina, and Jamnia. Those who lived in Azotus and Ashkelon were seized with terrible panic.

The People Plead for Peace

3 These people sent messengers to Holofernes with this petition for peace:

²"We, the servants of Nebuchadnezzar,
the great king, fall humbly before you.
Do with us whatever you will. ³See, all we
have is at your disposal—our buildings,
our land, our wheat fields, our flocks
and herds, and our sheepfolds and their
surrounding tents. Do with them as you
please. ⁴The people of our towns will all
be your slaves. Come and deal with us
and all we own as you see fit."

⁵The messengers went to Holofernes and told him all this.

⁶Then Holofernes went down to the seacoast with his army, stationed garrisons in all the fortified towns, and drafted the best men there as reserve troops. ⁷All the people along the coast and in the surrounding areas welcomed him, wearing garlands, dancing, and playing tambourines. ⁸But Holofernes demolished all their shrines* and cut down their sacred groves. For King Nebuchadnezzar had commanded him to destroy all the gods of the land so that he alone might be served as a god in the nations conquered by Holofernes. ⁹Then he came to the plain of Esdraelon, near Dothan, a village facing the great ridge of Judea. ¹⁰He camped between Geba and Scythopolis, and he stayed there for a whole month to collect all the provisions his army needed.

Judea Prepares for the Attack

4 The Israelites throughout Judea heard that Holofernes, the commander serving Nebuchadnezzar, king of the Assyrians, had plundered all the other nations and destroyed their temples. ²As he approached, they became terrified for Jerusalem and for the Temple of the Lord their God, ³for they had only recently returned from captivity. (All the people of Judea had recently resettled the city and rededicated the sacred vessels and the altar and the Temple, all of which had been defiled.)

⁴So the Israelites in Judea sent word to every district of Samaria and to Kona, Beth-horon, Belmain, Jericho, Choba, Aesora, and the Salem Valley. ⁵They occupied all the high hilltops and fortified the villages there. They also stored up food to prepare for war, for their fields had recently been harvested. ⁶Joakim, the high priest, was in Jerusalem at the time and wrote to the people of Bethulia and Betomesthaim, towns facing Esdraelon across the plain near Dothan. ⁷He told them to guard the mountain passes, for it was only through these passes that Judea could be invaded. It would be easy to stop any forces trying to enter because the passage was narrow, wide enough for only two soldiers to pass at a time. ⁸The Israelites did as they had been ordered by the high priest Joakim and the high council* of all the people of Israel, which was in session at Jerusalem.

⁹All the people cried out earnestly to God and humbled themselves by intense fasting. ¹⁰All the men, their wives, their children, and every resident foreigner (both hired workers and slaves) put on sackcloth to show they were in mourning. They even put sackcloth on their livestock. ¹¹And all the Israelite men, women, and children living in Jerusalem lay face down in front of the Temple, and with ashes on their heads, they spread out their sackcloth before the Lord. ¹²They even draped the altar with sackcloth. They cried out together, earnestly asking the God of Israel not to allow their infants to be carried off, their wives to be taken captive, their towns to be destroyed, and the sanctuary to be desecrated. They knew the Gentiles around them would be overjoyed at their defeat.

¹³The Lord heard their prayers and acknowledged their distress—for the people fasted many days throughout Judea and in Jerusalem before the sanctuary of the Lord Almighty. ¹⁴Joakim the high priest and all the priests who ministered before the Lord wore sackcloth as

3:8 As in Syriac version; Greek reads *borders.*   4:8 Greek *the senate.*

they offered the people's daily burnt offerings, offerings to fulfill vows, and freewill offerings. [15] With ashes on their turbans, they earnestly called on the Lord, asking him to look kindly on the people of Israel.

A Council of War

5 Holofernes, the commander of the Assyrian army, was told that the people of Israel had prepared for battle by closing the mountain passes, fortifying all the high hilltops, and placing obstructions in the plains. [2] Holofernes was very angry at this and called together all the princes of Moab, the commanders of Ammon, and all the governors of the coastlands. [3] He asked them, "Tell me, you Canaanites, who are these people that occupy the hill country? What towns do they live in? How large is their army? What is the source of their power and strength? Who is the king that leads their army? [4] Why is it that, of all the nations in this western region, they are the only ones who refuse to surrender to me?"

[5] Then Achior, leader of the Ammonites, answered, "My lord, if you wish, I will tell you the truth about these people who live in the hills nearby. I will not lie. [6] The ancestors of these people were Chaldeans. [7] For a time they settled in Mesopotamia because they refused to worship the gods their ancestors had worshiped in Chaldea. [8] Since they had abandoned their ancestors' ways and worshiped the God of heaven, the God they had come to know, their neighbors expelled them from the presence of their gods. So they fled to Mesopotamia, where they lived for a long time. [9] Then their God commanded them to leave that place and go to the land of Canaan. They settled there and acquired great wealth in gold, silver, and livestock.

[10] "When a famine spread over the land of Canaan, they went down to Egypt and lived there as long as there was food. They became such a great multitude that their race could not be counted, [11] so the king of Egypt became hostile toward them. He exploited them by making them slaves who produced bricks for him. [12] They cried out to their God, who punished all of Egypt with incurable plagues. So the Egyptians drove them out of their sight. [13] Then God dried up the Red Sea before them, [14] and he led them forward to Sinai and Kadeshbarnea. They drove out all the people living in the desert [15] and settled in the land of the Amorites. With great force they destroyed all

5:15 Greek *inherited*.

the inhabitants of Heshbon. Then they crossed over the Jordan River and took control of* all the hill country. [16] They drove out the Canaanites, Perizzites, Jebusites, Shechemites, and all the Girgashites. Then the Israelites lived there a long time.

[17] "As long as they did not sin against their God, they prospered, for the God who is with them hates sin. [18] But when they disobeyed him, they were defeated in many battles and were taken captive to foreign lands. The Temple of their God was demolished, and their towns were taken by their enemies. [19] But now they have returned to their God and have come back from the places where they were scattered. Some of them have occupied Jerusalem, the site of their Temple, while others settled in the unoccupied hill country.

[20] "So now, master and lord, we must find out if these people have sinned against their God. If so, we can go up and defeat them. [21] But if they are not guilty, my lord, you would do better to leave them alone and move on. For their Lord and God will protect them, and we would become the laughingstock of the whole world."

[22] When Achior had finished his talk, all the people standing around the tent began to disagree with him. Holofernes' officers, together with the people from the coastal area and from Moab, insisted that Achior should be killed. [23] "Why should we be afraid of the Israelites?" they said. "They are weak and powerless, incapable of withstanding any sort of attack. [24] Let's go ahead! Your great army, master Holofernes, will swallow them up!"

Achior Is Released to the Israelites

6 When the uproar made by the men outside the council died down, Holofernes, commander of the Assyrian army, spoke to Achior in the presence of all the foreigners and Moabites. [2] He said, "Achior, who do you think you are—you and the other mercenaries of Ephraim? Who are you to tell us like some prophet not to make war against the people of Israel? Do you think their God will defend them? What god is there except Nebuchadnezzar? He will send his forces to wipe them from the face of the earth! Their God will not rescue them. [3] We, the king's servants, will destroy them as if they were but one man. They could never resist the force of our horsemen. [4] We will burn them completely. Their mountains will be drunk with their blood, and their plains will be filled with their dead. Not a single trace

of them will survive our attack; they will all die. So says King Nebuchadnezzar, lord of the whole earth, for he has spoken, and he makes no empty threats.

5"As for you, Achior, you Ammonite mercenary, you have spoken these words rashly. You will not see my face again until I take revenge on these people who came out of Egypt. 6When I return, the swords of my soldiers and the spears* of my servants will pierce your sides, and you will fall among their wounded. 7Now my slaves are going to take you into the hill country and leave you in one of the towns near the mountain passes. 8You will not die until you are destroyed along with these people. 9If you really believe in your heart that they will not be conquered, don't look so sad! But I have spoken, and none of my words will fail to come true."

10Then Holofernes commanded his personal slaves to seize Achior and take him away to Bethulia, where they would hand him over to the Israelites. 11So the slaves led him out of the camp into the plain. From there they went up into the hill country and came to the springs below Bethulia. 12When the men of the town saw them, they picked up their weapons and ran from the town to the top of the hill. All the slingers prevented Holofernes' slaves from coming up because they kept slinging stones at them. 13So the slaves took shelter below the hill. Then they tied Achior, left him lying at the foot of the hill, and returned to their master.

14The Israelites came down from their town and found Achior. After untying him, they brought him into Bethulia, where he could speak to the leaders of their town. 15The leaders in those days were Uzziah son of Micah (of the tribe of Simeon), Chabris son of Gothoniel, and Charmis son of Melchiel. 16They called together all the elders of the town, and all the young men and women hurried to the assembly as well. Achior stood in the middle of all the people, and Uzziah questioned him about what had happened. 17Achior answered by telling them what had taken place at Holofernes' council. He told them everything he had said to the Assyrian leaders and how Holofernes had bragged about what he would do to the people of Israel.

18Then all the people fell down and worshiped God. They cried out, 19"O Lord God of heaven, see their pride, and be merciful to our humble race. Show your kindness to those who are dedicated to you."

20Then they reassured Achior and praised him warmly. 21Uzziah took him from the assembly to his own house and gave a banquet for the elders. All that night they called on the God of Israel for help.

The Campaign against Israel Begins

7 The next day Holofernes ordered his whole army and all the reserve troops who had joined him to break camp and march against Bethulia. He told them to take over the mountain passes as the first step in their attack on the Israelites. 2The army began to march that very day; it numbered at 148,000 foot soldiers and 12,000 horsemen, not counting the baggage carts and the soldiers handling the supplies. 3They set up camp in the valley near Bethulia beside the spring. They covered the whole land from Dothan to Balbaim and from Bethulia to Cyamon, which faces Esdraelon. 4When the Israelites saw this huge army, they were terrified and said to each other, "They will strip the whole land clean. The mountains, valleys, and hills cannot bear their weight." 5Yet they all took up their weapons and lit fires on their towers, where they remained on guard all night.

6On the second day Holofernes led all his horsemen out in full view of the Israelites in Bethulia. 7He scouted out the slopes leading up to the town and located the springs that supplied their water. So he took control of these springs and set guards of soldiers over them. Then he returned to his army.

8Then all the leaders of the Edomites and the Moabites and the commanders of the coastal area came to him and said, 9"Listen to what we have to say, our master, and your army will suffer no casualties. 10These Israelites do not have to rely on their spears, for they live in safety in the high mountains. 11Therefore, master, you do not have to fight against them in the normal way, and you will not lose a single man of your army. 12Simply stay in your camp and keep all your forces with you. Let your men keep control of the spring of water at the foot of the mountain, 13for this is where all the people of Bethulia get their water. Eventually their thirst will force them to surrender their town. Meanwhile, we and our people will go up to the tops of the nearest mountains. We will camp there to keep watch and to prevent anyone from leaving the town. 14All the men, women, and children will waste away from thirst, and you won't even need to attack them. Their bodies

6:6 As in Latin Vulgate and Syriac version; Greek reads *and the people*.

will be scattered about in the streets outside their houses. ¹⁵Thus, you will pay them back for their defiance and for refusing to receive you peaceably."

¹⁶This suggestion pleased Holofernes and all his officers, and he gave orders to do as they had said. ¹⁷So the army of the Ammonites moved forward along with five thousand Assyrians. They set up camp in the valley and seized the Israelites' water sources and springs. ¹⁸Meanwhile, the Edomites and Ammonites went up and camped in the hill country opposite Dothan. They sent some of their men southeast toward Acraba, near Chusi, which is beside Mochmur Brook. The rest of the Assyrian army camped in the plain. Their tents and supply wagons spread out in great numbers, and they covered the entire area.

¹⁹The Israelites lost their courage and cried out to the Lord their God for help. All their enemies had surrounded them, and there was no way of escape. ²⁰The whole Assyrian army, including their foot soldiers, chariots, and horsemen, surrounded them for thirty-four days. Eventually, all the water jars of every house in Bethulia became empty. ²¹Their cisterns were going dry, and no one had enough water to drink, for their water was rationed. ²²The children wasted away, and the women and young men, faint from thirst, were collapsing in the streets of the town and in the gateways. No one had any strength left.

²³Then all the people—including the young men, the women, and the children—gathered around Uzziah and the rulers of the town. They shouted at the elders, ²⁴"Let God judge between you and us! We are suffering because you wouldn't make peace with the Assyrians. ²⁵Now we have no one to help us. God has handed us over to them, thirsty and helpless. ²⁶Call them immediately, and surrender the whole town as a prize to the army of Holofernes, ²⁷for it would be better for us to be captured by them. We will be forced to become their slaves, but at least our lives will be spared. And we won't have to see our infants dying before our eyes or see our wives and children taking their last breath. ²⁸We call on heaven and earth and God to be our witnesses. The Lord of our ancestors is punishing us for our sins and the sins of our ancestors. Do what we have asked for today!" ²⁹Then the entire assembly began to weep, and they cried out to the Lord God with a loud voice.

³⁰But Uzziah said to them, "Take heart, my brothers and sisters.* Let's hold out for five more days. By then the Lord our God will show us his mercy again, for he will not completely forsake us. ³¹But if no help comes during that time, I will do as you say." ³²Then he dismissed the people to their various quarters. The men returned to their stations on the walls and towers of the town. The women and children went home. And everyone in the town was miserable and discouraged.

Judith

8 Now Judith heard about what had happened. She was the daughter of Merari son of Ox, son of Joseph, son of Oziel, son of Elkiah, son of Ananias, son of Gideon, son of Raphain, son of Ahitub, son of Elijah, son of Hilkiah, son of Eliab, son of Nathanael, son of Salamiel, son of Sarasadai, son of Israel. ²Her husband, Manasseh, who was from the same tribe and family, had died several years earlier during the barley harvest. ³As he supervised the workers who were binding sheaves of grain in the field, he was overcome by the burning heat and was confined to his bed. He died in Bethulia, his hometown, and was buried with his ancestors in the field between Dothan and Balamon. ⁴Judith had remained a widow for three years and four months. ⁵She stayed at home, where she set up a room* for herself on the roof of her house. She wore sackcloth around her waist and dressed in widow's clothing. ⁶She fasted every day except on the day before the Sabbath, the Sabbath itself, the day before the new moon, the festival of the new moon, and all the joyful festivals of Israel. ⁷She was a beautiful woman, very lovely in appearance. Her husband, Manasseh, had left her gold and silver, male and female servants, herds, and cultivated land, and she managed the entire estate. ⁸No one spoke a bad word about her, for she was devout and feared God.

Judith Consults the Elders

⁹Judith heard how the people, who were fainting because they had no water, had spoken against Uzziah, the ruler. And she heard all that Uzziah had promised them, even that he had sworn to surrender the town to the Assyrians after five days. ¹⁰So she sent her maid, who was in charge of all she owned, to summon Uzziah and* Chabris and Charmis, the elders of the town.

¹¹When the elders came to Judith, she said,

"Listen to me, rulers of the people of Bethulia! What you have said to the people today is wrong. You have bound yourselves by an oath to God, promising to surrender the town to our enemies unless the Lord helps us within a certain number of days. ¹²Who are you to test God? Who are you to set yourselves above him? ¹³You are testing the Lord Almighty, but you will never learn anything! ¹⁴If you cannot discover the depths of the human heart or understand the thoughts of the human mind, how can you search out God, who made these things? How can you grasp his mind or comprehend his thoughts? No, my brothers, do not make the Lord our God angry. ¹⁵For if he doesn't choose to help us within these five days, he still has the power to protect us for as long as he pleases. Or he could decide to destroy us in the presence of our enemies. ¹⁶Do not try to control the plans of the Lord our God, for God is not like a human being, to be manipulated. He is not like a mere mortal, who can be persuaded. ¹⁷Therefore, while we wait for him to rescue us, let us call on him for help. He will hear us, if it pleases him.

¹⁸"In these days there are no tribes, families, clans, or towns among us that worship gods they themselves have made, as was done before. ¹⁹That was why God allowed our ancestors to be killed, plundered, and humiliated by our enemies. ²⁰But now we worship no other gods but him, and so we hope that he will not abandon us or any of our people. ²¹For if we are captured, all Judea will be captured, and our Temple will be plundered. God will make us pay for its desecration with our very lives. ²²Our relatives will be slaughtered, our land will be taken over, and our inheritance will be destroyed—and all this in the presence of the Gentiles, to whom we will be slaves. We will be disgraced before these masters. ²³For our slavery will not bring us into their favor; rather, the Lord our God will make our slavery shameful.

²⁴"Therefore, fellow Israelites, let us be an example to our relatives, for their lives depend on us. And so does the Temple—even the holy places and the altar. ²⁵In spite of everything, we should thank the Lord our God, who is testing us, just as he tested our ancestors. ²⁶Remember how he tested Abraham and Isaac. And remember what happened to Jacob in Syrian Mesopotamia while he was taking care of the sheep of Laban, his mother's brother. ²⁷The Lord tried them with fire to test their hearts. But he is not

9:4 Greek *on their blood.*

punishing us. He punishes those who are close to him in order to warn them."

²⁸Then Uzziah said to her, "Everything you have said was spoken with a good heart, and there is no one who can disagree with your words. ²⁹Today is not the first time you have shown your wisdom, for the people have recognized your understanding and integrity from the time you were a small girl. ³⁰But the people were so thirsty that they forced us to make this promise, and they made us take an oath that cannot be broken. ³¹Now, since you are a devout woman, pray for us, that the Lord may send rain to fill our cisterns. Then we will no longer die of thirst."

³²Then Judith said to them, "Listen to me. I am about to do something that will be remembered by all our descendants. ³³Tonight, stand by the gate, where I will leave with my maid. Within five days—the period after which you have promised to surrender the town to our enemies—the Lord will rescue Israel through me. ³⁴But don't try to find out what I am doing, for I will not tell you until I have done it."

³⁵Uzziah and the rulers said to her, "Go in peace. May the Lord God go before you and take revenge on our enemies." ³⁶Then they left her room and returned to their quarters.

Judith's Prayer

9 Then Judith fell face down on the ground, put ashes on her head, and removed her clothing, leaving only the sackcloth she was wearing. At the very time the evening incense was being offered in the Temple of God in Jerusalem, Judith cried out to the Lord with a loud voice. She said, ²"O Lord God of my ancestor Simeon, you gave Simeon a sword to take revenge on the foreigners who had defiled a virgin by stripping off her clothes, exposing her thighs to put her to shame, and raping her. You said, 'Such a thing must not be done.' Yet they did it. ³So you allowed their rulers to be killed and their bed to be stained with blood, for it was covered with the shame of their deceitful deed. You struck down slaves along with princes and killed even the princes on their thrones. ⁴You let their wives be captured and their daughters be taken into captivity, and you gave all their possessions be divided among your beloved children. Your children burned with zeal for you and abhorred the stain on their sister,* so they called on you for help. Listen to me and answer me, O God, my God, for I am a widow. ⁵You made the things of the

past, and you designed everything that now exists and everything that is to come. What you planned has all happened. ⁶Everything you decided on has taken place just as you said it would. For all your ways are prepared in advance, and you make your judgments with knowledge of what will happen in the future.

⁷"Here now are the Assyrians, a great force, who take pride in their horses and riders. They boast in the strength of their foot soldiers and trust in shield and spear, bow and sling. They do not know that you are the Lord who crushes armies. ⁸Your name is the Lord. Break their strength by your might. Subdue their power in your anger. For they intend to defile your sanctuary, to pollute the Temple,* where your glorious name resides, and to break off the horns of your altar with their powerful swords. ⁹Look at their pride. Send your fury on their heads. Give strength to a widow's hand to do what I plan. ¹⁰When I trick them with my words, strike down the slave with the ruler and the ruler with his servant. Break their pride by the hand of a woman.

¹¹"For your strength does not depend on numbers nor your might on the powerful. But you are the God of the humble, helper of the oppressed, supporter of the weak, protector of the forsaken, deliverer of those without hope. ¹²Please, please, O God of my ancestor, God of Israel's heritage, Lord of heaven and earth, Creator of the seas, King of your whole creation—hear my prayer! ¹³Help my deceitful tongue to wound and bruise those who have planned cruel things against your covenant, against your holy dwelling place on top of Mount Zion, and against this land* that your children possess. ¹⁴Show your whole nation and every tribe that you are God, the God of all power and might. You are the only one who protects the people of Israel!"

Judith Goes to See Holofernes

10 When Judith finished pleading to the God of Israel, ²she got up from where she was lying face down before the Lord. She called her maid and went down into her house, where she lived on Sabbaths and festival days. ³Then she took off her sackcloth and the clothes that showed she was a widow in mourning. She took a bath, anointed herself with the finest lotion, braided her hair, put a tiara on her head, and dressed in her most beautiful clothing— things she had often worn when her husband, Manasseh, was still alive. ⁴Then she put sandals

on her feet and put on anklets, bracelets, rings, and earrings. She made herself very beautiful to catch the attention of any man who might see her.

⁵She gave her maid a wineskin filled with wine and a flask of oil to carry. She also filled a bag with roasted grain, dried fig cakes, and fine bread, and she filled a sack with her dishes and gave them to the maid to carry. ⁶Then they went to the town gate of Bethulia, where Uzziah and the elders of the town, Chabris and Charmis, were waiting. ⁷They were astonished when they saw her so transformed, and they greatly admired her beauty. They said to her, ⁸"May the God of our ancestors bring you favor and fulfill your plans, bringing glory to the Israelites and exaltation to Jerusalem."

Judith bowed down before God. Then she said to them, ⁹"Order the town gate to be opened, and I will go out and do what you have just said." So they ordered the young men to open the gate for her. ¹⁰Then Judith went out, accompanied by her maid. The men of the town watched her while she went down the mountain and passed through the valley. Then they lost sight of her.

¹¹As Judith and her maid went straight through the valley, an Assyrian patrol met her ¹²and took her into custody. They asked her, "To what people do you belong? Where are you coming from? Where are you going?"

Judith answered, "I am a daughter of the Hebrews, but I am fleeing from them because I know you will soon defeat them. ¹³I want to see your commander, Holofernes, so I can tell him their secrets and show him a way to take the hill country without losing a single life."

¹⁴When the men heard her words and saw her face—for she was incredibly beautiful— they said to her, ¹⁵"You have saved your life by choosing to surrender to our lord. Go to his tent immediately. Some of us will escort you to him. ¹⁶Don't be afraid when you tell him what you just told us, for he will treat you well." ¹⁷Then they chose a hundred men to accompany her and her maid, and they brought them to the tent of Holofernes.

¹⁸The whole camp was very excited, for news of her arrival spread from tent to tent. They came and gathered around her as she stood outside the tent of Holofernes, waiting to be invited in. ¹⁹They were amazed at her beauty and admired the Israelites, judging them by her. They said to one another, "Who can look down on the Jews when they have such

9:8 Greek *tabernacle.*   9:13 Greek *against the house.*

beautiful women? We must destroy them all, for any that escape could captivate the whole world."

20Then Holofernes' guards and servants came out and led her into the tent. 21Holofernes was resting on his bed under a purple canopy that was decorated with gold, emeralds, and other precious stones. 22When they told him about her, he came to the front of the tent, accompanied by servants with silver lamps. 23And when Holofernes and his servants saw Judith, they were all amazed at the beauty of her face. She showed honor by bowing low before him, but his slaves lifted her to her feet.

Judith's First Meeting with Holofernes

11 Then Holofernes said to Judith, "Take courage and don't be afraid. I have never hurt anyone who was willing to serve Nebuchadnezzar, king of all the earth. 2If your people from the hill country had not resisted me, I would never have attacked them. They have brought this on themselves. 3But tell me why you fled from them and came over to us. In any event, you have come to safety. Take courage! You will live tonight and ever after. 4No one will hurt you. In fact, everyone will treat you well, just as they treat all the servants of my lord, King Nebuchadnezzar."

5Judith replied, "I am your servant. Please let me speak to you, and I will not lie to you. 6If you follow my advice, God will accomplish great things through you, and you will achieve your goals. 7For I swear this by Nebuchadnezzar, king of all the earth, and by his great power, which he has given you to bring order to every living being. And because of you, not only people serve him, but even the wild animals, the livestock, and the birds live under Nebuchadnezzar's rule. 8We have all heard of your wisdom and skill, and everyone throughout the whole world knows that you alone are the most capable man in the whole kingdom, the most knowledgeable and brilliant in military strategy.

9"We have heard about what Achior said at your council meeting, for the people of Bethulia spared him, and he told them what he told you. 10Lord and master, do not disregard what he said, for it is true. Indeed, our nation cannot be punished, nor can the sword conquer the people if they have not sinned against their God.

11"But as it is now, my lord will not be defeated by them. Death will surely fall on them,

for they have been overtaken by sin and provoked the anger of their God. 12Since their food supply is depleted and their water is almost gone, they have planned to kill their livestock and eat all the parts that God has forbidden them to eat. 13And they have decided to eat the first part of the grain harvest and the tithes of the wine and oil, which they had dedicated and set aside for the priests in Jerusalem who minister in the presence of our God. It is not lawful for any of the people to even touch these things. 14But the elders of our town have sent men to Jerusalem (where they have been doing the same thing) to get permission from the high council* of elders there. 15When they get this permission and act upon it, on that very day they will be handed over to you to be destroyed.

16"When I, your slave, learned all this, I fled from them. God has sent me to accomplish with you things that will astonish everyone in the world who hears about them. 17I revere and serve the God of heaven night and day. So, my lord, I would like to remain with you, but every night I must go out into the valley and pray to God. He will let me know when my people have committed their sins. 18Then I will come and tell you so that you may go out with your whole army, and not one of the Israelites will be able to stand against you. 19Then I will guide you through Judea until you reach Jerusalem, where you will be enthroned. You will round up the people like sheep without a shepherd, and no dog will so much as bark at you. I was sent to tell you all this, which has been shown to me before it even happens."

20Judith's words pleased Holofernes and all his servants. They were amazed at her wisdom and said, 21"No other woman on earth looks so beautiful or speaks so wisely!" 22Then Holofernes said to her, "God has done well to send you ahead of the others. This strengthens our hands to bring destruction on those who have insulted my lord. 23You are as wise as you are beautiful. If you do as you have said, your God will be my God, and you will live in the palace of King Nebuchadnezzar and be famous throughout the whole world."

Judith Resides as Holofernes' Guest

12 Holofernes commanded his servants to bring Judith inside the tent, where his silver dinnerware was set on a table with some of his own delicacies and his own wine. 2But Judith said, "I cannot eat and drink these

11:14 Greek lacks *high council*.

things without sinning. But I have enough to eat from the supply I brought with me."

³Holofernes said to her, "If your supply runs out, where can we get you more? For none of your people are here."

⁴Judith replied, "As surely as you live, my lord, I will not use up my supplies before the Lord uses me to carry out what he has planned."

⁵Then the servants of Holofernes took her to her own tent. She slept until midnight and then got up about two o'clock in the morning. ⁶She sent a message to Holofernes asking permission to be allowed to go out and pray. ⁷Holofernes commanded his personal bodyguards not to stop her. She was at the camp three days, and each night she went out to the valley of Bethulia and bathed at the spring. ⁸After bathing, she asked the Lord, the God of Israel, to show her how to achieve victory for his people. ⁹When she had purified herself, she returned and stayed in the tent all day until she ate her evening meal.

Judith at Holofernes' Banquet

¹⁰On the fourth day Holofernes held a private banquet for his personal staff. He did not invite any of his officers. ¹¹He said to Bagoas, the eunuch in charge of his personal affairs, "Persuade the Hebrew woman to join us, for I want her to eat and drink with us. ¹²It would be a shame to let such a beautiful woman go without sleeping with her. If we fail to seduce her, she will laugh at us."

¹³So Bagoas went out to see Judith and said, "Would this lovely woman come to my lord as his guest of honor? Please come and enjoy our wine, and you will be treated like one of the Assyrian women who serve in the palace of Nebuchadnezzar."

¹⁴Judith replied, "Who am I to refuse my lord? I will do whatever he wants me to do, and it will be a joy to me until my dying day." ¹⁵So she dressed herself in all her beautiful clothing and feminine finery. Her maid went ahead and spread before Holofernes the lambskins Bagoas had provided for Judith's bed and dining couch.

¹⁶When Judith went in and lay down, Holofernes' heart burned with passion, for he had been waiting for a chance to seduce her ever since he first saw her. ¹⁷So Holofernes said to her, "Please, enjoy yourself! Have a drink!"

¹⁸Judith said, "I will gladly drink, my lord, because today is the best day of my life." ¹⁹Then she took the food and drink her maid had prepared and ate and drank with him.

²⁰Holofernes was so pleased with her that he drank a great quantity of wine, much more than he had ever drunk before.

Judith Kills Holofernes

13 When evening came, Holofernes' slaves left quickly. Bagoas closed the tent from the outside and sent the attendants away. They went to their beds, for they were all weary from the long banquet. ²Judith was left alone in the tent with Holofernes, who had collapsed on his bed in a drunken stupor. ³Judith told her maid to stand outside Holofernes' sleeping quarters and wait for her to come out, as she had done on the other days, for Judith said she would be going out for her prayers. (She had told Bagoas the same thing.) ⁴So now everyone had left, and she was alone in the tent.

Then Judith, standing beside Holofernes' bed, said in her heart, "O Lord, God of all power, bless what I am about to do for the glory of Jerusalem. ⁵Now is the time to help your people and to carry out my plan to destroy the enemies who have attacked us."

⁶She went up to the bedpost near Holofernes' head and took down his sword that hung there. ⁷She came close to his bed, took hold of his hair, and said, "Make me strong today, Lord God of Israel!" ⁸Then she struck his neck twice with all her might and cut off his head. ⁹Next she rolled his body off the bed and pulled the canopy down from the posts. Then she quickly went out and gave Holofernes' head to her maid, ¹⁰who put it in her food bag. Then the two of them left camp together, as they usually did when they went to pray.

As soon as they passed through the camp, they circled around the valley, went up the mountain toward Bethulia, and then headed for its gates. ¹¹From a distance Judith called out to the guards at the gates, "Please, open the gate! Open! God, our God, is still with us. He has shown his power in Israel and his strength against our enemies on this very day!"

¹²When the people of the town heard her voice, they hurried down to the town gate and summoned the elders of the town. ¹³The leaders and the rest of the people all ran to the gate, for it seemed unbelievable that she had returned. They opened the gate and welcomed the two women. Then they lit a fire for light and gathered around them.

¹⁴With a loud voice, Judith said to them, "Praise God! Praise him! Praise God, who has not withdrawn his mercy from the people of Israel. He has helped me destroy our enemies

this very night!" [15]Then she pulled the head out of the bag and showed it to them. "Look," she said. "This is the head of Holofernes, the commander of the Assyrian army. Here is the canopy beneath which he lay drunk. The Lord has struck him down by the hand of a woman! [16]The Lord protected me in this mission, and as the Lord lives, I swear that it was my beauty* that seduced him to his destruction. But he committed no sin with me so as to disgrace and shame me."

[17]All the people were completely amazed. They bowed down and worshiped God, saying with one voice, "We bless you, our God, for on this day you have humiliated the enemies of your people."

[18]Then Uzziah said to Judith, "Daughter, may you be blessed by the Most High God above all women on earth. Praise to the Lord God, who created the heavens and the earth, who has guided you to cut off the head of the leader of our enemies. [19]Those who acknowledge the power of God will forever find hope in him.* [20]May God give you honor forever, and may he reward you with blessings, for you did not think about your own life when our nation was brought to its knees. You prevented our ruin by walking in the straight path of our God."

And all the people said, "Amen! Amen!"

Judith's Plan

14 Then Judith said to them, "Listen to me, brothers and sisters.* Take this head and hang it on the battlements of your wall. [2]When morning comes and the sun is up, every able-bodied man should go out of the town with his weapons. Appoint a leader over them, as if you were going down to the plain to attack the Assyrian scouts—only don't really go. [3]The scouts will grab their weapons and run into the camp and wake up the officers. They will all rush to the tent of Holofernes, but when they cannot find him, they will panic and flee before you. [4]Then you and all who live within the borders of Israel will chase them and cut them down in their tracks. [5]But before you do all this, bring Achior the Ammonite to identify this man who despised the people of Israel and who thought he was sending Achior to his death by sending him to us."

[6]So they called Achior, who was staying in the home of Uzziah. When he came and saw one of the men holding Holofernes' head, he fell to the ground in a faint. [7]When they

revived him, he threw himself at Judith's feet and honored her. He said, "May you be blessed by every family of Judah! In every nation, those who hear your name will be afraid. [8]How in the world did you do this?"

So Judith, surrounded by all the people, told him everything she had done, from the day she left until that moment. [9]When she finished, the people cheered, rejoicing throughout the town. [10]When Achior saw all that the God of Israel had done, he became a firm believer in God. So he was circumcised and joined the people of Israel, remaining so to this day.

Holofernes Is Discovered Dead

[11]As soon as it was dawn, the people of Bethulia hung Holofernes' head on the wall. Then they all took their weapons and went in companies to the mountain passes. [12]When the Assyrians saw them, they sent word to their commanders, who reported the news to the generals and captains and all their other officers. [13]The officers went to Holofernes' tent and said to the man in charge of Holofernes' personal affairs, "Wake up our lord, for those slaves are so bold they are attacking us—but we will destroy them!"

[14]Bagoas went inside and knocked at the inner entrance of the tent, for he thought Holofernes was sleeping with Judith. [15]But when no one answered, he opened it and went into the bedchamber and found Holofernes' dead body lying on the floor with his head cut off. [16]Bagoas cried out in anguish, wept, moaned, shouted, and tore his clothes. [17]Then he ran to the tent where Judith had stayed. When he saw that she was gone, he ran out to the people and shouted, [18]"Those slaves have tricked us! A single Hebrew woman has disgraced the whole house of King Nebuchadnezzar. Look, Holofernes is lying dead on the ground, and his head is missing!"

[19]When the leaders of the Assyrian army heard this, they tore their clothing in terror and distress, and their loud cries and shouts rang throughout the camp.

The Assyrians Flee

15 When the men in the tents heard about it, they were astonished at what had happened. [2]Panic-stricken, they didn't wait for each other but rushed out and fled across the plain and through the hill country on any available road or path. [3]Those who were camped in the hills around Bethulia also fled. Then all the Israelite soldiers charged after them.

13:16 Greek *my face.*   13:19 Some manuscripts read *will forever praise him.*   14:1 Greek *brothers.*

4Uzziah sent messengers to Betomasthaim, Bebai,* Choba, Kola, and all the territory of Israel to tell what had happened and to urge everyone to pursue and destroy the enemy. 5When the Israelites heard it, they joined together to fight the enemy, cutting them down all the way to Choba. Those in Jerusalem and in all the hill country also came, for they were told what had happened in the enemy camp. The men of Gilead and Galilee repeatedly attacked the enemy from the flank and slaughtered them, pursuing them even to the borders of Damascus. 6The people of Bethulia plundered the Assyrian camp and carried off great riches. 7And when the other Israelites returned from the slaughter, they took what remained. There was such a huge amount of plunder that even the villages and towns in the hill country and in the plain received much of it.

Victory Celebration

8Then Joakim the high priest and the high council* of the Israelites in Jerusalem came to see the good things that the Lord had done for Israel. They also wanted to see Judith and congratulate her. 9When they met her, they all blessed her and said to her, "You are the glory of Jerusalem; all Israel boasts about you! You are the great pride of our nation! 10You have done all this with your own hand. You have done a great thing for Israel, and God is well pleased with it. May the Almighty Lord bless you forever!" And all the people said, "Amen."

11The people plundered the Assyrian camp for thirty days. They gave Holofernes' tent and all his silver dinnerware, his beds, his bowls, and his furniture to Judith. She loaded her mules, hitched up her carts, and piled up all the plunder. 12All the women of Israel hurried to see her and bless her. They danced in her honor, and Judith gave them ivy-covered wands. 13Then the women crowned themselves with olive wreaths. Judith led all the women in a dance procession, and the men of Israel followed, carrying their weapons, wearing garlands, and singing hymns. 14With all Israel surrounding her, Judith sang a song of thanksgiving. And all the people joined in her song of praise.

A Song of Praise

16 This is Judith's song:

Sing to my God with tambourines.
Sing to my Lord with cymbals.
Lift up to him a psalm of praise.

15:4 Some manuscripts lack *Bebai.*   15:8 Greek *the elders.*

Exalt him and call upon his name.
2 For the Lord is a God who crushes warfare.
He set up his camp in the midst of his people;
he rescued me from the hands of my oppressors.
3 Assyria came down from the mountains of the north.
They came with many thousands of warriors.
Their soldiers filled the valleys.
Their horsemen covered the hills.
4 They boasted that they would set my land on fire,
kill my young men with the sword,
throw my infants to the ground,
seize my children as prizes of war,
and take my virgins as captives.
5 But the Lord Almighty has defeated them by the hand of a woman.
6 Their mighty leader was not struck down by young men,
nor did the sons of the Titans bring him down,
nor did tall giants put him away.
It was Judith, daughter of Merari,
who disarmed him with her beauty.

7 She put away her widow's clothing to rescue the oppressed in Israel.
She put on sweet perfume
8 and fastened her hair with a tiara.
She put on a linen gown to seduce him,
9 and a glimpse of her sandal aroused him.
Her beauty captivated his soul,
but the sword severed his neck!
10 The Persians trembled at her boldness,
the Medes were stunned by her daring.

11 Then my oppressed people shouted a war cry.
My weak people cried out, and the enemy trembled;
they raised their voices, and the enemy turned back.
12 Sons of slave girls pierced the enemy and wounded them like deserters.
They perished before the army of my Lord.

13 I will sing a new song to my God:
O Lord, you are great and glorious,
wonderfully strong, invincible.

[14] May all your creatures serve you,
    for when you spoke, they came into
        being.
You sent your breath,* and it formed
    them;
    no one can resist your voice.
[15] The mountains and oceans will shake in
        your presence,
    and rocks will melt like wax before you,
but to those who fear you,
    you show mercy.
[16] Sweet-smelling sacrifices are a small thing
        to you.
    The fat of whole burnt offerings means
        little to you.
    But those who fear the Lord are great
        forever.

[17] Destruction is certain for the nations that
        rise up against my people!
    The Lord Almighty will punish them in
        the day of judgment.
    He will send fire and worms into their
        flesh,
        and they will cry in pain forever.

[18]Eventually the entire group arrived at Jerusalem, where they worshiped God. As soon

16:14 Or *spirit.*

as the people were purified, they offered burnt offerings, freewill offerings, and gifts. [19]Judith dedicated to God all the possessions of Holofernes she had been given, and she gave the canopy from his sleeping quarters as an offering to fulfill a vow. [20]For three months the people enjoyed the festivities in Jerusalem before the Temple. And Judith was with them the whole time.

Conclusion

[21]After these events, the people all went home. Judith returned to Bethulia and lived on her estate, and she was esteemed throughout the country for the rest of her life. [22]Many men wanted to marry her, but she never gave herself to another man after the death of her husband, Manasseh. [23]She became more and more famous through the years. She grew old in her husband's house, reaching the age of 105. She set her maid free, and then she died in Bethulia. She was buried in a cave beside her husband, Manasseh, [24]and all Israel mourned for seven days. Before she died she distributed her property to all of her relatives and to Manasseh's relatives.

[25]No one troubled the Israelites during Judith's lifetime or for a long time afterward.

Esther

WITH DRAMA, INTRIGUE, ROMANCE, and murder, the book of Esther tells of the near destruction of the Jewish people. It tells how a young Jewish woman named Esther risked her life to save her people. Esther and her cousin, Mordecai, lived in the land of Persia, where the Jews were in exile. After Vashti, queen of Persia, insulted her husband, she was deposed, and the king began looking for a new queen. Esther was selected for her beauty, but she kept her Jewish nationality a secret. Meanwhile, a wicked man named Haman became the king's adviser and began plotting the extermination of all Jews in the empire. Mordecai learned of the plot and begged Esther to intervene, asking, "Who knows if perhaps you were made queen for just such a time as this?" (4:14). So Esther risked her life and approached the king about the matter. The king heard her plea and the Jews were saved, while Haman was executed on a pole he had prepared especially for Mordecai. This remarkable deliverance of the Jews is celebrated by the Jewish feast of Purim.

- **Author:** Mordecai, according to Jewish tradition
- **Date Written:** Around 470 BC
- **Purpose:** To demonstrate God's sovereignty and his loving care for his people
- **Themes:** God's sovereignty; loyalty to the true faith; God can use faithful people in dramatic ways
- **Outline**
  A:1–2:23 Esther becomes queen
  3:1–4:3 Haman's plan to destroy the Jews
  4:4–7:10 Esther's plan to save the Jews
  8:1–10:3 The deliverance of the Jews and the feast of Purim

---

The Greek additions to Esther are traditionally designated by the letters A, B, C, D, E, and F, and this translation follows that tradition. Accordingly, the reader can readily distinguish between the content of the Hebrew text of Esther and the expansions found in Greek versions.

Mordecai's Dream

A In* the second year of the reign of King Xerxes* the Great, on the first day of the new year,* Mordecai son of Jair, son of Shimei, son of Kish, of the tribe of Benjamin, had a dream. ²He was a Jew living in the city of Susa, and he was an important man who worked in the king's palace. ³He was a descendant* of the captives whom King Nebuchadnezzar of Babylon had taken from Jerusalem when he took King Jehoiachin* of Judea, captive.

⁴This was Mordecai's dream: There was clamor and confusion, thunder and earthquakes, and tumult upon the earth! ⁵Two great dragons came forward, ready to fight one another. ⁶At their terrible roar, every nation prepared for war, to fight against the righteous nation. ⁷It was a day of darkness and gloom, of troubles and distress, of suffering and great confusion upon the earth. ⁸The entire righteous nation was distraught; the people feared impending evil and prepared for death. ⁹But then the people cried to God, and a great overflowing river burst forth from a tiny spring. ¹⁰Light from the rising sun burst forth, and the humble were exalted and destroyed the nobles.

A:1a The portions designated as chapters A, B, C, D, E, and F are not included in the Hebrew text of Esther. They are here translated from the Greek version. A:1b Greek *Ahasuerus*, another name for Xerxes; also throughout the book of Esther. A:1c Greek *On the first day of the month of Nisan.* A number of dates in the book of Esther can be cross-checked with dates in surviving Persian records and related accurately to our modern calendar. This dream occurred on March 26, 484 B.C. A:3a Greek *He was one.* A:3b Greek *Jeconiah*, a variant name for Jehoiachin.

11When he woke up from this dream that revealed what God was going to do, Mordecai began thinking about what it might mean. He kept turning it over in his mind, anxious to understand every detail of the dream.

12One time Mordecai was resting in the king's courtyard with Bigthana and Teresh,* the king's eunuchs who were guards of the courtyard. 13He overheard them discussing a conspiracy, so he investigated their plans and discovered that they were about to kill King Xerxes. So Mordecai warned the king about the plot. 14The king had the two men interrogated, and after they confessed, he had them executed. 15The king made an official record of what had happened, and Mordecai also wrote down the events. 16The king ordered Mordecai to serve in the palace and gave him a reward. 17But Haman son of Hammedatha the Agagite,* a man highly regarded by the king, sought to harm Mordecai and his people because of what had happened to the king's two eunuchs.

The King's Banquet

1 These events happened in the days of King Xerxes,* who reigned over 127 provinces stretching from India to Ethiopia.* 2At that time Xerxes ruled his empire from his royal throne at the fortress of Susa. 3In the third year of his reign, he gave a banquet for all his nobles and officials. He invited all the military officers of Persia and Media as well as the princes and nobles of the provinces. 4The celebration lasted 180 days—a tremendous display of the opulent wealth of his empire and the pomp and splendor of his majesty.

5When it was all over, the king gave a banquet for all the people, from the greatest to the least, who were in the fortress of Susa. It lasted for seven days and was held in the courtyard of the palace garden. 6The courtyard was beautifully decorated with white cotton curtains and blue hangings, which were fastened with white linen cords and purple ribbons to silver rings embedded in marble pillars. Gold and silver couches stood on a mosaic pavement of porphyry, marble, mother-of-pearl, and other costly stones.

7Drinks were served in gold goblets of many designs, and there was an abundance of royal wine, reflecting the king's generosity. 8By edict of the king, no limits were placed on the drinking, for the king had instructed all his palace officials to serve each man as much as he wanted.

9At the same time, Queen Vashti gave a banquet for the women in the royal palace of King Xerxes.

Queen Vashti Deposed

10On the seventh day of the feast, when King Xerxes was in high spirits because of the wine, he told the seven eunuchs who attended him— Mehuman, Biztha, Harbona, Bigtha, Abagtha, Zethar, and Carcas—11to bring Queen Vashti to him with the royal crown on her head. He wanted the nobles and all the other men to gaze on her beauty, for she was a very beautiful woman. 12But when they conveyed the king's order to Queen Vashti, she refused to come. This made the king furious, and he burned with anger.

13He immediately consulted with his wise advisers, who knew all the Persian laws and customs, for he always asked their advice. 14The names of these men were Carshena, Shethar, Admatha, Tarshish, Meres, Marsena, and Memucan—seven nobles of Persia and Media. They met with the king regularly and held the highest positions in the empire.

15"What must be done to Queen Vashti?" the king demanded. "What penalty does the law provide for a queen who refuses to obey the king's orders, properly sent through his eunuchs?"

16Memucan answered the king and his nobles, "Queen Vashti has wronged not only the king but also every noble and citizen throughout your empire. 17Women everywhere will begin to despise their husbands when they learn that Queen Vashti has refused to appear before the king. 18Before this day is out, the wives of all the king's nobles throughout Persia and Media will hear what the queen did and will start treating their husbands the same way. There will be no end to their contempt and anger.

19"So if it please the king, we suggest that you issue a written decree, a law of the Persians and Medes that cannot be revoked. It should order that Queen Vashti be forever banished from the presence of King Xerxes, and that the king should choose another queen more worthy than she. 20When this decree is published throughout the king's vast empire, husbands everywhere, whatever their rank, will receive proper respect from their wives!"

A:12 Greek *Gabatha and Tharra;* compare 2:21 and 6:2.   A:17 Greek *a Bougean.*   1:1a Hebrew *Ahasuerus,* another name for Xerxes; also throughout the book of Esther. Xerxes reigned 486–465 B.C.   1:1b Hebrew *to Cush.*

²¹The king and his nobles thought this made good sense, so he followed Memucan's counsel. ²²He sent letters to all parts of the empire, to each province in its own script and language, proclaiming that every man should be the ruler of his own home and should say whatever he pleases.*

Esther Becomes Queen

2 But after Xerxes' anger had subsided, he began thinking about Vashti and what she had done and the decree he had made. ²So his personal attendants suggested, "Let us search the empire to find beautiful young virgins for the king. ³Let the king appoint agents in each province to bring these beautiful young women into the royal harem at the fortress of Susa. Hegai, the king's eunuch in charge of the harem, will see that they are all given beauty treatments. ⁴After that, the young woman who most pleases the king will be made queen instead of Vashti." This advice was very appealing to the king, so he put the plan into effect.

⁵At that time there was a Jewish man in the fortress of Susa whose name was Mordecai son of Jair. He was from the tribe of Benjamin and was a descendant of Kish and Shimei. ⁶His family* had been among those who, with King Jehoiachin* of Judah, had been exiled from Jerusalem to Babylon by King Nebuchadnezzar. ⁷This man had a very beautiful and lovely young cousin, Hadassah, who was also called Esther. When her father and mother died, Mordecai adopted her into his family and raised her as his own daughter.

⁸As a result of the king's decree, Esther, along with many other young women, was brought to the king's harem at the fortress of Susa and placed in Hegai's care. ⁹Hegai was very impressed with Esther and treated her kindly. He quickly ordered a special menu for her and provided her with beauty treatments. He also assigned her seven maids specially chosen from the king's palace, and he moved her and her maids into the best place in the harem.

¹⁰Esther had not told anyone of her nationality and family background, because Mordecai had directed her not to do so. ¹¹Every day Mordecai would take a walk near the courtyard of the harem to find out about Esther and what was happening to her.

¹²Before each young woman was taken to the king's bed, she was given the prescribed twelve months of beauty treatments—six months with oil of myrrh, followed by six months with special perfumes and ointments. ¹³When it was time for her to go to the king's palace, she was given her choice of whatever clothing or jewelry she wanted to take from the harem. ¹⁴That evening she was taken to the king's private rooms, and the next morning she was brought to the second harem,* where the king's wives lived. There she would be under the care of Shaashgaz, the king's eunuch in charge of the concubines. She would never go to the king again unless he had especially enjoyed her and requested her by name.

¹⁵Esther was the daughter of Abihail, who was Mordecai's uncle. (Mordecai had adopted his younger cousin Esther.) When it was Esther's turn to go to the king, she accepted the advice of Hegai, the eunuch in charge of the harem. She asked for nothing except what he suggested, and she was admired by everyone who saw her.

¹⁶Esther was taken to King Xerxes at the royal palace in early winter* of the seventh year of his reign. ¹⁷And the king loved Esther more than any of the other young women. He was so delighted with her that he set the royal crown on her head and declared her queen instead of Vashti. ¹⁸To celebrate the occasion, he gave a great banquet in Esther's honor for all his nobles and officials, declaring a public holiday for the provinces and giving generous gifts to everyone.

¹⁹Even after all the young women had been transferred to the second harem* and Mordecai had become a palace official,* ²⁰Esther continued to keep her family background and nationality a secret. She was still following Mordecai's directions, just as she did when she lived in his home.

Mordecai's Loyalty to the King

²¹One day as Mordecai was on duty at the king's gate, two of the king's eunuchs, Bigthana* and Teresh—who were guards at the door of the king's private quarters—became angry at King Xerxes and plotted to assassinate him. ²²But Mordecai heard about the plot and gave the information to Queen Esther. She then told

---

1:22 Or *and should speak in the language of his own people.*   **2:6a** Hebrew *He.*   **2:6b** Hebrew *Jeconiah,* a variant spelling of Jehoiachin.   **2:14** Or *to another part of the harem.*   **2:16** Hebrew *in the tenth month, the month of Tebeth.* A number of dates in the book of Esther can be cross-checked with dates in surviving Persian records and related accurately to our modern calendar. This month of the ancient Hebrew lunar calendar occurred within the months of December 479 B.C. and January 478 B.C.   **2:19a** The meaning of the Hebrew is uncertain.   **2:19b** Hebrew *and Mordecai was sitting in the gate of the king.*   **2:21** Hebrew *Bigthan;* compare 6:2.

the king about it and gave Mordecai credit for the report. ²³When an investigation was made and Mordecai's story was found to be true, the two men were impaled on a sharpened pole. This was all recorded in *The Book of the History of King Xerxes' Reign.*

Haman's Plot against the Jews

3 Some time later King Xerxes promoted Haman son of Hammedatha the Agagite over all the other nobles, making him the most powerful official in the empire. ²All the king's officials would bow down before Haman to show him respect whenever he passed by, for so the king had commanded. But Mordecai refused to bow down or show him respect.

³Then the palace officials at the king's gate asked Mordecai, "Why are you disobeying the king's command?" ⁴They spoke to him day after day, but still he refused to comply with the order. So they spoke to Haman about this to see if he would tolerate Mordecai's conduct, since Mordecai had told them he was a Jew.

⁵When Haman saw that Mordecai would not bow down or show him respect, he was filled with rage. ⁶He had learned of Mordecai's nationality, so he decided it was not enough to lay hands on Mordecai alone. Instead, he looked for a way to destroy all the Jews throughout the entire empire of Xerxes.

⁷So in the month of April,* during the twelfth year of King Xerxes' reign, lots were cast in Haman's presence (the lots were called *purim*) to determine the best day and month to take action. And the day selected was March 7, nearly a year later.*

⁸Then Haman approached King Xerxes and said, "There is a certain race of people scattered through all the provinces of your empire who keep themselves separate from everyone else. Their laws are different from those of any other people, and they refuse to obey the laws of the king. So it is not in the king's interest to let them live. ⁹If it please the king, issue a decree that they be destroyed, and I will give 10,000 large sacks* of silver to the government administrators to be deposited in the royal treasury."

¹⁰The king agreed, confirming his decision by removing his signet ring from his finger and giving it to Haman son of Hammedatha the Agagite, the enemy of the Jews. ¹¹The king said, "The money and the people are both yours to do with as you see fit."

¹²So on April 17* the king's secretaries were summoned, and a decree was written exactly as Haman dictated. It was sent to the king's highest officers, the governors of the respective provinces, and the nobles of each province in their own scripts and languages. The decree was written in the name of King Xerxes and sealed with the king's signet ring. ¹³Dispatches were sent by swift messengers into all the provinces of the empire, giving the order that all Jews—young and old, including women and children—must be killed, slaughtered, and annihilated on a single day. This was scheduled to happen on March 7 of the next year.* The property of the Jews would be given to those who killed them.

Haman's Letter

B This is a copy of Haman's letter:

"This letter is from the great King Xerxes to the governors of his 127 provinces from India to Ethiopia and to the officials under them.*

²"I rule over many nations and have brought all the world under my dominion, but in spite of my power, I have not grown arrogant. Instead, I choose to govern my subjects with fairness and kindness so that they may live quietly without any fear. Then they can travel safely throughout the kingdom and enjoy peace, as all people desire.

³"When I asked my advisers how this might be accomplished, I received excellent counsel from Haman. He is a wise, kind, and faithful leader who is second in command of my kingdom. ⁴He told me that there is a hostile race of people scattered among all the nations and that the laws of these people are contrary to those of all nations. They despise the commands of kings and disrupt our attempt to unify our kingdom. ⁵This group constantly opposes all humanity by following strange lifestyles and laws, going against our commands,

3:7a Hebrew *in the first month, the month of Nisan.* This month of the ancient Hebrew lunar calendar occurred within the months of April and May 474 B.C.; also see note on 2:16.   3:7b As in 3:13, which reads *the thirteenth day of the twelfth month, the month of Adar;* Hebrew reads *in the twelfth month,* of the ancient Hebrew lunar calendar. The date selected was March 7, 473 B.C.; also see note on 2:16.   3:9 Hebrew *10,000 talents,* about 375 tons or 340 metric tons in weight.   3:12 Hebrew *On the thirteenth day of the first month,* of the ancient Hebrew lunar calendar. This day was April 17, 474 B.C.; also see note on 2:16. 3:13 Hebrew *on the thirteenth day of the twelfth month, the month of Adar,* of the ancient Hebrew lunar calendar. The date selected was March 7, 473 B.C.; also see note on 2:16.   B:1 See note at A:1a.

and disturbing the peace and unity of all our provinces. [6]Therefore, we have decreed that everyone must follow the instructions given by Haman, who is in charge of the government and second in power only to the king, for we honor Haman as a second father to us. All members of this race he has identified are to be completely destroyed by their enemies, together with their wives and children, and no one is to have pity on them. This is to happen next spring on March 8.* [7]So in a single day, all these people who have been hostile for so long come to a violent end,* and we will restore to our empire the peace they have disturbed."

3 (continued)

The King's Decree Is Published

[14]A copy of this decree was to be issued as law in every province and proclaimed to all peoples, so that they would be ready to do their duty on the appointed day. [15]At the king's command, the decree went out by swift messengers, and it was also proclaimed in the fortress of Susa. Then the king and Haman sat down to drink, but the city of Susa fell into confusion.

Mordecai Requests Esther's Help

4 When Mordecai learned about all that had been done, he tore his clothes, put on burlap and ashes, and went out into the city, crying with a loud and bitter wail. [2]He went as far as the gate of the palace, for no one was allowed to enter the palace gate while wearing clothes of mourning. [3]And as news of the king's decree reached all the provinces, there was great mourning among the Jews. They fasted, wept, and wailed, and many people lay in burlap and ashes.

[4]When Queen Esther's maids and eunuchs came and told her about Mordecai, she was deeply distressed. She sent clothing to him to replace the burlap, but he refused it. [5]Then Esther sent for Hathach, one of the king's eunuchs who had been appointed as her attendant. She ordered him to go to Mordecai and find out what was troubling him and why he was in mourning. [6]So Hathach went out to Mordecai in the square in front of the palace gate.

[7]Mordecai told him the whole story, including the exact amount of money Haman had promised to pay into the royal treasury for the destruction of the Jews. [8]Mordecai gave Hathach a copy of the decree issued in Susa that called for the death of all Jews. He asked Hathach to show it to Esther and explain the situation to her. He also asked Hathach to direct her to go to the king to beg for mercy and plead for her people. [9]So Hathach returned to Esther with Mordecai's message.

[10]Then Esther told Hathach to go back and relay this message to Mordecai: [11]"All the king's officials and even the people in the provinces know that anyone who appears before the king in his inner court without being invited is doomed to die unless the king holds out his gold scepter. And the king has not called for me to come to him for thirty days." [12]So Hathach* gave Esther's message to Mordecai.

[13]Mordecai sent this reply to Esther: "Don't think for a moment that because you're in the palace you will escape when all other Jews are killed. [14]If you keep quiet at a time like this, deliverance and relief for the Jews will arise from some other place, but you and your relatives will die. Who knows if perhaps you were made queen for just such a time as this?"

[15]Then Esther sent this reply to Mordecai: [16]"Go and gather together all the Jews of Susa and fast for me. Do not eat or drink for three days, night or day. My maids and I will do the same. And then, though it is against the law, I will go in to see the king. If I must die, I must die." [17]So Mordecai went away and did everything as Esther had ordered him.

Mordecai's Prayer

C Mordecai thought about all that the Lord had done, and then he began to pray.* [2]He said:

"O Lord, Lord, almighty King, you rule over all things, and no one can resist your will if you decide to save Israel. [3]You made heaven and earth and all the wonders under heaven. [4]You are Lord of all, and there is none who can resist you, Lord. [5]You know all things, and you know that it was not out of pride or contempt or desire for glory that I refused to bow down to proud Haman. [6]For I would willingly have kissed his feet to save Israel. [7]But I did this so I would not place human glory before the glory of God. And I will not bow down to anyone except you, my Lord. [8]And now, O Lord God and

---

B:6 Greek *On the fourteenth day of the twelfth month, Adar,* of the ancient Hebrew lunar calendar. This date was March 8, 473 B.C.; also see note on A:1c.   B:7 Greek *will go down in violence to Hades.*   4:12 As in Greek version; Hebrew reads *they.* C:1 See note at A:1a.

King, God of Abraham, spare your people, because our enemies are determined to destroy us and to wipe out the people who have been your possession from the beginning. ⁹Do not neglect us, your own people, whom you redeemed for yourself out of Egypt. ¹⁰Hear my prayer, and be merciful to us—your possession. Turn our mourning into joyful feasting so that we may live and praise your name. O Lord, do not destroy those who sing to you."

¹¹And all Israel cried out in prayer to the Lord, for death was staring them in the face.

¹²Queen Esther, fearing the mortal danger that was at hand, also turned to the Lord for help. ¹³Taking off her royal robes, she put on garments suitable for weeping and mourning. Instead of precious ointments, she covered her head with ashes and dung. She purposely made herself unattractive and covered her beauty with her tangled and disheveled hair.

Esther's Prayer

¹⁴Esther began to pray to the Lord, the God of Israel. She said:

"O my Lord, you alone are our King. Help me, since I am alone and have no other helper but you—¹⁵and I am about to risk my life. ¹⁶From my earliest days my family and tribe have taught me that you, O Lord, chose Israel from among all nations. You chose our ancestors from those who came before them so that they would be your special possession forever. And you have done all that you promised them. ¹⁷We have sinned in your sight. You have handed us over to our enemies ¹⁸because we have worshiped their gods. You are just, O Lord. ¹⁹But now our enemies are not content to oppress us with bitter slavery. They have vowed* ²⁰to abolish the decree you yourself made, to destroy your special possession, to close the mouths of those who praise you, and to extinguish the fire on the altar and the glory of your Temple. ²¹By doing this, they will give the Gentiles cause to praise their worthless idols and to exalt a mortal king forever.

²²"O Lord, do not surrender the scepter of your rule to gods that do not even exist. Do not let them laugh at our ruin. Turn their plan against them and destroy the man* who began this attack against us. ²³Remember us, O Lord! Show yourself to us in this time of trouble, and give me boldness, O King of gods and ruler of every power. ²⁴Put eloquent words in my mouth in the presence of the lion, and cause him to hate our enemy so that he may be destroyed along with those who agree with him. ²⁵But rescue us by your hand, and help me, O Lord, for I have no other helper but you.

²⁶"You know all things. You know that I hate the splendor of the wicked, and I abhor the bed of the uncircumcised and of any foreigner. ²⁷You know what a bind I am in. I hate my crown—that sign of my proud position—yet I must wear it on my head when I appear in public. I detest it as a filthy rag and never wear it in private. ²⁸I, your servant, have never eaten at Haman's table, nor have the king's banquets ever pleased me, nor have I drunk wine offered to idols. ²⁹I am your servant, O Lord God of Abraham. Ever since I was brought here, I have rejoiced only in you—even to this day. ³⁰O God, whose might is greater than all, hear the voice of those in despair, rescue us from the power of the wicked, and save me from my fear!"

Esther Visits the King

D On the third day of the fast, Esther ended her prayers. She took off the garments she wore for worship and put on her royal robes.* ²Dressed in all her splendor, she first called upon the All-Seeing God and Savior. Then she took two maids with her. ³She leaned gently upon one of the maids for support, ⁴while the other followed behind, carrying Esther's flowing train. ⁵Her radiant and beautiful countenance made her look happy, but Esther's heart was filled with fear. ⁶She passed through all the doors of the court and stood before the king. He was sitting upon his royal throne, clothed in his royal robes, resplendent with gold and precious stones. He was awesome to behold. ⁷Looking up, his face blazed with both royal splendor and fierce anger. The queen staggered, turning pale and faint, and then leaned weakly upon the shoulder of the maid in front of her. ⁸Then God changed the king's spirit to become gentle. He hurried from his throne with concern and lifted her up in his arms until she came to. He comforted her

C:19 Greek *have made a covenant with their idols.*　　C:22 Greek *make an example of the man.*　　D:1 See note at A:1a.

by saying, 9"What is the matter, Esther? I am your husband.* Don't be afraid. 10You will not die, for this law was made for others, not for you. 11You may approach the throne.*" 12The king raised the gold scepter and touched her neck with it. He embraced her and said, "Speak to me."

13She answered, "I saw you, my lord, as an angel of God, and my heart was fearful because of your glory. 14For you are wonderful, my lord, and your face reflects such grace." 15While she was speaking, she fainted and collapsed. 16The king was very concerned, and all his servants tried to help her.

Esther's Request to the King

5 On the third day of the fast, Esther put on her royal robes and entered the inner court of the palace, just across from the king's hall. The king was sitting on his royal throne, facing the entrance. 2When he saw Queen Esther standing there in the inner court, he welcomed her and held out the gold scepter to her. So Esther approached and touched the end of the scepter.

3Then the king asked her, "What do you want, Queen Esther? What is your request? I will give it to you, even if it is half the kingdom!"

4And Esther replied, "If it please the king, let the king and Haman come today to a banquet I have prepared for the king."

5The king turned to his attendants and said, "Tell Haman to come quickly to a banquet, as Esther has requested." So the king and Haman went to Esther's banquet.

6And while they were drinking wine, the king said to Esther, "Now tell me what you really want. What is your request? I will give it to you, even if it is half the kingdom!"

7Esther replied, "This is my request and deepest wish. 8If I have found favor with the king, and if it pleases the king to grant my request and do what I ask, please come with Haman tomorrow to the banquet I will prepare for you. Then I will explain what this is all about."

Haman's Plan to Kill Mordecai

9Haman was a happy man as he left the banquet! But when he saw Mordecai sitting at the palace gate, not standing up or trembling nervously before him, Haman became furious. 10However, he restrained himself and went on home.

Then Haman gathered together his friends and Zeresh, his wife, 11and boasted to them about his great wealth and his many children. He bragged about the honors the king had given him and how he had been promoted over all the other nobles and officials.

12Then Haman added, "And that's not all! Queen Esther invited only me and the king himself to the banquet she prepared for us. And she has invited me to dine with her and the king again tomorrow!" 13Then he added, "But this is all worth nothing as long as I see Mordecai the Jew just sitting there at the palace gate."

14So Haman's wife, Zeresh, and all his friends suggested, "Set up a sharpened pole that stands seventy-five feet* tall, and in the morning ask the king to impale Mordecai on it. When this is done, you can go on your merry way to the banquet with the king." This pleased Haman, and he ordered the pole set up.

The King Honors Mordecai

6 That night the king had trouble sleeping, so he ordered an attendant to bring the book of the history of his reign so it could be read to him. 2In those records he discovered an account of how Mordecai had exposed the plot of Bigthana and Teresh, two of the eunuchs who guarded the door to the king's private quarters. They had plotted to assassinate King Xerxes.

3"What reward or recognition did we ever give Mordecai for this?" the king asked.

His attendants replied, "Nothing has been done for him."

4"Who is that in the outer court?" the king inquired. As it happened, Haman had just arrived in the outer court of the palace to ask the king to impale Mordecai on the pole he had prepared.

5So the attendants replied to the king, "Haman is out in the court."

"Bring him in," the king ordered. 6So Haman came in, and the king said, "What should I do to honor a man who truly pleases me?"

Haman thought to himself, "Whom would the king wish to honor more than me?" 7So he replied, "If the king wishes to honor someone, 8he should bring out one of the king's own royal robes, as well as a horse that the king himself has ridden—one with a royal emblem on its head. 9Let the robes and the horse be handed over to one of the king's most noble officials.

D:9 Greek *your brother.*   D:11 Greek *Come near.*   5:14 Hebrew *50 cubits* [23 meters].

And let him see that the man whom the king wishes to honor is dressed in the king's robes and led through the city square on the king's horse. Have the official shout as they go, 'This is what the king does for someone he wishes to honor!'"

¹⁰"Excellent!" the king said to Haman. "Quick! Take the robes and my horse, and do just as you have said for Mordecai the Jew, who sits at the gate of the palace. Leave out nothing you have suggested!"

¹¹So Haman took the robes and put them on Mordecai, placed him on the king's own horse, and led him through the city square, shouting, "This is what the king does for someone he wishes to honor!" ¹²Afterward Mordecai returned to the palace gate, but Haman hurried home dejected and completely humiliated.

¹³When Haman told his wife, Zeresh, and all his friends what had happened, his wise advisers and his wife said, "Since Mordecai—this man who has humiliated you—is of Jewish birth, you will never succeed in your plans against him. It will be fatal to continue opposing him."

¹⁴While they were still talking, the king's eunuchs arrived and quickly took Haman to the banquet Esther had prepared.

The King Executes Haman

7 So the king and Haman went to Queen Esther's banquet. ²On this second occasion, while they were drinking wine, the king again said to Esther, "Tell me what you want, Queen Esther. What is your request? I will give it to you, even if it is half the kingdom!"

³Queen Esther replied, "If I have found favor with the king, and if it pleases the king to grant my request, I ask that my life and the lives of my people will be spared. ⁴For my people and I have been sold to those who would kill, slaughter, and annihilate us. If we had merely been sold as slaves, I could remain quiet, for that would be too trivial a matter to warrant disturbing the king."

⁵"Who would do such a thing?" King Xerxes demanded. "Who would be so presumptuous as to touch you?"

⁶Esther replied, "This wicked Haman is our adversary and our enemy." Haman grew pale with fright before the king and queen. ⁷Then the king jumped to his feet in a rage and went out into the palace garden.

Haman, however, stayed behind to plead for his life with Queen Esther, for he knew that the king intended to kill him. ⁸In despair he fell on the couch where Queen Esther was reclining, just as the king was returning from the palace garden.

The king exclaimed, "Will he even assault the queen right here in the palace, before my very eyes?" And as soon as the king spoke, his attendants covered Haman's face, signaling his doom.

⁹Then Harbona, one of the king's eunuchs, said, "Haman has set up a sharpened pole that stands seventy-five feet* tall in his own courtyard. He intended to use it to impale Mordecai, the man who saved the king from assassination."

"Then impale Haman on it!" the king ordered. ¹⁰So they impaled Haman on the pole he had set up for Mordecai, and the king's anger subsided.

A Decree to Help the Jews

8 On that same day King Xerxes gave the property of Haman, the enemy of the Jews, to Queen Esther. Then Mordecai was brought before the king, for Esther had told the king how they were related. ²The king took off his signet ring—which he had taken back from Haman—and gave it to Mordecai. And Esther appointed Mordecai to be in charge of Haman's property.

³Then Esther went again before the king, falling down at his feet and begging him with tears to stop the evil plot devised by Haman the Agagite against the Jews. ⁴Again the king held out the gold scepter to Esther. So she rose and stood before him.

⁵Esther said, "If it please the king, and if I have found favor with him, and if he thinks it is right, and if I am pleasing to him, let there be a decree that reverses the orders of Haman son of Hammedatha the Agagite, who ordered that Jews throughout all the king's provinces should be destroyed. ⁶For how can I endure to see my people and my family slaughtered and destroyed?"

⁷Then King Xerxes said to Queen Esther and Mordecai the Jew, "I have given Esther the property of Haman, and he has been impaled on a pole because he tried to destroy the Jews. ⁸Now go ahead and send a message to the Jews in the king's name, telling them whatever you want, and seal it with the king's signet ring. But remember that whatever has already been written in the king's name and sealed with his signet ring can never be revoked."

7:9 Hebrew *50 cubits* [23 meters].

⁹So on June 25* the king's secretaries were summoned, and a decree was written exactly as Mordecai dictated. It was sent to the Jews and to the highest officers, the governors, and the nobles of all the 127 provinces stretching from India to Ethiopia.* The decree was written in the scripts and languages of all the peoples of the empire, including that of the Jews. ¹⁰The decree was written in the name of King Xerxes and sealed with the king's signet ring. Mordecai sent the dispatches by swift messengers, who rode fast horses especially bred for the king's service.

¹¹The king's decree gave the Jews in every city authority to unite to defend their lives. They were allowed to kill, slaughter, and annihilate anyone of any nationality or province who might attack them or their children and wives, and to take the property of their enemies. ¹²The day chosen for this event throughout all the provinces of King Xerxes was March 7 of the next year.*

Mordecai's Letter

This is a copy of Mordecai's letter:

"This letter is from the great King Xerxes to the governors of his 127 provinces from India to Ethiopia and to our loyal subjects.* Greetings.

²"For many people, the more good things they receive from their benefactors, the more proud they become. ³Not only do they seek to oppress the king's subjects, but they are unable to enjoy the success given them. So they turn against their own benefactors. ⁴Not only do they drive out gratitude from others, but they also become proud from the flattery of those who don't know what good really is. They think they can escape the justice of God, who sees all things and hates evil. ⁵Often higher authorities are sweet-talked into granting public offices to friends, who then use their position to kill innocent people. In this way they involve the higher authority in irreparable tragedies, ⁶for they deceive the well-meaning rulers with false trickery.

⁷"Now this is proved both from ancient records and even more by recent events, which show the kind of evil that results from the destructive behavior of unworthy rulers. ⁸In the future we must provide for the peace and quiet of all the people of the kingdom. ⁹We must change our methods and use a more just process for judging matters that are brought to our attention.

¹⁰"For example, we received Haman son of Hammedatha, a Macedonian (so he was not even Persian and did not share in our kind nature), as a guest. ¹¹He benefited from the kindness that we show toward all people—so much so that everyone called him "father" and bowed down to him, regarding him as second in power only to the king. ¹²But he was so filled with arrogance that he tried to deprive us of our kingdom and our lives. ¹³With unbelievable craftiness and deceit, he has sought the destruction of Mordecai, our constant benefactor who saved our lives; of Esther, the blameless royal partner; and of their entire nation. ¹⁴In this way, Haman thought that he could make us defenseless and then transfer the kingdom of the Persians to the Macedonians. ¹⁵But we have found that the Jews, who were slated to be slain by that most hated man, are not evil. In fact, they have just laws, ¹⁶and they are the children of the living God, the Most High and greatest God. It is by this God's direction that the kingdom has been excellently maintained for us as well as for our ancestors.

¹⁷"Therefore, you should disregard the letters sent by Haman son of Hammedatha. ¹⁸He and all his household were impaled for this crime at the gates of Susa. God, who rules over all things, has swiftly repaid him as he deserved. ¹⁹Post a copy of this letter in all public places, and let the Jews follow their own laws. ²⁰On March 7* you must aid them in their time of hardship so that they may defend themselves against those who will attack them. ²¹For the all-powerful God has turned this day of destruction into a day of joy for his chosen people. ²²You will celebrate this day as another important festival. ²³From now on, Jews and loyal Persians will remember this day as a time of deliverance, but those who plot against us will only be reminded of their downfall.

8:9a Hebrew *on the twenty-third day of the third month, the month of Sivan,* of the ancient Hebrew lunar calendar. This day was June 25, 474 B.C.; also see note on 2:16.   8:9b Hebrew *to Cush.*   8:12 Hebrew *the thirteenth day of the twelfth month, the month of Adar,* of the ancient Hebrew lunar calendar. The date selected was March 7, 473 B.C.; also see note on 2:16.   E:1 See note at A:1a.   E:20 Greek *the thirteenth day of the twelfth month, which is Adar,* of the ancient Hebrew lunar calendar. This date was March 7, 473 B.C.; also see note on A:1c.

24Every single province and city that does not obey these orders will be viciously destroyed by spear and fire. Their land will become uninhabitable for human beings, and even the wild animals and birds will stay away."

8 (continued)

The King's New Decree Is Published

13A copy of this decree was to be issued as law in every province and proclaimed to all peoples, so that the Jews would be ready to take revenge on their enemies on the appointed day. 14So urged on by the king's command, the messengers rode out swiftly on fast horses bred for the king's service. The same decree was also proclaimed in the fortress of Susa.

15Then Mordecai left the king's presence, wearing the royal robe of blue and white, the great crown of gold, and an outer cloak of fine linen and purple. And the people of Susa celebrated the new decree. 16The Jews were filled with joy and gladness and were honored everywhere. 17In every province and city, wherever the king's decree arrived, the Jews rejoiced and had a great celebration and declared a public festival and holiday. And many of the people of the land became Jews themselves, for they feared what the Jews might do to them.

The Victory of the Jews

9 So on March 7* the two decrees of the king were put into effect. On that day, the enemies of the Jews had hoped to overpower them, but quite the opposite happened. It was the Jews who overpowered their enemies. 2The Jews gathered in their cities throughout all the king's provinces to attack anyone who tried to harm them. But no one could make a stand against them, for everyone was afraid of them. 3And all the nobles of the provinces, the highest officers, the governors, and the royal officials helped the Jews for fear of Mordecai. 4For Mordecai had been promoted in the king's palace, and his fame spread throughout all the provinces as he became more and more powerful.

5So the Jews went ahead on the appointed day and struck down their enemies with the sword. They killed and annihilated their enemies and did as they pleased with those who hated them. 6In the fortress of Susa itself, the Jews killed 500 men. 7They also killed Parshandatha, Dalphon, Aspatha, 8Poratha, Adalia, Aridatha, 9Parmashta, Arisai, Aridai, and Vaizatha—10the ten sons of Haman son of Hammedatha, the enemy of the Jews. But they did not take any plunder.

11That very day, when the king was informed of the number of people killed in the fortress of Susa, 12he called for Queen Esther. He said, "The Jews have killed 500 men in the fortress of Susa alone, as well as Haman's ten sons. If they have done that here, what has happened in the rest of the provinces? But now, what more do you want? It will be granted to you; tell me and I will do it."

13Esther responded, "If it please the king, give the Jews in Susa permission to do again tomorrow as they have done today, and let the bodies of Haman's ten sons be impaled on a pole."

14So the king agreed, and the decree was announced in Susa. And they impaled the bodies of Haman's ten sons. 15Then the Jews at Susa gathered together on March 8* and killed 300 more men, and again they took no plunder.

16Meanwhile, the other Jews throughout the king's provinces had gathered together to defend their lives. They gained relief from all their enemies, killing 75,000 of those who hated them. But they did not take any plunder. 17This was done throughout the provinces on March 7, and on March 8 they rested,* celebrating their victory with a day of feasting and gladness. 18(The Jews at Susa killed their enemies on March 7 and again on March 8, then rested on March 9,* making that their day of feasting and gladness.) 19So to this day, rural Jews living in remote villages celebrate an annual festival and holiday on the appointed day in late winter,* when they rejoice and send gifts of food to each other.

The Festival of Purim

20Mordecai recorded these events and sent letters to the Jews near and far, throughout all the provinces of King Xerxes, 21calling on them to celebrate an annual festival on these two days.* 22He told them to celebrate these

---

9:1 Hebrew *on the thirteenth day of the twelfth month, the month of Adar,* of the ancient Hebrew lunar calendar. This day was March 7, 473 B.C.; also see note on 2:16. 9:15 Hebrew *the fourteenth day of the month of Adar,* of the ancient Hebrew lunar calendar. This day was March 8, 473 B.C.; also see note on 2:16. 9:17 Hebrew *on the thirteenth day of the month of Adar, and on the fourteenth day they rested.* These days were March 7 and 8, 473 B.C.; also see note on 2:16. 9:18 Hebrew *killed their enemies on the thirteenth day and the fourteenth day, and then rested on the fifteenth day,* of the Hebrew month of Adar. 9:19 Hebrew *on the fourteenth day of the month of Adar.* This day of the ancient Hebrew lunar calendar occurs in February or March. 9:21 Hebrew *on the fourteenth and fifteenth days of Adar,* of the ancient Hebrew lunar calendar.

days with feasting and gladness and by giving gifts of food to each other and presents to the poor. This would commemorate a time when the Jews gained relief from their enemies, when their sorrow was turned into gladness and their mourning into joy.

²³So the Jews accepted Mordecai's proposal and adopted this annual custom. ²⁴Haman son of Hammedatha the Agagite, the enemy of the Jews, had plotted to crush and destroy them on the date determined by casting lots (the lots were called *purim*). ²⁵But when Esther came before the king, he issued a decree causing Haman's evil plot to backfire, and Haman and his sons were impaled on a sharpened pole. ²⁶That is why this celebration is called Purim, because it is the ancient word for casting lots.

So because of Mordecai's letter and because of what they had experienced, ²⁷the Jews throughout the realm agreed to inaugurate this tradition and to pass it on to their descendants and to all who became Jews. They declared they would never fail to celebrate these two prescribed days at the appointed time each year. ²⁸These days would be remembered and kept from generation to generation and celebrated by every family throughout the provinces and cities of the empire. This Festival of Purim would never cease to be celebrated among the Jews, nor would the memory of what happened ever die out among their descendants.

²⁹Then Queen Esther, the daughter of Abihail, along with Mordecai the Jew, wrote another letter putting the queen's full authority behind Mordecai's letter to establish the Festival of Purim. ³⁰Letters wishing peace and security were sent to the Jews throughout the 127 provinces of the empire of Xerxes. ³¹These letters established the Festival of Purim—an annual celebration of these days at the appointed time, decreed by both Mordecai the Jew and Queen Esther. (The people decided to observe this festival, just as they had decided for themselves and their descendants to establish the times of fasting and mourning.) ³²So the command of Esther confirmed the practices of Purim, and it was all written down in the records.

The Greatness of Xerxes and Mordecai

10 King Xerxes imposed a tribute throughout his empire, even to the distant coastlands. ²His great achievements and the full account of the greatness of Mordecai, whom the king had promoted, are recorded in *The Book of the History of the Kings of Media and Persia.* ³Mordecai the Jew became the prime minister, with authority next to that of King Xerxes himself. He was very great among the Jews, who held him in high esteem, because he continued to work for the good of his people and to speak up for the welfare of all their descendants.

Mordecai Interprets His Dream

Mordecai said, "God has done these things.* ²I remember the dream I had concerning these same things, and all of it has been fulfilled. ³There was a small spring that grew into a river, and there was light and sun and plenty of water. The river is Esther, whom the king married and made queen. ⁴The two dragons are Haman and myself. ⁵The nations are those who banded together to wipe out the Jews. ⁶My nation is Israel, who cried out to God and was saved. The Lord delivered us from all these evil schemes; God has performed great signs and wonders among the Gentiles. ⁷For this reason he made two lots (called *purim*), one for the people of God and the other for all the Gentiles. ⁸When the appointed day, hour, and moment came for the lots to be cast as God and all the Gentiles watched, ⁹God remembered his people and vindicated his special possession. ¹⁰So people will gather together for two specified days in late winter* and celebrate this day with joy and gladness before God. This festival will be celebrated from generation to generation forever among God's people, Israel."

Postscript

¹¹In the fourth year of the reign of Ptolemy Soter* and Cleopatra, Dositheus and his son Ptolemy brought to Egypt* the preceding letter about Purim. Dositheus said he was a priest and a Levite, and his son was a resident of Jerusalem. They asserted that the letter was authentic and that it had been translated by Lysimachus, Ptolemy's son.

F:1 See note at A:11a.   F:10 Greek *in the month of Adar, on the fourteenth and fifteenth of that month.* These two days of the ancient Hebrew lunar calendar usually occur in March.   F:11a Greek lacks *Soter.* The fourth year of Ptolemy Soter's reign was 113 B.C.   F:11b Greek lacks *to Egypt.*

1 Maccabees

UNFOLDING LIKE THE PLOT of a modern-day novel, the story of the family of Mattathias is filled with tales of heroic exploits, thrilling victories, and heartbreaking defeats. It opens with a description of the Jewish predicament around 167 BC, when the Jews were struggling for national and religious survival against their chief enemy—the Seleucid division of the divided Greek Empire. The ruler, Antiochus IV Epiphanes (175–164 BC), was trying to stamp out any sense of Jewish identity by forbidding all the practices established in the law of Moses, such as circumcision and observance of the Sabbath. But Mattathias and his sons, who came to be referred to as the Maccabees (thought to mean "hammerers"), rose up against the Greeks and eventually gained independence for the Jews. The book of 1 Maccabees recounts many of the twists and turns involved in their story and ends with the death of Simon, the last survivor among Mattathias's sons.

- **Author:** Unknown
- **Date Written:** Around 100 BC, recording events that occurred around 169 to 134 BC
- **Purpose:** To encourage Jews to continue to remain faithful to God and to resist those who oppose the laws of Moses
- **Themes:** The importance of godly leadership; courage and faith in the face of evil
- **Outline**
1:1-66 The danger to Judea
2:1-69 The determination of Mattathias
3:1–9:22 The leadership of Judas
9:23–12:54 The leadership of Judas's brother Jonathan
13:1–16:24 The leadership of Simon

Alexander and His Successors

1 Alexander the Macedonian, the son of Philip, was king of Greece. Alexander marched from the land of Greece* and conquered Darius, king of the Persians and Medes, and became king in his place. ²He fought in many campaigns, captured many fortresses, and put the local kings to death. ³He campaigned throughout the known world, plundering the nations, and all the nations of the world submitted to him. Alexander's heart was filled with pride, ⁴for he had gathered a powerful and mighty army and now ruled many nations and kingdoms, all of which paid him a tribute tax.

⁵But after all his great conquests, Alexander became very sick and was confined to his bed. When he knew he was dying, ⁶he called for his close friends—noblemen who had grown up with him—and he divided his kingdom among them while he was still alive. ⁷At his death, Alexander had reigned for twelve years.* ⁸Each of his close friends took over the region assigned to him, ⁹and each one crowned himself after Alexander's death. They and their descendants ruled for many years, spreading evil throughout the earth.

Antiochus IV Epiphanes

¹⁰Antiochus Epiphanes, son of King Antiochus, was a sinful descendant of these rulers. He had been a hostage in Rome before rising to the throne in the one hundred thirty-seventh year of Greek rule.*

¹¹In those days there were some ungodly Jews who tried to lead many astray. They said, "Let's make an agreement with the Gentiles around us, for since we separated ourselves from them, disaster has followed after

1:1 Greek *the land of Kittim*.   1:7 Alexander died in 323 B.C.   1:10 The dates in 1 Maccabees are calculated from 312 B.C., the year Seleucus I Nicator began his reign over a territory that included the land of Israel. The 137th year of Greek rule was 175 B.C.

disaster." [12]Many thought this was good advice, [13]so they went to the king, who authorized them to introduce Gentile practices. [14]In Jerusalem they built an education complex for promoting Greek culture,* as was customarily done among the Gentiles. [15]They hid the fact that they were circumcised,* abandoned their holy covenant with God, and joined with the Gentiles,* becoming slaves to evil.

The First Egyptian Campaign

[16]Once Antiochus Epiphanes consolidated his power, he decided to make himself king of Egypt as well so that he might rule over two kingdoms. [17]He invaded Egypt with a massive army—chariots, elephants, and horsemen—and a large fleet. [18]He attacked Ptolemy Philometor, king of Egypt, who turned and fled in terror, leaving behind many casualties. [19]Antiochus captured the fortified cities of Egypt and plundered the entire land.

[20]After conquering Egypt in the one hundred forty-third year of Greek rule,* Antiochus returned to Israel [21]with his powerful force and marched into Jerusalem. He arrogantly entered the Temple sanctuary and carried away the gold incense altar, the lampstand for light and all its accessories, [22]the table of the Bread of the Presence, the cups used for making drink offerings, the bowls, the gold incense burners, the curtain, the crowns, and the gold decoration that was on the front of the Temple. He stripped the Temple of everything of value. [23]He took the silver and gold and the precious vessels as well as all the hidden treasures he could find. [24]When he had gathered everything of value, he returned to his own country. He had murdered many people and arrogantly bragged about it.

[25] Throughout Israel, people mourned
    deeply,
[26]   and the rulers and elders grieved.
    Young women and young men grew weak,
        and the beauty of women faded.
[27] Every bridegroom began to lament,
        and every bride mourned in her bridal
        chamber.
[28] The land trembled for its residents,
        and all Israel* was filled with shame.

Construction of the Citadel

[29]Two years later King Antiochus sent his chief tax collector to the towns of Judea,* and he arrived at Jerusalem with a massive force. [30]He deceived the people by speaking peaceful words, thus gaining their trust. But suddenly he attacked the city and killed many of the Israelites. [31]He plundered the city, set it on fire, and tore down its houses and walls. [32]He took women and children captive and carried away their livestock. [33]He rebuilt and fortified the City of David with a great wall and strong towers, and it became their citadel. [34]He manned and strengthened the fortifications with sinful and wicked men. [35]They stored up weapons and provisions and collected there the wealth he and his men plundered from Jerusalem. And so they became a perpetual threat to Israel.

[36] The citadel became an ambush for the
        Temple,
    an ever present evil in Israel.
[37] They murdered the innocent all around
        the sanctuary;
    they even defiled the Holy Place.
[38] Because of them the residents of Jerusalem
        fled,
    and the city became the home of
        foreigners.
    Jerusalem became a stranger to her own
        offspring,
    and her children abandoned her.
[39] Her Temple became as barren as a desert;
        her festivals were turned to mourning.
    Her Sabbaths were turned to days of
        shame;
    her honor was turned to reproach.
[40] Her dishonor was as great as her former
        glory;
    her happiness was turned to grief.

Pagan Worship Instituted

[41]King Antiochus issued a proclamation that his entire kingdom should be united as one people [42]and that each nation should renounce its own customs. [43]The Gentiles accepted this command of the king, and many Israelites also willingly followed his religion. They offered sacrifices to idols and no longer observed the Sabbath. [44]The king sent messengers with letters to Jerusalem and to all the towns of Judea, ordering the people to follow the foreign customs of his kingdom. [45]He banned burnt offerings, sacrifices, and drink offerings in the Temple, and he prohibited keeping the Sabbath and celebrating religious festivals. [46]He

---

1:14 Greek *a gymnasium.* 1:15a Greek *made themselves uncircumcised.* 1:15b Or *intermarried with Gentiles.* 1:20 The 143rd year of Greek rule was 169 B.C. 1:28 Greek *all the house of Jacob.* 1:29 Greek *of Judah;* also in 1:44, 51, 54.

defiled the Temple and the priests. ⁴⁷He ordered altars, temples, and idols to be built and pigs and other ceremonially unclean animals to be sacrificed. ⁴⁸Their sons were not to be circumcised, and they were to practice all kinds of unclean and vile customs ⁴⁹so that they would forget to keep the law of Moses. ⁵⁰Anyone who failed to obey the king's command would be put to death.

⁵¹Antiochus sent this command to his whole kingdom. He appointed officers to enforce his policies, and he commanded all the towns of Judea to take turns offering pagan sacrifices. ⁵²Many of the people who abandoned the law of Moses joined in these sacrifices and committed evil deeds. ⁵³They forced the faithful Israelites to hide in any possible place of refuge.

The Sacrilegious Object

⁵⁴On December 6* in the one hundred forty-fifth year of Greek rule, the king and his forces* set up a sacrilegious object causing desecration* on top of the altar for burnt offerings, and they built pagan altars in the surrounding Judean towns. ⁵⁵They burned incense and offered sacrifices at the doors of the houses and in the streets. ⁵⁶Whenever a copy of the Book of the Law was found, it was torn up and burned. ⁵⁷By the king's decree, they put to death anyone found with a copy of the Book of the Covenant or anyone discovered following the law of Moses. ⁵⁸Each month they punished any Israelites who were caught remaining in the towns, ⁵⁹for on the twenty-fifth day of each month they offered sacrifices on the pagan altar that stood on top of the altar of burnt offering. ⁶⁰By order of the king, women who had their sons circumcised were put to death ⁶¹with their babies hung around their necks. And all their families and everyone else who took part in the circumcisions were killed with them.

⁶²Yet there were many Israelites who refused to eat unclean food ⁶³and who welcomed death rather than be defiled by food, profaning the holy covenant. ⁶⁴So a time of great trouble had come upon Israel.

Mattathias and His Sons

2 In those days Mattathias son of John, son of Simeon, a priest in the line of Joarib, had left Jerusalem to make his home in the town of Modein. ²He had five sons: John, who was known as Gaddi; ³Simon, who was called Thassi; ⁴Judas, who was called Maccabeus; ⁵Eleazar, who was called Avaran; and Jonathan, who was called Apphus.*

⁶When Mattathias saw the sacrilegious acts done in Judea* and Jerusalem, ⁷he said,

"How terrible that I was born to see this,
  the destruction of my people,
  the ruin of the holy city!
How terrible to stand by while Jerusalem
  is given to enemies,
  while the sanctuary is handed over to
  foreigners.
⁸ Her Temple is like a man who has lost his
  honor;
⁹ the glorious vessels have been carried
  into exile.
Her infants have been murdered in the
  streets,
  and her young men have been killed by
  the enemy's sword.
¹⁰ What nation has not taken its share of her
  realm?
  What nation has not plundered her?
¹¹ All her ornaments have been taken away.
  No longer free, she has become a slave.
¹² Look at our sanctuary and see how our
  beauty
  and our glory are laid waste.
They have been defiled by the Gentiles.
¹³ What is left to live for?"

¹⁴To show their grief, Mattathias and his sons tore their clothing, dressed themselves in sackcloth, and mourned deeply.

Pagan Sacrifices at Modein

¹⁵Officers of the king arrived in Modein to force the people to abandon Judaism and to offer pagan sacrifices. ¹⁶Many of the Israelites went along with these men, but Mattathias and his sons refused to go near the pagan altar. ¹⁷In response, the king's officers said to Mattathias, "You are an honored leader and an important man in this town. Your sons and brothers follow you. ¹⁸Therefore, be the first in your town to obey the king's command, just as all the Gentiles and the people of Judea* and those living in Jerusalem have done. Then you and your sons will be counted among the king's

1:54a Greek *On the fifteenth day of Kislev,* of the Hebrew lunar calendar. This event occurred on December 6, 167 B.C.
1:54b Greek *they.*   1:54c Greek *an abomination of desolation.*   2:4-5 The surnames of Mattathias's sons mean, respectively, "fortunate," "burning," "the hammerer" (or possibly "designated by Yahweh"), "awake," and "favorite."   2:6 Greek *in Judah.*   2:18 Greek *of Judah.*

favored leaders and be made rich with gold, silver, and many gifts."

[19]But Mattathias loudly replied, "Even if every nation in the kingdom obeys the king, yielding to his decrees and forsaking their own ancestral religion, [20]I and my sons and my brothers will still follow the covenant of our ancestors. [21]Heaven forbid that we should abandon the law of Moses and the commandments! [22]We will never obey the orders of the king, nor will we stray from our religion— either to the right or to the left."

[23]As he finished speaking, a certain Jew came forward to offer sacrifices on the pagan altar in the town of Modein, according to the king's regulations. [24]When Mattathias saw this, he burned with passion. Then driven by righteous fury, he ran at the man and slaughtered him on the altar. [25]At the same time, he killed the officer the king had sent to enforce the pagan sacrifices, and he pulled down the altar. [26]In his zeal for the law of Moses, he showed the spirit Phinehas had shown against Zimri son of Salu.

[27]Mattathias then went through the town, shouting loudly, "Everyone who is zealous for the law of Moses and wants to obey the covenant, follow me!" [28]Then he and his sons escaped into the hills, leaving behind everything they owned.

Martyrdom in the Wilderness

[29]Many who were committed to righteousness and justice retreated into the wilderness and lived there [30]with their children, their wives, and their livestock because their troubles had become so difficult to bear.

[31]The king's officers and soldiers in Jerusalem, in the City of David, heard about these Jews who had defied the king's commands and gone into hiding in the wilderness. [32]Soldiers were sent after them, and when they found them, they set up camp across from them and prepared to attack them on the Sabbath. [33]But first the soldiers said to them, "Enough of this! Come forward and obey the king's command, and you will live."

[34]But the Jews replied, "We will not come forward, nor will we desecrate the Sabbath by obeying the king's orders."

[35]Without hesitation the soldiers attacked, [36]but the Jews offered no resistance, refusing to throw stones at them or even to barricade their hideouts. [37]They said, "Let us all die in innocence. Heaven and earth will witness to the fact that you are killing us unjustly." [38]So the foreigners attacked them on the Sabbath, and they were killed, together with their wives, their children, and their livestock. A thousand people died that day.

Mattathias Chooses to Fight

[39]When Mattathias and his friends heard this news, they mourned deeply. [40]They said to one another, "If we all do as our fellow Israelites have done and refuse to fight the Gentiles for our lives and beliefs, they will quickly wipe us off the face of the earth." [41]So that day they decided, "If anyone attacks us on the Sabbath day, we will fight them. We will not die in our hiding places as our fellow Israelites did."

[42]They were joined at that time by a group of Hasideans,* strong Israelite warriors who were deeply committed to the law of Moses. [43]And all those who fled from persecution joined them, giving them added support. [44]They formed an organized army and in their anger killed guilty and ungodly Jews. The survivors fled to the Gentiles for safety. [45]Mattathias and his friends went around and tore down the pagan altars, [46]and they forcibly circumcised any boys in the hill country of Israel who had not been circumcised. [47]They hunted down the arrogant and were successful in their fight. [48]They rescued the law of Moses from the control of the Gentiles and their kings, and they never gave in to those who were guilty.

The Final Words of Mattathias

[49]As the time of Mattathias' death drew near, he said to his sons, "Pride and scorn have become rampant; it is a time of violence and fury. [50]Therefore, my sons, be zealous for the law of Moses and give your lives for the covenant of your ancestors. [51]If you remember the deeds our ancestors did for each of their generations, you will receive great honor and everlasting fame. [52]Wasn't Abraham found faithful when he was tested? And wasn't he declared to be righteous? [53]Joseph kept the law through trying times, and he became master over Egypt. [54]As a reward for his zeal, our ancestor Phinehas was granted a covenant that his descendants would be priests for all time. [55]For fulfilling his duty, Joshua became a judge in Israel. [56]For giving a positive report to the people, Caleb received an inheritance in the land. [57]For showing mercy, David received

---

2:42 This Jewish group, whose name means "The Devout," strongly supported the law of Moses and opposed foreign influence. They later split into two groups, the Pharisees and the Essenes.

the promise that his descendants would rule for all time. [58]Because of his zeal for the law of Moses, Elijah was taken up into heaven. [59]Because they had faith, Hananiah, Azariah, and Mishael* were rescued from the flames. [60]Because he was innocent, Daniel was delivered from the lions' jaws.

[61]"Take notice how, in every generation, all who trust in God* are strong. [62]Do not fear the threats of sinners, for their glory will turn to dung and worms. [63]Today they are exalted, but tomorrow they cannot be found, because they will return to dust, and their planning will come to nothing. [64]Therefore, my sons, be courageous and strong in keeping the law of Moses, for by obeying it you will gain glory. [65]"Your brother Simon* is a wise man, so listen to him always, for he will take my place. [66]Let Judas Maccabeus, who has always been valiant and strong, be the leader of your army and direct the war against the Gentiles. [67]Gather together all who observe the law of Moses, and avenge the wrong of your people. [68]Pay back the Gentiles in full, and always obey the law of Moses."

[69]Mattathias blessed his sons, and then he died [70]in the one hundred forty-sixth year of Greek rule.* He was buried in the tomb of his ancestors in Modein, and all Israel mourned deeply for him.

Judas Maccabeus

3 Judas, who was called Maccabeus, took the place of his father, Mattathias. [2]His brothers and all who had joined his father helped him, and they gladly fought for Israel.

[3] Judas brought great honor to his people.
   Like a giant he put on his body armor.
He armed himself with weapons of war
   and protected his camps with his sword.
[4] He was like a lion in his actions,
   like a lion's cub roaring for prey.
[5] He hunted down the wicked and pursued them,
   and he set on fire those who harmed his people.
[6] The wicked fled in fear,
   and all the ungodly were frightened.
The cause of liberation prospered under his planning;
[7]   he bitterly angered many kings.
He brought Israel* joy by his deeds;
   his memory will be blessed forever.
[8] He went throughout the towns of Judea*
   and destroyed the wicked,
   turning away punishment from Israel.
[9] He was famous even to the ends of the earth,
   and he helped those facing death.

Judas Begins to Fight

[10]Apollonius gathered a large army of Gentiles and Samaritans to attack Israel. [11]When Judas heard this, he went out to meet him, and he defeated and killed him. Many were wounded and fell, and the survivors fled. [12]Judas plundered their belongings, including the sword of Apollonius, which he used the rest of his life.

[13]When Seron, commander of the Syrian forces, heard that Judas had formed a large army of faithful men, [14]he said, "I will make a reputation for myself and become famous in my kingdom by crushing Judas and his followers, who have scorned the king's command."

[15]So Seron organized his troops, a large number of wicked men who sought vengeance on the Israelites. [16]They marched as far as Bethhoron, where Judas went out to meet him with only a few men. [17]When the Israelites saw the advancing army, they said to Judas, "How can so few of us fight against an army that is so large and strong? And we are weak, for we have eaten nothing today."

[18]Judas replied, "It is easy for many to be overpowered by a few, for it makes no difference in God's sight* whether we are saved by few or many. [19]Success in battle depends not on the size of the army but on strength that comes from God.* [20]This arrogant and wicked army has come to destroy us, our wives, and our children and to take our belongings. [21]But we will fight for our lives and our laws, [22]and the Lord* himself will crush them as we watch. So don't be afraid of them."

[23]As soon as Judas had finished speaking, he and his troops suddenly charged Seron and his army and overpowered them. [24]They pursued them from Beth-horon down to the plain; there they killed eight hundred soldiers, and the rest fled into Philistia.

[25]Then the Gentiles in the area feared Judas and his brothers. [26]Even the king heard of his reputation, and all the Gentiles talked about his battles.

2:59 *Hananiah, Azariah,* and *Mishael* were the original Hebrew names of Shadrach, Abednego, and Meshach.   2:61 Greek *in him.*   2:65 Greek *Simeon,* a variant name for Simon.   2:70 The 146th year of Greek rule was 166 B.C.   3:7 Greek *Jacob.*   3:8 Greek *the towns of Judah.*   3:18 Greek *in the sight of heaven.*   3:19 Greek *from heaven.*   3:22 Greek *he.*

Antiochus Epiphanes Invades Persia and Judea

27When King Antiochus Epiphanes heard these reports, he became angry. He formed a very strong army from the forces of his entire kingdom. 28Opening his treasury, he paid his troops a year's wages and told them to be ready for anything. 29In this way he exhausted the money in his treasury. Antiochus realized that his tax revenues were small because he had antagonized and impoverished the people when he abolished the ancient laws. 30He feared that he would not have enough money for all his expenses and for the gifts he liked to give. (He gave more lavishly than any of the kings who had preceded him.) 31He was very perplexed about this, so he decided to go to Persia to collect a large tax fund from those regions.

32So King Antiochus left Lysias, a nobleman of the royal family, to oversee the affairs of the kingdom—from the Euphrates River to the border of Egypt. 33Lysias was also supposed to take care of the king's son Antiochus until he returned. 34The king gave Lysias half his soldiers and all his elephants and gave him orders concerning the people of Judea and Jerusalem. 35Lysias was instructed to attack them in order to crush the strength of Israel and to wipe out the people left in Jerusalem. He was to erase even the memory of them from that place. 36He was instructed to settle foreigners in their territory and redistribute the land to them. 37Then the king took the other half of the army and left Antioch, his capital city, in the one hundred forty-seventh year of Greek rule.* He crossed the Euphrates River and went through the upper provinces.

38Lysias chose Ptolemy Macron son of Dorymenes along with Nicanor and Gorgias, all capable men who were among the king's favored leaders, 39and sent them with forty thousand foot soldiers and seven thousand horsemen to destroy the land of Judea,* as the king had ordered. 40So the powerful army marched out and set up camp in the plain near Emmaus. 41When the merchants of the surrounding area heard about it, they brought chains and large amounts of silver and gold to the camp to buy as slaves any Israelites who might be captured. Then forces from Syria and Philistia joined the army in its camp.

42Judas and his brothers saw that the situation was desperate, for the army had camped in their territory. They also knew that the king had given orders to completely destroy the Israelites. 43They said to each other, "Let us fight for our people and for our Temple; let us rescue them from ruin." 44Then they assembled the people for battle and prayed for God's mercy and compassion.

45 Jerusalem was abandoned like a
       wilderness;
     none of her children entered or exited
       the city.
   The Temple was trampled down.
     Foreigners occupied the citadel,
       and Gentiles made their homes there.
   There was no joy for Israel*;
       the flute and harp were silent.

46The Israelites assembled at Mizpah near Jerusalem, since it was a traditional place of prayer for them. 47That day they fasted and dressed in sackcloth. They also put ashes on their heads and tore their clothes in grief. 48And in contrast to the Gentiles, who search for answers from the idols of their gods, the Israelites opened the Book of the Law to find guidance. 49They brought out the priestly garments, the gifts that represented the first portion of the harvest, and the tithes, and they summoned the Nazirites, who had completed their vows. 50They cried loudly to heaven, "What can we do with these Nazirites? Where can we take them to fulfill the law of Moses? 51For your Temple is torn down and defiled. Your priests mourn in humiliation. 52The Gentiles have gathered together to destroy us. You know what their intentions are. 53How can we stand against them if you do not help us?" 54Then they sounded the trumpets and loudly cried out.

55After this, Judas appointed officers over the people to command groups of one thousand, one hundred, fifty, and ten. 56(He told those who were building houses and those soon to be married, as well as those who were planting vineyards and those who were afraid, that they should go home, just as the law of Moses instructed.) 57Then the army moved out and set up a new camp on the south side of Emmaus. 58Judas said, "Prepare yourselves and be brave. Be ready early in the morning to fight these Gentiles, for they want to destroy us and our Temple. 59It is better for us to die in battle than to see the ruin of our nation and our Temple. May God's will* be done."

3:37 The 147th year of Greek rule was 165 B.C.   3:39 Greek of Judah.   3:45 Greek for Jacob.   3:59 Greek Whatever is the will of heaven.

The Battle at Emmaus

4 Gorgias took a detachment of five thousand foot soldiers and a thousand select horsemen and moved out of the camp by night. ²Their plan was for the men of the citadel in Jerusalem to guide them to the camp of the Jews, and then they would launch a surprise attack. ³But Judas heard of their plan, so he and his soldiers prepared to attack the king's forces in Emmaus ⁴while the army was divided. ⁵When Gorgias reached Judas's camp that night, he found no one there, so he began looking for them in the hills, saying, "They ran away from us."

⁶Daybreak found Judas on the plain with three thousand men, but they lacked the armor and swords they needed. ⁷They saw that the camp of the Gentiles was well fortified, with men wearing body armor and horsemen patrolling it. These were trained soldiers. ⁸But Judas told his soldiers, "Don't be frightened by their numbers. Don't flinch at their attack. ⁹Remember how our ancestors were saved at the Red Sea when Pharaoh pursued them with his army. ¹⁰Now let us call upon God* with the hope that he will think of us, remembering his covenant with our ancestors, and that he will destroy this army facing us today. ¹¹Then all the Gentiles will know that there is one who redeems and rescues Israel."

¹²The foreigners looked up and saw Judas's army advancing against them, ¹³so they rushed out of the camp to engage them in battle. The trumpet sounded for Judas's army, ¹⁴and they began fighting. The Gentiles were routed and fled across the plain, ¹⁵and their rear guard was destroyed. Judas and his army chased them as far as Gazara and even to Azotus and Jamnia and the plains of Idumea. The enemy lost about three thousand men.

¹⁶Judas stopped the pursuit and returned with his men. ¹⁷He said to the people, "Forget the plunder. We have another battle to face. ¹⁸Gorgias and his detachment are in the hills nearby. First stand firm against our enemies and crush them. Then you may take as much plunder as you want." ¹⁹While Judas was still speaking, the enemy was spotted coming out of the hills. ²⁰But Gorgias saw that the soldiers he left in Emmaus had fled, and the smoke rising from his camp showed that Judas's men had set fire to it. ²¹When Gorgias's troops saw this, they were terrified. Then they saw Judas and his army in battle formation on the plain, ²²so they all fled into Philistia.

⁴:10 Greek *heaven;* also in 4:24, 55.

²³Then Judas turned back to plunder the camp. He and his men carried away a great amount of gold and silver, blue and purple silks, and other valuables. ²⁴On the way home they sang hymns of praise to God, singing, "He is good, and his faithful love endures forever." ²⁵So Israel experienced great deliverance that day.

²⁶The Gentiles who escaped reported to Lysias all that had happened. ²⁷He was shocked and upset when he heard about it, because things had not turned out as he had planned for Israel, and he had failed to fulfill the king's command.

Lysias's First Campaign

²⁸So the next year Lysias gathered sixty thousand select troops and five thousand horsemen in order to subdue the Jews. ²⁹This army marched into Idumea and set up camp in Beth-zur, where Judas faced them with ten thousand men.

³⁰When Judas saw their military might, he prayed, "Blessed are you, O Savior of Israel, for you stopped the giant warrior by your servant David and handed over the Philistine camp to Jonathan son of Saul and his armor bearer. ³¹Now let this army be surrounded by your people Israel, and let their many soldiers and horsemen become confused. ³²Strike them with fear, and undermine their confidence in their own strength. Give them fear for their own destruction. ³³Let those who love you strike them down with swords so that your followers may praise you with hymns."

³⁴The opposing forces engaged in hand-to-hand combat, and five thousand men of the army of Lysias were killed. ³⁵Lysias saw his men in retreat, and he also saw that Judas's followers were very bold and ready to live or die bravely. So he withdrew to Antioch to recruit mercenary soldiers; then he planned to return to Judea with an even larger army.

Purification of the Temple

³⁶Judas and his brothers said, "Our enemies have been utterly defeated. Now let us go up to purify the Temple and dedicate it." ³⁷So all the army was assembled, and they went up to Mount Zion. ³⁸There they saw the empty sanctuary, the desecrated altar, the gates burned down, the weeds growing in the courtyards as in a forest or on a hill, and the priests' rooms next to the Temple in ruins. ³⁹They tore their garments and mourned deeply, putting ashes

on their heads 40and falling face down on the ground. When the trumpets gave the signal, the people cried out to God.*

41Then Judas sent troops to attack the defenders of the citadel while he purified the Temple. 42He chose blameless priests, who were devoted to the law of Moses. 43They cleansed the sanctuary, and the stones that had been defiled were carried away to an unclean place. 44They discussed what should be done about the altar of burnt offering, for it had been defiled. 45Someone suggested that it be torn down so it would not become a lasting shame to them, for the Gentiles had defiled it. So they pulled the altar down 46and put the stones in a suitable place on the Temple hill until a prophet could come someday and tell them what to do with them. 47Then they took uncut stones, as required in the law of Moses, and built a new altar like the old one. 48They restored the sanctuary and all the things inside the Temple. Finally, they sanctified the Temple and its courtyards. 49They made new sacred vessels and took into the Temple the lampstand, the altar of incense, and the table for the Bread of the Presence. 50They burned incense on the altar and lit the lamps on the lampstand, which gave light in the Temple. 51Then they set the Bread of the Presence on the table, hung up the curtains, and finished all the work they had set out to do.

52On December 14* in the one hundred forty-eighth year of Greek rule, they arose early in the morning 53and offered sacrifices on the new altar of burnt offering, as the law of Moses directed. 54On the day of the month that the Gentiles regularly defiled it,* the altar was dedicated anew with songs, harps, lutes, and cymbals. 55And all the people fell face down in adoration and blessed God, who had given them success.

56For eight days they celebrated the dedication of the altar, and they joyfully offered burnt offerings, praise, and thanksgiving for their deliverance. 57They adorned the front of the Temple with gold crowns and shields, and they repaired the gates and restored the priests' rooms, furnishing them with doors. 58The people were very joyful because the disgrace caused by the Gentiles had been removed. 59Judas and his brothers and all Israel decreed that the dedication of the altar should be celebrated every year with joy and gladness for eight days, beginning on December 14.*

60They then built high walls and fortified towers around Mount Zion to stop the Gentiles from attacking and destroying it as they did before. 61Judas assigned a garrison to guard Mount Zion, and he fortified Beth-zur, so that the people would have a defense against Idumea.

Fighting the Idumeans and Ammonites

5 When the surrounding Gentile peoples heard that the altar and sanctuary had been restored, they became very angry. 2Determined to destroy all of Jacob's descendants living among them, they began to persecute and kill the people.

3Judas fought against Esau's descendants at Akrabattene in Idumea because they were attacking the Israelites there. The Idumeans were thoroughly humiliated in defeat and were stripped of their valuables and weapons. 4Judas also avenged the evil deeds of the sons of Baean, who constantly threatened travelers by ambushing them along the roads. 5Judas chased them into their fortified towers and surrounded them. Then, calling a curse down on them,* he set the towers on fire and burned them down with everyone inside.

6Next, Judas crossed over to attack the Ammonites and found a strong and numerous army under the command of Timothy. 7After fighting many battles with them, he routed them and cut them to pieces. 8He captured the town of Jazer and its nearby villages. Then he returned to Judea.

War with the Gentiles of Galilee and Gilead

9Now the Gentiles in Gilead banded together against the Israelites in their area and plotted to destroy them. But these Israelites fled to the fortress of Dathema. 10From there they sent this letter to Judas and his brothers:

"The Gentiles around us have banded together to destroy us. 11They are preparing to come and capture the fortress where we have taken refuge. Timothy is the leader of their army. 12Please come at once and rescue us from them, for many of us have already been killed or wounded. 13All our fellow Israelites in the land of Tob* are

4:40 Greek *to heaven.*   4:52 Greek *On the twenty-fifth day of the ninth month, which is Kislev,* of the Hebrew lunar calendar. This event occurred on December 14, 164 B.C.; see also 4:59.   4:54 See 1:59.   4:59 Greek *On the twenty-fifth day of the month of Kislev,* of the Hebrew lunar calendar. This is the origin of the Festival of Dedication, or the Festival of Lights, also known as Hanukkah. The 25th day of Kislev occurs every year in December.   5:5 Or *vowing their destruction.*   5:13 Or *our brothers among the Tobiads.*

dead. Their wives and children have been taken captive, and their goods have been confiscated. The enemy has killed almost a thousand men there."

[14]While this letter was being read, other messengers came from Galilee with their clothes torn. They had similar news: [15]"Everyone in Ptolemais, Tyre, and Sidon has joined with the Gentiles of Galilee to destroy us."

[16]When Judas and the people heard these reports, they held a large meeting to decide how to help their fellow Israelites who were being attacked by their enemies. [17]Judas said to his brother Simon, "Choose your men and rescue your fellow Israelites in Galilee; Jonathan and I will go to Gilead." [18]He left Joseph son of Zechariah and Azariah, a leader of the people, to guard Judea with the rest of the army. [19]He gave them these instructions: "Take charge of these people, but do not begin fighting the Gentiles until we return." [20]Three thousand men were assigned to accompany Simon into Galilee, and Judas led eight thousand men into Gilead.

[21]Simon invaded Galilee, and after fighting many battles, he completely crushed the Gentile forces there. [22]He chased them all the way to the gate of Ptolemais. Almost three thousand Gentiles were killed, and Simon captured all their belongings. [23]He led the Jews who were in Galilee and in Arbatta—together with their wives, children, and possessions—to Judea with great celebration.

[24]Judas Maccabeus and his brother Jonathan crossed the Jordan River and marched for three days into the wilderness. [25]There they met the Nabateans,* who received them peacefully. The Nabateans told them all that had been happening to the Israelites in Gilead. [26]They related that many had been trapped in Bozrah, Bosor, Alema, Chaspho, Maked, and Karnaim (all of which were large and fortified cities). [27]They said that Jews were also being held captive in the other towns of Gilead. The enemy planned to attack these towns the next day, and then they would capture and destroy all the Jews at once.

[28]Judas and his army quickly marched back by the wilderness road to Bozrah and captured that town. They killed every male by the sword, carried away all their goods, and burned the town. [29]They left Bozrah by night and marched until they came to the fortress of Dathema.*

[30]At dawn they saw a great number of soldiers carrying ladders and battering rams to attack the fortress and capture the Jews. [31]Judas saw that the fight had just begun and that the battle cry of the people was going up to heaven with trumpet blasts and shouts. [32]He shouted to his army, "Fight today for your fellow Israelites!" [33]Then Judas's men advanced from behind the enemy in three companies while sounding trumpets and crying aloud in prayer. [34]When the men of Timothy's army realized it was Maccabeus, they fled from him. Judas's army inflicted a crushing defeat, killing about eight thousand men that day.

[35]Judas then turned to Alema,* assaulted and captured it, killed all the males, carried away all the goods, and burned it. [36]From there he marched on and captured Chaspho, Maked, Bosor, and the rest of the towns of Gilead.

[37]Following his defeat, Timothy assembled another army and set up camp just across the streambed from Raphon. [38]Judas sent scouts to survey the enemy camp, and they returned to report, "All the Gentiles from the region have gathered to form a great army under Timothy's command; [39]they have also hired Arab reinforcements. They are camped on the opposite side of the streambed, ready to fight you." So Judas went forward to attack them.

[40]As Judas approached, Timothy said to his officers, "If Judas comes to the streambed and crosses it, we will not be able to resist him; he will certainly get the better of us. [41]But if his courage fails and he sets up camp on the other side, we will cross over and crush him."

[42]When Judas came near the stream, he stationed the officers of the army* on the bank, ordering them, "Don't let anyone stay behind to set up camp. Send everyone into battle." [43]Judas himself led the charge across the streambed, and his entire army followed. They routed the Gentile forces, who fled to the temple area in Karnaim, discarding their weapons as they ran. [44]But Judas captured Karnaim and burned out the temple area with everyone in it. So Karnaim was subdued, and all resistance against Judas ceased.

[45]Then Judas gathered together all the Israelites who were in Gilead, from the least to the greatest—with their wives, children, and possessions—and he led this large company back to Judea.* [46]Along the way they came to Ephron, a large city that was strongly fortified. They could not go around it, either to the

---

5:25 The Nabateans were from Arabia.   5:29 Greek lacks *of Dathema*; see 5:9.   5:35 Some manuscripts read *to Maapha*.
5:42 Greek *scribes of the people*.   5:45 Greek *to the land of Judah*; also in 5:53, 68.

right or left, so they had to go through it. ⁴⁷But the people in the city shut themselves in and barricaded the gates with stones. ⁴⁸Judas sent them a message of peace, saying, "Let us pass through your territory to get to our own. No one will harm you. We will only pass through on foot." But they refused to open the gates for him. ⁴⁹So Judas issued orders for all his troops to set up where they were. ⁵⁰His army prepared for battle and attacked the city all that day and through the night until the city fell to them. ⁵¹Judas and his men killed every male by the sword, carried away their possessions, and completely destroyed the city. Then they marched through the city over the bodies of the dead.

⁵²They crossed the Jordan River to the great plain near Beth-shan. ⁵³Judas hurried the stragglers and encouraged the people all the way until they reached Judea. ⁵⁴Then with joy and gladness they climbed Mount Zion, where they offered burnt offerings, for none of them had been killed and all had returned safely.

Tragedy at Jamnia

⁵⁵Now while Judas and Jonathan were in Gilead and their brother Simon was in Galilee outside Ptolemais, ⁵⁶Joseph son of Zechariah and Azariah, commanders of the soldiers in Judea,* heard of the victories and the battles that had been fought. ⁵⁷They said, "Let's also make a name for ourselves by fighting the Gentiles around us." ⁵⁸So Joseph gave orders to his troops, and they marched against Jamnia. ⁵⁹Gorgias and his men came out of the town to fight them. ⁶⁰Joseph and Azariah were routed, and they were chased all the way to the borders of Judea. About two thousand Israelites were killed that day. ⁶¹This great defeat took place because they did not listen to Judas and his brothers. They thought they would do brave deeds themselves, ⁶²but they were not from the family through whom deliverance was to come to Israel.

Success at Idumea and Philistia

⁶³Valiant Judas and his brothers, however, were greatly honored by all Israel, and their fame spread among the Gentiles. ⁶⁴People rallied around and cheered for them.

⁶⁵Judas and his brothers marched out and attacked the descendants of Esau in the land to the south. They captured Hebron and its surrounding towns, destroying their fortifications and burning down their perimeter towers.

⁶⁶As Judas and his army headed for Philistia, they passed through Marisa.* ⁶⁷That day some priests were killed in battle, for they had foolishly decided to make a name for themselves in battle. ⁶⁸Judas turned and marched to Azotus in Philistia. He tore down their altars, burned the statues of their gods, and carried away their possessions. Then he returned to Judea.

The Last Days of Antiochus Epiphanes

6 King Antiochus was passing through the upper provinces when he heard that the city of Elymais in Persia was famous for its rich stores of silver and gold. ²The temple in this city was very rich, containing gold armor, shields, and weapons left there by Alexander the Macedonian, son of Philip, the first ruler of Greece. ³Antiochus came and tried to capture the city and strip it of its wealth, but he did not succeed because its citizens had learned of his plans to attack. ⁴They resisted him in battle, so he retreated and returned to Babylon greatly disappointed.

⁵While Antiochus was still in Persia, someone told him that his armies had been defeated in Judea.* ⁶He was told that Lysias had attacked them with a strong force but had been defeated by the Jews. The Jews had now grown strong by capturing armor, war supplies, and stores of goods from the armies they destroyed. ⁷Antiochus was told that the Jews had thrown down the sacrilegious object he had set up on the altar in Jerusalem, had surrounded the Temple with high walls as in the past, and had fortified Beth-zur, his town.

⁸When the king heard this news, he was astounded and badly shaken. He became so sick with grief that he was confined to his bed, for things had not worked out as he had planned. ⁹He lay there for many days, overcome with bitterness and constant grief, until finally he realized he was dying.

¹⁰The king called for his favored leaders and said to them, "I can't sleep, and my heart has been broken with worry. ¹¹At first I said to myself, 'How could I have come to such distress and deep sorrow? I have been kind, and my people have always loved me.' ¹²But now I remember the wrongs I committed in Jerusalem—how I seized all the vessels of gold and silver and ordered the slaughter of the people of Judea* without just cause. ¹³I know now that this is why these evils have fallen on me. Now I will die of great sorrow in a foreign land."

5:56 Greek lacks *in Judea.*   5:66 Some manuscripts read *Samaria.*   6:5 Greek *in the land of Judah.*   6:12 Greek *of Judah.*

Philip Is Appointed Regent

[14]King Antiochus then called for Philip, one of his favored leaders, and put him in command of all his kingdom. [15]He gave Philip the royal crown, his robe, and his signet ring, with the understanding that Philip would be guardian to his son Antiochus and train him to become king. [16]Antiochus Epiphanes died there in Persia in the one hundred forty-ninth year of Greek rule.*

[17]Now when Lysias learned that the king was dead, he went ahead and crowned the king's son Antiochus as the new king. Lysias had raised him from childhood and gave him the title Eupator.

Judas Attacks the Citadel

[18]Meanwhile, the soldiers from the garrison in the Jerusalem citadel were harassing the Israelites near the sanctuary. They tried in every way they could to harm the Jews and strengthen the Gentiles. [19]Judas decided to destroy them, so he gathered all the people to besiege the citadel. [20]They joined together and attacked the citadel in the one hundred fiftieth year of Greek rule,* using siege weapons and battering rams.

[21]Some of the people in the citadel escaped from the siege, and some ungodly Israelites joined them. [22]They went to King Antiochus Eupator* and said, "How long will you refuse to do justice and avenge the attacks on our people? [23]We were content to serve your father, doing all he ordered and obeying his commands. [24]But because of this, the other Israelites are angry with us and have besieged the citadel. They have killed as many of us as they could catch and have seized our inheritances. [25]They have opposed not only us but also people in all the surrounding territories. [26]Now they have besieged the citadel in Jerusalem and have fortified the Temple and the stronghold of Beth-zur. [27]Unless you act quickly, they will do worse things than these, and you will not be able to stop them."

The Battle at Beth-zechariah

[28]The king became angry when he heard this. He called together all his favored leaders, the commanders of his army, and the officers over his horsemen. [29]He also hired mercenaries from various places, including the Mediterranean islands. [30]His army numbered one hundred thousand foot soldiers, twenty thousand horsemen, and thirty-two elephants trained in warfare. [31]After marching through Idumea, they came to Beth-zur and attacked it for many days. They even used battering rams in the attack, but the Jews bravely ran out of the town and set the battering rams on fire.

[32]Judas and his army left the siege of the citadel in Jerusalem and moved their camp to Beth-zechariah, opposite the camp of the king's army. [33]The king rose before daylight and marched his men toward Beth-zechariah, where they prepared for battle and sounded the trumpets. [34]The elephants were given grape juice and mulberry juice to provoke them to fight. [35]The elephants were distributed among the ranks of foot soldiers, each elephant to a thousand men, who were dressed in coats of mail and wearing bronze helmets. Five hundred select horsemen were assigned to each elephant. [36]These horsemen anticipated the moves of the elephants and went with them, never leaving them. [37]Fastened to each elephant by a harness was a sturdy wooden tower. A team of men* fought from each tower while an Indian driver directed the beast. [38]The rest of the horsemen were placed on either flank of the army to harass the enemy while being protected by the ranks of foot soldiers. [39]When the sun reflected from the shields of gold and bronze, the hills caught the glare and gleamed as if on fire. [40]Part of the king's army was deployed on the high hills, while the other part was on the plain. The soldiers advanced steadily and in solid formation. [41]Everyone trembled at the noise of this great multitude, for the powerful and numerous army thundered as it marched in its clanging armor.

[42]Judas and his army marched forward, and six hundred of the king's men were killed. [43]Judas's brother Eleazar, who was called Avaran, saw that one of the elephants was larger than the other beasts and was equipped with royal armor. He thought that the king was on it, [44]so he sacrificed himself to win the battle and earn everlasting fame. [45]As Eleazar fought his way boldly through the middle of the enemy ranks, killing men left and right, the troops parted as he came. [46]He got under the elephant, plunged his sword into it, and killed it; but the elephant collapsed on him and he died. [47]When the Jews saw the strength and determination of the king's army, however, they retreated.

The Siege of the Temple

[48]The king's army followed them to Jerusalem, where it set up camp to blockade Judea and

---

6:16 The 149th year of Greek rule was 163 B.C.   6:20 The 150th year of Greek rule was 162 B.C.   6:22 Greek *the king*.
6:37 Some manuscripts read *32*; others read *30*. The text could also be understood to read *4*.

Mount Zion. [49]The king granted terms of peace to the people of Beth-zur, and they evacuated the town. (They had no food to withstand a siege, since it was a Sabbath year for the land.) [50]So the king captured Beth-zur and stationed a garrison there to hold it. [51]Then he began a long siege of the Temple. He set up siege weapons, battering rams, machines to hurl fire and stones, machines to shoot arrows, and catapults. [52]The Jews also constructed weapons of war to match these, and they fought for many days. [53]But since it was the Sabbath year, there was no food in the town. Those who had sought refuge in Judea from the Gentiles had eaten all the stored food. [54]Because of the food shortage, only a few men stayed in the Temple; all the others had scattered to their own homes.

[55]Before he died, Antiochus Epiphanes had appointed Philip to raise his son, Antiochus Eupator, and to prepare him to be king. Lysias now heard that Philip [56]had returned from Persia and Media with the late king's army and was trying to seize control. [57]So Lysias gave orders to withdraw from attacking the Temple, and he went to King Antiochus Eupator and told him and his commanders, "We are growing weaker every day, we are short of food, and the place we are attacking is strong. Besides, the other affairs of the kingdom demand urgent attention. [58]Therefore, let us make a peace treaty with these people and their nation. [59]Let us agree that they may live according to their own laws once again. It is because we abolished their laws that they became angry and rebelled like this."

[60]The proposal pleased the king and his commanders. He sent the Jews an offer of peace, and they accepted it. [61]So the king and his commanders gave their word, and the defenders left the stronghold.

[62]But when the king went up to Mount Zion, he saw that its defenses were very strong, so he broke his word and gave orders to tear down the wall around the Temple. [63]Then he quickly left and returned to Antioch. There he found Philip in control of the city, so he attacked the city and captured it.

Demetrius I Soter Becomes King

7 In the one hundred fifty-first year of Greek rule,* Demetrius son of Seleucus left Rome* with a few men and arrived at a coastal city. There he proclaimed himself king. [2]As he was

entering the royal palace of his ancestors, the armies there captured Antiochus Eupator and Lysias, intending to bring them to him. [3]When Demetrius heard this, he said, "I don't even want to see them!" [4]So the army killed them, and Demetrius assumed the throne of his kingdom.

[5]Then all the ungodly and wicked Israelites came to Demetrius. They were led by Alcimus, who wanted to be made high priest. [6]They accused their own people, saying, "Judas and his brothers have killed all your favored leaders and have driven us from our land. [7]Therefore, send someone you trust who can survey all the damage that Judas has caused us and the king's lands. Let him punish Judas and his men and all who help them."

[8]So the king chose Bacchides, one of his favored leaders who governed the province west of the Euphrates River. He was a prominent figure in the kingdom and was faithful to King Demetrius. [9]He sent Bacchides and the wicked Alcimus, whom he made high priest, to take revenge on the Israelites. [10]They set out and arrived in Judea* with a large army. Alcimus sent messengers to Judas and his brothers with deceitful words of peace, [11]but Judas did not believe them, for he saw that the enemy had come with a large army.

[12]Nevertheless, some teachers of religious law went to Alcimus and Bacchides to inquire about just terms. [13]These Hasidean teachers* were the first to seek peace from the two men. [14]They reasoned, "A priest of the line of Aaron has come with the army. He will not deceive us."

[15]Alcimus spoke words of peace and vowed to them, "We will do no harm to you or your friends," [16]and they believed him. But he took sixty of them in one day and killed them, as had been written in the Scriptures:

[17] "They have scattered the bodies of your
    holy ones.
Their blood has been shed all around
    Jerusalem,
    and no one is left to bury the dead."*

[18]Then all the people became very fearful. They said, "They don't know what it means to be truthful, for they have broken the agreement that they guaranteed with an oath." [19]Bacchides moved the camp from Jerusalem

7:1a The 151st year of Greek rule was 161 B.C.   7:1b Demetrius was the rightful heir to the Seleucid throne. He had been held hostage in Rome, because his uncle, Antiochus Epiphanes, had usurped the throne from him.   7:10 Greek *the land of Judah;* also in 7:22, 50.   7:13 Greek *The Devout;* see note on 2:42.   7:17 Ps 79:2-3.

to Beth-zaith. He seized many of those who deserted to him* and also some Jews,* and he slaughtered them all and threw them into a large pit. 20He entrusted the country to Alcimus and left some troops to help him. Then Bacchides went back to the king.

21Alcimus continually fought to maintain his position as high priest, 22and some Jewish dissenters joined his cause. They took control of Judea and did much harm to Israel. 23Judas saw all the evils that Alcimus and his companions did to the Israelites. They were worse than the Gentiles. 24So Judas marched throughout the whole territory of Judea, taking revenge on those who had deserted and preventing them from leaving their towns. 25Alcimus realized that Judas and his companions were gaining control, and he knew he could not stand against them. So he went back to the king and accused Judas and his men of many serious crimes.

The Battle at Caphar-salama

26Nicanor, one of the king's most honored generals, despised Israel, so the king sent him to destroy the people there. 27Nicanor came to Jerusalem with a large army, and he sent Judas and his brothers a deceitful message of peace: 28"There is no need for us to fight each other. I will come with a few men to speak to you in peace." 29So he came to see Judas, and they greeted each other peaceably. All the while, Nicanor's men were preparing to kidnap Judas. 30But Judas learned of this deceitful plot, so he was cautious and would not meet Nicanor again. 31When Nicanor realized his plot had been discovered, he went out to fight against Judas near Caphar-salama. 32But about five hundred of Nicanor's men were killed, and the survivors fled into the City of David.

Threats against the Temple

33After this, Nicanor went up to Mount Zion. Some of the priests and elders came out to meet him peaceably. They showed him the burnt offerings that were being offered on behalf of the king. 34But he mocked and derided them, cursing and spitting at them as he angrily swore, 35"Unless Judas and his army are handed over to me, I will burn this house down when I return." Then he left in a terrible rage.

36The priests went into the Temple and stood facing the altar and the sanctuary. They wept and prayed,

37 "You have chosen this house to honor your
    name
    and to be a house of prayer and petition
      for your people.
38 Take vengeance on this man and his army;
    let them die by the sword.
   Remember their blasphemies;
    let them live no longer."

Nicanor Is Defeated

39Nicanor and his army left Jerusalem and set up camp near Beth-horon, where the Syrian army joined him. 40Judas and 3,000 of his troops set up camp in Adasa. He prayed, 41"When the messengers of King Sennacherib blasphemed you, your angel went out and killed 185,000 of the Assyrians. 42In the same way, utterly destroy this army before us today. Let everyone still alive know that Nicanor has blasphemed your sanctuary, and judge him as his wickedness deserves."

43The armies attacked each other on March 8.* Nicanor's army was completely defeated, and he himself was the first to fall in battle. 44When Nicanor's men saw that he was dead, they threw down their weapons and fled. 45The Jews chased them for about eighteen miles,* from Adasa as far as Gazara, and their trumpets kept sounding the battle call. 46People came out of all the towns of Judea and drove the enemy back to the pursuing Jewish army, which killed them all by the sword—not a single one was left alive. 47The Jews carried away all the goods, and they cut off Nicanor's head and his right hand, which he had so arrogantly raised against them. They brought his head and hand to Jerusalem and put them on display for all to see. 48The people were overjoyed and spent that day in festive celebration. 49Judas decreed that there should be a celebration each spring* to commemorate the victory. 50So Judea enjoyed peace and quiet for a short time.

Rome's Fame

8 Judas had heard of the Romans' famous reputation, that they were powerful and strong and good to those with whom they held alliances. They promised friendship to any who

---

7:19a Or *many of his own soldiers who had deserted.*   7:19b Greek *some of the people.*   7:43 Greek *on the thirteenth day of the month of Adar,* of the Hebrew lunar calendar. The text does not specify the year, but this battle probably occurred on March 8, 161 B.C. or March 27, 160 B.C.   7:45 Greek *a day's journey.*   7:49 Greek *each year on the thirteenth day of Adar,* of the Hebrew lunar calendar; see note on 7:43.

joined them, [2]and they were very powerful. Judas had heard of their battles and their heroic deeds against the Gauls—how they had conquered them and forced them to pay a tribute tax. [3]He had also heard of the great things they had done in Spain—how they had gained control of the silver and gold mines there [4]and taken possession of the whole region by their wisdom and patience, even though Spain was quite far from them. In every part of the world, kings who opposed the Romans had been overthrown with great losses, while others paid them a tribute tax every year. [5]Philip and Perseus, kings of the Macedonians, and others who had fought against the Romans had been conquered. [6]The Romans had also defeated Antiochus the Great, king of Asia, who had fought against them with 120 elephants and with horsemen, chariots, and a very large army. [7]The Romans took Antiochus alive and ordered that he and those who would reign after him should pay a large tribute tax and give them hostages. [8]Antiochus was also forced to give them India, Media, and Lydia.* These were then given to King Eumenes.

[9]The Greeks planned to attack and destroy the Romans, [10]but the Romans heard about it and sent a single general to attack them. In the ensuing battle, many Greeks were killed or wounded, and the Romans took their wives and children captive, carried away their possessions, annexed their territory, tore down their fortresses, and made them their slaves, as they are to this day. [11]They destroyed and enslaved all other kingdoms and islands that resisted them. [12]The Romans have maintained a firm friendship, however, with all their friends and allies.

So the Romans have conquered kingdoms both far and near, and all who have heard of them fear them. [13]They make kings of anyone they wish, and they depose anyone they wish; in this way, they have become very great. [14]Yet no Roman has ever crowned himself king or displayed his grandeur by wearing purple. [15]They have formed a senate of 320 people, who meet daily to decide what is best for the people and how to govern them. [16]Their government is directed by entrusting one man each year to rule over the whole country. They all obey him, and there is no envy or jealousy among them.

Alliance between the Jews and the Romans

[17]Judas chose Eupolemus son of John, son of Accos, and Jason son of Eleazar to go to Rome and establish a friendship and an alliance with the Romans. [18]Judas did this so the Jews could get out from under oppression, for it was obvious that the Greeks were reducing Israel to slavery. [19]Eupolemus and Jason traveled to Rome, which was a very long journey. When they arrived, they entered the senate chamber and said, [20]"Judas Maccabeus, his brothers, and the Jewish people have sent us to establish an alliance and a peace treaty with you. We want to be formally considered your friends and allies." [21]The senate was pleased to accept their proposal. [22]The senate sent a proclamation back to Jerusalem, engraved on bronze tablets so that it might be kept there as a permanent record of their peace treaty and alliance:

[23]"May the Romans and the Jewish nation meet with success forever, both at sea and on land. May sword and enemy be far from them. [24]If war should come to the Romans or to any of their allies in all their dominion, [25]the Jewish nation will wholeheartedly act as their allies in whatever way the occasion requires. [26]If an enemy is at war with the Romans, the Jews will not supply them with grain, arms, money, or ships, just as Rome has decided. They will keep these obligations without any compensation. [27]Likewise, if war should come to the Jewish nation, the Romans will willingly act as their allies in whatever way the occasion requires. [28]If the Jews have an enemy, the Romans will not supply them with grain, arms, money, or ships, just as Rome has decided. The Romans will keep these obligations without deception. [29]On these terms the Romans make an agreement with the Jewish people. [30]If both parties agree to add or delete anything in this agreement, they may do so, and whatever changes they make will be valid.

[31]"Concerning the wrongs that King Demetrius is committing against the Jews, we have written to him as follows: 'Why are you making things so hard for our friends and allies the Jews? [32]If they come to us again and complain about you, we will defend their rights. We will make war against you by sea and on land.'"

The Death of Judas Maccabeus

9 Meanwhile, when Demetrius heard that Nicanor and his army had fallen in battle, he sent Bacchides and Alcimus back into Judea,*

8:8 Or *Ionia, Mysia, and Lydia.*   9:1 Greek *the land of Judah;* also in 9:57, 72.

along with the right wing of his army. ²They marched along the road that leads to Gilgal and set up camp at the ascent to Arbela. They then captured the town and killed many of its people. ³In early spring* during the one hundred fifty-second year of Greek rule, they set up camp outside Jerusalem. ⁴Then they marched on to Berea near Jerusalem with twenty thousand foot soldiers and two thousand horsemen.

⁵Now Judas and three thousand of his select troops had set up camp in Elasa. ⁶When they saw the size of the enemy army, they became very frightened. Many deserted the camp until no more than eight hundred men remained. ⁷Seeing that only a fraction of his army was left and that the battle was imminent, Judas became discouraged because he had no time to gather more forces. ⁸But even though he was dismayed, he said to those who remained, "Let us get up and face our enemies. We may still have the strength to fight them."

⁹His men tried to dissuade him, saying, "We don't have the strength! We should save our lives and return to fight them with more of our fellow Israelites. There are too few of us now."

¹⁰But Judas said, "I would never think of running from them. If our time has come, let us die bravely for our people and leave no blemish on our reputation."

¹¹The army of Bacchides moved out of camp and took positions for combat. The horsemen were divided into two groups, and the slingers and the archers went ahead of the army, as did the best fighters. ¹²The ranks of foot soldiers were flanked by horsemen on either side, and Bacchides was on the right flank. The army advanced as it sounded its trumpets, and Judas's soldiers sounded their trumpets as well. ¹³The earth shook at the noise of the armies, and the battle continued from morning until evening. ¹⁴Judas saw that Bacchides and the stronger part of his army was on the right, so Judas led his bravest men ¹⁵and drove back the right flank, chasing them to Mount Azotus. ¹⁶The soldiers on the left flank realized that the right flank was beaten, so they turned to chase Judas and those who were with him, attacking them from the rear. ¹⁷The fighting became very intense, and both sides lost many men. ¹⁸Then Judas was killed, and the rest of his men fled.

¹⁹Jonathan and Simon took their brother Judas and buried him in the tomb of their ancestors at Modein. ²⁰For many days, all Israel mourned deeply for him, saying, ²¹"The mighty hero—the savior of Israel—has fallen!"

²²The rest of the deeds of Judas—his battles, his heroic acts, and his great achievements—have not been recorded here, but there were many of them.

Jonathan Becomes the New Leader

²³After the death of Judas, the ungodly came out of hiding throughout Israel, and evildoers reappeared. ²⁴In those days there was a very severe famine, and the country eventually sided with the ungodly. ²⁵Bacchides chose wicked men to administer the affairs of the country. ²⁶These people searched out Judas's friends and brought them to Bacchides, who punished and publicly humiliated them. ²⁷There had not been such distress in Israel since the day the last prophet was seen in Israel.

²⁸All Judas's friends said to Jonathan, ²⁹"Ever since your brother Judas died, there has been no one like him to fight Bacchides and our enemies and to deal with our own people who despise us. ³⁰Therefore, we have chosen you today to succeed him as our ruler and commander, so that you can lead us into battle." ³¹So Jonathan became leader in place of his brother Judas.

The Battle at Medeba

³²When Bacchides heard about this, he tried to kill Jonathan. ³³But Jonathan and his brother Simon and the others who were with them learned of the plot, and they fled into the wilderness of Tekoa. They set up camp by the pool of Asphar. ³⁴Bacchides learned of this on the Sabbath, so he and his army crossed the Jordan.

³⁵Jonathan sent his brother John to lead a convoy to ask their friends the Nabateans if they would store the Israelites' sizable amount of baggage. ³⁶The sons of Jambri, however, came from Medeba and seized John and all his possessions and took him away.

³⁷Sometime later Jonathan and his brother Simon learned that the sons of Jambri had planned a large wedding. The bride was the daughter of one of the great princes of Canaan, and they were planning to bring her from Nadabath in a splendid procession. ³⁸Remembering the bloody death of their brother John, Jonathan and Simon went up and hid themselves in the hills. ³⁹As they peered out, they saw a great crowd and a caravan loaded with possessions. The bridegroom came out with his relatives and friends to meet the procession with tambourines and musical instruments and a pompous military display. ⁴⁰Then the Israelites rushed from their ambush and

---

9:3 Greek *In the first month*. This month of the Hebrew lunar calendar occurred in March and April 160 B.C.

began killing them, and many of them died. The survivors fled into the mountains, leaving all their possessions behind to be captured by the Jews. ⁴¹So the wedding was turned into an occasion for mourning, and the joyful music into a dirge.

Crossing the Jordan

⁴²When Jonathan and Simon had taken revenge for the death of their brother, they returned to the marshes of the Jordan. ⁴³As soon as Bacchides heard about this, he came on the Sabbath to the banks of the Jordan with a large army. ⁴⁴Jonathan said to his men, "Get up! We must fight for our lives, for this is a new and desperate situation. ⁴⁵The battle is now in front of us, the Jordan River is behind us, and marshes and woods are on either side of us. There is no escape! ⁴⁶Therefore, pray to God* that you may be rescued from your enemies." ⁴⁷Then they began to fight.

Jonathan's army attacked the forces of Bacchides, but then Jonathan and his men retreated and escaped. ⁴⁸Jonathan and his men jumped into the Jordan and swam over to the other side, but the enemy did not follow. ⁴⁹That day a thousand of Bacchides' men were killed.

The Death of Alcimus

⁵⁰After returning to Jerusalem, Bacchides built strongholds throughout Judea. He built fortresses with high walls and gates and bars in Jericho, Emmaus, Beth-horon, Bethel, Timnath, Pharathon, and Tephon. ⁵¹Bacchides placed garrisons in them to harass the Israelites. ⁵²He fortified the towns of Beth-zur and Gazara and also the citadel, and he put troops in them, along with provisions. ⁵³He took as hostages the sons of the leading men of the country and imprisoned them in the citadel at Jerusalem.

⁵⁴In midspring* of the one hundred fifty-third year of Greek rule, Alcimus ordered that the walls separating the Gentiles from the inner court of the Temple be torn down, thereby destroying the works of the prophets. But he had hardly started this ⁵⁵when he suffered a stroke. Paralyzed and speechless, he could no longer give commands even in his own home, so the work stopped. ⁵⁶Then Alcimus died in great agony.

⁵⁷After he learned that Alcimus had died, Bacchides returned to the king, and Judea had peace for two years.

The Battle at Bethbasi

⁵⁸Then the ungodly began to plot, saying, "Jonathan and those with him live in peace and are full of confidence. Let us bring Bacchides back, and he can capture them all in one night." ⁵⁹So they went to Bacchides and advised him to carry out this plan. ⁶⁰Bacchides set out with a large army, and he sent secret letters to his military allies in Judea, instructing them to seize Jonathan and his men. But this failed because Jonathan learned of the plot. ⁶¹His men captured about fifty people in Judea who were the ringleaders of the plot, and they killed them. ⁶²Then Jonathan, Simon, and their followers withdrew to Bethbasi in the wilderness, and they rebuilt and fortified it.

⁶³When Bacchides found out what they had done, he gathered his entire army and sent word to his allies in Judea. ⁶⁴They set up camp outside Bethbasi, and they made siege weapons and attacked the town for many days. ⁶⁵Jonathan left his brother Simon in the town and went out into the country with a few men. ⁶⁶He struck down Odomera and his family and the sons of Phasiron in their tents. Then he attacked Bacchides' army. ⁶⁷Simon and his troops rushed out of the town and set the siege weapons on fire. ⁶⁸They fought against Bacchides and overcame him, inflicting great losses on him, and his planning and effort came to nothing.

⁶⁹Bacchides was angry with the renegades who had advised him to come into their country, so he killed many of them. Then he decided to return to his own country. ⁷⁰When Jonathan heard about this retreat, he sent ambassadors to Bacchides to offer peace and obtain release of the captives. ⁷¹Bacchides accepted the terms and kept his word, swearing that he would do Jonathan no harm as long as he lived. ⁷²Bacchides released the prisoners he had taken previously from Judea, returned to his own country, and never again set foot in Judea. ⁷³So war ended in Israel, and Jonathan settled in Michmash, where he judged the people and rooted out the wicked from Israel.

Jonathan Is Appointed High Priest

10 In the one hundred sixtieth year of Greek rule,* Alexander Epiphanes, the son of Antiochus Epiphanes, arrived and occupied Ptolemais. The people accepted him, and he began his reign there. ²When King Demetrius Soter heard of this, he gathered together a very large army and went to fight him.

9:46 Greek *to heaven.* 9:54 Greek *In the second month.* This month of the Hebrew lunar calendar occurred in April and May 159 B.C. 10:1 The 160th year of Greek rule was 152 B.C.

³Demetrius sent Jonathan a letter containing words of peace and promises to honor him. ⁴He reasoned, "We need to make peace with him before he makes an alliance with Alexander against us. ⁵For he will remember all the harm we have done to him, to his brothers, and to his nation." ⁶So Demetrius gave Jonathan authority to recruit and equip an army, hoping to make him a military ally. He also ordered that the hostages in the citadel should be released to Jonathan.

⁷Jonathan came to Jerusalem and read the letters to all the people and to those in the citadel. ⁸They were greatly alarmed when they heard that the king had given him authority to recruit an army, ⁹but the guards at the citadel released the hostages to Jonathan, and he returned them to their parents. ¹⁰Thereafter, Jonathan lived in Jerusalem and began to rebuild and repair the city. ¹¹He ordered workers to build walls around Mount Zion, using squared stones for better fortification. ¹²The foreigners living in the strongholds built by Bacchides fled, ¹³each one leaving his place and returning to his own country. ¹⁴Only in Bethzur did some remain who had forsaken the law of Moses and the commandments, for this was a place of refuge for them.

¹⁵King Alexander heard of the promises that Demetrius had made to Jonathan. He was told of the battles fought and the brave deeds done by Jonathan and his brothers, as well as the hardships they had endured. ¹⁶He said, "Could we ever find another man like this? We should make him our friend and our ally." ¹⁷So the king sent Jonathan a letter that read:

¹⁸"This letter is from King Alexander to his brother Jonathan. Greetings.

¹⁹"We have heard that you are a valiant warrior who is worthy to be our friend. ²⁰Therefore, today we make you high priest of your nation, and you will be one of the king's favored leaders and will promote our interests and keep our friendship."

Alexander also sent him a purple robe and a crown of gold.

²¹So in midautumn* of the one hundred sixtieth year of Greek rule, at the Festival of Shelters, Jonathan put on the holy vestments, and he recruited troops and heavily armed them.

A Letter from Demetrius Soter to Jonathan

²²When Demetrius heard about this, he was very distressed and said, ²³"What have we done that Alexander has thwarted our plans? He has gotten ahead of us and strengthened himself by gaining the friendship of the Jews. ²⁴I'll do the same thing; I'll send a letter of friendship to them and offer them honor and gifts so that they will help me." ²⁵So he sent this letter to them:

"This letter is from King Demetrius to the nation of the Jews. Greetings.

²⁶"We have heard that you have kept your agreement with us and have continued our friendship and have not sided with our enemies. This makes us glad. ²⁷Now continue to keep good faith with us, and we will richly reward you for all your efforts on our behalf. ²⁸We will grant you many privileges and give you many gifts.

²⁹"I now exempt you and all the Jews from all the tribute taxes. I also release you from the tax on salt and the crown taxes. ³⁰And from this day forward, I release you from paying the standard tax of one-third of all grain and half of all fruit that is harvested. I will not collect this from Judea* or from the three districts that were added to it from Samaria and Galilee from this day and forever. ³¹Jerusalem and its surrounding towns will be exempted from paying taxes on the tithes and revenues it receives. ³²I release my control of the citadel in Jerusalem and give it to the high priest so that he can station his own guards in it. ³³I am setting free, without ransom, every one of the Jews who has been brought captive from Judea into my kingdom, and all their taxes—even on their cattle—are remitted.

³⁴"I order that all festivals, Sabbaths, new moon celebrations, and appointed days, along with three days before and after each festival, are days of immunity and freedom for all the Jews in my kingdom. ³⁵On these days, no one will have authority to take anything from the Jews or harass them.

³⁶"Thirty thousand Jews will be allowed to enroll in the king's army; provisions will be provided for them as for all the king's troops. ³⁷Some of them will be

10:21 Greek *in the seventh month.* This month of the Hebrew lunar calendar occurred in September and October 152 B.C.
10:30 Greek *the land of Judah;* also in 10:33, 37.

assigned to the great fortresses of the king. Others will be given positions of trust within the kingdom. I will allow their officers and leaders to be chosen from their own ranks, and I will let them live according to their own laws, just as the king has commanded for those in Judea. 38The three districts that have been added to Judea from Samaria will be fully annexed, so that they may answer to only one authority—the high priest.

39"I give Ptolemais and its adjoining lands to the Temple in Jerusalem in order to meet the expenses of public worship. 40I grant 375 pounds* of silver annually from the king's treasury. 41All the additional funds that were denied in previous years will be given from now on for the upkeep of the Temple. 42In addition, my officials will no longer collect the tribute tax of 125 pounds* of silver from the income of the Temple; it will belong to the priests who minister there. 43If anyone flees into the Temple in Jerusalem or into its surrounding territory because of a debt owed to the king or anyone else, that person will be released from the debt and will receive back all property taken as collateral. 44The costs for rebuilding and restoring the Temple will be taken from the king's revenues. 45The king will also cover the cost of rebuilding the walls and fortifications of Jerusalem and the rest of Judea."

The Death of Demetrius Soter

46When Jonathan and the people heard this message, they did not believe it, because they remembered the tremendous harm that Demetrius had done to Israel and how much he had oppressed the people. 47They continued to side with Alexander, because he had been the first to offer them a peace treaty. So they remained his ally as long as he lived.

48King Alexander gathered a large army and moved his camp near the army of Demetrius. 49Then the armies of the two kings began to fight each other. The army of Demetrius fled, and Alexander's army pursued them and won the battle.* 50They continued to pursue them until sundown, and Demetrius was killed that day.

Alexander Marries Cleopatra

51Alexander sent ambassadors to Ptolemy Philometor, king of Egypt, with this message:

52"I have returned to my kingdom and regained the throne of my ancestors. I have secured my reign by defeating Demetrius. I have regained control of our country 53by destroying Demetrius and his army in battle, and now we have seized the throne of his kingdom. 54Therefore, let us make a mutual pact of friendship. Give me your daughter in marriage, and I will become your son-in-law. Then I will give you and your daughter gifts that are worthy of your position."

55King Ptolemy answered,

"It was a happy day when you returned to the land of your ancestors and regained the throne of their kingdom. 56Now I will do what you asked, but meet me at Ptolemais so that we may see one another. Then I will give you my daughter and become your father-in-law as you requested."

57So Ptolemy left Egypt with his daughter Cleopatra and came to Ptolemais in the one hundred sixty-second year of Greek rule.* 58King Alexander met him on friendly terms there, and Ptolemy gave Alexander his daughter Cleopatra in marriage. Ptolemy celebrated her marriage at Ptolemais with great and royal splendor.

59King Alexander wrote to Jonathan that he should come and meet him. 60So Jonathan went in stately ceremony to Ptolemais and met the two kings there. Jonathan gave them and their favored leaders silver, gold, and many other gifts and thereby gained their favor. 61Some ungodly troublemakers from Israel gathered together to bring accusations against him, but the king paid no attention to them. 62Alexander commanded that Jonathan should be clothed with a royal purple robe instead of his ordinary clothes, and it was done. 63Then the king gave him a seat of honor at his side. He said to his officers, "Escort Jonathan to the middle of the city and proclaim that no one is to bring charges against him for any reason, nor should anyone even annoy him." 64When Jonathan's accusers saw that he was being honored and that he was clothed in a royal purple robe, they all fled. 65So the king honored him and declared in writing that he was one of his most favored leaders, and he made

---

10:40 Greek 15,000 shekels [171 kilograms].   10:42 Greek 5,000 shekels [57 kilograms].   10:49 Some manuscripts read The army of Alexander fled, and Demetrius's army pursued them and won the battle.   10:57 The 162nd year of Greek rule was 150 B.C.

him general and governor of Judea.* ⁶⁶Then Jonathan returned to Jerusalem with a sense of peace and joy.

Demetrius II Nicator and Apollonius

⁶⁷In the one hundred sixty-fifth year of Greek rule,* Demetrius Nicator, the son of Demetrius Soter, came from Crete to the land of his ancestors. ⁶⁸When King Alexander heard about it, he was very troubled and returned to Antioch. ⁶⁹Demetrius appointed Apollonius governor of Coelesyria. Apollonius then gathered together a large army and set up camp outside Jamnia. He sent this message to Jonathan, the high priest:

⁷⁰"You are the only one who opposes us. People laugh at me and reproach me because of you. Why should you dominate us in the hill country? ⁷¹If you are so confident in your forces, come down and meet us on the plain. There we can test each other's strength, for I have the power of the cities behind me. ⁷²Ask and learn who I am and who my allies are, and you will find that you cannot stand up to us. After all, your relatives have already been put to flight twice in their own land. ⁷³You will not be able to defend yourselves against my horsemen and my army on the plain, where there are no rocks, or even pebbles, to hide behind or any place to which you can escape."

⁷⁴When Jonathan heard the message from Apollonius, he was stirred to action. He chose ten thousand men and marched out from Jerusalem, and his brother Simon met him to help him. ⁷⁵They set up camp outside Joppa, for the gates of the town had been closed because a garrison of Apollonius was in Joppa. When Jonathan's army began to attack it, ⁷⁶those in the town became terrified. So they opened the gates to him, and Jonathan captured Joppa. ⁷⁷When Apollonius heard about this, he assembled three thousand horsemen and a large army and marched to Azotus, as though he were going to pass through the area. But immediately he went out on to the plain because he had many horsemen he could rely on. ⁷⁸Jonathan pursued him to Azotus, and they fought there. ⁷⁹Apollonius had secretly left a thousand horsemen behind Jonathan's army. ⁸⁰Jonathan realized that there was an ambush behind him, for they surrounded his army and

shot arrows at his soldiers from morning until evening. ⁸¹But his men stood firm, as Jonathan had ordered them, while the enemy's horses grew tired.

⁸²Then Simon brought his army forward and attacked the enemy's ranks of foot soldiers, for their horsemen had become exhausted. He crushed the enemy, and they fled. ⁸³The horsemen scattered across the plain and fled to Azotus, where they took refuge in Beth-dagon, the temple of their idol. ⁸⁴But Jonathan set fire to Azotus and the surrounding towns. He carried away their possessions and burned down the temple of Dagon, along with all who had fled into it. ⁸⁵Almost eight thousand people were killed, whether by sword or by fire. ⁸⁶Then Jonathan moved his army and set up camp outside Ashkelon. The people came out of the town to greet him with great ceremony. ⁸⁷After this, Jonathan returned to Jerusalem with his people and a large amount of plunder.

⁸⁸When King Alexander heard about these deeds, he honored Jonathan even more. ⁸⁹He sent him a buckle of gold, a gift that is customarily given only to those whom the king regards as members of the royal family. He also gave Jonathan the town of Ekron and all its surrounding villages.

The Death of Ptolemy VI Philometor

11 Then King Ptolemy Philometor of Egypt gathered together an army as innumerable as the sands of the seashore, along with many ships. He planned to seize Alexander's kingdom by treachery and add it to his own kingdom. ²He marched into Syria with peaceful words, and the people opened the gates of their cities and greeted him. They did this because King Alexander had ordered them to welcome him, since Ptolemy was his father-in-law.

³As Ptolemy entered each town, he stationed a garrison of soldiers there. ⁴When he approached Azotus, the people showed him the ruins of the temple of Dagon, which Jonathan had destroyed by fire. They also showed him the town and its surroundings, which had been leveled, and the corpses lying about. Lining the road were the charred bodies of those whom Jonathan had burned in the battle, for the people had piled them along Ptolemy's route in heaps. ⁵They told King Ptolemy that Jonathan had done these things, for they wanted the king to dislike him. But the king said nothing. ⁶Jonathan met Ptolemy at Joppa with great

---

10:65 Greek lacks *of Judea.*   **10:67** The 165th year of Greek rule was 147 B.C.

ceremony, and they greeted one another and spent the night there. [7]Jonathan accompanied the king as far as the Eleutherus River; then he returned to Jerusalem.

[8]Continuing in his plot against Alexander, King Ptolemy gained control of the coastal cities, as far as Seleucia on the coast. [9]He sent ambassadors to King Demetrius to say, "Come, let us make a pact with each other. I will give you my daughter, who is now married to Alexander, and you will reign over your father's kingdom. [10]For I regret that I gave Alexander my daughter, since he has tried to kill me." [11]He accused Alexander because he coveted his kingdom. [12]So he took his daughter from Alexander and gave her to Demetrius, and it was now obvious that Ptolemy and Alexander were enemies. [13]Then Ptolemy Philometor entered Antioch and crowned himself king of Asia; so now he wore two crowns, that of Egypt and that of Asia.

[14]At this time King Alexander was in Cilicia because there was a rebellion there. [15]But when Alexander heard what had happened, he marched out to fight against Ptolemy, who met him with a strong force and routed Alexander's armies. [16]Alexander fled to Arabia to seek protection. King Ptolemy's triumph was complete [17]when Zabdiel the Arab cut off Alexander's head and sent it back to Ptolemy. [18]However, King Ptolemy died three days later, and his troops in each of the strongholds were killed by the local residents. [19]As a result, Demetrius Nicator became king in the one hundred sixty-seventh year of Greek rule.*

Peace between Demetrius Nicator and Jonathan

[20]In those days Jonathan gathered forces from Judea to seize the citadel in Jerusalem. They built many war machines to besiege it. [21]But some renegades who hated their own nation went to King Demetrius Nicator and told him that Jonathan was attacking the citadel. [22]When Demetrius heard this, he was angry and set out at once for Ptolemais. He wrote to Jonathan, demanding that he end the siege and meet him for a conference in Ptolemais as soon as possible. [23]When Jonathan heard this, he ordered the siege to continue. Then, despite the danger, he set out with some of the priests and elders of Israel. [24]He took gold, silver, rich garments, and many other presents and went to meet the king at Ptolemais, and there he won the king's favor. [25]Even though certain renegades of his nation made complaints against Jonathan, [26]the king treated him as his predecessors had done, and he exalted Jonathan in the sight of all his favored leaders. [27]The king confirmed Jonathan's position as high priest and all his previous distinctions, and he declared him to be one of his most favored leaders.

[28]Jonathan requested that the king exempt Judea and the three districts of Samaria from taxes, and he promised the king eleven tons of silver* in return. [29]The king consented and wrote this letter to Jonathan about all these things:

[30]"This letter is from King Demetrius to his brother Jonathan and to the nation of the Jews. Greetings.

[31]"This is a copy of a letter I am sending to our relative Lasthenes concerning you. I am sending it so that you might know the contents of the letter.

[32]"This letter is from King Demetrius to his esteemed relative* Lasthenes. Greetings.

[33]"We are determined to do good to the nation of the Jews, for they show their goodwill toward us by being our friends and keeping their agreements with us. [34]We have confirmed that they possess all the territory of Judea and the three districts of Aphairema, Lydda, and Ramathaim,* which were taken from Samaria and added to Judea. For all who offer sacrifices in Jerusalem, we have granted freedom from the annual royal tax and from taxes on their crops and fruit. [35]From this moment on, we release them from taxes on tithes, the tax on salt, and the crown tax. [36]Not a single one of these exemptions will ever be revoked. [37]See that you make a copy of these instructions and give it to Jonathan. Then post this where people can see it on the holy mountain of Zion.'"

Jonathan Rescues Demetrius Nicator

[38]King Demetrius Nicator saw that peace reigned throughout the land and that no one resisted him, so he dismissed all his troops, sending each to his own home. He retained the foreign soldiers, however, whom he had recruited from Gentile islands. As a result, he

---

11:19 The 167th year of Greek rule was 145 B.C.   11:28 Or *11 tons of gold;* Greek reads *300 talents* [10.2 metric tons].   11:32 Greek *his father.*   11:34 Greek *Rathamin,* a variant name for Ramathaim.

was hated by all the dismissed troops, who had served under his predecessors.

³⁹There was a man named Trypho, who had been one of Alexander's supporters. When he saw that all the dismissed troops were grumbling against Demetrius, he went to Imalkue the Arab, who was raising Antiochus, Alexander's young son. ⁴⁰Trypho urged the Arab to let him take Antiochus and make him king in his father's place. Trypho related to him all that Demetrius had done and how his soldiers hated him. Trypho remained there for many days.

⁴¹Meanwhile, Jonathan sent word to King Demetrius, asking him to remove the soldiers from the citadel at Jerusalem and from the strongholds, because they were constantly fighting against the Israelites. ⁴²Demetrius sent this message back to Jonathan: "I will gladly do this for you and your people, and I will also greatly honor you and your nation when the opportunity arises. ⁴³Therefore, please help yourself and me by sending some of your men to support me, because my troops have revolted." ⁴⁴So Jonathan sent 3,000 seasoned troops to him at Antioch, and the king was glad at their arrival.

⁴⁵Then 120,000 people of the city gathered together to kill the king, ⁴⁶but he fled into his palace. The people seized control of the streets and began to fight, ⁴⁷so the king called the Jewish troops to his aid. They rallied to assist him and spread out through the city. They killed about 100,000 people that day ⁴⁸and set fire to the city. They also seized a large amount of plunder and saved the king's life. ⁴⁹When the citizens saw that the Jews controlled the city and could do as they pleased, their courage failed, and they cried to the king. They begged him, ⁵⁰"Grant us peace, and make the Jews stop attacking us and our city." ⁵¹Then the citizens threw down their arms and made peace. So the Jews were honored by the king and all the people of his kingdom, and they returned to Jerusalem with a large amount of plunder. ⁵²But when King Demetrius's rule was secure and the land was peaceful under his government, ⁵³he broke his promises and alienated himself to Jonathan. Instead of repaying Jonathan for the favors he had been given, the king caused him much trouble.

Jonathan Opposes Demetrius Nicator

⁵⁴After this, Trypho returned with Antiochus, Alexander's young son, who was then crowned

11:59 Greek *the Ladder of Tyre.*

as king. ⁵⁵All the troops that Demetrius had dismissed joined Antiochus's forces and fought against Demetrius, who was routed. ⁵⁶Trypho captured the elephants and gained control of Antioch.

⁵⁷Then young Antiochus wrote to Jonathan, saying, "I confirm your position as high priest. I appoint you as ruler over the four districts and confirm you as one of the king's favored leaders." ⁵⁸He sent him a gold plate from his table service and gave him permission to drink from a gold cup and to be clothed in purple and wear a gold buckle. ⁵⁹Antiochus appointed Jonathan's brother Simon to be governor from the borders of Tyre* to the borders of Egypt.

⁶⁰Jonathan left and visited cities west of the Euphrates River, and all the armies of Syria joined forces with him. When he came to Ashkelon, the people came out to honor him. ⁶¹He went from there to Gaza, where he was denied admission, so he attacked it and burned its surrounding towns and carried away their possessions. ⁶²The people of Gaza pleaded with Jonathan, and he made peace with them. But he took the sons of their rulers as hostages and sent them to Jerusalem. Then he continued northward as far as Damascus.

⁶³Jonathan heard that the officers of Demetrius had come to Kadesh in Galilee with a large army, intending to remove him from power. ⁶⁴Jonathan went to fight them, leaving his brother Simon in Judea. ⁶⁵Simon set up camp outside Beth-zur, surrounded it, and besieged it for many days. ⁶⁶The people asked for terms of peace, and he granted them. But he removed the people from the town, took control of it, and placed a garrison in it.

⁶⁷Jonathan and his army set up camp by the Sea of Galilee. Early in the morning they marched on to the plain of Hazor. ⁶⁸The army of foreigners hid a contingent of soldiers in the mountains. Then they met Jonathan's army face to face on the plain. ⁶⁹When the soldiers in the mountains came out of hiding and joined the battle, ⁷⁰everyone on Jonathan's side fled. The only ones who remained were Mattathias son of Absalom and Judas son of Chalphi, commanders of the army. ⁷¹Jonathan tore his clothes in grief and put dust upon his head and prayed. ⁷²Then he returned to the battle and sent the enemy running.

⁷³When Jonathan's soldiers who were fleeing saw this, they returned to the battle to help him, and together they chased the enemy all the way to the enemy camp at Kadesh. There

Jonathan and his men set up their camp as well. [74]That day about three thousand enemy soldiers were killed. Then Jonathan returned to Jerusalem.

Jonathan's Relations with Rome and Sparta

12 Jonathan saw that the time was right to confirm his friendship with the Romans, so he chose certain men and sent them to Rome with this mission. [2]He also sent letters to the Spartans and to other places for the same purpose.

[3]When the men arrived in Rome, they entered the senate chamber and said, "Jonathan the high priest and the Jewish nation have sent us to renew our former friendship and alliance." [4]So the Romans provided these men with letters addressed to the authorities of each place, instructing them to provide safe conduct for them as they made their way back to Judea.*

[5]This is a copy of the letter Jonathan wrote to the Spartans:

[6]"This letter is from Jonathan the high priest, the high council,* the priests, and the rest of the Jewish people. It is addressed to our brothers the Spartans. Greetings.

[7]"Long ago your king Arius* sent a letter to our high priest Onias, stating that you are our brothers, as the attached copy shows. [8]Onias received your ambassador with honor and accepted the letter, which declared our alliance and friendship. [9]We do not need such alliances, since we find encouragement in our sacred books. [10]Nevertheless, we have chosen to renew our family ties and friendship with you so that we don't become strangers to you, for a long time has passed since you wrote to us. [11]We think of you on every special occasion. At our festivals and on other special days we remember you as we offer sacrifices and prayers, for it is fitting to remember brothers at these times. [12]We rejoice at your fame.

[13]"We have had many troubles and wars on every side because the neighboring kings have attacked us. [14]We did not want to trouble you or our allies and friends during these wars, [15]for our help comes from God.* We have been rescued from our enemies, and they have been humbled. [16]Nevertheless, we have selected Numenius son of Antiochus and Antipater son of Jason and have sent them to Rome to renew our former friendship and alliance with the Romans. [17]We have also instructed them to visit you and bring our greetings and to give you this letter concerning the renewal of our family ties. [18]We will be grateful for your response to it."

[19]Following is a copy of the letter the Spartans* had previously sent to Onias:

[20]"This letter is from Arius, king of the Spartans, to Onias the high priest. Greetings.

[21]"We have discovered a document that states that the Spartans and the Jews are brothers and that they are all descendants of Abraham. [22]Now that we have learned this, write to us and let us know how you are doing. [23]For our part, we declare to you that what is yours—your cattle and your possessions—is ours, and what is ours is yours. This is what we have ordered our envoys to report to you."

Demetrius Nicator Encounters Jonathan

[24]Jonathan then heard that Demetrius's commanders had returned with an even larger army than before to wage war against him. [25]So Jonathan marched out from Jerusalem and met them in the region of Hamath, for he did not want to give them a chance to invade his own country. [26]He sent scouts into their camp, who returned and reported that the enemy was preparing to attack that night. [27]When the sun set, Jonathan commanded his men to be on guard all night and to keep their weapons at hand, and he posted sentries around the camp. [28]When the enemy learned that Jonathan and his men were ready for battle, they were filled with dread. They lit fires in their camp and then retreated. [29]But Jonathan and his army did not know until morning that the enemy had retreated, because they had seen their campfires burning. [30]Jonathan chased them but did not catch them because they had crossed the Eleutherus River. [31]Jonathan then went after the Arabs called Zabadeans. He defeated them and carried away their possessions. [32]He marched on and came to Damascus and passed through all that country.

[33]Simon also marched out and went as far as

12:4 Greek *to the land of Judah*; also in 12:46, 52.   12:6 Greek *the senate of the nation*.   12:7 As in Latin Vulgate (see also 12:20); Greek reads *Darius*.   12:15 Greek *from heaven*.   12:19 Greek *they*.

Ashkelon and the neighboring fortresses. Then he turned to Joppa and took possession of it, ³⁴for he heard that the people were planning to hand their stronghold over to the supporters of Demetrius. Simon then stationed a garrison there to guard it.

³⁵When Jonathan returned, he officially called together the high council* and made plans with them to build fortresses in Judea. ³⁶They planned to heighten the walls of Jerusalem and erect a barrier to separate the citadel from the city, so that the soldiers in the citadel could neither buy nor sell. ³⁷So the people worked together to rebuild the city. They repaired a collapsed section of the wall that bordered the Kidron Valley on the east side of the city. Jonathan also repaired the section called Chaphenatha. ³⁸Simon built Adida in the western foothills*; he fortified it and erected gates that locked with bars.

Jonathan Is Deceived and Captured

³⁹Trypho was determined to make himself king of Asia and to assume the crown and overthrow King Antiochus. ⁴⁰But he was afraid that Jonathan would prevent him and fight against him, so he marched out to Beth-shan looking for some way to capture Jonathan and kill him.

⁴¹Jonathan went with forty thousand select troops to meet Trypho in battle at Beth-shan. ⁴²When Trypho saw that Jonathan had come with a large army, he was afraid to fight against him. ⁴³So he received him with honor, commended him to all his favored leaders, and gave him presents. Trypho ordered his favored leaders and his troops to obey him as they would himself. ⁴⁴He said to Jonathan, "Why have you troubled all these people when you and I are not at war? ⁴⁵Choose a few men to stay with you and send the rest home, and then come with me to Ptolemais. I will give you that city and the rest of the fortresses, along with their garrisons and officials. Then I will go home, for that is why I came here."

⁴⁶Jonathan believed him and did as he had suggested. He sent most of his army back to Judea, ⁴⁷keeping three thousand men with him. Then he sent two thousand of them into Galilee and kept only one thousand for himself. ⁴⁸But as soon as Jonathan entered Ptolemais, the people of the city shut the gates and captured him; then they killed everyone who had entered with him.

⁴⁹Trypho dispatched foot soldiers and horsemen to Galilee and the great plain of Esdraelon to destroy all of Jonathan's soldiers. ⁵⁰After Jonathan's soldiers concluded that Jonathan and his troops had been captured and killed, they encouraged one another and marched in close formation, ready for battle. ⁵¹When Trypho's troops realized that Jonathan's men were ready to fight for their lives, they turned back. ⁵²So Jonathan's men returned safely to Judea. They mourned for Jonathan and those who died with him, and all Israel grieved deeply.

⁵³Then all the nations surrounding them sought to destroy them. They said, "Israel has no leader and no one to help them. Now is the time to fight against them and blot out all memory of them from the world."

Simon Becomes the New Leader

13 Simon heard that Trypho was assembling a very large army to invade Judea* and destroy it. ²Seeing that the people were trembling with fear, Simon went up to Jerusalem and assembled the people. ³He encouraged them, saying, "You know what great things my brothers and my father's family and I have done for the laws and the Temple. You know the wars we have waged and the hardships we have experienced. ⁴For this cause—for the sake of Israel—all my brothers have lost their lives, and I alone am left. ⁵Far be it from me to spare my own life in time of trouble, for I am no better than my brothers. ⁶Nevertheless, I will avenge my nation and the Temple and your wives and children, for all the Gentiles have gathered together in hatred to destroy us."

⁷The people were inspired once again when they heard these words. ⁸They cried out to Simon, "You are our leader in place of your brothers Judas and Jonathan. ⁹Lead us in battle, and we will obey your every word." ¹⁰So Simon assembled the army and hurried to complete the walls of Jerusalem, fortifying it on all sides. ¹¹He sent a large force to Joppa under the command of Jonathan son of Absalom, and they drove out the residents and remained there.

Trypho Kills Jonathan

¹²Trypho and his large army left Ptolemais to invade Judea, and they took Jonathan along under guard. ¹³Simon set up camp in Adida, facing the plain. ¹⁴When Trypho learned that Simon had taken the place of his brother Jonathan and was preparing to fight against him,

12:35 Greek *the elders of the people.*　　**12:38** Greek *in the Shephelah.*　　**13:1** Greek *the land of Judah;* also in 13:12.

he sent envoys to Simon with this message: [15]"We have detained your brother Jonathan for the money that he owed the king's treasury when he was managing the king's affairs in Judea. [16]Send 7,500 pounds* of silver and two of his sons as hostages, so that when he is set free, he will not revolt against us. Then we will release him."

[17]Although Simon did not believe that Trypho could be trusted, he ordered the money and the children to be sent. He did not want the people of Israel to hate him and say, [18]"Jonathan died because Simon did not send the money and the children." [19]So he sent the children and the 7,500 pounds of silver. But Trypho broke his word and did not release Jonathan.

[20]After this, Trypho entered the country to destroy it. His troops took a detour along the road that leads to Adora, but Simon and his army countered them wherever they went. [21]The soldiers in the citadel sent envoys to Trypho, asking him to hurry to them through the wilderness to bring them food. [22]So Trypho got all his horsemen ready to leave; but that night a very heavy snow fell, and he could not go. Instead he went into Gilead. [23]As he neared Baskama, he killed Jonathan and buried him there. [24]Then Trypho changed course and returned to his own country.

Jonathan Is Buried

[25]Simon sent for the remains of his brother Jonathan and buried him in Modein, the town of his ancestors. [26]All Israel wept loudly for him, and they mourned for him many days. [27]Over the tomb of his father and his brothers, Simon built a tall monument with polished stone at the front and back. [28]He also erected seven pyramids facing each other for his father, his mother, and his four brothers. [29]He surrounded these with an elaborate arrangement of large pillars, upon which he hung armor as an eternal memorial. Beside the armor he carved ships large enough to be visible to those at sea. [30]This tomb remains in Modein even to this day.

Demetrius Nicator Supports Simon

[31]Trypho conspired against young King Antiochus and killed him. [32]He became king in his place, assuming the crown of Asia, and brought great evils upon the kingdom. [33]But Simon strengthened the strongholds of Judea, fortifying them with high towers, massive walls, and gates locked with bars. He also stored food in the strongholds.

[34]Simon selected ambassadors and sent them to King Demetrius Nicator, hoping to gain relief from taxes for his nation, since Trypho had plundered the land. [35]King Demetrius answered this request with the following letter:

[36]"This letter is from King Demetrius to Simon, the high priest and favored leader of kings, and to the high council* and the Jewish nation. Greetings. [37]"We have received the gold crown and the palm branch that you sent. We are ready to establish a lasting peace with you and to write to our officials, instructing them to release you from the tribute tax. [38]All that was previously agreed upon remains in force, and the fortresses you have built are yours to keep. [39]We forgive any oversights or faults you have committed to this day, and we cancel the crown tax that you owe. If there are any other taxes in Jerusalem, they are now canceled. [40]If any of you are qualified to join the royal guard, you will be allowed to enroll. Let there be peace between us."

[41]In the one hundred seventieth year of Greek rule,* the yoke of the Gentiles was removed from Israel. [42]At that time the people of Israel began to date their documents and public records in this way: "In the first year of Simon the great high priest, the commander and leader of the Jews."

Simon Captures Gazara

[43]In those days Simon set up camp outside Gazara and surrounded it with troops. He constructed a siege machine and directed it against the town. He attacked one tower and captured it. [44]The soldiers inside the siege machine entered the town, creating a great uproar. [45]The men in the town, together with their wives and children, went up to the wall, tore their clothes, and cried out with a loud voice, asking Simon to grant them terms of peace. [46]They said, "Do not treat us as our evil deeds deserve but according to your mercy." [47]So Simon reached an agreement with them. He did not destroy them, but he expelled them from the town and purified the houses where there had been idols. Then he entered the town, singing hymns of

13:16 Greek *100 talents* [3,400 kilograms]; also in 13:19. 13:36 Greek *to the elders.* 13:41 The 170th year of Greek rule was 142 B.C.

praise. ⁴⁸Having cleansed the town of all impurity, Simon appointed people to live there who would observe the law of Moses. He also fortified the town and built a house for himself there.

Simon Captures the Citadel

⁴⁹Then Simon prevented those who were in the citadel at Jerusalem from going in and out and from buying and selling in the countryside. So they became very hungry, and many of them died from famine. ⁵⁰They begged Simon for terms of peace, which he granted. Then he expelled them from the citadel and cleansed it from impurity. ⁵¹On June 3* in the one hundred seventy-first year of Greek rule, the Jews entered the citadel with thanksgiving, waving palm branches and playing harps and cymbals and stringed instruments. They sang hymns and songs, because Israel's great enemy had finally been destroyed. ⁵²Simon decreed that this occasion should be celebrated every year with gladness. He strengthened the fortifications of the Temple hill near the citadel, and he and his men lived there.

⁵³Since Simon's son John had now reached manhood, Simon made him commander of all the armies. John kept his residence in Gazara.

Simon's Success

14 In the one hundred seventy-second year of Greek rule,* King Demetrius assembled his army and marched into Media. He was hoping to gain support for a war against Trypho. ²When Arsaces, king of Persia and Media, heard that Demetrius had invaded his territory, he sent one of his commanders to capture him alive and bring him to him. ³The commander defeated the army of Demetrius, captured him, and brought him to Arsaces, who kept him prisoner.

⁴ Judea was at rest as long as Simon ruled,
    for he sought the good of his nation.
  The people were pleased with his authority,
    with the honor he received throughout his days.
⁵ To crown his glory, he captured Joppa for a seaport
    and opened a gateway to the Mediterranean islands.
⁶ He extended the borders of his nation
    and gained control of all the land.

⁷ Simon captured many prisoners of war
    and ruled over Gazara, Beth-zur, and the citadel.
  He removed the impurities from the citadel;
    no one could stand against him.
⁸ The people farmed the land in peace.
  The land yielded its produce,
    and the trees of the plains bore fruit.
⁹ Old men sat in the squares and talked of good times,
    while the young men dressed in splendid military style.
¹⁰ Simon provided food for the towns
    and furnished them with fortresses for defense.
  His name became famous, even to the ends of the earth.
¹¹ He established peace in the land,
    and Israel experienced great joy.
¹² The people relaxed under their own vines and fig trees.
    and no one gave them reason to fear.
¹³ No enemy remained in the land to fight them;
    their kings were crushed in those days.
¹⁴ Simon strengthened the lowly
    and was zealous for the law of Moses.
  He did away with the ungodly and evildoers.
¹⁵ He made the sanctuary glorious
    and furnished it with new utensils.

Renewed Alliances with Sparta and Rome

¹⁶News of Jonathan's death reached as far as Rome and Sparta, and they were deeply grieved. ¹⁷They heard that his brother Simon had become high priest in his place and was ruling over the nation and the cities there. ¹⁸So they wrote to Simon on bronze tablets to renew the friendship and alliance they had made with his brothers Judas and Jonathan. ¹⁹The letter from the Spartans was presented to the high council* in Jerusalem. It read as follows:

²⁰"This letter is from the rulers and the people of Sparta to the high priest Simon, the high council,* the priests, and the rest of the Jewish people, our brothers and sisters. Greetings. ²¹"The ambassadors you sent to us have told us of your glory and honor, and we have enjoyed their visit. ²²We have

---

13:51 Greek *On the twenty-third day of the second month,* of the Hebrew lunar calendar. This event occurred on June 3, 141 B.C.
14:1 The 172nd year of Greek rule was 140 B.C.   **14:19** Greek *the assembly.*   **14:20** Greek *the elders.*

recorded their message in our public archives as follows: 'Numenius son of Antiochus and Antipater son of Jason, ambassadors of the Jews, have come to us to renew their friendship with us. ²³Our people were pleased to receive the men with honor and to put a copy of their message in the public archives as a record for the Spartan people. We have also sent a copy of their message to Simon the high priest.'"

²⁴After this, Simon confirmed the alliance with the Romans by sending Numenius to Rome with a large gold shield weighing 1,250 pounds.*

²⁵When the people of Israel* heard about all this, they said, "How can we thank Simon and his sons? ²⁶For he and his brothers and his father's family have stood firm; they have repelled the enemies of Israel and established freedom for the nation." ²⁷So they made an inscription on bronze tablets and mounted them on pillars on Mount Zion. This is a copy of what they wrote:

"On September 13* in the one hundred seventy-second year of Greek rule, which is the third year of Simon the great high priest, ²⁸in Asaramel,* the following proclamations were made in the high council of the priests, the people, the rulers of the nation, and the elders of the country:

²⁹"'Because of the constant warfare in our country, Simon and his brothers, sons of Mattathias, a priest in the line of Joarib, have become great leaders among us. They have put themselves in danger and resisted the enemies of their nation in order to preserve the Temple and the law of Moses. They have brought great glory to their nation.

³⁰"'Jonathan rallied his nation together and became the high priest; now he is dead. ³¹When the enemies of Israel decided to invade the country and capture the Temple, ³²Simon came forward to fight for his nation. He spent much of his own money to arm the soldiers of his nation and pay them wages. ³³He fortified the towns of Judea, including Beth-zur, which lies on the border of Judea. At one time, the weapons of the enemies were stored there, but he defeated the enemy troops and replaced them with a garrison of Jews. ³⁴Simon fortified the coastal town of Joppa and also Gazara, which borders upon Azotus, where the enemy formerly lived. He settled Jews there and furnished those towns with everything needed to restore them.

³⁵"'When the people saw Simon's faithfulness and his determination to win glory for his nation, they made him their leader and high priest. They did this in return for all the things he had done and because of the justice and loyalty he showed his nation. In every way he sought to enhance his people's power.

³⁶"'During Simon's reign, the country prospered under his guidance. He drove the Gentiles from the land, and he also drove them from the City of David in Jerusalem. From this citadel they had gone out to defile the Temple, ruining its purity. ³⁷But Simon settled Jews in the citadel and fortified it for the safety of the country and the city. He also heightened the walls of Jerusalem.

³⁸"'Because of these things, King Demetrius confirmed Simon's position as high priest, ³⁹made him one of his favored leaders, and granted him great honor. ⁴⁰For Demetrius had heard that the Romans regarded the Jews as their friends, military allies, and brothers, and that the Romans had received Simon's ambassadors with honor.

⁴¹"'The Jews and their priests have decided that Simon should remain their leader and high priest until a true prophet should arise. ⁴²Simon should be their governor and take charge of the Temple. He should appoint officials over the Temple duties and over the country, the weapons, and the fortresses. ⁴³He should be obeyed by all, and all official documents in the country should be made in his name. And he should be clothed with purple and wear gold.

⁴⁴"'None of the people or priests may nullify any of these decisions, nor may they oppose Simon's orders. They may not gather an assembly in the country without his permission, nor may they be clothed in

14:24 Greek *1,000 minas* [570 kilograms].   **14:25** Greek lacks *of Israel.*   **14:27** Greek *On the eighteenth day of Elul,* of the Hebrew lunar calendar. This event occurred on September 13, 140 B.C.   **14:28** *In Asaramel* resembles the Hebrew words for "the prince of the people of God."

purple or wear a gold buckle. [45]Whoever violates or rejects any of these decisions will be liable to punishment.'"

[46]All the people agreed to allow Simon to act in accordance with these decisions. [47]Simon accepted this and agreed to be high priest, commander, and leader of the Jews and priests, and to exercise supreme authority over them all. [48]The people ordered that this proclamation be engraved on bronze tablets and set up where people could see it in the Temple area. [49]They also ordered that copies be deposited in the treasury so that Simon and his sons could access them.

A Letter from Antiochus VII Sidetes

15 Antiochus Sidetes,* the son of King Demetrius Soter, sent a letter from the Mediterranean islands to Simon, the priest and leader of the Jews, and to all the people. [2]The letter read as follows:

"This letter is from King Antiochus to Simon, high priest and leader, and to the Jewish nation. Greetings.

[3]"Certain rebels have seized control of the kingdom of our ancestors, but I intend to reclaim it and restore it to its former state. I have recruited a large army of foreign troops and have built warships, [4]and I plan to arrive in my country and take revenge on those who have destroyed our country and devastated many cities in my kingdom. [5]Therefore, I confirm all tax exemptions that the kings before me granted you, along with any other promises of release from payments. [6]I give you permission to mint your own coins in your country. [7]I declare Jerusalem and the Temple to be free. All the weapons you have made and the fortresses you have built and occupy are to remain yours. [8]Any debts owed to the king, including future obligations, are canceled from this moment and for all time. [9]When we regain control of our kingdom, we will highly honor you, your nation, and your Temple, so that your glory may be known throughout the world."

[10]In the one hundred seventy-fourth year of Greek rule,* Antiochus Sidetes entered the land of his ancestors. All the troops rallied to his support so that only a few people supported Trypho. [11]King Antiochus pursued him, and Trypho fled to the coastal town of Dor. [12]Antiochus realized that Trypho* was in deep trouble and that his troops had deserted him, [13]so Antiochus set up camp near Dor with 120,000 soldiers and 8,000 horsemen. [14]He surrounded the town, and his ships took up positions offshore. Antiochus shut off the town by land and sea so that no one could go in or out.

Alliance with Rome Proclaimed

[15]Meanwhile, Numenius and his companions arrived from Rome with letters to various kings and countries. The letters read as follows:

[16]"This letter is from Lucius, consul of the Romans, to King Ptolemy Physcon. Greetings.

[17]"Ambassadors of the Jews have come to us as friends and allies, and they wanted to renew our former friendship and alliance. They had been sent by the high priest Simon and by the Jewish people. [18]They also brought a gold shield weighing 1,250 pounds.* [19]Therefore, we have decided without hesitation to send these instructions to many kings and countries: Do not harm the Jews or attack their cities or their land. Do not make alliances with anyone who wages war against the Jews. [20]As a token of our friendship, we have decided to accept the shield from them. [21]Therefore, if any troublemakers have fled to you from Judea,* return them to the high priest Simon, so that he may punish them according to their law."

[22]This same message was sent to King Demetrius, Attalus, Ariarathes, and Arsaces [23]and to all the countries, including Sampsames, Sparta, Delos, Myndos, Sicyon, Caria, Samos, Pamphylia, Lycia, Halicarnassus, Rhodes, Phaselis, Cos, Side, Aradus, Gortyna, Cnidus, Cyprus, and Cyrene. [24]A copy of the letter was also sent to Simon the high priest.

Antiochus Sidetes Becomes Simon's Enemy

[25]King Antiochus Sidetes continued in his siege of Dor, assaulting it continually and building war machines to use against it. He

---

15:1 Antiochus VII Sidetes was the son of Demetrius I Soter and the brother of Demetrius II Nicator.   15:10 The 174th year of Greek rule was 138 B.C.   15:12 Or *Trypho realized that Antiochus;* Greek reads *He realized that he.*   15:18 Greek *1,000 minas* [570 kilograms].   15:21 Greek *from their country.*

trapped Trypho inside, and he could not escape. [26]Simon sent Antiochus two thousand select troops to help him, along with silver, gold, and a large amount of military equipment. [27]But Antiochus refused to receive them. Instead, he renounced all agreements he had made with Simon and alienated himself from him. [28]He sent Athenobius, one of his favored leaders, to meet with Simon and say, "You are occupying Joppa, Gazara, and the citadel in Jerusalem, which are cities of my kingdom. [29]You have devasted their territories, inflicted great damage on the land, and taken control of many places in my kingdom. [30]Therefore, give back the cities you have taken and the tribute taxes from the places you control beyond the borders of Judea. [31]Otherwise, give me nineteen tons* of silver for the destruction that you have caused, along with nineteen tons more to reimburse me for the tribute taxes of the cities. If you fail to do this, we will come and attack you."

[32]So Athenobius, the king's favored leader, came to Jerusalem. He was astonished when he saw Simon's splendor—his cabinet with the gold and silver plate and his great magnificence. Then he delivered the king's message.

[33]Simon responded, "We have not taken anyone else's land or property. Rather, we have taken what is the inheritance of our ancestors, which had been unjustly occupied by our enemies. [34]Now that we have the opportunity, we are merely recovering this inheritance. [35]Joppa and Gazara inflicted great harm on our people and our land, but we will give you 7,500 pounds of silver* for them."

[36]Athenobius did not answer a single word in reply. He returned angrily to the king with this message and told him about Simon's great splendor. The king was enraged.

Cendebeus Troubles Judea

[37]Meanwhile, Trypho escaped by ship to Orthosia. [38]The king appointed Cendebeus commander of the coastal areas and gave him an army of foot soldiers and horsemen. [39]The king ordered him to set up camp outside Judea. He ordered him to build up Kedron, to fortify its gates, and to attack the Jews. But the king himself pursued Trypho.

[40]So Cendebeus came to Jamnia and began to harass the people by raiding Judea, taking prisoners, and then killing them. [41]He built up Kedron and stationed horsemen and foot soldiers there so that they might make raids along the highways of Judea, as the king had commanded him.

Simon's Sons Defeat Cendebeus

16 Simon's son John came up from Gazara and told his father what Cendebeus had done. [2]Simon called for his two eldest sons, Judas and John, and said to them, "My brothers and my father's family and I have spent our whole lives fighting Israel's battles. Things have gone well under our leadership, for we have rescued Israel many times. [3]Now I am old, but by God's grace* you have matured to manhood. You must replace me and my brother and continue fighting for our nation. May God* help you."

[4]John chose twenty thousand soldiers and horsemen from Judea, and they marched out to fight Cendebeus. They camped for the night in Modein. [5]Then they got up early in the morning and moved out on to the plain, where they faced a large army of foot soldiers and horsemen. A stream separated the two armies. [6]As John and his troops lined up against the enemy, he saw that his troops were afraid to cross the stream. So he went over first. When his men saw him lead the way, they crossed over behind him. [7]John divided his army, positioning the horsemen in the center of the foot soldiers, for the enemy also had a large cavalry. [8]John's men sounded the trumpets and attacked, and Cendebeus and his army fled. Many of the enemy were wounded and fell, and the rest fled into the fortress. [9]At the same time, John's brother Judas was wounded, but John chased the enemy as far as Kedron, which Cendebeus had built up. [10]Some also fled into the towers in the fields of Azotus, but John burned these down. About two thousand enemy soldiers were killed, and John returned safely to Judea.

Simon's Tragic Death

[11]Ptolemy son of Abubus had been appointed governor over the plain of Jericho. He had a large amount of silver and gold, [12]for he was a son-in-law of Simon the high priest. [13]He became overly ambitious and wanted to gain control of the whole country. So he plotted against Simon and his sons to get rid of them by treachery.

[14]As Simon was going through the towns of Judea and attending to their needs, he and

---

15:31 Greek *500 talents* [17 metric tons]; also in 15:31b.   15:35 Greek *100 talents* [3,400 kilograms].   16:3a Greek *by heaven's mercy.*   16:3b Greek *May heaven.*

his sons Mattathias and Judas went down to Jericho in late winter* of the one hundred seventy-seventh year of Greek rule. ¹⁵At Dok, a small fortress he had built, Ptolemy* welcomed them with a deceptive display of friendliness. He invited them to a great banquet, but he hid his men in the fortress. ¹⁶When Simon and his sons were drunk, Ptolemy and his men jumped up, grabbed their weapons, and rushed into the banquet hall, killing Simon and his two sons and some of his servants. ¹⁷In this way, Ptolemy committed an act of great treachery, repaying evil for good.

Simon's Son John Becomes the New Leader

¹⁸Ptolemy wrote a report of his actions and sent it to King Antiochus Sidetes, asking him to send soldiers to help him. He also asked the king to place the towns and the country under his authority. ¹⁹Ptolemy also sent soldiers to Gazara to kill Simon's son John, and he sent letters to the army officers, asking them to come to him so he could give them silver and gold and gifts. ²⁰He sent other soldiers to capture Jerusalem and the Temple mount as well.

²¹But someone ran ahead to Gazara and told John that his father and his brothers were dead and that Ptolemy had sent men to kill him, too. ²²When John heard this, he was astounded. He captured the men that came to kill him, and he killed them instead, for he knew their intentions.

²³The rest of John's deeds, his battles, his brave accomplishments, his rebuilding of the walls, and his achievements, ²⁴are all recorded in the history of his high priesthood, beginning from the time he succeeded his father as high priest.

16:14 Greek *in the eleventh month, which is the month of Shebat.* This month of the Hebrew lunar calendar occurred in February 134 B.C.   16:15 Greek *the son of Abubus; see 16:11.*

2 Maccabees

THE BOOK OF 2 MACCABEES gives an overview and explanation of the Jewish struggle for independence during the turbulent era of the Seleucids and Ptolemies of the divided Greek Empire. In refined rhetorical style, the book of 2 Maccabees begins its account at the time of Seleucus IV (187–175 BC) and chronicles the events leading up to the Maccabean revolt. It describes various Jewish factions at the time and the efforts of Antiochus IV Epiphanes (175–164 BC) to abolish Judaism throughout Israel. The book then recounts the exploits of Judas Maccabeus, ending the account after his defeat of Nicanor in 161 BC. The entire span of the period covered by the book is approximately sixteen years. Unlike 1 Maccabees, this book attempts to give theological perspective to the deeds of the Jewish patriots.

■ **Author:** Unknown

■ **Date Written:** Around 100 BC, recording events that occurred around 180 to 164 BC

■ **Purpose:** To encourage Jews to remain faithful to the laws of Moses by noting God's marvelous interventions in the lives of those who honour him and seek to do his will

■ **Themes:** God's sovereignty and power; the importance of godly leadership; courage and faith in the face of evil

■ **Outline**
1:1–2:33 Letters to Jews and preface
3:1–39 Simon betrays his country
4:1–7:42 The Temple desecrated
8:1–9:8 Purification of the Temple
10:9–15:39 More persecution

First Letter to the Jews in Egypt

1 "This letter is from the Jews in Jerusalem and Judea to their fellow Jews in Egypt. Greetings and true peace to you.

2"May God be good to you and remember the covenant he made with Abraham, Isaac, and Jacob, his faithful servants. 3May God give you a desire to worship him and to do his will with a loving heart and a generous spirit. 4May he open your heart to his law and his commandments, and may he grant you peace. 5May he hear your prayers and be reconciled to you, and may he never forsake you in the time of evil. 6We are now praying for you here.

7"When Demetrius Nicator reigned in the one hundred sixty-ninth year of Greek rule,* we wrote to you of the trouble and intense conflict we experienced in the years after Jason defected from the holy land and from the kingdom. 8He burned the Temple gate and killed innocent people. So we prayed to the Lord, and our prayers were answered. We offered sacrifices and fine flour, and we lit the lamps and set the Bread of the Presence on the table. 9We are writing to remind you to commemorate this event by celebrating a second Festival of Shelters each year in the month of Kislev.*

"This letter was written in the one hundred eighty-eighth year of Greek rule.*"

Second Letter to the Jews

10"This letter is from the people of Jerusalem and Judea, from the high council,* and from Judas. It is written to

---

1:7 The dates in 2 Maccabees are calculated from 312 B.C., the year Seleucus I Nicator began his reign over a territory that included the land of Israel. The 169th year of Greek rule was 143 B.C.   **1:9a** The Festival of Shelters was held two months earlier, in the 7th month (see Lev 23:33-36). The reference here is to the Festival of Dedication, also known as the Festival of Lights, or Hanukkah. The Hebrew month Kislev occurs within our months of November and December; also in 1:18.   **1:9b** The 188th year of Greek rule was 124 B.C.   **1:10** Greek *the senate.*

Aristobulus, a member of the family of anointed priests and a teacher of King Ptolemy Physcon. This letter is also written to the Jews in Egypt. Greetings and good health to you.

11"Having been rescued by God from dangerous times, we give him great thanks for championing our cause against the king. 12God was the one who drove out those who fought against the holy city. 13When their leader, Antiochus, was in Persia with what seemed to be an invincible army, he and his men were killed in the temple of the goddess Nanea, for he was deceived by her priests. 14Hoping to secure large sums of money as a dowry, Antiochus led everyone to believe that he was going to marry Nanea. When he and his men arrived in Persia 15and the priests of Nanea set out the treasure, Antiochus and a few men entered the interior of the temple. The priests closed the door, trapping them inside. 16Then, opening a secret trapdoor in the ceiling, the priests threw stones down on Antiochus and his men, killing them. The priests then dismembered them, cutting off their heads and throwing the body parts outside. 17May God, who has judged the wicked, be blessed in all things!

18"Therefore, since we will be commemorating the purification of the Temple on the twenty-fifth day of the month of Kislev, we thought we should remind you also to celebrate this second Festival of Shelters, which also commemorates the day when the fire was given to Nehemiah to offer sacrifices. This fire was given to Nehemiah after he rebuilt the Temple and the altar.

19"When our ancestors were taken captive into Persia, the devout priests at that time secretly took the live coals from the altar and hid them deep in a dry cistern. There they kept the holy fire safe in a place unknown to anyone. 20When many years had passed, it pleased God to send Nehemiah back to Israel by order of the king of Persia. Nehemiah sent some of the descendants of those priests who had previously hidden the fire to look for it. They reported that they found no fire but instead found a thick liquid in the cistern. Nehemiah told them to draw it up and bring it to him. 21Then he commanded the priests to pour this liquid over the wood and sacrifices placed on the wood. 22This was done and sometime later, when the sun came out from behind a cloud, and a great fire broke out on the altar. Everyone was amazed, 23and all the priests and the people prayed while the sacrifice was burning. Jonathan took the lead, and the others joined Nehemiah in a response.

24"Their prayer went like this: 'O Lord, Lord God, Creator of all things, you are awesome and strong, just and merciful. You alone are king, and you are kind; 25you alone are gracious; you alone are just and almighty and eternal. It was you who saved Israel from all evil and chose our ancestors, setting them apart. 26Accept this sacrifice for all your people Israel, and preserve your own inheritance and make it holy. 27Gather together our scattered people. Free those who are slaves to the Gentiles. Look favorably on those who are despised and rejected, and let the Gentiles know that you are our God. 28Torment our insolent oppressors. 29Firmly plant your people in your Holy Place, as Moses said.*'

30"Then the priests sang hymns. 31When the sacrifice was fully burned, Nehemiah ordered the remaining liquid to be poured over large stones. 32When this was done, flames burst forth on them, but the light that blazed from the altar was even brighter.

33"This became a well-known event. The king of Persia heard that a thick liquid had appeared in the place where the exiled priests had hidden the fire and that Nehemiah and those with him had used the liquid to burn the sacrifices. 34The king verified the matter and then enclosed the place, declaring it sacred. 35The king gained a great deal of revenue from the place, and he used this money to give gifts to people he favored. 36Nehemiah and his people called this liquid nephthar, which means 'purification,' but many call it naphtha.*

2 "The records show that it was Jeremiah the prophet who commanded those who went into captivity to hide some of the fire of the altar. 2He also ordered them not to forget the commandments of the Lord and warned them not to be deceived in their thinking when they saw the gold and

1:29 See Exod 15:17.   1:36 *Naphtha* is the Greek word for petroleum.

silver idols with their ornaments. ³With similar speeches he told them to keep the law of Moses in their hearts.

⁴"The same records tell us how God told the prophet to take the Tabernacle and the Ark with him until he came to the mountain where Moses had looked out over the land God had promised to give his people. ⁵When Jeremiah arrived there, he found an empty cave into which he carried the Tabernacle, the Ark, and the altar of incense. Then he blocked the entrance. ⁶Some of those who followed him wanted to mark the place, but they could not find it. ⁷When Jeremiah heard this, he rebuked them, saying, 'The place will be hidden until God gathers his people together again and shows them his mercy. ⁸Then the Lord will reveal these things, and the glory of the Lord will appear in a cloud, as in the days of Moses and again when Solomon prayed that the Temple* might be specially set apart for God.'

⁹"It is also recorded how Solomon in his wisdom offered sacrifices for the dedication and completion of the Temple. ¹⁰Just as Moses prayed to the Lord and fire came down from heaven and consumed the sacrifice, so also Solomon prayed and fire came down from heaven and consumed the sacrifice. ¹¹And Moses said, 'Because the sin offering was not eaten, it was consumed.'* ¹²Solomon also celebrated the dedication for eight days.

¹³"These same things were written in the records and in the memoirs of Nehemiah. It is recorded that Nehemiah established a library by collecting the books about the kings and the prophets, the writings of David, and the letters of the kings concerning offerings to fulfill vows. ¹⁴Likewise, Judas collected all the books that were lost in our war, and now they are in our possession. ¹⁵If you need these things, send someone to get them for you.

¹⁶"We are writing to you because we are about to celebrate the purification of the Temple, and we would like you to celebrate this same festival. ¹⁷It is God who has saved his people and returned to us our inheritance, our kingdom, our priesthood, and our holiness, ¹⁸as he promised in the law of Moses.* We trust that God will soon have mercy on us and

gather us together from every land under heaven to the Holy Place. For he has saved us from great dangers and purified the Temple."

Preface to the Story of the Maccabees

¹⁹This is the story of Judas Maccabeus and his brothers, including an account of the purification of the great Temple and the dedication of the altar. ²⁰This story recounts the wars against Antiochus Epiphanes and his son Eupator ²¹and the heavenly apparitions seen by those heroes who fought bravely for Judaism. These heroes, though few in number, took the whole land and routed the barbarian hordes. ²²They regained the Temple renowned in all the world, liberated the city, and restored the laws of Moses, which were nearly abolished. The Lord showed great kindness and mercy to them.

²³All these things were recorded in five books by Jason of Cyrene, but we will attempt to condense them into one. ²⁴There are so many statistics—a veritable flood of material—that anyone who wants to study the narratives of history has a difficult job. ²⁵Therefore, our goal has been to make it easy for those who simply wish to read about these things and to help the studious to memorize more easily. We want all who read these things to profit. ²⁶As for ourselves, this work of condensing the records is a difficult task, yes, one of hard work and loss of sleep, ²⁷much like it is for those who prepare a banquet and try to please others. Yet we willingly undertake this labor for the sake of many. ²⁸We leave to compilers the exact handling of every detail, intending here to outline a brief digest. ²⁹The contractor of a new house must take care of the whole building, while the painter is concerned only with its decoration. So I think it is with us. ³⁰It is the historian's duty to collect all that is known, to put the events in order, and to search out and discuss every detail. ³¹But one who makes a digest is allowed to pursue brevity of speech and avoid lengthy explanations. ³²So let us begin the narrative without adding any further comment, for it would be foolish to make a long preface and then cut short the story itself!

The Story of Heliodorus

3 In the days of Onias the high priest, the holy city of Jerusalem was at peace, and the laws of Moses were diligently observed, because Onias obeyed God and hated evil.

2:8 Greek *the place;* also in 2:18.   2:11 Lev 10:16-18.   2:18 See Exod 19:5-6.

²So even the kings honored the sanctuary and embellished the Temple with wonderful gifts. ³Even Seleucus, king of Asia, paid from his own revenues all the expenses connected with offering the sacrifices.

⁴But a man named Simon from the tribe of Benjamin* opposed the high priest because he disagreed about how the city markets should be administered. Simon had been appointed manager of the Temple. ⁵When he could not win his dispute with Onias, he went to Apollonius of Tarsus, who was governor of Coelesyria and Phoenicia. ⁶Simon told him that the treasury in Jerusalem was so full of wealth that it couldn't be counted. Since this money did not belong to the account set aside for the sacrifices, Simon suggested that this money be brought under the king's control.

⁷When Apollonius saw the king, he told him about this money. Then the king called Heliodorus, who was in charge of his affairs, and ordered him to bring it back to him. ⁸So Heliodorus immediately set out on his journey, under the guise of visiting the cities of Coelesyria and Phoenicia. But his real purpose was to fulfill the king's order.

⁹When Heliodorus came to Jerusalem, the high priest received him courteously. Heliodorus told him what he had heard about this large sum of money and asked if it was true. ¹⁰The high priest told him that there were sums deposited to provide for widows and orphans. ¹¹He also stated that the rest belonged to Hyrcanus son of Tobiah, a man of prominent position. Contrary to what the wicked Simon had reported, the total amount was fifteen tons of silver and seven and a half tons of gold.* ¹²The high priest said he could not touch these deposits, for they had been brought for safekeeping to the Temple—the holy and sacred place that is honored throughout the whole world. ¹³But because of the orders he had received from the king, Heliodorus said he had no choice but to take the money for the royal treasury. ¹⁴So he set a day and entered the treasury to take inventory.

The people throughout the city were very upset, ¹⁵and the priests, dressed in their special clothing, threw themselves face down before the altar. They called upon God in heaven, who had given the law concerning the deposits, asking him to preserve the money for those who had deposited it. ¹⁶Everyone who saw the high priest became heartbroken, for his face

showed the inward anguish of his soul. ¹⁷His body trembled with horror, making the sorrow in his heart clear to all who saw him. ¹⁸Many of the people hurried from their homes to join in corporate prayer because the sanctuary was about to be defiled. ¹⁹The women, dressed in sackcloth, gathered in the streets. The young women ran from their homes—some to the gates and some to the walls—while others peered out of windows. ²⁰All of them stretched their hands toward heaven in prayer. ²¹It was pitiful to see everyone lying face down in anguish and to see the high priest in his agony.

²²While the people were calling to the almighty Lord to keep the deposits safe and secure for those who had given them, ²³Heliodorus went on with his plan. ²⁴But as he arrived at the treasury with his guard, the Lord of all spirits and all authority caused such an awesome heavenly apparition that all who had boldly accompanied Heliodorus collapsed in terror, overwhelmed by God's power. ²⁵Before them appeared a horse splendidly decorated, and on the horse sat a fearsome rider clad in gold armor. The horse charged and reared fiercely, striking Heliodorus with its front hooves. ²⁶At the same time, two young men of amazing strength and striking beauty, dressed in magnificent clothing, appeared to Heliodorus. They stood on either side of him and whipped him continuously, striking him with blow after blow. ²⁷Heliodorus suddenly fell to the ground, overwhelmed by a deep darkness. His men came to his rescue. They picked him up, put him on a stretcher, ²⁸and carried him away. He had come into that treasury with a large retinue of servants and all his guard, but now he was carried away helpless. He had experienced the power of God. ²⁹Indeed, because of God's intervention, he lay speechless and without hope of recovery. ³⁰The people praised the Lord because he had marvelously honored his sanctuary. And the Temple, which a short time before had been full of fear and commotion, was filled with joy and gladness because of the almighty Lord's appearance.

³¹Because Heliodorus was dying, some of his friends urged Onias to call upon the Most High to spare his life. ³²So the high priest, fearing that the king would suspect the Jews of foul play, offered a sacrifice for Heliodorus's recovery. ³³While the high priest was making a sacrifice for atonement, the same young men, dressed in the same clothing, appeared

3:4 Some manuscripts read *of the family of Bilgah.*   3:11 Greek *400 talents* [13.6 metric tons] *of silver and 200 talents* [6.8 metric tons] *of gold.*

to Heliodorus once again. They stood before him and said, "Give thanks to Onias the high priest, because for his sake the Lord has spared your life. 34And you, having been whipped by God,* should tell everyone of the great works and power of God." Then they vanished.

35Heliodorus offered a sacrifice to the Lord and made great vows to him, for he had spared his life. Then he said good-bye to Onias, and he and his troops returned to the king. 36He told everyone about the works of the supreme God, whom he had seen with his own eyes. 37Then the king asked Heliodorus what kind of person he should send to Jerusalem. Heliodorus replied, 38"If you have any enemy or conspirator in your country, send him there. He will return to you whipped, if he survives at all, for there is undoubtedly a certain power of God in that place. 39For the one who dwells in heaven is the guardian and protector of that place, and he strikes and destroys those who come to harm it."

This is the story about Heliodorus and how the treasury was saved.

Jason Hellenizes the Jews

4 Previously we told the story about Simon, who betrayed his country by informing about the money in the sanctuary. Then he blamed Onias for what had happened to Heliodorus, as if he had caused all the trouble. 2Simon even dared to accuse Onias of being a conspirator against the government, despite the fact that he was the benefactor of Jerusalem, the defender of his people, and a man zealous for the laws of Moses. 3When Simon's hatred got to such a point that his followers even committed murders, 4Onias realized the danger of this rivalry. He also could see that Apollonius son of Menestheus, governor of Coelesyria and Phoenicia, was encouraging Simon in his hatred. 5So Onias appealed to the king, not to accuse any of his own people, but with their good in mind, both as individuals and as a nation. 6He saw that unless the king intervened, conditions would go from bad to worse because Simon would not stop his foolish actions.

7When Seleucus died and Antiochus Epiphanes became king, Onias's brother Jason became the high priest by corrupt means. 8He went to the king, promising him thirteen and a half tons of silver immediately and another three tons from future revenue.* 9Besides this, he promised another five and a half tons of silver* if the king would grant him a license to set up a school to promote Greek culture* and a youth center and allow him to enroll people from Jerusalem as citizens of Antioch. 10When the king approved this and Jason took office, he immediately began to force the Greek lifestyle on his people. 11Jason rescinded the freedoms that the kings had granted the Jews through the mediation of John, the father of Eupolemus. (Eupolemus later went to Rome as ambassador to make a treaty of peace and alliance.) Jason also prohibited the people from keeping the law of Moses and introduced customs that were contrary to God's law. 12He went so far as to build a Greek school near the citadel, and he made the most outstanding young men wear hats that were usually worn by Greek students.

13Jason was extremely successful in his efforts to introduce foreign and pagan customs, for he was a man of incredible evil who lacked every virtue to be a true high priest. 14The priests were no longer concerned with the duties of the altar. Despising the Temple and neglecting the sacrifices, they hurried off to take part in the sinful athletic events whenever there was a call for the games to begin.* 15Looking down on the values of their ancestors, they held Greek customs in the highest regard. 16But disaster overtook them in the end, and the very ones whose values they desired and whose lifestyles they imitated were to become their enemies and tormentors. 17For contempt for the laws of God does not go unpunished, a fact that time would prove.

18Now when the games that were held every four years* took place at Tyre in the king's presence, 19the evil Jason sent Hellenized* citizens from Jerusalem to carry three hundred silver coins* for the sacrifice to Hercules. But even the envoys considered it inappropriate to use the money for the sacrifice and decided it should be used for something else. 20So the money intended by Jason for the sacrifice to Hercules was contributed by the envoys for the construction of some ships.

Antiochus IV Epiphanes Welcomed in Jerusalem

21Apollonius son of Menestheus went to Egypt as an ambassador to attend the coronation of

---

3:34 Greek *by heaven.*   4:8 Greek *360 talents* [12.2 metric tons] *of silver and other revenues of 80 talents* [2.7 metric tons].
4:9a Greek *another 150 talents* [5.1 metric tons].   4:9b Greek *a gymnasium;* also in 4:12.   4:14 Greek *a call for discus-throwing.*
4:18 Or *every five years.*   4:19a Greek *Antiochian.*   4:19b Greek *300 silver drachmas.*

Ptolemy Philometor. Antiochus Epiphanes heard from Apollonius that Ptolemy was hostile toward him, so he took measures for the king's security, going first to Joppa and then on to Jerusalem. 22In Jerusalem, Jason and the people received him in magnificent style, welcoming him with torchlights and shouts of praise. From there, Antiochus returned with his army to Phoenicia.

Menelaus Becomes High Priest

23Three years later Jason sent Menelaus, brother of the previously mentioned Simon, to carry money to the king and bring back the king's decisions regarding certain important affairs. 24But when Menelaus met with the king, he exaggerated his own authority and obtained the high priesthood for himself by offering eleven and a half tons* of silver more than Jason paid.

25Having received the king's authorization, Menelaus returned home, but he was not worthy to be high priest. He had the hot temper of a cruel tyrant and the rage of a savage beast. 26So Jason, who had undermined his own brother Onias, was undermined himself. He fled as a fugitive into the land of Ammon.

27Menelaus continued to hold the position of high priest, but he did not send the king any of the payments he had promised. 28He repeatedly ignored the requests for payment made by Sostratus, the commander of the citadel and the one in charge of collecting the king's revenues. So both men were summoned by the king. 29Menelaus left his brother Lysimachus as deputy high priest, and Sostratus left Crates as commander of the troops from Cyprus.

Onias III Is Murdered

30Meanwhile, a revolt broke out in Tarsus and Mallus because those areas had been given as a gift to Antiochis, the king's concubine. 31The king went immediately to settle the problem, leaving Andronicus, one of his nobles, to act in his place.

32Menelaus saw an opportunity to strengthen his position, so he presented Andronicus with some gold vessels he had stolen from the Temple. He also sold some other vessels in Tyre and the surrounding towns. 33When Onias became aware of what Menelaus was doing, he publicly exposed him, but he did it from the safety of the temple of Daphne near Antioch. 34So Menelaus took Andronicus aside and urged him to kill Onias. Andronicus went

to Onias and deceitfully offered him his right hand as a pledge that he would not kill him. Onias had some suspicions, but Andronicus persuaded him to leave the sanctuary. Then he immediately killed Onias without any regard to justice.

35Both the Jews and the other nations were angry and very saddened by the unjust murder. 36When King Antiochus Epiphanes returned from Cilicia, the Jews at Antioch went to him and complained about the unjust murder of Onias. The Greeks shared the Jews' anger over this crime, 37and Antiochus was deeply saddened by the news of Onias's death. He even shed tears, remembering the wisdom and noble character of the dead man. 38Inflamed with anger at the injustice, Antiochus commanded that Andronicus be stripped of his purple robe and be led naked through the city to the very place he had so shamelessly murdered Onias. There the wicked murderer was put to death. In this way the Lord repaid him with the punishment he deserved.

Lysimachus Is Killed

39In Jerusalem, Lysimachus, the deputy high priest, committed many sacrilegious acts, which were planned by Menelaus. Reports of his actions spread abroad, and the people turned against Lysimachus, who had already stolen many gold items from the Temple. 40Because the people were angry and ready to riot, Lysimachus armed about three thousand men and launched an unjust attack under the command of Auranus, a man as advanced in foolishness as he was in age. 41When the Jews saw what was happening, they attacked Lysimachus and his men with stones and blocks of wood. In wild confusion they threw ashes at the men to blind them. 42As a result, many of Lysimachus's men were wounded, some were killed, and the rest fled for their lives. As for the Temple robber himself, he was killed outside the treasury.

Menelaus's Bribery

43Charges about this affair were filed against Menelaus, the high priest. 44When the king came to Tyre, the Jewish high council* sent three men to plead their cause. 45Menelaus, knowing he would be defeated, promised Ptolemy Macron son of Dorymenes a large bribe if he would persuade the king to favor him. 46So Ptolemy, as though to get a breath of fresh air, took the king aside in a colonnade

4:24 Greek 300 talents [10.2 metric tons]. 4:44 Greek the senate.

and persuaded him to change his mind. ⁴⁷Because of this, Menelaus, who was guilty of all this evil, was acquitted by the king, and those poor souls who had brought the charges were condemned to death. It was so obvious that the three men were right, however, that even barbarian Scythians would have acquitted them. ⁴⁸So those who argued the cause for Jerusalem, for the Jewish people, and for the sacred vessels suffered unjust punishment. ⁴⁹Even some people from Tyre were indignant over the deed and buried the three men with great ceremony. ⁵⁰But Menelaus, through the greed of those in power, remained the high priest and grew even more wicked. He became the chief conspirator against his own people.

Second Egyptian Campaign

5 About this time Antiochus Epiphanes prepared for his second invasion of Egypt. ²For nearly forty days, apparitions were seen in the sky over Jerusalem. Horsemen in gold armor charged through the air, armed with lances and swords. ³Ranks of horsemen were seen with swords drawn—attacking and counterattacking, with flashing shields and numerous spears and flying arrows and shining gold armor of every sort. ⁴All the people prayed that this amazing apparition might be a good sign.

Jason's Revolt

⁵A false rumor began to circulate that Antiochus had died in Egypt, so Jason returned and assaulted Jerusalem with a force of no less than a thousand men. As the defenders on the wall were being defeated and the city was open to attack, Menelaus took refuge in the citadel. ⁶Jason killed his own people in Jerusalem without mercy, not realizing that success at the expense of relatives is the greatest of failures. He imagined that he was winning victories over his enemies rather than over his own people. ⁷But he did not gain control of the government, and in the end he was disgraced as the reward for his treachery. He was forced to flee again into the land of the Ammonites.

⁸Jason's life had a miserable end. After being imprisoned for a time by Aretas, king of the Arabians, he fled from town to town. He was pursued and hated by everyone as a despicable betrayer of the laws of Moses, a butcher of his own country and people. Finally, he was driven into Egypt. ⁹From there he went to live with the Spartans,* hoping they would give him

refuge because of their family ties with the Jews.* Then Jason, who had exiled so many others, died in a foreign land. ¹⁰The man who had thrown out so many corpses to lie unburied had no one to mourn his death, no funeral, and no place in the tomb of his ancestors.

The Sacrilege of Antiochus Epiphanes

¹¹When the news of fighting between Jason and the Jews in Jerusalem reached King Antiochus, he suspected that the Jews had revolted. So he left Egypt in a furious state of mind and took Jerusalem back by force. ¹²He commanded the soldiers to kill everyone they met and even to hunt down people hiding in their houses and kill them. ¹³They slaughtered young and old, women and children, young girls and infants. ¹⁴Within three days, there were eighty thousand victims—forty thousand killed and forty thousand sold into slavery.

¹⁵But this was not enough for Antiochus. He dared to enter the Temple, the most holy place in all the world. Menelaus, a traitor to the laws of Moses and to his country, was his guide. ¹⁶That filthy Antiochus seized the holy vessels; with defiled hands he took the ornaments that had been given as offerings by other kings to glorify and honor the Temple. ¹⁷Deluded by his pride, Antiochus did not realize he was successful only because the Lord was angry for a time with the sinful residents of Jerusalem. It was the Lord who permitted this contempt for the Holy Place. ¹⁸If the Jews had not been involved in many sins, Antiochus would have been immediately whipped for his presumption and turned back—as Heliodorus was when King Seleucus sent him to inspect the treasury. ¹⁹But the Lord did not choose the nation for the sake of the Holy Place; rather, he chose the Holy Place for the sake of the nation. ²⁰So the Holy Place itself suffered evils inflicted on the people, just as later it participated in their good fortune. As it was forsaken by the Almighty in his anger, so it would be restored again with great glory when the people were reconciled to the great Lord.

²¹After Antiochus had taken at least sixty-eight tons of silver* from the Temple, he hurried back to Antioch. Carried away with pride, he believed he could sail on the land and walk on the sea. ²²He left governors to oppress the people. He left Philip, a Phrygian by birth, at Jerusalem. But Philip was even more barbaric than the one who appointed him. ²³Antiochus left Andronicus at Mount Gerizim. And

5:9a Greek *the Lacedemonians,* another name for the Spartans. 5:9b See 1 Macc 12:21. 5:21 Greek *1,800 talents* [61 metric tons].

Menelaus remained high priest, oppressing his own people even more than the others did.

To appease his hatred of the Jews, 24Antiochus sent Apollonius, the captain of the Mysians, with an army of twenty-two thousand men and commanded him to kill all the grown men and to sell the women and children into slavery. 25Apollonius came to Jerusalem under the pretense of peace and waited until the holy day of the Sabbath. Then, as the Jews observed the holy day of rest, he ordered his men to parade around fully armed. 26After a crowd had gathered to watch them, he killed everyone who had come there. Dashing through the city with his armed men, he destroyed many others as well.

27But Judas Maccabeus and nine others escaped into the wilderness. They stayed in the hills, where they lived off the land like wild animals. They ate nothing but wild plants to avoid defiling themselves by eating forbidden animals.

Hellenism Enforced on the Jews

6 Not long afterward the king sent an influential Athenian citizen* to force the Jews to abandon the laws of God and their ancestors 2and to defile the Temple in Jerusalem. They were to call it the temple of Olympian Zeus, and the temple on Mount Gerazim was to be called the temple of Zeus the Hospitable, just as it was by those who lived there. 3This intensification of evil was hard for everyone to bear. 4The Temple was filled with Gentiles getting drunk at wild parties. They took their pleasure in prostitutes and had intercourse with women in the sacred Temple area. And for sacrifices they brought in things that were prohibited by the law of Moses. 5The altar was covered with offerings that were strictly forbidden by the laws. 6The Sabbath was not allowed to be kept as a holy day, and the people were prohibited from celebrating the festivals instituted by their ancestors. They were not even allowed to identify themselves as Jews. 7Each month at the king's birthday celebration, they were forced to participate in the pagan sacrifices. And when the festival of Dionysus was celebrated, they were forced to wear ivy wreaths in honor of the pagan god.

8At the suggestion of the people of Ptolemais,* a decree was sent to neighboring Greek cities that all Jews should be forced to participate in the sacrifices 9and that anyone who refused to conform to Gentile customs should be executed. The misery of the Jews was obvious. 10For example, two women were accused of having circumcised their children. They were seized and paraded through the city, clutching their infants to their breasts. Then they were thrown down from the city walls. 11Others who met secretly in nearby caves to keep the Sabbath day were betrayed to Philip. Then, because it was the holy Sabbath, they refused to resist their attackers, and they were all burned to death.

The Reason for Persecution

12Now, I urge those who read this book not to be disheartened by these calamities. Look at these, not as being for the destruction, but for the correction of our people. 13For it is a sign of great kindness when sinners are not allowed to continue in their sin for a long time but are immediately punished. 14In the case of other nations, the Lord waits patiently to judge them so that their punishment will be based on the full measure of their sins. 15But that's not how he deals with us. He punishes us before our sins reach their limit. 16That way he never withdraws his mercy from us. Although he chastises his people with adversity, he never abandons them. 17But let these words be sufficient warning to the readers. Now we must go on with the story.

The Martyrdom of Eleazar

18Eleazar, one of the leading teachers of religious law and an elderly man of noble appearance, was being forced to eat pork. 19But he preferred an honorable death to a defiled life, so he spit out the pork and went voluntarily to be beaten and tortured. 20He acted as all people should who have the courage to refuse to eat forbidden food, even if it means ignoring their natural instincts for staying alive. 21The officials in charge of the pagan sacrificial meal were old friends of Eleazar. In private they urged him to secretly bring meat he was allowed to eat by the law of Moses and only pretend to eat the pork from the king's sacrificial meal. 22In this way they were trying to be kind to Eleazar and help him save himself from death.

23But Eleazar had firmly decided to do otherwise. He was a gray-haired old man, who had lived an honorable life since childhood. He was worthy of the distinction that comes with such age and reputation, and he wanted to obey God's holy law. So he answered

6:1 Some manuscripts read *an influential citizen of Antioch.*   6:8 Or *At the suggestion of Ptolemy.*

immediately that they should send him to his death.* [24]"It is not right to pretend at my age," he said. "And I don't want to give young people the idea that Eleazar, at the age of ninety, has converted to a foreign religion. [25]I could gain a few more days of life by pretending to eat the pork, but I would also lead young people astray and defile and disgrace my old age. [26]For even if I should escape human punishment, whether I live or die, I will not escape the hands of the Almighty. [27]Therefore, by giving up my life bravely, I show myself worthy of my old age. [28]I also will give the young people a good example of how to die an honorable death willingly and bravely for the revered and holy laws of Moses." Then he was immediately taken to be tortured to death.

[29]Those who had just acted kindly toward Eleazar suddenly turned on him because what he had said seemed to them to be utter madness. [30]When he was about to die from the blows, he moaned, "The Lord knows all things. He knows I could have saved my life, but instead I suffer this agonizing pain. He also knows I am happy to suffer these things because I worship and fear him."

[31]So this was how Eleazar died, leaving a memorial of virtue and courage not only for the young but also for the greater part of the nation.

The Martyrdom of Seven Brothers

7 Another time seven brothers, together with their mother, were arrested by the king. They were tortured with whips to make them violate the law of Moses by eating pork. [2]One of them, speaking for all of them, asked, "What are you trying to find out from us? We are ready to die rather than sin against the laws of our ancestors."

[3]The king became enraged, and he ordered that pans and cauldrons be heated. [4]When they were hot, he ordered that the tongue of the spokesman be cut out, that he be scalped, and that his hands and feet be cut off. His brothers and his mother were forced to watch all this. [5]When the young man was completely helpless, the king commanded that he should be fried alive in the pan. As smoke rose from the sizzling pan, his brothers and his mother strongly urged each other to die bravely. [6]They said, "The Lord God is watching over us, and he will surely have compassion on us. As Moses declared in the hymn that he sang before the people, 'He will have compassion on his servants.'*"

[7]After the first brother died this way, they brought forward the second to continue their cruel sport. When they had scalped him, they asked him, "Will you eat pork, or do we have to tear you apart limb from limb?" [8]He replied in Hebrew, the language of his ancestors, "Never!" So he suffered the same torment as his brother. [9]And with his last breath, he said, "You wicked tormentor! You may be sending us from this present life, but the King of the world will raise us up again to live forever because we have died for his laws."

[10]After him the third brother was sent to the same torture. When he was ordered to do so, he quickly stuck out his tongue and courageously stretched out his hands. [11]Then he said with boldness, "I received these hands from God,* but for his laws I will gladly give them up, for I hope to receive them again from him." [12]The king and his men were amazed at the young man's courage because he regarded his suffering as nothing.

[13]After he was dead, they tortured the fourth brother in the same way. [14]When he was near death, he said, "It is better to die by human hands while clinging to the hope that God will raise us up again. But for you, there will be no resurrection to life!"

[15]Then they brought the fifth brother and tortured him as well. But he looked at the king [16]and said, "You have power among mortals, even though you are also mortal, so do whatever you want. But do not think that God has forsaken our people. [17]Wait, and you will see how his great power will torment you and your descendants."

[18]After him they brought the sixth brother. Just before he died, he declared, "Do not deceive yourself. It is our own fault that we suffer these things, for we have sinned against our God. Appalling things have happened to us. [19]But do not think that you will escape unpunished for trying to fight against God."

[20]The mother was particularly admirable and worthy of honorable memory. Although she saw her seven sons killed in the space of one day, she bore it with great courage because of her hope in the Lord. [21]She bravely encouraged each of them in Hebrew, the language of their ancestors. Joining a man's courage to a woman's insight, she said to them, [22]"I do not know how you were formed in my womb. I wasn't the one who gave you breath and life, nor did I shape any part of you. [23]But the Creator of the world, who formed the human race,

6:23 Greek *to Hades.*   7:6 See Deut 32:36.   7:11 Greek *from heaven.*

devised the origin of us all. In his mercy, he will restore both breath and life to you because you are obeying his laws and showing no concern for yourselves."

24Antiochus, suspecting insult in her tone of voice, thought she was mocking him. The youngest brother was still alive, so Antiochus assured him with an oath that he would make him a rich and happy man if he would abandon the traditions of his ancestors. Antiochus said he would make him one of his favored leaders and give him a high office. 25But the young man was not moved by these offers, so the king called for the mother and told her to persuade the youth to save his life. 26After Antiochus had argued with her for a long time, she said that she would try to persuade her son. 27Then, bending over him, she made a fool of the cruel tyrant and spoke to her son in their native language. "My son, have pity on me. I carried you nine months in my womb, nursed you three years, nourished you, and raised you to this age. 28I urge you, my child, look at heaven and earth and all that is in them, and remember that God made them out of nothing. He made all human beings in this way as well. 29So do not fear this butcher, but show yourself worthy of your brothers. Accept death, so that by God's mercy I may receive you back again along with your brothers."

30While the mother was still speaking, the young man said to his tormentors, "What are you waiting for? I will not obey the king's command but only the law that was given to our ancestors by Moses. 31Antiochus, you have contrived all sorts of evil against the Hebrews, but you will never escape the hand of God. 32We are suffering for our own sins. 33Though the living Lord is angry with us for a little while and punishes us, we, his servants, will be reconciled to him in the end. 34But you are wicked and most unmerciful. Do not let your vain hopes make you proud because you have the power to torture God's people,* 35for you have not yet escaped the judgment of the sovereign God who sees all things. 36My brothers suffered briefly for the sake of the covenant, and now they have drunk of eternal life. But God will justly punish you for your arrogance. 37But I, like my brothers, offer my body and my life for the laws of our ancestors. And I call upon God to show mercy to our nation quickly. And may you be tormented and filled with pain until you confess that he alone is God. 38Perhaps because of my brothers and myself, the

just wrath of the Almighty against our nation will cease."

39This made the king extremely angry, and he tortured him more cruelly than he had the others, for he bitterly resented his ridicule. 40So the youth died without being defiled, trusting wholly in the Lord.

41Last of all, after her sons, the mother died. 42But this is enough about the eating of pagan sacrifices and of the extreme cruelties.

Judas Maccabeus Leads the Resistance

8 Meanwhile, Judas Maccabeus and those who were with him went secretly through the towns, calling together their relatives and friends and enlisting those who continued in the Jewish faith. They gathered six thousand men. 2Then they called on the Lord to look down upon his oppressed people and to have pity on the Temple, which had been defiled by wicked men. 3They asked the Lord to have mercy on Jerusalem, which was being destroyed and was soon to be leveled to the ground, and to listen to the blood crying out to him. 4They begged him to remember the wicked slaughter of innocent children and the blasphemies spoken against his name and to show his hatred for evil.

5Once Maccabeus had organized his army, the Gentiles could not stand against him because the anger of the Lord was turned to mercy. 6So Maccabeus took the towns and villages by surprise and set them on fire. He captured strategic places and sent many enemies fleeing, 7usually making his strikes during the night. The reports of his bravery spread far and wide.

8Philip could see that Maccabeus was gaining ground little by little and that his victories were becoming more frequent, making him a real threat. So he wrote to Ptolemy Macron, the governor of Coelesyria and Phoenicia, asking him to send aid to the king's garrisons. 9Immediately Ptolemy sent Nicanor son of Patroclus, one of the king's most favored leaders, giving him no less than twenty thousand Gentile troops from different nations to wipe out the whole Jewish race. He also sent Gorgias, a general who was very experienced in matters of war.

10The king owed a large sum of money to the Romans, so Nicanor proposed to raise seventy-five tons of silver* by selling captured Jews into slavery. 11So he sent invitations to dealers in the coastal cities, offering to sell Jewish slaves

7:34 Greek *the children of heaven.*   8:10 Greek *2,000 talents* [68 metric tons].

at the price of ninety slaves for seventy-five pounds of silver.* Little did he know that the vengeance of the Almighty was about to catch up to him.

¹²When Judas learned that Nicanor was invading, he told those who were with him that the enemy was near. ¹³Some of them were afraid and did not trust the justice of God, so they ran away. ¹⁴Others sold all their possessions and prayed to the Lord that he would save them from the wicked Nicanor, who had already sold them even before meeting them. ¹⁵They asked the Lord to do this, if not for their own sakes, then for the sake of the covenant he had made with their ancestors and for the honor of his holy and glorious name, by which they were called.

¹⁶Maccabeus called together the six thousand that were now with him, encouraging them to fight bravely and not to be afraid of the enemy or discouraged at the vast horde of Gentiles who were wickedly advancing against them. ¹⁷He vividly reminded them of the sinful and outrageous acts done to the Holy Place and of the way Jerusalem had been attacked and humiliated, not to mention the destruction of the ancestral customs. ¹⁸"They trust in their weapons and their boldness," Maccabeus said, "but we trust in almighty God, who with a single nod can completely destroy both those that fight against us and the whole world." ¹⁹He also reminded them of the help their ancestors had received from God.* Once in the days of Sennacherib, 185,000 enemy soldiers were destroyed. ²⁰Maccabeus also recalled the battle when 8,000 Jews and 4,000 Macedonians fought against the Galatians in Babylonia. When the Macedonians were in danger, the Jews received help from God* and killed 120,000 of the enemy. Then they carried off many of the Galatians' possessions. ²¹The soldiers were greatly encouraged by these words and resolved even to die for their laws and country.

Maccabeus divided his army into four divisions ²²and appointed his brothers—Simon, Joseph, and Jonathan—to be captains over three of the divisions. Maccabeus assigned fifteen hundred men to each division. ²³He instructed Eleazar, another one of his brothers, to read to them from the holy book, and then he gave them their battle cry: "God is our help!" Then Maccabeus himself led the first division in an attack against Nicanor. ²⁴With the Almighty as their helper, they killed more than nine thousand of the enemy. They also wounded and disabled the greater part of Nicanor's army and forced them to flee. ²⁵They seized the money of those who had come to buy them as slaves. They also pursued the enemy for a considerable distance, but they had to call off the chase because it was getting late. ²⁶The Sabbath would begin that evening, and for that reason, they could not continue in pursuit. ²⁷When they had gathered together the weapons and captured the spoils of their enemy, they observed the Sabbath. They greatly praised and thanked the Lord, who had saved them that day and had chosen to begin showing his mercy to them. ²⁸After the Sabbath, they gave some of the spoils to those who had been tortured and to orphans and widows. The rest they took for themselves and their children. ²⁹When this was done, they all prayed together, asking the merciful Lord to be fully reconciled to his servants, the Jews.

The Defeat of Timothy and Bacchides

³⁰In confrontations with Timothy and Bacchides, the Jews killed more than twenty thousand of the enemy. They captured the high strongholds, and then they divided a great amount of plunder among those who had been tortured and to orphans and widows and the elderly. ³¹When they had carefully gathered together the enemy's weapons, they stored them in strategic places. They carried the rest of the plunder to Jerusalem. ³²They also killed the commander of Timothy's forces, a wicked man who had harmed the Jews in many ways. ³³As they celebrated the victory in Jerusalem, the city of their ancestors, they burned Callisthenes and some others who had been hiding in a certain house. These men had set fire to the sacred gates of the Temple, so they were justly repaid for their sacrilege.

The Defeat of Nicanor

³⁴But Nicanor—that most hated man, who had brought a thousand merchants to buy the Jews as slaves—³⁵was humiliated, with the Lord's help, by the very ones he considered insignificant. He took off his brilliant uniform and fled like a runaway slave through the open country. He was fortunate to even arrive at Antioch, for his entire army had been destroyed.* ³⁶He had promised to raise the tribute money for the Romans by capturing people from Jerusalem,

---

8:11 Greek *1 talent* [34 kilograms].   **8:19** Greek lacks *from God.*   **8:20** Greek *from heaven.*   **8:35** Or *He arrived in Antioch, having been very successful in destroying his own army.*

but now he proclaimed that the Jews had a Defender and that they could not be harmed, for they were following the laws God had given them.

The Last Days of Antiochus Epiphanes

9 About that time Antiochus Epiphanes returned from Persia with his armies in disarray. ²He had entered the city of Persepolis and attempted to plunder its temples and bring the town under his control. However, the people there had rushed to arms and routed the invaders, forcing them into a humiliating defeat.

³When Antiochus arrived at Ecbatana, he received the news of what had happened to Nicanor and to Timothy's forces. ⁴He became furious and decided to make the Jews pay for the humiliation he had just suffered. So he commanded his chariot driver to take him to Jerusalem without stopping. But God's judgment* went with him because in his arrogance he had said, "When I get to Jerusalem, I will make it a mass grave for the Jews!"

⁵But the Lord, the God of Israel who sees all things, struck Antiochus with an incurable and mysterious disease. For as soon as he had said these words, a dreadful pain seized his intestines—an excruciating intestinal torture that could not be stopped. ⁶This was a very just punishment indeed, considering he had tormented the intestines of others with many barbaric tortures. ⁷But not even this stopped his arrogance; he was still filled with pride. Breathing fire in his rage against the Jews, he commanded the driver to go even faster. But as they were hurrying along, he was thrown from the chariot and fell so hard that his every limb was in agony. ⁸In his superhuman arrogance, he had thought he could command the waves of the sea and weigh tall mountains on a scale, but now he was thrown to the ground and had to be carried on a stretcher. This was a clear manifestation of God's power. ⁹Maggots swarmed out of the wicked man's body, and while he still lived in grief and pain, his flesh rotted away. The stench of his decaying flesh made his army sick. ¹⁰No one could stand to carry the stretcher of this man who had thought only a little while earlier that he could touch the stars of heaven.

¹¹As a result of God's curse, Antiochus was humbled and began to come to his senses, for his agony grew by the minute. ¹²When he himself could no longer stand his own stench, he said, "It is right to be subject to God, and

9:4 Greek *the judgment of heaven.* 9:20 Greek *in heaven.*

mere humans should not think they are equal to God." ¹³Then this wicked man vowed to the Lord (who would not show him any mercy) ¹⁴that he would set Jerusalem free rather than level it and make it a mass grave. ¹⁵He had previously said that the Jews and their children were not worthy to be buried but only to have their bodies thrown out to be eaten by wild animals and vultures. But now he promised to grant them rights equaling those of the Athenians. ¹⁶He had previously desecrated the holy Temple, but now he promised to decorate it with the finest gifts, to lavishly replace the holy vessels in it, and to pay from his own resources all the expenses connected with offering the sacrifices. ¹⁷He even said that he would become a Jew himself and go throughout the earth declaring the power of God.

¹⁸But his agony continued, for the just judgment of God had come upon him. Then, realizing he was going to die, he wrote a letter of request to the Jews:

¹⁹"Antiochus, king and commander, sends hearty greetings to his excellent citizens, the Jews, and wishes them health and prosperity. ²⁰If you and your children are well and everything is going as you wish, I am thankful, for my hope is in God.*

²¹"As for me, I have fond memories of you. When I returned from the regions of Persia, I became seriously ill and thought it necessary to make plans for everybody's welfare. ²²Not that I despair of my health, for I have every expectation of recovering from my illness. ²³But I noticed that my father always appointed a successor whenever he led an army into the upper provinces. ²⁴He wanted to leave everything in order in case anything unexpected happened to him. That way the kingdom would not degenerate into chaos because the people would know who was to lead the government. ²⁵And I know that the rulers of the neighboring nations watch for opportunities to take advantage of us, so I have appointed my son Antiochus Eupator to succeed me as king. When traveling in the upper provinces, I have often left him in charge. I have sent him a copy of what I have written here. ²⁶So I urge and beg you to recall the public and private favors given to you and to continue to be faithful to me and to my son. ²⁷For I am confident that

he will follow my instructions to be fair and kind to you."

²⁸So the murderer and blasphemer suffered terribly, much as he had made others suffer. And he died a miserable death in the mountains of a foreign country. ²⁹Philip, his close friend, carried his body home. Then, fearing the son of Antiochus, Philip went to stay with King Ptolemy Philometor in Egypt.

Judas Maccabeus Purifies the Temple

10 Now Maccabeus and those who were with him, by the protection of the Lord, recovered the Temple and Jerusalem. ²They tore down the altars the Gentiles had set up in the public square and destroyed their pagan shrines. ³After they had purified the Temple, they made another altar. Striking new fire from flint, they offered the first sacrifice in two years. They burned incense, lit the lamps, and set out the Bread of the Presence. ⁴When they had done all these things, they fell face down on the ground and asked the Lord to keep them safe from any further disasters. They also asked that he punish them more gently if they did sin again and that he not hand them over to barbarians and blasphemous people.

⁵The purification of the Temple occurred on the anniversary of the day it had been polluted by foreigners—that is, on the twenty-fifth day of the month of Kislev.*

⁶They celebrated with joy for eight days, as is the custom for the Festival of Shelters. They remembered how they had recently kept the Festival of Shelters when they were living in caves in the mountains like wild animals. ⁷So they carried garlanded wands, green branches, and palm branches and sang hymns to the one who had given them success in purifying his Holy Place. ⁸They voted to pass a public decree that the entire Jewish nation should observe these days every year.

The Reign of Antiochus V Eupator

⁹We have finished recounting the death of Antiochus, who was called Epiphanes. ¹⁰We will now relate the events that took place during the reign of Antiochus Eupator, the son of that wicked man. We will give a brief summary of the evils brought about by his wars.

¹¹When Eupator became king, he appointed a man named Lysias to administer the affairs of his kingdom. Before this, Lysias had succeeded

Ptolemy Macron as governor of Coelesyria and Phoenicia. ¹²Ptolemy was determined to act justly toward the Jews and to deal with them peacefully, especially because of the wrongs that had been done to them. ¹³But the king's favored leaders came and accused Ptolemy Macron because of his policy toward the Jews. On every side he was called a traitor because he had also left Cyprus, where King Ptolemy Philometor had put him in charge, and had defected to Antiochus Epiphanes. Since Ptolemy Macron had no support, he committed suicide by taking poison.

Confrontations between Gorgias and Maccabeus

¹⁴When Gorgias replaced Lysias as governor of Coelesyria and Phoenicia,* he hired mercenaries and continually fought the Jews. ¹⁵At the same time, the Idumeans, who controlled important fortified strongholds, were also harassing the Jews. They welcomed renegade Jews from Jerusalem and did everything to keep the war going.

¹⁶After seeking God's help through prayer, Maccabeus and his troops launched an assault against the Idumean strongholds. ¹⁷They attacked vigorously and captured them, driving back those who fought on the walls and slaughtering everyone they encountered. They killed at least twenty thousand men. ¹⁸At least nine thousand men took refuge in two very strong towers with plenty of food and weapons to withstand a siege. ¹⁹So Maccabeus left Simon and Joseph, along with Zacchaeus and his troops, to command an army that was large enough to besiege them. Then he left to take care of more urgent matters. ²⁰But some of Simon's men were greedy, and they accepted a bribe of seventy thousand silver coins* to let the men in the tower escape. ²¹When Maccabeus was told what had happened, he gathered the leaders of the people and accused them of selling out their fellow Jews for money by letting their enemies escape. ²²Then he put those traitors to death and quickly captured the two towers. ²³He was successful in battle and in everything else he did, and he killed more than twenty thousand men in the two fortresses.

Maccabeus Defeats Timothy

²⁴Timothy, who had already been defeated once by the Jews, gathered a large army of mercenaries and assembled many horsemen from Asia.

10:5 The 25th day of the Hebrew month Kislev occurs in December.   **10:14** Greek *When Gorgias became governor of the region.*
10:20 Greek *70,000 drachmas.*

He approached Judea, intending to take it by force. 25But Maccabeus and his men prayed to God as Timothy drew near. To show their humility, they sprinkled dust on their heads and wore sackcloth. 26They lay face down at the foot of the altar and asked God to be merciful to them and to be an enemy to their enemies, an opponent to their opponents,* as the law of Moses says. 27After they had prayed, they took up their weapons and marched from the town until they came near their enemies. 28As soon as the sun came up, the two forces attacked each other. One army had not only courage but also confidence in the Lord as its guarantee for victory and success; the other army made rage its leader in the battle. 29When they were in the heat of battle, the enemy saw five men from heaven riding on brilliant horses with golden bridles. These heavenly horsemen were leading the Jews. 30Two of them stood on either side of Maccabeus, shielding him with their armor and keeping him safe. They shot arrows and thunderbolts at the enemy, making them blind and confused and throwing them into chaos. 31The Jews killed 20,500 troops and 600 horsemen. 32Timothy fled to Gazara, a heavily guarded stronghold where Chaereas was governor.

33Maccabeus and his army eagerly laid siege to the fortress for four days. 34Those who were inside, trusting in the strength of the place, kept shouting blasphemies and profanities. 35On the morning of the fifth day, twenty young men who were with Maccabeus became furious because of the blasphemy. They bravely stormed the wall and fiercely cut down the enemy. 36Then others followed them and set fire to the towers, burning the blasphemers alive. Still others broke open the gates and let in the rest of the army so they could capture the town. 37They killed Timothy, who was found hiding in a cistern, his brother Chaereas, and Apollophanes. 38After their victory, they sang hymns of thanksgiving, praising the Lord who had shown great kindness to Israel and given them the victory.

The First Campaign of Lysias

11 A short time after this, Lysias became very displeased with what had happened. Lysias was the king's guardian and second-in-command, and he was a member of the royal family. 2He gathered eighty thousand soldiers and all his horsemen with the intention of capturing Jerusalem and making it a Greek settlement. 3He intended to tax the Temple, as he did the shrines of other nations, and to auction off the office of high priest every year. 4He had no regard for the power of God but proudly trusted in his numerous foot soldiers, thousands of horsemen, and eighty elephants.

5He came into Judea and approached Bethzur, a fortified place about twenty miles* from Jerusalem. He began to vigorously attack it. 6When Maccabeus and his men learned that the strongholds were under siege, everyone cried out to the Lord. With tears they begged him to send a good angel to rescue Israel. 7Maccabeus himself was the first to take up arms, and he urged the others to follow him into battle in order to help their fellow Jews. So they rushed out together. 8While they were still near Jerusalem, a horseman in white clothing appeared to them brandishing gold weapons. 9Together they praised the merciful God and took such courage that they were ready to assault not only the men but also the fiercest beasts and walls of iron. 10So they advanced in battle formation, having a heavenly ally, the merciful Lord. 11Like lions they leaped on the enemy, killing eleven thousand foot soldiers and sixteen hundred horsemen and sending all the rest fleeing for their lives. 12Most of those who fled were wounded and without weapons. Even Lysias was forced to flee in shame.

13But Lysias was not stupid. He saw the loss he had suffered and realized that the Hebrews could not be overcome, because the mighty God fought along with them. So Lysias sent a message to them, 14urging them to settle everything on just terms and promising to make the king their friend. 15Maccabeus thought about what would be best for everyone, so he accepted Lysias's offer. The king, in turn, consented to all the Jews' requests, which Maccabeus had submitted in writing to Lysias.

16Lysias wrote the following letter to the Jews:

"This letter is from Lysias to the Jewish people. Greetings.

17"John and Absalom, your messengers, have delivered your written terms and requested that I grant them. 18I have reported all the necessary details to the king, and he has granted as much as he can. 19If, therefore, you will remain loyal to the

---

10:26 See Exod 23:22.   11:5 Greek 5 *stadia*. The meaning of 5 *stadia* here is uncertain, since it would normally equal about half a mile and the actual distance between Beth-zur and Jerusalem is about 20 miles [32 kilometers].

government, I will endeavor to help you from now on. ²⁰I have given verbal orders that my officials and your messengers should talk with you about the details. ²¹"Farewell. This letter was written on April 20* in the one hundred forty-eighth year of Greek rule."

²²The king had written this letter to Lysias:

"This letter is from King Antiochus to his brother Lysias. Greetings.

²³"Now that our father has taken his place among the gods, we desire that those in our realm should be left undisturbed in caring for their own affairs. ²⁴We understand that the Jews will not accept the Greek customs of our father. They prefer to keep their own ways and have asked us to allow them to follow their own customs. ²⁵Since we desire that this nation should be at peace, we have decided that their Temple should be restored to them and that they may live according to the custom of their ancestors. ²⁶You will do well, therefore, to write to them and pledge them your friendship. When they have heard this decision, they will be able to rest easy and take care of their own business."

²⁷The king's letter to the Jews was as follows:

"This letter is from King Antiochus to the Jewish high council* and to the Jewish people. Greetings.

²⁸"We hope you are well, as we ourselves are well. ²⁹Menelaus told us that you wish to return home and care for your own affairs. ³⁰We therefore grant safe conduct to all who go home by April 26.* ³¹We also decree that the Jews may follow their own food laws, as they did before, and that none of them will be harassed in any way for things they may have done in ignorance. ³²I have sent Menelaus to reassure you.

³³"Farewell. This letter was written on April 11* in the one hundred forty-eighth year of Greek rule."

³⁴The Romans also sent a letter to the Jews, which reads as follows:

"This letter is from Quintus Memmius and Titus Manius, ambassadors of the Romans, to the Jewish people. Greetings.

³⁵"Whatever Lysias, a member of the royal family, has granted you, we also grant. ³⁶But he thought some things should be referred to the king. So confer among yourselves on these issues, and then send someone with a message. That way we can make good proposals on your behalf, for we are going to Antioch. ³⁷Write back immediately so that we may know what you are thinking.

³⁸"Farewell. This letter was written on April 11 in the one hundred forty-eighth year."

Judas Maccabeus Continues to Fight

12 When these agreements were made, Lysias returned to the king and the Jews turned their attention to farming. ²However, some of the governors would not let them live in peace. These governors were Timothy, Apollonius son of Genneus, Hieronymus, Demophon, and Nicanor the governor of Cyprus.

³The people of Joppa also committed an evil deed. They invited the Jews who lived among them (men, women, and children) to go for a boat ride. Since this was an obvious sign of friendship, the Jews publicly voted to accept the offer. ⁴They did not suspect a thing and wanted to be on friendly terms. But when the boats were some distance from the shore, the people of Joppa drowned at least two hundred of the Jews.

⁵As soon as Judas heard about this cruelty to his fellow Jews, he assembled his men for action. ⁶After calling upon God, the just Judge, he attacked those murderers of his fellow Jews. He set the port on fire in the night, burned the boats, and killed with the sword those who had taken refuge there. ⁷Then he left, since the town's gates were closed. But he planned to return again to completely destroy all the people of Joppa.

⁸When he learned that the people of Jamnia also planned to wipe out the Jews who lived among them, ⁹he attacked Jamnia at night and set the port and its ships on fire. The light of the blaze was seen in Jerusalem twenty-eight miles* away.

11:21 Greek *Dioscorinthius the twenty-fourth.* The meaning of *Dioscorinthius* is uncertain, but it is taken here to mean the first month of the ancient Hebrew lunar calendar. This day occurred on April 20, 164 B.C.   11:27 Greek *the senate of the Jews.*   11:30 Greek *by the thirtieth of Xanthicus,* of the Macedonian calendar. Xanthicus corresponds to the first month of the ancient Hebrew lunar calendar; also in 11:33, 38. This day occurred on April 26, 164 B.C.   11:33 Greek *Xanthicus the fifteenth,* of the Macedonian calendar. This day occurred on April 11, 164 B.C.; also in 11:38.   12:9 Greek *240 stadia* [45 kilometers].

¹⁰When they had gone about a mile* from Jamnia and were marching toward Timothy, over five thousand Arabian foot soldiers and more than five hundred horsemen attacked them. ¹¹After a hard fight and with the help of God, Judas and his men won the victory. The defeated nomads asked Judas for a peace treaty, promising to give him livestock and to help the Jews in every other way. ¹²Thinking that they might indeed be useful in many ways, Judas promised them peace. After an exchange of pledges, the Arabians returned to their tents.

¹³Judas also attacked Caspin, a certain town that was surrounded by fortifications and walls and inhabited by all sorts of Gentiles. ¹⁴Confident in the strength of the walls and their supply of food, the people there became insolent, and they taunted Judas with mockery, blasphemy, and all sorts of evil words. ¹⁵But Judas and his men called upon the great Ruler of the world, for in the time of Joshua, the Lord had crumbled the walls of Jericho without the use of battering rams or war machines. Then Judas fiercely assaulted the walls. ¹⁶By God's will Judas and his men captured the town. They slaughtered so many people—a countless number—that a nearby lake that was about a quarter of a mile* wide seemed to overflow with blood.

¹⁷From there they marched eighty-seven miles* to Charax, to the Jews living in the land of Tob.* ¹⁸But they did not find Timothy there, for he had left the area without doing anything, except that he left a very strong garrison in a certain fortress. ¹⁹Dositheus and Sosipater, who were captains under Maccabeus, went and killed the men Timothy had left in the fortress—over ten thousand in all.

²⁰Maccabeus separated his men into divisions and appointed officers over them. He hurried after Timothy, who had with him 120,000 foot soldiers and 2,500 horsemen. ²¹When Timothy learned that Judas was coming after him, he sent the women and children and also the baggage to a fortress called Karnaim. This fortress was hard to besiege or attack because all the approaches were so narrow. ²²But when Judas's first band of soldiers came into sight, their enemies were struck with fear because of an apparition sent by the All-Seeing One. The enemies fled in such confusion that many of them were injured by their own companions and wounded with their own swords. ²³Judas

went after them vigorously, killing the sinners by the sword, and he destroyed about 30,000 men. ²⁴Timothy himself was captured by the soldiers of Dositheus and Sosipater. With great cunning, he begged them to let him live, for he held the parents and brothers of many of them, and if he died, they would also perish. ²⁵When he had solemnly promised to return them unharmed, they released him in order to save their relatives.

²⁶Judas then went to Karnaim and the temple of Atargatis. There he killed twenty-five thousand people. ²⁷After he had destroyed these and put the rest to flight, Judas led his army to Ephron, a fortified town where Lysias and many people from various nations lived. Strong young men guarding the walls made a vigorous resistance, and they had many catapults and plenty of ammunition. ²⁸But when the Jews invoked the name of the Sovereign One, whose power breaks the strength of his enemies, they captured the town and killed twenty-five thousand of those who were inside.

²⁹From there they pressed on to Scythopolis, which lies seventy miles* from Jerusalem. ³⁰But the Jews who lived in Scythopolis testified that the people of the town were kind to them, especially during times of adversity. ³¹So Judas thanked the people, strongly urging them to remain friendly to Jews in the future. They arrived back at Jerusalem just before the Festival of Pentecost.*

³²After the Festival of Pentecost, Judas and his men marched out to attack Gorgias, the governor of Idumea. ³³Gorgias met them with three thousand foot soldiers and four hundred horsemen. ³⁴When the battle began, a few of the Jews were killed. ³⁵Then a certain Dositheus, one of Bacenor's men and a strong horseman, caught hold of Gorgias and began to drag him by his cloak. Dositheus would have taken the accursed man alive, but a Thracian horseman rushed at him and cut off his arm, and so Gorgias escaped to Marisa. ³⁶Meanwhile, since Esdris and his men had fought a long time and were weary, Judas called upon the Lord to be their helper and their leader in battle. ³⁷After he chanted the battle cry in Hebrew, the language of their ancestors, accompanied by hymns, they made a surprise attack on Gorgias's troops and caused them to flee. ³⁸Judas then assembled his army and went to the town of Adullam. Since the seventh

day was approaching, they remained there to purify themselves according to custom and to keep the Sabbath.

39 By the day after the Sabbath, it had become urgent that the bodies of the Jews who had been killed be removed, so Judas and his men went to bury them with their relatives in the tombs of their ancestors. 40 But under the clothing of the dead they found some sacred amulets of the idols of Jamnia. The law forbids Jews to wear such things, so it was obvious to all that this was why these men had died. 41 Then they all blessed the ways of the Lord, the just Judge, who reveals things that are hidden.

42 They spent time in prayer, asking the Lord to completely forgive the sin that had been committed. Then the noble Judas strongly urged the people to keep themselves free from sin, since they saw with their own eyes what happens to people who sin in the same way as those who had died. 43 Taking up a collection from each person, Judas sent two thousand silver coins* to Jerusalem for a sacrifice to be offered for the sins of those who had died. In so doing he acted well and honorably, for he kept the resurrection in mind. 44 If he had not expected that those who had died would rise again, it would have been useless and foolish to pray for the dead. 45 But since he had in mind the splendid reward that awaits those who die a godly death, his thought in doing this was holy and devout. Therefore, he made this atoning sacrifice for the dead so that they might be released from their sin.

The Campaign of Antiochus Eupator

13 In the one hundred forty-ninth year of Greek rule,* Judas learned that Antiochus Eupator was marching with a great army toward Judea. 2 He had with him Lysias, his guardian and second-in-command, and each had an army of 110,000 foot soldiers, 5,300 horsemen, 22 elephants, and 300 chariots armed with deadly blades to cut down foot soldiers.

3 Menelaus joined them, and with great pretense he urged Antiochus on. But he was not really looking out for the welfare of his country; he simply hoped to strengthen his political position. 4 The King of kings caused Antiochus to become angry at the wicked man. So when Lysias suggested that Menelaus was the cause of all their trouble, Antiochus commanded that Menelaus be taken to Berea in Syria and executed according to their local custom. 5 For in Berea there was a tower seventy-five feet* high, with sides steeply sloping down to piles of ashes all around it. 6 Anyone guilty of sacrilege or notorious for other crimes is taken to the top of the tower and thrown down into the ashes to die. 7 That was the fate of sinful Menelaus, and he was not even given a decent burial. 8 It was only fitting that he die in ashes because he had committed many sins against the altar of the Temple, the fire and ashes of which are holy.

9 The king was consumed with savage arrogance, and he had plans, even worse than his father's, to devastate the Jews. 10 When Judas learned of these plans, he ordered the people to pray to the Lord day and night, asking him to help them now more than ever. For they feared that they would be deprived of the law of Moses, their land, and the holy Temple. 11 They prayed that God would not let his people be overtaken again by blasphemous Gentiles, for they were only now recovering from past troubles. 12 They all joined in this prayer and begged the Lord to be merciful. For three days they continually wept, fasted, and lay face down before the Lord, and then Judas encouraged them and ordered them to stand ready.

13 After consulting with the high council,* Judas decided not to wait for the king to lead his army into Judea to make himself master of the city. Judas decided instead to rely on the Lord to help them defeat the king's army in open warfare. 14 So Judas committed everything to the Creator of the world and encouraged his troops to fight bravely, even to death, in defense of the laws of Moses, the Temple, the city of Jerusalem, and their country and its citizens. Judas set up camp near Modein, 15 and he gave his soldiers their battle cry, "God brings us victory!" Then, with a select contingent of brave young men, he attacked the king's camp at night and killed as many as two thousand men in the camp. He also killed the lead elephant with its driver. 16 Having created great fear and confusion in the enemy camp, they left with great success 17 just as dawn was breaking. This all happened because the Lord helped and protected them.

18 The king, having seen the daring of the Jews, resorted to making strategic attacks against their positions. 19 He advanced with his army against Beth-zur, a strong fortress

---

12:43 Greek 2,000 drachmas of silver.   13:1 The 149th year of Greek rule was 163 B.C.   13:5 Greek 50 cubits [23 meters].
13:13 Greek with the elders.

of the Jews, but he was held off and defeated. [20]Judas was able to send supplies to reinforce the defenders. [21]And though Rhodocus, a Jewish soldier, supplied the enemy with secret information, his fellow soldiers discovered the plot, hunted him down, and took him to prison. [22]Then once more the king made a treaty with the people of Beth-zur, and they exchanged pledges of peace. When the king left them, he went to fight Judas and his men, but he was beaten again.

[23]Then the king learned that Philip, who had been left in charge of the government by Antiochus Epiphanes,* had rebelled at Antioch. The king was worried and made peace with the Jews, promising to honor their demands. When the peace treaty was finalized, the king offered sacrifices and honored the Temple by leaving generous gifts for the Holy Place. [24]He accepted Maccabeus with kindness and appointed Hegemonides as governor of the region stretching from Ptolemais in the north to Gerar in the south.

[25]Then the king visited Ptolemais, but the people of that city were very unhappy with the peace treaty. They were so angry that they wanted to cancel its terms. [26]But Lysias went up to the speaker's platform and argued in favor of the treaty the best he could. Finally, he convinced the people, and they were satisfied. Then the king returned to Antioch. This was how the king's invasion and withdrawal turned out.

Conflict with Nicanor

14 Three years later Judas and his men heard that Demetrius son of Seleucus had sailed into the port of Tripolis with a powerful army and navy. [2]He had killed Antiochus Eupator and his guardian Lysias and then declared himself king.

[3]Now Alcimus had been the high priest, but he voluntarily participated in sinful practices during the time of the revolt. He realized he was now in danger and there was no way for him to regain his position at the holy altar. [4]So he went to King Demetrius in the one hundred fifty-first year of Greek rule* and presented him with a gold crown and a palm branch as well as a customary gift of olive branches from the Temple. On that day he kept quiet about his intentions. [5]But Alcimus eventually found an opportunity to further his mad plans, for Demetrius called him to a meeting and asked about the attitudes and intentions of the Jews. [6]Alcimus answered, "Those Jews called Hasideans,* who are led by Judas Maccabeus, keep stirring up wars and rebellions and will not allow the country to enjoy peace. [7]That is why I have been deprived of my ancestors' glory—I mean the high priesthood. So now I have come here—[8]first out of loyalty to the king's interests but also to provide for the good of my own people. Our entire nation suffers terribly from the unreasonable conduct of those men. [9]Since you know all these things, O king, I beg you to show kindness to our country and our people, for your generosity and kindness are known to everyone. [10]As long as Judas lives, it is not possible for the country to enjoy peace."

[11]When he had said all this, the rest of the king's favored leaders, who were also enemies of Judas, furthered stirred up Demetrius's anger against Judas. [12]Immediately the king selected Nicanor, who was commander of the elephants, and appointed him governor of Judea. [13]He gave him orders to kill Judas, scatter his troops, and make Alcimus the high priest of the great Temple. [14]The Gentiles who had fled from Judea to escape from Judas joined Nicanor in large numbers, for they thought that defeating and harming the Jews would serve their own good.

[15]When the Jews heard that Nicanor was coming and that the Gentiles were assembled to attack them, they put dust on their heads to express their grief. Then they prayed to the One who established his own people forever and who always protects them by revealing his presence with them. [16]Then, at the order of their leader, the Jews moved out and went to the town of Dessau* to meet the enemy.

[17]Judas's brother Simon had once fought against Nicanor but was stopped suddenly when he saw so many enemies. [18]But Nicanor had heard of the bravery of Judas and his men. He had seen their courage as they fought for their country, so he was afraid and chose not to resolve the issue in battle. [19]Instead, he sent Posidonius, Theodotus, and Mattathias ahead to offer and receive pledges of peace. [20]After the terms of the treaty had been fully considered, both leaders informed their troops. Everyone seemed in favor of the treaty, so they consented to the agreement. [21]Then a day was

13:23 Greek lacks *Antiochus Epiphanes;* see 1 Macc 6:14-15.   14:4 The 151st year of Greek rule was 161 B.C.   14:6 This Jewish group, whose name means "the Devout," strongly supported the law of Moses and opposed foreign influence. They later split into two groups, the Pharisees and the Essenes.   14:16 Or *the town of Adasa.*

chosen when the leaders could meet together, and chariots brought them to seats of honor set up between the two armies. ²²Judas positioned armed men in strategic places to be ready for any treachery attempted by the enemy, but the conference went smoothly. ²³After this, Nicanor stayed in Jerusalem and did not cause trouble, dismissing the Gentiles who had joined him. ²⁴Nicanor kept Judas close to him because he had become warmly attached to him. ²⁵He urged Judas to marry and raise a family. So Judas married, settled down, and lived a normal life.

²⁶When Alcimus saw that the two men had become friends, he went to Demetrius with a copy of the treaty. Alcimus complained that Nicanor was being disloyal because he had appointed Judas, a conspirator against them, to succeed him as one of the king's favored leaders. ²⁷Roused by Alcimus's false accusations, the king became angry. He wrote to Nicanor saying that he was displeased with the terms of the treaty, and he ordered him to immediately send Maccabeus to Antioch as a prisoner. ²⁸Nicanor was disturbed when he received the message, for he did not want to break his agreement with a man who had done him no wrong. ²⁹But because he could not oppose the king, he waited for an opportunity to carry out the orders by some clever scheme. ³⁰When Maccabeus saw that Nicanor was no longer friendly to him and was actually rude when they met, he sensed trouble brewing. So he gathered together many of his men and hid himself from Nicanor.

³¹When Nicanor realized that Judas had outwitted him, he went to the great and holy Temple and commanded the priests who were offering the customary sacrifices to hand Judas over to him. ³²When they swore to him that they did not know where Judas was, ³³he stretched out his right hand toward the sanctuary and swore this oath: "If you do not hand over Judas to me as a prisoner, I will level this Temple of God to the ground and tear down the altar. Then I will erect a new temple to Dionysus." ³⁴After saying this, he left.

The priests raised their hands toward heaven and called upon the One who has always defended our nation. They prayed, ³⁵"O Lord of all things, you need nothing, yet you were pleased to give us a Temple so that you could live among us. ³⁶So now, O Lord of all holiness, keep this house forever undefiled, for it has only recently been purified."

The Martyrdom of Razis

³⁷Razis, a member of the high council* in Jerusalem, was a man who loved his people and was highly esteemed. Because of his kindness toward them, he was called the father of the Jews. But Razis was denounced to Nicanor. ³⁸In the early days of the revolt, Razis had been accused of practicing the traditions of the Jewish faith, for which he was ready to give body and soul. ³⁹Nicanor was determined to show his hatred for the Jews, so he sent five hundred soldiers to arrest Razis. ⁴⁰Nicanor thought that by taking him into custody he would be dealing the Jews a severe blow.

⁴¹The soldiers trapped Razis in a tower and tried to set fire to the door in order to gain entrance. But just as he was about to be captured, Razis threw himself on his own sword. ⁴²He chose to die a noble death rather than to fall into the hands of wicked men who would abuse and humiliate him in ways that a man of his stature should never have to endure. ⁴³But in all the excitement, he failed to make his wound fatal. With the mob rushing in through the door, Razis courageously ran to the top of the wall and threw himself down on the crowd. ⁴⁴But the people quickly jumped out of his way, and he landed on the ground. ⁴⁵Then, still breathing and inflamed with rage, he got up and ran through the crowd with blood gushing from his terrible wound. ⁴⁶He climbed a steep rock and, nearly drained of blood, tore out his intestines with both hands and threw them into the crowd. He then called on the Lord of life and spirit to allow him to live again.* This was how he died.

Nicanor's Fall

15 When Nicanor learned that Judas was in the vicinity of Samaria, he decided to attack him on the Sabbath day, since this day of rest would give Nicanor's troops complete safety. ²The Jews who had been forced to join his army protested, "Don't destroy them in such a barbaric and savage way. Respect the Sabbath, for it has been declared holy by the One who sees all things."

³But that most hated wretch mocked, "Is there some ruler in heaven who has commanded that the Sabbath be observed as a special day?"

⁴They replied, "It is the living Lord, the Ruler in heaven, who commands the observance of the Sabbath."

⁵But Nicanor said, "Well, I am sovereign

14:37 Greek *one of the elders.*   **14:46** Greek *to give these back to him again.*

upon earth, and I command you to take up arms and carry out your duty to the king." Even so he was not able to carry out his cruel plan.

⁶Nicanor was filled with immense pride, and he thought he would erect a public monument to commemorate his victory over Judas and his army. ⁷But Maccabeus never lost his trust that the Lord would help them. ⁸He urged his people not to fear the attack of the Gentiles but to remember the help they had previously received from God.* The Almighty would surely give them victory. ⁹He encouraged them with passages from the law and the prophets and recalled the battles they had won before, so they became enthusiastic. ¹⁰Then, after he had encouraged them, he issued his orders. At the same time, he pointed out that the Gentiles had lied and broken their oaths. ¹¹He armed all his people, not so much with the protection of shields and spears, but with the inspiration of his bold speech. He inspired them even more by telling them about a dream—a vision, as it were—worthy to be believed.

¹²This was the vision: "Onias, who was formerly the high priest, was a good and virtuous man. He was modest in appearance, gentle in manner, and graceful in speech, and he had been trained in every virtue from the time he was a child. One day he was praying with lifted hands for the whole Jewish community. ¹³At that moment another man appeared whose age and dignity made him look very distinguished and whose presence conveyed a noble authority. ¹⁴When Onias saw him, he said, 'This is a man who loves his fellow Jews. He prays often for his people and for the holy city. It is Jeremiah, the prophet of God.' ¹⁵Then Jeremiah reached out his right hand and gave Judas a gold sword, saying, ¹⁶'Take this holy sword, a gift from God, and use it to kill your enemies.'"

¹⁷That was all the people needed. Judas had stirred up the courage and strengthened the hearts of the young men. They now were eager to make this a quick fight and to attack bravely, deciding the matter in courageous hand-to-hand combat, for the holy city and the Temple were in danger. ¹⁸Their concern for their wives, children, brothers, and relatives paled in comparison to their first and foremost concern: the holy Temple. ¹⁹And everyone in the city was very concerned for those who were going to fight in the open country.

²⁰Everyone was ready for a decisive battle. Nearby, the enemy was set in formation, with the elephants in strategic position and the horsemen on the flanks. ²¹Maccabeus looked at the advancing army with its many types of armor and its savage elephants. Then he raised his hands toward heaven and called upon the Lord, who works wonders and gives victory to those who deserve it. For Maccabeus knew that battles are not won merely by weapons but according to the Lord's plan. ²²In his prayer Maccabeus said, "O Lord, you sent your angel in the days of Hezekiah, king of Judah,* and he killed 185,000 people in Sennacherib's camp. ²³Now, O Ruler of heaven, send a good angel to spread fear and dread before us. ²⁴With your mighty arm, strike down those who come with blasphemy against your holy people." And so he concluded his prayer.

²⁵Nicanor and his soldiers advanced with trumpets and marching songs. ²⁶Judas and his men met the enemy with prayers and cries to God. ²⁷Fighting with their hands while praying to God with their hearts, they killed at least thirty-five thousand men. They were ecstatic over this display of God's power. ²⁸And when the battle was over and they were returning with joy, they discovered Nicanor, lying dead in full armor. ²⁹With wild shouts, they blessed the Sovereign Lord in Hebrew, the language of their ancestors.

³⁰Judas had completely devoted himself, body and soul, to defending his people, and he loved his fellow Jews ever since childhood. Now he ordered that Nicanor's head and arm be cut off and carried to Jerusalem. ³¹When he arrived there, he called all the people together and stationed the priests before the altar. Then he sent for the remaining troops in the citadel. ³²He showed them the head of that evil and profane Nicanor and the arm he had raised with proud boasts against the holy Temple of the Almighty. ³³Then he cut out the tongue of the wicked Nicanor and ordered that it be fed piece by piece to the vultures. And to show what had happened to Nicanor for his foolish deeds, Judas hung Nicanor's arm in front of the sanctuary.

³⁴Then everyone looked toward heaven and blessed the Lord, who displayed his power. They said, "Blessed is he who has kept his Temple undefiled." ³⁵Finally, Judas hung Nicanor's head from the citadel as an obvious reminder of how the Lord had helped them.

³⁶The people voted to institute an annual celebration on this day, the thirteenth day of the twelfth month, which in Aramaic is called

15:8 Greek *from heaven.*   15:22 Greek *king of Judea.*

Adar.* (This is the day before Purim, the annual celebration of Mordecai's victory.*)

37 So this is how things turned out with Nicanor. From that time until now, Jerusalem has been in the possession of the Hebrews. Now I will also make an end of my narration here. 38 My goal was to make it well written and concise, but if it is poorly done or just mediocre, it is the best I could do. 39 It is disagreeable to drink only wine or only water, but wine mixed with water is a pleasant drink that increases our enjoyment. In the same way, a story that is well written is pleasantly received by its readers. Let this, then, be the end.

15:36a This day of the ancient Hebrew lunar calendar usually occurs in March.   15:36b See Esth 9:19.

Job

THE PROBLEM OF HUMAN SUFFERING is contemplated by almost everyone at some time or another. The book of Job addresses this ancient and difficult problem. It tells the story of Job, a godly man who endured an enormous amount of suffering while remaining faithful to God. The story begins with Job's losing his children, his possessions, and even his health—all within a very short period of time. Only Job and his wife survived the ruin that Satan inflicted upon him. Job's three friends came to comfort him and reflect on the purpose of his suffering. They each considered the basic question: Why must we endure suffer-

■ **Author:** Uncertain; Jewish tradition regards Moses as the author; others have suggested Job himself as the author

■ **Date Written:** Uncertain, though events alluded to and vocabulary used suggest it was written during the time of the patriarchs, between 2000 and 1800 BC

■ **Purpose:** To demonstrate God's sovereignty and address the problem of suffering

■ **Themes:** Innocent suffering, God's sovereignty, God's goodness, human arrogance

■ **Outline**
1:1–2:13 The onset of Job's misery
3:1–14:22 First set of speeches
15:1–21:34 Second set of speeches
22:1–31:40 Third set of speeches
32:1–37:24 Elihu's speech
38:1–41:34 The Lord's response to Job
42:1-17 Job's restoration

ing when God is powerful enough to do something about it? Job's wife simply declared it all unfair, advising Job, "Curse God and die" (2:9). Each of Job's three friends—Eliphaz, Bildad, and Zophar—delivered speeches accounting for Job's misery. A fourth young man, Elihu, tried to summarize the situation with yet another explanation. But all of them failed to provide Job with a satisfactory answer. Finally, God himself spoke directly to Job, asking him questions that forced him to recognize his finite understanding of life. Job realized that God is ultimately in charge and knows what he is doing. So Job remained silent and stood in awe of God's sovereignty. In the end, God restored Job's health, possessions, and family.

Prologue

1 There once was a man named Job who lived in the land of Uz. He was blameless—a man of complete integrity. He feared God and stayed away from evil. ²He had seven sons and three daughters. ³He owned 7,000 sheep, 3,000 camels, 500 teams of oxen, and 500 female donkeys. He also had many servants. He was, in fact, the richest person in that entire area.

⁴Job's sons would take turns preparing feasts in their homes, and they would also invite their three sisters to celebrate with them. ⁵When these celebrations ended—sometimes after

several days—Job would purify his children. He would get up early in the morning and offer a burnt offering for each of them. For Job said to himself, "Perhaps my children have sinned and have cursed God in their hearts." This was Job's regular practice.

Job's First Test

⁶One day the members of the heavenly court* came to present themselves before the LORD, and the Accuser, Satan,* came with them. ⁷"Where have you come from?" the LORD asked Satan.

Satan answered the LORD, "I have been

1:6a Hebrew *the sons of God.*   **1:6b** Hebrew *and the satan;* similarly throughout this chapter.

patrolling the earth, watching everything that's going on."

⁸Then the LORD asked Satan, "Have you noticed my servant Job? He is the finest man in all the earth. He is blameless—a man of complete integrity. He fears God and stays away from evil."

⁹Satan replied to the LORD, "Yes, but Job has good reason to fear God. ¹⁰You have always put a wall of protection around him and his home and his property. You have made him prosper in everything he does. Look how rich he is! ¹¹But reach out and take away everything he has, and he will surely curse you to your face!"

¹²"All right, you may test him," the LORD said to Satan. "Do whatever you want with everything he possesses, but don't harm him physically." So Satan left the LORD's presence.

¹³One day when Job's sons and daughters were feasting at the oldest brother's house, ¹⁴a messenger arrived at Job's home with this news: "Your oxen were plowing, with the donkeys feeding beside them, ¹⁵when the Sabeans raided us. They stole all the animals and killed all the farmhands. I am the only one who escaped to tell you."

¹⁶While he was still speaking, another messenger arrived with this news: "The fire of God has fallen from heaven and burned up your sheep and all the shepherds. I am the only one who escaped to tell you."

¹⁷While he was still speaking, a third messenger arrived with this news: "Three bands of Chaldean raiders have stolen your camels and killed your servants. I am the only one who escaped to tell you."

¹⁸While he was still speaking, another messenger arrived with this news: "Your sons and daughters were feasting in their oldest brother's home. ¹⁹Suddenly, a powerful wind swept in from the wilderness and hit the house on all sides. The house collapsed, and all your children are dead. I am the only one who escaped to tell you."

²⁰Job stood up and tore his robe in grief. Then he shaved his head and fell to the ground to worship. ²¹He said,

> "I came naked from my mother's womb,
>   and I will be naked when I leave.
> The LORD gave me what I had,
>   and the LORD has taken it away.
> Praise the name of the LORD!"

²²In all of this, Job did not sin by blaming God.

Job's Second Test

2 One day the members of the heavenly court* came again to present themselves before the LORD, and the Accuser, Satan,* came with them. ²"Where have you come from?" the LORD asked Satan.

Satan answered the LORD, "I have been patrolling the earth, watching everything that's going on."

³Then the LORD asked Satan, "Have you noticed my servant Job? He is the finest man in all the earth. He is blameless—a man of complete integrity. He fears God and stays away from evil. And he has maintained his integrity, even though you urged me to harm him without cause."

⁴Satan replied to the LORD, "Skin for skin! A man will give up everything he has to save his life. ⁵But reach out and take away his health, and he will surely curse you to your face!"

⁶"All right, do with him as you please," the LORD said to Satan. "But spare his life." ⁷So Satan left the LORD's presence, and he struck Job with terrible boils from head to foot.

⁸Job scraped his skin with a piece of broken pottery as he sat among the ashes. ⁹His wife said to him, "Are you still trying to maintain your integrity? Curse God and die."

¹⁰But Job replied, "You talk like a foolish woman. Should we accept only good things from the hand of God and never anything bad?" So in all this, Job said nothing wrong.

Job's Three Friends Share His Anguish

¹¹When three of Job's friends heard of the tragedy he had suffered, they got together and traveled from their homes to comfort and console him. Their names were Eliphaz the Temanite, Bildad the Shuhite, and Zophar the Naamathite. ¹²When they saw Job from a distance, they scarcely recognized him. Wailing loudly, they tore their robes and threw dust into the air over their heads to show their grief. ¹³Then they sat on the ground with him for seven days and nights. No one said a word to Job, for they saw that his suffering was too great for words.

Job's First Speech

3 At last Job spoke, and he cursed the day of his birth. ²He said:

³ "Let the day of my birth be erased,
    and the night I was conceived.
⁴ Let that day be turned to darkness.
    Let it be lost even to God on high,

2:1a Hebrew *the sons of God.*   2:1b Hebrew *and the satan;* similarly throughout this chapter.

and let no light shine on it.
5 Let the darkness and utter gloom claim
that day for its own.
Let a black cloud overshadow it,
and let the darkness terrify it.
6 Let that night be blotted off the calendar,
never again to be counted among the
days of the year,
never again to appear among the months.
7 Let that night be childless.
Let it have no joy.
8 Let those who are experts at cursing—
whose cursing could rouse Leviathan*—
curse that day.
9 Let its morning stars remain dark.
Let it hope for light, but in vain;
may it never see the morning light.
10 Curse that day for failing to shut my
mother's womb,
for letting me be born to see all this
trouble.

11 "Why wasn't I born dead?
Why didn't I die as I came from the
womb?
12 Why was I laid on my mother's lap?
Why did she nurse me at her breasts?
13 Had I died at birth, I would now be at
peace.
I would be asleep and at rest.
14 I would rest with the world's kings and
prime ministers,
whose great buildings now lie in ruins.
15 I would rest with princes, rich in gold,
whose palaces were filled with silver.
16 Why wasn't I buried like a stillborn child,
like a baby who never lives to see the
light?
17 For in death the wicked cause no trouble,
and the weary are at rest.
18 Even captives are at ease in death,
with no guards to curse them.
19 Rich and poor are both there,
and the slave is free from his master.

20 "Oh, why give light to those in misery,
and life to those who are bitter?
21 They long for death, and it won't come.
They search for death more eagerly than
for hidden treasure.
22 They're filled with joy when they finally
die,
and rejoice when they find the grave.
23 Why is life given to those with no future,

those God has surrounded with
difficulties?
24 I cannot eat for sighing;
my groans pour out like water.
25 What I always feared has happened to me.
What I dreaded has come true.
26 I have no peace, no quietness.
I have no rest; only trouble comes."

Eliphaz's First Response to Job

4 Then Eliphaz the Temanite replied to Job:

2 "Will you be patient and let me say a
word?
For who could keep from speaking out?

3 "In the past you have encouraged many
people;
you have strengthened those who were
weak.
4 Your words have supported those who
were falling;
you encouraged those with shaky knees.
5 But now when trouble strikes, you lose
heart.
You are terrified when it touches you.
6 Doesn't your reverence for God give you
confidence?
Doesn't your life of integrity give you
hope?

7 "Stop and think! Do the innocent die?
When have the upright been destroyed?
8 My experience shows that those who plant
trouble
and cultivate evil will harvest the same.
9 A breath from God destroys them.
They vanish in a blast of his anger.
10 The lion roars and the wildcat snarls,
but the teeth of strong lions will be
broken.
11 The fierce lion will starve for lack of prey,
and the cubs of the lioness will be
scattered.

12 "This truth was given to me in secret,
as though whispered in my ear.
13 It came to me in a disturbing vision at
night,
when people are in a deep sleep.
14 Fear gripped me,
and my bones trembled.
15 A spirit* swept past my face,
and my hair stood on end.*

3:8 The identification of Leviathan is disputed, ranging from an earthly creature to a mythical sea monster in ancient literature. 4:15a Or *wind;* also in 4:16. 4:15b Or *its wind sent shivers up my spine.*

16 The spirit stopped, but I couldn't see its
     shape.
   There was a form before my eyes.
   In the silence I heard a voice say,
17 'Can a mortal be innocent before God?
   Can anyone be pure before the
     Creator?'

18 "If God does not trust his own angels
     and has charged his messengers with
     foolishness,
19 how much less will he trust people made
     of clay!
   They are made of dust, crushed as easily
     as a moth.
20 They are alive in the morning but dead by
     evening,
   gone forever without a trace.
21 Their tent-cords are pulled and the tent
     collapses,
   and they die in ignorance.

Eliphaz's Response Continues

5 1 "Cry for help, but will anyone answer
      you?
    Which of the angels* will help you?
2 Surely resentment destroys the fool,
    and jealousy kills the simple.
3 I have seen that fools may be successful for
    the moment,
  but then comes sudden disaster.
4 Their children are abandoned far from
    help;
  they are crushed in court with no one
    to defend them.
5 The hungry devour their harvest,
    even when it is guarded by brambles.*
  The thirsty pant after their wealth.*
6 But evil does not spring from the soil,
    and trouble does not sprout from the
    earth.
7 People are born for trouble
    as readily as sparks fly up from a fire.

8 "If I were you, I would go to God
    and present my case to him.
9 He does great things too marvelous to
    understand.
  He performs countless miracles.
10 He gives rain for the earth
    and water for the fields.
11 He gives prosperity to the poor
    and protects those who suffer.
12 He frustrates the plans of schemers

so the work of their hands will not
  succeed.
13 He traps the wise in their own cleverness
   so their cunning schemes are
   thwarted.
14 They find it is dark in the daytime,
   and they grope at noon as if it were
   night.
15 He rescues the poor from the cutting
   words of the strong,
   and rescues them from the clutches of
   the powerful.
16 And so at last the poor have hope,
   and the snapping jaws of the wicked
   are shut.

17 "But consider the joy of those corrected
   by God!
  Do not despise the discipline of the
   Almighty when you sin.
18 For though he wounds, he also
   bandages.
  He strikes, but his hands also heal.
19 From six disasters he will rescue you;
   even in the seventh, he will keep you
   from evil.
20 He will save you from death in time of
   famine,
   from the power of the sword in time
   of war.
21 You will be safe from slander
   and have no fear when destruction
   comes.
22 You will laugh at destruction and
   famine;
   wild animals will not terrify you.
23 You will be at peace with the stones of the
   field,
   and its wild animals will be at peace
   with you.
24 You will know that your home is safe.
   When you survey your possessions,
   nothing will be missing.
25 You will have many children;
   your descendants will be as plentiful as
   grass!
26 You will go to the grave at a ripe old age,
   like a sheaf of grain harvested at the
   proper time!

27 "We have studied life and found all this
   to be true.
  Listen to my counsel, and apply it to
   yourself."

5:1 Hebrew *the holy ones.*   5:5a The meaning of the Hebrew for this phrase is uncertain.   5:5b As in Greek and Syriac versions; Hebrew reads *A snare snatches their wealth.*

Job's Second Speech: A Response to Eliphaz

6 Then Job spoke again:

2 "If my misery could be weighed
and my troubles be put on the scales,
3 they would outweigh all the sands of the
sea.
That is why I spoke impulsively.
4 For the Almighty has struck me down with
his arrows.
Their poison infects my spirit.
God's terrors are lined up against me.
5 Don't I have a right to complain?
Don't wild donkeys bray when they find
no grass,
and oxen bellow when they have no
food?
6 Don't people complain about unsalted
food?
Does anyone want the tasteless white of
an egg?*
7 My appetite disappears when I look at it;
I gag at the thought of eating it!

8 "Oh, that I might have my request,
that God would grant my desire.
9 I wish he would crush me.
I wish he would reach out his hand and
kill me.
10 At least I can take comfort in this:
Despite the pain,
I have not denied the words of the Holy
One.
11 But I don't have the strength to endure.
I have nothing to live for.
12 Do I have the strength of a stone?
Is my body made of bronze?
13 No, I am utterly helpless,
without any chance of success.

14 "One should be kind to a fainting friend,
but you accuse me without any fear of
the Almighty.*
15 My brothers, you have proved as
unreliable as a seasonal brook
that overflows its banks in the spring
16 when it is swollen with ice and melting
snow.
17 But when the hot weather arrives, the
water disappears.
The brook vanishes in the heat.
18 The caravans turn aside to be refreshed,
but there is nothing to drink, so they
die.

19 The caravans from Tema search for this
water;
the travelers from Sheba hope to find it.
20 They count on it but are disappointed.
When they arrive, their hopes are dashed.
21 You, too, have given no help.
You have seen my calamity, and you are
afraid.
22 But why? Have I ever asked you for a gift?
Have I begged for anything of yours for
myself?
23 Have I asked you to rescue me from my
enemies,
or to save me from ruthless people?
24 Teach me, and I will keep quiet.
Show me what I have done wrong.
25 Honest words can be painful,
but what do your criticisms amount to?
26 Do you think your words are convincing
when you disregard my cry of
desperation?
27 You would even send an orphan into
slavery*
or sell a friend.
28 Look at me!
Would I lie to your face?
29 Stop assuming my guilt,
for I have done no wrong.
30 Do you think I am lying?
Don't I know the difference between
right and wrong?

7 1 "Is not all human life a struggle?
Our lives are like that of a hired
hand,
2 like a worker who longs for the shade,
like a servant waiting to be paid.
3 I, too, have been assigned months of
futility,
long and weary nights of misery.
4 Lying in bed, I think, 'When will it be
morning?'
But the night drags on, and I toss till
dawn.
5 My body is covered with maggots and
scabs.
My skin breaks open, oozing with pus.

Job Cries Out to God

6 "My days fly faster than a weaver's shuttle.
They end without hope.
7 O God, remember that my life is but a
breath,
and I will never again feel happiness.

6:6 Or *the tasteless juice of the mallow plant?*   6:14 Or *friend, / or he might lose his fear of the Almighty.*   6:27 Hebrew *even gamble over an orphan.*

8 You see me now, but not for long.
  You will look for me, but I will be gone.
9 Just as a cloud dissipates and vanishes,
  those who die* will not come back.
10 They are gone forever from their home—
   never to be seen again.

11 "I cannot keep from speaking.
   I must express my anguish.
   My bitter soul must complain.
12 Am I a sea monster or a dragon
   that you must place me under guard?
13 I think, 'My bed will comfort me,
   and sleep will ease my misery,'
14 but then you shatter me with dreams
   and terrify me with visions.
15 I would rather be strangled—
   rather die than suffer like this.
16 I hate my life and don't want to go on
   living.
   Oh, leave me alone for my few
   remaining days.

17 "What are people, that you should make
   so much of us,
   that you should think of us so often?
18 For you examine us every morning
   and test us every moment.
19 Why won't you leave me alone,
   at least long enough for me to swallow!
20 If I have sinned, what have I done to you,
   O watcher of all humanity?
   Why make me your target?
   Am I a burden to you?*
21 Why not just forgive my sin
   and take away my guilt?
   For soon I will lie down in the dust
   and die.
   When you look for me, I will be gone."

Bildad's First Response to Job

8 Then Bildad the Shuhite replied to Job:

2 "How long will you go on like this?
  You sound like a blustering wind.
3 Does God twist justice?
  Does the Almighty twist what is right?
4 Your children must have sinned against
  him,
  so their punishment was well deserved.
5 But if you pray to God
  and seek the favor of the Almighty,
6 and if you are pure and live with integrity,
  he will surely rise up and restore your
  happy home.

7 And though you started with little,
  you will end with much.

8 "Just ask the previous generation.
  Pay attention to the experience of our
  ancestors.
9 For we were born but yesterday and know
  nothing.
  Our days on earth are as fleeting as a
  shadow.
10 But those who came before us will teach
   you.
   They will teach you the wisdom of old.

11 "Can papyrus reeds grow tall without a
   marsh?
   Can marsh grass flourish without
   water?
12 While they are still flowering, not ready to
   be cut,
   they begin to wither more quickly than
   grass.
13 The same happens to all who forget
   God.
   The hopes of the godless evaporate.
14 Their confidence hangs by a thread.
   They are leaning on a spider's web.
15 They cling to their home for security, but
   it won't last.
   They try to hold it tight, but it will not
   endure.
16 The godless seem like a lush plant growing
   in the sunshine,
   its branches spreading across the
   garden.
17 Its roots grow down through a pile of
   stones;
   it takes hold on a bed of rocks.
18 But when it is uprooted,
   it's as though it never existed!
19 That's the end of its life,
   and others spring up from the earth to
   replace it.

20 "But look, God will not reject a person
   of integrity,
   nor will he lend a hand to the
   wicked.
21 He will once again fill your mouth with
   laughter
   and your lips with shouts of joy.
22 Those who hate you will be clothed with
   shame,
   and the home of the wicked will be
   destroyed."

7:9 Hebrew *who go down to Sheol.*   7:20 As in Greek version; Hebrew reads *target, so that I am a burden to myself?*

Job's Third Speech: A Response to Bildad

9 Then Job spoke again:

2 "Yes, I know all this is true in principle.
But how can a person be declared
innocent in God's sight?
3 If someone wanted to take God to court,*
would it be possible to answer him even
once in a thousand times?
4 For God is so wise and so mighty.
Who has ever challenged him
successfully?

5 "Without warning, he moves the
mountains,
overturning them in his anger.
6 He shakes the earth from its place,
and its foundations tremble.
7 If he commands it, the sun won't rise
and the stars won't shine.
8 He alone has spread out the heavens
and marches on the waves of the sea.
9 He made all the stars—the Bear and
Orion,
the Pleiades and the constellations of
the southern sky.
10 He does great things too marvelous to
understand.
He performs countless miracles.

11 "Yet when he comes near, I cannot see him.
When he moves by, I do not see him go.
12 If he snatches someone in death, who can
stop him?
Who dares to ask, 'What are you
doing?'
13 And God does not restrain his anger.
Even the monsters of the sea* are
crushed beneath his feet.

14 "So who am I, that I should try to answer
God
or even reason with him?
15 Even if I were right, I would have no
defense.
I could only plead for mercy.
16 And even if I summoned him and he
responded,
I'm not sure he would listen to me.
17 For he attacks me with a storm
and repeatedly wounds me without
cause.
18 He will not let me catch my breath,
but fills me instead with bitter sorrows.

19 If it's a question of strength, he's the
strong one.
If it's a matter of justice, who dares to
summon him* to court?
20 Though I am innocent, my own mouth
would pronounce me guilty.
Though I am blameless, it* would prove
me wicked.

21 "I am innocent,
but it makes no difference to me—
I despise my life.
22 Innocent or wicked, it is all the same to
God.
That's why I say, 'He destroys both the
blameless and the wicked.'
23 When a plague* sweeps through,
he laughs at the death of the innocent.
24 The whole earth is in the hands of the
wicked,
and God blinds the eyes of the judges.
If he's not the one who does it, who is?

25 "My life passes more swiftly than a
runner.
It flees away without a glimpse of
happiness.
26 It disappears like a swift papyrus boat,
like an eagle swooping down on its prey.
27 If I decided to forget my complaints,
to put away my sad face and be cheerful,
28 I would still dread all the pain,
for I know you will not find me
innocent, O God.
29 Whatever happens, I will be found guilty.
So what's the use of trying?
30 Even if I were to wash myself with soap
and clean my hands with lye,
31 you would plunge me into a muddy ditch,
and my own filthy clothing would
hate me.

32 "God is not a mortal like me,
so I cannot argue with him or take him
to trial.
33 If only there were a mediator between us,
someone who could bring us together.
34 The mediator could make God stop
beating me,
and I would no longer live in terror of
his punishment.
35 Then I could speak to him without fear,
but I cannot do that in my own
strength.

9:3 Or *If God wanted to take someone to court.*   9:13 Hebrew *the helpers of Rahab,* the name of a mythical sea monster that represents chaos in ancient literature.   9:19 As in Greek version; Hebrew reads *me.*   9:20 Or *he.*   9:23 Or *disaster.*

Job Frames His Plea to God

10 ¹ "I am disgusted with my life.
Let me complain freely.
My bitter soul must complain.
² I will say to God, 'Don't simply condemn
me—
tell me the charge you are bringing
against me.
³ What do you gain by oppressing me?
Why do you reject me, the work of your
own hands,
while smiling on the schemes of the
wicked?
⁴ Are your eyes like those of a human?
Do you see things only as people see
them?
⁵ Is your lifetime only as long as ours?
Is your life so short
⁶ that you must quickly probe for my guilt
and search for my sin?
⁷ Although you know I am not guilty,
no one can rescue me from your
hands.

⁸ "'You formed me with your hands; you
made me,
yet now you completely destroy me.
⁹ Remember that you made me from
dust—
will you turn me back to dust so soon?
¹⁰ You guided my conception
and formed me in the womb.*
¹¹ You clothed me with skin and flesh,
and you knit my bones and sinews
together.
¹² You gave me life and showed me your
unfailing love.
My life was preserved by your care.

¹³ "'Yet your real motive—
your true intent—
¹⁴ was to watch me, and if I sinned,
you would not forgive my guilt.
¹⁵ If I am guilty, too bad for me;
and even if I'm innocent, I can't hold my
head high,
because I am filled with shame and
misery.
¹⁶ And if I hold my head high, you hunt me
like a lion
and display your awesome power
against me.
¹⁷ Again and again you witness against me.
You pour out your growing anger on me
and bring fresh armies against me.

¹⁸ "'Why, then, did you deliver me from my
mother's womb?
Why didn't you let me die at birth?
¹⁹ It would be as though I had never existed,
going directly from the womb to the
grave.
²⁰ I have only a few days left, so leave me
alone,
that I may have a moment of comfort
²¹ before I leave—never to return—
for the land of darkness and utter
gloom.
²² It is a land as dark as midnight,
a land of gloom and confusion,
where even the light is dark as
midnight.'"

Zophar's First Response to Job

11 Then Zophar the Naamathite replied
to Job:

² "Shouldn't someone answer this torrent
of words?
Is a person proved innocent just by a lot
of talking?
³ Should I remain silent while you
babble on?
When you mock God, shouldn't
someone make you ashamed?
⁴ You claim, 'My beliefs are pure,'
and 'I am clean in the sight of God.'
⁵ If only God would speak;
if only he would tell you what he
thinks!
⁶ If only he would tell you the secrets of
wisdom,
for true wisdom is not a simple matter.
Listen! God is doubtless punishing you
far less than you deserve!

⁷ "Can you solve the mysteries of God?
Can you discover everything about the
Almighty?
⁸ Such knowledge is higher than the
heavens—
and who are you?
It is deeper than the underworld*—
what do you know?
⁹ It is broader than the earth
and wider than the sea.
¹⁰ If God comes and puts a person in prison
or calls the court to order, who can stop
him?
¹¹ For he knows those who are false,
and he takes note of all their sins.

10:10 Hebrew *You poured me out like milk / and curdled me like cheese.*   **11:8** Hebrew *than Sheol.*

¹² An empty-headed person won't become
       wise
    any more than a wild donkey can bear a
       human child.*

¹³ "If only you would prepare your heart
    and lift up your hands to him in
       prayer!
¹⁴ Get rid of your sins,
    and leave all iniquity behind you.
¹⁵ Then your face will brighten with
       innocence.
    You will be strong and free of fear.
¹⁶ You will forget your misery;
    it will be like water flowing away.
¹⁷ Your life will be brighter than the
       noonday.
    Even darkness will be as bright as
       morning.
¹⁸ Having hope will give you courage.
    You will be protected and will rest in
       safety.
¹⁹ You will lie down unafraid,
    and many will look to you for help.
²⁰ But the wicked will be blinded.
    They will have no escape.
    Their only hope is death."

Job's Fourth Speech: A Response to Zophar

12 Then Job spoke again:

² "You people really know everything,
       don't you?
    And when you die, wisdom will die with
       you!
³ Well, I know a few things myself—
    and you're no better than I am.
    Who doesn't know these things you've
       been saying?
⁴ Yet my friends laugh at me,
    for I call on God and expect an answer.
    I am a just and blameless man,
       yet they laugh at me.
⁵ People who are at ease mock those in
       trouble.
    They give a push to people who are
       stumbling.
⁶ But robbers are left in peace,
    and those who provoke God live in
       safety—
    though God keeps them in his power.*

⁷ "Just ask the animals, and they will teach
       you.

    Ask the birds of the sky, and they will
       tell you.
⁸ Speak to the earth, and it will instruct you.
    Let the fish in the sea speak to you.
⁹ For they all know
    that my disaster* has come from the
       hand of the LORD.
¹⁰ For the life of every living thing is in his
       hand,
    and the breath of every human being.
¹¹ The ear tests the words it hears
    just as the mouth distinguishes between
       foods.
¹² Wisdom belongs to the aged,
    and understanding to the old.

¹³ "But true wisdom and power are found in
       God;
    counsel and understanding are his.
¹⁴ What he destroys cannot be rebuilt.
    When he puts someone in prison, there
       is no escape.
¹⁵ If he holds back the rain, the earth
       becomes a desert.
    If he releases the waters, they flood the
       earth.
¹⁶ Yes, strength and wisdom are his;
    deceivers and deceived are both in his
       power.
¹⁷ He leads counselors away, stripped of good
       judgment;
    wise judges become fools.
¹⁸ He removes the royal robe of kings.
    They are led away with ropes around
       their waist.
¹⁹ He leads priests away, stripped of status;
    he overthrows those with long years in
       power.
²⁰ He silences the trusted adviser
    and removes the insight of the elders.
²¹ He pours disgrace upon princes
    and disarms the strong.

²² "He uncovers mysteries hidden in
       darkness;
    he brings light to the deepest
       gloom.
²³ He builds up nations, and he destroys
       them.
    He expands nations, and he abandons
       them.
²⁴ He strips kings of understanding
    and leaves them wandering in a pathless
       wasteland.

11:12 Or *than a wild male donkey can bear a tame colt.*   12:6 Or *safety—those who try to manipulate God.* The meaning of the
Hebrew is uncertain.   12:9 Hebrew *that this.*

25 They grope in the darkness without a
      light.
   He makes them stagger like drunkards.

Job Wants to Argue His Case with God

13 1 "Look, I have seen all this with my
         own eyes
   and heard it with my own ears, and now
      I understand.
2 I know as much as you do.
   You are no better than I am.
3 As for me, I would speak directly to the
      Almighty.
   I want to argue my case with God
      himself.
4 As for you, you smear me with lies.
   As physicians, you are worthless
      quacks.
5 If only you could be silent!
   That's the wisest thing you could do.
6 Listen to my charge;
   pay attention to my arguments.

7 "Are you defending God with lies?
   Do you make your dishonest arguments
      for his sake?
8 Will you slant your testimony in his
      favor?
   Will you argue God's case for him?
9 What will happen when he finds out what
      you are doing?
   Can you fool him as easily as you fool
      people?
10 No, you will be in trouble with him
      if you secretly slant your testimony in
      his favor.
11 Doesn't his majesty terrify you?
   Doesn't your fear of him overwhelm
      you?
12 Your platitudes are as valuable as ashes.
   Your defense is as fragile as a clay pot.

13 "Be silent now and leave me alone.
   Let me speak, and I will face the
      consequences.
14 Why should I put myself in mortal
      danger*
   and take my life in my own hands?
15 God might kill me, but I have no other
      hope.*
   I am going to argue my case with him.
16 But this is what will save me—I am not
      godless.
   If I were, I could not stand before him.

17 "Listen closely to what I am about to say.
   Hear me out.
18 I have prepared my case;
   I will be proved innocent.
19 Who can argue with me over this?
   And if you prove me wrong, I will
      remain silent and die.

Job Asks How He Has Sinned

20 "O God, grant me these two things,
   and then I will be able to face you.
21 Remove your heavy hand from me,
   and don't terrify me with your awesome
      presence.
22 Now summon me, and I will answer!
   Or let me speak to you, and you reply.
23 Tell me, what have I done wrong?
   Show me my rebellion and my sin.
24 Why do you turn away from me?
   Why do you treat me as your enemy?
25 Would you terrify a leaf blown by the wind?
   Would you chase dry straw?

26 "You write bitter accusations against me
   and bring up all the sins of my youth.
27 You put my feet in stocks.
   You examine all my paths.
   You trace all my footprints.
28 I waste away like rotting wood,
   like a moth-eaten coat.

14 1 "How frail is humanity!
         How short is life, how full of
         trouble!
2 We blossom like a flower and then wither.
   Like a passing shadow, we quickly
      disappear.
3 Must you keep an eye on such a frail
      creature
   and demand an accounting from me?
4 Who can bring purity out of an impure
      person?
   No one!
5 You have decided the length of our lives.
   You know how many months we will
      live,
   and we are not given a minute longer.
6 So leave us alone and let us rest!
   We are like hired hands, so let us finish
      our work in peace.

7 "Even a tree has more hope!
   If it is cut down, it will sprout again
      and grow new branches.

13:14 Hebrew *Why should I take my flesh in my teeth.*   13:15 An alternate reading in the Masoretic Text reads *God might kill me, but I hope in him.*

⁸ Though its roots have grown old in the
        earth
    and its stump decays,
⁹ at the scent of water it will bud
    and sprout again like a new
        seedling.

¹⁰ "But when people die, their strength is
        gone.
    They breathe their last, and then where
        are they?
¹¹ As water evaporates from a lake
    and a river disappears in drought,
¹² people are laid to rest and do not rise
        again.
    Until the heavens are no more, they
        will not wake up
    nor be roused from their sleep.

¹³ "I wish you would hide me in the
        grave*
    and forget me there until your anger
        has passed.
    But mark your calendar to think of me
        again!
¹⁴ Can the dead live again?
    If so, this would give me hope through
        all my years of struggle,
    and I would eagerly await the release
        of death.
¹⁵ You would call and I would answer,
    and you would yearn for me, your
        handiwork.
¹⁶ For then you would guard my
        steps,
    instead of watching for my sins.
¹⁷ My sins would be sealed in a pouch,
    and you would cover my guilt.

¹⁸ "But instead, as mountains fall and
        crumble
    and as rocks fall from a cliff,
¹⁹ as water wears away the stones
    and floods wash away the soil,
    so you destroy people's hope.
²⁰ You always overpower them, and they
        pass from the scene.
    You disfigure them in death and send
        them away.
²¹ They never know if their children grow
        up in honor
    or sink to insignificance.
²² They suffer painfully;
    their life is full of trouble."

Eliphaz's Second Response to Job

15 Then Eliphaz the Temanite replied:

² "A wise man wouldn't answer with
        such empty talk!
    You are nothing but a windbag.
³ The wise don't engage in empty chatter.
    What good are such words?
⁴ Have you no fear of God,
    no reverence for him?
⁵ Your sins are telling your mouth what
        to say.
    Your words are based on clever
        deception.
⁶ Your own mouth condemns you, not I.
    Your own lips testify against you.

⁷ "Were you the first person ever born?
    Were you born before the hills were
        made?
⁸ Were you listening at God's secret council?
    Do you have a monopoly on wisdom?
⁹ What do you know that we don't?
    What do you understand that we
        do not?
¹⁰ On our side are aged, gray-haired men
    much older than your father!

¹¹ "Is God's comfort too little for you?
    Is his gentle word not enough?
¹² What has taken away your reason?
    What has weakened your vision,*
¹³ that you turn against God
    and say all these evil things?
¹⁴ Can any mortal be pure?
    Can anyone born of a woman be
        just?
¹⁵ Look, God does not even trust the
        angels.*
    Even the heavens are not absolutely
        pure in his sight.
¹⁶ How much less pure is a corrupt and sinful
        person
    with a thirst for wickedness!

¹⁷ "If you will listen, I will show you.
    I will answer you from my own
        experience.
¹⁸ And it is confirmed by the reports of wise
        men
    who have heard the same thing from
        their fathers—
¹⁹ from those to whom the land was given
    long before any foreigners arrived.

14:13 Hebrew *in Sheol.*   15:12 Or *Why do your eyes flash with anger;* Hebrew reads *Why do your eyes blink.*   15:15 Hebrew *the holy ones.*

²⁰ "The wicked writhe in pain throughout
their lives.
Years of trouble are stored up for the
ruthless.
²¹ The sound of terror rings in their ears,
and even on good days they fear the
attack of the destroyer.
²² They dare not go out into the darkness
for fear they will be murdered.
²³ They wander around, saying, 'Where can
I find bread?'*
They know their day of destruction is
near.
²⁴ That dark day terrifies them.
They live in distress and anguish,
like a king preparing for battle.
²⁵ For they shake their fists at God,
defying the Almighty.
²⁶ Holding their strong shields,
they defiantly charge against him.

²⁷ "These wicked people are heavy and
prosperous;
their waists bulge with fat.
²⁸ But their cities will be ruined.
They will live in abandoned houses
that are ready to tumble down.
²⁹ Their riches will not last,
and their wealth will not endure.
Their possessions will no longer spread
across the horizon.

³⁰ "They will not escape the darkness.
The burning sun will wither their shoots,
and the breath of God will destroy them.
³¹ Let them no longer fool themselves by
trusting in empty riches,
for emptiness will be their only reward.
³² They will be cut down in the prime of life;
their branches will never again be green.
³³ They will be like a vine whose grapes are
harvested too early,
like an olive tree that loses its blossoms
before the fruit can form.
³⁴ For the godless are barren.
Their homes, enriched through bribery,
will burn.
³⁵ They conceive trouble and give birth to
evil.
Their womb produces deceit."

Job's Fifth Speech: A Response to Eliphaz

16 Then Job spoke again:

² "I have heard all this before.

What miserable comforters you
are!
³ Won't you ever stop blowing hot air?
What makes you keep on talking?
⁴ I could say the same things if you were
in my place.
I could spout off criticism and shake
my head at you.
⁵ But if it were me, I would encourage you.
I would try to take away your grief.
⁶ Instead, I suffer if I defend myself,
and I suffer no less if I refuse to speak.

⁷ "O God, you have ground me down
and devastated my family.
⁸ As if to prove I have sinned, you've
reduced me to skin and bones.
My gaunt flesh testifies against me.
⁹ God hates me and angrily tears me apart.
He snaps his teeth at me
and pierces me with his eyes.
¹⁰ People jeer and laugh at me.
They slap my cheek in contempt.
A mob gathers against me.
¹¹ God has handed me over to sinners.
He has tossed me into the hands of the
wicked.

¹² "I was living quietly until he shattered me.
He took me by the neck and broke me
in pieces.
Then he set me up as his target,
¹³   and now his archers surround me.
His arrows pierce me without mercy.
The ground is wet with my blood.*
¹⁴ Again and again he smashes against me,
charging at me like a warrior.
¹⁵ I wear burlap to show my grief.
My pride lies in the dust.
¹⁶ My eyes are red with weeping;
dark shadows circle my eyes.
¹⁷ Yet I have done no wrong,
and my prayer is pure.

¹⁸ "O earth, do not conceal my blood.
Let it cry out on my behalf.
¹⁹ Even now my witness is in heaven.
My advocate is there on high.
²⁰ My friends scorn me,
but I pour out my tears to God.
²¹ I need someone to mediate between
God and me,
as a person mediates between friends.
²² For soon I must go down that road
from which I will never return.

15:23 Greek version reads *He is appointed to be food for a vulture.* 16:13 Hebrew *my gall.*

Job Continues to Defend His Innocence

17 ¹ "My spirit is crushed,
and my life is nearly snuffed out.
The grave is ready to receive me.
² I am surrounded by mockers.
I watch how bitterly they taunt me.

³ "You must defend my innocence, O God,
since no one else will stand up for me.
⁴ You have closed their minds to
understanding,
but do not let them triumph.
⁵ They betray their friends for their own
advantage,
so let their children faint with hunger.

⁶ "God has made a mockery of me among
the people;
they spit in my face.
⁷ My eyes are swollen with weeping,
and I am but a shadow of my former self.
⁸ The virtuous are horrified when they
see me.
The innocent rise up against the
ungodly.
⁹ The righteous keep moving forward,
and those with clean hands become
stronger and stronger.

¹⁰ "As for all of you, come back with a better
argument,
though I still won't find a wise man
among you.
¹¹ My days are over.
My hopes have disappeared.
My heart's desires are broken.
¹² These men say that night is day;
they claim that the darkness is light.
¹³ What if I go to the grave*
and make my bed in darkness?
¹⁴ What if I call the grave my father,
and the maggot my mother or my sister?
¹⁵ Where then is my hope?
Can anyone find it?
¹⁶ No, my hope will go down with me to the
grave.
We will rest together in the dust!"

Bildad's Second Response to Job

18 Then Bildad the Shuhite replied:

² "How long before you stop talking?
Speak sense if you want us to answer!
³ Do you think we are mere animals?
Do you think we are stupid?

⁴ You may tear out your hair in anger,
but will that destroy the earth?
Will it make the rocks tremble?

⁵ "Surely the light of the wicked will be
snuffed out.
The sparks of their fire will not glow.
⁶ The light in their tent will grow dark.
The lamp hanging above them will be
quenched.
⁷ The confident stride of the wicked will
be shortened.
Their own schemes will be their downfall.
⁸ The wicked walk into a net.
They fall into a pit.
⁹ A trap grabs them by the heel.
A snare holds them tight.
¹⁰ A noose lies hidden on the ground.
A rope is stretched across their path.

¹¹ "Terrors surround the wicked
and trouble them at every step.
¹² Hunger depletes their strength,
and calamity waits for them to stumble.
¹³ Disease eats their skin;
death devours their limbs.
¹⁴ They are torn from the security of their
homes
and are brought down to the king of
terrors.
¹⁵ The homes of the wicked will burn down;
burning sulfur rains on their houses.
¹⁶ Their roots will dry up,
and their branches will wither.
¹⁷ All memory of their existence will fade
from the earth;
no one will remember their names.
¹⁸ They will be thrust from light into darkness,
driven from the world.
¹⁹ They will have neither children nor
grandchildren,
nor any survivor in the place where they
lived.
²⁰ People in the west are appalled at their fate;
people in the east are horrified.
²¹ They will say, 'This was the home of a
wicked person,
the place of one who rejected God.'"

Job's Sixth Speech: A Response to Bildad

19 Then Job spoke again:

² "How long will you torture me?
How long will you try to crush me with
your words?

17:13 Hebrew *to Sheol;* also in 17:16.

³ You have already insulted me ten times.
    You should be ashamed of treating me
        so badly.
⁴ Even if I have sinned,
    that is my concern, not yours.
⁵ You think you're better than I am,
    using my humiliation as evidence of
        my sin.
⁶ But it is God who has wronged me,
    capturing me in his net.*

⁷ "I cry out, 'Help!' but no one answers me.
    I protest, but there is no justice.
⁸ God has blocked my way so I cannot
        move.
    He has plunged my path into
        darkness.
⁹ He has stripped me of my honor
    and removed the crown from my head.
¹⁰ He has demolished me on every side, and I
        am finished.
    He has uprooted my hope like a fallen
        tree.
¹¹ His fury burns against me;
    he counts me as an enemy.
¹² His troops advance.
    They build up roads to attack me.
    They camp all around my tent.

¹³ "My relatives stay far away,
    and my friends have turned against me.
¹⁴ My family is gone,
    and my close friends have forgotten me.
¹⁵ My servants and maids consider me a
        stranger.
    I am like a foreigner to them.
¹⁶ When I call my servant, he doesn't come;
    I have to plead with him!
¹⁷ My breath is repulsive to my wife.
    I am rejected by my own family.
¹⁸ Even young children despise me.
    When I stand to speak, they turn their
        backs on me.
¹⁹ My close friends detest me.
    Those I loved have turned against me.
²⁰ I have been reduced to skin and bones
    and have escaped death by the skin of
        my teeth.

²¹ "Have mercy on me, my friends, have
        mercy,
    for the hand of God has struck me.
²² Must you also persecute me, like God
        does?
    Haven't you chewed me up enough?

²³ "Oh, that my words could be recorded.
    Oh, that they could be inscribed on a
        monument,
²⁴ carved with an iron chisel and filled with
        lead,
    engraved forever in the rock.

²⁵ "But as for me, I know that my Redeemer
        lives,
    and he will stand upon the earth at
        last.
²⁶ And after my body has decayed,
    yet in my body I will see God!*
²⁷ I will see him for myself.
    Yes, I will see him with my own eyes.
    I am overwhelmed at the thought!

²⁸ "How dare you go on persecuting me,
    saying, 'It's his own fault'?
²⁹ You should fear punishment yourselves,
    for your attitude deserves punishment.
    Then you will know that there is indeed
        a judgment."

Zophar's Second Response to Job

20 Then Zophar the Naamathite replied:

² "I must reply
    because I am greatly disturbed.
³ I've had to endure your insults,
    but now my spirit prompts me to reply.

⁴ "Don't you realize that from the beginning
        of time,
    ever since people were first placed on
        the earth,
⁵ the triumph of the wicked has been short
        lived
    and the joy of the godless has been only
        temporary?
⁶ Though the pride of the godless reaches to
        the heavens
    and their heads touch the clouds,
⁷ yet they will vanish forever,
    thrown away like their own dung.
    Those who knew them will ask,
        'Where are they?'
⁸ They will fade like a dream and not be
        found.
    They will vanish like a vision in the
        night.
⁹ Those who once saw them will see them no
        more.
    Their families will never see them again.
¹⁰ Their children will beg from the poor,

19:6 Or *for I am like a city under siege.* 19:26 Or *without my body I will see God.* The meaning of the Hebrew is uncertain.

for they must give back their stolen
    riches.
11 Though they are young,
    their bones will lie in the dust.

12 "They enjoyed the sweet taste of
    wickedness,
    letting it melt under their tongue.
13 They savored it,
    holding it long in their mouths.
14 But suddenly the food in their bellies
    turns sour,
    a poisonous venom in their stomach.
15 They will vomit the wealth they
    swallowed.
    God won't let them keep it down.
16 They will suck the poison of cobras.
    The viper will kill them.
17 They will never again enjoy streams of
    olive oil
    or rivers of milk and honey.
18 They will give back everything they
    worked for.
    Their wealth will bring them no joy.
19 For they oppressed the poor and left them
    destitute.
    They foreclosed on their homes.
20 They were always greedy and never
    satisfied.
    Nothing remains of all the things they
    dreamed about.
21 Nothing is left after they finish gorging
    themselves.
    Therefore, their prosperity will not
    endure.

22 "In the midst of plenty, they will run into
    trouble
    and be overcome by misery.
23 May God give them a bellyful of trouble.
    May God rain down his anger upon
    them.
24 When they try to escape an iron weapon,
    a bronze-tipped arrow will pierce them.
25 The arrow is pulled from their back,
    and the arrowhead glistens with
    blood.*
    The terrors of death are upon them.
26   Their treasures will be thrown into
    deepest darkness.
    A wildfire will devour their goods,
    consuming all they have left.
27 The heavens will reveal their guilt,
    and the earth will testify against them.
28 A flood will sweep away their house.

God's anger will descend on them in
    torrents.
29 This is the reward that God gives the
    wicked.
    It is the inheritance decreed by God."

Job's Seventh Speech: A Response to Zophar

21 Then Job spoke again:

2 "Listen closely to what I am saying.
    That's one consolation you can give me.
3 Bear with me, and let me speak.
    After I have spoken, you may resume
    mocking me.

4 "My complaint is with God, not with
    people.
    I have good reason to be so impatient.
5 Look at me and be stunned.
    Put your hand over your mouth in
    shock.
6 When I think about what I am saying,
    I shudder.
    My body trembles.

7 "Why do the wicked prosper,
    growing old and powerful?
8 They live to see their children grow up and
    settle down,
    and they enjoy their grandchildren.
9 Their homes are safe from every fear,
    and God does not punish them.
10 Their bulls never fail to breed.
    Their cows bear calves and never
    miscarry.
11 They let their children frisk about like
    lambs.
    Their little ones skip and dance.
12 They sing with tambourine and harp.
    They celebrate to the sound of the flute.
13 They spend their days in prosperity,
    then go down to the grave* in peace.
14 And yet they say to God, 'Go away.
    We want no part of you and your ways.
15 Who is the Almighty, and why should we
    obey him?
    What good will it do us to pray?'
16 (They think their prosperity is of their
    own doing,
    but I will have nothing to do with that
    kind of thinking.)

17 "Yet the light of the wicked never seems to
    be extinguished.
    Do they ever have trouble?

20:25 Hebrew *with gall.*   21:13 Hebrew *to Sheol.*

Does God distribute sorrows to them
in anger?
18 Are they driven before the wind like
straw?
Are they carried away by the storm like
chaff?
Not at all!

19 "'Well,' you say, 'at least God will punish
their children!'
But I say he should punish the ones who
sin,
so that they understand his judgment.
20 Let them see their destruction with their
own eyes.
Let them drink deeply of the anger of
the Almighty.
21 For they will not care what happens to
their family
after they are dead.

22 "But who can teach a lesson to God,
since he judges even the most
powerful?
23 One person dies in prosperity,
completely comfortable and secure,
24 the picture of good health,
vigorous and fit.
25 Another person dies in bitter poverty,
never having tasted the good life.
26 But both are buried in the same dust,
both eaten by the same maggots.

27 "Look, I know what you're thinking.
I know the schemes you plot against me.
28 You will tell me of rich and wicked people
whose houses have vanished because of
their sins.
29 But ask those who have been around,
and they will tell you the truth.
30 Evil people are spared in times of calamity
and are allowed to escape disaster.
31 No one criticizes them openly
or pays them back for what they have
done.
32 When they are carried to the grave,
an honor guard keeps watch at their
tomb.
33 A great funeral procession goes to the
cemetery.
Many pay their respects as the body is
laid to rest,
and the earth gives sweet repose.

34 "How can your empty clichés comfort me?
All your explanations are lies!"

Eliphaz's Third Response to Job

22 Then Eliphaz the Temanite replied:

2 "Can a person do anything to help
God?
Can even a wise person be helpful to
him?
3 Is it any advantage to the Almighty if you
are righteous?
Would it be any gain to him if you were
perfect?
4 Is it because you're so pious that he accuses
you
and brings judgment against you?
5 No, it's because of your wickedness!
There's no limit to your sins.

6 "For example, you must have lent money
to your friend
and demanded clothing as security.
Yes, you stripped him to the bone.
7 You must have refused water for the
thirsty
and food for the hungry.
8 You probably think the land belongs to the
powerful
and only the privileged have a right
to it!
9 You must have sent widows away
empty-handed
and crushed the hopes of orphans.
10 That is why you are surrounded by traps
and tremble from sudden fears.
11 That is why you cannot see in the
darkness,
and waves of water cover you.

12 "God is so great—higher than the heavens,
higher than the farthest stars.
13 But you reply, 'That's why God can't see
what I am doing!
How can he judge through the thick
darkness?
14 For thick clouds swirl about him, and he
cannot see us.
He is way up there, walking on the vault
of heaven.'

15 "Will you continue on the old paths
where evil people have walked?
16 They were snatched away in the prime of
life,
the foundations of their lives washed
away.
17 For they said to God, 'Leave us alone!
What can the Almighty do to us?'

18 Yet he was the one who filled their homes
    with good things,
        so I will have nothing to do with that
        kind of thinking.

19 "The righteous will be happy to see the
    wicked destroyed,
        and the innocent will laugh in
        contempt.
20 They will say, 'See how our enemies have
    been destroyed.
        The last of them have been consumed
        in the fire.'

21 "Submit to God, and you will have peace;
    then things will go well for you.
22 Listen to his instructions,
    and store them in your heart.
23 If you return to the Almighty, you will be
    restored—
        so clean up your life.
24 If you give up your lust for money
    and throw your precious gold into the
    river,
25 the Almighty himself will be your
    treasure.
        He will be your precious silver!

26 "Then you will take delight in the
    Almighty
        and look up to God.
27 You will pray to him, and he will hear you,
    and you will fulfill your vows to him.
28 You will succeed in whatever you choose
    to do,
        and light will shine on the road ahead
        of you.
29 If people are in trouble and you say, 'Help
    them,'
        God will save them.
30 Even sinners will be rescued;
    they will be rescued because your hands
    are pure."

Job's Eighth Speech: A Response to Eliphaz

23 Then Job spoke again:

2 "My complaint today is still a bitter
    one,
        and I try hard not to groan aloud.
3 If only I knew where to find God,
    I would go to his court.
4 I would lay out my case
    and present my arguments.
5 Then I would listen to his reply
    and understand what he says to me.

6 Would he use his great power to argue
    with me?
        No, he would give me a fair hearing.
7 Honest people can reason with him,
    so I would be forever acquitted by my
    judge.
8 I go east, but he is not there.
    I go west, but I cannot find him.
9 I do not see him in the north, for he is
    hidden.
        I look to the south, but he is concealed.

10 "But he knows where I am going.
    And when he tests me, I will come out as
    pure as gold.
11 For I have stayed on God's paths;
    I have followed his ways and not turned
    aside.
12 I have not departed from his commands,
    but have treasured his words more than
    daily food.
13 But once he has made his decision, who
    can change his mind?
        Whatever he wants to do, he does.
14 So he will do to me whatever he has
    planned.
        He controls my destiny.
15 No wonder I am so terrified in his
    presence.
        When I think of it, terror grips me.
16 God has made me sick at heart;
    the Almighty has terrified me.
17 Darkness is all around me;
    thick, impenetrable darkness is
    everywhere.

Job Asks Why the Wicked Are Not Punished

24 1 "Why doesn't the Almighty bring
        the wicked to judgment?
    Why must the godly wait for him in
    vain?
2 Evil people steal land by moving the
    boundary markers.
        They steal livestock and put them in
        their own pastures.
3 They take the orphan's donkey
    and demand the widow's ox as security
    for a loan.
4 The poor are pushed off the path;
    the needy must hide together for safety.
5 Like wild donkeys in the wilderness,
    the poor must spend all their time
    looking for food,
        searching even in the desert for food for
        their children.
6 They harvest a field they do not own,

and they glean in the vineyards of the
wicked.
⁷ All night they lie naked in the cold,
without clothing or covering.
⁸ They are soaked by mountain showers,
and they huddle against the rocks for
want of a home.

⁹ "The wicked snatch a widow's child from
her breast,
taking the baby as security for a loan.
¹⁰ The poor must go about naked, without
any clothing.
They harvest food for others while they
themselves are starving.
¹¹ They press out olive oil without being
allowed to taste it,
and they tread in the winepress as they
suffer from thirst.
¹² The groans of the dying rise from the city,
and the wounded cry for help,
yet God ignores their moaning.

¹³ "Wicked people rebel against the light.
They refuse to acknowledge its ways
or stay in its paths.
¹⁴ The murderer rises in the early dawn
to kill the poor and needy;
at night he is a thief.
¹⁵ The adulterer waits for the twilight,
saying, 'No one will see me then.'
He hides his face so no one will know
him.
¹⁶ Thieves break into houses at night
and sleep in the daytime.
They are not acquainted with the light.
¹⁷ The black night is their morning.
They ally themselves with the terrors
of the darkness.

¹⁸ "But they disappear like foam down a
river.
Everything they own is cursed,
and they are afraid to enter their own
vineyards.
¹⁹ The grave* consumes sinners
just as drought and heat consume snow.
²⁰ Their own mothers will forget them.
Maggots will find them sweet to eat.
No one will remember them.
Wicked people are broken like a tree in
the storm.
²¹ They cheat the woman who has no son to
help her.
They refuse to help the needy widow.

²² "God, in his power, drags away the rich.
They may rise high, but they have no
assurance of life.
²³ They may be allowed to live in security,
but God is always watching them.
²⁴ And though they are great now,
in a moment they will be gone like all
others,
cut off like heads of grain.
²⁵ Can anyone claim otherwise?
Who can prove me wrong?"

Bildad's Third Response to Job

25 Then Bildad the Shuhite replied:

² "God is powerful and dreadful.
He enforces peace in the heavens.
³ Who is able to count his heavenly army?
Doesn't his light shine on all the earth?
⁴ How can a mortal be innocent before God?
Can anyone born of a woman be pure?
⁵ God is more glorious than the moon;
he shines brighter than the stars.
⁶ In comparison, people are maggots;
we mortals are mere worms."

Job's Ninth Speech: A Response to Bildad

26 Then Job spoke again:

² "How you have helped the
powerless!
How you have saved the weak!
³ How you have enlightened my stupidity!
What wise advice you have offered!
⁴ Where have you gotten all these wise
sayings?
Whose spirit speaks through you?

⁵ "The dead tremble—
those who live beneath the waters.
⁶ The underworld* is naked in God's
presence.
The place of destruction* is uncovered.
⁷ God stretches the northern sky over empty
space
and hangs the earth on nothing.
⁸ He wraps the rain in his thick clouds,
and the clouds don't burst with the
weight.
⁹ He covers the face of the moon,*
shrouding it with his clouds.
¹⁰ He created the horizon when he separated
the waters;
he set the boundary between day and
night.

24:19 Hebrew *Sheol.*   26:6a Hebrew *Sheol.*   26:6b Hebrew *Abaddon.*   26:9 Or *covers his throne.*

11 The foundations of heaven tremble;
      they shudder at his rebuke.
12 By his power the sea grew calm.
      By his skill he crushed the great sea
         monster.*
13 His Spirit made the heavens beautiful,
      and his power pierced the gliding
         serpent.
14 These are just the beginning of all that
      he does,
      merely a whisper of his power.
      Who, then, can comprehend the
         thunder of his power?"

Job's Final Speech

27 Job continued speaking:

2 "I vow by the living God, who has
      taken away my rights,
      by the Almighty who has embittered
         my soul—
3 As long as I live,
      while I have breath from God,
4 my lips will speak no evil,
      and my tongue will speak no lies.
5 I will never concede that you are right;
      I will defend my integrity until
         I die.
6 I will maintain my innocence without
      wavering.
      My conscience is clear for as long as
         I live.

7 "May my enemy be punished like the
      wicked,
      my adversary like those who do evil.
8 For what hope do the godless have when
      God cuts them off
      and takes away their life?
9 Will God listen to their cry
      when trouble comes upon them?
10 Can they take delight in the Almighty?
      Can they call to God at any time?
11 I will teach you about God's power.
      I will not conceal anything concerning
         the Almighty.
12 But you have seen all this,
      yet you say all these useless things
         to me.

13 "This is what the wicked will receive from
      God;
      this is their inheritance from the
         Almighty.

14 They may have many children,
      but the children will die in war or starve
         to death.
15 Those who survive will die of a plague,
      and not even their widows will mourn
         them.

16 "Evil people may have piles of money
      and may store away mounds of clothing.
17 But the righteous will wear that clothing,
      and the innocent will divide that money.
18 The wicked build houses as fragile as a
      spider's web,*
      as flimsy as a shelter made of branches.
19 The wicked go to bed rich
      but wake to find that all their wealth is
         gone.
20 Terror overwhelms them like a flood,
      and they are blown away in the storms
         of the night.
21 The east wind carries them away, and they
      are gone.
      It sweeps them away.
22 It whirls down on them without mercy.
      They struggle to flee from its power.
23 But everyone jeers at them
      and mocks them.

Job Speaks of Wisdom and Understanding

28 1 "People know where to mine silver
      and how to refine gold.
2 They know where to dig iron from the
      earth
      and how to smelt copper from rock.
3 They know how to shine light in the
      darkness
      and explore the farthest regions of the
         earth
      as they search in the dark for ore.
4 They sink a mine shaft into the earth
      far from where anyone lives.
      They descend on ropes, swinging back
         and forth.
5 Food is grown on the earth above,
      but down below, the earth is melted as
         by fire.
6 Here the rocks contain precious lapis
      lazuli,
      and the dust contains gold.
7 These are treasures no bird of prey can see,
      no falcon's eye observe.
8 No wild animal has walked upon these
      treasures;
      no lion has ever set his paw there.

26:12 Hebrew *Rahab*, the name of a mythical sea monster that represents chaos in ancient literature.   **27:18** As in Greek and
Syriac versions (see also 8:14); Hebrew reads *a moth*.

9 People know how to tear apart flinty rocks
and overturn the roots of mountains.
10 They cut tunnels in the rocks
and uncover precious stones.
11 They dam up the trickling streams
and bring to light the hidden treasures.

12 "But do people know where to find
wisdom?
Where can they find understanding?
13 No one knows where to find it,*
for it is not found among the living.
14 'It is not here,' says the ocean.
'Nor is it here,' says the sea.
15 It cannot be bought with gold.
It cannot be purchased with silver.
16 It's worth more than all the gold of Ophir,
greater than precious onyx or lapis
lazuli.
17 Wisdom is more valuable than gold and
crystal.
It cannot be purchased with jewels
mounted in fine gold.
18 Coral and jasper are worthless in trying to
get it.
The price of wisdom is far above rubies.
19 Precious peridot from Ethiopia* cannot be
exchanged for it.
It's worth more than the purest gold.

20 "But do people know where to find
wisdom?
Where can they find understanding?
21 It is hidden from the eyes of all humanity.
Even the sharp-eyed birds in the sky
cannot discover it.
22 Destruction* and Death say,
'We've heard only rumors of where
wisdom can be found.'

23 "God alone understands the way to
wisdom;
he knows where it can be found,
24 for he looks throughout the whole earth
and sees everything under the heavens.
25 He decided how hard the winds should
blow
and how much rain should fall.
26 He made the laws for the rain
and laid out a path for the lightning.
27 Then he saw wisdom and evaluated it.
He set it in place and examined it
thoroughly.
28 And this is what he says to all humanity:

'The fear of the Lord is true wisdom;
to forsake evil is real understanding.'"

Job Speaks of His Former Blessings

29 Job continued speaking:

2 "I long for the years gone by
when God took care of me,
3 when he lit up the way before me
and I walked safely through the
darkness.
4 When I was in my prime,
God's friendship was felt in my home.
5 The Almighty was still with me,
and my children were around me.
6 My steps were awash in cream,
and the rocks gushed olive oil for me.

7 "Those were the days when I went to the
city gate
and took my place among the honored
leaders.
8 The young stepped aside when they
saw me,
and even the aged rose in respect at my
coming.
9 The princes stood in silence
and put their hands over their mouths.
10 The highest officials of the city stood
quietly,
holding their tongues in respect.

11 "All who heard me praised me.
All who saw me spoke well of me.
12 For I assisted the poor in their need
and the orphans who required help.
13 I helped those without hope, and they
blessed me.
And I caused the widows' hearts to sing
for joy.
14 Everything I did was honest.
Righteousness covered me like a robe,
and I wore justice like a turban.
15 I served as eyes for the blind
and feet for the lame.
16 I was a father to the poor
and assisted strangers who needed help.
17 I broke the jaws of godless oppressors
and plucked their victims from their
teeth.

18 "I thought, 'Surely I will die surrounded
by my family
after a long, good life.*

28:13 As in Greek version; Hebrew reads *knows its value.*   28:19 Hebrew *from Cush.*   28:22 Hebrew *Abaddon.*   29:18 Hebrew
after I have counted my days like sand.

19 For I am like a tree whose roots reach the
        water,
    whose branches are refreshed with
        the dew.
20 New honors are constantly bestowed
        on me,
    and my strength is continually
        renewed.'

21 "Everyone listened to my advice.
    They were silent as they waited for me
        to speak.
22 And after I spoke, they had nothing to add,
    for my counsel satisfied them.
23 They longed for me to speak as people
        long for rain.
    They drank my words like a refreshing
        spring rain.
24 When they were discouraged, I smiled at
        them.
    My look of approval was precious to
        them.
25 Like a chief, I told them what to do.
    I lived like a king among his troops
    and comforted those who mourned.

Job Speaks of His Anguish

30 1 "But now I am mocked by people
        younger than I,
    by young men whose fathers are not
        worthy to run with my sheepdogs.
2 A lot of good they are to me—
    those worn-out wretches!
3 They are gaunt from poverty and hunger.
    They claw the dry ground in desolate
        wastelands.
4 They pluck wild greens from among the
        bushes
    and eat from the roots of broom trees.
5 They are driven from human society,
    and people shout at them as if they were
        thieves.
6 So now they live in frightening ravines,
    in caves and among the rocks.
7 They sound like animals howling among
        the bushes,
    huddled together beneath the nettles.
8 They are nameless fools,
    outcasts from society.

9 "And now they mock me with vulgar
        songs!
    They taunt me!
10 They despise me and won't come near me,
    except to spit in my face.

11 For God has cut my bowstring.
    He has humbled me,
    so they have thrown off all restraint.
12 These outcasts oppose me to my face.
    They send me sprawling
    and lay traps in my path.
13 They block my road
    and do everything they can to
        destroy me.
    They know I have no one to help me.
14   They come at me from all directions.
    They jump on me when I am down.
15   I live in terror now.
    My honor has blown away in the wind,
    and my prosperity has vanished like
        a cloud.

16 "And now my life seeps away.
    Depression haunts my days.
17 At night my bones are filled with pain,
    which gnaws at me relentlessly.
18 With a strong hand, God grabs my shirt.*
    He grips me by the collar of my coat.
19 He has thrown me into the mud.
    I'm nothing more than dust and ashes.

20 "I cry to you, O God, but you don't answer.
    I stand before you, but you don't even
        look.
21 You have become cruel toward me.
    You use your power to persecute me.
22 You throw me into the whirlwind
    and destroy me in the storm.
23 And I know you are sending me to my
        death—
    the destination of all who live.

24 "Surely no one would turn against the
        needy
    when they cry for help in their trouble.
25 Did I not weep for those in trouble?
    Was I not deeply grieved for the needy?
26 So I looked for good, but evil came instead.
    I waited for the light, but darkness fell.
27 My heart is troubled and restless.
    Days of suffering torment me.
28 I walk in gloom, without sunlight.
    I stand in the public square and cry
        for help.
29 Instead, I am considered a brother to
        jackals
    and a companion to owls.
30 My skin has turned dark,
    and my bones burn with fever.
31 My harp plays sad music,

30:18 As in Greek version; Hebrew reads *hand, my garment is disfigured.*

and my flute accompanies those who
weep.

Job's Final Protest of Innocence

31 ¹ "I made a covenant with my eyes
not to look with lust at a young
woman.
² For what has God above chosen for us?
What is our inheritance from the
Almighty on high?
³ Isn't it calamity for the wicked
and misfortune for those who do evil?
⁴ Doesn't he see everything I do
and every step I take?

⁵ "Have I lied to anyone
or deceived anyone?
⁶ Let God weigh me on the scales of justice,
for he knows my integrity.
⁷ If I have strayed from his pathway,
or if my heart has lusted for what my
eyes have seen,
or if I am guilty of any other sin,
⁸ then let someone else eat the crops I have
planted.
Let all that I have planted be uprooted.

⁹ "If my heart has been seduced by a woman,
or if I have lusted for my neighbor's
wife,
¹⁰ then let my wife serve* another man;
let other men sleep with her.
¹¹ For lust is a shameful sin,
a crime that should be punished.
¹² It is a fire that burns all the way to hell.*
It would wipe out everything I own.

¹³ "If I have been unfair to my male or female
servants
when they brought their complaints
to me,
¹⁴ how could I face God?
What could I say when he
questioned me?
¹⁵ For God created both me and my
servants.
He created us both in the womb.

¹⁶ "Have I refused to help the poor,
or crushed the hopes of widows?
¹⁷ Have I been stingy with my food
and refused to share it with orphans?
¹⁸ No, from childhood I have cared for
orphans like a father,
and all my life I have cared for widows.

¹⁹ Whenever I saw the homeless without
clothes
and the needy with nothing to wear,
²⁰ did they not praise me
for providing wool clothing to keep
them warm?

²¹ "If I raised my hand against an orphan,
knowing the judges would take my side,
²² then let my shoulder be wrenched out of
place!
Let my arm be torn from its socket!
²³ That would be better than facing God's
judgment.
For if the majesty of God opposes me,
what hope is there?

²⁴ "Have I put my trust in money
or felt secure because of my gold?
²⁵ Have I gloated about my wealth
and all that I own?

²⁶ "Have I looked at the sun shining in the
skies,
or the moon walking down its silver
pathway,
²⁷ and been secretly enticed in my heart
to throw kisses at them in worship?
²⁸ If so, I should be punished by the judges,
for it would mean I had denied the God
of heaven.

²⁹ "Have I ever rejoiced when disaster struck
my enemies,
or become excited when harm came
their way?
³⁰ No, I have never sinned by cursing anyone
or by asking for revenge.
³¹ "My servants have never said,
'He let others go hungry.'
³² I have never turned away a stranger
but have opened my doors to everyone.

³³ "Have I tried to hide my sins like other
people do,
concealing my guilt in my heart?
³⁴ Have I feared the crowd
or the contempt of the masses,
so that I kept quiet and stayed indoors?

³⁵ "If only someone would listen to me!
Look, I will sign my name to my
defense.
Let the Almighty answer me.

31:10 Hebrew *grind for*.   31:12 Hebrew *to Abaddon*.

Let my accuser write out the charges
    against me.
36 I would face the accusation proudly.
    I would wear it like a crown.
37 For I would tell him exactly what I have
        done.
    I would come before him like a prince.

38 "If my land accuses me
    and all its furrows cry out together,
39 or if I have stolen its crops
    or murdered its owners,
40 then let thistles grow on that land instead
        of wheat,
    and weeds instead of barley."

Job's words are ended.

Elihu Responds to Job's Friends

32 Job's three friends refused to reply further to him because he kept insisting on his innocence.

2 Then Elihu son of Barakel the Buzite, of the clan of Ram, became angry. He was angry because Job refused to admit that he had sinned and that God was right in punishing him. 3 He was also angry with Job's three friends, for they made God* appear to be wrong by their inability to answer Job's arguments. 4 Elihu had waited for the others to speak to Job because they were older than he. 5 But when he saw that they had no further reply, he spoke out angrily. 6 Elihu son of Barakel the Buzite said,

"I am young and you are old,
    so I held back from telling you what
        I think.
7 I thought, 'Those who are older should
        speak,
    for wisdom comes with age.'
8 But there is a spirit* within people,
    the breath of the Almighty within them,
    that makes them intelligent.
9 Sometimes the elders are not wise.
    Sometimes the aged do not understand
        justice.
10 So listen to me,
    and let me tell you what I think.

11 "I have waited all this time,
    listening very carefully to your
        arguments,
    listening to you grope for words.
12 I have listened,
    but not one of you has refuted Job

or answered his arguments.
13 And don't tell me, 'He is too wise for us.
    Only God can convince him.'
14 If Job had been arguing with me,
    I would not answer with your kind of
        logic!
15 You sit there baffled,
    with nothing more to say.
16 Should I continue to wait, now that you
        are silent?
    Must I also remain silent?
17 No, I will say my piece.
    I will speak my mind.
18 For I am full of pent-up words,
    and the spirit within me urges me on.
19 I am like a cask of wine without a vent,
    like a new wineskin ready to burst!
20 I must speak to find relief,
    so let me give my answers.
21 I won't play favorites
    or try to flatter anyone.
22 For if I tried flattery,
    my Creator would soon destroy me.

Elihu Presents His Case against Job

33 1 "Listen to my words, Job;
        pay attention to what I have
            to say.
2 Now that I have begun to speak,
    let me continue.
3 I speak with all sincerity;
    I speak the truth.
4 For the Spirit of God has made me,
    and the breath of the Almighty gives
        me life.
5 Answer me, if you can;
    make your case and take your stand.
6 Look, you and I both belong to God.
    I, too, was formed from clay.
7 So you don't need to be afraid of me.
    I won't come down hard on you.

8 "You have spoken in my hearing,
    and I have heard your very words.
9 You said, 'I am pure; I am without sin;
    I am innocent; I have no guilt.
10 God is picking a quarrel with me,
    and he considers me his enemy.
11 He puts my feet in the stocks
    and watches my every move.'

12 "But you are wrong, and I will show you
        why.
    For God is greater than any human
        being.

32:3 As in ancient Hebrew scribal tradition; the Masoretic Text reads *Job*.   32:8 Or *Spirit;* also in 32:18.

13 So why are you bringing a charge against
   him?
   Why say he does not respond to people's
   complaints?
14 For God speaks again and again,
   though people do not recognize it.
15 He speaks in dreams, in visions of the
   night,
   when deep sleep falls on people
   as they lie in their beds.
16 He whispers in their ears
   and terrifies them with warnings.
17 He makes them turn from doing wrong;
   he keeps them from pride.
18 He protects them from the grave,
   from crossing over the river of death.

19 "Or God disciplines people with pain on
   their sickbeds,
   with ceaseless aching in their bones.
20 They lose their appetite
   for even the most delicious food.
21 Their flesh wastes away,
   and their bones stick out.
22 They are at death's door;
   the angels of death wait for them.

23 "But if an angel from heaven appears—
   a special messenger to intercede for a
   person
   and declare that he is upright—
24 he will be gracious and say,
   'Rescue him from the grave,
   for I have found a ransom for his life.'
25 Then his body will become as healthy as
   a child's,
   firm and youthful again.
26 When he prays to God,
   he will be accepted.
   And God will receive him with joy
   and restore him to good standing.
27 He will declare to his friends,
   'I sinned and twisted the truth,
   but it was not worth it.*
28 God rescued me from the grave,
   and now my life is filled with light.'

29 "Yes, God does these things
   again and again for people.
30 He rescues them from the grave
   so they may enjoy the light of life.
31 Mark this well, Job. Listen to me,
   for I have more to say.
32 But if you have anything to say, go
   ahead.

Speak, for I am anxious to see you
   justified.
33 But if not, then listen to me.
   Keep silent and I will teach you
   wisdom!"

Elihu Accuses Job of Arrogance

34 Then Elihu said:

2 "Listen to me, you wise men.
   Pay attention, you who have knowledge.
3 Job said, 'The ear tests the words it hears
   just as the mouth distinguishes between
   foods.'
4 So let us discern for ourselves what is
   right;
   let us learn together what is good.
5 For Job also said, 'I am innocent,
   but God has taken away my rights.
6 I am innocent, but they call me a liar.
   My suffering is incurable, though I have
   not sinned.'

7 "Tell me, has there ever been a man like
   Job,
   with his thirst for irreverent talk?
8 He chooses evil people as companions.
   He spends his time with wicked men.
9 He has even said, 'Why waste time
   trying to please God?'

10 "Listen to me, you who have
   understanding.
   Everyone knows that God doesn't sin!
   The Almighty can do no wrong.
11 He repays people according to their deeds.
   He treats people as they deserve.
12 Truly, God will not do wrong.
   The Almighty will not twist justice.
13 Did someone else put the world in his
   care?
   Who set the whole world in place?
14 If God were to take back his spirit
   and withdraw his breath,
15 all life would cease,
   and humanity would turn again
   to dust.

16 "Now listen to me if you are wise.
   Pay attention to what I say.
17 Could God govern if he hated justice?
   Are you going to condemn the almighty
   judge?
18 For he says to kings, 'You are wicked,'
   and to nobles, 'You are unjust.'

33:27 Greek version reads *but he* [God] *did not punish me as my sin deserved.*

19 He doesn't care how great a person
          may be,
     and he pays no more attention to the
          rich than to the poor.
     He made them all.
20 In a moment they die.
     In the middle of the night they pass
          away;
     the mighty are removed without human
          hand.

21 "For God watches how people live;
     he sees everything they do.
22 No darkness is thick enough
     to hide the wicked from his eyes.
23 We don't set the time
     when we will come before God in
          judgment.
24 He brings the mighty to ruin without
          asking anyone,
     and he sets up others in their place.
25 He knows what they do,
     and in the night he overturns and
          destroys them.
26 He strikes them down because they are
          wicked,
     doing it openly for all to see.
27 For they turned away from following him.
     They have no respect for any of his ways.
28 They cause the poor to cry out, catching
          God's attention.
     He hears the cries of the needy.
29 But if he chooses to remain quiet,
     who can criticize him?
     When he hides his face, no one can find
          him,
     whether an individual or a nation.
30 He prevents the godless from ruling
     so they cannot be a snare to the
          people.

31 "Why don't people say to God, 'I have
          sinned,
     but I will sin no more'?
32 Or 'I don't know what evil I have done—
          tell me.
     If I have done wrong, I will stop at
          once'?

33 "Must God tailor his justice to your
          demands?
     But you have rejected him!
     The choice is yours, not mine.
     Go ahead, share your wisdom with us.

34 After all, bright people will tell me,
     and wise people will hear me say,
35 'Job speaks out of ignorance;
     his words lack insight.'
36 Job, you deserve the maximum penalty
     for the wicked way you have talked.
37 For you have added rebellion to your sin;
     you show no respect,
     and you speak many angry words
          against God."

Elihu Reminds Job of God's Justice

35 Then Elihu said:

2 "Do you think it is right for you to
          claim,
     'I am righteous before God'?
3 For you also ask, 'What's in it for me?
     What's the use of living a righteous life?'

4 "I will answer you
     and all your friends, too.
5 Look up into the sky,
     and see the clouds high above you.
6 If you sin, how does that affect God?
     Even if you sin again and again,
     what effect will it have on him?
7 If you are good, is this some great gift to
          him?
     What could you possibly give him?
8 No, your sins affect only people like
          yourself,
     and your good deeds also affect only
          humans.

9 "People cry out when they are oppressed.
     They groan beneath the power of the
          mighty.
10 Yet they don't ask, 'Where is God my
          Creator,
     the one who gives songs in the night?
11 Where is the one who makes us smarter
          than the animals
     and wiser than the birds of the sky?'
12 And when they cry out, God does not
          answer
     because of their pride.
13 But it is wrong to say God doesn't listen,
     to say the Almighty isn't concerned.
14 You say you can't see him,
     but he will bring justice if you will
          only wait.*
15 You say he does not respond to sinners
     with anger

35:13-14 These verses can also be translated as follows: ¹³Indeed, God doesn't listen to their empty plea; / the Almighty is not concerned. / ¹⁴How much less will he listen when you say you don't see him, / and that your case is before him and you're waiting for justice.

and is not greatly concerned about wickedness.*

16 But you are talking nonsense, Job.
You have spoken like a fool."

36 Elihu continued speaking:

2 "Let me go on, and I will show you the truth.
For I have not finished defending God!
3 I will present profound arguments
for the righteousness of my Creator.
4 I am telling you nothing but the truth,
for I am a man of great knowledge.

5 "God is mighty, but he does not despise anyone!
He is mighty in both power and understanding.
6 He does not let the wicked live
but gives justice to the afflicted.
7 He never takes his eyes off the innocent,
but he sets them on thrones with kings
and exalts them forever.
8 If they are bound in chains
and caught up in a web of trouble,
9 he shows them the reason.
He shows them their sins of pride.
10 He gets their attention
and commands that they turn from evil.

11 "If they listen and obey God,
they will be blessed with prosperity throughout their lives.
All their years will be pleasant.
12 But if they refuse to listen to him,
they will cross over the river of death,
dying from lack of understanding.
13 For the godless are full of resentment.
Even when he punishes them,
they refuse to cry out to him for help.
14 They die when they are young,
after wasting their lives in immoral living.
15 But by means of their suffering, he rescues those who suffer.
For he gets their attention through adversity.

16 "God is leading you away from danger, Job,
to a place free from distress.

He is setting your table with the best food.
17 But you are obsessed with whether the godless will be judged.
Don't worry, judgment and justice will be upheld.
18 But watch out, or you may be seduced by wealth.*
Don't let yourself be bribed into sin.
19 Could all your wealth*
or all your mighty efforts
keep you from distress?
20 Do not long for the cover of night,
for that is when people will be destroyed.*
21 Be on guard! Turn back from evil,
for God sent this suffering
to keep you from a life of evil.

Elihu Reminds Job of God's Power

22 "Look, God is all-powerful.
Who is a teacher like him?
23 No one can tell him what to do,
or say to him, 'You have done wrong.'
24 Instead, glorify his mighty works,
singing songs of praise.
25 Everyone has seen these things,
though only from a distance.

26 "Look, God is greater than we can understand.
His years cannot be counted.
27 He draws up the water vapor
and then distills it into rain.
28 The rain pours down from the clouds,
and everyone benefits.
29 Who can understand the spreading of the clouds
and the thunder that rolls forth from heaven?
30 See how he spreads the lightning around him
and how it lights up the depths of the sea.
31 By these mighty acts he nourishes* the people,
giving them food in abundance.
32 He fills his hands with lightning bolts
and hurls each at its target.
33 The thunder announces his presence;
the storm announces his indignant anger.*

35:15 As in Greek and Latin versions; the meaning of this Hebrew word is uncertain.   36:18 Or But don't let your anger lead you to mockery.   36:19 Or Could all your cries for help.   36:16-20 The meaning of the Hebrew in this passage is uncertain.   36:31 Or he governs.   36:33 Or even the cattle know when a storm is coming. The meaning of the Hebrew is uncertain.

37

1 "My heart pounds as I think of this.
It trembles within me.
2 Listen carefully to the thunder of God's
voice
as it rolls from his mouth.
3 It rolls across the heavens,
and his lightning flashes in every
direction.
4 Then comes the roaring of the thunder—
the tremendous voice of his majesty.
He does not restrain it when he speaks.
5 God's voice is glorious in the thunder.
We can't even imagine the greatness of
his power.

6 "He directs the snow to fall on the earth
and tells the rain to pour down.
7 Then everyone stops working
so they can watch his power.
8 The wild animals take cover
and stay inside their dens.
9 The stormy wind comes from its
chamber,
and the driving winds bring the cold.
10 God's breath sends the ice,
freezing wide expanses of water.
11 He loads the clouds with moisture,
and they flash with his lightning.
12 The clouds churn about at his direction.
They do whatever he commands
throughout the earth.
13 He makes these things happen either to
punish people
or to show his unfailing love.

14 "Pay attention to this, Job.
Stop and consider the wonderful
miracles of God!
15 Do you know how God controls the storm
and causes the lightning to flash from
his clouds?
16 Do you understand how he moves the
clouds
with wonderful perfection and skill?
17 When you are sweltering in your clothes
and the south wind dies down and
everything is still,
18 he makes the skies reflect the heat like a
bronze mirror.
Can you do that?

19 "So teach the rest of us what to say to God.
We are too ignorant to make our own
arguments.
20 Should God be notified that I want to
speak?
Can people even speak when they are
confused?*
21 We cannot look at the sun,
for it shines brightly in the sky
when the wind clears away the
clouds.
22 So also, golden splendor comes from
the mountain of God.*
He is clothed in dazzling splendor.
23 We cannot imagine the power of the
Almighty;
but even though he is just and
righteous,
he does not destroy us.
24 No wonder people everywhere fear him.
All who are wise show him reverence.*"

The Lord Challenges Job

38

Then the Lord answered Job from the
whirlwind:

2 "Who is this that questions my wisdom
with such ignorant words?
3 Brace yourself like a man,
because I have some questions for you,
and you must answer them.

4 "Where were you when I laid the
foundations of the earth?
Tell me, if you know so much.
5 Who determined its dimensions
and stretched out the surveying line?
6 What supports its foundations,
and who laid its cornerstone
7 as the morning stars sang together
and all the angels* shouted for joy?

8 "Who kept the sea inside its boundaries
as it burst from the womb,
9 and as I clothed it with clouds
and wrapped it in thick darkness?
10 For I locked it behind barred gates,
limiting its shores.
11 I said, 'This far and no farther will you
come.
Here your proud waves must stop!'

12 "Have you ever commanded the morning
to appear
and caused the dawn to rise in the east?
13 Have you made daylight spread to the
ends of the earth,

37:20 Or speak without being swallowed up?　37:22 Or from the north; or from the abode.　37:24 As in Greek version; Hebrew
reads He is not impressed by the wise.　38:7 Hebrew the sons of God.

to bring an end to the night's
wickedness?
14 As the light approaches,
the earth takes shape like clay pressed
beneath a seal;
it is robed in brilliant colors.*
15 The light disturbs the wicked
and stops the arm that is raised in
violence.

16 "Have you explored the springs from
which the seas come?
Have you explored their depths?
17 Do you know where the gates of death are
located?
Have you seen the gates of utter gloom?
18 Do you realize the extent of the earth?
Tell me about it if you know!

19 "Where does light come from,
and where does darkness go?
20 Can you take each to its home?
Do you know how to get there?
21 But of course you know all this!
For you were born before it was all created,
and you are so very experienced!

22 "Have you visited the storehouses of the
snow
or seen the storehouses of hail?
23 (I have reserved them as weapons for the
time of trouble,
for the day of battle and war.)
24 Where is the path to the source of light?
Where is the home of the east wind?

25 "Who created a channel for the torrents of
rain?
Who laid out the path for the lightning?
26 Who makes the rain fall on barren land,
in a desert where no one lives?
27 Who sends rain to satisfy the parched
ground
and make the tender grass spring up?

28 "Does the rain have a father?
Who gives birth to the dew?
29 Who is the mother of the ice?
Who gives birth to the frost from the
heavens?
30 For the water turns to ice as hard as rock,
and the surface of the water freezes.

31 "Can you direct the movement of the
stars—

binding the cluster of the Pleiades
or loosening the cords of Orion?
32 Can you direct the constellations through
the seasons
or guide the Bear with her cubs across
the heavens?
33 Do you know the laws of the universe?
Can you use them to regulate the
earth?

34 "Can you shout to the clouds
and make it rain?
35 Can you make lightning appear
and cause it to strike as you direct?
36 Who gives intuition to the heart
and instinct to the mind?
37 Who is wise enough to count all the
clouds?
Who can tilt the water jars of heaven
38 when the parched ground is dry
and the soil has hardened into clods?

39 "Can you stalk prey for a lioness
and satisfy the young lions' appetites
40 as they lie in their dens
or crouch in the thicket?
41 Who provides food for the ravens
when their young cry out to God
and wander about in hunger?

The LORD's Challenge Continues

39

1 "Do you know when the wild goats
give birth?
Have you watched as deer are born in
the wild?
2 Do you know how many months they
carry their young?
Are you aware of the time of their
delivery?
3 They crouch down to give birth to their
young
and deliver their offspring.
4 Their young grow up in the open fields,
then leave home and never return.

5 "Who gives the wild donkey its
freedom?
Who untied its ropes?
6 I have placed it in the wilderness;
its home is the wasteland.
7 It hates the noise of the city
and has no driver to shout at it.
8 The mountains are its pastureland,
where it searches for every blade
of grass.

38:14 Or *its features stand out like folds in a robe.*

⁹ "Will the wild ox consent to being tamed?
  Will it spend the night in your stall?
¹⁰ Can you hitch a wild ox to a plow?
  Will it plow a field for you?
¹¹ Given its strength, can you trust it?
  Can you leave and trust the ox to do
    your work?
¹² Can you rely on it to bring home your
    grain
  and deliver it to your threshing floor?

¹³ "The ostrich flaps her wings grandly,
  but they are no match for the feathers
    of the stork.
¹⁴ She lays her eggs on top of the earth,
  letting them be warmed in the dust.
¹⁵ She doesn't worry that a foot might crush
    them
  or a wild animal might destroy them.
¹⁶ She is harsh toward her young,
  as if they were not her own.
  She doesn't care if they die.
¹⁷ For God has deprived her of wisdom.
  He has given her no understanding.
¹⁸ But whenever she jumps up to run,
  she passes the swiftest horse with its
    rider.

¹⁹ "Have you given the horse its strength
  or clothed its neck with a flowing mane?
²⁰ Did you give it the ability to leap like a
    locust?
  Its majestic snorting is terrifying!
²¹ It paws the earth and rejoices in its
    strength
  when it charges out to battle.
²² It laughs at fear and is unafraid.
  It does not run from the sword.
²³ The arrows rattle against it,
  and the spear and javelin flash.
²⁴ It paws the ground fiercely
  and rushes forward into battle when
    the ram's horn blows.
²⁵ It snorts at the sound of the horn.
  It senses the battle in the distance.
  It quivers at the captain's commands
    and the noise of battle.

²⁶ "Is it your wisdom that makes the hawk
    soar
  and spread its wings toward the south?
²⁷ Is it at your command that the eagle rises
  to the heights to make its nest?
²⁸ It lives on the cliffs,

making its home on a distant, rocky
  crag.
²⁹ From there it hunts its prey,
  keeping watch with piercing eyes.
³⁰ Its young gulp down blood.
  Where there's a carcass, there you'll
    find it."

40 Then the LORD said to Job,

² "Do you still want to argue with
    the Almighty?
  You are God's critic, but do you have
    the answers?"

Job Responds to the LORD
³Then Job replied to the LORD,

⁴ "I am nothing—how could I ever find the
    answers?
  I will cover my mouth with my hand.
⁵ I have said too much already.
  I have nothing more to say."

The LORD Challenges Job Again
⁶Then the LORD answered Job from the whirlwind:

⁷ "Brace yourself like a man,
  because I have some questions for you,
  and you must answer them.

⁸ "Will you discredit my justice
  and condemn me just to prove you are
    right?
⁹ Are you as strong as God?
  Can you thunder with a voice like his?
¹⁰ All right, put on your glory and splendor,
  your honor and majesty.
¹¹ Give vent to your anger.
  Let it overflow against the proud.
¹² Humiliate the proud with a glance;
  walk on the wicked where they stand.
¹³ Bury them in the dust.
  Imprison them in the world of the dead.
¹⁴ Then even I would praise you,
  for your own strength would save you.

¹⁵ "Take a look at Behemoth,*
  which I made, just as I made you.
  It eats grass like an ox.
¹⁶ See its powerful loins
  and the muscles of its belly.
¹⁷ Its tail is as strong as a cedar.

40:15 The identification of Behemoth is disputed, ranging from an earthly creature to a mythical sea monster in ancient literature.

The sinews of its thighs are knit tightly
   together.
18 Its bones are tubes of bronze.
   Its limbs are bars of iron.
19 It is a prime example of God's handiwork,
   and only its Creator can threaten it.
20 The mountains offer it their best food,
   where all the wild animals play.
21 It lies under the lotus plants,*
   hidden by the reeds in the marsh.
22 The lotus plants give it shade
   among the willows beside the stream.
23 It is not disturbed by the raging river,
   not concerned when the swelling Jordan
      rushes around it.
24 No one can catch it off guard
   or put a ring in its nose and lead it away.

The LORD's Challenge Continues

41 1*"Can you catch Leviathan* with a
      hook
   or put a noose around its jaw?
2 Can you tie it with a rope through the
      nose
   or pierce its jaw with a spike?
3 Will it beg you for mercy
   or implore you for pity?
4 Will it agree to work for you,
   to be your slave for life?
5 Can you make it a pet like a bird,
   or give it to your little girls to play with?
6 Will merchants try to buy it
   to sell it in their shops?
7 Will its hide be hurt by spears
   or its head by a harpoon?
8 If you lay a hand on it,
   you will certainly remember the battle
      that follows.
   You won't try that again!
9*No, it is useless to try to capture it.
   The hunter who attempts it will be
      knocked down.
10 And since no one dares to disturb it,
   who then can stand up to me?
11 Who has given me anything that I need
      to pay back?
   Everything under heaven is mine.

12 "I want to emphasize Leviathan's limbs
   and its enormous strength and graceful
      form.
13 Who can strip off its hide,

and who can penetrate its double layer
   of armor?*
14 Who could pry open its jaws?
   For its teeth are terrible!
15 The scales on its back are like* rows of
      shields
   tightly sealed together.
16 They are so close together
   that no air can get between them.
17 Each scale sticks tight to the next.
   They interlock and cannot be
      penetrated.

18 "When it sneezes, it flashes light!
   Its eyes are like the red of dawn.
19 Lightning leaps from its mouth;
   flames of fire flash out.
20 Smoke streams from its nostrils
   like steam from a pot heated over
      burning rushes.
21 Its breath would kindle coals,
   for flames shoot from its mouth.

22 "The tremendous strength in Leviathan's
      neck
   strikes terror wherever it goes.
23 Its flesh is hard and firm
   and cannot be penetrated.
24 Its heart is hard as rock,
   hard as a millstone.
25 When it rises, the mighty are afraid,
   gripped by terror.
26 No sword can stop it,
   no spear, dart, or javelin.
27 Iron is nothing but straw to that creature,
   and bronze is like rotten wood.
28 Arrows cannot make it flee.
   Stones shot from a sling are like bits
      of grass.
29 Clubs are like a blade of grass,
   and it laughs at the swish of javelins.
30 Its belly is covered with scales as sharp
      as glass.
   It plows up the ground as it drags
      through the mud.

31 "Leviathan makes the water boil with its
      commotion.
   It stirs the depths like a pot of
      ointment.
32 The water glistens in its wake,
   making the sea look white.

40:21 Or *bramble bushes;* also in 40:22.   41:1a Verses 41:1-8 are numbered 40:25-32 in Hebrew text.   41:1b The identification
of Leviathan is disputed, ranging from an earthly creature to a mythical sea monster in ancient literature.   41:9 Verses
41:9-34 are numbered 41:1-26 in Hebrew text.   41:13 As in Greek version; Hebrew reads *its bridle?*   41:15 As in some Greek
manuscripts and Latin Vulgate; Hebrew reads *Its pride is in its.*

³³ Nothing on earth is its equal,
no other creature so fearless.
³⁴ Of all the creatures, it is the proudest.
It is the king of beasts."

Job Responds to the LORD

42 Then Job replied to the LORD:

² "I know that you can do anything,
and no one can stop you.
³ You asked, 'Who is this that questions my
wisdom with such ignorance?'
It is I—and I was talking about things
I knew nothing about,
things far too wonderful for me.
⁴ You said, 'Listen and I will speak!
I have some questions for you,
and you must answer them.'
⁵ I had only heard about you before,
but now I have seen you with my own
eyes.
⁶ I take back everything I said,
and I sit in dust and ashes to show my
repentance."

Conclusion: The LORD Blesses Job

⁷After the LORD had finished speaking to Job, he said to Eliphaz the Temanite: "I am angry with you and your two friends, for you have not spoken accurately about me, as my servant Job has. ⁸So take seven bulls and seven rams and go to my servant Job and offer a burnt offering for yourselves. My servant Job will pray for you, and I will accept his prayer on your behalf. I will not treat you as you deserve, for you have not spoken accurately about me, as my servant Job has." ⁹So Eliphaz the Temanite, Bildad the Shuhite, and Zophar the Naamathite did as the LORD commanded them, and the LORD accepted Job's prayer.

¹⁰When Job prayed for his friends, the LORD restored his fortunes. In fact, the LORD gave him twice as much as before! ¹¹Then all his brothers, sisters, and former friends came and feasted with him in his home. And they consoled him and comforted him because of all the trials the LORD had brought against him. And each of them brought him a gift of money* and a gold ring.

¹²So the LORD blessed Job in the second half of his life even more than in the beginning. For now he had 14,000 sheep, 6,000 camels, 1,000 teams of oxen, and 1,000 female donkeys. ¹³He also gave Job seven more sons and three more daughters. ¹⁴He named his first daughter Jemimah, the second Keziah, and the third Keren-happuch. ¹⁵In all the land no women were as lovely as the daughters of Job. And their father put them into his will along with their brothers.

¹⁶Job lived 140 years after that, living to see four generations of his children and grandchildren. ¹⁷Then he died, an old man who had lived a long, full life.

42:11 Hebrew *a kesitah;* the value or weight of the kesitah is no longer known.

Psalms

THROUGHOUT OUR LIVES, we experience a wide range of emotions, such as joy, anger, peacefulness, frustration, despair, happiness, and anxiety. These feelings don't typically obey carefully scripted creeds. Music and poetry often seem to be the only way to express them fully. The book of Psalms speaks to this part of human experience through the poetic words of people who offered their feelings to God. Are you angry about something? The book of Psalms includes several prayers that express this same emotion (see Psalm 35). Are you afraid? So was David when he wrote Psalm 2. Are you frustrated by injustice? Psalm 79 laments this same situation. Likewise, Psalm 19 and Psalm 104 celebrate the incredible power of God as it is revealed in his creation. This collection of hymns and prayers touches every corner of the human soul. As with the psalm writers themselves, these honest expressions of feeling will draw you closer to the God who made you.

■ **Author:** According to Jewish tradition, David wrote seventy-three Psalms; Asaph wrote twelve; the sons of Korah wrote nine; Solomon wrote two; Heman (with the sons of Korah), Ethan, and Moses each wrote one; and fifty-one psalms are anonymous. The New Testament ascribes two of the anonymous psalms (Psalms 2 and 95) to David (see Acts 4:25; Hebrews 4:7).

■ **Date Written:** Between the time of Moses (about 1440 BC) and the Babylonian captivity (586 BC)

■ **Purpose:** To provide poetry for the expression of praise, worship, and confession to God

■ **Themes:** Praise, forgiveness, thankfulness, trust, reverence for God and his creation

■ **Outline**
1–41 The first book of Psalms
42–72 The second book of Psalms
73–89 The third book of Psalms
90–106 The fourth book of Psalms
107–150 The fifth book of Psalms

BOOK ONE (Psalms 1–41)

1 ¹ Oh, the joys of those who do not
follow the advice of the wicked,
or stand around with sinners,
or join in with mockers.
² But they delight in the law of the LORD,
meditating on it day and night.
³ They are like trees planted along the
riverbank,
bearing fruit each season.
Their leaves never wither,
and they prosper in all they do.

⁴ But not the wicked!
They are like worthless chaff, scattered
by the wind.
⁵ They will be condemned at the time of
judgment.

Sinners will have no place among the
godly.
⁶ For the LORD watches over the path of
the godly,
but the path of the wicked leads to
destruction.

2 ¹ Why are the nations so angry?
Why do they waste their time with
futile plans?
² The kings of the earth prepare for battle;
the rulers plot together
against the LORD
and against his anointed one.
³ "Let us break their chains," they cry,
"and free ourselves from slavery to God."

⁴ But the one who rules in heaven laughs.
The Lord scoffs at them.

5 Then in anger he rebukes them,
  terrifying them with his fierce fury.
6 For the Lord declares, "I have placed my
  chosen king on the throne
  in Jerusalem,* on my holy mountain."

7 The king proclaims the LORD's decree:
  "The LORD said to me, 'You are my son.*
  Today I have become your Father.*
8 Only ask, and I will give you the nations
  as your inheritance,
  the whole earth as your possession.
9 You will break* them with an iron rod
  and smash them like clay pots.'"

10 Now then, you kings, act wisely!
  Be warned, you rulers of the earth!
11 Serve the LORD with reverent fear,
  and rejoice with trembling.
12 Submit to God's royal son,* or he will
  become angry,
  and you will be destroyed in the midst
  of all your activities—
  for his anger flares up in an instant.
  But what joy for all who take refuge
  in him!

3 A psalm of David, regarding the time David fled from
his son Absalom.

1 O LORD, I have so many enemies;
  so many are against me.
2 So many are saying,
  "God will never rescue him!"   Interlude*

3 But you, O LORD, are a shield
  around me;
  you are my glory, the one who holds
  my head high.
4 I cried out to the LORD,
  and he answered me from his holy
  mountain.   Interlude

5 I lay down and slept,
  yet I woke up in safety,
  for the LORD was watching over me.
6 I am not afraid of ten thousand enemies
  who surround me on every side.

7 Arise, O LORD!
  Rescue me, my God!
  Slap all my enemies in the face!
  Shatter the teeth of the wicked!

8 Victory comes from you, O LORD.
  May you bless your people.   Interlude

4 For the choir director: A psalm of David,
to be accompanied by stringed instruments.

1 Answer me when I call to you,
  O God who declares me innocent.
  Free me from my troubles.
  Have mercy on me and hear my prayer.

2 How long will you people ruin my
  reputation?
  How long will you make groundless
  accusations?
  How long will you continue your lies?
                                     Interlude
3 You can be sure of this:
  The LORD set apart the godly for
  himself.
  The LORD will answer when I call to
  him.

4 Don't sin by letting anger control you.
  Think about it overnight and remain
  silent.   Interlude
5 Offer sacrifices in the right spirit,
  and trust the LORD.

6 Many people say, "Who will show us better
  times?"
  Let your face smile on us, LORD.
7 You have given me greater joy
  than those who have abundant harvests
  of grain and new wine.
8 In peace I will lie down and sleep,
  for you alone, O LORD, will keep me
  safe.

5 For the choir director: A psalm of David, to be
accompanied by the flute.

1 O LORD, hear me as I pray;
  pay attention to my groaning.
2 Listen to my cry for help, my King and
  my God,
  for I pray to no one but you.
3 Listen to my voice in the morning, LORD.
  Each morning I bring my requests to
  you and wait expectantly.

4 O God, you take no pleasure in
  wickedness;

2:6 Hebrew *on Zion.* 2:7a Or *Son;* also in 2:12. 2:7b Or *Today I reveal you as my son.* 2:9 Greek version reads *rule.* Compare
Rev 2:27. 2:12 The meaning of the Hebrew is uncertain. 3:2 Hebrew *Selah.* The meaning of this word is uncertain,
though it is probably a musical or literary term. It is rendered *Interlude* throughout the Psalms.

you cannot tolerate the sins of the
wicked.
5 Therefore, the proud may not stand in
your presence,
for you hate all who do evil.
6 You will destroy those who tell lies.
The LORD detests murderers and
deceivers.

7 Because of your unfailing love, I can enter
your house;
I will worship at your Temple with
deepest awe.
8 Lead me in the right path, O LORD,
or my enemies will conquer me.
Make your way plain for me to follow.

9 My enemies cannot speak a truthful word.
Their deepest desire is to destroy others.
Their talk is foul, like the stench from an
open grave.
Their tongues are filled with flattery.*
10 O God, declare them guilty.
Let them be caught in their own traps.
Drive them away because of their many
sins,
for they have rebelled against you.

11 But let all who take refuge in you rejoice;
let them sing joyful praises forever.
Spread your protection over them,
that all who love your name may be
filled with joy.
12 For you bless the godly, O LORD;
you surround them with your shield
of love.

6 For the choir director: A psalm of David, to be
accompanied by an eight-stringed instrument.*

1 O LORD, don't rebuke me in your anger
or discipline me in your rage.
2 Have compassion on me, LORD, for I am
weak.
Heal me, LORD, for my bones are in
agony.
3 I am sick at heart.
How long, O LORD, until you
restore me?

4 Return, O LORD, and rescue me.
Save me because of your unfailing love.
5 For the dead do not remember you.
Who can praise you from the grave?*

6 I am worn out from sobbing.
All night I flood my bed with weeping,
drenching it with my tears.
7 My vision is blurred by grief;
my eyes are worn out because of all my
enemies.

8 Go away, all you who do evil,
for the LORD has heard my weeping.
9 The LORD has heard my plea;
the LORD will answer my prayer.
10 May all my enemies be disgraced and
terrified.
May they suddenly turn back in shame.

7 A psalm* of David, which he sang to the LORD
concerning Cush of the tribe of Benjamin.

1 I come to you for protection, O LORD
my God.
Save me from my persecutors—
rescue me!
2 If you don't, they will maul me like a lion,
tearing me to pieces with no one to
rescue me.
3 O LORD my God, if I have done wrong
or am guilty of injustice,
4 if I have betrayed a friend
or plundered my enemy without cause,
5 then let my enemies capture me.
Let them trample me into the ground
and drag my honor in the dust.
Interlude

6 Arise, O LORD, in anger!
Stand up against the fury of my
enemies!
Wake up, my God, and bring justice!
7 Gather the nations before you.
Rule over them from on high.
8 The LORD judges the nations.
Declare me righteous, O LORD,
for I am innocent, O Most High!
9 End the evil of those who are wicked,
and defend the righteous.
For you look deep within the mind
and heart,
O righteous God.

10 God is my shield,
saving those whose hearts are true
and right.
11 God is an honest judge.
He is angry with the wicked every day.

5:9 Greek version reads *with lies.* Compare Rom 3:13. **6:title** Hebrew *with stringed instruments; according to the sheminith.*
6:5 Hebrew *from Sheol?* 7:title Hebrew *A shiggaion,* probably indicating a musical setting for the psalm.

¹² If a person does not repent,
 God* will sharpen his sword;
 he will bend and string his bow.
¹³ He will prepare his deadly weapons
 and shoot his flaming arrows.

¹⁴ The wicked conceive evil;
 they are pregnant with trouble
 and give birth to lies.
¹⁵ They dig a deep pit to trap others,
 then fall into it themselves.
¹⁶ The trouble they make for others backfires
 on them.
 The violence they plan falls on their
 own heads.

¹⁷ I will thank the LORD because he is just;
 I will sing praise to the name of the
 LORD Most High.

8 *For the choir director: A psalm of David, to be accompanied by a stringed instrument.**

¹ O LORD, our Lord, your majestic name fills
 the earth!
 Your glory is higher than the heavens.
² You have taught children and infants
 to tell of your strength,*
silencing your enemies
 and all who oppose you.

³ When I look at the night sky and see the
 work of your fingers—
 the moon and the stars you set in
 place—
⁴ what are mere mortals that you should
 think about them,
 human beings that you should care for
 them?*
⁵ Yet you made them only a little lower than
 God*
 and crowned them* with glory and
 honor.
⁶ You gave them charge of everything you
 made,
 putting all things under their
 authority—
⁷ the flocks and the herds
 and all the wild animals,
⁸ the birds in the sky, the fish in the sea,
 and everything that swims the ocean
 currents.

⁹ O LORD, our Lord, your majestic name fills
 the earth!

9 *For the choir director: A psalm of David, to be sung to the tune "Death of the Son."*

¹ I will praise you, LORD, with all my heart;
 I will tell of all the marvelous things you
 have done.
² I will be filled with joy because of you.
 I will sing praises to your name,
 O Most High.

³ My enemies retreated;
 they staggered and died when you
 appeared.
⁴ For you have judged in my favor;
 from your throne you have judged with
 fairness.
⁵ You have rebuked the nations and
 destroyed the wicked;
 you have erased their names forever.
⁶ The enemy is finished, in endless ruins;
 the cities you uprooted are now
 forgotten.

⁷ But the LORD reigns forever,
 executing judgment from his throne.
⁸ He will judge the world with justice
 and rule the nations with fairness.
⁹ The LORD is a shelter for the oppressed,
 a refuge in times of trouble.
¹⁰ Those who know your name trust in you,
 for you, O LORD, do not abandon those
 who search for you.

¹¹ Sing praises to the LORD who reigns in
 Jerusalem.*
 Tell the world about his unforgettable
 deeds.
¹² For he who avenges murder cares for the
 helpless.
 He does not ignore the cries of those
 who suffer.

¹³ LORD, have mercy on me.
 See how my enemies torment me.
 Snatch me back from the jaws of death.
¹⁴ Save me so I can praise you publicly at
 Jerusalem's gates,
 so I can rejoice that you have
 rescued me.

7:12 Hebrew *he.*   8:title Hebrew *according to the gittith.*   8:2 Greek version reads *to give you praise.* Compare Matt 21:16.
8:4 Hebrew *what is man that you should think of him, / the son of man that you should care for him?*   8:5a Or *Yet you made them only a little lower than the angels;* Hebrew reads *Yet you made him* [i.e., man] *a little lower than Elohim.*   8:5b Hebrew *him* [i.e., man]; similarly in 8:6.   9:11 Hebrew *Zion;* also in 9:14.

15 The nations have fallen into the pit they
        dug for others.
    Their own feet have been caught in the
        trap they set.
16 The LORD is known for his justice.
    The wicked are trapped by their
        own deeds.   *Quiet Interlude**

17 The wicked will go down to the grave.*
    This is the fate of all the nations who
        ignore God.
18 But the needy will not be ignored forever;
    the hopes of the poor will not always be
        crushed.

19 Arise, O LORD!
    Do not let mere mortals defy you!
    Judge the nations!
20 Make them tremble in fear, O LORD.
    Let the nations know they are merely
        human.   *Interlude*

10

1 O LORD, why do you stand so far
        away?
    Why do you hide when I am in trouble?
2 The wicked arrogantly hunt down the poor.
    Let them be caught in the evil they plan
        for others.
3 For they brag about their evil desires;
    they praise the greedy and curse the
        LORD.

4 The wicked are too proud to seek God.
    They seem to think that God is dead.
5 Yet they succeed in everything they do.
    They do not see your punishment
        awaiting them.
    They sneer at all their enemies.
6 They think, "Nothing bad will ever
        happen to us!
    We will be free of trouble forever!"

7 Their mouths are full of cursing, lies, and
        threats.*
    Trouble and evil are on the tips of their
        tongues.
8 They lurk in ambush in the villages,
    waiting to murder innocent people.
    They are always searching for helpless
        victims.
9 Like lions crouched in hiding,
    they wait to pounce on the helpless.
    Like hunters they capture the helpless
    and drag them away in nets.

10 Their helpless victims are crushed;
    they fall beneath the strength of the
        wicked.
11 The wicked think, "God isn't watching us!
    He has closed his eyes and won't even
        see what we do!"

12 Arise, O LORD!
    Punish the wicked, O God!
    Do not ignore the helpless!
13 Why do the wicked get away with
        despising God?
    They think, "God will never call us
        to account."
14 But you see the trouble and grief they
        cause.
    You take note of it and punish them.
    The helpless put their trust in you.
    You defend the orphans.

15 Break the arms of these wicked, evil
        people!
    Go after them until the last one is
        destroyed.
16 The LORD is king forever and ever!
    The godless nations will vanish from
        the land.
17 LORD, you know the hopes of the
        helpless.
    Surely you will hear their cries and
        comfort them.
18 You will bring justice to the orphans and
        the oppressed,
    so mere people can no longer terrify
        them.

11

For the choir director: A psalm of David.

1 I trust in the LORD for protection.
    So why do you say to me,
        "Fly like a bird to the mountains for
        safety!
2 The wicked are stringing their bows
    and fitting their arrows on the
        bowstrings.
    They shoot from the shadows
        at those whose hearts are right.
3 The foundations of law and order have
        collapsed.
    What can the righteous do?"

4 But the LORD is in his holy Temple;
    the LORD still rules from heaven.

9:16 Hebrew *Higgaion Selah.* The meaning of this phrase is uncertain.   9:17 Hebrew *to Sheol.*   10:7 Greek version reads
cursing and bitterness. Compare Rom 3:14.

He watches everyone closely,
    examining every person on earth.
5 The LORD examines both the righteous
        and the wicked.
    He hates those who love violence.
6 He will rain down blazing coals and
        burning sulfur on the wicked,
    punishing them with scorching winds.
7 For the righteous LORD loves justice.
    The virtuous will see his face.

12 *For the choir director: A psalm of David, to be accompanied by an eight-stringed instrument.**

1 Help, O LORD, for the godly are fast
        disappearing!
    The faithful have vanished from the
        earth!
2 Neighbors lie to each other,
    speaking with flattering lips and
        deceitful hearts.
3 May the LORD cut off their flattering lips
    and silence their boastful tongues.
4 They say, "We will lie to our hearts'
        content.
    Our lips are our own—who can
        stop us?"

5 The LORD replies, "I have seen violence
        done to the helpless,
    and I have heard the groans of the poor.
    Now I will rise up to rescue them,
        as they have longed for me to do."
6 The LORD's promises are pure,
    like silver refined in a furnace,
        purified seven times over.
7 Therefore, LORD, we know you will protect
        the oppressed,
    preserving them forever from this lying
        generation,
8 even though the wicked strut about,
    and evil is praised throughout the
        land.

13 *For the choir director: A psalm of David.*

1 O LORD, how long will you forget me?
        Forever?
    How long will you look the other way?
2 How long must I struggle with anguish in
        my soul,
    with sorrow in my heart every day?
    How long will my enemy have the
        upper hand?

3 Turn and answer me, O LORD my God!
    Restore the sparkle to my eyes, or I will
        die.
4 Don't let my enemies gloat, saying, "We
        have defeated him!"
    Don't let them rejoice at my downfall.

5 But I trust in your unfailing love.
    I will rejoice because you have
        rescued me.
6 I will sing to the LORD
    because he is good to me.

14 *For the choir director: A psalm of David.*

1 Only fools say in their hearts,
    "There is no God."
    They are corrupt, and their actions are evil;
    not one of them does good!

2 The LORD looks down from heaven
        on the entire human race;
    he looks to see if anyone is truly wise,
        if anyone seeks God.
3 But no, all have turned away;
    all have become corrupt.*
    No one does good,
        not a single one!

4 Will those who do evil never learn?
    They eat up my people like bread
    and wouldn't think of praying to the
        LORD.
5 Terror will grip them,
    for God is with those who obey him.
6 The wicked frustrate the plans of the
        oppressed,
    but the LORD will protect his people.

7 Who will come from Mount Zion to rescue
        Israel?
    When the LORD restores his people,
    Jacob will shout with joy, and Israel will
        rejoice.

15 *A psalm of David.*

1 Who may worship in your sanctuary, LORD?
    Who may enter your presence on your
        holy hill?
2 Those who lead blameless lives and do
        what is right,
    speaking the truth from sincere hearts.

12:title Hebrew *according to the sheminith.*   14:3 Greek version reads *have become useless.* Compare Rom 3:12.

3 Those who refuse to gossip
　　or harm their neighbors
　　or speak evil of their friends.
4 Those who despise flagrant sinners,
　　and honor the faithful followers of
　　　the LORD,
　　and keep their promises even when
　　　it hurts.
5 Those who lend money without charging
　　interest,
　　and who cannot be bribed to lie about
　　　the innocent.
　Such people will stand firm forever.

16 A psalm* of David.

1 Keep me safe, O God,
　　for I have come to you for refuge.

2 I said to the LORD, "You are my Master!
　　Every good thing I have comes from
　　　you."
3 The godly people in the land
　　are my true heroes!
　　I take pleasure in them!
4 Troubles multiply for those who chase
　　after other gods.
　　I will not take part in their sacrifices
　　　of blood
　　or even speak the names of their gods.

5 LORD, you alone are my inheritance, my
　　cup of blessing.
　　You guard all that is mine.
6 The land you have given me is a pleasant
　　land.
　　What a wonderful inheritance!

7 I will bless the LORD who guides me;
　　even at night my heart instructs me.
8 I know the LORD is always with me.
　　I will not be shaken, for he is right
　　　beside me.

9 No wonder my heart is glad, and I rejoice.*
　　My body rests in safety.
10 For you will not leave my soul among the
　　dead*
　　or allow your holy one* to rot in the
　　　grave.
11 You will show me the way of life,
　　granting me the joy of your presence

and the pleasures of living with you
　　forever.*

17 A prayer of David.

1 O LORD, hear my plea for justice.
　　Listen to my cry for help.
　　Pay attention to my prayer,
　　for it comes from honest lips.
2 Declare me innocent,
　　for you see those who do right.

3 You have tested my thoughts and
　　examined my heart in the night.
　　You have scrutinized me and found
　　　nothing wrong.
　　I am determined not to sin in what I say.
4 I have followed your commands,
　　which keep me from following cruel
　　　and evil people.
5 My steps have stayed on your path;
　　I have not wavered from following you.

6 I am praying to you because I know you
　　will answer, O God.
　　Bend down and listen as I pray.
7 Show me your unfailing love in wonderful
　　ways.
　　By your mighty power you rescue
　　those who seek refuge from their
　　　enemies.
8 Guard me as you would guard your own
　　eyes.*
　　Hide me in the shadow of your wings.
9 Protect me from wicked people who
　　attack me,
　　from murderous enemies who
　　surround me.
10 They are without pity.
　　Listen to their boasting!
11 They track me down and surround me,
　　watching for the chance to throw me to
　　the ground.
12 They are like hungry lions, eager to tear
　　me apart—
　　like young lions hiding in ambush.

13 Arise, O LORD!
　　Stand against them, and bring them to
　　their knees!
　　Rescue me from the wicked with your
　　sword!

16:title Hebrew miktam. This may be a literary or musical term.　16:9 Greek version reads and my tongue shouts his praises.
Compare Acts 2:26.　16:10a Hebrew in Sheol.　16:10b Or your Holy One.　16:11 Greek version reads You have shown me the way
of life, / and you will fill me with the joy of your presence. Compare Acts 2:28.　17:8 Hebrew as the pupil of your eye.

14 By the power of your hand, O LORD,
    destroy those who look to this world for
      their reward.
   But satisfy the hunger of your treasured
      ones.
   May their children have plenty,
      leaving an inheritance for their
        descendants.
15 Because I am righteous, I will see you.
   When I awake, I will see you face to face
      and be satisfied.

18 *For the choir director: A psalm of David, the
    servant of the LORD. He sang this song to the
LORD on the day the LORD rescued him from all his
enemies and from Saul. He sang:*

1 I love you, LORD;
    you are my strength.
2 The LORD is my rock, my fortress, and my
      savior;
   my God is my rock, in whom I find
      protection.
   He is my shield, the power that saves me,
      and my place of safety.
3 I called on the LORD, who is worthy of
      praise,
   and he saved me from my enemies.

4 The ropes of death entangled me;
    floods of destruction swept over me.
5 The grave* wrapped its ropes around me;
    death laid a trap in my path.
6 But in my distress I cried out to the LORD;
    yes, I prayed to my God for help.
   He heard me from his sanctuary;
      my cry to him reached his ears.

7 Then the earth quaked and trembled.
   The foundations of the mountains
      shook;
   they quaked because of his anger.
8 Smoke poured from his nostrils;
    fierce flames leaped from his mouth.
   Glowing coals blazed forth from him.
9 He opened the heavens and came down;
    dark storm clouds were beneath his feet.
10 Mounted on a mighty angelic being,* he
      flew,
   soaring on the wings of the wind.
11 He shrouded himself in darkness,
    veiling his approach with dark rain
      clouds.
12 Thick clouds shielded the brightness
      around him

and rained down hail and burning
   coals.*
13 The LORD thundered from heaven;
    the voice of the Most High resounded
      amid the hail and burning coals.
14 He shot his arrows and scattered his
      enemies;
   great bolts of lightning flashed, and
      they were confused.
15 Then at your command, O LORD,
    at the blast of your breath,
   the bottom of the sea could be seen,
    and the foundations of the earth were
      laid bare.

16 He reached down from heaven and
      rescued me;
   he drew me out of deep waters.
17 He rescued me from my powerful enemies,
    from those who hated me and were too
      strong for me.
18 They attacked me at a moment when I was
      in distress,
   but the LORD supported me.
19 He led me to a place of safety;
    he rescued me because he delights
      in me.
20 The LORD rewarded me for doing right;
    he restored me because of my innocence.
21 For I have kept the ways of the LORD;
    I have not turned from my God to
      follow evil.
22 I have followed all his regulations;
    I have never abandoned his decrees.
23 I am blameless before God;
    I have kept myself from sin.
24 The LORD rewarded me for doing right.
   He has seen my innocence.

25 To the faithful you show yourself faithful;
    to those with integrity you show
      integrity.
26 To the pure you show yourself pure,
    but to the crooked you show yourself
      shrewd.
27 You rescue the humble,
    but you humiliate the proud.
28 You light a lamp for me.
   The LORD, my God, lights up my
      darkness.
29 In your strength I can crush an army;
    with my God I can scale any wall.

30 God's way is perfect.
   All the LORD's promises prove true.

18:5 Hebrew *Sheol.*   18:10 Hebrew *a cherub.*   18:12 Or *and lightning bolts;* also in 18:13.

He is a shield for all who look to him for
protection.
31 For who is God except the LORD?
Who but our God is a solid rock?
32 God arms me with strength,
and he makes my way perfect.
33 He makes me as surefooted as a deer,
enabling me to stand on mountain
heights.
34 He trains my hands for battle;
he strengthens my arm to draw a
bronze bow.
35 You have given me your shield of victory.
Your right hand supports me;
your help* has made me great.
36 You have made a wide path for my feet
to keep them from slipping.

37 I chased my enemies and caught them;
I did not stop until they were
conquered.
38 I struck them down so they could not
get up;
they fell beneath my feet.
39 You have armed me with strength for the
battle;
you have subdued my enemies under
my feet.
40 You placed my foot on their necks.
I have destroyed all who hated me.
41 They called for help, but no one came to
their rescue.
They even cried to the LORD, but he
refused to answer.
42 I ground them as fine as dust in the wind.
I swept them into the gutter like dirt.
43 You gave me victory over my accusers.
You appointed me ruler over nations;
people I don't even know now serve me.
44 As soon as they hear of me, they submit;
foreign nations cringe before me.
45 They all lose their courage
and come trembling from their
strongholds.

46 The LORD lives! Praise to my Rock!
May the God of my salvation be exalted!
47 He is the God who pays back those who
harm me;
he subdues the nations under me
48 and rescues me from my enemies.
You hold me safe beyond the reach of my
enemies;
you save me from violent opponents.

49 For this, O LORD, I will praise you among
the nations;
I will sing praises to your name.
50 You give great victories to your king;
you show unfailing love to your
anointed,
to David and all his descendants forever.

19
For the choir director: A psalm of David.

1 The heavens proclaim the glory of God.
The skies display his craftsmanship.
2 Day after day they continue to speak;
night after night they make him known.
3 They speak without a sound or word;
their voice is never heard.*
4 Yet their message has gone throughout the
earth,
and their words to all the world.

God has made a home in the heavens for
the sun.
5 It bursts forth like a radiant bridegroom
after his wedding.
It rejoices like a great athlete eager to
run the race.
6 The sun rises at one end of the heavens
and follows its course to the other end.
Nothing can hide from its heat.

7 The instructions of the LORD are perfect,
reviving the soul.
The decrees of the LORD are trustworthy,
making wise the simple.
8 The commandments of the LORD are right,
bringing joy to the heart.
The commands of the LORD are clear,
giving insight for living.
9 Reverence for the LORD is pure,
lasting forever.
The laws of the LORD are true;
each one is fair.
10 They are more desirable than gold,
even the finest gold.
They are sweeter than honey,
even honey dripping from the comb.
11 They are a warning to your servant,
a great reward for those who obey them.
12 How can I know all the sins lurking in my
heart?
Cleanse me from these hidden faults.
13 Keep your servant from deliberate sins!
Don't let them control me.

18:35 Hebrew *your humility;* compare 2 Sam 22:36.   19:3 Or *There is no speech or language where their voice is not heard.*

Then I will be free of guilt
and innocent of great sin.

14 May the words of my mouth
and the meditation of my heart
be pleasing to you,
O LORD, my rock and my redeemer.

20 *For the choir director: A psalm of David.*

1 In times of trouble, may the LORD answer
your cry.
May the name of the God of Jacob keep
you safe from all harm.

2 May he send you help from his sanctuary
and strengthen you from Jerusalem.*

3 May he remember all your gifts
and look favorably on your burnt
offerings.   *Interlude*

4 May he grant your heart's desires
and make all your plans succeed.

5 May we shout for joy when we hear of your
victory
and raise a victory banner in the name
of our God.
May the LORD answer all your prayers.

6 Now I know that the LORD rescues his
anointed king.
He will answer him from his holy
heaven
and rescue him by his great power.

7 Some nations boast of their chariots and
horses,
but we boast in the name of the LORD
our God.

8 Those nations will fall down and collapse,
but we will rise up and stand firm.

9 Give victory to our king, O LORD!
Answer our cry for help.

21 *For the choir director: A psalm of David.*

1 How the king rejoices in your strength,
O LORD!
He shouts with joy because you give
him victory.

2 For you have given him his heart's desire;
you have withheld nothing he
requested.   *Interlude*

3 You welcomed him back with success and
prosperity.
You placed a crown of finest gold on his
head.

4 He asked you to preserve his life,
and you granted his request.
The days of his life stretch on forever.

5 Your victory brings him great honor,
and you have clothed him with splendor
and majesty.

6 You have endowed him with eternal
blessings
and given him the joy of your presence.

7 For the king trusts in the LORD.
The unfailing love of the Most High will
keep him from stumbling.

8 You will capture all your enemies.
Your strong right hand will seize all
who hate you.

9 You will throw them in a flaming furnace
when you appear.
The LORD will consume them in his anger;
fire will devour them.

10 You will wipe their children from the face
of the earth;
they will never have descendants.

11 Although they plot against you,
their evil schemes will never succeed.

12 For they will turn and run
when they see your arrows aimed at
them.

13 Rise up, O LORD, in all your power.
With music and singing we celebrate
your mighty acts.

22 *For the choir director: A psalm of David, to be*
sung to the tune "Doe of the Dawn."

1 My God, my God, why have you
abandoned me?
Why are you so far away when I groan
for help?

2 Every day I call to you, my God, but you do
not answer.
Every night I lift my voice, but I find no
relief.

3 Yet you are holy,
enthroned on the praises of Israel.

4 Our ancestors trusted in you,
and you rescued them.

5 They cried out to you and were saved.
They trusted in you and were never
disgraced.

20:2 Hebrew *Zion.*

6 But I am a worm and not a man.
	I am scorned and despised by all!
7 Everyone who sees me mocks me.
	They sneer and shake their heads,
		saying,
8 "Is this the one who relies on the LORD?
	Then let the LORD save him!
	If the LORD loves him so much,
		let the LORD rescue him!"

9 Yet you brought me safely from my
		mother's womb
	and led me to trust you at my mother's
		breast.
10 I was thrust into your arms at my birth.
	You have been my God from the
		moment I was born.

11 Do not stay so far from me,
	for trouble is near,
	and no one else can help me.
12 My enemies surround me like a herd of
		bulls;
	fierce bulls of Bashan have hemmed
		me in!
13 Like lions they open their jaws against me,
	roaring and tearing into their prey.
14 My life is poured out like water,
	and all my bones are out of joint.
	My heart is like wax,
		melting within me.
15 My strength has dried up like sunbaked
		clay.
	My tongue sticks to the roof of my
		mouth.
	You have laid me in the dust and left me
		for dead.
16 My enemies surround me like a pack of
		dogs;
	an evil gang closes in on me.
	They have pierced* my hands and feet.
17 I can count all my bones.
	My enemies stare at me and gloat.
18 They divide my garments among
		themselves
	and throw dice* for my clothing.

19 O LORD, do not stay far away!
	You are my strength; come quickly to
		my aid!
20 Save me from the sword;
	spare my precious life from these dogs.
21 Snatch me from the lion's jaws
	and from the horns of these wild oxen.

22 I will proclaim your name to my brothers
		and sisters.*
	I will praise you among your assembled
		people.
23 Praise the LORD, all you who fear him!
	Honor him, all you descendants of Jacob!
	Show him reverence, all you
		descendants of Israel!
24 For he has not ignored or belittled the
		suffering of the needy.
	He has not turned his back on them,
	but has listened to their cries for help.

25 I will praise you in the great assembly.
	I will fulfill my vows in the presence of
		those who worship you.
26 The poor will eat and be satisfied.
	All who seek the LORD will praise him.
	Their hearts will rejoice with everlasting
		joy.
27 The whole earth will acknowledge the
		LORD and return to him.
	All the families of the nations will bow
		down before him.
28 For royal power belongs to the LORD.
	He rules all the nations.

29 Let the rich of the earth feast and worship.
	Bow before him, all who are mortal,
	all whose lives will end as dust.
30 Our children will also serve him.
	Future generations will hear about the
		wonders of the Lord.
31 His righteous acts will be told to those not
		yet born.
	They will hear about everything he has
		done.

23 *A psalm of David.*

1 The LORD is my shepherd;
	I have all that I need.
2 He lets me rest in green meadows;
	he leads me beside peaceful streams.
3 He renews my strength.
	He guides me along right paths,
		bringing honor to his name.
4 Even when I walk
		through the darkest valley,*
	I will not be afraid,
	for you are close beside me.
	Your rod and your staff
		protect and comfort me.

22:16 As in some Hebrew manuscripts and Greek and Syriac versions; most Hebrew manuscripts read *They are like a lion at.*
22:18 Hebrew *cast lots.*   22:22 Hebrew *my brothers.*   23:4 Or *the dark valley of death.*

⁵ You prepare a feast for me
in the presence of my enemies.
You honor me by anointing my head
with oil.
My cup overflows with blessings.
⁶ Surely your goodness and unfailing love
will pursue me
all the days of my life,
and I will live in the house of the LORD
forever.

24 A psalm of David.

¹ The earth is the LORD's, and everything
in it.
The world and all its people belong
to him.
² For he laid the earth's foundation on
the seas
and built it on the ocean depths.

³ Who may climb the mountain of the
LORD?
Who may stand in his holy place?
⁴ Only those whose hands and hearts are
pure,
who do not worship idols
and never tell lies.
⁵ They will receive the LORD's blessing
and have a right relationship with God
their savior.
⁶ Such people may seek you
and worship in your presence,
O God of Jacob.*   *Interlude*

⁷ Open up, ancient gates!
Open up, ancient doors,
and let the King of glory enter.
⁸ Who is the King of glory?
The LORD, strong and mighty;
the LORD, invincible in battle.
⁹ Open up, ancient gates!
Open up, ancient doors,
and let the King of glory enter.
¹⁰ Who is the King of glory?
The LORD of Heaven's Armies—
he is the King of glory.   *Interlude*

25 * A psalm of David.

¹ O LORD, I give my life to you.
² I trust in you, my God!

Do not let me be disgraced,
or let my enemies rejoice in my defeat.
³ No one who trusts in you will ever be
disgraced,
but disgrace comes to those who try to
deceive others.

⁴ Show me the right path, O LORD;
point out the road for me to follow.
⁵ Lead me by your truth and teach me,
for you are the God who saves me.
All day long I put my hope in you.
⁶ Remember, O LORD, your compassion and
unfailing love,
which you have shown from long ages
past.
⁷ Do not remember the rebellious sins of my
youth.
Remember me in the light of your
unfailing love,
for you are merciful, O LORD.

⁸ The LORD is good and does what is right;
he shows the proper path to those who
go astray.
⁹ He leads the humble in doing right,
teaching them his way.
¹⁰ The LORD leads with unfailing love and
faithfulness
all who keep his covenant and obey his
demands.

¹¹ For the honor of your name, O LORD,
forgive my many, many sins.
¹² Who are those who fear the LORD?
He will show them the path they should
choose.
¹³ They will live in prosperity,
and their children will inherit the land.
¹⁴ The LORD is a friend to those who fear him.
He teaches them his covenant.
¹⁵ My eyes are always on the LORD,
for he rescues me from the traps of my
enemies.

¹⁶ Turn to me and have mercy,
for I am alone and in deep distress.
¹⁷ My problems go from bad to worse.
Oh, save me from them all!
¹⁸ Feel my pain and see my trouble.
Forgive all my sins.
¹⁹ See how many enemies I have
and how viciously they hate me!
²⁰ Protect me! Rescue my life from them!

24:6 As in two Hebrew manuscripts and Greek and Syriac versions; most Hebrew manuscripts read *O Jacob.*   25 This psalm
is a Hebrew acrostic poem; each verse begins with a successive letter of the Hebrew alphabet.

Do not let me be disgraced, for in you I
     take refuge.
21 May integrity and honesty protect me,
     for I put my hope in you.

22 O God, ransom Israel
     from all its troubles.

26 A psalm of David.

1 Declare me innocent, O LORD,
     for I have acted with integrity;
     I have trusted in the LORD without
          wavering.
2 Put me on trial, LORD, and
          cross-examine me.
     Test my motives and my heart.
3 For I am always aware of your unfailing
          love,
     and I have lived according to your truth.
4 I do not spend time with liars
     or go along with hypocrites.
5 I hate the gatherings of those who do evil,
     and I refuse to join in with the wicked.
6 I wash my hands to declare my innocence.
     I come to your altar, O LORD,
7 singing a song of thanksgiving
     and telling of all your wonders.
8 I love your sanctuary, LORD,
     the place where your glorious presence
          dwells.

9 Don't let me suffer the fate of sinners.
     Don't condemn me along with
          murderers.
10 Their hands are dirty with evil schemes,
     and they constantly take bribes.
11 But I am not like that; I live with integrity.
     So redeem me and show me mercy.
12 Now I stand on solid ground,
     and I will publicly praise the LORD.

27 A psalm of David.

1 The LORD is my light and my salvation—
     so why should I be afraid?
   The LORD is my fortress, protecting me
          from danger,
     so why should I tremble?
2 When evil people come to devour me,
     when my enemies and foes attack me,
     they will stumble and fall.
3 Though a mighty army surrounds me,
     my heart will not be afraid.

Even if I am attacked,
     I will remain confident.

4 The one thing I ask of the LORD—
     the thing I seek most—
   is to live in the house of the LORD all the
          days of my life,
     delighting in the LORD's perfections
     and meditating in his Temple.
5 For he will conceal me there when troubles
          come;
     he will hide me in his sanctuary.
   He will place me out of reach on a high
          rock.
6 Then I will hold my head high
     above my enemies who surround me.
   At his sanctuary I will offer sacrifices with
          shouts of joy,
     singing and praising the LORD with
          music.

7 Hear me as I pray, O LORD.
     Be merciful and answer me!
8 My heart has heard you say, "Come and
          talk with me."
     And my heart responds, "LORD, I am
          coming."
9 Do not turn your back on me.
     Do not reject your servant in anger.
     You have always been my helper.
   Don't leave me now; don't abandon me,
     O God of my salvation!
10 Even if my father and mother abandon me,
     the LORD will hold me close.

11 Teach me how to live, O LORD.
     Lead me along the right path,
     for my enemies are waiting for me.
12 Do not let me fall into their hands.
     For they accuse me of things I've never
          done;
     with every breath they threaten me with
          violence.
13 Yet I am confident I will see the LORD's
          goodness
     while I am here in the land of the living.

14 Wait patiently for the LORD.
     Be brave and courageous.
     Yes, wait patiently for the LORD.

28 A psalm of David.

1 I pray to you, O LORD, my rock.
     Do not turn a deaf ear to me.

For if you are silent,
  I might as well give up and die.
2 Listen to my prayer for mercy
    as I cry out to you for help,
    as I lift my hands toward your holy
      sanctuary.

3 Do not drag me away with the wicked—
    with those who do evil—
  those who speak friendly words to their
      neighbors
    while planning evil in their hearts.
4 Give them the punishment they so richly
      deserve!
    Measure it out in proportion to their
      wickedness.
  Pay them back for all their evil deeds!
    Give them a taste of what they have
      done to others.
5 They care nothing for what the LORD has
      done
    or for what his hands have made.
  So he will tear them down,
    and they will never be rebuilt!

6 Praise the LORD!
    For he has heard my cry for mercy.
7 The LORD is my strength and shield.
    I trust him with all my heart.
  He helps me, and my heart is filled
      with joy.
    I burst out in songs of thanksgiving.

8 The LORD gives his people strength.
    He is a safe fortress for his anointed
      king.
9 Save your people!
    Bless Israel, your special possession.*
  Lead them like a shepherd,
    and carry them in your arms forever.

29 *A psalm of David.*

1 Honor the LORD, you heavenly beings*;
    honor the LORD for his glory and
      strength.
2 Honor the LORD for the glory of his name.
    Worship the LORD in the splendor of his
      holiness.

3 The voice of the LORD echoes above the sea.
    The God of glory thunders.
  The LORD thunders over the mighty sea.

4 The voice of the LORD is powerful;
    the voice of the LORD is majestic.
5 The voice of the LORD splits the mighty
      cedars;
    the LORD shatters the cedars of
      Lebanon.
6 He makes Lebanon's mountains skip like
      a calf;
    he makes Mount Hermon* leap like
      a young wild ox.
7 The voice of the LORD strikes
    with bolts of lightning.
8 The voice of the LORD makes the barren
      wilderness quake;
    the LORD shakes the wilderness of
      Kadesh.
9 The voice of the LORD twists mighty oaks*
    and strips the forests bare.
  In his Temple everyone shouts, "Glory!"

10 The LORD rules over the floodwaters.
    The LORD reigns as king forever.
11 The LORD gives his people strength.
    The LORD blesses them with peace.

30 *A psalm of David. A song for the dedication of the Temple.*

1 I will exalt you, LORD, for you rescued me.
    You refused to let my enemies triumph
      over me.
2 O LORD my God, I cried to you for help,
    and you restored my health.
3 You brought me up from the grave,*
    O LORD.
  You kept me from falling into the pit
      of death.

4 Sing to the LORD, all you godly ones!
    Praise his holy name.
5 For his anger lasts only a moment,
    but his favor lasts a lifetime!
  Weeping may last through the night,
    but joy comes with the morning.

6 When I was prosperous, I said,
    "Nothing can stop me now!"
7 Your favor, O LORD, made me as secure
      as a mountain.
    Then you turned away from me, and
      I was shattered.

8 I cried out to you, O LORD.
    I begged the Lord for mercy, saying,

28:9 Hebrew *Bless your inheritance.*   29:1 Hebrew *you sons of God.*   29:6 Hebrew *Sirion,* another name for Mount Hermon.
29:9 Or *causes the deer to writhe in labor.*   30:3 Hebrew *from Sheol.*

9 "What will you gain if I die,
   if I sink into the grave?
Can my dust praise you?
   Can it tell of your faithfulness?
10 Hear me, Lord, and have mercy on me.
   Help me, O Lord."

11 You have turned my mourning into joyful
      dancing.
   You have taken away my clothes of
      mourning and clothed me with joy,
12 that I might sing praises to you and not
      be silent.
   O Lord my God, I will give you thanks
      forever!

31 *For the choir director: A psalm of David.*

1 O Lord, I have come to you for protection;
   don't let me be disgraced.
Save me, for you do what is right.
2 Turn your ear to listen to me;
   rescue me quickly.
Be my rock of protection,
   a fortress where I will be safe.
3 You are my rock and my fortress.
   For the honor of your name, lead me
      out of this danger.
4 Pull me from the trap my enemies set
      for me,
   for I find protection in you alone.
5 I entrust my spirit into your hand.
   Rescue me, Lord, for you are a faithful
      God.

6 I hate those who worship worthless idols.
   I trust in the Lord.
7 I will be glad and rejoice in your unfailing
      love,
   for you have seen my troubles,
   and you care about the anguish of my
      soul.
8 You have not handed me over to my
      enemies
   but have set me in a safe place.

9 Have mercy on me, Lord, for I am in
      distress.
   Tears blur my eyes.
   My body and soul are withering away.
10 I am dying from grief;
   my years are shortened by sadness.
Sin has drained my strength;
   I am wasting away from within.

11 I am scorned by all my enemies
   and despised by my neighbors—
   even my friends are afraid to come
      near me.
When they see me on the street,
   they run the other way.
12 I am ignored as if I were dead,
   as if I were a broken pot.
13 I have heard the many rumors about me,
   and I am surrounded by terror.
My enemies conspire against me,
   plotting to take my life.

14 But I am trusting you, O Lord,
   saying, "You are my God!"
15 My future is in your hands.
   Rescue me from those who hunt me
      down relentlessly.
16 Let your favor shine on your servant.
   In your unfailing love, rescue me.
17 Don't let me be disgraced, O Lord,
   for I call out to you for help.
Let the wicked be disgraced;
   let them lie silent in the grave.*
18 Silence their lying lips—
   those proud and arrogant lips that
      accuse the godly.

19 How great is the goodness
   you have stored up for those who fear
      you.
You lavish it on those who come to you
      for protection,
   blessing them before the watching
      world.
20 You hide them in the shelter of your
      presence,
   safe from those who conspire against
      them.
You shelter them in your presence,
   far from accusing tongues.

21 Praise the Lord,
   for he has shown me the wonders of his
      unfailing love.
He kept me safe when my city was under
      attack.
22 In panic I cried out,
   "I am cut off from the Lord!"
But you heard my cry for mercy
   and answered my call for help.

23 Love the Lord, all you godly ones!
   For the Lord protects those who are
      loyal to him,

31:17 Hebrew *in Sheol.*

but he harshly punishes the
arrogant.
²⁴ So be strong and courageous,
all you who put your hope in
the LORD!

32 A psalm* of David.

¹ Oh, what joy for those
whose disobedience is forgiven,
whose sin is put out of sight!
² Yes, what joy for those
whose record the LORD has cleared
of guilt,*
whose lives are lived in complete
honesty!
³ When I refused to confess my sin,
my body wasted away,
and I groaned all day long.
⁴ Day and night your hand of discipline
was heavy on me.
My strength evaporated like water in
the summer heat.   *Interlude*

⁵ Finally, I confessed all my sins to you
and stopped trying to hide my guilt.
I said to myself, "I will confess my
rebellion to the LORD."
And you forgave me! All my guilt
is gone.   *Interlude*

⁶ Therefore, let all the godly pray to you
while there is still time,
that they may not drown in the
floodwaters of judgment.
⁷ For you are my hiding place;
you protect me from trouble.
You surround me with songs of victory. *Interlude*

⁸ The LORD says, "I will guide you along the
best pathway for your life.
I will advise you and watch over you.
⁹ Do not be like a senseless horse or mule
that needs a bit and bridle to keep it
under control."

¹⁰ Many sorrows come to the wicked,
but unfailing love surrounds those who
trust the LORD.
¹¹ So rejoice in the LORD and be glad, all you
who obey him!
Shout for joy, all you whose hearts are
pure!

33 ¹ Let the godly sing for joy to the
LORD;
it is fitting for the pure to praise him.
² Praise the LORD with melodies on the lyre;
make music for him on the ten-stringed
harp.
³ Sing a new song of praise to him;
play skillfully on the harp, and sing
with joy.
⁴ For the word of the LORD holds true,
and we can trust everything he does.
⁵ He loves whatever is just and good;
the unfailing love of the LORD fills the
earth.

⁶ The LORD merely spoke,
and the heavens were created.
He breathed the word,
and all the stars were born.
⁷ He assigned the sea its boundaries
and locked the oceans in vast
reservoirs.
⁸ Let the whole world fear the LORD,
and let everyone stand in awe of him.
⁹ For when he spoke, the world began!
It appeared at his command.

¹⁰ The LORD frustrates the plans of the
nations
and thwarts all their schemes.
¹¹ But the LORD's plans stand firm forever;
his intentions can never be shaken.

¹² What joy for the nation whose God is the
LORD,
whose people he has chosen as his
inheritance.

¹³ The LORD looks down from heaven
and sees the whole human race.
¹⁴ From his throne he observes
all who live on the earth.
¹⁵ He made their hearts,
so he understands everything they do.
¹⁶ The best-equipped army cannot save a
king,
nor is great strength enough to save a
warrior.
¹⁷ Don't count on your warhorse to give you
victory—
for all its strength, it cannot save you.

¹⁸ But the LORD watches over those who fear
him,
those who rely on his unfailing love.

32:title Hebrew *maskil*. This may be a literary or musical term.   32:2 Greek version reads *of sin*. Compare Rom 4:8.

¹⁹ He rescues them from death
and keeps them alive in times
of famine.

²⁰ We put our hope in the LORD.
He is our help and our shield.
²¹ In him our hearts rejoice,
for we trust in his holy name.
²² Let your unfailing love surround us, LORD,
for our hope is in you alone.

34 *A psalm of David, regarding the time he pretended to be insane in front of Abimelech, who sent him away.

¹ I will praise the LORD at all times.
I will constantly speak his praises.
² I will boast only in the LORD;
let all who are helpless take heart.
³ Come, let us tell of the LORD's greatness;
let us exalt his name together.

⁴ I prayed to the LORD, and he answered me.
He freed me from all my fears.
⁵ Those who look to him for help will be
radiant with joy;
no shadow of shame will darken their
faces.
⁶ In my desperation I prayed, and the LORD
listened;
he saved me from all my troubles.
⁷ For the angel of the LORD is a guard;
he surrounds and defends all who
fear him.

⁸ Taste and see that the LORD is good.
Oh, the joys of those who take refuge
in him!
⁹ Fear the LORD, you his godly people,
for those who fear him will have all they
need.
¹⁰ Even strong young lions sometimes go
hungry,
but those who trust in the LORD will
lack no good thing.

¹¹ Come, my children, and listen to me,
and I will teach you to fear the LORD.
¹² Does anyone want to live a life
that is long and prosperous?
¹³ Then keep your tongue from speaking evil
and your lips from telling lies!
¹⁴ Turn away from evil and do good.
Search for peace, and work to
maintain it.

¹⁵ The eyes of the LORD watch over those
who do right;
his ears are open to their cries for help.
¹⁶ But the LORD turns his face against those
who do evil;
he will erase their memory from the
earth.
¹⁷ The LORD hears his people when they call
to him for help.
He rescues them from all their troubles.
¹⁸ The LORD is close to the brokenhearted;
he rescues those whose spirits are
crushed.

¹⁹ The righteous person faces many troubles,
but the LORD comes to the rescue each
time.
²⁰ For the LORD protects the bones of the
righteous;
not one of them is broken!

²¹ Calamity will surely destroy the wicked,
and those who hate the righteous will
be punished.
²² But the LORD will redeem those who serve
him.
No one who takes refuge in him will be
condemned.

35 A psalm of David.

¹ O LORD, oppose those who oppose me.
Fight those who fight against me.
² Put on your armor, and take up your
shield.
Prepare for battle, and come to my aid.
³ Lift up your spear and javelin
against those who pursue me.
Let me hear you say,
"I will give you victory!"
⁴ Bring shame and disgrace on those trying
to kill me;
turn them back and humiliate those
who want to harm me.
⁵ Blow them away like chaff in the wind—
a wind sent by the angel of the LORD.
⁶ Make their path dark and slippery,
with the angel of the LORD pursuing
them.
⁷ I did them no wrong, but they laid a trap
for me.
I did them no wrong, but they dug a pit
to catch me.
⁸ So let sudden ruin come upon them!

34 This psalm is a Hebrew acrostic poem; each verse begins with a successive letter of the Hebrew alphabet.

Let them be caught in the trap they set
for me!
Let them be destroyed in the pit they
dug for me.

9 Then I will rejoice in the LORD.
I will be glad because he rescues me.
10 With every bone in my body I will praise
him:
"LORD, who can compare with you?
Who else rescues the helpless from the
strong?
Who else protects the helpless and poor
from those who rob them?"

11 Malicious witnesses testify against me.
They accuse me of crimes I know
nothing about.
12 They repay me evil for good.
I am sick with despair.
13 Yet when they were ill, I grieved for them.
I denied myself by fasting for them,
but my prayers returned unanswered.
14 I was sad, as though they were my friends
or family,
as if I were grieving for my own mother.
15 But they are glad now that I am in trouble;
they gleefully join together against me.
I am attacked by people I don't even know;
they slander me constantly.
16 They mock me and call me names;
they snarl at me.

17 How long, O Lord, will you look on and
do nothing?
Rescue me from their fierce attacks.
Protect my life from these lions!
18 Then I will thank you in front of the great
assembly.
I will praise you before all the people.
19 Don't let my treacherous enemies rejoice
over my defeat.
Don't let those who hate me without
cause gloat over my sorrow.
20 They don't talk of peace;
they plot against innocent people who
mind their own business.
21 They shout, "Aha! Aha!
With our own eyes we saw him do it!"

22 O LORD, you know all about this.
Do not stay silent.
Do not abandon me now, O Lord.
23 Wake up! Rise to my defense!
Take up my case, my God and my Lord.

24 Declare me not guilty, O LORD my God, for
you give justice.
Don't let my enemies laugh about me in
my troubles.
25 Don't let them say, "Look, we got what we
wanted!
Now we will eat him alive!"

26 May those who rejoice at my troubles
be humiliated and disgraced.
May those who triumph over me
be covered with shame and dishonor.
27 But give great joy to those who came to my
defense.
Let them continually say, "Great is the
LORD,
who delights in blessing his servant
with peace!"
28 Then I will proclaim your justice,
and I will praise you all day long.

36 For the choir director: A psalm of David,
the servant of the LORD.

1 Sin whispers to the wicked, deep within
their hearts.*
They have no fear of God at all.
2 In their blind conceit,
they cannot see how wicked they really
are.
3 Everything they say is crooked and
deceitful.
They refuse to act wisely or do good.
4 They lie awake at night, hatching sinful
plots.
Their actions are never good.
They make no attempt to turn from evil.

5 Your unfailing love, O LORD, is as vast as
the heavens;
your faithfulness reaches beyond the
clouds.
6 Your righteousness is like the mighty
mountains,
your justice like the ocean depths.
You care for people and animals alike,
O LORD.
7 How precious is your unfailing love,
O God!
All humanity finds shelter
in the shadow of your wings.
8 You feed them from the abundance of your
own house,
letting them drink from your river of
delights.

36:1 As in some Hebrew manuscripts and Syriac version, which read *in his heart.* Masoretic Text reads *in my heart.*

⁹ For you are the fountain of life,
    the light by which we see.

¹⁰ Pour out your unfailing love on those who
    love you;
    give justice to those with honest hearts.
¹¹ Don't let the proud trample me
    or the wicked push me around.
¹² Look! Those who do evil have fallen!
    They are thrown down, never to rise
    again.

37* A psalm of David.

¹ Don't worry about the wicked
    or envy those who do wrong.
² For like grass, they soon fade away.
    Like spring flowers, they soon wither.

³ Trust in the LORD and do good.
    Then you will live safely in the land and
    prosper.
⁴ Take delight in the LORD,
    and he will give you your heart's desires.

⁵ Commit everything you do to the LORD.
    Trust him, and he will help you.
⁶ He will make your innocence radiate like
    the dawn,
    and the justice of your cause will shine
    like the noonday sun.

⁷ Be still in the presence of the LORD,
    and wait patiently for him to act.
    Don't worry about evil people who prosper
    or fret about their wicked schemes.

⁸ Stop being angry!
    Turn from your rage!
    Do not lose your temper—
    it only leads to harm.
⁹ For the wicked will be destroyed,
    but those who trust in the LORD will
    possess the land.

¹⁰ Soon the wicked will disappear.
    Though you look for them, they will
    be gone.
¹¹ The lowly will possess the land
    and will live in peace and prosperity.

¹² The wicked plot against the godly;
    they snarl at them in defiance.
¹³ But the Lord just laughs,

for he sees their day of judgment
    coming.

¹⁴ The wicked draw their swords
    and string their bows
    to kill the poor and the oppressed,
    to slaughter those who do right.
¹⁵ But their swords will stab their own hearts,
    and their bows will be broken.

¹⁶ It is better to be godly and have little
    than to be evil and rich.
¹⁷ For the strength of the wicked will be
    shattered,
    but the LORD takes care of the godly.

¹⁸ Day by day the LORD takes care of the
    innocent,
    and they will receive an inheritance that
    lasts forever.
¹⁹ They will not be disgraced in hard times;
    even in famine they will have more than
    enough.

²⁰ But the wicked will die.
    The LORD's enemies are like flowers in
    a field—
    they will disappear like smoke.

²¹ The wicked borrow and never repay,
    but the godly are generous givers.
²² Those the LORD blesses will possess the
    land,
    but those he curses will die.

²³ The LORD directs the steps of the godly.
    He delights in every detail of their lives.
²⁴ Though they stumble, they will never fall,
    for the LORD holds them by the hand.

²⁵ Once I was young, and now I am old.
    Yet I have never seen the godly
    abandoned
    or their children begging for bread.
²⁶ The godly always give generous loans to
    others,
    and their children are a blessing.

²⁷ Turn from evil and do good,
    and you will live in the land forever.
²⁸ For the LORD loves justice,
    and he will never abandon the godly.

He will keep them safe forever,
    but the children of the wicked will die.

37 This psalm is a Hebrew acrostic poem; each stanza begins with a successive letter of the Hebrew alphabet.

²⁹ The godly will possess the land
    and will live there forever.

³⁰ The godly offer good counsel;
    they teach right from wrong.
³¹ They have made God's law their own,
    so they will never slip from his path.

³² The wicked wait in ambush for the godly,
    looking for an excuse to kill them.
³³ But the LORD will not let the wicked
        succeed
    or let the godly be condemned when
        they are put on trial.

³⁴ Put your hope in the LORD.
    Travel steadily along his path.
    He will honor you by giving you the land.
    You will see the wicked destroyed.

³⁵ I have seen wicked and ruthless people
    flourishing like a tree in its native soil.
³⁶ But when I looked again, they were gone!
    Though I searched for them, I could not
        find them!

³⁷ Look at those who are honest and good,
    for a wonderful future awaits those who
        love peace.
³⁸ But the rebellious will be destroyed;
    they have no future.

³⁹ The LORD rescues the godly;
    he is their fortress in times of trouble.
⁴⁰ The LORD helps them,
    rescuing them from the wicked.
    He saves them,
    and they find shelter in him.

38 A psalm of David, asking God to remember him.

¹ O LORD, don't rebuke me in your anger
    or discipline me in your rage!
² Your arrows have struck deep,
    and your blows are crushing me.
³ Because of your anger, my whole body
        is sick;
    my health is broken because of my sins.
⁴ My guilt overwhelms me—
    it is a burden too heavy to bear.
⁵ My wounds fester and stink
    because of my foolish sins.
⁶ I am bent over and racked with pain.
    All day long I walk around filled with
        grief.

⁷ A raging fever burns within me,
    and my health is broken.
⁸ I am exhausted and completely crushed.
    My groans come from an anguished
        heart.

⁹ You know what I long for, Lord;
    you hear my every sigh.
¹⁰ My heart beats wildly, my strength fails,
    and I am going blind.
¹¹ My loved ones and friends stay away,
        fearing my disease.
    Even my own family stands at a
        distance.
¹² Meanwhile, my enemies lay traps to
        kill me.
    Those who wish me harm make plans
        to ruin me.
    All day long they plan their
        treachery.

¹³ But I am deaf to all their threats.
    I am silent before them as one who
        cannot speak.
¹⁴ I choose to hear nothing,
    and I make no reply.
¹⁵ For I am waiting for you, O LORD.
    You must answer for me, O Lord
        my God.
¹⁶ I prayed, "Don't let my enemies gloat
        over me
    or rejoice at my downfall."

¹⁷ I am on the verge of collapse,
    facing constant pain.
¹⁸ But I confess my sins;
    I am deeply sorry for what I have done.
¹⁹ I have many aggressive enemies;
    they hate me without reason.
²⁰ They repay me evil for good
    and oppose me for pursuing good.
²¹ Do not abandon me, O LORD.
    Do not stand at a distance, my God.
²² Come quickly to help me,
    O Lord my savior.

39 For Jeduthun, the choir director: A psalm of David.

¹ I said to myself, "I will watch what I do
    and not sin in what I say.
    I will hold my tongue
    when the ungodly are around me."
² But as I stood there in silence—
    not even speaking of good things—
    the turmoil within me grew worse.

³ The more I thought about it,
     the hotter I got,
     igniting a fire of words:
⁴ "LORD, remind me how brief my time on
         earth will be.
     Remind me that my days are
         numbered—
     how fleeting my life is.
⁵ You have made my life no longer than the
         width of my hand.
     My entire lifetime is just a moment to
         you;
     at best, each of us is but a breath."
                                              Interlude

⁶ We are merely moving shadows,
     and all our busy rushing ends in
         nothing.
     We heap up wealth,
     not knowing who will spend it.
⁷ And so, Lord, where do I put my hope?
     My only hope is in you.
⁸ Rescue me from my rebellion.
     Do not let fools mock me.
⁹ I am silent before you; I won't say a word,
     for my punishment is from you.
¹⁰ But please stop striking me!
     I am exhausted by the blows from your
         hand.
¹¹ When you discipline us for our sins,
     you consume like a moth what is
         precious to us.
     Each of us is but a breath.   *Interlude*

¹² Hear my prayer, O LORD!
     Listen to my cries for help!
     Don't ignore my tears.
     For I am your guest—
     a traveler passing through,
     as my ancestors were before me.
¹³ Leave me alone so I can smile again
     before I am gone and exist no more.

40 *For the choir director: A psalm of David.*

¹ I waited patiently for the LORD to
         help me,
     and he turned to me and heard my cry.
² He lifted me out of the pit of despair,
     out of the mud and the mire.
     He set my feet on solid ground
     and steadied me as I walked along.
³ He has given me a new song to sing,
     a hymn of praise to our God.

Many will see what he has done and be
         amazed.
     They will put their trust in the LORD.

⁴ Oh, the joys of those who trust the LORD,
     who have no confidence in the proud
     or in those who worship idols.
⁵ O LORD my God, you have performed
         many wonders for us.
     Your plans for us are too numerous
         to list.
     You have no equal.
     If I tried to recite all your wonderful deeds,
     I would never come to the end of them.

⁶ You take no delight in sacrifices or
         offerings.
     Now that you have made me listen,
         I finally understand*—
     you don't require burnt offerings or sin
         offerings.
⁷ Then I said, "Look, I have come.
     As is written about me in the Scriptures:
⁸ I take joy in doing your will, my God,
     for your instructions are written on my
         heart."

⁹ I have told all your people about your
         justice.
     I have not been afraid to speak out,
     as you, O LORD, well know.
¹⁰ I have not kept the good news of your
         justice hidden in my heart;
     I have talked about your faithfulness
         and saving power.
     I have told everyone in the great assembly
     of your unfailing love and faithfulness.

¹¹ LORD, don't hold back your tender mercies
         from me.
     Let your unfailing love and faithfulness
         always protect me.
¹² For troubles surround me—
         too many to count!
     My sins pile up so high
         I can't see my way out.
     They outnumber the hairs on my head.
     I have lost all courage.

¹³ Please, LORD, rescue me!
     Come quickly, LORD, and help me.
¹⁴ May those who try to destroy me
     be humiliated and put to shame.
     May those who take delight in my trouble
     be turned back in disgrace.

40:6 Greek version reads *You have given me a body.* Compare Heb 10:5.

15 Let them be horrified by their shame,
   for they said, "Aha! We've got him now!"

16 But may all who search for you
   be filled with joy and gladness in you.
   May those who love your salvation
   repeatedly shout, "The LORD is great!"

17 As for me, since I am poor and needy,
   let the Lord keep me in his thoughts.
   You are my helper and my savior.
   O my God, do not delay.

41
For the choir director: A psalm of David.

1 Oh, the joys of those who are kind to the
     poor!
   The LORD rescues them when they are
     in trouble.

2 The LORD protects them
     and keeps them alive.
   He gives them prosperity in the land
     and rescues them from their enemies.

3 The LORD nurses them when they are sick
     and restores them to health.

4 "O LORD," I prayed, "have mercy on me.
     Heal me, for I have sinned against you."

5 But my enemies say nothing but evil
     about me.
   "How soon will he die and be
     forgotten?" they ask.

6 They visit me as if they were my friends,
     but all the while they gather gossip,
     and when they leave, they spread it
     everywhere.

7 All who hate me whisper about me,
     imagining the worst.

8 "He has some fatal disease," they say.
   "He will never get out of that bed!"

9 Even my best friend, the one I trusted
     completely,
     the one who shared my food, has turned
     against me.

10 LORD, have mercy on me.
     Make me well again, so I can pay them
     back!

11 I know you are pleased with me,
     for you have not let my enemies
     triumph over me.

12 You have preserved my life because I am
     innocent;
     you have brought me into your presence
     forever.

13 Praise the LORD, the God of Israel,
     who lives from everlasting to
     everlasting.
   Amen and amen!

BOOK TWO (Psalms 42–72)

42
For the choir director: A psalm* of the descendants of Korah.

1 As the deer longs for streams of water,
     so I long for you, O God.

2 I thirst for God, the living God.
   When can I go and stand before him?

3 Day and night I have only tears for food,
     while my enemies continually taunt me,
     saying,
   "Where is this God of yours?"

4 My heart is breaking
     as I remember how it used to be:
   I walked among the crowds of worshipers,
     leading a great procession to the house
     of God,
   singing for joy and giving thanks
     amid the sound of a great celebration!

5 Why am I discouraged?
     Why is my heart so sad?
   I will put my hope in God!
     I will praise him again—
     my Savior and ⁶my God!

   Now I am deeply discouraged,
     but I will remember you—
   even from distant Mount Hermon, the
     source of the Jordan,
     from the land of Mount Mizar.

7 I hear the tumult of the raging seas
     as your waves and surging tides sweep
     over me.

8 But each day the LORD pours his unfailing
     love upon me,
     and through each night I sing his songs,
     praying to God who gives me life.

9 "O God my rock," I cry,
   "Why have you forgotten me?
   Why must I wander around in grief,
     oppressed by my enemies?"

10 Their taunts break my bones.
     They scoff, "Where is this God of yours?"

11 Why am I discouraged?
     Why is my heart so sad?

42:title Hebrew *maskil*. This may be a literary or musical term.

I will put my hope in God!
  I will praise him again—
  my Savior and my God!

43

¹ Declare me innocent, O God!
  Defend me against these ungodly
  people.
Rescue me from these unjust liars.
² For you are God, my only safe haven.
  Why have you tossed me aside?
Why must I wander around in grief,
  oppressed by my enemies?
³ Send out your light and your truth;
  let them guide me.
Let them lead me to your holy mountain,
  to the place where you live.
⁴ There I will go to the altar of God,
  to God—the source of all my joy.
I will praise you with my harp,
  O God, my God!

⁵ Why am I discouraged?
  Why is my heart so sad?
I will put my hope in God!
  I will praise him again—
  my Savior and my God!

44

For the choir director: A psalm* of the descendants of Korah.

¹ O God, we have heard it with our own
  ears—
  our ancestors have told us
of all you did in their day,
  in days long ago:
² You drove out the pagan nations by your
  power
  and gave all the land to our ancestors.
You crushed their enemies
  and set our ancestors free.
³ They did not conquer the land with their
  swords;
  it was not their own strong arm that
  gave them victory.
It was your right hand and strong arm
  and the blinding light from your face
  that helped them,
  for you loved them.

⁴ You are my King and my God.
  You command victories for Israel.*
⁵ Only by your power can we push back our
  enemies;

only in your name can we trample our
  foes.
⁶ I do not trust in my bow;
  I do not count on my sword to save me.
⁷ You are the one who gives us victory over
  our enemies;
  you disgrace those who hate us.
⁸ O God, we give glory to you all day long
  and constantly praise your name.

                      Interlude

⁹ But now you have tossed us aside in
  dishonor.
  You no longer lead our armies to battle.
¹⁰ You make us retreat from our enemies
  and allow those who hate us to plunder
  our land.
¹¹ You have butchered us like sheep
  and scattered us among the nations.
¹² You sold your precious people for a pittance,
  making nothing on the sale.
¹³ You let our neighbors mock us.
  We are an object of scorn and derision to
  those around us.
¹⁴ You have made us the butt of their jokes;
  they shake their heads at us in scorn.
¹⁵ We can't escape the constant humiliation;
  shame is written across our faces.
¹⁶ All we hear are the taunts of our mockers.
  All we see are our vengeful enemies.

¹⁷ All this has happened though we have not
  forgotten you.
  We have not violated your covenant.
¹⁸ Our hearts have not deserted you.
  We have not strayed from your path.
¹⁹ Yet you have crushed us in the jackal's
  desert home.
  You have covered us with darkness and
  death.
²⁰ If we had forgotten the name of our God
  or spread our hands in prayer to foreign
  gods,
²¹ God would surely have known it,
  for he knows the secrets of every heart.
²² But for your sake we are killed every day;
  we are being slaughtered like sheep.

²³ Wake up, O Lord! Why do you sleep?
  Get up! Do not reject us forever.
²⁴ Why do you look the other way?
  Why do you ignore our suffering and
  oppression?

44:title Hebrew *maskil*. This may be a literary or musical term.   **44:4** Hebrew *for Jacob.* The names "Jacob" and "Israel" are often interchanged throughout the Old Testament, referring sometimes to the individual patriarch and sometimes to the nation.

25 We collapse in the dust,
   lying face down in the dirt.
26 Rise up! Help us!
   Ransom us because of your unfailing
      love.

45
For the choir director: A love song to be sung to the tune "Lilies." A psalm* of the descendants of Korah.

1 Beautiful words stir my heart.
   I will recite a lovely poem about the
      king,
   for my tongue is like the pen of a skillful
      poet.

2 You are the most handsome of all.
   Gracious words stream from your lips.
   God himself has blessed you forever.
3 Put on your sword, O mighty warrior!
   You are so glorious, so majestic!
4 In your majesty, ride out to victory,
   defending truth, humility, and justice.
   Go forth to perform awe-inspiring
      deeds!
5 Your arrows are sharp, piercing your
      enemies' hearts.
   The nations fall beneath your feet.

6 Your throne, O God,* endures forever and
      ever.
   You rule with a scepter of justice.
7 You love justice and hate evil.
   Therefore God, your God, has anointed
      you,
   pouring out the oil of joy on you more
      than on anyone else.
8 Myrrh, aloes, and cassia perfume your
      robes.
   In ivory palaces the music of strings
      entertains you.
9 Kings' daughters are among your noble
      women.
   At your right side stands the queen,
      wearing jewelry of finest gold from
      Ophir!

10 Listen to me, O royal daughter; take to
      heart what I say.
   Forget your people and your family far
      away.
11 For your royal husband delights in your
      beauty;
   honor him, for he is your lord.

12 The princess of Tyre* will shower you with
      gifts.
   The wealthy will beg your favor.
13 The bride, a princess, looks glorious
   in her golden gown.
14 In her beautiful robes, she is led to the
      king,
   accompanied by her bridesmaids.
15 What a joyful and enthusiastic procession
   as they enter the king's palace!

16 Your sons will become kings like their
      father.
   You will make them rulers over many
      lands.
17 I will bring honor to your name in every
      generation.
   Therefore, the nations will praise you
      forever and ever.

46
For the choir director: A song of the descendants of Korah, to be sung by soprano voices.*

1 God is our refuge and strength,
   always ready to help in times of trouble.
2 So we will not fear when earthquakes
      come
   and the mountains crumble into the sea.
3 Let the oceans roar and foam.
   Let the mountains tremble as the
      waters surge!   *Interlude*

4 A river brings joy to the city of our God,
   the sacred home of the Most High.
5 God dwells in that city; it cannot be
      destroyed.
   From the very break of day, God will
      protect it.
6 The nations are in chaos,
   and their kingdoms crumble!
   God's voice thunders,
   and the earth melts!
7 The LORD of Heaven's Armies is here
      among us;
   the God of Israel* is our fortress.
                                      Interlude

8 Come, see the glorious works of the LORD:
   See how he brings destruction upon the
      world.
9 He causes wars to end throughout the
      earth.
   He breaks the bow and snaps the spear;
   he burns the shields with fire.

45:title Hebrew *maskil.* This may be a literary or musical term.   45:6 Or *Your divine throne.*   45:12 Hebrew *The daughter of Tyre.*   46:title Hebrew *according to alamoth.*   46:7 Hebrew *of Jacob;* also in 46:11. See note on 44:4.

¹⁰ "Be still, and know that I am God!
    I will be honored by every nation.
    I will be honored throughout the
        world."

¹¹ The LORD of Heaven's Armies is here
        among us;
    the God of Israel is our fortress.

Interlude

47

For the choir director: A psalm of the descendants of Korah.

¹ Come, everyone! Clap your hands!
    Shout to God with joyful praise!
² For the LORD Most High is awesome.
    He is the great King of all the earth.
³ He subdues the nations before us,
    putting our enemies beneath our feet.
⁴ He chose the Promised Land as our
        inheritance,
    the proud possession of Jacob's
        descendants, whom he loves.

Interlude

⁵ God has ascended with a mighty shout.
    The LORD has ascended with trumpets
        blaring.
⁶ Sing praises to God, sing praises;
    sing praises to our King, sing
        praises!
⁷ For God is the King over all the earth.
    Praise him with a psalm.*
⁸ God reigns above the nations,
    sitting on his holy throne.
⁹ The rulers of the world have gathered
        together
    with the people of the God of
        Abraham.
    For all the kings of the earth belong
        to God.
    He is highly honored everywhere.

48

A song. A psalm of the descendants of Korah.

¹ How great is the LORD,
    how deserving of praise,
    in the city of our God,
    which sits on his holy mountain!
² It is high and magnificent;
    the whole earth rejoices to see it!
    Mount Zion, the holy mountain,*
    is the city of the great King!

³ God himself is in Jerusalem's towers,
    revealing himself as its defender.

⁴ The kings of the earth joined forces
    and advanced against the city.
⁵ But when they saw it, they were stunned;
    they were terrified and ran away.
⁶ They were gripped with terror
    and writhed in pain like a woman in
        labor.
⁷ You destroyed them like the mighty ships
        of Tarshish
    shattered by a powerful east wind.

⁸ We had heard of the city's glory,
    but now we have seen it ourselves—
    the city of the LORD of Heaven's Armies.
    It is the city of our God;
    he will make it safe forever.

Interlude

⁹ O God, we meditate on your unfailing love
    as we worship in your Temple.
¹⁰ As your name deserves, O God,
    you will be praised to the ends of the
        earth.
    Your strong right hand is filled with
        victory.
¹¹ Let the people on Mount Zion rejoice.
    Let all the towns of Judah be glad
    because of your justice.

¹² Go, inspect the city of Jerusalem.*
    Walk around and count the many
        towers.
¹³ Take note of the fortified walls,
    and tour all the citadels,
    that you may describe them
    to future generations.
¹⁴ For that is what God is like.
    He is our God forever and ever,
    and he will guide us until we die.

49

For the choir director: A psalm of the descendants of Korah.

¹ Listen to this, all you people!
    Pay attention, everyone in the world!
² High and low,
    rich and poor—listen!
³ For my words are wise,
    and my thoughts are filled with insight.
⁴ I listen carefully to many proverbs
    and solve riddles with inspiration
        from a harp.

47:7 Hebrew *maskil*. This may be a literary or musical term.   48:2 Or *Mount Zion, in the far north*; Hebrew reads *Mount Zion, the heights of Zaphon*.   48:12 Hebrew *Zion*.

5 Why should I fear when trouble comes,
    when enemies surround me?
6 They trust in their wealth
    and boast of great riches.
7 Yet they cannot redeem themselves from
        death*
    by paying a ransom to God.
8 Redemption does not come so easily,
    for no one can ever pay enough
9 to live forever
    and never see the grave.

10 Those who are wise must finally die,
    just like the foolish and senseless,
    leaving all their wealth behind.
11 The grave* is their eternal home,
    where they will stay forever.
   They may name their estates after
        themselves,
12 but their fame will not last.
    They will die, just like animals.
13 This is the fate of fools,
    though they are remembered
        as being wise.*   *Interlude*

14 Like sheep, they are led to the
        grave,*
    where death will be their shepherd.
   In the morning the godly will rule over
        them.
    Their bodies will rot in the grave,
        far from their grand estates.
15 But as for me, God will redeem my
        life.
    He will snatch me from the
        power of the grave.   *Interlude*

16 So don't be dismayed when the wicked
        grow rich
    and their homes become ever more
        splendid.
17 For when they die, they take nothing with
        them.
    Their wealth will not follow them into
        the grave.
18 In this life they consider themselves
        fortunate
    and are applauded for their
        success.
19 But they will die like all before them
    and never again see the light of day.
20 People who boast of their wealth don't
        understand;
    they will die, just like animals.

50 *A psalm of Asaph.*

1 The LORD, the Mighty One, is God,
    and he has spoken;
   he has summoned all humanity
    from where the sun rises to where
        it sets.
2 From Mount Zion, the perfection of
        beauty,
    God shines in glorious radiance.
3 Our God approaches,
    and he is not silent.
   Fire devours everything in his way,
    and a great storm rages around him.
4 He calls on the heavens above and earth
        below
    to witness the judgment of his people.
5 "Bring my faithful people to me—
    those who made a covenant with me by
        giving sacrifices."
6 Then let the heavens proclaim his justice,
    for God himself will be the judge.
                                     Interlude

7 "O my people, listen as I speak.
    Here are my charges against you,
        O Israel:
    I am God, your God!
8 I have no complaint about your sacrifices
    or the burnt offerings you constantly
        offer.
9 But I do not need the bulls from your
        barns
    or the goats from your pens.
10 For all the animals of the forest are mine,
    and I own the cattle on a thousand hills.
11 I know every bird on the mountains,
    and all the animals of the field are mine.
12 If I were hungry, I would not tell you,
    for all the world is mine and everything
        in it.
13 Do I eat the meat of bulls?
    Do I drink the blood of goats?
14 Make thankfulness your sacrifice to God,
    and keep the vows you made to the Most
        High.
15 Then call on me when you are in trouble,
    and I will rescue you,
    and you will give me glory."

16 But God says to the wicked:
   "Why bother reciting my decrees
    and pretending to obey my covenant?

49:7 Some Hebrew manuscripts read *no one can redeem the life of another.*   49:11 As in Greek and Syriac versions; Hebrew reads *Their inward [thought].*   49:13 The meaning of the Hebrew is uncertain.   49:14 Hebrew *Sheol;* also in 49:14b, 15.

¹⁷ For you refuse my discipline
   and treat my words like trash.
¹⁸ When you see thieves, you approve of
      them,
   and you spend your time with
      adulterers.
¹⁹ Your mouth is filled with wickedness,
   and your tongue is full of lies.
²⁰ You sit around and slander your brother—
   your own mother's son.
²¹ While you did all this, I remained silent,
   and you thought I didn't care.
But now I will rebuke you,
   listing all my charges against you.
²² Repent, all of you who forget me,
   or I will tear you apart,
   and no one will help you.
²³ But giving thanks is a sacrifice that truly
      honors me.
   If you keep to my path,
   I will reveal to you the salvation of God."

51 *For the choir director: A psalm of David, regarding the time Nathan the prophet came to him after David had committed adultery with Bathsheba.*

¹ Have mercy on me, O God,
   because of your unfailing love.
Because of your great compassion,
   blot out the stain of my sins.
² Wash me clean from my guilt.
   Purify me from my sin.
³ For I recognize my rebellion;
   it haunts me day and night.
⁴ Against you, and you alone, have I sinned;
   I have done what is evil in your sight.
You will be proved right in what you say,
   and your judgment against me is just.*
⁵ For I was born a sinner—
   yes, from the moment my mother
      conceived me.
⁶ But you desire honesty from the womb,*
   teaching me wisdom even there.

⁷ Purify me from my sins,* and I will be
      clean;
   wash me, and I will be whiter than
      snow.
⁸ Oh, give me back my joy again;
   you have broken me—
   now let me rejoice.
⁹ Don't keep looking at my sins.
   Remove the stain of my guilt.

¹⁰ Create in me a clean heart, O God.
   Renew a loyal spirit within me.
¹¹ Do not banish me from your presence,
   and don't take your Holy Spirit*
      from me.
¹² Restore to me the joy of your salvation,
   and make me willing to obey you.
¹³ Then I will teach your ways to rebels,
   and they will return to you.
¹⁴ Forgive me for shedding blood, O God
      who saves;
   then I will joyfully sing of your
      forgiveness.
¹⁵ Unseal my lips, O Lord,
   that my mouth may praise you.

¹⁶ You do not desire a sacrifice, or I would
      offer one.
   You do not want a burnt offering.
¹⁷ The sacrifice you desire is a broken spirit.
   You will not reject a broken and
      repentant heart, O God.
¹⁸ Look with favor on Zion and help her;
   rebuild the walls of Jerusalem.
¹⁹ Then you will be pleased with sacrifices
      offered in the right spirit—
   with burnt offerings and whole burnt
      offerings.
   Then bulls will again be sacrificed on
      your altar.

52 *For the choir director: A psalm* of David, regarding the time Doeg the Edomite said to Saul, "David has gone to see Ahimelech."*

¹ Why do you boast about your crimes, great
      warrior?
   Don't you realize God's justice
      continues forever?
² All day long you plot destruction.
   Your tongue cuts like a sharp razor;
   you're an expert at telling lies.
³ You love evil more than good
   and lies more than truth.   *Interlude*

⁴ You love to destroy others with your words,
   you liar!
⁵ But God will strike you down once and
      for all.
   He will pull you from your home
   and uproot you from the land of the
      living.   *Interlude*

51:4 Greek version reads *and you will win your case in court.* Compare Rom 3:4.   51:6 Or *from the heart;* Hebrew reads *in the inward parts.*   51:7 Hebrew *Purify me with the hyssop branch.*   51:11 Or *your spirit of holiness.*   52:title Hebrew *maskil.* This may be a literary or musical term.

6 The righteous will see it and be amazed.
    They will laugh and say,
7 "Look what happens to mighty warriors
    who do not trust in God.
  They trust their wealth instead
    and grow more and more bold in their
      wickedness."

8 But I am like an olive tree, thriving in the
    house of God.
  I will always trust in God's unfailing
    love.
9 I will praise you forever, O God,
    for what you have done.
  I will trust in your good name
    in the presence of your faithful
      people.

53 *For the choir director: A meditation; a psalm**
of David.

1 Only fools say in their hearts,
    "There is no God."
  They are corrupt, and their actions are
    evil;
      not one of them does good!

2 God looks down from heaven
    on the entire human race;
  he looks to see if anyone is truly wise,
    if anyone seeks God.
3 But no, all have turned away;
    all have become corrupt.*
  No one does good,
    not a single one!

4 Will those who do evil never learn?
    They eat up my people like bread
    and wouldn't think of praying to
      God.
5 Terror will grip them,
    terror like they have never known
      before.
  God will scatter the bones of your
    enemies.
      You will put them to shame, for God has
        rejected them.

6 Who will come from Mount Zion to rescue
    Israel?
  When God restores his people,
    Jacob will shout with joy, and Israel will
      rejoice.

54 *For the choir director: A psalm* of David,*
regarding the time the Ziphites came and
said to Saul, "We know where David is hiding."
To be accompanied by stringed instruments.

1 Come with great power, O God, and
    rescue me!
  Defend me with your might.
2 Listen to my prayer, O God.
    Pay attention to my plea.
3 For strangers are attacking me;
    violent people are trying to kill me.
  They care nothing for God.   *Interlude*

4 But God is my helper.
    The Lord keeps me alive!
5 May the evil plans of my enemies be
    turned against them.
  Do as you promised and put an end
    to them.

6 I will sacrifice a voluntary offering to you;
    I will praise your name, O Lord,
      for it is good.
7 For you have rescued me from my
    troubles
  and helped me to triumph over my
    enemies.

55 *For the choir director: A psalm* of David,*
to be accompanied by stringed instruments.

1 Listen to my prayer, O God.
    Do not ignore my cry for help!
2 Please listen and answer me,
    for I am overwhelmed by my
      troubles.
3 My enemies shout at me,
    making loud and wicked threats.
  They bring trouble on me
    and angrily hunt me down.

4 My heart pounds in my chest.
    The terror of death assaults me.
5 Fear and trembling overwhelm me,
    and I can't stop shaking.
6 Oh, that I had wings like a dove;
    then I would fly away and rest!
7 I would fly far away
    to the quiet of the wilderness.   *Interlude*

8 How quickly I would escape—
    far from this wild storm of hatred.

53:title Hebrew *According to mahalath; a maskil.* These may be literary or musical terms.   53:3 Greek version reads *have become*
useless. Compare Rom 3:12.   54:title Hebrew *maskil.* This may be a literary or musical term.   55:title Hebrew *maskil.* This
may be a literary or musical term.

⁹ Confuse them, Lord, and frustrate their
    plans,
    for I see violence and conflict in the
        city.
¹⁰ Its walls are patrolled day and night
    against invaders,
    but the real danger is wickedness within
        the city.
¹¹ Everything is falling apart;
    threats and cheating are rampant in the
        streets.

¹² It is not an enemy who taunts me—
    I could bear that.
    It is not my foes who so arrogantly insult
        me—
    I could have hidden from them.
¹³ Instead, it is you—my equal,
    my companion and close friend.
¹⁴ What good fellowship we once enjoyed
    as we walked together to the house
        of God.

¹⁵ Let death stalk my enemies;
    let the grave* swallow them alive,
    for evil makes its home within
        them.

¹⁶ But I will call on God,
    and the LORD will rescue me.
¹⁷ Morning, noon, and night
    I cry out in my distress,
    and the LORD hears my voice.
¹⁸ He ransoms me and keeps me safe
    from the battle waged against me,
    though many still oppose me.
¹⁹ God, who has ruled forever,
    will hear me and humble them.

                                    Interlude
For my enemies refuse to change their
        ways;
    they do not fear God.

²⁰ As for my companion, he betrayed his
        friends;
    he broke his promises.
²¹ His words are as smooth as butter,
    but in his heart is war.
    His words are as soothing as lotion,
    but underneath are daggers!

²² Give your burdens to the LORD,
    and he will take care of you.
    He will not permit the godly to slip
        and fall.

²³ But you, O God, will send the wicked
    down to the pit of destruction.
    Murderers and liars will die young,
    but I am trusting you to save me.

56

For the choir director: A psalm of David,
regarding the time the Philistines seized him
in Gath. To be sung to the tune "Dove on Distant Oaks."*

¹ O God, have mercy on me,
    for people are hounding me.
    My foes attack me all day long.
² I am constantly hounded by those who
        slander me,
    and many are boldly attacking me.
³ But when I am afraid,
    I will put my trust in you.
⁴ I praise God for what he has promised.
    I trust in God, so why should I be afraid?
    What can mere mortals do to me?

⁵ They are always twisting what I say;
    they spend their days plotting to
        harm me.
⁶ They come together to spy on me—
    watching my every step, eager to
        kill me.
⁷ Don't let them get away with their
        wickedness;
    in your anger, O God, bring them
        down.

⁸ You keep track of all my sorrows.*
    You have collected all my tears in your
        bottle.
    You have recorded each one in your
        book.

⁹ My enemies will retreat when I call to you
        for help.
    This I know: God is on my side!
¹⁰ I praise God for what he has promised;
    yes, I praise the LORD for what he has
        promised.

¹¹ I trust in God, so why should I be afraid?
    What can mere mortals do to me?

¹² I will fulfill my vows to you, O God,
    and will offer a sacrifice of thanks for
        your help.
¹³ For you have rescued me from death;
    you have kept my feet from slipping.
    So now I can walk in your presence,
        O God,
    in your life-giving light.

55:15 Hebrew *let Sheol*.   56:title Hebrew *miktam*. This may be a literary or musical term.   56:8 Or *my wanderings*.

57

For the choir director: A psalm* of David, regarding the time he fled from Saul and went into the cave. To be sung to the tune "Do Not Destroy!"

1 Have mercy on me, O God, have mercy!
    I look to you for protection.
I will hide beneath the shadow of your
        wings
    until the danger passes by.
2 I cry out to God Most High,*
    to God who will fulfill his purpose
        for me.
3 He will send help from heaven to
        rescue me,
    disgracing those who hound me.
                                        Interlude
My God will send forth his unfailing love
    and faithfulness.

4 I am surrounded by fierce lions
    who greedily devour human prey—
whose teeth pierce like spears and arrows,
    and whose tongues cut like swords.

5 Be exalted, O God, above the highest
        heavens!
    May your glory shine over all the earth.

6 My enemies have set a trap for me.
    I am weary from distress.
They have dug a deep pit in my path,
    but they themselves have fallen into it.
                                        Interlude

7 My heart is confident in you, O God;
    my heart is confident.
    No wonder I can sing your praises!
8 Wake up, my heart!
    Wake up, O lyre and harp!
    I will wake the dawn with my song.
9 I will thank you, Lord, among all the
        people.
    I will sing your praises among the
        nations.
10 For your unfailing love is as high as the
        heavens.
    Your faithfulness reaches to the
        clouds.

11 Be exalted, O God, above the highest
        heavens.
    May your glory shine over all the
        earth.

58

For the choir director: A psalm* of David, to be sung to the tune "Do Not Destroy!"

1 Justice—do you rulers* know the meaning
        of the word?
    Do you judge the people fairly?
2 No! You plot injustice in your hearts.
    You spread violence throughout the
        land.
3 These wicked people are born sinners;
    even from birth they have lied and gone
        their own way.
4 They spit venom like deadly snakes;
    they are like cobras that refuse to listen,
5 ignoring the tunes of the snake charmers,
    no matter how skillfully they play.

6 Break off their fangs, O God!
    Smash the jaws of these lions, O LORD!
7 May they disappear like water into thirsty
        ground.
    Make their weapons useless in their
        hands.*
8 May they be like snails that dissolve into
        slime,
    like a stillborn child who will never see
        the sun.
9 God will sweep them away, both young
        and old,
    faster than a pot heats over burning
        thorns.

10 The godly will rejoice when they see
        injustice avenged.
    They will wash their feet in the blood
        of the wicked.
11 Then at last everyone will say,
    "There truly is a reward for those who
        live for God;
    surely there is a God who judges justly
        here on earth."

59

For the choir director: A psalm* of David, regarding the time Saul sent soldiers to watch David's house in order to kill him. To be sung to the tune "Do Not Destroy!"

1 Rescue me from my enemies, O God.
    Protect me from those who have come
        to destroy me.
2 Rescue me from these criminals;
    save me from these murderers.
3 They have set an ambush for me.

57:title Hebrew *miktam*. This may be a literary or musical term.   57:2 Hebrew *Elohim-Elyon*.   58:title Hebrew *miktam*. This may be a literary or musical term.   58:1 Or *you gods*.   58:7 Or *Let them be trodden down and wither like grass.* The meaning of the Hebrew is uncertain.   59:title Hebrew *miktam*. This may be a literary or musical term.

Fierce enemies are out there waiting,
   Lord,
      though I have not sinned or offended
      them.
⁴ I have done nothing wrong,
      yet they prepare to attack me.
   Wake up! See what is happening and
      help me!
⁵ O Lord God of Heaven's Armies, the God
      of Israel,
      wake up and punish those hostile
      nations.
   Show no mercy to wicked traitors.

                                                            Interlude

⁶ They come out at night,
      snarling like vicious dogs
      as they prowl the streets.
⁷ Listen to the filth that comes from their
      mouths;
      their words cut like swords.
   "After all, who can hear us?" they sneer.
⁸ But Lord, you laugh at them.
      You scoff at all the hostile nations.
⁹ You are my strength; I wait for you to
      rescue me,
      for you, O God, are my fortress.
¹⁰ In his unfailing love, my God will stand
      with me.
      He will let me look down in triumph on
      all my enemies.

¹¹ Don't kill them, for my people soon forget
      such lessons;
      stagger them with your power, and
      bring them to their knees,
      O Lord our shield.
¹² Because of the sinful things they say,
      because of the evil that is on their lips,
   let them be captured by their pride,
      their curses, and their lies.
¹³ Destroy them in your anger!
      Wipe them out completely!
   Then the whole world will know
      that God reigns in Israel.*   *Interlude*

¹⁴ My enemies come out at night,
      snarling like vicious dogs
      as they prowl the streets.
¹⁵ They scavenge for food
      but go to sleep unsatisfied.*

¹⁶ But as for me, I will sing about your
      power.

Each morning I will sing with joy about
      your unfailing love.
   For you have been my refuge,
      a place of safety when I am in distress.
¹⁷ O my Strength, to you I sing praises,
      for you, O God, are my refuge,
      the God who shows me unfailing love.

60 *For the choir director: A psalm* of David useful
for teaching, regarding the time David fought
Aram-naharaim and Aram-zobah, and Joab returned and
killed 12,000 Edomites in the Valley of Salt. To be sung to
the tune "Lily of the Testimony."*

¹ You have rejected us, O God, and broken
      our defenses.
   You have been angry with us; now
      restore us to your favor.
² You have shaken our land and split it
      open.
   Seal the cracks, for the land trembles.
³ You have been very hard on us,
      making us drink wine that sent us
      reeling.
⁴ But you have raised a banner for those who
      fear you—
      a rallying point in the face of attack.

                                                            Interlude

⁵ Now rescue your beloved people.
      Answer and save us by your power.
⁶ God has promised this by his holiness*:
   "I will divide up Shechem with joy.
      I will measure out the valley of Succoth.
⁷ Gilead is mine,
      and Manasseh, too.
   Ephraim, my helmet, will produce my
      warriors,
      and Judah, my scepter, will produce my
      kings.
⁸ But Moab, my washbasin, will become my
      servant,
      and I will wipe my feet on Edom
      and shout in triumph over Philistia."

⁹ Who will bring me into the fortified city?
      Who will bring me victory over Edom?
¹⁰ Have you rejected us, O God?
      Will you no longer march with our
      armies?
¹¹ Oh, please help us against our enemies,
      for all human help is useless.
¹² With God's help we will do mighty things,
      for he will trample down our foes.

59:13 Hebrew *in Jacob.* See note on 44:4.   **59:15** Or *and growl if they don't get enough.*   **60:title** Hebrew *miktam.* This may be
a literary or musical term.   **60:6** Or *in his sanctuary.*

61

For the choir director: A psalm of David, to be accompanied by stringed instruments.

1 O God, listen to my cry!
Hear my prayer!
2 From the ends of the earth,
I cry to you for help
when my heart is overwhelmed.
Lead me to the towering rock of safety,
3 for you are my safe refuge,
a fortress where my enemies cannot
reach me.
4 Let me live forever in your sanctuary,
safe beneath the shelter of your wings!
Interlude

5 For you have heard my vows, O God.
You have given me an inheritance
reserved for those who fear your
name.
6 Add many years to the life of the king!
May his years span the generations!
7 May he reign under God's protection
forever.
May your unfailing love and
faithfulness watch over him.
8 Then I will sing praises to your name
forever
as I fulfill my vows each day.

62

*For Jeduthun, the choir director:
A psalm of David.*

1 I wait quietly before God,
for my victory comes from him.
2 He alone is my rock and my salvation,
my fortress where I will never be
shaken.

3 So many enemies against one man—
all of them trying to kill me.
To them I'm just a broken-down wall
or a tottering fence.
4 They plan to topple me from my high
position.
They delight in telling lies about me.
They praise me to my face
but curse me in their hearts.   *Interlude*

5 Let all that I am wait quietly before God,
for my hope is in him.
6 He alone is my rock and my salvation,
my fortress where I will not be
shaken.
7 My victory and honor come from
God alone.

He is my refuge, a rock where no enemy
can reach me.
8 O my people, trust in him at all times.
Pour out your heart to him,
for God is our refuge.   *Interlude*

9 Common people are as worthless as a puff
of wind,
and the powerful are not what they
appear to be.
If you weigh them on the scales,
together they are lighter than a breath
of air.

10 Don't make your living by extortion
or put your hope in stealing.
And if your wealth increases,
don't make it the center of your life.

11 God has spoken plainly,
and I have heard it many times:
Power, O God, belongs to you;
12 unfailing love, O Lord, is yours.
Surely you repay all people
according to what they have done.

63

*A psalm of David, regarding a time when David
was in the wilderness of Judah.*

1 O God, you are my God;
I earnestly search for you.
My soul thirsts for you;
my whole body longs for you
in this parched and weary land
where there is no water.
2 I have seen you in your sanctuary
and gazed upon your power and glory.
3 Your unfailing love is better than life
itself;
how I praise you!
4 I will praise you as long as I live,
lifting up my hands to you in prayer.
5 You satisfy me more than the richest feast.
I will praise you with songs of joy.
6 I lie awake thinking of you,
meditating on you through the night.
7 Because you are my helper,
I sing for joy in the shadow of your
wings.
8 I cling to you;
your strong right hand holds me
securely.

9 But those plotting to destroy me will come
to ruin.

They will go down into the depths of
    the earth.
¹⁰ They will die by the sword
    and become the food of jackals.
¹¹ But the king will rejoice in God.
    All who swear to tell the truth will
        praise him,
    while liars will be silenced.

64
For the choir director: A psalm of David.

¹ O God, listen to my complaint.
    Protect my life from my enemies'
        threats.
² Hide me from the plots of this evil mob,
    from this gang of wrongdoers.
³ They sharpen their tongues like swords
    and aim their bitter words like arrows.
⁴ They shoot from ambush at the innocent,
    attacking suddenly and fearlessly.
⁵ They encourage each other to do evil
    and plan how to set their traps in
        secret.
    "Who will ever notice?" they ask.
⁶ As they plot their crimes, they say,
    "We have devised the perfect plan!"
    Yes, the human heart and mind are
        cunning.

⁷ But God himself will shoot them with his
        arrows,
    suddenly striking them down.
⁸ Their own tongues will ruin them,
    and all who see them will shake their
        heads in scorn.
⁹ Then everyone will be afraid;
    they will proclaim the mighty acts
        of God
    and realize all the amazing things
        he does.
¹⁰ The godly will rejoice in the LORD
    and find shelter in him.
    And those who do what is right
        will praise him.

65
For the choir director: A song. A psalm of David.

¹ What mighty praise, O God,
    belongs to you in Zion.
    We will fulfill our vows to you,
² for you answer our prayers.
    All of us must come to you.
³ Though we are overwhelmed by our sins,
    you forgive them all.

⁴ What joy for those you choose to bring
        near,
    those who live in your holy courts.
    What festivities await us
        inside your holy Temple.

⁵ You faithfully answer our prayers with
        awesome deeds,
    O God our savior.
    You are the hope of everyone on earth,
        even those who sail on distant seas.
⁶ You formed the mountains by your power
    and armed yourself with mighty
        strength.
⁷ You quieted the raging oceans
    with their pounding waves
    and silenced the shouting of the nations.
⁸ Those who live at the ends of the earth
    stand in awe of your wonders.
    From where the sun rises to where it sets,
        you inspire shouts of joy.

⁹ You take care of the earth and water it,
    making it rich and fertile.
    The river of God has plenty of water;
        it provides a bountiful harvest of grain,
    for you have ordered it so.
¹⁰ You drench the plowed ground with rain,
    melting the clods and leveling the ridges.
    You soften the earth with showers
        and bless its abundant crops.
¹¹ You crown the year with a bountiful
        harvest;
    even the hard pathways overflow with
        abundance.
¹² The grasslands of the wilderness become
        a lush pasture,
    and the hillsides blossom with joy.
¹³ The meadows are clothed with flocks of
        sheep,
    and the valleys are carpeted with grain.
    They all shout and sing for joy!

66
For the choir director: A song. A psalm.

¹ Shout joyful praises to God, all the earth!
²   Sing about the glory of his name!
    Tell the world how glorious he is.
³ Say to God, "How awesome are your deeds!
    Your enemies cringe before your mighty
        power.
⁴ Everything on earth will worship you;
    they will sing your praises,
    shouting your name in glorious songs."
                                                Interlude

5 Come and see what our God has done,
   what awesome miracles he performs
      for people!
6 He made a dry path through the Red Sea,*
   and his people went across on foot.
      There we rejoiced in him.
7 For by his great power he rules forever.
   He watches every movement of the
      nations;
   let no rebel rise in defiance.   *Interlude*

8 Let the whole world bless our God
   and loudly sing his praises.
9 Our lives are in his hands,
   and he keeps our feet from stumbling.
10 You have tested us, O God;
   you have purified us like silver.
11 You captured us in your net
   and laid the burden of slavery on our
      backs.
12 Then you put a leader over us.*
   We went through fire and flood,
   but you brought us to a place of great
      abundance.

13 Now I come to your Temple with burnt
      offerings
   to fulfill the vows I made to you—
14 yes, the sacred vows that I made
   when I was in deep trouble.
15 That is why I am sacrificing burnt
      offerings to you—
   the best of my rams as a pleasing
      aroma,
   and a sacrifice of bulls and male goats.
                                        Interlude

16 Come and listen, all you who fear God,
   and I will tell you what he did for me.
17 For I cried out to him for help,
   praising him as I spoke.
18 If I had not confessed the sin in my heart,
   the Lord would not have listened.
19 But God did listen!
   He paid attention to my prayer.
20 Praise God, who did not ignore my prayer
   or withdraw his unfailing love
      from me.

67
*For the choir director: A song. A psalm, to be
accompanied by stringed instruments.*

1 May God be merciful and bless us.
   May his face smile with favor on us.
                                        Interlude

2 May your ways be known throughout the
      earth,
   your saving power among people
      everywhere.
3 May the nations praise you, O God.
   Yes, may all the nations praise you.
4 Let the whole world sing for joy,
   because you govern the nations with
      justice
   and guide the people of the whole
      world.   *Interlude*

5 May the nations praise you, O God.
   Yes, may all the nations praise you.
6 Then the earth will yield its harvests,
   and God, our God, will richly bless us.
7 Yes, God will bless us,
   and people all over the world will fear
      him.

68
For the choir director: A song. A psalm of David.

1 Rise up, O God, and scatter your enemies.
   Let those who hate God run for their lives.
2 Blow them away like smoke.
   Melt them like wax in a fire.
   Let the wicked perish in the presence
      of God.
3 But let the godly rejoice.
   Let them be glad in God's presence.
   Let them be filled with joy.
4 Sing praises to God and to his name!
   Sing loud praises to him who rides the
      clouds.*
   His name is the LORD—
   rejoice in his presence!

5 Father to the fatherless, defender of
      widows—
   this is God, whose dwelling is holy.
6 God places the lonely in families;
   he sets the prisoners free and gives
      them joy.
   But he makes the rebellious live in a sun-
      scorched land.

7 O God, when you led your people out from
      Egypt,
   when you marched through the dry
      wasteland,   *Interlude*
8 the earth trembled, and the heavens
      poured down rain
   before you, the God of Sinai,
   before God, the God of Israel.

66:6 Hebrew *the sea.*   66:12 Or *You made people ride over our heads.*   68:4 Or *rides through the deserts.*

⁹ You sent abundant rain, O God,
    to refresh the weary land.
¹⁰ There your people finally settled,
    and with a bountiful harvest, O God,
    you provided for your needy people.

¹¹ The Lord gives the word,
    and a great army* brings the good news.
¹² Enemy kings and their armies flee,
    while the women of Israel divide the
    plunder.
¹³ Even those who lived among the
    sheepfolds found treasures—
    doves with wings of silver
    and feathers of gold.
¹⁴ The Almighty scattered the enemy kings
    like a blowing snowstorm on Mount
    Zalmon.

¹⁵ The mountains of Bashan are majestic,
    with many peaks stretching high into
    the sky.
¹⁶ Why do you look with envy, O rugged
    mountains,
    at Mount Zion, where God has chosen
    to live,
    where the LORD himself will live forever?

¹⁷ Surrounded by unnumbered thousands
    of chariots,
    the Lord came from Mount Sinai into
    his sanctuary.
¹⁸ When you ascended to the heights,
    you led a crowd of captives.
    You received gifts from the people,
    even from those who rebelled against
    you.
    Now the LORD God will live among us
    there.

¹⁹ Praise the Lord; praise God our savior!
    For each day he carries us in his arms.
                              Interlude
²⁰ Our God is a God who saves!
    The Sovereign LORD rescues us from
    death.

²¹ But God will smash the heads of his
    enemies,
    crushing the skulls of those who love
    their guilty ways.
²² The Lord says, "I will bring my enemies
    down from Bashan;

    I will bring them up from the depths
    of the sea.
²³ You, my people, will wash* your feet in
    their blood,
    and even your dogs will get their share!"

²⁴ Your procession has come into view,
    O God—
    the procession of my God and King as
    he goes into the sanctuary.
²⁵ Singers are in front, musicians behind;
    between them are young women
    playing tambourines.
²⁶ Praise God, all you people of Israel;
    praise the LORD, the source of Israel's
    life.
²⁷ Look, the little tribe of Benjamin leads
    the way.
    Then comes a great throng of rulers
    from Judah
    and all the rulers of Zebulun and
    Naphtali.

²⁸ Summon your might, O God.*
    Display your power, O God, as you have
    in the past.
²⁹ The kings of the earth are bringing
    tribute
    to your Temple in Jerusalem.
³⁰ Rebuke these enemy nations—
    these wild animals lurking in the reeds,
    this herd of bulls among the weaker
    calves.
    Make them bring bars of silver in humble
    tribute.
    Scatter the nations that delight in war.
³¹ Let Egypt come with gifts of precious
    metals*;
    let Ethiopia* bring tribute to God.
³² Sing to God, you kingdoms of the earth.
    Sing praises to the Lord.   Interlude
³³ Sing to the one who rides across the
    ancient heavens,
    his mighty voice thundering from
    the sky.
³⁴ Tell everyone about God's power.
    His majesty shines down on Israel;
    his strength is mighty in the heavens.
³⁵ God is awesome in his sanctuary.
    The God of Israel gives power and
    strength to his people.

    Praise be to God!

68:11 Or *a host of women.*   68:23 As in Greek and Syriac versions; Hebrew reads *shatter.*   68:28 As in some Hebrew
manuscripts and Greek and Syriac versions; most Hebrew manuscripts read *Your God has commanded your strength.*
68:31a Or *of rich cloth.*   68:31b Hebrew *Cush.*

69

For the choir director: A psalm of David, to be sung to the tune "Lilies."

1 Save me, O God,
   for the floodwaters are up to my neck.
2 Deeper and deeper I sink into the mire;
   I can't find a foothold.
 I am in deep water,
   and the floods overwhelm me.
3 I am exhausted from crying for help;
   my throat is parched.
 My eyes are swollen with weeping,
   waiting for my God to help me.
4 Those who hate me without cause
   outnumber the hairs on my head.
 Many enemies try to destroy me with lies,
   demanding that I give back what I
   didn't steal.

5 O God, you know how foolish I am;
   my sins cannot be hidden from you.
6 Don't let those who trust in you be
   ashamed because of me,
   O Sovereign LORD of Heaven's Armies.
 Don't let me cause them to be humiliated,
   O God of Israel.
7 For I endure insults for your sake;
   humiliation is written all over my face.
8 Even my own brothers pretend they don't
   know me;
   they treat me like a stranger.

9 Passion for your house has consumed me,
   and the insults of those who insult you
   have fallen on me.
10 When I weep and fast,
   they scoff at me.
11 When I dress in burlap to show sorrow,
   they make fun of me.
12 I am the favorite topic of town gossip,
   and all the drunks sing about me.

13 But I keep praying to you, LORD,
   hoping this time you will show me
   favor.
 In your unfailing love, O God,
   answer my prayer with your sure
   salvation.
14 Rescue me from the mud;
   don't let me sink any deeper!
 Save me from those who hate me,
   and pull me from these deep waters.
15 Don't let the floods overwhelm me,
   or the deep waters swallow me,
   or the pit of death devour me.

16 Answer my prayers, O LORD,
   for your unfailing love is wonderful.
 Take care of me,
   for your mercy is so plentiful.
17 Don't hide from your servant;
   answer me quickly, for I am in deep
   trouble!
18 Come and redeem me;
   free me from my enemies.

19 You know of my shame, scorn, and
   disgrace.
   You see all that my enemies are doing.
20 Their insults have broken my heart,
   and I am in despair.
 If only one person would show some pity;
   if only one would turn and comfort me.
21 But instead, they give me poison* for food;
   they offer me sour wine for my thirst.

22 Let the bountiful table set before them
   become a snare
   and their prosperity become a trap.*
23 Let their eyes go blind so they cannot see,
   and make their bodies shake
   continually.*
24 Pour out your fury on them;
   consume them with your burning
   anger.
25 Let their homes become desolate
   and their tents be deserted.
26 To the one you have punished, they add
   insult to injury;
   they add to the pain of those you have
   hurt.
27 Pile their sins up high,
   and don't let them go free.
28 Erase their names from the Book of Life;
   don't let them be counted among the
   righteous.

29 I am suffering and in pain.
   Rescue me, O God, by your saving
   power.

30 Then I will praise God's name with
   singing,
   and I will honor him with thanksgiving.
31 For this will please the LORD more than
   sacrificing cattle,

69:21 Or *gall.*   **69:22** Greek version reads *Let their bountiful table set before them become a snare, / a trap that makes them think all is well. / Let their blessings cause them to stumble, / and let them get what they deserve.* Compare Rom 11:9.   **69:23** Greek version reads *and let their backs be bent forever.* Compare Rom 11:10.

more than presenting a bull with its
  horns and hooves.
32 The humble will see their God at work and
  be glad.
  Let all who seek God's help be
  encouraged.
33 For the LORD hears the cries of the needy;
  he does not despise his imprisoned
  people.

34 Praise him, O heaven and earth,
  the seas and all that move in them.
35 For God will save Jerusalem*
  and rebuild the towns of Judah.
  His people will live there
  and settle in their own land.
36 The descendants of those who obey him
  will inherit the land,
  and those who love him will live there
  in safety.

70 *For the choir director: A psalm of David, asking
God to remember him.*

1 Please, God, rescue me!
  Come quickly, LORD, and help me.
2 May those who try to kill me
  be humiliated and put to shame.
  May those who take delight in my trouble
  be turned back in disgrace.
3 Let them be horrified by their shame,
  for they said, "Aha! We've got him now!"
4 But may all who search for you
  be filled with joy and gladness in you.
  May those who love your salvation
  repeatedly shout, "God is great!"
5 But as for me, I am poor and needy;
  please hurry to my aid, O God.
  You are my helper and my savior;
  O LORD, do not delay.

71 1 O LORD, I have come to you for
  protection;
  don't let me be disgraced.
2 Save me and rescue me,
  for you do what is right.
  Turn your ear to listen to me,
  and set me free.
3 Be my rock of safety
  where I can always hide.
  Give the order to save me,
  for you are my rock and my fortress.
4 My God, rescue me from the power of the
  wicked,
  from the clutches of cruel oppressors.

5 O Lord, you alone are my hope.
  I've trusted you, O LORD, from
  childhood.
6 Yes, you have been with me from birth;
  from my mother's womb you have cared
  for me.
  No wonder I am always praising you!

7 My life is an example to many,
  because you have been my strength and
  protection.
8 That is why I can never stop praising you;
  I declare your glory all day long.
9 And now, in my old age, don't set me
  aside.
  Don't abandon me when my strength
  is failing.
10 For my enemies are whispering
  against me.
  They are plotting together to kill me.
11 They say, "God has abandoned him.
  Let's go and get him,
  for no one will help him now."

12 O God, don't stay away.
  My God, please hurry to help me.
13 Bring disgrace and destruction on my
  accusers.
  Humiliate and shame those who want
  to harm me.
14 But I will keep on hoping for your help;
  I will praise you more and more.
15 I will tell everyone about your
  righteousness.
  All day long I will proclaim your saving
  power,
  though I am not skilled with words.*
16 I will praise your mighty deeds,
  O Sovereign LORD.
  I will tell everyone that you alone
  are just.

17 O God, you have taught me from my
  earliest childhood,
  and I constantly tell others about the
  wonderful things you do.
18 Now that I am old and gray,
  do not abandon me, O God.
  Let me proclaim your power to this new
  generation,
  your mighty miracles to all who come
  after me.

19 Your righteousness, O God, reaches to the
  highest heavens.

69:35 Hebrew *Zion.*   **71:15** Or *though I cannot count it.*

You have done such wonderful things.
Who can compare with you, O God?
20 You have allowed me to suffer much
hardship,
but you will restore me to life again
and lift me up from the depths of the
earth.
21 You will restore me to even greater honor
and comfort me once again.

22 Then I will praise you with music on the
harp,
because you are faithful to your
promises, O my God.
I will sing praises to you with a lyre,
O Holy One of Israel.
23 I will shout for joy and sing your praises,
for you have ransomed me.
24 I will tell about your righteous deeds
all day long,
for everyone who tried to hurt me
has been shamed and humiliated.

72 A psalm of Solomon.

1 Give your love of justice to the king,
O God,
and righteousness to the king's son.
2 Help him judge your people in the right
way;
let the poor always be treated fairly.
3 May the mountains yield prosperity for all,
and may the hills be fruitful.
4 Help him to defend the poor,
to rescue the children of the needy,
and to crush their oppressors.
5 May they fear you* as long as the sun
shines,
as long as the moon remains in the sky.
Yes, forever!

6 May the king's rule be refreshing like
spring rain on freshly cut grass,
like the showers that water the earth.
7 May all the godly flourish during his
reign.
May there be abundant prosperity until
the moon is no more.
8 May he reign from sea to sea,
and from the Euphrates River* to the
ends of the earth.
9 Desert nomads will bow before him;
his enemies will fall before him in the
dust.

10 The western kings of Tarshish and other
distant lands
will bring him tribute.
The eastern kings of Sheba and Seba
will bring him gifts.
11 All kings will bow before him,
and all nations will serve him.

12 He will rescue the poor when they cry to
him;
he will help the oppressed, who have no
one to defend them.
13 He feels pity for the weak and the needy,
and he will rescue them.
14 He will redeem them from oppression and
violence,
for their lives are precious to him.

15 Long live the king!
May the gold of Sheba be given to him.
May the people always pray for him
and bless him all day long.
16 May there be abundant grain throughout
the land,
flourishing even on the hilltops.
May the fruit trees flourish like the trees
of Lebanon,
and may the people thrive like grass in
a field.
17 May the king's name endure forever;
may it continue as long as the sun
shines.
May all nations be blessed through him
and bring him praise.

18 Praise the LORD God, the God of Israel,
who alone does such wonderful things.
19 Praise his glorious name forever!
Let the whole earth be filled with his
glory.
Amen and amen!

20 (This ends the prayers of David son of
Jesse.)

BOOK THREE (Psalms 73–89)

73 A psalm of Asaph.

1 Truly God is good to Israel,
to those whose hearts are pure.
2 But as for me, I almost lost my footing.
My feet were slipping, and I was almost
gone.

72:5 Greek version reads *May they endure.*   72:8 Hebrew *the river.*

3 For I envied the proud
  when I saw them prosper despite their
    wickedness.
4 They seem to live such painless lives;
  their bodies are so healthy and strong.
5 They don't have troubles like other
    people;
  they're not plagued with problems like
    everyone else.
6 They wear pride like a jeweled necklace
  and clothe themselves with cruelty.
7 These fat cats have everything
  their hearts could ever wish for!
8 They scoff and speak only evil;
  in their pride they seek to crush others.
9 They boast against the very heavens,
  and their words strut throughout the
    earth.
10 And so the people are dismayed and
    confused,
  drinking in all their words.
11 "What does God know?" they ask.
  "Does the Most High even know what's
    happening?"
12 Look at these wicked people—
  enjoying a life of ease while their riches
    multiply.

13 Did I keep my heart pure for nothing?
  Did I keep myself innocent for no
    reason?
14 I get nothing but trouble all day long;
  every morning brings me pain.

15 If I had really spoken this way to others,
  I would have been a traitor to your
    people.
16 So I tried to understand why the wicked
    prosper.
  But what a difficult task it is!
17 Then I went into your sanctuary, O God,
  and I finally understood the destiny of
    the wicked.
18 Truly, you put them on a slippery path
  and send them sliding over the cliff to
    destruction.
19 In an instant they are destroyed,
  completely swept away by terrors.
20 When you arise, O Lord,
  you will laugh at their silly ideas
  as a person laughs at dreams in the
    morning.

21 Then I realized that my heart was bitter,
  and I was all torn up inside.

22 I was so foolish and ignorant—
  I must have seemed like a senseless
    animal to you.
23 Yet I still belong to you;
  you hold my right hand.
24 You guide me with your counsel,
  leading me to a glorious destiny.
25 Whom have I in heaven but you?
  I desire you more than anything on
    earth.
26 My health may fail, and my spirit may
    grow weak,
  but God remains the strength of my
    heart;
  he is mine forever.

27 Those who desert him will perish,
  for you destroy those who abandon you.
28 But as for me, how good it is to be near
    God!
  I have made the Sovereign LORD my
    shelter,
  and I will tell everyone about the
    wonderful things you do.

74 A psalm* of Asaph.

1 O God, why have you rejected us so long?
  Why is your anger so intense against the
    sheep of your own pasture?
2 Remember that we are the people you
    chose long ago,
  the tribe you redeemed as your own
    special possession!
  And remember Jerusalem,* your home
    here on earth.
3 Walk through the awful ruins of the city;
  see how the enemy has destroyed your
    sanctuary.

4 There your enemies shouted their
    victorious battle cries;
  there they set up their battle
    standards.
5 They swung their axes
  like woodcutters in a forest.
6 With axes and picks,
  they smashed the carved paneling.
7 They burned your sanctuary to the
    ground.
  They defiled the place that bears your
    name.
8 Then they thought, "Let's destroy
    everything!"

74:title Hebrew *maskil*. This may be a literary or musical term. **74:2** Hebrew *Mount Zion*.

So they burned down all the places
    where God was worshiped.

9 We no longer see your miraculous signs.
    All the prophets are gone,
    and no one can tell us when it will end.
10 How long, O God, will you allow our
    enemies to insult you?
    Will you let them dishonor your name
    forever?
11 Why do you hold back your strong right
    hand?
    Unleash your powerful fist and destroy
    them.

12 You, O God, are my king from ages past,
    bringing salvation to the earth.
13 You split the sea by your strength
    and smashed the heads of the sea
    monsters.
14 You crushed the heads of Leviathan*
    and let the desert animals eat him.
15 You caused the springs and streams to
    gush forth,
    and you dried up rivers that never
    run dry.
16 Both day and night belong to you;
    you made the starlight* and the sun.
17 You set the boundaries of the earth,
    and you made both summer and winter.

18 See how these enemies insult you, LORD.
    A foolish nation has dishonored your
    name.
19 Don't let these wild beasts destroy your
    turtledoves.
    Don't forget your suffering people
    forever.

20 Remember your covenant promises,
    for the land is full of darkness and
    violence!
21 Don't let the downtrodden be humiliated
    again.
    Instead, let the poor and needy praise
    your name.

22 Arise, O God, and defend your cause.
    Remember how these fools insult you
    all day long.
23 Don't overlook what your enemies have
    said
    or their growing uproar.

75

For the choir director: A psalm of Asaph. A song to be sung to the tune "Do Not Destroy!"

1 We thank you, O God!
    We give thanks because you are near.
    People everywhere tell of your
    wonderful deeds.

2 God says, "At the time I have planned,
    I will bring justice against the wicked.
3 When the earth quakes and its people live
    in turmoil,
    I am the one who keeps its foundations
    firm.   *Interlude*

4 "I warned the proud, 'Stop your
    boasting!'
    I told the wicked, 'Don't raise your
    fists!
5 Don't raise your fists in defiance at the
    heavens
    or speak with such arrogance.'"

6 For no one on earth—from east or west,
    or even from the wilderness—
    should raise a defiant fist.*
7 It is God alone who judges;
    he decides who will rise and who will
    fall.
8 For the LORD holds a cup in his hand
    that is full of foaming wine mixed with
    spices.
He pours out the wine in judgment,
    and all the wicked must drink it,
    draining it to the dregs.

9 But as for me, I will always proclaim what
    God has done;
    I will sing praises to the God of Jacob.
10 For God says, "I will break the strength of
    the wicked,
    but I will increase the power of the
    godly."

76

For the choir director: A psalm of Asaph. A song to be accompanied by stringed instruments.

1 God is honored in Judah;
    his name is great in Israel.
2 Jerusalem* is where he lives;
    Mount Zion is his home.
3 There he has broken the fiery arrows of
    the enemy,
    the shields and swords and weapons
    of war.   *Interlude*

74:14 The identification of Leviathan is disputed, ranging from an earthly creature to a mythical sea monster in ancient literature.   74:16 Or *moon*; Hebrew reads *light*.   75:6 Hebrew *should lift*.   76:2 Hebrew *Salem*, another name for Jerusalem.

⁴ You are glorious and more majestic
    than the everlasting mountains.*
⁵ Our boldest enemies have been plundered.
    They lie before us in the sleep of death.
    No warrior could lift a hand against us.
⁶ At the blast of your breath, O God of Jacob,
    their horses and chariots lay still.

⁷ No wonder you are greatly feared!
    Who can stand before you when your
        anger explodes?
⁸ From heaven you sentenced your enemies;
    the earth trembled and stood silent
        before you.
⁹ You stand up to judge those who do evil,
        O God,
    and to rescue the oppressed of the earth.
                                    Interlude
¹⁰ Human defiance only enhances your glory,
    for you use it as a weapon.*

¹¹ Make vows to the LORD your God, and
        keep them.
    Let everyone bring tribute to the
        Awesome One.
¹² For he breaks the pride of princes,
    and the kings of the earth fear him.

77 For Jeduthun, the choir director: A psalm of Asaph.

¹ I cry out to God; yes, I shout.
    Oh, that God would listen to me!
² When I was in deep trouble,
    I searched for the Lord.
    All night long I prayed, with hands lifted
        toward heaven,
    but my soul was not comforted.
³ I think of God, and I moan,
    overwhelmed with longing for his help.
                                    Interlude

⁴ You don't let me sleep.
    I am too distressed even to pray!
⁵ I think of the good old days,
    long since ended,
⁶ when my nights were filled with joyful
        songs.
    I search my soul and ponder the
        difference now.
⁷ Has the Lord rejected me forever?
    Will he never again be kind to me?
⁸ Is his unfailing love gone forever?
    Have his promises permanently failed?

⁹ Has God forgotten to be gracious?
    Has he slammed the door on his
        compassion?   Interlude
¹⁰ And I said, "This is my fate;
    the Most High has turned his hand
        against me."
¹¹ But then I recall all you have done,
        O LORD;
    I remember your wonderful deeds
        of long ago.
¹² They are constantly in my thoughts.
    I cannot stop thinking about your
        mighty works.

¹³ O God, your ways are holy.
    Is there any god as mighty as you?
¹⁴ You are the God of great wonders!
    You demonstrate your awesome power
        among the nations.
¹⁵ By your strong arm, you redeemed your
        people,
    the descendants of Jacob and Joseph.
                                    Interlude

¹⁶ When the Red Sea* saw you, O God,
    its waters looked and trembled!
    The sea quaked to its very depths.
¹⁷ The clouds poured down rain;
    the thunder rumbled in the sky.
    Your arrows of lightning flashed.
¹⁸ Your thunder roared from the whirlwind;
    the lightning lit up the world!
    The earth trembled and shook.
¹⁹ Your road led through the sea,
    your pathway through the mighty
        waters—
    a pathway no one knew was there!
²⁰ You led your people along that road like
        a flock of sheep,
    with Moses and Aaron as their
        shepherds.

78 A psalm* of Asaph.

¹ O my people, listen to my instructions.
    Open your ears to what I am saying,
² for I will speak to you in a parable.
    I will teach you hidden lessons from our
        past—
³ stories we have heard and known,
    stories our ancestors handed down to us.

76:4 As in Greek version; Hebrew reads *than mountains filled with beasts of prey.* 76:10 The meaning of the Hebrew is uncertain. 77:16 Hebrew *the waters.* 78:title Hebrew *maskil.* This may be a literary or musical term.

4 We will not hide these truths from our
     children;
  we will tell the next generation
about the glorious deeds of the Lord,
     about his power and his mighty
     wonders.
5 For he issued his laws to Jacob;
     he gave his instructions to Israel.
He commanded our ancestors
     to teach them to their children,
6 so the next generation might know
     them—
  even the children not yet born—
  and they in turn will teach their own
     children.
7 So each generation should set its hope
     anew on God,
  not forgetting his glorious miracles
  and obeying his commands.
8 Then they will not be like their
     ancestors—
  stubborn, rebellious, and unfaithful,
  refusing to give their hearts to God.

9 The warriors of Ephraim, though armed
     with bows,
  turned their backs and fled on the day
     of battle.
10 They did not keep God's covenant
     and refused to live by his instructions.
11 They forgot what he had done—
     the great wonders he had shown them,
12 the miracles he did for their ancestors
     on the plain of Zoan in the land of
     Egypt.
13 For he divided the sea and led them
     through,
  making the water stand up like walls!
14 In the daytime he led them by a cloud,
     and all night by a pillar of fire.
15 He split open the rocks in the wilderness
     to give them water, as from a gushing
     spring.
16 He made streams pour from the rock,
     making the waters flow down like a
     river!

17 Yet they kept on sinning against him,
     rebelling against the Most High in the
     desert.
18 They stubbornly tested God in their
     hearts,
  demanding the foods they craved.
19 They even spoke against God himself,
     saying,

  "God can't give us food in the
     wilderness.
20 Yes, he can strike a rock so water gushes
     out,
  but he can't give his people bread and
     meat."
21 When the Lord heard them, he was furious.
  The fire of his wrath burned against
     Jacob.
  Yes, his anger rose against Israel,
22 for they did not believe God
     or trust him to care for them.
23 But he commanded the skies to open;
     he opened the doors of heaven.
24 He rained down manna for them to eat;
     he gave them bread from heaven.
25 They ate the food of angels!
     God gave them all they could hold.
26 He released the east wind in the heavens
     and guided the south wind by his
     mighty power.
27 He rained down meat as thick as dust—
     birds as plentiful as the sand on the
     seashore!
28 He caused the birds to fall within their
     camp
  and all around their tents.
29 The people ate their fill.
     He gave them what they craved.
30 But before they satisfied their craving,
     while the meat was yet in their mouths,
31 the anger of God rose against them,
     and he killed their strongest men.
  He struck down the finest of Israel's
     young men.

32 But in spite of this, the people kept
     sinning.
  Despite his wonders, they refused to
     trust him.
33 So he ended their lives in failure,
     their years in terror.
34 When God began killing them,
     they finally sought him.
  They repented and took God seriously.
35 Then they remembered that God was their
     rock,
  that God Most High* was their
     redeemer.
36 But all they gave him was lip service;
     they lied to him with their tongues.
37 Their hearts were not loyal to him.
     They did not keep his covenant.
38 Yet he was merciful and forgave their sins
     and did not destroy them all.

78:35 Hebrew El-Elyon.

Many times he held back his anger
and did not unleash his fury!

³⁹ For he remembered that they were merely
mortal,
gone like a breath of wind that never
returns.

⁴⁰ Oh, how often they rebelled against him
in the wilderness
and grieved his heart in that dry
wasteland.

⁴¹ Again and again they tested God's
patience
and provoked the Holy One of Israel.

⁴² They did not remember his power
and how he rescued them from their
enemies.

⁴³ They did not remember his miraculous
signs in Egypt,
his wonders on the plain of Zoan.

⁴⁴ For he turned their rivers into blood,
so no one could drink from the streams.

⁴⁵ He sent vast swarms of flies to consume
them
and hordes of frogs to ruin them.

⁴⁶ He gave their crops to caterpillars;
their harvest was consumed by locusts.

⁴⁷ He destroyed their grapevines with hail
and shattered their sycamore-figs with
sleet.

⁴⁸ He abandoned their cattle to the hail,
their livestock to bolts of lightning.

⁴⁹ He loosed on them his fierce anger—
all his fury, rage, and hostility.
He dispatched against them
a band of destroying angels.

⁵⁰ He turned his anger against them;
he did not spare the Egyptians' lives
but ravaged them with the plague.

⁵¹ He killed the oldest son in each Egyptian
family,
the flower of youth throughout the land
of Egypt.*

⁵² But he led his own people like a flock of
sheep,
guiding them safely through the
wilderness.

⁵³ He kept them safe so they were not afraid;
but the sea covered their enemies.

⁵⁴ He brought them to the border of his holy
land,
to this land of hills he had won for
them.

⁵⁵ He drove out the nations before them;
he gave them their inheritance by lot.

He settled the tribes of Israel into their
homes.

⁵⁶ But they kept testing and rebelling against
God Most High.
They did not obey his laws.

⁵⁷ They turned back and were as faithless as
their parents.
They were as undependable as a crooked
bow.

⁵⁸ They angered God by building shrines to
other gods;
they made him jealous with their idols.

⁵⁹ When God heard them, he was very angry,
and he completely rejected Israel.

⁶⁰ Then he abandoned his dwelling at Shiloh,
the Tabernacle where he had lived
among the people.

⁶¹ He allowed the Ark of his might to be
captured;
he surrendered his glory into enemy
hands.

⁶² He gave his people over to be butchered by
the sword,
because he was so angry with his own
people—his special possession.

⁶³ Their young men were killed by fire;
their young women died before singing
their wedding songs.

⁶⁴ Their priests were slaughtered,
and their widows could not mourn their
deaths.

⁶⁵ Then the Lord rose up as though waking
from sleep,
like a warrior aroused from a drunken
stupor.

⁶⁶ He routed his enemies
and sent them to eternal shame.

⁶⁷ But he rejected Joseph's descendants;
he did not choose the tribe of Ephraim.

⁶⁸ He chose instead the tribe of Judah,
and Mount Zion, which he loved.

⁶⁹ There he built his sanctuary as high as the
heavens,
as solid and enduring as the earth.

⁷⁰ He chose his servant David,
calling him from the sheep pens.

⁷¹ He took David from tending the ewes and
lambs
and made him the shepherd of Jacob's
descendants—
God's own people, Israel.

⁷² He cared for them with a true heart
and led them with skillful hands.

78:51 Hebrew *in the tents of Ham.*

79

A psalm of Asaph.

1 O God, pagan nations have conquered
your land,
your special possession.
They have defiled your holy Temple
and made Jerusalem a heap of ruins.
2 They have left the bodies of your servants
as food for the birds of heaven.
The flesh of your godly ones
has become food for the wild animals.
3 Blood has flowed like water all around
Jerusalem;
no one is left to bury the dead.
4 We are mocked by our neighbors,
an object of scorn and derision to those
around us.

5 O LORD, how long will you be angry with
us? Forever?
How long will your jealousy burn like
fire?
6 Pour out your wrath on the nations that
refuse to acknowledge you—
on kingdoms that do not call upon your
name.
7 For they have devoured your people
Israel,*
making the land a desolate wilderness.
8 Do not hold us guilty for the sins of our
ancestors!
Let your compassion quickly meet our
needs,
for we are on the brink of despair.

9 Help us, O God of our salvation!
Help us for the glory of your name.
Save us and forgive our sins
for the honor of your name.
10 Why should pagan nations be allowed
to scoff,
asking, "Where is their God?"
Show us your vengeance against the
nations,
for they have spilled the blood of your
servants.
11 Listen to the moaning of the prisoners.
Demonstrate your great power by
saving those condemned to die.
12 O Lord, pay back our neighbors seven
times
for the scorn they have hurled at you.

13 Then we your people, the sheep of your
pasture,
will thank you forever and ever,
praising your greatness from generation
to generation.

80

*For the choir director: A psalm of Asaph,
to be sung to the tune "Lilies of the Covenant."*

1 Please listen, O Shepherd of Israel,
you who lead Joseph's descendants like
a flock.
O God, enthroned above the cherubim,
display your radiant glory
2 to Ephraim, Benjamin, and Manasseh.
Show us your mighty power.
Come to rescue us!

3 Turn us again to yourself, O God.
Make your face shine down upon us.
Only then will we be saved.
4 O LORD God of Heaven's Armies,
how long will you be angry with our
prayers?
5 You have fed us with sorrow
and made us drink tears by the
bucketful.
6 You have made us the scorn* of
neighboring nations.
Our enemies treat us as a joke.

7 Turn us again to yourself, O God of
Heaven's Armies.
Make your face shine down upon us.
Only then will we be saved.
8 You brought us from Egypt like a
grapevine;
you drove away the pagan nations and
transplanted us into your land.
9 You cleared the ground for us,
and we took root and filled the land.
10 Our shade covered the mountains;
our branches covered the mighty
cedars.
11 We spread our branches west to the
Mediterranean Sea;
our shoots spread east to the Euphrates
River.*
12 But now, why have you broken down our
walls
so that all who pass by may steal our
fruit?
13 The wild boar from the forest devours it,
and the wild animals feed on it.

79:7 Hebrew *devoured Jacob.* See note on 44:4.   80:6 As in Syriac version; Hebrew reads *the strife.*   80:11 Hebrew *west to the sea, . . . east to the river.*

14 Come back, we beg you, O God of Heaven's
   Armies.
  Look down from heaven and see our
   plight.
  Take care of this grapevine
15   that you yourself have planted,
  this son you have raised for yourself.
16 For we are chopped up and burned by our
   enemies.
  May they perish at the sight of your
   frown.
17 Strengthen the man you love,
  the son of your choice.
18 Then we will never abandon you again.
  Revive us so we can call on your name
   once more.

19 Turn us again to yourself, O Lord God
  of Heaven's Armies.
  Make your face shine down upon us.
  Only then will we be saved.

81
*For the choir director: A psalm of Asaph, to be accompanied by a stringed instrument.**

1 Sing praises to God, our strength.
  Sing to the God of Jacob.
2 Sing! Beat the tambourine.
  Play the sweet lyre and the harp.
3 Blow the ram's horn at new moon,
  and again at full moon to call a festival!
4 For this is required by the decrees of
   Israel;
  it is a regulation of the God of Jacob.
5 He made it a law for Israel*
  when he attacked Egypt to set us free.

  I heard an unknown voice say,
6 "Now I will take the load from your
   shoulders;
  I will free your hands from their heavy
   tasks.
7 You cried to me in trouble, and I saved
   you;
  I answered out of the thundercloud
  and tested your faith when there was
   no water at Meribah.   *Interlude*

8 "Listen to me, O my people, while I give
  you stern warnings.
  O Israel, if you would only listen
   to me!
9 You must never have a foreign god;
  you must not bow down before a false
   god.

10 For it was I, the Lord your God,
  who rescued you from the land of
   Egypt.
  Open your mouth wide, and I will fill
   it with good things.

11 "But no, my people wouldn't listen.
  Israel did not want me around.
12 So I let them follow their own stubborn
   desires,
  living according to their own ideas.
13 Oh, that my people would listen to me!
  Oh, that Israel would follow me,
   walking in my paths!
14 How quickly I would then subdue their
   enemies!
  How soon my hands would be upon
   their foes!
15 Those who hate the Lord would cringe
   before him;
  they would be doomed forever.
16 But I would feed you with the finest
   wheat.
  I would satisfy you with wild honey
   from the rock."

82
A psalm of Asaph.

1 God presides over heaven's court;
  he pronounces judgment on the
   heavenly beings:
2 "How long will you hand down unjust
   decisions
  by favoring the wicked?   *Interlude*

3 "Give justice to the poor and the
   orphan;
  uphold the rights of the oppressed
   and the destitute.
4 Rescue the poor and helpless;
  deliver them from the grasp of evil
   people.
5 But these oppressors know nothing;
  they are so ignorant!
  They wander about in darkness,
  while the whole world is shaken to
   the core.
6 I say, 'You are gods;
  you are all children of the Most High.
7 But you will die like mere mortals
  and fall like every other ruler.'"

8 Rise up, O God, and judge the earth,
  for all the nations belong to you.

81:title Hebrew *according to the gittith.*   81:5 Hebrew *for Joseph.*

83

A song. A psalm of Asaph.

1 O God, do not be silent!
  Do not be deaf.
  Do not be quiet, O God.
2 Don't you hear the uproar of your
    enemies?
  Don't you see that your arrogant
    enemies are rising up?
3 They devise crafty schemes against your
    people;
  they conspire against your precious
    ones.
4 "Come," they say, "let us wipe out Israel
    as a nation.
  We will destroy the very memory of its
    existence."
5 Yes, this was their unanimous decision.
  They signed a treaty as allies against
    you—
6 these Edomites and Ishmaelites;
  Moabites and Hagrites;
7 Gebalites, Ammonites, and Amalekites;
  and people from Philistia and Tyre.
8 Assyria has joined them, too,
  and is allied with the descendants
    of Lot.   *Interlude*

9 Do to them as you did to the Midianites
  and as you did to Sisera and Jabin at the
    Kishon River.
10 They were destroyed at Endor,
  and their decaying corpses fertilized
    the soil.
11 Let their mighty nobles die as Oreb and
    Zeeb did.
  Let all their princes die like Zebah and
    Zalmunna,
12 for they said, "Let us seize for our own use
    these pasturelands of God!"
13 O my God, scatter them like tumbleweed,
  like chaff before the wind!
14 As a fire burns a forest
  and as a flame sets mountains ablaze,
15 chase them with your fierce storm;
  terrify them with your tempest.
16 Utterly disgrace them
  until they submit to your name,
    O LORD.
17 Let them be ashamed and terrified
    forever.
  Let them die in disgrace.
18 Then they will learn that you alone are
    called the LORD,

that you alone are the Most High,
  supreme over all the earth.

84

*For the choir director: A psalm of the descendants
of Korah, to be accompanied by a stringed
instrument.**

1 How lovely is your dwelling place,
  O LORD of Heaven's Armies.
2 I long, yes, I faint with longing
  to enter the courts of the LORD.
With my whole being, body and soul,
  I will shout joyfully to the living God.
3 Even the sparrow finds a home,
  and the swallow builds her nest and
    raises her young
at a place near your altar,
  O LORD of Heaven's Armies, my King
    and my God!
4 What joy for those who can live in your
    house,
  always singing your praises.   *Interlude*

5 What joy for those whose strength comes
    from the LORD,
  who have set their minds on a
    pilgrimage to Jerusalem.
6 When they walk through the Valley of
    Weeping,*
  it will become a place of refreshing
    springs.
  The autumn rains will clothe it with
    blessings.
7 They will continue to grow stronger,
  and each of them will appear before God
    in Jerusalem.*

8 O LORD God of Heaven's Armies, hear my
    prayer.
  Listen, O God of Jacob.   *Interlude*

9 O God, look with favor upon the king, our
    shield!
  Show favor to the one you have
    anointed.

10 A single day in your courts
  is better than a thousand anywhere else!
I would rather be a gatekeeper in the
    house of my God
  than live the good life in the homes of
    the wicked.
11 For the LORD God is our sun and our
    shield.
  He gives us grace and glory.

84:title Hebrew *according to the gittith.*   84:6 Or *Valley of Poplars;* Hebrew reads *valley of Baca.*   84:7 Hebrew *Zion.*

The LORD will withhold no good thing
from those who do what is right.
12 O LORD of Heaven's Armies,
what joy for those who trust in you.

85

For the choir director: A psalm of the descendants of Korah.

1 LORD, you poured out blessings on your
land!
You restored the fortunes of Israel.*
2 You forgave the guilt of your people—
yes, you covered all their sins.

Interlude

3 You held back your fury.
You kept back your blazing anger.

4 Now restore us again, O God of our
salvation.
Put aside your anger against us once
more.
5 Will you be angry with us always?
Will you prolong your wrath to all
generations?
6 Won't you revive us again,
so your people can rejoice in you?
7 Show us your unfailing love, O LORD,
and grant us your salvation.

8 I listen carefully to what God the LORD is
saying,
for he speaks peace to his faithful
people.
But let them not return to their foolish
ways.
9 Surely his salvation is near to those who
fear him,
so our land will be filled with his glory.

10 Unfailing love and truth have met
together.
Righteousness and peace have kissed!
11 Truth springs up from the earth,
and righteousness smiles down from
heaven.
12 Yes, the LORD pours down his blessings.
Our land will yield its bountiful harvest.
13 Righteousness goes as a herald before him,
preparing the way for his steps.

86

A prayer of David.

1 Bend down, O LORD, and hear my prayer;
answer me, for I need your help.

2 Protect me, for I am devoted to you.
Save me, for I serve you and trust you.
You are my God.
3 Be merciful to me, O Lord,
for I am calling on you constantly.
4 Give me happiness, O Lord,
for I give myself to you.
5 O Lord, you are so good, so ready to
forgive,
so full of unfailing love for all who ask
for your help.
6 Listen closely to my prayer, O LORD;
hear my urgent cry.
7 I will call to you whenever I'm in
trouble,
and you will answer me.

8 No pagan god is like you, O Lord.
None can do what you do!
9 All the nations you made
will come and bow before you, Lord;
they will praise your holy name.
10 For you are great and perform wonderful
deeds.
You alone are God.

11 Teach me your ways, O LORD,
that I may live according to your
truth!
Grant me purity of heart,
so that I may honor you.
12 With all my heart I will praise you, O Lord
my God.
I will give glory to your name
forever,
13 for your love for me is very great.
You have rescued me from the depths
of death.*

14 O God, insolent people rise up
against me;
a violent gang is trying to kill me.
You mean nothing to them.
15 But you, O Lord,
are a God of compassion and mercy,
slow to get angry
and filled with unfailing love and
faithfulness.
16 Look down and have mercy on me.
Give your strength to your servant;
save me, the son of your servant.
17 Send me a sign of your favor.
Then those who hate me will be put to
shame,
for you, O LORD, help and comfort me.

85:1 Hebrew *of Jacob.* See note on 44:4.   86:13 Hebrew *of Sheol.*

87

A song. A psalm of the descendants of Korah.

¹ On the holy mountain
    stands the city founded by the LORD.
² He loves the city of Jerusalem
    more than any other city in Israel.*
³ O city of God,
    what glorious things are said of you!
                                           Interlude

⁴ I will count Egypt* and Babylon among
        those who know me—
    also Philistia and Tyre, and even distant
        Ethiopia.*
    They have all become citizens of
        Jerusalem!
⁵ Regarding Jerusalem* it will be said,
    "Everyone enjoys the rights of
        citizenship there."
    And the Most High will personally bless
        this city.
⁶ When the LORD registers the nations, he
        will say,
    "They have all become citizens of
        Jerusalem."   *Interlude*

⁷ The people will play flutes* and sing,
    "The source of my life springs from
        Jerusalem!"

88

*For the choir director: A psalm of the descendants
of Korah. A song to be sung to the tune "The
Suffering of Affliction." A psalm* of Heman the Ezrahite.*

¹ O LORD, God of my salvation,
    I cry out to you by day.
    I come to you at night.
² Now hear my prayer;
    listen to my cry.
³ For my life is full of troubles,
    and death* draws near.
⁴ I am as good as dead,
    like a strong man with no strength
        left.
⁵ They have left me among the dead,
    and I lie like a corpse in a grave.
    I am forgotten,
        cut off from your care.
⁶ You have thrown me into the lowest pit,
    into the darkest depths.
⁷ Your anger weighs me down;

with wave after wave you have
    engulfed me.   *Interlude*

⁸ You have driven my friends away
    by making me repulsive to them.
    I am in a trap with no way of escape.
⁹ My eyes are blinded by my tears.
    Each day I beg for your help,
        O LORD;
    I lift my hands to you for mercy.
¹⁰ Are your wonderful deeds of any use to
        the dead?
    Do the dead rise up and praise you?
                                           Interlude

¹¹ Can those in the grave declare your
        unfailing love?
    Can they proclaim your faithfulness in
        the place of destruction?*
¹² Can the darkness speak of your wonderful
        deeds?
    Can anyone in the land of forgetfulness
        talk about your righteousness?
¹³ O LORD, I cry out to you.
    I will keep on pleading day by day.
¹⁴ O LORD, why do you reject me?
    Why do you turn your face
        from me?

¹⁵ I have been sick and close to death since
        my youth.
    I stand helpless and desperate before
        your terrors.
¹⁶ Your fierce anger has overwhelmed me.
    Your terrors have paralyzed me.
¹⁷ They swirl around me like floodwaters all
        day long.
    They have engulfed me completely.
¹⁸ You have taken away my companions and
        loved ones.
    Darkness is my closest friend.

89

A psalm of Ethan the Ezrahite.*

¹ I will sing of the LORD's unfailing love
        forever!
    Young and old will hear of your
        faithfulness.
² Your unfailing love will last forever.
    Your faithfulness is as enduring as the
        heavens.

87:2 Hebrew *He loves the gates of Zion more than all the dwellings of Jacob.* See note on 44:4.   87:4a Hebrew *Rahab,* the name
of a mythical sea monster that represents chaos in ancient literature. The name is used here as a poetic name for Egypt.
87:4b Hebrew *Cush.*   87:5 Hebrew *Zion.*   87:7 Or *will dance.*   88:title Hebrew *maskil.* This may be a literary or musical
term.   88:3 Hebrew *Sheol.*   88:11 Hebrew *in Abaddon?*   89:title Hebrew *maskil.* This may be a literary or musical term.

³ The LORD said, "I have made a covenant
 with David, my chosen servant.
 I have sworn this oath to him:
⁴ 'I will establish your descendants as kings
  forever;
 they will sit on your throne from now
  until eternity.'"   *Interlude*
⁵ All heaven will praise your great wonders,
 LORD;
 myriads of angels will praise you for
  your faithfulness.
⁶ For who in all of heaven can compare with
  the LORD?
 What mightiest angel is anything like
  the LORD?
⁷ The highest angelic powers stand in awe
  of God.
 He is far more awesome than all who
  surround his throne.
⁸ O LORD God of Heaven's Armies!
 Where is there anyone as mighty as you,
  O LORD?
 You are entirely faithful.

⁹ You rule the oceans.
 You subdue their storm-tossed
  waves.
¹⁰ You crushed the great sea monster.*
 You scattered your enemies with your
  mighty arm.
¹¹ The heavens are yours, and the earth is
  yours;
 everything in the world is yours—you
  created it all.
¹² You created north and south.
 Mount Tabor and Mount Hermon
  praise your name.
¹³ Powerful is your arm!
 Strong is your hand!
 Your right hand is lifted high in
  glorious strength.
¹⁴ Righteousness and justice are the
  foundation of your throne.
 Unfailing love and truth walk before
  you as attendants.
¹⁵ Happy are those who hear the joyful call
  to worship,
 for they will walk in the light of your
  presence, LORD.
¹⁶ They rejoice all day long in your
  wonderful reputation.
 They exult in your righteousness.
¹⁷ You are their glorious strength.
 It pleases you to make us strong.
¹⁸ Yes, our protection comes from the LORD,

and he, the Holy One of Israel, has given
 us our king.

¹⁹ Long ago you spoke in a vision to your
  faithful people.
 You said, "I have raised up a warrior.
 I have selected him from the common
  people to be king.
²⁰ I have found my servant David.
 I have anointed him with my holy oil.
²¹ I will steady him with my hand;
 with my powerful arm I will make him
  strong.
²² His enemies will not defeat him,
 nor will the wicked overpower him.
²³ I will beat down his adversaries before him
 and destroy those who hate him.
²⁴ My faithfulness and unfailing love will be
  with him,
 and by my authority he will grow in
  power.
²⁵ I will extend his rule over the sea,
 his dominion over the rivers.
²⁶ And he will call out to me, 'You are my
  Father,
 my God, and the Rock of my salvation.'
²⁷ I will make him my firstborn son,
 the mightiest king on earth.
²⁸ I will love him and be kind to him forever;
 my covenant with him will never end.
²⁹ I will preserve an heir for him;
 his throne will be as endless as the days
  of heaven.
³⁰ But if his descendants forsake my
  instructions
 and fail to obey my regulations,
³¹ if they do not obey my decrees
 and fail to keep my commands,
³² then I will punish their sin with the rod,
 and their disobedience with beating.
³³ But I will never stop loving him
 nor fail to keep my promise to him.
³⁴ No, I will not break my covenant;
 I will not take back a single word I said.
³⁵ I have sworn an oath to David,
 and in my holiness I cannot lie:
³⁶ His dynasty will go on forever;
 his kingdom will endure as the sun.
³⁷ It will be as eternal as the moon,
 my faithful witness in the sky!"
                                      Interlude

³⁸ But now you have rejected him and cast
  him off.
 You are angry with your anointed king.

89:10 Hebrew *Rahab*, the name of a mythical sea monster that represents chaos in ancient literature.

³⁹ You have renounced your covenant with
    him;
  you have thrown his crown in the dust.
⁴⁰ You have broken down the walls
    protecting him
  and ruined every fort defending him.
⁴¹ Everyone who comes along has robbed
    him,
  and he has become a joke to his
    neighbors.
⁴² You have strengthened his enemies
  and made them all rejoice.
⁴³ You have made his sword useless
  and refused to help him in battle.
⁴⁴ You have ended his splendor
  and overturned his throne.
⁴⁵ You have made him old before his time
  and publicly disgraced him.   *Interlude*

⁴⁶ O LORD, how long will this go on?
  Will you hide yourself forever?
  How long will your anger burn like
    fire?
⁴⁷ Remember how short my life is,
  how empty and futile this human
    existence!
⁴⁸ No one can live forever; all will die.
  No one can escape the power of the
    grave.*   *Interlude*

⁴⁹ Lord, where is your unfailing love?
  You promised it to David with a faithful
    pledge.
⁵⁰ Consider, Lord, how your servants are
    disgraced!
  I carry in my heart the insults of so
    many people.
⁵¹ Your enemies have mocked me, O LORD;
  they mock your anointed king wherever
    he goes.

⁵² Praise the LORD forever!
  Amen and amen!

BOOK FOUR (Psalms 90–106)

90
A prayer of Moses, the man of God.

¹ Lord, through all the generations
  you have been our home!
² Before the mountains were born,
  before you gave birth to the earth and
    the world,
  from beginning to end, you are God.

89:48 Hebrew *of Sheol.*

³ You turn people back to dust, saying,
  "Return to dust, you mortals!"
⁴ For you, a thousand years are as a
    passing day,
  as brief as a few night hours.
⁵ You sweep people away like dreams that
    disappear.
  They are like grass that springs up in
    the morning.
⁶ In the morning it blooms and flourishes,
  but by evening it is dry and withered.
⁷ We wither beneath your anger;
  we are overwhelmed by your fury.
⁸ You spread out our sins before you—
  our secret sins—and you see them all.
⁹ We live our lives beneath your wrath,
  ending our years with a groan.
¹⁰ Seventy years are given to us!
  Some even live to eighty.
  But even the best years are filled with pain
    and trouble;
  soon they disappear, and we fly away.
¹¹ Who can comprehend the power of your
    anger?
  Your wrath is as awesome as the fear you
    deserve.
¹² Teach us to realize the brevity of life,
  so that we may grow in wisdom.

¹³ O LORD, come back to us!
  How long will you delay?
  Take pity on your servants!
¹⁴ Satisfy us each morning with your
    unfailing love,
  so we may sing for joy to the end of our
    lives.
¹⁵ Give us gladness in proportion to our
    former misery!
  Replace the evil years with good.
¹⁶ Let us, your servants, see you work again;
  let our children see your glory.
¹⁷ And may the Lord our God show us his
    approval
  and make our efforts successful.
  Yes, make our efforts successful!

91
¹ Those who live in the shelter of the
    Most High
  will find rest in the shadow of the
    Almighty.
² This I declare about the LORD:
  He alone is my refuge, my place of
    safety;
  he is my God, and I trust him.

3 For he will rescue you from every trap
  and protect you from deadly disease.
4 He will cover you with his feathers.
  He will shelter you with his wings.
  His faithful promises are your armor
    and protection.
5 Do not be afraid of the terrors of the night,
  nor the arrow that flies in the day.
6 Do not dread the disease that stalks in
    darkness,
  nor the disaster that strikes at midday.
7 Though a thousand fall at your side,
  though ten thousand are dying around
    you,
  these evils will not touch you.
8 Just open your eyes,
  and see how the wicked are punished.

9 If you make the LORD your refuge,
  if you make the Most High your shelter,
10 no evil will conquer you;
  no plague will come near your home.
11 For he will order his angels
  to protect you wherever you go.
12 They will hold you up with their hands
  so you won't even hurt your foot on a
    stone.
13 You will trample upon lions and cobras;
  you will crush fierce lions and serpents
    under your feet!

14 The LORD says, "I will rescue those who
    love me.
  I will protect those who trust in my name.
15 When they call on me, I will answer;
  I will be with them in trouble.
  I will rescue and honor them.
16 I will reward them with a long life
  and give them my salvation."

92 *A psalm. A song to be sung on the Sabbath Day.*

1 It is good to give thanks to the LORD,
  to sing praises to the Most High.
2 It is good to proclaim your unfailing love
    in the morning,
  your faithfulness in the evening,
3 accompanied by a ten-stringed
    instrument, a harp,
  and the melody of a lyre.

4 You thrill me, LORD, with all you have
    done for me!
  I sing for joy because of what you have
    done.

5 O LORD, what great works you do!
  And how deep are your thoughts.
6 Only a simpleton would not know,
  and only a fool would not understand
    this:
7 Though the wicked sprout like weeds
  and evildoers flourish,
  they will be destroyed forever.

8 But you, O LORD, will be exalted forever.
9 Your enemies, LORD, will surely perish;
  all evildoers will be scattered.
10 But you have made me as strong as a
    wild ox.
  You have anointed me with the finest
    oil.
11 My eyes have seen the downfall of my
    enemies;
  my ears have heard the defeat of my
    wicked opponents.
12 But the godly will flourish like palm trees
  and grow strong like the cedars of
    Lebanon.
13 For they are transplanted to the LORD's
    own house.
  They flourish in the courts of our God.
14 Even in old age they will still produce
    fruit;
  they will remain vital and green.
15 They will declare, "The LORD is just!
  He is my rock!
  There is no evil in him!"

93 1 The LORD is king! He is robed in
    majesty.
  Indeed, the LORD is robed in majesty
    and armed with strength.
  The world stands firm
    and cannot be shaken.

2 Your throne, O LORD, has stood from time
    immemorial.
  You yourself are from the everlasting
    past.
3 The floods have risen up, O LORD.
  The floods have roared like thunder;
  the floods have lifted their pounding
    waves.
4 But mightier than the violent raging of
    the seas,
  mightier than the breakers on the
    shore—
  the LORD above is mightier than these!
5 Your royal laws cannot be changed.
  Your reign, O LORD, is holy forever and
    ever.

94

¹ O Lord, the God of vengeance,
    O God of vengeance, let your
    glorious justice shine forth!
² Arise, O Judge of the earth.
    Give the proud what they deserve.
³ How long, O Lord?
    How long will the wicked be allowed
    to gloat?
⁴ How long will they speak with
    arrogance?
    How long will these evil people boast?
⁵ They crush your people, Lord,
    hurting those you claim as your own.
⁶ They kill widows and foreigners
    and murder orphans.
⁷ "The Lord isn't looking," they say,
    "and besides, the God of Israel* doesn't
    care."

⁸ Think again, you fools!
    When will you finally catch on?
⁹ Is he deaf—the one who made your ears?
    Is he blind—the one who formed your
    eyes?
¹⁰ He punishes the nations—won't he also
    punish you?
    He knows everything—doesn't he also
    know what you are doing?
¹¹ The Lord knows people's thoughts;
    he knows they are worthless!

¹² Joyful are those you discipline, Lord,
    those you teach with your instructions.
¹³ You give them relief from troubled times
    until a pit is dug to capture the wicked.
¹⁴ The Lord will not reject his people;
    he will not abandon his special
    possession.
¹⁵ Judgment will again be founded on
    justice,
    and those with virtuous hearts will
    pursue it.

¹⁶ Who will protect me from the wicked?
    Who will stand up for me against
    evildoers?
¹⁷ Unless the Lord had helped me,
    I would soon have settled in the silence
    of the grave.
¹⁸ I cried out, "I am slipping!"
    but your unfailing love, O Lord,
    supported me.
¹⁹ When doubts filled my mind,
    your comfort gave me renewed hope
    and cheer.

²⁰ Can unjust leaders claim that God is on
    their side—
    leaders whose decrees permit injustice?
²¹ They gang up against the righteous
    and condemn the innocent to death.
²² But the Lord is my fortress;
    my God is the mighty rock where I hide.
²³ God will turn the sins of evil people back
    on them.
    He will destroy them for their sins.
    The Lord our God will destroy them.

95

¹ Come, let us sing to the Lord!
    Let us shout joyfully to the Rock
    of our salvation.
² Let us come to him with thanksgiving.
    Let us sing psalms of praise to him.
³ For the Lord is a great God,
    a great King above all gods.
⁴ He holds in his hands the depths of the
    earth
    and the mightiest mountains.
⁵ The sea belongs to him, for he made it.
    His hands formed the dry land, too.

⁶ Come, let us worship and bow down.
    Let us kneel before the Lord our
    maker,
⁷   for he is our God.
We are the people he watches over,
    the flock under his care.

If only you would listen to his voice today!
⁸ The Lord says, "Don't harden your hearts
    as Israel did at Meribah,
    as they did at Massah in the wilderness.
⁹ For there your ancestors tested and tried
    my patience,
    even though they saw everything I did.
¹⁰ For forty years I was angry with them, and
    I said,
'They are a people whose hearts turn away
    from me.
    They refuse to do what I tell them.'
¹¹ So in my anger I took an oath:
    'They will never enter my place of rest.'"

96

¹ Sing a new song to the Lord!
    Let the whole earth sing to the
        Lord!
² Sing to the Lord; praise his name.
    Each day proclaim the good news that
    he saves.
³ Publish his glorious deeds among the
    nations.

94:7 Hebrew *of Jacob.* See note on 44:4.

Tell everyone about the amazing things
he does.
⁴ Great is the LORD! He is most worthy of
praise!
He is to be feared above all gods.
⁵ The gods of other nations are mere idols,
but the LORD made the heavens!
⁶ Honor and majesty surround him;
strength and beauty fill his sanctuary.

⁷ O nations of the world, recognize the
LORD;
recognize that the LORD is glorious and
strong.
⁸ Give to the LORD the glory he deserves!
Bring your offering and come into his
courts.
⁹ Worship the LORD in all his holy splendor.
Let all the earth tremble before him.
¹⁰ Tell all the nations, "The LORD reigns!"
The world stands firm and cannot be
shaken.
He will judge all peoples fairly.

¹¹ Let the heavens be glad, and the earth
rejoice!
Let the sea and everything in it shout his
praise!
¹² Let the fields and their crops burst out
with joy!
Let the trees of the forest sing for joy
¹³ before the LORD, for he is coming!
He is coming to judge the earth.
He will judge the world with justice,
and the nations with his truth.

97

¹ The LORD is king!
Let the earth rejoice!
Let the farthest coastlands be glad.
² Dark clouds surround him.
Righteousness and justice are the
foundation of his throne.
³ Fire spreads ahead of him
and burns up all his foes.
⁴ His lightning flashes out across the world.
The earth sees and trembles.
⁵ The mountains melt like wax before the
LORD,
before the Lord of all the earth.
⁶ The heavens proclaim his righteousness;
every nation sees his glory.
⁷ Those who worship idols are disgraced—
all who brag about their worthless
gods—
for every god must bow to him.

97:8 Hebrew *Zion.*

⁸ Jerusalem* has heard and rejoiced,
and all the towns of Judah are glad
because of your justice, O LORD!
⁹ For you, O LORD, are supreme over all the
earth;
you are exalted far above all gods.

¹⁰ You who love the LORD, hate evil!
He protects the lives of his godly
people
and rescues them from the power of the
wicked.
¹¹ Light shines on the godly,
and joy on those whose hearts are right.
¹² May all who are godly rejoice in the LORD
and praise his holy name!

98

A psalm.

¹ Sing a new song to the LORD,
for he has done wonderful deeds.
His right hand has won a mighty
victory;
his holy arm has shown his saving
power!
² The LORD has announced his victory
and has revealed his righteousness to
every nation!
³ He has remembered his promise to love
and be faithful to Israel.
The ends of the earth have seen the
victory of our God.

⁴ Shout to the LORD, all the earth;
break out in praise and sing for joy!
⁵ Sing your praise to the LORD with the
harp,
with the harp and melodious song,
⁶ with trumpets and the sound of the ram's
horn.
Make a joyful symphony before the
LORD, the King!

⁷ Let the sea and everything in it shout
his praise!
Let the earth and all living things
join in.
⁸ Let the rivers clap their hands in glee!
Let the hills sing out their songs
of joy
⁹ before the LORD,
for he is coming to judge the earth.
He will judge the world with justice,
and the nations with fairness.

99

¹ The LORD is king!
Let the nations tremble!
He sits on his throne between the
cherubim.
Let the whole earth quake!
² The LORD sits in majesty in Jerusalem,*
exalted above all the nations.
³ Let them praise your great and awesome
name.
Your name is holy!
⁴ Mighty King, lover of justice,
you have established fairness.
You have acted with justice
and righteousness throughout Israel.*
⁵ Exalt the LORD our God!
Bow low before his feet, for he is holy!

⁶ Moses and Aaron were among his
priests;
Samuel also called on his name.
They cried to the LORD for help,
and he answered them.
⁷ He spoke to Israel from the pillar of
cloud,
and they followed the laws and decrees
he gave them.
⁸ O LORD our God, you answered them.
You were a forgiving God to them,
but you punished them when they
went wrong.

⁹ Exalt the LORD our God,
and worship at his holy mountain in
Jerusalem,
for the LORD our God is holy!

100

A psalm of thanksgiving.

¹ Shout with joy to the LORD, all the earth!
² Worship the LORD with gladness.
Come before him, singing with joy.
³ Acknowledge that the LORD is God!
He made us, and we are his.*
We are his people, the sheep of his
pasture.
⁴ Enter his gates with thanksgiving;
go into his courts with praise.
Give thanks to him and praise his
name.
⁵ For the LORD is good.
His unfailing love continues forever,
and his faithfulness continues to each
generation.

101

A psalm of David.

¹ I will sing of your love and justice, LORD.
I will praise you with songs.
² I will be careful to live a blameless life—
when will you come to help me?
I will lead a life of integrity
in my own home.
³ I will refuse to look at
anything vile and vulgar.
I hate all who deal crookedly;
I will have nothing to do with them.
⁴ I will reject perverse ideas
and stay away from every evil.
⁵ I will not tolerate people who slander
their neighbors.
I will not endure conceit and pride.

⁶ I will search for faithful people
to be my companions.
Only those who are above reproach
will be allowed to serve me.
⁷ I will not allow deceivers to serve in my
house,
and liars will not stay in my presence.
⁸ My daily task will be to ferret out the
wicked
and free the city of the LORD from their
grip.

102

*A prayer of one overwhelmed with trouble,
pouring out problems before the LORD.*

¹ LORD, hear my prayer!
Listen to my plea!
² Don't turn away from me
in my time of distress.
Bend down to listen,
and answer me quickly when I call to
you.
³ For my days disappear like smoke,
and my bones burn like red-hot coals.
⁴ My heart is sick, withered like grass,
and I have lost my appetite.
⁵ Because of my groaning,
I am reduced to skin and bones.
⁶ I am like an owl in the desert,
like a little owl in a far-off
wilderness.
⁷ I lie awake,
lonely as a solitary bird on the roof.
⁸ My enemies taunt me day after day.
They mock and curse me.

99:2 Hebrew *Zion.* 99:4 Hebrew *Jacob.* See note on 44:4. 100:3 As in an alternate reading in the Masoretic Text; the other
alternate and some ancient versions read *and not we ourselves.*

⁹ I eat ashes for food.
  My tears run down into my drink
¹⁰ because of your anger and wrath.
  For you have picked me up and thrown
  me out.
¹¹ My life passes as swiftly as the evening
  shadows.
  I am withering away like grass.

¹² But you, O LORD, will sit on your throne
  forever.
  Your fame will endure to every
  generation.
¹³ You will arise and have mercy on
  Jerusalem*—
  and now is the time to pity her,
  now is the time you promised to help.
¹⁴ For your people love every stone in her
  walls
  and cherish even the dust in her streets.
¹⁵ Then the nations will tremble before the
  LORD.
  The kings of the earth will tremble
  before his glory.
¹⁶ For the LORD will rebuild Jerusalem.
  He will appear in his glory.
¹⁷ He will listen to the prayers of the
  destitute.
  He will not reject their pleas.

¹⁸ Let this be recorded for future generations,
  so that a people not yet born will praise
  the LORD.
¹⁹ Tell them the LORD looked down
  from his heavenly sanctuary.
  He looked down to earth from heaven
²⁰ to hear the groans of the prisoners,
  to release those condemned to die.
²¹ And so the LORD's fame will be celebrated
  in Zion,
  his praises in Jerusalem,
²² when multitudes gather together
  and kingdoms come to worship the
  LORD.

²³ He broke my strength in midlife,
  cutting short my days.
²⁴ But I cried to him, "O my God, who lives
  forever,
  don't take my life while I am so young!
²⁵ Long ago you laid the foundation of the
  earth
  and made the heavens with your hands.
²⁶ They will perish, but you remain forever;
  they will wear out like old clothing.

102:13 Hebrew *Zion;* also in 102:16.

You will change them like a garment
  and discard them.
²⁷ But you are always the same;
  you will live forever.
²⁸ The children of your people
  will live in security.
  Their children's children
  will thrive in your presence."

103 *A psalm of David.*

¹ Let all that I am praise the LORD;
  with my whole heart, I will praise his
  holy name.
² Let all that I am praise the LORD;
  may I never forget the good things he
  does for me.
³ He forgives all my sins
  and heals all my diseases.
⁴ He redeems me from death
  and crowns me with love and tender
  mercies.
⁵ He fills my life with good things.
  My youth is renewed like the eagle's!

⁶ The LORD gives righteousness
  and justice to all who are treated
  unfairly.

⁷ He revealed his character to Moses
  and his deeds to the people of Israel.
⁸ The LORD is compassionate and merciful,
  slow to get angry and filled with
  unfailing love.
⁹ He will not constantly accuse us,
  nor remain angry forever.
¹⁰ He does not punish us for all our sins;
  he does not deal harshly with us, as we
  deserve.
¹¹ For his unfailing love toward those who
  fear him
  is as great as the height of the heavens
  above the earth.
¹² He has removed our sins as far from us
  as the east is from the west.
¹³ The LORD is like a father to his children,
  tender and compassionate to those who
  fear him.
¹⁴ For he knows how weak we are;
  he remembers we are only dust.
¹⁵ Our days on earth are like grass;
  like wildflowers, we bloom and die.
¹⁶ The wind blows, and we are gone—
  as though we had never been here.

¹⁷ But the love of the LORD remains forever
  with those who fear him.
His salvation extends to the children's
  children
¹⁸   of those who are faithful to his
     covenant,
  of those who obey his commandments!

¹⁹ The LORD has made the heavens his
     throne;
  from there he rules over everything.

²⁰ Praise the LORD, you angels,
  you mighty ones who carry out his
     plans,
  listening for each of his commands.
²¹ Yes, praise the LORD, you armies of angels
  who serve him and do his will!
²² Praise the LORD, everything he has created,
  everything in all his kingdom.

Let all that I am praise the LORD.

104

¹ Let all that I am praise the LORD.

O LORD my God, how great you
  are!
You are robed with honor and majesty.
²   You are dressed in a robe of light.
You stretch out the starry curtain of the
  heavens;
³   you lay out the rafters of your home in
     the rain clouds.
You make the clouds your chariot;
  you ride upon the wings of the wind.
⁴ The winds are your messengers;
  flames of fire are your servants.*

⁵ You placed the world on its foundation
  so it would never be moved.
⁶ You clothed the earth with floods of water,
  water that covered even the mountains.
⁷ At your command, the water fled;
  at the sound of your thunder, it hurried
     away.
⁸ Mountains rose and valleys sank
  to the levels you decreed.
⁹ Then you set a firm boundary for the seas,
  so they would never again cover the
     earth.

¹⁰ You make springs pour water into the
  ravines,

so streams gush down from the
  mountains.
¹¹ They provide water for all the animals,
  and the wild donkeys quench their
     thirst.
¹² The birds nest beside the streams
  and sing among the branches of the
     trees.
¹³ You send rain on the mountains from your
     heavenly home,
  and you fill the earth with the fruit of
     your labor.
¹⁴ You cause grass to grow for the livestock
  and plants for people to use.
You allow them to produce food from the
  earth—
¹⁵   wine to make them glad,
olive oil to soothe their skin,
  and bread to give them strength.
¹⁶ The trees of the LORD are well cared for—
  the cedars of Lebanon that he planted.
¹⁷ There the birds make their nests,
  and the storks make their homes in the
     cypresses.
¹⁸ High in the mountains live the wild goats,
  and the rocks form a refuge for the
     hyraxes.*

¹⁹ You made the moon to mark the seasons,
  and the sun knows when to set.
²⁰ You send the darkness, and it becomes
     night,
  when all the forest animals prowl about.
²¹ Then the young lions roar for their prey,
  stalking the food provided by God.
²² At dawn they slink back
  into their dens to rest.
²³ Then people go off to their work,
  where they labor until evening.

²⁴ O LORD, what a variety of things you have
     made!
  In wisdom you have made them all.
  The earth is full of your creatures.
²⁵ Here is the ocean, vast and wide,
  teeming with life of every kind,
  both large and small.
²⁶ See the ships sailing along,
  and Leviathan,* which you made to play
     in the sea.

²⁷ They all depend on you
  to give them food as they need it.

104:4 Greek version reads *He sends his angels like the winds, / his servants like flames of fire.* Compare Heb 1:7.   104:18 Or *coneys,*
or *rock badgers.*   104:26 The identification of Leviathan is disputed, ranging from an earthly creature to a mythical sea
monster in ancient literature.

²⁸ When you supply it, they gather it.
  You open your hand to feed them,
  and they are richly satisfied.
²⁹ But if you turn away from them, they
    panic.
  When you take away their breath,
  they die and turn again to dust.
³⁰ When you give them your breath,* life is
    created,
  and you renew the face of the earth.

³¹ May the glory of the LORD continue
    forever!
  The LORD takes pleasure in all he has
    made!
³² The earth trembles at his glance;
  the mountains smoke at his touch.

³³ I will sing to the LORD as long as I live.
  I will praise my God to my last breath!
³⁴ May all my thoughts be pleasing to him,
  for I rejoice in the LORD.
³⁵ Let all sinners vanish from the face of the
    earth;
  let the wicked disappear forever.

Let all that I am praise the LORD.

Praise the LORD!

105

¹ Give thanks to the LORD and
    proclaim his greatness.
  Let the whole world know what he has
    done.
² Sing to him; yes, sing his praises.
  Tell everyone about his wonderful
    deeds.
³ Exult in his holy name;
  rejoice, you who worship the LORD.
⁴ Search for the LORD and for his strength;
  continually seek him.
⁵ Remember the wonders he has
    performed,
  his miracles, and the rulings he has
    given,
⁶ you children of his servant Abraham,
  you descendants of Jacob, his chosen
    ones.

⁷ He is the LORD our God.
  His justice is seen throughout the land.
⁸ He always stands by his covenant—
  the commitment he made to a thousand
    generations.

⁹ This is the covenant he made with
    Abraham
  and the oath he swore to Isaac.
¹⁰ He confirmed it to Jacob as a decree,
  and to the people of Israel as a never-
    ending covenant:
¹¹ "I will give you the land of Canaan
  as your special possession."

¹² He said this when they were few in
    number,
  a tiny group of strangers in Canaan.
¹³ They wandered from nation to nation,
  from one kingdom to another.
¹⁴ Yet he did not let anyone oppress
    them.
  He warned kings on their behalf:
¹⁵ "Do not touch my chosen people,
  and do not hurt my prophets."

¹⁶ He called for a famine on the land of
    Canaan,
  cutting off its food supply.
¹⁷ Then he sent someone to Egypt ahead
    of them—
  Joseph, who was sold as a slave.
¹⁸ They bruised his feet with fetters
  and placed his neck in an iron collar.
¹⁹ Until the time came to fulfill his
    dreams,*
  the LORD tested Joseph's character.
²⁰ Then Pharaoh sent for him and set him
    free;
  the ruler of the nation opened his prison
    door.
²¹ Joseph was put in charge of all the king's
    household;
  he became ruler over all the king's
    possessions.
²² He could instruct* the king's aides as he
    pleased
  and teach the king's advisers.

²³ Then Israel arrived in Egypt;
  Jacob lived as a foreigner in the land
    of Ham.
²⁴ And the LORD multiplied the people of
    Israel
  until they became too mighty for their
    enemies.
²⁵ Then he turned the Egyptians against the
    Israelites,
  and they plotted against the LORD's
    servants.

104:30 Or *When you send your Spirit.*   **105:19** Hebrew *his word.*   **105:22** As in Greek and Syriac versions; Hebrew reads *bind*
or *imprison.*

26 But the LORD sent his servant Moses,
     along with Aaron, whom he had
     chosen.
27 They performed miraculous signs among
     the Egyptians,
     and wonders in the land of Ham.
28 The LORD blanketed Egypt in darkness,
     for they had defied* his commands to
     let his people go.
29 He turned their water into blood,
     poisoning all the fish.
30 Then frogs overran the land
     and even invaded the king's bedrooms.
31 When the LORD spoke, flies descended on
     the Egyptians,
     and gnats swarmed across Egypt.
32 He sent them hail instead of rain,
     and lightning flashed over the land.
33 He ruined their grapevines and fig trees
     and shattered all the trees.
34 He spoke, and hordes of locusts came—
     young locusts beyond number.
35 They ate up everything green in the land,
     destroying all the crops in their fields.
36 Then he killed the oldest son in each
     Egyptian home,
     the pride and joy of each family.
37 The LORD brought his people out of
     Egypt, loaded with silver and gold;
     and not one among the tribes of Israel
     even stumbled.
38 Egypt was glad when they were gone,
     for they feared them greatly.
39 The LORD spread a cloud above them as a
     covering
     and gave them a great fire to light the
     darkness.
40 They asked for meat, and he sent them
     quail;
     he satisfied their hunger with manna—
     bread from heaven.
41 He split open a rock, and water gushed out
     to form a river through the dry
     wasteland.
42 For he remembered his sacred promise
     to his servant Abraham.
43 So he brought his people out of Egypt
     with joy,
     his chosen ones with rejoicing.
44 He gave his people the lands of pagan
     nations,
     and they harvested crops that others
     had planted.

45 All this happened so they would follow his
     decrees
     and obey his instructions.

Praise the LORD!

106 ¹ Praise the LORD!

     Give thanks to the LORD, for he
          is good!
     His faithful love endures forever.
² Who can list the glorious miracles of the
     LORD?
     Who can ever praise him enough?
³ There is joy for those who deal justly with
     others
     and always do what is right.

⁴ Remember me, LORD, when you show
     favor to your people;
     come near and rescue me.
⁵ Let me share in the prosperity of your
     chosen ones.
     Let me rejoice in the joy of your people;
     let me praise you with those who are
          your heritage.

⁶ Like our ancestors, we have sinned.
     We have done wrong! We have acted
          wickedly!
⁷ Our ancestors in Egypt
     were not impressed by the LORD's
          miraculous deeds.
     They soon forgot his many acts of
          kindness to them.
     Instead, they rebelled against him at the
          Red Sea.*
⁸ Even so, he saved them—
     to defend the honor of his name
     and to demonstrate his mighty power.
⁹ He commanded the Red Sea* to dry up.
     He led Israel across the sea as if it were
          a desert.
¹⁰ So he rescued them from their enemies
     and redeemed them from their foes.
¹¹ Then the water returned and covered their
     enemies;
     not one of them survived.
¹² Then his people believed his promises.
     Then they sang his praise.

¹³ Yet how quickly they forgot what he had
     done!
     They wouldn't wait for his counsel!

105:28 As in Greek and Syriac versions; Hebrew reads *had not defied*.   106:7 Hebrew *at the sea, the sea of reeds*.   106:9 Hebrew
sea of reeds; also in 106:22.

14 In the wilderness their desires ran wild,
  testing God's patience in that dry
    wasteland.
15 So he gave them what they asked for,
  but he sent a plague along with it.
16 The people in the camp were jealous of
    Moses
  and envious of Aaron, the LORD's holy
    priest.
17 Because of this, the earth opened up;
  it swallowed Dathan
  and buried Abiram and the other rebels.
18 Fire fell upon their followers;
  a flame consumed the wicked.

19 The people made a calf at Mount Sinai*;
  they bowed before an image made of
    gold.
20 They traded their glorious God
  for a statue of a grass-eating bull.
21 They forgot God, their savior,
  who had done such great things in
    Egypt—
22 such wonderful things in the land of Ham,
  such awesome deeds at the Red Sea.
23 So he declared he would destroy them.
  But Moses, his chosen one, stepped
  between the LORD and the people.
  He begged him to turn from his anger
  and not destroy them.

24 The people refused to enter the pleasant
    land,
  for they wouldn't believe his promise to
    care for them.
25 Instead, they grumbled in their tents
  and refused to obey the LORD.
26 Therefore, he solemnly swore
  that he would kill them in the
    wilderness,
27 that he would scatter their descendants*
  among the nations,
  exiling them to distant lands.

28 Then our ancestors joined in the worship
  of Baal at Peor;
  they even ate sacrifices offered to the
    dead!
29 They angered the LORD with all these
    things,
  so a plague broke out among them.
30 But Phinehas had the courage to
    intervene,
  and the plague was stopped.

31 So he has been regarded as a righteous
    man
  ever since that time.
32 At Meribah, too, they angered the LORD,
  causing Moses serious trouble.
33 They made Moses angry,*
  and he spoke foolishly.

34 Israel failed to destroy the nations in the
    land,
  as the LORD had commanded them.
35 Instead, they mingled among the pagans
  and adopted their evil customs.
36 They worshiped their idols,
  which led to their downfall.
37 They even sacrificed their sons
  and their daughters to the demons.
38 They shed innocent blood,
  the blood of their sons and daughters.
  By sacrificing them to the idols of Canaan,
  they polluted the land with murder.
39 They defiled themselves by their evil
    deeds,
  and their love of idols was adultery in
    the LORD's sight.

40 That is why the LORD's anger burned
  against his people,
  and he abhorred his own special
    possession.
41 He handed them over to pagan nations,
  and they were ruled by those who hated
    them.
42 Their enemies crushed them
  and brought them under their cruel
    power.
43 Again and again he rescued them,
  but they chose to rebel against him,
  and they were finally destroyed by
    their sin.
44 Even so, he pitied them in their distress
  and listened to their cries.
45 He remembered his covenant with them
  and relented because of his unfailing
    love.
46 He even caused their captors
  to treat them with kindness.

47 Save us, O LORD our God!
  Gather us back from among the
    nations,
  so we can thank your holy name
  and rejoice and praise you.

106:19 Hebrew *at Horeb,* another name for Sinai.   106:27 As in Syriac version; Hebrew reads *he would cause their descendants to fall.*   106:33 Hebrew *They embittered his spirit.*

⁴⁸ Praise the LORD, the God of Israel,
    who lives from everlasting to
        everlasting!
    Let all the people say, "Amen!"

    Praise the LORD!

BOOK FIVE (Psalms 107–150)

107 ¹ Give thanks to the LORD, for he
        is good!
    His faithful love endures forever.
² Has the LORD redeemed you? Then speak
        out!
    Tell others he has redeemed you from
        your enemies.
³ For he has gathered the exiles from many
        lands,
    from east and west,
    from north and south.*

⁴ Some wandered in the wilderness,
    lost and homeless.
⁵ Hungry and thirsty,
    they nearly died.
⁶ "LORD, help!" they cried in their trouble,
    and he rescued them from their
        distress.
⁷ He led them straight to safety,
    to a city where they could live.
⁸ Let them praise the LORD for his great love
    and for the wonderful things he has
        done for them.
⁹ For he satisfies the thirsty
    and fills the hungry with good things.

¹⁰ Some sat in darkness and deepest gloom,
    imprisoned in iron chains of misery.
¹¹ They rebelled against the words of God,
    scorning the counsel of the Most High.
¹² That is why he broke them with hard
        labor;
    they fell, and no one was there to help
        them.
¹³ "LORD, help!" they cried in their trouble,
    and he saved them from their distress.
¹⁴ He led them from the darkness and
        deepest gloom;
    he snapped their chains.
¹⁵ Let them praise the LORD for his great love
    and for the wonderful things he has
        done for them.
¹⁶ For he broke down their prison gates of
        bronze;
    he cut apart their bars of iron.

107:3 Hebrew and sea.

¹⁷ Some were fools; they rebelled
    and suffered for their sins.
¹⁸ They couldn't stand the thought of food,
    and they were knocking on death's door.
¹⁹ "LORD, help!" they cried in their trouble,
    and he saved them from their distress.
²⁰ He sent out his word and healed them,
    snatching them from the door of death.
²¹ Let them praise the LORD for his great love
    and for the wonderful things he has
        done for them.
²² Let them offer sacrifices of thanksgiving
    and sing joyfully about his glorious acts.

²³ Some went off to sea in ships,
    plying the trade routes of the world.
²⁴ They, too, observed the LORD's power in
        action,
    his impressive works on the deepest
        seas.
²⁵ He spoke, and the winds rose,
    stirring up the waves.
²⁶ Their ships were tossed to the heavens
    and plunged again to the depths;
    the sailors cringed in terror.
²⁷ They reeled and staggered like drunkards
    and were at their wits' end.
²⁸ "LORD, help!" they cried in their trouble,
    and he saved them from their distress.
²⁹ He calmed the storm to a whisper
    and stilled the waves.
³⁰ What a blessing was that stillness
    as he brought them safely into harbor!
³¹ Let them praise the LORD for his great love
    and for the wonderful things he has
        done for them.
³² Let them exalt him publicly before the
        congregation
    and before the leaders of the nation.

³³ He changes rivers into deserts,
    and springs of water into dry, thirsty
        land.
³⁴ He turns the fruitful land into salty
        wastelands,
    because of the wickedness of those who
        live there.
³⁵ But he also turns deserts into pools of
        water,
    the dry land into springs of water.
³⁶ He brings the hungry to settle there
    and to build their cities.
³⁷ They sow their fields, plant their
        vineyards,
    and harvest their bumper crops.

³⁸ How he blesses them!
They raise large families there,
and their herds of livestock increase.

³⁹ When they decrease in number and
become impoverished
through oppression, trouble, and
sorrow,
⁴⁰ the LORD pours contempt on their
princes,
causing them to wander in trackless
wastelands.
⁴¹ But he rescues the poor from trouble
and increases their families like flocks
of sheep.
⁴² The godly will see these things and be
glad,
while the wicked are struck silent.
⁴³ Those who are wise will take all this to
heart;
they will see in our history the faithful
love of the LORD.

108 *A song. A psalm of David.*

¹ My heart is confident in you, O God;
no wonder I can sing your praises with
all my heart!
² Wake up, lyre and harp!
I will wake the dawn with my song.
³ I will thank you, LORD, among all the
people.
I will sing your praises among the
nations.
⁴ For your unfailing love is higher than the
heavens.
Your faithfulness reaches to the clouds.
⁵ Be exalted, O God, above the highest
heavens.
May your glory shine over all the
earth.

⁶ Now rescue your beloved people.
Answer and save us by your power.
⁷ God has promised this by his holiness*:
"I will divide up Shechem with joy.
I will measure out the valley of
Succoth.
⁸ Gilead is mine,
and Manasseh, too.
Ephraim, my helmet, will produce my
warriors,
and Judah, my scepter, will produce
my kings.

⁹ But Moab, my washbasin, will become my
servant,
and I will wipe my feet on Edom
and shout in triumph over Philistia."

¹⁰ Who will bring me into the fortified city?
Who will bring me victory over Edom?
¹¹ Have you rejected us, O God?
Will you no longer march with our
armies?
¹² Oh, please help us against our enemies,
for all human help is useless.
¹³ With God's help we will do mighty
things,
for he will trample down our foes.

109 *For the choir director: A psalm of David.*

¹ O God, whom I praise,
don't stand silent and aloof
² while the wicked slander me
and tell lies about me.
³ They surround me with hateful words
and fight against me for no reason.
⁴ I love them, but they try to destroy me
with accusations
even as I am praying for them!
⁵ They repay evil for good,
and hatred for my love.

⁶ They say,* "Get an evil person to turn
against him.
Send an accuser to bring him to trial.
⁷ When his case comes up for judgment,
let him be pronounced guilty.
Count his prayers as sins.
⁸ Let his years be few;
let someone else take his position.
⁹ May his children become fatherless,
and his wife a widow.
¹⁰ May his children wander as beggars
and be driven from* their ruined
homes.
¹¹ May creditors seize his entire estate,
and strangers take all he has earned.
¹² Let no one be kind to him;
let no one pity his fatherless children.
¹³ May all his offspring die.
May his family name be blotted out in
the next generation.
¹⁴ May the LORD never forget the sins of his
fathers;
may his mother's sins never be erased
from the record.

108:7 Or *in his sanctuary.*   109:6 Hebrew lacks *They say.*   109:10 As in Greek version; Hebrew reads *and seek.*

¹⁵ May the LORD always remember these sins,
and may his name disappear from
human memory.
¹⁶ For he refused all kindness to others;
he persecuted the poor and needy,
and he hounded the brokenhearted
to death.
¹⁷ He loved to curse others;
now you curse him.
He never blessed others;
now don't you bless him.
¹⁸ Cursing is as natural to him as his
clothing,
or the water he drinks,
or the rich food he eats.
¹⁹ Now may his curses return and cling to
him like clothing;
may they be tied around him like a
belt."

²⁰ May those curses become the LORD's
punishment
for my accusers who speak evil of me.
²¹ But deal well with me, O Sovereign LORD,
for the sake of your own reputation!
Rescue me
because you are so faithful and good.
²² For I am poor and needy,
and my heart is full of pain.
²³ I am fading like a shadow at dusk;
I am brushed off like a locust.
²⁴ My knees are weak from fasting,
and I am skin and bones.
²⁵ I am a joke to people everywhere;
when they see me, they shake their
heads in scorn.

²⁶ Help me, O LORD my God!
Save me because of your unfailing love.
²⁷ Let them see that this is your doing,
that you yourself have done it, LORD.
²⁸ Then let them curse me if they like,
but you will bless me!
When they attack me, they will be
disgraced!
But I, your servant, will go right on
rejoicing!
²⁹ May my accusers be clothed with
disgrace;
may their humiliation cover them like
a cloak.
³⁰ But I will give repeated thanks to the
LORD,
praising him to everyone.

³¹ For he stands beside the needy,
ready to save them from those who
condemn them.

110 *A psalm of David.*

¹ The LORD said to my Lord,*
"Sit in the place of honor at my right
hand
until I humble your enemies,
making them a footstool under your
feet."

² The LORD will extend your powerful
kingdom from Jerusalem*;
you will rule over your enemies.
³ When you go to war,
your people will serve you willingly.
You are arrayed in holy garments,
and your strength will be renewed each
day like the morning dew.

⁴ The LORD has taken an oath and will not
break his vow:
"You are a priest forever in the order of
Melchizedek."

⁵ The Lord stands at your right hand to
protect you.
He will strike down many kings when
his anger erupts.
⁶ He will punish the nations
and fill their lands with corpses;
he will shatter heads over the whole
earth.
⁷ But he himself will be refreshed from
brooks along the way.
He will be victorious.

111 *¹ Praise the LORD!

I will thank the LORD with all
my heart
as I meet with his godly people.
² How amazing are the deeds of the LORD!
All who delight in him should ponder
them.
³ Everything he does reveals his glory and
majesty.
His righteousness never fails.
⁴ He causes us to remember his wonderful
works.
How gracious and merciful is our LORD!

110:1 Or *my lord.* 110:2 Hebrew *Zion.* 111 This psalm is a Hebrew acrostic poem; after the introductory note of praise, each
line begins with a successive letter of the Hebrew alphabet.

5 He gives food to those who fear him;
   he always remembers his covenant.
6 He has shown his great power to his
      people
   by giving them the lands of other
      nations.
7 All he does is just and good,
   and all his commandments are
      trustworthy.
8 They are forever true,
   to be obeyed faithfully and with
      integrity.
9 He has paid a full ransom for his people.
   He has guaranteed his covenant with
      them forever.
   What a holy, awe-inspiring name he has!
10 Fear of the LORD is the foundation of true
      wisdom.
   All who obey his commandments will
      grow in wisdom.

Praise him forever!

112 *1 Praise the LORD!

      How joyful are those who fear
         the LORD
   and delight in obeying his commands.
2 Their children will be successful
      everywhere;
   an entire generation of godly people
      will be blessed.
3 They themselves will be wealthy,
   and their good deeds will last forever.
4 Light shines in the darkness for the
      godly.
   They are generous, compassionate,
      and righteous.
5 Good comes to those who lend money
      generously
   and conduct their business fairly.
6 Such people will not be overcome by evil.
   Those who are righteous will be long
      remembered.
7 They do not fear bad news;
   they confidently trust the LORD to care
      for them.
8 They are confident and fearless
   and can face their foes triumphantly.
9 They share freely and give generously to
      those in need.
   Their good deeds will be remembered
      forever.
   They will have influence and honor.

10 The wicked will see this and be infuriated.
   They will grind their teeth in anger;
   they will slink away, their hopes
      thwarted.

113 1 Praise the LORD!

      Yes, give praise, O servants of the
         LORD.
   Praise the name of the LORD!
2 Blessed be the name of the LORD
   now and forever.
3 Everywhere—from east to west—
   praise the name of the LORD.
4 For the LORD is high above the nations;
   his glory is higher than the heavens.

5 Who can be compared with the LORD
      our God,
   who is enthroned on high?
6 He stoops to look down
   on heaven and on earth.
7 He lifts the poor from the dust
   and the needy from the garbage dump.
8 He sets them among princes,
   even the princes of his own people!
9 He gives the childless woman a family,
   making her a happy mother.

Praise the LORD!

114 1 When the Israelites escaped from
         Egypt—
   when the family of Jacob left that
      foreign land—
2 the land of Judah became God's sanctuary,
   and Israel became his kingdom.

3 The Red Sea* saw them coming and
      hurried out of their way!
   The water of the Jordan River turned
      away.
4 The mountains skipped like rams,
   the hills like lambs!
5 What's wrong, Red Sea, that made you
      hurry out of their way?
   What happened, Jordan River, that you
      turned away?
6 Why, mountains, did you skip like rams?
   Why, hills, like lambs?

7 Tremble, O earth, at the presence of the
      Lord,
   at the presence of the God of Jacob.

112 This psalm is a Hebrew acrostic poem; after the introductory note of praise, each line begins with a successive letter
of the Hebrew alphabet.   114:3 Hebrew *the sea;* also in 114:5.

8 He turned the rock into a pool of water;
  yes, a spring of water flowed from solid
  rock.

115

¹ Not to us, O LORD, not to us,
  but to your name goes all the
  glory
for your unfailing love and faithfulness.
² Why let the nations say,
  "Where is their God?"
³ Our God is in the heavens,
  and he does as he wishes.
⁴ Their idols are merely things of silver and
  gold,
  shaped by human hands.
⁵ They have mouths but cannot speak,
  and eyes but cannot see.
⁶ They have ears but cannot hear,
  and noses but cannot smell.
⁷ They have hands but cannot feel,
  and feet but cannot walk,
  and throats but cannot make a sound.
⁸ And those who make idols are just like
  them,
  as are all who trust in them.

⁹ O Israel, trust the LORD!
  He is your helper and your shield.
¹⁰ O priests, descendants of Aaron, trust the
  LORD!
  He is your helper and your shield.
¹¹ All you who fear the LORD, trust the LORD!
  He is your helper and your shield.

¹² The LORD remembers us and will bless us.
  He will bless the people of Israel
  and bless the priests, the descendants
  of Aaron.
¹³ He will bless those who fear the LORD,
  both great and lowly.

¹⁴ May the LORD richly bless
  both you and your children.
¹⁵ May you be blessed by the LORD,
  who made heaven and earth.
¹⁶ The heavens belong to the LORD,
  but he has given the earth to all
  humanity.
¹⁷ The dead cannot sing praises to the LORD,
  for they have gone into the silence of the
  grave.
¹⁸ But we can praise the LORD
  both now and forever!

Praise the LORD!

116:3 Hebrew *of Sheol.*

116

¹ I love the LORD because he hears
  my voice
and my prayer for mercy.
² Because he bends down to listen,
  I will pray as long as I have breath!
³ Death wrapped its ropes around me;
  the terrors of the grave* overtook me.
  I saw only trouble and sorrow.
⁴ Then I called on the name of the LORD:
  "Please, LORD, save me!"
⁵ How kind the LORD is! How good he is!
  So merciful, this God of ours!
⁶ The LORD protects those of childlike faith;
  I was facing death, and he saved me.
⁷ Let my soul be at rest again,
  for the LORD has been good to me.
⁸ He has saved me from death,
  my eyes from tears,
  my feet from stumbling.
⁹ And so I walk in the LORD's presence
  as I live here on earth!
¹⁰ I believed in you, so I said,
  "I am deeply troubled, LORD."
¹¹ In my anxiety I cried out to you,
  "These people are all liars!"
¹² What can I offer the LORD
  for all he has done for me?
¹³ I will lift up the cup of salvation
  and praise the LORD's name for
  saving me.
¹⁴ I will keep my promises to the LORD
  in the presence of all his people.

¹⁵ The LORD cares deeply
  when his loved ones die.
¹⁶ O LORD, I am your servant;
  yes, I am your servant, born into your
  household;
  you have freed me from my chains.
¹⁷ I will offer you a sacrifice of thanksgiving
  and call on the name of the LORD.
¹⁸ I will fulfill my vows to the LORD
  in the presence of all his people—
¹⁹ in the house of the LORD
  in the heart of Jerusalem.

Praise the LORD!

117

¹ Praise the LORD, all you nations.
  Praise him, all you people of
  the earth.
² For his unfailing love for us is powerful;
  the LORD's faithfulness endures forever.

Praise the LORD!

118

¹ Give thanks to the LORD, for he
   is good!
His faithful love endures forever.

² Let all Israel repeat:
   "His faithful love endures forever."
³ Let Aaron's descendants, the priests, repeat:
   "His faithful love endures forever."
⁴ Let all who fear the LORD repeat:
   "His faithful love endures forever."

⁵ In my distress I prayed to the LORD,
   and the LORD answered me and set
   me free.
⁶ The LORD is for me, so I will have no fear.
   What can mere people do to me?
⁷ Yes, the LORD is for me; he will help me.
   I will look in triumph at those who
   hate me.
⁸ It is better to take refuge in the LORD
   than to trust in people.
⁹ It is better to take refuge in the LORD
   than to trust in princes.

¹⁰ Though hostile nations surrounded me,
   I destroyed them all with the authority
   of the LORD.
¹¹ Yes, they surrounded and attacked me,
   but I destroyed them all with the
   authority of the LORD.
¹² They swarmed around me like bees;
   they blazed against me like a crackling
   fire.
   But I destroyed them all with the
   authority of the LORD.
¹³ My enemies did their best to kill me,
   but the LORD rescued me.
¹⁴ The LORD is my strength and my song;
   he has given me victory.
¹⁵ Songs of joy and victory are sung in the
   camp of the godly.
   The strong right arm of the LORD has
   done glorious things!
¹⁶ The strong right arm of the LORD is raised
   in triumph.
   The strong right arm of the LORD has
   done glorious things!
¹⁷ I will not die; instead, I will live
   to tell what the LORD has done.
¹⁸ The LORD has punished me severely,
   but he did not let me die.

¹⁹ Open for me the gates where the righteous
   enter,

and I will go in and thank the LORD.
²⁰ These gates lead to the presence of the
   LORD,
   and the godly enter there.
²¹ I thank you for answering my prayer
   and giving me victory!

²² The stone that the builders rejected
   has now become the cornerstone.
²³ This is the LORD's doing,
   and it is wonderful to see.
²⁴ This is the day the LORD has made.
   We will rejoice and be glad in it.
²⁵ Please, LORD, please save us.
   Please, LORD, please give us success.
²⁶ Bless the one who comes in the name of
   the LORD.
   We bless you from the house of the
   LORD.
²⁷ The LORD is God, shining upon us.
   Take the sacrifice and bind it with cords
   on the altar.
²⁸ You are my God, and I will praise you!
   You are my God, and I will exalt you!

²⁹ Give thanks to the LORD, for he is good!
   His faithful love endures forever.

Aleph

119

*¹ Joyful are people of integrity,
   who follow the instructions
   of the LORD.
² Joyful are those who obey his laws
   and search for him with all their hearts.
³ They do not compromise with evil,
   and they walk only in his paths.
⁴ You have charged us
   to keep your commandments carefully.
⁵ Oh, that my actions would consistently
   reflect your decrees!
⁶ Then I will not be ashamed
   when I compare my life with your
   commands.
⁷ As I learn your righteous regulations,
   I will thank you by living as I should!
⁸ I will obey your decrees.
   Please don't give up on me!

Beth

⁹ How can a young person stay pure?
   By obeying your word.
¹⁰ I have tried hard to find you—
   don't let me wander from your
   commands.

119 This psalm is a Hebrew acrostic poem; there are twenty-two stanzas, one for each successive letter of the Hebrew alphabet. Each of the eight verses within each stanza begins with the Hebrew letter named in its heading.

11 I have hidden your word in my heart,
   that I might not sin against you.
12 I praise you, O LORD;
   teach me your decrees.
13 I have recited aloud
   all the regulations you have given us.
14 I have rejoiced in your laws
   as much as in riches.
15 I will study your commandments
   and reflect on your ways.
16 I will delight in your decrees
   and not forget your word.

Gimel

17 Be good to your servant,
   that I may live and obey your word.
18 Open my eyes to see
   the wonderful truths in your
   instructions.
19 I am only a foreigner in the land.
   Don't hide your commands from me!
20 I am always overwhelmed
   with a desire for your regulations.
21 You rebuke the arrogant;
   those who wander from your commands
   are cursed.
22 Don't let them scorn and insult me,
   for I have obeyed your laws.
23 Even princes sit and speak against me,
   but I will meditate on your decrees.
24 Your laws please me;
   they give me wise advice.

Daleth

25 I lie in the dust;
   revive me by your word.
26 I told you my plans, and you answered.
   Now teach me your decrees.
27 Help me understand the meaning of your
   commandments,
   and I will meditate on your wonderful
   deeds.
28 I weep with sorrow;
   encourage me by your word.
29 Keep me from lying to myself;
   give me the privilege of knowing your
   instructions.
30 I have chosen to be faithful;
   I have determined to live by your
   regulations.
31 I cling to your laws.
   LORD, don't let me be put to
   shame!
32 I will pursue your commands,
   for you expand my understanding.

119:37 Some manuscripts read *in your ways.*

He

33 Teach me your decrees, O LORD;
   I will keep them to the end.
34 Give me understanding and I will obey
   your instructions;
   I will put them into practice with all my
   heart.
35 Make me walk along the path of your
   commands,
   for that is where my happiness is found.
36 Give me an eagerness for your laws
   rather than a love for money!
37 Turn my eyes from worthless things,
   and give me life through your word.*
38 Reassure me of your promise,
   made to those who fear you.
39 Help me abandon my shameful ways;
   for your regulations are good.
40 I long to obey your commandments!
   Renew my life with your goodness.

Waw

41 LORD, give me your unfailing love,
   the salvation that you promised me.
42 Then I can answer those who taunt me,
   for I trust in your word.
43 Do not snatch your word of truth from me,
   for your regulations are my only hope.
44 I will keep on obeying your instructions
   forever and ever.
45 I will walk in freedom,
   for I have devoted myself to your
   commandments.
46 I will speak to kings about your laws,
   and I will not be ashamed.
47 How I delight in your commands!
   How I love them!
48 I honor and love your commands.
   I meditate on your decrees.

Zayin

49 Remember your promise to me;
   it is my only hope.
50 Your promise revives me;
   it comforts me in all my troubles.
51 The proud hold me in utter contempt,
   but I do not turn away from your
   instructions.
52 I meditate on your age-old regulations;
   O LORD, they comfort me.
53 I become furious with the wicked,
   because they reject your instructions.
54 Your decrees have been the theme of my
   songs
   wherever I have lived.

⁵⁵ I reflect at night on who you are, O LORD;
therefore, I obey your instructions.
⁵⁶ This is how I spend my life:
obeying your commandments.

Heth

⁵⁷ LORD, you are mine!
I promise to obey your words!
⁵⁸ With all my heart I want your blessings.
Be merciful as you promised.
⁵⁹ I pondered the direction of my life,
and I turned to follow your laws.
⁶⁰ I will hurry, without delay,
to obey your commands.
⁶¹ Evil people try to drag me into sin,
but I am firmly anchored to your
instructions.
⁶² I rise at midnight to thank you
for your just regulations.
⁶³ I am a friend to anyone who fears you—
anyone who obeys your
commandments.
⁶⁴ O LORD, your unfailing love fills the
earth;
teach me your decrees.

Teth

⁶⁵ You have done many good things for me,
LORD,
just as you promised.
⁶⁶ I believe in your commands;
now teach me good judgment and
knowledge.
⁶⁷ I used to wander off until you
disciplined me;
but now I closely follow your word.
⁶⁸ You are good and do only good;
teach me your decrees.
⁶⁹ Arrogant people smear me with lies,
but in truth I obey your commandments
with all my heart.
⁷⁰ Their hearts are dull and stupid,
but I delight in your instructions.
⁷¹ My suffering was good for me,
for it taught me to pay attention to your
decrees.
⁷² Your instructions are more valuable to me
than millions in gold and silver.

Yodh

⁷³ You made me; you created me.
Now give me the sense to follow your
commands.
⁷⁴ May all who fear you find in me a cause
for joy,
for I have put my hope in your word.

⁷⁵ I know, O LORD, that your regulations
are fair;
you disciplined me because I needed it.
⁷⁶ Now let your unfailing love comfort me,
just as you promised me, your servant.
⁷⁷ Surround me with your tender mercies so
I may live,
for your instructions are my delight.
⁷⁸ Bring disgrace upon the arrogant people
who lied about me;
meanwhile, I will concentrate on your
commandments.
⁷⁹ Let me be united with all who fear you,
with those who know your laws.
⁸⁰ May I be blameless in keeping your
decrees;
then I will never be ashamed.

Kaph

⁸¹ I am worn out waiting for your rescue,
but I have put my hope in your word.
⁸² My eyes are straining to see your promises
come true.
When will you comfort me?
⁸³ I am shriveled like a wineskin in the
smoke,
but I have not forgotten to obey your
decrees.
⁸⁴ How long must I wait?
When will you punish those who
persecute me?
⁸⁵ These arrogant people who hate your
instructions
have dug deep pits to trap me.
⁸⁶ All your commands are trustworthy.
Protect me from those who hunt me
down without cause.
⁸⁷ They almost finished me off,
but I refused to abandon your
commandments.
⁸⁸ In your unfailing love, spare my life;
then I can continue to obey your laws.

Lamedh

⁸⁹ Your eternal word, O LORD,
stands firm in heaven.
⁹⁰ Your faithfulness extends to every
generation,
as enduring as the earth you created.
⁹¹ Your regulations remain true to this day,
for everything serves your plans.
⁹² If your instructions hadn't sustained me
with joy,
I would have died in my misery.
⁹³ I will never forget your commandments,
for by them you give me life.

94 I am yours; rescue me!
    For I have worked hard at obeying your
      commandments.
95 Though the wicked hide along the way to
      kill me,
    I will quietly keep my mind on your
      laws.
96 Even perfection has its limits,
    but your commands have no limit.

Mem

97 Oh, how I love your instructions!
    I think about them all day long.
98 Your commands make me wiser than my
      enemies,
    for they are my constant guide.
99 Yes, I have more insight than my teachers,
    for I am always thinking of your laws.
100 I am even wiser than my elders,
    for I have kept your commandments.
101 I have refused to walk on any evil path,
    so that I may remain obedient to your
      word.
102 I haven't turned away from your
      regulations,
    for you have taught me well.
103 How sweet your words taste to me;
    they are sweeter than honey.
104 Your commandments give me
      understanding;
    no wonder I hate every false way of life.

Nun

105 Your word is a lamp to guide my feet
    and a light for my path.
106 I've promised it once, and I'll promise it
      again:
    I will obey your righteous regulations.
107 I have suffered much, O LORD;
    restore my life again as you promised.
108 LORD, accept my offering of praise,
    and teach me your regulations.
109 My life constantly hangs in the balance,
    but I will not stop obeying your
      instructions.
110 The wicked have set their traps for me,
    but I will not turn from your
      commandments.
111 Your laws are my treasure;
    they are my heart's delight.
112 I am determined to keep your decrees
    to the very end.

Samekh

113 I hate those with divided loyalties,
    but I love your instructions.

114 You are my refuge and my shield;
    your word is my source of hope.
115 Get out of my life, you evil-minded people,
    for I intend to obey the commands of
      my God.
116 LORD, sustain me as you promised, that
      I may live!
    Do not let my hope be crushed.
117 Sustain me, and I will be rescued;
    then I will meditate continually on
      your decrees.
118 But you have rejected all who stray from
      your decrees.
    They are only fooling themselves.
119 You skim off the wicked of the earth like
      scum;
    no wonder I love to obey your laws!
120 I tremble in fear of you;
    I stand in awe of your regulations.

Ayin

121 Don't leave me to the mercy of my
      enemies,
    for I have done what is just and right.
122 Please guarantee a blessing for me.
    Don't let the arrogant oppress me!
123 My eyes strain to see your rescue,
    to see the truth of your promise
      fulfilled.
124 I am your servant; deal with me in
      unfailing love,
    and teach me your decrees.
125 Give discernment to me, your servant;
    then I will understand your laws.
126 LORD, it is time for you to act,
    for these evil people have violated your
      instructions.
127 Truly, I love your commands
    more than gold, even the finest gold.
128 Each of your commandments is right.
    That is why I hate every false way.

Pe

129 Your laws are wonderful.
    No wonder I obey them!
130 The teaching of your word gives light,
    so even the simple can understand.
131 I pant with expectation,
    longing for your commands.
132 Come and show me your mercy,
    as you do for all who love your name.
133 Guide my steps by your word,
    so I will not be overcome by evil.
134 Ransom me from the oppression of evil
      people;
    then I can obey your commandments.

135 Look upon me with love;
    teach me your decrees.
136 Rivers of tears gush from my eyes
    because people disobey your
    instructions.

Tsadhe

137 O LORD, you are righteous,
    and your regulations are fair.
138 Your laws are perfect
    and completely trustworthy.
139 I am overwhelmed with indignation,
    for my enemies have disregarded your
    words.
140 Your promises have been thoroughly
    tested;
    that is why I love them so much.
141 I am insignificant and despised,
    but I don't forget your commandments.
142 Your justice is eternal,
    and your instructions are perfectly
    true.
143 As pressure and stress bear down on me,
    I find joy in your commands.
144 Your laws are always right;
    help me to understand them so I may
    live.

Qoph

145 I pray with all my heart; answer me,
    LORD!
    I will obey your decrees.
146 I cry out to you; rescue me,
    that I may obey your laws.
147 I rise early, before the sun is up;
    I cry out for help and put my hope in
    your words.
148 I stay awake through the night,
    thinking about your promise.
149 In your faithful love, O LORD, hear
    my cry;
    let me be revived by following your
    regulations.
150 Lawless people are coming to attack me;
    they live far from your instructions.
151 But you are near, O LORD,
    and all your commands are true.
152 I have known from my earliest days
    that your laws will last forever.

Resh

153 Look upon my suffering and rescue me,
    for I have not forgotten your
    instructions.
154 Argue my case; take my side!
    Protect my life as you promised.

155 The wicked are far from rescue,
    for they do not bother with your
    decrees.
156 LORD, how great is your mercy;
    let me be revived by following your
    regulations.
157 Many persecute and trouble me,
    yet I have not swerved from your laws.
158 Seeing these traitors makes me sick at
    heart,
    because they care nothing for your
    word.
159 See how I love your commandments,
    LORD.
    Give back my life because of your
    unfailing love.
160 The very essence of your words is truth;
    all your just regulations will stand
    forever.

Shin

161 Powerful people harass me without
    cause,
    but my heart trembles only at your
    word.
162 I rejoice in your word
    like one who discovers a great treasure.
163 I hate and abhor all falsehood,
    but I love your instructions.
164 I will praise you seven times a day
    because all your regulations are just.
165 Those who love your instructions have
    great peace
    and do not stumble.
166 I long for your rescue, LORD,
    so I have obeyed your commands.
167 I have obeyed your laws,
    for I love them very much.
168 Yes, I obey your commandments and laws
    because you know everything I do.

Taw

169 O LORD, listen to my cry;
    give me the discerning mind you
    promised.
170 Listen to my prayer;
    rescue me as you promised.
171 Let praise flow from my lips,
    for you have taught me your decrees.
172 Let my tongue sing about your word,
    for all your commands are right.
173 Give me a helping hand,
    for I have chosen to follow your
    commandments.
174 O LORD, I have longed for your rescue,
    and your instructions are my delight.

175 Let me live so I can praise you,
   and may your regulations help me.
176 I have wandered away like a lost sheep;
   come and find me,
   for I have not forgotten your
      commands.

120

A song for pilgrims ascending to Jerusalem.

1 I took my troubles to the LORD;
   I cried out to him, and he answered
      my prayer.
2 Rescue me, O LORD, from liars
   and from all deceitful people.
3 O deceptive tongue, what will God do
      to you?
   How will he increase your
      punishment?
4 You will be pierced with sharp arrows
   and burned with glowing coals.

5 How I suffer in far-off Meshech.
   It pains me to live in distant Kedar.
6 I am tired of living
   among people who hate peace.
7 I search for peace;
   but when I speak of peace, they want
      war!

121

A song for pilgrims ascending to Jerusalem.

1 I look up to the mountains—
   does my help come from there?
2 My help comes from the LORD,
   who made heaven and earth!

3 He will not let you stumble;
   the one who watches over you will not
      slumber.
4 Indeed, he who watches over Israel
   never slumbers or sleeps.

5 The LORD himself watches over
      you!
   The LORD stands beside you as
      your protective shade.
6 The sun will not harm you by day,
   nor the moon at night.

7 The LORD keeps you from all harm
   and watches over your life.
8 The LORD keeps watch over you as
      you come and go,
   both now and forever.

122

*A song for pilgrims ascending to Jerusalem.
A psalm of David.*

1 I was glad when they said to me,
   "Let us go to the house of the LORD."
2 And now here we are,
   standing inside your gates, O Jerusalem.
3 Jerusalem is a well-built city;
   its seamless walls cannot be breached.
4 All the tribes of Israel—the LORD's
      people—
   make their pilgrimage here.
   They come to give thanks to the name of
      the LORD,
   as the law requires of Israel.
5 Here stand the thrones where judgment
      is given,
   the thrones of the dynasty of David.

6 Pray for peace in Jerusalem.
   May all who love this city prosper.
7 O Jerusalem, may there be peace within
      your walls
   and prosperity in your palaces.
8 For the sake of my family and friends,
      I will say,
   "May you have peace."
9 For the sake of the house of the LORD our
      God,
   I will seek what is best for you,
      O Jerusalem.

123

A song for pilgrims ascending to Jerusalem.

1 I lift my eyes to you,
   O God, enthroned in heaven.
2 We keep looking to the LORD our God for
      his mercy,
   just as servants keep their eyes on their
      master,
   as a slave girl watches her mistress for
      the slightest signal.
3 Have mercy on us, LORD, have mercy,
   for we have had our fill of contempt.
4 We have had more than our fill of the
      scoffing of the proud
   and the contempt of the arrogant.

124

*A song for pilgrims ascending to Jerusalem.
A psalm of David.*

1 What if the LORD had not been on our side?
   Let all Israel repeat:
2 What if the LORD had not been on our side
   when people attacked us?

3 They would have swallowed us alive
    in their burning anger.
4 The waters would have engulfed us;
    a torrent would have overwhelmed us.
5 Yes, the raging waters of their fury
    would have overwhelmed our very lives.

6 Praise the LORD,
    who did not let their teeth tear us apart!
7 We escaped like a bird from a hunter's trap.
    The trap is broken, and we are free!
8 Our help is from the LORD,
    who made heaven and earth.

125 *A song for pilgrims ascending to Jerusalem.*

1 Those who trust in the LORD are as secure
    as Mount Zion;
    they will not be defeated but will
    endure forever.
2 Just as the mountains surround Jerusalem,
    so the LORD surrounds his people, both
    now and forever.
3 The wicked will not rule the land of the
    godly,
    for then the godly might be tempted to
    do wrong.
4 O LORD, do good to those who are good,
    whose hearts are in tune with you.
5 But banish those who turn to crooked
    ways, O LORD.
    Take them away with those who do evil.

May Israel have peace!

126 *A song for pilgrims ascending to Jerusalem.*

1 When the LORD brought back his exiles
    to Jerusalem,*
    it was like a dream!
2 We were filled with laughter,
    and we sang for joy.
    And the other nations said,
    "What amazing things the LORD has
    done for them."
3 Yes, the LORD has done amazing things
    for us!
    What joy!

4 Restore our fortunes, LORD,
    as streams renew the desert.
5 Those who plant in tears
    will harvest with shouts of joy.

126:1 Hebrew *Zion.*

6 They weep as they go to plant their seed,
    but they sing as they return with the
    harvest.

127 *A song for pilgrims ascending to Jerusalem.*
A psalm of Solomon.

1 Unless the LORD builds a house,
    the work of the builders is wasted.
    Unless the LORD protects a city,
    guarding it with sentries will do no
    good.
2 It is useless for you to work so hard
    from early morning until late at night,
    anxiously working for food to eat;
    for God gives rest to his loved ones.

3 Children are a gift from the LORD;
    they are a reward from him.
4 Children born to a young man
    are like arrows in a warrior's hands.
5 How joyful is the man whose quiver is full
    of them!
    He will not be put to shame when he
    confronts his accusers at the city
    gates.

128 *A song for pilgrims ascending to Jerusalem.*

1 How joyful are those who fear the LORD—
    all who follow his ways!
2 You will enjoy the fruit of your labor.
    How joyful and prosperous you will be!
3 Your wife will be like a fruitful grapevine,
    flourishing within your home.
    Your children will be like vigorous young
    olive trees
    as they sit around your table.
4 That is the LORD's blessing
    for those who fear him.

5 May the LORD continually bless you from
    Zion.
    May you see Jerusalem prosper as long
    as you live.
6 May you live to enjoy your grandchildren.
    May Israel have peace!

129 *A song for pilgrims ascending to Jerusalem.*

1 From my earliest youth my enemies have
    persecuted me.
    Let all Israel repeat this:

2 From my earliest youth my enemies have
　　persecuted me,
　　but they have never defeated me.
3 My back is covered with cuts,
　　as if a farmer had plowed long
　　　furrows.
4 But the LORD is good;
　　he has cut me free from the ropes of the
　　　ungodly.

5 May all who hate Jerusalem*
　　be turned back in shameful defeat.
6 May they be as useless as grass on a
　　rooftop,
　　turning yellow when only half grown,
7 ignored by the harvester,
　　despised by the binder.
8 And may those who pass by
　　refuse to give them this blessing:
　"The LORD bless you;
　　we bless you in the LORD's name."

130 *A song for pilgrims ascending to Jerusalem.*

1 From the depths of despair, O LORD,
　　I call for your help.
2 Hear my cry, O Lord.
　　Pay attention to my prayer.

3 LORD, if you kept a record of our sins,
　　who, O Lord, could ever survive?
4 But you offer forgiveness,
　　that we might learn to fear you.

5 I am counting on the LORD;
　　yes, I am counting on him.
　　I have put my hope in his word.
6 I long for the Lord
　　more than sentries long for the dawn,
　　yes, more than sentries long for the
　　　dawn.

7 O Israel, hope in the LORD;
　　for with the LORD there is unfailing
　　　love.
　　His redemption overflows.
8 He himself will redeem Israel
　　from every kind of sin.

131 *A song for pilgrims ascending to Jerusalem.*
A psalm of David.

1 LORD, my heart is not proud;
　　my eyes are not haughty.

I don't concern myself with matters too
　　great
　　or too awesome for me to grasp.
2 Instead, I have calmed and quieted myself,
　　like a weaned child who no longer cries
　　for its mother's milk.
　　Yes, like a weaned child is my soul
　　within me.

3 O Israel, put your hope in the LORD—
　　now and always.

132 *A song for pilgrims ascending to Jerusalem.*

1 LORD, remember David
　　and all that he suffered.
2 He made a solemn promise to the LORD.
　　He vowed to the Mighty One of Israel,*
3 "I will not go home;
　　I will not let myself rest.
4 I will not let my eyes sleep
　　nor close my eyelids in slumber
5 until I find a place to build a house for the
　　LORD,
　　a sanctuary for the Mighty One of
　　　Israel."

6 We heard that the Ark was in Ephrathah;
　　then we found it in the distant
　　countryside of Jaar.
7 Let us go to the sanctuary of the LORD;
　　let us worship at the footstool of his
　　　throne.
8 Arise, O LORD, and enter your resting
　　place,
　　along with the Ark, the symbol of your
　　　power.
9 May your priests be clothed in godliness;
　　may your loyal servants sing for joy.
10 For the sake of your servant David,
　　do not reject the king you have
　　　anointed.
11 The LORD swore an oath to David
　　with a promise he will never take back:
　"I will place one of your descendants
　　on your throne.
12 If your descendants obey the terms of my
　　covenant
　　and the laws that I teach them,
　then your royal line
　　will continue forever and ever."

13 For the LORD has chosen Jerusalem*;
　　he has desired it for his home.

129:5 Hebrew *Zion.*　132:2 Hebrew *of Jacob;* also in 132:5. See note on 44:4.　132:13 Hebrew *Zion.*

14 "This is my resting place forever," he said.
    "I will live here, for this is the home I
    desired.
15 I will bless this city and make it
    prosperous;
    I will satisfy its poor with food.
16 I will clothe its priests with godliness;
    its faithful servants will sing for joy.
17 Here I will increase the power of David;
    my anointed one will be a light for my
    people.
18 I will clothe his enemies with shame,
    but he will be a glorious king."

133 *A song for pilgrims ascending to Jerusalem. A psalm of David.*

1 How wonderful and pleasant it is
    when brothers live together in
    harmony!
2 For harmony is as precious as the
    anointing oil
    that was poured over Aaron's head,
    that ran down his beard
    and onto the border of his robe.
3 Harmony is as refreshing as the dew from
    Mount Hermon
    that falls on the mountains of Zion.
    And there the LORD has pronounced his
    blessing,
    even life everlasting.

134 *A song for pilgrims ascending to Jerusalem.*

1 Oh, praise the LORD, all you servants of the
    LORD,
    you who serve at night in the house of
    the LORD.
2 Lift your hands toward the sanctuary,
    and praise the LORD.

3 May the LORD, who made heaven and
    earth,
    bless you from Jerusalem.*

135 1 Praise the LORD!

    Praise the name of the LORD!
    Praise him, you who serve the LORD,
2 you who serve in the house of the LORD,
    in the courts of the house of our God.

3 Praise the LORD, for the LORD is good;
    celebrate his lovely name with music.

134:3 Hebrew *Zion.*

4 For the LORD has chosen Jacob for himself,
    Israel for his own special treasure.

5 I know the greatness of the LORD—
    that our Lord is greater than any other
    god.
6 The LORD does whatever pleases him
    throughout all heaven and earth,
    and on the seas and in their depths.
7 He causes the clouds to rise over the whole
    earth.
    He sends the lightning with the rain
    and releases the wind from his
    storehouses.

8 He destroyed the firstborn in each
    Egyptian home,
    both people and animals.
9 He performed miraculous signs and
    wonders in Egypt
    against Pharaoh and all his people.
10 He struck down great nations
    and slaughtered mighty kings—
11 Sihon king of the Amorites,
    Og king of Bashan,
    and all the kings of Canaan.
12 He gave their land as an inheritance,
    a special possession to his people Israel.

13 Your name, O LORD, endures forever;
    your fame, O LORD, is known to every
    generation.
14 For the LORD will give justice to his people
    and have compassion on his servants.

15 The idols of the nations are merely things
    of silver and gold,
    shaped by human hands.
16 They have mouths but cannot speak,
    and eyes but cannot see.
17 They have ears but cannot hear,
    and mouths but cannot breathe.
18 And those who make idols are just like them,
    as are all who trust in them.

19 O Israel, praise the LORD!
    O priests—descendants of Aaron—
    praise the LORD!
20 O Levites, praise the LORD!
    All you who fear the LORD, praise the
    LORD!
21 The LORD be praised from Zion,
    for he lives here in Jerusalem.

    Praise the LORD!

136

¹ Give thanks to the LORD, for he is good!

His faithful love endures forever.

² Give thanks to the God of gods.

His faithful love endures forever.

³ Give thanks to the Lord of lords.

His faithful love endures forever.

⁴ Give thanks to him who alone does mighty miracles.

His faithful love endures forever.

⁵ Give thanks to him who made the heavens so skillfully.

His faithful love endures forever.

⁶ Give thanks to him who placed the earth among the waters.

His faithful love endures forever.

⁷ Give thanks to him who made the heavenly lights—

His faithful love endures forever.

⁸ the sun to rule the day,

His faithful love endures forever.

⁹ and the moon and stars to rule the night.

His faithful love endures forever.

¹⁰ Give thanks to him who killed the firstborn of Egypt.

His faithful love endures forever.

¹¹ He brought Israel out of Egypt.

His faithful love endures forever.

¹² He acted with a strong hand and powerful arm.

His faithful love endures forever.

¹³ Give thanks to him who parted the Red Sea.*

His faithful love endures forever.

¹⁴ He led Israel safely through,

His faithful love endures forever.

¹⁵ but he hurled Pharaoh and his army into the Red Sea.

His faithful love endures forever.

¹⁶ Give thanks to him who led his people through the wilderness.

His faithful love endures forever.

¹⁷ Give thanks to him who struck down mighty kings.

His faithful love endures forever.

¹⁸ He killed powerful kings—

His faithful love endures forever.

¹⁹ Sihon king of the Amorites,

His faithful love endures forever.

²⁰ and Og king of Bashan.

His faithful love endures forever.

²¹ God gave the land of these kings as an inheritance—

His faithful love endures forever.

²² a special possession to his servant Israel.

His faithful love endures forever.

²³ He remembered us in our weakness.

His faithful love endures forever.

²⁴ He saved us from our enemies.

His faithful love endures forever.

²⁵ He gives food to every living thing.

His faithful love endures forever.

²⁶ Give thanks to the God of heaven.

His faithful love endures forever.

137

¹ Beside the rivers of Babylon, we sat and wept

as we thought of Jerusalem.*

² We put away our harps,

hanging them on the branches of poplar trees.

³ For our captors demanded a song from us.

Our tormentors insisted on a joyful hymn:

"Sing us one of those songs of Jerusalem!"

⁴ But how can we sing the songs of the LORD while in a pagan land?

⁵ If I forget you, O Jerusalem,

let my right hand forget how to play the harp.

⁶ May my tongue stick to the roof of my mouth

if I fail to remember you,

if I don't make Jerusalem my greatest joy.

⁷ O LORD, remember what the Edomites did

on the day the armies of Babylon captured Jerusalem.

"Destroy it!" they yelled.

"Level it to the ground!"

⁸ O Babylon, you will be destroyed.

Happy is the one who pays you back

for what you have done to us.

⁹ Happy is the one who takes your babies

and smashes them against the rocks!

138

A psalm of David.

¹ I give you thanks, O LORD, with all my heart;

I will sing your praises before the gods.

136:13 Hebrew *sea of reeds;* also in 136:15.   137:1 Hebrew *Zion;* also in 137:3.

2 I bow before your holy Temple as I
   worship.
   I praise your name for your unfailing
      love and faithfulness;
   for your promises are backed
      by all the honor of your name.
3 As soon as I pray, you answer me;
   you encourage me by giving me
      strength.

4 Every king in all the earth will thank you,
      LORD,
   for all of them will hear your words.
5 Yes, they will sing about the LORD's ways,
   for the glory of the LORD is very great.
6 Though the LORD is great, he cares for the
      humble,
   but he keeps his distance from the
      proud.

7 Though I am surrounded by troubles,
   you will protect me from the anger of
      my enemies.
   You reach out your hand,
      and the power of your right hand
         saves me.
8 The LORD will work out his plans for my
      life—
   for your faithful love, O LORD, endures
      forever.
   Don't abandon me, for you made me.

139 *For the choir director: A psalm of David.*

1 O LORD, you have examined my heart
   and know everything about me.
2 You know when I sit down or stand up.
   You know my thoughts even when I'm
      far away.
3 You see me when I travel
   and when I rest at home.
   You know everything I do.
4 You know what I am going to say
   even before I say it, LORD.
5 You go before me and follow me.
   You place your hand of blessing on
      my head.
6 Such knowledge is too wonderful for me,
   too great for me to understand!

7 I can never escape from your Spirit!
   I can never get away from your presence!
8 If I go up to heaven, you are there;
   if I go down to the grave,* you are there.

9 If I ride the wings of the morning,
   if I dwell by the farthest oceans,
10 even there your hand will guide me,
   and your strength will support me.
11 I could ask the darkness to hide me
   and the light around me to become
      night—
12 but even in darkness I cannot hide
      from you.
To you the night shines as bright as day.
   Darkness and light are the same to you.

13 You made all the delicate, inner parts of
      my body
   and knit me together in my mother's
      womb.
14 Thank you for making me so wonderfully
      complex!
   Your workmanship is marvelous—how
      well I know it.
15 You watched me as I was being formed in
      utter seclusion,
   as I was woven together in the dark of
      the womb.
16 You saw me before I was born.
   Every day of my life was recorded in
      your book.
   Every moment was laid out
      before a single day had passed.

17 How precious are your thoughts about
      me,* O God.
   They cannot be numbered!
18 I can't even count them;
   they outnumber the grains of sand!
And when I wake up,
   you are still with me!

19 O God, if only you would destroy the
      wicked!
   Get out of my life, you murderers!
20 They blaspheme you;
   your enemies misuse your name.
21 O LORD, shouldn't I hate those who hate
      you?
   Shouldn't I despise those who oppose
      you?
22 Yes, I hate them with total hatred,
   for your enemies are my enemies.

23 Search me, O God, and know my heart;
   test me and know my anxious thoughts.
24 Point out anything in me that offends you,
   and lead me along the path of
      everlasting life.

139:8 Hebrew *to Sheol.*   **139:17** Or *How precious to me are your thoughts.*

140
For the choir director: A psalm of David.

1 O Lord, rescue me from evil people.
   Protect me from those who are violent,
2 those who plot evil in their hearts
   and stir up trouble all day long.
3 Their tongues sting like a snake;
   the venom of a viper drips from
      their lips.   *Interlude*

4 O Lord, keep me out of the hands of the
   wicked.
   Protect me from those who are violent,
   for they are plotting against me.
5 The proud have set a trap to catch me;
   they have stretched out a net;
   they have placed traps all along the way.
                                    Interlude

6 I said to the Lord, "You are my God!"
   Listen, O Lord, to my cries for mercy!
7 O Sovereign Lord, the strong one who
      rescued me,
   you protected me on the day of battle.
8 Lord, do not let evil people have their way.
   Do not let their evil schemes succeed,
   or they will become proud.   *Interlude*

9 Let my enemies be destroyed
   by the very evil they have planned
      for me.
10 Let burning coals fall down on their heads.
   Let them be thrown into the fire
   or into watery pits from which they
      can't escape.
11 Don't let liars prosper here in our land.
   Cause great disasters to fall on the
      violent.

12 But I know the Lord will help those they
      persecute;
   he will give justice to the poor.
13 Surely righteous people are praising your
      name;
   the godly will live in your presence.

141
A psalm of David.

1 O Lord, I am calling to you. Please hurry!
   Listen when I cry to you for help!
2 Accept my prayer as incense offered to you,
   and my upraised hands as an evening
      offering.

3 Take control of what I say, O Lord,
   and guard my lips.
4 Don't let me drift toward evil
   or take part in acts of wickedness.
   Don't let me share in the delicacies
   of those who do wrong.

5 Let the godly strike me!
   It will be a kindness!
   If they correct me, it is soothing medicine.
   Don't let me refuse it.

   But I pray constantly
   against the wicked and their deeds.
6 When their leaders are thrown down from
      a cliff,
   the wicked will listen to my words and
      find them true.
7 Like rocks brought up by a plow,
   the bones of the wicked will lie scattered
      without burial.*

8 I look to you for help, O Sovereign Lord.
   You are my refuge; don't let them
      kill me.
9 Keep me from the traps they have set
      for me,
   from the snares of those who do wrong.
10 Let the wicked fall into their own nets,
   but let me escape.

142
A psalm of David, regarding his experience
in the cave. A prayer.*

1 I cry out to the Lord;
   I plead for the Lord's mercy.
2 I pour out my complaints before him
   and tell him all my troubles.
3 When I am overwhelmed,
   you alone know the way I should turn.
   Wherever I go,
   my enemies have set traps for me.
4 I look for someone to come and help me,
   but no one gives me a passing thought!
   No one will help me;
   no one cares a bit what happens to me.
5 Then I pray to you, O Lord.
   I say, "You are my place of refuge.
   You are all I really want in life.
6 Hear my cry,
   for I am very low.
   Rescue me from my persecutors,
   for they are too strong for me.
7 Bring me out of prison
   so I can thank you.

141:7 Hebrew *our bones will be scattered at the mouth of Sheol.*   142:title Hebrew *maskil.* This may be a literary or musical term.

The godly will crowd around me,
　　for you are good to me."

143 *A psalm of David.*

1 Hear my prayer, O Lᴏʀᴅ;
　　listen to my plea!
　　Answer me because you are faithful and
　　　righteous.
2 Don't put your servant on trial,
　　for no one is innocent before you.
3 My enemy has chased me.
　　He has knocked me to the ground
　　and forces me to live in darkness like
　　　those in the grave.
4 I am losing all hope;
　　I am paralyzed with fear.
5 I remember the days of old.
　　I ponder all your great works
　　and think about what you have done.
6 I lift my hands to you in prayer.
　　I thirst for you as parched land thirsts
　　　for rain. 　　　　　　　　　*Interlude*

7 Come quickly, Lᴏʀᴅ, and answer me,
　　for my depression deepens.
　　Don't turn away from me,
　　　or I will die.
8 Let me hear of your unfailing love each
　　　morning,
　　for I am trusting you.
　　Show me where to walk,
　　　for I give myself to you.
9 Rescue me from my enemies, Lᴏʀᴅ;
　　I run to you to hide me.
10 Teach me to do your will,
　　for you are my God.
　　May your gracious Spirit lead me forward
　　　on a firm footing.
11 For the glory of your name, O Lᴏʀᴅ,
　　preserve my life.
　　Because of your faithfulness, bring me
　　　out of this distress.
12 In your unfailing love, silence all my
　　　enemies
　　and destroy all my foes,
　　　for I am your servant.

144 *A psalm of David.*

1 Praise the Lᴏʀᴅ, who is my rock.
　　He trains my hands for war
　　and gives my fingers skill for battle.

144:2 Some manuscripts read *my people.*

2 He is my loving ally and my fortress,
　　my tower of safety, my rescuer.
　　He is my shield, and I take refuge in him.
　　He makes the nations* submit to me.

3 O Lᴏʀᴅ, what are human beings that you
　　　should notice them,
　　mere mortals that you should think
　　　about them?
4 For they are like a breath of air;
　　their days are like a passing shadow.

5 Open the heavens, Lᴏʀᴅ, and come
　　　down.
　　Touch the mountains so they billow
　　　smoke.
6 Hurl your lightning bolts and scatter your
　　　enemies!
　　Shoot your arrows and confuse them!
7 Reach down from heaven and rescue me;
　　rescue me from deep waters,
　　from the power of my enemies.
8 Their mouths are full of lies;
　　they swear to tell the truth, but they lie
　　　instead.

9 I will sing a new song to you, O God!
　　I will sing your praises with a ten-
　　　stringed harp.
10 For you grant victory to kings!
　　You rescued your servant David from
　　　the fatal sword.
11 Save me!
　　Rescue me from the power of my
　　　enemies.
　　Their mouths are full of lies;
　　they swear to tell the truth, but they lie
　　　instead.

12 May our sons flourish in their youth
　　like well-nurtured plants.
　　May our daughters be like graceful
　　　pillars,
　　carved to beautify a palace.
13 May our barns be filled
　　with crops of every kind.
　　May the flocks in our fields multiply by the
　　　thousands,
　　　even tens of thousands,
14 　and may our oxen be loaded down with
　　　produce.
　　May there be no enemy breaking through
　　　our walls,
　　no going into captivity,
　　no cries of alarm in our town squares.

¹⁵ Yes, joyful are those who live like this!
   Joyful indeed are those whose God is the
   LORD.

145 *
A psalm of praise of David.

¹ I will exalt you, my God and King,
   and praise your name forever and ever.
² I will praise you every day;
   yes, I will praise you forever.
³ Great is the LORD! He is most worthy of
   praise!
   No one can measure his greatness.

⁴ Let each generation tell its children of your
   mighty acts;
   let them proclaim your power.
⁵ I will meditate on your majestic, glorious
   splendor
   and your wonderful miracles.
⁶ Your awe-inspiring deeds will be on every
   tongue;
   I will proclaim your greatness.
⁷ Everyone will share the story of your
   wonderful goodness;
   they will sing with joy about your
   righteousness.

⁸ The LORD is merciful and compassionate,
   slow to get angry and filled with
   unfailing love.
⁹ The LORD is good to everyone.
   He showers compassion on all his
   creation.
¹⁰ All of your works will thank you, LORD,
   and your faithful followers will praise
   you.
¹¹ They will speak of the glory of your
   kingdom;
   they will give examples of your power.
¹² They will tell about your mighty deeds
   and about the majesty and glory of your
   reign.
¹³ For your kingdom is an everlasting
   kingdom.
   You rule throughout all generations.

   The LORD always keeps his promises;
   he is gracious in all he does.*
¹⁴ The LORD helps the fallen
   and lifts those bent beneath their loads.
¹⁵ The eyes of all look to you in hope;

you give them their food as they
   need it.
¹⁶ When you open your hand,
   you satisfy the hunger and thirst of
   every living thing.
¹⁷ The LORD is righteous in everything he
   does;
   he is filled with kindness.
¹⁸ The LORD is close to all who call on him,
   yes, to all who call on him in truth.
¹⁹ He grants the desires of those who fear
   him;
   he hears their cries for help and rescues
   them.
²⁰ The LORD protects all those who love him,
   but he destroys the wicked.

²¹ I will praise the LORD,
   and may everyone on earth bless his
   holy name
   forever and ever.

146 ¹ Praise the LORD!

      Let all that I am praise the LORD.
² I will praise the LORD as long as I live.
   I will sing praises to my God with my
   dying breath.

³ Don't put your confidence in powerful
   people;
   there is no help for you there.
⁴ When they breathe their last, they return
   to the earth,
   and all their plans die with them.
⁵ But joyful are those who have the God of
   Israel* as their helper,
   whose hope is in the LORD their God.
⁶ He made heaven and earth,
   the sea, and everything in them.
   He keeps every promise forever.
⁷ He gives justice to the oppressed
   and food to the hungry.
   The LORD frees the prisoners.
⁸ The LORD opens the eyes of the blind.
   The LORD lifts up those who are weighed
   down.
   The LORD loves the godly.
⁹ The LORD protects the foreigners
   among us.
   He cares for the orphans and widows,
   but he frustrates the plans of the
   wicked.

145 This psalm is a Hebrew acrostic poem; each verse (including 13b) begins with a successive letter of the Hebrew alphabet.
145:13 As in Dead Sea Scrolls and Greek and Syriac versions; the Masoretic Text lacks the final two lines of this verse.
146:5 Hebrew *of Jacob.* See note on 44:4.

¹⁰ The LORD will reign forever.
   He will be your God, O Jerusalem,*
      throughout the generations.

Praise the LORD!

147 ¹ Praise the LORD!

   How good to sing praises to our
      God!
   How delightful and how fitting!
² The LORD is rebuilding Jerusalem
   and bringing the exiles back to Israel.
³ He heals the brokenhearted
   and bandages their wounds.
⁴ He counts the stars
   and calls them all by name.
⁵ How great is our Lord! His power is
      absolute!
   His understanding is beyond
      comprehension!
⁶ The LORD supports the humble,
   but he brings the wicked down into the
      dust.

⁷ Sing out your thanks to the LORD;
   sing praises to our God with a harp.
⁸ He covers the heavens with clouds,
   provides rain for the earth,
   and makes the grass grow in mountain
      pastures.
⁹ He gives food to the wild animals
   and feeds the young ravens when they cry.
¹⁰ He takes no pleasure in the strength of
      a horse
   or in human might.
¹¹ No, the LORD's delight is in those who fear
      him,
   those who put their hope in his
      unfailing love.

¹² Glorify the LORD, O Jerusalem!
   Praise your God, O Zion!
¹³ For he has strengthened the bars of your
      gates
   and blessed your children within your
      walls.
¹⁴ He sends peace across your nation
   and satisfies your hunger with the finest
      wheat.
¹⁵ He sends his orders to the world—
   how swiftly his word flies!
¹⁶ He sends the snow like white wool;
   he scatters frost upon the ground like
      ashes.

¹⁷ He hurls the hail like stones.*
   Who can stand against his freezing
      cold?
¹⁸ Then, at his command, it all melts.
   He sends his winds, and the ice thaws.
¹⁹ He has revealed his words to Jacob,
   his decrees and regulations to Israel.
²⁰ He has not done this for any other nation;
   they do not know his regulations.

Praise the LORD!

148 ¹ Praise the LORD!

   Praise the LORD from the
      heavens!
   Praise him from the skies!
² Praise him, all his angels!
   Praise him, all the armies of heaven!
³ Praise him, sun and moon!
   Praise him, all you twinkling stars!
⁴ Praise him, skies above!
   Praise him, vapors high above the
      clouds!
⁵ Let every created thing give praise to the
      LORD,
   for he issued his command, and they
      came into being.
⁶ He set them in place forever and ever.
   His decree will never be revoked.

⁷ Praise the LORD from the earth,
   you creatures of the ocean depths,
⁸ fire and hail, snow and clouds,*
   wind and weather that obey him,
⁹ mountains and all hills,
   fruit trees and all cedars,
¹⁰ wild animals and all livestock,
   small scurrying animals and birds,
¹¹ kings of the earth and all people,
   rulers and judges of the earth,
¹² young men and young women,
   old men and children.

¹³ Let them all praise the name of the
      LORD.
   For his name is very great;
   his glory towers over the earth and
      heaven!
¹⁴ He has made his people strong,
   honoring his faithful ones—
   the people of Israel who are close
      to him.

Praise the LORD!

146:10 Hebrew *Zion.*   147:17 Hebrew *like bread crumbs.*   148:8 Or *mist,* or *smoke.*

149

¹ Praise the LORD!

Sing to the LORD a new song.
Sing his praises in the assembly of the
faithful.

² O Israel, rejoice in your Maker.
O people of Jerusalem,* exult in your
King.

³ Praise his name with dancing,
accompanied by tambourine and harp.

⁴ For the LORD delights in his people;
he crowns the humble with victory.

⁵ Let the faithful rejoice that he honors
them.
Let them sing for joy as they lie on their
beds.

⁶ Let the praises of God be in their mouths,
and a sharp sword in their hands—

⁷ to execute vengeance on the nations
and punishment on the peoples,

⁸ to bind their kings with shackles
and their leaders with iron chains,

149:2 Hebrew *Zion.*

⁹ to execute the judgment written against
them.
This is the glorious privilege of his
faithful ones.

Praise the LORD!

150

¹ Praise the LORD!

Praise God in his sanctuary;
praise him in his mighty heaven!

² Praise him for his mighty works;
praise his unequaled greatness!

³ Praise him with a blast of the ram's horn;
praise him with the lyre and harp!

⁴ Praise him with the tambourine and
dancing;
praise him with strings and flutes!

⁵ Praise him with a clash of cymbals;
praise him with loud clanging cymbals.

⁶ Let everything that breathes sing praises
to the LORD!

Praise the LORD!

Proverbs

KNOWLEDGE IS GOOD, but wisdom is even better. Knowledge can help you pass tests and accomplish tasks, but wisdom will guide you through the most important decisions in life. The book of Proverbs was written by Solomon, the wisest man who ever lived. It contains hundreds of short, simple statements about how to live wisely and an assortment of longer passages that express wisdom with a bit more detail. These proverbs, however, are more than just wise sayings of the sort we find in most cultures. They are not a haphazard collection of commonsense directives. These proverbs expressly state, "Fear of the Lord is the foundation of true knowledge" (1:7). Respect for God is the foundation for these wise sayings. They help the reader to distinguish between two paths: the way of the wise and the way of the fool. They deal with almost all the major areas of life, including growing up, parenting, social justice, wise speech, work, marriage, sexuality, and money.

■ **Authors:** Solomon, Agur, and Lemuel, according to Jewish tradition

■ **Date Written:** Uncertain, perhaps around 960 BC, early in Solomon's reign

■ **Purpose:** To apply divine wisdom to daily life and to provide moral instruction

■ **Themes:** Wisdom, relationships, speech, work, success

■ **Outline**

1:1-7 Introduction and theme of Proverbs
1:8–9:18 Proverbs mainly for parents and children
10:1–22:16 The first collection of Solomon's wisdom
22:17–24:34 Two collections of wise sayings
25:1–29:27 The second collection of Solomon's wisdom
30:1–31:9 The wisdom of Agur and Lemuel
31:10-31 A portrait of a truly good wife

The Purpose of Proverbs

1 These are the proverbs of Solomon, David's son, king of Israel.

2 Their purpose is to teach people wisdom and discipline,
  to help them understand the insights of the wise.
3 Their purpose is to teach people to live disciplined and successful lives,
  to help them do what is right, just, and fair.
4 These proverbs will give insight to the simple,
  knowledge and discernment to the young.

5 Let the wise listen to these proverbs and become even wiser.

Let those with understanding receive guidance
6 by exploring the meaning in these proverbs and parables,
  the words of the wise and their riddles.

7 Fear of the LORD is the foundation of true knowledge,
  but fools despise wisdom and discipline.

A Father's Exhortation: Acquire Wisdom

8 My child,* listen when your father corrects you.
  Don't neglect your mother's instruction.
9 What you learn from them will crown you with grace
  and be a chain of honor around your neck.

1:8 Hebrew *My son*; also in 1:10, 15.

¹⁰ My child, if sinners entice you,
  turn your back on them!
¹¹ They may say, "Come and join us.
  Let's hide and kill someone!
  Just for fun, let's ambush the innocent!
¹² Let's swallow them alive, like the grave*;
  let's swallow them whole, like those
    who go down to the pit of death.
¹³ Think of the great things we'll get!
  We'll fill our houses with all the stuff
    we take.
¹⁴ Come, throw in your lot with us;
  we'll all share the loot."

¹⁵ My child, don't go along with them!
  Stay far away from their paths.
¹⁶ They rush to commit evil deeds.
  They hurry to commit murder.
¹⁷ If a bird sees a trap being set,
  it knows to stay away.
¹⁸ But these people set an ambush for
    themselves;
  they are trying to get themselves killed.
¹⁹ Such is the fate of all who are greedy for
    money;
  it robs them of life.

Wisdom Shouts in the Streets
²⁰ Wisdom shouts in the streets.
  She cries out in the public square.
²¹ She calls to the crowds along the main
    street,
  to those gathered in front of the city
    gate:
²² "How long, you simpletons,
  will you insist on being simpleminded?
  How long will you mockers relish your
    mocking?
  How long will you fools hate
    knowledge?
²³ Come and listen to my counsel.
  I'll share my heart with you
    and make you wise.

²⁴ "I called you so often, but you wouldn't
    come.
  I reached out to you, but you paid no
    attention.
²⁵ You ignored my advice
  and rejected the correction I offered.
²⁶ So I will laugh when you are in trouble!
  I will mock you when disaster overtakes
    you—
²⁷ when calamity overtakes you like a storm,
  when disaster engulfs you like a cyclone,

and anguish and distress overwhelm
  you.

²⁸ "When they cry for help, I will not
    answer.
  Though they anxiously search for me,
    they will not find me.
²⁹ For they hated knowledge
  and chose not to fear the LORD.
³⁰ They rejected my advice
  and paid no attention when I corrected
    them.
³¹ Therefore, they must eat the bitter fruit
    of living their own way,
  choking on their own schemes.
³² For simpletons turn away from me—to
    death.
  Fools are destroyed by their own
    complacency.
³³ But all who listen to me will live in peace,
  untroubled by fear of harm."

The Benefits of Wisdom
2 ¹ My child,* listen to what I say,
  and treasure my commands.
² Tune your ears to wisdom,
  and concentrate on understanding.
³ Cry out for insight,
  and ask for understanding.
⁴ Search for them as you would for silver;
  seek them like hidden treasures.
⁵ Then you will understand what it means
    to fear the LORD,
  and you will gain knowledge of God.
⁶ For the LORD grants wisdom!
  From his mouth come knowledge and
    understanding.
⁷ He grants a treasure of common sense to
    the honest.
  He is a shield to those who walk with
    integrity.
⁸ He guards the paths of the just
  and protects those who are faithful
    to him.

⁹ Then you will understand what is right,
    just, and fair,
  and you will find the right way to go.
¹⁰ For wisdom will enter your heart,
  and knowledge will fill you with joy.
¹¹ Wise choices will watch over you.
  Understanding will keep you safe.

¹² Wisdom will save you from evil people,
  from those whose words are twisted.

1:12 Hebrew *like Sheol.*   2:1 Hebrew *My son.*

13 These men turn from the right way
    to walk down dark paths.
14 They take pleasure in doing wrong,
    and they enjoy the twisted ways of evil.
15 Their actions are crooked,
    and their ways are wrong.

16 Wisdom will save you from the immoral
    woman,
    from the seductive words of the
    promiscuous woman.
17 She has abandoned her husband
    and ignores the covenant she made
    before God.
18 Entering her house leads to death;
    it is the road to the grave.*
19 The man who visits her is doomed.
    He will never reach the paths of life.

20 So follow the steps of the good,
    and stay on the paths of the righteous.
21 For only the godly will live in the land,
    and those with integrity will remain
    in it.
22 But the wicked will be removed from the
    land,
    and the treacherous will be uprooted.

Trusting in the LORD

3 1 My child,* never forget the things I have
    taught you.
    Store my commands in your heart.
2 If you do this, you will live many years,
    and your life will be satisfying.
3 Never let loyalty and kindness leave you!
    Tie them around your neck as a
    reminder.
    Write them deep within your heart.
4 Then you will find favor with both God
    and people,
    and you will earn a good reputation.

5 Trust in the LORD with all your heart;
    do not depend on your own
    understanding.
6 Seek his will in all you do,
    and he will show you which path to take.

7 Don't be impressed with your own
    wisdom.
    Instead, fear the LORD and turn away
    from evil.
8 Then you will have healing for your body
    and strength for your bones.

9 Honor the LORD with your wealth
    and with the best part of everything
    you produce.
10 Then he will fill your barns with grain,
    and your vats will overflow with good
    wine.

11 My child, don't reject the LORD's
    discipline,
    and don't be upset when he corrects
    you.
12 For the LORD corrects those he loves,
    just as a father corrects a child in whom
    he delights.*

13 Joyful is the person who finds wisdom,
    the one who gains understanding.
14 For wisdom is more profitable than silver,
    and her wages are better than gold.
15 Wisdom is more precious than rubies;
    nothing you desire can compare
    with her.
16 She offers you long life in her right hand,
    and riches and honor in her left.
17 She will guide you down delightful
    paths;
    all her ways are satisfying.
18 Wisdom is a tree of life to those who
    embrace her;
    happy are those who hold her tightly.

19 By wisdom the LORD founded the earth;
    by understanding he created the
    heavens.
20 By his knowledge the deep fountains of
    the earth burst forth,
    and the dew settles beneath the night
    sky.

21 My child, don't lose sight of common sense
    and discernment.
    Hang on to them,
22 for they will refresh your soul.
    They are like jewels on a necklace.
23 They keep you safe on your way,
    and your feet will not stumble.
24 You can go to bed without fear;
    you will lie down and sleep soundly.
25 You need not be afraid of sudden disaster
    or the destruction that comes upon the
    wicked,
26 for the LORD is your security.
    He will keep your foot from being
    caught in a trap.

2:18 Hebrew *to the spirits of the dead.*   **3:1** Hebrew *My son;* also in 3:11, 21.   **3:12** Greek version reads *loves, / and he punishes those he accepts as his children.* Compare Heb 12:6.

27 Do not withhold good from those who
   deserve it
   when it's in your power to help them.
28 If you can help your neighbor now,
   don't say,
   "Come back tomorrow, and then I'll
   help you."

29 Don't plot harm against your neighbor,
   for those who live nearby trust you.
30 Don't pick a fight without reason,
   when no one has done you harm.

31 Don't envy violent people
   or copy their ways.
32 Such wicked people are detestable to the
   LORD,
   but he offers his friendship to the godly.

33 The LORD curses the house of the wicked,
   but he blesses the home of the upright.

34 The LORD mocks the mockers
   but is gracious to the humble.*

35 The wise inherit honor,
   but fools are put to shame!

A Father's Wise Advice

4 ¹ My children,* listen when your father
   corrects you.
   Pay attention and learn good judgment,
2 for I am giving you good guidance.
   Don't turn away from my instructions.
3 For I, too, was once my father's son,
   tenderly loved as my mother's only
   child.

4 My father taught me,
   "Take my words to heart.
   Follow my commands, and you will live.
5 Get wisdom; develop good judgment.
   Don't forget my words or turn away
   from them.
6 Don't turn your back on wisdom, for she
   will protect you.
   Love her, and she will guard you.
7 Getting wisdom is the wisest thing you
   can do!
   And whatever else you do, develop good
   judgment.
8 If you prize wisdom, she will make you
   great.
   Embrace her, and she will honor you.

9 She will place a lovely wreath on your
   head;
   she will present you with a beautiful
   crown."

10 My child,* listen to me and do as I say,
   and you will have a long, good life.
11 I will teach you wisdom's ways
   and lead you in straight paths.
12 When you walk, you won't be held back;
   when you run, you won't stumble.
13 Take hold of my instructions; don't let
   them go.
   Guard them, for they are the key to life.

14 Don't do as the wicked do,
   and don't follow the path of evildoers.
15 Don't even think about it; don't go that
   way.
   Turn away and keep moving.
16 For evil people can't sleep until they've
   done their evil deed for the day.
   They can't rest until they've caused
   someone to stumble.
17 They eat the food of wickedness
   and drink the wine of violence!

18 The way of the righteous is like the first
   gleam of dawn,
   which shines ever brighter until the full
   light of day.
19 But the way of the wicked is like total
   darkness.
   They have no idea what they are
   stumbling over.

20 My child, pay attention to what I say.
   Listen carefully to my words.
21 Don't lose sight of them.
   Let them penetrate deep into your heart,
22 for they bring life to those who find them,
   and healing to their whole body.

23 Guard your heart above all else,
   for it determines the course of your life.

24 Avoid all perverse talk;
   stay away from corrupt speech.

25 Look straight ahead,
   and fix your eyes on what lies before
   you.
26 Mark out a straight path for your feet;
   stay on the safe path.

3:34 Greek version reads The LORD opposes the proud / but gives grace to the humble. Compare Jas 4:6; 1 Pet 5:5.   4:1 Hebrew My sons.
4:10 Hebrew My son; also in 4:20.

27 Don't get sidetracked;
   keep your feet from following evil.

Avoid Immoral Women

5 1 My son, pay attention to my wisdom;
       listen carefully to my wise counsel.
2 Then you will show discernment,
   and your lips will express what you've
   learned.
3 For the lips of an immoral woman are as
   sweet as honey,
   and her mouth is smoother than oil.
4 But in the end she is as bitter as poison,
   as dangerous as a double-edged sword.
5 Her feet go down to death;
   her steps lead straight to the grave.*
6 For she cares nothing about the path
   to life.
   She staggers down a crooked trail and
   doesn't realize it.

7 So now, my sons, listen to me.
   Never stray from what I am about
   to say:
8 Stay away from her!
   Don't go near the door of her house!
9 If you do, you will lose your honor
   and will lose to merciless people all you
   have achieved.
10 Strangers will consume your wealth,
   and someone else will enjoy the fruit
   of your labor.
11 In the end you will groan in anguish
   when disease consumes your body.
12 You will say, "How I hated discipline!
   If only I had not ignored all the
   warnings!
13 Oh, why didn't I listen to my teachers?
   Why didn't I pay attention to my
   instructors?
14 I have come to the brink of utter ruin,
   and now I must face public disgrace."

15 Drink water from your own well—
   share your love only with your wife.*
16 Why spill the water of your springs in the
   streets,
   having sex with just anyone?*
17 You should reserve it for yourselves.
   Never share it with strangers.

18 Let your wife be a fountain of blessing
   for you.
   Rejoice in the wife of your youth.

19 She is a loving deer, a graceful doe.
   Let her breasts satisfy you always.
   May you always be captivated by her
   love.
20 Why be captivated, my son, by an immoral
   woman,
   or fondle the breasts of a promiscuous
   woman?
21 For the LORD sees clearly what a man does,
   examining every path he takes.
22 An evil man is held captive by his own
   sins;
   they are ropes that catch and hold him.
23 He will die for lack of self-control;
   he will be lost because of his great
   foolishness.

Lessons for Daily Life

6 1 My child,* if you have put up security
       for a friend's debt
   or agreed to guarantee the debt of a
   stranger—
2 if you have trapped yourself by your
   agreement
   and are caught by what you said—
3 follow my advice and save yourself,
   for you have placed yourself at your
   friend's mercy.
   Now swallow your pride;
   go and beg to have your name erased.
4 Don't put it off; do it now!
   Don't rest until you do.
5 Save yourself like a gazelle escaping from
   a hunter,
   like a bird fleeing from a net.

6 Take a lesson from the ants, you lazybones.
   Learn from their ways and become
   wise!
7 Though they have no prince
   or governor or ruler to make them
   work,
8 they labor hard all summer,
   gathering food for the winter.
9 But you, lazybones, how long will you
   sleep?
   When will you wake up?
10 A little extra sleep, a little more slumber,
   a little folding of the hands to rest—
11 then poverty will pounce on you like a
   bandit;
   scarcity will attack you like an armed
   robber.

5:5 Hebrew *to Sheol.*   5:15 Hebrew *Drink water from your own cistern, / flowing water from your own well.*   5:16 Hebrew *Why spill your springs in the streets, / your streams in the city squares?*   6:1 Hebrew *My son.*

¹² What are worthless and wicked people
    like?
  They are constant liars,
¹³ signaling their deceit with a wink of
    the eye,
  a nudge of the foot, or the wiggle of
    fingers.
¹⁴ Their perverted hearts plot evil,
  and they constantly stir up trouble.
¹⁵ But they will be destroyed suddenly,
  broken in an instant beyond all hope
    of healing.

¹⁶ There are six things the LORD hates—
  no, seven things he detests:
¹⁷ haughty eyes,
  a lying tongue,
  hands that kill the innocent,
¹⁸ a heart that plots evil,
  feet that race to do wrong,
¹⁹ a false witness who pours out lies,
  a person who sows discord in a family.

²⁰ My son, obey your father's commands,
  and don't neglect your mother's
    instruction.
²¹ Keep their words always in your heart.
  Tie them around your neck.
²² When you walk, their counsel will lead
    you.
  When you sleep, they will protect you.
  When you wake up, they will advise you.
²³ For their command is a lamp
  and their instruction a light;
  their corrective discipline
  is the way to life.
²⁴ It will keep you from the immoral woman,
  from the smooth tongue of a
    promiscuous woman.
²⁵ Don't lust for her beauty.
  Don't let her coy glances seduce you.
²⁶ For a prostitute will bring you to poverty,*
  but sleeping with another man's wife
    will cost you your life.
²⁷ Can a man scoop a flame into his lap
  and not have his clothes catch on fire?
²⁸ Can he walk on hot coals
  and not blister his feet?
²⁹ So it is with the man who sleeps with
    another man's wife.
  He who embraces her will not go
    unpunished.

³⁰ Excuses might be found for a thief
  who steals because he is starving.

³¹ But if he is caught, he must pay back seven
    times what he stole,
  even if he has to sell everything in his
    house.
³² But the man who commits adultery is an
    utter fool,
  for he destroys himself.
³³ He will be wounded and disgraced.
  His shame will never be erased.
³⁴ For the woman's jealous husband will be
    furious,
  and he will show no mercy when he
    takes revenge.
³⁵ He will accept no compensation,
  nor be satisfied with a payoff of any
    size.

Another Warning about Immoral Women

7 ¹ Follow my advice, my son;
  always treasure my commands.
² Obey my commands and live!
  Guard my instructions as you guard
    your own eyes.*
³ Tie them on your fingers as a reminder.
  Write them deep within your heart.
⁴ Love wisdom like a sister;
  make insight a beloved member of your
    family.
⁵ Let them protect you from an affair with
    an immoral woman,
  from listening to the flattery of a
    promiscuous woman.

⁶ While I was at the window of my house,
  looking through the curtain,
⁷ I saw some naive young men,
  and one in particular who lacked
    common sense.
⁸ He was crossing the street near the house
    of an immoral woman,
  strolling down the path by her house.
⁹ It was at twilight, in the evening,
  as deep darkness fell.
¹⁰ The woman approached him,
  seductively dressed and sly of heart.
¹¹ She was the brash, rebellious type,
  never content to stay at home.
¹² She is often in the streets and markets,
  soliciting at every corner.
¹³ She threw her arms around him and
    kissed him,
  and with a brazen look she said,
¹⁴ "I've just made my peace offerings
  and fulfilled my vows.

6:26 Hebrew *to a loaf of bread.*   7:2 Hebrew *as the pupil of your eye.*

¹⁵ You're the one I was looking for!
    I came out to find you, and here you are!
¹⁶ My bed is spread with beautiful blankets,
    with colored sheets of Egyptian linen.
¹⁷ I've perfumed my bed
    with myrrh, aloes, and cinnamon.
¹⁸ Come, let's drink our fill of love until
    morning.
    Let's enjoy each other's caresses,
¹⁹ for my husband is not home.
    He's away on a long trip.
²⁰ He has taken a wallet full of money
    with him
    and won't return until later this
    month.*"

²¹ So she seduced him with her pretty speech
    and enticed him with her flattery.
²² He followed her at once,
    like an ox going to the slaughter.
    He was like a stag caught in a trap,*
²³   awaiting the arrow that would pierce
    its heart.
    He was like a bird flying into a snare,
    little knowing it would cost him his life.

²⁴ So listen to me, my sons,
    and pay attention to my words.
²⁵ Don't let your hearts stray away
    toward her.
    Don't wander down her wayward path.
²⁶ For she has been the ruin of many;
    many men have been her victims.
²⁷ Her house is the road to the grave.*
    Her bedroom is the den of death.

Wisdom Calls for a Hearing

8 ¹ Listen as Wisdom calls out!
    Hear as understanding raises her
    voice!
² On the hilltop along the road,
    she takes her stand at the crossroads.
³ By the gates at the entrance to the town,
    on the road leading in, she cries aloud,
⁴ "I call to you, to all of you!
    I raise my voice to all people.
⁵ You simple people, use good judgment.
    You foolish people, show some
    understanding.
⁶ Listen to me! For I have important things
    to tell you.
    Everything I say is right,
⁷ for I speak the truth
    and detest every kind of deception.

⁸ My advice is wholesome.
    There is nothing devious or crooked
    in it.
⁹ My words are plain to anyone with
    understanding,
    clear to those with knowledge.
¹⁰ Choose my instruction rather than silver,
    and knowledge rather than pure gold.
¹¹ For wisdom is far more valuable than
    rubies.
    Nothing you desire can compare with it.

¹² "I, Wisdom, live together with good
    judgment.
    I know where to discover knowledge
    and discernment.
¹³ All who fear the LORD will hate evil.
    Therefore, I hate pride and arrogance,
    corruption and perverse speech.
¹⁴ Common sense and success belong to me.
    Insight and strength are mine.
¹⁵ Because of me, kings reign,
    and rulers make just decrees.
¹⁶ Rulers lead with my help,
    and nobles make righteous judgments.*

¹⁷ "I love all who love me.
    Those who search will surely find me.
¹⁸ I have riches and honor,
    as well as enduring wealth and justice.
¹⁹ My gifts are better than gold, even the
    purest gold,
    my wages better than sterling silver!
²⁰ I walk in righteousness,
    in paths of justice.
²¹ Those who love me inherit wealth.
    I will fill their treasuries.

²² "The LORD formed me from the
    beginning,
    before he created anything else.
²³ I was appointed in ages past,
    at the very first, before the earth began.
²⁴ I was born before the oceans were created,
    before the springs bubbled forth their
    waters.
²⁵ Before the mountains were formed,
    before the hills, I was born—
²⁶ before he had made the earth and fields
    and the first handfuls of soil.
²⁷ I was there when he established the
    heavens,
    when he drew the horizon on the
    oceans.

7:20 Hebrew *until the moon is full.*   **7:22** As in Greek and Syriac versions; Hebrew reads *slaughter, as shackles are for the discipline of a fool.*   **7:27** Hebrew *to Sheol.*   **8:16** Some Hebrew manuscripts and Greek version read *and nobles are judges over the earth.*

28 I was there when he set the clouds above,
  when he established springs deep in the
    earth.
29 I was there when he set the limits of the
    seas,
  so they would not spread beyond their
    boundaries.
And when he marked off the earth's
    foundations,
30   I was the architect at his side.
I was his constant delight,
  rejoicing always in his presence.
31 And how happy I was with the world he
    created;
  how I rejoiced with the human family!

32 "And so, my children,* listen to me,
  for all who follow my ways are joyful.
33 Listen to my instruction and be wise.
  Don't ignore it.
34 Joyful are those who listen to me,
  watching for me daily at my gates,
  waiting for me outside my home!
35 For whoever finds me finds life
  and receives favor from the LORD.
36 But those who miss me injure themselves.
  All who hate me love death."

9 ¹ Wisdom has built her house;
    she has carved its seven columns.
2 She has prepared a great banquet,
  mixed the wines, and set the table.
3 She has sent her servants to invite
    everyone to come.
  She calls out from the heights
    overlooking the city.
4 "Come in with me," she urges the simple.
  To those who lack good judgment, she
    says,
5 "Come, eat my food,
  and drink the wine I have mixed.
6 Leave your simple ways behind, and begin
    to live;
  learn to use good judgment."

7 Anyone who rebukes a mocker will get an
    insult in return.
  Anyone who corrects the wicked will
    get hurt.
8 So don't bother correcting mockers;
  they will only hate you.
  But correct the wise,
    and they will love you.
9 Instruct the wise,
  and they will be even wiser.

Teach the righteous,
  and they will learn even more.
10 Fear of the LORD is the foundation of
    wisdom.
  Knowledge of the Holy One results in
    good judgment.
11 Wisdom will multiply your days
  and add years to your life.
12 If you become wise, you will be the one to
    benefit.
  If you scorn wisdom, you will be the one
    to suffer.

Folly Calls for a Hearing

13 The woman named Folly is brash.
  She is ignorant and doesn't know it.
14 She sits in her doorway
  on the heights overlooking the city.
15 She calls out to men going by
  who are minding their own business.
16 "Come in with me," she urges the simple.
  To those who lack good judgment,
    she says,
17 "Stolen water is refreshing;
  food eaten in secret tastes the best!"
18 But little do they know that the dead
    are there.
  Her guests are in the depths of the
    grave.*

The Proverbs of Solomon

10 The proverbs of Solomon:

A wise child* brings joy to a father;
  a foolish child brings grief to a mother.

2 Tainted wealth has no lasting value,
  but right living can save your life.

3 The LORD will not let the godly go hungry,
  but he refuses to satisfy the craving of
    the wicked.

4 Lazy people are soon poor;
  hard workers get rich.

5 A wise youth harvests in the summer,
  but one who sleeps during harvest is a
    disgrace.

6 The godly are showered with blessings;
  the words of the wicked conceal violent
    intentions.

8:32 Hebrew my sons. 9:18 Hebrew in Sheol. 10:1 Hebrew son; also in 10:1b.

7 We have happy memories of the godly,
   but the name of a wicked person rots
   away.

8 The wise are glad to be instructed,
   but babbling fools fall flat on their
   faces.

9 People with integrity walk safely,
   but those who follow crooked paths will
   be exposed.

10 People who wink at wrong cause trouble,
   but a bold reproof promotes peace.*

11 The words of the godly are a life-giving
   fountain;
   the words of the wicked conceal violent
   intentions.

12 Hatred stirs up quarrels,
   but love makes up for all offenses.

13 Wise words come from the lips of people
   with understanding,
   but those lacking sense will be beaten
   with a rod.

14 Wise people treasure knowledge,
   but the babbling of a fool invites
   disaster.

15 The wealth of the rich is their fortress;
   the poverty of the poor is their
   destruction.

16 The earnings of the godly enhance their
   lives,
   but evil people squander their money
   on sin.

17 People who accept discipline are on the
   pathway to life,
   but those who ignore correction will
   go astray.

18 Hiding hatred makes you a liar;
   slandering others makes you a fool.

19 Too much talk leads to sin.
   Be sensible and keep your mouth shut.

20 The words of the godly are like sterling
   silver;
   the heart of a fool is worthless.

21 The words of the godly encourage many,
   but fools are destroyed by their lack of
   common sense.

22 The blessing of the LORD makes a person
   rich,
   and he adds no sorrow with it.

23 Doing wrong is fun for a fool,
   but living wisely brings pleasure to the
   sensible.

24 The fears of the wicked will be fulfilled;
   the hopes of the godly will be granted.

25 When the storms of life come, the wicked
   are whirled away,
   but the godly have a lasting
   foundation.

26 Lazy people irritate their employers,
   like vinegar to the teeth or smoke in
   the eyes.

27 Fear of the LORD lengthens one's life,
   but the years of the wicked are cut
   short.

28 The hopes of the godly result in happiness,
   but the expectations of the wicked come
   to nothing.

29 The way of the LORD is a stronghold to
   those with integrity,
   but it destroys the wicked.

30 The godly will never be disturbed,
   but the wicked will be removed from
   the land.

31 The mouth of the godly person gives wise
   advice,
   but the tongue that deceives will be
   cut off.

32 The lips of the godly speak helpful words,
   but the mouth of the wicked speaks
   perverse words.

11

1 The LORD detests the use of
   dishonest scales,
   but he delights in accurate weights.

2 Pride leads to disgrace,
   but with humility comes wisdom.

10:10 As in Greek version; Hebrew reads *but babbling fools fall flat on their faces.*

³ Honesty guides good people;
　　dishonesty destroys treacherous
　　people.

⁴ Riches won't help on the day of judgment,
　　but right living can save you from death.

⁵ The godly are directed by honesty;
　　the wicked fall beneath their load
　　of sin.

⁶ The godliness of good people rescues
　　them;
　　the ambition of treacherous people
　　traps them.

⁷ When the wicked die, their hopes die with
　　them,
　　for they rely on their own feeble
　　strength.

⁸ The godly are rescued from trouble,
　　and it falls on the wicked instead.

⁹ With their words, the godless destroy their
　　friends,
　　but knowledge will rescue the
　　righteous.

¹⁰ The whole city celebrates when the godly
　　succeed;
　　they shout for joy when the wicked die.

¹¹ Upright citizens are good for a city and
　　make it prosper,
　　but the talk of the wicked tears it apart.

¹² It is foolish to belittle one's neighbor;
　　a sensible person keeps quiet.

¹³ A gossip goes around telling secrets,
　　but those who are trustworthy can keep
　　a confidence.

¹⁴ Without wise leadership, a nation falls;
　　there is safety in having many advisers.

¹⁵ There's danger in putting up security for
　　a stranger's debt;
　　it's safer not to guarantee another
　　person's debt.

¹⁶ A gracious woman gains respect,
　　but ruthless men gain only wealth.

¹⁷ Your kindness will reward you,
　　but your cruelty will destroy you.

¹⁸ Evil people get rich for the moment,
　　but the reward of the godly will last.

¹⁹ Godly people find life;
　　evil people find death.

²⁰ The LORD detests people with crooked
　　hearts,
　　but he delights in those with integrity.

²¹ Evil people will surely be punished,
　　but the children of the godly will go
　　free.

²² A beautiful woman who lacks discretion
　　is like a gold ring in a pig's snout.

²³ The godly can look forward to a reward,
　　while the wicked can expect only
　　judgment.

²⁴ Give freely and become more wealthy;
　　be stingy and lose everything.

²⁵ The generous will prosper;
　　those who refresh others will
　　themselves be refreshed.

²⁶ People curse those who hoard their grain,
　　but they bless the one who sells in time
　　of need.

²⁷ If you search for good, you will find favor;
　　but if you search for evil, it will find
　　you!

²⁸ Trust in your money and down you go!
　　But the godly flourish like leaves in
　　spring.

²⁹ Those who bring trouble on their families
　　inherit the wind.
　　The fool will be a servant to the wise.

³⁰ The seeds of good deeds become a tree
　　of life;
　　a wise person wins friends.*

³¹ If the righteous are rewarded here on
　　earth,
　　what will happen to wicked sinners?*

11:30 Or *and those who win souls are wise.*　　11:31 Greek version reads *If the righteous are barely saved, / what will happen to godless sinners?* Compare 1 Pet 4:18.

12

¹ To learn, you must love discipline;
    it is stupid to hate correction.

² The LORD approves of those who are
        good,
    but he condemns those who plan
        wickedness.

³ Wickedness never brings stability,
    but the godly have deep roots.

⁴ A worthy wife is a crown for her husband,
    but a disgraceful woman is like cancer
        in his bones.

⁵ The plans of the godly are just;
    the advice of the wicked is treacherous.

⁶ The words of the wicked are like a
        murderous ambush,
    but the words of the godly save lives.

⁷ The wicked die and disappear,
    but the family of the godly stands
        firm.

⁸ A sensible person wins admiration,
    but a warped mind is despised.

⁹ Better to be an ordinary person with a
        servant
    than to be self-important but have no
        food.

¹⁰ The godly care for their animals,
    but the wicked are always cruel.

¹¹ A hard worker has plenty of food,
    but a person who chases fantasies has
        no sense.

¹² Thieves are jealous of each other's loot,
    but the godly are well rooted and bear
        their own fruit.

¹³ The wicked are trapped by their own
        words,
    but the godly escape such trouble.

¹⁴ Wise words bring many benefits,
    and hard work brings rewards.

¹⁵ Fools think their own way is right,
    but the wise listen to others.

¹⁶ A fool is quick-tempered,
    but a wise person stays calm when
        insulted.

¹⁷ An honest witness tells the truth;
    a false witness tells lies.

¹⁸ Some people make cutting remarks,
    but the words of the wise bring
        healing.

¹⁹ Truthful words stand the test of time,
    but lies are soon exposed.

²⁰ Deceit fills hearts that are plotting evil;
    joy fills hearts that are planning peace!

²¹ No harm comes to the godly,
    but the wicked have their fill of trouble.

²² The LORD detests lying lips,
    but he delights in those who tell the
        truth.

²³ The wise don't make a show of their
        knowledge,
    but fools broadcast their foolishness.

²⁴ Work hard and become a leader;
    be lazy and become a slave.

²⁵ Worry weighs a person down;
    an encouraging word cheers a
        person up.

²⁶ The godly give good advice to their
        friends;*
    the wicked lead them astray.

²⁷ Lazy people don't even cook the game they
        catch,
    but the diligent make use of everything
        they find.

²⁸ The way of the godly leads to life;
    that path does not lead to death.

13

¹ A wise child accepts a parent's
        discipline;*
    a mocker refuses to listen to correction.

² Wise words will win you a good meal,
    but treacherous people have an appetite
        for violence.

12:26 Or *The godly are cautious in friendship;* or *The godly are freed from evil.* The meaning of the Hebrew is uncertain.
13:1 Hebrew *A wise son accepts his father's discipline.*

³ Those who control their tongue will have
a long life;
opening your mouth can ruin
everything.

⁴ Lazy people want much but get little,
but those who work hard will prosper.

⁵ The godly hate lies;
the wicked cause shame and disgrace.

⁶ Godliness guards the path of the
blameless,
but the evil are misled by sin.

⁷ Some who are poor pretend to be rich;
others who are rich pretend to be poor.

⁸ The rich can pay a ransom for their lives,
but the poor won't even get threatened.

⁹ The life of the godly is full of light and joy,
but the light of the wicked will be
snuffed out.

¹⁰ Pride leads to conflict;
those who take advice are wise.

¹¹ Wealth from get-rich-quick schemes
quickly disappears;
wealth from hard work grows over time.

¹² Hope deferred makes the heart sick,
but a dream fulfilled is a tree of life.

¹³ People who despise advice are asking for
trouble;
those who respect a command will
succeed.

¹⁴ The instruction of the wise is like a life-
giving fountain;
those who accept it avoid the snares
of death.

¹⁵ A person with good sense is respected;
a treacherous person is headed for
destruction.*

¹⁶ Wise people think before they act;
fools don't—and even brag about their
foolishness.

¹⁷ An unreliable messenger stumbles into
trouble,

but a reliable messenger brings
healing.

¹⁸ If you ignore criticism, you will end in
poverty and disgrace;
if you accept correction, you will be
honored.

¹⁹ It is pleasant to see dreams come true,
but fools refuse to turn from evil to
attain them.

²⁰ Walk with the wise and become wise;
associate with fools and get in trouble.

²¹ Trouble chases sinners,
while blessings reward the righteous.

²² Good people leave an inheritance to their
grandchildren,
but the sinner's wealth passes to the
godly.

²³ A poor person's farm may produce much
food,
but injustice sweeps it all away.

²⁴ Those who spare the rod of discipline hate
their children.
Those who love their children care
enough to discipline them.

²⁵ The godly eat to their hearts' content,
but the belly of the wicked goes hungry.

14

¹ A wise woman builds her home,
but a foolish woman tears it down
with her own hands.

² Those who follow the right path fear the
LORD;
those who take the wrong path despise
him.

³ A fool's proud talk becomes a rod that
beats him,
but the words of the wise keep them
safe.

⁴ Without oxen a stable stays clean,
but you need a strong ox for a large
harvest.

⁵ An honest witness does not lie;
a false witness breathes lies.

13:15 As in Greek version; Hebrew reads *the way of the treacherous is lasting.*

⁶ A mocker seeks wisdom and never
        finds it,
    but knowledge comes easily to those
        with understanding.

⁷ Stay away from fools,
    for you won't find knowledge on their
        lips.

⁸ The prudent understand where they are
        going,
    but fools deceive themselves.

⁹ Fools make fun of guilt,
    but the godly acknowledge it and seek
        reconciliation.

¹⁰ Each heart knows its own bitterness,
    and no one else can fully share
        its joy.

¹¹ The house of the wicked will be destroyed,
    but the tent of the godly will flourish.

¹² There is a path before each person that
        seems right,
    but it ends in death.

¹³ Laughter can conceal a heavy heart,
    but when the laughter ends, the grief
        remains.

¹⁴ Backsliders get what they deserve;
    good people receive their reward.

¹⁵ Only simpletons believe everything
        they're told!
    The prudent carefully consider their
        steps.

¹⁶ The wise are cautious* and avoid
        danger;
    fools plunge ahead with reckless
        confidence.

¹⁷ Short-tempered people do foolish things,
    and schemers are hated.

¹⁸ Simpletons are clothed with foolishness,*
    but the prudent are crowned with
        knowledge.

¹⁹ Evil people will bow before good people;
    the wicked will bow at the gates of the
        godly.

²⁰ The poor are despised even by their
        neighbors,
    while the rich have many "friends."

²¹ It is a sin to belittle one's neighbor;
    blessed are those who help the poor.

²² If you plan to do evil, you will be lost;
    if you plan to do good, you will receive
        unfailing love and faithfulness.

²³ Work brings profit,
    but mere talk leads to poverty!

²⁴ Wealth is a crown for the wise;
    the effort of fools yields only
        foolishness.

²⁵ A truthful witness saves lives,
    but a false witness is a traitor.

²⁶ Those who fear the LORD are secure;
    he will be a refuge for their children.

²⁷ Fear of the LORD is a life-giving fountain;
    it offers escape from the snares of death.

²⁸ A growing population is a king's glory;
    a prince without subjects has nothing.

²⁹ People with understanding control their
        anger;
    a hot temper shows great foolishness.

³⁰ A peaceful heart leads to a healthy body;
    jealousy is like cancer in the bones.

³¹ Those who oppress the poor insult their
        Maker,
    but helping the poor honors him.

³² The wicked are crushed by disaster,
    but the godly have a refuge when
        they die.

³³ Wisdom is enshrined in an understanding
        heart;
    wisdom is not* found among fools.

³⁴ Godliness makes a nation great,
    but sin is a disgrace to any people.

³⁵ A king rejoices in wise servants
    but is angry with those who disgrace
        him.

14:16 Hebrew *The wise fear.*   14:18 Or *inherit foolishness.*   14:33 As in Greek and Syriac versions; Hebrew lacks *not.*

15

¹ A gentle answer deflects anger,
but harsh words make tempers
flare.

² The tongue of the wise makes knowledge
appealing,
but the mouth of a fool belches out
foolishness.

³ The LORD is watching everywhere,
keeping his eye on both the evil and the
good.

⁴ Gentle words are a tree of life;
a deceitful tongue crushes the spirit.

⁵ Only a fool despises a parent's* discipline;
whoever learns from correction is wise.

⁶ There is treasure in the house of the godly,
but the earnings of the wicked bring
trouble.

⁷ The lips of the wise give good advice;
the heart of a fool has none to give.

⁸ The LORD detests the sacrifice of the
wicked,
but he delights in the prayers of the
upright.

⁹ The LORD detests the way of the wicked,
but he loves those who pursue
godliness.

¹⁰ Whoever abandons the right path will be
severely disciplined;
whoever hates correction will die.

¹¹ Even Death and Destruction* hold no
secrets from the LORD.
How much more does he know the
human heart!

¹² Mockers hate to be corrected,
so they stay away from the wise.

¹³ A glad heart makes a happy face;
a broken heart crushes the spirit.

¹⁴ A wise person is hungry for knowledge,
while the fool feeds on trash.

¹⁵ For the despondent, every day brings
trouble;

for the happy heart, life is a continual
feast.

¹⁶ Better to have little, with fear for the
LORD,
than to have great treasure and inner
turmoil.

¹⁷ A bowl of vegetables with someone
you love
is better than steak with someone
you hate.

¹⁸ A hot-tempered person starts fights;
a cool-tempered person stops them.

¹⁹ A lazy person's way is blocked with briers,
but the path of the upright is an open
highway.

²⁰ Sensible children bring joy to their father;
foolish children despise their mother.

²¹ Foolishness brings joy to those with no
sense;
a sensible person stays on the right path.

²² Plans go wrong for lack of advice;
many advisers bring success.

²³ Everyone enjoys a fitting reply;
it is wonderful to say the right thing at
the right time!

²⁴ The path of life leads upward for the wise;
they leave the grave* behind.

²⁵ The LORD tears down the house of the
proud,
but he protects the property of widows.

²⁶ The LORD detests evil plans,
but he delights in pure words.

²⁷ Greed brings grief to the whole family,
but those who hate bribes will live.

²⁸ The heart of the godly thinks carefully
before speaking;
the mouth of the wicked overflows with
evil words.

²⁹ The LORD is far from the wicked,
but he hears the prayers of the
righteous.

15:5 Hebrew *father's.*   15:11 Hebrew *Sheol and Abaddon.*   15:24 Hebrew *Sheol.*

30 A cheerful look brings joy to the heart;
  good news makes for good health.

31 If you listen to constructive criticism,
  you will be at home among the wise.

32 If you reject discipline, you only harm
    yourself;
  but if you listen to correction, you grow
    in understanding.

33 Fear of the LORD teaches wisdom;
  humility precedes honor.

16

1 We can make our own plans,
  but the LORD gives the right
    answer.

2 People may be pure in their own eyes,
  but the LORD examines their
    motives.

3 Commit your actions to the LORD,
  and your plans will succeed.

4 The LORD has made everything for his
    own purposes,
  even the wicked for a day of disaster.

5 The LORD detests the proud;
  they will surely be punished.

6 Unfailing love and faithfulness make
    atonement for sin.
  By fearing the LORD, people avoid
    evil.

7 When people's lives please the LORD,
  even their enemies are at peace with
    them.

8 Better to have little, with godliness,
  than to be rich and dishonest.

9 We can make our plans,
  but the LORD determines our steps.

10 The king speaks with divine wisdom;
  he must never judge unfairly.

11 The LORD demands accurate scales and
    balances;
  he sets the standards for fairness.

12 A king detests wrongdoing,
  for his rule is built on justice.

13 The king is pleased with words from
    righteous lips;
  he loves those who speak honestly.

14 The anger of the king is a deadly threat;
  the wise will try to appease it.

15 When the king smiles, there is life;
  his favor refreshes like a spring rain.

16 How much better to get wisdom than
    gold,
  and good judgment than silver!

17 The path of the virtuous leads away from
    evil;
  whoever follows that path is safe.

18 Pride goes before destruction,
  and haughtiness before a fall.

19 Better to live humbly with the poor
  than to share plunder with the proud.

20 Those who listen to instruction will
    prosper;
  those who trust the LORD will be
    joyful.

21 The wise are known for their
    understanding,
  and pleasant words are persuasive.

22 Discretion is a life-giving fountain to
    those who possess it,
  but discipline is wasted on fools.

23 From a wise mind comes wise speech;
  the words of the wise are persuasive.

24 Kind words are like honey—
  sweet to the soul and healthy for the
    body.

25 There is a path before each person that
    seems right,
  but it ends in death.

26 It is good for workers to have an appetite;
  an empty stomach drives them on.

27 Scoundrels create trouble;
  their words are a destructive blaze.

28 A troublemaker plants seeds of strife;
  gossip separates the best of friends.

29 Violent people mislead their companions,
   leading them down a harmful path.

30 With narrowed eyes, people plot evil;
   with a smirk, they plan their mischief.

31 Gray hair is a crown of glory;
   it is gained by living a godly life.

32 Better to be patient than powerful;
   better to have self-control than to
   conquer a city.

33 We may throw the dice,*
   but the LORD determines how they
   fall.

17

1 Better a dry crust eaten in peace
   than a house filled with
   feasting—and conflict.

2 A wise servant will rule over the master's
   disgraceful son
   and will share the inheritance of the
   master's children.

3 Fire tests the purity of silver and gold,
   but the LORD tests the heart.

4 Wrongdoers eagerly listen to gossip;
   liars pay close attention to slander.

5 Those who mock the poor insult their
   Maker;
   those who rejoice at the misfortune
   of others will be punished.

6 Grandchildren are the crowning glory
   of the aged;
   parents* are the pride of their children.

7 Eloquent words are not fitting for a fool;
   even less are lies fitting for a ruler.

8 A bribe is like a lucky charm;
   whoever gives one will prosper!

9 Love prospers when a fault is forgiven,
   but dwelling on it separates close
   friends.

10 A single rebuke does more for a person
   of understanding
   than a hundred lashes on the back
   of a fool.

11 Evil people are eager for rebellion,
   but they will be severely punished.

12 It is safer to meet a bear robbed of her cubs
   than to confront a fool caught in
   foolishness.

13 If you repay good with evil,
   evil will never leave your house.

14 Starting a quarrel is like opening a
   floodgate,
   so stop before a dispute breaks out.

15 Acquitting the guilty and condemning the
   innocent—
   both are detestable to the LORD.

16 It is senseless to pay to educate a fool,
   since he has no heart for learning.

17 A friend is always loyal,
   and a brother is born to help in time
   of need.

18 It's poor judgment to guarantee another
   person's debt
   or put up security for a friend.

19 Anyone who loves to quarrel loves sin;
   anyone who trusts in high walls invites
   disaster.

20 The crooked heart will not prosper;
   the lying tongue tumbles into trouble.

21 It is painful to be the parent of a fool;
   there is no joy for the father of a rebel.

22 A cheerful heart is good medicine,
   but a broken spirit saps a person's
   strength.

23 The wicked take secret bribes
   to pervert the course of justice.

24 Sensible people keep their eyes glued on
   wisdom,
   but a fool's eyes wander to the ends of
   the earth.

25 Foolish children* bring grief to their
   father
   and bitterness to the one who gave them
   birth.

16:33 Hebrew *We may cast lots.*   17:6 Hebrew *fathers.*   17:25 Hebrew *A foolish son.*

²⁶ It is wrong to punish the godly for being
good
 or to flog leaders for being
honest.

²⁷ A truly wise person uses few words;
 a person with understanding is
even-tempered.

²⁸ Even fools are thought wise when they
keep silent;
 with their mouths shut, they seem
intelligent.

18

¹ Unfriendly people care only about
themselves;
 they lash out at common sense.

² Fools have no interest in understanding;
 they only want to air their own
opinions.

³ Doing wrong leads to disgrace,
 and scandalous behavior brings
contempt.

⁴ Wise words are like deep waters;
 wisdom flows from the wise like a
bubbling brook.

⁵ It is not right to acquit the guilty
 or deny justice to the innocent.

⁶ Fools' words get them into constant
quarrels;
 they are asking for a beating.

⁷ The mouths of fools are their ruin;
 they trap themselves with their
lips.

⁸ Rumors are dainty morsels
 that sink deep into one's heart.

⁹ A lazy person is as bad as
 someone who destroys things.

¹⁰ The name of the LORD is a strong
fortress;
 the godly run to him and are safe.

¹¹ The rich think of their wealth as a strong
defense;
 they imagine it to be a high wall of
safety.

¹² Haughtiness goes before destruction;
 humility precedes honor.

¹³ Spouting off before listening to the facts
 is both shameful and foolish.

¹⁴ The human spirit can endure a sick body,
 but who can bear a crushed spirit?

¹⁵ Intelligent people are always ready to
learn.
 Their ears are open for knowledge.

¹⁶ Giving a gift can open doors;
 it gives access to important people!

¹⁷ The first to speak in court sounds right—
 until the cross-examination begins.

¹⁸ Flipping a coin* can end arguments;
 it settles disputes between powerful
opponents.

¹⁹ An offended friend is harder to win back
 than a fortified city.
 Arguments separate friends like a gate
locked with bars.

²⁰ Wise words satisfy like a good meal;
 the right words bring satisfaction.

²¹ The tongue can bring death or life;
 those who love to talk will reap the
consequences.

²² The man who finds a wife finds a treasure,
 and he receives favor from the LORD.

²³ The poor plead for mercy;
 the rich answer with insults.

²⁴ There are "friends" who destroy each
other,
 but a real friend sticks closer than a
brother.

19

¹ Better to be poor and honest
 than to be dishonest and a fool.

² Enthusiasm without knowledge is no good;
 haste makes mistakes.

³ People ruin their lives by their own
foolishness
 and then are angry at the LORD.

18:18 Hebrew *Casting lots.*

4 Wealth makes many "friends";
  poverty drives them all away.

5 A false witness will not go unpunished,
  nor will a liar escape.

6 Many seek favors from a ruler;
  everyone is the friend of a person who
    gives gifts!

7 The relatives of the poor despise them;
  how much more will their friends avoid
    them!
  Though the poor plead with them,
    their friends are gone.

8 To acquire wisdom is to love yourself;
  people who cherish understanding will
    prosper.

9 A false witness will not go unpunished,
  and a liar will be destroyed.

10 It isn't right for a fool to live in luxury
   or for a slave to rule over princes!

11 Sensible people control their temper;
   they earn respect by overlooking wrongs.

12 The king's anger is like a lion's roar,
   but his favor is like dew on the grass.

13 A foolish child* is a calamity to a father;
   a quarrelsome wife is as annoying as
     constant dripping.

14 Fathers can give their sons an inheritance
     of houses and wealth,
   but only the LORD can give an
     understanding wife.

15 Lazy people sleep soundly,
   but idleness leaves them hungry.

16 Keep the commandments and keep your
     life;
   despising them leads to death.

17 If you help the poor, you are lending to the
     LORD—
   and he will repay you!

18 Discipline your children while there is
     hope.
   Otherwise you will ruin their lives.

19:13 Hebrew *son;* also in 19:27.

19 Hot-tempered people must pay the
     penalty.
   If you rescue them once, you will have to
     do it again.

20 Get all the advice and instruction you can,
   so you will be wise the rest of your life.

21 You can make many plans,
   but the LORD's purpose will prevail.

22 Loyalty makes a person attractive.
   It is better to be poor than dishonest.

23 Fear of the LORD leads to life,
   bringing security and protection from
     harm.

24 Lazy people take food in their hand
   but don't even lift it to their mouth.

25 If you punish a mocker, the simpleminded
     will learn a lesson;
   if you correct the wise, they will be all
     the wiser.

26 Children who mistreat their father or
     chase away their mother
   are an embarrassment and a public
     disgrace.

27 If you stop listening to instruction, my
     child,
   you will turn your back on knowledge.

28 A corrupt witness makes a mockery of
     justice;
   the mouth of the wicked gulps down
     evil.

29 Punishment is made for mockers,
   and the backs of fools are made to
     be beaten.

20

1 Wine produces mockers; alcohol
    leads to brawls.
  Those led astray by drink cannot be
    wise.

2 The king's fury is like a lion's roar;
  to rouse his anger is to risk your
    life.

3 Avoiding a fight is a mark of honor;
  only fools insist on quarreling.

⁴ Those too lazy to plow in the right season
    will have no food at the harvest.

⁵ Though good advice lies deep within the
        heart,
    a person with understanding will draw
        it out.

⁶ Many will say they are loyal friends,
    but who can find one who is truly
        reliable?

⁷ The godly walk with integrity;
    blessed are their children who follow
        them.

⁸ When a king sits in judgment, he weighs
        all the evidence,
    distinguishing the bad from the
        good.

⁹ Who can say, "I have cleansed my heart;
    I am pure and free from sin"?

¹⁰ False weights and unequal measures*—
    the LORD detests double standards of
        every kind.

¹¹ Even children are known by the way
        they act,
    whether their conduct is pure, and
        whether it is right.

¹² Ears to hear and eyes to see—
    both are gifts from the LORD.

¹³ If you love sleep, you will end in poverty.
    Keep your eyes open, and there will be
        plenty to eat!

¹⁴ The buyer haggles over the price, saying,
        "It's worthless,"
    then brags about getting a bargain!

¹⁵ Wise words are more valuable
    than much gold and many rubies.

¹⁶ Get security from someone who
        guarantees a stranger's debt.
    Get a deposit if he does it for
        foreigners.*

¹⁷ Stolen bread tastes sweet,
    but it turns to gravel in the mouth.

¹⁸ Plans succeed through good counsel;
    don't go to war without wise advice.

¹⁹ A gossip goes around telling secrets,
    so don't hang around with chatterers.

²⁰ If you insult your father or mother,
    your light will be snuffed out in total
        darkness.

²¹ An inheritance obtained too early in life
    is not a blessing in the end.

²² Don't say, "I will get even for this wrong."
    Wait for the LORD to handle the matter.

²³ The LORD detests double standards;
    he is not pleased by dishonest scales.

²⁴ The LORD directs our steps,
    so why try to understand everything
        along the way?

²⁵ Don't trap yourself by making a rash
        promise to God
    and only later counting the cost.

²⁶ A wise king scatters the wicked like
        wheat,
    then runs his threshing wheel over
        them.

²⁷ The LORD's light penetrates the human
        spirit,*
    exposing every hidden motive.

²⁸ Unfailing love and faithfulness protect
        the king;
    his throne is made secure through
        love.

²⁹ The glory of the young is their strength;
    the gray hair of experience is the
        splendor of the old.

³⁰ Physical punishment cleanses away evil;*
    such discipline purifies the heart.

21 ¹ The king's heart is like a stream of
        water directed by the LORD;
    he guides it wherever he pleases.

² People may be right in their own eyes,
    but the LORD examines their heart.

20:10 Hebrew *A stone and a stone, an ephah and an ephah.*   20:16 An alternate reading in the Masoretic Text is *for a promiscuous woman.*   20:27 Or *The human spirit is the LORD's light.*   20:30 The meaning of the Hebrew is uncertain.

3 The LORD is more pleased when we do
    what is right and just
    than when we offer him sacrifices.

4 Haughty eyes, a proud heart,
    and evil actions are all sin.

5 Good planning and hard work lead to
    prosperity,
    but hasty shortcuts lead to poverty.

6 Wealth created by a lying tongue
    is a vanishing mist and a deadly
    trap.*

7 The violence of the wicked sweeps them
    away,
    because they refuse to do what is just.

8 The guilty walk a crooked path;
    the innocent travel a straight road.

9 It's better to live alone in the corner of an
    attic
    than with a quarrelsome wife in a lovely
    home.

10 Evil people desire evil;
    their neighbors get no mercy from
    them.

11 If you punish a mocker, the simpleminded
    become wise;
    if you instruct the wise, they will be all
    the wiser.

12 The Righteous One* knows what is going
    on in the homes of the wicked;
    he will bring disaster on them.

13 Those who shut their ears to the cries
    of the poor
    will be ignored in their own time
    of need.

14 A secret gift calms anger;
    a bribe under the table pacifies fury.

15 Justice is a joy to the godly,
    but it terrifies evildoers.

16 The person who strays from common
    sense
    will end up in the company of the
    dead.

17 Those who love pleasure become poor;
    those who love wine and luxury will
    never be rich.

18 The wicked are punished in place of the
    godly,
    and traitors in place of the honest.

19 It's better to live alone in the desert
    than with a quarrelsome, complaining
    wife.

20 The wise have wealth and luxury,
    but fools spend whatever they get.

21 Whoever pursues righteousness and
    unfailing love
    will find life, righteousness, and
    honor.

22 The wise conquer the city of the strong
    and level the fortress in which they
    trust.

23 Watch your tongue and keep your mouth
    shut,
    and you will stay out of trouble.

24 Mockers are proud and haughty;
    they act with boundless arrogance.

25 Despite their desires, the lazy will come
    to ruin,
    for their hands refuse to work.

26 Some people are always greedy for more,
    but the godly love to give!

27 The sacrifice of an evil person is detestable,
    especially when it is offered with wrong
    motives.

28 A false witness will be cut off,
    but a credible witness will be allowed
    to speak.

29 The wicked bluff their way through,
    but the virtuous think before they act.

30 No human wisdom or understanding
    or plan
    can stand against the LORD.

31 The horse is prepared for the day of battle,
    but the victory belongs to the LORD.

21:6 As in Greek version; Hebrew reads *mist for those who seek death.*   21:12 Or *The righteous man.*

22

¹ Choose a good reputation over great
    riches;
  being held in high esteem is better than
    silver or gold.

² The rich and poor have this in common:
  The LORD made them both.

³ A prudent person foresees danger and
    takes precautions.
  The simpleton goes blindly on and
    suffers the consequences.

⁴ True humility and fear of the LORD
  lead to riches, honor, and long life.

⁵ Corrupt people walk a thorny, treacherous
    road;
  whoever values life will avoid it.

⁶ Direct your children onto the right path,
    and when they are older, they will not
    leave it.

⁷ Just as the rich rule the poor,
  so the borrower is servant to the lender.

⁸ Those who plant injustice will harvest
    disaster,
  and their reign of terror will come to
    an end.*

⁹ Blessed are those who are generous,
  because they feed the poor.

¹⁰ Throw out the mocker, and fighting
    goes, too.
  Quarrels and insults will disappear.

¹¹ Whoever loves a pure heart and gracious
    speech
  will have the king as a friend.

¹² The LORD preserves those with
    knowledge,
  but he ruins the plans of the
    treacherous.

¹³ The lazy person claims, "There's a lion out
    there!
  If I go outside, I might be killed!"

¹⁴ The mouth of an immoral woman is a
    dangerous trap;

those who make the LORD angry will
    fall into it.

¹⁵ A youngster's heart is filled with
    foolishness,
  but physical discipline will drive it far
    away.

¹⁶ A person who gets ahead by oppressing
    the poor
  or by showering gifts on the rich will
    end in poverty.

Sayings of the Wise

¹⁷ Listen to the words of the wise;
  apply your heart to my instruction.
¹⁸ For it is good to keep these sayings in
    your heart
  and always ready on your lips.
¹⁹ I am teaching you today—yes, you—
  so you will trust in the LORD.
²⁰ I have written thirty sayings* for you,
  filled with advice and knowledge.
²¹ In this way, you may know the truth
  and take an accurate report to those
    who sent you.

²² Don't rob the poor just because you
    can,
  or exploit the needy in court.
²³ For the LORD is their defender.
  He will ruin anyone who ruins
    them.

²⁴ Don't befriend angry people
  or associate with hot-tempered people,
²⁵ or you will learn to be like them
  and endanger your soul.

²⁶ Don't agree to guarantee another person's
    debt
  or put up security for someone else.
²⁷ If you can't pay it,
  even your bed will be snatched from
    under you.

²⁸ Don't cheat your neighbor by moving the
    ancient boundary markers
  set up by previous generations.

²⁹ Do you see any truly competent workers?
  They will serve kings
  rather than working for ordinary
    people.

22:8 The Greek version includes an additional proverb: *God blesses a man who gives cheerfully, / but his worthless deeds will come to an end.* Compare 2 Cor 9:7. 22:20 Or *excellent sayings;* the meaning of the Hebrew is uncertain.

23

¹ While dining with a ruler,
pay attention to what is put
before you.
² If you are a big eater,
put a knife to your throat;
³ don't desire all the delicacies,
for he might be trying to trick you.

⁴ Don't wear yourself out trying to get rich.
Be wise enough to know when to quit.
⁵ In the blink of an eye wealth disappears,
for it will sprout wings
and fly away like an eagle.

⁶ Don't eat with people who are stingy;
don't desire their delicacies.
⁷ They are always thinking about how much
it costs.*
"Eat and drink," they say, but they don't
mean it.
⁸ You will throw up what little you've eaten,
and your compliments will be wasted.

⁹ Don't waste your breath on fools,
for they will despise the wisest advice.

¹⁰ Don't cheat your neighbor by moving the
ancient boundary markers;
don't take the land of defenseless
orphans.
¹¹ For their Redeemer* is strong;
he himself will bring their charges
against you.

¹² Commit yourself to instruction;
listen carefully to words of knowledge.

¹³ Don't fail to discipline your children.
The rod of punishment won't kill them.
¹⁴ Physical discipline
may well save them from death.*

¹⁵ My child,* if your heart is wise,
my own heart will rejoice!
¹⁶ Everything in me will celebrate
when you speak what is right.

¹⁷ Don't envy sinners,
but always continue to fear the LORD.
¹⁸ You will be rewarded for this;
your hope will not be disappointed.

¹⁹ My child, listen and be wise:
Keep your heart on the right course.

²⁰ Do not carouse with drunkards
or feast with gluttons,
²¹ for they are on their way to poverty,
and too much sleep clothes them
in rags.

²² Listen to your father, who gave you life,
and don't despise your mother when she
is old.
²³ Get the truth and never sell it;
also get wisdom, discipline, and good
judgment.

²⁴ The father of godly children has cause
for joy.
What a pleasure to have children who
are wise.*
²⁵ So give your father and mother joy!
May she who gave you birth be happy.

²⁶ O my son, give me your heart.
May your eyes take delight in following
my ways.
²⁷ A prostitute is a dangerous trap;
a promiscuous woman is as dangerous
as falling into a narrow well.
²⁸ She hides and waits like a robber,
eager to make more men unfaithful.

²⁹ Who has anguish? Who has sorrow?
Who is always fighting? Who is always
complaining?
Who has unnecessary bruises? Who has
bloodshot eyes?
³⁰ It is the one who spends long hours in the
taverns,
trying out new drinks.
³¹ Don't gaze at the wine, seeing how red
it is,
how it sparkles in the cup, how
smoothly it goes down.
³² For in the end it bites like a poisonous
snake;
it stings like a viper.
³³ You will see hallucinations,
and you will say crazy things.
³⁴ You will stagger like a sailor tossed
at sea,
clinging to a swaying mast.
³⁵ And you will say, "They hit me, but I didn't
feel it.
I didn't even know it when they beat
me up.
When will I wake up
so I can look for another drink?"

23:7 The meaning of the Hebrew is uncertain.   23:11 Or redeemer.   23:14 Hebrew from Sheol.   23:15 Hebrew My son; also
in 23:19.   23:24 Hebrew to have a wise son.

24

¹ Don't envy evil people
or desire their company.
² For their hearts plot violence,
and their words always stir up trouble.

³ A house is built by wisdom
and becomes strong through good
sense.
⁴ Through knowledge its rooms are filled
with all sorts of precious riches and
valuables.

⁵ The wise are mightier than the strong,*
and those with knowledge grow
stronger and stronger.
⁶ So don't go to war without wise guidance;
victory depends on having many
advisers.

⁷ Wisdom is too lofty for fools.
Among leaders at the city gate, they
have nothing to say.

⁸ A person who plans evil
will get a reputation as a troublemaker.
⁹ The schemes of a fool are sinful;
everyone detests a mocker.

¹⁰ If you fail under pressure,
your strength is too small.

¹¹ Rescue those who are unjustly sentenced
to die;
save them as they stagger to their death.
¹² Don't excuse yourself by saying, "Look, we
didn't know."
For God understands all hearts, and he
sees you.
He who guards your soul knows you knew.
He will repay all people as their actions
deserve.

¹³ My child,* eat honey, for it is good,
and the honeycomb is sweet to the
taste.
¹⁴ In the same way, wisdom is sweet to your
soul.
If you find it, you will have a bright
future,
and your hopes will not be cut short.

¹⁵ Don't wait in ambush at the home of the
godly,
and don't raid the house where the
godly live.
¹⁶ The godly may trip seven times, but they
will get up again.
But one disaster is enough to overthrow
the wicked.

¹⁷ Don't rejoice when your enemies fall;
don't be happy when they stumble.
¹⁸ For the LORD will be displeased with you
and will turn his anger away from
them.

¹⁹ Don't fret because of evildoers;
don't envy the wicked.
²⁰ For evil people have no future;
the light of the wicked will be snuffed
out.

²¹ My child, fear the LORD and the king.
Don't associate with rebels,
²² for disaster will hit them suddenly.
Who knows what punishment will come
from the LORD and the king?

More Sayings of the Wise

²³Here are some further sayings of the wise:

It is wrong to show favoritism when
passing judgment.
²⁴ A judge who says to the wicked, "You are
innocent,"
will be cursed by many people and
denounced by the nations.
²⁵ But it will go well for those who convict
the guilty;
rich blessings will be showered on them.

²⁶ An honest answer
is like a kiss of friendship.

²⁷ Do your planning and prepare your fields
before building your house.

²⁸ Don't testify against your neighbors
without cause;
don't lie about them.
²⁹ And don't say, "Now I can pay them back
for what they've done to me!
I'll get even with them!"

³⁰ I walked by the field of a lazy person,
the vineyard of one with no common
sense.
³¹ I saw that it was overgrown with nettles.
It was covered with weeds,
and its walls were broken down.

24:5 As in Greek version; Hebrew reads *A wise man is strength.* 24:13 Hebrew *My son;* also in 24:21.

³² Then, as I looked and thought about it,
   I learned this lesson:
³³ A little extra sleep, a little more slumber,
   a little folding of the hands to rest—
³⁴ then poverty will pounce on you like a
      bandit;
   scarcity will attack you like an armed
      robber.

More Proverbs of Solomon

25 These are more proverbs of Solomon,
collected by the advisers of King Hezekiah of Judah.

² It is God's privilege to conceal things
   and the king's privilege to discover them.

³ No one can comprehend the height of
      heaven, the depth of the earth,
   or all that goes on in the king's mind!

⁴ Remove the impurities from silver,
   and the sterling will be ready for the
      silversmith.
⁵ Remove the wicked from the king's court,
   and his reign will be made secure by
      justice.

⁶ Don't demand an audience with the king
   or push for a place among the great.
⁷ It's better to wait for an invitation to the
      head table
   than to be sent away in public disgrace.

Just because you've seen something,
⁸   don't be in a hurry to go to court.
For what will you do in the end
   if your neighbor deals you a shameful
      defeat?

⁹ When arguing with your neighbor,
   don't betray another person's secret.
¹⁰ Others may accuse you of gossip,
   and you will never regain your good
      reputation.

¹¹ Timely advice is lovely,
   like golden apples in a silver basket.

¹² To one who listens, valid criticism
   is like a gold earring or other gold jewelry.

¹³ Trustworthy messengers refresh like snow
      in summer.
   They revive the spirit of their employer.

¹⁴ A person who promises a gift but doesn't
      give it
   is like clouds and wind that bring no
      rain.

¹⁵ Patience can persuade a prince,
   and soft speech can break bones.

¹⁶ Do you like honey?
   Don't eat too much, or it will make
      you sick!

¹⁷ Don't visit your neighbors too often,
   or you will wear out your welcome.

¹⁸ Telling lies about others
   is as harmful as hitting them with
      an ax,
wounding them with a sword,
   or shooting them with a sharp
      arrow.

¹⁹ Putting confidence in an unreliable
      person in times of trouble
   is like chewing with a broken tooth
   or walking on a lame foot.

²⁰ Singing cheerful songs to a person with
      a heavy heart
   is like taking someone's coat in cold
      weather
   or pouring vinegar in a wound.*

²¹ If your enemies are hungry, give them food
      to eat.
   If they are thirsty, give them water to
      drink.
²² You will heap burning coals of shame on
      their heads,
   and the LORD will reward you.

²³ As surely as a north wind brings rain,
   so a gossiping tongue causes anger!

²⁴ It's better to live alone in the corner of an
      attic
   than with a quarrelsome wife in a lovely
      home.

²⁵ Good news from far away
   is like cold water to the thirsty.

²⁶ If the godly give in to the wicked,
   it's like polluting a fountain or
      muddying a spring.

25:20 As in Greek version; Hebrew reads *pouring vinegar on soda*.

27 It's not good to eat too much honey,
  and it's not good to seek honors for
    yourself.

28 A person without self-control
  is like a city with broken-down walls.

26

¹ Honor is no more associated
    with fools
  than snow with summer or rain
  with harvest.

² Like a fluttering sparrow or a darting
    swallow,
  an undeserved curse will not land on its
    intended victim.

³ Guide a horse with a whip, a donkey with
    a bridle,
  and a fool with a rod to his back!

⁴ Don't answer the foolish arguments of
    fools,
  or you will become as foolish as they are.

⁵ Be sure to answer the foolish arguments
    of fools,
  or they will become wise in their own
    estimation.

⁶ Trusting a fool to convey a message
  is like cutting off one's feet or drinking
    poison!

⁷ A proverb in the mouth of a fool
  is as useless as a paralyzed leg.

⁸ Honoring a fool
  is as foolish as tying a stone to a
    slingshot.

⁹ A proverb in the mouth of a fool
  is like a thorny branch brandished by
    a drunk.

¹⁰ An employer who hires a fool or a
    bystander
  is like an archer who shoots at random.

¹¹ As a dog returns to its vomit,
  so a fool repeats his foolishness.

¹² There is more hope for fools
  than for people who think they are
    wise.

¹³ The lazy person claims, "There's a lion on
    the road!
  Yes, I'm sure there's a lion out there!"

¹⁴ As a door swings back and forth on its
    hinges,
  so the lazy person turns over in bed.

¹⁵ Lazy people take food in their hand
  but don't even lift it to their mouth.

¹⁶ Lazy people consider themselves smarter
  than seven wise counselors.

¹⁷ Interfering in someone else's argument
  is as foolish as yanking a dog's ears.

¹⁸ Just as damaging
  as a madman shooting a deadly
    weapon
¹⁹ is someone who lies to a friend
  and then says, "I was only joking."

²⁰ Fire goes out without wood,
  and quarrels disappear when gossip
    stops.

²¹ A quarrelsome person starts fights
  as easily as hot embers light charcoal
  or fire lights wood.

²² Rumors are dainty morsels
  that sink deep into one's heart.

²³ Smooth* words may hide a wicked heart,
  just as a pretty glaze covers a clay pot.

²⁴ People may cover their hatred with
    pleasant words,
  but they're deceiving you.
²⁵ They pretend to be kind, but don't believe
    them.
  Their hearts are full of many evils.*
²⁶ While their hatred may be concealed by
    trickery,
  their wrongdoing will be exposed in
    public.

²⁷ If you set a trap for others,
  you will get caught in it yourself.
  If you roll a boulder down on others,
  it will crush you instead.

²⁸ A lying tongue hates its victims,
  and flattering words cause ruin.

26:23 As in Greek version; Hebrew reads *Burning.*   **26:25** Hebrew *seven evils.*

27

¹ Don't brag about tomorrow,
   since you don't know what the
   day will bring.

² Let someone else praise you, not your own
   mouth—
   a stranger, not your own lips.

³ A stone is heavy and sand is weighty,
   but the resentment caused by a fool is
   even heavier.

⁴ Anger is cruel, and wrath is like a flood,
   but jealousy is even more dangerous.

⁵ An open rebuke
   is better than hidden love!

⁶ Wounds from a sincere friend
   are better than many kisses from an
   enemy.

⁷ A person who is full refuses honey,
   but even bitter food tastes sweet to the
   hungry.

⁸ A person who strays from home
   is like a bird that strays from its nest.

⁹ The heartfelt counsel of a friend
   is as sweet as perfume and incense.

¹⁰ Never abandon a friend—
   either yours or your father's.
   When disaster strikes, you won't have to
   ask your brother for assistance.
   It's better to go to a neighbor than to a
   brother who lives far away.

¹¹ Be wise, my child,* and make my heart glad.
   Then I will be able to answer my critics.

¹² A prudent person foresees danger and
   takes precautions.
   The simpleton goes blindly on and
   suffers the consequences.

¹³ Get security from someone who
   guarantees a stranger's debt.
   Get a deposit if he does it for foreigners.*

¹⁴ A loud and cheerful greeting early in the
   morning
   will be taken as a curse!

¹⁵ A quarrelsome wife is as annoying
   as constant dripping on a rainy day.

¹⁶ Stopping her complaints is like trying to
   stop the wind
   or trying to hold something with
   greased hands.

¹⁷ As iron sharpens iron,
   so a friend sharpens a friend.

¹⁸ As workers who tend a fig tree are allowed
   to eat the fruit,
   so workers who protect their employer's
   interests will be rewarded.

¹⁹ As a face is reflected in water,
   so the heart reflects the real person.

²⁰ Just as Death and Destruction* are never
   satisfied,
   so human desire is never satisfied.

²¹ Fire tests the purity of silver and gold,
   but a person is tested by being praised.*

²² You cannot separate fools from their
   foolishness,
   even though you grind them like grain
   with mortar and pestle.

²³ Know the state of your flocks,
   and put your heart into caring for your
   herds,

²⁴ for riches don't last forever,
   and the crown might not be passed to
   the next generation.

²⁵ After the hay is harvested and the new
   crop appears
   and the mountain grasses are
   gathered in,

²⁶ your sheep will provide wool for
   clothing,
   and your goats will provide the price
   of a field.

²⁷ And you will have enough goats' milk for
   yourself,
   your family, and your servant girls.

28

¹ The wicked run away when no one
   is chasing them,
   but the godly are as bold as lions.

² When there is moral rot within a nation,
   its government topples easily.

27:11 Hebrew *my son.*   27:13 As in Greek and Latin versions (see also 20:16); Hebrew reads *for a promiscuous woman.*
27:20 Hebrew *Sheol and Abaddon.*   27:21 Or *by flattery.*

But wise and knowledgeable leaders
bring stability.

3 A poor person who oppresses the poor
is like a pounding rain that destroys the
crops.

4 To reject the law is to praise the wicked;
to obey the law is to fight them.

5 Evil people don't understand justice,
but those who follow the LORD
understand completely.

6 Better to be poor and honest
than to be dishonest and rich.

7 Young people who obey the law are wise;
those with wild friends bring shame to
their parents.*

8 Income from charging high interest rates
will end up in the pocket of someone
who is kind to the poor.

9 God detests the prayers
of a person who ignores the law.

10 Those who lead good people along an evil
path
will fall into their own trap,
but the honest will inherit good things.

11 Rich people may think they are wise,
but a poor person with discernment can
see right through them.

12 When the godly succeed, everyone is glad.
When the wicked take charge, people go
into hiding.

13 People who conceal their sins will not
prosper,
but if they confess and turn from them,
they will receive mercy.

14 Blessed are those who fear to do wrong,*
but the stubborn are headed for serious
trouble.

15 A wicked ruler is as dangerous to the poor
as a roaring lion or an attacking bear.

16 A ruler with no understanding will
oppress his people,

but one who hates corruption will have
a long life.

17 A murderer's tormented conscience will
drive him into the grave.
Don't protect him!

18 The blameless will be rescued from
harm,
but the crooked will be suddenly
destroyed.

19 A hard worker has plenty of food,
but a person who chases fantasies ends
up in poverty.

20 The trustworthy person will get a rich
reward,
but a person who wants quick riches
will get into trouble.

21 Showing partiality is never good,
yet some will do wrong for a mere piece
of bread.

22 Greedy people try to get rich quick
but don't realize they're headed for
poverty.

23 In the end, people appreciate honest
criticism
far more than flattery.

24 Anyone who steals from his father and
mother
and says, "What's wrong with that?"
is no better than a murderer.

25 Greed causes fighting;
trusting the LORD leads to prosperity.

26 Those who trust their own insight are
foolish,
but anyone who walks in wisdom
is safe.

27 Whoever gives to the poor will lack
nothing,
but those who close their eyes to poverty
will be cursed.

28 When the wicked take charge, people go
into hiding.
When the wicked meet disaster, the
godly flourish.

28:7 Hebrew *their father.*   28:14 Or *those who fear the LORD*; Hebrew reads *those who fear.*

29

¹ Whoever stubbornly refuses to
accept criticism
will suddenly be destroyed beyond
recovery.

² When the godly are in authority, the
people rejoice.
But when the wicked are in power, they
groan.

³ The man who loves wisdom brings joy to
his father,
but if he hangs around with prostitutes,
his wealth is wasted.

⁴ A just king gives stability to his nation,
but one who demands bribes destroys it.

⁵ To flatter friends
is to lay a trap for their feet.

⁶ Evil people are trapped by sin,
but the righteous escape, shouting for
joy.

⁷ The godly care about the rights of the
poor;
the wicked don't care at all.

⁸ Mockers can get a whole town agitated,
but the wise will calm anger.

⁹ If a wise person takes a fool to court,
there will be ranting and ridicule but no
satisfaction.

¹⁰ The bloodthirsty hate blameless people,
but the upright seek to help them.*

¹¹ Fools vent their anger,
but the wise quietly hold it back.

¹² If a ruler pays attention to liars,
all his advisers will be wicked.

¹³ The poor and the oppressor have this in
common—
the LORD gives sight to the eyes of both.

¹⁴ If a king judges the poor fairly,
his throne will last forever.

¹⁵ To discipline a child produces wisdom,
but a mother is disgraced by an
undisciplined child.

¹⁶ When the wicked are in authority, sin
flourishes,
but the godly will live to see their
downfall.

¹⁷ Discipline your children, and they will
give you peace of mind
and will make your heart glad.

¹⁸ When people do not accept divine
guidance, they run wild.
But whoever obeys the law is joyful.

¹⁹ Words alone will not discipline a servant;
the words may be understood, but they
are not heeded.

²⁰ There is more hope for a fool
than for someone who speaks without
thinking.

²¹ A servant pampered from childhood
will become a rebel.

²² An angry person starts fights;
a hot-tempered person commits all
kinds of sin.

²³ Pride ends in humiliation,
while humility brings honor.

²⁴ If you assist a thief, you only hurt yourself.
You are sworn to tell the truth, but you
dare not testify.

²⁵ Fearing people is a dangerous trap,
but trusting the LORD means safety.

²⁶ Many seek the ruler's favor,
but justice comes from the LORD.

²⁷ The righteous despise the unjust;
the wicked despise the godly.

The Sayings of Agur

30

The sayings of Agur son of Jakeh contain this message.*

I am weary, O God;
I am weary and worn out, O God.*

29:10 Or *The bloodthirsty hate blameless people, / and they seek to kill the upright;* Hebrew reads *The bloodthirsty hate blameless people;
/ as for the upright, they seek their life.*   30:1a Or *son of Jakeh from Massa;* or *son of Jakeh, an oracle.*   30:1b The Hebrew can also be
translated *The man declares this to Ithiel, / to Ithiel and to Ucal.*

2 I am too stupid to be human,
  and I lack common sense.
3 I have not mastered human wisdom,
  nor do I know the Holy One.

4 Who but God goes up to heaven and comes
    back down?
  Who holds the wind in his fists?
  Who wraps up the oceans in his cloak?
  Who has created the whole wide world?
  What is his name—and his son's name?
  Tell me if you know!

5 Every word of God proves true.
  He is a shield to all who come to him for
    protection.
6 Do not add to his words,
  or he may rebuke you and expose you
    as a liar.

7 O God, I beg two favors from you;
  let me have them before I die.
8 First, help me never to tell a lie.
  Second, give me neither poverty nor
    riches!
  Give me just enough to satisfy my
    needs.
9 For if I grow rich, I may deny you and say,
  "Who is the LORD?"
  And if I am too poor, I may steal and
    thus insult God's holy name.

10 Never slander a worker to the employer,
   or the person will curse you, and you
     will pay for it.

11 Some people curse their father
   and do not thank their mother.
12 They are pure in their own eyes,
   but they are filthy and unwashed.
13 They look proudly around,
   casting disdainful glances.
14 They have teeth like swords
   and fangs like knives.
   They devour the poor from the earth
   and the needy from among humanity.

15 The leech has two suckers
   that cry out, "More, more!"*

   There are three things that are never
     satisfied—
   no, four that never say, "Enough!":
16 the grave,*
   the barren womb,

the thirsty desert,
the blazing fire.

17 The eye that mocks a father
   and despises a mother's instructions
will be plucked out by ravens of the
     valley
   and eaten by vultures.

18 There are three things that amaze me—
   no, four things that I don't understand:
19 how an eagle glides through the sky,
   how a snake slithers on a rock,
   how a ship navigates the ocean,
   how a man loves a woman.

20 An adulterous woman consumes a man,
   then wipes her mouth and says,
   "What's wrong with that?"

21 There are three things that make the earth
     tremble—
   no, four it cannot endure:
22 a slave who becomes a king,
   an overbearing fool who prospers,
23   a bitter woman who finally gets a
     husband,
   a servant girl who supplants her
     mistress.

24 There are four things on earth that are
     small but unusually wise:
25 Ants—they aren't strong,
   but they store up food all summer.
26 Hyraxes*—they aren't powerful,
   but they make their homes among the
     rocks.
27 Locusts—they have no king,
   but they march in formation.
28 Lizards—they are easy to catch,
   but they are found even in kings'
     palaces.

29 There are three things that walk with
     stately stride—
   no, four that strut about:
30 the lion, king of animals, who won't turn
     aside for anything,
31   the strutting rooster,
   the male goat,
   a king as he leads his army.

32 If you have been a fool by being proud or
     plotting evil,
   cover your mouth in shame.

30:15 Hebrew *two daughters who cry out, "Give, give!"*   30:16 Hebrew *Sheol.*   30:26 Or *Coneys,* or *Rock badgers.*

³³ As the beating of cream yields butter
    and striking the nose causes bleeding,
    so stirring up anger causes quarrels.

The Sayings of King Lemuel

31 The sayings of King Lemuel contain this message,* which his mother taught him.

² O my son, O son of my womb,
    O son of my vows,
³ do not waste your strength on women,
    on those who ruin kings.

⁴ It is not for kings, O Lemuel, to guzzle
    wine.
    Rulers should not crave alcohol.
⁵ For if they drink, they may forget the law
    and not give justice to the oppressed.
⁶ Alcohol is for the dying,
    and wine for those in bitter distress.
⁷ Let them drink to forget their poverty
    and remember their troubles no more.

⁸ Speak up for those who cannot speak for
    themselves;
    ensure justice for those being crushed.
⁹ Yes, speak up for the poor and helpless,
    and see that they get justice.

A Wife of Noble Character

¹⁰*Who can find a virtuous and capable wife?
    She is more precious than rubies.
¹¹ Her husband can trust her,
    and she will greatly enrich his life.
¹² She brings him good, not harm,
    all the days of her life.

¹³ She finds wool and flax
    and busily spins it.
¹⁴ She is like a merchant's ship,
    bringing her food from afar.
¹⁵ She gets up before dawn to prepare
    breakfast for her household
    and plan the day's work for her servant
    girls.

¹⁶ She goes to inspect a field and buys it;
    with her earnings she plants a vineyard.

¹⁷ She is energetic and strong,
    a hard worker.
¹⁸ She makes sure her dealings are
    profitable;
    her lamp burns late into the night.

¹⁹ Her hands are busy spinning thread,
    her fingers twisting fiber.
²⁰ She extends a helping hand to the poor
    and opens her arms to the needy.
²¹ She has no fear of winter for her
    household,
    for everyone has warm* clothes.

²² She makes her own bedspreads.
    She dresses in fine linen and purple
    gowns.
²³ Her husband is well known at the city
    gates,
    where he sits with the other civic
    leaders.
²⁴ She makes belted linen garments
    and sashes to sell to the merchants.

²⁵ She is clothed with strength and
    dignity,
    and she laughs without fear of the
    future.
²⁶ When she speaks, her words are wise,
    and she gives instructions with
    kindness.
²⁷ She carefully watches everything in her
    household
    and suffers nothing from laziness.

²⁸ Her children stand and bless her.
    Her husband praises her:
²⁹ "There are many virtuous and capable
    women in the world,
    but you surpass them all!"

³⁰ Charm is deceptive, and beauty does not
    last;
    but a woman who fears the LORD will
    be greatly praised.
³¹ Reward her for all she has done.
    Let her deeds publicly declare her
    praise.

31:1 Or *of Lemuel, king of Massa*; or *of King Lemuel, an oracle.* **31:10** Verses 10-31 comprise a Hebrew acrostic poem; each verse begins with a successive letter of the Hebrew alphabet. **31:21** As in Greek and Latin versions; Hebrew reads *scarlet.*

Ecclesiastes

THERE ARE FEW EXPERIENCES in life that are more universal than disappointment. It seems as if everyone has experienced a broken promise, an unfulfilled expectation, or a shattered belief. The "Teacher" in the book of Ecclesiastes recorded his own experiences with disappointment as he tried to find peace apart from God. The Teacher uses a series of examples—wealth, wisdom, popularity, pleasure—and shows how each of them ultimately ends in disappointment if it becomes the sole reason for one's existence. After pondering this for several chapters, the author finally offers

- **Author:** Solomon, according to Jewish tradition
- **Date Written:** Uncertain, perhaps around 935 BC, late in Solomon's life
- **Purpose:** To teach that life is meaningless apart from God
- **Themes:** Searching, emptiness, injustice, work, death, wisdom
- **Outline**
  1:1-11 The pointless cycle of life
  1:12–2:23 The futility of life
  2:24–4:12 Weariness, oppression, and inhumanity
  4:13–6:12 The futility of popularity, religiosity, and wealth
  7:1–11:10 The futility of life
  12:1-14 Conclusion: Fear God and obey his commands

his conclusion: "Fear God and obey his commands, for this is everyone's duty" (12:13). It appears that the Teacher abandoned any hope in worldly pursuits and decided that glorifying God provides the only lasting meaning in life.

---

1 These are the words of the Teacher,* King David's son, who ruled in Jerusalem.

Everything Is Meaningless
2"Everything is meaningless," says the Teacher, "completely meaningless!"

3What do people get for all their hard work under the sun? 4Generations come and generations go, but the earth never changes. 5The sun rises and the sun sets, then hurries around to rise again. 6The wind blows south, and then turns north. Around and around it goes, blowing in circles. 7Rivers run into the sea, but the sea is never full. Then the water returns again to the rivers and flows out again to the sea. 8Everything is wearisome beyond description. No matter how much we see, we are never satisfied. No matter how much we hear, we are not content.

9History merely repeats itself. It has all been done before. Nothing under the sun is truly new. 10Sometimes people say, "Here is

something new!" But actually it is old; nothing is ever truly new. 11We don't remember what happened in the past, and in future generations, no one will remember what we are doing now.

The Teacher Speaks: The Futility of Wisdom
12I, the Teacher, was king of Israel, and I lived in Jerusalem. 13I devoted myself to search for understanding and to explore by wisdom everything being done under heaven. I soon discovered that God has dealt a tragic existence to the human race. 14I observed everything going on under the sun, and really, it is all meaningless—like chasing the wind.

15 What is wrong cannot be made right.
What is missing cannot be recovered.

16I said to myself, "Look, I am wiser than any of the kings who ruled in Jerusalem before me. I have greater wisdom and knowledge than any

1:1 Hebrew *Qoheleth*; this term is rendered "the Teacher" throughout this book.

of them." [17]So I set out to learn everything from wisdom to madness and folly. But I learned firsthand that pursuing all this is like chasing the wind.

[18] The greater my wisdom, the greater my grief.
To increase knowledge only increases sorrow.

The Futility of Pleasure

2 I said to myself, "Come on, let's try pleasure. Let's look for the 'good things' in life." But I found that this, too, was meaningless. [2]So I said, "Laughter is silly. What good does it do to seek pleasure?" [3]After much thought, I decided to cheer myself with wine. And while still seeking wisdom, I clutched at foolishness. In this way, I tried to experience the only happiness most people find during their brief life in this world.

[4]I also tried to find meaning by building huge homes for myself and by planting beautiful vineyards. [5]I made gardens and parks, filling them with all kinds of fruit trees. [6]I built reservoirs to collect the water to irrigate my many flourishing groves. [7]I bought slaves, both men and women, and others were born into my household. I also owned large herds and flocks, more than any of the kings who had lived in Jerusalem before me. [8]I collected great sums of silver and gold, the treasure of many kings and provinces. I hired wonderful singers, both men and women, and had many beautiful concubines. I had everything a man could desire!

[9]So I became greater than all who had lived in Jerusalem before me, and my wisdom never failed me. [10]Anything I wanted, I would take. I denied myself no pleasure. I even found great pleasure in hard work, a reward for all my labors. [11]But as I looked at everything I had worked so hard to accomplish, it was all so meaningless—like chasing the wind. There was nothing really worthwhile anywhere.

The Wise and the Foolish

[12]So I decided to compare wisdom with foolishness and madness (for who can do this better than I, the king?*). [13]I thought, "Wisdom is better than foolishness, just as light is better than darkness. [14]For the wise can see where they are going, but fools walk in the dark." Yet I saw that the wise and the foolish share the same fate. [15]Both will die. So I said to myself, "Since I will end up the same as the fool, what's the value of all my wisdom? This is all so meaningless!" [16]For the wise and the foolish both die. The wise will not be remembered any longer than the fool. In the days to come, both will be forgotten.

[17]So I came to hate life because everything done here under the sun is so troubling. Everything is meaningless—like chasing the wind.

The Futility of Work

[18]I came to hate all my hard work here on earth, for I must leave to others everything I have earned. [19]And who can tell whether my successors will be wise or foolish? Yet they will control everything I have gained by my skill and hard work under the sun. How meaningless! [20]So I gave up in despair, questioning the value of all my hard work in this world.

[21]Some people work wisely with knowledge and skill, then must leave the fruit of their efforts to someone who hasn't worked for it. This, too, is meaningless, a great tragedy. [22]So what do people get in this life for all their hard work and anxiety? [23]Their days of labor are filled with pain and grief; even at night their minds cannot rest. It is all meaningless.

[24]So I decided there is nothing better than to enjoy food and drink and to find satisfaction in work. Then I realized that these pleasures are from the hand of God. [25]For who can eat or enjoy anything apart from him?* [26]God gives wisdom, knowledge, and joy to those who please him. But if a sinner becomes wealthy, God takes the wealth away and gives it to those who please him. This, too, is meaningless—like chasing the wind.

A Time for Everything

3 [1] For everything there is a season,
    a time for every activity under
        heaven.
[2] A time to be born and a time to die.
    A time to plant and a time to harvest.
[3] A time to kill and a time to heal.
    A time to tear down and a time to
        build up.
[4] A time to cry and a time to laugh.
    A time to grieve and a time to dance.
[5] A time to scatter stones and a time to
        gather stones.
    A time to embrace and a time to turn
        away.
[6] A time to search and a time to quit
        searching.
    A time to keep and a time to throw away.

2:12 The meaning of the Hebrew is uncertain.   2:25 As in Greek and Syriac versions; Hebrew reads *apart from me?*

7 A time to tear and a time to mend.
  A time to be quiet and a time to speak.
8 A time to love and a time to hate.
  A time for war and a time for peace.

9What do people really get for all their hard work? 10I have seen the burden God has placed on us all. 11Yet God has made everything beautiful for its own time. He has planted eternity in the human heart, but even so, people cannot see the whole scope of God's work from beginning to end. 12So I concluded there is nothing better than to be happy and enjoy ourselves as long as we can. 13And people should eat and drink and enjoy the fruits of their labor, for these are gifts from God.

14And I know that whatever God does is final. Nothing can be added to it or taken from it. God's purpose is that people should fear him. 15What is happening now has happened before, and what will happen in the future has happened before, because God makes the same things happen over and over again.

The Injustices of Life

16I also noticed that under the sun there is evil in the courtroom. Yes, even the courts of law are corrupt! 17I said to myself, "In due season God will judge everyone, both good and bad, for all their deeds."

18I also thought about the human condition—how God proves to people that they are like animals. 19For people and animals share the same fate—both breathe* and both must die. So people have no real advantage over the animals. How meaningless! 20Both go to the same place—they came from dust and they return to dust. 21For who can prove that the human spirit goes up and the spirit of animals goes down into the earth? 22So I saw that there is nothing better for people than to be happy in their work. That is our lot in life. And no one can bring us back to see what happens after we die.

4 Again, I observed all the oppression that takes place under the sun. I saw the tears of the oppressed, with no one to comfort them. The oppressors have great power, and their victims are helpless. 2So I concluded that the dead are better off than the living. 3But most fortunate of all are those who are not yet born. For they have not seen all the evil that is done under the sun.

4Then I observed that most people are motivated to success because they envy their neighbors. But this, too, is meaningless—like chasing the wind.

5 "Fools fold their idle hands,
  leading them to ruin."

6And yet,

  "Better to have one handful with quietness
    than two handfuls with hard work
    and chasing the wind."

The Advantages of Companionship

7I observed yet another example of something meaningless under the sun. 8This is the case of a man who is all alone, without a child or a brother, yet who works hard to gain as much wealth as he can. But then he asks himself, "Who am I working for? Why am I giving up so much pleasure now?" It is all so meaningless and depressing.

9Two people are better off than one, for they can help each other succeed. 10If one person falls, the other can reach out and help. But someone who falls alone is in real trouble. 11Likewise, two people lying close together can keep each other warm. But how can one be warm alone? 12A person standing alone can be attacked and defeated, but two can stand back-to-back and conquer. Three are even better, for a triple-braided cord is not easily broken.

The Futility of Political Power

13It is better to be a poor but wise youth than an old and foolish king who refuses all advice. 14Such a youth could rise from poverty and succeed. He might even become king, though he has been in prison. 15But then everyone rushes to the side of yet another youth* who replaces him. 16Endless crowds stand around him,* but then another generation grows up and rejects him, too. So it is all meaningless—like chasing the wind.

Approaching God with Care

5 1*As you enter the house of God, keep your ears open and your mouth shut. It is evil to make mindless offerings to God. 2*Don't make rash promises, and don't be hasty in bringing matters before God. After all, God is in heaven, and you are here on earth. So let your words be few.

3:19 Or *both have the same spirit.* 4:15 Hebrew *the second youth.* 4:16 Hebrew *There is no end to all the people, to all those who are before them.* 5:1 Verse 5:1 is numbered 4:17 in Hebrew text. 5:2 Verses 5:2-20 are numbered 5:1-19 in Hebrew text.

³Too much activity gives you restless dreams; too many words make you a fool.

⁴When you make a promise to God, don't delay in following through, for God takes no pleasure in fools. Keep all the promises you make to him. ⁵It is better to say nothing than to make a promise and not keep it. ⁶Don't let your mouth make you sin. And don't defend yourself by telling the Temple messenger that the promise you made was a mistake. That would make God angry, and he might wipe out everything you have achieved.

⁷Talk is cheap, like daydreams and other useless activities. Fear God instead.

The Futility of Wealth

⁸Don't be surprised if you see a poor person being oppressed by the powerful and if justice is being miscarried throughout the land. For every official is under orders from higher up, and matters of justice get lost in red tape and bureaucracy. ⁹Even the king milks the land for his own profit!*

¹⁰Those who love money will never have enough. How meaningless to think that wealth brings true happiness! ¹¹The more you have, the more people come to help you spend it. So what good is wealth—except perhaps to watch it slip through your fingers!

¹²People who work hard sleep well, whether they eat little or much. But the rich seldom get a good night's sleep.

¹³There is another serious problem I have seen under the sun. Hoarding riches harms the saver. ¹⁴Money is put into risky investments that turn sour, and everything is lost. In the end, there is nothing left to pass on to one's children. ¹⁵We all come to the end of our lives as naked and empty-handed as on the day we were born. We can't take our riches with us.

¹⁶And this, too, is a very serious problem. People leave this world no better off than when they came. All their hard work is for nothing—like working for the wind. ¹⁷Throughout their lives, they live under a cloud—frustrated, discouraged, and angry.

¹⁸Even so, I have noticed one thing, at least, that is good. It is good for people to eat, drink, and enjoy their work under the sun during the short life God has given them, and to accept their lot in life. ¹⁹And it is a good thing to receive wealth from God and the good health to enjoy it. To enjoy your work and accept your lot in life—this is indeed a gift from God. ²⁰God keeps such people so busy

enjoying life that they take no time to brood over the past.

6 There is another serious tragedy I have seen under the sun, and it weighs heavily on humanity. ²God gives some people great wealth and honor and everything they could ever want, but then he doesn't give them the chance to enjoy these things. They die, and someone else, even a stranger, ends up enjoying their wealth! This is meaningless—a sickening tragedy.

³A man might have a hundred children and live to be very old. But if he finds no satisfaction in life and doesn't even get a decent burial, it would have been better for him to be born dead. ⁴His birth would have been meaningless, and he would have ended in darkness. He wouldn't even have had a name, ⁵and he would never have seen the sun or known of its existence. Yet he would have had more peace than in growing up to be an unhappy man. ⁶He might live a thousand years twice over but still not find contentment. And since he must die like everyone else—well, what's the use?

⁷All people spend their lives scratching for food, but they never seem to have enough. ⁸So are wise people really better off than fools? Do poor people gain anything by being wise and knowing how to act in front of others?

⁹Enjoy what you have rather than desiring what you don't have. Just dreaming about nice things is meaningless—like chasing the wind.

The Future—Determined and Unknown

¹⁰Everything has already been decided. It was known long ago what each person would be. So there's no use arguing with God about your destiny.

¹¹The more words you speak, the less they mean. So what good are they?

¹²In the few days of our meaningless lives, who knows how our days can best be spent? Our lives are like a shadow. Who can tell what will happen on this earth after we are gone?

Wisdom for Life

7 ¹ A good reputation is more valuable
　　than costly perfume.
　　And the day you die is better than the
　　　　day you are born.
² Better to spend your time at funerals than
　　　　at parties.
　　After all, everyone dies—
　　so the living should take this to heart.

5:9 The meaning of the Hebrew in verses 8 and 9 is uncertain.

³ Sorrow is better than laughter,
    for sadness has a refining influence
      on us.
⁴ A wise person thinks a lot about death,
    while a fool thinks only about having
      a good time.

⁵ Better to be criticized by a wise person
    than to be praised by a fool.
⁶ A fool's laughter is quickly gone,
    like thorns crackling in a fire.
    This also is meaningless.

⁷ Extortion turns wise people into fools,
    and bribes corrupt the heart.

⁸ Finishing is better than starting.
    Patience is better than pride.

⁹ Control your temper,
    for anger labels you a fool.

¹⁰ Don't long for "the good old days."
    This is not wise.

¹¹ Wisdom is even better when you have
    money.
    Both are a benefit as you go through life.
¹² Wisdom and money can get you almost
    anything,
    but only wisdom can save your life.

¹³ Accept the way God does things,
    for who can straighten what he has
      made crooked?
¹⁴ Enjoy prosperity while you can,
    but when hard times strike, realize that
      both come from God.
    Remember that nothing is certain in
      this life.

The Limits of Human Wisdom

¹⁵I have seen everything in this meaningless life, including the death of good young people and the long life of wicked people. ¹⁶So don't be too good or too wise! Why destroy yourself? ¹⁷On the other hand, don't be too wicked either. Don't be a fool! Why die before your time? ¹⁸Pay attention to these instructions, for anyone who fears God will avoid both extremes.*

¹⁹One wise person is stronger than ten leading citizens of a town!

²⁰Not a single person on earth is always good and never sins.

²¹Don't eavesdrop on others—you may hear

your servant curse you. ²²For you know how often you yourself have cursed others.

²³I have always tried my best to let wisdom guide my thoughts and actions. I said to myself, "I am determined to be wise." But it didn't work. ²⁴Wisdom is always distant and difficult to find. ²⁵I searched everywhere, determined to find wisdom and to understand the reason for things. I was determined to prove to myself that wickedness is stupid and that foolishness is madness.

²⁶I discovered that a seductive woman* is a trap more bitter than death. Her passion is a snare, and her soft hands are chains. Those who are pleasing to God will escape her, but sinners will be caught in her snare.

²⁷"This is my conclusion," says the Teacher. "I discovered this after looking at the matter from every possible angle. ²⁸Though I have searched repeatedly, I have not found what I was looking for. Only one out of a thousand men is virtuous, but not one woman! ²⁹But I did find this: God created people to be virtuous, but they have each turned to follow their own downward path."

8 ¹ How wonderful to be wise,
    to analyze and interpret things.
  Wisdom lights up a person's face,
    softening its harshness.

Obedience to the King

²Obey the king since you vowed to God that you would. ³Don't try to avoid doing your duty, and don't stand with those who plot evil, for the king can do whatever he wants. ⁴His command is backed by great power. No one can resist or question it. ⁵Those who obey him will not be punished. Those who are wise will find a time and a way to do what is right, ⁶for there is a time and a way for everything, even when a person is in trouble.

⁷Indeed, how can people avoid what they don't know is going to happen? ⁸None of us can hold back our spirit from departing. None of us has the power to prevent the day of our death. There is no escaping that obligation, that dark battle. And in the face of death, wickedness will certainly not rescue the wicked.

The Wicked and the Righteous

⁹I have thought deeply about all that goes on here under the sun, where people have the power to hurt each other. ¹⁰I have seen wicked people buried with honor. Yet they were the

7:18 Or *will follow them both.*   7:26 Hebrew *a woman.*

very ones who frequented the Temple and are now praised* in the same city where they committed their crimes! This, too, is meaningless. ¹¹When a crime is not punished quickly, people feel it is safe to do wrong. ¹²But even though a person sins a hundred times and still lives a long time, I know that those who fear God will be better off. ¹³The wicked will not prosper, for they do not fear God. Their days will never grow long like the evening shadows.

¹⁴And this is not all that is meaningless in our world. In this life, good people are often treated as though they were wicked, and wicked people are often treated as though they were good. This is so meaningless!

¹⁵So I recommend having fun, because there is nothing better for people in this world than to eat, drink, and enjoy life. That way they will experience some happiness along with all the hard work God gives them under the sun.

¹⁶In my search for wisdom and in my observation of people's burdens here on earth, I discovered that there is ceaseless activity, day and night. ¹⁷I realized that no one can discover everything God is doing under the sun. Not even the wisest people discover everything, no matter what they claim.

Death Comes to All

9 ¹This, too, I carefully explored: Even though the actions of godly and wise people are in God's hands, no one knows whether God will show them favor. ²The same destiny ultimately awaits everyone, whether righteous or wicked, good or bad,* ceremonially clean or unclean, religious or irreligious. Good people receive the same treatment as sinners, and people who make promises to God are treated like people who don't.

³It seems so wrong that everyone under the sun suffers the same fate. Already twisted by evil, people choose their own mad course, for they have no hope. There is nothing ahead but death anyway. ⁴There is hope only for the living. As they say, "It's better to be a live dog than a dead lion!"

⁵The living at least know they will die, but the dead know nothing. They have no further reward, nor are they remembered. ⁶Whatever they did in their lifetime—loving, hating, envying—is all long gone. They no longer play a part in anything here on earth. ⁷So go ahead. Eat your food with joy, and drink your

wine with a happy heart, for God approves of this! ⁸Wear fine clothes, with a splash of cologne!

⁹Live happily with the woman you love through all the meaningless days of life that God has given you under the sun. The wife God gives you is your reward for all your earthly toil. ¹⁰Whatever you do, do well. For when you go to the grave,* there will be no work or planning or knowledge or wisdom.

¹¹I have observed something else under the sun. The fastest runner doesn't always win the race, and the strongest warrior doesn't always win the battle. The wise sometimes go hungry, and the skillful are not necessarily wealthy. And those who are educated don't always lead successful lives. It is all decided by chance, by being in the right place at the right time.

¹²People can never predict when hard times might come. Like fish in a net or birds in a trap, people are caught by sudden tragedy.

Thoughts on Wisdom and Folly

¹³Here is another bit of wisdom that has impressed me as I have watched the way our world works. ¹⁴There was a small town with only a few people, and a great king came with his army and besieged it. ¹⁵A poor, wise man knew how to save the town, and so it was rescued. But afterward no one thought to thank him. ¹⁶So even though wisdom is better than strength, those who are wise will be despised if they are poor. What they say will not be appreciated for long.

¹⁷ Better to hear the quiet words of a wise
    person
        than the shouts of a foolish king.
¹⁸ Better to have wisdom than weapons
      of war,
        but one sinner can destroy much that
        is good.

10 ¹ As dead flies cause even a bottle
      of perfume to stink,
  so a little foolishness spoils great
    wisdom and honor.

² A wise person chooses the right road;
    a fool takes the wrong one.

³ You can identify fools
    just by the way they walk down the
      street!

8:10 As in some Hebrew manuscripts and Greek version; many Hebrew manuscripts read *and are forgotten.* 9:2 As in Greek and Syriac versions and Latin Vulgate; Hebrew lacks *or bad.* 9:10 Hebrew *to Sheol.*

4 If your boss is angry at you, don't quit!
  A quiet spirit can overcome even great
    mistakes.

The Ironies of Life

5There is another evil I have seen under the
sun. Kings and rulers make a grave mistake
6when they give great authority to foolish
people and low positions to people of proven
worth. 7I have even seen servants riding horseback like princes—and princes walking like
servants!

8 When you dig a well,
    you might fall in.
  When you demolish an old wall,
    you could be bitten by a snake.
9 When you work in a quarry,
    stones might fall and crush you.
  When you chop wood,
    there is danger with each stroke of
      your ax.

10 Using a dull ax requires great strength,
    so sharpen the blade.
  That's the value of wisdom;
    it helps you succeed.

11 If a snake bites before you charm it,
    what's the use of being a snake charmer?

12 Wise words bring approval,
    but fools are destroyed by their own
      words.

13 Fools base their thoughts on foolish
      assumptions,
    so their conclusions will be wicked
      madness;
14   they chatter on and on.

  No one really knows what is going to
      happen;
    no one can predict the future.

15 Fools are so exhausted by a little work
    that they can't even find their way
      home.

16 What sorrow for the land ruled by a
      servant,*
    the land whose leaders feast in the
      morning.

17 Happy is the land whose king is a noble
      leader
    and whose leaders feast at the proper
      time
    to gain strength for their work, not to
      get drunk.

18 Laziness leads to a sagging roof;
    idleness leads to a leaky house.

19 A party gives laughter,
    wine gives happiness,
    and money gives everything!

20 Never make light of the king, even in your
      thoughts.
    And don't make fun of the powerful,
      even in your own bedroom.
    For a little bird might deliver your
      message
    and tell them what you said.

The Uncertainties of Life

11 1 Send your grain across the seas,
    and in time, profits will flow back
      to you.*
2 But divide your investments among many
      places,*
    for you do not know what risks might
      lie ahead.

3 When clouds are heavy, the rains come
      down.
    Whether a tree falls north or south, it
      stays where it falls.

4 Farmers who wait for perfect weather
    never plant.
  If they watch every cloud, they never
    harvest.

5Just as you cannot understand the path of
the wind or the mystery of a tiny baby growing
in its mother's womb,* so you cannot understand the activity of God, who does all things.
6Plant your seed in the morning and keep
busy all afternoon, for you don't know if profit
will come from one activity or another—or
maybe both.

Advice for Young and Old

7Light is sweet; how pleasant to see a new day
dawning.

10:16 Or a child.   11:1 Or Give generously, / for your gifts will return to you later. Hebrew reads Throw your bread on the waters, / for
after many days you will find it again.   11:2 Hebrew among seven or even eight.   11:5 Some manuscripts read Just as you cannot
understand how breath comes to a tiny baby in its mother's womb.

8When people live to be very old, let them rejoice in every day of life. But let them also remember there will be many dark days. Everything still to come is meaningless.

9Young people,* it's wonderful to be young! Enjoy every minute of it. Do everything you want to do; take it all in. But remember that you must give an account to God for everything you do. 10So refuse to worry, and keep your body healthy. But remember that youth, with a whole life before you, is meaningless.

12 Don't let the excitement of youth cause you to forget your Creator. Honor him in your youth before you grow old and say, "Life is not pleasant anymore." 2Remember him before the light of the sun, moon, and stars is dim to your old eyes, and rain clouds continually darken your sky. 3Remember him before your legs—the guards of your house—start to tremble; and before your shoulders—the strong men—stoop. Remember him before your teeth—your few remaining servants—stop grinding; and before your eyes—the women looking through the windows—see dimly.

4Remember him before the door to life's opportunities is closed and the sound of work fades. Now you rise at the first chirping of the birds, but then all their sounds will grow faint.

5Remember him before you become fearful of falling and worry about danger in the streets; before your hair turns white like an almond tree in bloom, and you drag along without energy like a dying grasshopper, and the caperberry no longer inspires sexual desire. Remember him before you near the grave, your everlasting home, when the mourners will weep at your funeral.

6Yes, remember your Creator now while you are young, before the silver cord of life snaps and the golden bowl is broken. Don't wait until the water jar is smashed at the spring and the pulley is broken at the well. 7For then the dust will return to the earth, and the spirit will return to God who gave it.

Concluding Thoughts about the Teacher

8"Everything is meaningless," says the Teacher, "completely meaningless."

9Keep this in mind: The Teacher was considered wise, and he taught the people everything he knew. He listened carefully to many proverbs, studying and classifying them. 10The Teacher sought to find just the right words to express truths clearly.*

11The words of the wise are like cattle prods—painful but helpful. Their collected sayings are like a nail-studded stick with which a shepherd* drives the sheep.

12But, my child,* let me give you some further advice: Be careful, for writing books is endless, and much study wears you out.

13That's the whole story. Here now is my final conclusion: Fear God and obey his commands, for this is everyone's duty. 14God will judge us for everything we do, including every secret thing, whether good or bad.

11:9 Hebrew Young man.   12:10 Or sought to write what was upright and true.   12:11 Or one shepherd.   12:12 Hebrew my son.

Song of Songs

POPULAR SEXUAL BEHAVIOR today is a sad distortion of the plan God established in the Garden of Eden. Contrary to God's design, sex has become a freely traded commodity rather than an exclusive, private treasure shared between a committed husband and wife. God values romantic love and sexual union, and the Song of Songs expresses the beauty of this love as God intended it. The headings identifying the various speakers are not in the original text but were added by the editors to show the interactions between Solomon and the young woman. This is a song that uses vivid metaphors to describe love, courtship, and marriage. These poetic verses

- **Author:** Solomon, according to Jewish tradition
- **Date Written:** Uncertain, perhaps around 960 BC, early in Solomon's reign
- **Purpose:** To celebrate romantic love as God intended it and to picture God's love for his people
- **Themes:** The joys of romantic love, commitment, beauty, intimacy
- **Outline**
  1:1–2:7 The bride describes herself and her feelings for her fiancé
  2:8–3:11 The king invites his bride for a springtime trip; the bride dreams of losing the king
  4:1–5:1 Solomon describes his bride
  5:2–6:3 The bride describes her husband
  6:4–7:9 The king describes his wife
  7:10–8:4 The desires of the woman
  8:5-14 The power of love and the rewards of purity

describe a couple's desire for each other, the struggles they overcome, the tender feelings love awakens in them, and the joy they find in being together. The young women of Jerusalem also add some observations of their own. Many scholars believe this poem should also be understood as an illustration of Christ's love for the Church.

---

1 This is Solomon's song of songs, more wonderful than any other.

*Young Woman**
2 Kiss me and kiss me again,
  for your love is sweeter than wine.
3 How pleasing is your fragrance;
  your name is like the spreading fragrance of scented oils.
  No wonder all the young women love you!
4 Take me with you; come, let's run!
  The king has brought me into his bedroom.

Young Women of Jerusalem
  How happy we are for you, O king.
  We praise your love even more than wine.

Young Woman
  How right they are to adore you.

5 I am dark but beautiful,
  O women of Jerusalem—
dark as the tents of Kedar,
  dark as the curtains of Solomon's tents.
6 Don't stare at me because I am dark—
  the sun has darkened my skin.
  My brothers were angry with me;

1:1 The headings identifying the speakers are not in the original text, though the Hebrew usually gives clues by means of the gender of the person speaking.

they forced me to care for their
  vineyards,
so I couldn't care for myself—my own
  vineyard.

7 Tell me, my love, where are you leading
  your flock today?
Where will you rest your sheep at noon?
For why should I wander like a prostitute*
  among your friends and their flocks?

Young Man
8 If you don't know, O most beautiful
  woman,
  follow the trail of my flock,
  and graze your young goats by the
    shepherds' tents.
9 You are as exciting, my darling,
  as a mare among Pharaoh's stallions.
10 How lovely are your cheeks;
  your earrings set them afire!
How lovely is your neck,
  enhanced by a string of jewels.
11 We will make for you earrings of gold
  and beads of silver.

Young Woman
12 The king is lying on his couch,
  enchanted by the fragrance of my
    perfume.
13 My lover is like a sachet of myrrh
  lying between my breasts.
14 He is like a bouquet of sweet henna
  blossoms
  from the vineyards of En-gedi.

Young Man
15 How beautiful you are, my darling,
  how beautiful!
Your eyes are like doves.

Young Woman
16 You are so handsome, my love,
  pleasing beyond words!
The soft grass is our bed;
17 fragrant cedar branches are the beams
    of our house,
  and pleasant smelling firs are the
    rafters.

Young Woman
2 1 I am the spring crocus blooming on the
    Sharon Plain,*
  the lily of the valley.

Young Man
2 Like a lily among thistles
  is my darling among young women.

Young Woman
3 Like the finest apple tree in the orchard
  is my lover among other young men.
I sit in his delightful shade
  and taste his delicious fruit.
4 He escorts me to the banquet hall;
  it's obvious how much he loves me.
5 Strengthen me with raisin cakes,
  refresh me with apples,
  for I am weak with love.
6 His left arm is under my head,
  and his right arm embraces me.

7 Promise me, O women of Jerusalem,
  by the gazelles and wild deer,
  not to awaken love until the time is
    right.*

8 Ah, I hear my lover coming!
  He is leaping over the mountains,
  bounding over the hills.
9 My lover is like a swift gazelle
  or a young stag.
Look, there he is behind the wall,
  looking through the window,
  peering into the room.

10 My lover said to me,
  "Rise up, my darling!
  Come away with me, my fair one!
11 Look, the winter is past,
  and the rains are over and gone.
12 The flowers are springing up,
  the season of singing birds* has
    come,
  and the cooing of turtledoves fills
    the air.
13 The fig trees are forming young fruit,
  and the fragrant grapevines are
    blossoming.
  Rise up, my darling!
  Come away with me, my fair one!"

Young Man
14 My dove is hiding behind the rocks,
  behind an outcrop on the cliff.
Let me see your face;
  let me hear your voice.
For your voice is pleasant,
  and your face is lovely.

1:7 Hebrew *like a veiled woman.*   2:1 Traditionally rendered *I am the rose of Sharon.* Sharon Plain is a region in the coastal plain
of Palestine.   2:7 Or *not to awaken love until it is ready.*   2:12 Or *the season of pruning vines.*

Young Women of Jerusalem
15 Catch all the foxes,
    those little foxes,
before they ruin the vineyard of love,
    for the grapevines are blossoming!

Young Woman
16 My lover is mine, and I am his.
    He browses among the lilies.
17 Before the dawn breezes blow
    and the night shadows flee,
return to me, my love, like a gazelle
    or a young stag on the rugged
        mountains.*

Young Woman
3 1 One night as I lay in bed, I yearned for
    my lover.
I yearned for him, but he did not come.
2 So I said to myself, "I will get up and roam
    the city,
searching in all its streets and squares.
I will search for the one I love."
    So I searched everywhere but did not
        find him.
3 The watchmen stopped me as they made
    their rounds,
and I asked, "Have you seen the one
    I love?"
4 Then scarcely had I left them
    when I found my love!
I caught and held him tightly,
    then I brought him to my mother's
        house,
    into my mother's bed, where I had been
        conceived.

5 Promise me, O women of Jerusalem,
    by the gazelles and wild deer,
not to awaken love until the time is
    right.*

Young Women of Jerusalem
6 Who is this sweeping in from the
    wilderness
    like a cloud of smoke?
Who is it, fragrant with myrrh and
    frankincense
    and every kind of spice?
7 Look, it is Solomon's carriage,
    surrounded by sixty heroic men,
    the best of Israel's soldiers.
8 They are all skilled swordsmen,
    experienced warriors.

Each wears a sword on his thigh,
    ready to defend the king against an
        attack in the night.
9 King Solomon's carriage is built
    of wood imported from Lebanon.
10 Its posts are silver,
    its canopy gold;
    its cushions are purple.
It was decorated with love
    by the young women of Jerusalem.

Young Woman
11 Come out to see King Solomon,
    young women of Jerusalem.*
He wears the crown his mother gave him
    on his wedding day,
    his most joyous day.

Young Man
4 1 You are beautiful, my darling,
    beautiful beyond words.
Your eyes are like doves
    behind your veil.
Your hair falls in waves,
    like a flock of goats winding down the
        slopes of Gilead.
2 Your teeth are as white as sheep,
    recently shorn and freshly washed.
Your smile is flawless,
    each tooth matched with its twin.*
3 Your lips are like scarlet ribbon;
    your mouth is inviting.
Your cheeks are like rosy pomegranates
    behind your veil.
4 Your neck is as beautiful as the tower of
    David,
    jeweled with the shields of a thousand
        heroes.
5 Your breasts are like two fawns,
    twin fawns of a gazelle grazing among
        the lilies.
6 Before the dawn breezes blow
    and the night shadows flee,
I will hurry to the mountain of myrrh
    and to the hill of frankincense.
7 You are altogether beautiful, my darling,
    beautiful in every way.

8 Come with me from Lebanon, my bride,
    come with me from Lebanon.
Come down* from Mount Amana,
    from the peaks of Senir and Hermon,
where the lions have their dens
    and leopards live among the hills.

2:17 Or *on the hills of Bether.*   3:5 Or *not to awaken love until it is ready.*   3:11 Hebrew *of Zion.*   4:2 Hebrew *Not one is missing; each has a twin.*   4:8 Or *Look down.*

⁹ You have captured my heart,
    my treasure,* my bride.
You hold it hostage with one glance of
    your eyes,
    with a single jewel of your necklace.
¹⁰ Your love delights me,
    my treasure, my bride.
Your love is better than wine,
    your perfume more fragrant than
    spices.
¹¹ Your lips are as sweet as nectar, my bride.
    Honey and milk are under your tongue.
Your clothes are scented
    like the cedars of Lebanon.

¹² You are my private garden, my treasure,
    my bride,
    a secluded spring, a hidden fountain.
¹³ Your thighs shelter a paradise of
    pomegranates
    with rare spices—
henna with nard,
¹⁴   nard and saffron,
    fragrant calamus and cinnamon,
with all the trees of frankincense, myrrh,
    and aloes,
    and every other lovely spice.
¹⁵ You are a garden fountain,
    a well of fresh water
    streaming down from Lebanon's
    mountains.

Young Woman
¹⁶ Awake, north wind!
    Rise up, south wind!
Blow on my garden
    and spread its fragrance all around.
Come into your garden, my love;
    taste its finest fruits.

Young Man
5 ¹ I have entered my garden, my treasure,*
    my bride!
I gather myrrh with my spices
and eat honeycomb with my honey.
    I drink wine with my milk.

Young Women of Jerusalem
    Oh, lover and beloved, eat and drink!
    Yes, drink deeply of your love!

Young Woman
² I slept, but my heart was awake,
    when I heard my lover knocking and
    calling:

"Open to me, my treasure, my darling,
    my dove, my perfect one.
My head is drenched with dew,
    my hair with the dampness of the
    night."

³ But I responded,
    "I have taken off my robe.
    Should I get dressed again?
I have washed my feet.
    Should I get them soiled?"

⁴ My lover tried to unlatch the door,
    and my heart thrilled within me.
⁵ I jumped up to open the door for my love,
    and my hands dripped with perfume.
My fingers dripped with lovely myrrh
    as I pulled back the bolt.
⁶ I opened to my lover,
    but he was gone!
    My heart sank.
I searched for him
    but could not find him anywhere.
I called to him,
    but there was no reply.
⁷ The night watchmen found me
    as they made their rounds.
They beat and bruised me
    and stripped off my veil,
    those watchmen on the walls.

⁸ Make this promise, O women of
    Jerusalem—
    If you find my lover,
    tell him I am weak with love.

Young Women of Jerusalem
⁹ Why is your lover better than all others,
    O woman of rare beauty?
What makes your lover so special
    that we must promise this?

Young Woman
¹⁰ My lover is dark and dazzling,
    better than ten thousand others!
¹¹ His head is finest gold,
    his wavy hair is black as a raven.
¹² His eyes sparkle like doves
    beside springs of water;
they are set like jewels
    washed in milk.
¹³ His cheeks are like gardens of spices
    giving off fragrance.
His lips are like lilies,
    perfumed with myrrh.

4:9 Hebrew *my sister;* also in 4:10, 12.   5:1 Hebrew *my sister;* also in 5:2.

14 His arms are like rounded bars of gold,
      set with beryl.
   His body is like bright ivory,
      glowing with lapis lazuli.
15 His legs are like marble pillars
      set in sockets of finest gold.
   His posture is stately,
      like the noble cedars of Lebanon.
16 His mouth is sweetness itself;
      he is desirable in every way.
   Such, O women of Jerusalem,
      is my lover, my friend.

Young Women of Jerusalem

6 1 Where has your lover gone,
         O woman of rare beauty?
   Which way did he turn
      so we can help you find him?

Young Woman

2 My lover has gone down to his garden,
      to his spice beds,
   to browse in the gardens
      and gather the lilies.
3 I am my lover's, and my lover is mine.
   He browses among the lilies.

Young Man

4 You are beautiful, my darling,
      like the lovely city of Tirzah.
   Yes, as beautiful as Jerusalem,
      as majestic as an army with billowing
      banners.
5 Turn your eyes away,
      for they overpower me.
   Your hair falls in waves,
      like a flock of goats winding down the
      slopes of Gilead.
6 Your teeth are as white as sheep
      that are freshly washed.
   Your smile is flawless,
      each tooth matched with its twin.*
7 Your cheeks are like rosy pomegranates
      behind your veil.

8 Even among sixty queens
      and eighty concubines
      and countless young women,
9 I would still choose my dove, my perfect
      one—
   the favorite of her mother,
      dearly loved by the one who bore her.

   The young women see her and praise her;
      even queens and royal concubines sing
      her praises:
10 "Who is this, arising like the dawn,
      as fair as the moon,
   as bright as the sun,
      as majestic as an army with billowing
      banners?"

Young Woman

11 I went down to the grove of walnut trees
      and out to the valley to see the new
         spring growth,
   to see whether the grapevines had budded
      or the pomegranates were in bloom.
12 Before I realized it,
      my strong desires had taken me to the
         chariot of a noble man.*

Young Women of Jerusalem

13*Return, return to us, O maid of Shulam.
      Come back, come back, that we may see
         you again.

Young Man

   Why do you stare at this young woman of
      Shulam,
      as she moves so gracefully between two
         lines of dancers?*

7 1*How beautiful are your sandaled feet,
         O queenly maiden.
   Your rounded thighs are like jewels,
      the work of a skilled craftsman.
2 Your navel is perfectly formed
      like a goblet filled with mixed wine.
   Between your thighs lies a mound of
      wheat
      bordered with lilies.
3 Your breasts are like two fawns,
      twin fawns of a gazelle.
4 Your neck is as beautiful as an ivory
      tower.
   Your eyes are like the sparkling pools
      in Heshbon
      by the gate of Bath-rabbim.
   Your nose is as fine as the tower of Lebanon
      overlooking Damascus.
5 Your head is as majestic as Mount Carmel,
      and the sheen of your hair radiates
         royalty.
   The king is held captive by its tresses.

6:6 Hebrew *Not one is missing; each has a twin.*   6:12 Or *to the royal chariots of my people,* or *to the chariots of Amminadab.* The
meaning of the Hebrew is uncertain.   6:13a Verse 6:13 is numbered 7:1 in Hebrew text.   6:13b Or *as you would at the*
movements of two armies? or *as you would at the dance of Mahanaim?* The meaning of the Hebrew is uncertain.   7:1 Verses 7:1-13
are numbered 7:2-14 in Hebrew text.

⁶ Oh, how beautiful you are!
How pleasing, my love, how full of
delights!
⁷ You are slender like a palm tree,
and your breasts are like its clusters
of fruit.
⁸ I said, "I will climb the palm tree
and take hold of its fruit."
May your breasts be like grape clusters,
and the fragrance of your breath like
apples.
⁹ May your kisses be as exciting as the best
wine—

Young Woman
Yes, wine that goes down smoothly for my
lover,
flowing gently over lips and teeth.*
¹⁰ I am my lover's,
and he claims me as his own.
¹¹ Come, my love, let us go out to the fields
and spend the night among the
wildflowers.*
¹² Let us get up early and go to the vineyards
to see if the grapevines have budded,
if the blossoms have opened,
and if the pomegranates have bloomed.
There I will give you my love.
¹³ There the mandrakes give off their
fragrance,
and the finest fruits are at our door,
new delights as well as old,
which I have saved for you, my lover.

Young Woman
8 ¹ Oh, I wish you were my brother,
who nursed at my mother's breasts.
Then I could kiss you no matter who was
watching,
and no one would criticize me.
² I would bring you to my childhood home,
and there you would teach me.*
I would give you spiced wine to drink,
my sweet pomegranate wine.
³ Your left arm would be under my head,
and your right arm would embrace me.
⁴ Promise me, O women of Jerusalem,
not to awaken love until the time is
right.*

Young Women of Jerusalem
⁵ Who is this sweeping in from the desert,
leaning on her lover?

Young Woman
I aroused you under the apple tree,
where your mother gave you birth,
where in great pain she delivered you.
⁶ Place me like a seal over your heart,
like a seal on your arm.
For love is as strong as death,
its jealousy* as enduring as the grave.*
Love flashes like fire,
the brightest kind of flame.
⁷ Many waters cannot quench love,
nor can rivers drown it.
If a man tried to buy love
with all his wealth,
his offer would be utterly scorned.

The Young Woman's Brothers
⁸ We have a little sister
too young to have breasts.
What will we do for our sister
if someone asks to marry her?
⁹ If she is a virgin, like a wall,
we will protect her with a silver tower.
But if she is promiscuous, like a swinging
door,
we will block her door with a cedar bar.

Young Woman
¹⁰ I was a virgin, like a wall;
now my breasts are like towers.
When my lover looks at me,
he is delighted with what he sees.

¹¹ Solomon has a vineyard at Baal-hamon,
which he leases out to tenant farmers.
Each of them pays a thousand pieces
of silver
for harvesting its fruit.
¹² But my vineyard is mine to give,
and Solomon need not pay a thousand
pieces of silver.
But I will give two hundred pieces
to those who care for its vines.

Young Man
¹³ O my darling, lingering in the gardens,
your companions are fortunate to hear
your voice.
Let me hear it, too!

Young Woman
¹⁴ Come away, my love! Be like a gazelle
or a young stag on the mountains
of spices.

7:9 As in Greek and Syriac versions and Latin Vulgate; Hebrew reads *over lips of sleepers.*   **7:11** Or *in the villages.*   **8:2** Or *there she will teach me.*   **8:4** Or *not to awaken love until it is ready.*   **8:6a** Or *its passion.*   **8:6b** Hebrew *as Sheol.*

Wisdom

SOMETIMES CALLED the Wisdom of Solomon from its internal references, this book is believed to belong to the years of Jewish persecution by Greek and Roman invaders in the second and first centuries BC. Combining the poetic beauty of Psalms with the earthy wisdom of Proverbs, the book of Wisdom sings the praises of wisdom and righteous living, contrasting the destinies of the righteous and the wicked. It majestically describes the glories of wisdom and recounts its deeds from the beginning of time. The author also reveals the foolishness of idolatry and seeks to rekindle the religious zeal of his fellow Jews who have departed from the faith of their fathers. He calls upon them to live a life of faith and godliness in the midst of perplexities and persecution. In many ways, this book forms a helpful bridge between the Old and New Testaments.

- **Author:** Unknown
- **Date Written:** First century BC
- **Purpose:** To encourage readers to live righteously, to seek wisdom, and to shun idolatry
- **Themes:** The nature of wisdom; the importance of righteous living; enduring through times of testing
- **Outline**
  1:1–5:24 The need for justice
  6:1–9:19 The desirability of wisdom
  10:1–19:22 Examples from history of how God saved his people

Wisdom Forsakes the Wicked

1 ¹ Love justice, you rulers of the earth.
　　Think of the Lord in the right way,
　and seek him with a sincere heart,
² for he is found by those who trust him,
　　and he shows himself to those who have faith in him.

³ Dishonest thinking separates people from God.
　　When his power is put to the test,
　it exposes fools for what they are.
⁴ Wisdom will not enter an evil person,
　　nor will it dwell in a person enslaved by sin.
⁵ Someone with a disciplined, holy spirit will flee from deceit,
　　abandon foolish thoughts,
　and withdraw when sin intrudes.

⁶ Wisdom is a spirit that is kind to humanity,
　　but it holds blasphemers accountable for what they say.

God knows their innermost being;
　　he sees what is truly in their hearts
　and listens to them speak.
⁷ The Spirit of the Lord fills the whole world;
　　he holds all things together
　and knows every word that is spoken.
⁸ Therefore, those who speak unjustly cannot escape notice.
　　Justice will certainly punish them.
⁹ The thoughts of the ungodly will be carefully examined;
　　their words will be reported to the Lord,
　and he will convict them of their sins.
¹⁰ His jealous ear hears all things;
　　he does not ignore the sound of complaining.
¹¹ So be sure you don't engage in pointless grumbling,
　　and keep your tongue from finding fault.
　Even what you say in private has consequences,
　　and a lying tongue destroys the soul.

¹² Do not court death by living a life of error;
  do not destroy yourself by your own
    actions.
¹³ God did not make death,
  and he takes no pleasure in the
    destruction of the living.
¹⁴ He created all things so that they could
    exist,
  and everything he created is inclined
    toward wellness.*
  There is no destructive poison in them.
  The grave* has no power on earth,
¹⁵   for righteousness is immortal.
¹⁶ But the wicked invite death by their deeds
    and words.
  They consider death a friend, so they
    long for him.
  They have made a covenant with him
  because they belong together.

The Wicked Say Life Is for Pleasure

2 ¹ The wicked have reached this irrational
    conclusion:
  "Our life is short and sad.
  There is no remedy for death;
  no one has returned from the grave.*
² We are born by chance,
  and when we die, it is as though we
    never existed.
  The breath in our nostrils is but a puff of
    smoke,
  and our reason is merely a spark kept
    alive by our beating hearts.
³ When that spark is extinguished, it will
    leave the body in ashes;
  our spirit will dissipate like a vapor.
⁴ In time even our name will be forgotten,
  and no one will remember anything we
    have done.
  Our life will pass away
    like the last wisp of a cloud;
  it will dissipate like mist
    that is driven away by sunlight
    and overcome by its heat.
⁵ For our days are but the passing of a
    shadow,
  and there is no return from death.
  Our fate is sealed,
    and no one can come back.

⁶ "Come, then, let's enjoy the good things
    around us
  and take pleasure in creation with
    youthful zeal.

⁷ Let's take our fill of costly wines and
    perfumes;
  let's take time to enjoy the spring
    flowers.
⁸ Let's crown ourselves with rosebuds before
    they wilt;
⁹   let's stop in every meadow for joyous
    play.*
  Let's leave signs of our enjoyment
    everywhere,
  for this life is what we have inherited.

¹⁰ "Let's oppress the righteous poor man
  and not spare the widow.
  Let's dishonor the aged, whose hair is
    gray.
¹¹ Let's consider our might to be right,
  for the weak prove to be useless.
¹² Let's lie in wait for righteous people,
  for they are an embarrassment to us.
  They oppose our actions;
  they reproach us for breaking the law
    of Moses
  and rebelling against our upbringing.
¹³ They claim to know God
  and call themselves servants* of God.
¹⁴ They tell us our thoughts are sinful;
  the very sight of these people bothers us.
¹⁵ They are not like other people;
  their ways are very different.
¹⁶ They regard us as insignificant
  and avoid our ways, calling them
    unclean.
  They say that the final destiny of the
    righteous is blessed,
  and they boast that God is their Father.
¹⁷ Let's see then if their words are true;
  let's watch what happens to them in
    the end.
¹⁸ If the righteous are the children of God,
  God will defend them
  and rescue them from their enemies'
    control.
¹⁹ Let's insult and torture them;
  then we will find out how meek and
    patient they are.
²⁰ Let's condemn them to a most shameful
    death,
  for they say God will protect them."

²¹ They reasoned this way, but they were
    deceived,
  for their own evil blinded them.

²² They did not know the secret plan of God.
    They never expected that a holy life
        would have its rewards.
²³ For God created people to be immortal;
    he made us in his own eternal image.
²⁴ But because of the envy of the Devil,
    death came into the world,
        and all who belong to him experience it.

The Destiny of the Righteous

3 ¹ But the souls of the righteous are in the
        hand of God,
    and no torment will ever touch them.
² In the eyes of the foolish, the righteous
        appear to die;
    their passing is considered a misfortune.
³ They seem to be on their way to
        destruction,
    but they are really at peace.
⁴ And though they appear to suffer
        punishment,
    immortality has made their hope
        complete.
⁵ The righteous may suffer a little in this
        life,
    but they will be well rewarded,
    for God has tested them
    and found them worthy to join him.
⁶ He has tried them like gold purified by fire
    and has accepted them as he accepts a
        whole burnt offering.
⁷ In their time of judgment, the righteous
        will shine;
    they will destroy their enemies.*
⁸ They will govern nations and rule over
        people,
    and the Lord will reign over them
        forever.
⁹ Those who trust in the Lord will
        understand truth,
    and the faithful will live with him
        in love.
    For he shows grace and mercy to his
        chosen ones.

The Destiny of the Wicked

¹⁰ But the wicked will be punished as their
        thoughts deserve,
    for they neglected justice and rebelled
        against the Lord.
¹¹ Those who reject wisdom and instruction
        are miserable;
    their hope is in vain,
    their labors bear no fruit,
    and their work is pointless.

¹² Their wives are foolish,
    their children are depraved,
    and their offspring are cursed.

The Rewards of Righteousness

¹³ God blesses the childless woman who
        remains pure,
    who has not entered into a sinful sexual
        relationship.
    She will be rewarded when God comes
        to judge people.
¹⁴ God also blesses the eunuch whose hands
        have done no wrong,
    who has no wicked thoughts against the
        Lord.
    Special favor will be given to him for his
        faithfulness,
    and he will be given a place of honor in
        the Lord's Temple.
¹⁵ For everyone knows that good labor yields
        good fruit,
    and wisdom is a strong and nourishing
        root.
¹⁶ But the children of adulterers will not
        reach maturity;
    the offspring of a sinful relationship
        will disappear.
¹⁷ Even if they live long, they will not be
        esteemed;
    they will receive no honor in their
        old age.
¹⁸ And if they die young, they will have
        no hope
    and no consolation on the day of
        judgment,
¹⁹ for harsh is the end of a wicked
        generation.

4 ¹ It is better to be childless
        than to lack virtue.
    For virtuous people will live on forever
        since they are honored by God and by
        people.
² When virtue is present, people imitate it,
    and when it is absent, they long for it.
    Forever it marches, crowned in triumph,
    honorably winning lasting rewards.
³ The numerous offspring of the ungodly
        will not thrive;
    their illegitimate seedlings will not take
        deep root
    or gain a firm hold.
⁴ They may flourish for a time,
    but they will be shaken by the wind
    because of their shallow roots

3:7 Greek *they will run like fire through stubble.*

and uprooted by the force of the
storm.
5 The young branches will be broken off,
and their fruit will be useless,
not ripe enough to eat and good for
nothing.
6 For children who are born of sinful
relationships
will be evidence of their parents'
wickedness when judgment comes.
7 But the righteous, though they may die
young,
will be at rest.
8 Honor is not gained merely by a long life,
nor is it measured by a person's age;
9 but understanding comes with gray hair,
and a blameless life brings the honor of
ripe old age.

10 Once such a man pleased God and was
loved by him.
While living among sinners, he was
taken from the earth.
11 He was taken away so evil could not
undermine his judgment
nor deceit seduce his soul.
12 For fascination with wickedness obscures
what is truly good,
and unrestrained desire perverts the
innocent mind.
13 He was made perfect in his few short years,
as though he had lived a long life.
14 Since his soul pleased the Lord,
the Lord quickly took him from the
wickedness around him.
15 Yet the people saw this and did not
understand it;
they did not take these things to heart:
that God shows grace and mercy to his
chosen ones
and that he watches over his holy ones.

Terror for the Wicked

16 The righteous who have died
condemn the wicked who are living,
and the youth who is made perfect in a
short life
condemns the long life of the unjust.
17 The unjust will see the end of the wise,
but they will not understand what the
Lord has designed for them
and why he has taken them to safety.
18 The unjust will see them and despise
them,
but the Lord will laugh at the unjust.
19 They will become dishonored corpses;

they will be a reproach among the dead
forever.
He will throw them down speechless
and will shake them from their
foundations.
They will be completely abandoned and
left to suffer grief.
Even the memory of them will perish.

20 They will be filled with dread when their
sins are recounted,
and their crimes will convict them.

5 ¹ Then the righteous will stand up with
great confidence
to confront those who have persecuted
them
and ridiculed their actions.
2 Those who see the righteous will tremble
with terrible fear
and will be surprised and amazed at
their salvation.
3 They will speak to each other with words
of repentance.
They will groan in anguish and say,
4 "These are the people we once derided!
We were fools to reproach them.
We thought they were crazy;
we thought they died without honor.
5 Look, now they are regarded as children
of God.
They are listed among the saints.
6 We were the ones who strayed from the
truth.
The light of righteousness has not
shined on us,
and the sun has not risen upon us.
7 We took all the paths of wickedness and
destruction
and walked through the wilderness,
but we did not find the way of the Lord.

8 "But how has our pride helped us?
What has our boasting about riches
gained us?
9 All those things have passed away like a
shadow
and like a fleeting rumor.
10 They have vanished like a ship passing
through the waves,
leaving no trace of its passage,
no track of its path in the waves.
11 They are like a bird flying through the air,
leaving no evidence of its passage—
only the sound of wings beating the light
air,

parting the air by the force of its
    flight.
It moves its wings and passes through,
    yet it leaves no trace of its path.
12 They are like an arrow shot at a target.
    The air divides and comes together
        again,
    so that no one knows its route.
13 So it is with us; we die almost as soon as we
        are born.
    And we have left nothing of virtue
        behind,
    for we were consumed by our
        wickedness."
14 The hope of the wicked is like thistledown
        blown by the wind
    or like foam blown by a storm.
It is like smoke dissipated by the wind.
    It is soon forgotten like the memory of
        a one-day guest.

15 But the righteous will live forever,
    and their reward is in the Lord's
        keeping.
    The Most High takes care of them.
16 Therefore, they will receive a glorious
        crown,
    a beautiful diadem from the Lord.
For he will cover them with his right hand,
    and he will shield them with his arm.
17 The Lord will use his zeal as armor
    and all creation as a weapon against his
        enemies.
18 He will put on righteousness as body armor,
    and he will wear impartial justice as
        a helmet.
19 He will take holiness for an invincible
        shield,
20   and he will sharpen his stern wrath as
        a sword.
All creation will join his fight against his
    frantic enemies.
21 Shafts of lightning will strike with
        pinpoint accuracy,
    shooting from the clouds like arrows
        from a fully drawn bow.
22 Hailstones of wrath will be catapulted
        upon the enemy.
The sea will rage against them,
    and the rivers will flood them in a
        torrent.
23 A mighty wind will blow over them,
    and like a whirlwind it will winnow
        them.
So lawlessness will destroy the earth,
    and wickedness will overthrow rulers.

Kings Should Seek Wisdom

6 ¹ Hear, then, you kings, and understand;
    learn, you who judge everyone on
        earth.
2 Listen, you who rule over many people
    and govern numerous nations.
3 Your authority was given to you by the
        Lord,
    and your power comes from the Most
        High.
He will examine your works
    and scrutinize your plans.
4 You are the servants of his kingdom,
    but you have not judged justly.
You have not upheld the law of Moses
    or lived according to the will of God.
5 He will come against you terribly and
        quickly,
    because severe judgment falls on those
        with great authority.
6 To the lowly, mercy may be granted;
    but those who are great will be greatly
        tested.
7 For the Lord will not stand in awe of
        anyone,
    nor will he step aside for greatness.
He made both the small and the great,
    and he regards them all the same.
8 But greater scrutiny awaits the powerful.
9 So my words are directed to you, O kings,
    in order that you may learn wisdom and
        not depart from it.
10 For those who have treated the sacred with
        holiness
    will be considered holy,
and those who have learned these things
    will know how to defend themselves.
11 Therefore, be eager to hear my words;
    long for them, and you will be
        instructed.

The Way to Wisdom

12 Wisdom is glorious and never fades away.
    She is easily seen by those who love her;
    she is found by those who seek her.
13 She is quick to show herself to all who
        desire her.
14   Those who rise early to seek her will not
        find it difficult,
    for they will find her sitting at the gate.
15 Meditating upon wisdom brings perfect
        understanding,
    and those who watch for her will soon
        be free from care.
16 For she goes about seeking those who are
        worthy of her;

she graciously shows herself to them in
their daily activities
and meets them in every thought they
have.

17 The beginning of wisdom is a sincere
desire for instruction,
and concern for instruction shows a love
of wisdom.
18 To love wisdom is to keep her laws,
and obeying her laws guarantees
immortality.
19 Immortality brings one near to God;
20 so the desire for wisdom is the way to
acquire a kingdom.
21 So if you kings desire thrones and scepters,
honor wisdom, and you will reign
forever.

Wisdom's Riches

22 Now I will tell what wisdom is
and how she came to be.
I will hide no secrets from you
but will trace her steps from the
beginning.
I will bring knowledge of her to light
and not bypass the truth.
23 I will not allow myself to be consumed
with envy,
for envy has nothing in common with
wisdom.
24 A multitude of wise counselors brings
salvation to the world,
and a wise king brings stability to his
people.
25 Therefore, be instructed by my words,
and you will profit from them.

7 ¹ I, too, am mortal, like everyone else.
I am a descendant of the first man
formed from the earth;
in my mother's womb I was fashioned
into a body.
² For nine months* I developed,
having come from the seed of man and
the pleasure of marriage.
³ When I was born, I breathed the air we all
breathe
and was laid upon the earth that bears
us all.
The first sound I uttered was a cry, as is
true with everyone else.
⁴ Snugly wrapped in strips of cloth, I was
nursed with care.

5 And no king had a beginning that was
any different.
6 For all people have one entrance into life,
and all have a common exit.
7 So I prayed, and I was given
understanding;
I pleaded, and the spirit of wisdom came
upon me.
8 I preferred wisdom to power and
kingship;
riches were as nothing compared to her.
9 I did not compare her to any precious
stone,
for gold is but a little sand in
comparison to her,
and silver is as clay.
10 I loved her more than health and beauty;
I preferred her even to light,
for her light cannot be extinguished.
11 All good things came to me along with
her;
innumerable riches accompanied her.
12 I rejoiced in all these things, because
wisdom brought them to me,
though I did not know that wisdom
was the mother of them all.
13 I learned diligently, and I teach others
freely.
I do not hide wisdom's riches,
14 for they are an infinite treasure to
people.
Those who use wisdom's riches become
friends of God
and are commended for the benefits
of learning.

15 May God grant me the ability to speak
wisely
and to think thoughts worthy of all
I have learned.
He is the guide of wisdom
and the director of the wise.
16 We and our words are in his hands
along with all knowledge and skills.
17 For he has given me true knowledge of
what exists.
I know how the world and the elements
work.
18 I know all the ages from beginning
to end,
the movements of the sun and the
changes of seasons.
19 I know the cycles of the year and the
various constellations,

7:2 Greek *For ten months*. Ten months of the ancient Hebrew lunar calendar is about equal to 9 months of the modern
solar calendar.

20 the nature of animals and the instincts
       of wild beasts.
    I know the power of spirits and the way
       people think,
       the varieties of plants, and the roots
          that are beneficial.
21 I know what is hidden and what is
       visible,
       for wisdom, the designer of all things,
          taught me.

The Nature of Wisdom

22 Wisdom's spirit is intelligent, holy,
       unique,
       many-faceted, subtle, active,
       clear, undefiled, certain,
       sweet, benevolent, sharp,
       irresistible, 23helpful, kind,
       firm, sure, and secure.
    Wisdom's spirit is all-powerful and
       oversees all things.
    It permeates every intelligent, pure, and
       perceptive spirit.
24 Wisdom is more active than motion itself.
    She pervades and permeates everything
       by her purity.
25 For she is a breath of God's power,
    a pure revelation of the glory of the
       Almighty.
    Therefore, nothing that is defiled can
       reach her.
26 For she is the reflection of eternal light,
    the spotless mirror of God's power,
    and the image of his goodness.
27 She is only one, but she can do all things.
    She herself remains the same, but she
       renews all things.
    In every generation she gives herself to
       holy souls,
       making them prophets and friends of
          God.
28 For God loves none as much as those who
       dwell with wisdom.
29 She is more beautiful than the sun,
    more wonderful than all the
       constellations of stars.
    She is superior even to the sun's light,
30 for daylight is followed by night,
    but no evil can overcome wisdom.

The Rewards of Wisdom

8 ¹ Wisdom reaches from one end of the
       earth to the other
    and governs all things well.
 2 I have loved her and sought her from my
       youth.

I have desired to take her for my bride,
    for I am enamored with her beauty.
3 She enhances her noble birth by living
       with God,
    and the Lord of all loves her.
4 For she has received the knowledge of
       God;
    she is his helper in all he does.
5 If you desire riches in life,
    what is richer than wisdom, who is the
       cause of all things?
6 If understanding is effective,
    what about wisdom, who designed all
       things?
7 And if a person loves righteousness,
    wisdom's labors have great virtue,
    for she teaches self-control, prudence,
       justice, and courage—
    the most valuable attributes in life.
8 And if a person desires much knowledge,
    wisdom knows the past and foresees the
       future.
    She knows the subtleties of speech and the
       solutions of riddles.
    She foreknows signs and wonders
    and the outcome of times and ages yet
       to come.
9 So I determined to take wisdom to live
       with me,
    knowing that she would give me good
       instruction
    and comfort me in my cares and grief.
10 Because of her, the multitudes honor me,
    and the elders esteem me, though I am
       young.
11 I will be found wise in judgment,
    and I will be admired by the mighty.
12 They will wait for me when I am silent,
    and they will pay attention when I speak.
    And if I talk at length,
    they will not interrupt me.
13 Because of wisdom I will be immortal;
    I will leave an everlasting memory to
       those who come after me.
14 I will rule the people,
    and nations will be subject to me.
15 Tyrants will quake when they hear my
       name;
    my people will find that I am good and
       valiant in war.
16 When I go into my home, I will find rest
       with wisdom,
    for companionship with her has no
       bitterness.
    To live with her is to live without pain
       in joy and gladness.

A Prayer for Wisdom

17 I pondered these things and weighed
them in my mind—
that associating with wisdom brings
immortality,
18 that her friendship is pure delight,
that her activities bring great wealth,
that her companionship brings
understanding,
and that a person gains respect by
sharing her words.
Then I went about seeking how I might
get wisdom for myself.
19 I was born a gifted child,
and I was naturally good.*
20 Better yet, since I was good,
I was given an undefiled body.
21 But I knew I could not possess wisdom
unless God gave her to me.
It was a sign of intelligence that I knew
who had given me wisdom.
So I went to the Lord and pleaded with
him.
With my whole heart I said:

9 1 "O God of my ancestors and Lord of
mercy,
you have made all things by your word.
2 In your wisdom you formed people
to be masters over the creatures you
made,
3 to rule the world in holiness and
justice,
and to pronounce judgment with a
righteous heart.
4 Give me the wisdom that sits by your
throne,
and do not exclude me from being one
of your servants.
5 For I am your servant and the son of your
servant girl,
a weak man with a short life
and little understanding of justice and
laws.
6 Even if there were a perfect human being,
without wisdom he would be regarded
as nothing.
7 You have chosen me to be king of your
people
and judge over your sons and daughters.
8 You told me to build a Temple on your
holy mountain
and an altar in the city of your dwelling
place—

a copy of the holy Tabernacle you
prepared from the beginning.
9 Wisdom, who resides with you, knows
your works;
she was present when you made the
world.
She knows what is pleasant in your sight
and what is right according to your
commandments.
10 Send her out from your holy heaven
and from the throne of your glory
so that she may work with me
and teach me what is pleasing to you.
11 For wisdom knows and understands all
things;
she will guide me wisely in my actions
and guard me with her glory.
12 Then my works will be acceptable,
and I will govern your people justly.
I will be worthy of the throne of my
father.
13 For what human being can know the
counsel of God?
Who can discern the will of the Lord?
14 The thoughts of mortals are fallible,
and our plans are uncertain.
15 The mortal body weighs down the soul.
This earthly tent burdens the active
mind.
16 We can scarcely guess at what is on earth;
we struggle to understand what is
within our reach.
So who can search out the things in
heaven?
17 Who could have known your plan
if you had not given wisdom
and sent your Holy Spirit from above?
18 Through them, people on earth were
guided on the right path.
The people were taught the things that
please you,
and they were saved by wisdom."

The Deeds of Wisdom throughout History

10 1 Wisdom protected Adam,* the first
father of the world,
when he alone had been created.
Wisdom freed him from his sin
2 and gave him power to be master over
all things.
3 But when Cain, an unrighteous man,
abandoned wisdom in his anger,
he was destroyed because he murdered
his brother in a fit of rage.

8:19 Greek *I was given a good soul.* 10:1 In 10:1-16, *Adam, Cain, Noah, Abraham, Lot, Lot's wife, Jacob, Joseph, the Israelites,* and *Moses* are alluded to but not explicitly named in the Greek text.

⁴ When water flooded the earth because of
    Cain's sin,
    wisdom saved it again,
    steering Noah, a righteous man, by a
      mere piece of wood.

⁵ When the nations were thrown into
    confusion for planning wicked things
    together,
    wisdom recognized Abraham, a
      righteous man.
She protected him from sin before God
    and gave him strength to be willing to
      sacrifice his son, whom he loved.

⁶ She delivered Lot, a righteous man,
    when the wicked were being destroyed.
He escaped the fire that destroyed
    Sodom and Gomorrah.*
⁷ Evidence of their wickedness still remains:
    a smoking, desolate land,
    trees bearing fruit that never ripens,
    and a pillar of salt—a monument to
      Lot's unbelieving wife.
⁸ By forsaking wisdom,
    the people of those cities failed to
      recognize good things.
But they also left us a memorial to their
    foolish actions,
    so that their failures would always be
      remembered.

⁹ Yet wisdom rescued those who served her.
¹⁰ When Jacob, a righteous man, fled from
    his brother's anger,
    Wisdom guided him well.
She showed him the kingdom of God
    and gave him knowledge of holy
      things.
She made him successful in his work
    and blessed him for his efforts.
¹¹ While others tried to defraud him,
    wisdom stood by him and made him
      wealthy.
¹² She kept him safe from his enemies
    and defended him from those who
      wanted to ambush him.
In his difficult fight she gave him victory,
    so that he might know that godliness is
      more powerful than anything.

¹³ Wisdom did not forsake Joseph, a
    righteous man, when he was sold
    but delivered him from sin.

¹⁴ She went with him down into the
    dungeon
    and did not abandon him in prison.
In time, she made him the ruler of a
    kingdom
    and gave him authority over those who
      oppressed him.
Then she exposed his accusers as liars
    and gave him everlasting honor.

Wisdom Rescued the Israelites

¹⁵ Wisdom rescued the Israelites, a holy and
    blameless people,
    from the nations that oppressed them.
¹⁶ She entered the soul of Moses, a servant
    of the Lord,
    and resisted dreaded kings with
      wonders and signs.
¹⁷ She rewarded the holy people for their
    work
    and guided them on an amazing
      journey.
She was a shelter for them by day
    and a starry beacon in the night.
¹⁸ She brought them through the Red Sea
    and led them through deep waters.
¹⁹ But she drowned their enemies
    and cast them up from the watery
      depths.
²⁰ Therefore the righteous plundered the
    wicked.
They sang hymns to your holy name,
    O Lord,
    and together they praised your
      victorious hand.
²¹ For wisdom opened the mouths of the
    mute
    and made the tongues of infants
      eloquent.

The Lord Provided for His People

11 ¹ Wisdom gave his people success
    under the leadership of Moses,*
    a holy prophet.
² They traveled through uninhabited
    desert
    and pitched their tents in the frontier.
³ They withstood attacks by their enemies
    and defended themselves against their
      adversaries.
⁴ When they were thirsty, they called upon
    you, Lord,
    and you gave them water from the sheer
      rock.

10:6 Greek *the fire that came down on the Five Cities.* **11:1** *Moses* is alluded to but not explicitly named in the Greek text; also in 11:14.

Refreshment for their thirst came from
hard stone.
5 The very things that punished their
enemies
became a benefit to the Israelites when
they needed help.
6 Their enemies had only an ever-flowing
river polluted with blood—
7 their punishment for ordering that the
infants be killed.
But you gave the Israelites abundant
water from an unexpected source.
8 So the thirst of the Israelites
reminded them how you had once
punished their enemies.
9 For when they were tested, though only by
merciful discipline,
they learned how the ungodly were
judged in anger and tormented.
10 For you tested the Israelites as a father
warns his children,
but you examined and condemned the
others like a stern king.

The Wicked Were Punished

11 For whether they were at home or abroad,
the ungodly were equally distressed.
12 They were doubly grieved
and groaned at the memory of what had
happened.
13 For when the ungodly heard that their
punishments benefited the righteous,
they recognized that the Lord had
caused these things to happen.
14 They had scorned and rejected Moses,
whom they had cast out as a child much
earlier and left to die.
But in the end they were amazed at him,
for they were thirsty in a different way
than the righteous.

15 But the foolish and evil thoughts of the
ungodly
deceived them to worship irrational
serpents and worthless animals.
In return, you sent hordes of irrational
animals to punish them.
16 This was done to teach them that people
are punished by the very sins they
commit.
17 For your almighty hand,
which created the world out of formless
matter,
was able to send upon the ungodly
many bears or fierce lions,

18 or newly created, unknown beasts filled
with rage,
breathing out fiery breath,
belching forth acrid smoke,
and flashing terrible sparks from their
eyes.
19 Not only could these savage beasts destroy
people,
but the very sight of them could scare
people to death.
20 Even besides these animals, people could
be killed by a single breath of the
Lord,
when they are pursued by justice and
scattered by the breath of your power.
But you have arranged all things by
measure, number, and weight.
21 For you are always able to display your
great power.
Who can resist your mighty arm?
22 For the whole world before you is as the
smallest grain that tips the scales,
or as a drop of morning dew that lies
upon the ground.

The Mercy of the Lord

23 But you have mercy on all, because you can
do all things;
you overlook people's sins so that they
might repent.
24 For you love everything that exists.
You hate none of the things you have
made,
for you would not have made anything
you hated.
25 And how could anything last if you had
not wanted it?
How could it endure if you had not
called it into being?
26 But you spare all things because they are
yours,
O Lord, who loves everything that lives.

12 1 For your immortal spirit is in
everything.
2 Therefore, little by little you correct those
who disobey,
and you warn them about the way they
are sinning.
You do this so they will be freed from their
wickedness
and trust in you, O Lord.

3 Those Canaanites* who lived long ago in
your holy land

12:3 The *Canaanites* are alluded to but not explicitly named in the Greek text; also in 12:8, 11.

⁴ were hated by you because of their
  detestable practices,
  their sorceries, and their wicked
  rituals.
⁵ They mercilessly slaughtered their own
  children
  and feasted on sacrifices of human flesh
  and blood during their pagan rituals.
⁶ You told our ancestors to destroy
  those parents who sacrificed innocent
  lives,
⁷ for you wanted the land most dear to you
  to receive a worthy colony of God's
  servants.*
⁸ Yet you spared even these Canaanites,
  since they were merely human beings,
  but you sent hornets as forerunners of
  your army,
  to destroy them little by little.
⁹ You could have handed over the wicked to
  the righteous by means of war
  or destroyed them in one fell swoop by
  fearsome animals or your stern word.
¹⁰ But you judged them little by little to give
  them a chance to repent,
  although you knew that they were evil
  by nature
  and that their way of thinking would
  never change.
¹¹ The Canaanites were a cursed race from
  the beginning.
  It was your kindness, not fear of anyone,
  that you did not punish them for
  their sins.

The Justice of the Lord
¹² For who will say to you: "What have you
  done?"
  Or who will challenge your judgment?
  Who will accuse you for destroying the
  nations you have made?
  Or who will face you to avenge the death
  of the unrighteous?
¹³ For there is no other God but you, and you
  care for all,
  proving that you have not judged
  unjustly.
¹⁴ No king or ruler can confront you
  about those you have punished.
¹⁵ You are righteous, and you rule over all
  things righteously.
  You consider it uncharacteristic of your
  power
  to condemn anyone who does not
  deserve to be punished.

¹⁶ Your strength is the source of
  righteousness;
  because you rule over all, you are
  gracious to all.
¹⁷ You show your strength when people
  doubt your absolute power,
  and you rebuke those who do believe in
  your power but are arrogant.
¹⁸ Although you are sovereign in strength,
  you judge mildly,
  and you govern us leniently,
  for your power is at hand when you
  choose to use it.
¹⁹ In this way you have taught your people
  that the righteous must be kind.
  You have given your children good reason
  for hope
  because you make room for repentance
  of sins.
²⁰ After showing great care and leniency, you
  finally punished
  your servants' enemies, who deserved
  to die.
  You had given them time and
  opportunity to repent of their
  wickedness.
²¹ So you have judged your own children
  even more strictly,
  for you swore oaths and covenants of
  good promises to their ancestors.
²² Therefore, while you merely discipline us,
  you punish our enemies ten thousand
  times more,
  so that when we judge others, we may
  keep your goodness in mind,
  and when we are judged, we may hope
  for mercy.

²³ So those who foolishly live unrighteous
  lives
  are tormented by you through their
  own sins.
²⁴ For the Egyptians* strayed far down the
  path of error
  and worshiped the most despised
  animals;
  they were deceived like foolish children.
²⁵ Therefore, as with senseless children,
  you punished them in a way that made
  them look ridiculous.
²⁶ But those who do not heed gentle
  warnings
  experience the just punishment
  of God.

12:7 Or *children.*   12:24 *The Egyptians* are alluded to but not explicitly named in the Greek text; also in 12:27.

27 The Egyptians became angry because they
      suffered
   and were punished by the very animals
      they considered gods.
   So they realized and confessed that the
      One they had formerly rejected was
      the true God.
   For this reason they had been
      completely condemned.

The Foolishness of Nature Worship

13 ¹ All people who were unaware of
      God were foolish by nature.
   Despite the good things they could see,
      they were unable to perceive the God
      who is,*
   nor did they recognize the craftsman,
      though they observe his works.
² But they imagined that fire or wind or
      swift air
   or the movement of the stars or rushing
      water
   or the heavenly lights are the gods that
      rule the world.
³ If mere beauty caused people to believe
      these things were gods,
   let them know how much more
      beautiful is their Lord,
   for the author of all beauty created these
      things.
⁴ Or if people were amazed by their power
      and energy,
   let them learn from these things how
      much more powerful is the One who
      made them.
⁵ For the Creator can be seen and
      understood
   through the greatness and beauty of
      creation.
⁶ But yet such people should not be blamed
      very harshly,
   for perhaps they went astray while
      seeking God and desiring to find
      him.
⁷ For they are familiar with his works and
      search diligently,
   but they fall victim to mere appearances,
      for the things they see are
      beautiful.
⁸ But even so, they are not to be excused.
⁹ For if they know so much
      that they can speculate about the
      world,
   how have they been so slow to find the
      Lord of creation?

13:1 See Exod 3:14.

The Foolishness of Idolatry

¹⁰ But those who set their hopes on dead
      things are miserable.
   They worship "gods" made by human
      beings—
   works of gold and silver skillfully shaped
      to resemble animals,
   or useless stone, the work of someone
      long ago.
¹¹ A skilled woodcarver cuts down a suitable
      tree
   and deftly strips off all the bark.
   Then with admirable precision
      he forms a bowl that is useful in daily
      life.
¹² He burns the fallen chips from his work
      to heat his food so that he can eat his fill.
¹³ But one stick is left over, seemingly good
      for nothing,
   since it is crooked and full of knots.
   This he carefully carves in his spare time.
      With leisurely skill he fashions it;
   he gives it the shape of a human
¹⁴   or of some worthless animal.
   He coats it with crimson paint and colors
      it red,
   covering every blemish with paint.
¹⁵ Then he makes a special place to put it
      and sets it in a wall, fastening it with
      iron.
¹⁶ He must take care of it so it doesn't fall
      because he knows it cannot help itself;
   it is only an image and needs his help.
¹⁷ But then he prays to it about his
      possessions, his marriage, or his
      children;
   he is not ashamed to speak to a lifeless
      object.
   For health, he appeals to a thing that has
      no strength;
¹⁸   for life, he prays to a thing that is dead;
   for help, he calls upon a thing that is
      completely helpless;
   for a successful journey, he petitions a
      thing that cannot take a single step;
¹⁹   for money, work, and success in
      business
   he asks for strength from a thing that is
      unable to help itself.

Trust in God, Not Idols

14 ¹ Again, a person preparing to set sail
      on a voyage over raging waves
   calls upon a piece of wood more fragile
      than the ship that carries him.

² For it was the desire for profit that planned
 the vessel,
  and wisdom was the craftsmen who
  built it.
³ But it is steered by your providence,
 O Father,
  for you have made a path for it even in
  the sea,
  and a safe way over the waves.
⁴ This shows that you can save people from
 every danger,
  so that even an inexperienced person
  can make a sea voyage.
⁵ For you want people to use the objects
 produced through your wisdom.
  So people trust their lives even to the
  smallest piece of wood;
  they pass over the waves on a raft and
  arrive safely on land.
⁶ Even from the beginning, when the proud
 giants were being destroyed,
  Noah,* the hope of the world, took
  refuge on a raft,
  and you led him to produce a new
  human race.
⁷ For blessed is the wooden object by which
 righteousness comes.

⁸ But the idol that is made by hands is
 cursed,
  and so is the one who made it.
 The person is cursed because he made the
 idol,
  and the perishable idol is cursed because
  it is called a god.
⁹ For equally hateful to God are the wicked
 and their wicked deeds.
¹⁰ Both the thing that was made and the one
 who made it will be punished.
¹¹ Therefore, pagan idols will be condemned
 because they have become a terrible sin,
  even though they belong to God's
  creation.
 They are snares for human souls,
  and a trap for the feet of the foolish.

The Origin of Idolatry

¹² Immorality came about when idols were
 first made,
  and life was corrupted by their
  invention.
¹³ They did not exist from the beginning,
 nor will they last forever.
¹⁴ Futile thinking brought them into the
 world,

and swift destruction is planned for
 them.

¹⁵ For a father, mourning the untimely death
 of his child,
  made an image of the child who had
  been suddenly snatched from him.
 He then worshiped as a god the image of
 a corpse
  and devised secret rites and initiations
  for his household.
¹⁶ The wicked custom became established
 over time and was regarded as a law.
 Carved images of tyrants were
  worshiped at their command.
¹⁷ Some people could not honor the rulers in
 person since they lived far away.
 So they imagined what the rulers looked
 like
  and made a visible image of the king
  they wished to honor.
 They did this to flatter the king as
  though he were present.
¹⁸ Then even those who did not know the
 king
  were spurred on to worship him—all
  because of the artisan's ambition.
¹⁹ For he, perhaps wishing to please his ruler,
  labored with all his skill to make the
  likeness even more beautiful than the
  actual person.
²⁰ Then the masses, carried away by the
 beauty of the work,
  decided to worship the one they had
  honored as a mere mortal just a short
  time before.
²¹ And this became a trap for people;
 in their bondage to misfortune or
 tyranny,
 they gave objects of stone or wood the
  name "God"—
 a name that is not to be shared with
  others.

The Evils of Idolatry

²² It was not enough for them to hold
 misconceptions about God.
  They also live in great conflict due to
  ignorance,
  and they call such evils peace.
²³ For they kill children in their initiation
 rituals and celebrate secret mysteries;
 they hold frenzied orgies with strange
 practices.

14:6 *Noah* is alluded to but not explicitly named in the Greek text.

24 They keep neither their own lives nor their
    marriages pure,
  for they treacherously kill each other or
    harm each other by adultery.
25 Everything is chaos—
  blood and murder, theft and deceit,
  corruption, unfaithfulness, riots, lying,
26   confusion over what is good, neglect of
    favors,
  corruption of souls, sexual perversion,
    disorder in marriages, adultery, and
    shameless living.
27 For the worship of nameless idols is the
    source and cause and result of every
    evil.
28 The worshipers become intoxicated with
    festivity,
  or they prophesy lies, live wicked lives,
    or readily break oaths.
29 Because they trust in lifeless idols,
  they swear falsely and expect to suffer
    no harm for it.
30 But for two things they will be justly
    punished:
  because they misunderstood God when
    they worshiped idols,
  and because they made false oaths since
    they despised what is holy.
31 For the wicked and their sins are pursued
  not by the power of the things by which
    people swear
  but by the just punishment of sinners.

Worship of the True God

15 1 But you, our God, are kind and
    true—
  a patient and merciful ruler over all
    things.
2 Even if we sin, we are still yours and
    acknowledge your power.
  But we will not sin, because we know
    that you acknowledge us as your own.
3 For perfect righteousness comes from
    knowing you,
  and knowledge of your power is the root
    of immortality.
4 The evil intent of human art has not
    deceived us,
  nor has the fruitless work of painters—
  a statue stained with various colors.
5 The appearance of such works excites
    fools
  and causes them to desire the lifeless
    form of a dead image.
6 Those who make or desire or worship such
    idols

love evil things and deserve no better
    hope
  than that offered by the idols.

More Examples of Foolish Idolatry

7 The potter works the soft clay
  and laboriously shapes each piece of
    pottery for our use.
  From the same clay he makes some pots
    for clean uses
  and some for unclean uses.
  They are all made alike,
  and the potter decides how each will
    be used.
8 He then wastes his time by making a
    useless god from the same clay,
  though he himself, only a short time
    before, was also made from earth.
  After a little while he will return to the
    earth from which he came,
  when he is asked to return the life that
    was lent to him.
9 But he is not concerned that he will die
    one day or that his life is short.
  Instead, he competes with the
    goldsmiths and silversmiths and
    imitates the bronzeworkers.
  He takes pride in fashioning counterfeit
    gods.
10 His heart is ashes, his hope is worth less
    than dirt,
  and his life is of less value than clay.
11 For he did not know the One who formed
    him,
  who infused him with an active soul
  and breathed into him a living spirit.
12 He considered our existence to be a
    meaningless game
  and life merely a festival for making
    profit.
  He says people must make money
    however they can—even by evil
    means.
13 Yet this man, above all others, knows that
    he sins
  when he makes fragile pots and carved
    images from earthly clay.
14 But those who are most foolish and more
    miserable than infants
  are the enemies who oppress your
    people.
15 They thought all their pagan idols were
    gods,
  though these idols have no eyes for
    seeing,

nor noses for breathing,
nor ears for hearing,
nor fingers for grasping.
Even their feet are useless for
walking.
16 They were made by a human being;
they were formed by someone whose
own life is borrowed.
People cannot make true gods that are like
themselves,
17 for people are mortal and can form only
dead things with their wicked hands.
They are better than the objects they
worship,
for they, at least, are alive; the idols will
never live.

The Plagues of Small Animals
18 These people worship even the most
detestable creatures,
which are worse than all others because
they lack intelligence.
19 In comparison to other animals, they are
not beautiful or desirable.
They were excluded both from the
praise and blessing of God.

16 1 Therefore the Egyptians* were
rightly punished by such
creatures;
they were tormented by a great number
of animals.
2 But instead of punishing your people in
this way, you showed them kindness.
You sent a delicacy to satisfy their
hungry appetites—
quail for them to eat.
3 You did this so that when the Egyptians
wanted food,
they would think of the repulsive
creatures you sent
and would lose their appetites.
But your people, after going hungry for a
short time, would eat delicacies.
4 The Egyptian oppressors had to be made
permanently needy,
but your people only had to see their
enemies being tormented.

5 When your people were attacked by raging
wild animals
and were being destroyed by the bites of
writhing serpents,
you did not stay angry until they were
completely destroyed.

6 They were troubled for a short time as a
warning,
but they received a symbol of
deliverance to remind them of your
law's commandment.

7 Anyone who turned toward it was healed,
not by the visible object,
but by you, the Savior of all.
8 And by this you showed our enemies
that you are the one who rescues from
every evil.
9 They were killed by the bites of locusts
and flies,
for there was no remedy to save them;
they deserved to be punished by such
things.
10 But not even the fangs of venomous
serpents overcame your children,
for your mercy came to their aid and
healed them.
11 They were bitten to remind them of your
words,
and then they were quickly rescued
so that they would not completely forget
and become unresponsive to your
kindness.
12 For neither herb nor ointment healed
them;
it is your word, O Lord, that heals all
things.
13 You have power over life and death.
You take people down to the gates of
death* and bring them back again.
14 A person who maliciously kills another
cannot bring back the departed spirit
or release the soul that has been
captured by death.

15 It is impossible to escape your hand.
16 The wicked Egyptians who refused to
acknowledge you
were flogged by your strong arm.
They were pursued by extraordinary rains,
hail, and relentless storms
and completely consumed by fire.
17 Most incredible of all was that the fire was
even more effective
in water, which normally extinguishes
everything,
for the universe fights for the
righteous.
18 At one point the fire died down
so that the creatures sent against the
wicked would not be burned.

16:1 *The Egyptians* are alluded to but not explicitly named in the Greek text; also in 16:4, 16.   16:13 Greek *of Hades*.

Then the people could see and understand
that they were pursued by God's
judgment.

¹⁹ And at another point, the fire burned
in the rain even hotter than it is
naturally able,
in order to destroy the crops of a wicked
land.

Rewards for True Worship

²⁰ Instead of these punishments, you fed
your people with manna,* the food
of angels.
Without their help you prepared bread
from heaven for your people,
and everything it contained was
delicious and tasty to everyone.

²¹ The food you gave your children showed
your sweetness toward them.
The bread satisfied everyone who ate it
and changed to suit each person's taste.

²² Snow and ice resisted fire without
melting,
so your people would see that their
enemies' crops
were being destroyed by the fire that
burned in the hail
and flashed in the rain.

²³ But this same fire forgot the limits of its
own power
in order that the righteous might be
nourished.

²⁴ For creation serves you, the Creator,
and strives to punish the wicked,
but it relaxes for the benefit of those
who trust in you.

²⁵ Therefore, even creation changed into all
sorts of forms
and was obedient to your generosity,
which nourished all people
according to their needs and desires.

²⁶ This happened, O Lord, so that your
beloved children might learn
that it is not by crops that people are
nourished
but by your word, which sustains those
who trust in you.

²⁷ The manna that was not destroyed by fire
melted after being warmed by a passing
ray from the sun.

²⁸ So the people learned that they must rise
before dawn to give you thanks
and pray to you at daybreak.

²⁹ For the hope of the ungrateful will melt
away like a winter frost
and drain away like waste water.

The Plague of Darkness

17 ¹ Your judgments are great and
difficult to describe;
so the unlearned have gone astray.

² The wicked Egyptians* thought they held
the holy nation in their power,
but they themselves were captives of
darkness and prisoners of unending
night.
They were confined under their
own roofs and exiled from eternal
providence.

³ While they thought their secret sins were
concealed
behind a dark curtain of forgetfulness,
they were scattered and terrified;
they were frightened by apparitions.

⁴ Not even the most secluded room they hid
in protected them from fear.
Terrifying noises echoed around them
and somber, gloomy-faced phantoms
appeared to them.

⁵ No fire, no matter how intense, could give
them light,
and the bright glow of the stars
were unable to illuminate that gloomy
night.

⁶ Nothing gave the Egyptians light
except a spontaneous, dreadful flash.
In their fear, they thought they saw things
even worse than the things they had
imagined.

⁷ The tricks of their magic art were
humbled,
and the wisdom they boasted about was
scornfully rebuked.

⁸ Those who promised to drive away the
fears and troubles of a sick soul
were now sick themselves with
ludicrous fear.

⁹ No terrible thing actually attacked them,
but they were frightened by hissing
serpents and wild animals passing by.

¹⁰ The Egyptians died of fright
as they futilely tried even to ignore the
very air around them.

¹¹ For wickedness is cowardly and condemns
itself
because a troubled conscience always
assumes the worst.

16:20 *Manna* is alluded to but not explicitly named in the Greek text; also in 16:27.   17:2 The *Egyptians* are alluded to but not explicitly named in the Greek text; also in 17:6, 10, 14, 21.

¹² Fear is nothing but the surrender of
　　assistance from reason.
¹³ And after hope has been defeated
　　within,
　　people imagine the cause of their
　　　torment to be worse than it
　　　actually is.
¹⁴ That terrifying night was really powerless,
　　since it came from the powerless place
　　　of the dead,*
　　but the Egyptians all slept in terror.
¹⁵　They were chased by monstrous
　　　apparitions,
　　yet they were also paralyzed by their
　　　fainting souls,
　　for sudden and unexpected fear
　　　overwhelmed them.
¹⁶ People everywhere fell down
　　and were shut up in a prison without
　　　bars.
¹⁷ Whether they were farmers or shepherds
　　or people working in the desert,
　　they were suddenly snatched up and
　　　suffered an inescapable fate.
　　They were all bound together with
　　　a chain of darkness.
¹⁸ Whether it was the whistling wind,
　　or the melodious sound of birds in
　　　the trees,
　　or the steady noise of rushing water,
¹⁹　or the mighty crash of rocks hurled
　　　down,
　　or the sound of animals running along
　　　unseen,
　　or the roar of the most savage beasts,
　　or an echo rebounding from a mountain
　　　hollow—
　　the noise paralyzed them with fear.
²⁰ The rest of the world was illumined with
　　bright light,
　　and people went about their work
　　　unhindered.
²¹ But a dark night descended upon the
　　Egyptians alone,
　　an image of another darkness that
　　　would one day come upon them.
　　Yet more heavy than this darkness was
　　　the burden they were to themselves.

The Pillar of Light

18 ¹ Your holy ones, however, saw a
　　　bright light;
　　the Egyptians* heard their voices but
　　　could not see them.

They realized that your holy ones were
　　happy because they did not suffer the
　　same things.
² They were thankful that your people did
　　not repay them for past injuries.
　　They asked forgiveness for past
　　　conflicts.
³ Therefore, you sent a flaming pillar of fire
　　to guide your people on an unknown
　　journey.
　　It acted as a harmless sun for their
　　　celebrated wandering.
⁴ The Egyptians deserved to be deprived of
　　light and imprisoned in darkness,
　　for they had imprisoned your children,
　　through whom the unfading light of
　　　the law would be given to the
　　　world.

The Plague upon the Firstborn

⁵ When the Egyptians decided to kill the
　　infants of your holy ones,
　　one child, Moses, was abandoned and
　　　then rescued.
　　You punished them by taking away many
　　　of their children.
　　Then you destroyed them all at once in
　　　a mighty flood.
⁶ You had warned our ancestors ahead of
　　time about that night,
　　so they might rejoice and know that
　　　your promise could be trusted.
⁷ Your people expected to see
　　the salvation of the righteous and the
　　　destruction of their enemies.
⁸ You used this event to punish our
　　adversaries
　　and also call us to yourself and bring us
　　　glory.
⁹ For during this time, the holy children of
　　good people secretly offered sacrifices
　　and unanimously agreed upon this
　　　divine institution of Passover.
　　In this way they would share in good
　　　things and dangers alike
　　while already singing the praises of the
　　　ancestors.
¹⁰ But the discordant cry of their enemies
　　echoed back,
　　and a mournful lament for their
　　　children sounded throughout the
　　　land.
¹¹ The slave suffered the same punishment
　　as the master,

17:14 Greek *from the recesses of powerless Hades.* **18:1** In 18:1-25, *the Egyptians, Moses, Passover,* and *Aaron* are alluded to but not
explicitly named in the Greek text.

and commoners experienced the same
loss as the king.
¹² By the death of the firstborn, they all
had countless dead.
There were not enough living to bury the
dead,
for in one moment their most favored
children were destroyed.
¹³ Earlier, they would not have believed this
could happen,
for they trusted in their magic arts.
But when their firstborn were destroyed,
they acknowledged your people to be
God's child.
¹⁴ While all things were wrapped in utter
silence
and the night was halfway through its
swift course,
¹⁵ your almighty word leaped down from
your royal throne in heaven
and entered the doomed land like a
fierce warrior.
¹⁶ Carrying the sharp sword of your
unchanging command,
it stood and spread death everywhere.
While standing on earth it reached to
heaven.
¹⁷ Apparitions in horrible dreams terrified
the people,
and unexpected fears came over them.
¹⁸ As people everywhere were hurled to the
ground half dead,
they testified as to the reason they were
dying.
¹⁹ For their nightmares had forewarned
them about this,
so that they would not die without
knowing why they suffered.

God Punished His People

²⁰ But even the righteous experienced death.
In the desert you struck the people with
a plague.
But your wrath did not continue long,
²¹ for Aaron, a blameless man, hurried to
the people's defense.
Bringing forth the shield of his ministry—
prayer and incense that satisfies you—
he withstood your wrath and put an end
to the disaster.
This showed that he was your servant.
²² He overcame the destruction,*
but not by physical strength or force
of arms;

with a word he subdued the one who
punished them,
invoking the oaths and covenants given
to our ancestors.
²³ After the dead had fallen on one another
in heaps,
Aaron intervened and stopped the
wrath,
cutting off its access to the living.
²⁴ On his long robe the whole world was
depicted,
and the glories of the ancestors were
engraved on the four rows of stones
on his ephod.
Your majesty was written on the diadem,
the turban on his head.
²⁵ To these the destroyer yielded for he feared
them.
This single test of wrath was enough.

God Destroyed the Egyptians

19 ¹ But the wicked Egyptians* were
assailed with merciless wrath to
the very end,
for God knew in advance what they
would do.
² He knew that they would let your people
leave
and anxiously send them on their way,
but he also knew they would change
their minds and pursue your people.
³ While the Egyptians were still mourning
and lamenting at the graves of their
dead,
they reached another foolish decision
and pursued the very ones they had
urged to leave.
⁴ Their well-deserved fate led them to this
end,
causing them to forget all that had
happened
so they would complete their torments
with one final punishment.
⁵ Then your people could experience an
amazing journey,
but the Egyptians would meet an
extraordinary death.

Nature Obeyed God's Commands

⁶ All creation had its very nature recreated
in obedience to your commands,
so that your servants* might be
protected from harm.
⁷ A cloud overshadowed their camp,

18:22 Greek *crowd.* 19:1 In 19:1-22, *the Egyptians, the residents of Sodom, Lot,* and *manna* are alluded to but not explicitly named
in the Greek text. 19:6 Or *children.*

and dry land appeared where water had
    stood before.
This provided a clear path through the
    Red Sea—
    a grassy plain instead of raging waves.
8 The whole nation passed through under
    your protection
    after they had witnessed amazing
    miracles.
9 They ranged like horses and skipped like
    lambs,
    praising you, O Lord, who had delivered
    them.
10 They still remembered what had
    happened while they were living in
    Egypt as foreigners—
    how the ground brought forth flies
    instead of animals
    and the river teemed with vast numbers
    of frogs instead of fish.
11 Later they saw a new kind of bird
    when their cravings led them to ask for
    delicacies.
12 To satisfy their desires, quail came to them
    from the sea.

13 Punishments came upon the sinners,
    but not without prior signs from
    crashing thunder.
They suffered justly because of their
    wicked deeds,
    for they had shown more hatred of
    strangers than even the residents of
    Sodom had shown.
14 The residents of Sodom refused to
    welcome strangers when they arrived,
    but the Egyptians made slaves of guests
    who had served them well.
15 And besides this, while the residents
    of Sodom will receive some sort of
    punishment

    for being hostile toward strangers,
16 the Egyptians were worse, for first they
    welcomed the strangers with a
    celebration,
    but then they enslaved the very people
    they had first received with joy.
They harshly afflicted them even
    though they shared the same rights.
17 The Egyptians were struck with
    blindness,
    like those at the door of Lot, the
    righteous man.
They were surrounded by deep darkness
    and groped to find the door to their own
    house.

18 For the elements changed places with each
    other,
    just as on a harp the tune is varied by
    rearranging the notes,
    yet each note keeps its same sound.
This may be clearly deduced by looking
    at what happened.
19 Land animals were turned into water
    creatures,
    and creatures that swim walked on
    land.
20 Fire kept its normal power even in water,
    and water forgot its fire-quenching
    nature.
21 But the flames did not consume the flesh
    of perishable animals that walked
    through the fire.
Nor did the flames melt the manna—that
    heavenly food that melts as easily
    as ice.

22 For in all things, O Lord, you have exalted
    and glorified your people.
    You have never failed to help them at
    any time or place.

Sirach (Ecclesiasticus)

SOMETIMES CALLED Ecclesiasticus, or the Wisdom of Jesus son of Eleazar, this book contains a wealth of maxims and proverbs that reflect the religious and social concerns of the second century BC. The book was composed in Hebrew by Joshua (Jesus) ben Sira, a scribe living in Jerusalem, and was brought to the Jewish community in Alexandria, Egypt, by his grandson, where it was translated into Greek. Ben Sira called his pupils to live, first and foremost, by the laws of

- **Author:** Joshua (Jesus) ben Sira
- **Date Written:** Around 175 BC
- **Purpose:** To assist people in living a righteous life according to the law of Moses
- **Themes:** The nature of wisdom and its virtues, including patience, humility, mercy, generosity, trust in God, and just living; the effects of wisdom on society; the connection between wisdom and God's law

■ **Outline**
Translator's prologue
1:1–43:33 Wisdom and advice
44:1–50:26 Praise of the ancients
50:27–51:30 Postscript and Appendix

the God of Israel, even as foreign Greek values were being forced upon them by Antiochus IV Epiphanes (175–164 BC). Ben Sira reminded his people that the path to wisdom and success was in following God's law rather than the "wisdom" of the Greeks. The first section considers wisdom's relationship to God and its effects upon human conduct. The second section praises the righteous who lived long ago and reviews the history of salvation. The appendix gives a prayer and hymn of thanksgiving.

Translator's Prologue
The knowledge of many great things has been given to us through the Law, the Prophets, and the other books that followed them. In light of these books, Israel should be commended for its learning and wisdom. But those who read the Scriptures must do more than simply understand them for themselves. Since they love learning, they must also be able to teach outsiders through speaking and writing. My grandfather Jeshua* was a great student of the Law, the Prophets, and the other books of our ancestors. He decided to write something himself pertaining to instruction and wisdom so that those who want to learn may make progress in living according to the law of Moses.

I urge you, therefore, to come with a charitable attitude and to read with attention. Pardon us if, despite our careful work, we seem to have mistranslated anything, for the Hebrew words lose some of their meaning when they are translated into another language. And this is not the only book in which that happens; the translation of the Law, the Prophets, and the other books differs considerably when compared to the original text.

I came to Egypt in the thirty-eighth year of the reign of Ptolemy Physcon* and stayed for some time. There I came across this book of great learning and wisdom. I felt it was important that I devote myself to translating it, so I worked day and night to complete it. Now it is published for the benefit of those living abroad who want to learn how to conduct themselves in accordance with the law of Moses.

In Praise of Wisdom

1 ¹ All wisdom comes from the Lord,
   and wisdom is with him for eternity.
² Who has numbered the sands of the sea,

the drops of rain, and the days of
    eternity?
³ Who has measured the height of heaven,
    the width of the earth, and the depth of
    the abyss?
⁴ Wisdom was created before all things;
    prudent understanding is from
    eternity.*
⁶ To whom has the root of wisdom been
    revealed,
    and who has known all that she does?*
⁸ There is but one who is wise and greatly to
    be feared—
    he sits upon his throne.
⁹ Yes, it is the Lord who created wisdom.
    He saw her and measured her.
He poured her out upon all his works;
¹⁰   to each living creature he gave a certain
    amount.
    He has lavished her on those who love
    him.

Fear of the Lord

¹¹ Fear of the Lord brings honor, glory,
    gladness, and a crown of joy.
¹² Fear of the Lord delights the heart
    and gives gladness, joy, and long life.*
¹³ Those who fear the Lord will have a happy
    end;
    even on the day of death they will be
    blessed.
¹⁴ Fear of the Lord is the beginning of
    wisdom;
    she is instilled in the faithful even in the
    womb.
¹⁵ She has made an everlasting home among
    the human race,
    and she will faithfully stay with our
    descendants.
¹⁶ Fear of the Lord is the fullness of wisdom;
    she deeply satisfies people with her
    fruits.
¹⁷ She fills their houses with good things
    and their storehouses with her harvest.
¹⁸ Fear of the Lord is a crown of wisdom,
    making peace and health to flourish.
¹⁹ Knowledge and discernment shower down
    from wisdom;
    she brings glory to those who cling to
    her.
²⁰ Fear of the Lord is the root of wisdom,
    and long life stems from her.*

²² Unjust anger can never be excused,
    for anger tips the scales to a person's
    own destruction.
²³ Patient people endure for a time,
    and joy is later restored to them.
²⁴ They hold back their words until the right
    time;
    then everyone praises their good works.
²⁵ The treasuries of wisdom hold wise
    sayings,
    but godly living is detestable to a sinner.
²⁶ If you desire wisdom, keep the
    commandments,
    and the Lord will freely give her to you.
²⁷ For fear of the Lord is wisdom and
    instruction,
    and he applauds faithfulness and
    humility.
²⁸ Don't refuse to fear the Lord,
    and don't come to him unless you are
    sincere.
²⁹ Don't be a hypocrite before others;
    be careful of what you say.
³⁰ Don't exalt yourself, or you might fall
    and disgrace yourself.
The Lord will expose your secrets
    and humble you before the whole
    community
because you did not come to him in the
    fear of the Lord,
    and your heart was full of deceit.

Coping with Troubles

2 ¹ My child, when you come to serve the
    Lord,
    expect to encounter troubles.
² Firmly resolve to go in the right
    direction,
    and don't flinch in the face of
    adversity.
³ Cling to the Lord and do not leave him
    so that your last days may be
    prosperous.
⁴ Accept whatever comes your way,
    and be patient in times of humiliation.
⁵ For gold is tested in the fire,
    and worthy souls in the furnace of
    humiliation.
⁶ Trust in the Lord, and he will help you.
    Follow a straight path, and hope
    in him.

1:4 Some manuscripts add verse 5, *The word of God on high is the fountain of wisdom, and wisdom's ways are the everlasting commandments.*   1:6 Some manuscripts add verse 7, *To whom has the instruction of wisdom been revealed? And who has grasped her wealth of experience?*   1:12 Some manuscripts add *Fear of the Lord is a gift from him; because of his love, he makes our paths firm.* 1:20 Some manuscripts add verse 21, *The fear of the Lord drives out sin; and where it resides, it will turn away all anger.*

7 You who fear the Lord, wait for his mercy;
    don't turn away from him, or you may
    fall.
8 You who fear the Lord, trust in him,
    and you will not lose your reward.
9 You who fear the Lord, hope for good
    things
    and for lasting joy and mercy.
10 Look at the generations of old and
    consider:
    Has anyone trusted in the Lord and been
    disappointed?
    Has anyone stood firm in the fear of him
    and been forsaken?
    Has anyone called upon him and been
    ignored by him?
11 For the Lord is compassionate and merciful;
    he forgives sins and saves in times of
    distress.

12 How terrible it will be for the fearful and
    cowardly
    and for the sinner who leads a double
    life!
13 How terrible it will be for the fainthearted
    who have no trust,
    for they will not be protected!
14 How terrible it will be for you who have
    lost your nerve!
    What will you do when the Lord brings
    about justice?

15 Those who fear the Lord do not disobey his
    words,
    and those who love him keep his ways.
16 Those who fear the Lord try to please him,
    and those who love him are filled with
    his law.
17 Those who fear the Lord prepare their
    hearts
    and humble themselves in his presence.
18 Let us fall into the hands of the Lord
    rather than into the hands of people,
    for his mercy is equal to his majesty.

Children and Parents

3 ¹ Children, listen to me, for I am your
    father;
    do what I tell you, so that you may be
    kept safe.
2 The Lord has given the father a place of
    honor before his children
    and has confirmed the mother's
    authority over her children.

3 Those who honor their father will have
    their sins forgiven,
4 and those who respect their mother
    store up treasure.
5 Those who honor their father will have joy
    in their own children,
    and their prayers will be heard.
6 Those who respect their father will enjoy a
    long life,
    and those who comfort their mother
    obey the Lord.*
7 They submit to their parents as a servant
    would to his master.

8 Honor your father by word and deed
    so that you may receive his blessing.
9 A father's blessing strengthens the homes
    of his children,
    but a mother's curse tears out their
    foundations.
10 Don't seek to glorify yourself by
    dishonoring your father,
    for his shame is no glory to you.
11 For people are glorified when their father
    is glorified,
    and it is disgraceful for children not to
    honor their mother.

12 My child, help your father in his old age,
    and do not cause him grief during his
    life.
13 Even if his mind fails, have patience with
    him,
    and do not despise him when you are in
    your prime.
14 For kindness to a father will not be
    forgotten
    and will be recorded in your favor
    against your sins.
15 When you are in trouble, your kindness
    will be remembered;
    your sins will melt away like frost in the
    sunshine.
16 Those who forsake their father are like
    blasphemers,
    and those who anger their mother are
    cursed by the Lord.

Humility

17 My child, do your work with humility,
    and God's people will love you.
18 The greater you are, the more you should
    humble yourself;
    then you will find favor with the Lord.*

3:6 Some manuscripts add verse 7a, *Those who fear the Lord honor their father.*   3:18 Some manuscripts add verse 19, *Many are high and renowned, but he reveals his secrets to the humble.*

20 The Lord is great and powerful,
   but he is honored by the humble.
21 Don't try to understand things that are too
      difficult for you
   or search into things beyond your
      ability.
22 Focus instead on what God has given you,
   for what is hidden is not your concern.
23 Don't meddle in matters that are beyond
      you,
   for even what you see is more than you
      can grasp.
24 For many have been deceived by their own
      reasoning,
   and false assumptions have impaired
      their judgment.*
26 A stubborn heart will come to a bad end,
   and those who love danger will perish
      in it.
27 A stubborn heart will be weighed down
      with sorrows,
   and the sinner heaps up sin upon sin.
28 There is no cure when disaster falls upon
      the proud,
   for an evil plant has taken root in them.
29 Sensible people will reflect on proverbs,
   and an attentive listener delights the
      wise teacher.

Kindness to the Poor

30 Just as water quenches a flaming fire,
   helping the poor atones for sins.
31 Those who repay favors are thinking
      ahead,
   for they will be supported when they
      fall.

4 ¹ My child, don't cheat the poor out of
      their livelihood,
   and don't hold back from helping the
      destitute.
2 Don't aggravate the hungry,
   and don't provoke the needy.
3 Don't cause more troubles for the
      desperate,
   and don't delay in giving to those in
      need.
4 Don't ignore the pleas of those in distress,
   and don't turn your face away from the
      poor.
5 Don't turn your eyes away from the
      needy,
   and give no one a reason to curse you.
6 For if people curse you out of bitterness,
   their Creator will hear them.

7 Make yourself welcome in your
      congregation;
   show respect to the great.
8 Listen to the poor,
   and return their greetings courteously.
9 Rescue the oppressed from the oppressor,
   and don't be fainthearted when giving
      a verdict.
10 Be a father to the fatherless,
   and act as a husband to their mother.
   You will be like an obedient son of the
      Most High,
   and he will love you more than your
      own mother does.

The Rewards of Wisdom

11 Wisdom exalts her children
   and helps those who seek her.
12 Anyone who loves her loves life;
   those who look for her early in the
      morning will be filled with joy.
13 Anyone who holds tight to her will inherit
      honor;
   the Lord blesses every place she enters.
14 Those who serve her are really serving the
      Holy One;
   the Lord loves those who love her.
15 Those who obey her will judge the
      nations,
   and those who listen to her will remain
      secure.
16 If they trust in wisdom, they will inherit
      her,
   and their descendants will also possess
      her.
17 At first she will lead people down winding
      trails,
   causing them fear and apprehension.
   She will discipline them and test them
   until they come to trust her.
18 Then she will immediately return to them
      and give them joy;
   she will reveal her secrets to them.
19 But if they go astray, wisdom will forsake
      them
   and hand them over to destruction.

Wisdom in Speech

20 Be on guard all the time, and watch out
      for evil,
   but don't be overly modest about
      yourself.
21 For one kind of modesty leads to sin,
   but another kind leads to honor and
      favor.

3:24 Some manuscripts add verse 25, *Without eyes there is no light; without knowledge there is no wisdom.*

²² Don't favor others so much that you harm
yourself
  or defer to others to the point that you
  cause your own downfall.
²³ Don't hesitate to speak at the proper
moment.
  And don't hide your wisdom.*
²⁴ For wisdom is revealed by what you say,
  and instruction by the words you speak.
²⁵ Never contradict the truth;
  instead, be ashamed of your own
  ignorance.
²⁶ Don't be ashamed to confess your sins,
  and don't fight against the current of
  a river.
²⁷ Don't let a fool tell you what to do,
  but don't show favor to the powerful.
²⁸ Fight for truth even to the point of death,
  and the Lord God will fight for you.

Guarding against Overconfidence

²⁹ Don't be hasty in your speech
  or slow and lazy in your actions.
³⁰ Don't be like a lion in your home
  or suspicious of your servants.
³¹ Don't open your hands to receive from
  others
  and then close them when it is time
  to give.

5 ¹ Don't put your confidence in wealth
  or say, "I have enough—I'm set for
  life."
² Don't follow your inclinations and
  strength
  and pursue all the desires of your heart.
³ Don't say, "No one is more powerful than
  I am,"
  for the Lord will surely punish you.
⁴ Don't say, "I have sinned, yet nothing has
  happened to me,"
  for the Lord is simply being patient
  with you.
⁵ Don't be so sure your sin is forgiven
  that you continue to heap up sin
  upon sin.
⁶ Don't say, "The mercy of the Lord is great,
  so I can keep sinning and receive
  forgiveness."
  For the Lord shows both mercy and anger,
  and he will become angry with sinners.
⁷ Don't wait to return to the Lord;
  don't put it off one day longer.
  For the Lord's anger will come suddenly
  upon you,

and in the time of punishment you will
  be destroyed.
⁸ Don't take comfort in ill-gotten wealth,
  for it will not help you on the day of
  disaster.

Sincerity in Speech

⁹ Don't winnow in every wind
  or follow every path.*
¹⁰ Stand firm for what you know,
  and be a person of your word.
¹¹ Be quick to hear
  and slow to answer.
¹² If you know what to say, answer your
  neighbors' questions;
  but if you don't, keep quiet.
¹³ What you say brings either honor or
  dishonor,
  and the tongue may bring about a
  person's downfall.
¹⁴ Don't gain a reputation as a slanderer,
  and don't try to trap people by what
  you say.
  For shame awaits the thief,
  and condemnation will come to those
  who speak out of both sides of their
  mouth.
¹⁵ Be careful not to offend others in matters
  great or small,
  and don't be an enemy instead of a friend.

6 ¹ For a bad name will bring reproach and
  shame,
  as happens to every double-tongued
  sinner.

² Don't let passion completely overtake you,
  or it will tear you apart like an angry
  bull.
³ It will eat your leaves and destroy your
  fruit
  so that you are left as a withered tree.
⁴ Those who are filled with evil passion are
  destroyed by it,
  causing their enemies to laugh at them.

Regarding Friendship

⁵ A gentle word wins friends,
  and gracious speech prompts kindness.
⁶ Have many friends,
  but let only one in a thousand be your
  adviser.
⁷ When you are looking to gain friends, test
  them first,
  and do not trust them too quickly.

4:23 Some manuscripts do not include this sentence.   **5:9** Some manuscripts add, *This is the way lying sinners behave.*

8 Some friends are loyal only when it suits
them,
and they will not stand with you when
trouble comes.
9 Some friends become your enemies
and shame you by publicizing your
quarrel.
10 Other friends will dine at your table
but will not stand with you when
trouble comes.
11 When things are going well for you, they
make themselves your equal,
bossing your servants around.
12 But when times are tough, they turn
against you
and hide themselves from you.
13 Avoid your enemies,
and be on guard even with your
friends.

14 A faithful friend is a strong refuge,
and anyone who has found one has
found a treasure.
15 Faithful friends are priceless;
their worth can't be measured.
16 A faithful friend is a lifesaving remedy,
and those who fear the Lord will find
one.
17 Those who fear the Lord will make good
friends,
for they will find friends among others
of like mind.

Seeking Wisdom

18 My child, receive instruction in your
youth,
and you will still possess her when your
hair turns gray.
19 Come to wisdom as one who plows and
plants;
then wait for her good harvest.
You will labor a little as you cultivate her
soil,
but you will soon eat of her harvest.
20 Wisdom seems harsh to the unlearned!
The foolish will not put up with her.
21 She will weigh them down as a heavy
stone,
and they will quickly abandon her.
22 For wisdom is true to her name,
and she is not attained by many.

23 Listen, my child, and take my advice;
do not discard my instruction.
24 Put your feet into wisdom's fetters
and your neck into her collar.

25 Bow down your shoulders and carry her,
and do not resent her bonds.
26 Come to her with all your being,
and keep her ways with all your power.
27 Search intently for her, and she will reveal
herself to you;
when you have taken hold of her, do not
let her go.
28 In the end you will find rest in her,
and she will become your joy.
29 Then her fetters will give you a strong
defense,
and her collar will be your robe of
glory.
30 Her yoke will be a gold ornament,
and her bonds a royal purple cord.
31 You will wear her like a robe of glory
and put her on your head like a crown
of joy.

32 My child, if you will listen to me, you will
learn;
if you will apply yourself, you will be
intelligent.
33 If you love to listen, you will gain
knowledge;
if you pay attention, you will become
wise.
34 Stand in the company of wise elders;
find out who is wise and stay close to
them.
35 Be ready to listen to every godly
conversation,
and let no wise sayings be missed.
36 If you find an intelligent man, get up early
each day to visit him;
let your feet wear out his doorstep.
37 Let your thoughts dwell on the laws of the
Lord,
and meditate continually on his
commandments.
He will affirm your thinking,
and the wisdom you desire will be
granted.

Proverbs for Life

7 1 Do no evil, and no evil will happen to
you;
2 avoid wickedness, and it will stay away
from you.
3 My child, don't plant in the field of
injustice;
otherwise you will harvest its crop
sevenfold.
4 Don't ask the Lord for a high position,
or the king for the seat of honor.

5 Don't try to justify yourself before
 the Lord
  or try to appear wise before the
   king.
6 Don't seek to be made a judge,
  for you may not be able to root out
   injustice,
 or you may be partial to the powerful.
  Then you would lose your integrity.
7 Don't commit an injustice against the
  community;
  don't disgrace yourself before the
   people.

8 Don't plan to repeat a sin,
  for you will be punished even for
   one sin.
9 Don't say, "God will respect my many
  offerings;
  the Most High God will accept what
   I offer."
10 Don't grow weary of praying,
  and don't neglect to give to the poor.
11 Don't ridicule someone who is bitter
   about something,
  for the same God who humbles a person
   can also exalt him.
12 Don't make up lies about your brother
   or about your friend.
13 Refuse to tell any lie,
  for it is a habit that does no good.
14 Don't talk on and on before the elders
   or repeat yourself in prayer.

15 Don't despise hard work or farm work,
  which was ordained by the Most High.
16 Don't join the ranks of sinners;
  remember, punishment will soon
   follow.
17 Humble yourself as much as you can,
  for the ungodly will be punished by fire
   and worms.

Regarding Relationships

18 Don't betray a friend for money
   or despise a true brother for all the gold
    of Ophir.
19 Don't leave a wise and good wife,
  for her gracious presence is worth more
   than gold.
20 Don't hurt servants who work faithfully
   or hired laborers who are devoted to
    their work.
21 Love wise servants as you love yourself;
   don't deny them their freedom.

22 Do you have livestock? Look after them,
  and if they are profitable, keep them.
23 Do you have children? Instruct them,
  and make them obedient from
   childhood.
24 Do you have daughters? Be concerned for
   their chastity,*
  and don't be too indulgent with them.
25 Giving your daughter in marriage is the
   culmination of a great task;
  but be sure to give her to a sensible man.
26 If you have a wife who pleases you, don't
   divorce her;
  but if you don't love her, don't trust her.

27 Honor your father with your whole heart,
  and don't forget the pain your mother
   endured to give you birth.
28 Remember that you owe your very life to
   them;
  how can you repay them for all they
   have done?

29 Fear the Lord with all your soul,
  and revere his priests.
30 Love your Creator with all your strength,
  and don't forsake his servants.
31 Fear the Lord and honor the priest.
  As it is commanded, give the priest his
   portion:
 firstfruits, guilt offerings, shoulder
   offerings,*
 sanctification sacrifices, and firstfruits
   of the holy things.

32 Stretch out your hand to help the poor,
  so your blessing may be complete.
33 Be generous to all the living,
  and honor even the dead.*
34 Don't turn away from those who weep;
  share the grief of those who mourn.
35 Don't hesitate to visit the sick,
  because you will be loved for doing such
   things.
36 If you always live in light of your
   approaching death,
  you will never sin.

More Proverbs for Life

8 1 Don't fight against the powerful,
   or you might fall into their hands.
 2 Don't quarrel with the rich;
  their resources may outweigh yours.
 For gold has destroyed many
  and corrupted the hearts of kings.

7:24 Greek *their bodies.*   7:31 See Deut 18:3.   7:33 Greek *and do not withhold kindness from the dead.*

³ Don't argue with loudmouths;
  don't heap fuel on their fire.

⁴ Don't make fun of an ignorant man,
  for he may insult your ancestors.
⁵ Don't criticize a repentant sinner;
  remember, we are all guilty.
⁶ Don't despise anyone who is old,
  for some of us are also growing old.
⁷ Don't rejoice at anyone's death;
  remember, we all have to die.

⁸ Don't despise the counsel of the wise,
  but strive to learn their proverbs.
From them you can gain instruction
  and learn how to serve the great.
⁹ Don't ignore what elderly people have
    to say,
  for they themselves learned from their
    parents.*
From them you can learn how to
    understand
  and give a timely answer.

¹⁰ Don't kindle the coals of sinners,
   or you may be burned in the fire of their
     sins.
¹¹ Don't let insolent people provoke you,
   or they will trap you in your own words.
¹² Don't lend to a person who is stronger
     than you—
   but if you do lend something, count it
     as lost.
¹³ Don't give a guarantee beyond your
     means;
   and if you put up bond money for
     someone, presume you will have to
     pay it.

¹⁴ Don't file suit against a judge;
   the ruling will favor him because of his
     position.
¹⁵ Don't go on a journey with irresponsible
     people,
   for their mischief will become your
     burden.
They will do what they wish,
   and you will be ruined by their
     foolishness.
¹⁶ Don't quarrel with those who have short
     tempers,
   and don't go with them into the desert,
for bloodshed is nothing to them,
   and they will strike you down when no
     one is near to help you.

¹⁷ Don't discuss your plans with fools,
   for they can't keep anything secret.
¹⁸ Be careful what you do around strangers,
   for you do not know what they will tell.
¹⁹ Don't open your heart to just anyone,
   and don't accept favors from such a
     person.

Regarding Women

9 ¹ Don't be jealous of the wife you love
       or teach her wicked ways she can use
         to repay you.
² Don't give yourself to a woman,
   for she may dominate you completely.
³ Don't go near a promiscuous woman,
   or you will fall into her snares.
⁴ Don't spend time with a dancing girl,
   or you will succumb to her charms.
⁵ Don't stare at a young girl,
   or you might sleep with her and have
     to pay a penalty.*
⁶ Don't sleep with prostitutes,
   or you might lose your inheritance.
⁷ Don't look around the streets of a city
   or wander up and down in its deserted
     places.
⁸ Turn your eyes away from a shapely woman,
   and don't stare at beauty that belongs to
     another.
For many have been seduced by a woman's
     beauty,
   and passion then becomes a roaring fire.
⁹ Don't have dinner with another man's wife
   or spend time with her drinking wine,
for you might fall in love with her
   and come to ruin because of your
     passion.

Keeping Good Company

¹⁰ Don't forsake old friends,
   for new ones will not compare to them.
A new friend is like new wine;
   when it has aged, you drink it with
     pleasure.
¹¹ Don't envy the success of sinners,
   for you don't know what is in store for
     them.
¹² Don't seek after the pleasures of the
     ungodly;
   remember, they will eventually be
     punished before they die.

¹³ Keep far from those who have the power
     to kill,
   and you will have no worry about death.

8:9 Greek *their fathers.*   9:5 See Exod 22:16-17; Deut 22:28-29.

But if you must approach them, be careful
    not to offend them,
  or they may kill you.
Realize that you are stepping among
    traps
  and walking along the edge of a cliff.*

14 Know your neighbor as well as you can,
  and consult with the wise.
15 Look for intelligent people to talk with;
  always discuss the law of the Most High.
16 Choose the righteous to be your dinner
    companions,
  and let your boasting be in the fear of
    the Lord.
17 A work is praised for the skill of the
    artisan,
  and a leader is praised for the wisdom
    of his speech.
18 Loudmouths are feared in their city,
  and those who speak recklessly are
    hated.

Regarding Government

10

1 A wise ruler educates his people,
  and the administration of a
    prudent ruler is well ordered.
2 The judge of the people sets the example,
  and all his officials follow his lead.
The mayor of a city sets the tone, and
    the people follow.
3 An unlearned king will be the ruin of his
    people,
  but a city prospers through its leaders'
    knowledge.
4 The Lord is in charge of the whole earth.
  He establishes the right leader at the
    right time.
5 The Lord is in charge of human success,
  and he is the one who honors the
    legislator.*

The Evils of Pride

6 Don't get angry at your neighbor for every
    little injury,
  and don't behave rashly.
7 Pride is hateful to the Lord and humanity,
  and injustice is outrageous to both.
8 Control of a kingdom passes from one
    group of people to another
  because of injustice, arrogance, and
    greed.
9 How can we—dust and ashes—be proud?
  Even during life a person's body decays.

10 A long sickness baffles the physician;
  a king today is a corpse tomorrow.
11 When people die,
  they inherit maggots, wild animals, and
    worms.
12 Pride begins when a person abandons the
    Lord
  and turns away from his Maker.
13 Pride begins with sin;
  those who remain proud are
    abominable.
For this reason the Lord brings them
    unexpected disasters,
  which completely destroy them.
14 The Lord overturns the thrones of princes
  and sets up the meek in their place.
15 The Lord plucks up the roots of proud
    nations
  and plants the humble in their place.
16 The Lord overthrows the nations
  and destroys them to their very
    foundations.
17 He removes some of them and destroys
    them.
He erases their memory from the
    earth.

Those Worthy of Honor

18 Pride was not created for mortals,
  or furious anger for those born of
    women.
19 Who is worthy of honor?
  The human race.
Who is worthy of honor?
  Those who fear the Lord.
Who is not worthy of honor?
  The human race.
Who is not worthy of honor?
  Those who break the commandments.
20 Among family members, their leader is
    worthy of honor,
  but with the Lord, anyone who fears
    him is worthy of honor.*
22 The rich, the noble, the poor—
  let them pride themselves in fearing
    the Lord.
23 It is not right to despise an intelligent
    person who is poor,
  and it is not good to honor a sinful
    person.
24 The prince, the judge, and the ruler are
    honored,
  yet there is none greater than the person
    who fears the Lord.

9:13 Greek *along the battlements of the city.*   10:5 As in Hebrew; Greek reads *scribe.*   10:20 Some manuscripts add verse 21,
The fear of the Lord is the beginning of acceptance; obstinacy and pride are the beginning of rejection.

25 Those who are free will serve a wise slave,
      and the intelligent will not protest.

26 Don't show off your wisdom when doing
        your work
      or boast in the time of need.
27 Better are those who work and have plenty
      than those who brag but need bread.
28 My child, think well of yourself but with
        modesty;
      be honest in assessing your worth.
29 Who can acquit those who condemn
        themselves?
      And who can honor those who devalue
        their own lives?
30 The poor are honored for their
        understanding,
      and the rich are honored for their
        wealth.
31 If a person is honored in poverty,
      how much more in wealth!
    If a person is dishonored in wealth,
      how much more in poverty!

Appearances Are Deceiving

11 1 The wisdom of the humble raises
          their heads high
      and causes them to sit among the great.
2 Don't praise people for their good looks
      or despise them for their appearance.
3 The bee is small among flying creatures,
      but what it produces is the sweetest.
4 Don't boast about your fine clothes,
      or become proud when you are
        honored;
    for the works of the Lord are wonderful,
      and his works are hidden from people.
5 Many kings have been deposed,*
      and an unlikely person has been given
        the crown.
6 Many rulers have been completely
        disgraced,
      and the prominent have been placed at
        the mercy of others.

Acting with Caution

7 Don't place blame before you investigate;
      when you have finished your inquiry,
        then criticize.
8 Listen before you answer,
      and don't interrupt others while they
        are talking.

9 Don't get involved in a matter that doesn't
        concern you
      or sit with sinners involved in a dispute.
10 My child, don't take on too many
        responsibilities;
      if you get overcommitted, you will still
        be held accountable.
    In all your hurrying, you will not catch up,
      and you will not escape by running
        away.
11 Some people labor and struggle and rush,
      only to fall farther behind.
12 Others are slow and need help.
      They lack strength and are plagued by
        poverty.
    Yet the Lord looks upon them with
        kindness;
      he lifts them from their lowly
        condition.
13 He gives them honor—
      to the amazement of most everyone.

14 Good and bad, life and death, poverty and
        riches—
      all are from the Lord.*
17 The gift of the Lord remains with the
        devout,
      and the Lord's favor brings lasting
        success.
18 People become rich by living frugally,
      and this is their reward:
19 They say, "I have found rest,
      and now I will enjoy my possessions."
    But they do not know how much time is
        left
      until they die and leave all their wealth
        to others.

20 Stand by your contracts and fulfill them.
      Grow old in your work.
21 Don't be amazed at what sinners do.
      Trust in the Lord, and stick to your job.
    In the Lord's sight it is easy
      to make a poor person suddenly rich.
22 The Lord rewards the devout by blessing
        them,
      and his blessing flourishes fruit quickly.
23 Don't say, "What do I need,
      and how will I benefit from this?"
24 Don't say, "I am self-sufficient;
      what could possibly go wrong?"
25 In times of prosperity we forget adversity,

11:5 Greek *made to sit on the ground.*   11:14 Some manuscripts add verses 15-16, *15Wisdom and understanding and knowledge of the law come from the Lord. 16Love and good works come from him. Error and darkness were created with sinners, and evil grows old with those who delight in it.*

and in times of adversity we forget
  prosperity.
²⁶ It is easy for the Lord on the day of death
  to reward a person's conduct.
²⁷ An hour's misery makes a person forget
  past delights.
  The last hour of life reveals a person's
  deeds.
²⁸ Don't call anyone blessed before that
  person dies,
  for people are known by their children.

²⁹ Don't bring just anyone into your home,
  for the deceitful have many tricks.
³⁰ The proud act like decoy partridges in
  a cage.
  Like spies, they look for what could
  make you fall.
³¹ They lie in wait, turning good into evil,
  and find fault with what is praiseworthy.
³² A blazing fire comes from one spark,
  and a sinner looks for a chance to shed
  blood.
³³ Beware of scoundrels and their evil
  schemes,
  for they could ruin your reputation
  forever.
³⁴ If you receive strangers into your home,
  they will cause trouble and make you
  a stranger in your own home.

Rules for Doing Good

12 ¹ If you do good to others, give
  thought to the people you select;
  then your good deeds will be
  appreciated.
² Do good to the devout, and you will be
  rewarded—
  if not by them, then certainly by the
  Most High.
³ No good comes to those who continue to
  do evil
  or to those who do not give to the poor.
⁴ Give to the godly but not to the sinner.
⁵ Do good to the humble, but do not give
  to the ungodly.
  Keep your bread, and don't give it to the
  ungodly,
  for they might grow stronger than you
  because of it.
  Then you will receive twice as much evil
  for all the good you have done to them.
⁶ The Most High hates sinners
  and will punish the ungodly.*
⁷ Give to the good,

but don't help the sinner.
⁸ A friend will not ask for favors when you
  are doing well,
  but an enemy won't stay away when you
  are in trouble.
⁹ When people are prosperous, their
  enemies act like friends,
  but when trouble comes, even one's
  friends disappear.

Guarding against Enemies

¹⁰ Never trust your enemies,
  for they will turn wicked as surely as
  copper tarnishes.
¹¹ Even if they humble themselves and come
  begging,
  be on guard—beware of them.
  Treat them carefully, as though you were
  polishing a metal mirror
  to be sure it doesn't tarnish.
¹² Don't give your enemies a position next
  to you,
  or they may overthrow you and take
  your place.
  Don't seat them at your right hand,
  or they may try to take your seat.
  And then you will see that I was right
  and be stung by what I told you.

¹³ Who feels sorry for snake charmers when
  they are bitten?
  Or for those who go near savage beasts?
¹⁴ So it is with those who keep bad company
  and participate in their sins.
¹⁵ Sinners will stand by you for a while,
  but if you slip, they will abandon you.
¹⁶ Enemies speak sweetly with their lips,
  but in their hearts they plot to throw
  you into a pit.
  Enemies weep with their eyes,
  but they will use every opportunity to
  cause as much bloodshed as they can.
¹⁷ If trouble comes, enemies will be there
  ahead of you.
  They will pretend to help you, but they
  will trip you up.
¹⁸ They will shake their heads and clap their
  hands to mock you,
  and they will whisper about you,
  showing their true feelings toward you.

The Rich and the Poor

13 ¹ As those who touch pitch get dirty,
  so those who associate with the
  proud will become proud.

12:6 Some manuscripts add *and he is keeping them for their day of punishment.*

2 Don't try to carry a burden too heavy
for you
or associate with someone mightier or
richer than you.
How can you put a clay jar next to an iron
kettle?
If they knock against one another, the
jar will be smashed.
3 If rich people do wrong, they blame
others,
but if poor people are wronged, they
must apologize over and over.
4 Rich people will exploit you if you have
anything to give,
but they will abandon you if you have
nothing.
5 If you have anything, the rich will live
with you
and consume your goods without
remorse.
6 If they need you, they will deceive you.
They will smile at you and encourage
you.
They will speak gently to you,
asking, "What do you need?"
7 The rich will shame you by their fine
meals
until you are drained two or three times
by returning the favor.
Finally, they will laugh at you.
Afterward when they see you,
they will avoid you and deride you.
8 Beware that you are not deceived
and humiliated by your stupidity.
9 If you are invited to dinner by the
influential, be reluctant to accept;
then they will be even more
insistent.
10 Don't push yourself forward, or you
might be pushed back;
but don't stand aloof, or you may be
forgotten.
11 Don't speak to the influential as equals
or believe their many words,
for they will test you with their long
discourses
and probe you with their smiles.
12 Those who betray your confidence are
cruel.
They will not hesitate to harm or
imprison you.
13 Keep quiet and be very careful,
for you are flirting with disaster.*

15 Every creature loves its own kind,
so every person should love his
neighbor.
16 Every creature associates with those like
itself,
and people are drawn to others like
themselves.
17 What does a wolf have in common with
a lamb?
So it is with the sinner and the godly.
18 What peace can there be between a hyena
and a dog?
Or what peace can there be between the
rich and the poor?
19 The wild donkey is a lion's prey in the
wilderness;
so also the poor are devoured by the rich.
20 Humility is an abomination to the proud,
just as the poor are abhorred by the rich.
21 When the rich fail, their friends support
them;
but when the poor fall, their friends
push them away.
22 When the rich falter, many come to their
aid;
when they speak inappropriately, they
are justified by others.
But if the poor slip, they are criticized.
They may speak wisely, but no one
listens.
23 The rich speak, and everyone stops
talking;
their speech is praised to the heavens.
The poor person speaks, and people ask,
"Who is this?"
If the poor stumble, they are pushed
down.
24 Riches are good for those without sin,
and poverty is evil only to the ungodly.

True Happiness

25 The heart changes one's countenance—
for better or for worse.
26 The sign of a good heart is a happy face,
but composing proverbs is painful work.

14 ¹ Blessed are those who have not erred
in their speech
and who are not plagued by remorse
for sin.
2 Blessed are those who are not wracked by
guilt
and who have not given up hope.

13:13 Some manuscripts add verse 14, *When you hear these things in your sleep, wake up! Love the Lord all your life and call upon him
for your salvation.*

3 Riches are not appropriate for those who
  think small.
  What use is money to a miser?
4 By depriving himself, he is only storing up
  for others,
  and they will enjoy a life of luxury with
  his possessions.
5 If people are stingy toward themselves, to
  whom will they be generous?
  They don't even enjoy their own
  wealth.
6 No one is worse than those who are stingy
  with themselves;
  they punish themselves by their own
  stinginess.
7 If they do good, it is by mistake;
  in the end they show that they are
  mean.
8 Misers are wicked;
  they turn away from people and
  disregard them.
9 Greedy people are never satisfied with
  their share;
  their souls will shrivel up from greed.
10 Misers are reluctant to share food,
  and even their own meals are meager.

11 My child, be good to yourself with what
  you have,
  and give worthy offerings to the Lord.
12 Remember that death advances steadily
  and that the decree* of the grave* has
  not been shown to you.
13 Be good to your friends while you are still
  alive;
  reach out and give to them as much as
  you can.
14 Don't forget to enjoy the good things each
  day brings,
  and don't let your part of a good gift
  pass you by.
15 When you die, others will receive your
  hard-earned possessions;
  everything you worked for will be
  randomly distributed to others.
16 Give, take, and be good to yourself,
  for you cannot find luxury in the place
  of the dead.*
17 Like a garment, all living beings grow old,
  for the age-old decree is: "You will die."*
18 The generations of flesh and blood
  are like the many leaves of a growing
  tree.
  The tree sheds some leaves and puts forth
  new ones.

So also one generation dies and another
  is born.
19 All things made by people decay and
  disappear,
  and those who made them will
  eventually pass away with them.

The Pursuit of Wisdom
20 Blessed are those who meditate on wisdom
  and reflect on knowledge.
21 They consider wisdom's ways
  and ponder her secrets.
22 They pursue her like a hunter
  and wait to ambush her along her paths.
23 They look for her through her windows
  and listen for her at her doors.
24 They camp near her house
  and fasten their tent pegs to her wall.
25 They pitch their tent near her;
  in this way they find a good place to live.
26 They place their children under her shelter
  and camp under her branches.
27 She protects them from the heat,
  and they live amidst her glory.

The Blessings of Wisdom
15 1 Whoever fears God will do these
  things;
  whoever follows the law of Moses will
  gain wisdom.
2 Like a mother, she will come to meet him;
  like a young bride, she will welcome
  him.
3 She will feed him with the bread of
  understanding
  and give him the water of wisdom to
  drink.
4 He will lean on her and not fall;
  he will depend on her and not be
  humiliated.
5 She will exalt him above his neighbors
  and make him eloquent among the
  congregation.
6 He will be crowned with joy and gladness
  and inherit an everlasting name.
7 The foolish will not obtain wisdom,
  nor will sinners ever see her.
8 Wisdom will have nothing to do with
  arrogance,
  and liars never give thought to her.
9 Praise from sinners is out of place,
  for it has not been given to them by the
  Lord.
10 For praise must flow from wisdom,
  and the Lord must prompt it.

14:12a Greek *covenant;* also in 14:17.   14:12b Greek *of Hades.*   14:16 Greek *in Hades.*   14:17 See Gen 2:16-17; 3:19.

Freedom to Choose

11 Don't say, "It is the Lord's fault that I
        sinned,"
    for he does not do what he hates.
12 Don't say, "It was the Lord who led me
        astray,"
    for he does not need sinful people.
13 The Lord hates every kind of detestable sin,
    and those who fear him will not love
        it either.
14 In the beginning he made people
    and allowed them to do whatever they
        planned.
15 If you choose, you can obey the
        commandments;
    you have the freedom to act faithfully.
16 He has set before you fire and water;
    reach out and select whichever one you
        choose.
17 Before each person are life and death;*
    you will receive whichever one you
        choose.
18 For the wisdom of the Lord is great;
    he is powerful and sees all things.
19 The Lord watches over those who fear him,
    and he knows everything we do.
20 He has not commanded anyone to be
        wicked;
    he has given no one permission to sin.

Ungodly Children

16 1 Do not desire to have many children
        if they are worthless;
    do not delight in godless offspring.
2 No matter how many children you have,
        don't rejoice over them
    unless they are godly.
3 Don't count on them living a long time
    or take confidence in how many
        there are.
    For one can be better than a thousand,
        and it is better to die childless than to
        have ungodly children.
4 One intelligent person can cause a city to
        become populated,
    but a clan of rebels causes it to become
        deserted.

The Lord Punishes Sinners

5 My eyes have seen many things like this,
    and my ears have heard things even
        more astounding.

6 A fire was kindled in Korah's* group of
        sinners,
    and the Lord's wrath blazed up within
        the disobedient nation.
7 The Lord did not forgive the ancient
        giants,
    who used their strength to rebel.
8 He did not spare Lot's neighbors;
    he detested them for their pride.
9 The Lord showed no pity for the doomed
        nation of Canaanites,
    who were uprooted for their sins.
10 Nor did he have pity on the 600,000
        Israelite foot soldiers
    that gathered together in their
        stubbornness.
11 Even if there had been only one stubborn
        person,
    it would have been amazing if he had
        escaped unpunished.
    For the Lord possesses both mercy and
        wrath;
    he forgives a great deal, but he also
        pours out wrath.
12 His mercy is great, but so is his
        punishment.
    He judges people according to their
        deeds.
13 He does not let sinners escape with their
        plunder
    or allow the patience of the godly to go
        unrewarded.
14 He credits every act of mercy in a person's
        favor,*
    and all are treated as their deeds
        deserve.*

17 Don't say, "I am hidden from the Lord.
    Who will remember me from on high?
    No one will notice me in such a large
        crowd.
    What do I amount to in such an
        immense creation?
18 Look! The very highest heavens,
    the watery depths, and the earth
    tremble at the Lord's coming.
19 The mountains and the foundations of the
        earth
    tremble and shake when he looks at
        them.
20 But no mind thinks about these things,
    for who can comprehend his ways?

15:17 See Deut 30:19.   16:6 In 16:6-10, Korah, Canaanites and Israelites are alluded to but not explicitly named in the
Greek text.   16:14a Or He shows mercy wherever he can.   16:14b Some manuscripts add verses 15-16, 15The Lord caused Pharaoh
to become stubborn so that he would not acknowledge him; in this way the Lord's works could become known throughout the world. 16His
mercy is revealed to all the world, and he divided his light and darkness with a plumb line.

21 Just as the wind of a storm cannot be seen,
  so most of the Lord's works are hidden.
22 Who will announce his acts of justice?
  Or who will wait for them to happen?
  It will be a long time before he carries
  out what he has decreed."
23 This is how people who lack
  understanding think.
  They are foolish, senseless, and
  misguided.

The Lord Created with Order
24 Listen to me, my child, and gain knowledge.
  Focus your thoughts on my words.
25 I will measure out my learning
  and declare knowledge accurately.

26 When the Lord created his works in the
  beginning
  and determined the natural laws of
  creation,
27 he arranged things in a certain order
  forever
  and assigned their dominion for all
  generations.
  They do not grow hungry or weary,
  nor do they shirk their duties.
28 They do not crowd each other,
  and they never disobey his word.
29 After this the Lord looked at the earth
  and filled it with his good things.
30 He covered its surface with all kinds of
  living things,
  and to the earth they must return.

17 ¹ The Lord created human beings
  from the earth,
  and he makes them return to it.
² He gave them a certain number of days
  to live
  but also granted them authority over
  everything on earth.
³ He gave them strength like his own
  and created them in his own image.
⁴ He put the fear of them in all living
  creatures
  and gave them dominion over animals
  and birds.*
⁶ The Lord gave people discretion, a tongue,
  eyes,
  ears, and a mind for thinking.

⁷ He filled them with knowledge and
  understanding
  and showed them the difference
  between good and evil.
⁸ He kept his eye on their hearts
  to show them the greatness of his
  works.*
¹⁰ People will praise the holy name of the
  Lord
  as they proclaim the glory of his
  works.
¹¹ He gave them knowledge
  and the law of life for an inheritance.
¹² He made an everlasting covenant with
  them
  and showed them his decrees.
¹³ Their eyes saw his glorious majesty,
  and their ears heard his glorious voice.
¹⁴ The Lord said to them, "Beware of all evil."
  And he gave all of them a
  commandment about their
  neighbors.
¹⁵ Their ways are always known to him;
  they are not hidden from his eyes.*
¹⁷ Over each nation he appointed a ruler.
  But Israel is the Lord's own possession.*
¹⁹ To him, all their actions are as plain as
  the sun,
  and his eyes continually watch how
  they live.
²⁰ Their evil deeds are not hidden from him;
  the Lord sees all their sins.*
²² Gifts to the needy are like a signet ring to
  the Lord,
  and kind acts are the apple of his eye.
²³ Afterward he will rise up and repay the
  wicked;
  he will bring his retribution down on
  their heads.
²⁴ But to those who repent he grants a return
  to his favor,
  and he encourages those who have lost
  hope.

A Call to Repentance
²⁵ Return to the Lord, and forsake your sins.
  Pray in his presence, and stop offending
  him.*
²⁶ Return to the Most High, and turn away
  from evil;
  completely detest what he hates.

17:4 Some manuscripts add verse 5, *The Lord gave them the use of the five senses. He also gave them a mind as the sixth gift and reason, which interprets for the senses, as the seventh.* **17:8** Some manuscripts add verse 9, *He enabled them to boast of his marvels forever.* **17:15** Some manuscripts add verse 16, *From the time they were young, their ways tended toward evil, and they are unable to turn their hard hearts into soft ones.* **17:17** Some manuscripts add verse 18, *He brings them up with discipline because they are his firstborn. He gives them the light of love and never neglects them.* **17:20** Some manuscripts add verse 21, *But the gracious Lord knows what they are made of, so he has neither rejected them nor abandoned them. Rather, he has spared them.* **17:25** Or *and thereby reduce your guilt.*

27 Who will praise the Most High from the
  place of the dead?*
    Will they replace the living who give
    thanks?
28 Once people die, they can no longer give
  thanks,
    but those who are alive and well can
    sing praises to the Lord.
29 How great is the mercy of the Lord
    and his forgiveness for those who return
    to him!
30 Human beings cannot do everything,
    for they are not immortal.
31 There is nothing brighter than the sun, is
  there? Yet even it can be eclipsed.
    In the same way, human beings falter by
    devising evil.
32 The sun* watches over the powers of the
  heavens,
    but all humans are merely dust and
    ashes.

The Greatness of God

18 1 He who lives forever created all the
    universe.
2   The Lord alone is just.*
4 He has given no one the power to fully
  proclaim his works.
    Who can search out his mighty deeds?
5 Who can measure his majestic power?
    And who is able to tell about his
    mercy?
6 None of these things can be diminished
  or enlarged.
    No one can search out the wonders of
    the Lord.
7 When people finish recounting them, they
  are still at the beginning;
    when they stop, they are still puzzled.
8 What are mere mortals, and what is their
  purpose?
    What is good in them, and what is evil?
9 The lifespan of a person
    is a hundred years at most.
10 Like a drop of water from the sea or a grain
  of sand,
    so are these few years compared to
    eternity.
11 For this reason the Lord is patient with
  them
    and pours out his mercy on them.
12 He recognizes how harsh their end is,
    so he grants them forgiveness all the
    more.

13 Human compassion extends to one's
  neighbor,
    but the Lord's mercy reaches every
    living thing.
  He trains, corrects, and teaches them;
    he brings them back as a shepherd does
    with his flock.
14 He has compassion on all who accept his
  guidance
    and who are eager to obey his laws.

Using Caution and Good Judgment

15 My child, don't scold while doing good
  deeds
    or ruin your generous deeds by speaking
    harshly.
16 Doesn't the dew relieve the scorching heat?
    So also a word is better than a gift.
17 Certainly a word is worth more than a
  good gift, isn't it?
    A gracious person gives both.
18 A fool is ungracious and offensive.
    The gift of a stingy person is an eyesore.

19 Learn before you speak.
    Take care of your health before you get
    sick.
20 Examine yourself before judgment comes,
    and you will receive forgiveness in the
    time of reckoning.
21 Humble yourself before you get sick,
    and when you sin, repent.
22 Don't let anything keep you from fulfilling
  a vow promptly,
    and don't go to your grave before you
    have fulfilled your vow.
23 Before you make a vow, prepare yourself,
    and don't be like a person who tries the
    Lord's patience.
24 Think about the wrath that awaits you at
  death
    and the time of vengeance when the
    Lord turns away his face.
25 Remember times of hunger during times
  of plenty,
    and remember times of poverty and
    need when you are wealthy.
26 From dawn to dusk conditions change,
    and the Lord watches all things move
    swiftly.

27 Wise people are cautious in everything
    and take care not to participate in the
    sins that surround them.

17:27 Greek *from Hades.*   17:32 Or *The Lord.*   18:2 Some manuscripts add verses 2b-3, *and there is no other beside him.* 3He steers the
world with the touch of his hand, and all things obey his will. For he is king of all things; by his power he can separate the holy from the profane.

28 Every sensible person recognizes wisdom
    and praises the one who finds her.
29 Those who are skilled with words become
        wise
    and pour out fitting proverbs.

Self-Control

30 Don't be ruled by your passions;
    restrain your desires.
31 If you give in to your passions,
    they will make a mockery of you before
        your enemies.
32 Don't indulge in great luxury,
    for you may go broke from the cost.
33 Do not make yourself poor by feasting
        with borrowed money
    when you have nothing in your pocket.

19 ¹ A drunken worker will not become
        rich,
    and those who don't take care of the
        little they have will fail little by little.
² Wine and women corrupt intelligent men,
    and the man who frequents prostitutes
        is reckless.
³ Rottenness and worms will consume him,
    and the reckless person will be snatched
        away.

Caution in Speech

⁴ One who trusts others too easily has a
        shallow mind,
    and those who sin hurt themselves.
⁵ Those who take pleasure in evil will be
        condemned.
⁶ Those who hate gossip are guarding
        against evil.
⁷ Do not repeat what you hear,
    and you will never let anything slip.
⁸ Do not tell it to friend or foe;
    do not disclose it, unless keeping it a
        secret would be a sin.
⁹ For someone may watch you and hear you,
    and over time they will come to hate you.
¹⁰ Have you heard something? Let it die with
        you.
    Be strong! It will not make you burst!
¹¹ When something is told to fools, they
        suffer agony
    like a woman in labor with a child.
¹² Like an arrow stuck in someone's thigh,
    so is gossip in the heart of a fool.

¹³ If you hear a rumor, question your friends
        about it.
    They may have not done anything.
    Or if they did, question them so that
        they may not do it again.
¹⁴ Question your neighbors, for they may not
        have said anything;
    but if they have, question them so that
        they may not repeat it.
¹⁵ Question your friends about any rumor,
    for it may only be slander against them.
    Do not believe everything you hear.
¹⁶ A person may make a slip in speech
        without intending it.
    For who has never sinned by something
        they have said?
¹⁷ Question your neighbors before you
        threaten them,
    and let the law of the Most High take its
        course.*

Wisdom Is Better Than Craftiness

²⁰ All wisdom comes from fearing the Lord
    and always involves practicing the law
        of Moses.*
²² Knowledge about wickedness is not wisdom,
    and there is no prudence in the advice
        of sinners.
²³ Certain kinds of cleverness are detestable,
    and some people are fools simply
        because they lack wisdom.
²⁴ But better are those who lack wisdom and
        yet fear God
    than those who are brilliant and yet
        disobey the law of Moses.
²⁵ Some cleverness is keen but unjust,
    while on the other hand some people
        pervert the system to get justice.
²⁶ There are villains who appear stooped over
        in grief,
    while inwardly they are full of deceit.
²⁷ They cover their faces and pretend not to
        hear,
    but once no one is looking, they will
        take advantage of you.
²⁸ Though their lack of strength may keep
        them from sinning,
    if they find an opportunity to do evil,
        they will do it.
²⁹ People are known by their appearance,
    and sensible people can be recognized
        at first sight.

19:17 Some manuscripts add verses 18-19, *¹⁸Fear of the Lord is the beginning of gaining his acceptance, and wisdom obtains his love.*
¹⁹Knowing the Lord's commandments is a discipline that brings life, and those who do what pleases him enjoy fruit of the tree of immortality.
19:20 Some manuscripts add verses 20b-21, *and acknowledging the Lord's omnipotence. ²¹When a slave says to his master, "I will not do
as you wish," he angers the one who supports him even if he does it later.*

30 The way they dress, laugh heartily,
  and walk tells you what kind of people
      they are.

The Wise Know When to Keep Silent

20 ¹ Certain kinds of rebuke are out
      of place,
  and a wise person knows when to
      keep quiet.
2 But how much better it is to rebuke
      someone
  than to stay angry with that person.
3 The person who admits a mistake
  will avoid being disgraced.
4 Like a eunuch lusting after a girl,
  so is the person who does what is right
      only under compulsion.
5 Some people are thought to be wise
  because they remain silent,
  while others are despised because they
      are talkative.
6 Some people keep quiet because they have
      no answer,
  while others keep quiet because they
      know when to speak.
7 A wise person keeps quiet until the right
      opportunity,
  but an arrogant fool is completely
      unaware of the right moment.
8 Whoever talks too much is hated,
  and those who act as if they are
      important are detested.

Some Paradoxes of Life

9 Sometimes hard times can bring good
      fortune,
  while a windfall may turn into a loss.
10 Some gifts are not profitable
  and others must be paid back double.
11 There are losses because of honor,
  and some people of lowly status have
      gained prestige.
12 Some people buy much for little,
  but then they pay for it seven times over.
13 The wise gain favor with their words,
  but fools waste their compliments to
      others.
14 Gifts from fools will do you no good,
  for they are looking to be repaid
      sevenfold.
15 Fools give little and berate much.
  They announce things like the town
      crier.
  Today they lend, and tomorrow they ask
      for it back;
  such people are detestable.

16 The fool says, "I have no friends,
  and no one thanks me for my good
      deeds.
17 The very people I feed speak maliciously
      about me."
  How often—and by how many—will
      such a person be laughed at!

Shameful Speech

18 A slip on the pavement is better than a slip
      of the tongue.
  That is how fast the wicked will fall.
19 An ill-mannered person is like an
      indiscreet story
  that is continually repeated by fools.
20 A proverb told by a fool will be rejected
  because he does not tell it at the right
      moment.
21 Poverty may prevent some people from
      sinning;
  when they try to sleep, they will not be
      restless with remorse.
22 People can be destroyed because they are
      modest
  or because they look foolish.
23 A person may be shamed into making
      promises to a friend
  and thereby gains an enemy for no good
      reason.
24 A lie is an ugly stain on a person,
  and the foolish will constantly talk
      about it.
25 A thief is better than a constant liar,
  but both are headed for destruction.
26 Lying leads to disgrace,
  and such shame stays with a person
      constantly.

Displaying Wisdom

27 Wise people gain prestige by their words,
  and sensible people please the
      powerful.
28 Those who till their land will harvest a
      good crop,
  and those who please the powerful
      make up for injustice.
29 Favors and gifts blind the eyes of the
      wise;
  like a muzzle over their mouths, they
      keep them from criticizing.
30 What profit is there in wisdom that is
      hidden
  and in treasure that no one has
      discovered?

31 Better are those who hide their foolishness
than those who hide their wisdom.*

Warnings against Sin

21 1 My child, have you sinned? Don't sin
anymore.
But ask forgiveness for your past sins.
2 Flee from sin as from a snake,
for if you come near sin, it will bite you.
Its teeth are the teeth of a lion,
which can destroy human lives.
3 All lawlessness is like a two-edged sword;
the wound it inflicts will never heal.

4 Terror and arrogance will cause riches to
waste away.
In this way the household of the proud
will be reduced to nothing.
5 The prayer of the poor will be heard by the
Lord,
and his judgment comes quickly.
6 Those who hate correction follow in the
footsteps of sinners,
but those who fear the Lord repent in
their heart.
7 The eloquent are heard by everyone,
but the sensible person notices when
such people slip.

8 To build a house with borrowed money
is like gathering stones for your own
tomb.
9 A band of wicked people is like a bundle
of fibers;
they are destined to be thrown into a
blazing fire.
10 The way of sinners is paved with smooth
stones,
but eventually it leads to death.*

The Wise and the Foolish

11 Those who observe the law will control
their thinking.
The fear of the Lord results in
wisdom.
12 Those who are not clever cannot be
taught,
but a certain kind of cleverness makes
a person bitter.
13 The knowledge of the wise will swell like
a flood,
and their advice is like a living spring.
14 The mind of a fool is like a broken jar;
it cannot hold any knowledge.

15 When intelligent people hear a wise saying,
they applaud it and add to it.
When fools hear it, they sneer at it
and throw it away.
16 The talk of a fool is like a burden on a
journey,
but it is delightful to hear the
intelligent speak.
17 The words of a sensible person are sought
after in the congregation,
and they will ponder the words in their
minds.

18 Like a house that lies in ruins, so is wisdom
to a fool,
and to the ignorant, knowledge is
merely babbling speech.
19 To a senseless person, education is like
fetters on the feet
and shackles on the right hand.
20 Fools laugh loudly,
but the clever smile quietly.
21 To the sensible person, education is like
a gold ornament
or a bracelet on the right arm.

22 A fool rushes into a house,
but an experienced person waits
respectfully outside.
23 An ill-mannered person peers into a house
from the doorway,
but one who is well-taught waits
outside.
24 It is bad manners for a person to listen
outside someone's door.
The discreet would be upset by such
a disgrace.

25 Babblers merely repeat what others have
said,
but the wise carefully measure their
words.
26 Fools blurt out whatever they are thinking,
but the wise think before they speak.
27 When the ungodly curse their adversaries,
they are cursing themselves.
28 Gossips degrade themselves
and gain the hatred of the whole
neighborhood.

Foolishness Brings Grief

22 1 Lazy people are like filthy stones.
Everyone jeers at their disgrace.
2 Lazy people are like a lump of dung;

20:31 Some manuscripts add verse 32, *Tireless persistence in seeking the Lord is better than trying to steer your own life without a leader.*
21:10 Greek *to the pit of Hades.*

everyone who picks it up will shake it
from his hand.

3 A father is disgraced by an undisciplined
son,
and the birth of a daughter means loss.
4 A sensible daughter is sure to find a
husband,
but a shameful daughter is a grief to her
father.
5 A brazen daughter makes both her father
and her husband ashamed,
and she is despised by both.
6 Untimely speech is like music during a
time of mourning,
but punishment and discipline are
always wise.*

9 Teaching a fool is like gluing broken
pottery back together
or like rousing a sleeper from deep
slumber.
10 Whoever tells a story to a fool
might as well be speaking to someone
who is asleep.
At the end of the story, the fool will say,
"What was that?"
11 Weep for the dead, for they left the light
behind;
and weep for fools, for they have left
intelligence behind.
Do not weep as much for the dead, for they
are at rest.
But the life of the fool is worse than
death.
12 Mourning for the dead lasts seven days,
but for fools and the ungodly it lasts a
lifetime.

13 Do not talk much with a fool
or visit those who lack common
sense.
Keep away from them, or you will have
trouble
and be spattered when they shake
themselves off.
Avoid such people, and you will find rest.
You will not be exhausted by their
foolishness.
14 What is heavier than lead?
The same one who is called "Fool."
15 Sand, salt, and a piece of iron
are less of a burden than a stupid
person.

16 A wooden beam firmly secured in the
frame of a building
will not be loosed by an earthquake.
In the same way, a mind made up after
thoughtful reflection
will not be shaken during a time of
crisis.
17 A mind solidified with intelligent
thought
is like stucco decoration on a smooth
wall.
18 A fence set on a high place
will not stand against the force of the
wind.
Likewise, a timid mind with the resolve
of a fool
will not stand firm in the face of fear.

Preserving Friendships

19 Prick an eye and tears will come;
prick the heart and feelings pour
forth.
20 One who throws stones at birds scares
them off,
and one who insults a friend destroys
a friendship.
21 But even if you have drawn a sword on
a friend,
do not despair; there is a way back.
22 If you have said something to a friend,
don't worry; you can still be reconciled.
Only insults, arrogance, disclosing of
secrets,
or a treacherous blow will cause a friend
to flee from you.

23 Gain your neighbors' trust when they are
poor
so that you may rejoice with them when
they are prosperous.
In the time of trouble continue to be
faithful to them
so that they may share with you when
they receive an inheritance.
24 As fumes and smoke precede a fire in a
furnace,
so also insults precede bloodshed.
25 I am not ashamed to give shelter to
friends,
nor will I hide from them.
26 But if any harm should come to me
because of them,
everyone who hears of it will watch out
for them.

22:6 Some manuscripts add verses 7-8, *7Children nurtured in a good life do not show the lowly birth of their parents, 8but those who
are rebellious, undisciplined, and arrogant tarnish the good name of their family.*

Guarding against Sin

27 Who will set up a guard over my mouth
     and a tight seal on my lips
  to keep them from becoming my
        downfall
     and my tongue from destroying me?

23 1 O Lord, Father, and Ruler of my life,
        do not abandon me to their
           schemes
     or allow me to fall because of them.
2 Who will punish my thoughts to correct
        them
     and discipline my mind with wisdom
  so that I am not left unpunished for my
        errors
     and my sins are not overlooked?
3 Otherwise my mistakes may increase
     and my sins may multiply,
  and I may fall before my enemies,
     allowing them to rejoice over me.
4 O Lord, Father and God of my life,
     do not let me become proud,
5   and take away all my evil desires.
6 Do not let gluttony or lust consume me,
     and do not abandon me to shameless
        passions.

Controlling the Tongue

7 My child, listen to instruction concerning
        the things you say.
     The one who obeys it will never be
        tripped up.
8 Sinners are ensnared by their own words;
     scoffers and the proud fall by what
        they say.
9 Don't make a habit of swearing an oath
        after everything you say
     or of using the name of the Holy One.
10 Just as a slave who is constantly monitored
        is always bruised,
     so everyone who takes God's name in vain
        will not be free from sin.
11 Those who constantly swear oaths are
        sinful;
     their households will continually be
        punished.
  If they go back on their oaths, their sin will
        not be overlooked.
     If they disregard their oaths, their guilt
        is doubled.
  If they swear an oath that is not true, they
        will not be acquitted.
     Their house will be filled with troubles.
12 There is also a manner of speaking that
        equals death.

May it never be found among Jacob's
        descendants!
  The godly will steer clear of such conduct
     and will not wallow in sin.
13 Don't get used to speaking lewd
        vulgarities,
     for this is sinful speech.
14 Remember who your father and mother
        are
     when you sit among the great.
  Otherwise you may forget who you are in
        their presence
     and behave like a fool.
  Then you will wish you had never been
        born,
     and you will curse the day of your
        birth.
15 Those who are accustomed to vulgarity
     will never correct the habit as long as
        they live.

Regarding Sexual Sins

16 There are two kinds of people who pile
        up sins
     and a third who brings wrath upon
        themselves.
17 Hot passion that burns fire
     cannot be quenched until it burns itself
        out.
  Those who have sexual relations with their
        own family members
     will not give up until they are devoured
        by fire.
  To the sexually immoral all that they
        devour is sweet;
     they will not be weary of sinning until
        they die.
18 The man who is unfaithful in marriage
     says to himself, "Who can see me?
  Darkness covers me, and the walls
        hide me.
     No one sees me, so why should I fear?
  The Most High will not remember my
        sins."
19 But his fears concern only human eyes.
     He does not realize that the eyes of the
        Lord
  are ten thousand times more intense
        than the sun.
  They perceive every aspect of human
        behavior
     and see into the most hidden places.
20 For all things were known to the Lord
        before they were created,
     and he has known them since they were
        finished.

21 This unfaithful man will be punished in
    the streets of the city,
  and when he least suspects it, he will
    be captured.

22 The same thing will happen to every
    woman who leaves her husband
  and presents him with an heir by
    another man.

23 First of all, she has disobeyed the law of
    the Most High.
  Second, she has sinned against her
    husband.
  Third, she has committed the sin of
    adultery
  and has given birth to children by
    another man.

24 This woman will be brought before the
    congregation,
  and her punishment will be inherited
    by her children.

25 Her children will not become firmly rooted,
  and her branches will not bear fruit.

26 People will curse the very memory of her,
  and her disgrace will never be removed.

27 Those who live on after her will realize
    that there is nothing better than to fear
    the Lord
  and nothing sweeter than to obey his
    commandments.*

The Praise of Wisdom

24 1 Wisdom praises herself
    and proclaims her glory in the
    midst of her people.

2 In the assembly of the Most High she
    speaks,
  and before his heavenly armies she
    declares her glory.

3 "I came forth when the Most High spoke,
  and I covered the earth like a mist.

4 I lived in the highest places,
  and my throne was in a pillar of clouds.

5 I alone have traveled across the heavens
  and have walked on the bottom of the
    watery depths.

6 Over the waves of the sea, over the whole
    earth,
  and over every people and nation I have
    held power.

7 Among all these I looked for a place to rest.
  I wondered, 'In whose territory should
    I settle?'

8 "Then the Creator of all things gave me
    a command.
  My Creator chose the place for me to
    live.*
  He said, 'Live among Jacob's descendants,
    and make Israel the permanent home of
    your family.'

9 Before the dawn of time and creation, the
    Lord created me,
  and I will never cease to exist.

10 In the holy Tabernacle I ministered before
    him,
  and so I was established in the Temple
    on Mount Zion.

11 Therefore, the Lord gave me a resting place
    in the beloved city.
  In Jerusalem I held authority.

12 I took root among an honored people
  and in the portion of the Lord, his
    special possession.

13 "I grew tall like a cedar in Lebanon
  and like a cypress on Mount Hermon.

14 I grew tall like a palm tree in En-gedi
  and like a rosebush in Jericho.
  Like a beautiful olive tree in a field
  or a plane tree beside water, I grew tall.

15 I gave off a pleasant aroma like cinnamon
    and camel's thorn.
  I yielded a fragrance like the finest
    myrrh.
  My aroma was like galbanum, mollusk
    scent, and resin droplets
  and like the incense of the Tabernacle.

16 I stretch out my branches like a tree
  and my branches are splendid and
    graceful.

17 Like a vine I put forth pleasant buds,
  and my blossoms become splendid and
    abundant fruit.*

19 "Come to me, all you who desire me,
  and eat as many of my fruits as you wish.

20 For remembering me is sweeter than
    honey,
  and possessing me is sweeter than the
    honeycomb.

21 Those who eat me will hunger for more,
  and those who drink me will thirst for
    more.

22 Those who obey me will not be ashamed,
  and those who work with me will not
    sin."

23:27 Some manuscripts add verse 28, *It is a great honor to follow God. Gaining his approval ensures a long life.* 24:8 Greek *chose the place for my tent.* 24:17 Some manuscripts add verse 18, *I am the mother of beautiful love, of fear, of knowledge, and of holy hope. Since I am eternal, I am given to all my children, who are called by the Lord.*

Wisdom Flows from the Law

23 All this is the Book of the Covenant of the
  Most High God,
    the law that Moses commanded us
    as an inheritance for the congregations
    of Israel.*

25 Wisdom overflows like the Pishon River
    and like the Tigris during the season
    of the first crops.

26 Like the Euphrates, it runs over with
  understanding,
    and like the Jordan at harvesttime.

27 Like the Nile,* it pours out knowledge.
  It is like the Gihon at the time of the
    grape harvest.

28 The first man did not know wisdom fully,
    nor will the last one understand.

29 For her thoughts are more vast than the
    sea,
    and her counsel deeper than the great
    abyss.

30 As for me, I was like a canal from a river,
    and an irrigation ditch into a garden.

31 I said, "I will water my garden
    and irrigate my flower beds."
  Then my canal became a river,
    and my river became a sea.

32 I will make teaching shine like the dawn,
    and it will be clearly visible from far
    away.

33 Once again I will pour out teaching like
    prophecy
    and leave it for all future generations.

34 Take note that I have not labored for
    myself alone
    but for all who seek wisdom.

Reasons for Happiness

25 1 There are three things that
      please me,
    for they are delightful to God and to all
    people:
    harmony between brothers and sisters,*
    friendship among neighbors,
    and a wife and husband who live well
    together.

2 There are three kinds of people I hate,
    and I am disgusted by the way they live:
    a poor person who boasts, a rich person
    who lies,
    and an old fool who commits adultery.

3 If you have gathered nothing in your youth,
    how will you get anything in your old
    age?

4 How beautiful it is to see sound judgment
    coming from gray-haired people
    and good advice from the aged!

5 How beautiful it is to see wisdom coming
    from the aged
    and understanding and advice from the
    honorable!

6 The crown of the aged is their ample
    experience,
    and they take pride in their fear of the
    Lord.

7 I can think of nine people whom I would
    call blessed
    and a tenth, whom I will speak of:
  a man who can rejoice in his children
    and one who lives to see the downfall
    of his enemies.

8 Blessed is the man who lives with a
    sensible wife.
  Blessed is the one who does not sin
    by what he says
    and the one who has not served a person
    who is inferior to himself.

9 Blessed is the one who finds a friend*
    and the one who has good listeners as
    his audience.

10 How great is the one who finds wisdom!
    But no one is superior to the person who
    fears the Lord.

11 Fear of the Lord surpasses all things.
    Those who have it are beyond compare.*

Warnings against Wicked Women

13 No wound is worse than a wound of the
    heart!
  No wickedness is worse than the
    wickedness of a woman!

14 No affliction is worse than the affliction
    from those who hate you!
  And no vengeance is worse than the
    vengeance of your enemies!

15 No poison* is worse than that of a snake,
    and no anger worse than a woman's
    anger.

16 I would rather live with a lion and a
    dragon
    than live with an evil woman.

24:23 Some manuscripts add verse 24, *Never stop being strong in the Lord. Cling to him so that he may strengthen you. The Lord Almighty alone is God; there is no other Savior besides him.*   24:27 As in Syriac; Greek reads *Like light.*   25:1 Greek *brothers.* 25:9 As in Syriac; Greek reads *good sense.*   25:11 Some manuscripts add verse 12, *Fearing the Lord is the way to begin loving him, and faith is the way to begin staying close to him.*   25:15 As in Syriac; Greek reads *No head.*

17 A woman's wickedness changes her
    appearance
    and darkens her face like that of a bear.
18 When her husband sits down to eat with
    neighbors,
    he cannot restrain his bitter sighs.
19 Any evil is insignificant compared to that
    of a woman.
    May the fate of sinners overtake her!
20 Just as climbing a sandy hill is difficult for
    the aged,
    so is a talkative wife to a quiet man.
21 Don't be taken in by a woman's beauty,
    and don't desire her for her possessions.
22 There is anger, shamefulness, and great
    disgrace
    when a wife must support her husband.
23 Depression, sadness,
    and a wounded heart are caused by an
    evil wife.
    Feeble hands and weak knees
    are caused by the wife who does not
    make her husband happy.
24 Sin came about because of a woman,
    and because of her we all die.
25 Don't allow a cistern to leak water
    or an evil wife to speak arrogantly.
26 If she does not follow your instructions,
    send her away from you.

The Blessings of a Good Wife

26 1 Blessed is the husband of a good
            wife,
    for his lifespan will be doubled.
2 A virtuous wife brings joy to her husband,
    and he will live out his years in peace.
3 A good wife is a great blessing;
    she will be one of the blessings given to
    the man who fears the Lord.
4 Whether rich or poor, his heart is content,
    and his face is always cheerful.
5 Three things frighten my heart,
    and a fourth makes me afraid:
    slander in a city, the gathering of
    a mob,
    and false accusation—all these are
    worse than death.
6 But there is grief and heartache when a
    wife is jealous over another woman,
    and her tongue-lashing will let everyone
    know about it.
7 A bad wife chafes like a poorly fitted yoke;
    trying to control her is like grasping a
    scorpion.
8 A drunken wife makes her husband very
    angry,

for she cannot hide her shameful
    behavior.
9 An unfaithful wife is revealed by her bold
    stare,
    and her glances give her away.
10 Keep a strict watch over a strong-willed
    daughter,
    or else, when she gets a chance, she will
    take advantage of it.
11 Watch out for her immodest glances,
    and do not be surprised if she disobeys
    you.
12 Like a thirsty traveler who is eager
    to drink from any water nearby,
    she will sleep with anyone
    and open her quiver to any arrow.
13 A wife's charm pleases her husband,
    and her skill puts meat on his bones.
14 A silent wife is a gift from the Lord,
    and nothing is worth more than her
    good character.
15 A modest wife becomes ever more
    pleasing,
    and no price can be placed on her
    faithfulness.
16 Like the sun rising in the Lord's heavens,
    so is the beauty of a good wife in her
    well-kept home.
17 Like the shining lamp on the holy
    lampstand,
    so is a beautiful face on a graceful
    figure.
18 Like golden pillars on silver bases,
    so are shapely legs and steady feet.

[*The most reliable Greek manuscripts do not include
Sirach 26:19-27.*]

Warnings against Ungodly Women

19 My child, be careful not to ruin yourself in
    the prime of your life,
    and do not spend your strength on
    women you don't even know.
20 With regard to women, look for a fertile
    field within the whole plain,
    and plant it with your own seed,
    trusting in your fine stock.
21 Your offspring will grow strong,
    and they will become great, since they
    know they come from a good family.
22 People regard a prostitute as spittle,
    and a married woman as a tower of
    death for her lovers.
23 The wicked man inherits an ungodly wife,

while the man who fears the Lord
   receives a devout wife.
24 A shameless woman constantly acts
   disgracefully,
   but a humble daughter will act
   modestly even around her husband.
25 People regard a stubborn wife as a dog,
   but a wife who possesses modesty fears
   the Lord.
26 Everyone regards as wise a wife who
   honors her husband,
   but everyone will think she is ungodly
   if she pridefully dishonors him.
Blessed is the husband of a good wife,
   for his lifespan will be doubled.
27 A loud, talkative wife is like a trumpet
   sounding the charge,
   and everyone like this experiences all
   the upheavals of war.

Miscellaneous Instruction
28 Two things grieve my heart,
   and a third arouses my anger:
   a warrior in poverty, an intelligent
   person who is despised,
   and someone who turns from
   righteousness to sin.
The Lord will prepare this last person for
   a violent death.

29 It is difficult for a merchant to keep from
   doing wrong
   and for a shopkeeper to keep from
   sinning.

27 ¹ Many sin for profit,
   and those who seek riches will
   look the other way.
2 As a stake is driven between stones,
   so also is sin wedged between selling
   and buying.
3 Unless people continually fear the Lord,
   their house will quickly collapse.

4 When a sieve is shaken, the chaff remains;
   likewise, a person's faults are revealed
   when he speaks.
5 Just as a furnace tests the potter's vessels,
   so also people are tested by their
   speech.
6 As the fruit of a tree shows the quality
   of its cultivation,
   so also people's speech shows their true
   character.
7 Do not praise people before they speak,
   for this is how they are tested.

8 If you pursue justice, you will obtain it
   and wear it as a splendid robe.
9 Just as birds roost with their own kind,
   so honesty is repaid to those who
   practice it.
10 The lion lies in wait for prey,
   and so do sins for those who practice
   evil.

Wise Conversation
11 The godly always speak wisely,
   but a fool is as changeable as the moon.
12 Don't spend much time with foolish
   people,
   but stay among those who are
   thoughtful.
13 Fools always say offensive things,
   and they laugh at sinful practices.
14 Their swearing makes your hair stand on
   end,
   and their quarrels make people hold
   their ears.
15 The quarrels of the proud lead to
   bloodshed,
   and their insults are grievous to hear.

16 Whoever betrays secrets destroys trust
   and will never find a close friend.
17 Love your friend and maintain his trust.
   But if you betray his secrets, stay away
   from him.
18 For as a person destroys an enemy,
   so you have destroyed friendship with
   your neighbor.
19 And as you let a bird escape from your
   hand,
   so you have let your friend go and will
   not recapture him.
20 Do not chase after him, for he is gone.
   He has escaped like a gazelle from a
   snare.
21 A wound can be bandaged,
   and insults can be forgiven,
   but those who betray secrets have
   no hope.

Regarding Those Who Plot Evil
22 Those who slyly wink are planning
   mischief,
   and those who know them will keep
   their distance.
23 In your presence they are sweet tongued,
   and they admire your words.
But later they will change their story
   and use your own words to condemn
   you.

24 I have hated many things, but I hate them
    the most.
  The Lord even hates such people, too.
25 To throw a stone straight up is to throw
    it on your own head,
  and backstabbing will wound many.
26 Those who dig a pit will fall into it,
  and those who set a snare will be caught
    in it.
27 Those who do evil will be crushed by it
  and not know where it came from.
28 Mockery and insults come from the
    proud,
  yet vengeance lies in wait for them like
    a lion.
29 Those who rejoice in the fall of the godly
    will be caught in a snare,
  and pain will overwhelm them before
    they die.

Anger and Forgiveness

30 Anger and fury are also detestable,
  but the sinner is a master at both
    of them.

28

1 Those who seek revenge will
    experience vengeance from
    the Lord,
  who keeps a strict account of their sins.
2 Forgive those neighbors who have
    wronged you,
  and then your sins will be forgiven
    when you pray.
3 If people harbor anger against each other,
  how can they expect healing from the
    Lord?
4 If they do not show mercy toward people
    like themselves,
  how can they seek pardon for their own
    sins?
5 If mere human beings harbor anger,
  who will make an atoning sacrifice for
    their sins?
6 Think of your approaching death,
  and choose not to act as an enemy.
  Think of your mortality and death,
  and be faithful to the commandments.
7 Think of the commandments,
  and don't be angry with your neighbor.
  Think of the covenant of the Most High,
  and overlook the faults of others.

Quarrels and Slander

8 Refrain from quarreling, and you will
    sin less,

for a hot-tempered person provokes
    arguments.
9 A sinner causes trouble among friends
  and plants discord among those who are
    at peace.
10 The more the fuel, the greater the fire;
  the stronger the stubbornness, the more
    the quarreling;
  and the greater the wealth, the hotter
    the anger.
11 A quarrel that begins easily kindles a fire,
  and a hasty dispute sheds blood.
12 If you blow on a spark, it flares up,
  and if you spit upon it, it will be
    quenched;
  yet both come from your mouth.

13 May the gossips and the double-tongued
    be cursed,
  for they have troubled many who were
    at peace.
14 The slanderer* has upset many
  and scattered them from nation to
    nation.
  Slander has destroyed strong cities
  and overthrown the houses of the great.
15 Slander has driven virtuous women from
    their homes
  and deprived them of the rewards for
    their work.
16 Those who listen to slander will never find
    rest,
  nor will they relax in peace.
17 The lash of a whip makes a bruise,
  but a lash of the tongue breaks bones.
18 Many have been killed by the sword,
  but even more have been destroyed by
    the tongue.
19 Happy are those who are protected from
    the tongue,
  who have not experienced its anger,
  who have not been burdened with its yoke
  and bound with its chains.
20 For its yoke is a yoke of iron,
  and its chains are chains of bronze.
21 The death that the tongue brings is evil,
  and the grave* is preferable to it.
22 The tongue has no power over the godly;
  they will not be burned by its flame.
23 Those who forsake the Lord will fall into
    its power.
  Its fire will burn among them and not
    be quenched.
  This fire will be sent upon them as a lion;
  like a leopard it will tear them apart.

28:14 Greek A third tongue.   28:21 Greek Hades.

²⁴ Just as you hedge your property with
  thorns
  and lock up your silver and gold,
²⁵ so also make a door and bolt for your
  mouth
  and a scale to carefully measure your
  words.
²⁶ Take care not to slip with your tongue
  and fall victim to those waiting to catch
  you.

Lending and Borrowing

29 ¹ Those who show mercy lend to their
  neighbors.
  By giving them help, they are obeying
  the commandments.
² Lend to your neighbors in their time of
  need,
  and pay your neighbor when your loan
  is due.
³ Keep your word and be honest with them,
  and you will always find what you need.
⁴ Many look upon a loan as a windfall
  and give trouble to those who help them.
⁵ They kiss someone's hand until they get
  a loan from them,
  and they make themselves appear
  humble as they speak of their
  neighbor's wealth.
  But when the time comes to repay, they
  put it off
  by repaying with only empty promises
  and complaining about the lack of time.
⁶ And if they are able to pay, the lender will
  hardly get back half
  and will consider himself fortunate to
  get that much.
  They will repay the creditor with insults
  and curses
  and with dishonor rather than praise.
⁷ Many have refused to lend, not out of their
  own meanness,
  but simply because they are afraid of
  being defrauded without reason.
⁸ Nevertheless, be patient with those in
  poverty,
  and do not keep them waiting for your
  gifts of charity.
⁹ Help the poor in obedience to the
  commandment,
  and do not send the needy away
  empty-handed.
¹⁰ Lose your money for the sake of your
  brother or your friend.
  Don't let it rust away under a stone.

¹¹ Store up your treasure according to the
  commandments of the Most High,
  and it will bring you more profit than
  gold.
¹² Store up gifts for charity in your treasury,
  and they will bring you help in every
  disaster.
¹³ Such gifts are better than a strong shield
  and a sturdy spear.
  They will fight for you against your
  enemy.
¹⁴ A good person will cosign a loan for his
  neighbor,
  but a shameless person will let his
  neighbor down.
¹⁵ Never forget the kindness of your
  guarantor,
  for he has given his life for you.
¹⁶ The sinner wastes the property of his
  guarantor,
  and the ungrateful person abandons
  his rescuer.
¹⁷ Cosigning for others has ruined many
  wealthy people
  and tossed them about like waves of
  the sea.
¹⁸ It has driven the powerful into exile,
  and they have wandered in foreign
  lands.
¹⁹ Sinners fall into trouble by cosigning.
  Their pursuit for profit leads to lawsuits.
²⁰ Assist your neighbor as best you can,
  but be careful that you don't fall
  yourself.

Contentment

²¹ The essentials for life are water, bread, and
  clothing,
  and a house for privacy.
²² Better is the life of the poor under their
  own simple roof
  than lavish banquets among strangers.
²³ Be content with little or plenty;
  then you will not be known for living on
  others' hospitality.
²⁴ It is a miserable life to go from house to
  house,
  for as a guest, you can't say anything.
²⁵ You must act as a host and provide drinks
  without being thanked,
  and you even hear rude words like:
²⁶ "Come here, stranger, and set the table.
  Let me eat whatever you have."
²⁷ "You must leave now. An honored guest is
  coming.

My brother has come to visit, and I need
the guest room."
28 Two things are upsetting to a
conscientious person:
to be scolded about lodging and to be
reproached by creditors.

Regarding Children

30 1 Whoever loves his son will
frequently discipline him
so that he may rejoice in the way his son
turns out.
2 Whoever disciplines his son will benefit
from him
and boast about him to people he
knows.
3 Whoever educates his son will make his
enemy jealous
and glory in him among his friends.
4 When the father dies, it will be as if he
were not dead;
for he has left behind a man like
himself.
5 While the father lived, he rejoiced at the
sight of his son;
and when he died, he had no regrets.
6 He has left behind an avenger against his
enemies
and one to repay kindness to his
friends.

7 Whoever spoils his son will bandage his
every wound
and be heartbroken at every cry.
8 A horse that is not broken becomes
stubborn,
and a child left to himself becomes
headstrong.
9 Pamper a child, and he will be a terror
for you;
join in with his games, and he will cause
you grief.
10 Do not laugh with him, or you will be
sorry
and gnash your teeth in anguish in
the end.
11 Give him no freedom while he is young,
and don't overlook his mistakes.
12 Break him in while he is young,
and punish him while he is a child.
Otherwise he will grow stubborn and
disobey you,
and your heart will grieve over him.
13 Discipline your son and be hard on him
so that he will not offend you by acting
shamelessly.

Health and Cheerfulness

14 Better to be a poor person who is healthy
and physically fit
than a rich person who is sick.
15 Health and strength are better than gold,
and a sound body is better than
immense riches.
16 No treasure is greater than a healthy body,
and no pleasure is greater than a joyful
heart.
17 Death is better than a miserable life,
and eternal sleep than continual
sickness.

18 Good things lavished upon someone who
will not eat
are like offerings of food placed upon a
grave.
19 What good does an offering do for an
idol?
For the idol can neither eat nor smell.
It is the same for a person who is being
punished by the Lord.
20 He sees the food and groans
like a eunuch groans when embracing
a young woman.

21 Don't let yourself become sad,
and don't intentionally make yourself
upset.
22 A joyful heart is life itself,
and rejoicing lengthens a person's life.
23 Indulge yourself and take it easy;
drive sadness far away from you.
For sadness has destroyed many,
and there is no benefit from it.
24 Envy and anger shorten a person's life,
and anxiety brings on premature
old age.
25 Those who are cheerful while feasting
will benefit from their food.

Proper Attitudes toward Wealth

31 1 Losing sleep over wealth wears out
the body,
and anxiety about it drives away rest.
2 Sleepless worry prevents a person from
resting,
and a severe illness steals away sleep.
3 The rich struggle to amass a fortune,
and when they relax, they enjoy luxury.
4 The poor struggle to barely make a living,
and if they ever rest, they become poor.

5 Those who love gold will not be regarded
as righteous,

and those who pursue wealth will be led
    astray by it.*
6 Many have come to ruin because of gold
    and come face to face with destruction.
7 Gold causes those who are devoted to it to
        stumble;
    every fool gets tripped up by it.
8 Blessed are the rich who are found
        blameless
    and do not chase after gold.
9 Who are they? We want to praise them,
    for they have achieved wonderful things
        among their people.
10 Who have been tested in this way and
        found perfect?
    Let them boast about it.
    Who could have sinned and chose not to
        do so?
    Who could have done evil but did not
        do it?
11 They will be made secure in their wealth,
    and the congregation will praise their
        acts of charity.

Practicing Temperance

12 Are you seated at a grand table?
    Don't show that you are greedy,
    and don't say, "There is so much here
        to eat!"
13 Remember that a greedy eye is evil.
    Is anything in creation more greedy
        than the eye?
    That is why it cries so easily.
14 Don't reach for everything you see,
    and don't crowd the one sitting next to
        you at a meal.
15 Be considerate of your neighbors' feelings
    by thinking about how you would
        feel,
    and be thoughtful in everything.
16 Show your good upbringing as you eat
        what is set before you.
    Don't gorge yourself, or you will offend
        someone.
17 Be the first to stop eating, as good manners
        demand,
    and don't be a glutton, or you will
        offend someone.
18 And if you are sitting with many people,
    don't be the first to reach for the food.

19 Well-disciplined people are more than
        satisfied with only a little food.
    They have no trouble breathing when
        they lie in bed.

20 Moderate eating ensures sound sleep.
    Those who practice it rise early and feel
        well.
    But sleeplessness, nausea, and colic
        cause distress for the glutton.
21 If you eat too much,
    go vomit, and you will be relieved.
22 Listen to me, my child, and don't
        ignore me,
    and in the end you will find my words
        to be true.
    Practice moderation in all you do,
    and you will never get sick.
23 People bless those who are generous with
        food,
    and their testimony to such generosity
        can be trusted.
24 But the whole city complains about those
        who are stingy with food,
    and their testimony to such selfishness
        is accurate.

25 Do not try to prove your strength by
        drinking wine,
    for wine has destroyed many.
26 As fire tests metal,
    so wine tests people's hearts when
        braggarts begin to argue.
27 Wine gives a person life
    if it is drunk in moderation.
    What is life without wine?
    It was created to make people happy.
28 Wine drunk with moderation at
        appropriate times
    gives joy to the heart and soul.
29 Wine drunk to excess produces bitter
        attitudes,
    quarrels, and brawls.
30 Drunkenness fuels the anger of a fool to
        his own harm,
    sapping his strength and causing
        wounds.
31 Don't correct your neighbor at a banquet,
    and don't mock him when he is
        enjoying himself.
    Don't say anything nasty to him
    or pressure him for anything.

Proper Conduct at a Banquet

32 1 If they make you the master of
        ceremonies for a banquet, don't
        become proud.
    Act simply as one of the crowd.
2 Take care of them first, and then sit
        down;

31:5 As in Hebrew; Greek reads *and those who pursue destruction will be filled by it.*

when you have fulfilled all your duties,
    take your seat.
Then you can celebrate with them
    and receive a wreath for your fine
        leadership.

3 You who are older should speak, for this
    is fitting.
    But speak accurately, and don't
        interrupt the music.
4 If entertainment is going on, don't keep
    talking.
    Don't show off your wisdom at the
        wrong time.
5 A concert of music at a banquet
    is like a ruby set in gold.
6 Melodious music with good wine
    is like an emerald seal set in gold.

7 You who are young should only speak
    when necessary.
    But never speak more than twice, and
        only when asked.
8 Be brief; say much in only a few words.
    Act like a person who can hold his
        tongue, even though he knows the
        answer.
9 When you are around prestigious people,
    don't act like their equal.
    Don't chatter on while another is
        speaking.

10 Lightning comes before thunder,
    and approval goes before a modest
        person.
11 Leave the banquet in good time, and don't
    be the last to leave.
    Go straight home; don't linger on at the
        banquet.
12 Enjoy yourself at the banquet to your
    heart's content,
    but don't sin by speaking arrogantly.
13 Above all, bless your Maker,
    who causes you to experience his good
        gifts.

Obeying the Lord and His Law

14 The one who fears the Lord will accept his
    discipline,
    and those who rise early to seek him
        will find favor.
15 The one who seeks the law will be filled
    with it,
    but the hypocrite will stumble
        over it.

16 Those who fear the Lord will think
    correctly;
    their good deeds will shine forth like
        a fire.
17 Sinners will ignore correction
    and find a way to justify what they want
        to do.

18 A sensible person will not neglect a
    thoughtful suggestion,
    but not even fear will change the mind
        of an arrogant and proud person.
19 Never do anything without getting advice;
    then when you do something, don't
        change your mind.
20 Don't travel on a hazardous path,
    and don't stumble over its stones.
21 Don't be careless even on a smooth road;
22 watch where you are going.*
23 Be careful* in everything you do,
    for this is how a person keeps the
        commandments.

24 The one who believes the law is careful to
    obey the commandments,
    and the one who trusts in the Lord will
        never fare for the worse.

33 1 Nothing bad will happen to those
            who fear the Lord;
    he will rescue them from trials again
        and again.
2 The wise do not hate the law,
    but those who are insincere about it are
        tossed about like a boat in a storm.
3 A sensible person trusts in the law,
    for it is as dependable as a divine oracle.

4 Carefully prepare what you will say,
    and people will listen to you.
    Make use of your learning as you give
        your answer.
5 The heart of a fool turns like a wheel of
    a cart,
    and his thoughts spin like an axle.
6 Mocking friends are like stallions;
    they neigh no matter who is on their
        back.

Creation Was Established by the Lord's Wisdom

7 Why is one day more important than
    another
    when every day receives its light from
        the sun?

32:22 As in Hebrew; Greek reads *beware of your children.*   **32:23** As in Hebrew; Greek reads *Trust yourself.*

8 By the Lord's wisdom they are different;
   he established the various seasons and
      festivals.
9 The Lord made some days important and
      holy,
   and some of them he made ordinary.
10 And all humans come from the ground,
      the dust from which Adam was created.
11 With perfect knowledge the Lord
      distinguished people from each other
   and assigned them their various ways
      of life.
12 Some people he has blessed and exalted;
   some he has made holy and drawn to
      himself;
   and some he has cursed and humbled,
      removing them from the place they once
      lived.
13 As the potter's clay is in his hand
      to be shaped as he pleases,
   so all people are in the hand of their
      Maker,
   and they will be given whatever he
      decides.
14 Good is the opposite of evil, and life is the
      opposite of death.
   In the same way, sinners are the
      opposite of the godly.
15 Look at everything the Most High has
      made;
   they come in pairs, one opposite the
      other.

The Author Comments on His Work

16 I, Sirach, kept watch at the end
   like one who gleans what the grape
      gatherers have left behind.
17 By God's blessing I arrived before the other
      gleaners,
   and I filled my winepress as full as any
      of the grape pickers' presses.
18 Notice that I have not labored only for
      myself
   but for all who seek learning.
19 Listen to me, you who hold prestige
      among the people,
   and pay attention, you leaders of the
      congregation.

Managing a Household Wisely

20 Don't give to your son or wife, brother or
      friend
   power over yourself as long as you live.
   Don't give your property to someone else,

for you might change your mind and
      have to ask for it back.
21 As long as you live and have breath in you,
   don't let anyone take over your position.
22 It is better for your children to ask from
      you
   than for you to depend on your
      children.
23 Maintain the upper hand in all you do,
   and never allow your honor to be
      stained.
24 When you come to the end of your life,
   then, at the hour of your death,
      distribute your inheritance.

25 Fodder, the stick, and burdens are for a
      donkey;
   bread, discipline, and work are for a
      slave.
26 Keep your slaves busy at work, and you
      will find rest.
   Allow them to be idle, and they will seek
      freedom.
27 The yoke and the harness make an ox obey,
   and torture and pain are for a wicked
      slave.
28 Put him to work so that he will not be idle,
29   for idleness trains a person to be very
      evil.
30 Put him to work, as is fitting for him,
   and if he does not obey, make his fetters
      heavy.
   But don't be too demanding of anyone,
   and do nothing unjust.
31 If you have only one slave, treat him like
      yourself,
   for you have bought him at a high price.*
   If you have only one slave, treat him like a
      brother,
   for you need him as much as you need
      your own life.
32 If you mistreat him, and he runs away,
33 where will you go to find him?

Regarding Dreams

34 ¹ Vain and false hopes are for the
      senseless,
   and dreams lend wings to fools.
2 The person who believes in dreams
   is like one who grabs at shadows
   and chases after the wind.
3 What is seen in a dream is simply a
      reflection,
   a face looking at itself in a mirror.

33:31 Greek *bought him with blood.*

⁴ Nothing clean can come from something
   unclean, can it?
   In the same way, truth cannot come
   from something false.
⁵ Divinations, omens, and dreams are
   unreal.
   The mind has fantasies just like a
   woman in labor hopes for something.
⁶ Unless they are sent as visions from the
   Most High,
   pay no attention to them.
⁷ For dreams have deceived many,
   and those who have trusted in them
   have been disappointed.
⁸ The law is perfect without such deceptions
   as dreams.
   Wisdom is complete when it is spoken
   by the faithful.

Experience and Travel Bring Knowledge

⁹ A person who has traveled much will know
   many things,
   and a person of experience knows what
   he is talking about.
¹⁰ A person with little experience knows
   little,
   but a person grows more resourceful as
   he travels.
¹¹ I have seen many things by traveling
   and learned more than I could ever say.
¹² I have often been in mortal danger
   but have escaped because of my many
   experiences.

Fear of the Lord Brings Blessing

¹³ Those who fear the Lord will live,
   for their hope is in him who has saved
   them.
¹⁴ Those who fear the Lord will not be
   timid.
   They will not be afraid for the Lord
   is their hope.
¹⁵ Blessed are those who fear the Lord.
   Just think whom they look to for
   support!
¹⁶ The Lord watches over those who love
   him.
   He is their mighty shield and strong
   support,
   a shelter from the scorching wind and
   midday sun,
   a safeguard against stumbling, and a
   help against falling.
¹⁷ He revives the soul and makes the eyes
   sparkle;
   he gives health and life and blessing.

Insincere Worship

¹⁸ The sacrifice of something wrongfully
   obtained is blemished,
   and the gifts of the lawless are not
   acceptable.
¹⁹ The Most High does not accept the gifts
   of the wicked
   or forgive their sins for a multitude
   of sacrifices.
²⁰ Those who offer a sacrifice seized from the
   poor
   are like those who slaughter a son before
   his father's eyes.
²¹ Bread is life for the needy and the poor.
   Whoever deprives them of it is a
   murderer.
²² Those who take away a person's livelihood
   are murderers.
   Those who deprive an employee of
   wages shed blood.
²³ When one builds up and another tears
   down,
   what do they gain except hard work?
²⁴ When one prays for something and
   another curses it,
   which request will the Lord honor?
²⁵ If a person touches a corpse, washes, and
   then touches it again,
   what good did washing do?
²⁶ In the same way, if people fast over their
   sins
   and then commit them again,
   who will listen to their prayers?
   What good does their act of humility do?

Sincere Worship

35 ¹ Keeping the law is the same as
         making many offerings.
   Heeding the commandments is like
   making a peace offering.
² To repay a kind deed is to offer fine flour,
   and to give charitable gifts is to sacrifice
   an offering of thanksgiving.
³ To avoid wickedness is to please the Lord,
   and to abandon injustice is to make an
   atoning sacrifice.
⁴ But do not come before the Lord without
   anything to offer,
   for making these offerings fulfills the
   Lord's commandment.
⁵ The offering of the righteous enriches the
   altar;
   its pleasing aroma rises to the Most High.
⁶ The sacrifice of the righteous is acceptable;
   the Lord will never forget it.

7 Be generous when you worship the Lord.
  Do not hold back the firstfruits of your
    labor.
8 Be cheerful as you give each gift,
  and be joyful as you dedicate your
    tithes.
9 Give to the Most High as he has given
    to you
  and as generously as you can afford.
10 For the Lord always repays,
  and he will repay you seven times over.

The Lord Repays Injustice
11 Do not offer him a bribe, for he will not
    accept it.
  Do not rely on a wrongly obtained
    sacrifice.
12 For the Lord is the judge,
  and he does not show favoritism.
13 The Lord is not prejudiced against* the
    poor,
  and he will listen to the prayer of the
    one who is wronged.
14 He will not ignore the requests of the
    orphan
  or the widow when she pours out her
    complaint.
15 Look how the widow's tears run down
    her cheek
  as she cries out against the one who
    causes them to fall!
16 Those who serve the Lord in a way that
    pleases him will be accepted,
  and their prayers will reach even to the
    clouds.
17 The prayer of the humble penetrates the
    clouds,
  and they* will not rest until the prayer
    has been answered.
18 They will not stop until the Most High
    responds,
  enforcing justice for the righteous and
    executing judgment.
19 The Lord will not delay;
  he will not be patient.
20 He will crush the loins of the unmerciful
  and take vengeance on the nations.
21 He will destroy all of the arrogant
  and shatter the power of the wicked.
22 He will repay all people as their deeds
    deserve
  and judge their actions by their
    intentions.
23 He will rule in favor of his people
  and cause them to rejoice in his mercy.

24 His mercy is as welcome in a time of
    distress
  as clouds of rain in a time of drought.

A Prayer for Israel
36 1 "Have mercy upon us, O Lord, the
  God of all.
  Make all the nations fear you.
2 Punish the foreign nations,
  and let them see your power.
3 Use them to show your glory to us,
  just as you have used us to show your
    holiness to them.
4 Let them know, as we have known,
  that there is no God besides you, O Lord.
5 Give new signs and work other miracles,
  showing the glory of your hand and
    right arm.
6 Stir up your anger and pour out your
    wrath.
  Destroy the adversary and crush the
    enemy.
7 Remember the time appointed for this,
  and make it come quickly.
  Let people recount your mighty deeds.
8 Let those who escape be consumed in fiery
    wrath,
  and let those who oppress your people
    be destroyed.
9 Crush the heads of hostile rulers
  who say, "We are the only ones who
    matter."
10 Gather all the tribes of Jacob,
  and give them their inheritance as you
    did at the beginning.
11 Show mercy to the people called by your
    name,
  on Israel, whom you have made your
    firstborn.
12 Have pity on the city of your sanctuary,
  Jerusalem, the place where you reside.
13 Fill Zion with praise for your wonderful
    deeds,
  and fill your Temple* with your glory.
14 Acknowledge those you created in the
    beginning,
  and fulfill the prophecies spoken in
    your name.
15 Reward those who wait for you,
  and show that your prophets can be
    trusted.
16 Respond to the prayers of your servants,
    O Lord,
  in the manner that Aaron blessed your
    people.

35:13 Or *is not partial toward.* 35:17 Or *it;* also in 35:18. 36:13 As in Hebrew; Greek reads *your people.*

¹⁷ Then everyone on earth will know
that you are the Lord, the eternal
God."

The Need for Discretion

¹⁸ The stomach will accept any food,
yet one food is better than another.
¹⁹ As the palate recognizes the type of wild
animal by the flavor of the meat,
so the intelligent mind discerns lies.
²⁰ Those with perverse minds will cause
grief,
but a person with experience will pay
them back.
²¹ A woman will accept any man as a
husband,
but a man will prefer one girl over
another.
²² A woman's beauty lights up a man's face,
and there is nothing he desires more.
²³ If her words convey kindness and
humility,
her husband is the happiest of men.
²⁴ He who finds a good wife finds his best
possession.
She is a helper fit for him and a pillar
of support.
²⁵ Where there is no fence,
the property will be plundered;
where there is no wife,
a man will become a wandering
fugitive.
²⁶ Who would trust a fleet-footed bandit
that goes from city to city?
²⁷ So it is with the man who has no home
and who lodges wherever the night
finds him.

37

¹ Every friend says, "I, too, am your
friend."
But some are friends in name only.
² When a close friend turns into an enemy,
it is as sad as someone's death.
³ O evil inclination, why were you created?
You cover the earth with deceitfulness.
⁴ Some companions rejoice with a friend
when times are joyful,
but they turn against him when times
are hard.
⁵ Some companions help a friend for their
stomachs' sake,
but then in battle they carry his shield.
⁶ Do not forget a close friend,
and do not overlook him when you
distribute your wealth.

Being Cautious of Advice

⁷ All counselors think their own advice
is good,
but some are only looking out for
themselves.
⁸ So be careful about those who offer you
advice.
First find out what they want
because they might be thinking of their
own interests.
They may set you up for a fall
⁹ and tell you, "Your way is good,"
and then stand aside to see what
happens to you.
¹⁰ Don't seek advice from anyone who is
suspicious of you
or reveal your intentions to those who
envy you.
¹¹ Don't consult with a woman about her
rival;
or with a coward concerning war;
or with a merchant about commerce;
or with a buyer about selling;
or with a stingy person about generosity;*
or with the merciless about kindness;
or with a lazy person about work;
or with a seasonal worker about staying
on to finish a task;
or with an idle servant about a big job.
Pay no attention to the advice they give.
¹² But spend time with a godly person,
whom you know obeys the
commandments.
Make sure he thinks like you do
and that he will sympathize with you if
you fail.
¹³ Follow the advice of your own heart,
for it is devoted to you more than
anyone is.
¹⁴ Sometimes our own mind does a better job
of keeping us informed
than seven watchmen sitting in a
watchtower.
¹⁵ But above all these things pray to the Most
High
that he may direct you along the path
of truth.

True Wisdom Yields Good Results

¹⁶ Let discussion precede every undertaking
and counsel precede every action.
¹⁷ The mind is the root of all behavior.
Out of it come four branches:
¹⁸ good and evil, life and death.
And the tongue continually rules them.

37:11 As in Hebrew; Greek reads *about gratitude.*

19 Some people are good at teaching others
    yet are of no use to themselves.
20 Others are very eloquent, but if detested,
    they will starve to death.
21 Charm was not given to them from the
    Lord,
    for they are lacking in all wisdom.
22 Those who use wisdom to better
    themselves
    will produce results that are
    praiseworthy.
23 But the wise instruct their own people,
    producing results that will last.
24 The wise will be highly praised,
    and all who see them will call them
    blessed.
25 The length of a person's life is limited,
    but the number of Israel's days is
    infinite.
26 The wise will inherit honor among their
    people,
    and their name will live forever.

27 My child, test yourself all your life;
    learn what is bad for you, and do not
    give in to it.
28 For not everything is good for everyone,
    nor is everything enjoyable to
    everyone.
29 Don't be greedy for luxury,
    and don't be a glutton.
30 For overeating causes sickness,
    and gluttony leads to nausea.
31 Many have died of gluttony,
    but avoiding it will prolong your life.

Honoring Physicians

38 ¹ Honor physicians for their services,
    for the Lord has created them.
2 Their skill with healing comes from the
    Most High,
    and they are rewarded by kings.
3 The skill of physicians makes them
    distinguished,
    and they are admired by the great.
4 The Lord has created medicines from the
    earth,
    and the sensible will not despise them.
5 Wasn't bitter water made sweet by a tree
    so that its power might be known?
6 The Lord has given skill to people
    so that he might be honored through
    his marvelous works.
7 By these works the physician cures and
    removes pain,

    and from them the pharmacist makes
    medicine.
8 There is no end to God's works,
    and he spreads health all over the
    earth.
9 My child, when you are sick, do not wait;
    pray to the Lord, and he will heal you.
10 Renounce your errors, amend your ways,
    and cleanse your heart from all sin.
11 Offer a sweet-smelling sacrifice and a
    memorial of fine flour,
    and pour oil on your offering—as much
    as you can afford.
12 Then let the physician take his place, for
    the Lord created him.
    Don't let him leave you, for you need
    him.
13 A time will come when you must commit
    yourself to physicians.
    Then they will pray to the Lord,
14 asking for success in diagnosis*
    and in healing so that your life will
    be saved.
15 Those who sin against their Maker
    will not listen to the physician.*

Mourning for the Dead
16 My child, shed tears for the dead
    and lament for them to show your great
    sorrow.
    Prepare the body with proper ceremony,
    and provide for a decent burial.
17 Weep bitterly and wail fervently;
    make your mourning worthy of the
    deceased.
    Mourn for at least one or two days to avoid
    criticism,
    and then let yourself be comforted
    during your grief.
18 For grief can lead to death,
    and a heavy heart saps a person's
    strength.
19 When a person is buried, the time of
    mourning is over,
    but a life of poverty continues to weigh
    down the heart.
20 Do not be consumed with grieving for
    others.
    Drive grief from you, and think about
    your own approaching death.
21 Do not forget that there is no returning
    from death.
    Grieving does the dead no good and
    harms the one who grieves.

38:14 As in Hebrew; Greek reads *in rest.*   38:15 As in Hebrew; Greek reads *may he fall into the hands of the physician.*

22 Remember this fate, for yours is the same;
  yesterday it was for that person, and
  today it is for you.
23 When the dead are at rest, let the memory
  of them also end.
  Take comfort that their spirit has
  departed.

The Worker Has Little Time for Wisdom

24 The scribe possesses wisdom because he
  possesses leisure time.
  Only those who have few
  responsibilities can become wise.
25 How can a person become wise who directs
  the plow
  or who glories in the goad,
  who drives oxen or keeps busy with work
  or whose conversation is always about
  bulls?
26 His mind is fixed on plowing furrows,
  and his concerns are about giving his
  cows fodder.
27 It is the same for every craftsman and
  designer,
  who labors night and day.
  So also for those who cut engraved seals.
  Each is diligent to make the image
  unique.
  Their minds are fixed on making a lifelike
  image,
  they are concerned about completing
  the task.
28 It is also the same for the blacksmith who
  sits by the anvil,
  concentrating on his ironwork.
  The heat from the fire melts his flesh
  as he works with the heat of the furnace.
  The noise of the hammer rings in his ears,
  and he keeps his eyes on the pattern of
  the object.
  His mind is fixed on finishing his work,
  and he is concerned about giving it a
  perfect finish.
29 It is also the same for the potter, who sits
  at his work,
  turning the wheel with his feet.
  He always takes great care with his work
  and makes many vessels.
30 He fashions the clay with his hands
  and kneads it beneath his feet.
  His mind is fixed on finishing the glazing,
  and he is concerned about keeping the
  furnace clean.
31 All these people rely on their hands,
  and all are skilled in their own craft.

32 Without them a city could not be
  inhabited,
  for people could not live or walk in it.
33 Yet they are not chosen for the council of
  the people
  or hold high rank in the congregation.
  They do not occupy the judge's seat,
  nor do they understand the laws of the
  courts.
  They cannot explain moral or legal
  principles,
  and they are not familiar with proverbs.
34 But they sustain the structure of society,
  and their concern is for the practice of
  their craft.

The Student of the Law Gains Wisdom

39 1 How different it is for the one who
  devotes himself
  to studying the law of the Most High.
  He seeks out the wisdom of all the ancients
  and is occupied with the prophets'
  writings.
2 He is careful to remember the sayings
  of the famous,
  and he can perceive the subtle truths
  of parables.
3 He searches out the hidden meanings
  of proverbs
  and is very familiar with the secrets
  of parables.
4 His services are employed by the great,
  and he appears before the rulers.
  He travels in foreign countries
  and witnesses good and evil among
  humanity.
5 He determines to rise early
  to seek the Lord who made him
  and to pray to the Most High.
  He opens his mouth in prayer
  and asks forgiveness for his sins.
6 If it pleases the great Lord,
  such a person will be filled with the
  spirit of understanding.
  He will pour forth his own words of
  wisdom
  and give thanks to the Lord in prayer.
7 The Lord will direct his counsel and his
  knowledge
  as he meditates on the Lord's mysteries.
8 He will display the wisdom he has gained
  and glory in the law of the Lord's
  covenant.
9 Many will praise his understanding,
  and he will never be forgotten.

People will always remember him,
    and his name will be honored for all
        generations.
10 Nations will declare his wisdom,
    and the congregation will proclaim his
        praise.
11 If he lives long, he will leave a name that
        surpasses a thousand;
    if he dies, he has lived a full life.

A Hymn of Praise to the Lord

12 I, Sirach, have yet more on my mind to
        express,
    for I am as full as the full moon.
13 Listen to me, my faithful children, and
        blossom
    like a rose planted by a stream.
14 Give off fragrance like frankincense,
        and bloom like a lily.
    Spread fragrance, and sing a hymn of
        praise;
    bless the Lord for all his works.
15 Give glory to his name;
    give praise and thanks to the Lord.
    As you sing and play harps,
        thank him with these words:

16 "All the works of the Lord are very good,
    and everything he commands is done at
        the appointed time.
17 You must not say, 'What is this?' or 'Why
        is that?'—
    for all such questions will be answered
        at the appointed time.
    At the Lord's word the waters stood in a
        heap,
    and reservoirs of water were created.
18 When he commands, his will is carried out
        entirely,
    and no one can hold back his saving
        power.
19 He sees what everyone does,
    and nothing can be hidden from his
        eyes.
20 He sees everything throughout all eternity,
    and nothing is too amazing for him.
21 You must not say, 'What is this?' or 'Why
        is that?'—
    for everything has been created for a
        purpose.

22 "The Lord's blessing overflows like a river
    and soaks the earth like a flood.
23 His anger drives out the nations
    just as he turned irrigated land into a
        salty desert.

24 To the faithful, his journey is smooth,
    but for sinners, the way is full of
        obstacles.
25 From the beginning, good things were
        created for good people,
    while bad things were created for
        sinners.
26 The basic necessities of life
    are water, fire, iron, salt,
        flour, milk, honey,
        juice from the grape, olive oil, and
        clothing.
27 All these things are good for the godly,
    but they turn out bad for sinners.

28 "Some winds are created for vengeance,
    and in their fury they can inflict terrible
        punishment.
    On the day of judgment they will pour out
        their force
    and give vent to the anger of their
        Maker.
29 Fire, hail, famine, and disease—
    all these were created for punishment.
30 So also the fangs of wild animals,
        scorpions, and serpents,
    and the sword that punishes the
        ungodly by destroying them.
31 These things delight in doing the Lord's
        bidding,
    and they are always ready to serve him
        on earth.
    When the time comes, they never
        disobey him."

32 I, Sirach, have been sure of all this from the
        beginning;
    I have meditated on these things and
        put them in writing.
33 All the works of the Lord are good,
    and he will fully supply every need in
        due time.
34 No one can say, "This is not as good as
        that,"
    for all things will prove good at their
        proper time.
35 So now sing praise with all your heart and
        voice,
    and bless the name of the Lord.

Hardships of Life

40 1 Hard work was created for everyone,
    and a heavy yoke has been laid on
        the children of Adam—
from the day they emerge from their
        mother's womb

to the day they return to the mother
of all.

2 They are filled with thoughts and fears
of the heart
and anxiety over the day they will die.

3 From the one who sits on a glorious throne
to the one who lies humbled in dust and
ashes,

4 from the one who wears a purple robe and
a crown
to the one who is dressed in sackcloth,
there is anger, envy, trouble, unrest,
fear of death, fury, and quarreling.

5 And when such people rest in bed,
their sleep causes them confusion.

6 They get little or no rest,
and they are as troubled in sleep as they
are in the daytime.
They are troubled by their dreams,
imagining that they were escaping from
battle.

7 The instant they reach safety, they wake up
and are astonished that there is nothing
to fear.

8 For all creatures, both human and
animal—
but seven times more for sinners—

9 come death and bloodshed, quarrels and
war,
disasters and famine, havoc and plague.

10 All these were created for the wicked,
and because of them the flood came.

11 All that is from the earth returns to the
earth,
and all that is from water returns
to the sea.

Goodness Outlasts Evil

12 All bribery and injustice will be blotted
out,
but faithfulness will last forever.

13 The riches of the unjust will dry up like
a seasonal brook
and fade away like a clap of thunder in
a storm.

14 A generous person will rejoice,
but lawbreakers will be completely
ruined.

15 The children of sinners put forth few
branches.
They are withered roots on sheer rock.

16 The reeds growing along any riverbank
wither before any grass.

17 But kindness is like a garden of blessings,
and acts of charity last forever.

Joys of Life

18 Wealth and wages can make life sweet,*
but finding treasure is better than
either.

19 A person's name is established through
children and through building a city,
but a blameless wife will be counted
better than either.

20 Wine and music cheer the heart,
but the love of wisdom is better than
either.

21 The flute and the harp make a sweet
melody,
but a pleasant voice is better than either.

22 The eye seeks grace and beauty,
but green, sprouting grain is better than
either.

23 A friend or companion is always welcome,
but a wife with her husband is better
than either.

24 Family and friends are for times of trouble,
but acts of charity rescue better than
either.

25 Gold and silver give a person security,
but good advice is more valued than
either.

26 Wealth and strength make a person
confident,
but the fear of the Lord is better than
either.
Those who fear the Lord lack nothing;
they do not need to look for help.

27 The fear of the Lord is like a garden of
blessing;
it covers a person better than any
glory.

28 My child, do not live like a beggar,
for it is better to die than to beg.

29 When people must depend on another
for food,
their existence is hardly to be called
living.
People lose self-respect by living off
another person's food.
An intelligent, learned person guards
against this.

30 For the shameless, begging is sweet in the
mouth,
but it burns them within like a fire.

Welcoming Death

41 1 O death, how bitter is the reminder
of you
to people who enjoy their possessions—

40:18 As in Hebrew; Greek reads *Life is sweet for the self-reliant worker.*

to those who are prosperous in everything
  and have no worries
  and who are still able to enjoy food.
² O death, how welcome your sentence is
    to those who are needy and losing
    strength!
  For they are worn out by old age and
    endless anxiety
  and have become grumpy and
    impatient.
³ Do not fear the sentence of death.
    Remember those who went before you
    and those who will come after you.
⁴ This sentence is from the Lord to
    everyone.
  So why object to the will of the Most
    High?
  Whether your life lasts ten or a hundred
    or a thousand years,
  no one will ask about it in the place of
    the dead.*

The Wicked and the Righteous

⁵ The children of sinners are detestable,
    and they are found among the
    ungodly.
⁶ The inheritance of sinners' children will
    perish,
  and perpetual shame will plague their
    offspring.
⁷ Children will blame their ungodly father,
    for they endure shame because of him.
⁸ How terrible it will be for you ungodly,
    for you have abandoned the law of the
    Most High God.
⁹ When you were born, you were born under
    a curse;
  when you die, a curse will be your
    inheritance.
¹⁰ All things from the earth return to the
    earth;
  so the ungodly pass from curse to
    destruction.

¹¹ Physical death brings grief,
  but sinners and their bad reputation
    will also be forgotten.
¹² Be careful of your reputation, for it will
    live on after you.
  It will last longer than a thousand
    treasures of gold.
¹³ The actual life span of a good person is
    limited,
  but a good reputation lasts forever.

Things That Warrant Shame

¹⁴ My children, be true to your upbringing
    and be at peace,
  for hidden wisdom is as useless as a
    treasure that lies undiscovered.
¹⁵ Better are those who hide their foolishness
    than those who hide their wisdom.
¹⁶ Therefore, show respect for what I say,
  for it is not always appropriate to be
    ashamed,
  nor is everything regarded with the
    same respect by everyone.

¹⁷ Be ashamed of sexual immorality before
    your father or mother
  and of a lie before a prince or ruler;
¹⁸ of a crime before a judge or official;
  of sin before the congregation and
    community;
¹⁹ of dishonest dealings before a partner
    or friend;
  and of theft in your neighborhood.
²⁰ Be ashamed of breaking an oath or
    covenant*
  and of reclining* at meals;
²¹ of receiving or giving ungraciously;
  of ignoring those who greet you;
²² of looking at a prostitute;
  of rejecting a request from your
    relative;
²³ of taking away someone's inheritance
    or gift;
  and of gazing at another man's wife.
²⁴ Be ashamed of making advances toward
    a man's servant girl;
  don't go near her bed.
²⁵ Be ashamed of reprimanding friends,
  and do not insult someone after you
    give them a gift.
²⁶ Be ashamed of repeating what you have
    heard
  and of betraying confidences.
²⁷ Then you will display a proper sense of
    shame
  and be well liked by everyone.

Things That Do Not Warrant Shame

42 ¹ Don't sin to maintain your dignity,
    and don't be ashamed of any of
    the following:
² of the law of the Most High and of his
    covenant;
  of rendering judgment that acquits the
    ungodly;

41:4 Greek *In Hades.*   41:20a As in Hebrew; Greek reads *Be ashamed before God's truth and the covenant.*   41:20b Greek *of leaning on your elbow.*

3 of sharing expenses with partners and fellow travelers;
of dividing a friend's inheritance;
4 of using accurate scales and weights;
of gaining much or little profit;
5 of making profit from trade;
of frequently disciplining your children;
and of lashing a wicked slave until he bleeds.
6 Bolting the door is wise when you have an untrustworthy wife.
Where there are many hands, lock everything up.
7 Keep careful records of your deposits,
and put in writing any donations you give or receive.
8 Do not be ashamed to correct the ignorant and foolish
or the aged who are found guilty before the young.
Then you will show that you are well instructed,
and you will gain everyone's approval.

Regarding Daughters

9 A daughter causes her father unspoken anxiety,
and worry over her robs him of sleep.
When she is young, he worries that she may not find a husband.
When she is married, he worries that her husband may be displeased with her.
10 While she is a virgin, her father worries that she may be seduced
and become pregnant while living in his house.
When she has a husband, her father worries that she may be unfaithful
or, though she is married, that she may be childless.
11 Keep strict watch over a headstrong daughter,
or else she might make you a laughingstock to your enemies.
You would become the talk of the town and a reproach among the people,
and she would make you ashamed to appear in public.
12 Don't let her display her beauty to any man,
and don't let her socialize with married women.
13 For as from clothes comes the moth,
so from a woman comes a woman's wickedness.

14 The wickedness of a man is better than the goodness of a woman.
A woman brings shame and disgrace.

The Works of the Lord

15 I will now recall the works of the Lord
and declare what I have seen.
His works were made by the word of the Lord.
16 The sun shines down on all things,
and the work of the Lord is full of his glory.
17 Not even the holy ones were empowered by the Lord
to declare all his wonderful works.
The Lord Almighty has established these works
so that the universe may stand firm in his glory.
18 He searches out the watery depths and the human heart,
and he understands their innermost secrets.
For the Most High knows all that there is to know.
He perceives the signs of the times.
19 He discloses the past and the future
and reveals the traces of hidden things.
20 No thought escapes his notice,
and nothing is hidden from him.
21 He has set in order the glorious works of his wisdom,
and he is the same for all eternity.
Nothing can be added to him or subtracted from him,
and he has no need of any counselor.
22 How desirable are all the Lord's works,
and even the smallest spark deserves attention.
23 All these things live and remain forever,
and they obey him regarding every need.
24 All things come in pairs, one opposite the other,
and he has made nothing incomplete.
25 Each adds to the good things of another.
Who could ever see enough of his glory?

43 1 The clear firmament of the sky is the pride of the higher realms.
The beauty of heaven is glorious to see.
2 The rising sun testifies
that it is a wonderful work of the Most High.
3 At noon it parches the land.
Who can endure its burning heat?

⁴ A person must tend a furnace to get any
    heat,
    but the sun burns three times as hot
        when it shines upon the mountains.
    It breathes out fiery vapors,
    and its bright rays blind the eyes.
⁵ Great is the Lord who made it,
    and at his command the sun speeds
        along its course.

⁶ He created the moon to mark the seasons.
    It acts as an eternal sign to regulate the
        times.
⁷ The moon sets apart the days for festivals.
    It is a light that wanes as it completes its
        course.
⁸ The month is named after the moon.
    It is marvelous as it changes in its phases.
    It is a beacon to the stars in the sky,
    shining in the heavenly firmament.

⁹ The glory of the stars makes the heavens
    beautiful;
    they are a sparkling array in the heights
        of the Lord.
¹⁰ They stand in their appointed places, just
        as the Holy One has ordered them,
    and they are never lax on their watch.
¹¹ Look at the rainbow, and praise him who
        made it;
    it is very beautiful in its brightness.
¹² It spans the heavens with its glorious arc.
    The hands of the Most High have bent it
        like a bow.

¹³ By his command he sends snowstorms
    and shoots out lightning to execute
        judgment.
¹⁴ The storehouses of heaven are opened at
        his command as well,
    and the clouds fly out like birds.
¹⁵ By his greatness he gives the clouds their
        strength,
    and the hailstones are formed.
¹⁶ At his sight the mountains shake,
    and at his will the south wind blows.
¹⁷ The noise of his thunder causes the earth
        to recoil,
    and the northern storm and the
        whirlwind to blow.
    He makes the snow fall like birds
        fluttering down;
    it settles like a swarm of locusts.
¹⁸ The eye admires the beauty of snow's
        whiteness,
    and the mind is amazed as it falls.

¹⁹ The Most High pours frost upon the earth
        like salt,
    and icicles become sharp thorns.
²⁰ The cold north wind blows,
    and ice forms on the water.
    It freezes over every pool of water
    and clothes it like armor.
²¹ The Most High levels the mountains,
        burns up the wilderness,
    and shrivels the grass like fire.
²² Then a cloud soon heals everything,
    and the falling dew brings relief from
        the heat.

²³ By his design the Most High calmed the
        watery depths
    and planted islands in it.
²⁴ When those who sail on the sea tell of its
        dangers,
    we are amazed at what we hear.
²⁵ The sea contains strange and amazing
        creatures,
    all kinds of living things and great sea
        monsters.
²⁶ It is by the Most High that each messenger
        reaches his destination,
    and by his word all things hold together.

²⁷ We could say more but could never say
        enough.
    But the sum of our words is, "He is all."
²⁸ Where can we find the ability to praise
        him?
    For he is greater than all his works.
²⁹ The Lord is awesome and very great,
    and his power is amazing.
³⁰ Glorify the Lord as much as you can,
    yet he will far exceed your praise.
    When you exalt him, put forth all your
        strength.
    Don't become weary, for you can never
        praise him enough.
³¹ Who has seen him and can describe him?
    Who can praise him for who he really is?
³² Many things greater than these lie hidden
        from us,
    for we have seen but a few of his works.
³³ The Lord has made all things,
    and to the godly he has given wisdom.

In Praise of the Earliest Ancestors

44 ¹ Let us now praise famous men,
    our ancestors in their successive
        generations.
² The Lord has created great glory,
    his majesty from the beginning.

3 There were those who ruled in their
    kingdoms;
  they were renowned for their valor.
  Others were intelligent advisers
    or those who spoke prophecies.
4 Some led the people by advising them
    and by knowing the writings of the
    people.
  They gave wise instruction.
5 Some composed musical tunes
    or wrote poetic lyrics.
6 Others were rich and powerful,
    living peacefully in their homes.
7 All these men gained glory in their
    generations;
  they were the pride of their times.
8 Some of them have left behind a famous
    name,
  so that others tell of their praises.
9 But others are not remembered at all;
    they have completely perished as if they
    had never existed.
  They have become as if they had never
    been born,
  and their children are forgotten as
    well.
10 But these were godly men,
    whose righteous deeds have not been
    forgotten.
11 Their wealth will remain in the family,
    and their inheritance will pass to their
    descendants.
12 Their children have kept the covenants,
    and their grandchildren also, for their
    sake.
13 Their line of descendants will continue
    forever,
  and their glory will not diminish.
14 Their bodies are buried in peace,
    but their name lives on from generation
    to generation.
15 The people tell about their wisdom,
    and the congregation declares their
    praise.
16 Enoch pleased the Lord and was taken
    up to heaven
  as an example of repentance to all
    generations.
17 Noah was found perfect and righteous.
    In the time of wrath he was chosen to
    begin a new human race.*
  Therefore, a remnant was left on earth
    after the flood came.

44:17 As in Hebrew; Greek reads *was taken in exchange.*

18 Everlasting covenants were made with
    him
  that all flesh should never again be
    destroyed by a flood.

In Praise of the Patriarchs
19 Abraham was the great father of many
    nations,
  and there has never been anyone equal
    to him in honor.
20 He obeyed the law of the Most High
    and entered into a covenant with him.
  He ratified the covenant by undergoing
    circumcision,
  and when he was tested he was found
    faithful.
21 Therefore, the Lord promised him with
    an oath
  that the nations would be blessed
    through his descendants.
  He promised to make them as numerous
    as the dust of the earth,
  to exalt them like the stars.
  He promised to give them an inheritance
    from sea to sea
  and from the Euphrates River to the
    ends of the earth.
22 He gave Isaac the same assurance
    for the sake of his father, Abraham.
  The Lord caused Jacob to receive
    the blessing of all people and the
    covenant.
23 He confirmed Jacob's position by blessing
    him,
  and he gave him his inheritance.
  He divided his portions
    and distributed them among twelve
    tribes.

In Praise of Moses
45 1 From Jacob's descendants the Lord
    brought forth a godly man,
  who gained everyone's favor.
  This man was Moses, who was beloved by
    God and people
  and blessed whenever people remember
    him.
2 The Lord made Moses' glory equal to that
    of the holy ones.
  He made him great, terrifying his
    enemies.
3 With his words Moses put a stop to the
    miracles of others,
  and the Lord glorified him in the sight
    of kings.

The Lord gave Moses commandments for
    his people
and revealed to him his glory.
4 Because of Moses' faithfulness and
    meekness, the Lord set him apart
    as holy,
    choosing him from among all people.
5 The Lord allowed him to hear his voice
    and led him into the dark cloud.
He gave him the commandments face
    to face,
    the law of life and knowledge,
so that he might teach Jacob the covenant
    and Israel his decrees.

In Praise of Aaron

6 The Lord exalted Aaron, a holy man like
    Moses.
    Moses was Aaron's brother and came
    from the tribe of Levi.
7 The Lord made an everlasting covenant
    with Aaron,
    and he made him and his descendants
    priests over the people.
He honored and adorned him,
    giving him a glorious robe.
8 He clothed him with majestic attire
    and established him with the symbols
    of authority—
    the linen undergarments, the long robe,
    and the ephod.
9 The Lord encircled Aaron's attire with
    pomegranates,
    along with many gold bells.
These would sound with every step,
    ringing throughout the Temple
    as a reminder to his people.
10 He gave Aaron a sacred garment of gold,
    blue, and purple,
    the work of an embroiderer.
The Lord gave him the oracle of judgment,
    Urim and Thummim,
11   with twisted scarlet, the work of an
    artisan.
He gave Aaron precious stones engraved
    like signets
    and set in gold, the work of a jeweler.
These stones contained inscriptions
    that denoted each of the tribes of Israel.
12 The Lord also gave Aaron a gold crown to
    put over his turban.
    It was engraved like a signet with the
    word *Holiness*.
The crown was an ornament of honor, the
    work of an expert
    and a richly adorned delight to the eyes.

13 Before Aaron's time none of these
    beautiful things existed,
    and no stranger was ever clothed with
    them.
    Only Aaron's sons and his descendants
    would ever be allowed to wear them.
14 Aaron's sacrifices were to be completely
    consumed with fire,
    twice every day forever.
15 Moses ordained Aaron
    and anointed him with holy oil.
This was an everlasting covenant for him
    and for his descendants as long as the
    heavens endure.
He was supposed to serve the Lord as
    priest
    and bless his people in the name of the
    Lord.
16 The Lord chose Aaron out of all the living
    to offer sacrifice to the Lord.
He chose him to offer incense and a
    pleasing aroma as a memorial
    offering
    to make atonement for his people.
17 The Lord entrusted Aaron with his
    commandments
    and with the authority of law and
    judgment.
He instructed Aaron to teach Jacob his
    decrees
    and enlighten Israel concerning his law.
18 Strangers conspired against Aaron
    and envied him in the wilderness.
Dathan and Abiram and their followers,
    along with the company of Korah, acted
    in anger against him.
19 The Lord saw their actions and was
    displeased,
    so he destroyed them in anger.
He performed wonders against them
    and consumed them in flaming fire.
20 He increased Aaron's glory
    and gave him an inheritance.
He prescribed that Aaron should receive
    the best of the firstfruits
    so that he would have plenty of bread.
21 For the priests eat the sacrifices of the
    Lord,
    which he gave to Aaron and his
    descendants.
22 But Aaron did not receive any of the land
    as an inheritance.
    He was allotted no portion among the
    people,
    for the Lord himself was his portion and
    inheritance.

In Praise of Phinehas

23 Phinehas son of Eleazar ranks third in
glory
because of his zeal in fearing the Lord.
He stood firm when the people turned
away.
He acted with noble courage
and made atonement for Israel.

24 Therefore, the Lord made a covenant of
peace with him.
He made him the leader of the sanctuary
and of his people,
and Phinehas and his descendants were
given
the honor of the priesthood forever.

25 In the covenant that was given to David,
who was the son of Jesse and a
descendant of Judah,
royalty passed only from son to son.
In the same way, Aaron's priestly
inheritance was for his descendants
alone.

26 May the Lord grant you wisdom of mind
to judge his people with justice
so that their prosperity may never fade
and their glory may endure for all
generations.

In Praise of Joshua

46 1 Joshua was mighty in war.
He succeeded Moses as a
prophet
and was worthy of his name,
for he was a great savior* of the Lord's
chosen ones.
Joshua took vengeance on the enemies
who rose up against them
so that he might give Israel its
inheritance.

2 How glorious he was when he raised his
arm
and brandished his sword against the
cities!

3 Before Joshua's time, who ever stood so
firmly?
He fought the Lord's battles.

4 Wasn't he the one through whom the sun
stood still
and one day became as long as two?

5 He called upon the Most High, the Mighty
One,
when enemies assaulted him on every
side.
The great Lord answered him

by sending a terrible storm of
hailstones.

6 Joshua overwhelmed that nation in battle.
He destroyed his adversaries as they
were going down the pass
so that the nations might know the Lord's
power
and that he was fighting as the Lord
watched over him.
Joshua was a devoted follower of the
Mighty One,

7 and he showed his allegiance in the days
of Moses.
Joshua and Caleb son of Jephunneh
opposed the congregation,
kept them from sinning,
and halted their wicked complaining.

8 These two alone were spared
out of six hundred thousand infantry.
They led the people into their inheritance,
the land flowing with milk and honey.

9 The Lord gave strength to Caleb,
and he remained strong even in his
old age.
He went up into the hill country,
and his descendants obtained it for an
inheritance.

10 He did this so the Israelites might see
that it is good to follow the Lord.

In Praise of the Judges and Samuel

11 Let us also consider all the judges with
their respective names,
whose hearts did not fall into idolatry
or turn away from the Lord.
May their memory be blessed!

12 May their bones, wherever they lie, give
life to others,
and may their honored names
continue to live on in their children.

13 Samuel was beloved by his Lord,
and this prophet of the Lord established
the kingdom
and anointed leaders over his people.

14 By the law of the Lord he judged the
people,
and the Lord watched over Israel.*

15 His faithfulness proved that he was a
prophet,
and his messages showed that he was a
trustworthy seer.

16 He called upon the Lord, the Mighty One,
when his enemies were attacking him
on every side,

46:1 *Joshua* means "The LORD saves." 46:14 Greek *Jacob.*

and he offered a young lamb as a
　　sacrifice.
17 Then the Lord thundered from heaven
　　and made his voice heard with a great
　　　noise.
18 Samuel conquered the leaders of Tyre
　　and all the rulers of the Philistines.
19 Before he died he proclaimed
　　before the Lord and his anointed:
　　"I have not taken anything from anyone,
　　not even a pair of shoes."
　　And no one accused him.
20 Even after Samuel died, he prophesied,
　　revealing to the king that he, too,
　　　would die.
　　Samuel spoke from the grave
　　　to prophesy and blot out the wickedness
　　　of the people.

In Praise of Nathan and David

47　¹ Then Nathan came along
　　　to prophesy in the days of David.
² As the fat is set aside in preparing a peace
　　offering,
　　so David was set apart from the
　　Israelites.
³ He played with lions, as though they were
　　young goats,
　　and with bears, as though they were
　　lambs of the flock.
⁴ When David was young, did he not kill a
　　giant
　　and get rid of his people's shame?
　　He hurled a stone from his sling
　　and struck down that boastful Goliath.
⁵ David called upon the Lord Most High,
　　who strengthened his right hand
　　to kill the mighty warrior
　　and exalt the power of his nation.
⁶ They glorified him for the tens of
　　thousands he had conquered
　　and praised him for the blessings
　　received from the Lord.
　　When a glorious crown was given to him,
⁷ 　David annihilated his enemies on
　　every side.
　　He crushed the Philistines, his
　　adversaries,
　　and destroyed their power even
　　to this day.
⁸ In all that he did David gave thanks,
　　giving glory to the Holy One, the
　　Most High.
　　He sang praises with all his heart
　　because he loved his Maker.

⁹ David stationed singers before the altar
　　to make sweet melody.
¹⁰ He gave fitting dignity to the festivals
　　and established their appointed days
　　throughout the year.
　　Everyone praised the Lord's holy name,
　　and the sanctuary resounded from the
　　break of dawn.
¹¹ The Lord removed David's sins
　　and exalted his power forever.
　　The Lord made a covenant with him that
　　made him king,
　　and he gave him a throne of glory in
　　Israel.

In Praise of Solomon

¹² After David, a wise son came along
　　who lived in security* because of David.
¹³ Solomon reigned in an age of peace
　　because God allowed no border disputes
　　to happen.
　　God did this so that Solomon might build
　　a Temple to his name
　　and prepare an eternal sanctuary.
¹⁴ O Solomon, how wise you were when you
　　were young!
　　You overflowed like the Nile* with
　　understanding.
¹⁵ Your understanding spread throughout
　　the earth;
　　you filled it with riddles and proverbs.
¹⁶ Your fame spread to distant islands,
　　and you were loved for your peaceful
　　reign.
¹⁷ Your answers astounded the nations,
　　as did your songs, proverbs, and stories.
¹⁸ In the name of the Lord God,
　　who is known as the God of Israel,
　　you gathered gold like tin
　　and amassed silver like lead.
¹⁹ But you brought in women to sleep with
　　and let others rule over you by means
　　of your body.
²⁰ You stained your honor
　　and defiled your posterity.
　　You brought God's wrath on your
　　children,
　　who had to suffer for your foolishness.
²¹ You caused the kingdom to be divided.
　　Out of Ephraim a rebellious kingdom
　　came into power.
²² But the Lord will never cease to be
　　merciful
　　or cause any of his works to be
　　destroyed.

47:12 As in Hebrew; Greek reads *in a broad place*.   47:14 As in Hebrew; Greek reads *like a river*.

He will never cause his chosen one's
    descendants to be eliminated
or destroy the family line of him who
    loved the Lord.
So he provided Jacob with a remnant
    and gave David a root from his family.

23 Solomon died
    and left behind a son.
This son was foolish in many ways and
    lacked sense.
    His name was Rehoboam, and his
        policies caused the people to rebel.
Jeroboam son of Nebat caused Israel to sin
    and led Ephraim down the path of sin.
24 Their sins piled up more and more
    until they were exiled from their land.
25 For they explored every kind of evil
    until vengeance overtook them.

In Praise of Elijah

48 ¹ Then Elijah the prophet arose like a
    fire,
    and his word burned like a torch.
2 He brought a famine upon Israel,
    and he reduced them to a small number
    by his zeal.
3 By the word of the Lord he held back the
    rain
    and three times brought down fire from
    heaven.
4 How glorious your amazing deeds made
    you, Elijah!
    Who else can boast such deeds?
5 You raised a corpse from death
    and the grave* by the word of the Most
    High.
6 You brought down kings to destruction
    as well as the famous from their
    sickbeds.
7 You heard rebuke at Mount Sinai
    and judgments of vengeance at Mount
    Horeb.
8 You anointed kings to mete out
    retribution
    and prophets to succeed you.
9 You were taken up in a whirlwind of fire,
    in a chariot with fiery horses.
10 The Scriptures say that you are to come at
    the appointed time
    to calm the anger of the Lord before it
    furiously breaks out.
He will turn the hearts of parents to
    their children
and restore the tribes of Jacob.

11 Blessed are they who saw you
    and were honored with your love.
    For now we also will certainly live.

In Praise of Elisha
12 When Elijah was enveloped in the
    whirlwind,
    Elisha was filled with his spirit.
Throughout his life, Elisha never feared
    any ruler,
    and no one could even intimidate him.
13 Nothing was too difficult for him,
    and his body retained prophetic power
    even after death.
14 During his lifetime, Elisha performed
    wonders,
    and after death he performed amazing
    deeds.

15 Despite all this the people did not
    repent.
They did not abandon their sins
until they were carried from their land
    as captives
    and scattered throughout the whole
    world.
Only a small number of people were
    left,
    but one of them was a ruler from
    David's royal line.
16 Some of them did what was right,
    but others heaped up sins.

In Praise of Hezekiah
17 Hezekiah fortified his city
    and brought water within its walls.
He tunneled through solid rock with iron
    tools
    and made cisterns to collect the water.
18 During Hezekiah's reign Sennacherib
    invaded the country.
He sent his commander and then left.
He threatened Jerusalem*
    and arrogantly made great boasts.
19 The hearts of the people were shaken, and
    their hands trembled.
They were in anguish like women in
    labor.
20 But they called upon the Lord, who is
    merciful,
    spreading out their hands toward him
    in prayer.
The Holy One quickly heard them from
    heaven
    and rescued them through Isaiah.

48:5 Greek *and Hades.*   48:18 Greek *Zion;* also in 48:24.

21 The Lord attacked the army of the
     Assyrians,
   and his angel destroyed them.
22 For Hezekiah did what pleased the Lord
   and walked faithfully in the ways of his
     ancestor David.
   Hezekiah had been commanded to do this
     by Isaiah,
   the great and trustworthy prophet.
23 During Isaiah's time the sun went
     backward,
   and he lengthened the king's life.
24 Empowered by the Spirit,* he saw the
     future
   and comforted the mourners of
     Jerusalem.
25 He showed what would happen until the
     end of time
   and revealed hidden events before they
     even occurred.

In Praise of Josiah

49 1 The memories of Josiah are like
        blended incense
   made by the skill of a perfumer.
   The remembrance of him is as sweet as
     honey in every mouth
   and like music at a banquet.
2 He did the right thing by reforming the
     people
   and removing wicked and loathsome
     practices.
3 He kept his heart directed toward the
     Lord,
   and in lawless times he promoted
     godliness.

In Praise of Other Leaders

4 Except for David, Hezekiah, and
     Josiah,
   all the kings were very sinful.
   All of them abandoned the law of the
     Most High,
   so the royal line of Judah came to
     an end.
5 They gave their power to others
   and their glory to a foreign nation.
6 These nations burned Jerusalem, the
     chosen city of the sanctuary.
   They made its streets desolate,
   just as Jeremiah prophesied.
7 For they had mistreated Jeremiah,
   who was set apart to be a prophet while
     still in his mother's womb.

He was sent to uproot, to ruin, and to
   destroy,
   but also to build and to plant.
8 Ezekiel saw the vision of glory,
   which the Lord showed him above the
     chariot of the cherubim.
9 For the Lord remembered his enemies and
     sent a storm,
   and he helped those who followed in the
     right path.
10 May the bones of the twelve prophets
     give life to others wherever they lie.
   For they encouraged the people of Israel*
     and rescued them with confident hope.

11 How will we praise Zerubbabel?
   He was like a signet ring on the right
     hand,
12 and so was Jeshua son of Jehozadak.*
   In their days they built the house,
     raising up a Temple holy to the Lord
     and destined for everlasting glory.
13 Nehemiah is often remembered
   because he raised up our fallen walls,
   put gates and bars in place,
     and rebuilt our ruined houses.

14 No one on earth has ever been created who
     was comparable to Enoch,
   for he was taken up from the earth.
15 Nor has anyone like Joseph ever been born.
   He was a leader of his brothers and the
     support of his people.
   Even his bones were cared for.
16 Shem and Seth were honored among people,
   but Adam stands above every other
     created living being.

In Praise of Simon the High Priest

50 1 Simon the high priest,* the son of
        Onias,
   was the leader of his brothers and the
     pride of his people.*
   During his lifetime he repaired the Lord's
     house;
   in his day he fortified the Temple.
2 He laid the foundations for the high
     double walls,
   the high retaining walls of the Temple
     area.
3 During Simon's time a water cistern
     was dug,
   a reservoir as broad as the sea.

48:24 Or *Empowered in his spirit.*   49:10 Greek *of Jacob.*   49:12 Greek *Jozadak,* a variant name for Jehozadak.   50:1a Probably
Simon II, who died around 195 B.C.   50:1b As in Hebrew; Greek lacks *was the leader of his brothers and the pride of his people.*

4 He devised a plan to save his people from
    destruction
        and fortified the city against siege.
5 How glorious Simon was when the people
    would surround him
        as he came out of the veiled sanctuary.
6 He shone like the morning star among the
    clouds,
        like the moon at its fullest.
7 He was like the sun when it shines on the
    Temple of the Most High,
        like the rainbow gleaming in beautiful
        clouds.
8 He was like roses in the springtime,
    like lilies by a spring of water,
        like a green shoot on Mount Lebanon on
        a summer day.
9 Simon was like fire and incense in the
    censer,
        like a vessel of hammered gold
        adorned with every kind of precious
        stone.
10 He was like an olive tree weighed down
    with fruit,
        like a cypress tree reaching up to the
        clouds.
11 When he put on his glorious robe
    and dressed himself in all his
        splendor,
    he made the court of the sanctuary
        glorious
        as he went up to the holy altar.
12 When he received the sacrifices from the
    priests
        and stood by the hearth of the altar,
    he was surrounded by brothers as with
        a garland,
    and he was like a young cedar on
        Mount Lebanon
        surrounded by palm trees.
13 All the sons of Aaron in their glory
    held offerings for the Lord in their
        hands
        as they stood before the entire
        congregation of Israel.
14 When Simon finished the service at the
    altar,
        he would arrange the offering to the
        Most High, the Almighty.
15 Simon would reach out to receive the cup
    and pour out a drink offering of wine.*
    He would pour it out at the foot of the
        altar,

a pleasing aroma to the Most High, the
    King of all.
16 Then the sons of Aaron would shout
    and blow their trumpets of hammered
        metal.
    They made a mighty fanfare
        as a reminder to those in the presence
        of the Most High.
17 Then all the people would quickly
    fall with their faces to the ground
    and worship their Lord,
        the Almighty, God Most High.
18 Then the singers would praise him with
        their voices,
        making a sweet, resounding melody
        throughout the Temple.
19 The people of the Lord Most High would
    offer
        their prayers to the Merciful One.
    This was done until the order of the
        worship of the Lord was completed,
        and they finished his ritual.
20 Then Simon would come down and raise
    his hands
        over the entire congregation of
        Israelites.
    He would pronounce the blessing of
        the Lord
        and glorify his name.
21 The people would bow down again to
        worship
        and receive the blessing from the Most
        High.

A Blessing and a Curse

22 Now bless the God of all,
    who works great wonders
        everywhere,
    who has caused us to grow from the
        day we were born,
        and who deals with us according to
        his mercy.
23 May he grant us joyfulness of heart,
    and may there be peace in our time
        in Israel, just as there was long ago.
24 May he confirm his mercy toward us
        by rescuing us in our time.

25 There are two nations my soul abhors
    and the third is not even a nation:
26 those who live in Edom* and Philistia
    and those foolish Samaritans who live
        in Shechem.

50:15 Greek *of the blood of the grape.*   50:26 As in Hebrew, which reads, *in Seir,* another name for Edom. Greek reads *on the mountain of Samaria.*

Postscript

27 I, Jeshua* son of Eleazar
  son of Sirach of Jerusalem (whose mind
    overflowed with wisdom),
  have written instruction in
    understanding and knowledge in this
    book.

28 Blessed are those who ponder these things,
  and those who take them to heart will
    become wise.

29 For if they put them into practice, they
    will be equal to any task,
  for the fear* of the Lord guides their
    steps.

A Prayer of Jeshua Son of Sirach

51 ¹ I give thanks to you, O Lord and
    King,
  and I praise you, O God my Savior.
  I give thanks to your name,
2   for you have been my protector and
      helper.
  You have rescued me from destruction,
    from the traps set for me by slanderers,
    by those who make up lies.
  In the sight of my enemies
3   you have been my helper and rescued me.
  In keeping with your abundant kindness
      and great name,
    you rescued me from gnashing teeth
      about to devour me,
    from the hands of those wanting to
      kill me,
  and from my many troubles.
4 You rescued me from the choking flames
      that surrounded me,
    from the fire that I had not kindled,
5   from deep in the belly of Hades,
    and from a filthy tongue and lying
      words,
    for wicked people have slandered me
      before the king.
6 My soul was approaching death;
    my life was on the brink of the grave.*
7 My enemies surrounded me on every side,
    and there was no one to help me.
  I looked for someone to assist me,
    but there was no one.
8 Then I remembered your mercy, O Lord,
    and your deeds from long ago.
  You rescue those who wait for you
    and save them from their enemies.
9 I called out in prayer from the earth.
    I pleaded to be rescued from death.

10 I cried, "Lord, you are my Father.
    Don't abandon me in the times of
      trouble,
    when there is no help against the
      proud.
11 I will praise your name continually
    and sing hymns of thanksgiving."
  My prayer was heard.
12   You saved me from destruction
    and rescued me in the time of trouble.
  Therefore, I give you thanks and praise,
    and I bless the name of the Lord.

[Hebrew manuscripts of Sirach include the
following hymn between verses 12 and 13.]

A Hymn of Thanksgiving to the LORD

Give thanks to the LORD, for he is good;
    his mercy endures forever.
Give thanks to the God of praises;
    his mercy endures forever.
Give thanks to the guardian of Israel;
    his mercy endures forever.
Give thanks to him who formed all things;
    his mercy endures forever.
Give thanks to the Redeemer of Israel;
    his mercy endures forever.
Give thanks to him who gathers those
      dispersed from Israel;
    his mercy endures forever.
Give thanks to him who rebuilt his city
      and his Temple;
    his mercy endures forever.
Give thanks to him who increases the
      power of David's family;*
    his mercy endures forever.
Give thanks to him who has chosen the
      sons of Zadok to be priests;
    his mercy endures forever.
Give thanks to the shield of Abraham;
    his mercy endures forever.
Give thanks to the rock of Isaac;
    his mercy endures forever.
Give thanks to the Mighty One of Jacob;
    his mercy endures forever.
Give thanks to him who has chosen Zion;
    his mercy endures forever.
Give thanks to the greatest King of kings;
    his mercy endures forever.
He has increased the power of his people.
Praise for all his loyal ones—
    for the children of Israel, the people
      close to him.
Praise the LORD!

50:27 Greek *Jesus.*   50:29 Some manuscripts read *light.*   51:6 Greek *on the brink of Hades below.*   HYMN Hebrew *who makes
a horn to sprout for the house of David.*

The Author's Search for Wisdom

13 When I was still young, before I had
  traveled much,
  I openly sought wisdom in my prayer.
14 At the Temple I prayed to receive her,
  and I will seek her to the end.

15 My heart delighted in wisdom
  from the time she first blossomed to the
  time she ripened into fruit.
  My feet followed the right path.
  I followed wisdom from the time I was
  young.

16 I made some effort to listen and received
  wisdom.
  I found a great deal of instruction.
17 I have advanced in wisdom;
  I give glory to the Lord, who gives me
  wisdom.

18 For I have determined to live according to
  wisdom.
  I was zealous for the good
  and will never be disappointed.
19 My soul has fought to possess wisdom,
  and I tried to strictly control my
  conduct.
  I spread out my hands to the heavens
  and was grieved over my ignorance
  of her.
20 I directed my soul toward wisdom,
  and I found her as I lived purely.
  Through wisdom I gained understanding
  right from the start;
  therefore, I will not be forsaken.

21 My heart was stirred to seek her;
  therefore, I have gained a valuable
  prize.
22 The Lord has rewarded me with things
  to say,
  so I will praise him by speaking.

23 Draw near to me, you unlearned,
  and live in the house of instruction.
24 Why do you complain of lacking these
  things,
  and why do you let yourselves be so
  thirsty?
25 I have declared,
  "Buy wisdom for yourselves without
  money."

26 Submit your neck to wisdom's yoke,
  and let your soul receive instruction,
  for it is easily found.
27 See with your own eyes how I have not
  worked hard
  and have found great peace in my
  life.
28 Acquire instruction with a large sum
  of silver,
  and you will use it to gain a great deal
  of gold.

29 May your soul rejoice in the Lord's mercy,
  and may you never be ashamed to praise
  him.
30 Do your work before the assigned time,
  and the Lord will reward you in his
  time.

Isaiah

ISAIAH'S LONG MINISTRY lasted almost sixty years and covered the reigns of four kings, including Hezekiah. The prophecies of Isaiah spoke primarily to the people of Judah, although his messages applied to the northern kingdom of Israel as well. Isaiah lived through the dark days of the civil war between Israel and Judah (734–732 BC) and saw the destruction of Israel by Assyria in 722 BC. Isaiah used the grim lesson of Israel's fall to teach King Hezekiah of Judah to trust in the Lord. Isaiah also spoke about events that would take place after his own time, including the coming exile of Judah to Babylon and the deliverance that God would provide afterward. Isaiah warned the nations surrounding Israel and Judah that they, too, would be judged for their actions. In the end, however, Isaiah offered a message of hope and comfort for the entire world, promising that God would restore the nations after their punishment was completed. Isaiah's messages, like those of most prophets, made him few friends during his lifetime. Nevertheless, he faithfully continued to bring God's message to the world.

■ **Author:** Isaiah or his followers

■ **Date Written:** The events of chapters 1–39 occurred during Isaiah's ministry, so they were probably written around 700 BC. Chapters 40–66, however, may have been written near the end of his life, around 681 BC.

■ **Purpose:** To call the nation of Judah back to God and to tell of God's plan of salvation through the Messiah

■ **Themes:** Holiness, punishment, salvation, the coming Messiah, hope

■ **Outline**
1:1–23:18 Prophecies concerning Judah and the nations
24:1–27:13 God's judgment upon the world's sin
28:1–35:10 Prophecies concerning Judah and Israel
36:1–39:8 Events during Hezekiah's reign
40:1–66:24 Judah's future comfort and God's salvation

---

1 These are the visions that Isaiah son of Amoz saw concerning Judah and Jerusalem. He saw these visions during the years when Uzziah, Jotham, Ahaz, and Hezekiah were kings of Judah.*

A Message for Rebellious Judah
² Listen, O heavens! Pay attention, earth!
This is what the LORD says:
"The children I raised and cared for have rebelled against me.
³ Even an ox knows its owner, and a donkey recognizes its master's care—
but Israel doesn't know its master.

1:1 These kings reigned from 792 to 686 B.C.

My people don't recognize my care for them."
⁴ Oh, what a sinful nation they are—
loaded down with a burden of guilt.
They are evil people,
corrupt children who have rejected the LORD.
They have despised the Holy One of Israel
and turned their backs on him.

⁵ Why do you continue to invite punishment?
Must you rebel forever?
Your head is injured,
and your heart is sick.

6 You are battered from head to foot—
   covered with bruises, welts, and infected
      wounds—
   without any soothing ointments or
      bandages.
7 Your country lies in ruins,
   and your towns are burned.
   Foreigners plunder your fields before
      your eyes
   and destroy everything they see.
8 Beautiful Jerusalem* stands abandoned
   like a watchman's shelter in a vineyard,
   like a lean-to in a cucumber field after the
      harvest,
   like a helpless city under siege.
9 If the LORD of Heaven's Armies
   had not spared a few of us,*
   we would have been wiped out like Sodom,
   destroyed like Gomorrah.

10 Listen to the LORD, you leaders of
   "Sodom."
   Listen to the law of our God, people
   of "Gomorrah."
11 "What makes you think I want all your
      sacrifices?"
   says the LORD.
   "I am sick of your burnt offerings of rams
   and the fat of fattened cattle.
   I get no pleasure from the blood
   of bulls and lambs and goats.
12 When you come to worship me,
   who asked you to parade through my
      courts with all your ceremony?
13 Stop bringing me your meaningless gifts;
   the incense of your offerings
      disgusts me!
   As for your celebrations of the new moon
      and the Sabbath
   and your special days for fasting—
   they are all sinful and false.
   I want no more of your pious meetings.
14 I hate your new moon celebrations and
      your annual festivals.
   They are a burden to me. I cannot stand
      them!
15 When you lift up your hands in prayer,
   I will not look.
   Though you offer many prayers, I will
      not listen,
   for your hands are covered with the
      blood of innocent victims.
16 Wash yourselves and be clean!
   Get your sins out of my sight.
   Give up your evil ways.

17 Learn to do good.
   Seek justice.
   Help the oppressed.
   Defend the cause of orphans.
   Fight for the rights of widows.

18 "Come now, let's settle this,"
   says the LORD.
   "Though your sins are like scarlet,
   I will make them as white as snow.
   Though they are red like crimson,
   I will make them as white as wool.
19 If you will only obey me,
   you will have plenty to eat.
20 But if you turn away and refuse to listen,
   you will be devoured by the sword of
      your enemies.
   I, the LORD, have spoken!"

Unfaithful Jerusalem
21 See how Jerusalem, once so faithful,
   has become a prostitute.
   Once the home of justice and
      righteousness,
   she is now filled with murderers.
22 Once like pure silver,
   you have become like worthless slag.
   Once so pure,
   you are now like watered-down wine.
23 Your leaders are rebels,
   the companions of thieves.
   All of them love bribes
   and demand payoffs,
   but they refuse to defend the cause of
      orphans
   or fight for the rights of widows.

24 Therefore, the Lord, the LORD of Heaven's
      Armies,
   the Mighty One of Israel, says,
   "I will take revenge on my enemies
   and pay back my foes!
25 I will raise my fist against you.
   I will melt you down and skim off your
      slag.
   I will remove all your impurities.
26 Then I will give you good judges again
   and wise counselors like you used to have.
   Then Jerusalem will again be called the
      Home of Justice
   and the Faithful City."

27 Zion will be restored by justice;
   those who repent will be revived by
      righteousness.

1:8 Hebrew *The daughter of Zion.*   1:9 Greek version reads *a few of our children.* Compare Rom 9:29.

²⁸ But rebels and sinners will be completely
      destroyed,
   and those who desert the LORD will be
      consumed.

²⁹ You will be ashamed of your idol worship
      in groves of sacred oaks.
   You will blush because you worshiped
      in gardens dedicated to idols.
³⁰ You will be like a great tree with withered
      leaves,
   like a garden without water.
³¹ The strongest among you will disappear
      like straw;
   their evil deeds will be the spark that
      sets it on fire.
   They and their evil works will burn up
      together,
   and no one will be able to put out the
      fire.

The LORD's Future Reign

2 This is a vision that Isaiah son of Amoz saw
   concerning Judah and Jerusalem:

² In the last days, the mountain of the
      LORD's house
   will be the highest of all—
      the most important place on earth.
   It will be raised above the other hills,
      and people from all over the world will
      stream there to worship.
³ People from many nations will come and
      say,
   "Come, let us go up to the mountain of the
      LORD,
   to the house of Jacob's God.
   There he will teach us his ways,
      and we will walk in his paths."
   For the LORD's teaching will go out from
      Zion;
   his word will go out from Jerusalem.
⁴ The LORD will mediate between nations
      and will settle international disputes.
   They will hammer their swords into
      plowshares
   and their spears into pruning hooks.
   Nation will no longer fight against nation,
      nor train for war anymore.

A Warning of Judgment

⁵ Come, descendants of Jacob,
      let us walk in the light of the LORD!
⁶ For the LORD has rejected his people,
      the descendants of Jacob,

because they have filled their land with
      practices from the East
   and with sorcerers, as the Philistines do.
   They have made alliances with pagans.
⁷ Israel is full of silver and gold;
      there is no end to its treasures.
   Their land is full of warhorses;
      there is no end to its chariots.
⁸ Their land is full of idols;
      the people worship things they have
      made
   with their own hands.
⁹ So now they will be humbled,
      and all will be brought low—
      do not forgive them.
¹⁰ Crawl into caves in the rocks.
      Hide in the dust
   from the terror of the LORD
      and the glory of his majesty.
¹¹ Human pride will be brought down,
      and human arrogance will be
      humbled.
   Only the LORD will be exalted
      on that day of judgment.

¹² For the LORD of Heaven's Armies
      has a day of reckoning.
   He will punish the proud and mighty
      and bring down everything that is
      exalted.
¹³ He will cut down the tall cedars of
      Lebanon
   and all the mighty oaks of Bashan.
¹⁴ He will level all the high mountains
      and all the lofty hills.
¹⁵ He will break down every high tower
      and every fortified wall.
¹⁶ He will destroy all the great trading ships*
      and every magnificent vessel.
¹⁷ Human pride will be humbled,
      and human arrogance will be brought
      down.
   Only the LORD will be exalted
      on that day of judgment.

¹⁸ Idols will completely disappear.
¹⁹ When the LORD rises to shake the earth,
      his enemies will crawl into holes in the
      ground.
   They will hide in caves in the rocks
      from the terror of the LORD
      and the glory of his majesty.
²⁰ On that day of judgment they will
      abandon the gold and silver idols
      they made for themselves to worship.

2:16 Hebrew *every ship of Tarshish.*

They will leave their gods to the rodents
and bats,
²¹ while they crawl away into caverns
and hide among the jagged rocks in the
cliffs.
They will try to escape the terror of the
LORD
and the glory of his majesty
as he rises to shake the earth.
²² Don't put your trust in mere humans.
They are as frail as breath.
What good are they?

Judgment against Judah

3 ¹ The Lord, the LORD of Heaven's Armies,
will take away from Jerusalem and
Judah
everything they depend on:
every bit of bread
and every drop of water,
² all their heroes and soldiers,
judges and prophets,
fortune-tellers and elders,
³ army officers and high officials,
advisers, skilled sorcerers, and
astrologers.

⁴ I will make boys their leaders,
and toddlers their rulers.
⁵ People will oppress each other—
man against man,
neighbor against neighbor.
Young people will insult their elders,
and vulgar people will sneer at the
honorable.

⁶ In those days a man will say to his brother,
"Since you have a coat, you be our leader!
Take charge of this heap of ruins!"
⁷ But he will reply,
"No! I can't help.
I don't have any extra food or clothes.
Don't put me in charge!"

⁸ For Jerusalem will stumble,
and Judah will fall,
because they speak out against the LORD
and refuse to obey him.
They provoke him to his face.
⁹ The very look on their faces gives them
away.
They display their sin like the people
of Sodom
and don't even try to hide it.

They are doomed!
They have brought destruction upon
themselves.

¹⁰ Tell the godly that all will be well for
them.
They will enjoy the rich reward they
have earned!
¹¹ But the wicked are doomed,
for they will get exactly what they
deserve.

¹² Childish leaders oppress my people,
and women rule over them.
O my people, your leaders mislead you;
they send you down the wrong road.

¹³ The LORD takes his place in court
and presents his case against his
people.*
¹⁴ The LORD comes forward to pronounce
judgment
on the elders and rulers of his people:
"You have ruined Israel, my vineyard.
Your houses are filled with things stolen
from the poor.
¹⁵ How dare you crush my people,
grinding the faces of the poor into the
dust?"
demands the Lord, the LORD of
Heaven's Armies.

A Warning to Jerusalem

¹⁶ The LORD says, "Beautiful Zion* is
haughty:
craning her elegant neck,
flirting with her eyes,
walking with dainty steps,
tinkling her ankle bracelets.
¹⁷ So the Lord will send scabs on her head;
the LORD will make beautiful Zion
bald."

¹⁸ On that day of judgment
the Lord will strip away everything that
makes her beautiful:
ornaments, headbands, crescent necklaces,
¹⁹ earrings, bracelets, and veils;
²⁰ scarves, ankle bracelets, sashes,
perfumes, and charms;
²¹ rings, jewels,
²² party clothes, gowns, capes, and purses;
²³ mirrors, fine linen garments,
head ornaments, and shawls.

3:13 As in Greek and Syriac versions; Hebrew reads *against the peoples*.   3:16 Or *The women of Zion* (with corresponding changes to plural forms through verse 24); Hebrew reads *The daughters of Zion*; also in 3:17.

²⁴ Instead of smelling of sweet perfume, she
will stink.
  She will wear a rope for a sash,
    and her elegant hair will fall out.
  She will wear rough burlap instead of rich
    robes.
  Shame will replace her beauty.*
²⁵ The men of the city will be killed with the
    sword,
  and her warriors will die in battle.
²⁶ The gates of Zion will weep and mourn.
  The city will be like a ravaged woman,
    huddled on the ground.

4 In that day so few men will be left that
seven women will fight for each man, saying, "Let us all marry you! We will provide our
own food and clothing. Only let us take your
name so we won't be mocked as old maids."

A Promise of Restoration

² But in that day, the branch* of the LORD
  will be beautiful and glorious;
  the fruit of the land will be the pride and
    glory
  of all who survive in Israel.
³ All who remain in Zion
  will be a holy people—
  those who survive the destruction of
    Jerusalem
  and are recorded among the living.
⁴ The Lord will wash the filth from beautiful
    Zion*
  and cleanse Jerusalem of its bloodstains
  with the hot breath of fiery judgment.
⁵ Then the LORD will provide shade for
    Mount Zion
  and all who assemble there.
  He will provide a canopy of cloud during
    the day
  and smoke and flaming fire at night,
    covering the glorious land.
⁶ It will be a shelter from daytime heat
  and a hiding place from storms and rain.

A Song about the LORD's Vineyard

5 ¹ Now I will sing for the one I love
  a song about his vineyard:
  My beloved had a vineyard
  on a rich and fertile hill.
² He plowed the land, cleared its stones,
  and planted it with the best vines.

In the middle he built a watchtower
  and carved a winepress in the nearby
    rocks.
  Then he waited for a harvest of sweet
    grapes,
  but the grapes that grew were bitter.

³ Now, you people of Jerusalem and Judah,
  you judge between me and my vineyard.
⁴ What more could I have done for my
    vineyard
  that I have not already done?
  When I expected sweet grapes,
  why did my vineyard give me bitter
    grapes?

⁵ Now let me tell you
  what I will do to my vineyard:
  I will tear down its hedges
  and let it be destroyed.
  I will break down its walls
  and let the animals trample it.
⁶ I will make it a wild place
  where the vines are not pruned and the
    ground is not hoed,
  a place overgrown with briers and thorns.
  I will command the clouds
  to drop no rain on it.

⁷ The nation of Israel is the vineyard of the
    LORD of Heaven's Armies.
  The people of Judah are his pleasant
    garden.
  He expected a crop of justice,
  but instead he found oppression.
  He expected to find righteousness,
  but instead he heard cries of violence.

Judah's Guilt and Judgment

⁸ What sorrow for you who buy up house
  after house and field after field,
  until everyone is evicted and you live
    alone in the land.
⁹ But I have heard the LORD of Heaven's
    Armies
  swear a solemn oath:
  "Many houses will stand deserted;
  even beautiful mansions will be empty.
¹⁰ Ten acres* of vineyard will not produce
  even six gallons* of wine.
  Ten baskets of seed will yield only one
    basket* of grain."

3:24 As in Dead Sea Scrolls; Masoretic Text reads *robes / because instead of beauty.*   4:2 Or *the Branch.*   4:4 Or *from the women of Zion;* Hebrew reads *from the daughters of Zion.*   5:10a Hebrew *A ten yoke,* that is, the area of land plowed by ten teams of oxen in one day.   5:10b Hebrew *a bath* [21 liters].   5:10c Hebrew *A homer* [5 bushels or 220 liters] *of seed will yield only an ephah* [20 quarts or 22 liters].

11 What sorrow for those who get up early
in the morning
looking for a drink of alcohol
and spend long evenings drinking wine
to make themselves flaming drunk.
12 They furnish wine and lovely music at
their grand parties—
lyre and harp, tambourine and flute—
but they never think about the LORD
or notice what he is doing.

13 So my people will go into exile far away
because they do not know me.
Those who are great and honored will
starve,
and the common people will die of
thirst.
14 The grave* is licking its lips in
anticipation,
opening its mouth wide.
The great and the lowly
and all the drunken mob will be
swallowed up.
15 Humanity will be destroyed, and people
brought down;
even the arrogant will lower their eyes
in humiliation.
16 But the LORD of Heaven's Armies will be
exalted by his justice.
The holiness of God will be displayed
by his righteousness.
17 In that day lambs will find good
pastures,
and fattened sheep and young goats*
will feed among the ruins.

18 What sorrow for those who drag their sins
behind them
with ropes made of lies,
who drag wickedness behind them like
a cart!
19 They even mock God and say,
"Hurry up and do something!
We want to see what you can do.
Let the Holy One of Israel carry out his
plan,
for we want to know what it is."

20 What sorrow for those who say
that evil is good and good is evil,
that dark is light and light is dark,
that bitter is sweet and sweet is bitter.
21 What sorrow for those who are wise in
their own eyes
and think themselves so clever.

22 What sorrow for those who are heroes at
drinking wine
and boast about all the alcohol they can
hold.
23 They take bribes to let the wicked go free,
and they punish the innocent.

24 Therefore, just as fire licks up stubble
and dry grass shrivels in the flame,
so their roots will rot
and their flowers wither.
For they have rejected the law of the LORD
of Heaven's Armies;
they have despised the word of the Holy
One of Israel.
25 That is why the LORD's anger burns
against his people,
and why he has raised his fist to crush
them.
The mountains tremble,
and the corpses of his people litter the
streets like garbage.
But even then the LORD's anger is not
satisfied.
His fist is still poised to strike!

26 He will send a signal to distant nations
far away
and whistle to those at the ends of the
earth.
They will come racing toward
Jerusalem.
27 They will not get tired or stumble.
They will not stop for rest or sleep.
Not a belt will be loose,
not a sandal strap broken.
28 Their arrows will be sharp
and their bows ready for battle.
Sparks will fly from their horses' hooves,
and the wheels of their chariots will
spin like a whirlwind.
29 They will roar like lions,
like the strongest of lions.
Growling, they will pounce on their
victims and carry them off,
and no one will be there to rescue
them.
30 They will roar over their victims on that
day of destruction
like the roaring of the sea.
If someone looks across the land,
only darkness and distress will be
seen;
even the light will be darkened by
clouds.

5:14 Hebrew *Sheol.*   5:17 As in Greek version; Hebrew reads *and strangers.*

Isaiah's Cleansing and Call

6 It was in the year King Uzziah died* that I saw the Lord. He was sitting on a lofty throne, and the train of his robe filled the Temple. [2] Attending him were mighty seraphim, each having six wings. With two wings they covered their faces, with two they covered their feet, and with two they flew. [3] They were calling out to each other,

"Holy, holy, holy is the LORD of Heaven's
    Armies!
The whole earth is filled with his glory!"

[4] Their voices shook the Temple to its foundations, and the entire building was filled with smoke. [5] Then I said, "It's all over! I am doomed, for I am a sinful man. I have filthy lips, and I live among a people with filthy lips. Yet I have seen the King, the LORD of Heaven's Armies."

[6] Then one of the seraphim flew to me with a burning coal he had taken from the altar with a pair of tongs. [7] He touched my lips with it and said, "See, this coal has touched your lips. Now your guilt is removed, and your sins are forgiven."

[8] Then I heard the Lord asking, "Whom should I send as a messenger to this people? Who will go for us?"

I said, "Here I am. Send me."

[9] And he said, "Yes, go, and say to this people,

'Listen carefully, but do not understand.
    Watch closely, but learn nothing.'
[10] Harden the hearts of these people.
    Plug their ears and shut their eyes.
That way, they will not see with their eyes,
    nor hear with their ears,
nor understand with their hearts
    and turn to me for healing."*

[11] Then I said, "Lord, how long will this go on?"

And he replied,

"Until their towns are empty,
    their houses are deserted,
    and the whole country is a wasteland;
[12] until the LORD has sent everyone away,
    and the entire land of Israel lies deserted.

[13] If even a tenth—a remnant—survive,
    it will be invaded again and burned.
But as a terebinth or oak tree leaves a
    stump when it is cut down,
so Israel's stump will be a holy seed."

A Message for Ahaz

7 When Ahaz, son of Jotham and grandson of Uzziah, was king of Judah, King Rezin of Syria* and Pekah son of Remaliah, the king of Israel, set out to attack Jerusalem. However, they were unable to carry out their plan.

[2] The news had come to the royal court of Judah: "Syria is allied with Israel* against us!" So the hearts of the king and his people trembled with fear, like trees shaking in a storm.

[3] Then the LORD said to Isaiah, "Take your son Shear-jashub* and go out to meet King Ahaz. You will find him at the end of the aqueduct that feeds water into the upper pool, near the road leading to the field where cloth is washed.* [4] Tell him to stop worrying. Tell him he doesn't need to fear the fierce anger of those two burned-out embers, King Rezin of Syria and Pekah son of Remaliah. [5] Yes, the kings of Syria and Israel are plotting against him, saying, [6] 'We will attack Judah and capture it for ourselves. Then we will install the son of Tabeel as Judah's king.' [7] But this is what the Sovereign LORD says:

"This invasion will never happen;
    it will never take place;
[8] for Syria is no stronger than its capital,
        Damascus,
    and Damascus is no stronger than its
        king, Rezin.
As for Israel, within sixty-five years
    it will be crushed and completely
        destroyed.
[9] Israel is no stronger than its capital,
        Samaria,
    and Samaria is no stronger than its king,
        Pekah son of Remaliah.
Unless your faith is firm,
    I cannot make you stand firm."

The Sign of Immanuel

[10] Later, the LORD sent this message to King Ahaz: [11] "Ask the LORD your God for a sign of confirmation, Ahaz. Make it as difficult as you

---

6:1 King Uzziah died in 740 B.C.   6:9-10 Greek version reads *And he said, "Go and say to this people, / 'When you hear what I say, you will not understand. / When you see what I do, you will not comprehend.' / For the hearts of these people are hardened, / and their ears cannot hear, and they have closed their eyes—/ so their eyes cannot see, / and their ears cannot hear, / and their hearts cannot understand, / and they cannot turn to me and let me heal them.*" Compare Matt 13:14-15; Mark 4:12; Luke 8:10; Acts 28:26-27.   7:1 Hebrew *Aram;* also in 7:2, 4, 5, 8.   7:2 Hebrew *Ephraim,* referring to the northern kingdom of Israel; also in 7:5, 8, 9, 17.   7:3a *Shear-jashub* means "A remnant will return."   7:3b Or *bleached.*

want—as high as heaven or as deep as the place of the dead.*"

12But the king refused. "No," he said, "I will not test the LORD like that."

13Then Isaiah said, "Listen well, you royal family of David! Isn't it enough to exhaust human patience? Must you exhaust the patience of my God as well? 14All right then, the Lord himself will give you the sign. Look! The virgin* will conceive a child! She will give birth to a son and will call him Immanuel (which means 'God is with us'). 15By the time this child is old enough to choose what is right and reject what is wrong, he will be eating yogurt* and honey. 16For before the child is that old, the lands of the two kings you fear so much will both be deserted.

17"Then the LORD will bring things on you, your nation, and your family unlike anything since Israel broke away from Judah. He will bring the king of Assyria upon you!"

18In that day the LORD will whistle for the army of southern Egypt and for the army of Assyria. They will swarm around you like flies and bees. 19They will come in vast hordes and settle in the fertile areas and also in the desolate valleys, caves, and thorny places. 20In that day the Lord will hire a "razor" from beyond the Euphrates River*—the king of Assyria—and use it to shave off everything: your land, your crops, and your people.*

21In that day a farmer will be fortunate to have a cow and two sheep or goats left. 22Nevertheless, there will be enough milk for everyone because so few people will be left in the land. They will eat their fill of yogurt and honey. 23In that day the lush vineyards, now worth 1,000 pieces of silver,* will become patches of briers and thorns. 24The entire land will become a vast expanse of briers and thorns, a hunting ground overrun by wildlife. 25No one will go to the fertile hillsides where the gardens once grew, for briers and thorns will cover them. Cattle, sheep, and goats will graze there.

The Coming Assyrian Invasion

8 Then the LORD said to me, "Make a large signboard and clearly write this name on it: Maher-shalal-hash-baz.*" 2I asked Uriah the priest and Zechariah son of Jeberekiah, both known as honest men, to witness my doing this.

3Then I slept with my wife, and she became pregnant and gave birth to a son. And the LORD said, "Call him Maher-shalal-hash-baz. 4For before this child is old enough to say 'Papa' or 'Mama,' the king of Assyria will carry away both the abundance of Damascus and the riches of Samaria."

5Then the LORD spoke to me again and said, 6"My care for the people of Judah is like the gently flowing waters of Shiloah, but they have rejected it. They are rejoicing over what will happen to* King Rezin and King Pekah.* 7Therefore, the Lord will overwhelm them with a mighty flood from the Euphrates River*—the king of Assyria and all his glory. This flood will overflow all its channels 8and sweep into Judah until it is chin deep. It will spread its wings, submerging your land from one end to the other, O Immanuel.

9 "Huddle together, you nations, and be terrified.
  Listen, all you distant lands.
  Prepare for battle, but you will be crushed!
  Yes, prepare for battle, but you will be crushed!
10 Call your councils of war, but they will be worthless.
  Develop your strategies, but they will not succeed.
  For God is with us!*"

A Call to Trust the LORD

11The LORD has given me a strong warning not to think like everyone else does. He said,

12 "Don't call everything a conspiracy, like they do,
  and don't live in dread of what frightens them.
13 Make the LORD of Heaven's Armies holy in your life.
  He is the one you should fear.
  He is the one who should make you tremble.
14 He will keep you safe.
  But to Israel and Judah
  he will be a stone that makes people stumble,
  a rock that makes them fall.
  And for the people of Jerusalem
  he will be a trap and a snare.

7:11 Hebrew *as deep as Sheol.* 7:14 Or *young woman.* 7:15 Or *curds;* also in 7:22. 7:20a Hebrew *the river.* 7:20b Hebrew *shave off the head, the hair of the legs, and the beard.* 7:23 Hebrew *1,000 [shekels] of silver,* about 25 pounds or 11.4 kilograms in weight. 8:1 *Maher-shalal-hash-baz* means "Swift to plunder and quick to carry away." 8:6a Or *They are rejoicing because of.* 8:6b Hebrew *and the son of Remaliah.* 8:7 Hebrew *the river.* 8:10 Hebrew *Immanuel!*

15 Many will stumble and fall,
   never to rise again.
   They will be snared and captured."

16 Preserve the teaching of God;
   entrust his instructions to those who
      follow me.
17 I will wait for the LORD,
   who has turned away from the
      descendants of Jacob.
   I will put my hope in him.

18 I and the children the LORD has given me serve as signs and warnings to Israel from the LORD of Heaven's Armies who dwells in his Temple on Mount Zion.

19 Someone may say to you, "Let's ask the mediums and those who consult the spirits of the dead. With their whisperings and mutterings, they will tell us what to do." But shouldn't people ask God for guidance? Should the living seek guidance from the dead?

20 Look to God's instructions and teachings! People who contradict his word are completely in the dark. 21 They will go from one place to another, weary and hungry. And because they are hungry, they will rage and curse their king and their God. They will look up to heaven 22 and down at the earth, but wherever they look, there will be trouble and anguish and dark despair. They will be thrown out into the darkness.

Hope in the Messiah

9 1*Nevertheless, that time of darkness and despair will not go on forever. The land of Zebulun and Naphtali will be humbled, but there will be a time in the future when Galilee of the Gentiles, which lies along the road that runs between the Jordan and the sea, will be filled with glory.

2 *The people who walk in darkness
   will see a great light.
   For those who live in a land of deep
      darkness,*
   a light will shine.
3 You will enlarge the nation of Israel,
   and its people will rejoice.
   They will rejoice before you
      as people rejoice at the harvest
      and like warriors dividing the
         plunder.

4 For you will break the yoke of their slavery
   and lift the heavy burden from their
      shoulders.
   You will break the oppressor's rod,
      just as you did when you destroyed the
         army of Midian.
5 The boots of the warrior
   and the uniforms bloodstained by war
   will all be burned.
   They will be fuel for the fire.

6 For a child is born to us,
   a son is given to us.
   The government will rest on his shoulders.
   And he will be called:
   Wonderful Counselor,* Mighty God,
   Everlasting Father, Prince of Peace.
7 His government and its peace
   will never end.
   He will rule with fairness and justice from
      the throne of his ancestor David
      for all eternity.
   The passionate commitment of the LORD
      of Heaven's Armies
   will make this happen!

The LORD's Anger against Israel

8 The Lord has spoken out against Jacob;
   his judgment has fallen upon Israel.
9 And the people of Israel* and Samaria,
   who spoke with such pride and
      arrogance,
   will soon know it.
10 They said, "We will replace the broken
      bricks of our ruins with finished
      stone,
   and replant the felled sycamore-fig trees
      with cedars."

11 But the LORD will bring Rezin's enemies
      against Israel
   and stir up all their foes.
12 The Syrians* from the east and the
      Philistines from the west
   will bare their fangs and devour Israel.
   But even then the LORD's anger will not be
      satisfied.
   His fist is still poised to strike.

13 For after all this punishment, the people
      will still not repent.
   They will not seek the LORD of Heaven's
      Armies.

9:1 Verse 9:1 is numbered 8:23 in Hebrew text.   9:2a Verses 9:2-21 are numbered 9:1-20 in Hebrew text.   9:2b Greek version reads *a land where death casts its shadow.* Compare Matt 4:16.   9:6 Or *Wonderful, Counselor.*   9:9 Hebrew *of Ephraim,* referring to the northern kingdom of Israel.   9:12 Hebrew *Arameans.*

14 Therefore, in a single day the LORD will
 destroy both the head and the tail,
 the noble palm branch and the lowly
 reed.
15 The leaders of Israel are the head,
 and the lying prophets are the tail.
16 For the leaders of the people have misled
 them.
 They have led them down the path of
 destruction.
17 That is why the Lord takes no pleasure in
 the young men
 and shows no mercy even to the widows
 and orphans.
 For they are all wicked hypocrites,
 and they all speak foolishness.
 But even then the LORD's anger will not
 be satisfied.
 His fist is still poised to strike.
18 This wickedness is like a brushfire.
 It burns not only briers and thorns
 but also sets the forests ablaze.
 Its burning sends up clouds of smoke.
19 The land will be blackened
 by the fury of the LORD of Heaven's
 Armies.
 The people will be fuel for the fire,
 and no one will spare even his own
 brother.
20 They will attack their neighbor on the
 right
 but will still be hungry.
 They will devour their neighbor on the left
 but will not be satisfied.
 In the end they will even eat their own
 children.*
21 Manasseh will feed on Ephraim,
 Ephraim will feed on Manasseh,
 and both will devour Judah.
 But even then the LORD's anger will not be
 satisfied.
 His fist is still poised to strike.

10

1 What sorrow awaits the unjust
 judges
 and those who issue unfair laws.
2 They deprive the poor of justice
 and deny the rights of the needy among
 my people.
 They prey on widows
 and take advantage of orphans.
3 What will you do when I punish you,
 when I send disaster upon you from a
 distant land?

9:20 Or *eat their own arms.*

To whom will you turn for help?
 Where will your treasures be safe?
4 You will stumble along as prisoners
 or lie among the dead.
 But even then the LORD's anger will not
 be satisfied.
 His fist is still poised to strike.

Judgment against Assyria

5 "What sorrow awaits Assyria, the rod of
 my anger.
 I use it as a club to express my anger.
6 I am sending Assyria against a godless
 nation,
 against a people with whom I am angry.
 Assyria will plunder them,
 trampling them like dirt beneath its
 feet.
7 But the king of Assyria will not
 understand that he is my tool;
 his mind does not work that way.
 His plan is simply to destroy,
 to cut down nation after nation.
8 He will say,
 'Each of my princes will soon be a king.
9 We destroyed Calno just as we did
 Carchemish.
 Hamath fell before us as Arpad did.
 And we destroyed Samaria just as we did
 Damascus.
10 Yes, we have finished off many a kingdom
 whose gods were greater than those in
 Jerusalem and Samaria.
11 So we will defeat Jerusalem and her gods,
 just as we destroyed Samaria with
 hers.'"

12After the Lord has used the king of Assyria
to accomplish his purposes on Mount Zion and
in Jerusalem, he will turn against the king of
Assyria and punish him—for he is proud and
arrogant. 13He boasts,

"By my own powerful arm I have done
 this.
 With my own shrewd wisdom I
 planned it.
 I have broken down the defenses of
 nations
 and carried off their treasures.
 I have knocked down their kings like
 a bull.
14 I have robbed their nests of riches
 and gathered up kingdoms as a farmer
 gathers eggs.

No one can even flap a wing against me
   or utter a peep of protest.”

15 But can the ax boast greater power than
   the person who uses it?
  Is the saw greater than the person who
   saws?
  Can a rod strike unless a hand moves it?
  Can a wooden cane walk by itself?
16 Therefore, the Lord, the LORD of Heaven’s
   Armies,
  will send a plague among Assyria’s
   proud troops,
  and a flaming fire will consume its glory.
17 The LORD, the Light of Israel, will be a fire;
   the Holy One will be a flame.
  He will devour the thorns and briers with
   fire,
  burning up the enemy in a single night.
18 The LORD will consume Assyria’s glory
   like a fire consumes a forest in a fruitful
   land;
  it will waste away like sick people in a
   plague.
19 Of all that glorious forest, only a few trees
   will survive—
  so few that a child could count them!

Hope for the LORD’s People

20 In that day the remnant left in Israel,
   the survivors in the house of Jacob,
  will no longer depend on allies
   who seek to destroy them.
  But they will faithfully trust the LORD,
   the Holy One of Israel.
21 A remnant will return;*
   yes, the remnant of Jacob will return to
   the Mighty God.
22 But though the people of Israel are as
   numerous
   as the sand of the seashore,
  only a remnant of them will return.
  The LORD has rightly decided to destroy
   his people.
23 Yes, the Lord, the LORD of Heaven’s
   Armies,
  has already decided to destroy the entire
   land.*

24So this is what the Lord, the LORD of Heaven’s Armies, says: “O my people in Zion, do not be afraid of the Assyrians when they oppress you with rod and club as the Egyptians did long ago. 25In a little while my anger against you will end, and then my anger will rise up to destroy them.” 26The LORD of Heaven’s Armies will lash them with his whip, as he did when Gideon triumphed over the Midianites at the rock of Oreb, or when the LORD’s staff was raised to drown the Egyptian army in the sea.

27 In that day the LORD will end the bondage
   of his people.
  He will break the yoke of slavery
   and lift it from their shoulders.*

28 Look, the Assyrians are now at Aiath.
  They are passing through Migron
  and are storing their equipment at
   Micmash.
29 They are crossing the pass
   and are camping at Geba.
  Fear strikes the town of Ramah.
  All the people of Gibeah, the hometown
   of Saul,
  are running for their lives.
30 Scream in terror,
   you people of Gallim!
  Shout out a warning to Laishah.
   Oh, poor Anathoth!
31 There go the people of Madmenah, all
   fleeing.
  The citizens of Gebim are trying to
   hide.
32 The enemy stops at Nob for the rest of
   that day.
  He shakes his fist at beautiful Mount
   Zion, the mountain of Jerusalem.

33 But look! The Lord, the LORD of Heaven’s
   Armies,
  will chop down the mighty tree of
   Assyria with great power!
  He will cut down the proud.
   That lofty tree will be brought down.
34 He will cut down the forest trees with
   an ax.
  Lebanon will fall to the Mighty One.*

A Branch from David’s Line

11 1 Out of the stump of David’s family*
   will grow a shoot—
  yes, a new Branch bearing fruit from the
   old root.

10:21 Hebrew *Shear-jashub*; see 7:3; 8:18. **10:22-23** Greek version reads *only a remnant of them will be saved. / For he will carry out his sentence quickly and with finality and righteousness; / for God will carry out his sentence upon all the world with finality.* Compare Rom 9:27-28. **10:27** As in Greek version; Hebrew reads *The yoke will be broken, / for you have grown so fat.* **10:34** Or *with an ax / as even the mighty trees of Lebanon fall.* **11:1** Hebrew *the stump of the line of Jesse.* Jesse was King David’s father.

2 And the Spirit of the LORD will rest on
    him—
    the Spirit of wisdom and
       understanding,
  the Spirit of counsel and might,
    the Spirit of knowledge and the fear
      of the LORD.
3 He will delight in obeying the LORD.
    He will not judge by appearance
    nor make a decision based on
      hearsay.
4 He will give justice to the poor
    and make fair decisions for the
      exploited.
  The earth will shake at the force of his
      word,
    and one breath from his mouth will
      destroy the wicked.
5 He will wear righteousness like a belt
    and truth like an undergarment.

6 In that day the wolf and the lamb will live
    together;
    the leopard will lie down with the baby
      goat.
  The calf and the yearling will be safe with
      the lion,
    and a little child will lead them all.
7 The cow will graze near the bear.
    The cub and the calf will lie down
      together.
    The lion will eat hay like a cow.
8 The baby will play safely near the hole of
    a cobra.
    Yes, a little child will put its hand in a
      nest of deadly snakes without harm.
9 Nothing will hurt or destroy in all my holy
    mountain,
    for as the waters fill the sea,
  so the earth will be filled with people
    who know the LORD.

10 In that day the heir to David's throne*
    will be a banner of salvation to all the
    world.
  The nations will rally to him,
    and the land where he lives will be a
      glorious place.*
11 In that day the Lord will reach out his
    hand a second time
    to bring back the remnant of his
      people—

  those who remain in Assyria and northern
    Egypt;
  in southern Egypt, Ethiopia,* and Elam;
  in Babylonia,* Hamath, and all the
    distant coastlands.
12 He will raise a flag among the nations
    and assemble the exiles of Israel.
  He will gather the scattered people of
    Judah
    from the ends of the earth.

13 Then at last the jealousy between Israel*
    and Judah will end.
    They will not be rivals anymore.
14 They will join forces to swoop down on
    Philistia to the west.
  Together they will attack and plunder
    the nations to the east.
  They will occupy the lands of Edom and
    Moab,
    and Ammon will obey them.
15 The LORD will make a dry path through
    the gulf of the Red Sea.*
  He will wave his hand over the
    Euphrates River,*
  sending a mighty wind to divide it into
    seven streams
    so it can easily be crossed on foot.
16 He will make a highway for the remnant
    of his people,
    the remnant coming from Assyria,
  just as he did for Israel long ago
    when they returned from Egypt.

Songs of Praise for Salvation

12 1 In that day you will sing:
    "I will praise you, O LORD!
  You were angry with me, but not any
    more.
    Now you comfort me.
2 See, God has come to save me.
    I will trust in him and not be afraid.
  The LORD GOD is my strength and my
    song;
    he has given me victory."

3 With joy you will drink deeply
    from the fountain of salvation!
4 In that wonderful day you will sing:
    "Thank the LORD! Praise his name!
  Tell the nations what he has done.
    Let them know how mighty he is!

11:10a Hebrew *the root of Jesse.*   11:10b Greek version reads *In that day the heir to David's throne* [literally *the root of Jesse*] *will
come, / and he will rule over the Gentiles. / They will place their hopes on him.* Compare Rom 15:12.   11:11a Hebrew *in Pathros, Cush.*
11:11b Hebrew *in Shinar.*   11:13 Hebrew *Ephraim,* referring to the northern kingdom of Israel.   11:15a Hebrew *will destroy
the tongue of the sea of Egypt.*   11:15b Hebrew *the river.*

⁵ Sing to the LORD, for he has done
   wonderful things.
 Make known his praise around the
   world.
⁶ Let all the people of Jerusalem* shout his
   praise with joy!
 For great is the Holy One of Israel who
   lives among you."

A Message about Babylon

13 Isaiah son of Amoz received this message concerning the destruction of
Babylon:

² "Raise a signal flag on a bare hilltop.
   Call up an army against Babylon.
 Wave your hand to encourage them
   as they march into the palaces of the
   high and mighty.
³ I, the LORD, have dedicated these soldiers
   for this task.
 Yes, I have called mighty warriors to
   express my anger,
   and they will rejoice when I am
   exalted."

⁴ Hear the noise on the mountains!
   Listen, as the vast armies march!
 It is the noise and shouting of many
   nations.
 The LORD of Heaven's Armies has called
   this army together.
⁵ They come from distant countries,
   from beyond the farthest horizons.
 They are the LORD's weapons to carry out
   his anger.
 With them he will destroy the whole
   land.

⁶ Scream in terror, for the day of the LORD
   has arrived—
   the time for the Almighty to destroy.
⁷ Every arm is paralyzed with fear.
   Every heart melts,
⁸   and people are terrified.
 Pangs of anguish grip them,
   like those of a woman in labor.
 They look helplessly at one another,
   their faces aflame with fear.

⁹ For see, the day of the LORD is coming—
   the terrible day of his fury and fierce
   anger.
 The land will be made desolate,
   and all the sinners destroyed with it.

12:6 Hebrew *Zion.*

¹⁰ The heavens will be black above them;
   the stars will give no light.
 The sun will be dark when it rises,
   and the moon will provide no light.

¹¹ "I, the LORD, will punish the world for
   its evil
   and the wicked for their sin.
 I will crush the arrogance of the proud
   and humble the pride of the mighty.
¹² I will make people scarcer than gold—
   more rare than the fine gold of Ophir.
¹³ For I will shake the heavens.
   The earth will move from its place
 when the LORD of Heaven's Armies
   displays his wrath
   in the day of his fierce anger."

¹⁴ Everyone in Babylon will run about like a
   hunted gazelle,
   like sheep without a shepherd.
 They will try to find their own people
   and flee to their own land.
¹⁵ Anyone who is captured will be cut
   down—
   run through with a sword.
¹⁶ Their little children will be dashed to
   death before their eyes.
 Their homes will be sacked, and their
   wives will be raped.

¹⁷ "Look, I will stir up the Medes against
   Babylon.
 They cannot be tempted by silver
   or bribed with gold.
¹⁸ The attacking armies will shoot down the
   young men with arrows.
 They will have no mercy on helpless
   babies
 and will show no compassion for
   children."

¹⁹ Babylon, the most glorious of kingdoms,
   the flower of Chaldean pride,
 will be devastated like Sodom and
   Gomorrah
   when God destroyed them.
²⁰ Babylon will never be inhabited again.
   It will remain empty for generation
   after generation.
 Nomads will refuse to camp there,
   and shepherds will not bed down their
   sheep.
²¹ Desert animals will move into the ruined
   city,

and the houses will be haunted by
　　howling creatures.
Owls will live among the ruins,
　　and wild goats will go there to dance.
22 Hyenas will howl in its fortresses,
　　and jackals will make dens in its
　　　luxurious palaces.
Babylon's days are numbered;
　　its time of destruction will soon arrive.

A Taunt for Babylon's King

14 But the LORD will have mercy on the
descendants of Jacob. He will choose
Israel as his special people once again. He will
bring them back to settle once again in their
own land. And people from many different nations will come and join them there and unite
with the people of Israel.* 2 The nations of the
world will help the people of Israel to return,
and those who come to live in the LORD's land
will serve them. Those who captured Israel will
themselves be captured, and Israel will rule
over its enemies.

3 In that wonderful day when the LORD gives
his people rest from sorrow and fear, from slavery and chains, 4 you will taunt the king of Babylon. You will say,

"The mighty man has been destroyed.
　　Yes, your insolence* is ended.
5 For the LORD has crushed your wicked
　　power
　　and broken your evil rule.
6 You struck the people with endless blows
　　of rage
　　and held the nations in your angry grip
　　with unrelenting tyranny.
7 But finally the earth is at rest and quiet.
　　Now it can sing again!
8 Even the trees of the forest—
　　the cypress trees and the cedars of
　　　Lebanon—
　　sing out this joyous song:
'Since you have been cut down,
　　no one will come now to cut us down!'

9 "In the place of the dead* there is
　　excitement
　　over your arrival.
The spirits of world leaders and mighty
　　kings long dead
　　stand up to see you.

10 With one voice they all cry out,
　　'Now you are as weak as we are!
11 Your might and power were buried with
　　you.*
The sound of the harp in your palace
　　has ceased.
Now maggots are your sheet,
　　and worms your blanket.'

12 "How you are fallen from heaven,
　　O shining star, son of the morning!
You have been thrown down to the earth,
　　you who destroyed the nations of the
　　　world.
13 For you said to yourself,
　　'I will ascend to heaven and set my
　　　throne above God's stars.
I will preside on the mountain of the
　　gods
　　far away in the north.*
14 I will climb to the highest heavens
　　and be like the Most High.'
15 Instead, you will be brought down to the
　　place of the dead,
　　down to its lowest depths.
16 Everyone there will stare at you and ask,
　　'Can this be the one who shook the earth
　　and made the kingdoms of the world
　　　tremble?
17 Is this the one who destroyed the world
　　and made it into a wasteland?
Is this the king who demolished the
　　world's greatest cities
　　and had no mercy on his prisoners?'

18 "The kings of the nations lie in stately
　　glory,
　　each in his own tomb,
19 but you will be thrown out of your grave
　　like a worthless branch.
Like a corpse trampled underfoot,
　　you will be dumped into a mass grave
　　with those killed in battle.
You will descend to the pit.
20 You will not be given a proper burial,
　　for you have destroyed your nation
　　and slaughtered your people.
The descendants of such an evil person
　　will never again receive honor.
21 Kill this man's children!
　　Let them die because of their father's
　　　sins!

14:1 Hebrew *the house of Jacob.* The names "Jacob" and "Israel" are often interchanged throughout the Old Testament,
referring sometimes to the individual patriarch and sometimes to the nation.　14:4 As in Dead Sea Scrolls; the meaning
of the Masoretic Text is uncertain.　14:9 Hebrew *Sheol;* also in 14:15.　14:11 Hebrew *were brought down to Sheol.*　14:13 Or *on
the heights of Zaphon.*

They must not rise and conquer the earth,
    filling the world with their cities."

²² This is what the LORD of Heaven's Armies
    says:
"I, myself, have risen against Babylon!
I will destroy its children and its children's
    children,"
    says the LORD.
²³ "I will make Babylon a desolate place of
    owls,
    filled with swamps and marshes.
I will sweep the land with the broom of
    destruction.
    I, the LORD of Heaven's Armies, have
    spoken!"

A Message about Assyria

²⁴The LORD of Heaven's Armies has sworn this
oath:

"It will all happen as I have planned.
    It will be as I have decided.
²⁵ I will break the Assyrians when they are in
    Israel;
    I will trample them on my mountains.
My people will no longer be their slaves
    nor bow down under their heavy
    loads.
²⁶ I have a plan for the whole earth,
    a hand of judgment upon all the
    nations.
²⁷ The LORD of Heaven's Armies has
    spoken—
    who can change his plans?
When his hand is raised,
    who can stop him?"

A Message about Philistia

²⁸This message came to me the year King Ahaz
died:*

²⁹ Do not rejoice, you Philistines,
    that the rod that struck you is broken—
    that the king who attacked you is dead.
For from that snake a more poisonous
    snake will be born,
    a fiery serpent to destroy you!
³⁰ I will feed the poor in my pasture;
    the needy will lie down in peace.
But as for you, I will wipe you out with
    famine
    and destroy the few who remain.
³¹ Wail at the gates! Weep in the cities!
    Melt with fear, you Philistines!

14:28 King Ahaz died in 715 B.C.   14:32 Hebrew *Zion.*

A powerful army comes like smoke from
    the north.
    Each soldier rushes forward eager to
    fight.

³²What should we tell the Philistine messengers? Tell them,

"The LORD has built Jerusalem*;
    its walls will give refuge to his
    oppressed people."

A Message about Moab

15 This message came to me concerning
Moab:

In one night the town of Ar will be leveled,
    and the city of Kir will be destroyed.
² Your people will go to their temple in
    Dibon to mourn.
    They will go to their sacred shrines to
    weep.
They will wail for the fate of Nebo and
    Medeba,
    shaving their heads in sorrow and
    cutting off their beards.
³ They will wear burlap as they wander the
    streets.
    From every home and public square will
    come the sound of wailing.
⁴ The people of Heshbon and Elealeh will
    cry out;
    their voices will be heard as far away as
    Jahaz!
The bravest warriors of Moab will cry out
    in utter terror.
    They will be helpless with fear.

⁵ My heart weeps for Moab.
    Its people flee to Zoar and
    Eglath-shelishiyah.
Weeping, they climb the road to Luhith.
    Their cries of distress can be heard all
    along the road to Horonaim.
⁶ Even the waters of Nimrim are dried up!
    The grassy banks are scorched.
The tender plants are gone;
    nothing green remains.
⁷ The people grab their possessions
    and carry them across the Ravine of
    Willows.
⁸ A cry of distress echoes through the land
    of Moab
    from one end to the other—
    from Eglaim to Beer-elim.

⁹ The stream near Dibon* runs red with
    blood,
  but I am still not finished with
      Dibon!
  Lions will hunt down the survivors—
      both those who try to escape
      and those who remain behind.

16

¹ Send lambs from Sela as tribute
    to the ruler of the land.
  Send them through the desert
    to the mountain of beautiful Zion.
² The women of Moab are left like homeless
      birds
    at the shallow crossings of the Arnon
        River.
³ "Help us," they cry.
  "Defend us against our enemies.
  Protect us from their relentless attack.
  Do not betray us now that we have
      escaped.
⁴ Let our refugees stay among you.
    Hide them from our enemies until the
        terror is past."

  When oppression and destruction have
      ended
    and enemy raiders have disappeared,
⁵ then God will establish one of David's
      descendants as king.
  He will rule with mercy and truth.
  He will always do what is just
    and be eager to do what is right.

⁶ We have heard about proud Moab—
    about its pride and arrogance and rage.
  But all that boasting has disappeared.
⁷ The entire land of Moab weeps.
    Yes, everyone in Moab mourns
  for the cakes of raisins from Kir-hareseth.
    They are all gone now.
⁸ The farms of Heshbon are abandoned;
    the vineyards at Sibmah are deserted.
  The rulers of the nations have broken
      down Moab—
    that beautiful grapevine.
  Its tendrils spread north as far as the town
      of Jazer
    and trailed eastward into the
        wilderness.
  Its shoots reached so far west
    that they crossed over the Dead Sea.*

⁹ So now I weep for Jazer and the vineyards
    of Sibmah;
  my tears will flow for Heshbon and
      Elealeh.
  There are no more shouts of joy
    over your summer fruits and harvest.
¹⁰ Gone now is the gladness,
    gone the joy of harvest.
  There will be no singing in the vineyards,
    no more happy shouts,
  no treading of grapes in the winepresses.
    I have ended all their harvest joys.
¹¹ My heart's cry for Moab is like a lament
      on a harp.
  I am filled with anguish for
      Kir-hareseth.*
¹² The people of Moab will worship at their
      pagan shrines,
    but it will do them no good.
  They will cry to the gods in their temples,
    but no one will be able to save them.

¹³The LORD has already said these things
about Moab in the past. ¹⁴But now the LORD
says, "Within three years, counting each
day,* the glory of Moab will be ended. From
its great population, only a feeble few will be
left alive."

A Message about Damascus and Israel

17

This message came to me concerning
Damascus:

  "Look, the city of Damascus will
      disappear!
    It will become a heap of ruins.
² The towns of Aroer will be deserted.
    Flocks will graze in the streets and lie
        down undisturbed,
    with no one to chase them away.
³ The fortified towns of Israel* will also be
      destroyed,
    and the royal power of Damascus will
        end.
  All that remains of Syria*
    will share the fate of Israel's departed
        glory,"
  declares the LORD of Heaven's Armies.

⁴ "In that day Israel's* glory will grow dim;
    its robust body will waste away.
⁵ The whole land will look like a grainfield

15:9 As in Dead Sea Scrolls, some Greek manuscripts, and Latin Vulgate; Masoretic Text reads *Dimon;* also in 15:9b.
16:8 Hebrew *the sea.*   16:11 Hebrew *Kir-heres,* a variant spelling of Kir-hareseth.   16:14 Hebrew *Within three years, as a servant
bound by contract would count them.*   17:3a Hebrew *of Ephraim,* referring to the northern kingdom of Israel.   17:3b Hebrew
Aram.   17:4 Hebrew *Jacob's.* See note on 14:1.

after the harvesters have gathered the
grain.
It will be desolate,
like the fields in the valley of Rephaim
after the harvest.
6 Only a few of its people will be left,
like stray olives left on a tree after the
harvest.
Only two or three remain in the highest
branches,
four or five scattered here and there on
the limbs,"
declares the Lord, the God of Israel.

7 Then at last the people will look to their
Creator
and turn their eyes to the Holy One
of Israel.
8 They will no longer look to their idols
for help
or worship what their own hands have
made.
They will never again bow down to their
Asherah poles
or worship at the pagan shrines they
have built.
9 Their largest cities will be like a deserted
forest,
like the land the Hivites and Amorites
abandoned*
when the Israelites came here so long
ago.
It will be utterly desolate.
10 Why? Because you have turned from the
God who can save you.
You have forgotten the Rock who can
hide you.
So you may plant the finest grapevines
and import the most expensive
seedlings.
11 They may sprout on the day you set them
out;
yes, they may blossom on the very
morning you plant them,
but you will never pick any grapes from
them.
Your only harvest will be a load of grief
and unrelieved pain.

12 Listen! The armies of many nations
roar like the roaring of the sea.
Hear the thunder of the mighty forces
as they rush forward like thundering
waves.

13 But though they thunder like breakers on
a beach,
God will silence them, and they will run
away.
They will flee like chaff scattered by the
wind,
like a tumbleweed whirling before a
storm.
14 In the evening Israel waits in terror,
but by dawn its enemies are dead.
This is the just reward of those who
plunder us,
a fitting end for those who destroy us.

A Message about Ethiopia

18 ¹ Listen, Ethiopia*—land of
fluttering sails*
that lies at the headwaters of the Nile,
2 that sends ambassadors
in swift boats down the river.

Go, swift messengers!
Take a message to a tall, smooth-skinned
people,
who are feared far and wide
for their conquests and destruction,
and whose land is divided by
rivers.

3 All you people of the world,
everyone who lives on the earth—
when I raise my battle flag on the
mountain, look!
When I blow the ram's horn, listen!
4 For the Lord has told me this:
"I will watch quietly from my dwelling
place—
as quietly as the heat rises on a summer
day,
or as the morning dew forms during the
harvest."
5 Even before you begin your attack,
while your plans are ripening like
grapes,
the Lord will cut off your new growth
with pruning shears.
He will snip off and discard your
spreading branches.
6 Your mighty army will be left dead in the
fields
for the mountain vultures and wild
animals.
The vultures will tear at the corpses all
summer.

17:9 As in Greek version; Hebrew reads *like places of the wood and the highest bough.*   18:1a Hebrew *Cush.*   18:1b Or *land of many locusts;* Hebrew reads *land of whirring wings.*

The wild animals will gnaw at the bones
all winter.

7 At that time the LORD of Heaven's Armies
will receive gifts
from this land divided by rivers,
from this tall, smooth-skinned people,
who are feared far and wide for their
conquests and destruction.
They will bring the gifts to Jerusalem,*
where the LORD of Heaven's Armies
dwells.

A Message about Egypt

19 This message came to me concerning
Egypt:

Look! The LORD is advancing against
Egypt,
riding on a swift cloud.
The idols of Egypt tremble.
The hearts of the Egyptians melt with
fear.

2 "I will make Egyptian fight against
Egyptian—
brother against brother,
neighbor against neighbor,
city against city,
province against province.
3 The Egyptians will lose heart,
and I will confuse their plans.
They will plead with their idols for wisdom
and call on spirits, mediums, and those
who consult the spirits of the dead.
4 I will hand Egypt over
to a hard, cruel master.
A fierce king will rule them,"
says the Lord, the LORD of Heaven's
Armies.

5 The waters of the Nile will fail to rise and
flood the fields.
The riverbed will be parched and dry.
6 The canals of the Nile will dry up,
and the streams of Egypt will stink
with rotting reeds and rushes.
7 All the greenery along the riverbank
and all the crops along the river
will dry up and blow away.
8 The fishermen will lament for lack of
work.
Those who cast hooks into the Nile will
groan,
and those who use nets will lose heart.

9 There will be no flax for the harvesters,
no thread for the weavers.
10 They will be in despair,
and all the workers will be sick at heart.

11 What fools are the officials of Zoan!
Their best counsel to the king of Egypt
is stupid and wrong.
Will they still boast to Pharaoh of their
wisdom?
Will they dare brag about all their wise
ancestors?
12 Where are your wise counselors, Pharaoh?
Let them tell you what God plans,
what the LORD of Heaven's Armies is
going to do to Egypt.
13 The officials of Zoan are fools,
and the officials of Memphis* are
deluded.
The leaders of the people
have led Egypt astray.
14 The LORD has sent a spirit of foolishness
on them,
so all their suggestions are wrong.
They cause Egypt to stagger
like a drunk in his vomit.
15 There is nothing Egypt can do.
All are helpless—
the head and the tail,
the noble palm branch and the lowly
reed.

16In that day the Egyptians will be as weak
as women. They will cower in fear beneath the
upraised fist of the LORD of Heaven's Armies.
17Just to speak the name of Israel will terrorize
them, for the LORD of Heaven's Armies has laid
out his plans against them.

18In that day five of Egypt's cities will follow the LORD of Heaven's Armies. They will
even begin to speak Hebrew, the language of
Canaan. One of these cities will be Heliopolis,
the City of the Sun.*

19In that day there will be an altar to the
LORD in the heart of Egypt, and there will be
a monument to the LORD at its border. 20It
will be a sign and a witness that the LORD of
Heaven's Armies is worshiped in the land of
Egypt. When the people cry to the LORD for
help against those who oppress them, he will
send them a savior who will rescue them. 21The
LORD will make himself known to the Egyptians. Yes, they will know the LORD and will
give their sacrifices and offerings to him. They
will make a vow to the LORD and will keep it.

18:7 Hebrew *to Mount Zion.*   19:13 Hebrew *Noph.*   19:18 Or *will be the City of Destruction.*

²²The LORD will strike Egypt, and then he will bring healing. For the Egyptians will turn to the LORD, and he will listen to their pleas and heal them.

²³In that day Egypt and Assyria will be connected by a highway. The Egyptians and Assyrians will move freely between their lands, and they will both worship God. ²⁴In that day Israel will be the third, along with Egypt and Assyria, a blessing in the midst of the earth. ²⁵For the LORD of Heaven's Armies will say, "Blessed be Egypt, my people. Blessed be Assyria, the land I have made. Blessed be Israel, my special possession!"

A Message about Egypt and Ethiopia

20 In the year when King Sargon of Assyria sent his commander in chief to capture the Philistine city of Ashdod,* ²the LORD told Isaiah son of Amoz, "Take off the burlap you have been wearing, and remove your sandals." Isaiah did as he was told and walked around naked and barefoot.

³Then the LORD said, "My servant Isaiah has been walking around naked and barefoot for the last three years. This is a sign—a symbol of the terrible troubles I will bring upon Egypt and Ethiopia.* ⁴For the king of Assyria will take away the Egyptians and Ethiopians* as prisoners. He will make them walk naked and barefoot, both young and old, their buttocks bared, to the shame of Egypt. ⁵Then the Philistines will be thrown into panic, for they counted on the power of Ethiopia and boasted of their allies in Egypt! ⁶They will say, 'If this can happen to Egypt, what chance do we have? We were counting on Egypt to protect us from the king of Assyria.'"

A Message about Babylon

21 This message came to me concerning Babylon—the desert by the sea*:

Disaster is roaring down on you from the desert,
    like a whirlwind sweeping in from the Negev.
² I see a terrifying vision:
    I see the betrayer betraying,
    the destroyer destroying.
Go ahead, you Elamites and Medes,
    attack and lay siege.

I will make an end
    to all the groaning Babylon caused.
³ My stomach aches and burns with pain.
    Sharp pangs of anguish are upon me,
    like those of a woman in labor.
I grow faint when I hear what God is planning;
    I am too afraid to look.
⁴ My mind reels and my heart races.
    I longed for evening to come,
    but now I am terrified of the dark.

⁵ Look! They are preparing a great feast.
    They are spreading rugs for people to sit on.
Everyone is eating and drinking.
But quick! Grab your shields and prepare for battle.
    You are being attacked!

⁶ Meanwhile, the Lord said to me,
    "Put a watchman on the city wall.
    Let him shout out what he sees.
⁷ He should look for chariots
    drawn by pairs of horses,
and for riders on donkeys and camels.
    Let the watchman be fully alert."

⁸ Then the watchman* called out,
    "Day after day I have stood on the watchtower, my lord.
    Night after night I have remained at my post.
⁹ Now at last—look!
Here comes a man in a chariot
    with a pair of horses!"
Then the watchman said,
    "Babylon is fallen, fallen!
All the idols of Babylon
    lie broken on the ground!"
¹⁰ O my people, threshed and winnowed,
    I have told you everything the LORD of Heaven's Armies has said,
    everything the God of Israel has told me.

A Message about Edom
¹¹This message came to me concerning Edom*:

Someone from Edom* keeps calling to me,
    "Watchman, how much longer until morning?
    When will the night be over?"

20:1 Ashdod was captured by Assyria in 711 B.C.   20:3 Hebrew *Cush;* also in 20:5.   20:4 Hebrew *Cushites.*   21:1 Hebrew *concerning the desert by the sea.*   21:8 As in Dead Sea Scrolls and Syriac version; Masoretic Text reads *a lion.*   21:11a Hebrew *Dumah,* which means "silence" or "stillness." It is a wordplay on the word *Edom.*   21:11b Hebrew *Seir,* another name for Edom.

¹² The watchman replies,
  "Morning is coming, but night will soon
    return.
  If you wish to ask again, then come back
    and ask."

A Message about Arabia

¹³This message came to me concerning Arabia:

O caravans from Dedan,
  hide in the deserts of Arabia.
¹⁴ O people of Tema,
  bring water to these thirsty people,
  food to these weary refugees.
¹⁵ They have fled from the sword,
  from the drawn sword,
from the bent bow
  and the terrors of battle.

¹⁶The Lord said to me, "Within a year, counting each day,* all the glory of Kedar will come to
an end. ¹⁷Only a few of its courageous archers
will survive. I, the LORD, the God of Israel, have
spoken!"

A Message about Jerusalem

22 This message came to me concerning
Jerusalem—the Valley of Vision*:

What is happening?
  Why is everyone running to the
    rooftops?
² The whole city is in a terrible uproar.
  What do I see in this reveling city?
Bodies are lying everywhere,
  killed not in battle but by famine and
    disease.
³ All your leaders have fled.
  They surrendered without resistance.
The people tried to slip away,
  but they were captured, too.
⁴ That's why I said, "Leave me alone to
    weep;
  do not try to comfort me.
Let me cry for my people
  as I watch them being destroyed."

⁵ Oh, what a day of crushing defeat!
  What a day of confusion and terror
brought by the Lord, the LORD of Heaven's
    Armies,
  upon the Valley of Vision!
The walls of Jerusalem have been broken,

and cries of death echo from the
    mountainsides.
⁶ Elamites are the archers,
  with their chariots and charioteers.
  The men of Kir hold up the shields.
⁷ Chariots fill your beautiful valleys,
  and charioteers storm your gates.
⁸ Judah's defenses have been stripped away.
  You run to the armory* for your
    weapons.
⁹ You inspect the breaks in the walls of
    Jerusalem.*
  You store up water in the lower pool.
¹⁰ You survey the houses and tear some down
  for stone to strengthen the walls.
¹¹ Between the city walls, you build a
    reservoir
  for water from the old pool.
But you never ask for help from the One
  who did all this.
You never considered the One who
  planned this long ago.

¹² At that time the Lord, the LORD of
    Heaven's Armies,
  called you to weep and mourn.
He told you to shave your heads in sorrow
  for your sins
and to wear clothes of burlap to show
  your remorse.
¹³ But instead, you dance and play;
  you slaughter cattle and kill sheep.
  You feast on meat and drink wine.
You say, "Let's feast and drink,
  for tomorrow we die!"

¹⁴The LORD of Heaven's Armies has revealed
this to me: "Till the day you die, you will never
be forgiven for this sin." That is the judgment
of the Lord, the LORD of Heaven's Armies.

A Message for Shebna

¹⁵This is what the Lord, the LORD of Heaven's
Armies, said to me: "Confront Shebna, the palace administrator, and give him this message:

¹⁶ "Who do you think you are,
  and what are you doing here,
building a beautiful tomb for yourself—
  a monument high up in the rock?
¹⁷ For the LORD is about to hurl you away,
  mighty man.
He is going to grab you,

21:16 Hebrew *Within a year, as a servant bound by contract would count it.* Some ancient manuscripts read *Within three years,* as
in 16:14.   22:1 Hebrew *concerning the Valley of Vision.*   22:8 Hebrew *to the House of the Forest;* see 1 Kgs 7:2-5.   22:9 Hebrew
the city of David.

18 crumple you into a ball,
   and toss you away into a distant, barren
      land.
There you will die,
   and your glorious chariots will be
      broken and useless.
You are a disgrace to your master!

19"Yes, I will drive you out of office," says the
LORD. "I will pull you down from your high
position. 20And then I will call my servant Eliakim son of Hilkiah to replace you. 21I will dress
him in your royal robes and will give him your
title and your authority. And he will be a father
to the people of Jerusalem and Judah. 22I will
give him the key to the house of David—the
highest position in the royal court. When he
opens doors, no one will be able to close them;
when he closes doors, no one will be able to
open them. 23He will bring honor to his family
name, for I will drive him firmly in place like
a nail in the wall. 24They will give him great
responsibility, and he will bring honor to even
the lowliest members of his family.*"

25But the LORD of Heaven's Armies also says:
"The time will come when I will pull out the
nail that seemed so firm. It will come out and
fall to the ground. Everything it supports will
fall with it. I, the LORD, have spoken!"

A Message about Tyre

23 This message came to me concerning
Tyre:

Wail, you trading ships of Tarshish,
   for the harbor and houses of Tyre are
      gone!
The rumors you heard in Cyprus*
   are all true.
2 Mourn in silence, you people of the coast
   and you merchants of Sidon.
Your traders crossed the sea,*
3   sailing over deep waters.
They brought you grain from Egypt*
   and harvests from along the Nile.
You were the marketplace of the world.

4 But now you are put to shame, city of
      Sidon,
   for Tyre, the fortress of the sea, says,*
"Now I am childless;
   I have no sons or daughters."

5 When Egypt hears the news about Tyre,
   there will be great sorrow.
6 Send word now to Tarshish!
   Wail, you people who live in distant
      lands!
7 Is this silent ruin all that is left of your
   once joyous city?
What a long history was yours!
   Think of all the colonists you sent to
      distant places.

8 Who has brought this disaster on Tyre,
   that great creator of kingdoms?
Her traders were all princes,
   her merchants were nobles.
9 The LORD of Heaven's Armies has done it
   to destroy your pride
   and bring low all earth's nobility.

10 Come, people of Tarshish,
   sweep over the land like the flooding
      Nile,
   for Tyre is defenseless.*
11 The LORD held out his hand over the sea
   and shook the kingdoms of the earth.
He has spoken out against Phoenicia,*
   ordering that her fortresses be
      destroyed.
12 He says, "Never again will you rejoice,
   O daughter of Sidon, for you have been
      crushed.
Even if you flee to Cyprus,
   you will find no rest."

13 Look at the land of Babylonia*—
   the people of that land are gone!
The Assyrians have handed Babylon over
   to the wild animals of the desert.
They have built siege ramps against its
      walls,
   torn down its palaces,
   and turned it to a heap of rubble.

14 Wail, you ships of Tarshish,
   for your harbor is destroyed!

15For seventy years, the length of a king's
life, Tyre will be forgotten. But then the city
will come back to life as in the song about the
prostitute:

16 Take a harp and walk the streets,
   you forgotten harlot.

22:24 Hebrew *They will hang on him all the glory of his father's house: its offspring and offshoots, all its lesser vessels, from the bowls to all the jars.*   23:1 Hebrew *Kittim;* also in 23:12.   23:2 As in Dead Sea Scrolls and Greek version; Masoretic Text reads *Those who have gone over the sea have filled you.*   23:3 Hebrew *from Shihor,* a branch of the Nile River.   23:4 Or *for the god of the sea says;* Hebrew reads *for the sea, the fortress of the sea, says.*   23:10 The meaning of the Hebrew in this verse is uncertain. 23:11 Hebrew *Canaan.*   23:13 Or *Chaldea.*

Make sweet melody and sing your songs
　so you will be remembered again.

17 Yes, after seventy years the LORD will revive Tyre. But she will be no different than she
was before. She will again be a prostitute to
all kingdoms around the world. 18 But in the
end her profits will be given to the LORD. Her
wealth will not be hoarded but will provide
good food and fine clothing for the LORD's
priests.

Destruction of the Earth

24 1 Look! The LORD is about to destroy
　　the earth
and make it a vast wasteland.
He devastates the surface of the earth
　and scatters the people.
2 Priests and laypeople,
　　servants and masters,
　　maids and mistresses,
　　buyers and sellers,
　　lenders and borrowers,
　　bankers and debtors—none will be
　　　spared.
3 The earth will be completely emptied and
　　looted.
　The LORD has spoken!

4 The earth mourns and dries up,
　and the land wastes away and withers.
　Even the greatest people on earth waste
　　away.
5 The earth suffers for the sins of its people,
　　for they have twisted God's instructions,
　violated his laws,
　　and broken his everlasting covenant.
6 Therefore, a curse consumes the earth.
　　Its people must pay the price for their
　　　sin.
　They are destroyed by fire,
　　and only a few are left alive.
7 The grapevines waste away,
　　and there is no new wine.
　All the merrymakers sigh and mourn.
8 The cheerful sound of tambourines is
　　stilled;
　　the happy cries of celebration are heard
　　　no more.
　The melodious chords of the harp are
　　silent.
9 Gone are the joys of wine and song;
　　alcoholic drink turns bitter in the mouth.
10 The city writhes in chaos;
　　every home is locked to keep out
　　　intruders.

11 Mobs gather in the streets, crying out for
　　wine.
　Joy has turned to gloom.
　Gladness has been banished from the
　　land.
12 The city is left in ruins,
　　its gates battered down.
13 Throughout the earth the story is the
　　same—
　only a remnant is left,
　like the stray olives left on the tree
　　or the few grapes left on the vine after
　　　harvest.

14 But all who are left shout and sing for joy.
　　Those in the west praise the LORD's
　　majesty.
15 In eastern lands, give glory to the LORD.
　　In the lands beyond the sea, praise the
　　　name of the LORD, the God of Israel.
16 We hear songs of praise from the ends of
　　the earth,
　songs that give glory to the Righteous
　　One!

But my heart is heavy with grief.
　Weep for me, for I wither away.
Deceit still prevails,
　and treachery is everywhere.
17 Terror and traps and snares will be
　　your lot,
　you people of the earth.
18 Those who flee in terror will fall into a
　　trap,
　and those who escape the trap will be
　　caught in a snare.

Destruction falls like rain from the
　　heavens;
　the foundations of the earth shake.
19 The earth has broken up.
　It has utterly collapsed;
　it is violently shaken.
20 The earth staggers like a drunk.
　It trembles like a tent in a storm.
　It falls and will not rise again,
　　for the guilt of its rebellion is very heavy.

21 In that day the LORD will punish the gods
　　in the heavens
　and the proud rulers of the nations on
　　earth.
22 They will be rounded up and put in
　　prison.
　They will be shut up in prison
　　and will finally be punished.

23 Then the glory of the moon will wane,
    and the brightness of the sun will fade,
for the LORD of Heaven's Armies will rule
    on Mount Zion.
He will rule in great glory in Jerusalem,
    in the sight of all the leaders of his
    people.

Praise for Judgment and Salvation

25 1 O LORD, I will honor and praise your
    name,
    for you are my God.
You do such wonderful things!
    You planned them long ago,
    and now you have accomplished them.
2 You turn mighty cities into heaps of ruins.
    Cities with strong walls are turned to
    rubble.
Beautiful palaces in distant lands
    disappear
    and will never be rebuilt.
3 Therefore, strong nations will declare your
    glory;
    ruthless nations will fear you.

4 But you are a tower of refuge to the poor,
    O LORD,
    a tower of refuge to the needy in
    distress.
You are a refuge from the storm
    and a shelter from the heat.
For the oppressive acts of ruthless people
    are like a storm beating against a wall,
5   or like the relentless heat of the desert.
But you silence the roar of foreign nations.
    As the shade of a cloud cools relentless
    heat,
    so the boastful songs of ruthless people
    are stilled.

6 In Jerusalem,* the LORD of Heaven's
    Armies
    will spread a wonderful feast
    for all the people of the world.
It will be a delicious banquet
    with clear, well-aged wine and choice
    meat.
7 There he will remove the cloud of gloom,
    the shadow of death that hangs over the
    earth.
8 He will swallow up death forever!
    The Sovereign LORD will wipe away all
    tears.
He will remove forever all insults and
    mockery

25:6 Hebrew *On this mountain;* also in 25:10.

against his land and people.
    The LORD has spoken!

9 In that day the people will proclaim,
    "This is our God!
    We trusted in him, and he saved us!
This is the LORD, in whom we trusted.
    Let us rejoice in the salvation he
    brings!"
10 For the LORD's hand of blessing will rest
    on Jerusalem.
    But Moab will be crushed.
    It will be like straw trampled down and
    left to rot.
11 God will push down Moab's people
    as a swimmer pushes down water with
    his hands.
He will end their pride
    and all their evil works.
12 The high walls of Moab will be
    demolished.
    They will be brought down to the
    ground,
    down into the dust.

A Song of Praise to the LORD

26 In that day, everyone in the land of
Judah will sing this song:

Our city is strong!
    We are surrounded by the walls of God's
    salvation.
2 Open the gates to all who are righteous;
    allow the faithful to enter.
3 You will keep in perfect peace
    all who trust in you,
    all whose thoughts are fixed on you!
4 Trust in the LORD always,
    for the LORD GOD is the eternal Rock.
5 He humbles the proud
    and brings down the arrogant city.
    He brings it down to the dust.
6 The poor and oppressed trample it
    underfoot,
    and the needy walk all over it.

7 But for those who are righteous,
    the way is not steep and rough.
You are a God who does what is right,
    and you smooth out the path ahead of
    them.
8 LORD, we show our trust in you by obeying
    your laws;
    our heart's desire is to glorify your
    name.

⁹ In the night I search for you;
   in the morning* I earnestly seek you.
For only when you come to judge the earth
   will people learn what is right.
¹⁰ Your kindness to the wicked
   does not make them do good.
Although others do right, the wicked keep
      doing wrong
   and take no notice of the LORD's
      majesty.
¹¹ O LORD, they pay no attention to your
      upraised fist.
Show them your eagerness to defend
   your people.
Then they will be ashamed.
   Let your fire consume your enemies.

¹² LORD, you will grant us peace;
   all we have accomplished is really from
      you.
¹³ O LORD our God, others have ruled us,
   but you alone are the one we worship.
¹⁴ Those we served before are dead and gone.
   Their departed spirits will never return!
You attacked them and destroyed them,
   and they are long forgotten.
¹⁵ O LORD, you have made our nation great;
   yes, you have made us great.
You have extended our borders,
   and we give you the glory!

¹⁶ LORD, in distress we searched for you.
   We prayed beneath the burden of your
      discipline.
¹⁷ Just as a pregnant woman
   writhes and cries out in pain as she gives
      birth,
   so were we in your presence, LORD.
¹⁸ We, too, writhe in agony,
   but nothing comes of our suffering.
We have not given salvation to the earth,
   nor brought life into the world.
¹⁹ But those who die in the LORD will live;
   their bodies will rise again!
Those who sleep in the earth
   will rise up and sing for joy!
For your life-giving light will fall like dew
   on your people in the place of the dead!

Restoration for Israel

²⁰ Go home, my people,
   and lock your doors!
Hide yourselves for a little while
   until the LORD's anger has passed.

²¹ Look! The LORD is coming from heaven
   to punish the people of the earth for
      their sins.
The earth will no longer hide those
   who have been killed.
They will be brought out for all
   to see.

27 In that day the LORD will take his terrible, swift sword and punish Leviathan,* the swiftly moving serpent, the coiling,
writhing serpent. He will kill the dragon of
the sea.

² "In that day,
   sing about the fruitful vineyard.
³ I, the LORD, will watch over it,
   watering it carefully.
Day and night I will watch so no one can
   harm it.
⁴   My anger will be gone.
If I find briers and thorns growing,
   I will attack them;
I will burn them up—
⁵   unless they turn to me for help.
Let them make peace with me;
   yes, let them make peace with me."
⁶ The time is coming when Jacob's
   descendants will take root.
Israel will bud and blossom
   and fill the whole earth with fruit!

⁷ Has the LORD struck Israel
   as he struck her enemies?
Has he punished her
   as he punished them?
⁸ No, but he exiled Israel to call her to
      account.
   She was exiled from her land
   as though blown away in a storm from
      the east.
⁹ The LORD did this to purge Israel's*
      wickedness,
   to take away all her sin.
As a result, all the pagan altars will be
   crushed to dust.
   No Asherah pole or pagan shrine will
   be left standing.
¹⁰ The fortified towns will be silent and
      empty,
   the houses abandoned, the streets
      overgrown with weeds.
Calves will graze there,
   chewing on twigs and branches.

26:9 Hebrew *within me.*   27:1 The identification of Leviathan is disputed, ranging from an earthly creature to a mythical sea monster in ancient literature.   27:9 Hebrew *Jacob's.* See note on 14:1.

11 The people are like the dead branches
　　of a tree,
　　broken off and used for kindling
　　beneath the cooking pots.
Israel is a foolish and stupid nation,
　　for its people have turned away from
　　God.
Therefore, the one who made them
　　will show them no pity or mercy.

12Yet the time will come when the LORD will
gather them together like handpicked grain.
One by one he will gather them—from the
Euphrates River* in the east to the Brook of
Egypt in the west. 13In that day the great trumpet will sound. Many who were dying in exile
in Assyria and Egypt will return to Jerusalem
to worship the LORD on his holy mountain.

A Message about Samaria

28 ¹ What sorrow awaits the proud city
　　of Samaria—
　　the glorious crown of the drunks of
　　Israel.*
It sits at the head of a fertile valley,
　　but its glorious beauty will fade like a
　　flower.
It is the pride of a people
　　brought down by wine.
2 For the Lord will send a mighty army
　　against it.
Like a mighty hailstorm and a torrential
　　rain,
they will burst upon it like a surging flood
　　and smash it to the ground.
3 The proud city of Samaria—
　　the glorious crown of the drunks of
　　Israel*—
will be trampled beneath its enemies'
　　feet.
4 It sits at the head of a fertile valley,
　　but its glorious beauty will fade like a
　　flower.
Whoever sees it will snatch it up,
　　as an early fig is quickly picked and
　　eaten.

5 Then at last the LORD of Heaven's Armies
　　will himself be Israel's glorious crown.
He will be the pride and joy
　　of the remnant of his people.
6 He will give a longing for justice
　　to their judges.

He will give great courage
　　to their warriors who stand at the
　　gates.

7 Now, however, Israel is led by drunks
　　who reel with wine and stagger with
　　alcohol.
The priests and prophets stagger with
　　alcohol
　　and lose themselves in wine.
They reel when they see visions
　　and stagger as they render decisions.
8 Their tables are covered with vomit;
　　filth is everywhere.
9 "Who does the LORD think we are?"
　　they ask.
　　"Why does he speak to us like this?
Are we little children,
　　just recently weaned?
10 He tells us everything over and over—
　　one line at a time,
　　one line at a time,
　　a little here,
　　and a little there!"

11 So now God will have to speak to his
　　people
　　through foreign oppressors who speak
　　a strange language!
12 God has told his people,
　　"Here is a place of rest;
　　let the weary rest here.
This is a place of quiet rest."
　　But they would not listen.
13 So the LORD will spell out his message for
　　them again,
one line at a time,
　　one line at a time,
a little here,
　　and a little there,
so that they will stumble and fall.
　　They will be injured, trapped, and
　　captured.

14 Therefore, listen to this message from the
　　LORD,
　　you scoffing rulers in Jerusalem.
15 You boast, "We have struck a bargain to
　　cheat death
　　and have made a deal to dodge the
　　grave.*
The coming destruction can never
　　touch us,

27:12 Hebrew the river.　28:1 Hebrew What sorrow awaits the crowning glory of the drunks of Ephraim, referring to Samaria, capital
of the northern kingdom of Israel.　28:3 Hebrew The crowning glory of the drunks of Ephraim; see note on 28:1.　28:15 Hebrew
Sheol; also in 28:18.

for we have built a strong refuge made
of lies and deception."

16 Therefore, this is what the Sovereign LORD
says:
"Look! I am placing a foundation stone in
Jerusalem,*
a firm and tested stone.
It is a precious cornerstone that is safe to
build on.
Whoever believes need never be shaken.*
17 I will test you with the measuring line of
justice
and the plumb line of righteousness.
Since your refuge is made of lies,
a hailstorm will knock it down.
Since it is made of deception,
a flood will sweep it away.
18 I will cancel the bargain you made to cheat
death,
and I will overturn your deal to dodge
the grave.
When the terrible enemy sweeps through,
you will be trampled into the ground.
19 Again and again that flood will come,
morning after morning,
day and night,
until you are carried away."

This message will bring terror to your
people.
20 The bed you have made is too short to
lie on.
The blankets are too narrow to cover
you.
21 The LORD will come as he did against the
Philistines at Mount Perazim
and against the Amorites at Gibeon.
He will come to do a strange thing;
he will come to do an unusual deed:
22 For the Lord, the LORD of Heaven's Armies,
has plainly said that he is determined to
crush the whole land.
So scoff no more,
or your punishment will be even
greater.

23 Listen to me;
listen, and pay close attention.
24 Does a farmer always plow and never sow?
Is he forever cultivating the soil and
never planting?
25 Does he not finally plant his seeds—

black cumin, cumin, wheat, barley, and
emmer wheat—
each in its proper way,
and each in its proper place?
26 The farmer knows just what to do,
for God has given him understanding.
27 A heavy sledge is never used to thresh
black cumin;
rather, it is beaten with a light stick.
A threshing wheel is never rolled on
cumin;
instead, it is beaten lightly with a flail.
28 Grain for bread is easily crushed,
so he doesn't keep on pounding it.
He threshes it under the wheels of a cart,
but he doesn't pulverize it.
29 The LORD of Heaven's Armies is a
wonderful teacher,
and he gives the farmer great wisdom.

A Message about Jerusalem

29 1 "What sorrow awaits Ariel,* the City
of David.
Year after year you celebrate your feasts.
2 Yet I will bring disaster upon you,
and there will be much weeping and
sorrow.
For Jerusalem will become what her name
Ariel means—
an altar covered with blood.
3 I will be your enemy,
surrounding Jerusalem and attacking
its walls.
I will build siege towers
and destroy it.
4 Then deep from the earth you will speak;
from low in the dust your words will
come.
Your voice will whisper from the ground
like a ghost conjured up from the grave.

5 "But suddenly, your ruthless enemies will
be crushed
like the finest of dust.
Your many attackers will be driven away
like chaff before the wind.
Suddenly, in an instant,
6 I, the LORD of Heaven's Armies, will act
for you
with thunder and earthquake and great
noise,
with whirlwind and storm and
consuming fire.

28:16a Hebrew in Zion.   28:16b Greek version reads Look! I am placing a stone in the foundation of Jerusalem [literally Zion], /
a precious cornerstone for its foundation, chosen for great honor. / Anyone who trusts in him will never be disgraced. Compare Rom 9:33; /
1 Pet 2:6.   29:1 Ariel sounds like a Hebrew term that means "hearth" or "altar."

7 All the nations fighting against Jerusalem*
    will vanish like a dream!
Those who are attacking her walls
    will vanish like a vision in the night.
8 A hungry person dreams of eating
    but wakes up still hungry.
A thirsty person dreams of drinking
    but is still faint from thirst when
        morning comes.
So it will be with your enemies,
    with those who attack Mount Zion."

9 Are you amazed and incredulous?
    Don't you believe it?
Then go ahead and be blind.
    You are stupid, but not from wine!
    You stagger, but not from liquor!
10 For the LORD has poured out on you a
        spirit of deep sleep.
    He has closed the eyes of your prophets
        and visionaries.

11All the future events in this vision are like a
sealed book to them. When you give it to those
who can read, they will say, "We can't read it
because it is sealed." 12When you give it to those
who cannot read, they will say, "We don't know
how to read."

13 And so the Lord says,
    "These people say they are mine.
They honor me with their lips,
    but their hearts are far from me.
And their worship of me
    is nothing but man-made rules learned
        by rote.*
14 Because of this, I will once again astound
        these hypocrites
    with amazing wonders.
The wisdom of the wise will pass away,
    and the intelligence of the intelligent
        will disappear."

15 What sorrow awaits those who try to hide
        their plans from the LORD,
    who do their evil deeds in the dark!
"The LORD can't see us," they say.
    "He doesn't know what's going on!"
16 How foolish can you be?
    He is the Potter, and he is certainly
        greater than you, the clay!
Should the created thing say of the one
        who made it,
    "He didn't make me"?

Does a jar ever say,
    "The potter who made me is stupid"?

17 Soon—and it will not be very long—
    the forests of Lebanon will become a
        fertile field,
    and the fertile field will yield bountiful
        crops.
18 In that day the deaf will hear words read
        from a book,
    and the blind will see through the
        gloom and darkness.
19 The humble will be filled with fresh joy
        from the LORD.
    The poor will rejoice in the Holy One
        of Israel.
20 The scoffer will be gone,
    the arrogant will disappear,
    and those who plot evil will be killed.
21 Those who convict the innocent
        by their false testimony will disappear.
A similar fate awaits those who use
        trickery to pervert justice
    and who tell lies to destroy the innocent.

22That is why the LORD, who redeemed Abraham, says to the people of Israel,*

"My people will no longer be ashamed
    or turn pale with fear.
23 For when they see their many children
        and all the blessings I have given them,
    they will recognize the holiness of the
        Holy One of Jacob.
    They will stand in awe of the God of
        Israel.
24 Then the wayward will gain
        understanding,
    and complainers will accept
        instruction.

Judah's Worthless Treaty with Egypt

30

1 "What sorrow awaits my rebellious
        children,"
    says the LORD.
"You make plans that are contrary to mine.
    You make alliances not directed by my
        Spirit,
    thus piling up your sins.
2 For without consulting me,
    you have gone down to Egypt for help.
You have put your trust in Pharaoh's
        protection.
    You have tried to hide in his shade.

29:7 Hebrew *Ariel.*   29:13 Greek version reads *Their worship is a farce, / for they teach man-made ideas as commands from God.*
Compare Mark 7:7.   29:22 Hebrew *of Jacob.* See note on 14:1.

3 But by trusting Pharaoh, you will be
    humiliated,
  and by depending on him, you will be
    disgraced.
4 For though his power extends to Zoan
  and his officials have arrived in Hanes,
5 all who trust in him will be ashamed.
  He will not help you.
  Instead, he will disgrace you."

6 This message came to me concerning the animals in the Negev:

The caravan moves slowly
  across the terrible desert to Egypt—
donkeys weighed down with riches
  and camels loaded with treasure—
all to pay for Egypt's protection.
They travel through the wilderness,
  a place of lionesses and lions,
  a place where vipers and poisonous
    snakes live.
All this, and Egypt will give you nothing
  in return.
7 Egypt's promises are worthless!
Therefore, I call her Rahab—
  the Harmless Dragon.*

A Warning for Rebellious Judah

8 Now go and write down these words.
  Write them in a book.
They will stand until the end of time
  as a witness
9 that these people are stubborn rebels
  who refuse to pay attention to the
    LORD's instructions.
10 They tell the seers,
  "Stop seeing visions!"
They tell the prophets,
  "Don't tell us what is right.
Tell us nice things.
  Tell us lies.
11 Forget all this gloom.
  Get off your narrow path.
Stop telling us about your
  'Holy One of Israel.'"

12 This is the reply of the Holy One of Israel:

"Because you despise what I tell you
  and trust instead in oppression and lies,
13 calamity will come upon you suddenly—
  like a bulging wall that bursts and falls.
In an instant it will collapse

and come crashing down.
14 You will be smashed like a piece of
    pottery—
  shattered so completely that
there won't be a piece big enough
  to carry coals from a fireplace
  or a little water from the well."

15 This is what the Sovereign LORD,
  the Holy One of Israel, says:
"Only in returning to me
  and resting in me will you be saved.
In quietness and confidence is your
    strength.
  But you would have none of it.
16 You said, 'No, we will get our help from
    Egypt.
  They will give us swift horses for riding
    into battle.'
But the only swiftness you are going to see
  is the swiftness of your enemies chasing
    you!
17 One of them will chase a thousand of you.
  Five of them will make all of you flee.
You will be left like a lonely flagpole on
    a hill
  or a tattered banner on a distant
    mountaintop."

Blessings for the LORD's People

18 So the LORD must wait for you to come
    to him
  so he can show you his love and
    compassion.
For the LORD is a faithful God.
  Blessed are those who wait for his help.

19 O people of Zion, who live in Jerusalem,
  you will weep no more.
He will be gracious if you ask for help.
  He will surely respond to the sound of
    your cries.
20 Though the Lord gave you adversity for
    food
  and suffering for drink,
he will still be with you to teach you.
  You will see your teacher with your own
    eyes.
21 Your own ears will hear him.
  Right behind you a voice will say,
"This is the way you should go,"
  whether to the right or to the left.
22 Then you will destroy all your silver idols
  and your precious gold images.

30:7 Hebrew *Rahab who sits still*. Rahab is the name of a mythical sea monster that represents chaos in ancient literature.
The name is used here as a poetic name for Egypt.

You will throw them out like filthy rags,
saying to them, "Good riddance!"

23Then the LORD will bless you with rain at planting time. There will be wonderful harvests and plenty of pastureland for your livestock. 24The oxen and donkeys that till the ground will eat good grain, its chaff blown away by the wind. 25In that day, when your enemies are slaughtered and the towers fall, there will be streams of water flowing down every mountain and hill. 26The moon will be as bright as the sun, and the sun will be seven times brighter—like the light of seven days in one! So it will be when the LORD begins to heal his people and cure the wounds he gave them.

27 Look! The LORD is coming from far away,
burning with anger,
surrounded by thick, rising smoke.
His lips are filled with fury;
his words consume like fire.
28 His hot breath pours out like a flood
up to the neck of his enemies.
He will sift out the proud nations for
destruction.
He will bridle them and lead them away
to ruin.

29 But the people of God will sing a song
of joy,
like the songs at the holy festivals.
You will be filled with joy,
as when a flutist leads a group of
pilgrims
to Jerusalem, the mountain of the LORD—
to the Rock of Israel.
30 And the LORD will make his majestic voice
heard.
He will display the strength of his
mighty arm.
It will descend with devouring flames,
with cloudbursts, thunderstorms, and
huge hailstones.
31 At the LORD's command, the Assyrians will
be shattered.
He will strike them down with his royal
scepter.
32 And as the LORD strikes them with his rod
of punishment,*
his people will celebrate with
tambourines and harps.
Lifting his mighty arm, he will fight the
Assyrians.

33 Topheth—the place of burning—
has long been ready for the Assyrian
king;
the pyre is piled high with wood.
The breath of the LORD, like fire from a
volcano,
will set it ablaze.

The Futility of Relying on Egypt

31 1 What sorrow awaits those who look
to Egypt for help,
trusting their horses, chariots, and
charioteers
and depending on the strength of human
armies
instead of looking to the LORD,
the Holy One of Israel.
2 In his wisdom, the LORD will send great
disaster;
he will not change his mind.
He will rise against the wicked
and against their helpers.
3 For these Egyptians are mere humans,
not God!
Their horses are puny flesh, not mighty
spirits!
When the LORD raises his fist against
them,
those who help will stumble,
and those being helped will fall.
They will all fall down and die together.

4But this is what the LORD has told me:

"When a strong young lion
stands growling over a sheep it has
killed,
it is not frightened by the shouts and noise
of a whole crowd of shepherds.
In the same way, the LORD of Heaven's
Armies
will come down and fight on Mount
Zion.
5 The LORD of Heaven's Armies will hover
over Jerusalem
and protect it like a bird protecting its
nest.
He will defend and save the city;
he will pass over it and rescue it."

6Though you are such wicked rebels, my people, come and return to the LORD. 7I know the glorious day will come when each of you will throw away the gold idols and silver images your sinful hands have made.

30:32 As in some Hebrew manuscripts and Syriac version; Masoretic Text reads *with the founded rod.*

8 "The Assyrians will be destroyed,
  but not by the swords of men.
The sword of God will strike them,
  and they will panic and flee.
The strong young Assyrians
  will be taken away as captives.
9 Even the strongest will quake with terror,
  and princes will flee when they see your
    battle flags,"
says the LORD, whose fire burns in Zion,
  whose flame blazes from Jerusalem.

Israel's Ultimate Deliverance

32 ¹ Look, a righteous king is coming!
  And honest princes will rule
    under him.
2 Each one will be like a shelter from the
    wind
  and a refuge from the storm,
like streams of water in the desert
  and the shadow of a great rock in a
    parched land.

3 Then everyone who has eyes will be able
    to see the truth,
  and everyone who has ears will be able
    to hear it.
4 Even the hotheads will be full of sense and
    understanding.
  Those who stammer will speak out
    plainly.
5 In that day ungodly fools will not be
    heroes.
  Scoundrels will not be respected.
6 For fools speak foolishness
  and make evil plans.
They practice ungodliness
  and spread false teachings about the
    LORD.
They deprive the hungry of food
  and give no water to the thirsty.
7 The smooth tricks of scoundrels are evil.
  They plot crooked schemes.
They lie to convict the poor,
  even when the cause of the poor is just.
8 But generous people plan to do what is
    generous,
  and they stand firm in their generosity.

9 Listen, you women who lie around in
    ease.
  Listen to me, you who are so smug.
10 In a short time—just a little more than
    a year—

you careless ones will suddenly begin
    to care.
For your fruit crops will fail,
  and the harvest will never take place.
11 Tremble, you women of ease;
  throw off your complacency.
Strip off your pretty clothes,
  and put on burlap to show your grief.
12 Beat your breasts in sorrow for your
    bountiful farms
  and your fruitful grapevines.
13 For your land will be overgrown with
    thorns and briers.
  Your joyful homes and happy towns will
    be gone.
14 The palace and the city will be deserted,
  and busy towns will be empty.
Wild donkeys will frolic and flocks will
    graze
  in the empty forts* and watchtowers
15 until at last the Spirit is poured out
  on us from heaven.
Then the wilderness will become a fertile
    field,
  and the fertile field will yield bountiful
    crops.

16 Justice will rule in the wilderness
  and righteousness in the fertile field.
17 And this righteousness will bring peace.
  Yes, it will bring quietness and
    confidence forever.
18 My people will live in safety, quietly at
    home.
  They will be at rest.
19 Even if the forest should be destroyed
  and the city torn down,
20 the LORD will greatly bless his people.
  Wherever they plant seed, bountiful
    crops will spring up.
  Their cattle and donkeys will graze
    freely.

A Message about Assyria

33 ¹ What sorrow awaits you Assyrians,
  who have destroyed others*
but have never been destroyed
    yourselves.
You betray others,
  but you have never been betrayed.
When you are done destroying,
  you will be destroyed.
When you are done betraying,
  you will be betrayed.

32:14 Hebrew *the Ophel.*   **33:1** Hebrew *What sorrow awaits you, O destroyer.* The Hebrew text does not specifically name Assyria as the object of the prophecy in this chapter.

2 But Lord, be merciful to us,
    for we have waited for you.
Be our strong arm each day
    and our salvation in times of trouble.
3 The enemy runs at the sound of your voice.
    When you stand up, the nations flee!
4 Just as caterpillars and locusts strip the
    fields and vines,
    so the fallen army of Assyria will be
    stripped!

5 Though the Lord is very great and lives
    in heaven,
    he will make Jerusalem* his home of
    justice and righteousness.
6 In that day he will be your sure
    foundation,
    providing a rich store of salvation,
    wisdom, and knowledge.
The fear of the Lord will be your
    treasure.

7 But now your brave warriors weep in
    public.
Your ambassadors of peace cry in bitter
    disappointment.
8 Your roads are deserted;
    no one travels them anymore.
The Assyrians have broken their peace
    treaty
    and care nothing for the promises they
    made before witnesses.*
They have no respect for anyone.
9 The land of Israel wilts in mourning.
    Lebanon withers with shame.
The plain of Sharon is now a wilderness.
    Bashan and Carmel have been
    plundered.

10 But the Lord says: "Now I will stand up.
    Now I will show my power and might.
11 You Assyrians produce nothing but dry
    grass and stubble.
Your own breath will turn to fire and
    consume you.
12 Your people will be burned up completely,
    like thornbushes cut down and tossed
    in a fire.
13 Listen to what I have done, you nations far
    away!
    And you that are near, acknowledge my
    might!"

14 The sinners in Jerusalem shake with fear.
    Terror seizes the godless.

"Who can live with this devouring fire?"
    they cry.
"Who can survive this all-consuming
    fire?"
15 Those who are honest and fair,
    who refuse to profit by fraud,
    who stay far away from bribes,
who refuse to listen to those who plot
    murder,
who shut their eyes to all enticement to
    do wrong—
16 these are the ones who will dwell on high.
    The rocks of the mountains will be their
    fortress.
Food will be supplied to them,
    and they will have water in abundance.

17 Your eyes will see the king in all his
    splendor,
    and you will see a land that stretches
    into the distance.
18 You will think back to this time of terror,
    asking,
"Where are the Assyrian officers
    who counted our towers?
Where are the bookkeepers
    who recorded the plunder taken from
    our fallen city?"
19 You will no longer see these fierce, violent
    people
    with their strange, unknown
    language.

20 Instead, you will see Zion as a place of holy
    festivals.
    You will see Jerusalem, a city quiet and
    secure.
It will be like a tent whose ropes are taut
    and whose stakes are firmly fixed.
21 The Lord will be our Mighty One.
    He will be like a wide river of
    protection
that no enemy can cross,
    that no enemy ship can sail upon.
22 For the Lord is our judge,
    our lawgiver, and our king.
    He will care for us and save us.
23 The enemies' sails hang loose
    on broken masts with useless tackle.
Their treasure will be divided by the
    people of God.
    Even the lame will take their share!
24 The people of Israel will no longer say,
    "We are sick and helpless,"
    for the Lord will forgive their sins.

33:5 Hebrew *Zion;* also in 33:14.   **33:8** As in Dead Sea Scrolls; Masoretic Text reads *care nothing for the cities.*

A Message for the Nations

34 ¹ Come here and listen, O nations of
the earth.
Let the world and everything in it hear
my words.
² For the LORD is enraged against the
nations.
His fury is against all their armies.
He will completely destroy* them,
dooming them to slaughter.
³ Their dead will be left unburied,
and the stench of rotting bodies will fill
the land.
The mountains will flow with their
blood.
⁴ The heavens above will melt away
and disappear like a rolled-up scroll.
The stars will fall from the sky
like withered leaves from a grapevine,
or shriveled figs from a fig tree.

⁵ And when my sword has finished its work
in the heavens,
it will fall upon Edom,
the nation I have marked for
destruction.
⁶ The sword of the LORD is drenched with
blood
and covered with fat—
with the blood of lambs and goats,
with the fat of rams prepared for
sacrifice.
Yes, the LORD will offer a sacrifice in the
city of Bozrah.
He will make a mighty slaughter in
Edom.
⁷ Even men as strong as wild oxen will
die—
the young men alongside the veterans.
The land will be soaked with blood
and the soil enriched with fat.

⁸ For it is the day of the LORD's revenge,
the year when Edom will be paid back
for all it did to Israel.*
⁹ The streams of Edom will be filled with
burning pitch,
and the ground will be covered with
fire.
¹⁰ This judgment on Edom will never end;
the smoke of its burning will rise
forever.

The land will lie deserted from generation
to generation.
No one will live there anymore.
¹¹ It will be haunted by the desert owl and
the screech owl,
the great owl and the raven.*
For God will measure that land carefully;
he will measure it for chaos and
destruction.
¹² It will be called the Land of Nothing,
and all its nobles will soon be gone.*
¹³ Thorns will overrun its palaces;
nettles and thistles will grow in its forts.
The ruins will become a haunt for jackals
and a home for owls.
¹⁴ Desert animals will mingle there with
hyenas,
their howls filling the night.
Wild goats will bleat at one another among
the ruins,
and night creatures* will come there to
rest.
¹⁵ There the owl will make her nest and lay
her eggs.
She will hatch her young and cover
them with her wings.
And the buzzards will come,
each one with its mate.

¹⁶ Search the book of the LORD,
and see what he will do.
Not one of these birds and animals will be
missing,
and none will lack a mate,
for the LORD has promised this.
His Spirit will make it all come true.
¹⁷ He has surveyed and divided the land
and deeded it over to those creatures.
They will possess it forever,
from generation to generation.

Hope for Restoration

35 ¹ Even the wilderness and desert will
be glad in those days.
The wasteland will rejoice and blossom
with spring crocuses.
² Yes, there will be an abundance of flowers
and singing and joy!
The deserts will become as green as the
mountains of Lebanon,
as lovely as Mount Carmel or the plain
of Sharon.

34:2 The Hebrew term used here refers to the complete consecration of things or people to the LORD, either by destroying them or by giving them as an offering; similarly in 34:5. 34:8 Hebrew *to Zion.* 34:11 The identification of some of these birds is uncertain. 34:12 The meaning of the Hebrew is uncertain. 34:14 Hebrew *Lilith,* possibly a reference to a mythical demon of the night.

There the LORD will display his glory,
  the splendor of our God.
³ With this news, strengthen those who
    have tired hands,
  and encourage those who have weak
    knees.
⁴ Say to those with fearful hearts,
  "Be strong, and do not fear,
for your God is coming to destroy your
    enemies.
  He is coming to save you."

⁵ And when he comes, he will open the eyes
    of the blind
  and unplug the ears of the deaf.
⁶ The lame will leap like a deer,
  and those who cannot speak will sing
    for joy!
Springs will gush forth in the wilderness,
  and streams will water the wasteland.
⁷ The parched ground will become a pool,
  and springs of water will satisfy the
    thirsty land.
Marsh grass and reeds and rushes will
    flourish
  where desert jackals once lived.

⁸ And a great road will go through that once
    deserted land.
  It will be named the Highway of
    Holiness.
Evil-minded people will never travel on it.
  It will be only for those who walk in
    God's ways;
  fools will never walk there.
⁹ Lions will not lurk along its course,
  nor any other ferocious beasts.
There will be no other dangers.
  Only the redeemed will walk on it.
¹⁰ Those who have been ransomed by the
    LORD will return.
  They will enter Jerusalem* singing,
    crowned with everlasting joy.
Sorrow and mourning will disappear,
  and they will be filled with joy and
    gladness.

Assyria Invades Judah

36 In the fourteenth year of King Hezekiah's reign,* King Sennacherib of Assyria came to attack the fortified towns of Judah and conquered them. ²Then the king of Assyria sent his chief of staff* from Lachish

with a huge army to confront King Hezekiah in Jerusalem. The Assyrians took up a position beside the aqueduct that feeds water into the upper pool, near the road leading to the field where cloth is washed.* ³These are the officials who went out to meet with them: Eliakim son of Hilkiah, the palace administrator; Shebna the court secretary; and Joah son of Asaph, the royal historian.

Sennacherib Threatens Jerusalem

⁴Then the Assyrian king's chief of staff told them to give this message to Hezekiah:

"This is what the great king of Assyria says: What are you trusting in that makes you so confident? ⁵Do you think* that mere words can substitute for military skill and strength? Who are you counting on, that you have rebelled against me? ⁶On Egypt? If you lean on Egypt, it will be like a reed that splinters beneath your weight and pierces your hand. Pharaoh, the king of Egypt, is completely unreliable!

⁷"But perhaps you will say to me, 'We are trusting in the LORD our God!' But isn't he the one who was insulted by Hezekiah? Didn't Hezekiah tear down his shrines and altars and make everyone in Judah and Jerusalem worship only at the altar here in Jerusalem?

⁸"I'll tell you what! Strike a bargain with my master, the king of Assyria. I will give you 2,000 horses if you can find that many men to ride on them! ⁹With your tiny army, how can you think of challenging even the weakest contingent of my master's troops, even with the help of Egypt's chariots and charioteers? ¹⁰What's more, do you think we have invaded your land without the LORD's direction? The LORD himself told us, 'Attack this land and destroy it!'"

¹¹Then Eliakim, Shebna, and Joah said to the Assyrian chief of staff, "Please speak to us in Aramaic, for we understand it well. Don't speak in Hebrew,* for the people on the wall will hear."

¹²But Sennacherib's chief of staff replied, "Do you think my master sent this message only to you and your master? He wants all the people to hear it, for when we put this city

---

35:10 Hebrew *Zion.* 36:1 The fourteenth year of Hezekiah's reign was 701 B.C. 36:2a Or *the rabshakeh;* also in 36:4, 11, 12, 22. 36:2b Or *bleached.* 36:5 As in Dead Sea Scrolls (see also 2 Kgs 18:20); Masoretic Text reads *Do I think.* 36:11 Hebrew *in the dialect of Judah;* also in 36:13.

under siege, they will suffer along with you. They will be so hungry and thirsty that they will eat their own dung and drink their own urine."

¹³Then the chief of staff stood and shouted in Hebrew to the people on the wall, "Listen to this message from the great king of Assyria! ¹⁴This is what the king says: Don't let Hezekiah deceive you. He will never be able to rescue you. ¹⁵Don't let him fool you into trusting in the LORD by saying, 'The LORD will surely rescue us. This city will never fall into the hands of the Assyrian king!'

¹⁶"Don't listen to Hezekiah! These are the terms the king of Assyria is offering: Make peace with me—open the gates and come out. Then each of you can continue eating from your own grapevine and fig tree and drinking from your own well. ¹⁷Then I will arrange to take you to another land like this one—a land of grain and new wine, bread and vineyards.

¹⁸"Don't let Hezekiah mislead you by saying, 'The LORD will rescue us!' Have the gods of any other nations ever saved their people from the king of Assyria? ¹⁹What happened to the gods of Hamath and Arpad? And what about the gods of Sepharvaim? Did any god rescue Samaria from my power? ²⁰What god of any nation has ever been able to save its people from my power? So what makes you think that the LORD can rescue Jerusalem from me?"

²¹But the people were silent and did not utter a word because Hezekiah had commanded them, "Do not answer him."

²²Then Eliakim son of Hilkiah, the palace administrator; Shebna the court secretary; and Joah son of Asaph, the royal historian, went back to Hezekiah. They tore their clothes in despair, and they went in to see the king and told him what the Assyrian chief of staff had said.

Hezekiah Seeks the LORD's Help

37 When King Hezekiah heard their report, he tore his clothes and put on burlap and went into the Temple of the LORD. ²And he sent Eliakim the palace administrator, Shebna the court secretary, and the leading priests, all dressed in burlap, to the prophet Isaiah son of Amoz. ³They told him, "This is what King Hezekiah says: Today is a day of trouble, insults, and disgrace. It is like when a child is ready to be born, but the mother has no strength to deliver the baby. ⁴But perhaps the LORD your God has heard the Assyrian chief of staff,* sent by the king to defy the living God,

and will punish him for his words. Oh, pray for those of us who are left!"

⁵After King Hezekiah's officials delivered the king's message to Isaiah, ⁶the prophet replied, "Say to your master, 'This is what the LORD says: Do not be disturbed by this blasphemous speech against me from the Assyrian king's messengers. ⁷Listen! I myself will move against him,* and the king will receive a message that he is needed at home. So he will return to his land, where I will have him killed with a sword.'"

⁸Meanwhile, the Assyrian chief of staff left Jerusalem and went to consult the king of Assyria, who had left Lachish and was attacking Libnah.

⁹Soon afterward King Sennacherib received word that King Tirhakah of Ethiopia* was leading an army to fight against him. Before leaving to meet the attack, he sent messengers back to Hezekiah in Jerusalem with this message:

¹⁰"This message is for King Hezekiah of Judah. Don't let your God, in whom you trust, deceive you with promises that Jerusalem will not be captured by the king of Assyria. ¹¹You know perfectly well what the kings of Assyria have done wherever they have gone. They have completely destroyed everyone who stood in their way! Why should you be any different? ¹²Have the gods of other nations rescued them—such nations as Gozan, Haran, Rezeph, and the people of Eden who were in Tel-assar? My predecessors destroyed them all! ¹³What happened to the king of Hamath and the king of Arpad? What happened to the kings of Sepharvaim, Hena, and Ivvah?"

¹⁴After Hezekiah received the letter from the messengers and read it, he went up to the LORD's Temple and spread it out before the LORD. ¹⁵And Hezekiah prayed this prayer before the LORD: ¹⁶"O LORD of Heaven's Armies, God of Israel, you are enthroned between the mighty cherubim! You alone are God of all the kingdoms of the earth. You alone created the heavens and the earth. ¹⁷Bend down, O LORD, and listen! Open your eyes, O LORD, and see! Listen to Sennacherib's words of defiance against the living God.

¹⁸"It is true, LORD, that the kings of Assyria have destroyed all these nations. ¹⁹And they have thrown the gods of these nations into the

37:4 Or *the rabshakeh;* also in 37:8. 37:7 Hebrew *I will put a spirit in him.* 37:9 Hebrew *of Cush.*

fire and burned them. But of course the Assyrians could destroy them! They were not gods at all—only idols of wood and stone shaped by human hands. ²⁰Now, O LORD our God, rescue us from his power; then all the kingdoms of the earth will know that you alone, O LORD, are God.*"

Isaiah Predicts Judah's Deliverance

²¹Then Isaiah son of Amoz sent this message to Hezekiah: "This is what the LORD, the God of Israel, says: Because you prayed about King Sennacherib of Assyria, ²²the LORD has spoken this word against him:

"The virgin daughter of Zion
    despises you and laughs at you.
The daughter of Jerusalem
    shakes her head in derision as you flee.

²³ "Whom have you been defying and
        ridiculing?
    Against whom did you raise your voice?
At whom did you look with such haughty
        eyes?
    It was the Holy One of Israel!
²⁴ By your messengers you have defied the
        Lord.
    You have said, 'With my many chariots
I have conquered the highest mountains—
    yes, the remotest peaks of Lebanon.
I have cut down its tallest cedars
    and its finest cypress trees.
I have reached its farthest heights
    and explored its deepest forests.
²⁵ I have dug wells in many foreign lands*
    and refreshed myself with their water.
With the sole of my foot,
    I stopped up all the rivers of Egypt!'

²⁶ "But have you not heard?
    I decided this long ago.
Long ago I planned it,
    and now I am making it happen.
I planned for you to crush fortified
        cities
    into heaps of rubble.
²⁷ That is why their people have so little
        power
    and are so frightened and confused.
They are as weak as grass,
    as easily trampled as tender green
        shoots.

They are like grass sprouting on a
        housetop,
    scorched* before it can grow lush
        and tall.

²⁸ "But I know you well—
    where you stay
and when you come and go.
    I know the way you have raged
        against me.
²⁹ And because of your raging against me
    and your arrogance, which I have heard
        for myself,
I will put my hook in your nose
    and my bit in your mouth.
I will make you return
    by the same road on which you came."

³⁰Then Isaiah said to Hezekiah, "Here is the proof that what I say is true:

"This year you will eat only what grows up
        by itself,
    and next year you will eat what springs
        up from that.
But in the third year you will plant crops
        and harvest them;
    you will tend vineyards and eat their
        fruit.
³¹ And you who are left in Judah,
    who have escaped the ravages of the
        siege,
will put roots down in your own soil
    and grow up and flourish.
³² For a remnant of my people will spread
        out from Jerusalem,
    a group of survivors from Mount Zion.
The passionate commitment of the LORD
        of Heaven's Armies
    will make this happen!

³³"And this is what the LORD says about the king of Assyria:

"'His armies will not enter Jerusalem.
    They will not even shoot an arrow at it.
They will not march outside its gates with
        their shields
    nor build banks of earth against its walls.
³⁴ The king will return to his own country
    by the same road on which he came.
He will not enter this city,'
    says the LORD.

37:20 As in Dead Sea Scrolls (see also 2 Kgs 19:19); Masoretic Text reads *you alone are the LORD*. 37:25 As in Dead Sea Scrolls (see also 2 Kgs 19:24); Masoretic Text lacks *in many foreign lands*. 37:27 As in Dead Sea Scrolls and some Greek manuscripts (see also 2 Kgs 19:26); most Hebrew manuscripts read *like a terraced field*.

35 'For my own honor and for the sake
  of my servant David,
  I will defend this city and
    protect it.'"

36That night the angel of the LORD went out to the Assyrian camp and killed 185,000 Assyrian soldiers. When the surviving Assyrians* woke up the next morning, they found corpses everywhere. 37Then King Sennacherib of Assyria broke camp and returned to his own land. He went home to his capital of Nineveh and stayed there.

38One day while he was worshiping in the temple of his god Nisroch, his sons Adrammelech and Sharezer killed him with their swords. They then escaped to the land of Ararat, and another son, Esarhaddon, became the next king of Assyria.

Hezekiah's Sickness and Recovery

38 About that time Hezekiah became deathly ill, and the prophet Isaiah son of Amoz went to visit him. He gave the king this message: "This is what the LORD says: 'Set your affairs in order, for you are going to die. You will not recover from this illness.'"

2When Hezekiah heard this, he turned his face to the wall and prayed to the LORD, 3"Remember, O LORD, how I have always been faithful to you and have served you singlemindedly, always doing what pleases you." Then he broke down and wept bitterly.

4Then this message came to Isaiah from the LORD: 5"Go back to Hezekiah and tell him, 'This is what the LORD, the God of your ancestor David, says: I have heard your prayer and seen your tears. I will add fifteen years to your life, 6and I will rescue you and this city from the king of Assyria. Yes, I will defend this city.

7"'And this is the sign from the LORD to prove that he will do as he promised: 8I will cause the sun's shadow to move ten steps backward on the sundial* of Ahaz!'" So the shadow on the sundial moved backward ten steps.

Hezekiah's Poem of Praise

9When King Hezekiah was well again, he wrote this poem:

10 I said, "In the prime of my life,
  must I now enter the place of the
    dead?*
  Am I to be robbed of the rest of my
    years?"

11 I said, "Never again will I see the LORD
    GOD
  while still in the land of the living.
  Never again will I see my friends
  or be with those who live in this world.
12 My life has been blown away
  like a shepherd's tent in a storm.
  It has been cut short,
  as when a weaver cuts cloth from a loom.
  Suddenly, my life was over.
13 I waited patiently all night,
  but I was torn apart as though by lions.
  Suddenly, my life was over.
14 Delirious, I chattered like a swallow or a
    crane,
  and then I moaned like a mourning
    dove.
  My eyes grew tired of looking to heaven
    for help.
  I am in trouble, Lord. Help me!"

15 But what could I say?
  For he himself sent this sickness.
  Now I will walk humbly throughout my
    years
  because of this anguish I have felt.
16 Lord, your discipline is good,
  for it leads to life and health.
  You restore my health
  and allow me to live!
17 Yes, this anguish was good for me,
  for you have rescued me from death
  and forgiven all my sins.
18 For the dead* cannot praise you;
  they cannot raise their voices in praise.
  Those who go down to the grave
  can no longer hope in your faithfulness.
19 Only the living can praise you as I do today.
  Each generation tells of your
    faithfulness to the next.
20 Think of it—the LORD is ready to heal me!
  I will sing his praises with instruments
  every day of my life
  in the Temple of the LORD.

21Isaiah had said to Hezekiah's servants, "Make an ointment from figs and spread it over the boil, and Hezekiah will recover."

22And Hezekiah had asked, "What sign will prove that I will go to the Temple of the LORD?"

Envoys from Babylon

39 Soon after this, Merodach-baladan son of Baladan, king of Babylon, sent Hezekiah his best wishes and a gift. He had heard

37:36 Hebrew *When they.*   38:8 Hebrew *the steps.*   38:10 Hebrew *enter the gates of Sheol?*   38:18 Hebrew *Sheol.*

that Hezekiah had been very sick and that he had recovered. [2]Hezekiah was delighted with the Babylonian envoys and showed them everything in his treasure-houses—the silver, the gold, the spices, and the aromatic oils. He also took them to see his armory and showed them everything in his royal treasuries! There was nothing in his palace or kingdom that Hezekiah did not show them.

[3]Then Isaiah the prophet went to King Hezekiah and asked him, "What did those men want? Where were they from?"

Hezekiah replied, "They came from the distant land of Babylon."

[4]"What did they see in your palace?" asked Isaiah.

"They saw everything," Hezekiah replied. "I showed them everything I own—all my royal treasuries."

[5]Then Isaiah said to Hezekiah, "Listen to this message from the LORD of Heaven's Armies: [6]'The time is coming when everything in your palace—all the treasures stored up by your ancestors until now—will be carried off to Babylon. Nothing will be left,' says the LORD. [7]'Some of your very own sons will be taken away into exile. They will become eunuchs who will serve in the palace of Babylon's king.'"

[8]Then Hezekiah said to Isaiah, "This message you have given me from the LORD is good." For the king was thinking, "At least there will be peace and security during my lifetime."

Comfort for God's People

40

[1]"Comfort, comfort my people,"
    says your God.
[2]"Speak tenderly to Jerusalem.
Tell her that her sad days are gone
    and her sins are pardoned.
Yes, the LORD has punished her twice over
    for all her sins."

[3]Listen! It's the voice of someone shouting,
"Clear the way through the wilderness
    for the LORD!
Make a straight highway through the
    wasteland
    for our God!
[4]Fill in the valleys,
    and level the mountains and hills.
Straighten the curves,
    and smooth out the rough places.

[5]Then the glory of the LORD will be
    revealed,
and all people will see it together.
The LORD has spoken!"*

[6]A voice said, "Shout!"
I asked, "What should I shout?"

"Shout that people are like the grass.
Their beauty fades as quickly
    as the flowers in a field.
[7]The grass withers and the flowers fade
    beneath the breath of the LORD.
And so it is with people.
[8]The grass withers and the flowers fade,
    but the word of our God stands forever."

[9]O Zion, messenger of good news,
    shout from the mountaintops!
Shout it louder, O Jerusalem.*
    Shout, and do not be afraid.
Tell the towns of Judah,
    "Your God is coming!"
[10]Yes, the Sovereign LORD is coming in power.
    He will rule with a powerful arm.
See, he brings his reward with him as
    he comes.
[11]He will feed his flock like a shepherd.
    He will carry the lambs in his arms,
holding them close to his heart.
    He will gently lead the mother sheep
    with their young.

The LORD Has No Equal

[12]Who else has held the oceans in his hand?
    Who has measured off the heavens with
    his fingers?
Who else knows the weight of the earth
    or has weighed the mountains and hills
    on a scale?
[13]Who is able to advise the Spirit of the
    LORD?*
Who knows enough to give him advice
    or teach him?
[14]Has the LORD ever needed anyone's advice?
    Does he need instruction about what is
    good?
Did someone teach him what is right
    or show him the path of justice?

[15]No, for all the nations of the world
    are but a drop in the bucket.

40:3-5 Greek version reads *He is a voice shouting in the wilderness,* / *"Prepare the way for the LORD's coming!* / *Clear a road for our God!* / *Fill in the valleys,* / *and level the mountains and hills.* / *And then the glory of the LORD will be revealed,* / *and all people will see the salvation sent from God.* / *The LORD has spoken!"* Compare Matt 3:3; Mark 1:3; Luke 3:4-6. **40:9** Or *O messenger of good news, shout to Zion from the mountaintops! Shout it louder to Jerusalem.* **40:13** Greek version reads *Who can know the LORD's thoughts?* Compare Rom 11:34; 1 Cor 2:16.

They are nothing more
　　than dust on the scales.
He picks up the whole earth
　　as though it were a grain of sand.
16 All the wood in Lebanon's forests
　　and all Lebanon's animals would not
　　　　be enough
　　to make a burnt offering worthy of
　　　　our God.
17 The nations of the world are worth
　　　　nothing to him.
　　In his eyes they count for less than
　　　　nothing—
　　mere emptiness and froth.

18 To whom can you compare God?
　　What image can you find to resemble
　　　　him?
19 Can he be compared to an idol formed in
　　　　a mold,
　　overlaid with gold, and decorated with
　　　　silver chains?
20 Or if people are too poor for that,
　　they might at least choose wood that
　　　　won't decay
　　and a skilled craftsman
　　　　to carve an image that won't fall down!

21 Haven't you heard? Don't you understand?
　　Are you deaf to the words of God—
　　the words he gave before the world began?
　　Are you so ignorant?
22 God sits above the circle of the earth.
　　The people below seem like
　　　　grasshoppers to him!
　　He spreads out the heavens like a curtain
　　and makes his tent from them.
23 He judges the great people of the world
　　and brings them all to nothing.
24 They hardly get started, barely taking
　　　　root,
　　when he blows on them and they
　　　　wither.
　　The wind carries them off like chaff.

25 "To whom will you compare me?
　　Who is my equal?" asks the Holy One.

26 Look up into the heavens.
　　Who created all the stars?
　　He brings them out like an army, one after
　　　　another,
　　calling each by its name.
　　Because of his great power and
　　　　incomparable strength,
　　not a single one is missing.

27 O Jacob, how can you say the LORD does
　　　　not see your troubles?
　　O Israel, how can you say God ignores
　　　　your rights?
28 Have you never heard?
　　Have you never understood?
　　The LORD is the everlasting God,
　　　　the Creator of all the earth.
　　He never grows weak or weary.
　　No one can measure the depths of his
　　　　understanding.
29 He gives power to the weak
　　　　and strength to the powerless.
30 Even youths will become weak and tired,
　　and young men will fall in exhaustion.
31 But those who trust in the LORD will find
　　　　new strength.
　　They will soar high on wings like eagles.
　　They will run and not grow weary.
　　They will walk and not faint.

God's Help for Israel

41 ¹ "Listen in silence before me, you
　　　　lands beyond the sea.
　　Bring your strongest arguments.
　　Come now and speak.
　　The court is ready for your case.

2 "Who has stirred up this king from the
　　　　east,
　　rightly calling him to God's service?
　　Who gives this man victory over many
　　　　nations
　　and permits him to trample their kings
　　　　underfoot?
　　With his sword, he reduces armies to dust.
　　　　With his bow, he scatters them like chaff
　　　　before the wind.
3 He chases them away and goes on safely,
　　though he is walking over unfamiliar
　　　　ground.
4 Who has done such mighty deeds,
　　summoning each new generation from
　　　　the beginning of time?
　　It is I, the LORD, the First and the Last.
　　I alone am he."

5 The lands beyond the sea watch in fear.
　　Remote lands tremble and mobilize
　　　　for war.
6 The idol makers encourage one another,
　　saying to each other, "Be strong!"
7 The carver encourages the goldsmith,
　　and the molder helps at the anvil.
　　"Good," they say. "It's coming along
　　　　fine."

Carefully they join the parts together,
then fasten the thing in place so it won't
fall over.

8 "But as for you, Israel my servant,
Jacob my chosen one,
descended from Abraham my friend,
9 I have called you back from the ends of the
earth,
saying, 'You are my servant.'
For I have chosen you
and will not throw you away.
10 Don't be afraid, for I am with you.
Don't be discouraged, for I am your God.
I will strengthen you and help you.
I will hold you up with my victorious
right hand.

11 "See, all your angry enemies lie there,
confused and humiliated.
Anyone who opposes you will die
and come to nothing.
12 You will look in vain
for those who tried to conquer you.
Those who attack you
will come to nothing.
13 For I hold you by your right hand—
I, the LORD your God.
And I say to you,
'Don't be afraid. I am here to help you.
14 Though you are a lowly worm, O Jacob,
don't be afraid, people of Israel, for I
will help you.
I am the LORD, your Redeemer.
I am the Holy One of Israel.'

15 You will be a new threshing instrument
with many sharp teeth.
You will tear your enemies apart,
making chaff of mountains.
16 You will toss them into the air,
and the wind will blow them all away;
a whirlwind will scatter them.
Then you will rejoice in the LORD.
You will glory in the Holy One of
Israel.

17 "When the poor and needy search for
water and there is none,
and their tongues are parched from
thirst,
then I, the LORD, will answer them.
I, the God of Israel, will never abandon
them.
18 I will open up rivers for them on the high
plateaus.

I will give them fountains of water in
the valleys.
I will fill the desert with pools of water.
Rivers fed by springs will flow across the
parched ground.
19 I will plant trees in the barren desert—
cedar, acacia, myrtle, olive, cypress, fir,
and pine.
20 I am doing this so all who see this miracle
will understand what it means—
that it is the LORD who has done this,
the Holy One of Israel who created it.

21 "Present the case for your idols,"
says the LORD.
"Let them show what they can do,"
says the King of Israel.*
22 "Let them try to tell us what happened
long ago
so that we may consider the evidence.
Or let them tell us what the future holds,
so we can know what's going to
happen.
23 Yes, tell us what will occur in the days
ahead.
Then we will know you are gods.
In fact, do anything—good or bad!
Do something that will amaze and
frighten us.
24 But no! You are less than nothing and can
do nothing at all.
Those who choose you pollute
themselves.

25 "But I have stirred up a leader who will
approach from the north.
From the east he will call on my name.
I will give him victory over kings and
princes.
He will trample them as a potter treads
on clay.

26 "Who told you from the beginning
that this would happen?
Who predicted this,
making you admit that he was right?
No one said a word!
27 I was the first to tell Zion,
'Look! Help is on the way!'*
I will send Jerusalem a messenger with
good news.
28 Not one of your idols told you this.
Not one gave any answer when I asked.
29 See, they are all foolish, worthless things.
All your idols are as empty as the wind.

41:21 Hebrew *the King of Jacob.* See note on 14:1.   41:27 Or *'Look! They are coming home.'*

The Lord's Chosen Servant

42 1 "Look at my servant, whom I
strengthen.
He is my chosen one, who pleases me.
I have put my Spirit upon him.
He will bring justice to the nations.
2 He will not shout
or raise his voice in public.
3 He will not crush the weakest reed
or put out a flickering candle.
He will bring justice to all who have
been wronged.
4 He will not falter or lose heart
until justice prevails throughout the
earth.
Even distant lands beyond the sea will
wait for his instruction.*"

5 God, the Lord, created the heavens and
stretched them out.
He created the earth and everything
in it.
He gives breath to everyone,
life to everyone who walks the earth.
And it is he who says,
6 "I, the Lord, have called you to
demonstrate my righteousness.
I will take you by the hand and guard
you,
and I will give you to my people, Israel,
as a symbol of my covenant with them.
And you will be a light to guide the
nations.
7 You will open the eyes of the blind.
You will free the captives from prison,
releasing those who sit in dark
dungeons.

8 "I am the Lord; that is my name!
I will not give my glory to anyone else,
nor share my praise with carved idols.
9 Everything I prophesied has come true,
and now I will prophesy again.
I will tell you the future before it happens."

A Song of Praise to the Lord

10 Sing a new song to the Lord!
Sing his praises from the ends of the
earth!
Sing, all you who sail the seas,
all you who live in distant coastlands.
11 Join in the chorus, you desert towns;
let the villages of Kedar rejoice!
Let the people of Sela sing for joy;
shout praises from the mountaintops!

12 Let the whole world glorify the Lord;
let it sing his praise.
13 The Lord will march forth like a mighty
hero;
he will come out like a warrior, full
of fury.
He will shout his battle cry
and crush all his enemies.

14 He will say, "I have long been silent;
yes, I have restrained myself.
But now, like a woman in labor,
I will cry and groan and pant.
15 I will level the mountains and hills
and blight all their greenery.
I will turn the rivers into dry land
and will dry up all the pools.
16 I will lead blind Israel down a new path,
guiding them along an unfamiliar way.
I will brighten the darkness before them
and smooth out the road ahead of them.
Yes, I will indeed do these things;
I will not forsake them.
17 But those who trust in idols,
who say, 'You are our gods,'
will be turned away in shame.

Israel's Failure to Listen and See

18 "Listen, you who are deaf!
Look and see, you blind!
19 Who is as blind as my own people, my
servant?
Who is as deaf as my messenger?
Who is as blind as my chosen people,
the servant of the Lord?
20 You see and recognize what is right
but refuse to act on it.
You hear with your ears,
but you don't really listen."

21 Because he is righteous,
the Lord has exalted his glorious law.
22 But his own people have been robbed and
plundered,
enslaved, imprisoned, and trapped.
They are fair game for anyone
and have no one to protect them,
no one to take them back home.

23 Who will hear these lessons from the past
and see the ruin that awaits you in the
future?
24 Who allowed Israel to be robbed and hurt?
It was the Lord, against whom we
sinned,

42:4 Greek version reads *And his name will be the hope of all the world.* Compare Matt 12:21.

for the people would not walk in his path,
  nor would they obey his law.
²⁵ Therefore, he poured out his fury on them
  and destroyed them in battle.
They were enveloped in flames,
  but they still refused to understand.
They were consumed by fire,
  but they did not learn their lesson.

The Savior of Israel

43 ¹ But now, O Jacob, listen to the LORD
  who created you.
O Israel, the one who formed you says,
"Do not be afraid, for I have ransomed you.
  I have called you by name; you are
  mine.
² When you go through deep waters,
  I will be with you.
When you go through rivers of difficulty,
  you will not drown.
When you walk through the fire of
  oppression,
  you will not be burned up;
  the flames will not consume you.
³ For I am the LORD, your God,
  the Holy One of Israel, your Savior.
I gave Egypt as a ransom for your freedom;
  I gave Ethiopia* and Seba in your place.
⁴ Others were given in exchange for you.
  I traded their lives for yours
because you are precious to me.
  You are honored, and I love you.

⁵ "Do not be afraid, for I am with you.
  I will gather you and your children from
  east and west.
⁶ I will say to the north and south,
  'Bring my sons and daughters back to
  Israel
  from the distant corners of the earth.
⁷ Bring all who claim me as their God,
  for I have made them for my glory.
  It was I who created them.'"

⁸ Bring out the people who have eyes but
  are blind,
  who have ears but are deaf.
⁹ Gather the nations together!
  Assemble the peoples of the world!
Which of their idols has ever foretold such
  things?
  Which can predict what will happen
  tomorrow?
Where are the witnesses of such
  predictions?

Who can verify that they spoke the
  truth?
¹⁰ "But you are my witnesses, O Israel!" says
  the LORD.
  "You are my servant.
You have been chosen to know me, believe
  in me,
  and understand that I alone am God.
There is no other God—
  there never has been, and there never
  will be.
¹¹ I, yes I, am the LORD,
  and there is no other Savior.
¹² First I predicted your rescue,
  then I saved you and proclaimed it to
  the world.
No foreign god has ever done this.
  You are witnesses that I am the only
  God,"
  says the LORD.
¹³ "From eternity to eternity I am God.
  No one can snatch anyone out of my
  hand.
  No one can undo what I have done."

The LORD's Promise of Victory

¹⁴This is what the LORD says—your Redeemer,
the Holy One of Israel:

"For your sakes I will send an army against
  Babylon,
  forcing the Babylonians* to flee in those
  ships they are so proud of.
¹⁵ I am the LORD, your Holy One,
  Israel's Creator and King.
¹⁶ I am the LORD, who opened a way through
  the waters,
  making a dry path through the sea.
¹⁷ I called forth the mighty army of Egypt
  with all its chariots and horses.
I drew them beneath the waves, and they
  drowned,
  their lives snuffed out like a smoldering
  candlewick.

¹⁸ "But forget all that—
  it is nothing compared to what I am
  going to do.
¹⁹ For I am about to do something new.
  See, I have already begun! Do you not
  see it?
I will make a pathway through the
  wilderness.
  I will create rivers in the dry wasteland.

43:3 Hebrew *Cush*.   43:14 Or *Chaldeans*.

20 The wild animals in the fields will thank me,
   the jackals and owls, too,
for giving them water in the desert.
Yes, I will make rivers in the dry wasteland
   so my chosen people can be refreshed.
21 I have made Israel for myself,
   and they will someday honor me before
      the whole world.

22 "But, dear family of Jacob, you refuse to
      ask for my help.
   You have grown tired of me, O Israel!
23 You have not brought me sheep or goats
      for burnt offerings.
   You have not honored me with
      sacrifices,
though I have not burdened and wearied
      you
   with requests for grain offerings and
      frankincense.
24 You have not brought me fragrant calamus
      or pleased me with the fat from
         sacrifices.
   Instead, you have burdened me with your
      sins
   and wearied me with your faults.

25 "I—yes, I alone—will blot out your sins
      for my own sake
   and will never think of them again.
26 Let us review the situation together,
      and you can present your case to prove
         your innocence.
27 From the very beginning, your first
      ancestor sinned against me;
   all your leaders broke my laws.
28 That is why I have disgraced your priests;
   I have decreed complete destruction*
      for Jacob
   and shame for Israel.

44

1 "But now, listen to me, Jacob my
      servant,
   Israel my chosen one.
2 The LORD who made you and helps you
      says:
   Do not be afraid, O Jacob, my servant,
   O dear Israel,* my chosen one.
3 For I will pour out water to quench your
      thirst
      and to irrigate your parched fields.
   And I will pour out my Spirit on your
      descendants,
      and my blessing on your children.

4 They will thrive like watered grass,
   like willows on a riverbank.
5 Some will proudly claim, 'I belong to the
      LORD.'
   Others will say, 'I am a descendant of
      Jacob.'
   Some will write the LORD's name on their
      hands
      and will take the name of Israel as their
         own."

The Foolishness of Idols

6 This is what the LORD says—Israel's King and
Redeemer, the LORD of Heaven's Armies:

   "I am the First and the Last;
      there is no other God.
7 Who is like me?
   Let him step forward and prove to you
      his power.
   Let him do as I have done since ancient
      times
      when I established a people and
         explained its future.
8 Do not tremble; do not be afraid.
   Did I not proclaim my purposes for you
      long ago?
   You are my witnesses—is there any other
      God?
   No! There is no other Rock—not one!"

9 How foolish are those who manufacture
      idols.
   These prized objects are really
      worthless.
   The people who worship idols don't know
      this,
      so they are all put to shame.
10 Who but a fool would make his own
      god—
      an idol that cannot help him one bit?
11 All who worship idols will be disgraced
      along with all these craftsmen—mere
         humans—
      who claim they can make a god.
   They may all stand together,
      but they will stand in terror and shame.

12 The blacksmith stands at his forge to make
      a sharp tool,
      pounding and shaping it with all his
         might.
   His work makes him hungry and weak.
   It makes him thirsty and faint.

43:28 The Hebrew term used here refers to the complete consecration of things or people to the LORD, either by destroying them or by giving them as an offering.   44:2 Hebrew *Jeshurun,* a term of endearment for Israel.

13 Then the wood-carver measures a block
      of wood
   and draws a pattern on it.
He works with chisel and plane
   and carves it into a human figure.
He gives it human beauty
   and puts it in a little shrine.
14 He cuts down cedars;
   he selects the cypress and the oak;
he plants the pine in the forest
   to be nourished by the rain.
15 Then he uses part of the wood to make
      a fire.
   With it he warms himself and bakes
      his bread.
Then—yes, it's true—he takes the rest
      of it
   and makes himself a god to worship!
He makes an idol
   and bows down in front of it!
16 He burns part of the tree to roast his
      meat
   and to keep himself warm.
He says, "Ah, that fire feels good."
17 Then he takes what's left
   and makes his god: a carved idol!
He falls down in front of it,
   worshiping and praying to it.
"Rescue me!" he says.
   "You are my god!"

18 Such stupidity and ignorance!
   Their eyes are closed, and they cannot
      see.
   Their minds are shut, and they cannot
      think.
19 The person who made the idol never stops
      to reflect,
   "Why, it's just a block of wood!
I burned half of it for heat
   and used it to bake my bread and roast
      my meat.
How can the rest of it be a god?
   Should I bow down to worship a piece
      of wood?"
20 The poor, deluded fool feeds on ashes.
   He trusts something that can't help him
      at all.
Yet he cannot bring himself to ask,
   "Is this idol that I'm holding in my
      hand a lie?"

Restoration for Jerusalem

21 "Pay attention, O Jacob,
   for you are my servant, O Israel.
I, the LORD, made you,
   and I will not forget you.
22 I have swept away your sins like a cloud.
   I have scattered your offenses like the
      morning mist.
Oh, return to me,
   for I have paid the price to set you free."

23 Sing, O heavens, for the LORD has done
      this wondrous thing.
   Shout for joy, O depths of the earth!
Break into song,
   O mountains and forests and every tree!
For the LORD has redeemed Jacob
   and is glorified in Israel.

24 This is what the LORD says—
   your Redeemer and Creator:
"I am the LORD, who made all things.
   I alone stretched out the heavens.
Who was with me
   when I made the earth?
25 I expose the false prophets as liars
   and make fools of fortune-tellers.
I cause the wise to give bad advice,
   thus proving them to be fools.
26 But I carry out the predictions of my
      prophets!
   By them I say to Jerusalem, 'People will
      live here again,'
and to the towns of Judah, 'You will be
      rebuilt;
   I will restore all your ruins!'
27 When I speak to the rivers and say,
   'Dry up!'
they will be dry.
28 When I say of Cyrus, 'He is my shepherd,'
   he will certainly do as I say.
He will command, 'Rebuild Jerusalem';
   he will say, 'Restore the Temple.'"

Cyrus, the LORD's Chosen One

45 1 This is what the LORD says to Cyrus,
      his anointed one,
   whose right hand he will empower.
Before him, mighty kings will be
      paralyzed with fear.
   Their fortress gates will be opened,
      never to shut again.
2 This is what the LORD says:

"I will go before you, Cyrus,
   and level the mountains.*
I will smash down gates of bronze
   and cut through bars of iron.

45:2 As in Dead Sea Scrolls and Greek version; Masoretic Text reads *the swellings.*

³ And I will give you treasures hidden in the
darkness—
secret riches.
I will do this so you may know that I am
the LORD,
the God of Israel, the one who calls you
by name.

⁴ "And why have I called you for this work?
Why did I call you by name when you
did not know me?
It is for the sake of Jacob my servant,
Israel my chosen one.
⁵ I am the LORD;
there is no other God.
I have equipped you for battle,
though you don't even know me,
⁶ so all the world from east to west
will know there is no other God.
I am the LORD, and there is no other.
⁷ I create the light and make the darkness.
I send good times and bad times.
I, the LORD, am the one who does these
things.

⁸ "Open up, O heavens,
and pour out your righteousness.
Let the earth open wide
so salvation and righteousness can
sprout up together.
I, the LORD, created them.

⁹ "What sorrow awaits those who argue
with their Creator.
Does a clay pot argue with its maker?
Does the clay dispute with the one who
shapes it, saying,
'Stop, you're doing it wrong!'
Does the pot exclaim,
'How clumsy can you be?'
¹⁰ How terrible it would be if a newborn
baby said to its father,
'Why was I born?'
or if it said to its mother,
'Why did you make me this way?'"

¹¹ This is what the LORD says—
the Holy One of Israel and your
Creator:
"Do you question what I do for my
children?
Do you give me orders about the work
of my hands?
¹² I am the one who made the earth
and created people to live on it.

With my hands I stretched out the
heavens.
All the stars are at my command.
¹³ I will raise up Cyrus to fulfill my righteous
purpose,
and I will guide his actions.
He will restore my city and free my captive
people—
without seeking a reward!
I, the LORD of Heaven's Armies, have
spoken!"

Future Conversion of Gentiles
¹⁴This is what the LORD says:

"You will rule the Egyptians,
the Ethiopians,* and the Sabeans.
They will come to you with all their
merchandise,
and it will all be yours.
They will follow you as prisoners in chains.
They will fall to their knees in front of
you and say,
'God is with you, and he is the only God.
There is no other.'"

¹⁵ Truly, O God of Israel, our Savior,
you work in mysterious ways.
¹⁶ All craftsmen who make idols will be
humiliated.
They will all be disgraced together.
¹⁷ But the LORD will save the people of Israel
with eternal salvation.
Throughout everlasting ages,
they will never again be humiliated and
disgraced.

¹⁸ For the LORD is God,
and he created the heavens and earth
and put everything in place.
He made the world to be lived in,
not to be a place of empty chaos.
"I am the LORD," he says,
"and there is no other.
¹⁹ I publicly proclaim bold promises.
I do not whisper obscurities in some
dark corner.
I would not have told the people of Israel*
to seek me
if I could not be found.
I, the LORD, speak only what is true
and declare only what is right.

²⁰ "Gather together and come,
you fugitives from surrounding nations.

45:14 Hebrew *Cushites.*   45:19 Hebrew *of Jacob.* See note on 14:1.

What fools they are who carry around their
 wooden idols
and pray to gods that cannot save!
²¹ Consult together, argue your case.
 Get together and decide what to say.
Who made these things known so long ago?
 What idol ever told you they would
 happen?
Was it not I, the LORD?
 For there is no other God but me,
a righteous God and Savior.
 There is none but me.
²² Let all the world look to me for salvation!
 For I am God; there is no other.
²³ I have sworn by my own name;
 I have spoken the truth,
 and I will never go back on my word:
Every knee will bend to me,
 and every tongue will declare allegiance
 to me.*"
²⁴ The people will declare,
 "The LORD is the source of all my
 righteousness and strength."
And all who were angry with him
 will come to him and be ashamed.
²⁵ In the LORD all the generations of Israel
 will be justified,
 and in him they will boast.

Babylon's False Gods

46

¹ Bel and Nebo, the gods of Babylon,
 bow as they are lowered to the
 ground.
They are being hauled away on ox carts.
 The poor beasts stagger under the
 weight.
² Both the idols and their owners are bowed
 down.
 The gods cannot protect the people,
and the people cannot protect the gods.
 They go off into captivity together.

³ "Listen to me, descendants of Jacob,
 all you who remain in Israel.
I have cared for you since you were born.
 Yes, I carried you before you were born.
⁴ I will be your God throughout your
 lifetime—
 until your hair is white with age.
I made you, and I will care for you.
 I will carry you along and save you.

⁵ "To whom will you compare me?
 Who is my equal?

⁶ Some people pour out their silver and gold
 and hire a craftsman to make a god
 from it.
Then they bow down and worship it!
⁷ They carry it around on their shoulders,
 and when they set it down, it stays there.
 It can't even move!
And when someone prays to it, there is no
 answer.
 It can't rescue anyone from trouble.

⁸ "Do not forget this! Keep it in mind!
 Remember this, you guilty ones.
⁹ Remember the things I have done in the
 past.
 For I alone am God!
I am God, and there is none like me.
¹⁰ Only I can tell you the future
 before it even happens.
Everything I plan will come to pass,
 for I do whatever I wish.
¹¹ I will call a swift bird of prey from the
 east—
 a leader from a distant land to come and
 do my bidding.
I have said what I would do,
 and I will do it.

¹² "Listen to me, you stubborn people
 who are so far from doing right.
¹³ For I am ready to set things right,
 not in the distant future, but right now!
I am ready to save Jerusalem*
 and show my glory to Israel.

Prediction of Babylon's Fall

47

¹ "Come down, virgin daughter
 of Babylon, and sit in the dust.
For your days of sitting on a throne have
 ended.
O daughter of Babylonia,* never again will
 you be
the lovely princess, tender and delicate.
² Take heavy millstones and grind flour.
 Remove your veil, and strip off your robe.
 Expose yourself to public view.*
³ You will be naked and burdened with
 shame.
 I will take vengeance against you
 without pity."

⁴ Our Redeemer, whose name is the LORD of
 Heaven's Armies,
 is the Holy One of Israel.

45:23 Hebrew *will confess*; Greek version reads *will declare allegiance to God.* Compare Rom 14:11.   46:13 Hebrew *Zion.*   47:1 Or
Chaldea; also in 47:5.   47:2 Hebrew *Bare your legs; pass through the rivers.*

⁵ "O beautiful Babylon, sit now in darkness
and silence.
Never again will you be known as the
queen of kingdoms.
⁶ For I was angry with my chosen people
and punished them by letting them fall
into your hands.
But you, Babylon, showed them no
mercy.
You oppressed even the elderly.
⁷ You said, 'I will reign forever as queen of
the world!'
You did not reflect on your actions
or think about their consequences.

⁸ "Listen to this, you pleasure-loving
kingdom,
living at ease and feeling secure.
You say, 'I am the only one, and there is no
other.
I will never be a widow or lose my
children.'
⁹ Well, both these things will come upon
you in a moment:
widowhood and the loss of your
children.
Yes, these calamities will come upon you,
despite all your witchcraft and magic.

¹⁰ "You felt secure in your wickedness.
'No one sees me,' you said.
But your 'wisdom' and 'knowledge' have
led you astray,
and you said, 'I am the only one, and
there is no other.'
¹¹ So disaster will overtake you,
and you won't be able to charm it away.
Calamity will fall upon you,
and you won't be able to buy your
way out.
A catastrophe will strike you suddenly,
one for which you are not prepared.

¹² "Now use your magical charms!
Use the spells you have worked at all
these years!
Maybe they will do you some good.
Maybe they can make someone afraid
of you.
¹³ All the advice you receive has made you
tired.
Where are all your astrologers,
those stargazers who make predictions
each month?
Let them stand up and save you from
what the future holds.

¹⁴ But they are like straw burning in a fire;
they cannot save themselves from the
flame.
You will get no help from them at all;
their hearth is no place to sit for
warmth.
¹⁵ And all your friends,
those with whom you've done business
since childhood,
will go their own ways,
turning a deaf ear to your cries.

God's Stubborn People

48 ¹ "Listen to me, O family of Jacob,
you who are called by the name
of Israel
and born into the family of Judah.
Listen, you who take oaths in the name
of the LORD
and call on the God of Israel.
You don't keep your promises,
²   even though you call yourself the holy
city
and talk about depending on the God
of Israel,
whose name is the LORD of Heaven's
Armies.
³ Long ago I told you what was going to
happen.
Then suddenly I took action,
and all my predictions came true.
⁴ For I know how stubborn and obstinate
you are.
Your necks are as unbending as iron.
Your heads are as hard as bronze.
⁵ That is why I told you what would happen;
I told you beforehand what I was going
to do.
Then you could never say, 'My idols did it.
My wooden image and metal god
commanded it to happen!'
⁶ You have heard my predictions and seen
them fulfilled,
but you refuse to admit it.
Now I will tell you new things,
secrets you have not yet heard.
⁷ They are brand new, not things from
the past.
So you cannot say, 'We knew that all
the time!'

⁸ "Yes, I will tell you of things that are
entirely new,
things you never heard of before.
For I know so well what traitors you are.
You have been rebels from birth.

⁹ Yet for my own sake and for the honor of
  my name,
  I will hold back my anger and not wipe
  you out.
¹⁰ I have refined you, but not as silver is
  refined.
  Rather, I have refined you in the furnace
  of suffering.
¹¹ I will rescue you for my sake—
  yes, for my own sake!
  I will not let my reputation be tarnished,
  and I will not share my glory with
  idols!

Freedom from Babylon

¹² "Listen to me, O family of Jacob,
  Israel my chosen one!
  I alone am God,
  the First and the Last.
¹³ It was my hand that laid the foundations
  of the earth,
  my right hand that spread out the
  heavens above.
  When I call out the stars,
  they all appear in order."

¹⁴ Have any of your idols ever told you this?
  Come, all of you, and listen:
  The Lord has chosen Cyrus as his ally.
  He will use him to put an end to the
  empire of Babylon
  and to destroy the Babylonian* armies.

¹⁵ "I have said it: I am calling Cyrus!
  I will send him on this errand and will
  help him succeed.
¹⁶ Come closer, and listen to this.
  From the beginning I have told you
  plainly what would happen."

And now the Sovereign Lord and his
  Spirit
  have sent me with this message.
¹⁷ This is what the Lord says—
  your Redeemer, the Holy One of Israel:
  "I am the Lord your God,
  who teaches you what is good for you
  and leads you along the paths you
  should follow.
¹⁸ Oh, that you had listened to my
  commands!
  Then you would have had peace flowing
  like a gentle river
  and righteousness rolling over you like
  waves in the sea.

¹⁹ Your descendants would have been like
  the sands along the seashore—
  too many to count!
  There would have been no need for your
  destruction,
  or for cutting off your family name."

²⁰ Yet even now, be free from your captivity!
  Leave Babylon and the Babylonians.*
  Sing out this message!
  Shout it to the ends of the earth!
  The Lord has redeemed his servants,
  the people of Israel.*
²¹ They were not thirsty
  when he led them through the desert.
  He divided the rock,
  and water gushed out for them to drink.
²² "But there is no peace for the wicked,"
  says the Lord.

The Lord's Servant Commissioned

49 ¹ Listen to me, all you in distant
  lands!
  Pay attention, you who are far away!
  The Lord called me before my birth;
  from within the womb he called me
  by name.
² He made my words of judgment as sharp
  as a sword.
  He has hidden me in the shadow of his
  hand.
  I am like a sharp arrow in his quiver.

³ He said to me, "You are my servant,
  Israel,
  and you will bring me glory."

⁴ I replied, "But my work seems so useless!
  I have spent my strength for nothing
  and to no purpose.
  Yet I leave it all in the Lord's hand;
  I will trust God for my reward."

⁵ And now the Lord speaks—
  the one who formed me in my mother's
  womb to be his servant,
  who commissioned me to bring Israel
  back to him.
  The Lord has honored me,
  and my God has given me strength.
⁶ He says, "You will do more than restore
  the people of Israel to me.
  I will make you a light to the Gentiles,
  and you will bring my salvation to the
  ends of the earth."

48:14 Or *Chaldean.*   48:20a Or *the Chaldeans.*   48:20b Hebrew *his servant, Jacob.* See note on 14:1.

⁷ The LORD, the Redeemer
    and Holy One of Israel,
says to the one who is despised and
    rejected by the nations,
to the one who is the servant of rulers:
"Kings will stand at attention when you
    pass by.
Princes will also bow low
because of the LORD, the faithful one,
    the Holy One of Israel, who has chosen
    you."

Promises of Israel's Restoration

⁸This is what the LORD says:

"At just the right time, I will respond to
    you.*
    On the day of salvation I will help you.
I will protect you and give you to the
    people
    as my covenant with them.
Through you I will reestablish the land
    of Israel
    and assign it to its own people again.
⁹ I will say to the prisoners, 'Come out in
    freedom,'
    and to those in darkness, 'Come into the
    light.'
They will be my sheep, grazing in green
    pastures
    and on hills that were previously bare.
¹⁰ They will neither hunger nor thirst.
    The searing sun will not reach them
    anymore.
For the LORD in his mercy will lead them;
    he will lead them beside cool waters.
¹¹ And I will make my mountains into level
    paths for them.
    The highways will be raised above the
    valleys.
¹² See, my people will return from far away,
    from lands to the north and west,
    and from as far south as Egypt.*

¹³ Sing for joy, O heavens!
    Rejoice, O earth!
    Burst into song, O mountains!
For the LORD has comforted his people
    and will have compassion on them in
    their suffering.

¹⁴ Yet Jerusalem* says, "The LORD has
    deserted us;
    the Lord has forgotten us."

¹⁵ "Never! Can a mother forget her nursing
    child?
    Can she feel no love for the child she has
    borne?
But even if that were possible,
    I would not forget you!
¹⁶ See, I have written your name on the palms
    of my hands.
    Always in my mind is a picture of
    Jerusalem's walls in ruins.
¹⁷ Soon your descendants will come back,
    and all who are trying to destroy you
    will go away.
¹⁸ Look around you and see,
    for all your children will come back
    to you.
As surely as I live," says the LORD,
    "they will be like jewels or bridal
    ornaments for you to display.

¹⁹ "Even the most desolate parts of your
    abandoned land
    will soon be crowded with your people.
Your enemies who enslaved you
    will be far away.
²⁰ The generations born in exile will return
    and say,
    'We need more room! It's crowded
    here!'
²¹ Then you will think to yourself,
    'Who has given me all these
    descendants?
For most of my children were killed,
    and the rest were carried away into
    exile.
I was left here all alone.
    Where did all these people come from?
Who bore these children?
    Who raised them for me?'"

²² This is what the Sovereign LORD says:
    "See, I will give a signal to the godless
    nations.
They will carry your little sons back to you
    in their arms;
    they will bring your daughters on their
    shoulders.
²³ Kings and queens will serve you
    and care for all your needs.
They will bow to the earth before you
    and lick the dust from your feet.
Then you will know that I am the LORD.
    Those who trust in me will never be put
    to shame."

49:8 Greek version reads *I heard you*. Compare 2 Cor 6:2.   49:12 As in Dead Sea Scrolls, which read *from the region of Aswan*, which is in southern Egypt. Masoretic Text reads *from the region of Sinim*.   49:14 Hebrew *Zion*.

²⁴ Who can snatch the plunder of war from
the hands of a warrior?
Who can demand that a tyrant* let his
captives go?
²⁵ But the LORD says,
"The captives of warriors will be released,
and the plunder of tyrants will be
retrieved.
For I will fight those who fight you,
and I will save your children.
²⁶ I will feed your enemies with their own
flesh.
They will be drunk with rivers of their
own blood.
All the world will know that I, the LORD,
am your Savior and your Redeemer,
the Mighty One of Israel.*"

50

This is what the LORD says:

"Was your mother sent away because
I divorced her?
Did I sell you as slaves to my creditors?
No, you were sold because of your sins.
And your mother, too, was taken
because of your sins.
² Why was no one there when I came?
Why didn't anyone answer when I
called?
Is it because I have no power to rescue?
No, that is not the reason!
For I can speak to the sea and make it
dry up!
I can turn rivers into deserts covered
with dying fish.
³ I dress the skies in darkness,
covering them with clothes of
mourning."

The LORD's Obedient Servant

⁴ The Sovereign LORD has given me his
words of wisdom,
so that I know how to comfort the
weary.
Morning by morning he wakens me
and opens my understanding to his will.
⁵ The Sovereign LORD has spoken to me,
and I have listened.
I have not rebelled or turned away.
⁶ I offered my back to those who beat me
and my cheeks to those who pulled out
my beard.
I did not hide my face
from mockery and spitting.

⁷ Because the Sovereign LORD helps me,
I will not be disgraced.
Therefore, I have set my face like a stone,
determined to do his will.
And I know that I will not be put to
shame.
⁸ He who gives me justice is near.
Who will dare to bring charges against
me now?
Where are my accusers?
Let them appear!
⁹ See, the Sovereign LORD is on my side!
Who will declare me guilty?
All my enemies will be destroyed
like old clothes that have been eaten
by moths!

¹⁰ Who among you fears the LORD
and obeys his servant?
If you are walking in darkness,
without a ray of light,
trust in the LORD
and rely on your God.
¹¹ But watch out, you who live in your own
light
and warm yourselves by your own
fires.
This is the reward you will receive
from me:
You will soon fall down in great
torment.

A Call to Trust the LORD

51

¹ "Listen to me, all who hope for
deliverance—
all who seek the LORD!
Consider the rock from which you were
cut,
the quarry from which you were mined.
² Yes, think about Abraham, your ancestor,
and Sarah, who gave birth to your
nation.
Abraham was only one man when I called
him.
But when I blessed him, he became a
great nation."

³ The LORD will comfort Israel* again
and have pity on her ruins.
Her desert will blossom like Eden,
her barren wilderness like the garden
of the LORD.
Joy and gladness will be found there.
Songs of thanksgiving will fill the air.

49:24 As in Dead Sea Scrolls, Syriac version, and Latin Vulgate (also see 49:25); Masoretic Text reads *a righteous person.*
49:26 Hebrew *of Jacob.* See note on 14:1.   51:3 Hebrew *Zion;* also in 51:16.

4 "Listen to me, my people.
  Hear me, Israel,
for my law will be proclaimed,
  and my justice will become a light to
    the nations.
5 My mercy and justice are coming soon.
  My salvation is on the way.
  My strong arm will bring justice to the
    nations.
All distant lands will look to me
  and wait in hope for my powerful arm.
6 Look up to the skies above,
  and gaze down on the earth below.
For the skies will disappear like smoke,
  and the earth will wear out like a piece
    of clothing.
The people of the earth will die like flies,
  but my salvation lasts forever.
My righteous rule will never end!

7 "Listen to me, you who know right from
    wrong,
  you who cherish my law in your
    hearts.
Do not be afraid of people's scorn,
  nor fear their insults.
8 For the moth will devour them as it
    devours clothing.
  The worm will eat at them as it eats
    wool.
But my righteousness will last forever.
  My salvation will continue from
    generation to generation."

9 Wake up, wake up, O LORD! Clothe
    yourself with strength!
  Flex your mighty right arm!
Rouse yourself as in the days of old
  when you slew Egypt, the dragon
    of the Nile.*
10 Are you not the same today,
    the one who dried up the sea,
  making a path of escape through the
    depths
  so that your people could cross over?
11 Those who have been ransomed by the
    LORD will return.
  They will enter Jerusalem* singing,
    crowned with everlasting joy.
  Sorrow and mourning will disappear,
    and they will be filled with joy and
      gladness.

12 "I, yes I, am the one who comforts you.
  So why are you afraid of mere humans,
    who wither like the grass and
      disappear?
13 Yet you have forgotten the LORD, your
    Creator,
  the one who stretched out the sky like
    a canopy
  and laid the foundations of the earth.
Will you remain in constant dread of
    human oppressors?
  Will you continue to fear the anger of
    your enemies?
Where is their fury and anger now?
  It is gone!
14 Soon all you captives will be released!
  Imprisonment, starvation, and death
    will not be your fate!
15 For I am the LORD your God,
  who stirs up the sea, causing its waves
    to roar.
  My name is the LORD of Heaven's Armies.
16 And I have put my words in your mouth
    and hidden you safely in my hand.
  I stretched out* the sky like a canopy
    and laid the foundations of the earth.
  I am the one who says to Israel,
    'You are my people!'"

17 Wake up, wake up, O Jerusalem!
  You have drunk the cup of the LORD's
    fury.
  You have drunk the cup of terror,
    tipping out its last drops.
18 Not one of your children is left alive
    to take your hand and guide you.
19 These two calamities have fallen on you:
    desolation and destruction, famine
      and war.
  And who is left to sympathize with you?
    Who is left to comfort you?*
20 For your children have fainted and lie in
    the streets,
  helpless as antelopes caught in a net.
  The LORD has poured out his fury;
    God has rebuked them.

21 But now listen to this, you afflicted ones
    who sit in a drunken stupor,
  though not from drinking wine.
22 This is what the Sovereign LORD,
    your God and Defender, says:

51:9 Hebrew *You slew Rahab; you pierced the dragon.* Rahab is the name of a mythical sea monster that represents chaos in ancient literature. The name is used here as a poetic name for Egypt.   51:11 Hebrew *Zion.*   51:16 As in Syriac version (see also 51:13); Hebrew reads *planted.*   51:19 As in Dead Sea Scrolls and Greek, Latin, and Syriac versions; Masoretic Text reads *How can I comfort you?*

"See, I have taken the terrible cup from
your hands.
You will drink no more of my fury.
²³ Instead, I will hand that cup to your
tormentors,
those who said, 'We will trample you
into the dust
and walk on your backs.'"

Deliverance for Jerusalem

52 ¹ Wake up, wake up, O Zion!
Clothe yourself with strength.
Put on your beautiful clothes, O holy city
of Jerusalem,
for unclean and godless people will
enter your gates no longer.
² Rise from the dust, O Jerusalem.
Sit in a place of honor.
Remove the chains of slavery from your
neck,
O captive daughter of Zion.
³ For this is what the LORD says:
"When I sold you into exile,
I received no payment.
Now I can redeem you
without having to pay for you."

⁴This is what the Sovereign LORD says:
"Long ago my people chose to live in Egypt.
Now they are oppressed by Assyria. ⁵What is
this?" asks the LORD. "Why are my people enslaved again? Those who rule them shout in
exultation.* My name is blasphemed all day
long.* ⁶But I will reveal my name to my people,
and they will come to know its power. Then at
last they will recognize that I am the one who
speaks to them."

⁷ How beautiful on the mountains
are the feet of the messenger who brings
good news,
the good news of peace and salvation,
the news that the God of Israel*
reigns!
⁸ The watchmen shout and sing with joy,
for before their very eyes
they see the LORD returning to
Jerusalem.*
⁹ Let the ruins of Jerusalem break into
joyful song,
for the LORD has comforted his people.
He has redeemed Jerusalem.

¹⁰ The LORD has demonstrated his holy power
before the eyes of all the nations.
All the ends of the earth will see
the victory of our God.

¹¹ Get out! Get out and leave your captivity,
where everything you touch is unclean.
Get out of there and purify yourselves,
you who carry home the sacred objects
of the LORD.
¹² You will not leave in a hurry,
running for your lives.
For the LORD will go ahead of you;
yes, the God of Israel will protect you
from behind.

The LORD's Suffering Servant

¹³ See, my servant will prosper;
he will be highly exalted.
¹⁴ But many were amazed when they saw
him.*
His face was so disfigured he seemed
hardly human,
and from his appearance, one would
scarcely know he was a man.
¹⁵ And he will startle* many nations.
Kings will stand speechless in his
presence.
For they will see what they had not been
told;
they will understand what they had not
heard about.*

53 ¹ Who has believed our message?
To whom has the LORD revealed
his powerful arm?
² My servant grew up in the LORD's presence
like a tender green shoot,
like a root in dry ground.
There was nothing beautiful or majestic
about his appearance,
nothing to attract us to him.
³ He was despised and rejected—
a man of sorrows, acquainted with
deepest grief.
We turned our backs on him and looked
the other way.
He was despised, and we did not care.

⁴ Yet it was our weaknesses he carried;
it was our sorrows* that weighed him
down.

52:5a As in Dead Sea Scrolls; Masoretic Text reads *Those who rule them wail.* **52:5b** Greek version reads *The Gentiles
continually blaspheme my name because of you.* Compare Rom 2:24. **52:7** Hebrew *of Zion.* **52:8** Hebrew *to Zion.* **52:14** As in
Syriac version; Hebrew reads *you.* **52:15a** Or *cleanse.* **52:15b** Greek version reads *Those who have never been told about him will
see, / and those who have never heard of him will understand.* Compare Rom 15:21. **53:4** Or *Yet it was our sicknesses he carried; / it was
our diseases.*

And we thought his troubles were a
    punishment from God,
    a punishment for his own sins!
5 But he was pierced for our rebellion,
    crushed for our sins.
He was beaten so we could be whole.
    He was whipped so we could be
    healed.
6 All of us, like sheep, have strayed away.
    We have left God's paths to follow
    our own.
Yet the LORD laid on him
    the sins of us all.

7 He was oppressed and treated harshly,
    yet he never said a word.
He was led like a lamb to the slaughter.
    And as a sheep is silent before the
    shearers,
    he did not open his mouth.
8 Unjustly condemned,
    he was led away.*
No one cared that he died without
    descendants,
    that his life was cut short in midstream.*
But he was struck down
    for the rebellion of my people.
9 He had done no wrong
    and had never deceived anyone.
But he was buried like a criminal;
    he was put in a rich man's grave.

10 But it was the LORD's good plan to crush
    him
    and cause him grief.
Yet when his life is made an offering
    for sin,
    he will have many descendants.
He will enjoy a long life,
    and the LORD's good plan will prosper
    in his hands.
11 When he sees all that is accomplished by
    his anguish,
    he will be satisfied.
And because of his experience,
    my righteous servant will make it
    possible
for many to be counted righteous,
    for he will bear all their sins.
12 I will give him the honors of a victorious
    soldier,
    because he exposed himself to death.
He was counted among the rebels.

He bore the sins of many and interceded
    for rebels.

Future Glory for Jerusalem

54 1 "Sing, O childless woman,
    you who have never given birth!
Break into loud and joyful song,
    O Jerusalem,
you who have never been in labor.
For the desolate woman now has more
    children
    than the woman who lives with her
    husband,"
    says the LORD.
2 "Enlarge your house; build an addition.
    Spread out your home, and spare no
    expense!
3 For you will soon be bursting at the seams.
    Your descendants will occupy other
    nations
    and resettle the ruined cities.

4 "Fear not; you will no longer live in
    shame.
    Don't be afraid; there is no more
    disgrace for you.
You will no longer remember the shame
    of your youth
    and the sorrows of widowhood.
5 For your Creator will be your husband;
    the LORD of Heaven's Armies is his
    name!
He is your Redeemer, the Holy One of
    Israel,
    the God of all the earth.
6 For the LORD has called you back from
    your grief—
    as though you were a young wife
    abandoned by her husband,"
    says your God.
7 "For a brief moment I abandoned you,
    but with great compassion I will take
    you back.
8 In a burst of anger I turned my face away
    for a little while.
But with everlasting love I will have
    compassion on you,"
    says the LORD, your Redeemer.

9 "Just as I swore in the time of Noah
    that I would never again let a flood cover
    the earth,
so now I swear

53:8a Greek version reads *He was humiliated and received no justice.* Compare Acts 8:33.   53:8b Or *As for his contemporaries, / who cared that his life was cut short in midstream?* Greek version reads *Who can speak of his descendants? / For his life was taken from the earth.* Compare Acts 8:33.

that I will never again be angry and
   punish you.
10 For the mountains may move
   and the hills disappear,
but even then my faithful love for you will
   remain.
   My covenant of blessing will never be
     broken,"
   says the LORD, who has mercy on you.

11 "O storm-battered city,
   troubled and desolate!
I will rebuild you with precious jewels
   and make your foundations from lapis
     lazuli.
12 I will make your towers of sparkling
     rubies,
   your gates of shining gems,
   and your walls of precious stones.
13 I will teach all your children,
   and they will enjoy great peace.
14 You will be secure under a government
     that is just and fair.
   Your enemies will stay far away.
You will live in peace,
   and terror will not come near.
15 If any nation comes to fight you,
   it is not because I sent them.
   Whoever attacks you will go down in
     defeat.

16 "I have created the blacksmith
   who fans the coals beneath the forge
and makes the weapons of destruction.
   And I have created the armies that
     destroy.
17 But in that coming day
   no weapon turned against you will
     succeed.
You will silence every voice
   raised up to accuse you.
These benefits are enjoyed by the servants
     of the LORD;
   their vindication will come from me.
   I, the LORD, have spoken!

Invitation to the LORD's Salvation

55 ¹ "Is anyone thirsty?
     Come and drink—
even if you have no money!
Come, take your choice of wine or milk—
   it's all free!
² Why spend your money on food that does
     not give you strength?
   Why pay for food that does you no
     good?

Listen to me, and you will eat what is
     good.
   You will enjoy the finest food.

³ "Come to me with your ears wide open.
   Listen, and you will find life.
I will make an everlasting covenant with
     you.
   I will give you all the unfailing love I
     promised to David.
⁴ See how I used him to display my power
     among the peoples.
   I made him a leader among the nations.
⁵ You also will command nations you do not
     know,
   and peoples unknown to you will come
     running to obey,
because I, the LORD your God,
   the Holy One of Israel, have made you
     glorious."

⁶ Seek the LORD while you can find him.
   Call on him now while he is near.
⁷ Let the wicked change their ways
   and banish the very thought of doing
     wrong.
Let them turn to the LORD that he may
     have mercy on them.
   Yes, turn to our God, for he will forgive
     generously.

⁸ "My thoughts are nothing like your
     thoughts," says the LORD.
   "And my ways are far beyond anything
     you could imagine.
⁹ For just as the heavens are higher than the
     earth,
   so my ways are higher than your ways
   and my thoughts higher than your
     thoughts.

10 "The rain and snow come down from the
     heavens
   and stay on the ground to water the
     earth.
They cause the grain to grow,
   producing seed for the farmer
   and bread for the hungry.
11 It is the same with my word.
   I send it out, and it always produces
     fruit.
It will accomplish all I want it to,
   and it will prosper everywhere I send it.
12 You will live in joy and peace.
   The mountains and hills will burst into
     song,

and the trees of the field will clap their
hands!
13 Where once there were thorns, cypress
trees will grow.
Where nettles grew, myrtles will
sprout up.
These events will bring great honor to the
LORD's name;
they will be an everlasting sign of his
power and love."

Blessings for All Nations

56 This is what the LORD says:

"Be just and fair to all.
Do what is right and good,
for I am coming soon to rescue you
and to display my righteousness among
you.
2 Blessed are all those
who are careful to do this.
Blessed are those who honor my Sabbath
days of rest
and keep themselves from doing wrong.

3 "Don't let foreigners who commit
themselves to the LORD say,
'The LORD will never let me be part of
his people.'
And don't let the eunuchs say,
'I'm a dried-up tree with no children
and no future.'
4 For this is what the LORD says:
I will bless those eunuchs
who keep my Sabbath days holy
and who choose to do what pleases me
and commit their lives to me.
5 I will give them—within the walls of my
house—
a memorial and a name
far greater than sons and daughters
could give.
For the name I give them is an everlasting
one.
It will never disappear!

6 "I will also bless the foreigners who
commit themselves to the LORD,
who serve him and love his name,
who worship him and do not desecrate the
Sabbath day of rest,
and who hold fast to my covenant.
7 I will bring them to my holy mountain of
Jerusalem
and will fill them with joy in my house
of prayer.

I will accept their burnt offerings and
sacrifices,
because my Temple will be called a
house of prayer for all nations.
8 For the Sovereign LORD,
who brings back the outcasts of Israel,
says:
I will bring others, too,
besides my people Israel."

Sinful Leaders Condemned

9 Come, wild animals of the field!
Come, wild animals of the forest!
Come and devour my people!
10 For the leaders of my people—
the LORD's watchmen, his shepherds—
are blind and ignorant.
They are like silent watchdogs
that give no warning when danger
comes.
They love to lie around, sleeping and
dreaming.
11 Like greedy dogs, they are never
satisfied.
They are ignorant shepherds,
all following their own path
and intent on personal gain.
12 "Come," they say, "let's get some wine and
have a party.
Let's all get drunk.
Then tomorrow we'll do it again
and have an even bigger party!"

57 1 Good people pass away;
the godly often die before their
time.
But no one seems to care or wonder why.
No one seems to understand
that God is protecting them from the
evil to come.
2 For those who follow godly paths
will rest in peace when they die.

Idolatrous Worship Condemned

3 "But you—come here, you witches'
children,
you offspring of adulterers and
prostitutes!
4 Whom do you mock,
making faces and sticking out your
tongues?
You children of sinners and liars!
5 You worship your idols with great
passion
beneath the oaks and under every
green tree.

You sacrifice your children down in the
valleys,
among the jagged rocks in the cliffs.
⁶ Your gods are the smooth stones in the
valleys.
You worship them with liquid offerings
and grain offerings.
They, not I, are your inheritance.
Do you think all this makes me happy?
⁷ You have committed adultery on every
high mountain.
There you have worshiped idols
and have been unfaithful to me.
⁸ You have put pagan symbols
on your doorposts and behind your
doors.
You have left me
and climbed into bed with these
detestable gods.
You have committed yourselves to them.
You love to look at their naked bodies.
⁹ You have gone to Molech*
with olive oil and many perfumes,
sending your agents far and wide,
even to the world of the dead.*
¹⁰ You grew weary in your search,
but you never gave up.
Desire gave you renewed strength,
and you did not grow weary.

¹¹ "Are you afraid of these idols?
Do they terrify you?
Is that why you have lied to me
and forgotten me and my words?
Is it because of my long silence
that you no longer fear me?
¹² Now I will expose your so-called good
deeds.
None of them will help you.
¹³ Let's see if your idols can save you
when you cry to them for help.
Why, a puff of wind can knock them down!
If you just breathe on them, they fall
over!
But whoever trusts in me will inherit the
land
and possess my holy mountain."

God Forgives the Repentant

¹⁴ God says, "Rebuild the road!
Clear away the rocks and stones
so my people can return from captivity."
¹⁵ The high and lofty one who lives in
eternity,
the Holy One, says this:

"I live in the high and holy place
with those whose spirits are contrite
and humble.
I restore the crushed spirit of the humble
and revive the courage of those with
repentant hearts.
¹⁶ For I will not fight against you forever;
I will not always be angry.
If I were, all people would pass away—
all the souls I have made.
¹⁷ I was angry,
so I punished these greedy people.
I withdrew from them,
but they kept going on their own
stubborn way.
¹⁸ I have seen what they do,
but I will heal them anyway!
I will lead them.
I will comfort those who mourn,
¹⁹ bringing words of praise to their lips.
May they have abundant peace, both near
and far,"
says the LORD, who heals them.
²⁰ "But those who still reject me are like the
restless sea,
which is never still
but continually churns up mud and
dirt.
²¹ There is no peace for the wicked,"
says my God.

True and False Worship

58 ¹ "Shout with the voice of a trumpet
blast.
Shout aloud! Don't be timid.
Tell my people Israel* of their sins!
² Yet they act so pious!
They come to the Temple every day
and seem delighted to learn all
about me.
They act like a righteous nation
that would never abandon the laws of
its God.
They ask me to take action on their behalf,
pretending they want to be near me.
³ 'We have fasted before you!' they say.
'Why aren't you impressed?
We have been very hard on ourselves,
and you don't even notice it!'

"I will tell you why!" I respond.
"It's because you are fasting to please
yourselves.
Even while you fast,
you keep oppressing your workers.

57:9a Or *to the king.*   57:9b Hebrew *to Sheol.*   58:1 Hebrew *Jacob.* See note on 14:1.

⁴ What good is fasting
　　when you keep on fighting and
　　　quarreling?
　This kind of fasting
　　will never get you anywhere with me.
⁵ You humble yourselves
　　by going through the motions of
　　　penance,
　bowing your heads
　　like reeds bending in the wind.
　You dress in burlap
　　and cover yourselves with ashes.
　Is this what you call fasting?
　　Do you really think this will please the
　　　LORD?

⁶ "No, this is the kind of fasting I want:
　Free those who are wrongly imprisoned;
　　lighten the burden of those who work
　　　for you.
　Let the oppressed go free,
　　and remove the chains that bind people.
⁷ Share your food with the hungry,
　　and give shelter to the homeless.
　Give clothes to those who need them,
　　and do not hide from relatives who need
　　　your help.

⁸ "Then your salvation will come like the
　　dawn,
　　and your wounds will quickly heal.
　Your godliness will lead you forward,
　　and the glory of the LORD will protect
　　　you from behind.
⁹ Then when you call, the LORD will answer.
　　'Yes, I am here,' he will quickly reply.

　"Remove the heavy yoke of oppression.
　　Stop pointing your finger and spreading
　　　vicious rumors!
¹⁰ Feed the hungry,
　　and help those in trouble.
　Then your light will shine out from the
　　darkness,
　　and the darkness around you will be as
　　　bright as noon.
¹¹ The LORD will guide you continually,
　　giving you water when you are dry
　　and restoring your strength.
　You will be like a well-watered garden,
　　like an ever-flowing spring.
¹² Some of you will rebuild the deserted
　　ruins of your cities.
　　Then you will be known as a rebuilder
　　　of walls
　　and a restorer of homes.

¹³ "Keep the Sabbath day holy.
　　Don't pursue your own interests on
　　　that day,
　but enjoy the Sabbath
　　and speak of it with delight as the
　　　LORD's holy day.
　Honor the Sabbath in everything you do
　　on that day,
　　and don't follow your own desires or
　　　talk idly.
¹⁴ Then the LORD will be your delight.
　　I will give you great honor
　and satisfy you with the inheritance I
　　promised to your ancestor Jacob.
　　I, the LORD, have spoken!"

Warnings against Sin

59 ¹ Listen! The LORD's arm is not too
　　　weak to save you,
　　nor is his ear too deaf to hear you call.
² It's your sins that have cut you off from
　　God.
　Because of your sins, he has turned
　　away
　　and will not listen anymore.
³ Your hands are the hands of murderers,
　　and your fingers are filthy with sin.
　Your lips are full of lies,
　　and your mouth spews corruption.

⁴ No one cares about being fair and honest.
　　The people's lawsuits are based on lies.
　They conceive evil deeds
　　and then give birth to sin.
⁵ They hatch deadly snakes
　　and weave spiders' webs.
　Whoever eats their eggs will die;
　　whoever cracks them will hatch a viper.
⁶ Their webs can't be made into clothing,
　　and nothing they do is productive.
　All their activity is filled with sin,
　　and violence is their trademark.
⁷ Their feet run to do evil,
　　and they rush to commit murder.
　They think only about sinning.
　　Misery and destruction always follow
　　　them.
⁸ They don't know where to find peace
　　or what it means to be just and good.
　They have mapped out crooked roads,
　　and no one who follows them knows
　　　a moment's peace.

⁹ So there is no justice among us,
　　and we know nothing about right
　　　living.

We look for light but find only darkness.
We look for bright skies but walk in
gloom.
10 We grope like the blind along a wall,
feeling our way like people without eyes.
Even at brightest noontime,
we stumble as though it were dark.
Among the living,
we are like the dead.
11 We growl like hungry bears;
we moan like mournful doves.
We look for justice, but it never comes.
We look for rescue, but it is far away
from us.
12 For our sins are piled up before God
and testify against us.
Yes, we know what sinners we are.
13 We know we have rebelled and have
denied the LORD.
We have turned our backs on our God.
We know how unfair and oppressive we
have been,
carefully planning our deceitful lies.
14 Our courts oppose the righteous,
and justice is nowhere to be found.
Truth stumbles in the streets,
and honesty has been outlawed.
15 Yes, truth is gone,
and anyone who renounces evil is
attacked.

The LORD looked and was displeased
to find there was no justice.
16 He was amazed to see that no one
intervened
to help the oppressed.
So he himself stepped in to save them with
his strong arm,
and his justice sustained him.
17 He put on righteousness as his body armor
and placed the helmet of salvation on
his head.
He clothed himself with a robe of vengeance
and wrapped himself in a cloak of
divine passion.
18 He will repay his enemies for their evil
deeds.
His fury will fall on his foes.
He will pay them back even to the ends
of the earth.
19 In the west, people will respect the name
of the LORD;
in the east, they will glorify him.

For he will come like a raging flood tide
driven by the breath of the LORD.*

20 "The Redeemer will come to Jerusalem
to buy back those in Israel
who have turned from their sins,"*
says the LORD.

21 "And this is my covenant with them," says
the LORD. "My Spirit will not leave them, and
neither will these words I have given you. They
will be on your lips and on the lips of your children and your children's children forever. I, the
LORD, have spoken!

Future Glory for Jerusalem

60 1 "Arise, Jerusalem! Let your light
shine for all to see.
For the glory of the LORD rises to shine
on you.
2 Darkness as black as night covers all the
nations of the earth,
but the glory of the LORD rises and
appears over you.
3 All nations will come to your light;
mighty kings will come to see your
radiance.

4 "Look and see, for everyone is coming
home!
Your sons are coming from distant lands;
your little daughters will be carried
home.
5 Your eyes will shine,
and your heart will thrill with joy,
for merchants from around the world will
come to you.
They will bring you the wealth of many
lands.
6 Vast caravans of camels will converge on
you,
the camels of Midian and Ephah.
The people of Sheba will bring gold and
frankincense
and will come worshiping the LORD.
7 The flocks of Kedar will be given to you,
and the rams of Nebaioth will be
brought for my altars.
I will accept their offerings,
and I will make my Temple glorious.

8 "And what do I see flying like clouds to
Israel,

59:19 Or When the enemy comes like a raging flood tide, / the Spirit of the LORD will drive him back.   **59:20** Hebrew The Redeemer will
come to Zion / to buy back those in Jacob / who have turned from their sins. Greek version reads The one who rescues will come on behalf
of Zion, / and he will turn Jacob away from ungodliness. Compare Rom 11:26.

like doves to their nests?

⁹ They are ships from the ends of the
earth,
from lands that trust in me,
led by the great ships of Tarshish.
They are bringing the people of Israel
home from far away,
carrying their silver and gold.
They will honor the LORD your God,
the Holy One of Israel,
for he has filled you with splendor.

¹⁰ "Foreigners will come to rebuild your
towns,
and their kings will serve you.
For though I have destroyed you in my
anger,
I will now have mercy on you through
my grace.
¹¹ Your gates will stay open day and night
to receive the wealth of many lands.
The kings of the world will be led as
captives
in a victory procession.
¹² For the nations that refuse to serve you
will be destroyed.

¹³ "The glory of Lebanon will be yours—
the forests of cypress, fir, and pine—
to beautify my sanctuary.
My Temple will be glorious!
¹⁴ The descendants of your tormentors
will come and bow before you.
Those who despised you
will kiss your feet.
They will call you the City of the LORD,
and Zion of the Holy One of Israel.

¹⁵ "Though you were once despised and
hated,
with no one traveling through you,
I will make you beautiful forever,
a joy to all generations.
¹⁶ Powerful kings and mighty nations
will satisfy your every need,
as though you were a child
nursing at the breast of a queen.
You will know at last that I, the LORD,
am your Savior and your Redeemer,
the Mighty One of Israel.*
¹⁷ I will exchange your bronze for gold,
your iron for silver,
your wood for bronze,
and your stones for iron.

I will make peace your leader
and righteousness your ruler.
¹⁸ Violence will disappear from your land;
the desolation and destruction of war
will end.
Salvation will surround you like city walls,
and praise will be on the lips of all who
enter there.

¹⁹ "No longer will you need the sun to shine
by day,
nor the moon to give its light by night,
for the LORD your God will be your
everlasting light,
and your God will be your glory.
²⁰ Your sun will never set;
your moon will not go down.
For the LORD will be your everlasting
light.
Your days of mourning will come to
an end.
²¹ All your people will be righteous.
They will possess their land forever,
for I will plant them there with my own
hands
in order to bring myself glory.
²² The smallest family will become a
thousand people,
and the tiniest group will become a
mighty nation.
At the right time, I, the LORD, will
make it happen."

Good News for the Oppressed

61 ¹ The Spirit of the Sovereign LORD
is upon me,
for the LORD has anointed me
to bring good news to the poor.
He has sent me to comfort the
brokenhearted
and to proclaim that captives will be
released
and prisoners will be freed.*
² He has sent me to tell those who mourn
that the time of the LORD's favor has
come,*
and with it, the day of God's anger
against their enemies.
³ To all who mourn in Israel,*
he will give a crown of beauty for ashes,
a joyous blessing instead of mourning,
festive praise instead of despair.
In their righteousness, they will be like
great oaks

60:16 Hebrew *of Jacob.* See note on 14:1. **61:1** Greek version reads *and the blind will see.* Compare Luke 4:18. **61:2** Or *to proclaim the acceptable year of the LORD.* **61:3** Hebrew *in Zion.*

that the LORD has planted for his own
glory.

4 They will rebuild the ancient ruins,
repairing cities destroyed long ago.
They will revive them,
though they have been deserted for
many generations.
5 Foreigners will be your servants.
They will feed your flocks
and plow your fields
and tend your vineyards.
6 You will be called priests of the LORD,
ministers of our God.
You will feed on the treasures of the nations
and boast in their riches.
7 Instead of shame and dishonor,
you will enjoy a double share of honor.
You will possess a double portion of
prosperity in your land,
and everlasting joy will be yours.

8 "For I, the LORD, love justice.
I hate robbery and wrongdoing.
I will faithfully reward my people for their
suffering
and make an everlasting covenant with
them.
9 Their descendants will be recognized
and honored among the nations.
Everyone will realize that they are a people
the LORD has blessed."

10 I am overwhelmed with joy in the LORD
my God!
For he has dressed me with the clothing
of salvation
and draped me in a robe of
righteousness.
I am like a bridegroom dressed for his
wedding
or a bride with her jewels.
11 The Sovereign LORD will show his justice
to the nations of the world.
Everyone will praise him!
His righteousness will be like a garden in
early spring,
with plants springing up everywhere.

Isaiah's Prayer for Jerusalem

62 1 Because I love Zion,
I will not keep still.
Because my heart yearns for Jerusalem,
I cannot remain silent.

I will not stop praying for her
until her righteousness shines like the
dawn,
and her salvation blazes like a burning
torch.
2 The nations will see your righteousness.
World leaders will be blinded by your
glory.
And you will be given a new name
by the LORD's own mouth.
3 The LORD will hold you in his hand for all
to see—
a splendid crown in the hand of God.
4 Never again will you be called "The
Forsaken City"*
or "The Desolate Land."*
Your new name will be "The City of God's
Delight"*
and "The Bride of God,"*
for the LORD delights in you
and will claim you as his bride.
5 Your children will commit themselves to
you, O Jerusalem,
just as a young man commits himself
to his bride.
Then God will rejoice over you
as a bridegroom rejoices over his
bride.

6 O Jerusalem, I have posted watchmen
on your walls;
they will pray day and night,
continually.
Take no rest, all you who pray to the
LORD.
7 Give the LORD no rest until he completes
his work,
until he makes Jerusalem the pride of
the earth.
8 The LORD has sworn to Jerusalem by his
own strength:
"I will never again hand you over to
your enemies.
Never again will foreign warriors come
and take away your grain and new wine.
9 You raised the grain, and you will eat it,
praising the LORD.
Within the courtyards of the Temple,
you yourselves will drink the wine you
have pressed."

10 Go out through the gates!
Prepare the highway for my people to
return!

62:4a Hebrew *Azubah*, which means "forsaken."   62:4b Hebrew *Shemamah*, which means "desolate."   62:4c Hebrew
Hephzibah, which means "my delight is in her."   62:4d Hebrew *Beulah*, which means "married."

Smooth out the road; pull out the
boulders;
raise a flag for all the nations to see.
[11] The LORD has sent this message to every
land:
"Tell the people of Israel,*
'Look, your Savior is coming.
See, he brings his reward with him as
he comes.'"
[12] They will be called "The Holy People"
and "The People Redeemed by the
LORD."
And Jerusalem will be known as "The
Desirable Place"
and "The City No Longer Forsaken."

Judgment against the LORD's Enemies

63
[1] Who is this who comes from Edom,
from the city of Bozrah,
with his clothing stained red?
Who is this in royal robes,
marching in his great strength?

"It is I, the LORD, announcing your
salvation!
It is I, the LORD, who has the power
to save!"

[2] Why are your clothes so red,
as if you have been treading out
grapes?

[3] "I have been treading the winepress alone;
no one was there to help me.
In my anger I have trampled my enemies
as if they were grapes.
In my fury I have trampled my foes.
Their blood has stained my clothes.
[4] For the time has come for me to avenge my
people,
to ransom them from their oppressors.
[5] I was amazed to see that no one intervened
to help the oppressed.
So I myself stepped in to save them with
my strong arm,
and my wrath sustained me.
[6] I crushed the nations in my anger
and made them stagger and fall to the
ground,
spilling their blood upon the earth."

Praise for Deliverance

[7] I will tell of the LORD's unfailing love.
I will praise the LORD for all he has
done.

I will rejoice in his great goodness to
Israel,
which he has granted according to his
mercy and love.
[8] He said, "They are my very own people.
Surely they will not betray me again."
And he became their Savior.
[9] In all their suffering he also suffered,
and he personally* rescued them.
In his love and mercy he redeemed them.
He lifted them up and carried them
through all the years.
[10] But they rebelled against him
and grieved his Holy Spirit.
So he became their enemy
and fought against them.

[11] Then they remembered those days of old
when Moses led his people out of Egypt.
They cried out, "Where is the one who
brought Israel through the sea,
with Moses as their shepherd?
Where is the one who sent his Holy Spirit
to be among his people?
[12] Where is the one whose power was
displayed
when Moses lifted up his hand—
the one who divided the sea before them,
making himself famous forever?
[13] Where is the one who led them through
the bottom of the sea?
They were like fine stallions
racing through the desert, never
stumbling.
[14] As with cattle going down into a peaceful
valley,
the Spirit of the LORD gave them rest.
You led your people, LORD,
and gained a magnificent reputation."

Prayer for Mercy and Pardon

[15] LORD, look down from heaven;
look from your holy, glorious home,
and see us.
Where is the passion and the might
you used to show on our behalf?
Where are your mercy and compassion
now?
[16] Surely you are still our Father!
Even if Abraham and Jacob* would
disown us,
LORD, you would still be our Father.
You are our Redeemer from ages past.
[17] LORD, why have you allowed us to turn
from your path?

62:11 Hebrew *Tell the daughter of Zion.*   63:9 Hebrew *and the angel of his presence.*   63:16 Hebrew *Israel.* See note on 14:1.

Why have you given us stubborn hearts
so we no longer fear you?
Return and help us, for we are your
servants,
the tribes that are your special
possession.
18 How briefly your holy people possessed
your holy place,
and now our enemies have destroyed it.
19 Sometimes it seems as though we never
belonged to you,
as though we had never been known as
your people.

64

1*Oh, that you would burst from the
heavens and come down!
How the mountains would quake in
your presence!
2*As fire causes wood to burn
and water to boil,
your coming would make the nations
tremble.
Then your enemies would learn the
reason for your fame!
3 When you came down long ago,
you did awesome deeds beyond our
highest expectations.
And oh, how the mountains quaked!
4 For since the world began,
no ear has heard
and no eye has seen a God like you,
who works for those who wait for him!
5 You welcome those who gladly do good,
who follow godly ways.
But you have been very angry with us,
for we are not godly.
We are constant sinners;
how can people like us be saved?
6 We are all infected and impure with sin.
When we display our righteous deeds,
they are nothing but filthy rags.
Like autumn leaves, we wither and fall,
and our sins sweep us away like the
wind.
7 Yet no one calls on your name
or pleads with you for mercy.
Therefore, you have turned away from us
and turned us over* to our sins.

8 And yet, O LORD, you are our Father.
We are the clay, and you are the potter.
We all are formed by your hand.

9 Don't be so angry with us, LORD.
Please don't remember our sins forever.
Look at us, we pray,
and see that we are all your people.
10 Your holy cities are destroyed.
Zion is a wilderness;
yes, Jerusalem is a desolate ruin.
11 The holy and beautiful Temple
where our ancestors praised you
has been burned down,
and all the things of beauty are
destroyed.
12 After all this, LORD, must you still refuse
to help us?
Will you continue to be silent and
punish us?

Judgment and Final Salvation

65

The LORD says,

"I was ready to respond, but no one
asked for help.
I was ready to be found, but no one was
looking for me.
I said, 'Here I am, here I am!'
to a nation that did not call on my
name.*
2 All day long I opened my arms to a
rebellious people.*
But they follow their own evil paths
and their own crooked schemes.
3 All day long they insult me to my face
by worshiping idols in their sacred
gardens.
They burn incense on pagan altars.
4 At night they go out among the graves,
worshiping the dead.
They eat the flesh of pigs
and make stews with other forbidden
foods.
5 Yet they say to each other,
'Don't come too close or you will
defile me!
I am holier than you!'
These people are a stench in my nostrils,
an acrid smell that never goes away.

6 "Look, my decree is written out* in front
of me:
I will not stand silent;
I will repay them in full!
Yes, I will repay them—

64:1 In the Hebrew text this verse is included in 63:19.   64:2 Verses 64:2-12 are numbered 64:1-11 in Hebrew text.   64:7 As in Greek, Syriac, and Aramaic versions; Hebrew reads *melted us*.   65:1 Or *to a nation that did not bear my name*.   65:1-2 Greek version reads *I was found by people who were not looking for me. / I showed myself to those who were not asking for me. / All day long I opened my arms to them, / but they were disobedient and rebellious.* Compare Rom 10:20-21.   65:6 Or *their sins are written out;* Hebrew reads *it stands written*.

⁷ both for their own sins
      and for those of their ancestors,"
   says the LORD.
"For they also burned incense on the
      mountains
   and insulted me on the hills.
   I will pay them back in full!

⁸ "But I will not destroy them all,"
   says the LORD.
"For just as good grapes are found among
      a cluster of bad ones
   (and someone will say, 'Don't throw
      them all away—
   some of those grapes are good!'),
   so I will not destroy all Israel.
   For I still have true servants there.
⁹ I will preserve a remnant of the people
      of Israel*
   and of Judah to possess my land.
   Those I choose will inherit it,
      and my servants will live there.
¹⁰ The plain of Sharon will again be filled
      with flocks
   for my people who have searched for me,
   and the valley of Achor will be a place
      to pasture herds.

¹¹ "But because the rest of you have forsaken
      the LORD
   and have forgotten his Temple,
   and because you have prepared feasts to
      honor the god of Fate
   and have offered mixed wine to the god
      of Destiny,
¹² now I will 'destine' you for the sword.
   All of you will bow down before the
      executioner.
   For when I called, you did not answer.
      When I spoke, you did not listen.
   You deliberately sinned—before my very
      eyes—
   and chose to do what you know I
      despise."

¹³ Therefore, this is what the Sovereign LORD
      says:
"My servants will eat,
      but you will starve.
   My servants will drink,
      but you will be thirsty.
   My servants will rejoice,
      but you will be sad and ashamed.
¹⁴ My servants will sing for joy,
      but you will cry in sorrow and despair.

¹⁵ Your name will be a curse word among my
      people,
   for the Sovereign LORD will destroy you
      and will call his true servants by another
      name.
¹⁶ All who invoke a blessing or take an oath
      will do so by the God of truth.
   For I will put aside my anger
      and forget the evil of earlier days.

¹⁷ "Look! I am creating new heavens and a
      new earth,
   and no one will even think about the old
      ones anymore.
¹⁸ Be glad; rejoice forever in my creation!
   And look! I will create Jerusalem as a
      place of happiness.
   Her people will be a source of joy.
¹⁹ I will rejoice over Jerusalem
      and delight in my people.
   And the sound of weeping and crying
      will be heard in it no more.

²⁰ "No longer will babies die when only a few
      days old.
   No longer will adults die before they
      have lived a full life.
   No longer will people be considered old at
      one hundred!
   Only the cursed will die that young!
²¹ In those days people will live in the houses
      they build
   and eat the fruit of their own vineyards.
²² Unlike the past, invaders will not take
      their houses
   and confiscate their vineyards.
   For my people will live as long as trees,
   and my chosen ones will have time to
      enjoy their hard-won gains.
²³ They will not work in vain,
   and their children will not be doomed
      to misfortune.
   For they are people blessed by the LORD,
   and their children, too, will be blessed.
²⁴ I will answer them before they even call
      to me.
   While they are still talking about their
      needs,
   I will go ahead and answer their prayers!
²⁵ The wolf and the lamb will feed together.
   The lion will eat hay like a cow.
      But the snakes will eat dust.
   In those days no one will be hurt or
      destroyed on my holy mountain.
   I, the LORD, have spoken!"

65:9 Hebrew *remnant of Jacob.* See note on 14:1.

66

This is what the LORD says:

"Heaven is my throne,
and the earth is my footstool.
Could you build me a temple as good
as that?
Could you build me such a resting
place?
² My hands have made both heaven and
earth;
they and everything in them are
mine.*
I, the LORD, have spoken!

"I will bless those who have humble and
contrite hearts,
who tremble at my word.
³ But those who choose their own ways—
delighting in their detestable sins—
will not have their offerings accepted.
When such people sacrifice a bull,
it is no more acceptable than a human
sacrifice.
When they sacrifice a lamb,
it's as though they had sacrificed a dog!
When they bring an offering of grain,
they might as well offer the blood of
a pig.
When they burn frankincense,
it's as if they had blessed an idol.
⁴ I will send them great trouble—
all the things they feared.
For when I called, they did not answer.
When I spoke, they did not listen.
They deliberately sinned before my
very eyes
and chose to do what they know
I despise."

⁵ Hear this message from the LORD,
all you who tremble at his words:
"Your own people hate you
and throw you out for being loyal to
my name.
'Let the LORD be honored!' they scoff.
'Be joyful in him!'
But they will be put to shame.
⁶ What is all the commotion in the city?
What is that terrible noise from the
Temple?
It is the voice of the LORD
taking vengeance against his enemies.

⁷ "Before the birth pains even begin,
Jerusalem gives birth to a son.

⁸ Who has ever seen anything as strange as
this?
Who ever heard of such a thing?
Has a nation ever been born in a single day?
Has a country ever come forth in a mere
moment?
But by the time Jerusalem's* birth pains
begin,
her children will be born.
⁹ Would I ever bring this nation to the point
of birth
and then not deliver it?" asks the LORD.
"No! I would never keep this nation
from being born,"
says your God.

¹⁰ "Rejoice with Jerusalem!
Be glad with her, all you who love her
and all you who mourn for her.
¹¹ Drink deeply of her glory
even as an infant drinks at its mother's
comforting breasts."

¹² This is what the LORD says:
"I will give Jerusalem a river of peace and
prosperity.
The wealth of the nations will flow
to her.
Her children will be nursed at her breasts,
carried in her arms, and held on her lap.
¹³ I will comfort you there in Jerusalem
as a mother comforts her child."

¹⁴ When you see these things, your heart will
rejoice.
You will flourish like the grass!
Everyone will see the LORD's hand of
blessing on his servants—
and his anger against his enemies.
¹⁵ See, the LORD is coming with fire,
and his swift chariots roar like a
whirlwind.
He will bring punishment with the fury
of his anger
and the flaming fire of his hot rebuke.
¹⁶ The LORD will punish the world by fire
and by his sword.
He will judge the earth,
and many will be killed by him.

¹⁷"Those who 'consecrate' and 'purify' themselves in a sacred garden with its idol in the
center—feasting on pork and rats and other
detestable meats—will come to a terrible end,"
says the LORD.

66:2 As in Greek, Latin, and Syriac versions; Hebrew reads *these things are.*   66:8 Hebrew *Zion's.*

18"I can see what they are doing, and I know what they are thinking. So I will gather all nations and peoples together, and they will see my glory. 19I will perform a sign among them. And I will send those who survive to be messengers to the nations—to Tarshish, to the Libyans* and Lydians* (who are famous as archers), to Tubal and Greece,* and to all the lands beyond the sea that have not heard of my fame or seen my glory. There they will declare my glory to the nations. 20They will bring the remnant of your people back from every nation. They will bring them to my holy mountain in Jerusalem as an offering to the LORD. They will ride on horses, in chariots and wagons, and on mules and camels," says the LORD. 21"And I will appoint some of them to be my priests and Levites. I, the LORD, have spoken!

22 "As surely as my new heavens and earth
        will remain,
    so will you always be my people,
    with a name that will never disappear,"
        says the LORD.
23 "All humanity will come to
        worship me
    from week to week
    and from month to month.
24 And as they go out, they will see
        the dead bodies of those who have
        rebelled against me.
    For the worms that devour them will
        never die,
    and the fire that burns them will never
        go out.
    All who pass by
        will view them with utter horror."

66:19a As in some Greek manuscripts, which read *Put* [that is, *Libya*]; Hebrew reads *Pul*.   66:19b Hebrew *Lud*.
66:19c Hebrew *Javan*.

Jeremiah

BY ANY HUMAN MEASURE, the prophet Jeremiah was a colossal failure. For most of his life he was poor, unpopular, isolated, and persecuted. Because of his troubles and sorrow for his land, Jeremiah has often been called "the weeping prophet." Jeremiah lived in Judah for forty years just before the people were exiled to Babylon, and his prophecies were collected into the book that bears his name. The main message of his prophecies is simple: It is too late to avoid God's discipline, so accept it and turn from your sins. After a time of punishment, however, God would restore Israel and Judah. Jeremiah often used figurative actions to communicate this message, such as shattering a clay jar to show how God would shatter Jerusalem. Unfortunately, Jeremiah's messages were not well received. His audience discounted his warnings, locked him up in stocks, and even threatened his life. Jeremiah lived to see the Babylonian armies' invasion, the deportation of his people, the slaughter of Jerusalem's inhabitants, and the destruction of the Temple.

■ **Author:** Jeremiah or his followers

■ **Date Written:** During Jeremiah's ministry, about 627 to 586 BC

■ **Purpose:** To urge people to repent of their sins and turn back to God

■ **Themes:** Consequences of sin, impending judgment, God's dominion, new hearts, restoration

■ **Outline**
1:1–25:38 Prophecies concerning Judah
26:1–42:22 Prophecies at the end of Judah's existence
43:1–45:5 Jeremiah's prophecies in Egypt
46:1–51:64 Prophecies concerning the nations
52:1-34 Historical appendix

---

1 These are the words of Jeremiah son of Hilkiah, one of the priests from the town of Anathoth in the land of Benjamin. ²The LORD first gave messages to Jeremiah during the thirteenth year of the reign of Josiah son of Amon, king of Judah.* ³The LORD's messages continued throughout the reign of King Jehoiakim, Josiah's son, until the eleventh year of the reign of King Zedekiah, another of Josiah's sons. In August* of that eleventh year the people of Jerusalem were taken away as captives.

Jeremiah's Call and First Visions
⁴The LORD gave me this message:

5 "I knew you before I formed you in your
   mother's womb.

Before you were born I set you
   apart
and appointed you as my prophet to
   the nations."

⁶"O Sovereign LORD," I said, "I can't speak for you! I'm too young!"
⁷The LORD replied, "Don't say, 'I'm too young,' for you must go wherever I send you and say whatever I tell you. ⁸And don't be afraid of the people, for I will be with you and will protect you. I, the LORD, have spoken!" ⁹Then the LORD reached out and touched my mouth and said,

"Look, I have put my words in your
   mouth!

1:2 The thirteenth year of Josiah's reign was 627 B.C. 1:3 Hebrew *In the fifth month,* of the ancient Hebrew lunar calendar. A number of events in Jeremiah can be cross-checked with dates in surviving Babylonian records and related accurately to our modern calendar. The fifth month in the eleventh year of Zedekiah's reign occurred within the months of August and September 586 B.C. Also see 52:12 and the note there.

¹⁰ Today I appoint you to stand up
    against nations and kingdoms.
Some you must uproot and tear
    down,
    destroy and overthrow.
Others you must build up
    and plant."

¹¹Then the LORD said to me, "Look, Jeremiah! What do you see?"

And I replied, "I see a branch from an almond tree."

¹²And the LORD said, "That's right, and it means that I am watching,* and I will certainly carry out all my plans."

¹³Then the LORD spoke to me again and asked, "What do you see now?"

And I replied, "I see a pot of boiling water, spilling from the north."

¹⁴"Yes," the LORD said, "for terror from the north will boil out on the people of this land. ¹⁵Listen! I am calling the armies of the kingdoms of the north to come to Jerusalem. I, the LORD, have spoken!

"They will set their thrones
    at the gates of the city.
They will attack its walls
    and all the other towns of Judah.
¹⁶ I will pronounce judgment
    on my people for all their evil—
for deserting me and burning incense
    to other gods.
    Yes, they worship idols made with their
    own hands!

¹⁷ "Get up and prepare for action.
    Go out and tell them everything I tell
    you to say.
Do not be afraid of them,
    or I will make you look foolish in front
    of them.
¹⁸ For see, today I have made you strong
    like a fortified city that cannot be
    captured,
    like an iron pillar or a bronze wall.
You will stand against the whole
    land—
    the kings, officials, priests, and people
    of Judah.
¹⁹ They will fight you, but they will fail.
    For I am with you, and I will take care
    of you.
I, the LORD, have spoken!"

The LORD's Case against His People

2 The LORD gave me another message. He said, ²"Go and shout this message to Jerusalem. This is what the LORD says:

"I remember how eager you were to
    please me
    as a young bride long ago,
how you loved me and followed me
    even through the barren wilderness.
³ In those days Israel was holy to the LORD,
    the first of his children.*
All who harmed his people were declared
    guilty,
    and disaster fell on them.
I, the LORD, have spoken!"

⁴Listen to the word of the LORD, people of Jacob—all you families of Israel! ⁵This is what the LORD says:

"What did your ancestors find wrong
    with me
    that led them to stray so far from me?
They worshiped worthless idols,
    only to become worthless themselves.
⁶ They did not ask, 'Where is the LORD
    who brought us safely out of Egypt
and led us through the barren
    wilderness—
    a land of deserts and pits,
a land of drought and death,
    where no one lives or even travels?'

⁷ "And when I brought you into a fruitful
    land
    to enjoy its bounty and goodness,
you defiled my land and
    corrupted the possession I had
    promised you.
⁸ The priests did not ask,
    'Where is the LORD?'
Those who taught my word ignored me,
    the rulers turned against me,
and the prophets spoke in the name of
    Baal,
    wasting their time on worthless
    idols.
⁹ Therefore, I will bring my case against
    you,"
    says the LORD.
"I will even bring charges against your
    children's children
    in the years to come.

1:12 The Hebrew word for "watching" (*shoqed*) sounds like the word for "almond tree" (*shaqed*).   2:3 Hebrew *the firstfruits of his harvest.*

10 "Go west and look in the land of Cyprus*;
    go east and search through the land
        of Kedar.
Has anyone ever heard of anything
    as strange as this?
11 Has any nation ever traded its gods for
        new ones,
    even though they are not gods at all?
Yet my people have exchanged their
        glorious God*
    for worthless idols!
12 The heavens are shocked at such a thing
    and shrink back in horror and dismay,"
    says the LORD.
13 "For my people have done two evil things:
They have abandoned me—
    the fountain of living water.
And they have dug for themselves cracked
        cisterns
    that can hold no water at all!

The Results of Israel's Sin

14 "Why has Israel become a slave?
    Why has he been carried away as
        plunder?
15 Strong lions have roared against him,
    and the land has been destroyed.
The towns are now in ruins,
    and no one lives in them anymore.
16 Egyptians, marching from their cities
        of Memphis* and Tahpanhes,
    have destroyed Israel's glory and
        power.
17 And you have brought this upon
        yourselves
    by rebelling against the LORD your
        God,
    even though he was leading you on
        the way!

18 "What have you gained by your alliances
        with Egypt
    and your covenants with Assyria?
What good to you are the streams of the
        Nile*
    or the waters of the Euphrates River?*
19 Your wickedness will bring its own
        punishment.
    Your turning from me will shame you.
You will see what an evil, bitter thing it is
    to abandon the LORD your God and not
        to fear him.
    I, the Lord, the LORD of Heaven's
        Armies, have spoken!

20 "Long ago I broke the yoke that oppressed
        you
    and tore away the chains of your
        slavery,
but still you said,
    'I will not serve you.'
On every hill and under every green tree,
    you have prostituted yourselves by
        bowing down to idols.
21 But I was the one who planted you,
    choosing a vine of the purest stock—the
        very best.
How did you grow into this corrupt
    wild vine?
22 No amount of soap or lye can make you
        clean.
    I still see the stain of your guilt.
    I, the Sovereign LORD, have spoken!

Israel, an Unfaithful Wife

23 "You say, 'That's not true!
    I haven't worshiped the images
        of Baal!'
But how can you say that?
    Go and look in any valley in the land!
Face the awful sins you have done.
    You are like a restless female camel
        desperately searching for a mate.
24 You are like a wild donkey,
    sniffing the wind at mating time.
Who can restrain her lust?
    Those who desire her don't need to
        search,
    for she goes running to them!
25 When will you stop running?
    When will you stop panting after other
        gods?
But you say, 'Save your breath.
    I'm in love with these foreign gods,
    and I can't stop loving them now!'

26 "Israel is like a thief
    who feels shame only when he gets
        caught.
They, their kings, officials, priests, and
        prophets—
    all are alike in this.
27 To an image carved from a piece of wood
        they say,
    'You are my father.'
To an idol chiseled from a block of stone
        they say,
    'You are my mother.'
They turn their backs on me,

2:10 Hebrew *Kittim.*   2:11 Hebrew *their glory.*   2:16 Hebrew *Noph.*   2:18a Hebrew *of Shihor,* a branch of the Nile River.
2:18b Hebrew *the river?*

but in times of trouble they cry out
to me,
'Come and save us!'
28 But why not call on these gods you have
made?
When trouble comes, let them save you
if they can!
For you have as many gods
as there are towns in Judah.
29 Why do you accuse me of doing wrong?
You are the ones who have rebelled,"
says the LORD.
30 "I have punished your children,
but they did not respond to my
discipline.
You yourselves have killed your prophets
as a lion kills its prey.

31 "O my people, listen to the words of the
LORD!
Have I been like a desert to Israel?
Have I been to them a land of darkness?
Why then do my people say, 'At last we are
free from God!
We don't need him anymore!'
32 Does a young woman forget her jewelry,
or a bride her wedding dress?
Yet for years on end
my people have forgotten me.

33 "How you plot and scheme to win your
lovers.
Even an experienced prostitute could
learn from you!
34 Your clothing is stained with the blood of
the innocent and the poor,
though you didn't catch them breaking
into your houses!
35 And yet you say,
'I have done nothing wrong.
Surely God isn't angry with me!'
But now I will punish you severely
because you claim you have not
sinned.
36 First here, then there—
you flit from one ally to another asking
for help.
But your new friends in Egypt will let you
down,
just as Assyria did before.
37 In despair, you will be led into exile
with your hands on your heads,
for the LORD has rejected the nations you
trust.
They will not help you at all.

3 1 "If a man divorces a woman
and she goes and marries someone
else,
he will not take her back again,
for that would surely corrupt the
land.
But you have prostituted yourself with
many lovers,
so why are you trying to come back
to me?"
says the LORD.
2 "Look at the shrines on every
hilltop.
Is there any place you have not
been defiled
by your adultery with other gods?
You sit like a prostitute beside the road
waiting for a customer.
You sit alone like a nomad in the
desert.
You have polluted the land with your
prostitution
and your wickedness.
3 That's why even the spring rains have
failed.
For you are a brazen prostitute and
completely shameless.
4 Yet you say to me,
'Father, you have been my guide since
my youth.
5 Surely you won't be angry forever!
Surely you can forget about it!'
So you talk,
but you keep on doing all the evil
you can."

Judah Follows Israel's Example

6 During the reign of King Josiah, the LORD said to me, "Have you seen what fickle Israel has done? Like a wife who commits adultery, Israel has worshiped other gods on every hill and under every green tree. 7 I thought, 'After she has done all this, she will return to me.' But she did not return, and her faithless sister Judah saw this. 8 She saw* that I divorced faithless Israel because of her adultery. But that treacherous sister Judah had no fear, and now she, too, has left me and given herself to prostitution. 9 Israel treated it all so lightly—she thought nothing of committing adultery by worshiping idols made of wood and stone. So now the land has been polluted. 10 But despite all this, her faithless sister Judah has never sincerely returned to me. She has only pretended to be sorry. I, the LORD, have spoken!"

3:8 As in Dead Sea Scrolls, one Greek manuscript, and Syriac version; Masoretic Text reads *I saw.*

Hope for Wayward Israel

¹¹Then the LORD said to me, "Even faithless Israel is less guilty than treacherous Judah! ¹²Therefore, go and give this message to Israel.* This is what the LORD says:

"O Israel, my faithless people,
    come home to me again,
for I am merciful.
    I will not be angry with you forever.
¹³ Only acknowledge your guilt.
    Admit that you rebelled against the
        LORD your God
and committed adultery against him
    by worshiping idols under every green
        tree.
Confess that you refused to listen to my
    voice.
    I, the LORD, have spoken!

¹⁴ "Return home, you wayward
        children,"
    says the LORD,
    "for I am your master.
I will bring you back to the land of
        Israel*—
    one from this town and two from
        that family—
    from wherever you are scattered.
¹⁵ And I will give you shepherds after my
        own heart,
    who will guide you with knowledge
        and understanding.

¹⁶"And when your land is once more filled with people," says the LORD, "you will no longer wish for 'the good old days' when you possessed the Ark of the LORD's Covenant. You will not miss those days or even remember them, and there will be no need to rebuild the Ark. ¹⁷In that day Jerusalem will be known as 'The Throne of the LORD.' All nations will come there to honor the LORD. They will no longer stubbornly follow their own evil desires. ¹⁸In those days the people of Judah and Israel will return together from exile in the north. They will return to the land I gave your ancestors as an inheritance forever.

¹⁹ "I thought to myself,
    'I would love to treat you as my own
        children!'
I wanted nothing more than to give you
        this beautiful land—
    the finest possession in the world.

I looked forward to your calling me
        'Father,'
    and I wanted you never to turn from me.
²⁰ But you have been unfaithful to me, you
        people of Israel!
    You have been like a faithless wife who
        leaves her husband.
    I, the LORD, have spoken."

²¹ Voices are heard high on the windswept
        mountains,
    the weeping and pleading of Israel's
        people.
For they have chosen crooked paths
    and have forgotten the LORD their God.

²² "My wayward children," says the LORD,
    "come back to me, and I will heal your
        wayward hearts."

"Yes, we're coming," the people reply,
    "for you are the LORD our God.
²³ Our worship of idols on the hills
    and our religious orgies on the
        mountains
    are a delusion.
Only in the LORD our God
    will Israel ever find salvation.
²⁴ From childhood we have watched
    as everything our ancestors worked
        for—
    their flocks and herds, their sons and
        daughters—
    was squandered on a delusion.
²⁵ Let us now lie down in shame
    and cover ourselves with dishonor,
for we and our ancestors have sinned
    against the LORD our God.
From our childhood to this day
    we have never obeyed him."

4 ¹ "O Israel," says the LORD,
    "if you wanted to return to me, you
        could.
You could throw away your detestable
        idols
    and stray away no more.
² Then when you swear by my name, saying,
    'As surely as the LORD lives,'
you could do so
    with truth, justice, and righteousness.
Then you would be a blessing to the
        nations of the world,
    and all people would come and praise
        my name."

3:12 Hebrew *toward the north*.   **3:14** Hebrew *to Zion*.

Coming Judgment against Judah

³This is what the LORD says to the people of Judah and Jerusalem:

> "Plow up the hard ground of your hearts!
>   Do not waste your good seed among
>   thorns.
> ⁴ O people of Judah and Jerusalem,
>   surrender your pride and power.
> Change your hearts before the LORD,*
>   or my anger will burn like an
>   unquenchable fire
>   because of all your sins.
>
> ⁵ "Shout to Judah, and broadcast to
>   Jerusalem!
>   Tell them to sound the alarm
>   throughout the land:
> 'Run for your lives!
>   Flee to the fortified cities!'
> ⁶ Raise a signal flag as a warning for
>   Jerusalem*:
> 'Flee now! Do not delay!'
> For I am bringing terrible destruction
>   upon you
>   from the north."
>
> ⁷ A lion stalks from its den,
>   a destroyer of nations.
> It has left its lair and is headed your way.
>   It's going to devastate your land!
> Your towns will lie in ruins,
>   with no one living in them anymore.
> ⁸ So put on clothes of mourning
>   and weep with broken hearts,
> for the fierce anger of the LORD
>   is still upon us.
>
> ⁹ "In that day," says the LORD,
>   "the king and the officials will tremble
>   in fear.
> The priests will be struck with horror,
>   and the prophets will be appalled."
>
> ¹⁰ Then I said, "O Sovereign LORD,
>   the people have been deceived by what
>   you said,
> for you promised peace for Jerusalem.
>   But the sword is held at their throats!"
>
> ¹¹ The time is coming when the LORD will
>   say
>   to the people of Jerusalem,
> "My dear people, a burning wind is
>   blowing in from the desert,

> and it's not a gentle breeze useful for
>   winnowing grain.
> ¹² It is a roaring blast sent by me!
>   Now I will pronounce your
>   destruction!"
>
> ¹³ Our enemy rushes down on us like storm
>   clouds!
>   His chariots are like whirlwinds.
> His horses are swifter than eagles.
>   How terrible it will be, for we are
>   doomed!
> ¹⁴ O Jerusalem, cleanse your heart
>   that you may be saved.
> How long will you harbor
>   your evil thoughts?
> ¹⁵ Your destruction has been announced
>   from Dan and the hill country of
>   Ephraim.
>
> ¹⁶ "Warn the surrounding nations
>   and announce this to Jerusalem:
> The enemy is coming from a distant land,
>   raising a battle cry against the towns
>   of Judah.
> ¹⁷ They surround Jerusalem like watchmen
>   around a field,
>   for my people have rebelled against me,"
>   says the LORD.
> ¹⁸ "Your own actions have brought this
>   upon you.
>   This punishment is bitter, piercing you
>   to the heart!"

Jeremiah Weeps for His People

> ¹⁹ My heart, my heart—I writhe in pain!
>   My heart pounds within me! I cannot
>   be still.
> For I have heard the blast of enemy
>   trumpets
>   and the roar of their battle cries.
> ²⁰ Waves of destruction roll over the land,
>   until it lies in complete desolation.
> Suddenly my tents are destroyed;
>   in a moment my shelters are crushed.
> ²¹ How long must I see the battle flags
>   and hear the trumpets of war?
>
> ²² "My people are foolish
>   and do not know me," says the LORD.
> "They are stupid children
>   who have no understanding.
> They are clever enough at doing wrong,
>   but they have no idea how to do
>   right!"

4:4 Hebrew *Circumcise yourselves to the LORD, and take away the foreskins of your heart.*   4:6 Hebrew *Zion.*

Jeremiah's Vision of Coming Disaster

23 I looked at the earth, and it was empty and
      formless.
   I looked at the heavens, and there was
      no light.
24 I looked at the mountains and hills,
      and they trembled and shook.
25 I looked, and all the people were gone.
      All the birds of the sky had flown away.
26 I looked, and the fertile fields had become
      a wilderness.
   The towns lay in ruins,
      crushed by the LORD's fierce anger.

27 This is what the LORD says:
   "The whole land will be ruined,
      but I will not destroy it completely.
28 The earth will mourn
      and the heavens will be draped in black
   because of my decree against my people.
   I have made up my mind and will not
      change it."

29 At the noise of charioteers and archers,
      the people flee in terror.
   They hide in the bushes
      and run for the mountains.
   All the towns have been abandoned—
      not a person remains!
30 What are you doing,
      you who have been plundered?
   Why do you dress up in beautiful
      clothing
      and put on gold jewelry?
   Why do you brighten your eyes with
      mascara?
   Your primping will do you no good!
   The allies who were your lovers
      despise you and seek to kill you.

31 I hear a cry, like that of a woman in labor,
      the groans of a woman giving birth to
      her first child.
   It is beautiful Jerusalem*
      gasping for breath and crying out,
      "Help! I'm being murdered!"

The Sins of Judah

5 ¹ "Run up and down every street in
      Jerusalem," says the LORD.
   "Look high and low; search throughout
      the city!
   If you can find even one just and honest
      person,
      I will not destroy the city.

4:31 Hebrew *the daughter of Zion.*

2 But even when they are under oath,
      saying, 'As surely as the LORD lives,'
      they are still telling lies!"

3 LORD, you are searching for honesty.
   You struck your people,
      but they paid no attention.
   You crushed them,
      but they refused to be corrected.
   They are determined, with faces set like
      stone;
      they have refused to repent.

4 Then I said, "But what can we expect from
      the poor?
   They are ignorant.
   They don't know the ways of the LORD.
   They don't understand God's laws.
5 So I will go and speak to their leaders.
   Surely they know the ways of the
      LORD
      and understand God's laws."
   But the leaders, too, as one man,
      had thrown off God's yoke
      and broken his chains.
6 So now a lion from the forest will attack
      them;
   a wolf from the desert will pounce on
      them.
   A leopard will lurk near their towns,
      tearing apart any who dare to venture
      out.
   For their rebellion is great,
      and their sins are many.

7 "How can I pardon you?
   For even your children have turned
      from me.
   They have sworn by gods that are not gods
      at all!
   I fed my people until they were full.
   But they thanked me by committing
      adultery
      and lining up at the brothels.
8 They are well-fed, lusty stallions,
      each neighing for his neighbor's wife.
9 Should I not punish them for this?" says
      the LORD.
   "Should I not avenge myself against
      such a nation?

10 "Go down the rows of the vineyards and
      destroy the grapevines,
      leaving a scattered few alive.
   Strip the branches from the vines,

for these people do not belong to the
LORD.

11 The people of Israel and Judah
    are full of treachery against me,"
    says the LORD.
12 "They have lied about the LORD
    and said, 'He won't bother us!
No disasters will come upon us.
    There will be no war or famine.
13 God's prophets are all windbags
    who don't really speak for him.
Let their predictions of disaster fall on
    themselves!' "

14Therefore, this is what the LORD God of
Heaven's Armies says:

"Because the people are talking like this,
    my messages will flame out of your
        mouth
and burn the people like kindling wood.
15 O Israel, I will bring a distant nation
    against you,"
    says the LORD.
"It is a mighty nation,
    an ancient nation,
a people whose language you do not know,
    whose speech you cannot understand.
16 Their weapons are deadly;
    their warriors are mighty.
17 They will devour the food of your harvest;
    they will devour your sons and
        daughters.
They will devour your flocks and herds;
    they will devour your grapes and figs.
And they will destroy your fortified towns,
    which you think are so safe.

18"Yet even in those days I will not blot you
out completely," says the LORD. 19"And when
your people ask, 'Why did the LORD our God do
all this to us?' you must reply, 'You rejected him
and gave yourselves to foreign gods in your
own land. Now you will serve foreigners in a
land that is not your own.'

A Warning for God's People

20 "Make this announcement to Israel,*
    and say this to Judah:
21 Listen, you foolish and senseless people,
    with eyes that do not see
    and ears that do not hear.
22 Have you no respect for me?
    Why don't you tremble in my presence?

I, the LORD, define the ocean's sandy
    shoreline
    as an everlasting boundary that the
        waters cannot cross.
The waves may toss and roar,
    but they can never pass the boundaries
        I set.
23 But my people have stubborn and
    rebellious hearts.
They have turned away and
    abandoned me.
24 They do not say from the heart,
    'Let us live in awe of the LORD our God,
for he gives us rain each spring and fall,
    assuring us of a harvest when the time
        is right.'
25 Your wickedness has deprived you of these
    wonderful blessings.
Your sin has robbed you of all these
    good things.

26 "Among my people are wicked men
    who lie in wait for victims like a hunter
        hiding in a blind.
They continually set traps
    to catch people.
27 Like a cage filled with birds,
    their homes are filled with evil plots.
And now they are great and rich.
28 They are fat and sleek,
    and there is no limit to their wicked deeds.
They refuse to provide justice to orphans
    and deny the rights of the poor.
29 Should I not punish them for this?" says
    the LORD.
"Should I not avenge myself against
    such a nation?
30 A horrible and shocking thing
    has happened in this land—
31 the prophets give false prophecies,
    and the priests rule with an iron hand.
Worse yet, my people like it that way!
    But what will you do when the end
        comes?

Jerusalem's Last Warning

6 1 "Run for your lives, you people of
    Benjamin!
Get out of Jerusalem!
Sound the alarm in Tekoa!
    Send up a signal at Beth-hakkerem!
A powerful army is coming from the
    north,
    coming with disaster and destruction.

5:20 Hebrew *to the house of Jacob*. The names "Jacob" and "Israel" are often interchanged throughout the Old Testament,
referring sometimes to the individual patriarch and sometimes to the nation.

2 O Jerusalem,* you are my beautiful and
    delicate daughter—
  but I will destroy you!
3 Enemies will surround you, like shepherds
    camped around the city.
  Each chooses a place for his troops to
    devour.
4 They shout, 'Prepare for battle!
    Attack at noon!'
  'No, it's too late; the day is fading,
    and the evening shadows are falling.'
5 'Well then, let's attack at night
    and destroy her palaces!'"

6 This is what the LORD of Heaven's Armies
    says:
  "Cut down the trees for battering rams.
    Build siege ramps against the walls of
      Jerusalem.
  This is the city to be punished,
    for she is wicked through and
      through.
7 She spouts evil like a fountain.
    Her streets echo with the sounds of
      violence and destruction.
  I always see her sickness and sores.
8 Listen to this warning, Jerusalem,
    or I will turn from you in disgust.
  Listen, or I will turn you into a heap of
    ruins,
    a land where no one lives."

9 This is what the LORD of Heaven's Armies
    says:
  "Even the few who remain in Israel
    will be picked over again,
  as when a harvester checks each vine a
    second time
    to pick the grapes that were missed."

Judah's Constant Rebellion

10 To whom can I give warning?
    Who will listen when I speak?
  Their ears are closed,
    and they cannot hear.
  They scorn the word of the LORD.
    They don't want to listen at all.
11 So now I am filled with the LORD's fury.
    Yes, I am tired of holding it in!

  "I will pour out my fury on children
    playing in the streets
    and on gatherings of young men,
  on husbands and wives
    and on those who are old and gray.

12 Their homes will be turned over to their
    enemies,
    as will their fields and their wives.
  For I will raise my powerful fist
    against the people of this land,"
    says the LORD.
13 "From the least to the greatest,
    their lives are ruled by greed.
  From prophets to priests,
    they are all frauds.
14 They offer superficial treatments
    for my people's mortal wound.
  They give assurances of peace
    when there is no peace.
15 Are they ashamed of their disgusting
    actions?
  Not at all—they don't even know how
    to blush!
  Therefore, they will lie among the
    slaughtered.
  They will be brought down when I
    punish them,"
    says the LORD.

Judah Rejects the LORD's Way

16 This is what the LORD says:
  "Stop at the crossroads and look around.
    Ask for the old, godly way, and walk
      in it.
  Travel its path, and you will find rest for
    your souls.
  But you reply, 'No, that's not the road
    we want!'
17 I posted watchmen over you who said,
    'Listen for the sound of the alarm.'
  But you replied,
    'No! We won't pay attention!'

18 "Therefore, listen to this, all you nations.
    Take note of my people's situation.
19 Listen, all the earth!
  I will bring disaster on my people.
  It is the fruit of their own schemes,
    because they refuse to listen to me.
  They have rejected my word.
20 There's no use offering me sweet
    frankincense from Sheba.
  Keep your fragrant calamus imported
    from distant lands!
  I will not accept your burnt offerings.
    Your sacrifices have no pleasing aroma
      for me."

21 Therefore, this is what the LORD says:
  "I will put obstacles in my people's path.

6:2 Hebrew *Daughter of Zion*.

Fathers and sons will both fall over them.
Neighbors and friends will die
together."

An Invasion from the North

22 This is what the LORD says:
"Look! A great army coming from the
north!
A great nation is rising against you from
far-off lands.
23 They are armed with bows and spears.
They are cruel and show no mercy.
They sound like a roaring sea
as they ride forward on horses.
They are coming in battle formation,
planning to destroy you, beautiful
Jerusalem.*"

24 We have heard reports about the enemy,
and we wring our hands in fright.
Pangs of anguish have gripped us,
like those of a woman in labor.
25 Don't go out to the fields!
Don't travel on the roads!
The enemy's sword is everywhere
and terrorizes us at every turn!
26 Oh, my people, dress yourselves in
burlap
and sit among the ashes.
Mourn and weep bitterly, as for the loss
of an only son.
For suddenly the destroying armies
will be upon you!

27 "Jeremiah, I have made you a tester of
metals,*
that you may determine the quality
of my people.
28 They are the worst kind of rebel,
full of slander.
They are as hard as bronze and iron,
and they lead others into corruption.
29 The bellows fiercely fan the flames
to burn out the corruption.
But it does not purify them,
for the wickedness remains.
30 I will label them 'Rejected Silver,'
for I, the LORD, am discarding them."

Jeremiah Speaks at the Temple

7 The LORD gave another message to Jeremiah. He said, 2"Go to the entrance of the LORD's Temple, and give this message to the people: 'O Judah, listen to this message from the LORD! Listen to it, all of you who worship here! 3This is what the LORD of Heaven's Armies, the God of Israel, says:

"'Even now, if you quit your evil ways, I will let you stay in your own land. 4But don't be fooled by those who promise you safety simply because the LORD's Temple is here. They chant, "The LORD's Temple is here! The LORD's Temple is here!" 5But I will be merciful only if you stop your evil thoughts and deeds and start treating each other with justice; 6only if you stop exploiting foreigners, orphans, and widows; only if you stop your murdering; and only if you stop harming yourselves by worshiping idols. 7Then I will let you stay in this land that I gave to your ancestors to keep forever.

8"'Don't be fooled into thinking that you will never suffer because the Temple is here. It's a lie! 9Do you really think you can steal, murder, commit adultery, lie, and burn incense to Baal and all those other new gods of yours, 10and then come here and stand before me in my Temple and chant, "We are safe!"—only to go right back to all those evils again? 11Don't you yourselves admit that this Temple, which bears my name, has become a den of thieves? Surely I see all the evil going on there. I, the LORD, have spoken!

12"'Go now to the place at Shiloh where I once put the Tabernacle that bore my name. See what I did there because of all the wickedness of my people, the Israelites. 13While you were doing these wicked things, says the LORD, I spoke to you about it repeatedly, but you would not listen. I called out to you, but you refused to answer. 14So just as I destroyed Shiloh, I will now destroy this Temple that bears my name, this Temple that you trust in for help, this place that I gave to you and your ancestors. 15And I will send you out of my sight into exile, just as I did your relatives, the people of Israel.*'

Judah's Persistent Idolatry

16"Pray no more for these people, Jeremiah. Do not weep or pray for them, and don't beg me to help them, for I will not listen to you. 17Don't you see what they are doing throughout the towns of Judah and in the streets of Jerusalem? 18No wonder I am so angry! Watch how the children gather wood and the fathers build sacrificial fires. See how the women knead dough and make cakes to offer to the Queen of Heaven. And they pour out liquid offerings to their other idol gods! 19Am I the one they

6:23 Hebrew *daughter of Zion.*   6:27 As in Greek version; Hebrew reads *a tester of my people a fortress.*   7:15 Hebrew *of Ephraim,* referring to the northern kingdom of Israel.

are hurting?" asks the LORD. "Most of all, they hurt themselves, to their own shame."

²⁰So this is what the Sovereign LORD says: "I will pour out my terrible fury on this place. Its people, animals, trees, and crops will be consumed by the unquenchable fire of my anger."

²¹This is what the LORD of Heaven's Armies, the God of Israel, says: "Take your burnt offerings and your other sacrifices and eat them yourselves! ²²When I led your ancestors out of Egypt, it was not burnt offerings and sacrifices I wanted from them. ²³This is what I told them: 'Obey me, and I will be your God, and you will be my people. Do everything as I say, and all will be well!'

²⁴"But my people would not listen to me. They kept doing whatever they wanted, following the stubborn desires of their evil hearts. They went backward instead of forward. ²⁵From the day your ancestors left Egypt until now, I have continued to send my servants, the prophets—day in and day out. ²⁶But my people have not listened to me or even tried to hear. They have been stubborn and sinful—even worse than their ancestors.

²⁷"Tell them all this, but do not expect them to listen. Shout out your warnings, but do not expect them to respond. ²⁸Say to them, 'This is the nation whose people will not obey the LORD their God and who refuse to be taught. Truth has vanished from among them; it is no longer heard on their lips. ²⁹Shave your head in mourning, and weep alone on the mountains. For the LORD has rejected and forsaken this generation that has provoked his fury.'

The Valley of Slaughter

³⁰"The people of Judah have sinned before my very eyes," says the LORD. "They have set up their abominable idols right in the Temple that bears my name, defiling it. ³¹They have built pagan shrines at Topheth, the garbage dump in the valley of Ben-Hinnom, and there they burn their sons and daughters in the fire. I have never commanded such a horrible deed; it never even crossed my mind to command such a thing! ³²So beware, for the time is coming," says the LORD, "when that garbage dump will no longer be called Topheth or the valley of Ben-Hinnom, but the Valley of Slaughter. They will bury the bodies in Topheth until there is no more room for them. ³³The bodies of my people will be food for the vultures and wild animals, and no one will be left to scare them away. ³⁴I will put an end to the

8:7 The identification of some of these birds is uncertain.

happy singing and laughter in the streets of Jerusalem. The joyful voices of bridegrooms and brides will no longer be heard in the towns of Judah. The land will lie in complete desolation.

8 "In that day," says the LORD, "the enemy will break open the graves of the kings and officials of Judah, and the graves of the priests, prophets, and common people of Jerusalem. ²They will spread out their bones on the ground before the sun, moon, and stars—the gods my people have loved, served, and worshiped. Their bones will not be gathered up again or buried but will be scattered on the ground like manure. ³And the people of this evil nation who survive will wish to die rather than live where I will send them. I, the LORD of Heaven's Armies, have spoken!

Deception by False Prophets

⁴"Jeremiah, say to the people, 'This is what the LORD says:

"'When people fall down, don't they get
    up again?
When they discover they're on the
    wrong road, don't they turn back?
⁵ Then why do these people stay on their
    self-destructive path?
Why do the people of Jerusalem refuse
    to turn back?
They cling tightly to their lies
    and will not turn around.
⁶ I listen to their conversations
    and don't hear a word of truth.
Is anyone sorry for doing wrong?
Does anyone say, "What a terrible thing
    I have done"?
No! All are running down the path of sin
    as swiftly as a horse galloping into
    battle!
⁷ Even the stork that flies across the sky
    knows the time of her migration,
as do the turtledove, the swallow, and the
    crane.*
They all return at the proper time each
    year.
But not my people!
    They do not know the LORD's laws.

⁸ "'How can you say, "We are wise because
    we have the word of the LORD,"
when your teachers have twisted it by
    writing lies?

⁹ These wise teachers will fall
　　into the trap of their own foolishness,
　for they have rejected the word of the
　　LORD.
　　Are they so wise after all?
¹⁰ I will give their wives to others
　　and their farms to strangers.
　From the least to the greatest,
　　their lives are ruled by greed.
　Yes, even my prophets and priests are like
　　that.
　　They are all frauds.
¹¹ They offer superficial treatments
　　for my people's mortal wound.
　They give assurances of peace
　　when there is no peace.
¹² Are they ashamed of these disgusting
　　actions?
　　Not at all—they don't even know how
　　　to blush!
　Therefore, they will lie among the
　　slaughtered.
　　They will be brought down when I
　　　punish them,
　　says the LORD.
¹³ I will surely consume them.
　　There will be no more harvests of figs
　　　and grapes.
　Their fruit trees will all die.
　　Whatever I gave them will soon be gone.
　　I, the LORD, have spoken!'

¹⁴ "Then the people will say,
　　'Why should we wait here to die?
　Come, let's go to the fortified towns and
　　die there.
　For the LORD our God has decreed our
　　destruction
　and has given us a cup of poison to drink
　　because we sinned against the LORD.
¹⁵ We hoped for peace, but no peace came.
　　We hoped for a time of healing, but
　　　found only terror.'

¹⁶ "The snorting of the enemies' warhorses
　　can be heard
　all the way from the land of Dan in the
　　north!
　The neighing of their stallions makes the
　　whole land tremble.
　　They are coming to devour the land and
　　　everything in it—
　　cities and people alike.
¹⁷ I will send these enemy troops
　　among you

like poisonous snakes you cannot
　　charm.
　They will bite you, and you will die.
　　I, the LORD, have spoken!"

Jeremiah Weeps for Sinful Judah

¹⁸ My grief is beyond healing;
　　my heart is broken.
¹⁹ Listen to the weeping of my people;
　　it can be heard all across the land.
　"Has the LORD abandoned Jerusalem?*"
　　the people ask.
　"Is her King no longer there?"

　"Oh, why have they provoked my anger
　　with their carved idols
　and their worthless foreign gods?" says
　　the LORD.

²⁰ "The harvest is finished,
　　and the summer is gone," the people cry,
　　"yet we are not saved!"

²¹ I hurt with the hurt of my people.
　　I mourn and am overcome with grief.
²² Is there no medicine in Gilead?
　　Is there no physician there?
　Why is there no healing
　　for the wounds of my people?

9 ¹*If only my head were a pool of water
　　and my eyes a fountain of tears,
　I would weep day and night
　　for all my people who have been
　　　slaughtered.
²*Oh, that I could go away and forget my
　　people
　and live in a travelers' shack in the
　　desert.
　For they are all adulterers—
　　a pack of treacherous liars.

Judgment for Disobedience

³ "My people bend their tongues like
　　bows
　　to shoot out lies.
　They refuse to stand up for the truth.
　　They only go from bad to worse.
　They do not know me,"
　　says the LORD.

⁴ "Beware of your neighbor!
　　Don't even trust your brother!
　For brother takes advantage of brother,
　　and friend slanders friend.

⁵ They all fool and defraud each other;
  no one tells the truth.
 With practiced tongues they tell lies;
  they wear themselves out with all their
   sinning.
⁶ They pile lie upon lie
  and utterly refuse to acknowledge me,"
 says the LORD.

⁷ Therefore, this is what the LORD of
   Heaven's Armies says:
 "See, I will melt them down in a crucible
  and test them like metal.
 What else can I do with my people?*
⁸   For their tongues shoot lies like
   poisoned arrows.
 They speak friendly words to their
   neighbors
  while scheming in their heart to kill
   them.
⁹ Should I not punish them for this?" says
   the LORD.
  "Should I not avenge myself against
   such a nation?"

¹⁰ I will weep for the mountains
  and wail for the wilderness pastures.
 For they are desolate and empty of life;
  the lowing of cattle is heard no more;
  the birds and wild animals have all fled.

¹¹ "I will make Jerusalem into a heap of
   ruins," says the LORD.
  "It will be a place haunted by jackals.
 The towns of Judah will be ghost towns,
  with no one living in them."

¹²Who is wise enough to understand all this?
Who has been instructed by the LORD and can
explain it to others? Why has the land been so
ruined that no one dares to travel through it?
¹³The LORD replies, "This has happened because my people have abandoned my instructions; they have refused to obey what I said.
¹⁴Instead, they have stubbornly followed their
own desires and worshiped the images of Baal,
as their ancestors taught them. ¹⁵So now, this
is what the LORD of Heaven's Armies, the God
of Israel, says: Look! I will feed them with bitterness and give them poison to drink. ¹⁶I will
scatter them around the world, in places they
and their ancestors never heard of, and even
there I will chase them with the sword until I
have destroyed them completely."

Weeping in Jerusalem

¹⁷ This is what the LORD of Heaven's Armies
   says:
 "Consider all this, and call for the mourners.
  Send for the women who mourn at
   funerals.
¹⁸ Quick! Begin your weeping!
  Let the tears flow from your eyes.
¹⁹ Hear the people of Jerusalem* crying in
   despair,
  'We are ruined! We are completely
   humiliated!
 We must leave our land,
  because our homes have been torn
   down.'"

²⁰ Listen, you women, to the words of the
   LORD;
  open your ears to what he has to say.
 Teach your daughters to wail;
  teach one another how to lament.
²¹ For death has crept in through our
   windows
  and has entered our mansions.
 It has killed off the flower of our youth:
  Children no longer play in the streets,
  and young men no longer gather in the
   squares.

²² This is what the LORD says:
 "Bodies will be scattered across the fields
  like clumps of manure,
  like bundles of grain after the harvest.
  No one will be left to bury them."

²³ This is what the LORD says:
 "Don't let the wise boast in their wisdom,
  or the powerful boast in their power,
  or the rich boast in their riches.
²⁴ But those who wish to boast
  should boast in this alone:
 that they truly know me and understand
   that I am the LORD
 who demonstrates unfailing love
  and who brings justice and
   righteousness to the earth,
 and that I delight in these things.
  I, the LORD, have spoken!

²⁵"A time is coming," says the LORD, "when
I will punish all those who are circumcised
in body but not in spirit—²⁶the Egyptians,
Edomites, Ammonites, Moabites, the people
who live in the desert in remote places,* and

9:7 Hebrew *with the daughter of my people?* Greek version reads *with the evil daughter of my people?*   9:19 Hebrew *Zion.*   9:26 Or
in the desert and clip the corners of their hair.

yes, even the people of Judah. And like all these pagan nations, the people of Israel also have uncircumcised hearts."

Idolatry Brings Destruction

10 Hear the word that the LORD speaks to you, O Israel! [2] This is what the LORD says:

"Do not act like the other nations,
  who try to read their future in the stars.
Do not be afraid of their predictions,
  even though other nations are terrified
    by them.
[3] Their ways are futile and foolish.
  They cut down a tree, and a craftsman
    carves an idol.
[4] They decorate it with gold and silver
  and then fasten it securely with hammer
    and nails
  so it won't fall over.
[5] Their gods are like
  helpless scarecrows in a cucumber
    field!
They cannot speak,
  and they need to be carried because
    they cannot walk.
Do not be afraid of such gods,
  for they can neither harm you nor do
    you any good."

[6] LORD, there is no one like you!
  For you are great, and your name is full
    of power.
[7] Who would not fear you, O King of
    nations?
  That title belongs to you alone!
Among all the wise people of the earth
  and in all the kingdoms of the world,
    there is no one like you.

[8] People who worship idols are stupid and
    foolish.
  The things they worship are made of
    wood!
[9] They bring beaten sheets of silver from
    Tarshish
  and gold from Uphaz,
and they give these materials to skillful
    craftsmen
  who make their idols.
Then they dress these gods in royal blue
  and purple robes
    made by expert tailors.
[10] But the LORD is the only true God.

He is the living God and the everlasting
    King!
The whole earth trembles at his anger.
  The nations cannot stand up to his
    wrath.

[11] Say this to those who worship other gods:
"Your so-called gods, who did not make the heavens and earth, will vanish from the earth and from under the heavens."*

[12] But the LORD made the earth by his power,
  and he preserves it by his wisdom.
With his own understanding
  he stretched out the heavens.
[13] When he speaks in the thunder,
  the heavens roar with rain.
He causes the clouds to rise over the earth.
  He sends the lightning with the rain
  and releases the wind from his
    storehouses.
[14] The whole human race is foolish and has
    no knowledge!
  The craftsmen are disgraced by the idols
    they make,
for their carefully shaped works are a
    fraud.
  These idols have no breath or power.
[15] Idols are worthless; they are ridiculous
    lies!
  On the day of reckoning they will all
    be destroyed.
[16] But the God of Israel* is no idol!
  He is the Creator of everything that
    exists,
including Israel, his own special
    possession.
  The LORD of Heaven's Armies is his
    name!

The Coming Destruction

[17] Pack your bags and prepare to leave;
  the siege is about to begin.
[18] For this is what the LORD says:
"Suddenly, I will fling out
  all you who live in this land.
I will pour great troubles upon you,
  and at last you will feel my anger."

[19] My wound is severe,
  and my grief is great.
My sickness is incurable,
  but I must bear it.
[20] My home is gone,
  and no one is left to help me rebuild it.

10:11 The original text of this verse is in Aramaic.   10:16 Hebrew *the Portion of Jacob*. See note on 5:20.

My children have been taken away,
    and I will never see them again.
21 The shepherds of my people have lost
    their senses.
    They no longer seek wisdom from the
        LORD.
    Therefore, they fail completely,
    and their flocks are scattered.
22 Listen! Hear the terrifying roar of great
    armies
    as they roll down from the north.
    The towns of Judah will be destroyed
    and become a haunt for jackals.

Jeremiah's Prayer

23 I know, LORD, that our lives are not our
    own.
    We are not able to plan our own course.
24 So correct me, LORD, but please be gentle.
    Do not correct me in anger, for I would
    die.
25 Pour out your wrath on the nations that
    refuse to acknowledge you—
    on the peoples that do not call upon
    your name.
    For they have devoured your people
    Israel*;
    they have devoured and consumed
    them,
    making the land a desolate
    wilderness.

Judah's Broken Covenant

11 The LORD gave another message to Jeremiah. He said, 2"Remind the people of Judah and Jerusalem about the terms of my covenant with them. 3Say to them, 'This is what the LORD, the God of Israel, says: Cursed is anyone who does not obey the terms of my covenant! 4For I said to your ancestors when I brought them out of the iron-smelting furnace of Egypt, "If you obey me and do whatever I command you, then you will be my people, and I will be your God." 5I said this so I could keep my promise to your ancestors to give you a land flowing with milk and honey—the land you live in today.'"

Then I replied, "Amen, LORD! May it be so."

6Then the LORD said, "Broadcast this message in the streets of Jerusalem. Go from town to town throughout the land and say, 'Remember the ancient covenant, and do everything it requires. 7For I solemnly warned your ancestors when I brought them out of Egypt, "Obey me!" I have repeated this warning over and over to

10:25 Hebrew *devoured Jacob.* See note on 5:20.

this day, 8but your ancestors did not listen or even pay attention. Instead, they stubbornly followed their own evil desires. And because they refused to obey, I brought upon them all the curses described in this covenant.'"

9Again the LORD spoke to me and said, "I have discovered a conspiracy against me among the people of Judah and Jerusalem. 10They have returned to the sins of their ancestors. They have refused to listen to me and are worshiping other gods. Israel and Judah have both broken the covenant I made with their ancestors. 11Therefore, this is what the LORD says: I am going to bring calamity upon them, and they will not escape. Though they beg for mercy, I will not listen to their cries. 12Then the people of Judah and Jerusalem will pray to their idols and burn incense before them. But the idols will not save them when disaster strikes! 13Look now, people of Judah; you have as many gods as you have towns. You have as many altars of shame—altars for burning incense to your god Baal—as there are streets in Jerusalem.

14"Pray no more for these people, Jeremiah. Do not weep or pray for them, for I will not listen to them when they cry out to me in distress.

15 "What right do my beloved people have to
    come to my Temple,
    when they have done so many immoral
    things?
    Can their vows and sacrifices prevent their
    destruction?
    They actually rejoice in doing evil!
16 I, the LORD, once called them a thriving
    olive tree,
    beautiful to see and full of good fruit.
    But now I have sent the fury of their
    enemies
    to burn them with fire,
    leaving them charred and broken.

17"I, the LORD of Heaven's Armies, who planted this olive tree, have ordered it destroyed. For the people of Israel and Judah have done evil, arousing my anger by burning incense to Baal."

A Plot against Jeremiah

18Then the LORD told me about the plots my enemies were making against me. 19I was like a lamb being led to the slaughter. I had no idea that they were planning to kill me! "Let's destroy this man and all his words," they said.

"Let's cut him down, so his name will be forgotten forever."

20 O LORD of Heaven's Armies,
  you make righteous judgments,
    and you examine the deepest thoughts
      and secrets.
  Let me see your vengeance against them,
    for I have committed my cause to you.

21This is what the LORD says about the men of Anathoth who wanted me dead. They had said, "We will kill you if you do not stop prophesying in the LORD's name." 22So this is what the LORD of Heaven's Armies says about them: "I will punish them! Their young men will die in battle, and their boys and girls will starve to death. 23Not one of these plotters from Anathoth will survive, for I will bring disaster upon them when their time of punishment comes."

Jeremiah Questions the LORD's Justice

12 1 LORD, you always give me justice
      when I bring a case before you.
  So let me bring you this complaint:
    Why are the wicked so prosperous?
      Why are evil people so happy?
2 You have planted them,
    and they have taken root and prospered.
  Your name is on their lips,
    but you are far from their hearts.
3 But as for me, LORD, you know my heart.
    You see me and test my thoughts.
  Drag these people away like sheep to be
      butchered!
    Set them aside to be slaughtered!

4 How long must this land mourn?
    Even the grass in the fields has
      withered.
  The wild animals and birds have
      disappeared
    because of the evil in the land.
  For the people have said,
    "The LORD doesn't see what's ahead
      for us!"

The LORD's Reply to Jeremiah

5 "If racing against mere men makes you
      tired,
    how will you race against horses?
  If you stumble and fall on open ground,
    what will you do in the thickets near the
      Jordan?

12:9 Or *speckled hyenas.*

6 Even your brothers, members of your own
      family,
    have turned against you.
  They plot and raise complaints against
      you.
  Do not trust them,
    no matter how pleasantly they speak.

7 "I have abandoned my people, my special
      possession.
  I have surrendered my dearest ones to
      their enemies.
8 My chosen people have roared at me like
      a lion of the forest,
    so I have treated them with contempt.
9 My chosen people act like speckled
      vultures,*
    but they themselves are surrounded by
      vultures.
  Bring on the wild animals to pick their
      corpses clean!

10 "Many rulers have ravaged my vineyard,
    trampling down the vines
      and turning all its beauty into a barren
        wilderness.
11 They have made it an empty wasteland;
    I hear its mournful cry.
  The whole land is desolate,
    and no one even cares.
12 On all the bare hilltops,
    destroying armies can be seen.
  The sword of the LORD devours people
    from one end of the nation to the other.
      No one will escape!
13 My people have planted wheat
    but are harvesting thorns.
  They have worn themselves out,
    but it has done them no good.
  They will harvest a crop of shame
    because of the fierce anger of the
      LORD."

A Message for Israel's Neighbors

14Now this is what the LORD says: "I will uproot from their land all the evil nations reaching out for the possession I gave my people Israel. And I will uproot Judah from among them. 15But afterward I will return and have compassion on all of them. I will bring them home to their own lands again, each nation to its own possession. 16And if these nations truly learn the ways of my people, and if they learn to swear by my name, saying, 'As surely as the LORD lives' (just as they taught my people to swear by the name of Baal), then they will be given a place among my people. [17]But any nation who refuses to obey me will be uprooted and destroyed. I, the LORD, have spoken!"

Jeremiah's Linen Loincloth

13 This is what the LORD said to me: "Go and buy a linen loincloth and put it on, but do not wash it." [2]So I bought the loincloth as the LORD directed me, and I put it on.

[3]Then the LORD gave me another message: [4]"Take the linen loincloth you are wearing, and go to the Euphrates River.* Hide it there in a hole in the rocks." [5]So I went and hid it by the Euphrates as the LORD had instructed me.

[6]A long time afterward the LORD said to me, "Go back to the Euphrates and get the loincloth I told you to hide there." [7]So I went to the Euphrates and dug it out of the hole where I had hidden it. But now it was rotting and falling apart. The loincloth was good for nothing.

[8]Then I received this message from the LORD: [9]"This is what the LORD says: This shows how I will rot away the pride of Judah and Jerusalem. [10]These wicked people refuse to listen to me. They stubbornly follow their own desires and worship other gods. Therefore, they will become like this loincloth—good for nothing! [11]As a loincloth clings to a man's waist, so I created Judah and Israel to cling to me, says the LORD. They were to be my people, my pride, my glory—an honor to my name. But they would not listen to me.

[12]"So tell them, 'This is what the LORD, the God of Israel, says: May all your jars be filled with wine.' And they will reply, 'Of course! Jars are made to be filled with wine!' [13]Then tell them, 'No, this is what the LORD means: I will fill everyone in this land with drunkenness—from the king sitting on David's throne to the priests and the prophets, right down to the common people of Jerusalem. [14]I will smash them against each other, even parents against children, says the LORD. I will not let my pity or mercy or compassion keep me from destroying them.'"

A Warning against Pride

[15] Listen and pay attention!
      Do not be arrogant, for the LORD has
            spoken.
[16] Give glory to the LORD your God
            before it is too late.
      Acknowledge him before he brings
            darkness upon you,

causing you to stumble and fall on the
      darkening mountains.
For then, when you look for light,
      you will find only terrible darkness and
            gloom.
[17] And if you still refuse to listen,
      I will weep alone because of your pride.
My eyes will overflow with tears,
      because the LORD's flock will be led
            away into exile.

[18] Say to the king and his mother,
      "Come down from your thrones
            and sit in the dust,
for your glorious crowns
      will soon be snatched from your heads."
[19] The towns of the Negev will close their
            gates,
      and no one will be able to open them.
The people of Judah will be taken away as
            captives.
      All will be carried into exile.

[20] Open up your eyes and see
      the armies marching down from the
            north!
Where is your flock—
      your beautiful flock—
      that he gave you to care for?
[21] What will you say when the LORD takes
            the allies you have cultivated
      and appoints them as your rulers?
Pangs of anguish will grip you,
      like those of a woman in labor!
[22] You may ask yourself,
      "Why is all this happening to me?"
      It is because of your many sins!
That is why you have been stripped
      and raped by invading armies.
[23] Can an Ethiopian* change the color of
            his skin?
      Can a leopard take away its spots?
Neither can you start doing good,
      for you have always done evil.

[24] "I will scatter you like chaff
      that is blown away by the desert winds.
[25] This is your allotment,
      the portion I have assigned to you,"
      says the LORD,
"for you have forgotten me,
      putting your trust in false gods.
[26] I myself will strip you
      and expose you to shame.
[27] I have seen your adultery and lust,

13:4 Hebrew *Perath*; also in 13:5, 6, 7.   13:23 Hebrew *a Cushite*.

and your disgusting idol worship out in
the fields and on the hills.
What sorrow awaits you, Jerusalem!
How long before you are pure?"

Judah's Terrible Drought

14 This message came to Jeremiah from the
LORD, explaining why he was holding
back the rain:

2 "Judah wilts;
commerce at the city gates grinds to a
halt.
All the people sit on the ground in
mourning,
and a great cry rises from Jerusalem.
3 The nobles send servants to get water,
but all the wells are dry.
The servants return with empty pitchers,
confused and desperate,
covering their heads in grief.
4 The ground is parched
and cracked for lack of rain.
The farmers are deeply troubled;
they, too, cover their heads.
5 Even the doe abandons her newborn fawn
because there is no grass in the field.
6 The wild donkeys stand on the bare hills
panting like thirsty jackals.
They strain their eyes looking for grass,
but there is none to be found."

7 The people say, "Our wickedness has
caught up with us, LORD,
but help us for the sake of your own
reputation.
We have turned away from you
and sinned against you again and again.
8 O Hope of Israel, our Savior in times of
trouble,
why are you like a stranger to us?
Why are you like a traveler passing
through the land,
stopping only for the night?
9 Are you also confused?
Is our champion helpless to save us?
You are right here among us, LORD.
We are known as your people.
Please don't abandon us now!"

10 So this is what the LORD says to his people:
"You love to wander far from me
and do not restrain yourselves.
Therefore, I will no longer accept you as
my people.

14:19 Hebrew *Zion?*

Now I will remember all your
wickedness
and will punish you for your sins."

The LORD Forbids Jeremiah to Intercede

11 Then the LORD said to me, "Do not pray for
these people anymore. 12 When they fast, I will
pay no attention. When they present their
burnt offerings and grain offerings to me, I will
not accept them. Instead, I will devour them
with war, famine, and disease."

13 Then I said, "O Sovereign LORD, their
prophets are telling them, 'All is well—no war
or famine will come. The LORD will surely send
you peace.'"

14 Then the LORD said, "These prophets are
telling lies in my name. I did not send them
or tell them to speak. I did not give them any
messages. They prophesy of visions and revelations they have never seen or heard. They speak
foolishness made up in their own lying hearts.
15 Therefore, this is what the LORD says: I will
punish these lying prophets, for they have spoken in my name even though I never sent them.
They say that no war or famine will come, but
they themselves will die by war and famine!
16 As for the people to whom they prophesy—
their bodies will be thrown out into the streets
of Jerusalem, victims of famine and war. There
will be no one left to bury them. Husbands,
wives, sons, and daughters—all will be gone.
For I will pour out their own wickedness on
them. 17 Now, Jeremiah, say this to them:

"Night and day my eyes overflow with
tears.
I cannot stop weeping,
for my virgin daughter—my precious
people—
has been struck down
and lies mortally wounded.
18 If I go out into the fields,
I see the bodies of people slaughtered
by the enemy.
If I walk the city streets,
I see people who have died of starvation.
The prophets and priests continue with
their work,
but they don't know what they're
doing."

A Prayer for Healing

19 LORD, have you completely rejected
Judah?
Do you really hate Jerusalem?*

Why have you wounded us past all hope
of healing?
We hoped for peace, but no peace came.
We hoped for a time of healing, but
found only terror.

20 LORD, we confess our wickedness
and that of our ancestors, too.
We all have sinned against you.

21 For the sake of your reputation, LORD,
do not abandon us.
Do not disgrace your own glorious
throne.
Please remember us,
and do not break your covenant
with us.

22 Can any of the worthless foreign gods
send us rain?
Does it fall from the sky by itself?
No, you are the one, O LORD our God!
Only you can do such things.
So we will wait for you to help us.

Judah's Inevitable Doom

15 Then the LORD said to me, "Even if
Moses and Samuel stood before me
pleading for these people, I wouldn't help
them. Away with them! Get them out of my
sight! 2And if they say to you, 'But where can
we go?' tell them, 'This is what the LORD says:

"'Those who are destined for death, to
death;
those who are destined for war, to war;
those who are destined for famine, to
famine;
those who are destined for captivity, to
captivity.'

3"I will send four kinds of destroyers against
them," says the LORD. "I will send the sword
to kill, the dogs to drag away, the vultures to
devour, and the wild animals to finish up what
is left. 4Because of the wicked things Manasseh
son of Hezekiah, king of Judah, did in Jerusalem, I will make my people an object of horror
to all the kingdoms of the earth.

5 "Who will feel sorry for you, Jerusalem?
Who will weep for you?
Who will even bother to ask how you
are?

6 You have abandoned me
and turned your back on me,"
says the LORD.

"Therefore, I will raise my fist to destroy
you.
I am tired of always giving you another
chance.

7 I will winnow you like grain at the gates
of your cities
and take away the children you hold dear.
I will destroy my own people,
because they refuse to change their evil
ways.

8 There will be more widows
than the grains of sand on the seashore.
At noontime I will bring a destroyer
against the mothers of young men.
I will cause anguish and terror
to come upon them suddenly.

9 The mother of seven grows faint and gasps
for breath;
her sun has gone down while it is still
day.
She sits childless now,
disgraced and humiliated.
And I will hand over those who are left
to be killed by the enemy.
I, the LORD, have spoken!"

Jeremiah's Complaint

10Then I said,

"What sorrow is mine, my mother.
Oh, that I had died at birth!
I am hated everywhere I go.
I am neither a lender who threatens to
foreclose
nor a borrower who refuses to pay—
yet they all curse me."

11The LORD replied,

"I will take care of you, Jeremiah.
Your enemies will ask you to plead on
their behalf
in times of trouble and distress.

12 Can a man break a bar of iron from the
north,
or a bar of bronze?

13 At no cost to them,
I will hand over your wealth and
treasures
as plunder to your enemies,
for sin runs rampant in your land.

14 I will tell your enemies to take you
as captives to a foreign land.
For my anger blazes like a fire
that will burn forever.*"

15:14 As in some Hebrew manuscripts (see also 17:4); most Hebrew manuscripts read *will burn against you.*

¹⁵Then I said,

"LORD, you know what's happening to me.
  Please step in and help me. Punish my
  persecutors!
Please give me time; don't let me die
  young.
It's for your sake that I am suffering.
¹⁶ When I discovered your words, I devoured
  them.
They are my joy and my heart's delight,
for I bear your name,
O LORD God of Heaven's Armies.
¹⁷ I never joined the people in their merry
  feasts.
I sat alone because your hand was
  on me.
I was filled with indignation at their
  sins.
¹⁸ Why then does my suffering continue?
Why is my wound so incurable?
Your help seems as uncertain as a seasonal
  brook,
like a spring that has gone dry."

¹⁹This is how the LORD responds:

"If you return to me, I will restore you
  so you can continue to serve me.
If you speak good words rather than
  worthless ones,
you will be my spokesman.
You must influence them;
  do not let them influence you!
²⁰ They will fight against you like an
  attacking army,
but I will make you as secure as a
  fortified wall of bronze.
They will not conquer you,
for I am with you to protect and
  rescue you.
I, the LORD, have spoken!
²¹ Yes, I will certainly keep you safe from
  these wicked men.
I will rescue you from their cruel
  hands."

Jeremiah Forbidden to Marry

16 The LORD gave me another message. He said, ²"Do not get married or have children in this place. ³For this is what the LORD says about the children born here in this city and about their mothers and fathers: ⁴They will die from terrible diseases. No one will mourn for them or bury them, and they will lie scattered on the ground like manure. They will die from war and famine, and their bodies will be food for the vultures and wild animals."

Judah's Coming Punishment

⁵This is what the LORD says: "Do not go to funerals to mourn and show sympathy for these people, for I have removed my protection and peace from them. I have taken away my unfailing love and my mercy. ⁶Both the great and the lowly will die in this land. No one will bury them or mourn for them. Their friends will not cut themselves in sorrow or shave their heads in sadness. ⁷No one will offer a meal to comfort those who mourn for the dead—not even at the death of a mother or father. No one will send a cup of wine to console them.

⁸"And do not go to their feasts and parties. Do not eat and drink with them at all. ⁹For this is what the LORD of Heaven's Armies, the God of Israel, says: In your own lifetime, before your very eyes, I will put an end to the happy singing and laughter in this land. The joyful voices of bridegrooms and brides will no longer be heard.

¹⁰"When you tell the people all these things, they will ask, 'Why has the LORD decreed such terrible things against us? What have we done to deserve such treatment? What is our sin against the LORD our God?' ¹¹"Then you will give them the LORD's reply: 'It is because your ancestors were unfaithful to me. They worshiped other gods and served them. They abandoned me and did not obey my word. ¹²And you are even worse than your ancestors! You stubbornly follow your own evil desires and refuse to listen to me. ¹³So I will throw you out of this land and send you into a foreign land where you and your ancestors have never been. There you can worship idols day and night—and I will grant you no favors!'

Hope despite the Disaster

¹⁴"But the time is coming," says the LORD, "when people who are taking an oath will no longer say, 'As surely as the LORD lives, who rescued the people of Israel from the land of Egypt.' ¹⁵Instead, they will say, 'As surely as the LORD lives, who brought the people of Israel back to their own land from the land of the north and from all the countries to which he had exiled them.' For I will bring them back to this land that I gave their ancestors.

¹⁶"But now I am sending for many fishermen who will catch them," says the LORD. "I am sending for hunters who will hunt them down in the mountains, hills, and caves. ¹⁷I am

watching them closely, and I see every sin. They cannot hope to hide from me. ¹⁸I will double their punishment for all their sins, because they have defiled my land with lifeless images of their detestable gods and have filled my territory with their evil deeds."

Jeremiah's Prayer of Confidence

¹⁹ LORD, you are my strength and fortress,
　my refuge in the day of trouble!
Nations from around the world
　will come to you and say,
"Our ancestors left us a foolish heritage,
　for they worshiped worthless idols.
²⁰ Can people make their own gods?
　These are not real gods at all!"

²¹ The LORD says,
"Now I will show them my power;
　now I will show them my might.
At last they will know and understand
　that I am the LORD.

Judah's Sin and Punishment

17 ¹ "The sin of Judah
　is inscribed with an iron chisel—
engraved with a diamond point on their
　stony hearts
and on the corners of their altars.
² Even their children go to worship
　at their pagan altars and Asherah poles,
beneath every green tree
　and on every high hill.
³ So I will hand over my holy mountain—
　along with all your wealth and treasures
　and your pagan shrines—
as plunder to your enemies,
　for sin runs rampant in your land.
⁴ The wonderful possession I have reserved
　for you
　will slip from your hands.
I will tell your enemies to take you
　as captives to a foreign land.
For my anger blazes like a fire
　that will burn forever."

Wisdom from the LORD

⁵ This is what the LORD says:
"Cursed are those who put their trust in
　mere humans,
　who rely on human strength
　and turn their hearts away from the LORD.
⁶ They are like stunted shrubs in the desert,
　with no hope for the future.
They will live in the barren wilderness,
　in an uninhabited salty land.

⁷ "But blessed are those who trust in the
　LORD
　and have made the LORD their hope and
　confidence.
⁸ They are like trees planted along a
　riverbank,
　with roots that reach deep into the water.
Such trees are not bothered by the heat
　or worried by long months of drought.
Their leaves stay green,
　and they never stop producing fruit.

⁹ "The human heart is the most deceitful
　of all things,
　and desperately wicked.
Who really knows how bad it is?
¹⁰ But I, the LORD, search all hearts
　and examine secret motives.
I give all people their due rewards,
　according to what their actions
　deserve."

Jeremiah's Trust in the LORD

¹¹ Like a partridge that hatches eggs she has
　not laid,
　so are those who get their wealth by
　unjust means.
At midlife they will lose their riches;
　in the end, they will become poor
　old fools.
¹² But we worship at your throne—
　eternal, high, and glorious!
¹³ O LORD, the hope of Israel,
　all who turn away from you will be
　disgraced.
They will be buried in the dust of the
　earth,
　for they have abandoned the LORD,
　the fountain of living water.

¹⁴ O LORD, if you heal me, I will be truly
　healed;
　if you save me, I will be truly saved.
　My praises are for you alone!
¹⁵ People scoff at me and say,
"What is this 'message from the LORD' you
　talk about?
Why don't your predictions come true?"

¹⁶ LORD, I have not abandoned my job
　as a shepherd for your people.
I have not urged you to send disaster.
　You have heard everything I've said.
¹⁷ LORD, don't terrorize me!
　You alone are my hope in the day of
　disaster.

¹⁸ Bring shame and dismay on all who
    persecute me,
  but don't let me experience shame and
    dismay.
Bring a day of terror on them.
Yes, bring double destruction upon
    them!

Observing the Sabbath

¹⁹This is what the LORD said to me: "Go and stand in the gates of Jerusalem, first in the gate where the king goes in and out, and then in each of the other gates. ²⁰Say to all the people, 'Listen to this message from the LORD, you kings of Judah and all you people of Judah and everyone living in Jerusalem. ²¹This is what the LORD says: Listen to my warning! Stop carrying on your trade at Jerusalem's gates on the Sabbath day. ²²Do not do your work on the Sabbath, but make it a holy day. I gave this command to your ancestors, ²³but they did not listen or obey. They stubbornly refused to pay attention or accept my discipline.

²⁴"'But if you obey me, says the LORD, and do not carry on your trade at the gates or work on the Sabbath day, and if you keep it holy, ²⁵then kings and their officials will go in and out of these gates forever. There will always be a descendant of David sitting on the throne here in Jerusalem. Kings and their officials will always ride in and out among the people of Judah in chariots and on horses, and this city will remain forever. ²⁶And from all around Jerusalem, from the towns of Judah and Benjamin, from the western foothills* and the hill country and the Negev, the people will come with their burnt offerings and sacrifices. They will bring their grain offerings, frankincense, and thanksgiving offerings to the LORD's Temple. ²⁷"'But if you do not listen to me and refuse to keep the Sabbath holy, and if on the Sabbath day you bring loads of merchandise through the gates of Jerusalem just as on other days, then I will set fire to these gates. The fire will spread to the palaces, and no one will be able to put out the roaring flames.'"

The Potter and the Clay

18 The LORD gave another message to Jeremiah. He said, ²"Go down to the potter's shop, and I will speak to you there." ³So I did as he told me and found the potter working at his wheel. ⁴But the jar he was making did not turn out as he had hoped, so he crushed it into a lump of clay again and started over.

17:26 Hebrew *the Shephelah.*

⁵Then the LORD gave me this message: ⁶"O Israel, can I not do to you as this potter has done to his clay? As the clay is in the potter's hand, so are you in my hand. ⁷If I announce that a certain nation or kingdom is to be uprooted, torn down, and destroyed, ⁸but then that nation renounces its evil ways, I will not destroy it as I had planned. ⁹And if I announce that I will plant and build up a certain nation or kingdom, ¹⁰but then that nation turns to evil and refuses to obey me, I will not bless it as I said I would.

¹¹"Therefore, Jeremiah, go and warn all Judah and Jerusalem. Say to them, 'This is what the LORD says: I am planning disaster for you instead of good. So turn from your evil ways, each of you, and do what is right.'"

¹²But the people replied, "Don't waste your breath. We will continue to live as we want to, stubbornly following our own evil desires."

¹³So this is what the LORD says:

"Has anyone ever heard of such a thing,
  even among the pagan nations?
My virgin daughter Israel
  has done something terrible!
¹⁴ Does the snow ever disappear from the
    mountaintops of Lebanon?
  Do the cold streams flowing from those
    distant mountains ever run dry?
¹⁵ But my people are not so reliable, for they
    have deserted me;
  they burn incense to worthless idols.
They have stumbled off the ancient
    highways
  and walk in muddy paths.
¹⁶ Therefore, their land will become desolate,
    a monument to their stupidity.
All who pass by will be astonished
  and will shake their heads in
    amazement.
¹⁷ I will scatter my people before their
    enemies
  as the east wind scatters dust.
And in all their trouble I will turn my back
    on them
  and refuse to notice their distress."

A Plot against Jeremiah

¹⁸Then the people said, "Come on, let's plot a way to stop Jeremiah. We have plenty of priests and wise men and prophets. We don't need him to teach the word and give us advice and prophecies. Let's spread rumors about him and ignore what he says."

¹⁹ LORD, hear me and help me!
  Listen to what my enemies are saying.
²⁰ Should they repay evil for good?
  They have dug a pit to kill me,
  though I pleaded for them
  and tried to protect them from your
    anger.
²¹ So let their children starve!
  Let them die by the sword!
  Let their wives become childless widows.
  Let their old men die in a plague,
  and let their young men be killed in
    battle!
²² Let screaming be heard from their homes
  as warriors come suddenly upon them.
  For they have dug a pit for me
  and have hidden traps along my path.
²³ LORD, you know all about their murderous
    plots against me.
  Don't forgive their crimes and blot out
    their sins.
  Let them die before you.
  Deal with them in your anger.

Jeremiah's Shattered Jar

19 This is what the LORD said to me: "Go and buy a clay jar. Then ask some of the leaders of the people and of the priests to follow you. ²Go out through the Gate of Broken Pots to the garbage dump in the valley of Ben-Hinnom, and give them this message. ³Say to them, 'Listen to this message from the LORD, you kings of Judah and citizens of Jerusalem! This is what the LORD of Heaven's Armies, the God of Israel, says: I will bring a terrible disaster on this place, and the ears of those who hear about it will ring!

⁴"'For Israel has forsaken me and turned this valley into a place of wickedness. The people burn incense to foreign gods—idols never before acknowledged by this generation, by their ancestors, or by the kings of Judah. And they have filled this place with the blood of innocent children. ⁵They have built pagan shrines to Baal, and there they burn their sons as sacrifices to Baal. I have never commanded such a horrible deed; it never even crossed my mind to command such a thing! ⁶So beware, for the time is coming, says the LORD, when this garbage dump will no longer be called Topheth or the valley of Ben-Hinnom, but the Valley of Slaughter.

⁷"'For I will upset the careful plans of Judah and Jerusalem. I will allow the people to be slaughtered by invading armies, and I will leave their dead bodies as food for the vultures and wild animals. ⁸I will reduce Jerusalem to ruins, making it a monument to their stupidity. All who pass by will be astonished and will gasp at the destruction they see there. ⁹I will see to it that your enemies lay siege to the city until all the food is gone. Then those trapped inside will eat their own sons and daughters and friends. They will be driven to utter despair.'

¹⁰"As these men watch you, Jeremiah, smash the jar you brought. ¹¹Then say to them, 'This is what the LORD of Heaven's Armies says: As this jar lies shattered, so I will shatter the people of Judah and Jerusalem beyond all hope of repair. They will bury the bodies here in Topheth, the garbage dump, until there is no more room for them. ¹²This is what I will do to this place and its people, says the LORD. I will cause this city to become defiled like Topheth. ¹³Yes, all the houses in Jerusalem, including the palace of Judah's kings, will become like Topheth—all the houses where you burned incense on the rooftops to your star gods, and where liquid offerings were poured out to your idols.'"

¹⁴Then Jeremiah returned from Topheth, the garbage dump where he had delivered this message, and he stopped in front of the Temple of the LORD. He said to the people there, ¹⁵"This is what the LORD of Heaven's Armies, the God of Israel, says: 'I will bring disaster upon this city and its surrounding towns as I promised, because you have stubbornly refused to listen to me.'"

Jeremiah and Pashhur

20 Now Pashhur son of Immer, the priest in charge of the Temple of the LORD, heard what Jeremiah was prophesying. ²So he arrested Jeremiah the prophet and had him whipped and put in stocks at the Benjamin Gate of the LORD's Temple.

³The next day, when Pashhur finally released him, Jeremiah said, "Pashhur, the LORD has changed your name. From now on you are to be called 'The Man Who Lives in Terror.'* ⁴For this is what the LORD says: 'I will send terror upon you and all your friends, and you will watch as they are slaughtered by the swords of the enemy. I will hand the people of Judah over to the king of Babylon. He will take them captive to Babylon or run them through with the sword. ⁵And I will let your enemies plunder Jerusalem. All the famed treasures of the city—the precious jewels and gold and silver of your kings—will be carried off to Babylon. ⁶As

20:3 Hebrew *Magor-missabib*, which means "surrounded by terror"; also in 20:10.

for you, Pashhur, you and all your household will go as captives to Babylon. There you will die and be buried, you and all your friends to whom you prophesied that everything would be all right.'"

Jeremiah's Complaint

7 O Lord, you misled me,
    and I allowed myself to be misled.
You are stronger than I am,
    and you overpowered me.
Now I am mocked every day;
    everyone laughs at me.
8 When I speak, the words burst out.
    "Violence and destruction!" I shout.
So these messages from the Lord
    have made me a household joke.
9 But if I say I'll never mention the Lord
    or speak in his name,
his word burns in my heart like a fire.
    It's like a fire in my bones!
I am worn out trying to hold it in!
    I can't do it!
10 I have heard the many rumors about me.
    They call me "The Man Who Lives in
        Terror."
They threaten, "If you say anything, we
        will report it."
    Even my old friends are watching me,
        waiting for a fatal slip.
"He will trap himself," they say,
    "and then we will get our revenge on
        him."

11 But the Lord stands beside me like a great
        warrior.
    Before him my persecutors will stumble.
    They cannot defeat me.
They will fail and be thoroughly
        humiliated.
    Their dishonor will never be forgotten.
12 O Lord of Heaven's Armies,
    you test those who are righteous,
    and you examine the deepest thoughts
        and secrets.
Let me see your vengeance against them,
    for I have committed my cause to you.
13 Sing to the Lord!
    Praise the Lord!
For though I was poor and needy,
    he rescued me from my oppressors.

14 Yet I curse the day I was born!
    May no one celebrate the day of my
        birth.

15 I curse the messenger who told my father,
    "Good news—you have a son!"
16 Let him be destroyed like the cities of old
    that the Lord overthrew without mercy.
Terrify him all day long with battle shouts,
17   because he did not kill me at birth.
Oh, that I had died in my mother's womb,
    that her body had been my grave!
18 Why was I ever born?
    My entire life has been filled
    with trouble, sorrow, and shame.

No Deliverance from Babylon

21 The Lord spoke through Jeremiah when King Zedekiah sent Pashhur son of Malkijah and Zephaniah son of Maaseiah, the priest, to speak with him. They begged Jeremiah, 2"Please speak to the Lord for us and ask him to help us. King Nebuchadnezzar* of Babylon is attacking Judah. Perhaps the Lord will be gracious and do a mighty miracle as he has done in the past. Perhaps he will force Nebuchadnezzar to withdraw his armies."

3Jeremiah replied, "Go back to King Zedekiah and tell him, 4'This is what the Lord, the God of Israel, says: I will make your weapons useless against the king of Babylon and the Babylonians* who are outside your walls attacking you. In fact, I will bring your enemies right into the heart of this city. 5I myself will fight against you with a strong hand and a powerful arm, for I am very angry. You have made me furious! 6I will send a terrible plague upon this city, and both people and animals will die. 7And after all that, says the Lord, I will hand over King Zedekiah, his staff, and everyone else in the city who survives the disease, war, and famine. I will hand them over to King Nebuchadnezzar of Babylon and to their other enemies. He will slaughter them and show them no mercy, pity, or compassion.'

8"Tell all the people, 'This is what the Lord says: Take your choice of life or death! 9Everyone who stays in Jerusalem will die from war, famine, or disease, but those who go out and surrender to the Babylonians will live. Their reward will be life! 10For I have decided to bring disaster and not good upon this city, says the Lord. It will be handed over to the king of Babylon, and he will reduce it to ashes.'

Judgment on Judah's Kings

11"Say to the royal family of Judah, 'Listen to this message from the Lord! 12This is what the Lord says to the dynasty of David:

21:2 Hebrew *Nebuchadrezzar*, a variant spelling of Nebuchadnezzar; also in 21:7.   21:4 Or *Chaldeans*; also in 21:9.

"'Give justice each morning to the people
 you judge!
Help those who have been robbed;
 rescue them from their oppressors.
Otherwise, my anger will burn like an
 unquenchable fire
because of all your sins.
13 I will personally fight against the people
 in Jerusalem,
  that mighty fortress—
the people who boast, "No one can touch
 us here.
No one can break in here."
14 And I myself will punish you for your
 sinfulness,
  says the LORD.
I will light a fire in your forests
 that will burn up everything around
  you.'"

A Message for Judah's Kings

22 This is what the LORD said to me: "Go
over and speak directly to the king of
Judah. Say to him, 2'Listen to this message
from the LORD, you king of Judah, sitting on
David's throne. Let your attendants and your
people listen, too. 3This is what the LORD says:
Be fair-minded and just. Do what is right! Help
those who have been robbed; rescue them from
their oppressors. Quit your evil deeds! Do not
mistreat foreigners, orphans, and widows. Stop
murdering the innocent! 4If you obey me, there
will always be a descendant of David sitting on
the throne here in Jerusalem. The king will
ride through the palace gates in chariots and
on horses, with his parade of attendants and
subjects. 5But if you refuse to pay attention to
this warning, I swear by my own name, says
the LORD, that this palace will become a pile
of rubble.'"

A Message about the Palace

6Now this is what the LORD says concerning
Judah's royal palace:

"I love you as much as fruitful Gilead
 and the green forests of Lebanon.
But I will turn you into a desert,
 with no one living within your walls.
7 I will call for wreckers,
 who will bring out their tools to
  dismantle you.
They will tear out all your fine cedar beams
 and throw them on the fire.

8"People from many nations will pass by the
ruins of this city and say to one another, 'Why
did the LORD destroy such a great city?' 9And
the answer will be, 'Because they violated their
covenant with the LORD their God by worshiping other gods.'"

A Message about Jehoahaz

10 Do not weep for the dead king or mourn
 his loss.
  Instead, weep for the captive king being
  led away!
  For he will never return to see his native
  land again.

11For this is what the LORD says about Jehoahaz,* who succeeded his father, King Josiah,
and was taken away as a captive: "He will never
return. 12He will die in a distant land and will
never again see his own country."

A Message about Jehoiakim

13 And the LORD says, "What sorrow awaits
 Jehoiakim,*
 who builds his palace with forced
  labor.*
He builds injustice into its walls,
 for he makes his neighbors work for
  nothing.
He does not pay them for their labor.
14 He says, 'I will build a magnificent palace
 with huge rooms and many windows.
I will panel it throughout with fragrant
 cedar
 and paint it a lovely red.'
15 But a beautiful cedar palace does not make
 a great king!
Your father, Josiah, also had plenty to
 eat and drink.
But he was just and right in all his
 dealings.
That is why God blessed him.
16 He gave justice and help to the poor and
 needy,
 and everything went well for him.
Isn't that what it means to know me?"
 says the LORD.
17 "But you! You have eyes only for greed and
 dishonesty!
You murder the innocent,
 oppress the poor, and reign ruthlessly."

18Therefore, this is what the LORD says about
Jehoiakim, son of King Josiah:

22:11 Hebrew *Shallum*, another name for Jehoahaz. 22:13a The brother and successor of the exiled Jehoahaz. See 22:18.
22:13b Hebrew *by unrighteousness*.

"The people will not mourn for him,
　　crying to one another,
　　'Alas, my brother! Alas, my sister!'
His subjects will not mourn for him,
　　crying,
　　'Alas, our master is dead! Alas, his
　　splendor is gone!'
19 He will be buried like a dead donkey—
　　dragged out of Jerusalem and dumped
　　outside the gates!
20 Weep for your allies in Lebanon.
　　Shout for them in Bashan.
　　Search for them in the regions east of the
　　river.*
　　See, they are all destroyed.
　　Not one is left to help you.
21 I warned you when you were prosperous,
　　but you replied, 'Don't bother me.'
　　You have been that way since childhood—
　　you simply will not obey me!
22 And now the wind will blow away your
　　allies.
　　All your friends will be taken away as
　　captives.
　　Surely then you will see your
　　wickedness and be ashamed.
23 It may be nice to live in a beautiful palace
　　paneled with wood from the cedars of
　　Lebanon,
　but soon you will groan with pangs of
　　anguish—
　　anguish like that of a woman in labor.

A Message for Jehoiachin

24 "As surely as I live," says the LORD, "I will
abandon you, Jehoiachin* son of Jehoiakim,
king of Judah. Even if you were the signet
ring on my right hand, I would pull you off.
25 I will hand you over to those who seek to
kill you, those you so desperately fear—to
King Nebuchadnezzar* of Babylon and the
mighty Babylonian* army. 26 I will expel you
and your mother from this land, and you will
die in a foreign country, not in your native
land. 27 You will never again return to the land
you yearn for.

28 "Why is this man Jehoiachin like a
　　discarded, broken jar?
　　Why are he and his children to be exiled
　　to a foreign land?
29 O earth, earth, earth!
　　Listen to this message from the LORD!
30 This is what the LORD says:

'Let the record show that this man
　　Jehoiachin was childless.
He is a failure,
for none of his children will succeed him
　　on the throne of David
　　to rule over Judah.'

The Righteous Descendant

23 "What sorrow awaits the leaders of my
people—the shepherds of my sheep—
for they have destroyed and scattered the very
ones they were expected to care for," says the
LORD.

2 Therefore, this is what the LORD, the God
of Israel, says to these shepherds: "Instead of
caring for my flock and leading them to safety,
you have deserted them and driven them to
destruction. Now I will pour out judgment on
you for the evil you have done to them. 3 But I
will gather together the remnant of my flock
from the countries where I have driven them.
I will bring them back to their own sheepfold,
and they will be fruitful and increase in number. 4 Then I will appoint responsible shepherds
who will care for them, and they will never be
afraid again. Not a single one will be lost or
missing. I, the LORD, have spoken!

5 "For the time is coming,"
　　says the LORD,
　"when I will raise up a righteous
　　descendant*
　　from King David's line.
He will be a King who rules with wisdom.
　　He will do what is just and right
　　throughout the land.
6 And this will be his name:
　　'The LORD Is Our Righteousness.'*
In that day Judah will be saved,
　　and Israel will live in safety.

7 "In that day," says the LORD, "when people
are taking an oath, they will no longer say,
'As surely as the LORD lives, who rescued the
people of Israel from the land of Egypt.' 8 Instead, they will say, 'As surely as the LORD lives,
who brought the people of Israel back to their
own land from the land of the north and from
all the countries to which he had exiled them.'
Then they will live in their own land."

Judgment on False Prophets

9 My heart is broken because of the false
　　prophets,

22:20 Or *in Abarim*.　22:24 Hebrew *Coniah*, a variant spelling of Jehoiachin; also in 22:28.　22:25a Hebrew *Nebuchadrezzar*, a
variant spelling of Nebuchadnezzar.　22:25b Or *Chaldean*.　23:5 Hebrew *a righteous branch*.　23:6 Hebrew *Yahweh Tsidqenu*.

and my bones tremble.
I stagger like a drunkard,
    like someone overcome by wine,
because of the holy words
    the LORD has spoken against them.
10 For the land is full of adultery,
    and it lies under a curse.
The land itself is in mourning—
    its wilderness pastures are dried up.
For they all do evil
    and abuse what power they have.

11 "Even the priests and prophets
    are ungodly, wicked men.
I have seen their despicable acts
    right here in my own Temple,"
says the LORD.
12 "Therefore, the paths they take
    will become slippery.
They will be chased through the dark,
    and there they will fall.
For I will bring disaster upon them
    at the time fixed for their punishment.
I, the LORD, have spoken!

13 "I saw that the prophets of Samaria were
    terribly evil,
for they prophesied in the name of Baal
    and led my people of Israel into sin.
14 But now I see that the prophets of
    Jerusalem are even worse!
They commit adultery and love
    dishonesty.
They encourage those who are doing evil
    so that no one turns away from their
    sins.
These prophets are as wicked
    as the people of Sodom and Gomorrah
    once were."

15Therefore, this is what the LORD of Heaven's Armies says concerning the prophets:

"I will feed them with bitterness
    and give them poison to drink.
For it is because of Jerusalem's prophets
    that wickedness has filled this land."

16This is what the LORD of Heaven's Armies says to his people:

"Do not listen to these prophets when they
    prophesy to you,
filling you with futile hopes.
They are making up everything they say.
    They do not speak for the LORD!

17 They keep saying to those who despise my
    word,
    'Don't worry! The LORD says you will
    have peace!'
And to those who stubbornly follow their
    own desires,
    they say, 'No harm will come your way!'

18 "Have any of these prophets been in the
    LORD's presence
    to hear what he is really saying?
    Has even one of them cared enough to
    listen?
19 Look! The LORD's anger bursts out like a
    storm,
    a whirlwind that swirls down on the
    heads of the wicked.
20 The anger of the LORD will not diminish
    until it has finished all he has planned.
In the days to come
    you will understand all this very clearly.

21 "I have not sent these prophets,
    yet they run around claiming to speak
    for me.
I have given them no message,
    yet they go on prophesying.
22 If they had stood before me and listened
    to me,
    they would have spoken my words,
and they would have turned my people
    from their evil ways and deeds.
23 Am I a God who is only close at hand?"
    says the LORD.
    "No, I am far away at the same time.
24 Can anyone hide from me in a secret place?
    Am I not everywhere in all the heavens
    and earth?"
says the LORD.

25"I have heard these prophets say, 'Listen to the dream I had from God last night.' And then they proceed to tell lies in my name. 26How long will this go on? If they are prophets, they are prophets of deceit, inventing everything they say. 27By telling these false dreams, they are trying to get my people to forget me, just as their ancestors did by worshiping the idols of Baal.

28 "Let these false prophets tell their dreams,
    but let my true messengers faithfully
    proclaim my every word.
There is a difference between straw and
    grain!
29 Does not my word burn like fire?"
    says the LORD.

"Is it not like a mighty hammer
that smashes a rock to pieces?

[30] "Therefore," says the LORD, "I am against these prophets who steal messages from each other and claim they are from me. [31] I am against these smooth-tongued prophets who say, 'This prophecy is from the LORD!' [32] I am against these false prophets. Their imaginary dreams are flagrant lies that lead my people into sin. I did not send or appoint them, and they have no message at all for my people. I, the LORD, have spoken!

False Prophecies and False Prophets

[33] "Suppose one of the people or one of the prophets or priests asks you, 'What prophecy has the LORD burdened you with now?' You must reply, 'You are the burden!* The LORD says he will abandon you!'

[34] "If any prophet, priest, or anyone else says, 'I have a prophecy from the LORD,' I will punish that person along with his entire family. [35] You should keep asking each other, 'What is the LORD's answer?' or 'What is the LORD saying?' [36] But stop using this phrase, 'prophecy from the LORD.' For people are using it to give authority to their own ideas, turning upside down the words of our God, the living God, the LORD of Heaven's Armies.

[37] "This is what you should say to the prophets: 'What is the LORD's answer?' or 'What is the LORD saying?' [38] But suppose they respond, 'This is a prophecy from the LORD!' Then you should say, 'This is what the LORD says: Because you have used this phrase, "prophecy from the LORD," even though I warned you not to use it, [39] I will forget you completely.* I will expel you from my presence, along with this city that I gave to you and your ancestors. [40] And I will make you an object of ridicule, and your name will be infamous throughout the ages.'"

Good and Bad Figs

24 After King Nebuchadnezzar* of Babylon exiled Jehoiachin* son of Jehoiakim, king of Judah, to Babylon along with the officials of Judah and all the craftsmen and artisans, the LORD gave me this vision. I saw two baskets of figs placed in front of the LORD's Temple in Jerusalem. [2] One basket was filled with fresh, ripe figs, while the other was filled with bad figs that were too rotten to eat. [3] Then the LORD said to me, "What do you see, Jeremiah?"

I replied, "Figs, some very good and some very bad, too rotten to eat."

[4] Then the LORD gave me this message: [5] "This is what the LORD, the God of Israel, says: The good figs represent the exiles I sent from Judah to the land of the Babylonians.* [6] I will watch over and care for them, and I will bring them back here again. I will build them up and not tear them down. I will plant them and not uproot them. [7] I will give them hearts that recognize me as the LORD. They will be my people, and I will be their God, for they will return to me wholeheartedly.

[8] "But the bad figs," the LORD said, "represent King Zedekiah of Judah, his officials, all the people left in Jerusalem, and those who live in Egypt. I will treat them like bad figs, too rotten to eat. [9] I will make them an object of horror and a symbol of evil to every nation on earth. They will be disgraced and mocked, taunted and cursed, wherever I scatter them. [10] And I will send war, famine, and disease until they have vanished from the land of Israel, which I gave to them and their ancestors."

Seventy Years of Captivity

25 This message for all the people of Judah came to Jeremiah from the LORD during the fourth year of Jehoiakim's reign over Judah.* This was the year when King Nebuchadnezzar* of Babylon began his reign.

[2] Jeremiah the prophet said to all the people in Judah and Jerusalem, [3] "For the past twenty-three years—from the thirteenth year of the reign of Josiah son of Amon,* king of Judah, until now—the LORD has been giving me his messages. I have faithfully passed them on to you, but you have not listened.

[4] "Again and again the LORD has sent you his servants, the prophets, but you have not listened or even paid attention. [5] Each time the message was this: 'Turn from the evil road you are traveling and from the evil things you are doing. Only then will I let you live in this land that the LORD gave to you and your ancestors forever. [6] Do not provoke my anger by worshiping idols you made with your own hands. Then I will not harm you.'

23:33 As in Greek version and Latin Vulgate; Hebrew reads *What burden?*   23:39 Some Hebrew manuscripts and Greek version read *I will surely lift you up.*   24:1a Hebrew *Nebuchadrezzar,* a variant spelling of Nebuchadnezzar.   24:1b Hebrew *Jeconiah,* a variant spelling of Jehoiachin.   24:5 Or *Chaldeans.*   25:1a The fourth year of Jehoiakim's reign and the accession year of Nebuchadnezzar's reign was 605 B.C.   25:1b Hebrew *Nebuchadrezzar,* a variant spelling of Nebuchadnezzar; also in 25:9.   25:3 The thirteenth year of Josiah's reign was 627 B.C.

⁷"But you would not listen to me," says the Lord. "You made me furious by worshiping idols you made with your own hands, bringing on yourselves all the disasters you now suffer. ⁸And now the Lord of Heaven's Armies says: Because you have not listened to me, ⁹I will gather together all the armies of the north under King Nebuchadnezzar of Babylon, whom I have appointed as my deputy. I will bring them all against this land and its people and against the surrounding nations. I will completely destroy* you and make you an object of horror and contempt and a ruin forever. ¹⁰I will take away your happy singing and laughter. The joyful voices of bridegrooms and brides will no longer be heard. Your millstones will fall silent, and the lights in your homes will go out. ¹¹This entire land will become a desolate wasteland. Israel and her neighboring lands will serve the king of Babylon for seventy years.

¹²"Then, after the seventy years of captivity are over, I will punish the king of Babylon and his people for their sins," says the Lord. "I will make the country of the Babylonians* a wasteland forever. ¹³I will bring upon them all the terrors I have promised in this book— all the penalties announced by Jeremiah against the nations. ¹⁴Many nations and great kings will enslave the Babylonians, just as they enslaved my people. I will punish them in proportion to the suffering they cause my people."

The Cup of the Lord's Anger

¹⁵This is what the Lord, the God of Israel, said to me: "Take from my hand this cup filled to the brim with my anger, and make all the nations to whom I send you drink from it. ¹⁶When they drink from it, they will stagger, crazed by the warfare I will send against them."

¹⁷So I took the cup of anger from the Lord and made all the nations drink from it—every nation to which the Lord sent me. ¹⁸I went to Jerusalem and the other towns of Judah, and their kings and officials drank from the cup. From that day until this, they have been a desolate ruin, an object of horror, contempt, and cursing. ¹⁹I gave the cup to Pharaoh, king of Egypt, his attendants, his officials, and all his people, ²⁰along with all the foreigners living in that land. I also gave it to all the kings of the land of Uz and the kings of the Philistine cities of Ashkelon, Gaza, Ekron, and what

remains of Ashdod. ²¹Then I gave the cup to the nations of Edom, Moab, and Ammon, ²²and the kings of Tyre and Sidon, and the kings of the regions across the sea. ²³I gave it to Dedan, Tema, and Buz, and to the people who live in distant places.* ²⁴I gave it to the kings of Arabia, the kings of the nomadic tribes of the desert, ²⁵and to the kings of Zimri, Elam, and Media. ²⁶And I gave it to the kings of the northern countries, far and near, one after the other— all the kingdoms of the world. And finally, the king of Babylon* himself drank from the cup of the Lord's anger.

²⁷Then the Lord said to me, "Now tell them, 'This is what the Lord of Heaven's Armies, the God of Israel, says: Drink from this cup of my anger. Get drunk and vomit; fall to rise no more, for I am sending terrible wars against you.' ²⁸And if they refuse to accept the cup, tell them, 'The Lord of Heaven's Armies says: You have no choice but to drink from it. ²⁹I have begun to punish Jerusalem, the city that bears my name. Now should I let you go unpunished? No, you will not escape disaster. I will call for war against all the nations of the earth. I, the Lord of Heaven's Armies, have spoken!'

³⁰"Now prophesy all these things, and say to them,

"'The Lord will roar against his own land
    from his holy dwelling in heaven.
He will shout like those who tread grapes;
    he will shout against everyone on earth.
³¹ His cry of judgment will reach the ends of
        the earth,
    for the Lord will bring his case against
        all the nations.
He will judge all the people of the earth,
    slaughtering the wicked with the sword.
    I, the Lord, have spoken!'"

³² This is what the Lord of Heaven's Armies
        says:
    "Look! Disaster will fall upon nation
        after nation!
A great whirlwind of fury is rising
    from the most distant corners of the
        earth!"

³³In that day those the Lord has slaughtered will fill the earth from one end to the other. No one will mourn for them or gather up their

25:9 The Hebrew term used here refers to the complete consecration of things or people to the Lord, either by destroying them or by giving them as an offering.   25:12 Or Chaldeans.   25:23 Or who clip the corners of their hair.   25:26 Hebrew of Sheshach, a code name for Babylon.

bodies to bury them. They will be scattered on the ground like manure.

³⁴ Weep and moan, you evil shepherds!
   Roll in the dust, you leaders of the flock!
   The time of your slaughter has arrived;
      you will fall and shatter like a fragile
         vase.
³⁵ You will find no place to hide;
      there will be no way to escape.
³⁶ Listen to the frantic cries of the shepherds.
   The leaders of the flock are wailing in
      despair,
   for the LORD is ruining their pastures.
³⁷ Peaceful meadows will be turned into a
      wasteland
   by the LORD's fierce anger.
³⁸ He has left his den like a strong lion
      seeking its prey,
   and their land will be made desolate
   by the sword* of the enemy
   and the LORD's fierce anger.

Jeremiah's Escape from Death

26 This message came to Jeremiah from the LORD early in the reign of Jehoiakim son of Josiah,* king of Judah. ²"This is what the LORD says: Stand in the courtyard in front of the Temple of the LORD, and make an announcement to the people who have come there to worship from all over Judah. Give them my entire message; include every word. ³Perhaps they will listen and turn from their evil ways. Then I will change my mind about the disaster I am ready to pour out on them because of their sins.

⁴"Say to them, 'This is what the LORD says: If you will not listen to me and obey my word I have given you, ⁵and if you will not listen to my servants, the prophets—for I sent them again and again to warn you, but you would not listen to them—⁶then I will destroy this Temple as I destroyed Shiloh, the place where the Tabernacle was located. And I will make Jerusalem an object of cursing in every nation on earth.'"

⁷The priests, the prophets, and all the people listened to Jeremiah as he spoke in front of the LORD's Temple. ⁸But when Jeremiah had finished his message, saying everything the LORD had told him to say, the priests and prophets and all the people at the Temple mobbed him. "Kill him!" they shouted. ⁹"What right do you have to prophesy in the LORD's name that this Temple will be destroyed like Shiloh? What do you mean, saying that Jerusalem will be destroyed and left with no inhabitants?" And all the people threatened him as he stood in front of the Temple.

¹⁰When the officials of Judah heard what was happening, they rushed over from the palace and sat down at the New Gate of the Temple to hold court. ¹¹The priests and prophets presented their accusations to the officials and the people. "This man should die!" they said. "You have heard with your own ears what a traitor he is, for he has prophesied against this city."

¹²Then Jeremiah spoke to the officials and the people in his own defense. "The LORD sent me to prophesy against this Temple and this city," he said. "The LORD gave me every word that I have spoken. ¹³But if you stop your sinning and begin to obey the LORD your God, he will change his mind about this disaster that he has announced against you. ¹⁴As for me, I am in your hands—do with me as you think best. ¹⁵But if you kill me, rest assured that you will be killing an innocent man! The responsibility for such a deed will lie on you, on this city, and on every person living in it. For it is absolutely true that the LORD sent me to speak every word you have heard."

¹⁶Then the officials and the people said to the priests and prophets, "This man does not deserve the death sentence, for he has spoken to us in the name of the LORD our God."

¹⁷Then some of the wise old men stood and spoke to all the people assembled there. ¹⁸They said, "Remember when Micah of Moresheth prophesied during the reign of King Hezekiah of Judah. He told the people of Judah,

'This is what the LORD of Heaven's Armies
   says:
Mount Zion will be plowed like an open
   field;
   Jerusalem will be reduced to ruins!
A thicket will grow on the heights
   where the Temple now stands.'*

¹⁹But did King Hezekiah and the people kill him for saying this? No, they turned from their sins and worshiped the LORD. They begged him for mercy. Then the LORD changed his mind about the terrible disaster he had pronounced against them. So we are about to do ourselves great harm."

²⁰At this time Uriah son of Shemaiah from

25:38 As in some Hebrew manuscripts and Greek version; Masoretic Text reads *by the anger.*   26:1 The first year of Jehoiakim's reign was 608 B.C.   26:18 Mic 3:12.

Kiriath-jearim was also prophesying for the LORD. And he predicted the same terrible disaster against the city and nation as Jeremiah did. [21]When King Jehoiakim and the army officers and officials heard what he was saying, the king sent someone to kill him. But Uriah heard about the plan and escaped in fear to Egypt. [22]Then King Jehoiakim sent Elnathan son of Acbor to Egypt along with several other men to capture Uriah. [23]They took him prisoner and brought him back to King Jehoiakim. The king then killed Uriah with a sword and had him buried in an unmarked grave.

[24]Nevertheless, Ahikam son of Shaphan stood up for Jeremiah and persuaded the court not to turn him over to the mob to be killed.

Jeremiah Wears an Ox Yoke

27 This message came to Jeremiah from the LORD early in the reign of Zedekiah* son of Josiah, king of Judah.

[2]This is what the LORD said to me: "Make a yoke, and fasten it on your neck with leather straps. [3]Then send messages to the kings of Edom, Moab, Ammon, Tyre, and Sidon through their ambassadors who have come to see King Zedekiah in Jerusalem. [4]Give them this message for their masters: 'This is what the LORD of Heaven's Armies, the God of Israel, says: [5]With my great strength and powerful arm I made the earth and all its people and every animal. I can give these things of mine to anyone I choose. [6]Now I will give your countries to King Nebuchadnezzar of Babylon, who is my servant. I have put everything, even the wild animals, under his control. [7]All the nations will serve him, his son, and his grandson until his time is up. Then many nations and great kings will conquer and rule over Babylon. [8]So you must submit to Babylon's king and serve him; put your neck under Babylon's yoke! I will punish any nation that refuses to be his slave, says the LORD. I will send war, famine, and disease upon that nation until Babylon has conquered it.

[9]"'Do not listen to your false prophets, fortune-tellers, interpreters of dreams, mediums, and sorcerers who say, "The king of Babylon will not conquer you." [10]They are all liars, and their lies will lead to your being driven out of your land. I will drive you out and send you far away to die. [11]But the people of any nation that submits to the king of Babylon will be allowed to stay in their own country to farm the land as usual. I, the LORD, have spoken!'"

[12]Then I repeated this same message to King Zedekiah of Judah. "If you want to live, submit to the yoke of the king of Babylon and his people. [13]Why do you insist on dying—you and your people? Why should you choose war, famine, and disease, which the LORD will bring against every nation that refuses to submit to Babylon's king? [14]Do not listen to the false prophets who keep telling you, 'The king of Babylon will not conquer you.' They are liars. [15]This is what the LORD says: 'I have not sent these prophets! They are telling you lies in my name, so I will drive you from this land. You will all die—you and all these prophets, too.'"

[16]Then I spoke to the priests and the people and said, "This is what the LORD says: 'Do not listen to your prophets who claim that soon the gold articles taken from my Temple will be returned from Babylon. It is all a lie! [17]Do not listen to them. Surrender to the king of Babylon, and you will live. Why should this whole city be destroyed? [18]If they really are prophets and speak the LORD's messages, let them pray to the LORD of Heaven's Armies. Let them pray that the articles remaining in the LORD's Temple and in the king's palace and in the palaces of Jerusalem will not be carried away to Babylon!'

[19]"For the LORD of Heaven's Armies has spoken about the pillars in front of the Temple, the great bronze basin called the Sea, the water carts, and all the other ceremonial articles. [20]King Nebuchadnezzar of Babylon left them here when he exiled Jehoiachin* son of Jehoiakim, king of Judah, to Babylon, along with all the other nobles of Judah and Jerusalem. [21]Yes, this is what the LORD of Heaven's Armies, the God of Israel, says about the precious things still in the Temple, in the palace of Judah's king, and in Jerusalem: [22]'They will all be carried away to Babylon and will stay there until I send for them,' says the LORD. 'Then I will bring them back to Jerusalem again.'"

Jeremiah Condemns Hananiah

28 One day in late summer* of that same year—the fourth year of the reign of Zedekiah, king of Judah—Hananiah son of Azzur, a prophet from Gibeon, addressed me

---

27:1 As in some Hebrew manuscripts and Syriac version (see also 27:3, 12); most Hebrew manuscripts read *Jehoiakim*. 27:20 Hebrew *Jeconiah*, a variant spelling of Jehoiachin. 28:1 Hebrew *In the fifth month*, of the ancient Hebrew lunar calendar. The fifth month in the fourth year of Zedekiah's reign occurred within the months of August and September 593 B.C. Also see note on 1:3.

publicly in the Temple while all the priests and people listened. He said, ²"This is what the LORD of Heaven's Armies, the God of Israel, says: 'I will remove the yoke of the king of Babylon from your necks. ³Within two years I will bring back all the Temple treasures that King Nebuchadnezzar carried off to Babylon. ⁴And I will bring back Jehoiachin* son of Jehoiakim, king of Judah, and all the other captives that were taken to Babylon. I will surely break the yoke that the king of Babylon has put on your necks. I, the LORD, have spoken!'"

⁵Jeremiah responded to Hananiah as they stood in front of all the priests and people at the Temple. ⁶He said, "Amen! May your prophecies come true! I hope the LORD does everything you say. I hope he does bring back from Babylon the treasures of this Temple and all the captives. ⁷But listen now to the solemn words I speak to you in the presence of all these people. ⁸The ancient prophets who preceded you and me spoke against many nations, always warning of war, disaster, and disease. ⁹So a prophet who predicts peace must show he is right. Only when his predictions come true can we know that he is really from the LORD."

¹⁰Then Hananiah the prophet took the yoke off Jeremiah's neck and broke it in pieces. ¹¹And Hananiah said again to the crowd that had gathered, "This is what the LORD says: 'Just as this yoke has been broken, within two years I will break the yoke of oppression from all the nations now subject to King Nebuchadnezzar of Babylon.'" With that, Jeremiah left the Temple area.

¹²Soon after this confrontation with Hananiah, the LORD gave this message to Jeremiah: ¹³"Go and tell Hananiah, 'This is what the LORD says: You have broken a wooden yoke, but you have replaced it with a yoke of iron. ¹⁴The LORD of Heaven's Armies, the God of Israel, says: I have put a yoke of iron on the necks of all these nations, forcing them into slavery under King Nebuchadnezzar of Babylon. I have put everything, even the wild animals, under his control.'"

¹⁵Then Jeremiah the prophet said to Hananiah, "Listen, Hananiah! The LORD has not sent you, but the people believe your lies. ¹⁶Therefore, this is what the LORD says: 'You must die. Your life will end this very year because you have rebelled against the LORD.'"

¹⁷Two months later* the prophet Hananiah died.

A Letter to the Exiles

29 Jeremiah wrote a letter from Jerusalem to the elders, priests, prophets, and all the people who had been exiled to Babylon by King Nebuchadnezzar. ²This was after King Jehoiachin,* the queen mother, the court officials, the other officials of Judah, and all the craftsmen and artisans had been deported from Jerusalem. ³He sent the letter with Elasah son of Shaphan and Gemariah son of Hilkiah when they went to Babylon as King Zedekiah's ambassadors to Nebuchadnezzar. This is what Jeremiah's letter said:

⁴This is what the LORD of Heaven's Armies, the God of Israel, says to all the captives he has exiled to Babylon from Jerusalem: ⁵"Build homes, and plan to stay. Plant gardens, and eat the food they produce. ⁶Marry and have children. Then find spouses for them so that you may have many grandchildren. Multiply! Do not dwindle away! ⁷And work for the peace and prosperity of the city where I sent you into exile. Pray to the LORD for it, for its welfare will determine your welfare."

⁸This is what the LORD of Heaven's Armies, the God of Israel, says: "Do not let your prophets and fortune-tellers who are with you in the land of Babylon trick you. Do not listen to their dreams, ⁹because they are telling you lies in my name. I have not sent them," says the LORD.

¹⁰This is what the LORD says: "You will be in Babylon for seventy years. But then I will come and do for you all the good things I have promised, and I will bring you home again. ¹¹For I know the plans I have for you," says the LORD. "They are plans for good and not for disaster, to give you a future and a hope. ¹²In those days when you pray, I will listen. ¹³If you look for me wholeheartedly, you will find me. ¹⁴I will be found by you," says the LORD. "I will end your captivity and restore your fortunes. I will gather you out of the nations where I sent you and will bring you home again to your own land."

¹⁵You claim that the LORD has raised up prophets for you in Babylon. ¹⁶But this is what the LORD says about the king who sits on David's throne and all those still living here in Jerusalem—your relatives who were not exiled to Babylon. ¹⁷This is

---

28:4 Hebrew *Jeconiah*, a variant spelling of Jehoiachin.   28:17 Hebrew *In the seventh month of that same year.* See 28:1 and the note there.   29:2 Hebrew *Jeconiah*, a variant spelling of Jehoiachin.

what the LORD of Heaven's Armies says: "I will send war, famine, and disease upon them and make them like bad figs, too rotten to eat. 18Yes, I will pursue them with war, famine, and disease, and I will scatter them around the world. In every nation where I send them, I will make them an object of damnation, horror, contempt, and mockery. 19For they refuse to listen to me, though I have spoken to them repeatedly through the prophets I sent. And you who are in exile have not listened either," says the LORD.

20Therefore, listen to this message from the LORD, all you captives there in Babylon. 21This is what the LORD of Heaven's Armies, the God of Israel, says about your prophets—Ahab son of Kolaiah and Zedekiah son of Maaseiah—who are telling you lies in my name: "I will turn them over to Nebuchadnezzar* for execution before your eyes. 22Their terrible fate will become proverbial, so that the Judean exiles will curse someone by saying, 'May the LORD make you like Zedekiah and Ahab, whom the king of Babylon burned alive!' 23For these men have done terrible things among my people. They have committed adultery with their neighbors' wives and have lied in my name, saying things I did not command. I am a witness to this. I, the LORD, have spoken."

A Message for Shemaiah

24The LORD sent this message to Shemaiah the Nehelamite in Babylon: 25"This is what the LORD of Heaven's Armies, the God of Israel, says: You wrote a letter on your own authority to Zephaniah son of Maaseiah, the priest, and you sent copies to the other priests and people in Jerusalem. You wrote to Zephaniah,

26"The LORD has appointed you to replace Jehoiada as the priest in charge of the house of the LORD. You are responsible to put into stocks and neck irons any crazy man who claims to be a prophet. 27So why have you done nothing to stop Jeremiah from Anathoth, who pretends to be a prophet among you? 28Jeremiah sent a letter here to Babylon, predicting that our captivity will be a long one. He said, 'Build homes, and plan to stay. Plant gardens, and eat the food they produce.'"

29But when Zephaniah the priest received Shemaiah's letter, he took it to Jeremiah and read it to him. 30Then the LORD gave this message to Jeremiah: 31"Send an open letter to all the exiles in Babylon. Tell them, 'This is what the LORD says concerning Shemaiah the Nehelamite: Since he has prophesied to you when I did not send him and has tricked you into believing his lies, 32I will punish him and his family. None of his descendants will see the good things I will do for my people, for he has incited you to rebel against me. I, the LORD, have spoken!'"

Promises of Deliverance

30 The LORD gave another message to Jeremiah. He said, 2"This is what the LORD, the God of Israel, says: Write down for the record everything I have said to you, Jeremiah. 3For the time is coming when I will restore the fortunes of my people of Israel and Judah. I will bring them home to this land that I gave to their ancestors, and they will possess it again. I, the LORD, have spoken!"

4This is the message the LORD gave concerning Israel and Judah. 5This is what the LORD says:

"I hear cries of fear;
　　there is terror and no peace.
6 Now let me ask you a question:
　　Do men give birth to babies?
Then why do they stand there,
　　　　ashen-faced,
hands pressed against their sides
　　like a woman in labor?
7 In all history there has never been such
　　a time of terror.
It will be a time of trouble for my
　　people Israel.*
Yet in the end they will be saved!
8 For in that day,"
　　says the LORD of Heaven's Armies,
"I will break the yoke from their necks
　　and snap their chains.
Foreigners will no longer be their
　　masters.
9 For my people will serve the LORD their
　　God
and their king descended from David—
　　the king I will raise up for them.

10 "So do not be afraid, Jacob, my servant;
　　do not be dismayed, Israel,"
　　says the LORD.

29:21 Hebrew *Nebuchadrezzar,* a variant spelling of Nebuchadnezzar.　30:7 Hebrew *Jacob;* also in 30:10b, 18. See note on 5:20.

"For I will bring you home again from
    distant lands,
  and your children will return from their
    exile.
Israel will return to a life of peace and
    quiet,
  and no one will terrorize them.
¹¹ For I am with you and will save you,"
    says the LORD.
"I will completely destroy the nations
    where I have scattered you,
  but I will not completely destroy you.
I will discipline you, but with justice;
  I cannot let you go unpunished."

¹² This is what the LORD says:
"Your injury is incurable—
    a terrible wound.
¹³ There is no one to help you
    or to bind up your injury.
  No medicine can heal you.
¹⁴ All your lovers—your allies—have left you
    and do not care about you anymore.
I have wounded you cruelly,
    as though I were your enemy.
For your sins are many,
    and your guilt is great.
¹⁵ Why do you protest your punishment—
    this wound that has no cure?
I have had to punish you
    because your sins are many
    and your guilt is great.

¹⁶ "But all who devour you will be
    devoured,
  and all your enemies will be sent
    into exile.
All who plunder you will be plundered,
  and all who attack you will be attacked.
¹⁷ I will give you back your health
    and heal your wounds," says the LORD.
"For you are called an outcast—
    'Jerusalem* for whom no one cares.'"

¹⁸ This is what the LORD says:
"When I bring Israel home again from
    captivity
  and restore their fortunes,
Jerusalem will be rebuilt on its ruins,
  and the palace reconstructed as before.
¹⁹ There will be joy and songs of
    thanksgiving,
  and I will multiply my people, not
    diminish them;
I will honor them, not despise them.

²⁰ Their children will prosper as they did
    long ago.
I will establish them as a nation before me,
  and I will punish anyone who hurts
    them.
²¹ They will have their own ruler again,
  and he will come from their own
    people.
I will invite him to approach me," says
    the LORD,
  "for who would dare to come unless
    invited?
²² You will be my people,
  and I will be your God."

²³ Look! The LORD's anger bursts out like a
    storm,
  a driving wind that swirls down on the
    heads of the wicked.
²⁴ The fierce anger of the LORD will not
    diminish
  until it has finished all he has planned.
In the days to come
  you will understand all this.

Hope for Restoration

31 "In that day," says the LORD, "I will be
the God of all the families of Israel, and
they will be my people. ²This is what the LORD
says:

"Those who survive the coming
    destruction
  will find blessings even in the barren
    land,
  for I will give rest to the people of
    Israel."

³ Long ago the LORD said to Israel:
"I have loved you, my people, with an
    everlasting love.
  With unfailing love I have drawn you
    to myself.
⁴ I will rebuild you, my virgin Israel.
  You will again be happy
    and dance merrily with your
    tambourines.
⁵ Again you will plant your vineyards on
    the mountains of Samaria
  and eat from your own gardens there.
⁶ The day will come when watchmen will
    shout
  from the hill country of Ephraim,
'Come, let us go up to Jerusalem*
  to worship the LORD our God.'"

30:17 Hebrew *Zion.*   31:6 Hebrew *Zion;* also in 31:12.

7 Now this is what the LORD says:
"Sing with joy for Israel.*
  Shout for the greatest of nations!
Shout out with praise and joy:
'Save your people, O LORD,
  the remnant of Israel!'
8 For I will bring them from the north
  and from the distant corners of the earth.
I will not forget the blind and lame,
  the expectant mothers and women in
    labor.
A great company will return!
9 Tears of joy will stream down their faces,
  and I will lead them home with great
    care.
They will walk beside quiet streams
  and on smooth paths where they will
    not stumble.
For I am Israel's father,
  and Ephraim is my oldest child.

10 "Listen to this message from the LORD,
  you nations of the world;
  proclaim it in distant coastlands:
The LORD, who scattered his people,
  will gather them and watch over them
  as a shepherd does his flock.
11 For the LORD has redeemed Israel
  from those too strong for them.
12 They will come home and sing songs of joy
  on the heights of Jerusalem.
  They will be radiant because of the
    LORD's good gifts—
  the abundant crops of grain, new wine,
    and olive oil,
  and the healthy flocks and herds.
Their life will be like a watered garden,
  and all their sorrows will be gone.
13 The young women will dance for joy,
  and the men—old and young—will
    join in the celebration.
I will turn their mourning into joy.
  I will comfort them and exchange their
    sorrow for rejoicing.
14 The priests will enjoy abundance,
  and my people will feast on my good
    gifts.
I, the LORD, have spoken!"

Rachel's Sadness Turns to Joy
15 This is what the LORD says:

"A cry is heard in Ramah—
  deep anguish and bitter weeping.

Rachel weeps for her children,
  refusing to be comforted—
  for her children are gone."

16 But now this is what the LORD says:
"Do not weep any longer,
  for I will reward you," says the LORD.
"Your children will come back to you
  from the distant land of the enemy.
17 There is hope for your future," says the
  LORD.
"Your children will come again to their
  own land.
18 I have heard Israel* saying,
'You disciplined me severely,
  like a calf that needs training for the
    yoke.
Turn me again to you and restore me,
  for you alone are the LORD my God.
19 I turned away from God,
  but then I was sorry.
I kicked myself for my stupidity!
  I was thoroughly ashamed of all I did
  in my younger days.'
20 "Is not Israel still my son,
  my darling child?" says the LORD.
"I often have to punish him,
  but I still love him.
That's why I long for him
  and surely will have mercy on him.
21 Set up road signs;
  put up guideposts.
Mark well the path
  by which you came.
Come back again, my virgin Israel;
  return to your towns here.
22 How long will you wander,
  my wayward daughter?
For the LORD will cause something new
    to happen—
  Israel will embrace her God.*"

23 This is what the LORD of Heaven's Armies,
the God of Israel, says: "When I bring them
back from captivity, the people of Judah and
its towns will again say, 'The LORD bless you,
O righteous home, O holy mountain!' 24 Townspeople and farmers and shepherds alike will
live together in peace and happiness. 25 For
I have given rest to the weary and joy to the
sorrowing."

26 At this, I woke up and looked around. My
sleep had been very sweet.

31:7 Hebrew *Jacob;* also in 31:11. See note on 5:20.   31:18 Hebrew *Ephraim,* referring to the northern kingdom of Israel;
also in 31:20.   31:22 Hebrew *a woman will surround a man.*

27"The day is coming," says the LORD, "when I will greatly increase the human population and the number of animals here in Israel and Judah. 28In the past I deliberately uprooted and tore down this nation. I overthrew it, destroyed it, and brought disaster upon it. But in the future I will just as deliberately plant it and build it up. I, the LORD, have spoken!

29"The people will no longer quote this proverb:

'The parents have eaten sour grapes,
     but their children's mouths pucker at
          the taste.'

30All people will die for their own sins—those who eat the sour grapes will be the ones whose mouths will pucker.

31"The day is coming," says the LORD, "when I will make a new covenant with the people of Israel and Judah. 32This covenant will not be like the one I made with their ancestors when I took them by the hand and brought them out of the land of Egypt. They broke that covenant, though I loved them as a husband loves his wife," says the LORD.

33"But this is the new covenant I will make with the people of Israel after those days," says the LORD. "I will put my instructions deep within them, and I will write them on their hearts. I will be their God, and they will be my people. 34And they will not need to teach their neighbors, nor will they need to teach their relatives, saying, 'You should know the LORD.' For everyone, from the least to the greatest, will know me already," says the LORD. "And I will forgive their wickedness, and I will never again remember their sins."

35 It is the LORD who provides the sun to
          light the day
     and the moon and stars to light the
          night,
     and who stirs the sea into roaring waves.
His name is the LORD of Heaven's Armies,
     and this is what he says:
36 "I am as likely to reject my people Israel
     as I am to abolish the laws of nature!"
37 This is what the LORD says:
"Just as the heavens cannot be measured
     and the foundations of the earth cannot
          be explored,
so I will not consider casting them away

for the evil they have done.
     I, the LORD, have spoken!

38"The day is coming," says the LORD, "when all Jerusalem will be rebuilt for me, from the Tower of Hananel to the Corner Gate. 39A measuring line will be stretched out over the hill of Gareb and across to Goah. 40And the entire area—including the graveyard and ash dump in the valley, and all the fields out to the Kidron Valley on the east as far as the Horse Gate—will be holy to the LORD. The city will never again be captured or destroyed."

Jeremiah's Land Purchase

32 The following message came to Jeremiah from the LORD in the tenth year of the reign of Zedekiah,* king of Judah. This was also the eighteenth year of the reign of King Nebuchadnezzar.* 2Jerusalem was then under siege from the Babylonian army, and Jeremiah was imprisoned in the courtyard of the guard in the royal palace. 3King Zedekiah had put him there, asking why he kept giving this prophecy: "This is what the LORD says: 'I am about to hand this city over to the king of Babylon, and he will take it. 4King Zedekiah will be captured by the Babylonians* and taken to meet the king of Babylon face to face. 5He will take Zedekiah to Babylon, and I will deal with him there,' says the LORD. 'If you fight against the Babylonians, you will never succeed.'"

6At that time the LORD sent me a message. He said, 7"Your cousin Hanamel son of Shallum will come and say to you, 'Buy my field at Anathoth. By law you have the right to buy it before it is offered to anyone else.'"

8Then, just as the LORD had said he would, my cousin Hanamel came and visited me in the prison. He said, "Please buy my field at Anathoth in the land of Benjamin. By law you have the right to buy it before it is offered to anyone else, so buy it for yourself." Then I knew that the message I had heard was from the LORD.

9So I bought the field at Anathoth, paying Hanamel seventeen pieces* of silver for it. 10I signed and sealed the deed of purchase before witnesses, weighed out the silver, and paid him. 11Then I took the sealed deed and an unsealed copy of the deed, which contained the terms and conditions of the purchase, 12and I handed them to Baruch son of Neriah and

32:1a The tenth year of Zedekiah's reign and the eighteenth year of Nebuchadnezzar's reign was 587 B.C.   32:1b Hebrew *Nebuchadrezzar,* a variant spelling of Nebuchadnezzar; also in 32:28.   32:4 Or *Chaldeans;* also in 32:5, 24, 25, 28, 29, 43. 32:9 Hebrew *17 shekels,* about 7 ounces or 194 grams in weight.

grandson of Mahseiah. I did all this in the presence of my cousin Hanamel, the witnesses who had signed the deed, and all the men of Judah who were there in the courtyard of the guardhouse.

¹³Then I said to Baruch as they all listened, ¹⁴"This is what the LORD of Heaven's Armies, the God of Israel, says: 'Take both this sealed deed and the unsealed copy, and put them into a pottery jar to preserve them for a long time.' ¹⁵For this is what the LORD of Heaven's Armies, the God of Israel, says: 'Someday people will again own property here in this land and will buy and sell houses and vineyards and fields.'"

Jeremiah's Prayer

¹⁶Then after I had given the papers to Baruch, I prayed to the LORD:

¹⁷"O Sovereign LORD! You made the heavens and earth by your strong hand and powerful arm. Nothing is too hard for you! ¹⁸You show unfailing love to thousands, but you also bring the consequences of one generation's sin upon the next. You are the great and powerful God, the LORD of Heaven's Armies. ¹⁹You have all wisdom and do great and mighty miracles. You see the conduct of all people, and you give them what they deserve. ²⁰You performed miraculous signs and wonders in the land of Egypt—things still remembered to this day! And you have continued to do great miracles in Israel and all around the world. You have made your name famous to this day.

²¹"You brought Israel out of Egypt with mighty signs and wonders, with a strong hand and powerful arm, and with overwhelming terror. ²²You gave the people of Israel this land that you had promised their ancestors long before—a land flowing with milk and honey. ²³Our ancestors came and conquered it and lived in it, but they refused to obey you or follow your word. They have not done anything you commanded. That is why you have sent this terrible disaster upon them.

²⁴"See how the siege ramps have been built against the city walls! Through war, famine, and disease, the city will be handed over to the Babylonians, who will conquer it. Everything has happened just as you said. ²⁵And yet, O Sovereign LORD, you have told me to buy the field—paying good money for it before these

witnesses—even though the city will soon be handed over to the Babylonians."

A Prediction of Jerusalem's Fall

²⁶Then this message came to Jeremiah from the LORD: ²⁷"I am the LORD, the God of all the peoples of the world. Is anything too hard for me? ²⁸Therefore, this is what the LORD says: I will hand this city over to the Babylonians and to Nebuchadnezzar, king of Babylon, and he will capture it. ²⁹The Babylonians outside the walls will come in and set fire to the city. They will burn down all these houses where the people provoked my anger by burning incense to Baal on the rooftops and by pouring out liquid offerings to other gods. ³⁰Israel and Judah have done nothing but wrong since their earliest days. They have infuriated me with all their evil deeds," says the LORD. ³¹"From the time this city was built until now, it has done nothing but anger me, so I am determined to get rid of it.

³²"The sins of Israel and Judah—the sins of the people of Jerusalem, the kings, the officials, the priests, and the prophets—have stirred up my anger. ³³My people have turned their backs on me and have refused to return. Even though I diligently taught them, they would not receive instruction or obey. ³⁴They have set up their abominable idols right in my own Temple, defiling it. ³⁵They have built pagan shrines to Baal in the valley of Ben-Hinnom, and there they sacrifice their sons and daughters to Molech. I have never commanded such a horrible deed; it never even crossed my mind to command such a thing. What an incredible evil, causing Judah to sin so greatly!

A Promise of Restoration

³⁶"Now I want to say something more about this city. You have been saying, 'It will fall to the king of Babylon through war, famine, and disease.' But this is what the LORD, the God of Israel, says: ³⁷I will certainly bring my people back again from all the countries where I will scatter them in my fury. I will bring them back to this very city and let them live in peace and safety. ³⁸They will be my people, and I will be their God. ³⁹And I will give them one heart and one purpose: to worship me forever, for their own good and for the good of all their descendants. ⁴⁰And I will make an everlasting covenant with them: I will never stop doing good for them. I will put a desire in their hearts to worship me, and they will never leave me. ⁴¹I will find joy doing good for them and will

faithfully and wholeheartedly replant them in this land.

⁴²"This is what the LORD says: Just as I have brought all these calamities on them, so I will do all the good I have promised them. ⁴³Fields will again be bought and sold in this land about which you now say, 'It has been ravaged by the Babylonians, a desolate land where people and animals have all disappeared.' ⁴⁴Yes, fields will once again be bought and sold—deeds signed and sealed and witnessed—in the land of Benjamin and here in Jerusalem, in the towns of Judah and in the hill country, in the foothills of Judah* and in the Negev, too. For someday I will restore prosperity to them. I, the LORD, have spoken!"

Promises of Peace and Prosperity

33 While Jeremiah was still confined in the courtyard of the guard, the LORD gave him this second message: ²"This is what the LORD says—the LORD who made the earth, who formed and established it, whose name is the LORD: ³Ask me and I will tell you remarkable secrets you do not know about things to come. ⁴For this is what the LORD, the God of Israel, says: You have torn down the houses of this city and even the king's palace to get materials to strengthen the walls against the siege ramps and swords of the enemy. ⁵You expect to fight the Babylonians,* but the men of this city are already as good as dead, for I have determined to destroy them in my terrible anger. I have abandoned them because of all their wickedness.

⁶"Nevertheless, the time will come when I will heal Jerusalem's wounds and give it prosperity and true peace. ⁷I will restore the fortunes of Judah and Israel and rebuild their towns. ⁸I will cleanse them of their sins against me and forgive all their sins of rebellion. ⁹Then this city will bring me joy, glory, and honor before all the nations of the earth! The people of the world will see all the good I do for my people, and they will tremble with awe at the peace and prosperity I provide for them.

¹⁰"This is what the LORD says: You have said, 'This is a desolate land where people and animals have all disappeared.' Yet in the empty streets of Jerusalem and Judah's other towns, there will be heard once more ¹¹the sounds of joy and laughter. The joyful voices of bridegrooms and brides will be heard again, along with the joyous songs of people bringing

thanksgiving offerings to the LORD. They will sing,

'Give thanks to the LORD of Heaven's
    Armies,
    for the LORD is good.
His faithful love endures forever!'

For I will restore the prosperity of this land to what it was in the past, says the LORD.

¹²"This is what the LORD of Heaven's Armies says: This land—though it is now desolate and has no people and animals—will once more have pastures where shepherds can lead their flocks. ¹³Once again shepherds will count their flocks in the towns of the hill country, the foothills of Judah,* the Negev, the land of Benjamin, the vicinity of Jerusalem, and all the towns of Judah. I, the LORD, have spoken!

¹⁴"The day will come, says the LORD, when I will do for Israel and Judah all the good things I have promised them.

¹⁵ "In those days and at that time
    I will raise up a righteous descendant*
        from King David's line.
    He will do what is just and right
        throughout the land.
¹⁶ In that day Judah will be saved,
        and Jerusalem will live in safety.
    And this will be its name:
        'The LORD Is Our Righteousness.'*

¹⁷For this is what the LORD says: David will have a descendant sitting on the throne of Israel forever. ¹⁸And there will always be Levitical priests to offer burnt offerings and grain offerings and sacrifices to me."

¹⁹Then this message came to Jeremiah from the LORD: ²⁰"This is what the LORD says: If you can break my covenant with the day and the night so that one does not follow the other, ²¹only then will my covenant with my servant David be broken. Only then will he no longer have a descendant to reign on his throne. The same is true for my covenant with the Levitical priests who minister before me. ²²And as the stars of the sky cannot be counted and the sand on the seashore cannot be measured, so I will multiply the descendants of my servant David and the Levites who minister before me."

²³The LORD gave another message to Jeremiah. He said, ²⁴"Have you noticed what people are saying?—'The LORD chose Judah

---

32:44 Hebrew *the Shephelah.*   33:5 Or *Chaldeans.*   33:13 Hebrew *the Shephelah.*   33:15 Hebrew *a righteous branch.*
33:16 Hebrew *Yahweh Tsidqenu.*

and Israel and then abandoned them!' They are sneering and saying that Israel is not worthy to be counted as a nation. 25But this is what the LORD says: I would no more reject my people than I would change my laws that govern night and day, earth and sky. 26I will never abandon the descendants of Jacob or David, my servant, or change the plan that David's descendants will rule the descendants of Abraham, Isaac, and Jacob. Instead, I will restore them to their land and have mercy on them."

A Warning for Zedekiah

34 King Nebuchadnezzar* of Babylon came with all the armies from the kingdoms he ruled, and he fought against Jerusalem and the towns of Judah. At that time this message came to Jeremiah from the LORD: 2"Go to King Zedekiah of Judah, and tell him, 'This is what the LORD, the God of Israel, says: I am about to hand this city over to the king of Babylon, and he will burn it down. 3You will not escape his grasp but will be captured and taken to meet the king of Babylon face to face. Then you will be exiled to Babylon.

4"'But listen to this promise from the LORD, O Zedekiah, king of Judah. This is what the LORD says: You will not be killed in war 5but will die peacefully. People will burn incense in your memory, just as they did for your ancestors, the kings who preceded you. They will mourn for you, crying, "Alas, our master is dead!" This I have decreed, says the LORD.'"

6So Jeremiah the prophet delivered the message to King Zedekiah of Judah. 7At this time the Babylonian army was besieging Jerusalem, Lachish, and Azekah—the only fortified cities of Judah not yet captured.

Freedom for Hebrew Slaves

8This message came to Jeremiah from the LORD after King Zedekiah made a covenant with the people, proclaiming freedom for the slaves. 9He had ordered all the people to free their Hebrew slaves—both men and women. No one was to keep a fellow Judean in bondage. 10The officials and all the people had obeyed the king's command, 11but later they changed their minds. They took back the men and women they had freed, forcing them to be slaves again.

12So the LORD gave them this message through Jeremiah: 13"This is what the LORD, the God of Israel, says: I made a covenant with your ancestors long ago when I rescued them from their slavery in Egypt. 14I told them that every Hebrew slave must be freed after serving six years. But your ancestors paid no attention to me. 15Recently you repented and did what was right, following my command. You freed your slaves and made a solemn covenant with me in the Temple that bears my name. 16But now you have shrugged off your oath and defiled my name by taking back the men and women you had freed, forcing them to be slaves once again.

17"Therefore, this is what the LORD says: Since you have not obeyed me by setting your countrymen free, I will set you free to be destroyed by war, disease, and famine. You will be an object of horror to all the nations of the earth. 18Because you have broken the terms of our covenant, I will cut you apart just as you cut apart the calf when you walked between its halves to solemnize your vows. 19Yes, I will cut you apart, whether you are officials of Judah or Jerusalem, court officials, priests, or common people—for you have broken your oath. 20I will give you to your enemies, and they will kill you. Your bodies will be food for the vultures and wild animals.

21"I will hand over King Zedekiah of Judah and his officials to the army of the king of Babylon. And although they have left Jerusalem for a while, 22I will call the Babylonian armies back again. They will fight against this city and will capture it and burn it down. I will see to it that all the towns of Judah are destroyed, with no one living there."

The Faithful Recabites

35 This is the message the LORD gave Jeremiah when Jehoiakim son of Josiah was king of Judah: 2"Go to the settlement where the families of the Recabites live, and invite them to the LORD's Temple. Take them into one of the inner rooms, and offer them some wine."

3So I went to see Jaazaniah son of Jeremiah and grandson of Habazziniah and all his brothers and sons—representing all the Recabite families. 4I took them to the Temple, and we went into the room assigned to the sons of Hanan son of Igdaliah, a man of God. This room was located next to the one used by the Temple officials, directly above the room of Maaseiah son of Shallum, the Temple gatekeeper. 5I set cups and jugs of wine before them and invited them to have a drink, 6but they refused. "No," they said, "we don't drink wine, because our ancestor Jehonadab* son of Recab gave us this command: 'You and your descendants must never drink wine. ⁷And do not build houses or plant crops or vineyards, but always live in tents. If you follow these commands, you will live long, good lives in the land.' ⁸So we have obeyed him in all these things. We have never had a drink of wine to this day, nor have our wives, our sons, or our daughters. ⁹We haven't built houses or owned vineyards or farms or planted crops. ¹⁰We have lived in tents and have fully obeyed all the commands of Jehonadab, our ancestor. ¹¹But when King Nebuchadnezzar* of Babylon attacked this country, we were afraid of the Babylonian and Syrian* armies. So we decided to move to Jerusalem. That is why we are here."

¹²Then the LORD gave this message to Jeremiah: ¹³"This is what the LORD of Heaven's Armies, the God of Israel, says: Go and say to the people in Judah and Jerusalem, 'Come and learn a lesson about how to obey me. ¹⁴The Recabites do not drink wine to this day because their ancestor Jehonadab told them not to. But I have spoken to you again and again, and you refuse to obey me. ¹⁵Time after time I sent you prophets, who told you, "Turn from your wicked ways, and start doing things right. Stop worshiping other gods so that you might live in peace here in the land I have given to you and your ancestors." But you would not listen to me or obey me. ¹⁶The descendants of Jehonadab son of Recab have obeyed their ancestor completely, but you have refused to listen to me.'

¹⁷"Therefore, this is what the LORD God of Heaven's Armies, the God of Israel, says: 'Because you refuse to listen or answer when I call, I will send upon Judah and Jerusalem all the disasters I have threatened.'"

¹⁸Then Jeremiah turned to the Recabites and said, "This is what the LORD of Heaven's Armies, the God of Israel, says: 'You have obeyed your ancestor Jehonadab in every respect, following all his instructions.' ¹⁹Therefore, this is what the LORD of Heaven's Armies, the God of Israel, says: 'Jehonadab son of Recab will always have descendants who serve me.'"

Baruch Reads the LORD's Messages

36 During the fourth year that Jehoiakim son of Josiah was king in Judah,* the LORD gave this message to Jeremiah: ²"Get a scroll, and write down all my messages against

Israel, Judah, and the other nations. Begin with the first message back in the days of Josiah, and write down every message, right up to the present time. ³Perhaps the people of Judah will repent when they hear again all the terrible things I have planned for them. Then I will be able to forgive their sins and wrongdoings."

⁴So Jeremiah sent for Baruch son of Neriah, and as Jeremiah dictated all the prophecies that the LORD had given him, Baruch wrote them on a scroll. ⁵Then Jeremiah said to Baruch, "I am a prisoner here and unable to go to the Temple. ⁶So you go to the Temple on the next day of fasting, and read the messages from the LORD that I have had you write on this scroll. Read them so the people who are there from all over Judah will hear them. ⁷Perhaps even yet they will turn from their evil ways and ask the LORD's forgiveness before it is too late. For the LORD has threatened them with his terrible anger."

⁸Baruch did as Jeremiah told him and read these messages from the LORD to the people at the Temple. ⁹He did this on a day of sacred fasting held in late autumn,* during the fifth year of the reign of Jehoiakim son of Josiah. People from all over Judah had come to Jerusalem to attend the services at the Temple on that day. ¹⁰Baruch read Jeremiah's words on the scroll to all the people. He stood in front of the Temple room of Gemariah, son of Shaphan the secretary. This room was just off the upper courtyard of the Temple, near the New Gate entrance.

¹¹When Micaiah son of Gemariah and grandson of Shaphan heard the messages from the LORD, ¹²he went down to the secretary's room in the palace where the administrative officials were meeting. Elishama the secretary was there, along with Delaiah son of Shemaiah, Elnathan son of Acbor, Gemariah son of Shaphan, Zedekiah son of Hananiah, and all the other officials. ¹³When Micaiah told them about the messages Baruch was reading to the people, ¹⁴the officials sent Jehudi son of Nethaniah, grandson of Shelemiah and great-grandson of Cushi, to ask Baruch to come and read the messages to them, too. So Baruch took the scroll and went to them. ¹⁵"Sit down and read the scroll to us," the officials said, and Baruch did as they requested.

¹⁶When they heard all the messages, they

35:11a Hebrew *Nebuchadrezzar,* a variant spelling of Nebuchadnezzar.   35:11b Or *Chaldean and Aramean.*   36:1 The fourth year of Jehoiakim's reign was 605 B.C.   36:9 Hebrew *in the ninth month,* of the ancient Hebrew lunar calendar (also in 36:22). The ninth month in the fifth year of Jehoiakim's reign occurred within the months of November and December 604 B.C. Also see note on 1:3.

looked at one another in alarm. "We must tell the king what we have heard," they said to Baruch. [17]"But first, tell us how you got these messages. Did they come directly from Jeremiah?"

[18]So Baruch explained, "Jeremiah dictated them, and I wrote them down in ink, word for word, on this scroll."

[19]"You and Jeremiah should both hide," the officials told Baruch. "Don't tell anyone where you are!" [20]Then the officials left the scroll for safekeeping in the room of Elishama the secretary and went to tell the king what had happened.

King Jehoiakim Burns the Scroll

[21]The king sent Jehudi to get the scroll. Jehudi brought it from Elishama's room and read it to the king as all his officials stood by. [22]It was late autumn, and the king was in a winterized part of the palace, sitting in front of a fire to keep warm. [23]Each time Jehudi finished reading three or four columns, the king took a knife and cut off that section of the scroll. He then threw it into the fire, section by section, until the whole scroll was burned up. [24]Neither the king nor his attendants showed any signs of fear or repentance at what they heard. [25]Even when Elnathan, Delaiah, and Gemariah begged the king not to burn the scroll, he wouldn't listen.

[26]Then the king commanded his son Jerahmeel, Seraiah son of Azriel, and Shelemiah son of Abdeel to arrest Baruch and Jeremiah. But the LORD had hidden them.

Jeremiah Rewrites the Scroll

[27]After the king had burned the scroll on which Baruch had written Jeremiah's words, the LORD gave Jeremiah another message. He said, [28]"Get another scroll, and write everything again just as you did on the scroll King Jehoiakim burned. [29]Then say to the king, 'This is what the LORD says: You burned the scroll because it said the king of Babylon would destroy this land and empty it of people and animals. [30]Now this is what the LORD says about King Jehoiakim of Judah: He will have no heirs to sit on the throne of David. His dead body will be thrown out to lie unburied—exposed to the heat of the day and the frost of the night. [31]I will punish him and his family and his attendants for their sins. I will pour out on them and on all the people of Jerusalem and Judah

all the disasters I promised, for they would not listen to my warnings.'"

[32]So Jeremiah took another scroll and dictated again to his secretary, Baruch. He wrote everything that had been on the scroll King Jehoiakim had burned in the fire. Only this time he added much more!

Zedekiah Calls for Jeremiah

37 Zedekiah son of Josiah succeeded Jehoiachin* son of Jehoiakim as the king of Judah. He was appointed by King Nebuchadnezzar* of Babylon. [2]But neither King Zedekiah nor his attendants nor the people who were left in the land listened to what the LORD said through Jeremiah.

[3]Nevertheless, King Zedekiah sent Jehucal son of Shelemiah, and Zephaniah the priest, son of Maaseiah, to ask Jeremiah, "Please pray to the LORD our God for us." [4]Jeremiah had not yet been imprisoned, so he could come and go among the people as he pleased.

[5]At this time the army of Pharaoh Hophra* of Egypt appeared at the southern border of Judah. When the Babylonian* army heard about it, they withdrew from their siege of Jerusalem.

[6]Then the LORD gave this message to Jeremiah: [7]"This is what the LORD, the God of Israel, says: The king of Judah sent you to ask me what is going to happen. Tell him, 'Pharaoh's army is about to return to Egypt, though he came here to help you. [8]Then the Babylonians* will come back and capture this city and burn it to the ground.'

[9]"This is what the LORD says: Do not fool yourselves into thinking that the Babylonians are gone for good. They aren't! [10]Even if you were to destroy the entire Babylonian army, leaving only a handful of wounded survivors, they would still stagger from their tents and burn this city to the ground!"

Jeremiah Is Imprisoned

[11]When the Babylonian army left Jerusalem because of Pharaoh's approaching army, [12]Jeremiah started to leave the city on his way to the territory of Benjamin, to claim his share of the property among his relatives there.* [13]But as he was walking through the Benjamin Gate, a sentry arrested him and said, "You are defecting to the Babylonians!" The sentry making the arrest was Irijah son of Shelemiah, grandson of Hananiah.

37:1a Hebrew *Coniah,* a variant spelling of Jehoiachin.   37:1b Hebrew *Nebuchadrezzar,* a variant spelling of Nebuchadnezzar.
37:5a Hebrew *army of Pharaoh;* see 44:30.   37:5b Or *Chaldean;* also in 37:10, 11.   37:8 Or *Chaldeans;* also in 37:9, 13.
37:12 Hebrew *to separate from there in the midst of the people.*

14"That's not true!" Jeremiah protested. "I had no intention of doing any such thing." But Irijah wouldn't listen, and he took Jeremiah before the officials. 15They were furious with Jeremiah and had him flogged and imprisoned in the house of Jonathan the secretary. Jonathan's house had been converted into a prison. 16Jeremiah was put into a dungeon cell, where he remained for many days.

17Later King Zedekiah secretly requested that Jeremiah come to the palace, where the king asked him, "Do you have any messages from the LORD?"

"Yes, I do!" said Jeremiah. "You will be defeated by the king of Babylon."

18Then Jeremiah asked the king, "What crime have I committed? What have I done against you, your attendants, or the people that I should be imprisoned like this? 19Where are your prophets now who told you the king of Babylon would not attack you or this land? 20Listen, my lord the king, I beg you. Don't send me back to the dungeon in the house of Jonathan the secretary, for I will die there."

21So King Zedekiah commanded that Jeremiah not be returned to the dungeon. Instead, he was imprisoned in the courtyard of the guard in the royal palace. The king also commanded that Jeremiah be given a loaf of fresh bread every day as long as there was any left in the city. So Jeremiah was put in the palace prison.

Jeremiah in a Cistern

38 Now Shephatiah son of Mattan, Gedaliah son of Pashhur, Jehucal* son of Shelemiah, and Pashhur son of Malkijah heard what Jeremiah had been telling the people. He had been saying, 2"This is what the LORD says: 'Everyone who stays in Jerusalem will die from war, famine, or disease, but those who surrender to the Babylonians* will live. Their reward will be life. They will live!' 3The LORD also says: 'The city of Jerusalem will certainly be handed over to the army of the king of Babylon, who will capture it.'"

4So these officials went to the king and said, "Sir, this man must die! That kind of talk will undermine the morale of the few fighting men we have left, as well as that of all the people. This man is a traitor!"

5King Zedekiah agreed. "All right," he said. "Do as you like. I can't stop you."

6So the officials took Jeremiah from his cell and lowered him by ropes into an empty cistern in the prison yard. It belonged to Malkijah, a member of the royal family. There was no water in the cistern, but there was a thick layer of mud at the bottom, and Jeremiah sank down into it.

7But Ebed-melech the Ethiopian,* an important court official, heard that Jeremiah was in the cistern. At that time the king was holding court at the Benjamin Gate, 8so Ebed-melech rushed from the palace to speak with him. 9"My lord the king," he said, "these men have done a very evil thing in putting Jeremiah the prophet into the cistern. He will soon die of hunger, for almost all the bread in the city is gone."

10So the king told Ebed-melech, "Take thirty of my men with you, and pull Jeremiah out of the cistern before he dies."

11So Ebed-melech took the men with him and went to a room in the palace beneath the treasury, where he found some old rags and discarded clothing. He carried these to the cistern and lowered them to Jeremiah on a rope. 12Ebed-melech called down to Jeremiah, "Put these rags under your armpits to protect you from the ropes." Then when Jeremiah was ready, 13they pulled him out. So Jeremiah was returned to the courtyard of the guard—the palace prison—where he remained.

Zedekiah Questions Jeremiah

14One day King Zedekiah sent for Jeremiah and had him brought to the third entrance of the LORD's Temple. "I want to ask you something," the king said. "And don't try to hide the truth."

15Jeremiah said, "If I tell you the truth, you will kill me. And if I give you advice, you won't listen to me anyway."

16So King Zedekiah secretly promised him, "As surely as the LORD our Creator lives, I will not kill you or hand you over to the men who want you dead."

17Then Jeremiah said to Zedekiah, "This is what the LORD God of Heaven's Armies, the God of Israel, says: 'If you surrender to the Babylonian officers, you and your family will live, and the city will not be burned down. 18But if you refuse to surrender, you will not escape! This city will be handed over to the Babylonians, and they will burn it to the ground.'"

19"But I am afraid to surrender," the king said, "for the Babylonians may hand me over to the Judeans who have defected to them. And who knows what they will do to me!"

20Jeremiah replied, "You won't be handed over to them if you choose to obey the LORD.

38:1 Hebrew *Jucal,* a variant spelling of Jehucal; see 37:3.   38:2 Or *Chaldeans;* also in 38:18, 19, 23.   38:7 Hebrew *the Cushite.*

Your life will be spared, and all will go well for you. ²¹But if you refuse to surrender, this is what the LORD has revealed to me: ²²All the women left in your palace will be brought out and given to the officers of the Babylonian army. Then the women will taunt you, saying,

'What fine friends you have!
They have betrayed and misled you.
When your feet sank in the mud,
they left you to your fate!'

²³All your wives and children will be led out to the Babylonians, and you will not escape. You will be seized by the king of Babylon, and this city will be burned down."

²⁴Then Zedekiah said to Jeremiah, "Don't tell anyone you told me this, or you will die! ²⁵My officials may hear that I spoke to you, and they may say, 'Tell us what you and the king were talking about. If you don't tell us, we will kill you.' ²⁶If this happens, just tell them you begged me not to send you back to Jonathan's dungeon, for fear you would die there."

²⁷Sure enough, it wasn't long before the king's officials came to Jeremiah and asked him why the king had called for him. But Jeremiah followed the king's instructions, and they left without finding out the truth. No one had overheard the conversation between Jeremiah and the king. ²⁸And Jeremiah remained a prisoner in the courtyard of the guard until the day Jerusalem was captured.

The Fall of Jerusalem

39 In January* of the ninth year of King Zedekiah's reign, King Nebuchadnezzar* of Babylon came with his entire army to besiege Jerusalem. ²Two and a half years later, on July 18* in the eleventh year of Zedekiah's reign, a section of the city wall was broken down. ³All the officers of the Babylonian army came in and sat in triumph at the Middle Gate: Nergal-sharezer of Samgar, and Nebo-sarsekim,* a chief officer, and Nergal-sharezer, the king's adviser, and all the other officers of the king of Babylon.

⁴When King Zedekiah of Judah and all the soldiers saw that the Babylonians had broken into the city, they fled. They waited for nightfall and then slipped through the gate between the two walls behind the king's garden and headed toward the Jordan Valley.*

⁵But the Babylonian* troops chased them and overtook Zedekiah on the plains of Jericho. They captured him and took him to King Nebuchadnezzar of Babylon, who was at Riblah in the land of Hamath. There the king of Babylon pronounced judgment upon Zedekiah. ⁶The king of Babylon made Zedekiah watch as he slaughtered his sons at Riblah. The king of Babylon also slaughtered all the nobles of Judah. ⁷Then he gouged out Zedekiah's eyes and bound him in bronze chains to lead him away to Babylon.

⁸Meanwhile, the Babylonians burned Jerusalem, including the royal palace and the houses of the people, and they tore down the walls of the city. ⁹Then Nebuzaradan, the captain of the guard, took as exiles to Babylon the rest of the people who remained in the city, those who had defected to him, and everyone else who remained. ¹⁰But Nebuzaradan allowed some of the poorest people to stay behind in the land of Judah, and he assigned them to care for the vineyards and fields.

Jeremiah Remains in Judah

¹¹King Nebuchadnezzar had told Nebuzaradan, the captain of the guard, to find Jeremiah. ¹²"See that he isn't hurt," he said. "Look after him well, and give him anything he wants." ¹³So Nebuzaradan, the captain of the guard; Nebushazban, a chief officer; Nergal-sharezer, the king's adviser; and the other officers of Babylon's king ¹⁴sent messengers to bring Jeremiah out of the prison. They put him under the care of Gedaliah son of Ahikam and grandson of Shaphan, who took him back to his home. So Jeremiah stayed in Judah among his own people.

¹⁵The LORD had given the following message to Jeremiah while he was still in prison: ¹⁶"Say to Ebed-melech the Ethiopian,* 'This is what the LORD of Heaven's Armies, the God of Israel, says: I will do to this city everything I have threatened. I will send disaster, not prosperity. You will see its destruction, ¹⁷but I will rescue you from those you fear so much. ¹⁸Because you trusted me, I will give you your life as a reward. I will rescue you and keep you safe. I, the LORD, have spoken!'"

39:1a Hebrew *In the tenth month,* of the ancient Hebrew lunar calendar. A number of events in Jeremiah can be cross-checked with dates in surviving Babylonian records and related accurately to our modern calendar. This event occurred on January 15, 588 B.C.; see 52:4a and the note there.   39:1b Hebrew *Nebuchadrezzar,* a variant spelling of Nebuchadnezzar; also in 39:5, 11.   39:2 Hebrew *On the ninth day of the fourth month.* This day was July 18, 586 B.C.; also see note on 39:1a.   39:3 Or *Nergal-sharezer, Samgar-nebo, Sarsekim.*   39:4 Hebrew *the Arabah.*   39:5 Or *Chaldean;* similarly in 39:8.   39:16 Hebrew *the Cushite.*

40

The LORD gave a message to Jeremiah after Nebuzaradan, the captain of the guard, had released him at Ramah. He had found Jeremiah bound in chains among all the other captives of Jerusalem and Judah who were being sent to exile in Babylon.

2The captain of the guard called for Jeremiah and said, "The LORD your God has brought this disaster on this land, 3just as he said he would. For these people have sinned against the LORD and disobeyed him. That is why it happened. 4But I am going to take off your chains and let you go. If you want to come with me to Babylon, you are welcome. I will see that you are well cared for. But if you don't want to come, you may stay here. The whole land is before you—go wherever you like. 5If you decide to stay, then return to Gedaliah son of Ahikam and grandson of Shaphan. He has been appointed governor of Judah by the king of Babylon. Stay there with the people he rules. But it's up to you; go wherever you like."

Then Nebuzaradan, the captain of the guard, gave Jeremiah some food and money and let him go. 6So Jeremiah returned to Gedaliah son of Ahikam at Mizpah, and he lived in Judah with the few who were still left in the land.

Gedaliah Governs in Judah

7The leaders of the Judean military groups in the countryside heard that the king of Babylon had appointed Gedaliah son of Ahikam as governor over the poor people who were left behind in Judah—the men, women, and children who hadn't been exiled to Babylon. 8So they went to see Gedaliah at Mizpah. These included: Ishmael son of Nethaniah, Johanan and Jonathan sons of Kareah, Seraiah son of Tanhumeth, the sons of Ephai the Netophathite, Jezaniah son of the Maacathite, and all their men.

9Gedaliah vowed to them that the Babylonians* meant them no harm. "Don't be afraid to serve them. Live in the land and serve the king of Babylon, and all will go well for you," he promised. 10"As for me, I will stay at Mizpah to represent you before the Babylonians who come to meet with us. Settle in the towns you have taken, and live off the land. Harvest the grapes and summer fruits and olives, and store them away."

11When the Judeans in Moab, Ammon, Edom, and the other nearby countries heard that the king of Babylon had left a few people in Judah and that Gedaliah was the governor, 12they began to return to Judah from the places to which they had fled. They stopped at Mizpah to meet with Gedaliah and then went into the Judean countryside to gather a great harvest of grapes and other crops.

A Plot against Gedaliah

13Soon after this, Johanan son of Kareah and the other military leaders came to Gedaliah at Mizpah. 14They said to him, "Did you know that Baalis, king of Ammon, has sent Ishmael son of Nethaniah to assassinate you?" But Gedaliah refused to believe them.

15Later Johanan had a private conference with Gedaliah and volunteered to kill Ishmael secretly. "Why should we let him come and murder you?" Johanan asked. "What will happen then to the Judeans who have returned? Why should the few of us who are still left be scattered and lost?"

16But Gedaliah said to Johanan, "I forbid you to do any such thing, for you are lying about Ishmael."

The Murder of Gedaliah

41

But in midautumn of that year,* Ishmael son of Nethaniah and grandson of Elishama, who was a member of the royal family and had been one of the king's high officials, went to Mizpah with ten men to meet Gedaliah. While they were eating together, 2Ishmael and his ten men suddenly jumped up, drew their swords, and killed Gedaliah, whom the king of Babylon had appointed governor. 3Ishmael also killed all the Judeans and the Babylonian* soldiers who were with Gedaliah at Mizpah.

4The next day, before anyone had heard about Gedaliah's murder, 5eighty men arrived from Shechem, Shiloh, and Samaria to worship at the Temple of the LORD. They had shaved off their beards, torn their clothes, and cut themselves, and had brought along grain offerings and frankincense. 6Ishmael left Mizpah to meet them, weeping as he went. When he reached them, he said, "Oh, come and see what has happened to Gedaliah!"

7But as soon as they were all inside the town, Ishmael and his men killed all but ten of them and threw their bodies into a cistern. 8The other ten had talked Ishmael into letting

40:9 Or Chaldeans; also in 40:10.   41:1 Hebrew in the seventh month, of the ancient Hebrew lunar calendar. This month occurred within the months of October and November 586 B.C.; also see note on 39:1a.   41:3 Or Chaldean.

them go by promising to bring him their stores of wheat, barley, olive oil, and honey that they had hidden away. [9]The cistern where Ishmael dumped the bodies of the men he murdered was the large one* dug by King Asa when he fortified Mizpah to protect himself against King Baasha of Israel. Ishmael son of Nethaniah filled it with corpses.

[10]Then Ishmael made captives of the king's daughters and the other people who had been left under Gedaliah's care in Mizpah by Nebuzaradan, the captain of the guard. Taking them with him, he started back toward the land of Ammon.

[11]But when Johanan son of Kareah and the other military leaders heard about Ishmael's crimes, [12]they took all their men and set out to stop him. They caught up with him at the large pool near Gibeon. [13]The people Ishmael had captured shouted for joy when they saw Johanan and the other military leaders. [14]And all the captives from Mizpah escaped and began to help Johanan. [15]Meanwhile, Ishmael and eight of his men escaped from Johanan into the land of Ammon.

[16]Then Johanan son of Kareah and the other military leaders took all the people they had rescued in Gibeon—the soldiers, women, children, and court officials* whom Ishmael had captured after he killed Gedaliah. [17]They took them all to the village of Geruth-kimham near Bethlehem, where they prepared to leave for Egypt. [18]They were afraid of what the Babylonians* would do when they heard that Ishmael had killed Gedaliah, the governor appointed by the Babylonian king.

Warning to Stay in Judah

42 Then all the military leaders, including Johanan son of Kareah and Jezaniah* son of Hoshaiah, and all the people, from the least to the greatest, approached [2]Jeremiah the prophet. They said, "Please pray to the LORD your God for us. As you can see, we are only a tiny remnant compared to what we were before. [3]Pray that the LORD your God will show us what to do and where to go."

[4]"All right," Jeremiah replied. "I will pray to the LORD your God, as you have asked, and I will tell you everything he says. I will hide nothing from you."

[5]Then they said to Jeremiah, "May the LORD your God be a faithful witness against us if we refuse to obey whatever he tells us to do!

[6]Whether we like it or not, we will obey the LORD our God to whom we are sending you with our plea. For if we obey him, everything will turn out well for us."

[7]Ten days later the LORD gave his reply to Jeremiah. [8]So he called for Johanan son of Kareah and the other military leaders, and for all the people, from the least to the greatest. [9]He said to them, "You sent me to the LORD, the God of Israel, with your request, and this is his reply: [10]'Stay here in this land. If you do, I will build you up and not tear you down; I will plant you and not uproot you. For I am sorry about all the punishment I have had to bring upon you. [11]Do not fear the king of Babylon anymore,' says the LORD. 'For I am with you and will save you and rescue you from his power. [12]I will be merciful to you by making him kind, so he will let you stay here in your land.'

[13]"But if you refuse to obey the LORD your God, and if you say, 'We will not stay here; [14]instead, we will go to Egypt where we will be free from war, the call to arms, and hunger,' [15]then hear the LORD's message to the remnant of Judah. This is what the LORD of Heaven's Armies, the God of Israel, says: 'If you are determined to go to Egypt and live there, [16]the very war and famine you fear will catch up to you, and you will die there. [17]That is the fate awaiting every one of you who insists on going to live in Egypt. Yes, you will die from war, famine, and disease. None of you will escape the disaster I will bring upon you there.'

[18]"This is what the LORD of Heaven's Armies, the God of Israel, says: 'Just as my anger and fury have been poured out on the people of Jerusalem, so they will be poured out on you when you enter Egypt. You will be an object of damnation, horror, cursing, and mockery. And you will never see your homeland again.'

[19]"Listen, you remnant of Judah. The LORD has told you: 'Do not go to Egypt!' Don't forget this warning I have given you today. [20]For you were not being honest when you sent me to pray to the LORD your God for you. You said, 'Just tell us what the LORD our God says, and we will do it!' [21]And today I have told you exactly what he said, but you will not obey the LORD your God any better now than you have in the past. [22]So you can be sure that you will die from war, famine, and disease in Egypt, where you insist on going."

41:9 As in Greek version; Hebrew reads *murdered because of Gedaliah was one.*   41:16 Or *eunuchs.*   41:18 Or *Chaldeans.*
42:1 Greek version reads *Azariah;* compare 43:2.

Jeremiah Taken to Egypt

43 When Jeremiah had finished giving this message from the LORD their God to all the people, ²Azariah son of Hoshaiah and Johanan son of Kareah and all the other proud men said to Jeremiah, "You lie! The LORD our God hasn't forbidden us to go to Egypt! ³Baruch son of Neriah has convinced you to say this, because he wants us to stay here and be killed by the Babylonians* or be carried off into exile."

⁴So Johanan and the other military leaders and all the people refused to obey the LORD's command to stay in Judah. ⁵Johanan and the other leaders took with them all the people who had returned from the nearby countries to which they had fled. ⁶In the crowd were men, women, and children, the king's daughters, and all those whom Nebuzaradan, the captain of the guard, had left with Gedaliah. The prophet Jeremiah and Baruch were also included. ⁷The people refused to obey the voice of the LORD and went to Egypt, going as far as the city of Tahpanhes.

⁸Then at Tahpanhes, the LORD gave another message to Jeremiah. He said, ⁹"While the people of Judah are watching, take some large rocks and bury them under the pavement stones at the entrance of Pharaoh's palace here in Tahpanhes. ¹⁰Then say to the people of Judah, 'This is what the LORD of Heaven's Armies, the God of Israel, says: I will certainly bring my servant Nebuchadnezzar,* king of Babylon, here to Egypt. I will set his throne over these stones that I have hidden. He will spread his royal canopy over them. ¹¹And when he comes, he will destroy the land of Egypt. He will bring death to those destined for death, captivity to those destined for captivity, and war to those destined for war. ¹²He will set fire to the temples of Egypt's gods; he will burn the temples and carry the idols away as plunder. He will pick clean the land of Egypt as a shepherd picks fleas from his cloak. And he himself will leave unharmed. ¹³He will break down the sacred pillars standing in the temple of the sun* in Egypt, and he will burn down the temples of Egypt's gods.'"

Judgment for Idolatry

44 This is the message Jeremiah received concerning the Judeans living in northern Egypt in the cities of Migdol, Tahpanhes, and Memphis,* and in southern Egypt* as well: ²"This is what the LORD of Heaven's Armies, the God of Israel, says: You saw the calamity I brought on Jerusalem and all the towns of Judah. They now lie deserted and in ruins. ³They provoked my anger with all their wickedness. They burned incense and worshiped other gods—gods that neither they nor you nor any of your ancestors had ever even known.

⁴"Again and again I sent my servants, the prophets, to plead with them, 'Don't do these horrible things that I hate so much.' ⁵But my people would not listen or turn back from their wicked ways. They kept on burning incense to these gods. ⁶And so my fury boiled over and fell like fire on the towns of Judah and into the streets of Jerusalem, and they are still a desolate ruin today.

⁷"And now the LORD God of Heaven's Armies, the God of Israel, asks you: Why are you destroying yourselves? For not one of you will survive—not a man, woman, or child among you who has come here from Judah, not even the babies in your arms. ⁸Why provoke my anger by burning incense to the idols you have made here in Egypt? You will only destroy yourselves and make yourselves an object of cursing and mockery for all the nations of the earth. ⁹Have you forgotten the sins of your ancestors, the sins of the kings and queens of Judah, and the sins you and your wives committed in Judah and Jerusalem? ¹⁰To this very hour you have shown no remorse or reverence. No one has chosen to follow my word and the decrees I gave to you and your ancestors before you.

¹¹"Therefore, this is what the LORD of Heaven's Armies, the God of Israel, says: I am determined to destroy every one of you! ¹²I will take this remnant of Judah—those who were determined to come here and live in Egypt—and I will consume them. They will fall here in Egypt, killed by war and famine. All will die, from the least to the greatest. They will be an object of damnation, horror, cursing, and mockery. ¹³I will punish them in Egypt just as I punished them in Jerusalem, by war, famine, and disease. ¹⁴Of that remnant who fled to Egypt, hoping someday to return to Judah, there will be no survivors. Even though they long to return home, only a handful will do so."

¹⁵Then all the women present and all the men who knew that their wives had burned incense to idols—a great crowd of all the Judeans living in northern Egypt and southern Egypt*—answered Jeremiah, ¹⁶"We will not listen to your messages from the LORD! ¹⁷We

43:3 Or *Chaldeans.*   43:10 Hebrew *Nebuchadrezzar,* a variant spelling of Nebuchadnezzar.   43:13 Or *in Heliopolis.*
44:1a Hebrew *Noph.*   44:1b Hebrew *in Pathros.*   44:15 Hebrew *in Egypt, in Pathros.*

will do whatever we want. We will burn incense and pour out liquid offerings to the Queen of Heaven just as much as we like—just as we, and our ancestors, and our kings and officials have always done in the towns of Judah and in the streets of Jerusalem. For in those days we had plenty to eat, and we were well off and had no troubles! 18But ever since we quit burning incense to the Queen of Heaven and stopped worshiping her with liquid offerings, we have been in great trouble and have been dying from war and famine."

19"Besides," the women added, "do you suppose that we were burning incense and pouring out liquid offerings to the Queen of Heaven, and making cakes marked with her image, without our husbands knowing it and helping us? Of course not!"

20Then Jeremiah said to all of them, men and women alike, who had given him that answer, 21"Do you think the LORD did not know that you and your ancestors, your kings and officials, and all the people were burning incense to idols in the towns of Judah and in the streets of Jerusalem? 22It was because the LORD could no longer bear all the disgusting things you were doing that he made your land an object of cursing—a desolate ruin without inhabitants—as it is today. 23All these terrible things happened to you because you have burned incense to idols and sinned against the LORD. You have refused to obey him and have not followed his instructions, his decrees, and his laws."

24Then Jeremiah said to them all, including the women, "Listen to this message from the LORD, all you citizens of Judah who live in Egypt. 25This is what the LORD of Heaven's Armies, the God of Israel, says: 'You and your wives have said, "We will keep our promises to burn incense and pour out liquid offerings to the Queen of Heaven," and you have proved by your actions that you meant it. So go ahead and carry out your promises and vows to her!'

26"But listen to this message from the LORD, all you Judeans now living in Egypt: 'I have sworn by my great name,' says the LORD, 'that my name will no longer be spoken by any of the Judeans in the land of Egypt. None of you may invoke my name or use this oath: "As surely as the Sovereign LORD lives." 27For I will watch over you to bring you disaster and not good. Everyone from Judah who is now living in Egypt will suffer war and famine until all of you are dead. 28Only a small number will escape death and return to Judah from Egypt. Then all those who came to Egypt will find out whose words are true—mine or theirs!

29"'And this is the proof I give you,' says the LORD, 'that all I have threatened will happen to you and that I will punish you here.' 30This is what the LORD says: 'I will turn Pharaoh Hophra, king of Egypt, over to his enemies who want to kill him, just as I turned King Zedekiah of Judah over to King Nebuchadnezzar* of Babylon.'"

A Message for Baruch

45 The prophet Jeremiah gave a message to Baruch son of Neriah in the fourth year of the reign of Jehoiakim son of Josiah,* after Baruch had written down everything Jeremiah had dictated to him. He said, 2"This is what the LORD, the God of Israel, says to you, Baruch: 3You have said, 'I am overwhelmed with trouble! Haven't I had enough pain already? And now the LORD has added more! I am worn out from sighing and can find no rest.'

4"Baruch, this is what the LORD says: 'I will destroy this nation that I built. I will uproot what I planted. 5Are you seeking great things for yourself? Don't do it! I will bring great disaster upon all these people; but I will give you your life as a reward wherever you go. I, the LORD, have spoken!'"

Messages for the Nations

46 The following messages were given to Jeremiah the prophet from the LORD concerning foreign nations.

Messages about Egypt

2This message concerning Egypt was given in the fourth year of the reign of Jehoiakim son of Josiah, the king of Judah, on the occasion of the battle of Carchemish* when Pharaoh Neco, king of Egypt, and his army were defeated beside the Euphrates River by King Nebuchadnezzar* of Babylon.

3 "Prepare your shields,
　　and advance into battle!
4 Harness the horses,
　　and mount the stallions.
　Take your positions.
　　Put on your helmets.

44:30 Hebrew *Nebuchadrezzar*, a variant spelling of Nebuchadnezzar.   45:1 The fourth year of Jehoiakim's reign was 605 B.C.
46:2a This event occurred in 605 B.C., during the fourth year of Jehoiakim's reign (according to the calendar system in which the new year begins in the spring).   46:2b Hebrew *Nebuchadrezzar*, a variant spelling of Nebuchadnezzar; also in 46:13, 26.

Sharpen your spears,
and prepare your armor.
⁵ But what do I see?
The Egyptian army flees in terror.
The bravest of its fighting men run
without a backward glance.
They are terrorized at every turn,"
says the LORD.
⁶ "The swiftest runners cannot flee;
the mightiest warriors cannot escape.
By the Euphrates River to the north,
they stumble and fall.

⁷ "Who is this, rising like the Nile at
floodtime,
overflowing all the land?
⁸ It is the Egyptian army,
overflowing all the land,
boasting that it will cover the earth like a
flood,
destroying cities and their people.
⁹ Charge, you horses and chariots;
attack, you mighty warriors of Egypt!
Come, all you allies from Ethiopia, Libya,
and Lydia*
who are skilled with the shield and
bow!
¹⁰ For this is the day of the Lord, the LORD
of Heaven's Armies,
a day of vengeance on his enemies.
The sword will devour until it is satisfied,
yes, until it is drunk with your blood!
The Lord, the LORD of Heaven's Armies,
will receive a sacrifice today
in the north country beside the
Euphrates River.

¹¹ "Go up to Gilead to get medicine,
O virgin daughter of Egypt!
But your many treatments
will bring you no healing.
¹² The nations have heard of your shame.
The earth is filled with your cries of
despair.
Your mightiest warriors will run into each
other
and fall down together."

¹³Then the LORD gave the prophet Jeremiah
this message about King Nebuchadnezzar's
plans to attack Egypt.

¹⁴ "Shout it out in Egypt!
Publish it in the cities of Migdol,
Memphis,* and Tahpanhes!

Mobilize for battle,
for the sword will devour everyone
around you.
¹⁵ Why have your warriors fallen?
They cannot stand, for the LORD has
knocked them down.
¹⁶ They stumble and fall over each other
and say among themselves,
'Come, let's go back to our people,
to the land of our birth.
Let's get away from the sword of the
enemy!'
¹⁷ There they will say,
'Pharaoh, the king of Egypt, is a
loudmouth
who missed his opportunity!'

¹⁸ "As surely as I live," says the King,
whose name is the LORD of Heaven's
Armies,
"one is coming against Egypt
who is as tall as Mount Tabor,
or as Mount Carmel by the sea!
¹⁹ Pack up! Get ready to leave for exile,
you citizens of Egypt!
The city of Memphis will be destroyed,
without a single inhabitant.
²⁰ Egypt is as sleek as a beautiful heifer,
but a horsefly from the north is on its
way!
²¹ Egypt's mercenaries have become like
fattened calves.
They, too, will turn and run,
for it is a day of great disaster for Egypt,
a time of great punishment.
²² Egypt flees, silent as a serpent gliding
away.
The invading army marches in;
they come against her with axes like
woodsmen.
²³ They will cut down her people like trees,"
says the LORD,
"for they are more numerous than
locusts.
²⁴ Egypt will be humiliated;
she will be handed over to people from
the north."

²⁵The LORD of Heaven's Armies, the God of
Israel, says: "I will punish Amon, the god of
Thebes,* and all the other gods of Egypt. I will
punish its rulers and Pharaoh, too, and all who
trust in him. ²⁶I will hand them over to those
who want them killed—to King Nebuchadnezzar of Babylon and his army. But afterward

46:9 Hebrew *from Cush, Put, and Lud.*   46:14 Hebrew *Noph; also in 46:19.*   46:25 Hebrew *of No.*

the land will recover from the ravages of war.
I, the LORD, have spoken!

27 "But do not be afraid, Jacob, my servant;
  do not be dismayed, Israel.
For I will bring you home again from
    distant lands,
  and your children will return from their
    exile.
Israel* will return to a life of peace and
    quiet,
  and no one will terrorize them.
28 Do not be afraid, Jacob, my servant,
  for I am with you," says the LORD.
"I will completely destroy the nations to
    which I have exiled you,
  but I will not completely destroy you.
I will discipline you, but with justice;
  I cannot let you go unpunished."

A Message about Philistia

47 This is the LORD's message to the
prophet Jeremiah concerning the Philistines of Gaza, before it was captured by the
Egyptian army. 2This is what the LORD says:

"A flood is coming from the north
  to overflow the land.
It will destroy the land and everything
    in it—
  cities and people alike.
People will scream in terror,
  and everyone in the land will wail.
3 Hear the clatter of stallions' hooves
  and the rumble of wheels as the chariots
    rush by.
Terrified fathers run madly,
  without a backward glance at their
    helpless children.

4 "The time has come for the Philistines to
    be destroyed,
  along with their allies from Tyre and
    Sidon.
Yes, the LORD is destroying the remnant
    of the Philistines,
  those colonists from the island of Crete.*
5 Gaza will be humiliated, its head shaved
    bald;
  Ashkelon will lie silent.
You remnant from the Mediterranean
    coast,*

how long will you cut yourselves in
    mourning?
6 "Now, O sword of the LORD,
  when will you be at rest again?
Go back into your sheath;
  rest and be still.
7 "But how can it be still
  when the LORD has sent it on a mission?
For the city of Ashkelon
  and the people living along the sea
  must be destroyed."

A Message about Moab

48 This message was given concerning
Moab. This is what the LORD of Heav-
en's Armies, the God of Israel, says:

"What sorrow awaits the city of Nebo;
  it will soon lie in ruins.
The city of Kiriathaim will be humiliated
    and captured;
  the fortress will be humiliated and
    broken down.
2 No one will ever brag about Moab again,
  for in Heshbon there is a plot to destroy
    her.
'Come,' they say, 'we will cut her off from
    being a nation.'
The town of Madmen,* too, will be
    silenced;
  the sword will follow you there.
3 Listen to the cries from Horonaim,
  cries of devastation and great destruction.
4 All Moab is destroyed.
  Her little ones will cry out.*
5 Her refugees weep bitterly,
  climbing the slope to Luhith.
They cry out in terror,
  descending the slope to Horonaim.
6 Flee for your lives!
  Hide* in the wilderness!
7 Because you have trusted in your wealth
    and skill,
  you will be taken captive.
Your god Chemosh, with his priests and
    officials,
  will be hauled off to distant lands!

8 "All the towns will be destroyed,
  and no one will escape—

46:27 Hebrew *Jacob.* See note on 5:20.   47:4 Hebrew *from Caphtor.*   47:5 Hebrew *the plain.*   48:2 *Madmen* sounds like the
Hebrew word for "silence"; it should not be confused with the English word *madmen.*   48:4 Greek version reads *Her cries are
heard as far away as Zoar.*   48:6 Or *Hide like a wild donkey;* or *Hide like a juniper shrub;* or *Be like* [the town of] *Aroer.* The meaning
of the Hebrew is uncertain.

either on the plateaus or in the valleys,
    for the LORD has spoken.
9 Oh, that Moab had wings
    so she could fly away,*
for her towns will be left empty,
    with no one living in them.
10 Cursed are those who refuse to do the
    LORD's work,
    who hold back their swords from
      shedding blood!

11 "From his earliest history, Moab has lived
    in peace,
    never going into exile.
He is like wine that has been allowed to
    settle.
He has not been poured from flask to
    flask,
    and he is now fragrant and smooth.
12 But the time is coming soon," says the
    LORD,
    "when I will send men to pour him from
    his jar.
They will pour him out,
    then shatter the jar!
13 At last Moab will be ashamed of his idol
    Chemosh,
    as the people of Israel were ashamed
    of their gold calf at Bethel.*

14 "You used to boast, 'We are heroes,
    mighty men of war.'
15 But now Moab and his towns will be
    destroyed.
    His most promising youth are doomed
      to slaughter,"
    says the King, whose name is the LORD
      of Heaven's Armies.
16 "Destruction is coming fast for Moab;
    calamity threatens ominously.
17 You friends of Moab,
    weep for him and cry!
See how the strong scepter is broken,
    how the beautiful staff is shattered!

18 "Come down from your glory
    and sit in the dust, you people of
      Dibon,
for those who destroy Moab will shatter
    Dibon, too.
    They will tear down all your towers.
19 You people of Aroer,
    stand beside the road and watch.

Shout to those who flee from Moab,
    'What has happened there?'

20 "And the reply comes back,
    'Moab lies in ruins, disgraced;
    weep and wail!
Tell it by the banks of the Arnon River:
    Moab has been destroyed!'
21 Judgment has been poured out on the
    towns of the plateau—
    on Holon and Jahaz* and Mephaath,
22 on Dibon and Nebo and Beth-diblathaim,
23   on Kiriathaim and Beth-gamul and
      Beth-meon,
24 on Kerioth and Bozrah—
    all the towns of Moab, far and near.

25 "The strength of Moab has ended.
    His arm has been broken," says the
      LORD.
26 "Let him stagger and fall like a drunkard,
    for he has rebelled against the LORD.
Moab will wallow in his own vomit,
    ridiculed by all.
27 Did you not ridicule the people of Israel?
    Were they caught in the company of
      thieves
    that you should despise them as you do?

28 "You people of Moab,
    flee from your towns and live in the
      caves.
Hide like doves that nest
    in the clefts of the rocks.
29 We have all heard of the pride of Moab,
    for his pride is very great.
We know of his lofty pride,
    his arrogance, and his haughty heart.
30 I know about his insolence,"
    says the LORD,
    "but his boasts are empty—
    as empty as his deeds.
31 So now I wail for Moab;
    yes, I will mourn for Moab.
My heart is broken for the men of
    Kir-hareseth.*

32 "You people of Sibmah, rich in vineyards,
    I will weep for you even more than I did
      for Jazer.
Your spreading vines once reached as far as
    the Dead Sea,*
    but the destroyer has stripped you bare!

48:9 Or Put salt on Moab, / for she will be laid waste.   48:13 Hebrew ashamed when they trusted in Bethel.   48:21 Hebrew Jahzah, a variant spelling of Jahaz.   48:31 Hebrew Kir-heres, a variant spelling of Kir-hareseth; also in 48:36.   48:32 Hebrew the sea of Jazer.

He has harvested your grapes and
    summer fruits.
33 Joy and gladness are gone from fruitful
    Moab.
The presses yield no wine.
No one treads the grapes with shouts
    of joy.
There is shouting, yes, but not of
    joy.

34"Instead, their awful cries of terror can be heard from Heshbon clear across to Elealeh and Jahaz; from Zoar all the way to Horonaim and Eglath-shelishiyah. Even the waters of Nimrim are dried up now.

35"I will put an end to Moab," says the LORD, "for the people offer sacrifices at the pagan shrines and burn incense to their false gods. 36My heart moans like a flute for Moab and Kirhareseth, for all their wealth has disappeared. 37The people shave their heads and beards in mourning. They slash their hands and put on clothes made of burlap. 38There is crying and sorrow in every Moabite home and on every street. For I have smashed Moab like an old, unwanted jar. 39How it is shattered! Hear the wailing! See the shame of Moab! It has become an object of ridicule, an example of ruin to all its neighbors."

40This is what the LORD says:

"Look! The enemy swoops down like an
    eagle,
  spreading his wings over Moab.
41 Its cities will fall,
    and its strongholds will be seized.
Even the mightiest warriors will be in
    anguish
    like a woman in labor.
42 Moab will no longer be a nation,
    for it has boasted against the LORD.

43 "Terror and traps and snares will be your
    lot,
    O Moab," says the LORD.
44 "Those who flee in terror will fall into a
    trap,
    and those who escape the trap will step
    into a snare.
I will see to it that you do not get away,
    for the time of your judgment has
    come,"
    says the LORD.
45 "The people flee as far as Heshbon
    but are unable to go on.

For a fire comes from Heshbon,
    King Sihon's ancient home,
to devour the entire land
    with all its rebellious people.

46 "What sorrow awaits you, O people of
    Moab!
The people of the god Chemosh are
    destroyed!
Your sons and your daughters
    have been taken away as captives.
47 But I will restore the fortunes of Moab
    in days to come.
I, the LORD, have spoken!"

This is the end of Jeremiah's prophecy concerning Moab.

A Message about Ammon

49 This message was given concerning the Ammonites. This is what the LORD says:

"Are there no descendants of Israel
    to inherit the land of Gad?
Why are you, who worship Molech,*
    living in its towns?
2 In the days to come," says the LORD,
    "I will sound the battle cry against your
    city of Rabbah.
It will become a desolate heap of ruins,
    and the neighboring towns will be
    burned.
Then Israel will take back the land
    you took from her," says the LORD.

3 "Cry out, O Heshbon,
    for the town of Ai is destroyed.
Weep, O people of Rabbah!
    Put on your clothes of mourning.
Weep and wail, hiding in the hedges,
    for your god Molech, with his priests
    and officials,
    will be hauled off to distant lands.
4 You are proud of your fertile valleys,
    but they will soon be ruined.
You trusted in your wealth,
    you rebellious daughter,
    and thought no one could ever harm
    you.
5 But look! I will bring terror upon you,"
    says the Lord, the LORD of Heaven's
    Armies.
"Your neighbors will chase you from your
    land,

49:1 Hebrew *Malcam*, a variant spelling of Molech; also in 49:3.

and no one will help your exiles as they
　　flee.
⁶ But I will restore the fortunes of the
　　Ammonites
　　in days to come.
　　I, the LORD, have spoken."

Messages about Edom

⁷This message was given concerning Edom.
This is what the LORD of Heaven's Armies says:

"Is there no wisdom in Teman?
　　Is no one left to give wise counsel?
⁸ Turn and flee!
　　Hide in deep caves, you people of
　　　Dedan!
　　For when I bring disaster on Edom,*
　　　I will punish you, too!
⁹ Those who harvest grapes
　　always leave a few for the poor.
　　If thieves came at night,
　　they would not take everything.
¹⁰ But I will strip bare the land of Edom,
　　and there will be no place left to hide.
　　Its children, its brothers, and its
　　　neighbors
　　will all be destroyed,
　　and Edom itself will be no more.
¹¹ But I will protect the orphans who remain
　　among you.
　　Your widows, too, can depend on me for
　　　help."

¹²And this is what the LORD says: "If the innocent must suffer, how much more must you!
You will not go unpunished! You must drink
this cup of judgment! ¹³For I have sworn by my
own name," says the LORD, "that Bozrah will
become an object of horror and a heap of ruins;
it will be mocked and cursed. All its towns and
villages will be desolate forever."

¹⁴ I have heard a message from the LORD
　　that an ambassador was sent to the
　　　nations to say,
　　"Form a coalition against Edom,
　　and prepare for battle!"

¹⁵ The LORD says to Edom,
　　"I will cut you down to size among the
　　　nations.
　　You will be despised by all.
¹⁶ You have been deceived
　　by the fear you inspire in others
　　and by your own pride.

You live in a rock fortress
　　and control the mountain heights.
　　But even if you make your nest among the
　　　peaks with the eagles,
　　I will bring you crashing down,"
　　says the LORD.

¹⁷ "Edom will be an object of horror.
　　All who pass by will be appalled
　　and will gasp at the destruction they
　　　see there.
¹⁸ It will be like the destruction of Sodom
　　and Gomorrah
　　and their neighboring towns," says the
　　　LORD.
　　"No one will live there;
　　no one will inhabit it.
¹⁹ I will come like a lion from the thickets of
　　the Jordan,
　　leaping on the sheep in the pasture.
　　I will chase Edom from its land,
　　and I will appoint the leader of my
　　　choice.
　　For who is like me, and who can
　　　challenge me?
　　What ruler can oppose my will?"

²⁰ Listen to the LORD's plans against Edom
　　and the people of Teman.
　　Even the little children will be dragged off
　　　like sheep,
　　and their homes will be destroyed.
²¹ The earth will shake with the noise of
　　Edom's fall,
　　and its cry of despair will be heard all
　　　the way to the Red Sea.*
²² Look! The enemy swoops down like an
　　eagle,
　　spreading his wings over Bozrah.
　　Even the mightiest warriors will be in
　　　anguish
　　like a woman in labor.

A Message about Damascus

²³This message was given concerning Damascus. This is what the LORD says:

"The towns of Hamath and Arpad are
　　struck with fear,
　　for they have heard the news of their
　　　destruction.
　　Their hearts are troubled
　　like a wild sea in a raging storm.
²⁴ Damascus has become feeble,
　　and all her people turn to flee.

49:8 Hebrew *Esau;* also in 49:10.　　49:21 Hebrew *sea of reeds.*

Fear, anguish, and pain have gripped her
as they grip a woman in labor.
25 That famous city, a city of joy,
will be forsaken!
26 Her young men will fall in the streets
and die.
Her soldiers will all be killed,"
says the LORD of Heaven's Armies.
27 "And I will set fire to the walls of Damascus
that will burn up the palaces of
Ben-hadad."

A Message about Kedar and Hazor

28This message was given concerning Kedar
and the kingdoms of Hazor, which were attacked by King Nebuchadnezzar* of Babylon.
This is what the LORD says:

"Advance against Kedar!
Destroy the warriors from the East!
29 Their flocks and tents will be captured,
and their household goods and camels
will be taken away.
Everywhere shouts of panic will be heard:
'We are terrorized at every turn!'
30 Run for your lives," says the LORD.
"Hide yourselves in deep caves, you
people of Hazor,
for King Nebuchadnezzar of Babylon has
plotted against you
and is preparing to destroy you.

31 "Go up and attack that complacent nation,"
says the LORD.
"Its people live alone in the desert
without walls or gates.
32 Their camels and other livestock will all
be yours.
I will scatter to the winds these people
who live in remote places.*
I will bring calamity upon them
from every direction," says the LORD.
33 "Hazor will be inhabited by jackals,
and it will be desolate forever.
No one will live there;
no one will inhabit it."

A Message about Elam

34This message concerning Elam came to the
prophet Jeremiah from the LORD at the beginning of the reign of King Zedekiah of Judah.
35This is what the LORD of Heaven's Armies
says:

"I will destroy the archers of Elam—
the best of their forces.
36 I will bring enemies from all directions,
and I will scatter the people of Elam to
the four winds.
They will be exiled to countries around
the world.
37 I myself will go with Elam's enemies to
shatter it.
In my fierce anger, I will bring great
disaster
upon the people of Elam," says the LORD.
"Their enemies will chase them with the
sword
until I have destroyed them completely.
38 I will set my throne in Elam," says the
LORD,
"and I will destroy its king and officials.
39 But I will restore the fortunes of Elam
in days to come.
I, the LORD, have spoken!"

A Message about Babylon

50 The LORD gave Jeremiah the prophet
this message concerning Babylon and
the land of the Babylonians.* 2This is what the
LORD says:

"Tell the whole world,
and keep nothing back.
Raise a signal flag
to tell everyone that Babylon will fall!
Her images and idols* will be shattered.
Her gods Bel and Marduk will be utterly
disgraced.
3 For a nation will attack her from the north
and bring such destruction that no one
will live there again.
Everything will be gone;
both people and animals will flee.

Hope for Israel and Judah

4 "In those coming days,"
says the LORD,
"the people of Israel will return home
together with the people of Judah.
They will come weeping
and seeking the LORD their God.
5 They will ask the way to Jerusalem*
and will start back home again.
They will bind themselves to the LORD
with an eternal covenant that will never
be forgotten.

49:28 Hebrew *Nebuchadrezzar*, a variant spelling of Nebuchadnezzar; also in 49:30. 49:32 Or *who clip the corners of their hair.* 50:1 Or *Chaldeans*; also in 50:8, 25, 35, 45. 50:2 The Hebrew term (literally *round things*) probably alludes to dung. 50:5 Hebrew *Zion*; also in 50:28.

6 "My people have been lost sheep.
  Their shepherds have led them astray
  and turned them loose in the
    mountains.
They have lost their way
  and can't remember how to get back to
    the sheepfold.
7 All who found them devoured them.
  Their enemies said,
'We did nothing wrong in attacking them,
  for they sinned against the LORD,
their true place of rest,
  and the hope of their ancestors.'

8 "But now, flee from Babylon!
  Leave the land of the Babylonians.
Like male goats at the head of the flock,
  lead my people home again.
9 For I am raising up an army
  of great nations from the north.
They will join forces to attack Babylon,
  and she will be captured.
The enemies' arrows will go straight to the
    mark;
  they will not miss!
10 Babylonia* will be looted
  until the attackers are glutted with loot.
  I, the LORD, have spoken!

Babylon's Sure Fall

11 "You rejoice and are glad,
  you who plundered my chosen people.
You frisk about like a calf in a meadow
  and neigh like a stallion.
12 But your homeland* will be overwhelmed
    with shame and disgrace.
You will become the least of nations—
  a wilderness, a dry and desolate land.
13 Because of the LORD's anger,
  Babylon will become a deserted
    wasteland.
All who pass by will be horrified
  and will gasp at the destruction they see
    there.

14 "Yes, prepare to attack Babylon,
  all you surrounding nations.
Let your archers shoot at her; spare no
    arrows.
  For she has sinned against the LORD.
15 Shout war cries against her from every
    side.
  Look! She surrenders!

Her walls have fallen.
  It is the LORD's vengeance,
  so take vengeance on her.
  Do to her as she has done to others!
16 Take from Babylon all those who plant
    crops;
  send all the harvesters away.
Because of the sword of the enemy,
  everyone will run away and rush back
    to their own lands.

Hope for God's People

17 "The Israelites are like sheep
  that have been scattered by lions.
First the king of Assyria ate them up.
  Then King Nebuchadnezzar* of Babylon
    cracked their bones."
18 Therefore, this is what the LORD of
    Heaven's Armies,
  the God of Israel, says:
"Now I will punish the king of Babylon
    and his land,
  just as I punished the king of Assyria.
19 And I will bring Israel home again to its
    own land,
  to feed in the fields of Carmel and
    Bashan,
and to be satisfied once more
  in the hill country of Ephraim and
    Gilead.
20 In those days," says the LORD,
  "no sin will be found in Israel or in
    Judah,
  for I will forgive the remnant I preserve.

The LORD's Judgment on Babylon

21 "Go up, my warriors, against the land of
    Merathaim
  and against the people of Pekod.
Pursue, kill, and completely destroy*
    them,
  as I have commanded you," says the
    LORD.
22 "Let the battle cry be heard in the land,
  a shout of great destruction.
23 Babylon, the mightiest hammer in all the
    earth,
  lies broken and shattered.
  Babylon is desolate among the nations!
24 Listen, Babylon, for I have set a trap for
    you.
  You are caught, for you have fought
    against the LORD.

50:10 Or Chaldea.   50:12 Hebrew your mother.   50:17 Hebrew Nebuchadrezzar, a variant spelling of Nebuchadnezzar.
50:21 The Hebrew term used here refers to the complete consecration of things or people to the LORD, either by destroying
them or by giving them as an offering.

25 The LORD has opened his armory
    and brought out weapons to vent his
        fury.
The terror that falls upon the Babylonians
    will be the work of the Sovereign LORD
        of Heaven's Armies.
26 Yes, come against her from distant lands.
    Break open her granaries.
Crush her walls and houses into heaps of
    rubble.
Destroy her completely, and leave
    nothing!
27 Destroy even her young bulls—
    it will be terrible for them, too!
Slaughter them all!
    For Babylon's day of reckoning has
        come.
28 Listen to the people who have escaped
        from Babylon,
    as they tell in Jerusalem
how the LORD our God has taken
        vengeance
    against those who destroyed his Temple.

29 "Send out a call for archers to come to
        Babylon.
    Surround the city so none can escape.
Do to her as she has done to others,
    for she has defied the LORD, the Holy
        One of Israel.
30 Her young men will fall in the streets
        and die.
    Her soldiers will all be killed,"
    says the LORD.

31 "See, I am your enemy, you arrogant
        people,"
    says the Lord, the LORD of Heaven's
        Armies.
"Your day of reckoning has arrived—
    the day when I will punish you.
32 O land of arrogance, you will stumble and
        fall,
    and no one will raise you up.
For I will light a fire in the cities of
        Babylon
    that will burn up everything around
        them."

33 This is what the LORD of Heaven's Armies
    says:
"The people of Israel and Judah have been
    wronged.
    Their captors hold them and refuse to
        let them go.

34 But the one who redeems them is strong.
    His name is the LORD of Heaven's Armies.
He will defend them
    and give them rest again in Israel.
But for the people of Babylon
    there will be no rest!

35 "The sword of destruction will strike the
        Babylonians,"
    says the LORD.
"It will strike the people of Babylon—
    her officials and wise men, too.
36 The sword will strike her wise counselors,
    and they will become fools.
The sword will strike her mightiest
        warriors,
    and panic will seize them.
37 The sword will strike her horses and
        chariots
    and her allies from other lands,
    and they will all become like women.
The sword will strike her treasures,
    and they all will be plundered.
38 A drought* will strike her water supply,
    causing it to dry up.
And why? Because the whole land is filled
        with idols,
    and the people are madly in love with
        them.

39 "Soon Babylon will be inhabited by desert
        animals and hyenas.
    It will be a home for owls.
Never again will people live there;
    it will lie desolate forever.
40 I will destroy it as I* destroyed Sodom and
        Gomorrah
    and their neighboring towns," says the
        LORD.
"No one will live there;
    no one will inhabit it.

41 "Look! A great army is coming from the
        north.
    A great nation and many kings
    are rising against you from far-off lands.
42 They are armed with bows and spears.
    They are cruel and show no mercy.
As they ride forward on horses,
    they sound like a roaring sea.
They are coming in battle formation,
    planning to destroy you, Babylon.
43 The king of Babylon has heard reports
        about the enemy,
    and he is weak with fright.

50:38 Or *sword;* the Hebrew words for *drought* and *sword* are very similar.   50:40 Hebrew *as God.*

Pangs of anguish have gripped him,
like those of a woman in labor.

44 "I will come like a lion from the thickets
of the Jordan,
leaping on the sheep in the pasture.
I will chase Babylon from its land,
and I will appoint the leader of my
choice.
For who is like me, and who can
challenge me?
What ruler can oppose my will?"

45 Listen to the LORD's plans against
Babylon
and the land of the Babylonians.
Even the little children will be dragged
off like sheep,
and their homes will be destroyed.

46 The earth will shake with the shout,
"Babylon has been taken!"
and its cry of despair will be heard
around the world.

51

1 This is what the LORD says:
"I will stir up a destroyer against
Babylon
and the people of Babylonia.*

2 Foreigners will come and winnow her,
blowing her away as chaff.
They will come from every side
to rise against her in her day of trouble.

3 Don't let the archers put on their armor
or draw their bows.
Don't spare even her best soldiers!
Let her army be completely destroyed.*

4 They will fall dead in the land of the
Babylonians,*
slashed to death in her streets.

5 For the LORD of Heaven's Armies
has not abandoned Israel and Judah.
He is still their God,
even though their land was filled
with sin
against the Holy One of Israel."

6 Flee from Babylon! Save yourselves!
Don't get trapped in her punishment!
It is the LORD's time for vengeance;
he will repay her in full.

7 Babylon has been a gold cup in the LORD's
hands,
a cup that made the whole earth drunk.

The nations drank Babylon's wine,
and it drove them all mad.

8 But suddenly Babylon, too, has fallen.
Weep for her.
Give her medicine.
Perhaps she can yet be healed.

9 We would have helped her if we could,
but nothing can save her now.
Let her go; abandon her.
Return now to your own land.
For her punishment reaches to the
heavens;
it is so great it cannot be measured.

10 The LORD has vindicated us.
Come, let us announce in Jerusalem*
everything the LORD our God has done.

11 Sharpen the arrows!
Lift up the shields!*
For the LORD has inspired the kings of
the Medes
to march against Babylon and destroy
her.
This is his vengeance against those
who desecrated his Temple.

12 Raise the battle flag against Babylon!
Reinforce the guard and station the
watchmen.
Prepare an ambush,
for the LORD will fulfill all his plans
against Babylon.

13 You are a city by a great river,
a great center of commerce,
but your end has come.
The thread of your life is cut.

14 The LORD of Heaven's Armies has taken
this vow
and has sworn to it by his own name:
"Your cities will be filled with enemies,
like fields swarming with locusts,
and they will shout in triumph over you."

A Hymn of Praise to the LORD

15 The LORD made the earth by his power,
and he preserves it by his wisdom.
With his own understanding
he stretched out the heavens.

16 When he speaks in the thunder,
the heavens roar with rain.
He causes the clouds to rise over the earth.
He sends the lightning with the rain
and releases the wind from his
storehouses.

51:1 Hebrew *of Leb-kamai,* a code name for Babylonia.   51:3 The Hebrew term used here refers to the complete consecration
of things or people to the LORD, either by destroying them or by giving them as an offering.   51:4 Or *Chaldeans;* also
in 51:54.   51:10 Hebrew *Zion;* also in 51:24.   51:11 Greek version reads *Fill up the quivers.*

17 The whole human race is foolish and has
    no knowledge!
  The craftsmen are disgraced by the idols
    they make,
for their carefully shaped works are a
    fraud.
  These idols have no breath or power.
18 Idols are worthless; they are ridiculous
    lies!
  On the day of reckoning they will all
    be destroyed.
19 But the God of Israel* is no idol!
  He is the Creator of everything that
    exists,
including his people, his own special
    possession.
  The LORD of Heaven's Armies is his
    name!

Babylon's Great Punishment

20 "You* are my battle-ax and sword,"
    says the LORD.
"With you I will shatter nations
  and destroy many kingdoms.
21 With you I will shatter armies—
  destroying the horse and rider,
  the chariot and charioteer.
22 With you I will shatter men and women,
  old people and children,
  young men and young women.
23 With you I will shatter shepherds and
    flocks,
  farmers and oxen,
  captains and officers.

24 "I will repay Babylon
  and the people of Babylonia*
for all the wrong they have done
  to my people in Jerusalem," says the
    LORD.

25 "Look, O mighty mountain, destroyer of
    the earth!
  I am your enemy," says the LORD.
"I will raise my fist against you,
  to knock you down from the heights.
When I am finished,
  you will be nothing but a heap of burnt
    rubble.
26 You will be desolate forever.
  Even your stones will never again be
    used for building.
You will be completely wiped out,"
  says the LORD.

27 Raise a signal flag to the nations.
  Sound the battle cry!
Mobilize them all against Babylon.
  Prepare them to fight against her!
Bring out the armies of Ararat, Minni,
    and Ashkenaz.
  Appoint a commander,
  and bring a multitude of horses like
    swarming locusts!
28 Bring against her the armies of the
    nations—
  led by the kings of the Medes
  and all their captains and officers.

29 The earth trembles and writhes in pain,
  for everything the LORD has planned
    against Babylon stands unchanged.
Babylon will be left desolate without a
    single inhabitant.
30 Her mightiest warriors no longer fight.
They stay in their barracks, their courage
    gone.
  They have become like women.
The invaders have burned the houses
  and broken down the city gates.
31 The news is passed from one runner to the
    next
  as the messengers hurry to tell the king
  that his city has been captured.
32 All the escape routes are blocked.
  The marshes have been set aflame,
  and the army is in a panic.

33 This is what the LORD of Heaven's Armies,
    the God of Israel, says:
"Babylon is like wheat on a threshing
    floor,
  about to be trampled.
In just a little while
  her harvest will begin."

34 "King Nebuchadnezzar* of Babylon has
    eaten and crushed us
  and drained us of strength.
He has swallowed us like a great monster
  and filled his belly with our riches.
  He has thrown us out of our own
    country.
35 Make Babylon suffer as she made us
    suffer,"
  say the people of Zion.
"Make the people of Babylonia pay for
    spilling our blood,"
  says Jerusalem.

51:19 Hebrew *the Portion of Jacob.* See note on 5:20.   51:20 Possibly Cyrus, whom God used to conquer Babylon. Compare
Isa 44:28; 45:1.   51:24 Or *Chaldea;* also in 51:35.   51:34 Hebrew *Nebuchadrezzar,* a variant spelling of Nebuchadnezzar.

The Lord's Vengeance on Babylon

³⁶ This is what the Lord says to Jerusalem:

"I will be your lawyer to plead your case,
and I will avenge you.
I will dry up her river,
as well as her springs,
³⁷ and Babylon will become a heap of ruins,
haunted by jackals.
She will be an object of horror and
contempt,
a place where no one lives.
³⁸ Her people will roar together like strong
lions.
They will growl like lion cubs.
³⁹ And while they lie inflamed with all their
wine,
I will prepare a different kind of feast
for them.
I will make them drink until they fall
asleep,
and they will never wake up again,"
says the Lord.
⁴⁰ "I will bring them down
like lambs to the slaughter,
like rams and goats to be sacrificed.

⁴¹ "How Babylon* is fallen—
great Babylon, praised throughout the
earth!
Now she has become an object of horror
among the nations.
⁴² The sea has risen over Babylon;
she is covered by its crashing waves.
⁴³ Her cities now lie in ruins;
she is a dry wasteland
where no one lives or even passes by.
⁴⁴ And I will punish Bel, the god of Babylon,
and make him vomit up all he has eaten.
The nations will no longer come and
worship him.
The wall of Babylon has fallen!

A Message for the Exiles

⁴⁵ "Come out, my people, flee from Babylon.
Save yourselves! Run from the Lord's
fierce anger.
⁴⁶ But do not panic; don't be afraid
when you hear the first rumor of
approaching forces.
For rumors will keep coming year by
year.
Violence will erupt in the land
as the leaders fight against each other.
⁴⁷ For the time is surely coming

51:41 Hebrew *Sheshach*, a code name for Babylon.

when I will punish this great city and
all her idols.
Her whole land will be disgraced,
and her dead will lie in the streets.
⁴⁸ Then the heavens and earth will rejoice,
for out of the north will come
destroying armies
against Babylon," says the Lord.
⁴⁹ "Just as Babylon killed the people of
Israel
and others throughout the world,
so must her people be killed.
⁵⁰ Get out, all you who have escaped the
sword!
Do not stand and watch—flee while
you can!
Remember the Lord, though you are in
a far-off land,
and think about your home in
Jerusalem."

⁵¹ "We are ashamed," the people say.
"We are insulted and disgraced
because the Lord's Temple
has been defiled by foreigners."

⁵² "Yes," says the Lord, "but the time is
coming
when I will destroy Babylon's idols.
The groans of her wounded people
will be heard throughout the land.
⁵³ Though Babylon reaches as high as the
heavens
and makes her fortifications incredibly
strong,
I will still send enemies to plunder her.
I, the Lord, have spoken!

Babylon's Complete Destruction

⁵⁴ "Listen! Hear the cry of Babylon,
the sound of great destruction from the
land of the Babylonians.
⁵⁵ For the Lord is destroying Babylon.
He will silence her loud voice.
Waves of enemies pound against her;
the noise of battle rings through the
city.
⁵⁶ Destroying armies come against Babylon.
Her mighty men are captured,
and their weapons break in their hands.
For the Lord is a God who gives just
punishment;
he always repays in full.
⁵⁷ I will make her officials and wise men
drunk,

along with her captains, officers, and
warriors.
They will fall asleep
and never wake up again!"
says the King, whose name is
the LORD of Heaven's Armies.

58 This is what the LORD of Heaven's Armies
says:
"The thick walls of Babylon will be leveled
to the ground,
and her massive gates will be burned.
The builders from many lands have
worked in vain,
for their work will be destroyed by
fire!"

Jeremiah's Message Sent to Babylon

59The prophet Jeremiah gave this message to
Seraiah son of Neriah and grandson of Mahseiah, a staff officer, when Seraiah went to Babylon with King Zedekiah of Judah. This was
during the fourth year of Zedekiah's reign.*
60Jeremiah had recorded on a scroll all the terrible disasters that would soon come upon Babylon—all the words written here. 61He said to
Seraiah, "When you get to Babylon, read aloud
everything on this scroll. 62Then say, 'LORD,
you have said that you will destroy Babylon
so that neither people nor animals will remain
here. She will lie empty and abandoned forever.' 63When you have finished reading the
scroll, tie it to a stone and throw it into the
Euphrates River. 64Then say, 'In this same way
Babylon and her people will sink, never again
to rise, because of the disasters I will bring
upon her.'"

This is the end of Jeremiah's messages.

The Fall of Jerusalem

52 Zedekiah was twenty-one years old
when he became king, and he reigned
in Jerusalem eleven years. His mother was Hamutal, the daughter of Jeremiah from Libnah.
2But Zedekiah did what was evil in the LORD's
sight, just as Jehoiakim had done. 3These
things happened because of the LORD's anger
against the people of Jerusalem and Judah,
until he finally banished them from his presence and sent them into exile.

Zedekiah rebelled against the king of Babylon. 4So on January 15,* during the ninth year
of Zedekiah's reign, King Nebuchadnezzar* of
Babylon led his entire army against Jerusalem.
They surrounded the city and built siege ramps
against its walls. 5Jerusalem was kept under
siege until the eleventh year of King Zedekiah's reign.

6By July 18 in the eleventh year of Zedekiah's reign,* the famine in the city had become
very severe, and the last of the food was entirely gone. 7Then a section of the city wall was
broken down, and all the soldiers fled. Since
the city was surrounded by the Babylonians,*
they waited for nightfall. Then they slipped
through the gate between the two walls behind
the king's garden and headed toward the Jordan Valley.*

8But the Babylonian troops chased King
Zedekiah and overtook him on the plains of
Jericho, for his men had all deserted him and
scattered. 9They captured the king and took
him to the king of Babylon at Riblah in the
land of Hamath. There the king of Babylon
pronounced judgment upon Zedekiah. 10The
king of Babylon made Zedekiah watch as he
slaughtered his sons. He also slaughtered
all the officials of Judah at Riblah. 11Then he
gouged out Zedekiah's eyes and bound him in
bronze chains, and the king of Babylon led him
away to Babylon. Zedekiah remained there in
prison until the day of his death.

The Temple Destroyed

12On August 17 of that year,* which was the
nineteenth year of King Nebuchadnezzar's
reign, Nebuzaradan, the captain of the guard
and an official of the Babylonian king, arrived
in Jerusalem. 13He burned down the Temple of
the LORD, the royal palace, and all the houses
of Jerusalem. He destroyed all the important
buildings* in the city. 14Then he supervised the
entire Babylonian* army as they tore down the
walls of Jerusalem on every side. 15Then Nebuzaradan, the captain of the guard, took as
exiles some of the poorest of the people, the
rest of the people who remained in the city, the
defectors who had declared their allegiance to
the king of Babylon, and the rest of the craftsmen. 16But Nebuzaradan allowed some of the

---

51:59 The fourth year of Zedekiah's reign was 593 B.C.   52:4a Hebrew *on the tenth day of the tenth month,* of the ancient
Hebrew lunar calendar. A number of events in Jeremiah can be cross-checked with dates in surviving Babylonian records
and related accurately to our modern calendar. This day was January 15, 588 B.C.   52:4b Hebrew *Nebuchadrezzar,* a variant
spelling of Nebuchadnezzar; also in 52:12, 28, 29, 30.   52:6 Hebrew *By the ninth day of the fourth month* [in the eleventh year
of Zedekiah's reign]. This day was July 18, 586 B.C.; also see note on 52:4a.   52:7a Or *the Chaldeans;* similarly in 52:8, 17.
52:7b Hebrew *the Arabah.*   52:12 Hebrew *On the tenth day of the fifth month,* of the ancient Hebrew lunar calendar. This day
was August 17, 586 B.C.; also see note on 52:4a.   52:13 Or *destroyed the houses of all the important people.*   52:14 Or *Chaldean.*

poorest people to stay behind to care for the vineyards and fields.

¹⁷The Babylonians broke up the bronze pillars in front of the LORD's Temple, the bronze water carts, and the great bronze basin called the Sea, and they carried all the bronze away to Babylon. ¹⁸They also took all the ash buckets, shovels, lamp snuffers, basins, dishes, and all the other bronze articles used for making sacrifices at the Temple. ¹⁹The captain of the guard also took the small bowls, incense burners, basins, pots, lampstands, ladles, bowls used for liquid offerings, and all the other articles made of pure gold or silver.

²⁰The weight of the bronze from the two pillars, the Sea with the twelve bronze oxen beneath it, and the water carts was too great to be measured. These things had been made for the LORD's Temple in the days of King Solomon. ²¹Each of the pillars was 27 feet tall and 18 feet in circumference.* They were hollow, with walls 3 inches thick.* ²²The bronze capital on top of each pillar was 7½ feet* high and was decorated with a network of bronze pomegranates all the way around. ²³There were 96 pomegranates on the sides, and a total of 100 pomegranates on the network around the top.

²⁴Nebuzaradan, the captain of the guard, took with him as prisoners Seraiah the high priest, Zephaniah the priest of the second rank, and the three chief gatekeepers. ²⁵And from among the people still hiding in the city, he took an officer who had been in charge of the Judean army; seven of the king's personal advisers; the army commander's chief secretary, who was in charge of recruitment; and sixty other citizens. ²⁶Nebuzaradan, the captain of the guard, took them all to the king of Babylon at Riblah. ²⁷And there at Riblah, in the land of Hamath, the king of Babylon had them all put to death. So the people of Judah were sent into exile from their land.

²⁸The number of captives taken to Babylon in the seventh year of Nebuchadnezzar's reign* was 3,023. ²⁹Then in Nebuchadnezzar's eighteenth year* he took 832 more. ³⁰In Nebuchadnezzar's twenty-third year* he sent Nebuzaradan, the captain of the guard, who took 745 more—a total of 4,600 captives in all.

Hope for Israel's Royal Line

³¹In the thirty-seventh year of the exile of King Jehoiachin of Judah, Evil-merodach ascended to the Babylonian throne. He was kind to* Jehoiachin and released him from prison on March 31 of that year.* ³²He spoke kindly to Jehoiachin and gave him a higher place than all the other exiled kings in Babylon. ³³He supplied Jehoiachin with new clothes to replace his prison garb and allowed him to dine in the king's presence for the rest of his life. ³⁴So the Babylonian king gave him a regular food allowance as long as he lived. This continued until the day of his death.

52:21a Hebrew *18 cubits* [8.3 meters] *tall and 12 cubits* [5.5 meters] *in circumference.*   52:21b Hebrew *4 fingers thick* [8 centimeters]. 52:22 Hebrew *5 cubits* [2.3 meters].   52:28 This exile in the seventh year of Nebuchadnezzar's reign occurred in 597 B.C. 52:29 This exile in the eighteenth year of Nebuchadnezzar's reign occurred in 586 B.C.   52:30 This exile in the twenty-third year of Nebuchadnezzar's reign occurred in 581 B.C.   52:31a Hebrew *He raised the head of.*   52:31b Hebrew *on the twenty-fifth day of the twelfth month,* of the ancient Hebrew lunar calendar. This day was March 31, 561 B.C.; also see note on 52:4a.

Lamentations

A LAMENTATION is a sad funeral song. Jeremiah recorded these lamentations to express his grief over the tragic destruction of Jerusalem and the exile of its inhabitants to Babylon. Through acrostic poetry, the book of Lamentations graphically describes the destruction of Jerusalem and the exile of its people. Jeremiah spared his readers little detail as he recalled the horrible tragedy. There is very little comfort in Jeremiah's lament, though in chapter 5 his prayer does look beyond the desolate ashes of Jerusalem as he pleads to God, whose throne endures forever.

■ **Author:** Jeremiah, according to Jewish tradition

■ **Date Written:** Soon after the fall of Jerusalem in 586 BC

■ **Purpose:** To record in graphic detail the consequences of sin and to show that God suffers along with his people

■ **Themes:** Destruction of Jerusalem, consequences of sin, God's mercy

■ **Outline**

1:1-22 Jeremiah's sorrow over Jerusalem's desolation
2:1-22 God's anger at Jerusalem's sin
3:1-66 Jerusalem's only hope is God's mercy
4:1-22 Jerusalem's former glory and present humiliation
5:1-22 Jeremiah's prayer for Jerusalem's restoration

Sorrow in Jerusalem

1 *¹ Jerusalem, once so full of people,
    is now deserted.
She who was once great among the
    nations
    now sits alone like a widow.
Once the queen of all the earth,
    she is now a slave.

² She sobs through the night;
    tears stream down her cheeks.
Among all her lovers,
    there is no one left to comfort her.
All her friends have betrayed her
    and become her enemies.

³ Judah has been led away into
    captivity,
    oppressed with cruel slavery.
She lives among foreign nations
    and has no place of rest.
Her enemies have chased her down,
    and she has nowhere to turn.

⁴ The roads to Jerusalem* are in mourning,
    for crowds no longer come to celebrate
    the festivals.
The city gates are silent,
    her priests groan,
her young women are crying—
    how bitter is her fate!

⁵ Her oppressors have become her
    masters,
    and her enemies prosper,
for the LORD has punished Jerusalem
    for her many sins.
Her children have been captured
    and taken away to distant lands.

⁶ All the majesty of beautiful
    Jerusalem*
    has been stripped away.
Her princes are like starving deer
    searching for pasture.
They are too weak to run
    from the pursuing enemy.

1 Each of the first four chapters of this book is an acrostic, laid out in the order of the Hebrew alphabet. The first word of each verse begins with a successive Hebrew letter. Chapters 1, 2, and 4 have one verse for each of the 22 Hebrew letters. Chapter 3 contains 22 stanzas of three verses each. Though chapter 5 has 22 verses, it is not an acrostic.   1:4 Hebrew *Zion;* also in 1:17.   1:6 Hebrew *of the daughter of Zion.*

7 In the midst of her sadness and
    wandering,
  Jerusalem remembers her ancient
    splendor.
But now she has fallen to her enemy,
  and there is no one to help her.
Her enemy struck her down
  and laughed as she fell.

8 Jerusalem has sinned greatly,
  so she has been tossed away like a filthy
    rag.
All who once honored her now despise her,
  for they have seen her stripped naked
    and humiliated.
All she can do is groan
  and hide her face.

9 She defiled herself with immorality
  and gave no thought to her future.
Now she lies in the gutter
  with no one to lift her out.
"LORD, see my misery," she cries.
  "The enemy has triumphed."

10 The enemy has plundered her completely,
  taking every precious thing she owns.
She has seen foreigners violate her sacred
    Temple,
  the place the LORD had forbidden them
    to enter.

11 Her people groan as they search for bread.
  They have sold their treasures for food
    to stay alive.
"O LORD, look," she mourns,
  "and see how I am despised.

12 "Does it mean nothing to you, all you who
    pass by?
  Look around and see if there is any
    suffering like mine,
which the LORD brought on me
  when he erupted in fierce anger.

13 "He has sent fire from heaven that burns
    in my bones.
He has placed a trap in my path and
    turned me back.
He has left me devastated,
  racked with sickness all day long.

14 "He wove my sins into ropes
  to hitch me to a yoke of captivity.

The Lord sapped my strength and turned
    me over to my enemies;
  I am helpless in their hands.

15 "The Lord has treated my mighty men
    with contempt.
At his command a great army has come
    to crush my young warriors.
The Lord has trampled his beloved city*
  like grapes are trampled in a winepress.

16 "For all these things I weep;
  tears flow down my cheeks.
No one is here to comfort me;
  any who might encourage me are far
    away.
My children have no future,
  for the enemy has conquered us."

17 Jerusalem reaches out for help,
  but no one comforts her.
Regarding his people Israel,*
  the LORD has said,
"Let their neighbors be their enemies!
  Let them be thrown away like a filthy
    rag!"

18 "The LORD is right," Jerusalem says,
  "for I rebelled against him.
Listen, people everywhere;
  look upon my anguish and despair,
for my sons and daughters
  have been taken captive to distant lands.

19 "I begged my allies for help,
  but they betrayed me.
My priests and leaders
  starved to death in the city,
even as they searched for food
  to save their lives.

20 "LORD, see my anguish!
  My heart is broken
and my soul despairs,
  for I have rebelled against you.
In the streets the sword kills,
  and at home there is only death.

21 "Others heard my groans,
  but no one turned to comfort me.
When my enemies heard about my
    troubles,
  they were happy to see what you had
    done.

1:15 Hebrew *the virgin daughter of Judah.* 1:17 Hebrew *Jacob.* The names "Jacob" and "Israel" are often interchanged throughout the Old Testament, referring sometimes to the individual patriarch and sometimes to the nation.

Oh, bring the day you promised,
  when they will suffer as I have suffered.

22 "Look at all their evil deeds, LORD.
    Punish them,
  as you have punished me
    for all my sins.
  My groans are many,
    and I am sick at heart."

God's Anger at Sin

2 ¹ The Lord in his anger
      has cast a dark shadow over beautiful
        Jerusalem.*
  The fairest of Israel's cities lies in the dust,
    thrown down from the heights of
      heaven.
  In his day of great anger,
    the Lord has shown no mercy even to his
      Temple.*

² Without mercy the Lord has destroyed
    every home in Israel.*
  In his anger he has broken down
    the fortress walls of beautiful
      Jerusalem.*
  He has brought them to the ground,
    dishonoring the kingdom and its rulers.

³ All the strength of Israel
    vanishes beneath his fierce anger.
  The Lord has withdrawn his protection
    as the enemy attacks.
  He consumes the whole land of Israel
    like a raging fire.

⁴ He bends his bow against his people,
    as though he were their enemy.
  His strength is used against them
    to kill their finest youth.
  His fury is poured out like fire
    on beautiful Jerusalem.*

⁵ Yes, the Lord has vanquished Israel
    like an enemy.
  He has destroyed her palaces
    and demolished her fortresses.
  He has brought unending sorrow and
      tears
    upon beautiful Jerusalem.

⁶ He has broken down his Temple
    as though it were merely a garden
      shelter.

The LORD has blotted out all memory
  of the holy festivals and Sabbath days.
Kings and priests fall together
  before his fierce anger.

⁷ The Lord has rejected his own altar;
    he despises his own sanctuary.
  He has given Jerusalem's palaces
    to her enemies.
  They shout in the LORD's Temple
    as though it were a day of celebration.

⁸ The LORD was determined
    to destroy the walls of beautiful
      Jerusalem.
  He made careful plans for their
      destruction,
    then did what he had planned.
  Therefore, the ramparts and walls
    have fallen down before him.

⁹ Jerusalem's gates have sunk into the
      ground.
    He has smashed their locks and bars.
  Her kings and princes have been exiled
    to distant lands;
    her law has ceased to exist.
  Her prophets receive
    no more visions from the LORD.

¹⁰ The leaders of beautiful Jerusalem
    sit on the ground in silence.
  They are clothed in burlap
    and throw dust on their heads.
  The young women of Jerusalem
    hang their heads in shame.

¹¹ I have cried until the tears no longer come;
    my heart is broken.
  My spirit is poured out in agony
    as I see the desperate plight of my people.
  Little children and tiny babies
    are fainting and dying in the streets.

¹² They cry out to their mothers,
    "We need food and drink!"
  Their lives ebb away in the streets
    like the life of a warrior wounded in
      battle.
  They gasp for life
    as they collapse in their mothers' arms.

¹³ What can I say about you?
    Who has ever seen such sorrow?

2:1a Hebrew *the daughter of Zion;* also in 2:8, 10, 18. 2:1b Hebrew *his footstool.* 2:2a Hebrew *Jacob;* also in 2:3b. See note
on 1:17. 2:2b Hebrew *the daughter of Judah;* also in 2:5. 2:4 Hebrew *on the tent of the daughter of Zion.*

O daughter of Jerusalem,
  to what can I compare your anguish?
O virgin daughter of Zion,
  how can I comfort you?
For your wound is as deep as the sea.
  Who can heal you?

14 Your prophets have said
  so many foolish things, false to the core.
They did not save you from exile
  by pointing out your sins.
Instead, they painted false pictures,
  filling you with false hope.

15 All who pass by jeer at you.
  They scoff and insult beautiful
    Jerusalem,* saying,
"Is this the city called 'Most Beautiful in
    All the World'
  and 'Joy of All the Earth'?"

16 All your enemies mock you.
  They scoff and snarl and say,
"We have destroyed her at last!
  We have long waited for this day,
  and it is finally here!"

17 But it is the LORD who did just as he
    planned.
He has fulfilled the promises of disaster
  he made long ago.
He has destroyed Jerusalem without
    mercy.
He has caused her enemies to gloat over
    her
  and has given them power over her.

18 Cry aloud* before the Lord,
  O walls of beautiful Jerusalem!
Let your tears flow like a river
  day and night.
Give yourselves no rest;
  give your eyes no relief.

19 Rise during the night and cry out.
  Pour out your hearts like water to the
    Lord.
Lift up your hands to him in prayer,
  pleading for your children,
for in every street
  they are faint with hunger.

20 "O LORD, think about this!
  Should you treat your own people this
    way?

Should mothers eat their own children,
  those they once bounced on their knees?
Should priests and prophets be killed
  within the Lord's Temple?

21 "See them lying in the streets—
    young and old,
boys and girls,
  killed by the swords of the enemy.
You have killed them in your anger,
  slaughtering them without mercy.

22 "You have invited terrors from all
    around,
  as though you were calling them
    to a day of feasting.
In the day of the LORD's anger,
  no one has escaped or survived.
The enemy has killed all the children
  whom I carried and raised."

Hope in the LORD's Faithfulness

3 ¹ I am the one who has seen the afflictions
    that come from the rod of the LORD's
    anger.
2 He has led me into darkness,
  shutting out all light.
3 He has turned his hand against me
  again and again, all day long.

4 He has made my skin and flesh grow old.
  He has broken my bones.
5 He has besieged and surrounded me
  with anguish and distress.
6 He has buried me in a dark place,
  like those long dead.

7 He has walled me in, and I cannot escape.
  He has bound me in heavy chains.
8 And though I cry and shout,
  he has shut out my prayers.
9 He has blocked my way with a high stone
    wall;
  he has made my road crooked.

10 He has hidden like a bear or a lion,
  waiting to attack me.
11 He has dragged me off the path and torn
    me in pieces,
  leaving me helpless and devastated.
12 He has drawn his bow
  and made me the target for his arrows.

13 He shot his arrows
  deep into my heart.

2:15 Hebrew *the daughter of Jerusalem.*   2:18 Hebrew *Their heart cried.*

¹⁴ My own people laugh at me.
  All day long they sing their mocking
      songs.
¹⁵ He has filled me with bitterness
  and given me a bitter cup of sorrow
      to drink.

¹⁶ He has made me chew on gravel.
  He has rolled me in the dust.
¹⁷ Peace has been stripped away,
  and I have forgotten what prosperity is.
¹⁸ I cry out, "My splendor is gone!
  Everything I had hoped for from the
      LORD is lost!"

¹⁹ The thought of my suffering and
      homelessness
  is bitter beyond words.*
²⁰ I will never forget this awful time,
  as I grieve over my loss.
²¹ Yet I still dare to hope
  when I remember this:

²² The faithful love of the LORD never ends!*
  His mercies never cease.
²³ Great is his faithfulness;
  his mercies begin afresh each morning.
²⁴ I say to myself, "The LORD is my inheritance;
  therefore, I will hope in him!"

²⁵ The LORD is good to those who depend
      on him,
  to those who search for him.
²⁶ So it is good to wait quietly
  for salvation from the LORD.
²⁷ And it is good for people to submit at an
      early age
  to the yoke of his discipline:

²⁸ Let them sit alone in silence
  beneath the LORD's demands.
²⁹ Let them lie face down in the dust,
  for there may be hope at last.
³⁰ Let them turn the other cheek to those
      who strike them
  and accept the insults of their enemies.

³¹ For no one is abandoned
  by the Lord forever.
³² Though he brings grief, he also shows
      compassion
  because of the greatness of his unfailing
      love.
³³ For he does not enjoy hurting people
  or causing them sorrow.

³⁴ If people crush underfoot
  all the prisoners of the land,
³⁵ if they deprive others of their rights
  in defiance of the Most High,
³⁶ if they twist justice in the courts—
  doesn't the Lord see all these things?

³⁷ Who can command things to happen
  without the Lord's permission?
³⁸ Does not the Most High
  send both calamity and good?
³⁹ Then why should we, mere humans,
      complain
  when we are punished for our sins?

⁴⁰ Instead, let us test and examine our ways.
  Let us turn back to the LORD.
⁴¹ Let us lift our hearts and hands
  to God in heaven and say,
⁴² "We have sinned and rebelled,
  and you have not forgiven us.

⁴³ "You have engulfed us with your anger,
      chased us down,
  and slaughtered us without mercy.
⁴⁴ You have hidden yourself in a cloud
  so our prayers cannot reach you.
⁴⁵ You have discarded us as refuse and
      garbage
  among the nations.

⁴⁶ "All our enemies
  have spoken out against us.
⁴⁷ We are filled with fear,
  for we are trapped, devastated,
      and ruined."
⁴⁸ Tears stream from my eyes
  because of the destruction of my
      people!

⁴⁹ My tears flow endlessly;
  they will not stop
⁵⁰ until the LORD looks down
  from heaven and sees.
⁵¹ My heart is breaking
  over the fate of all the women of
      Jerusalem.

⁵² My enemies, whom I have never
      harmed,
  hunted me down like a bird.
⁵³ They threw me into a pit
  and dropped stones on me.
⁵⁴ The water rose over my head,
  and I cried out, "This is the end!"

3:19 Or *is wormwood and gall.*   3:22 As in Syriac version; Hebrew reads *of the LORD keeps us from destruction.*

55 But I called on your name, LORD,
     from deep within the pit.
56 You heard me when I cried, "Listen to my
     pleading!
     Hear my cry for help!"
57 Yes, you came when I called;
     you told me, "Do not fear."

58 Lord, you have come to my defense;
     you have redeemed my life.
59 You have seen the wrong they have done
     to me, LORD.
     Be my judge, and prove me right.
60 You have seen the vengeful plots
     my enemies have laid against me.

61 LORD, you have heard the vile names they
     call me.
     You know all about the plans they have
     made.
62 My enemies whisper and mutter
     as they plot against me all day long.
63 Look at them! Whether they sit or stand,
     I am the object of their mocking songs.

64 Pay them back, LORD,
     for all the evil they have done.
65 Give them hard and stubborn hearts,
     and then let your curse fall on them!
66 Chase them down in your anger,
     destroying them beneath the LORD's
     heavens.

God's Anger Satisfied

4 ¹ How the gold has lost its luster!
     Even the finest gold has become dull.
   The sacred gemstones
     lie scattered in the streets!

² See how the precious children of
     Jerusalem,*
     worth their weight in fine gold,
   are now treated like pots of clay
     made by a common potter.

³ Even the jackals feed their young,
     but not my people Israel.
   They ignore their children's cries,
     like ostriches in the desert.

⁴ The parched tongues of their little ones
     stick to the roofs of their mouths in
     thirst.
   The children cry for bread,
     but no one has any to give them.

⁵ The people who once ate the richest foods
     now beg in the streets for anything they
     can get.
   Those who once wore the finest clothes
     now search the garbage dumps for food.

⁶ The guilt* of my people
     is greater than that of Sodom,
   where utter disaster struck in a moment
     and no hand offered help.

⁷ Our princes once glowed with health—
     brighter than snow, whiter than milk.
   Their faces were as ruddy as rubies,
     their appearance like fine jewels.*

⁸ But now their faces are blacker than soot.
     No one recognizes them in the streets.
   Their skin sticks to their bones;
     it is as dry and hard as wood.

⁹ Those killed by the sword are better off
     than those who die of hunger.
   Starving, they waste away
     for lack of food from the fields.

¹⁰ Tenderhearted women
     have cooked their own children.
   They have eaten them
     to survive the siege.

¹¹ But now the anger of the LORD is satisfied.
     His fierce anger has been poured out.
   He started a fire in Jerusalem*
     that burned the city to its foundations.

¹² Not a king in all the earth—
     no one in all the world—
   would have believed that an enemy
     could march through the gates of
     Jerusalem.

¹³ Yet it happened because of the sins of her
     prophets
     and the sins of her priests,
   who defiled the city
     by shedding innocent blood.

¹⁴ They wandered blindly
     through the streets,
   so defiled by blood
     that no one dared touch them.

¹⁵ "Get away!" the people shouted at them.
     "You're defiled! Don't touch us!"

4:2 Hebrew precious sons of Zion.   4:6 Or punishment.   4:7 Hebrew like lapis lazuli.   4:11 Hebrew in Zion.

So they fled to distant lands
and wandered among foreign nations,
but none would let them stay.

16 The LORD himself has scattered them,
and he no longer helps them.
People show no respect for the priests
and no longer honor the leaders.

17 We looked in vain for our allies
to come and save us,
but we were looking to nations
that could not help us.

18 We couldn't go into the streets
without danger to our lives.
Our end was near; our days were
numbered.
We were doomed!

19 Our enemies were swifter than eagles
in flight.
If we fled to the mountains, they
found us.
If we hid in the wilderness,
they were waiting for us there.

20 Our king—the LORD's anointed, the very
life of our nation—
was caught in their snares.
We had thought that his shadow
would protect us against any nation
on earth!

21 Are you rejoicing in the land of Uz,
O people of Edom?
But you, too, must drink from the cup of
the LORD's anger.
You, too, will be stripped naked in your
drunkenness.

22 O beautiful Jerusalem,* your punishment
will end;
you will soon return from exile.
But Edom, your punishment is just
beginning;
soon your many sins will be exposed.

Prayer for Restoration

5 1 LORD, remember what has happened
to us.
See how we have been disgraced!
2 Our inheritance has been turned over to
strangers,
our homes to foreigners.

3 We are orphaned and fatherless.
Our mothers are widowed.
4 We have to pay for water to drink,
and even firewood is expensive.
5 Those who pursue us are at our heels;
we are exhausted but are given no
rest.
6 We submitted to Egypt and Assyria
to get enough food to survive.
7 Our ancestors sinned, but they have
died—
and we are suffering the punishment
they deserved!

8 Slaves have now become our masters;
there is no one left to rescue us.
9 We hunt for food at the risk of our lives,
for violence rules the countryside.
10 The famine has blackened our skin
as though baked in an oven.
11 Our enemies rape the women in
Jerusalem*
and the young girls in all the towns
of Judah.
12 Our princes are being hanged by their
thumbs,
and our elders are treated with
contempt.
13 Young men are led away to work at
millstones,
and boys stagger under heavy loads
of wood.
14 The elders no longer sit in the city gates;
the young men no longer dance and
sing.
15 Joy has left our hearts;
our dancing has turned to mourning.
16 The garlands have* fallen from our heads.
Weep for us because we have sinned.
17 Our hearts are sick and weary,
and our eyes grow dim with tears.
18 For Jerusalem* is empty and desolate,
a place haunted by jackals.

19 But LORD, you remain the same forever!
Your throne continues from generation
to generation.
20 Why do you continue to forget us?
Why have you abandoned us for so
long?
21 Restore us, O LORD, and bring us back
to you again!
Give us back the joys we once had!
22 Or have you utterly rejected us?
Are you angry with us still?

4:22 Hebrew O daughter of Zion.   5:11 Hebrew in Zion.   5:16 Or The crown has.   5:18 Hebrew Mount Zion.

Baruch

THE JEWS WERE IN CAPTIVITY in Babylon and sought to understand why they, God's chosen people, should endure such a trial. The book of Baruch gives the answer: the infidelity of the Jews to the laws of God. Even so, Baruch contends, God will keep his covenant with his people, and they will return to Jerusalem. Baruch exhorts God's people to strictly follow God's laws and rediscover the wisdom that they alone possess. The book ends with a brief glimpse of the glory and deliverance that God has in store for a repentant Israel.

- **Author:** Ascribed to Baruch, secretary of the prophet Jeremiah
- **Date Written:** Sixth century BC
- **Purpose:** To show that God is righteous and wise in his mercy and that he will answer the prayers of those who repent
- **Themes:** The reasons for God's judgment; the importance of repentance; hope for Israel's restoration; the mercy of God
- **Outline**
1:1–3:8 The exiles' prayer
3:9–4:4 Praise of wisdom
4:5–5:9 Jerusalem's hope
6:1-72 Jeremiah's letter

Baruch and the Jews in Babylon

1 These are the words that Baruch son of Neriah, son of Mahseiah, son of Zedekiah, son of Hasadiah, son of Hilkiah, wrote in Babylon. ²He wrote it on the seventh day of the month during the fifth year after the Babylonians* captured Jerusalem and destroyed it by fire.* ³Baruch read this book to Jehoiachin* son of Jehoiakim, the king of Judah, and to all the people who came to hear it. ⁴He also read it to the nobles, the princes of Judah, the elders, and everyone else, from the least to the greatest, who lived in Babylon by the Sud River.

⁵When the people heard what Baruch wrote, they wept, fasted, and prayed to the Lord. ⁶Then they collected all the money they could afford to give ⁷and sent it to Jerusalem to the high priest, Jehoiakim son of Hilkiah, son of Shallum, and to all the other priests, and to all the Jews who were still with them in Jerusalem.

⁸At about this time in early summer,* Baruch recovered the silver utensils that had been looted from the Temple, in order to return them to the land of Judah. Zedekiah son

of Josiah, the king of Judah, had made these silver utensils ⁹after Nebuchadnezzar, the king of Babylon, had deported Jehoiachin, the princes, the skilled workers,* the nobles, and other people from Jerusalem and had taken them as captives to Babylon.

¹⁰They sent this message to the people in Jerusalem:

"We are sending you money to buy incense, burnt offerings, sin offerings, and grain offerings to be offered on the altar of the Lord our God. ¹¹Pray for the health* of King Nebuchadnezzar of Babylon and for his son Belshazzar so that their days on earth may last as long as heaven itself lasts. ¹²And pray that the Lord will give us strength and wisdom as we live under the protective shadow of King Nebuchadnezzar and his son Belshazzar. May we serve them for a long time and win their favor. ¹³Also, pray to the Lord our God for us, for we have sinned against him, and even to this day the anger of

---

1:2a Greek *Chaldeans.* 1:2b The first capture of Jerusalem occurred in 597 B.C. The city was captured again and burned in 586 B.C. 1:3 Greek *Jeconiah,* a variant name for Jehoiachin; also in 1:9. 1:8 Greek *On the tenth day of Sivan,* of the ancient Hebrew lunar calendar. The year is not specified, but this date usually occurs in June. 1:9 As in Syriac version (see also Jer 24:1); Greek reads *the prisoners.* 1:11 Greek *the life.*

the Lord has not turned away from us. [14]Finally, we send you this book to read aloud as your confession in the Lord's Temple during the special feasts and sacred festivals.

Instruction for Confession of Sins

[15]"This is what you will say: Lord, you are in the right, and our faces are covered with shame. This is true of us all, including the people of Judah and Jerusalem, [16]our kings, our rulers, our priests, our prophets, and our ancestors. [17]We have sinned before the Lord. [18]We have not obeyed him, nor have we listened to the voice of the Lord our God, nor kept the commandments that the Lord gave us. [19]From the day the Lord brought our ancestors out of Egypt until today, we have disobeyed the Lord our God. We have acted thoughtlessly and have not listened to his voice. [20]So to this day we have experienced many disasters as well as the curses spoken by the Lord* when his servant Moses brought our ancestors out of Egypt into a land flowing with milk and honey. [21]Despite all the warnings of the prophets he sent us, we have not listened to the voice of the Lord our God. [22]We have each followed the inclinations of our own wicked heart, serving other gods and doing evil in the sight of the Lord our God.

2 "As a result, the Lord has carried out his threat on our kings, our rulers, and each person of Israel and Judah. [2]As it is written in the law of Moses, the atrocities we experienced in Jerusalem have never before been witnessed under heaven. [3]Some people even ate the flesh of their own sons and daughters. [4]God allowed us to be captured by the kingdoms around us. Our land became a desert, and we were scorned by the surrounding nations where the Lord has scattered us. [5]Instead of being exalted, we were humiliated because we sinned against the Lord our God by not obeying what he said.

[6]"Even now the Lord our God is in the right, and our faces are covered with shame, just like our ancestors. [7]All the disasters that the Lord threatened have happened to us. [8]Yet we have not renounced our wicked thoughts to win back the favor of the Lord our God. [9]The Lord has kept the disasters ready for

just the right moment and then allowed them to fall on us. But we deserved them, for the Lord is just in all that he has commanded us to do. [10]We have not listened to his voice, nor have we obeyed the commandments he gave us.

Prayer for Restoration

[11]"O Lord God of Israel, you brought your people out of Egypt with amazing power, miraculous signs and wonders, and overwhelming terror. Because of this, you have brought lasting honor to your name. [12]Now we acknowledge that we have sinned by being ungodly and doing wrong; we have disobeyed all your commands, O Lord our God. [13]But please let your anger turn away from us, for we are but a small group among the nations where you have scattered us. [14]Hear our prayers and petitions, O Lord. Deliver us for your own sake, and grant us favor with those who have taken us as captives. [15]Then the whole world will know that you are the Lord our God, for Israel and his descendants bear your name. [16]Look down upon us from your holy dwelling place, O Lord; think of us and hear us. [17]Open your eyes and look at us. Those who are dead,* whose spirits have been taken from their bodies, cannot give glory and recognition to the Lord. [18]But the person* who is deeply sorrowful, who walks bowed down, who is feeble and has failing eyes, and who has spiritual hunger—such a person gives glory to the Lord and acknowledges his righteousness.

[19]"It is not because of the merits of our ancestors or kings that we pour out our prayers and beg your mercy, O Lord our God, [20]for you have punished us because of your anger and indignation with us. You revealed this through your servants the prophets, who told us, [21]'This message is from the Lord: If you work hard and serve the king of Babylon, you will remain in the land I promised to your ancestors. [22]But if you do not listen to the voice of the Lord and do not serve the king of Babylon, [23]I will remove all happy and joyful voices from the towns of Judah and from those surrounding Jerusalem. I will silence the voice of the bridegroom and the bride, and the land will become a desert with no people living in it.'

1:20 See Lev 26:14-39; Deut 28:15-68.   2:17 Greek *who are in Hades.*   2:18 Greek *soul;* also in 2:18b.

24"But we did not listen to your command that we should serve the king of Babylon. As a result, you carried out what you had threatened through your servants the prophets. The bones of our rulers and our ancestors have been scattered from their tombs, as you said. 25Indeed, they have been thrown out into the heat of the day and the frost of the night. People have died in severe pain by famine, by sword, and by plague. 26Because of the wickedness of the people of Israel and Judah, you have humbled your Temple and left it as it is today.

27"And yet, O Lord our God, you have dealt with us according to your kindness and great mercy. 28Everything has happened exactly as you warned us when you commanded your servant Moses to write your law in the presence of the people of Israel. 29This law says, 'If you do not obey my voice, this great multitude will be turned into a very small number among the nations where I will scatter them. 30But I know they will not listen to me, for they are stubborn. In their exile they will finally come to their senses, 31and then they will realize that I am the Lord their God. I will give them an understanding heart and an attentive ear. 32Then they will praise me in the land of their captivity and will recall my name. 33Remembering the sins of their ancestors, they will turn away from their own wickedness and stubborn ways. 34Then I will bring them back again to the land that I promised to Abraham, Isaac, and Jacob, and they will rule over it. Their numbers will not grow smaller, for I will increase their population. 35I will make an everlasting covenant with them to be their God, and they will be my people. I will never again remove my people Israel out of the land that I have given them.'*

Prayer for Restoration Continues

3 "And now, O Lord Almighty, God of Israel, our souls are in pain. With troubled spirits, we cry out to you. 2Listen, O Lord, and have mercy on us who have sinned against you. 3You will reign forever, but we will remain dead forever. 4O Lord Almighty, God of Israel, hear the prayer of those who have died in Israel and of their children, who have sinned against

you. They failed to listen to the voice of the Lord their God, and so disaster fell upon us. 5Do not dwell on the sins of our ancestors, but for now think only of your power and your name. 6You are the Lord our God, and we will praise you, O Lord. 7For you have caused us to fear you so that we will call upon your name. We praise you in our captivity, for we have turned from the evil of our ancestors, who sinned against you. 8Look at us today in our land of exile, where you have scattered us to be reproached, cursed, and punished for all the sins of our ancestors who deserted you, O Lord our God."

In Praise of Wisdom

9 Listen, O Israel, to the commandments
   of life;
   pay attention, that you may learn
      wisdom.
10 How did it happen, O Israel,
   that you are in the land of your
      enemies,
   that you have grown old in a foreign
      country?
11 You are defiled with the dead;
   you are counted among those who have
      gone to the grave.*
12 It is because you have abandoned the
      fountain of wisdom.
13 If you had walked in the way of God,
   you would have lived in peace forever.
14 Learn where understanding resides,
   where to find strength and insight.
   Then you will know where to find a long
      life—
   and life itself.
   You will know what makes the eyes shine
   and where to find peace.

15 Who has discovered wisdom's dwelling
      place?
   Who has gone into the place where
      wisdom is stored?
16 Where are the leaders of the nations?
   Where are those who rule over the
      animals on earth
17 and entertain themselves with birds?
   Where are those who hoard silver and
      gold?
   They place their trust in such things,
   yet they have no end to their wants.
18 Where are the careful craftsmen of silver?
   There is no trace of their works.

2:29-35 See Deut 31:24-27.   3:11 Greek *who are in Hades.*

19 They have vanished into the place of the
  dead,*
  and others have risen up in their place.

20 Generations have seen the light of day
  and inhabited the earth,
but they have not learned the way to
  knowledge.
21 They do not know the path,
  so their children have strayed from the
  truth.
22 Wisdom has not been heard of in Canaan;
  neither has she been seen in Teman.
23 The descendants of Hagar search after
  worldly wisdom,
  as do the merchants of Merran and
  Teman,
  the storytellers, and the philosophers.
None have found the way to wisdom;
  neither have they discovered her
  paths.

24 O Israel, how great is the world God
  created;
  how vast is his domain!
25 It is great and has no end;
  it is high and immeasurable.
26 In it were born giants,
  men renowned from the beginning,
  great in stature, expert in war.
27 Yet God did not choose them,
  neither did they find the paths of
  knowledge.
28 And because they did not have wisdom,
  they perished through their own
  foolishness.

29 Who has gone up into heaven and seized
  wisdom?
  Who has brought her down from the
  clouds?
30 Who has sailed across the sea and found
  her?
  Who could buy her for gold?
31 No one can know the way to wisdom
  nor search out the paths she takes.
32 But God, who knows all, knows her;
  he has mastered her by his own
  intelligence.
  God is the one who constructed the earth
  for all time
  and filled it with four-footed animals.
33 He sends forth the light, and it speeds
  away.
  He recalls it, and it obeys trembling.

3:19 Greek *into Hades.*

34 The stars shine joyfully in their appointed
  places.
35 When he calls to them, they reply: "Here
  we are!"
  And they cheerfully shine for their
  Creator.
36 This is our God,
  and no one else can be compared
  to him.
37 He who holds all knowledge
  has given her to his servant Jacob
  and to Israel, whom he loved.
38 Then wisdom came to earth
  and lived among people.

4 ¹ Wisdom is the book of God's
  commandments,
  the law that endures forever.
Those who keep her will live;
  those who forsake her will die.
² Come back, O Jacob, and take hold of
  wisdom;
  walk in the light of her brightness.
³ Do not give your honor to another,
  nor your privileges to a foreign people.
⁴ We rejoice, O Israel,
  because we know what pleases God.

Jerusalem Consoles the Exiled People
⁵ Take courage, my people,
  who keep Israel's name alive.
⁶ It was not for your destruction
  that you were sold to the Gentiles.
It was because you provoked God
  that you were handed over to your
  enemies.
⁷ You angered your Creator
  by sacrificing to demons rather than
  to God.
⁸ You have forgotten the eternal God, who
  brought you up,
  and you have grieved Jerusalem, the city
  that reared you.
⁹ For Jerusalem saw the wrath of God that
  came upon you,
  and she said, "Listen, all you who live
  near Zion.
God has brought great sorrow upon me,
¹⁰ for I have seen my sons and daughters
  being taken captive.
  The Eternal One allowed them to suffer
  this.
¹¹ I nourished them with joy,
  but I sent them away weeping and
  mourning.

¹² Let no one rejoice over me, a widow
　　forsaken by many.
　I was left alone because of the sins of my
　　children,
　for they abandoned the law of God.
¹³ They have not heeded his laws
　　or followed his commandments
　　or taken the paths of justice that God
　　showed them.
¹⁴ Let those who live near Zion come
　　and remember the captivity of my sons
　　and daughters,
　　which the Eternal One allowed them to
　　suffer.
¹⁵ For he brought a distant nation against
　　them,
　　a wicked nation that spoke a strange
　　language.
　They had no respect for the aged
　　and no pity on children.
¹⁶ They carried away the widow's beloved
　　sons
　　and deprived her of her daughters.

¹⁷ "But as for my part, what help can I give
　　you?
¹⁸ Only he who allowed you to suffer these
　　disasters
　　can deliver you from your enemies.
¹⁹ Go your way, my children, go your way,
　　for I am left alone.
²⁰ I have taken off the robe of peace
　　and put on the sackcloth of one crying
　　out to God.
　I will cry to the Eternal One all my
　　days.

²¹ "Take courage, my children, and cry out
　　to God.
　He will deliver you from the oppression
　　of your enemies.
²² For I have put my hope in the Eternal One
　　to save you.
　Joy has come upon me from the Holy
　　One
　because of the mercy that will soon come
　　to you
　from your everlasting Savior.
²³ Although I sent you away with mourning
　　and weeping,
　God will bring you back to me
　　with joy and gladness forever.
²⁴ For as those who live near Zion have
　　seen your captivity,
　so will they soon see God's
　　deliverance.

It will come to you with great glory
　　and with the splendor of the Eternal One.
²⁵ My children, endure patiently the
　　punishment
　　that has come upon you from God.
　Although your enemies persecute you,
　　you will soon see their destruction,
　　and you will conquer them.
²⁶ My tender children have walked rough
　　paths,
　　for they were taken away like a flock
　　seized by raiders.

²⁷ "Take courage, my children, and cry out
　　to God,
　　for he who brought this upon you will
　　remember you.
²⁸ Just you chose to stray from God,
　　you can seek him again with ten times
　　the zeal.
²⁹ For he who allowed you to suffer these
　　disasters
　　will bring you everlasting joy through
　　salvation."

Consolation for Jerusalem

³⁰ Take courage, O Jerusalem,
　　for he who named you will comfort you.
³¹ Misery will come to those who have
　　harmed you
　　and to those who rejoiced at your fall.
³² Misery will come to the cities that enslaved
　　your children,
　　to those who took your sons and
　　daughters.
³³ Just as they rejoiced at your fall
　　and were made happy by your ruin,
　　so will they grieve when they
　　themselves are made desolate.
³⁴ I will rob them of their pride in their great
　　numbers,
　　and their arrogance will be turned to
　　grief.
³⁵ Fire from the Eternal One will fall on them
　　for many days,
　　and for a long time their city will be
　　inhabited only by demons.

³⁶ Look to the east, O Jerusalem,
　　and see the joy that is coming from God.
³⁷ Look! The children you sent away are now
　　returning,
　　coming from the east to the west.
　They are coming at the command of the
　　Holy One,
　　rejoicing in the glory of God.

5 ¹ O Jerusalem, take off the garment of
    your sadness and pain.
  Put on forever the beautiful glory that
    comes from God.
² Wrap the cloak of God's righteousness
    around you,
  and crown yourself with glory from
    the Eternal One.
³ For God will reveal your splendor
    to everyone under heaven.
⁴ God will give you a name that will last
    forever:
  "The Peace of Justice, and the Glory
    of Godliness."

⁵ Arise, Jerusalem! Go to a high point
    and look toward the east.
  See your children gathered together from
    west and east
    by the command of the Holy One.
  Rejoice that God has remembered them.
⁶ Although they left you on foot,
    led away by their enemies,
  God will bring them back to you,
    carried in glory as on a royal throne.
⁷ For God has ordered the leveling of every
    high mountain
  and of the everlasting hills.
  The valleys will be filled up to make the
    ground level
    so that Israel may walk safely in God's
      glory.
⁸ The forests and every fragrant tree
    will give Israel shade at God's command.
⁹ For God will lead Israel with joy,
    in the light of his glory,
    with his mercy and righteousness.

The Letter of Jeremiah

6 This is a copy of the letter* that Jeremiah
  sent to those who were to be taken to Babylon as captives by the king of the Babylonians.
Jeremiah gave them the message that God had
given him.

"Because of the sins you have committed
before God, you will be taken as captives
to Babylon by Nebuchadnezzar, king of
Babylon. ²You will have to spend many
years in Babylon—as much as seven
generations. After that captivity, I, the
Lord, will bring you home in peace. ³In
Babylon you will see gods of silver, gold,
and wood—gods that are carried about

on people's shoulders and that cause
other nations to fear. ⁴Be careful that you
do not imitate these pagan acts, and do
not become fearful of pagan gods. ⁵When
you see crowds carrying the images in a
procession and worshiping them, you
must say in your hearts, 'O Lord, we must
worship you alone.' ⁶For my angel is with
you, and he will watch over your lives.

⁷"The pagan gods are overlaid with
gold and silver, and their tongues are
polished by woodcarvers, but they are
fake and cannot speak. ⁸The people make
gold crowns for their gods as if they
were dressing up a girl who loves fancy
clothing. ⁹Sometimes the priests steal the
gold and silver for themselves ¹⁰or give it
to the temple prostitutes. They put clothes
on these gods of gold, silver, and wood as if
they were human. ¹¹Yet these gods, dressed
in purple robes, cannot protect themselves
from tarnish or decay. ¹²Even the temple
dust needs to be cleaned from their faces.
¹³One god holds a scepter, like a district
judge, yet it is powerless to condemn an
offender to death. ¹⁴Another holds a sword
or an ax in its hand but cannot protect
itself from war or thieves. Therefore, it is
evident that they are not gods, so do not
fear them.

¹⁵"Just as a pot becomes worthless when
it is broken, ¹⁶so these gods are worthless
as they sit in their temples. Their eyes are
full of dust kicked up by the feet of those
who enter the temple. ¹⁷A person who is
awaiting execution for offending the king
must be securely locked up. In the same
way, the priests must secure their temples
with bars and locks, lest their gods be
taken by thieves. ¹⁸The priests light more
lamps than they themselves would ever
need, but their gods cannot see the light.
¹⁹The gods are like the wooden beams
in the temple, for termites eat out their
hearts from within. Even their garments
are devoured, but the gods do not even
notice. ²⁰Their faces are black from the
smoke that rises in the temple. ²¹Bats,
swallows, and other birds perch on their
bodies and heads, and so do cats. ²²All this
is evidence that they are not gods, so do
not fear them.

²³"They may be adorned with gold, but
unless someone cleans off the tarnish,

6:1 The Latin Vulgate and the King James Version include "The Letter of Jeremiah" as chapter 6 of Baruch. In the Greek
version, it follows Lamentations.

they will not shine. And they felt nothing when they were being molded. 24Even though they cost much money, there is no spirit* in them. 25Because they cannot walk, they must be carried on people's shoulders, which proves how worthless they are. People who worship them are put to shame, 26for if these idols topple over, their worshipers must stand them up again. And even when they are set upright, they cannot move. Offering gifts to them is like offering gifts to the dead. 27Everything offered as a sacrifice to these idols is taken by the priests for their own use. The wives of the priests take their share of the food, storing it for later use, but they never give even part of it to the poor or the helpless. 28Even women who are ceremonially unclean because of menstruation or childbirth handle the sacrifices. Thus you can see that they are not gods; do not fear them.

29"How can they even be called gods? They allow women to place offerings before these idols made of silver, gold, and wood! 30The priests sit in their temples with torn clothing, with heads and beards shaved, and with their heads uncovered! 31The priests moan and shriek before their gods as if they were wailing for a dead person at a funeral. 32The priests even take the clothing of the idols to give to their wives and children. 33And whether these gods are treated well or poorly, they cannot repay in kind. They don't have the power to appoint a king or to depose him. 34Likewise, they cannot give wealth or money to anyone. If someone makes a vow to them and does not keep it, these idols cannot hold that person accountable. 35They cannot prevent a person from dying or protect the weak from the strong. 36They cannot restore sight to the blind or rescue a person in distress. 37They cannot show concern for widows or help orphans. 38These wooden idols that are overlaid with gold and silver are as powerless as a block of stone from a mountain quarry! Anyone who worships idols will be put to shame. 39So how can anyone claim, or even think, that such idols are gods?

40"Even the Babylonians* themselves dishonor them. When they find a person who cannot speak, they present him to Bel, asking him for the gift of speech, as though Bel understands them! 41Yet the people fail to understand the contradiction, for they have no common sense. So they do not abandon these gods. 42Women sit in their roped-off area along the passageways,* burning grain as incense. 43And when one of them is selected by a man to sleep with him, she mocks the women next to her who are less attractive and were not selected.* 44Everything that takes place around these idols is false. So how can anyone claim, or even think, that these idols are gods?

45"Made by carvers and goldsmiths, these idols can be only what the artisans want them to be. 46And the very craftsmen who make them don't live very long themselves. So how can the things made by mortals be gods? 47The only legacy they leave is lies and disgrace. 48If war comes or a disaster occurs, the priests discuss where they can hide with their gods. 49How can anyone think these idols are gods when they cannot even save themselves from war or disaster? 50Considering that they are only wood covered with gold or silver, it will become obvious that they are not gods; every nation and king will realize that they are merely human creations without any divine power* in them. 51Don't the people realize that these idols are not gods?

52"These idols cannot appoint a king or send rain to people. 53They cannot regulate their own affairs or vindicate someone who has been wronged. They are as useless as crows that fly across the sky. 54If fire breaks out in the temple of these gods made of wood and covered with gold or silver, their priests run to safety, but the gods burn up like the temple beams. 55They cannot stop an enemy king and his armies. 56So why should anyone say, or even think, that they are gods?

"These wooden gods, overlaid with silver and gold, are unable to save themselves from thieves or robbers. 57Those who steal the gold and silver and clothing of the idols are not stopped, for the gods are helpless. 58Therefore, it is better to be a king who shows his courage, or even a kitchen pot that is used by its owner, than to be one of these false gods.

6:24 Or breath. 6:40 Greek Chaldeans. 6:42 Greek sit in the passageways with cords about them. 6:43 Greek did not have their cords broken. 6:50 Greek work of God.

It is even better to be a door that protects a house or a wooden pillar in a palace than to be one of these false gods. ⁵⁹The sun, moon, and stars shine brightly, fulfilling the purpose for which God made them. ⁶⁰Lightning flashes across the sky and is seen by many people. The winds blow in every land. ⁶¹The clouds obey God's orders to float over all the earth. ⁶²Fire falls from the sky and burns up mountainsides and woods, just as it is commanded to do. But idols cannot compare to such glory or power. ⁶³So no one should think or say these idols are gods, for they cannot decide a case or do any good to anyone. ⁶⁴Since you know then that these idols are not gods, do not fear them.

⁶⁵"They can neither curse kings nor bless them. ⁶⁶They cannot produce signs in the heavens for nations to see. They neither shine like the sun nor give light like the moon. ⁶⁷Wild animals are better off than idols because they can flee to shelter and take care of themselves. ⁶⁸No one can produce evidence that they are gods, so do not fear them.

⁶⁹"These wooden gods, overlaid with silver and gold, are as powerless as a scarecrow in a cucumber patch. ⁷⁰They are no better than a thornbush in a garden—which birds perch on anyway! These wooden gods, overlaid with gold and silver, are like a corpse thrown out into the darkness. ⁷¹The purple robes and silk* garments rot as they hang upon the idols, so you can tell that these idols are not gods. In the end they themselves will be destroyed as well and will become a disgrace to their country. ⁷²Therefore, it is better to be an upright person who has no idols; such a person will never be in danger of disgrace."

6:71 As in Syriac version; Greek reads *marble*.

Ezekiel

LIKE STUBBORN CHILDREN refusing to obey their father, the people of Israel often refused to listen to God. And like a loving parent, God repeatedly called his people back to obedience. He sent prophets, like Ezekiel, to preach messages of judgment and restoration. According to his book, Ezekiel was a priest who was among the captives taken to Babylon when the Jews were deported in 597 BC. There in Babylon, God called Ezekiel to be a prophet, and Ezekiel forewarned his people that Jerusalem's judgment was not yet complete. His

- **Author:** Ezekiel, a Zadokite priest
- **Date Written:** Around 571 BC
- **Purpose:** To announce God's judgment on Israel and other nations and to proclaim restoration for God's people
- **Themes:** God's holiness, sin, restoration, worship, the new Temple
- **Outline**
  1:1–3:27 The call of Ezekiel
  4:1–24:27 Prophecies against Israel and Jerusalem
  25:1–32:32 Prophecies against the foreign nations
  33:1–39:29 The promise of return and restoration
  40:1–48:35 The renewed Temple in the New Jerusalem

preaching was not well received by the Jews who were with him in captivity. They thought he should be giving messages of comfort and hope, not judgment. But Ezekiel's dire predictions came true as Jerusalem was destroyed in 586 BC. From then on, the people listened carefully to his preaching. After Ezekiel's predictions of doom were proved, however, his message changed from one of judgment to one of comfort and hope. The worst was past; it was time to begin again.

A Vision of Living Beings

1 On July 31* of my thirtieth year,* while I was with the Judean exiles beside the Kebar River in Babylon, the heavens were opened and I saw visions of God. ²This happened during the fifth year of King Jehoiachin's captivity. ³(The LORD gave this message to Ezekiel son of Buzi, a priest, beside the Kebar River in the land of the Babylonians,* and he felt the hand of the LORD take hold of him.)

⁴As I looked, I saw a great storm coming from the north, driving before it a huge cloud that flashed with lightning and shone with brilliant light. There was fire inside the cloud, and in the middle of the fire glowed something like gleaming amber.* ⁵From the center of the cloud came four living beings that looked human, ⁶except that each had four faces and four wings.

⁷Their legs were straight, and their feet had hooves like those of a calf and shone like burnished bronze. ⁸Under each of their four wings I could see human hands. So each of the four beings had four faces and four wings. ⁹The wings of each living being touched the wings of the beings beside it. Each one moved straight forward in any direction without turning around.

¹⁰Each had a human face in the front, the face of a lion on the right side, the face of an ox on the left side, and the face of an eagle at the back. ¹¹Each had two pairs of outstretched wings—one pair stretched out to touch the wings of the living beings on either side of it, and the other pair covered its body. ¹²They went in whatever direction the spirit chose, and they moved straight forward in any direction without turning around.

1:1a Hebrew *On the fifth day of the fourth month,* of the ancient Hebrew lunar calendar. A number of dates in Ezekiel can be cross-checked with dates in surviving Babylonian records and related accurately to our modern calendar. This event occurred on July 31, 593 B.C.   1:1b Or *in the thirtieth year.*   1:3 Or *Chaldeans.*   1:4 Or *like burnished metal;* also in 1:27.

¹³The living beings looked like bright coals of fire or brilliant torches, and lightning seemed to flash back and forth among them. ¹⁴And the living beings darted to and fro like flashes of lightning.

¹⁵As I looked at these beings, I saw four wheels touching the ground beside them, one wheel belonging to each. ¹⁶The wheels sparkled as if made of beryl. All four wheels looked alike and were made the same; each wheel had a second wheel turning crosswise within it. ¹⁷The beings could move in any of the four directions they faced, without turning as they moved. ¹⁸The rims of the four wheels were tall and frightening, and they were covered with eyes all around.

¹⁹When the living beings moved, the wheels moved with them. When they flew upward, the wheels went up, too. ²⁰The spirit of the living beings was in the wheels. So wherever the spirit went, the wheels and the living beings also went. ²¹When the beings moved, the wheels moved. When the beings stopped, the wheels stopped. When the beings flew upward, the wheels rose up, for the spirit of the living beings was in the wheels.

²²Spread out above them was a surface like the sky, glittering like crystal. ²³Beneath this surface the wings of each living being stretched out to touch the others' wings, and each had two wings covering its body. ²⁴As they flew, their wings sounded to me like waves crashing against the shore or like the voice of the Almighty* or like the shouting of a mighty army. When they stopped, they let down their wings. ²⁵As they stood with wings lowered, a voice spoke from beyond the crystal surface above them.

²⁶Above this surface was something that looked like a throne made of blue lapis lazuli. And on this throne high above was a figure whose appearance resembled a man. ²⁷From what appeared to be his waist up, he looked like gleaming amber, flickering like a fire. And from his waist down, he looked like a burning flame, shining with splendor. ²⁸All around him was a glowing halo, like a rainbow shining in the clouds on a rainy day. This is what the glory of the LORD looked like to me. When I saw it, I fell face down on the ground, and I heard someone's voice speaking to me.

Ezekiel's Call and Commission

2 "Stand up, son of man," said the voice. "I want to speak with you." ²The Spirit came into me as he spoke, and he set me on my feet. I listened carefully to his words. ³"Son of man," he said, "I am sending you to the nation of Israel, a rebellious nation that has rebelled against me. They and their ancestors have been rebelling against me to this very day. ⁴They are a stubborn and hard-hearted people. But I am sending you to say to them, 'This is what the Sovereign LORD says!' ⁵And whether they listen or refuse to listen—for remember, they are rebels—at least they will know they have had a prophet among them.

⁶"Son of man, do not fear them or their words. Don't be afraid even though their threats surround you like nettles and briers and stinging scorpions. Do not be dismayed by their dark scowls, even though they are rebels. ⁷You must give them my messages whether they listen or not. But they won't listen, for they are completely rebellious! ⁸Son of man, listen to what I say to you. Do not join them in their rebellion. Open your mouth, and eat what I give you."

⁹Then I looked and saw a hand reaching out to me. It held a scroll, ¹⁰which he unrolled. And I saw that both sides were covered with funeral songs, words of sorrow, and pronouncements of doom.

3 The voice said to me, "Son of man, eat what I am giving you—eat this scroll! Then go and give its message to the people of Israel." ²So I opened my mouth, and he fed me the scroll. ³"Fill your stomach with this," he said. And when I ate it, it tasted as sweet as honey in my mouth.

⁴Then he said, "Son of man, go to the people of Israel and give them my messages. ⁵I am not sending you to a foreign people whose language you cannot understand. ⁶No, I am not sending you to people with strange and difficult speech. If I did, they would listen! ⁷But the people of Israel won't listen to you any more than they listen to me! For the whole lot of them are hard-hearted and stubborn. ⁸But look, I have made you as obstinate and hard-hearted as they are. ⁹I have made your forehead as hard as the hardest rock! So don't be afraid of them or fear their angry looks, even though they are rebels."

¹⁰Then he added, "Son of man, let all my words sink deep into your own heart first. Listen to them carefully for yourself. ¹¹Then go to your people in exile and say to them, 'This is what the Sovereign LORD says!' Do this whether they listen to you or not."

1:24 Hebrew *Shaddai.*

¹²Then the Spirit lifted me up, and I heard a loud rumbling sound behind me. (May the glory of the LORD be praised in his place!)* ¹³It was the sound of the wings of the living beings as they brushed against each other and the rumbling of their wheels beneath them.

¹⁴The Spirit lifted me up and took me away. I went in bitterness and turmoil, but the LORD's hold on me was strong. ¹⁵Then I came to the colony of Judean exiles in Tel-abib, beside the Kebar River. I was overwhelmed and sat among them for seven days.

A Watchman for Israel

¹⁶After seven days the LORD gave me a message. He said, ¹⁷"Son of man, I have appointed you as a watchman for Israel. Whenever you receive a message from me, warn people immediately. ¹⁸If I warn the wicked, saying, 'You are under the penalty of death,' but you fail to deliver the warning, they will die in their sins. And I will hold you responsible for their deaths. ¹⁹If you warn them and they refuse to repent and keep on sinning, they will die in their sins. But you will have saved yourself because you obeyed me.

²⁰"If righteous people turn away from their righteous behavior and ignore the obstacles I put in their way, they will die. And if you do not warn them, they will die in their sins. None of their righteous acts will be remembered, and I will hold you responsible for their deaths. ²¹But if you warn righteous people not to sin and they listen to you and do not sin, they will live, and you will have saved yourself, too."

²²Then the LORD took hold of me and said, "Get up and go out into the valley, and I will speak to you there." ²³So I got up and went, and there I saw the glory of the LORD, just as I had seen in my first vision by the Kebar River. And I fell face down on the ground.

²⁴Then the Spirit came into me and set me on my feet. He spoke to me and said, "Go to your house and shut yourself in. ²⁵There, son of man, you will be tied with ropes so you cannot go out among the people. ²⁶And I will make your tongue stick to the roof of your mouth so that you will be speechless and unable to rebuke them, for they are rebels. ²⁷But when I give you a message, I will loosen your tongue and let you speak. Then you will say to them, 'This is what the Sovereign LORD says!' Those who choose to listen will listen, but those who refuse will refuse, for they are rebels.

A Sign of the Coming Siege

4 "And now, son of man, take a large clay brick and set it down in front of you. Then draw a map of the city of Jerusalem on it. ²Show the city under siege. Build a wall around it so no one can escape. Set up the enemy camp, and surround the city with siege ramps and battering rams. ³Then take an iron griddle and place it between you and the city. Turn toward the city and demonstrate how harsh the siege will be against Jerusalem. This will be a warning to the people of Israel.

⁴"Now lie on your left side and place the sins of Israel on yourself. You are to bear their sins for the number of days you lie there on your side. ⁵I am requiring you to bear Israel's sins for 390 days—one day for each year of their sin. ⁶After that, turn over and lie on your right side for 40 days—one day for each year of Judah's sin.

⁷"Meanwhile, keep staring at the siege of Jerusalem. Lie there with your arm bared and prophesy her destruction. ⁸I will tie you up with ropes so you won't be able to turn from side to side until the days of your siege have been completed.

⁹"Now go and get some wheat, barley, beans, lentils, millet, and emmer wheat, and mix them together in a storage jar. Use them to make bread for yourself during the 390 days you will be lying on your side. ¹⁰Ration this out to yourself, eight ounces* of food for each day, and eat it at set times. ¹¹Then measure out a jar* of water for each day, and drink it at set times. ¹²Prepare and eat this food as you would barley cakes. While all the people are watching, bake it over a fire using dried human dung as fuel and then eat the bread." ¹³Then the LORD said, "This is how Israel will eat defiled bread in the Gentile lands to which I will banish them!"

¹⁴Then I said, "O Sovereign LORD, must I be defiled by using human dung? For I have never been defiled before. From the time I was a child until now I have never eaten any animal that died of sickness or was killed by other animals. I have never eaten any meat forbidden by the law."

¹⁵"All right," the LORD said. "You may bake your bread with cow dung instead of human dung." ¹⁶Then he told me, "Son of man, I will make food very scarce in Jerusalem. It will be weighed out with great care and eaten fearfully. The water will be rationed out drop by drop, and the people will drink it with dismay.

3:12 A possible reading for this verse is *Then the Spirit lifted me up, and as the glory of the LORD rose from its place, I heard a loud rumbling sound behind me.* 4:10 Hebrew *20 shekels* [228 grams]. 4:11 Hebrew ⅙ *of a hin* [about 1 pint or 0.6 liters].

[17]Lacking food and water, people will look at one another in terror, and they will waste away under their punishment.

A Sign of the Coming Judgment

5 "Son of man, take a sharp sword and use it as a razor to shave your head and beard. Use a scale to weigh the hair into three equal parts. [2]Place a third of it at the center of your map of Jerusalem. After acting out the siege, burn it there. Scatter another third across your map and chop it with a sword. Scatter the last third to the wind, for I will scatter my people with the sword. [3]Keep just a bit of the hair and tie it up in your robe. [4]Then take some of these hairs out and throw them into the fire, burning them up. A fire will then spread from this remnant and destroy all of Israel.

[5]"This is what the Sovereign LORD says: This is an illustration of what will happen to Jerusalem. I placed her at the center of the nations, [6]but she has rebelled against my regulations and decrees and has been even more wicked than the surrounding nations. She has refused to obey the regulations and decrees I gave her to follow.

[7]"Therefore, this is what the Sovereign LORD says: You people have behaved worse than your neighbors and have refused to obey my decrees and regulations. You have not even lived up to the standards of the nations around you. [8]Therefore, I myself, the Sovereign LORD, am now your enemy. I will punish you publicly while all the nations watch. [9]Because of your detestable idols, I will punish you like I have never punished anyone before or ever will again. [10]Parents will eat their own children, and children will eat their parents. I will punish you and scatter to the winds the few who survive.

[11]"As surely as I live, says the Sovereign LORD, I will cut you off completely. I will show you no pity at all because you have defiled my Temple with your vile images and detestable sins. [12]A third of your people will die in the city from disease and famine. A third of them will be slaughtered by the enemy outside the city walls. And I will scatter a third to the winds, chasing them with my sword. [13]Then at last my anger will be spent, and I will be satisfied. And when my fury against them has subsided, all Israel will know that I, the LORD, have spoken to them in my jealous anger.

[14]"So I will turn you into a ruin, a mockery in the eyes of the surrounding nations and to all who pass by. [15]You will become an object of mockery and taunting and horror. You will be a warning to all the nations around you. They will see what happens when the LORD punishes a nation in anger and rebukes it, says the LORD.

[16]"I will shower you with the deadly arrows of famine to destroy you. The famine will become more and more severe until every crumb of food is gone. [17]And along with the famine, wild animals will attack you and rob you of your children. Disease and war will stalk your land, and I will bring the sword of the enemy against you. I, the LORD, have spoken!"

Judgment against Israel's Mountains

6 Again a message came to me from the LORD: [2]"Son of man, turn and face the mountains of Israel and prophesy against them. [3]Proclaim this message from the Sovereign LORD against the mountains of Israel. This is what the Sovereign LORD says to the mountains and hills and to the ravines and valleys: I am about to bring war upon you, and I will smash your pagan shrines. [4]All your altars will be demolished, and your places of worship will be destroyed. I will kill your people in front of your idols.* [5]I will lay your corpses in front of your idols and scatter your bones around your altars. [6]Wherever you live there will be desolation, and I will destroy your pagan shrines. Your altars will be demolished, your idols will be smashed, your places of worship will be torn down, and all the religious objects you have made will be destroyed. [7]The place will be littered with corpses, and you will know that I alone am the LORD.

[8]"But I will let a few of my people escape destruction, and they will be scattered among the nations of the world. [9]Then when they are exiled among the nations, they will remember me. They will recognize how hurt I am by their unfaithful hearts and lustful eyes that long for their idols. Then at last they will hate themselves for all their detestable sins. [10]They will know that I alone am the LORD and that I was serious when I said I would bring this calamity on them.

[11]"This is what the Sovereign LORD says: Clap your hands in horror, and stamp your feet. Cry out because of all the detestable sins the people of Israel have committed. Now they are going to die from war and famine and disease. [12]Disease will strike down those who are far away in exile. War will destroy those who

6:4 The Hebrew term (literally *round things*) probably alludes to dung; also in 6:5, 6, 9, 13.

are nearby. And anyone who survives will be killed by famine. So at last I will spend my fury on them. [13]They will know that I am the LORD when their dead lie scattered among their idols and altars on every hill and mountain and under every green tree and every great shade tree—the places where they offered sacrifices to their idols. [14]I will crush them and make their cities desolate from the wilderness in the south to Riblah* in the north. Then they will know that I am the LORD."

The Coming of the End

7 Then this message came to me from the LORD: [2]"Son of man, this is what the Sovereign LORD says to Israel:

"The end is here!
  Wherever you look—
east, west, north, or south—
  your land is finished.
[3] No hope remains,
  for I will unleash my anger against you.
I will call you to account
  for all your detestable sins.
[4] I will turn my eyes away and show no pity.
  I will repay you for all your detestable
    sins.
Then you will know that I am the LORD.

[5] "This is what the Sovereign LORD says:
Disaster after disaster
  is coming your way!
[6] The end has come.
  It has finally arrived.
  Your final doom is waiting!
[7] O people of Israel, the day of your
    destruction is dawning.
  The time has come; the day of trouble
    is near.
Shouts of anguish will be heard on the
    mountains,
  not shouts of joy.
[8] Soon I will pour out my fury on you
  and unleash my anger against you.
I will call you to account
  for all your detestable sins.
[9] I will turn my eyes away and show no pity.
  I will repay you for all your detestable
    sins.
Then you will know that it is I, the LORD,
  who is striking the blow.

[10] "The day of judgment is here;
  your destruction awaits!

The people's wickedness and pride
  have blossomed to full flower.
[11] Their violence has grown into a rod
  that will beat them for their wickedness.
None of these proud and wicked people
  will survive.
All their wealth and prestige will be
  swept away.
[12] Yes, the time has come;
  the day is here!
Buyers should not rejoice over bargains,
  nor sellers grieve over losses,
for all of them will fall
  under my terrible anger.
[13] Even if the merchants survive,
  they will never return to their business.
For what God has said applies to
    everyone—
  it will not be changed!
Not one person whose life is twisted by sin
  will ever recover.

The Desolation of Israel

[14] "The trumpet calls Israel's army to
    mobilize,
  but no one listens,
  for my fury is against them all.
[15] There is war outside the city
  and disease and famine within.
Those outside the city walls
  will be killed by enemy swords.
Those inside the city
  will die of famine and disease.
[16] The survivors who escape to the mountains
  will moan like doves, weeping for
    their sins.
[17] Their hands will hang limp,
  their knees will be weak as water.
[18] They will dress themselves in burlap;
  horror and shame will cover them.
They will shave their heads
  in sorrow and remorse.

[19] "They will throw their money in the
    streets,
  tossing it out like worthless trash.
Their silver and gold won't save them
  on that day of the LORD's anger.
It will neither satisfy nor feed them,
  for their greed can only trip them up.
[20] They were proud of their beautiful jewelry
  and used it to make detestable idols and
    vile images.
Therefore, I will make all their wealth
  disgusting to them.

6:14 As in some Hebrew manuscripts; most Hebrew manuscripts read *Diblah.*

²¹ I will give it as plunder to foreigners,
to the most wicked of nations,
and they will defile it.
²² I will turn my eyes from them
as these robbers invade and defile my
treasured land.

²³ "Prepare chains for my people,
for the land is bloodied by terrible
crimes.
Jerusalem is filled with violence.
²⁴ I will bring the most ruthless of nations
to occupy their homes.
I will break down their proud fortresses
and defile their sanctuaries.
²⁵ Terror and trembling will overcome my
people.
They will look for peace but not find it.
²⁶ Calamity will follow calamity;
rumor will follow rumor.
They will look in vain
for a vision from the prophets.
They will receive no teaching from the
priests
and no counsel from the leaders.
²⁷ The king and the prince will stand
helpless,
weeping in despair,
and the people's hands
will tremble with fear.
I will bring on them
the evil they have done to others,
and they will receive the punishment
they so richly deserve.
Then they will know that I am the LORD."

Idolatry in the Temple

8 Then on September 17,* during the sixth
year of King Jehoiachin's captivity, while
the leaders of Judah were in my home, the Sovereign LORD took hold of me. ²I saw a figure
that appeared to be a man.* From what appeared to be his waist down, he looked like a
burning flame. From the waist up he looked
like gleaming amber.* ³He reached out what
seemed to be a hand and took me by the hair.
Then the Spirit lifted me up into the sky and
transported me to Jerusalem in a vision from
God. I was taken to the north gate of the inner
courtyard of the Temple, where there is a large
idol that has made the LORD very jealous. ⁴Sud-
denly, the glory of the God of Israel was there,
just as I had seen it before in the valley.

⁵Then the LORD said to me, "Son of man,
look toward the north." So I looked, and there
to the north, beside the entrance to the gate
near the altar, stood the idol that had made
the LORD so jealous.

⁶"Son of man," he said, "do you see what
they are doing? Do you see the detestable
sins the people of Israel are committing to
drive me from my Temple? But come, and
you will see even more detestable sins than
these!" ⁷Then he brought me to the door of
the Temple courtyard, where I could see a hole
in the wall. ⁸He said to me, "Now, son of man,
dig into the wall." So I dug into the wall and
found a hidden doorway.

⁹"Go in," he said, "and see the wicked and
detestable sins they are committing in there!"
¹⁰So I went in and saw the walls covered with
engravings of all kinds of crawling animals
and detestable creatures. I also saw the various idols* worshiped by the people of Israel.
¹¹Seventy leaders of Israel were standing there
with Jaazaniah son of Shaphan in the center.
Each of them held an incense burner, from
which a cloud of incense rose above their
heads.

¹²Then the LORD said to me, "Son of man,
have you seen what the leaders of Israel are
doing with their idols in dark rooms? They
are saying, 'The LORD doesn't see us; he has
deserted our land!'" ¹³Then the LORD added,
"Come, and I will show you even more detestable sins than these!"

¹⁴He brought me to the north gate of the
LORD's Temple, and some women were sitting
there, weeping for the god Tammuz. ¹⁵"Have
you seen this?" he asked. "But I will show you
even more detestable sins than these!"

¹⁶Then he brought me into the inner courtyard of the LORD's Temple. At the entrance to
the sanctuary, between the entry room and
the bronze altar, there were about twenty-five
men with their backs to the sanctuary of the
LORD. They were facing east, bowing low to
the ground, worshiping the sun!

¹⁷"Have you seen this, son of man?" he
asked. "Is it nothing to the people of Judah
that they commit these detestable sins, leading the whole nation into violence, thumbing
their noses at me, and provoking my anger?
¹⁸Therefore, I will respond in fury. I will neither
pity nor spare them. And though they cry for
mercy, I will not listen."

8:1 Hebrew *on the fifth [day] of the sixth month,* of the ancient Hebrew lunar calendar. This event occurred on September 17,
592 B.C.; also see note on 1:1.   8:2a As in Greek version; Hebrew reads *appeared to be fire.*   8:2b Or *like burnished metal.*
8:10 The Hebrew term (literally *round things*) probably alludes to dung.

The Slaughter of Idolaters

9 Then the LORD thundered, "Bring on the men appointed to punish the city! Tell them to bring their weapons with them!" ²Six men soon appeared from the upper gate that faces north, each carrying a deadly weapon in his hand. With them was a man dressed in linen, who carried a writer's case at his side. They all went into the Temple courtyard and stood beside the bronze altar.

³Then the glory of the God of Israel rose up from between the cherubim, where it had rested, and moved to the entrance of the Temple. And the LORD called to the man dressed in linen who was carrying the writer's case. ⁴He said to him, "Walk through the streets of Jerusalem and put a mark on the foreheads of all who weep and sigh because of the detestable sins being committed in their city."

⁵Then I heard the LORD say to the other men, "Follow him through the city and kill everyone whose forehead is not marked. Show no mercy; have no pity! ⁶Kill them all—old and young, girls and women and little children. But do not touch anyone with the mark. Begin right here at the Temple." So they began by killing the seventy leaders.

⁷"Defile the Temple!" the LORD commanded. "Fill its courtyards with corpses. Go!" So they went and began killing throughout the city.

⁸While they were out killing, I was all alone. I fell face down on the ground and cried out, "O Sovereign LORD! Will your fury against Jerusalem wipe out everyone left in Israel?"

⁹Then he said to me, "The sins of the people of Israel and Judah are very, very great. The entire land is full of murder; the city is filled with injustice. They are saying, 'The LORD doesn't see it! The LORD has abandoned the land!' ¹⁰So I will not spare them or have any pity on them. I will fully repay them for all they have done."

¹¹Then the man in linen clothing, who carried the writer's case, reported back and said, "I have done as you commanded."

The LORD's Glory Leaves the Temple

10 In my vision I saw what appeared to be a throne of blue lapis lazuli above the crystal surface over the heads of the cherubim. ²Then the LORD spoke to the man in linen clothing and said, "Go between the whirling wheels beneath the cherubim, and take a handful of burning coals and scatter them over the city." He did this as I watched.

³The cherubim were standing at the south end of the Temple when the man went in, and the cloud of glory filled the inner courtyard. ⁴Then the glory of the LORD rose up from above the cherubim and went over to the entrance of the Temple. The Temple was filled with this cloud of glory, and the courtyard glowed brightly with the glory of the LORD. ⁵The moving wings of the cherubim sounded like the voice of God Almighty* and could be heard even in the outer courtyard.

⁶The LORD said to the man in linen clothing, "Go between the cherubim and take some burning coals from between the wheels." So the man went in and stood beside one of the wheels. ⁷Then one of the cherubim reached out his hand and took some live coals from the fire burning among them. He put the coals into the hands of the man in linen clothing, and the man took them and went out. ⁸(All the cherubim had what looked like human hands under their wings.)

⁹I looked, and each of the four cherubim had a wheel beside him, and the wheels sparkled like beryl. ¹⁰All four wheels looked alike and were made the same; each wheel had a second wheel turning crosswise within it. ¹¹The cherubim could move in any of the four directions they faced, without turning as they moved. They went straight in the direction they faced, never turning aside. ¹²Both the cherubim and the wheels were covered with eyes. The cherubim had eyes all over their bodies, including their hands, their backs, and their wings. ¹³I heard someone refer to the wheels as "the whirling wheels." ¹⁴Each of the four cherubim had four faces: the first was the face of an ox,* the second was a human face, the third was the face of a lion, and the fourth was the face of an eagle.

¹⁵Then the cherubim rose upward. These were the same living beings I had seen beside the Kebar River. ¹⁶When the cherubim moved, the wheels moved with them. When they lifted their wings to fly, the wheels stayed beside them. ¹⁷When the cherubim stopped, the wheels stopped. When they flew upward, the wheels rose up, for the spirit of the living beings was in the wheels.

¹⁸Then the glory of the LORD moved out from the entrance of the Temple and hovered above the cherubim. ¹⁹And as I watched, the cherubim flew with their wheels to the east gate of the LORD's Temple. And the glory of the God of Israel hovered above them.

²⁰These were the same living beings I had

10:5 Hebrew *El-Shaddai.*   10:14 Hebrew *the face of a cherub;* compare 1:10.

seen beneath the God of Israel when I was by the Kebar River. I knew they were cherubim, 21for each had four faces and four wings and what looked like human hands under their wings. 22And their faces were just like the faces of the beings I had seen at the Kebar, and they traveled straight ahead, just as the others had.

Judgment on Israel's Leaders

11 Then the Spirit lifted me and brought me to the east gateway of the LORD's Temple, where I saw twenty-five prominent men of the city. Among them were Jaazaniah son of Azzur and Pelatiah son of Benaiah, who were leaders among the people.

2The Spirit said to me, "Son of man, these are the men who are planning evil and giving wicked counsel in this city. 3They say to the people, 'Is it not a good time to build houses? This city is like an iron pot. We are safe inside it like meat in a pot.*' 4Therefore, son of man, prophesy against them loudly and clearly."

5Then the Spirit of the LORD came upon me, and he told me to say, "This is what the LORD says to the people of Israel: I know what you are saying, for I know every thought that comes into your minds. 6You have murdered many in this city and filled its streets with the dead.

7"Therefore, this is what the Sovereign LORD says: This city is an iron pot all right, but the pieces of meat are the victims of your injustice. As for you, I will soon drag you from this pot. 8I will bring on you the sword of war you so greatly fear, says the Sovereign LORD. 9I will drive you out of Jerusalem and hand you over to foreigners, who will carry out my judgments against you. 10You will be slaughtered all the way to the borders of Israel. I will execute judgment on you, and you will know that I am the LORD. 11No, this city will not be an iron pot for you, and you will not be like meat safe inside it. I will judge you even to the borders of Israel, 12and you will know that I am the LORD. For you have refused to obey my decrees and regulations; instead, you have copied the standards of the nations around you."

13While I was still prophesying, Pelatiah son of Benaiah suddenly died. Then I fell face down on the ground and cried out, "O Sovereign LORD, are you going to kill everyone in Israel?"

Hope for Exiled Israel

14Then this message came to me from the LORD: 15"Son of man, the people still left in Jerusalem are talking about you and your relatives and

all the people of Israel who are in exile. They are saying, 'Those people are far away from the LORD, so now he has given their land to us!'

16"Therefore, tell the exiles, 'This is what the Sovereign LORD says: Although I have scattered you in the countries of the world, I will be a sanctuary to you during your time in exile. 17I, the Sovereign LORD, will gather you back from the nations where you have been scattered, and I will give you the land of Israel once again.'

18"When the people return to their homeland, they will remove every trace of their vile images and detestable idols. 19And I will give them singleness of heart and put a new spirit within them. I will take away their stony, stubborn heart and give them a tender, responsive heart,* 20so they will obey my decrees and regulations. Then they will truly be my people, and I will be their God. 21But as for those who long for vile images and detestable idols, I will repay them fully for their sins. I, the Sovereign LORD, have spoken!"

The LORD's Glory Leaves Jerusalem

22Then the cherubim lifted their wings and rose into the air with their wheels beside them, and the glory of the God of Israel hovered above them. 23Then the glory of the LORD went up from the city and stopped above the mountain to the east.

24Afterward the Spirit of God carried me back again to Babylonia,* to the people in exile there. And so ended the vision of my visit to Jerusalem. 25And I told the exiles everything the LORD had shown me.

Signs of the Coming Exile

12 Again a message came to me from the LORD: 2"Son of man, you live among rebels who have eyes but refuse to see. They have ears but refuse to hear. For they are a rebellious people.

3"So now, son of man, pretend you are being sent into exile. Pack the few items an exile could carry, and leave your home to go somewhere else. Do this right in front of the people so they can see you. For perhaps they will pay attention to this, even though they are such rebels. 4Bring your baggage outside during the day so they can watch you. Then in the evening, as they are watching, leave your house as captives do when they begin a long march to distant lands. 5Dig a hole through the wall while they are watching and go out

11:3 Hebrew *This city is the pot, and we are the meat.*   11:19 Hebrew *a heart of flesh.*   11:24 Or *Chaldea.*

through it. ⁶As they watch, lift your pack to your shoulders and walk away into the night. Cover your face so you cannot see the land you are leaving. For I have made you a sign for the people of Israel."

⁷So I did as I was told. In broad daylight I brought my pack outside, filled with the things I might carry into exile. Then in the evening while the people looked on, I dug through the wall with my hands and went out into the night with my pack on my shoulder.

⁸The next morning this message came to me from the LORD: ⁹"Son of man, these rebels, the people of Israel, have asked you what all this means. ¹⁰Say to them, 'This is what the Sovereign LORD says: These actions contain a message for King Zedekiah in Jerusalem* and for all the people of Israel.' ¹¹Explain that your actions are a sign to show what will soon happen to them, for they will be driven into exile as captives.

¹²"Even Zedekiah will leave Jerusalem at night through a hole in the wall, taking only what he can carry with him. He will cover his face, and his eyes will not see the land he is leaving. ¹³Then I will throw my net over him and capture him in my snare. I will bring him to Babylon, the land of the Babylonians,* though he will never see it, and he will die there. ¹⁴I will scatter his servants and warriors to the four winds and send the sword after them. ¹⁵And when I scatter them among the nations, they will know that I am the LORD. ¹⁶But I will spare a few of them from death by war, famine, or disease, so they can confess all their detestable sins to their captors. Then they will know that I am the LORD."

¹⁷Then this message came to me from the LORD: ¹⁸"Son of man, tremble as you eat your food. Shake with fear as you drink your water. ¹⁹Tell the people, 'This is what the Sovereign LORD says concerning those living in Israel and Jerusalem: They will eat their food with trembling and sip their water in despair, for their land will be stripped bare because of their violence. ²⁰The cities will be destroyed and the farmland made desolate. Then you will know that I am the LORD.'"

A New Proverb for Israel

²¹Again a message came to me from the LORD: ²²"Son of man, you've heard that proverb they quote in Israel: 'Time passes, and prophecies come to nothing.' ²³Tell the people, 'This is what the Sovereign LORD says: I will put an end to this proverb, and you will soon stop quoting it.' Now give them this new proverb to replace the old one: 'The time has come for every prophecy to be fulfilled!'

²⁴"There will be no more false visions and flattering predictions in Israel. ²⁵For I am the LORD! If I say it, it will happen. There will be no more delays, you rebels of Israel. I will fulfill my threat of destruction in your own lifetime. I, the Sovereign LORD, have spoken!"

²⁶Then this message came to me from the LORD: ²⁷"Son of man, the people of Israel are saying, 'He's talking about the distant future. His visions won't come true for a long, long time.' ²⁸Therefore, tell them, 'This is what the Sovereign LORD says: No more delay! I will now do everything I have threatened. I, the Sovereign LORD, have spoken!'"

Judgment against False Prophets

13 Then this message came to me from the LORD: ²"Son of man, prophesy against the false prophets of Israel who are inventing their own prophecies. Say to them, 'Listen to the word of the LORD. ³This is what the Sovereign LORD says: What sorrow awaits the false prophets who are following their own imaginations and have seen nothing at all!'

⁴"O people of Israel, these prophets of yours are like jackals digging in the ruins. ⁵They have done nothing to repair the breaks in the walls around the nation. They have not helped it to stand firm in battle on the day of the LORD. ⁶Instead, they have told lies and made false predictions. They say, 'This message is from the LORD,' even though the LORD never sent them. And yet they expect him to fulfill their prophecies! ⁷Can your visions be anything but false if you claim, 'This message is from the LORD,' when I have not even spoken to you?

⁸"Therefore, this is what the Sovereign LORD says: Because what you say is false and your visions are a lie, I will stand against you, says the Sovereign LORD. ⁹I will raise my fist against all the prophets who see false visions and make lying predictions, and they will be banished from the community of Israel. I will blot their names from Israel's record books, and they will never again set foot in their own land. Then you will know that I am the Sovereign LORD.

¹⁰"This will happen because these evil prophets deceive my people by saying, 'All is peaceful' when there is no peace at all! It's as if

12:10 Hebrew *the prince in Jerusalem;* similarly in 12:12.   12:13 Or *Chaldeans.*

the people have built a flimsy wall, and these prophets are trying to reinforce it by covering it with whitewash! [11]Tell these whitewashers that their wall will soon fall down. A heavy rainstorm will undermine it; great hailstones and mighty winds will knock it down. [12]And when the wall falls, the people will cry out, 'What happened to your whitewash?'

[13]"Therefore, this is what the Sovereign LORD says: I will sweep away your whitewashed wall with a storm of indignation, with a great flood of anger, and with hailstones of fury. [14]I will break down your wall right to its foundation, and when it falls, it will crush you. Then you will know that I am the LORD. [15]At last my anger against the wall and those who covered it with whitewash will be satisfied. Then I will say to you: 'The wall and those who whitewashed it are both gone. [16]They were lying prophets who claimed peace would come to Jerusalem when there was no peace. I, the Sovereign LORD, have spoken!'

Judgment against False Women Prophets

[17]"Now, son of man, speak out against the women who prophesy from their own imaginations. [18]This is what the Sovereign LORD says: What sorrow awaits you women who are ensnaring the souls of my people, young and old alike. You tie magic charms on their wrists and furnish them with magic veils. Do you think you can trap others without bringing destruction on yourselves? [19]You bring shame on me among my people for a few handfuls of barley or a piece of bread. By lying to my people who love to listen to lies, you kill those who should not die, and you promise life to those who should not live.

[20]"This is what the Sovereign LORD says: I am against all your magic charms, which you use to ensnare my people like birds. I will tear them from your arms, setting my people free like birds set free from a cage. [21]I will tear off the magic veils and save my people from your grasp. They will no longer be your victims. Then you will know that I am the LORD. [22]You have discouraged the righteous with your lies, but I didn't want them to be sad. And you have encouraged the wicked by promising them life, even though they continue in their sins. [23]Because of all this, you will no longer talk of seeing visions that you never saw, nor will you make predictions. For I will rescue my people from your grasp. Then you will know that I am the LORD."

The Idolatry of Israel's Leaders

14 Then some of the leaders of Israel visited me, and while they were sitting with me, [2]this message came to me from the LORD: [3]"Son of man, these leaders have set up idols* in their hearts. They have embraced things that will make them fall into sin. Why should I listen to their requests? [4]Tell them, 'This is what the Sovereign LORD says: The people of Israel have set up idols in their hearts and fallen into sin, and then they go to a prophet asking for a message. So I, the LORD, will give them the kind of answer their great idolatry deserves. [5]I will do this to capture the minds and hearts of all my people who have turned from me to worship their detestable idols.'

[6]"Therefore, tell the people of Israel, 'This is what the Sovereign LORD says: Repent and turn away from your idols, and stop all your detestable sins. [7]I, the LORD, will answer all those, both Israelites and foreigners, who reject me and set up idols in their hearts and so fall into sin, and who then come to a prophet asking for my advice. [8]I will turn against such people and make a terrible example of them, eliminating them from among my people. Then you will know that I am the LORD.

[9]"'And if a prophet is deceived into giving a message, it is because I, the LORD, have deceived that prophet. I will lift my fist against such prophets and cut them off from the community of Israel. [10]False prophets and those who seek their guidance will all be punished for their sins. [11]In this way, the people of Israel will learn not to stray from me, polluting themselves with sin. They will be my people, and I will be their God. I, the Sovereign LORD, have spoken!'"

The Certainty of the LORD's Judgment

[12]Then this message came to me from the LORD: [13]"Son of man, suppose the people of a country were to sin against me, and I lifted my fist to crush them, cutting off their food supply and sending a famine to destroy both people and animals. [14]Even if Noah, Daniel, and Job were there, their righteousness would save no one but themselves, says the Sovereign LORD.

[15]"Or suppose I were to send wild animals to invade the country, kill the people, and make the land too desolate and dangerous to pass through. [16]As surely as I live, says the Sovereign LORD, even if those three men were there, they wouldn't be able to save their own sons or

14:3 The Hebrew term (literally *round things*) probably alludes to dung; also in 14:4, 5, 6, 7.

daughters. They alone would be saved, but the land would be made desolate.

17"Or suppose I were to bring war against the land, and I sent enemy armies to destroy both people and animals. 18As surely as I live, says the Sovereign LORD, even if those three men were there, they wouldn't be able to save their own sons or daughters. They alone would be saved.

19"Or suppose I were to pour out my fury by sending an epidemic into the land, and the disease killed people and animals alike. 20As surely as I live, says the Sovereign LORD, even if Noah, Daniel, and Job were there, they wouldn't be able to save their own sons or daughters. They alone would be saved by their righteousness.

21"Now this is what the Sovereign LORD says: How terrible it will be when all four of these dreadful punishments fall upon Jerusalem—war, famine, wild animals, and disease—destroying all her people and animals. 22Yet there will be survivors, and they will come here to join you as exiles in Babylon. You will see with your own eyes how wicked they are, and then you will feel better about what I have done to Jerusalem. 23When you meet them and see their behavior, you will understand that these things are not being done to Israel without cause. I, the Sovereign LORD, have spoken!"

Jerusalem—a Useless Vine

15 Then this message came to me from the LORD: 2"Son of man, how does a grapevine compare to a tree? Is a vine's wood as useful as the wood of a tree? 3Can its wood be used for making things, like pegs to hang up pots and pans? 4No, it can only be used for fuel, and even as fuel, it burns too quickly. 5Vines are useless both before and after being put into the fire!

6"And this is what the Sovereign LORD says: The people of Jerusalem are like grapevines growing among the trees of the forest. Since they are useless, I have thrown them on the fire to be burned. 7And I will see to it that if they escape from one fire, they will fall into another. When I turn against them, you will know that I am the LORD. 8And I will make the land desolate because my people have been unfaithful to me. I, the Sovereign LORD, have spoken!"

Jerusalem—an Unfaithful Wife

16 Then another message came to me from the LORD: 2"Son of man, confront Jerusalem with her detestable sins. 3Give her this message from the Sovereign LORD: You are nothing but a Canaanite! Your father was an Amorite and your mother a Hittite. 4On the day you were born, no one cared about you. Your umbilical cord was not cut, and you were never washed, rubbed with salt, and wrapped in cloth. 5No one had the slightest interest in you; no one pitied you or cared for you. On the day you were born, you were unwanted, dumped in a field and left to die.

6"But I came by and saw you there, helplessly kicking about in your own blood. As you lay there, I said, 'Live!' 7And I helped you to thrive like a plant in the field. You grew up and became a beautiful jewel. Your breasts became full, and your body hair grew, but you were still naked. 8And when I passed by again, I saw that you were old enough for love. So I wrapped my cloak around you to cover your nakedness and declared my marriage vows. I made a covenant with you, says the Sovereign LORD, and you became mine.

9"Then I bathed you and washed off your blood, and I rubbed fragrant oils into your skin. 10I gave you expensive clothing of fine linen and silk, beautifully embroidered, and sandals made of fine goatskin leather. 11I gave you lovely jewelry, bracelets, beautiful necklaces, 12a ring for your nose, earrings for your ears, and a lovely crown for your head. 13And so you were adorned with gold and silver. Your clothes were made of fine linen and costly fabric and were beautifully embroidered. You ate the finest foods—choice flour, honey, and olive oil—and became more beautiful than ever. You looked like a queen, and so you were! 14Your fame soon spread throughout the world because of your beauty. I dressed you in my splendor and perfected your beauty, says the Sovereign LORD.

15"But you thought your fame and beauty were your own. So you gave yourself as a prostitute to every man who came along. Your beauty was theirs for the asking. 16You used the lovely things I gave you to make shrines for idols, where you played the prostitute. Unbelievable! How could such a thing ever happen? 17You took the very jewels and gold and silver ornaments I had given you and made statues of men and worshiped them. This is adultery against me! 18You used the beautifully embroidered clothes I gave you to dress your idols. Then you used my special oil and my incense to worship them. 19Imagine it! You set before them as a sacrifice the choice flour, olive oil, and honey I had given you, says the Sovereign LORD.

²⁰"Then you took your sons and daughters—the children you had borne to me—and sacrificed them to your gods. Was your prostitution not enough? ²¹Must you also slaughter my children by sacrificing them to idols? ²²In all your years of adultery and detestable sin, you have not once remembered the days long ago when you lay naked in a field, kicking about in your own blood.

²³"What sorrow awaits you, says the Sovereign LORD. In addition to all your other wickedness, ²⁴you built a pagan shrine and put altars to idols in every town square. ²⁵On every street corner you defiled your beauty, offering your body to every passerby in an endless stream of prostitution. ²⁶Then you added lustful Egypt to your lovers, provoking my anger with your increasing promiscuity. ²⁷That is why I struck you with my fist and reduced your boundaries. I handed you over to your enemies, the Philistines, and even they were shocked by your lewd conduct. ²⁸You have prostituted yourself with the Assyrians, too. It seems you can never find enough new lovers! And after your prostitution there, you still were not satisfied. ²⁹You added to your lovers by embracing Babylonia,* the land of merchants, but you still weren't satisfied.

³⁰"What a sick heart you have, says the Sovereign LORD, to do such things as these, acting like a shameless prostitute. ³¹You build your pagan shrines on every street corner and your altars to idols in every square. In fact, you have been worse than a prostitute, so eager for sin that you have not even demanded payment. ³²Yes, you are an adulterous wife who takes in strangers instead of her own husband. ³³Prostitutes charge for their services—but not you! You give gifts to your lovers, bribing them to come and have sex with you. ³⁴So you are the opposite of other prostitutes. You pay your lovers instead of their paying you!

Judgment on Jerusalem's Prostitution

³⁵"Therefore, you prostitute, listen to this message from the LORD! ³⁶This is what the Sovereign LORD says: Because you have poured out your lust and exposed yourself in prostitution to all your lovers, and because you have worshiped detestable idols,* and because you have slaughtered your children as sacrifices to your gods, ³⁷this is what I am going to do. I will gather together all your allies—the lovers with whom you have sinned, both those you loved and those you hated—and I will strip you naked in front of them so they can stare at you. ³⁸I will punish you for your murder and adultery. I will cover you with blood in my jealous fury. ³⁹Then I will give you to these many nations who are your lovers, and they will destroy you. They will knock down your pagan shrines and the altars to your idols. They will strip you and take your beautiful jewels, leaving you stark naked. ⁴⁰They will band together in a mob to stone you and cut you up with swords. ⁴¹They will burn your homes and punish you in front of many women. I will stop your prostitution and end your payments to your many lovers.

⁴²"Then at last my fury against you will be spent, and my jealous anger will subside. I will be calm and will not be angry with you anymore. ⁴³But first, because you have not remembered your youth but have angered me by doing all these evil things, I will fully repay you for all of your sins, says the Sovereign LORD. For you have added lewd acts to all your detestable sins. ⁴⁴Everyone who makes up proverbs will say of you, 'Like mother, like daughter.' ⁴⁵For your mother loathed her husband and her children, and so do you. And you are exactly like your sisters, for they despised their husbands and their children. Truly your mother was a Hittite and your father an Amorite.

⁴⁶"Your older sister was Samaria, who lived with her daughters in the north. Your younger sister was Sodom, who lived with her daughters in the south. ⁴⁷But you have not merely sinned as they did. You quickly surpassed them in corruption. ⁴⁸As surely as I live, says the Sovereign LORD, Sodom and her daughters were never as wicked as you and your daughters. ⁴⁹Sodom's sins were pride, gluttony, and laziness, while the poor and needy suffered outside her door. ⁵⁰She was proud and committed detestable sins, so I wiped her out, as you have seen.*

⁵¹"Even Samaria did not commit half your sins. You have done far more detestable things than your sisters ever did. They seem righteous compared to you. ⁵²Shame on you! Your sins are so terrible that you make your sisters seem righteous, even virtuous.

⁵³"But someday I will restore the fortunes of Sodom and Samaria, and I will restore you, too. ⁵⁴Then you will be truly ashamed of everything you have done, for your sins make them feel good in comparison. ⁵⁵Yes, your sisters,

16:29 Or *Chaldea.* 16:36 The Hebrew term (literally *round things*) probably alludes to dung. 16:50 As in a few Hebrew manuscripts and Greek version; Masoretic Text reads *as I have seen.*

Sodom and Samaria, and all their people will be restored, and at that time you also will be restored. ⁵⁶In your proud days you held Sodom in contempt. ⁵⁷But now your greater wickedness has been exposed to all the world, and you are the one who is scorned—by Edom* and all her neighbors and by Philistia. ⁵⁸This is your punishment for all your lewdness and detestable sins, says the LORD.

⁵⁹"Now this is what the Sovereign LORD says: I will give you what you deserve, for you have taken your solemn vows lightly by breaking your covenant. ⁶⁰Yet I will remember the covenant I made with you when you were young, and I will establish an everlasting covenant with you. ⁶¹Then you will remember with shame all the evil you have done. I will make your sisters, Samaria and Sodom, to be your daughters, even though they are not part of our covenant. ⁶²And I will reaffirm my covenant with you, and you will know that I am the LORD. ⁶³You will remember your sins and cover your mouth in silent shame when I forgive you of all that you have done. I, the Sovereign LORD, have spoken!"

A Story of Two Eagles

17 Then this message came to me from the LORD: ²"Son of man, give this riddle, and tell this story to the people of Israel. ³Give them this story from the Sovereign LORD:

"A great eagle with broad wings and long
    feathers,
    covered with many-colored plumage,
    came to Lebanon.
He seized the top of a cedar tree
⁴   and plucked off its highest branch.
He carried it away to a city filled with
    merchants.
    He planted it in a city of traders.
⁵ He also took a seedling from the land
    and planted it in fertile soil.
He placed it beside a broad river,
    where it could grow like a willow tree.
⁶ It took root there and
    grew into a low, spreading vine.
Its branches turned up toward the
    eagle,
    and its roots grew down into the
    ground.
It produced strong branches
    and put out shoots.
⁷ But then another great eagle came
    with broad wings and full plumage.

So the vine now sent its roots and branches
    toward him for water,
⁸ even though it was already planted in
    good soil
    and had plenty of water
so it could grow into a splendid vine
    and produce rich leaves and luscious
    fruit.

⁹ "So now the Sovereign LORD asks:
Will this vine grow and prosper?
    No! I will pull it up, roots and all!
I will cut off its fruit
    and let its leaves wither and die.
I will pull it up easily
    without a strong arm or a large army.
¹⁰ But when the vine is transplanted,
    will it thrive?
No, it will wither away
    when the east wind blows against it.
It will die in the same good soil
    where it had grown so well."

The Riddle Explained

¹¹Then this message came to me from the LORD: ¹²"Say to these rebels of Israel: Don't you understand the meaning of this riddle of the eagles? The king of Babylon came to Jerusalem, took away her king and princes, and brought them to Babylon. ¹³He made a treaty with a member of the royal family and forced him to take an oath of loyalty. He also exiled Israel's most influential leaders, ¹⁴so Israel would not become strong again and revolt. Only by keeping her treaty with Babylon could Israel survive.

¹⁵"Nevertheless, this man of Israel's royal family rebelled against Babylon, sending ambassadors to Egypt to request a great army and many horses. Can Israel break her sworn treaties like that and get away with it? ¹⁶No! For as surely as I live, says the Sovereign LORD, the king of Israel will die in Babylon, the land of the king who put him in power and whose treaty he disregarded and broke. ¹⁷Pharaoh and all his mighty army will fail to help Israel when the king of Babylon lays siege to Jerusalem again and destroys many lives. ¹⁸For the king of Israel disregarded his treaty and broke it after swearing to obey; therefore, he will not escape.

¹⁹"So this is what the Sovereign LORD says: As surely as I live, I will punish him for breaking my covenant and disregarding the solemn oath he made in my name. ²⁰I will throw my net over him and capture him in my snare.

16:57 As in many Hebrew manuscripts and Syriac version; Masoretic Text reads *Aram.*

I will bring him to Babylon and put him on trial for this treason against me. [21]And all his best warriors* will be killed in battle, and those who survive will be scattered to the four winds. Then you will know that I, the LORD, have spoken.

[22]"This is what the Sovereign LORD says: I will take a branch from the top of a tall cedar, and I will plant it on the top of Israel's highest mountain. [23]It will become a majestic cedar, sending forth its branches and producing seed. Birds of every sort will nest in it, finding shelter in the shade of its branches. [24]And all the trees will know that it is I, the LORD, who cuts the tall tree down and makes the short tree grow tall. It is I who makes the green tree wither and gives the dead tree new life. I, the LORD, have spoken, and I will do what I said!"

The Justice of a Righteous God

18 Then another message came to me from the LORD: [2]"Why do you quote this proverb concerning the land of Israel: 'The parents have eaten sour grapes, but their children's mouths pucker at the taste'? [3]As surely as I live, says the Sovereign LORD, you will not quote this proverb anymore in Israel. [4]For all people are mine to judge—both parents and children alike. And this is my rule: The person who sins is the one who will die.

[5]"Suppose a certain man is righteous and does what is just and right. [6]He does not feast in the mountains before Israel's idols* or worship them. He does not commit adultery or have intercourse with a woman during her menstrual period. [7]He is a merciful creditor, not keeping the items given as security by poor debtors. He does not rob the poor but instead gives food to the hungry and provides clothes for the needy. [8]He grants loans without interest, stays away from injustice, is honest and fair when judging others, [9]and faithfully obeys my decrees and regulations. Anyone who does these things is just and will surely live, says the Sovereign LORD.

[10]"But suppose that man has a son who grows up to be a robber or murderer and refuses to do what is right. [11]And that son does all the evil things his father would never do—he worships idols on the mountains, commits adultery, [12]oppresses the poor and helpless, steals from debtors by refusing to let them redeem their security, worships idols, commits detestable sins, [13]and lends money at excessive

interest. Should such a sinful person live? No! He must die and must take full blame.

[14]"But suppose that sinful son, in turn, has a son who sees his father's wickedness and decides against that kind of life. [15]This son refuses to worship idols on the mountains and does not commit adultery. [16]He does not exploit the poor, but instead is fair to debtors and does not rob them. He gives food to the hungry and provides clothes for the needy. [17]He helps the poor,* does not lend money at interest, and obeys all my regulations and decrees. Such a person will not die because of his father's sins; he will surely live. [18]But the father will die for his many sins—for being cruel, robbing people, and doing what was clearly wrong among his people.

[19]"'What?' you ask. 'Doesn't the child pay for the parent's sins?' No! For if the child does what is just and right and keeps my decrees, that child will surely live. [20]The person who sins is the one who will die. The child will not be punished for the parent's sins, and the parent will not be punished for the child's sins. Righteous people will be rewarded for their own righteous behavior, and wicked people will be punished for their own wickedness. [21]But if wicked people turn away from all their sins and begin to obey my decrees and do what is just and right, they will surely live and not die. [22]All their past sins will be forgotten, and they will live because of the righteous things they have done.

[23]"Do you think that I like to see wicked people die? says the Sovereign LORD. Of course not! I want them to turn from their wicked ways and live. [24]However, if righteous people turn from their righteous behavior and start doing sinful things and act like other sinners, should they be allowed to live? No, of course not! All their righteous acts will be forgotten, and they will die for their sins.

[25]"Yet you say, 'The Lord isn't doing what's right!' Listen to me, O people of Israel. Am I the one not doing what's right, or is it you? [26]When righteous people turn from their righteous behavior and start doing sinful things, they will die for it. Yes, they will die because of their sinful deeds. [27]And if wicked people turn from their wickedness, obey the law, and do what is just and right, they will save their lives. [28]They will live because they thought it over and decided to turn from their sins. Such people will not die. [29]And yet the people of

---

17:21 As in many Hebrew manuscripts; Masoretic Text reads *his fleeing warriors.* The meaning is uncertain.   18:6 The Hebrew term (literally *round things*) probably alludes to dung; also in 18:12, 15.   18:17 Greek version reads *He refuses to do evil.*

Israel keep saying, 'The Lord isn't doing what's right!' O people of Israel, it is you who are not doing what's right, not I.

³⁰ "Therefore, I will judge each of you, O people of Israel, according to your actions, says the Sovereign LORD. Repent, and turn from your sins. Don't let them destroy you! ³¹Put all your rebellion behind you, and find yourselves a new heart and a new spirit. For why should you die, O people of Israel? ³²I don't want you to die, says the Sovereign LORD. Turn back and live!

A Funeral Song for Israel's Kings

19 "Sing this funeral song for the princes of Israel:

² "What is your mother?
A lioness among lions!
She lay down among the young lions
and reared her cubs.
³ She raised one of her cubs
to become a strong young lion.
He learned to hunt and devour prey,
and he became a man-eater.
⁴ Then the nations heard about him,
and he was trapped in their pit.
They led him away with hooks
to the land of Egypt.

⁵ "When the lioness saw
that her hopes for him were gone,
she took another of her cubs
and taught him to be a strong young
lion.
⁶ He prowled among the other lions
and stood out among them in his
strength.
He learned to hunt and devour prey,
and he, too, became a man-eater.
⁷ He demolished fortresses*
and destroyed their towns and cities.
Their farms were desolated,
and their crops were destroyed.
The land and its people trembled in fear
when they heard him roar.
⁸ Then the armies of the nations attacked
him,
surrounding him from every direction.
They threw a net over him
and captured him in their pit.
⁹ With hooks, they dragged him into a cage
and brought him before the king of
Babylon.

They held him in captivity,
so his voice could never again be heard
on the mountains of Israel.

¹⁰ "Your mother was like a vine
planted by the water's edge.
It had lush, green foliage
because of the abundant water.
¹¹ Its branches became strong—
strong enough to be a ruler's scepter.
It grew very tall,
towering above all others.
It stood out because of its height
and its many lush branches.
¹² But the vine was uprooted in fury
and thrown down to the ground.
The desert wind dried up its fruit
and tore off its strong branches,
so that it withered
and was destroyed by fire.
¹³ Now the vine is transplanted to the
wilderness,
where the ground is hard and dry.
¹⁴ A fire has burst out from its branches
and devoured its fruit.
Its remaining limbs are not
strong enough to be a ruler's scepter.

"This is a funeral song, and it will be used in a funeral."

The Rebellion of Israel

20 On August 14,* during the seventh year of King Jehoiachin's captivity, some of the leaders of Israel came to request a message from the LORD. They sat down in front of me to wait for his reply. ²Then this message came to me from the LORD: ³"Son of man, tell the leaders of Israel, 'This is what the Sovereign LORD says: How dare you come to ask me for a message? As surely as I live, says the Sovereign LORD, I will tell you nothing!'

⁴"Son of man, bring charges against them and condemn them. Make them realize how detestable the sins of their ancestors really were. ⁵Give them this message from the Sovereign LORD: When I chose Israel—when I revealed myself to the descendants of Jacob in Egypt—I took a solemn oath that I, the LORD, would be their God. ⁶I took a solemn oath that day that I would bring them out of Egypt to a land I had discovered and explored for them—a good land, a land flowing with milk and honey, the best of all lands anywhere.

19:7 As in Greek version; Hebrew reads *He knew widows.* 20:1 Hebrew *In the fifth month, on the tenth day,* of the ancient Hebrew lunar calendar. This day was August 14, 591 B.C.; also see note on 1:1.

⁷Then I said to them, 'Each of you, get rid of the vile images you are so obsessed with. Do not defile yourselves with the idols* of Egypt, for I am the LORD your God.'

⁸"But they rebelled against me and would not listen. They did not get rid of the vile images they were obsessed with, or forsake the idols of Egypt. Then I threatened to pour out my fury on them to satisfy my anger while they were still in Egypt. ⁹But I didn't do it, for I acted to protect the honor of my name. I would not allow shame to be brought on my name among the surrounding nations who saw me reveal myself by bringing the Israelites out of Egypt. ¹⁰So I brought them out of Egypt and led them into the wilderness. ¹¹There I gave them my decrees and regulations so they could find life by keeping them. ¹²And I gave them my Sabbath days of rest as a sign between them and me. It was to remind them that I am the LORD, who had set them apart to be holy.

¹³"But the people of Israel rebelled against me, and they refused to obey my decrees there in the wilderness. They wouldn't obey my regulations even though obedience would have given them life. They also violated my Sabbath days. So I threatened to pour out my fury on them, and I made plans to utterly consume them in the wilderness. ¹⁴But again I held back in order to protect the honor of my name before the nations who had seen my power in bringing Israel out of Egypt. ¹⁵But I took a solemn oath against them in the wilderness. I swore I would not bring them into the land I had given them, a land flowing with milk and honey, the most beautiful place on earth. ¹⁶For they had rejected my regulations, refused to follow my decrees, and violated my Sabbath days. Their hearts were given to their idols. ¹⁷Nevertheless, I took pity on them and held back from destroying them in the wilderness.

¹⁸"Then I warned their children not to follow in their parents' footsteps, defiling themselves with their idols. ¹⁹'I am the LORD your God,' I told them. 'Follow my decrees, pay attention to my regulations, ²⁰and keep my Sabbath days holy, for they are a sign to remind you that I am the LORD your God.'

²¹"But their children, too, rebelled against me. They refused to keep my decrees and follow my regulations, even though obedience would have given them life. And they also violated my Sabbath days. So again I threatened to pour out my fury on them in the wilderness. ²²Nevertheless, I withdrew my judgment against them to protect the honor of my name before the nations that had seen my power in bringing them out of Egypt. ²³But I took a solemn oath against them in the wilderness. I swore I would scatter them among all the nations ²⁴because they did not obey my regulations. They scorned my decrees by violating my Sabbath days and longing for the idols of their ancestors. ²⁵I gave them over to worthless decrees and regulations that would not lead to life. ²⁶I let them pollute themselves* with the very gifts I had given them, and I allowed them to give their firstborn children as offerings to their gods—so I might devastate them and remind them that I alone am the LORD.

Judgment and Restoration

²⁷"Therefore, son of man, give the people of Israel this message from the Sovereign LORD: Your ancestors continued to blaspheme and betray me, ²⁸for when I brought them into the land I had promised them, they offered sacrifices on every high hill and under every green tree they saw! They roused my fury as they offered up sacrifices to their gods. They brought their perfumes and incense and poured out their liquid offerings to them. ²⁹I said to them, 'What is this high place where you are going?' (This kind of pagan shrine has been called Bamah—'high place'—ever since.)

³⁰"Therefore, give the people of Israel this message from the Sovereign LORD: Do you plan to pollute yourselves just as your ancestors did? Do you intend to keep prostituting yourselves by worshiping vile images? ³¹For when you offer gifts to them and give your little children to be burned as sacrifices,* you continue to pollute yourselves with idols to this day. Should I allow you to ask for a message from me, O people of Israel? As surely as I live, says the Sovereign LORD, I will tell you nothing.

³²"You say, 'We want to be like the nations all around us, who serve idols of wood and stone.' But what you have in mind will never happen. ³³As surely as I live, says the Sovereign LORD, I will rule over you with an iron fist in great anger and with awesome power. ³⁴And in anger I will reach out with my strong hand and powerful arm, and I will bring you back* from the lands where you are scattered. ³⁵I will bring you into the wilderness of the nations,

---

20:7 The Hebrew term (literally *round things*) probably alludes to dung; also in 20:8, 16, 18, 24, 31, 39.   20:25-26 Or *I gave them worthless decrees and regulations. . . . I polluted them.*   20:31 Or *and make your little children pass through the fire.*   20:34 Greek version reads *I will welcome you.* Compare 2 Cor 6:17.

and there I will judge you face to face. ³⁶I will judge you there just as I did your ancestors in the wilderness after bringing them out of Egypt, says the Sovereign LORD. ³⁷I will examine you carefully and hold you to the terms of the covenant. ³⁸I will purge you of all those who rebel and revolt against me. I will bring them out of the countries where they are in exile, but they will never enter the land of Israel. Then you will know that I am the LORD.

³⁹"As for you, O people of Israel, this is what the Sovereign LORD says: Go right ahead and worship your idols, but sooner or later you will obey me and will stop bringing shame on my holy name by worshiping idols. ⁴⁰For on my holy mountain, the great mountain of Israel, says the Sovereign LORD, the people of Israel will someday worship me, and I will accept them. There I will require that you bring me all your offerings and choice gifts and sacrifices. ⁴¹When I bring you home from exile, you will be like a pleasing sacrifice to me. And I will display my holiness through you as all the nations watch. ⁴²Then when I have brought you home to the land I promised with a solemn oath to give to your ancestors, you will know that I am the LORD. ⁴³You will look back on all the ways you defiled yourselves and will hate yourselves because of the evil you have done. ⁴⁴You will know that I am the LORD, O people of Israel, when I have honored my name by treating you mercifully in spite of your wickedness. I, the Sovereign LORD, have spoken!"

Judgment against the Negev

⁴⁵*Then this message came to me from the LORD: ⁴⁶"Son of man, turn and face the south* and speak out against it; prophesy against the brushlands of the Negev. ⁴⁷Tell the southern wilderness, 'This is what the Sovereign LORD says: Hear the word of the LORD! I will set you on fire, and every tree, both green and dry, will be burned. The terrible flames will not be quenched and will scorch everything from south to north. ⁴⁸And everyone in the world will see that I, the LORD, have set this fire. It will not be put out.'"

⁴⁹Then I said, "O Sovereign LORD, they are saying of me, 'He only talks in riddles!'"

The LORD's Sword of Judgment

21 ¹*Then this message came to me from the LORD: ²"Son of man, turn and face Jerusalem and prophesy against Israel and

her sanctuaries. ³Tell her, 'This is what the LORD says: I am your enemy, O Israel, and I am about to unsheath my sword to destroy your people—the righteous and the wicked alike. ⁴Yes, I will cut off both the righteous and the wicked! I will draw my sword against everyone in the land from south to north. ⁵Everyone in the world will know that I am the LORD. My sword is in my hand, and it will not return to its sheath until its work is finished.'

⁶"Son of man, groan before the people! Groan before them with bitter anguish and a broken heart. ⁷When they ask why you are groaning, tell them, 'I groan because of the terrifying news I have heard. When it comes true, the boldest heart will melt with fear; all strength will disappear. Every spirit will faint; strong knees will become as weak as water. And the Sovereign LORD says: It is coming! It's on its way!'"

⁸Then the LORD said to me, ⁹"Son of man, give the people this message from the Lord:

"A sword, a sword
    is being sharpened and polished.
¹⁰ It is sharpened for terrible slaughter
    and polished to flash like lightning!
Now will you laugh?
    Those far stronger than you have fallen
        beneath its power!*
¹¹ Yes, the sword is now being sharpened and
        polished;
    it is being prepared for the executioner.

¹² "Son of man, cry out and wail;
    pound your thighs in anguish,
for that sword will slaughter my people
    and their leaders—
        everyone will die!
¹³ It will put them all to the test.
    What chance do they have?*
    says the Sovereign LORD.

¹⁴ "Son of man, prophesy to them
    and clap your hands.
Then take the sword and brandish it twice,
    even three times,
to symbolize the great massacre,
    the great massacre facing them on every
        side.
¹⁵ Let their hearts melt with terror,
    for the sword glitters at every gate.
It flashes like lightning
    and is polished for slaughter!

20:45 Verses 20:45-49 are numbered 21:1-5 in Hebrew text.   **20:46** Hebrew *toward Teman.*   **21:1** Verses 21:1-32 are numbered 21:6-37 in Hebrew text.   **21:10** The meaning of the Hebrew is uncertain.   **21:13** The meaning of the Hebrew is uncertain.

16 O sword, slash to the right,
  then slash to the left,
  wherever you will,
  wherever you want.
17 I, too, will clap my hands,
  and I will satisfy my fury.
  I, the LORD, have spoken!"

Omens for Babylon's King

18 Then this message came to me from the LORD: 19 "Son of man, make a map and trace two routes on it for the sword of Babylon's king to follow. Put a signpost on the road that comes out of Babylon where the road forks into two—20 one road going to Ammon and its capital, Rabbah, and the other to Judah and fortified Jerusalem. 21 The king of Babylon now stands at the fork, uncertain whether to attack Jerusalem or Rabbah. He calls his magicians to look for omens. They cast lots by shaking arrows from the quiver. They inspect the livers of animal sacrifices. 22 The omen in his right hand says, 'Jerusalem!' With battering rams his soldiers will go against the gates, shouting for the kill. They will put up siege towers and build ramps against the walls. 23 The people of Jerusalem will think it is a false omen, because of their treaty with the Babylonians. But the king of Babylon will remind the people of their rebellion. Then he will attack and capture them.

24 "Therefore, this is what the Sovereign LORD says: Again and again you remind me of your sin and your guilt. You don't even try to hide it! In everything you do, your sins are obvious for all to see. So now the time of your punishment has come!

25 "O you corrupt and wicked prince of Israel, your final day of reckoning is here! 26 This is what the Sovereign LORD says:

"Take off your jeweled crown,
  for the old order changes.
Now the lowly will be exalted,
  and the mighty will be brought down.
27 Destruction! Destruction!
  I will surely destroy the kingdom.
And it will not be restored until the one
    appears
  who has the right to judge it.
Then I will hand it over to him.

A Message for the Ammonites

28 "And now, son of man, prophesy concerning the Ammonites and their mockery. Give them this message from the Sovereign LORD:

"A sword, a sword
  is drawn for your slaughter.
It is polished to destroy,
  flashing like lightning!
29 Your prophets have given false visions,
  and your fortune-tellers have told lies.
The sword will fall on the necks of the
    wicked
  for whom the day of final reckoning
    has come.

30 "Now return the sword to its sheath,
  for in your own country,
the land of your birth,
  I will pass judgment upon you.
31 I will pour out my fury on you
  and blow on you with the fire of my
    anger.
I will hand you over to cruel men
  who are skilled in destruction.
32 You will be fuel for the fire,
  and your blood will be spilled in your
    own land.
You will be utterly wiped out,
  your memory lost to history,
  for I, the LORD, have spoken!"

The Sins of Jerusalem

22 Now this message came to me from the LORD: 2 "Son of man, are you ready to judge Jerusalem? Are you ready to judge this city of murderers? Publicly denounce her detestable sins, 3 and give her this message from the Sovereign LORD: O city of murderers, doomed and damned—city of idols,* filthy and foul—4 you are guilty because of the blood you have shed. You are defiled because of the idols you have made. Your day of destruction has come! You have reached the end of your years. I will make you an object of mockery throughout the world. 5 O infamous city, filled with confusion, you will be mocked by people far and near.

6 "Every leader in Israel who lives within your walls is bent on murder. 7 Fathers and mothers are treated with contempt. Foreigners are forced to pay for protection. Orphans and widows are wronged and oppressed among you. 8 You despise my holy things and violate my Sabbath days of rest. 9 People accuse others falsely and send them to their death. You are filled with idol worshipers and people who do obscene things. 10 Men sleep with their fathers' wives and force themselves on women who are menstruating. 11 Within your walls live men

22:3 The Hebrew term (literally *round things*) probably alludes to dung; also in 22:4.

who commit adultery with their neighbors' wives, who defile their daughters-in-law, or who rape their own sisters. ¹²There are hired murderers, loan racketeers, and extortionists everywhere. They never even think of me and my commands, says the Sovereign LORD.

¹³"But now I clap my hands in indignation over your dishonest gain and bloodshed. ¹⁴How strong and courageous will you be in my day of reckoning? I, the LORD, have spoken, and I will do what I said. ¹⁵I will scatter you among the nations and purge you of your wickedness. ¹⁶And when I have been dishonored among the nations because of you,* you will know that I am the LORD."

The LORD's Refining Furnace

¹⁷Then this message came to me from the LORD: ¹⁸"Son of man, the people of Israel are the worthless slag that remains after silver is smelted. They are the dross that is left over—a useless mixture of copper, tin, iron, and lead. ¹⁹So tell them, 'This is what the Sovereign LORD says: Because you are all worthless slag, I will bring you to my crucible in Jerusalem. ²⁰Just as silver, copper, iron, lead, and tin are melted down in a furnace, I will melt you down in the heat of my fury. ²¹I will gather you together and blow the fire of my anger upon you, ²²and you will melt like silver in fierce heat. Then you will know that I, the LORD, have poured out my fury on you.'"

The Sins of Israel's Leaders

²³Again a message came to me from the LORD: ²⁴"Son of man, give the people of Israel this message: In the day of my indignation, you will be like a polluted land, a land without rain. ²⁵Your princes* plot conspiracies just as lions stalk their prey. They devour innocent people, seizing treasures and extorting wealth. They make many widows in the land. ²⁶Your priests have violated my instructions and defiled my holy things. They make no distinction between what is holy and what is not. And they do not teach my people the difference between what is ceremonially clean and unclean. They disregard my Sabbath days so that I am dishonored among them. ²⁷Your leaders are like wolves who tear apart their victims. They actually destroy people's lives for money! ²⁸And your prophets cover up for them by announcing false visions and making lying predictions.

They say, 'My message is from the Sovereign LORD,' when the LORD hasn't spoken a single word to them. ²⁹Even common people oppress the poor, rob the needy, and deprive foreigners of justice.

³⁰"I looked for someone who might rebuild the wall of righteousness that guards the land. I searched for someone to stand in the gap in the wall so I wouldn't have to destroy the land, but I found no one. ³¹So now I will pour out my fury on them, consuming them with the fire of my anger. I will heap on their heads the full penalty for all their sins. I, the Sovereign LORD, have spoken!"

The Adultery of Two Sisters

23 This message came to me from the LORD: ²"Son of man, once there were two sisters who were daughters of the same mother. ³They became prostitutes in Egypt. Even as young girls, they allowed men to fondle their breasts. ⁴The older girl was named Oholah, and her sister was Oholibah. I married them, and they bore me sons and daughters. I am speaking of Samaria and Jerusalem, for Oholah is Samaria and Oholibah is Jerusalem.

⁵"Then Oholah lusted after other lovers instead of me, and she gave her love to the Assyrian officers. ⁶They were all attractive young men, captains and commanders dressed in handsome blue, charioteers driving their horses. ⁷And so she prostituted herself with the most desirable men of Assyria, worshiping their idols* and defiling herself. ⁸For when she left Egypt, she did not leave her spirit of prostitution behind. She was still as lewd as in her youth, when the Egyptians slept with her, fondled her breasts, and used her as a prostitute.

⁹"And so I handed her over to her Assyrian lovers, whom she desired so much. ¹⁰They stripped her, took away her children as their slaves, and then killed her. After she received her punishment, her reputation was known to every woman in the land.

¹¹"Yet even though Oholibah saw what had happened to Oholah, her sister, she followed right in her footsteps. And she was even more depraved, abandoning herself to her lust and prostitution. ¹²She fawned over all the Assyrian officers—those captains and commanders in handsome uniforms, those charioteers driving their horses—all of them attractive young

22:16 As in one Hebrew manuscript and Greek and Syriac versions; Masoretic Text reads *when you have been dishonored among the nations.*   22:25 As in Greek version; Hebrew reads *prophets.*   23:7 The Hebrew term (literally *round things*) probably alludes to dung; also in 23:30, 37, 39, 49.

men. ¹³I saw the way she was going, defiling herself just like her older sister.

¹⁴"Then she carried her prostitution even further. She fell in love with pictures that were painted on a wall—pictures of Babylonian* military officers, outfitted in striking red uniforms. ¹⁵Handsome belts encircled their waists, and flowing turbans crowned their heads. They were dressed like chariot officers from the land of Babylonia.* ¹⁶When she saw these paintings, she longed to give herself to them, so she sent messengers to Babylonia to invite them to come to her. ¹⁷So they came and committed adultery with her, defiling her in the bed of love. After being defiled, however, she rejected them in disgust.

¹⁸"In the same way, I became disgusted with Oholibah and rejected her, just as I had rejected her sister, because she flaunted herself before them and gave herself to satisfy their lusts. ¹⁹Yet she turned to even greater prostitution, remembering her youth when she was a prostitute in Egypt. ²⁰She lusted after lovers with genitals as large as a donkey's and emissions like those of a horse. ²¹And so, Oholibah, you relived your former days as a young girl in Egypt, when you first allowed your breasts to be fondled.

The LORD's Judgment of Oholibah

²²"Therefore, Oholibah, this is what the Sovereign LORD says: I will send your lovers against you from every direction—those very nations from which you turned away in disgust. ²³For the Babylonians will come with all the Chaldeans from Pekod and Shoa and Koa. And all the Assyrians will come with them—handsome young captains, commanders, chariot officers, and other high-ranking officers, all riding their horses. ²⁴They will all come against you from the north* with chariots, wagons, and a great army prepared for attack. They will take up positions on every side, surrounding you with men armed with shields and helmets. And I will hand you over to them for punishment so they can do with you as they please. ²⁵I will turn my jealous anger against you, and they will deal harshly with you. They will cut off your nose and ears, and any survivors will then be slaughtered by the sword. Your children will be taken away as captives, and everything that is left will be burned. ²⁶They will strip you of your beautiful clothes and jewels. ²⁷In this way, I will put a stop to the lewdness and prostitution you brought from Egypt. You will never again cast longing eyes on those things or fondly remember your time in Egypt.

²⁸"For this is what the Sovereign LORD says: I will surely hand you over to your enemies, to those you loathe, those you rejected. ²⁹They will treat you with hatred and rob you of all you own, leaving you stark naked. The shame of your prostitution will be exposed to all the world. ³⁰You brought all this on yourself by prostituting yourself to other nations, defiling yourself with all their idols. ³¹Because you have followed in your sister's footsteps, I will force you to drink the same cup of terror she drank.

³²"Yes, this is what the Sovereign LORD says:

"You will drink from your sister's cup
   of terror,
   a cup that is large and deep.
It is filled to the brim
   with scorn and derision.
³³ Drunkenness and anguish will fill you,
   for your cup is filled to the brim with
      distress and desolation,
   the same cup your sister Samaria drank.
³⁴ You will drain that cup of terror
   to the very bottom.
Then you will smash it to pieces
   and beat your breast in anguish.
   I, the Sovereign LORD, have spoken!

³⁵"And because you have forgotten me and turned your back on me, this is what the Sovereign LORD says: You must bear the consequences of all your lewdness and prostitution."

The LORD's Judgment on Both Sisters

³⁶The LORD said to me, "Son of man, you must accuse Oholah and Oholibah of all their detestable sins. ³⁷They have committed both adultery and murder—adultery by worshiping idols and murder by burning as sacrifices the children they bore to me. ³⁸Furthermore, they have defiled my Temple and violated my Sabbath day! ³⁹On the very day that they sacrificed their children to their idols, they boldly came into my Temple to worship! They came in and defiled my house.

⁴⁰"You sisters sent messengers to distant lands to get men. Then when they arrived, you bathed yourselves, painted your eyelids, and put on your finest jewels for them. ⁴¹You sat with them on a beautifully embroidered couch and put my incense and my special oil on a table that was spread before you. ⁴²From your room came the sound of many men carousing.

23:14 Or *Chaldean.*   23:15 Or *Chaldea;* also in 23:16.   23:24 As in Greek version; the meaning of the Hebrew is uncertain.

They were lustful men and drunkards* from the wilderness, who put bracelets on your wrists and beautiful crowns on your heads. ⁴³Then I said, 'If they really want to have sex with old worn-out prostitutes like these, let them!' ⁴⁴And that is what they did. They had sex with Oholah and Oholibah, these shameless prostitutes. ⁴⁵But righteous people will judge these sister cities for what they really are—adulterers and murderers.

⁴⁶"Now this is what the Sovereign LORD says: Bring an army against them and hand them over to be terrorized and plundered. ⁴⁷For their enemies will stone them and kill them with swords. They will butcher their sons and daughters and burn their homes. ⁴⁸In this way, I will put an end to lewdness and idolatry in the land, and my judgment will be a warning to all women not to follow your wicked example. ⁴⁹You will be fully repaid for all your prostitution—your worship of idols. Yes, you will suffer the full penalty. Then you will know that I am the Sovereign LORD."

The Sign of the Cooking Pot

24 On January 15,* during the ninth year of King Jehoiachin's captivity, this message came to me from the LORD: ²"Son of man, write down today's date, because on this very day the king of Babylon is beginning his attack against Jerusalem. ³Then give these rebels an illustration with this message from the Sovereign LORD:

"Put a pot on the fire,
  and pour in some water.
⁴ Fill it with choice pieces of meat—
  the rump and the shoulder
  and all the most tender cuts.
⁵ Use only the best sheep from the flock,
  and heap fuel on the fire beneath
    the pot.
Bring the pot to a boil,
  and cook the bones along with
    the meat.

⁶ "Now this is what the Sovereign LORD
    says:
What sorrow awaits Jerusalem,
  the city of murderers!
She is a cooking pot
  whose corruption can't be cleaned out.
Take the meat out in random order,
  for no piece is better than another.

⁷ For the blood of her murders
  is splashed on the rocks.
It isn't even spilled on the ground,
  where the dust could cover it!
⁸ So I will splash her blood on a rock
  for all to see,
an expression of my anger
  and vengeance against her.

⁹ "This is what the Sovereign LORD says:
What sorrow awaits Jerusalem,
  the city of murderers!
I myself will pile up the fuel beneath
    her.
¹⁰ Yes, heap on the wood!
  Let the fire roar to make the pot boil.
Cook the meat with many spices,
  and afterward burn the bones.
¹¹ Now set the empty pot on the coals.
  Heat it red hot!
Burn away the filth and corruption.
¹² But it's hopeless;
  the corruption can't be cleaned out.
  So throw it into the fire.
¹³ Your impurity is your lewdness
  and the corruption of your idolatry.
I tried to cleanse you,
  but you refused.
So now you will remain in your filth
  until my fury against you has been
    satisfied.

¹⁴"I, the LORD, have spoken! The time has come, and I won't hold back. I will not change my mind, and I will have no pity on you. You will be judged on the basis of all your wicked actions, says the Sovereign LORD."

The Death of Ezekiel's Wife

¹⁵Then this message came to me from the LORD: ¹⁶"Son of man, with one blow I will take away your dearest treasure. Yet you must not show any sorrow at her death. Do not weep; let there be no tears. ¹⁷Groan silently, but let there be no wailing at her grave. Do not uncover your head or take off your sandals. Do not perform the usual rituals of mourning or accept any food brought to you by consoling friends."

¹⁸So I proclaimed this to the people the next morning, and in the evening my wife died. The next morning I did everything I had been told to do. ¹⁹Then the people asked, "What does all this mean? What are you trying to tell us?"

²⁰So I said to them, "A message came to me

23:42 Or *Sabeans.* 24:1 Hebrew *On the tenth day of the tenth month,* of the ancient Hebrew lunar calendar. This event occurred on January 15, 588 B.C.; also see note on 1:1.

from the LORD, 21and I was told to give this message to the people of Israel. This is what the Sovereign LORD says: I will defile my Temple, the source of your security and pride, the place your heart delights in. Your sons and daughters whom you left behind in Judah will be slaughtered by the sword. 22Then you will do as Ezekiel has done. You will not mourn in public or console yourselves by eating the food brought by friends. 23Your heads will remain covered, and your sandals will not be taken off. You will not mourn or weep, but you will waste away because of your sins. You will groan among yourselves for all the evil you have done. 24Ezekiel is an example for you; you will do just as he has done. And when that time comes, you will know that I am the Sovereign LORD."

25Then the LORD said to me, "Son of man, on the day I take away their stronghold—their joy and glory, their heart's desire, their dearest treasure—I will also take away their sons and daughters. 26And on that day a survivor from Jerusalem will come to you in Babylon and tell you what has happened. 27And when he arrives, your voice will suddenly return so you can talk to him, and you will be a symbol for these people. Then they will know that I am the LORD."

A Message for Ammon

25 Then this message came to me from the LORD: 2"Son of man, turn and face the land of Ammon and prophesy against its people. 3Give the Ammonites this message from the Sovereign LORD: Hear the word of the Sovereign LORD! Because you cheered when my Temple was defiled, mocked Israel in her desolation, and laughed at Judah as she went away into exile, 4I will allow nomads from the eastern deserts to overrun your country. They will set up their camps among you and pitch their tents on your land. They will harvest all your fruit and drink the milk from your livestock. 5And I will turn the city of Rabbah into a pasture for camels, and all the land of the Ammonites into a resting place for sheep and goats. Then you will know that I am the LORD.

6"This is what the Sovereign LORD says: Because you clapped and danced and cheered with glee at the destruction of my people, 7I will raise my fist of judgment against you. I will give you as plunder to many nations. I will

cut you off from being a nation and destroy you completely. Then you will know that I am the LORD.

A Message for Moab

8"This is what the Sovereign LORD says: Because the people of Moab* have said that Judah is just like all the other nations, 9I will open up their eastern flank and wipe out their glorious frontier towns—Beth-jeshimoth, Baal-meon, and Kiriathaim. 10And I will hand Moab over to nomads from the eastern deserts, just as I handed over Ammon. Yes, the Ammonites will no longer be counted among the nations. 11In the same way, I will bring my judgment down on the Moabites. Then they will know that I am the LORD.

A Message for Edom

12"This is what the Sovereign LORD says: The people of Edom have sinned greatly by avenging themselves against the people of Judah. 13Therefore, says the Sovereign LORD, I will raise my fist of judgment against Edom. I will wipe out its people and animals with the sword. I will make a wasteland of everything from Teman to Dedan. 14I will accomplish this by the hand of my people of Israel. They will carry out my vengeance with anger, and Edom will know that this vengeance is from me. I, the Sovereign LORD, have spoken!

A Message for Philistia

15"This is what the Sovereign LORD says: The people of Philistia have acted against Judah out of bitter revenge and long-standing contempt. 16Therefore, this is what the Sovereign LORD says: I will raise my fist of judgment against the land of the Philistines. I will wipe out the Kerethites and utterly destroy the people who live by the sea. 17I will execute terrible vengeance against them to punish them for what they have done. And when I have inflicted my revenge, they will know that I am the LORD."

A Message for Tyre

26 On February 3, during the twelfth year of King Jehoiachin's captivity,* this message came to me from the LORD: 2"Son of man, Tyre has rejoiced over the fall of Jerusalem, saying, 'Ha! She who was the gateway to the rich trade routes to the east has been broken,

---

25:8 As in Greek version; Hebrew reads *Moab and Seir.*   26:1 Hebrew *In the eleventh year, on the first day of the month,* of the ancient Hebrew lunar calendar year. Since an element is missing in the date formula here, scholars have reconstructed this probable reading: *In the eleventh [month of the twelfth] year, on the first day of the month.* This reading would put this message on February 3, 585 B.C.; also see note on 1:1.

and I am the heir! Because she has been made desolate, I will become wealthy!'

³"Therefore, this is what the Sovereign LORD says: I am your enemy, O Tyre, and I will bring many nations against you, like the waves of the sea crashing against your shoreline. ⁴They will destroy the walls of Tyre and tear down its towers. I will scrape away its soil and make it a bare rock! ⁵It will be just a rock in the sea, a place for fishermen to spread their nets, for I have spoken, says the Sovereign LORD. Tyre will become the prey of many nations, ⁶and its mainland villages will be destroyed by the sword. Then they will know that I am the LORD.

⁷"This is what the Sovereign LORD says: From the north I will bring King Nebuchadnezzar* of Babylon against Tyre. He is king of kings and brings his horses, chariots, charioteers, and great army. ⁸First he will destroy your mainland villages. Then he will attack you by building a siege wall, constructing a ramp, and raising a roof of shields against you. ⁹He will pound your walls with battering rams and demolish your towers with sledgehammers. ¹⁰The hooves of his horses will choke the city with dust, and the noise of the charioteers and chariot wheels will shake your walls as they storm through your broken gates. ¹¹His horsemen will trample through every street in the city. They will butcher your people, and your strong pillars will topple.

¹²"They will plunder all your riches and merchandise and break down your walls. They will destroy your lovely homes and dump your stones and timbers and even your dust into the sea. ¹³I will stop the music of your songs. No more will the sound of harps be heard among your people. ¹⁴I will make your island a bare rock, a place for fishermen to spread their nets. You will never be rebuilt, for I, the LORD, have spoken. Yes, the Sovereign LORD has spoken!

The Effect of Tyre's Destruction

¹⁵"This is what the Sovereign LORD says to Tyre: The whole coastline will tremble at the sound of your fall, as the screams of the wounded echo in the continuing slaughter. ¹⁶All the seaport rulers will step down from their thrones and take off their royal robes and beautiful clothing. They will sit on the ground trembling with horror at your destruction. ¹⁷Then they will wail for you, singing this funeral song:

"O famous island city,
  once ruler of the sea,

how you have been destroyed!
Your people, with their naval power,
  once spread fear around the world.
¹⁸ Now the coastlands tremble at your fall.
  The islands are dismayed as you
    disappear.

¹⁹"This is what the Sovereign LORD says: I will make Tyre an uninhabited ruin, like many others. I will bury you beneath the terrible waves of enemy attack. Great seas will swallow you. ²⁰I will send you to the pit to join those who descended there long ago. Your city will lie in ruins, buried beneath the earth, like those in the pit who have entered the world of the dead. You will have no place of respect here in the land of the living. ²¹I will bring you to a terrible end, and you will exist no more. You will be looked for, but you will never again be found. I, the Sovereign LORD, have spoken!"

The End of Tyre's Glory

27 Then this message came to me from the LORD: ²"Son of man, sing a funeral song for Tyre, ³that mighty gateway to the sea, the trading center of the world. Give Tyre this message from the Sovereign LORD:

"You boasted, O Tyre,
  'My beauty is perfect!'
⁴ You extended your boundaries into the
    sea.
  Your builders made your beauty perfect.
⁵ You were like a great ship
    built of the finest cypress from Senir.*
  They took a cedar from Lebanon
    to make a mast for you.
⁶ They carved your oars
    from the oaks of Bashan.
  Your deck of pine from the coasts of Cyprus*
    was inlaid with ivory.
⁷ Your sails were made of Egypt's finest
    linen,
    and they flew as a banner above you.
  You stood beneath blue and purple
    awnings
    made bright with dyes from the coasts
      of Elishah.
⁸ Your oarsmen came from Sidon and Arvad;
    your helmsmen were skilled men from
      Tyre itself.
⁹ Wise old craftsmen from Gebal did the
    caulking.
  Ships from every land came with goods
    to barter for your trade.

26:7 Hebrew *Nebuchadrezzar*, a variant spelling of Nebuchadnezzar.   27:5 Or *Hermon*.   27:6 Hebrew *Kittim*.

10"Men from distant Persia, Lydia, and Libya* served in your great army. They hung their shields and helmets on your walls, giving you great honor. 11Men from Arvad and Helech stood on your walls. Your towers were manned by men from Gammad. Their shields hung on your walls, completing your beauty.

12"Tarshish sent merchants to buy your wares in exchange for silver, iron, tin, and lead. 13Merchants from Greece,* Tubal, and Meshech brought slaves and articles of bronze to trade with you.

14"From Beth-togarmah came riding horses, chariot horses, and mules, all in exchange for your goods. 15Merchants came to you from Dedan.* Numerous coastlands were your captive markets; they brought payment in ivory tusks and ebony wood.

16"Syria* sent merchants to buy your rich variety of goods. They traded turquoise, purple dyes, embroidery, fine linen, and jewelry of coral and rubies. 17Judah and Israel traded for your wares, offering wheat from Minnith, figs,* honey, olive oil, and balm.

18"Damascus sent merchants to buy your rich variety of goods, bringing wine from Helbon and white wool from Zahar. 19Greeks from Uzal* came to trade for your merchandise. Wrought iron, cassia, and fragrant calamus were bartered for your wares.

20"Dedan sent merchants to trade their expensive saddle blankets with you. 21The Arabians and the princes of Kedar sent merchants to trade lambs and rams and male goats in exchange for your goods. 22The merchants of Sheba and Raamah came with all kinds of spices, jewels, and gold in exchange for your wares.

23"Haran, Canneh, Eden, Sheba, Asshur, and Kilmad came with their merchandise, too. 24They brought choice fabrics to trade—blue cloth, embroidery, and multicolored carpets rolled up and bound with cords. 25The ships of Tarshish were your ocean caravans. Your island warehouse was filled to the brim!

The Destruction of Tyre

26 "But look! Your oarsmen
have taken you into stormy seas!
A mighty eastern gale
has wrecked you in the heart of the sea!
27 Everything is lost—
your riches and wares,
your sailors and pilots,
your ship builders, merchants, and
warriors.
On the day of your ruin,
everyone on board sinks into the depths
of the sea.
28 Your cities by the sea tremble
as your pilots cry out in terror.
29 All the oarsmen abandon their ships;
the sailors and pilots stand on the shore.
30 They cry aloud over you
and weep bitterly.
They throw dust on their heads
and roll in ashes.
31 They shave their heads in grief for you
and dress themselves in burlap.
They weep for you with bitter anguish
and deep mourning.
32 As they wail and mourn over you,
they sing this sad funeral song:
'Was there ever such a city as Tyre,
now silent at the bottom of the sea?
33 The merchandise you traded
satisfied the desires of many nations.
Kings at the ends of the earth
were enriched by your trade.
34 Now you are a wrecked ship,
broken at the bottom of the sea.
All your merchandise and crew
have gone down with you.
35 All who live along the coastlands
are appalled at your terrible fate.
Their kings are filled with horror
and look on with twisted faces.
36 The merchants among the nations
shake their heads at the sight of you,*
for you have come to a horrible end
and will exist no more.'"

A Message for Tyre's King

28 Then this message came to me from the LORD: 2"Son of man, give the prince of Tyre this message from the Sovereign LORD:

"In your great pride you claim, 'I am a god!
I sit on a divine throne in the heart of
the sea.'
But you are only a man and not a god,
though you boast that you are a god.
3 You regard yourself as wiser than Daniel
and think no secret is hidden from you.
4 With your wisdom and understanding you
have amassed great wealth—
gold and silver for your treasuries.

27:10 Hebrew *Paras, Lud, and Put.*   27:13 Hebrew *Javan.*   27:15 Greek version reads *Rhodes.*   27:16 Hebrew *Aram;* some manuscripts read *Edom.*   27:17 The meaning of the Hebrew is uncertain.   27:19 Hebrew *Vedan and Javan from Uzal.* The meaning of the Hebrew is uncertain.   27:36 Hebrew *hiss at you.*

⁵ Yes, your wisdom has made you very rich,
    and your riches have made you very
      proud.

⁶ "Therefore, this is what the Sovereign
    LORD says:
  Because you think you are as wise as a god,
⁷   I will now bring against you a foreign
      army,
    the terror of the nations.
  They will draw their swords against your
      marvelous wisdom
    and defile your splendor!
⁸ They will bring you down to the pit,
    and you will die in the heart of the sea,
      pierced with many wounds.
⁹ Will you then boast, 'I am a god!'
    to those who kill you?
  To them you will be no god
    but merely a man!
¹⁰ You will die like an outcast*
    at the hands of foreigners.
  I, the Sovereign LORD, have spoken!"

¹¹Then this further message came to me
from the LORD: ¹²"Son of man, sing this funeral song for the king of Tyre. Give him this
message from the Sovereign LORD:

  "You were the model of perfection,
    full of wisdom and exquisite in beauty.
¹³ You were in Eden,
    the garden of God.
  Your clothing was adorned with every
      precious stone*—
    red carnelian, pale-green peridot, white
      moonstone,
    blue-green beryl, onyx, green jasper,
    blue lapis lazuli, turquoise, and
      emerald—
  all beautifully crafted for you
    and set in the finest gold.
  They were given to you
    on the day you were created.
¹⁴ I ordained and anointed you
    as the mighty angelic guardian.*
  You had access to the holy mountain of God
    and walked among the stones of fire.

¹⁵ "You were blameless in all you did
    from the day you were created
      until the day evil was found in you.
¹⁶ Your rich commerce led you to violence,
    and you sinned.

  So I banished you in disgrace
    from the mountain of God.
  I expelled you, O mighty guardian,
    from your place among the stones
      of fire.
¹⁷ Your heart was filled with pride
    because of all your beauty.
  Your wisdom was corrupted
    by your love of splendor.
  So I threw you to the ground
    and exposed you to the curious gaze
      of kings.
¹⁸ You defiled your sanctuaries
    with your many sins and your dishonest
      trade.
  So I brought fire out from within you,
    and it consumed you.
  I reduced you to ashes on the ground
    in the sight of all who were watching.
¹⁹ All who knew you are appalled at your
      fate.
  You have come to a terrible end,
    and you will exist no more."

A Message for Sidon

²⁰Then another message came to me from the
LORD: ²¹"Son of man, turn and face the city
of Sidon and prophesy against it. ²²Give the
people of Sidon this message from the Sovereign LORD:

  "I am your enemy, O Sidon,
    and I will reveal my glory by what I do
      to you.
  When I bring judgment against you
    and reveal my holiness among you,
  everyone watching will know
    that I am the LORD.
²³ I will send a plague against you,
    and blood will be spilled in your streets.
  The attack will come from every direction,
    and your people will lie slaughtered
      within your walls.
  Then everyone will know
    that I am the LORD.
²⁴ No longer will Israel's scornful neighbors
    prick and tear at her like briers and
      thorns.
  For then they will know
    that I am the Sovereign LORD.

Restoration for Israel

²⁵"This is what the Sovereign LORD says: The
people of Israel will again live in their own

28:10 Hebrew *will die the death of the uncircumcised.*   28:13 The identification of some of these gemstones is uncertain.
28:14 Hebrew *guardian cherub;* similarly in 28:16.

land, the land I gave my servant Jacob. For I will gather them from the distant lands where I have scattered them. I will reveal to the nations of the world my holiness among my people. ²⁶They will live safely in Israel and build homes and plant vineyards. And when I punish the neighboring nations that treated them with contempt, they will know that I am the LORD their God."

A Message for Egypt

29 On January 7,* during the tenth year of King Jehoiachin's captivity, this message came to me from the LORD: ²"Son of man, turn and face Egypt and prophesy against Pharaoh the king and all the people of Egypt. ³Give them this message from the Sovereign LORD:

"I am your enemy, O Pharaoh, king of
 Egypt—
 you great monster, lurking in the
 streams of the Nile.
For you have said, 'The Nile River is mine;
 I made it for myself.'
⁴ I will put hooks in your jaws
 and drag you out on the land
 with fish sticking to your scales.
⁵ I will leave you and all your fish
 stranded in the wilderness to die.
You will lie unburied on the open ground,
 for I have given you as food to the wild
 animals and birds.
⁶ All the people of Egypt will know that I
 am the LORD,
 for to Israel you were just a staff made
 of reeds.
⁷ When Israel leaned on you,
 you splintered and broke
 and stabbed her in the armpit.
When she put her weight on you,
 you collapsed, and her legs gave way.

⁸"Therefore, this is what the Sovereign LORD says: I will bring an army against you, O Egypt, and destroy both people and animals. ⁹The land of Egypt will become a desolate wasteland, and the Egyptians will know that I am the LORD.

"Because you said, 'The Nile River is mine; I made it,' ¹⁰I am now the enemy of both you and your river. I will make the land of Egypt a totally desolate wasteland, from Migdol to Aswan, as far south as the border of Ethiopia.* ¹¹For forty years not a soul will pass that way, neither people nor animals. It will be completely uninhabited. ¹²I will make Egypt desolate, and it will be surrounded by other desolate nations. Its cities will be empty and desolate for forty years, surrounded by other ruined cities. I will scatter the Egyptians to distant lands.

¹³"But this is what the Sovereign LORD also says: At the end of the forty years I will bring the Egyptians home again from the nations to which they have been scattered. ¹⁴I will restore the prosperity of Egypt and bring its people back to the land of Pathros in southern Egypt from which they came. But Egypt will remain an unimportant, minor kingdom. ¹⁵It will be the lowliest of all the nations, never again great enough to rise above its neighbors.

¹⁶"Then Israel will no longer be tempted to trust in Egypt for help. Egypt's shattered condition will remind Israel of how sinful she was to trust Egypt in earlier days. Then Israel will know that I am the Sovereign LORD."

Nebuchadnezzar to Conquer Egypt

¹⁷On April 26, the first day of the new year,* during the twenty-seventh year of King Jehoiachin's captivity, this message came to me from the LORD: ¹⁸"Son of man, the army of King Nebuchadnezzar* of Babylon fought so hard against Tyre that the warriors' heads were rubbed bare and their shoulders were raw and blistered. Yet Nebuchadnezzar and his army won no plunder to compensate them for all their work. ¹⁹Therefore, this is what the Sovereign LORD says: I will give the land of Egypt to Nebuchadnezzar, king of Babylon. He will carry off its wealth, plundering everything it has so he can pay his army. ²⁰Yes, I have given him the land of Egypt as a reward for his work, says the Sovereign LORD, because he was working for me when he destroyed Tyre.

²¹"And the day will come when I will cause the ancient glory of Israel to revive,* and then, Ezekiel, your words will be respected. Then they will know that I am the LORD."

A Sad Day for Egypt

30 This is another message that came to me from the LORD: ²"Son of man, prophesy and give this message from the Sovereign LORD:

"Weep and wail
    for that day,
3 for the terrible day is almost here—
    the day of the LORD!
It is a day of clouds and gloom,
    a day of despair for the nations.
4 A sword will come against Egypt,
    and those who are slaughtered will
        cover the ground.
Its wealth will be carried away
    and its foundations destroyed.
The land of Ethiopia* will be ravished.
5   Ethiopia, Libya, Lydia, all Arabia,*
    and all their other allies
        will be destroyed in that war.

6 "For this is what the LORD says:
All of Egypt's allies will fall,
    and the pride of her power will end.
From Migdol to Aswan*
    they will be slaughtered by the sword,
    says the Sovereign LORD.
7 Egypt will be desolate,
    surrounded by desolate nations,
and its cities will be in ruins,
    surrounded by other ruined cities.
8 And the people of Egypt will know that
        I am the LORD
    when I have set Egypt on fire
    and destroyed all their allies.
9 At that time I will send swift messengers
        in ships
    to terrify the complacent Ethiopians.
Great panic will come upon them
    on that day of Egypt's certain
        destruction.
Watch for it!
    It is sure to come!

10 "For this is what the Sovereign LORD says:
By the power of King Nebuchadnezzar*
        of Babylon,
    I will destroy the hordes of Egypt.
11 He and his armies—the most ruthless
        of all—
    will be sent to demolish the land.
They will make war against Egypt
    until slaughtered Egyptians cover the
        ground.
12 I will dry up the Nile River
    and sell the land to wicked men.

I will destroy the land of Egypt and
        everything in it
    by the hands of foreigners.
    I, the LORD, have spoken!

13 "This is what the Sovereign LORD says:
I will smash the idols* of Egypt
    and the images at Memphis.*
There will be no rulers left in Egypt;
    terror will sweep the land.
14 I will destroy southern Egypt,*
    set fire to Zoan,
    and bring judgment against Thebes.*
15 I will pour out my fury on Pelusium,*
    the strongest fortress of Egypt,
and I will stamp out
    the hordes of Thebes.
16 Yes, I will set fire to all Egypt!
    Pelusium will be racked with pain;
Thebes will be torn apart;
    Memphis will live in constant terror.
17 The young men of Heliopolis and
        Bubastis* will die in battle,
    and the women* will be taken away
        as slaves.
18 When I come to break the proud strength
        of Egypt,
    it will be a dark day for Tahpanhes, too.
A dark cloud will cover Tahpanhes,
    and its daughters will be led away as
        captives.
19 And so I will greatly punish Egypt,
    and they will know that I am the LORD."

The Broken Arms of Pharaoh

20 On April 29,* during the eleventh year of King
Jehoiachin's captivity, this message came to me
from the LORD: 21 "Son of man, I have broken
the arm of Pharaoh, the king of Egypt. His arm
has not been put in a cast so that it may heal.
Neither has it been bound up with a splint
to make it strong enough to hold a sword.
22 Therefore, this is what the Sovereign LORD
says: I am the enemy of Pharaoh, the king of
Egypt! I will break both of his arms—the good
arm along with the broken one—and I will
make his sword clatter to the ground. 23 I will
scatter the Egyptians to many lands throughout the world. 24 I will strengthen the arms of
Babylon's king and put my sword in his hand.
But I will break the arms of Pharaoh, king of

30:4 Hebrew *Cush;* similarly in 30:9.   30:5 Hebrew *Cush, Put, Lud, all Arabia, Cub. Cub* is otherwise unknown and
may be another spelling for *Lub* (Libya).   30:6 Hebrew *to Syene.*   30:10 Hebrew *Nebuchadrezzar,* a variant spelling of
Nebuchadnezzar.   30:13a The Hebrew term (literally *round things*) probably alludes to dung.   30:13b Hebrew *Noph;* also
in 30:16.   30:14a Hebrew *Pathros.*   30:14b Hebrew *No;* also in 30:15, 16.   30:15 Hebrew *Sin;* also in 30:16.   30:17a Hebrew
of Awen and Pi-beseth.   30:17b Or *and her cities.*   30:20 Hebrew *On the seventh day of the first month,* of the ancient Hebrew lunar
calendar. This event occurred on April 29, 587 B.C.; also see note on 1:1.

Egypt, and he will lie there mortally wounded, groaning in pain. 25I will strengthen the arms of the king of Babylon, while the arms of Pharaoh fall useless to his sides. And when I put my sword in the hand of Babylon's king and he brings it against the land of Egypt, Egypt will know that I am the LORD. 26I will scatter the Egyptians among the nations, dispersing them throughout the earth. Then they will know that I am the LORD."

Egypt Compared to Fallen Assyria

31 On June 21,* during the eleventh year of King Jehoiachin's captivity, this message came to me from the LORD: 2"Son of man, give this message to Pharaoh, king of Egypt, and all his hordes:

"To whom would you compare your
     greatness?
3 You are like mighty Assyria,
     which was once like a cedar of Lebanon,
with beautiful branches that cast deep
          forest shade
     and with its top high among the clouds.
4 Deep springs watered it
     and helped it to grow tall and luxuriant.
The water flowed around it like a river,
     streaming to all the trees nearby.
5 This great tree towered high,
     higher than all the other trees around it.
It prospered and grew long thick branches
     because of all the water at its roots.
6 The birds nested in its branches,
     and in its shade all the wild animals
          gave birth.
All the great nations of the world
     lived in its shadow.
7 It was strong and beautiful,
     with wide-spreading branches,
for its roots went deep
     into abundant water.
8 No other cedar in the garden of God
     could rival it.
No cypress had branches to equal it;
     no plane tree had boughs to compare.
No tree in the garden of God
     came close to it in beauty.
9 Because I made this tree so beautiful,
     and gave it such magnificent foliage,
it was the envy of all the other trees of Eden,
     the garden of God.

10"Therefore, this is what the Sovereign LORD says: Because Egypt* became proud and arrogant, and because it set itself so high above the others, with its top reaching to the clouds, 11I will hand it over to a mighty nation that will destroy it as its wickedness deserves. I have already discarded it. 12A foreign army—the terror of the nations—has cut it down and left it fallen on the ground. Its branches are scattered across the mountains and valleys and ravines of the land. All those who lived in its shadow have gone away and left it lying there.

13 "The birds roost on its fallen trunk,
     and the wild animals lie among its
          branches.
14 Let the tree of no other nation
     proudly exult in its own prosperity,
though it be higher than the clouds
     and it be watered from the depths.
For all are doomed to die,
     to go down to the depths of the earth.
They will land in the pit
     along with everyone else on earth.

15"This is what the Sovereign LORD says: When Assyria went down to the grave,* I made the deep springs mourn. I stopped its rivers and dried up its abundant water. I clothed Lebanon in black and caused the trees of the field to wilt. 16I made the nations shake with fear at the sound of its fall, for I sent it down to the grave with all the others who descend to the pit. And all the other proud trees of Eden, the most beautiful and the best of Lebanon, the ones whose roots went deep into the water, took comfort to find it there with them in the depths of the earth. 17Its allies, too, were all destroyed and had passed away. They had gone down to the grave—all those nations that had lived in its shade.

18"O Egypt, to which of the trees of Eden will you compare your strength and glory? You, too, will be brought down to the depths with all these other nations. You will lie there among the outcasts* who have died by the sword. This will be the fate of Pharaoh and all his hordes. I, the Sovereign LORD, have spoken!"

A Warning for Pharaoh

32 On March 3,* during the twelfth year of King Jehoiachin's captivity, this

---

31:1 Hebrew *On the first day of the third month,* of the ancient Hebrew lunar calendar. This event occurred on June 21, 587 B.C.; also see note on 1:1.   31:10 Hebrew *you.*   31:15 Hebrew *to Sheol;* also in 31:16, 17.   31:18 Hebrew *among the uncircumcised.*
32:1 Hebrew *On the first day of the twelfth month,* of the ancient Hebrew lunar calendar. This event occurred on March 3, 585 B.C.; also see note on 1:1.

message came to me from the LORD: ²"Son of man, mourn for Pharaoh, king of Egypt, and give him this message:

"You think of yourself as a strong young
   lion among the nations,
   but you are really just a sea monster,
heaving around in your own rivers,
   stirring up mud with your feet.
³ Therefore, this is what the Sovereign LORD
   says:
I will send many people
   to catch you in my net
   and haul you out of the water.
⁴ I will leave you stranded on the land to die.
   All the birds of the heavens will land on
      you,
and the wild animals of the whole earth
   will gorge themselves on you.
⁵ I will scatter your flesh on the hills
   and fill the valleys with your bones.
⁶ I will drench the earth with your gushing
      blood
   all the way to the mountains,
   filling the ravines to the brim.
⁷ When I blot you out,
   I will veil the heavens and darken the
      stars.
I will cover the sun with a cloud,
   and the moon will not give you its light.
⁸ I will darken the bright stars overhead
   and cover your land in darkness.
   I, the Sovereign LORD, have spoken!

⁹"I will disturb many hearts when I bring news of your downfall to distant nations you have never seen. ¹⁰Yes, I will shock many lands, and their kings will be terrified at your fate. They will shudder in fear for their lives as I brandish my sword before them on the day of your fall. ¹¹For this is what the Sovereign LORD says:

"The sword of the king of Babylon
   will come against you.
¹² I will destroy your hordes with the swords
      of mighty warriors—
   the terror of the nations.
They will shatter the pride of Egypt,
   and all its hordes will be destroyed.
¹³ I will destroy all your flocks and herds
   that graze beside the streams.

Never again will people or animals
   muddy those waters with their feet.
¹⁴ Then I will let the waters of Egypt become
      calm again,
   and they will flow as smoothly as olive
      oil,
   says the Sovereign LORD.
¹⁵ And when I destroy Egypt
   and strip you of everything you own
   and strike down all your people,
   then you will know that I am the
      LORD.
¹⁶ Yes, this is the funeral song
   they will sing for Egypt.
Let all the nations mourn.
   Let them mourn for Egypt and its
      hordes.
   I, the Sovereign LORD, have spoken!"

Egypt Falls into the Pit

¹⁷On March 17,* during the twelfth year, another message came to me from the LORD: ¹⁸"Son of man, weep for the hordes of Egypt and for the other mighty nations.* For I will send them down to the world below in company with those who descend to the pit. ¹⁹Say to them,

'O Egypt, are you lovelier than the other
      nations?
No! So go down to the pit and lie there
      among the outcasts.*'

²⁰The Egyptians will fall with the many who have died by the sword, for the sword is drawn against them. Egypt and its hordes will be dragged away to their judgment. ²¹Down in the grave* mighty leaders will mockingly welcome Egypt and its allies, saying, 'They have come down; they lie among the outcasts, hordes slaughtered by the sword.'

²²"Assyria lies there surrounded by the graves of its army, those who were slaughtered by the sword. ²³Their graves are in the depths of the pit, and they are surrounded by their allies. They struck terror in the hearts of people everywhere, but now they have been slaughtered by the sword.

²⁴"Elam lies there surrounded by the graves of all its hordes, those who were slaughtered by the sword. They struck terror in the hearts of people everywhere, but now they have

32:17 Hebrew *On the fifteenth day of the month,* presumably in the twelfth month of the ancient Hebrew lunar calendar (see 32:1). This would put this message at the end of King Jehoiachin's twelfth year of captivity, on March 17, 585 B.C.; also see note on 1:1. Greek version reads *On the fifteenth day of the first month,* which would put this message on April 27, 586 B.C., at the beginning of Jehoiachin's twelfth year. 32:18 The meaning of the Hebrew is uncertain. 32:19 Hebrew *the uncircumcised;* also in 32:21, 24, 25, 26, 28, 29, 30, 32. 32:21 Hebrew *in Sheol.*

descended as outcasts to the world below. Now they lie in the pit and share the shame of those who have gone before them. 25They have a resting place among the slaughtered, surrounded by the graves of all their hordes. Yes, they terrorized the nations while they lived, but now they lie in shame with others in the pit, all of them outcasts, slaughtered by the sword.

26"Meshech and Tubal are there, surrounded by the graves of all their hordes. They once struck terror in the hearts of people everywhere. But now they are outcasts, all slaughtered by the sword. 27They are not buried in honor like their fallen heroes, who went down to the grave* with their weapons—their shields covering their bodies* and their swords beneath their heads. Their guilt rests upon them because they brought terror to everyone while they were still alive.

28"You too, Egypt, will lie crushed and broken among the outcasts, all slaughtered by the sword.

29"Edom is there with its kings and princes. Mighty as they were, they also lie among those slaughtered by the sword, with the outcasts who have gone down to the pit.

30"All the princes of the north and the Sidonians are there with others who have died. Once a terror, they have been put to shame. They lie there as outcasts with others who were slaughtered by the sword. They share the shame of all who have descended to the pit.

31"When Pharaoh and his entire army arrive, he will take comfort that he is not alone in having his hordes killed, says the Sovereign LORD. 32Although I have caused his terror to fall upon all the living, Pharaoh and his hordes will lie there among the outcasts who were slaughtered by the sword. I, the Sovereign LORD, have spoken!"

Ezekiel as Israel's Watchman

33 Once again a message came to me from the LORD: 2"Son of man, give your people this message: 'When I bring an army against a country, the people of that land choose one of their own to be a watchman. 3When the watchman sees the enemy coming, he sounds the alarm to warn the people. 4Then if those who hear the alarm refuse to take action, it is their own fault if they die. 5They heard the alarm but ignored it, so the responsibility is theirs. If they had listened to the warning, they could have saved their lives. 6But if the watchman sees the enemy coming and

doesn't sound the alarm to warn the people, he is responsible for their captivity. They will die in their sins, but I will hold the watchman responsible for their deaths.'

7"Now, son of man, I am making you a watchman for the people of Israel. Therefore, listen to what I say and warn them for me. 8If I announce that some wicked people are sure to die and you fail to tell them to change their ways, then they will die in their sins, and I will hold you responsible for their deaths. 9But if you warn them to repent and they don't repent, they will die in their sins, but you will have saved yourself.

The Watchman's Message

10"Son of man, give the people of Israel this message: You are saying, 'Our sins are heavy upon us; we are wasting away! How can we survive?' 11As surely as I live, says the Sovereign LORD, I take no pleasure in the death of wicked people. I only want them to turn from their wicked ways so they can live. Turn! Turn from your wickedness, O people of Israel! Why should you die?

12"Son of man, give your people this message: The righteous behavior of righteous people will not save them if they turn to sin, nor will the wicked behavior of wicked people destroy them if they repent and turn from their sins. 13When I tell righteous people that they will live, but then they sin, expecting their past righteousness to save them, then none of their righteous acts will be remembered. I will destroy them for their sins. 14And suppose I tell some wicked people that they will surely die, but then they turn from their sins and do what is just and right. 15For instance, they might give back a debtor's security, return what they have stolen, and obey my life-giving laws, no longer doing what is evil. If they do this, then they will surely live and not die. 16None of their past sins will be brought up again, for they have done what is just and right, and they will surely live.

17"Your people are saying, 'The Lord isn't doing what's right,' but it is they who are not doing what's right. 18For again I say, when righteous people turn away from their righteous behavior and turn to evil, they will die. 19But if wicked people turn from their wickedness and do what is just and right, they will live. 20O people of Israel, you are saying, 'The Lord isn't doing what's right.' But I judge each of you according to your deeds."

32:27a Hebrew *to Sheol*.   32:27b The meaning of the Hebrew is uncertain.

Explanation of Jerusalem's Fall

²¹On January 8,* during the twelfth year of our captivity, a survivor from Jerusalem came to me and said, "The city has fallen!" ²²The previous evening the LORD had taken hold of me and given me back my voice. So I was able to speak when this man arrived the next morning.

²³Then this message came to me from the LORD: ²⁴"Son of man, the scattered remnants of Israel living among the ruined cities keep saying, 'Abraham was only one man, yet he gained possession of the entire land. We are many; surely the land has been given to us as a possession.' ²⁵So tell these people, 'This is what the Sovereign LORD says: You eat meat with blood in it, you worship idols,* and you murder the innocent. Do you really think the land should be yours? ²⁶Murderers! Idolaters! Adulterers! Should the land belong to you?'

²⁷"Say to them, 'This is what the Sovereign LORD says: As surely as I live, those living in the ruins will die by the sword. And I will send wild animals to eat those living in the open fields. Those hiding in the forts and caves will die of disease. ²⁸I will completely destroy the land and demolish her pride. Her arrogant power will come to an end. The mountains of Israel will be so desolate that no one will even travel through them. ²⁹When I have completely destroyed the land because of their detestable sins, then they will know that I am the LORD.'

³⁰"Son of man, your people talk about you in their houses and whisper about you at the doors. They say to each other, 'Come on, let's go hear the prophet tell us what the LORD is saying!' ³¹So my people come pretending to be sincere and sit before you. They listen to your words, but they have no intention of doing what you say. Their mouths are full of lustful words, and their hearts seek only after money. ³²You are very entertaining to them, like someone who sings love songs with a beautiful voice or plays fine music on an instrument. They hear what you say, but they don't act on it! ³³But when all these terrible things happen to them—as they certainly will—then they will know a prophet has been among them."

The Shepherds of Israel

34 Then this message came to me from the LORD: ²"Son of man, prophesy against the shepherds, the leaders of Israel. Give them this message from the Sovereign LORD: What sorrow awaits you shepherds who feed yourselves instead of your flocks. Shouldn't shepherds feed their sheep? ³You drink the milk, wear the wool, and butcher the best animals, but you let your flocks starve. ⁴You have not taken care of the weak. You have not tended the sick or bound up the injured. You have not gone looking for those who have wandered away and are lost. Instead, you have ruled them with harshness and cruelty. ⁵So my sheep have been scattered without a shepherd, and they are easy prey for any wild animal. ⁶They have wandered through all the mountains and all the hills, across the face of the earth, yet no one has gone to search for them.

⁷"Therefore, you shepherds, hear the word of the LORD: ⁸As surely as I live, says the Sovereign LORD, you abandoned my flock and left them to be attacked by every wild animal. And though you were my shepherds, you didn't search for my sheep when they were lost. You took care of yourselves and left the sheep to starve. ⁹Therefore, you shepherds, hear the word of the LORD. ¹⁰This is what the Sovereign LORD says: I now consider these shepherds my enemies, and I will hold them responsible for what has happened to my flock. I will take away their right to feed the flock, and I will stop them from feeding themselves. I will rescue my flock from their mouths; the sheep will no longer be their prey.

The Good Shepherd

¹¹"For this is what the Sovereign LORD says: I myself will search and find my sheep. ¹²I will be like a shepherd looking for his scattered flock. I will find my sheep and rescue them from all the places where they were scattered on that dark and cloudy day. ¹³I will bring them back home to their own land of Israel from among the peoples and nations. I will feed them on the mountains of Israel and by the rivers and in all the places where people live. ¹⁴Yes, I will give them good pastureland on the high hills of Israel. There they will lie down in pleasant places and feed in the lush pastures of the hills. ¹⁵I myself will tend my sheep and give them a place to lie down in peace, says the Sovereign LORD. ¹⁶I will search for my lost ones who strayed away, and I will bring them safely home again. I will bandage the injured and strengthen the weak. But I will destroy those who are fat and powerful. I will feed them, yes—feed them justice!

¹⁷"And as for you, my flock, this is what the

33:21 Hebrew *On the fifth day of the tenth month,* of the ancient Hebrew lunar calendar. This event occurred on January 8, 585 B.C.; also see note on 1:1.   33:25 The Hebrew term (literally *round things*) probably alludes to dung.

Sovereign LORD says to his people: I will judge between one animal of the flock and another, separating the sheep from the goats. ¹⁸Isn't it enough for you to keep the best of the pastures for yourselves? Must you also trample down the rest? Isn't it enough for you to drink clear water for yourselves? Must you also muddy the rest with your feet? ¹⁹Why must my flock eat what you have trampled down and drink water you have fouled?

²⁰"Therefore, this is what the Sovereign LORD says: I will surely judge between the fat sheep and the scrawny sheep. ²¹For you fat sheep pushed and butted and crowded my sick and hungry flock until you scattered them to distant lands. ²²So I will rescue my flock, and they will no longer be abused. I will judge between one animal of the flock and another. ²³And I will set over them one shepherd, my servant David. He will feed them and be a shepherd to them. ²⁴And I, the LORD, will be their God, and my servant David will be a prince among my people. I, the LORD, have spoken!

The LORD's Covenant of Peace

²⁵"I will make a covenant of peace with my people and drive away the dangerous animals from the land. Then they will be able to camp safely in the wildest places and sleep in the woods without fear. ²⁶I will bless my people and their homes around my holy hill. And in the proper season I will send the showers they need. There will be showers of blessing. ²⁷The orchards and fields of my people will yield bumper crops, and everyone will live in safety. When I have broken their chains of slavery and rescued them from those who enslaved them, then they will know that I am the LORD. ²⁸They will no longer be prey for other nations, and wild animals will no longer devour them. They will live in safety, and no one will frighten them.

²⁹"And I will make their land famous for its crops, so my people will never again suffer from famines or the insults of foreign nations. ³⁰In this way, they will know that I, the LORD their God, am with them. And they will know that they, the people of Israel, are my people, says the Sovereign LORD. ³¹You are my flock, the sheep of my pasture. You are my people, and I am your God. I, the Sovereign LORD, have spoken!"

A Message for Edom

35 Again a message came to me from the LORD: ²"Son of man, turn and face Mount Seir, and prophesy against its people.

³Give them this message from the Sovereign LORD:

"I am your enemy, O Mount Seir,
    and I will raise my fist against you
    to destroy you completely.
⁴ I will demolish your cities
    and make you desolate.
Then you will know that I am the LORD.

⁵"Your eternal hatred for the people of Israel led you to butcher them when they were helpless, when I had already punished them for all their sins. ⁶As surely as I live, says the Sovereign LORD, since you show no distaste for blood, I will give you a bloodbath of your own. Your turn has come! ⁷I will make Mount Seir utterly desolate, killing off all who try to escape and any who return. ⁸I will fill your mountains with the dead. Your hills, your valleys, and your ravines will be filled with people slaughtered by the sword. ⁹I will make you desolate forever. Your cities will never be rebuilt. Then you will know that I am the LORD.

¹⁰"For you said, 'The lands of Israel and Judah will be ours. We will take possession of them. What do we care that the LORD is there!' ¹¹Therefore, as surely as I live, says the Sovereign LORD, I will pay back your angry deeds with my own. I will punish you for all your acts of anger, envy, and hatred. And I will make myself known to Israel* by what I do to you. ¹²Then you will know that I, the LORD, have heard every contemptuous word you spoke against the mountains of Israel. For you said, 'They are desolate; they have been given to us as food to eat!' ¹³In saying that, you boasted proudly against me, and I have heard it all!

¹⁴"This is what the Sovereign LORD says: The whole world will rejoice when I make you desolate. ¹⁵You rejoiced at the desolation of Israel's territory. Now I will rejoice at yours! You will be wiped out, you people of Mount Seir and all who live in Edom! Then you will know that I am the LORD.

Restoration for Israel

36 "Son of man, prophesy to Israel's mountains. Give them this message: O mountains of Israel, hear the word of the LORD! ²This is what the Sovereign LORD says: Your enemies have taunted you, saying, 'Aha! Now the ancient heights belong to us!' ³Therefore, son of man, give the mountains of Israel this message from the Sovereign LORD: Your enemies have

35:11 Hebrew *to them*; Greek version reads *to you.*

attacked you from all directions, making you the property of many nations and the object of much mocking and slander. ⁴Therefore, O mountains of Israel, hear the word of the Sovereign LORD. He speaks to the hills and mountains, ravines and valleys, and to ruined wastes and long-deserted cities that have been destroyed and mocked by the surrounding nations. ⁵This is what the Sovereign LORD says: My jealous anger burns against these nations, especially Edom, because they have shown utter contempt for me by gleefully taking my land for themselves as plunder.

⁶"Therefore, prophesy to the hills and mountains, the ravines and valleys of Israel. This is what the Sovereign LORD says: I am furious that you have suffered shame before the surrounding nations. ⁷Therefore, this is what the Sovereign LORD says: I have taken a solemn oath that those nations will soon have their own shame to endure.

⁸"But the mountains of Israel will produce heavy crops of fruit for my people—for they will be coming home again soon! ⁹See, I care about you, and I will pay attention to you. Your ground will be plowed and your crops planted. ¹⁰I will greatly increase the population of Israel, and the ruined cities will be rebuilt and filled with people. ¹¹I will increase not only the people, but also your animals. O mountains of Israel, I will bring people to live on you once again. I will make you even more prosperous than you were before. Then you will know that I am the LORD. ¹²I will cause my people to walk on you once again, and you will be their territory. You will never again rob them of their children.

¹³"This is what the Sovereign LORD says: The other nations taunt you, saying, 'Israel is a land that devours its own people and robs them of their children!' ¹⁴But you will never again devour your people or rob them of their children, says the Sovereign LORD. ¹⁵I will not let you hear those other nations insult you, and you will no longer be mocked by them. You will not be a land that causes its nation to fall, says the Sovereign LORD."

¹⁶Then this further message came to me from the LORD: ¹⁷"Son of man, when the people of Israel were living in their own land, they defiled it by the evil way they lived. To me their conduct was as unclean as a woman's menstrual cloth. ¹⁸They polluted the land with murder and the worship of idols,* so I poured out my fury on them. ¹⁹I scattered them to many lands to punish them for the evil way they had lived. ²⁰But when they were scattered among the nations, they brought shame on my holy name. For the nations said, 'These are the people of the LORD, but he couldn't keep them safe in his own land!' ²¹Then I was concerned for my holy name, on which my people brought shame among the nations.

²²"Therefore, give the people of Israel this message from the Sovereign LORD: I am bringing you back, but not because you deserve it. I am doing it to protect my holy name, on which you brought shame while you were scattered among the nations. ²³I will show how holy my great name is—the name on which you brought shame among the nations. And when I reveal my holiness through you before their very eyes, says the Sovereign LORD, then the nations will know that I am the LORD. ²⁴For I will gather you up from all the nations and bring you home again to your land.

²⁵"Then I will sprinkle clean water on you, and you will be clean. Your filth will be washed away, and you will no longer worship idols. ²⁶And I will give you a new heart, and I will put a new spirit in you. I will take out your stony, stubborn heart and give you a tender, responsive heart.* ²⁷And I will put my Spirit in you so that you will follow my decrees and be careful to obey my regulations.

²⁸"And you will live in Israel, the land I gave your ancestors long ago. You will be my people, and I will be your God. ²⁹I will cleanse you of your filthy behavior. I will give you good crops of grain, and I will send no more famines on the land. ³⁰I will give you great harvests from your fruit trees and fields, and never again will the surrounding nations be able to scoff at your land for its famines. ³¹Then you will remember your past sins and despise yourselves for all the detestable things you did. ³²But remember, says the Sovereign LORD, I am not doing this because you deserve it. O my people of Israel, you should be utterly ashamed of all you have done!

³³"This is what the Sovereign LORD says: When I cleanse you from your sins, I will repopulate your cities, and the ruins will be rebuilt. ³⁴The fields that used to lie empty and desolate in plain view of everyone will again be farmed. ³⁵And when I bring you back, people will say, 'This former wasteland is now like the Garden of Eden! The abandoned and ruined cities now have strong walls and are filled with people!' ³⁶Then the surrounding nations that survive will know that I, the LORD, have rebuilt

36:18 The Hebrew term (literally *round things*) probably alludes to dung; also in 36:25.   36:26 Hebrew *a heart of flesh*.

the ruins and replanted the wasteland. For I, the LORD, have spoken, and I will do what I say.

37"This is what the Sovereign LORD says: I am ready to hear Israel's prayers and to increase their numbers like a flock. 38They will be as numerous as the sacred flocks that fill Jerusalem's streets at the time of her festivals. The ruined cities will be crowded with people once more, and everyone will know that I am the LORD."

A Valley of Dry Bones

37 The LORD took hold of me, and I was carried away by the Spirit of the LORD to a valley filled with bones. 2He led me all around among the bones that covered the valley floor. They were scattered everywhere across the ground and were completely dried out. 3Then he asked me, "Son of man, can these bones become living people again?"

"O Sovereign LORD," I replied, "you alone know the answer to that."

4Then he said to me, "Speak a prophetic message to these bones and say, 'Dry bones, listen to the word of the LORD! 5This is what the Sovereign LORD says: Look! I am going to put breath into you and make you live again! 6I will put flesh and muscles on you and cover you with skin. I will put breath into you, and you will come to life. Then you will know that I am the LORD.'"

7So I spoke this message, just as he told me. Suddenly as I spoke, there was a rattling noise all across the valley. The bones of each body came together and attached themselves as complete skeletons. 8Then as I watched, muscles and flesh formed over the bones. Then skin formed to cover their bodies, but they still had no breath in them.

9Then he said to me, "Speak a prophetic message to the winds, son of man. Speak a prophetic message and say, 'This is what the Sovereign LORD says: Come, O breath, from the four winds! Breathe into these dead bodies so they may live again.'"

10So I spoke the message as he commanded me, and breath came into their bodies. They all came to life and stood up on their feet—a great army.

11Then he said to me, "Son of man, these bones represent the people of Israel. They are saying, 'We have become old, dry bones— all hope is gone. Our nation is finished.'

12Therefore, prophesy to them and say, 'This is what the Sovereign LORD says: O my people, I will open your graves of exile and cause you to rise again. Then I will bring you back to the land of Israel. 13When this happens, O my people, you will know that I am the LORD. 14I will put my Spirit in you, and you will live again and return home to your own land. Then you will know that I, the LORD, have spoken, and I have done what I said. Yes, the LORD has spoken!'"

Reunion of Israel and Judah

15Again a message came to me from the LORD: 16"Son of man, take a piece of wood and carve on it these words: 'This represents Judah and its allied tribes.' Then take another piece and carve these words on it: 'This represents Ephraim and the northern tribes of Israel.'* 17Now hold them together in your hand as if they were one piece of wood. 18When your people ask you what your actions mean, 19say to them, 'This is what the Sovereign LORD says: I will take Ephraim and the northern tribes and join them to Judah. I will make them one piece of wood in my hand.'

20"Then hold out the pieces of wood you have inscribed, so the people can see them. 21And give them this message from the Sovereign LORD: I will gather the people of Israel from among the nations. I will bring them home to their own land from the places where they have been scattered. 22I will unify them into one nation on the mountains of Israel. One king will rule them all; no longer will they be divided into two nations or into two kingdoms. 23They will never again pollute themselves with their idols* and vile images and rebellion, for I will save them from their sinful apostasy.* I will cleanse them. Then they will truly be my people, and I will be their God.

24"My servant David will be their king, and they will have only one shepherd. They will obey my regulations and be careful to keep my decrees. 25They will live in the land I gave my servant Jacob, the land where their ancestors lived. They and their children and their grandchildren after them will live there forever, generation after generation. And my servant David will be their prince forever. 26And I will make a covenant of peace with them, an everlasting covenant. I will give them their land and increase their numbers,* and I will put my

---

37:16 Hebrew *This is Ephraim's wood, representing Joseph and all the house of Israel;* similarly in 37:19.   37:23a The Hebrew term (literally *round things*) probably alludes to dung.   37:23b As in many Hebrew manuscripts and Greek version; Masoretic Text reads *from all their dwelling places where they sinned.*   37:26 Hebrew reads *I will give them and increase their numbers;* Greek version lacks the entire phrase.

Temple among them forever. 27I will make my home among them. I will be their God, and they will be my people. 28And when my Temple is among them forever, the nations will know that I am the LORD, who makes Israel holy."

A Message for Gog

38 This is another message that came to me from the LORD: 2"Son of man, turn and face Gog of the land of Magog, the prince who rules over the nations of Meshech and Tubal, and prophesy against him. 3Give him this message from the Sovereign LORD: Gog, I am your enemy! 4I will turn you around and put hooks in your jaws to lead you out with your whole army—your horses and charioteers in full armor and a great horde armed with shields and swords. 5Persia, Ethiopia, and Libya* will join you, too, with all their weapons. 6Gomer and all its armies will also join you, along with the armies of Beth-togarmah from the distant north, and many others.

7"Get ready; be prepared! Keep all the armies around you mobilized, and take command of them. 8A long time from now you will be called into action. In the distant future you will swoop down on the land of Israel, which will be enjoying peace after recovering from war and after its people have returned from many lands to the mountains of Israel. 9You and all your allies—a vast and awesome army—will roll down on them like a storm and cover the land like a cloud.

10"This is what the Sovereign LORD says: At that time evil thoughts will come to your mind, and you will devise a wicked scheme. 11You will say, 'Israel is an unprotected land filled with unwalled villages! I will march against her and destroy these people who live in such confidence! 12I will go to those formerly desolate cities that are now filled with people who have returned from exile in many nations. I will capture vast amounts of plunder, for the people are rich with livestock and other possessions now. They think the whole world revolves around them!' 13But Sheba and Dedan and the merchants of Tarshish will ask, 'Do you really think the armies you have gathered can rob them of silver and gold? Do you think you can drive away their livestock and seize their goods and carry off plunder?'

14"Therefore, son of man, prophesy against Gog. Give him this message from the Sovereign LORD: When my people are living in peace in their land, then you will rouse yourself.* 15You

will come from your homeland in the distant north with your vast cavalry and your mighty army, 16and you will attack my people Israel, covering their land like a cloud. At that time in the distant future, I will bring you against my land as everyone watches, and my holiness will be displayed by what happens to you, Gog. Then all the nations will know that I am the LORD.

17"This is what the Sovereign LORD asks: Are you the one I was talking about long ago, when I announced through Israel's prophets that in the future I would bring you against my people? 18But this is what the Sovereign LORD says: When Gog invades the land of Israel, my fury will boil over! 19In my jealousy and blazing anger, I promise a mighty shaking in the land of Israel on that day. 20All living things—the fish in the sea, the birds of the sky, the animals of the field, the small animals that scurry along the ground, and all the people on earth—will quake in terror at my presence. Mountains will be thrown down; cliffs will crumble; walls will fall to the earth. 21I will summon the sword against you on all the hills of Israel, says the Sovereign LORD. Your men will turn their swords against each other. 22I will punish you and your armies with disease and bloodshed; I will send torrential rain, hailstones, fire, and burning sulfur! 23In this way, I will show my greatness and holiness, and I will make myself known to all the nations of the world. Then they will know that I am the LORD.

The Slaughter of Gog's Hordes

39 "Son of man, prophesy against Gog. Give him this message from the Sovereign LORD: I am your enemy, O Gog, ruler of the nations of Meshech and Tubal. 2I will turn you around and drive you toward the mountains of Israel, bringing you from the distant north. 3I will knock the bow from your left hand and the arrows from your right hand, and I will leave you helpless. 4You and your army and your allies will all die on the mountains. I will feed you to the vultures and wild animals. 5You will fall in the open fields, for I have spoken, says the Sovereign LORD. 6And I will rain down fire on Magog and on all your allies who live safely on the coasts. Then they will know that I am the LORD.

7"In this way, I will make known my holy name among my people of Israel. I will not let anyone bring shame on it. And the nations, too, will know that I am the LORD, the Holy One of Israel. 8That day of judgment will come, says

38:5 Hebrew *Paras, Cush, and Put.*   38:14 As in Greek version; Hebrew reads *then you will know.*

the Sovereign LORD. Everything will happen just as I have declared it.

9"Then the people in the towns of Israel will go out and pick up your small and large shields, bows and arrows, javelins and spears, and they will use them for fuel. There will be enough to last them seven years! 10They won't need to cut wood from the fields or forests, for these weapons will give them all the fuel they need. They will plunder those who planned to plunder them, and they will rob those who planned to rob them, says the Sovereign LORD.

11"And I will make a vast graveyard for Gog and his hordes in the Valley of the Travelers, east of the Dead Sea.* It will block the way of those who travel there, and they will change the name of the place to the Valley of Gog's Hordes. 12It will take seven months for the people of Israel to bury the bodies and cleanse the land. 13Everyone in Israel will help, for it will be a glorious victory for Israel when I demonstrate my glory on that day, says the Sovereign LORD.

14"After seven months, teams of men will be appointed to search the land for skeletons to bury, so the land will be made clean again. 15Whenever bones are found, a marker will be set up so the burial crews will take them to be buried in the Valley of Gog's Hordes. 16(There will be a town there named Hamonah, which means 'horde.') And so the land will finally be cleansed.

17"And now, son of man, this is what the Sovereign LORD says: Call all the birds and wild animals. Say to them: Gather together for my great sacrificial feast. Come from far and near to the mountains of Israel, and there eat flesh and drink blood! 18Eat the flesh of mighty men and drink the blood of princes as though they were rams, lambs, goats, and bulls—all fattened animals from Bashan! 19Gorge yourselves with flesh until you are glutted; drink blood until you are drunk. This is the sacrificial feast I have prepared for you. 20Feast at my banquet table—feast on horses and charioteers, on mighty men and all kinds of valiant warriors, says the Sovereign LORD.

21"In this way, I will demonstrate my glory to the nations. Everyone will see the punishment I have inflicted on them and the power of my fist when I strike. 22And from that time on the people of Israel will know that I am the LORD

their God. 23The nations will then know why Israel was sent away to exile—it was punishment for sin, for they were unfaithful to their God. Therefore, I turned away from them and let their enemies destroy them. 24I turned my face away and punished them because of their defilement and their sins.

Restoration for God's People

25"So now, this is what the Sovereign LORD says: I will end the captivity of my people*; I will have mercy on all Israel, for I jealously guard my holy reputation! 26They will accept responsibility for* their past shame and unfaithfulness after they come home to live in peace in their own land, with no one to bother them. 27When I bring them home from the lands of their enemies, I will display my holiness among them for all the nations to see. 28Then my people will know that I am the LORD their God, because I sent them away to exile and brought them home again. I will leave none of my people behind. 29And I will never again turn my face from them, for I will pour out my Spirit upon the people of Israel. I, the Sovereign LORD, have spoken!"

The New Temple Area

40 On April 28,* during the twenty-fifth year of our captivity—fourteen years after the fall of Jerusalem—the LORD took hold of me. 2In a vision from God he took me to the land of Israel and set me down on a very high mountain. From there I could see toward the south what appeared to be a city. 3As he brought me nearer, I saw a man whose face shone like bronze standing beside a gateway entrance. He was holding in his hand a linen measuring cord and a measuring rod.

4He said to me, "Son of man, watch and listen. Pay close attention to everything I show you. You have been brought here so I can show you many things. Then you will return to the people of Israel and tell them everything you have seen."

The East Gateway

5I could see a wall completely surrounding the Temple area. The man took a measuring rod that was 10½ feet* long and measured the wall, and the wall was 10½ feet* thick and 10½ feet high.

39:11 Hebrew *the sea*.   39:25 Hebrew *of Jacob*.   39:26 A few Hebrew manuscripts read *They will forget*.   40:1 Hebrew *At the beginning of the year, on the tenth day of the month*, of the ancient Hebrew lunar calendar. This event occurred on April 28, 573 B.C.; also see note on 1:1.   40:5a Hebrew *6 long cubits* [3.2 meters], *each being a cubit* [18 inches or 45 centimeters] *and a handbreadth* [3 inches or 8 centimeters] *in length*.   40:5b Hebrew *1 rod* [3.2 meters]; also in 40:5c, 7.

⁶Then he went over to the eastern gateway. He climbed the steps and measured the threshold of the gateway; it was 10½ feet front to back.* ⁷There were guard alcoves on each side built into the gateway passage. Each of these alcoves was 10½ feet square, with a distance between them of 8¾ feet* along the passage wall. The gateway's inner threshold, which led to the entry room at the inner end of the gateway passage, was 10½ feet front to back. ⁸He also measured the entry room of the gateway.* ⁹It was 14 feet* across, with supporting columns 3½ feet* thick. This entry room was at the inner end of the gateway structure, facing toward the Temple.

¹⁰There were three guard alcoves on each side of the gateway passage. Each had the same measurements, and the dividing walls separating them were also identical. ¹¹The man measured the gateway entrance, which was 17½ feet* wide at the opening and 22¾ feet* wide in the gateway passage. ¹²In front of each of the guard alcoves was a 21-inch* curb. The alcoves themselves were 10½ feet* on each side.

¹³Then he measured the entire width of the gateway, measuring the distance between the back walls of facing guard alcoves; this distance was 43¾ feet.* ¹⁴He measured the dividing walls all along the inside of the gateway up to the entry room of the gateway; this distance was 105 feet.* ¹⁵The full length of the gateway passage was 87½ feet* from one end to the other. ¹⁶There were recessed windows that narrowed inward through the walls of the guard alcoves and their dividing walls. There were also windows in the entry room. The surfaces of the dividing walls were decorated with carved palm trees.

The Outer Courtyard

¹⁷Then the man brought me through the gateway into the outer courtyard of the Temple. A stone pavement ran along the walls of the courtyard, and thirty rooms were built against the walls, opening onto the pavement. ¹⁸This pavement flanked the gates and extended out from the walls into the courtyard the same distance as the gateway entrance. This was the lower pavement. ¹⁹Then the man measured across the Temple's outer courtyard between the outer and inner gateways; the distance was 175 feet.*

The North Gateway

²⁰The man measured the gateway on the north just like the one on the east. ²¹Here, too, there were three guard alcoves on each side, with dividing walls and an entry room. All the measurements matched those of the east gateway. The gateway passage was 87½ feet long and 43¾ feet wide between the back walls of facing guard alcoves. ²²The windows, the entry room, and the palm tree decorations were identical to those in the east gateway. There were seven steps leading up to the gateway entrance, and the entry room was at the inner end of the gateway passage. ²³Here on the north side, just as on the east, there was another gateway leading to the Temple's inner courtyard directly opposite this outer gateway. The distance between the two gateways was 175 feet.

The South Gateway

²⁴Then the man took me around to the south gateway and measured its various parts, and they were exactly the same as in the others. ²⁵It had windows along the walls as the others did, and there was an entry room where the gateway passage opened into the outer courtyard. And like the others, the gateway passage was 87½ feet long and 43¾ feet wide between the back walls of facing guard alcoves. ²⁶This gateway also had a stairway of seven steps leading up to it, and an entry room at the inner end, and palm tree decorations along the dividing walls. ²⁷And here again, directly opposite the outer gateway, was another gateway that led into the inner courtyard. The distance between the two gateways was 175 feet.

Gateways to the Inner Courtyard

²⁸Then the man took me to the south gateway leading into the inner courtyard. He measured it, and it had the same measurements as the other gateways. ²⁹Its guard alcoves, dividing walls, and entry room were the same size as those in the others. It also had windows along its walls and in the entry room. And like the others, the gateway passage was 87½ feet long and 43¾ feet wide. ³⁰(The entry rooms of the

---

40:6 As in Greek version, which reads *1 rod* [3.2 meters] *deep;* Hebrew reads *1 rod deep, and 1 threshold, 1 rod deep.*   40:7 Hebrew *5 cubits* [2.7 meters]; also in 40:48.   40:8 As in many Hebrew manuscripts and Syriac version; other Hebrew manuscripts add *which faced inward toward the Temple; it was 1 rod* [10.5 feet or 3.2 meters] *deep. ⁹Then he measured the entry room of the gateway.*   40:9a Hebrew *8 cubits* [4.2 meters].   40:9b Hebrew *2 cubits* [1.1 meters].   40:11a Hebrew *10 cubits* [5.3 meters].   40:11b Hebrew *13 cubits* [6.9 meters].   40:12a Hebrew *1 cubit* [53 centimeters].   40:12b Hebrew *6 cubits* [3.2 meters].   40:13 Hebrew *25 cubits* [13.3 meters]; also in 40:21, 25, 29, 30, 33, 36.   40:14 Hebrew *60 cubits* [31.8 meters]. Greek version reads *20 cubits* [35 feet or 10.6 meters]. The meaning of the Hebrew in this verse is uncertain.   40:15 Hebrew *50 cubits* [26.5 meters]; also in 40:21, 25, 29, 33, 36.   40:19 Hebrew *100 cubits* [53 meters]; also in 40:23, 27, 47.

gateways leading into the inner courtyard were 14 feet* across and 43¾ feet wide.) ³¹The entry room to the south gateway faced into the outer courtyard. It had palm tree decorations on its columns, and there were eight steps leading to its entrance.

³²Then he took me to the east gateway leading to the inner courtyard. He measured it, and it had the same measurements as the other gateways. ³³Its guard alcoves, dividing walls, and entry room were the same size as those of the others, and there were windows along the walls and in the entry room. The gateway passage measured 87½ feet long and 43¾ feet wide. ³⁴Its entry room faced into the outer courtyard. It had palm tree decorations on its columns, and there were eight steps leading to its entrance.

³⁵Then he took me around to the north gateway leading to the inner courtyard. He measured it, and it had the same measurements as the other gateways. ³⁶The guard alcoves, dividing walls, and entry room of this gateway had the same measurements as in the others and the same window arrangements. The gateway passage measured 87½ feet long and 43¾ feet wide. ³⁷Its entry room* faced into the outer courtyard, and it had palm tree decorations on the columns. There were eight steps leading to its entrance.

Rooms for Preparing Sacrifices

³⁸A door led from the entry room of one of the inner gateways into a side room, where the meat for sacrifices was washed. ³⁹On each side of this entry room were two tables, where the sacrificial animals were slaughtered for the burnt offerings, sin offerings, and guilt offerings. ⁴⁰Outside the entry room, on each side of the stairs going up to the north entrance, were two more tables. ⁴¹So there were eight tables in all—four inside and four outside—where the sacrifices were cut up and prepared. ⁴²There were also four tables of finished stone for preparation of the burnt offerings, each 31½ inches square and 21 inches high.* On these tables were placed the butchering knives and other implements for slaughtering the sacrificial animals. ⁴³There were hooks, each 3 inches* long, fastened all around the foyer walls. The sacrificial meat was laid on the tables.

Rooms for the Priests

⁴⁴Inside the inner courtyard were two rooms,* one beside the north gateway, facing south, and the other beside the south* gateway, facing north. ⁴⁵And the man said to me, "The room beside the north inner gate is for the priests who supervise the Temple maintenance. ⁴⁶The room beside the south inner gate is for the priests in charge of the altar—the descendants of Zadok—for they alone of all the Levites may approach the LORD to minister to him."

The Inner Courtyard and Temple

⁴⁷Then the man measured the inner courtyard, and it was a square, 175 feet wide and 175 feet across. The altar stood in the courtyard in front of the Temple. ⁴⁸Then he brought me to the entry room of the Temple. He measured the walls on either side of the opening to the entry room, and they were 8¾ feet thick. The entrance itself was 24½ feet wide, and the walls on each side of the entrance were an additional 5¼ feet long.* ⁴⁹The entry room was 35 feet* wide and 21 feet* deep. There were ten steps* leading up to it, with a column on each side.

41 After that, the man brought me into the sanctuary of the Temple. He measured the walls on either side of its doorway,* and they were 10½ feet* thick. ²The doorway was 17½ feet* wide, and the walls on each side of it were 8¾ feet* long. The sanctuary itself was 70 feet long and 35 feet wide.*

³Then he went beyond the sanctuary into the inner room. He measured the walls on either side of its entrance, and they were 3½ feet* thick. The entrance was 10½ feet wide, and the walls on each side of the entrance were 12¼ feet* long. ⁴The inner room of the sanctuary was 35 feet* long and 35 feet wide. "This," he told me, "is the Most Holy Place."

⁵Then he measured the wall of the Temple,

40:30 As in 40:9, which reads *8 cubits* [14 feet or 4.2 meters]; here the Hebrew reads *5 cubits* [8¾ feet or 2.7 meters]. Some Hebrew manuscripts and the Greek version lack this entire verse.   40:37 As in Greek version (compare parallels at 40:26, 31, 34); Hebrew reads *Its dividing wall.*   40:42 Hebrew *1½ cubits* [80 centimeters] *long and 1½ cubits wide and 1 cubit* [53 centimeters] *high.*   40:43 Hebrew *a handbreadth* [8 centimeters].   40:44a As in Greek version; Hebrew reads *rooms for singers.*   40:44b As in Greek version; Hebrew reads *east.*   40:48 As in Greek version, which reads *The entrance was 14 cubits* [7.4 meters] *wide, and the walls of the entrance were 3 cubits* [1.6 meters] *on each side;* Hebrew lacks *14 cubits wide, and the walls of the entrance were.*   40:49a Hebrew *20 cubits* [10.6 meters].   40:49b As in Greek version, which reads *12 cubits* [21 feet or 6.4 meters]; Hebrew reads *11 cubits* [19¼ feet or 5.8 meters].   40:49c As in Greek version; Hebrew reads *There were steps that were.*   41:1a As in Greek version; the meaning of the Hebrew is uncertain.   41:1b Hebrew *6 cubits* [3.2 meters]; also in 41:3, 5.   41:2a Hebrew *10 cubits* [5.3 meters].   41:2b Hebrew *5 cubits* [2.7 meters]; also in 41:9, 11.   41:2c Hebrew *40 cubits* [21.2 meters] *long and 20 cubits* [10.6 meters] *wide.*   41:3a Hebrew *2 cubits* [1.1 meters].   41:3b Hebrew *7 cubits* [3.7 meters]. 41:4 Hebrew *20 cubits* [10.6 meters]; also in 41:4b, 10.

and it was 10½ feet thick. There was a row of rooms along the outside wall; each room was 7 feet* wide. ⁶These side rooms were built in three levels, one above the other, with thirty rooms on each level. The supports for these side rooms rested on exterior ledges on the Temple wall; they did not extend into the wall. ⁷Each level was wider than the one below it, corresponding to the narrowing of the Temple wall as it rose higher. A stairway led up from the bottom level through the middle level to the top level.

⁸I saw that the Temple was built on a terrace, which provided a foundation for the side rooms. This terrace was 10½ feet* high. ⁹The outer wall of the Temple's side rooms was 8¾ feet thick. This left an open area between these side rooms ¹⁰and the row of rooms along the outer wall of the inner courtyard. This open area was 35 feet wide, and it went all the way around the Temple. ¹¹Two doors opened from the side rooms into the terrace yard, which was 8¾ feet wide. One door faced north and the other south.

¹²A large building stood on the west, facing the Temple courtyard. It was 122½ feet wide and 157½ feet long, and its walls were 8¾ feet* thick. ¹³Then the man measured the Temple, and it was 175 feet* long. The courtyard around the building, including its walls, was an additional 175 feet in length. ¹⁴The inner courtyard to the east of the Temple was also 175 feet wide. ¹⁵The building to the west, including its two walls, was also 175 feet wide.

The sanctuary, the inner room, and the entry room of the Temple ¹⁶were all paneled with wood, as were the frames of the recessed windows. The inner walls of the Temple were paneled with wood above and below the windows. ¹⁷The space above the door leading into the inner room, and its walls inside and out, were also paneled. ¹⁸All the walls were decorated with carvings of cherubim, each with two faces, and there was a carving of a palm tree between each of the cherubim. ¹⁹One face—that of a man—looked toward the palm tree on one side. The other face—that of a young lion—looked toward the palm tree on the other side. The figures were carved all along the inside of the Temple, ²⁰from the floor to the top of the walls, including the outer wall of the sanctuary.

²¹There were square columns at the entrance to the sanctuary, and the ones at the entrance of the Most Holy Place were similar. ²²There was an altar made of wood, 5¼ feet high and 3½ feet across.* Its corners, base, and sides were all made of wood. "This," the man told me, "is the table that stands in the LORD's presence."

²³Both the sanctuary and the Most Holy Place had double doorways, ²⁴each with two swinging doors. ²⁵The doors leading into the sanctuary were decorated with carved cherubim and palm trees, just as on the walls. And there was a wooden roof at the front of the entry room to the Temple. ²⁶On both sides of the entry room were recessed windows decorated with carved palm trees. The side rooms along the outside wall also had roofs.

Rooms for the Priests

42 Then the man led me out of the Temple courtyard by way of the north gateway. We entered the outer courtyard and came to a group of rooms against the north wall of the inner courtyard. ²This structure, whose entrance opened toward the north, was 175 feet* long and 87½ feet* wide. ³One block of rooms overlooked the 35-foot* width of the inner courtyard. Another block of rooms looked out onto the pavement of the outer courtyard. The two blocks were built three levels high and stood across from each other. ⁴Between the two blocks of rooms ran a walkway 17½ feet* wide. It extended the entire 175 feet of the complex,* and all the doors faced north. ⁵Each of the two upper levels of rooms was narrower than the one beneath it because the upper levels had to allow space for walkways in front of them. ⁶Since there were three levels and they did not have supporting columns as in the courtyards, each of the upper levels was set back from the level beneath it. ⁷There was an outer wall that separated the rooms from the outer courtyard; it was 87½ feet long. ⁸This wall added length to the outer block of rooms, which extended for only 87½ feet, while the inner block—the rooms toward the Temple—extended for 175 feet. ⁹There was an eastern entrance from the outer courtyard to these rooms.

¹⁰On the south* side of the Temple there were two blocks of rooms just south of the inner courtyard between the Temple and the

---

41:5 Hebrew *4 cubits* [2.1 meters].   41:8 Hebrew *1 rod, 6 cubits* [3.2 meters].   41:12 Hebrew *70 cubits* [37.1 meters] *wide and 90 cubits* [47.7 meters] *long, and its walls were 5 cubits* [2.7 meters] *thick.*   41:13 Hebrew *100 cubits* [53 meters]; also in 41:13b, 14, 15.   41:22 Hebrew *3 cubits* [1.6 meters] *high and 2 cubits* [1.1 meters] *across.*   42:2a Hebrew *100 cubits* [53 meters]; also in 42:8.   42:2b Hebrew *50 cubits* [26.5 meters]; also in 42:7, 8.   42:3 Hebrew *20[-cubit]* [10.6-meter].   42:4a Hebrew *10 cubits* [5.3 meters].   42:4b As in Greek and Syriac versions, which read *Its length was 100 cubits* [53 meters]; Hebrew reads *and a passage 1 cubit* [21 inches or 53 centimeters] *wide.*   42:10 As in Greek version; Hebrew reads *east.*

outer courtyard. These rooms were arranged just like the rooms on the north. ¹¹There was a walkway between the two blocks of rooms just like the complex on the north side of the Temple. This complex of rooms was the same length and width as the other one, and it had the same entrances and doors. The dimensions of each were identical. ¹²So there was an entrance in the wall facing the doors of the inner block of rooms, and another on the east at the end of the interior walkway.

¹³Then the man told me, "These rooms that overlook the Temple from the north and south are holy. Here the priests who offer sacrifices to the LORD will eat the most holy offerings. And because these rooms are holy, they will be used to store the sacred offerings—the grain offerings, sin offerings, and guilt offerings. ¹⁴When the priests leave the sanctuary, they must not go directly to the outer courtyard. They must first take off the clothes they wore while ministering, because these clothes are holy. They must put on other clothes before entering the parts of the building complex open to the public."

¹⁵When the man had finished measuring the inside of the Temple area, he led me out through the east gateway to measure the entire perimeter. ¹⁶He measured the east side with his measuring rod, and it was 875 feet long.* ¹⁷Then he measured the north side, and it was also 875 feet. ¹⁸The south side was also 875 feet, ¹⁹and the west side was also 875 feet. ²⁰So the area was 875 feet on each side with a wall all around it to separate what was holy from what was common.

The LORD's Glory Returns

43 After this, the man brought me back around to the east gateway. ²Suddenly, the glory of the God of Israel appeared from the east. The sound of his coming was like the roar of rushing waters, and the whole landscape shone with his glory. ³This vision was just like the others I had seen, first by the Kebar River and then when he came* to destroy Jerusalem. I fell face down on the ground. ⁴And the glory of the LORD came into the Temple through the east gateway.

⁵Then the Spirit took me up and brought me into the inner courtyard, and the glory of the LORD filled the Temple. ⁶And I heard someone speaking to me from within the Temple, while the man who had been measuring stood beside me. ⁷The LORD said to me, "Son of man, this is the place of my throne and the place where I will rest my feet. I will live here forever among the people of Israel. They and their kings will not defile my holy name any longer by their adulterous worship of other gods or by honoring the relics of their kings who have died.* ⁸They put their idol altars right next to mine with only a wall between them and me. They defiled my holy name by such detestable sin, so I consumed them in my anger. ⁹Now let them stop worshiping other gods and honoring the relics of their kings, and I will live among them forever.

¹⁰"Son of man, describe to the people of Israel the Temple I have shown you, so they will be ashamed of all their sins. Let them study its plan, ¹¹and they will be ashamed* of what they have done. Describe to them all the specifications of the Temple—including its entrances and exits—and everything else about it. Tell them about its decrees and laws. Write down all these specifications and decrees as they watch so they will be sure to remember and follow them. ¹²And this is the basic law of the Temple: absolute holiness! The entire top of the mountain where the Temple is built is holy. Yes, this is the basic law of the Temple.

The Altar

¹³"These are the measurements of the altar*: There is a gutter all around the altar 21 inches deep and 21 inches wide,* with a curb 9 inches* wide around its edge. And this is the height* of the altar: ¹⁴From the gutter the altar rises 3½ feet* to a lower ledge that surrounds the altar and is 21 inches* wide. From the lower ledge the altar rises 7 feet* to the upper ledge that is also 21 inches wide. ¹⁵The top of the altar, the hearth, rises another 7 feet higher, with a horn rising up from each of the four corners. ¹⁶The top of the altar is square, measuring 21 feet by 21 feet.* ¹⁷The upper ledge also forms a square, measuring 24½ feet by 24½ feet,* with a 21-inch gutter and a 10½-inch curb* all

---

42:16 As in 45:2 and in Greek version at 42:17, which reads *500 cubits* [265 meters]; Hebrew reads *500 rods* [5,250 feet or 1,590 meters]; similarly in 42:17, 18, 19, 20.   42:3 As in some Hebrew manuscripts and Latin Vulgate; Masoretic Text reads *I came.* 43:7 Or *kings on their high places.*   43:11 As in Greek version; Hebrew reads *if they are ashamed.*   43:13a Hebrew *measurements of the altar in long cubits, each being a cubit* [18 inches or 45 centimeters] *and a handbreadth* [3 inches or 8 centimeters] *in length.* 43:13b Hebrew *a cubit* [53 centimeters] *deep and a cubit wide.*   43:13c Hebrew *1 span* [23 centimeters].   43:13d As in Greek version; Hebrew reads *base.*   43:14a Hebrew *2 cubits* [1.1 meters].   43:14b Hebrew *1 cubit* [53 centimeters]; also in 43:14d. 43:14c Hebrew *4 cubits* [2.1 meters]; also in 43:15.   43:16 Hebrew *12* [cubits] [6.4 meters] *long and 12* [cubits] *wide.*   43:17a Hebrew *14* [cubits] [7.4 meters] *long and 14* [cubits] *wide.*   43:17b Hebrew *a gutter of 1 cubit* [53 centimeters] *and a curb of ½ a cubit* [27 centimeters].

around the edge. There are steps going up the east side of the altar."

¹⁸Then he said to me, "Son of man, this is what the Sovereign LORD says: These will be the regulations for the burning of offerings and the sprinkling of blood when the altar is built. ¹⁹At that time, the Levitical priests of the family of Zadok, who minister before me, are to be given a young bull for a sin offering, says the Sovereign LORD. ²⁰You will take some of its blood and smear it on the four horns of the altar, the four corners of the upper ledge, and the curb that runs around that ledge. This will cleanse and make atonement for the altar. ²¹Then take the young bull for the sin offering and burn it at the appointed place outside the Temple area.

²²"On the second day, sacrifice as a sin offering a young male goat that has no physical defects. Then cleanse and make atonement for the altar again, just as you did with the young bull. ²³When you have finished the cleansing ceremony, offer another young bull that has no defects and a perfect ram from the flock. ²⁴You are to present them to the LORD, and the priests are to sprinkle salt on them and offer them as a burnt offering to the LORD.

²⁵"Every day for seven days a male goat, a young bull, and a ram from the flock will be sacrificed as a sin offering. None of these animals may have physical defects of any kind. ²⁶Do this each day for seven days to cleanse and make atonement for the altar, thus setting it apart for holy use. ²⁷On the eighth day, and on each day afterward, the priests will sacrifice on the altar the burnt offerings and peace offerings of the people. Then I will accept you. I, the Sovereign LORD, have spoken!"

The Prince, Levites, and Priests

44 Then the man brought me back to the east gateway in the outer wall of the Temple area, but it was closed. ²And the LORD said to me, "This gate must remain closed; it will never again be opened. No one will ever open it and pass through, for the LORD, the God of Israel, has entered here. Therefore, it must always remain shut. ³Only the prince himself may sit inside this gateway to feast in the LORD's presence. But he may come and go only through the entry room of the gateway."

⁴Then the man brought me through the north gateway to the front of the Temple. I looked and saw that the glory of the LORD filled the Temple of the LORD, and I fell face down on the ground.

⁵And the LORD said to me, "Son of man, take careful notice. Use your eyes and ears, and listen to everything I tell you about the regulations concerning the LORD's Temple. Take careful note of the procedures for using the Temple's entrances and exits. ⁶And give these rebels, the people of Israel, this message from the Sovereign LORD: O people of Israel, enough of your detestable sins! ⁷You have brought uncircumcised foreigners into my sanctuary—people who have no heart for God. In this way, you defiled my Temple even as you offered me my food, the fat and blood of sacrifices. In addition to all your other detestable sins, you have broken my covenant. ⁸Instead of safeguarding my sacred rituals, you have hired foreigners to take charge of my sanctuary.

⁹"So this is what the Sovereign LORD says: No foreigners, including those who live among the people of Israel, will enter my sanctuary if they have not been circumcised and have not surrendered themselves to the LORD. ¹⁰And the men of the tribe of Levi who abandoned me when Israel strayed away from me to worship idols* must bear the consequences of their unfaithfulness. ¹¹They may still be Temple guards and gatekeepers, and they may slaughter the animals brought for burnt offerings and be present to help the people. ¹²But they encouraged my people to worship idols, causing Israel to fall into deep sin. So I have taken a solemn oath that they must bear the consequences for their sins, says the Sovereign LORD. ¹³They may not approach me to minister as priests. They may not touch any of my holy things or the holy offerings, for they must bear the shame of all the detestable sins they have committed. ¹⁴They are to serve as the Temple caretakers, taking charge of the maintenance work and performing general duties.

¹⁵"However, the Levitical priests of the family of Zadok continued to minister faithfully in the Temple when Israel abandoned me for idols. These men will serve as my ministers. They will stand in my presence and offer the fat and blood of the sacrifices, says the Sovereign LORD. ¹⁶They alone will enter my sanctuary and approach my table to serve me. They will fulfill all my requirements.

¹⁷"When they enter the gateway to the inner courtyard, they must wear only linen clothing. They must wear no wool while on duty in the inner courtyard or in the Temple itself. ¹⁸They

44:10 The Hebrew term (literally *round things*) probably alludes to dung; also in 44:12.

must wear linen turbans and linen undergarments. They must not wear anything that would cause them to perspire. ¹⁹When they return to the outer courtyard where the people are, they must take off the clothes they wear while ministering to me. They must leave them in the sacred rooms and put on other clothes so they do not endanger anyone by transmitting holiness to them through this clothing.

²⁰"They must neither shave their heads nor let their hair grow too long. Instead, they must trim it regularly. ²¹The priests must not drink wine before entering the inner courtyard. ²²They may choose their wives only from among the virgins of Israel or the widows of the priests. They may not marry other widows or divorced women. ²³They will teach my people the difference between what is holy and what is common, what is ceremonially clean and unclean.

²⁴"They will serve as judges to resolve any disagreements among my people. Their decisions must be based on my regulations. And the priests themselves must obey my instructions and decrees at all the sacred festivals, and see to it that the Sabbaths are set apart as holy days.

²⁵"A priest must not defile himself by being in the presence of a dead person unless it is his father, mother, child, brother, or unmarried sister. In such cases it is permitted. ²⁶Even then, he can return to his Temple duties only after being ceremonially cleansed and then waiting for seven days. ²⁷The first day he returns to work and enters the inner courtyard and the sanctuary, he must offer a sin offering for himself, says the Sovereign LORD.

²⁸"The priests will not have any property or possession of land, for I alone am their special possession. ²⁹Their food will come from the gifts and sacrifices brought to the Temple by the people—the grain offerings, the sin offerings, and the guilt offerings. Whatever anyone sets apart* for the LORD will belong to the priests. ³⁰The first of the ripe fruits and all the gifts brought to the LORD will go to the priests. The first batch of dough must also be given to the priests so the LORD will bless your homes. ³¹The priests may not eat meat from any bird or animal that dies a natural death or that dies after being attacked by another animal.

Division of the Land

45 "When you divide the land among the tribes of Israel, you must set aside a section for the LORD as his holy portion. This piece of land will be 8⅓ miles long and 6⅔ miles wide.* The entire area will be holy. ²A section of this land, measuring 875 feet by 875 feet,* will be set aside for the Temple. An additional strip of land 87½ feet* wide is to be left empty all around it. ³Within the larger sacred area, measure out a portion of land 8⅓ miles long and 3⅓ miles wide.* Within it the sanctuary of the Most Holy Place will be located. ⁴This area will be holy, set aside for the priests who minister to the LORD in the sanctuary. They will use it for their homes, and my Temple will be located within it. ⁵The strip of sacred land next to it, also 8⅓ miles long and 3⅓ miles wide, will be a living area for the Levites who work at the Temple. It will be their possession and a place for their towns.*

⁶"Adjacent to the larger sacred area will be a section of land 8⅓ miles long and 1⅔ miles wide.* This will be set aside for a city where anyone in Israel can live.

⁷"Two special sections of land will be set apart for the prince. One section will share a border with the east side of the sacred lands and city, and the second section will share a border on the west side. Then the far eastern and western borders of the prince's lands will line up with the eastern and western boundaries of the tribal areas. ⁸These sections of land will be the prince's allotment. Then my princes will no longer oppress and rob my people; they will assign the rest of the land to the people, giving an allotment to each tribe.

Rules for the Princes

⁹"For this is what the Sovereign LORD says: Enough, you princes of Israel! Stop your violence and oppression and do what is just and right. Quit robbing and cheating my people out of their land. Stop expelling them from their homes, says the Sovereign LORD. ¹⁰Use only honest weights and scales and honest measures, both dry and liquid.* ¹¹The homer* will be your standard unit for measuring volume. The ephah and the bath* will each measure one-tenth of a homer. ¹²The standard unit

---

44:29 The Hebrew term used here refers to the complete consecration of things or people to the LORD, either by destroying them or by giving them as an offering.   45:1 As in Greek version, which reads 25,000 [cubits] [13.3 kilometers] long and 20,000 [cubits] [10.6 kilometers] wide; Hebrew reads 25,000 [cubits] long and 10,000 [cubits] [3⅓ miles or 5.3 kilometers] wide. Compare 45:3, 5; 48:9.   45:2a Hebrew 500 [cubits] [265 meters] by 500 [cubits], a square.   45:2b Hebrew 50 cubits [26.5 meters].   45:3 Hebrew 25,000 [cubits] [13.3 kilometers] long and 10,000 [cubits] [5.3 kilometers] wide; also in 45:5.   45:5 As in Greek version; Hebrew reads They will have as their possession 20 rooms.   45:6 Hebrew 25,000 [cubits] [13.3 kilometers] long and 5,000 [cubits] [2.65 kilometers] wide.   45:10 Hebrew Use honest scales, an honest ephah, and an honest bath.   45:11a The homer measures about 50 gallons or 220 liters.   45:11b The ephah is a dry measure; the bath is a liquid measure.

for weight will be the silver shekel.* One shekel will consist of twenty gerahs, and sixty shekels will be equal to one mina.*

Special Offerings and Celebrations

13"You must give this tax to the prince: one bushel of wheat or barley for every 60* you harvest, 14one percent of your olive oil,* 15and one sheep or goat for every 200 in your flocks in Israel. These will be the grain offerings, burnt offerings, and peace offerings that will make atonement for the people who bring them, says the Sovereign LORD. 16All the people of Israel must join in bringing these offerings to the prince. 17The prince will be required to provide offerings that are given at the religious festivals, the new moon celebrations, the Sabbath days, and all other similar occasions. He will provide the sin offerings, burnt offerings, grain offerings, liquid offerings, and peace offerings to purify the people of Israel, making them right with the LORD.*

18"This is what the Sovereign LORD says: In early spring, on the first day of each new year,* sacrifice a young bull with no defects to purify the Temple. 19The priest will take blood from this sin offering and put it on the doorposts of the Temple, the four corners of the upper ledge of the altar, and the gateposts at the entrance to the inner courtyard. 20Do this also on the seventh day of the new year for anyone who has sinned through error or ignorance. In this way, you will purify* the Temple.

21"On the fourteenth day of the first month,* you must celebrate the Passover. This festival will last for seven days. The bread you eat during that time must be made without yeast. 22On the day of Passover the prince will provide a young bull as a sin offering for himself and the people of Israel. 23On each of the seven days of the feast he will prepare a burnt offering to the LORD, consisting of seven young bulls and seven rams without defects. A male goat will also be given each day for a sin offering. 24The prince will provide a basket of flour as a grain offering and a gallon of olive oil* with each young bull and ram.

25"During the seven days of the Festival of Shelters, which occurs every year in early autumn,* the prince will provide these same sacrifices for the sin offering, the burnt offering, and the grain offering, along with the required olive oil.

46 "This is what the Sovereign LORD says: The east gateway of the inner courtyard will be closed during the six workdays each week, but it will be open on Sabbath days and the days of new moon celebrations. 2The prince will enter the entry room of the gateway from the outside. Then he will stand by the gatepost while the priest offers his burnt offering and peace offering. He will bow down in worship inside the gateway passage and then go back out the way he came. The gateway will not be closed until evening. 3The common people will bow down and worship the LORD in front of this gateway on Sabbath days and the days of new moon celebrations.

4"Each Sabbath day the prince will present to the LORD a burnt offering of six lambs and one ram, all with no defects. 5He will present a grain offering of a basket of choice flour to go with the ram and whatever amount of flour he chooses to go with each lamb, and he is to offer one gallon of olive oil* for each basket of flour. 6At the new moon celebrations, he will bring one young bull, six lambs, and one ram, all with no defects. 7With the young bull he must bring a basket of choice flour for a grain offering. With the ram he must bring another basket of flour. And with each lamb he is to bring whatever amount of flour he chooses to give. With each basket of flour he must offer one gallon of olive oil.

8"The prince must enter the gateway through the entry room, and he must leave the same way. 9But when the people come in through the north gateway to worship the LORD during the religious festivals, they must leave by the south gateway. And those who entered through the south gateway must leave by the north gateway. They must never leave by the same gateway they came in, but must always use the opposite gateway. 10The prince will enter and leave with the people on these occasions.

11"So at the special feasts and sacred festivals, the grain offering will be a basket of choice

45:12a The *shekel* weighs about 0.4 ounces or 11 grams.   45:12b Elsewhere the *mina* is equated to 50 shekels.   45:13 Hebrew ⅙ of an ephah from each homer of wheat and ⅙ of an ephah from each homer of barley.   45:14 Hebrew the portion of oil, measured by the bath, is ¹⁄₁₀ of a bath from each cor, which consists of 10 baths or 1 homer, for 10 baths are equivalent to a homer.   45:17 Or to make atonement for the people of Israel.   45:18 Hebrew On the first day of the first month, of the Hebrew calendar. This day in the ancient Hebrew lunar calendar occurred in March or April.   45:20 Or will make atonement for.   45:21 This day in the ancient Hebrew lunar calendar occurred in late March, April, or early May.   45:24 Hebrew an ephah [20 quarts or 22 liters] of flour . . . and a hin [3.8 liters] of olive oil.   45:25 Hebrew the festival which begins on the fifteenth day of the seventh month (see Lev 23:34). This day in the ancient Hebrew lunar calendar occurred in late September, October, or early November.   46:5 Hebrew an ephah [20 quarts or 22 liters] of choice flour . . . a hin [3.8 liters] of olive oil; similarly in 46:7, 11.

flour with each young bull, another basket of flour with each ram, and as much flour as the worshiper chooses to give with each lamb. Give one gallon of olive oil with each basket of flour. ¹²When the prince offers a voluntary burnt offering or peace offering to the LORD, the east gateway to the inner courtyard will be opened for him, and he will offer his sacrifices as he does on Sabbath days. Then he will leave, and the gateway will be shut behind him.

¹³"Each morning you must sacrifice a one-year-old lamb with no defects as a burnt offering to the LORD. ¹⁴With the lamb, a grain offering must also be given to the LORD— about three quarts of flour with a third of a gallon of olive oil* to moisten the choice flour. This will be a permanent law for you. ¹⁵The lamb, the grain offering, and the olive oil must be given as a daily sacrifice every morning without fail.

¹⁶"This is what the Sovereign LORD says: If the prince gives a gift of land to one of his sons as his inheritance, it will belong to him and his descendants forever. ¹⁷But if the prince gives a gift of land from his inheritance to one of his servants, the servant may keep it only until the Year of Jubilee, which comes every fiftieth year.* At that time the land will return to the prince. But when the prince gives gifts to his sons, those gifts will be permanent. ¹⁸And the prince may never take anyone's property by force. If he gives property to his sons, it must be from his own land, for I do not want any of my people unjustly evicted from their property."

The Temple Kitchens

¹⁹In my vision, the man brought me through the entrance beside the gateway and led me to the sacred rooms assigned to the priests, which faced toward the north. He showed me a place at the extreme west end of these rooms. ²⁰He explained, "This is where the priests will cook the meat from the guilt offerings and sin offerings and bake the flour from the grain offerings into bread. They will do it here to avoid carrying the sacrifices through the outer courtyard and endangering the people by transmitting holiness to them."

²¹Then he brought me back to the outer courtyard and led me to each of its four corners. In each corner I saw an enclosure. ²²Each of these enclosures was 70 feet long and 52½

feet wide,* surrounded by walls. ²³Along the inside of these walls was a ledge of stone with fireplaces under the ledge all the way around. ²⁴The man said to me, "These are the kitchens to be used by the Temple assistants to boil the sacrifices offered by the people."

The River of Healing

47 In my vision, the man brought me back to the entrance of the Temple. There I saw a stream flowing east from beneath the door of the Temple and passing to the right of the altar on its south side. ²The man brought me outside the wall through the north gateway and led me around to the eastern entrance. There I could see the water flowing out through the south side of the east gateway.

³Measuring as he went, he took me along the stream for 1,750 feet* and then led me across. The water was up to my ankles. ⁴He measured off another 1,750 feet and led me across again. This time the water was up to my knees. After another 1,750 feet, it was up to my waist. ⁵Then he measured another 1,750 feet, and the river was too deep to walk across. It was deep enough to swim in, but too deep to walk through.

⁶He asked me, "Have you been watching, son of man?" Then he led me back along the riverbank. ⁷When I returned, I was surprised by the sight of many trees growing on both sides of the river. ⁸Then he said to me, "This river flows east through the desert into the valley of the Dead Sea.* The waters of this stream will make the salty waters of the Dead Sea fresh and pure. ⁹There will be swarms of living things wherever the water of this river flows.* Fish will abound in the Dead Sea, for its waters will become fresh. Life will flourish wherever this water flows. ¹⁰Fishermen will stand along the shores of the Dead Sea. All the way from En-gedi to En-eglaim, the shores will be covered with nets drying in the sun. Fish of every kind will fill the Dead Sea, just as they fill the Mediterranean.* ¹¹But the marshes and swamps will not be purified; they will still be salty. ¹²Fruit trees of all kinds will grow along both sides of the river. The leaves of these trees will never turn brown and fall, and there will always be fruit on their branches. There will be a new crop every month, for they are watered by the river flowing from the Temple. The fruit will be for food and the leaves for healing."

46:14 Hebrew ⅙ of an ephah [3.7 liters] of flour with ⅓ of a hin [1.3 liters] of olive oil.   46:17 Hebrew until the Year of Release; see Lev 25:8-17.   46:22 Hebrew 40 [cubits] [21.2 meters] long and 30 [cubits] [15.9 meters] wide.   47:3 Hebrew 1,000 cubits [530 meters]; also in 47:4, 5.   47:8 Hebrew the sea.   47:9 As in Greek and Syriac versions; Hebrew reads of these two rivers flow.   47:10 Hebrew the Great Sea; also in 47:15, 17, 19, 20.

Boundaries for the Land

13This is what the Sovereign LORD says: "Divide the land in this way for the twelve tribes of Israel: The descendants of Joseph will be given two shares of land.* 14Otherwise each tribe will receive an equal share. I took a solemn oath and swore that I would give this land to your ancestors, and it will now come to you as your possession.

15"These are the boundaries of the land: The northern border will run from the Mediterranean toward Hethlon, then on through Lebo-hamath to Zedad; 16then it will run to Berothah and Sibraim,* which are on the border between Damascus and Hamath, and finally to Hazer-hatticon, on the border of Hauran. 17So the northern border will run from the Mediterranean to Hazar-enan, on the border between Hamath to the north and Damascus to the south.

18"The eastern border starts at a point between Hauran and Damascus and runs south along the Jordan River between Israel and Gilead, past the Dead Sea* and as far south as Tamar.* This will be the eastern border.

19"The southern border will go west from Tamar to the waters of Meribah at Kadesh* and then follow the course of the Brook of Egypt to the Mediterranean. This will be the southern border.

20"On the west side, the Mediterranean itself will be your border from the southern border to the point where the northern border begins, opposite Lebo-hamath.

21"Divide the land within these boundaries among the tribes of Israel. 22Distribute the land as an allotment for yourselves and for the foreigners who have joined you and are raising their families among you. They will be like native-born Israelites to you and will receive an allotment among the tribes. 23These foreigners are to be given land within the territory of the tribe with whom they now live. I, the Sovereign LORD, have spoken!

Division of the Land

48 "Here is the list of the tribes of Israel and the territory each is to receive. The territory of Dan is in the extreme north. Its boundary line follows the Hethlon road to Lebo-hamath and then runs on to Hazar-enan on the border of Damascus, with Hamath to the north. Dan's territory extends all the way across the land of Israel from east to west.

2"Asher's territory lies south of Dan's and also extends from east to west. 3Naphtali's land lies south of Asher's, also extending from east to west. 4Then comes Manasseh south of Naphtali, and its territory also extends from east to west. 5South of Manasseh is Ephraim, 6and then Reuben, 7and then Judah, all of whose boundaries extend from east to west.

8"South of Judah is the land set aside for a special purpose. It will be 8⅓ miles* wide and will extend as far east and west as the tribal territories, with the Temple at the center.

9"The area set aside for the LORD's Temple will be 8⅓ miles long and 6⅔ miles wide.* 10For the priests there will be a strip of land measuring 8⅓ miles long by 3⅓ miles wide,* with the LORD's Temple at the center. 11This area is set aside for the ordained priests, the descendants of Zadok who served me faithfully and did not go astray with the people of Israel and the rest of the Levites. 12It will be their special portion when the land is distributed, the most sacred land of all. Next to the priests' territory will lie the land where the other Levites will live.

13"The land allotted to the Levites will be the same size and shape as that belonging to the priests—8⅓ miles long and 3⅓ miles wide. Together these portions of land will measure 8⅓ miles long by 6⅔ miles wide.* 14None of this special land may ever be sold or traded or used by others, for it belongs to the LORD; it is set apart as holy.

15"An additional strip of land 8⅓ miles long by 1⅔ miles wide,* south of the sacred Temple area, will be allotted for public use—homes, pasturelands, and common lands, with a city at the center. 16The city will measure 1½ miles* on each side—north, south, east, and west. 17Open lands will surround the city for 150 yards* in

---

47:13 It was important to retain twelve portions of land. Since Levi had no portion, the descendants of Joseph's sons, Ephraim and Manasseh, received land as two tribes.   47:15-16 As in Greek version; Masoretic Text reads *then on through Lebo to Zedad; 16then it will run to Hamath, Berothah, and Sibraim.*   47:18a Hebrew *the eastern sea.*   47:18b As in Greek version; Hebrew reads *you will measure.*   47:19 Hebrew *waters of Meribath-kadesh.*   48:8 Hebrew *25,000 [cubits]* [13.3 kilometers].   48:9 As in one Greek manuscript and the Greek reading in 45:11: *25,000 [cubits]* [13.3 kilometers] *long and 20,000 [cubits]* [10.6 kilometers] *wide;* Hebrew reads *25,000 [cubits] long and 10,000 [cubits]* [3⅓ miles or 5.3 kilometers] *wide.* Similarly in 48:13b. Compare 45:1-5; 48:10-13.   48:10 Hebrew *25,000 [cubits]* [13.3 kilometers] *long by 10,000 [cubits]* [5.3 kilometers] *wide;* also in 48:13a.   48:13 See note on 48:9.   48:15 Hebrew *25,000 [cubits]* [13.3 kilometers] *long by 5,000 [cubits]* [2.65 kilometers] *wide.*   48:16 Hebrew *4,500 [cubits]* [2.4 kilometers]; also in 48:30, 32, 33, 34.   48:17 Hebrew *250 [cubits]* [133 meters].

every direction. ¹⁸Outside the city there will be a farming area that stretches 3⅓ miles to the east and 3⅓ miles to the west* along the border of the sacred area. This farmland will produce food for the people working in the city. ¹⁹Those who come from the various tribes to work in the city may farm it. ²⁰This entire area—including the sacred lands and the city—is a square that measures 8⅓ miles* on each side.

²¹"The areas that remain, to the east and to the west of the sacred lands and the city, will belong to the prince. Each of these areas will be 8⅓ miles wide, extending in opposite directions to the eastern and western borders of Israel, with the sacred lands and the sanctuary of the Temple in the center. ²²So the prince's land will include everything between the territories allotted to Judah and Benjamin, except for the areas set aside for the sacred lands and the city.

²³"These are the territories allotted to the rest of the tribes. Benjamin's territory lies just south of the prince's lands, and it extends across the entire land of Israel from east to west. ²⁴South of Benjamin's territory lies that of Simeon, also extending across the land from east to west. ²⁵Next is the territory of Issachar with the same eastern and western boundaries.

²⁶"Then comes the territory of Zebulun, which also extends across the land from east to west. ²⁷The territory of Gad is just south of Zebulun with the same borders to the east and west. ²⁸The southern border of Gad runs from Tamar to the waters of Meribah at Kadesh* and then follows the Brook of Egypt to the Mediterranean.*

²⁹"These are the allotments that will be set aside for each tribe's exclusive possession. I, the Sovereign LORD, have spoken!

The Gates of the City

³⁰"These will be the exits to the city: On the north wall, which is 1½ miles long, ³¹there will be three gates, each one named after a tribe of Israel. The first will be named for Reuben, the second for Judah, and the third for Levi. ³²On the east wall, also 1½ miles long, the gates will be named for Joseph, Benjamin, and Dan. ³³The south wall, also 1½ miles long, will have gates named for Simeon, Issachar, and Zebulun. ³⁴And on the west wall, also 1½ miles long, the gates will be named for Gad, Asher, and Naphtali.

³⁵"The distance around the entire city will be 6 miles.* And from that day the name of the city will be 'The LORD Is There.'*"

48:18 Hebrew *10,000 [cubits]* [5.3 kilometers] *to the east and 10,000 [cubits] to the west.*   48:20 Hebrew *25,000 [cubits]* [13.3 kilometers]; also in 48:21.   48:28a Hebrew *waters of Meribath-kadesh.*   48:28b Hebrew *the Great Sea.*   48:35a Hebrew *18,000 [cubits]* [9.6 kilometers].   48:35b Hebrew *Yahweh Shammah.*

Daniel

A STRANGER IN A STRANGE LAND,
Daniel lived during a time when the Jewish people seemed to have little hope. They were living as captives in Babylon, hundreds of miles from home, with only promises from God that they would ever see their homeland again. As this book records, Daniel and his friends were taken to Babylon as young men. Although they were captives, they received an excellent education and rose to high positions in the Babylonian and Persian governments. Because of their faith in the God of Israel, they were persecuted and even sentenced to die. But

■ **Author:** Daniel, according to Jewish tradition

■ **Date Written:** Around 535 BC, recording events that occurred from about 605 to 535 BC

■ **Purpose:** To demonstrate through Daniel's experiences that God is sovereign over the whole earth and to encourage the Jews to remain faithful to God despite persecution

■ **Themes:** God's sovereignty; God's faithfulness to his people; the importance of faithfulness and perseverance under persecution

■ **Outline**
1:1–6:28 Daniel's life in Babylon
7:1–8:27 Daniel's visions of the beasts
9:1-27 Daniel's prayer and prophecies
10:1–12:13 Daniel's vision of God and the future
13:1-64 Susanna and the elders
14:1-42 Bel and the dragon

God rewarded them for their faithfulness, and they were rescued from certain death. Daniel had several encounters with King Nebuchadnezzar, and God revealed his sovereignty in each instance. The second half of the book records Daniel's visions of future events. These apocalyptic dreams and the stories of Daniel and his friends provided encouragement for the Jews to remain faithful to God in the midst of persecution.

Daniel in Nebuchadnezzar's Court

1 During the third year of King Jehoiakim's reign in Judah,* King Nebuchadnezzar of Babylon came to Jerusalem and besieged it. ²The Lord gave him victory over King Jehoiakim of Judah and permitted him to take some of the sacred objects from the Temple of God. So Nebuchadnezzar took them back to the land of Babylonia* and placed them in the treasure-house of his god.

³Then the king ordered Ashpenaz, his chief of staff, to bring to the palace some of the young men of Judah's royal family and other noble families, who had been brought to Babylon as captives. ⁴"Select only strong, healthy, and good-looking young men," he said. "Make sure they are well versed in every

branch of learning, are gifted with knowledge and good judgment, and are suited to serve in the royal palace. Train these young men in the language and literature of Babylon.*" ⁵The king assigned them a daily ration of food and wine from his own kitchens. They were to be trained for three years, and then they would enter the royal service.

⁶Daniel, Hananiah, Mishael, and Azariah were four of the young men chosen, all from the tribe of Judah. ⁷The chief of staff renamed them with these Babylonian names:

Daniel was called Belteshazzar.
Hananiah was called Shadrach.
Mishael was called Meshach.
Azariah was called Abednego.

1:1 This event occurred in 605 B.C., during the third year of Jehoiakim's reign (according to the calendar system in which the new year begins in the spring). 1:2 Hebrew *the land of Shinar.* 1:4 Or *of the Chaldeans.*

⁸But Daniel was determined not to defile himself by eating the food and wine given to them by the king. He asked the chief of staff for permission not to eat these unacceptable foods. ⁹Now God had given the chief of staff both respect and affection for Daniel. ¹⁰But he responded, "I am afraid of my lord the king, who has ordered that you eat this food and wine. If you become pale and thin compared to the other youths your age, I am afraid the king will have me beheaded."

¹¹Daniel spoke with the attendant who had been appointed by the chief of staff to look after Daniel, Hananiah, Mishael, and Azariah. ¹²"Please test us for ten days on a diet of vegetables and water," Daniel said. ¹³"At the end of the ten days, see how we look compared to the other young men who are eating the king's food. Then make your decision in light of what you see." ¹⁴The attendant agreed to Daniel's suggestion and tested them for ten days.

¹⁵At the end of the ten days, Daniel and his three friends looked healthier and better nourished than the young men who had been eating the food assigned by the king. ¹⁶So after that, the attendant fed them only vegetables instead of the food and wine provided for the others.

¹⁷God gave these four young men an unusual aptitude for understanding every aspect of literature and wisdom. And God gave Daniel the special ability to interpret the meanings of visions and dreams.

¹⁸When the training period ordered by the king was completed, the chief of staff brought all the young men to King Nebuchadnezzar. ¹⁹The king talked with them, and no one impressed him as much as Daniel, Hananiah, Mishael, and Azariah. So they entered the royal service. ²⁰Whenever the king consulted them in any matter requiring wisdom and balanced judgment, he found them ten times more capable than any of the magicians and enchanters in his entire kingdom.

²¹Daniel remained in the royal service until the first year of the reign of King Cyrus.*

Nebuchadnezzar's Dream

2 One night during the second year of his reign,* Nebuchadnezzar had such disturbing dreams that he couldn't sleep. ²He called in his magicians, enchanters, sorcerers, and astrologers,* and he demanded that they tell him what he had dreamed. As they

stood before the king, ³he said, "I have had a dream that deeply troubles me, and I must know what it means."

⁴Then the astrologers answered the king in Aramaic,* "Long live the king! Tell us the dream, and we will tell you what it means."

⁵But the king said to the astrologers, "I am serious about this. If you don't tell me what my dream was and what it means, you will be torn limb from limb, and your houses will be turned into heaps of rubble! ⁶But if you tell me what I dreamed and what the dream means, I will give you many wonderful gifts and honors. Just tell me the dream and what it means!"

⁷They said again, "Please, Your Majesty. Tell us the dream, and we will tell you what it means."

⁸The king replied, "I know what you are doing! You're stalling for time because you know I am serious when I say, ⁹'If you don't tell me the dream, you are doomed.' So you have conspired to tell me lies, hoping I will change my mind. But tell me the dream, and then I'll know that you can tell me what it means."

¹⁰The astrologers replied to the king, "No one on earth can tell the king his dream! And no king, however great and powerful, has ever asked such a thing of any magician, enchanter, or astrologer! ¹¹The king's demand is impossible. No one except the gods can tell you your dream, and they do not live here among people."

¹²The king was furious when he heard this, and he ordered that all the wise men of Babylon be executed. ¹³And because of the king's decree, men were sent to find and kill Daniel and his friends.

¹⁴When Arioch, the commander of the king's guard, came to kill them, Daniel handled the situation with wisdom and discretion. ¹⁵He asked Arioch, "Why has the king issued such a harsh decree?" So Arioch told him all that had happened. ¹⁶Daniel went at once to see the king and requested more time to tell the king what the dream meant.

¹⁷Then Daniel went home and told his friends Hananiah, Mishael, and Azariah what had happened. ¹⁸He urged them to ask the God of heaven to show them his mercy by telling them the secret, so they would not be executed along with the other wise men of Babylon. ¹⁹That night the secret was revealed to Daniel in a vision. Then Daniel praised the God of heaven. ²⁰He said,

1:21 Cyrus began his reign (over Babylon) in 539 B.C.   2:1 The second year of Nebuchadnezzar's reign was 603 B.C.
2:2 Or *Chaldeans;* also in 2:4, 5, 10.   2:4 The original text from this point through chapter 7 is in Aramaic.

"Praise the name of God forever and ever,
for he has all wisdom and power.
21 He controls the course of world events;
he removes kings and sets up other
kings.
He gives wisdom to the wise
and knowledge to the scholars.
22 He reveals deep and mysterious things
and knows what lies hidden in darkness,
though he is surrounded by light.
23 I thank and praise you, God of my
ancestors,
for you have given me wisdom and
strength.
You have told me what we asked of you
and revealed to us what the king
demanded."

Daniel Interprets the Dream

24Then Daniel went in to see Arioch, whom the king had ordered to execute the wise men of Babylon. Daniel said to him, "Don't kill the wise men. Take me to the king, and I will tell him the meaning of his dream."

25Arioch quickly took Daniel to the king and said, "I have found one of the captives from Judah who will tell the king the meaning of his dream!"

26The king said to Daniel (also known as Belteshazzar), "Is this true? Can you tell me what my dream was and what it means?"

27Daniel replied, "There are no wise men, enchanters, magicians, or fortune-tellers who can reveal the king's secret. 28But there is a God in heaven who reveals secrets, and he has shown King Nebuchadnezzar what will happen in the future. Now I will tell you your dream and the visions you saw as you lay on your bed.

29"While Your Majesty was sleeping, you dreamed about coming events. He who reveals secrets has shown you what is going to happen. 30And it is not because I am wiser than anyone else that I know the secret of your dream, but because God wants you to understand what was in your heart.

31"In your vision, Your Majesty, you saw standing before you a huge, shining statue of a man. It was a frightening sight. 32The head of the statue was made of fine gold. Its chest and arms were silver, its belly and thighs were bronze, 33its legs were iron, and its feet were a combination of iron and baked clay. 34As you watched, a rock was cut from a mountain,* but not by human hands. It struck the feet of iron and clay, smashing them to bits. 35The whole statue was crushed into small pieces of iron, clay, bronze, silver, and gold. Then the wind blew them away without a trace, like chaff on a threshing floor. But the rock that knocked the statue down became a great mountain that covered the whole earth.

36"That was the dream. Now we will tell the king what it means. 37Your Majesty, you are the greatest of kings. The God of heaven has given you sovereignty, power, strength, and honor. 38He has made you the ruler over all the inhabited world and has put even the wild animals and birds under your control. You are the head of gold.

39"But after your kingdom comes to an end, another kingdom, inferior to yours, will rise to take your place. After that kingdom has fallen, yet a third kingdom, represented by bronze, will rise to rule the world. 40Following that kingdom, there will be a fourth one, as strong as iron. That kingdom will smash and crush all previous empires, just as iron smashes and crushes everything it strikes. 41The feet and toes you saw were a combination of iron and baked clay, showing that this kingdom will be divided. Like iron mixed with clay, it will have some of the strength of iron. 42But while some parts of it will be as strong as iron, other parts will be as weak as clay. 43This mixture of iron and clay also shows that these kingdoms will try to strengthen themselves by forming alliances with each other through intermarriage. But they will not hold together, just as iron and clay do not mix.

44"During the reigns of those kings, the God of heaven will set up a kingdom that will never be destroyed or conquered. It will crush all these kingdoms into nothingness, and it will stand forever. 45That is the meaning of the rock cut from the mountain, though not by human hands, that crushed to pieces the statue of iron, bronze, clay, silver, and gold. The great God was showing the king what will happen in the future. The dream is true, and its meaning is certain."

Nebuchadnezzar Rewards Daniel

46Then King Nebuchadnezzar threw himself down before Daniel and worshiped him, and he commanded his people to offer sacrifices and burn sweet incense before him. 47The king said to Daniel, "Truly, your God is the greatest of gods, the Lord over kings, a revealer of mysteries, for you have been able to reveal this secret."

2:34 As in Greek version (see also 2:45); Hebrew lacks *from a mountain.*

48Then the king appointed Daniel to a high position and gave him many valuable gifts. He made Daniel ruler over the whole province of Babylon, as well as chief over all his wise men. 49At Daniel's request, the king appointed Shadrach, Meshach, and Abednego to be in charge of all the affairs of the province of Babylon, while Daniel remained in the king's court.

Nebuchadnezzar's Gold Statue

3 King Nebuchadnezzar made a gold statue ninety feet tall and nine feet wide* and set it up on the plain of Dura in the province of Babylon. 2Then he sent messages to the high officers, officials, governors, advisers, treasurers, judges, magistrates, and all the provincial officials to come to the dedication of the statue he had set up. 3So all these officials* came and stood before the statue King Nebuchadnezzar had set up.

4Then a herald shouted out, "People of all races and nations and languages, listen to the king's command! 5When you hear the sound of the horn, flute, zither, lyre, harp, pipes, and other musical instruments,* bow to the ground to worship King Nebuchadnezzar's gold statue. 6Anyone who refuses to obey will immediately be thrown into a blazing furnace."

7So at the sound of the musical instruments,* all the people, whatever their race or nation or language, bowed to the ground and worshiped the gold statue that King Nebuchadnezzar had set up.

8But some of the astrologers* went to the king and informed on the Jews. 9They said to King Nebuchadnezzar, "Long live the king! 10You issued a decree requiring all the people to bow down and worship the gold statue when they hear the sound of the horn, flute, zither, lyre, harp, pipes, and other musical instruments. 11That decree also states that those who refuse to obey must be thrown into a blazing furnace. 12But there are some Jews—Shadrach, Meshach, and Abednego—whom you have put in charge of the province of Babylon. They pay no attention to you, Your Majesty. They refuse to serve your gods and do not worship the gold statue you have set up."

13Then Nebuchadnezzar flew into a rage and ordered that Shadrach, Meshach, and Abednego be brought before him. When they were brought in, 14Nebuchadnezzar said to them, "Is it true, Shadrach, Meshach, and Abednego, that you refuse to serve my gods or to worship the gold statue I have set up? 15I will give you one more chance to bow down and worship the statue I have made when you hear the sound of the musical instruments.* But if you refuse, you will be thrown immediately into the blazing furnace. And then what god will be able to rescue you from my power?"

16Shadrach, Meshach, and Abednego replied, "O Nebuchadnezzar, we do not need to defend ourselves before you. 17If we are thrown into the blazing furnace, the God whom we serve is able to save us. He will rescue us from your power, Your Majesty. 18But even if he doesn't, we want to make it clear to you, Your Majesty, that we will never serve your gods or worship the gold statue you have set up."

The Blazing Furnace

19Nebuchadnezzar was so furious with Shadrach, Meshach, and Abednego that his face became distorted with rage. He commanded that the furnace be heated seven times hotter than usual. 20Then he ordered some of the strongest men of his army to bind Shadrach, Meshach, and Abednego and throw them into the blazing furnace. 21So they tied them up and threw them into the furnace, fully dressed in their pants, turbans, robes, and other garments. 22And because the king, in his anger, had demanded such a hot fire in the furnace, the flames killed the soldiers as they threw the three men in. 23So Shadrach, Meshach, and Abednego, securely tied, fell into the roaring flames.

The Prayer of Azariah

24The three men walked around in the fire, singing hymns to God and praising the Lord.* 25Then Azariah* stood still in the fire and prayed aloud:

26 "You are worthy of praise, O Lord, the God of our ancestors.
    Your name is glorious forever!
27 For you are just in everything you have done.
    All your works are true, your ways are right,
    and all your judgments reflect the truth.

3:1 Aramaic 60 cubits [27.6 meters] tall and 6 cubits [2.8 meters] wide.   3:3 Aramaic the high officers, officials, governors, advisers, treasurers, judges, magistrates, and all the provincial officials.   3:5 The identification of some of these musical instruments is uncertain.   3:7 Aramaic the horn, flute, zither, lyre, harp, and other musical instruments.   3:8 Aramaic Chaldeans.   3:15 Aramaic the horn, flute, zither, lyre, harp, pipes, and other musical instruments.   3:24 Verses 3:24-90 and chapters 13 and 14 are not included in the Hebrew and Aramaic text of Daniel. They are here translated from Theodotion's Greek text.   3:25 Azariah was the original Hebrew name of Abednego. See 1:6-7.

28 You acted justly when you caused all these
     things to happen to us
     and to Jerusalem, the holy city of our
       ancestors.
   Because of our sins, you acted justly,
     causing all this to happen.
29 For we have sinned and broken your law
     by deserting you.
   We sinned greatly in everything.
30 We have not obeyed your commandments.
   We have not done what you commanded
     for our own good.
31 So in everything you have brought
     upon us
   and everything you have done to us,
   you have acted justly.
32 You have handed us over to our enemies—
     lawless and detested rebels—
   and to an unjust king, the worst in all
     the world.
33 And now there is nothing we can say.
   We, your servants who worship you,
     have been shamed and disgraced.

34 "But for your name's sake do not abandon
     us forever;
   do not discard your covenant.
35 Do not withdraw your mercy from us—
     for the sake of Abraham, your beloved
       friend;
   Isaac your servant; and Israel, your holy
     one.
36 For you promised them as many
     descendants
   as the stars of heaven
   and the sand on the seashore.
37 Lord, we have become the smallest of all
     nations,
   and now we are humiliated in all the
     world
   because of our sins.
38 We have no ruler or prophet or leader,
   no burnt offering, sacrifice, drink
     offering, or incense.
   We have no place to make an offering
     before you and find mercy.
39 Yet because of our contrite heart and
     humble spirit, please accept us
40 as if we had sacrificed burnt offerings
     of rams and bulls
   or thousands of fat lambs.
   Please regard our sacrifice this way today,
   and may we follow you completely,
     for those who trust in you will not be
       put to shame.

41 And now we follow you with all our heart.
   We fear you and seek your presence.
42 Do not let us be put to shame,
   but deal with us in your patience
   and in your great mercy.
43 Rescue us, just as you have done many
     other marvelous works,
   and bring glory to your name, O Lord.
44 Let all who harm your servants be put to
     shame;
   let them be humbled and deprived of
     all power,
   and let their strength be broken.
45 Teach them that you alone are the Lord God,
   glorious over the whole world."

The Song of the Three Young Men
46Now the king's servants who had thrown
them into the furnace continued to stoke it
with oil, pitch, flax fibers, and brush, 47and the
flames shot seventy-five feet* into the air above
the furnace. 48The flames also leaped out and
burned some of the Babylonians* who were
near the furnace. 49But the angel of the Lord
went down into the furnace to be with Azariah
and his friends. He drove the flames out of the
furnace 50so that the middle of the furnace was
as cool as a dew-laden breeze. The fire did not
touch them or even bother them, nor did it
harm them in any way.

51Then the three men praised, glorified, and
blessed God together in the furnace. They said,

52 "Blessed are you, O Lord, the God of our
     ancestors,
   and worthy to be praised and exalted
     above all forever.
   Blessed is your glorious, holy name
   and worthy to be praised and exalted
     above all forever.
53 Blessed are you in the Temple, where your
     holy glory is,
   and worthy to be honored and glorified
     forever.
54 Blessed are you, ruling from the throne of
     your kingdom,
   and worthy to be honored and exalted
     above all forever.
55 Blessed are you, who looks into the depths
     from your throne between the cherubim,
   and worthy to be praised and exalted
     above all forever.
56 Blessed are you in the expanse of heaven
   and worthy to be honored and glorified
     forever.

3:47 Greek 49 cubits [22.5 meters].   3:48 Greek Chaldeans.

57 "Bless the Lord, all you works of the Lord.
  Sing praise to him, and exalt him above
    all forever.
58 Bless the Lord, you angels of the Lord.
  Sing praise to him, and exalt him above
    all forever.
59 Bless the Lord, you heavens.
  Sing praise to him, and exalt him above
    all forever.
60 Bless the Lord, all you clouds in the sky.*
  Sing praise to him, and exalt him above
    all forever.
61 Bless the Lord, all you heavenly works of
    the Lord.
  Sing praise to him, and exalt him above
    all forever.
62 Bless the Lord, sun and moon.
  Sing praise to him, and exalt him above
    all forever.
63 Bless the Lord, stars of heaven.
  Sing praise to him, and exalt him above
    all forever.
64 "Bless the Lord, all rain and dew.
  Sing praise to him, and exalt him above
    all forever.
65 Bless the Lord, all you winds.
  Sing praise to him, and exalt him above
    all forever.
66 Bless the Lord, fire and heat.
  Sing praise to him, and exalt him above
    all forever.
67 Bless the Lord, winter cold and summer
    heat.
  Sing praise to him, and exalt him above
    all forever.
68 Bless the Lord, dew and snow.
  Sing praise to him, and exalt him above
    all forever.
69 Bless the Lord, frost and cold.
  Sing praise to him, and exalt him above
    all forever.
70 Bless the Lord, ice and snow.
  Sing praise to him, and exalt him above
    all forever.
71 Bless the Lord, nights and days.
  Sing praise to him, and exalt him above
    all forever.
72 Bless the Lord, light and darkness.
  Sing praise to him, and exalt him above
    all forever.
73 Bless the Lord, lightning and clouds.
  Sing praise to him, and exalt him above
    all forever.

74 "Let the earth bless the Lord.
  Let it sing praise to him and exalt him
    above all forever.
75 Bless the Lord, you mountains and hills.
  Sing praise to him, and exalt him above
    all forever.
76 Bless the Lord, all that grows in the
    ground.
  Sing praise to him, and exalt him above
    all forever.
77 Bless the Lord, you springs of the earth.
  Sing praise to him, and exalt him above
    all forever.
78 Bless the Lord, you seas and rivers.
  Sing praise to him, and exalt him above
    all forever.
79 Bless the Lord, you whales and fish.
  Sing praise to him, and exalt him above
    all forever.
80 Bless the Lord, you flying birds.
  Sing praise to him, and exalt him above
    all forever.
81 Bless the Lord, all you animals, wild and
    tame.
  Sing praise to him, and exalt him above
    all forever.
82 "Bless the Lord, all you people on earth.
  Sing praise to him, and exalt him above
    all forever.
83 Bless the Lord, you people of Israel.
  Sing praise to him, and exalt him above
    all forever.
84 Bless the Lord, you priests of the Lord.
  Sing praise to him, and exalt him above
    all forever.
85 Bless the Lord, you servants of the Lord.
  Sing praise to him, and exalt him above
    all forever.
86 Bless the Lord, you righteous ones.*
  Sing praise to him, and exalt him above
    all forever.
87 Bless the Lord, you who are holy and
    humble of heart.
  Sing praise to him, and exalt him above
    all forever.
88 "Bless the Lord, Hananiah, Azariah, and
    Mishael.*
  Sing praise to him, and exalt him above
    all forever.
  For he has rescued us from the grave*
    and saved us from the power of death.
  He delivered us from the fiery furnace;

3:60 Greek *you waters above the heavens.*   3:86 Greek *you spirits and souls of the righteous.*   3:88a *Hananiah, Azariah,* and *Mishael*
were the original Hebrew names of Shadrach, Abednego, and Meshach. See 1:6-7.   3:88b Greek *from Hades.*

from the midst of the fire he has
delivered us.
89 Give thanks to the Lord, for he is good,
for his mercy endures forever.
90 All you who worship the Lord, bless the
God of gods.
Sing praise to him, and give him thanks,
for his mercy endures forever."

The Three Young Men Are Delivered

91 But suddenly, Nebuchadnezzar jumped up
in amazement and exclaimed to his advisers,
"Didn't we tie up three men and throw them
into the furnace?"

"Yes, Your Majesty, we certainly did," they
replied.

92 "Look!" Nebuchadnezzar shouted. "I see
four men, unbound, walking around in the fire
unharmed! And the fourth looks like a god*!"

93 Then Nebuchadnezzar came as close as
he could to the door of the flaming furnace
and shouted: "Shadrach, Meshach, and Abednego, servants of the Most High God, come
out! Come here!"

So Shadrach, Meshach, and Abednego
stepped out of the fire. 94 Then the high officers, officials, governors, and advisers crowded
around them and saw that the fire had not
touched them. Not a hair on their heads was
singed, and their clothing was not scorched.
They didn't even smell of smoke!

95 Then Nebuchadnezzar said, "Praise to the
God of Shadrach, Meshach, and Abednego! He
sent his angel to rescue his servants who trusted
in him. They defied the king's command and
were willing to die rather than serve or worship
any god except their own God. 96 Therefore, I
make this decree: If any people, whatever their
race or nation or language, speak a word against
the God of Shadrach, Meshach, and Abednego,
they will be torn limb from limb, and their
houses will be turned into heaps of rubble.
There is no other god who can rescue like this!"

97 Then the king promoted Shadrach, Meshach, and Abednego to even higher positions
in the province of Babylon.

Nebuchadnezzar's Dream about a Tree

4 1*King Nebuchadnezzar sent this message
to the people of every race and nation and
language throughout the world:

"Peace and prosperity to you!
2 "I want you all to know about the

miraculous signs and wonders the Most
High God has performed for me.

3 How great are his signs,
how powerful his wonders!
His kingdom will last forever,
his rule through all generations.

4* "I, Nebuchadnezzar, was living in my
palace in comfort and prosperity. 5 But one
night I had a dream that frightened me; I
saw visions that terrified me as I lay in my
bed. 6 So I issued an order calling in all the
wise men of Babylon, so they could tell
me what my dream meant. 7 When all the
magicians, enchanters, astrologers,* and
fortune-tellers came in, I told them the
dream, but they could not tell me what it
meant. 8 At last Daniel came in before me,
and I told him the dream. (He was named
Belteshazzar after my god, and the spirit
of the holy gods is in him.)

9 "I said to him, 'Belteshazzar, chief of
the magicians, I know that the spirit of the
holy gods is in you and that no mystery
is too great for you to solve. Now tell me
what my dream means.

10 "While I was lying in my bed, this is
what I dreamed. I saw a large tree in the
middle of the earth. 11 The tree grew very
tall and strong, reaching high into the
heavens for all the world to see. 12 It had
fresh green leaves, and it was loaded with
fruit for all to eat. Wild animals lived in its
shade, and birds nested in its branches. All
the world was fed from this tree.

13 "Then as I lay there dreaming, I saw a
messenger,* a holy one, coming down from
heaven. 14 The messenger shouted,

"Cut down the tree and lop off its
branches!
Shake off its leaves and scatter its
fruit!
Chase the wild animals from its shade
and the birds from its branches.
15 But leave the stump and the roots in the
ground,
bound with a band of iron and bronze
and surrounded by tender grass.
Now let him be drenched with the dew
of heaven,
and let him live with the wild animals
among the plants of the field.

3:92 Aramaic like a son of the gods.   4:1 Verses 4:1-3 are numbered 3:31-33 in Aramaic text.   4:4 Verses 4:4-37 are numbered
4:1-34 in Aramaic text.   4:7 Or Chaldeans.   4:13 Aramaic a watcher; also in 4:23.

16 For seven periods of time,
  let him have the mind of a wild
    animal
  instead of the mind of a human.
17 For this has been decreed by the
    messengers*;
  it is commanded by the holy ones,
so that everyone may know
  that the Most High rules over the
    kingdoms of the world.
He gives them to anyone he chooses—
  even to the lowliest of people."

18 "'Belteshazzar, that was the dream
that I, King Nebuchadnezzar, had. Now
tell me what it means, for none of the wise
men of my kingdom can do so. But you can
tell me because the spirit of the holy gods
is in you.'

Daniel Explains the Dream

19 "Upon hearing this, Daniel (also known
as Belteshazzar) was overcome for a time,
frightened by the meaning of the dream.
Then the king said to him, 'Belteshazzar,
don't be alarmed by the dream and what
it means.'

"Belteshazzar replied, 'I wish the
events foreshadowed in this dream would
happen to your enemies, my lord, and not
to you! 20 The tree you saw was growing
very tall and strong, reaching high into
the heavens for all the world to see. 21 It
had fresh green leaves and was loaded
with fruit for all to eat. Wild animals
lived in its shade, and birds nested in its
branches. 22 That tree, Your Majesty, is you.
For you have grown strong and great; your
greatness reaches up to heaven, and your
rule to the ends of the earth.

23 "'Then you saw a messenger, a holy
one, coming down from heaven and
saying, "Cut down the tree and destroy it.
But leave the stump and the roots in the
ground, bound with a band of iron and
bronze and surrounded by tender grass.
Let him be drenched with the dew of
heaven. Let him live with the animals of
the field for seven periods of time."

24 "'This is what the dream means,
Your Majesty, and what the Most High
has declared will happen to my lord the
king. 25 You will be driven from human
society, and you will live in the fields with
the wild animals. You will eat grass like

a cow, and you will be drenched with the
dew of heaven. Seven periods of time will
pass while you live this way, until you
learn that the Most High rules over the
kingdoms of the world and gives them to
anyone he chooses. 26 But the stump and
roots of the tree were left in the ground.
This means that you will receive your
kingdom back again when you have
learned that heaven rules.

27 "'King Nebuchadnezzar, please accept
my advice. Stop sinning and do what is
right. Break from your wicked past and be
merciful to the poor. Perhaps then you will
continue to prosper.'

The Dream's Fulfillment

28 "But all these things did happen to King
Nebuchadnezzar. 29 Twelve months later
he was taking a walk on the flat roof of the
royal palace in Babylon. 30 As he looked
out across the city, he said, 'Look at this
great city of Babylon! By my own mighty
power, I have built this beautiful city as
my royal residence to display my majestic
splendor.'

31 "While these words were still in his
mouth, a voice called down from heaven,
'O King Nebuchadnezzar, this message
is for you! You are no longer ruler of
this kingdom. 32 You will be driven from
human society. You will live in the fields
with the wild animals, and you will eat
grass like a cow. Seven periods of time
will pass while you live this way, until you
learn that the Most High rules over the
kingdoms of the world and gives them to
anyone he chooses.'

33 "That same hour the judgment was
fulfilled, and Nebuchadnezzar was driven
from human society. He ate grass like a
cow, and he was drenched with the dew
of heaven. He lived this way until his hair
was as long as eagles' feathers and his nails
were like birds' claws.

Nebuchadnezzar Praises God

34 "After this time had passed, I,
Nebuchadnezzar, looked up to heaven.
My sanity returned, and I praised and
worshiped the Most High and honored
the one who lives forever.

His rule is everlasting,
  and his kingdom is eternal.

4:17 Aramaic *the watchers.*

35 All the people of the earth
 are nothing compared to him.
He does as he pleases
 among the angels of heaven
 and among the people of the earth.
No one can stop him or say to him,
 'What do you mean by doing these
  things?'

36 "When my sanity returned to me, so did my honor and glory and kingdom. My advisers and nobles sought me out, and I was restored as head of my kingdom, with even greater honor than before. 37 "Now I, Nebuchadnezzar, praise and glorify and honor the King of heaven. All his acts are just and true, and he is able to humble the proud."

The Writing on the Wall

5 Many years later King Belshazzar gave a great feast for 1,000 of his nobles, and he drank wine with them. 2 While Belshazzar was drinking the wine, he gave orders to bring in the gold and silver cups that his predecessor,* Nebuchadnezzar, had taken from the Temple in Jerusalem. He wanted to drink from them with his nobles, his wives, and his concubines. 3 So they brought these gold cups taken from the Temple, the house of God in Jerusalem, and the king and his nobles, his wives, and his concubines drank from them. 4 While they drank from them they praised their idols made of gold, silver, bronze, iron, wood, and stone.

5 Suddenly, they saw the fingers of a human hand writing on the plaster wall of the king's palace, near the lampstand. The king himself saw the hand as it wrote, 6 and his face turned pale with fright. His knees knocked together in fear and his legs gave way beneath him.

7 The king shouted for the enchanters, astrologers,* and fortune-tellers to be brought before him. He said to these wise men of Babylon, "Whoever can read this writing and tell me what it means will be dressed in purple robes of royal honor and will have a gold chain placed around his neck. He will become the third highest ruler in the kingdom!"

8 But when all the king's wise men had come in, none of them could read the writing or tell him what it meant. 9 So the king grew even more alarmed, and his face turned pale. His nobles, too, were shaken.

10 But when the queen mother heard what was happening, she hurried to the banquet hall. She said to Belshazzar, "Long live the king! Don't be so pale and frightened. 11 There is a man in your kingdom who has within him the spirit of the holy gods. During Nebuchadnezzar's reign, this man was found to have insight, understanding, and wisdom like that of the gods. Your predecessor, the king—your predecessor King Nebuchadnezzar—made him chief over all the magicians, enchanters, astrologers, and fortune-tellers of Babylon. 12 This man Daniel, whom the king named Belteshazzar, has exceptional ability and is filled with divine knowledge and understanding. He can interpret dreams, explain riddles, and solve difficult problems. Call for Daniel, and he will tell you what the writing means."

Daniel Explains the Writing

13 So Daniel was brought in before the king. The king asked him, "Are you Daniel, one of the exiles brought from Judah by my predecessor, King Nebuchadnezzar? 14 I have heard that you have the spirit of the gods within you and that you are filled with insight, understanding, and wisdom. 15 My wise men and enchanters have tried to read the words on the wall and tell me their meaning, but they cannot do it. 16 I am told that you can give interpretations and solve difficult problems. If you can read these words and tell me their meaning, you will be clothed in purple robes of royal honor, and you will have a gold chain placed around your neck. You will become the third highest ruler in the kingdom."

17 Daniel answered the king, "Keep your gifts or give them to someone else, but I will tell you what the writing means. 18 Your Majesty, the Most High God gave sovereignty, majesty, glory, and honor to your predecessor, Nebuchadnezzar. 19 He made him so great that people of all races and nations and languages trembled before him in fear. He killed those he wanted to kill and spared those he wanted to spare. He honored those he wanted to honor and disgraced those he wanted to disgrace. 20 But when his heart and mind were puffed up with arrogance, he was brought down from his royal throne and stripped of his glory. 21 He was driven from human society. He was given the mind of a wild animal, and he lived among the wild donkeys. He ate grass like a cow, and he was drenched with the dew of heaven, until he learned that the Most High God rules over the kingdoms of the world and appoints anyone he desires to rule over them.

5:2 Aramaic *father;* also in 5:11, 13, 18. 5:7 Or *Chaldeans;* also in 5:11.

²²"You are his successor,* O Belshazzar, and you knew all this, yet you have not humbled yourself. ²³For you have proudly defied the Lord of heaven and have had these cups from his Temple brought before you. You and your nobles and your wives and concubines have been drinking wine from them while praising gods of silver, gold, bronze, iron, wood, and stone—gods that neither see nor hear nor know anything at all. But you have not honored the God who gives you the breath of life and controls your destiny! ²⁴So God has sent this hand to write this message.

²⁵"This is the message that was written: MENE, MENE, TEKEL, and PARSIN. ²⁶This is what these words mean:

> Mene means 'numbered'—God has numbered the days of your reign and has brought it to an end.
> ²⁷ Tekel means 'weighed'—you have been weighed on the balances and have not measured up.
> ²⁸ Parsin* means 'divided'—your kingdom has been divided and given to the Medes and Persians."

²⁹Then at Belshazzar's command, Daniel was dressed in purple robes, a gold chain was hung around his neck, and he was proclaimed the third highest ruler in the kingdom.

³⁰That very night Belshazzar, the Babylonian* king, was killed.*

³¹*And Darius the Mede took over the kingdom at the age of sixty-two.

Daniel in the Lions' Den

6 ¹*Darius the Mede decided to divide the kingdom into 120 provinces, and he appointed a high officer to rule over each province. ²The king also chose Daniel and two others as administrators to supervise the high officers and protect the king's interests. ³Daniel soon proved himself more capable than all the other administrators and high officers. Because of Daniel's great ability, the king made plans to place him over the entire empire.

⁴Then the other administrators and high officers began searching for some fault in the way Daniel was handling government affairs, but they couldn't find anything to criticize or condemn. He was faithful, always responsible, and completely trustworthy. ⁵So they concluded, "Our only chance of finding grounds for accusing Daniel will be in connection with the rules of his religion."

⁶So the administrators and high officers went to the king and said, "Long live King Darius! ⁷We are all in agreement—we administrators, officials, high officers, advisers, and governors—that the king should make a law that will be strictly enforced. Give orders that for the next thirty days any person who prays to anyone, divine or human—except to you, Your Majesty—will be thrown into the den of lions. ⁸And now, Your Majesty, issue and sign this law so it cannot be changed, an official law of the Medes and Persians that cannot be revoked." ⁹So King Darius signed the law.

¹⁰But when Daniel learned that the law had been signed, he went home and knelt down as usual in his upstairs room, with its windows open toward Jerusalem. He prayed three times a day, just as he had always done, giving thanks to his God. ¹¹Then the officials went together to Daniel's house and found him praying and asking for God's help. ¹²So they went straight to the king and reminded him about his law. "Did you not sign a law that for the next thirty days any person who prays to anyone, divine or human—except to you, Your Majesty—will be thrown into the den of lions?"

"Yes," the king replied, "that decision stands; it is an official law of the Medes and Persians that cannot be revoked."

¹³Then they told the king, "That man Daniel, one of the captives from Judah, is ignoring you and your law. He still prays to his God three times a day."

¹⁴Hearing this, the king was deeply troubled, and he tried to think of a way to save Daniel. He spent the rest of the day looking for a way to get Daniel out of this predicament.

¹⁵In the evening the men went together to the king and said, "Your Majesty, you know that according to the law of the Medes and the Persians, no law that the king signs can be changed."

¹⁶So at last the king gave orders for Daniel to be arrested and thrown into the den of lions. The king said to him, "May your God, whom you serve so faithfully, rescue you."

¹⁷A stone was brought and placed over the mouth of the den. The king sealed the stone with his own royal seal and the seals of his nobles, so that no one could rescue Daniel.

5:22 Aramaic son.   5:28 Aramaic Peres, the singular of Parsin.   5:30a Or Chaldean.   5:30b The Persians and Medes conquered Babylon in October 539 B.C.   5:31 Verse 5:31 is numbered 6:1 in Aramaic text.   6:1 Verses 6:1-28 are numbered 6:2-29 in Aramaic text.

18Then the king returned to his palace and spent the night fasting. He refused his usual entertainment and couldn't sleep at all that night.

19Very early the next morning, the king got up and hurried out to the lions' den. 20When he got there, he called out in anguish, "Daniel, servant of the living God! Was your God, whom you serve so faithfully, able to rescue you from the lions?"

21Daniel answered, "Long live the king! 22My God sent his angel to shut the lions' mouths so that they would not hurt me, for I have been found innocent in his sight. And I have not wronged you, Your Majesty."

23The king was overjoyed and ordered that Daniel be lifted from the den. Not a scratch was found on him, for he had trusted in his God.

24Then the king gave orders to arrest the men who had maliciously accused Daniel. He had them thrown into the lions' den, along with their wives and children. The lions leaped on them and tore them apart before they even hit the floor of the den.

25Then King Darius sent this message to the people of every race and nation and language throughout the world:

"Peace and prosperity to you!

26"I decree that everyone throughout my kingdom should tremble with fear before the God of Daniel.

For he is the living God,
    and he will endure forever.
His kingdom will never be destroyed,
    and his rule will never end.
27 He rescues and saves his people;
    he performs miraculous signs and
        wonders
    in the heavens and on earth.
He has rescued Daniel
    from the power of the lions."

28So Daniel prospered during the reign of Darius and the reign of Cyrus the Persian.*

Daniel's Vision of Four Beasts

7 Earlier, during the first year of King Belshazzar's reign in Babylon,* Daniel had a dream and saw visions as he lay in his bed. He wrote down the dream, and this is what he saw.

2In my vision that night, I, Daniel, saw a great storm churning the surface of a great sea, with strong winds blowing from every direction. 3Then four huge beasts came up out of the water, each different from the others.

4The first beast was like a lion with eagles' wings. As I watched, its wings were pulled off, and it was left standing with its two hind feet on the ground, like a human being. And it was given a human mind.

5Then I saw a second beast, and it looked like a bear. It was rearing up on one side, and it had three ribs in its mouth between its teeth. And I heard a voice saying to it, "Get up! Devour the flesh of many people!"

6Then the third of these strange beasts appeared, and it looked like a leopard. It had four bird's wings on its back, and it had four heads. Great authority was given to this beast.

7Then in my vision that night, I saw a fourth beast—terrifying, dreadful, and very strong. It devoured and crushed its victims with huge iron teeth and trampled their remains beneath its feet. It was different from any of the other beasts, and it had ten horns.

8As I was looking at the horns, suddenly another small horn appeared among them. Three of the first horns were torn out by the roots to make room for it. This little horn had eyes like human eyes and a mouth that was boasting arrogantly.

9 I watched as thrones were put in place
    and the Ancient One* sat down to judge.
His clothing was as white as snow,
    his hair like purest wool.
He sat on a fiery throne
    with wheels of blazing fire,
10 and a river of fire was pouring out,
    flowing from his presence.
Millions of angels ministered to him;
    many millions stood to attend him.
Then the court began its session,
    and the books were opened.

11I continued to watch because I could hear the little horn's boastful speech. I kept watching until the fourth beast was killed and its body was destroyed by fire. 12The other three beasts had their authority taken from them, but they were allowed to live a while longer.* 13As my vision continued that night, I saw someone like a son of man* coming with the clouds of heaven. He approached the Ancient

---

6:28 Or of Darius, that is, the reign of Cyrus the Persian.   7:1 The first year of Belshazzar's reign (who was co-regent with his father, Nabonidus) was 556 B.C. (or perhaps as late as 553 B.C.).   7:9 Aramaic an Ancient of Days; also in 7:13, 22.
7:12 Aramaic for a season and a time.   7:13 Or like a Son of Man.

One and was led into his presence. ¹⁴He was given authority, honor, and sovereignty over all the nations of the world, so that people of every race and nation and language would obey him. His rule is eternal—it will never end. His kingdom will never be destroyed.

The Vision Is Explained

¹⁵I, Daniel, was troubled by all I had seen, and my visions terrified me. ¹⁶So I approached one of those standing beside the throne and asked him what it all meant. He explained it to me like this: ¹⁷"These four huge beasts represent four kingdoms that will arise from the earth. ¹⁸But in the end, the holy people of the Most High will be given the kingdom, and they will rule forever and ever."

¹⁹Then I wanted to know the true meaning of the fourth beast, the one so different from the others and so terrifying. It had devoured and crushed its victims with iron teeth and bronze claws, trampling their remains beneath its feet. ²⁰I also asked about the ten horns on the fourth beast's head and the little horn that came up afterward and destroyed three of the other horns. This horn had seemed greater than the others, and it had human eyes and a mouth that was boasting arrogantly. ²¹As I watched, this horn was waging war against God's holy people and was defeating them, ²²until the Ancient One—the Most High—came and judged in favor of his holy people. Then the time arrived for the holy people to take over the kingdom.

²³Then he said to me, "This fourth beast is the fourth world power that will rule the earth. It will be different from all the others. It will devour the whole world, trampling and crushing everything in its path. ²⁴Its ten horns are ten kings who will rule that empire. Then another king will arise, different from the other ten, who will subdue three of them. ²⁵He will defy the Most High and oppress the holy people of the Most High. He will try to change their sacred festivals and laws, and they will be placed under his control for a time, times, and half a time.

²⁶"But then the court will pass judgment, and all his power will be taken away and completely destroyed. ²⁷Then the sovereignty, power, and greatness of all the kingdoms under heaven will be given to the holy people of the Most High. His kingdom will last forever, and all rulers will serve and obey him."

²⁸That was the end of the vision. I, Daniel, was terrified by my thoughts and my face was pale with fear, but I kept these things to myself.

Daniel's Vision of a Ram and Goat

8 ¹*During the third year of King Belshazzar's reign, I, Daniel, saw another vision, following the one that had already appeared to me. ²In this vision I was at the fortress of Susa, in the province of Elam, standing beside the Ulai River.*

³As I looked up, I saw a ram with two long horns standing beside the river.* One of the horns was longer than the other, even though it had grown later than the other one. ⁴The ram butted everything out of his way to the west, to the north, and to the south, and no one could stand against him or help his victims. He did as he pleased and became very great.

⁵While I was watching, suddenly a male goat appeared from the west, crossing the land so swiftly that he didn't even touch the ground. This goat, which had one very large horn between its eyes, ⁶headed toward the two-horned ram that I had seen standing beside the river, rushing at him in a rage. ⁷The goat charged furiously at the ram and struck him, breaking off both his horns. Now the ram was helpless, and the goat knocked him down and trampled him. No one could rescue the ram from the goat's power.

⁸The goat became very powerful. But at the height of his power, his large horn was broken off. In the large horn's place grew four prominent horns pointing in the four directions of the earth. ⁹Then from one of the prominent horns came a small horn whose power grew very great. It extended toward the south and the east and toward the glorious land of Israel. ¹⁰Its power reached to the heavens, where it attacked the heavenly army, throwing some of the heavenly beings and some of the stars to the ground and trampling them. ¹¹It even challenged the Commander of heaven's army by canceling the daily sacrifices offered to him and by destroying his Temple. ¹²The army of heaven was restrained from responding to this rebellion. So the daily sacrifice was halted, and truth was overthrown. The horn succeeded in everything it did.*

¹³Then I heard two holy ones talking to each other. One of them asked, "How long will the events of this vision last? How long will the

---

8:1 The original text from this point through chapter 12 is in Hebrew. See note at 2:4.   8:2 Or *the Ulai Gate*; also in 8:16.
8:3 Or *the gate*; also in 8:6.   8:11-12 The meaning of the Hebrew for these verses is uncertain.

rebellion that causes desecration stop the daily sacrifices? How long will the Temple and heaven's army be trampled on?"

¹⁴The other replied, "It will take 2,300 evenings and mornings; then the Temple will be made right again."

Gabriel Explains the Vision

¹⁵As I, Daniel, was trying to understand the meaning of this vision, someone who looked like a man stood in front of me. ¹⁶And I heard a human voice calling out from the Ulai River, "Gabriel, tell this man the meaning of his vision."

¹⁷As Gabriel approached the place where I was standing, I became so terrified that I fell with my face to the ground. "Son of man," he said, "you must understand that the events you have seen in your vision relate to the time of the end."

¹⁸While he was speaking, I fainted and lay there with my face to the ground. But Gabriel roused me with a touch and helped me to my feet.

¹⁹Then he said, "I am here to tell you what will happen later in the time of wrath. What you have seen pertains to the very end of time. ²⁰The two-horned ram represents the kings of Media and Persia. ²¹The shaggy male goat represents the king of Greece,* and the large horn between his eyes represents the first king of the Greek Empire. ²²The four prominent horns that replaced the one large horn show that the Greek Empire will break into four kingdoms, but none as great as the first.

²³"At the end of their rule, when their sin is at its height, a fierce king, a master of intrigue, will rise to power. ²⁴He will become very strong, but not by his own power. He will cause a shocking amount of destruction and succeed in everything he does. He will destroy powerful leaders and devastate the holy people. ²⁵He will be a master of deception and will become arrogant; he will destroy many without warning. He will even take on the Prince of princes in battle, but he will be broken, though not by human power.

²⁶"This vision about the 2,300 evenings and mornings* is true. But none of these things will happen for a long time, so keep this vision a secret."

²⁷Then I, Daniel, was overcome and lay sick for several days. Afterward I got up and performed my duties for the king, but I was greatly troubled by the vision and could not understand it.

Daniel's Prayer for His People

9 It was the first year of the reign of Darius the Mede, the son of Ahasuerus, who became king of the Babylonians.* ²During the first year of his reign, I, Daniel, learned from reading the word of the LORD, as revealed to Jeremiah the prophet, that Jerusalem must lie desolate for seventy years.* ³So I turned to the Lord God and pleaded with him in prayer and fasting. I also wore rough burlap and sprinkled myself with ashes.

⁴I prayed to the LORD my God and confessed:

"O Lord, you are a great and awesome God! You always fulfill your covenant and keep your promises of unfailing love to those who love you and obey your commands. ⁵But we have sinned and done wrong. We have rebelled against you and scorned your commands and regulations. ⁶We have refused to listen to your servants the prophets, who spoke on your authority to our kings and princes and ancestors and to all the people of the land.

⁷"Lord, you are in the right; but as you see, our faces are covered with shame. This is true of all of us, including the people of Judah and Jerusalem and all Israel, scattered near and far, wherever you have driven us because of our disloyalty to you. ⁸O LORD, we and our kings, princes, and ancestors are covered with shame because we have sinned against you. ⁹But the Lord our God is merciful and forgiving, even though we have rebelled against him. ¹⁰We have not obeyed the LORD our God, for we have not followed the instructions he gave us through his servants the prophets. ¹¹All Israel has disobeyed your instruction and turned away, refusing to listen to your voice.

"So now the solemn curses and judgments written in the Law of Moses, the servant of God, have been poured down on us because of our sin. ¹²You have kept your word and done to us and our rulers exactly as you warned. Never has there been such a disaster as happened in Jerusalem. ¹³Every curse written against us in the Law of Moses has come true. Yet we have refused to seek mercy from the LORD our God by

---

8:21 Hebrew *of Javan*.   8:26 Hebrew *about the evenings and mornings;* compare 8:14.   9:1 Or *the Chaldeans.*
9:2 See Jer 25:11-12; 29:10.

turning from our sins and recognizing his truth. [14]Therefore, the LORD has brought upon us the disaster he prepared. The LORD our God was right to do all of these things, for we did not obey him.

[15]"O Lord our God, you brought lasting honor to your name by rescuing your people from Egypt in a great display of power. But we have sinned and are full of wickedness. [16]In view of all your faithful mercies, Lord, please turn your furious anger away from your city Jerusalem, your holy mountain. All the neighboring nations mock Jerusalem and your people because of our sins and the sins of our ancestors.

[17]"O our God, hear your servant's prayer! Listen as I plead. For your own sake, Lord, smile again on your desolate sanctuary.

[18]"O my God, lean down and listen to me. Open your eyes and see our despair. See how your city—the city that bears your name—lies in ruins. We make this plea, not because we deserve help, but because of your mercy.

[19]"O Lord, hear. O Lord, forgive. O Lord, listen and act! For your own sake, do not delay, O my God, for your people and your city bear your name."

Gabriel's Message about the Anointed One

[20]I went on praying and confessing my sin and the sin of my people, pleading with the LORD my God for Jerusalem, his holy mountain. [21]As I was praying, Gabriel, whom I had seen in the earlier vision, came swiftly to me at the time of the evening sacrifice. [22]He explained to me, "Daniel, I have come here to give you insight and understanding. [23]The moment you began praying, a command was given. And now I am here to tell you what it was, for you are very precious to God. Listen carefully so that you can understand the meaning of your vision.

[24]"A period of seventy sets of seven* has been decreed for your people and your holy city to finish their rebellion, to put an end to their sin, to atone for their guilt, to bring in everlasting righteousness, to confirm the prophetic vision, and to anoint the Most Holy Place.* [25]Now listen and understand! Seven sets of seven plus sixty-two sets of seven* will pass from the time the command is given to rebuild Jerusalem until a ruler—the Anointed One*—comes. Jerusalem will be rebuilt with streets and strong defenses,* despite the perilous times.

[26]"After this period of sixty-two sets of seven,* the Anointed One will be killed, appearing to have accomplished nothing, and a ruler will arise whose armies will destroy the city and the Temple. The end will come with a flood, and war and its miseries are decreed from that time to the very end. [27]The ruler will make a treaty with the people for a period of one set of seven,* but after half this time, he will put an end to the sacrifices and offerings. And as a climax to all his terrible deeds,* he will set up a sacrilegious object that causes desecration,* until the fate decreed for this defiler is finally poured out on him."

Daniel's Vision of a Messenger

10 In the third year of the reign of King Cyrus of Persia,* Daniel (also known as Belteshazzar) had another vision. He understood that the vision concerned events certain to happen in the future—times of war and great hardship.

[2]When this vision came to me, I, Daniel, had been in mourning for three whole weeks. [3]All that time I had eaten no rich food. No meat or wine crossed my lips, and I used no fragrant lotions until those three weeks had passed.

[4]On April 23,* as I was standing on the bank of the great Tigris River, [5]I looked up and saw a man dressed in linen clothing, with a belt of pure gold around his waist. [6]His body looked like a precious gem. His face flashed like lightning, and his eyes flamed like torches. His arms and feet shone like polished bronze, and his voice roared like a vast multitude of people.

[7]Only I, Daniel, saw this vision. The men with me saw nothing, but they were suddenly terrified and ran away to hide. [8]So I was left there all alone to see this amazing vision. My strength left me, my face grew deathly pale, and I felt very weak. [9]Then I heard the man speak, and when I heard the sound of his voice, I fainted and lay there with my face to the ground.

[10]Just then a hand touched me and lifted me,

9:24a Hebrew *seventy sevens.*   9:24b Or *the Most Holy One.*   9:25a Hebrew *Seven sevens plus sixty-two sevens.*   9:25b Or *an anointed one;* similarly in 9:26. Hebrew reads *a messiah.*   9:25c Or *and a moat,* or *and trenches.*   9:26 Hebrew *After sixty-two sevens.*   9:27a Hebrew *for one seven.*   9:27b Hebrew *And on the wing;* the meaning of the Hebrew is uncertain. 9:27c Hebrew *an abomination of desolation.*   10:1 The third year of Cyrus's reign was 536 B.C.   10:4 Hebrew *On the twenty-fourth day of the first month,* of the ancient Hebrew lunar calendar. This date in the book of Daniel can be cross-checked with dates in surviving Persian records and can be related accurately to our modern calendar. This event occurred on April 23, 536 B.C.

still trembling, to my hands and knees. ¹¹And the man said to me, "Daniel, you are very precious to God, so listen carefully to what I have to say to you. Stand up, for I have been sent to you." When he said this to me, I stood up, still trembling.

¹²Then he said, "Don't be afraid, Daniel. Since the first day you began to pray for understanding and to humble yourself before your God, your request has been heard in heaven. I have come in answer to your prayer. ¹³But for twenty-one days the spirit prince* of the kingdom of Persia blocked my way. Then Michael, one of the archangels,* came to help me, and I left him there with the spirit prince of the kingdom of Persia.* ¹⁴Now I am here to explain what will happen to your people in the future, for this vision concerns a time yet to come."

¹⁵While he was speaking to me, I looked down at the ground, unable to say a word. ¹⁶Then the one who looked like a man* touched my lips, and I opened my mouth and began to speak. I said to the one standing in front of me, "I am filled with anguish because of the vision I have seen, my lord, and I am very weak. ¹⁷How can someone like me, your servant, talk to you, my lord? My strength is gone, and I can hardly breathe."

¹⁸Then the one who looked like a man touched me again, and I felt my strength returning. ¹⁹"Don't be afraid," he said, "for you are very precious to God. Peace! Be encouraged! Be strong!"

As he spoke these words to me, I suddenly felt stronger and said to him, "Please speak to me, my lord, for you have strengthened me."

²⁰He replied, "Do you know why I have come? Soon I must return to fight against the spirit prince of the kingdom of Persia, and after that the spirit prince of the kingdom of Greece* will come. ²¹Meanwhile, I will tell you what is written in the Book of Truth. (No one helps me against these spirit princes except Michael, your spirit prince.* ¹¹:¹I have been standing beside Michael* to support and strengthen him since the first year of the reign of Darius the Mede.)

Kings of the South and North

11 ²"Now then, I will reveal the truth to you. Three more Persian kings will reign, to be succeeded by a fourth, far richer than the others. He will use his wealth to stir up everyone to fight against the kingdom of Greece.*

³"Then a mighty king will rise to power who will rule with great authority and accomplish everything he sets out to do. ⁴But at the height of his power, his kingdom will be broken apart and divided into four parts. It will not be ruled by the king's descendants, nor will the kingdom hold the authority it once had. For his empire will be uprooted and given to others.

⁵"The king of the south will increase in power, but one of his own officials will become more powerful than he and will rule his kingdom with great strength.

⁶"Some years later an alliance will be formed between the king of the north and the king of the south. The daughter of the king of the south will be given in marriage to the king of the north to secure the alliance, but she will lose her influence over him, and so will her father. She will be abandoned along with her supporters. ⁷But when one of her relatives* becomes king of the south, he will raise an army and enter the fortress of the king of the north and defeat him. ⁸When he returns to Egypt, he will carry back their idols with him, along with priceless articles of gold and silver. For some years afterward he will leave the king of the north alone.

⁹"Later the king of the north will invade the realm of the king of the south but will soon return to his own land. ¹⁰However, the sons of the king of the north will assemble a mighty army that will advance like a flood and carry the battle as far as the enemy's fortress.

¹¹"Then, in a rage, the king of the south will rally against the vast forces assembled by the king of the north and will defeat them. ¹²After the enemy army is swept away, the king of the south will be filled with pride and will execute many thousands of his enemies. But his success will be short lived.

¹³"A few years later the king of the north will return with a fully equipped army far greater than before. ¹⁴At that time there will be a general uprising against the king of the south. Violent men among your own people will join them in fulfillment of this vision, but they will not succeed. ¹⁵Then the king of the north will come and lay siege to a fortified city and capture it. The best troops of the

10:13a Hebrew *the prince*; also in 10:13c, 20.   10:13b Hebrew *the chief princes*.   10:13c As in one Greek version; Hebrew reads *and I was left there with the kings of Persia*. The meaning of the Hebrew is uncertain.   10:16 As in most manuscripts of the Masoretic Text; one manuscript of the Masoretic Text and one Greek version read *Then something that looked like a human hand*.   10:20 Hebrew *of Javan*.   10:21 Hebrew *against these except Michael, your prince*.   11:1 Hebrew *him*.   11:2 Hebrew *of Javan*.   11:7 Hebrew *a branch from her roots*.

south will not be able to stand in the face of the onslaught.

¹⁶"The king of the north will march onward unopposed; none will be able to stop him. He will pause in the glorious land of Israel,* intent on destroying it. ¹⁷He will make plans to come with the might of his entire kingdom and will form an alliance with the king of the south. He will give him a daughter in marriage in order to overthrow the kingdom from within, but his plan will fail.

¹⁸"After this, he will turn his attention to the coastland and conquer many cities. But a commander from another land will put an end to his insolence and cause him to retreat in shame. ¹⁹He will take refuge in his own fortresses but will stumble and fall and be seen no more.

²⁰"His successor will send out a tax collector to maintain the royal splendor. But after a very brief reign, he will die, though not from anger or in battle.

²¹"The next to come to power will be a despicable man who is not in line for royal succession. He will slip in when least expected and take over the kingdom by flattery and intrigue. ²²Before him great armies will be swept away, including a covenant prince. ²³With deceitful promises, he will make various alliances. He will become strong despite having only a handful of followers. ²⁴Without warning he will enter the richest areas of the land. Then he will distribute among his followers the plunder and wealth of the rich—something his predecessors had never done. He will plot the overthrow of strongholds, but this will last for only a short while.

²⁵"Then he will stir up his courage and raise a great army against the king of the south. The king of the south will go to battle with a mighty army, but to no avail, for there will be plots against him. ²⁶His own household will cause his downfall. His army will be swept away, and many will be killed. ²⁷Seeking nothing but each other's harm, these kings will plot against each other at the conference table, attempting to deceive each other. But it will make no difference, for the end will come at the appointed time.

²⁸"The king of the north will then return home with great riches. On the way he will set himself against the people of the holy covenant, doing much damage before continuing his journey.

²⁹"Then at the appointed time he will once again invade the south, but this time the result will be different. ³⁰For warships from western coastlands* will scare him off, and he will withdraw and return home. But he will vent his anger against the people of the holy covenant and reward those who forsake the covenant.

³¹"His army will take over the Temple fortress, pollute the sanctuary, put a stop to the daily sacrifices, and set up the sacrilegious object that causes desecration.* ³²He will flatter and win over those who have violated the covenant. But the people who know their God will be strong and will resist him.

³³"Wise leaders will give instruction to many, but these teachers will die by fire and sword, or they will be jailed and robbed. ³⁴During these persecutions, little help will arrive, and many who join them will not be sincere. ³⁵And some of the wise will fall victim to persecution. In this way, they will be refined and cleansed and made pure until the time of the end, for the appointed time is still to come.

³⁶"The king will do as he pleases, exalting himself and claiming to be greater than every god, even blaspheming the God of gods. He will succeed, but only until the time of wrath is completed. For what has been determined will surely take place. ³⁷He will have no respect for the gods of his ancestors, or for the god loved by women, or for any other god, for he will boast that he is greater than them all. ³⁸Instead of these, he will worship the god of fortresses—a god his ancestors never knew—and lavish on him gold, silver, precious stones, and expensive gifts. ³⁹Claiming this foreign god's help, he will attack the strongest fortresses. He will honor those who submit to him, appointing them to positions of authority and dividing the land among them as their reward.*

⁴⁰"Then at the time of the end, the king of the south will attack the king of the north. The king of the north will storm out with chariots, charioteers, and a vast navy. He will invade various lands and sweep through them like a flood. ⁴¹He will enter the glorious land of Israel,* and many nations will fall, but Moab, Edom, and the best part of Ammon will escape. ⁴²He will conquer many countries, and even Egypt will not escape. ⁴³He will gain control over the gold, silver, and treasures of Egypt, and the Libyans and Ethiopians* will be his servants.

⁴⁴"But then news from the east and the north will alarm him, and he will set out in great anger to destroy and obliterate many. ⁴⁵He will

---

11:16 Hebrew *the glorious land.*   11:30 Hebrew *from Kittim.*   11:31 Hebrew *the abomination of desolation.*   11:39 Or *at a price.*
11:41 Hebrew *the glorious land.*   11:43 Hebrew *Cushites.*

stop between the glorious holy mountain and the sea and will pitch his royal tents. But while he is there, his time will suddenly run out, and no one will help him.

The Time of the End

12 "At that time Michael, the archangel* who stands guard over your nation, will arise. Then there will be a time of anguish greater than any since nations first came into existence. But at that time every one of your people whose name is written in the book will be rescued. ²Many of those whose bodies lie dead and buried will rise up, some to everlasting life and some to shame and everlasting disgrace. ³Those who are wise will shine as bright as the sky, and those who lead many to righteousness will shine like the stars forever. ⁴But you, Daniel, keep this prophecy a secret; seal up the book until the time of the end, when many will rush here and there, and knowledge will increase."

⁵Then I, Daniel, looked and saw two others standing on opposite banks of the river. ⁶One of them asked the man dressed in linen, who was now standing above the river, "How long will it be until these shocking events are over?"

⁷The man dressed in linen, who was standing above the river, raised both his hands toward heaven and took a solemn oath by the One who lives forever, saying, "It will go on for a time, times, and half a time. When the shattering of the holy people has finally come to an end, all these things will have happened."

⁸I heard what he said, but I did not understand what he meant. So I asked, "How will all this finally end, my lord?"

⁹But he said, "Go now, Daniel, for what I have said is kept secret and sealed until the time of the end. ¹⁰Many will be purified, cleansed, and refined by these trials. But the wicked will continue in their wickedness, and none of them will understand. Only those who are wise will know what it means.

¹¹"From the time the daily sacrifice is stopped and the sacrilegious object that causes desecration* is set up to be worshiped, there will be 1,290 days. ¹²And blessed are those who wait and remain until the end of the 1,335 days!

¹³"As for you, go your way until the end. You will rest, and then at the end of the days, you will rise again to receive the inheritance set aside for you."

Susanna and the Elders

13 There was a man named Joakim who lived in Babylon.* ²He married a woman named Susanna, the daughter of Hilkiah. She was very beautiful and feared the Lord. ³Susanna's parents were righteous people, so they had raised her to follow the law of Moses. ⁴Joakim was very rich and had a garden near his house, and the Jews came to him for counsel because he was the most honored member of their community.

⁵Two elders were appointed to be judges that year, but the Lord said about them: "Wickedness has come from Babylon, from the elders who were supposed to govern the people."* ⁶These men came frequently to Joakim's house, and anyone who needed a dispute settled came to them.

⁷When the people left each day at noon, Susanna would go out and walk in her husband's garden. ⁸The two elders saw her going out to walk in the garden every day, and they began to lust for her. ⁹They ignored their consciences, shutting out any thoughts of God* and disregarding justice. ¹⁰So they were both overcome with passion for her, but neither one revealed his feelings to the other, ¹¹for they were ashamed to let anyone know about their desire to seduce her. ¹²Every day they eagerly waited for the opportunity to watch her.

¹³One day they said to each other, "Let's go home now. It's time for dinner." So they left and went their separate ways. ¹⁴But then they each circled back to spy on Susanna, and each discovered the other. After questioning each other, they both admitted their lust for Susanna. Then they cooked up a plan to find her alone.

¹⁵Once, as they were watching for a chance to find her alone, Susanna went out at the regular time. She was accompanied by only two servant girls, for the day was hot, and she wanted to bathe in the garden. ¹⁶No one else was there except the two elders, who had hidden in the garden and were watching her. ¹⁷Susanna said to her servants, "Bring me olive oil and ointments, and shut the gates of the garden so I can bathe in privacy." ¹⁸They did as she told them. They shut the gates of the garden and went out by a side gate to get what she had asked for. They didn't know that the elders were hiding inside.

¹⁹When the servant girls had left, the two

12:1 Hebrew *the great prince.*   12:11 Hebrew *the abomination of desolation.*   13:1 Chapter 13 is not included in the Hebrew and Aramaic text of Daniel. It is here translated from Theodotion's Greek text.   13:5 See Jer 29:20-23.   13:9 Greek *turning their eyes away from heaven.*

elders ran over to Susanna and said, 20"Look, the gates of the garden are shut, and no one can see us. We want to have sex with you. 21If you don't cooperate, we will testify against you in court and say that you sent your servants away because you had arranged to meet a young man in the garden."

22Susanna groaned in despair and said, "I am trapped no matter what I do. If I agree to have sex with you, it is a sin punishable by death. But if I refuse, I will still not escape your power. 23I choose not to do it! I choose to suffer innocently at your hands rather than to sin against the Lord."

24With that, Susanna cried out for help, but the two elders began shouting, putting the blame on her. 25Then one of the elders ran to open the front gate of the garden. 26When the servants in the house heard the commotion in the garden, they rushed through the side gate to see what had happened to Susanna. 27As the elders told their story, the servants were dismayed, for no one had ever accused Susanna of such a sin.

The False Accusation

28The next day the people came as usual to Joakim's house. The two elders also came, fully determined to carry out their wicked plot to have Susanna put to death. 29In the presence of all the people, they said, "Send for Hilkiah's daughter Susanna, the wife of Joakim." So they sent for her at once. 30And she came to the assembly with her parents, her children, and all her relatives. 31Now Susanna was very refined and beautiful. 32Her face was veiled, but those wicked men commanded that she take off her veil. They did this so that they could at least feast their eyes on her beauty.

33While all Susanna's friends and everyone else wept, 34the two elders stood up before the assembly to lay hands on her head and accuse her of sin. 35Through her tears, Susanna looked up toward heaven, for she trusted in the Lord. 36Then the elders said: "As we walked in the garden alone, this woman came in with two servant girls and shut the gates of the garden, and then she sent the servants away. 37Then a young man who was hiding there came out and had sex with her. 38We were in a corner of the garden, and when we saw this crime, we ran over to them. 39Although we had seen them lying together, we could not catch the young man because he was too strong for us.

He opened the gates and ran off. 40But we did catch this woman. When we asked her who the young man was, 41she would not tell us. We testify that this is what we saw."

Since the two men were elders and judges, the crowd believed them and condemned Susanna to death. 42Then Susanna cried out with a loud voice: "Eternal God, you know things that are hidden, and you foresee all things. 43You know that these men have testified falsely against me. And now I am going to die, even though I have done none of the things these wicked men have said about me."

Daniel Exposes the Elders' Lie

44The Lord heard Susanna's cry, 45so when she was being led away to her execution, God stirred up the righteous* spirit of a young man named Daniel. 46He shouted, "I will have no part in the shedding of this woman's blood!"

47Then all the people turned to Daniel and said, "What are you talking about?"

48So he stood before them and said, "Are you so foolish, you people of Israel, that you have condemned a daughter of Israel without a proper trial? 49Return to the court, for these witnesses have given false testimony against her."

50So all the people quickly returned, and the other elders said to Daniel, "Come, sit here among us, and show us your reasoning, since God has given you the wisdom of old age."

51Daniel said to them, "Separate these two witnesses, and I will cross-examine them separately." 52So when they had been separated, he called for one of them and said to him, "How evil you have grown in your old age! Now the sins of your earlier days have caught up with you. 53You made unjust judgments, condemned the innocent, and let the guilty go free, though the Lord said, 'Never put an innocent or honest person to death.'* 54Now then, if you really saw what happened, tell me what kind of tree the couple was lying under when you saw them together."

The elder answered, "Under a mastic tree."

55Then Daniel said, "Well, now, this lie has cost you your head. The angel of God has already received the sentence from God and will cut you in two."*

56Then Daniel dismissed the first elder and called for the second. He said to him, "You filthy Canaanite,* beauty has deceived you, and lust has perverted your heart. 57This is how

---

13:45 Greek *holy.*   13:53 Exod 23:7.   13:55 The Greek words for *mastic tree* and *cut* are similar.   13:56 Greek *O you seed of Canaan and not of Judah.*

you sinned with the daughters of Israel, and in their fear they gave in to you. But here is a daughter of Judah who would not tolerate your wickedness. 58Now then, tell me what kind of tree the couple was lying under when you saw them together."

The second elder answered, "Under an oak tree."

59Then Daniel said to him, "Well, now, this lie has cost you your head as well. The angel of God is waiting with his sword to split you in two.* Then both of you elders will be destroyed."

60Then the entire assembly gave a great shout and blessed God, who saves those who trust in him. 61And they rose up against the two elders, for Daniel had used their own words to convict them of giving false testimony. In keeping with the law of Moses, the elders received the same punishment they were about to inflict on their neighbor: 62They were put to death. And so an innocent life was saved that day.

63Hilkiah and his wife praised God for their daughter Susanna, as did her husband, Joakim, and all her relatives, because she was found innocent of a shameful crime. 64And Daniel was greatly esteemed by the people from that day forward.

Daniel Destroys Bel the Idol

14 After King Astyages joined his ancestors in death, Cyrus the Persian took over his kingdom.* 2Daniel was the king's companion and was honored above all the king's favored leaders.

3Now the Babylonians had an idol named Bel. Every day, twelve large measures of fine flour, forty sheep, and six measures of wine were offered to the idol. 4The king also adored it and went every day to worship it. But Daniel worshiped his own God.

5So the king said to Daniel: "Why don't you worship Bel?"

Daniel answered: "I do not worship idols made by human hands. I worship the living God, who created heaven and earth and rules over every living being."

6The king said to him, "Don't you think Bel is a living god? Don't you see how much he eats and drinks every day?"

7But Daniel smirked and said: "O King, don't be deceived, for that idol is only clay on the inside and bronze on the outside. It has never eaten or drunk anything."

8Then the king became angry, and he called for his priests and said to them, "If you do not tell me who eats all the food, you will die. 9But if you can show that Bel eats it, Daniel will die because he has blasphemed Bel."

And Daniel said to the king, "Let it be as you say."

Now there were seventy priests of Bel in all, besides their wives and children. 10The king went with Daniel into the temple of Bel. 11The priests of Bel said, "See, we are leaving now. You yourself, O King, can set out the food and prepare the wine. Then lock the door and seal it with your own signet. 12If you do not find that Bel has eaten and drunk everything when you return in the morning, we will be put to death. But if Bel has eaten and drunk everything, this will prove that Daniel has lied about us and must die." 13They were not worried because they had made a secret entrance under the altar, and they always went in that way and ate all the food themselves.

14So after the priests had left, the king set the food before Bel. Then Daniel ordered his servants to bring ashes, and they spread them all over the temple floor while only the king watched. Then they left and shut the door, sealing it with the king's signet. 15As usual, the priests and their wives and children went in during the night and ate and drank everything.

16The king went to the temple early in the morning, and Daniel went with him. 17The king asked, "Are the seals unbroken, Daniel?"

He answered, "They are unbroken, O King."

18As soon as he had opened the door, the king saw that the table was empty. Then he exclaimed, "You are great, O Bel; there is not one deceitful thing about you!"

19Daniel laughed, and he kept the king from entering. "Look at the floor," he said, "and tell me whose footprints these are."

20The king said, "I see the footprints of men, women, and children." 21Then the king became angry and arrested the priests and their wives and children. They showed him the secret doors through which they entered to eat the food that was on the table. 22So the king put them to death, and he gave Daniel permission to do whatever he wanted with Bel. So Daniel destroyed both the idol and its temple.

Daniel Destroys the Dragon

23There was also a great dragon that the Babylonians worshiped. 24The king said to Daniel,

13:59 The Greek words for *oak tree* and *split* are similar.   14:1 Chapter 14 is not included in the Hebrew and Aramaic text of Daniel. It is here translated from Theodotion's Greek text.

"Look, you cannot deny that this is a living god. So worship it."

²⁵But Daniel said, "I worship only the Lord my God, for he is the living God. With your permission, O King, I will kill this dragon without sword or club."

²⁶The king said, "I give you permission." ²⁷So Daniel took pitch, fat, and hair, and he boiled it all together. Then he made it into cakes and fed them to the dragon. After the dragon ate them, it burst open. Then Daniel said, "Look at this one you worshiped!"

²⁸When the Babylonians heard about it, they became very angry and rebelled against the king. They said, "The king has become a Jew. He has destroyed Bel, he has killed the dragon, and he has slaughtered the priests." ²⁹So they went to the king and said, "Hand Daniel over to us, or we will destroy you and your household." ³⁰The king saw that he was in danger, so he was forced to hand Daniel over to them.

Daniel in the Lions' Den Again

³¹The people threw Daniel into the lions' den, and he was there six days. ³²In the den were seven lions that were fed each day with two human bodies and two sheep. But during this time they were not fed at all to ensure that they would devour Daniel.

³³Now there was a prophet named Habakkuk who lived in Judea. He had made some stew and put some bread in a basket. He was on his way to the fields to give the food to the harvesters. ³⁴But an angel of the Lord said to Habakkuk, "Take this food to Daniel in Babylon because he is in the lions' den."

³⁵Habakkuk responded, "Lord, I've never been to Babylon, and I don't know where to find the lions' den." ³⁶Then the angel of the Lord grabbed him by the hair and carried him as fast as the wind all the way to Babylon. The angel of the Lord set him down just above the lions' den. ³⁷Habakkuk called out, "Daniel, Daniel! Take the meal God has sent you."

³⁸And Daniel said, "You have remembered me, O God. You have not abandoned those who love you." ³⁹So Daniel got up and ate, and the angel of the Lord immediately carried Habakkuk back to his own place.

⁴⁰On the seventh day the king went to the den to mourn for Daniel. But when he arrived at the den and looked in, he saw Daniel sitting there! ⁴¹The king exclaimed, "You are great, O Lord, the God of Daniel! There is no God but you!" ⁴²Then he pulled Daniel out, and those who had tried to destroy Daniel were thrown into the den. They were devoured in a moment as the king watched.

Hosea

THE BOOK OF HOSEA is a tragic love story with a happy ending. Hosea was a prophet to the northern kingdom of Israel before its fall in 722 BC, and his ministry spanned forty years. He was a contemporary of Amos, Isaiah, and Micah. In his book, Hosea was called by God to marry an unfaithful woman, and so he married Gomer. After bearing three children to Hosea, Gomer acted unfaithfully, and the marriage was shattered. In the end, however, Hosea urged Gomer to repent and receive forgiveness and restoration. Hosea used this experience with Gomer to illustrate God's experience with Israel. The first half of Hosea's book describes his marriage to Gomer, the birth of their children, and her unfaithfulness. The second half of the book draws lessons from the symbolic story. Hosea warned of stern judgment for Israel's unfaithfulness, for Israel had turned to other gods, just as Gomer had left Hosea for other men. Like Gomer, Israel would receive forgiveness and restoration if the people returned to God.

- **Author:** Hosea
- **Date Written:** Around 715 BC, recording events between 753 and 715 BC
- **Purpose:** To illustrate God's love for his sinful people
- **Themes:** Israel's unfaithfulness, God's judgment, God's love, restoration
- **Outline**
  1:1–3:5 Hosea's tragic home life
  4:1–8:14 Israel's rebellion against God
  9:1–13:16 The judgment to come
  14:1-9 The promised restoration

---

1 The LORD gave this message to Hosea son of Beeri during the years when Uzziah, Jotham, Ahaz, and Hezekiah were kings of Judah, and Jeroboam son of Jehoash* was king of Israel.

Hosea's Wife and Children

²When the LORD first began speaking to Israel through Hosea, he said to him, "Go and marry a prostitute,* so that some of her children will be conceived in prostitution. This will illustrate how Israel has acted like a prostitute by turning against the LORD and worshiping other gods."

³So Hosea married Gomer, the daughter of Diblaim, and she became pregnant and gave Hosea a son. ⁴And the LORD said, "Name the child Jezreel, for I am about to punish King Jehu's dynasty to avenge the murders he committed at Jezreel. In fact, I will bring an end to

Israel's independence. ⁵I will break its military power in the Jezreel Valley."

⁶Soon Gomer became pregnant again and gave birth to a daughter. And the LORD said to Hosea, "Name your daughter Loruhamah—'Not loved'—for I will no longer show love to the people of Israel or forgive them. ⁷But I will show love to the people of Judah. I will free them from their enemies—not with weapons and armies or horses and charioteers, but by my power as the LORD their God."

⁸After Gomer had weaned Lo-ruhamah, she again became pregnant and gave birth to a second son. ⁹And the LORD said, "Name him Lo-ammi—'Not my people'—for Israel is not my people, and I am not their God.

¹⁰*"Yet the time will come when Israel's people will be like the sands of the seashore—too many to count! Then, at the place where

---

1:1 Hebrew *Joash*, a variant spelling of Jehoash. 1:2 Or *a promiscuous woman.* 1:10 Verses 1:10-11 are numbered 2:1-2 in Hebrew text.

they were told, 'You are not my people,' it will be said, 'You are children of the living God.' ¹¹Then the people of Judah and Israel will unite together. They will choose one leader for themselves, and they will return from exile together. What a day that will be—the day of Jezreel*— when God will again plant his people in his land.

2:1*"In that day you will call your brothers Ammi—'My people.' And you will call your sisters Ruhamah—'The ones I love.'

Charges against an Unfaithful Wife

2 ² "But now bring charges against
Israel—your mother—
for she is no longer my wife,
and I am no longer her husband.
Tell her to remove the prostitute's
makeup from her face
and the clothing that exposes her
breasts.
³ Otherwise, I will strip her as naked
as she was on the day she was born.
I will leave her to die of thirst,
as in a dry and barren wilderness.
⁴ And I will not love her children,
for they were conceived in
prostitution.
⁵ Their mother is a shameless prostitute
and became pregnant in a shameful
way.
She said, 'I'll run after other lovers
and sell myself to them for food and
water,
for clothing of wool and linen,
and for olive oil and drinks.'

⁶ "For this reason I will fence her in with
thornbushes.
I will block her path with a wall
to make her lose her way.
⁷ When she runs after her lovers,
she won't be able to catch them.
She will search for them
but not find them.
Then she will think,
'I might as well return to my husband,
for I was better off with him than I am
now.'
⁸ She doesn't realize it was I who gave her
everything she has—
the grain, the new wine, the olive oil;
I even gave her silver and gold.
But she gave all my gifts to Baal.

⁹ "But now I will take back the ripened
grain and new wine
I generously provided each harvest
season.
I will take away the wool and linen
clothing
I gave her to cover her nakedness.
¹⁰ I will strip her naked in public,
while all her lovers look on.
No one will be able
to rescue her from my hands.
¹¹ I will put an end to her annual festivals,
her new moon celebrations, and her
Sabbath days—
all her appointed festivals.
¹² I will destroy her grapevines and fig trees,
things she claims her lovers gave her.
I will let them grow into tangled thickets,
where only wild animals will eat the
fruit.
¹³ I will punish her for all those times
when she burned incense to her images
of Baal,
when she put on her earrings and jewels
and went out to look for her lovers
but forgot all about me,"
says the LORD.

The LORD's Love for Unfaithful Israel

¹⁴ "But then I will win her back once again.
I will lead her into the desert
and speak tenderly to her there.
¹⁵ I will return her vineyards to her
and transform the Valley of Trouble*
into a gateway of hope.
She will give herself to me there,
as she did long ago when she was young,
when I freed her from her captivity in
Egypt.
¹⁶ When that day comes," says the LORD,
"you will call me 'my husband'
instead of 'my master.'*
¹⁷ O Israel, I will wipe the many names of
Baal from your lips,
and you will never mention them again.
¹⁸ On that day I will make a covenant
with all the wild animals and the birds
of the sky
and the animals that scurry along the
ground
so they will not harm you.
I will remove all weapons of war from the
land,
all swords and bows,

1:11 *Jezreel* means "God plants."   2:1 Verses 2:1-23 are numbered 2:3-25 in Hebrew text.   2:15 Hebrew *valley of Achor.*
2:16 Hebrew *my baal.*

so you can live unafraid
    in peace and safety.
19 I will make you my wife forever,
    showing you righteousness and justice,
    unfailing love and compassion.
20 I will be faithful to you and make you
        mine,
    and you will finally know me as the
        LORD.

21 "In that day, I will answer,"
        says the LORD.
    "I will answer the sky as it pleads for
        clouds.
    And the sky will answer the earth with
        rain.
22 Then the earth will answer the thirsty cries
    of the grain, the grapevines, and the
        olive trees.
    And they in turn will answer,
        'Jezreel'—'God plants!'
23 At that time I will plant a crop of Israelites
    and raise them for myself.
    I will show love
        to those I called 'Not loved.'*
    And to those I called 'Not my people,'*
        I will say, 'Now you are my people.'
    And they will reply, 'You are our God!'"

Hosea's Wife Is Redeemed

3 Then the LORD said to me, "Go and love
your wife again, even though she* commits
adultery with another lover. This will illustrate
that the LORD still loves Israel, even though the
people have turned to other gods and love to
worship them.*"

2 So I bought her back for fifteen pieces of
silver* and five bushels of barley and a measure of wine.* 3 Then I said to her, "You must
live in my house for many days and stop your
prostitution. During this time, you will not
have sexual relations with anyone, not even
with me.*"

4 This shows that Israel will go a long time
without a king or prince, and without sacrifices, sacred pillars, priests,* or even idols! 5 But
afterward the people will return and devote
themselves to the LORD their God and to David's descendant, their king.* In the last days,
they will tremble in awe of the LORD and of
his goodness.

The LORD's Case against Israel

4 ¹ Hear the word of the LORD, O people
    of Israel!
    The LORD has brought charges against
        you, saying:
    "There is no faithfulness, no kindness,
        no knowledge of God in your land.
2 You make vows and break them;
    you kill and steal and commit adultery.
    There is violence everywhere—
        one murder after another.
3 That is why your land is in mourning,
    and everyone is wasting away.
    Even the wild animals, the birds of the sky,
        and the fish of the sea are
        disappearing.

4 "Don't point your finger at someone else
    and try to pass the blame!
    My complaint, you priests,
        is with you.*
5 So you will stumble in broad daylight,
    and your false prophets will fall with
        you in the night.
    And I will destroy Israel, your mother.
6 My people are being destroyed
    because they don't know me.
    Since you priests refuse to know me,
        I refuse to recognize you as my priests.
    Since you have forgotten the laws of your
        God,
    I will forget to bless your children.
7 The more priests there are,
    the more they sin against me.
    They have exchanged the glory of God
        for the shame of idols.*

8 "When the people bring their sin
        offerings, the priests get fed.
    So the priests are glad when the
        people sin!
9 'And what the priests do, the people
        also do.'
    So now I will punish both priests and
        people
    for their wicked deeds.
10 They will eat and still be hungry.
    They will play the prostitute and gain
        nothing from it,
    for they have deserted the LORD
11   to worship other gods.

2:23a Hebrew *Lo-ruhamah;* see 1:6.   2:23b Hebrew *Lo-ammi;* see 1:9.   3:1a Or *Go and love a woman who.*   3:1b Hebrew *love
their raisin cakes.*   3:2a Hebrew *15 [shekels] of silver,* about 6 ounces or 171 grams in weight.   3:2b As in Greek version, which
reads *a homer of barley and a wineskin full of wine;* Hebrew reads *a homer* [5 bushels or 220 liters] *of barley and a lethek* [2.5 bushels
or 110 liters] *of barley.*   3:3 Or *and I will live with you.*   3:4 Hebrew *ephod,* the vest worn by the priest.   3:5 Hebrew *to David
their king.*   4:4 Hebrew *Your people are like those with a complaint against the priests.*   4:7 As in Syriac version and an ancient
Hebrew tradition; Masoretic Text reads *I will turn their glory into shame.*

"Wine has robbed my people
of their understanding.
¹² They ask a piece of wood for advice!
They think a stick can tell them the
future!
Longing after idols
has made them foolish.
They have played the prostitute,
serving other gods and deserting their
God.
¹³ They offer sacrifices to idols on the
mountaintops.
They go up into the hills to burn
incense
in the pleasant shade of oaks, poplars,
and terebinth trees.

"That is why your daughters turn to
prostitution,
and your daughters-in-law commit
adultery.
¹⁴ But why should I punish them
for their prostitution and adultery?
For your men are doing the same thing,
sinning with whores and shrine
prostitutes.
O foolish people! You refuse to
understand,
so you will be destroyed.

¹⁵ "Though you, Israel, are a prostitute,
may Judah not be guilty of such
things.
Do not join the false worship at Gilgal
or Beth-aven,*
and do not take oaths there in the
LORD's name.
¹⁶ Israel is stubborn,
like a stubborn heifer.
So should the LORD feed her
like a lamb in a lush pasture?
¹⁷ Leave Israel* alone,
because she is married to idolatry.
¹⁸ When the rulers of Israel finish their
drinking,
off they go to find some prostitutes.
They love shame more than honor.*
¹⁹ So a mighty wind will sweep them
away.
Their sacrifices to idols will bring
them shame.

The Failure of Israel's Leaders

5 ¹ "Hear this, you priests.
Pay attention, you leaders of Israel.
Listen, you members of the royal family.
Judgment has been handed down
against you.
For you have led the people into a snare
by worshiping the idols at Mizpah and
Tabor.
² You have dug a deep pit to trap them at
Acacia Grove.*
But I will settle with you for what you
have done.
³ I know what you are like, O Ephraim.
You cannot hide yourself from me,
O Israel.
You have left me as a prostitute leaves
her husband;
you are utterly defiled.
⁴ Your deeds won't let you return to your
God.
You are a prostitute through and
through,
and you do not know the LORD.

⁵ "The arrogance of Israel testifies against
her;
Israel and Ephraim will stumble under
their load of guilt.
Judah, too, will fall with them.
⁶ When they come with their flocks and
herds
to offer sacrifices to the LORD,
they will not find him,
because he has withdrawn from them.
⁷ They have betrayed the honor of the LORD,
bearing children that are not his.
Now their false religion will devour them
along with their wealth.*

⁸ "Sound the alarm in Gibeah!
Blow the trumpet in Ramah!
Raise the battle cry in Beth-aven*!
Lead on into battle, O warriors of
Benjamin!
⁹ One thing is certain, Israel*:
On your day of punishment,
you will become a heap of rubble.

¹⁰ "The leaders of Judah have become like
thieves.*

4:15 Beth-aven means "house of wickedness"; it is being used as another name for Bethel, which means "house of God."
4:17 Hebrew Ephraim, referring to the northern kingdom of Israel.   4:18 As in Greek version; the meaning of the Hebrew
is uncertain.   5:2 Hebrew at Shittim. The meaning of the Hebrew for this sentence is uncertain.   5:7 The meaning
of the Hebrew is uncertain.   5:8 Beth-aven means "house of wickedness"; it is being used as another name for Bethel,
which means "house of God."   5:9 Hebrew Ephraim, referring to the northern kingdom of Israel; also in 5:11, 12, 13, 14.
5:10 Hebrew like those who move a boundary marker.

So I will pour my anger on them like
a waterfall.
¹¹ The people of Israel will be crushed and
broken by my judgment
because they are determined to worship
idols.*
¹² I will destroy Israel as a moth consumes
wool.
I will make Judah as weak as rotten
wood.

¹³ "When Israel and Judah saw how sick
they were,
Israel turned to Assyria—
to the great king there—
but he could neither help nor cure them.
¹⁴ I will be like a lion to Israel,
like a strong young lion to Judah.
I will tear them to pieces!
I will carry them off,
and no one will be left to rescue them.
¹⁵ Then I will return to my place
until they admit their guilt and turn
to me.
For as soon as trouble comes,
they will earnestly search for me."

A Call to Repentance

6 ¹ "Come, let us return to the LORD.
He has torn us to pieces;
now he will heal us.
He has injured us;
now he will bandage our wounds.
² In just a short time he will restore us,
so that we may live in his presence.
³ Oh, that we might know the LORD!
Let us press on to know him.
He will respond to us as surely as the
arrival of dawn
or the coming of rains in early spring."

⁴ "O Israel* and Judah,
what should I do with you?" asks the
LORD.
"For your love vanishes like the morning
mist
and disappears like dew in the sunlight.
⁵ I sent my prophets to cut you to pieces—
to slaughter you with my words,
with judgments as inescapable as light.
⁶ I want you to show love,*
not offer sacrifices.

I want you to know me*
more than I want burnt offerings.
⁷ But like Adam,* you broke my covenant
and betrayed my trust.

⁸ "Gilead is a city of sinners,
tracked with footprints of blood.
⁹ Priests form bands of robbers,
waiting in ambush for their victims.
They murder travelers along the road to
Shechem
and practice every kind of sin.
¹⁰ Yes, I have seen something horrible in
Ephraim and Israel:
My people are defiled by prostituting
themselves with other gods!

¹¹ "O Judah, a harvest of punishment is also
waiting for you,
though I wanted to restore the fortunes
of my people.

Israel's Love for Wickedness

7 ¹ "I want to heal Israel, but its* sins are
too great.
Samaria is filled with liars.
Thieves are on the inside
and bandits on the outside!
² Its people don't realize
that I am watching them.
Their sinful deeds are all around them,
and I see them all.

³ "The people entertain the king with their
wickedness,
and the princes laugh at their lies.
⁴ They are all adulterers,
always aflame with lust.
They are like an oven that is kept hot
while the baker is kneading the dough.
⁵ On royal holidays, the princes get drunk
with wine,
carousing with those who mock them.
⁶ Their hearts are like an oven
blazing with intrigue.
Their plot smolders* through the night,
and in the morning it breaks out like
a raging fire.
⁷ Burning like an oven,
they consume their leaders.
They kill their kings one after another,
and no one cries to me for help.

5:11 Or *determined to follow human commands.* The meaning of the Hebrew is uncertain.   6:4 Hebrew *Ephraim,* referring to
the northern kingdom of Israel.   6:6a Greek version translates this Hebrew term as *to show mercy.* Compare Matt 9:13; 12:7.
6:6b Hebrew *to know God.*   6:7 Or *But at Adam.*   7:1 Hebrew *Ephraim's,* referring to the northern kingdom of Israel;
similarly in 7:8, 11.   7:6 Hebrew *Their baker sleeps.*

8 "The people of Israel mingle with godless
　　foreigners,
　　making themselves as worthless as a
　　　half-baked cake!
9 Worshiping foreign gods has sapped their
　　strength,
　　but they don't even know it.
　Their hair is gray,
　　but they don't realize they're old and
　　　weak.
10 Their arrogance testifies against them,
　　yet they don't return to the LORD their
　　　God
　　or even try to find him.

11 "The people of Israel have become like
　　silly, witless doves,
　　first calling to Egypt, then flying to
　　　Assyria for help.
12 But as they fly about,
　　I will throw my net over them
　and bring them down like a bird from
　　the sky.
　　I will punish them for all the evil
　　　they do.*

13 "What sorrow awaits those who have
　　deserted me!
　　Let them die, for they have rebelled
　　　against me.
　I wanted to redeem them,
　　but they have told lies about me.
14 They do not cry out to me with sincere
　　hearts.
　　Instead, they sit on their couches and
　　　wail.
　They cut themselves,* begging foreign
　　gods for grain and new wine,
　　and they turn away from me.
15 I trained them and made them strong,
　　yet now they plot evil against me.
16 They look everywhere except to the Most
　　High.
　　They are as useless as a crooked bow.
　Their leaders will be killed by their
　　enemies
　　because of their insolence toward me.
　Then the people of Egypt
　　will laugh at them.

Israel Harvests the Whirlwind

8 1 "Sound the alarm!
　　The enemy descends like an eagle on
　　　the people of the LORD,

for they have broken my covenant
　　and revolted against my law.
2 Now Israel pleads with me,
　　'Help us, for you are our God!'
3 But it is too late.
　The people of Israel have rejected what is
　　good,
　　and now their enemies will chase after
　　　them.
4 The people have appointed kings without
　　my consent,
　　and princes without my approval.
　By making idols for themselves from their
　　silver and gold,
　　they have brought about their own
　　　destruction.

5 "O Samaria, I reject this calf—
　　this idol you have made.
　My fury burns against you.
　　How long will you be incapable of
　　　innocence?
6 This calf you worship, O Israel,
　　was crafted by your own hands!
　It is not God!
　　Therefore, it must be smashed
　　　to bits.

7 "They have planted the wind
　　and will harvest the whirlwind.
　The stalks of grain wither
　　and produce nothing to eat.
　And even if there is any grain,
　　foreigners will eat it.
8 The people of Israel have been
　　swallowed up;
　　they lie among the nations like an old
　　　discarded pot.
9 Like a wild donkey looking for a mate,
　　they have gone up to Assyria.
　The people of Israel* have sold
　　themselves—
　　sold themselves to many lovers.
10 But though they have sold themselves to
　　many allies,
　　I will now gather them together for
　　　judgment.
　Then they will writhe
　　under the burden of the great king.

11 "Israel has built many altars to take away
　　sin,
　　but these very altars became places for
　　　sinning!

7:12 Hebrew *I will punish them because of what was reported against them in the assembly.*　7:14 As in Greek version; Hebrew reads *They gather together.*　8:9 Hebrew *Ephraim,* referring to the northern kingdom of Israel; also in 8:11.

¹² Even though I gave them all my laws,
  they act as if those laws don't apply to
  them.
¹³ The people love to offer sacrifices to me,
  feasting on the meat,
  but I do not accept their sacrifices.
  I will hold my people accountable for their
  sins,
  and I will punish them.
  They will return to Egypt.
¹⁴ Israel has forgotten its Maker and built
  great palaces,
  and Judah has fortified its cities.
  Therefore, I will send down fire on their
  cities
  and will burn up their fortresses."

Hosea Announces Israel's Punishment

9 ¹ O people of Israel,
    do not rejoice as other nations do.
  For you have been unfaithful to your
    God,
    hiring yourselves out like prostitutes,
    worshiping other gods on every
      threshing floor.
² So now your harvests will be too small to
    feed you.
    There will be no grapes for making new
      wine.
³ You may no longer stay here in the LORD's
    land.
    Instead, you will return to Egypt,
  and in Assyria you will eat food
    that is ceremonially unclean.
⁴ There you will make no offerings of wine
    to the LORD.
    None of your sacrifices there will please
      him.
  They will be unclean, like food touched
    by a person in mourning.
    All who present such sacrifices will be
      defiled.
  They may eat this food themselves,
    but they may not offer it to the LORD.
⁵ What then will you do on festival days?
    How will you observe the LORD's
      festivals?
⁶ Even if you escape destruction from
    Assyria,
    Egypt will conquer you, and Memphis*
      will bury you.
  Nettles will take over your treasures of
    silver;
    thistles will invade your ruined homes.

⁷ The time of Israel's punishment has come;
  the day of payment is here.
  Soon Israel will know this all too well.
  Because of your great sin and hostility,
  you say, "The prophets are crazy
  and the inspired men are fools!"
⁸ The prophet is a watchman over Israel*
  for my God,
  yet traps are laid for him wherever he
    goes.
  He faces hostility even in the house
    of God.
⁹ The things my people do are as depraved
  as what they did in Gibeah long ago.
  God will not forget.
  He will surely punish them for their
    sins.
¹⁰ The LORD says, "O Israel, when I first
  found you,
  it was like finding fresh grapes in the
    desert.
  When I saw your ancestors,
  it was like seeing the first ripe figs of the
    season.
  But then they deserted me for Baal-peor,
  giving themselves to that shameful idol.
  Soon they became vile,
  as vile as the god they worshiped.
¹¹ The glory of Israel will fly away like a bird,
  for your children will not be born
  or grow in the womb
  or even be conceived.
¹² Even if you do have children who grow up,
  I will take them from you.
  It will be a terrible day when I turn away
  and leave you alone.
¹³ I have watched Israel become as beautiful
  as Tyre.
  But now Israel will bring out her
  children for slaughter."
¹⁴ O LORD, what should I request for your
  people?
  I will ask for wombs that don't give birth
  and breasts that give no milk.
¹⁵ The LORD says, "All their wickedness
  began at Gilgal;
  there I began to hate them.
  I will drive them from my land
  because of their evil actions.
  I will love them no more
  because all their leaders are rebels.

9:6 Memphis was the capital of northern Egypt.   9:8 Hebrew *Ephraim,* referring to the northern kingdom of Israel; also in 9:11, 13, 16.

16 The people of Israel are struck down.
    Their roots are dried up,
    and they will bear no more fruit.
And if they give birth,
    I will slaughter their beloved children."

17 My God will reject the people of Israel
    because they will not listen or obey.
They will be wanderers,
    homeless among the nations.

The LORD's Judgment against Israel

10 ¹ How prosperous Israel is—
    a luxuriant vine loaded with fruit.
But the richer the people get,
    the more pagan altars they build.
The more bountiful their harvests,
    the more beautiful their sacred pillars.
² The hearts of the people are fickle;
    they are guilty and must be punished.
The LORD will break down their altars
    and smash their sacred pillars.
³ Then they will say, "We have no king
    because we didn't fear the LORD.
But even if we had a king,
    what could he do for us anyway?"
⁴ They spout empty words
    and make covenants they don't intend
        to keep.
So injustice springs up among them
    like poisonous weeds in a farmer's field.

⁵ The people of Samaria tremble in fear
    for their calf idol at Beth-aven,*
    and they mourn for it.
Though its priests rejoice over it,
    its glory will be stripped away.*
⁶ This idol will be carted away to Assyria,
    a gift to the great king there.
Ephraim will be ridiculed and Israel will
        be shamed,
    because its people have trusted in this
        idol.
⁷ Samaria and its king will be cut off;
    they will float away like driftwood on
        an ocean wave.
⁸ And the pagan shrines of Aven,* the place
    of Israel's sin, will crumble.
Thorns and thistles will grow up around
    their altars.
They will beg the mountains, "Bury us!"
    and plead with the hills, "Fall on us!"

⁹ The LORD says, "O Israel, ever since
        Gibeah,
    there has been only sin and more sin!
You have made no progress whatsoever.
    Was it not right that the wicked men
        of Gibeah were attacked?
¹⁰ Now whenever it fits my plan,
    I will attack you, too.
I will call out the armies of the nations
    to punish you for your multiplied sins.

¹¹ "Israel* is like a trained heifer treading out
        the grain—
    an easy job she loves.
But I will put a heavy yoke on her tender
        neck.
I will force Judah to pull the plow
    and Israel* to break up the hard
        ground.
¹² I said, 'Plant the good seeds of
        righteousness,
    and you will harvest a crop of love.
Plow up the hard ground of your hearts,
    for now is the time to seek the LORD,
that he may come
    and shower righteousness upon you.'

¹³ "But you have cultivated wickedness
    and harvested a thriving crop of sins.
You have eaten the fruit of lies—
    trusting in your military might,
believing that great armies
    could make your nation safe.
¹⁴ Now the terrors of war
    will rise among your people.
All your fortifications will fall,
    just as when Shalman destroyed
        Beth-arbel.
Even mothers and children
    were dashed to death there.
¹⁵ You will share that fate, Bethel,
    because of your great wickedness.
When the day of judgment dawns,
    the king of Israel will be completely
        destroyed.

The LORD's Love for Israel

11 ¹ "When Israel was a child, I loved
        him,
    and I called my son out of Egypt.
² But the more I called to him,
    the farther he moved from me,*

10:5a Beth-aven means "house of wickedness"; it is being used as another name for Bethel, which means "house of God."
10:5b Or will be taken away into exile.   10:8 Aven is a reference to Beth-aven; see 10:5a and the note there.   10:11a Hebrew
Ephraim, referring to the northern kingdom of Israel.   10:11b Hebrew Jacob. The names "Jacob" and "Israel" are often
interchanged throughout the Old Testament, referring sometimes to the individual patriarch and sometimes to the
nation.   11:2 As in Greek version; Hebrew reads the more they called to him, the farther he moved from them.

offering sacrifices to the images of Baal
and burning incense to idols.
3 I myself taught Israel* how to walk,
leading him along by the hand.
But he doesn't know or even care
that it was I who took care of him.
4 I led Israel along
with my ropes of kindness and love.
I lifted the yoke from his neck,
and I myself stooped to feed him.

5 "But since my people refuse to return
to me,
they will return to Egypt
and will be forced to serve Assyria.
6 War will swirl through their cities;
their enemies will crash through their
gates.
They will destroy them,
trapping them in their own evil plans.
7 For my people are determined to
desert me.
They call me the Most High,
but they don't truly honor me.

8 "Oh, how can I give you up, Israel?
How can I let you go?
How can I destroy you like Admah
or demolish you like Zeboiim?
My heart is torn within me,
and my compassion overflows.
9 No, I will not unleash my fierce anger.
I will not completely destroy Israel,
for I am God and not a mere mortal.
I am the Holy One living among you,
and I will not come to destroy.
10 For someday the people will follow me.
I, the LORD, will roar like a lion.
And when I roar,
my people will return trembling from
the west.
11 Like a flock of birds, they will come from
Egypt.
Trembling like doves, they will return
from Assyria.
And I will bring them home again,"
says the LORD.

Charges against Israel and Judah

12*Israel surrounds me with lies and deceit,
but Judah still obeys God
and is faithful to the Holy One.*

12 1*The people of Israel* feed on the
wind;
they chase after the east wind all day
long.
They pile up lies and violence;
they are making an alliance with Assyria
while sending olive oil to buy support
from Egypt.

2 Now the LORD is bringing charges against
Judah.
He is about to punish Jacob* for all his
deceitful ways,
and pay him back for all he has done.
3 Even in the womb,
Jacob struggled with his brother;
when he became a man,
he even fought with God.
4 Yes, he wrestled with the angel and won.
He wept and pleaded for a blessing from
him.
There at Bethel he met God face to face,
and God spoke to him*—
5 the LORD God of Heaven's Armies,
the LORD is his name!
6 So now, come back to your God.
Act with love and justice,
and always depend on him.

7 But no, the people are like crafty
merchants
selling from dishonest scales—
they love to cheat.
8 Israel boasts, "I am rich!
I've made a fortune all by myself!
No one has caught me cheating!
My record is spotless!"

9 "But I am the LORD your God,
who rescued you from slavery in Egypt.
And I will make you live in tents again,
as you do each year at the Festival of
Shelters.*
10 I sent my prophets to warn you
with many visions and parables."

11 But the people of Gilead are worthless
because of their idol worship.
And in Gilgal, too, they sacrifice bulls;
their altars are lined up like the heaps
of stone
along the edges of a plowed field.

11:3 Hebrew *Ephraim*, referring to the northern kingdom of Israel; also in 11:8, 9, 12.   11:12a Verse 11:12 is numbered 12:1
in Hebrew text.   11:12b Or *and Judah is unruly against God, the faithful Holy One.* The meaning of the Hebrew is uncertain.
12:1a Verses 12:1-14 are numbered 12:2-15 in Hebrew text.   12:1b Hebrew *Ephraim*, referring to the northern kingdom
of Israel; also in 12:8, 14.   12:2 *Jacob* sounds like the Hebrew word for "deceiver."   12:4 As in Greek and Syriac versions;
Hebrew reads *to us.*   12:9 Hebrew *as in the days of your appointed feast.*

¹² Jacob fled to the land of Aram,
     and there he* earned a wife by tending
         sheep.
¹³ Then by a prophet
     the LORD brought Jacob's descendants*
         out of Egypt;
and by that prophet
     they were protected.
¹⁴ But the people of Israel
     have bitterly provoked the LORD,
so their Lord will now sentence them to
     death
     in payment for their sins.

The LORD's Anger against Israel

13 ¹ When the tribe of Ephraim spoke,
         the people shook with fear,
for that tribe was important in Israel.
But the people of Ephraim sinned by
     worshiping Baal
and thus sealed their destruction.
² Now they continue to sin by making silver
     idols,
     images shaped skillfully with human
         hands.
"Sacrifice to these," they cry,
     "and kiss the calf idols!"
³ Therefore, they will disappear like the
     morning mist,
     like dew in the morning sun,
like chaff blown by the wind,
     like smoke from a chimney.

⁴ "I have been the LORD your God
     ever since I brought you out of Egypt.
You must acknowledge no God but me,
     for there is no other savior.
⁵ I took care of you in the wilderness,
     in that dry and thirsty land.
⁶ But when you had eaten and were
     satisfied,
     you became proud and forgot me.
⁷ So now I will attack you like a lion,
     like a leopard that lurks along the road.
⁸ Like a bear whose cubs have been taken
     away,
     I will tear out your heart.
I will devour you like a hungry lioness
     and mangle you like a wild animal.

⁹ "You are about to be destroyed, O Israel—
     yes, by me, your only helper.

¹⁰ Now where is* your king?
     Let him save you!
Where are all the leaders of the land,
     the king and the officials you demanded
         of me?
¹¹ In my anger I gave you kings,
     and in my fury I took them away.

¹² "Ephraim's guilt has been collected,
     and his sin has been stored up for
         punishment.
¹³ Pain has come to the people
     like the pain of childbirth,
but they are like a child
     who resists being born.
The moment of birth has arrived,
     but they stay in the womb!

¹⁴ "Should I ransom them from the grave*?
     Should I redeem them from death?
O death, bring on your terrors!
     O grave, bring on your plagues!*
For I will not take pity on them.
¹⁵ Ephraim was the most fruitful of all his
     brothers,
     but the east wind—a blast from the
         LORD—
will arise in the desert.
All their flowing springs will run dry,
     and all their wells will disappear.
Every precious thing they own
     will be plundered and carried away.
¹⁶*The people of Samaria
     must bear the consequences of their
         guilt
     because they rebelled against their God.
They will be killed by an invading army,
     their little ones dashed to death against
         the ground,
     their pregnant women ripped open by
         swords."

Healing for the Repentant

14 ¹*Return, O Israel, to the LORD your
         God,
     for your sins have brought you down.
² Bring your confessions, and return to the
     LORD.
Say to him,
"Forgive all our sins and graciously
     receive us,
     so that we may offer you our praises.*

12:12 Hebrew *Israel.* See note on 10:11b.   12:13 Hebrew *brought Israel.* See note on 10:11b.   13:10 As in Greek and Syriac versions and Latin Vulgate; Hebrew reads *I will be.*   13:14a Hebrew *Sheol;* also in 13:14b.   13:14b Greek version reads *O death, where is your punishment? / O grave* [Hades], *where is your sting?* Compare 1 Cor 15:55.   13:16 Verse 16 is numbered 14:1 in Hebrew text.   14:1 Verses 14:1-9 are numbered 14:2-10 in Hebrew text.   14:2 As in Greek and Syriac versions, which read *may repay the fruit of our lips;* Hebrew reads *may repay the bulls of our lips.*

³ Assyria cannot save us,
   nor can our warhorses.
Never again will we say to the idols we
      have made,
   'You are our gods.'
No, in you alone
   do the orphans find mercy."

⁴ The LORD says,
   "Then I will heal you of your
      faithlessness;
   my love will know no bounds,
   for my anger will be gone forever.
⁵ I will be to Israel
   like a refreshing dew from heaven.
Israel will blossom like the lily;
   it will send roots deep into the soil
   like the cedars in Lebanon.
⁶ Its branches will spread out like beautiful
      olive trees,
   as fragrant as the cedars of Lebanon.

14:8 Hebrew *Ephraim,* referring to the northern kingdom of Israel.

⁷ My people will again live under my shade.
   They will flourish like grain and
      blossom like grapevines.
   They will be as fragrant as the wines
      of Lebanon.

⁸ "O Israel,* stay away from idols!
   I am the one who answers your prayers
      and cares for you.
   I am like a tree that is always green;
      all your fruit comes from me."

⁹ Let those who are wise understand these
      things.
   Let those with discernment listen
      carefully.
The paths of the LORD are true and right,
   and righteous people live by walking
      in them.
   But in those paths sinners stumble
      and fall.

Joel

DISPLAYS OF POWER can be impressive, but none will be more impressive than the coming "day of the LORD." On that day God will call all to account for their rebellion and sin. For those who have forsaken God, it will be a terrible day of judgment. This great day is the focus of Joel's prophecies. Joel used a plague of locusts to illustrate the coming of this terrible judgment, and he urged God's people to listen—how much better to repent and live! But Joel's

- **Author:** Joel
- **Date Written:** During Joel's ministry, either between 835 and 796 BC, or possibly after 538 BC. There is uncertainty about the timeframe of Joel's ministry.
- **Purpose:** To warn people of God's impending judgment unless they turned from their sins
- **Themes:** Punishment, forgiveness, promise of the Spirit
- **Outline**
  1:1–2:17 The plague of locusts and its meaning
  2:18-27 Immediate blessing promised
  2:28-32 Future blessing promised
  3:1-21 The judgment of Israel's enemies

prophecies contain messages of hope as well as warning. If the people responded to his warning, God would be merciful. God promised, "I will give you back what you lost to the swarming locusts" (2:25). God's desire was to bless his people, not to destroy them. That was the reason for the locusts: to make people see while there was still time.

---

1 The LORD gave this message to Joel son of Pethuel.

Mourning over the Locust Plague

2 Hear this, you leaders of the people.
  Listen, all who live in the land.
In all your history,
  has anything like this happened before?
3 Tell your children about it in the years to come,
  and let your children tell their children.
Pass the story down from generation to generation.
4 After the cutting locusts finished eating the crops,
  the swarming locusts took what was left!
After them came the hopping locusts,
  and then the stripping locusts,* too!

5 Wake up, you drunkards, and weep!
  Wail, all you wine-drinkers!
All the grapes are ruined,
  and all your sweet wine is gone.

6 A vast army of locusts* has invaded my land,
  a terrible army too numerous to count.
Its teeth are like lions' teeth,
  its fangs like those of a lioness.
7 It has destroyed my grapevines
  and ruined my fig trees,
stripping their bark and destroying it,
  leaving the branches white and bare.

8 Weep like a bride dressed in black,
  mourning the death of her husband.
9 For there is no grain or wine
  to offer at the Temple of the LORD.
So the priests are in mourning.
  The ministers of the LORD are weeping.
10 The fields are ruined,
  the land is stripped bare.
The grain is destroyed,
  the grapes have shriveled,
  and the olive oil is gone.

11 Despair, all you farmers!
  Wail, all you vine growers!

1:4 The precise identification of the four kinds of locusts mentioned here is uncertain.   1:6 Hebrew *A nation.*

Weep, because the wheat and barley—
    all the crops of the field—are
        ruined.
¹² The grapevines have dried up,
    and the fig trees have withered.
The pomegranate trees, palm trees, and
        apple trees—
    all the fruit trees—have dried up.
And the people's joy has dried up with
        them.

¹³ Dress yourselves in burlap and weep,
        you priests!
    Wail, you who serve before the altar!
Come, spend the night in burlap,
    you ministers of my God.
For there is no grain or wine
    to offer at the Temple of your God.
¹⁴ Announce a time of fasting;
    call the people together for a solemn
        meeting.
Bring the leaders
    and all the people of the land
into the Temple of the LORD your
        God,
    and cry out to him there.
¹⁵ The day of the LORD is near,
    the day when destruction comes
        from the Almighty.
    How terrible that day will be!

¹⁶ Our food disappears before our very
        eyes.
    No joyful celebrations are held in the
        house of our God.
¹⁷ The seeds die in the parched ground,
    and the grain crops fail.
The barns stand empty,
    and granaries are abandoned.
¹⁸ How the animals moan with hunger!
    The herds of cattle wander about
        confused,
    because they have no pasture.
    The flocks of sheep and goats bleat
        in misery.

¹⁹ LORD, help us!
    The fire has consumed the wilderness
        pastures,
    and flames have burned up all the
        trees.
²⁰ Even the wild animals cry out to you
    because the streams have dried up,
    and fire has consumed the wilderness
        pastures.

Locusts Invade like an Army

2 ¹ Sound the trumpet in Jerusalem*!
        Raise the alarm on my holy
            mountain!
    Let everyone tremble in fear
        because the day of the LORD is upon us.
² It is a day of darkness and gloom,
    a day of thick clouds and deep blackness.
Suddenly, like dawn spreading across the
        mountains,
    a great and mighty army appears.
Nothing like it has been seen before
    or will ever be seen again.

³ Fire burns in front of them,
    and flames follow after them.
Ahead of them the land lies
    as beautiful as the Garden of Eden.
Behind them is nothing but desolation;
    not one thing escapes.
⁴ They look like horses;
    they charge forward like warhorses.*
⁵ Look at them as they leap along the
        mountaintops.
    Listen to the noise they make—like the
        rumbling of chariots,
like the roar of fire sweeping across a field
        of stubble,
    or like a mighty army moving into
        battle.

⁶ Fear grips all the people;
    every face grows pale with terror.
⁷ The attackers march like warriors
    and scale city walls like soldiers.
Straight forward they march,
    never breaking rank.
⁸ They never jostle each other;
    each moves in exactly the right position.
They break through defenses
    without missing a step.
⁹ They swarm over the city
    and run along its walls.
They enter all the houses,
    climbing like thieves through the
        windows.
¹⁰ The earth quakes as they advance,
    and the heavens tremble.
The sun and moon grow dark,
    and the stars no longer shine.

¹¹ The LORD is at the head of the column.
    He leads them with a shout.
This is his mighty army,
    and they follow his orders.

2:1 Hebrew *Zion;* also in 2:15, 23.   2:4 Or *like charioteers.*

The day of the LORD is an awesome,
  terrible thing.
Who can possibly survive?

A Call to Repentance

12 That is why the LORD says,
  "Turn to me now, while there is time.
Give me your hearts.
  Come with fasting, weeping, and
    mourning.
13 Don't tear your clothing in your grief,
  but tear your hearts instead."
Return to the LORD your God,
  for he is merciful and compassionate,
slow to get angry and filled with unfailing
    love.
He is eager to relent and not punish.
14 Who knows? Perhaps he will give you a
    reprieve,
  sending you a blessing instead of this
    curse.
Perhaps you will be able to offer grain and
    wine
  to the LORD your God as before.

15 Blow the ram's horn in Jerusalem!
  Announce a time of fasting;
call the people together
  for a solemn meeting.
16 Gather all the people—
  the elders, the children, and even the
    babies.
Call the bridegroom from his quarters
  and the bride from her private room.
17 Let the priests, who minister in the LORD's
    presence,
  stand and weep between the entry room
    to the Temple and the altar.
Let them pray, "Spare your people, LORD!
  Don't let your special possession become
    an object of mockery.
Don't let them become a joke for
  unbelieving foreigners who say,
    'Has the God of Israel left them?'"

The LORD's Promise of Restoration

18 Then the LORD will pity his people
  and jealously guard the honor of his land.
19 The LORD will reply,
  "Look! I am sending you grain and new
    wine and olive oil,
  enough to satisfy your needs.
You will no longer be an object of mockery
  among the surrounding nations.

20 I will drive away these armies from the
    north.
  I will send them into the parched
    wastelands.
Those in the front will be driven into the
    Dead Sea,
  and those at the rear into the
    Mediterranean.*
The stench of their rotting bodies will rise
  over the land."

Surely the LORD has done great things!
21   Don't be afraid, O land.
Be glad now and rejoice,
  for the LORD has done great things.
22 Don't be afraid, you animals of the field,
  for the wilderness pastures will soon
    be green.
The trees will again be filled with fruit;
  fig trees and grapevines will be loaded
    down once more.
23 Rejoice, you people of Jerusalem!
  Rejoice in the LORD your God!
For the rain he sends demonstrates his
    faithfulness.
  Once more the autumn rains will
    come,
  as well as the rains of spring.
24 The threshing floors will again be piled
    high with grain,
  and the presses will overflow with new
    wine and olive oil.

25 The LORD says, "I will give you back what
    you lost
  to the swarming locusts, the hopping
    locusts,
  the stripping locusts, and the cutting
    locusts.*
  It was I who sent this great destroying
    army against you.
26 Once again you will have all the food you
    want,
  and you will praise the LORD your
    God,
who does these miracles for you.
  Never again will my people be
    disgraced.
27 Then you will know that I am among my
    people Israel,
  that I am the LORD your God, and there
    is no other.
Never again will my people be
  disgraced.

2:20 Hebrew *into the eastern sea, . . . into the western sea.*   2:25 The precise identification of the four kinds of locusts mentioned here is uncertain.

The LORD's Promise of His Spirit

28*"Then, after doing all those things,
  I will pour out my Spirit upon all
    people.
  Your sons and daughters will prophesy.
  Your old men will dream dreams,
    and your young men will see visions.
29 In those days I will pour out my Spirit
    even on servants—men and women
      alike.
30 And I will cause wonders in the heavens
    and on the earth—
  blood and fire and columns of smoke.
31 The sun will become dark,
    and the moon will turn blood red
  before that great and terrible* day of
    the LORD arrives.
32 But everyone who calls on the name of
    the LORD
  will be saved,
  for some on Mount Zion in Jerusalem will
    escape,
  just as the LORD has said.
  These will be among the survivors
    whom the LORD has called.

Judgment against Enemy Nations

3 1*"At the time of those events," says the
    LORD,
  "when I restore the prosperity of Judah
    and Jerusalem,
2 I will gather the armies of the world
    into the valley of Jehoshaphat.*
  There I will judge them
    for harming my people, my special
      possession,
  for scattering my people among the nations,
    and for dividing up my land.
3 They threw dice* to decide which of my
    people
  would be their slaves.
  They traded boys to obtain prostitutes
    and sold girls for enough wine to get
      drunk.

4 "What do you have against me, Tyre and
Sidon and you cities of Philistia? Are you trying
to take revenge on me? If you are, then watch
out! I will strike swiftly and pay you back for
everything you have done. 5 You have taken
my silver and gold and all my precious treasures, and have carried them off to your pagan
temples. 6 You have sold the people of Judah

and Jerusalem to the Greeks,* so they could
take them far from their homeland.

7 "But I will bring them back from all the
places to which you sold them, and I will pay
you back for everything you have done. 8 I will
sell your sons and daughters to the people of
Judah, and they will sell them to the people
of Arabia,* a nation far away. I, the LORD, have
spoken!"

9 Say to the nations far and wide:
    "Get ready for war!
  Call out your best warriors.
  Let all your fighting men advance for
    the attack.
10 Hammer your plowshares into swords
    and your pruning hooks into spears.
  Train even your weaklings to be
    warriors.
11 Come quickly, all you nations everywhere.
    Gather together in the valley."

  And now, O LORD, call out your warriors!

12 "Let the nations be called to arms.
  Let them march to the valley of
    Jehoshaphat.
  There I, the LORD, will sit
    to pronounce judgment on them all.
13 Swing the sickle,
    for the harvest is ripe.*
  Come, tread the grapes,
    for the winepress is full.
  The storage vats are overflowing
    with the wickedness of these people."

14 Thousands upon thousands are waiting
    in the valley of decision.
  There the day of the LORD will soon
    arrive.
15 The sun and moon will grow dark,
    and the stars will no longer shine.
16 The LORD's voice will roar from Zion
    and thunder from Jerusalem,
  and the heavens and the earth will shake.
  But the LORD will be a refuge for his
    people,
  a strong fortress for the people of Israel.

Blessings for God's People

17 "Then you will know that I, the LORD your
    God,
  live in Zion, my holy mountain.

2:28 Verses 2:28-32 are numbered 3:1-5 in Hebrew text.   2:31 Greek version reads *glorious*.   3:1 Verses 3:1-21 are numbered
4:1-21 in Hebrew text.   3:2 *Jehoshaphat* means "the LORD judges."   3:3 Hebrew *They cast lots*.   3:6 Hebrew *to the peoples
of Javan*.   3:8 Hebrew *to the Sabeans*.   3:13 Greek version reads *for the harvest time has come*. Compare Mark 4:29.

Jerusalem will be holy forever,
    and foreign armies will never conquer
      her again.
18 In that day the mountains will drip with
      sweet wine,
    and the hills will flow with milk.
Water will fill the streambeds of
      Judah,
    and a fountain will burst forth from the
      LORD's Temple,
    watering the arid valley of acacias.*
19 But Egypt will become a wasteland
    and Edom will become a wilderness,

3:18 Hebrew *valley of Shittim.*   3:21 Hebrew *Zion.*

because they attacked the people of
      Judah
    and killed innocent people in their
      land.

20 "But Judah will be filled with people
      forever,
    and Jerusalem will endure through
      all generations.
21 I will pardon my people's crimes,
    which I have not yet pardoned;
and I, the LORD, will make my home
    in Jerusalem* with my people."

Amos

WHEN WE THINK of the first prophets God called to preach against the northern kingdom of Israel, Amos is not someone we would normally imagine as a candidate. Amos was a shepherd and a sycamore-fig farmer, not an educated priest or a religious servant. But Amos was faithful to his calling, and he delivered God's message to the people. Amos was a contemporary of the prophets Hosea, Isaiah, and Micah. Like Hosea, Amos's message was directed mainly to the northern kingdom of Israel,

- **Author:** Amos
- **Date Written:** Probably during the reigns of Jeroboam II of Israel and Uzziah of Judah, between around 760 and 750 BC
- **Purpose:** To pronounce God's judgment upon Israel for its complacency, idolatry, and oppression of the poor
- **Themes:** Complacency, social justice, superficial religion
- **Outline**
  1:1-2 Introduction
  1:3–2:16 Judgment upon the nations and Israel
  3:1–6:14 The prophet's message of judgment
  7:1–9:10 Five visions of judgment
  9:11-15 A future hope

although he himself was from the southern kingdom of Judah. Amos's prophecy begins by pronouncing judgment upon the surrounding nations; then the prophecy focuses on Israel itself. Amos denounced the injustice, corruption, greed, and false worship that were rampant in Israel. Amos's prophecy continues with a series of visions, and the book ends with the hope that Israel will heed these warnings.

---

1 This message was given to Amos, a shepherd from the town of Tekoa in Judah. He received this message in visions two years before the earthquake, when Uzziah was king of Judah and Jeroboam II, the son of Jehoash,* was king of Israel.

²This is what he saw and heard:

"The LORD's voice will roar from Zion
and thunder from Jerusalem!
The lush pastures of the shepherds will
dry up;
the grass on Mount Carmel will wither
and die."

God's Judgment on Israel's Neighbors
³This is what the LORD says:

"The people of Damascus have sinned
again and again,*
and I will not let them go unpunished!
They beat down my people in Gilead

as grain is threshed with iron sledges.
⁴ So I will send down fire on King Hazael's
palace,
and the fortresses of King Ben-hadad
will be destroyed.
⁵ I will break down the gates of Damascus
and slaughter the people in the valley
of Aven.
I will destroy the ruler in Beth-eden,
and the people of Aram will go as
captives to Kir,"
says the LORD.

⁶This is what the LORD says:

"The people of Gaza have sinned again
and again,
and I will not let them go unpunished!
They sent whole villages into exile,
selling them as slaves to Edom.
⁷ So I will send down fire on the walls of
Gaza,

1:1 Hebrew *Joash*, a variant spelling of Jehoash.   1:3 Hebrew *have committed three sins, even four*; also in 1:6, 9, 11, 13.

and all its fortresses will be destroyed.
8 I will slaughter the people of Ashdod
    and destroy the king of Ashkelon.
Then I will turn to attack Ekron,
    and the few Philistines still left will be
        killed,"
    says the Sovereign LORD.

9This is what the LORD says:

"The people of Tyre have sinned again and
    again,
    and I will not let them go unpunished!
They broke their treaty of brotherhood
    with Israel,
    selling whole villages as slaves to
        Edom.
10 So I will send down fire on the walls of
    Tyre,
    and all its fortresses will be destroyed."

11This is what the LORD says:

"The people of Edom have sinned again
    and again,
    and I will not let them go unpunished!
They chased down their relatives, the
    Israelites, with swords,
    showing them no mercy.
In their rage, they slashed them
    continually
    and were unrelenting in their anger.
12 So I will send down fire on Teman,
    and the fortresses of Bozrah will be
        destroyed."

13This is what the LORD says:

"The people of Ammon have sinned again
    and again,
    and I will not let them go unpunished!
When they attacked Gilead to extend their
    borders,
    they ripped open pregnant women with
        their swords.
14 So I will send down fire on the walls of
    Rabbah,
    and all its fortresses will be destroyed.
The battle will come upon them with
    shouts,
    like a whirlwind in a mighty storm.
15 And their king* and his princes will go
    into exile together,"
    says the LORD.

2 This is what the LORD says:

"The people of Moab have sinned again
    and again,*
    and I will not let them go unpunished!
They desecrated the bones of Edom's king,
    burning them to ashes.
2 So I will send down fire on the land of
    Moab,
    and all the fortresses in Kerioth will be
        destroyed.
The people will fall in the noise of battle,
    as the warriors shout and the ram's horn
        sounds.
3 And I will destroy their king
    and slaughter all their princes,"
    says the LORD.

God's Judgment on Judah and Israel

4This is what the LORD says:

"The people of Judah have sinned again
    and again,
    and I will not let them go unpunished!
They have rejected the instruction of the
    LORD,
    refusing to obey his decrees.
They have been led astray by the same lies
    that deceived their ancestors.
5 So I will send down fire on Judah,
    and all the fortresses of Jerusalem will
        be destroyed."

6This is what the LORD says:

"The people of Israel have sinned again
    and again,
    and I will not let them go unpunished!
They sell honorable people for silver
    and poor people for a pair of sandals.
7 They trample helpless people in the dust
    and shove the oppressed out of the way.
Both father and son sleep with the same
    woman,
    corrupting my holy name.
8 At their religious festivals,
    they lounge in clothing their debtors
        put up as security.
In the house of their gods,*
    they drink wine bought with unjust
        fines.

9 "But as my people watched,
    I destroyed the Amorites,

1:15 Hebrew *malcam*, possibly referring to their god Molech.   2:1 Hebrew *have committed three sins, even four*; also in 2:4, 6.
2:8 Or *their God*.

though they were as tall as cedars
    and as strong as oaks.
I destroyed the fruit on their branches
    and dug out their roots.
10 It was I who rescued you from Egypt
    and led you through the desert for
        forty years,
    so you could possess the land of the
        Amorites.
11 I chose some of your sons to be prophets
    and others to be Nazirites.
    Can you deny this, my people of Israel?”
        asks the LORD.
12 “But you caused the Nazirites to sin by
        making them drink wine,
    and you commanded the prophets,
        ‘Shut up!’

13 “So I will make you groan
    like a wagon loaded down with sheaves
        of grain.
14 Your fastest runners will not get away.
    The strongest among you will become
        weak.
    Even mighty warriors will be unable to
        save themselves.
15   The archers will not stand their ground.
    The swiftest runners won’t be fast enough
        to escape.
    Even those riding horses won’t be able
        to save themselves.
16 On that day the most courageous of your
        fighting men
    will drop their weapons and run for
        their lives,”
    says the LORD.

3 Listen to this message that the LORD has
   spoken against you, O people of Israel—
against the entire family I rescued from Egypt:

2 “From among all the families on the earth,
    I have been intimate with you alone.
    That is why I must punish you
        for all your sins.”

Witnesses against Guilty Israel
3 Can two people walk together
    without agreeing on the direction?
4 Does a lion ever roar in a thicket
    without first finding a victim?
    Does a young lion growl in its den
    without first catching its prey?

5 Does a bird ever get caught in a trap
    that has no bait?
    Does a trap spring shut
    when there’s nothing to catch?
6 When the ram’s horn blows a warning,
    shouldn’t the people be alarmed?
    Does disaster come to a city
    unless the LORD has planned it?

7 Indeed, the Sovereign LORD never does
        anything
    until he reveals his plans to his servants
        the prophets.

8 The lion has roared—
    so who isn’t frightened?
    The Sovereign LORD has spoken—
    so who can refuse to proclaim his
        message?
9 Announce this to the leaders of Philistia*
    and to the great ones of Egypt:
    “Take your seats now on the hills around
        Samaria,
    and witness the chaos and oppression
        in Israel.”

10 “My people have forgotten how to do right,”
    says the LORD.
    “Their fortresses are filled with wealth
    taken by theft and violence.
11 Therefore,” says the Sovereign LORD,
    “an enemy is coming!
    He will surround them and shatter their
        defenses.
    Then he will plunder all their fortresses.”

12 This is what the LORD says:

    “A shepherd who tries to rescue a sheep
        from a lion’s mouth
    will recover only two legs or a piece of
        an ear.
    So it will be for the Israelites in Samaria
        lying on luxurious beds,
    and for the people of Damascus
        reclining on couches.*

13 “Now listen to this, and announce it
throughout all Israel,*” says the Lord, the LORD
God of Heaven’s Armies.

14 “On the very day I punish Israel for its sins,
    I will destroy the pagan altars at Bethel.

3:9 Hebrew *Ashdod*.   **3:12** The meaning of the Hebrew in this sentence is uncertain.   **3:13** Hebrew *the house of Jacob*. The names “Jacob” and “Israel” are often interchanged throughout the Old Testament, referring sometimes to the individual patriarch and sometimes to the nation.

The horns of the altar will be cut off
  and fall to the ground.
15 And I will destroy the beautiful homes
    of the wealthy—
  their winter mansions and their
    summer houses, too—
  all their palaces filled with ivory,"
    says the LORD.

Israel's Failure to Learn

4 ¹ Listen to me, you fat cows*
    living in Samaria,
you women who oppress the poor
  and crush the needy,
and who are always calling to your
    husbands,
  "Bring us another drink!"
² The Sovereign LORD has sworn this by his
    holiness:
"The time will come when you will be led
    away
  with hooks in your noses.
Every last one of you will be dragged
    away
  like a fish on a hook!
³ You will be led out through the ruins of
    the wall;
  you will be thrown from your
    fortresses,*"
    says the LORD.

⁴ "Go ahead and offer sacrifices to the idols
    at Bethel.
  Keep on disobeying at Gilgal.
Offer sacrifices each morning,
  and bring your tithes every three days.
⁵ Present your bread made with yeast
  as an offering of thanksgiving.
Then give your extra voluntary offerings
  so you can brag about it everywhere!
This is the kind of thing you Israelites
    love to do,"
    says the Sovereign LORD.

⁶ "I brought hunger to every city
  and famine to every town.
But still you would not return to me,"
    says the LORD.

⁷ "I kept the rain from falling
  when your crops needed it the
    most.
I sent rain on one town
  but withheld it from another.

Rain fell on one field,
  while another field withered away.
⁸ People staggered from town to town
  looking for water,
  but there was never enough.
But still you would not return to me,"
    says the LORD.

⁹ "I struck your farms and vineyards with
    blight and mildew.
  Locusts devoured all your fig and olive
    trees.
But still you would not return to me,"
    says the LORD.

¹⁰ "I sent plagues on you
  like the plagues I sent on Egypt
    long ago.
I killed your young men in war
  and led all your horses away.*
The stench of death filled the air!
But still you would not return to me,"
    says the LORD.

¹¹ "I destroyed some of your cities,
  as I destroyed* Sodom and Gomorrah.
Those of you who survived
  were like charred sticks pulled from
    a fire.
But still you would not return to me,"
    says the LORD.

¹² "Therefore, I will bring upon you all the
    disasters I have announced.
  Prepare to meet your God in judgment,
    you people of Israel!"

¹³ For the LORD is the one who shaped the
    mountains,
  stirs up the winds, and reveals his
    thoughts to mankind.
He turns the light of dawn into darkness
  and treads on the heights of the earth.
  The LORD God of Heaven's Armies is his
    name!

A Call to Repentance

5 Listen, you people of Israel! Listen to this
    funeral song I am singing:

² "The virgin Israel has fallen,
    never to rise again!
  She lies abandoned on the ground,
    with no one to help her up."

4:1 Hebrew *you cows of Bashan.*   4:3 Or *thrown out toward Harmon*, possibly a reference to Mount Hermon.   4:10 Or *and
slaughtered your captured horses.*   4:11 Hebrew *as when God destroyed.*

³The Sovereign LORD says:

"When a city sends a thousand men to battle,
only a hundred will return.
When a town sends a hundred,
only ten will come back alive."

⁴Now this is what the LORD says to the family of Israel:

"Come back to me and live!
⁵ Don't worship at the pagan altars at Bethel;
don't go to the shrines at Gilgal or Beersheba.
For the people of Gilgal will be dragged off into exile,
and the people of Bethel will be reduced to nothing."
⁶ Come back to the LORD and live!
Otherwise, he will roar through Israel*
like a fire,
devouring you completely.
Your gods in Bethel
won't be able to quench the flames.
⁷ You twist justice, making it a bitter pill for the oppressed.
You treat the righteous like dirt.

⁸ It is the LORD who created the stars,
the Pleiades and Orion.
He turns darkness into morning
and day into night.
He draws up water from the oceans
and pours it down as rain on the land.
The LORD is his name!
⁹ With blinding speed and power he destroys the strong,
crushing all their defenses.

¹⁰ How you hate honest judges!
How you despise people who tell the truth!
¹¹ You trample the poor,
stealing their grain through taxes and unfair rent.
Therefore, though you build beautiful stone houses,
you will never live in them.
Though you plant lush vineyards,
you will never drink wine from them.
¹² For I know the vast number of your sins
and the depth of your rebellions.

You oppress good people by taking bribes
and deprive the poor of justice in the courts.
¹³ So those who are smart keep their mouths shut,
for it is an evil time.

¹⁴ Do what is good and run from evil
so that you may live!
Then the LORD God of Heaven's Armies
will be your helper,
just as you have claimed.
¹⁵ Hate evil and love what is good;
turn your courts into true halls of justice.
Perhaps even yet the LORD God of Heaven's Armies
will have mercy on the remnant of his people.*

¹⁶Therefore, this is what the Lord, the LORD God of Heaven's Armies, says:

"There will be crying in all the public squares
and mourning in every street.
Call for the farmers to weep with you,
and summon professional mourners to wail.
¹⁷ There will be wailing in every vineyard,
for I will destroy them all,"
says the LORD.

Warning of Coming Judgment

¹⁸ What sorrow awaits you who say,
"If only the day of the LORD were here!"
You have no idea what you are wishing for.
That day will bring darkness, not light.
¹⁹ In that day you will be like a man who runs from a lion—
only to meet a bear.
Escaping from the bear, he leans his hand against a wall in his house—
and he's bitten by a snake.
²⁰ Yes, the day of the LORD will be dark and hopeless,
without a ray of joy or hope.

²¹ "I hate all your show and pretense—
the hypocrisy of your religious festivals
and solemn assemblies.
²² I will not accept your burnt offerings and grain offerings.
I won't even notice all your choice peace offerings.

5:6 Hebrew *the house of Joseph.*   5:15 Hebrew *the remnant of Joseph.*

23 Away with your noisy hymns of
    praise!
    I will not listen to the music of your
    harps.
24 Instead, I want to see a mighty flood of
    justice,
    an endless river of righteous living.

25 "Was it to me you were bringing sacrifices and offerings during the forty years in
the wilderness, Israel? 26 No, you served your
pagan gods—Sakkuth your king god and Kai-
wan your star god—the images you made for
yourselves. 27 So I will send you into exile, to a
land east of Damascus,* says the LORD, whose
name is the God of Heaven's Armies.

6 1 What sorrow awaits you who lounge in
    luxury in Jerusalem,*
    and you who feel secure in Samaria!
    You are famous and popular in Israel,
    and people go to you for help.
2 But go over to Calneh
    and see what happened there.
    Then go to the great city of Hamath
    and down to the Philistine city of
    Gath.
    You are no better than they were,
    and look at how they were destroyed.
3 You push away every thought of coming
    disaster,
    but your actions only bring the day of
    judgment closer.
4 How terrible for you who sprawl on ivory
    beds
    and lounge on your couches,
    eating the meat of tender lambs from the
    flock
    and of choice calves fattened in the
    stall.
5 You sing trivial songs to the sound of
    the harp
    and fancy yourselves to be great
    musicians like David.
6 You drink wine by the bowlful
    and perfume yourselves with fragrant
    lotions.
    You care nothing about the ruin of your
    nation.*
7 Therefore, you will be the first to be led
    away as captives.
    Suddenly, all your parties will end.

8 The Sovereign LORD has sworn by his own
name, and this is what he, the LORD God of
Heaven's Armies, says:

"I despise the arrogance of Israel,*
    and I hate their fortresses.
I will give this city
    and everything in it to their enemies."

9 (If there are ten men left in one house, they
will all die. 10 And when a relative who is responsible to dispose of the dead* goes into the
house to carry out the bodies, he will ask the
last survivor, "Is anyone else with you?" When
the person begins to swear, "No, by . . . ," he will
interrupt and say, "Stop! Don't even mention
the name of the LORD.")

11 When the LORD gives the command,
    homes both great and small will be
    smashed to pieces.

12 Can horses gallop over boulders?
    Can oxen be used to plow them?
    But that's how foolish you are when you
    turn justice into poison
    and the sweet fruit of righteousness into
    bitterness.

13 And you brag about your conquest of
    Lo-debar.*
    You boast, "Didn't we take Karnaim* by
    our own strength?"

14 "O people of Israel, I am about to bring an
    enemy nation against you,"
    says the LORD God of Heaven's Armies.
    "They will oppress you throughout your
    land—
    from Lebo-hamath in the north
    to the Arabah Valley in the south."

A Vision of Locusts

7 The Sovereign LORD showed me a vision. I
    saw him preparing to send a vast swarm of
locusts over the land. This was after the king's
share had been harvested from the fields and
as the main crop was coming up. 2 In my vision
the locusts ate every green plant in sight. Then
I said, "O Sovereign LORD, please forgive us
or we will not survive, for Israel* is so small."

3 So the LORD relented from this plan. "I will
not do it," he said.

5:26-27 Greek version reads No, you carried your pagan gods—the shrine of Molech, the star of your god Rephan, and the images you
made for yourselves. So I will send you into exile, to a land east of Damascus. Compare Acts 7:43.   6:1 Hebrew in Zion.   6:6 Hebrew
of Joseph.   6:8 Hebrew Jacob. See note on 3:13.   6:10 Or to burn the dead. The meaning of the Hebrew is uncertain.
6:13a Lo-debar means "nothing."   6:13b Karnaim means "horns," a term that symbolizes strength.   7:2 Hebrew Jacob;
also in 7:5. See note on 3:13.

A Vision of Fire

4Then the Sovereign LORD showed me another vision. I saw him preparing to punish his people with a great fire. The fire had burned up the depths of the sea and was devouring the entire land. 5Then I said, "O Sovereign LORD, please stop or we will not survive, for Israel is so small."

6Then the LORD relented from this plan, too. "I will not do that either," said the Sovereign LORD.

A Vision of a Plumb Line

7Then he showed me another vision. I saw the Lord standing beside a wall that had been built using a plumb line. He was using a plumb line to see if it was still straight. 8And the LORD said to me, "Amos, what do you see?"

I answered, "A plumb line."

And the Lord replied, "I will test my people with this plumb line. I will no longer ignore all their sins. 9The pagan shrines of your ancestors* will be ruined, and the temples of Israel will be destroyed; I will bring the dynasty of King Jeroboam to a sudden end."

Amos and Amaziah

10Then Amaziah, the priest of Bethel, sent a message to Jeroboam, king of Israel: "Amos is hatching a plot against you right here on your very doorstep! What he is saying is intolerable. 11He is saying, 'Jeroboam will soon be killed, and the people of Israel will be sent away into exile.'"

12Then Amaziah sent orders to Amos: "Get out of here, you prophet! Go on back to the land of Judah, and earn your living by prophesying there! 13Don't bother us with your prophecies here in Bethel. This is the king's sanctuary and the national place of worship!"

14But Amos replied, "I'm not a professional prophet, and I was never trained to be one.* I'm just a shepherd, and I take care of sycamore-fig trees. 15But the LORD called me away from my flock and told me, 'Go and prophesy to my people in Israel.' 16Now then, listen to this message from the LORD:

"You say,
'Don't prophesy against Israel.
    Stop preaching against my
        people.*'
17 But this is what the LORD says:

'Your wife will become a prostitute in
    this city,
and your sons and daughters will be
    killed.
Your land will be divided up,
    and you yourself will die in a foreign
    land.
And the people of Israel will certainly
    become captives in exile,
far from their homeland.'"

A Vision of Ripe Fruit

8 Then the Sovereign LORD showed me another vision. In it I saw a basket filled with ripe fruit. 2"What do you see, Amos?" he asked.

I replied, "A basket full of ripe fruit."

Then the LORD said, "Like this fruit, Israel is ripe for punishment! I will not delay their punishment again. 3In that day the singing in the temple will turn to wailing. Dead bodies will be scattered everywhere. They will be carried out of the city in silence. I, the Sovereign LORD, have spoken!"

4 Listen to this, you who rob the poor
    and trample down the needy!
5 You can't wait for the Sabbath day to
    be over
    and the religious festivals to end
    so you can get back to cheating the
        helpless.
You measure out grain with dishonest
        measures
    and cheat the buyer with dishonest
        scales.*
6 And you mix the grain you sell
    with chaff swept from the floor.
Then you enslave poor people
    for one piece of silver or a pair of
        sandals.

7 Now the LORD has sworn this oath
    by his own name, the Pride of Israel*:
"I will never forget
    the wicked things you have done!
8 The earth will tremble for your deeds,
    and everyone will mourn.
The ground will rise like the Nile River
        at floodtime;
    it will heave up, then sink again.

9 "In that day," says the Sovereign LORD,
    "I will make the sun go down at noon

7:9 Hebrew of Isaac.   7:14 Or I'm not a prophet nor the son of a prophet.   7:16 Hebrew against the house of Isaac.   8:5 Hebrew You make the ephah [a unit for measuring grain] small and the shekel [a unit of weight] great, and you deal falsely by using deceitful balances.   8:7 Hebrew the pride of Jacob. See note on 3:13.

and darken the earth while it is
     still day.
¹⁰ I will turn your celebrations into times
          of mourning
     and your singing into weeping.
You will wear funeral clothes
     and shave your heads to show your
          sorrow—
     as if your only son had died.
     How very bitter that day will be!

¹¹ "The time is surely coming," says the
          Sovereign LORD,
     "when I will send a famine on the land—
not a famine of bread or water
     but of hearing the words of the LORD.
¹² People will stagger from sea to sea
     and wander from border to border*
searching for the word of the LORD,
     but they will not find it.
¹³ Beautiful girls and strong young men
     will grow faint in that day,
     thirsting for the LORD's word.
¹⁴ And those who swear by the shameful
          idols of Samaria—
     who take oaths in the name of the god
          of Dan
     and make vows in the name of the god
          of Beersheba*—
they will all fall down,
     never to rise again."

A Vision of God at the Altar

9 Then I saw a vision of the Lord standing beside the altar. He said,

"Strike the tops of the Temple columns,
     so that the foundation will shake.
Bring down the roof
     on the heads of the people below.
I will kill with the sword those who
          survive.
     No one will escape!

² "Even if they dig down to the place of the
          dead,*
     I will reach down and pull them up.
Even if they climb up into the heavens,
     I will bring them down.
³ Even if they hide at the very top of Mount
          Carmel,
     I will search them out and capture them.
Even if they hide at the bottom of the
          ocean,

I will send the sea serpent after them
     to bite them.
⁴ Even if their enemies drive them into
          exile,
     I will command the sword to kill them
          there.
I am determined to bring disaster upon
          them
     and not to help them."

⁵ The Lord, the LORD of Heaven's Armies,
     touches the land and it melts,
     and all its people mourn.
The ground rises like the Nile River at
          floodtime,
     and then it sinks again.
⁶ The LORD's home reaches up to the
          heavens,
     while its foundation is on the earth.
He draws up water from the oceans
     and pours it down as rain on the land.
     The LORD is his name!

⁷ "Are you Israelites more important to me
     than the Ethiopians?*" asks the LORD.
"I brought Israel out of Egypt,
     but I also brought the Philistines from
          Crete*
     and led the Arameans out of Kir.

⁸ "I, the Sovereign LORD,
     am watching this sinful nation of Israel.
I will destroy it
     from the face of the earth.
But I will never completely destroy the
          family of Israel,*"
     says the LORD.
⁹ "For I will give the command
     and will shake Israel along with the
          other nations
as grain is shaken in a sieve,
     yet not one true kernel will be lost.
¹⁰ But all the sinners will die by the sword—
     all those who say, 'Nothing bad will
          happen to us.'

A Promise of Restoration

¹¹ "In that day I will restore the fallen house*
          of David.
     I will repair its damaged walls.
From the ruins I will rebuild it
     and restore its former glory.
¹² And Israel will possess what is left of
          Edom

8:12 Hebrew *from north to east.*   8:14 Hebrew *the way of Beersheba.*   9:2 Hebrew *to Sheol.*   9:7a Hebrew *the Cushites?*
9:7b Hebrew *Caphtor.*   9:8 Hebrew *the house of Jacob.* See note on 3:13.   9:11a Or *kingdom;* Hebrew reads *tent.*

and all the nations I have called to be
   mine.*"
The LORD has spoken,
   and he will do these things.

13 "The time will come," says the LORD,
   "when the grain and grapes will grow
      faster
   than they can be harvested.
Then the terraced vineyards on the hills
      of Israel
   will drip with sweet wine!

14 I will bring my exiled people of Israel
   back from distant lands,
and they will rebuild their ruined cities
   and live in them again.
They will plant vineyards and gardens;
   they will eat their crops and drink their
      wine.
15 I will firmly plant them there
   in their own land.
They will never again be uprooted
   from the land I have given them,"
   says the LORD your God.

9:11b-12 Greek version reads *and restore its former glory, / so that the rest of humanity, including the Gentiles— / all those I have called to be mine—might seek me.* Compare Acts 15:16-17.

Obadiah

OFTEN THE MOST PAINFUL betrayals come from those who are closest to us. At least this was how Obadiah felt about the Edomites' attack on Jerusalem. In this short book, Obadiah foretold Edom's doom for treacherously plundering Jerusalem after its fall to the Babylonians in 586 BC. The Edomites were descendants of Esau, Jacob's brother, so they were related by blood to the Israelites who inhabited Jerusalem. Of all people, the Edomites should have come to Jerusalem's aid. Instead, they took part in the destruction and gloated over Jerusalem's demise. The Edomites failed to realize that their survival depended upon their humility before almighty God and not upon their "invincible" mountain fortresses.

- **Author:** Obadiah
- **Date Written:** Uncertain, perhaps shortly after the fall of Jerusalem in 586 BC
- **Purpose:** To condemn Edom for its cruel treachery toward Jerusalem
- **Themes:** Treachery, justice, pride
- **Outline**
  1:1-9 Edom's destruction foretold
  1:10-14 The sins of Edom
  1:15-21 The day of the Lord, and Judah's restoration

This is the vision that the Sovereign LORD revealed to Obadiah concerning the land of Edom.

Edom's Judgment Announced

We have heard a message from the LORD
that an ambassador was sent to the
    nations to say,
"Get ready, everyone!
    Let's assemble our armies and attack
    Edom!"

² The LORD says to Edom,
"I will cut you down to size among the
    nations;
    you will be greatly despised.
³ You have been deceived by your own
    pride
because you live in a rock fortress
    and make your home high in the
    mountains.
'Who can ever reach us way up here?'
    you ask boastfully.
⁴ But even if you soar as high as eagles
    and build your nest among the stars,
I will bring you crashing down,"
    says the LORD.

⁵ "If thieves came at night and robbed you
    (what a disaster awaits you!),
    they would not take everything.
Those who harvest grapes
    always leave a few for the poor.
But your enemies will wipe you out
    completely!
⁶ Every nook and cranny of Edom*
    will be searched and looted.
    Every treasure will be found and taken.

⁷ "All your allies will turn against you.
    They will help to chase you from your
    land.
They will promise you peace
    while plotting to deceive and destroy
    you.
Your trusted friends will set traps for you,
    and you won't even know about it.
⁸ At that time not a single wise person
    will be left in the whole land of Edom,"
    says the LORD.
"For on the mountains of Edom
    I will destroy everyone who has
    understanding.
⁹ The mightiest warriors of Teman
    will be terrified,

6 Hebrew *Esau*; also in 8b, 9, 18, 19, 21.

and everyone on the mountains of Edom
    will be cut down in the slaughter.

Reasons for Edom's Punishment

10 "Because of the violence you did
    to your close relatives in Israel,*
you will be filled with shame
    and destroyed forever.
11 When they were invaded,
    you stood aloof, refusing to help them.
Foreign invaders carried off their wealth
    and cast lots to divide up Jerusalem,
but you acted like one of Israel's
    enemies.

12 "You should not have gloated
    when they exiled your relatives to
    distant lands.
You should not have rejoiced
    when the people of Judah suffered such
    misfortune.
You should not have spoken arrogantly
    in that terrible time of trouble.
13 You should not have plundered the land
    of Israel
    when they were suffering such calamity.
You should not have gloated over their
    destruction
    when they were suffering such calamity.
You should not have seized their wealth
    when they were suffering such calamity.
14 You should not have stood at the
    crossroads,
    killing those who tried to escape.
You should not have captured the
    survivors
    and handed them over in their terrible
    time of trouble.

Edom Destroyed, Israel Restored

15 "The day is near when I, the LORD,
    will judge all godless nations!
As you have done to Israel,
    so it will be done to you.

All your evil deeds
    will fall back on your own heads.
16 Just as you swallowed up my people
    on my holy mountain,
so you and the surrounding nations
    will swallow the punishment I pour
    out on you.
Yes, all you nations will drink and
    stagger
    and disappear from history.

17 "But Jerusalem* will become a refuge for
    those who escape;
    it will be a holy place.
And the people of Israel* will come back
    to reclaim their inheritance.
18 The people of Israel will be a raging fire,
    and Edom a field of dry stubble.
The descendants of Joseph will be a flame
    roaring across the field, devouring
    everything.
There will be no survivors in Edom.
    I, the LORD, have spoken!

19 "Then my people living in the Negev
    will occupy the mountains of Edom.
Those living in the foothills of Judah*
    will possess the Philistine plains
    and take over the fields of Ephraim
    and Samaria.
And the people of Benjamin
    will occupy the land of Gilead.
20 The exiles of Israel will return to their
    land
    and occupy the Phoenician coast as far
    north as Zarephath.
The captives from Jerusalem exiled in the
    north*
    will return home and resettle the towns
    of the Negev.
21 Those who have been rescued* will go up
    to* Mount Zion in Jerusalem
    to rule over the mountains of Edom.
And the LORD himself will be king!"

10 Hebrew *your brother Jacob.* The names "Jacob" and "Israel" are often interchanged throughout the Old Testament, referring sometimes to the individual patriarch and sometimes to the nation. 17a Hebrew *Mount Zion.* 17b Hebrew *house of Jacob;* also in 18. See note on 10. 19 Hebrew *the Shephelah.* 20 Hebrew *in Sepharad.* 21a As in Greek and Syriac versions; Hebrew reads *Rescuers.* 21b Or *from.*

Jonah

IF YOU WERE GIVEN an assignment to preach the gospel to a band of convicted killers, would you do it? This is similar to the assignment God gave Jonah. Jonah was a prophet born in Israel (see 2 Kings 14:25) and called by God to preach to the people of Nineveh, the capital city of Assyria. Not only was Assyria the most powerful empire in that day, it was also ruthlessly violent toward its conquered enemies. So it is unlikely that many Is-

- **Author:** Jonah, according to Jewish tradition
- **Date Written:** Between 785 and 760 BC
- **Purpose:** To show that God wants all people to come to know him
- **Themes:** God's sovereignty, repentance, God's universal compassion
- **Outline**
  1:1-17 Jonah's fall and flight from God
  2:1-10 Jonah's prayer in the fish's belly
  3:1-10 Jonah's renewed commission and success
  4:1-11 Jonah's reaction and God's concern

raelites would have accepted Jonah's task. The book of Jonah relates how Jonah tried to flee his calling and travel by ship to another country. But God sent a storm to change his plans; Jonah was thrown overboard, and a giant fish swallowed him. The fish then spewed Jonah back onto the shore, and Jonah went to Assyria. To Jonah's dismay, the king and citizens of Nineveh heard his message and repented, and God spared them from their promised destruction. In disgust, Jonah went outside the city and wished it would be destroyed. God rebuked Jonah, however, and expressed his desire for all people, Jews and Gentiles alike, to come to know him.

Jonah Runs from the LORD

1 The LORD gave this message to Jonah son of Amittai: 2"Get up and go to the great city of Nineveh. Announce my judgment against it because I have seen how wicked its people are."

3But Jonah got up and went in the opposite direction to get away from the LORD. He went down to the port of Joppa, where he found a ship leaving for Tarshish. He bought a ticket and went on board, hoping to escape from the LORD by sailing to Tarshish.

4But the LORD hurled a powerful wind over the sea, causing a violent storm that threatened to break the ship apart. 5Fearing for their lives, the desperate sailors shouted to their gods for help and threw the cargo overboard to lighten the ship.

But all this time Jonah was sound asleep down in the hold. 6So the captain went down after him. "How can you sleep at a time like this?" he shouted. "Get up and pray to your god! Maybe he will pay attention to us and spare our lives."

7Then the crew cast lots to see which of them had offended the gods and caused the terrible storm. When they did this, the lots identified Jonah as the culprit. 8"Why has this awful storm come down on us?" they demanded. "Who are you? What is your line of work? What country are you from? What is your nationality?"

9Jonah answered, "I am a Hebrew, and I worship the LORD, the God of heaven, who made the sea and the land."

10The sailors were terrified when they heard this, for he had already told them he was running away from the LORD. "Oh, why did you do it?" they groaned. 11And since the storm was getting worse all the time, they asked him, "What should we do to you to stop this storm?"

12"Throw me into the sea," Jonah said, "and

it will become calm again. I know that this terrible storm is all my fault."

[13]Instead, the sailors rowed even harder to get the ship to the land. But the stormy sea was too violent for them, and they couldn't make it. [14]Then they cried out to the LORD, Jonah's God. "O LORD," they pleaded, "don't make us die for this man's sin. And don't hold us responsible for his death. O LORD, you have sent this storm upon him for your own good reasons."

[15]Then the sailors picked Jonah up and threw him into the raging sea, and the storm stopped at once! [16]The sailors were awestruck by the LORD's great power, and they offered him a sacrifice and vowed to serve him.

[17]*Now the LORD had arranged for a great fish to swallow Jonah. And Jonah was inside the fish for three days and three nights.

Jonah's Prayer

2 [1]*Then Jonah prayed to the LORD his God from inside the fish. [2]He said,

"I cried out to the LORD in my great
    trouble,
    and he answered me.
I called to you from the land of the dead,*
    and LORD, you heard me!
[3] You threw me into the ocean depths,
    and I sank down to the heart of the sea.
The mighty waters engulfed me;
    I was buried beneath your wild and
        stormy waves.
[4] Then I said, 'O LORD, you have driven me
        from your presence.
    Yet I will look once more toward your
        holy Temple.'
[5] "I sank beneath the waves,
    and the waters closed over me.
    Seaweed wrapped itself around my
        head.
[6] I sank down to the very roots of the
        mountains.
    I was imprisoned in the earth,
        whose gates lock shut forever.
    But you, O LORD my God,
        snatched me from the jaws of death!
[7] As my life was slipping away,
    I remembered the LORD.
    And my earnest prayer went out to you
        in your holy Temple.
[8] Those who worship false gods
        turn their backs on all God's mercies.

[9] But I will offer sacrifices to you with songs
        of praise,
    and I will fulfill all my vows.
    For my salvation comes from the LORD
        alone."

[10]Then the LORD ordered the fish to spit Jonah out onto the beach.

Jonah Goes to Nineveh

3 Then the LORD spoke to Jonah a second time: [2]"Get up and go to the great city of Nineveh, and deliver the message I have given you."

[3]This time Jonah obeyed the LORD's command and went to Nineveh, a city so large that it took three days to see it all.* [4]On the day Jonah entered the city, he shouted to the crowds: "Forty days from now Nineveh will be destroyed!" [5]The people of Nineveh believed God's message, and from the greatest to the least, they declared a fast and put on burlap to show their sorrow.

[6]When the king of Nineveh heard what Jonah was saying, he stepped down from his throne and took off his royal robes. He dressed himself in burlap and sat on a heap of ashes. [7]Then the king and his nobles sent this decree throughout the city:

"No one, not even the animals from
your herds and flocks, may eat or drink
anything at all. [8]People and animals alike
must wear garments of mourning, and
everyone must pray earnestly to God. They
must turn from their evil ways and stop all
their violence. [9]Who can tell? Perhaps even
yet God will change his mind and hold
back his fierce anger from destroying us."

[10]When God saw what they had done and how they had put a stop to their evil ways, he changed his mind and did not carry out the destruction he had threatened.

Jonah's Anger at the LORD's Mercy

4 This change of plans greatly upset Jonah, and he became very angry. [2]So he complained to the LORD about it: "Didn't I say before I left home that you would do this, LORD? That is why I ran away to Tarshish! I knew that you are a merciful and compassionate God, slow to get angry and filled with unfailing love. You are eager to turn back from

1:17 Verse 1:17 is numbered 2:1 in Hebrew text.   2:1 Verses 2:1-10 are numbered 2:2-11 in Hebrew text.   2:2 Hebrew *from Sheol.*   3:3 Hebrew *a great city to God, of three days' journey.*

destroying people. ³Just kill me now, Lord! I'd rather be dead than alive if what I predicted will not happen."

⁴The Lord replied, "Is it right for you to be angry about this?"

⁵Then Jonah went out to the east side of the city and made a shelter to sit under as he waited to see what would happen to the city. ⁶And the Lord God arranged for a leafy plant to grow there, and soon it spread its broad leaves over Jonah's head, shading him from the sun. This eased his discomfort, and Jonah was very grateful for the plant.

⁷But God also arranged for a worm! The next morning at dawn the worm ate through the stem of the plant so that it withered away.

⁸And as the sun grew hot, God arranged for a scorching east wind to blow on Jonah. The sun beat down on his head until he grew faint and wished to die. "Death is certainly better than living like this!" he exclaimed.

⁹Then God said to Jonah, "Is it right for you to be angry because the plant died?"

"Yes," Jonah retorted, "even angry enough to die!"

¹⁰Then the Lord said, "You feel sorry about the plant, though you did nothing to put it there. It came quickly and died quickly. ¹¹But Nineveh has more than 120,000 people living in spiritual darkness,* not to mention all the animals. Shouldn't I feel sorry for such a great city?"

4:11 Hebrew *people who don't know their right hand from their left.*

Micah

CAN A LOVING GOD HATE SIN? According to the prophet Micah, God most certainly can—and does. Micah was a contemporary of Isaiah who preached to Israel and Judah during the 700s BC. He lived in a small town called Moresheth, which lay south of Jerusalem. Micah denounced the oppression, pride, greed, corruption, false piety, and arrogance of the two kingdoms. He summoned the priests and leaders to appear before God and plead their case, for they were about to be judged for their wicked-

- **Author:** Micah
- **Date Written:** Possibly during the reigns of Jotham, Ahaz, and Hezekiah, between 742 and 687 BC
- **Purpose:** To warn God's people that judgment is coming and to offer pardon to all who repent
- **Themes:** Wicked leaders, injustice, the coming Messiah, restoration
- **Outline**
  1:1-16 The judgment of God
  2:1–3:12 God's hatred of sin
  4:1–5:1 Future blessings
  5:2-15 The coming Messiah
  6:1–7:20 God's judgment on Israel

ness. God would indeed hold everyone accountable for his or her actions. But Micah also made it clear that God's love never dies. Judgment often comes after we have been given many opportunities to repent. And once God's punishment has been given, he will restore his people to himself again and will forgive their sins.

---

1 The LORD gave this message to Micah of Moresheth during the years when Jotham, Ahaz, and Hezekiah were kings of Judah. The visions he saw concerned both Samaria and Jerusalem.

Grief over Samaria and Jerusalem
² Attention! Let all the people of the world
   listen!
Let the earth and everything in it hear.
The Sovereign LORD is making accusations
   against you;
   the Lord speaks from his holy Temple.
³ Look! The LORD is coming!
   He leaves his throne in heaven
   and tramples the heights of the earth.
⁴ The mountains melt beneath his feet
   and flow into the valleys
like wax in a fire,
   like water pouring down a hill.
⁵ And why is this happening?
   Because of the rebellion of Israel*—
   yes, the sins of the whole nation.

Who is to blame for Israel's rebellion?
   Samaria, its capital city!
Where is the center of idolatry in Judah?
   In Jerusalem, its capital!

⁶ "So I, the LORD, will make the city of
      Samaria
   a heap of ruins.
Her streets will be plowed up
   for planting vineyards.
I will roll the stones of her walls into the
      valley below,
   exposing her foundations.
⁷ All her carved images will be smashed.
   All her sacred treasures will be burned.
These things were bought with the money
   earned by her prostitution,
and they will now be carried away
   to pay prostitutes elsewhere."

⁸ Therefore, I will mourn and lament.
   I will walk around barefoot and
      naked.

1:5 Hebrew *Jacob*; also in 1:5b. The names "Jacob" and "Israel" are often interchanged throughout the Old Testament, referring sometimes to the individual patriarch and sometimes to the nation.

I will howl like a jackal
　and moan like an owl.
9 For my people's wound
　is too deep to heal.
It has reached into Judah,
　even to the gates of Jerusalem.

10 Don't tell our enemies in Gath*;
　don't weep at all.
You people in Beth-leaphrah,*
　roll in the dust to show your despair.
11 You people in Shaphir,*
　go as captives into exile—naked and
　　ashamed.
The people of Zaanan*
　dare not come outside their walls.
The people of Beth-ezel* mourn,
　for their house has no support.
12 The people of Maroth* anxiously wait for
　　relief,
　but only bitterness awaits them
as the LORD's judgment reaches
　even to the gates of Jerusalem.

13 Harness your chariot horses and flee,
　you people of Lachish.*
You were the first city in Judah
　to follow Israel in her rebellion,
　and you led Jerusalem* into sin.
14 Send farewell gifts to Moresheth-gath*;
　there is no hope of saving it.
The town of Aczib*
　has deceived the kings of Israel.
15 O people of Mareshah,*
　I will bring a conqueror to capture
　　your town.
And the leaders* of Israel
　will go to Adullam.

16 Oh, people of Judah, shave your heads
　　in sorrow,
　for the children you love will be
　　snatched away.
Make yourselves as bald as a vulture,
　for your little ones will be exiled to
　　distant lands.

Judgment against Wealthy Oppressors

2 ¹ What sorrow awaits you who lie awake
　　at night,
　thinking up evil plans.

You rise at dawn and hurry to carry them
　　out,
　simply because you have the power to
　　do so.
2 When you want a piece of land,
　you find a way to seize it.
When you want someone's house,
　you take it by fraud and violence.
You cheat a man of his property,
　stealing his family's inheritance.

3 But this is what the LORD says:
"I will reward your evil with evil;
　you won't be able to pull your neck out
　　of the noose.
You will no longer walk around proudly,
　for it will be a terrible time."

4 In that day your enemies will make fun
　　of you
　by singing this song of despair about
　　you:
"We are finished,
　completely ruined!
God has confiscated our land,
　taking it from us.
He has given our fields
　to those who betrayed us.*"

5 Others will set your boundaries then,
　and the LORD's people will have no say
　in how the land is divided.

True and False Prophets
6 "Don't say such things,"
　the people respond.*
"Don't prophesy like that.
　Such disasters will never come our way!"

7 Should you talk that way, O family of
　　Israel?*
　Will the LORD's Spirit have patience
　　with such behavior?
If you would do what is right,
　you would find my words comforting.
8 Yet to this very hour
　my people rise against me like an
　　enemy!
You steal the shirts right off the backs
　of those who trusted you,
making them as ragged as men
　returning from battle.

1:10a *Gath* sounds like the Hebrew term for "tell." 1:10b *Beth-leaphrah* means "house of dust." 1:11a *Shaphir* means
"pleasant." 1:11b *Zaanan* sounds like the Hebrew term for "come out." 1:11c *Beth-ezel* means "adjoining house."
1:12 *Maroth* sounds like the Hebrew term for "bitter." 1:13a *Lachish* sounds like the Hebrew term for "team of horses."
1:13b Hebrew *the daughter of Zion.* 1:14a *Moresheth* sounds like the Hebrew term for "gift" or "dowry." 1:14b *Aczib* means
"deception." 1:15a *Mareshah* sounds like the Hebrew term for "conqueror." 1:15b Hebrew *the glory.* 2:4 Or *to those who
took us captive.* 2:6 Or *the prophets respond;* Hebrew reads *they prophesy.* 2:7 Hebrew *O house of Jacob?* See note on 1:5a.

⁹ You have evicted women from their
      pleasant homes
   and forever stripped their children of
      all that God would give them.
¹⁰ Up! Begone!
   This is no longer your land and home,
   for you have filled it with sin
      and ruined it completely.

¹¹ Suppose a prophet full of lies would say
      to you,
   "I'll preach to you the joys of wine and
      alcohol!"
   That's just the kind of prophet you would
      like!

Hope for Restoration

¹² "Someday, O Israel, I will gather you;
   I will gather the remnant who are left.
   I will bring you together again like sheep
      in a pen,
      like a flock in its pasture.
   Yes, your land will again
      be filled with noisy crowds!
¹³ Your leader will break out
      and lead you out of exile,
   out through the gates of the enemy
      cities,
      back to your own land.
   Your king will lead you;
      the LORD himself will guide you."

Judgment against Israel's Leaders

3 ¹ I said, "Listen, you leaders of Israel!
      You are supposed to know right
         from wrong,
² but you are the very ones
      who hate good and love evil.
   You skin my people alive
      and tear the flesh from their bones.
³ Yes, you eat my people's flesh,
      strip off their skin,
      and break their bones.
   You chop them up
      like meat for the cooking pot.
⁴ Then you beg the LORD for help in times
      of trouble!
   Do you really expect him to answer?
   After all the evil you have done,
      he won't even look at you!"

⁵ This is what the LORD says:
   "You false prophets are leading my
      people astray!
   You promise peace for those who give
      you food,

but you declare war on those who refuse
   to feed you.
⁶ Now the night will close around you,
   cutting off all your visions.
   Darkness will cover you,
      putting an end to your predictions.
   The sun will set for you prophets,
      and your day will come to an end.
⁷ Then you seers will be put to shame,
      and you fortune-tellers will be
         disgraced.
   And you will cover your faces
      because there is no answer from God."

⁸ But as for me, I am filled with power—
   with the Spirit of the LORD.
   I am filled with justice and strength
      to boldly declare Israel's sin and
         rebellion.
⁹ Listen to me, you leaders of Israel!
      You hate justice and twist all that is
         right.
¹⁰ You are building Jerusalem
      on a foundation of murder and
         corruption.
¹¹ You rulers make decisions based on
         bribes;
      you priests teach God's laws only for
         a price;
   you prophets won't prophesy unless you
      are paid.
   Yet all of you claim to depend on the
      LORD.
   "No harm can come to us," you say,
      "for the LORD is here among us."
¹² Because of you, Mount Zion will be
         plowed like an open field;
   Jerusalem will be reduced to ruins!
   A thicket will grow on the heights
      where the Temple now stands.

The LORD's Future Reign

4 ¹ In the last days, the mountain of the
         LORD's house
   will be the highest of all—
   the most important place on earth.
   It will be raised above the other hills,
      and people from all over the world will
         stream there to worship.
² People from many nations will come and
      say,
   "Come, let us go up to the mountain of the
      LORD,
   to the house of Jacob's God.
   There he will teach us his ways,
      and we will walk in his paths."

For the LORD's teaching will go out from
Zion;
his word will go out from Jerusalem.
³ The LORD will mediate between peoples
and will settle disputes between strong
nations far away.
They will hammer their swords into
plowshares
and their spears into pruning hooks.
Nation will no longer fight against nation,
nor train for war anymore.
⁴ Everyone will live in peace and prosperity,
enjoying their own grapevines and fig
trees,
for there will be nothing to fear.
The LORD of Heaven's Armies
has made this promise!
⁵ Though the nations around us follow their
idols,
we will follow the LORD our God forever
and ever.

Israel's Return from Exile

⁶ "In that coming day," says the LORD,
"I will gather together those who are lame,
those who have been exiles,
and those whom I have filled with grief.
⁷ Those who are weak will survive as a
remnant;
those who were exiles will become a
strong nation.
Then I, the LORD, will rule from
Jerusalem*
as their king forever."
⁸ As for you, Jerusalem,
the citadel of God's people,*
your royal might and power
will come back to you again.
The kingship will be restored
to my precious Jerusalem.

⁹ But why are you now screaming in terror?
Have you no king to lead you?
Have your wise people all died?
Pain has gripped you like a woman in
childbirth.
¹⁰ Writhe and groan like a woman in labor,
you people of Jerusalem,*
for now you must leave this city
to live in the open country.
You will soon be sent in exile
to distant Babylon.
But the LORD will rescue you there;

he will redeem you from the grip of
your enemies.
¹¹ Now many nations have gathered against
you.
"Let her be desecrated," they say.
"Let us see the destruction of
Jerusalem.*"
¹² But they do not know the LORD's thoughts
or understand his plan.
These nations don't know
that he is gathering them together
to be beaten and trampled
like sheaves of grain on a threshing
floor.
¹³ "Rise up and crush the nations,
O Jerusalem!"*
says the LORD.
"For I will give you iron horns and bronze
hooves,
so you can trample many nations to
pieces.
You will present their stolen riches to the
LORD,
their wealth to the Lord of all the earth."

5
¹*Mobilize! Marshal your troops!
The enemy is laying siege to
Jerusalem.
They will strike Israel's leader
in the face with a rod.

A Ruler from Bethlehem

²*But you, O Bethlehem Ephrathah,
are only a small village among all the
people of Judah.
Yet a ruler of Israel,
whose origins are in the distant past,
will come from you on my behalf.
³ The people of Israel will be abandoned to
their enemies
until the woman in labor gives birth.
Then at last his fellow countrymen
will return from exile to their own land.
⁴ And he will stand to lead his flock with the
LORD's strength,
in the majesty of the name of the LORD
his God.
Then his people will live there
undisturbed,
for he will be highly honored around
the world.
⁵ And he will be the source of peace.

4:7 Hebrew *Mount Zion.*   4:8 Hebrew *As for you, Migdal-eder, / the Ophel of the daughter of Zion.*   4:10 Hebrew *O daughter of Zion.*
4:11 Hebrew *of Zion.*   4:13 Hebrew "Rise up and thresh, O daughter of Zion."   5:1 Verse 5:1 is numbered 4:14 in Hebrew text.
5:2 Verses 5:2-15 are numbered 5:1-14 in Hebrew text.

When the Assyrians invade our land
  and break through our defenses,
we will appoint seven rulers to watch
      over us,
  eight princes to lead us.
6 They will rule Assyria with drawn swords
    and enter the gates of the land of
      Nimrod.
  He will rescue us from the Assyrians
    when they pour over the borders to
      invade our land.

The Remnant Purified
7 Then the remnant left in Israel*
    will take their place among the nations.
  They will be like dew sent by the LORD
    or like rain falling on the grass,
  which no one can hold back
    and no one can restrain.
8 The remnant left in Israel
    will take their place among the nations.
  They will be like a lion among the animals
      of the forest,
    like a strong young lion among flocks of
      sheep and goats,
  pouncing and tearing as they go
    with no rescuer in sight.
9 The people of Israel will stand up to their
      foes,
    and all their enemies will be wiped out.

10 "In that day," says the LORD,
  "I will slaughter your horses
    and destroy your chariots.
11 I will tear down your walls
    and demolish your defenses.
12 I will put an end to all witchcraft,
    and there will be no more
      fortune-tellers.
13 I will destroy all your idols and sacred
      pillars,
    so you will never again worship the
      work of your own hands.
14 I will abolish your idol shrines with their
      Asherah poles
    and destroy your pagan cities.
15 I will pour out my vengeance
    on all the nations that refuse to
      obey me."

The LORD's Case against Israel
6 Listen to what the LORD is saying:

  "Stand up and state your case against me.

Let the mountains and hills be called to
      witness your complaints.
2 And now, O mountains,
    listen to the LORD's complaint!
  He has a case against his people.
    He will bring charges against Israel.

3 "O my people, what have I done to you?
    What have I done to make you tired
      of me?
    Answer me!
4 For I brought you out of Egypt
    and redeemed you from slavery.
  I sent Moses, Aaron, and Miriam to help
      you.
5 Don't you remember, my people,
    how King Balak of Moab tried to have
      you cursed
    and how Balaam son of Beor blessed you
      instead?
  And remember your journey from Acacia
      Grove* to Gilgal,
    when I, the LORD, did everything I could
      to teach you about my faithfulness."

6 What can we bring to the LORD?
    Should we bring him burnt offerings?
  Should we bow before God Most High
    with offerings of yearling calves?
7 Should we offer him thousands of rams
    and ten thousand rivers of olive oil?
  Should we sacrifice our firstborn children
    to pay for our sins?

8 No, O people, the LORD has told you what
      is good,
    and this is what he requires of you:
  to do what is right, to love mercy,
    and to walk humbly with your God.

Israel's Guilt and Punishment
9 Fear the LORD if you are wise!
    His voice calls to everyone in Jerusalem:
  "The armies of destruction are coming;
    the LORD is sending them.*
10 What shall I say about the homes of the
      wicked
    filled with treasures gained by
      cheating?
  What about the disgusting practice
    of measuring out grain with dishonest
      measures?*
11 How can I tolerate your merchants
    who use dishonest scales and weights?

5:7 Hebrew *in Jacob;* also in 5:8. See note on 1:5a.   **6:5** Hebrew *Shittim.*   **6:9** Hebrew *"Listen to the rod. / Who appointed it?"*
6:10 Hebrew *of using the short ephah?* The ephah was a unit for measuring grain.

¹² The rich among you have become wealthy
    through extortion and violence.
Your citizens are so used to lying
    that their tongues can no longer tell the
    truth.

¹³ "Therefore, I will wound you!
    I will bring you to ruin for all your sins.
¹⁴ You will eat but never have enough.
    Your hunger pangs and emptiness will
    remain.
And though you try to save your money,
    it will come to nothing in the end.
You will save a little,
    but I will give it to those who conquer
    you.
¹⁵ You will plant crops
    but not harvest them.
You will press your olives
    but not get enough oil to anoint
    yourselves.
You will trample the grapes
    but get no juice to make your wine.
¹⁶ You keep only the laws of evil King Omri;
    you follow only the example of wicked
    King Ahab!
Therefore, I will make an example of you,
    bringing you to complete ruin.
You will be treated with contempt,
    mocked by all who see you."

Misery Turned to Hope

7 ¹ How miserable I am!
    I feel like the fruit picker after the
    harvest
    who can find nothing to eat.
Not a cluster of grapes or a single early fig
    can be found to satisfy my hunger.
² The godly people have all disappeared;
    not one honest person is left on the
    earth.
They are all murderers,
    setting traps even for their own
    brothers.
³ Both their hands are equally skilled at
    doing evil!
    Officials and judges alike demand
    bribes.
The people with influence get what they
    want,
    and together they scheme to twist
    justice.
⁴ Even the best of them is like a brier;
    the most honest is as dangerous as a
    hedge of thorns.

But your judgment day is coming swiftly
    now.
Your time of punishment is here, a time
    of confusion.
⁵ Don't trust anyone—
    not your best friend or even your wife!
⁶ For the son despises his father.
    The daughter defies her mother.
The daughter-in-law defies her
    mother-in-law.
Your enemies are right in your own
    household!

⁷ As for me, I look to the LORD for help.
    I wait confidently for God to save me,
    and my God will certainly hear me.
⁸ Do not gloat over me, my enemies!
    For though I fall, I will rise again.
Though I sit in darkness,
    the LORD will be my light.
⁹ I will be patient as the LORD punishes me,
    for I have sinned against him.
But after that, he will take up my case
    and give me justice for all I have
    suffered from my enemies.
The LORD will bring me into the light,
    and I will see his righteousness.
¹⁰ Then my enemies will see that the LORD is
    on my side.
    They will be ashamed that they taunted
    me, saying,
"So where is the LORD—
    that God of yours?"
With my own eyes I will see their downfall;
    they will be trampled like mud in the
    streets.

¹¹ In that day, Israel, your cities will be
    rebuilt,
    and your borders will be extended.
¹² People from many lands will come and
    honor you—
    from Assyria all the way to the towns
    of Egypt,
from Egypt all the way to the Euphrates
    River,*
    and from distant seas and mountains.
¹³ But the land* will become empty and
    desolate
    because of the wickedness of those who
    live there.

The LORD's Compassion on Israel

¹⁴ O LORD, protect your people with your
    shepherd's staff;

7:12 Hebrew *the river.*   7:13 Or *earth.*

lead your flock, your special possession.
Though they live alone in a thicket
    on the heights of Mount Carmel,*
let them graze in the fertile pastures of
        Bashan and Gilead
    as they did long ago.

15 "Yes," says the LORD,
    "I will do mighty miracles for you,
like those I did when I rescued you
    from slavery in Egypt."

16 All the nations of the world will stand
        amazed
    at what the LORD will do for you.
They will be embarrassed
    at their feeble power.
They will cover their mouths in silent awe,
    deaf to everything around them.
17 Like snakes crawling from their holes,
    they will come out to meet the LORD
        our God.

7:14 Or *surrounded by a fruitful land.*

They will fear him greatly,
    trembling in terror at his presence.

18 Where is another God like you,
    who pardons the guilt of the
        remnant,
    overlooking the sins of his special
        people?
You will not stay angry with your people
        forever,
    because you delight in showing
        unfailing love.
19 Once again you will have compassion
        on us.
    You will trample our sins under your
        feet
    and throw them into the depths of the
        ocean!
20 You will show us your faithfulness and
        unfailing love
    as you promised to our ancestors
        Abraham and Jacob long ago.

Nahum

BE WARNED: God will indeed repay those who have inflicted terrible suffering on others. This was the message Nahum spoke against Nineveh, the capital of Assyria. The Assyrians had destroyed Samaria, the capital of the northern kingdom of Israel, in 722 BC and exiled its inhabitants to distant lands throughout the empire. They were ruthlessly violent to their enemies and showed them no mercy. They were guilty of arrogance, cruelty, idolatry, murder, deceit, treachery, superstition, and oppression. The book of Nahum rails against the people of Nineveh for this wickedness and pronounces God's judgment upon them.

■ **Author:** Nahum

■ **Date Written:** During Nahum's prophetic ministry, between 663 and 654 BC

■ **Purpose:** To pronounce God's judgment upon Assyria

■ **Themes:** Judgment, vengeance, justice

■ **Outline**
1:1-15 God and his punishment for evil
2:1-13 The destruction of Nineveh
3:1-19 The sin of Nineveh

---

1 This message concerning Nineveh came as a vision to Nahum, who lived in Elkosh.

The LORD's Anger against Nineveh

² The LORD is a jealous God,
   filled with vengeance and rage.
He takes revenge on all who oppose him
   and continues to rage against his
     enemies!
³ The LORD is slow to get angry, but his
     power is great,
   and he never lets the guilty go
     unpunished.
He displays his power in the whirlwind
   and the storm.
   The billowing clouds are the dust
     beneath his feet.
⁴ At his command the oceans dry up,
   and the rivers disappear.
   The lush pastures of Bashan and Carmel
     fade,
   and the green forests of Lebanon
     wither.
⁵ In his presence the mountains quake,
   and the hills melt away;
the earth trembles,
   and its people are destroyed.
⁶ Who can stand before his fierce anger?
   Who can survive his burning fury?

His rage blazes forth like fire,
   and the mountains crumble to dust in
     his presence.

⁷ The LORD is good,
   a strong refuge when trouble comes.
He is close to those who trust in him.
⁸ But he will sweep away his enemies*
   in an overwhelming flood.
He will pursue his foes
   into the darkness of night.

⁹ Why are you scheming against the LORD?
   He will destroy you with one blow;
   he won't need to strike twice!
¹⁰ His enemies, tangled like thornbushes
   and staggering like drunks,
   will be burned up like dry stubble in
     a field.
¹¹ Who is this wicked counselor of yours
   who plots evil against the LORD?

¹² This is what the LORD says:
"Though the Assyrians have many allies,
   they will be destroyed and disappear.
O my people, I have punished you before,
   but I will not punish you again.
¹³ Now I will break the yoke of bondage from
   your neck

1:8 As in Greek version; Hebrew reads *sweep away her place.*

and tear off the chains of Assyrian
oppression."

14 And this is what the LORD says concerning
the Assyrians in Nineveh:
"You will have no more children to carry
on your name.
I will destroy all the idols in the temples
of your gods.
I am preparing a grave for you
because you are despicable!"

15*Look! A messenger is coming over the
mountains with good news!
He is bringing a message of peace.
Celebrate your festivals, O people of
Judah,
and fulfill all your vows,
for your wicked enemies will never invade
your land again.
They will be completely destroyed!

The Fall of Nineveh

2 1*Your enemy is coming to crush you,
Nineveh.
Man the ramparts! Watch the roads!
Prepare your defenses! Call out your
forces!

2 Even though the destroyer has destroyed
Judah,
the LORD will restore its honor.
Israel's vine has been stripped of
branches,
but he will restore its splendor.

3 Shields flash red in the sunlight!
See the scarlet uniforms of the valiant
troops!
Watch as their glittering chariots move
into position,
with a forest of spears waving above
them.*
4 The chariots race recklessly along the
streets
and rush wildly through the squares.
They flash like firelight
and move as swiftly as lightning.
5 The king shouts to his officers;
they stumble in their haste,
rushing to the walls to set up their
defenses.
6 The river gates have been torn open!
The palace is about to collapse!

7 Nineveh's exile has been decreed,
and all the servant girls mourn its
capture.
They moan like doves
and beat their breasts in sorrow.
8 Nineveh is like a leaking water reservoir!
The people are slipping away.
"Stop, stop!" someone shouts,
but no one even looks back.
9 Loot the silver!
Plunder the gold!
There's no end to Nineveh's treasures—
its vast, uncounted wealth.
10 Soon the city is plundered, empty, and
ruined.
Hearts melt and knees shake.
The people stand aghast,
their faces pale and trembling.

11 Where now is that great Nineveh,
that den filled with young lions?
It was a place where people—like lions
and their cubs—
walked freely and without fear.
12 The lion tore up meat for his cubs
and strangled prey for his mate.
He filled his den with prey,
his caverns with his plunder.

13 "I am your enemy!"
says the LORD of Heaven's Armies.
"Your chariots will soon go up in smoke.
Your young men* will be killed in battle.
Never again will you plunder conquered
nations.
The voices of your proud messengers
will be heard no more."

The LORD's Judgment against Nineveh

3 1 What sorrow awaits Nineveh,
the city of murder and lies!
She is crammed with wealth
and is never without victims.
2 Hear the crack of whips,
the rumble of wheels!
Horses' hooves pound,
and chariots clatter wildly.
3 See the flashing swords and glittering
spears
as the charioteers charge past!
There are countless casualties,
heaps of bodies—
so many bodies that
people stumble over them.

1:15 Verse 1:15 is numbered 2:1 in Hebrew text.   2:1 Verses 2:1-13 are numbered 2:2-14 in Hebrew text.   2:3 Greek and Syriac
versions read *into position, / the horses whipped into a frenzy.*   2:13 Hebrew *young lions.*

4 All this because Nineveh,
    the beautiful and faithless city,
mistress of deadly charms,
    enticed the nations with her beauty.
She taught them all her magic,
    enchanting people everywhere.

5 "I am your enemy!"
    says the LORD of Heaven's Armies.
"And now I will lift your skirts
    and show all the earth your nakedness
        and shame.
6 I will cover you with filth
    and show the world how vile you
        really are.
7 All who see you will shrink back and say,
    'Nineveh lies in ruins.
Where are the mourners?'
    Does anyone regret your destruction?"

8 Are you any better than the city of
        Thebes,*
    situated on the Nile River, surrounded
        by water?
She was protected by the river on all
        sides,
    walled in by water.
9 Ethiopia* and the land of Egypt
    gave unlimited assistance.
The nations of Put and Libya
    were among her allies.
10 Yet Thebes fell,
    and her people were led away as
        captives.
Her babies were dashed to death
    against the stones of the streets.
Soldiers threw dice* to get Egyptian
    officers as servants.
All their leaders were bound in chains.

11 And you, Nineveh, will also stagger like
        a drunkard.
    You will hide for fear of the attacking
        enemy.
12 All your fortresses will fall.
    They will be devoured like the ripe figs
that fall into the mouths
    of those who shake the trees.
13 Your troops will be as weak
    and helpless as women.
The gates of your land will be opened wide
        to the enemy
    and set on fire and burned.
14 Get ready for the siege!
    Store up water!
    Strengthen the defenses!
Go into the pits to trample clay,
    and pack it into molds,
        making bricks to repair the walls.

15 But the fire will devour you;
    the sword will cut you down.
The enemy will consume you like locusts,
    devouring everything they see.
There will be no escape,
    even if you multiply like swarming
        locusts.
16 Your merchants have multiplied
    until they outnumber the stars.
But like a swarm of locusts,
    they strip the land and fly away.
17 Your guards* and officials are also like
        swarming locusts
    that crowd together in the hedges on a
        cold day.
But like locusts that fly away when the sun
        comes up,
    all of them will fly away and disappear.

18 Your shepherds are asleep, O Assyrian
        king;
    your princes lie dead in the dust.
Your people are scattered across the
        mountains
    with no one to gather them together.
19 There is no healing for your wound;
    your injury is fatal.
All who hear of your destruction
    will clap their hands for joy.
Where can anyone be found
    who has not suffered from your
        continual cruelty?

3:8 Hebrew *No-amon;* also in 3:10. 3:9 Hebrew *Cush.* 3:10 Hebrew *They cast lots.* 3:17 Or *princes.*

Habakkuk

"IF GOD EXISTS, why do the wicked so often prosper?" This question is commonly asked by those who are sensitive to social justice. The prophet Habakkuk was quite sympathetic to such concerns. Habakkuk preached during the last days of Judah, before its fall to Babylon in 586 BC. He foresaw the impending doom and was troubled by two things: why God allowed the people of Judah to sin and how God could use a sinful nation like Babylon to punish Judah. Desperate for answers, Habakkuk boldly and confidently took his complaints directly to God. God answers Habakkuk's questions in this book, asserting that he will judge all people but that righteousness will ultimately prevail. It may not happen immediately, but it will happen. This assurance, along with his glimpse of God's sovereign rule, gave Habakkuk the courage and hope to trust in God's plans regarding the dark days ahead.

- **Author:** Habakkuk
- **Date Written:** Between 612 and 589 BC
- **Purpose:** To show that God is still sovereign despite the apparent triumph of evil
- **Themes:** Questioning God, God's sovereignty, hope
- **Outline**
  1:1-11 Sin and punishment
  1:12–2:20 Babylon, and God's answer
  3:1-19 Habakkuk's triumphant faith

---

1 This is the message that the prophet Habakkuk received in a vision.

Habakkuk's Complaint

2 How long, O LORD, must I call for help?
   But you do not listen!
"Violence is everywhere!" I cry,
   but you do not come to save.
3 Must I forever see these evil deeds?
   Why must I watch all this misery?
Wherever I look,
   I see destruction and violence.
I am surrounded by people
   who love to argue and fight.
4 The law has become paralyzed,
   and there is no justice in the courts.
The wicked far outnumber the
   righteous,
   so that justice has become perverted.

The LORD's Reply

5 The LORD replied,

"Look around at the nations;
   look and be amazed!*

For I am doing something in your own
   day,
   something you wouldn't believe
   even if someone told you about it.
6 I am raising up the Babylonians,*
   a cruel and violent people.
They will march across the world
   and conquer other lands.
7 They are notorious for their cruelty
   and do whatever they like.
8 Their horses are swifter than cheetahs*
   and fiercer than wolves at dusk.
Their charioteers charge from far away.
   Like eagles, they swoop down to devour
   their prey.

9 "On they come, all bent on violence.
   Their hordes advance like a desert
   wind,
   sweeping captives ahead of them like
   sand.
10 They scoff at kings and princes
   and scorn all their fortresses.
They simply pile ramps of earth
   against their walls and capture them!

1:5 Greek version reads *Look, you mockers; / look and be amazed and die.* Compare Acts 13:41.   **1:6** Or *Chaldeans.*   **1:8** Or *leopards.*

¹¹ They sweep past like the wind
    and are gone.
But they are deeply guilty,
    for their own strength is their god."

Habakkuk's Second Complaint

¹² O LORD my God, my Holy One, you who
    are eternal—
    surely you do not plan to wipe us out?
O LORD, our Rock, you have sent these
    Babylonians to correct us,
    to punish us for our many sins.
¹³ But you are pure and cannot stand the
    sight of evil.
    Will you wink at their treachery?
Should you be silent while the wicked
    swallow up people more righteous than
    they?

¹⁴ Are we only fish to be caught and killed?
    Are we only sea creatures that have no
    leader?
¹⁵ Must we be strung up on their hooks
    and caught in their nets while they
    rejoice and celebrate?
¹⁶ Then they will worship their nets
    and burn incense in front of them.
"These nets are the gods who have made
    us rich!"
    they will claim.
¹⁷ Will you let them get away with this
    forever?
    Will they succeed forever in their
    heartless conquests?

2
¹ I will climb up to my watchtower
    and stand at my guardpost.
There I will wait to see what the LORD says
    and how he* will answer my complaint.

The LORD's Second Reply

²Then the LORD said to me,

"Write my answer plainly on tablets,
    so that a runner can carry the correct
    message to others.
³ This vision is for a future time.
    It describes the end, and it will be
    fulfilled.
If it seems slow in coming, wait
    patiently,
    for it will surely take place.
It will not be delayed.

⁴ "Look at the proud!
    They trust in themselves, and their lives
    are crooked.
But the righteous will live by their
    faithfulness to God.*
⁵ Wealth* is treacherous,
    and the arrogant are never at rest.
They open their mouths as wide as the
    grave,*
    and like death, they are never satisfied.
In their greed they have gathered up many
    nations
    and swallowed many peoples.

⁶ "But soon their captives will taunt them.
    They will mock them, saying,
'What sorrow awaits you thieves!
    Now you will get what you deserve!
You've become rich by extortion,
    but how much longer can this go on?'
⁷ Suddenly, your debtors will take action.
    They will turn on you and take all you
    have,
    while you stand trembling and
    helpless.
⁸ Because you have plundered many
    nations,
    now all the survivors will plunder you.
You committed murder throughout the
    countryside
    and filled the towns with violence.

⁹ "What sorrow awaits you who build big
    houses
    with money gained dishonestly!
You believe your wealth will buy security,
    putting your family's nest beyond the
    reach of danger.
¹⁰ But by the murders you committed,
    you have shamed your name and
    forfeited your lives.
¹¹ The very stones in the walls cry out against
    you,
    and the beams in the ceilings echo the
    complaint.

¹² "What sorrow awaits you who build cities
    with money gained through murder
    and corruption!
¹³ Has not the LORD of Heaven's Armies
    promised
    that the wealth of nations will turn to
    ashes?

2:1 As in Syriac version; Hebrew reads *I.*   2:3b-4 Greek version reads *If the vision is delayed, wait patiently, / for it will surely come
and not delay. / ⁴I will take no pleasure in anyone who turns away. / But the righteous person will live by my faith.* Compare Rom 1:17; Gal
3:11; Heb 10:37-38.   2:5a As in Dead Sea Scroll 1QpHab; other Hebrew manuscripts read *Wine.*   2:5b Hebrew *as Sheol.*

They work so hard,
    but all in vain!
¹⁴ For as the waters fill the sea,
    the earth will be filled with an
        awareness
    of the glory of the LORD.

¹⁵ "What sorrow awaits you who make your
        neighbors drunk!
    You force your cup on them
    so you can gloat over their shameful
        nakedness.
¹⁶ But soon it will be your turn to be
        disgraced.
    Come, drink and be exposed!*
Drink from the cup of the LORD's
        judgment,
    and all your glory will be turned to
        shame.
¹⁷ You cut down the forests of Lebanon.
    Now you will be cut down.
You destroyed the wild animals,
    so now their terror will be yours.
You committed murder throughout the
        countryside
    and filled the towns with violence.

¹⁸ "What good is an idol carved by man,
    or a cast image that deceives you?
How foolish to trust in your own
        creation—
    a god that can't even talk!
¹⁹ What sorrow awaits you who say to
        wooden idols,
    'Wake up and save us!'
To speechless stone images you say,
    'Rise up and teach us!'
    Can an idol tell you what to do?
They may be overlaid with gold and silver,
    but they are lifeless inside.
²⁰ But the LORD is in his holy Temple.
    Let all the earth be silent before him."

Habakkuk's Prayer

3 This prayer was sung by the prophet
Habakkuk*:

² I have heard all about you, LORD.
    I am filled with awe by your amazing
        works.
In this time of our deep need,
    help us again as you did in years
        gone by.

And in your anger,
    remember your mercy.

³ I see God moving across the deserts from
        Edom,*
    the Holy One coming from Mount
        Paran.*
His brilliant splendor fills the heavens,
    and the earth is filled with his praise.
⁴ His coming is as brilliant as the sunrise.
    Rays of light flash from his hands,
    where his awesome power is hidden.
⁵ Pestilence marches before him;
    plague follows close behind.
⁶ When he stops, the earth shakes.
    When he looks, the nations tremble.
He shatters the everlasting mountains
    and levels the eternal hills.
    He is the Eternal One!*
⁷ I see the people of Cushan in distress,
    and the nation of Midian trembling in
        terror.

⁸ Was it in anger, LORD, that you struck the
        rivers
    and parted the sea?
Were you displeased with them?
    No, you were sending your chariots of
        salvation!
⁹ You brandished your bow
    and your quiver of arrows.
    You split open the earth with flowing
        rivers.
¹⁰ The mountains watched and trembled.
    Onward swept the raging waters.
The mighty deep cried out,
    lifting its hands in submission.
¹¹ The sun and moon stood still in the sky
    as your brilliant arrows flew
    and your glittering spear flashed.

¹² You marched across the land in anger
    and trampled the nations in your fury.
¹³ You went out to rescue your chosen
        people,
    to save your anointed ones.
You crushed the heads of the wicked
    and stripped their bones from head
        to toe.
¹⁴ With his own weapons,
    you destroyed the chief of those
who rushed out like a whirlwind,
    thinking Israel would be easy prey.

2:16 Dead Sea Scrolls and Greek and Syriac versions read *and stagger!*   3:1 Hebrew adds *according to shigionoth,* probably
indicating the musical setting for the prayer.   3:3a Hebrew *Teman.*   3:3b Hebrew adds *selah;* also in 3:9, 13. The meaning
of this Hebrew term is uncertain; it is probably a musical or literary term.   3:6 Or *The ancient paths belong to him.*

15 You trampled the sea with your horses,
  and the mighty waters piled high.

16 I trembled inside when I heard this;
  my lips quivered with fear.
  My legs gave way beneath me,*
  and I shook in terror.
  I will wait quietly for the coming day
  when disaster will strike the people who
  invade us.

17 Even though the fig trees have no
  blossoms,
  and there are no grapes on the vines;

even though the olive crop fails,
  and the fields lie empty and barren;
even though the flocks die in the fields,
  and the cattle barns are empty,

18 yet I will rejoice in the LORD!
  I will be joyful in the God of my
  salvation!

19 The Sovereign LORD is my strength!
  He makes me as surefooted as a deer,*
  able to tread upon the heights.

(For the choir director: This prayer is to be accompanied by stringed instruments.)

3:16 Hebrew *Decay entered my bones.*   3:19 Or *He gives me the speed of a deer.*

Zephaniah

THOUGH DARK DAYS loomed ahead, there was hope for the future. This was Zephaniah's basic message to the people of Judah. Zephaniah was a prophet in the last decades before Jerusalem was destroyed by the Babylonians. The opening stanzas of his prophecies bring bad news. The people of Judah had completely abandoned the Lord and had chosen to worship false gods. In addition, they dismissed obedience to God as irrelevant. They were materially prosperous and saw no need to repent of their sins in order to please God. Consequently, Zephaniah's message to them was harsh: When the "day of the Lord" would come, Judah would be completely destroyed. Even the animals would be killed as the Babylonian troops pillaged the land. This dreadful day would also visit several nations surrounding Judah. But God would not leave them without hope. Judah would eventually be restored and return to the Lord.

■ **Author:** Zephaniah

■ **Date Written:** Probably near the end of Zephaniah's ministry (between 640 and 621 BC), when King Josiah's great reforms began

■ **Purpose:** To shake the people of Judah out of their complacency and urge them to return to God

■ **Themes:** Day of the Lord, religious complacency, restoration

■ **Outline**
1:1–2:3 The coming judgment of God
2:4–3:8 Judgment upon the nations and Jerusalem
3:9-20 Blessing promised to Judah

---

1 The LORD gave this message to Zephaniah when Josiah son of Amon was king of Judah. Zephaniah was the son of Cushi, son of Gedaliah, son of Amariah, son of Hezekiah.

Coming Judgment against Judah
2 "I will sweep away everything
   from the face of the earth," says the
   LORD.
3 "I will sweep away people and animals
   alike.
   I will sweep away the birds of the sky
   and the fish in the sea.
   I will reduce the wicked to heaps of
   rubble,*
   and I will wipe humanity from the face
   of the earth," says the LORD.
4 "I will crush Judah and Jerusalem with
   my fist
   and destroy every last trace of their Baal
   worship.

   I will put an end to all the idolatrous
   priests,
   so that even the memory of them will
   disappear.
5 For they go up to their roofs
   and bow down to the sun, moon, and
   stars.
   They claim to follow the LORD,
   but then they worship Molech,*
   too.
6 And I will destroy those who used to
   worship me
   but now no longer do.
   They no longer ask for the LORD's
   guidance
   or seek my blessings."

7 Stand in silence in the presence of the
   Sovereign LORD,
   for the awesome day of the LORD's
   judgment is near.

1:3 The meaning of the Hebrew is uncertain.   1:5 Hebrew *Malcam,* a variant spelling of Molech; or it could possibly mean *their king.*

The LORD has prepared his people for a
  great slaughter
and has chosen their executioners.*

8 "On that day of judgment,"
    says the LORD,
  "I will punish the leaders and princes of
    Judah
  and all those following pagan customs.

9 Yes, I will punish those who participate in
    pagan worship ceremonies,
  and those who fill their masters' houses
    with violence and deceit.

10 "On that day," says the LORD,
    "a cry of alarm will come from the Fish
      Gate
  and echo throughout the New Quarter of
    the city.*
  And a great crash will sound from the
    hills.

11 Wail in sorrow, all you who live in the
    market area,*
  for all the merchants and traders will
    be destroyed.

12 "I will search with lanterns in Jerusalem's
    darkest corners
  to punish those who sit complacent
    in their sins.
  They think the LORD will do nothing
    to them,
  either good or bad.

13 So their property will be plundered,
    their homes will be ransacked.
  They will build new homes
    but never live in them.
  They will plant vineyards
    but never drink wine from them.

14 "That terrible day of the LORD is near.
    Swiftly it comes—
  a day of bitter tears,
    a day when even strong men will
      cry out.

15 It will be a day when the LORD's anger
    is poured out—
  a day of terrible distress and anguish,
  a day of ruin and desolation,
  a day of darkness and gloom,
  a day of clouds and blackness,

16   a day of trumpet calls and battle cries.
  Down go the walled cities
    and the strongest battlements!

17 "Because you have sinned against the LORD,
  I will make you grope around like the
    blind.
  Your blood will be poured into the dust,
    and your bodies will lie rotting on the
      ground."

18 Your silver and gold will not save you
    on that day of the LORD's anger.
  For the whole land will be devoured
    by the fire of his jealousy.
  He will make a terrifying end
    of all the people on earth.*

A Call to Repentance

2 1 Gather together—yes, gather together,
    you shameless nation.

2 Gather before judgment begins,
    before your time to repent is blown
      away like chaff.
  Act now, before the fierce fury of the LORD
    falls
  and the terrible day of the LORD's anger
    begins.

3 Seek the LORD, all who are humble,
    and follow his commands.
  Seek to do what is right
    and to live humbly.
  Perhaps even yet the LORD will protect
    you—
  protect you from his anger on that day
    of destruction.

Judgment against Philistia

4 Gaza and Ashkelon will be abandoned,
    Ashdod and Ekron torn down.

5 And what sorrow awaits you Philistines*
    who live along the coast and in the land
      of Canaan,
  for this judgment is against you, too!
  The LORD will destroy you
    until not one of you is left.

6 The Philistine coast will become a
    wilderness pasture,
  a place of shepherd camps
    and enclosures for sheep and goats.

7 The remnant of the tribe of Judah will
    pasture there.
  They will rest at night in the abandoned
    houses in Ashkelon.
  For the LORD their God will visit his
    people in kindness
  and restore their prosperity again.

1:7 Hebrew *has prepared a sacrifice and sanctified his guests.*   1:10 Or *the Second Quarter,* a newer section of Jerusalem. Hebrew reads *the Mishneh.*   1:11 Or *in the valley,* a lower section of Jerusalem. Hebrew reads *the Maktesh.*   1:18 Or *the people living in the land.*   2:5 Hebrew *Kerethites.*

Judgment against Moab and Ammon

8 "I have heard the taunts of the Moabites
    and the insults of the Ammonites,
mocking my people
    and invading their borders.
9 Now, as surely as I live,"
    says the LORD of Heaven's Armies, the
        God of Israel,
"Moab and Ammon will be destroyed—
    destroyed as completely as Sodom and
        Gomorrah.
Their land will become a place of stinging
    nettles,
    salt pits, and eternal desolation.
The remnant of my people will plunder
    them
    and take their land."

10 They will receive the wages of their pride,
    for they have scoffed at the people of the
        LORD of Heaven's Armies.
11 The LORD will terrify them
    as he destroys all the gods in the land.
Then nations around the world will
        worship the LORD,
    each in their own land.

Judgment against Ethiopia and Assyria

12 "You Ethiopians* will also be slaughtered
    by my sword," says the LORD.

13 And the LORD will strike the lands of the
        north with his fist,
    destroying the land of Assyria.
He will make its great capital, Nineveh,
    a desolate wasteland,
    parched like a desert.
14 The proud city will become a pasture for
        flocks and herds,
    and all sorts of wild animals will settle
        there.
The desert owl and screech owl will roost
        on its ruined columns,
    their calls echoing through the gaping
        windows.
Rubble will block all the doorways,
    and the cedar paneling will be exposed
        to the weather.
15 This is the boisterous city,
    once so secure.
"I am the greatest!" it boasted.
    "No other city can compare with me!"
But now, look how it has become an utter
    ruin,
    a haven for wild animals.

2:12 Hebrew *Cushites*.

Everyone passing by will laugh in derision
    and shake a defiant fist.

Jerusalem's Rebellion and Redemption

3 1 What sorrow awaits rebellious, polluted
        Jerusalem,
    the city of violence and crime!
2 No one can tell it anything;
    it refuses all correction.
It does not trust in the LORD
    or draw near to its God.
3 Its leaders are like roaring lions
    hunting for their victims.
Its judges are like ravenous wolves at
        evening time,
    who by dawn have left no trace of their
        prey.
4 Its prophets are arrogant liars seeking
        their own gain.
    Its priests defile the Temple by
        disobeying God's instructions.
5 But the LORD is still there in the city,
    and he does no wrong.
Day by day he hands down justice,
    and he does not fail.
But the wicked know no shame.

6 "I have wiped out many nations,
    devastating their fortress walls and
        towers.
Their streets are now deserted;
    their cities lie in silent ruin.
There are no survivors—
    none at all.
7 I thought, 'Surely they will have reverence
        for me now!
    Surely they will listen to my warnings.
Then I won't need to strike again,
    destroying their homes.'
But no, they get up early
    to continue their evil deeds.
8 Therefore, be patient," says the LORD.
    "Soon I will stand and accuse these evil
        nations.
For I have decided to gather the kingdoms
        of the earth
    and pour out my fiercest anger and fury
        on them.
All the earth will be devoured
    by the fire of my jealousy.

9 "Then I will purify the speech of all
        people,
    so that everyone can worship the LORD
        together.

10 My scattered people who live beyond the
  rivers of Ethiopia*
 will come to present their offerings.
11 On that day you will no longer need to
  be ashamed,
 for you will no longer be rebels
  against me.
 I will remove all proud and arrogant
  people from among you.
 There will be no more haughtiness on
  my holy mountain.
12 Those who are left will be the lowly and
  humble,
 for it is they who trust in the name of
  the LORD.
13 The remnant of Israel will do no wrong;
 they will never tell lies or deceive one
  another.
 They will eat and sleep in safety,
 and no one will make them afraid."

14 Sing, O daughter of Zion;
 shout aloud, O Israel!
 Be glad and rejoice with all your heart,
 O daughter of Jerusalem!
15 For the LORD will remove his hand of
  judgment
 and will disperse the armies of your
  enemy.
 And the LORD himself, the King of Israel,
 will live among you!
 At last your troubles will be over,
 and you will never again fear disaster.

16 On that day the announcement to
  Jerusalem will be,
 "Cheer up, Zion! Don't be afraid!
17 For the LORD your God is living among
  you.
 He is a mighty savior.
 He will take delight in you with
  gladness.
 With his love, he will calm all your
  fears.*
 He will rejoice over you with joyful
  songs."

18 "I will gather you who mourn for the
  appointed festivals;
 you will be disgraced no more.*
19 And I will deal severely with all who have
  oppressed you.
 I will save the weak and helpless ones;
 I will bring together
  those who were chased away.
 I will give glory and fame to my former
  exiles,
 wherever they have been mocked and
  shamed.
20 On that day I will gather you together
  and bring you home again.
 I will give you a good name, a name of
  distinction,
  among all the nations of the earth,
 as I restore your fortunes before their
  very eyes.
 I, the LORD, have spoken!"

3:10 Hebrew *Cush.*   3:17 Or *He will be silent in his love.* Greek and Syriac versions read *He will renew you with his love.*   3:18 The
meaning of the Hebrew for this verse is uncertain.

Haggai

DO YOU HAVE TROUBLE finishing the projects you start? This was a definite problem for the people of Haggai's day. Haggai lived in Jerusalem shortly after many Jews had returned from exile in Babylonia. Those who returned had begun to rebuild the Temple, but opposition from local enemies soon mounted. Eventually the Jews abandoned the project when it was only half finished. After several years, Haggai, along with

- **Author:** Haggai
- **Date Written:** 520 BC
- **Purpose:** To call the people to finish rebuilding the Temple
- **Themes:** Right priorities, finishing the Temple
- **Outline**
  1:1-11 The prophet's rebuke for neglecting the Temple
  1:12-15 God's favor
  2:1-9 Encouragement for the builders
  2:10-19 Blessings to follow the work
  2:20-23 God's judgment on the nations

a prophet/priest named Zechariah, began a campaign to continue work on the Temple. In this book, Haggai admonishes the governor, Zerubbabel, and the high priest, Jeshua, to finish building a house for the Lord. The combined efforts of Haggai and Zechariah worked, and the Temple was completed and rededicated in 516 BC.

A Call to Rebuild the Temple

1 On August 29* of the second year of King Darius's reign, the LORD gave a message through the prophet Haggai to Zerubbabel son of Shealtiel, governor of Judah, and to Jeshua* son of Jehozadak, the high priest.

2 "This is what the LORD of Heaven's Armies says: The people are saying, 'The time has not yet come to rebuild the house of the LORD.'"

3 Then the LORD sent this message through the prophet Haggai: 4 "Why are you living in luxurious houses while my house lies in ruins? 5 This is what the LORD of Heaven's Armies says: Look at what's happening to you! 6 You have planted much but harvest little. You eat but are not satisfied. You drink but are still thirsty. You put on clothes but cannot keep warm. Your wages disappear as though you were putting them in pockets filled with holes!

7 "This is what the LORD of Heaven's Armies says: Look at what's happening to you! 8 Now go up into the hills, bring down timber, and

rebuild my house. Then I will take pleasure in it and be honored, says the LORD. 9 You hoped for rich harvests, but they were poor. And when you brought your harvest home, I blew it away. Why? Because my house lies in ruins, says the LORD of Heaven's Armies, while all of you are busy building your own fine houses. 10 It's because of you that the heavens withhold the dew and the earth produces no crops. 11 I have called for a drought on your fields and hills—a drought to wither the grain and grapes and olive trees and all your other crops, a drought to starve you and your livestock and to ruin everything you have worked so hard to get."

Obedience to God's Call

12 Then Zerubbabel son of Shealtiel, and Jeshua son of Jehozadak, the high priest, and the whole remnant of God's people began to obey the message from the LORD their God. When they heard the words of the prophet Haggai, whom the LORD their God had sent, the people

---

1:1a Hebrew *On the first day of the sixth month*, of the ancient Hebrew lunar calendar. A number of dates in Haggai can be cross-checked with dates in surviving Persian records and related accurately to our modern calendar. This event occurred on August 29, 520 B.C.   1:1b Hebrew *Joshua*, a variant spelling of Jeshua; also in 1:12, 14.

feared the LORD. ¹³Then Haggai, the LORD's messenger, gave the people this message from the LORD: "I am with you, says the LORD!"

¹⁴So the LORD sparked the enthusiasm of Zerubbabel son of Shealtiel, governor of Judah, and the enthusiasm of Jeshua son of Jehozadak, the high priest, and the enthusiasm of the whole remnant of God's people. They began to work on the house of their God, the LORD of Heaven's Armies, ¹⁵on September 21* of the second year of King Darius's reign.

The New Temple's Diminished Splendor

2 Then on October 17 of that same year,* the LORD sent another message through the prophet Haggai. ²"Say this to Zerubbabel son of Shealtiel, governor of Judah, and to Jeshua* son of Jehozadak, the high priest, and to the remnant of God's people there in the land: ³'Does anyone remember this house—this Temple—in its former splendor? How, in comparison, does it look to you now? It must seem like nothing at all! ⁴But now the LORD says: Be strong, Zerubbabel. Be strong, Jeshua son of Jehozadak, the high priest. Be strong, all you people still left in the land. And now get to work, for I am with you, says the LORD of Heaven's Armies. ⁵My Spirit remains among you, just as I promised when you came out of Egypt. So do not be afraid.'

⁶"For this is what the LORD of Heaven's Armies says: In just a little while I will again shake the heavens and the earth, the oceans and the dry land. ⁷I will shake all the nations, and the treasures of all the nations will be brought to this Temple. I will fill this place with glory, says the LORD of Heaven's Armies. ⁸The silver is mine, and the gold is mine, says the LORD of Heaven's Armies. ⁹The future glory of this Temple will be greater than its past glory, says the LORD of Heaven's Armies. And in this place I will bring peace. I, the LORD of Heaven's Armies, have spoken!"

Blessings Promised for Obedience

¹⁰On December 18* of the second year of King Darius's reign, the LORD sent this message to the prophet Haggai: ¹¹"This is what the LORD of Heaven's Armies says. Ask the priests this question about the law: ¹²'If one of you is carrying some meat from a holy sacrifice in his robes and his robe happens to brush against some bread or stew, wine or olive oil, or any other kind of food, will it also become holy?'"

The priests replied, "No."

¹³Then Haggai asked, "If someone becomes ceremonially unclean by touching a dead person and then touches any of these foods, will the food be defiled?"

And the priests answered, "Yes."

¹⁴Then Haggai responded, "That is how it is with this people and this nation, says the LORD. Everything they do and everything they offer is defiled by their sin. ¹⁵Look at what was happening to you before you began to lay the foundation of the LORD's Temple. ¹⁶When you hoped for a twenty-bushel crop, you harvested only ten. When you expected to draw fifty gallons from the winepress, you found only twenty. ¹⁷I sent blight and mildew and hail to destroy everything you worked so hard to produce. Even so, you refused to return to me, says the LORD.

¹⁸"Think about this eighteenth day of December, the day* when the foundation of the LORD's Temple was laid. Think carefully. ¹⁹I am giving you a promise now while the seed is still in the barn.* You have not yet harvested your grain, and your grapevines, fig trees, pomegranates, and olive trees have not yet produced their crops. But from this day onward I will bless you."

Promises for Zerubbabel

²⁰On that same day, December 18,* the LORD sent this second message to Haggai: ²¹"Tell Zerubbabel, the governor of Judah, that I am about to shake the heavens and the earth. ²²I will overthrow royal thrones and destroy the power of foreign kingdoms. I will overturn their chariots and riders. The horses will fall, and their riders will kill each other.

²³"But when this happens, says the LORD of Heaven's Armies, I will honor you, Zerubbabel son of Shealtiel, my servant. I will make you like a signet ring on my finger, says the LORD, for I have chosen you. I, the LORD of Heaven's Armies, have spoken!"

1:15 Hebrew *on the twenty-fourth day of the sixth month,* of the ancient Hebrew lunar calendar. This event occurred on September 21, 520 B.C.; also see note on 1:1a.   2:1 Hebrew *on the twenty-first day of the seventh month,* of the ancient Hebrew lunar calendar. This event (in the second year of Darius's reign) occurred on October 17, 520 B.C.; also see note on 1:1a. 2:2 Hebrew *Joshua,* a variant spelling of Jeshua; also in 2:4.   2:10 Hebrew *On the twenty-fourth day of the ninth month,* of the ancient Hebrew lunar calendar (similarly in 2:18). This event occurred on December 18, 520 B.C.; also see note on 1:1a. 2:18 Or *On this eighteenth day of December, think about the day.*   2:19 Hebrew *Is the seed yet in the barn?*   2:20 Hebrew *On the twenty-fourth day of the [ninth] month;* see note on 2:10.

Zechariah

FROM TIME TO TIME God gives us glimpses of the future. Usually these glimpses come through the words of prophets like Zechariah. His book includes some of the most graphic images of the future found in the Bible. Zechariah was both a priest and a prophet to the Jews living in Palestine after their exile in Babylonia. He was a contemporary of the prophet Haggai and assisted him in campaigning to finish rebuilding the Temple. In his book, Zechariah explains that Israel was exiled for its sinful practices, but he promises that God himself will eventually transform his people and usher in a new age of holiness throughout the earth. The first half of Zechariah's book describes eight night visions and discusses the ritual of fasting. Several of the visions focus on the reconstruction of the Temple and the re-institution of the priesthood. The second half of Zechariah's book describes the age to come when God will transform Israel into a truly holy society and when the nations will come to worship God in Jerusalem. Zechariah saw the Temple's reconstruction as the dawn of this new era. Zechariah also told of a great "shepherd," or Messiah, who would come to reign over a new kingdom of perfect harmony.

■ **Author:** Zechariah

■ **Date Written:** Chapters 1–8 were written from about 520 to 518 BC. Chapters 9–14 were written about 480 BC.

■ **Purpose:** To give hope to God's people by revealing God's future deliverance through the Messiah

■ **Themes:** Rebuilding the Temple, restoration, the coming Messiah

■ **Outline**
1:1-6 Introduction
1:7–6:8 Eight prophetic visions
6:9-15 The prophetic coronation of Jeshua
7:1–10:12 Various messages of judgment
　and hope
11:1–13:9 The coming Messiah and his rejection
14:1-21 The ultimate triumph of the Messiah

A Call to Return to the LORD

1 In November* of the second year of King Darius's reign, the LORD gave this message to the prophet Zechariah son of Berekiah and grandson of Iddo:

²"I, the LORD, was very angry with your ancestors. ³Therefore, say to the people, 'This is what the LORD of Heaven's Armies says: Return to me, and I will return to you, says the LORD of Heaven's Armies.' ⁴Don't be like your ancestors who would not listen or pay attention when the earlier prophets said to them, 'This is what the LORD of Heaven's Armies says: Turn from your evil ways, and stop all your evil practices.'

⁵"Where are your ancestors now? They and the prophets are long dead. ⁶But everything I said through my servants the prophets happened to your ancestors, just as I said. As a result, they repented and said, 'We have received what we deserved from the LORD of Heaven's Armies. He has done what he said he would do.'"

A Man among the Myrtle Trees

⁷Three months later, on February 15,* the LORD sent another message to the prophet Zechariah son of Berekiah and grandson of Iddo.

⁸In a vision during the night, I saw a man

1:1 Hebrew *In the eighth month.* A number of dates in Zechariah can be cross-checked with dates in surviving Persian records and related accurately to our modern calendar. This month of the ancient Hebrew lunar calendar occurred within the months of October and November 520 B.C.　1:7 Hebrew *On the twenty-fourth day of the eleventh month, the month of Shebat, in the second year of Darius.* This event occurred on February 15, 519 B.C.; also see note on 1:1.

sitting on a red horse that was standing among some myrtle trees in a small valley. Behind him were riders on red, brown, and white horses. [9]I asked the angel who was talking with me, "My lord, what do these horses mean?"

"I will show you," the angel replied.

[10]The rider standing among the myrtle trees then explained, "They are the ones the LORD has sent out to patrol the earth."

[11]Then the other riders reported to the angel of the LORD, who was standing among the myrtle trees, "We have been patrolling the earth, and the whole earth is at peace."

[12]Upon hearing this, the angel of the LORD prayed this prayer: "O LORD of Heaven's Armies, for seventy years now you have been angry with Jerusalem and the towns of Judah. How long until you again show mercy to them?" [13]And the LORD spoke kind and comforting words to the angel who talked with me.

[14]Then the angel said to me, "Shout this message for all to hear: 'This is what the LORD of Heaven's Armies says: My love for Jerusalem and Mount Zion is passionate and strong. [15]But I am very angry with the other nations that are now enjoying peace and security. I was only a little angry with my people, but the nations inflicted harm on them far beyond my intentions.

[16]"'Therefore, this is what the LORD says: I have returned to show mercy to Jerusalem. My Temple will be rebuilt, says the LORD of Heaven's Armies, and measurements will be taken for the reconstruction of Jerusalem.*'

[17]"Say this also: 'This is what the LORD of Heaven's Armies says: The towns of Israel will again overflow with prosperity, and the LORD will again comfort Zion and choose Jerusalem as his own.'"

Four Horns and Four Blacksmiths

[18]*Then I looked up and saw four animal horns. [19]"What are these?" I asked the angel who was talking with me.

He replied, "These horns represent the nations that scattered Judah, Israel, and Jerusalem."

[20]Then the LORD showed me four blacksmiths. [21]"What are these men coming to do?" I asked.

The angel replied, "These four horns—these

nations—scattered and humbled Judah. Now these blacksmiths have come to terrify those nations and throw them down and destroy them."

Future Prosperity of Jerusalem

2 [1]*When I looked again, I saw a man with a measuring line in his hand. [2]"Where are you going?" I asked.

He replied, "I am going to measure Jerusalem, to see how wide and how long it is."

[3]Then the angel who was with me went to meet a second angel who was coming toward him. [4]The other angel said, "Hurry, and say to that young man, 'Jerusalem will someday be so full of people and livestock that there won't be room enough for everyone! Many will live outside the city walls. [5]Then I, myself, will be a protective wall of fire around Jerusalem, says the LORD. And I will be the glory inside the city!'"

The Exiles Are Called Home

[6]The LORD says, "Come away! Flee from Babylon in the land of the north, for I have scattered you to the four winds. [7]Come away, people of Zion, you who are exiled in Babylon!"

[8]After a period of glory, the LORD of Heaven's Armies sent me* against the nations who plundered you. For he said, "Anyone who harms you harms my most precious possession.* [9]I will raise my fist to crush them, and their own slaves will plunder them." Then you will know that the LORD of Heaven's Armies has sent me.

[10]The LORD says, "Shout and rejoice, O beautiful Jerusalem,* for I am coming to live among you. [11]Many nations will join themselves to the LORD on that day, and they, too, will be my people. I will live among you, and you will know that the LORD of Heaven's Armies sent me to you. [12]The land of Judah will be the LORD's special possession in the holy land, and he will once again choose Jerusalem to be his own city. [13]Be silent before the LORD, all humanity, for he is springing into action from his holy dwelling."

Cleansing for the High Priest

3 Then the angel showed me Jeshua* the high priest standing before the angel of the LORD. The Accuser, Satan,* was there at the angel's right hand, making accusations

---

1:16 Hebrew *and the measuring line will be stretched out over Jerusalem.*   1:18 Verses 1:18-21 are numbered 2:1-4 in Hebrew text.
2:1 Verses 2:1-13 are numbered 2:5-17 in Hebrew text.   2:8a The meaning of the Hebrew is uncertain.   2:8b Hebrew *Anyone who touches you touches the pupil of his eye.*   2:10 Hebrew *O daughter of Zion.*   3:1a Hebrew *Joshua,* a variant spelling of Jeshua; also in 3:3, 4, 6, 8, 9.   3:1b Hebrew *The satan;* similarly in 3:2.

against Jeshua. ²And the LORD said to Satan, "I, the LORD, reject your accusations, Satan. Yes, the LORD, who has chosen Jerusalem, rebukes you. This man is like a burning stick that has been snatched from the fire."

³Jeshua's clothing was filthy as he stood there before the angel. ⁴So the angel said to the others standing there, "Take off his filthy clothes." And turning to Jeshua he said, "See, I have taken away your sins, and now I am giving you these fine new clothes."

⁵Then I said, "They should also place a clean turban on his head." So they put a clean priestly turban on his head and dressed him in new clothes while the angel of the LORD stood by.

⁶Then the angel of the LORD spoke very solemnly to Jeshua and said, ⁷"This is what the LORD of Heaven's Armies says: If you follow my ways and carefully serve me, then you will be given authority over my Temple and its courtyards. I will let you walk among these others standing here.

⁸"Listen to me, O Jeshua the high priest, and all you other priests. You are symbols of things to come. Soon I am going to bring my servant, the Branch. ⁹Now look at the jewel I have set before Jeshua, a single stone with seven facets.* I will engrave an inscription on it, says the LORD of Heaven's Armies, and I will remove the sins of this land in a single day.

¹⁰"And on that day, says the LORD of Heaven's Armies, each of you will invite your neighbor to sit with you peacefully under your own grapevine and fig tree."

A Lampstand and Two Olive Trees

4 Then the angel who had been talking with me returned and woke me, as though I had been asleep. ²"What do you see now?" he asked.

I answered, "I see a solid gold lampstand with a bowl of oil on top of it. Around the bowl are seven lamps, each having seven spouts with wicks. ³And I see two olive trees, one on each side of the bowl." ⁴Then I asked the angel, "What are these, my lord? What do they mean?"

⁵"Don't you know?" the angel asked.

"No, my lord," I replied.

⁶Then he said to me, "This is what the LORD says to Zerubbabel: It is not by force nor by strength, but by my Spirit, says the LORD of Heaven's Armies. ⁷Nothing, not even a mighty mountain, will stand in Zerubbabel's way; it will become a level plain before him! And when Zerubbabel sets the final stone of the Temple in place, the people will shout: 'May God bless it! May God bless it!'*"

⁸Then another message came to me from the LORD: ⁹"Zerubbabel is the one who laid the foundation of this Temple, and he will complete it. Then you will know that the LORD of Heaven's Armies has sent me. ¹⁰Do not despise these small beginnings, for the LORD rejoices to see the work begin, to see the plumb line in Zerubbabel's hand."

(The seven lamps* represent the eyes of the LORD that search all around the world.)

¹¹Then I asked the angel, "What are these two olive trees on each side of the lampstand, ¹²and what are the two olive branches that pour out golden oil through two gold tubes?"

¹³"Don't you know?" he asked.

"No, my lord," I replied.

¹⁴Then he said to me, "They represent the two anointed ones* who stand in the court of the Lord of all the earth."

A Flying Scroll

5 I looked up again and saw a scroll flying through the air.

²"What do you see?" the angel asked.

"I see a flying scroll," I replied. "It appears to be about 30 feet long and 15 feet wide.*"

³Then he said to me, "This scroll contains the curse that is going out over the entire land. One side of the scroll says that those who steal will be banished from the land; the other side says that those who swear falsely will be banished from the land. ⁴And this is what the LORD of Heaven's Armies says: I am sending this curse into the house of every thief and into the house of everyone who swears falsely using my name. And my curse will remain in that house and completely destroy it—even its timbers and stones."

A Woman in a Basket

⁵Then the angel who was talking with me came forward and said, "Look up and see what's coming."

⁶"What is it?" I asked.

He replied, "It is a basket for measuring grain,* and it's filled with the sins* of everyone throughout the land."

3:9 Hebrew *seven eyes.*   4:7 Hebrew '*Grace, grace to it.*'   4:10 Or *The seven facets* (see 3:9); Hebrew reads *These seven.*   4:14 Or *two heavenly beings;* Hebrew reads *two sons of fresh oil.*   5:2 Hebrew *20 cubits* [9.2 meters] *long and 10 cubits* [4.6 meters] *wide.*   5:6a Hebrew *an ephah* [20 quarts or 22 liters]; also in 5:7, 8, 9, 10, 11.   5:6b As in Greek version; Hebrew reads *the appearance.*

⁷Then the heavy lead cover was lifted off the basket, and there was a woman sitting inside it. ⁸The angel said, "The woman's name is Wickedness," and he pushed her back into the basket and closed the heavy lid again.

⁹Then I looked up and saw two women flying toward us, gliding on the wind. They had wings like a stork, and they picked up the basket and flew into the sky.

¹⁰"Where are they taking the basket?" I asked the angel.

¹¹He replied, "To the land of Babylonia,* where they will build a temple for the basket. And when the temple is ready, they will set the basket there on its pedestal."

Four Chariots

6 Then I looked up again and saw four chariots coming from between two bronze mountains. ²The first chariot was pulled by red horses, the second by black horses, ³the third by white horses, and the fourth by powerful dappled-gray horses. ⁴"And what are these, my lord?" I asked the angel who was talking with me.

⁵The angel replied, "These are the four spirits* of heaven who stand before the Lord of all the earth. They are going out to do his work. ⁶The chariot with black horses is going north, the chariot with white horses is going west,* and the chariot with dappled-gray horses is going south."

⁷The powerful horses were eager to set out to patrol the earth. And the LORD said, "Go and patrol the earth!" So they left at once on their patrol.

⁸Then the LORD summoned me and said, "Look, those who went north have vented the anger of my Spirit* there in the land of the north."

The Crowning of Jeshua

⁹Then I received another message from the LORD: ¹⁰"Heldai, Tobijah, and Jedaiah will bring gifts of silver and gold from the Jews exiled in Babylon. As soon as they arrive, meet them at the home of Josiah son of Zephaniah. ¹¹Accept their gifts, and make a crown from the silver and gold. Then put the crown on the head of Jeshua* son of Jehozadak, the high priest. ¹²Tell him, 'This is what the LORD of Heaven's Armies says: Here is the man called the Branch. He will branch out from where he is and build the Temple of the LORD. ¹³Yes, he will build the Temple of the LORD. Then he will receive royal honor and will rule as king from his throne. He will also serve as priest from his throne,* and there will be perfect harmony between his two roles.'

¹⁴"The crown will be a memorial in the Temple of the LORD to honor those who gave it—Heldai,* Tobijah, Jedaiah, and Josiah* son of Zephaniah."

¹⁵People will come from distant lands to rebuild the Temple of the LORD. And when this happens, you will know that my messages have been from the LORD of Heaven's Armies. All this will happen if you carefully obey what the LORD your God says.

A Call to Justice and Mercy

7 On December 7* of the fourth year of King Darius's reign, another message came to Zechariah from the LORD. ²The people of Bethel had sent Sharezer and Regemmelech,* along with their attendants, to seek the LORD's favor. ³They were to ask this question of the prophets and the priests at the Temple of the LORD of Heaven's Armies: "Should we continue to mourn and fast each summer on the anniversary of the Temple's destruction,* as we have done for so many years?"

⁴The LORD of Heaven's Armies sent me this message in reply: ⁵"Say to all your people and your priests, 'During these seventy years of exile, when you fasted and mourned in the summer and in early autumn,* was it really for me that you were fasting? ⁶And even now in your holy festivals, aren't you eating and drinking just to please yourselves? ⁷Isn't this the same message the LORD proclaimed through the prophets in years past when Jerusalem and the towns of Judah were bustling with people, and the Negev and the foothills of Judah* were well populated?'"

⁸Then this message came to Zechariah from the LORD: ⁹"This is what the LORD of Heaven's Armies says: Judge fairly, and show mercy and

---

6:11 Hebrew *the land of Shinar.*   6:5 Or *the four winds.*   6:6 Hebrew *is going after them.*   6:8 Hebrew *have given my Spirit rest.*
6:11 Hebrew *Joshua,* a variant spelling of Jeshua.   6:13 Or *There will be a priest by his throne.*   6:14a As in Syriac version
(compare 6:10); Hebrew reads *Helem.*   6:14b As in Syriac version (compare 6:10); Hebrew reads *Hen.*   7:1 Hebrew *On the fourth
day of the ninth month, the month of Kislev,* of the ancient Hebrew lunar calendar. This event occurred on December 7, 518 B.C.;
also see note on 1:1.   7:2 Or *Bethel-sharezer had sent Regemmelech.*   7:3 Hebrew *mourn and fast in the fifth month.* The Temple had
been destroyed in the fifth month of the ancient Hebrew lunar calendar (August 586 B.C.); see 2 Kgs 25:8.   7:5 Hebrew *fasted
and mourned in the fifth and seventh months.* The fifth month of the ancient Hebrew lunar calendar usually occurs within the
months of July and August. The seventh month usually occurs within the months of September and October; both the Day
of Atonement and the Festival of Shelters were celebrated in the seventh month.   7:7 Hebrew *the Shephelah.*

kindness to one another. ¹⁰Do not oppress widows, orphans, foreigners, and the poor. And do not scheme against each other.

¹¹"Your ancestors refused to listen to this message. They stubbornly turned away and put their fingers in their ears to keep from hearing. ¹²They made their hearts as hard as stone, so they could not hear the instructions or the messages that the LORD of Heaven's Armies had sent them by his Spirit through the earlier prophets. That is why the LORD of Heaven's Armies was so angry with them.

¹³"Since they refused to listen when I called to them, I would not listen when they called to me, says the LORD of Heaven's Armies. ¹⁴As with a whirlwind, I scattered them among the distant nations, where they lived as strangers. Their land became so desolate that no one even traveled through it. They turned their pleasant land into a desert."

Promised Blessings for Jerusalem

8 Then another message came to me from the LORD of Heaven's Armies: ²"This is what the LORD of Heaven's Armies says: My love for Mount Zion is passionate and strong; I am consumed with passion for Jerusalem!

³"And now the LORD says: I am returning to Mount Zion, and I will live in Jerusalem. Then Jerusalem will be called the Faithful City; the mountain of the LORD of Heaven's Armies will be called the Holy Mountain.

⁴"This is what the LORD of Heaven's Armies says: Once again old men and women will walk Jerusalem's streets with their canes and will sit together in the city squares. ⁵And the streets of the city will be filled with boys and girls at play.

⁶"This is what the LORD of Heaven's Armies says: All this may seem impossible to you now, a small remnant of God's people. But is it impossible for me? says the LORD of Heaven's Armies.

⁷"This is what the LORD of Heaven's Armies says: You can be sure that I will rescue my people from the east and from the west. ⁸I will bring them home again to live safely in Jerusalem. They will be my people, and I will be faithful and just toward them as their God.

⁹"This is what the LORD of Heaven's Armies says: Be strong and finish the task! Ever since the laying of the foundation of the Temple of the LORD of Heaven's Armies, you have heard what the prophets have been saying about completing the building. ¹⁰Before the work on the Temple began, there were no jobs and no money to hire people or animals. No traveler was safe from the enemy, for there were enemies on all sides. I had turned everyone against each other.

¹¹"But now I will not treat the remnant of my people as I treated them before, says the LORD of Heaven's Armies. ¹²For I am planting seeds of peace and prosperity among you. The grapevines will be heavy with fruit. The earth will produce its crops, and the heavens will release the dew. Once more I will cause the remnant in Judah and Israel to inherit these blessings. ¹³Among the other nations, Judah and Israel became symbols of a cursed nation. But no longer! Now I will rescue you and make you both a symbol and a source of blessing. So don't be afraid. Be strong, and get on with rebuilding the Temple!

¹⁴"For this is what the LORD of Heaven's Armies says: I was determined to punish you when your ancestors angered me, and I did not change my mind, says the LORD of Heaven's Armies. ¹⁵But now I am determined to bless Jerusalem and the people of Judah. So don't be afraid. ¹⁶But this is what you must do: Tell the truth to each other. Render verdicts in your courts that are just and that lead to peace. ¹⁷Don't scheme against each other. Stop your love of telling lies that you swear are the truth. I hate all these things, says the LORD."

¹⁸Here is another message that came to me from the LORD of Heaven's Armies. ¹⁹"This is what the LORD of Heaven's Armies says: The traditional fasts and times of mourning you have kept in early summer, midsummer, autumn, and winter* are now ended. They will become festivals of joy and celebration for the people of Judah. So love truth and peace.

²⁰"This is what the LORD of Heaven's Armies says: People from nations and cities around the world will travel to Jerusalem. ²¹The people of one city will say to the people of another, 'Come with us to Jerusalem to ask the LORD to bless us. Let's worship the LORD of Heaven's Armies. I'm determined to go.' ²²Many peoples and powerful nations will come to Jerusalem to seek the LORD of Heaven's Armies and to ask for his blessing.

²³"This is what the LORD of Heaven's Armies

8:19 Hebrew *in the fourth, fifth, seventh, and tenth months.* The fourth month of the ancient Hebrew lunar calendar usually occurs within the months of June and July. The fifth month usually occurs within the months of July and August. The seventh month usually occurs within the months of September and October. The tenth month usually occurs within the months of December and January.

says: In those days ten men from different nations and languages of the world will clutch at the sleeve of one Jew. And they will say, 'Please let us walk with you, for we have heard that God is with you.'"

Judgment against Israel's Enemies

9 This is the message* from the LORD against the land of Aram* and the city of Damascus, for the eyes of humanity, including all the tribes of Israel, are on the LORD.

2 Doom is certain for Hamath,
    near Damascus,
and for the cities of Tyre and Sidon,
    though they are so clever.
3 Tyre has built a strong fortress
    and has made silver and gold
    as plentiful as dust in the streets!
4 But now the Lord will strip away Tyre's
        possessions
    and hurl its fortifications into the sea,
    and it will be burned to the ground.
5 The city of Ashkelon will see Tyre fall
    and will be filled with fear.
Gaza will shake with terror,
    as will Ekron, for their hopes will be
        dashed.
Gaza's king will be killed,
    and Ashkelon will be deserted.
6 Foreigners will occupy the city of Ashdod.
    I will destroy the pride of the
        Philistines.
7 I will grab the bloody meat from their
        mouths
    and snatch the detestable sacrifices from
        their teeth.
Then the surviving Philistines will
        worship our God
    and become like a clan in Judah.*
The Philistines of Ekron will join my
        people,
    as the ancient Jebusites once did.
8 I will guard my Temple
    and protect it from invading armies.
I am watching closely to ensure
    that no more foreign oppressors
        overrun my people's land.

Zion's Coming King

9 Rejoice, O people of Zion!*
    Shout in triumph, O people of
        Jerusalem!

Look, your king is coming to you.
    He is righteous and victorious,*
yet he is humble, riding on a
        donkey—
    riding on a donkey's colt.
10 I will remove the battle chariots from
        Israel*
    and the warhorses from Jerusalem.
I will destroy all the weapons used in
        battle,
    and your king will bring peace to the
        nations.
His realm will stretch from sea to sea
    and from the Euphrates River* to the
        ends of the earth.*
11 Because of the covenant I made with
        you,
    sealed with blood,
I will free your prisoners
    from death in a waterless dungeon.
12 Come back to the place of safety,
    all you prisoners who still have hope!
I promise this very day
    that I will repay two blessings for each
        of your troubles.
13 Judah is my bow,
    and Israel is my arrow.
Jerusalem* is my sword,
    and like a warrior, I will brandish it
        against the Greeks.*
14 The LORD will appear above his
        people;
    his arrows will fly like lightning!
The Sovereign LORD will sound the ram's
        horn
    and attack like a whirlwind from the
        southern desert.
15 The LORD of Heaven's Armies will protect
        his people,
    and they will defeat their enemies by
        hurling great stones.
They will shout in battle as though drunk
        with wine.
    They will be filled with blood like a
        bowl,
    drenched with blood like the corners
        of the altar.
16 On that day the LORD their God will rescue
        his people,
    just as a shepherd rescues his sheep.
They will sparkle in his land
    like jewels in a crown.

9:1a Hebrew *An Oracle: The message.*   9:1b Hebrew *land of Hadrach.*   9:7 Hebrew *like a leader in Judah.*   9:9a Hebrew *O daughter of Zion!*   9:9b Hebrew *and is being vindicated.*   9:10a Hebrew *Ephraim,* referring to the northern kingdom of Israel; also in 9:13.   9:10b Hebrew *the river.*   9:10c Or *the end of the land.*   9:13a Hebrew *Zion.*   9:13b Hebrew *the sons of Javan.*

¹⁷ How wonderful and beautiful they will be!
  The young men will thrive on abundant
    grain,
  and the young women will flourish on
    new wine.

The LORD Will Restore His People

10

¹ Ask the LORD for rain in the spring,
    for he makes the storm clouds.
And he will send showers of rain
  so every field becomes a lush pasture.
² Household gods give worthless advice,
    fortune-tellers predict only lies,
  and interpreters of dreams pronounce
    falsehoods that give no comfort.
So my people are wandering like lost
    sheep;
  they are attacked because they have no
    shepherd.

³ "My anger burns against your shepherds,
    and I will punish these leaders.*
For the LORD of Heaven's Armies has
    arrived
  to look after Judah, his flock.
He will make them strong and glorious,
  like a proud warhorse in battle.
⁴ From Judah will come the cornerstone,
    the tent peg,
  the bow for battle,
    and all the rulers.
⁵ They will be like mighty warriors in battle,
    trampling their enemies in the mud
      under their feet.
Since the LORD is with them as they fight,
    they will overthrow even the enemy's
      horsemen.

⁶ "I will strengthen Judah and save Israel*;
    I will restore them because of my
      compassion.
It will be as though I had never rejected
    them,
  for I am the LORD their God, who will
    hear their cries.
⁷ The people of Israel* will become like
    mighty warriors,
  and their hearts will be made happy as
    if by wine.
Their children, too, will see it and be glad;
  their hearts will rejoice in the LORD.
⁸ When I whistle to them, they will come
    running,
  for I have redeemed them.

From the few who are left,
  they will grow as numerous as they were
    before.
⁹ Though I have scattered them like seeds
    among the nations,
  they will still remember me in distant
    lands.
They and their children will survive
  and return again to Israel.
¹⁰ I will bring them back from Egypt
    and gather them from Assyria.
I will resettle them in Gilead and Lebanon
    until there is no more room for them all.
¹¹ They will pass safely through the sea of
    distress,*
  for the waves of the sea will be held
    back,
  and the waters of the Nile will dry up.
The pride of Assyria will be crushed,
  and the rule of Egypt will end.
¹² By my power* I will make my people
    strong,
  and by my authority they will go
    wherever they wish.
I, the LORD, have spoken!"

11

¹ Open your doors, Lebanon,
    so that fire may devour your cedar
      forests.
² Weep, you cypress trees, for all the ruined
    cedars;
  the most majestic ones have fallen.
Weep, you oaks of Bashan,
  for the thick forests have been cut down.
³ Listen to the wailing of the shepherds,
  for their rich pastures are destroyed.
Hear the young lions roaring,
  for their thickets in the Jordan Valley are
    ruined.

The Good and Evil Shepherds

⁴This is what the LORD my God says: "Go and
care for the flock that is intended for slaughter. ⁵The buyers slaughter their sheep without
remorse. The sellers say, 'Praise the LORD! Now
I'm rich!' Even the shepherds have no compassion for them. ⁶Likewise, I will no longer have
pity on the people of the land," says the LORD.
"I will let them fall into each other's hands and
into the hands of their king. They will turn the
land into a wilderness, and I will not rescue
them."

⁷So I cared for the flock intended for
slaughter—the flock that was oppressed. Then

10:3 Or *these male goats.*   **10:6** Hebrew *save the house of Joseph.*   **10:7** Hebrew *of Ephraim.*   **10:11** Or *the sea of Egypt,* referring to
the Red Sea.   **10:12** Hebrew *In the LORD.*

I took two shepherd's staffs and named one Favor and the other Union. [8]I got rid of their three evil shepherds in a single month.

But I became impatient with these sheep, and they hated me, too. [9]So I told them, "I won't be your shepherd any longer. If you die, you die. If you are killed, you are killed. And let those who remain devour each other!"

[10]Then I took my staff called Favor and cut it in two, showing that I had revoked the covenant I had made with all the nations. [11]That was the end of my covenant with them. The suffering flock was watching me, and they knew that the LORD was speaking through my actions.

[12]And I said to them, "If you like, give me my wages, whatever I am worth; but only if you want to." So they counted out for my wages thirty pieces of silver.

[13]And the LORD said to me, "Throw it to the potter*"—this magnificent sum at which they valued me! So I took the thirty coins and threw them to the potter in the Temple of the LORD.

[14]Then I took my other staff, Union, and cut it in two, showing that the bond of unity between Judah and Israel was broken.

[15]Then the LORD said to me, "Go again and play the part of a worthless shepherd. [16]This illustrates how I will give this nation a shepherd who will not care for those who are dying, nor look after the young, nor heal the injured, nor feed the healthy. Instead, this shepherd will eat the meat of the fattest sheep and tear off their hooves.

[17] "What sorrow awaits this worthless
         shepherd
    who abandons the flock!
The sword will cut his arm
    and pierce his right eye.
His arm will become useless,
    and his right eye completely
         blind."

Future Deliverance for Jerusalem

12 This* message concerning the fate of Israel came from the LORD: "This message is from the LORD, who stretched out the heavens, laid the foundations of the earth, and formed the human spirit. [2]I will make Jerusalem like an intoxicating drink that makes the nearby nations stagger when they send their armies to besiege Jerusalem and Judah. [3]On that day I will make Jerusalem an immovable rock. All the nations will gather against it to try to move it, but they will only hurt themselves.

[4]"On that day," says the LORD, "I will cause every horse to panic and every rider to lose his nerve. I will watch over the people of Judah, but I will blind all the horses of their enemies. [5]And the clans of Judah will say to themselves, 'The people of Jerusalem have found strength in the LORD of Heaven's Armies, their God.'

[6]"On that day I will make the clans of Judah like a flame that sets a woodpile ablaze or like a burning torch among sheaves of grain. They will burn up all the neighboring nations right and left, while the people living in Jerusalem remain secure.

[7]"The LORD will give victory to the rest of Judah first, before Jerusalem, so that the people of Jerusalem and the royal line of David will not have greater honor than the rest of Judah. [8]On that day the LORD will defend the people of Jerusalem; the weakest among them will be as mighty as King David! And the royal descendants will be like God, like the angel of the LORD who goes before them! [9]For on that day I will begin to destroy all the nations that come against Jerusalem.

[10]"Then I will pour out a spirit* of grace and prayer on the family of David and on the people of Jerusalem. They will look on me whom they have pierced and mourn for him as for an only son. They will grieve bitterly for him as for a firstborn son who has died. [11]The sorrow and mourning in Jerusalem on that day will be like the great mourning for Hadad-rimmon in the valley of Megiddo.

[12]"All Israel will mourn, each clan by itself, and with the husbands separate from their wives. The clan of David will mourn alone, as will the clan of Nathan, [13]the clan of Levi, and the clan of Shimei. [14]Each of the surviving clans from Judah will mourn separately, and with the husbands separate from their wives.

A Fountain of Cleansing

13 "On that day a fountain will be opened for the dynasty of David and for the people of Jerusalem, a fountain to cleanse them from all their sins and impurity.

[2]"And on that day," says the LORD of Heaven's Armies, "I will erase idol worship throughout the land, so that even the names of the idols will be forgotten. I will remove from the land both the false prophets and the spirit of impurity that came with them. [3]If

11:13 Syriac version reads *into the treasury;* also in 11:13b. Compare Matt 27:6-10.   12:1 Hebrew *An Oracle: This.*   12:10 Or *the Spirit.*

anyone continues to prophesy, his own father and mother will tell him, 'You must die, for you have prophesied lies in the name of the LORD.' And as he prophesies, his own father and mother will stab him.

4"On that day people will be ashamed to claim the prophetic gift. No one will pretend to be a prophet by wearing prophet's clothes. 5He will say, 'I'm no prophet; I'm a farmer. I began working for a farmer as a boy.' 6And if someone asks, 'Then what about those wounds on your chest?*' he will say, 'I was wounded at my friends' house!'

The Scattering of the Sheep

7 "Awake, O sword, against my shepherd,
 the man who is my partner,"
 says the LORD of Heaven's Armies.
"Strike down the shepherd,
 and the sheep will be scattered,
 and I will turn against the lambs.
8 Two-thirds of the people in the land
 will be cut off and die," says the LORD.
 "But one-third will be left in the land.
9 I will bring that group through the fire
 and make them pure.
I will refine them like silver
 and purify them like gold.
They will call on my name,
 and I will answer them.
I will say, 'These are my people,'
 and they will say, 'The LORD is our
 God.'"

The LORD Will Rule the Earth

14 Watch, for the day of the LORD is coming when your possessions will be plundered right in front of you! 2I will gather all the nations to fight against Jerusalem. The city will be taken, the houses looted, and the women raped. Half the population will be taken into captivity, and the rest will be left among the ruins of the city.

3Then the LORD will go out to fight against those nations, as he has fought in times past. 4On that day his feet will stand on the Mount of Olives, east of Jerusalem. And the Mount of Olives will split apart, making a wide valley running from east to west. Half the mountain will move toward the north and half toward the south. 5You will flee through this valley, for it will reach across to Azal.* Yes, you will

flee as you did from the earthquake in the days of King Uzziah of Judah. Then the LORD my God will come, and all his holy ones with him.*

6On that day the sources of light will no longer shine,* 7yet there will be continuous day! Only the LORD knows how this could happen. There will be no normal day and night, for at evening time it will still be light.

8On that day life-giving waters will flow out from Jerusalem, half toward the Dead Sea and half toward the Mediterranean,* flowing continuously in both summer and winter.

9And the LORD will be king over all the earth. On that day there will be one LORD—his name alone will be worshiped.

10All the land from Geba, north of Judah, to Rimmon, south of Jerusalem, will become one vast plain. But Jerusalem will be raised up in its original place and will be inhabited all the way from the Benjamin Gate over to the site of the old gate, then to the Corner Gate, and from the Tower of Hananel to the king's winepresses. 11And Jerusalem will be filled, safe at last, never again to be cursed and destroyed.

12And the LORD will send a plague on all the nations that fought against Jerusalem. Their people will become like walking corpses, their flesh rotting away. Their eyes will rot in their sockets, and their tongues will rot in their mouths. 13On that day they will be terrified, stricken by the LORD with great panic. They will fight their neighbors hand to hand. 14Judah, too, will be fighting at Jerusalem. The wealth of all the neighboring nations will be captured—great quantities of gold and silver and fine clothing. 15This same plague will strike the horses, mules, camels, donkeys, and all the other animals in the enemy camps.

16In the end, the enemies of Jerusalem who survive the plague will go up to Jerusalem each year to worship the King, the LORD of Heaven's Armies, and to celebrate the Festival of Shelters. 17Any nation in the world that refuses to come to Jerusalem to worship the King, the LORD of Heaven's Armies, will have no rain. 18If the people of Egypt refuse to attend the festival, the LORD will punish* them with the same plague that he sends on the other nations who refuse to go. 19Egypt and the other nations will all be punished if they don't go to celebrate the Festival of Shelters.

20On that day even the harness bells of the

13:6 Hebrew *wounds between your hands?* 14:5a The meaning of the Hebrew is uncertain. 14:5b As in Greek version; Hebrew reads *with you.* 14:6 Hebrew *the precious ones shall diminish;* or *the precious ones and frost.* The meaning of the Hebrew is uncertain. 14:8 Hebrew *half toward the eastern sea and half toward the western sea.* 14:18 As in some Hebrew manuscripts and Greek and Syriac versions; Masoretic Text reads *will not punish.*

horses will be inscribed with these words: HOLY TO THE LORD. And the cooking pots in the Temple of the LORD will be as sacred as the basins used beside the altar. [21]In fact, every cooking pot in Jerusalem and Judah will be

14:21 Hebrew *Canaanites*.

holy to the LORD of Heaven's Armies. All who come to worship will be free to use any of these pots to boil their sacrifices. And on that day there will no longer be traders* in the Temple of the LORD of Heaven's Armies.

Malachi

SPIRITUAL HEALTH requires constant maintenance. Otherwise we quickly lapse into apathy and insincerity. This was a problem in the time of Malachi, as well. After returning from exile in Babylonia, the Jews rebuilt the Temple and reinstated the priesthood. Everything seemed to be going well. But after a few generations passed, many Jews became complacent in their faith. Even the priests became corrupt and careless in carrying out their duties. So Malachi prophesied against the people's insincere worship, their refusal to tithe the full amount, and their lack of concern for God's commands. He did not just condemn them for their failures, however; he also promised them great blessings for their obedience. Malachi also foretold the coming of Elijah, who would prepare the way for the great "day of the LORD."

- **Author:** Malachi
- **Date Written:** Around 430 BC
- **Purpose:** To confront the people with their sins of insincere worship and corruption and to restore their relationship with God
- **Themes:** God's love, the corruption of the priests, the sins of the people, the day of the LORD
- **Outline**
  1:1–2:9 God's love and Israel's shame
  2:10-17 Israel's sins denounced
  3:1-6 Future judgment predicted
  3:7-18 The neglected tithe
  4:1-6 The coming of Elijah foretold

1 This is the message* that the LORD gave to Israel through the prophet Malachi.*

The LORD's Love for Israel
2 "I have always loved you," says the LORD.

But you retort, "Really? How have you loved us?"

And the LORD replies, "This is how I showed my love for you: I loved your ancestor Jacob, 3 but I rejected his brother, Esau, and devastated his hill country. I turned Esau's inheritance into a desert for jackals."

4 Esau's descendants in Edom may say, "We have been shattered, but we will rebuild the ruins."

But the LORD of Heaven's Armies replies, "They may try to rebuild, but I will demolish them again. Their country will be known as 'The Land of Wickedness,' and their people will be called 'The People with Whom the LORD Is Forever Angry.' 5 When you see the destruction for yourselves, you will say, 'Truly, the LORD's greatness reaches far beyond Israel's borders!'"

Unworthy Sacrifices
6 The LORD of Heaven's Armies says to the priests: "A son honors his father, and a servant respects his master. If I am your father and master, where are the honor and respect I deserve? You have shown contempt for my name!

"But you ask, 'How have we ever shown contempt for your name?'

7 "You have shown contempt by offering defiled sacrifices on my altar.

"Then you ask, 'How have we defiled the sacrifices?*'

"You defile them by saying the altar of the LORD deserves no respect. 8 When you give blind animals as sacrifices, isn't that wrong? And isn't it wrong to offer animals that are crippled and diseased? Try giving gifts like that to your governor, and see how pleased he is!" says the LORD of Heaven's Armies.

9 "Go ahead, beg God to be merciful to you! But when you bring that kind of offering, why should he show you any favor at all?" asks the LORD of Heaven's Armies.

1:1a Hebrew *An Oracle: The message.* 1:1b *Malachi* means "my messenger." 1:7 As in Greek version; Hebrew reads *defiled you?*

¹⁰"How I wish one of you would shut the Temple doors so that these worthless sacrifices could not be offered! I am not pleased with you," says the LORD of Heaven's Armies, "and I will not accept your offerings. ¹¹But my name is honored* by people of other nations from morning till night. All around the world they offer* sweet incense and pure offerings in honor of my name. For my name is great among the nations," says the LORD of Heaven's Armies.

¹²"But you dishonor my name with your actions. By bringing contemptible food, you are saying it's all right to defile the Lord's table. ¹³You say, 'It's too hard to serve the LORD,' and you turn up your noses at my commands," says the LORD of Heaven's Armies. "Think of it! Animals that are stolen and crippled and sick are being presented as offerings! Should I accept from you such offerings as these?" asks the LORD.

¹⁴"Cursed is the cheat who promises to give a fine ram from his flock but then sacrifices a defective one to the Lord. For I am a great king," says the LORD of Heaven's Armies, "and my name is feared among the nations!

A Warning to the Priests

2 "Listen, you priests—this command is for you! ²Listen to me and make up your minds to honor my name," says the LORD of Heaven's Armies, "or I will bring a terrible curse against you. I will curse even the blessings you receive. Indeed, I have already cursed them, because you have not taken my warning to heart. ³I will punish your descendants and splatter your faces with the manure from your festival sacrifices, and I will throw you on the manure pile. ⁴Then at last you will know it was I who sent you this warning so that my covenant with the Levites can continue," says the LORD of Heaven's Armies.

⁵"The purpose of my covenant with the Levites was to bring life and peace, and that is what I gave them. This required reverence from them, and they greatly revered me and stood in awe of my name. ⁶They passed on to the people the truth of the instructions they received from me. They did not lie or cheat; they walked with me, living good and righteous lives, and they turned many from lives of sin.

⁷"The words of a priest's lips should preserve knowledge of God, and people should go to him for instruction, for the priest is the messenger of the LORD of Heaven's Armies. ⁸But you priests have left God's paths. Your instructions have caused many to stumble into sin. You have corrupted the covenant I made with the Levites," says the LORD of Heaven's Armies. ⁹"So I have made you despised and humiliated in the eyes of all the people. For you have not obeyed me but have shown favoritism in the way you carry out my instructions."

A Call to Faithfulness

¹⁰Are we not all children of the same Father? Are we not all created by the same God? Then why do we betray each other, violating the covenant of our ancestors?

¹¹Judah has been unfaithful, and a detestable thing has been done in Israel and in Jerusalem. The men of Judah have defiled the LORD's beloved sanctuary by marrying women who worship idols. ¹²May the LORD cut off from the nation of Israel* every last man who has done this and yet brings an offering to the LORD of Heaven's Armies.

¹³Here is another thing you do. You cover the LORD's altar with tears, weeping and groaning because he pays no attention to your offerings and doesn't accept them with pleasure. ¹⁴You cry out, "Why doesn't the LORD accept my worship?" I'll tell you why! Because the LORD witnessed the vows you and your wife made when you were young. But you have been unfaithful to her, though she remained your faithful partner, the wife of your marriage vows.

¹⁵Didn't the LORD make you one with your wife? In body and spirit you are his.* And what does he want? Godly children from your union. So guard your heart; remain loyal to the wife of your youth. ¹⁶"For I hate divorce!"* says the LORD, the God of Israel. "To divorce your wife is to overwhelm her with cruelty,*" says the LORD of Heaven's Armies. "So guard your heart; do not be unfaithful to your wife."

¹⁷You have wearied the LORD with your words.

"How have we wearied him?" you ask.

You have wearied him by saying that all who do evil are good in the LORD's sight, and he is pleased with them. You have wearied him by asking, "Where is the God of justice?"

1:11a Or *will be honored.*   1:11b Or *will offer.*   2:12 Hebrew *from the tents of Jacob.* The names "Jacob" and "Israel" are often interchanged throughout the Old Testament, referring sometimes to the individual patriarch and sometimes to the nation.   2:15 Or *Didn't the one LORD make us and preserve our life and breath?* or *Didn't the one LORD make her, both flesh and spirit?* The meaning of the Hebrew is uncertain.   2:16a Hebrew *For he hates divorcing.*   2:16b Hebrew *to cover one's garment with violence.*

The Coming Day of Judgment

3 "Look! I am sending my messenger, and he will prepare the way before me. Then the Lord you are seeking will suddenly come to his Temple. The messenger of the covenant, whom you look for so eagerly, is surely coming," says the LORD of Heaven's Armies.

2"But who will be able to endure it when he comes? Who will be able to stand and face him when he appears? For he will be like a blazing fire that refines metal, or like a strong soap that bleaches clothes. 3He will sit like a refiner of silver, burning away the dross. He will purify the Levites, refining them like gold and silver, so that they may once again offer acceptable sacrifices to the LORD. 4Then once more the LORD will accept the offerings brought to him by the people of Judah and Jerusalem, as he did in the past.

5"At that time I will put you on trial. I am eager to witness against all sorcerers and adulterers and liars. I will speak against those who cheat employees of their wages, who oppress widows and orphans, or who deprive the foreigners living among you of justice, for these people do not fear me," says the LORD of Heaven's Armies.

A Call to Repentance

6"I am the LORD, and I do not change. That is why you descendants of Jacob are not already destroyed. 7Ever since the days of your ancestors, you have scorned my decrees and failed to obey them. Now return to me, and I will return to you," says the LORD of Heaven's Armies.

"But you ask, 'How can we return when we have never gone away?'

8"Should people cheat God? Yet you have cheated me!

"But you ask, 'What do you mean? When did we ever cheat you?'

"You have cheated me of the tithes and offerings due to me. 9You are under a curse, for your whole nation has been cheating me. 10Bring all the tithes into the storehouse so there will be enough food in my Temple. If you do," says the LORD of Heaven's Armies, "I will open the windows of heaven for you. I will pour out a blessing so great you won't have enough room to take it in! Try it! Put me to the test! 11Your crops will be abundant, for I will guard them from insects and disease.* Your grapes will not fall from the vine before they are ripe," says the LORD of Heaven's Armies.

12"Then all nations will call you blessed, for your land will be such a delight," says the LORD of Heaven's Armies.

13"You have said terrible things about me," says the LORD.

"But you say, 'What do you mean? What have we said against you?'

14"You have said, 'What's the use of serving God? What have we gained by obeying his commands or by trying to show the LORD of Heaven's Armies that we are sorry for our sins? 15From now on we will call the arrogant blessed. For those who do evil get rich, and those who dare God to punish them suffer no harm.'"

The LORD's Promise of Mercy

16Then those who feared the LORD spoke with each other, and the LORD listened to what they said. In his presence, a scroll of remembrance was written to record the names of those who feared him and always thought about the honor of his name.

17"They will be my people," says the LORD of Heaven's Armies. "On the day when I act in judgment, they will be my own special treasure. I will spare them as a father spares an obedient child. 18Then you will again see the difference between the righteous and the wicked, between those who serve God and those who do not."

The Coming Day of Judgment

4 1*The LORD of Heaven's Armies says, "The day of judgment is coming, burning like a furnace. On that day the arrogant and the wicked will be burned up like straw. They will be consumed—roots, branches, and all.

2"But for you who fear my name, the Sun of Righteousness will rise with healing in his wings.* And you will go free, leaping with joy like calves let out to pasture. 3On the day when I act, you will tread upon the wicked as if they were dust under your feet," says the LORD of Heaven's Armies.

4"Remember to obey the Law of Moses, my servant—all the decrees and regulations that I gave him on Mount Sinai* for all Israel.

5"Look, I am sending you the prophet Elijah before the great and dreadful day of the LORD arrives. 6His preaching will turn the hearts of fathers to their children, and the hearts of children to their fathers. Otherwise I will come and strike the land with a curse."

3:11 Hebrew *from the devourer.*   4:1 Verses 4:1-6 are numbered 3:19-24 in Hebrew text.   4:2 Or *the sun of righteousness will rise with healing in its wings.*   4:4 Hebrew *Horeb,* another name for Sinai.

New Testament

Matthew

THE BIRTH OF JESUS OF NAZARETH
ushered in the long-awaited age of a
new kingdom on earth—the Kingdom
of Heaven. Matthew's Gospel records
the advent of this new Kingdom through
the teachings and actions of Jesus, the
Messiah. Since the Kingdom of Heaven
is a major theme throughout this Gospel,
Matthew was careful to show how Jesus
fulfilled the Old Testament passages that
speak of the Messiah, the ruler of the
Kingdom. He recounted Jesus' family
history to show his royal lineage. After
describing the virgin birth of Jesus, Matthew detailed Jesus' messianic baptism,

- **Author:** Matthew (Levi)
- **Date Written:** Probably between AD 60 and 65, perhaps from the city of Antioch
- **Purpose:** To present Jesus as the Messiah, who has brought the Kingdom of Heaven to earth
- **Themes:** Jesus the Messiah, the Kingdom of Heaven, Gentiles' inclusion in the Kingdom of Heaven
- **Outline**
  1:1–4:25 The early life and ministry of Jesus
  5:1–7:29 The Sermon on the Mount
  8:1–18:35 General teaching, parables, and discourses
  19:1–23:39 Journey to Jerusalem and final warnings
  24:1–25:46 Prophecies of things to come
  26:1–28:20 Jesus' death and resurrection

his temptation in the wilderness, and the early days of his ministry. In the Sermon on
the Mount, Jesus taught his disciples how life in the Kingdom should be lived. Jesus
also performed many miracles and taught the people various parables, or stories,
that further illustrated what the Kingdom of Heaven is like. Matthew was careful to
point out that the Gentiles, as well as the Jews, would be included in the Kingdom
of Heaven. Matthew's Gospel concludes with Jesus' death and resurrection and his
command to make disciples from every nation.

The Ancestors of Jesus the Messiah

1 This is a record of the ancestors of Jesus the Messiah, a descendant of David and of Abraham*:

2 Abraham was the father of Isaac.
Isaac was the father of Jacob.
Jacob was the father of Judah and his brothers.
3 Judah was the father of Perez and Zerah (whose mother was Tamar).
Perez was the father of Hezron.
Hezron was the father of Ram.*
4 Ram was the father of Amminadab.
Amminadab was the father of Nahshon.
Nahshon was the father of Salmon.
5 Salmon was the father of Boaz (whose mother was Rahab).
Boaz was the father of Obed (whose mother was Ruth).
Obed was the father of Jesse.
6 Jesse was the father of King David.
David was the father of Solomon (whose mother was Bathsheba, the widow of Uriah).
7 Solomon was the father of Rehoboam.
Rehoboam was the father of Abijah.
Abijah was the father of Asa.*
8 Asa was the father of Jehoshaphat.
Jehoshaphat was the father of Jehoram.*

1:1 Greek *Jesus the Messiah, Son of David and son of Abraham.* 1:3 Greek *Aram*, a variant spelling of Ram; also in 1:4. See 1 Chr 2:9-10. 1:7 Greek *Asaph*, a variant spelling of Asa; also in 1:8. See 1 Chr 3:10. 1:8a Greek *Joram*, a variant spelling of Jehoram; also in 1:8b. See 1 Kgs 22:50 and note at 1 Chr 3:11.

Jehoram was the father* of Uzziah.
9 Uzziah was the father of Jotham.
Jotham was the father of Ahaz.
Ahaz was the father of Hezekiah.
10 Hezekiah was the father of Manasseh.
Manasseh was the father of Amon.*
Amon was the father of Josiah.
11 Josiah was the father of Jehoiachin* and
his brothers (born at the time of the
exile to Babylon).
12 After the Babylonian exile:
Jehoiachin was the father of Shealtiel.
Shealtiel was the father of Zerubbabel.
13 Zerubbabel was the father of Abiud.
Abiud was the father of Eliakim.
Eliakim was the father of Azor.
14 Azor was the father of Zadok.
Zadok was the father of Akim.
Akim was the father of Eliud.
15 Eliud was the father of Eleazar.
Eleazar was the father of Matthan.
Matthan was the father of Jacob.
16 Jacob was the father of Joseph, the
husband of Mary.
Mary gave birth to Jesus, who is called the
Messiah.

17All those listed above include fourteen generations from Abraham to David, fourteen from David to the Babylonian exile, and fourteen from the Babylonian exile to the Messiah.

The Birth of Jesus the Messiah

18This is how Jesus the Messiah was born. His mother, Mary, was engaged to be married to Joseph. But before the marriage took place, while she was still a virgin, she became pregnant through the power of the Holy Spirit. 19Joseph, to whom she was engaged, was a righteous man and did not want to disgrace her publicly, so he decided to break the engagement* quietly.

20As he considered this, an angel of the Lord appeared to him in a dream. "Joseph, son of David," the angel said, "do not be afraid to take Mary as your wife. For the child within her was conceived by the Holy Spirit. 21And she will have a son, and you are to name him Jesus,* for he will save his people from their sins."

22All of this occurred to fulfill the Lord's message through his prophet:

23 "Look! The virgin will conceive a child!
She will give birth to a son,
and they will call him Immanuel,*
which means 'God is with us.'"

24When Joseph woke up, he did as the angel of the Lord commanded and took Mary as his wife. 25But he did not have sexual relations with her until her son was born. And Joseph named him Jesus.

Visitors from the East

2 Jesus was born in Bethlehem in Judea, during the reign of King Herod. About that time some wise men* from eastern lands arrived in Jerusalem, asking, 2"Where is the newborn king of the Jews? We saw his star as it rose,* and we have come to worship him."

3King Herod was deeply disturbed when he heard this, as was everyone in Jerusalem. 4He called a meeting of the leading priests and teachers of religious law and asked, "Where is the Messiah supposed to be born?"

5"In Bethlehem in Judea," they said, "for this is what the prophet wrote:

6 'And you, O Bethlehem in the land of Judah,
are not least among the ruling cities*
of Judah,
for a ruler will come from you
who will be the shepherd for my people
Israel.'*"

7Then Herod called for a private meeting with the wise men, and he learned from them the time when the star first appeared. 8Then he told them, "Go to Bethlehem and search carefully for the child. And when you find him, come back and tell me so that I can go and worship him, too!"

9After this interview the wise men went their way. And the star they had seen in the east guided them to Bethlehem. It went ahead of them and stopped over the place where the child was. 10When they saw the star, they were filled with joy! 11They entered the house and saw the child with his mother, Mary, and they bowed down and worshiped him. Then they opened their treasure chests and gave him gifts of gold, frankincense, and myrrh.

12When it was time to leave, they returned to their own country by another route, for God

1:8b Or ancestor; also in 1:11.   1:10 Greek Amos, a variant spelling of Amon; also in 1:10b. See 1 Chr 3:14.   1:11 Greek Jeconiah, a variant spelling of Jehoiachin; also in 1:12. See 2 Kgs 24:6 and note at 1 Chr 3:16.   1:19 Greek to divorce her.   1:21 Jesus means "The LORD saves."   1:23 Isa 7:14; 8:8, 10 (Greek version).   2:1 Or royal astrologers; Greek reads magi; also in 2:7, 16.   2:2 Or star in the east.   2:6a Greek the rulers.   2:6b Mic 5:2; 2 Sam 5:2.

had warned them in a dream not to return to Herod.

The Escape to Egypt

13After the wise men were gone, an angel of the Lord appeared to Joseph in a dream. "Get up! Flee to Egypt with the child and his mother," the angel said. "Stay there until I tell you to return, because Herod is going to search for the child to kill him."

14That night Joseph left for Egypt with the child and Mary, his mother, 15and they stayed there until Herod's death. This fulfilled what the Lord had spoken through the prophet: "I called my Son out of Egypt."*

16Herod was furious when he realized that the wise men had outwitted him. He sent soldiers to kill all the boys in and around Bethlehem who were two years old and under, based on the wise men's report of the star's first appearance. 17Herod's brutal action fulfilled what God had spoken through the prophet Jeremiah:

18 "A cry was heard in Ramah—
    weeping and great mourning.
Rachel weeps for her children,
    refusing to be comforted,
    for they are dead."*

The Return to Nazareth

19When Herod died, an angel of the Lord appeared in a dream to Joseph in Egypt. 20"Get up!" the angel said. "Take the child and his mother back to the land of Israel, because those who were trying to kill the child are dead."

21So Joseph got up and returned to the land of Israel with Jesus and his mother. 22But when he learned that the new ruler of Judea was Herod's son Archelaus, he was afraid to go there. Then, after being warned in a dream, he left for the region of Galilee. 23So the family went and lived in a town called Nazareth. This fulfilled what the prophets had said: "He will be called a Nazarene."

John the Baptist Prepares the Way

3 In those days John the Baptist came to the Judean wilderness and began preaching. His message was, 2"Repent of your sins and turn to God, for the Kingdom of Heaven is near.*" 3The prophet Isaiah was speaking about John when he said,

"He is a voice shouting in the wilderness,
'Prepare the way for the LORD's coming!
    Clear the road for him!'"*

4John's clothes were woven from coarse camel hair, and he wore a leather belt around his waist. For food he ate locusts and wild honey. 5People from Jerusalem and from all of Judea and all over the Jordan Valley went out to see and hear John. 6And when they confessed their sins, he baptized them in the Jordan River.

7But when he saw many Pharisees and Sadducees coming to watch him baptize,* he denounced them. "You brood of snakes!" he exclaimed. "Who warned you to flee the coming wrath? 8Prove by the way you live that you have repented of your sins and turned to God. 9Don't just say to each other, 'We're safe, for we are descendants of Abraham.' That means nothing, for I tell you, God can create children of Abraham from these very stones. 10Even now the ax of God's judgment is poised, ready to sever the roots of the trees. Yes, every tree that does not produce good fruit will be chopped down and thrown into the fire.

11"I baptize with* water those who repent of their sins and turn to God. But someone is coming soon who is greater than I am—so much greater that I'm not worthy even to be his slave and carry his sandals. He will baptize you with the Holy Spirit and with fire.* 12He is ready to separate the chaff from the wheat with his winnowing fork. Then he will clean up the threshing area, gathering the wheat into his barn but burning the chaff with never-ending fire."

The Baptism of Jesus

13Then Jesus went from Galilee to the Jordan River to be baptized by John. 14But John tried to talk him out of it. "I am the one who needs to be baptized by you," he said, "so why are you coming to me?"

15But Jesus said, "It should be done, for we must carry out all that God requires.*" So John agreed to baptize him.

16After his baptism, as Jesus came up out of the water, the heavens were opened* and he saw the Spirit of God descending like a dove and settling on him. 17And a voice from heaven said, "This is my dearly loved Son, who brings me great joy."

2:15 Hos 11:1.   2:18 Jer 31:15.   3:2 Or has come, or is coming soon.   3:3 Isa 40:3 (Greek version).   3:7 Or coming to be baptized.   3:11a Or in.   3:11b Or in the Holy Spirit and in fire.   3:15 Or for we must fulfill all righteousness.   3:16 Some manuscripts read opened to him.

The Temptation of Jesus

4 Then Jesus was led by the Spirit into the wilderness to be tempted there by the devil. ²For forty days and forty nights he fasted and became very hungry.

³During that time the devil* came and said to him, "If you are the Son of God, tell these stones to become loaves of bread."

⁴But Jesus told him, "No! The Scriptures say,

'People do not live by bread alone,
    but by every word that comes from the
        mouth of God.'*"

⁵Then the devil took him to the holy city, Jerusalem, to the highest point of the Temple, ⁶and said, "If you are the Son of God, jump off! For the Scriptures say,

'He will order his angels to protect you.
And they will hold you up with their
        hands
    so you won't even hurt your foot on a
        stone.'*"

⁷Jesus responded, "The Scriptures also say, 'You must not test the LORD your God.'*"

⁸Next the devil took him to the peak of a very high mountain and showed him all the kingdoms of the world and their glory. ⁹"I will give it all to you," he said, "if you will kneel down and worship me."

¹⁰"Get out of here, Satan," Jesus told him. "For the Scriptures say,

'You must worship the LORD your God
    and serve only him.'*"

¹¹Then the devil went away, and angels came and took care of Jesus.

The Ministry of Jesus Begins

¹²When Jesus heard that John had been arrested, he left Judea and returned to Galilee. ¹³He went first to Nazareth, then left there and moved to Capernaum, beside the Sea of Galilee, in the region of Zebulun and Naphtali. ¹⁴This fulfilled what God said through the prophet Isaiah:

¹⁵ "In the land of Zebulun and of Naphtali,
        beside the sea, beyond the Jordan River,
        in Galilee where so many Gentiles live,

¹⁶ the people who sat in darkness
        have seen a great light.
    And for those who lived in the land where
        death casts its shadow,
        a light has shined."*

¹⁷From then on Jesus began to preach, "Repent of your sins and turn to God, for the Kingdom of Heaven is near.*"

The First Disciples

¹⁸One day as Jesus was walking along the shore of the Sea of Galilee, he saw two brothers—Simon, also called Peter, and Andrew—throwing a net into the water, for they fished for a living. ¹⁹Jesus called out to them, "Come, follow me, and I will show you how to fish for people!" ²⁰And they left their nets at once and followed him.

²¹A little farther up the shore he saw two other brothers, James and John, sitting in a boat with their father, Zebedee, repairing their nets. And he called them to come, too. ²²They immediately followed him, leaving the boat and their father behind.

Crowds Follow Jesus

²³Jesus traveled throughout the region of Galilee, teaching in the synagogues and announcing the Good News about the Kingdom. And he healed every kind of disease and illness. ²⁴News about him spread as far as Syria, and people soon began bringing to him all who were sick. And whatever their sickness or disease, or if they were demon possessed or epileptic or paralyzed—he healed them all. ²⁵Large crowds followed him wherever he went—people from Galilee, the Ten Towns,* Jerusalem, from all over Judea, and from east of the Jordan River.

The Sermon on the Mount

5 One day as he saw the crowds gathering, Jesus went up on the mountainside and sat down. His disciples gathered around him, ²and he began to teach them.

The Beatitudes

³ "God blesses those who are poor and
        realize their need for him,*
        for the Kingdom of Heaven is theirs.

⁴ God blesses those who mourn,
        for they will be comforted.

⁵ God blesses those who are humble,
        for they will inherit the whole earth.

4:3 Greek *the tempter.* 4:4 Deut 8:3. 4:6 Ps 91:11-12. 4:7 Deut 6:16. 4:10 Deut 6:13. 4:15-16 Isa 9:1-2 (Greek version).
4:17 Or *has come,* or *is coming soon.* 4:25 Greek *Decapolis.* 5:3 Greek *poor in spirit.*

⁶ God blesses those who hunger and thirst
    for justice,*
    for they will be satisfied.
⁷ God blesses those who are merciful,
    for they will be shown mercy.
⁸ God blesses those whose hearts are pure,
    for they will see God.
⁹ God blesses those who work for peace,
    for they will be called the children of God.
¹⁰ God blesses those who are persecuted for
    doing right,
    for the Kingdom of Heaven is theirs.

¹¹"God blesses you when people mock you and persecute you and lie about you and say all sorts of evil things against you because you are my followers. ¹²Be happy about it! Be very glad! For a great reward awaits you in heaven. And remember, the ancient prophets were persecuted in the same way.

Teaching about Salt and Light

¹³"You are the salt of the earth. But what good is salt if it has lost its flavor? Can you make it salty again? It will be thrown out and trampled underfoot as worthless.

¹⁴"You are the light of the world—like a city on a hilltop that cannot be hidden. ¹⁵No one lights a lamp and then puts it under a basket. Instead, a lamp is placed on a stand, where it gives light to everyone in the house. ¹⁶In the same way, let your good deeds shine out for all to see, so that everyone will praise your heavenly Father.

Teaching about the Law

¹⁷"Don't misunderstand why I have come. I did not come to abolish the law of Moses or the writings of the prophets. No, I came to accomplish their purpose. ¹⁸I tell you the truth, until heaven and earth disappear, not even the smallest detail of God's law will disappear until its purpose is achieved. ¹⁹So if you ignore the least commandment and teach others to do the same, you will be called the least in the Kingdom of Heaven. But anyone who obeys God's laws and teaches them will be called great in the Kingdom of Heaven.

²⁰"But I warn you—unless your righteousness is better than the righteousness of the teachers of religious law and the Pharisees, you will never enter the Kingdom of Heaven!

Teaching about Anger

²¹"You have heard that our ancestors were told, 'You must not murder. If you commit murder, you are subject to judgment.'* ²²But I say, if you are even angry with someone,* you are subject to judgment! If you call someone an idiot,* you are in danger of being brought before the court. And if you curse someone,* you are in danger of the fires of hell.*

²³"So if you are presenting a sacrifice* at the altar in the Temple and you suddenly remember that someone has something against you, ²⁴leave your sacrifice there at the altar. Go and be reconciled to that person. Then come and offer your sacrifice to God.

²⁵"When you are on the way to court with your adversary, settle your differences quickly. Otherwise, your accuser may hand you over to the judge, who will hand you over to an officer, and you will be thrown into prison. ²⁶And if that happens, you surely won't be free again until you have paid the last penny.*

Teaching about Adultery

²⁷"You have heard the commandment that says, 'You must not commit adultery.'* ²⁸But I say, anyone who even looks at a woman with lust has already committed adultery with her in his heart. ²⁹So if your eye—even your good eye*—causes you to lust, gouge it out and throw it away. It is better for you to lose one part of your body than for your whole body to be thrown into hell. ³⁰And if your hand—even your stronger hand*—causes you to sin, cut it off and throw it away. It is better for you to lose one part of your body than for your whole body to be thrown into hell.

Teaching about Divorce

³¹"You have heard the law that says, 'A man can divorce his wife by merely giving her a written notice of divorce.'* ³²But I say that a man who divorces his wife, unless she has been unfaithful, causes her to commit adultery. And anyone who marries a divorced woman also commits adultery.

Teaching about Vows

³³"You have also heard that our ancestors were told, 'You must not break your vows; you must carry out the vows you make to the LORD.'* ³⁴But I say, do not make any vows! Do not say,

---

5:6 Or for righteousness.   5:21 Exod 20:13; Deut 5:17.   5:22a Some manuscripts add without cause.   5:22b Greek uses an Aramaic term of contempt: If you say to your brother, 'Raca.'   5:22c Greek if you say, 'You fool.'   5:22d Greek Gehenna; also in 5:29, 30.   5:23 Greek gift; also in 5:24.   5:26 Greek the last kodrantes [i.e., quadrans].   5:27 Exod 20:14; Deut 5:18. 5:29 Greek your right eye.   5:30 Greek your right hand.   5:31 Deut 24:1.   5:33 Num 30:2.

'By heaven!' because heaven is God's throne. ³⁵And do not say, 'By the earth!' because the earth is his footstool. And do not say, 'By Jerusalem!' for Jerusalem is the city of the great King. ³⁶Do not even say, 'By my head!' for you can't turn one hair white or black. ³⁷Just say a simple, 'Yes, I will,' or 'No, I won't.' Anything beyond this is from the evil one.

Teaching about Revenge

³⁸"You have heard the law that says the punishment must match the injury: 'An eye for an eye, and a tooth for a tooth.'* ³⁹But I say, do not resist an evil person! If someone slaps you on the right cheek, offer the other cheek also. ⁴⁰If you are sued in court and your shirt is taken from you, give your coat, too. ⁴¹If a soldier demands that you carry his gear for a mile,* carry it two miles. ⁴²Give to those who ask, and don't turn away from those who want to borrow.

Teaching about Love for Enemies

⁴³"You have heard the law that says, 'Love your neighbor'* and hate your enemy. ⁴⁴But I say, love your enemies!* Pray for those who persecute you! ⁴⁵In that way, you will be acting as true children of your Father in heaven. For he gives his sunlight to both the evil and the good, and he sends rain on the just and the unjust alike. ⁴⁶If you love only those who love you, what reward is there for that? Even corrupt tax collectors do that much. ⁴⁷If you are kind only to your friends,* how are you different from anyone else? Even pagans do that. ⁴⁸But you are to be perfect, even as your Father in heaven is perfect.

Teaching about Giving to the Needy

6 "Watch out! Don't do your good deeds publicly, to be admired by others, for you will lose the reward from your Father in heaven. ²When you give to someone in need, don't do as the hypocrites do—blowing trumpets in the synagogues and streets to call attention to their acts of charity! I tell you the truth, they have received all the reward they will ever get. ³But when you give to someone in need, don't let your left hand know what your right hand is doing. ⁴Give your gifts in private, and your Father, who sees everything, will reward you.

Teaching about Prayer and Fasting

⁵"When you pray, don't be like the hypocrites who love to pray publicly on street corners and in the synagogues where everyone can see them. I tell you the truth, that is all the reward they will ever get. ⁶But when you pray, go away by yourself, shut the door behind you, and pray to your Father in private. Then your Father, who sees everything, will reward you.

⁷"When you pray, don't babble on and on as the Gentiles do. They think their prayers are answered merely by repeating their words again and again. ⁸Don't be like them, for your Father knows exactly what you need even before you ask him! ⁹Pray like this:

Our Father in heaven,
    may your name be kept holy.
¹⁰ May your Kingdom come soon.
May your will be done on earth,
    as it is in heaven.
¹¹ Give us today the food we need,*
¹² and forgive us our sins,
    as we have forgiven those who sin
      against us.
¹³ And don't let us yield to temptation,*
    but rescue us from the evil one.*

¹⁴"If you forgive those who sin against you, your heavenly Father will forgive you. ¹⁵But if you refuse to forgive others, your Father will not forgive your sins.

¹⁶"And when you fast, don't make it obvious, as the hypocrites do, for they try to look miserable and disheveled so people will admire them for their fasting. I tell you the truth, that is the only reward they will ever get. ¹⁷But when you fast, comb your hair* and wash your face. ¹⁸Then no one will notice that you are fasting, except your Father, who knows what you do in private. And your Father, who sees everything, will reward you.

Teaching about Money and Possessions

¹⁹"Don't store up treasures here on earth, where moths eat them and rust destroys them, and where thieves break in and steal. ²⁰Store your treasures in heaven, where moths and rust cannot destroy, and thieves do not break in and steal. ²¹Wherever your treasure is, there the desires of your heart will also be.

²²"Your eye is like a lamp that provides light

5:38 Greek *the law that says: 'An eye for an eye and a tooth for a tooth.'* Exod 21:24; Lev 24:20; Deut 19:21.   5:41 Greek *milion* [4,854 feet or 1,478 meters].   5:43 Lev 19:18.   5:44 Some manuscripts add *Bless those who curse you. Do good to those who hate you.* Compare Luke 6:27-28.   5:47 Greek *your brothers.*   6:11 Or *Give us today our food for the day;* or *Give us today our food for tomorrow.*   6:13a Or *And keep us from being tested.*   6:13b Or *from evil.* Some manuscripts add *For yours is the kingdom and the power and the glory forever. Amen.*   6:17 Greek *anoint your head.*

for your body. When your eye is healthy, your whole body is filled with light. 23But when your eye is unhealthy, your whole body is filled with darkness. And if the light you think you have is actually darkness, how deep that darkness is!

24"No one can serve two masters. For you will hate one and love the other; you will be devoted to one and despise the other. You cannot serve God and be enslaved to money.

25"That is why I tell you not to worry about everyday life—whether you have enough food and drink, or enough clothes to wear. Isn't life more than food, and your body more than clothing? 26Look at the birds. They don't plant or harvest or store food in barns, for your heavenly Father feeds them. And aren't you far more valuable to him than they are? 27Can all your worries add a single moment to your life?

28"And why worry about your clothing? Look at the lilies of the field and how they grow. They don't work or make their clothing, 29yet Solomon in all his glory was not dressed as beautifully as they are. 30And if God cares so wonderfully for wildflowers that are here today and thrown into the fire tomorrow, he will certainly care for you. Why do you have so little faith?

31"So don't worry about these things, saying, 'What will we eat? What will we drink? What will we wear?' 32These things dominate the thoughts of unbelievers, but your heavenly Father already knows all your needs. 33Seek the Kingdom of God* above all else, and live righteously, and he will give you everything you need.

34"So don't worry about tomorrow, for tomorrow will bring its own worries. Today's trouble is enough for today.

Do Not Judge Others

7 "Do not judge others, and you will not be judged. 2For you will be treated as you treat others.* The standard you use in judging is the standard by which you will be judged.*

3"And why worry about a speck in your friend's eye* when you have a log in your own? 4How can you think of saying to your friend,* 'Let me help you get rid of that speck in your eye,' when you can't see past the log in your own eye? 5Hypocrite! First get rid of the log in your own eye; then you will see well enough to deal with the speck in your friend's eye.

6"Don't waste what is holy on people who

are unholy.* Don't throw your pearls to pigs! They will trample the pearls, then turn and attack you.

Effective Prayer

7"Keep on asking, and you will receive what you ask for. Keep on seeking, and you will find. Keep on knocking, and the door will be opened to you. 8For everyone who asks, receives. Everyone who seeks, finds. And to everyone who knocks, the door will be opened.

9"You parents—if your children ask for a loaf of bread, do you give them a stone instead? 10Or if they ask for a fish, do you give them a snake? Of course not! 11So if you sinful people know how to give good gifts to your children, how much more will your heavenly Father give good gifts to those who ask him.

The Golden Rule

12"Do to others whatever you would like them to do to you. This is the essence of all that is taught in the law and the prophets.

The Narrow Gate

13"You can enter God's Kingdom only through the narrow gate. The highway to hell* is broad, and its gate is wide for the many who choose that way. 14But the gateway to life is very narrow and the road is difficult, and only a few ever find it.

The Tree and Its Fruit

15"Beware of false prophets who come disguised as harmless sheep but are really vicious wolves. 16You can identify them by their fruit, that is, by the way they act. Can you pick grapes from thornbushes, or figs from thistles? 17A good tree produces good fruit, and a bad tree produces bad fruit. 18A good tree can't produce bad fruit, and a bad tree can't produce good fruit. 19So every tree that does not produce good fruit is chopped down and thrown into the fire. 20Yes, just as you can identify a tree by its fruit, so you can identify people by their actions.

True Disciples

21"Not everyone who calls out to me, 'Lord! Lord!' will enter the Kingdom of Heaven. Only those who actually do the will of my Father in heaven will enter. 22On judgment day many will say to me, 'Lord! Lord! We prophesied in

6:33 Some manuscripts do not include of God.   7:2a Or For God will judge you as you judge others.   7:2b Or The measure you give will be the measure you get back.   7:3 Greek your brother's eye; also in 7:5.   7:4 Greek your brother.   7:6 Greek Don't give the sacred to dogs.   7:13 Greek The road that leads to destruction.

your name and cast out demons in your name and performed many miracles in your name.' ²³But I will reply, 'I never knew you. Get away from me, you who break God's laws.'

Building on a Solid Foundation

²⁴"Anyone who listens to my teaching and follows it is wise, like a person who builds a house on solid rock. ²⁵Though the rain comes in torrents and the floodwaters rise and the winds beat against that house, it won't collapse because it is built on bedrock. ²⁶But anyone who hears my teaching and doesn't obey it is foolish, like a person who builds a house on sand. ²⁷When the rains and floods come and the winds beat against that house, it will collapse with a mighty crash."

²⁸When Jesus had finished saying these things, the crowds were amazed at his teaching, ²⁹for he taught with real authority—quite unlike their teachers of religious law.

Jesus Heals a Man with Leprosy

8 Large crowds followed Jesus as he came down the mountainside. ²Suddenly, a man with leprosy approached him and knelt before him. "Lord," the man said, "if you are willing, you can heal me and make me clean."

³Jesus reached out and touched him. "I am willing," he said. "Be healed!" And instantly the leprosy disappeared. ⁴Then Jesus said to him, "Don't tell anyone about this. Instead, go to the priest and let him examine you. Take along the offering required in the law of Moses for those who have been healed of leprosy.* This will be a public testimony that you have been cleansed."

The Faith of a Roman Officer

⁵When Jesus returned to Capernaum, a Roman officer* came and pleaded with him, ⁶"Lord, my young servant* lies in bed, paralyzed and in terrible pain."

⁷Jesus said, "I will come and heal him."

⁸But the officer said, "Lord, I am not worthy to have you come into my home. Just say the word from where you are, and my servant will be healed. ⁹I know this because I am under the authority of my superior officers, and I have authority over my soldiers. I only need to say, 'Go,' and they go, or 'Come,' and they come. And if I say to my slaves, 'Do this,' they do it."

¹⁰When Jesus heard this, he was amazed. Turning to those who were following him, he said, "I tell you the truth, I haven't seen faith like this in all Israel! ¹¹And I tell you this, that many Gentiles will come from all over the world—from east and west—and sit down with Abraham, Isaac, and Jacob at the feast in the Kingdom of Heaven. ¹²But many Israelites—those for whom the Kingdom was prepared—will be thrown into outer darkness, where there will be weeping and gnashing of teeth."

¹³Then Jesus said to the Roman officer, "Go back home. Because you believed, it has happened." And the young servant was healed that same hour.

Jesus Heals Many People

¹⁴When Jesus arrived at Peter's house, Peter's mother-in-law was sick in bed with a high fever. ¹⁵But when Jesus touched her hand, the fever left her. Then she got up and prepared a meal for him.

¹⁶That evening many demon-possessed people were brought to Jesus. He cast out the evil spirits with a simple command, and he healed all the sick. ¹⁷This fulfilled the word of the Lord through the prophet Isaiah, who said,

"He took our sicknesses
    and removed our diseases."*

The Cost of Following Jesus

¹⁸When Jesus saw the crowd around him, he instructed his disciples to cross to the other side of the lake.

¹⁹Then one of the teachers of religious law said to him, "Teacher, I will follow you wherever you go."

²⁰But Jesus replied, "Foxes have dens to live in, and birds have nests, but the Son of Man* has no place even to lay his head."

²¹Another of his disciples said, "Lord, first let me return home and bury my father."

²²But Jesus told him, "Follow me now. Let the spiritually dead bury their own dead.*"

Jesus Calms the Storm

²³Then Jesus got into the boat and started across the lake with his disciples. ²⁴Suddenly, a fierce storm struck the lake, with waves breaking into the boat. But Jesus was sleeping. ²⁵The disciples went and woke him up, shouting, "Lord, save us! We're going to drown!"

²⁶Jesus responded, "Why are you afraid? You have so little faith!" Then he got up and

---

8:4 See Lev 14:2-32.   8:5 Greek *a centurion;* similarly in 8:8, 13.   8:6 Or *child;* also in 8:13.   8:17 Isa 53:4.   8:20 "Son of Man" is a title Jesus used for himself.   8:22 Greek *Let the dead bury their own dead.*

rebuked the wind and waves, and suddenly there was a great calm.

27The disciples were amazed. "Who is this man?" they asked. "Even the winds and waves obey him!"

Jesus Heals Two Demon-Possessed Men

28When Jesus arrived on the other side of the lake, in the region of the Gadarenes,* two men who were possessed by demons met him. They came out of the tombs and were so violent that no one could go through that area.

29They began screaming at him, "Why are you interfering with us, Son of God? Have you come here to torture us before God's appointed time?"

30There happened to be a large herd of pigs feeding in the distance. 31So the demons begged, "If you cast us out, send us into that herd of pigs."

32"All right, go!" Jesus commanded them. So the demons came out of the men and entered the pigs, and the whole herd plunged down the steep hillside into the lake and drowned in the water.

33The herdsmen fled to the nearby town, telling everyone what happened to the demon-possessed men. 34Then the entire town came out to meet Jesus, but they begged him to go away and leave them alone.

Jesus Heals a Paralyzed Man

9 Jesus climbed into a boat and went back across the lake to his own town. 2Some people brought to him a paralyzed man on a mat. Seeing their faith, Jesus said to the paralyzed man, "Be encouraged, my child! Your sins are forgiven."

3But some of the teachers of religious law said to themselves, "That's blasphemy! Does he think he's God?"

4Jesus knew* what they were thinking, so he asked them, "Why do you have such evil thoughts in your hearts? 5Is it easier to say 'Your sins are forgiven,' or 'Stand up and walk'? 6So I will prove to you that the Son of Man* has the authority on earth to forgive sins." Then Jesus turned to the paralyzed man and said, "Stand up, pick up your mat, and go home!"

7And the man jumped up and went home! 8Fear swept through the crowd as they saw this happen. And they praised God for giving humans such authority.

Jesus Calls Matthew

9As Jesus was walking along, he saw a man named Matthew sitting at his tax collector's booth. "Follow me and be my disciple," Jesus said to him. So Matthew got up and followed him.

10Later, Matthew invited Jesus and his disciples to his home as dinner guests, along with many tax collectors and other disreputable sinners. 11But when the Pharisees saw this, they asked his disciples, "Why does your teacher eat with such scum?*"

12When Jesus heard this, he said, "Healthy people don't need a doctor—sick people do." 13Then he added, "Now go and learn the meaning of this Scripture: 'I want you to show mercy, not offer sacrifices.'* For I have come to call not those who think they are righteous, but those who know they are sinners."

A Discussion about Fasting

14One day the disciples of John the Baptist came to Jesus and asked him, "Why don't your disciples fast* like we do and the Pharisees do?"

15Jesus replied, "Do wedding guests mourn while celebrating with the groom? Of course not. But someday the groom will be taken away from them, and then they will fast.

16"Besides, who would patch old clothing with new cloth? For the new patch would shrink and rip away from the old cloth, leaving an even bigger tear than before.

17"And no one puts new wine into old wineskins. For the old skins would burst from the pressure, spilling the wine and ruining the skins. New wine is stored in new wineskins so that both are preserved."

Jesus Heals in Response to Faith

18As Jesus was saying this, the leader of a synagogue came and knelt before him. "My daughter has just died," he said, "but you can bring her back to life again if you just come and lay your hand on her."

19So Jesus and his disciples got up and went with him. 20Just then a woman who had suffered for twelve years with constant bleeding came up behind him. She touched the fringe of his robe, 21for she thought, "If I can just touch his robe, I will be healed."

22Jesus turned around, and when he saw her he said, "Daughter, be encouraged! Your

---

8:28 Other manuscripts read *Gerasenes;* still others read *Gergesenes.* Compare Mark 5:1; Luke 8:26.   9:4 Some manuscripts read *saw.*   9:6 "Son of Man" is a title Jesus used for himself.   9:11 Greek *with tax collectors and sinners?*   9:13 Hos 6:6 (Greek version).   9:14 Some manuscripts read *fast often.*

faith has made you well." And the woman was healed at that moment.

²³When Jesus arrived at the official's home, he saw the noisy crowd and heard the funeral music. ²⁴"Get out!" he told them. "The girl isn't dead; she's only asleep." But the crowd laughed at him. ²⁵After the crowd was put outside, however, Jesus went in and took the girl by the hand, and she stood up! ²⁶The report of this miracle swept through the entire countryside.

Jesus Heals the Blind

²⁷After Jesus left the girl's home, two blind men followed along behind him, shouting, "Son of David, have mercy on us!"

²⁸They went right into the house where he was staying, and Jesus asked them, "Do you believe I can make you see?"

"Yes, Lord," they told him, "we do."

²⁹Then he touched their eyes and said, "Because of your faith, it will happen." ³⁰Then their eyes were opened, and they could see! Jesus sternly warned them, "Don't tell anyone about this." ³¹But instead, they went out and spread his fame all over the region.

³²When they left, a demon-possessed man who couldn't speak was brought to Jesus. ³³So Jesus cast out the demon, and then the man began to speak. The crowds were amazed. "Nothing like this has ever happened in Israel!" they exclaimed.

³⁴But the Pharisees said, "He can cast out demons because he is empowered by the prince of demons."

The Need for Workers

³⁵Jesus traveled through all the towns and villages of that area, teaching in the synagogues and announcing the Good News about the Kingdom. And he healed every kind of disease and illness. ³⁶When he saw the crowds, he had compassion on them because they were confused and helpless, like sheep without a shepherd. ³⁷He said to his disciples, "The harvest is great, but the workers are few. ³⁸So pray to the Lord who is in charge of the harvest; ask him to send more workers into his fields."

Jesus Sends Out the Twelve Apostles

10 Jesus called his twelve disciples together and gave them authority to cast out evil* spirits and to heal every kind of disease and illness. ²Here are the names of the twelve apostles:

first, Simon (also called Peter),
then Andrew (Peter's brother),
James (son of Zebedee),
John (James's brother),
³ Philip,
Bartholomew,
Thomas,
Matthew (the tax collector),
James (son of Alphaeus),
Thaddaeus,*
⁴ Simon (the zealot*),
Judas Iscariot (who later betrayed him).

⁵Jesus sent out the twelve apostles with these instructions: "Don't go to the Gentiles or the Samaritans, ⁶but only to the people of Israel—God's lost sheep. ⁷Go and announce to them that the Kingdom of Heaven is near.* ⁸Heal the sick, raise the dead, cure those with leprosy, and cast out demons. Give as freely as you have received!

⁹"Don't take any money in your money belts—no gold, silver, or even copper coins. ¹⁰Don't carry a traveler's bag with a change of clothes and sandals or even a walking stick. Don't hesitate to accept hospitality, because those who work deserve to be fed.

¹¹"Whenever you enter a city or village, search for a worthy person and stay in his home until you leave town. ¹²When you enter the home, give it your blessing. ¹³If it turns out to be a worthy home, let your blessing stand; if it is not, take back the blessing. ¹⁴If any household or town refuses to welcome you or listen to your message, shake its dust from your feet as you leave. ¹⁵I tell you the truth, the wicked cities of Sodom and Gomorrah will be better off than such a town on the judgment day.

¹⁶"Look, I am sending you out as sheep among wolves. So be as shrewd as snakes and harmless as doves. ¹⁷But beware! For you will be handed over to the courts and will be flogged with whips in the synagogues. ¹⁸You will stand trial before governors and kings because you are my followers. But this will be your opportunity to tell the rulers and other unbelievers about me.* ¹⁹When you are arrested, don't worry about how to respond or what to say. God will give you the right words at the right time. ²⁰For it is not you who will be speaking—it will be the Spirit of your Father speaking through you.

²¹"A brother will betray his brother to death,

10:1 Greek *unclean.*   10:3 Other manuscripts read *Lebbaeus;* still others read *Lebbaeus who is called Thaddaeus.*   10:4 Greek *the Cananean,* an Aramaic term for Jewish nationalists.   10:7 Or *has come,* or *is coming soon.*   10:18 Or *But this will be your testimony against the rulers and other unbelievers.*

a father will betray his own child, and children will rebel against their parents and cause them to be killed. 22And all nations will hate you because you are my followers.* But everyone who endures to the end will be saved. 23When you are persecuted in one town, flee to the next. I tell you the truth, the Son of Man* will return before you have reached all the towns of Israel.

24"Students* are not greater than their teacher, and slaves are not greater than their master. 25Students are to be like their teacher, and slaves are to be like their master. And since I, the master of the household, have been called the prince of demons,* the members of my household will be called by even worse names!

26"But don't be afraid of those who threaten you. For the time is coming when everything that is covered will be revealed, and all that is secret will be made known to all. 27What I tell you now in the darkness, shout abroad when daybreak comes. What I whisper in your ear, shout from the housetops for all to hear!

28"Don't be afraid of those who want to kill your body; they cannot touch your soul. Fear only God, who can destroy both soul and body in hell.* 29What is the price of two sparrows— one copper coin*? But not a single sparrow can fall to the ground without your Father knowing it. 30And the very hairs on your head are all numbered. 31So don't be afraid; you are more valuable to God than a whole flock of sparrows.

32"Everyone who acknowledges me publicly here on earth, I will also acknowledge before my Father in heaven. 33But everyone who denies me here on earth, I will also deny before my Father in heaven.

34"Don't imagine that I came to bring peace to the earth! I came not to bring peace, but a sword.

35 'I have come to set a man against his father,
　　a daughter against her mother,
and a daughter-in-law against her
　　mother-in-law.
36　Your enemies will be right in your own
　　household!'*

37"If you love your father or mother more than you love me, you are not worthy of being mine; or if you love your son or daughter more than me, you are not worthy of being mine. 38If you refuse to take up your cross and follow me,

you are not worthy of being mine. 39If you cling to your life, you will lose it; but if you give up your life for me, you will find it.

40"Anyone who receives you receives me, and anyone who receives me receives the Father who sent me. 41If you receive a prophet as one who speaks for God,* you will be given the same reward as a prophet. And if you receive righteous people because of their righteousness, you will be given a reward like theirs. 42And if you give even a cup of cold water to one of the least of my followers, you will surely be rewarded."

Jesus and John the Baptist

11 When Jesus had finished giving these instructions to his twelve disciples, he went out to teach and preach in towns throughout the region.

2John the Baptist, who was in prison, heard about all the things the Messiah was doing. So he sent his disciples to ask Jesus, 3"Are you the Messiah we've been expecting,* or should we keep looking for someone else?"

4Jesus told them, "Go back to John and tell him what you have heard and seen—5the blind see, the lame walk, those with leprosy are cured, the deaf hear, the dead are raised to life, and the Good News is being preached to the poor." 6And he added, "God blesses those who do not fall away because of me.*"

7As John's disciples were leaving, Jesus began talking about him to the crowds. "What kind of man did you go into the wilderness to see? Was he a weak reed, swayed by every breath of wind? 8Or were you expecting to see a man dressed in expensive clothes? No, people with expensive clothes live in palaces. 9Were you looking for a prophet? Yes, and he is more than a prophet. 10John is the man to whom the Scriptures refer when they say,

'Look, I am sending my messenger ahead
　　of you,
　and he will prepare your way before
　　you.'*

11"I tell you the truth, of all who have ever lived, none is greater than John the Baptist. Yet even the least person in the Kingdom of Heaven is greater than he is! 12And from the time John the Baptist began preaching until

10:22 Greek *on account of my name.*　10:23 "Son of Man" is a title Jesus used for himself.　10:24 Or *Disciples.*　10:25 Greek *Beelzeboul;* other manuscripts read *Beezeboul;* Latin version reads *Beelzebub.*　10:28 Greek *Gehenna.*　10:29 Greek *one assarion* [i.e., one "as," a Roman coin equal to ¹⁄₁₆ of a denarius].　10:35-36 Mic 7:6.　10:41 Greek *receive a prophet in the name of a prophet.*　11:3 Greek *Are you the one who is coming?*　11:6 Or *who are not offended by me.*　11:10 Mal 3:1.

now, the Kingdom of Heaven has been forcefully advancing,* and violent people are attacking it. [13]For before John came, all the prophets and the law of Moses looked forward to this present time. [14]And if you are willing to accept what I say, he is Elijah, the one the prophets said would come.* [15]Anyone with ears to hear should listen and understand!

[16]"To what can I compare this generation? It is like children playing a game in the public square. They complain to their friends,

[17] 'We played wedding songs,
      and you didn't dance,
   so we played funeral songs,
      and you didn't mourn.'

[18]For John didn't spend his time eating and drinking, and you say, 'He's possessed by a demon.' [19]The Son of Man,* on the other hand, feasts and drinks, and you say, 'He's a glutton and a drunkard, and a friend of tax collectors and other sinners!' But wisdom is shown to be right by its results."

Judgment for the Unbelievers

[20]Then Jesus began to denounce the towns where he had done so many of his miracles, because they hadn't repented of their sins and turned to God. [21]"What sorrow awaits you, Korazin and Bethsaida! For if the miracles I did in you had been done in wicked Tyre and Sidon, their people would have repented of their sins long ago, clothing themselves in burlap and throwing ashes on their heads to show their remorse. [22]I tell you, Tyre and Sidon will be better off on judgment day than you.

[23]"And you people of Capernaum, will you be honored in heaven? No, you will go down to the place of the dead.* For if the miracles I did for you had been done in wicked Sodom, it would still be here today. [24]I tell you, even Sodom will be better off on judgment day than you."

Jesus' Prayer of Thanksgiving

[25]At that time Jesus prayed this prayer: "O Father, Lord of heaven and earth, thank you for hiding these things from those who think themselves wise and clever, and for revealing them to the childlike. [26]Yes, Father, it pleased you to do it this way!

[27]"My Father has entrusted everything to me. No one truly knows the Son except the Father, and no one truly knows the Father except the Son and those to whom the Son chooses to reveal him."

[28]Then Jesus said, "Come to me, all of you who are weary and carry heavy burdens, and I will give you rest. [29]Take my yoke upon you. Let me teach you, because I am humble and gentle at heart, and you will find rest for your souls. [30]For my yoke is easy to bear, and the burden I give you is light."

A Discussion about the Sabbath

12 At about that time Jesus was walking through some grainfields on the Sabbath. His disciples were hungry, so they began breaking off some heads of grain and eating them. [2]But some Pharisees saw them do it and protested, "Look, your disciples are breaking the law by harvesting grain on the Sabbath."

[3]Jesus said to them, "Haven't you read in the Scriptures what David did when he and his companions were hungry? [4]He went into the house of God, and he and his companions broke the law by eating the sacred loaves of bread that only the priests are allowed to eat. [5]And haven't you read in the law of Moses that the priests on duty in the Temple may work on the Sabbath? [6]I tell you, there is one here who is even greater than the Temple! [7]But you would not have condemned my innocent disciples if you knew the meaning of this Scripture: 'I want you to show mercy, not offer sacrifices.'* [8]For the Son of Man* is Lord, even over the Sabbath!"

Jesus Heals on the Sabbath

[9]Then Jesus went over to their synagogue, [10]where he noticed a man with a deformed hand. The Pharisees asked Jesus, "Does the law permit a person to work by healing on the Sabbath?" (They were hoping he would say yes, so they could bring charges against him.)

[11]And he answered, "If you had a sheep that fell into a well on the Sabbath, wouldn't you work to pull it out? Of course you would. [12]And how much more valuable is a person than a sheep! Yes, the law permits a person to do good on the Sabbath."

[13]Then he said to the man, "Hold out your hand." So the man held out his hand, and it was restored, just like the other one! [14]Then the Pharisees called a meeting to plot how to kill Jesus.

11:12 Or *the Kingdom of Heaven has suffered from violence.*   11:14 See Mal 4:5.   11:19 "Son of Man" is a title Jesus used for himself.   11:23 Greek *to Hades.*   12:7 Hos 6:6 (Greek version).   12:8 "Son of Man" is a title Jesus used for himself.

Jesus, God's Chosen Servant

¹⁵But Jesus knew what they were planning. So he left that area, and many people followed him. He healed all the sick among them, ¹⁶but he warned them not to reveal who he was. ¹⁷This fulfilled the prophecy of Isaiah concerning him:

¹⁸ "Look at my Servant, whom I have chosen.
　He is my Beloved, who pleases me.
　I will put my Spirit upon him,
　　and he will proclaim justice to the
　　nations.
¹⁹ He will not fight or shout
　　or raise his voice in public.
²⁰ He will not crush the weakest reed
　　or put out a flickering candle.
　Finally he will cause justice to be
　　victorious.
²¹ And his name will be the hope
　　of all the world."*

Jesus and the Prince of Demons

²²Then a demon-possessed man, who was blind and couldn't speak, was brought to Jesus. He healed the man so that he could both speak and see. ²³The crowd was amazed and asked, "Could it be that Jesus is the Son of David, the Messiah?"

²⁴But when the Pharisees heard about the miracle, they said, "No wonder he can cast out demons. He gets his power from Satan,* the prince of demons."

²⁵Jesus knew their thoughts and replied, "Any kingdom divided by civil war is doomed. A town or family splintered by feuding will fall apart. ²⁶And if Satan is casting out Satan, he is divided and fighting against himself. His own kingdom will not survive. ²⁷And if I am empowered by Satan, what about your own exorcists? They cast out demons, too, so they will condemn you for what you have said. ²⁸But if I am casting out demons by the Spirit of God, then the Kingdom of God has arrived among you. ²⁹For who is powerful enough to enter the house of a strong man and plunder his goods? Only someone even stronger—someone who could tie him up and then plunder his house.

³⁰"Anyone who isn't with me opposes me, and anyone who isn't working with me is actually working against me.

³¹"So I tell you, every sin and blasphemy can be forgiven—except blasphemy against the Holy Spirit, which will never be forgiven. ³²Anyone who speaks against the Son of Man can be forgiven, but anyone who speaks against the Holy Spirit will never be forgiven, either in this world or in the world to come.

³³"A tree is identified by its fruit. If a tree is good, its fruit will be good. If a tree is bad, its fruit will be bad. ³⁴You brood of snakes! How could evil men like you speak what is good and right? For whatever is in your heart determines what you say. ³⁵A good person produces good things from the treasury of a good heart, and an evil person produces evil things from the treasury of an evil heart. ³⁶And I tell you this, you must give an account on judgment day for every idle word you speak. ³⁷The words you say will either acquit you or condemn you."

The Sign of Jonah

³⁸One day some teachers of religious law and Pharisees came to Jesus and said, "Teacher, we want you to show us a miraculous sign to prove your authority."

³⁹But Jesus replied, "Only an evil, adulterous generation would demand a miraculous sign; but the only sign I will give them is the sign of the prophet Jonah. ⁴⁰For as Jonah was in the belly of the great fish for three days and three nights, so will the Son of Man be in the heart of the earth for three days and three nights.

⁴¹"The people of Nineveh will stand up against this generation on judgment day and condemn it, for they repented of their sins at the preaching of Jonah. Now someone greater than Jonah is here—but you refuse to repent. ⁴²The queen of Sheba* will also stand up against this generation on judgment day and condemn it, for she came from a distant land to hear the wisdom of Solomon. Now someone greater than Solomon is here—but you refuse to listen.

⁴³"When an evil* spirit leaves a person, it goes into the desert, seeking rest but finding none. ⁴⁴Then it says, 'I will return to the person I came from.' So it returns and finds its former home empty, swept, and in order. ⁴⁵Then the spirit finds seven other spirits more evil than itself, and they all enter the person and live there. And so that person is worse off than before. That will be the experience of this evil generation."

The True Family of Jesus

⁴⁶As Jesus was speaking to the crowd, his mother and brothers stood outside, asking

---

12:18-21 Isa 42:1-4 (Greek version for 42:4). 　12:24 Greek *Beelzeboul;* also in 12:27. Other manuscripts read *Beezeboul;* Latin version reads *Beelzebub.* 　12:42 Greek *The queen of the south.* 　12:43 Greek *unclean.*

to speak to him. 47Someone told Jesus, "Your mother and your brothers are standing outside, and they want to speak to you."*

48Jesus asked, "Who is my mother? Who are my brothers?" 49Then he pointed to his disciples and said, "Look, these are my mother and brothers. 50Anyone who does the will of my Father in heaven is my brother and sister and mother!"

Parable of the Farmer Scattering Seed

13 Later that same day Jesus left the house and sat beside the lake. 2A large crowd soon gathered around him, so he got into a boat. Then he sat there and taught as the people stood on the shore. 3He told many stories in the form of parables, such as this one:

"Listen! A farmer went out to plant some seeds. 4As he scattered them across his field, some seeds fell on a footpath, and the birds came and ate them. 5Other seeds fell on shallow soil with underlying rock. The seeds sprouted quickly because the soil was shallow. 6But the plants soon wilted under the hot sun, and since they didn't have deep roots, they died. 7Other seeds fell among thorns that grew up and choked out the tender plants. 8Still other seeds fell on fertile soil, and they produced a crop that was thirty, sixty, and even a hundred times as much as had been planted! 9Anyone with ears to hear should listen and understand."

10His disciples came and asked him, "Why do you use parables when you talk to the people?"

11He replied, "You are permitted to understand the secrets* of the Kingdom of Heaven, but others are not. 12To those who listen to my teaching, more understanding will be given, and they will have an abundance of knowledge. But for those who are not listening, even what little understanding they have will be taken away from them. 13That is why I use these parables,

For they look, but they don't really see.
    They hear, but they don't really listen or
        understand.

14This fulfills the prophecy of Isaiah that says,

'When you hear what I say,
    you will not understand.
When you see what I do,
    you will not comprehend.

15 For the hearts of these people are hardened,
    and their ears cannot hear,
and they have closed their eyes—
    so their eyes cannot see,
and their ears cannot hear,
    and their hearts cannot understand,
and they cannot turn to me
    and let me heal them.'*

16"But blessed are your eyes, because they see; and your ears, because they hear. 17I tell you the truth, many prophets and righteous people longed to see what you see, but they didn't see it. And they longed to hear what you hear, but they didn't hear it.

18"Now listen to the explanation of the parable about the farmer planting seeds: 19The seed that fell on the footpath represents those who hear the message about the Kingdom and don't understand it. Then the evil one comes and snatches away the seed that was planted in their hearts. 20The seed on the rocky soil represents those who hear the message and immediately receive it with joy. 21But since they don't have deep roots, they don't last long. They fall away as soon as they have problems or are persecuted for believing God's word. 22The seed that fell among the thorns represents those who hear God's word, but all too quickly the message is crowded out by the worries of this life and the lure of wealth, so no fruit is produced. 23The seed that fell on good soil represents those who truly hear and understand God's word and produce a harvest of thirty, sixty, or even a hundred times as much as had been planted!"

Parable of the Wheat and Weeds

24Here is another story Jesus told: "The Kingdom of Heaven is like a farmer who planted good seed in his field. 25But that night as the workers slept, his enemy came and planted weeds among the wheat, then slipped away. 26When the crop began to grow and produce grain, the weeds also grew.

27"The farmer's workers went to him and said, 'Sir, the field where you planted that good seed is full of weeds! Where did they come from?'

28"'An enemy has done this!' the farmer exclaimed.

"'Should we pull out the weeds?' they asked.

29"'No,' he replied, 'you'll uproot the wheat if you do. 30Let both grow together until the harvest. Then I will tell the harvesters to sort

12:47 Some manuscripts do not include verse 47. Compare Mark 3:32 and Luke 8:20. 13:11 Greek *the mysteries.* 13:14-15 Isa 6:9-10 (Greek version).

out the weeds, tie them into bundles, and burn them, and to put the wheat in the barn.'"

Parable of the Mustard Seed

31Here is another illustration Jesus used: "The Kingdom of Heaven is like a mustard seed planted in a field. 32It is the smallest of all seeds, but it becomes the largest of garden plants; it grows into a tree, and birds come and make nests in its branches."

Parable of the Yeast

33Jesus also used this illustration: "The Kingdom of Heaven is like the yeast a woman used in making bread. Even though she put only a little yeast in three measures of flour, it permeated every part of the dough."

34Jesus always used stories and illustrations like these when speaking to the crowds. In fact, he never spoke to them without using such parables. 35This fulfilled what God had spoken through the prophet:

"I will speak to you in parables.
    I will explain things hidden since the
        creation of the world.*"

Parable of the Wheat and Weeds Explained

36Then, leaving the crowds outside, Jesus went into the house. His disciples said, "Please explain to us the story of the weeds in the field."

37Jesus replied, "The Son of Man* is the farmer who plants the good seed. 38The field is the world, and the good seed represents the people of the Kingdom. The weeds are the people who belong to the evil one. 39The enemy who planted the weeds among the wheat is the devil. The harvest is the end of the world,* and the harvesters are the angels.

40"Just as the weeds are sorted out and burned in the fire, so it will be at the end of the world. 41The Son of Man will send his angels, and they will remove from his Kingdom everything that causes sin and all who do evil. 42And the angels will throw them into the fiery furnace, where there will be weeping and gnashing of teeth. 43Then the righteous will shine like the sun in their Father's Kingdom. Anyone with ears to hear should listen and understand!

Parables of the Hidden Treasure and the Pearl

44"The Kingdom of Heaven is like a treasure that a man discovered hidden in a field. In his excitement, he hid it again and sold everything he owned to get enough money to buy the field.

45"Again, the Kingdom of Heaven is like a merchant on the lookout for choice pearls. 46When he discovered a pearl of great value, he sold everything he owned and bought it!

Parable of the Fishing Net

47"Again, the Kingdom of Heaven is like a fishing net that was thrown into the water and caught fish of every kind. 48When the net was full, they dragged it up onto the shore, sat down, and sorted the good fish into crates, but threw the bad ones away. 49That is the way it will be at the end of the world. The angels will come and separate the wicked people from the righteous, 50throwing the wicked into the fiery furnace, where there will be weeping and gnashing of teeth. 51Do you understand all these things?"

"Yes," they said, "we do."

52Then he added, "Every teacher of religious law who becomes a disciple in the Kingdom of Heaven is like a homeowner who brings from his storeroom new gems of truth as well as old."

Jesus Rejected at Nazareth

53When Jesus had finished telling these stories and illustrations, he left that part of the country. 54He returned to Nazareth, his hometown. When he taught there in the synagogue, everyone was amazed and said, "Where does he get this wisdom and the power to do miracles?" 55Then they scoffed, "He's just the carpenter's son, and we know Mary, his mother, and his brothers—James, Joseph,* Simon, and Judas. 56All his sisters live right here among us. Where did he learn all these things?" 57And they were deeply offended and refused to believe in him.

Then Jesus told them, "A prophet is honored everywhere except in his own hometown and among his own family." 58And so he did only a few miracles there because of their unbelief.

The Death of John the Baptist

14 When Herod Antipas, the ruler of Galilee,* heard about Jesus, 2he said to his advisers, "This must be John the Baptist raised from the dead! That is why he can do such miracles."

3For Herod had arrested and imprisoned John as a favor to his wife Herodias (the former

---

13:35 Some manuscripts do not include *of the world.* Ps 78:2.   13:37 "Son of Man" is a title Jesus used for himself.   13:39 Or *the age;* also in 13:40, 49.   13:55 Other manuscripts read *Joses;* still others read *John.*   14:1 Greek *Herod the tetrarch.* Herod Antipas was a son of King Herod and was ruler over Galilee.

wife of Herod's brother Philip). ⁴John had been telling Herod, "It is against God's law for you to marry her." ⁵Herod wanted to kill John, but he was afraid of a riot, because all the people believed John was a prophet.

⁶But at a birthday party for Herod, Herodias's daughter performed a dance that greatly pleased him, ⁷so he promised with a vow to give her anything she wanted. ⁸At her mother's urging, the girl said, "I want the head of John the Baptist on a tray!" ⁹Then the king regretted what he had said; but because of the vow he had made in front of his guests, he issued the necessary orders. ¹⁰So John was beheaded in the prison, ¹¹and his head was brought on a tray and given to the girl, who took it to her mother. ¹²Later, John's disciples came for his body and buried it. Then they went and told Jesus what had happened.

Jesus Feeds Five Thousand

¹³As soon as Jesus heard the news, he left in a boat to a remote area to be alone. But the crowds heard where he was headed and followed on foot from many towns. ¹⁴Jesus saw the huge crowd as he stepped from the boat, and he had compassion on them and healed their sick.

¹⁵That evening the disciples came to him and said, "This is a remote place, and it's already getting late. Send the crowds away so they can go to the villages and buy food for themselves."

¹⁶But Jesus said, "That isn't necessary—you feed them."

¹⁷"But we have only five loaves of bread and two fish!" they answered.

¹⁸"Bring them here," he said. ¹⁹Then he told the people to sit down on the grass. Jesus took the five loaves and two fish, looked up toward heaven, and blessed them. Then, breaking the loaves into pieces, he gave the bread to the disciples, who distributed it to the people. ²⁰They all ate as much as they wanted, and afterward, the disciples picked up twelve baskets of leftovers. ²¹About 5,000 men were fed that day, in addition to all the women and children!

Jesus Walks on Water

²²Immediately after this, Jesus insisted that his disciples get back into the boat and cross to the other side of the lake, while he sent the people home. ²³After sending them home, he went up into the hills by himself to pray. Night fell while he was there alone.

²⁴Meanwhile, the disciples were in trouble far away from land, for a strong wind had risen, and they were fighting heavy waves. ²⁵About three o'clock in the morning* Jesus came toward them, walking on the water. ²⁶When the disciples saw him walking on the water, they were terrified. In their fear, they cried out, "It's a ghost!"

²⁷But Jesus spoke to them at once. "Don't be afraid," he said. "Take courage. I am here!*"

²⁸Then Peter called to him, "Lord, if it's really you, tell me to come to you, walking on the water."

²⁹"Yes, come," Jesus said.

So Peter went over the side of the boat and walked on the water toward Jesus. ³⁰But when he saw the strong* wind and the waves, he was terrified and began to sink. "Save me, Lord!" he shouted.

³¹Jesus immediately reached out and grabbed him. "You have so little faith," Jesus said. "Why did you doubt me?"

³²When they climbed back into the boat, the wind stopped. ³³Then the disciples worshiped him. "You really are the Son of God!" they exclaimed.

³⁴After they had crossed the lake, they landed at Gennesaret. ³⁵When the people recognized Jesus, the news of his arrival spread quickly throughout the whole area, and soon people were bringing all their sick to be healed. ³⁶They begged him to let the sick touch at least the fringe of his robe, and all who touched him were healed.

Jesus Teaches about Inner Purity

15 Some Pharisees and teachers of religious law now arrived from Jerusalem to see Jesus. They asked him, ²"Why do your disciples disobey our age-old tradition? For they ignore our tradition of ceremonial hand washing before they eat."

³Jesus replied, "And why do you, by your traditions, violate the direct commandments of God? ⁴For instance, God says, 'Honor your father and mother,'* and 'Anyone who speaks disrespectfully of father or mother must be put to death.'* ⁵But you say it is all right for people to say to their parents, 'Sorry, I can't help you. For I have vowed to give to God what I would have given to you.' ⁶In this way, you say they don't need to honor their parents.* And so you cancel the word of God for the sake of

14:25 Greek *In the fourth watch of the night.*   14:27 Or *The 'I AM' is here;* Greek reads *I am.* See Exod 3:14.   14:30 Some manuscripts do not include *strong.*   15:4a Exod 20:12; Deut 5:16.   15:4b Exod 21:17 (Greek version); Lev 20:9 (Greek version).   15:6 Greek *their father;* other manuscripts read *their father or their mother.*

your own tradition. [7]You hypocrites! Isaiah was right when he prophesied about you, for he wrote,

[8] 'These people honor me with their lips,
    but their hearts are far from me.
[9] Their worship is a farce,
    for they teach man-made ideas as
        commands from God.'*"

[10]Then Jesus called to the crowd to come and hear. "Listen," he said, "and try to understand. [11]It's not what goes into your mouth that defiles you; you are defiled by the words that come out of your mouth."

[12]Then the disciples came to him and asked, "Do you realize you offended the Pharisees by what you just said?"

[13]Jesus replied, "Every plant not planted by my heavenly Father will be uprooted, [14]so ignore them. They are blind guides leading the blind, and if one blind person guides another, they will both fall into a ditch."

[15]Then Peter said to Jesus, "Explain to us the parable that says people aren't defiled by what they eat."

[16]"Don't you understand yet?" Jesus asked. [17]"Anything you eat passes through the stomach and then goes into the sewer. [18]But the words you speak come from the heart—that's what defiles you. [19]For from the heart come evil thoughts, murder, adultery, all sexual immorality, theft, lying, and slander. [20]These are what defile you. Eating with unwashed hands will never defile you."

The Faith of a Gentile Woman

[21]Then Jesus left Galilee and went north to the region of Tyre and Sidon. [22]A Gentile* woman who lived there came to him, pleading, "Have mercy on me, O Lord, Son of David! For my daughter is possessed by a demon that torments her severely."

[23]But Jesus gave her no reply, not even a word. Then his disciples urged him to send her away. "Tell her to go away," they said. "She is bothering us with all her begging."

[24]Then Jesus said to the woman, "I was sent only to help God's lost sheep—the people of Israel."

[25]But she came and worshiped him, pleading again, "Lord, help me!"

[26]Jesus responded, "It isn't right to take food from the children and throw it to the dogs."

[27]She replied, "That's true, Lord, but even dogs are allowed to eat the scraps that fall beneath their masters' table."

[28]"Dear woman," Jesus said to her, "your faith is great. Your request is granted." And her daughter was instantly healed.

Jesus Heals Many People

[29]Jesus returned to the Sea of Galilee and climbed a hill and sat down. [30]A vast crowd brought to him people who were lame, blind, crippled, those who couldn't speak, and many others. They laid them before Jesus, and he healed them all. [31]The crowd was amazed! Those who hadn't been able to speak were talking, the crippled were made well, the lame were walking, and the blind could see again! And they praised the God of Israel.

Jesus Feeds Four Thousand

[32]Then Jesus called his disciples and told them, "I feel sorry for these people. They have been here with me for three days, and they have nothing left to eat. I don't want to send them away hungry, or they will faint along the way."

[33]The disciples replied, "Where would we get enough food here in the wilderness for such a huge crowd?"

[34]Jesus asked, "How much bread do you have?"

They replied, "Seven loaves, and a few small fish."

[35]So Jesus told all the people to sit down on the ground. [36]Then he took the seven loaves and the fish, thanked God for them, and broke them into pieces. He gave them to the disciples, who distributed the food to the crowd. [37]They all ate as much as they wanted. Afterward, the disciples picked up seven large baskets of leftover food. [38]There were 4,000 men who were fed that day, in addition to all the women and children. [39]Then Jesus sent the people home, and he got into a boat and crossed over to the region of Magadan.

Leaders Demand a Miraculous Sign

16 One day the Pharisees and Sadducees came to test Jesus, demanding that he show them a miraculous sign from heaven to prove his authority.

[2]He replied, "You know the saying, 'Red sky at night means fair weather tomorrow; [3]red sky in the morning means foul weather all day.' You know how to interpret the weather signs in the sky, but you don't know how to interpret

15:8-9 Isa 29:13 (Greek version).　　15:22 Greek *Canaanite*.

the signs of the times!* 4Only an evil, adulterous generation would demand a miraculous sign, but the only sign I will give them is the sign of the prophet Jonah.*" Then Jesus left them and went away.

Yeast of the Pharisees and Sadducees

5Later, after they crossed to the other side of the lake, the disciples discovered they had forgotten to bring any bread. 6"Watch out!" Jesus warned them. "Beware of the yeast of the Pharisees and Sadducees."

7At this they began to argue with each other because they hadn't brought any bread. 8Jesus knew what they were saying, so he said, "You have so little faith! Why are you arguing with each other about having no bread? 9Don't you understand even yet? Don't you remember the 5,000 I fed with five loaves, and the baskets of leftovers you picked up? 10Or the 4,000 I fed with seven loaves, and the large baskets of leftovers you picked up? 11Why can't you understand that I'm not talking about bread? So again I say, 'Beware of the yeast of the Pharisees and Sadducees.'"

12Then at last they understood that he wasn't speaking about the yeast in bread, but about the deceptive teaching of the Pharisees and Sadducees.

Peter's Declaration about Jesus

13When Jesus came to the region of Caesarea Philippi, he asked his disciples, "Who do people say that the Son of Man is?"*

14"Well," they replied, "some say John the Baptist, some say Elijah, and others say Jeremiah or one of the other prophets."

15Then he asked them, "But who do you say I am?"

16Simon Peter answered, "You are the Messiah,* the Son of the living God."

17Jesus replied, "You are blessed, Simon son of John,* because my Father in heaven has revealed this to you. You did not learn this from any human being. 18Now I say to you that you are Peter (which means 'rock'),* and upon this rock I will build my church, and all the powers of hell* will not conquer it. 19And I will give you the keys of the Kingdom of Heaven. Whatever you forbid* on earth will be forbidden in heaven, and whatever you permit* on earth will be permitted in heaven."

20Then he sternly warned the disciples not to tell anyone that he was the Messiah.

Jesus Predicts His Death

21From then on Jesus* began to tell his disciples plainly that it was necessary for him to go to Jerusalem, and that he would suffer many terrible things at the hands of the elders, the leading priests, and the teachers of religious law. He would be killed, but on the third day he would be raised from the dead.

22But Peter took him aside and began to reprimand him* for saying such things. "Heaven forbid, Lord," he said. "This will never happen to you!"

23Jesus turned to Peter and said, "Get away from me, Satan! You are a dangerous trap to me. You are seeing things merely from a human point of view, not from God's."

24Then Jesus said to his disciples, "If any of you wants to be my follower, you must give up your own way, take up your cross, and follow me. 25If you try to hang on to your life, you will lose it. But if you give up your life for my sake, you will save it. 26And what do you benefit if you gain the whole world but lose your own soul?* Is anything worth more than your soul? 27For the Son of Man will come with his angels in the glory of his Father and will judge all people according to their deeds. 28And I tell you the truth, some standing here right now will not die before they see the Son of Man coming in his Kingdom."

The Transfiguration

17 Six days later Jesus took Peter and the two brothers, James and John, and led them up a high mountain to be alone. 2As the men watched, Jesus' appearance was transformed so that his face shone like the sun, and his clothes became as white as light. 3Suddenly, Moses and Elijah appeared and began talking with Jesus.

4Peter exclaimed, "Lord, it's wonderful for us to be here! If you want, I'll make three shelters as memorials*—one for you, one for Moses, and one for Elijah."

5But even as he spoke, a bright cloud overshadowed them, and a voice from the cloud said, "This is my dearly loved Son, who brings me great joy. Listen to him." 6The disciples were terrified and fell face down on the ground.

16:2-3 Several manuscripts do not include any of the words in 16:2-3 after He replied.   16:4 Greek the sign of Jonah.
16:13 "Son of Man" is a title Jesus used for himself.   16:16 Or the Christ. Messiah (a Hebrew term) and Christ (a Greek term) both mean "anointed one."   16:17 Greek Simon bar-Jonah; see John 1:42; 21:15-17.   16:18a Greek that you are Peter.
16:18b Greek and the gates of Hades.   16:19a Or bind, or lock.   16:19b Or loose, or open.   16:21 Some manuscripts read Jesus the Messiah.   16:22 Or began to correct him.   16:26 Or your self? also in 16:26b.   17:4 Greek three tabernacles.

⁷Then Jesus came over and touched them. "Get up," he said. "Don't be afraid." ⁸And when they looked up, Moses and Elijah were gone, and they saw only Jesus.

⁹As they went back down the mountain, Jesus commanded them, "Don't tell anyone what you have seen until the Son of Man* has been raised from the dead."

¹⁰Then his disciples asked him, "Why do the teachers of religious law insist that Elijah must return before the Messiah comes?*"

¹¹Jesus replied, "Elijah is indeed coming first to get everything ready. ¹²But I tell you, Elijah has already come, but he wasn't recognized, and they chose to abuse him. And in the same way they will also make the Son of Man suffer." ¹³Then the disciples realized he was talking about John the Baptist.

Jesus Heals a Demon-Possessed Boy

¹⁴At the foot of the mountain, a large crowd was waiting for them. A man came and knelt before Jesus and said, ¹⁵"Lord, have mercy on my son. He has seizures and suffers terribly. He often falls into the fire or into the water. ¹⁶So I brought him to your disciples, but they couldn't heal him."

¹⁷Jesus said, "You faithless and corrupt people! How long must I be with you? How long must I put up with you? Bring the boy here to me." ¹⁸Then Jesus rebuked the demon in the boy, and it left him. From that moment the boy was well.

¹⁹Afterward the disciples asked Jesus privately, "Why couldn't we cast out that demon?"

²⁰"You don't have enough faith," Jesus told them. "I tell you the truth, if you had faith even as small as a mustard seed, you could say to this mountain, 'Move from here to there,' and it would move. Nothing would be impossible.*"

Jesus Again Predicts His Death

²²After they gathered again in Galilee, Jesus told them, "The Son of Man is going to be betrayed into the hands of his enemies. ²³He will be killed, but on the third day he will be raised from the dead." And the disciples were filled with grief.

Payment of the Temple Tax

²⁴On their arrival in Capernaum, the collectors of the Temple tax* came to Peter and asked him, "Doesn't your teacher pay the Temple tax?"

²⁵"Yes, he does," Peter replied. Then he went into the house.

But before he had a chance to speak, Jesus asked him, "What do you think, Peter?* Do kings tax their own people or the people they have conquered?*"

²⁶"They tax the people they have conquered," Peter replied.

"Well, then," Jesus said, "the citizens are free! ²⁷However, we don't want to offend them, so go down to the lake and throw in a line. Open the mouth of the first fish you catch, and you will find a large silver coin.* Take it and pay the tax for both of us."

The Greatest in the Kingdom

18 About that time the disciples came to Jesus and asked, "Who is greatest in the Kingdom of Heaven?"

²Jesus called a little child to him and put the child among them. ³Then he said, "I tell you the truth, unless you turn from your sins and become like little children, you will never get into the Kingdom of Heaven. ⁴So anyone who becomes as humble as this little child is the greatest in the Kingdom of Heaven.

⁵"And anyone who welcomes a little child like this on my behalf* is welcoming me. ⁶But if you cause one of these little ones who trusts in me to fall into sin, it would be better for you to have a large millstone tied around your neck and be drowned in the depths of the sea.

⁷"What sorrow awaits the world, because it tempts people to sin. Temptations are inevitable, but what sorrow awaits the person who does the tempting. ⁸So if your hand or foot causes you to sin, cut it off and throw it away. It's better to enter eternal life with only one hand or one foot than to be thrown into eternal fire with both of your hands and feet. ⁹And if your eye causes you to sin, gouge it out and throw it away. It's better to enter eternal life with only one eye than to have two eyes and be thrown into the fire of hell.*

¹⁰"Beware that you don't look down on any of these little ones. For I tell you that in heaven their angels are always in the presence of my heavenly Father.*

Parable of the Lost Sheep

¹²"If a man has a hundred sheep and one of them wanders away, what will he do? Won't he

---

17:9 "Son of Man" is a title Jesus used for himself.   17:10 Greek *that Elijah must come first?*   17:20 Some manuscripts add verse 21, *But this kind of demon won't leave except by prayer and fasting.* Compare Mark 9:29.   17:24 Greek *the two-drachma [tax];* also in 17:24b. See Exod 30:13-16; Neh 10:32-33.   17:25a Greek *Simon?*   17:25b Greek *their sons or others?*   17:27 Greek *a stater* [a Greek coin equivalent to four drachmas].   18:5 Greek *in my name.*   18:9 Greek *the Gehenna of fire.*   18:10 Some manuscripts add verse 11, *And the Son of Man came to save those who are lost.* Compare Luke 19:10.

leave the ninety-nine others on the hills and go out to search for the one that is lost? ¹³And if he finds it, I tell you the truth, he will rejoice over it more than over the ninety-nine that didn't wander away! ¹⁴In the same way, it is not my heavenly Father's will that even one of these little ones should perish.

Correcting Another Believer

¹⁵"If another believer* sins against you,* go privately and point out the offense. If the other person listens and confesses it, you have won that person back. ¹⁶But if you are unsuccessful, take one or two others with you and go back again, so that everything you say may be confirmed by two or three witnesses. ¹⁷If the person still refuses to listen, take your case to the church. Then if he or she won't accept the church's decision, treat that person as a pagan or a corrupt tax collector.

¹⁸"I tell you the truth, whatever you forbid* on earth will be forbidden in heaven, and whatever you permit* on earth will be permitted in heaven.

¹⁹"I also tell you this: If two of you agree here on earth concerning anything you ask, my Father in heaven will do it for you. ²⁰For where two or three gather together as my followers,* I am there among them."

Parable of the Unforgiving Debtor

²¹Then Peter came to him and asked, "Lord, how often should I forgive someone* who sins against me? Seven times?"

²²"No, not seven times," Jesus replied, "but seventy times seven!*

²³"Therefore, the Kingdom of Heaven can be compared to a king who decided to bring his accounts up to date with servants who had borrowed money from him. ²⁴In the process, one of his debtors was brought in who owed him millions of dollars.* ²⁵He couldn't pay, so his master ordered that he be sold—along with his wife, his children, and everything he owned—to pay the debt.

²⁶"But the man fell down before his master and begged him, 'Please, be patient with me, and I will pay it all.' ²⁷Then his master was filled with pity for him, and he released him and forgave his debt.

²⁸"But when the man left the king, he went to a fellow servant who owed him a few thousand dollars.* He grabbed him by the throat and demanded instant payment.

²⁹"His fellow servant fell down before him and begged for a little more time. 'Be patient with me, and I will pay it,' he pleaded. ³⁰But his creditor wouldn't wait. He had the man arrested and put in prison until the debt could be paid in full.

³¹"When some of the other servants saw this, they were very upset. They went to the king and told him everything that had happened. ³²Then the king called in the man he had forgiven and said, 'You evil servant! I forgave you that tremendous debt because you pleaded with me. ³³Shouldn't you have mercy on your fellow servant, just as I had mercy on you?' ³⁴Then the angry king sent the man to prison to be tortured until he had paid his entire debt.

³⁵"That's what my heavenly Father will do to you if you refuse to forgive your brothers and sisters* from your heart."

Discussion about Divorce and Marriage

19 When Jesus had finished saying these things, he left Galilee and went down to the region of Judea east of the Jordan River. ²Large crowds followed him there, and he healed their sick.

³Some Pharisees came and tried to trap him with this question: "Should a man be allowed to divorce his wife for just any reason?"

⁴"Haven't you read the Scriptures?" Jesus replied. "They record that from the beginning 'God made them male and female.'*" ⁵And he said, "'This explains why a man leaves his father and mother and is joined to his wife, and the two are united into one.'* ⁶Since they are no longer two but one, let no one split apart what God has joined together."

⁷"Then why did Moses say in the law that a man could give his wife a written notice of divorce and send her away?"* they asked.

⁸Jesus replied, "Moses permitted divorce only as a concession to your hard hearts, but it was not what God had originally intended. ⁹And I tell you this, whoever divorces his wife and marries someone else commits adultery—unless his wife has been unfaithful.*"

¹⁰Jesus' disciples then said to him, "If this is the case, it is better not to marry!"

¹¹"Not everyone can accept this statement," Jesus said. "Only those whom God helps.

18:15a Greek *If your brother.*   18:15b Some manuscripts do not include *against you.*   18:18a Or *bind,* or *lock.*   18:18b Or *loose,* or *open.*   18:20 Greek *gather together in my name.*   18:21 Greek *my brother.*   18:22 Or *seventy-seven times.*   18:24 Greek 10,000 *talents* [375 tons or 340 metric tons of silver].   18:28 Greek 100 *denarii.* A denarius was equivalent to a laborer's full day's wage.   18:35 Greek *your brother.*   19:4 Gen 1:27; 5:2.   19:5 Gen 2:24.   19:7 See Deut 24:1.   19:9 Some manuscripts add *And anyone who marries a divorced woman commits adultery.* Compare Matt 5:32.

¹²Some are born as eunuchs, some have been made eunuchs by others, and some choose not to marry* for the sake of the Kingdom of Heaven. Let anyone accept this who can."

Jesus Blesses the Children

¹³One day some parents brought their children to Jesus so he could lay his hands on them and pray for them. But the disciples scolded the parents for bothering him.

¹⁴But Jesus said, "Let the children come to me. Don't stop them! For the Kingdom of Heaven belongs to those who are like these children." ¹⁵And he placed his hands on their heads and blessed them before he left.

The Rich Man

¹⁶Someone came to Jesus with this question: "Teacher,* what good deed must I do to have eternal life?"

¹⁷"Why ask me about what is good?" Jesus replied. "There is only One who is good. But to answer your question—if you want to receive eternal life, keep* the commandments."

¹⁸"Which ones?" the man asked.

And Jesus replied: "'You must not murder. You must not commit adultery. You must not steal. You must not testify falsely. ¹⁹Honor your father and mother. Love your neighbor as yourself.'*"

²⁰"I've obeyed all these commandments," the young man replied. "What else must I do?"

²¹Jesus told him, "If you want to be perfect, go and sell all your possessions and give the money to the poor, and you will have treasure in heaven. Then come, follow me."

²²But when the young man heard this, he went away sad, for he had many possessions.

²³Then Jesus said to his disciples, "I tell you the truth, it is very hard for a rich person to enter the Kingdom of Heaven. ²⁴I'll say it again—it is easier for a camel to go through the eye of a needle than for a rich person to enter the Kingdom of God!"

²⁵The disciples were astounded. "Then who in the world can be saved?" they asked.

²⁶Jesus looked at them intently and said, "Humanly speaking, it is impossible. But with God everything is possible."

²⁷Then Peter said to him, "We've given up everything to follow you. What will we get?"

²⁸Jesus replied, "I assure you that when the world is made new* and the Son of Man* sits upon his glorious throne, you who have been my followers will also sit on twelve thrones, judging the twelve tribes of Israel. ²⁹And everyone who has given up houses or brothers or sisters or father or mother or children or property, for my sake, will receive a hundred times as much in return and will inherit eternal life. ³⁰But many who are the greatest now will be least important then, and those who seem least important now will be the greatest then.*

Parable of the Vineyard Workers

20 "For the Kingdom of Heaven is like the landowner who went out early one morning to hire workers for his vineyard. ²He agreed to pay the normal daily wage* and sent them out to work.

³"At nine o'clock in the morning he was passing through the marketplace and saw some people standing around doing nothing. ⁴So he hired them, telling them he would pay them whatever was right at the end of the day. ⁵So they went to work in the vineyard. At noon and again at three o'clock he did the same thing.

⁶"At five o'clock that afternoon he was in town again and saw some more people standing around. He asked them, 'Why haven't you been working today?'

⁷"They replied, 'Because no one hired us.'

"The landowner told them, 'Then go out and join the others in my vineyard.'

⁸"That evening he told the foreman to call the workers in and pay them, beginning with the last workers first. ⁹When those hired at five o'clock were paid, each received a full day's wage. ¹⁰When those hired first came to get their pay, they assumed they would receive more. But they, too, were paid a day's wage. ¹¹When they received their pay, they protested to the owner, ¹²'Those people worked only one hour, and yet you've paid them just as much as you paid us who worked all day in the scorching heat.'

¹³"He answered one of them, 'Friend, I haven't been unfair! Didn't you agree to work all day for the usual wage? ¹⁴Take your money and go. I wanted to pay this last worker the same as you. ¹⁵Is it against the law for me to do what I want with my money? Should you be jealous because I am kind to others?'

19:12 Greek *and some make themselves eunuchs.*　**19:16** Some manuscripts read *Good Teacher.*　**19:17** Some manuscripts read *continue to keep.*　**19:18-19** Exod 20:12-16; Deut 5:16-20; Lev 19:18.　**19:28a** Or *in the regeneration.*　**19:28b** "Son of Man" is a title Jesus used for himself.　**19:30** Greek *But many who are first will be last; and the last, first.*　**20:2** Greek *a denarius,* the payment for a full day's labor; similarly in 20:9, 10, 13.

¹⁶"So those who are last now will be first then, and those who are first will be last."

Jesus Again Predicts His Death

¹⁷As Jesus was going up to Jerusalem, he took the twelve disciples aside privately and told them what was going to happen to him. ¹⁸"Listen," he said, "we're going up to Jerusalem, where the Son of Man* will be betrayed to the leading priests and the teachers of religious law. They will sentence him to die. ¹⁹Then they will hand him over to the Romans* to be mocked, flogged with a whip, and crucified. But on the third day he will be raised from the dead."

Jesus Teaches about Serving Others

²⁰Then the mother of James and John, the sons of Zebedee, came to Jesus with her sons. She knelt respectfully to ask a favor. ²¹"What is your request?" he asked.

She replied, "In your Kingdom, please let my two sons sit in places of honor next to you, one on your right and the other on your left."

²²But Jesus answered by saying to them, "You don't know what you are asking! Are you able to drink from the bitter cup of suffering I am about to drink?"

"Oh yes," they replied, "we are able!"

²³Jesus told them, "You will indeed drink from my bitter cup. But I have no right to say who will sit on my right or my left. My Father has prepared those places for the ones he has chosen."

²⁴When the ten other disciples heard what James and John had asked, they were indignant. ²⁵But Jesus called them together and said, "You know that the rulers in this world lord it over their people, and officials flaunt their authority over those under them. ²⁶But among you it will be different. Whoever wants to be a leader among you must be your servant, ²⁷and whoever wants to be first among you must become your slave. ²⁸For even the Son of Man came not to be served but to serve others and to give his life as a ransom for many."

Jesus Heals Two Blind Men

²⁹As Jesus and the disciples left the town of Jericho, a large crowd followed behind. ³⁰Two blind men were sitting beside the road. When they heard that Jesus was coming that way, they began shouting, "Lord, Son of David, have mercy on us!"

³¹"Be quiet!" the crowd yelled at them.

But they only shouted louder, "Lord, Son of David, have mercy on us!"

³²When Jesus heard them, he stopped and called, "What do you want me to do for you?"

³³"Lord," they said, "we want to see!" ³⁴Jesus felt sorry for them and touched their eyes. Instantly they could see! Then they followed him.

Jesus' Triumphant Entry

21 As Jesus and the disciples approached Jerusalem, they came to the town of Bethphage on the Mount of Olives. Jesus sent two of them on ahead. ²"Go into the village over there," he said. "As soon as you enter it, you will see a donkey tied there, with its colt beside it. Untie them and bring them to me. ³If anyone asks what you are doing, just say, 'The Lord needs them,' and he will immediately let you take them."

⁴This took place to fulfill the prophecy that said,

⁵ "Tell the people of Jerusalem,*
    'Look, your King is coming to you.
    He is humble, riding on a donkey—
      riding on a donkey's colt.'"*

⁶The two disciples did as Jesus commanded. ⁷They brought the donkey and the colt to him and threw their garments over the colt, and he sat on it.* ⁸Most of the crowd spread their garments on the road ahead of him, and others cut branches from the trees and spread them on the road. ⁹Jesus was in the center of the procession, and the people all around him were shouting,

"Praise God* for the Son of David!
   Blessings on the one who comes in the
      name of the Lord!
   Praise God in highest heaven!"*

¹⁰The entire city of Jerusalem was in an uproar as he entered. "Who is this?" they asked.

¹¹And the crowds replied, "It's Jesus, the prophet from Nazareth in Galilee."

Jesus Clears the Temple

¹²Jesus entered the Temple and began to drive out all the people buying and selling animals for sacrifice. He knocked over the tables of the

---

20:18 "Son of Man" is a title Jesus used for himself.   20:19 Greek *the Gentiles.*   21:5a Greek *Tell the daughter of Zion.* Isa 62:11.
21:5b Zech 9:9.   21:7 Greek *over them, and he sat on them.*   21:9a Greek *Hosanna,* an exclamation of praise that literally means "save now"; also in 21:9b, 15.   21:9b Pss 118:25-26; 148:1.

money changers and the chairs of those selling doves. [13]He said to them, "The Scriptures declare, 'My Temple will be called a house of prayer,' but you have turned it into a den of thieves!"*

[14]The blind and the lame came to him in the Temple, and he healed them. [15]The leading priests and the teachers of religious law saw these wonderful miracles and heard even the children in the Temple shouting, "Praise God for the Son of David."

But the leaders were indignant. [16]They asked Jesus, "Do you hear what these children are saying?"

"Yes," Jesus replied. "Haven't you ever read the Scriptures? For they say, 'You have taught children and infants to give you praise.'*"
[17]Then he returned to Bethany, where he stayed overnight.

Jesus Curses the Fig Tree

[18]In the morning, as Jesus was returning to Jerusalem, he was hungry, [19]and he noticed a fig tree beside the road. He went over to see if there were any figs, but there were only leaves. Then he said to it, "May you never bear fruit again!" And immediately the fig tree withered up.

[20]The disciples were amazed when they saw this and asked, "How did the fig tree wither so quickly?"

[21]Then Jesus told them, "I tell you the truth, if you have faith and don't doubt, you can do things like this and much more. You can even say to this mountain, 'May you be lifted up and thrown into the sea,' and it will happen. [22]You can pray for anything, and if you have faith, you will receive it."

The Authority of Jesus Challenged

[23]When Jesus returned to the Temple and began teaching, the leading priests and elders came up to him. They demanded, "By what authority are you doing all these things? Who gave you the right?"

[24]"I'll tell you by what authority I do these things if you answer one question," Jesus replied. [25]"Did John's authority to baptize come from heaven, or was it merely human?"

They talked it over among themselves. "If we say it was from heaven, he will ask us why we didn't believe John. [26]But if we say it was merely human, we'll be mobbed because the people believe John was a prophet." [27]So they finally replied, "We don't know."

And Jesus responded, "Then I won't tell you by what authority I do these things.

Parable of the Two Sons

[28]"But what do you think about this? A man with two sons told the older boy, 'Son, go out and work in the vineyard today.' [29]The son answered, 'No, I won't go,' but later he changed his mind and went anyway. [30]Then the father told the other son, 'You go,' and he said, 'Yes, sir, I will.' But he didn't go.

[31]"Which of the two obeyed his father?"

They replied, "The first."*

Then Jesus explained his meaning: "I tell you the truth, corrupt tax collectors and prostitutes will get into the Kingdom of God before you do. [32]For John the Baptist came and showed you the right way to live, but you didn't believe him, while tax collectors and prostitutes did. And even when you saw this happening, you refused to believe him and repent of your sins.

Parable of the Evil Farmers

[33]"Now listen to another story. A certain landowner planted a vineyard, built a wall around it, dug a pit for pressing out the grape juice, and built a lookout tower. Then he leased the vineyard to tenant farmers and moved to another country. [34]At the time of the grape harvest, he sent his servants to collect his share of the crop. [35]But the farmers grabbed his servants, beat one, killed one, and stoned another. [36]So the landowner sent a larger group of his servants to collect for him, but the results were the same.

[37]"Finally, the owner sent his son, thinking, 'Surely they will respect my son.'

[38]"But when the tenant farmers saw his son coming, they said to one another, 'Here comes the heir to this estate. Come on, let's kill him and get the estate for ourselves!' [39]So they grabbed him, dragged him out of the vineyard, and murdered him.

[40]"When the owner of the vineyard returns," Jesus asked, "what do you think he will do to those farmers?"

[41]The religious leaders replied, "He will put the wicked men to a horrible death and lease the vineyard to others who will give him his share of the crop after each harvest."

21:13 Isa 56:7; Jer 7:11.   21:16 Ps 8:2 (Greek version).   21:29-31 Other manuscripts read *"The second."* In still other manuscripts the first son says "Yes" but does nothing, the second son says "No" but then repents and goes, and the answer to Jesus' question is that the second son obeyed his father.

⁴²Then Jesus asked them, "Didn't you ever read this in the Scriptures?

'The stone that the builders rejected
    has now become the cornerstone.
This is the Lord's doing,
    and it is wonderful to see.'*

⁴³I tell you, the Kingdom of God will be taken away from you and given to a nation that will produce the proper fruit. ⁴⁴Anyone who stumbles over that stone will be broken to pieces, and it will crush anyone it falls on.*"

⁴⁵When the leading priests and Pharisees heard this parable, they realized he was telling the story against them—they were the wicked farmers. ⁴⁶They wanted to arrest him, but they were afraid of the crowds, who considered Jesus to be a prophet.

Parable of the Great Feast

22 Jesus also told them other parables. He said, ²"The Kingdom of Heaven can be illustrated by the story of a king who prepared a great wedding feast for his son. ³When the banquet was ready, he sent his servants to notify those who were invited. But they all refused to come!

⁴"So he sent other servants to tell them, 'The feast has been prepared. The bulls and fattened cattle have been killed, and everything is ready. Come to the banquet!' ⁵But the guests he had invited ignored them and went their own way, one to his farm, another to his business. ⁶Others seized his messengers and insulted them and killed them.

⁷"The king was furious, and he sent out his army to destroy the murderers and burn their town. ⁸And he said to his servants, 'The wedding feast is ready, and the guests I invited aren't worthy of the honor. ⁹Now go out to the street corners and invite everyone you see.' ¹⁰So the servants brought in everyone they could find, good and bad alike, and the banquet hall was filled with guests.

¹¹"But when the king came in to meet the guests, he noticed a man who wasn't wearing the proper clothes for a wedding. ¹²'Friend,' he asked, 'how is it that you are here without wedding clothes?' But the man had no reply. ¹³Then the king said to his aides, 'Bind his hands and feet and throw him into the outer darkness, where there will be weeping and gnashing of teeth.'

¹⁴"For many are called, but few are chosen."

Taxes for Caesar

¹⁵Then the Pharisees met together to plot how to trap Jesus into saying something for which he could be arrested. ¹⁶They sent some of their disciples, along with the supporters of Herod, to meet with him. "Teacher," they said, "we know how honest you are. You teach the way of God truthfully. You are impartial and don't play favorites. ¹⁷Now tell us what you think about this: Is it right to pay taxes to Caesar or not?"

¹⁸But Jesus knew their evil motives. "You hypocrites!" he said. "Why are you trying to trap me? ¹⁹Here, show me the coin used for the tax." When they handed him a Roman coin,* ²⁰he asked, "Whose picture and title are stamped on it?"

²¹"Caesar's," they replied.

"Well, then," he said, "give to Caesar what belongs to Caesar, and give to God what belongs to God."

²²His reply amazed them, and they went away.

Discussion about Resurrection

²³That same day Jesus was approached by some Sadducees—religious leaders who say there is no resurrection from the dead. They posed this question: ²⁴"Teacher, Moses said, 'If a man dies without children, his brother should marry the widow and have a child who will carry on the brother's name.'* ²⁵Well, suppose there were seven brothers. The oldest one married and then died without children, so his brother married the widow. ²⁶But the second brother also died, and the third brother married her. This continued with all seven of them. ²⁷Last of all, the woman also died. ²⁸So tell us, whose wife will she be in the resurrection? For all seven were married to her."

²⁹Jesus replied, "Your mistake is that you don't know the Scriptures, and you don't know the power of God. ³⁰For when the dead rise, they will neither marry nor be given in marriage. In this respect they will be like the angels in heaven.

³¹"But now, as to whether there will be a resurrection of the dead—haven't you ever read about this in the Scriptures? Long after Abraham, Isaac, and Jacob had died, God said,* ³²'I am the God of Abraham, the God of Isaac, and the God of Jacob.'* So he is the God of the living, not the dead."

³³When the crowds heard him, they were astounded at his teaching.

21:42 Ps 118:22-23.   21:44 This verse is not included in some early manuscripts. Compare Luke 20:18.   22:19 Greek *a denarius*.   22:24 Deut 25:5-6.   22:31 Greek *read about this? God said.*   22:32 Exod 3:6.

The Most Important Commandment

³⁴But when the Pharisees heard that he had silenced the Sadducees with his reply, they met together to question him again. ³⁵One of them, an expert in religious law, tried to trap him with this question: ³⁶"Teacher, which is the most important commandment in the law of Moses?"

³⁷Jesus replied, "'You must love the LORD your God with all your heart, all your soul, and all your mind.'* ³⁸This is the first and greatest commandment. ³⁹A second is equally important: 'Love your neighbor as yourself.'* ⁴⁰The entire law and all the demands of the prophets are based on these two commandments."

Whose Son Is the Messiah?

⁴¹Then, surrounded by the Pharisees, Jesus asked them a question: ⁴²"What do you think about the Messiah? Whose son is he?"

They replied, "He is the son of David."

⁴³Jesus responded, "Then why does David, speaking under the inspiration of the Spirit, call the Messiah 'my Lord'? For David said,

⁴⁴ 'The LORD said to my Lord,
Sit in the place of honor at my right hand
until I humble your enemies beneath
your feet.'*

⁴⁵Since David called the Messiah 'my Lord,' how can the Messiah be his son?"

⁴⁶No one could answer him. And after that, no one dared to ask him any more questions.

Jesus Criticizes the Religious Leaders

23 Then Jesus said to the crowds and to his disciples, ²"The teachers of religious law and the Pharisees are the official interpreters of the law of Moses.* ³So practice and obey whatever they tell you, but don't follow their example. For they don't practice what they teach. ⁴They crush people with unbearable religious demands and never lift a finger to ease the burden.

⁵"Everything they do is for show. On their arms they wear extra wide prayer boxes with Scripture verses inside, and they wear robes with extra long tassels.* ⁶And they love to sit at the head table at banquets and in the seats of honor in the synagogues. ⁷They love to re-ceive respectful greetings as they walk in the marketplaces, and to be called 'Rabbi.'*

⁸"Don't let anyone call you 'Rabbi,' for you have only one teacher, and all of you are equal as brothers and sisters.* ⁹And don't address anyone here on earth as 'Father,' for only God in heaven is your Father. ¹⁰And don't let anyone call you 'Teacher,' for you have only one teacher, the Messiah. ¹¹The greatest among you must be a servant. ¹²But those who exalt themselves will be humbled, and those who humble themselves will be exalted.

¹³"What sorrow awaits you teachers of religious law and you Pharisees. Hypocrites! For you shut the door of the Kingdom of Heaven in people's faces. You won't go in yourselves, and you don't let others enter either.*

¹⁵"What sorrow awaits you teachers of religious law and you Pharisees. Hypocrites! For you cross land and sea to make one convert, and then you turn that person into twice the child of hell* you yourselves are!

¹⁶"Blind guides! What sorrow awaits you! For you say that it means nothing to swear 'by God's Temple,' but that it is binding to swear 'by the gold in the Temple.' ¹⁷Blind fools! Which is more important—the gold or the Temple that makes the gold sacred? ¹⁸And you say that to swear 'by the altar' is not binding, but to swear 'by the gifts on the altar' is binding. ¹⁹How blind! For which is more important—the gift on the altar or the altar that makes the gift sacred? ²⁰When you swear 'by the altar,' you are swearing by it and by everything on it. ²¹And when you swear 'by the Temple,' you are swearing by it and by God, who lives in it. ²²And when you swear 'by heaven,' you are swearing by the throne of God and by God, who sits on the throne.

²³"What sorrow awaits you teachers of religious law and you Pharisees. Hypocrites! For you are careful to tithe even the tiniest income from your herb gardens,* but you ignore the more important aspects of the law—justice, mercy, and faith. You should tithe, yes, but do not neglect the more important things. ²⁴Blind guides! You strain your water so you won't accidentally swallow a gnat, but you swallow a camel!*

²⁵"What sorrow awaits you teachers of religious law and you Pharisees. Hypocrites! For you are so careful to clean the outside of the cup

---

22:37 Deut 6:5. 22:39 Lev 19:18. 22:44 Ps 110:1. 23:2 Greek *and the Pharisees sit in the seat of Moses.* 23:5 Greek *They enlarge their phylacteries and lengthen their tassels.* 23:7 *Rabbi,* from Aramaic, means "master" or "teacher." 23:8 Greek *brothers.* 23:13 Some manuscripts add verse 14, *What sorrow awaits you teachers of religious law and you Pharisees. Hypocrites! You shamelessly cheat widows out of their property and then pretend to be pious by making long prayers in public. Because of this, you will be severely punished.* Compare Mark 12:40 and Luke 20:47. 23:15 Greek *of Gehenna;* also in 23:33. 23:23 Greek *tithe the mint, the dill, and the cumin.* 23:24 See Lev 11:4, 23, where gnats and camels are both forbidden as food.

and the dish, but inside you are filthy—full of greed and self-indulgence! [26]You blind Pharisee! First wash the inside of the cup and the dish,* and then the outside will become clean, too.

[27]"What sorrow awaits you teachers of religious law and you Pharisees. Hypocrites! For you are like whitewashed tombs—beautiful on the outside but filled on the inside with dead people's bones and all sorts of impurity. [28]Outwardly you look like righteous people, but inwardly your hearts are filled with hypocrisy and lawlessness.

[29]"What sorrow awaits you teachers of religious law and you Pharisees. Hypocrites! For you build tombs for the prophets your ancestors killed, and you decorate the monuments of the godly people your ancestors destroyed. [30]Then you say, 'If we had lived in the days of our ancestors, we would never have joined them in killing the prophets.'

[31]"But in saying that, you testify against yourselves that you are indeed the descendants of those who murdered the prophets. [32]Go ahead and finish what your ancestors started. [33]Snakes! Sons of vipers! How will you escape the judgment of hell?

[34]"Therefore, I am sending you prophets and wise men and teachers of religious law. But you will kill some by crucifixion, and you will flog others with whips in your synagogues, chasing them from city to city. [35]As a result, you will be held responsible for the murder of all godly people of all time—from the murder of righteous Abel to the murder of Zechariah son of Berekiah, whom you killed in the Temple between the sanctuary and the altar. [36]I tell you the truth, this judgment will fall on this very generation.

Jesus Grieves over Jerusalem

[37]"O Jerusalem, Jerusalem, the city that kills the prophets and stones God's messengers! How often I have wanted to gather your children together as a hen protects her chicks beneath her wings, but you wouldn't let me. [38]And now, look, your house is abandoned and desolate.* [39]For I tell you this, you will never see me again until you say, 'Blessings on the one who comes in the name of the LORD!'*"

Jesus Speaks about the Future

24 As Jesus was leaving the Temple grounds, his disciples pointed out to him the various Temple buildings. [2]But he responded, "Do you see all these buildings? I tell you the truth, they will be completely demolished. Not one stone will be left on top of another!"

[3]Later, Jesus sat on the Mount of Olives. His disciples came to him privately and said, "Tell us, when will all this happen? What sign will signal your return and the end of the world?*"

[4]Jesus told them, "Don't let anyone mislead you, [5]for many will come in my name, claiming, 'I am the Messiah.' They will deceive many. [6]And you will hear of wars and threats of wars, but don't panic. Yes, these things must take place, but the end won't follow immediately. [7]Nation will go to war against nation, and kingdom against kingdom. There will be famines and earthquakes in many parts of the world. [8]But all this is only the first of the birth pains, with more to come.

[9]"Then you will be arrested, persecuted, and killed. You will be hated all over the world because you are my followers.* [10]And many will turn away from me and betray and hate each other. [11]And many false prophets will appear and will deceive many people. [12]Sin will be rampant everywhere, and the love of many will grow cold. [13]But the one who endures to the end will be saved. [14]And the Good News about the Kingdom will be preached throughout the whole world, so that all nations* will hear it; and then the end will come.

[15]"The day is coming when you will see what Daniel the prophet spoke about—the sacrilegious object that causes desecration* standing in the Holy Place." (Reader, pay attention!) [16]"Then those in Judea must flee to the hills. [17]A person out on the deck of a roof must not go down into the house to pack. [18]A person out in the field must not return even to get a coat. [19]How terrible it will be for pregnant women and for nursing mothers in those days. [20]And pray that your flight will not be in winter or on the Sabbath. [21]For there will be greater anguish than at any time since the world began. And it will never be so great again. [22]In fact, unless that time of calamity is shortened, not a single person will survive. But it will be shortened for the sake of God's chosen ones.

[23]"Then if anyone tells you, 'Look, here is the Messiah,' or 'There he is,' don't believe it. [24]For false messiahs and false prophets will rise up and perform great signs and wonders so as to deceive, if possible, even God's chosen ones. [25]See, I have warned you about this ahead of time.

23:26 Some manuscripts do not include *and the dish.*   23:38 Some manuscripts do not include *and desolate.*   23:39 Ps 118:26.
24:3 Or *the age?*   24:9 Greek *on account of my name.*   24:14 Or *all peoples.*   24:15 Greek *the abomination of desolation.* See Dan 9:27; 11:31; 12:11.

26"So if someone tells you, 'Look, the Messiah is out in the desert,' don't bother to go and look. Or, 'Look, he is hiding here,' don't believe it! 27For as the lightning flashes in the east and shines to the west, so it will be when the Son of Man* comes. 28Just as the gathering of vultures shows there is a carcass nearby, so these signs indicate that the end is near.*

29"Immediately after the anguish of those days,

the sun will be darkened,
    the moon will give no light,
the stars will fall from the sky,
    and the powers in the heavens will
    be shaken.*

30And then at last, the sign that the Son of Man is coming will appear in the heavens, and there will be deep mourning among all the peoples of the earth. And they will see the Son of Man coming on the clouds of heaven with power and great glory.* 31And he will send out his angels with the mighty blast of a trumpet, and they will gather his chosen ones from all over the world*—from the farthest ends of the earth and heaven.

32"Now learn a lesson from the fig tree. When its branches bud and its leaves begin to sprout, you know that summer is near. 33In the same way, when you see all these things, you can know his return is very near, right at the door. 34I tell you the truth, this generation* will not pass from the scene until all these things take place. 35Heaven and earth will disappear, but my words will never disappear.

36"However, no one knows the day or hour when these things will happen, not even the angels in heaven or the Son himself.* Only the Father knows.

37"When the Son of Man returns, it will be like it was in Noah's day. 38In those days before the flood, the people were enjoying banquets and parties and weddings right up to the time Noah entered his boat. 39People didn't realize what was going to happen until the flood came and swept them all away. That is the way it will be when the Son of Man comes.

40"Two men will be working together in the field; one will be taken, the other left. 41Two women will be grinding flour at the mill; one will be taken, the other left.

42"So you, too, must keep watch! For you don't know what day your Lord is coming. 43Understand this: If a homeowner knew exactly when a burglar was coming, he would keep watch and not permit his house to be broken into. 44You also must be ready all the time, for the Son of Man will come when least expected.

45"A faithful, sensible servant is one to whom the master can give the responsibility of managing his other household servants and feeding them. 46If the master returns and finds that the servant has done a good job, there will be a reward. 47I tell you the truth, the master will put that servant in charge of all he owns. 48But what if the servant is evil and thinks, 'My master won't be back for a while,' 49and he begins beating the other servants, partying, and getting drunk? 50The master will return unannounced and unexpected, 51and he will cut the servant to pieces and assign him a place with the hypocrites. In that place there will be weeping and gnashing of teeth.

Parable of the Ten Bridesmaids

25 "Then the Kingdom of Heaven will be like ten bridesmaids* who took their lamps and went to meet the bridegroom. 2Five of them were foolish, and five were wise. 3The five who were foolish didn't take enough olive oil for their lamps, 4but the other five were wise enough to take along extra oil. 5When the bridegroom was delayed, they all became drowsy and fell asleep.

6"At midnight they were roused by the shout, 'Look, the bridegroom is coming! Come out and meet him!'

7"All the bridesmaids got up and prepared their lamps. 8Then the five foolish ones asked the others, 'Please give us some of your oil because our lamps are going out.'

9"But the others replied, 'We don't have enough for all of us. Go to a shop and buy some for yourselves.'

10"But while they were gone to buy oil, the bridegroom came. Then those who were ready went in with him to the marriage feast, and the door was locked. 11Later, when the other five bridesmaids returned, they stood outside, calling, 'Lord! Lord! Open the door for us!'

12"But he called back, 'Believe me, I don't know you!'

13"So you, too, must keep watch! For you do not know the day or hour of my return.

24:27 "Son of Man" is a title Jesus used for himself.   24:28 Greek *Wherever the carcass is, the vultures gather.*   24:29 See Isa 13:10; 34:4; Joel 2:10.   24:30 See Dan 7:13.   24:31 Greek *from the four winds.*   24:34 Or *this age,* or *this nation.*   24:36 Some manuscripts do not include *or the Son himself.*   25:1 Or *virgins;* also in 25:7, 11.

Parable of the Three Servants

14 "Again, the Kingdom of Heaven can be illustrated by the story of a man going on a long trip. He called together his servants and entrusted his money to them while he was gone. 15He gave five bags of silver* to one, two bags of silver to another, and one bag of silver to the last—dividing it in proportion to their abilities. He then left on his trip.

16 "The servant who received the five bags of silver began to invest the money and earned five more. 17The servant with two bags of silver also went to work and earned two more. 18But the servant who received the one bag of silver dug a hole in the ground and hid the master's money.

19 "After a long time their master returned from his trip and called them to give an account of how they had used his money. 20The servant to whom he had entrusted the five bags of silver came forward with five more and said, 'Master, you gave me five bags of silver to invest, and I have earned five more.'

21 "The master was full of praise. 'Well done, my good and faithful servant. You have been faithful in handling this small amount, so now I will give you many more responsibilities. Let's celebrate together!*'

22 "The servant who had received the two bags of silver came forward and said, 'Master, you gave me two bags of silver to invest, and I have earned two more.'

23 "The master said, 'Well done, my good and faithful servant. You have been faithful in handling this small amount, so now I will give you many more responsibilities. Let's celebrate together!'

24 "Then the servant with the one bag of silver came and said, 'Master, I knew you were a harsh man, harvesting crops you didn't plant and gathering crops you didn't cultivate. 25I was afraid I would lose your money, so I hid it in the earth. Look, here is your money back.'

26 "But the master replied, 'You wicked and lazy servant! If you knew I harvested crops I didn't plant and gathered crops I didn't cultivate, 27why didn't you deposit my money in the bank? At least I could have gotten some interest on it.'

28 "Then he ordered, 'Take the money from this servant, and give it to the one with the ten bags of silver. 29To those who use well what they are given, even more will be given, and they will have an abundance. But from those who do nothing, even what little they have will be taken away. 30Now throw this useless servant into outer darkness, where there will be weeping and gnashing of teeth.'

The Final Judgment

31 "But when the Son of Man* comes in his glory, and all the angels with him, then he will sit upon his glorious throne. 32All the nations* will be gathered in his presence, and he will separate the people as a shepherd separates the sheep from the goats. 33He will place the sheep at his right hand and the goats at his left.

34 "Then the King will say to those on his right, 'Come, you who are blessed by my Father, inherit the Kingdom prepared for you from the creation of the world. 35For I was hungry, and you fed me. I was thirsty, and you gave me a drink. I was a stranger, and you invited me into your home. 36I was naked, and you gave me clothing. I was sick, and you cared for me. I was in prison, and you visited me.'

37 "Then these righteous ones will reply, 'Lord, when did we ever see you hungry and feed you? Or thirsty and give you something to drink? 38Or a stranger and show you hospitality? Or naked and give you clothing? 39When did we ever see you sick or in prison and visit you?'

40 "And the King will say, 'I tell you the truth, when you did it to one of the least of these my brothers and sisters,* you were doing it to me!'

41 "Then the King will turn to those on the left and say, 'Away with you, you cursed ones, into the eternal fire prepared for the devil and his demons.* 42For I was hungry, and you didn't feed me. I was thirsty, and you didn't give me a drink. 43I was a stranger, and you didn't invite me into your home. I was naked, and you didn't give me clothing. I was sick and in prison, and you didn't visit me.'

44 "Then they will reply, 'Lord, when did we ever see you hungry or thirsty or a stranger or naked or sick or in prison, and not help you?'

45 "And he will answer, 'I tell you the truth, when you refused to help the least of these my brothers and sisters, you were refusing to help me.'

46 "And they will go away into eternal punishment, but the righteous will go into eternal life."

25:15 Greek *talents;* also throughout the story. A talent is equal to 75 pounds or 34 kilograms.   25:21 Greek *Enter into the joy of your master* [or *your Lord*]; also in 25:23.   25:31 "Son of Man" is a title Jesus used for himself.   25:32 Or *peoples.* 25:40 Greek *my brothers.*   25:41 Greek *his angels.*

The Plot to Kill Jesus

26 When Jesus had finished saying all these things, he said to his disciples, ²"As you know, Passover begins in two days, and the Son of Man* will be handed over to be crucified."

³At that same time the leading priests and elders were meeting at the residence of Caiaphas, the high priest, ⁴plotting how to capture Jesus secretly and kill him. ⁵"But not during the Passover celebration," they agreed, "or the people may riot."

Jesus Anointed at Bethany

⁶Meanwhile, Jesus was in Bethany at the home of Simon, a man who had previously had leprosy. ⁷While he was eating,* a woman came in with a beautiful alabaster jar of expensive perfume and poured it over his head.

⁸The disciples were indignant when they saw this. "What a waste!" they said. ⁹"It could have been sold for a high price and the money given to the poor."

¹⁰But Jesus, aware of this, replied, "Why criticize this woman for doing such a good thing to me? ¹¹You will always have the poor among you, but you will not always have me. ¹²She has poured this perfume on me to prepare my body for burial. ¹³I tell you the truth, wherever the Good News is preached throughout the world, this woman's deed will be remembered and discussed."

Judas Agrees to Betray Jesus

¹⁴Then Judas Iscariot, one of the twelve disciples, went to the leading priests ¹⁵and asked, "How much will you pay me to betray Jesus to you?" And they gave him thirty pieces of silver. ¹⁶From that time on, Judas began looking for an opportunity to betray Jesus.

The Last Supper

¹⁷On the first day of the Festival of Unleavened Bread, the disciples came to Jesus and asked, "Where do you want us to prepare the Passover meal for you?"

¹⁸"As you go into the city," he told them, "you will see a certain man. Tell him, 'The Teacher says: My time has come, and I will eat the Passover meal with my disciples at your house.'" ¹⁹So the disciples did as Jesus told them and prepared the Passover meal there.

²⁰When it was evening, Jesus sat down at the table* with the Twelve. ²¹While they were eating, he said, "I tell you the truth, one of you will betray me."

²²Greatly distressed, each one asked in turn, "Am I the one, Lord?"

²³He replied, "One of you who has just eaten from this bowl with me will betray me. ²⁴For the Son of Man must die, as the Scriptures declared long ago. But how terrible it will be for the one who betrays him. It would be far better for that man if he had never been born!"

²⁵Judas, the one who would betray him, also asked, "Rabbi, am I the one?"

And Jesus told him, "You have said it."

²⁶As they were eating, Jesus took some bread and blessed it. Then he broke it in pieces and gave it to the disciples, saying, "Take this and eat it, for this is my body."

²⁷And he took a cup of wine and gave thanks to God for it. He gave it to them and said, "Each of you drink from it, ²⁸for this is my blood, which confirms the covenant* between God and his people. It is poured out as a sacrifice to forgive the sins of many. ²⁹Mark my words—I will not drink wine again until the day I drink it new with you in my Father's Kingdom."

³⁰Then they sang a hymn and went out to the Mount of Olives.

Jesus Predicts Peter's Denial

³¹On the way, Jesus told them, "Tonight all of you will desert me. For the Scriptures say,

'God will strike* the Shepherd,
    and the sheep of the flock will be
        scattered.'

³²But after I have been raised from the dead, I will go ahead of you to Galilee and meet you there."

³³Peter declared, "Even if everyone else deserts you, I will never desert you."

³⁴Jesus replied, "I tell you the truth, Peter—this very night, before the rooster crows, you will deny three times that you even know me."

³⁵"No!" Peter insisted. "Even if I have to die with you, I will never deny you!" And all the other disciples vowed the same.

Jesus Prays in Gethsemane

³⁶Then Jesus went with them to the olive grove called Gethsemane, and he said, "Sit here while I go over there to pray." ³⁷He took Peter and Zebedee's two sons, James and John, and he became anguished and distressed. ³⁸He

---

26:2 "Son of Man" is a title Jesus used for himself. 26:7 Or *reclining.* 26:20 Or *Jesus reclined.* 26:28 Some manuscripts read *the new covenant.* 26:31 Greek *I will strike.* Zech 13:7.

told them, "My soul is crushed with grief to the point of death. Stay here and keep watch with me."

39He went on a little farther and bowed with his face to the ground, praying, "My Father! If it is possible, let this cup of suffering be taken away from me. Yet I want your will to be done, not mine."

40Then he returned to the disciples and found them asleep. He said to Peter, "Couldn't you watch with me even one hour? 41Keep watch and pray, so that you will not give in to temptation. For the spirit is willing, but the body is weak!"

42Then Jesus left them a second time and prayed, "My Father! If this cup cannot be taken away* unless I drink it, your will be done." 43When he returned to them again, he found them sleeping, for they couldn't keep their eyes open.

44So he went to pray a third time, saying the same things again. 45Then he came to the disciples and said, "Go ahead and sleep. Have your rest. But look—the time has come. The Son of Man is betrayed into the hands of sinners. 46Up, let's be going. Look, my betrayer is here!"

Jesus Is Betrayed and Arrested

47And even as Jesus said this, Judas, one of the twelve disciples, arrived with a crowd of men armed with swords and clubs. They had been sent by the leading priests and elders of the people. 48The traitor, Judas, had given them a prearranged signal: "You will know which one to arrest when I greet him with a kiss." 49So Judas came straight to Jesus. "Greetings, Rabbi!" he exclaimed and gave him the kiss.

50Jesus said, "My friend, go ahead and do what you have come for."

Then the others grabbed Jesus and arrested him. 51But one of the men with Jesus pulled out his sword and struck the high priest's slave, slashing off his ear.

52"Put away your sword," Jesus told him. "Those who use the sword will die by the sword. 53Don't you realize that I could ask my Father for thousands* of angels to protect us, and he would send them instantly? 54But if I did, how would the Scriptures be fulfilled that describe what must happen now?"

55Then Jesus said to the crowd, "Am I some dangerous revolutionary, that you come with swords and clubs to arrest me? Why didn't you arrest me in the Temple? I was there teaching every day. 56But this is all happening to fulfill the words of the prophets as recorded in the Scriptures." At that point, all the disciples deserted him and fled.

Jesus before the Council

57Then the people who had arrested Jesus led him to the home of Caiaphas, the high priest, where the teachers of religious law and the elders had gathered. 58Meanwhile, Peter followed him at a distance and came to the high priest's courtyard. He went in and sat with the guards and waited to see how it would all end.

59Inside, the leading priests and the entire high council* were trying to find witnesses who would lie about Jesus, so they could put him to death. 60But even though they found many who agreed to give false witness, they could not use anyone's testimony. Finally, two men came forward 61who declared, "This man said, 'I am able to destroy the Temple of God and rebuild it in three days.'"

62Then the high priest stood up and said to Jesus, "Well, aren't you going to answer these charges? What do you have to say for yourself?" 63But Jesus remained silent. Then the high priest said to him, "I demand in the name of the living God—tell us if you are the Messiah, the Son of God."

64Jesus replied, "You have said it. And in the future you will see the Son of Man seated in the place of power at God's right hand* and coming on the clouds of heaven."*

65Then the high priest tore his clothing to show his horror and said, "Blasphemy! Why do we need other witnesses? You have all heard his blasphemy. 66What is your verdict?"

"Guilty!" they shouted. "He deserves to die!"

67Then they began to spit in Jesus' face and beat him with their fists. And some slapped him, 68jeering, "Prophesy to us, you Messiah! Who hit you that time?"

Peter Denies Jesus

69Meanwhile, Peter was sitting outside in the courtyard. A servant girl came over and said to him, "You were one of those with Jesus the Galilean."

70But Peter denied it in front of everyone. "I don't know what you're talking about," he said.

71Later, out by the gate, another servant girl noticed him and said to those standing around, "This man was with Jesus of Nazareth.*"

26:42 Greek *If this cannot pass.*   26:53 Greek *twelve legions.*   26:59 Greek *the Sanhedrin.*   26:64a Greek *seated at the right hand of the power.* See Ps 110:1.   26:64b See Dan 7:13.   26:71 Or *Jesus the Nazarene.*

72Again Peter denied it, this time with an oath. "I don't even know the man," he said.

73A little later some of the other bystanders came over to Peter and said, "You must be one of them; we can tell by your Galilean accent."

74Peter swore, "A curse on me if I'm lying—I don't know the man!" And immediately the rooster crowed.

75Suddenly, Jesus' words flashed through Peter's mind: "Before the rooster crows, you will deny three times that you even know me." And he went away, weeping bitterly.

Judas Hangs Himself

27 Very early in the morning the leading priests and the elders of the people met again to lay plans for putting Jesus to death. 2Then they bound him, led him away, and took him to Pilate, the Roman governor.

3When Judas, who had betrayed him, realized that Jesus had been condemned to die, he was filled with remorse. So he took the thirty pieces of silver back to the leading priests and the elders. 4"I have sinned," he declared, "for I have betrayed an innocent man."

"What do we care?" they retorted. "That's your problem."

5Then Judas threw the silver coins down in the Temple and went out and hanged himself.

6The leading priests picked up the coins. "It wouldn't be right to put this money in the Temple treasury," they said, "since it was payment for murder."* 7After some discussion they finally decided to buy the potter's field, and they made it into a cemetery for foreigners. 8That is why the field is still called the Field of Blood. 9This fulfilled the prophecy of Jeremiah that says,

"They took* the thirty pieces of silver—
the price at which he was valued by the
people of Israel,
10 and purchased the potter's field,
as the LORD directed.*"

Jesus' Trial before Pilate

11Now Jesus was standing before Pilate, the Roman governor. "Are you the king of the Jews?" the governor asked him.

Jesus replied, "You have said it."

12But when the leading priests and the elders made their accusations against him, Jesus remained silent. 13"Don't you hear all these charges they are bringing against you?" Pilate demanded. 14But Jesus made no response to any of the charges, much to the governor's surprise.

15Now it was the governor's custom each year during the Passover celebration to release one prisoner to the crowd—anyone they wanted. 16This year there was a notorious prisoner, a man named Barabbas.* 17As the crowds gathered before Pilate's house that morning, he asked them, "Which one do you want me to release to you—Barabbas, or Jesus who is called the Messiah?" 18(He knew very well that the religious leaders had arrested Jesus out of envy.)

19Just then, as Pilate was sitting on the judgment seat, his wife sent him this message: "Leave that innocent man alone. I suffered through a terrible nightmare about him last night."

20Meanwhile, the leading priests and the elders persuaded the crowd to ask for Barabbas to be released and for Jesus to be put to death. 21So the governor asked again, "Which of these two do you want me to release to you?"

The crowd shouted back, "Barabbas!"

22Pilate responded, "Then what should I do with Jesus who is called the Messiah?"

They shouted back, "Crucify him!"

23"Why?" Pilate demanded. "What crime has he committed?"

But the mob roared even louder, "Crucify him!"

24Pilate saw that he wasn't getting anywhere and that a riot was developing. So he sent for a bowl of water and washed his hands before the crowd, saying, "I am innocent of this man's blood. The responsibility is yours!"

25And all the people yelled back, "We will take responsibility for his death—we and our children!"*

26So Pilate released Barabbas to them. He ordered Jesus flogged with a lead-tipped whip, then turned him over to the Roman soldiers to be crucified.

The Soldiers Mock Jesus

27Some of the governor's soldiers took Jesus into their headquarters* and called out the entire regiment. 28They stripped him and put a scarlet robe on him. 29They wove thorn branches into a crown and put it on his head, and they placed a reed stick in his right hand

---

27:6 Greek *since it is the price for blood.*   27:9 Or *I took.*   27:9-10 Greek *as the LORD directed me.* Zech 11:12-13; Jer 32:6-9.
27:16 Some manuscripts read *Jesus Barabbas;* also in 27:17.   27:25 Greek *"His blood be on us and on our children."*   27:27 Or *into the Praetorium.*

as a scepter. Then they knelt before him in mockery and taunted, "Hail! King of the Jews!" [30]And they spit on him and grabbed the stick and struck him on the head with it. [31]When they were finally tired of mocking him, they took off the robe and put his own clothes on him again. Then they led him away to be crucified.

The Crucifixion

[32]Along the way, they came across a man named Simon, who was from Cyrene,* and the soldiers forced him to carry Jesus' cross. [33]And they went out to a place called Golgotha (which means "Place of the Skull"). [34]The soldiers gave Jesus wine mixed with bitter gall, but when he had tasted it, he refused to drink it.

[35]After they had nailed him to the cross, the soldiers gambled for his clothes by throwing dice.* [36]Then they sat around and kept guard as he hung there. [37]A sign was fastened above Jesus' head, announcing the charge against him. It read: "This is Jesus, the King of the Jews." [38]Two revolutionaries* were crucified with him, one on his right and one on his left.

[39]The people passing by shouted abuse, shaking their heads in mockery. [40]"Look at you now!" they yelled at him. "You said you were going to destroy the Temple and rebuild it in three days. Well then, if you are the Son of God, save yourself and come down from the cross!"

[41]The leading priests, the teachers of religious law, and the elders also mocked Jesus. [42]"He saved others," they scoffed, "but he can't save himself! So he is the King of Israel, is he? Let him come down from the cross right now, and we will believe in him! [43]He trusted God, so let God rescue him now if he wants him! For he said, 'I am the Son of God.'" [44]Even the revolutionaries who were crucified with him ridiculed him in the same way.

The Death of Jesus

[45]At noon, darkness fell across the whole land until three o'clock. [46]At about three o'clock, Jesus called out with a loud voice, "Eli, Eli,* lema sabachthani?" which means "My God, my God, why have you abandoned me?"* [47]Some of the bystanders misunderstood and thought he was calling for the prophet Elijah. [48]One of them ran and filled a sponge with sour wine, holding it up to him on a reed stick so he could drink. [49]But the rest said, "Wait! Let's see whether Elijah comes to save him."*

[50]Then Jesus shouted out again, and he released his spirit. [51]At that moment the curtain in the sanctuary of the Temple was torn in two, from top to bottom. The earth shook, rocks split apart, [52]and tombs opened. The bodies of many godly men and women who had died were raised from the dead. [53]They left the cemetery after Jesus' resurrection, went into the holy city of Jerusalem, and appeared to many people.

[54]The Roman officer* and the other soldiers at the crucifixion were terrified by the earthquake and all that had happened. They said, "This man truly was the Son of God!"

[55]And many women who had come from Galilee with Jesus to care for him were watching from a distance. [56]Among them were Mary Magdalene, Mary (the mother of James and Joseph), and the mother of James and John, the sons of Zebedee.

The Burial of Jesus

[57]As evening approached, Joseph, a rich man from Arimathea who had become a follower of Jesus, [58]went to Pilate and asked for Jesus' body. And Pilate issued an order to release it to him. [59]Joseph took the body and wrapped it in a long sheet of clean linen cloth. [60]He placed it in his own new tomb, which had been carved out of the rock. Then he rolled a great stone across the entrance and left. [61]Both Mary Magdalene and the other Mary were sitting across from the tomb and watching.

The Guard at the Tomb

[62]The next day, on the Sabbath,* the leading priests and Pharisees went to see Pilate. [63]They told him, "Sir, we remember what that deceiver once said while he was still alive: 'After three days I will rise from the dead.' [64]So we request that you seal the tomb until the third day. This will prevent his disciples from coming and stealing his body and then telling everyone he was raised from the dead! If that happens, we'll be worse off than we were at first."

[65]Pilate replied, "Take guards and secure it the best you can." [66]So they sealed the tomb and posted guards to protect it.

27:32 Cyrene was a city in northern Africa.   27:35 Greek by casting lots. A few late manuscripts add This fulfilled the word of the prophet: "They divided my garments among themselves and cast lots for my robe." See Ps 22:18.   27:38 Or criminals; also in 27:44. 27:46a Some manuscripts read Eloi, Eloi.   27:46b Ps 22:1.   27:49 Some manuscripts add And another took a spear and pierced his side, and out flowed water and blood. Compare John 19:34.   27:54 Greek The centurion.   27:62 Or On the next day, which is after the Preparation.

The Resurrection

28 Early on Sunday morning,* as the new day was dawning, Mary Magdalene and the other Mary went out to visit the tomb.

²Suddenly there was a great earthquake! For an angel of the Lord came down from heaven, rolled aside the stone, and sat on it. ³His face shone like lightning, and his clothing was as white as snow. ⁴The guards shook with fear when they saw him, and they fell into a dead faint.

⁵Then the angel spoke to the women. "Don't be afraid!" he said. "I know you are looking for Jesus, who was crucified. ⁶He isn't here! He is risen from the dead, just as he said would happen. Come, see where his body was lying. ⁷And now, go quickly and tell his disciples that he has risen from the dead, and he is going ahead of you to Galilee. You will see him there. Remember what I have told you."

⁸The women ran quickly from the tomb. They were very frightened but also filled with great joy, and they rushed to give the disciples the angel's message. ⁹And as they went, Jesus met them and greeted them. And they ran to him, grasped his feet, and worshiped him. ¹⁰Then Jesus said to them, "Don't be afraid! Go tell my brothers to leave for Galilee, and they will see me there."

The Report of the Guard

¹¹As the women were on their way, some of the guards went into the city and told the leading priests what had happened. ¹²A meeting with the elders was called, and they decided to give the soldiers a large bribe. ¹³They told the soldiers, "You must say, 'Jesus' disciples came during the night while we were sleeping, and they stole his body.' ¹⁴If the governor hears about it, we'll stand up for you so you won't get in trouble." ¹⁵So the guards accepted the bribe and said what they were told to say. Their story spread widely among the Jews, and they still tell it today.

The Great Commission

¹⁶Then the eleven disciples left for Galilee, going to the mountain where Jesus had told them to go. ¹⁷When they saw him, they worshiped him—but some of them doubted!

¹⁸Jesus came and told his disciples, "I have been given all authority in heaven and on earth. ¹⁹Therefore, go and make disciples of all the nations,* baptizing them in the name of the Father and the Son and the Holy Spirit. ²⁰Teach these new disciples to obey all the commands I have given you. And be sure of this: I am with you always, even to the end of the age."

28:1 Greek *After the Sabbath, on the first day of the week.* 28:19 Or *all peoples.*

Mark

MANY PASSAGES OF SCRIPTURE speak of Jesus as the exalted Lord, but Mark's Gospel presents another side of Jesus, as well: his servanthood. Mark was not one of the twelve disciples, but it is traditionally believed that his Gospel was compiled from the sermons of the apostle Peter. Mark set the pace for his Gospel from the very start, forgoing the details of Jesus' birth and moving straight into his baptism and ministry. Throughout this Gospel, Jesus is constantly on the move, healing the sick, confronting demons, feeding large crowds, giving time to "outsiders," and tirelessly responding to requests for help and guidance. Mark included several passages of teaching as well, but these are largely overshadowed by the accounts of Jesus' actions. Mark made it clear that Jesus is indeed the Son of God; no one else could have done what Jesus did. But Jesus' actions and teaching also point toward a core theme of the book: "For even the Son of Man came not to be served but to serve others and to give his life as a ransom for many" (10:45). The book closes with Jesus' death and resurrection, thus completing a basic outline of the life of Jesus Christ.

■ **Author:** John Mark. He was not one of the twelve disciples, but it is traditionally believed that his Gospel is compiled from the sermons of the apostle Peter.

■ **Date Written:** Probably between AD 55 and 65, from the city of Rome

■ **Purpose:** To present Jesus Christ as both servant and Son of God by recounting his ministry and teachings in a basic biographical outline

■ **Themes:** Jesus the Messiah, servanthood/ministry, miracles

■ **Outline**
1:1-13 John the Baptist and the baptism of Jesus
1:14–9:50 The Galilean ministry of Jesus
10:1–11:25 Trip to Jerusalem and entrance into the city
11:27–12:44 Conflicts in the city
13:1-37 Prophecies of things to come
14:1–16:20 Jesus' death and resurrection

John the Baptist Prepares the Way

1 This is the Good News about Jesus the Messiah, the Son of God.* It began ²just as the prophet Isaiah had written:

"Look, I am sending my messenger ahead of you,
and he will prepare your way.*
³ He is a voice shouting in the wilderness,
'Prepare the way for the LORD's coming!
Clear the road for him!'*"

⁴This messenger was John the Baptist. He was in the wilderness and preached that people should be baptized to show that they had repented of their sins and turned to God to be forgiven. ⁵All of Judea, including all the people of Jerusalem, went out to see and hear John. And when they confessed their sins, he baptized them in the Jordan River. ⁶His clothes were woven from coarse camel hair, and he wore a leather belt around his waist. For food he ate locusts and wild honey.

⁷John announced: "Someone is coming soon who is greater than I am—so much greater that I'm not even worthy to stoop down like a slave and untie the straps of his sandals. ⁸I baptize you with* water, but he will baptize you with the Holy Spirit!"

1:1 Some manuscripts do not include *the Son of God.*   1:2 Mal 3:1.   1:3 Isa 40:3 (Greek version).   1:8 Or *in*; also in 1:8b.

The Baptism and Temptation of Jesus

⁹One day Jesus came from Nazareth in Galilee, and John baptized him in the Jordan River. ¹⁰As Jesus came up out of the water, he saw the heavens splitting apart and the Holy Spirit descending on him* like a dove. ¹¹And a voice from heaven said, "You are my dearly loved Son, and you bring me great joy."

¹²The Spirit then compelled Jesus to go into the wilderness, ¹³where he was tempted by Satan for forty days. He was out among the wild animals, and angels took care of him.

¹⁴Later on, after John was arrested, Jesus went into Galilee, where he preached God's Good News.* ¹⁵"The time promised by God has come at last!" he announced. "The Kingdom of God is near! Repent of your sins and believe the Good News!"

The First Disciples

¹⁶One day as Jesus was walking along the shore of the Sea of Galilee, he saw Simon* and his brother Andrew throwing a net into the water, for they fished for a living. ¹⁷Jesus called out to them, "Come, follow me, and I will show you how to fish for people!" ¹⁸And they left their nets at once and followed him.

¹⁹A little farther up the shore Jesus saw Zebedee's sons, James and John, in a boat repairing their nets. ²⁰He called them at once, and they also followed him, leaving their father, Zebedee, in the boat with the hired men.

Jesus Casts Out an Evil Spirit

²¹Jesus and his companions went to the town of Capernaum. When the Sabbath day came, he went into the synagogue and began to teach. ²²The people were amazed at his teaching, for he taught with real authority—quite unlike the teachers of religious law.

²³Suddenly, a man in the synagogue who was possessed by an evil* spirit cried out, ²⁴"Why are you interfering with us, Jesus of Nazareth? Have you come to destroy us? I know who you are—the Holy One of God!"

²⁵But Jesus reprimanded him. "Be quiet! Come out of the man," he ordered. ²⁶At that, the evil spirit screamed, threw the man into a convulsion, and then came out of him.

²⁷Amazement gripped the audience, and they began to discuss what had happened. "What sort of new teaching is this?" they asked excitedly. "It has such authority! Even evil spirits obey his orders!" ²⁸The news about Jesus spread quickly throughout the entire region of Galilee.

Jesus Heals Many People

²⁹After Jesus left the synagogue with James and John, they went to Simon and Andrew's home. ³⁰Now Simon's mother-in-law was sick in bed with a high fever. They told Jesus about her right away. ³¹So he went to her bedside, took her by the hand, and helped her sit up. Then the fever left her, and she prepared a meal for them.

³²That evening after sunset, many sick and demon-possessed people were brought to Jesus. ³³The whole town gathered at the door to watch. ³⁴So Jesus healed many people who were sick with various diseases, and he cast out many demons. But because the demons knew who he was, he did not allow them to speak.

Jesus Preaches in Galilee

³⁵Before daybreak the next morning, Jesus got up and went out to an isolated place to pray. ³⁶Later Simon and the others went out to find him. ³⁷When they found him, they said, "Everyone is looking for you."

³⁸But Jesus replied, "We must go on to other towns as well, and I will preach to them, too. That is why I came." ³⁹So he traveled throughout the region of Galilee, preaching in the synagogues and casting out demons.

Jesus Heals a Man with Leprosy

⁴⁰A man with leprosy came and knelt in front of Jesus, begging to be healed. "If you are willing, you can heal me and make me clean," he said.

⁴¹Moved with compassion,* Jesus reached out and touched him. "I am willing," he said. "Be healed!" ⁴²Instantly the leprosy disappeared, and the man was healed. ⁴³Then Jesus sent him on his way with a stern warning: ⁴⁴"Don't tell anyone about this. Instead, go to the priest and let him examine you. Take along the offering required in the law of Moses for those who have been healed of leprosy.* This will be a public testimony that you have been cleansed."

⁴⁵But the man went and spread the word, proclaiming to everyone what had happened. As a result, large crowds soon surrounded Jesus, and he couldn't publicly enter a town anywhere. He had to stay out in the secluded places, but people from everywhere kept coming to him.

1:10 Or *toward him,* or *into him.*   1:14 Some manuscripts read *the Good News of the Kingdom of God.*   1:16 *Simon* is called "Peter" in 3:16 and thereafter.   1:23 Greek *unclean;* also in 1:26, 27.   1:41 Some manuscripts read *Moved with anger.*   1:44 See Lev 14:2-32.

Jesus Heals a Paralyzed Man

2 When Jesus returned to Capernaum several days later, the news spread quickly that he was back home. ²Soon the house where he was staying was so packed with visitors that there was no more room, even outside the door. While he was preaching God's word to them, ³four men arrived carrying a paralyzed man on a mat. ⁴They couldn't bring him to Jesus because of the crowd, so they dug a hole through the roof above his head. Then they lowered the man on his mat, right down in front of Jesus. ⁵Seeing their faith, Jesus said to the paralyzed man, "My child, your sins are forgiven."

⁶But some of the teachers of religious law who were sitting there thought to themselves, ⁷"What is he saying? This is blasphemy! Only God can forgive sins!"

⁸Jesus knew immediately what they were thinking, so he asked them, "Why do you question this in your hearts? ⁹Is it easier to say to the paralyzed man 'Your sins are forgiven,' or 'Stand up, pick up your mat, and walk'? ¹⁰So I will prove to you that the Son of Man* has the authority on earth to forgive sins." Then Jesus turned to the paralyzed man and said, ¹¹"Stand up, pick up your mat, and go home!"

¹²And the man jumped up, grabbed his mat, and walked out through the stunned onlookers. They were all amazed and praised God, exclaiming, "We've never seen anything like this before!"

Jesus Calls Levi (Matthew)

¹³Then Jesus went out to the lakeshore again and taught the crowds that were coming to him. ¹⁴As he walked along, he saw Levi son of Alphaeus sitting at his tax collector's booth. "Follow me and be my disciple," Jesus said to him. So Levi got up and followed him.

¹⁵Later, Levi invited Jesus and his disciples to his home as dinner guests, along with many tax collectors and other disreputable sinners. (There were many people of this kind among Jesus' followers.) ¹⁶But when the teachers of religious law who were Pharisees* saw him eating with tax collectors and other sinners, they asked his disciples, "Why does he eat with such scum?*"

¹⁷When Jesus heard this, he told them, "Healthy people don't need a doctor—sick people do. I have come to call not those who think they are righteous, but those who know they are sinners."

A Discussion about Fasting

¹⁸Once when John's disciples and the Pharisees were fasting, some people came to Jesus and asked, "Why don't your disciples fast like John's disciples and the Pharisees do?"

¹⁹Jesus replied, "Do wedding guests fast while celebrating with the groom? Of course not. They can't fast while the groom is with them. ²⁰But someday the groom will be taken away from them, and then they will fast.

²¹"Besides, who would patch old clothing with new cloth? For the new patch would shrink and rip away from the old cloth, leaving an even bigger tear than before.

²²"And no one puts new wine into old wineskins. For the wine would burst the wineskins, and the wine and the skins would both be lost. New wine calls for new wineskins."

A Discussion about the Sabbath

²³One Sabbath day as Jesus was walking through some grainfields, his disciples began breaking off heads of grain to eat. ²⁴But the Pharisees said to Jesus, "Look, why are they breaking the law by harvesting grain on the Sabbath?"

²⁵Jesus said to them, "Haven't you ever read in the Scriptures what David did when he and his companions were hungry? ²⁶He went into the house of God (during the days when Abiathar was high priest) and broke the law by eating the sacred loaves of bread that only the priests are allowed to eat. He also gave some to his companions."

²⁷Then Jesus said to them, "The Sabbath was made to meet the needs of people, and not people to meet the requirements of the Sabbath. ²⁸So the Son of Man is Lord, even over the Sabbath!"

Jesus Heals on the Sabbath

3 Jesus went into the synagogue again and noticed a man with a deformed hand. ²Since it was the Sabbath, Jesus' enemies watched him closely. If he healed the man's hand, they planned to accuse him of working on the Sabbath.

³Jesus said to the man with the deformed hand, "Come and stand in front of everyone." ⁴Then he turned to his critics and asked, "Does the law permit good deeds on the Sabbath, or is it a day for doing evil? Is this a day to save life or to destroy it?" But they wouldn't answer him.

⁵He looked around at them angrily and was

2:10 "Son of Man" is a title Jesus used for himself. 2:16a Greek *the scribes of the Pharisees.* 2:16b Greek *with tax collectors and sinners?*

deeply saddened by their hard hearts. Then he said to the man, "Hold out your hand." So the man held out his hand, and it was restored! ⁶At once the Pharisees went away and met with the supporters of Herod to plot how to kill Jesus.

Crowds Follow Jesus

⁷Jesus went out to the lake with his disciples, and a large crowd followed him. They came from all over Galilee, Judea, ⁸Jerusalem, Idumea, from east of the Jordan River, and even from as far north as Tyre and Sidon. The news about his miracles had spread far and wide, and vast numbers of people came to see him.

⁹Jesus instructed his disciples to have a boat ready so the crowd would not crush him. ¹⁰He had healed many people that day, so all the sick people eagerly pushed forward to touch him. ¹¹And whenever those possessed by evil* spirits caught sight of him, the spirits would throw them to the ground in front of him shrieking, "You are the Son of God!" ¹²But Jesus sternly commanded the spirits not to reveal who he was.

Jesus Chooses the Twelve Apostles

¹³Afterward Jesus went up on a mountain and called out the ones he wanted to go with him. And they came to him. ¹⁴Then he appointed twelve of them and called them his apostles.* They were to accompany him, and he would send them out to preach, ¹⁵giving them authority to cast out demons. ¹⁶These are the twelve he chose:

Simon (whom he named Peter),
¹⁷ James and John (the sons of Zebedee, but Jesus nicknamed them "Sons of Thunder"*),
¹⁸ Andrew,
Philip,
Bartholomew,
Matthew,
Thomas,
James (son of Alphaeus),
Thaddaeus,
Simon (the zealot*),
¹⁹ Judas Iscariot (who later betrayed him).

Jesus and the Prince of Demons

²⁰One time Jesus entered a house, and the crowds began to gather again. Soon he and his disciples couldn't even find time to eat. ²¹When his family heard what was happening, they tried to take him away. "He's out of his mind," they said.

²²But the teachers of religious law who had arrived from Jerusalem said, "He's possessed by Satan,* the prince of demons. That's where he gets the power to cast out demons."

²³Jesus called them over and responded with an illustration. "How can Satan cast out Satan?" he asked. ²⁴"A kingdom divided by civil war will collapse. ²⁵Similarly, a family splintered by feuding will fall apart. ²⁶And if Satan is divided and fights against himself, how can he stand? He would never survive. ²⁷Let me illustrate this further. Who is powerful enough to enter the house of a strong man and plunder his goods? Only someone even stronger—someone who could tie him up and then plunder his house.

²⁸"I tell you the truth, all sin and blasphemy can be forgiven, ²⁹but anyone who blasphemes the Holy Spirit will never be forgiven. This is a sin with eternal consequences." ³⁰He told them this because they were saying, "He's possessed by an evil spirit."

The True Family of Jesus

³¹Then Jesus' mother and brothers came to see him. They stood outside and sent word for him to come out and talk with them. ³²There was a crowd sitting around Jesus, and someone said, "Your mother and your brothers* are outside asking for you."

³³Jesus replied, "Who is my mother? Who are my brothers?" ³⁴Then he looked at those around him and said, "Look, these are my mother and brothers. ³⁵Anyone who does God's will is my brother and sister and mother."

Parable of the Farmer Scattering Seed

4 Once again Jesus began teaching by the lakeshore. A very large crowd soon gathered around him, so he got into a boat. Then he sat in the boat while all the people remained on the shore. ²He taught them by telling many stories in the form of parables, such as this one:

³"Listen! A farmer went out to plant some seed. ⁴As he scattered it across his field, some of the seed fell on a footpath, and the birds came and ate it. ⁵Other seed fell on shallow soil with underlying rock. The seed sprouted

3:11 Greek *unclean;* also in 3:30.   3:14 Some manuscripts do not include *and called them his apostles.*   3:17 Greek *whom he named Boanerges, which means Sons of Thunder.*   3:18 Greek *the Cananean,* an Aramaic term for Jewish nationalists.   3:22 Greek *Beelzeboul;* other manuscripts read *Beezeboul;* Latin version reads *Beelzebub.*   3:32 Some manuscripts add *and sisters.*

quickly because the soil was shallow. 6But the plant soon wilted under the hot sun, and since it didn't have deep roots, it died. 7Other seed fell among thorns that grew up and choked out the tender plants so they produced no grain. 8Still other seeds fell on fertile soil, and they sprouted, grew, and produced a crop that was thirty, sixty, and even a hundred times as much as had been planted!" 9Then he said, "Anyone with ears to hear should listen and understand."

10Later, when Jesus was alone with the twelve disciples and with the others who were gathered around, they asked him what the parables meant.

11He replied, "You are permitted to understand the secret* of the Kingdom of God. But I use parables for everything I say to outsiders, 12so that the Scriptures might be fulfilled:

'When they see what I do,
    they will learn nothing.
When they hear what I say,
    they will not understand.
Otherwise, they will turn to me
    and be forgiven.'*"

13Then Jesus said to them, "If you can't understand the meaning of this parable, how will you understand all the other parables? 14The farmer plants seed by taking God's word to others. 15The seed that fell on the footpath represents those who hear the message, only to have Satan come at once and take it away. 16The seed on the rocky soil represents those who hear the message and immediately receive it with joy. 17But since they don't have deep roots, they don't last long. They fall away as soon as they have problems or are persecuted for believing God's word. 18The seed that fell among the thorns represents others who hear God's word, 19but all too quickly the message is crowded out by the worries of this life, the lure of wealth, and the desire for other things, so no fruit is produced. 20And the seed that fell on good soil represents those who hear and accept God's word and produce a harvest of thirty, sixty, or even a hundred times as much as had been planted!"

Parable of the Lamp

21Then Jesus asked them, "Would anyone light a lamp and then put it under a basket or under a bed? Of course not! A lamp is placed on a stand, where its light will shine. 22For everything that is hidden will eventually be brought into the open, and every secret will be brought to light. 23Anyone with ears to hear should listen and understand."

24Then he added, "Pay close attention to what you hear. The closer you listen, the more understanding you will be given*—and you will receive even more. 25To those who listen to my teaching, more understanding will be given. But for those who are not listening, even what little understanding they have will be taken away from them."

Parable of the Growing Seed

26Jesus also said, "The Kingdom of God is like a farmer who scatters seed on the ground. 27Night and day, while he's asleep or awake, the seed sprouts and grows, but he does not understand how it happens. 28The earth produces the crops on its own. First a leaf blade pushes through, then the heads of wheat are formed, and finally the grain ripens. 29And as soon as the grain is ready, the farmer comes and harvests it with a sickle, for the harvest time has come."

Parable of the Mustard Seed

30Jesus said, "How can I describe the Kingdom of God? What story should I use to illustrate it? 31It is like a mustard seed planted in the ground. It is the smallest of all seeds, 32but it becomes the largest of all garden plants; it grows long branches, and birds can make nests in its shade."

33Jesus used many similar stories and illustrations to teach the people as much as they could understand. 34In fact, in his public ministry he never taught without using parables; but afterward, when he was alone with his disciples, he explained everything to them.

Jesus Calms the Storm

35As evening came, Jesus said to his disciples, "Let's cross to the other side of the lake." 36So they took Jesus in the boat and started out, leaving the crowds behind (although other boats followed). 37But soon a fierce storm came up. High waves were breaking into the boat, and it began to fill with water.

38Jesus was sleeping at the back of the boat with his head on a cushion. The disciples woke him up, shouting, "Teacher, don't you care that we're going to drown?"

39When Jesus woke up, he rebuked the wind and said to the waves, "Silence! Be still!"

4:11 Greek *mystery*.   4:12 Isa 6:9-10 (Greek version).   4:24 Or *The measure you give will be the measure you get back.*

Suddenly the wind stopped, and there was a great calm. ⁴⁰Then he asked them, "Why are you afraid? Do you still have no faith?"

⁴¹The disciples were absolutely terrified. "Who is this man?" they asked each other. "Even the wind and waves obey him!"

Jesus Heals a Demon-Possessed Man

5 So they arrived at the other side of the lake, in the region of the Gerasenes.* ²When Jesus climbed out of the boat, a man possessed by an evil* spirit came out from the tombs to meet him. ³This man lived in the burial caves and could no longer be restrained, even with a chain. ⁴Whenever he was put into chains and shackles—as he often was—he snapped the chains from his wrists and smashed the shackles. No one was strong enough to subdue him. ⁵Day and night he wandered among the burial caves and in the hills, howling and cutting himself with sharp stones.

⁶When Jesus was still some distance away, the man saw him, ran to meet him, and bowed low before him. ⁷With a shriek, he screamed, "Why are you interfering with me, Jesus, Son of the Most High God? In the name of God, I beg you, don't torture me!" ⁸For Jesus had already said to the spirit, "Come out of the man, you evil spirit."

⁹Then Jesus demanded, "What is your name?"

And he replied, "My name is Legion, because there are many of us inside this man." ¹⁰Then the evil spirits begged him again and again not to send them to some distant place.

¹¹There happened to be a large herd of pigs feeding on the hillside nearby. ¹²"Send us into those pigs," the spirits begged. "Let us enter them."

¹³So Jesus gave them permission. The evil spirits came out of the man and entered the pigs, and the entire herd of about 2,000 pigs plunged down the steep hillside into the lake and drowned in the water.

¹⁴The herdsmen fled to the nearby town and the surrounding countryside, spreading the news as they ran. People rushed out to see what had happened. ¹⁵A crowd soon gathered around Jesus, and they saw the man who had been possessed by the legion of demons. He was sitting there fully clothed and perfectly sane, and they were all afraid. ¹⁶Then those who had seen what happened told the others about the demon-possessed man and the pigs.

¹⁷And the crowd began pleading with Jesus to go away and leave them alone.

¹⁸As Jesus was getting into the boat, the man who had been demon possessed begged to go with him. ¹⁹But Jesus said, "No, go home to your family, and tell them everything the Lord has done for you and how merciful he has been." ²⁰So the man started off to visit the Ten Towns* of that region and began to proclaim the great things Jesus had done for him; and everyone was amazed at what he told them.

Jesus Heals in Response to Faith

²¹Jesus got into the boat again and went back to the other side of the lake, where a large crowd gathered around him on the shore. ²²Then a leader of the local synagogue, whose name was Jairus, arrived. When he saw Jesus, he fell at his feet, ²³pleading fervently with him. "My little daughter is dying," he said. "Please come and lay your hands on her; heal her so she can live."

²⁴Jesus went with him, and all the people followed, crowding around him. ²⁵A woman in the crowd had suffered for twelve years with constant bleeding. ²⁶She had suffered a great deal from many doctors, and over the years she had spent everything she had to pay them, but she had gotten no better. In fact, she had gotten worse. ²⁷She had heard about Jesus, so she came up behind him through the crowd and touched his robe. ²⁸For she thought to herself, "If I can just touch his robe, I will be healed." ²⁹Immediately the bleeding stopped, and she could feel in her body that she had been healed of her terrible condition.

³⁰Jesus realized at once that healing power had gone out from him, so he turned around in the crowd and asked, "Who touched my robe?"

³¹His disciples said to him, "Look at this crowd pressing around you. How can you ask, 'Who touched me?'"

³²But he kept on looking around to see who had done it. ³³Then the frightened woman, trembling at the realization of what had happened to her, came and fell to her knees in front of him and told him what she had done. ³⁴And he said to her, "Daughter, your faith has made you well. Go in peace. Your suffering is over."

³⁵While he was still speaking to her, messengers arrived from the home of Jairus, the leader of the synagogue. They told him, "Your daughter is dead. There's no use troubling the Teacher now."

5:1 Other manuscripts read *Gadarenes;* still others read *Gergesenes.* See Matt 8:28; Luke 8:26.   5:2 Greek *unclean;* also in 5:8, 13.   5:20 Greek *Decapolis.*

³⁶But Jesus overheard* them and said to Jairus, "Don't be afraid. Just have faith."

³⁷Then Jesus stopped the crowd and wouldn't let anyone go with him except Peter, James, and John (the brother of James). ³⁸When they came to the home of the synagogue leader, Jesus saw much commotion and weeping and wailing. ³⁹He went inside and asked, "Why all this commotion and weeping? The child isn't dead; she's only asleep."

⁴⁰The crowd laughed at him. But he made them all leave, and he took the girl's father and mother and his three disciples into the room where the girl was lying. ⁴¹Holding her hand, he said to her, "Talitha koum," which means "Little girl, get up!" ⁴²And the girl, who was twelve years old, immediately stood up and walked around! They were overwhelmed and totally amazed. ⁴³Jesus gave them strict orders not to tell anyone what had happened, and then he told them to give her something to eat.

Jesus Rejected at Nazareth

6 Jesus left that part of the country and returned with his disciples to Nazareth, his hometown. ²The next Sabbath he began teaching in the synagogue, and many who heard him were amazed. They asked, "Where did he get all this wisdom and the power to perform such miracles?" ³Then they scoffed, "He's just a carpenter, the son of Mary* and the brother of James, Joseph,* Judas, and Simon. And his sisters live right here among us." They were deeply offended and refused to believe in him.

⁴Then Jesus told them, "A prophet is honored everywhere except in his own hometown and among his relatives and his own family." ⁵And because of their unbelief, he couldn't do any miracles among them except to place his hands on a few sick people and heal them. ⁶And he was amazed at their unbelief.

Jesus Sends Out the Twelve Disciples

Then Jesus went from village to village, teaching the people. ⁷And he called his twelve disciples together and began sending them out two by two, giving them authority to cast out evil* spirits. ⁸He told them to take nothing for their journey except a walking stick—no food, no traveler's bag, no money.* ⁹He allowed them to wear sandals but not to take a change of clothes. ¹⁰"Wherever you go," he said, "stay in the same house until you leave town. ¹¹But if any

place refuses to welcome you or listen to you, shake its dust from your feet as you leave to show that you have abandoned those people to their fate."

¹²So the disciples went out, telling everyone they met to repent of their sins and turn to God. ¹³And they cast out many demons and healed many sick people, anointing them with olive oil.

The Death of John the Baptist

¹⁴Herod Antipas, the king, soon heard about Jesus, because everyone was talking about him. Some were saying,* "This must be John the Baptist raised from the dead. That is why he can do such miracles." ¹⁵Others said, "He's the prophet Elijah." Still others said, "He's a prophet like the other great prophets of the past."

¹⁶When Herod heard about Jesus, he said, "John, the man I beheaded, has come back from the dead."

¹⁷For Herod had sent soldiers to arrest and imprison John as a favor to Herodias. She had been his brother Philip's wife, but Herod had married her. ¹⁸John had been telling Herod, "It is against God's law for you to marry your brother's wife." ¹⁹So Herodias bore a grudge against John and wanted to kill him. But without Herod's approval she was powerless, ²⁰for Herod respected John; and knowing that he was a good and holy man, he protected him. Herod was greatly disturbed whenever he talked with John, but even so, he liked to listen to him.

²¹Herodias's chance finally came on Herod's birthday. He gave a party for his high government officials, army officers, and the leading citizens of Galilee. ²²Then his daughter, also named Herodias,* came in and performed a dance that greatly pleased Herod and his guests. "Ask me for anything you like," the king said to the girl, "and I will give it to you." ²³He even vowed, "I will give you whatever you ask, up to half my kingdom!"

²⁴She went out and asked her mother, "What should I ask for?"

Her mother told her, "Ask for the head of John the Baptist!"

²⁵So the girl hurried back to the king and told him, "I want the head of John the Baptist, right now, on a tray!"

²⁶Then the king deeply regretted what he had said; but because of the vows he had made in front of his guests, he couldn't refuse her.

5:36 Or ignored. 6:3a Some manuscripts read He's just the son of the carpenter and of Mary. 6:3b Most manuscripts read Joses; see Matt 13:55. 6:7 Greek unclean. 6:8 Greek no copper coins in their money belts. 6:14 Some manuscripts read He was saying. 6:22 Some manuscripts read the daughter of Herodias herself.

²⁷So he immediately sent an executioner to the prison to cut off John's head and bring it to him. The soldier beheaded John in the prison, ²⁸brought his head on a tray, and gave it to the girl, who took it to her mother. ²⁹When John's disciples heard what had happened, they came to get his body and buried it in a tomb.

Jesus Feeds Five Thousand

³⁰The apostles returned to Jesus from their ministry tour and told him all they had done and taught. ³¹Then Jesus said, "Let's go off by ourselves to a quiet place and rest awhile." He said this because there were so many people coming and going that Jesus and his apostles didn't even have time to eat.

³²So they left by boat for a quiet place, where they could be alone. ³³But many people recognized them and saw them leaving, and people from many towns ran ahead along the shore and got there ahead of them. ³⁴Jesus saw the huge crowd as he stepped from the boat, and he had compassion on them because they were like sheep without a shepherd. So he began teaching them many things.

³⁵Late in the afternoon his disciples came to him and said, "This is a remote place, and it's already getting late. ³⁶Send the crowds away so they can go to the nearby farms and villages and buy something to eat."

³⁷But Jesus said, "You feed them."

"With what?" they asked. "We'd have to work for months to earn enough money* to buy food for all these people!"

³⁸"How much bread do you have?" he asked. "Go and find out."

They came back and reported, "We have five loaves of bread and two fish."

³⁹Then Jesus told the disciples to have the people sit down in groups on the green grass. ⁴⁰So they sat down in groups of fifty or a hundred.

⁴¹Jesus took the five loaves and two fish, looked up toward heaven, and blessed them. Then, breaking the loaves into pieces, he kept giving the bread to the disciples so they could distribute it to the people. He also divided the fish for everyone to share. ⁴²They all ate as much as they wanted, ⁴³and afterward, the disciples picked up twelve baskets of leftover bread and fish. ⁴⁴A total of 5,000 men and their families were fed.*

Jesus Walks on Water

⁴⁵Immediately after this, Jesus insisted that his disciples get back into the boat and head across the lake to Bethsaida, while he sent the people home. ⁴⁶After telling everyone goodbye, he went up into the hills by himself to pray.

⁴⁷Late that night, the disciples were in their boat in the middle of the lake, and Jesus was alone on land. ⁴⁸He saw that they were in serious trouble, rowing hard and struggling against the wind and waves. About three o'clock in the morning* Jesus came toward them, walking on the water. He intended to go past them, ⁴⁹but when they saw him walking on the water, they cried out in terror, thinking he was a ghost. ⁵⁰They were all terrified when they saw him.

But Jesus spoke to them at once. "Don't be afraid," he said. "Take courage! I am here!*" ⁵¹Then he climbed into the boat, and the wind stopped. They were totally amazed, ⁵²for they still didn't understand the significance of the miracle of the loaves. Their hearts were too hard to take it in.

⁵³After they had crossed the lake, they landed at Gennesaret. They brought the boat to shore ⁵⁴and climbed out. The people recognized Jesus at once, ⁵⁵and they ran throughout the whole area, carrying sick people on mats to wherever they heard he was. ⁵⁶Wherever he went—in villages, cities, or the countryside—they brought the sick out to the marketplaces. They begged him to let the sick touch at least the fringe of his robe, and all who touched him were healed.

Jesus Teaches about Inner Purity

7 One day some Pharisees and teachers of religious law arrived from Jerusalem to see Jesus. ²They noticed that some of his disciples failed to follow the Jewish ritual of hand washing before eating. ³(The Jews, especially the Pharisees, do not eat until they have poured water over their cupped hands,* as required by their ancient traditions. ⁴Similarly, they don't eat anything from the market until they immerse their hands* in water. This is but one of many traditions they have clung to—such as their ceremonial washing of cups, pitchers, and kettles.*)

⁵So the Pharisees and teachers of religious

6:37 Greek *It would take 200 denarii.* A denarius was equivalent to a laborer's full day's wage.   6:44 Some manuscripts read *fed from the loaves.*   6:48 Greek *About the fourth watch of the night.*   6:50 Or *The 'I AM' is here;* Greek reads *I am.* See Exod 3:14.   7:3 Greek *have washed with the fist.*   7:4a Some manuscripts read *sprinkle themselves.*   7:4b Some manuscripts add *and dining couches.*

law asked him, "Why don't your disciples follow our age-old tradition? They eat without first performing the hand-washing ceremony."

6Jesus replied, "You hypocrites! Isaiah was right when he prophesied about you, for he wrote,

'These people honor me with their lips,
    but their hearts are far from me.
7 Their worship is a farce,
    for they teach man-made ideas as
        commands from God.'*

8For you ignore God's law and substitute your own tradition."

9Then he said, "You skillfully sidestep God's law in order to hold on to your own tradition. 10For instance, Moses gave you this law from God: 'Honor your father and mother,'* and 'Anyone who speaks disrespectfully of father or mother must be put to death.'* 11But you say it is all right for people to say to their parents, 'Sorry, I can't help you. For I have vowed to give to God what I would have given to you.'* 12In this way, you let them disregard their needy parents. 13And so you cancel the word of God in order to hand down your own tradition. And this is only one example among many others."

14Then Jesus called to the crowd to come and hear. "All of you listen," he said, "and try to understand. 15It's not what goes into your body that defiles you; you are defiled by what comes from your heart.*"

17Then Jesus went into a house to get away from the crowd, and his disciples asked him what he meant by the parable he had just used. 18"Don't you understand either?" he asked. "Can't you see that the food you put into your body cannot defile you? 19Food doesn't go into your heart, but only passes through the stomach and then goes into the sewer." (By saying this, he declared that every kind of food is acceptable in God's eyes.)

20And then he added, "It is what comes from inside that defiles you. 21For from within, out of a person's heart, come evil thoughts, sexual immorality, theft, murder, 22adultery, greed, wickedness, deceit, lustful desires, envy, slander, pride, and foolishness. 23All these vile things come from within; they are what defile you."

The Faith of a Gentile Woman

24Then Jesus left Galilee and went north to the region of Tyre.* He didn't want anyone to know which house he was staying in, but he couldn't keep it a secret. 25Right away a woman who had heard about him came and fell at his feet. Her little girl was possessed by an evil* spirit, 26and she begged him to cast out the demon from her daughter.

Since she was a Gentile, born in Syrian Phoenicia, 27Jesus told her, "First I should feed the children—my own family, the Jews.* It isn't right to take food from the children and throw it to the dogs."

28She replied, "That's true, Lord, but even the dogs under the table are allowed to eat the scraps from the children's plates."

29"Good answer!" he said. "Now go home, for the demon has left your daughter." 30And when she arrived home, she found her little girl lying quietly in bed, and the demon was gone.

Jesus Heals a Deaf Man

31Jesus left Tyre and went up to Sidon before going back to the Sea of Galilee and the region of the Ten Towns.* 32A deaf man with a speech impediment was brought to him, and the people begged Jesus to lay his hands on the man to heal him.

33Jesus led him away from the crowd so they could be alone. He put his fingers into the man's ears. Then, spitting on his own fingers, he touched the man's tongue. 34Looking up to heaven, he sighed and said, "Ephphatha," which means, "Be opened!" 35Instantly the man could hear perfectly, and his tongue was freed so he could speak plainly!

36Jesus told the crowd not to tell anyone, but the more he told them not to, the more they spread the news. 37They were completely amazed and said again and again, "Everything he does is wonderful. He even makes the deaf to hear and gives speech to those who cannot speak."

Jesus Feeds Four Thousand

8 About this time another large crowd had gathered, and the people ran out of food again. Jesus called his disciples and told them, 2"I feel sorry for these people. They have been here with me for three days, and they have

7:7 Isa 29:13 (Greek version).   7:10a Exod 20:12; Deut 5:16.   7:10b Exod 21:17 (Greek version); Lev 20:9 (Greek version). 7:11 Greek 'What I would have given to you is Corban' (that is, a gift).   7:15 Some manuscripts add verse 16, Anyone with ears to hear should listen and understand. Compare 4:9, 23.   7:24 Some manuscripts add and Sidon.   7:25 Greek unclean.   7:27 Greek Let the children eat first.   7:31 Greek Decapolis.

nothing left to eat. ³If I send them home hungry, they will faint along the way. For some of them have come a long distance."

⁴His disciples replied, "How are we supposed to find enough food to feed them out here in the wilderness?"

⁵Jesus asked, "How much bread do you have?"

"Seven loaves," they replied.

⁶So Jesus told all the people to sit down on the ground. Then he took the seven loaves, thanked God for them, and broke them into pieces. He gave them to his disciples, who distributed the bread to the crowd. ⁷A few small fish were found, too, so Jesus also blessed these and told the disciples to distribute them.

⁸They ate as much as they wanted. Afterward, the disciples picked up seven large baskets of leftover food. ⁹There were about 4,000 men in the crowd that day, and Jesus sent them home after they had eaten. ¹⁰Immediately after this, he got into a boat with his disciples and crossed over to the region of Dalmanutha.

Pharisees Demand a Miraculous Sign

¹¹When the Pharisees heard that Jesus had arrived, they came and started to argue with him. Testing him, they demanded that he show them a miraculous sign from heaven to prove his authority.

¹²When he heard this, he sighed deeply in his spirit and said, "Why do these people keep demanding a miraculous sign? I tell you the truth, I will not give this generation any such sign." ¹³So he got back into the boat and left them, and he crossed to the other side of the lake.

Yeast of the Pharisees and Herod

¹⁴But the disciples had forgotten to bring any food. They had only one loaf of bread with them in the boat. ¹⁵As they were crossing the lake, Jesus warned them, "Watch out! Beware of the yeast of the Pharisees and of Herod."

¹⁶At this they began to argue with each other because they hadn't brought any bread. ¹⁷Jesus knew what they were saying, so he said, "Why are you arguing about having no bread? Don't you know or understand even yet? Are your hearts too hard to take it in? ¹⁸'You have eyes—can't you see? You have ears—can't you hear?'* Don't you remember anything at all? ¹⁹When I fed the 5,000 with five loaves of bread, how many baskets of leftovers did you pick up afterward?"

"Twelve," they said.

²⁰"And when I fed the 4,000 with seven loaves, how many large baskets of leftovers did you pick up?"

"Seven," they said.

²¹"Don't you understand yet?" he asked them.

Jesus Heals a Blind Man

²²When they arrived at Bethsaida, some people brought a blind man to Jesus, and they begged him to touch the man and heal him. ²³Jesus took the blind man by the hand and led him out of the village. Then, spitting on the man's eyes, he laid his hands on him and asked, "Can you see anything now?"

²⁴The man looked around. "Yes," he said, "I see people, but I can't see them very clearly. They look like trees walking around."

²⁵Then Jesus placed his hands on the man's eyes again, and his eyes were opened. His sight was completely restored, and he could see everything clearly. ²⁶Jesus sent him away, saying, "Don't go back into the village on your way home."

Peter's Declaration about Jesus

²⁷Jesus and his disciples left Galilee and went up to the villages near Caesarea Philippi. As they were walking along, he asked them, "Who do people say I am?"

²⁸"Well," they replied, "some say John the Baptist, some say Elijah, and others say you are one of the other prophets."

²⁹Then he asked them, "But who do you say I am?"

Peter replied, "You are the Messiah.*"

³⁰But Jesus warned them not to tell anyone about him.

Jesus Predicts His Death

³¹Then Jesus began to tell them that the Son of Man* must suffer many terrible things and be rejected by the elders, the leading priests, and the teachers of religious law. He would be killed, but three days later he would rise from the dead. ³²As he talked about this openly with his disciples, Peter took him aside and began to reprimand him for saying such things.*

³³Jesus turned around and looked at his disciples, then reprimanded Peter. "Get away from me, Satan!" he said. "You are seeing things merely from a human point of view, not from God's."

8:18 Jer 5:21.　8:29 Or *the Christ. Messiah* (a Hebrew term) and *Christ* (a Greek term) both mean "anointed one."　8:31 "Son of Man" is a title Jesus used for himself.　8:32 Or *began to correct him.*

³⁴Then, calling the crowd to join his disciples, he said, "If any of you wants to be my follower, you must give up your own way, take up your cross, and follow me. ³⁵If you try to hang on to your life, you will lose it. But if you give up your life for my sake and for the sake of the Good News, you will save it. ³⁶And what do you benefit if you gain the whole world but lose your own soul?* ³⁷Is anything worth more than your soul? ³⁸If anyone is ashamed of me and my message in these adulterous and sinful days, the Son of Man will be ashamed of that person when he returns in the glory of his Father with the holy angels."

9 Jesus went on to say, "I tell you the truth, some standing here right now will not die before they see the Kingdom of God arrive in great power!"

The Transfiguration

²Six days later Jesus took Peter, James, and John, and led them up a high mountain to be alone. As the men watched, Jesus' appearance was transformed, ³and his clothes became dazzling white, far whiter than any earthly bleach could ever make them. ⁴Then Elijah and Moses appeared and began talking with Jesus.

⁵Peter exclaimed, "Rabbi, it's wonderful for us to be here! Let's make three shelters as memorials*—one for you, one for Moses, and one for Elijah." ⁶He said this because he didn't really know what else to say, for they were all terrified.

⁷Then a cloud overshadowed them, and a voice from the cloud said, "This is my dearly loved Son. Listen to him." ⁸Suddenly, when they looked around, Moses and Elijah were gone, and they saw only Jesus with them.

⁹As they went back down the mountain, he told them not to tell anyone what they had seen until the Son of Man* had risen from the dead. ¹⁰So they kept it to themselves, but they often asked each other what he meant by "rising from the dead."

¹¹Then they asked him, "Why do the teachers of religious law insist that Elijah must return before the Messiah comes?*"

¹²Jesus responded, "Elijah is indeed coming first to get everything ready. Yet why do the Scriptures say that the Son of Man must suffer greatly and be treated with utter contempt? ¹³But I tell you, Elijah has already come, and

they chose to abuse him, just as the Scriptures predicted."

Jesus Heals a Demon-Possessed Boy

¹⁴When they returned to the other disciples, they saw a large crowd surrounding them, and some teachers of religious law were arguing with them. ¹⁵When the crowd saw Jesus, they were overwhelmed with awe, and they ran to greet him.

¹⁶"What is all this arguing about?" Jesus asked.

¹⁷One of the men in the crowd spoke up and said, "Teacher, I brought my son so you could heal him. He is possessed by an evil spirit that won't let him talk. ¹⁸And whenever this spirit seizes him, it throws him violently to the ground. Then he foams at the mouth and grinds his teeth and becomes rigid.* So I asked your disciples to cast out the evil spirit, but they couldn't do it."

¹⁹Jesus said to them,* "You faithless people! How long must I be with you? How long must I put up with you? Bring the boy to me."

²⁰So they brought the boy. But when the evil spirit saw Jesus, it threw the child into a violent convulsion, and he fell to the ground, writhing and foaming at the mouth.

²¹"How long has this been happening?" Jesus asked the boy's father.

He replied, "Since he was a little boy. ²²The spirit often throws him into the fire or into water, trying to kill him. Have mercy on us and help us, if you can."

²³"What do you mean, 'If I can'?" Jesus asked. "Anything is possible if a person believes."

²⁴The father instantly cried out, "I do believe, but help me overcome my unbelief!"

²⁵When Jesus saw that the crowd of onlookers was growing, he rebuked the evil* spirit. "Listen, you spirit that makes this boy unable to hear and speak," he said. "I command you to come out of this child and never enter him again!"

²⁶Then the spirit screamed and threw the boy into another violent convulsion and left him. The boy appeared to be dead. A murmur ran through the crowd as people said, "He's dead." ²⁷But Jesus took him by the hand and helped him to his feet, and he stood up.

²⁸Afterward, when Jesus was alone in the house with his disciples, they asked him, "Why couldn't we cast out that evil spirit?"

8:36 Or *your self?* also in 8:37.   9:5 Greek *three tabernacles.*   9:9 "Son of Man" is a title Jesus used for himself.   9:11 Greek *that Elijah must come first?*   9:18 Or *becomes weak.*   9:19 Or *said to his disciples.*   9:25 Greek *unclean.*

²⁹Jesus replied, "This kind can be cast out only by prayer.*"

Jesus Again Predicts His Death

³⁰Leaving that region, they traveled through Galilee. Jesus didn't want anyone to know he was there, ³¹for he wanted to spend more time with his disciples and teach them. He said to them, "The Son of Man is going to be betrayed into the hands of his enemies. He will be killed, but three days later he will rise from the dead." ³²They didn't understand what he was saying, however, and they were afraid to ask him what he meant.

The Greatest in the Kingdom

³³After they arrived at Capernaum and settled in a house, Jesus asked his disciples, "What were you discussing out on the road?" ³⁴But they didn't answer, because they had been arguing about which of them was the greatest. ³⁵He sat down, called the twelve disciples over to him, and said, "Whoever wants to be first must take last place and be the servant of everyone else."

³⁶Then he put a little child among them. Taking the child in his arms, he said to them, ³⁷"Anyone who welcomes a little child like this on my behalf* welcomes me, and anyone who welcomes me welcomes not only me but also my Father who sent me."

Using the Name of Jesus

³⁸John said to Jesus, "Teacher, we saw someone using your name to cast out demons, but we told him to stop because he wasn't in our group."

³⁹"Don't stop him!" Jesus said. "No one who performs a miracle in my name will soon be able to speak evil of me. ⁴⁰Anyone who is not against us is for us. ⁴¹If anyone gives you even a cup of water because you belong to the Messiah, I tell you the truth, that person will surely be rewarded.

⁴²"But if you cause one of these little ones who trusts in me to fall into sin, it would be better for you to be thrown into the sea with a large millstone hung around your neck. ⁴³If your hand causes you to sin, cut it off. It's better to enter eternal life with only one hand than to go into the unquenchable fires of hell* with two hands.* ⁴⁵If your foot causes you to sin, cut

it off. It's better to enter eternal life with only one foot than to be thrown into hell with two feet.* ⁴⁷And if your eye causes you to sin, gouge it out. It's better to enter the Kingdom of God with only one eye than to have two eyes and be thrown into hell, ⁴⁸'where the maggots never die and the fire never goes out.'*

⁴⁹"For everyone will be tested with fire.* ⁵⁰Salt is good for seasoning. But if it loses its flavor, how do you make it salty again? You must have the qualities of salt among yourselves and live in peace with each other."

Discussion about Divorce and Marriage

10 Then Jesus left Capernaum and went down to the region of Judea and into the area east of the Jordan River. Once again crowds gathered around him, and as usual he was teaching them.

²Some Pharisees came and tried to trap him with this question: "Should a man be allowed to divorce his wife?"

³Jesus answered them with a question: "What did Moses say in the law about divorce?"

⁴"Well, he permitted it," they replied. "He said a man can give his wife a written notice of divorce and send her away."*

⁵But Jesus responded, "He wrote this commandment only as a concession to your hard hearts. ⁶But 'God made them male and female'* from the beginning of creation. ⁷'This explains why a man leaves his father and mother and is joined to his wife,* ⁸and the two are united into one.'* Since they are no longer two but one, ⁹let no one split apart what God has joined together."

¹⁰Later, when he was alone with his disciples in the house, they brought up the subject again. ¹¹He told them, "Whoever divorces his wife and marries someone else commits adultery against her. ¹²And if a woman divorces her husband and marries someone else, she commits adultery."

Jesus Blesses the Children

¹³One day some parents brought their children to Jesus so he could touch and bless them. But the disciples scolded the parents for bothering him.

¹⁴When Jesus saw what was happening, he was angry with his disciples. He said to them, "Let the children come to me. Don't

---

9:29 Some manuscripts read *by prayer and fasting.* 9:37 Greek *in my name.* 9:43a Greek *Gehenna;* also in 9:45, 47. 9:43b Some manuscripts add verse 44, *'where the maggots never die and the fire never goes out.'* See 9:48. 9:45 Some manuscripts add verse 46, *'where the maggots never die and the fire never goes out.'* See 9:48. 9:48 Isa 66:24. 9:49 Greek *salted with fire;* other manuscripts add *and every sacrifice will be salted with salt.* 10:4 See Deut 24:1. 10:6 Gen 1:27; 5:2. 10:7 Some manuscripts do not include *and is joined to his wife.* 10:7-8 Gen 2:24.

stop them! For the Kingdom of God belongs to those who are like these children. ¹⁵I tell you the truth, anyone who doesn't receive the Kingdom of God like a child will never enter it." ¹⁶Then he took the children in his arms and placed his hands on their heads and blessed them.

The Rich Man

¹⁷As Jesus was starting out on his way to Jerusalem, a man came running up to him, knelt down, and asked, "Good Teacher, what must I do to inherit eternal life?"

¹⁸"Why do you call me good?" Jesus asked. "Only God is truly good. ¹⁹But to answer your question, you know the commandments: 'You must not murder. You must not commit adultery. You must not steal. You must not testify falsely. You must not cheat anyone. Honor your father and mother.'*"

²⁰"Teacher," the man replied, "I've obeyed all these commandments since I was young."

²¹Looking at the man, Jesus felt genuine love for him. "There is still one thing you haven't done," he told him. "Go and sell all your possessions and give the money to the poor, and you will have treasure in heaven. Then come, follow me."

²²At this the man's face fell, and he went away sad, for he had many possessions.

²³Jesus looked around and said to his disciples, "How hard it is for the rich to enter the Kingdom of God!" ²⁴This amazed them. But Jesus said again, "Dear children, it is very hard* to enter the Kingdom of God. ²⁵In fact, it is easier for a camel to go through the eye of a needle than for a rich person to enter the Kingdom of God!"

²⁶The disciples were astounded. "Then who in the world can be saved?" they asked.

²⁷Jesus looked at them intently and said, "Humanly speaking, it is impossible. But not with God. Everything is possible with God."

²⁸Then Peter began to speak up. "We've given up everything to follow you," he said.

²⁹"Yes," Jesus replied, "and I assure you that everyone who has given up house or brothers or sisters or mother or father or children or property, for my sake and for the Good News, ³⁰will receive now in return a hundred times as many houses, brothers, sisters, mothers, children, and property—along with persecution. And in the world to come that person will have eternal life. ³¹But many who are the greatest now will be least important then, and those who seem least important now will be the greatest then.*"

Jesus Again Predicts His Death

³²They were now on the way up to Jerusalem, and Jesus was walking ahead of them. The disciples were filled with awe, and the people following behind were overwhelmed with fear. Taking the twelve disciples aside, Jesus once more began to describe everything that was about to happen to him. ³³"Listen," he said, "we're going up to Jerusalem, where the Son of Man* will be betrayed to the leading priests and the teachers of religious law. They will sentence him to die and hand him over to the Romans.* ³⁴They will mock him, spit on him, flog him with a whip, and kill him, but after three days he will rise again."

Jesus Teaches about Serving Others

³⁵Then James and John, the sons of Zebedee, came over and spoke to him. "Teacher," they said, "we want you to do us a favor."

³⁶"What is your request?" he asked.

³⁷They replied, "When you sit on your glorious throne, we want to sit in places of honor next to you, one on your right and the other on your left."

³⁸But Jesus said to them, "You don't know what you are asking! Are you able to drink from the bitter cup of suffering I am about to drink? Are you able to be baptized with the baptism of suffering I must be baptized with?"

³⁹"Oh yes," they replied, "we are able!"

Then Jesus told them, "You will indeed drink from my bitter cup and be baptized with my baptism of suffering. ⁴⁰But I have no right to say who will sit on my right or my left. God has prepared those places for the ones he has chosen."

⁴¹When the ten other disciples heard what James and John had asked, they were indignant. ⁴²So Jesus called them together and said, "You know that the rulers in this world lord it over their people, and officials flaunt their authority over those under them. ⁴³But among you it will be different. Whoever wants to be a leader among you must be your servant, ⁴⁴and whoever wants to be first among you must be the slave of everyone else. ⁴⁵For even the Son of Man came not to be served but to serve others and to give his life as a ransom for many."

10:19 Exod 20:12-16; Deut 5:16-20. 10:24 Some manuscripts read very hard for those who trust in riches. 10:31 Greek But many who are first will be last; and the last, first. 10:33a "Son of Man" is a title Jesus used for himself. 10:33b Greek the Gentiles.

Jesus Heals Blind Bartimaeus

⁴⁶Then they reached Jericho, and as Jesus and his disciples left town, a large crowd followed him. A blind beggar named Bartimaeus (son of Timaeus) was sitting beside the road. ⁴⁷When Bartimaeus heard that Jesus of Nazareth was nearby, he began to shout, "Jesus, Son of David, have mercy on me!"

⁴⁸"Be quiet!" many of the people yelled at him.

But he only shouted louder, "Son of David, have mercy on me!"

⁴⁹When Jesus heard him, he stopped and said, "Tell him to come here."

So they called the blind man. "Cheer up," they said. "Come on, he's calling you!" ⁵⁰Bartimaeus threw aside his coat, jumped up, and came to Jesus.

⁵¹"What do you want me to do for you?" Jesus asked.

"My Rabbi,*" the blind man said, "I want to see!"

⁵²And Jesus said to him, "Go, for your faith has healed you." Instantly the man could see, and he followed Jesus down the road.*

Jesus' Triumphant Entry

11 As Jesus and his disciples approached Jerusalem, they came to the towns of Bethphage and Bethany on the Mount of Olives. Jesus sent two of them on ahead. ²"Go into that village over there," he told them. "As soon as you enter it, you will see a young donkey tied there that no one has ever ridden. Untie it and bring it here. ³If anyone asks, 'What are you doing?' just say, 'The Lord needs it and will return it soon.'"

⁴The two disciples left and found the colt standing in the street, tied outside the front door. ⁵As they were untying it, some bystanders demanded, "What are you doing, untying that colt?" ⁶They said what Jesus had told them to say, and they were permitted to take it. ⁷Then they brought the colt to Jesus and threw their garments over it, and he sat on it.

⁸Many in the crowd spread their garments on the road ahead of him, and others spread leafy branches they had cut in the fields. ⁹Jesus was in the center of the procession, and the people all around him were shouting,

"Praise God!*
    Blessings on the one who comes in the
        name of the LORD!

¹⁰ Blessings on the coming Kingdom of our
        ancestor David!
    Praise God in highest heaven!"*

¹¹So Jesus came to Jerusalem and went into the Temple. After looking around carefully at everything, he left because it was late in the afternoon. Then he returned to Bethany with the twelve disciples.

Jesus Curses the Fig Tree

¹²The next morning as they were leaving Bethany, Jesus was hungry. ¹³He noticed a fig tree in full leaf a little way off, so he went over to see if he could find any figs. But there were only leaves because it was too early in the season for fruit. ¹⁴Then Jesus said to the tree, "May no one ever eat your fruit again!" And the disciples heard him say it.

Jesus Clears the Temple

¹⁵When they arrived back in Jerusalem, Jesus entered the Temple and began to drive out the people buying and selling animals for sacrifices. He knocked over the tables of the money changers and the chairs of those selling doves, ¹⁶and he stopped everyone from using the Temple as a marketplace.* ¹⁷He said to them, "The Scriptures declare, 'My Temple will be called a house of prayer for all nations,' but you have turned it into a den of thieves."*

¹⁸When the leading priests and teachers of religious law heard what Jesus had done, they began planning how to kill him. But they were afraid of him because the people were so amazed at his teaching.

¹⁹That evening Jesus and the disciples left* the city.

²⁰The next morning as they passed by the fig tree he had cursed, the disciples noticed it had withered from the roots up. ²¹Peter remembered what Jesus had said to the tree on the previous day and exclaimed, "Look, Rabbi! The fig tree you cursed has withered and died!"

²²Then Jesus said to the disciples, "Have faith in God. ²³I tell you the truth, you can say to this mountain, 'May you be lifted up and thrown into the sea,' and it will happen. But you must really believe it will happen and have no doubt in your heart. ²⁴I tell you, you can pray for anything, and if you believe that you've received it, it will be yours. ²⁵But when you are

---

10:51 Greek uses the Hebrew term *Rabboni*.   10:52 Or *on the way*.   11:9 Greek *Hosanna*, an exclamation of praise that literally means "save now"; also in 11:10.   11:9-10 Pss 118:25-26; 148:1.   11:16 Or *from carrying merchandise through the Temple*.   11:17 Isa 56:7; Jer 7:11.   11:19 Greek *they left*; other manuscripts read *he left*.

praying, first forgive anyone you are holding a grudge against, so that your Father in heaven will forgive your sins, too.*"

The Authority of Jesus Challenged

27Again they entered Jerusalem. As Jesus was walking through the Temple area, the leading priests, the teachers of religious law, and the elders came up to him. 28They demanded, "By what authority are you doing all these things? Who gave you the right to do them?"

29"I'll tell you by what authority I do these things if you answer one question," Jesus replied. 30"Did John's authority to baptize come from heaven, or was it merely human? Answer me!"

31They talked it over among themselves. "If we say it was from heaven, he will ask why we didn't believe John. 32But do we dare say it was merely human?" For they were afraid of what the people would do, because everyone believed that John was a prophet. 33So they finally replied, "We don't know."

And Jesus responded, "Then I won't tell you by what authority I do these things."

Parable of the Evil Farmers

12 Then Jesus began teaching them with stories: "A man planted a vineyard. He built a wall around it, dug a pit for pressing out the grape juice, and built a lookout tower. Then he leased the vineyard to tenant farmers and moved to another country. 2At the time of the grape harvest, he sent one of his servants to collect his share of the crop. 3But the farmers grabbed the servant, beat him up, and sent him back empty-handed. 4The owner then sent another servant, but they insulted him and beat him over the head. 5The next servant he sent was killed. Others he sent were either beaten or killed, 6until there was only one left—his son whom he loved dearly. The owner finally sent him, thinking, 'Surely they will respect my son.'

7"But the tenant farmers said to one another, 'Here comes the heir to this estate. Let's kill him and get the estate for ourselves!' 8So they grabbed him and murdered him and threw his body out of the vineyard.

9"What do you suppose the owner of the vineyard will do?" Jesus asked. "I'll tell you—he will come and kill those farmers and lease the vineyard to others. 10Didn't you ever read this in the Scriptures?

'The stone that the builders rejected
has now become the cornerstone.
11 This is the LORD's doing,
and it is wonderful to see.'*"

12The religious leaders* wanted to arrest Jesus because they realized he was telling the story against them—they were the wicked farmers. But they were afraid of the crowd, so they left him and went away.

Taxes for Caesar

13Later the leaders sent some Pharisees and supporters of Herod to trap Jesus into saying something for which he could be arrested. 14"Teacher," they said, "we know how honest you are. You are impartial and don't play favorites. You teach the way of God truthfully. Now tell us—is it right to pay taxes to Caesar or not? 15Should we pay them, or shouldn't we?"

Jesus saw through their hypocrisy and said, "Why are you trying to trap me? Show me a Roman coin,* and I'll tell you." 16When they handed it to him, he asked, "Whose picture and title are stamped on it?"

"Caesar's," they replied.

17"Well, then," Jesus said, "give to Caesar what belongs to Caesar, and give to God what belongs to God."

His reply completely amazed them.

Discussion about Resurrection

18Then Jesus was approached by some Sadducees—religious leaders who say there is no resurrection from the dead. They posed this question: 19"Teacher, Moses gave us a law that if a man dies, leaving a wife without children, his brother should marry the widow and have a child who will carry on the brother's name.* 20Well, suppose there were seven brothers. The oldest one married and then died without children. 21So the second brother married the widow, but he also died without children. Then the third brother married her. 22This continued with all seven of them, and still there were no children. Last of all, the woman also died. 23So tell us, whose wife will she be in the resurrection? For all seven were married to her."

24Jesus replied, "Your mistake is that you don't know the Scriptures, and you don't know the power of God. 25For when the dead rise, they will neither marry nor be given in marriage. In this respect they will be like the angels in heaven.

11:25 Some manuscripts add verse 26, *But if you refuse to forgive, your Father in heaven will not forgive your sins.* Compare Matt 6:15.   12:10-11 Ps 118:22-23.   12:12 Greek *They.*   12:15 Greek *a denarius.*   12:19 See Deut 25:5-6.

26"But now, as to whether the dead will be raised—haven't you ever read about this in the writings of Moses, in the story of the burning bush? Long after Abraham, Isaac, and Jacob had died, God said to Moses,* 'I am the God of Abraham, the God of Isaac, and the God of Jacob.'* 27So he is the God of the living, not the dead. You have made a serious error."

The Most Important Commandment

28One of the teachers of religious law was standing there listening to the debate. He realized that Jesus had answered well, so he asked, "Of all the commandments, which is the most important?"

29Jesus replied, "The most important commandment is this: 'Listen, O Israel! The LORD our God is the one and only LORD. 30And you must love the LORD your God with all your heart, all your soul, all your mind, and all your strength.'* 31The second is equally important: 'Love your neighbor as yourself.'* No other commandment is greater than these."

32The teacher of religious law replied, "Well said, Teacher. You have spoken the truth by saying that there is only one God and no other. 33And I know it is important to love him with all my heart and all my understanding and all my strength, and to love my neighbor as myself. This is more important than to offer all of the burnt offerings and sacrifices required in the law."

34Realizing how much the man understood, Jesus said to him, "You are not far from the Kingdom of God." And after that, no one dared to ask him any more questions.

Whose Son Is the Messiah?

35Later, as Jesus was teaching the people in the Temple, he asked, "Why do the teachers of religious law claim that the Messiah is the son of David? 36For David himself, speaking under the inspiration of the Holy Spirit, said,

'The LORD said to my Lord,
Sit in the place of honor at my right
    hand
until I humble your enemies beneath
    your feet.'*

37Since David himself called the Messiah 'my Lord,' how can the Messiah be his son?" The large crowd listened to him with great delight.

38Jesus also taught: "Beware of these teachers of religious law! For they like to parade around in flowing robes and receive respectful greetings as they walk in the marketplaces. 39And how they love the seats of honor in the synagogues and the head table at banquets. 40Yet they shamelessly cheat widows out of their property and then pretend to be pious by making long prayers in public. Because of this, they will be more severely punished."

The Widow's Offering

41Jesus sat down near the collection box in the Temple and watched as the crowds dropped in their money. Many rich people put in large amounts. 42Then a poor widow came and dropped in two small coins.*

43Jesus called his disciples to him and said, "I tell you the truth, this poor widow has given more than all the others who are making contributions. 44For they gave a tiny part of their surplus, but she, poor as she is, has given everything she had to live on."

Jesus Speaks about the Future

13 As Jesus was leaving the Temple that day, one of his disciples said, "Teacher, look at these magnificent buildings! Look at the impressive stones in the walls."

2Jesus replied, "Yes, look at these great buildings. But they will be completely demolished. Not one stone will be left on top of another!"

3Later, Jesus sat on the Mount of Olives across the valley from the Temple. Peter, James, John, and Andrew came to him privately and asked him, 4"Tell us, when will all this happen? What sign will show us that these things are about to be fulfilled?"

5Jesus replied, "Don't let anyone mislead you, 6for many will come in my name, claiming, 'I am the Messiah.'* They will deceive many. 7And you will hear of wars and threats of wars, but don't panic. Yes, these things must take place, but the end won't follow immediately. 8Nation will go to war against nation, and kingdom against kingdom. There will be earthquakes in many parts of the world, as well as famines. But this is only the first of the birth pains, with more to come.

9"When these things begin to happen, watch out! You will be handed over to the local councils and beaten in the synagogues. You will stand trial before governors and kings

---

12:26a Greek *in the story of the bush? God said to him.*   12:26b Exod 3:6.   12:29-30 Deut 6:4-5.   12:31 Lev 19:18.   12:36 Ps 110:1.
12:42 Greek *two lepta, which is a kodrantes* [i.e., a quadrans].   13:6 Greek *claiming, 'I am.'*

because you are my followers. But this will be your opportunity to tell them about me.* ¹⁰For the Good News must first be preached to all nations.* ¹¹But when you are arrested and stand trial, don't worry in advance about what to say. Just say what God tells you at that time, for it is not you who will be speaking, but the Holy Spirit.

¹²"A brother will betray his brother to death, a father will betray his own child, and children will rebel against their parents and cause them to be killed. ¹³And everyone will hate you because you are my followers.* But the one who endures to the end will be saved.

¹⁴"The day is coming when you will see the sacrilegious object that causes desecration* standing where he* should not be." (Reader, pay attention!) "Then those in Judea must flee to the hills. ¹⁵A person out on the deck of a roof must not go down into the house to pack. ¹⁶A person out in the field must not return even to get a coat. ¹⁷How terrible it will be for pregnant women and for nursing mothers in those days. ¹⁸And pray that your flight will not be in winter. ¹⁹For there will be greater anguish in those days than at any time since God created the world. And it will never be so great again. ²⁰In fact, unless the Lord shortens that time of calamity, not a single person will survive. But for the sake of his chosen ones he has shortened those days.

²¹"Then if anyone tells you, 'Look, here is the Messiah,' or 'There he is,' don't believe it. ²²For false messiahs and false prophets will rise up and perform signs and wonders so as to deceive, if possible, even God's chosen ones. ²³Watch out! I have warned you about this ahead of time!

²⁴"At that time, after the anguish of those days,

the sun will be darkened,
　　the moon will give no light,
²⁵ the stars will fall from the sky,
　　and the powers in the heavens will
　　　　be shaken.*

²⁶Then everyone will see the Son of Man* coming on the clouds with great power and glory.* ²⁷And he will send out his angels to gather his chosen ones from all over the world*—from the farthest ends of the earth and heaven.

²⁸"Now learn a lesson from the fig tree. When its branches bud and its leaves begin to sprout, you know that summer is near. ²⁹In the same way, when you see all these things taking place, you can know that his return is very near, right at the door. ³⁰I tell you the truth, this generation* will not pass from the scene before all these things take place. ³¹Heaven and earth will disappear, but my words will never disappear.

³²"However, no one knows the day or hour when these things will happen, not even the angels in heaven or the Son himself. Only the Father knows. ³³And since you don't know when that time will come, be on guard! Stay alert*!

³⁴"The coming of the Son of Man can be illustrated by the story of a man going on a long trip. When he left home, he gave each of his slaves instructions about the work they were to do, and he told the gatekeeper to watch for his return. ³⁵You, too, must keep watch! For you don't know when the master of the household will return—in the evening, at midnight, before dawn, or at daybreak. ³⁶Don't let him find you sleeping when he arrives without warning. ³⁷I say to you what I say to everyone: Watch for him!"

Jesus Anointed at Bethany

14 It was now two days before Passover and the Festival of Unleavened Bread. The leading priests and the teachers of religious law were still looking for an opportunity to capture Jesus secretly and kill him. ²"But not during the Passover celebration," they agreed, "or the people may riot."

³Meanwhile, Jesus was in Bethany at the home of Simon, a man who had previously had leprosy. While he was eating,* a woman came in with a beautiful alabaster jar of expensive perfume made from essence of nard. She broke open the jar and poured the perfume over his head.

⁴Some of those at the table were indignant. "Why waste such expensive perfume?" they asked. ⁵"It could have been sold for a year's wages* and the money given to the poor!" So they scolded her harshly.

⁶But Jesus replied, "Leave her alone. Why criticize her for doing such a good thing to me? ⁷You will always have the poor among you, and

---

13:9 Or *But this will be your testimony against them.* **13:10** Or *all peoples.* **13:13** Greek *on account of my name.* **13:14a** Greek *the abomination of desolation.* See Dan 9:27; 11:31; 12:11. **13:14b** Or *it.* **13:24-25** See Isa 13:10; 34:4; Joel 2:10. **13:26a** "Son of Man" is a title Jesus used for himself. **13:26b** See Dan 7:13. **13:27** Greek *from the four winds.* **13:30** Or *this age,* or *this nation.* **13:33** Some manuscripts add *and pray.* **14:3** Or *reclining.* **14:5** Greek *for 300 denarii.* A denarius was equivalent to a laborer's full day's wage.

you can help them whenever you want to. But you will not always have me. ⁸She has done what she could and has anointed my body for burial ahead of time. ⁹I tell you the truth, wherever the Good News is preached throughout the world, this woman's deed will be remembered and discussed."

Judas Agrees to Betray Jesus

¹⁰Then Judas Iscariot, one of the twelve disciples, went to the leading priests to arrange to betray Jesus to them. ¹¹They were delighted when they heard why he had come, and they promised to give him money. So he began looking for an opportunity to betray Jesus.

The Last Supper

¹²On the first day of the Festival of Unleavened Bread, when the Passover lamb is sacrificed, Jesus' disciples asked him, "Where do you want us to go to prepare the Passover meal for you?"

¹³So Jesus sent two of them into Jerusalem with these instructions: "As you go into the city, a man carrying a pitcher of water will meet you. Follow him. ¹⁴At the house he enters, say to the owner, 'The Teacher asks: Where is the guest room where I can eat the Passover meal with my disciples?' ¹⁵He will take you upstairs to a large room that is already set up. That is where you should prepare our meal." ¹⁶So the two disciples went into the city and found everything just as Jesus had said, and they prepared the Passover meal there.

¹⁷In the evening Jesus arrived with the Twelve. ¹⁸As they were at the table* eating, Jesus said, "I tell you the truth, one of you eating with me here will betray me."

¹⁹Greatly distressed, each one asked in turn, "Am I the one?"

²⁰He replied, "It is one of you twelve who is eating from this bowl with me. ²¹For the Son of Man* must die, as the Scriptures declared long ago. But how terrible it will be for the one who betrays him. It would be far better for that man if he had never been born!"

²²As they were eating, Jesus took some bread and blessed it. Then he broke it in pieces and gave it to the disciples, saying, "Take it, for this is my body."

²³And he took a cup of wine and gave thanks to God for it. He gave it to them, and they all drank from it. ²⁴And he said to them, "This is my blood, which confirms the covenant* between God and his people. It is poured out as a sacrifice for many. ²⁵I tell you the truth, I will not drink wine again until the day I drink it new in the Kingdom of God."

²⁶Then they sang a hymn and went out to the Mount of Olives.

Jesus Predicts Peter's Denial

²⁷On the way, Jesus told them, "All of you will desert me. For the Scriptures say,

'God will strike* the Shepherd,
      and the sheep will be scattered.'

²⁸But after I am raised from the dead, I will go ahead of you to Galilee and meet you there."

²⁹Peter said to him, "Even if everyone else deserts you, I never will."

³⁰Jesus replied, "I tell you the truth, Peter—this very night, before the rooster crows twice, you will deny three times that you even know me."

³¹"No!" Peter declared emphatically. "Even if I have to die with you, I will never deny you!" And all the others vowed the same.

Jesus Prays in Gethsemane

³²They went to the olive grove called Gethsemane, and Jesus said, "Sit here while I go and pray." ³³He took Peter, James, and John with him, and he became deeply troubled and distressed. ³⁴He told them, "My soul is crushed with grief to the point of death. Stay here and keep watch with me."

³⁵He went on a little farther and fell to the ground. He prayed that, if it were possible, the awful hour awaiting him might pass him by. ³⁶"Abba, Father,"* he cried out, "everything is possible for you. Please take this cup of suffering away from me. Yet I want your will to be done, not mine."

³⁷Then he returned and found the disciples asleep. He said to Peter, "Simon, are you asleep? Couldn't you watch with me even one hour? ³⁸Keep watch and pray, so that you will not give in to temptation. For the spirit is willing, but the body is weak."

³⁹Then Jesus left them again and prayed the same prayer as before. ⁴⁰When he returned to them again, he found them sleeping, for they couldn't keep their eyes open. And they didn't know what to say.

⁴¹When he returned to them the third time,

14:18 Or As they reclined.   14:21 "Son of Man" is a title Jesus used for himself.   14:24 Some manuscripts read the new covenant.
14:27 Greek I will strike. Zech 13:7.   14:36 Abba is an Aramaic term for "father."

he said, "Go ahead and sleep. Have your rest. But no—the time has come. The Son of Man is betrayed into the hands of sinners. ⁴²Up, let's be going. Look, my betrayer is here!"

Jesus Is Betrayed and Arrested

⁴³And immediately, even as Jesus said this, Judas, one of the twelve disciples, arrived with a crowd of men armed with swords and clubs. They had been sent by the leading priests, the teachers of religious law, and the elders. ⁴⁴The traitor, Judas, had given them a prearranged signal: "You will know which one to arrest when I greet him with a kiss. Then you can take him away under guard." ⁴⁵As soon as they arrived, Judas walked up to Jesus. "Rabbi!" he exclaimed, and gave him the kiss.

⁴⁶Then the others grabbed Jesus and arrested him. ⁴⁷But one of the men with Jesus pulled out his sword and struck the high priest's slave, slashing off his ear.

⁴⁸Jesus asked them, "Am I some dangerous revolutionary, that you come with swords and clubs to arrest me? ⁴⁹Why didn't you arrest me in the Temple? I was there among you teaching every day. But these things are happening to fulfill what the Scriptures say about me."

⁵⁰Then all his disciples deserted him and ran away. ⁵¹One young man following behind was clothed only in a long linen shirt. When the mob tried to grab him, ⁵²he slipped out of his shirt and ran away naked.

Jesus before the Council

⁵³They took Jesus to the high priest's home where the leading priests, the elders, and the teachers of religious law had gathered. ⁵⁴Meanwhile, Peter followed him at a distance and went right into the high priest's courtyard. There he sat with the guards, warming himself by the fire.

⁵⁵Inside, the leading priests and the entire high council* were trying to find evidence against Jesus, so they could put him to death. But they couldn't find any. ⁵⁶Many false witnesses spoke against him, but they contradicted each other. ⁵⁷Finally, some men stood up and gave this false testimony: ⁵⁸"We heard him say, 'I will destroy this Temple made with human hands, and in three days I will build another, made without human hands.'" ⁵⁹But even then they didn't get their stories straight!

⁶⁰Then the high priest stood up before the others and asked Jesus, "Well, aren't you going to answer these charges? What do you have to say for yourself?" ⁶¹But Jesus was silent and made no reply. Then the high priest asked him, "Are you the Messiah, the Son of the Blessed One?"

⁶²Jesus said, "I AM.* And you will see the Son of Man seated in the place of power at God's right hand* and coming on the clouds of heaven.*"

⁶³Then the high priest tore his clothing to show his horror and said, "Why do we need other witnesses? ⁶⁴You have all heard his blasphemy. What is your verdict?"

"Guilty!" they all cried. "He deserves to die!"

⁶⁵Then some of them began to spit at him, and they blindfolded him and beat him with their fists. "Prophesy to us," they jeered. And the guards slapped him as they took him away.

Peter Denies Jesus

⁶⁶Meanwhile, Peter was in the courtyard below. One of the servant girls who worked for the high priest came by ⁶⁷and noticed Peter warming himself at the fire. She looked at him closely and said, "You were one of those with Jesus of Nazareth.*"

⁶⁸But Peter denied it. "I don't know what you're talking about," he said, and he went out into the entryway. Just then, a rooster crowed.*

⁶⁹When the servant girl saw him standing there, she began telling the others, "This man is definitely one of them!" ⁷⁰But Peter denied it again.

A little later some of the other bystanders confronted Peter and said, "You must be one of them, because you are a Galilean."

⁷¹Peter swore, "A curse on me if I'm lying—I don't know this man you're talking about!" ⁷²And immediately the rooster crowed the second time.

Suddenly, Jesus' words flashed through Peter's mind: "Before the rooster crows twice, you will deny three times that you even know me." And he broke down and wept.

Jesus' Trial before Pilate

15 Very early in the morning the leading priests, the elders, and the teachers of religious law—the entire high council*—met

---

14:55 Greek *the Sanhedrin.*   **14:62a** Or *The 'I AM' is here;* or *I am the* LORD. See Exod 3:14.   **14:62b** Greek *seated at the right hand of the power.* See Ps 110:1.   **14:62c** See Dan 7:13.   **14:67** Or *Jesus the Nazarene.*   **14:68** Some manuscripts do not include *Just then, a rooster crowed.*   **15:1** Greek *the Sanhedrin;* also in 15:43.

to discuss their next step. They bound Jesus, led him away, and took him to Pilate, the Roman governor.

²Pilate asked Jesus, "Are you the king of the Jews?"

Jesus replied, "You have said it."

³Then the leading priests kept accusing him of many crimes, ⁴and Pilate asked him, "Aren't you going to answer them? What about all these charges they are bringing against you?" ⁵But Jesus said nothing, much to Pilate's surprise.

⁶Now it was the governor's custom each year during the Passover celebration to release one prisoner—anyone the people requested. ⁷One of the prisoners at that time was Barabbas, a revolutionary who had committed murder in an uprising. ⁸The crowd went to Pilate and asked him to release a prisoner as usual.

⁹"Would you like me to release to you this 'King of the Jews'?" Pilate asked. ¹⁰(For he realized by now that the leading priests had arrested Jesus out of envy.) ¹¹But at this point the leading priests stirred up the crowd to demand the release of Barabbas instead of Jesus. ¹²Pilate asked them, "Then what should I do with this man you call the king of the Jews?"

¹³They shouted back, "Crucify him!"

¹⁴"Why?" Pilate demanded. "What crime has he committed?"

But the mob roared even louder, "Crucify him!"

¹⁵So to pacify the crowd, Pilate released Barabbas to them. He ordered Jesus flogged with a lead-tipped whip, then turned him over to the Roman soldiers to be crucified.

The Soldiers Mock Jesus

¹⁶The soldiers took Jesus into the courtyard of the governor's headquarters (called the Praetorium) and called out the entire regiment. ¹⁷They dressed him in a purple robe, and they wove thorn branches into a crown and put it on his head. ¹⁸Then they saluted him and taunted, "Hail! King of the Jews!" ¹⁹And they struck him on the head with a reed stick, spit on him, and dropped to their knees in mock worship. ²⁰When they were finally tired of mocking him, they took off the purple robe and put his own clothes on him again. Then they led him away to be crucified.

The Crucifixion

²¹A passerby named Simon, who was from Cyrene,* was coming in from the countryside just then, and the soldiers forced him to carry Jesus' cross. (Simon was the father of Alexander and Rufus.) ²²And they brought Jesus to a place called Golgotha (which means "Place of the Skull"). ²³They offered him wine drugged with myrrh, but he refused it.

²⁴Then the soldiers nailed him to the cross. They divided his clothes and threw dice* to decide who would get each piece. ²⁵It was nine o'clock in the morning when they crucified him. ²⁶A sign announced the charge against him. It read, "The King of the Jews." ²⁷Two revolutionaries* were crucified with him, one on his right and one on his left.*

²⁹The people passing by shouted abuse, shaking their heads in mockery. "Ha! Look at you now!" they yelled at him. "You said you were going to destroy the Temple and rebuild it in three days. ³⁰Well then, save yourself and come down from the cross!"

³¹The leading priests and teachers of religious law also mocked Jesus. "He saved others," they scoffed, "but he can't save himself! ³²Let this Messiah, this King of Israel, come down from the cross so we can see it and believe him!" Even the men who were crucified with Jesus ridiculed him.

The Death of Jesus

³³At noon, darkness fell across the whole land until three o'clock. ³⁴Then at three o'clock Jesus called out with a loud voice, *"Eloi, Eloi, lema sabachthani?"* which means "My God, my God, why have you abandoned me?"*

³⁵Some of the bystanders misunderstood and thought he was calling for the prophet Elijah. ³⁶One of them ran and filled a sponge with sour wine, holding it up to him on a reed stick so he could drink. "Wait!" he said. "Let's see whether Elijah comes to take him down!"

³⁷Then Jesus uttered another loud cry and breathed his last. ³⁸And the curtain in the sanctuary of the Temple was torn in two, from top to bottom.

³⁹When the Roman officer* who stood facing him* saw how he had died, he exclaimed, "This man truly was the Son of God!"

⁴⁰Some women were there, watching from

---

a distance, including Mary Magdalene, Mary (the mother of James the younger and of Joseph*), and Salome. ⁴¹They had been followers of Jesus and had cared for him while he was in Galilee. Many other women who had come with him to Jerusalem were also there.

The Burial of Jesus

⁴²This all happened on Friday, the day of preparation,* the day before the Sabbath. As evening approached, ⁴³Joseph of Arimathea took a risk and went to Pilate and asked for Jesus' body. (Joseph was an honored member of the high council, and he was waiting for the Kingdom of God to come.) ⁴⁴Pilate couldn't believe that Jesus was already dead, so he called for the Roman officer and asked if he had died yet. ⁴⁵The officer confirmed that Jesus was dead, so Pilate told Joseph he could have the body. ⁴⁶Joseph bought a long sheet of linen cloth. Then he took Jesus' body down from the cross, wrapped it in the cloth, and laid it in a tomb that had been carved out of the rock. Then he rolled a stone in front of the entrance. ⁴⁷Mary Magdalene and Mary the mother of Joseph saw where Jesus' body was laid.

The Resurrection

16 Saturday evening, when the Sabbath ended, Mary Magdalene, Mary the mother of James, and Salome went out and purchased burial spices so they could anoint Jesus' body. ²Very early on Sunday morning,* just at sunrise, they went to the tomb. ³On the way they were asking each other, "Who will roll away the stone for us from the entrance to the tomb?" ⁴But as they arrived, they looked up and saw that the stone, which was very large, had already been rolled aside.

⁵When they entered the tomb, they saw a young man clothed in a white robe sitting on the right side. The women were shocked, ⁶but the angel said, "Don't be alarmed. You are looking for Jesus of Nazareth,* who was crucified. He isn't here! He is risen from the dead! Look, this is where they laid his body. ⁷Now go and tell his disciples, including Peter, that Jesus is going ahead of you to Galilee. You

will see him there, just as he told you before he died."

⁸The women fled from the tomb, trembling and bewildered, and they said nothing to anyone because they were too frightened.*

[*The most ancient manuscripts of Mark conclude with verse 16:8. Later manuscripts add one or both of the following endings.*]

[*Shorter Ending of Mark*]

Then they briefly reported all this to Peter and his companions. Afterward Jesus himself sent them out from east to west with the sacred and unfailing message of salvation that gives eternal life. Amen.

[*Longer Ending of Mark*]

⁹After Jesus rose from the dead early on Sunday morning, the first person who saw him was Mary Magdalene, the woman from whom he had cast out seven demons. ¹⁰She went to the disciples, who were grieving and weeping, and told them what had happened. ¹¹But when she told them that Jesus was alive and she had seen him, they didn't believe her.

¹²Afterward he appeared in a different form to two of his followers who were walking from Jerusalem into the country. ¹³They rushed back to tell the others, but no one believed them.

¹⁴Still later he appeared to the eleven disciples as they were eating together. He rebuked them for their stubborn unbelief because they refused to believe those who had seen him after he had been raised from the dead.*

¹⁵And then he told them, "Go into all the world and preach the Good News to everyone. ¹⁶Anyone who believes and is baptized will be saved. But anyone who refuses to believe will be condemned. ¹⁷These miraculous signs will accompany those who believe: They will cast out demons in my name, and they will speak in new languages.* ¹⁸They will be able to handle snakes with safety, and if they drink anything

---

15:40 Greek *Joses*; also in 15:47. See Matt 27:56.   15:42 Greek *It was the day of preparation*.   16:2 Greek *on the first day of the week*; also in 16:9.   16:6 Or *Jesus the Nazarene*.   16:8 The most reliable early manuscripts of the Gospel of Mark end at verse 8. Other manuscripts include various endings to the Gospel. A few include both the "shorter ending" and the "longer ending." The majority of manuscripts include the "longer ending" immediately after verse 8.   16:14 Some early manuscripts add: *And they excused themselves, saying, "This age of lawlessness and unbelief is under Satan, who does not permit God's truth and power to conquer the evil [unclean] spirits. Therefore, reveal your justice now." This is what they said to Christ. And Christ replied to them, "The period of years of Satan's power has been fulfilled, but other dreadful things will happen soon. And I was handed over to death for those who have sinned, so that they may return to the truth and sin no more, and so they may inherit the spiritual, incorruptible, and righteous glory in heaven."*   16:17 Or *new tongues*; some manuscripts do not include *new*.

poisonous, it won't hurt them. They will be able to place their hands on the sick, and they will be healed."

[19]When the Lord Jesus had finished talking with them, he was taken up into heaven and sat down in the place of honor at God's right hand. [20]And the disciples went everywhere and preached, and the Lord worked through them, confirming what they said by many miraculous signs.

Luke

LIKE AN INVESTIGATIVE JOURNALIST compiling a story from several informants, Luke composed his Gospel from the accounts of several eyewitnesses to Jesus Christ. Luke, a Gentile physician who traveled extensively with the apostle Paul, wrote his Gospel for a man named Theophilus (1:1-4), most likely another Gentile believer. After consulting several eyewitnesses and accounts of Jesus' life, Luke wrote this fresh account of Jesus' life and ministry. Since both Luke and Theophilus were Gentiles, it is not surprising that this Gospel has a very universal flavor to its stories and teachings of Jesus. Luke also highlighted Jesus' concern for the oppressed and outcast, such as women and the poor, and there is a notable emphasis on the role of the Holy Spirit. Luke was careful to give precise dates for the events recorded in his Gospel, beginning with an extensive record of Jesus' birth and the only canonical story from Jesus' childhood years. Luke arranged his outline of Jesus' ministry in the same general order as the Gospels of Matthew and Mark, and he added a lengthy account of Jesus' trip to Jerusalem. After Jesus' death and resurrection, the book leaves the disciples rejoicing and waiting for the promised power of God to fill them.

- **Author:** Luke, a Gentile physician and Paul's associate
- **Date Written:** Around AD 60, perhaps from the city of Caesarea
- **Purpose:** To present an accurate account of the life and ministry of Jesus Christ
- **Themes:** Jesus Christ the Savior, the Holy Spirit, compassion for the oppressed, salvation for Gentiles
- **Outline**
  1:1–2:52 Jesus' birth and boyhood
  3:1–4:13 Jesus' baptism and temptation
  4:14–9:50 Jesus' Galilean ministry
  9:51–19:27 Jesus' ministry on the way to Jerusalem
  19:28–20:47 Jesus' ministry in Jerusalem
  21:1-38 Prophecies of things to come
  22:1–24:53 Jesus' death and resurrection

Introduction

1 Many people have set out to write accounts about the events that have been fulfilled among us. ²They used the eyewitness reports circulating among us from the early disciples.* ³Having carefully investigated everything from the beginning, I also have decided to write an accurate account for you, most honorable Theophilus, ⁴so you can be certain of the truth of everything you were taught.

The Birth of John the Baptist Foretold

⁵When Herod was king of Judea, there was a Jewish priest named Zechariah. He was a member of the priestly order of Abijah, and his wife, Elizabeth, was also from the priestly line of Aaron. ⁶Zechariah and Elizabeth were righteous in God's eyes, careful to obey all of the Lord's commandments and regulations. ⁷They had no children because Elizabeth was unable to conceive, and they were both very old.

⁸One day Zechariah was serving God in the Temple, for his order was on duty that week. ⁹As was the custom of the priests, he was chosen by lot to enter the sanctuary of the Lord and burn incense. ¹⁰While the incense was being burned, a great crowd stood outside, praying.

¹¹While Zechariah was in the sanctuary, an angel of the Lord appeared to him, standing to the right of the incense altar. ¹²Zechariah was shaken and overwhelmed with fear when he saw him. ¹³But the angel said, "Don't be afraid,

1:2 Greek *from those who from the beginning were servants of the word.*

Zechariah! God has heard your prayer. Your wife, Elizabeth, will give you a son, and you are to name him John. 14You will have great joy and gladness, and many will rejoice at his birth, 15for he will be great in the eyes of the Lord. He must never touch wine or other alcoholic drinks. He will be filled with the Holy Spirit, even before his birth.* 16And he will turn many Israelites to the Lord their God. 17He will be a man with the spirit and power of Elijah. He will prepare the people for the coming of the Lord. He will turn the hearts of the fathers to their children,* and he will cause those who are rebellious to accept the wisdom of the godly."

18Zechariah said to the angel, "How can I be sure this will happen? I'm an old man now, and my wife is also well along in years."

19Then the angel said, "I am Gabriel! I stand in the very presence of God. It was he who sent me to bring you this good news! 20But now, since you didn't believe what I said, you will be silent and unable to speak until the child is born. For my words will certainly be fulfilled at the proper time."

21Meanwhile, the people were waiting for Zechariah to come out of the sanctuary, wondering why he was taking so long. 22When he finally did come out, he couldn't speak to them. Then they realized from his gestures and his silence that he must have seen a vision in the sanctuary.

23When Zechariah's week of service in the Temple was over, he returned home. 24Soon afterward his wife, Elizabeth, became pregnant and went into seclusion for five months. 25"How kind the Lord is!" she exclaimed. "He has taken away my disgrace of having no children."

The Birth of Jesus Foretold

26In the sixth month of Elizabeth's pregnancy, God sent the angel Gabriel to Nazareth, a village in Galilee, 27to a virgin named Mary. She was engaged to be married to a man named Joseph, a descendant of King David. 28Gabriel appeared to her and said, "Greetings,* favored woman! The Lord is with you!*"

29Confused and disturbed, Mary tried to think what the angel could mean. 30"Don't be afraid, Mary," the angel told her, "for you have found favor with God! 31You will conceive and give birth to a son, and you will name him Jesus. 32He will be very great and will be called the Son of the Most High. The Lord God will give him the throne of his ancestor David. 33And he will reign over Israel* forever; his Kingdom will never end!"

34Mary asked the angel, "But how can this happen? I am a virgin."

35The angel replied, "The Holy Spirit will come upon you, and the power of the Most High will overshadow you. So the baby to be born will be holy, and he will be called the Son of God. 36What's more, your relative Elizabeth has become pregnant in her old age! People used to say she was barren, but she has conceived a son and is now in her sixth month. 37For the word of God will never fail.*"

38Mary responded, "I am the Lord's servant. May everything you have said about me come true." And then the angel left her.

Mary Visits Elizabeth

39A few days later Mary hurried to the hill country of Judea, to the town 40where Zechariah lived. She entered the house and greeted Elizabeth. 41At the sound of Mary's greeting, Elizabeth's child leaped within her, and Elizabeth was filled with the Holy Spirit.

42Elizabeth gave a glad cry and exclaimed to Mary, "God has blessed you above all women, and your child is blessed. 43Why am I so honored, that the mother of my Lord should visit me? 44When I heard your greeting, the baby in my womb jumped for joy. 45You are blessed because you believed that the Lord would do what he said."

The Magnificat: Mary's Song of Praise

46Mary responded,

"Oh, how my soul praises the Lord.
47   How my spirit rejoices in God my Savior!
48 For he took notice of his lowly servant girl,
        and from now on all generations will
        call me blessed.
49 For the Mighty One is holy,
        and he has done great things for me.
50 He shows mercy from generation to
        generation
        to all who fear him.
51 His mighty arm has done tremendous
        things!
    He has scattered the proud and haughty
        ones.
52 He has brought down princes from their
        thrones
        and exalted the humble.

1:15 Or even from birth.   1:17 See Mal 4:5-6.   1:28a Or Rejoice.   1:28b Some manuscripts add Blessed are you among women.
1:33 Greek over the house of Jacob.   1:37 Some manuscripts read For nothing is impossible with God.

53 He has filled the hungry with good things
    and sent the rich away with empty hands.
54 He has helped his servant Israel
    and remembered to be merciful.
55 For he made this promise to our ancestors,
    to Abraham and his children forever."

56Mary stayed with Elizabeth about three months and then went back to her own home.

The Birth of John the Baptist

57When it was time for Elizabeth's baby to be born, she gave birth to a son. 58And when her neighbors and relatives heard that the Lord had been very merciful to her, everyone rejoiced with her.

59When the baby was eight days old, they all came for the circumcision ceremony. They wanted to name him Zechariah, after his father. 60But Elizabeth said, "No! His name is John!"

61"What?" they exclaimed. "There is no one in all your family by that name." 62So they used gestures to ask the baby's father what he wanted to name him. 63He motioned for a writing tablet, and to everyone's surprise he wrote, "His name is John." 64Instantly Zechariah could speak again, and he began praising God.

65Awe fell upon the whole neighborhood, and the news of what had happened spread throughout the Judean hills. 66Everyone who heard about it reflected on these events and asked, "What will this child turn out to be?" For the hand of the Lord was surely upon him in a special way.

Zechariah's Prophecy

67Then his father, Zechariah, was filled with the Holy Spirit and gave this prophecy:

68 "Praise the Lord, the God of Israel,
    because he has visited and redeemed his
      people.
69 He has sent us a mighty Savior*
    from the royal line of his servant David,
70 just as he promised
    through his holy prophets long ago.
71 Now we will be saved from our enemies
    and from all who hate us.
72 He has been merciful to our ancestors
    by remembering his sacred covenant—
73 the covenant he swore with an oath
    to our ancestor Abraham.
74 We have been rescued from our enemies
    so we can serve God without fear,
75 in holiness and righteousness
    for as long as we live.
76 "And you, my little son,
    will be called the prophet of the Most
      High,
    because you will prepare the way for the
      Lord.
77 You will tell his people how to find
      salvation
    through forgiveness of their sins.
78 Because of God's tender mercy,
    the morning light from heaven is about
      to break upon us,*
79 to give light to those who sit in darkness
    and in the shadow of death,
    and to guide us to the path of peace."

80John grew up and became strong in spirit. And he lived in the wilderness until he began his public ministry to Israel.

The Birth of Jesus

2 At that time the Roman emperor, Augustus, decreed that a census should be taken throughout the Roman Empire. 2(This was the first census taken when Quirinius was governor of Syria.) 3All returned to their own ancestral towns to register for this census. 4And because Joseph was a descendant of King David, he had to go to Bethlehem in Judea, David's ancient home. He traveled there from the village of Nazareth in Galilee. 5He took with him Mary, to whom he was engaged, who was now expecting a child.

6And while they were there, the time came for her baby to be born. 7She gave birth to her firstborn son. She wrapped him snugly in strips of cloth and laid him in a manger, because there was no lodging available for them.

The Shepherds and Angels

8That night there were shepherds staying in the fields nearby, guarding their flocks of sheep. 9Suddenly, an angel of the Lord appeared among them, and the radiance of the Lord's glory surrounded them. They were terrified, 10but the angel reassured them. "Don't be afraid!" he said. "I bring you good news that will bring great joy to all people. 11The Savior—yes, the Messiah, the Lord—has been born today in Bethlehem, the city of David! 12And you will recognize him by this sign: You will find a baby wrapped snugly in strips of cloth, lying in a manger."

1:69 Greek *has raised up a horn of salvation for us.*   1:78 Or *the Morning Light from Heaven is about to visit us.*

[13]Suddenly, the angel was joined by a vast host of others—the armies of heaven—praising God and saying,

[14] "Glory to God in highest heaven,
    and peace on earth to those with whom
    God is pleased."

[15]When the angels had returned to heaven, the shepherds said to each other, "Let's go to Bethlehem! Let's see this thing that has happened, which the Lord has told us about."
[16]They hurried to the village and found Mary and Joseph. And there was the baby, lying in the manger. [17]After seeing him, the shepherds told everyone what had happened and what the angel had said to them about this child. [18]All who heard the shepherds' story were astonished, [19]but Mary kept all these things in her heart and thought about them often. [20]The shepherds went back to their flocks, glorifying and praising God for all they had heard and seen. It was just as the angel had told them.

Jesus Is Presented in the Temple
[21]Eight days later, when the baby was circumcised, he was named Jesus, the name given him by the angel even before he was conceived.

[22]Then it was time for their purification offering, as required by the law of Moses after the birth of a child; so his parents took him to Jerusalem to present him to the Lord. [23]The law of the Lord says, "If a woman's first child is a boy, he must be dedicated to the LORD."* [24]So they offered the sacrifice required in the law of the Lord—"either a pair of turtledoves or two young pigeons."*

The Prophecy of Simeon
[25]At that time there was a man in Jerusalem named Simeon. He was righteous and devout and was eagerly waiting for the Messiah to come and rescue Israel. The Holy Spirit was upon him [26]and had revealed to him that he would not die until he had seen the Lord's Messiah. [27]That day the Spirit led him to the Temple. So when Mary and Joseph came to present the baby Jesus to the Lord as the law required, [28]Simeon was there. He took the child in his arms and praised God, saying,

[29] "Sovereign Lord, now let your servant die
    in peace,
    as you have promised.
[30] I have seen your salvation,

[31]   which you have prepared for all people.
[32] He is a light to reveal God to the nations,
    and he is the glory of your people
        Israel!"

[33]Jesus' parents were amazed at what was being said about him. [34]Then Simeon blessed them, and he said to Mary, the baby's mother, "This child is destined to cause many in Israel to fall, and many others to rise. He has been sent as a sign from God, but many will oppose him. [35]As a result, the deepest thoughts of many hearts will be revealed. And a sword will pierce your very soul."

The Prophecy of Anna
[36]Anna, a prophet, was also there in the Temple. She was the daughter of Phanuel from the tribe of Asher, and she was very old. Her husband died when they had been married only seven years. [37]Then she lived as a widow to the age of eighty-four.* She never left the Temple but stayed there day and night, worshiping God with fasting and prayer. [38]She came along just as Simeon was talking with Mary and Joseph, and she began praising God. She talked about the child to everyone who had been waiting expectantly for God to rescue Jerusalem.

[39]When Jesus' parents had fulfilled all the requirements of the law of the Lord, they returned home to Nazareth in Galilee. [40]There the child grew up healthy and strong. He was filled with wisdom, and God's favor was on him.

Jesus Speaks with the Teachers
[41]Every year Jesus' parents went to Jerusalem for the Passover festival. [42]When Jesus was twelve years old, they attended the festival as usual. [43]After the celebration was over, they started home to Nazareth, but Jesus stayed behind in Jerusalem. His parents didn't miss him at first, [44]because they assumed he was among the other travelers. But when he didn't show up that evening, they started looking for him among their relatives and friends.

[45]When they couldn't find him, they went back to Jerusalem to search for him there. [46]Three days later they finally discovered him in the Temple, sitting among the religious teachers, listening to them and asking questions. [47]All who heard him were amazed at his understanding and his answers.

[48]His parents didn't know what to think. "Son," his mother said to him, "why have you

2:23 Exod 13:2.   2:24 Lev 12:8.   2:37 Or *She had been a widow for eighty-four years.*

done this to us? Your father and I have been frantic, searching for you everywhere."

49"But why did you need to search?" he asked. "Didn't you know that I must be in my Father's house?"* 50But they didn't understand what he meant.

51Then he returned to Nazareth with them and was obedient to them. And his mother stored all these things in her heart.

52Jesus grew in wisdom and in stature and in favor with God and all the people.

John the Baptist Prepares the Way

3 It was now the fifteenth year of the reign of Tiberius, the Roman emperor. Pontius Pilate was governor over Judea; Herod Antipas was ruler* over Galilee; his brother Philip was ruler* over Iturea and Traconitis; Lysanias was ruler over Abilene. 2Annas and Caiaphas were the high priests. At this time a message from God came to John son of Zechariah, who was living in the wilderness. 3Then John went from place to place on both sides of the Jordan River, preaching that people should be baptized to show that they had repented of their sins and turned to God to be forgiven. 4Isaiah had spoken of John when he said,

"He is a voice shouting in the wilderness,
'Prepare the way for the LORD's coming!
    Clear the road for him!
5 The valleys will be filled,
    and the mountains and hills made level.
The curves will be straightened,
    and the rough places made smooth.
6 And then all people will see
    the salvation sent from God.'"*

7When the crowds came to John for baptism, he said, "You brood of snakes! Who warned you to flee the coming wrath? 8Prove by the way you live that you have repented of your sins and turned to God. Don't just say to each other, 'We're safe, for we are descendants of Abraham.' That means nothing, for I tell you, God can create children of Abraham from these very stones. 9Even now the ax of God's judgment is poised, ready to sever the roots of the trees. Yes, every tree that does not produce good fruit will be chopped down and thrown into the fire."

10The crowds asked, "What should we do?"
11John replied, "If you have two shirts, give one to the poor. If you have food, share it with those who are hungry."

12Even corrupt tax collectors came to be baptized and asked, "Teacher, what should we do?"

13He replied, "Collect no more taxes than the government requires."

14"What should we do?" asked some soldiers.

John replied, "Don't extort money or make false accusations. And be content with your pay."

15Everyone was expecting the Messiah to come soon, and they were eager to know whether John might be the Messiah. 16John answered their questions by saying, "I baptize you with* water; but someone is coming soon who is greater than I am—so much greater that I'm not even worthy to be his slave and untie the straps of his sandals. He will baptize you with the Holy Spirit and with fire.* 17He is ready to separate the chaff from the wheat with his winnowing fork. Then he will clean up the threshing area, gathering the wheat into his barn but burning the chaff with never-ending fire." 18John used many such warnings as he announced the Good News to the people.

19John also publicly criticized Herod Antipas, the ruler of Galilee,* for marrying Herodias, his brother's wife, and for many other wrongs he had done. 20So Herod put John in prison, adding this sin to his many others.

The Baptism of Jesus

21One day when the crowds were being baptized, Jesus himself was baptized. As he was praying, the heavens opened, 22and the Holy Spirit, in bodily form, descended on him like a dove. And a voice from heaven said, "You are my dearly loved Son, and you bring me great joy.*"

The Ancestors of Jesus

23Jesus was about thirty years old when he began his public ministry.

Jesus was known as the son of Joseph.
    Joseph was the son of Heli.
24 Heli was the son of Matthat.
    Matthat was the son of Levi.
    Levi was the son of Melki.
    Melki was the son of Jannai.
    Jannai was the son of Joseph.
25 Joseph was the son of Mattathias.
    Mattathias was the son of Amos.
    Amos was the son of Nahum.

2:49 Or "Didn't you realize that I should be involved with my Father's affairs?"   3:1a Greek Herod was tetrarch. Herod Antipas was a son of King Herod.   3:1b Greek tetrarch; also in 3:1c.   3:4-6 Isa 40:3-5 (Greek version).   3:16a Or in.   3:16b Or in the Holy Spirit and in fire.   3:19 Greek Herod the tetrarch.   3:22 Some manuscripts read my Son, and today I have become your Father.

Nahum was the son of Esli.
Esli was the son of Naggai.
²⁶ Naggai was the son of Maath.
Maath was the son of Mattathias.
Mattathias was the son of Semein.
Semein was the son of Josech.
Josech was the son of Joda.
²⁷ Joda was the son of Joanan.
Joanan was the son of Rhesa.
Rhesa was the son of Zerubbabel.
Zerubbabel was the son of Shealtiel.
Shealtiel was the son of Neri.
²⁸ Neri was the son of Melki.
Melki was the son of Addi.
Addi was the son of Cosam.
Cosam was the son of Elmadam.
Elmadam was the son of Er.
²⁹ Er was the son of Joshua.
Joshua was the son of Eliezer.
Eliezer was the son of Jorim.
Jorim was the son of Matthat.
Matthat was the son of Levi.
³⁰ Levi was the son of Simeon.
Simeon was the son of Judah.
Judah was the son of Joseph.
Joseph was the son of Jonam.
Jonam was the son of Eliakim.
³¹ Eliakim was the son of Melea.
Melea was the son of Menna.
Menna was the son of Mattatha.
Mattatha was the son of Nathan.
Nathan was the son of David.
³² David was the son of Jesse.
Jesse was the son of Obed.
Obed was the son of Boaz.
Boaz was the son of Salmon.*
Salmon was the son of Nahshon.
³³ Nahshon was the son of Amminadab.
Amminadab was the son of Admin.
Admin was the son of Arni.*
Arni was the son of Hezron.
Hezron was the son of Perez.
Perez was the son of Judah.
³⁴ Judah was the son of Jacob.
Jacob was the son of Isaac.
Isaac was the son of Abraham.
Abraham was the son of Terah.
Terah was the son of Nahor.
³⁵ Nahor was the son of Serug.
Serug was the son of Reu.
Reu was the son of Peleg.
Peleg was the son of Eber.

Eber was the son of Shelah.
³⁶ Shelah was the son of Cainan.
Cainan was the son of Arphaxad.
Arphaxad was the son of Shem.
Shem was the son of Noah.
Noah was the son of Lamech.
³⁷ Lamech was the son of Methuselah.
Methuselah was the son of Enoch.
Enoch was the son of Jared.
Jared was the son of Mahalalel.
Mahalalel was the son of Kenan.
³⁸ Kenan was the son of Enosh.*
Enosh was the son of Seth.
Seth was the son of Adam.
Adam was the son of God.

The Temptation of Jesus

4 Then Jesus, full of the Holy Spirit, returned from the Jordan River. He was led by the Spirit in the wilderness,* ²where he was tempted by the devil for forty days. Jesus ate nothing all that time and became very hungry.

³Then the devil said to him, "If you are the Son of God, tell this stone to become a loaf of bread."

⁴But Jesus told him, "No! The Scriptures say, 'People do not live by bread alone.'*"

⁵Then the devil took him up and revealed to him all the kingdoms of the world in a moment of time. ⁶"I will give you the glory of these kingdoms and authority over them," the devil said, "because they are mine to give to anyone I please. ⁷I will give it all to you if you will worship me."

⁸Jesus replied, "The Scriptures say,

'You must worship the LORD your God
    and serve only him.'*"

⁹Then the devil took him to Jerusalem, to the highest point of the Temple, and said, "If you are the Son of God, jump off! ¹⁰For the Scriptures say,

'He will order his angels to protect and
    guard you.
¹¹ And they will hold you up with their hands
    so you won't even hurt your foot on a
    stone.'*"

¹²Jesus responded, "The Scriptures also say, 'You must not test the LORD your God.'*"

3:32 Greek *Sala,* a variant spelling of Salmon; also in 3:32b. See Ruth 4:20-21.   3:33 Some manuscripts read *Amminadab was the son of Aram. Arni* and *Aram* are alternate spellings of Ram. See 1 Chr 2:9-10.   3:38 Greek *Enos,* a variant spelling of Enosh; also in 3:38b. See Gen 5:6.   4:1 Some manuscripts read *into the wilderness.*   4:4 Deut 8:3.   4:8 Deut 6:13.   4:10-11 Ps 91:11-12. 4:12 Deut 6:16.

13When the devil had finished tempting Jesus, he left him until the next opportunity came.

Jesus Rejected at Nazareth

14Then Jesus returned to Galilee, filled with the Holy Spirit's power. Reports about him spread quickly through the whole region. 15He taught regularly in their synagogues and was praised by everyone.

16When he came to the village of Nazareth, his boyhood home, he went as usual to the synagogue on the Sabbath and stood up to read the Scriptures. 17The scroll of Isaiah the prophet was handed to him. He unrolled the scroll and found the place where this was written:

18 "The Spirit of the LORD is upon me,
      for he has anointed me to bring Good
      News to the poor.
   He has sent me to proclaim that captives
      will be released,
   that the blind will see,
   that the oppressed will be set free,
19   and that the time of the LORD's favor
      has come.*"

20He rolled up the scroll, handed it back to the attendant, and sat down. All eyes in the synagogue looked at him intently. 21Then he began to speak to them. "The Scripture you've just heard has been fulfilled this very day!"

22Everyone spoke well of him and was amazed by the gracious words that came from his lips. "How can this be?" they asked. "Isn't this Joseph's son?"

23Then he said, "You will undoubtedly quote me this proverb: 'Physician, heal yourself'—meaning, 'Do miracles here in your hometown like those you did in Capernaum.' 24But I tell you the truth, no prophet is accepted in his own hometown.

25"Certainly there were many needy widows in Israel in Elijah's time, when the heavens were closed for three and a half years, and a severe famine devastated the land. 26Yet Elijah was not sent to any of them. He was sent instead to a foreigner—a widow of Zarephath in the land of Sidon. 27And many in Israel had leprosy in the time of the prophet Elisha, but the only one healed was Naaman, a Syrian."

28When they heard this, the people in the synagogue were furious. 29Jumping up, they mobbed him and forced him to the edge of the hill on which the town was built. They intended to push him over the cliff, 30but he passed right through the crowd and went on his way.

Jesus Casts Out a Demon

31Then Jesus went to Capernaum, a town in Galilee, and taught there in the synagogue every Sabbath day. 32There, too, the people were amazed at his teaching, for he spoke with authority.

33Once when he was in the synagogue, a man possessed by a demon—an evil* spirit—cried out, shouting, 34"Go away! Why are you interfering with us, Jesus of Nazareth? Have you come to destroy us? I know who you are—the Holy One of God!"

35But Jesus reprimanded him. "Be quiet! Come out of the man," he ordered. At that, the demon threw the man to the floor as the crowd watched; then it came out of him without hurting him further.

36Amazed, the people exclaimed, "What authority and power this man's words possess! Even evil spirits obey him, and they flee at his command!" 37The news about Jesus spread through every village in the entire region.

Jesus Heals Many People

38After leaving the synagogue that day, Jesus went to Simon's home, where he found Simon's mother-in-law very sick with a high fever. "Please heal her," everyone begged. 39Standing at her bedside, he rebuked the fever, and it left her. And she got up at once and prepared a meal for them.

40As the sun went down that evening, people throughout the village brought sick family members to Jesus. No matter what their diseases were, the touch of his hand healed every one. 41Many were possessed by demons; and the demons came out at his command, shouting, "You are the Son of God!" But because they knew he was the Messiah, he rebuked them and refused to let them speak.

Jesus Continues to Preach

42Early the next morning Jesus went out to an isolated place. The crowds searched everywhere for him, and when they finally found him, they begged him not to leave them. 43But he replied, "I must preach the Good News of the Kingdom of God in other towns, too, because that is why I was sent." 44So he continued

4:18-19 Or and to proclaim the acceptable year of the LORD. Isa 61:1-2 (Greek version); 58:6.   4:33 Greek unclean; also in 4:36.

to travel around, preaching in synagogues throughout Judea.*

The First Disciples

5 One day as Jesus was preaching on the shore of the Sea of Galilee,* great crowds pressed in on him to listen to the word of God. [2]He noticed two empty boats at the water's edge, for the fishermen had left them and were washing their nets. [3]Stepping into one of the boats, Jesus asked Simon,* its owner, to push it out into the water. So he sat in the boat and taught the crowds from there.

[4]When he had finished speaking, he said to Simon, "Now go out where it is deeper, and let down your nets to catch some fish."

[5]"Master," Simon replied, "we worked hard all last night and didn't catch a thing. But if you say so, I'll let the nets down again." [6]And this time their nets were so full of fish they began to tear! [7]A shout for help brought their partners in the other boat, and soon both boats were filled with fish and on the verge of sinking.

[8]When Simon Peter realized what had happened, he fell to his knees before Jesus and said, "Oh, Lord, please leave me—I'm such a sinful man." [9]For he was awestruck by the number of fish they had caught, as were the others with him. [10]His partners, James and John, the sons of Zebedee, were also amazed.

Jesus replied to Simon, "Don't be afraid! From now on you'll be fishing for people!" [11]And as soon as they landed, they left everything and followed Jesus.

Jesus Heals a Man with Leprosy

[12]In one of the villages, Jesus met a man with an advanced case of leprosy. When the man saw Jesus, he bowed with his face to the ground, begging to be healed. "Lord," he said, "if you are willing, you can heal me and make me clean."

[13]Jesus reached out and touched him. "I am willing," he said. "Be healed!" And instantly the leprosy disappeared. [14]Then Jesus instructed him not to tell anyone what had happened. He said, "Go to the priest and let him examine you. Take along the offering required in the law of Moses for those who have been healed of leprosy.* This will be a public testimony that you have been cleansed."

[15]But despite Jesus' instructions, the report of his power spread even faster, and vast crowds came to hear him preach and to be healed of their diseases. [16]But Jesus often withdrew to the wilderness for prayer.

Jesus Heals a Paralyzed Man

[17]One day while Jesus was teaching, some Pharisees and teachers of religious law were sitting nearby. (It seemed that these men showed up from every village in all Galilee and Judea, as well as from Jerusalem.) And the Lord's healing power was strongly with Jesus.

[18]Some men came carrying a paralyzed man on a sleeping mat. They tried to take him inside to Jesus, [19]but they couldn't reach him because of the crowd. So they went up to the roof and took off some tiles. Then they lowered the sick man on his mat down into the crowd, right in front of Jesus. [20]Seeing their faith, Jesus said to the man, "Young man, your sins are forgiven."

[21]But the Pharisees and teachers of religious law said to themselves, "Who does he think he is? That's blasphemy! Only God can forgive sins!"

[22]Jesus knew what they were thinking, so he asked them, "Why do you question this in your hearts? [23]Is it easier to say 'Your sins are forgiven,' or 'Stand up and walk'? [24]So I will prove to you that the Son of Man* has the authority on earth to forgive sins." Then Jesus turned to the paralyzed man and said, "Stand up, pick up your mat, and go home!"

[25]And immediately, as everyone watched, the man jumped up, picked up his mat, and went home praising God. [26]Everyone was gripped with great wonder and awe, and they praised God, exclaiming, "We have seen amazing things today!"

Jesus Calls Levi (Matthew)

[27]Later, as Jesus left the town, he saw a tax collector named Levi sitting at his tax collector's booth. "Follow me and be my disciple," Jesus said to him. [28]So Levi got up, left everything, and followed him.

[29]Later, Levi held a banquet in his home with Jesus as the guest of honor. Many of Levi's fellow tax collectors and other guests also ate with them. [30]But the Pharisees and their teachers of religious law complained bitterly to Jesus' disciples, "Why do you eat and drink with such scum?*"

[31]Jesus answered them, "Healthy people don't need a doctor—sick people do. [32]I have

---

4:44 Some manuscripts read *Galilee.*   5:1 Greek *Lake Gennesaret,* another name for the Sea of Galilee.   5:3 *Simon* is called "Peter" in 6:14 and thereafter.   5:14 See Lev 14:2-32.   5:24 "Son of Man" is a title Jesus used for himself.   5:30 Greek *with tax collectors and sinners?*

come to call not those who think they are righteous, but those who know they are sinners and need to repent."

A Discussion about Fasting

33One day some people said to Jesus, "John the Baptist's disciples fast and pray regularly, and so do the disciples of the Pharisees. Why are your disciples always eating and drinking?"

34Jesus responded, "Do wedding guests fast while celebrating with the groom? Of course not. 35But someday the groom will be taken away from them, and then they will fast."

36Then Jesus gave them this illustration: "No one tears a piece of cloth from a new garment and uses it to patch an old garment. For then the new garment would be ruined, and the new patch wouldn't even match the old garment.

37"And no one puts new wine into old wineskins. For the new wine would burst the wineskins, spilling the wine and ruining the skins. 38New wine must be stored in new wineskins. 39But no one who drinks the old wine seems to want the new wine. 'The old is just fine,' they say."

A Discussion about the Sabbath

6 One Sabbath day as Jesus was walking through some grainfields, his disciples broke off heads of grain, rubbed off the husks in their hands, and ate the grain. 2But some Pharisees said, "Why are you breaking the law by harvesting grain on the Sabbath?"

3Jesus replied, "Haven't you read in the Scriptures what David did when he and his companions were hungry? 4He went into the house of God and broke the law by eating the sacred loaves of bread that only the priests can eat. He also gave some to his companions." 5And Jesus added, "The Son of Man* is Lord, even over the Sabbath."

Jesus Heals on the Sabbath

6On another Sabbath day, a man with a deformed right hand was in the synagogue while Jesus was teaching. 7The teachers of religious law and the Pharisees watched Jesus closely. If he healed the man's hand, they planned to accuse him of working on the Sabbath.

8But Jesus knew their thoughts. He said to the man with the deformed hand, "Come and stand in front of everyone." So the man came forward. 9Then Jesus said to his critics, "I have a question for you. Does the law permit good deeds on the Sabbath, or is it a day for doing evil? Is this a day to save life or to destroy it?"

10He looked around at them one by one and then said to the man, "Hold out your hand." So the man held out his hand, and it was restored! 11At this, the enemies of Jesus were wild with rage and began to discuss what to do with him.

Jesus Chooses the Twelve Apostles

12One day soon afterward Jesus went up on a mountain to pray, and he prayed to God all night. 13At daybreak he called together all of his disciples and chose twelve of them to be apostles. Here are their names:

14 Simon (whom he named Peter),
   Andrew (Peter's brother),
   James,
   John,
   Philip,
   Bartholomew,
15 Matthew,
   Thomas,
   James (son of Alphaeus),
   Simon (who was called the zealot),
16 Judas (son of James),
   Judas Iscariot (who later betrayed him).

Crowds Follow Jesus

17When they came down from the mountain, the disciples stood with Jesus on a large, level area, surrounded by many of his followers and by the crowds. There were people from all over Judea and from Jerusalem and from as far north as the seacoasts of Tyre and Sidon. 18They had come to hear him and to be healed of their diseases; and those troubled by evil* spirits were healed. 19Everyone tried to touch him, because healing power went out from him, and he healed everyone.

The Beatitudes

20Then Jesus turned to his disciples and said,

"God blesses you who are poor,
   for the Kingdom of God is yours.
21 God blesses you who are hungry now,
   for you will be satisfied.
God blesses you who weep now,
   for in due time you will laugh.

22What blessings await you when people hate you and exclude you and mock you and curse you as evil because you follow the Son of Man.

6:5 "Son of Man" is a title Jesus used for himself.   6:18 Greek *unclean*.

23When that happens, be happy! Yes, leap for joy! For a great reward awaits you in heaven. And remember, their ancestors treated the ancient prophets that same way.

Sorrows Foretold

24 "What sorrow awaits you who are rich,
  for you have your only happiness now.
25 What sorrow awaits you who are fat and prosperous now,
  for a time of awful hunger awaits you.
What sorrow awaits you who laugh now,
  for your laughing will turn to mourning and sorrow.
26 What sorrow awaits you who are praised by the crowds,
  for their ancestors also praised false prophets.

Love for Enemies

27"But to you who are willing to listen, I say, love your enemies! Do good to those who hate you. 28Bless those who curse you. Pray for those who hurt you. 29If someone slaps you on one cheek, offer the other cheek also. If someone demands your coat, offer your shirt also. 30Give to anyone who asks; and when things are taken away from you, don't try to get them back. 31Do to others as you would like them to do to you.

32"If you love only those who love you, why should you get credit for that? Even sinners love those who love them! 33And if you do good only to those who do good to you, why should you get credit? Even sinners do that much! 34And if you lend money only to those who can repay you, why should you get credit? Even sinners will lend to other sinners for a full return.

35"Love your enemies! Do good to them. Lend to them without expecting to be repaid. Then your reward from heaven will be very great, and you will truly be acting as children of the Most High, for he is kind to those who are unthankful and wicked. 36You must be compassionate, just as your Father is compassionate.

Do Not Judge Others

37"Do not judge others, and you will not be judged. Do not condemn others, or it will all come back against you. Forgive others, and you will be forgiven. 38Give, and you will receive. Your gift will return to you in full—pressed down, shaken together to make room for more, running over, and poured into your lap. The amount you give will determine the amount you get back.*"

39Then Jesus gave the following illustration: "Can one blind person lead another? Won't they both fall into a ditch? 40Students* are not greater than their teacher. But the student who is fully trained will become like the teacher.

41"And why worry about a speck in your friend's eye* when you have a log in your own? 42How can you think of saying, 'Friend,* let me help you get rid of that speck in your eye,' when you can't see past the log in your own eye? Hypocrite! First get rid of the log in your own eye; then you will see well enough to deal with the speck in your friend's eye.

The Tree and Its Fruit

43"A good tree can't produce bad fruit, and a bad tree can't produce good fruit. 44A tree is identified by its fruit. Figs are never gathered from thornbushes, and grapes are not picked from bramble bushes. 45A good person produces good things from the treasury of a good heart, and an evil person produces evil things from the treasury of an evil heart. What you say flows from what is in your heart.

Building on a Solid Foundation

46"So why do you keep calling me 'Lord, Lord!' when you don't do what I say? 47I will show you what it's like when someone comes to me, listens to my teaching, and then follows it. 48It is like a person building a house who digs deep and lays the foundation on solid rock. When the floodwaters rise and break against that house, it stands firm because it is well built. 49But anyone who hears and doesn't obey is like a person who builds a house right on the ground, without a foundation. When the floods sweep down against that house, it will collapse into a heap of ruins."

The Faith of a Roman Officer

7 When Jesus had finished saying all this to the people, he returned to Capernaum. 2At that time the highly valued slave of a Roman officer* was sick and near death. 3When the officer heard about Jesus, he sent some respected Jewish elders to ask him to come and heal his slave. 4So they earnestly begged Jesus to help the man. "If anyone deserves your help,

---

6:38 Or *The measure you give will be the measure you get back.*   6:40 Or *Disciples.*   6:41 Greek *your brother's eye;* also in 6:42.
6:42 Greek *Brother.*   7:2 Greek *a centurion;* similarly in 7:6.

he does," they said, [5]"for he loves the Jewish people and even built a synagogue for us."

[6]So Jesus went with them. But just before they arrived at the house, the officer sent some friends to say, "Lord, don't trouble yourself by coming to my home, for I am not worthy of such an honor. [7]I am not even worthy to come and meet you. Just say the word from where you are, and my servant will be healed. [8]I know this because I am under the authority of my superior officers, and I have authority over my soldiers. I only need to say, 'Go,' and they go, or 'Come,' and they come. And if I say to my slaves, 'Do this,' they do it."

[9]When Jesus heard this, he was amazed. Turning to the crowd that was following him, he said, "I tell you, I haven't seen faith like this in all Israel!" [10]And when the officer's friends returned to his house, they found the slave completely healed.

Jesus Raises a Widow's Son

[11]Soon afterward Jesus went with his disciples to the village of Nain, and a large crowd followed him. [12]A funeral procession was coming out as he approached the village gate. The young man who had died was a widow's only son, and a large crowd from the village was with her. [13]When the Lord saw her, his heart overflowed with compassion. "Don't cry!" he said. [14]Then he walked over to the coffin and touched it, and the bearers stopped. "Young man," he said, "I tell you, get up." [15]Then the dead boy sat up and began to talk! And Jesus gave him back to his mother.

[16]Great fear swept the crowd, and they praised God, saying, "A mighty prophet has risen among us," and "God has visited his people today." [17]And the news about Jesus spread throughout Judea and the surrounding countryside.

Jesus and John the Baptist

[18]The disciples of John the Baptist told John about everything Jesus was doing. So John called for two of his disciples, [19]and he sent them to the Lord to ask him, "Are you the Messiah we've been expecting,* or should we keep looking for someone else?"

[20]John's two disciples found Jesus and said to him, "John the Baptist sent us to ask, 'Are you the Messiah we've been expecting, or should we keep looking for someone else?'"

[21]At that very time, Jesus cured many people of their diseases, illnesses, and evil spirits, and he restored sight to many who were blind. [22]Then he told John's disciples, "Go back to John and tell him what you have seen and heard—the blind see, the lame walk, those with leprosy are cured, the deaf hear, the dead are raised to life, and the Good News is being preached to the poor." [23]And he added, "God blesses those who do not fall away because of me.*"

[24]After John's disciples left, Jesus began talking about him to the crowds. "What kind of man did you go into the wilderness to see? Was he a weak reed, swayed by every breath of wind? [25]Or were you expecting to see a man dressed in expensive clothes? No, people who wear beautiful clothes and live in luxury are found in palaces. [26]Were you looking for a prophet? Yes, and he is more than a prophet. [27]John is the man to whom the Scriptures refer when they say,

'Look, I am sending my messenger ahead
    of you,
    and he will prepare your way before you.'*

[28]I tell you, of all who have ever lived, none is greater than John. Yet even the least person in the Kingdom of God is greater than he is!"

[29]When they heard this, all the people—even the tax collectors—agreed that God's way was right,* for they had been baptized by John. [30]But the Pharisees and experts in religious law rejected God's plan for them, for they had refused John's baptism.

[31]"To what can I compare the people of this generation?" Jesus asked. "How can I describe them? [32]They are like children playing a game in the public square. They complain to their friends,

'We played wedding songs,
    and you didn't dance,
so we played funeral songs,
    and you didn't weep.'

[33]For John the Baptist didn't spend his time eating bread or drinking wine, and you say, 'He's possessed by a demon.' [34]The Son of Man,* on the other hand, feasts and drinks, and you say, 'He's a glutton and a drunkard, and a friend of tax collectors and other sinners!' [35]But wisdom is shown to be right by the lives of those who follow it.*"

7:19 Greek *Are you the one who is coming?* Also in 7:20.   7:23 Or *who are not offended by me.*   7:27 Mal 3:1.   7:29 Or *praised God for his justice.*   7:34 "Son of Man" is a title Jesus used for himself.   7:35 Or *But wisdom is justified by all her children.*

Jesus Anointed by a Sinful Woman

36One of the Pharisees asked Jesus to have dinner with him, so Jesus went to his home and sat down to eat.* 37When a certain immoral woman from that city heard he was eating there, she brought a beautiful alabaster jar filled with expensive perfume. 38Then she knelt behind him at his feet, weeping. Her tears fell on his feet, and she wiped them off with her hair. Then she kept kissing his feet and putting perfume on them.

39When the Pharisee who had invited him saw this, he said to himself, "If this man were a prophet, he would know what kind of woman is touching him. She's a sinner!"

40Then Jesus answered his thoughts. "Simon," he said to the Pharisee, "I have something to say to you."

"Go ahead, Teacher," Simon replied.

41Then Jesus told him this story: "A man loaned money to two people—500 pieces of silver* to one and 50 pieces to the other. 42But neither of them could repay him, so he kindly forgave them both, canceling their debts. Who do you suppose loved him more after that?"

43Simon answered, "I suppose the one for whom he canceled the larger debt."

"That's right," Jesus said. 44Then he turned to the woman and said to Simon, "Look at this woman kneeling here. When I entered your home, you didn't offer me water to wash the dust from my feet, but she has washed them with her tears and wiped them with her hair. 45You didn't greet me with a kiss, but from the time I first came in, she has not stopped kissing my feet. 46You neglected the courtesy of olive oil to anoint my head, but she has anointed my feet with rare perfume.

47"I tell you, her sins—and they are many— have been forgiven, so she has shown me much love. But a person who is forgiven little shows only little love." 48Then Jesus said to the woman, "Your sins are forgiven."

49The men at the table said among themselves, "Who is this man, that he goes around forgiving sins?"

50And Jesus said to the woman, "Your faith has saved you; go in peace."

Women Who Followed Jesus

8 Soon afterward Jesus began a tour of the nearby towns and villages, preaching and announcing the Good News about the Kingdom of God. He took his twelve disciples with him, 2along with some women who had been cured of evil spirits and diseases. Among them were Mary Magdalene, from whom he had cast out seven demons; 3Joanna, the wife of Chuza, Herod's business manager; Susanna; and many others who were contributing from their own resources to support Jesus and his disciples.

Parable of the Farmer Scattering Seed

4One day Jesus told a story in the form of a parable to a large crowd that had gathered from many towns to hear him: 5"A farmer went out to plant his seed. As he scattered it across his field, some seed fell on a footpath, where it was stepped on, and the birds ate it. 6Other seed fell among rocks. It began to grow, but the plant soon wilted and died for lack of moisture. 7Other seed fell among thorns that grew up with it and choked out the tender plants. 8Still other seed fell on fertile soil. This seed grew and produced a crop that was a hundred times as much as had been planted!" When he had said this, he called out, "Anyone with ears to hear should listen and understand."

9His disciples asked him what this parable meant. 10He replied, "You are permitted to understand the secrets* of the Kingdom of God. But I use parables to teach the others so that the Scriptures might be fulfilled:

'When they look, they won't really see.
    When they hear, they won't understand.'*

11"This is the meaning of the parable: The seed is God's word. 12The seeds that fell on the footpath represent those who hear the message, only to have the devil come and take it away from their hearts and prevent them from believing and being saved. 13The seeds on the rocky soil represent those who hear the message and receive it with joy. But since they don't have deep roots, they believe for a while, then they fall away when they face temptation. 14The seeds that fell among the thorns represent those who hear the message, but all too quickly the message is crowded out by the cares and riches and pleasures of this life. And so they never grow into maturity. 15And the seeds that fell on the good soil represent honest, good-hearted people who hear God's word, cling to it, and patiently produce a huge harvest.

Parable of the Lamp

16"No one lights a lamp and then covers it with a bowl or hides it under a bed. A lamp is placed

---

7:36 Or and reclined.   7:41 Greek 500 denarii. A denarius was equivalent to a laborer's full day's wage.   8:10a Greek mysteries.
8:10b Isa 6:9 (Greek version).

on a stand, where its light can be seen by all who enter the house. ¹⁷For all that is secret will eventually be brought into the open, and everything that is concealed will be brought to light and made known to all.

¹⁸"So pay attention to how you hear. To those who listen to my teaching, more understanding will be given. But for those who are not listening, even what they think they understand will be taken away from them."

The True Family of Jesus

¹⁹Then Jesus' mother and brothers came to see him, but they couldn't get to him because of the crowd. ²⁰Someone told Jesus, "Your mother and your brothers are standing outside, and they want to see you."

²¹Jesus replied, "My mother and my brothers are all those who hear God's word and obey it."

Jesus Calms the Storm

²²One day Jesus said to his disciples, "Let's cross to the other side of the lake." So they got into a boat and started out. ²³As they sailed across, Jesus settled down for a nap. But soon a fierce storm came down on the lake. The boat was filling with water, and they were in real danger.

²⁴The disciples went and woke him up, shouting, "Master, Master, we're going to drown!"

When Jesus woke up, he rebuked the wind and the raging waves. Suddenly the storm stopped and all was calm. ²⁵Then he asked them, "Where is your faith?"

The disciples were terrified and amazed. "Who is this man?" they asked each other. "When he gives a command, even the wind and waves obey him!"

Jesus Heals a Demon-Possessed Man

²⁶So they arrived in the region of the Gerasenes,* across the lake from Galilee. ²⁷As Jesus was climbing out of the boat, a man who was possessed by demons came out to meet him. For a long time he had been homeless and naked, living in the tombs outside the town.

²⁸As soon as he saw Jesus, he shrieked and fell down in front of him. Then he screamed, "Why are you interfering with me, Jesus, Son of the Most High God? Please, I beg you, don't torture me!" ²⁹For Jesus had already commanded the evil* spirit to come out of him. This spirit had often taken control of the man. Even when he

was placed under guard and put in chains and shackles, he simply broke them and rushed out into the wilderness, completely under the demon's power.

³⁰Jesus demanded, "What is your name?"

"Legion," he replied, for he was filled with many demons. ³¹The demons kept begging Jesus not to send them into the bottomless pit.*

³²There happened to be a large herd of pigs feeding on the hillside nearby, and the demons begged him to let them enter into the pigs.

So Jesus gave them permission. ³³Then the demons came out of the man and entered the pigs, and the entire herd plunged down the steep hillside into the lake and drowned.

³⁴When the herdsmen saw it, they fled to the nearby town and the surrounding countryside, spreading the news as they ran. ³⁵People rushed out to see what had happened. A crowd soon gathered around Jesus, and they saw the man who had been freed from the demons. He was sitting at Jesus' feet, fully clothed and perfectly sane, and they were all afraid. ³⁶Then those who had seen what happened told the others how the demon-possessed man had been healed. ³⁷And all the people in the region of the Gerasenes begged Jesus to go away and leave them alone, for a great wave of fear swept over them.

So Jesus returned to the boat and left, crossing back to the other side of the lake. ³⁸The man who had been freed from the demons begged to go with him. But Jesus sent him home, saying, ³⁹"No, go back to your family, and tell them everything God has done for you." So he went all through the town proclaiming the great things Jesus had done for him.

Jesus Heals in Response to Faith

⁴⁰On the other side of the lake the crowds welcomed Jesus, because they had been waiting for him. ⁴¹Then a man named Jairus, a leader of the local synagogue, came and fell at Jesus' feet, pleading with him to come home with him. ⁴²His only daughter,* who was about twelve years old, was dying.

As Jesus went with him, he was surrounded by the crowds. ⁴³A woman in the crowd had suffered for twelve years with constant bleeding,* and she could find no cure. ⁴⁴Coming up behind Jesus, she touched the fringe of his robe. Immediately, the bleeding stopped.

8:26 Other manuscripts read *Gadarenes;* still others read *Gergesenes;* also in 8:37. See Matt 8:28; Mark 5:1.   8:29 Greek *unclean.*
8:31 Or *the abyss,* or *the underworld.*   8:42 Or *His only child, a daughter.*   8:43 Some manuscripts add *having spent everything she had on doctors.*

⁴⁵"Who touched me?" Jesus asked.

Everyone denied it, and Peter said, "Master, this whole crowd is pressing up against you."

⁴⁶But Jesus said, "Someone deliberately touched me, for I felt healing power go out from me." ⁴⁷When the woman realized that she could not stay hidden, she began to tremble and fell to her knees in front of him. The whole crowd heard her explain why she had touched him and that she had been immediately healed. ⁴⁸"Daughter," he said to her, "your faith has made you well. Go in peace."

⁴⁹While he was still speaking to her, a messenger arrived from the home of Jairus, the leader of the synagogue. He told him, "Your daughter is dead. There's no use troubling the Teacher now."

⁵⁰But when Jesus heard what had happened, he said to Jairus, "Don't be afraid. Just have faith, and she will be healed."

⁵¹When they arrived at the house, Jesus wouldn't let anyone go in with him except Peter, John, James, and the little girl's father and mother. ⁵²The house was filled with people weeping and wailing, but he said, "Stop the weeping! She isn't dead; she's only asleep."

⁵³But the crowd laughed at him because they all knew she had died. ⁵⁴Then Jesus took her by the hand and said in a loud voice, "My child, get up!" ⁵⁵And at that moment her life* returned, and she immediately stood up! Then Jesus told them to give her something to eat. ⁵⁶Her parents were overwhelmed, but Jesus insisted that they not tell anyone what had happened.

Jesus Sends Out the Twelve Disciples

9 One day Jesus called together his twelve disciples* and gave them power and authority to cast out all demons and to heal all diseases. ²Then he sent them out to tell everyone about the Kingdom of God and to heal the sick. ³"Take nothing for your journey," he instructed them. "Don't take a walking stick, a traveler's bag, food, money,* or even a change of clothes. ⁴Wherever you go, stay in the same house until you leave town. ⁵And if a town refuses to welcome you, shake its dust from your feet as you leave to show that you have abandoned those people to their fate."

⁶So they began their circuit of the villages, preaching the Good News and healing the sick.

Herod's Confusion

⁷When Herod Antipas, the ruler of Galilee,* heard about everything Jesus was doing, he was puzzled. Some were saying that John the Baptist had been raised from the dead. ⁸Others thought Jesus was Elijah or one of the other prophets risen from the dead.

⁹"I beheaded John," Herod said, "so who is this man about whom I hear such stories?" And he kept trying to see him.

Jesus Feeds Five Thousand

¹⁰When the apostles returned, they told Jesus everything they had done. Then he slipped quietly away with them toward the town of Bethsaida. ¹¹But the crowds found out where he was going, and they followed him. He welcomed them and taught them about the Kingdom of God, and he healed those who were sick.

¹²Late in the afternoon the twelve disciples came to him and said, "Send the crowds away to the nearby villages and farms, so they can find food and lodging for the night. There is nothing to eat here in this remote place."

¹³But Jesus said, "You feed them."

"But we have only five loaves of bread and two fish," they answered. "Or are you expecting us to go and buy enough food for this whole crowd?" ¹⁴For there were about 5,000 men there.

Jesus replied, "Tell them to sit down in groups of about fifty each." ¹⁵So the people all sat down. ¹⁶Jesus took the five loaves and two fish, looked up toward heaven, and blessed them. Then, breaking the loaves into pieces, he kept giving the bread and fish to the disciples so they could distribute it to the people. ¹⁷They all ate as much as they wanted, and afterward, the disciples picked up twelve baskets of leftovers!

Peter's Declaration about Jesus

¹⁸One day Jesus left the crowds to pray alone. Only his disciples were with him, and he asked them, "Who do people say I am?"

¹⁹"Well," they replied, "some say John the Baptist, some say Elijah, and others say you are one of the other ancient prophets risen from the dead."

²⁰Then he asked them, "But who do you say I am?"

Peter replied, "You are the Messiah* sent from God!"

8:55 Or *her spirit.* 9:1 Greek *the Twelve;* other manuscripts read *the twelve apostles.* 9:3 Or *silver coins.* 9:7 Greek *Herod the tetrarch.* Herod Antipas was a son of King Herod and was ruler over Galilee. 9:20 Or *the Christ. Messiah* (a Hebrew term) and *Christ* (a Greek term) both mean "anointed one."

Jesus Predicts His Death

21Jesus warned his disciples not to tell anyone who he was. 22"The Son of Man* must suffer many terrible things," he said. "He will be rejected by the elders, the leading priests, and the teachers of religious law. He will be killed, but on the third day he will be raised from the dead."

23Then he said to the crowd, "If any of you wants to be my follower, you must give up your own way, take up your cross daily, and follow me. 24If you try to hang on to your life, you will lose it. But if you give up your life for my sake, you will save it. 25And what do you benefit if you gain the whole world but are yourself lost or destroyed? 26If anyone is ashamed of me and my message, the Son of Man will be ashamed of that person when he returns in his glory and in the glory of the Father and the holy angels. 27I tell you the truth, some standing here right now will not die before they see the Kingdom of God."

The Transfiguration

28About eight days later Jesus took Peter, John, and James up on a mountain to pray. 29And as he was praying, the appearance of his face was transformed, and his clothes became dazzling white. 30Suddenly, two men, Moses and Elijah, appeared and began talking with Jesus. 31They were glorious to see. And they were speaking about his exodus from this world, which was about to be fulfilled in Jerusalem.

32Peter and the others had fallen asleep. When they woke up, they saw Jesus' glory and the two men standing with him. 33As Moses and Elijah were starting to leave, Peter, not even knowing what he was saying, blurted out, "Master, it's wonderful for us to be here! Let's make three shelters as memorials*—one for you, one for Moses, and one for Elijah." 34But even as he was saying this, a cloud overshadowed them, and terror gripped them as the cloud covered them.

35Then a voice from the cloud said, "This is my Son, my Chosen One.* Listen to him." 36When the voice finished, Jesus was there alone. They didn't tell anyone at that time what they had seen.

Jesus Heals a Demon-Possessed Boy

37The next day, after they had come down the mountain, a large crowd met Jesus. 38A man in the crowd called out to him, "Teacher, I beg you to look at my son, my only child. 39An evil spirit keeps seizing him, making him scream. It throws him into convulsions so that he foams at the mouth. It batters him and hardly ever leaves him alone. 40I begged your disciples to cast out the spirit, but they couldn't do it."

41Jesus said, "You faithless and corrupt people! How long must I be with you and put up with you?" Then he said to the man, "Bring your son here."

42As the boy came forward, the demon knocked him to the ground and threw him into a violent convulsion. But Jesus rebuked the evil* spirit and healed the boy. Then he gave him back to his father. 43Awe gripped the people as they saw this majestic display of God's power.

Jesus Again Predicts His Death

While everyone was marveling at everything he was doing, Jesus said to his disciples, 44"Listen to me and remember what I say. The Son of Man is going to be betrayed into the hands of his enemies." 45But they didn't know what he meant. Its significance was hidden from them, so they couldn't understand it, and they were afraid to ask him about it.

The Greatest in the Kingdom

46Then his disciples began arguing about which of them was the greatest. 47But Jesus knew their thoughts, so he brought a little child to his side. 48Then he said to them, "Anyone who welcomes a little child like this on my behalf* welcomes me, and anyone who welcomes me also welcomes my Father who sent me. Whoever is the least among you is the greatest."

Using the Name of Jesus

49John said to Jesus, "Master, we saw someone using your name to cast out demons, but we told him to stop because he isn't in our group."

50But Jesus said, "Don't stop him! Anyone who is not against you is for you."

Opposition from Samaritans

51As the time drew near for him to ascend to heaven, Jesus resolutely set out for Jerusalem. 52He sent messengers ahead to a Samaritan village to prepare for his arrival. 53But the people of the village did not welcome Jesus because he was on his way to Jerusalem. 54When James and John saw this, they said to Jesus, "Lord, should

9:22 "Son of Man" is a title Jesus used for himself.   9:33 Greek *three tabernacles*.   9:35 Some manuscripts read *This is my dearly loved Son*.   9:42 Greek *unclean*.   9:48 Greek *in my name*.

we call down fire from heaven to burn them up*?" [55]But Jesus turned and rebuked them.* [56]So they went on to another village.

The Cost of Following Jesus

[57]As they were walking along, someone said to Jesus, "I will follow you wherever you go."

[58]But Jesus replied, "Foxes have dens to live in, and birds have nests, but the Son of Man has no place even to lay his head."

[59]He said to another person, "Come, follow me."

The man agreed, but he said, "Lord, first let me return home and bury my father."

[60]But Jesus told him, "Let the spiritually dead bury their own dead!* Your duty is to go and preach about the Kingdom of God."

[61]Another said, "Yes, Lord, I will follow you, but first let me say good-bye to my family."

[62]But Jesus told him, "Anyone who puts a hand to the plow and then looks back is not fit for the Kingdom of God."

Jesus Sends Out His Disciples

10 The Lord now chose seventy-two* other disciples and sent them ahead in pairs to all the towns and places he planned to visit. [2]These were his instructions to them: "The harvest is great, but the workers are few. So pray to the Lord who is in charge of the harvest; ask him to send more workers into his fields. [3]Now go, and remember that I am sending you out as lambs among wolves. [4]Don't take any money with you, nor a traveler's bag, nor an extra pair of sandals. And don't stop to greet anyone on the road.

[5]"Whenever you enter someone's home, first say, 'May God's peace be on this house.' [6]If those who live there are peaceful, the blessing will stand; if they are not, the blessing will return to you. [7]Don't move around from home to home. Stay in one place, eating and drinking what they provide. Don't hesitate to accept hospitality, because those who work deserve their pay.

[8]"If you enter a town and it welcomes you, eat whatever is set before you. [9]Heal the sick, and tell them, 'The Kingdom of God is near you now.' [10]But if a town refuses to welcome you, go out into its streets and say, [11]'We wipe even the dust of your town from our feet to show that we have abandoned you to your fate. And know this—the Kingdom of God is near!' [12]I assure

you, even wicked Sodom will be better off than such a town on judgment day.

[13]"What sorrow awaits you, Korazin and Bethsaida! For if the miracles I did in you had been done in wicked Tyre and Sidon, their people would have repented of their sins long ago, clothing themselves in burlap and throwing ashes on their heads to show their remorse. [14]Yes, Tyre and Sidon will be better off on judgment day than you. [15]And you people of Capernaum, will you be honored in heaven? No, you will go down to the place of the dead.*"

[16]Then he said to the disciples, "Anyone who accepts your message is also accepting me. And anyone who rejects you is rejecting me. And anyone who rejects me is rejecting God, who sent me."

[17]When the seventy-two disciples returned, they joyfully reported to him, "Lord, even the demons obey us when we use your name!"

[18]"Yes," he told them, "I saw Satan fall from heaven like lightning! [19]Look, I have given you authority over all the power of the enemy, and you can walk among snakes and scorpions and crush them. Nothing will injure you. [20]But don't rejoice because evil spirits obey you; rejoice because your names are registered in heaven."

Jesus' Prayer of Thanksgiving

[21]At that same time Jesus was filled with the joy of the Holy Spirit, and he said, "O Father, Lord of heaven and earth, thank you for hiding these things from those who think themselves wise and clever, and for revealing them to the childlike. Yes, Father, it pleased you to do it this way.

[22]"My Father has entrusted everything to me. No one truly knows the Son except the Father, and no one truly knows the Father except the Son and those to whom the Son chooses to reveal him."

[23]Then when they were alone, he turned to the disciples and said, "Blessed are the eyes that see what you have seen. [24]I tell you, many prophets and kings longed to see what you see, but they didn't see it. And they longed to hear what you hear, but they didn't hear it."

The Most Important Commandment

[25]One day an expert in religious law stood up to test Jesus by asking him this question: "Teacher, what should I do to inherit eternal life?"

9:54 Some manuscripts add *as Elijah did.*   **9:55** Some manuscripts add an expanded conclusion to verse 55 and an additional sentence in verse 56: *And he said, "You don't realize what your hearts are like. [56]For the Son of Man has not come to destroy people's lives, but to save them."*   **9:60** Greek *Let the dead bury their own dead.*   **10:1** Some manuscripts read *seventy;* also in 10:17. **10:15** Greek *to Hades.*

²⁶Jesus replied, "What does the law of Moses say? How do you read it?"

²⁷The man answered, "'You must love the LORD your God with all your heart, all your soul, all your strength, and all your mind.' And, 'Love your neighbor as yourself.'"*

²⁸"Right!" Jesus told him. "Do this and you will live!"

²⁹The man wanted to justify his actions, so he asked Jesus, "And who is my neighbor?"

Parable of the Good Samaritan

³⁰Jesus replied with a story: "A Jewish man was traveling from Jerusalem down to Jericho, and he was attacked by bandits. They stripped him of his clothes, beat him up, and left him half dead beside the road.

³¹"By chance a priest came along. But when he saw the man lying there, he crossed to the other side of the road and passed him by. ³²A Temple assistant* walked over and looked at him lying there, but he also passed by on the other side.

³³"Then a despised Samaritan came along, and when he saw the man, he felt compassion for him. ³⁴Going over to him, the Samaritan soothed his wounds with olive oil and wine and bandaged them. Then he put the man on his own donkey and took him to an inn, where he took care of him. ³⁵The next day he handed the innkeeper two silver coins,* telling him, 'Take care of this man. If his bill runs higher than this, I'll pay you the next time I'm here.'

³⁶"Now which of these three would you say was a neighbor to the man who was attacked by bandits?" Jesus asked.

³⁷The man replied, "The one who showed him mercy."

Then Jesus said, "Yes, now go and do the same."

Jesus Visits Martha and Mary

³⁸As Jesus and the disciples continued on their way to Jerusalem, they came to a certain village where a woman named Martha welcomed him into her home. ³⁹Her sister, Mary, sat at the Lord's feet, listening to what he taught. ⁴⁰But Martha was distracted by the big dinner she was preparing. She came to Jesus and said, "Lord, doesn't it seem unfair to you that my sister just sits here while I do all the work? Tell her to come and help me."

⁴¹But the Lord said to her, "My dear Martha, you are worried and upset over all these details! ⁴²There is only one thing worth being concerned about. Mary has discovered it, and it will not be taken away from her."

Teaching about Prayer

11 Once Jesus was in a certain place praying. As he finished, one of his disciples came to him and said, "Lord, teach us to pray, just as John taught his disciples."

²Jesus said, "This is how you should pray:*

"Father, may your name be kept holy.
    May your Kingdom come soon.
³ Give us each day the food we need,*
⁴ and forgive us our sins,
    as we forgive those who sin against us.
And don't let us yield to temptation.*"

⁵Then, teaching them more about prayer, he used this story: "Suppose you went to a friend's house at midnight, wanting to borrow three loaves of bread. You say to him, ⁶'A friend of mine has just arrived for a visit, and I have nothing for him to eat.' ⁷And suppose he calls out from his bedroom, 'Don't bother me. The door is locked for the night, and my family and I are all in bed. I can't help you.' ⁸But I tell you this—though he won't do it for friendship's sake, if you keep knocking long enough, he will get up and give you whatever you need because of your shameless persistence.*

⁹"And so I tell you, keep on asking, and you will receive what you ask for. Keep on seeking, and you will find. Keep on knocking, and the door will be opened to you. ¹⁰For everyone who asks, receives. Everyone who seeks, finds. And to everyone who knocks, the door will be opened.

¹¹"You fathers—if your children ask* for a fish, do you give them a snake instead? ¹²Or if they ask for an egg, do you give them a scorpion? Of course not! ¹³So if you sinful people know how to give good gifts to your children, how much more will your heavenly Father give the Holy Spirit to those who ask him."

Jesus and the Prince of Demons

¹⁴One day Jesus cast out a demon from a man who couldn't speak, and when the demon was gone, the man began to speak. The crowds were

---

10:27 Deut 6:5; Lev 19:18. **10:32** Greek *A Levite.* **10:35** Greek *two denarii.* A denarius was equivalent to a laborer's full day's wage. **11:2** Some manuscripts add additional phrases from the Lord's Prayer as it reads in Matt 6:9-13. **11:3** Or *Give us each day our food for the day;* or *Give us each day our food for tomorrow.* **11:4** Or *And keep us from being tested.* **11:8** Or *in order to avoid shame,* or *so his reputation won't be damaged.* **11:11** Some manuscripts add *for bread, do you give them a stone? Or [if they ask].*

amazed, [15]but some of them said, "No wonder he can cast out demons. He gets his power from Satan,* the prince of demons." [16]Others, trying to test Jesus, demanded that he show them a miraculous sign from heaven to prove his authority.

[17]He knew their thoughts, so he said, "Any kingdom divided by civil war is doomed. A family splintered by feuding will fall apart. [18]You say I am empowered by Satan. But if Satan is divided and fighting against himself, how can his kingdom survive? [19]And if I am empowered by Satan, what about your own exorcists? They cast out demons, too, so they will condemn you for what you have said. [20]But if I am casting out demons by the power of God,* then the Kingdom of God has arrived among you. [21]For when a strong man is fully armed and guards his palace, his possessions are safe—[22]until someone even stronger attacks and overpowers him, strips him of his weapons, and carries off his belongings.

[23]"Anyone who isn't with me opposes me, and anyone who isn't working with me is actually working against me.

[24]"When an evil* spirit leaves a person, it goes into the desert, searching for rest. But when it finds none, it says, 'I will return to the person I came from.' [25]So it returns and finds that its former home is all swept and in order. [26]Then the spirit finds seven other spirits more evil than itself, and they all enter the person and live there. And so that person is worse off than before."

[27]As he was speaking, a woman in the crowd called out, "God bless your mother—the womb from which you came, and the breasts that nursed you!"

[28]Jesus replied, "But even more blessed are all who hear the word of God and put it into practice."

The Sign of Jonah

[29]As the crowd pressed in on Jesus, he said, "This evil generation keeps asking me to show them a miraculous sign. But the only sign I will give them is the sign of Jonah. [30]What happened to him was a sign to the people of Nineveh that God had sent him. What happens to the Son of Man* will be a sign to these people that he was sent by God.

[31]"The queen of Sheba* will stand up against this generation on judgment day and condemn it, for she came from a distant land to hear the wisdom of Solomon. Now someone greater than Solomon is here—but you refuse to listen. [32]The people of Nineveh will also stand up against this generation on judgment day and condemn it, for they repented of their sins at the preaching of Jonah. Now someone greater than Jonah is here—but you refuse to repent.

Receiving the Light

[33]"No one lights a lamp and then hides it or puts it under a basket.* Instead, a lamp is placed on a stand, where its light can be seen by all who enter the house.

[34]"Your eye is like a lamp that provides light for your body. When your eye is healthy, your whole body is filled with light. But when it is unhealthy, your body is filled with darkness. [35]Make sure that the light you think you have is not actually darkness. [36]If you are filled with light, with no dark corners, then your whole life will be radiant, as though a floodlight were filling you with light."

Jesus Criticizes the Religious Leaders

[37]As Jesus was speaking, one of the Pharisees invited him home for a meal. So he went in and took his place at the table.* [38]His host was amazed to see that he sat down to eat without first performing the hand-washing ceremony required by Jewish custom. [39]Then the Lord said to him, "You Pharisees are so careful to clean the outside of the cup and the dish, but inside you are filthy—full of greed and wickedness! [40]Fools! Didn't God make the inside as well as the outside? [41]So clean the inside by giving gifts to the poor, and you will be clean all over.

[42]"What sorrow awaits you Pharisees! For you are careful to tithe even the tiniest income from your herb gardens,* but you ignore justice and the love of God. You should tithe, yes, but do not neglect the more important things.

[43]"What sorrow awaits you Pharisees! For you love to sit in the seats of honor in the synagogues and receive respectful greetings as you walk in the marketplaces. [44]Yes, what sorrow awaits you! For you are like hidden graves in a field. People walk over them without knowing the corruption they are stepping on."

[45]"Teacher," said an expert in religious law,

11:15 Greek *Beelzeboul;* also in 11:18, 19. Other manuscripts read *Beezeboul;* Latin version reads *Beelzebub.*   11:20 Greek *by the finger of God.*   11:24 Greek *unclean.*   11:30 "Son of Man" is a title Jesus used for himself.   11:31 Greek *The queen of the south.*   11:33 Some manuscripts do not include *or puts it under a basket.*   11:37 Or *and reclined.*   11:42 Greek *tithe the mint, the rue, and every herb.*

"you have insulted us, too, in what you just said."

46"Yes," said Jesus, "what sorrow also awaits you experts in religious law! For you crush people with unbearable religious demands, and you never lift a finger to ease the burden. 47What sorrow awaits you! For you build monuments for the prophets your own ancestors killed long ago. 48But in fact, you stand as witnesses who agree with what your ancestors did. They killed the prophets, and you join in their crime by building the monuments! 49This is what God in his wisdom said about you:* 'I will send prophets and apostles to them, but they will kill some and persecute the others.'

50"As a result, this generation will be held responsible for the murder of all God's prophets from the creation of the world—51from the murder of Abel to the murder of Zechariah, who was killed between the altar and the sanctuary. Yes, it will certainly be charged against this generation.

52"What sorrow awaits you experts in religious law! For you remove the key to knowledge from the people. You don't enter the Kingdom yourselves, and you prevent others from entering."

53As Jesus was leaving, the teachers of religious law and the Pharisees became hostile and tried to provoke him with many questions. 54They wanted to trap him into saying something they could use against him.

A Warning against Hypocrisy

12 Meanwhile, the crowds grew until thousands were milling about and stepping on each other. Jesus turned first to his disciples and warned them, "Beware of the yeast of the Pharisees—their hypocrisy. 2The time is coming when everything that is covered up will be revealed, and all that is secret will be made known to all. 3Whatever you have said in the dark will be heard in the light, and what you have whispered behind closed doors will be shouted from the housetops for all to hear!

4"Dear friends, don't be afraid of those who want to kill your body; they cannot do any more to you after that. 5But I'll tell you whom to fear. Fear God, who has the power to kill you and then throw you into hell.* Yes, he's the one to fear.

6"What is the price of five sparrows—two copper coins*? Yet God does not forget a single one of them. 7And the very hairs on your head are all numbered. So don't be afraid; you are more valuable to God than a whole flock of sparrows.

8"I tell you the truth, everyone who acknowledges me publicly here on earth, the Son of Man* will also acknowledge in the presence of God's angels. 9But anyone who denies me here on earth will be denied before God's angels. 10Anyone who speaks against the Son of Man can be forgiven, but anyone who blasphemes the Holy Spirit will not be forgiven.

11"And when you are brought to trial in the synagogues and before rulers and authorities, don't worry about how to defend yourself or what to say, 12for the Holy Spirit will teach you at that time what needs to be said."

Parable of the Rich Fool

13Then someone called from the crowd, "Teacher, please tell my brother to divide our father's estate with me."

14Jesus replied, "Friend, who made me a judge over you to decide such things as that?" 15Then he said, "Beware! Guard against every kind of greed. Life is not measured by how much you own."

16Then he told them a story: "A rich man had a fertile farm that produced fine crops. 17He said to himself, 'What should I do? I don't have room for all my crops.' 18Then he said, 'I know! I'll tear down my barns and build bigger ones. Then I'll have room enough to store all my wheat and other goods. 19And I'll sit back and say to myself, "My friend, you have enough stored away for years to come. Now take it easy! Eat, drink, and be merry!"'

20"But God said to him, 'You fool! You will die this very night. Then who will get everything you worked for?'

21"Yes, a person is a fool to store up earthly wealth but not have a rich relationship with God."

Teaching about Money and Possessions

22Then, turning to his disciples, Jesus said, "That is why I tell you not to worry about everyday life—whether you have enough food to eat or enough clothes to wear. 23For life is more than food, and your body more than clothing. 24Look at the ravens. They don't plant or harvest or store food in barns, for God feeds them. And you are far more valuable to him than any birds! 25Can all your worries add a

---

11:49 Greek *Therefore, the wisdom of God said.* 12:5 Greek *Gehenna.* 12:6 Greek *two assaria* [Roman coins equal to ¹⁄₁₆ of a denarius]. 12:8 "Son of Man" is a title Jesus used for himself.

single moment to your life? ²⁶And if worry can't accomplish a little thing like that, what's the use of worrying over bigger things?

²⁷"Look at the lilies and how they grow. They don't work or make their clothing, yet Solomon in all his glory was not dressed as beautifully as they are. ²⁸And if God cares so wonderfully for flowers that are here today and thrown into the fire tomorrow, he will certainly care for you. Why do you have so little faith?

²⁹"And don't be concerned about what to eat and what to drink. Don't worry about such things. ³⁰These things dominate the thoughts of unbelievers all over the world, but your Father already knows your needs. ³¹Seek the Kingdom of God above all else, and he will give you everything you need.

³²"So don't be afraid, little flock. For it gives your Father great happiness to give you the Kingdom.

³³"Sell your possessions and give to those in need. This will store up treasure for you in heaven! And the purses of heaven never get old or develop holes. Your treasure will be safe; no thief can steal it and no moth can destroy it. ³⁴Wherever your treasure is, there the desires of your heart will also be.

Be Ready for the Lord's Coming

³⁵"Be dressed for service and keep your lamps burning, ³⁶as though you were waiting for your master to return from the wedding feast. Then you will be ready to open the door and let him in the moment he arrives and knocks. ³⁷The servants who are ready and waiting for his return will be rewarded. I tell you the truth, he himself will seat them, put on an apron, and serve them as they sit and eat! ³⁸He may come in the middle of the night or just before dawn.* But whenever he comes, he will reward the servants who are ready.

³⁹"Understand this: If a homeowner knew exactly when a burglar was coming, he would not permit his house to be broken into. ⁴⁰You also must be ready all the time, for the Son of Man will come when least expected."

⁴¹Peter asked, "Lord, is that illustration just for us or for everyone?"

⁴²And the Lord replied, "A faithful, sensible servant is one to whom the master can give the responsibility of managing his other household servants and feeding them. ⁴³If the master returns and finds that the servant has done a good job, there will be a reward. ⁴⁴I tell you

the truth, the master will put that servant in charge of all he owns. ⁴⁵But what if the servant thinks, 'My master won't be back for a while,' and he begins beating the other servants, partying, and getting drunk? ⁴⁶The master will return unannounced and unexpected, and he will cut the servant in pieces and banish him with the unfaithful.

⁴⁷"And a servant who knows what the master wants, but isn't prepared and doesn't carry out those instructions, will be severely punished. ⁴⁸But someone who does not know, and then does something wrong, will be punished only lightly. When someone has been given much, much will be required in return; and when someone has been entrusted with much, even more will be required.

Jesus Causes Division

⁴⁹"I have come to set the world on fire, and I wish it were already burning! ⁵⁰I have a terrible baptism of suffering ahead of me, and I am under a heavy burden until it is accomplished. ⁵¹Do you think I have come to bring peace to the earth? No, I have come to divide people against each other! ⁵²From now on families will be split apart, three in favor of me, and two against—or two in favor and three against.

⁵³ 'Father will be divided against son
    and son against father;
 mother against daughter
    and daughter against mother;
 and mother-in-law against
        daughter-in-law
    and daughter-in-law against
        mother-in-law.'*"

⁵⁴Then Jesus turned to the crowd and said, "When you see clouds beginning to form in the west, you say, 'Here comes a shower.' And you are right. ⁵⁵When the south wind blows, you say, 'Today will be a scorcher.' And it is. ⁵⁶You fools! You know how to interpret the weather signs of the earth and sky, but you don't know how to interpret the present times.

⁵⁷"Why can't you decide for yourselves what is right? ⁵⁸When you are on the way to court with your accuser, try to settle the matter before you get there. Otherwise, your accuser may drag you before the judge, who will hand you over to an officer, who will throw you into prison. ⁵⁹And if that happens, you won't be free again until you have paid the very last penny.*"

12:38 Greek *in the second or third watch.*   12:53 Mic 7:6.   12:59 Greek *last lepton* [the smallest Jewish coin].

A Call to Repentance

13 About this time Jesus was informed that Pilate had murdered some people from Galilee as they were offering sacrifices at the Temple. ²"Do you think those Galileans were worse sinners than all the other people from Galilee?" Jesus asked. "Is that why they suffered? ³Not at all! And you will perish, too, unless you repent of your sins and turn to God. ⁴And what about the eighteen people who died when the tower in Siloam fell on them? Were they the worst sinners in Jerusalem? ⁵No, and I tell you again that unless you repent, you will perish, too."

Parable of the Barren Fig Tree

⁶Then Jesus told this story: "A man planted a fig tree in his garden and came again and again to see if there was any fruit on it, but he was always disappointed. ⁷Finally, he said to his gardener, 'I've waited three years, and there hasn't been a single fig! Cut it down. It's just taking up space in the garden.'

⁸"The gardener answered, 'Sir, give it one more chance. Leave it another year, and I'll give it special attention and plenty of fertilizer. ⁹If we get figs next year, fine. If not, then you can cut it down.'"

Jesus Heals on the Sabbath

¹⁰One Sabbath day as Jesus was teaching in a synagogue, ¹¹he saw a woman who had been crippled by an evil spirit. She had been bent double for eighteen years and was unable to stand up straight. ¹²When Jesus saw her, he called her over and said, "Dear woman, you are healed of your sickness!" ¹³Then he touched her, and instantly she could stand straight. How she praised God!

¹⁴But the leader in charge of the synagogue was indignant that Jesus had healed her on the Sabbath day. "There are six days of the week for working," he said to the crowd. "Come on those days to be healed, not on the Sabbath."

¹⁵But the Lord replied, "You hypocrites! Each of you works on the Sabbath day! Don't you untie your ox or your donkey from its stall on the Sabbath and lead it out for water? ¹⁶This dear woman, a daughter of Abraham, has been held in bondage by Satan for eighteen years. Isn't it right that she be released, even on the Sabbath?"

¹⁷This shamed his enemies, but all the people rejoiced at the wonderful things he did.

Parable of the Mustard Seed

¹⁸Then Jesus said, "What is the Kingdom of God like? How can I illustrate it? ¹⁹It is like a tiny mustard seed that a man planted in a garden; it grows and becomes a tree, and the birds make nests in its branches."

Parable of the Yeast

²⁰He also asked, "What else is the Kingdom of God like? ²¹It is like the yeast a woman used in making bread. Even though she put only a little yeast in three measures of flour, it permeated every part of the dough."

The Narrow Door

²²Jesus went through the towns and villages, teaching as he went, always pressing on toward Jerusalem. ²³Someone asked him, "Lord, will only a few be saved?"

He replied, ²⁴"Work hard to enter the narrow door to God's Kingdom, for many will try to enter but will fail. ²⁵When the master of the house has locked the door, it will be too late. You will stand outside knocking and pleading, 'Lord, open the door for us!' But he will reply, 'I don't know you or where you come from.' ²⁶Then you will say, 'But we ate and drank with you, and you taught in our streets.' ²⁷And he will reply, 'I tell you, I don't know you or where you come from. Get away from me, all you who do evil.'

²⁸"There will be weeping and gnashing of teeth, for you will see Abraham, Isaac, Jacob, and all the prophets in the Kingdom of God, but you will be thrown out. ²⁹And people will come from all over the world—from east and west, north and south—to take their places in the Kingdom of God. ³⁰And note this: Some who seem least important now will be the greatest then, and some who are the greatest now will be least important then.*"

Jesus Grieves over Jerusalem

³¹At that time some Pharisees said to him, "Get away from here if you want to live! Herod Antipas wants to kill you!"

³²Jesus replied, "Go tell that fox that I will keep on casting out demons and healing people today and tomorrow; and the third day I will accomplish my purpose. ³³Yes, today, tomorrow, and the next day I must proceed on my way. For it wouldn't do for a prophet of God to be killed except in Jerusalem!

³⁴"O Jerusalem, Jerusalem, the city that kills the prophets and stones God's messengers!

13:30 Greek *Some are last who will be first, and some are first who will be last.*

How often I have wanted to gather your children together as a hen protects her chicks beneath her wings, but you wouldn't let me. [35]And now, look, your house is abandoned. And you will never see me again until you say, 'Blessings on the one who comes in the name of the LORD!'*"

Jesus Heals on the Sabbath

14 One Sabbath day Jesus went to eat dinner in the home of a leader of the Pharisees, and the people were watching him closely. [2]There was a man there whose arms and legs were swollen.* [3]Jesus asked the Pharisees and experts in religious law, "Is it permitted in the law to heal people on the Sabbath day, or not?" [4]When they refused to answer, Jesus touched the sick man and healed him and sent him away. [5]Then he turned to them and said, "Which of you doesn't work on the Sabbath? If your son* or your cow falls into a pit, don't you rush to get him out?" [6]Again they could not answer.

Jesus Teaches about Humility

[7]When Jesus noticed that all who had come to the dinner were trying to sit in the seats of honor near the head of the table, he gave them this advice: [8]"When you are invited to a wedding feast, don't sit in the seat of honor. What if someone who is more distinguished than you has also been invited? [9]The host will come and say, 'Give this person your seat.' Then you will be embarrassed, and you will have to take whatever seat is left at the foot of the table!

[10]"Instead, take the lowest place at the foot of the table. Then when your host sees you, he will come and say, 'Friend, we have a better place for you!' Then you will be honored in front of all the other guests. [11]For those who exalt themselves will be humbled, and those who humble themselves will be exalted."

[12]Then he turned to his host. "When you put on a luncheon or a banquet," he said, "don't invite your friends, brothers, relatives, and rich neighbors. For they will invite you back, and that will be your only reward. [13]Instead, invite the poor, the crippled, the lame, and the blind. [14]Then at the resurrection of the righteous, God will reward you for inviting those who could not repay you."

Parable of the Great Feast

[15]Hearing this, a man sitting at the table with Jesus exclaimed, "What a blessing it will be to attend a banquet* in the Kingdom of God!"

[16]Jesus replied with this story: "A man prepared a great feast and sent out many invitations. [17]When the banquet was ready, he sent his servant to tell the guests, 'Come, the banquet is ready.' [18]But they all began making excuses. One said, 'I have just bought a field and must inspect it. Please excuse me.' [19]Another said, 'I have just bought five pairs of oxen, and I want to try them out. Please excuse me.' [20]Another said, 'I just got married, so I can't come.'

[21]"The servant returned and told his master what they had said. His master was furious and said, 'Go quickly into the streets and alleys of the town and invite the poor, the crippled, the blind, and the lame.' [22]After the servant had done this, he reported, 'There is still room for more.' [23]So his master said, 'Go out into the country lanes and behind the hedges and urge anyone you find to come, so that the house will be full. [24]For none of those I first invited will get even the smallest taste of my banquet.'"

The Cost of Being a Disciple

[25]A large crowd was following Jesus. He turned around and said to them, [26]"If you want to be my disciple, you must, by comparison, hate everyone else—your father and mother, wife and children, brothers and sisters—yes, even your own life. Otherwise, you cannot be my disciple. [27]And if you do not carry your own cross and follow me, you cannot be my disciple.

[28]"But don't begin until you count the cost. For who would begin construction of a building without first calculating the cost to see if there is enough money to finish it? [29]Otherwise, you might complete only the foundation before running out of money, and then everyone would laugh at you. [30]They would say, 'There's the person who started that building and couldn't afford to finish it!'

[31]"Or what king would go to war against another king without first sitting down with his counselors to discuss whether his army of 10,000 could defeat the 20,000 soldiers marching against him? [32]And if he can't, he will send a delegation to discuss terms of peace while the enemy is still far away. [33]So you cannot become my disciple without giving up everything you own.

[34]"Salt is good for seasoning. But if it loses its flavor, how do you make it salty again? [35]Flavorless salt is good neither for the soil nor for the manure pile. It is thrown away. Anyone with ears to hear should listen and understand!"

13:35 Ps 118:26.   14:2 Or *who had dropsy.*   14:5 Some manuscripts read *donkey.*   14:15 Greek *to eat bread.*

Parable of the Lost Sheep

15 Tax collectors and other notorious sinners often came to listen to Jesus teach. ²This made the Pharisees and teachers of religious law complain that he was associating with such sinful people—even eating with them!

³So Jesus told them this story: ⁴"If a man has a hundred sheep and one of them gets lost, what will he do? Won't he leave the ninety-nine others in the wilderness and go to search for the one that is lost until he finds it? ⁵And when he has found it, he will joyfully carry it home on his shoulders. ⁶When he arrives, he will call together his friends and neighbors, saying, 'Rejoice with me because I have found my lost sheep.' ⁷In the same way, there is more joy in heaven over one lost sinner who repents and returns to God than over ninety-nine others who are righteous and haven't strayed away!

Parable of the Lost Coin

⁸"Or suppose a woman has ten silver coins* and loses one. Won't she light a lamp and sweep the entire house and search carefully until she finds it? ⁹And when she finds it, she will call in her friends and neighbors and say, 'Rejoice with me because I have found my lost coin.' ¹⁰In the same way, there is joy in the presence of God's angels when even one sinner repents."

Parable of the Lost Son

¹¹To illustrate the point further, Jesus told them this story: "A man had two sons. ¹²The younger son told his father, 'I want my share of your estate now before you die.' So his father agreed to divide his wealth between his sons.

¹³"A few days later this younger son packed all his belongings and moved to a distant land, and there he wasted all his money in wild living. ¹⁴About the time his money ran out, a great famine swept over the land, and he began to starve. ¹⁵He persuaded a local farmer to hire him, and the man sent him into his fields to feed the pigs. ¹⁶The young man became so hungry that even the pods he was feeding the pigs looked good to him. But no one gave him anything.

¹⁷"When he finally came to his senses, he said to himself, 'At home even the hired servants have food enough to spare, and here I am dying of hunger! ¹⁸I will go home to my father and say, "Father, I have sinned against both heaven and you, ¹⁹and I am no longer worthy of being called your son. Please take me on as a hired servant."'

²⁰"So he returned home to his father. And while he was still a long way off, his father saw him coming. Filled with love and compassion, he ran to his son, embraced him, and kissed him. ²¹His son said to him, 'Father, I have sinned against both heaven and you, and I am no longer worthy of being called your son.*'

²²"But his father said to the servants, 'Quick! Bring the finest robe in the house and put it on him. Get a ring for his finger and sandals for his feet. ²³And kill the calf we have been fattening. We must celebrate with a feast, ²⁴for this son of mine was dead and has now returned to life. He was lost, but now he is found.' So the party began.

²⁵"Meanwhile, the older son was in the fields working. When he returned home, he heard music and dancing in the house, ²⁶and he asked one of the servants what was going on. ²⁷'Your brother is back,' he was told, 'and your father has killed the fattened calf. We are celebrating because of his safe return.'

²⁸"The older brother was angry and wouldn't go in. His father came out and begged him, ²⁹but he replied, 'All these years I've slaved for you and never once refused to do a single thing you told me to. And in all that time you never gave me even one young goat for a feast with my friends. ³⁰Yet when this son of yours comes back after squandering your money on prostitutes, you celebrate by killing the fattened calf!'

³¹"His father said to him, 'Look, dear son, you have always stayed by me, and everything I have is yours. ³²We had to celebrate this happy day. For your brother was dead and has come back to life! He was lost, but now he is found!'"

Parable of the Shrewd Manager

16 Jesus told this story to his disciples: "There was a certain rich man who had a manager handling his affairs. One day a report came that the manager was wasting his employer's money. ²So the employer called him in and said, 'What's this I hear about you? Get your report in order, because you are going to be fired.'

³"The manager thought to himself, 'Now what? My boss has fired me. I don't have the strength to dig ditches, and I'm too proud to beg. ⁴Ah, I know how to ensure that I'll have

plenty of friends who will give me a home when I am fired.'

5 "So he invited each person who owed money to his employer to come and discuss the situation. He asked the first one, 'How much do you owe him?' 6 The man replied, 'I owe him 800 gallons of olive oil.' So the manager told him, 'Take the bill and quickly change it to 400 gallons.*'

7 "'And how much do you owe my employer?' he asked the next man. 'I owe him 1,000 bushels of wheat,' was the reply. 'Here,' the manager said, 'take the bill and change it to 800 bushels.*'

8 "The rich man had to admire the dishonest rascal for being so shrewd. And it is true that the children of this world are more shrewd in dealing with the world around them than are the children of the light. 9 Here's the lesson: Use your worldly resources to benefit others and make friends. Then, when your possessions are gone, they will welcome you to an eternal home.*

10 "If you are faithful in little things, you will be faithful in large ones. But if you are dishonest in little things, you won't be honest with greater responsibilities. 11 And if you are untrustworthy about worldly wealth, who will trust you with the true riches of heaven? 12 And if you are not faithful with other people's things, why should you be trusted with things of your own?

13 "No one can serve two masters. For you will hate one and love the other; you will be devoted to one and despise the other. You cannot serve God and be enslaved to money."

14 The Pharisees, who dearly loved their money, heard all this and scoffed at him. 15 Then he said to them, "You like to appear righteous in public, but God knows your hearts. What this world honors is detestable in the sight of God.

16 "Until John the Baptist, the law of Moses and the messages of the prophets were your guides. But now the Good News of the Kingdom of God is preached, and everyone is eager to get in.* 17 But that doesn't mean that the law has lost its force. It is easier for heaven and earth to disappear than for the smallest point of God's law to be overturned.

18 "For example, a man who divorces his wife and marries someone else commits adultery. And anyone who marries a woman divorced from her husband commits adultery."

Parable of the Rich Man and Lazarus

19 Jesus said, "There was a certain rich man who was splendidly clothed in purple and fine linen and who lived each day in luxury. 20 At his gate lay a poor man named Lazarus who was covered with sores. 21 As Lazarus lay there longing for scraps from the rich man's table, the dogs would come and lick his open sores.

22 "Finally, the poor man died and was carried by the angels to sit beside Abraham at the heavenly banquet.* The rich man also died and was buried, 23 and he went to the place of the dead.* There, in torment, he saw Abraham in the far distance with Lazarus at his side.

24 "The rich man shouted, 'Father Abraham, have some pity! Send Lazarus over here to dip the tip of his finger in water and cool my tongue. I am in anguish in these flames.'

25 "But Abraham said to him, 'Son, remember that during your lifetime you had everything you wanted, and Lazarus had nothing. So now he is here being comforted, and you are in anguish. 26 And besides, there is a great chasm separating us. No one can cross over to you from here, and no one can cross over to us from there.'

27 "Then the rich man said, 'Please, Father Abraham, at least send him to my father's home. 28 For I have five brothers, and I want him to warn them so they don't end up in this place of torment.'

29 "But Abraham said, 'Moses and the prophets have warned them. Your brothers can read what they wrote.'

30 "The rich man replied, 'No, Father Abraham! But if someone is sent to them from the dead, then they will repent of their sins and turn to God.'

31 "But Abraham said, 'If they won't listen to Moses and the prophets, they won't be persuaded even if someone rises from the dead.'"

Teachings about Forgiveness and Faith

17 One day Jesus said to his disciples, "There will always be temptations to sin, but what sorrow awaits the person who does the tempting! 2 It would be better to be thrown into the sea with a millstone hung around your neck than to cause one of these little ones to fall into sin. 3 So watch yourselves!

"If another believer* sins, rebuke that person; then if there is repentance, forgive. 4 Even if that person wrongs you seven times a day

16:6 Greek 100 baths . . . 50 [baths].   16:7 Greek 100 korous . . . 80 [korous].   16:9 Or you will be welcomed into eternal homes.
16:16 Or everyone is urged to enter in.   16:22 Greek to Abraham's bosom.   16:23 Greek to Hades.   17:3 Greek If your brother.

and each time turns again and asks forgiveness, you must forgive."

⁵The apostles said to the Lord, "Show us how to increase our faith."

⁶The Lord answered, "If you had faith even as small as a mustard seed, you could say to this mulberry tree, 'May you be uprooted and be planted in the sea,' and it would obey you!

⁷"When a servant comes in from plowing or taking care of sheep, does his master say, 'Come in and eat with me'? ⁸No, he says, 'Prepare my meal, put on your apron, and serve me while I eat. Then you can eat later.' ⁹And does the master thank the servant for doing what he was told to do? Of course not. ¹⁰In the same way, when you obey me you should say, 'We are unworthy servants who have simply done our duty.'"

Ten Healed of Leprosy

¹¹As Jesus continued on toward Jerusalem, he reached the border between Galilee and Samaria. ¹²As he entered a village there, ten men with leprosy stood at a distance, ¹³crying out, "Jesus, Master, have mercy on us!"

¹⁴He looked at them and said, "Go show yourselves to the priests."* And as they went, they were cleansed of their leprosy.

¹⁵One of them, when he saw that he was healed, came back to Jesus, shouting, "Praise God!" ¹⁶He fell to the ground at Jesus' feet, thanking him for what he had done. This man was a Samaritan.

¹⁷Jesus asked, "Didn't I heal ten men? Where are the other nine? ¹⁸Has no one returned to give glory to God except this foreigner?" ¹⁹And Jesus said to the man, "Stand up and go. Your faith has healed you.*"

The Coming of the Kingdom

²⁰One day the Pharisees asked Jesus, "When will the Kingdom of God come?"

Jesus replied, "The Kingdom of God can't be detected by visible signs.* ²¹You won't be able to say, 'Here it is!' or 'It's over there!' For the Kingdom of God is already among you.*"

²²Then he said to his disciples, "The time is coming when you will long to see the day when the Son of Man returns,* but you won't see it. ²³People will tell you, 'Look, there is the Son of Man,' or 'Here he is,' but don't go out and follow them. ²⁴For as the lightning flashes and

lights up the sky from one end to the other, so it will be on the day* when the Son of Man comes. ²⁵But first the Son of Man must suffer terribly* and be rejected by this generation.

²⁶"When the Son of Man returns, it will be like it was in Noah's day. ²⁷In those days, the people enjoyed banquets and parties and weddings right up to the time Noah entered his boat and the flood came and destroyed them all.

²⁸"And the world will be as it was in the days of Lot. People went about their daily business—eating and drinking, buying and selling, farming and building—²⁹until the morning Lot left Sodom. Then fire and burning sulfur rained down from heaven and destroyed them all. ³⁰Yes, it will be 'business as usual' right up to the day when the Son of Man is revealed. ³¹On that day a person out on the deck of a roof must not go down into the house to pack. A person out in the field must not return home. ³²Remember what happened to Lot's wife! ³³If you cling to your life, you will lose it, and if you let your life go, you will save it. ³⁴That night two people will be asleep in one bed; one will be taken, the other left. ³⁵Two women will be grinding flour together at the mill; one will be taken, the other left.*"

³⁷"Where will this happen, Lord?"* the disciples asked.

Jesus replied, "Just as the gathering of vultures shows there is a carcass nearby, so these signs indicate that the end is near."*

Parable of the Persistent Widow

18 One day Jesus told his disciples a story to show that they should always pray and never give up. ²"There was a judge in a certain city," he said, "who neither feared God nor cared about people. ³A widow of that city came to him repeatedly, saying, 'Give me justice in this dispute with my enemy.' ⁴The judge ignored her for a while, but finally he said to himself, 'I don't fear God or care about people, ⁵but this woman is driving me crazy. I'm going to see that she gets justice, because she is wearing me out with her constant requests!'"

⁶Then the Lord said, "Learn a lesson from this unjust judge. ⁷Even he rendered a just decision in the end. So don't you think God will surely give justice to his chosen people who cry out to him day and night? Will he keep putting

---

17:14 See Lev 14:2-32.   17:19 Or *Your faith has saved you.*   17:20 Or *by your speculations.*   17:21 Or *is within you,* or *is in your grasp.* 17:22 Or *long for even one day with the Son of Man.* "Son of Man" is a title Jesus used for himself.   17:24 Some manuscripts do not include *on the day.*   17:25 Or *suffer many things.*   17:35 Some manuscripts add verse 36, *Two men will be working in the field; one will be taken, the other left.* Compare Matt 24:40.   17:37a Greek *"Where, Lord?"*   17:37b Greek *"Wherever the carcass is, the vultures gather."*

them off? [8]I tell you, he will grant justice to them quickly! But when the Son of Man* returns, how many will he find on the earth who have faith?"

Parable of the Pharisee and Tax Collector

[9]Then Jesus told this story to some who had great confidence in their own righteousness and scorned everyone else: [10]"Two men went to the Temple to pray. One was a Pharisee, and the other was a despised tax collector. [11]The Pharisee stood by himself and prayed this prayer*: 'I thank you, God, that I am not like other people—cheaters, sinners, adulterers. I'm certainly not like that tax collector! [12]I fast twice a week, and I give you a tenth of my income.'

[13]"But the tax collector stood at a distance and dared not even lift his eyes to heaven as he prayed. Instead, he beat his chest in sorrow, saying, 'O God, be merciful to me, for I am a sinner.' [14]I tell you, this sinner, not the Pharisee, returned home justified before God. For those who exalt themselves will be humbled, and those who humble themselves will be exalted."

Jesus Blesses the Children

[15]One day some parents brought their little children to Jesus so he could touch and bless them. But when the disciples saw this, they scolded the parents for bothering him.

[16]Then Jesus called for the children and said to the disciples, "Let the children come to me. Don't stop them! For the Kingdom of God belongs to those who are like these children. [17]I tell you the truth, anyone who doesn't receive the Kingdom of God like a child will never enter it."

The Rich Man

[18]Once a religious leader asked Jesus this question: "Good Teacher, what should I do to inherit eternal life?"

[19]"Why do you call me good?" Jesus asked him. "Only God is truly good. [20]But to answer your question, you know the commandments: 'You must not commit adultery. You must not murder. You must not steal. You must not testify falsely. Honor your father and mother.'*"

[21]The man replied, "I've obeyed all these commandments since I was young."

[22]When Jesus heard his answer, he said, "There is still one thing you haven't done. Sell all your possessions and give the money to the poor, and you will have treasure in heaven. Then come, follow me."

[23]But when the man heard this he became very sad, for he was very rich.

[24]When Jesus saw this,* he said, "How hard it is for the rich to enter the Kingdom of God! [25]In fact, it is easier for a camel to go through the eye of a needle than for a rich person to enter the Kingdom of God!"

[26]Those who heard this said, "Then who in the world can be saved?"

[27]He replied, "What is impossible for people is possible with God."

[28]Peter said, "We've left our homes to follow you."

[29]"Yes," Jesus replied, "and I assure you that everyone who has given up house or wife or brothers or parents or children, for the sake of the Kingdom of God, [30]will be repaid many times over in this life, and will have eternal life in the world to come."

Jesus Again Predicts His Death

[31]Taking the twelve disciples aside, Jesus said, "Listen, we're going up to Jerusalem, where all the predictions of the prophets concerning the Son of Man will come true. [32]He will be handed over to the Romans,* and he will be mocked, treated shamefully, and spit upon. [33]They will flog him with a whip and kill him, but on the third day he will rise again."

[34]But they didn't understand any of this. The significance of his words was hidden from them, and they failed to grasp what he was talking about.

Jesus Heals a Blind Beggar

[35]As Jesus approached Jericho, a blind beggar was sitting beside the road. [36]When he heard the noise of a crowd going past, he asked what was happening. [37]They told him that Jesus the Nazarene* was going by. [38]So he began shouting, "Jesus, Son of David, have mercy on me!"

[39]"Be quiet!" the people in front yelled at him.

But he only shouted louder, "Son of David, have mercy on me!"

[40]When Jesus heard him, he stopped and ordered that the man be brought to him. As the man came near, Jesus asked him, [41]"What do you want me to do for you?"

"Lord," he said, "I want to see!"

[42]And Jesus said, "All right, receive your

18:8 "Son of Man" is a title Jesus used for himself.   18:11 Some manuscripts read *stood and prayed this prayer to himself.*
18:20 Exod 20:12-16; Deut 5:16-20.   18:24 Some manuscripts read *When Jesus saw how sad the man was.*   18:32 Greek *the Gentiles.*   18:37 Or *Jesus of Nazareth.*

sight! Your faith has healed you." ⁴³Instantly the man could see, and he followed Jesus, praising God. And all who saw it praised God, too.

Jesus and Zacchaeus

19 Jesus entered Jericho and made his way through the town. ²There was a man there named Zacchaeus. He was the chief tax collector in the region, and he had become very rich. ³He tried to get a look at Jesus, but he was too short to see over the crowd. ⁴So he ran ahead and climbed a sycamore-fig tree beside the road, for Jesus was going to pass that way.

⁵When Jesus came by, he looked up at Zacchaeus and called him by name. "Zacchaeus!" he said. "Quick, come down! I must be a guest in your home today."

⁶Zacchaeus quickly climbed down and took Jesus to his house in great excitement and joy. ⁷But the people were displeased. "He has gone to be the guest of a notorious sinner," they grumbled.

⁸Meanwhile, Zacchaeus stood before the Lord and said, "I will give half my wealth to the poor, Lord, and if I have cheated people on their taxes, I will give them back four times as much!"

⁹Jesus responded, "Salvation has come to this home today, for this man has shown himself to be a true son of Abraham. ¹⁰For the Son of Man* came to seek and save those who are lost."

Parable of the Ten Servants

¹¹The crowd was listening to everything Jesus said. And because he was nearing Jerusalem, he told them a story to correct the impression that the Kingdom of God would begin right away. ¹²He said, "A nobleman was called away to a distant empire to be crowned king and then return. ¹³Before he left, he called together ten of his servants and divided among them ten pounds of silver,* saying, 'Invest this for me while I am gone.' ¹⁴But his people hated him and sent a delegation after him to say, 'We do not want him to be our king.'

¹⁵"After he was crowned king, he returned and called in the servants to whom he had given the money. He wanted to find out what their profits were. ¹⁶The first servant reported, 'Master, I invested your money and made ten times the original amount!'

¹⁷"'Well done!' the king exclaimed. 'You are a good servant. You have been faithful with the little I entrusted to you, so you will be governor of ten cities as your reward.'

¹⁸"The next servant reported, 'Master, I invested your money and made five times the original amount.'

¹⁹"'Well done!' the king said. 'You will be governor over five cities.'

²⁰"But the third servant brought back only the original amount of money and said, 'Master, I hid your money and kept it safe. ²¹I was afraid because you are a hard man to deal with, taking what isn't yours and harvesting crops you didn't plant.'

²²"'You wicked servant!' the king roared. 'Your own words condemn you. If you knew that I'm a hard man who takes what isn't mine and harvests crops I didn't plant, ²³why didn't you deposit my money in the bank? At least I could have gotten some interest on it.'

²⁴"Then, turning to the others standing nearby, the king ordered, 'Take the money from this servant, and give it to the one who has ten pounds.'

²⁵"'But, master,' they said, 'he already has ten pounds!'

²⁶"'Yes,' the king replied, 'and to those who use well what they are given, even more will be given. But from those who do nothing, even what little they have will be taken away. ²⁷And as for these enemies of mine who didn't want me to be their king—bring them in and execute them right here in front of me.'"

Jesus' Triumphant Entry

²⁸After telling this story, Jesus went on toward Jerusalem, walking ahead of his disciples. ²⁹As he came to the towns of Bethphage and Bethany on the Mount of Olives, he sent two disciples ahead. ³⁰"Go into that village over there," he told them. "As you enter it, you will see a young donkey tied there that no one has ever ridden. Untie it and bring it here. ³¹If anyone asks, 'Why are you untying that colt?' just say, 'The Lord needs it.'"

³²So they went and found the colt, just as Jesus had said. ³³And sure enough, as they were untying it, the owners asked them, "Why are you untying that colt?"

³⁴And the disciples simply replied, "The Lord needs it." ³⁵So they brought the colt to Jesus and threw their garments over it for him to ride on.

³⁶As he rode along, the crowds spread out their garments on the road ahead of him. ³⁷When he reached the place where the road

19:10 "Son of Man" is a title Jesus used for himself.   **19:13** Greek *ten minas;* one mina was worth about three months' wages.

started down the Mount of Olives, all of his followers began to shout and sing as they walked along, praising God for all the wonderful miracles they had seen.

38 "Blessings on the King who comes in the
        name of the LORD!
    Peace in heaven, and glory in highest
        heaven!"*

39But some of the Pharisees among the crowd said, "Teacher, rebuke your followers for saying things like that!"

40He replied, "If they kept quiet, the stones along the road would burst into cheers!"

Jesus Weeps over Jerusalem

41But as he came closer to Jerusalem and saw the city ahead, he began to weep. 42"How I wish today that you of all people would understand the way to peace. But now it is too late, and peace is hidden from your eyes. 43Before long your enemies will build ramparts against your walls and encircle you and close in on you from every side. 44They will crush you into the ground, and your children with you. Your enemies will not leave a single stone in place, because you did not recognize it when God visited you.*"

Jesus Clears the Temple

45Then Jesus entered the Temple and began to drive out the people selling animals for sacrifices. 46He said to them, "The Scriptures declare, 'My Temple will be a house of prayer,' but you have turned it into a den of thieves."*

47After that, he taught daily in the Temple, but the leading priests, the teachers of religious law, and the other leaders of the people began planning how to kill him. 48But they could think of nothing, because all the people hung on every word he said.

The Authority of Jesus Challenged

20 One day as Jesus was teaching the people and preaching the Good News in the Temple, the leading priests, the teachers of religious law, and the elders came up to him. 2They demanded, "By what authority are you doing all these things? Who gave you the right?"

3"Let me ask you a question first," he replied. 4"Did John's authority to baptize come from heaven, or was it merely human?"

5They talked it over among themselves. "If we say it was from heaven, he will ask why we didn't believe John. 6But if we say it was merely human, the people will stone us because they are convinced John was a prophet." 7So they finally replied that they didn't know.

8And Jesus responded, "Then I won't tell you by what authority I do these things."

Parable of the Evil Farmers

9Now Jesus turned to the people again and told them this story: "A man planted a vineyard, leased it to tenant farmers, and moved to another country to live for several years. 10At the time of the grape harvest, he sent one of his servants to collect his share of the crop. But the farmers attacked the servant, beat him up, and sent him back empty-handed. 11So the owner sent another servant, but they also insulted him, beat him up, and sent him away empty-handed. 12A third man was sent, and they wounded him and chased him away.

13"'What will I do?' the owner asked himself. 'I know! I'll send my cherished son. Surely they will respect him.'

14"But when the tenant farmers saw his son, they said to each other, 'Here comes the heir to this estate. Let's kill him and get the estate for ourselves!' 15So they dragged him out of the vineyard and murdered him.

"What do you suppose the owner of the vineyard will do to them?" Jesus asked. 16"I'll tell you—he will come and kill those farmers and lease the vineyard to others."

"How terrible that such a thing should ever happen," his listeners protested.

17Jesus looked at them and said, "Then what does this Scripture mean?

'The stone that the builders rejected
    has now become the cornerstone.'*

18Everyone who stumbles over that stone will be broken to pieces, and it will crush anyone it falls on."

19The teachers of religious law and the leading priests wanted to arrest Jesus immediately because they realized he was telling the story against them—they were the wicked farmers. But they were afraid of the people's reaction.

Taxes for Caesar

20Watching for their opportunity, the leaders sent spies pretending to be honest men.

19:38 Pss 118:26; 148:1.   19:44 Greek *did not recognize the time of your visitation*, a reference to the Messiah's coming.
19:46 Isa 56:7; Jer 7:11.   20:17 Ps 118:22.

They tried to get Jesus to say something that could be reported to the Roman governor so he would arrest Jesus. ²¹"Teacher," they said, "we know that you speak and teach what is right and are not influenced by what others think. You teach the way of God truthfully. ²²Now tell us—is it right for us to pay taxes to Caesar or not?"

²³He saw through their trickery and said, ²⁴"Show me a Roman coin.* Whose picture and title are stamped on it?"

"Caesar's," they replied.

²⁵"Well then," he said, "give to Caesar what belongs to Caesar, and give to God what belongs to God."

²⁶So they failed to trap him by what he said in front of the people. Instead, they were amazed by his answer, and they became silent.

Discussion about Resurrection

²⁷Then Jesus was approached by some Sadducees—religious leaders who say there is no resurrection from the dead. ²⁸They posed this question: "Teacher, Moses gave us a law that if a man dies, leaving a wife but no children, his brother should marry the widow and have a child who will carry on the brother's name.* ²⁹Well, suppose there were seven brothers. The oldest one married and then died without children. ³⁰So the second brother married the widow, but he also died. ³¹Then the third brother married her. This continued with all seven of them, who died without children. ³²Finally, the woman also died. ³³So tell us, whose wife will she be in the resurrection? For all seven were married to her!"

³⁴Jesus replied, "Marriage is for people here on earth. ³⁵But in the age to come, those worthy of being raised from the dead will neither marry nor be given in marriage. ³⁶And they will never die again. In this respect they will be like angels. They are children of God and children of the resurrection.

³⁷"But now, as to whether the dead will be raised—even Moses proved this when he wrote about the burning bush. Long after Abraham, Isaac, and Jacob had died, he referred to the Lord* as 'the God of Abraham, the God of Isaac, and the God of Jacob.'* ³⁸So he is the God of the living, not the dead, for they are all alive to him."

³⁹"Well said, Teacher!" remarked some of the teachers of religious law who were standing

there. ⁴⁰And then no one dared to ask him any more questions.

Whose Son Is the Messiah?

⁴¹Then Jesus presented them with a question. "Why is it," he asked, "that the Messiah is said to be the son of David? ⁴²For David himself wrote in the book of Psalms:

'The LORD said to my Lord,
    Sit in the place of honor at my right
        hand
⁴³ until I humble your enemies,
        making them a footstool under your
            feet.'*

⁴⁴Since David called the Messiah 'Lord,' how can the Messiah be his son?"

⁴⁵Then, with the crowds listening, he turned to his disciples and said, ⁴⁶"Beware of these teachers of religious law! For they like to parade around in flowing robes and love to receive respectful greetings as they walk in the marketplaces. And how they love the seats of honor in the synagogues and the head table at banquets. ⁴⁷Yet they shamelessly cheat widows out of their property and then pretend to be pious by making long prayers in public. Because of this, they will be severely punished."

The Widow's Offering

21 While Jesus was in the Temple, he watched the rich people dropping their gifts in the collection box. ²Then a poor widow came by and dropped in two small coins.*

³"I tell you the truth," Jesus said, "this poor widow has given more than all the rest of them. ⁴For they have given a tiny part of their surplus, but she, poor as she is, has given everything she has."

Jesus Speaks about the Future

⁵Some of his disciples began talking about the majestic stonework of the Temple and the memorial decorations on the walls. But Jesus said, ⁶"The time is coming when all these things will be completely demolished. Not one stone will be left on top of another!"

⁷"Teacher," they asked, "when will all this happen? What sign will show us that these things are about to take place?"

⁸He replied, "Don't let anyone mislead you, for many will come in my name, claiming, 'I am the Messiah,'* and saying, 'The time has

---

20:24 Greek *a denarius.*   20:28 See Deut 25:5-6.   20:37a Greek *when he wrote about the bush. He referred to the Lord.*
20:37b Exod 3:6.   20:42-43 Ps 110:1.   21:2 Greek *two lepta* [the smallest of Jewish coins].   21:8 Greek *claiming, 'I am.'*

come!' But don't believe them. ⁹And when you hear of wars and insurrections, don't panic. Yes, these things must take place first, but the end won't follow immediately." ¹⁰Then he added, "Nation will go to war against nation, and kingdom against kingdom. ¹¹There will be great earthquakes, and there will be famines and plagues in many lands, and there will be terrifying things and great miraculous signs from heaven.

¹²"But before all this occurs, there will be a time of great persecution. You will be dragged into synagogues and prisons, and you will stand trial before kings and governors because you are my followers. ¹³But this will be your opportunity to tell them about me.* ¹⁴So don't worry in advance about how to answer the charges against you, ¹⁵for I will give you the right words and such wisdom that none of your opponents will be able to reply or refute you! ¹⁶Even those closest to you—your parents, brothers, relatives, and friends—will betray you. They will even kill some of you. ¹⁷And everyone will hate you because you are my followers.* ¹⁸But not a hair of your head will perish! ¹⁹By standing firm, you will win your souls.

²⁰"And when you see Jerusalem surrounded by armies, then you will know that the time of its destruction has arrived. ²¹Then those in Judea must flee to the hills. Those in Jerusalem must get out, and those out in the country should not return to the city. ²²For those will be days of God's vengeance, and the prophetic words of the Scriptures will be fulfilled. ²³How terrible it will be for pregnant women and for nursing mothers in those days. For there will be disaster in the land and great anger against this people. ²⁴They will be killed by the sword or sent away as captives to all the nations of the world. And Jerusalem will be trampled down by the Gentiles until the period of the Gentiles comes to an end.

²⁵"And there will be strange signs in the sun, moon, and stars. And here on earth the nations will be in turmoil, perplexed by the roaring seas and strange tides. ²⁶People will be terrified at what they see coming upon the earth, for the powers in the heavens will be shaken. ²⁷Then everyone will see the Son of Man* coming on a cloud with power and great glory.* ²⁸So when all these things begin to happen, stand and look up, for your salvation is near!"

²⁹Then he gave them this illustration: "Notice the fig tree, or any other tree. ³⁰When the leaves come out, you know without being told that summer is near. ³¹In the same way, when you see all these things taking place, you can know that the Kingdom of God is near. ³²I tell you the truth, this generation will not pass from the scene until all these things have taken place. ³³Heaven and earth will disappear, but my words will never disappear.

³⁴"Watch out! Don't let your hearts be dulled by carousing and drunkenness, and by the worries of this life. Don't let that day catch you unaware, ³⁵like a trap. For that day will come upon everyone living on the earth. ³⁶Keep alert at all times. And pray that you might be strong enough to escape these coming horrors and stand before the Son of Man."

³⁷Every day Jesus went to the Temple to teach, and each evening he returned to spend the night on the Mount of Olives. ³⁸The crowds gathered at the Temple early each morning to hear him.

Judas Agrees to Betray Jesus

22 The Festival of Unleavened Bread, which is also called Passover, was approaching. ²The leading priests and teachers of religious law were plotting how to kill Jesus, but they were afraid of the people's reaction.

³Then Satan entered into Judas Iscariot, who was one of the twelve disciples, ⁴and he went to the leading priests and captains of the Temple guard to discuss the best way to betray Jesus to them. ⁵They were delighted, and they promised to give him money. ⁶So he agreed and began looking for an opportunity to betray Jesus so they could arrest him when the crowds weren't around.

The Last Supper

⁷Now the Festival of Unleavened Bread arrived, when the Passover lamb is sacrificed. ⁸Jesus sent Peter and John ahead and said, "Go and prepare the Passover meal, so we can eat it together."

⁹"Where do you want us to prepare it?" they asked him.

¹⁰He replied, "As soon as you enter Jerusalem, a man carrying a pitcher of water will meet you. Follow him. At the house he enters, ¹¹say to the owner, 'The Teacher asks: Where is the guest room where I can eat the Passover meal with my disciples?' ¹²He will take you upstairs to a large room that is already set up. That is where you should prepare our meal." ¹³They

21:13 Or *This will be your testimony against them.*   21:17 Greek *on account of my name.*   21:27a "Son of Man" is a title Jesus used for himself.   21:27b See Dan 7:13.

went off to the city and found everything just as Jesus had said, and they prepared the Passover meal there.

14When the time came, Jesus and the apostles sat down together at the table.* 15Jesus said, "I have been very eager to eat this Passover meal with you before my suffering begins. 16For I tell you now that I won't eat this meal again until its meaning is fulfilled in the Kingdom of God."

17Then he took a cup of wine and gave thanks to God for it. Then he said, "Take this and share it among yourselves. 18For I will not drink wine again until the Kingdom of God has come."

19He took some bread and gave thanks to God for it. Then he broke it in pieces and gave it to the disciples, saying, "This is my body, which is given for you. Do this in remembrance of me."

20After supper he took another cup of wine and said, "This cup is the new covenant between God and his people—an agreement confirmed with my blood, which is poured out as a sacrifice for you.*

21"But here at this table, sitting among us as a friend, is the man who will betray me. 22For it has been determined that the Son of Man* must die. But what sorrow awaits the one who betrays him." 23The disciples began to ask each other which of them would ever do such a thing.

24Then they began to argue among themselves about who would be the greatest among them. 25Jesus told them, "In this world the kings and great men lord it over their people, yet they are called 'friends of the people.' 26But among you it will be different. Those who are the greatest among you should take the lowest rank, and the leader should be like a servant. 27Who is more important, the one who sits at the table or the one who serves? The one who sits at the table, of course. But not here! For I am among you as one who serves.

28"You have stayed with me in my time of trial. 29And just as my Father has granted me a Kingdom, I now grant you the right 30to eat and drink at my table in my Kingdom. And you will sit on thrones, judging the twelve tribes of Israel.

Jesus Predicts Peter's Denial

31"Simon, Simon, Satan has asked to sift each of you like wheat. 32But I have pleaded in prayer for you, Simon, that your faith should not fail. So when you have repented and turned to me again, strengthen your brothers."

33Peter said, "Lord, I am ready to go to prison with you, and even to die with you."

34But Jesus said, "Peter, let me tell you something. Before the rooster crows tomorrow morning, you will deny three times that you even know me."

35Then Jesus asked them, "When I sent you out to preach the Good News and you did not have money, a traveler's bag, or an extra pair of sandals, did you need anything?"

"No," they replied.

36"But now," he said, "take your money and a traveler's bag. And if you don't have a sword, sell your cloak and buy one! 37For the time has come for this prophecy about me to be fulfilled: 'He was counted among the rebels.'* Yes, everything written about me by the prophets will come true."

38"Look, Lord," they replied, "we have two swords among us."

"That's enough," he said.

Jesus Prays on the Mount of Olives

39Then, accompanied by the disciples, Jesus left the upstairs room and went as usual to the Mount of Olives. 40There he told them, "Pray that you will not give in to temptation."

41He walked away, about a stone's throw, and knelt down and prayed, 42"Father, if you are willing, please take this cup of suffering away from me. Yet I want your will to be done, not mine." 43Then an angel from heaven appeared and strengthened him. 44He prayed more fervently, and he was in such agony of spirit that his sweat fell to the ground like great drops of blood.*

45At last he stood up again and returned to the disciples, only to find them asleep, exhausted from grief. 46"Why are you sleeping?" he asked them. "Get up and pray, so that you will not give in to temptation."

Jesus Is Betrayed and Arrested

47But even as Jesus said this, a crowd approached, led by Judas, one of the twelve disciples. Judas walked over to Jesus to greet him with a kiss. 48But Jesus said, "Judas, would you betray the Son of Man with a kiss?"

49When the other disciples saw what was about to happen, they exclaimed, "Lord,

---

22:14 Or reclined together. 22:19-20 Some manuscripts do not include 22:19b-20, which is given for you ... which is poured out as a sacrifice for you. 22:22 "Son of Man" is a title Jesus used for himself. 22:37 Isa 53:12. 22:43-44 Verses 43 and 44 are not included in the most ancient manuscripts.

should we fight? We brought the swords!"
⁵⁰And one of them struck at the high priest's
slave, slashing off his right ear.

⁵¹But Jesus said, "No more of this." And he
touched the man's ear and healed him.

⁵²Then Jesus spoke to the leading priests, the
captains of the Temple guard, and the elders
who had come for him. "Am I some dangerous
revolutionary," he asked, "that you come with
swords and clubs to arrest me? ⁵³Why didn't
you arrest me in the Temple? I was there every
day. But this is your moment, the time when
the power of darkness reigns."

Peter Denies Jesus

⁵⁴So they arrested him and led him to the high
priest's home. And Peter followed at a distance.
⁵⁵The guards lit a fire in the middle of the
courtyard and sat around it, and Peter joined
them there. ⁵⁶A servant girl noticed him in the
firelight and began staring at him. Finally she
said, "This man was one of Jesus' followers!"

⁵⁷But Peter denied it. "Woman," he said, "I
don't even know him!"

⁵⁸After a while someone else looked at him
and said, "You must be one of them!"

"No, man, I'm not!" Peter retorted.

⁵⁹About an hour later someone else insisted,
"This must be one of them, because he is a Galilean, too."

⁶⁰But Peter said, "Man, I don't know what
you are talking about." And immediately,
while he was still speaking, the rooster crowed.
⁶¹At that moment the Lord turned and
looked at Peter. Suddenly, the Lord's words
flashed through Peter's mind: "Before the
rooster crows tomorrow morning, you will
deny three times that you even know me."
⁶²And Peter left the courtyard, weeping bitterly.

⁶³The guards in charge of Jesus began mocking and beating him. ⁶⁴They blindfolded him
and said, "Prophesy to us! Who hit you that
time?" ⁶⁵And they hurled all sorts of terrible
insults at him.

Jesus before the Council

⁶⁶At daybreak all the elders of the people assembled, including the leading priests and the
teachers of religious law. Jesus was led before
this high council,* ⁶⁷and they said, "Tell us, are
you the Messiah?"

But he replied, "If I tell you, you won't believe me. ⁶⁸And if I ask you a question, you
won't answer. ⁶⁹But from now on the Son of

Man will be seated in the place of power at
God's right hand.*"

⁷⁰They all shouted, "So, are you claiming to
be the Son of God?"

And he replied, "You say that I am."

⁷¹"Why do we need other witnesses?" they
said. "We ourselves heard him say it."

Jesus' Trial before Pilate

23 Then the entire council took Jesus to Pilate, the Roman governor. ²They began
to state their case: "This man has been leading
our people astray by telling them not to pay
their taxes to the Roman government and by
claiming he is the Messiah, a king."

³So Pilate asked him, "Are you the king of
the Jews?"

Jesus replied, "You have said it."

⁴Pilate turned to the leading priests and to
the crowd and said, "I find nothing wrong with
this man!"

⁵Then they became insistent. "But he is causing riots by his teaching wherever he goes—all
over Judea, from Galilee to Jerusalem!"

⁶"Oh, is he a Galilean?" Pilate asked. ⁷When
they said that he was, Pilate sent him to Herod
Antipas, because Galilee was under Herod's
jurisdiction, and Herod happened to be in Jerusalem at the time.

⁸Herod was delighted at the opportunity to
see Jesus, because he had heard about him and
had been hoping for a long time to see him perform a miracle. ⁹He asked Jesus question after
question, but Jesus refused to answer. ¹⁰Mean-
while, the leading priests and the teachers of
religious law stood there shouting their accusations. ¹¹Then Herod and his soldiers began
mocking and ridiculing Jesus. Finally, they put
a royal robe on him and sent him back to Pilate.
¹²(Herod and Pilate, who had been enemies before, became friends that day.)

¹³Then Pilate called together the leading
priests and other religious leaders, along
with the people, ¹⁴and he announced his verdict. "You brought this man to me, accusing
him of leading a revolt. I have examined him
thoroughly on this point in your presence and
find him innocent. ¹⁵Herod came to the same
conclusion and sent him back to us. Nothing
this man has done calls for the death penalty.
¹⁶So I will have him flogged, and then I will
release him."*

¹⁸Then a mighty roar rose from the crowd,
and with one voice they shouted, "Kill him,

22:66 Greek *before their Sanhedrin.*   22:69 See Ps 110:1.   23:16 Some manuscripts add verse 17, *Now it was necessary for him to
release one prisoner to them during the Passover celebration.* Compare Matt 27:15; Mark 15:6; John 18:39.

and release Barabbas to us!" ¹⁹(Barabbas was in prison for taking part in an insurrection in Jerusalem against the government, and for murder.) ²⁰Pilate argued with them, because he wanted to release Jesus. ²¹But they kept shouting, "Crucify him! Crucify him!"

²²For the third time he demanded, "Why? What crime has he committed? I have found no reason to sentence him to death. So I will have him flogged, and then I will release him."

²³But the mob shouted louder and louder, demanding that Jesus be crucified, and their voices prevailed. ²⁴So Pilate sentenced Jesus to die as they demanded. ²⁵As they had requested, he released Barabbas, the man in prison for insurrection and murder. But he turned Jesus over to them to do as they wished.

The Crucifixion

²⁶As they led Jesus away, a man named Simon, who was from Cyrene,* happened to be coming in from the countryside. The soldiers seized him and put the cross on him and made him carry it behind Jesus. ²⁷A large crowd trailed behind, including many grief-stricken women. ²⁸But Jesus turned and said to them, "Daughters of Jerusalem, don't weep for me, but weep for yourselves and for your children. ²⁹For the days are coming when they will say, 'Fortunate indeed are the women who are childless, the wombs that have not borne a child and the breasts that have never nursed.' ³⁰People will beg the mountains, 'Fall on us,' and plead with the hills, 'Bury us.'* ³¹For if these things are done when the tree is green, what will happen when it is dry?*"

³²Two others, both criminals, were led out to be executed with him. ³³When they came to a place called The Skull,* they nailed him to the cross. And the criminals were also crucified— one on his right and one on his left.

³⁴Jesus said, "Father, forgive them, for they don't know what they are doing."* And the soldiers gambled for his clothes by throwing dice.*

³⁵The crowd watched and the leaders scoffed. "He saved others," they said, "let him save himself if he is really God's Messiah, the Chosen One." ³⁶The soldiers mocked him, too, by offering him a drink of sour wine. ³⁷They called out to him, "If you are the King of the Jews, save yourself!" ³⁸A sign was fastened above him with these words: "This is the King of the Jews."

³⁹One of the criminals hanging beside him scoffed, "So you're the Messiah, are you? Prove it by saving yourself—and us, too, while you're at it!"

⁴⁰But the other criminal protested, "Don't you fear God even when you have been sentenced to die? ⁴¹We deserve to die for our crimes, but this man hasn't done anything wrong." ⁴²Then he said, "Jesus, remember me when you come into your Kingdom."

⁴³And Jesus replied, "I assure you, today you will be with me in paradise."

The Death of Jesus

⁴⁴By this time it was about noon, and darkness fell across the whole land until three o'clock. ⁴⁵The light from the sun was gone. And suddenly, the curtain in the sanctuary of the Temple was torn down the middle. ⁴⁶Then Jesus shouted, "Father, I entrust my spirit into your hands!"* And with those words he breathed his last.

⁴⁷When the Roman officer* overseeing the execution saw what had happened, he worshiped God and said, "Surely this man was innocent.*" ⁴⁸And when all the crowd that came to see the crucifixion saw what had happened, they went home in deep sorrow.* ⁴⁹But Jesus' friends, including the women who had followed him from Galilee, stood at a distance watching.

The Burial of Jesus

⁵⁰Now there was a good and righteous man named Joseph. He was a member of the Jewish high council, ⁵¹but he had not agreed with the decision and actions of the other religious leaders. He was from the town of Arimathea in Judea, and he was waiting for the Kingdom of God to come. ⁵²He went to Pilate and asked for Jesus' body. ⁵³Then he took the body down from the cross and wrapped it in a long sheet of linen cloth and laid it in a new tomb that had been carved out of rock. ⁵⁴This was done late on Friday afternoon, the day of preparation,* as the Sabbath was about to begin.

⁵⁵As his body was taken away, the women from Galilee followed and saw the tomb where his body was placed. ⁵⁶Then they went home and prepared spices and ointments to anoint

23:26 *Cyrene* was a city in northern Africa.   23:30 Hos 10:8.   23:31 Or *If these things are done to me, the living tree, what will happen to you, the dry tree?*   23:33 Sometimes rendered *Calvary*, which comes from the Latin word for "skull."   23:34a This sentence is not included in many ancient manuscripts.   23:34b Greek *by casting lots.* See Ps 22:18.   23:46 Ps 31:5. 23:47a Greek *the centurion.*   23:47b Or *righteous.*   23:48 Greek *went home beating their breasts.*   23:54 Greek *It was the day of preparation.*

his body. But by the time they were finished the Sabbath had begun, so they rested as required by the law.

The Resurrection

24 But very early on Sunday morning* the women went to the tomb, taking the spices they had prepared. ²They found that the stone had been rolled away from the entrance. ³So they went in, but they didn't find the body of the Lord Jesus. ⁴As they stood there puzzled, two men suddenly appeared to them, clothed in dazzling robes.

⁵The women were terrified and bowed with their faces to the ground. Then the men asked, "Why are you looking among the dead for someone who is alive? ⁶He isn't here! He is risen from the dead! Remember what he told you back in Galilee, ⁷that the Son of Man* must be betrayed into the hands of sinful men and be crucified, and that he would rise again on the third day."

⁸Then they remembered that he had said this. ⁹So they rushed back from the tomb to tell his eleven disciples—and everyone else— what had happened. ¹⁰It was Mary Magdalene, Joanna, Mary the mother of James, and several other women who told the apostles what had happened. ¹¹But the story sounded like nonsense to the men, so they didn't believe it. ¹²However, Peter jumped up and ran to the tomb to look. Stooping, he peered in and saw the empty linen wrappings; then he went home again, wondering what had happened.

The Walk to Emmaus

¹³That same day two of Jesus' followers were walking to the village of Emmaus, seven miles* from Jerusalem. ¹⁴As they walked along they were talking about everything that had happened. ¹⁵As they talked and discussed these things, Jesus himself suddenly came and began walking with them. ¹⁶But God kept them from recognizing him.

¹⁷He asked them, "What are you discussing so intently as you walk along?"

They stopped short, sadness written across their faces. ¹⁸Then one of them, Cleopas, replied, "You must be the only person in Jerusalem who hasn't heard about all the things that have happened there the last few days."

¹⁹"What things?" Jesus asked.

"The things that happened to Jesus, the man from Nazareth," they said. "He was a prophet who did powerful miracles, and he was a mighty teacher in the eyes of God and all the people. ²⁰But our leading priests and other religious leaders handed him over to be condemned to death, and they crucified him. ²¹We had hoped he was the Messiah who had come to rescue Israel. This all happened three days ago.

²²"Then some women from our group of his followers were at his tomb early this morning, and they came back with an amazing report. ²³They said his body was missing, and they had seen angels who told them Jesus is alive! ²⁴Some of our men ran out to see, and sure enough, his body was gone, just as the women had said."

²⁵Then Jesus said to them, "You foolish people! You find it so hard to believe all that the prophets wrote in the Scriptures. ²⁶Wasn't it clearly predicted that the Messiah would have to suffer all these things before entering his glory?" ²⁷Then Jesus took them through the writings of Moses and all the prophets, explaining from all the Scriptures the things concerning himself.

²⁸By this time they were nearing Emmaus and the end of their journey. Jesus acted as if he were going on, ²⁹but they begged him, "Stay the night with us, since it is getting late." So he went home with them. ³⁰As they sat down to eat,* he took the bread and blessed it. Then he broke it and gave it to them. ³¹Suddenly, their eyes were opened, and they recognized him. And at that moment he disappeared!

³²They said to each other, "Didn't our hearts burn within us as he talked with us on the road and explained the Scriptures to us?" ³³And within the hour they were on their way back to Jerusalem. There they found the eleven disciples and the others who had gathered with them, ³⁴who said, "The Lord has really risen! He appeared to Peter.*"

Jesus Appears to the Disciples

³⁵Then the two from Emmaus told their story of how Jesus had appeared to them as they were walking along the road, and how they had recognized him as he was breaking the bread. ³⁶And just as they were telling about it, Jesus himself was suddenly standing there among them. "Peace be with you," he said. ³⁷But the whole group was startled and frightened, thinking they were seeing a ghost!

24:1 Greek *But on the first day of the week, very early in the morning.* 24:7 "Son of Man" is a title Jesus used for himself.
24:13 Greek *60 stadia* [11.1 kilometers]. 24:30 Or *As they reclined.* 24:34 Greek *Simon.*

[38] "Why are you frightened?" he asked. "Why are your hearts filled with doubt? [39] Look at my hands. Look at my feet. You can see that it's really me. Touch me and make sure that I am not a ghost, because ghosts don't have bodies, as you see that I do." [40] As he spoke, he showed them his hands and his feet.

[41] Still they stood there in disbelief, filled with joy and wonder. Then he asked them, "Do you have anything here to eat?" [42] They gave him a piece of broiled fish, [43] and he ate it as they watched.

[44] Then he said, "When I was with you before, I told you that everything written about me in the law of Moses and the prophets and in the Psalms must be fulfilled." [45] Then he opened their minds to understand the Scriptures. [46] And he said, "Yes, it was written long ago that the Messiah would suffer and die and

24:47 Or *all peoples.*

rise from the dead on the third day. [47] It was also written that this message would be proclaimed in the authority of his name to all the nations,* beginning in Jerusalem: 'There is forgiveness of sins for all who repent.' [48] You are witnesses of all these things.

[49] "And now I will send the Holy Spirit, just as my Father promised. But stay here in the city until the Holy Spirit comes and fills you with power from heaven."

The Ascension

[50] Then Jesus led them to Bethany, and lifting his hands to heaven, he blessed them. [51] While he was blessing them, he left them and was taken up to heaven. [52] So they worshiped him and then returned to Jerusalem filled with great joy. [53] And they spent all of their time in the Temple, praising God.

John

EACH GOSPEL WAS WRITTEN with a theological agenda in mind, but only John, "the disciple Jesus loved" (21:20), made his agenda explicit: "But these are written so that you may continue to believe that Jesus is the Messiah, the Son of God, and that by believing in him you will have life" (20:31). Because of this goal, John's Gospel takes on a different flavor than the other three accounts. John was less concerned with Jesus' actions than with what his actions said about him. John spoke of Jesus' miracles as "signs," and he recorded lengthy theological monologues by Jesus, including seven "I am" statements about himself. John opened his Gospel with an account of the preexistent Christ—"the Word," the unique Son of God—who became human and made God the Father known to us. After recounting details of John the Baptist and his ministry, John described Jesus' baptism. At this point the general outline of John's narrative breaks sharply from those of the other three accounts, rearranging some of the events and including different material. For instance, John's Gospel records more than one trip to Jerusalem by Jesus, unlike the other Gospels. After describing in detail Jesus' last supper with his disciples, John recounts Jesus' crucifixion and resurrection. The book closes with some post-resurrection encounters between Jesus and his disciples.

- **Author:** John the apostle, son of Zebedee and brother of James the apostle
- **Date Written:** Around AD 90, from the city of Ephesus
- **Purpose:** To show that Jesus is the Messiah, the Son of God, and that all who believe in him will have eternal life
- **Themes:** Jesus as the unique Son of God, eternal life, the Holy Spirit, light vs. darkness, Jesus' "I am" declarations

- **Outline**

1:1-18 Prologue
1:19–4:54 Jesus' pre-Galilean ministry
5:1–10:42 Jesus' Galilean ministry and conflicts in Jerusalem
11:1-57 The raising of Lazarus from the dead and the plot to kill Jesus
12:1–17:26 Jesus' triumphal entry into Jerusalem and final teachings
18:1–20:10 Jesus' death and resurrection
20:11–21:25 Jesus' resurrection appearances

Prologue: Christ, the Eternal Word

1 ¹ In the beginning the Word already existed.
The Word was with God,
and the Word was God.
² He existed in the beginning with God.
³ God created everything through him,
and nothing was created except through him.
⁴ The Word gave life to everything that was created,*

and his life brought light to everyone.
⁵ The light shines in the darkness,
and the darkness can never extinguish it.*

⁶God sent a man, John the Baptist,* ⁷to tell about the light so that everyone might believe because of his testimony. ⁸John himself was not the light; he was simply a witness to tell about the light. ⁹The one who is the true light,

1:3-4 Or *and nothing that was created was created except through him. The Word gave life to everything.* 1:5 Or *and the darkness has not understood it.* 1:6 Greek *a man named John.*

who gives light to everyone, was coming into the world.

¹⁰He came into the very world he created, but the world didn't recognize him. ¹¹He came to his own people, and even they rejected him. ¹²But to all who believed him and accepted him, he gave the right to become children of God. ¹³They are reborn—not with a physical birth resulting from human passion or plan, but a birth that comes from God.

¹⁴So the Word became human* and made his home among us. He was full of unfailing love and faithfulness.* And we have seen his glory, the glory of the Father's one and only Son.

¹⁵John testified about him when he shouted to the crowds, "This is the one I was talking about when I said, 'Someone is coming after me who is far greater than I am, for he existed long before me.'"

¹⁶From his abundance we have all received one gracious blessing after another.* ¹⁷For the law was given through Moses, but God's unfailing love and faithfulness came through Jesus Christ. ¹⁸No one has ever seen God. But the unique One, who is himself God,* is near to the Father's heart. He has revealed God to us.

The Testimony of John the Baptist

¹⁹This was John's testimony when the Jewish leaders sent priests and Temple assistants* from Jerusalem to ask John, "Who are you?" ²⁰He came right out and said, "I am not the Messiah."

²¹"Well then, who are you?" they asked. "Are you Elijah?"

"No," he replied.

"Are you the Prophet we are expecting?"* "No."

²²"Then who are you? We need an answer for those who sent us. What do you have to say about yourself?"

²³John replied in the words of the prophet Isaiah:

"I am a voice shouting in the wilderness,
    'Clear the way for the LORD's coming!'"*

²⁴Then the Pharisees who had been sent ²⁵asked him, "If you aren't the Messiah or Elijah or the Prophet, what right do you have to baptize?"

²⁶John told them, "I baptize with* water, but right here in the crowd is someone you do not recognize. ²⁷Though his ministry follows mine, I'm not even worthy to be his slave and untie the straps of his sandal."

²⁸This encounter took place in Bethany, an area east of the Jordan River, where John was baptizing.

Jesus, the Lamb of God

²⁹The next day John saw Jesus coming toward him and said, "Look! The Lamb of God who takes away the sin of the world! ³⁰He is the one I was talking about when I said, 'A man is coming after me who is far greater than I am, for he existed long before me.' ³¹I did not recognize him as the Messiah, but I have been baptizing with water so that he might be revealed to Israel."

³²Then John testified, "I saw the Holy Spirit descending like a dove from heaven and resting upon him. ³³I didn't know he was the one, but when God sent me to baptize with water, he told me, 'The one on whom you see the Spirit descend and rest is the one who will baptize with the Holy Spirit.' ³⁴I saw this happen to Jesus, so I testify that he is the Chosen One of God.*"

The First Disciples

³⁵The following day John was again standing with two of his disciples. ³⁶As Jesus walked by, John looked at him and declared, "Look! There is the Lamb of God!" ³⁷When John's two disciples heard this, they followed Jesus.

³⁸Jesus looked around and saw them following. "What do you want?" he asked them.

They replied, "Rabbi" (which means "Teacher"), "where are you staying?"

³⁹"Come and see," he said. It was about four o'clock in the afternoon when they went with him to the place where he was staying, and they remained with him the rest of the day.

⁴⁰Andrew, Simon Peter's brother, was one of these men who heard what John said and then followed Jesus. ⁴¹Andrew went to find his brother, Simon, and told him, "We have found the Messiah" (which means "Christ"*).

⁴²Then Andrew brought Simon to meet Jesus. Looking intently at Simon, Jesus said, "Your name is Simon, son of John—but you will be called Cephas" (which means "Peter"*).

⁴³The next day Jesus decided to go to Galilee.

1:14a Greek *became flesh.* 1:14b Or *grace and truth;* also in 1:17. 1:16 Or *received the grace of Christ rather than the grace of the law;* Greek reads *received grace upon grace.* 1:18 Some manuscripts read *But the one and only Son.* 1:19 Greek *and Levites.* 1:21 Greek *Are you the Prophet?* See Deut 18:15, 18; Mal 4:5-6. 1:23 Isa 40:3. 1:26 Or *in;* also in 1:31, 33. 1:34 Some manuscripts read *the Son of God.* 1:41 *Messiah* (a Hebrew term) and *Christ* (a Greek term) both mean "anointed one." 1:42 The names *Cephas* (from Aramaic) and *Peter* (from Greek) both mean "rock."

He found Philip and said to him, "Come, follow me." 44Philip was from Bethsaida, Andrew and Peter's hometown.

45Philip went to look for Nathanael and told him, "We have found the very person Moses* and the prophets wrote about! His name is Jesus, the son of Joseph from Nazareth."

46"Nazareth!" exclaimed Nathanael. "Can anything good come from Nazareth?"

"Come and see for yourself," Philip replied.

47As they approached, Jesus said, "Now here is a genuine son of Israel—a man of complete integrity."

48"How do you know about me?" Nathanael asked.

Jesus replied, "I could see you under the fig tree before Philip found you."

49Then Nathanael exclaimed, "Rabbi, you are the Son of God—the King of Israel!"

50Jesus asked him, "Do you believe this just because I told you I had seen you under the fig tree? You will see greater things than this." 51Then he said, "I tell you the truth, you will all see heaven open and the angels of God going up and down on the Son of Man, the one who is the stairway between heaven and earth.*"

The Wedding at Cana

2 The next day* there was a wedding celebration in the village of Cana in Galilee. Jesus' mother was there, 2and Jesus and his disciples were also invited to the celebration. 3The wine supply ran out during the festivities, so Jesus' mother told him, "They have no more wine."

4"Dear woman, that's not our problem," Jesus replied. "My time has not yet come."

5But his mother told the servants, "Do whatever he tells you."

6Standing nearby were six stone water jars, used for Jewish ceremonial washing. Each could hold twenty to thirty gallons.* 7Jesus told the servants, "Fill the jars with water." When the jars had been filled, 8he said, "Now dip some out, and take it to the master of ceremonies." So the servants followed his instructions.

9When the master of ceremonies tasted the water that was now wine, not knowing where it had come from (though, of course, the servants knew), he called the bridegroom over. 10"A host always serves the best wine first," he said. "Then, when everyone has had a lot to drink, he brings out the less expensive wine. But you have kept the best until now!"

11This miraculous sign at Cana in Galilee was the first time Jesus revealed his glory. And his disciples believed in him.

12After the wedding he went to Capernaum for a few days with his mother, his brothers, and his disciples.

Jesus Clears the Temple

13It was nearly time for the Jewish Passover celebration, so Jesus went to Jerusalem. 14In the Temple area he saw merchants selling cattle, sheep, and doves for sacrifices; he also saw dealers at tables exchanging foreign money. 15Jesus made a whip from some ropes and chased them all out of the Temple. He drove out the sheep and cattle, scattered the money changers' coins over the floor, and turned over their tables. 16Then, going over to the people who sold doves, he told them, "Get these things out of here. Stop turning my Father's house into a marketplace!"

17Then his disciples remembered this prophecy from the Scriptures: "Passion for God's house will consume me."*

18But the Jewish leaders demanded, "What are you doing? If God gave you authority to do this, show us a miraculous sign to prove it."

19"All right," Jesus replied. "Destroy this temple, and in three days I will raise it up."

20"What!" they exclaimed. "It has taken forty-six years to build this Temple, and you can rebuild it in three days?" 21But when Jesus said "this temple," he meant his own body. 22After he was raised from the dead, his disciples remembered he had said this, and they believed both the Scriptures and what Jesus had said.

Jesus and Nicodemus

23Because of the miraculous signs Jesus did in Jerusalem at the Passover celebration, many began to trust in him. 24But Jesus didn't trust them, because he knew all about people. 25No one needed to tell him about human nature, for he knew what was in each person's heart.

3 There was a man named Nicodemus, a Jewish religious leader who was a Pharisee. 2After dark one evening, he came to speak with Jesus. "Rabbi," he said, "we all know that God has sent you to teach us. Your miraculous signs are evidence that God is with you."

3Jesus replied, "I tell you the truth, unless

1:45 Greek *Moses in the law.*   1:51 Greek *going up and down on the Son of Man;* see Gen 28:10-17. "Son of Man" is a title Jesus used for himself.   2:1 Greek *On the third day;* see 1:35, 43.   2:6 Greek *2 or 3 measures* [75 to 113 liters].   2:17 Or *"Concern for God's house will be my undoing."* Ps 69:9.

you are born again,* you cannot see the Kingdom of God."

4"What do you mean?" exclaimed Nicodemus. "How can an old man go back into his mother's womb and be born again?"

5Jesus replied, "I assure you, no one can enter the Kingdom of God without being born of water and the Spirit.* 6Humans can reproduce only human life, but the Holy Spirit gives birth to spiritual life.* 7So don't be surprised when I say, 'You* must be born again.' 8The wind blows wherever it wants. Just as you can hear the wind but can't tell where it comes from or where it is going, so you can't explain how people are born of the Spirit."

9"How are these things possible?" Nicodemus asked.

10Jesus replied, "You are a respected Jewish teacher, and yet you don't understand these things? 11I assure you, we tell you what we know and have seen, and yet you won't believe our testimony. 12But if you don't believe me when I tell you about earthly things, how can you possibly believe if I tell you about heavenly things? 13No one has ever gone to heaven and returned. But the Son of Man* has come down from heaven. 14And as Moses lifted up the bronze snake on a pole in the wilderness, so the Son of Man must be lifted up, 15so that everyone who believes in him will have eternal life.*

16"For this is how God loved the world: He gave* his one and only Son, so that everyone who believes in him will not perish but have eternal life. 17God sent his Son into the world not to judge the world, but to save the world through him.

18"There is no judgment against anyone who believes in him. But anyone who does not believe in him has already been judged for not believing in God's one and only Son. 19And the judgment is based on this fact: God's light came into the world, but people loved the darkness more than the light, for their actions were evil. 20All who do evil hate the light and refuse to go near it for fear their sins will be exposed. 21But those who do what is right come to the light so others can see that they are doing what God wants.*"

John the Baptist Exalts Jesus

22Then Jesus and his disciples left Jerusalem and went into the Judean countryside. Jesus spent some time with them there, baptizing people.

23At this time John the Baptist was baptizing at Aenon, near Salim, because there was plenty of water there; and people kept coming to him for baptism. 24(This was before John was thrown into prison.) 25A debate broke out between John's disciples and a certain Jew* over ceremonial cleansing. 26So John's disciples came to him and said, "Rabbi, the man you met on the other side of the Jordan River, the one you identified as the Messiah, is also baptizing people. And everybody is going to him instead of coming to us."

27John replied, "No one can receive anything unless God gives it from heaven. 28You yourselves know how plainly I told you, 'I am not the Messiah. I am only here to prepare the way for him.' 29It is the bridegroom who marries the bride, and the bridegroom's friend is simply glad to stand with him and hear his vows. Therefore, I am filled with joy at his success. 30He must become greater and greater, and I must become less and less.

31"He has come from above and is greater than anyone else. We are of the earth, and we speak of earthly things, but he has come from heaven and is greater than anyone else.* 32He testifies about what he has seen and heard, but how few believe what he tells them! 33Anyone who accepts his testimony can affirm that God is true. 34For he is sent by God. He speaks God's words, for God gives him the Spirit without limit. 35The Father loves his Son and has put everything into his hands. 36And anyone who believes in God's Son has eternal life. Anyone who doesn't obey the Son will never experience eternal life but remains under God's angry judgment."

Jesus and the Samaritan Woman

4 Jesus* knew the Pharisees had heard that he was baptizing and making more disciples than John 2(though Jesus himself didn't baptize them—his disciples did). 3So he left Judea and returned to Galilee.

4He had to go through Samaria on the way. 5Eventually he came to the Samaritan village of Sychar, near the field that Jacob gave to his son Joseph. 6Jacob's well was there; and Jesus, tired from the long walk, sat wearily beside the well about noontime. 7Soon a Samaritan

---

3:3 Or born from above; also in 3:7.   3:5 Or and spirit. The Greek word for Spirit can also be translated wind; see 3:8.   3:6 Greek what is born of the Spirit is spirit.   3:7 The Greek word for you is plural; also in 3:12.   3:13 Some manuscripts add who lives in heaven. "Son of Man" is a title Jesus used for himself.   3:15 Or everyone who believes will have eternal life in him.   3:16 Or For God loved the world so much that he gave.   3:21 Or can see God at work in what he is doing.   3:25 Some manuscripts read some Jews.   3:31 Some manuscripts do not include and is greater than anyone else.   4:1 Some manuscripts read The Lord.

woman came to draw water, and Jesus said to her, "Please give me a drink." 8He was alone at the time because his disciples had gone into the village to buy some food.

9The woman was surprised, for Jews refuse to have anything to do with Samaritans.* She said to Jesus, "You are a Jew, and I am a Samaritan woman. Why are you asking me for a drink?"

10Jesus replied, "If you only knew the gift God has for you and who you are speaking to, you would ask me, and I would give you living water."

11"But sir, you don't have a rope or a bucket," she said, "and this well is very deep. Where would you get this living water? 12And besides, do you think you're greater than our ancestor Jacob, who gave us this well? How can you offer better water than he and his sons and his animals enjoyed?"

13Jesus replied, "Anyone who drinks this water will soon become thirsty again. 14But those who drink the water I give will never be thirsty again. It becomes a fresh, bubbling spring within them, giving them eternal life."

15"Please, sir," the woman said, "give me this water! Then I'll never be thirsty again, and I won't have to come here to get water."

16"Go and get your husband," Jesus told her.

17"I don't have a husband," the woman replied.

Jesus said, "You're right! You don't have a husband—18for you have had five husbands, and you aren't even married to the man you're living with now. You certainly spoke the truth!"

19"Sir," the woman said, "you must be a prophet. 20So tell me, why is it that you Jews insist that Jerusalem is the only place of worship, while we Samaritans claim it is here at Mount Gerizim,* where our ancestors worshiped?"

21Jesus replied, "Believe me, dear woman, the time is coming when it will no longer matter whether you worship the Father on this mountain or in Jerusalem. 22You Samaritans know very little about the one you worship, while we Jews know all about him, for salvation comes through the Jews. 23But the time is coming—indeed it's here now—when true worshipers will worship the Father in spirit and in truth. The Father is looking for those who will worship him that way. 24For God is Spirit, so those who worship him must worship in spirit and in truth."

25The woman said, "I know the Messiah is coming—the one who is called Christ. When he comes, he will explain everything to us."

26Then Jesus told her, "I AM the Messiah!"*

27Just then his disciples came back. They were shocked to find him talking to a woman, but none of them had the nerve to ask, "What do you want with her?" or "Why are you talking to her?" 28The woman left her water jar beside the well and ran back to the village, telling everyone, 29"Come and see a man who told me everything I ever did! Could he possibly be the Messiah?" 30So the people came streaming from the village to see him.

31Meanwhile, the disciples were urging Jesus, "Rabbi, eat something."

32But Jesus replied, "I have a kind of food you know nothing about."

33"Did someone bring him food while we were gone?" the disciples asked each other.

34Then Jesus explained: "My nourishment comes from doing the will of God, who sent me, and from finishing his work. 35You know the saying, 'Four months between planting and harvest.' But I say, wake up and look around. The fields are already ripe* for harvest. 36The harvesters are paid good wages, and the fruit they harvest is people brought to eternal life. What joy awaits both the planter and the harvester alike! 37You know the saying, 'One plants and another harvests.' And it's true. 38I sent you to harvest where you didn't plant; others had already done the work, and now you will get to gather the harvest."

Many Samaritans Believe

39Many Samaritans from the village believed in Jesus because the woman had said, "He told me everything I ever did!" 40When they came out to see him, they begged him to stay in their village. So he stayed for two days, 41long enough for many more to hear his message and believe. 42Then they said to the woman, "Now we believe, not just because of what you told us, but because we have heard him ourselves. Now we know that he is indeed the Savior of the world."

Jesus Heals an Official's Son

43At the end of the two days, Jesus went on to Galilee. 44He himself had said that a prophet is not honored in his own hometown. 45Yet the Galileans welcomed him, for they had been in Jerusalem at the Passover celebration and had seen everything he did there.

46As he traveled through Galilee, he came

4:9 Some manuscripts do not include this sentence.   4:20 Greek *on this mountain.*   4:26 Or *"The 'I AM' is here"*; or *"I am the* LORD*"*; Greek reads *"I am, the one speaking to you."* See Exod 3:14.   4:35 Greek *white.*

to Cana, where he had turned the water into wine. There was a government official in nearby Capernaum whose son was very sick. ⁴⁷When he heard that Jesus had come from Judea to Galilee, he went and begged Jesus to come to Capernaum to heal his son, who was about to die.

⁴⁸Jesus asked, "Will you never believe in me unless you see miraculous signs and wonders?"

⁴⁹The official pleaded, "Lord, please come now before my little boy dies."

⁵⁰Then Jesus told him, "Go back home. Your son will live!" And the man believed what Jesus said and started home.

⁵¹While the man was on his way, some of his servants met him with the news that his son was alive and well. ⁵²He asked them when the boy had begun to get better, and they replied, "Yesterday afternoon at one o'clock his fever suddenly disappeared!" ⁵³Then the father realized that that was the very time Jesus had told him, "Your son will live." And he and his entire household believed in Jesus. ⁵⁴This was the second miraculous sign Jesus did in Galilee after coming from Judea.

Jesus Heals a Lame Man

5 Afterward Jesus returned to Jerusalem for one of the Jewish holy days. ²Inside the city, near the Sheep Gate, was the pool of Bethesda,* with five covered porches. ³Crowds of sick people—blind, lame, or paralyzed—lay on the porches.* ⁵One of the men lying there had been sick for thirty-eight years. ⁶When Jesus saw him and knew he had been ill for a long time, he asked him, "Would you like to get well?"

⁷"I can't, sir," the sick man said, "for I have no one to put me into the pool when the water bubbles up. Someone else always gets there ahead of me."

⁸Jesus told him, "Stand up, pick up your mat, and walk!"

⁹Instantly, the man was healed! He rolled up his sleeping mat and began walking! But this miracle happened on the Sabbath, ¹⁰so the Jewish leaders objected. They said to the man who was cured, "You can't work on the Sabbath! The law doesn't allow you to carry that sleeping mat!"

¹¹But he replied, "The man who healed me told me, 'Pick up your mat and walk.'"

¹²"Who said such a thing as that?" they demanded.

¹³The man didn't know, for Jesus had disappeared into the crowd. ¹⁴But afterward Jesus found him in the Temple and told him, "Now you are well; so stop sinning, or something even worse may happen to you." ¹⁵Then the man went and told the Jewish leaders that it was Jesus who had healed him.

Jesus Claims to Be the Son of God

¹⁶So the Jewish leaders began harassing* Jesus for breaking the Sabbath rules. ¹⁷But Jesus replied, "My Father is always working, and so am I." ¹⁸So the Jewish leaders tried all the harder to find a way to kill him. For he not only broke the Sabbath, he called God his Father, thereby making himself equal with God.

¹⁹So Jesus explained, "I tell you the truth, the Son can do nothing by himself. He does only what he sees the Father doing. Whatever the Father does, the Son also does. ²⁰For the Father loves the Son and shows him everything he is doing. In fact, the Father will show him how to do even greater works than healing this man. Then you will truly be astonished. ²¹For just as the Father gives life to those he raises from the dead, so the Son gives life to anyone he wants. ²²In addition, the Father judges no one. Instead, he has given the Son absolute authority to judge, ²³so that everyone will honor the Son, just as they honor the Father. Anyone who does not honor the Son is certainly not honoring the Father who sent him.

²⁴"I tell you the truth, those who listen to my message and believe in God who sent me have eternal life. They will never be condemned for their sins, but they have already passed from death into life.

²⁵"And I assure you that the time is coming, indeed it's here now, when the dead will hear my voice—the voice of the Son of God. And those who listen will live. ²⁶The Father has life in himself, and he has granted that same life-giving power to his Son. ²⁷And he has given him authority to judge everyone because he is the Son of Man.* ²⁸Don't be so surprised! Indeed, the time is coming when all the dead in their graves will hear the voice of God's Son, ²⁹and they will rise again. Those who have done good will rise to experience eternal life, and those who have continued in evil will rise to

---

5:2 Other manuscripts read *Beth-zatha*; still others read *Bethsaida*. 5:3 Some manuscripts add an expanded conclusion to verse 3 and all of verse 4: *waiting for a certain movement of the water, ⁴for an angel of the Lord came from time to time and stirred up the water. And the first person to step in after the water was stirred was healed of whatever disease he had.* 5:16 Or *persecuting*. 5:27 "Son of Man" is a title Jesus used for himself.

experience judgment. ³⁰I can do nothing on my own. I judge as God tells me. Therefore, my judgment is just, because I carry out the will of the one who sent me, not my own will.

Witnesses to Jesus

³¹"If I were to testify on my own behalf, my testimony would not be valid. ³²But someone else is also testifying about me, and I assure you that everything he says about me is true. ³³In fact, you sent investigators to listen to John the Baptist, and his testimony about me was true. ³⁴Of course, I have no need of human witnesses, but I say these things so you might be saved. ³⁵John was like a burning and shining lamp, and you were excited for a while about his message. ³⁶But I have a greater witness than John—my teachings and my miracles. The Father gave me these works to accomplish, and they prove that he sent me. ³⁷And the Father who sent me has testified about me himself. You have never heard his voice or seen him face to face, ³⁸and you do not have his message in your hearts, because you do not believe me—the one he sent to you.

³⁹"You search the Scriptures because you think they give you eternal life. But the Scriptures point to me! ⁴⁰Yet you refuse to come to me to receive this life.

⁴¹"Your approval means nothing to me, ⁴²because I know you don't have God's love within you. ⁴³For I have come to you in my Father's name, and you have rejected me. Yet if others come in their own name, you gladly welcome them. ⁴⁴No wonder you can't believe! For you gladly honor each other, but you don't care about the honor that comes from the one who alone is God.*

⁴⁵"Yet it isn't I who will accuse you before the Father. Moses will accuse you! Yes, Moses, in whom you put your hopes. ⁴⁶If you really believed Moses, you would believe me, because he wrote about me. ⁴⁷But since you don't believe what he wrote, how will you believe what I say?"

Jesus Feeds Five Thousand

6 After this, Jesus crossed over to the far side of the Sea of Galilee, also known as the Sea of Tiberias. ²A huge crowd kept following him wherever he went, because they saw his miraculous signs as he healed the sick. ³Then Jesus climbed a hill and sat down with his disciples around him. ⁴(It was nearly time for the Jewish Passover celebration.) ⁵Jesus soon saw a huge crowd of people coming to look for him. Turning to Philip, he asked, "Where can we buy bread to feed all these people?" ⁶He was testing Philip, for he already knew what he was going to do.

⁷Philip replied, "Even if we worked for months, we wouldn't have enough money* to feed them!"

⁸Then Andrew, Simon Peter's brother, spoke up. ⁹"There's a young boy here with five barley loaves and two fish. But what good is that with this huge crowd?"

¹⁰"Tell everyone to sit down," Jesus said. So they all sat down on the grassy slopes. (The men alone numbered about 5,000.) ¹¹Then Jesus took the loaves, gave thanks to God, and distributed them to the people. Afterward he did the same with the fish. And they all ate as much as they wanted. ¹²After everyone was full, Jesus told his disciples, "Now gather the leftovers, so that nothing is wasted." ¹³So they picked up the pieces and filled twelve baskets with scraps left by the people who had eaten from the five barley loaves.

¹⁴When the people saw him* do this miraculous sign, they exclaimed, "Surely, he is the Prophet we have been expecting!"* ¹⁵When Jesus saw that they were ready to force him to be their king, he slipped away into the hills by himself.

Jesus Walks on Water

¹⁶That evening Jesus' disciples went down to the shore to wait for him. ¹⁷But as darkness fell and Jesus still hadn't come back, they got into the boat and headed across the lake toward Capernaum. ¹⁸Soon a gale swept down upon them, and the sea grew very rough. ¹⁹They had rowed three or four miles* when suddenly they saw Jesus walking on the water toward the boat. They were terrified, ²⁰but he called out to them, "Don't be afraid. I am here!"* ²¹Then they were eager to let him in the boat, and immediately they arrived at their destination!

Jesus, the Bread of Life

²²The next day the crowd that had stayed on the far shore saw that the disciples had taken the only boat, and they realized Jesus had not gone with them. ²³Several boats from Tiberias landed near the place where the Lord had

---

5:44 Some manuscripts read *from the only One.*   6:7 Greek *Two hundred denarii would not be enough.* A denarius was equivalent to a laborer's full day's wage.   6:14a Some manuscripts read *Jesus.*   6:14b See Deut 18:15, 18; Mal 4:5-6.   6:19 Greek *25 or 30 stadia* [4.6 or 5.5 kilometers].   6:20 Or *The 'I AM' is here;* Greek reads *I am.* See Exod 3:14.

blessed the bread and the people had eaten. 24So when the crowd saw that neither Jesus nor his disciples were there, they got into the boats and went across to Capernaum to look for him. 25They found him on the other side of the lake and asked, "Rabbi, when did you get here?"

26Jesus replied, "I tell you the truth, you want to be with me because I fed you, not because you understood the miraculous signs. 27But don't be so concerned about perishable things like food. Spend your energy seeking the eternal life that the Son of Man* can give you. For God the Father has given me the seal of his approval."

28They replied, "We want to perform God's works, too. What should we do?"

29Jesus told them, "This is the only work God wants from you: Believe in the one he has sent."

30They answered, "Show us a miraculous sign if you want us to believe in you. What can you do? 31After all, our ancestors ate manna while they journeyed through the wilderness! The Scriptures say, 'Moses gave them bread from heaven to eat.'*"

32Jesus said, "I tell you the truth, Moses didn't give you bread from heaven. My Father did. And now he offers you the true bread from heaven. 33The true bread of God is the one who comes down from heaven and gives life to the world."

34"Sir," they said, "give us that bread every day."

35Jesus replied, "I am the bread of life. Whoever comes to me will never be hungry again. Whoever believes in me will never be thirsty. 36But you haven't believed in me even though you have seen me. 37However, those the Father has given me will come to me, and I will never reject them. 38For I have come down from heaven to do the will of God who sent me, not to do my own will. 39And this is the will of God, that I should not lose even one of all those he has given me, but that I should raise them up at the last day. 40For it is my Father's will that all who see his Son and believe in him should have eternal life. I will raise them up at the last day."

41Then the people* began to murmur in disagreement because he had said, "I am the bread that came down from heaven." 42They said, "Isn't this Jesus, the son of Joseph? We know his father and mother. How can he say, 'I came down from heaven'?"

43But Jesus replied, "Stop complaining about what I said. 44For no one can come to me unless the Father who sent me draws them to me, and at the last day I will raise them up. 45As it is written in the Scriptures,* 'They will all be taught by God.' Everyone who listens to the Father and learns from him comes to me. 46(Not that anyone has ever seen the Father; only I, who was sent from God, have seen him.)

47"I tell you the truth, anyone who believes has eternal life. 48Yes, I am the bread of life! 49Your ancestors ate manna in the wilderness, but they all died. 50Anyone who eats the bread from heaven, however, will never die. 51I am the living bread that came down from heaven. Anyone who eats this bread will live forever; and this bread, which I will offer so the world may live, is my flesh."

52Then the people began arguing with each other about what he meant. "How can this man give us his flesh to eat?" they asked.

53So Jesus said again, "I tell you the truth, unless you eat the flesh of the Son of Man and drink his blood, you cannot have eternal life within you. 54But anyone who eats my flesh and drinks my blood has eternal life, and I will raise that person at the last day. 55For my flesh is true food, and my blood is true drink. 56Anyone who eats my flesh and drinks my blood remains in me, and I in him. 57I live because of the living Father who sent me; in the same way, anyone who feeds on me will live because of me. 58I am the true bread that came down from heaven. Anyone who eats this bread will not die as your ancestors did (even though they ate the manna) but will live forever."

59He said these things while he was teaching in the synagogue in Capernaum.

Many Disciples Desert Jesus

60Many of his disciples said, "This is very hard to understand. How can anyone accept it?"

61Jesus was aware that his disciples were complaining, so he said to them, "Does this offend you? 62Then what will you think if you see the Son of Man ascend to heaven again? 63The Spirit alone gives eternal life. Human effort accomplishes nothing. And the very words I have spoken to you are spirit and life. 64But some of you do not believe me." (For Jesus knew from the beginning which ones didn't believe, and he knew who would betray him.) 65Then he said, "That is why I said that people can't come to me unless the Father gives them to me."

66At this point many of his disciples turned away and deserted him. 67Then Jesus turned

6:27 "Son of Man" is a title Jesus used for himself.   6:31 Exod 16:4; Ps 78:24.   6:41 Greek *Jewish people; also in 6:52.*
6:45 Greek *in the prophets.* Isa 54:13.

to the Twelve and asked, "Are you also going to leave?"

⁶⁸Simon Peter replied, "Lord, to whom would we go? You have the words that give eternal life. ⁶⁹We believe, and we know you are the Holy One of God.*"

⁷⁰Then Jesus said, "I chose the twelve of you, but one is a devil." ⁷¹He was speaking of Judas, son of Simon Iscariot, one of the Twelve, who would later betray him.

Jesus and His Brothers

7 After this, Jesus traveled around Galilee. He wanted to stay out of Judea, where the Jewish leaders were plotting his death. ²But soon it was time for the Jewish Festival of Shelters, ³and Jesus' brothers said to him, "Leave here and go to Judea, where your followers can see your miracles! ⁴You can't become famous if you hide like this! If you can do such wonderful things, show yourself to the world!" ⁵For even his brothers didn't believe in him.

⁶Jesus replied, "Now is not the right time for me to go, but you can go anytime. ⁷The world can't hate you, but it does hate me because I accuse it of doing evil. ⁸You go on. I'm not going* to this festival, because my time has not yet come." ⁹After saying these things, Jesus remained in Galilee.

Jesus Teaches Openly at the Temple

¹⁰But after his brothers left for the festival, Jesus also went, though secretly, staying out of public view. ¹¹The Jewish leaders tried to find him at the festival and kept asking if anyone had seen him. ¹²There was a lot of grumbling about him among the crowds. Some argued, "He's a good man," but others said, "He's nothing but a fraud who deceives the people." ¹³But no one had the courage to speak favorably about him in public, for they were afraid of getting in trouble with the Jewish leaders.

¹⁴Then, midway through the festival, Jesus went up to the Temple and began to teach. ¹⁵The people* were surprised when they heard him. "How does he know so much when he hasn't been trained?" they asked.

¹⁶So Jesus told them, "My message is not my own; it comes from God who sent me. ¹⁷Anyone who wants to do the will of God will know whether my teaching is from God or is merely my own. ¹⁸Those who speak for themselves want glory only for themselves, but a person who seeks to honor the one who sent him speaks truth, not lies. ¹⁹Moses gave you the law, but none of you obeys it! In fact, you are trying to kill me."

²⁰The crowd replied, "You're demon possessed! Who's trying to kill you?"

²¹Jesus replied, "I did one miracle on the Sabbath, and you were amazed. ²²But you work on the Sabbath, too, when you obey Moses' law of circumcision. (Actually, this tradition of circumcision began with the patriarchs, long before the law of Moses.) ²³For if the correct time for circumcising your son falls on the Sabbath, you go ahead and do it so as not to break the law of Moses. So why should you be angry with me for healing a man on the Sabbath? ²⁴Look beneath the surface so you can judge correctly."

Is Jesus the Messiah?

²⁵Some of the people who lived in Jerusalem started to ask each other, "Isn't this the man they are trying to kill? ²⁶But here he is, speaking in public, and they say nothing to him. Could our leaders possibly believe that he is the Messiah? ²⁷But how could he be? For we know where this man comes from. When the Messiah comes, he will simply appear; no one will know where he comes from."

²⁸While Jesus was teaching in the Temple, he called out, "Yes, you know me, and you know where I come from. But I'm not here on my own. The one who sent me is true, and you don't know him. ²⁹But I know him because I come from him, and he sent me to you." ³⁰Then the leaders tried to arrest him; but no one laid a hand on him, because his time* had not yet come.

³¹Many among the crowds at the Temple believed in him. "After all," they said, "would you expect the Messiah to do more miraculous signs than this man has done?"

³²When the Pharisees heard that the crowds were whispering such things, they and the leading priests sent Temple guards to arrest Jesus. ³³But Jesus told them, "I will be with you only a little longer. Then I will return to the one who sent me. ³⁴You will search for me but not find me. And you cannot go where I am going."

³⁵The Jewish leaders were puzzled by this statement. "Where is he planning to go?" they asked. "Is he thinking of leaving the country and going to the Jews in other lands?* Maybe he will even teach the Greeks! ³⁶What does he mean when he says, 'You will search for me

---

6:69 Other manuscripts read *you are the Christ, the Holy One of God;* still others read *you are the Christ, the Son of God;* and still others read *you are the Christ, the Son of the living God.* 7:8 Some manuscripts read *not yet going.* 7:15 Greek *Jewish people.* 7:30 Greek *his hour.* 7:35 Or *the Jews who live among the Greeks?*

but not find me,' and 'You cannot go where I am going'?"

Jesus Promises Living Water

37On the last day, the climax of the festival, Jesus stood and shouted to the crowds, "Anyone who is thirsty may come to me! 38Anyone who believes in me may come and drink! For the Scriptures declare, 'Rivers of living water will flow from his heart.'"* 39(When he said "living water," he was speaking of the Spirit, who would be given to everyone believing in him. But the Spirit had not yet been given,* because Jesus had not yet entered into his glory.)

Division and Unbelief

40When the crowds heard him say this, some of them declared, "Surely this man is the Prophet we've been expecting."* 41Others said, "He is the Messiah." Still others said, "But he can't be! Will the Messiah come from Galilee? 42For the Scriptures clearly state that the Messiah will be born of the royal line of David, in Bethlehem, the village where King David was born."* 43So the crowd was divided about him. 44Some even wanted him arrested, but no one laid a hand on him.

45When the Temple guards returned without having arrested Jesus, the leading priests and Pharisees demanded, "Why didn't you bring him in?"

46"We have never heard anyone speak like this!" the guards responded.

47"Have you been led astray, too?" the Pharisees mocked. 48"Is there a single one of us rulers or Pharisees who believes in him? 49This foolish crowd follows him, but they are ignorant of the law. God's curse is on them!"

50Then Nicodemus, the leader who had met with Jesus earlier, spoke up. 51"Is it legal to convict a man before he is given a hearing?" he asked.

52They replied, "Are you from Galilee, too? Search the Scriptures and see for yourself—no prophet ever comes* from Galilee!"

[The most ancient Greek manuscripts do not include John 7:53–8:11.]

53Then the meeting broke up, and everybody went home.

A Woman Caught in Adultery

8 Jesus returned to the Mount of Olives, 2but early the next morning he was back again at the Temple. A crowd soon gathered, and he sat down and taught them. 3As he was speaking, the teachers of religious law and the Pharisees brought a woman who had been caught in the act of adultery. They put her in front of the crowd.

4"Teacher," they said to Jesus, "this woman was caught in the act of adultery. 5The law of Moses says to stone her. What do you say?"

6They were trying to trap him into saying something they could use against him, but Jesus stooped down and wrote in the dust with his finger. 7They kept demanding an answer, so he stood up again and said, "All right, but let the one who has never sinned throw the first stone!" 8Then he stooped down again and wrote in the dust.

9When the accusers heard this, they slipped away one by one, beginning with the oldest, until only Jesus was left in the middle of the crowd with the woman. 10Then Jesus stood up again and said to the woman, "Where are your accusers? Didn't even one of them condemn you?"

11"No, Lord," she said.

And Jesus said, "Neither do I. Go and sin no more."

Jesus, the Light of the World

12Jesus spoke to the people once more and said, "I am the light of the world. If you follow me, you won't have to walk in darkness, because you will have the light that leads to life."

13The Pharisees replied, "You are making those claims about yourself! Such testimony is not valid."

14Jesus told them, "These claims are valid even though I make them about myself. For I know where I came from and where I am going, but you don't know this about me. 15You judge me by human standards, but I do not judge anyone. 16And if I did, my judgment would be correct in every respect because I am not alone. The Father* who sent me is with me. 17Your own law says that if two people agree about something, their witness is accepted as fact.* 18I am one witness, and my Father who sent me is the other."

7:37-38 Or "Let anyone who is thirsty come to me and drink. 38For the Scriptures declare, 'Rivers of living water will flow from the heart of anyone who believes in me.'" 7:39 Several early manuscripts read But as yet there was no Spirit. Still others read But as yet there was no Holy Spirit. 7:40 See Deut 18:15, 18; Mal 4:5-6. 7:42 See Mic 5:2. 7:52 Some manuscripts read the prophet does not come. 8:16 Some manuscripts read The One. 8:17 See Deut 19:15.

¹⁹"Where is your father?" they asked.

Jesus answered, "Since you don't know who I am, you don't know who my Father is. If you knew me, you would also know my Father." ²⁰Jesus made these statements while he was teaching in the section of the Temple known as the Treasury. But he was not arrested, because his time* had not yet come.

The Unbelieving People Warned

²¹Later Jesus said to them again, "I am going away. You will search for me but will die in your sin. You cannot come where I am going."

²²The people* asked, "Is he planning to commit suicide? What does he mean, 'You cannot come where I am going'?"

²³Jesus continued, "You are from below; I am from above. You belong to this world; I do not. ²⁴That is why I said that you will die in your sins; for unless you believe that I AM who I claim to be,* you will die in your sins."

²⁵"Who are you?" they demanded.

Jesus replied, "The one I have always claimed to be.* ²⁶I have much to say about you and much to condemn, but I won't. For I say only what I have heard from the one who sent me, and he is completely truthful." ²⁷But they still didn't understand that he was talking about his Father.

²⁸So Jesus said, "When you have lifted up the Son of Man on the cross, then you will understand that I AM he.* I do nothing on my own but say only what the Father taught me. ²⁹And the one who sent me is with me—he has not deserted me. For I always do what pleases him." ³⁰Then many who heard him say these things believed in him.

Jesus and Abraham

³¹Jesus said to the people who believed in him, "You are truly my disciples if you remain faithful to my teachings. ³²And you will know the truth, and the truth will set you free."

³³"But we are descendants of Abraham," they said. "We have never been slaves to anyone. What do you mean, 'You will be set free'?"

³⁴Jesus replied, "I tell you the truth, everyone who sins is a slave of sin. ³⁵A slave is not a permanent member of the family, but a son is part of the family forever. ³⁶So if the Son sets you free, you are truly free. ³⁷Yes, I realize that you are descendants of Abraham. And yet some

of you are trying to kill me because there's no room in your hearts for my message. ³⁸I am telling you what I saw when I was with my Father. But you are following the advice of your father."

³⁹"Our father is Abraham!" they declared.

"No," Jesus replied, "for if you were really the children of Abraham, you would follow his example.* ⁴⁰Instead, you are trying to kill me because I told you the truth, which I heard from God. Abraham never did such a thing. ⁴¹No, you are imitating your real father."

They replied, "We aren't illegitimate children! God himself is our true Father."

⁴²Jesus told them, "If God were your Father, you would love me, because I have come to you from God. I am not here on my own, but he sent me. ⁴³Why can't you understand what I am saying? It's because you can't even hear me! ⁴⁴For you are the children of your father the devil, and you love to do the evil things he does. He was a murderer from the beginning. He has always hated the truth, because there is no truth in him. When he lies, it is consistent with his character; for he is a liar and the father of lies. ⁴⁵So when I tell the truth, you just naturally don't believe me! ⁴⁶Which of you can truthfully accuse me of sin? And since I am telling you the truth, why don't you believe me? ⁴⁷Anyone who belongs to God listens gladly to the words of God. But you don't listen because you don't belong to God."

⁴⁸The people retorted, "You Samaritan devil! Didn't we say all along that you were possessed by a demon?"

⁴⁹"No," Jesus said, "I have no demon in me. For I honor my Father—and you dishonor me. ⁵⁰And though I have no wish to glorify myself, God is going to glorify me. He is the true judge. ⁵¹I tell you the truth, anyone who obeys my teaching will never die!"

⁵²The people said, "Now we know you are possessed by a demon. Even Abraham and the prophets died, but you say, 'Anyone who obeys my teaching will never die!' ⁵³Are you greater than our father Abraham? He died, and so did the prophets. Who do you think you are?"

⁵⁴Jesus answered, "If I want glory for myself, it doesn't count. But it is my Father who will glorify me. You say, 'He is our God,'* ⁵⁵but you don't even know him. I know him. If I said otherwise, I would be as great a liar as you! But

8:20 Greek *his hour.*   8:22 Greek *Jewish people; also in 8:31, 48, 52, 57.*   8:24 Greek *unless you believe that I am. See Exod 3:14.*
8:25 Or *Why do I speak to you at all?*   8:28 Greek *When you have lifted up the Son of Man, then you will know that I am.* "Son of Man" is a title Jesus used for himself.   8:39 Some manuscripts read *if you are really the children of Abraham, follow his example.*
8:54 Some manuscripts read *You say he is your God.*

I do know him and obey him. ⁵⁶Your father Abraham rejoiced as he looked forward to my coming. He saw it and was glad."

⁵⁷The people said, "You aren't even fifty years old. How can you say you have seen Abraham?*"

⁵⁸Jesus answered, "I tell you the truth, before Abraham was even born, I AM!*" ⁵⁹At that point they picked up stones to throw at him. But Jesus was hidden from them and left the Temple.

Jesus Heals a Man Born Blind

9 As Jesus was walking along, he saw a man who had been blind from birth. ²"Rabbi," his disciples asked him, "why was this man born blind? Was it because of his own sins or his parents' sins?"

³"It was not because of his sins or his parents' sins," Jesus answered. "This happened so the power of God could be seen in him. ⁴We must quickly carry out the tasks assigned us by the one who sent us.* The night is coming, and then no one can work. ⁵But while I am here in the world, I am the light of the world."

⁶Then he spit on the ground, made mud with the saliva, and spread the mud over the blind man's eyes. ⁷He told him, "Go wash yourself in the pool of Siloam" (Siloam means "sent"). So the man went and washed and came back seeing!

⁸His neighbors and others who knew him as a blind beggar asked each other, "Isn't this the man who used to sit and beg?" ⁹Some said he was, and others said, "No, he just looks like him!"

But the beggar kept saying, "Yes, I am the same one!"

¹⁰They asked, "Who healed you? What happened?"

¹¹He told them, "The man they call Jesus made mud and spread it over my eyes and told me, 'Go to the pool of Siloam and wash yourself.' So I went and washed, and now I can see!"

¹²"Where is he now?" they asked.

"I don't know," he replied.

¹³Then they took the man who had been blind to the Pharisees, ¹⁴because it was on the Sabbath that Jesus had made the mud and healed him. ¹⁵The Pharisees asked the man all about it. So he told them, "He put the mud over my eyes, and when I washed it away, I could see!"

¹⁶Some of the Pharisees said, "This man Jesus is not from God, for he is working on the Sabbath." Others said, "But how could an ordinary sinner do such miraculous signs?" So there was a deep division of opinion among them.

¹⁷Then the Pharisees again questioned the man who had been blind and demanded, "What's your opinion about this man who healed you?"

The man replied, "I think he must be a prophet."

¹⁸The Jewish leaders still refused to believe the man had been blind and could now see, so they called in his parents. ¹⁹They asked them, "Is this your son? Was he born blind? If so, how can he now see?"

²⁰His parents replied, "We know this is our son and that he was born blind, ²¹but we don't know how he can see or who healed him. Ask him. He is old enough to speak for himself." ²²His parents said this because they were afraid of the Jewish leaders, who had announced that anyone saying Jesus was the Messiah would be expelled from the synagogue. ²³That's why they said, "He is old enough. Ask him."

²⁴So for the second time they called in the man who had been blind and told him, "God should get the glory for this,* because we know this man Jesus is a sinner."

²⁵"I don't know whether he is a sinner," the man replied. "But I know this: I was blind, and now I can see!"

²⁶"But what did he do?" they asked. "How did he heal you?"

²⁷"Look!" the man exclaimed. "I told you once. Didn't you listen? Why do you want to hear it again? Do you want to become his disciples, too?"

²⁸Then they cursed him and said, "You are his disciple, but we are disciples of Moses! ²⁹We know God spoke to Moses, but we don't even know where this man comes from."

³⁰"Why, that's very strange!" the man replied. "He healed my eyes, and yet you don't know where he comes from? ³¹We know that God doesn't listen to sinners, but he is ready to hear those who worship him and do his will. ³²Ever since the world began, no one has been able to open the eyes of someone born blind. ³³If this man were not from God, he couldn't have done it."

8:57 Some manuscripts read *How can you say Abraham has seen you?* 8:58 Or *before Abraham was even born, I have always been alive;* Greek reads *before Abraham was, I am.* See Exod 3:14. 9:4 Other manuscripts read *I must quickly carry out the tasks assigned me by the one who sent me;* still others read *We must quickly carry out the tasks assigned us by the one who sent me.* 9:24 Or *Give glory to God, not to Jesus;* Greek reads *Give glory to God.*

³⁴"You were born a total sinner!" they answered. "Are you trying to teach us?" And they threw him out of the synagogue.

Spiritual Blindness

³⁵When Jesus heard what had happened, he found the man and asked, "Do you believe in the Son of Man?*"

³⁶The man answered, "Who is he, sir? I want to believe in him."

³⁷"You have seen him," Jesus said, "and he is speaking to you!"

³⁸"Yes, Lord, I believe!" the man said. And he worshiped Jesus.

³⁹Then Jesus told him,* "I entered this world to render judgment—to give sight to the blind and to show those who think they see* that they are blind."

⁴⁰Some Pharisees who were standing nearby heard him and asked, "Are you saying we're blind?"

⁴¹"If you were blind, you wouldn't be guilty," Jesus replied. "But you remain guilty because you claim you can see.

The Good Shepherd and His Sheep

10 "I tell you the truth, anyone who sneaks over the wall of a sheepfold, rather than going through the gate, must surely be a thief and a robber! ²But the one who enters through the gate is the shepherd of the sheep. ³The gatekeeper opens the gate for him, and the sheep recognize his voice and come to him. He calls his own sheep by name and leads them out. ⁴After he has gathered his own flock, he walks ahead of them, and they follow him because they know his voice. ⁵They won't follow a stranger; they will run from him because they don't know his voice."

⁶Those who heard Jesus use this illustration didn't understand what he meant, ⁷so he explained it to them: "I tell you the truth, I am the gate for the sheep. ⁸All who came before me* were thieves and robbers. But the true sheep did not listen to them. ⁹Yes, I am the gate. Those who come in through me will be saved.* They will come and go freely and will find good pastures. ¹⁰The thief's purpose is to steal and kill and destroy. My purpose is to give them a rich and satisfying life.

¹¹"I am the good shepherd. The good shepherd sacrifices his life for the sheep. ¹²A hired hand will run when he sees a wolf coming. He will abandon the sheep because they don't belong to him and he isn't their shepherd. And so the wolf attacks them and scatters the flock. ¹³The hired hand runs away because he's working only for the money and doesn't really care about the sheep.

¹⁴"I am the good shepherd; I know my own sheep, and they know me, ¹⁵just as my Father knows me and I know the Father. So I sacrifice my life for the sheep. ¹⁶I have other sheep, too, that are not in this sheepfold. I must bring them also. They will listen to my voice, and there will be one flock with one shepherd.

¹⁷"The Father loves me because I sacrifice my life so I may take it back again. ¹⁸No one can take my life from me. I sacrifice it voluntarily. For I have the authority to lay it down when I want to and also to take it up again. For this is what my Father has commanded."

¹⁹When he said these things, the people* were again divided in their opinions about him. ²⁰Some said, "He's demon possessed and out of his mind. Why listen to a man like that?" ²¹Others said, "This doesn't sound like a man possessed by a demon! Can a demon open the eyes of the blind?"

Jesus Claims to Be the Son of God

²²It was now winter, and Jesus was in Jerusalem at the time of Hanukkah, the Festival of Dedication. ²³He was in the Temple, walking through the section known as Solomon's Colonnade. ²⁴The people surrounded him and asked, "How long are you going to keep us in suspense? If you are the Messiah, tell us plainly."

²⁵Jesus replied, "I have already told you, and you don't believe me. The proof is the work I do in my Father's name. ²⁶But you don't believe me because you are not my sheep. ²⁷My sheep listen to my voice; I know them, and they follow me. ²⁸I give them eternal life, and they will never perish. No one can snatch them away from me, ²⁹for my Father has given them to me, and he is more powerful than anyone else.* No one can snatch them from the Father's hand. ³⁰The Father and I are one."

³¹Once again the people picked up stones to kill him. ³²Jesus said, "At my Father's direction I have done many good works. For which one are you going to stone me?"

9:35 Some manuscripts read *the Son of God?* "Son of Man" is a title Jesus used for himself. **9:38-39a** Some manuscripts do not include *"Yes, Lord, I believe!" the man said. And he worshiped Jesus. Then Jesus told him.* **9:39b** Greek *those who see.* **10:8** Some manuscripts do not include *before me.* **10:9** Or *will find safety.* **10:19** Greek *Jewish people;* also in 10:24, 31. **10:29** Other manuscripts read *for what my Father has given me is more powerful than anything;* still others read *for regarding that which my Father has given me, he is greater than all.*

³³They replied, "We're stoning you not for any good work, but for blasphemy! You, a mere man, claim to be God."

³⁴Jesus replied, "It is written in your own Scriptures* that God said to certain leaders of the people, 'I say, you are gods!'* ³⁵And you know that the Scriptures cannot be altered. So if those people who received God's message were called 'gods,' ³⁶why do you call it blasphemy when I say, 'I am the Son of God'? After all, the Father set me apart and sent me into the world. ³⁷Don't believe me unless I carry out my Father's work. ³⁸But if I do his work, believe in the evidence of the miraculous works I have done, even if you don't believe me. Then you will know and understand that the Father is in me, and I am in the Father."

³⁹Once again they tried to arrest him, but he got away and left them. ⁴⁰He went beyond the Jordan River near the place where John was first baptizing and stayed there awhile. ⁴¹And many followed him. "John didn't perform miraculous signs," they remarked to one another, "but everything he said about this man has come true." ⁴²And many who were there believed in Jesus.

The Raising of Lazarus

11 A man named Lazarus was sick. He lived in Bethany with his sisters, Mary and Martha. ²This is the Mary who later poured the expensive perfume on the Lord's feet and wiped them with her hair.* Her brother, Lazarus, was sick. ³So the two sisters sent a message to Jesus telling him, "Lord, your dear friend is very sick."

⁴But when Jesus heard about it he said, "Lazarus's sickness will not end in death. No, it happened for the glory of God so that the Son of God will receive glory from this." ⁵So although Jesus loved Martha, Mary, and Lazarus, ⁶he stayed where he was for the next two days. ⁷Finally, he said to his disciples, "Let's go back to Judea."

⁸But his disciples objected. "Rabbi," they said, "only a few days ago the people* in Judea were trying to stone you. Are you going there again?"

⁹Jesus replied, "There are twelve hours of daylight every day. During the day people can walk safely. They can see because they have the light of this world. ¹⁰But at night there is danger of stumbling because they have no light."

¹¹Then he said, "Our friend Lazarus has fallen asleep, but now I will go and wake him up."

¹²The disciples said, "Lord, if he is sleeping, he will soon get better!" ¹³They thought Jesus meant Lazarus was simply sleeping, but Jesus meant Lazarus had died.

¹⁴So he told them plainly, "Lazarus is dead. ¹⁵And for your sakes, I'm glad I wasn't there, for now you will really believe. Come, let's go see him."

¹⁶Thomas, nicknamed the Twin,* said to his fellow disciples, "Let's go, too—and die with Jesus."

¹⁷When Jesus arrived at Bethany, he was told that Lazarus had already been in his grave for four days. ¹⁸Bethany was only a few miles* down the road from Jerusalem, ¹⁹and many of the people had come to console Martha and Mary in their loss. ²⁰When Martha got word that Jesus was coming, she went to meet him. But Mary stayed in the house. ²¹Martha said to Jesus, "Lord, if only you had been here, my brother would not have died. ²²But even now I know that God will give you whatever you ask."

²³Jesus told her, "Your brother will rise again."

²⁴"Yes," Martha said, "he will rise when everyone else rises, at the last day."

²⁵Jesus told her, "I am the resurrection and the life.* Anyone who believes in me will live, even after dying. ²⁶Everyone who lives in me and believes in me will never ever die. Do you believe this, Martha?"

²⁷"Yes, Lord," she told him. "I have always believed you are the Messiah, the Son of God, the one who has come into the world from God." ²⁸Then she returned to Mary. She called Mary aside from the mourners and told her, "The Teacher is here and wants to see you." ²⁹So Mary immediately went to him.

³⁰Jesus had stayed outside the village, at the place where Martha met him. ³¹When the people who were at the house consoling Mary saw her leave so hastily, they assumed she was going to Lazarus's grave to weep. So they followed her there. ³²When Mary arrived and saw Jesus, she fell at his feet and said, "Lord, if only you had been here, my brother would not have died."

³³When Jesus saw her weeping and saw the other people wailing with her, a deep anger welled up within him,* and he was deeply

10:34a Greek *your own law.*   10:34b Ps 82:6.   11:2 This incident is recorded in chapter 12.   11:8 Greek *Jewish people;* also in 11:19, 31, 33, 36, 45, 54.   11:16 Greek *Thomas, who was called Didymus.*   11:18 Greek *was about 15 stadia* [about 2.8 kilometers]. 11:25 Some manuscripts do not include *and the life.*   11:33 Or *he was angry in his spirit.*

troubled. 34"Where have you put him?" he asked them.

They told him, "Lord, come and see." 35Then Jesus wept. 36The people who were standing nearby said, "See how much he loved him!" 37But some said, "This man healed a blind man. Couldn't he have kept Lazarus from dying?"

38Jesus was still angry as he arrived at the tomb, a cave with a stone rolled across its entrance. 39"Roll the stone aside," Jesus told them.

But Martha, the dead man's sister, protested, "Lord, he has been dead for four days. The smell will be terrible."

40Jesus responded, "Didn't I tell you that you would see God's glory if you believe?" 41So they rolled the stone aside. Then Jesus looked up to heaven and said, "Father, thank you for hearing me. 42You always hear me, but I said it out loud for the sake of all these people standing here, so that they will believe you sent me." 43Then Jesus shouted, "Lazarus, come out!" 44And the dead man came out, his hands and feet bound in graveclothes, his face wrapped in a headcloth. Jesus told them, "Unwrap him and let him go!"

The Plot to Kill Jesus

45Many of the people who were with Mary believed in Jesus when they saw this happen. 46But some went to the Pharisees and told them what Jesus had done. 47Then the leading priests and Pharisees called the high council* together. "What are we going to do?" they asked each other. "This man certainly performs many miraculous signs. 48If we allow him to go on like this, soon everyone will believe in him. Then the Roman army will come and destroy both our Temple* and our nation."

49Caiaphas, who was high priest at that time,* said, "You don't know what you're talking about! 50You don't realize that it's better for you that one man should die for the people than for the whole nation to be destroyed."

51He did not say this on his own; as high priest at that time he was led to prophesy that Jesus would die for the entire nation. 52And not only for that nation, but to bring together and unite all the children of God scattered around the world.

53So from that time on, the Jewish leaders began to plot Jesus' death. 54As a result, Jesus stopped his public ministry among the people and left Jerusalem. He went to a place near the wilderness, to the village of Ephraim, and stayed there with his disciples.

55It was now almost time for the Jewish Passover celebration, and many people from all over the country arrived in Jerusalem several days early so they could go through the purification ceremony before Passover began. 56They kept looking for Jesus, but as they stood around in the Temple, they said to each other, "What do you think? He won't come for Passover, will he?" 57Meanwhile, the leading priests and Pharisees had publicly ordered that anyone seeing Jesus must report it immediately so they could arrest him.

Jesus Anointed at Bethany

12 Six days before the Passover celebration began, Jesus arrived in Bethany, the home of Lazarus—the man he had raised from the dead. 2A dinner was prepared in Jesus' honor. Martha served, and Lazarus was among those who ate* with him. 3Then Mary took a twelve-ounce jar* of expensive perfume made from essence of nard, and she anointed Jesus' feet with it, wiping his feet with her hair. The house was filled with the fragrance.

4But Judas Iscariot, the disciple who would soon betray him, said, 5"That perfume was worth a year's wages.* It should have been sold and the money given to the poor." 6Not that he cared for the poor—he was a thief, and since he was in charge of the disciples' money, he often stole some for himself.

7Jesus replied, "Leave her alone. She did this in preparation for my burial. 8You will always have the poor among you, but you will not always have me."

9When all the people* heard of Jesus' arrival, they flocked to see him and also to see Lazarus, the man Jesus had raised from the dead. 10Then the leading priests decided to kill Lazarus, too, 11for it was because of him that many of the people had deserted them* and believed in Jesus.

Jesus' Triumphant Entry

12The next day, the news that Jesus was on the way to Jerusalem swept through the city. A large crowd of Passover visitors 13took palm

---

11:47 Greek *the Sanhedrin.*   11:48 Or *our position;* Greek reads *our place.*   11:49 Greek *that year;* also in 11:51.   12:2 Or *who reclined.*   12:3 Greek *took 1 litra* [327 grams].   12:5 Greek *worth 300 denarii.* A denarius was equivalent to a laborer's full day's wage.   12:9 Greek *Jewish people;* also in 12:11.   12:11 Or *had deserted their traditions;* Greek reads *had deserted.*

branches and went down the road to meet him. They shouted,

> "Praise God!*
> Blessings on the one who comes in the
> name of the LORD!
> Hail to the King of Israel!"*

¹⁴Jesus found a young donkey and rode on it, fulfilling the prophecy that said:

> ¹⁵ "Don't be afraid, people of Jerusalem.*
> Look, your King is coming,
> riding on a donkey's colt."*

¹⁶His disciples didn't understand at the time that this was a fulfillment of prophecy. But after Jesus entered into his glory, they remembered what had happened and realized that these things had been written about him. ¹⁷Many in the crowd had seen Jesus call Lazarus from the tomb, raising him from the dead, and they were telling others* about it. ¹⁸That was the reason so many went out to meet him—because they had heard about this miraculous sign. ¹⁹Then the Pharisees said to each other, "There's nothing we can do. Look, everyone* has gone after him!"

Jesus Predicts His Death

²⁰Some Greeks who had come to Jerusalem for the Passover celebration ²¹paid a visit to Philip, who was from Bethsaida in Galilee. They said, "Sir, we want to meet Jesus." ²²Philip told Andrew about it, and they went together to ask Jesus.

²³Jesus replied, "Now the time has come for the Son of Man* to enter into his glory. ²⁴I tell you the truth, unless a kernel of wheat is planted in the soil and dies, it remains alone. But its death will produce many new kernels— a plentiful harvest of new lives. ²⁵Those who love their life in this world will lose it. Those who care nothing for their life in this world will keep it for eternity. ²⁶Anyone who wants to serve me must follow me, because my servants must be where I am. And the Father will honor anyone who serves me.

²⁷"Now my soul is deeply troubled. Should I pray, 'Father, save me from this hour'? But this is the very reason I came! ²⁸Father, bring glory to your name."

Then a voice spoke from heaven, saying, "I have already brought glory to my name, and I will do so again." ²⁹When the crowd heard the voice, some thought it was thunder, while others declared an angel had spoken to him.

³⁰Then Jesus told them, "The voice was for your benefit, not mine. ³¹The time for judging this world has come, when Satan, the ruler of this world, will be cast out. ³²And when I am lifted up from the earth, I will draw everyone to myself." ³³He said this to indicate how he was going to die.

³⁴The crowd responded, "We understood from Scripture* that the Messiah would live forever. How can you say the Son of Man will die? Just who is this Son of Man, anyway?"

³⁵Jesus replied, "My light will shine for you just a little longer. Walk in the light while you can, so the darkness will not overtake you. Those who walk in the darkness cannot see where they are going. ³⁶Put your trust in the light while there is still time; then you will become children of the light."

After saying these things, Jesus went away and was hidden from them.

The Unbelief of the People

³⁷But despite all the miraculous signs Jesus had done, most of the people still did not believe in him. ³⁸This is exactly what Isaiah the prophet had predicted:

> "LORD, who has believed our message?
> To whom has the LORD revealed his
> powerful arm?"*

³⁹But the people couldn't believe, for as Isaiah also said,

> ⁴⁰ "The Lord has blinded their eyes
> and hardened their hearts—
> so that their eyes cannot see,
> and their hearts cannot understand,
> and they cannot turn to me
> and have me heal them."*

⁴¹Isaiah was referring to Jesus when he said this, because he saw the future and spoke of the Messiah's glory. ⁴²Many people did believe in him, however, including some of the Jewish leaders. But they wouldn't admit it for fear that the Pharisees would expel them from the synagogue. ⁴³For they loved human praise more than the praise of God.

12:13a Greek *Hosanna,* an exclamation of praise adapted from a Hebrew expression that means "save now." 12:13b Ps 118:25-26; Zeph 3:15. 12:15a Greek *daughter of Zion.* 12:15b Zech 9:9. 12:17 Greek *were testifying.* 12:19 Greek *the world.* 12:23 "Son of Man" is a title Jesus used for himself. 12:34 Greek *from the law.* 12:38 Isa 53:1. 12:40 Isa 6:10.

⁴⁴Jesus shouted to the crowds, "If you trust me, you are trusting not only me, but also God who sent me. ⁴⁵For when you see me, you are seeing the one who sent me. ⁴⁶I have come as a light to shine in this dark world, so that all who put their trust in me will no longer remain in the dark. ⁴⁷I will not judge those who hear me but don't obey me, for I have come to save the world and not to judge it. ⁴⁸But all who reject me and my message will be judged on the day of judgment by the truth I have spoken. ⁴⁹I don't speak on my own authority. The Father who sent me has commanded me what to say and how to say it. ⁵⁰And I know his commands lead to eternal life; so I say whatever the Father tells me to say."

Jesus Washes His Disciples' Feet

13 Before the Passover celebration, Jesus knew that his hour had come to leave this world and return to his Father. He had loved his disciples during his ministry on earth, and now he loved them to the very end.* ²It was time for supper, and the devil had already prompted Judas,* son of Simon Iscariot, to betray Jesus. ³Jesus knew that the Father had given him authority over everything and that he had come from God and would return to God. ⁴So he got up from the table, took off his robe, wrapped a towel around his waist, ⁵and poured water into a basin. Then he began to wash the disciples' feet, drying them with the towel he had around him.

⁶When Jesus came to Simon Peter, Peter said to him, "Lord, are you going to wash my feet?"

⁷Jesus replied, "You don't understand now what I am doing, but someday you will."

⁸"No," Peter protested, "you will never ever wash my feet!"

Jesus replied, "Unless I wash you, you won't belong to me."

⁹Simon Peter exclaimed, "Then wash my hands and head as well, Lord, not just my feet!"

¹⁰Jesus replied, "A person who has bathed all over does not need to wash, except for the feet,* to be entirely clean. And you disciples are clean, but not all of you." ¹¹For Jesus knew who would betray him. That is what he meant when he said, "Not all of you are clean."

¹²After washing their feet, he put on his robe again and sat down and asked, "Do you understand what I was doing? ¹³You call me 'Teacher' and 'Lord,' and you are right, because that's what I am. ¹⁴And since I, your Lord and Teacher, have washed your feet, you ought to wash each other's feet. ¹⁵I have given you an example to follow. Do as I have done to you. ¹⁶I tell you the truth, slaves are not greater than their master. Nor is the messenger more important than the one who sends the message. ¹⁷Now that you know these things, God will bless you for doing them.

Jesus Predicts His Betrayal

¹⁸"I am not saying these things to all of you; I know the ones I have chosen. But this fulfills the Scripture that says, 'The one who eats my food has turned against me.'* ¹⁹I tell you this beforehand, so that when it happens you will believe that I Am the Messiah.* ²⁰I tell you the truth, anyone who welcomes my messenger is welcoming me, and anyone who welcomes me is welcoming the Father who sent me."

²¹Now Jesus was deeply troubled,* and he exclaimed, "I tell you the truth, one of you will betray me!"

²²The disciples looked at each other, wondering whom he could mean. ²³The disciple Jesus loved was sitting next to Jesus at the table.* ²⁴Simon Peter motioned to him to ask, "Who's he talking about?" ²⁵So that disciple leaned over to Jesus and asked, "Lord, who is it?"

²⁶Jesus responded, "It is the one to whom I give the bread I dip in the bowl." And when he had dipped it, he gave it to Judas, son of Simon Iscariot. ²⁷When Judas had eaten the bread, Satan entered into him. Then Jesus told him, "Hurry and do what you're going to do." ²⁸None of the others at the table knew what Jesus meant. ²⁹Since Judas was their treasurer, some thought Jesus was telling him to go and pay for the food or to give some money to the poor. ³⁰So Judas left at once, going out into the night.

Jesus Predicts Peter's Denial

³¹As soon as Judas left the room, Jesus said, "The time has come for the Son of Man* to enter into his glory, and God will be glorified because of him. ³²And since God receives glory because of the Son,* he will give his own glory to the Son, and he will do so at once. ³³Dear children, I will be with you only a little longer. And as I told the Jewish leaders, you will search for

---

13:1 Or *he showed them the full extent of his love.*   13:2 Or *the devil had already intended for Judas.*   13:10 Some manuscripts do not include *except for the feet.*   13:18 Ps 41:9.   13:19 Or *that the 'I Am' has come;* or *that I am the Lord;* Greek reads *that I am.* See Exod 3:14.   13:21 Greek *was troubled in his spirit.*   13:23 Greek *was reclining on Jesus' bosom.* The "disciple Jesus loved" was probably John.   13:31 "Son of Man" is a title Jesus used for himself.   13:32 Several early manuscripts do not include *And since God receives glory because of the Son.*

me, but you can't come where I am going. ³⁴So now I am giving you a new commandment: Love each other. Just as I have loved you, you should love each other. ³⁵Your love for one another will prove to the world that you are my disciples."

³⁶Simon Peter asked, "Lord, where are you going?"

And Jesus replied, "You can't go with me now, but you will follow me later."

³⁷"But why can't I come now, Lord?" he asked. "I'm ready to die for you."

³⁸Jesus answered, "Die for me? I tell you the truth, Peter—before the rooster crows tomorrow morning, you will deny three times that you even know me.

Jesus, the Way to the Father

14 "Don't let your hearts be troubled. Trust in God, and trust also in me. ²There is more than enough room in my Father's home.* If this were not so, would I have told you that I am going to prepare a place for you?* ³When everything is ready, I will come and get you, so that you will always be with me where I am. ⁴And you know the way to where I am going."

⁵"No, we don't know, Lord," Thomas said. "We have no idea where you are going, so how can we know the way?"

⁶Jesus told him, "I am the way, the truth, and the life. No one can come to the Father except through me. ⁷If you had really known me, you would know who my Father is.* From now on, you do know him and have seen him!"

⁸Philip said, "Lord, show us the Father, and we will be satisfied."

⁹Jesus replied, "Have I been with you all this time, Philip, and yet you still don't know who I am? Anyone who has seen me has seen the Father! So why are you asking me to show him to you? ¹⁰Don't you believe that I am in the Father and the Father is in me? The words I speak are not my own, but my Father who lives in me does his work through me. ¹¹Just believe that I am in the Father and the Father is in me. Or at least believe because of the work you have seen me do.

¹²"I tell you the truth, anyone who believes in me will do the same works I have done, and even greater works, because I am going to be with the Father. ¹³You can ask for anything in my name, and I will do it, so that the Son can bring glory to the Father. ¹⁴Yes, ask me for anything in my name, and I will do it!

Jesus Promises the Holy Spirit

¹⁵"If you love me, obey* my commandments. ¹⁶And I will ask the Father, and he will give you another Advocate,* who will never leave you. ¹⁷He is the Holy Spirit, who leads into all truth. The world cannot receive him, because it isn't looking for him and doesn't recognize him. But you know him, because he lives with you now and later will be in you.* ¹⁸No, I will not abandon you as orphans—I will come to you. ¹⁹Soon the world will no longer see me, but you will see me. Since I live, you also will live. ²⁰When I am raised to life again, you will know that I am in my Father, and you are in me, and I am in you. ²¹Those who accept my commandments and obey them are the ones who love me. And because they love me, my Father will love them. And I will love them and reveal myself to each of them."

²²Judas (not Judas Iscariot, but the other disciple with that name) said to him, "Lord, why are you going to reveal yourself only to us and not to the world at large?"

²³Jesus replied, "All who love me will do what I say. My Father will love them, and we will come and make our home with each of them. ²⁴Anyone who doesn't love me will not obey me. And remember, my words are not my own. What I am telling you is from the Father who sent me. ²⁵I am telling you these things now while I am still with you. ²⁶But when the Father sends the Advocate as my representative—that is, the Holy Spirit—he will teach you everything and will remind you of everything I have told you.

²⁷"I am leaving you with a gift—peace of mind and heart. And the peace I give is a gift the world cannot give. So don't be troubled or afraid. ²⁸Remember what I told you: I am going away, but I will come back to you again. If you really loved me, you would be happy that I am going to the Father, who is greater than I am. ²⁹I have told you these things before they happen so that when they do happen, you will believe.

³⁰"I don't have much more time to talk to you, because the ruler of this world approaches. He has no power over me, ³¹but I will do what the Father requires of me, so that the world

14:2a Or *There are many rooms in my Father's house.* **14:2b** Or *If this were not so, I would have told you that I am going to prepare a place for you.* Some manuscripts read *If this were not so, I would have told you. I am going to prepare a place for you.* **14:7** Some manuscripts read *If you have really known me, you will know who my Father is.* **14:15** Other manuscripts read *you will obey;* still others read *you should obey.* **14:16** Or *Comforter,* or *Encourager,* or *Counselor.* Greek reads *Paraclete;* also in 14:26. **14:17** Some manuscripts read *and is in you.*

will know that I love the Father. Come, let's be going.

Jesus, the True Vine

15 "I am the true grapevine, and my Father is the gardener. ²He cuts off every branch of mine that doesn't produce fruit, and he prunes the branches that do bear fruit so they will produce even more. ³You have already been pruned and purified by the message I have given you. ⁴Remain in me, and I will remain in you. For a branch cannot produce fruit if it is severed from the vine, and you cannot be fruitful unless you remain in me.

⁵"Yes, I am the vine; you are the branches. Those who remain in me, and I in them, will produce much fruit. For apart from me you can do nothing. ⁶Anyone who does not remain in me is thrown away like a useless branch and withers. Such branches are gathered into a pile to be burned. ⁷But if you remain in me and my words remain in you, you may ask for anything you want, and it will be granted! ⁸When you produce much fruit, you are my true disciples. This brings great glory to my Father.

⁹"I have loved you even as the Father has loved me. Remain in my love. ¹⁰When you obey my commandments, you remain in my love, just as I obey my Father's commandments and remain in his love. ¹¹I have told you these things so that you will be filled with my joy. Yes, your joy will overflow! ¹²This is my commandment: Love each other in the same way I have loved you. ¹³There is no greater love than to lay down one's life for one's friends. ¹⁴You are my friends if you do what I command. ¹⁵I no longer call you slaves, because a master doesn't confide in his slaves. Now you are my friends, since I have told you everything the Father told me. ¹⁶You didn't choose me. I chose you. I appointed you to go and produce lasting fruit, so that the Father will give you whatever you ask for, using my name. ¹⁷This is my command: Love each other.

The World's Hatred

¹⁸"If the world hates you, remember that it hated me first. ¹⁹The world would love you as one of its own if you belonged to it, but you are no longer part of the world. I chose you to come out of the world, so it hates you. ²⁰Do you remember what I told you? 'A slave is not greater than the master.' Since they persecuted me, naturally they will persecute you. And if

they had listened to me, they would listen to you. ²¹They will do all this to you because of me, for they have rejected the one who sent me. ²²They would not be guilty if I had not come and spoken to them. But now they have no excuse for their sin. ²³Anyone who hates me also hates my Father. ²⁴If I hadn't done such miraculous signs among them that no one else could do, they would not be guilty. But as it is, they have seen everything I did, yet they still hate me and my Father. ²⁵This fulfills what is written in their Scriptures*: 'They hated me without cause.'

²⁶"But I will send you the Advocate*—the Spirit of truth. He will come to you from the Father and will testify all about me. ²⁷And you must also testify about me because you have been with me from the beginning of my ministry.

16 "I have told you these things so that you won't abandon your faith. ²For you will be expelled from the synagogues, and the time is coming when those who kill you will think they are doing a holy service for God. ³This is because they have never known the Father or me. ⁴Yes, I'm telling you these things now, so that when they happen, you will remember my warning. I didn't tell you earlier because I was going to be with you for a while longer.

The Work of the Holy Spirit

⁵"But now I am going away to the one who sent me, and not one of you is asking where I am going. ⁶Instead, you grieve because of what I've told you. ⁷But in fact, it is best for you that I go away, because if I don't, the Advocate* won't come. If I do go away, then I will send him to you. ⁸And when he comes, he will convict the world of its sin, and of God's righteousness, and of the coming judgment. ⁹The world's sin is that it refuses to believe in me. ¹⁰Righteousness is available because I go to the Father, and you will see me no more. ¹¹Judgment will come because the ruler of this world has already been judged.

¹²"There is so much more I want to tell you, but you can't bear it now. ¹³When the Spirit of truth comes, he will guide you into all truth. He will not speak on his own but will tell you what he has heard. He will tell you about the future. ¹⁴He will bring me glory by telling you whatever he receives from me. ¹⁵All that belongs to the Father is mine; this is why I said,

---

15:25 Greek *in their law*. Pss 35:19; 69:4.   15:26 Or *Comforter*, or *Encourager*, or *Counselor*. Greek reads *Paraclete*.   16:7 Or *Comforter*, or *Encourager*, or *Counselor*. Greek reads *Paraclete*.

'The Spirit will tell you whatever he receives from me.'

Sadness Will Be Turned to Joy

¹⁶"In a little while you won't see me anymore. But a little while after that, you will see me again."

¹⁷Some of the disciples asked each other, "What does he mean when he says, 'In a little while you won't see me, but then you will see me,' and 'I am going to the Father'? ¹⁸And what does he mean by 'a little while'? We don't understand."

¹⁹Jesus realized they wanted to ask him about it, so he said, "Are you asking yourselves what I meant? I said in a little while you won't see me, but a little while after that you will see me again. ²⁰I tell you the truth, you will weep and mourn over what is going to happen to me, but the world will rejoice. You will grieve, but your grief will suddenly turn to wonderful joy. ²¹It will be like a woman suffering the pains of labor. When her child is born, her anguish gives way to joy because she has brought a new baby into the world. ²²So you have sorrow now, but I will see you again; then you will rejoice, and no one can rob you of that joy. ²³At that time you won't need to ask me for anything. I tell you the truth, you will ask the Father directly, and he will grant your request because you use my name. ²⁴You haven't done this before. Ask, using my name, and you will receive, and you will have abundant joy.

²⁵"I have spoken of these matters in figures of speech, but soon I will stop speaking figuratively and will tell you plainly all about the Father. ²⁶Then you will ask in my name. I'm not saying I will ask the Father on your behalf, ²⁷for the Father himself loves you dearly because you love me and believe that I came from God.* ²⁸Yes, I came from the Father into the world, and now I will leave the world and return to the Father."

²⁹Then his disciples said, "At last you are speaking plainly and not figuratively. ³⁰Now we understand that you know everything, and there's no need to question you. From this we believe that you came from God."

³¹Jesus asked, "Do you finally believe? ³²But the time is coming—indeed it's here now—when you will be scattered, each one going his own way, leaving me alone. Yet I am not alone because the Father is with me. ³³I have told you all this so that you may have peace in me. Here on earth you will have many trials and sorrows. But take heart, because I have overcome the world."

The Prayer of Jesus

17 After saying all these things, Jesus looked up to heaven and said, "Father, the hour has come. Glorify your Son so he can give glory back to you. ²For you have given him authority over everyone. He gives eternal life to each one you have given him. ³And this is the way to have eternal life—to know you, the only true God, and Jesus Christ, the one you sent to earth. ⁴I brought glory to you here on earth by completing the work you gave me to do. ⁵Now, Father, bring me into the glory we shared before the world began.

⁶"I have revealed you* to the ones you gave me from this world. They were always yours. You gave them to me, and they have kept your word. ⁷Now they know that everything I have is a gift from you, ⁸for I have passed on to them the message you gave me. They accepted it and know that I came from you, and they believe you sent me.

⁹"My prayer is not for the world, but for those you have given me, because they belong to you. ¹⁰All who are mine belong to you, and you have given them to me, so they bring me glory. ¹¹Now I am departing from the world; they are staying in this world, but I am coming to you. Holy Father, you have given me your name;* now protect them by the power of your name so that they will be united just as we are. ¹²During my time here, I protected them by the power of the name you gave me.* I guarded them so that not one was lost, except the one headed for destruction, as the Scriptures foretold.

¹³"Now I am coming to you. I told them many things while I was with them in this world so they would be filled with my joy. ¹⁴I have given them your word. And the world hates them because they do not belong to the world, just as I do not belong to the world. ¹⁵I'm not asking you to take them out of the world, but to keep them safe from the evil one. ¹⁶They do not belong to this world any more than I do. ¹⁷Make them holy by your truth; teach them your word, which is truth. ¹⁸Just as you sent me into the world, I am sending them into the world. ¹⁹And I give myself as a holy sacrifice for them so they can be made holy by your truth.

16:27 Some manuscripts read *from the Father.* 17:6 Greek *have revealed your name;* also in 17:26. 17:11 Some manuscripts read *you have given me these [disciples].* 17:12 Some manuscripts read *I protected those you gave me, by the power of your name.*

²⁰"I am praying not only for these disciples but also for all who will ever believe in me through their message. ²¹I pray that they will all be one, just as you and I are one—as you are in me, Father, and I am in you. And may they be in us so that the world will believe you sent me.

²²"I have given them the glory you gave me, so they may be one as we are one. ²³I am in them and you are in me. May they experience such perfect unity that the world will know that you sent me and that you love them as much as you love me. ²⁴Father, I want these whom you have given me to be with me where I am. Then they can see all the glory you gave me because you loved me even before the world began!

²⁵"O righteous Father, the world doesn't know you, but I do; and these disciples know you sent me. ²⁶I have revealed you to them, and I will continue to do so. Then your love for me will be in them, and I will be in them."

Jesus Is Betrayed and Arrested

18 After saying these things, Jesus crossed the Kidron Valley with his disciples and entered a grove of olive trees. ²Judas, the betrayer, knew this place, because Jesus had often gone there with his disciples. ³The leading priests and Pharisees had given Judas a contingent of Roman soldiers and Temple guards to accompany him. Now with blazing torches, lanterns, and weapons, they arrived at the olive grove.

⁴Jesus fully realized all that was going to happen to him, so he stepped forward to meet them. "Who are you looking for?" he asked.

⁵"Jesus the Nazarene,"* they replied.

"I AM he,"* Jesus said. (Judas, who betrayed him, was standing with them.) ⁶As Jesus said "I AM he," they all drew back and fell to the ground! ⁷Once more he asked them, "Who are you looking for?"

And again they replied, "Jesus the Nazarene."

⁸"I told you that I AM he," Jesus said. "And since I am the one you want, let these others go." ⁹He did this to fulfill his own statement: "I did not lose a single one of those you have given me."*

¹⁰Then Simon Peter drew a sword and slashed off the right ear of Malchus, the high priest's slave. ¹¹But Jesus said to Peter, "Put your sword back into its sheath. Shall I not drink from the cup of suffering the Father has given me?"

Jesus at the High Priest's House

¹²So the soldiers, their commanding officer, and the Temple guards arrested Jesus and tied him up. ¹³First they took him to Annas, since he was the father-in-law of Caiaphas, the high priest at that time.* ¹⁴Caiaphas was the one who had told the other Jewish leaders, "It's better that one man should die for the people."

Peter's First Denial

¹⁵Simon Peter followed Jesus, as did another of the disciples. That other disciple was acquainted with the high priest, so he was allowed to enter the high priest's courtyard with Jesus. ¹⁶Peter had to stay outside the gate. Then the disciple who knew the high priest spoke to the woman watching at the gate, and she let Peter in. ¹⁷The woman asked Peter, "You're not one of that man's disciples, are you?"

"No," he said, "I am not."

¹⁸Because it was cold, the household servants and the guards had made a charcoal fire. They stood around it, warming themselves, and Peter stood with them, warming himself.

The High Priest Questions Jesus

¹⁹Inside, the high priest began asking Jesus about his followers and what he had been teaching them. ²⁰Jesus replied, "Everyone knows what I teach. I have preached regularly in the synagogues and the Temple, where the people* gather. I have not spoken in secret. ²¹Why are you asking me this question? Ask those who heard me. They know what I said."

²²Then one of the Temple guards standing nearby slapped Jesus across the face. "Is that the way to answer the high priest?" he demanded.

²³Jesus replied, "If I said anything wrong, you must prove it. But if I'm speaking the truth, why are you beating me?"

²⁴Then Annas bound Jesus and sent him to Caiaphas, the high priest.

Peter's Second and Third Denials

²⁵Meanwhile, as Simon Peter was standing by the fire warming himself, they asked him again, "You're not one of his disciples, are you?"

He denied it, saying, "No, I am not."

²⁶But one of the household slaves of the high priest, a relative of the man whose ear Peter had cut off, asked, "Didn't I see you out there in the

18:5a Or *Jesus of Nazareth;* also in 18:7.   **18:5b** Or *"The 'I AM' is here";* or *"I am the LORD";* Greek reads *I am;* also in 18:6, 8. See Exod 3:14.   **18:9** See John 6:39 and 17:12.   **18:13** Greek *that year.*   **18:20** Greek *Jewish people;* also in 18:38.

olive grove with Jesus?" ²⁷Again Peter denied it. And immediately a rooster crowed.

Jesus' Trial before Pilate

²⁸Jesus' trial before Caiaphas ended in the early hours of the morning. Then he was taken to the headquarters of the Roman governor.* His accusers didn't go inside because it would defile them, and they wouldn't be allowed to celebrate the Passover. ²⁹So Pilate, the governor, went out to them and asked, "What is your charge against this man?"

³⁰"We wouldn't have handed him over to you if he weren't a criminal!" they retorted.

³¹"Then take him away and judge him by your own law," Pilate told them.

"Only the Romans are permitted to execute someone," the Jewish leaders replied. ³²(This fulfilled Jesus' prediction about the way he would die.*)

³³Then Pilate went back into his headquarters and called for Jesus to be brought to him. "Are you the king of the Jews?" he asked him.

³⁴Jesus replied, "Is this your own question, or did others tell you about me?"

³⁵"Am I a Jew?" Pilate retorted. "Your own people and their leading priests brought you to me for trial. Why? What have you done?"

³⁶Jesus answered, "My Kingdom is not an earthly kingdom. If it were, my followers would fight to keep me from being handed over to the Jewish leaders. But my Kingdom is not of this world."

³⁷Pilate said, "So you are a king?"

Jesus responded, "You say I am a king. Actually, I was born and came into the world to testify to the truth. All who love the truth recognize that what I say is true."

³⁸"What is truth?" Pilate asked. Then he went out again to the people and told them, "He is not guilty of any crime. ³⁹But you have a custom of asking me to release one prisoner each year at Passover. Would you like me to release this 'King of the Jews'?"

⁴⁰But they shouted back, "No! Not this man. We want Barabbas!" (Barabbas was a revolutionary.)

Jesus Sentenced to Death

19 Then Pilate had Jesus flogged with a lead-tipped whip. ²The soldiers wove a crown of thorns and put it on his head, and they put a purple robe on him. ³"Hail! King of the Jews!" they mocked, as they slapped him across the face.

⁴Pilate went outside again and said to the people, "I am going to bring him out to you now, but understand clearly that I find him not guilty." ⁵Then Jesus came out wearing the crown of thorns and the purple robe. And Pilate said, "Look, here is the man!"

⁶When they saw him, the leading priests and Temple guards began shouting, "Crucify him! Crucify him!"

"Take him yourselves and crucify him," Pilate said. "I find him not guilty."

⁷The Jewish leaders replied, "By our law he ought to die because he called himself the Son of God."

⁸When Pilate heard this, he was more frightened than ever. ⁹He took Jesus back into the headquarters* again and asked him, "Where are you from?" But Jesus gave no answer. ¹⁰"Why don't you talk to me?" Pilate demanded. "Don't you realize that I have the power to release you or crucify you?"

¹¹Then Jesus said, "You would have no power over me at all unless it were given to you from above. So the one who handed me over to you has the greater sin."

¹²Then Pilate tried to release him, but the Jewish leaders shouted, "If you release this man, you are no 'friend of Caesar.'* Anyone who declares himself a king is a rebel against Caesar."

¹³When they said this, Pilate brought Jesus out to them again. Then Pilate sat down on the judgment seat on the platform that is called the Stone Pavement (in Hebrew, *Gabbatha*). ¹⁴It was now about noon on the day of preparation for the Passover. And Pilate said to the people,* "Look, here is your king!"

¹⁵"Away with him," they yelled. "Away with him! Crucify him!"

"What? Crucify your king?" Pilate asked.

"We have no king but Caesar," the leading priests shouted back.

¹⁶Then Pilate turned Jesus over to them to be crucified.

The Crucifixion

So they took Jesus away. ¹⁷Carrying the cross by himself, he went to the place called Place of the Skull (in Hebrew, *Golgotha*). ¹⁸There they nailed him to the cross. Two others were crucified with him, one on either side, with Jesus between them. ¹⁹And Pilate posted a sign on the

---

18:28 Greek *to the Praetorium*; also in 18:33.   18:32 See John 12:32-33.   19:9 Greek *the Praetorium*.   19:12 "Friend of Caesar" is a technical term that refers to an ally of the emperor.   19:14 Greek *Jewish people*; also in 19:20.

cross that read, "Jesus of Nazareth,* the King of the Jews." 20The place where Jesus was crucified was near the city, and the sign was written in Hebrew, Latin, and Greek, so that many people could read it.

21Then the leading priests objected and said to Pilate, "Change it from 'The King of the Jews' to 'He said, I am King of the Jews.'"

22Pilate replied, "No, what I have written, I have written."

23When the soldiers had crucified Jesus, they divided his clothes among the four of them. They also took his robe, but it was seamless, woven in one piece from top to bottom. 24So they said, "Rather than tearing it apart, let's throw dice* for it." This fulfilled the Scripture that says, "They divided my garments among themselves and threw dice for my clothing."* So that is what they did.

25Standing near the cross were Jesus' mother, and his mother's sister, Mary (the wife of Clopas), and Mary Magdalene. 26When Jesus saw his mother standing there beside the disciple he loved, he said to her, "Dear woman, here is your son." 27And he said to this disciple, "Here is your mother." And from then on this disciple took her into his home.

The Death of Jesus

28Jesus knew that his mission was now finished, and to fulfill Scripture he said, "I am thirsty."* 29A jar of sour wine was sitting there, so they soaked a sponge in it, put it on a hyssop branch, and held it up to his lips. 30When Jesus had tasted it, he said, "It is finished!" Then he bowed his head and gave up his spirit.

31It was the day of preparation, and the Jewish leaders didn't want the bodies hanging there the next day, which was the Sabbath (and a very special Sabbath, because it was Passover week). So they asked Pilate to hasten their deaths by ordering that their legs be broken. Then their bodies could be taken down. 32So the soldiers came and broke the legs of the two men crucified with Jesus. 33But when they came to Jesus, they saw that he was already dead, so they didn't break his legs. 34One of the soldiers, however, pierced his side with a spear, and immediately blood and water flowed out. 35(This report is from an eyewitness giving an accurate account. He speaks the truth so that you also may continue to believe.*) 36These things happened in fulfillment of the Scriptures that say,

"Not one of his bones will be broken,"* 37and "They will look on the one they pierced."*

The Burial of Jesus

38Afterward Joseph of Arimathea, who had been a secret disciple of Jesus (because he feared the Jewish leaders), asked Pilate for permission to take down Jesus' body. When Pilate gave permission, Joseph came and took the body away. 39With him came Nicodemus, the man who had come to Jesus at night. He brought about seventy-five pounds* of perfumed ointment made from myrrh and aloes. 40Following Jewish burial custom, they wrapped Jesus' body with the spices in long sheets of linen cloth. 41The place of crucifixion was near a garden, where there was a new tomb, never used before. 42And so, because it was the day of preparation for the Jewish Passover* and since the tomb was close at hand, they laid Jesus there.

The Resurrection

20 Early on Sunday morning,* while it was still dark, Mary Magdalene came to the tomb and found that the stone had been rolled away from the entrance. 2She ran and found Simon Peter and the other disciple, the one whom Jesus loved. She said, "They have taken the Lord's body out of the tomb, and we don't know where they have put him!"

3Peter and the other disciple started out for the tomb. 4They were both running, but the other disciple outran Peter and reached the tomb first. 5He stooped and looked in and saw the linen wrappings lying there, but he didn't go in. 6Then Simon Peter arrived and went inside. He also noticed the linen wrappings lying there, 7while the cloth that had covered Jesus' head was folded up and lying apart from the other wrappings. 8Then the disciple who had reached the tomb first also went in, and he saw and believed—9for until then they still hadn't understood the Scriptures that said Jesus must rise from the dead. 10Then they went home.

Jesus Appears to Mary Magdalene

11Mary was standing outside the tomb crying, and as she wept, she stooped and looked in. 12She saw two white-robed angels, one sitting at the head and the other at the foot of the place where the body of Jesus had been lying. 13"Dear woman, why are you crying?" the angels asked her.

19:19 Or Jesus the Nazarene.   19:24a Greek cast lots.   19:24b Ps 22:18.   19:28 See Pss 22:15; 69:21.   19:35 Some manuscripts read that you also may believe.   19:36 Exod 12:46; Num 9:12; Ps 34:20.   19:37 Zech 12:10.   19:39 Greek 100 litras [32.7 kilograms].   19:42 Greek because of the Jewish day of preparation.   20:1 Greek On the first day of the week.

"Because they have taken away my Lord," she replied, "and I don't know where they have put him."

¹⁴She turned to leave and saw someone standing there. It was Jesus, but she didn't recognize him. ¹⁵"Dear woman, why are you crying?" Jesus asked her. "Who are you looking for?"

She thought he was the gardener. "Sir," she said, "if you have taken him away, tell me where you have put him, and I will go and get him."

¹⁶"Mary!" Jesus said.

She turned to him and cried out, "Rabboni!" (which is Hebrew for "Teacher").

¹⁷"Don't cling to me," Jesus said, "for I haven't yet ascended to the Father. But go find my brothers and tell them, 'I am ascending to my Father and your Father, to my God and your God.'"

¹⁸Mary Magdalene found the disciples and told them, "I have seen the Lord!" Then she gave them his message.

Jesus Appears to His Disciples

¹⁹That Sunday evening* the disciples were meeting behind locked doors because they were afraid of the Jewish leaders. Suddenly, Jesus was standing there among them! "Peace be with you," he said. ²⁰As he spoke, he showed them the wounds in his hands and his side. They were filled with joy when they saw the Lord! ²¹Again he said, "Peace be with you. As the Father has sent me, so I am sending you." ²²Then he breathed on them and said, "Receive the Holy Spirit. ²³If you forgive anyone's sins, they are forgiven. If you do not forgive them, they are not forgiven."

Jesus Appears to Thomas

²⁴One of the twelve disciples, Thomas (nicknamed the Twin),* was not with the others when Jesus came. ²⁵They told him, "We have seen the Lord!"

But he replied, "I won't believe it unless I see the nail wounds in his hands, put my fingers into them, and place my hand into the wound in his side."

²⁶Eight days later the disciples were together again, and this time Thomas was with them. The doors were locked; but suddenly, as before, Jesus was standing among them. "Peace be with you," he said. ²⁷Then he said to Thomas,

"Put your finger here, and look at my hands. Put your hand into the wound in my side. Don't be faithless any longer. Believe!"

²⁸"My Lord and my God!" Thomas exclaimed.

²⁹Then Jesus told him, "You believe because you have seen me. Blessed are those who believe without seeing me."

Purpose of the Book

³⁰The disciples saw Jesus do many other miraculous signs in addition to the ones recorded in this book. ³¹But these are written so that you may continue to believe* that Jesus is the Messiah, the Son of God, and that by believing in him you will have life by the power of his name.

Epilogue: Jesus Appears to Seven Disciples

21 Later, Jesus appeared again to the disciples beside the Sea of Galilee.* This is how it happened. ²Several of the disciples were there—Simon Peter, Thomas (nicknamed the Twin),* Nathanael from Cana in Galilee, the sons of Zebedee, and two other disciples.

³Simon Peter said, "I'm going fishing."

"We'll come, too," they all said. So they went out in the boat, but they caught nothing all night.

⁴At dawn Jesus was standing on the beach, but the disciples couldn't see who he was. ⁵He called out, "Fellows,* have you caught any fish?"

"No," they replied.

⁶Then he said, "Throw out your net on the right-hand side of the boat, and you'll get some!" So they did, and they couldn't haul in the net because there were so many fish in it.

⁷Then the disciple Jesus loved said to Peter, "It's the Lord!" When Simon Peter heard that it was the Lord, he put on his tunic (for he had stripped for work), jumped into the water, and headed to shore. ⁸The others stayed with the boat and pulled the loaded net to the shore, for they were only about a hundred yards* from shore. ⁹When they got there, they found breakfast waiting for them—fish cooking over a charcoal fire, and some bread.

¹⁰"Bring some of the fish you've just caught," Jesus said. ¹¹So Simon Peter went aboard and dragged the net to the shore. There were 153 large fish, and yet the net hadn't torn. ¹²"Now come and have some breakfast!" Jesus said. None of the disciples dared to ask

20:19 Greek *In the evening of that day, the first day of the week.*   **20:24** Greek *Thomas, who was called Didymus.*   **20:31** Some manuscripts read *that you may believe.*   **21:1** Greek *Sea of Tiberias,* another name for the Sea of Galilee.   **21:2** Greek *Thomas, who was called Didymus.*   **21:5** Greek *Children.*   **21:8** Greek *200 cubits* [90 meters].

him, "Who are you?" They knew it was the Lord. [13]Then Jesus served them the bread and the fish. [14]This was the third time Jesus had appeared to his disciples since he had been raised from the dead.

[15]After breakfast Jesus asked Simon Peter, "Simon son of John, do you love me more than these?*"

"Yes, Lord," Peter replied, "you know I love you."

"Then feed my lambs," Jesus told him.

[16]Jesus repeated the question: "Simon son of John, do you love me?"

"Yes, Lord," Peter said, "you know I love you."

"Then take care of my sheep," Jesus said.

[17]A third time he asked him, "Simon son of John, do you love me?"

Peter was hurt that Jesus asked the question a third time. He said, "Lord, you know everything. You know that I love you."

Jesus said, "Then feed my sheep.

[18]"I tell you the truth, when you were young, you were able to do as you liked; you dressed yourself and went wherever you wanted to go.

But when you are old, you will stretch out your hands, and others* will dress you and take you where you don't want to go." [19]Jesus said this to let him know by what kind of death he would glorify God. Then Jesus told him, "Follow me."

[20]Peter turned around and saw behind them the disciple Jesus loved—the one who had leaned over to Jesus during supper and asked, "Lord, who will betray you?" [21]Peter asked Jesus, "What about him, Lord?"

[22]Jesus replied, "If I want him to remain alive until I return, what is that to you? As for you, follow me." [23]So the rumor spread among the community of believers* that this disciple wouldn't die. But that isn't what Jesus said at all. He only said, "If I want him to remain alive until I return, what is that to you?"

[24]This disciple is the one who testifies to these events and has recorded them here. And we know that his account of these things is accurate.

[25]Jesus also did many other things. If they were all written down, I suppose the whole world could not contain the books that would be written.

21:15 Or *more than these others do?*   **21:18** Some manuscripts read *and another one.*   **21:23** Greek *the brothers.*

Acts of the Apostles

NEARLY TWO THOUSAND YEARS AGO, a match was struck in Palestine that would eventually ignite the whole world. Soon after Jesus' ascension into heaven, the Holy Spirit descended at Jerusalem, and about three thousand people became followers of Jesus Christ. This marked the birth of the Church. The book of Acts chronicles the birth and expansion of the early church, highlighting the deeds of some of its most influential leaders, such as Peter and Paul. Acts continues the story begun in the Gospel of Luke, showing how the Church continues the work that Jesus began. After

■ **Author:** Luke, a Gentile physician and Paul's associate

■ **Date Written:** Probably between AD 63 and 70

■ **Purpose:** To record the birth and growth of the Church

■ **Themes:** The Holy Spirit, the growth of the Church, opposition, inclusion of Gentile believers, the apostolic work of Peter and Paul

■ **Outline**
1:1–5:42 The early days of the Church
6:1–9:31 Persecution and expansion
9:32–12:25 Peter's missionary activity
13:1–14:28 Paul's first missionary journey
15:1-35 The meeting in Jerusalem
15:36–18:22 Paul's second missionary journey
18:23–21:14 Paul's third missionary journey
21:15–28:31 Paul's arrest and trip to Rome

recounting Peter's sermon and the birth of the Church, Acts describes the life of the church in Jerusalem, the spread of the gospel to Samaria, the activities of Peter, and the early persecution of the believers. After describing the death of James, the focus of the book shifts to the apostle Paul and his missionary work throughout the Gentile world. His three missionary journeys are described in detail, and the first major council in Jerusalem is recorded as well. Acts concludes with Paul's trip to Rome, where the book abruptly ends.

The Promise of the Holy Spirit

1 In my first book* I told you, Theophilus, about everything Jesus began to do and teach [2]until the day he was taken up to heaven after giving his chosen apostles further instructions through the Holy Spirit. [3]During the forty days after he suffered and died, he appeared to the apostles from time to time, and he proved to them in many ways that he was actually alive. And he talked to them about the Kingdom of God.

[4]Once when he was eating with them, he commanded them, "Do not leave Jerusalem until the Father sends you the gift he promised, as I told you before. [5]John baptized with* water, but in just a few days you will be baptized with the Holy Spirit."

The Ascension of Jesus

[6]So when the apostles were with Jesus, they kept asking him, "Lord, has the time come for you to free Israel and restore our kingdom?"

[7]He replied, "The Father alone has the authority to set those dates and times, and they are not for you to know. [8]But you will receive power when the Holy Spirit comes upon you. And you will be my witnesses, telling people about me everywhere—in Jerusalem, throughout Judea, in Samaria, and to the ends of the earth."

[9]After saying this, he was taken up into a cloud while they were watching, and they could no longer see him. [10]As they strained to see him rising into heaven, two white-robed men suddenly stood among them. [11]"Men

1:1 The reference is to the Gospel of Luke.   1:5 Or *in*; also in 1:5b.

of Galilee," they said, "why are you standing here staring into heaven? Jesus has been taken from you into heaven, but someday he will return from heaven in the same way you saw him go!"

Matthias Replaces Judas

¹²Then the apostles returned to Jerusalem from the Mount of Olives, a distance of half a mile.* ¹³When they arrived, they went to the upstairs room of the house where they were staying.

Here are the names of those who were present: Peter, John, James, Andrew, Philip, Thomas, Bartholomew, Matthew, James (son of Alphaeus), Simon (the zealot), and Judas (son of James). ¹⁴They all met together and were constantly united in prayer, along with Mary the mother of Jesus, several other women, and the brothers of Jesus.

¹⁵During this time, when about 120 believers* were together in one place, Peter stood up and addressed them. ¹⁶"Brothers," he said, "the Scriptures had to be fulfilled concerning Judas, who guided those who arrested Jesus. This was predicted long ago by the Holy Spirit, speaking through King David. ¹⁷Judas was one of us and shared in the ministry with us."

¹⁸(Judas had bought a field with the money he received for his treachery. Falling headfirst there, his body split open, spilling out all his intestines. ¹⁹The news of his death spread to all the people of Jerusalem, and they gave the place the Aramaic name *Akeldama,* which means "Field of Blood.")

²⁰Peter continued, "This was written in the book of Psalms, where it says, 'Let his home become desolate, with no one living in it.' It also says, 'Let someone else take his position.'*

²¹"So now we must choose a replacement for Judas from among the men who were with us the entire time we were traveling with the Lord Jesus—²²from the time he was baptized by John until the day he was taken from us. Whoever is chosen will join us as a witness of Jesus' resurrection."

²³So they nominated two men: Joseph called Barsabbas (also known as Justus) and Matthias. ²⁴Then they all prayed, "O Lord, you know every heart. Show us which of these men you have chosen ²⁵as an apostle to replace Judas in this ministry, for he has deserted us and gone where he belongs." ²⁶Then they cast lots, and Matthias was selected to become an apostle with the other eleven.

The Holy Spirit Comes

2 On the day of Pentecost* all the believers were meeting together in one place. ²Suddenly, there was a sound from heaven like the roaring of a mighty windstorm, and it filled the house where they were sitting. ³Then, what looked like flames or tongues of fire appeared and settled on each of them. ⁴And everyone present was filled with the Holy Spirit and began speaking in other languages,* as the Holy Spirit gave them this ability.

⁵At that time there were devout Jews from every nation living in Jerusalem. ⁶When they heard the loud noise, everyone came running, and they were bewildered to hear their own languages being spoken by the believers.

⁷They were completely amazed. "How can this be?" they exclaimed. "These people are all from Galilee, ⁸and yet we hear them speaking in our own native languages! ⁹Here we are—Parthians, Medes, Elamites, people from Mesopotamia, Judea, Cappadocia, Pontus, the province of Asia, ¹⁰Phrygia, Pamphylia, Egypt, and the areas of Libya around Cyrene, visitors from Rome ¹¹(both Jews and converts to Judaism), Cretans, and Arabs. And we all hear these people speaking in our own languages about the wonderful things God has done!" ¹²They stood there amazed and perplexed. "What can this mean?" they asked each other.

¹³But others in the crowd ridiculed them, saying, "They're just drunk, that's all!"

Peter Preaches to the Crowd

¹⁴Then Peter stepped forward with the eleven other apostles and shouted to the crowd, "Listen carefully, all of you, fellow Jews and residents of Jerusalem! Make no mistake about this. ¹⁵These people are not drunk, as some of you are assuming. Nine o'clock in the morning is much too early for that. ¹⁶No, what you see was predicted long ago by the prophet Joel:

¹⁷ 'In the last days,' God says,
    'I will pour out my Spirit upon all
       people.
   Your sons and daughters will
       prophesy.
    Your young men will see visions,
     and your old men will dream dreams.
¹⁸ In those days I will pour out my Spirit
    even on my servants—men and
      women alike—
    and they will prophesy.

1:12 Greek *a Sabbath day's journey.* 1:15 Greek *brothers.* 1:20 Pss 69:25; 109:8. 2:1 The Festival of Pentecost came 50 days after Passover (when Jesus was crucified). 2:4 Or *in other tongues.*

¹⁹ And I will cause wonders in the heavens
above
and signs on the earth below—
blood and fire and clouds of smoke.
²⁰ The sun will become dark,
and the moon will turn blood red
before that great and glorious day of
the LORD arrives.
²¹ But everyone who calls on the name of
the LORD
will be saved.'*

²²"People of Israel, listen! God publicly endorsed Jesus the Nazarene* by doing powerful miracles, wonders, and signs through him, as you well know. ²³But God knew what would happen, and his prearranged plan was carried out when Jesus was betrayed. With the help of lawless Gentiles, you nailed him to a cross and killed him. ²⁴But God released him from the horrors of death and raised him back to life, for death could not keep him in its grip. ²⁵King David said this about him:

'I see that the LORD is always with me.
I will not be shaken, for he is right
beside me.
²⁶ No wonder my heart is glad,
and my tongue shouts his praises!
My body rests in hope.
²⁷ For you will not leave my soul among the
dead*
or allow your Holy One to rot in the grave.
²⁸ You have shown me the way of life,
and you will fill me with the joy of your
presence.'*

²⁹"Dear brothers, think about this! You can be sure that the patriarch David wasn't referring to himself, for he died and was buried, and his tomb is still here among us. ³⁰But he was a prophet, and he knew God had promised with an oath that one of David's own descendants would sit on his throne. ³¹David was looking into the future and speaking of the Messiah's resurrection. He was saying that God would not leave him among the dead or allow his body to rot in the grave.

³²"God raised Jesus from the dead, and we are all witnesses of this. ³³Now he is exalted to the place of highest honor in heaven, at God's right hand. And the Father, as he had promised, gave him the Holy Spirit to pour out

upon us, just as you see and hear today. ³⁴For David himself never ascended into heaven, yet he said,

'The LORD said to my Lord,
"Sit in the place of honor at my right hand
³⁵ until I humble your enemies,
making them a footstool under your
feet."'*

³⁶"So let everyone in Israel know for certain that God has made this Jesus, whom you crucified, to be both Lord and Messiah!"

³⁷Peter's words pierced their hearts, and they said to him and to the other apostles, "Brothers, what should we do?"

³⁸Peter replied, "Each of you must repent of your sins and turn to God, and be baptized in the name of Jesus Christ for the forgiveness of your sins. Then you will receive the gift of the Holy Spirit. ³⁹This promise is to you, to your children, and to those far away*—all who have been called by the Lord our God." ⁴⁰Then Peter continued preaching for a long time, strongly urging all his listeners, "Save yourselves from this crooked generation!"

⁴¹Those who believed what Peter said were baptized and added to the church that day—about 3,000 in all.

The Believers Form a Community

⁴²All the believers devoted themselves to the apostles' teaching, and to fellowship, and to sharing in meals (including the Lord's Supper*), and to prayer.

⁴³A deep sense of awe came over them all, and the apostles performed many miraculous signs and wonders. ⁴⁴And all the believers met together in one place and shared everything they had. ⁴⁵They sold their property and possessions and shared the money with those in need. ⁴⁶They worshiped together at the Temple each day, met in homes for the Lord's Supper, and shared their meals with great joy and generosity*—⁴⁷all the while praising God and enjoying the goodwill of all the people. And each day the Lord added to their fellowship those who were being saved.

Peter Heals a Crippled Beggar

3 Peter and John went to the Temple one afternoon to take part in the three o'clock prayer service. ²As they approached the Temple,

---

2:17-21 Joel 2:28-32.   2:22 Or *Jesus of Nazareth.*   2:27 Greek *in Hades; also in 2:31.*   2:25-28 Ps 16:8-11 (Greek version).
2:34-35 Ps 110:1.   2:39 Or *and to people far in the future,* or *and to the Gentiles.*   2:42 Greek *the breaking of bread; also in 2:46.*
2:46 Or *and sincere hearts.*

a man lame from birth was being carried in. Each day he was put beside the Temple gate, the one called the Beautiful Gate, so he could beg from the people going into the Temple. ³When he saw Peter and John about to enter, he asked them for some money.

⁴Peter and John looked at him intently, and Peter said, "Look at us!" ⁵The lame man looked at them eagerly, expecting some money. ⁶But Peter said, "I don't have any silver or gold for you. But I'll give you what I have. In the name of Jesus Christ the Nazarene,* get up and* walk!"

⁷Then Peter took the lame man by the right hand and helped him up. And as he did, the man's feet and ankles were instantly healed and strengthened. ⁸He jumped up, stood on his feet, and began to walk! Then, walking, leaping, and praising God, he went into the Temple with them.

⁹All the people saw him walking and heard him praising God. ¹⁰When they realized he was the lame beggar they had seen so often at the Beautiful Gate, they were absolutely astounded! ¹¹They all rushed out in amazement to Solomon's Colonnade, where the man was holding tightly to Peter and John.

Peter Preaches in the Temple

¹²Peter saw his opportunity and addressed the crowd. "People of Israel," he said, "what is so surprising about this? And why stare at us as though we had made this man walk by our own power or godliness? ¹³For it is the God of Abraham, Isaac, and Jacob—the God of all our ancestors—who has brought glory to his servant Jesus by doing this. This is the same Jesus whom you handed over and rejected before Pilate, despite Pilate's decision to release him. ¹⁴You rejected this holy, righteous one and instead demanded the release of a murderer. ¹⁵You killed the author of life, but God raised him from the dead. And we are witnesses of this fact!

¹⁶"Through faith in the name of Jesus, this man was healed—and you know how crippled he was before. Faith in Jesus' name has healed him before your very eyes.

¹⁷"Friends,* I realize that what you and your leaders did to Jesus was done in ignorance. ¹⁸But God was fulfilling what all the prophets had foretold about the Messiah—that he must suffer these things. ¹⁹Now repent of your sins and turn to God, so that your sins may be wiped

away. ²⁰Then times of refreshment will come from the presence of the Lord, and he will again send you Jesus, your appointed Messiah. ²¹For he must remain in heaven until the time for the final restoration of all things, as God promised long ago through his holy prophets. ²²Moses said, 'The LORD your God will raise up for you a Prophet like me from among your own people. Listen carefully to everything he tells you.'* ²³Then Moses said, 'Anyone who will not listen to that Prophet will be completely cut off from God's people.'*

²⁴"Starting with Samuel, every prophet spoke about what is happening today. ²⁵You are the children of those prophets, and you are included in the covenant God promised to your ancestors. For God said to Abraham, 'Through your descendants* all the families on earth will be blessed.' ²⁶When God raised up his servant, Jesus, he sent him first to you people of Israel, to bless you by turning each of you back from your sinful ways."

Peter and John before the Council

4 While Peter and John were speaking to the people, they were confronted by the priests, the captain of the Temple guard, and some of the Sadducees. ²These leaders were very disturbed that Peter and John were teaching the people that through Jesus there is a resurrection of the dead. ³They arrested them and, since it was already evening, put them in jail until morning. ⁴But many of the people who heard their message believed it, so the number of men who believed now totaled about 5,000.

⁵The next day the council of all the rulers and elders and teachers of religious law met in Jerusalem. ⁶Annas the high priest was there, along with Caiaphas, John, Alexander, and other relatives of the high priest. ⁷They brought in the two disciples and demanded, "By what power, or in whose name, have you done this?"

⁸Then Peter, filled with the Holy Spirit, said to them, "Rulers and elders of our people, ⁹are we being questioned today because we've done a good deed for a crippled man? Do you want to know how he was healed? ¹⁰Let me clearly state to all of you and to all the people of Israel that he was healed by the powerful name of Jesus Christ the Nazarene,* the man you crucified but whom God raised from the dead. ¹¹For Jesus is the one referred to in the Scriptures, where it says,

---

3:6a Or Jesus Christ of Nazareth.   3:6b Some manuscripts do not include get up and.   3:17 Greek Brothers.   3:22 Deut 18:15.
3:23 Deut 18:19; Lev 23:29.   3:25 Greek your seed; see Gen 12:3; 22:18.   4:10 Or Jesus Christ of Nazareth.

'The stone that you builders rejected
has now become the cornerstone.'*

¹²There is salvation in no one else! God has given no other name under heaven by which we must be saved."

¹³The members of the council were amazed when they saw the boldness of Peter and John, for they could see that they were ordinary men with no special training in the Scriptures. They also recognized them as men who had been with Jesus. ¹⁴But since they could see the man who had been healed standing right there among them, there was nothing the council could say. ¹⁵So they ordered Peter and John out of the council chamber* and conferred among themselves.

¹⁶"What should we do with these men?" they asked each other. "We can't deny that they have performed a miraculous sign, and everybody in Jerusalem knows about it. ¹⁷But to keep them from spreading their propaganda any further, we must warn them not to speak to anyone in Jesus' name again." ¹⁸So they called the apostles back in and commanded them never again to speak or teach in the name of Jesus.

¹⁹But Peter and John replied, "Do you think God wants us to obey you rather than him? ²⁰We cannot stop telling about everything we have seen and heard."

²¹The council then threatened them further, but they finally let them go because they didn't know how to punish them without starting a riot. For everyone was praising God ²²for this miraculous sign—the healing of a man who had been lame for more than forty years.

The Believers Pray for Courage

²³As soon as they were freed, Peter and John returned to the other believers and told them what the leading priests and elders had said. ²⁴When they heard the report, all the believers lifted their voices together in prayer to God: "O Sovereign Lord, Creator of heaven and earth, the sea, and everything in them—²⁵you spoke long ago by the Holy Spirit through our ancestor David, your servant, saying,

'Why were the nations so angry?
Why did they waste their time with
futile plans?
²⁶ The kings of the earth prepared for battle;
the rulers gathered together
against the LORD
and against his Messiah.'*

²⁷"In fact, this has happened here in this very city! For Herod Antipas, Pontius Pilate the governor, the Gentiles, and the people of Israel were all united against Jesus, your holy servant, whom you anointed. ²⁸But everything they did was determined beforehand according to your will. ²⁹And now, O Lord, hear their threats, and give us, your servants, great boldness in preaching your word. ³⁰Stretch out your hand with healing power; may miraculous signs and wonders be done through the name of your holy servant Jesus."

³¹After this prayer, the meeting place shook, and they were all filled with the Holy Spirit. Then they preached the word of God with boldness.

The Believers Share Their Possessions

³²All the believers were united in heart and mind. And they felt that what they owned was not their own, so they shared everything they had. ³³The apostles testified powerfully to the resurrection of the Lord Jesus, and God's great blessing was upon them all. ³⁴There were no needy people among them, because those who owned land or houses would sell them ³⁵and bring the money to the apostles to give to those in need.

³⁶For instance, there was Joseph, the one the apostles nicknamed Barnabas (which means "Son of Encouragement"). He was from the tribe of Levi and came from the island of Cyprus. ³⁷He sold a field he owned and brought the money to the apostles.

Ananias and Sapphira

5 But there was a certain man named Ananias who, with his wife, Sapphira, sold some property. ²He brought part of the money to the apostles, claiming it was the full amount. With his wife's consent, he kept the rest. ³Then Peter said, "Ananias, why have you let Satan fill your heart? You lied to the Holy Spirit, and you kept some of the money for yourself. ⁴The property was yours to sell or not sell, as you wished. And after selling it, the money was also yours to give away. How could you do a thing like this? You weren't lying to us but to God!"

⁵As soon as Ananias heard these words, he fell to the floor and died. Everyone who heard about it was terrified. ⁶Then some young men got up, wrapped him in a sheet, and took him out and buried him.

⁷About three hours later his wife came in,

4:11 Ps 118:22. 4:15 Greek *the Sanhedrin.* 4:25-26 Or *his anointed one;* or *his Christ.* Ps 2:1-2.

not knowing what had happened. [8]Peter asked her, "Was this the price you and your husband received for your land?"

"Yes," she replied, "that was the price."

[9]And Peter said, "How could the two of you even think of conspiring to test the Spirit of the Lord like this? The young men who buried your husband are just outside the door, and they will carry you out, too."

[10]Instantly, she fell to the floor and died. When the young men came in and saw that she was dead, they carried her out and buried her beside her husband. [11]Great fear gripped the entire church and everyone else who heard what had happened.

The Apostles Heal Many

[12]The apostles were performing many miraculous signs and wonders among the people. And all the believers were meeting regularly at the Temple in the area known as Solomon's Colonnade. [13]But no one else dared to join them, even though all the people had high regard for them. [14]Yet more and more people believed and were brought to the Lord—crowds of both men and women. [15]As a result of the apostles' work, sick people were brought out into the streets on beds and mats so that Peter's shadow might fall across some of them as he went by. [16]Crowds came from the villages around Jerusalem, bringing their sick and those possessed by evil* spirits, and they were all healed.

The Apostles Meet Opposition

[17]The high priest and his officials, who were Sadducees, were filled with jealousy. [18]They arrested the apostles and put them in the public jail. [19]But an angel of the Lord came at night, opened the gates of the jail, and brought them out. Then he told them, [20]"Go to the Temple and give the people this message of life!"

[21]So at daybreak the apostles entered the Temple, as they were told, and immediately began teaching.

When the high priest and his officials arrived, they convened the high council*—the full assembly of the elders of Israel. Then they sent for the apostles to be brought from the jail for trial. [22]But when the Temple guards went to the jail, the men were gone. So they returned to the council and reported, [23]"The jail was securely locked, with the guards standing outside, but when we opened the gates, no one was there!"

[24]When the captain of the Temple guard and the leading priests heard this, they were perplexed, wondering where it would all end. [25]Then someone arrived with startling news: "The men you put in jail are standing in the Temple, teaching the people!"

[26]The captain went with his Temple guards and arrested the apostles, but without violence, for they were afraid the people would stone them. [27]Then they brought the apostles before the high council, where the high priest confronted them. [28]"We gave you strict orders never again to teach in this man's name!" he said. "Instead, you have filled all Jerusalem with your teaching about him, and you want to make us responsible for his death!"

[29]But Peter and the apostles replied, "We must obey God rather than any human authority. [30]The God of our ancestors raised Jesus from the dead after you killed him by hanging him on a cross.* [31]Then God put him in the place of honor at his right hand as Prince and Savior. He did this so the people of Israel would repent of their sins and be forgiven. [32]We are witnesses of these things and so is the Holy Spirit, who is given by God to those who obey him."

[33]When they heard this, the high council was furious and decided to kill them. [34]But one member, a Pharisee named Gamaliel, who was an expert in religious law and respected by all the people, stood up and ordered that the men be sent outside the council chamber for a while. [35]Then he said to his colleagues, "Men of Israel, take care what you are planning to do to these men! [36]Some time ago there was that fellow Theudas, who pretended to be someone great. About 400 others joined him, but he was killed, and all his followers went their various ways. The whole movement came to nothing. [37]After him, at the time of the census, there was Judas of Galilee. He got people to follow him, but he was killed, too, and all his followers were scattered.

[38]"So my advice is, leave these men alone. Let them go. If they are planning and doing these things merely on their own, it will soon be overthrown. [39]But if it is from God, you will not be able to overthrow them. You may even find yourselves fighting against God!"

[40]The others accepted his advice. They called in the apostles and had them flogged. Then they ordered them never again to speak in the name of Jesus, and they let them go.

[41]The apostles left the high council rejoicing that God had counted them worthy to suffer disgrace for the name of Jesus.* [42]And every day,

5:16 Greek *unclean.*   5:21 Greek *Sanhedrin;* also in 5:27, 41.   5:30 Greek *on a tree.*   5:41 Greek *for the name.*

in the Temple and from house to house, they continued to teach and preach this message: "Jesus is the Messiah."

Seven Men Chosen to Serve

6 But as the believers* rapidly multiplied, there were rumblings of discontent. The Greek-speaking believers complained about the Hebrew-speaking believers, saying that their widows were being discriminated against in the daily distribution of food.

²So the Twelve called a meeting of all the believers. They said, "We apostles should spend our time teaching the word of God, not running a food program. ³And so, brothers, select seven men who are well respected and are full of the Spirit and wisdom. We will give them this responsibility. ⁴Then we apostles can spend our time in prayer and teaching the word."

⁵Everyone liked this idea, and they chose the following: Stephen (a man full of faith and the Holy Spirit), Philip, Procorus, Nicanor, Timon, Parmenas, and Nicolas of Antioch (an earlier convert to the Jewish faith). ⁶These seven were presented to the apostles, who prayed for them as they laid their hands on them.

⁷So God's message continued to spread. The number of believers greatly increased in Jerusalem, and many of the Jewish priests were converted, too.

Stephen Is Arrested

⁸Stephen, a man full of God's grace and power, performed amazing miracles and signs among the people. ⁹But one day some men from the Synagogue of Freed Slaves, as it was called, started to debate with him. They were Jews from Cyrene, Alexandria, Cilicia, and the province of Asia. ¹⁰None of them could stand against the wisdom and the Spirit with which Stephen spoke.

¹¹So they persuaded some men to lie about Stephen, saying, "We heard him blaspheme Moses, and even God." ¹²This roused the people, the elders, and the teachers of religious law. So they arrested Stephen and brought him before the high council.*

¹³The lying witnesses said, "This man is always speaking against the holy Temple and against the law of Moses. ¹⁴We have heard him say that this Jesus of Nazareth* will destroy the Temple and change the customs Moses handed down to us."

¹⁵At this point everyone in the high council stared at Stephen, because his face became as bright as an angel's.

Stephen Addresses the Council

7 Then the high priest asked Stephen, "Are these accusations true?"

²This was Stephen's reply: "Brothers and fathers, listen to me. Our glorious God appeared to our ancestor Abraham in Mesopotamia before he settled in Haran.* ³God told him, 'Leave your native land and your relatives, and come into the land that I will show you.'* ⁴So Abraham left the land of the Chaldeans and lived in Haran until his father died. Then God brought him here to the land where you now live.

⁵"But God gave him no inheritance here, not even one square foot of land. God did promise, however, that eventually the whole land would belong to Abraham and his descendants—even though he had no children yet. ⁶God also told him that his descendants would live in a foreign land, where they would be oppressed as slaves for 400 years. ⁷'But I will punish the nation that enslaves them,' God said, 'and in the end they will come out and worship me here in this place.'*

⁸"God also gave Abraham the covenant of circumcision at that time. So when Abraham became the father of Isaac, he circumcised him on the eighth day. And the practice was continued when Isaac became the father of Jacob, and when Jacob became the father of the twelve patriarchs of the Israelite nation.

⁹"These patriarchs were jealous of their brother Joseph, and they sold him to be a slave in Egypt. But God was with him ¹⁰and rescued him from all his troubles. And God gave him favor before Pharaoh, king of Egypt. God also gave Joseph unusual wisdom, so that Pharaoh appointed him governor over all of Egypt and put him in charge of the palace.

¹¹"But a famine came upon Egypt and Canaan. There was great misery, and our ancestors ran out of food. ¹²Jacob heard that there was still grain in Egypt, so he sent his sons—our ancestors—to buy some. ¹³The second time they went, Joseph revealed his identity to his brothers,* and they were introduced to Pharaoh. ¹⁴Then Joseph sent for his father, Jacob, and all his relatives to come to Egypt, seventy-five persons in all. ¹⁵So Jacob went to Egypt. He died there, as did our ancestors. ¹⁶Their bodies

6:1 Greek disciples; also in 6:2, 7.   6:12 Greek Sanhedrin; also in 6:15.   6:14 Or Jesus the Nazarene.   7:2 Mesopotamia was the region now called Iraq. Haran was a city in what is now called Syria.   7:3 Gen 12:1.   7:5-7 Gen 12:7; 15:13-14; Exod 3:12. 7:13 Other manuscripts read Joseph was recognized by his brothers.

were taken to Shechem and buried in the tomb Abraham had bought for a certain price from Hamor's sons in Shechem.

17"As the time drew near when God would fulfill his promise to Abraham, the number of our people in Egypt greatly increased. 18But then a new king came to the throne of Egypt who knew nothing about Joseph. 19This king exploited our people and oppressed them, forcing parents to abandon their newborn babies so they would die.

20"At that time Moses was born—a beautiful child in God's eyes. His parents cared for him at home for three months. 21When they had to abandon him, Pharaoh's daughter adopted him and raised him as her own son. 22Moses was taught all the wisdom of the Egyptians, and he was powerful in both speech and action.

23"One day when Moses was forty years old, he decided to visit his relatives, the people of Israel. 24He saw an Egyptian mistreating an Israelite. So Moses came to the man's defense and avenged him, killing the Egyptian. 25Moses assumed his fellow Israelites would realize that God had sent him to rescue them, but they didn't.

26"The next day he visited them again and saw two men of Israel fighting. He tried to be a peacemaker. 'Men,' he said, 'you are brothers. Why are you fighting each other?'

27"But the man in the wrong pushed Moses aside. 'Who made you a ruler and judge over us?' he asked. 28'Are you going to kill me as you killed that Egyptian yesterday?' 29When Moses heard that, he fled the country and lived as a foreigner in the land of Midian. There his two sons were born.

30"Forty years later, in the desert near Mount Sinai, an angel appeared to Moses in the flame of a burning bush. 31When Moses saw it, he was amazed at the sight. As he went to take a closer look, the voice of the LORD called out to him, 32'I am the God of your ancestors—the God of Abraham, Isaac, and Jacob.' Moses shook with terror and did not dare to look.

33"Then the LORD said to him, 'Take off your sandals, for you are standing on holy ground. 34I have certainly seen the oppression of my people in Egypt. I have heard their groans and have come down to rescue them. Now go, for I am sending you back to Egypt.'*

35"So God sent back the same man his people had previously rejected when they demanded, 'Who made you a ruler and judge over us?'

Through the angel who appeared to him in the burning bush, God sent Moses to be their ruler and savior. 36And by means of many wonders and miraculous signs, he led them out of Egypt, through the Red Sea, and through the wilderness for forty years.

37"Moses himself told the people of Israel, 'God will raise up for you a Prophet like me from among your own people.'* 38Moses was with our ancestors, the assembly of God's people in the wilderness, when the angel spoke to him at Mount Sinai. And there Moses received life-giving words to pass on to us.*

39"But our ancestors refused to listen to Moses. They rejected him and wanted to return to Egypt. 40They told Aaron, 'Make us some gods who can lead us, for we don't know what has become of this Moses, who brought us out of Egypt.' 41So they made an idol shaped like a calf, and they sacrificed to it and celebrated over this thing they had made. 42Then God turned away from them and abandoned them to serve the stars of heaven as their gods! In the book of the prophets it is written,

'Was it to me you were bringing sacrifices
    and offerings
    during those forty years in the
    wilderness, Israel?
43 No, you carried your pagan gods—
    the shrine of Molech,
    the star of your god Rephan,
    and the images you made to worship
    them.
So I will send you into exile
    as far away as Babylon.'*

44"Our ancestors carried the Tabernacle* with them through the wilderness. It was constructed according to the plan God had shown to Moses. 45Years later, when Joshua led our ancestors in battle against the nations that God drove out of this land, the Tabernacle was taken with them into their new territory. And it stayed there until the time of King David.

46"David found favor with God and asked for the privilege of building a permanent Temple for the God of Jacob.* 47But it was Solomon who actually built it. 48However, the Most High doesn't live in temples made by human hands. As the prophet says,

49 'Heaven is my throne,
    and the earth is my footstool.

7:31-34 Exod 3:5-10.   7:37 Deut 18:15.   7:38 Some manuscripts read *to you.*   7:42-43 Amos 5:25-27 (Greek version).
7:44 Greek *the tent of witness.*   7:46 Some manuscripts read *the house of Jacob.*

Could you build me a temple as good as
that?'
asks the LORD.
'Could you build me such a resting place?
50   Didn't my hands make both heaven and
earth?'*

51"You stubborn people! You are heathen* at
heart and deaf to the truth. Must you forever
resist the Holy Spirit? That's what your ancestors did, and so do you! 52Name one prophet
your ancestors didn't persecute! They even
killed the ones who predicted the coming of
the Righteous One—the Messiah whom you
betrayed and murdered. 53You deliberately disobeyed God's law, even though you received it
from the hands of angels."

54The Jewish leaders were infuriated by Stephen's accusation, and they shook their fists at
him in rage.* 55But Stephen, full of the Holy
Spirit, gazed steadily into heaven and saw the
glory of God, and he saw Jesus standing in the
place of honor at God's right hand. 56And he
told them, "Look, I see the heavens opened
and the Son of Man standing in the place of
honor at God's right hand!"

57Then they put their hands over their ears
and began shouting. They rushed at him 58and
dragged him out of the city and began to stone
him. His accusers took off their coats and laid
them at the feet of a young man named Saul.*

59As they stoned him, Stephen prayed, "Lord
Jesus, receive my spirit." 60He fell to his knees,
shouting, "Lord, don't charge them with this
sin!" And with that, he died.

8 Saul was one of the witnesses, and he agreed
completely with the killing of Stephen.

Persecution Scatters the Believers
A great wave of persecution began that day,
sweeping over the church in Jerusalem; and
all the believers except the apostles were scattered through the regions of Judea and Samaria. 2(Some devout men came and buried
Stephen with great mourning.) 3But Saul was
going everywhere to destroy the church. He
went from house to house, dragging out both
men and women to throw them into prison.

Philip Preaches in Samaria
4But the believers who were scattered preached
the Good News about Jesus wherever they
went. 5Philip, for example, went to the city of
Samaria and told the people there about the
Messiah. 6Crowds listened intently to Philip
because they were eager to hear his message
and see the miraculous signs he did. 7Many
evil* spirits were cast out, screaming as they
left their victims. And many who had been
paralyzed or lame were healed. 8So there was
great joy in that city.

9A man named Simon had been a sorcerer
there for many years, amazing the people of
Samaria and claiming to be someone great.
10Everyone, from the least to the greatest, often
spoke of him as "the Great One—the Power of
God." 11They listened closely to him because
for a long time he had astounded them with
his magic.

12But now the people believed Philip's message of Good News concerning the Kingdom
of God and the name of Jesus Christ. As a result, many men and women were baptized.
13Then Simon himself believed and was baptized. He began following Philip wherever he
went, and he was amazed by the signs and great
miracles Philip performed.

14When the apostles in Jerusalem heard that
the people of Samaria had accepted God's message, they sent Peter and John there. 15As soon
as they arrived, they prayed for these new believers to receive the Holy Spirit. 16The Holy
Spirit had not yet come upon any of them, for
they had only been baptized in the name of
the Lord Jesus. 17Then Peter and John laid their
hands upon these believers, and they received
the Holy Spirit.

18When Simon saw that the Spirit was given
when the apostles laid their hands on people,
he offered them money to buy this power.
19"Let me have this power, too," he exclaimed,
"so that when I lay my hands on people, they
will receive the Holy Spirit!"

20But Peter replied, "May your money be destroyed with you for thinking God's gift can be
bought! 21You can have no part in this, for your
heart is not right with God. 22Repent of your
wickedness and pray to the Lord. Perhaps he
will forgive your evil thoughts, 23for I can see
that you are full of bitter jealousy and are held
captive by sin."

24"Pray to the Lord for me," Simon exclaimed, "that these terrible things you've said
won't happen to me!"

25After testifying and preaching the word of
the Lord in Samaria, Peter and John returned
to Jerusalem. And they stopped in many

7:49-50 Isa 66:1-2.   7:51 Greek uncircumcised.   7:54 Greek they were grinding their teeth against him.   7:58 Saul is later called
Paul; see 13:9.   8:7 Greek unclean.

Samaritan villages along the way to preach the Good News.

Philip and the Ethiopian Eunuch

26As for Philip, an angel of the Lord said to him, "Go south* down the desert road that runs from Jerusalem to Gaza." 27So he started out, and he met the treasurer of Ethiopia, a eunuch of great authority under the Kandake, the queen of Ethiopia. The eunuch had gone to Jerusalem to worship, 28and he was now returning. Seated in his carriage, he was reading aloud from the book of the prophet Isaiah.

29The Holy Spirit said to Philip, "Go over and walk along beside the carriage."

30Philip ran over and heard the man reading from the prophet Isaiah. Philip asked, "Do you understand what you are reading?"

31The man replied, "How can I, unless someone instructs me?" And he urged Philip to come up into the carriage and sit with him.

32The passage of Scripture he had been reading was this:

"He was led like a sheep to the slaughter.
    And as a lamb is silent before the shearers,
    he did not open his mouth.
33 He was humiliated and received no justice.
    Who can speak of his descendants?
    For his life was taken from the earth."*

34The eunuch asked Philip, "Tell me, was the prophet talking about himself or someone else?" 35So beginning with this same Scripture, Philip told him the Good News about Jesus.

36As they rode along, they came to some water, and the eunuch said, "Look! There's some water! Why can't I be baptized?"* 38He ordered the carriage to stop, and they went down into the water, and Philip baptized him. 39When they came up out of the water, the Spirit of the Lord snatched Philip away. The eunuch never saw him again but went on his way rejoicing. 40Meanwhile, Philip found himself farther north at the town of Azotus. He preached the Good News there and in every town along the way until he came to Caesarea.

Saul's Conversion

9 Meanwhile, Saul was uttering threats with every breath and was eager to kill the Lord's followers.* So he went to the high priest. 2He requested letters addressed to the synagogues in Damascus, asking for their cooperation in the arrest of any followers of the Way he found there. He wanted to bring them—both men and women—back to Jerusalem in chains.

3As he was approaching Damascus on this mission, a light from heaven suddenly shone down around him. 4He fell to the ground and heard a voice saying to him, "Saul! Saul! Why are you persecuting me?"

5"Who are you, lord?" Saul asked.

And the voice replied, "I am Jesus, the one you are persecuting! 6Now get up and go into the city, and you will be told what you must do."

7The men with Saul stood speechless, for they heard the sound of someone's voice but saw no one! 8Saul picked himself up off the ground, but when he opened his eyes he was blind. So his companions led him by the hand to Damascus. 9He remained there blind for three days and did not eat or drink.

10Now there was a believer* in Damascus named Ananias. The Lord spoke to him in a vision, calling, "Ananias!"

"Yes, Lord!" he replied.

11The Lord said, "Go over to Straight Street, to the house of Judas. When you get there, ask for a man from Tarsus named Saul. He is praying to me right now. 12I have shown him a vision of a man named Ananias coming in and laying hands on him so he can see again."

13"But Lord," exclaimed Ananias, "I've heard many people talk about the terrible things this man has done to the believers* in Jerusalem! 14And he is authorized by the leading priests to arrest everyone who calls upon your name."

15But the Lord said, "Go, for Saul is my chosen instrument to take my message to the Gentiles and to kings, as well as to the people of Israel. 16And I will show him how much he must suffer for my name's sake."

17So Ananias went and found Saul. He laid his hands on him and said, "Brother Saul, the Lord Jesus, who appeared to you on the road, has sent me so that you might regain your sight and be filled with the Holy Spirit." 18Instantly something like scales fell from Saul's eyes, and he regained his sight. Then he got up and was baptized. 19Afterward he ate some food and regained his strength.

Saul in Damascus and Jerusalem

Saul stayed with the believers* in Damascus for a few days. 20And immediately he began

---

8:26 Or Go at noon.   8:32-33 Isa 53:7-8 (Greek version).   8:36 Some manuscripts add verse 37, "You can," Philip answered, "if you believe with all your heart." And the eunuch replied, "I believe that Jesus Christ is the Son of God."   9:1 Greek disciples. 9:10 Greek disciple; also in 9:26, 36.   9:13 Greek God's holy people; also in 9:32, 41.   9:19 Greek disciples; also in 9:26, 38.

preaching about Jesus in the synagogues, saying, "He is indeed the Son of God!"

21All who heard him were amazed. "Isn't this the same man who caused such devastation among Jesus' followers in Jerusalem?" they asked. "And didn't he come here to arrest them and take them in chains to the leading priests?"

22Saul's preaching became more and more powerful, and the Jews in Damascus couldn't refute his proofs that Jesus was indeed the Messiah. 23After a while some of the Jews plotted together to kill him. 24They were watching for him day and night at the city gate so they could murder him, but Saul was told about their plot. 25So during the night, some of the other believers* lowered him in a large basket through an opening in the city wall.

26When Saul arrived in Jerusalem, he tried to meet with the believers, but they were all afraid of him. They did not believe he had truly become a believer! 27Then Barnabas brought him to the apostles and told them how Saul had seen the Lord on the way to Damascus and how the Lord had spoken to Saul. He also told them that Saul had preached boldly in the name of Jesus in Damascus.

28So Saul stayed with the apostles and went all around Jerusalem with them, preaching boldly in the name of the Lord. 29He debated with some Greek-speaking Jews, but they tried to murder him. 30When the believers* heard about this, they took him down to Caesarea and sent him away to Tarsus, his hometown.

31The church then had peace throughout Judea, Galilee, and Samaria, and it became stronger as the believers lived in the fear of the Lord. And with the encouragement of the Holy Spirit, it also grew in numbers.

Peter Heals Aeneas and Raises Dorcas

32Meanwhile, Peter traveled from place to place, and he came down to visit the believers in the town of Lydda. 33There he met a man named Aeneas, who had been paralyzed and bedridden for eight years. 34Peter said to him, "Aeneas, Jesus Christ heals you! Get up, and roll up your sleeping mat!" And he was healed instantly. 35Then the whole population of Lydda and Sharon saw Aeneas walking around, and they turned to the Lord.

36There was a believer in Joppa named Tabitha (which in Greek is Dorcas*). She was always doing kind things for others and helping the poor. 37About this time she became ill and died.

Her body was washed for burial and laid in an upstairs room. 38But the believers had heard that Peter was nearby at Lydda, so they sent two men to beg him, "Please come as soon as possible!"

39So Peter returned with them; and as soon as he arrived, they took him to the upstairs room. The room was filled with widows who were weeping and showing him the coats and other clothes Dorcas had made for them. 40But Peter asked them all to leave the room; then he knelt and prayed. Turning to the body he said, "Get up, Tabitha." And she opened her eyes! When she saw Peter, she sat up! 41He gave her his hand and helped her up. Then he called in the widows and all the believers, and he presented her to them alive.

42The news spread through the whole town, and many believed in the Lord. 43And Peter stayed a long time in Joppa, living with Simon, a tanner of hides.

Cornelius Calls for Peter

10 In Caesarea there lived a Roman army officer* named Cornelius, who was a captain of the Italian Regiment. 2He was a devout, God-fearing man, as was everyone in his household. He gave generously to the poor and prayed regularly to God. 3One afternoon about three o'clock, he had a vision in which he saw an angel of God coming toward him. "Cornelius!" the angel said.

4Cornelius stared at him in terror. "What is it, sir?" he asked the angel.

And the angel replied, "Your prayers and gifts to the poor have been received by God as an offering! 5Now send some men to Joppa, and summon a man named Simon Peter. 6He is staying with Simon, a tanner who lives near the seashore."

7As soon as the angel was gone, Cornelius called two of his household servants and a devout soldier, one of his personal attendants. 8He told them what had happened and sent them off to Joppa.

Peter Visits Cornelius

9The next day as Cornelius's messengers were nearing the town, Peter went up on the flat roof to pray. It was about noon, 10and he was hungry. But while a meal was being prepared, he fell into a trance. 11He saw the sky open, and something like a large sheet was let down by its four corners. 12In the sheet were all sorts

9:25 Greek *his disciples.*   9:30 Greek *brothers.*   9:36 The names *Tabitha* in Aramaic and *Dorcas* in Greek both mean "gazelle."
10:1 Greek *a centurion;* similarly in 10:22.

of animals, reptiles, and birds. [13]Then a voice said to him, "Get up, Peter; kill and eat them."

[14]"No, Lord," Peter declared. "I have never eaten anything that our Jewish laws have declared impure and unclean.*"

[15]But the voice spoke again: "Do not call something unclean if God has made it clean." [16]The same vision was repeated three times. Then the sheet was suddenly pulled up to heaven.

[17]Peter was very perplexed. What could the vision mean? Just then the men sent by Cornelius found Simon's house. Standing outside the gate, [18]they asked if a man named Simon Peter was staying there.

[19]Meanwhile, as Peter was puzzling over the vision, the Holy Spirit said to him, "Three men have come looking for you. [20]Get up, go downstairs, and go with them without hesitation. Don't worry, for I have sent them."

[21]So Peter went down and said, "I'm the man you are looking for. Why have you come?"

[22]They said, "We were sent by Cornelius, a Roman officer. He is a devout and God-fearing man, well respected by all the Jews. A holy angel instructed him to summon you to his house so that he can hear your message." [23]So Peter invited the men to stay for the night. The next day he went with them, accompanied by some of the brothers from Joppa.

[24]They arrived in Caesarea the following day. Cornelius was waiting for them and had called together his relatives and close friends. [25]As Peter entered his home, Cornelius fell at his feet and worshiped him. [26]But Peter pulled him up and said, "Stand up! I'm a human being just like you!" [27]So they talked together and went inside, where many others were assembled.

[28]Peter told them, "You know it is against our laws for a Jewish man to enter a Gentile home like this or to associate with you. But God has shown me that I should no longer think of anyone as impure or unclean. [29]So I came without objection as soon as I was sent for. Now tell me why you sent for me."

[30]Cornelius replied, "Four days ago I was praying in my house about this same time, three o'clock in the afternoon. Suddenly, a man in dazzling clothes was standing in front of me. [31]He told me, 'Cornelius, your prayer has been heard, and your gifts to the poor have been noticed by God! [32]Now send messengers to Joppa, and summon a man named Simon Peter. He is staying in the home of Simon, a tanner who lives near the seashore.' [33]So I sent for you at once, and it was good of you to come. Now we are all here, waiting before God to hear the message the Lord has given you."

The Gentiles Hear the Good News

[34]Then Peter replied, "I see very clearly that God shows no favoritism. [35]In every nation he accepts those who fear him and do what is right. [36]This is the message of Good News for the people of Israel—that there is peace with God through Jesus Christ, who is Lord of all. [37]You know what happened throughout Judea, beginning in Galilee, after John began preaching his message of baptism. [38]And you know that God anointed Jesus of Nazareth with the Holy Spirit and with power. Then Jesus went around doing good and healing all who were oppressed by the devil, for God was with him.

[39]"And we apostles are witnesses of all he did throughout Judea and in Jerusalem. They put him to death by hanging him on a cross,* [40]but God raised him to life on the third day. Then God allowed him to appear, [41]not to the general public,* but to us whom God had chosen in advance to be his witnesses. We were those who ate and drank with him after he rose from the dead. [42]And he ordered us to preach everywhere and to testify that Jesus is the one appointed by God to be the judge of all—the living and the dead. [43]He is the one all the prophets testified about, saying that everyone who believes in him will have their sins forgiven through his name."

The Gentiles Receive the Holy Spirit

[44]Even as Peter was saying these things, the Holy Spirit fell upon all who were listening to the message. [45]The Jewish believers* who came with Peter were amazed that the gift of the Holy Spirit had been poured out on the Gentiles, too. [46]For they heard them speaking in other tongues* and praising God.

Then Peter asked, [47]"Can anyone object to their being baptized, now that they have received the Holy Spirit just as we did?" [48]So he gave orders for them to be baptized in the name of Jesus Christ. Afterward Cornelius asked him to stay with them for several days.

Peter Explains His Actions

11 Soon the news reached the apostles and other believers* in Judea that the Gentiles had received the word of God. [2]But when

---

10:14 Greek *anything common and unclean.*   10:39 Greek *on a tree.*   10:41 Greek *the people.*   10:45 Greek *The faithful ones of the circumcision.*   10:46 Or *in other languages.*   11:1 Greek *brothers.*

Peter arrived back in Jerusalem, the Jewish believers* criticized him. ³"You entered the home of Gentiles* and even ate with them!" they said.

⁴Then Peter told them exactly what had happened. ⁵"I was in the town of Joppa," he said, "and while I was praying, I went into a trance and saw a vision. Something like a large sheet was let down by its four corners from the sky. And it came right down to me. ⁶When I looked inside the sheet, I saw all sorts of tame and wild animals, reptiles, and birds. ⁷And I heard a voice say, 'Get up, Peter; kill and eat them.'

⁸"'No, Lord,' I replied. 'I have never eaten anything that our Jewish laws have declared impure or unclean.*'

⁹"But the voice from heaven spoke again: 'Do not call something unclean if God has made it clean.' ¹⁰This happened three times before the sheet and all it contained was pulled back up to heaven.

¹¹"Just then three men who had been sent from Caesarea arrived at the house where we were staying. ¹²The Holy Spirit told me to go with them and not to worry that they were Gentiles. These six brothers here accompanied me, and we soon entered the home of the man who had sent for us. ¹³He told us how an angel had appeared to him in his home and had told him, 'Send messengers to Joppa, and summon a man named Simon Peter. ¹⁴He will tell you how you and everyone in your household can be saved!'

¹⁵"As I began to speak," Peter continued, "the Holy Spirit fell on them, just as he fell on us at the beginning. ¹⁶Then I thought of the Lord's words when he said, 'John baptized with* water, but you will be baptized with the Holy Spirit.' ¹⁷And since God gave these Gentiles the same gift he gave us when we believed in the Lord Jesus Christ, who was I to stand in God's way?"

¹⁸When the others heard this, they stopped objecting and began praising God. They said, "We can see that God has also given the Gentiles the privilege of repenting of their sins and receiving eternal life."

The Church in Antioch of Syria

¹⁹Meanwhile, the believers who had been scattered during the persecution after Stephen's death traveled as far as Phoenicia, Cyprus, and Antioch of Syria. They preached the word of God, but only to Jews. ²⁰However, some of the believers who went to Antioch from Cyprus and Cyrene began preaching to the Gentiles* about the Lord Jesus. ²¹The power of the Lord was with them, and a large number of these Gentiles believed and turned to the Lord.

²²When the church at Jerusalem heard what had happened, they sent Barnabas to Antioch. ²³When he arrived and saw this evidence of God's blessing, he was filled with joy, and he encouraged the believers to stay true to the Lord. ²⁴Barnabas was a good man, full of the Holy Spirit and strong in faith. And many people were brought to the Lord.

²⁵Then Barnabas went on to Tarsus to look for Saul. ²⁶When he found him, he brought him back to Antioch. Both of them stayed there with the church for a full year, teaching large crowds of people. (It was at Antioch that the believers* were first called Christians.)

²⁷During this time some prophets traveled from Jerusalem to Antioch. ²⁸One of them named Agabus stood up in one of the meetings and predicted by the Spirit that a great famine was coming upon the entire Roman world. (This was fulfilled during the reign of Claudius.) ²⁹So the believers in Antioch decided to send relief to the brothers and sisters* in Judea, everyone giving as much as they could. ³⁰This they did, entrusting their gifts to Barnabas and Saul to take to the elders of the church in Jerusalem.

James Is Killed and Peter Is Imprisoned

12 About that time King Herod Agrippa* began to persecute some believers in the church. ²He had the apostle James (John's brother) killed with a sword. ³When Herod saw how much this pleased the Jewish people, he also arrested Peter. (This took place during the Passover celebration.*) ⁴Then he imprisoned him, placing him under the guard of four squads of four soldiers each. Herod intended to bring Peter out for public trial after the Passover. ⁵But while Peter was in prison, the church prayed very earnestly for him.

Peter's Miraculous Escape from Prison

⁶The night before Peter was to be placed on trial, he was asleep, fastened with two chains between two soldiers. Others stood guard at the prison gate. ⁷Suddenly, there was a bright

---

11:2 Greek *those of the circumcision.*   11:3 Greek *of uncircumcised men.*   11:8 Greek *anything common or unclean.*   11:16 Or *in;* also in 11:16b.   11:20 Greek *the Hellenists* (i.e., those who speak Greek); other manuscripts read *the Greeks.*   11:26 Greek *disciples;* also in 11:29.   11:29 Greek *the brothers.*   12:1 Greek *Herod the king.* He was the nephew of Herod Antipas and a grandson of Herod the Great.   12:3 Greek *the days of unleavened bread.*

light in the cell, and an angel of the Lord stood before Peter. The angel struck him on the side to awaken him and said, "Quick! Get up!" And the chains fell off his wrists. ⁸Then the angel told him, "Get dressed and put on your sandals." And he did. "Now put on your coat and follow me," the angel ordered.

⁹So Peter left the cell, following the angel. But all the time he thought it was a vision. He didn't realize it was actually happening. ¹⁰They passed the first and second guard posts and came to the iron gate leading to the city, and this opened for them all by itself. So they passed through and started walking down the street, and then the angel suddenly left him.

¹¹Peter finally came to his senses. "It's really true!" he said. "The Lord has sent his angel and saved me from Herod and from what the Jewish leaders* had planned to do to me!"

¹²When he realized this, he went to the home of Mary, the mother of John Mark, where many were gathered for prayer. ¹³He knocked at the door in the gate, and a servant girl named Rhoda came to open it. ¹⁴When she recognized Peter's voice, she was so overjoyed that, instead of opening the door, she ran back inside and told everyone, "Peter is standing at the door!"

¹⁵"You're out of your mind!" they said. When she insisted, they decided, "It must be his angel."

¹⁶Meanwhile, Peter continued knocking. When they finally opened the door and saw him, they were amazed. ¹⁷He motioned for them to quiet down and told them how the Lord had led him out of prison. "Tell James and the other brothers what happened," he said. And then he went to another place.

¹⁸At dawn there was a great commotion among the soldiers about what had happened to Peter. ¹⁹Herod Agrippa ordered a thorough search for him. When he couldn't be found, Herod interrogated the guards and sentenced them to death. Afterward Herod left Judea to stay in Caesarea for a while.

The Death of Herod Agrippa

²⁰Now Herod was very angry with the people of Tyre and Sidon. So they sent a delegation to make peace with him because their cities were dependent upon Herod's country for food. The delegates won the support of Blastus, Herod's personal assistant, ²¹and an appointment with Herod was granted. When the day arrived,

Herod put on his royal robes, sat on his throne, and made a speech to them. ²²The people gave him a great ovation, shouting, "It's the voice of a god, not of a man!"

²³Instantly, an angel of the Lord struck Herod with a sickness, because he accepted the people's worship instead of giving the glory to God. So he was consumed with worms and died.

²⁴Meanwhile, the word of God continued to spread, and there were many new believers. ²⁵When Barnabas and Saul had finished their mission to Jerusalem, they returned,* taking John Mark with them.

Barnabas and Saul Are Commissioned

13 Among the prophets and teachers of the church at Antioch of Syria were Barnabas, Simeon (called "the black man"*), Lucius (from Cyrene), Manaen (the childhood companion of King Herod Antipas*), and Saul. ²One day as these men were worshiping the Lord and fasting, the Holy Spirit said, "Appoint Barnabas and Saul for the special work to which I have called them." ³So after more fasting and prayer, the men laid their hands on them and sent them on their way.

Paul's First Missionary Journey

⁴So Barnabas and Saul were sent out by the Holy Spirit. They went down to the seaport of Seleucia and then sailed for the island of Cyprus. ⁵There, in the town of Salamis, they went to the Jewish synagogues and preached the word of God. John Mark went with them as their assistant.

⁶Afterward they traveled from town to town across the entire island until finally they reached Paphos, where they met a Jewish sorcerer, a false prophet named Bar-Jesus. ⁷He had attached himself to the governor, Sergius Paulus, who was an intelligent man. The governor invited Barnabas and Saul to visit him, for he wanted to hear the word of God. ⁸But Elymas, the sorcerer (as his name means in Greek), interfered and urged the governor to pay no attention to what Barnabas and Saul said. He was trying to keep the governor from believing.

⁹Saul, also known as Paul, was filled with the Holy Spirit, and he looked the sorcerer in the eye. ¹⁰Then he said, "You son of the devil, full of every sort of deceit and fraud, and enemy of all that is good! Will you never stop perverting the true ways of the Lord? ¹¹Watch now, for the

12:11 Or *the Jewish people.*   12:25 Or *mission, they returned to Jerusalem.* Other manuscripts read *mission, they returned from Jerusalem; still others read mission, they returned from Jerusalem to Antioch.*   13:1a Greek *who was called Niger.*   13:1b Greek *Herod the tetrarch.*

Lord has laid his hand of punishment upon you, and you will be struck blind. You will not see the sunlight for some time." Instantly mist and darkness came over the man's eyes, and he began groping around begging for someone to take his hand and lead him.

¹²When the governor saw what had happened, he became a believer, for he was astonished at the teaching about the Lord.

Paul Preaches in Antioch of Pisidia

¹³Paul and his companions then left Paphos by ship for Pamphylia, landing at the port town of Perga. There John Mark left them and returned to Jerusalem. ¹⁴But Paul and Barnabas traveled inland to Antioch of Pisidia.*

On the Sabbath they went to the synagogue for the services. ¹⁵After the usual readings from the books of Moses* and the prophets, those in charge of the service sent them this message: "Brothers, if you have any word of encouragement for the people, come and give it."

¹⁶So Paul stood, lifted his hand to quiet them, and started speaking. "Men of Israel," he said, "and you God-fearing Gentiles, listen to me.

¹⁷"The God of this nation of Israel chose our ancestors and made them multiply and grow strong during their stay in Egypt. Then with a powerful arm he led them out of their slavery. ¹⁸He put up with them* through forty years of wandering in the wilderness. ¹⁹Then he destroyed seven nations in Canaan and gave their land to Israel as an inheritance. ²⁰All this took about 450 years.

"After that, God gave them judges to rule until the time of Samuel the prophet. ²¹Then the people begged for a king, and God gave them Saul son of Kish, a man of the tribe of Benjamin, who reigned for forty years. ²²But God removed Saul and replaced him with David, a man about whom God said, 'I have found David son of Jesse, a man after my own heart. He will do everything I want him to do.'*

²³"And it is one of King David's descendants, Jesus, who is God's promised Savior of Israel! ²⁴Before he came, John the Baptist preached that all the people of Israel needed to repent of their sins and turn to God and be baptized. ²⁵As John was finishing his ministry he asked, 'Do you think I am the Messiah? No, I am not! But he is coming soon—and I'm not even worthy to be his slave and untie the sandals on his feet.'

²⁶"Brothers—you sons of Abraham, and also you God-fearing Gentiles—this message of salvation has been sent to us! ²⁷The people in Jerusalem and their leaders did not recognize Jesus as the one the prophets had spoken about. Instead, they condemned him, and in doing this they fulfilled the prophets' words that are read every Sabbath. ²⁸They found no legal reason to execute him, but they asked Pilate to have him killed anyway.

²⁹"When they had done all that the prophecies said about him, they took him down from the cross* and placed him in a tomb. ³⁰But God raised him from the dead! ³¹And over a period of many days he appeared to those who had gone with him from Galilee to Jerusalem. They are now his witnesses to the people of Israel.

³²"And now we are here to bring you this Good News. The promise was made to our ancestors, ³³and God has now fulfilled it for us, their descendants, by raising Jesus. This is what the second psalm says about Jesus:

'You are my Son.
    Today I have become your Father.'*

³⁴For God had promised to raise him from the dead, not leaving him to rot in the grave. He said, 'I will give you the sacred blessings I promised to David.'* ³⁵Another psalm explains it more fully: 'You will not allow your Holy One to rot in the grave.'* ³⁶This is not a reference to David, for after David had done the will of God in his own generation, he died and was buried with his ancestors, and his body decayed. ³⁷No, it was a reference to someone else—someone whom God raised and whose body did not decay.

³⁸*"Brothers, listen! We are here to proclaim that through this man Jesus there is forgiveness for your sins. ³⁹Everyone who believes in him is made right in God's sight—something the law of Moses could never do. ⁴⁰Be careful! Don't let the prophets' words apply to you. For they said,

⁴¹ 'Look, you mockers,
    be amazed and die!
For I am doing something in your own
        day,
    something you wouldn't believe
    even if someone told you about it.'*"

13:13-14 *Pamphylia* and *Pisidia* were districts in what is now Turkey.   13:15 Greek *from the law.*   13:18 Some manuscripts read *He cared for them;* compare Deut 1:31.   13:22 1 Sam 13:14.   13:29 Greek *from the tree.*   13:33 Or *Today I reveal you as my Son.* Ps 2:7. 13:34 Isa 55:3.   13:35 Ps 16:10.   13:38 English translations divide verses 38 and 39 in various ways.   13:41 Hab 1:5 (Greek version).

[42]As Paul and Barnabas left the synagogue that day, the people begged them to speak about these things again the next week. [43]Many Jews and devout converts to Judaism followed Paul and Barnabas, and the two men urged them to continue to rely on the grace of God.

Paul Turns to the Gentiles

[44]The following week almost the entire city turned out to hear them preach the word of the Lord. [45]But when some of the Jews saw the crowds, they were jealous; so they slandered Paul and argued against whatever he said.

[46]Then Paul and Barnabas spoke out boldly and declared, "It was necessary that we first preach the word of God to you Jews. But since you have rejected it and judged yourselves unworthy of eternal life, we will offer it to the Gentiles. [47]For the Lord gave us this command when he said,

'I have made you a light to the Gentiles,
    to bring salvation to the farthest corners
        of the earth.'*"

[48]When the Gentiles heard this, they were very glad and thanked the Lord for his message; and all who were chosen for eternal life became believers. [49]So the Lord's message spread throughout that region.

[50]Then the Jews stirred up the influential religious women and the leaders of the city, and they incited a mob against Paul and Barnabas and ran them out of town. [51]So they shook the dust from their feet as a sign of rejection and went to the town of Iconium. [52]And the believers* were filled with joy and with the Holy Spirit.

Paul and Barnabas in Iconium

14 The same thing happened in Iconium.* Paul and Barnabas went to the Jewish synagogue and preached with such power that a great number of both Jews and Greeks became believers. [2]Some of the Jews, however, spurned God's message and poisoned the minds of the Gentiles against Paul and Barnabas. [3]But the apostles stayed there a long time, preaching boldly about the grace of the Lord. And the Lord proved their message was true by giving them power to do miraculous signs and wonders. [4]But the people of the town were divided in their opinion about them. Some sided with the Jews, and some with the apostles.

[5]Then a mob of Gentiles and Jews, along with their leaders, decided to attack and stone them. [6]When the apostles learned of it, they fled to the region of Lycaonia—to the towns of Lystra and Derbe and the surrounding area. [7]And there they preached the Good News.

Paul and Barnabas in Lystra and Derbe

[8]While they were at Lystra, Paul and Barnabas came upon a man with crippled feet. He had been that way from birth, so he had never walked. He was sitting [9]and listening as Paul preached. Looking straight at him, Paul realized he had faith to be healed. [10]So Paul called to him in a loud voice, "Stand up!" And the man jumped to his feet and started walking.

[11]When the crowd saw what Paul had done, they shouted in their local dialect, "These men are gods in human form!" [12]They decided that Barnabas was the Greek god Zeus and that Paul was Hermes, since he was the chief speaker. [13]Now the temple of Zeus was located just outside the town. So the priest of the temple and the crowd brought bulls and wreaths of flowers to the town gates, and they prepared to offer sacrifices to the apostles.

[14]But when the apostles Barnabas and Paul heard what was happening, they tore their clothing in dismay and ran out among the people, shouting, [15]"Friends,* why are you doing this? We are merely human beings—just like you! We have come to bring you the Good News that you should turn from these worthless things and turn to the living God, who made heaven and earth, the sea, and everything in them. [16]In the past he permitted all the nations to go their own ways, [17]but he never left them without evidence of himself and his goodness. For instance, he sends you rain and good crops and gives you food and joyful hearts." [18]But even with these words, Paul and Barnabas could scarcely restrain the people from sacrificing to them.

[19]Then some Jews arrived from Antioch and Iconium and won the crowds to their side. They stoned Paul and dragged him out of town, thinking he was dead. [20]But as the believers* gathered around him, he got up and went back into the town. The next day he left with Barnabas for Derbe.

Paul and Barnabas Return to Antioch of Syria

[21]After preaching the Good News in Derbe and making many disciples, Paul and Barnabas

13:47 Isa 49:6.   13:52 Greek *the disciples.*   14:1 *Iconium,* as well as *Lystra* and *Derbe* (14:6), were towns in what is now Turkey. 14:15 Greek *Men.*   14:20 Greek *disciples;* also in 14:22, 28.

returned to Lystra, Iconium, and Antioch of Pisidia, 22where they strengthened the believers. They encouraged them to continue in the faith, reminding them that we must suffer many hardships to enter the Kingdom of God. 23Paul and Barnabas also appointed elders in every church. With prayer and fasting, they turned the elders over to the care of the Lord, in whom they had put their trust. 24Then they traveled back through Pisidia to Pamphylia. 25They preached the word in Perga, then went down to Attalia.

26Finally, they returned by ship to Antioch of Syria, where their journey had begun. The believers there had entrusted them to the grace of God to do the work they had now completed. 27Upon arriving in Antioch, they called the church together and reported everything God had done through them and how he had opened the door of faith to the Gentiles, too. 28And they stayed there with the believers for a long time.

The Council at Jerusalem

15 While Paul and Barnabas were at Antioch of Syria, some men from Judea arrived and began to teach the believers*: "Unless you are circumcised as required by the law of Moses, you cannot be saved." 2Paul and Barnabas disagreed with them, arguing vehemently. Finally, the church decided to send Paul and Barnabas to Jerusalem, accompanied by some local believers, to talk to the apostles and elders about this question. 3The church sent the delegates to Jerusalem, and they stopped along the way in Phoenicia and Samaria to visit the believers. They told them—much to everyone's joy—that the Gentiles, too, were being converted.

4When they arrived in Jerusalem, Barnabas and Paul were welcomed by the whole church, including the apostles and elders. They reported everything God had done through them. 5But then some of the believers who belonged to the sect of the Pharisees stood up and insisted, "The Gentile converts must be circumcised and required to follow the law of Moses."

6So the apostles and elders met together to resolve this issue. 7At the meeting, after a long discussion, Peter stood and addressed them as follows: "Brothers, you all know that God chose me from among you some time ago to preach to the Gentiles so that they could hear the Good

News and believe. 8God knows people's hearts, and he confirmed that he accepts Gentiles by giving them the Holy Spirit, just as he did to us. 9He made no distinction between us and them, for he cleansed their hearts through faith. 10So why are you now challenging God by burdening the Gentile believers* with a yoke that neither we nor our ancestors were able to bear? 11We believe that we are all saved the same way, by the undeserved grace of the Lord Jesus."

12Everyone listened quietly as Barnabas and Paul told about the miraculous signs and wonders God had done through them among the Gentiles.

13When they had finished, James stood and said, "Brothers, listen to me. 14Peter* has told you about the time God first visited the Gentiles to take from them a people for himself. 15And this conversion of Gentiles is exactly what the prophets predicted. As it is written:

16 'Afterward I will return
    and restore the fallen house*
    of David.
  I will rebuild its ruins
    and restore it,
17 so that the rest of humanity might seek
    the LORD,
    including the Gentiles—
    all those I have called to be mine.
  The LORD has spoken—
18   he who made these things known so
    long ago.'*

19"And so my judgment is that we should not make it difficult for the Gentiles who are turning to God. 20Instead, we should write and tell them to abstain from eating food offered to idols, from sexual immorality, from eating the meat of strangled animals, and from consuming blood. 21For these laws of Moses have been preached in Jewish synagogues in every city on every Sabbath for many generations."

The Letter for Gentile Believers

22Then the apostles and elders together with the whole church in Jerusalem chose delegates, and they sent them to Antioch of Syria with Paul and Barnabas to report on this decision. The men chosen were two of the church leaders*—Judas (also called Barsabbas) and Silas. 23This is the letter they took with them:

15:1 Greek *brothers*; also in 15:3, 23, 32, 33, 36, 40.   15:10 Greek *disciples*.   15:14 Greek *Simeon*.   15:16 Or *kingdom*; Greek reads *tent*.   15:16-18 Amos 9:11-12 (Greek version); Isa 45:21.   15:22 Greek *were leaders among the brothers*.

"This letter is from the apostles and elders, your brothers in Jerusalem. It is written to the Gentile believers in Antioch, Syria, and Cilicia. Greetings!

²⁴"We understand that some men from here have troubled you and upset you with their teaching, but we did not send them! ²⁵So we decided, having come to complete agreement, to send you official representatives, along with our beloved Barnabas and Paul, ²⁶who have risked their lives for the name of our Lord Jesus Christ. ²⁷We are sending Judas and Silas to confirm what we have decided concerning your question.

²⁸"For it seemed good to the Holy Spirit and to us to lay no greater burden on you than these few requirements: ²⁹You must abstain from eating food offered to idols, from consuming blood or the meat of strangled animals, and from sexual immorality. If you do this, you will do well. Farewell."

³⁰The messengers went at once to Antioch, where they called a general meeting of the believers and delivered the letter. ³¹And there was great joy throughout the church that day as they read this encouraging message.

³²Then Judas and Silas, both being prophets, spoke at length to the believers, encouraging and strengthening their faith. ³³They stayed for a while, and then the believers sent them back to the church in Jerusalem with a blessing of peace.* ³⁵Paul and Barnabas stayed in Antioch. They and many others taught and preached the word of the Lord there.

Paul and Barnabas Separate

³⁶After some time Paul said to Barnabas, "Let's go back and visit each city where we previously preached the word of the Lord, to see how the new believers are doing." ³⁷Barnabas agreed and wanted to take along John Mark. ³⁸But Paul disagreed strongly, since John Mark had deserted them in Pamphylia and had not continued with them in their work. ³⁹Their disagreement was so sharp that they separated. Barnabas took John Mark with him and sailed for Cyprus. ⁴⁰Paul chose Silas, and as he left, the believers entrusted him to the Lord's gracious care. ⁴¹Then he traveled throughout Syria and Cilicia, strengthening the churches there.

Paul's Second Missionary Journey

16 Paul went first to Derbe and then to Lystra, where there was a young disciple named Timothy. His mother was a Jewish believer, but his father was a Greek. ²Timothy was well thought of by the believers* in Lystra and Iconium, ³so Paul wanted him to join them on their journey. In deference to the Jews of the area, he arranged for Timothy to be circumcised before they left, for everyone knew that his father was a Greek. ⁴Then they went from town to town, instructing the believers to follow the decisions made by the apostles and elders in Jerusalem. ⁵So the churches were strengthened in their faith and grew larger every day.

A Call from Macedonia

⁶Next Paul and Silas traveled through the area of Phrygia and Galatia, because the Holy Spirit had prevented them from preaching the word in the province of Asia at that time. ⁷Then coming to the borders of Mysia, they headed north for the province of Bithynia,* but again the Spirit of Jesus did not allow them to go there. ⁸So instead, they went on through Mysia to the seaport of Troas.

⁹That night Paul had a vision: A man from Macedonia in northern Greece was standing there, pleading with him, "Come over to Macedonia and help us!" ¹⁰So we* decided to leave for Macedonia at once, having concluded that God was calling us to preach the Good News there.

Lydia of Philippi Believes in Jesus

¹¹We boarded a boat at Troas and sailed straight across to the island of Samothrace, and the next day we landed at Neapolis. ¹²From there we reached Philippi, a major city of that district of Macedonia and a Roman colony. And we stayed there several days.

¹³On the Sabbath we went a little way outside the city to a riverbank, where we thought people would be meeting for prayer, and we sat down to speak with some women who had gathered there. ¹⁴One of them was Lydia from Thyatira, a merchant of expensive purple cloth, who worshiped God. As she listened to us, the Lord opened her heart, and she accepted what Paul was saying. ¹⁵She and her household were baptized, and she asked us to be her guests. "If you agree that I am a true believer in the Lord,"

15:33 Some manuscripts add verse 34, *But Silas decided to stay there.*   16:2 Greek *brothers;* also in 16:40.   16:6-7 *Phrygia, Galatia, Asia, Mysia,* and *Bithynia* were all districts in what is now Turkey.   16:10 Luke, the writer of this book, here joined Paul and accompanied him on his journey.

she said, "come and stay at my home." And she urged us until we agreed.

Paul and Silas in Prison

¹⁶One day as we were going down to the place of prayer, we met a slave girl who had a spirit that enabled her to tell the future. She earned a lot of money for her masters by telling fortunes. ¹⁷She followed Paul and the rest of us, shouting, "These men are servants of the Most High God, and they have come to tell you how to be saved."

¹⁸This went on day after day until Paul got so exasperated that he turned and said to the demon within her, "I command you in the name of Jesus Christ to come out of her." And instantly it left her.

¹⁹Her masters' hopes of wealth were now shattered, so they grabbed Paul and Silas and dragged them before the authorities at the marketplace. ²⁰"The whole city is in an uproar because of these Jews!" they shouted to the city officials. ²¹"They are teaching customs that are illegal for us Romans to practice."

²²A mob quickly formed against Paul and Silas, and the city officials ordered them stripped and beaten with wooden rods. ²³They were severely beaten, and then they were thrown into prison. The jailer was ordered to make sure they didn't escape. ²⁴So the jailer put them into the inner dungeon and clamped their feet in the stocks.

²⁵Around midnight Paul and Silas were praying and singing hymns to God, and the other prisoners were listening. ²⁶Suddenly, there was a massive earthquake, and the prison was shaken to its foundations. All the doors immediately flew open, and the chains of every prisoner fell off! ²⁷The jailer woke up to see the prison doors wide open. He assumed the prisoners had escaped, so he drew his sword to kill himself. ²⁸But Paul shouted to him, "Stop! Don't kill yourself! We are all here!"

²⁹The jailer called for lights and ran to the dungeon and fell down trembling before Paul and Silas. ³⁰Then he brought them out and asked, "Sirs, what must I do to be saved?"

³¹They replied, "Believe in the Lord Jesus and you will be saved, along with everyone in your household." ³²And they shared the word of the Lord with him and with all who lived in his household. ³³Even at that hour of the night, the jailer cared for them and washed their wounds. Then he and everyone in his household were immediately baptized. ³⁴He brought them into his house and set a meal before them, and he and his entire household rejoiced because they all believed in God.

³⁵The next morning the city officials sent the police to tell the jailer, "Let those men go!" ³⁶So the jailer told Paul, "The city officials have said you and Silas are free to leave. Go in peace."

³⁷But Paul replied, "They have publicly beaten us without a trial and put us in prison—and we are Roman citizens. So now they want us to leave secretly? Certainly not! Let them come themselves to release us!"

³⁸When the police reported this, the city officials were alarmed to learn that Paul and Silas were Roman citizens. ³⁹So they came to the jail and apologized to them. Then they brought them out and begged them to leave the city. ⁴⁰When Paul and Silas left the prison, they returned to the home of Lydia. There they met with the believers and encouraged them once more. Then they left town.

Paul Preaches in Thessalonica

17 Paul and Silas then traveled through the towns of Amphipolis and Apollonia and came to Thessalonica, where there was a Jewish synagogue. ²As was Paul's custom, he went to the synagogue service, and for three Sabbaths in a row he used the Scriptures to reason with the people. ³He explained the prophecies and proved that the Messiah must suffer and rise from the dead. He said, "This Jesus I'm telling you about is the Messiah." ⁴Some of the Jews who listened were persuaded and joined Paul and Silas, along with many God-fearing Greek men and quite a few prominent women.*

⁵But some of the Jews were jealous, so they gathered some troublemakers from the marketplace to form a mob and start a riot. They attacked the home of Jason, searching for Paul and Silas so they could drag them out to the crowd.* ⁶Not finding them there, they dragged out Jason and some of the other believers* instead and took them before the city council. "Paul and Silas have caused trouble all over the world," they shouted, "and now they are here disturbing our city, too. ⁷And Jason has welcomed them into his home. They are all guilty of treason against Caesar, for they profess allegiance to another king, named Jesus."

⁸The people of the city, as well as the city council, were thrown into turmoil by these reports. ⁹So the officials forced Jason and the

---

17:4 Some manuscripts read *quite a few of the wives of the leading men.*   17:5 Or *the city council.*   17:6 Greek *brothers;* also in 17:10, 14.

other believers to post bond, and then they released them.

Paul and Silas in Berea

¹⁰That very night the believers sent Paul and Silas to Berea. When they arrived there, they went to the Jewish synagogue. ¹¹And the people of Berea were more open-minded than those in Thessalonica, and they listened eagerly to Paul's message. They searched the Scriptures day after day to see if Paul and Silas were teaching the truth. ¹²As a result, many Jews believed, as did many of the prominent Greek women and men.

¹³But when some Jews in Thessalonica learned that Paul was preaching the word of God in Berea, they went there and stirred up trouble. ¹⁴The believers acted at once, sending Paul on to the coast, while Silas and Timothy remained behind. ¹⁵Those escorting Paul went with him all the way to Athens; then they returned to Berea with instructions for Silas and Timothy to hurry and join him.

Paul Preaches in Athens

¹⁶While Paul was waiting for them in Athens, he was deeply troubled by all the idols he saw everywhere in the city. ¹⁷He went to the synagogue to reason with the Jews and the God-fearing Gentiles, and he spoke daily in the public square to all who happened to be there.

¹⁸He also had a debate with some of the Epicurean and Stoic philosophers. When he told them about Jesus and his resurrection, they said, "What's this babbler trying to say with these strange ideas he's picked up?" Others said, "He seems to be preaching about some foreign gods."

¹⁹Then they took him to the high council of the city.* "Come and tell us about this new teaching," they said. ²⁰"You are saying some rather strange things, and we want to know what it's all about." ²¹(It should be explained that all the Athenians as well as the foreigners in Athens seemed to spend all their time discussing the latest ideas.)

²²So Paul, standing before the council,* addressed them as follows: "Men of Athens, I notice that you are very religious in every way, ²³for as I was walking along I saw your many shrines. And one of your altars had this inscription on it: 'To an Unknown God.' This God, whom you worship without knowing, is the one I'm telling you about.

²⁴"He is the God who made the world and everything in it. Since he is Lord of heaven and earth, he doesn't live in man-made temples, ²⁵and human hands can't serve his needs—for he has no needs. He himself gives life and breath to everything, and he satisfies every need. ²⁶From one man* he created all the nations throughout the whole earth. He decided beforehand when they should rise and fall, and he determined their boundaries.

²⁷"His purpose was for the nations to seek after God and perhaps feel their way toward him and find him—though he is not far from any one of us. ²⁸For in him we live and move and exist. As some of your* own poets have said, 'We are his offspring.' ²⁹And since this is true, we shouldn't think of God as an idol designed by craftsmen from gold or silver or stone.

³⁰"God overlooked people's ignorance about these things in earlier times, but now he commands everyone everywhere to repent of their sins and turn to him. ³¹For he has set a day for judging the world with justice by the man he has appointed, and he proved to everyone who this is by raising him from the dead."

³²When they heard Paul speak about the resurrection of the dead, some laughed in contempt, but others said, "We want to hear more about this later." ³³That ended Paul's discussion with them, ³⁴but some joined him and became believers. Among them were Dionysius, a member of the council,* a woman named Damaris, and others with them.

Paul Meets Priscilla and Aquila in Corinth

18 Then Paul left Athens and went to Corinth.* ²There he became acquainted with a Jew named Aquila, born in Pontus, who had recently arrived from Italy with his wife, Priscilla. They had left Italy when Claudius Caesar deported all Jews from Rome. ³Paul lived and worked with them, for they were tentmakers* just as he was.

⁴Each Sabbath found Paul at the synagogue, trying to convince the Jews and Greeks alike. ⁵And after Silas and Timothy came down from Macedonia, Paul spent all his time preaching the word. He testified to the Jews that Jesus was the Messiah. ⁶But when they opposed

---

17:19 Or the most learned society of philosophers in the city. Greek reads the Areopagus.   17:22 Traditionally rendered standing in the middle of Mars Hill; Greek reads standing in the middle of the Areopagus.   17:26 Greek From one; other manuscripts read From one blood.   17:28 Some manuscripts read our.   17:34 Greek an Areopagite.   18:1 Athens and Corinth were major cities in Achaia, the region in the southern portion of the Greek peninsula.   18:3 Or leatherworkers.

and insulted him, Paul shook the dust from his clothes and said, "Your blood is upon your own heads—I am innocent. From now on I will go preach to the Gentiles."

7Then he left and went to the home of Titius Justus, a Gentile who worshiped God and lived next door to the synagogue. 8Crispus, the leader of the synagogue, and everyone in his household believed in the Lord. Many others in Corinth also heard Paul, became believers, and were baptized.

9One night the Lord spoke to Paul in a vision and told him, "Don't be afraid! Speak out! Don't be silent! 10For I am with you, and no one will attack and harm you, for many people in this city belong to me." 11So Paul stayed there for the next year and a half, teaching the word of God.

12But when Gallio became governor of Achaia, some Jews rose up together against Paul and brought him before the governor for judgment. 13They accused Paul of "persuading people to worship God in ways that are contrary to our law."

14But just as Paul started to make his defense, Gallio turned to Paul's accusers and said, "Listen, you Jews, if this were a case involving some wrongdoing or a serious crime, I would have a reason to accept your case. 15But since it is merely a question of words and names and your Jewish law, take care of it yourselves. I refuse to judge such matters." 16And he threw them out of the courtroom.

17The crowd* then grabbed Sosthenes, the leader of the synagogue, and beat him right there in the courtroom. But Gallio paid no attention.

Paul Returns to Antioch of Syria

18Paul stayed in Corinth for some time after that, then said good-bye to the brothers and sisters* and went to nearby Cenchrea. There he shaved his head according to Jewish custom, marking the end of a vow. Then he set sail for Syria, taking Priscilla and Aquila with him.

19They stopped first at the port of Ephesus, where Paul left the others behind. While he was there, he went to the synagogue to reason with the Jews. 20They asked him to stay longer, but he declined. 21As he left, however, he said, "I will come back later,* God willing." Then he set sail from Ephesus. 22The next stop was at the port of Caesarea. From there he went up

and visited the church at Jerusalem* and then went back to Antioch.

23After spending some time in Antioch, Paul went back through Galatia and Phrygia, visiting and strengthening all the believers.*

Apollos Instructed at Ephesus

24Meanwhile, a Jew named Apollos, an eloquent speaker who knew the Scriptures well, had arrived in Ephesus from Alexandria in Egypt. 25He had been taught the way of the Lord, and he taught others about Jesus with an enthusiastic spirit* and with accuracy. However, he knew only about John's baptism. 26When Priscilla and Aquila heard him preaching boldly in the synagogue, they took him aside and explained the way of God even more accurately.

27Apollos had been thinking about going to Achaia, and the brothers and sisters in Ephesus encouraged him to go. They wrote to the believers in Achaia, asking them to welcome him. When he arrived there, he proved to be of great benefit to those who, by God's grace, had believed. 28He refuted the Jews with powerful arguments in public debate. Using the Scriptures, he explained to them that Jesus was the Messiah.

Paul's Third Missionary Journey

19 While Apollos was in Corinth, Paul traveled through the interior regions until he reached Ephesus, on the coast, where he found several believers.* 2"Did you receive the Holy Spirit when you believed?" he asked them.

"No," they replied, "we haven't even heard that there is a Holy Spirit."

3"Then what baptism did you experience?" he asked.

And they replied, "The baptism of John."

4Paul said, "John's baptism called for repentance from sin. But John himself told the people to believe in the one who would come later, meaning Jesus."

5As soon as they heard this, they were baptized in the name of the Lord Jesus. 6Then when Paul laid his hands on them, the Holy Spirit came on them, and they spoke in other tongues* and prophesied. 7There were about twelve men in all.

Paul Ministers in Ephesus

8Then Paul went to the synagogue and preached boldly for the next three months,

18:17 Greek Everyone; other manuscripts read All the Greeks. 18:18 Greek brothers; also in 18:27. 18:21 Some manuscripts read "I must by all means be at Jerusalem for the upcoming festival, but I will come back later." 18:22 Greek the church. 18:23 Greek disciples; also in 18:27. 18:25 Or with enthusiasm in the Spirit. 19:1 Greek disciples; also in 19:9, 30. 19:6 Or in other languages.

arguing persuasively about the Kingdom of God. 9But some became stubborn, rejecting his message and publicly speaking against the Way. So Paul left the synagogue and took the believers with him. Then he held daily discussions at the lecture hall of Tyrannus. 10This went on for the next two years, so that people throughout the province of Asia—both Jews and Greeks—heard the word of the Lord.

11God gave Paul the power to perform unusual miracles. 12When handkerchiefs or aprons that had merely touched his skin were placed on sick people, they were healed of their diseases, and evil spirits were expelled.

13A group of Jews was traveling from town to town casting out evil spirits. They tried to use the name of the Lord Jesus in their incantation, saying, "I command you in the name of Jesus, whom Paul preaches, to come out!" 14Seven sons of Sceva, a leading priest, were doing this. 15But one time when they tried it, the evil spirit replied, "I know Jesus, and I know Paul, but who are you?" 16Then the man with the evil spirit leaped on them, overpowered them, and attacked them with such violence that they fled from the house, naked and battered.

17The story of what happened spread quickly all through Ephesus, to Jews and Greeks alike. A solemn fear descended on the city, and the name of the Lord Jesus was greatly honored. 18Many who became believers confessed their sinful practices. 19A number of them who had been practicing sorcery brought their incantation books and burned them at a public bonfire. The value of the books was several million dollars.* 20So the message about the Lord spread widely and had a powerful effect.

21Afterward Paul felt compelled by the Spirit* to go over to Macedonia and Achaia before going to Jerusalem. "And after that," he said, "I must go on to Rome!" 22He sent his two assistants, Timothy and Erastus, ahead to Macedonia while he stayed awhile longer in the province of Asia.

The Riot in Ephesus

23About that time, serious trouble developed in Ephesus concerning the Way. 24It began with Demetrius, a silversmith who had a large business manufacturing silver shrines of the Greek goddess Artemis.* He kept many craftsmen busy. 25He called them together, along with others employed in similar trades, and addressed them as follows:

"Gentlemen, you know that our wealth comes from this business. 26But as you have seen and heard, this man Paul has persuaded many people that handmade gods aren't really gods at all. And he's done this not only here in Ephesus but throughout the entire province! 27Of course, I'm not just talking about the loss of public respect for our business. I'm also concerned that the temple of the great goddess Artemis will lose its influence and that Artemis—this magnificent goddess worshiped throughout the province of Asia and all around the world—will be robbed of her great prestige!"

28At this their anger boiled, and they began shouting, "Great is Artemis of the Ephesians!" 29Soon the whole city was filled with confusion. Everyone rushed to the amphitheater, dragging along Gaius and Aristarchus, who were Paul's traveling companions from Macedonia. 30Paul wanted to go in, too, but the believers wouldn't let him. 31Some of the officials of the province, friends of Paul, also sent a message to him, begging him not to risk his life by entering the amphitheater.

32Inside, the people were all shouting, some one thing and some another. Everything was in confusion. In fact, most of them didn't even know why they were there. 33The Jews in the crowd pushed Alexander forward and told him to explain the situation. He motioned for silence and tried to speak. 34But when the crowd realized he was a Jew, they started shouting again and kept it up for about two hours: "Great is Artemis of the Ephesians! Great is Artemis of the Ephesians!"

35At last the mayor was able to quiet them down enough to speak. "Citizens of Ephesus," he said. "Everyone knows that Ephesus is the official guardian of the temple of the great Artemis, whose image fell down to us from heaven. 36Since this is an undeniable fact, you should stay calm and not do anything rash. 37You have brought these men here, but they have stolen nothing from the temple and have not spoken against our goddess.

38"If Demetrius and the craftsmen have a case against them, the courts are in session and the officials can hear the case at once. Let them make formal charges. 39And if there are complaints about other matters, they can be settled in a legal assembly. 40I am afraid we are in danger of being charged with rioting by the Roman government, since there is no cause

---

19:19 Greek 50,000 pieces of silver, each of which was the equivalent of a day's wage.   19:21 Or decided in his spirit.
19:24 Artemis is otherwise known as Diana.

for all this commotion. And if Rome demands an explanation, we won't know what to say." ⁴¹*Then he dismissed them, and they dispersed.

Paul Goes to Macedonia and Greece

20 When the uproar was over, Paul sent for the believers* and encouraged them. Then he said good-bye and left for Macedonia. ²While there, he encouraged the believers in all the towns he passed through. Then he traveled down to Greece, ³where he stayed for three months. He was preparing to sail back to Syria when he discovered a plot by some Jews against his life, so he decided to return through Macedonia.

⁴Several men were traveling with him. They were Sopater son of Pyrrhus from Berea; Aristarchus and Secundus from Thessalonica; Gaius from Derbe; Timothy; and Tychicus and Trophimus from the province of Asia. ⁵They went on ahead and waited for us at Troas. ⁶After the Passover* ended, we boarded a ship at Philippi in Macedonia and five days later joined them in Troas, where we stayed a week.

Paul's Final Visit to Troas

⁷On the first day of the week, we gathered with the local believers to share in the Lord's Supper.* Paul was preaching to them, and since he was leaving the next day, he kept talking until midnight. ⁸The upstairs room where we met was lighted with many flickering lamps. ⁹As Paul spoke on and on, a young man named Eutychus, sitting on the windowsill, became very drowsy. Finally, he fell sound asleep and dropped three stories to his death below. ¹⁰Paul went down, bent over him, and took him into his arms. "Don't worry," he said, "he's alive!" ¹¹Then they all went back upstairs, shared in the Lord's Supper,* and ate together. Paul continued talking to them until dawn, and then he left. ¹²Meanwhile, the young man was taken home alive and well, and everyone was greatly relieved.

Paul Meets the Ephesian Elders

¹³Paul went by land to Assos, where he had arranged for us to join him, while we traveled by ship. ¹⁴He joined us there, and we sailed together to Mitylene. ¹⁵The next day we sailed past the island of Kios. The following day we crossed to the island of Samos, and* a day later we arrived at Miletus.

¹⁶Paul had decided to sail on past Ephesus, for he didn't want to spend any more time in the province of Asia. He was hurrying to get to Jerusalem, if possible, in time for the Festival of Pentecost. ¹⁷But when we landed at Miletus, he sent a message to the elders of the church at Ephesus, asking them to come and meet him.

¹⁸When they arrived he declared, "You know that from the day I set foot in the province of Asia until now ¹⁹I have done the Lord's work humbly and with many tears. I have endured the trials that came to me from the plots of the Jews. ²⁰I never shrank back from telling you what you needed to hear, either publicly or in your homes. ²¹I have had one message for Jews and Greeks alike—the necessity of repenting from sin and turning to God, and of having faith in our Lord Jesus.

²²"And now I am bound by the Spirit* to go to Jerusalem. I don't know what awaits me, ²³except that the Holy Spirit tells me in city after city that jail and suffering lie ahead. ²⁴But my life is worth nothing to me unless I use it for finishing the work assigned me by the Lord Jesus—the work of telling others the Good News about the wonderful grace of God.

²⁵"And now I know that none of you to whom I have preached the Kingdom will ever see me again. ²⁶I declare today that I have been faithful. If anyone suffers eternal death, it's not my fault,* ²⁷for I didn't shrink from declaring all that God wants you to know.

²⁸"So guard yourselves and God's people. Feed and shepherd God's flock—his church, purchased with his own blood*—over which the Holy Spirit has appointed you as leaders.* ²⁹I know that false teachers, like vicious wolves, will come in among you after I leave, not sparing the flock. ³⁰Even some men from your own group will rise up and distort the truth in order to draw a following. ³¹Watch out! Remember the three years I was with you—my constant watch and care over you night and day, and my many tears for you.

³²"And now I entrust you to God and the message of his grace that is able to build you up and give you an inheritance with all those he has set apart for himself.

³³"I have never coveted anyone's silver or gold or fine clothes. ³⁴You know that these hands of mine have worked to supply my own needs and even the needs of those who were

---

19:41 Some translations include verse 41 as part of verse 40. 20:1 Greek *disciples.* 20:6 Greek *the days of unleavened bread.* 20:7 Greek *to break bread.* 20:11 Greek *broke the bread.* 20:15 Some manuscripts read *and having stayed at Trogyllium.* 20:22 Or *by my spirit,* or *by an inner compulsion;* Greek reads *by the spirit.* 20:26 Greek *I am innocent of the blood of all.* 20:28a Or *with the blood of his own [Son].* 20:28b Or *overseers,* or *bishops.*

with me. [35]And I have been a constant example of how you can help those in need by working hard. You should remember the words of the Lord Jesus: 'It is more blessed to give than to receive.'"

[36]When he had finished speaking, he knelt and prayed with them. [37]They all cried as they embraced and kissed him good-bye. [38]They were sad most of all because he had said that they would never see him again. Then they escorted him down to the ship.

Paul's Journey to Jerusalem

21 After saying farewell to the Ephesian elders, we sailed straight to the island of Cos. The next day we reached Rhodes and then went to Patara. [2]There we boarded a ship sailing for Phoenicia. [3]We sighted the island of Cyprus, passed it on our left, and landed at the harbor of Tyre, in Syria, where the ship was to unload its cargo.

[4]We went ashore, found the local believers,* and stayed with them a week. These believers prophesied through the Holy Spirit that Paul should not go on to Jerusalem. [5]When we returned to the ship at the end of the week, the entire congregation, including women* and children, left the city and came down to the shore with us. There we knelt, prayed, [6]and said our farewells. Then we went aboard, and they returned home.

[7]The next stop after leaving Tyre was Ptolemais, where we greeted the brothers and sisters* and stayed for one day. [8]The next day we went on to Caesarea and stayed at the home of Philip the Evangelist, one of the seven men who had been chosen to distribute food. [9]He had four unmarried daughters who had the gift of prophecy.

[10]Several days later a man named Agabus, who also had the gift of prophecy, arrived from Judea. [11]He came over, took Paul's belt, and bound his own feet and hands with it. Then he said, "The Holy Spirit declares, 'So shall the owner of this belt be bound by the Jewish leaders in Jerusalem and turned over to the Gentiles.'" [12]When we heard this, we and the local believers all begged Paul not to go on to Jerusalem.

[13]But he said, "Why all this weeping? You are breaking my heart! I am ready not only to be jailed at Jerusalem but even to die for the sake of the Lord Jesus." [14]When it was clear that we couldn't persuade him, we gave up and said, "The Lord's will be done."

Paul Arrives at Jerusalem

[15]After this we packed our things and left for Jerusalem. [16]Some believers from Caesarea accompanied us, and they took us to the home of Mnason, a man originally from Cyprus and one of the early believers. [17]When we arrived, the brothers and sisters in Jerusalem welcomed us warmly.

[18]The next day Paul went with us to meet with James, and all the elders of the Jerusalem church were present. [19]After greeting them, Paul gave a detailed account of the things God had accomplished among the Gentiles through his ministry.

[20]After hearing this, they praised God. And then they said, "You know, dear brother, how many thousands of Jews have also believed, and they all follow the law of Moses very seriously. [21]But the Jewish believers here in Jerusalem have been told that you are teaching all the Jews who live among the Gentiles to turn their backs on the laws of Moses. They've heard that you teach them not to circumcise their children or follow other Jewish customs. [22]What should we do? They will certainly hear that you have come.

[23]"Here's what we want you to do. We have four men here who have completed their vow. [24]Go with them to the Temple and join them in the purification ceremony, paying for them to have their heads ritually shaved. Then everyone will know that the rumors are all false and that you yourself observe the Jewish laws. [25]"As for the Gentile believers, they should do what we already told them in a letter: They should abstain from eating food offered to idols, from consuming blood or the meat of strangled animals, and from sexual immorality."

Paul Is Arrested

[26]So Paul went to the Temple the next day with the other men. They had already started the purification ritual, so he publicly announced the date when their vows would end and sacrifices would be offered for each of them.

[27]The seven days were almost ended when some Jews from the province of Asia saw Paul in the Temple and roused a mob against him. They grabbed him, [28]yelling, "Men of Israel, help us! This is the man who preaches against our people everywhere and tells everybody to disobey the Jewish laws. He speaks against the Temple—and even defiles this holy place by bringing in Gentiles.*" [29](For earlier that day

21:4 Greek *disciples;* also in 21:16.   21:5 Or *wives.*   21:7 Greek *brothers;* also in 21:17.   21:28 Greek *Greeks.*

they had seen him in the city with Trophimus, a Gentile from Ephesus,* and they assumed Paul had taken him into the Temple.)

30 The whole city was rocked by these accusations, and a great riot followed. Paul was grabbed and dragged out of the Temple, and immediately the gates were closed behind him. 31 As they were trying to kill him, word reached the commander of the Roman regiment that all Jerusalem was in an uproar. 32 He immediately called out his soldiers and officers* and ran down among the crowd. When the mob saw the commander and the troops coming, they stopped beating Paul.

33 Then the commander arrested him and ordered him bound with two chains. He asked the crowd who he was and what he had done. 34 Some shouted one thing and some another. Since he couldn't find out the truth in all the uproar and confusion, he ordered that Paul be taken to the fortress. 35 As Paul reached the stairs, the mob grew so violent the soldiers had to lift him to their shoulders to protect him. 36 And the crowd followed behind, shouting, "Kill him, kill him!"

Paul Speaks to the Crowd

37 As Paul was about to be taken inside, he said to the commander, "May I have a word with you?"

"Do you know Greek?" the commander asked, surprised. 38 "Aren't you the Egyptian who led a rebellion some time ago and took 4,000 members of the Assassins out into the desert?"

39 "No," Paul replied, "I am a Jew and a citizen of Tarsus in Cilicia, which is an important city. Please, let me talk to these people." 40 The commander agreed, so Paul stood on the stairs and motioned to the people to be quiet. Soon a deep silence enveloped the crowd, and he addressed them in their own language, Aramaic.*

22 "Brothers and esteemed fathers," Paul said, "listen to me as I offer my defense." 2 When they heard him speaking in their own language,* the silence was even greater.

3 Then Paul said, "I am a Jew, born in Tarsus, a city in Cilicia, and I was brought up and educated here in Jerusalem under Gamaliel. As his student, I was carefully trained in our Jewish laws and customs. I became very zealous to honor God in everything I did, just like all of you today. 4 And I persecuted the followers of the Way, hounding some to death, arresting both men and women and throwing them in prison. 5 The high priest and the whole council of elders can testify that this is so. For I received letters from them to our Jewish brothers in Damascus, authorizing me to bring the followers of the Way from there to Jerusalem, in chains, to be punished.

6 "As I was on the road, approaching Damascus about noon, a very bright light from heaven suddenly shone down around me. 7 I fell to the ground and heard a voice saying to me, 'Saul, Saul, why are you persecuting me?'

8 "'Who are you, lord?' I asked.

"And the voice replied, 'I am Jesus the Nazarene,* the one you are persecuting.' 9 The people with me saw the light but didn't understand the voice speaking to me.

10 "I asked, 'What should I do, Lord?'

"And the Lord told me, 'Get up and go into Damascus, and there you will be told everything you are to do.'

11 "I was blinded by the intense light and had to be led by the hand to Damascus by my companions. 12 A man named Ananias lived there. He was a godly man, deeply devoted to the law, and well regarded by all the Jews of Damascus. 13 He came and stood beside me and said, 'Brother Saul, regain your sight.' And that very moment I could see him!

14 "Then he told me, 'The God of our ancestors has chosen you to know his will and to see the Righteous One and hear him speak. 15 For you are to be his witness, telling everyone what you have seen and heard. 16 What are you waiting for? Get up and be baptized. Have your sins washed away by calling on the name of the Lord.'

17 "After I returned to Jerusalem, I was praying in the Temple and fell into a trance. 18 I saw a vision of Jesus* saying to me, 'Hurry! Leave Jerusalem, for the people here won't accept your testimony about me.'

19 "'But Lord,' I argued, 'they certainly know that in every synagogue I imprisoned and beat those who believed in you. 20 And I was in complete agreement when your witness Stephen was killed. I stood by and kept the coats they took off when they stoned him.'

21 "But the Lord said to me, 'Go, for I will send you far away to the Gentiles!'"

22 The crowd listened until Paul said that word. Then they all began to shout, "Away with such a fellow! He isn't fit to live!" 23 They yelled,

---

21:29 Greek *Trophimus, the Ephesian.*   21:32 Greek *centurions.*   21:40 Or *Hebrew.*   22:2 Greek *in Aramaic,* or *in Hebrew.*
22:8 Or *Jesus of Nazareth.*   22:18 Greek *him.*

threw off their coats, and tossed handfuls of dust into the air.

Paul Reveals His Roman Citizenship

24The commander brought Paul inside and ordered him lashed with whips to make him confess his crime. He wanted to find out why the crowd had become so furious. 25When they tied Paul down to lash him, Paul said to the officer* standing there, "Is it legal for you to whip a Roman citizen who hasn't even been tried?"

26When the officer heard this, he went to the commander and asked, "What are you doing? This man is a Roman citizen!"

27So the commander went over and asked Paul, "Tell me, are you a Roman citizen?"

"Yes, I certainly am," Paul replied.

28"I am, too," the commander muttered, "and it cost me plenty!"

Paul answered, "But I am a citizen by birth!"

29The soldiers who were about to interrogate Paul quickly withdrew when they heard he was a Roman citizen, and the commander was frightened because he had ordered him bound and whipped.

Paul before the High Council

30The next day the commander ordered the leading priests into session with the Jewish high council.* He wanted to find out what the trouble was all about, so he released Paul to have him stand before them.

23 Gazing intently at the high council,* Paul began: "Brothers, I have always lived before God with a clear conscience!"

2Instantly Ananias the high priest commanded those close to Paul to slap him on the mouth. 3But Paul said to him, "God will slap you, you corrupt hypocrite!* What kind of judge are you to break the law yourself by ordering me struck like that?"

4Those standing near Paul said to him, "Do you dare to insult God's high priest?"

5"I'm sorry, brothers. I didn't realize he was the high priest," Paul replied, "for the Scriptures say, 'You must not speak evil of any of your rulers.'*"

6Paul realized that some members of the high council were Sadducees and some were Pharisees, so he shouted, "Brothers, I am a Pharisee, as were my ancestors! And I am on trial because my hope is in the resurrection of the dead!"

7This divided the council—the Pharisees against the Sadducees—8for the Sadducees say there is no resurrection or angels or spirits, but the Pharisees believe in all of these. 9So there was a great uproar. Some of the teachers of religious law who were Pharisees jumped up and began to argue forcefully. "We see nothing wrong with him," they shouted. "Perhaps a spirit or an angel spoke to him." 10As the conflict grew more violent, the commander was afraid they would tear Paul apart. So he ordered his soldiers to go and rescue him by force and take him back to the fortress.

11That night the Lord appeared to Paul and said, "Be encouraged, Paul. Just as you have been a witness to me here in Jerusalem, you must preach the Good News in Rome as well."

The Plan to Kill Paul

12The next morning a group of Jews* got together and bound themselves with an oath not to eat or drink until they had killed Paul. 13There were more than forty of them in the conspiracy. 14They went to the leading priests and elders and told them, "We have bound ourselves with an oath to eat nothing until we have killed Paul. 15So you and the high council should ask the commander to bring Paul back to the council again. Pretend you want to examine his case more fully. We will kill him on the way."

16But Paul's nephew—his sister's son—heard of their plan and went to the fortress and told Paul. 17Paul called for one of the Roman officers* and said, "Take this young man to the commander. He has something important to tell him."

18So the officer did, explaining, "Paul, the prisoner, called me over and asked me to bring this young man to you because he has something to tell you."

19The commander took his hand, led him aside, and asked, "What is it you want to tell me?"

20Paul's nephew told him, "Some Jews are going to ask you to bring Paul before the high council tomorrow, pretending they want to get some more information. 21But don't do it! There are more than forty men hiding along the way ready to ambush him. They have vowed not to eat or drink anything until they have killed him. They are ready now, just waiting for your consent."

22"Don't let anyone know you told me this," the commander warned the young man.

22:25 Greek *the centurion;* also in 22:26.   22:30 Greek *Sanhedrin.*   23:1 Greek *Sanhedrin;* also in 23:6, 15, 20, 28.   23:3 Greek *you whitewashed wall.*   23:5 Exod 22:28.   23:12 Greek *the Jews.*   23:17 Greek *centurions;* also in 23:23.

Paul Is Sent to Caesarea

23Then the commander called two of his officers and ordered, "Get 200 soldiers ready to leave for Caesarea at nine o'clock tonight. Also take 200 spearmen and 70 mounted troops. 24Provide horses for Paul to ride, and get him safely to Governor Felix." 25Then he wrote this letter to the governor:

26"From Claudius Lysias, to his Excellency, Governor Felix: Greetings!

27"This man was seized by some Jews, and they were about to kill him when I arrived with the troops. When I learned that he was a Roman citizen, I removed him to safety. 28Then I took him to their high council to try to learn the basis of the accusations against him. 29I soon discovered the charge was something regarding their religious law—certainly nothing worthy of imprisonment or death. 30But when I was informed of a plot to kill him, I immediately sent him on to you. I have told his accusers to bring their charges before you."

31So that night, as ordered, the soldiers took Paul as far as Antipatris. 32They returned to the fortress the next morning, while the mounted troops took him on to Caesarea. 33When they arrived in Caesarea, they presented Paul and the letter to Governor Felix. 34He read it and then asked Paul what province he was from. "Cilicia," Paul answered.

35"I will hear your case myself when your accusers arrive," the governor told him. Then the governor ordered him kept in the prison at Herod's headquarters.*

Paul Appears before Felix

24 Five days later Ananias, the high priest, arrived with some of the Jewish elders and the lawyer* Tertullus, to present their case against Paul to the governor. 2When Paul was called in, Tertullus presented the charges against Paul in the following address to the governor:

"You have provided a long period of peace for us Jews and with foresight have enacted reforms for us. 3For all of this, Your Excellency, we are very grateful to you. 4But I don't want to bore you, so please give me your attention for only a moment. 5We have found this man to be a troublemaker who is constantly stirring up riots among the Jews all over the world. He is a ringleader of the cult known as the Nazarenes. 6Furthermore, he was trying to desecrate the Temple when we arrested him.* 8You can find out the truth of our accusations by examining him yourself." 9Then the other Jews chimed in, declaring that everything Tertullus said was true.

10The governor then motioned for Paul to speak. Paul said, "I know, sir, that you have been a judge of Jewish affairs for many years, so I gladly present my defense before you. 11You can quickly discover that I arrived in Jerusalem no more than twelve days ago to worship at the Temple. 12My accusers never found me arguing with anyone in the Temple, nor stirring up a riot in any synagogue or on the streets of the city. 13These men cannot prove the things they accuse me of doing.

14"But I admit that I follow the Way, which they call a cult. I worship the God of our ancestors, and I firmly believe the Jewish law and everything written in the prophets. 15I have the same hope in God that these men have, that he will raise both the righteous and the unrighteous. 16Because of this, I always try to maintain a clear conscience before God and all people.

17"After several years away, I returned to Jerusalem with money to aid my people and to offer sacrifices to God. 18My accusers saw me in the Temple as I was completing a purification ceremony. There was no crowd around me and no rioting. 19But some Jews from the province of Asia were there—and they ought to be here to bring charges if they have anything against me! 20Ask these men here what crime the Jewish high council* found me guilty of, 21except for the one time I shouted out, 'I am on trial before you today because I believe in the resurrection of the dead!'"

22At that point Felix, who was quite familiar with the Way, adjourned the hearing and said, "Wait until Lysias, the garrison commander, arrives. Then I will decide the case." 23He ordered an officer* to keep Paul in custody but to give him some freedom and allow his friends to visit him and take care of his needs.

24A few days later Felix came back with his wife, Drusilla, who was Jewish. Sending for Paul, they listened as he told them about faith

23:35 Greek *Herod's Praetorium.*   24:1 Greek *some elders and an orator.*   24:6 Some manuscripts add an expanded conclusion to verse 6, all of verse 7, and an additional phrase in verse 8: *We would have judged him by our law,* 7*but Lysias, the commander of the garrison, came and violently took him away from us,* 8*commanding his accusers to come before you.*   24:20 Greek *Sanhedrin.* 24:23 Greek *a centurion.*

in Christ Jesus. ²⁵As he reasoned with them about righteousness and self-control and the coming day of judgment, Felix became frightened. "Go away for now," he replied. "When it is more convenient, I'll call for you again." ²⁶He also hoped that Paul would bribe him, so he sent for him quite often and talked with him.

²⁷After two years went by in this way, Felix was succeeded by Porcius Festus. And because Felix wanted to gain favor with the Jewish people, he left Paul in prison.

Paul Appears before Festus

25 Three days after Festus arrived in Caesarea to take over his new responsibilities, he left for Jerusalem, ²where the leading priests and other Jewish leaders met with him and made their accusations against Paul. ³They asked Festus as a favor to transfer Paul to Jerusalem (planning to ambush and kill him on the way). ⁴But Festus replied that Paul was at Caesarea and he himself would be returning there soon. ⁵So he said, "Those of you in authority can return with me. If Paul has done anything wrong, you can make your accusations."

⁶About eight or ten days later Festus returned to Caesarea, and on the following day he took his seat in court and ordered that Paul be brought in. ⁷When Paul arrived, the Jewish leaders from Jerusalem gathered around and made many serious accusations they couldn't prove.

⁸Paul denied the charges. "I am not guilty of any crime against the Jewish laws or the Temple or the Roman government," he said.

⁹Then Festus, wanting to please the Jews, asked him, "Are you willing to go to Jerusalem and stand trial before me there?"

¹⁰But Paul replied, "No! This is the official Roman court, so I ought to be tried right here. You know very well I am not guilty of harming the Jews. ¹¹If I have done something worthy of death, I don't refuse to die. But if I am innocent, no one has a right to turn me over to these men to kill me. I appeal to Caesar!"

¹²Festus conferred with his advisers and then replied, "Very well! You have appealed to Caesar, and to Caesar you will go!"

¹³A few days later King Agrippa arrived with his sister, Bernice,* to pay their respects to Festus. ¹⁴During their stay of several days, Festus discussed Paul's case with the king. "There is a prisoner here," he told him, "whose case was left for me by Felix. ¹⁵When I was in Jerusalem, the leading priests and Jewish elders pressed

charges against him and asked me to condemn him. ¹⁶I pointed out to them that Roman law does not convict people without a trial. They must be given an opportunity to confront their accusers and defend themselves.

¹⁷"When his accusers came here for the trial, I didn't delay. I called the case the very next day and ordered Paul brought in. ¹⁸But the accusations made against him weren't any of the crimes I expected. ¹⁹Instead, it was something about their religion and a dead man named Jesus, who Paul insists is alive. ²⁰I was at a loss to know how to investigate these things, so I asked him whether he would be willing to stand trial on these charges in Jerusalem. ²¹But Paul appealed to have his case decided by the emperor. So I ordered that he be held in custody until I could arrange to send him to Caesar."

²²"I'd like to hear the man myself," Agrippa said.

And Festus replied, "You will—tomorrow!"

Paul Speaks to Agrippa

²³So the next day Agrippa and Bernice arrived at the auditorium with great pomp, accompanied by military officers and prominent men of the city. Festus ordered that Paul be brought in. ²⁴Then Festus said, "King Agrippa and all who are here, this is the man whose death is demanded by all the Jews, both here and in Jerusalem. ²⁵But in my opinion he has done nothing deserving death. However, since he appealed his case to the emperor, I have decided to send him to Rome.

²⁶"But what shall I write the emperor? For there is no clear charge against him. So I have brought him before all of you, and especially you, King Agrippa, so that after we examine him, I might have something to write. ²⁷For it makes no sense to send a prisoner to the emperor without specifying the charges against him!"

26 Then Agrippa said to Paul, "You may speak in your defense."

So Paul, gesturing with his hand, started his defense: ²"I am fortunate, King Agrippa, that you are the one hearing my defense today against all these accusations made by the Jewish leaders, ³for I know you are an expert on all Jewish customs and controversies. Now please listen to me patiently!

⁴"As the Jewish leaders are well aware, I was given a thorough Jewish training from

25:13 Greek *Agrippa the king and Bernice arrived.*

my earliest childhood among my own people and in Jerusalem. ⁵If they would admit it, they know that I have been a member of the Pharisees, the strictest sect of our religion. ⁶Now I am on trial because of my hope in the fulfillment of God's promise made to our ancestors. ⁷In fact, that is why the twelve tribes of Israel zealously worship God night and day, and they share the same hope I have. Yet, Your Majesty, they accuse me for having this hope! ⁸Why does it seem incredible to any of you that God can raise the dead?

⁹"I used to believe that I ought to do everything I could to oppose the very name of Jesus the Nazarene.* ¹⁰Indeed, I did just that in Jerusalem. Authorized by the leading priests, I caused many believers* there to be sent to prison. And I cast my vote against them when they were condemned to death. ¹¹Many times I had them punished in the synagogues to get them to curse Jesus.* I was so violently opposed to them that I even chased them down in foreign cities.

¹²"One day I was on such a mission to Damascus, armed with the authority and commission of the leading priests. ¹³About noon, Your Majesty, as I was on the road, a light from heaven brighter than the sun shone down on me and my companions. ¹⁴We all fell down, and I heard a voice saying to me in Aramaic,* 'Saul, Saul, why are you persecuting me? It is useless for you to fight against my will.'*

¹⁵"'Who are you, lord?' I asked.

"And the Lord replied, 'I am Jesus, the one you are persecuting. ¹⁶Now get to your feet! For I have appeared to you to appoint you as my servant and witness. Tell people that you have seen me, and tell them what I will show you in the future. ¹⁷And I will rescue you from both your own people and the Gentiles. Yes, I am sending you to the Gentiles ¹⁸to open their eyes, so they may turn from darkness to light and from the power of Satan to God. Then they will receive forgiveness for their sins and be given a place among God's people, who are set apart by faith in me.'

¹⁹"And so, King Agrippa, I obeyed that vision from heaven. ²⁰I preached first to those in Damascus, then in Jerusalem and throughout all Judea, and also to the Gentiles, that all must repent of their sins and turn to God—and prove they have changed by the good things they do. ²¹Some Jews arrested me in the Temple for preaching this, and they tried to kill me. ²²But God has protected me right up to this present time so I can testify to everyone, from the least to the greatest. I teach nothing except what the prophets and Moses said would happen—²³that the Messiah would suffer and be the first to rise from the dead, and in this way announce God's light to Jews and Gentiles alike."

²⁴Suddenly, Festus shouted, "Paul, you are insane. Too much study has made you crazy!"

²⁵But Paul replied, "I am not insane, Most Excellent Festus. What I am saying is the sober truth. ²⁶And King Agrippa knows about these things. I speak boldly, for I am sure these events are all familiar to him, for they were not done in a corner! ²⁷King Agrippa, do you believe the prophets? I know you do—"

²⁸Agrippa interrupted him. "Do you think you can persuade me to become a Christian so quickly?"*

²⁹Paul replied, "Whether quickly or not, I pray to God that both you and everyone here in this audience might become the same as I am, except for these chains."

³⁰Then the king, the governor, Bernice, and all the others stood and left. ³¹As they went out, they talked it over and agreed, "This man hasn't done anything to deserve death or imprisonment."

³²And Agrippa said to Festus, "He could have been set free if he hadn't appealed to Caesar."

Paul Sails for Rome

27 When the time came, we set sail for Italy. Paul and several other prisoners were placed in the custody of a Roman officer* named Julius, a captain of the Imperial Regiment. ²Aristarchus, a Macedonian from Thessalonica, was also with us. We left on a ship whose home port was Adramyttium on the northwest coast of the province of Asia;* it was scheduled to make several stops at ports along the coast of the province.

³The next day when we docked at Sidon, Julius was very kind to Paul and let him go ashore to visit with friends so they could provide for his needs. ⁴Putting out to sea from there, we encountered strong headwinds that made it difficult to keep the ship on course, so we sailed north of Cyprus between the island and the mainland. ⁵Keeping to the open sea, we passed along the coast of Cilicia and

26:9 Or Jesus of Nazareth. 26:10 Greek many of God's holy people. 26:11 Greek to blaspheme. 26:14a Or Hebrew. 26:14b Greek It is hard for you to kick against the oxgoads. 26:28 Or "A little more, and your arguments would make me a Christian." 27:1 Greek centurion; similarly in 27:6, 11, 31, 43. 27:2 Asia was a Roman province in what is now western Turkey.

Pamphylia, landing at Myra, in the province of Lycia. [6]There the commanding officer found an Egyptian ship from Alexandria that was bound for Italy, and he put us on board.

[7]We had several days of slow sailing, and after great difficulty we finally neared Cnidus. But the wind was against us, so we sailed across to Crete and along the sheltered coast of the island, past the cape of Salmone. [8]We struggled along the coast with great difficulty and finally arrived at Fair Havens, near the town of Lasea. [9]We had lost a lot of time. The weather was becoming dangerous for sea travel because it was so late in the fall,* and Paul spoke to the ship's officers about it.

[10]"Men," he said, "I believe there is trouble ahead if we go on—shipwreck, loss of cargo, and danger to our lives as well." [11]But the officer in charge of the prisoners listened more to the ship's captain and the owner than to Paul. [12]And since Fair Havens was an exposed harbor—a poor place to spend the winter— most of the crew wanted to go on to Phoenix, farther up the coast of Crete, and spend the winter there. Phoenix was a good harbor with only a southwest and northwest exposure.

The Storm at Sea

[13]When a light wind began blowing from the south, the sailors thought they could make it. So they pulled up anchor and sailed close to the shore of Crete. [14]But the weather changed abruptly, and a wind of typhoon strength (called a "northeaster") burst across the island and blew us out to sea. [15]The sailors couldn't turn the ship into the wind, so they gave up and let it run before the gale.

[16]We sailed along the sheltered side of a small island named Cauda,* where with great difficulty we hoisted aboard the lifeboat being towed behind us. [17]Then the sailors bound ropes around the hull of the ship to strengthen it. They were afraid of being driven across to the sandbars of Syrtis off the African coast, so they lowered the sea anchor to slow the ship and were driven before the wind.

[18]The next day, as gale-force winds continued to batter the ship, the crew began throwing the cargo overboard. [19]The following day they even took some of the ship's gear and threw it overboard. [20]The terrible storm raged for many days, blotting out the sun and the stars, until at last all hope was gone.

[21]No one had eaten for a long time. Finally, Paul called the crew together and said, "Men, you should have listened to me in the first place and not left Crete. You would have avoided all this damage and loss. [22]But take courage! None of you will lose your lives, even though the ship will go down. [23]For last night an angel of the God to whom I belong and whom I serve stood beside me, [24]and he said, 'Don't be afraid, Paul, for you will surely stand trial before Caesar! What's more, God in his goodness has granted safety to everyone sailing with you.' [25]So take courage! For I believe God. It will be just as he said. [26]But we will be shipwrecked on an island."

The Shipwreck

[27]About midnight on the fourteenth night of the storm, as we were being driven across the Sea of Adria,* the sailors sensed land was near. [28]They dropped a weighted line and found that the water was 120 feet deep. But a little later they measured again and found it was only 90 feet deep.* [29]At this rate they were afraid we would soon be driven against the rocks along the shore, so they threw out four anchors from the back of the ship and prayed for daylight.

[30]Then the sailors tried to abandon the ship; they lowered the lifeboat as though they were going to put out anchors from the front of the ship. [31]But Paul said to the commanding officer and the soldiers, "You will all die unless the sailors stay aboard." [32]So the soldiers cut the ropes to the lifeboat and let it drift away.

[33]Just as day was dawning, Paul urged everyone to eat. "You have been so worried that you haven't touched food for two weeks," he said. [34]"Please eat something now for your own good. For not a hair of your heads will perish." [35]Then he took some bread, gave thanks to God before them all, and broke off a piece and ate it. [36]Then everyone was encouraged and began to eat—[37]all 276 of us who were on board. [38]After eating, the crew lightened the ship further by throwing the cargo of wheat overboard.

[39]When morning dawned, they didn't recognize the coastline, but they saw a bay with a beach and wondered if they could get to shore by running the ship aground. [40]So they cut off the anchors and left them in the sea. Then they lowered the rudders, raised the foresail, and headed toward shore. [41]But they hit a shoal and ran the ship aground too soon. The bow of the

27:9 Greek *because the fast was now already gone by.* This fast was associated with the Day of Atonement (*Yom Kippur*), which occurred in late September or early October.   27:16 Some manuscripts read *Clauda.*   27:27 The *Sea of Adria* includes the central portion of the Mediterranean.   27:28 Greek *20 fathoms . . . 15 fathoms* [37 meters . . . 27 meters].

ship stuck fast, while the stern was repeatedly smashed by the force of the waves and began to break apart.

⁴²The soldiers wanted to kill the prisoners to make sure they didn't swim ashore and escape. ⁴³But the commanding officer wanted to spare Paul, so he didn't let them carry out their plan. Then he ordered all who could swim to jump overboard first and make for land. ⁴⁴The others held on to planks or debris from the broken ship.* So everyone escaped safely to shore.

Paul on the Island of Malta

28 Once we were safe on shore, we learned that we were on the island of Malta. ²The people of the island were very kind to us. It was cold and rainy, so they built a fire on the shore to welcome us.

³As Paul gathered an armful of sticks and was laying them on the fire, a poisonous snake, driven out by the heat, bit him on the hand. ⁴The people of the island saw it hanging from his hand and said to each other, "A murderer, no doubt! Though he escaped the sea, justice will not permit him to live." ⁵But Paul shook off the snake into the fire and was unharmed. ⁶The people waited for him to swell up or suddenly drop dead. But when they had waited a long time and saw that he wasn't harmed, they changed their minds and decided he was a god.

⁷Near the shore where we landed was an estate belonging to Publius, the chief official of the island. He welcomed us and treated us kindly for three days. ⁸As it happened, Publius's father was ill with fever and dysentery. Paul went in and prayed for him, and laying his hands on him, he healed him. ⁹Then all the other sick people on the island came and were healed. ¹⁰As a result we were showered with honors, and when the time came to sail, people supplied us with everything we would need for the trip.

Paul Arrives at Rome

¹¹It was three months after the shipwreck that we set sail on another ship that had wintered at the island—an Alexandrian ship with the twin gods* as its figurehead. ¹²Our first stop was Syracuse,* where we stayed three days. ¹³From there we sailed across to Rhegium.* A day later a south wind began blowing, so the following day we sailed up the coast to Puteoli.

¹⁴There we found some believers,* who invited us to spend a week with them. And so we came to Rome.

¹⁵The brothers and sisters* in Rome had heard we were coming, and they came to meet us at the Forum* on the Appian Way. Others joined us at The Three Taverns.* When Paul saw them, he was encouraged and thanked God.

¹⁶When we arrived in Rome, Paul was permitted to have his own private lodging, though he was guarded by a soldier.

Paul Preaches at Rome under Guard

¹⁷Three days after Paul's arrival, he called together the local Jewish leaders. He said to them, "Brothers, I was arrested in Jerusalem and handed over to the Roman government, even though I had done nothing against our people or the customs of our ancestors. ¹⁸The Romans tried me and wanted to release me, because they found no cause for the death sentence. ¹⁹But when the Jewish leaders protested the decision, I felt it necessary to appeal to Caesar, even though I had no desire to press charges against my own people. ²⁰I asked you to come here today so we could get acquainted and so I could explain to you that I am bound with this chain because I believe that the hope of Israel—the Messiah—has already come."

²¹They replied, "We have had no letters from Judea or reports against you from anyone who has come here. ²²But we want to hear what you believe, for the only thing we know about this movement is that it is denounced everywhere."

²³So a time was set, and on that day a large number of people came to Paul's lodging. He explained and testified about the Kingdom of God and tried to persuade them about Jesus from the Scriptures. Using the law of Moses and the books of the prophets, he spoke to them from morning until evening. ²⁴Some were persuaded by the things he said, but others did not believe. ²⁵And after they had argued back and forth among themselves, they left with this final word from Paul: "The Holy Spirit was right when he said to your ancestors through Isaiah the prophet,

²⁶ 'Go and say to this people:
When you hear what I say,
    you will not understand.

27:44 Or *or were helped by members of the ship's crew.*   **28:11** The *twin gods* were the Roman gods Castor and Pollux.   **28:12** *Syracuse* was on the island of Sicily.   **28:13** *Rhegium* was on the southern tip of Italy.   **28:14** Greek *brothers.*   **28:15a** Greek *brothers.* **28:15b** *The Forum* was about 43 miles (70 kilometers) from Rome.   **28:15c** *The Three Taverns* was about 35 miles (57 kilometers) from Rome.

When you see what I do,
    you will not comprehend.
27 For the hearts of these people are
    hardened,
    and their ears cannot hear,
    and they have closed their
        eyes—
    so their eyes cannot see,
    and their ears cannot hear,
    and their hearts cannot
        understand,

and they cannot turn to me
    and let me heal them.'*

28So I want you to know that this salvation from God has also been offered to the Gentiles, and they will accept it.'*

30For the next two years, Paul lived in Rome at his own expense.* He welcomed all who visited him, 31boldly proclaiming the Kingdom of God and teaching about the Lord Jesus Christ. And no one tried to stop him.

28:26-27 Isa 6:9-10 (Greek version).   28:28 Some manuscripts add verse 29, *And when he had said these words, the Jews departed, greatly disagreeing with each other.*   28:30 Or *in his own rented quarters.*

Romans

LIKE A SKILLED LAWYER presenting his case, Paul established a solid framework for understanding the broad scope of the gospel in his letter to the Romans. Of all the epistles of Paul, this is the longest, most elaborate, and most systematic in design, reading more like a theological treatise than a personal letter. After a lofty introduction, Paul opened his discourse by discussing humanity's relationship to God. Once he established the basic concept that all human beings are violators of God's holy law, Paul offered the solution: the sacrifice of Jesus Christ.

- **Author:** Paul the apostle
- **Date Written:** Around AD 58, from the city of Corinth
- **Purpose:** To present a systematic explanation of the gospel of Jesus Christ to the church in Rome
- **Themes:** Sin, atonement, living according to the Holy Spirit, the place of Jews and Gentiles in God's plan
- **Outline**
  1:1-17 Introduction
  1:18–5:21 Humanity's sin and Christ's salvation
  6:1–8:39 Victory over sin by the power of Christ
  9:1–11:36 God's plan for the Jews
  12:1–15:13 Principles of Christian living
  15:14–16:27 Concluding remarks

Those who believe in Jesus Christ receive forgiveness for sin and gain new life in the Holy Spirit. Paul also examined Israel's place in God's grand scheme of history and discussed the future roles of Israel and Gentile nations in the Kingdom of God. Returning to his earlier train of thought, Paul discussed some practical applications of redemption through Jesus Christ. He concluded his letter with heartfelt salutations to several believers in Rome. Paul's epistle to the Roman believers provides the Church with a systematic presentation of the gospel of Jesus Christ.

Greetings from Paul

1 This letter is from Paul, a slave of Christ Jesus, chosen by God to be an apostle and sent out to preach his Good News. ²God promised this Good News long ago through his prophets in the holy Scriptures. ³The Good News is about his Son. In his earthly life he was born into King David's family line, ⁴and he was shown to be* the Son of God when he was raised from the dead by the power of the Holy Spirit.* He is Jesus Christ our Lord. ⁵Through Christ, God has given us the privilege* and authority as apostles to tell Gentiles everywhere what God has done for them, so that they will believe and obey him, bringing glory to his name.

⁶And you are included among those Gentiles who have been called to belong to Jesus Christ. ⁷I am writing to all of you in Rome who are loved by God and are called to be his own holy people.

May God our Father and the Lord Jesus Christ give you grace and peace.

God's Good News

⁸Let me say first that I thank my God through Jesus Christ for all of you, because your faith in him is being talked about all over the world. ⁹God knows how often I pray for you. Day and night I bring you and your needs in prayer to God, whom I serve with all my heart* by spreading the Good News about his Son.

¹⁰One of the things I always pray for is the opportunity, God willing, to come at last to see you. ¹¹For I long to visit you so I can bring you some spiritual gift that will help you grow

1:4a Or *and was designated.*   1:4b Or *by the Spirit of holiness; or in the new realm of the Spirit.*   1:5 Or *the grace.*   1:9 Or *in my spirit.*

strong in the Lord. ¹²When we get together, I want to encourage you in your faith, but I also want to be encouraged by yours.

¹³I want you to know, dear brothers and sisters,* that I planned many times to visit you, but I was prevented until now. I want to work among you and see spiritual fruit, just as I have seen among other Gentiles. ¹⁴For I have a great sense of obligation to people in both the civilized world and the rest of the world,* to the educated and uneducated alike. ¹⁵So I am eager to come to you in Rome, too, to preach the Good News.

¹⁶For I am not ashamed of this Good News about Christ. It is the power of God at work, saving everyone who believes—the Jew first and also the Gentile.* ¹⁷This Good News tells us how God makes us right in his sight. This is accomplished from start to finish by faith. As the Scriptures say, "It is through faith that a righteous person has life."*

God's Anger at Sin

¹⁸But God shows his anger from heaven against all sinful, wicked people who suppress the truth by their wickedness.* ¹⁹They know the truth about God because he has made it obvious to them. ²⁰For ever since the world was created, people have seen the earth and sky. Through everything God made, they can clearly see his invisible qualities—his eternal power and divine nature. So they have no excuse for not knowing God.

²¹Yes, they knew God, but they wouldn't worship him as God or even give him thanks. And they began to think up foolish ideas of what God was like. As a result, their minds became dark and confused. ²²Claiming to be wise, they instead became utter fools. ²³And instead of worshiping the glorious, ever-living God, they worshiped idols made to look like mere people and birds and animals and reptiles.

²⁴So God abandoned them to do whatever shameful things their hearts desired. As a result, they did vile and degrading things with each other's bodies. ²⁵They traded the truth about God for a lie. So they worshiped and served the things God created instead of the Creator himself, who is worthy of eternal praise! Amen. ²⁶That is why God abandoned them to their shameful desires. Even the women turned against the natural way to have sex and instead indulged in sex with each other. ²⁷And the men, instead of having normal sexual relations with women, burned with lust for each other. Men did shameful things with other men, and as a result of this sin, they suffered within themselves the penalty they deserved.

²⁸Since they thought it foolish to acknowledge God, he abandoned them to their foolish thinking and let them do things that should never be done. ²⁹Their lives became full of every kind of wickedness, sin, greed, hate, envy, murder, quarreling, deception, malicious behavior, and gossip. ³⁰They are backstabbers, haters of God, insolent, proud, and boastful. They invent new ways of sinning, and they disobey their parents. ³¹They refuse to understand, break their promises, are heartless, and have no mercy. ³²They know God's justice requires that those who do these things deserve to die, yet they do them anyway. Worse yet, they encourage others to do them, too.

God's Judgment of Sin

2 You may think you can condemn such people, but you are just as bad, and you have no excuse! When you say they are wicked and should be punished, you are condemning yourself, for you who judge others do these very same things. ²And we know that God, in his justice, will punish anyone who does such things. ³Since you judge others for doing these things, why do you think you can avoid God's judgment when you do the same things? ⁴Don't you see how wonderfully kind, tolerant, and patient God is with you? Does this mean nothing to you? Can't you see that his kindness is intended to turn you from your sin?

⁵But because you are stubborn and refuse to turn from your sin, you are storing up terrible punishment for yourself. For a day of anger is coming, when God's righteous judgment will be revealed. ⁶He will judge everyone according to what they have done. ⁷He will give eternal life to those who keep on doing good, seeking after the glory and honor and immortality that God offers. ⁸But he will pour out his anger and wrath on those who live for themselves, who refuse to obey the truth and instead live lives of wickedness. ⁹There will be trouble and calamity for everyone who keeps on doing what is evil—for the Jew first and also for the Gentile.* ¹⁰But there will be glory and honor and peace from God for all who do good—for the Jew first and also for the Gentile. ¹¹For God does not show favoritism.

1:13 Greek *brothers.* 1:14 Greek *to Greeks and barbarians.* 1:16 Greek *also the Greek.* 1:17 Or *"The righteous will live by faith."* Hab 2:4. 1:18 Or *who, by their wickedness, prevent the truth from being known.* 2:9 Greek *also for the Greek; also in 2:10.*

[12] When the Gentiles sin, they will be destroyed, even though they never had God's written law. And the Jews, who do have God's law, will be judged by that law when they fail to obey it. [13] For merely listening to the law doesn't make us right with God. It is obeying the law that makes us right in his sight. [14] Even Gentiles, who do not have God's written law, show that they know his law when they instinctively obey it, even without having heard it. [15] They demonstrate that God's law is written in their hearts, for their own conscience and thoughts either accuse them or tell them they are doing right. [16] And this is the message I proclaim—that the day is coming when God, through Christ Jesus, will judge everyone's secret life.

The Jews and the Law

[17] You who call yourselves Jews are relying on God's law, and you boast about your special relationship with him. [18] You know what he wants; you know what is right because you have been taught his law. [19] You are convinced that you are a guide for the blind and a light for people who are lost in darkness. [20] You think you can instruct the ignorant and teach children the ways of God. For you are certain that God's law gives you complete knowledge and truth.

[21] Well then, if you teach others, why don't you teach yourself? You tell others not to steal, but do you steal? [22] You say it is wrong to commit adultery, but do you commit adultery? You condemn idolatry, but do you use items stolen from pagan temples?* [23] You are so proud of knowing the law, but you dishonor God by breaking it. [24] No wonder the Scriptures say, "The Gentiles blaspheme the name of God because of you."*

[25] The Jewish ceremony of circumcision has value only if you obey God's law. But if you don't obey God's law, you are no better off than an uncircumcised Gentile. [26] And if the Gentiles obey God's law, won't God declare them to be his own people? [27] In fact, uncircumcised Gentiles who keep God's law will condemn you Jews who are circumcised and possess God's law but don't obey it.

[28] For you are not a true Jew just because you were born of Jewish parents or because you have gone through the ceremony of circumcision. [29] No, a true Jew is one whose heart is right with God. And true circumcision is not merely obeying the letter of the law; rather, it is a change of heart produced by the Spirit. And a person with a changed heart seeks praise* from God, not from people.

God Remains Faithful

3 Then what's the advantage of being a Jew? Is there any value in the ceremony of circumcision? [2] Yes, there are great benefits! First of all, the Jews were entrusted with the whole revelation of God.*

[3] True, some of them were unfaithful; but just because they were unfaithful, does that mean God will be unfaithful? [4] Of course not! Even if everyone else is a liar, God is true. As the Scriptures say about him,

"You will be proved right in what you say,
    and you will win your case in court."*

[5] "But," some might say, "our sinfulness serves a good purpose, for it helps people see how righteous God is. Isn't it unfair, then, for him to punish us?" (This is merely a human point of view.) [6] Of course not! If God were not entirely fair, how would he be qualified to judge the world? [7] "But," someone might still argue, "how can God condemn me as a sinner if my dishonesty highlights his truthfulness and brings him more glory?" [8] And some people even slander us by claiming that we say, "The more we sin, the better it is!" Those who say such things deserve to be condemned.

All People Are Sinners

[9] Well then, should we conclude that we Jews are better than others? No, not at all, for we have already shown that all people, whether Jews or Gentiles,* are under the power of sin. [10] As the Scriptures say,

"No one is righteous—
    not even one.
[11] No one is truly wise;
    no one is seeking God.
[12] All have turned away;
    all have become useless.
No one does good,
    not a single one."*
[13] "Their talk is foul, like the stench from
        an open grave.
    Their tongues are filled with lies."
"Snake venom drips from their
        lips."*

2:22 Greek *do you steal from temples?*   2:24 Isa 52:5 (Greek version).   2:29 Or *receives praise.*   3:2 Greek *the oracles of God.*
3:4 Ps 51:4 (Greek version).   3:9 Greek *or Greeks.*   3:10-12 Pss 14:1-3; 53:1-3 (Greek version).   3:13 Pss 5:9 (Greek version); 140:3.

14   "Their mouths are full of cursing and
          bitterness."*
15. "They rush to commit murder.
16   Destruction and misery always follow
          them.
17   They don't know where to find peace."*
18   "They have no fear of God at all."*

¹⁹Obviously, the law applies to those to
whom it was given, for its purpose is to keep
people from having excuses, and to show that
the entire world is guilty before God. ²⁰For no
one can ever be made right with God by doing
what the law commands. The law simply shows
us how sinful we are.

Christ Took Our Punishment

²¹But now God has shown us a way to be made
right with him without keeping the requirements of the law, as was promised in the writings of Moses* and the prophets long ago. ²²We
are made right with God by placing our faith in
Jesus Christ. And this is true for everyone who
believes, no matter who we are.

²³For everyone has sinned; we all fall short
of God's glorious standard. ²⁴Yet God, in his
grace, freely makes us right in his sight. He
did this through Christ Jesus when he freed
us from the penalty for our sins. ²⁵For God presented Jesus as the sacrifice for sin. People are
made right with God when they believe that
Jesus sacrificed his life, shedding his blood.
This sacrifice shows that God was being fair
when he held back and did not punish those
who sinned in times past, ²⁶for he was looking
ahead and including them in what he would
do in this present time. God did this to demonstrate his righteousness, for he himself is
fair and just, and he makes sinners right in his
sight when they believe in Jesus.

²⁷Can we boast, then, that we have done
anything to be accepted by God? No, because
our acquittal is not based on obeying the law.
It is based on faith. ²⁸So we are made right
with God through faith and not by obeying
the law.

²⁹After all, is God the God of the Jews
only? Isn't he also the God of the Gentiles?
Of course he is. ³⁰There is only one God, and
he makes people right with himself only by
faith, whether they are Jews or Gentiles.* ³¹Well
then, if we emphasize faith, does this mean
that we can forget about the law? Of course not!

In fact, only when we have faith do we truly
fulfill the law.

The Faith of Abraham

4 Abraham was, humanly speaking, the
founder of our Jewish nation. What did he
discover about being made right with God? ²If
his good deeds had made him something to boast
God, he would have had something to boast
about. But that was not God's way. ³For the
Scriptures tell us, "Abraham believed God,
and God counted him as righteous because of
his faith."*

⁴When people work, their wages are not a
gift, but something they have earned. ⁵But
people are counted as righteous, not because
of their work, but because of their faith in God
who forgives sinners. ⁶David also spoke of this
when he described the happiness of those who
are declared righteous without working for it:

7   "Oh, what joy for those
        whose disobedience is forgiven,
        whose sins are put out of sight.
8   Yes, what joy for those
        whose record the LORD has cleared
        of sin."*

⁹Now, is this blessing only for the Jews, or is
it also for uncircumcised Gentiles?* Well, we
have been saying that Abraham was counted
as righteous by God because of his faith. ¹⁰But
how did this happen? Was he counted as righteous only after he was circumcised, or was it
before he was circumcised? Clearly, God accepted Abraham before he was circumcised!

¹¹Circumcision was a sign that Abraham already had faith and that God had already accepted him and declared him to be
righteous—even before he was circumcised.
So Abraham is the spiritual father of those who
have faith but have not been circumcised. They
are counted as righteous because of their faith.
¹²And Abraham is also the spiritual father of
those who have been circumcised, but only if
they have the same kind of faith Abraham had
before he was circumcised.

¹³Clearly, God's promise to give the whole
earth to Abraham and his descendants was
based not on his obedience to God's law, but
on a right relationship with God that comes by
faith. ¹⁴If God's promise is only for those who
obey the law, then faith is not necessary and

3:14 Ps 10:7 (Greek version).   3:15-17 Isa 59:7-8.   3:18 Ps 36:1.   3:21 Greek *in the law*.   3:30 Greek *whether they are circumcised
or uncircumcised*.   4:3 Gen 15:6.   4:7-8 Ps 32:1-2 (Greek version).   4:9 Greek *is this blessing only for the circumcised, or is it also
for the uncircumcised?*

the promise is pointless. ¹⁵For the law always brings punishment on those who try to obey it. (The only way to avoid breaking the law is to have no law to break!)

¹⁶So the promise is received by faith. It is given as a free gift. And we are all certain to receive it, whether or not we live according to the law of Moses, if we have faith like Abraham's. For Abraham is the father of all who believe. ¹⁷That is what the Scriptures mean when God told him, "I have made you the father of many nations."* This happened because Abraham believed in the God who brings the dead back to life and who creates new things out of nothing.

¹⁸Even when there was no reason for hope, Abraham kept hoping—believing that he would become the father of many nations. For God had said to him, "That's how many descendants you will have!"* ¹⁹And Abraham's faith did not weaken, even though, at about 100 years of age, he figured his body was as good as dead—and so was Sarah's womb. ²⁰Abraham never wavered in believing God's promise. In fact, his faith grew stronger, and in this he brought glory to God. ²¹He was fully convinced that God is able to do whatever he promises. ²²And because of Abraham's faith, God counted him as righteous. ²³And when God counted him as righteous, it wasn't just for Abraham's benefit. It was recorded ²⁴for our benefit, too, assuring us that God will also count us as righteous if we believe in him, the one who raised Jesus our Lord from the dead. ²⁵He was handed over to die because of our sins, and he was raised to life to make us right with God.

Faith Brings Joy

5 Therefore, since we have been made right in God's sight by faith, we have peace* with God because of what Jesus Christ our Lord has done for us. ²Because of our faith, Christ has brought us into this place of undeserved privilege where we now stand, and we confidently and joyfully look forward to sharing God's glory.

³We can rejoice, too, when we run into problems and trials, for we know that they help us develop endurance. ⁴And endurance develops strength of character, and character strengthens our confident hope of salvation. ⁵And this hope will not lead to disappointment. For we know how dearly God loves us, because he has given us the Holy Spirit to fill our hearts with his love.

⁶When we were utterly helpless, Christ came at just the right time and died for us sinners. ⁷Now, most people would not be willing to die for an upright person, though someone might perhaps be willing to die for a person who is especially good. ⁸But God showed his great love for us by sending Christ to die for us while we were still sinners. ⁹And since we have been made right in God's sight by the blood of Christ, he will certainly save us from God's condemnation. ¹⁰For since our friendship with God was restored by the death of his Son while we were still his enemies, we will certainly be saved through the life of his Son. ¹¹So now we can rejoice in our wonderful new relationship with God because our Lord Jesus Christ has made us friends of God.

Adam and Christ Contrasted

¹²When Adam sinned, sin entered the world. Adam's sin brought death, so death spread to everyone, for everyone sinned. ¹³Yes, people sinned even before the law was given. But it was not counted as sin because there was not yet any law to break. ¹⁴Still, everyone died—from the time of Adam to the time of Moses—even those who did not disobey an explicit commandment of God, as Adam did. Now Adam is a symbol, a representation of Christ, who was yet to come. ¹⁵But there is a great difference between Adam's sin and God's gracious gift. For the sin of this one man, Adam, brought death to many. But even greater is God's wonderful grace and his gift of forgiveness to many through this other man, Jesus Christ. ¹⁶And the result of God's gracious gift is very different from the result of that one man's sin. For Adam's sin led to condemnation, but God's free gift leads to our being made right with God, even though we are guilty of many sins. ¹⁷For the sin of this one man, Adam, caused death to rule over many. But even greater is God's wonderful grace and his gift of righteousness, for all who receive it will live in triumph over sin and death through this one man, Jesus Christ.

¹⁸Yes, Adam's one sin brings condemnation for everyone, but Christ's one act of righteousness brings a right relationship with God and new life for everyone. ¹⁹Because one person disobeyed God, many became sinners. But because one other person obeyed God, many will be made righteous.

²⁰God's law was given so that all people could see how sinful they were. But as people sinned more and more, God's wonderful grace became

4:17 Gen 17:5.   4:18 Gen 15:5.   5:1 Some manuscripts read *let us have peace.*

more abundant. [21]So just as sin ruled over all people and brought them to death, now God's wonderful grace rules instead, giving us right standing with God and resulting in eternal life through Jesus Christ our Lord.

Sin's Power Is Broken

6 Well then, should we keep on sinning so that God can show us more and more of his wonderful grace? [2]Of course not! Since we have died to sin, how can we continue to live in it? [3]Or have you forgotten that when we were joined with Christ Jesus in baptism, we joined him in his death? [4]For we died and were buried with Christ by baptism. And just as Christ was raised from the dead by the glorious power of the Father, now we also may live new lives.

[5]Since we have been united with him in his death, we will also be raised to life as he was. [6]We know that our old sinful selves were crucified with Christ so that sin might lose its power in our lives. We are no longer slaves to sin. [7]For when we died with Christ we were set free from the power of sin. [8]And since we died with Christ, we know we will also live with him. [9]We are sure of this because Christ was raised from the dead, and he will never die again. Death no longer has any power over him. [10]When he died, he died once to break the power of sin. But now that he lives, he lives for the glory of God. [11]So you also should consider yourselves to be dead to the power of sin and alive to God through Christ Jesus.

[12]Do not let sin control the way you live;* do not give in to sinful desires. [13]Do not let any part of your body become an instrument of evil to serve sin. Instead, give yourselves completely to God, for you were dead, but now you have new life. So use your whole body as an instrument to do what is right for the glory of God. [14]Sin is no longer your master, for you no longer live under the requirements of the law. Instead, you live under the freedom of God's grace.

[15]Well then, since God's grace has set us free from the law, does that mean we can go on sinning? Of course not! [16]Don't you realize that you become the slave of whatever you choose to obey? You can be a slave to sin, which leads to death, or you can choose to obey God, which leads to righteous living. [17]Thank God! Once you were slaves of sin, but now you wholeheartedly obey this teaching we have given you. [18]Now you are free from your slavery to sin, and you have become slaves to righteous living.

[19]Because of the weakness of your human nature, I am using the illustration of slavery to help you understand all this. Previously, you let yourselves be slaves to impurity and lawlessness, which led ever deeper into sin. Now you must give yourselves to be slaves to righteous living so that you will become holy. [20]When you were slaves to sin, you were free from the obligation to do right. [21]And what was the result? You are now ashamed of the things you used to do, things that end in eternal doom. [22]But now you are free from the power of sin and have become slaves of God. Now you do those things that lead to holiness and result in eternal life. [23]For the wages of sin is death, but the free gift of God is eternal life through Christ Jesus our Lord.

No Longer Bound to the Law

7 Now, dear brothers and sisters*—you who are familiar with the law—don't you know that the law applies only while a person is living? [2]For example, when a woman marries, the law binds her to her husband as long as he is alive. But if he dies, the laws of marriage no longer apply to her. [3]So while her husband is alive, she would be committing adultery if she married another man. But if her husband dies, she is free from that law and does not commit adultery when she remarries.

[4]So, my dear brothers and sisters, this is the point: You died to the power of the law when you died with Christ. And now you are united with the one who was raised from the dead. As a result, we can produce a harvest of good deeds for God. [5]When we were controlled by our old nature,* sinful desires were at work within us, and the law aroused these evil desires that produced a harvest of sinful deeds, resulting in death. [6]But now we have been released from the law, for we died to it and are no longer captive to its power. Now we can serve God, not in the old way of obeying the letter of the law, but in the new way of living in the Spirit.

God's Law Reveals Our Sin

[7]Well then, am I suggesting that the law of God is sinful? Of course not! In fact, it was the law that showed me my sin. I would never have known that coveting is wrong if the law had not said, "You must not covet."* [8]But sin used this command to arouse all kinds of covetous desires within me! If there were no law, sin would not have that power. [9]At one time

---

6:12 Or *Do not let sin reign in your body, which is subject to death.*   7:1 Greek *brothers;* also in 7:4.   7:5 Greek *When we were in the flesh.*   7:7 Exod 20:17; Deut 5:21.

I lived without understanding the law. But when I learned the command not to covet, for instance, the power of sin came to life, 10and I died. So I discovered that the law's commands, which were supposed to bring life, brought spiritual death instead. 11Sin took advantage of those commands and deceived me; it used the commands to kill me. 12But still, the law itself is holy, and its commands are holy and right and good.

13But how can that be? Did the law, which is good, cause my death? Of course not! Sin used what was good to bring about my condemnation to death. So we can see how terrible sin really is. It uses God's good commands for its own evil purposes.

Struggling with Sin

14So the trouble is not with the law, for it is spiritual and good. The trouble is with me, for I am all too human, a slave to sin. 15I don't really understand myself, for I want to do what is right, but I don't do it. Instead, I do what I hate. 16But if I know that what I am doing is wrong, this shows that I agree that the law is good. 17So I am not the one doing wrong; it is sin living in me that does it.

18And I know that nothing good lives in me, that is, in my sinful nature.* I want to do what is right, but I can't. 19I want to do what is good, but I don't. I don't want to do what is wrong, but I do it anyway. 20But if I do what I don't want to do, I am not really the one doing wrong; it is sin living in me that does it.

21I have discovered this principle of life— that when I want to do what is right, I inevitably do what is wrong. 22I love God's law with all my heart. 23But there is another power* within me that is at war with my mind. This power makes me a slave to the sin that is still within me. 24Oh, what a miserable person I am! Who will free me from this life that is dominated by sin and death? 25Thank God! The answer is in Jesus Christ our Lord. So you see how it is: In my mind I really want to obey God's law, but because of my sinful nature I am a slave to sin.

Life in the Spirit

8 So now there is no condemnation for those who belong to Christ Jesus. 2And because you belong to him, the power* of the life-giving Spirit has freed you* from the power

of sin that leads to death. 3The law of Moses was unable to save us because of the weakness of our sinful nature.* So God did what the law could not do. He sent his own Son in a body like the bodies we sinners have. And in that body God declared an end to sin's control over us by giving his Son as a sacrifice for our sins. 4He did this so that the just requirement of the law would be fully satisfied for us, who no longer follow our sinful nature but instead follow the Spirit.

5Those who are dominated by the sinful nature think about sinful things, but those who are controlled by the Holy Spirit think about things that please the Spirit. 6So letting your sinful nature control your mind leads to death. But letting the Spirit control your mind leads to life and peace. 7For the sinful nature is always hostile to God. It never did obey God's laws, and it never will. 8That's why those who are still under the control of their sinful nature can never please God.

9But you are not controlled by your sinful nature. You are controlled by the Spirit if you have the Spirit of God living in you. (And remember that those who do not have the Spirit of Christ living in them do not belong to him at all.) 10And Christ lives within you, so even though your body will die because of sin, the Spirit gives you life* because you have been made right with God. 11The Spirit of God, who raised Jesus from the dead, lives in you. And just as God raised Christ Jesus from the dead, he will give life to your mortal bodies by this same Spirit living within you.

12Therefore, dear brothers and sisters,* you have no obligation to do what your sinful nature urges you to do. 13For if you live by its dictates, you will die. But if through the power of the Spirit you put to death the deeds of your sinful nature,* you will live. 14For all who are led by the Spirit of God are children* of God.

15So you have not received a spirit that makes you fearful slaves. Instead, you received God's Spirit when he adopted you as his own children.* Now we call him, "Abba, Father."* 16For his Spirit joins with our spirit to affirm that we are God's children. 17And since we are his children, we are his heirs. In fact, together with Christ we are heirs of God's glory. But if we are to share his glory, we must also share his suffering.

7:18 Greek *my flesh;* also in 7:25.   7:23 Greek *law;* also in 7:23b.   8:2a Greek *the law;* also in 8:2b.   8:2b Some manuscripts read *me.*   8:3 Greek *our flesh;* similarly in 8:4, 5, 6, 7, 8, 9, 12.   8:10 Or *your spirit is alive.*   8:12 Greek *brothers;* also in 8:29.   8:13 Greek *deeds of the body.*   8:14 Greek *sons;* also in 8:19.   8:15a Greek *you received a spirit of sonship.*   8:15b *Abba* is an Aramaic term for "father."

The Future Glory

¹⁸Yet what we suffer now is nothing compared to the glory he will reveal to us later. ¹⁹For all creation is waiting eagerly for that future day when God will reveal who his children really are. ²⁰Against its will, all creation was subjected to God's curse. But with eager hope, ²¹the creation looks forward to the day when it will join God's children in glorious freedom from death and decay. ²²For we know that all creation has been groaning as in the pains of childbirth right up to the present time. ²³And we believers also groan, even though we have the Holy Spirit within us as a foretaste of future glory, for we long for our bodies to be released from sin and suffering. We, too, wait with eager hope for the day when God will give us our full rights as his adopted children,* including the new bodies he has promised us. ²⁴We were given this hope when we were saved. (If we already have something, we don't need to hope* for it. ²⁵But if we look forward to something we don't yet have, we must wait patiently and confidently.)

²⁶And the Holy Spirit helps us in our weakness. For example, we don't know what God wants us to pray for. But the Holy Spirit prays for us with groanings that cannot be expressed in words. ²⁷And the Father who knows all hearts knows what the Spirit is saying, for the Spirit pleads for us believers* in harmony with God's own will. ²⁸And we know that God causes everything to work together* for the good of those who love God and are called according to his purpose for them. ²⁹For God knew his people in advance, and he chose them to become like his Son, so that his Son would be the firstborn* among many brothers and sisters. ³⁰And having chosen them, he called them to come to him. And having called them, he gave them right standing with himself. And having given them right standing, he gave them his glory.

Nothing Can Separate Us from God's Love

³¹What shall we say about such wonderful things as these? If God is for us, who can ever be against us? ³²Since he did not spare even his own Son but gave him up for us all, won't he also give us everything else? ³³Who dares accuse us whom God has chosen for his own? No one—for God himself has given us right standing with himself. ³⁴Who then will condemn us? No one—for Christ Jesus died for us and was raised to life for us, and he is sitting in the place of honor at God's right hand, pleading for us.

³⁵Can anything ever separate us from Christ's love? Does it mean he no longer loves us if we have trouble or calamity, or are persecuted, or hungry, or destitute, or in danger, or threatened with death? ³⁶(As the Scriptures say, "For your sake we are killed every day; we are being slaughtered like sheep."*) ³⁷No, despite all these things, overwhelming victory is ours through Christ, who loved us.

³⁸And I am convinced that nothing can ever separate us from God's love. Neither death nor life, neither angels nor demons,* neither our fears for today nor our worries about tomorrow—not even the powers of hell can separate us from God's love. ³⁹No power in the sky above or in the earth below—indeed, nothing in all creation will ever be able to separate us from the love of God that is revealed in Christ Jesus our Lord.

God's Selection of Israel

9 With Christ as my witness, I speak with utter truthfulness. My conscience and the Holy Spirit confirm it. ²My heart is filled with bitter sorrow and unending grief ³for my people, my Jewish brothers and sisters.* I would be willing to be forever cursed—cut off from Christ!—if that would save them. ⁴They are the people of Israel, chosen to be God's adopted children.* God revealed his glory to them. He made covenants with them and gave them his law. He gave them the privilege of worshiping him and receiving his wonderful promises. ⁵Abraham, Isaac, and Jacob are their ancestors, and Christ himself was an Israelite as far as his human nature is concerned. And he is God, the one who rules over everything and is worthy of eternal praise! Amen.*

⁶Well then, has God failed to fulfill his promise to Israel? No, for not all who are born into the nation of Israel are truly members of God's people! ⁷Being descendants of Abraham doesn't make them truly Abraham's children. For the Scriptures say, "Isaac is the son through whom your descendants will be counted,"* though Abraham had other children, too. ⁸This

8:23 Greek *wait anxiously for sonship.* 8:24 Some manuscripts read *wait.* 8:27 Greek *for God's holy people.* 8:28 Some manuscripts read *And we know that everything works together.* 8:29 Or *would be supreme.* 8:36 Ps 44:22. 8:38 Greek *nor rulers.* 9:3 Greek *my brothers.* 9:4 Greek *chosen for sonship.* 9:5 Or *May God, the one who rules over everything, be praised forever. Amen.* 9:7 Gen 21:12.

means that Abraham's physical descendants are not necessarily children of God. Only the children of the promise are considered to be Abraham's children. 9For God had promised, "I will return about this time next year, and Sarah will have a son."*

10This son was our ancestor Isaac. When he married Rebekah, she gave birth to twins.* 11But before they were born, before they had done anything good or bad, she received a message from God. (This message shows that God chooses people according to his own purposes; 12he calls people, but not according to their good or bad works.) She was told, "Your older son will serve your younger son."* 13In the words of the Scriptures, "I loved Jacob, but I rejected Esau."*

14Are we saying, then, that God was unfair? Of course not! 15For God said to Moses,

"I will show mercy to anyone I choose,
    and I will show compassion to anyone
        I choose."*

16So it is God who decides to show mercy. We can neither choose it nor work for it.

17For the Scriptures say that God told Pharaoh, "I have appointed you for the very purpose of displaying my power in you and to spread my fame throughout the earth."* 18So you see, God chooses to show mercy to some, and he chooses to harden the hearts of others so they refuse to listen.

19Well then, you might say, "Why does God blame people for not responding? Haven't they simply done what he makes them do?"

20No, don't say that. Who are you, a mere human being, to argue with God? Should the thing that was created say to the one who created it, "Why have you made me like this?" 21When a potter makes jars out of clay, doesn't he have a right to use the same lump of clay to make one jar for decoration and another to throw garbage into? 22In the same way, even though God has the right to show his anger and his power, he is very patient with those on whom his anger falls, who are destined for destruction. 23He does this to make the riches of his glory shine even brighter on those to whom he shows mercy, who were prepared in advance for glory. 24And we are among those whom he selected, both from the Jews and from the Gentiles.

25Concerning the Gentiles, God says in the prophecy of Hosea,

"Those who were not my people,
    I will now call my people.
And I will love those
    whom I did not love before."*

26And,

"Then, at the place where they were told,
    'You are not my people,'
there they will be called
    'children of the living God.'"*

27And concerning Israel, Isaiah the prophet cried out,

"Though the people of Israel are as
        numerous as the sand of the seashore,
    only a remnant will be saved.
28 For the LORD will carry out his sentence
        upon the earth
    quickly and with finality."*

29And Isaiah said the same thing in another place:

"If the LORD of Heaven's Armies
    had not spared a few of our
        children,
we would have been wiped out like
        Sodom,
    destroyed like Gomorrah."*

Israel's Unbelief

30What does all this mean? Even though the Gentiles were not trying to follow God's standards, they were made right with God. And it was by faith that this took place. 31But the people of Israel, who tried so hard to get right with God by keeping the law, never succeeded. 32Why not? Because they were trying to get right with God by keeping the law* instead of by trusting in him. They stumbled over the great rock in their path. 33God warned them of this in the Scriptures when he said,

"I am placing a stone in Jerusalem* that
        makes people stumble,
    a rock that makes them fall.
But anyone who trusts in him
    will never be disgraced."*

9:9 Gen 18:10, 14.   9:10 Greek *she conceived children through this one man.*   9:12 Gen 25:23.   9:13 Mal 1:2-3.   9:15 Exod 33:19.
9:17 Exod 9:16 (Greek version).   9:25 Hos 2:23.   9:26 Greek *sons of the living God.* Hos 1:10.   9:27-28 Isa 10:22-23 (Greek version).   9:29 Isa 1:9 (Greek version).   9:32 Greek *by works.*   9:33a Greek *in Zion.*   9:33b Isa 8:14; 28:16 (Greek version).

10 Dear brothers and sisters,* the longing of my heart and my prayer to God is for the people of Israel to be saved. ²I know what enthusiasm they have for God, but it is misdirected zeal. ³For they don't understand God's way of making people right with himself. Refusing to accept God's way, they cling to their own way of getting right with God by trying to keep the law. ⁴For Christ has already accomplished the purpose for which the law was given.* As a result, all who believe in him are made right with God.

Salvation Is for Everyone

⁵For Moses writes that the law's way of making a person right with God requires obedience to all of its commands.* ⁶But faith's way of getting right with God says, "Don't say in your heart, 'Who will go up to heaven?' (to bring Christ down to earth). ⁷And don't say, 'Who will go down to the place of the dead?' (to bring Christ back to life again)." ⁸In fact, it says,

"The message is very close at hand;
    it is on your lips and in your heart."*

And that message is the very message about faith that we preach: ⁹If you openly declare that Jesus is Lord and believe in your heart that God raised him from the dead, you will be saved. ¹⁰For it is by believing in your heart that you are made right with God, and it is by openly declaring your faith that you are saved. ¹¹As the Scriptures tell us, "Anyone who trusts in him will never be disgraced."* ¹²Jew and Gentile* are the same in this respect. They have the same Lord, who gives generously to all who call on him. ¹³For "Everyone who calls on the name of the LORD will be saved."*

¹⁴But how can they call on him to save them unless they believe in him? And how can they believe in him if they have never heard about him? And how can they hear about him unless someone tells them? ¹⁵And how will anyone go and tell them without being sent? That is why the Scriptures say, "How beautiful are the feet of messengers who bring good news!"*

¹⁶But not everyone welcomes the Good News, for Isaiah the prophet said, "LORD, who has believed our message?"* ¹⁷So faith comes from hearing, that is, hearing the Good News about Christ. ¹⁸But I ask, have the people of Israel actually heard the message? Yes, they have:

"The message has gone throughout the
    earth,
    and the words to all the world."*

¹⁹But I ask, did the people of Israel really understand? Yes, they did, for even in the time of Moses, God said,

"I will rouse your jealousy through people
    who are not even a nation.
I will provoke your anger through the
    foolish Gentiles."*

²⁰And later Isaiah spoke boldly for God, saying,

"I was found by people who were not
    looking for me.
I showed myself to those who were not
    asking for me."*

²¹But regarding Israel, God said,

"All day long I opened my arms to them,
    but they were disobedient and
    rebellious."*

God's Mercy on Israel

11 I ask, then, has God rejected his own people, the nation of Israel? Of course not! I myself am an Israelite, a descendant of Abraham and a member of the tribe of Benjamin.

²No, God has not rejected his own people, whom he chose from the very beginning. Do you realize what the Scriptures say about this? Elijah the prophet complained to God about the people of Israel and said, ³"LORD, they have killed your prophets and torn down your altars. I am the only one left, and now they are trying to kill me, too."*

⁴And do you remember God's reply? He said, "No, I have 7,000 others who have never bowed down to Baal!"*

⁵It is the same today, for a few of the people of Israel* have remained faithful because of God's grace—his undeserved kindness in choosing them. ⁶And since it is through God's kindness, then it is not by their good works. For in that case, God's grace would not be what it really is—free and undeserved.

10:1 Greek *Brothers.*   10:4 Or *For Christ is the end of the law.*   10:5 See Lev 18:5.   10:6-8 Deut 30:12-14.   10:11 Isa 28:16 (Greek version).   10:12 Greek *and Greek.*   10:13 Joel 2:32.   10:15 Isa 52:7.   10:16 Isa 53:1.   10:18 Ps 19:4.   10:19 Deut 32:21. 10:20 Isa 65:1 (Greek version).   10:21 Isa 65:2 (Greek version).   11:3 1 Kgs 19:10, 14.   11:4 1 Kgs 19:18.   11:5 Greek *for a remnant.*

[7] So this is the situation: Most of the people of Israel have not found the favor of God they are looking for so earnestly. A few have—the ones God has chosen—but the hearts of the rest were hardened. [8] As the Scriptures say,

"God has put them into a deep sleep.
To this day he has shut their eyes so they
    do not see,
    and closed their ears so they do not
        hear."*

[9] Likewise, David said,

"Let their bountiful table become a snare,
    a trap that makes them think all is well.
Let their blessings cause them to stumble,
    and let them get what they deserve.
[10] Let their eyes go blind so they cannot see,
    and let their backs be bent forever."*

[11] Did God's people stumble and fall beyond recovery? Of course not! They were disobedient, so God made salvation available to the Gentiles. But he wanted his own people to become jealous and claim it for themselves. [12] Now if the Gentiles were enriched because the people of Israel turned down God's offer of salvation, think how much greater a blessing the world will share when they finally accept it.

[13] I am saying all this especially for you Gentiles. God has appointed me as the apostle to the Gentiles. I stress this, [14] for I want somehow to make the people of Israel jealous of what you Gentiles have, so I might save some of them. [15] For since their rejection meant that God offered salvation to the rest of the world, their acceptance will be even more wonderful. It will be life for those who were dead! [16] And since Abraham and the other patriarchs were holy, their descendants will also be holy—just as the entire batch of dough is holy because the portion given as an offering is holy. For if the roots of the tree are holy, the branches will be, too.

[17] But some of these branches from Abraham's tree—some of the people of Israel—have been broken off. And you Gentiles, who were branches from a wild olive tree, have been grafted in. So now you also receive the blessing God has promised Abraham and his children, sharing in the rich nourishment from the root of God's special olive tree. [18] But you must not brag about being grafted in to replace the branches that were broken off. You are just a branch, not the root.

[19] "Well," you may say, "those branches were broken off to make room for me." [20] Yes, but remember—those branches were broken off because they didn't believe in Christ, and you are there because you do believe. So don't think highly of yourself, but fear what could happen. [21] For if God did not spare the original branches, he won't* spare you either.

[22] Notice how God is both kind and severe. He is severe toward those who disobeyed, but kind to you if you continue to trust in his kindness. But if you stop trusting, you also will be cut off. [23] And if the people of Israel turn from their unbelief, they will be grafted in again, for God has the power to graft them back into the tree. [24] You, by nature, were a branch cut from a wild olive tree. So if God was willing to do something contrary to nature by grafting you into his cultivated tree, he will be far more eager to graft the original branches back into the tree where they belong.

God's Mercy Is for Everyone

[25] I want you to understand this mystery, dear brothers and sisters,* so that you will not feel proud about yourselves. Some of the people of Israel have hard hearts, but this will last only until the full number of Gentiles comes to Christ. [26] And so all Israel will be saved. As the Scriptures say,

"The one who rescues will come from
    Jerusalem,*
    and he will turn Israel* away from
        ungodliness.
[27] And this is my covenant with them,
    that I will take away their sins."*

[28] Many of the people of Israel are now enemies of the Good News, and this benefits you Gentiles. Yet they are still the people he loves because he chose their ancestors Abraham, Isaac, and Jacob. [29] For God's gifts and his call can never be withdrawn. [30] Once, you Gentiles were rebels against God, but when the people of Israel rebelled against him, God was merciful to you instead. [31] Now they are the rebels, and God's mercy has come to you so that they, too, will share* in God's mercy. [32] For God has imprisoned everyone in disobedience so he could have mercy on everyone.

11:8 Isa 29:10; Deut 29:4.   11:9-10 Ps 69:22-23 (Greek version).   11:21 Some manuscripts read *perhaps he won't*.   11:25 Greek *brothers*.   11:26a Greek *from Zion*.   11:26b Greek *Jacob*.   11:26-27 Isa 59:20-21; 27:9 (Greek version).   11:31 Other manuscripts read *will now share*; still others read *will someday share*.

33Oh, how great are God's riches and wisdom and knowledge! How impossible it is for us to understand his decisions and his ways!

34 For who can know the LORD's thoughts?
    Who knows enough to give him advice?*
35 And who has given him so much
    that he needs to pay it back?*

36For everything comes from him and exists by his power and is intended for his glory. All glory to him forever! Amen.

A Living Sacrifice to God

12 And so, dear brothers and sisters,* I plead with you to give your bodies to God because of all he has done for you. Let them be a living and holy sacrifice—the kind he will find acceptable. This is truly the way to worship him.* 2Don't copy the behavior and customs of this world, but let God transform you into a new person by changing the way you think. Then you will learn to know God's will for you, which is good and pleasing and perfect.

3Because of the privilege and authority* God has given me, I give each of you this warning: Don't think you are better than you really are. Be honest in your evaluation of yourselves, measuring yourselves by the faith God has given us.* 4Just as our bodies have many parts and each part has a special function, 5so it is with Christ's body. We are many parts of one body, and we all belong to each other.

6In his grace, God has given us different gifts for doing certain things well. So if God has given you the ability to prophesy, speak out with as much faith as God has given you. 7If your gift is serving others, serve them well. If you are a teacher, teach well. 8If your gift is to encourage others, be encouraging. If it is giving, give generously. If God has given you leadership ability, take the responsibility seriously. And if you have a gift for showing kindness to others, do it gladly.

9Don't just pretend to love others. Really love them. Hate what is wrong. Hold tightly to what is good. 10Love each other with genuine affection,* and take delight in honoring each other. 11Never be lazy, but work hard and serve the Lord enthusiastically.* 12Rejoice in our confident hope. Be patient in trouble, and keep on praying. 13When God's people are in need, be ready to help them. Always be eager to practice hospitality.

14Bless those who persecute you. Don't curse them; pray that God will bless them. 15Be happy with those who are happy, and weep with those who weep. 16Live in harmony with each other. Don't be too proud to enjoy the company of ordinary people. And don't think you know it all!

17Never pay back evil with more evil. Do things in such a way that everyone can see you are honorable. 18Do all that you can to live in peace with everyone.

19Dear friends, never take revenge. Leave that to the righteous anger of God. For the Scriptures say,

"I will take revenge;
    I will pay them back,"*
    says the LORD.

20Instead,

"If your enemies are hungry, feed them.
    If they are thirsty, give them something
        to drink.
    In doing this, you will heap
        burning coals of shame on their heads."*

21Don't let evil conquer you, but conquer evil by doing good.

Respect for Authority

13 Everyone must submit to governing authorities. For all authority comes from God, and those in positions of authority have been placed there by God. 2So anyone who rebels against authority is rebelling against what God has instituted, and they will be punished. 3For the authorities do not strike fear in people who are doing right, but in those who are doing wrong. Would you like to live without fear of the authorities? Do what is right, and they will honor you. 4The authorities are God's servants, sent for your good. But if you are doing wrong, of course you should be afraid, for they have the power to punish you. They are God's servants, sent for the very purpose of punishing those who do what is wrong. 5So you must submit to them, not only

11:34 Isa 40:13 (Greek version).   11:35 See Job 41:11.   12:1a Greek brothers.   12:1b Or This is your spiritual worship; or This is your reasonable service.   12:3a Or Because of the grace; compare 1:5.   12:3b Or by the faith God has given you; or by the standard of our God-given faith.   12:10 Greek with brotherly love.   12:11 Or but serve the Lord with a zealous spirit; or but let the Spirit excite you as you serve the Lord.   12:19 Deut 32:35.   12:20 Prov 25:21-22.

to avoid punishment, but also to keep a clear conscience.

⁶Pay your taxes, too, for these same reasons. For government workers need to be paid. They are serving God in what they do. ⁷Give to everyone what you owe them: Pay your taxes and government fees to those who collect them, and give respect and honor to those who are in authority.

Love Fulfills God's Requirements

⁸Owe nothing to anyone—except for your obligation to love one another. If you love your neighbor, you will fulfill the requirements of God's law. ⁹For the commandments say, "You must not commit adultery. You must not murder. You must not steal. You must not covet."* These—and other such commandments—are summed up in this one commandment: "Love your neighbor as yourself."* ¹⁰Love does no wrong to others, so love fulfills the requirements of God's law.

¹¹This is all the more urgent, for you know how late it is; time is running out. Wake up, for our salvation is nearer now than when we first believed. ¹²The night is almost gone; the day of salvation will soon be here. So remove your dark deeds like dirty clothes, and put on the shining armor of right living. ¹³Because we belong to the day, we must live decent lives for all to see. Don't participate in the darkness of wild parties and drunkenness, or in sexual promiscuity and immoral living, or in quarreling and jealousy. ¹⁴Instead, clothe yourself with the presence of the Lord Jesus Christ. And don't let yourself think about ways to indulge your evil desires.

The Danger of Criticism

14 Accept other believers who are weak in faith, and don't argue with them about what they think is right or wrong. ²For instance, one person believes it's all right to eat anything. But another believer with a sensitive conscience will eat only vegetables. ³Those who feel free to eat anything must not look down on those who don't. And those who don't eat certain foods must not condemn those who do, for God has accepted them. ⁴Who are you to condemn someone else's servants? Their own master will judge whether they stand or fall. And with the Lord's help, they will stand and receive his approval.

⁵In the same way, some think one day is more holy than another day, while others think every day is alike. You should each be fully convinced that whichever day you choose is acceptable. ⁶Those who worship the Lord on a special day do it to honor him. Those who eat any kind of food do so to honor the Lord, since they give thanks to God before eating. And those who refuse to eat certain foods also want to please the Lord and give thanks to God. ⁷For we don't live for ourselves or die for ourselves. ⁸If we live, it's to honor the Lord. And if we die, it's to honor the Lord. So whether we live or die, we belong to the Lord. ⁹Christ died and rose again for this very purpose—to be Lord both of the living and of the dead.

¹⁰So why do you condemn another believer*? Why do you look down on another believer? Remember, we will all stand before the judgment seat of God. ¹¹For the Scriptures say,

"'As surely as I live,' says the LORD,
'every knee will bend to me,
   and every tongue will declare allegiance
      to God.'"*

¹²Yes, each of us will give a personal account to God. ¹³So let's stop condemning each other. Decide instead to live in such a way that you will not cause another believer to stumble and fall.

¹⁴I know and am convinced on the authority of the Lord Jesus that no food, in and of itself, is wrong to eat. But if someone believes it is wrong, then for that person it is wrong. ¹⁵And if another believer is distressed by what you eat, you are not acting in love if you eat it. Don't let your eating ruin someone for whom Christ died. ¹⁶Then you will not be criticized for doing something you believe is good. ¹⁷For the Kingdom of God is not a matter of what we eat or drink, but of living a life of goodness and peace and joy in the Holy Spirit. ¹⁸If you serve Christ with this attitude, you will please God, and others will approve of you, too. ¹⁹So then, let us aim for harmony in the church and try to build each other up.

²⁰Don't tear apart the work of God over what you eat. Remember, all foods are acceptable, but it is wrong to eat something if it makes another person stumble. ²¹It is better not to eat meat or drink wine or do anything else if it might cause another believer to stumble.* ²²You may believe there's nothing wrong with what you are doing, but keep it between yourself and God. Blessed are those who don't feel

13:9a Exod 20:13-15, 17.   13:9b Lev 19:18.   14:10 Greek *your brother;* also in 14:10b, 13, 15, 21.   14:11 Or *declare praise for God.* Isa 49:18; 45:23 (Greek version).   14:21 Some manuscripts read *to stumble or be offended or be weakened.*

guilty for doing something they have decided is right. 23But if you have doubts about whether or not you should eat something, you are sinning if you go ahead and do it. For you are not following your convictions. If you do anything you believe is not right, you are sinning.*

Living to Please Others

15 We who are strong must be considerate of those who are sensitive about things like this. We must not just please ourselves. 2We should help others do what is right and build them up in the Lord. 3For even Christ didn't live to please himself. As the Scriptures say, "The insults of those who insult you, O God, have fallen on me."* 4Such things were written in the Scriptures long ago to teach us. And the Scriptures give us hope and encouragement as we wait patiently for God's promises to be fulfilled.

5May God, who gives this patience and encouragement, help you live in complete harmony with each other, as is fitting for followers of Christ Jesus. 6Then all of you can join together with one voice, giving praise and glory to God, the Father of our Lord Jesus Christ.

7Therefore, accept each other just as Christ has accepted you so that God will be given glory. 8Remember that Christ came as a servant to the Jews* to show that God is true to the promises he made to their ancestors. 9He also came so that the Gentiles might give glory to God for his mercies to them. That is what the psalmist meant when he wrote:

"For this, I will praise you among the
  Gentiles;
 I will sing praises to your name."*

10And in another place it is written,

"Rejoice with his people,
 you Gentiles."*

11And yet again,

"Praise the LORD, all you Gentiles.
 Praise him, all you people of the
  earth."*

12And in another place Isaiah said,

"The heir to David's throne* will come,
 and he will rule over the Gentiles.
 They will place their hope on him."*

13I pray that God, the source of hope, will fill you completely with joy and peace because you trust in him. Then you will overflow with confident hope through the power of the Holy Spirit.

Paul's Reason for Writing

14I am fully convinced, my dear brothers and sisters,* that you are full of goodness. You know these things so well you can teach each other all about them. 15Even so, I have been bold enough to write about some of these points, knowing that all you need is this reminder. For by God's grace, 16I am a special messenger from Christ Jesus to you Gentiles. I bring you the Good News so that I might present you as an acceptable offering to God, made holy by the Holy Spirit. 17So I have reason to be enthusiastic about all Christ Jesus has done through me in my service to God. 18Yet I dare not boast about anything except what Christ has done through me, bringing the Gentiles to God by my message and by the way I worked among them. 19They were convinced by the power of miraculous signs and wonders and by the power of God's Spirit.* In this way, I have fully presented the Good News of Christ from Jerusalem all the way to Illyricum.*

20My ambition has always been to preach the Good News where the name of Christ has never been heard, rather than where a church has already been started by someone else. 21I have been following the plan spoken of in the Scriptures, where it says,

"Those who have never been told about
  him will see,
 and those who have never heard of him
  will understand."*

22In fact, my visit to you has been delayed so long because I have been preaching in these places.

Paul's Travel Plans

23But now I have finished my work in these regions, and after all these long years of waiting, I am eager to visit you. 24I am planning to

14:23 Some manuscripts place the text of 16:25-27 here.   15:3 Greek *who insult you have fallen on me.* Ps 69:9.   15:8 Greek *servant of circumcision.*   15:9 Ps 18:49.   15:10 Deut 32:43.   15:11 Ps 117:1.   15:12a Greek *The root of Jesse.* David was the son of Jesse.   15:12b Isa 11:10 (Greek version).   15:14 Greek *brothers;* also in 15:30.   15:19a Other manuscripts read *the Spirit;* still others read *the Holy Spirit.*   15:19b *Illyricum* was a region northeast of Italy.   15:21 Isa 52:15 (Greek version).

go to Spain, and when I do, I will stop off in Rome. And after I have enjoyed your fellowship for a little while, you can provide for my journey.

25But before I come, I must go to Jerusalem to take a gift to the believers* there. 26For you see, the believers in Macedonia and Achaia* have eagerly taken up an offering for the poor among the believers in Jerusalem. 27They were glad to do this because they feel they owe a real debt to them. Since the Gentiles received the spiritual blessings of the Good News from the believers in Jerusalem, they feel the least they can do in return is to help them financially. 28As soon as I have delivered this money and completed this good deed of theirs, I will come to see you on my way to Spain. 29And I am sure that when I come, Christ will richly bless our time together.

30Dear brothers and sisters, I urge you in the name of our Lord Jesus Christ to join in my struggle by praying to God for me. Do this because of your love for me, given to you by the Holy Spirit. 31Pray that I will be rescued from those in Judea who refuse to obey God. Pray also that the believers there will be willing to accept the donation* I am taking to Jerusalem. 32Then, by the will of God, I will be able to come to you with a joyful heart, and we will be an encouragement to each other.

33And now may God, who gives us his peace, be with you all. Amen.*

Paul Greets His Friends

16 I commend to you our sister Phoebe, who is a deacon in the church in Cenchrea. 2Welcome her in the Lord as one who is worthy of honor among God's people. Help her in whatever she needs, for she has been helpful to many, and especially to me.

3Give my greetings to Priscilla and Aquila, my co-workers in the ministry of Christ Jesus. 4In fact, they once risked their lives for me. I am thankful to them, and so are all the Gentile churches. 5Also give my greetings to the church that meets in their home.

Greet my dear friend Epenetus. He was the first person from the province of Asia to become a follower of Christ. 6Give my greetings to Mary, who has worked so hard for your benefit. 7Greet Andronicus and Junia,* my fellow Jews,* who were in prison with me. They are highly respected among the apostles and became followers of Christ before I did. 8Greet Ampliatus, my dear friend in the Lord. 9Greet Urbanus, our co-worker in Christ, and my dear friend Stachys.

10Greet Apelles, a good man whom Christ approves. And give my greetings to the believers from the household of Aristobulus. 11Greet Herodion, my fellow Jew.* Greet the Lord's people from the household of Narcissus. 12Give my greetings to Tryphena and Tryphosa, the Lord's workers, and to dear Persis, who has worked so hard for the Lord. 13Greet Rufus, whom the Lord picked out to be his very own; and also his dear mother, who has been a mother to me.

14Give my greetings to Asyncritus, Phlegon, Hermes, Patrobas, Hermas, and the brothers and sisters* who meet with them. 15Give my greetings to Philologus, Julia, Nereus and his sister, and to Olympas and all the believers* who meet with them. 16Greet each other with a sacred kiss. All the churches of Christ send you their greetings.

Paul's Final Instructions

17And now I make one more appeal, my dear brothers and sisters. Watch out for people who cause divisions and upset people's faith by teaching things contrary to what you have been taught. Stay away from them. 18Such people are not serving Christ our Lord; they are serving their own personal interests. By smooth talk and glowing words they deceive innocent people. 19But everyone knows that you are obedient to the Lord. This makes me very happy. I want you to be wise in doing right and to stay innocent of any wrong. 20The God of peace will soon crush Satan under your feet. May the grace of our Lord Jesus* be with you.

21Timothy, my fellow worker, sends you his greetings, as do Lucius, Jason, and Sosipater, my fellow Jews.

22I, Tertius, the one writing this letter for Paul, send my greetings, too, as one of the Lord's followers.

23Gaius says hello to you. He is my host and also serves as host to the whole church. Erastus, the city treasurer, sends you his greetings, and so does our brother Quartus.*

15:25 Greek God's holy people; also in 15:26, 31.   15:26 Macedonia and Achaia were the northern and southern regions of Greece.
15:31 Greek the ministry; other manuscripts read the gift.   15:33 Some manuscripts do not include Amen. One very early
manuscript places 16:25-27 here.   16:7a Junia is a feminine name. Some late manuscripts accent the word so it reads Junias,
a masculine name; still others read Julia (feminine).   16:7b Or compatriots; also in 16:21.   16:11 Or compatriot.   16:14 Greek
brothers; also in 16:17.   16:15 Greek all of God's holy people.   16:20 Some manuscripts read Lord Jesus Christ.   16:23 Some
manuscripts add verse 24, May the grace of our Lord Jesus Christ be with you all. Amen. Still others add this sentence after verse 27.

25Now all glory to God, who is able to make you strong, just as my Good News says. This message about Jesus Christ has revealed his plan for you Gentiles, a plan kept secret from the beginning of time. 26But now as the prophets* foretold and as the eternal God has commanded, this message is made known to all Gentiles everywhere, so that they too might believe and obey him. 27All glory to the only wise God, through Jesus Christ, forever. Amen.*

16:26 Greek *the prophetic writings.*   16:25-27 Various manuscripts place the doxology (shown here as 16:25-27) after 14:23 or after 15:33 or after 16:23.

1 Corinthians

SURROUNDED BY CORRUPTION and flagrant sin, the Christians in Corinth felt pressure to adapt to the low standards of those around them. Many who had already compromised asserted that they were free in Christ, but what did this freedom mean? To resolve this confusion, Paul wrote this letter to the Corinthian believers. The letter covers a wide variety of topics including rival factions within the local church, sexual immorality among believers, public lawsuits between fellow Christians, abuses of spiritual gifts, and disorderly conduct during worship meetings and the Lord's Supper. Paul addressed each of these problems, pointing to Christ as the ultimate solution. Paul also answered specific questions asked by the Corin-thians, questions related to marriage, eating food sacrificed to idols, and the resurrection of Christ and his followers. Throughout the letter, Paul emphasized that believers should be shaped by Christ, not by the world around them. First Corinthians provides the Church with an actual sample of how specific problems were addressed and corrected by the early believers.

■ **Author:** Paul the apostle

■ **Date Written:** Around AD 56, near the end of Paul's two- to three-year ministry in the city of Ephesus during his third missionary journey

■ **Purpose:** To identify problems in the Corin-thian church, to offer solutions, and to teach believers how to live as Christians in a corrupt society

■ **Themes:** Divisions, sexual immorality, free-dom in Christ, worship, resurrection

■ **Outline**

1:1-9 Paul's greetings
1:10–4:21 The problem of divisions
5:1-13 The problem of sexual sin
6:1-11 The problem of lawsuits
6:12-20 The problem of sexual immorality
7:1-40 Problems related to marriage
8:1–11:1 Problems concerning idols
11:2–14:40 Problems at worship, and spiritual gifts
15:1-58 Thoughts concerning the resurrection
16:1-24 Concluding remarks

Greetings from Paul

1 This letter is from Paul, chosen by the will of God to be an apostle of Christ Jesus, and from our brother Sosthenes.

2 I am writing to God's church in Corinth,* to you who have been called by God to be his own holy people. He made you holy by means of Christ Jesus,* just as he did for all people everywhere who call on the name of our Lord Jesus Christ, their Lord and ours.

3 May God our Father and the Lord Jesus Christ give you grace and peace.

Paul Gives Thanks to God

4 I always thank my God for you and for the gracious gifts he has given you, now that you belong to Christ Jesus. 5 Through him, God has enriched your church in every way—with all of your eloquent words and all of your knowledge. 6 This confirms that what I told you about Christ is true. 7 Now you have every spiritual gift you need as you eagerly wait for the return of our Lord Jesus Christ. 8 He will keep you strong to the end so that you will be free from all blame on the day when our Lord

1:2a *Corinth* was the capital city of Achaia, the southern region of the Greek peninsula.   1:2b Or *because you belong to Christ Jesus.*

Jesus Christ returns. 9God will do this, for he is faithful to do what he says, and he has invited you into partnership with his Son, Jesus Christ our Lord.

Divisions in the Church

10I appeal to you, dear brothers and sisters,* by the authority of our Lord Jesus Christ, to live in harmony with each other. Let there be no divisions in the church. Rather, be of one mind, united in thought and purpose. 11For some members of Chloe's household have told me about your quarrels, my dear brothers and sisters. 12Some of you are saying, "I am a follower of Paul." Others are saying, "I follow Apollos," or "I follow Peter,"* or "I follow only Christ."

13Has Christ been divided into factions? Was I, Paul, crucified for you? Were any of you baptized in the name of Paul? Of course not! 14I thank God that I did not baptize any of you except Crispus and Gaius, 15for now no one can say they were baptized in my name. 16(Oh yes, I also baptized the household of Stephanas, but I don't remember baptizing anyone else.) 17For Christ didn't send me to baptize, but to preach the Good News—and not with clever speech, for fear that the cross of Christ would lose its power.

The Wisdom of God

18The message of the cross is foolish to those who are headed for destruction! But we who are being saved know it is the very power of God. 19As the Scriptures say,

"I will destroy the wisdom of the wise
    and discard the intelligence of the
        intelligent."*

20So where does this leave the philosophers, the scholars, and the world's brilliant debaters? God has made the wisdom of this world look foolish. 21Since God in his wisdom saw to it that the world would never know him through human wisdom, he has used our foolish preaching to save those who believe. 22It is foolish to the Jews, who ask for signs from heaven. And it is foolish to the Greeks, who seek human wisdom. 23So when we preach that Christ was crucified, the Jews are offended and the Gentiles say it's all nonsense. 24But to those called by God to salvation, both Jews and Gentiles,* Christ is the power of God and the wisdom of God. 25This foolish plan of God is wiser than the wisest of human plans, and God's weakness is stronger than the greatest of human strength.

26Remember, dear brothers and sisters, that few of you were wise in the world's eyes or powerful or wealthy* when God called you. 27Instead, God chose things the world considers foolish in order to shame those who think they are wise. And he chose things that are powerless to shame those who are powerful. 28God chose things despised by the world,* things counted as nothing at all, and used them to bring to nothing what the world considers important. 29As a result, no one can ever boast in the presence of God.

30God has united you with Christ Jesus. For our benefit God made him to be wisdom itself. Christ made us right with God; he made us pure and holy, and he freed us from sin. 31Therefore, as the Scriptures say, "If you want to boast, boast only about the LORD."*

Paul's Message of Wisdom

2 When I first came to you, dear brothers and sisters,* I didn't use lofty words and impressive wisdom to tell you God's secret plan.* 2For I decided that while I was with you I would forget everything except Jesus Christ, the one who was crucified. 3I came to you in weakness—timid and trembling. 4And my message and my preaching were very plain. Rather than using clever and persuasive speeches, I relied only on the power of the Holy Spirit. 5I did this so you would trust not in human wisdom but in the power of God.

6Yet when I am among mature believers, I do speak with words of wisdom, but not the kind of wisdom that belongs to this world or to the rulers of this world, who are soon forgotten. 7No, the wisdom we speak of is the mystery of God*—his plan that was previously hidden, even though he made it for our ultimate glory before the world began. 8But the rulers of this world have not understood it; if they had, they would not have crucified our glorious Lord. 9That is what the Scriptures mean when they say,

"No eye has seen, no ear has heard,
    and no mind has imagined
what God has prepared
    for those who love him."*

1:10 Greek brothers; also in 1:11, 26.   1:12 Greek Cephas.   1:19 Isa 29:14.   1:24 Greek and Greeks.   1:26 Or high born.   1:28 Or God chose those who are low born.   1:31 Jer 9:24.   2:1a Greek brothers.   2:1b Greek God's mystery; other manuscripts read God's testimony.   2:7 Greek But we speak God's wisdom in a mystery.   2:9 Isa 64:4.

¹⁰But* it was to us that God revealed these things by his Spirit. For his Spirit searches out everything and shows us God's deep secrets. ¹¹No one can know a person's thoughts except that person's own spirit, and no one can know God's thoughts except God's own Spirit. ¹²And we have received God's Spirit (not the world's spirit), so we can know the wonderful things God has freely given us.

¹³When we tell you these things, we do not use words that come from human wisdom. Instead, we speak words given to us by the Spirit, using the Spirit's words to explain spiritual truths.* ¹⁴But people who aren't spiritual* can't receive these truths from God's Spirit. It all sounds foolish to them and they can't understand it, for only those who are spiritual can understand what the Spirit means. ¹⁵Those who are spiritual can evaluate all things, but they themselves cannot be evaluated by others. ¹⁶For,

"Who can know the LORD's thoughts?
    Who knows enough to teach him?"*

But we understand these things, for we have the mind of Christ.

Paul and Apollos, Servants of Christ

3 Dear brothers and sisters,* when I was with you I couldn't talk to you as I would to spiritual people.* I had to talk as though you belonged to this world or as though you were infants in Christ. ²I had to feed you with milk, not with solid food, because you weren't ready for anything stronger. And you still aren't ready, ³for you are still controlled by your sinful nature. You are jealous of one another and quarrel with each other. Doesn't that prove you are controlled by your sinful nature? Aren't you living like people of the world? ⁴When one of you says, "I am a follower of Paul," and another says, "I follow Apollos," aren't you acting just like people of the world?

⁵After all, who is Apollos? Who is Paul? We are only God's servants through whom you believed the Good News. Each of us did the work the Lord gave us. ⁶I planted the seed in your hearts, and Apollos watered it, but it was God who made it grow. ⁷It's not important who does the planting, or who does the watering. What's important is that God makes the seed grow. ⁸The one who plants and the one who

waters work together with the same purpose. And both will be rewarded for their own hard work. ⁹For we are both God's workers. And you are God's field. You are God's building.

¹⁰Because of God's grace to me, I have laid the foundation like an expert builder. Now others are building on it. But whoever is building on this foundation must be very careful. ¹¹For no one can lay any foundation other than the one we already have—Jesus Christ.

¹²Anyone who builds on that foundation may use a variety of materials—gold, silver, jewels, wood, hay, or straw. ¹³But on the judgment day, fire will reveal what kind of work each builder has done. The fire will show if a person's work has any value. ¹⁴If the work survives, that builder will receive a reward. ¹⁵But if the work is burned up, the builder will suffer great loss. The builder will be saved, but like someone barely escaping through a wall of flames.

¹⁶Don't you realize that all of you together are the temple of God and that the Spirit of God lives in* you? ¹⁷God will destroy anyone who destroys this temple. For God's temple is holy, and you are that temple.

¹⁸Stop deceiving yourselves. If you think you are wise by this world's standards, you need to become a fool to be truly wise. ¹⁹For the wisdom of this world is foolishness to God. As the Scriptures say,

"He traps the wise
    in the snare of their own cleverness."*

²⁰And again,

"The LORD knows the thoughts of the
        wise;
    he knows they are worthless."*

²¹So don't boast about following a particular human leader. For everything belongs to you—²²whether Paul or Apollos or Peter,* or the world, or life and death, or the present and the future. Everything belongs to you, ²³and you belong to Christ, and Christ belongs to God.

Paul's Relationship with the Corinthians

4 So look at Apollos and me as mere servants of Christ who have been put in charge of explaining God's mysteries. ²Now, a person

---

2:10 Some manuscripts read For.   2:13 Or explaining spiritual truths in spiritual language, or explaining spiritual truths to spiritual people.   2:14 Or who don't have the Spirit; or who have only physical life.   2:16 Isa 40:13 (Greek version).   3:1a Greek Brothers.   3:1b Or to people who have the Spirit.   3:16 Or among.   3:19 Job 5:13.   3:20 Ps 94:11.   3:22 Greek Cephas.

who is put in charge as a manager must be faithful. [3]As for me, it matters very little how I might be evaluated by you or by any human authority. I don't even trust my own judgment on this point. [4]My conscience is clear, but that doesn't prove I'm right. It is the Lord himself who will examine me and decide.

[5]So don't make judgments about anyone ahead of time—before the Lord returns. For he will bring our darkest secrets to light and will reveal our private motives. Then God will give to each one whatever praise is due.

[6]Dear brothers and sisters,* I have used Apollos and myself to illustrate what I've been saying. If you pay attention to what I have quoted from the Scriptures,* you won't be proud of one of your leaders at the expense of another. [7]For what gives you the right to make such a judgment? What do you have that God hasn't given you? And if everything you have is from God, why boast as though it were not a gift?

[8]You think you already have everything you need. You think you are already rich. You have begun to reign in God's kingdom without us! I wish you really were reigning already, for then we would be reigning with you. [9]Instead, I sometimes think God has put us apostles on display, like prisoners of war at the end of a victor's parade, condemned to die. We have become a spectacle to the entire world—to people and angels alike.

[10]Our dedication to Christ makes us look like fools, but you claim to be so wise in Christ! We are weak, but you are so powerful! You are honored, but we are ridiculed. [11]Even now we go hungry and thirsty, and we don't have enough clothes to keep warm. We are often beaten and have no home. [12]We work wearily with our own hands to earn our living. We bless those who curse us. We are patient with those who abuse us. [13]We appeal gently when evil things are said about us. Yet we are treated like the world's garbage, like everybody's trash—right up to the present moment.

[14]I am not writing these things to shame you, but to warn you as my beloved children. [15]For even if you had ten thousand others to teach you about Christ, you have only one spiritual father. For I became your father in Christ Jesus when I preached the Good News to you. [16]So I urge you to imitate me.

[17]That's why I have sent Timothy, my be-loved and faithful child in the Lord. He will remind you of how I follow Christ Jesus, just as I teach in all the churches wherever I go.

[18]Some of you have become arrogant, thinking I will not visit you again. [19]But I will come—and soon—if the Lord lets me, and then I'll find out whether these arrogant people just give pretentious speeches or whether they really have God's power. [20]For the Kingdom of God is not just a lot of talk; it is living by God's power. [21]Which do you choose? Should I come with a rod to punish you, or should I come with love and a gentle spirit?

Paul Condemns Spiritual Pride

5 I can hardly believe the report about the sexual immorality going on among you—something that even pagans don't do. I am told that a man in your church is living in sin with his stepmother.* [2]You are so proud of yourselves, but you should be mourning in sorrow and shame. And you should remove this man from your fellowship.

[3]Even though I am not with you in person, I am with you in the Spirit.* And as though I were there, I have already passed judgment on this man [4]in the name of the Lord Jesus. You must call a meeting of the church.* I will be present with you in spirit, and so will the power of our Lord Jesus. [5]Then you must throw this man out and hand him over to Satan so that his sinful nature will be destroyed* and he himself* will be saved on the day the Lord* returns.

[6]Your boasting about this is terrible. Don't you realize that this sin is like a little yeast that spreads through the whole batch of dough? [7]Get rid of the old "yeast" by removing this wicked person from among you. Then you will be like a fresh batch of dough made without yeast, which is what you really are. Christ, our Passover Lamb, has been sacrificed for us.* [8]So let us celebrate the festival, not with the old bread* of wickedness and evil, but with the new bread* of sincerity and truth.

[9]When I wrote to you before, I told you not to associate with people who indulge in sexual sin. [10]But I wasn't talking about unbelievers who indulge in sexual sin, or are greedy, or cheat people, or worship idols. You would have to leave this world to avoid people like that. [11]I meant that you are not to associate

---

4:6a Greek *Brothers.*   4:6b Or *If you learn not to go beyond "what is written."*   5:1 Greek *his father's wife.*   5:3 Or *in spirit.*
5:4 Or *In the name of the Lord Jesus, you must call a meeting of the church.*   5:5a Or *so that his body will be destroyed;* Greek reads *for the destruction of the flesh.*   5:5b Greek *and the spirit.*   5:5c Other manuscripts read *the Lord Jesus;* still others read *our Lord Jesus Christ.*   5:7 Greek *has been sacrificed.*   5:8a Greek *not with old leaven.*   5:8b Greek *but with unleavened [bread].*

with anyone who claims to be a believer* yet indulges in sexual sin, or is greedy, or worships idols, or is abusive, or is a drunkard, or cheats people. Don't even eat with such people.

¹²It isn't my responsibility to judge outsiders, but it certainly is your responsibility to judge those inside the church who are sinning. ¹³God will judge those on the outside; but as the Scriptures say, "You must remove the evil person from among you."*

Avoiding Lawsuits with Christians

6 When one of you has a dispute with another believer, how dare you file a lawsuit and ask a secular court to decide the matter instead of taking it to other believers*! ²Don't you realize that someday we believers will judge the world? And since you are going to judge the world, can't you decide even these little things among yourselves? ³Don't you realize that we will judge angels? So you should surely be able to resolve ordinary disputes in this life. ⁴If you have legal disputes about such matters, why go to outside judges who are not respected by the church? ⁵I am saying this to shame you. Isn't there anyone in all the church who is wise enough to decide these issues? ⁶But instead, one believer* sues another—right in front of unbelievers!

⁷Even to have such lawsuits with one another is a defeat for you. Why not just accept the injustice and leave it at that? Why not let yourselves be cheated? ⁸Instead, you yourselves are the ones who do wrong and cheat even your fellow believers.*

⁹Don't you realize that those who do wrong will not inherit the Kingdom of God? Don't fool yourselves. Those who indulge in sexual sin, or who worship idols, or commit adultery, or are male prostitutes, or practice homosexuality, ¹⁰or are thieves, or greedy people, or drunkards, or are abusive, or cheat people—none of these will inherit the Kingdom of God. ¹¹Some of you were once like that. But you were cleansed; you were made holy; you were made right with God by calling on the name of the Lord Jesus Christ and by the Spirit of our God.

Avoiding Sexual Sin

¹²You say, "I am allowed to do anything"—but not everything is good for you. And even though "I am allowed to do anything," I must not become a slave to anything. ¹³You say, "Food was made for the stomach, and the stomach for food." (This is true, though someday God will do away with both of them.) But you can't say that our bodies were made for sexual immorality. They were made for the Lord, and the Lord cares about our bodies. ¹⁴And God will raise us from the dead by his power, just as he raised our Lord from the dead.

¹⁵Don't you realize that your bodies are actually parts of Christ? Should a man take his body, which is part of Christ, and join it to a prostitute? Never! ¹⁶And don't you realize that if a man joins himself to a prostitute, he becomes one body with her? For the Scriptures say, "The two are united into one."* ¹⁷But the person who is joined to the Lord is one spirit with him.

¹⁸Run from sexual sin! No other sin so clearly affects the body as this one does. For sexual immorality is a sin against your own body. ¹⁹Don't you realize that your body is the temple of the Holy Spirit, who lives in you and was given to you by God? You do not belong to yourself, ²⁰for God bought you with a high price. So you must honor God with your body.

Instruction on Marriage

7 Now regarding the questions you asked in your letter. Yes, it is good to abstain from sexual relations.* ²But because there is so much sexual immorality, each man should have his own wife, and each woman should have her own husband.

³The husband should fulfill his wife's sexual needs, and the wife should fulfill her husband's needs. ⁴The wife gives authority over her body to her husband, and the husband gives authority over his body to his wife.

⁵Do not deprive each other of sexual relations, unless you both agree to refrain from sexual intimacy for a limited time so you can give yourselves more completely to prayer. Afterward, you should come together again so that Satan won't be able to tempt you because of your lack of self-control. ⁶I say this as a concession, not as a command. ⁷But I wish everyone were single, just as I am. Yet each person has a special gift from God, of one kind or another.

⁸So I say to those who aren't married and to widows—it's better to stay unmarried, just as I am. ⁹But if they can't control themselves, they should go ahead and marry. It's better to marry than to burn with lust.

¹⁰But for those who are married, I have a command that comes not from me, but from

the Lord.* A wife must not leave her husband. [11] But if she does leave him, let her remain single or else be reconciled to him. And the husband must not leave his wife.

[12] Now, I will speak to the rest of you, though I do not have a direct command from the Lord. If a fellow believer* has a wife who is not a believer and she is willing to continue living with him, he must not leave her. [13] And if a believing woman has a husband who is not a believer and he is willing to continue living with her, she must not leave him. [14] For the believing wife brings holiness to her marriage, and the believing husband* brings holiness to his marriage. Otherwise, your children would not be holy, but now they are holy. [15] (But if the husband or wife who isn't a believer insists on leaving, let them go. In such cases the believing husband or wife* is no longer bound to the other, for God has called you* to live in peace.) [16] Don't you wives realize that your husbands might be saved because of you? And don't you husbands realize that your wives might be saved because of you?

[17] Each of you should continue to live in whatever situation the Lord has placed you, and remain as you were when God first called you. This is my rule for all the churches. [18] For instance, a man who was circumcised before he became a believer should not try to reverse it. And the man who was uncircumcised when he became a believer should not be circumcised now. [19] For it makes no difference whether or not a man has been circumcised. The important thing is to keep God's commandments.

[20] Yes, each of you should remain as you were when God called you. [21] Are you a slave? Don't let that worry you—but if you get a chance to be free, take it. [22] And remember, if you were a slave when the Lord called you, you are now free in the Lord. And if you were free when the Lord called you, you are now a slave of Christ. [23] God paid a high price for you, so don't be enslaved by the world.* [24] Each of you, dear brothers and sisters,* should remain as you were when God first called you.

[25] Now regarding your question about the young women who are not yet married. I do not have a command from the Lord for them. But the Lord in his mercy has given me wisdom that can be trusted, and I will share it with you. [26] Because of the present crisis,* I think it is best to remain as you are. [27] If you have a wife, do not seek to end the marriage. If you do not have a wife, do not seek to get married. [28] But if you do get married, it is not a sin. And if a young woman gets married, it is not a sin. However, those who get married at this time will have troubles, and I am trying to spare you those problems.

[29] But let me say this, dear brothers and sisters: The time that remains is very short. So from now on, those with wives should not focus only on their marriage. [30] Those who weep or who rejoice or who buy things should not be absorbed by their weeping or their joy or their possessions. [31] Those who use the things of the world should not become attached to them. For this world as we know it will soon pass away.

[32] I want you to be free from the concerns of this life. An unmarried man can spend his time doing the Lord's work and thinking how to please him. [33] But a married man has to think about his earthly responsibilities and how to please his wife. [34] His interests are divided. In the same way, a woman who is no longer married or has never been married can be devoted to the Lord and holy in body and in spirit. But a married woman has to think about her earthly responsibilities and how to please her husband. [35] I am saying this for your benefit, not to place restrictions on you. I want you to do whatever will help you serve the Lord best, with as few distractions as possible.

[36] But if a man thinks that he's treating his fiancée improperly and will inevitably give in to his passion, let him marry her as he wishes. It is not a sin. [37] But if he has decided firmly not to marry and there is no urgency and he can control his passion, he does well not to marry. [38] So the person who marries his fiancée does well, and the person who doesn't marry does even better.

[39] A wife is bound to her husband as long as he lives. If her husband dies, she is free to marry anyone she wishes, but only if he loves the Lord.* [40] But in my opinion it would be better for her to stay single, and I think I am giving you counsel from God's Spirit when I say this.

Food Sacrificed to Idols

8 Now regarding your question about food that has been offered to idols. Yes, we know that "we all have knowledge" about this issue. But while knowledge makes us feel important, it is love that strengthens the church. [2] Anyone

---

7:10 See Matt 5:32; 19:9; Mark 10:11-12; Luke 16:18.   7:12 Greek *a brother.*   7:14 Greek *the brother.*   7:15a Greek *the brother or sister.*   7:15b Some manuscripts read *us.*   7:23 Greek *don't become slaves of people.*   7:24 Greek *brothers;* also in 7:29.
7:26 Or *the pressures of life.*   7:39 Greek *but only in the Lord.*

who claims to know all the answers doesn't really know very much. ³But the person who loves God is the one whom God recognizes.*

⁴So, what about eating meat that has been offered to idols? Well, we all know that an idol is not really a god and that there is only one God. ⁵There may be so-called gods both in heaven and on earth, and some people actually worship many gods and many lords. ⁶But for us,

There is one God, the Father,
   by whom all things were created,
   and for whom we live.
And there is one Lord, Jesus Christ,
   through whom all things were created,
   and through whom we live.

⁷However, not all believers know this. Some are accustomed to thinking of idols as being real, so when they eat food that has been offered to idols, they think of it as the worship of real gods, and their weak consciences are violated. ⁸It's true that we can't win God's approval by what we eat. We don't lose anything if we don't eat it, and we don't gain anything if we do.

⁹But you must be careful so that your freedom does not cause others with a weaker conscience to stumble. ¹⁰For if others see you—with your "superior knowledge"—eating in the temple of an idol, won't they be encouraged to violate their conscience by eating food that has been offered to an idol? ¹¹So because of your superior knowledge, a weak believer* for whom Christ died will be destroyed. ¹²And when you sin against other believers* by encouraging them to do something they believe is wrong, you are sinning against Christ. ¹³So if what I eat causes another believer to sin, I will never eat meat again as long as I live—for I don't want to cause another believer to stumble.

Paul Gives Up His Rights

9 Am I not as free as anyone else? Am I not an apostle? Haven't I seen Jesus our Lord with my own eyes? Isn't it because of my work that you belong to the Lord? ²Even if others think I am not an apostle, I certainly am to you. You yourselves are proof that I am the Lord's apostle.

³This is my answer to those who question my authority.* ⁴Don't we have the right to live in your homes and share your meals? ⁵Don't we

have the right to bring a believing wife* with us as the other apostles and the Lord's brothers do, and as Peter* does? ⁶Or is it only Barnabas and I who have to work to support ourselves?

⁷What soldier has to pay his own expenses? What farmer plants a vineyard and doesn't have the right to eat some of its fruit? What shepherd cares for a flock of sheep and isn't allowed to drink some of the milk? ⁸Am I expressing merely a human opinion, or does the law say the same thing? ⁹For the law of Moses says, "You must not muzzle an ox to keep it from eating as it treads out the grain."* Was God thinking only about oxen when he said this? ¹⁰Wasn't he actually speaking to us? Yes, it was written for us, so that the one who plows and the one who threshes the grain might both expect a share of the harvest.

¹¹Since we have planted spiritual seed among you, aren't we entitled to a harvest of physical food and drink? ¹²If you support others who preach to you, shouldn't we have an even greater right to be supported? But we have never used this right. We would rather put up with anything than be an obstacle to the Good News about Christ.

¹³Don't you realize that those who work in the temple get their meals from the offerings brought to the temple? And those who serve at the altar get a share of the sacrificial offerings. ¹⁴In the same way, the Lord ordered that those who preach the Good News should be supported by those who benefit from it. ¹⁵Yet I have never used any of these rights. And I am not writing this to suggest that I want to start now. In fact, I would rather die than lose my right to boast about preaching without charge. ¹⁶Yet preaching the Good News is not something I can boast about. I am compelled by God to do it. How terrible for me if I didn't preach the Good News!

¹⁷If I were doing this on my own initiative, I would deserve payment. But I have no choice, for God has given me this sacred trust. ¹⁸What then is my pay? It is the opportunity to preach the Good News without charging anyone. That's why I never demand my rights when I preach the Good News.

¹⁹Even though I am a free man with no master, I have become a slave to all people to bring many to Christ. ²⁰When I was with the Jews, I lived like a Jew to bring the Jews to Christ. When I was with those who follow the Jewish law, I too lived under that law. Even though I

8:3 Some manuscripts read *the person who loves has full knowledge.*   8:11 Greek *brother;* also in 8:13.   8:12 Greek *brothers.*
9:3 Greek *those who examine me.*   9:5a Greek *a sister a wife.*   9:5b Greek *Cephas.*   9:9 Deut 25:4.

am not subject to the law, I did this so I could bring to Christ those who are under the law. ²¹When I am with the Gentiles who do not follow the Jewish law,* I too live apart from that law so I can bring them to Christ. But I do not ignore the law of God; I obey the law of Christ. ²²When I am with those who are weak, I share their weakness, for I want to bring the weak to Christ. Yes, I try to find common ground with everyone, doing everything I can to save some. ²³I do everything to spread the Good News and share in its blessings.

²⁴Don't you realize that in a race everyone runs, but only one person gets the prize? So run to win! ²⁵All athletes are disciplined in their training. They do it to win a prize that will fade away, but we do it for an eternal prize. ²⁶So I run with purpose in every step. I am not just shadowboxing. ²⁷I discipline my body like an athlete, training it to do what it should. Otherwise, I fear that after preaching to others I myself might be disqualified.

Lessons from Israel's Idolatry

10 I don't want you to forget, dear brothers and sisters,* about our ancestors in the wilderness long ago. All of them were guided by a cloud that moved ahead of them, and all of them walked through the sea on dry ground. ²In the cloud and in the sea, all of them were baptized as followers of Moses. ³All of them ate the same spiritual food, ⁴and all of them drank the same spiritual water. For they drank from the spiritual rock that traveled with them, and that rock was Christ. ⁵Yet God was not pleased with most of them, and their bodies were scattered in the wilderness.

⁶These things happened as a warning to us, so that we would not crave evil things as they did, ⁷or worship idols as some of them did. As the Scriptures say, "The people celebrated with feasting and drinking, and they indulged in pagan revelry."* ⁸And we must not engage in sexual immorality as some of them did, causing 23,000 of them to die in one day. ⁹Nor should we put Christ* to the test, as some of them did and then died from snakebites. ¹⁰And don't grumble as some of them did, and then were destroyed by the angel of death. ¹¹These things happened to them as examples for us. They were written down to warn us who live at the end of the age.

¹²If you think you are standing strong, be careful not to fall. ¹³The temptations in your life are no different from what others experience. And God is faithful. He will not allow the temptation to be more than you can stand. When you are tempted, he will show you a way out so that you can endure.

¹⁴So, my dear friends, flee from the worship of idols. ¹⁵You are reasonable people. Decide for yourselves if what I am saying is true. ¹⁶When we bless the cup at the Lord's Table, aren't we sharing in the blood of Christ? And when we break the bread, aren't we sharing in the body of Christ? ¹⁷And though we are many, we all eat from one loaf of bread, showing that we are one body. ¹⁸Think about the people of Israel. Weren't they united by eating the sacrifices at the altar?

¹⁹What am I trying to say? Am I saying that food offered to idols has some significance, or that idols are real gods? ²⁰No, not at all. I am saying that these sacrifices are offered to demons, not to God. And I don't want you to participate with demons. ²¹You cannot drink from the cup of the Lord and from the cup of demons, too. You cannot eat at the Lord's Table and at the table of demons, too. ²²What? Do we dare to rouse the Lord's jealousy? Do you think we are stronger than he is?

²³You say, "I am allowed to do anything"*— but not everything is good for you. You say, "I am allowed to do anything"—but not everything is beneficial. ²⁴Don't be concerned for your own good but for the good of others.

²⁵So you may eat any meat that is sold in the marketplace without raising questions of conscience. ²⁶For "the earth is the LORD's, and everything in it."* ²⁷If someone who isn't a believer asks you home for dinner, accept the invitation if you want to. Eat whatever is offered to you without raising questions of conscience. ²⁸(But suppose someone tells you, "This meat was offered to an idol." Don't eat it, out of consideration for the conscience of the one who told you. ²⁹It might not be a matter of conscience for you, but it is for the other person.) For why should my freedom be limited by what someone else thinks? ³⁰If I can thank God for the food and enjoy it, why should I be condemned for eating it?

³¹So whether you eat or drink, or whatever you do, do it all for the glory of God. ³²Don't give offense to Jews or Gentiles* or the church of God. ³³I, too, try to please everyone in everything I do. I don't just do what is best for me; I do what is best for others so that many may

be saved. 11:1And you should imitate me, just as I imitate Christ.

Instructions for Public Worship

11 2I am so glad that you always keep me in your thoughts, and that you are following the teachings I passed on to you. 3But there is one thing I want you to know: The head of every man is Christ, the head of woman is man, and the head of Christ is God.* 4A man dishonors his head* if he covers his head while praying or prophesying. 5But a woman dishonors her head* if she prays or prophesies without a covering on her head, for this is the same as shaving her head. 6Yes, if she refuses to wear a head covering, she should cut off all her hair! But since it is shameful for a woman to have her hair cut or her head shaved, she should wear a covering.*

7A man should not wear anything on his head when worshiping, for man is made in God's image and reflects God's glory. And woman reflects man's glory. 8For the first man didn't come from woman, but the first woman came from man. 9And man was not made for woman, but woman was made for man. 10For this reason, and because the angels are watching, a woman should wear a covering on her head to show she is under authority.*

11But among the Lord's people, women are not independent of men, and men are not independent of women. 12For although the first woman came from man, every other man was born from a woman, and everything comes from God.

13Judge for yourselves. Is it right for a woman to pray to God in public without covering her head? 14Isn't it obvious that it's disgraceful for a man to have long hair? 15And isn't long hair a woman's pride and joy? For it has been given to her as a covering. 16But if anyone wants to argue about this, I simply say that we have no other custom than this, and neither do God's other churches.

Order at the Lord's Supper

17But in the following instructions, I cannot praise you. For it sounds as if more harm than good is done when you meet together. 18First, I hear that there are divisions among you when you meet as a church, and to some extent I believe it. 19But, of course, there must

be divisions among you so that you who have God's approval will be recognized!

20When you meet together, you are not really interested in the Lord's Supper. 21For some of you hurry to eat your own meal without sharing with others. As a result, some go hungry while others get drunk. 22What? Don't you have your own homes for eating and drinking? Or do you really want to disgrace God's church and shame the poor? What am I supposed to say? Do you want me to praise you? Well, I certainly will not praise you for this!

23For I pass on to you what I received from the Lord himself. On the night when he was betrayed, the Lord Jesus took some bread 24and gave thanks to God for it. Then he broke it in pieces and said, "This is my body, which is given for you.* Do this in remembrance of me." 25In the same way, he took the cup of wine after supper, saying, "This cup is the new covenant between God and his people—an agreement confirmed with my blood. Do this in remembrance of me as often as you drink it." 26For every time you eat this bread and drink this cup, you are announcing the Lord's death until he comes again.

27So anyone who eats this bread or drinks this cup of the Lord unworthily is guilty of sinning against* the body and blood of the Lord. 28That is why you should examine yourself before eating the bread and drinking the cup. 29For if you eat the bread or drink the cup without honoring the body of Christ,* you are eating and drinking God's judgment upon yourself. 30That is why many of you are weak and sick and some have even died.

31But if we would examine ourselves, we would not be judged by God in this way. 32Yet when we are judged by the Lord, we are being disciplined so that we will not be condemned along with the world.

33So, my dear brothers and sisters,* when you gather for the Lord's Supper, wait for each other. 34If you are really hungry, eat at home so you won't bring judgment upon yourselves when you meet together. I'll give you instructions about the other matters after I arrive.

Spiritual Gifts

12 Now, dear brothers and sisters,* regarding your question about the special abilities the Spirit gives us. I don't want you

11:3 Or to know: The source of every man is Christ, the source of woman is man, and the source of Christ is God. Or to know: Every man is responsible to Christ, a woman is responsible to her husband, and Christ is responsible to God.   11:4 Or dishonors Christ.   11:5 Or dishonors her husband.   11:6 Or should have long hair.   11:10 Greek should have an authority on her head.   11:24 Greek which is for you; other manuscripts read which is broken for you.   11:27 Or is responsible for.   11:29 Greek the body; other manuscripts read the Lord's body.   11:33 Greek brothers.   12:1 Greek brothers.

to misunderstand this. ²You know that when you were still pagans, you were led astray and swept along in worshiping speechless idols. ³So I want you to know that no one speaking by the Spirit of God will curse Jesus, and no one can say Jesus is Lord, except by the Holy Spirit.

⁴There are different kinds of spiritual gifts, but the same Spirit is the source of them all. ⁵There are different kinds of service, but we serve the same Lord. ⁶God works in different ways, but it is the same God who does the work in all of us.

⁷A spiritual gift is given to each of us so we can help each other. ⁸To one person the Spirit gives the ability to give wise advice*; to another the same Spirit gives a message of special knowledge.* ⁹The same Spirit gives great faith to another, and to someone else the one Spirit gives the gift of healing. ¹⁰He gives one person the power to perform miracles, and another the ability to prophesy. He gives someone else the ability to discern whether a message is from the Spirit of God or from another spirit. Still another person is given the ability to speak in unknown languages,* while another is given the ability to interpret what is being said. ¹¹It is the one and only Spirit who distributes all these gifts. He alone decides which gift each person should have.

One Body with Many Parts

¹²The human body has many parts, but the many parts make up one whole body. So it is with the body of Christ. ¹³Some of us are Jews, some are Gentiles,* some are slaves, and some are free. But we have all been baptized into one body by one Spirit, and we all share the same Spirit.*

¹⁴Yes, the body has many different parts, not just one part. ¹⁵If the foot says, "I am not a part of the body because I am not a hand," that does not make it any less a part of the body. ¹⁶And if the ear says, "I am not part of the body because I am not an eye," would that make it any less a part of the body? ¹⁷If the whole body were an eye, how would you hear? Or if your whole body were an ear, how would you smell anything?

¹⁸But our bodies have many parts, and God has put each part just where he wants it. ¹⁹How strange a body would be if it had only one part! ²⁰Yes, there are many parts, but only one body. ²¹The eye can never say to the hand, "I don't need you." The head can't say to the feet, "I don't need you."

²²In fact, some parts of the body that seem weakest and least important are actually the most necessary. ²³And the parts we regard as less honorable are those we clothe with the greatest care. So we carefully protect those parts that should not be seen, ²⁴while the more honorable parts do not require this special care. So God has put the body together such that extra honor and care are given to those parts that have less dignity. ²⁵This makes for harmony among the members, so that all the members care for each other. ²⁶If one part suffers, all the parts suffer with it, and if one part is honored, all the parts are glad.

²⁷All of you together are Christ's body, and each of you is a part of it. ²⁸Here are some of the parts God has appointed for the church:

first are apostles,
second are prophets,
third are teachers,
then those who do miracles,
those who have the gift of healing,
those who can help others,
those who have the gift of leadership,
those who speak in unknown languages.

²⁹Are we all apostles? Are we all prophets? Are we all teachers? Do we all have the power to do miracles? ³⁰Do we all have the gift of healing? Do we all have the ability to speak in unknown languages? Do we all have the ability to interpret unknown languages? Of course not! ³¹So you should earnestly desire the most helpful gifts.

But now let me show you a way of life that is best of all.

Love Is the Greatest

13 If I could speak all the languages of earth and of angels, but didn't love others, I would only be a noisy gong or a clanging cymbal. ²If I had the gift of prophecy, and if I understood all of God's secret plans and possessed all knowledge, and if I had such faith that I could move mountains, but didn't love others, I would be nothing. ³If I gave everything I have to the poor and even sacrificed my body, I could boast about it;* but if I didn't love others, I would have gained nothing.

⁴Love is patient and kind. Love is not jealous or boastful or proud ⁵or rude. It does not demand its own way. It is not irritable, and it keeps no record of being wronged. ⁶It does not

12:8a Or *gives a word of wisdom.*   12:8b Or *gives a word of knowledge.*   12:10 Or *in various tongues;* also in 12:28, 30.   12:13a Greek *some are Greeks.*   12:13b Greek *we were all given one Spirit to drink.*   13:3 Some manuscripts read *sacrificed my body to be burned.*

rejoice about injustice but rejoices whenever the truth wins out. ⁷Love never gives up, never loses faith, is always hopeful, and endures through every circumstance.

⁸Prophecy and speaking in unknown languages* and special knowledge will become useless. But love will last forever! ⁹Now our knowledge is partial and incomplete, and even the gift of prophecy reveals only part of the whole picture! ¹⁰But when the time of perfection comes, these partial things will become useless.

¹¹When I was a child, I spoke and thought and reasoned as a child. But when I grew up, I put away childish things. ¹²Now we see things imperfectly, like puzzling reflections in a mirror, but then we will see everything with perfect clarity.* All that I know now is partial and incomplete, but then I will know everything completely, just as God now knows me completely.

¹³Three things will last forever—faith, hope, and love—and the greatest of these is love.

Tongues and Prophecy

14 Let love be your highest goal! But you should also desire the special abilities the Spirit gives—especially the ability to prophesy. ²For if you have the ability to speak in tongues,* you will be talking only to God, since people won't be able to understand you. You will be speaking by the power of the Spirit,* but it will all be mysterious. ³But one who prophesies strengthens others, encourages them, and comforts them. ⁴A person who speaks in tongues is strengthened personally, but one who speaks a word of prophecy strengthens the entire church.

⁵I wish you could all speak in tongues, but even more I wish you could all prophesy. For prophecy is greater than speaking in tongues, unless someone interprets what you are saying so that the whole church will be strengthened.

⁶Dear brothers and sisters,* if I should come to you speaking in an unknown language,* how would that help you? But if I bring you a revelation or some special knowledge or prophecy or teaching, that will be helpful. ⁷Even lifeless instruments like the flute or the harp must play the notes clearly, or no one will recognize the melody. ⁸And if the bugler doesn't sound a clear call, how will the soldiers know they are being called to battle?

⁹It's the same for you. If you speak to people in words they don't understand, how will they know what you are saying? You might as well be talking into empty space.

¹⁰There are many different languages in the world, and every language has meaning. ¹¹But if I don't understand a language, I will be a foreigner to someone who speaks it, and the one who speaks it will be a foreigner to me. ¹²And the same is true for you. Since you are so eager to have the special abilities the Spirit gives, seek those that will strengthen the whole church.

¹³So anyone who speaks in tongues should pray also for the ability to interpret what has been said. ¹⁴For if I pray in tongues, my spirit is praying, but I don't understand what I am saying.

¹⁵Well then, what shall I do? I will pray in the spirit,* and I will also pray in words I understand. I will sing in the spirit, and I will also sing in words I understand. ¹⁶For if you praise God only in the spirit, how can those who don't understand you praise God along with you? How can they join you in giving thanks when they don't understand what you are saying? ¹⁷You will be giving thanks very well, but it won't strengthen the people who hear you.

¹⁸I thank God that I speak in tongues more than any of you. ¹⁹But in a church meeting I would rather speak five understandable words to help others than ten thousand words in an unknown language.

²⁰Dear brothers and sisters, don't be childish in your understanding of these things. Be innocent as babies when it comes to evil, but be mature in understanding matters of this kind. ²¹It is written in the Scriptures*:

"I will speak to my own people
    through strange languages
    and through the lips of foreigners.
But even then, they will not listen to me,"*
    says the LORD.

²²So you see that speaking in tongues is a sign, not for believers, but for unbelievers. Prophecy, however, is for the benefit of believers, not unbelievers. ²³Even so, if unbelievers or people who don't understand these things come into your church meeting and hear everyone speaking in an unknown language, they will think you are crazy. ²⁴But if all of you are

13:8 Or in tongues.   13:12 Greek see face to face.   14:2a Or in unknown languages; also in 14:4, 5, 13, 14, 18, 22, 26, 27, 28, 39.
14:2b Or speaking in your spirit.   14:6a Greek brothers; also in 14:20, 26, 39.   14:6b Or in tongues; also in 14:19, 23.   14:15 Or in the Spirit; also in 14:15b, 16.   14:21a Greek in the law.   14:21b Isa 28:11-12.

prophesying, and unbelievers or people who don't understand these things come into your meeting, they will be convicted of sin and judged by what you say. ²⁵As they listen, their secret thoughts will be exposed, and they will fall to their knees and worship God, declaring, "God is truly here among you."

A Call to Orderly Worship

²⁶Well, my brothers and sisters, let's summarize. When you meet together, one will sing, another will teach, another will tell some special revelation God has given, one will speak in tongues, and another will interpret what is said. But everything that is done must strengthen all of you.

²⁷No more than two or three should speak in tongues. They must speak one at a time, and someone must interpret what they say. ²⁸But if no one is present who can interpret, they must be silent in your church meeting and speak in tongues to God privately.

²⁹Let two or three people prophesy, and let the others evaluate what is said. ³⁰But if someone is prophesying and another person receives a revelation from the Lord, the one who is speaking must stop. ³¹In this way, all who prophesy will have a turn to speak, one after the other, so that everyone will learn and be encouraged. ³²Remember that people who prophesy are in control of their spirit and can take turns. ³³For God is not a God of disorder but of peace, as in all the meetings of God's holy people.*

³⁴Women should be silent during the church meetings. It is not proper for them to speak. They should be submissive, just as the law says. ³⁵If they have any questions, they should ask their husbands at home, for it is improper for women to speak in church meetings.*

³⁶Or do you think God's word originated with you Corinthians? Are you the only ones to whom it was given? ³⁷If you claim to be a prophet or think you are spiritual, you should recognize that what I am saying is a command from the Lord himself. ³⁸But if you do not recognize this, you yourself will not be recognized.*

³⁹So, my dear brothers and sisters, be eager to prophesy, and don't forbid speaking in tongues. ⁴⁰But be sure that everything is done properly and in order.

The Resurrection of Christ

15 Let me now remind you, dear brothers and sisters,* of the Good News I preached to you before. You welcomed it then, and you still stand firm in it. ²It is this Good News that saves you if you continue to believe the message I told you—unless, of course, you believed something that was never true in the first place.*

³I passed on to you what was most important and what had also been passed on to me. Christ died for our sins, just as the Scriptures said. ⁴He was buried, and he was raised from the dead on the third day, just as the Scriptures said. ⁵He was seen by Peter* and then by the Twelve. ⁶After that, he was seen by more than 500 of his followers* at one time, most of whom are still alive, though some have died. ⁷Then he was seen by James and later by all the apostles. ⁸Last of all, as though I had been born at the wrong time, I also saw him. ⁹For I am the least of all the apostles. In fact, I'm not even worthy to be called an apostle after the way I persecuted God's church.

¹⁰But whatever I am now, it is all because God poured out his special favor on me—and not without results. For I have worked harder than any of the other apostles; yet it was not I but God who was working through me by his grace. ¹¹So it makes no difference whether I preach or they preach, for we all preach the same message you have already believed.

The Resurrection of the Dead

¹²But tell me this—since we preach that Christ rose from the dead, why are some of you saying there will be no resurrection of the dead? ¹³For if there is no resurrection of the dead, then Christ has not been raised either. ¹⁴And if Christ has not been raised, then all our preaching is useless, and your faith is useless. ¹⁵And we apostles would all be lying about God—for we have said that God raised Christ from the grave. But that can't be true if there is no resurrection of the dead. ¹⁶And if there is no resurrection of the dead, then Christ has not been raised. ¹⁷And if Christ has not been raised, then your faith is useless and you are still guilty of your sins. ¹⁸In that case, all who have died believing in Christ are lost! ¹⁹And if our hope in Christ is

---

14:33 The phrase *as in all the meetings of God's holy people* could instead be joined to the beginning of 14:34.   14:35 Some manuscripts place verses 34-35 after 14:40.   14:38 Some manuscripts read *If you are ignorant of this, stay in your ignorance.*   15:1 Greek *brothers;* also in 15:31, 50, 58.   15:2 Or *unless you never believed it in the first place.*   15:5 Greek *Cephas.*   15:6 Greek *the brothers.*

only for this life, we are more to be pitied than anyone in the world.

20But in fact, Christ has been raised from the dead. He is the first of a great harvest of all who have died.

21So you see, just as death came into the world through a man, now the resurrection from the dead has begun through another man. 22Just as everyone dies because we all belong to Adam, everyone who belongs to Christ will be given new life. 23But there is an order to this resurrection: Christ was raised as the first of the harvest; then all who belong to Christ will be raised when he comes back.

24After that the end will come, when he will turn the Kingdom over to God the Father, having destroyed every ruler and authority and power. 25For Christ must reign until he humbles all his enemies beneath his feet. 26And the last enemy to be destroyed is death. 27For the Scriptures say, "God has put all things under his authority."* (Of course, when it says "all things are under his authority," that does not include God himself, who gave Christ his authority.) 28Then, when all things are under his authority, the Son will put himself under God's authority, so that God, who gave his Son authority over all things, will be utterly supreme over everything everywhere.

29If the dead will not be raised, what point is there in people being baptized for those who are dead? Why do it unless the dead will someday rise again?

30And why should we ourselves risk our lives hour by hour? 31For I swear, dear brothers and sisters, that I face death daily. This is as certain as my pride in what Christ Jesus our Lord has done in you. 32And what value was there in fighting wild beasts—those people of Ephesus*—if there will be no resurrection from the dead? And if there is no resurrection, "Let's feast and drink, for tomorrow we die!"* 33Don't be fooled by those who say such things, for "bad company corrupts good character." 34Think carefully about what is right, and stop sinning. For to your shame I say that some of you don't know God at all.

The Resurrection Body

35But someone may ask, "How will the dead be raised? What kind of bodies will they have?" 36What a foolish question! When you put a seed into the ground, it doesn't grow into a plant unless it dies first. 37And what you put in the ground is not the plant that will grow, but only a bare seed of wheat or whatever you are planting. 38Then God gives it the new body he wants it to have. A different plant grows from each kind of seed. 39Similarly there are different kinds of flesh—one kind for humans, another for animals, another for birds, and another for fish.

40There are also bodies in the heavens and bodies on the earth. The glory of the heavenly bodies is different from the glory of the earthly bodies. 41The sun has one kind of glory, while the moon and stars each have another kind. And even the stars differ from each other in their glory.

42It is the same way with the resurrection of the dead. Our earthly bodies are planted in the ground when we die, but they will be raised to live forever. 43Our bodies are buried in brokenness, but they will be raised in glory. They are buried in weakness, but they will be raised in strength. 44They are buried as natural human bodies, but they will be raised as spiritual bodies. For just as there are natural bodies, there are also spiritual bodies.

45The Scriptures tell us, "The first man, Adam, became a living person."* But the last Adam—that is, Christ—is a life-giving Spirit. 46What comes first is the natural body, then the spiritual body comes later. 47Adam, the first man, was made from the dust of the earth, while Christ, the second man, came from heaven. 48Earthly people are like the earthly man, and heavenly people are like the heavenly man. 49Just as we are now like the earthly man, we will someday be like* the heavenly man.

50What I am saying, dear brothers and sisters, is that our physical bodies cannot inherit the Kingdom of God. These dying bodies cannot inherit what will last forever.

51But let me reveal to you a wonderful secret. We will not all die, but we will all be transformed! 52It will happen in a moment, in the blink of an eye, when the last trumpet is blown. For when the trumpet sounds, those who have died will be raised to live forever. And we who are living will also be transformed. 53For our dying bodies must be transformed into bodies that will never die; our mortal bodies must be transformed into immortal bodies.

54Then, when our dying bodies have been transformed into bodies that will never die,* this Scripture will be fulfilled:

15:27 Ps 8:6.   15:32a Greek *fighting wild beasts in Ephesus.*   15:32b Isa 22:13.   15:45 Gen 2:7.   15:49 Some manuscripts read *let us be like.*   15:54a Some manuscripts add *and our mortal bodies have been transformed into immortal bodies.*

"Death is swallowed up in victory.*
55 O death, where is your victory?
O death, where is your sting?*"

56For sin is the sting that results in death, and the law gives sin its power. 57But thank God! He gives us victory over sin and death through our Lord Jesus Christ.

58So, my dear brothers and sisters, be strong and immovable. Always work enthusiastically for the Lord, for you know that nothing you do for the Lord is ever useless.

The Collection for Jerusalem

16 Now regarding your question about the money being collected for God's people in Jerusalem. You should follow the same procedure I gave to the churches in Galatia. 2On the first day of each week, you should each put aside a portion of the money you have earned. Don't wait until I get there and then try to collect it all at once. 3When I come, I will write letters of recommendation for the messengers you choose to deliver your gift to Jerusalem. 4And if it seems appropriate for me to go along, they can travel with me.

Paul's Final Instructions

5I am coming to visit you after I have been to Macedonia,* for I am planning to travel through Macedonia. 6Perhaps I will stay awhile with you, possibly all winter, and then you can send me on my way to my next destination. 7This time I don't want to make just a short visit and then go right on. I want to come and stay awhile, if the Lord will let me. 8In the meantime, I will be staying here at Ephesus until the Festival of Pentecost. 9There is a wide-open door for a great work here, although many oppose me.

10When Timothy comes, don't intimidate him. He is doing the Lord's work, just as I am. 11Don't let anyone treat him with contempt. Send him on his way with your blessing when he returns to me. I expect him to come with the other believers.*

12Now about our brother Apollos—I urged him to visit you with the other believers, but he was not willing to go right now. He will see you later when he has the opportunity.

13Be on guard. Stand firm in the faith. Be courageous.* Be strong. 14And do everything with love.

15You know that Stephanas and his household were the first of the harvest of believers in Greece,* and they are spending their lives in service to God's people. I urge you, dear brothers and sisters,* 16to submit to them and others like them who serve with such devotion. 17I am very glad that Stephanas, Fortunatus, and Achaicus have come here. They have been providing the help you weren't here to give me. 18They have been a wonderful encouragement to me, as they have been to you. You must show your appreciation to all who serve so well.

Paul's Final Greetings

19The churches here in the province of Asia* send greetings in the Lord, as do Aquila and Priscilla* and all the others who gather in their home for church meetings. 20All the brothers and sisters here send greetings to you. Greet each other with a sacred kiss.

21HERE IS MY GREETING IN MY OWN HAND-WRITING—PAUL.

22If anyone does not love the Lord, that person is cursed. Our Lord, come!*

23May the grace of the Lord Jesus be with you.

24My love to all of you in Christ Jesus.*

15:54b Isa 25:8.   15:55 Hos 13:14 (Greek version).   16:5 Macedonia was in the northern region of Greece.   16:11 Greek with the brothers; also in 16:12.   16:12 Greek Be men.   16:15a Greek in Achaia, the southern region of the Greek peninsula.   16:15b Greek brothers; also in 16:20.   16:19a Asia was a Roman province in what is now western Turkey.   16:19b Greek Prisca.   16:22 From Aramaic, Marana tha. Some manuscripts read Maran atha, "Our Lord has come."   16:24 Some manuscripts add Amen.

2 Corinthians

FOLLOWING CHRIST is a constant struggle. The church at Corinth knew this all too well. Though the believers were being renewed by the Holy Spirit, they still struggled against the immoral influences of the culture around them. Through personal visits and letters, Paul instructed the Corinthian believers in the faith and addressed several problems there. Most of the members received this instruction well, but a few false teachers slandered Paul and denied his authority over them. So Paul wrote this letter to defend his authority and denounce those who were twisting the truth. Paul's critics had attacked his motives, saying that he did not care for the Corinthians and used them only for his gain. So Paul pointed to evidence that showed how he had always been straightforward with the Corinthians and had worked tirelessly for their good. Paul also defended himself against charges of incompetence by comparing himself with the false teachers. Paul encouraged the Corinthians to continue following his example—to be holy, generous, and true to Christ.

- **Author:** Paul the apostle
- **Date Written:** Around AD 57, from the city of Ephesus
- **Purpose:** To defend his apostolic authority and ministry and to refute the false teachers in Corinth
- **Themes:** Apostolic authority and ministry, Church discipline, hope, giving, sound doctrine
- **Outline**
1:1-11 Paul's greetings
1:12–2:13 A summary of Paul's actions
2:14–6:10 A discourse on Paul's apostolic ministry
6:11-7:16 Paul's personal remarks
8:1–9:15 The collection for the poor in Jerusalem
10:1–13:10 Paul's defense of his apostolic authority
13:11-14 Concluding remarks

Greetings from Paul

1 This letter is from Paul, chosen by the will of God to be an apostle of Christ Jesus, and from our brother Timothy.

I am writing to God's church in Corinth and to all of his holy people throughout Greece.*

2 May God our Father and the Lord Jesus Christ give you grace and peace.

God Offers Comfort to All

3 All praise to God, the Father of our Lord Jesus Christ. God is our merciful Father and the source of all comfort. 4 He comforts us in all our troubles so that we can comfort others. When they are troubled, we will be able to give them the same comfort God has given us. 5 For the more we suffer for Christ, the more God will shower us with his comfort through Christ. 6 Even when we are weighed down with troubles, it is for your comfort and salvation! For when we ourselves are comforted, we will certainly comfort you. Then you can patiently endure the same things we suffer. 7 We are confident that as you share in our sufferings, you will also share in the comfort God gives us.

8 We think you ought to know, dear brothers and sisters,* about the trouble we went through in the province of Asia. We were crushed and overwhelmed beyond our ability to endure, and we thought we would never live through it. 9 In fact, we expected to die. But as a result, we stopped relying on ourselves and learned to rely only on God, who raises the dead. 10 And he did rescue us from mortal danger, and he will rescue us again. We have placed our confidence in him, and he will continue to rescue

1:1 Greek *Achaia,* the southern region of the Greek peninsula. 1:8 Greek *brothers.*

us. [11]And you are helping us by praying for us. Then many people will give thanks because God has graciously answered so many prayers for our safety.

Paul's Change of Plans

[12]We can say with confidence and a clear conscience that we have lived with a God-given holiness* and sincerity in all our dealings. We have depended on God's grace, not on our own human wisdom. That is how we have conducted ourselves before the world, and especially toward you. [13]Our letters have been straightforward, and there is nothing written between the lines and nothing you can't understand. I hope someday you will fully understand us, [14]even if you don't understand us now. Then on the day when the Lord Jesus* returns, you will be proud of us in the same way we are proud of you.

[15]Since I was so sure of your understanding and trust, I wanted to give you a double blessing by visiting you twice—[16]first on my way to Macedonia and again when I returned from Macedonia.* Then you could send me on my way to Judea.

[17]You may be asking why I changed my plan. Do you think I make my plans carelessly? Do you think I am like people of the world who say "Yes" when they really mean "No"? [18]As surely as God is faithful, our word to you does not waver between "Yes" and "No." [19]For Jesus Christ, the Son of God, does not waver between "Yes" and "No." He is the one whom Silas,* Timothy, and I preached to you, and as God's ultimate "Yes," he always does what he says. [20]For all of God's promises have been fulfilled in Christ with a resounding "Yes!" And through Christ, our "Amen" (which means "Yes") ascends to God for his glory.

[21]It is God who enables us, along with you, to stand firm for Christ. He has commissioned us, [22]and he has identified us as his own by placing the Holy Spirit in our hearts as the first installment that guarantees everything he has promised us.

[23]Now I call upon God as my witness that I am telling the truth. The reason I didn't return to Corinth was to spare you from a severe rebuke. [24]But that does not mean we want to dominate you by telling you how to put your faith into practice. We want to work together with you so you will be full of joy, for it is by your own faith that you stand firm.

2 So I decided that I would not bring you grief with another painful visit. [2]For if I cause you grief, who will make me glad? Certainly not someone I have grieved. [3]That is why I wrote to you as I did, so that when I do come, I won't be grieved by the very ones who ought to give me the greatest joy. Surely you all know that my joy comes from your being joyful. [4]I wrote that letter in great anguish, with a troubled heart and many tears. I didn't want to grieve you, but I wanted to let you know how much love I have for you.

Forgiveness for the Sinner

[5]I am not overstating it when I say that the man who caused all the trouble hurt all of you more than he hurt me. [6]Most of you opposed him, and that was punishment enough. [7]Now, however, it is time to forgive and comfort him. Otherwise he may be overcome by discouragement. [8]So I urge you now to reaffirm your love for him.

[9]I wrote to you as I did to test you and see if you would fully comply with my instructions. [10]When you forgive this man, I forgive him, too. And when I forgive whatever needs to be forgiven, I do so with Christ's authority for your benefit, [11]so that Satan will not outsmart us. For we are familiar with his evil schemes.

[12]When I came to the city of Troas to preach the Good News of Christ, the Lord opened a door of opportunity for me. [13]But I had no peace of mind because my dear brother Titus hadn't yet arrived with a report from you. So I said good-bye and went on to Macedonia to find him.

Ministers of the New Covenant

[14]But thank God! He has made us his captives and continues to lead us along in Christ's triumphal procession. Now he uses us to spread the knowledge of Christ everywhere, like a sweet perfume. [15]Our lives are a Christ-like fragrance rising up to God. But this fragrance is perceived differently by those who are being saved and by those who are perishing. [16]To those who are perishing, we are a dreadful smell of death and doom. But to those who are being saved, we are a life-giving perfume. And who is adequate for such a task as this?

[17]You see, we are not like the many hucksters* who preach for personal profit. We preach the word of God with sincerity and with Christ's authority, knowing that God is watching us.

1:12 Some manuscripts read *honesty.*   1:14 Some manuscripts read *our Lord Jesus.*   1:16 *Macedonia* was in the northern region of Greece.   1:19 Greek *Silvanus.*   2:17 Some manuscripts read *the rest of the hucksters.*

3 Are we beginning to praise ourselves again? Are we like others, who need to bring you letters of recommendation, or who ask you to write such letters on their behalf? Surely not! ²The only letter of recommendation we need is you yourselves. Your lives are a letter written in our* hearts; everyone can read it and recognize our good work among you. ³Clearly, you are a letter from Christ showing the result of our ministry among you. This "letter" is written not with pen and ink, but with the Spirit of the living God. It is carved not on tablets of stone, but on human hearts.

⁴We are confident of all this because of our great trust in God through Christ. ⁵It is not that we think we are qualified to do anything on our own. Our qualification comes from God. ⁶He has enabled us to be ministers of his new covenant. This is a covenant not of written laws, but of the Spirit. The old written covenant ends in death; but under the new covenant, the Spirit gives life.

The Glory of the New Covenant

⁷The old way,* with laws etched in stone, led to death, though it began with such glory that the people of Israel could not bear to look at Moses' face. For his face shone with the glory of God, even though the brightness was already fading away. ⁸Shouldn't we expect far greater glory under the new way, now that the Holy Spirit is giving life? ⁹If the old way, which brings condemnation, was glorious, how much more glorious is the new way, which makes us right with God! ¹⁰In fact, that first glory was not glorious at all compared with the overwhelming glory of the new way. ¹¹So if the old way, which has been replaced, was glorious, how much more glorious is the new, which remains forever!

¹²Since this new way gives us such confidence, we can be very bold. ¹³We are not like Moses, who put a veil over his face so the people of Israel would not see the glory, even though it was destined to fade away. ¹⁴But the people's minds were hardened, and to this day whenever the old covenant is being read, the same veil covers their minds so they cannot understand the truth. And this veil can be removed only by believing in Christ. ¹⁵Yes, even today when they read Moses' writings, their hearts are covered with that veil, and they do not understand.

¹⁶But whenever someone turns to the Lord, the veil is taken away. ¹⁷For the Lord is the Spirit, and wherever the Spirit of the Lord is, there is freedom. ¹⁸So all of us who have had that veil removed can see and reflect the glory of the Lord. And the Lord—who is the Spirit—makes us more and more like him as we are changed into his glorious image.

Treasure in Fragile Clay Jars

4 Therefore, since God in his mercy has given us this new way,* we never give up. ²We reject all shameful deeds and underhanded methods. We don't try to trick anyone or distort the word of God. We tell the truth before God, and all who are honest know this.

³If the Good News we preach is hidden behind a veil, it is hidden only from people who are perishing. ⁴Satan, who is the god of this world, has blinded the minds of those who don't believe. They are unable to see the glorious light of the Good News. They don't understand this message about the glory of Christ, who is the exact likeness of God.

⁵You see, we don't go around preaching about ourselves. We preach that Jesus Christ is Lord, and we ourselves are your servants for Jesus' sake. ⁶For God, who said, "Let there be light in the darkness," has made this light shine in our hearts so we could know the glory of God that is seen in the face of Jesus Christ.

⁷We now have this light shining in our hearts, but we ourselves are like fragile clay jars containing this great treasure.* This makes it clear that our great power is from God, not from ourselves.

⁸We are pressed on every side by troubles, but we are not crushed. We are perplexed, but not driven to despair. ⁹We are hunted down, but never abandoned by God. We get knocked down, but we are not destroyed. ¹⁰Through suffering, our bodies continue to share in the death of Jesus so that the life of Jesus may also be seen in our bodies.

¹¹Yes, we live under constant danger of death because we serve Jesus, so that the life of Jesus will be evident in our dying bodies. ¹²So we live in the face of death, but this has resulted in eternal life for you.

¹³But we continue to preach because we have the same kind of faith the psalmist had when he said, "I believed in God, so I spoke."* ¹⁴We know that God, who raised the Lord Jesus,* will also raise us with Jesus and present us to himself together with you. ¹⁵All of this is for your

---

3:2 Some manuscripts read *your.*   3:7 Or *ministry;* also in 3:8, 9, 10, 11, 12.   4:1 Or *ministry.*   4:7 Greek *We now have this treasure in clay jars.*   4:13 Ps 116:10.   4:14 Some manuscripts read *who raised Jesus.*

benefit. And as God's grace reaches more and more people, there will be great thanksgiving, and God will receive more and more glory.

¹⁶That is why we never give up. Though our bodies are dying, our spirits are* being renewed every day. ¹⁷For our present troubles are small and won't last very long. Yet they produce for us a glory that vastly outweighs them and will last forever! ¹⁸So we don't look at the troubles we can see now; rather, we fix our gaze on things that cannot be seen. For the things we see now will soon be gone, but the things we cannot see will last forever.

New Bodies

5 For we know that when this earthly tent we live in is taken down (that is, when we die and leave this earthly body), we will have a house in heaven, an eternal body made for us by God himself and not by human hands. ²We grow weary in our present bodies, and we long to put on our heavenly bodies like new clothing. ³For we will put on heavenly bodies; we will not be spirits without bodies.* ⁴While we live in these earthly bodies, we groan and sigh, but it's not that we want to die and get rid of these bodies that clothe us. Rather, we want to put on our new bodies so that these dying bodies will be swallowed up by life. ⁵God himself has prepared us for this, and as a guarantee he has given us his Holy Spirit.

⁶So we are always confident, even though we know that as long as we live in these bodies we are not at home with the Lord. ⁷For we live by believing and not by seeing. ⁸Yes, we are fully confident, and we would rather be away from these earthly bodies, for then we will be at home with the Lord. ⁹So whether we are here in this body or away from this body, our goal is to please him. ¹⁰For we must all stand before Christ to be judged. We will each receive whatever we deserve for the good or evil we have done in this earthly body.

We Are God's Ambassadors

¹¹Because we understand our fearful responsibility to the Lord, we work hard to persuade others. God knows we are sincere, and I hope you know this, too. ¹²Are we commending ourselves to you again? No, we are giving you a reason to be proud of us,* so you can answer those who brag about having a spectacular ministry rather than having a sincere heart.

¹³If it seems we are crazy, it is to bring glory to God. And if we are in our right minds, it is for your benefit. ¹⁴Either way, Christ's love controls us.* Since we believe that Christ died for all, we also believe that we have all died to our old life.* ¹⁵He died for everyone so that those who receive his new life will no longer live for themselves. Instead, they will live for Christ, who died and was raised for them.

¹⁶So we have stopped evaluating others from a human point of view. At one time we thought of Christ merely from a human point of view. How differently we know him now! ¹⁷This means that anyone who belongs to Christ has become a new person. The old life is gone; a new life has begun!

¹⁸And all of this is a gift from God, who brought us back to himself through Christ. And God has given us this task of reconciling people to him. ¹⁹For God was in Christ, reconciling the world to himself, no longer counting people's sins against them. And he gave us this wonderful message of reconciliation. ²⁰So we are Christ's ambassadors; God is making his appeal through us. We speak for Christ when we plead, "Come back to God!" ²¹For God made Christ, who never sinned, to be the offering for our sin,* so that we could be made right with God through Christ.

6 As God's partners,* we beg you not to accept this marvelous gift of God's kindness and then ignore it. ²For God says,

"At just the right time, I heard you.
    On the day of salvation, I helped you."*

Indeed, the "right time" is now. Today is the day of salvation.

Paul's Hardships

³We live in such a way that no one will stumble because of us, and no one will find fault with our ministry. ⁴In everything we do, we show that we are true ministers of God. We patiently endure troubles and hardships and calamities of every kind. ⁵We have been beaten, been put in prison, faced angry mobs, worked to exhaustion, endured sleepless nights, and gone without food. ⁶We prove ourselves by our purity, our understanding, our patience, our kindness, by the Holy Spirit within us,* and by our sincere love. ⁷We faithfully preach the

---

4:16 Greek *our inner being is.*   5:3 Greek *we will not be naked.*   5:12 Some manuscripts read *proud of yourselves.*   5:14a Or *urges us on.*   5:14b Greek *Since one died for all, then all died.*   5:21 Or *to become sin itself.*   6:1 Or *As we work together.*   6:2 Isa 49:8 (Greek version).   6:6 Or *by our holiness of spirit.*

truth. God's power is working in us. We use the weapons of righteousness in the right hand for attack and the left hand for defense. [8]We serve God whether people honor us or despise us, whether they slander us or praise us. We are honest, but they call us impostors. [9]We are ignored, even though we are well known. We live close to death, but we are still alive. We have been beaten, but we have not been killed. [10]Our hearts ache, but we always have joy. We are poor, but we give spiritual riches to others. We own nothing, and yet we have everything.

[11]Oh, dear Corinthian friends! We have spoken honestly with you, and our hearts are open to you. [12]There is no lack of love on our part, but you have withheld your love from us. [13]I am asking you to respond as if you were my own children. Open your hearts to us!

The Temple of the Living God

[14]Don't team up with those who are unbelievers. How can righteousness be a partner with wickedness? How can light live with darkness? [15]What harmony can there be between Christ and the devil*? How can a believer be a partner with an unbeliever? [16]And what union can there be between God's temple and idols? For we are the temple of the living God. As God said:

"I will live in them
    and walk among them.
I will be their God,
    and they will be my people.*
[17] Therefore, come out from among
    unbelievers,
    and separate yourselves from them, says
      the LORD.
Don't touch their filthy things,
    and I will welcome you.*
[18] And I will be your Father,
    and you will be my sons and daughters,
    says the LORD Almighty.*"

7 Because we have these promises, dear friends, let us cleanse ourselves from everything that can defile our body or spirit. And let us work toward complete holiness because we fear God.

[2]Please open your hearts to us. We have not done wrong to anyone, nor led anyone astray, nor taken advantage of anyone. [3]I'm not saying this to condemn you. I said before that you are in our hearts, and we live or die together

with you. [4]I have the highest confidence in you, and I take great pride in you. You have greatly encouraged me and made me happy despite all our troubles.

Paul's Joy at the Church's Repentance

[5]When we arrived in Macedonia, there was no rest for us. We faced conflict from every direction, with battles on the outside and fear on the inside. [6]But God, who encourages those who are discouraged, encouraged us by the arrival of Titus. [7]His presence was a joy, but so was the news he brought of the encouragement he received from you. When he told us how much you long to see me, and how sorry you are for what happened, and how loyal you are to me, I was filled with joy!

[8]I am not sorry that I sent that severe letter to you, though I was sorry at first, for I know it was painful to you for a little while. [9]Now I am glad I sent it, not because it hurt you, but because the pain caused you to repent and change your ways. It was the kind of sorrow God wants his people to have, so you were not harmed by us in any way. [10]For the kind of sorrow God wants us to experience leads us away from sin and results in salvation. There's no regret for that kind of sorrow. But worldly sorrow, which lacks repentance, results in spiritual death.

[11]Just see what this godly sorrow produced in you! Such earnestness, such concern to clear yourselves, such indignation, such alarm, such longing to see me, such zeal, and such a readiness to punish wrong. You showed that you have done everything necessary to make things right. [12]My purpose, then, was not to write about who did the wrong or who was wronged. I wrote to you so that in the sight of God you could see for yourselves how loyal you are to us. [13]We have been greatly encouraged by this.

In addition to our own encouragement, we were especially delighted to see how happy Titus was about the way all of you welcomed him and set his mind* at ease. [14]I had told him how proud I was of you—and you didn't disappoint me. I have always told you the truth, and now my boasting to Titus has also proved true! [15]Now he cares for you more than ever when he remembers the way all of you obeyed him and welcomed him with such fear and deep respect. [16]I am very happy now because I have complete confidence in you.

6:15 Greek *Beliar*; various other manuscripts render this proper name of the devil as *Belian, Beliab,* or *Belial.*   6:16 Lev 26:12; Ezek 37:27.   6:17 Isa 52:11; Ezek 20:34 (Greek version).   6:18 2 Sam 7:14.   7:13 Greek *his spirit.*

A Call to Generous Giving

8 Now I want you to know, dear brothers and sisters,* what God in his kindness has done through the churches in Macedonia. ²They are being tested by many troubles, and they are very poor. But they are also filled with abundant joy, which has overflowed in rich generosity.

³For I can testify that they gave not only what they could afford, but far more. And they did it of their own free will. ⁴They begged us again and again for the privilege of sharing in the gift for the believers in Jerusalem.* ⁵They even did more than we had hoped, for their first action was to give themselves to the Lord and to us, just as God wanted them to do.

⁶So we have urged Titus, who encouraged your giving in the first place, to return to you and encourage you to finish this ministry of giving. ⁷Since you excel in so many ways—in your faith, your gifted speakers, your knowledge, your enthusiasm, and your love from us*—I want you to excel also in this gracious act of giving.

⁸I am not commanding you to do this. But I am testing how genuine your love is by comparing it with the eagerness of the other churches. ⁹You know the generous grace of our Lord Jesus Christ. Though he was rich, yet for your sakes he became poor, so that by his poverty he could make you rich.

¹⁰Here is my advice: It would be good for you to finish what you started a year ago. Last year you were the first who wanted to give, and you were the first to begin doing it. ¹¹Now you should finish what you started. Let the eagerness you showed in the beginning be matched now by your giving. Give in proportion to what you have. ¹²Whatever you give is acceptable if you give it eagerly. And give according to what you have, not what you don't have. ¹³Of course, I don't mean your giving should make life easy for others and hard for yourselves. I only mean that there should be some equality. ¹⁴Right now you have plenty and can help those who are in need. Later, they will have plenty and can share with you when you need it. In this way, things will be equal. ¹⁵As the Scriptures say,

"Those who gathered a lot had nothing
  left over,
  and those who gathered only a little had
  enough."*

Titus and His Companions

¹⁶But thank God! He has given Titus the same enthusiasm for you that I have. ¹⁷Titus welcomed our request that he visit you again. In fact, he himself was very eager to go and see you. ¹⁸We are also sending another brother with Titus. All the churches praise him as a preacher of the Good News. ¹⁹He was appointed by the churches to accompany us as we take the offering to Jerusalem*—a service that glorifies the Lord and shows our eagerness to help.

²⁰We are traveling together to guard against any criticism for the way we are handling this generous gift. ²¹We are careful to be honorable before the Lord, but we also want everyone else to see that we are honorable.

²²We are also sending with them another of our brothers who has proven himself many times and has shown on many occasions how eager he is. He is now even more enthusiastic because of his great confidence in you. ²³If anyone asks about Titus, say that he is my partner who works with me to help you. And the brothers with him have been sent by the churches,* and they bring honor to Christ. ²⁴So show them your love, and prove to all the churches that our boasting about you is justified.

The Collection for Christians in Jerusalem

9 I really don't need to write to you about this ministry of giving for the believers in Jerusalem.* ²For I know how eager you are to help, and I have been boasting to the churches in Macedonia that you in Greece* were ready to send an offering a year ago. In fact, it was your enthusiasm that stirred up many of the Macedonian believers to begin giving.

³But I am sending these brothers to be sure you really are ready, as I have been telling them, and that your money is all collected. I don't want to be wrong in my boasting about you. ⁴We would be embarrassed—not to mention your own embarrassment—if some Macedonian believers came with me and found that you weren't ready after all I had told them! ⁵So I thought I should send these brothers ahead of me to make sure the gift you promised is ready. But I want it to be a willing gift, not one given grudgingly.

⁶Remember this—a farmer who plants only a few seeds will get a small crop. But the one who plants generously will get a generous

8:1 Greek *brothers.* 8:4 Greek *for God's holy people.* 8:7 Some manuscripts read *your love for us.* 8:15 Exod 16:18. 8:19 See 1 Cor 16:3-4. 8:23 Greek *are apostles of the churches.* 9:1 Greek *about the offering for God's holy people.* 9:2 Greek *in Achaia,* the southern region of the Greek peninsula. *Macedonia* was in the northern region of Greece.

crop. ⁷You must each decide in your heart how much to give. And don't give reluctantly or in response to pressure. "For God loves a person who gives cheerfully."* ⁸And God will generously provide all you need. Then you will always have everything you need and plenty left over to share with others. ⁹As the Scriptures say,

"They share freely and give generously to
      the poor.
   Their good deeds will be remembered
      forever."*

¹⁰For God is the one who provides seed for the farmer and then bread to eat. In the same way, he will provide and increase your resources and then produce a great harvest of generosity* in you.

¹¹Yes, you will be enriched in every way so that you can always be generous. And when we take your gifts to those who need them, they will thank God. ¹²So two good things will result from this ministry of giving—the needs of the believers in Jerusalem* will be met, and they will joyfully express their thanks to God.

¹³As a result of your ministry, they will give glory to God. For your generosity to them and to all believers will prove that you are obedient to the Good News of Christ. ¹⁴And they will pray for you with deep affection because of the overflowing grace God has given to you. ¹⁵Thank God for this gift* too wonderful for words!

Paul Defends His Authority

10 Now I, Paul, appeal to you with the gentleness and kindness of Christ—though I realize you think I am timid in person and bold only when I write from far away. ²Well, I am begging you now so that when I come I won't have to be bold with those who think we act from human motives.

³We are human, but we don't wage war as humans do. ⁴*We use God's mighty weapons, not worldly weapons, to knock down the strongholds of human reasoning and to destroy false arguments. ⁵We destroy every proud obstacle that keeps people from knowing God. We capture their rebellious thoughts and teach them to obey Christ. ⁶And after you have become fully obedient, we will punish everyone who remains disobedient.

⁷Look at the obvious facts.* Those who say they belong to Christ must recognize that we belong to Christ as much as they do. ⁸I may seem to be boasting too much about the authority given to us by the Lord. But our authority builds you up; it doesn't tear you down. So I will not be ashamed of using my authority.

⁹I'm not trying to frighten you by my letters. ¹⁰For some say, "Paul's letters are demanding and forceful, but in person he is weak, and his speeches are worthless!" ¹¹Those people should realize that our actions when we arrive in person will be as forceful as what we say in our letters from far away.

¹²Oh, don't worry; we wouldn't dare say that we are as wonderful as these other men who tell you how important they are! But they are only comparing themselves with each other, using themselves as the standard of measurement. How ignorant!

¹³We will not boast about things done outside our area of authority. We will boast only about what has happened within the boundaries of the work God has given us, which includes our working with you. ¹⁴We are not reaching beyond these boundaries when we claim authority over you, as if we had never visited you. For we were the first to travel all the way to Corinth with the Good News of Christ.

¹⁵Nor do we boast and claim credit for the work someone else has done. Instead, we hope that your faith will grow so that the boundaries of our work among you will be extended. ¹⁶Then we will be able to go and preach the Good News in other places far beyond you, where no one else is working. Then there will be no question of our boasting about work done in someone else's territory. ¹⁷As the Scriptures say, "If you want to boast, boast only about the LORD."*

¹⁸When people commend themselves, it doesn't count for much. The important thing is for the Lord to commend them.

Paul and the False Apostles

11 I hope you will put up with a little more of my foolishness. Please bear with me. ²For I am jealous for you with the jealousy of God himself. I promised you as a pure bride* to one husband—Christ. ³But I fear that somehow your pure and undivided devotion to Christ will be corrupted, just as Eve was deceived by the cunning ways of the serpent. ⁴You happily put up with whatever anyone tells you,

---

9:7 See footnote on Prov 22:8.   9:9 Ps 112:9.   9:10 Greek *righteousness*.   9:12 Greek *of God's holy people*.   9:15 Greek *his gift*.
10:4 English translations divide verses 4 and 5 in various ways.   10:7 Or *You look at things only on the basis of appearance*.
10:17 Jer 9:24.   11:2 Greek *a virgin*.

even if they preach a different Jesus than the one we preach, or a different kind of Spirit than the one you received, or a different kind of gospel than the one you believed.

5But I don't consider myself inferior in any way to these "super apostles" who teach such things. 6I may be unskilled as a speaker, but I'm not lacking in knowledge. We have made this clear to you in every possible way.

7Was I wrong when I humbled myself and honored you by preaching God's Good News to you without expecting anything in return? 8I "robbed" other churches by accepting their contributions so I could serve you at no cost. 9And when I was with you and didn't have enough to live on, I did not become a financial burden to anyone. For the brothers who came from Macedonia brought me all that I needed. I have never been a burden to you, and I never will be. 10As surely as the truth of Christ is in me, no one in all of Greece* will ever stop me from boasting about this. 11Why? Because I don't love you? God knows that I do.

12But I will continue doing what I have always done. This will undercut those who are looking for an opportunity to boast that their work is just like ours. 13These people are false apostles. They are deceitful workers who disguise themselves as apostles of Christ. 14But I am not surprised! Even Satan disguises himself as an angel of light. 15So it is no wonder that his servants also disguise themselves as servants of righteousness. In the end they will get the punishment their wicked deeds deserve.

Paul's Many Trials

16Again I say, don't think that I am a fool to talk like this. But even if you do, listen to me, as you would to a foolish person, while I also boast a little. 17Such boasting is not from the Lord, but I am acting like a fool. 18And since others boast about their human achievements, I will, too. 19After all, you think you are so wise, but you enjoy putting up with fools! 20You put up with it when someone enslaves you, takes everything you have, takes advantage of you, takes control of everything, and slaps you in the face. 21I'm ashamed to say that we've been too "weak" to do that!

But whatever they dare to boast about— I'm talking like a fool again—I dare to boast about it, too. 22Are they Hebrews? So am I. Are they Israelites? So am I. Are they descendants of Abraham? So am I. 23Are they servants of Christ? I know I sound like a madman, but I have served him far more! I have worked harder, been put in prison more often, been whipped times without number, and faced death again and again. 24Five different times the Jewish leaders gave me thirty-nine lashes. 25Three times I was beaten with rods. Once I was stoned. Three times I was shipwrecked. Once I spent a whole night and a day adrift at sea. 26I have traveled on many long journeys. I have faced danger from rivers and from robbers. I have faced danger from my own people, the Jews, as well as from the Gentiles. I have faced danger in the cities, in the deserts, and on the seas. And I have faced danger from men who claim to be believers but are not.* 27I have worked hard and long, enduring many sleepless nights. I have been hungry and thirsty and have often gone without food. I have shivered in the cold, without enough clothing to keep me warm.

28Then, besides all this, I have the daily burden of my concern for all the churches. 29Who is weak without my feeling that weakness? Who is led astray, and I do not burn with anger?

30If I must boast, I would rather boast about the things that show how weak I am. 31God, the Father of our Lord Jesus, who is worthy of eternal praise, knows I am not lying. 32When I was in Damascus, the governor under King Aretas kept guards at the city gates to catch me. 33I had to be lowered in a basket through a window in the city wall to escape from him.

Paul's Vision and His Thorn in the Flesh

12 This boasting will do no good, but I must go on. I will reluctantly tell about visions and revelations from the Lord. 2I* was caught up to the third heaven fourteen years ago. Whether I was in my body or out of my body, I don't know—only God knows. 3Yes, only God knows whether I was in my body or outside my body. But I do know 4that I was caught up* to paradise and heard things so astounding that they cannot be expressed in words, things no human is allowed to tell.

5That experience is worth boasting about, but I'm not going to do it. I will boast only about my weaknesses. 6If I wanted to boast, I would be no fool in doing so, because I would be telling the truth. But I won't do it, because I don't want anyone to give me credit beyond what they can see in my life or hear in my message, 7even though I have received such

---

11:10 Greek *Achaia*, the southern region of the Greek peninsula.   11:26 Greek *from false brothers.*   12:2 Greek *I know a man in Christ who.*   12:3-4 Greek *But I know such a man,* 4*that he was caught up.*

wonderful revelations from God. So to keep me from becoming proud, I was given a thorn in my flesh, a messenger from Satan to torment me and keep me from becoming proud.

⁸Three different times I begged the Lord to take it away. ⁹Each time he said, "My grace is all you need. My power works best in weakness." So now I am glad to boast about my weaknesses, so that the power of Christ can work through me. ¹⁰That's why I take pleasure in my weaknesses, and in the insults, hardships, persecutions, and troubles that I suffer for Christ. For when I am weak, then I am strong.

Paul's Concern for the Corinthians
¹¹You have made me act like a fool. You ought to be writing commendations for me, for I am not at all inferior to these "super apostles," even though I am nothing at all. ¹²When I was with you, I certainly gave you proof that I am an apostle. For I patiently did many signs and wonders and miracles among you. ¹³The only thing I failed to do, which I do in the other churches, was to become a financial burden to you. Please forgive me for this wrong!

¹⁴Now I am coming to you for the third time, and I will not be a burden to you. I don't want what you have—I want you. After all, children don't provide for their parents. Rather, parents provide for their children. ¹⁵I will gladly spend myself and all I have for you, even though it seems that the more I love you, the less you love me.

¹⁶Some of you admit I was not a burden to you. But others still think I was sneaky and took advantage of you by trickery. ¹⁷But how? Did any of the men I sent to you take advantage of you? ¹⁸When I urged Titus to visit you and sent our other brother with him, did Titus take advantage of you? No! For we have the same spirit and walk in each other's steps, doing things the same way.

¹⁹Perhaps you think we're saying these things just to defend ourselves. No, we tell you this as Christ's servants, and with God as our witness. Everything we do, dear friends, is to strengthen you. ²⁰For I am afraid that when I come I won't like what I find, and you won't like my response. I am afraid that I will find quarreling, jealousy, anger, selfishness, slander, gossip, arrogance, and disorderly behavior. ²¹Yes, I am afraid that when I come again, God will humble me in your presence. And I will be grieved because many of you have not given up

your old sins. You have not repented of your impurity, sexual immorality, and eagerness for lustful pleasure.

Paul's Final Advice
13 This is the third time I am coming to visit you (and as the Scriptures say, "The facts of every case must be established by the testimony of two or three witnesses"*). ²I have already warned those who had been sinning when I was there on my second visit. Now I again warn them and all others, just as I did before, that next time I will not spare them.

³I will give you all the proof you want that Christ speaks through me. Christ is not weak when he deals with you; he is powerful among you. ⁴Although he was crucified in weakness, he now lives by the power of God. We, too, are weak, just as Christ was, but when we deal with you we will be alive with him and will have God's power.

⁵Examine yourselves to see if your faith is genuine. Test yourselves. Surely you know that Jesus Christ is among you*; if not, you have failed the test of genuine faith. ⁶As you test yourselves, I hope you will recognize that we have not failed the test of apostolic authority.

⁷We pray to God that you will not do what is wrong by refusing our correction. I hope we won't need to demonstrate our authority when we arrive. Do the right thing before we come—even if that makes it look like we have failed to demonstrate our authority. ⁸For we cannot oppose the truth, but must always stand for the truth. ⁹We are glad to seem weak if it helps show that you are actually strong. We pray that you will become mature.

¹⁰I am writing this to you before I come, hoping that I won't need to deal severely with you when I do come. For I want to use the authority the Lord has given me to strengthen you, not to tear you down.

Paul's Final Greetings
¹¹Dear brothers and sisters,* I close my letter with these last words: Be joyful. Grow to maturity. Encourage each other. Live in harmony and peace. Then the God of love and peace will be with you.

¹²Greet each other with a sacred kiss. ¹³All of God's people here send you their greetings.

¹⁴*May the grace of the Lord Jesus Christ, the love of God, and the fellowship of the Holy Spirit be with you all.

13:1 Deut 19:15.   13:5 Or *in you*.   13:11 Greek *Brothers*.   13:14 Some English translations include verse 13 as part of verse 12, and then verse 14 becomes verse 13.

Galatians

WHO, AFTER BEING SET FREE, would ever willingly submit themselves to slavery again? This was Paul's question to the Galatians, who were giving up their freedom in Christ to serve the law again. It was clear to the early church that the sacrifice of Jesus Christ achieved salvation for all who believed, but what did this mean for the law of Moses? Should Christians continue observing the law or not? The Galatian church was divided over this question. Paul wrote this letter to the Galatians to settle the dispute. He

■ **Author:** Paul the apostle

■ **Date Written:** Around AD 49, prior to the Jerusalem council held in AD 50

■ **Purpose:** To refute those who insisted that Christians must obey the law of Moses and to remind Christians of their freedom in Christ

■ **Themes:** Law, faith, freedom, work of the Holy Spirit

■ **Outline**

1:1–2:21 Paul's defense of himself and the gospel
3:1-22 Freedom from the curse of the law
3:23–4:31 The gospel's superiority over the law
5:1-26 The freedom of the Christian
6:1-18 Practical exhortations

opened his letter with a very short introduction and then cut right to the heart of the matter: If believers are justified by grace through Christ, why were many Galatians insisting upon other requirements? Paul drew a lesson from Abraham, who lived more than four hundred years prior to the giving of the law. Paul showed that Abraham was justified by his faith, not his deeds. Likewise, the Galatians should see themselves as free from the law—free, that is, to serve Christ and be transformed by the Holy Spirit in the community of believers.

Greetings from Paul

1 This letter is from Paul, an apostle. I was not appointed by any group of people or any human authority, but by Jesus Christ himself and by God the Father, who raised Jesus from the dead.

2All the brothers and sisters* here join me in sending this letter to the churches of Galatia.

3May God the Father and our Lord Jesus Christ* give you grace and peace. 4Jesus gave his life for our sins, just as God our Father planned, in order to rescue us from this evil world in which we live. 5All glory to God forever and ever! Amen.

There Is Only One Good News

6I am shocked that you are turning away so soon from God, who called you to himself through the loving mercy of Christ.* You are following a different way that pretends to be the Good News 7but is not the Good News at all. You are being fooled by those who deliberately twist the truth concerning Christ.

8Let God's curse fall on anyone, including us or even an angel from heaven, who preaches a different kind of Good News than the one we preached to you. 9I say again what we have said before: If anyone preaches any other Good News than the one you welcomed, let that person be cursed.

10Obviously, I'm not trying to win the approval of people, but of God. If pleasing people were my goal, I would not be Christ's servant.

Paul's Message Comes from Christ

11Dear brothers and sisters, I want you to understand that the gospel message I preach is not based on mere human reasoning. 12I received

1:2 Greek *brothers;* also in 1:11.   1:3 Some manuscripts read *God our Father and the Lord Jesus Christ.*   1:6 Some manuscripts read *through loving mercy.*

my message from no human source, and no one taught me. Instead, I received it by direct revelation from Jesus Christ.*

13You know what I was like when I followed the Jewish religion—how I violently persecuted God's church. I did my best to destroy it. 14I was far ahead of my fellow Jews in my zeal for the traditions of my ancestors.

15But even before I was born, God chose me and called me by his marvelous grace. Then it pleased him 16to reveal his Son to me* so that I would proclaim the Good News about Jesus to the Gentiles.

When this happened, I did not rush out to consult with any human being.* 17Nor did I go up to Jerusalem to consult with those who were apostles before I was. Instead, I went away into Arabia, and later I returned to the city of Damascus.

18Then three years later I went to Jerusalem to get to know Peter,* and I stayed with him for fifteen days. 19The only other apostle I met at that time was James, the Lord's brother. 20I declare before God that what I am writing to you is not a lie.

21After that visit I went north into the provinces of Syria and Cilicia. 22And still the churches in Christ that are in Judea didn't know me personally. 23All they knew was that people were saying, "The one who used to persecute us is now preaching the very faith he tried to destroy!" 24And they praised God because of me.

The Apostles Accept Paul

2 Then fourteen years later I went back to Jerusalem again, this time with Barnabas; and Titus came along, too. 2I went there because God revealed to me that I should go. While I was there I met privately with those considered to be leaders of the church and shared with them the message I had been preaching to the Gentiles. I wanted to make sure that we were in agreement, for fear that all my efforts had been wasted and I was running the race for nothing. 3And they supported me and did not even demand that my companion Titus be circumcised, though he was a Gentile.*

4Even that question came up only because of some so-called believers there—false ones, really*—who were secretly brought in. They sneaked in to spy on us and take away the freedom we have in Christ Jesus. They wanted to enslave us and force us to follow their Jewish regulations. 5But we refused to give in to them for a single moment. We wanted to preserve the truth of the gospel message for you.

6And the leaders of the church had nothing to add to what I was preaching. (By the way, their reputation as great leaders made no difference to me, for God has no favorites.) 7Instead, they saw that God had given me the responsibility of preaching the gospel to the Gentiles, just as he had given Peter the responsibility of preaching to the Jews. 8For the same God who worked through Peter as the apostle to the Jews also worked through me as the apostle to the Gentiles.

9In fact, James, Peter,* and John, who were known as pillars of the church, recognized the gift God had given me, and they accepted Barnabas and me as their co-workers. They encouraged us to keep preaching to the Gentiles, while they continued their work with the Jews. 10Their only suggestion was that we keep on helping the poor, which I have always been eager to do.

Paul Confronts Peter

11But when Peter came to Antioch, I had to oppose him to his face, for what he did was very wrong. 12When he first arrived, he ate with the Gentile believers, who were not circumcised. But afterward, when some friends of James came, Peter wouldn't eat with the Gentiles anymore. He was afraid of criticism from these people who insisted on the necessity of circumcision. 13As a result, other Jewish believers followed Peter's hypocrisy, and even Barnabas was led astray by their hypocrisy.

14When I saw that they were not following the truth of the gospel message, I said to Peter in front of all the others, "Since you, a Jew by birth, have discarded the Jewish laws and are living like a Gentile, why are you now trying to make these Gentiles follow the Jewish traditions?

15"You and I are Jews by birth, not 'sinners' like the Gentiles. 16Yet we know that a person is made right with God by faith in Jesus Christ, not by obeying the law. And we have believed in Christ Jesus, so that we might be made right with God because of our faith in Christ, not because we have obeyed the law. For no one will ever be made right with God by obeying the law."*

1:12 Or by the revelation of Jesus Christ.   1:16a Or in me.   1:16b Greek with flesh and blood.   1:18 Greek Cephas.   2:3 Greek a Greek.
2:4 Greek some false brothers.   2:9 Greek Cephas; also in 2:11, 14.   2:16 Some translators hold that the quotation extends
through verse 14; others through verse 16; and still others through verse 21.

17But suppose we seek to be made right with God through faith in Christ and then we are found guilty because we have abandoned the law. Would that mean Christ has led us into sin? Absolutely not! 18Rather, I am a sinner if I rebuild the old system of law I already tore down. 19For when I tried to keep the law, it condemned me. So I died to the law—I stopped trying to meet all its requirements—so that I might live for God. 20My old self has been crucified with Christ.* It is no longer I who live, but Christ lives in me. So I live in this earthly body by trusting in the Son of God, who loved me and gave himself for me. 21I do not treat the grace of God as meaningless. For if keeping the law could make us right with God, then there was no need for Christ to die.

The Law and Faith in Christ

3 Oh, foolish Galatians! Who has cast an evil spell on you? For the meaning of Jesus Christ's death was made as clear to you as if you had seen a picture of his death on the cross. 2Let me ask you this one question: Did you receive the Holy Spirit by obeying the law of Moses? Of course not! You received the Spirit because you believed the message you heard about Christ. 3How foolish can you be? After starting your new lives in the Spirit, why are you now trying to become perfect by your own human effort? 4Have you experienced* so much for nothing? Surely it was not in vain, was it?

5I ask you again, does God give you the Holy Spirit and work miracles among you because you obey the law? Of course not! It is because you believe the message you heard about Christ.

6In the same way, "Abraham believed God, and God counted him as righteous because of his faith."* 7The real children of Abraham, then, are those who put their faith in God.

8What's more, the Scriptures looked forward to this time when God would make the Gentiles right in his sight because of their faith. God proclaimed this good news to Abraham long ago when he said, "All nations will be blessed through you."* 9So all who put their faith in Christ share the same blessing Abraham received because of his faith.

10But those who depend on the law to make them right with God are under his curse, for the Scriptures say, "Cursed is everyone who does not observe and obey all the commands that are written in God's Book of the Law."* 11So it is clear that no one can be made right with God by trying to keep the law. For the Scriptures say, "It is through faith that a righteous person has life."* 12This way of faith is very different from the way of law, which says, "It is through obeying the law that a person has life."*

13But Christ has rescued us from the curse pronounced by the law. When he was hung on the cross, he took upon himself the curse for our wrongdoing. For it is written in the Scriptures, "Cursed is everyone who is hung on a tree."* 14Through Christ Jesus, God has blessed the Gentiles with the same blessing he promised to Abraham, so that we who are believers might receive the promised* Holy Spirit through faith.

The Law and God's Promise

15Dear brothers and sisters,* here's an example from everyday life. Just as no one can set aside or amend an irrevocable agreement, so it is in this case. 16God gave the promises to Abraham and his child.* And notice that the Scripture doesn't say "to his children,*" as if it meant many descendants. Rather, it says "to his child"—and that, of course, means Christ. 17This is what I am trying to say: The agreement God made with Abraham could not be canceled 430 years later when God gave the law to Moses. God would be breaking his promise. 18For if the inheritance could be received by keeping the law, then it would not be the result of accepting God's promise. But God graciously gave it to Abraham as a promise.

19Why, then, was the law given? It was given alongside the promise to show people their sins. But the law was designed to last only until the coming of the child who was promised. God gave his law through angels to Moses, who was the mediator between God and the people. 20Now a mediator is helpful if more than one party must reach an agreement. But God, who is one, did not use a mediator when he gave his promise to Abraham.

21Is there a conflict, then, between God's law and God's promises?* Absolutely not! If the law could give us new life, we could be made right

2:20 Some English translations put this sentence in verse 19.   3:4 Or *Have you suffered.*   3:6 Gen 15:6.   3:8 Gen 12:3; 18:18; 22:18.   3:10 Deut 27:26.   3:11 Hab 2:4.   3:12 Lev 18:5.   3:13 Deut 21:23 (Greek version).   3:14 Some manuscripts read *the blessing of the.*   3:15 Greek *Brothers.*   3:16a Greek *seed;* also in 3:16c, 19. See notes on Gen 12:7 and 13:15.   3:16b Greek *seeds.*   3:21 Some manuscripts read *and the promises?*

with God by obeying it. ²²But the Scriptures declare that we are all prisoners of sin, so we receive God's promise of freedom only by believing in Jesus Christ.

God's Children through Faith

²³Before the way of faith in Christ was available to us, we were placed under guard by the law. We were kept in protective custody, so to speak, until the way of faith was revealed.

²⁴Let me put it another way. The law was our guardian until Christ came; it protected us until we could be made right with God through faith. ²⁵And now that the way of faith has come, we no longer need the law as our guardian.

²⁶For you are all children* of God through faith in Christ Jesus. ²⁷And all who have been united with Christ in baptism have put on Christ, like putting on new clothes.* ²⁸There is no longer Jew or Gentile,* slave or free, male and female. For you are all one in Christ Jesus. ²⁹And now that you belong to Christ, you are the true children* of Abraham. You are his heirs, and God's promise to Abraham belongs to you.

4 Think of it this way. If a father dies and leaves an inheritance for his young children, those children are not much better off than slaves until they grow up, even though they actually own everything their father had. ²They have to obey their guardians until they reach whatever age their father set. ³And that's the way it was with us before Christ came. We were like children; we were slaves to the basic spiritual principles* of this world.

⁴But when the right time came, God sent his Son, born of a woman, subject to the law. ⁵God sent him to buy freedom for us who were slaves to the law, so that he could adopt us as his very own children.* ⁶And because we* are his children, God has sent the Spirit of his Son into our hearts, prompting us to call out, "Abba, Father."* ⁷Now you are no longer a slave but God's own child.* And since you are his child, God has made you his heir.

Paul's Concern for the Galatians

⁸Before you Gentiles knew God, you were slaves to so-called gods that do not even exist. ⁹So now that you know God (or should I say, now that God knows you), why do you want to go back again and become slaves once more to the weak and useless spiritual principles of this world? ¹⁰You are trying to earn favor with God by observing certain days or months or seasons or years. ¹¹I fear for you. Perhaps all my hard work with you was for nothing. ¹²Dear brothers and sisters,* I plead with you to live as I do in freedom from these things, for I have become like you Gentiles—free from those laws.

You did not mistreat me when I first preached to you. ¹³Surely you remember that I was sick when I first brought you the Good News. ¹⁴But even though my condition tempted you to reject me, you did not despise me or turn me away. No, you took me in and cared for me as though I were an angel from God or even Christ Jesus himself. ¹⁵Where is that joyful and grateful spirit you felt then? I am sure you would have taken out your own eyes and given them to me if it had been possible. ¹⁶Have I now become your enemy because I am telling you the truth?

¹⁷Those false teachers are so eager to win your favor, but their intentions are not good. They are trying to shut you off from me so that you will pay attention only to them. ¹⁸If someone is eager to do good things for you, that's all right; but let them do it all the time, not just when I'm with you.

¹⁹Oh, my dear children! I feel as if I'm going through labor pains for you again, and they will continue until Christ is fully developed in your lives. ²⁰I wish I were with you right now so I could change my tone. But at this distance I don't know how else to help you.

Abraham's Two Children

²¹Tell me, you who want to live under the law, do you know what the law actually says? ²²The Scriptures say that Abraham had two sons, one from his slave wife and one from his freeborn wife.* ²³The son of the slave wife was born in a human attempt to bring about the fulfillment of God's promise. But the son of the freeborn wife was born as God's own fulfillment of his promise.

²⁴These two women serve as an illustration of God's two covenants. The first woman, Hagar, represents Mount Sinai where people received the law that enslaved them. ²⁵And now Jerusalem is just like Mount Sinai in Arabia,*

3:26 Greek *sons.* 3:27 Greek *have put on Christ.* 3:28 Greek *Jew or Greek.* 3:29 Greek *seed.* 4:3 Or *powers;* also in 4:9. 4:5 Greek *sons;* also in 4:6. 4:6a Greek *you.* 4:6b *Abba* is an Aramaic term for "father." 4:7 Greek *son;* also in 4:7b. 4:12 Greek *brothers;* also in 4:28, 31. 4:22 See Gen 16:15; 21:2-3. 4:25 Greek *And Hagar, which is Mount Sinai in Arabia, is now like Jerusalem;* other manuscripts read *And Mount Sinai in Arabia is now like Jerusalem.*

because she and her children live in slavery to the law. 26But the other woman, Sarah, represents the heavenly Jerusalem. She is the free woman, and she is our mother. 27As Isaiah said,

"Rejoice, O childless woman,
    you who have never given birth!
Break into a joyful shout,
    you who have never been in labor!
For the desolate woman now has more
        children
    than the woman who lives with her
        husband!"*

28And you, dear brothers and sisters, are children of the promise, just like Isaac. 29But you are now being persecuted by those who want you to keep the law, just as Ishmael, the child born by human effort, persecuted Isaac, the child born by the power of the Spirit. 30But what do the Scriptures say about that? "Get rid of the slave and her son, for the son of the slave woman will not share the inheritance with the free woman's son."* 31So, dear brothers and sisters, we are not children of the slave woman; we are children of the free woman.

Freedom in Christ

5 So Christ has truly set us free. Now make sure that you stay free, and don't get tied up again in slavery to the law.

2Listen! I, Paul, tell you this: If you are counting on circumcision to make you right with God, then Christ will be of no benefit to you. 3I'll say it again. If you are trying to find favor with God by being circumcised, you must obey every regulation in the whole law of Moses. 4For if you are trying to make yourselves right with God by keeping the law, you have been cut off from Christ! You have fallen away from God's grace.

5But we who live by the Spirit eagerly wait to receive by faith the righteousness God has promised to us. 6For when we place our faith in Christ Jesus, there is no benefit in being circumcised or being uncircumcised. What is important is faith expressing itself in love.

7You were running the race so well. Who has held you back from following the truth? 8It certainly isn't God, for he is the one who called you to freedom. 9This false teaching is like a little yeast that spreads through the whole batch of dough! 10I am trusting the Lord

to keep you from believing false teachings. God will judge that person, whoever he is, who has been confusing you.

11Dear brothers and sisters,* if I were still preaching that you must be circumcised—as some say I do—why am I still being persecuted? If I were no longer preaching salvation through the cross of Christ, no one would be offended. 12I just wish that those troublemakers who want to mutilate you by circumcision would mutilate themselves.*

13For you have been called to live in freedom, my brothers and sisters. But don't use your freedom to satisfy your sinful nature. Instead, use your freedom to serve one another in love. 14For the whole law can be summed up in this one command: "Love your neighbor as yourself."* 15But if you are always biting and devouring one another, watch out! Beware of destroying one another.

Living by the Spirit's Power

16So I say, let the Holy Spirit guide your lives. Then you won't be doing what your sinful nature craves. 17The sinful nature wants to do evil, which is just the opposite of what the Spirit wants. And the Spirit gives us desires that are the opposite of what the sinful nature desires. These two forces are constantly fighting each other, so you are not free to carry out your good intentions. 18But when you are directed by the Spirit, you are not under obligation to the law of Moses.

19When you follow the desires of your sinful nature, the results are very clear: sexual immorality, impurity, lustful pleasures, 20idolatry, sorcery, hostility, quarreling, jealousy, outbursts of anger, selfish ambition, dissension, division, 21envy, drunkenness, wild parties, and other sins like these. Let me tell you again, as I have before, that anyone living that sort of life will not inherit the Kingdom of God.

22But the Holy Spirit produces this kind of fruit in our lives: love, joy, peace, patience, kindness, goodness, faithfulness, 23gentleness, and self-control. There is no law against these things!

24Those who belong to Christ Jesus have nailed the passions and desires of their sinful nature to his cross and crucified them there. 25Since we are living by the Spirit, let us follow the Spirit's leading in every part of our lives. 26Let us not become conceited, or provoke one another, or be jealous of one another.

4:27 Isa 54:1.   4:30 Gen 21:10.   5:11 Greek *Brothers;* similarly in 5:13.   5:12 Or *castrate themselves,* or *cut themselves off from you;* Greek reads *cut themselves off.*   5:14 Lev 19:18.

We Harvest What We Plant

6 Dear brothers and sisters, if another believer* is overcome by some sin, you who are godly* should gently and humbly help that person back onto the right path. And be careful not to fall into the same temptation yourself. ²Share each other's burdens, and in this way obey the law of Christ. ³If you think you are too important to help someone, you are only fooling yourself. You are not that important.

⁴Pay careful attention to your own work, for then you will get the satisfaction of a job well done, and you won't need to compare yourself to anyone else. ⁵For we are each responsible for our own conduct.

⁶Those who are taught the word of God should provide for their teachers, sharing all good things with them.

⁷Don't be misled—you cannot mock the justice of God. You will always harvest what you plant. ⁸Those who live only to satisfy their own sinful nature will harvest decay and death from that sinful nature. But those who live to please the Spirit will harvest everlasting life from the Spirit. ⁹So let's not get tired of doing what is good. At just the right time we will reap a harvest of blessing if we don't give up. ¹⁰Therefore, whenever we have the opportunity, we should do good to everyone—especially to those in the family of faith.

Paul's Final Advice

¹¹Notice what large letters I use as I write these closing words in my own handwriting.

¹²Those who are trying to force you to be circumcised want to look good to others. They don't want to be persecuted for teaching that the cross of Christ alone can save. ¹³And even those who advocate circumcision don't keep the whole law themselves. They only want you to be circumcised so they can boast about it and claim you as their disciples.

¹⁴As for me, may I never boast about anything except the cross of our Lord Jesus Christ. Because of that cross,* my interest in this world has been crucified, and the world's interest in me has also died. ¹⁵It doesn't matter whether we have been circumcised or not. What counts is whether we have been transformed into a new creation. ¹⁶May God's peace and mercy be upon all who live by this principle; they are the new people of God.*

¹⁷From now on, don't let anyone trouble me with these things. For I bear on my body the scars that show I belong to Jesus.

¹⁸Dear brothers and sisters,* may the grace of our Lord Jesus Christ be with your spirit. Amen.

6:1a Greek *Brothers, if a man.*   6:1b Greek *spiritual.*   6:14 Or *Because of him.*   6:16 Greek *this principle, and upon the Israel of God.* 6:18 Greek *Brothers.*

Ephesians

EVERY ONCE IN A WHILE, God grants his people a glimpse of their place in the grand scheme of history. There is a brief moment when they can assess who they are, where they have come from, and where they are going. Paul's letter to the Ephesians provides the Church with such a vision. This letter, which was possibly intended to be circulated among several churches, was written while Paul was a prisoner in Rome. Paul began his lofty message with an overview of God's work in the past, where God worked out his plans for the world. Paul then moved to the present, where God was saving and transforming those who believed in Christ. Paul concluded this section with a vision of the future, when all evil will be overcome. He pointed out that in the present, however, we will continue to have conflicts because our battle is with the forces of evil. Paul ended the letter with directives for some practical matters of the Christian life, such as family life and work. The letter to the Ephesians provides the Church with a grand vision of itself toward which it can continually grow.

- **Author:** Paul the apostle
- **Date Written:** Around AD 61, during Paul's imprisonment in Rome
- **Purpose:** To strengthen believers by explaining the nature and purpose of the Church, the body of Christ
- **Themes:** The Church, the body of Christ, God's grand purpose in history, unity in the Church, Christian conduct
- **Outline**
  1:1–2:22 God's plan and the believer's salvation
  3:1-21 The mystery of the gospel
  4:1–5:20 The Christian's life in the world
  5:21–6:9 The Christian's relationships
  6:10-24 The Christian's battle with evil

Greetings from Paul

1 This letter is from Paul, chosen by the will of God to be an apostle of Christ Jesus.

I am writing to God's holy people in Ephesus,* who are faithful followers of Christ Jesus.

²May God our Father and the Lord Jesus Christ give you grace and peace.

Spiritual Blessings

³All praise to God, the Father of our Lord Jesus Christ, who has blessed us with every spiritual blessing in the heavenly realms because we are united with Christ. ⁴Even before he made the world, God loved us and chose us in Christ to be holy and without fault in his eyes. ⁵God decided in advance to adopt us into his own family by bringing us to himself through Jesus Christ. This is what he wanted to do, and it gave him great pleasure. ⁶So we praise God for the glorious grace he has poured out on us who belong to his dear Son.* ⁷He is so rich in kindness and grace that he purchased our freedom with the blood of his Son and forgave our sins. ⁸He has showered his kindness on us, along with all wisdom and understanding.

⁹God has now revealed to us his mysterious will regarding Christ—which is to fulfill his own good plan. ¹⁰And this is the plan: At the right time he will bring everything together under the authority of Christ—everything in heaven and on earth. ¹¹Furthermore, because we are united with Christ, we have received an inheritance from God,* for he chose us in advance, and he makes everything work out according to his plan.

¹²God's purpose was that we Jews who were the first to trust in Christ would bring praise and glory to God. ¹³And now you Gentiles have

---

1:1 The most ancient manuscripts do not include *in Ephesus.* 1:6 Greek *to us in the beloved.* 1:11 Or *we have become God's inheritance.*

also heard the truth, the Good News that God saves you. And when you believed in Christ, he identified you as his own* by giving you the Holy Spirit, whom he promised long ago. ¹⁴The Spirit is God's guarantee that he will give us the inheritance he promised and that he has purchased us to be his own people. He did this so we would praise and glorify him.

Paul's Prayer for Spiritual Wisdom

¹⁵Ever since I first heard of your strong faith in the Lord Jesus and your love for God's people everywhere,* ¹⁶I have not stopped thanking God for you. I pray for you constantly, ¹⁷asking God, the glorious Father of our Lord Jesus Christ, to give you spiritual wisdom* and insight so that you might grow in your knowledge of God. ¹⁸I pray that your hearts will be flooded with light so that you can understand the confident hope he has given to those he called—his holy people who are his rich and glorious inheritance.*

¹⁹I also pray that you will understand the incredible greatness of God's power for us who believe him. This is the same mighty power ²⁰that raised Christ from the dead and seated him in the place of honor at God's right hand in the heavenly realms. ²¹Now he is far above any ruler or authority or power or leader or anything else—not only in this world but also in the world to come. ²²God has put all things under the authority of Christ and has made him head over all things for the benefit of the church. ²³And the church is his body; it is made full and complete by Christ, who fills all things everywhere with himself.

Made Alive with Christ

2 Once you were dead because of your disobedience and your many sins. ²You used to live in sin, just like the rest of the world, obeying the devil—the commander of the powers in the unseen world.* He is the spirit at work in the hearts of those who refuse to obey God. ³All of us used to live that way, following the passionate desires and inclinations of our sinful nature. By our very nature we were subject to God's anger, just like everyone else.

⁴But God is so rich in mercy, and he loved us so much, ⁵that even though we were dead because of our sins, he gave us life when he raised Christ from the dead. (It is only by God's grace that you have been saved!) ⁶For he raised

us from the dead along with Christ and seated us with him in the heavenly realms because we are united with Christ Jesus. ⁷So God can point to us in all future ages as examples of the incredible wealth of his grace and kindness toward us, as shown in all he has done for us who are united with Christ Jesus.

⁸God saved you by his grace when you believed. And you can't take credit for this; it is a gift from God. ⁹Salvation is not a reward for the good things we have done, so none of us can boast about it. ¹⁰For we are God's masterpiece. He has created us anew in Christ Jesus, so we can do the good things he planned for us long ago.

Oneness and Peace in Christ

¹¹Don't forget that you Gentiles used to be outsiders. You were called "uncircumcised heathens" by the Jews, who were proud of their circumcision, even though it affected only their bodies and not their hearts. ¹²In those days you were living apart from Christ. You were excluded from citizenship among the people of Israel, and you did not know the covenant promises God had made to them. You lived in this world without God and without hope. ¹³But now you have been united with Christ Jesus. Once you were far away from God, but now you have been brought near to him through the blood of Christ.

¹⁴For Christ himself has brought peace to us. He united Jews and Gentiles into one people when, in his own body on the cross, he broke down the wall of hostility that separated us. ¹⁵He did this by ending the system of law with its commandments and regulations. He made peace between Jews and Gentiles by creating in himself one new people from the two groups. ¹⁶Together as one body, Christ reconciled both groups to God by means of his death on the cross, and our hostility toward each other was put to death.

¹⁷He brought this Good News of peace to you Gentiles who were far away from him, and peace to the Jews who were near. ¹⁸Now all of us can come to the Father through the same Holy Spirit because of what Christ has done for us.

A Temple for the Lord

¹⁹So now you Gentiles are no longer strangers and foreigners. You are citizens along with all of God's holy people. You are members of

---

1:13 Or *he put his seal on you.*   1:15 Some manuscripts read *your faithfulness to the Lord Jesus and to God's people everywhere.*   1:17 Or *to give you the Spirit of wisdom.*   1:18 Or *called, and the rich and glorious inheritance he has given to his holy people.*   2:2 Greek *obeying the commander of the power of the air.*

God's family. 20Together, we are his house, built on the foundation of the apostles and the prophets. And the cornerstone is Christ Jesus himself. 21We are carefully joined together in him, becoming a holy temple for the Lord. 22Through him you Gentiles are also being made part of this dwelling where God lives by his Spirit.

God's Mysterious Plan Revealed

3 When I think of all this, I, Paul, a prisoner of Christ Jesus for the benefit of you Gentiles* . . . 2assuming, by the way, that you know God gave me the special responsibility of extending his grace to you Gentiles. 3As I briefly wrote earlier, God himself revealed his mysterious plan to me. 4As you read what I have written, you will understand my insight into this plan regarding Christ. 5God did not reveal it to previous generations, but now by his Spirit he has revealed it to his holy apostles and prophets.

6And this is God's plan: Both Gentiles and Jews who believe the Good News share equally in the riches inherited by God's children. Both are part of the same body, and both enjoy the promise of blessings because they belong to Christ Jesus.* 7By God's grace and mighty power, I have been given the privilege of serving him by spreading this Good News.

8Though I am the least deserving of all God's people, he graciously gave me the privilege of telling the Gentiles about the endless treasures available to them in Christ. 9I was chosen to explain to everyone* this mysterious plan that God, the Creator of all things, had kept secret from the beginning. 10God's purpose in all this was to use the church to display his wisdom in its rich variety to all the unseen rulers and authorities in the heavenly places. 11This was his eternal plan, which he carried out through Christ Jesus our Lord. 12Because of Christ and our faith in him,* we can now come boldly and confidently into God's presence. 13So please don't lose heart because of my trials here. I am suffering for you, so you should feel honored.

Paul's Prayer for Spiritual Growth

14When I think of all this, I fall to my knees and pray to the Father,* 15the Creator of everything in heaven and on earth.* 16I pray that from his glorious, unlimited resources he will empower you with inner strength through his Spirit. 17Then Christ will make his home in your hearts as you trust in him. Your roots will grow down into God's love and keep you strong. 18And may you have the power to understand, as all God's people should, how wide, how long, how high, and how deep his love is. 19May you experience the love of Christ, though it is too great to understand fully. Then you will be made complete with all the fullness of life and power that comes from God.

20Now all glory to God, who is able, through his mighty power at work within us, to accomplish infinitely more than we might ask or think. 21Glory to him in the church and in Christ Jesus through all generations forever and ever! Amen.

Unity in the Body

4 Therefore I, a prisoner for serving the Lord, beg you to lead a life worthy of your calling, for you have been called by God. 2Always be humble and gentle. Be patient with each other, making allowance for each other's faults because of your love. 3Make every effort to keep yourselves united in the Spirit, binding yourselves together with peace. 4For there is one body and one Spirit, just as you have been called to one glorious hope for the future.

5 There is one Lord, one faith, one baptism,
6 one God and Father of all,
    who is over all, in all, and living through all.

7However, he has given each one of us a special gift* through the generosity of Christ. 8That is why the Scriptures say,

"When he ascended to the heights,
    he led a crowd of captives
    and gave gifts to his people."*

9Notice that it says "he ascended." This clearly means that Christ also descended to our lowly world.* 10And the same one who descended is the one who ascended higher than all the heavens, so that he might fill the entire universe with himself.

11Now these are the gifts Christ gave to the church: the apostles, the prophets, the

---

3:1 Paul resumes this thought in verse 14: "When I think of all this, I fall to my knees and pray to the Father."   3:6 Or *because they are united with Christ Jesus.*   3:9 Some manuscripts do not include *to everyone.*   3:12 Or *Because of Christ's faithfulness.*   3:14 Some manuscripts read *the Father of our Lord Jesus Christ.*   3:15 Or *from whom every family in heaven and on earth takes its name.*   4:7 Greek *a grace.*   4:8 Ps 68:18.   4:9 Some manuscripts read *to the lower parts of the earth.*

evangelists, and the pastors and teachers. [12]Their responsibility is to equip God's people to do his work and build up the church, the body of Christ. [13]This will continue until we all come to such unity in our faith and knowledge of God's Son that we will be mature in the Lord, measuring up to the full and complete standard of Christ.

[14]Then we will no longer be immature like children. We won't be tossed and blown about by every wind of new teaching. We will not be influenced when people try to trick us with lies so clever they sound like the truth. [15]Instead, we will speak the truth in love, growing in every way more and more like Christ, who is the head of his body, the church. [16]He makes the whole body fit together perfectly. As each part does its own special work, it helps the other parts grow, so that the whole body is healthy and growing and full of love.

Living as Children of Light

[17]With the Lord's authority I say this: Live no longer as the Gentiles do, for they are hopelessly confused. [18]Their minds are full of darkness; they wander far from the life God gives because they have closed their minds and hardened their hearts against him. [19]They have no sense of shame. They live for lustful pleasure and eagerly practice every kind of impurity.

[20]But that isn't what you learned about Christ. [21]Since you have heard about Jesus and have learned the truth that comes from him, [22]throw off your old sinful nature and your former way of life, which is corrupted by lust and deception. [23]Instead, let the Spirit renew your thoughts and attitudes. [24]Put on your new nature, created to be like God—truly righteous and holy.

[25]So stop telling lies. Let us tell our neighbors the truth, for we are all parts of the same body. [26]And "don't sin by letting anger control you."* Don't let the sun go down while you are still angry, [27]for anger gives a foothold to the devil.

[28]If you are a thief, quit stealing. Instead, use your hands for good hard work, and then give generously to others in need. [29]Don't use foul or abusive language. Let everything you say be good and helpful, so that your words will be an encouragement to those who hear them.

[30]And do not bring sorrow to God's Holy Spirit by the way you live. Remember, he has identified you as his own,* guaranteeing that you will be saved on the day of redemption.

[31]Get rid of all bitterness, rage, anger, harsh words, and slander, as well as all types of evil behavior. [32]Instead, be kind to each other, tenderhearted, forgiving one another, just as God through Christ has forgiven you.

Living in the Light

5 Imitate God, therefore, in everything you do, because you are his dear children. [2]Live a life filled with love, following the example of Christ. He loved us* and offered himself as a sacrifice for us, a pleasing aroma to God.

[3]Let there be no sexual immorality, impurity, or greed among you. Such sins have no place among God's people. [4]Obscene stories, foolish talk, and coarse jokes—these are not for you. Instead, let there be thankfulness to God. [5]You can be sure that no immoral, impure, or greedy person will inherit the Kingdom of Christ and of God. For a greedy person is an idolater, worshiping the things of this world.

[6]Don't be fooled by those who try to excuse these sins, for the anger of God will fall on all who disobey him. [7]Don't participate in the things these people do. [8]For once you were full of darkness, but now you have light from the Lord. So live as people of light! [9]For this light within you produces only what is good and right and true.

[10]Carefully determine what pleases the Lord. [11]Take no part in the worthless deeds of evil and darkness; instead, expose them. [12]It is shameful even to talk about the things that ungodly people do in secret. [13]But their evil intentions will be exposed when the light shines on them, [14]for the light makes everything visible. This is why it is said,

> "Awake, O sleeper,
>   rise up from the dead,
>   and Christ will give you light."

Living by the Spirit's Power

[15]So be careful how you live. Don't live like fools, but like those who are wise. [16]Make the most of every opportunity in these evil days. [17]Don't act thoughtlessly, but understand what the Lord wants you to do. [18]Don't be drunk with wine, because that will ruin your life. Instead, be filled with the Holy Spirit, [19]singing psalms and hymns and spiritual songs among yourselves, and making music to the Lord in your hearts. [20]And give thanks for everything to God the Father in the name of our Lord Jesus Christ.

4:26 Ps 4:4.   4:30 Or *has put his seal on you.*   5:2 Some manuscripts read *loved you.*

Spirit-Guided Relationships: Wives and Husbands

²¹And further, submit to one another out of reverence for Christ.

²²For wives, this means submit to your husbands as to the Lord. ²³For a husband is the head of his wife as Christ is the head of the church. He is the Savior of his body, the church. ²⁴As the church submits to Christ, so you wives should submit to your husbands in everything.

²⁵For husbands, this means love your wives, just as Christ loved the church. He gave up his life for her ²⁶to make her holy and clean, washed by the cleansing of God's word.* ²⁷He did this to present her to himself as a glorious church without a spot or wrinkle or any other blemish. Instead, she will be holy and without fault. ²⁸In the same way, husbands ought to love their wives as they love their own bodies. For a man who loves his wife actually shows love for himself. ²⁹No one hates his own body but feeds and cares for it, just as Christ cares for the church. ³⁰And we are members of his body.

³¹As the Scriptures say, "A man leaves his father and mother and is joined to his wife, and the two are united into one."* ³²This is a great mystery, but it is an illustration of the way Christ and the church are one. ³³So again I say, each man must love his wife as he loves himself, and the wife must respect her husband.

Children and Parents

6 Children, obey your parents because you belong to the Lord,* for this is the right thing to do. ²"Honor your father and mother." This is the first commandment with a promise: ³If you honor your father and mother, "things will go well for you, and you will have a long life on the earth."*

⁴Fathers,* do not provoke your children to anger by the way you treat them. Rather, bring them up with the discipline and instruction that comes from the Lord.

Slaves and Masters

⁵Slaves, obey your earthly masters with deep respect and fear. Serve them sincerely as you would serve Christ. ⁶Try to please them all the time, not just when they are watching you. As slaves of Christ, do the will of God with all your heart. ⁷Work with enthusiasm, as though you were working for the Lord rather than for people. ⁸Remember that the Lord will reward each one of us for the good we do, whether we are slaves or free.

⁹Masters, treat your slaves in the same way. Don't threaten them; remember, you both have the same Master in heaven, and he has no favorites.

The Whole Armor of God

¹⁰A final word: Be strong in the Lord and in his mighty power. ¹¹Put on all of God's armor so that you will be able to stand firm against all strategies of the devil. ¹²For we* are not fighting against flesh-and-blood enemies, but against evil rulers and authorities of the unseen world, against mighty powers in this dark world, and against evil spirits in the heavenly places.

¹³Therefore, put on every piece of God's armor so you will be able to resist the enemy in the time of evil. Then after the battle you will still be standing firm. ¹⁴Stand your ground, putting on the belt of truth and the body armor of God's righteousness. ¹⁵For shoes, put on the peace that comes from the Good News so that you will be fully prepared.* ¹⁶In addition to all of these, hold up the shield of faith to stop the fiery arrows of the devil.* ¹⁷Put on salvation as your helmet, and take the sword of the Spirit, which is the word of God.

¹⁸Pray in the Spirit at all times and on every occasion. Stay alert and be persistent in your prayers for all believers everywhere.*

¹⁹And pray for me, too. Ask God to give me the right words so I can boldly explain God's mysterious plan that the Good News is for Jews and Gentiles alike.* ²⁰I am in chains now, still preaching this message as God's ambassador. So pray that I will keep on speaking boldly for him, as I should.

Final Greetings

²¹To bring you up to date, Tychicus will give you a full report about what I am doing and how I am getting along. He is a beloved brother and faithful helper in the Lord's work. ²²I have sent him to you for this very purpose—to let you know how we are doing and to encourage you.

²³Peace be with you, dear brothers and sisters,* and may God the Father and the Lord Jesus Christ give you love with faithfulness. ²⁴May God's grace be eternally upon all who love our Lord Jesus Christ.

5:26 Greek *washed by water with the word.* 5:31 Gen 2:24. 6:1 Or *Children, obey your parents who belong to the Lord;* some manuscripts read simply *Children, obey your parents.* 6:2-3 Exod 20:12; Deut 5:16. 6:4 Or *Parents.* 6:12 Some manuscripts read *you.* 6:15 Or *For shoes, put on the readiness to preach the Good News of peace with God.* 6:16 Greek *the evil one.* 6:18 Greek *all of God's holy people.* 6:19 Greek *explain the mystery of the Good News;* some manuscripts read simply *explain the mystery.* 6:23 Greek *brothers.*

Philippians

CONTENTMENT. Paul had learned the secret of this attitude, and he revealed it to the Philippians. While under house arrest, Paul wrote this letter to the Philippians to thank some dear friends who had sent him money. In this letter he told them about a joy that does not depend upon external circumstances because it is rooted in Jesus Christ, who gives it freely. Paul began by expressing his thanks to the Philippians. After describing some problems he was facing in Rome, Paul revealed his uncertainty about his future, whether he would be executed or released. Despite his uncertainty, however, Paul remained confident in the face of death, for he trusted in Christ. Paul then painted a picture of Christ's humility and urged the Philippians to follow this example. Paul digressed for a bit and warned his readers against relying upon external qualifications for their faith. After a few personal comments, Paul closed his letter by thanking the Philippians again for their generosity.

■ **Author:** Paul the apostle

■ **Date Written:** Around AD 61, during Paul's imprisonment in Rome

■ **Purpose:** To thank the Philippians for the gift they had sent him and to encourage them by describing the contentment he had found in Jesus Christ

■ **Themes:** Contentment, humility, unity, generosity, joy

■ **Outline**

1:1-30 Paul's joy despite the problems at Rome
2:1-30 The example of Christ's humility
3:1-21 Warnings and direction for Christian living
4:1-23 God's peace and his provisions for the believer

Greetings from Paul

1 This letter is from Paul and Timothy, slaves of Christ Jesus.

I am writing to all of God's holy people in Philippi who belong to Christ Jesus, including the church leaders* and deacons.

²May God our Father and the Lord Jesus Christ give you grace and peace.

Paul's Thanksgiving and Prayer

³Every time I think of you, I give thanks to my God. ⁴Whenever I pray, I make my requests for all of you with joy, ⁵for you have been my partners in spreading the Good News about Christ from the time you first heard it until now. ⁶And I am certain that God, who began the good work within you, will continue his work until it is finally finished on the day when Christ Jesus returns.

⁷So it is right that I should feel as I do about all of you, for you have a special place in my heart. You share with me the special favor of God, both in my imprisonment and in defending and confirming the truth of the Good News. ⁸God knows how much I love you and long for you with the tender compassion of Christ Jesus.

⁹I pray that your love will overflow more and more, and that you will keep on growing in knowledge and understanding. ¹⁰For I want you to understand what really matters, so that you may live pure and blameless lives until the day of Christ's return. ¹¹May you always be filled with the fruit of your salvation—the righteous character produced in your life by Jesus Christ*—for this will bring much glory and praise to God.

1:1 Or *overseers,* or *bishops.*   1:11 Greek *with the fruit of righteousness through Jesus Christ.*

Paul's Joy That Christ Is Preached

12And I want you to know, my dear brothers and sisters,* that everything that has happened to me here has helped to spread the Good News. 13For everyone here, including the whole palace guard,* knows that I am in chains because of Christ. 14And because of my imprisonment, most of the believers* here have gained confidence and boldly speak God's message* without fear.

15It's true that some are preaching out of jealousy and rivalry. But others preach about Christ with pure motives. 16They preach because they love me, for they know I have been appointed to defend the Good News. 17Those others do not have pure motives as they preach about Christ. They preach with selfish ambition, not sincerely, intending to make my chains more painful to me. 18But that doesn't matter. Whether their motives are false or genuine, the message about Christ is being preached either way, so I rejoice. And I will continue to rejoice. 19For I know that as you pray for me and the Spirit of Jesus Christ helps me, this will lead to my deliverance.

Paul's Life for Christ

20For I fully expect and hope that I will never be ashamed, but that I will continue to be bold for Christ, as I have been in the past. And I trust that my life will bring honor to Christ, whether I live or die. 21For to me, living means living for Christ, and dying is even better. 22But if I live, I can do more fruitful work for Christ. So I really don't know which is better. 23I'm torn between two desires: I long to go and be with Christ, which would be far better for me. 24But for your sakes, it is better that I continue to live.

25Knowing this, I am convinced that I will remain alive so I can continue to help all of you grow and experience the joy of your faith. 26And when I come to you again, you will have even more reason to take pride in Christ Jesus because of what he is doing through me.

Live as Citizens of Heaven

27Above all, you must live as citizens of heaven, conducting yourselves in a manner worthy of the Good News about Christ. Then, whether I come and see you again or only hear about you, I will know that you are standing together with one spirit and one purpose, fighting together

for the faith, which is the Good News. 28Don't be intimidated in any way by your enemies. This will be a sign to them that they are going to be destroyed, but that you are going to be saved, even by God himself. 29For you have been given not only the privilege of trusting in Christ but also the privilege of suffering for him. 30We are in this struggle together. You have seen my struggle in the past, and you know that I am still in the midst of it.

Have the Attitude of Christ

2 Is there any encouragement from belonging to Christ? Any comfort from his love? Any fellowship together in the Spirit? Are your hearts tender and compassionate? 2Then make me truly happy by agreeing wholeheartedly with each other, loving one another, and working together with one mind and purpose.

3Don't be selfish; don't try to impress others. Be humble, thinking of others as better than yourselves. 4Don't look out only for your own interests, but take an interest in others, too.

5You must have the same attitude that Christ Jesus had.

6 Though he was God,*
    he did not think of equality with God
    as something to cling to.
7 Instead, he gave up his divine privileges*;
    he took the humble position of
        a slave*
    and was born as a human being.
    When he appeared in human form,*
8   he humbled himself in obedience to God
    and died a criminal's death on a cross.

9 Therefore, God elevated him to the place
        of highest honor
    and gave him the name above all other
        names,
10 that at the name of Jesus every knee
        should bow,
    in heaven and on earth and under the
        earth,
11 and every tongue declare that Jesus Christ
        is Lord,
    to the glory of God the Father.

Shine Brightly for Christ

12Dear friends, you always followed my instructions when I was with you. And now that I am

---

1:12 Greek brothers.   1:13 Greek including all the Praetorium.   1:14a Greek brothers in the Lord.   1:14b Some manuscripts read speak the message.   2:6 Or Being in the form of God.   2:7a Greek he emptied himself.   2:7b Or the form of a slave.   2:7c Some English translations put this phrase in verse 8.

away, it is even more important. Work hard to show the results of your salvation, obeying God with deep reverence and fear. ¹³For God is working in you, giving you the desire and the power to do what pleases him.

¹⁴Do everything without complaining and arguing, ¹⁵so that no one can criticize you. Live clean, innocent lives as children of God, shining like bright lights in a world full of crooked and perverse people. ¹⁶Hold firmly to the word of life; then, on the day of Christ's return, I will be proud that I did not run the race in vain and that my work was not useless. ¹⁷But I will rejoice even if I lose my life, pouring it out like a liquid offering to God,* just like your faithful service is an offering to God. And I want all of you to share that joy. ¹⁸Yes, you should rejoice, and I will share your joy.

Paul Commends Timothy

¹⁹If the Lord Jesus is willing, I hope to send Timothy to you soon for a visit. Then he can cheer me up by telling me how you are getting along. ²⁰I have no one else like Timothy, who genuinely cares about your welfare. ²¹All the others care only for themselves and not for what matters to Jesus Christ. ²²But you know how Timothy has proved himself. Like a son with his father, he has served with me in preaching the Good News. ²³I hope to send him to you just as soon as I find out what is going to happen to me here. ²⁴And I have confidence from the Lord that I myself will come to see you soon.

Paul Commends Epaphroditus

²⁵Meanwhile, I thought I should send Epaphroditus back to you. He is a true brother, coworker, and fellow soldier. And he was your messenger to help me in my need. ²⁶I am sending him because he has been longing to see you, and he was very distressed that you heard he was ill. ²⁷And he certainly was ill; in fact, he almost died. But God had mercy on him—and also on me, so that I would not have one sorrow after another.

²⁸So I am all the more anxious to send him back to you, for I know you will be glad to see him, and then I will not be so worried about you. ²⁹Welcome him in the Lord's love* and with great joy, and give him the honor that people like him deserve. ³⁰For he risked his life for the work of Christ, and he was at the point of death while doing for me what you couldn't do from far away.

The Priceless Value of Knowing Christ

3 Whatever happens, my dear brothers and sisters,* rejoice in the Lord. I never get tired of telling you these things, and I do it to safeguard your faith.

²Watch out for those dogs, those people who do evil, those mutilators who say you must be circumcised to be saved. ³For we who worship by the Spirit of God* are the ones who are truly circumcised. We rely on what Christ Jesus has done for us. We put no confidence in human effort, ⁴though I could have confidence in my own effort if anyone could. Indeed, if others have reason for confidence in their own efforts, I have even more!

⁵I was circumcised when I was eight days old. I am a pure-blooded citizen of Israel and a member of the tribe of Benjamin—a real Hebrew if there ever was one! I was a member of the Pharisees, who demand the strictest obedience to the Jewish law. ⁶I was so zealous that I harshly persecuted the church. And as for righteousness, I obeyed the law without fault.

⁷I once thought these things were valuable, but now I consider them worthless because of what Christ has done. ⁸Yes, everything else is worthless when compared with the infinite value of knowing Christ Jesus my Lord. For his sake I have discarded everything else, counting it all as garbage, so that I could gain Christ ⁹and become one with him. I no longer count on my own righteousness through obeying the law; rather, I become righteous through faith in Christ.* For God's way of making us right with himself depends on faith. ¹⁰I want to know Christ and experience the mighty power that raised him from the dead. I want to suffer with him, sharing in his death, ¹¹so that one way or another I will experience the resurrection from the dead!

Pressing toward the Goal

¹²I don't mean to say that I have already achieved these things or that I have already reached perfection. But I press on to possess that perfection for which Christ Jesus first possessed me. ¹³No, dear brothers and sisters, I have not achieved it,* but I focus on this one thing: Forgetting the past and looking forward to what lies ahead, ¹⁴I press on to reach the end

---

2:17 Greek *I will rejoice even if I am to be poured out as a liquid offering.*   2:29 Greek *in the Lord.*   3:1 Greek *brothers;* also in 3:13, 17.
3:3 Some manuscripts read *worship God in spirit;* one early manuscript reads *worship in spirit.*   3:9 Or *through the faithfulness of Christ.*   3:13 Some manuscripts read *not yet achieved it.*

of the race and receive the heavenly prize for which God, through Christ Jesus, is calling us.

[15]Let all who are spiritually mature agree on these things. If you disagree on some point, I believe God will make it plain to you. [16]But we must hold on to the progress we have already made.

[17]Dear brothers and sisters, pattern your lives after mine, and learn from those who follow our example. [18]For I have told you often before, and I say it again with tears in my eyes, that there are many whose conduct shows they are really enemies of the cross of Christ. [19]They are headed for destruction. Their god is their appetite, they brag about shameful things, and they think only about this life here on earth. [20]But we are citizens of heaven, where the Lord Jesus Christ lives. And we are eagerly waiting for him to return as our Savior. [21]He will take our weak mortal bodies and change them into glorious bodies like his own, using the same power with which he will bring everything under his control.

4 Therefore, my dear brothers and sisters,* stay true to the Lord. I love you and long to see you, dear friends, for you are my joy and the crown I receive for my work.

Words of Encouragement

[2]Now I appeal to Euodia and Syntyche. Please, because you belong to the Lord, settle your disagreement. [3]And I ask you, my true partner,* to help these two women, for they worked hard with me in telling others the Good News. They worked along with Clement and the rest of my co-workers, whose names are written in the Book of Life.

[4]Always be full of joy in the Lord. I say it again—rejoice! [5]Let everyone see that you are considerate in all you do. Remember, the Lord is coming soon.*

[6]Don't worry about anything; instead, pray about everything. Tell God what you need, and thank him for all he has done. [7]Then you will experience God's peace, which exceeds anything we can understand. His peace will guard your hearts and minds as you live in Christ Jesus.

[8]And now, dear brothers and sisters, one final thing. Fix your thoughts on what is true, and honorable, and right, and pure, and lovely, and admirable. Think about things that are excellent and worthy of praise. [9]Keep putting into practice all you learned and received from me—everything you heard from me and saw me doing. Then the God of peace will be with you.

Paul's Thanks for Their Gifts

[10]How I praise the Lord that you are concerned about me again. I know you have always been concerned for me, but you didn't have the chance to help me. [11]Not that I was ever in need, for I have learned how to be content with whatever I have. [12]I know how to live on almost nothing or with everything. I have learned the secret of living in every situation, whether it is with a full stomach or empty, with plenty or little. [13]For I can do everything through Christ,* who gives me strength. [14]Even so, you have done well to share with me in my present difficulty.

[15]As you know, you Philippians were the only ones who gave me financial help when I first brought you the Good News and then traveled on from Macedonia. No other church did this. [16]Even when I was in Thessalonica you sent help more than once. [17]I don't say this because I want a gift from you. Rather, I want you to receive a reward for your kindness.

[18]At the moment I have all I need—and more! I am generously supplied with the gifts you sent me with Epaphroditus. They are a sweet-smelling sacrifice that is acceptable and pleasing to God. [19]And this same God who takes care of me will supply all your needs from his glorious riches, which have been given to us in Christ Jesus.

[20]Now all glory to God our Father forever and ever! Amen.

Paul's Final Greetings

[21]Give my greetings to each of God's holy people—all who belong to Christ Jesus. The brothers who are with me send you their greetings. [22]And all the rest of God's people send you greetings, too, especially those in Caesar's household.

[23]May the grace of the Lord Jesus Christ be with your spirit.*

4:1 Greek *brothers;* also in 4:8.   4:3 Or *loyal Syzygus.*   4:5 Greek *the Lord is near.*   4:13 Greek *through the one.*   4:23 Some manuscripts add *Amen.*

Colossians

WHO IS JESUS? From the earliest days of Christianity, there has never been a shortage of answers and theories regarding this question. Paul's letter to the Colossians addressed this question as well, as he combatted pagan ideas that were creeping into the local church. Paul had never visited the church at Colosse, but he was concerned about its members and warned them against those who were promoting theories about Jesus that mixed pagan and scriptural ideas. These false teachers had taken elements of astrology, magic, and Judaism and produced a doctrine that regarded Jesus as merely an angelic being. To correct this view, Paul emphasized the deity of Christ and listed several attributes of Jesus that highlight his uniqueness: "the visible image of the invisible God," "through him God created everything," "the head of the church," and "supreme over all who rise from the dead." Then Paul instructed his readers in the new life they should lead in Christ. After several personal greetings, Paul concluded the letter.

- **Author:** Paul the apostle
- **Date Written:** Around AD 61, during Paul's imprisonment in Rome
- **Purpose:** To combat false doctrines about Jesus Christ and to show the sufficiency of Jesus Christ for the Colossians
- **Themes:** The person of Jesus Christ, false doctrines, new life in Christ
- **Outline**
  1:1-14 Paul's opening prayer
  1:15–2:3 The glory of Christ
  2:4-23 Warnings against false beliefs
  3:1–4:1 Instructions for Christian living
  4:2-18 Exhortations to prayer and concluding remarks

Greetings from Paul

1 This letter is from Paul, chosen by the will of God to be an apostle of Christ Jesus, and from our brother Timothy.

2 We are writing to God's holy people in the city of Colosse, who are faithful brothers and sisters* in Christ.

May God our Father give you grace and peace.

Paul's Thanksgiving and Prayer

3 We always pray for you, and we give thanks to God, the Father of our Lord Jesus Christ. 4 For we have heard of your faith in Christ Jesus and your love for all of God's people, 5 which come from your confident hope of what God has reserved for you in heaven. You have had this expectation ever since you first heard the truth of the Good News.

6 This same Good News that came to you is going out all over the world. It is bearing fruit everywhere by changing lives, just as it changed your lives from the day you first heard and understood the truth about God's wonderful grace.

7 You learned about the Good News from Epaphras, our beloved co-worker. He is Christ's faithful servant, and he is helping us on your behalf.* 8 He has told us about the love for others that the Holy Spirit has given you.

9 So we have not stopped praying for you since we first heard about you. We ask God to give you complete knowledge of his will and to give you spiritual wisdom and understanding. 10 Then the way you live will always honor and please the Lord, and your lives will produce every kind of good fruit. All the while, you will grow as you learn to know God better and better.

11 We also pray that you will be strengthened

1:2 Greek *faithful brothers.*   1:7 Or *he is ministering on your behalf;* some manuscripts read *he is ministering on our behalf.*

with all his glorious power so you will have all the endurance and patience you need. May you be filled with joy,* ¹²always thanking the Father. He has enabled you to share in the inheritance that belongs to his people, who live in the light. ¹³For he has rescued us from the kingdom of darkness and transferred us into the Kingdom of his dear Son, ¹⁴who purchased our freedom* and forgave our sins.

Christ Is Supreme

¹⁵ Christ is the visible image of the invisible God.
    He existed before anything was created
    and is supreme over all creation,*
¹⁶ for through him God created everything
    in the heavenly realms and on earth.
    He made the things we can see
    and the things we can't see—
    such as thrones, kingdoms, rulers, and authorities in the unseen world.
    Everything was created through him and for him.
¹⁷ He existed before anything else,
    and he holds all creation together.
¹⁸ Christ is also the head of the church,
    which is his body.
    He is the beginning,
    supreme over all who rise from the dead.*
    So he is first in everything.
¹⁹ For God in all his fullness
    was pleased to live in Christ,
²⁰ and through him God reconciled everything to himself.
    He made peace with everything in heaven and on earth
    by means of Christ's blood on the cross.

²¹This includes you who were once far away from God. You were his enemies, separated from him by your evil thoughts and actions. ²²Yet now he has reconciled you to himself through the death of Christ in his physical body. As a result, he has brought you into his own presence, and you are holy and blameless as you stand before him without a single fault. ²³But you must continue to believe this truth and stand firmly in it. Don't drift away from the assurance you received when you heard the Good News. The Good News has been preached all over the world, and I, Paul, have been appointed as God's servant to proclaim it.

Paul's Work for the Church

²⁴I am glad when I suffer for you in my body, for I am participating in the sufferings of Christ that continue for his body, the church. ²⁵God has given me the responsibility of serving his church by proclaiming his entire message to you. ²⁶This message was kept secret for centuries and generations past, but now it has been revealed to God's people. ²⁷For God wanted them to know that the riches and glory of Christ are for you Gentiles, too. And this is the secret: Christ lives in you. This gives you assurance of sharing his glory.

²⁸So we tell others about Christ, warning everyone and teaching everyone with all the wisdom God has given us. We want to present them to God, perfect* in their relationship to Christ. ²⁹That's why I work and struggle so hard, depending on Christ's mighty power that works within me.

2 I want you to know how much I have agonized for you and for the church at Laodicea, and for many other believers who have never met me personally. ²I want them to be encouraged and knit together by strong ties of love. I want them to have complete confidence that they understand God's mysterious plan, which is Christ himself. ³In him lie hidden all the treasures of wisdom and knowledge.

⁴I am telling you this so no one will deceive you with well-crafted arguments. ⁵For though I am far away from you, my heart is with you. And I rejoice that you are living as you should and that your faith in Christ is strong.

Freedom from Rules and New Life in Christ

⁶And now, just as you accepted Christ Jesus as your Lord, you must continue to follow him. ⁷Let your roots grow down into him, and let your lives be built on him. Then your faith will grow strong in the truth you were taught, and you will overflow with thankfulness.

⁸Don't let anyone capture you with empty philosophies and high-sounding nonsense that come from human thinking and from the spiritual powers* of this world, rather than from Christ. ⁹For in Christ lives all the fullness of God in a human body.* ¹⁰So you also are complete through your union with Christ, who is the head over every ruler and authority.

1:11 Or *all the patience and endurance you need with joy.*   1:14 Some manuscripts add *with his blood.*   1:15 Or *He is the firstborn of all creation.*   1:18 Or *the firstborn from the dead.*   1:28 Or *mature.*   2:8 Or *the spiritual principles;* also in 2:20.   2:9 Or *in him dwells all the completeness of the Godhead bodily.*

11When you came to Christ, you were "circumcised," but not by a physical procedure. Christ performed a spiritual circumcision—the cutting away of your sinful nature.* 12For you were buried with Christ when you were baptized. And with him you were raised to new life because you trusted the mighty power of God, who raised Christ from the dead.

13You were dead because of your sins and because your sinful nature was not yet cut away. Then God made you alive with Christ, for he forgave all our sins. 14He canceled the record of the charges against us and took it away by nailing it to the cross. 15In this way, he disarmed* the spiritual rulers and authorities. He shamed them publicly by his victory over them on the cross.

16So don't let anyone condemn you for what you eat or drink, or for not celebrating certain holy days or new moon ceremonies or Sabbaths. 17For these rules are only shadows of the reality yet to come. And Christ himself is that reality. 18Don't let anyone condemn you by insisting on pious self-denial or the worship of angels,* saying they have had visions about these things. Their sinful minds have made them proud, 19and they are not connected to Christ, the head of the body. For he holds the whole body together with its joints and ligaments, and it grows as God nourishes it.

20You have died with Christ, and he has set you free from the spiritual powers of this world. So why do you keep on following the rules of the world, such as, 21"Don't handle! Don't taste! Don't touch!"? 22Such rules are mere human teachings about things that deteriorate as we use them. 23These rules may seem wise because they require strong devotion, pious self-denial, and severe bodily discipline. But they provide no help in conquering a person's evil desires.

Living the New Life

3 Since you have been raised to new life with Christ, set your sights on the realities of heaven, where Christ sits in the place of honor at God's right hand. 2Think about the things of heaven, not the things of earth. 3For you died to this life, and your real life is hidden with Christ in God. 4And when Christ, who is your* life, is revealed to the whole world, you will share in all his glory.

5So put to death the sinful, earthly things lurking within you. Have nothing to do with sexual immorality, impurity, lust, and evil desires. Don't be greedy, for a greedy person is an idolater, worshiping the things of this world. 6Because of these sins, the anger of God is coming.* 7You used to do these things when your life was still part of this world. 8But now is the time to get rid of anger, rage, malicious behavior, slander, and dirty language. 9Don't lie to each other, for you have stripped off your old sinful nature and all its wicked deeds. 10Put on your new nature, and be renewed as you learn to know your Creator and become like him. 11In this new life, it doesn't matter if you are a Jew or a Gentile,* circumcised or uncircumcised, barbaric, uncivilized,* slave, or free. Christ is all that matters, and he lives in all of us.

12Since God chose you to be the holy people he loves, you must clothe yourselves with tenderhearted mercy, kindness, humility, gentleness, and patience. 13Make allowance for each other's faults, and forgive anyone who offends you. Remember, the Lord forgave you, so you must forgive others. 14Above all, clothe yourselves with love, which binds us all together in perfect harmony. 15And let the peace that comes from Christ rule in your hearts. For as members of one body you are called to live in peace. And always be thankful.

16Let the message about Christ, in all its richness, fill your lives. Teach and counsel each other with all the wisdom he gives. Sing psalms and hymns and spiritual songs to God with thankful hearts. 17And whatever you do or say, do it as a representative of the Lord Jesus, giving thanks through him to God the Father.

Instructions for Christian Households

18Wives, submit to your husbands, as is fitting for those who belong to the Lord.

19Husbands, love your wives and never treat them harshly.

20Children, always obey your parents, for this pleases the Lord. 21Fathers, do not aggravate your children, or they will become discouraged.

22Slaves, obey your earthly masters in everything you do. Try to please them all the time, not just when they are watching you. Serve them sincerely because of your reverent fear of the Lord. 23Work willingly at whatever you do, as though you were working for the Lord

---

2:11 Greek *the cutting away of the body of the flesh.*   2:15 Or *he stripped off.*   2:18 Or *or worshiping with angels.*   3:4 Some manuscripts read *our.*   3:6 Some manuscripts read *is coming on all who disobey him.*   3:11a Greek *a Greek.*   3:11b Greek *Barbarian, Scythian.*

rather than for people. [24]Remember that the Lord will give you an inheritance as your reward, and that the Master you are serving is Christ.* [25]But if you do what is wrong, you will be paid back for the wrong you have done. For God has no favorites.

4 Masters, be just and fair to your slaves. Remember that you also have a Master—in heaven.

An Encouragement for Prayer

[2]Devote yourselves to prayer with an alert mind and a thankful heart. [3]Pray for us, too, that God will give us many opportunities to speak about his mysterious plan concerning Christ. That is why I am here in chains. [4]Pray that I will proclaim this message as clearly as I should.

[5]Live wisely among those who are not believers, and make the most of every opportunity. [6]Let your conversation be gracious and attractive* so that you will have the right response for everyone.

Paul's Final Instructions and Greetings

[7]Tychicus will give you a full report about how I am getting along. He is a beloved brother and faithful helper who serves with me in the Lord's work. [8]I have sent him to you for this very purpose—to let you know how we are doing and to encourage you. [9]I am also sending Onesimus, a faithful and beloved brother,

one of your own people. He and Tychicus will tell you everything that's happening here.

[10]Aristarchus, who is in prison with me, sends you his greetings, and so does Mark, Barnabas's cousin. As you were instructed before, make Mark welcome if he comes your way. [11]Jesus (the one we call Justus) also sends his greetings. These are the only Jewish believers among my co-workers; they are working with me here for the Kingdom of God. And what a comfort they have been!

[12]Epaphras, a member of your own fellowship and a servant of Christ Jesus, sends you his greetings. He always prays earnestly for you, asking God to make you strong and perfect, fully confident that you are following the whole will of God. [13]I can assure you that he prays hard for you and also for the believers in Laodicea and Hierapolis.

[14]Luke, the beloved doctor, sends his greetings, and so does Demas. [15]Please give my greetings to our brothers and sisters* at Laodicea, and to Nympha and the church that meets in her house.

[16]After you have read this letter, pass it on to the church at Laodicea so they can read it, too. And you should read the letter I wrote to them.

[17]And say to Archippus, "Be sure to carry out the ministry the Lord gave you."

[18]HERE IS MY GREETING IN MY OWN HANDWRITING—PAUL.

Remember my chains.

May God's grace be with you.

3:24 Or *and serve Christ as your Master.*   4:6 Greek *and seasoned with salt.*   4:15 Greek *brothers.*

1 Thessalonians

LIKE A FATHER instructing his growing children, Paul urged the Thessalonians to lead lives worthy of Christ's Kingdom, which would soon be established. This was one of Paul's first epistles, and he wrote it shortly after the church was founded in Thessalonica (2:17). Paul opened the letter by commending the Thessalonians for their faith and eagerness to spread the gospel throughout their region. He encouraged them to remain strong for the sake of the gospel despite persecution. After expressing his longing to see them, Paul also guided the Thessalonian believers in a

- **Author:** Paul the apostle
- **Date Written:** Around AD 51, one of Paul's earliest letters, written from the city of Corinth
- **Purpose:** To encourage the Thessalonian believers in their faith and assure them of Christ's return
- **Themes:** Faith, persecution, hope in Christ's return, resurrection
- **Outline**
  1:1-10 Paul's heartfelt thanks for the Thessalonians
  2:1-16 Paul's personal defense
  2:17–3:13 Description of events since leaving Thessalonica
  4:1-12 Direction and encouragement to live a godly life
  4:13–5:11 The return of Christ
  5:12-28 Final admonitions

few practical matters, addressing adultery, revelry, disrespect, and obstruction of the Holy Spirit's work. Paul corrected these believers while affirming his love for them. Some believers whose relatives had died needed comfort and reassurance that their relatives would also be included in the Kingdom. Paul's discussion about Christ's return also encouraged the believers to live in constant hope.

Greetings from Paul

1 This letter is from Paul, Silas,* and Timothy.
We are writing to the church in Thessalonica, to you who belong to God the Father and the Lord Jesus Christ.

May God give you grace and peace.

The Faith of the Thessalonian Believers

2We always thank God for all of you and pray for you constantly. 3As we pray to our God and Father about you, we think of your faithful work, your loving deeds, and the enduring hope you have because of our Lord Jesus Christ.

4We know, dear brothers and sisters,* that God loves you and has chosen you to be his own people. 5For when we brought you the Good News, it was not only with words but also with power, for the Holy Spirit gave you full assurance* that what we said was true. And you

know of our concern for you from the way we lived when we were with you. 6So you received the message with joy from the Holy Spirit in spite of the severe suffering it brought you. In this way, you imitated both us and the Lord. 7As a result, you have become an example to all the believers in Greece—throughout both Macedonia and Achaia.*

8And now the word of the Lord is ringing out from you to people everywhere, even beyond Macedonia and Achaia, for wherever we go we find people telling us about your faith in God. We don't need to tell them about it, 9for they keep talking about the wonderful welcome you gave us and how you turned away from idols to serve the living and true God. 10And they speak of how you are looking forward to the coming of God's Son from heaven—Jesus, whom God raised from the dead. He is the one who

1:1 Greek *Silvanus*, the Greek form of the name. 1:4 Greek *brothers*. 1:5 Or *with the power of the Holy Spirit, so you can have full assurance.* 1:7 *Macedonia* and *Achaia* were the northern and southern regions of Greece.

has rescued us from the terrors of the coming judgment.

Paul Remembers His Visit

2 You yourselves know, dear brothers and sisters,* that our visit to you was not a failure. ²You know how badly we had been treated at Philippi just before we came to you and how much we suffered there. Yet our God gave us the courage to declare his Good News to you boldly, in spite of great opposition. ³So you can see we were not preaching with any deceit or impure motives or trickery.

⁴For we speak as messengers approved by God to be entrusted with the Good News. Our purpose is to please God, not people. He alone examines the motives of our hearts. ⁵Never once did we try to win you with flattery, as you well know. And God is our witness that we were not pretending to be your friends just to get your money! ⁶As for human praise, we have never sought it from you or anyone else.

⁷As apostles of Christ we certainly had a right to make some demands of you, but instead we were like children* among you. Or we were like a mother feeding and caring for her own children. ⁸We loved you so much that we shared with you not only God's Good News but our own lives, too.

⁹Don't you remember, dear brothers and sisters, how hard we worked among you? Night and day we toiled to earn a living so that we would not be a burden to any of you as we preached God's Good News to you. ¹⁰You yourselves are our witnesses—and so is God—that we were devout and honest and faultless toward all of you believers. ¹¹And you know that we treated each of you as a father treats his own children. ¹²We pleaded with you, encouraged you, and urged you to live your lives in a way that God would consider worthy. For he called you to share in his Kingdom and glory.

¹³Therefore, we never stop thanking God that when you received his message from us, you didn't think of our words as mere human ideas. You accepted what we said as the very word of God—which, of course, it is. And this word continues to work in you who believe.

¹⁴And then, dear brothers and sisters, you suffered persecution from your own countrymen. In this way, you imitated the believers in God's churches in Judea who, because of their belief in Christ Jesus, suffered from their own people, the Jews. ¹⁵For some of the Jews killed the prophets, and some even killed the Lord Jesus. Now they have persecuted us, too. They fail to please God and work against all humanity ¹⁶as they try to keep us from preaching the Good News of salvation to the Gentiles. By doing this, they continue to pile up their sins. But the anger of God has caught up with them at last.

Timothy's Good Report about the Church

¹⁷Dear brothers and sisters, after we were separated from you for a little while (though our hearts never left you), we tried very hard to come back because of our intense longing to see you again. ¹⁸We wanted very much to come to you, and I, Paul, tried again and again, but Satan prevented us. ¹⁹After all, what gives us hope and joy, and what will be our proud reward and crown as we stand before our Lord Jesus when he returns? It is you! ²⁰Yes, you are our pride and joy.

3 Finally, when we could stand it no longer, we decided to stay alone in Athens, ²and we sent Timothy to visit you. He is our brother and God's co-worker* in proclaiming the Good News of Christ. We sent him to strengthen you, to encourage you in your faith, ³and to keep you from being shaken by the troubles you were going through. But you know that we are destined for such troubles. ⁴Even while we were with you, we warned you that troubles would soon come—and they did, as you well know. ⁵That is why, when I could bear it no longer, I sent Timothy to find out whether your faith was still strong. I was afraid that the tempter had gotten the best of you and that our work had been useless.

⁶But now Timothy has just returned, bringing us good news about your faith and love. He reports that you always remember our visit with joy and that you want to see us as much as we want to see you. ⁷So we have been greatly encouraged in the midst of our troubles and suffering, dear brothers and sisters,* because you have remained strong in your faith. ⁸It gives us new life to know that you are standing firm in the Lord.

⁹How we thank God for you! Because of you we have great joy as we enter God's presence. ¹⁰Night and day we pray earnestly for you,

---

2:1 Greek *brothers;* also in 2:9, 14, 17.   2:7 Some manuscripts read *we were gentle.*   3:2 Other manuscripts read *and God's servant;* still others read *and a co-worker,* or *and a servant and co-worker for God,* or *and God's servant and our co-worker.*   3:7 Greek *brothers.*

asking God to let us see you again to fill the gaps in your faith.

¹¹May God our Father and our Lord Jesus bring us to you very soon. ¹²And may the Lord make your love for one another and for all people grow and overflow, just as our love for you overflows. ¹³May he, as a result, make your hearts strong, blameless, and holy as you stand before God our Father when our Lord Jesus comes again with all his holy people. Amen.

Live to Please God

4 Finally, dear brothers and sisters,* we urge you in the name of the Lord Jesus to live in a way that pleases God, as we have taught you. You live this way already, and we encourage you to do so even more. ²For you remember what we taught you by the authority of the Lord Jesus.

³God's will is for you to be holy, so stay away from all sexual sin. ⁴Then each of you will control his own body* and live in holiness and honor—⁵not in lustful passion like the pagans who do not know God and his ways. ⁶Never harm or cheat a fellow believer in this matter by violating his wife,* for the Lord avenges all such sins, as we have solemnly warned you before. ⁷God has called us to live holy lives, not impure lives. ⁸Therefore, anyone who refuses to live by these rules is not disobeying human teaching but is rejecting God, who gives his Holy Spirit to you.

⁹But we don't need to write to you about the importance of loving each other,* for God himself has taught you to love one another. ¹⁰Indeed, you already show your love for all the believers* throughout Macedonia. Even so, dear brothers and sisters, we urge you to love them even more.

¹¹Make it your goal to live a quiet life, minding your own business and working with your hands, just as we instructed you before. ¹²Then people who are not believers will respect the way you live, and you will not need to depend on others.

The Hope of the Resurrection

¹³And now, dear brothers and sisters, we want you to know what will happen to the believers who have died* so you will not grieve like people who have no hope. ¹⁴For since we believe that Jesus died and was raised to life again, we also believe that when Jesus returns, God will bring back with him the believers who have died.

¹⁵We tell you this directly from the Lord: We who are still living when the Lord returns will not meet him ahead of those who have died.* ¹⁶For the Lord himself will come down from heaven with a commanding shout, with the voice of the archangel, and with the trumpet call of God. First, the believers who have died* will rise from their graves. ¹⁷Then, together with them, we who are still alive and remain on the earth will be caught up in the clouds to meet the Lord in the air. Then we will be with the Lord forever. ¹⁸So encourage each other with these words.

5 Now concerning how and when all this will happen, dear brothers and sisters,* we don't really need to write to you. ²For you know quite well that the day of the Lord's return will come unexpectedly, like a thief in the night. ³When people are saying, "Everything is peaceful and secure," then disaster will fall on them as suddenly as a pregnant woman's labor pains begin. And there will be no escape.

⁴But you aren't in the dark about these things, dear brothers and sisters, and you won't be surprised when the day of the Lord comes like a thief.* ⁵For you are all children of the light and of the day; we don't belong to darkness and night. ⁶So be on your guard, not asleep like the others. Stay alert and be clearheaded. ⁷Night is the time when people sleep and drinkers get drunk. ⁸But let us who live in the light be clearheaded, protected by the armor of faith and love, and wearing as our helmet the confidence of our salvation.

⁹For God chose to save us through our Lord Jesus Christ, not to pour out his anger on us. ¹⁰Christ died for us so that, whether we are dead or alive when he returns, we can live with him forever. ¹¹So encourage each other and build each other up, just as you are already doing.

Paul's Final Advice

¹²Dear brothers and sisters, honor those who are your leaders in the Lord's work. They work hard among you and give you spiritual guidance. ¹³Show them great respect and wholehearted love because of their work. And live peacefully with each other.

4:1 Greek *brothers*; also in 4:10, 13.   4:4 Or *will know how to take a wife for himself*; or *will learn to live with his own wife*; Greek reads *will know how to possess his own vessel.*   4:6 Greek *Never harm or cheat a brother in this matter.*   4:9 Greek *about brotherly love.*   4:10 Greek *the brothers.*   4:13 Greek *those who have fallen asleep*; also in 4:14.   4:15 Greek *those who have fallen asleep.*   4:16 Greek *the dead in Christ.*   5:1 Greek *brothers*; also in 5:4, 12, 14, 25, 26, 27.   5:4 Some manuscripts read *comes upon you as if you were thieves.*

14Brothers and sisters, we urge you to warn those who are lazy. Encourage those who are timid. Take tender care of those who are weak. Be patient with everyone.

15See that no one pays back evil for evil, but always try to do good to each other and to all people.

16Always be joyful. 17Never stop praying. 18Be thankful in all circumstances, for this is God's will for you who belong to Christ Jesus.

19Do not stifle the Holy Spirit. 20Do not scoff at prophecies, 21but test everything that is said. Hold on to what is good. 22Stay away from every kind of evil.

Paul's Final Greetings

23Now may the God of peace make you holy in every way, and may your whole spirit and soul and body be kept blameless until our Lord Jesus Christ comes again. 24God will make this happen, for he who calls you is faithful.

25Dear brothers and sisters, pray for us. 26Greet all the brothers and sisters with a sacred kiss.

27I command you in the name of the Lord to read this letter to all the brothers and sisters.

28May the grace of our Lord Jesus Christ be with you.

2 Thessalonians

GOOD COMMUNICATION is essential for understanding one another's thoughts. Often the message we receive is not the message the other person intended to send. This is what happened with Paul's first letter to the Thessalonians. In his first letter, Paul had explained that Christ could return at any moment, but apparently some believers misunderstood this to mean that they should stop working and simply wait for Christ to come back. Paul meant to encourage them—not give them a detailed schedule for the future. So he wrote 2 Thessalonians to correct these misunderstandings. Paul began his second letter by encouraging those who were still enduring persecution for their faith. Moving quickly to the heart of the matter, Paul explained that no one knows the exact time of Christ's return, only that he will return. He explained that this great day of judgment would not take them by surprise but would be preceded by a series of recognizable events. Therefore, in the light of Christ's sure return, Christians should lead lives that are above reproach.

■ **Author:** Paul the apostle

■ **Date Written:** Around AD 51, written from Corinth a few months after 1 Thessalonians

■ **Purpose:** To clear up confusion about the day of Christ's return

■ **Themes:** Persecution, Christ's return, the man of lawlessness and the great rebellion, endurance

■ **Outline**

1:1-12 Encouragement from Christ's promised return

2:1-12 The events before Christ returns

2:13–3:5 Further instructions and admonitions

3:6-18 Christian behavior and final greetings

Greetings from Paul

1 This letter is from Paul, Silas,* and Timothy.

We are writing to the church in Thessalonica, to you who belong to God our Father and the Lord Jesus Christ.

2 May God our Father* and the Lord Jesus Christ give you grace and peace.

Encouragement during Persecution

3 Dear brothers and sisters,* we can't help but thank God for you, because your faith is flourishing and your love for one another is growing. 4 We proudly tell God's other churches about your endurance and faithfulness in all the persecutions and hardships you are suffering. 5 And God will use this persecution to show his justice and to make you worthy of his Kingdom, for which you are suffering. 6 In

his justice he will pay back those who persecute you.

7 And God will provide rest for you who are being persecuted and also for us when the Lord Jesus appears from heaven. He will come with his mighty angels, 8 in flaming fire, bringing judgment on those who don't know God and on those who refuse to obey the Good News of our Lord Jesus. 9 They will be punished with eternal destruction, forever separated from the Lord and from his glorious power. 10 When he comes on that day, he will receive glory from his holy people—praise from all who believe. And this includes you, for you believed what we told you about him.

11 So we keep on praying for you, asking our God to enable you to live a life worthy of his call. May he give you the power to accomplish

1:1 Greek *Silvanus*, the Greek form of the name.   1:2 Some manuscripts read *God the Father*.   1:3 Greek *Brothers*.

all the good things your faith prompts you to do. ¹²Then the name of our Lord Jesus will be honored because of the way you live, and you will be honored along with him. This is all made possible because of the grace of our God and Lord, Jesus Christ.*

Events prior to the Lord's Second Coming

2 Now, dear brothers and sisters,* let us clarify some things about the coming of our Lord Jesus Christ and how we will be gathered to meet him. ²Don't be so easily shaken or alarmed by those who say that the day of the Lord has already begun. Don't believe them, even if they claim to have had a spiritual vision, a revelation, or a letter supposedly from us. ³Don't be fooled by what they say. For that day will not come until there is a great rebellion against God and the man of lawlessness* is revealed—the one who brings destruction.* ⁴He will exalt himself and defy everything that people call god and every object of worship. He will even sit in the temple of God, claiming that he himself is God.

⁵Don't you remember that I told you about all this when I was with you? ⁶And you know what is holding him back, for he can be revealed only when his time comes. ⁷For this lawlessness is already at work secretly, and it will remain secret until the one who is holding it back steps out of the way. ⁸Then the man of lawlessness will be revealed, but the Lord Jesus will slay him with the breath of his mouth and destroy him by the splendor of his coming.

⁹This man will come to do the work of Satan with counterfeit power and signs and miracles. ¹⁰He will use every kind of evil deception to fool those on their way to destruction, because they refuse to love and accept the truth that would save them. ¹¹So God will cause them to be greatly deceived, and they will believe these lies. ¹²Then they will be condemned for enjoying evil rather than believing the truth.

Believers Should Stand Firm

¹³As for us, we can't help but thank God for you, dear brothers and sisters loved by the Lord. We are always thankful that God chose you to be among the first* to experience salvation—a salvation that came through the Spirit who makes you holy and through your belief in the truth. ¹⁴He called you to salvation when we told

you the Good News; now you can share in the glory of our Lord Jesus Christ.

¹⁵With all these things in mind, dear brothers and sisters, stand firm and keep a strong grip on the teaching we passed on to you both in person and by letter.

¹⁶Now may our Lord Jesus Christ himself and God our Father, who loved us and by his grace gave us eternal comfort and a wonderful hope, ¹⁷comfort you and strengthen you in every good thing you do and say.

Paul's Request for Prayer

3 Finally, dear brothers and sisters,* we ask you to pray for us. Pray that the Lord's message will spread rapidly and be honored wherever it goes, just as when it came to you. ²Pray, too, that we will be rescued from wicked and evil people, for not everyone is a believer. ³But the Lord is faithful; he will strengthen you and guard you from the evil one.* ⁴And we are confident in the Lord that you are doing and will continue to do the things we commanded you. ⁵May the Lord lead your hearts into a full understanding and expression of the love of God and the patient endurance that comes from Christ.

An Exhortation to Proper Living

⁶And now, dear brothers and sisters, we give you this command in the name of our Lord Jesus Christ: Stay away from all believers* who live idle lives and don't follow the tradition they received* from us. ⁷For you know that you ought to imitate us. We were not idle when we were with you. ⁸We never accepted food from anyone without paying for it. We worked hard day and night so we would not be a burden to any of you. ⁹We certainly had the right to ask you to feed us, but we wanted to give you an example to follow. ¹⁰Even while we were with you, we gave you this command: "Those unwilling to work will not get to eat."

¹¹Yet we hear that some of you are living idle lives, refusing to work and meddling in other people's business. ¹²We command such people and urge them in the name of the Lord Jesus Christ to settle down and work to earn their own living. ¹³As for the rest of you, dear brothers and sisters, never get tired of doing good.

¹⁴Take note of those who refuse to obey what we say in this letter. Stay away from them so they will be ashamed. ¹⁵Don't think of them as

---

1:12 Or of our God and our Lord Jesus Christ.   2:1 Greek brothers; also in 2:13, 15.   2:3a Some manuscripts read the man of sin. 2:3b Greek the son of destruction.   2:13 Some manuscripts read chose you from the very beginning.   3:1 Greek brothers; also in 3:6, 13.   3:3 Or from evil.   3:6a Greek from every brother.   3:6b Some manuscripts read you received.

enemies, but warn them as you would a brother or sister.*

Paul's Final Greetings

16Now may the Lord of peace himself give you his peace at all times and in every situation. The Lord be with you all.

3:15 Greek *as a brother.*

17HERE IS MY GREETING IN MY OWN HAND-WRITING—PAUL. I DO THIS IN ALL MY LETTERS TO PROVE THEY ARE FROM ME. 18May the grace of our Lord Jesus Christ be with you all.

1 Timothy

TIMOTHY IS THE FIRST "second-generation" Christian leader mentioned in the New Testament. He became Paul's protégé and a leader of the church in Ephesus. As a young minister, Timothy faced all sorts of pressures, conflicts, and challenges from the church and the surrounding culture. Paul sent this personal letter to counsel and encourage Timothy. Paul spent the final years of his life in prison (see Acts 25–28), but many scholars believe he enjoyed a period of freedom between AD 62 and 64, before he was imprisoned again and executed.

■ **Author:** Paul the apostle

■ **Date Written:** Around AD 64, probably just prior to Paul's final imprisonment in Rome

■ **Purpose:** To encourage and instruct Timothy, a young Church leader

■ **Themes:** Sound doctrine, public worship, Church leadership, personal discipline, a caring Church

■ **Outline**
1:1-20 Warnings about false doctrine
2:1-15 Instructions regarding prayer and worship
3:1-16 Concerning the ordination of leaders and deacons
4:1–5:25 Exhortations and ministry
6:1-21 The Christian ministry and Paul's charge to Timothy

He probably wrote this letter during his period of freedom. In his letter, Paul warned against false teachers and encouraged Timothy to remain strong in the faith. Paul also gave several directives for worship and for the ordination of Church officers. The letter tends to be fairly personal, but many of its instructions are still helpful for Church leaders today.

Greetings from Paul

1 This letter is from Paul, an apostle of Christ Jesus, appointed by the command of God our Savior and Christ Jesus, who gives us hope.

²I am writing to Timothy, my true son in the faith.

May God the Father and Christ Jesus our Lord give you grace, mercy, and peace.

Warnings against False Teachings

³When I left for Macedonia, I urged you to stay there in Ephesus and stop those whose teaching is contrary to the truth. ⁴Don't let them waste their time in endless discussion of myths and spiritual pedigrees. These things only lead to meaningless speculations,* which don't help people live a life of faith in God.*

⁵The purpose of my instruction is that all believers would be filled with love that comes from a pure heart, a clear conscience, and

genuine faith. ⁶But some people have missed this whole point. They have turned away from these things and spend their time in meaningless discussions. ⁷They want to be known as teachers of the law of Moses, but they don't know what they are talking about, even though they speak so confidently.

⁸We know that the law is good when used correctly. ⁹For the law was not intended for people who do what is right. It is for people who are lawless and rebellious, who are ungodly and sinful, who consider nothing sacred and defile what is holy, who kill their father or mother or commit other murders. ¹⁰The law is for people who are sexually immoral, or who practice homosexuality, or are slave traders,* liars, promise breakers, or who do anything else that contradicts the wholesome teaching ¹¹that comes from the glorious Good News entrusted to me by our blessed God.

1:4a Greek *in myths and endless genealogies, which cause speculation.* **1:4b** Greek *a stewardship of God in faith.* **1:10** Or *kidnappers.*

Paul's Gratitude for God's Mercy

[12]I thank Christ Jesus our Lord, who has given me strength to do his work. He considered me trustworthy and appointed me to serve him, [13]even though I used to blaspheme the name of Christ. In my insolence, I persecuted his people. But God had mercy on me because I did it in ignorance and unbelief. [14]Oh, how generous and gracious our Lord was! He filled me with the faith and love that come from Christ Jesus.

[15]This is a trustworthy saying, and everyone should accept it: "Christ Jesus came into the world to save sinners"—and I am the worst of them all. [16]But God had mercy on me so that Christ Jesus could use me as a prime example of his great patience with even the worst sinners. Then others will realize that they, too, can believe in him and receive eternal life. [17]All honor and glory to God forever and ever! He is the eternal King, the unseen one who never dies; he alone is God. Amen.

Timothy's Responsibility

[18]Timothy, my son, here are my instructions for you, based on the prophetic words spoken about you earlier. May they help you fight well in the Lord's battles. [19]Cling to your faith in Christ, and keep your conscience clear. For some people have deliberately violated their consciences; as a result, their faith has been shipwrecked. [20]Hymenaeus and Alexander are two examples. I threw them out and handed them over to Satan so they might learn not to blaspheme God.

Instructions about Worship

2 I urge you, first of all, to pray for all people. Ask God to help them; intercede on their behalf, and give thanks for them. [2]Pray this way for kings and all who are in authority so that we can live peaceful and quiet lives marked by godliness and dignity. [3]This is good and pleases God our Savior, [4]who wants everyone to be saved and to understand the truth. [5]For,

There is one God and one Mediator who can reconcile God and humanity—the man Christ Jesus. [6]He gave his life to purchase freedom for everyone.

This is the message God gave to the world at just the right time. [7]And I have been chosen as a preacher and apostle to teach the Gentiles this message about faith and truth. I'm not exaggerating—just telling the truth.

[8]In every place of worship, I want men to pray with holy hands lifted up to God, free from anger and controversy.

[9]And I want women to be modest in their appearance.* They should wear decent and appropriate clothing and not draw attention to themselves by the way they fix their hair or by wearing gold or pearls or expensive clothes. [10]For women who claim to be devoted to God should make themselves attractive by the good things they do.

[11]Women should learn quietly and submissively. [12]I do not let women teach men or have authority over them.* Let them listen quietly. [13]For God made Adam first, and afterward he made Eve. [14]And it was not Adam who was deceived by Satan. The woman was deceived, and sin was the result. [15]But women will be saved through childbearing,* assuming they continue to live in faith, love, holiness, and modesty.

Leaders in the Church

3 This is a trustworthy saying: "If someone aspires to be a church leader,* he desires an honorable position." [2]So a church leader must be a man whose life is above reproach. He must be faithful to his wife.* He must exercise self-control, live wisely, and have a good reputation. He must enjoy having guests in his home, and he must be able to teach. [3]He must not be a heavy drinker* or be violent. He must be gentle, not quarrelsome, and not love money. [4]He must manage his own family well, having children who respect and obey him. [5]For if a man cannot manage his own household, how can he take care of God's church?

[6]A church leader must not be a new believer, because he might become proud, and the devil would cause him to fall.* [7]Also, people outside the church must speak well of him so that he will not be disgraced and fall into the devil's trap.

[8]In the same way, deacons must be well respected and have integrity. They must not be heavy drinkers or dishonest with money. [9]They must be committed to the mystery of the faith

---

2:9 Or *to pray in modest apparel.* 2:12 Or *teach men or usurp their authority.* 2:15 Or *will be saved by accepting their role as mothers,* or *will be saved by the birth of the Child.* 3:1 Or *an overseer,* or *a bishop;* also in 3:2, 6. 3:2 Or *must have only one wife,* or *must be married only once;* Greek reads *must be the husband of one wife;* also in 3:12. 3:3 Greek *must not drink too much wine;* similarly in 3:8. 3:6 Or *he might fall into the same judgment as the devil.*

now revealed and must live with a clear conscience. [10]Before they are appointed as deacons, let them be closely examined. If they pass the test, then let them serve as deacons.

[11]In the same way, their wives* must be respected and must not slander others. They must exercise self-control and be faithful in everything they do.

[12]A deacon must be faithful to his wife, and he must manage his children and household well. [13]Those who do well as deacons will be rewarded with respect from others and will have increased confidence in their faith in Christ Jesus.

The Truths of Our Faith

[14]I am writing these things to you now, even though I hope to be with you soon, [15]so that if I am delayed, you will know how people must conduct themselves in the household of God. This is the church of the living God, which is the pillar and foundation of the truth.

[16]Without question, this is the great mystery of our faith*:

Christ* was revealed in a human body
    and vindicated by the Spirit.*
He was seen by angels
    and announced to the nations.
He was believed in throughout the
        world
    and taken to heaven in glory.

Warnings against False Teachers

4 Now the Holy Spirit tells us clearly that in the last times some will turn away from the true faith; they will follow deceptive spirits and teachings that come from demons. [2]These people are hypocrites and liars, and their consciences are dead.*

[3]They will say it is wrong to be married and wrong to eat certain foods. But God created those foods to be eaten with thanks by faithful people who know the truth. [4]Since everything God created is good, we should not reject any of it but receive it with thanks. [5]For we know it is made acceptable* by the word of God and prayer.

A Good Servant of Christ Jesus

[6]If you explain these things to the brothers and sisters,* Timothy, you will be a worthy servant of Christ Jesus, one who is nourished by the

message of faith and the good teaching you have followed. [7]Do not waste time arguing over godless ideas and old wives' tales. Instead, train yourself to be godly. [8]"Physical training is good, but training for godliness is much better, promising benefits in this life and in the life to come." [9]This is a trustworthy saying, and everyone should accept it. [10]This is why we work hard and continue to struggle,* for our hope is in the living God, who is the Savior of all people and particularly of all believers.

[11]Teach these things and insist that everyone learn them. [12]Don't let anyone think less of you because you are young. Be an example to all believers in what you say, in the way you live, in your love, your faith, and your purity. [13]Until I get there, focus on reading the Scriptures to the church, encouraging the believers, and teaching them.

[14]Do not neglect the spiritual gift you received through the prophecy spoken over you when the elders of the church laid their hands on you. [15]Give your complete attention to these matters. Throw yourself into your tasks so that everyone will see your progress. [16]Keep a close watch on how you live and on your teaching. Stay true to what is right for the sake of your own salvation and the salvation of those who hear you.

Advice about Widows, Elders, and Slaves

5 Never speak harshly to an older man,* but appeal to him respectfully as you would to your own father. Talk to younger men as you would to your own brothers. [2]Treat older women as you would your mother, and treat younger women with all purity as you would your own sisters.

[3]Take care of* any widow who has no one else to care for her. [4]But if she has children or grandchildren, their first responsibility is to show godliness at home and repay their parents by taking care of them. This is something that pleases God.

[5]Now a true widow, a woman who is truly alone in this world, has placed her hope in God. She prays night and day, asking God for his help. [6]But the widow who lives only for pleasure is spiritually dead even while she lives. [7]Give these instructions to the church so that no one will be open to criticism.

[8]But those who won't care for their relatives, especially those in their own household, have

---

3:11 Or the women deacons. The Greek word can be translated women or wives.   3:16a Or of godliness.   3:16b Greek He who; other manuscripts read God.   3:16c Or in his spirit.   4:2 Greek are seared.   4:5 Or made holy.   4:6 Greek brothers.   4:10 Some manuscripts read continue to suffer.   5:1 Or an elder.   5:3 Or Honor.

denied the true faith. Such people are worse than unbelievers.

9A widow who is put on the list for support must be a woman who is at least sixty years old and was faithful to her husband.* 10She must be well respected by everyone because of the good she has done. Has she brought up her children well? Has she been kind to strangers and served other believers humbly?* Has she helped those who are in trouble? Has she always been ready to do good?

11The younger widows should not be on the list, because their physical desires will overpower their devotion to Christ and they will want to remarry. 12Then they would be guilty of breaking their previous pledge. 13And if they are on the list, they will learn to be lazy and will spend their time gossiping from house to house, meddling in other people's business and talking about things they shouldn't. 14So I advise these younger widows to marry again, have children, and take care of their own homes. Then the enemy will not be able to say anything against them. 15For I am afraid that some of them have already gone astray and now follow Satan.

16If a woman who is a believer has relatives who are widows, she must take care of them and not put the responsibility on the church. Then the church can care for the widows who are truly alone.

17Elders who do their work well should be respected and paid well,* especially those who work hard at both preaching and teaching. 18For the Scripture says, "You must not muzzle an ox to keep it from eating as it treads out the grain." And in another place, "Those who work deserve their pay!"*

19Do not listen to an accusation against an elder unless it is confirmed by two or three witnesses. 20Those who sin should be reprimanded in front of the whole church; this will serve as a strong warning to others.

21I solemnly command you in the presence of God and Christ Jesus and the highest angels to obey these instructions without taking sides or showing favoritism to anyone.

22Never be in a hurry about appointing a church leader.* Do not share in the sins of others. Keep yourself pure.

23Don't drink only water. You ought to drink a little wine for the sake of your stomach because you are sick so often.

24Remember, the sins of some people are obvious, leading them to certain judgment. But there are others whose sins will not be revealed until later. 25In the same way, the good deeds of some people are obvious. And the good deeds done in secret will someday come to light.

6 All slaves should show full respect for their masters so they will not bring shame on the name of God and his teaching. 2If the masters are believers, that is no excuse for being disrespectful. Those slaves should work all the harder because their efforts are helping other believers* who are well loved.

False Teaching and True Riches

Teach these things, Timothy, and encourage everyone to obey them. 3Some people may contradict our teaching, but these are the wholesome teachings of the Lord Jesus Christ. These teachings promote a godly life. 4Anyone who teaches something different is arrogant and lacks understanding. Such a person has an unhealthy desire to quibble over the meaning of words. This stirs up arguments ending in jealousy, division, slander, and evil suspicions. 5These people always cause trouble. Their minds are corrupt, and they have turned their backs on the truth. To them, a show of godliness is just a way to become wealthy.

6Yet true godliness with contentment is itself great wealth. 7After all, we brought nothing with us when we came into the world, and we can't take anything with us when we leave it. 8So if we have enough food and clothing, let us be content.

9But people who long to be rich fall into temptation and are trapped by many foolish and harmful desires that plunge them into ruin and destruction. 10For the love of money is the root of all kinds of evil. And some people, craving money, have wandered from the true faith and pierced themselves with many sorrows.

Paul's Final Instructions

11But you, Timothy, are a man of God; so run from all these evil things. Pursue righteousness and a godly life, along with faith, love, perseverance, and gentleness. 12Fight the good fight for the true faith. Hold tightly to the eternal life to which God has called you, which you have declared so well before many witnesses. 13And I charge you before God, who gives life to all, and before Christ Jesus, who gave a good

---

5:9 Greek was the wife of one husband.   5:10 Greek and washed the feet of God's holy people?   5:17 Greek should be worthy of double honor.   5:18 Deut 25:4; Luke 10:7.   5:22 Greek about the laying on of hands.   6:2 Greek brothers.

testimony before Pontius Pilate, [14]that you obey this command without wavering. Then no one can find fault with you from now until our Lord Jesus Christ comes again. [15]For,

At just the right time Christ will be revealed from heaven by the blessed and only almighty God, the King of all kings and Lord of all lords. [16]He alone can never die, and he lives in light so brilliant that no human can approach him. No human eye has ever seen him, nor ever will. All honor and power to him forever! Amen.

[17]Teach those who are rich in this world not to be proud and not to trust in their money, which is so unreliable. Their trust should be in God, who richly gives us all we need for our enjoyment. [18]Tell them to use their money to do good. They should be rich in good works and generous to those in need, always being ready to share with others. [19]By doing this they will be storing up their treasure as a good foundation for the future so that they may experience true life.

[20]Timothy, guard what God has entrusted to you. Avoid godless, foolish discussions with those who oppose you with their so-called knowledge. [21]Some people have wandered from the faith by following such foolishness.

May God's grace be with you all.

2 Timothy

WE TEND TO PAY special attention to the words of a person who is very near death because we believe that those words will contain important wisdom, reflection, and advice. Paul's second letter to Timothy expresses Paul's thoughts and reflections shortly before his death. This letter is very personal and is probably the last letter Paul ever wrote. It expressed Paul's deepest feelings and his assurance that, though his earthly life might end soon, God had eternal life waiting for him in heaven (1:10-12). Paul also reflected on God's faithfulness and exhorted Timothy to remain faithful, though the days were coming when Christians would be persecuted and some would depart from the truth.

■ **Author:** Paul the apostle

■ **Date Written:** Around AD 66 or 67, from prison in Rome shortly before his execution

■ **Purpose:** To give final instructions and encouragement to Timothy, a young Church leader

■ **Themes:** Faithfulness, boldness in preaching, the coming rebellion against God

■ **Outline**
1:1-5 Paul's thanksgiving for Timothy
1:6–2:2 Paul's charge to Timothy
2:3-26 A description of a faithful servant
3:1-17 The coming rebellion against God
4:1-22 Paul's final words

Greetings from Paul

1 This letter is from Paul, chosen by the will of God to be an apostle of Christ Jesus. I have been sent out to tell others about the life he has promised through faith in Christ Jesus.

²I am writing to Timothy, my dear son.

May God the Father and Christ Jesus our Lord give you grace, mercy, and peace.

Encouragement to Be Faithful

³Timothy, I thank God for you—the God I serve with a clear conscience, just as my ancestors did. Night and day I constantly remember you in my prayers. ⁴I long to see you again, for I remember your tears as we parted. And I will be filled with joy when we are together again.

⁵I remember your genuine faith, for you share the faith that first filled your grandmother Lois and your mother, Eunice. And I know that same faith continues strong in you. ⁶This is why I remind you to fan into flames the spiritual gift God gave you when I laid my hands on you. ⁷For God has not given us a spirit of fear and timidity, but of power, love, and self-discipline.

⁸So never be ashamed to tell others about our Lord. And don't be ashamed of me, either, even though I'm in prison for him. With the strength God gives you, be ready to suffer with me for the sake of the Good News. ⁹For God saved us and called us to live a holy life. He did this, not because we deserved it, but because that was his plan from before the beginning of time—to show us his grace through Christ Jesus. ¹⁰And now he has made all of this plain to us by the appearing of Christ Jesus, our Savior. He broke the power of death and illuminated the way to life and immortality through the Good News. ¹¹And God chose me to be a preacher, an apostle, and a teacher of this Good News.

¹²That is why I am suffering here in prison. But I am not ashamed of it, for I know the one in whom I trust, and I am sure that he is able to guard what I have entrusted to him* until the day of his return.

¹³Hold on to the pattern of wholesome teaching you learned from me—a pattern shaped by the faith and love that you have in Christ Jesus. ¹⁴Through the power of the Holy Spirit who lives within us, carefully guard the precious truth that has been entrusted to you.

1:12 Or *what has been entrusted to me.*

¹⁵As you know, everyone from the province of Asia has deserted me—even Phygelus and Hermogenes.

¹⁶May the Lord show special kindness to Onesiphorus and all his family because he often visited and encouraged me. He was never ashamed of me because I was in chains. ¹⁷When he came to Rome, he searched everywhere until he found me. ¹⁸May the Lord show him special kindness on the day of Christ's return. And you know very well how helpful he was in Ephesus.

A Good Soldier of Christ Jesus

2 Timothy, my dear son, be strong through the grace that God gives you in Christ Jesus. ²You have heard me teach things that have been confirmed by many reliable witnesses. Now teach these truths to other trustworthy people who will be able to pass them on to others.

³Endure suffering along with me, as a good soldier of Christ Jesus. ⁴Soldiers don't get tied up in the affairs of civilian life, for then they cannot please the officer who enlisted them. ⁵And athletes cannot win the prize unless they follow the rules. ⁶And hardworking farmers should be the first to enjoy the fruit of their labor. ⁷Think about what I am saying. The Lord will help you understand all these things.

⁸Always remember that Jesus Christ, a descendant of King David, was raised from the dead. This is the Good News I preach. ⁹And because I preach this Good News, I am suffering and have been chained like a criminal. But the word of God cannot be chained. ¹⁰So I am willing to endure anything if it will bring salvation and eternal glory in Christ Jesus to those God has chosen.

¹¹This is a trustworthy saying:

If we die with him,
    we will also live with him.
¹² If we endure hardship,
    we will reign with him.
If we deny him,
    he will deny us.
¹³ If we are unfaithful,
    he remains faithful,
    for he cannot deny who he is.

¹⁴Remind everyone about these things, and command them in God's presence to stop fighting over words. Such arguments are useless, and they can ruin those who hear them.

2:17 Greek *gangrene*. 2:19a Num 16:5. 2:19b See Isa 52:11.

An Approved Worker

¹⁵Work hard so you can present yourself to God and receive his approval. Be a good worker, one who does not need to be ashamed and who correctly explains the word of truth. ¹⁶Avoid worthless, foolish talk that only leads to more godless behavior. ¹⁷This kind of talk spreads like cancer,* as in the case of Hymenaeus and Philetus. ¹⁸They have left the path of truth, claiming that the resurrection of the dead has already occurred; in this way, they have turned some people away from the faith.

¹⁹But God's truth stands firm like a foundation stone with this inscription: "The LORD knows those who are his,"* and "All who belong to the LORD must turn away from evil."*

²⁰In a wealthy home some utensils are made of gold and silver, and some are made of wood and clay. The expensive utensils are used for special occasions, and the cheap ones are for everyday use. ²¹If you keep yourself pure, you will be a special utensil for honorable use. Your life will be clean, and you will be ready for the Master to use you for every good work.

²²Run from anything that stimulates youthful lusts. Instead, pursue righteous living, faithfulness, love, and peace. Enjoy the companionship of those who call on the Lord with pure hearts.

²³Again I say, don't get involved in foolish, ignorant arguments that only start fights. ²⁴A servant of the Lord must not quarrel but must be kind to everyone, be able to teach, and be patient with difficult people. ²⁵Gently instruct those who oppose the truth. Perhaps God will change those people's hearts, and they will learn the truth. ²⁶Then they will come to their senses and escape from the devil's trap. For they have been held captive by him to do whatever he wants.

The Dangers of the Last Days

3 You should know this, Timothy, that in the last days there will be very difficult times. ²For people will love only themselves and their money. They will be boastful and proud, scoffing at God, disobedient to their parents, and ungrateful. They will consider nothing sacred. ³They will be unloving and unforgiving; they will slander others and have no self-control. They will be cruel and hate what is good. ⁴They will betray their friends, be reckless, be puffed up with pride, and love pleasure rather than God. ⁵They will act religious, but they will

reject the power that could make them godly. Stay away from people like that!

⁶They are the kind who work their way into people's homes and win the confidence of* vulnerable women who are burdened with the guilt of sin and controlled by various desires. ⁷(Such women are forever following new teachings, but they are never able to understand the truth.) ⁸These teachers oppose the truth just as Jannes and Jambres opposed Moses. They have depraved minds and a counterfeit faith. ⁹But they won't get away with this for long. Someday everyone will recognize what fools they are, just as with Jannes and Jambres.

Paul's Charge to Timothy

¹⁰But you, Timothy, certainly know what I teach, and how I live, and what my purpose in life is. You know my faith, my patience, my love, and my endurance. ¹¹You know how much persecution and suffering I have endured. You know all about how I was persecuted in Antioch, Iconium, and Lystra—but the Lord rescued me from all of it. ¹²Yes, and everyone who wants to live a godly life in Christ Jesus will suffer persecution. ¹³But evil people and impostors will flourish. They will deceive others and will themselves be deceived.

¹⁴But you must remain faithful to the things you have been taught. You know they are true, for you know you can trust those who taught you. ¹⁵You have been taught the holy Scriptures from childhood, and they have given you the wisdom to receive the salvation that comes by trusting in Christ Jesus. ¹⁶All Scripture is inspired by God and is useful to teach us what is true and to make us realize what is wrong in our lives. It corrects us when we are wrong and teaches us to do what is right. ¹⁷God uses it to prepare and equip his people to do every good work.

4 I solemnly urge you in the presence of God and Christ Jesus, who will someday judge the living and the dead when he comes to set up his Kingdom: ²Preach the word of God. Be prepared, whether the time is favorable or not. Patiently correct, rebuke, and encourage your people with good teaching.

³For a time is coming when people will no longer listen to sound and wholesome teaching. They will follow their own desires and will look for teachers who will tell them whatever their itching ears want to hear. ⁴They will reject the truth and chase after myths.

⁵But you should keep a clear mind in every situation. Don't be afraid of suffering for the Lord. Work at telling others the Good News, and fully carry out the ministry God has given you.

⁶As for me, my life has already been poured out as an offering to God. The time of my death is near. ⁷I have fought the good fight, I have finished the race, and I have remained faithful. ⁸And now the prize awaits me—the crown of righteousness, which the Lord, the righteous Judge, will give me on the day of his return. And the prize is not just for me but for all who eagerly look forward to his appearing.

Paul's Final Words

⁹Timothy, please come as soon as you can. ¹⁰Demas has deserted me because he loves the things of this life and has gone to Thessalonica. Crescens has gone to Galatia, and Titus has gone to Dalmatia. ¹¹Only Luke is with me. Bring Mark with you when you come, for he will be helpful to me in my ministry. ¹²I sent Tychicus to Ephesus. ¹³When you come, be sure to bring the coat I left with Carpus at Troas. Also bring my books, and especially my papers.*

¹⁴Alexander the coppersmith did me much harm, but the Lord will judge him for what he has done. ¹⁵Be careful of him, for he fought against everything we said.

¹⁶The first time I was brought before the judge, no one came with me. Everyone abandoned me. May it not be counted against them. ¹⁷But the Lord stood with me and gave me strength so that I might preach the Good News in its entirety for all the Gentiles to hear. And he rescued me from certain death.* ¹⁸Yes, and the Lord will deliver me from every evil attack and will bring me safely into his heavenly Kingdom. All glory to God forever and ever! Amen.

Paul's Final Greetings

¹⁹Give my greetings to Priscilla and Aquila and those living in the household of Onesiphorus. ²⁰Erastus stayed at Corinth, and I left Trophimus sick at Miletus.

²¹Do your best to get here before winter. Eubulus sends you greetings, and so do Pudens, Linus, Claudia, and all the brothers and sisters.*

²²May the Lord be with your spirit. And may his grace be with all of you.

3:6 Greek *and take captive.*   4:13 Greek *especially the parchments.*   4:17 Greek *from the mouth of a lion.*   4:21 Greek *brothers.*

Titus

LIKE TIMOTHY, Titus was one of Paul's trusted assistants who was commissioned to help lead a church. Paul wrote this letter to instruct Titus in his pastoral duties on the island of Crete. Paul advised Titus regarding the ordination of elders and the teaching of the basic doctrines of the faith. He went into some detail regarding the qualifications for the office of elder and gave instructions for others in the church as well. Paul directed Titus to encourage the people to be submissive to the governing authorities whenever possible. Paul also addressed problems that Church leaders often faced and instructed Titus in how to solve them.

■ **Author:** Paul the apostle

■ **Date Written:** Around AD 64, about the same time 1 Timothy was written

■ **Purpose:** To instruct Titus in his duties as a leader of the church in Crete

■ **Themes:** Church leadership, godly behavior in the Church and in society

■ **Outline**
1:1-4 Personal greeting
1:5-16 Concerning the ordination of leaders
2:1-15 General remarks for Church members
3:1-15 Exhortation to Christian living

Greetings from Paul

1 This letter is from Paul, a slave of God and an apostle of Jesus Christ. I have been sent to proclaim faith to* those God has chosen and to teach them to know the truth that shows them how to live godly lives. ²This truth gives them confidence that they have eternal life, which God—who does not lie—promised them before the world began. ³And now at just the right time he has revealed this message, which we announce to everyone. It is by the command of God our Savior that I have been entrusted with this work for him.

⁴I am writing to Titus, my true son in the faith that we share.

May God the Father and Christ Jesus our Savior give you grace and peace.

Titus's Work in Crete

⁵I left you on the island of Crete so you could complete our work there and appoint elders in each town as I instructed you. ⁶An elder must live a blameless life. He must be faithful to his wife,* and his children must be believers who don't have a reputation for being wild or rebellious. ⁷A church leader* is a manager of God's household, so he must live a blameless life. He must not be arrogant or quick-tempered; he must not be a heavy drinker,* violent, or dishonest with money.

⁸Rather, he must enjoy having guests in his home, and he must love what is good. He must live wisely and be just. He must live a devout and disciplined life. ⁹He must have a strong belief in the trustworthy message he was taught; then he will be able to encourage others with wholesome teaching and show those who oppose it where they are wrong.

¹⁰For there are many rebellious people who engage in useless talk and deceive others. This is especially true of those who insist on circumcision for salvation. ¹¹They must be silenced, because they are turning whole families away from the truth by their false teaching. And they do it only for money. ¹²Even one of their own men, a prophet from Crete, has said about them, "The people of Crete are all liars, cruel animals, and lazy gluttons."* ¹³This is true. So reprimand them sternly to make them strong in the faith. ¹⁴They must stop listening to Jewish myths and the commands of people who have turned away from the truth.

1:1 Or *to strengthen the faith of.*   1:6 Or *must have only one wife,* or *must be married only once;* Greek reads *must be the husband of one wife.*
1:7a Or *An overseer,* or *A bishop.*   1:7b Greek *must not drink too much wine.*   1:12 This quotation is from Epimenides of Knossos.

¹⁵Everything is pure to those whose hearts are pure. But nothing is pure to those who are corrupt and unbelieving, because their minds and consciences are corrupted. ¹⁶Such people claim they know God, but they deny him by the way they live. They are detestable and disobedient, worthless for doing anything good.

Promote Right Teaching

2 As for you, Titus, promote the kind of living that reflects wholesome teaching. ²Teach the older men to exercise self-control, to be worthy of respect, and to live wisely. They must have sound faith and be filled with love and patience.

³Similarly, teach the older women to live in a way that honors God. They must not slander others or be heavy drinkers.* Instead, they should teach others what is good. ⁴These older women must train the younger women to love their husbands and their children, ⁵to live wisely and be pure, to work in their homes,* to do good, and to be submissive to their husbands. Then they will not bring shame on the word of God.

⁶In the same way, encourage the young men to live wisely. ⁷And you yourself must be an example to them by doing good works of every kind. Let everything you do reflect the integrity and seriousness of your teaching. ⁸Teach the truth so that your teaching can't be criticized. Then those who oppose us will be ashamed and have nothing bad to say about us.

⁹Slaves must always obey their masters and do their best to please them. They must not talk back ¹⁰or steal, but must show themselves to be entirely trustworthy and good. Then they will make the teaching about God our Savior attractive in every way.

¹¹For the grace of God has been revealed, bringing salvation to all people. ¹²And we are instructed to turn from godless living and sinful pleasures. We should live in this evil world with wisdom, righteousness, and devotion to God, ¹³while we look forward with hope to that wonderful day when the glory of our great God and Savior, Jesus Christ, will be revealed. ¹⁴He gave his life to free us from every kind of sin, to cleanse us, and to make us his very own people, totally committed to doing good deeds.

¹⁵You must teach these things and encourage the believers to do them. You have the authority to correct them when necessary, so don't let anyone disregard what you say.

Do What Is Good

3 Remind the believers to submit to the government and its officers. They should be obedient, always ready to do what is good. ²They must not slander anyone and must avoid quarreling. Instead, they should be gentle and show true humility to everyone.

³Once we, too, were foolish and disobedient. We were misled and became slaves to many lusts and pleasures. Our lives were full of evil and envy, and we hated each other. ⁴But—

When God our Savior revealed his kindness and love, ⁵he saved us, not because of the righteous things we had done, but because of his mercy. He washed away our sins, giving us a new birth and new life through the Holy Spirit.* ⁶He generously poured out the Spirit upon us through Jesus Christ our Savior. ⁷Because of his grace he made us right in his sight and gave us confidence that we will inherit eternal life.

⁸This is a trustworthy saying, and I want you to insist on these teachings so that all who trust in God will devote themselves to doing good. These teachings are good and beneficial for everyone.

⁹Do not get involved in foolish discussions about spiritual pedigrees* or in quarrels and fights about obedience to Jewish laws. These things are useless and a waste of time. ¹⁰If people are causing divisions among you, give a first and second warning. After that, have nothing more to do with them. ¹¹For people like that have turned away from the truth, and their own sins condemn them.

Paul's Final Remarks and Greetings

¹²I am planning to send either Artemas or Tychicus to you. As soon as one of them arrives, do your best to meet me at Nicopolis, for I have decided to stay there for the winter. ¹³Do everything you can to help Zenas the lawyer and Apollos with their trip. See that they are given everything they need. ¹⁴Our people must learn to do good by meeting the urgent needs of others; then they will not be unproductive.

¹⁵Everybody here sends greetings. Please give my greetings to the believers—all who love us.

May God's grace be with you all.

2:3 Greek *be enslaved to much wine.*   2:5 Some manuscripts read *to care for their homes.*   3:5 Greek *He saved us through the washing of regeneration and renewing of the Holy Spirit.*   3:9 Or *spiritual genealogies.*

Philemon

FORGIVENESS. All Christians have received forgiveness from God, so we should forgive others as well. That is why Paul wrote to Philemon, a believer in the church at Colosse. Philemon owned a slave named Onesimus, who had fled from his master. Paul met Onesimus after he had fled, and Onesimus became a Christian. Paul then sent Onesimus back to his owner with this letter, asking Philemon to forgive Onesimus and treat him like a brother in Christ. It is very likely that this letter was sent along with Paul's letter to the Colossians.

■ **Author:** Paul the apostle

■ **Date Written:** Around AD 61, during Paul's imprisonment in Rome

■ **Purpose:** To convince Philemon to forgive his runaway slave and accept him as a brother in Christ

■ **Theme:** Forgiveness

■ **Outline**
1:1-3 Paul's greetings to Philemon
1:4-7 Paul's praise of Philemon
1:8-21 Paul's plea for Onesimus
1:22-25 Concluding remarks

Greetings from Paul

This letter is from Paul, a prisoner for preaching the Good News about Christ Jesus, and from our brother Timothy.

I am writing to Philemon, our beloved co-worker, 2and to our sister Apphia, and to our fellow soldier Archippus, and to the church that meets in your* house.

3May God our Father and the Lord Jesus Christ give you grace and peace.

Paul's Thanksgiving and Prayer

4I always thank my God when I pray for you, Philemon, 5because I keep hearing about your faith in the Lord Jesus and your love for all of God's people. 6And I am praying that you will put into action the generosity that comes from your faith as you understand and experience all the good things we have in Christ. 7Your love has given me much joy and comfort, my brother, for your kindness has often refreshed the hearts of God's people.

Paul's Appeal for Onesimus

8That is why I am boldly asking a favor of you. I could demand it in the name of Christ because it is the right thing for you to do. 9But because of our love, I prefer simply to ask you. Consider this as a request from me—Paul, an old man and now also a prisoner for the sake of Christ Jesus.*

10I appeal to you to show kindness to my child, Onesimus. I became his father in the faith while here in prison. 11Onesimus* hasn't been of much use to you in the past, but now he is very useful to both of us. 12I am sending him back to you, and with him comes my own heart.

13I wanted to keep him here with me while I am in these chains for preaching the Good News, and he would have helped me on your behalf. 14But I didn't want to do anything without your consent. I wanted you to help because you were willing, not because you were forced. 15It seems you lost Onesimus for a little while so that you could have him back forever. 16He is no longer like a slave to you. He is more than a slave, for he is a beloved brother, especially to me. Now he will mean much more to you, both as a man and as a brother in the Lord.

17So if you consider me your partner, welcome him as you would welcome me. 18If he has wronged you in any way or owes you anything,

2 Throughout this letter, *you* and *your* are singular except in verses 3, 22, and 25.   9 Or *a prisoner of Christ Jesus.*   11 *Onesimus* means "useful."

charge it to me. ¹⁹I, PAUL, WRITE THIS WITH MY OWN HAND: I WILL REPAY IT. AND I WON'T MENTION THAT YOU OWE ME YOUR VERY SOUL!

²⁰Yes, my brother, please do me this favor* for the Lord's sake. Give me this encouragement in Christ.

²¹I am confident as I write this letter that you will do what I ask and even more! ²²One more thing—please prepare a guest room for me, for

20 Greek *onaimen,* a play on the name Onesimus.

I am hoping that God will answer your prayers and let me return to you soon.

Paul's Final Greetings

²³Epaphras, my fellow prisoner in Christ Jesus, sends you his greetings. ²⁴So do Mark, Aristarchus, Demas, and Luke, my co-workers.

²⁵May the grace of the Lord Jesus Christ be with your spirit.

Hebrews

HAVE YOU EVER SECOND-GUESSED yourself on a major decision and wondered if you made a big mistake? The letter to the Hebrews deals with this concern among Jewish Christians. Apparently, after pressure and persecution, some believers were having second thoughts about their decision to leave Judaism to become Christians. So this letter shows how Christianity is superior to Judaism. In every way, Christ is shown to be better. As God, he is superior to angels, to Moses, and to the Old Testament priests. At the same time, Jesus Christ is fully human, so he is able to identify with our human struggles. Jesus Christ has sealed a new covenant that is

■ **Author:** Uncertain; some have suggested Paul, Barnabas, Apollos, Priscilla, Luke, and others

■ **Date Written:** Probably around AD 68, a few years before the destruction of the Temple in Jerusalem in AD 70

■ **Purpose:** To present Christianity as superior to Judaism and to show the sufficiency of Jesus Christ's work

■ **Themes:** Superiority of Christianity over Judaism, Jesus as High Priest, Jesus as the ultimate sacrifice, rest, maturity, faith, endurance

■ **Outline**
1:1–3:19 The superiority of Christ
4:1-16 The better life of the believer
5:1–8:13 Christ's superior priestly work
9:1–10:39 The better covenant
11:1-40 Great believers of old
12:1–13:19 Practical instructions for believers
13:20-25 Concluding words

far superior to the old covenant of Judaism. So the author admonished the believers to move beyond questions about the basics of the faith. The believers were encouraged to follow the many examples of faithful men and women of the past who followed God in the midst of persecution. The author concluded with personal greetings and thoughts.

Jesus Christ Is God's Son

1 Long ago God spoke many times and in many ways to our ancestors through the prophets. ²And now in these final days, he has spoken to us through his Son. God promised everything to the Son as an inheritance, and through the Son he created the universe. ³The Son radiates God's own glory and expresses the very character of God, and he sustains everything by the mighty power of his command. When he had cleansed us from our sins, he sat down in the place of honor at the right hand of the majestic God in heaven. ⁴This shows that the Son is far greater than the angels, just as the name God gave him is greater than their names.

The Son Is Greater Than the Angels

⁵For God never said to any angel what he said to Jesus:

"You are my Son.
   Today I have become your Father.*"

God also said,

"I will be his Father,
   and he will be my Son."*

⁶And when he brought his supreme* Son into the world, God said,*

"Let all of God's angels worship him."*

1:5a Or *Today I reveal you as my Son.* Ps 2:7.   1:5b 2 Sam 7:14.   1:6a Or *firstborn.*   1:6b Or *when he again brings his supreme Son* [or *firstborn Son*] *into the world, God will say.*   1:6c Deut 32:43.

[7]Regarding the angels, he says,

> "He sends his angels like the winds,
>   his servants like flames of fire."*

[8]But to the Son he says,

> "Your throne, O God, endures forever and
>   ever.
> You rule with a scepter of justice.
> [9] You love justice and hate evil.
>   Therefore, O God, your God has
>   anointed you,
>   pouring out the oil of joy on you more
>   than on anyone else."*

[10]He also says to the Son,

> "In the beginning, Lord, you laid the
>   foundation of the earth
> and made the heavens with your hands.
> [11] They will perish, but you remain forever.
>   They will wear out like old clothing.
> [12] You will fold them up like a cloak
>   and discard them like old clothing.
> But you are always the same;
>   you will live forever."*

[13]And God never said to any of the angels,

> "Sit in the place of honor at my right
>   hand
> until I humble your enemies,
>   making them a footstool under
>   your feet."*

[14]Therefore, angels are only servants—spirits sent to care for people who will inherit salvation.

A Warning against Drifting Away

2 So we must listen very carefully to the truth we have heard, or we may drift away from it. [2]For the message God delivered through angels has always stood firm, and every violation of the law and every act of disobedience was punished. [3]So what makes us think we can escape if we ignore this great salvation that was first announced by the Lord Jesus himself and then delivered to us by those who heard him speak? [4]And God confirmed the message by giving signs and wonders and various miracles and gifts of the Holy Spirit whenever he chose.

Jesus, the Man

[5]And furthermore, it is not angels who will control the future world we are talking about. [6]For in one place the Scriptures say,

> "What are mere mortals that you should
>   think about them,
>   or a son of man* that you should care
>   for him?
> [7] Yet for a little while you made them a little
>   lower than the angels
>   and crowned them with glory and honor.*
> [8] You gave them authority over all things."*

Now when it says "all things," it means nothing is left out. But we have not yet seen all things put under their authority. [9]What we do see is Jesus, who for a little while was given a position "a little lower than the angels"; and because he suffered death for us, he is now "crowned with glory and honor." Yes, by God's grace, Jesus tasted death for everyone. [10]God, for whom and through whom everything was made, chose to bring many children into glory. And it was only right that he should make Jesus, through his suffering, a perfect leader, fit to bring them into their salvation.

[11]So now Jesus and the ones he makes holy have the same Father. That is why Jesus is not ashamed to call them his brothers and sisters.* [12]For he said to God,

> "I will proclaim your name to my brothers
>   and sisters.
> I will praise you among your assembled
>   people."*

[13]He also said,

> "I will put my trust in him,"
>   that is, "I and the children God has
>   given me."*

[14]Because God's children are human beings—made of flesh and blood—the Son also became flesh and blood. For only as a human being could he die, and only by dying could he break the power of the devil, who had* the power of death. [15]Only in this way could he set free all who have lived their lives as slaves to the fear of dying.

[16]We also know that the Son did not come to help angels; he came to help the descendants of

Abraham. [17]Therefore, it was necessary for him to be made in every respect like us, his brothers and sisters,* so that he could be our merciful and faithful High Priest before God. Then he could offer a sacrifice that would take away the sins of the people. [18]Since he himself has gone through suffering and testing, he is able to help us when we are being tested.

Jesus Is Greater Than Moses

3 And so, dear brothers and sisters who belong to God and* are partners with those called to heaven, think carefully about this Jesus whom we declare to be God's messenger* and High Priest. [2]For he was faithful to God, who appointed him, just as Moses served faithfully when he was entrusted with God's entire* house.

[3]But Jesus deserves far more glory than Moses, just as a person who builds a house deserves more praise than the house itself. [4]For every house has a builder, but the one who built everything is God.

[5]Moses was certainly faithful in God's house as a servant. His work was an illustration of the truths God would reveal later. [6]But Christ, as the Son, is in charge of God's entire house. And we are God's house, if we keep our courage and remain confident in our hope in Christ.*

[7]That is why the Holy Spirit says,

"Today when you hear his voice,
[8]   don't harden your hearts
  as Israel did when they rebelled,
    when they tested me in the wilderness.
[9] There your ancestors tested and tried my
     patience,
    even though they saw my miracles for
     forty years.
[10] So I was angry with them, and I said,
  'Their hearts always turn away from me.
  They refuse to do what I tell them.'
[11] So in my anger I took an oath:
  'They will never enter my place of rest.'"*

[12]Be careful then, dear brothers and sisters.* Make sure that your own hearts are not evil and unbelieving, turning you away from the living God. [13]You must warn each other every day, while it is still "today," so that none of you will be deceived by sin and hardened against God. [14]For if we are faithful to the end, trusting God

just as firmly as when we first believed, we will share in all that belongs to Christ. [15]Remember what it says:

"Today when you hear his voice,
  don't harden your hearts
  as Israel did when they rebelled."*

[16]And who was it who rebelled against God, even though they heard his voice? Wasn't it the people Moses led out of Egypt? [17]And who made God angry for forty years? Wasn't it the people who sinned, whose corpses lay in the wilderness? [18]And to whom was God speaking when he took an oath that they would never enter his rest? Wasn't it the people who disobeyed him? [19]So we see that because of their unbelief they were not able to enter his rest.

Promised Rest for God's People

4 God's promise of entering his rest still stands, so we ought to tremble with fear that some of you might fail to experience it. [2]For this good news—that God has prepared this rest—has been announced to us just as it was to them. But it did them no good because they didn't share the faith of those who listened to God.* [3]For only we who believe can enter his rest. As for the others, God said,

"In my anger I took an oath:
  'They will never enter my place of rest,'"*

even though this rest has been ready since he made the world. [4]We know it is ready because of the place in the Scriptures where it mentions the seventh day: "On the seventh day God rested from all his work."* [5]But in the other passage God said, "They will never enter my place of rest."*

[6]So God's rest is there for people to enter, but those who first heard this good news failed to enter because they disobeyed God. [7]So God set another time for entering his rest, and that time is today. God announced this through David much later in the words already quoted:

"Today when you hear his voice,
  don't harden your hearts."*

[8]Now if Joshua had succeeded in giving them this rest, God would not have spoken about

---

2:17 Greek *like the brothers.*   3:1a Greek *And so, holy brothers who.*   3:1b Greek *God's apostle.*   3:2 Some manuscripts do not include *entire.*   3:6 Some manuscripts add *faithful to the end.*   3:7-11 Ps 95:7-11.   3:12 Greek *brothers.*   3:15 Ps 95:7-8.   4:2 Some manuscripts read *they didn't combine what they heard with faith.*   4:3 Ps 95:11.   4:4 Gen 2:2.   4:5 Ps 95:11.   4:7 Ps 95:7-8.

another day of rest still to come. ⁹So there is a special rest* still waiting for the people of God. ¹⁰For all who have entered into God's rest have rested from their labors, just as God did after creating the world. ¹¹So let us do our best to enter that rest. But if we disobey God, as the people of Israel did, we will fall.

¹²For the word of God is alive and powerful. It is sharper than the sharpest two-edged sword, cutting between soul and spirit, between joint and marrow. It exposes our innermost thoughts and desires. ¹³Nothing in all creation is hidden from God. Everything is naked and exposed before his eyes, and he is the one to whom we are accountable.

Christ Is Our High Priest

¹⁴So then, since we have a great High Priest who has entered heaven, Jesus the Son of God, let us hold firmly to what we believe. ¹⁵This High Priest of ours understands our weaknesses, for he faced all of the same testings we do, yet he did not sin. ¹⁶So let us come boldly to the throne of our gracious God. There we will receive his mercy, and we will find grace to help us when we need it most.

5 Every high priest is a man chosen to represent other people in their dealings with God. He presents their gifts to God and offers sacrifices for their sins. ²And he is able to deal gently with ignorant and wayward people because he himself is subject to the same weaknesses. ³That is why he must offer sacrifices for his own sins as well as theirs.

⁴And no one can become a high priest simply because he wants such an honor. He must be called by God for this work, just as Aaron was. ⁵That is why Christ did not honor himself by assuming he could become High Priest. No, he was chosen by God, who said to him,

"You are my Son.
Today I have become your Father.*"

⁶And in another passage God said to him,

"You are a priest forever in the order of
Melchizedek."*

⁷While Jesus was here on earth, he offered prayers and pleadings, with a loud cry and tears, to the one who could rescue him from death. And God heard his prayers because of

his deep reverence for God. ⁸Even though Jesus was God's Son, he learned obedience from the things he suffered. ⁹In this way, God qualified him as a perfect High Priest, and he became the source of eternal salvation for all those who obey him. ¹⁰And God designated him to be a High Priest in the order of Melchizedek.

A Call to Spiritual Growth

¹¹There is much more we would like to say about this, but it is difficult to explain, especially since you are spiritually dull and don't seem to listen. ¹²You have been believers so long now that you ought to be teaching others. Instead, you need someone to teach you again the basic things about God's word.* You are like babies who need milk and cannot eat solid food. ¹³For someone who lives on milk is still an infant and doesn't know how to do what is right. ¹⁴Solid food is for those who are mature, who through training have the skill to recognize the difference between right and wrong.

6 So let us stop going over the basic teachings about Christ again and again. Let us go on instead and become mature in our understanding. Surely we don't need to start again with the fundamental importance of repenting from evil deeds* and placing our faith in God. ²You don't need further instruction about baptisms, the laying on of hands, the resurrection of the dead, and eternal judgment. ³And so, God willing, we will move forward to further understanding.

⁴For it is impossible to bring back to repentance those who were once enlightened—those who have experienced the good things of heaven and shared in the Holy Spirit, ⁵who have tasted the goodness of the word of God and the power of the age to come—⁶and who then turn away from God. It is impossible to bring such people back to repentance; by rejecting the Son of God, they themselves are nailing him to the cross once again and holding him up to public shame.

⁷When the ground soaks up the falling rain and bears a good crop for the farmer, it has God's blessing. ⁸But if a field bears thorns and thistles, it is useless. The farmer will soon condemn that field and burn it.

⁹Dear friends, even though we are talking this way, we really don't believe it applies to you. We are confident that you are meant for

---

4:9 Or *a Sabbath rest.*   5:5 Or *Today I reveal you as my Son.* Ps 2:7.   5:6 Ps 110:4.   5:12 Or *about the oracles of God.*   6:1 Greek *from dead works.*

better things, things that come with salvation. ¹⁰For God is not unjust. He will not forget how hard you have worked for him and how you have shown your love to him by caring for other believers,* as you still do. ¹¹Our great desire is that you will keep on loving others as long as life lasts, in order to make certain that what you hope for will come true. ¹²Then you will not become spiritually dull and indifferent. Instead, you will follow the example of those who are going to inherit God's promises because of their faith and endurance.

God's Promises Bring Hope

¹³For example, there was God's promise to Abraham. Since there was no one greater to swear by, God took an oath in his own name, saying:

¹⁴ "I will certainly bless you,
and I will multiply your descendants
beyond number."*

¹⁵Then Abraham waited patiently, and he received what God had promised.

¹⁶Now when people take an oath, they call on someone greater than themselves to hold them to it. And without any question that oath is binding. ¹⁷God also bound himself with an oath, so that those who received the promise could be perfectly sure that he would never change his mind. ¹⁸So God has given both his promise and his oath. These two things are unchangeable because it is impossible for God to lie. Therefore, we who have fled to him for refuge can have great confidence as we hold to the hope that lies before us. ¹⁹This hope is a strong and trustworthy anchor for our souls. It leads us through the curtain into God's inner sanctuary. ²⁰Jesus has already gone in there for us. He has become our eternal High Priest in the order of Melchizedek.

Melchizedek Is Greater Than Abraham

7 This Melchizedek was king of the city of Salem and also a priest of God Most High. When Abraham was returning home after winning a great battle against the kings, Melchizedek met him and blessed him. ²Then Abraham took a tenth of all he had captured in battle and gave it to Melchizedek. The name Melchizedek means "king of justice," and king of Salem means "king of peace." ³There is no record of his father or mother or any of his ancestors— no beginning or end to his life. He remains a priest forever, resembling the Son of God.

⁴Consider then how great this Melchizedek was. Even Abraham, the great patriarch of Israel, recognized this by giving him a tenth of what he had taken in battle. ⁵Now the law of Moses required that the priests, who are descendants of Levi, must collect a tithe from the rest of the people of Israel,* who are also descendants of Abraham. ⁶But Melchizedek, who was not a descendant of Levi, collected a tenth from Abraham. And Melchizedek placed a blessing upon Abraham, the one who had already received the promises of God. ⁷And without question, the person who has the power to give a blessing is greater than the one who is blessed.

⁸The priests who collect tithes are men who die, so Melchizedek is greater than they are, because we are told that he lives on. ⁹In addition, we might even say that these Levites— the ones who collect the tithe—paid a tithe to Melchizedek when their ancestor Abraham paid a tithe to him. ¹⁰For although Levi wasn't born yet, the seed from which he came was in Abraham's body when Melchizedek collected the tithe from him.

¹¹So if the priesthood of Levi, on which the law was based, could have achieved the perfection God intended, why did God need to establish a different priesthood, with a priest in the order of Melchizedek instead of the order of Levi and Aaron?* ¹²And if the priesthood is changed, the law must also be changed to permit it. ¹³For the priest we are talking about belongs to a different tribe, whose members have never served at the altar as priests. ¹⁴What I mean is, our Lord came from the tribe of Judah, and Moses never mentioned priests coming from that tribe.

Jesus Is like Melchizedek

¹⁵This change has been made very clear since a different priest, who is like Melchizedek, has appeared. ¹⁶Jesus became a priest, not by meeting the physical requirement of belonging to the tribe of Levi, but by the power of a life that cannot be destroyed. ¹⁷And the psalmist pointed this out when he prophesied,

"You are a priest forever in the order of
Melchizedek."*

¹⁸Yes, the old requirement about the priesthood was set aside because it was weak and useless. ¹⁹For the law never made anything perfect. But now we have confidence in a better hope, through which we draw near to God.

6:10 Greek *for God's holy people.*   6:14 Gen 22:17.   7:5 Greek *from their brothers.*   7:11 Greek *the order of Aaron?*   7:17 Ps 110:4.

²⁰This new system was established with a solemn oath. Aaron's descendants became priests without such an oath, ²¹but there was an oath regarding Jesus. For God said to him,

"The LORD has taken an oath and will not
break his vow:
'You are a priest forever.'"*

²²Because of this oath, Jesus is the one who guarantees this better covenant with God.

²³There were many priests under the old system, for death prevented them from remaining in office. ²⁴But because Jesus lives forever, his priesthood lasts forever. ²⁵Therefore he is able, once and forever, to save* those who come to God through him. He lives forever to intercede with God on their behalf.

²⁶He is the kind of high priest we need because he is holy and blameless, unstained by sin. He has been set apart from sinners and has been given the highest place of honor in heaven.* ²⁷Unlike those other high priests, he does not need to offer sacrifices every day. They did this for their own sins first and then for the sins of the people. But Jesus did this once for all when he offered himself as the sacrifice for the people's sins. ²⁸The law appointed high priests who were limited by human weakness. But after the law was given, God appointed his Son with an oath, and his Son has been made the perfect High Priest forever.

Christ Is Our High Priest

8 Here is the main point: We have a High Priest who sat down in the place of honor beside the throne of the majestic God in heaven. ²There he ministers in the heavenly Tabernacle,* the true place of worship that was built by the Lord and not by human hands.

³And since every high priest is required to offer gifts and sacrifices, our High Priest must make an offering, too. ⁴If he were here on earth, he would not even be a priest, since there already are priests who offer the gifts required by the law. ⁵They serve in a system of worship that is only a copy, a shadow of the real one in heaven. For when Moses was getting ready to build the Tabernacle, God gave him this warning: "Be sure that you make everything according to the pattern I have shown you here on the mountain."*

⁶But now Jesus, our High Priest, has been given a ministry that is far superior to the old priesthood, for he is the one who mediates for us a far better covenant with God, based on better promises.

⁷If the first covenant had been faultless, there would have been no need for a second covenant to replace it. ⁸But when God found fault with the people, he said:

"The day is coming, says the LORD,
when I will make a new covenant
with the people of Israel and Judah.
⁹ This covenant will not be like the one
I made with their ancestors
when I took them by the hand
and led them out of the land of
Egypt.
They did not remain faithful to my
covenant,
so I turned my back on them, says the
LORD.
¹⁰ But this is the new covenant I will make
with the people of Israel on that day,*
says the LORD:
I will put my laws in their minds,
and I will write them on their hearts.
I will be their God,
and they will be my people.
¹¹ And they will not need to teach their
neighbors,
nor will they need to teach their
relatives,*
saying, 'You should know the LORD.'
For everyone, from the least to the
greatest,
will know me already.
¹² And I will forgive their wickedness,
and I will never again remember their
sins."*

¹³When God speaks of a "new" covenant, it means he has made the first one obsolete. It is now out of date and will soon disappear.

Old Rules about Worship

9 That first covenant between God and Israel had regulations for worship and a place of worship here on earth. ²There were two rooms in that Tabernacle.* In the first room were a lampstand, a table, and sacred loaves of bread on the table. This room was called the Holy Place. ³Then there was a curtain, and behind the curtain was the second room* called the

Most Holy Place. ⁴In that room were a gold incense altar and a wooden chest called the Ark of the Covenant, which was covered with gold on all sides. Inside the Ark were a gold jar containing manna, Aaron's staff that sprouted leaves, and the stone tablets of the covenant. ⁵Above the Ark were the cherubim of divine glory, whose wings stretched out over the Ark's cover, the place of atonement. But we cannot explain these things in detail now.

⁶When these things were all in place, the priests regularly entered the first room* as they performed their religious duties. ⁷But only the high priest ever entered the Most Holy Place, and only once a year. And he always offered blood for his own sins and for the sins the people had committed in ignorance. ⁸By these regulations the Holy Spirit revealed that the entrance to the Most Holy Place was not freely open as long as the Tabernacle* and the system it represented were still in use.

⁹This is an illustration pointing to the present time. For the gifts and sacrifices that the priests offer are not able to cleanse the consciences of the people who bring them. ¹⁰For that old system deals only with food and drink and various cleansing ceremonies—physical regulations that were in effect only until a better system could be established.

Christ Is the Perfect Sacrifice

¹¹So Christ has now become the High Priest over all the good things that have come.* He has entered that greater, more perfect Tabernacle in heaven, which was not made by human hands and is not part of this created world. ¹²With his own blood—not the blood of goats and calves—he entered the Most Holy Place once for all time and secured our redemption forever.

¹³Under the old system, the blood of goats and bulls and the ashes of a heifer could cleanse people's bodies from ceremonial impurity. ¹⁴Just think how much more the blood of Christ will purify our consciences from sinful deeds* so that we can worship the living God. For by the power of the eternal Spirit, Christ offered himself to God as a perfect sacrifice for our sins. ¹⁵That is why he is the one who mediates a new covenant between God and people, so that all who are called can receive the eternal inheritance God has promised them. For Christ died to set them free from the penalty of the sins they had committed under that first covenant.

¹⁶Now when someone leaves a will,* it is necessary to prove that the person who made it is dead.* ¹⁷The will goes into effect only after the person's death. While the person who made it is still alive, the will cannot be put into effect.

¹⁸That is why even the first covenant was put into effect with the blood of an animal. ¹⁹For after Moses had read each of God's commandments to all the people, he took the blood of calves and goats,* along with water, and sprinkled both the book of God's law and all the people, using hyssop branches and scarlet wool. ²⁰Then he said, "This blood confirms the covenant God has made with you."* ²¹And in the same way, he sprinkled blood on the Tabernacle and on everything used for worship. ²²In fact, according to the law of Moses, nearly everything was purified with blood. For without the shedding of blood, there is no forgiveness.

²³That is why the Tabernacle and everything in it, which were copies of things in heaven, had to be purified by the blood of animals. But the real things in heaven had to be purified with far better sacrifices than the blood of animals.

²⁴For Christ did not enter into a holy place made with human hands, which was only a copy of the true one in heaven. He entered into heaven itself to appear now before God on our behalf. ²⁵And he did not enter heaven to offer himself again and again, like the high priest here on earth who enters the Most Holy Place year after year with the blood of an animal. ²⁶If that had been necessary, Christ would have had to die again and again, ever since the world began. But now, once for all time, he has appeared at the end of the age* to remove sin by his own death as a sacrifice.

²⁷And just as each person is destined to die once and after that comes judgment, ²⁸so also Christ was offered once for all time as a sacrifice to take away the sins of many people. He will come again, not to deal with our sins, but to bring salvation to all who are eagerly waiting for him.

Christ's Sacrifice Once for All

10 The old system under the law of Moses was only a shadow, a dim preview of the good things to come, not the good things

---

9:6 Greek *first tent.* 9:8 Or *the first room;* Greek reads *the first tent.* 9:11 Some manuscripts read *that are about to come.* 9:14 Greek *from dead works.* 9:16a Or *covenant;* also in 9:17. 9:16b Or *Now when someone makes a covenant, it is necessary to ratify it with the death of a sacrifice.* 9:19 Some manuscripts do not include *and goats.* 9:20 Exod 24:8. 9:26 Greek *the ages.*

themselves. The sacrifices under that system were repeated again and again, year after year, but they were never able to provide perfect cleansing for those who came to worship. [2]If they could have provided perfect cleansing, the sacrifices would have stopped, for the worshipers would have been purified once for all time, and their feelings of guilt would have disappeared.

[3]But instead, those sacrifices actually reminded them of their sins year after year. [4]For it is not possible for the blood of bulls and goats to take away sins. [5]That is why, when Christ* came into the world, he said to God,

"You did not want animal sacrifices or sin offerings.
But you have given me a body to offer.
[6] You were not pleased with burnt offerings or other offerings for sin.
[7] Then I said, 'Look, I have come to do your will, O God—
as is written about me in the Scriptures.'"*

[8]First, Christ said, "You did not want animal sacrifices or sin offerings or burnt offerings or other offerings for sin, nor were you pleased with them" (though they are required by the law of Moses). [9]Then he said, "Look, I have come to do your will." He cancels the first covenant in order to put the second into effect. [10]For God's will was for us to be made holy by the sacrifice of the body of Jesus Christ, once for all time.

[11]Under the old covenant, the priest stands and ministers before the altar day after day, offering the same sacrifices again and again, which can never take away sins. [12]But our High Priest offered himself to God as a single sacrifice for sins, good for all time. Then he sat down in the place of honor at God's right hand. [13]There he waits until his enemies are humbled and made a footstool under his feet. [14]For by that one offering he forever made perfect those who are being made holy.

[15]And the Holy Spirit also testifies that this is so. For he says,

[16] "This is the new covenant I will make with my people on that day,* says the LORD:
I will put my laws in their hearts, and I will write them on their minds."*

[17]Then he says,

"I will never again remember their sins and lawless deeds."*

[18]And when sins have been forgiven, there is no need to offer any more sacrifices.

A Call to Persevere

[19]And so, dear brothers and sisters,* we can boldly enter heaven's Most Holy Place because of the blood of Jesus. [20]By his death,* Jesus opened a new and life-giving way through the curtain into the Most Holy Place. [21]And since we have a great High Priest who rules over God's house, [22]let us go right into the presence of God with sincere hearts fully trusting him. For our guilty consciences have been sprinkled with Christ's blood to make us clean, and our bodies have been washed with pure water.

[23]Let us hold tightly without wavering to the hope we affirm, for God can be trusted to keep his promise. [24]Let us think of ways to motivate one another to acts of love and good works. [25]And let us not neglect our meeting together, as some people do, but encourage one another, especially now that the day of his return is drawing near.

[26]Dear friends, if we deliberately continue sinning after we have received knowledge of the truth, there is no longer any sacrifice that will cover these sins. [27]There is only the terrible expectation of God's judgment and the raging fire that will consume his enemies. [28]For anyone who refused to obey the law of Moses was put to death without mercy on the testimony of two or three witnesses. [29]Just think how much worse the punishment will be for those who have trampled on the Son of God, and have treated the blood of the covenant, which made us holy, as if it were common and unholy, and have insulted and disdained the Holy Spirit who brings God's mercy to us. [30]For we know the one who said,

"I will take revenge.
I will pay them back."*

He also said,

"The LORD will judge his own people."*

[31]It is a terrible thing to fall into the hands of the living God.

10:5 Greek *he;* also in 10:8.   10:5-7 Ps 40:6-8 (Greek version).   10:16a Greek *after those days.*   10:16b Jer 31:33a.
10:17 Jer 31:34b.   10:19 Greek *brothers.*   10:20 Greek *Through his flesh.*   10:30a Deut 32:35.   10:30b Deut 32:36.

32Think back on those early days when you first learned about Christ.* Remember how you remained faithful even though it meant terrible suffering. 33Sometimes you were exposed to public ridicule and were beaten, and sometimes you helped others who were suffering the same things. 34You suffered along with those who were thrown into jail, and when all you owned was taken from you, you accepted it with joy. You knew there were better things waiting for you that will last forever.

35So do not throw away this confident trust in the Lord. Remember the great reward it brings you! 36Patient endurance is what you need now, so that you will continue to do God's will. Then you will receive all that he has promised.

37 "For in just a little while,
　　the Coming One will come and not
　　　delay.
38 And my righteous ones will live by faith.*
　　But I will take no pleasure in anyone
　　　who turns away."*

39But we are not like those who turn away from God to their own destruction. We are the faithful ones, whose souls will be saved.

Great Examples of Faith

11 Faith shows the reality of what we hope for; it is the evidence of things we cannot see. 2Through their faith, the people in days of old earned a good reputation.

3By faith we understand that the entire universe was formed at God's command, that what we now see did not come from anything that can be seen.

4It was by faith that Abel brought a more acceptable offering to God than Cain did. Abel's offering gave evidence that he was a righteous man, and God showed his approval of his gifts. Although Abel is long dead, he still speaks to us by his example of faith.

5It was by faith that Enoch was taken up to heaven without dying—"he disappeared, because God took him."* For before he was taken up, he was known as a person who pleased God. 6And it is impossible to please God without faith. Anyone who wants to come to him must believe that God exists and that he rewards those who sincerely seek him.

7It was by faith that Noah built a large boat to save his family from the flood. He obeyed God, who warned him about things that had never happened before. By his faith Noah condemned the rest of the world, and he received the righteousness that comes by faith.

8It was by faith that Abraham obeyed when God called him to leave home and go to another land that God would give him as his inheritance. He went without knowing where he was going. 9And even when he reached the land God promised him, he lived there by faith—for he was like a foreigner, living in tents. And so did Isaac and Jacob, who inherited the same promise. 10Abraham was confidently looking forward to a city with eternal foundations, a city designed and built by God.

11It was by faith that even Sarah was able to have a child, though she was barren and was too old. She believed* that God would keep his promise. 12And so a whole nation came from this one man who was as good as dead—a nation with so many people that, like the stars in the sky and the sand on the seashore, there is no way to count them.

13All these people died still believing what God had promised them. They did not receive what was promised, but they saw it all from a distance and welcomed it. They agreed that they were foreigners and nomads here on earth. 14Obviously people who say such things are looking forward to a country they can call their own. 15If they had longed for the country they came from, they could have gone back. 16But they were looking for a better place, a heavenly homeland. That is why God is not ashamed to be called their God, for he has prepared a city for them.

17It was by faith that Abraham offered Isaac as a sacrifice when God was testing him. Abraham, who had received God's promises, was ready to sacrifice his only son, Isaac, 18even though God had told him, "Isaac is the son through whom your descendants will be counted."* 19Abraham reasoned that if Isaac died, God was able to bring him back to life again. And in a sense, Abraham did receive his son back from the dead.

20It was by faith that Isaac promised blessings for the future to his sons, Jacob and Esau.

21It was by faith that Jacob, when he was old and dying, blessed each of Joseph's sons and bowed in worship as he leaned on his staff.

22It was by faith that Joseph, when he was

10:32 Greek when you were first enlightened.   10:38 Or my righteous ones will live by their faithfulness; Greek reads my righteous one will live by faith.   10:37-38 Hab 2:3-4.   11:5 Gen 5:24.   11:11 Or It was by faith that he [Abraham] was able to have a child, even though Sarah was barren and he was too old. He believed.   11:18 Gen 21:12.

about to die, said confidently that the people of Israel would leave Egypt. He even commanded them to take his bones with them when they left.

23It was by faith that Moses' parents hid him for three months when he was born. They saw that God had given them an unusual child, and they were not afraid to disobey the king's command.

24It was by faith that Moses, when he grew up, refused to be called the son of Pharaoh's daughter. 25He chose to share the oppression of God's people instead of enjoying the fleeting pleasures of sin. 26He thought it was better to suffer for the sake of Christ than to own the treasures of Egypt, for he was looking ahead to his great reward. 27It was by faith that Moses left the land of Egypt, not fearing the king's anger. He kept right on going because he kept his eyes on the one who is invisible. 28It was by faith that Moses commanded the people of Israel to keep the Passover and to sprinkle blood on the doorposts so that the angel of death would not kill their firstborn sons.

29It was by faith that the people of Israel went right through the Red Sea as though they were on dry ground. But when the Egyptians tried to follow, they were all drowned.

30It was by faith that the people of Israel marched around Jericho for seven days, and the walls came crashing down.

31It was by faith that Rahab the prostitute was not destroyed with the people in her city who refused to obey God. For she had given a friendly welcome to the spies.

32How much more do I need to say? It would take too long to recount the stories of the faith of Gideon, Barak, Samson, Jephthah, David, Samuel, and all the prophets. 33By faith these people overthrew kingdoms, ruled with justice, and received what God had promised them. They shut the mouths of lions, 34quenched the flames of fire, and escaped death by the edge of the sword. Their weakness was turned to strength. They became strong in battle and put whole armies to flight. 35Women received their loved ones back again from death.

But others were tortured, refusing to turn from God in order to be set free. They placed their hope in a better life after the resurrection. 36Some were jeered at, and their backs were cut open with whips. Others were chained in prisons. 37Some died by stoning, some were sawed

in half,* and others were killed with the sword. Some went about wearing skins of sheep and goats, destitute and oppressed and mistreated. 38They were too good for this world, wandering over deserts and mountains, hiding in caves and holes in the ground.

39All these people earned a good reputation because of their faith, yet none of them received all that God had promised. 40For God had something better in mind for us, so that they would not reach perfection without us.

God's Discipline Proves His Love

12 Therefore, since we are surrounded by such a huge crowd of witnesses to the life of faith, let us strip off every weight that slows us down, especially the sin that so easily trips us up. And let us run with endurance the race God has set before us. 2We do this by keeping our eyes on Jesus, the champion who initiates and perfects our faith.* Because of the joy* awaiting him, he endured the cross, disregarding its shame. Now he is seated in the place of honor beside God's throne. 3Think of all the hostility he endured from sinful people;* then you won't become weary and give up. 4After all, you have not yet given your lives in your struggle against sin.

5And have you forgotten the encouraging words God spoke to you as his children?* He said,

"My child,* don't make light of the LORD's
    discipline,
  and don't give up when he corrects you.
 6 For the LORD disciplines those he loves,
    and he punishes each one he accepts as
      his child."*

7As you endure this divine discipline, remember that God is treating you as his own children. Who ever heard of a child who is never disciplined by its father? 8If God doesn't discipline you as he does all of his children, it means that you are illegitimate and are not really his children at all. 9Since we respected our earthly fathers who disciplined us, shouldn't we submit even more to the discipline of the Father of our spirits, and live forever?*

10For our earthly fathers disciplined us for a few years, doing the best they knew how. But God's discipline is always good for us, so that we might share in his holiness. 11No discipline

---

11:37 Some manuscripts add *some were tested.*   12:2a Or *Jesus, the originator and perfecter of our faith.*   12:2b Or *Instead of the joy.*
12:3 Some manuscripts read *Think of how people hurt themselves by opposing him.*   12:5a Greek *sons;* also in 12:7, 8.   12:5b Greek
son; also in 12:6, 7.   12:5-6 Prov 3:11-12 (Greek version).   12:9 Or *and really live?*

is enjoyable while it is happening—it's painful! But afterward there will be a peaceful harvest of right living for those who are trained in this way.

¹²So take a new grip with your tired hands and strengthen your weak knees. ¹³Mark out a straight path for your feet so that those who are weak and lame will not fall but become strong.

A Call to Listen to God

¹⁴Work at living in peace with everyone, and work at living a holy life, for those who are not holy will not see the Lord. ¹⁵Look after each other so that none of you fails to receive the grace of God. Watch out that no poisonous root of bitterness grows up to trouble you, corrupting many. ¹⁶Make sure that no one is immoral or godless like Esau, who traded his birthright as the firstborn son for a single meal. ¹⁷You know that afterward, when he wanted his father's blessing, he was rejected. It was too late for repentance, even though he begged with bitter tears.

¹⁸You have not come to a physical mountain,* to a place of flaming fire, darkness, gloom, and whirlwind, as the Israelites did at Mount Sinai. ¹⁹For they heard an awesome trumpet blast and a voice so terrible that they begged God to stop speaking. ²⁰They staggered back under God's command: "If even an animal touches the mountain, it must be stoned to death."* ²¹Moses himself was so frightened at the sight that he said, "I am terrified and trembling."*

²²No, you have come to Mount Zion, to the city of the living God, the heavenly Jerusalem, and to countless thousands of angels in a joyful gathering. ²³You have come to the assembly of God's firstborn children, whose names are written in heaven. You have come to God himself, who is the judge over all things. You have come to the spirits of the righteous ones in heaven who have now been made perfect. ²⁴You have come to Jesus, the one who mediates the new covenant between God and people, and to the sprinkled blood, which speaks of forgiveness instead of crying out for vengeance like the blood of Abel.

²⁵Be careful that you do not refuse to listen to the One who is speaking. For if the people of Israel did not escape when they refused to listen to Moses, the earthly messenger, we will certainly not escape if we reject the One who speaks to us from heaven! ²⁶When God spoke from Mount Sinai his voice shook the earth, but now he makes another promise: "Once again I will shake not only the earth but the heavens also."* ²⁷This means that all of creation will be shaken and removed, so that only unshakable things will remain.

²⁸Since we are receiving a Kingdom that is unshakable, let us be thankful and please God by worshiping him with holy fear and awe. ²⁹For our God is a devouring fire.

Concluding Words

13 Keep on loving each other as brothers and sisters.* ²Don't forget to show hospitality to strangers, for some who have done this have entertained angels without realizing it! ³Remember those in prison, as if you were there yourself. Remember also those being mistreated, as if you felt their pain in your own bodies.

⁴Give honor to marriage, and remain faithful to one another in marriage. God will surely judge people who are immoral and those who commit adultery.

⁵Don't love money; be satisfied with what you have. For God has said,

"I will never fail you.
     I will never abandon you."*

⁶So we can say with confidence,

"The LORD is my helper,
     so I will have no fear.
     What can mere people do to me?"*

⁷Remember your leaders who taught you the word of God. Think of all the good that has come from their lives, and follow the example of their faith.

⁸Jesus Christ is the same yesterday, today, and forever. ⁹So do not be attracted by strange, new ideas. Your strength comes from God's grace, not from rules about food, which don't help those who follow them.

¹⁰We have an altar from which the priests in the Tabernacle* have no right to eat. ¹¹Under the old system, the high priest brought the blood of animals into the Holy Place as a sacrifice for sin, and the bodies of the animals were burned outside the camp. ¹²So also Jesus suffered and died outside the city gates to make his people holy by means of his own blood. ¹³So let us go out to him, outside the camp, and bear the disgrace he bore. ¹⁴For this world is not our

---

12:18 Greek *to something that can be touched.*   12:20 Exod 19:13.   12:21 Deut 9:19.   12:26 Hag 2:6.   13:1 Greek *Continue in brotherly love.*   13:5 Deut 31:6, 8.   13:6 Ps 118:6.   13:10 Or *tent.*

permanent home; we are looking forward to a home yet to come.

15Therefore, let us offer through Jesus a continual sacrifice of praise to God, proclaiming our allegiance to his name. 16And don't forget to do good and to share with those in need. These are the sacrifices that please God.

17Obey your spiritual leaders, and do what they say. Their work is to watch over your souls, and they are accountable to God. Give them reason to do this with joy and not with sorrow. That would certainly not be for your benefit.

18Pray for us, for our conscience is clear and we want to live honorably in everything we do. 19And especially pray that I will be able to come back to you soon.

20 Now may the God of peace—
   who brought up from the dead our Lord
      Jesus,

the great Shepherd of the sheep,
   and ratified an eternal covenant with his
      blood—
21 may he equip you with all you need
   for doing his will.
May he produce in you,*
   through the power of Jesus Christ,
every good thing that is pleasing to him.
   All glory to him forever and ever! Amen.

22I urge you, dear brothers and sisters,* to pay attention to what I have written in this brief exhortation.

23I want you to know that our brother Timothy has been released from jail. If he comes here soon, I will bring him with me to see you.

24Greet all your leaders and all the believers there.* The believers from Italy send you their greetings.

25May God's grace be with you all.

13:21 Some manuscripts read *in us.*   13:22 Greek *brothers.*   13:24 Greek *all of God's holy people.*

James

ACTIONS SPEAK LOUDER than words. That old adage is reflected well in the book of James. This book attacks the notion that becoming a Christian is simply a matter of assenting to a few spiritual truths without experiencing any real change in behavior or thought. James was a leader in the church at Jerusalem, so his book has a very Jewish flavor. It contains many short, proverbial sayings and resembles the teachings of Jesus, especially the Sermon on the Mount. James addressed several matters in which Christian behavior should reflect Christian faith. He discussed pride, discrimination, greed, lust, hypocrisy, worldliness, and slander. James used several analogies to show how true faith must evidence itself in good works. He compared believers to fruit trees bearing only the kind of fruit that belongs to them. Because of the book's emphasis on good works, it is a very practical book regarding the Christian life.

■ **Author:** James, a half-brother of Jesus, a leader in the Jerusalem church

■ **Date Written:** Probably around AD 49, prior to the Jerusalem Council held in AD 50

■ **Purpose:** To correct the false belief that a person can have faith without a change of behavior and to give practical instruction regarding the Christian life

■ **Themes:** Faith and deeds, trials of faith, controlling the tongue, the dangers of wealth

■ **Outline**
1:1-27 The true life of faith
2:1-13 The social implications of faith
2:14-26 Faith and works
3:1-18 A discourse on controlling the tongue
4:1-17 Practical exhortations
5:1-6 The rich rebuked
5:7-20 Concluding exhortations

Greetings from James

1 This letter is from James, a slave of God and of the Lord Jesus Christ.

I am writing to the "twelve tribes"—Jewish believers scattered abroad.

Greetings!

Faith and Endurance

²Dear brothers and sisters,* when troubles of any kind come your way, consider it an opportunity for great joy. ³For you know that when your faith is tested, your endurance has a chance to grow. ⁴So let it grow, for when your endurance is fully developed, you will be perfect and complete, needing nothing.

⁵If you need wisdom, ask our generous God, and he will give it to you. He will not rebuke you for asking. ⁶But when you ask him, be sure that your faith is in God alone. Do not waver, for a person with divided loyalty is as unsettled as a wave of the sea that is blown and tossed by the wind. ⁷Such people should not expect to receive anything from the Lord. ⁸Their loyalty is divided between God and the world, and they are unstable in everything they do.

⁹Believers who are* poor have something to boast about, for God has honored them. ¹⁰And those who are rich should boast that God has humbled them. They will fade away like a little flower in the field. ¹¹The hot sun rises and the grass withers; the little flower droops and falls, and its beauty fades away. In the same way, the rich will fade away with all of their achievements.

¹²God blesses those who patiently endure testing and temptation. Afterward they will receive the crown of life that God has promised to those who love him. ¹³And remember, when you are being tempted, do not say, "God is tempting me." God is never tempted to do wrong,* and he

1:2 Greek *brothers;* also in 1:16, 19. 1:9 Greek *The brother who is.* 1:13 Or *God should not be put to a test by evil people.*

never tempts anyone else. ¹⁴Temptation comes from our own desires, which entice us and drag us away. ¹⁵These desires give birth to sinful actions. And when sin is allowed to grow, it gives birth to death.

¹⁶So don't be misled, my dear brothers and sisters. ¹⁷Whatever is good and perfect is a gift coming down to us from God our Father, who created all the lights in the heavens.* He never changes or casts a shifting shadow.* ¹⁸He chose to give birth to us by giving us his true word. And we, out of all creation, became his prized possession.*

Listening and Doing

¹⁹Understand this, my dear brothers and sisters: You must all be quick to listen, slow to speak, and slow to get angry. ²⁰Human anger* does not produce the righteousness* God desires. ²¹So get rid of all the filth and evil in your lives, and humbly accept the word God has planted in your hearts, for it has the power to save your souls.

²²But don't just listen to God's word. You must do what it says. Otherwise, you are only fooling yourselves. ²³For if you listen to the word and don't obey, it is like glancing at your face in a mirror. ²⁴You see yourself, walk away, and forget what you look like. ²⁵But if you look carefully into the perfect law that sets you free, and if you do what it says and don't forget what you heard, then God will bless you for doing it.

²⁶If you claim to be religious but don't control your tongue, you are fooling yourself, and your religion is worthless. ²⁷Pure and genuine religion in the sight of God the Father means caring for orphans and widows in their distress and refusing to let the world corrupt you.

A Warning against Prejudice

2 My dear brothers and sisters,* how can you claim to have faith in our glorious Lord Jesus Christ if you favor some people over others?

²For example, suppose someone comes into your meeting* dressed in fancy clothes and expensive jewelry, and another comes in who is poor and dressed in dirty clothes. ³If you give special attention and a good seat to the rich person, but you say to the poor one, "You can stand over there, or else sit on the floor"—well, ⁴doesn't this discrimination show that your judgments are guided by evil motives?

⁵Listen to me, dear brothers and sisters. Hasn't God chosen the poor in this world to be rich in faith? Aren't they the ones who will inherit the Kingdom he promised to those who love him? ⁶But you dishonor the poor! Isn't it the rich who oppress you and drag you into court? ⁷Aren't they the ones who slander Jesus Christ, whose noble name* you bear?

⁸Yes indeed, it is good when you obey the royal law as found in the Scriptures: "Love your neighbor as yourself."* ⁹But if you favor some people over others, you are committing a sin. You are guilty of breaking the law.

¹⁰For the person who keeps all of the laws except one is as guilty as a person who has broken all of God's laws. ¹¹For the same God who said, "You must not commit adultery," also said, "You must not murder."* So if you murder someone but do not commit adultery, you have still broken the law.

¹²So whatever you say or whatever you do, remember that you will be judged by the law that sets you free. ¹³There will be no mercy for those who have not shown mercy to others. But if you have been merciful, God will be merciful when he judges you.

Faith without Good Deeds Is Dead

¹⁴What good is it, dear brothers and sisters, if you say you have faith but don't show it by your actions? Can that kind of faith save anyone? ¹⁵Suppose you see a brother or sister who has no food or clothing, ¹⁶and you say, "Good-bye and have a good day; stay warm and eat well"— but then you don't give that person any food or clothing. What good does that do?

¹⁷So you see, faith by itself isn't enough. Unless it produces good deeds, it is dead and useless.

¹⁸Now someone may argue, "Some people have faith; others have good deeds." But I say, "How can you show me your faith if you don't have good deeds? I will show you my faith by my good deeds."

¹⁹You say you have faith, for you believe that there is one God.* Good for you! Even the demons believe this, and they tremble in terror. ²⁰How foolish! Can't you see that faith without good deeds is useless?

²¹Don't you remember that our ancestor Abraham was shown to be right with God by his actions when he offered his son Isaac on

---

1:17a Greek *from above, from the Father of lights.*   1:17b Some manuscripts read *He never changes, as a shifting shadow does.*
1:18 Greek *we became a kind of firstfruit of his creatures.*   1:20a Greek *A man's anger.*   1:20b Or *the justice.*   2:1 Greek *brothers;* also in 2:5, 14.   2:2 Greek *your synagogue.*   2:7 Greek *slander the noble name.*   2:8 Lev 19:18.   2:11 Exod 20:13-14; Deut 5:17-18.
2:19 Some manuscripts read *that God is one;* see Deut 6:4.

the altar? 22You see, his faith and his actions worked together. His actions made his faith complete. 23And so it happened just as the Scriptures say: "Abraham believed God, and God counted him as righteous because of his faith."* He was even called the friend of God.* 24So you see, we are shown to be right with God by what we do, not by faith alone.

25Rahab the prostitute is another example. She was shown to be right with God by her actions when she hid those messengers and sent them safely away by a different road. 26Just as the body is dead without breath,* so also faith is dead without good works.

Controlling the Tongue

3 Dear brothers and sisters,* not many of you should become teachers in the church, for we who teach will be judged more strictly. 2Indeed, we all make many mistakes. For if we could control our tongues, we would be perfect and could also control ourselves in every other way.

3We can make a large horse go wherever we want by means of a small bit in its mouth. 4And a small rudder makes a huge ship turn wherever the pilot chooses to go, even though the winds are strong. 5In the same way, the tongue is a small thing that makes grand speeches.

But a tiny spark can set a great forest on fire. 6And among all the parts of the body, the tongue is a flame of fire. It is a whole world of wickedness, corrupting your entire body. It can set your whole life on fire, for it is set on fire by hell itself.*

7People can tame all kinds of animals, birds, reptiles, and fish, 8but no one can tame the tongue. It is restless and evil, full of deadly poison. 9Sometimes it praises our Lord and Father, and sometimes it curses those who have been made in the image of God. 10And so blessing and cursing come pouring out of the same mouth. Surely, my brothers and sisters, this is not right! 11Does a spring of water bubble out with both fresh water and bitter water? 12Does a fig tree produce olives, or a grapevine produce figs? No, and you can't draw fresh water from a salty spring.*

True Wisdom Comes from God

13If you are wise and understand God's ways, prove it by living an honorable life, doing good works with the humility that comes from wisdom. 14But if you are bitterly jealous and there is selfish ambition in your heart, don't cover up the truth with boasting and lying. 15For jealousy and selfishness are not God's kind of wisdom. Such things are earthly, unspiritual, and demonic. 16For wherever there is jealousy and selfish ambition, there you will find disorder and evil of every kind.

17But the wisdom from above is first of all pure. It is also peace loving, gentle at all times, and willing to yield to others. It is full of mercy and the fruit of good deeds. It shows no favoritism and is always sincere. 18And those who are peacemakers will plant seeds of peace and reap a harvest of righteousness.*

Drawing Close to God

4 What is causing the quarrels and fights among you? Don't they come from the evil desires at war within you? 2You want what you don't have, so you scheme and kill to get it. You are jealous of what others have, but you can't get it, so you fight and wage war to take it away from them. Yet you don't have what you want because you don't ask God for it. 3And even when you ask, you don't get it because your motives are all wrong—you want only what will give you pleasure.

4You adulterers!* Don't you realize that friendship with the world makes you an enemy of God? I say it again: If you want to be a friend of the world, you make yourself an enemy of God. 5Do you think the Scriptures have no meaning? They say that God is passionate that the spirit he has placed within us should be faithful to him.* 6And he gives grace generously. As the Scriptures say,

"God opposes the proud
    but gives grace to the humble."*

7So humble yourselves before God. Resist the devil, and he will flee from you. 8Come close to God, and God will come close to you. Wash your hands, you sinners; purify your hearts, for your loyalty is divided between God and the world. 9Let there be tears for what you have done. Let there be sorrow and deep grief. Let there be sadness instead of laughter, and gloom instead of joy. 10Humble yourselves before the Lord, and he will lift you up in honor.

2:23a Gen 15:6.   2:23b See Isa 41:8.   2:26 Or *without spirit.*   3:1 Greek *brothers;* also in 3:10.   3:6 Or *for it will burn in hell* (Greek *Gehenna*).   3:12 Greek *from salt.*   3:18 Or *of good things,* or *of justice.*   4:4 Greek *You adulteresses!*   4:5 Or *They say that the spirit God has placed within us is filled with envy;* or *They say that the Holy Spirit, whom God has placed within us, opposes our envy.* 4:6 Prov 3:34 (Greek version).

Warning against Judging Others

[11]Don't speak evil against each other, dear brothers and sisters.* If you criticize and judge each other, then you are criticizing and judging God's law. But your job is to obey the law, not to judge whether it applies to you. [12]God alone, who gave the law, is the Judge. He alone has the power to save or to destroy. So what right do you have to judge your neighbor?

Warning about Self-Confidence

[13]Look here, you who say, "Today or tomorrow we are going to a certain town and will stay there a year. We will do business there and make a profit." [14]How do you know what your life will be like tomorrow? Your life is like the morning fog—it's here a little while, then it's gone. [15]What you ought to say is, "If the Lord wants us to, we will live and do this or that." [16]Otherwise you are boasting about your own pretentious plans, and all such boasting is evil.

[17]Remember, it is sin to know what you ought to do and then not do it.

Warning to the Rich

5 Look here, you rich people: Weep and groan with anguish because of all the terrible troubles ahead of you. [2]Your wealth is rotting away, and your fine clothes are moth-eaten rags. [3]Your gold and silver are corroded. The very wealth you were counting on will eat away your flesh like fire. This corroded treasure you have hoarded will testify against you on the day of judgment. [4]For listen! Hear the cries of the field workers whom you have cheated of their pay. The cries of those who harvest your fields have reached the ears of the LORD of Heaven's Armies.

[5]You have spent your years on earth in luxury, satisfying your every desire. You have fattened yourselves for the day of slaughter. [6]You have condemned and killed innocent people,* who do not resist you.*

Patience and Endurance

[7]Dear brothers and sisters,* be patient as you wait for the Lord's return. Consider the farmers who patiently wait for the rains in the fall and in the spring. They eagerly look for the valuable harvest to ripen. [8]You, too, must be patient. Take courage, for the coming of the Lord is near.

[9]Don't grumble about each other, brothers and sisters, or you will be judged. For look—the Judge is standing at the door!

[10]For examples of patience in suffering, dear brothers and sisters, look at the prophets who spoke in the name of the Lord. [11]We give great honor to those who endure under suffering. For instance, you know about Job, a man of great endurance. You can see how the Lord was kind to him at the end, for the Lord is full of tenderness and mercy.

[12]But most of all, my brothers and sisters, never take an oath, by heaven or earth or anything else. Just say a simple yes or no, so that you will not sin and be condemned.

The Power of Prayer

[13]Are any of you suffering hardships? You should pray. Are any of you happy? You should sing praises. [14]Are any of you sick? You should call for the elders of the church to come and pray over you, anointing you with oil in the name of the Lord. [15]Such a prayer offered in faith will heal the sick, and the Lord will make you well. And if you have committed any sins, you will be forgiven.

[16]Confess your sins to each other and pray for each other so that you may be healed. The earnest prayer of a righteous person has great power and produces wonderful results. [17]Elijah was as human as we are, and yet when he prayed earnestly that no rain would fall, none fell for three and a half years! [18]Then, when he prayed again, the sky sent down rain and the earth began to yield its crops.

Restore Wandering Believers

[19]My dear brothers and sisters, if someone among you wanders away from the truth and is brought back, [20]you can be sure that whoever brings the sinner back from wandering will save that person from death and bring about the forgiveness of many sins.

4:11 Greek brothers. 5:6a Or killed the Righteous One. 5:6b Or Don't they resist you? or Doesn't God oppose you? or Aren't they now accusing you before God? 5:7 Greek brothers; also in 5:9, 10, 12, 19.

1 Peter

ABUSE AND PERSECUTION were par for the course for many who followed Christ in the first century AD. To comfort and encourage these persecuted believers, the apostle Peter wrote them a letter near the end of his life. The letter was addressed to believers in five different regions of Asia Minor, so it was probably routed among them. Peter opened his letter by reminding his readers of their precious hope in Jesus Christ. This hope far outweighed any sufferings they would endure for their faith. In light of this hope, Peter urged all believers—husbands and wives, masters and slaves, elders and laypeople—to live holy lives among unbelievers, thereby giving testimony to Jesus Christ. He comforted them regarding the abuse they had endured, noting that Jesus Christ had also suffered. But Peter also prepared his readers for even harder times. These sufferings would perfect the believers' faith and purify their souls.

■ **Author:** Peter the apostle

■ **Date Written:** Around AD 63, perhaps from the city of Rome

■ **Purpose:** To offer encouragement to suffering Christians

■ **Themes:** Salvation, persecution, believers as living building stones, obedience

■ **Outline**

1:1-25 The glory of salvation in Christ
2:1-10 Christians as God's chosen people
2:11-25 Suffering and the example of Christ
3:1-17 Christian living at home and in the world
3:18–4:19 Suffering and the example of Christ
5:1-14 Christian service and concluding words

Greetings from Peter

1 This letter is from Peter, an apostle of Jesus Christ.

I am writing to God's chosen people who are living as foreigners in the provinces of Pontus, Galatia, Cappadocia, Asia, and Bithynia.* ²God the Father knew you and chose you long ago, and his Spirit has made you holy. As a result, you have obeyed him and have been cleansed by the blood of Jesus Christ.

May God give you more and more grace and peace.

The Hope of Eternal Life

³All praise to God, the Father of our Lord Jesus Christ. It is by his great mercy that we have been born again, because God raised Jesus Christ from the dead. Now we live with great expectation, ⁴and we have a priceless inheritance—an inheritance that is kept in heaven for you, pure and undefiled, beyond the reach of change and decay. ⁵And through your faith, God is protecting you by his power until you receive this salvation, which is ready to be revealed on the last day for all to see.

⁶So be truly glad.* There is wonderful joy ahead, even though you must endure many trials for a little while. ⁷These trials will show that your faith is genuine. It is being tested as fire tests and purifies gold—though your faith is far more precious than mere gold. So when your faith remains strong through many trials, it will bring you much praise and glory and honor on the day when Jesus Christ is revealed to the whole world.

⁸You love him even though you have never seen him. Though you do not see him now, you trust him; and you rejoice with a glorious, inexpressible joy. ⁹The reward for trusting him will be the salvation of your souls.

¹⁰This salvation was something even the prophets wanted to know more about when they prophesied about this gracious salvation prepared for you. ¹¹They wondered what time

1:1 *Pontus, Galatia, Cappadocia, Asia,* and *Bithynia* were Roman provinces in what is now Turkey. 1:6 Or *So you are truly glad.*

or situation the Spirit of Christ within them was talking about when he told them in advance about Christ's suffering and his great glory afterward.

¹²They were told that their messages were not for themselves, but for you. And now this Good News has been announced to you by those who preached in the power of the Holy Spirit sent from heaven. It is all so wonderful that even the angels are eagerly watching these things happen.

A Call to Holy Living

¹³So prepare your minds for action and exercise self-control. Put all your hope in the gracious salvation that will come to you when Jesus Christ is revealed to the world. ¹⁴So you must live as God's obedient children. Don't slip back into your old ways of living to satisfy your own desires. You didn't know any better then. ¹⁵But now you must be holy in everything you do, just as God who chose you is holy. ¹⁶For the Scriptures say, "You must be holy because I am holy."*

¹⁷And remember that the heavenly Father to whom you pray has no favorites. He will judge or reward you according to what you do. So you must live in reverent fear of him during your time here as "temporary residents." ¹⁸For you know that God paid a ransom to save you from the empty life you inherited from your ancestors. And it was not paid with mere gold or silver, which lose their value. ¹⁹It was the precious blood of Christ, the sinless, spotless Lamb of God. ²⁰God chose him as your ransom long before the world began, but now in these last days he has been revealed for your sake.

²¹Through Christ you have come to trust in God. And you have placed your faith and hope in God because he raised Christ from the dead and gave him great glory.

²²You were cleansed from your sins when you obeyed the truth, so now you must show sincere love to each other as brothers and sisters.* Love each other deeply with all your heart.*

²³For you have been born again, but not to a life that will quickly end. Your new life will last forever because it comes from the eternal, living word of God. ²⁴As the Scriptures say,

"People are like grass;
    their beauty is like a flower in the field.
The grass withers and the flower fades.
²⁵   But the word of the Lord remains
        forever."*

And that word is the Good News that was preached to you.

2 So get rid of all evil behavior. Be done with all deceit, hypocrisy, jealousy, and all unkind speech. ²Like newborn babies, you must crave pure spiritual milk so that you will grow into a full experience of salvation. Cry out for this nourishment, ³now that you have had a taste of the Lord's kindness.

Living Stones for God's House

⁴You are coming to Christ, who is the living cornerstone of God's temple. He was rejected by people, but he was chosen by God for great honor.

⁵And you are living stones that God is building into his spiritual temple. What's more, you are his holy priests.* Through the mediation of Jesus Christ, you offer spiritual sacrifices that please God. ⁶As the Scriptures say,

"I am placing a cornerstone in Jerusalem,*
        chosen for great honor,
and anyone who trusts in him
        will never be disgraced."*

⁷Yes, you who trust him recognize the honor God has given him.* But for those who reject him,

"The stone that the builders rejected
        has now become the cornerstone."*

⁸And,

"He is the stone that makes people
        stumble,
    the rock that makes them fall."*

They stumble because they do not obey God's word, and so they meet the fate that was planned for them.

⁹But you are not like that, for you are a chosen people. You are royal priests,* a holy nation, God's very own possession. As a result, you can show others the goodness of God, for he called you out of the darkness into his wonderful light.

1:16 Lev 11:44-45; 19:2; 20:7.   1:22a Greek *must have brotherly love.*   1:22b Some manuscripts read *with a pure heart.*
1:24-25 Isa 40:6-8.   2:5 Greek *holy priesthood.*   2:6a Greek *in Zion.*   2:6b Isa 28:16 (Greek version).   2:7a Or *Yes, for you who believe, there is honor.*   2:7b Ps 118:22.   2:8 Isa 8:14.   2:9 Greek *a royal priesthood.*

¹⁰ "Once you had no identity as a people;
  now you are God's people.
Once you received no mercy;
  now you have received God's mercy."*

¹¹Dear friends, I warn you as "temporary residents and foreigners" to keep away from worldly desires that wage war against your very souls. ¹²Be careful to live properly among your unbelieving neighbors. Then even if they accuse you of doing wrong, they will see your honorable behavior, and they will give honor to God when he judges the world.*

Respecting People in Authority

¹³For the Lord's sake, submit to all human authority—whether the king as head of state, ¹⁴or the officials he has appointed. For the king has sent them to punish those who do wrong and to honor those who do right.

¹⁵It is God's will that your honorable lives should silence those ignorant people who make foolish accusations against you. ¹⁶For you are free, yet you are God's slaves, so don't use your freedom as an excuse to do evil. ¹⁷Respect everyone, and love the family of believers.* Fear God, and respect the king.

Slaves

¹⁸You who are slaves must submit to your masters with all respect.* Do what they tell you—not only if they are kind and reasonable, but even if they are cruel. ¹⁹For God is pleased when, conscious of his will, you patiently endure unjust treatment. ²⁰Of course, you get no credit for being patient if you are beaten for doing wrong. But if you suffer for doing good and endure it patiently, God is pleased with you.

²¹For God called you to do good, even if it means suffering, just as Christ suffered* for you. He is your example, and you must follow in his steps.

²² He never sinned,
  nor ever deceived anyone.*
²³ He did not retaliate when he was insulted,
  nor threaten revenge when he suffered.
He left his case in the hands of God,
  who always judges fairly.
²⁴ He personally carried our sins
  in his body on the cross
so that we can be dead to sin
  and live for what is right.

By his wounds
  you are healed.
²⁵ Once you were like sheep
  who wandered away.
But now you have turned to your Shepherd,
  the Guardian of your souls.

Wives

3 In the same way, you wives must accept the authority of your husbands. Then, even if some refuse to obey the Good News, your godly lives will speak to them without any words. They will be won over ²by observing your pure and reverent lives.

³Don't be concerned about the outward beauty of fancy hairstyles, expensive jewelry, or beautiful clothes. ⁴You should clothe yourselves instead with the beauty that comes from within, the unfading beauty of a gentle and quiet spirit, which is so precious to God. ⁵This is how the holy women of old made themselves beautiful. They put their trust in God and accepted the authority of their husbands. ⁶For instance, Sarah obeyed her husband, Abraham, and called him her master. You are her daughters when you do what is right without fear of what your husbands might do.

Husbands

⁷In the same way, you husbands must give honor to your wives. Treat your wife with understanding as you live together. She may be weaker than you are, but she is your equal partner in God's gift of new life. Treat her as you should so your prayers will not be hindered.

All Christians

⁸Finally, all of you should be of one mind. Sympathize with each other. Love each other as brothers and sisters.* Be tenderhearted, and keep a humble attitude. ⁹Don't repay evil for evil. Don't retaliate with insults when people insult you. Instead, pay them back with a blessing. That is what God has called you to do, and he will grant you his blessing. ¹⁰For the Scriptures say,

"If you want to enjoy life
  and see many happy days,
keep your tongue from speaking evil
  and your lips from telling lies.
¹¹ Turn away from evil and do good.
  Search for peace, and work to maintain it.

2:10 Hos 1:6, 9; 2:23.   2:12 Or *on the day of visitation.*   2:17 Greek *love the brotherhood.*   2:18 Or *because you fear God;* Greek reads *in all fear.*   2:21 Some manuscripts read *died.*   2:22 Isa 53:9.   3:8 Greek *Show brotherly love.*

¹² The eyes of the LORD watch over
those who do right,
and his ears are open to their
prayers.
But the LORD turns his face
against those who do evil."*

Suffering for Doing Good

¹³Now, who will want to harm you if you are eager to do good? ¹⁴But even if you suffer for doing what is right, God will reward you for it. So don't worry or be afraid of their threats. ¹⁵Instead, you must worship Christ as Lord of your life. And if someone asks about your hope as a believer, always be ready to explain it. ¹⁶But do this in a gentle and respectful way.* Keep your conscience clear. Then if people speak against you, they will be ashamed when they see what a good life you live because you belong to Christ. ¹⁷Remember, it is better to suffer for doing good, if that is what God wants, than to suffer for doing wrong!

¹⁸Christ suffered* for our sins once for all time. He never sinned, but he died for sinners to bring you safely home to God. He suffered physical death, but he was raised to life in the Spirit.*

¹⁹So he went and preached to the spirits in prison—²⁰those who disobeyed God long ago when God waited patiently while Noah was building his boat. Only eight people were saved from drowning in that terrible flood.* ²¹And that water is a picture of baptism, which now saves you, not by removing dirt from your body, but as a response to God from* a clean conscience. It is effective because of the resurrection of Jesus Christ.

²²Now Christ has gone to heaven. He is seated in the place of honor next to God, and all the angels and authorities and powers accept his authority.

Living for God

4 So then, since Christ suffered physical pain, you must arm yourselves with the same attitude he had, and be ready to suffer, too. For if you have suffered physically for Christ, you have finished with sin.* ²You won't spend the rest of your lives chasing your own desires, but you will be anxious to do the will of God. ³You have had enough in the past of the evil things that godless people

enjoy—their immorality and lust, their feasting and drunkenness and wild parties, and their terrible worship of idols.

⁴Of course, your former friends are surprised when you no longer plunge into the flood of wild and destructive things they do. So they slander you. ⁵But remember that they will have to face God, who stands ready to judge everyone, both the living and the dead. ⁶That is why the Good News was preached to those who are now dead*—so although they were destined to die like all people,* they now live forever with God in the Spirit.*

⁷The end of the world is coming soon. Therefore, be earnest and disciplined in your prayers. ⁸Most important of all, continue to show deep love for each other, for love covers a multitude of sins. ⁹Cheerfully share your home with those who need a meal or a place to stay.

¹⁰God has given each of you a gift from his great variety of spiritual gifts. Use them well to serve one another. ¹¹Do you have the gift of speaking? Then speak as though God himself were speaking through you. Do you have the gift of helping others? Do it with all the strength and energy that God supplies. Then everything you do will bring glory to God through Jesus Christ. All glory and power to him forever and ever! Amen.

Suffering for Being a Christian

¹²Dear friends, don't be surprised at the fiery trials you are going through, as if something strange were happening to you. ¹³Instead, be very glad—for these trials make you partners with Christ in his suffering, so that you will have the wonderful joy of seeing his glory when it is revealed to all the world.

¹⁴If you are insulted because you bear the name of Christ, you will be blessed, for the glorious Spirit of God* rests upon you.* ¹⁵If you suffer, however, it must not be for murder, stealing, making trouble, or prying into other people's affairs. ¹⁶But it is no shame to suffer for being a Christian. Praise God for the privilege of being called by his name! ¹⁷For the time has come for judgment, and it must begin with God's household. And if judgment begins with us, what terrible fate awaits those who have never obeyed God's Good News? ¹⁸And also,

3:10-12 Ps 34:12-16.   3:16 Some English translations put this sentence in verse 15.   3:18a Some manuscripts read died. 3:18b Or in spirit.   3:20 Greek saved through water.   3:21 Or as an appeal to God for.   4:1 Or For the one [or One] who has suffered physically has finished with sin.   4:6a Greek preached even to the dead.   4:6b Or so although people had judged them worthy of death. 4:6c Or in spirit.   4:14a Or for the glory of God, which is his Spirit.   4:14b Some manuscripts add On their part he is blasphemed, but on your part he is glorified.

"If the righteous are barely saved,
　　what will happen to godless sinners?"*

¹⁹So if you are suffering in a manner that pleases God, keep on doing what is right, and trust your lives to the God who created you, for he will never fail you.

Advice for Elders and Young Men

5 And now, a word to you who are elders in the churches. I, too, am an elder and a witness to the sufferings of Christ. And I, too, will share in his glory when he is revealed to the whole world. As a fellow elder, I appeal to you: ²Care for the flock that God has entrusted to you. Watch over it willingly, not grudgingly—not for what you will get out of it, but because you are eager to serve God. ³Don't lord it over the people assigned to your care, but lead them by your own good example. ⁴And when the Great Shepherd appears, you will receive a crown of never-ending glory and honor.

⁵In the same way, you who are younger must accept the authority of the elders. And all of you, dress yourselves in humility as you relate to one another, for

"God opposes the proud
　　but gives grace to the humble."*

⁶So humble yourselves under the mighty power of God, and at the right time he will lift you up in honor. ⁷Give all your worries and cares to God, for he cares about you.

⁸Stay alert! Watch out for your great enemy, the devil. He prowls around like a roaring lion, looking for someone to devour. ⁹Stand firm against him, and be strong in your faith. Remember that your family of believers* all over the world is going through the same kind of suffering you are.

¹⁰In his kindness God called you to share in his eternal glory by means of Christ Jesus. So after you have suffered a little while, he will restore, support, and strengthen you, and he will place you on a firm foundation. ¹¹All power to him forever! Amen.

Peter's Final Greetings

¹²I have written and sent this short letter to you with the help of Silas,* whom I commend to you as a faithful brother. My purpose in writing is to encourage you and assure you that what you are experiencing is truly part of God's grace for you. Stand firm in this grace.

¹³Your sister church here in Babylon* sends you greetings, and so does my son Mark. ¹⁴Greet each other with a kiss of love.

Peace be with all of you who are in Christ.

4:18 Prov 11:31 (Greek version).　5:5 Prov 3:34 (Greek version).　5:9 Greek *your brotherhood*.　5:12 Greek *Silvanus*.
5:13 Greek *The elect one in Babylon*. Babylon was probably symbolic for Rome.

2 Peter

LIKE A ROAD SIGN warning of things ahead, Peter's second letter, written shortly before his death, alerts readers to the coming return of the Lord. In light of the Lord's imminent return, Peter urged his readers to live lives that would glorify God. He also cautioned them to watch out for false teachers who would distort the gospel. These evil workers will receive their punishment when the Lord returns. Peter instructed his readers

- **Author:** Peter the apostle
- **Date Written:** Around AD 67, perhaps from the city of Rome, shortly before his execution
- **Purpose:** To warn believers about false teachers and to encourage them to grow in the grace and knowledge of Jesus Christ
- **Themes:** Diligence, false teachers, the Lord's return
- **Outline**
  1:1-21 Strategy for spiritual growth
  2:1-22 Warnings about false teachers
  3:1-18 Exhortations based on the Lord's return

to pay no attention to scoffers who cast doubt into the minds of believers regarding the return of the Lord. He assured them that the Lord would indeed return and establish a new heaven and a new earth. The letter closes with a comment about Paul's letters, noting that they are difficult to understand. Peter warned his readers about those who might twist Paul's words to justify their own lawless actions, and he encouraged believers to continually grow in their knowledge of Jesus Christ.

Greetings from Peter

1 This letter is from Simon* Peter, a slave and apostle of Jesus Christ.

I am writing to you who share the same precious faith we have. This faith was given to you because of the justice and fairness* of Jesus Christ, our God and Savior.

²May God give you more and more grace and peace as you grow in your knowledge of God and Jesus our Lord.

Growing in Faith

³By his divine power, God has given us everything we need for living a godly life. We have received all of this by coming to know him, the one who called us to himself by means of his marvelous glory and excellence. ⁴And because of his glory and excellence, he has given us great and precious promises. These are the promises that enable you to share his divine nature and escape the world's corruption caused by human desires.

⁵In view of all this, make every effort to respond to God's promises. Supplement your

faith with a generous provision of moral excellence, and moral excellence with knowledge, ⁶and knowledge with self-control, and self-control with patient endurance, and patient endurance with godliness, ⁷and godliness with brotherly affection, and brotherly affection with love for everyone.

⁸The more you grow like this, the more productive and useful you will be in your knowledge of our Lord Jesus Christ. ⁹But those who fail to develop in this way are shortsighted or blind, forgetting that they have been cleansed from their old sins.

¹⁰So, dear brothers and sisters,* work hard to prove that you really are among those God has called and chosen. Do these things, and you will never fall away. ¹¹Then God will give you a grand entrance into the eternal Kingdom of our Lord and Savior Jesus Christ.

Paying Attention to Scripture

¹²Therefore, I will always remind you about these things—even though you already know them and are standing firm in the truth you

1:1a Greek *Simeon.*   1:1b Or *to you in the righteousness.*   1:10 Greek *brothers.*

have been taught. [13]And it is only right that I should keep on reminding you as long as I live.* [14]For our Lord Jesus Christ has shown me that I must soon leave this earthly life,* [15]so I will work hard to make sure you always remember these things after I am gone.

[16]For we were not making up clever stories when we told you about the powerful coming of our Lord Jesus Christ. We saw his majestic splendor with our own eyes [17]when he received honor and glory from God the Father. The voice from the majestic glory of God said to him, "This is my dearly loved Son, who brings me great joy."* [18]We ourselves heard that voice from heaven when we were with him on the holy mountain.

[19]Because of that experience, we have even greater confidence in the message proclaimed by the prophets. You must pay close attention to what they wrote, for their words are like a lamp shining in a dark place—until the Day dawns, and Christ the Morning Star shines* in your hearts. [20]Above all, you must realize that no prophecy in Scripture ever came from the prophet's own understanding,* [21]or from human initiative. No, those prophets were moved by the Holy Spirit, and they spoke from God.

The Danger of False Teachers

2 But there were also false prophets in Israel, just as there will be false teachers among you. They will cleverly teach destructive heresies and even deny the Master who bought them. In this way, they will bring sudden destruction on themselves. [2]Many will follow their evil teaching and shameful immorality. And because of these teachers, the way of truth will be slandered. [3]In their greed they will make up clever lies to get hold of your money. But God condemned them long ago, and their destruction will not be delayed.

[4]For God did not spare even the angels who sinned. He threw them into hell,* in gloomy pits of darkness,* where they are being held until the day of judgment. [5]And God did not spare the ancient world—except for Noah and the seven others in his family. Noah warned the world of God's righteous judgment. So God protected Noah when he destroyed the world of ungodly people with a vast flood. [6]Later, God condemned the cities of Sodom and Gomorrah and turned them into heaps of ashes. He made them an example of what will happen to ungodly people. [7]But God also rescued Lot out of Sodom because he was a righteous man who was sick of the shameful immorality of the wicked people around him. [8]Yes, Lot was a righteous man who was tormented in his soul by the wickedness he saw and heard day after day. [9]So you see, the Lord knows how to rescue godly people from their trials, even while keeping the wicked under punishment until the day of final judgment. [10]He is especially hard on those who follow their own twisted sexual desire, and who despise authority.

These people are proud and arrogant, daring even to scoff at supernatural beings* without so much as trembling. [11]But the angels, who are far greater in power and strength, do not dare to bring from the Lord* a charge of blasphemy against those supernatural beings.

[12]These false teachers are like unthinking animals, creatures of instinct, born to be caught and destroyed. They scoff at things they do not understand, and like animals, they will be destroyed. [13]Their destruction is their reward for the harm they have done. They love to indulge in evil pleasures in broad daylight. They are a disgrace and a stain among you. They delight in deception* even as they eat with you in your fellowship meals. [14]They commit adultery with their eyes, and their desire for sin is never satisfied. They lure unstable people into sin, and they are well trained in greed. They live under God's curse. [15]They have wandered off the right road and followed the footsteps of Balaam son of Beor,* who loved to earn money by doing wrong. [16]But Balaam was stopped from his mad course when his donkey rebuked him with a human voice.

[17]These people are as useless as dried-up springs or as mist blown away by the wind. They are doomed to blackest darkness. [18]They brag about themselves with empty, foolish boasting. With an appeal to twisted sexual desires, they lure back into sin those who have barely escaped from a lifestyle of deception. [19]They promise freedom, but they themselves are slaves of sin and corruption. For you are a slave to whatever controls you. [20]And when people escape from the wickedness of the world by knowing our Lord and Savior Jesus

---

1:13 Greek *as long as I am in this tent* [or *tabernacle*]. 1:14 Greek *I must soon put off my tent* [or *tabernacle*]. 1:17 Matt 17:5; Mark 9:7; Luke 9:35. 1:19 Or *rises*. 1:20 Or *is a matter of one's own interpretation*. 2:4a Greek *Tartarus*. 2:4b Some manuscripts read *in chains of gloom*. 2:10 Greek *at glorious ones*, which are probably evil angels. 2:11 Other manuscripts read *to the Lord;* still others do not include this phrase at all. 2:13 Some manuscripts read *in fellowship meals*. 2:15 Some manuscripts read *Bosor*.

Christ and then get tangled up and enslaved by sin again, they are worse off than before. [21] It would be better if they had never known the way to righteousness than to know it and then reject the command they were given to live a holy life. [22] They prove the truth of this proverb: "A dog returns to its vomit."* And another says, "A washed pig returns to the mud."

The Day of the Lord Is Coming

3 This is my second letter to you, dear friends, and in both of them I have tried to stimulate your wholesome thinking and refresh your memory. [2] I want you to remember what the holy prophets said long ago and what our Lord and Savior commanded through your apostles.

[3] Most importantly, I want to remind you that in the last days scoffers will come, mocking the truth and following their own desires. [4] They will say, "What happened to the promise that Jesus is coming again? From before the times of our ancestors, everything has remained the same since the world was first created."

[5] They deliberately forget that God made the heavens long ago by the word of his command, and he brought the earth out from the water and surrounded it with water. [6] Then he used the water to destroy the ancient world with a mighty flood. [7] And by the same word, the present heavens and earth have been stored up for fire. They are being kept for the day of judgment, when ungodly people will be destroyed.

[8] But you must not forget this one thing, dear friends: A day is like a thousand years to the Lord, and a thousand years is like a day. [9] The Lord isn't really being slow about his promise, as some people think. No, he is being patient for your sake. He does not want anyone to be destroyed, but wants everyone to repent. [10] But the day of the Lord will come as unexpectedly as a thief. Then the heavens will pass away with a terrible noise, and the very elements themselves will disappear in fire, and the earth and everything on it will be found to deserve judgment.*

[11] Since everything around us is going to be destroyed like this, what holy and godly lives you should live, [12] looking forward to the day of God and hurrying it along. On that day, he will set the heavens on fire, and the elements will melt away in the flames. [13] But we are looking forward to the new heavens and new earth he has promised, a world filled with God's righteousness.

[14] And so, dear friends, while you are waiting for these things to happen, make every effort to be found living peaceful lives that are pure and blameless in his sight.

[15] And remember, our Lord's patience gives people time to be saved. This is what our beloved brother Paul also wrote to you with the wisdom God gave him—[16] speaking of these things in all of his letters. Some of his comments are hard to understand, and those who are ignorant and unstable have twisted his letters to mean something quite different, just as they do with other parts of Scripture. And this will result in their destruction.

Peter's Final Words

[17] You already know these things, dear friends. So be on guard; then you will not be carried away by the errors of these wicked people and lose your own secure footing. [18] Rather, you must grow in the grace and knowledge of our Lord and Savior Jesus Christ.

All glory to him, both now and forever! Amen.

2:22 Prov 26:11.   **3:10** Other manuscripts read *will be burned up;* one early manuscript reads *will be found destroyed.*

1 John

FOR THE MOST PART, seeing is believing. Learning something by word of mouth leaves room for misunderstanding, but witnessing an event firsthand gives a person's testimony special significance. John's first letter to the Church makes it clear that he had indeed seen Jesus Christ with his own two eyes and that he really knew Jesus. This epistle was prompted by a heretical faction that had developed within the Church. The faction distorted the apostles' teachings about the person of Christ, denying that Jesus Christ had actually come in the flesh. In order to counter these false assertions, John reaffirmed that he and the other apostles had actually seen and touched Jesus Christ. He exhorted his readers to do several things: walk in the light with God and fellow Christians, confess their sins, love God and others, purify themselves from worldly lusts, follow the Spirit of truth, and esteem Jesus Christ as God. John stressed the importance of fellowship in order to safeguard against further division and heresy.

- **Author:** John the apostle
- **Date Written:** Probably between AD 85 and 90, from the city of Ephesus
- **Purpose:** To reaffirm Jesus Christ's humanity and divinity and to instruct believers in their Christian walk
- **Themes:** Walking in the light, the family of God, truth and error, God is love, God is life
- **Outline**
  1:1-10 The believers' fellowship with God
  2:1-17 The new command to love
  2:18-27 Warnings against the Antichrist and evil
  2:28–3:24 Christian behavior
  4:1-6 False teachers
  4:7-21 The love of God
  5:1-21 The victory of faith

Introduction

1 We proclaim to you the one who existed from the beginning,* whom we have heard and seen. We saw him with our own eyes and touched him with our own hands. He is the Word of life. ²This one who is life itself was revealed to us, and we have seen him. And now we testify and proclaim to you that he is the one who is eternal life. He was with the Father, and then he was revealed to us. ³We proclaim to you what we ourselves have actually seen and heard so that you may have fellowship with us. And our fellowship is with the Father and with his Son, Jesus Christ. ⁴We are writing these things so that you may fully share our joy.*

Living in the Light

⁵This is the message we heard from Jesus* and now declare to you: God is light, and there is no darkness in him at all. ⁶So we are lying if we say we have fellowship with God but go on living in spiritual darkness; we are not practicing the truth. ⁷But if we are living in the light, as God is in the light, then we have fellowship with each other, and the blood of Jesus, his Son, cleanses us from all sin.

⁸If we claim we have no sin, we are only fooling ourselves and not living in the truth. ⁹But if we confess our sins to him, he is faithful and just to forgive us our sins and to cleanse us from all wickedness. ¹⁰If we claim we have not sinned, we are calling God a liar and showing that his word has no place in our hearts.

2 My dear children, I am writing this to you so that you will not sin. But if anyone does sin, we have an advocate who pleads our case before the Father. He is Jesus Christ, the one

1:1 Greek *What was from the beginning.* **1:4** Or *so that our joy may be complete;* some manuscripts read *your joy.* **1:5** Greek *from him.*

who is truly righteous. ²He himself is the sacrifice that atones for our sins—and not only our sins but the sins of all the world.

³And we can be sure that we know him if we obey his commandments. ⁴If someone claims, "I know God," but doesn't obey God's commandments, that person is a liar and is not living in the truth. ⁵But those who obey God's word truly show how completely they love him. That is how we know we are living in him. ⁶Those who say they live in God should live their lives as Jesus did.

A New Commandment

⁷Dear friends, I am not writing a new commandment for you; rather it is an old one you have had from the very beginning. This old commandment—to love one another—is the same message you heard before. ⁸Yet it is also new. Jesus lived the truth of this commandment, and you also are living it. For the darkness is disappearing, and the true light is already shining.

⁹If anyone claims, "I am living in the light," but hates a fellow believer,* that person is still living in darkness. ¹⁰Anyone who loves a fellow believer* is living in the light and does not cause others to stumble. ¹¹But anyone who hates a fellow believer is still living and walking in darkness. Such a person does not know the way to go, having been blinded by the darkness.

¹² I am writing to you who are God's children
   because your sins have been forgiven
      through Jesus.*
¹³ I am writing to you who are mature in the
      faith*
   because you know Christ, who existed
      from the beginning.
   I am writing to you who are young in the
      faith
   because you have won your battle with
      the evil one.
¹⁴ I have written to you who are God's children
   because you know the Father.
   I have written to you who are mature in
      the faith
   because you know Christ, who existed
      from the beginning.
   I have written to you who are young in the
      faith
   because you are strong.

God's word lives in your hearts,
   and you have won your battle with the
      evil one.

Do Not Love This World

¹⁵Do not love this world nor the things it offers you, for when you love the world, you do not have the love of the Father in you. ¹⁶For the world offers only a craving for physical pleasure, a craving for everything we see, and pride in our achievements and possessions. These are not from the Father, but are from this world. ¹⁷And this world is fading away, along with everything that people crave. But anyone who does what pleases God will live forever.

Warning about Antichrists

¹⁸Dear children, the last hour is here. You have heard that the Antichrist is coming, and already many such antichrists have appeared. From this we know that the last hour has come. ¹⁹These people left our churches, but they never really belonged with us; otherwise they would have stayed with us. When they left, it proved that they did not belong with us.

²⁰But you are not like that, for the Holy One has given you his Spirit,* and all of you know the truth. ²¹So I am writing to you not because you don't know the truth but because you know the difference between truth and lies. ²²And who is a liar? Anyone who says that Jesus is not the Christ.* Anyone who denies the Father and the Son is an antichrist.* ²³Anyone who denies the Son doesn't have the Father, either. But anyone who acknowledges the Son has the Father also.

²⁴So you must remain faithful to what you have been taught from the beginning. If you do, you will remain in fellowship with the Son and with the Father. ²⁵And in this fellowship we enjoy the eternal life he promised us.

²⁶I am writing these things to warn you about those who want to lead you astray. ²⁷But you have received the Holy Spirit,* and he lives within you, so you don't need anyone to teach you what is true. For the Spirit* teaches you everything you need to know, and what he teaches is true—it is not a lie. So just as he has taught you, remain in fellowship with Christ.

Living as Children of God

²⁸And now, dear children, remain in fellowship with Christ so that when he returns, you will

---

2:9 Greek *hates his brother;* also in 2:11. 2:10 Greek *loves his brother.* 2:12 Greek *through his name.* 2:13 Or *to you fathers;* also in 2:14. 2:20 Greek *But you have an anointing from the Holy One.* 2:22a Or *not the Messiah.* 2:22b Or *the antichrist.* 2:27a Greek *the anointing from him.* 2:27b Greek *the anointing.*

be full of courage and not shrink back from him in shame.

²⁹Since we know that Christ is righteous, we also know that all who do what is right are God's children.

3 See how very much our Father loves us, for he calls us his children, and that is what we are! But the people who belong to this world don't recognize that we are God's children because they don't know him. ²Dear friends, we are already God's children, but he has not yet shown us what we will be like when Christ appears. But we do know that we will be like him, for we will see him as he really is. ³And all who have this eager expectation will keep themselves pure, just as he is pure.

⁴Everyone who sins is breaking God's law, for all sin is contrary to the law of God. ⁵And you know that Jesus came to take away our sins, and there is no sin in him. ⁶Anyone who continues to live in him will not sin. But anyone who keeps on sinning does not know him or understand who he is.

⁷Dear children, don't let anyone deceive you about this: When people do what is right, it shows that they are righteous, even as Christ is righteous. ⁸But when people keep on sinning, it shows that they belong to the devil, who has been sinning since the beginning. But the Son of God came to destroy the works of the devil. ⁹Those who have been born into God's family do not make a practice of sinning, because God's life* is in them. So they can't keep on sinning, because they are children of God. ¹⁰So now we can tell who are children of God and who are children of the devil. Anyone who does not live righteously and does not love other believers* does not belong to God.

Love One Another

¹¹This is the message you have heard from the beginning: We should love one another. ¹²We must not be like Cain, who belonged to the evil one and killed his brother. And why did he kill him? Because Cain had been doing what was evil, and his brother had been doing what was righteous. ¹³So don't be surprised, dear brothers and sisters,* if the world hates you.

¹⁴If we love our brothers and sisters who are believers,* it proves that we have passed from death to life. But a person who has no love is still dead. ¹⁵Anyone who hates another brother or sister* is really a murderer at heart. And you know that murderers don't have eternal life within them.

¹⁶We know what real love is because Jesus gave up his life for us. So we also ought to give up our lives for our brothers and sisters. ¹⁷If someone has enough money to live well and sees a brother or sister* in need but shows no compassion—how can God's love be in that person?

¹⁸Dear children, let's not merely say that we love each other; let us show the truth by our actions. ¹⁹Our actions will show that we belong to the truth, so we will be confident when we stand before God. ²⁰Even if we feel guilty, God is greater than our feelings, and he knows everything.

²¹Dear friends, if we don't feel guilty, we can come to God with bold confidence. ²²And we will receive from him whatever we ask because we obey him and do the things that please him.

²³And this is his commandment: We must believe in the name of his Son, Jesus Christ, and love one another, just as he commanded us. ²⁴Those who obey God's commandments remain in fellowship with him, and he with them. And we know he lives in us because the Spirit he gave us lives in us.

Discerning False Prophets

4 Dear friends, do not believe everyone who claims to speak by the Spirit. You must test them to see if the spirit they have comes from God. For there are many false prophets in the world. ²This is how we know if they have the Spirit of God: If a person claiming to be a prophet* acknowledges that Jesus Christ came in a real body, that person has the Spirit of God. ³But if someone claims to be a prophet and does not acknowledge the truth about Jesus, that person is not from God. Such a person has the spirit of the Antichrist, which you heard is coming into the world and indeed is already here.

⁴But you belong to God, my dear children. You have already won a victory over those people, because the Spirit who lives in you is greater than the spirit who lives in the world. ⁵Those people belong to this world, so they speak from the world's viewpoint, and the world listens to them. ⁶But we belong to God, and those who know God listen to us. If they do not belong to God, they do not listen to us. That is how we know if someone has the Spirit of truth or the spirit of deception.

3:9 Greek *because his seed.*   3:10 Greek *does not love his brother.*   3:13 Greek *brothers.*   3:14 Greek *the brothers;* similarly in 3:16.
3:15 Greek *hates his brother.*   3:17 Greek *sees his brother.*   4:2 Greek *If a spirit;* similarly in 4:3.

Loving One Another

[7]Dear friends, let us continue to love one another, for love comes from God. Anyone who loves is a child of God and knows God. [8]But anyone who does not love does not know God, for God is love.

[9]God showed how much he loved us by sending his one and only Son into the world so that we might have eternal life through him. [10]This is real love—not that we loved God, but that he loved us and sent his Son as a sacrifice to take away our sins.

[11]Dear friends, since God loved us that much, we surely ought to love each other. [12]No one has ever seen God. But if we love each other, God lives in us, and his love is brought to full expression in us.

[13]And God has given us his Spirit as proof that we live in him and he in us. [14]Furthermore, we have seen with our own eyes and now testify that the Father sent his Son to be the Savior of the world. [15]All who declare that Jesus is the Son of God have God living in them, and they live in God. [16]We know how much God loves us, and we have put our trust in his love.

God is love, and all who live in love live in God, and God lives in them. [17]And as we live in God, our love grows more perfect. So we will not be afraid on the day of judgment, but we can face him with confidence because we live like Jesus here in this world.

[18]Such love has no fear, because perfect love expels all fear. If we are afraid, it is for fear of punishment, and this shows that we have not fully experienced his perfect love. [19]We love each other* because he loved us first.

[20]If someone says, "I love God," but hates a fellow believer,* that person is a liar; for if we don't love people we can see, how can we love God, whom we cannot see? [21]And he has given us this command: Those who love God must also love their fellow believers.*

Faith in the Son of God

5 Everyone who believes that Jesus is the Christ* has become a child of God. And everyone who loves the Father loves his children, too. [2]We know we love God's children if we love God and obey his commandments. [3]Loving God means keeping his commandments, and his commandments are not burdensome. [4]For every child of God defeats this evil world, and we achieve this victory through our faith. [5]And who can win this battle against the world? Only those who believe that Jesus is the Son of God.

[6]And Jesus Christ was revealed as God's Son by his baptism in water and by shedding his blood on the cross*—not by water only, but by water and blood. And the Spirit, who is truth, confirms it with his testimony. [7]So we have these three witnesses*—[8]the Spirit, the water, and the blood—and all three agree. [9]Since we believe human testimony, surely we can believe the greater testimony that comes from God. And God has testified about his Son. [10]All who believe in the Son of God know in their hearts that this testimony is true. Those who don't believe this are actually calling God a liar because they don't believe what God has testified about his Son.

[11]And this is what God has testified: He has given us eternal life, and this life is in his Son. [12]Whoever has the Son has life; whoever does not have God's Son does not have life.

Conclusion

[13]I have written this to you who believe in the name of the Son of God, so that you may know you have eternal life. [14]And we are confident that he hears us whenever we ask for anything that pleases him. [15]And since we know he hears us when we make our requests, we also know that he will give us what we ask for.

[16]If you see a fellow believer* sinning in a way that does not lead to death, you should pray, and God will give that person life. But there is a sin that leads to death, and I am not saying you should pray for those who commit it. [17]All wicked actions are sin, but not every sin leads to death.

[18]We know that God's children do not make a practice of sinning, for God's Son holds them securely, and the evil one cannot touch them. [19]We know that we are children of God and that the world around us is under the control of the evil one.

[20]And we know that the Son of God has come, and he has given us understanding so that we can know the true God.* And now we live in fellowship with the true God because we live in fellowship with his Son, Jesus Christ. He is the only true God, and he is eternal life.

[21]Dear children, keep away from anything that might take God's place in your hearts.*

4:19 Greek We love. Other manuscripts read We love God; still others read We love him.   4:20 Greek hates his brother.
4:21 Greek The one who loves God must also love his brother.   5:1 Or the Messiah.   5:6 Greek This is he who came by water and blood.
5:7 A few very late manuscripts add in heaven—the Father, the Word, and the Holy Spirit, and these three are one. And we have three witnesses on earth.   5:16 Greek a brother.   5:20 Greek the one who is true.   5:21 Greek keep yourselves from idols.

2 John

JOHN WROTE this short letter "to the chosen lady and to her children," probably meaning a local church and its members. It was written to encourage true Christian love and to warn against deceivers who might deny that Jesus Christ became truly human. John directed his readers to hold fast to the teachings of Jesus Christ and cautioned against hosting those who did not hold to these teachings. John closed his letter by telling them that he wished to see them soon.

- **Author:** John the apostle
- **Date Written:** Probably between AD 85 and 90, from the city of Ephesus, about the same time as 1 John
- **Purpose:** To emphasize truth and love among believers and to warn against false teachers
- **Themes:** Truth, love, false teachers
- **Outline**
  1:1-3 Introduction
  1:4-6 The life of love
  1:7-11 Rejecting false teachers
  1:12-13 Closing remarks

Greetings

This letter is from John, the elder.*

I am writing to the chosen lady and to her children,* whom I love in the truth—as does everyone else who knows the truth—²because the truth lives in us and will be with us forever.

³Grace, mercy, and peace, which come from God the Father and from Jesus Christ—the Son of the Father—will continue to be with us who live in truth and love.

Live in the Truth

⁴How happy I was to meet some of your children and find them living according to the truth, just as the Father commanded.

⁵I am writing to remind you, dear friends,* that we should love one another. This is not a new commandment, but one we have had from the beginning. ⁶Love means doing what God has commanded us, and he has commanded us to love one another, just as you heard from the beginning.

⁷I say this because many deceivers have gone out into the world. They deny that Jesus Christ came* in a real body. Such a person is a deceiver and an antichrist. ⁸Watch out that you do not lose what we* have worked so hard to achieve. Be diligent so that you receive your full reward. ⁹Anyone who wanders away from this teaching has no relationship with God. But anyone who remains in the teaching of Christ has a relationship with both the Father and the Son.

¹⁰If anyone comes to your meeting and does not teach the truth about Christ, don't invite that person into your home or give any kind of encouragement. ¹¹Anyone who encourages such people becomes a partner in their evil work.

Conclusion

¹²I have much more to say to you, but I don't want to do it with paper and ink. For I hope to visit you soon and talk with you face to face. Then our joy will be complete.

¹³Greetings from the children of your sister,* chosen by God.

1a Greek *From the elder.*　**1b** Or *the church God has chosen and its members.*　**5** Greek *I urge you, lady.*　**7** Or *will come.*　**8** Some manuscripts read *you.*　**13** Or *from the members of your sister church.*

3 John

THIS SHORT LETTER is a personal note from John the apostle to his friend Gaius. Apparently Gaius regularly welcomed traveling Christian workers into his home. John commended Gaius for his deeds and encouraged him to continue his ministry. John also denounced the actions of Diotrephes, who refused to acknowledge the authority of John and his associates; but he commended Demetrius, who followed the truth. John closed the letter by telling Gaius that he wanted to see him face to face.

■ **Author:** John the apostle

■ **Date Written:** Probably between AD 85 and 90, from the city of Ephesus, about the same time as 1 John

■ **Purpose:** To commend Gaius for his hospitality and to denounce the actions of Diotrephes

■ **Themes:** Hospitality, pride

■ **Outline**
1:1-4 Introduction
1:5-8 Christian hospitality
1:9-11 The evil work of Diotrephes
1:12 The good work of Demetrius
1:13-15 Closing remarks

Greetings

This letter is from John, the elder.*

I am writing to Gaius, my dear friend, whom I love in the truth.

²Dear friend, I hope all is well with you and that you are as healthy in body as you are strong in spirit. ³Some of the traveling teachers* recently returned and made me very happy by telling me about your faithfulness and that you are living according to the truth. ⁴I could have no greater joy than to hear that my children are following the truth.

Caring for the Lord's Workers

⁵Dear friend, you are being faithful to God when you care for the traveling teachers who pass through, even though they are strangers to you. ⁶They have told the church here of your loving friendship. Please continue providing for such teachers in a manner that pleases God. ⁷For they are traveling for the Lord,* and they accept nothing from people who are not believers.* ⁸So we ourselves should support them so that we can be their partners as they teach the truth.

⁹I wrote to the church about this, but Diotrephes, who loves to be the leader, refuses to have anything to do with us. ¹⁰When I come, I will report some of the things he is doing and the evil accusations he is making against us. Not only does he refuse to welcome the traveling teachers, he also tells others not to help them. And when they do help, he puts them out of the church.

¹¹Dear friend, don't let this bad example influence you. Follow only what is good. Remember that those who do good prove that they are God's children, and those who do evil prove that they do not know God.*

¹²Everyone speaks highly of Demetrius, as does the truth itself. We ourselves can say the same for him, and you know we speak the truth.

Conclusion

¹³I have much more to say to you, but I don't want to write it with pen and ink. ¹⁴For I hope to see you soon, and then we will talk face to face.

¹⁵*Peace be with you.

Your friends here send you their greetings. Please give my personal greetings to each of our friends there.

---

1 Greek *From the elder.* **3** Greek *the brothers;* also in verses 5 and 10. **7a** Greek *They went out on behalf of the Name.* **7b** Greek *from Gentiles.* **11** Greek *they have not seen God.* **15** Some English translations combine verses 14 and 15 into verse 14.

Jude

WHY DO LIES TICKLE our ears so much more than the truth? Often we allow false information to be spread among us because it is interesting, and we are slow to put an end to it. Jude was concerned about this problem as he wrote his letter. We do not know where he sent his letter, but the message is very clear: Christians must stand firm against false teachers and their false doctrines. Jude warned his readers that intruders had slipped in among them and spread false teachings.

■ **Author:** Jude, a half-brother of Jesus

■ **Date Written:** Around AD 65

■ **Purpose:** To warn believers about false teachers and to encourage believers to remain faithful to Jesus Christ

■ **Themes:** False teachers, rebellion against God

■ **Outline**
1:1-2 Introduction
1:3-7 Warnings concerning false teachers
1:8-19 The evil lives of false teachers
1:20-23 Exhortation to Christians
1:24-25 Doxology

He condemned these teachers and compared their fate to that of Cain, Balaam, and Sodom and Gomorrah. He described these teachers as lawless, lustful malcontents who schemed for their own gain. Jude challenged his readers to be faithful followers of Jesus Christ and to help others who were wavering in their faith.

Greetings from Jude

This letter is from Jude, a slave of Jesus Christ and a brother of James.

I am writing to all who have been called by God the Father, who loves you and keeps you safe in the care of Jesus Christ.*

²May God give you more and more mercy, peace, and love.

The Danger of False Teachers

³Dear friends, I had been eagerly planning to write to you about the salvation we all share. But now I find that I must write about something else, urging you to defend the faith that God has entrusted once for all time to his holy people. ⁴I say this because some ungodly people have wormed their way into your churches, saying that God's marvelous grace allows us to live immoral lives. The condemnation of such people was recorded long ago, for they have denied our only Master and Lord, Jesus Christ.

⁵So I want to remind you, though you already know these things, that Jesus* first

rescued the nation of Israel from Egypt, but later he destroyed those who did not remain faithful. ⁶And I remind you of the angels who did not stay within the limits of authority God gave them but left the place where they belonged. God has kept them securely chained in prisons of darkness, waiting for the great day of judgment. ⁷And don't forget Sodom and Gomorrah and their neighboring towns, which were filled with immorality and every kind of sexual perversion. Those cities were destroyed by fire and serve as a warning of the eternal fire of God's judgment.

⁸In the same way, these people—who claim authority from their dreams—live immoral lives, defy authority, and scoff at supernatural beings.* ⁹But even Michael, one of the mightiest of the angels,* did not dare accuse the devil of blasphemy, but simply said, "The Lord rebuke you!" (This took place when Michael was arguing with the devil about Moses' body.) ¹⁰But these people scoff at things they do not understand. Like unthinking animals,

---

1 Or *keeps you for Jesus Christ.*   5 Other manuscripts read *[the] Lord,* or *God,* or *God Christ.*   8 Greek *at glorious ones,* which are probably evil angels.   9 Greek *Michael, the archangel.*

they do whatever their instincts tell them, and so they bring about their own destruction. [11]What sorrow awaits them! For they follow in the footsteps of Cain, who killed his brother. Like Balaam, they deceive people for money. And like Korah, they perish in their rebellion.

[12]When these people eat with you in your fellowship meals commemorating the Lord's love, they are like dangerous reefs that can shipwreck you.* They are like shameless shepherds who care only for themselves. They are like clouds blowing over the land without giving any rain. They are like trees in autumn that are doubly dead, for they bear no fruit and have been pulled up by the roots. [13]They are like wild waves of the sea, churning up the foam of their shameful deeds. They are like wandering stars, doomed forever to blackest darkness.

[14]Enoch, who lived in the seventh generation after Adam, prophesied about these people. He said, "Listen! The Lord is coming with countless thousands of his holy ones [15]to execute judgment on the people of the world. He will convict every person of all the ungodly things they have done and for all the insults that ungodly sinners have spoken against him."*

[16]These people are grumblers and complainers, living only to satisfy their desires. They brag loudly about themselves, and they flatter others to get what they want.

A Call to Remain Faithful

[17]But you, my dear friends, must remember what the apostles of our Lord Jesus Christ predicted. [18]They told you that in the last times there would be scoffers whose purpose in life is to satisfy their ungodly desires. [19]These people are the ones who are creating divisions among you. They follow their natural instincts because they do not have God's Spirit in them.

[20]But you, dear friends, must build each other up in your most holy faith, pray in the power of the Holy Spirit,* [21]and await the mercy of our Lord Jesus Christ, who will bring you eternal life. In this way, you will keep yourselves safe in God's love.

[22]And you must show mercy to* those whose faith is wavering. [23]Rescue others by snatching them from the flames of judgment. Show mercy to still others,* but do so with great caution, hating the sins that contaminate their lives.*

A Prayer of Praise

[24]Now all glory to God, who is able to keep you from falling away and will bring you with great joy into his glorious presence without a single fault. [25]All glory to him who alone is God, our Savior through Jesus Christ our Lord. All glory, majesty, power, and authority are his before all time, and in the present, and beyond all time! Amen.

12 Or *they are contaminants among you;* or *they are stains.*   **14-15** The quotation comes from intertestamental literature: 1 Enoch 1:9.   **20** Greek *pray in the Holy Spirit.*   **22** Some manuscripts read *must reprove.*   **22-23a** Some manuscripts have only two categories of people: (1) those whose faith is wavering and therefore need to be snatched from the flames of judgment, and (2) those who need to be shown mercy.   **23b** Greek *with fear, hating even the clothing stained by the flesh.*

Revelation

WHEN FACED with fierce persecution and even death, how could Christians of the first century remain faithful to their Lord? The answer is simple: hope. Though the world around them was hostile and often appeared to be winning the battle, these Christians could stand firm because they knew the end of the story: Jesus Christ and his saints would be victorious in the end. This is the message of the book of Revelation. The first three chapters of the book are written as letters to various churches in Asia Minor, warning them about their specific shortcomings. The rest of the book recounts John's fantastic vision involving bizarre creatures, divine beings, symbolic signs and numbers, and various plagues and curses. The meaning of this vision is related to the final judgment. At God's appointed time, Jesus Christ will come in glory and reveal himself to the entire world as the sovereign Lord. Those who love him will be glad, and those who do not will be afraid, for they will be allied with Satan in a battle doomed to failure. Ultimately, Jesus Christ will defeat God's enemies and usher in his eternal Kingdom. The book of Revelation provides a fitting end to the Bible's grand story about God and humanity.

- **Author:** John the apostle
- **Date Written:** Around AD 95, from the island of Patmos
- **Purpose:** To encourage believers to remain faithful to Jesus Christ and to give them hope that they will ultimately be victorious
- **Themes:** God's sovereignty, Christ's return, God's faithful people, judgment, hope
- **Outline**
  1:1-20 The opening vision
  2:1–3:22 The letters to the seven churches
  4:1–5:14 The vision of God and the Lamb
  6:1–8:5 The seven seals of judgment
  8:6–11:19 The seven trumpets of judgment
  12:1–14:20 Visions of earthly and heavenly conflict
  15:1–16:21 The seven bowls of judgment
  17:1–19:21 The judgment of the prostitute and Babylon
  20:1–22:21 The end of the age and the age to come

Prologue

1 This is a revelation from* Jesus Christ, which God gave him to show his servants the events that must soon* take place. He sent an angel to present this revelation to his servant John, ²who faithfully reported everything he saw. This is his report of the word of God and the testimony of Jesus Christ.

³God blesses the one who reads the words of this prophecy to the church, and he blesses all who listen to its message and obey what it says, for the time is near.

John's Greeting to the Seven Churches

⁴This letter is from John to the seven churches in the province of Asia.*

Grace and peace to you from the one who is, who always was, and who is still to come; from the sevenfold Spirit* before his throne; ⁵and from Jesus Christ. He is the faithful witness to these things, the first to rise from the dead, and the ruler of all the kings of the world.

All glory to him who loves us and has freed us from our sins by shedding his blood for us. ⁶He has made us a Kingdom of priests for God

---

1:1a Or *of.*   1:1b Or *suddenly,* or *quickly.*   1:4a *Asia* was a Roman province in what is now western Turkey.   1:4b Greek *the seven spirits.*

his Father. All glory and power to him forever and ever! Amen.

7 Look! He comes with the clouds of heaven.
   And everyone will see him—
   even those who pierced him.
And all the nations of the world
   will mourn for him.
Yes! Amen!

8"I am the Alpha and the Omega—the beginning and the end,"* says the Lord God. "I am the one who is, who always was, and who is still to come—the Almighty One."

Vision of the Son of Man

9I, John, am your brother and your partner in suffering and in God's Kingdom and in the patient endurance to which Jesus calls us. I was exiled to the island of Patmos for preaching the word of God and for my testimony about Jesus. 10It was the Lord's Day, and I was worshiping in the Spirit.* Suddenly, I heard behind me a loud voice like a trumpet blast. 11It said, "Write in a book* everything you see, and send it to the seven churches in the cities of Ephesus, Smyrna, Pergamum, Thyatira, Sardis, Philadelphia, and Laodicea."

12When I turned to see who was speaking to me, I saw seven gold lampstands. 13And standing in the middle of the lampstands was someone like the Son of Man.* He was wearing a long robe with a gold sash across his chest. 14His head and his hair were white like wool, as white as snow. And his eyes were like flames of fire. 15His feet were like polished bronze refined in a furnace, and his voice thundered like mighty ocean waves. 16He held seven stars in his right hand, and a sharp two-edged sword came from his mouth. And his face was like the sun in all its brilliance.

17When I saw him, I fell at his feet as if I were dead. But he laid his right hand on me and said, "Don't be afraid! I am the First and the Last. 18I am the living one. I died, but look—I am alive forever and ever! And I hold the keys of death and the grave.*

19"Write down what you have seen—both the things that are now happening and the things that will happen.* 20This is the meaning of the mystery of the seven stars you saw in my right hand and the seven gold lampstands:

The seven stars are the angels* of the seven churches, and the seven lampstands are the seven churches.

The Message to the Church in Ephesus

2 "Write this letter to the angel* of the church in Ephesus. This is the message from the one who holds the seven stars in his right hand, the one who walks among the seven gold lampstands:

2"I know all the things you do. I have seen your hard work and your patient endurance. I know you don't tolerate evil people. You have examined the claims of those who say they are apostles but are not. You have discovered they are liars. 3You have patiently suffered for me without quitting.

4"But I have this complaint against you. You don't love me or each other as you did at first!* 5Look how far you have fallen! Turn back to me and do the works you did at first. If you don't repent, I will come and remove your lampstand from its place among the churches. 6But this is in your favor: You hate the evil deeds of the Nicolaitans, just as I do.

7"Anyone with ears to hear must listen to the Spirit and understand what he is saying to the churches. To everyone who is victorious I will give fruit from the tree of life in the paradise of God.

The Message to the Church in Smyrna

8"Write this letter to the angel of the church in Smyrna. This is the message from the one who is the First and the Last, who was dead but is now alive:

9"I know about your suffering and your poverty—but you are rich! I know the blasphemy of those opposing you. They say they are Jews, but they are not, because their synagogue belongs to Satan. 10Don't be afraid of what you are about to suffer. The devil will throw some of you into prison to test you. You will suffer for ten days. But if you remain faithful even when facing death, I will give you the crown of life.

11"Anyone with ears to hear must

1:8 Greek I am the Alpha and the Omega, referring to the first and last letters of the Greek alphabet.   1:10 Or in spirit.   1:11 Or on a scroll.   1:13 Or like a son of man. See Dan 7:13. "Son of Man" is a title Jesus used for himself.   1:18 Greek and Hades. 1:19 Or what you have seen and what they mean—the things that have already begun to happen.   1:20 Or the messengers.   2:1 Or the messenger; also in 2:8, 12, 18.   2:4 Greek You have lost your first love.

listen to the Spirit and understand what he is saying to the churches. Whoever is victorious will not be harmed by the second death.

The Message to the Church in Pergamum

12"Write this letter to the angel of the church in Pergamum. This is the message from the one with the sharp two-edged sword:

13"I know that you live in the city where Satan has his throne, yet you have remained loyal to me. You refused to deny me even when Antipas, my faithful witness, was martyred among you there in Satan's city. 14"But I have a few complaints against you. You tolerate some among you whose teaching is like that of Balaam, who showed Balak how to trip up the people of Israel. He taught them to sin by eating food offered to idols and by committing sexual sin. 15In a similar way, you have some Nicolaitans among you who follow the same teaching. 16Repent of your sin, or I will come to you suddenly and fight against them with the sword of my mouth. 17"Anyone with ears to hear must listen to the Spirit and understand what he is saying to the churches. To everyone who is victorious I will give some of the manna that has been hidden away in heaven. And I will give to each one a white stone, and on the stone will be engraved a new name that no one understands except the one who receives it.

The Message to the Church in Thyatira

18"Write this letter to the angel of the church in Thyatira. This is the message from the Son of God, whose eyes are like flames of fire, whose feet are like polished bronze:

19"I know all the things you do. I have seen your love, your faith, your service, and your patient endurance. And I can see your constant improvement in all these things. 20"But I have this complaint against you. You are permitting that woman—that Jezebel who calls herself a prophet—to lead my servants astray. She teaches them to commit sexual sin and to eat food offered to idols. 21I gave her time to repent, but she does not want to turn away from her immorality.

22"Therefore, I will throw her on a bed of suffering,* and those who commit adultery with her will suffer greatly unless they repent and turn away from her evil deeds. 23I will strike her children dead. Then all the churches will know that I am the one who searches out the thoughts and intentions of every person. And I will give to each of you whatever you deserve.

24"But I also have a message for the rest of you in Thyatira who have not followed this false teaching ('deeper truths,' as they call them—depths of Satan, actually). I will ask nothing more of you 25except that you hold tightly to what you have until I come. 26To all who are victorious, who obey me to the very end,

To them I will give authority over all the nations.
27 They will rule the nations with an iron rod
    and smash them like clay pots.*

28They will have the same authority I received from my Father, and I will also give them the morning star! 29"Anyone with ears to hear must listen to the Spirit and understand what he is saying to the churches.

The Message to the Church in Sardis

3 "Write this letter to the angel* of the church in Sardis. This is the message from the one who has the sevenfold Spirit* of God and the seven stars:

"I know all the things you do, and that you have a reputation for being alive—but you are dead. 2Wake up! Strengthen what little remains, for even what is left is almost dead. I find that your actions do not meet the requirements of my God. 3Go back to what you heard and believed at first; hold to it firmly. Repent and turn to me again. If you don't wake up, I will come to you suddenly, as unexpected as a thief.

4"Yet there are some in the church in Sardis who have not soiled their clothes with evil. They will walk with me in white, for they are worthy. 5All who are victorious will be clothed in white. I will never erase their names from the Book of Life, but I will announce before my Father and his angels that they are mine.

2:22 Greek *a bed*. 2:26-27 Ps 2:8-9 (Greek version). 3:1a Or *the messenger*; also in 3:7, 14. 3:1b Greek *the seven spirits*.

⁶"Anyone with ears to hear must listen to the Spirit and understand what he is saying to the churches.

The Message to the Church in Philadelphia

⁷"Write this letter to the angel of the church in Philadelphia.

This is the message from the one who is
    holy and true,
  the one who has the key of David.
What he opens, no one can close;
  and what he closes, no one can open:*

⁸"I know all the things you do, and I have opened a door for you that no one can close. You have little strength, yet you obeyed my word and did not deny me. ⁹Look, I will force those who belong to Satan's synagogue—those liars who say they are Jews but are not—to come and bow down at your feet. They will acknowledge that you are the ones I love.

¹⁰"Because you have obeyed my command to persevere, I will protect you from the great time of testing that will come upon the whole world to test those who belong to this world. ¹¹I am coming soon.* Hold on to what you have, so that no one will take away your crown. ¹²All who are victorious will become pillars in the Temple of my God, and they will never have to leave it. And I will write on them the name of my God, and they will be citizens in the city of my God—the new Jerusalem that comes down from heaven from my God. And I will also write on them my new name.

¹³"Anyone with ears to hear must listen to the Spirit and understand what he is saying to the churches.

The Message to the Church in Laodicea

¹⁴"Write this letter to the angel of the church in Laodicea. This is the message from the one who is the Amen—the faithful and true witness, the beginning* of God's new creation:

¹⁵"I know all the things you do, that you are neither hot nor cold. I wish that you were one or the other! ¹⁶But since you are like lukewarm water, neither hot nor cold, I will spit you out of my mouth! ¹⁷You say, 'I am rich. I have everything I want. I don't need a thing!' And you don't realize that you are wretched and miserable and poor and blind and naked. ¹⁸So I advise you to buy gold from me—gold that has been purified by fire. Then you will be rich. Also buy white garments from me so you will not be shamed by your nakedness, and ointment for your eyes so you will be able to see. ¹⁹I correct and discipline everyone I love. So be diligent and turn from your indifference.

²⁰"Look! I stand at the door and knock. If you hear my voice and open the door, I will come in, and we will share a meal together as friends. ²¹Those who are victorious will sit with me on my throne, just as I was victorious and sat with my Father on his throne.

²²"Anyone with ears to hear must listen to the Spirit and understand what he is saying to the churches."

Worship in Heaven

4 Then as I looked, I saw a door standing open in heaven, and the same voice I had heard before spoke to me like a trumpet blast. The voice said, "Come up here, and I will show you what must happen after this." ²And instantly I was in the Spirit,* and I saw a throne in heaven and someone sitting on it. ³The one sitting on the throne was as brilliant as gemstones—like jasper and carnelian. And the glow of an emerald circled his throne like a rainbow. ⁴Twenty-four thrones surrounded him, and twenty-four elders sat on them. They were all clothed in white and had gold crowns on their heads. ⁵From the throne came flashes of lightning and the rumble of thunder. And in front of the throne were seven torches with burning flames. This is the sevenfold Spirit* of God. ⁶In front of the throne was a shiny sea of glass, sparkling like crystal.

In the center and around the throne were four living beings, each covered with eyes, front and back. ⁷The first of these living beings was like a lion; the second was like an ox; the third had a human face; and the fourth was like an eagle in flight. ⁸Each of these living beings had six wings, and their wings were covered all over with eyes, inside and out. Day after day and night after night they keep on saying,

"Holy, holy, holy is the Lord God, the
    Almighty—
  the one who always was, who is, and
    who is still to come."

3:7 Isa 22:22.   3:11 Or *suddenly*, or *quickly*.   3:14 Or *the ruler*, or *the source*.   4:2 Or *in spirit*.   4:5 Greek *They are the seven spirits*.

9Whenever the living beings give glory and honor and thanks to the one sitting on the throne (the one who lives forever and ever), 10the twenty-four elders fall down and worship the one sitting on the throne (the one who lives forever and ever). And they lay their crowns before the throne and say,

11 "You are worthy, O Lord our God,
    to receive glory and honor and power.
  For you created all things,
    and they exist because you created what
      you pleased."

The Lamb Opens the Scroll

5 Then I saw a scroll* in the right hand of the one who was sitting on the throne. There was writing on the inside and the outside of the scroll, and it was sealed with seven seals. 2And I saw a strong angel, who shouted with a loud voice: "Who is worthy to break the seals on this scroll and open it?" 3But no one in heaven or on earth or under the earth was able to open the scroll and read it.

4Then I began to weep bitterly because no one was found worthy to open the scroll and read it. 5But one of the twenty-four elders said to me, "Stop weeping! Look, the Lion of the tribe of Judah, the heir to David's throne,* has won the victory. He is worthy to open the scroll and its seven seals."

6Then I saw a Lamb that looked as if it had been slaughtered, but it was now standing between the throne and the four living beings and among the twenty-four elders. He had seven horns and seven eyes, which represent the sevenfold Spirit* of God that is sent out into every part of the earth. 7He stepped forward and took the scroll from the right hand of the one sitting on the throne. 8And when he took the scroll, the four living beings and the twenty-four elders fell down before the Lamb. Each one had a harp, and they held gold bowls filled with incense, which are the prayers of God's people. 9And they sang a new song with these words:

"You are worthy to take the scroll
  and break its seals and open it.
For you were slaughtered, and your blood
  has ransomed people for God
  from every tribe and language and
    people and nation.

10 And you have caused them to become
  a Kingdom of priests for our God.
  And they will reign* on the earth."

11Then I looked again, and I heard the voices of thousands and millions of angels around the throne and of the living beings and the elders. 12And they sang in a mighty chorus:

"Worthy is the Lamb who was
    slaughtered—
  to receive power and riches
and wisdom and strength
  and honor and glory and blessing."

13And then I heard every creature in heaven and on earth and under the earth and in the sea. They sang:

"Blessing and honor and glory and power
  belong to the one sitting on the throne
  and to the Lamb forever and ever."

14And the four living beings said, "Amen!" And the twenty-four elders fell down and worshiped the Lamb.

The Lamb Breaks the First Six Seals

6 As I watched, the Lamb broke the first of the seven seals on the scroll.* Then I heard one of the four living beings say with a voice like thunder, "Come!" 2I looked up and saw a white horse standing there. Its rider carried a bow, and a crown was placed on his head. He rode out to win many battles and gain the victory.

3When the Lamb broke the second seal, I heard the second living being say, "Come!" 4Then another horse appeared, a red one. Its rider was given a mighty sword and the authority to take peace from the earth. And there was war and slaughter everywhere.

5When the Lamb broke the third seal, I heard the third living being say, "Come!" I looked up and saw a black horse, and its rider was holding a pair of scales in his hand. 6And I heard a voice from among the four living beings say, "A loaf of wheat bread or three loaves of barley will cost a day's pay.* And don't waste* the olive oil and wine."

7When the Lamb broke the fourth seal, I heard the fourth living being say, "Come!" 8I looked up and saw a horse whose color was pale green. Its rider was named Death, and his

---

5:1 Or book; also in 5:2, 3, 4, 5, 7, 8, 9.   5:5 Greek the root of David. See Isa 11:10.   5:6 Greek which are the seven spirits.
5:10 Some manuscripts read they are reigning.   6:1 Or book.   6:6a Greek A choinix [1 quart or 1 liter] of wheat for a denarius, and
3 choinix of barley for a denarius. A denarius was equivalent to a laborer's full day's wage.   6:6b Or harm.

companion was the Grave.* These two were given authority over one-fourth of the earth, to kill with the sword and famine and disease* and wild animals.

⁹When the Lamb broke the fifth seal, I saw under the altar the souls of all who had been martyred for the word of God and for being faithful in their testimony. ¹⁰They shouted to the Lord and said, "O Sovereign Lord, holy and true, how long before you judge the people who belong to this world and avenge our blood for what they have done to us?" ¹¹Then a white robe was given to each of them. And they were told to rest a little longer until the full number of their brothers and sisters*—their fellow servants of Jesus who were to be martyred—had joined them.

¹²I watched as the Lamb broke the sixth seal, and there was a great earthquake. The sun became as dark as black cloth, and the moon became as red as blood. ¹³Then the stars of the sky fell to the earth like green figs falling from a tree shaken by a strong wind. ¹⁴The sky was rolled up like a scroll, and all of the mountains and islands were moved from their places.

¹⁵Then everyone—the kings of the earth, the rulers, the generals, the wealthy, the powerful, and every slave and free person—all hid themselves in the caves and among the rocks of the mountains. ¹⁶And they cried to the mountains and the rocks, "Fall on us and hide us from the face of the one who sits on the throne and from the wrath of the Lamb. ¹⁷For the great day of their wrath has come, and who is able to survive?"

God's People Will Be Preserved

7 Then I saw four angels standing at the four corners of the earth, holding back the four winds so they did not blow on the earth or the sea, or even on any tree. ²And I saw another angel coming up from the east, carrying the seal of the living God. And he shouted to those four angels, who had been given power to harm land and sea, ³"Wait! Don't harm the land or the sea or the trees until we have placed the seal of God on the foreheads of his servants."

⁴And I heard how many were marked with the seal of God—144,000 were sealed from all the tribes of Israel:

⁵ from Judah.........................12,000
   from Reuben 12,000
   from Gad 12,000

⁶ from Asher 12,000
   from Naphtali 12,000
   from Manasseh 12,000
⁷ from Simeon 12,000
   from Levi 12,000
   from Issachar....................12,000
⁸ from Zebulun 12,000
   from Joseph 12,000
   from Benjamin 12,000

Praise from the Great Crowd

⁹After this I saw a vast crowd, too great to count, from every nation and tribe and people and language, standing in front of the throne and before the Lamb. They were clothed in white robes and held palm branches in their hands. ¹⁰And they were shouting with a great roar,

"Salvation comes from our God who sits
   on the throne
   and from the Lamb!"

¹¹And all the angels were standing around the throne and around the elders and the four living beings. And they fell before the throne with their faces to the ground and worshiped God. ¹²They sang,

"Amen! Blessing and glory and wisdom
   and thanksgiving and honor
and power and strength belong to our God
   forever and ever! Amen."

¹³Then one of the twenty-four elders asked me, "Who are these who are clothed in white? Where did they come from?"

¹⁴And I said to him, "Sir, you are the one who knows."

Then he said to me, "These are the ones who died in* the great tribulation.* They have washed their robes in the blood of the Lamb and made them white.

¹⁵ "That is why they stand in front of God's
   throne
   and serve him day and night in his
    Temple.
And he who sits on the throne
   will give them shelter.
¹⁶ They will never again be hungry or thirsty;
   they will never be scorched by the heat
    of the sun.
¹⁷ For the Lamb on the throne*
   will be their Shepherd.

6:8a Greek was Hades.   6:8b Greek death.   6:11 Greek their brothers.   7:14a Greek who came out of.   7:14b Or the great suffering.
7:17 Greek on the center of the throne.

He will lead them to springs of life-giving
water.
And God will wipe every tear from their
eyes."

The Lamb Breaks the Seventh Seal

8 When the Lamb broke the seventh seal on
the scroll,* there was silence throughout
heaven for about half an hour. ²I saw the seven
angels who stand before God, and they were
given seven trumpets.

³Then another angel with a gold incense
burner came and stood at the altar. And a great
amount of incense was given to him to mix
with the prayers of God's people as an offering on the gold altar before the throne. ⁴The
smoke of the incense, mixed with the prayers
of God's holy people, ascended up to God from
the altar where the angel had poured them out.
⁵Then the angel filled the incense burner with
fire from the altar and threw it down upon the
earth; and thunder crashed, lightning flashed,
and there was a terrible earthquake.

The First Four Trumpets

⁶Then the seven angels with the seven trumpets prepared to blow their mighty blasts.

⁷The first angel blew his trumpet, and hail
and fire mixed with blood were thrown down
on the earth. One-third of the earth was set on
fire, one-third of the trees were burned, and all
the green grass was burned.

⁸Then the second angel blew his trumpet,
and a great mountain of fire was thrown into
the sea. One-third of the water in the sea became blood, ⁹one-third of all things living in
the sea died, and one-third of all the ships on
the sea were destroyed.

¹⁰Then the third angel blew his trumpet,
and a great star fell from the sky, burning like
a torch. It fell on one-third of the rivers and
on the springs of water. ¹¹The name of the star
was Bitterness.* It made one-third of the water
bitter, and many people died from drinking
the bitter water.

¹²Then the fourth angel blew his trumpet,
and one-third of the sun was struck, and one-
third of the moon, and one-third of the stars,
and they became dark. And one-third of the
day was dark, and also one-third of the night.

¹³Then I looked, and I heard a single eagle
crying loudly as it flew through the air, "Terror,
terror, terror to all who belong to this world because of what will happen when the last three
angels blow their trumpets."

The Fifth Trumpet Brings the First Terror

9 Then the fifth angel blew his trumpet, and
I saw a star that had fallen to earth from the
sky, and he was given the key to the shaft of the
bottomless pit.* ²When he opened it, smoke
poured out as though from a huge furnace,
and the sunlight and air turned dark from the
smoke.

³Then locusts came from the smoke and
descended on the earth, and they were given
power to sting like scorpions. ⁴They were told
not to harm the grass or plants or trees, but
only the people who did not have the seal of
God on their foreheads. ⁵They were told not to
kill them but to torture them for five months
with pain like the pain of a scorpion sting. ⁶In
those days people will seek death but will not
find it. They will long to die, but death will
flee from them!

⁷The locusts looked like horses prepared
for battle. They had what looked like gold
crowns on their heads, and their faces looked
like human faces. ⁸They had hair like women's
hair and teeth like the teeth of a lion. ⁹They
wore armor made of iron, and their wings
roared like an army of chariots rushing into
battle. ¹⁰They had tails that stung like scorpions, and for five months they had the power to
torment people. ¹¹Their king is the angel from
the bottomless pit; his name in Hebrew is *Abaddon,* and in Greek, *Apollyon*—the Destroyer.

¹²The first terror is past, but look, two more
terrors are coming!

The Sixth Trumpet Brings the Second Terror

¹³Then the sixth angel blew his trumpet, and
I heard a voice speaking from the four horns
of the gold altar that stands in the presence
of God. ¹⁴And the voice said to the sixth angel
who held the trumpet, "Release the four angels who are bound at the great Euphrates
River." ¹⁵Then the four angels who had been
prepared for this hour and day and month
and year were turned loose to kill one-third
of all the people on earth. ¹⁶I heard the size of
their army, which was 200 million mounted
troops.

¹⁷And in my vision, I saw the horses and the
riders sitting on them. The riders wore armor
that was fiery red and dark blue and yellow.
The horses had heads like lions, and fire and
smoke and burning sulfur billowed from their
mouths. ¹⁸One-third of all the people on earth
were killed by these three plagues—by the fire
and smoke and burning sulfur that came from

8:1 Or *book.* 8:11 Greek *Wormwood.* 9:1 Or *the abyss,* or *the underworld;* also in 9:11.

the mouths of the horses. [19]Their power was in their mouths and in their tails. For their tails had heads like snakes, with the power to injure people.

[20]But the people who did not die in these plagues still refused to repent of their evil deeds and turn to God. They continued to worship demons and idols made of gold, silver, bronze, stone, and wood—idols that can neither see nor hear nor walk! [21]And they did not repent of their murders or their witchcraft or their sexual immorality or their thefts.

The Angel and the Small Scroll

10 Then I saw another mighty angel coming down from heaven, surrounded by a cloud, with a rainbow over his head. His face shone like the sun, and his feet were like pillars of fire. [2]And in his hand was a small scroll* that had been opened. He stood with his right foot on the sea and his left foot on the land. [3]And he gave a great shout like the roar of a lion. And when he shouted, the seven thunders answered.

[4]When the seven thunders spoke, I was about to write. But I heard a voice from heaven saying, "Keep secret* what the seven thunders said, and do not write it down."

[5]Then the angel I saw standing on the sea and on the land raised his right hand toward heaven. [6]He swore an oath in the name of the one who lives forever and ever, who created the heavens and everything in them, the earth and everything in it, and the sea and everything in it. He said, "There will be no more delay. [7]When the seventh angel blows his trumpet, God's mysterious plan will be fulfilled. It will happen just as he announced it to his servants the prophets."

[8]Then the voice from heaven spoke to me again: "Go and take the open scroll from the hand of the angel who is standing on the sea and on the land."

[9]So I went to the angel and told him to give me the small scroll. "Yes, take it and eat it," he said. "It will be sweet as honey in your mouth, but it will turn sour in your stomach!" [10]So I took the small scroll from the hand of the angel, and I ate it! It was sweet in my mouth, but when I swallowed it, it turned sour in my stomach.

[11]Then I was told, "You must prophesy again about many peoples, nations, languages, and kings."

The Two Witnesses

11 Then I was given a measuring stick, and I was told, "Go and measure the Temple of God and the altar, and count the number of worshipers. [2]But do not measure the outer courtyard, for it has been turned over to the nations. They will trample the holy city for 42 months. [3]And I will give power to my two witnesses, and they will be clothed in burlap and will prophesy during those 1,260 days."

[4]These two prophets are the two olive trees and the two lampstands that stand before the Lord of all the earth. [5]If anyone tries to harm them, fire flashes from their mouths and consumes their enemies. This is how anyone who tries to harm them must die. [6]They have power to shut the sky so that no rain will fall for as long as they prophesy. And they have the power to turn the rivers and oceans into blood, and to strike the earth with every kind of plague as often as they wish.

[7]When they complete their testimony, the beast that comes up out of the bottomless pit* will declare war against them, and he will conquer them and kill them. [8]And their bodies will lie in the main street of Jerusalem,* the city that is figuratively called "Sodom" and "Egypt," the city where their Lord was crucified. [9]And for three and a half days, all peoples, tribes, languages, and nations will stare at their bodies. No one will be allowed to bury them. [10]All the people who belong to this world will gloat over them and give presents to each other to celebrate the death of the two prophets who had tormented them.

[11]But after three and a half days, God breathed life into them, and they stood up! Terror struck all who were staring at them. [12]Then a loud voice from heaven called to the two prophets, "Come up here!" And they rose to heaven in a cloud as their enemies watched.

[13]At the same time there was a terrible earthquake that destroyed a tenth of the city. Seven thousand people died in that earthquake, and everyone else was terrified and gave glory to the God of heaven.

[14]The second terror is past, but look, the third terror is coming quickly.

The Seventh Trumpet Brings the Third Terror

[15]Then the seventh angel blew his trumpet, and there were loud voices shouting in heaven:

10:2 Or *book;* also in 10:8, 9, 10.   10:4 Greek *Seal up.*   11:7 Or *the abyss,* or *the underworld.*   11:8 Greek *the great city.*

"The world has now become the Kingdom
of our Lord and of his Christ,*
and he will reign forever and ever."

16The twenty-four elders sitting on their
thrones before God fell with their faces to the
ground and worshiped him. 17And they said,

"We give thanks to you, Lord God, the
Almighty,
the one who is and who always was,
for now you have assumed your great
power
and have begun to reign.
18 The nations were filled with wrath,
but now the time of your wrath has
come.
It is time to judge the dead
and reward your servants the
prophets,
as well as your holy people,
and all who fear your name,
from the least to the greatest.
It is time to destroy
all who have caused destruction on the
earth."

19Then, in heaven, the Temple of God was
opened and the Ark of his covenant could be
seen inside the Temple. Lightning flashed,
thunder crashed and roared, and there was an
earthquake and a terrible hailstorm.

The Woman and the Dragon

12 Then I witnessed in heaven an event
of great significance. I saw a woman
clothed with the sun, with the moon beneath
her feet, and a crown of twelve stars on her
head. 2She was pregnant, and she cried out
because of her labor pains and the agony of
giving birth.

3Then I witnessed in heaven another significant event. I saw a large red dragon with
seven heads and ten horns, with seven crowns
on his heads. 4His tail swept away one-third of
the stars in the sky, and he threw them to the
earth. He stood in front of the woman as she
was about to give birth, ready to devour her
baby as soon as it was born.

5She gave birth to a son who was to rule all
nations with an iron rod. And her child was
snatched away from the dragon and was caught
up to God and to his throne. 6And the woman

fled into the wilderness, where God had prepared a place to care for her for 1,260 days.

7Then there was war in heaven. Michael and
his angels fought against the dragon and his
angels. 8And the dragon lost the battle, and he
and his angels were forced out of heaven. 9This
great dragon—the ancient serpent called the
devil, or Satan, the one deceiving the whole
world—was thrown down to the earth with
all his angels.

10Then I heard a loud voice shouting across
the heavens,

"It has come at last—
salvation and power
and the Kingdom of our God,
and the authority of his Christ.*
For the accuser of our brothers and sisters*
has been thrown down to earth—
the one who accuses them
before our God day and night.
11 And they have defeated him by the blood
of the Lamb
and by their testimony.
And they did not love their lives so much
that they were afraid to die.
12 Therefore, rejoice, O heavens!
And you who live in the heavens, rejoice!
But terror will come on the earth and the
sea,
for the devil has come down to you in
great anger,
knowing that he has little time."

13When the dragon realized that he had
been thrown down to the earth, he pursued
the woman who had given birth to the male
child. 14But she was given two wings like
those of a great eagle so she could fly to the
place prepared for her in the wilderness. There
she would be cared for and protected from the
dragon* for a time, times, and half a time.

15Then the dragon tried to drown the
woman with a flood of water that flowed from
his mouth. 16But the earth helped her by opening its mouth and swallowing the river that
gushed out from the mouth of the dragon.
17And the dragon was angry at the woman and
declared war against the rest of her children—
all who keep God's commandments and maintain their testimony for Jesus.

18Then the dragon took his stand* on the
shore beside the sea.

11:15 Or his Messiah.   12:10a Or his Messiah.   12:10b Greek brothers.   12:14 Greek the serpent; also in 12:15. See 12:9.
12:18 Greek Then he took his stand; some manuscripts read Then I took my stand. Some translations put this entire sentence
into 13:1.

The Beast out of the Sea

13 Then I saw a beast rising up out of the sea. It had seven heads and ten horns, with ten crowns on its horns. And written on each head were names that blasphemed God. ²This beast looked like a leopard, but it had the feet of a bear and the mouth of a lion! And the dragon gave the beast his own power and throne and great authority.

³I saw that one of the heads of the beast seemed wounded beyond recovery—but the fatal wound was healed! The whole world marveled at this miracle and gave allegiance to the beast. ⁴They worshiped the dragon for giving the beast such power, and they also worshiped the beast. "Who is as great as the beast?" they exclaimed. "Who is able to fight against him?"

⁵Then the beast was allowed to speak great blasphemies against God. And he was given authority to do whatever he wanted for forty-two months. ⁶And he spoke terrible words of blasphemy against God, slandering his name and his dwelling—that is, those who dwell in heaven.* ⁷And the beast was allowed to wage war against God's holy people and to conquer them. And he was given authority to rule over every tribe and people and language and nation. ⁸And all the people who belong to this world worshiped the beast. They are the ones whose names were not written in the Book of Life that belongs to the Lamb who was slaughtered before the world was made.*

⁹ Anyone with ears to hear
    should listen and understand.
¹⁰ Anyone who is destined for prison
    will be taken to prison.
Anyone destined to die by the sword
    will die by the sword.

This means that God's holy people must endure persecution patiently and remain faithful.

The Beast out of the Earth

¹¹Then I saw another beast come up out of the earth. He had two horns like those of a lamb, but he spoke with the voice of a dragon. ¹²He exercised all the authority of the first beast. And he required all the earth and its people to worship the first beast, whose fatal wound had been healed. ¹³He did astounding miracles, even making fire flash down to earth from the sky while everyone was watching. ¹⁴And with all the miracles he was allowed to perform on behalf of the first beast, he deceived all the people who belong to this world. He ordered the people to make a great statue of the first beast, who was fatally wounded and then came back to life. ¹⁵He was then permitted to give life to this statue so that it could speak. Then the statue of the beast commanded that anyone refusing to worship it must die.

¹⁶He required everyone—small and great, rich and poor, free and slave—to be given a mark on the right hand or on the forehead. ¹⁷And no one could buy or sell anything without that mark, which was either the name of the beast or the number representing his name. ¹⁸Wisdom is needed here. Let the one with understanding solve the meaning of the number of the beast, for it is the number of a man.* His number is 666.*

The Lamb and the 144,000

14 Then I saw the Lamb standing on Mount Zion, and with him were 144,000 who had his name and his Father's name written on their foreheads. ²And I heard a sound from heaven like the roar of mighty ocean waves or the rolling of loud thunder. It was like the sound of many harpists playing together.

³This great choir sang a wonderful new song in front of the throne of God and before the four living beings and the twenty-four elders. No one could learn this song except the 144,000 who had been redeemed from the earth. ⁴They have kept themselves as pure as virgins,* following the Lamb wherever he goes. They have been purchased from among the people on the earth as a special offering* to God and to the Lamb. ⁵They have told no lies; they are without blame.

The Three Angels

⁶And I saw another angel flying through the sky, carrying the eternal Good News to proclaim to the people who belong to this world—to every nation, tribe, language, and people. ⁷"Fear God," he shouted. "Give glory to him. For the time has come when he will sit as judge. Worship him who made the heavens, the earth, the sea, and all the springs of water."

⁸Then another angel followed him through the sky, shouting, "Babylon is fallen—that great city is fallen—because she made all the

---

13:6 Some manuscripts read *and his dwelling and all who dwell in heaven.*   13:8 Or *not written in the Book of Life before the world was made—the Book that belongs to the Lamb who was slaughtered.*   13:18a Or *of humanity.*   13:18b Some manuscripts read *616.*
14:4a Greek *They are virgins who have not defiled themselves with women.*   14:4b Greek *as firstfruits.*

nations of the world drink the wine of her passionate immorality."

9Then a third angel followed them, shouting, "Anyone who worships the beast and his statue or who accepts his mark on the forehead or on the hand 10must drink the wine of God's anger. It has been poured full strength into God's cup of wrath. And they will be tormented with fire and burning sulfur in the presence of the holy angels and the Lamb. 11The smoke of their torment will rise forever and ever, and they will have no relief day or night, for they have worshiped the beast and his statue and have accepted the mark of his name."

12This means that God's holy people must endure persecution patiently, obeying his commands and maintaining their faith in Jesus.

13And I heard a voice from heaven saying, "Write this down: Blessed are those who die in the Lord from now on. Yes, says the Spirit, they are blessed indeed, for they will rest from their hard work; for their good deeds follow them!"

The Harvest of the Earth

14Then I saw a white cloud, and seated on the cloud was someone like the Son of Man.* He had a gold crown on his head and a sharp sickle in his hand.

15Then another angel came from the Temple and shouted to the one sitting on the cloud, "Swing the sickle, for the time of harvest has come; the crop on earth is ripe." 16So the one sitting on the cloud swung his sickle over the earth, and the whole earth was harvested.

17After that, another angel came from the Temple in heaven, and he also had a sharp sickle. 18Then another angel, who had power to destroy with fire, came from the altar. He shouted to the angel with the sharp sickle, "Swing your sickle now to gather the clusters of grapes from the vines of the earth, for they are ripe for judgment." 19So the angel swung his sickle over the earth and loaded the grapes into the great winepress of God's wrath. 20The grapes were trampled in the winepress outside the city, and blood flowed from the winepress in a stream about 180 miles* long and as high as a horse's bridle.

The Song of Moses and of the Lamb

15 Then I saw in heaven another marvelous event of great significance. Seven angels were holding the seven last plagues, which would bring God's wrath to completion. 2I saw before me what seemed to be a glass sea mixed with fire. And on it stood all the people who had been victorious over the beast and his statue and the number representing his name. They were all holding harps that God had given them. 3And they were singing the song of Moses, the servant of God, and the song of the Lamb:

"Great and marvelous are your works,
　O Lord God, the Almighty.
Just and true are your ways,
　O King of the nations.*
4 Who will not fear you, Lord,
　and glorify your name?
For you alone are holy.
All nations will come and worship before
　you,
　for your righteous deeds have been
　revealed."

The Seven Bowls of the Seven Plagues

5Then I looked and saw that the Temple in heaven, God's Tabernacle, was thrown wide open. 6The seven angels who were holding the seven plagues came out of the Temple. They were clothed in spotless white linen* with gold sashes across their chests. 7Then one of the four living beings handed each of the seven angels a gold bowl filled with the wrath of God, who lives forever and ever. 8The Temple was filled with smoke from God's glory and power. No one could enter the Temple until the seven angels had completed pouring out the seven plagues.

16 Then I heard a mighty voice from the Temple say to the seven angels, "Go your ways and pour out on the earth the seven bowls containing God's wrath."

2So the first angel left the Temple and poured out his bowl on the earth, and horrible, malignant sores broke out on everyone who had the mark of the beast and who worshiped his statue.

3Then the second angel poured out his bowl on the sea, and it became like the blood of a corpse. And everything in the sea died.

4Then the third angel poured out his bowl on the rivers and springs, and they became blood. 5And I heard the angel who had authority over all water saying,

14:14 Or *like a son of man.* See Dan 7:13. "Son of Man" is a title Jesus used for himself.　14:20 Greek *1,600 stadia* [300 kilometers].　15:3 Some manuscripts read *King of the ages.*　15:6 Other manuscripts read *white stone;* still others read *white [garments] made of linen.*

"You are just, O Holy One, who is and who
   always was,
   because you have sent these judgments.
6 Since they shed the blood
   of your holy people and your prophets,
   you have given them blood to drink.
   It is their just reward."

7And I heard a voice from the altar,* saying,

"Yes, O Lord God, the Almighty,
   your judgments are true and just."

8Then the fourth angel poured out his bowl
on the sun, causing it to scorch everyone with
its fire. 9Everyone was burned by this blast of
heat, and they cursed the name of God, who
had control over all these plagues. They did
not repent of their sins and turn to God and
give him glory.

10Then the fifth angel poured out his bowl on
the throne of the beast, and his kingdom was
plunged into darkness. His subjects ground
their teeth* in anguish, 11and they cursed the
God of heaven for their pains and sores. But
they did not repent of their evil deeds and turn
to God.

12Then the sixth angel poured out his bowl
on the great Euphrates River, and it dried up so
that the kings from the east could march their
armies toward the west without hindrance.
13And I saw three evil* spirits that looked like
frogs leap from the mouths of the dragon, the
beast, and the false prophet. 14They are demonic spirits who work miracles and go out
to all the rulers of the world to gather them for
battle against the Lord on that great judgment
day of God the Almighty.

15"Look, I will come as unexpectedly as a
   thief! Blessed are all who are watching for
   me, who keep their clothing ready so they
   will not have to walk around naked and
   ashamed."

16And the demonic spirits gathered all the
rulers and their armies to a place with the Hebrew name *Armageddon.**
17Then the seventh angel poured out his
bowl into the air. And a mighty shout came
from the throne in the Temple, saying, "It is
finished!" 18Then the thunder crashed and
rolled, and lightning flashed. And a great
earthquake struck—the worst since people

were placed on the earth. 19The great city of
Babylon split into three sections, and the cities
of many nations fell into heaps of rubble. So
God remembered all of Babylon's sins, and he
made her drink the cup that was filled with the
wine of his fierce wrath. 20And every island disappeared, and all the mountains were leveled.
21There was a terrible hailstorm, and hailstones
weighing as much as seventy-five pounds*
fell from the sky onto the people below. They
cursed God because of the terrible plague of
the hailstorm.

The Great Prostitute

17 One of the seven angels who had
poured out the seven bowls came over
and spoke to me. "Come with me," he said,
"and I will show you the judgment that is
going to come on the great prostitute, who
rules over many waters. 2The kings of the
world have committed adultery with her,
and the people who belong to this world
have been made drunk by the wine of her immorality."

3So the angel took me in the Spirit* into
the wilderness. There I saw a woman sitting
on a scarlet beast that had seven heads and
ten horns, and blasphemies against God
were written all over it. 4The woman wore
purple and scarlet clothing and beautiful
jewelry made of gold and precious gems and
pearls. In her hand she held a gold goblet full
of obscenities and the impurities of her immorality. 5A mysterious name was written on
her forehead: "Babylon the Great, Mother of
All Prostitutes and Obscenities in the World."
6I could see that she was drunk—drunk with
the blood of God's holy people who were witnesses for Jesus. I stared at her in complete
amazement.

7"Why are you so amazed?" the angel asked.
"I will tell you the mystery of this woman and
of the beast with seven heads and ten horns
on which she sits. 8The beast you saw was once
alive but isn't now. And yet he will soon come
up out of the bottomless pit* and go to eternal
destruction. And the people who belong to this
world, whose names were not written in the
Book of Life before the world was made, will
be amazed at the reappearance of this beast
who had died.

9"This calls for a mind with understanding:
The seven heads of the beast represent the
seven hills where the woman rules. They also

16:7 Greek *I heard the altar*.   16:10 Greek *gnawed their tongues*.   16:13 Greek *unclean*.   16:16 Or *Harmagedon*.   16:21 Greek
1 talent [34 kilograms].   17:3 Or *in spirit*.   17:8 Or *the abyss*, or *the underworld*.

represent seven kings. ¹⁰Five kings have already fallen, the sixth now reigns, and the seventh is yet to come, but his reign will be brief. ¹¹"The scarlet beast that was, but is no longer, is the eighth king. He is like the other seven, and he, too, is headed for destruction. ¹²The ten horns of the beast are ten kings who have not yet risen to power. They will be appointed to their kingdoms for one brief moment to reign with the beast. ¹³They will all agree to give him their power and authority. ¹⁴Together they will go to war against the Lamb, but the Lamb will defeat them because he is Lord of all lords and King of all kings. And his called and chosen and faithful ones will be with him."

¹⁵Then the angel said to me, "The waters where the prostitute is ruling represent masses of people of every nation and language. ¹⁶The scarlet beast and his ten horns all hate the prostitute. They will strip her naked, eat her flesh, and burn her remains with fire. ¹⁷For God has put a plan into their minds, a plan that will carry out his purposes. They will agree to give their authority to the scarlet beast, and so the words of God will be fulfilled. ¹⁸And this woman you saw in your vision represents the great city that rules over the kings of the world."

The Fall of Babylon

18 After all this I saw another angel come down from heaven with great authority, and the earth grew bright with his splendor. ²He gave a mighty shout:

"Babylon is fallen—that great city is
    fallen!
She has become a home for demons.
She is a hideout for every foul* spirit,
    a hideout for every foul vulture
    and every foul and dreadful animal.*
³ For all the nations have fallen*
    because of the wine of her passionate
    immorality.
The kings of the world
    have committed adultery with her.
Because of her desires for extravagant
    luxury,
    the merchants of the world have grown
    rich."

⁴Then I heard another voice calling from heaven,

"Come away from her, my people.
Do not take part in her sins,
    or you will be punished with her.
⁵ For her sins are piled as high as heaven,
    and God remembers her evil deeds.
⁶ Do to her as she has done to others.
    Double her penalty* for all her evil
    deeds.
She brewed a cup of terror for others,
    so brew twice as much* for her.
⁷ She glorified herself and lived in luxury,
    so match it now with torment and
    sorrow.
She boasted in her heart,
    'I am queen on my throne.
I am no helpless widow,
    and I have no reason to mourn.'
⁸ Therefore, these plagues will overtake her
    in a single day—
    death and mourning and famine.
She will be completely consumed by fire,
    for the Lord God who judges her is
    mighty."

⁹And the kings of the world who committed adultery with her and enjoyed her great luxury will mourn for her as they see the smoke rising from her charred remains. ¹⁰They will stand at a distance, terrified by her great torment. They will cry out,

"How terrible, how terrible for you,
    O Babylon, you great city!
In a single moment
    God's judgment came on you."

¹¹The merchants of the world will weep and mourn for her, for there is no one left to buy their goods. ¹²She bought great quantities of gold, silver, jewels, and pearls; fine linen, purple, silk, and scarlet cloth; things made of fragrant thyine wood, ivory goods, and objects made of expensive wood; and bronze, iron, and marble. ¹³She also bought cinnamon, spice, incense, myrrh, frankincense, wine, olive oil, fine flour, wheat, cattle, sheep, horses, wagons, and bodies—that is, human slaves.

¹⁴ "The fancy things you loved so much
    are gone," they cry.
"All your luxuries and splendor
    are gone forever,
    never to be yours again."

18:2a Greek *unclean;* also in each of the two following phrases.   18:2b Some manuscripts condense the last two lines to read *a hideout for every foul [unclean] and dreadful vulture.*   18:3 Some manuscripts read *have drunk.*   18:6a Or *Give her an equal penalty.*   18:6b Or *brew just as much.*

15The merchants who became wealthy by selling her these things will stand at a distance, terrified by her great torment. They will weep and cry out,

16 "How terrible, how terrible for that great
city!
She was clothed in finest purple and
scarlet linens,
decked out with gold and precious
stones and pearls!
17 In a single moment
all the wealth of the city is gone!"

And all the captains of the merchant ships and their passengers and sailors and crews will stand at a distance. 18They will cry out as they watch the smoke ascend, and they will say, "Where is there another city as great as this?" 19And they will weep and throw dust on their heads to show their grief. And they will cry out,

"How terrible, how terrible for that great
city!
The shipowners became wealthy
by transporting her great wealth on the
seas.
In a single moment it is all gone."

20 Rejoice over her fate, O heaven
and people of God and apostles and
prophets!
For at last God has judged her
for your sakes.

21Then a mighty angel picked up a boulder the size of a huge millstone. He threw it into the ocean and shouted,

"Just like this, the great city Babylon
will be thrown down with violence
and will never be found again.
22 The sound of harps, singers, flutes, and
trumpets
will never be heard in you again.
No craftsmen and no trades
will ever be found in you again.
The sound of the mill
will never be heard in you again.
23 The light of a lamp
will never shine in you again.
The happy voices of brides and
grooms
will never be heard in you again.

For your merchants were the greatest in
the world,
and you deceived the nations with your
sorceries.
24 In your* streets flowed the blood of the
prophets and of God's holy people
and the blood of people slaughtered all
over the world."

Songs of Victory in Heaven

19 After this, I heard what sounded like a vast crowd in heaven shouting,

"Praise the LORD!*
Salvation and glory and power belong to
our God.
2 His judgments are true and just.
He has punished the great prostitute
who corrupted the earth with her
immorality.
He has avenged the murder of his
servants."

3And again their voices rang out:

"Praise the LORD!
The smoke from that city ascends
forever and ever!"

4Then the twenty-four elders and the four living beings fell down and worshiped God, who was sitting on the throne. They cried out, "Amen! Praise the LORD!"

5And from the throne came a voice that said,

"Praise our God,
all his servants,
all who fear him,
from the least to the greatest."

6Then I heard again what sounded like the shout of a vast crowd or the roar of mighty ocean waves or the crash of loud thunder:

"Praise the LORD!
For the Lord our God,* the Almighty,
reigns.
7 Let us be glad and rejoice,
and let us give honor to him.
For the time has come for the wedding
feast of the Lamb,
and his bride has prepared herself.
8 She has been given the finest of pure white
linen to wear."

18:24 Greek her. 19:1 Greek Hallelujah; also in 19:3, 4, 6. Hallelujah is the transliteration of a Hebrew term that means "Praise the LORD." 19:6 Some manuscripts read the Lord God.

For the fine linen represents the good
deeds of God's holy people.

⁹And the angel said to me, "Write this:
Blessed are those who are invited to the wedding feast of the Lamb." And he added, "These
are true words that come from God."

¹⁰Then I fell down at his feet to worship
him, but he said, "No, don't worship me. I
am a servant of God, just like you and your
brothers and sisters* who testify about their
faith in Jesus. Worship only God. For the essence of prophecy is to give a clear witness
for Jesus.*"

The Rider on the White Horse

¹¹Then I saw heaven opened, and a white horse
was standing there. Its rider was named Faithful and True, for he judges fairly and wages
a righteous war. ¹²His eyes were like flames
of fire, and on his head were many crowns. A
name was written on him that no one understood except himself. ¹³He wore a robe dipped
in blood, and his title was the Word of God.
¹⁴The armies of heaven, dressed in the finest
of pure white linen, followed him on white
horses. ¹⁵From his mouth came a sharp sword
to strike down the nations. He will rule them
with an iron rod. He will release the fierce
wrath of God, the Almighty, like juice flowing
from a winepress. ¹⁶On his robe at his thigh*
was written this title: King of all kings and
Lord of all lords.

¹⁷Then I saw an angel standing in the sun,
shouting to the vultures flying high in the sky:
"Come! Gather together for the great banquet
God has prepared. ¹⁸Come and eat the flesh of
kings, generals, and strong warriors; of horses
and their riders; and of all humanity, both free
and slave, small and great."

¹⁹Then I saw the beast and the kings of the
world and their armies gathered together to
fight against the one sitting on the horse and
his army. ²⁰And the beast was captured, and
with him the false prophet who did mighty
miracles on behalf of the beast—miracles that
deceived all who had accepted the mark of the
beast and who worshiped his statue. Both the
beast and his false prophet were thrown alive
into the fiery lake of burning sulfur. ²¹Their
entire army was killed by the sharp sword
that came from the mouth of the one riding
the white horse. And the vultures all gorged
themselves on the dead bodies.

The Thousand Years

20 Then I saw an angel coming down from
heaven with the key to the bottomless
pit* and a heavy chain in his hand. ²He seized
the dragon—that old serpent, who is the devil,
Satan—and bound him in chains for a thousand
years. ³The angel threw him into the bottomless pit, which he then shut and locked so Satan
could not deceive the nations anymore until
the thousand years were finished. Afterward
he must be released for a little while.

⁴Then I saw thrones, and the people sitting
on them had been given the authority to judge.
And I saw the souls of those who had been beheaded for their testimony about Jesus and for
proclaiming the word of God. They had not
worshiped the beast or his statue, nor accepted
his mark on their foreheads or their hands.
They all came to life again, and they reigned
with Christ for a thousand years.

⁵This is the first resurrection. (The rest of
the dead did not come back to life until the
thousand years had ended.) ⁶Blessed and holy
are those who share in the first resurrection.
For them the second death holds no power, but
they will be priests of God and of Christ and
will reign with him a thousand years.

The Defeat of Satan

⁷When the thousand years come to an end, Satan will be let out of his prison. ⁸He will go
out to deceive the nations—called Gog and
Magog—in every corner of the earth. He will
gather them together for battle—a mighty
army, as numberless as sand along the seashore. ⁹And I saw them as they went up on
the broad plain of the earth and surrounded
God's people and the beloved city. But fire from
heaven came down on the attacking armies and
consumed them.

¹⁰Then the devil, who had deceived them,
was thrown into the fiery lake of burning sulfur, joining the beast and the false prophet.
There they will be tormented day and night
forever and ever.

The Final Judgment

¹¹And I saw a great white throne and the one
sitting on it. The earth and sky fled from his
presence, but they found no place to hide.
¹²I saw the dead, both great and small, standing before God's throne. And the books were
opened, including the Book of Life. And the
dead were judged according to what they had

19:10a Greek *brothers.*   19:10b Or *is the message confirmed by Jesus.*   19:16 Or *On his robe and thigh.*   20:1 Or *the abyss,* or *the underworld;* also in 20:3.

done, as recorded in the books. [13]The sea gave up its dead, and death and the grave* gave up their dead. And all were judged according to their deeds. [14]Then death and the grave were thrown into the lake of fire. This lake of fire is the second death. [15]And anyone whose name was not found recorded in the Book of Life was thrown into the lake of fire.

The New Jerusalem

21 Then I saw a new heaven and a new earth, for the old heaven and the old earth had disappeared. And the sea was also gone. [2]And I saw the holy city, the new Jerusalem, coming down from God out of heaven like a bride beautifully dressed for her husband.

[3]I heard a loud shout from the throne, saying, "Look, God's home is now among his people! He will live with them, and they will be his people. God himself will be with them.* [4]He will wipe every tear from their eyes, and there will be no more death or sorrow or crying or pain. All these things are gone forever."

[5]And the one sitting on the throne said, "Look, I am making everything new!" And then he said to me, "Write this down, for what I tell you is trustworthy and true." [6]And he also said, "It is finished! I am the Alpha and the Omega—the Beginning and the End. To all who are thirsty I will give freely from the springs of the water of life. [7]All who are victorious will inherit all these blessings, and I will be their God, and they will be my children.

[8]"But cowards, unbelievers, the corrupt, murderers, the immoral, those who practice witchcraft, idol worshipers, and all liars—their fate is in the fiery lake of burning sulfur. This is the second death."

[9]Then one of the seven angels who held the seven bowls containing the seven last plagues came and said to me, "Come with me! I will show you the bride, the wife of the Lamb."

[10]So he took me in the Spirit* to a great, high mountain, and he showed me the holy city, Jerusalem, descending out of heaven from God. [11]It shone with the glory of God and sparkled like a precious stone—like jasper as clear as crystal. [12]The city wall was broad and high, with twelve gates guarded by twelve angels. And the names of the twelve tribes of Israel were written on the gates. [13]There were three gates on each side—east, north, south, and west. [14]The wall of the city had twelve foundation stones, and on them were written the names of the twelve apostles of the Lamb.

[15]The angel who talked to me held in his hand a gold measuring stick to measure the city, its gates, and its wall. [16]When he measured it, he found it was a square, as wide as it was long. In fact, its length and width and height were each 1,400 miles.* [17]Then he measured the walls and found them to be 216 feet thick* (according to the human standard used by the angel).

[18]The wall was made of jasper, and the city was pure gold, as clear as glass. [19]The wall of the city was built on foundation stones inlaid with twelve precious stones:* the first was jasper, the second sapphire, the third agate, the fourth emerald, [20]the fifth onyx, the sixth carnelian, the seventh chrysolite, the eighth beryl, the ninth topaz, the tenth chrysoprase, the eleventh jacinth, the twelfth amethyst.

[21]The twelve gates were made of pearls—each gate from a single pearl! And the main street was pure gold, as clear as glass.

[22]I saw no temple in the city, for the Lord God Almighty and the Lamb are its temple. [23]And the city has no need of sun or moon, for the glory of God illuminates the city, and the Lamb is its light. [24]The nations will walk in its light, and the kings of the world will enter the city in all their glory. [25]Its gates will never be closed at the end of day because there is no night there. [26]And all the nations will bring their glory and honor into the city. [27]Nothing evil* will be allowed to enter, nor anyone who practices shameful idolatry and dishonesty—but only those whose names are written in the Lamb's Book of Life.

22 Then the angel showed me a river with the water of life, clear as crystal, flowing from the throne of God and of the Lamb. [2]It flowed down the center of the main street. On each side of the river grew a tree of life, bearing twelve crops of fruit,* with a fresh crop each month. The leaves were used for medicine to heal the nations.

[3]No longer will there be a curse upon anything. For the throne of God and of the Lamb will be there, and his servants will worship him. [4]And they will see his face, and his name will be written on their foreheads. [5]And there will be no night there—no need for lamps or sun—for the Lord God will shine on them. And they will reign forever and ever.

20:13 Greek *and Hades;* also in 20:14.   21:3 Some manuscripts read *God himself will be with them, their God.*   21:10 Or *in spirit.* 21:16 Greek *12,000 stadia* [2,220 kilometers].   21:17 Greek *144 cubits* [65 meters].   21:19 The identification of some of these gemstones is uncertain.   21:27 Or *ceremonially unclean.*   22:2 Or *twelve kinds of fruit.*

⁶Then the angel said to me, "Everything you have heard and seen is trustworthy and true. The Lord God, who inspires his prophets,* has sent his angel to tell his servants what will happen soon.*"

Jesus Is Coming

⁷"Look, I am coming soon! Blessed are those who obey the words of prophecy written in this book.*"

⁸I, John, am the one who heard and saw all these things. And when I heard and saw them, I fell down to worship at the feet of the angel who showed them to me. ⁹But he said, "No, don't worship me. I am a servant of God, just like you and your brothers the prophets, as well as all who obey what is written in this book. Worship only God!"

¹⁰Then he instructed me, "Do not seal up the prophetic words in this book, for the time is near. ¹¹Let the one who is doing harm continue to do harm; let the one who is vile continue to be vile; let the one who is righteous continue to live righteously; let the one who is holy continue to be holy."

¹²"Look, I am coming soon, bringing my reward with me to repay all people according to their deeds. ¹³I am the Alpha and the Omega, the First and the Last, the Beginning and the End."

¹⁴Blessed are those who wash their robes. They will be permitted to enter through the gates of the city and eat the fruit from the tree of life. ¹⁵Outside the city are the dogs—the sorcerers, the sexually immoral, the murderers, the idol worshipers, and all who love to live a lie.

¹⁶"I, Jesus, have sent my angel to give you this message for the churches. I am both the source of David and the heir to his throne.* I am the bright morning star."

¹⁷The Spirit and the bride say, "Come." Let anyone who hears this say, "Come." Let anyone who is thirsty come. Let anyone who desires drink freely from the water of life. ¹⁸And I solemnly declare to everyone who hears the words of prophecy written in this book: If anyone adds anything to what is written here, God will add to that person the plagues described in this book. ¹⁹And if anyone removes any of the words from this book of prophecy, God will remove that person's share in the tree of life and in the holy city that are described in this book.

²⁰He who is the faithful witness to all these things says, "Yes, I am coming soon!"

Amen! Come, Lord Jesus!

²¹May the grace of the Lord Jesus be with God's holy people.*

22:6a Or *The Lord, the God of the spirits of the prophets.*   22:6b Or *suddenly,* or *quickly;* also in 22:7, 12, 20.   22:7 Or *scroll;* also in 22:9, 10, 18, 19.   22:16 Greek *I am the root and offspring of David.*   22:21 Other manuscripts read *be with all;* still others read *be with all of God's holy people.* Some manuscripts add *Amen.*

WORLD OF THE PATRIARCHS

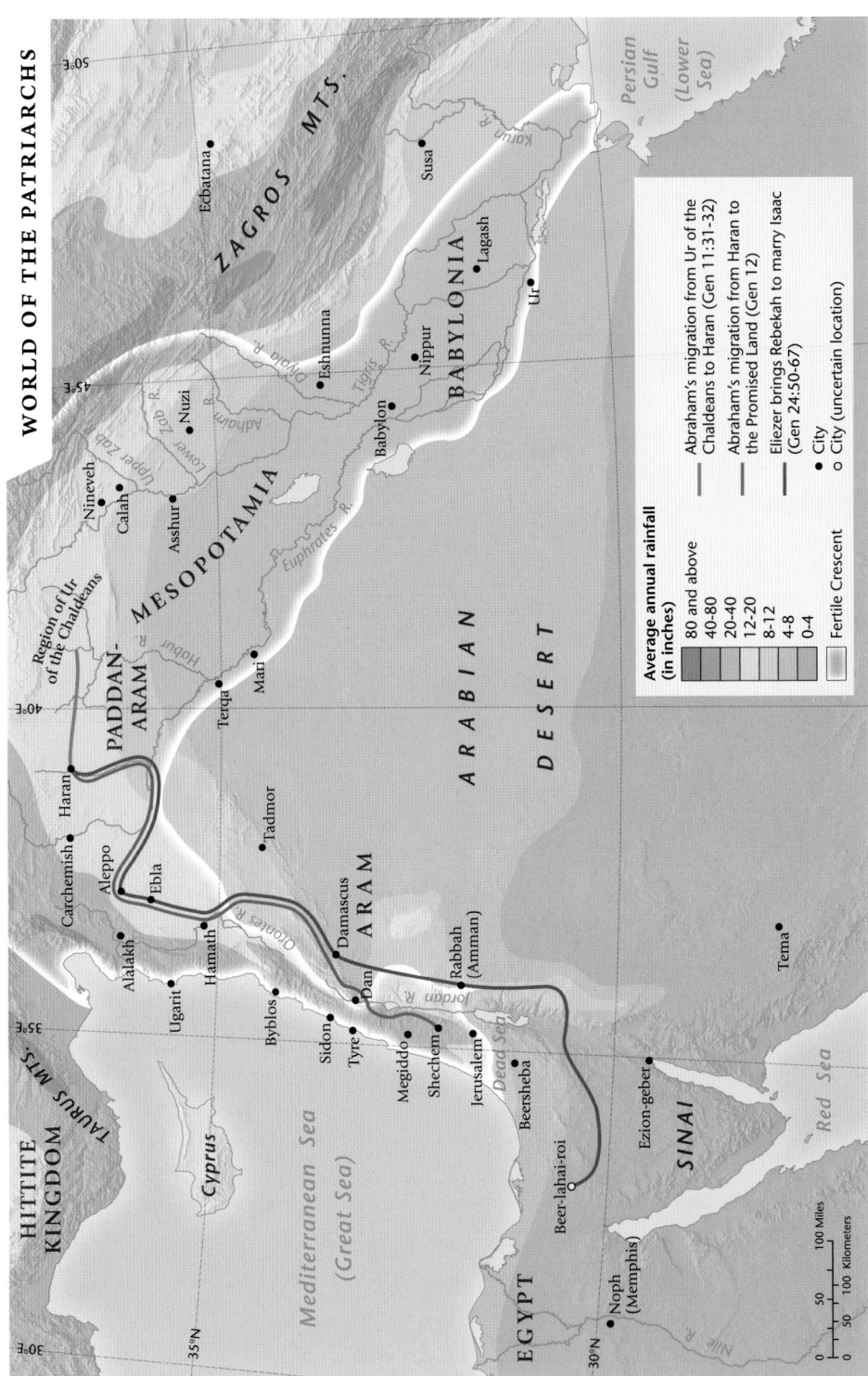

Average annual rainfall (in inches)

80 and above
40–80
20–40
12–20
8–12
4–8
0–4

Fertile Crescent

—— Abraham's migration from Ur of the Chaldeans to Haran (Gen 11:31-32)
—— Abraham's migration from Haran to the Promised Land (Gen 12)
—— Eliezer brings Rebekah to marry Isaac (Gen 24:50-67)

• City
○ City (uncertain location)

EXODUS FROM EGYPT

Legend:

- Route from Egypt to Mt. Sinai
- Route from Mt. Sinai to Kadesh-barnea
- Route from Kadesh-barnea to Acacia Grove
- Annual bird migration path
- Ancient roadway

- • City
- ○ City (modern name)
- ▲ Mountain peak (possible sites of Mt. Sinai)

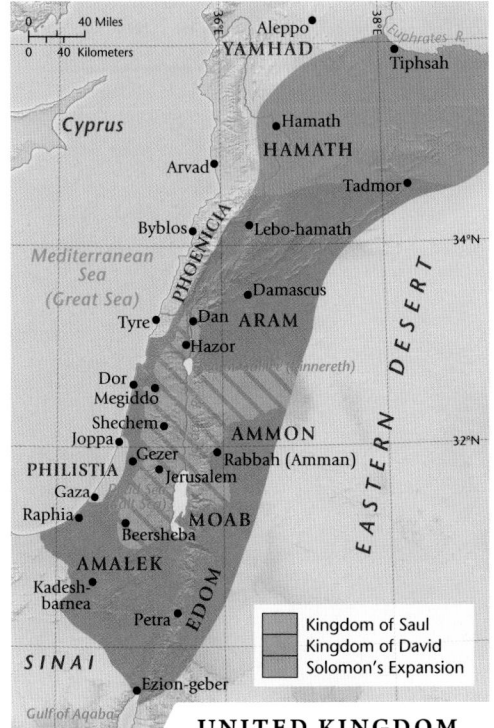

UNITED KINGDOM

KINGDOMS OF ISRAEL

The United Kingdom of Israel came into being at the coronation of Saul, grew in size and influence under David, and reached its height during Solomon's reign. Solomon inherited a powerful kingdom from his father David, covering the entire area inhabited by the 12 tribes of Israel. Throughout Solomon's reign, his power and influence increased as he also gained control over many of the surrounding nations.

After the death of Solomon, the kingdom of Israel divided. Solomon's son, Rehoboam, remained king of the southern kingdom of Judah, with Jerusalem as its capital. Jeroboam became the king of the northern kingdom of Israel and rebuilt Shechem as his capital. He also built new worship centers in Bethel and Dan, influencing his people to stay away from Jerusalem and its annual religious festivals. The division of the kingdom of Israel began a downward spiral into idolatry and godless leadership for both nations, eventually leading to the exile of the northern kingdom to Assyria and the southern kingdom to Babylon.

DIVIDED KINGDOM

ASSYRIAN AND BABYLONIAN EMPIRES

Assyria around 700 B.C.

Babylonia around 600 B.C.

Black Sea

Byzantium

LYDIA

URARTU

Araxes R.

Caspian Sea

40°N

Lake Van

Lake Urmia

Tarsus KUE Carchemish
Haran

Nineveh
Calah

Aleppo

Asshur Arrapha

MEDIA

Riblah

Cyprus

Ecbatana

Mediterranean Sea
(Great Sea)

Tadmor

Tyre

Damascus

Sippar

Samaria

KEDAR

Babylon Nippur

Susa

Jerusalem

Erech (Uruk)

Ur

ELAM

30°N

Memphis

Ezion-geber

Dumah

PERSIA

SAHARA
DESERT

ARABIAN
DESERT

Persian Gulf

0   100   200 Miles

0 100 200 Kilometers

Red
Sea

Tema

30°E

40°E

50°E

GREEK EMPIRE

Danube R.

MACEDONIA

Black Sea

CAUCASUS MTS.

Caspian Sea

Pella

THRACE

Sinope

40°N

Araxes R.

Athens

ASIA

ARMENIA

HELLAS

Ephesus

Sparta

Tarsus Carchemish
Haran

Crete

Aleppo

Gaugamela
Arbela

MEDIA

Mediterranean Sea
(Great Sea)

Cyprus

Tadmor

Ecbatana

Cyrene

Tyre

Damascus

BABYLONIA

Opis

LIBYA

Alexandria

Jerusalem

NABATEA

Babylon

Susa

EGYPT

Erech (Uruk)

Ur

30°N

Memphis

Ezion-geber

Extent of
Alexandrian empire

Ptolemaic realm

Seleucid realm

Antigonid realm

Minor Hellenistic provinces

SAHARA
DESERT

ARABIAN
DESERT

0   100   200 Miles

0 100 200 Kilometers

Thebes

Red
Sea

30°E

40°E

ROMAN DIVISION OF PALESTINE

ABILENE
Abila

Sidon
PHOENICIA
ITUREA
Mt. Hermon
Damascus
Abana R.
SYRIA

Tyre
Coastal Road
Litani R.
Caesarea Philippi
GAULANITIS
TRACONITIS
Raphana

33°N

Cadasa (Kedesh)
Thella
Lake Hala

Ptolemais (Acco)
GALILEE
Mt. Meron
Korazin
Capernaum
Gennesaret
Bethsaida
Sea of Galilee (Kinnereth)
BATANEA

Mediterranean Sea
(Great Sea)

Mt. Carmel
Gebae
Magdala
Tiberias
Gergesa
Hippos
Mt. Tabor
Nain
Abila
Dora
Gadara
Edrei
AURANITIS

Caesarea
DECAPOLIS

Scythopolis (Beth-shan)
Pella
Dion

Dothan
SAMARIA

Sebaste (Samaria)
Mt. Ebal
Sychar (Shechem)
Mt. Gerizim
Amathus
Gerasa

Antipatris (Aphek)
Jordan R.
Jabbok R.
Yarkon R.

Joppa
Alexandrium
PEREA

32°N

Lydda (Lod)
Bethel
Ephraim
Tyrus
Philadelphia (Amman)

Jamnia
Abila
Jericho
Cyprus
Esbus (Heshbon)

Azotus (Ashdod)
Mt. of Olives
Jerusalem
Bethany
Hyrcania
Medeba

Ascalon
Bethlehem
JUDEA
Herodium
Machaerus

Marisa
NABATEA

Gaza
Hebron
Dead Sea
(Salt Sea)
Arnon R.

Adora
En-gedi

IDUMEA
Masada
King's Highway

Raphia
Besor Brook
Beersheba
Malatha
Arad

31°N

0   10   20 Miles
0   10   20 Kilometers

Division of Herod's kingdom to his three sons

- Territory of Archelaus
- Territory of Herod Antipas
- Territory of Philip
- Territory of the Proconsul of Syria
- Extent of Herod the Great's kingdom

- ● City
- ○ Decapolis city
- ■ Herodian fortress
- ▲ Mountain peak

MINISTRY OF JESUS

Chronologically speaking, it is not possible to sequentially arrange the events in the life of Christ in any definitive way; none of the New Testament Gospels follows an overtly chronological pattern. Accordingly, the arrangement here follows a geographic order, basically proceeding from north to south on the map. Because the Gospel of Matthew most frequently contains information cited here, and because it is the most geographically particularistic Gospel, synoptic passages are keyed to the book of Matthew, except where they are unattested there or where more pertinent information about the event cited is available in another Gospel.

Ⓐ *Region of Tyre:* Gentile woman's daughter healed (Mt 15:21-28)

Ⓑ *Caesarea Philippi:* Peter's great declaration (Mt 16:13-20)

Ⓒ *Mt. Meron/Mt. Tabor/Mt. Hermon:* (1) possible location of Transfiguration (Mt 17:1-13); (2) demon-possessed boy healed nearby (Mt 17:14-21)

Ⓓ *Cana of Galilee:* (1) water changed to wine (Jn 2:1-11); (2) Capernaum official's son healed (Jn 4:46-54)

Ⓔ *Gennesaret:* (1) possible location of feeding of multitudes (Mt 14:13-21; 15:32-39); (2) many healings (Mk 6:53-56)

Ⓕ *Area of Korazin:* (1) judgment pronounced on the cities of Korazin, Bethsaida, and Capernaum (Mt 11:20-24); (2) possible area of Sermon on the Mount (Mt 5–7)

Ⓖ *Capernaum:* (1) catch of fish (Lk 5:1-11); (2) evil spirit cast out (Mk 1:21-28); (3) Sermon on the Mount (Mt 5–7); (4) Peter's mother-in-law healed (Mt 8:14-15); (5) Roman officer's servant healed (Mt 8:5-13); (6) paralyzed man healed (Mk 2:1-12); (7) woman with a hemorrhage healed (Mk 5:25-34); (8) Jairus's daughter raised (Lk 8:40-56); (9) two blind men healed (Mt 9:27-31); (10) a mute, demon-possessed man healed (Mt 9:32-34); (11) the twelve apostles sent out (Mt 10:1-15); (12) man with deformed hand healed (Mt 12:9-13); (13) another demon-possessed man healed (Mt 12:22-37); (14) Temple tax provided (Mt 17:24-27); (15) Bread of Life discourse (Jn 6:22-59)

Ⓗ *Bethsaida:* (1) possible location of feeding of multitudes (Mt 14:13-21; 15:32-39); (2) blind man healed (Mk 8:22-26)

Ⓘ *Sea of Galilee near Bethsaida:* walking on water (Mt 14:22-33)

Ⓘ *Sea of Galilee:* storm quieted (Mt 8:23-27)

Ⓚ *Gergesa/Gadara:* possible location of casting out demons, which enter pigs; the pigs then rush down a steep bank and drown (Lk 8:26-39)

Ⓛ *Nazareth:* (1) childhood home (Mt 2:19-23); (2) rejected by townspeople (Lk 4:16-30)

Ⓜ *Nain:* widow's son raised (Lk 7:11-17)

Ⓞ *Decapolis (Region of Ten Towns):* many healings (Mt 15:29-31; Mk 7:31-37)

Ⓟ *Region between Galilee and Samaria:* (1) refused entry into village (Lk 9:51-56); (2) ten lepers healed (Lk 17:11-19)

Ⓠ *Sychar:* woman at the well of Samaria (Jn 4:1-42)

Ⓡ *Ephraim:* enters into seclusion with the disciples (Jn 11:54)

Ⓢ *Region of Perea:* (1) teaching on marriage (Mt 19:1-12); (2) possible location of healing of woman with infirmity (Lk 13:10-13); (3) possible location of healing of man with swollen limbs (Lk 14:1-6); (4) possible location of the rich young ruler (Lk 18:18-30)

Ⓣ *Jericho:* (1) Bartimaeus healed (Mk 10:46-52); (2) Zacchaeus converted (Lk 19:1-10)

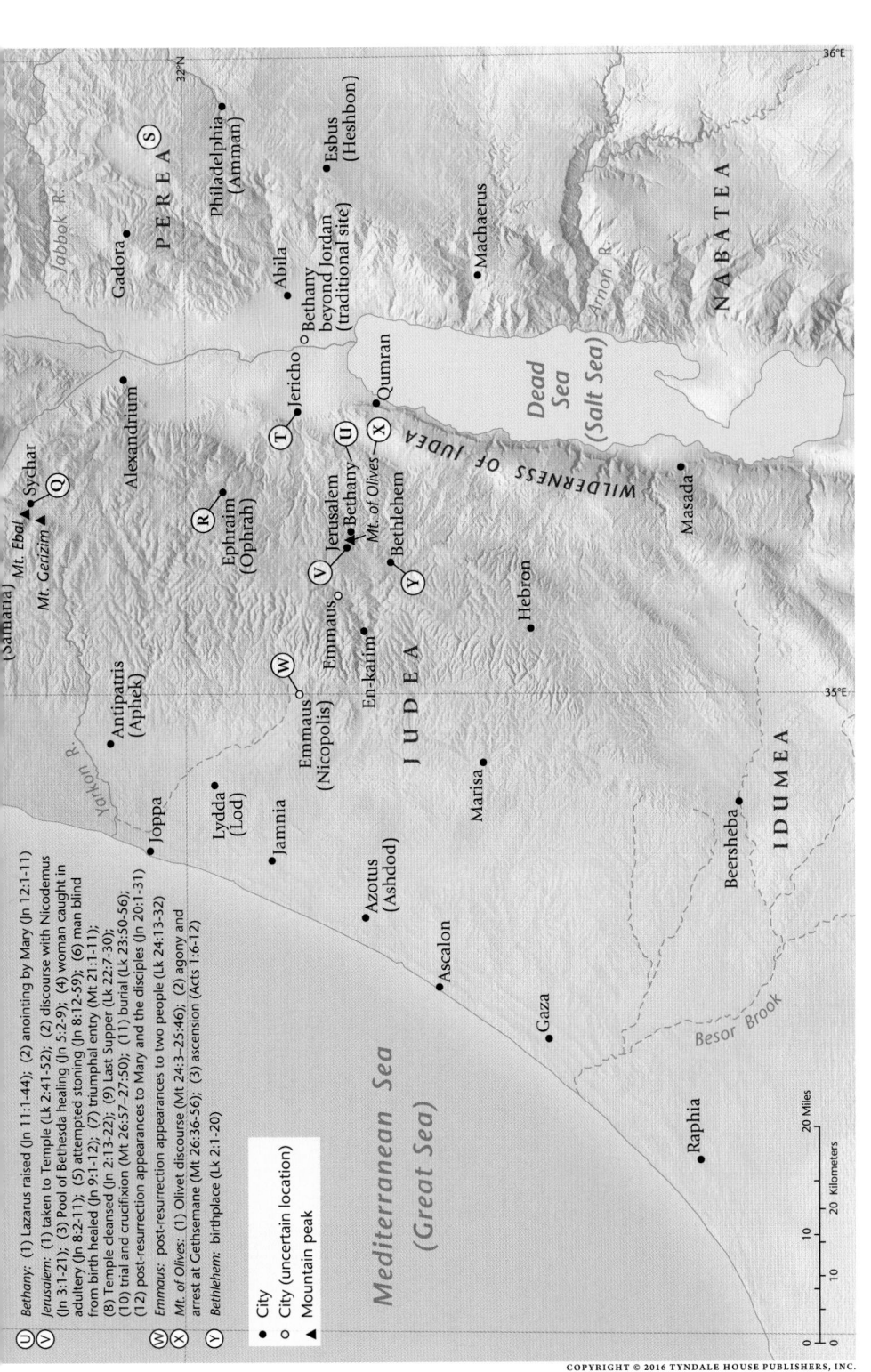

Ⓤ Ⓥ Ⓥ **Bethany:** (1) Lazarus raised (Jn 11:1-44); (2) anointing by Mary (Jn 12:1-11)
Jerusalem: (1) taken to Temple (Lk 2:41-52); (2) discourse with Nicodemus
(Jn 3:1-21); (3) Pool of Bethesda healing (Jn 5:2-9); (4) woman caught in
adultery (Jn 8:2-11); (5) attempted stoning (Jn 8:12-59); (6) man blind
from birth healed (Jn 9:1-12); (7) triumphal entry (Mt 21:1-11);
(8) Temple cleansed (Jn 2:13-22); (9) Last Supper (Lk 22:7-30);
(10) trial and crucifixion (Mt 26:57-27:50); (11) burial (Lk 23:50-56);
(12) post-resurrection appearances to Mary and the disciples (Jn 20:1-31)
Ⓦ **Emmaus:** post-resurrection appearances to two people (Lk 24:13-32)
Ⓧ **Mt. of Olives:** (1) Olivet discourse (Mt 24:3–25:46); (2) agony and
arrest at Gethsemane (Mt 26:36-56); (3) ascension (Acts 1:6-12)
Ⓨ **Bethlehem:** birthplace (Lk 2:1-20)

• City
○ City (uncertain location)
▲ Mountain peak

COPYRIGHT © 2016 TYNDALE HOUSE PUBLISHERS, INC.

PAUL'S MISSIONARY JOURNEYS